THE ENCYCLOPAEDIA OF WALES

The Welsh Academy

Encyclopaedia of Wales

CO-EDITORS

JOHN DAVIES, NIGEL JENKINS,
MENNA BAINES, PEREDUR I. LYNCH

UNIVERSITY OF WALES PRESS
CARDIFF
2008

Published by the University of Wales Press
10 Columbus Walk
Brigantine Place
Cardiff CF10 4UP

www.uwp.co.uk

Funded by the Arts Council of Wales

Hardback   ISBN 978-0-7083-1953-6
Paperback ISBN 978-0-7083-2154-6

British Library Cataloguing-in-Publication Data.
A catalogue record for this book is available from the British Library.

Production project management by Stuart Booth
Page creation and typesetting by Chris Bell, cbdesign
Proofreading by Rosie Anderson, Martin Bryant, David Pickering and Ann Leyshon
Indexing by Janet Davies, Hannah Austin and Alwen Lloyd-Wynne at Merrall-Ross
Cover designed by Clifford Hayes, based on an original concept by Nicky Roper
Picture research collation by Steven Gordon Goundrey at the University of Wales Press
Printed by Gutenberg Press, Tarxien, Malta

academi
hybu llên • literature promotion

CONTENTS

CONTENTS

FOREWORD

I am delighted to have been asked to provide a foreword for this, the first-ever single volume encyclopaedia in the history of Wales.

Within this ambitious new book are entries on all the people, places and events which make Wales so culturally, historically and geographically rich. I was particularly pleased to be able to turn to the letter B and read the entry about Betws-y-Coed, which is my home when I am in the north. Elsewhere in the book I find reference to Cardiff Bay and our magnificent Senedd building, home to the National Assembly, the presence of which, as the authors rightly point out, gives a fuller meaning to Cardiff's role as capital of Wales.

This is a fitting time for such an important book to be published. We have just celebrated ten years of devolution in Wales and our National Assembly has new enhanced legislative powers, giving us the opportunity of passing laws for Wales. With the introduction of these new powers the scope for doing things differently in Wales will increase. We are moving forward into a new phase of devolution, increasing in confidence as a nation. It is only right, therefore, that as a modern nation we should have our own Encyclopaedia, reminding us of our rich past, but also celebrating our vibrant present and pointing the way to our future direction.

LORD DAFYDD ELIS-THOMAS
Llywydd
National Assembly for Wales

FOREWORD

I am delighted to have been asked to provide a Foreword for this, the first-ever single volume encyclopedia in the history of Wales.

Within this ambitious new book are entries on all the people, places and events which make Wales so culturally, historically and geographically rich. I was particularly pleased to be able to turn to the letter B and read the entry about Betws-y-Coed, which is my home when I am in the north. Elsewhere in the book I find reference to Cardiff Bay and our magnificent Senedd building, home to the National Assembly, the presence of which, as the authors rightly point out, gives a fuller meaning to Cardiff's role as capital of Wales.

This is a fitting time for such an important book to be published. We have just celebrated ten years of devolution in Wales and our National Assembly has new enhanced legislative powers, giving us the opportunity of passing laws for Wales. With the introduction of these new powers the scope for doing things differently in Wales will increase. We are moving forward into a new phase of devolution, increasing in confidence as a nation. It is only right, therefore, that as a modern nation, we should have our own Encyclopaedia, reminding us of our rich past, but also celebrating our vibrant present and pointing the way to our future direction.

LORD DAFYDD ELIS-THOMAS
Llywydd
National Assembly for Wales

A WORD ON BEHALF OF THE WELSH ACADEMY

Yr Academi Gymreig / The Welsh Academy was founded in 1958 and has a long history of literary projects, including the pioneering *Welsh Academy English–Welsh Dictionary*, *The Oxford Companion to the Literature of Wales* and the *Cydymaith i Lenyddiaeth Cymru*. In the mid-90s, under the guidance of M. Wynn Thomas, Sally Roberts Jones and Nesta Wyn Jones, it was decided to press for the creation of an Encyclopaedia which would embrace the culture and achievements of one of Europe's oldest nations. Funded by the Arts Council of Wales through a significant Lottery grant, and with the support of Lottery Director Richard Turner, the foundations were laid for what has subsequently become a risk-taking, all-embracing and ultimately successful ten-year project.

The project began in 1998, when Yr Academi Gymreig was reformed and enlarged as the Welsh National Literature Promotion Agency and Society of Writers and I was appointed as Chief Executive. John Davies, Menna Baines and Nigel Jenkins were appointed editors, later to be joined by Peredur I. Lynch. Kevin Thomas, the old Academy's English section director in charge of the original funding application, became project manager. They were overseen by an Encyclopaedia management committee chaired by Brynley F. Roberts. After the project manager and committee completed their work, further detailed monitoring was undertaken by Tony Bianchi. Were it not for the commitment and enthusiasm of all these individuals, the project would not have borne fruit. Thanks are also due to the many others involved with the project: to Peter Tyndall, Chief Executive of the Arts Council of Wales, for his support in many difficult moments; to the Academi's Management Board, under its joint chairs Harri Pritchard Jones and John Pikoulis, for maintaining belief; to the staff of the Academi for managing the Encyclopaedia's complex and at times frustratingly difficult finances and organization; to Robin Gwyn, of the National Museum Wales, for his help with the project's education arm; to Susan Jenkins and her successor Ashley Drake, directors of the University of Wales Press, for their encouragement, and to the universities at Swansea and Bangor for providing editorial and other resources. Most of all, we wish to thank the editors. With painstaking attention to detail and flair and imagination, they have brought an important work into being.

PETER FINCH
Academi Chief Executive

ACADEMIC PARTNERS

hybu llên • literature promotion

Ysgol y Gymraeg / School of Welsh

Centre for Research into the English Literature
and Language of Wales

PRINCIPAL SPONSORS

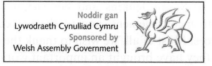

CORPORATE SPONSORS

www.icwales.co.uk

www.uwic.ac.uk

PUBLISHER'S NOTE

The *Welsh Academy Encyclopaedia of Wales* is a landmark publication for Wales and for the University of Wales Press, presenting to the people of Wales one of the largest and most important projects in the history of UWP. As it now, finally, sees the light of day I would like to take this opportunity to express my appreciation of the excellent working relationship that has developed between us and Yr Academi Gymreig, and in particular the latter's able and resourceful chief executive, Peter Finch.

I take this opportunity also to note the important role played by those who govern the University of Wales Press. UWP's management board has enthusiastically supported the project from the outset, and I thank in particular the three individuals who have chaired the board during the past decade – M. Wynn Thomas, Emyr Jenkins and Philip Allan. If ever the adage that an organization's greatest resource is its people needed to be proven, then this project has surely done so. The dedication and commitment of the UWP staff to this project, and their sustained enthusiasm for it, have been unfailing.

As the project has evolved, the Encyclopaedia has become a far more 'visual' proposition than it was originally, with inclusion of a greater number of images than first intended and the decision to publish, where possible, in colour. With each change has come the attendant increase in cost in order to make the Encyclopaedia the truly unique publication that it is: the corporate organizations opposite have all helped make those changes possible through their generous sponsorship of the book. The volume here presented embodies the commitment of the University of Wales Press to publishing work of the highest quality, and its commitment to Wales. I am delighted to affirm that these commitments are as central to our mission today as they were at our founding in 1922.

ASHLEY DRAKE
Director, University of Wales Press

THE ENCYCLOPAEDIA OF WALES

CO-EDITORS
John Davies, Nigel Jenkins, Menna Baines, Peredur I. Lynch

ASSISTANT EDITOR
Janet Davies

CHAIRMAN OF THE *ENCYCLOPAEDIA OF WALES* MANAGEMENT COMMITTEE
Brynley F. Roberts

Editorial Consultants and Advisers

(Those whose names are italicized, we regret to say, have since died.)

Jane Aaron
Douglas A. Bassett
Dave Berry
Kay Byrne
Stuart Cole
Hazel Walford Davies
Janet Davies
Tom Davies
Patrick Dobbs
Hywel Teifi Edwards
Dyfed Elis-Gruffydd

Meredydd Evans
Neville Evans
Trevor Herbert
John B. Hilling
W. Penri James
Dafydd Jenkins
J. Geraint Jenkins
Gareth Elwyn Jones
Emma Lile
Ceridwen Lloyd-Morgan

Hugh McKay
D. Densil Morgan
David Morris
Osi Rhys Osmond
Trefor M. Owen
Dylan Phillips
Glyn O. Phillips
Adam Price
Brynley F. Roberts
J. Beverley Smith
Peter Stead

Terry Stevens
Mared Wyn Sutherland
Arthur Thomas
Phil Thomas
Roy Thomas
Huw Walters
Gareth W. Williams
John Llewelyn Williams
L. John Williams
Phil Williams

Contributors

Jane Aaron
Rufus Adams
Pat Aithie
A. M. Allchin
David Allsobrook
Margaret Ames
Felix Aubel
Colin Baber
Menna Baines
John Barnie

Mario Basini
Douglas A. Bassett
Mike G. Bassett
T. M. Bassett
David Bateman
Hywel Bebb
Richard Bebb
Deirdre Beddoe
Martin Bell
Tom Bennett

Dave Berry
Gareth A. Bevan
Richard E. Bevins
D. Q. Bowen
Trevor Boyns
Peter Brabham
Mike Bridges
Gillian Bristow
Mariska van den Broek
Ian Brookfield

Duncan Brown
Roger L. Brown
M. Paul Bryant-Quinn
Kay Byrne
Ewen Cameron
Anthony D. Carr
Glenda Carr
Harold Carter
Richard Carter
Jane Cartwright
Nickie Charles
Lesley Cherns
Stuart Cole
Noel Cross
Richard Crowe
John Cule
Menna Cunningham
Dafydd Dafis
Lyn Lewis Dafis
Iestyn Daniel
Richard Daugherty
Rhys David
Aled Lloyd Davies
Brian Davies
Ceri Davies
Charlotte Aull Davies
Gwilym Prys Davies
Hazel Walford Davies
Hywel Davies
J. Reuben Davies
Janet Davies
John Davies
John Davies (Llandysul)
Ken Davies
Lyn Davies
Roy Davies
Tom Davies
David Dixon
Patrick Dobbs
Norman Doe
Ben Dressel
Catherine Duigan
David Dykes
Hywel Teifi Edwards
John Edwards
Nancy Edwards
Tony Edwards
David Egan
Twm Elias
Dyfed Elis-Gruffydd
Osian Ellis
Susan Ellis

Dafydd Huw Evans
Dan Evans
David Evans
Dylan Foster Evans
John Evans
Meredydd Evans
Neil Evans
Neville Evans
R. Alun Evans
Martyn Farr
Martin Fitzpatrick
Hywel Francis
Paddy French
Angela Gaffney
Mike Gash
Walford Gealy
Noel Gibbard
Terence Gilmore-James
Brian Glover
Jon Gower
Graham Greaves
Mike Greenow
William Greenway
Gwilym Griffith
W. P. Griffith
Bruce Griffiths
Matthew Griffiths
Ralph A. Griffiths
Rhidian Griffiths
Rhodri Griffiths
T. Elwyn Griffiths
Russell Grigg
Eirlys Gruffydd
R. Geraint Gruffydd
David Gwyn
Elinor Gwyn
William Haresign
Sally Harper
Tristan Hatton-Ellis
John Hefin
Trevor Herbert
Sarah Hill
John B. Hilling
Rhisiart Hincks
Deian Hopkin
Tony Howard
David Howell
Ray Howell
Brian Howells
Glyn Tegai Hughes
Heather Hughes
Iestyn Hughes

J. Elwyn Hughes
Lynn Hughes
R. Elwyn Hughes
Trystan Hughes
Pat Humphreys
Daniel Huws
Gwilym Huws
Richard Huws
Allan James
E. Wyn James
Penri James
Siân James
Watcyn James
Branwen Jarvis
Angharad Jenkins
Branwen Jenkins
Colin Jenkins
Dafydd Jenkins
Geraint H. Jenkins
Gwyn Jenkins
J. Geraint Jenkins
Nigel Jenkins
Myrddin John
Martin Johnes
Colin Johnson
Howard Johnson
Caroline Joll
Aled Gruffydd Jones
Alun Gwynedd Jones
Barbara Jones
Barrie Jones
Bill Jones
Dafydd Glyn Jones
David Jones
David Ceri Jones
Dot Jones
Emrys Jones
Gareth Elwyn Jones
Glyn Saunders Jones
Hefin Jones
Ilid Ann Jones
J. Anthony J. Jones
J. Graham Jones
J. Gwynfor Jones
Meinir Llwyd Jones
R. Merfyn Jones
Nerys Ann Jones
O. R. Jones
Peter Jones
Peter Hope Jones
Philip Henry Jones
R. Brinley Jones

Sally Roberts Jones
Tecwyn Vaughan Jones
Tegwyn Jones
Phyllis Kinney
Bernard Knight
David Lambert
Gwyneth Lewis
Lisa Lewis
Emma Lile
William Linnard
Dafydd Llewelyn
Dewi M. Lloyd
Nesta Lloyd
Ceridwen Lloyd-Morgan
Cen Llwyd
Rheinallt Llwyd
Marion Löffler
John Lovering
Roy Lowe
Frances Lynch
Peredur I. Lynch
Hugh Mackay
Gwenan Mared
E. Gwynn Matthews
Hugh Matthews
Danny McCaroll
Alec McKinty
Mandy McMath
Ruth Meadows
Eddie Melen
Pamela Michael
Peter Midmore
Bethan Miles
Dillwyn Miles
E. G. Millward
John Minkes
Richard Moore-Colyer
Matt Morden
D. Densil Morgan
Gerald Morgan
John Morgan
Kevin Morgan
Moc Morgan
Prys Morgan
Delyth Morgans
Bernard Morris
Gwyn Morris
Gerallt Nash
Jonathan Neale
Robert Nisbet
Keith Nurse
Paul O'Leary

John Osmond
Osi Rhys Osmond
Arwel Ellis Owen
Buddug Owen
D. Huw Owen
Goronwy P. Owen
Hywel Wyn Owen
Morfydd E. Owen
Trefor M. Owen
Stuart Owen-Jones
Bob Owens
Malcolm Parr
Bryn Parri
Harri Parri
Gwyn Parry
Malcolm Parry
R. Gwynedd Parry
R. Palmer Parry
Matthew Pearson
Jim Perrin
Allen Perry
Dewi Z. Phillips
Dylan Phillips
Robert Pope
David Powell
Nia Watkin Powell
W. Eifion Powell
David Pretty
Geraint Price
Richard D. Price
William Price
Huw Pryce
Richard D. Pryce
W. T. Rees Pryce
Barbara Prys-Williams
Glyn Pursglove
Peter Read
Phil Rees
Stephen Rees
Peter Rhind
Rhobert ap Steffan
Martin Rhys
Robert Rhys
Huw Richards
Alun Roberts
Alwyn Roberts
Bob Roberts
Brynley F. Roberts
Geraint Roberts
Glyn Roberts
Hywel E. Roberts
Tom Roberts

Paul Robertshaw
Dilwyn Roberts-Young
Gordon Roderick
Dyfed Rowlands
John Rowlands
Mike Ryan
D. Roy Saer
Austin Savage
Tom Sharpe
John Shorey
Chris Shumack
Michael Siddons
Pwyll ap Siôn
John Skone
Roy Sloan
Llinos Smith
Robert Smith
Jill Stallard
Peter Stead
Meic Stephens
Catrin Stevens
Christine Stevens
Terry Stevens
Ann Stone
Mike Sullivan
Mared Wyn Sutherland
Mick Tems
Alan R. Thomas
Arthur Thomas
Claire Thomas
Dennis Thomas
Graham C. G. Thomas
Gwyn Thomas
John Thomas
Kevin Thomas
M. Wynn Thomas
Patrick Thomas
Phil Thomas
Roger Thomas
Roy Thomas
Wyn Thomas
Steven Thompson
Geraint Tudur
Bob Turner
Richard Twining
Norman Vetter
Huw Walters
Thomas Glyn Watkin
Andrew Weltch
Eurwyn Wiliam
Mary Wiliam
Cathrin Williams

Chris Williams
Cyril Williams
David H. Williams
Gareth W. Williams
Gareth Haulfryn Williams
Gareth Vaughan Williams
George Campbell Williams
Glanmor Williams
Gruffydd Aled Williams
Herbert Williams

Huw Williams
Huw Glyn Williams
Ioan Williams
Iolo Williams
Iolo Wyn Williams
J. Gwynn Williams
John Williams
John Llewelyn Williams
L. John Williams
Lyndon Williams

Mari Angharad Williams
Mel Williams
Merfyn Williams
Phil Williams
William Jones Williams
Jen Wilson
Romilly Witts
Juliette Wood
Alex Woolf
Goronwy Wynne

INTRODUCTION AND ACKNOWLEDGEMENTS

The appearance of an encyclopaedia that aspires to encapsulate a country's material, natural and cultural essence is a significant – and sometimes controversial – event in the life of any nation. As Wales voted, hesitantly, for a future in the devolution referendum of 1997, the Welsh Academy was preparing to produce a pioneering work of reference – in both English and Welsh editions – that would take its place alongside *The Dictionary of Welsh Biography* (published first in Welsh in 1953), *The Companion to the Literature of Wales* (1986), *Geiriadur Prifysgol Cymru* (1950–2002), *The Welsh Academy English–Welsh Dictionary* (1995) and *The Buildings of Wales* (1979–) as a major building block of the resurgent nation. If Welsh historians, during much of the later 20th century, had been asking 'When was Wales?', it would be the task of this encyclopaedia in the early 21st century to answer the question, 'What is Wales?'.

Intended for the general reader, this book keeps in mind the kind of enquiry likely to arise among both Welsh people and those from other countries with an interest in the country, and it tries to maintain a balance between national subjects and those of more regional or local appeal. Although it contains material that has never before been published, this encyclopaedia, like most similar compendiums, synthesizes rather than extends existing scholarship. Occasionally, where interest in a topic is likely to be comparatively restricted, or where material has proved resistant to simple paraphrase, contributors have addressed themselves a little more to specialists, but this encyclopaedia has been designed mainly for readers requiring accessible information on any aspect of Wales and Welsh life, past and present – not only the nation's people and places, but its history and languages, its arts, religions, organizations, social movements, industries, politics, sports, pastimes and continuing traditions.

There are two kinds of national encyclopaedia. The earlier – following the example of Ephraim Chambers's *Cyclopaedia* (1728), the 'father of modern encyclopaedias' whose work was massively developed by Abraham Rees in the later 18th century – belongs to that period, 1850–1930, when encyclopaedias were published that communicated a particular country's interpretation of the world in general, often as a demonstration of that country's sophistication and maturity. Wales produced such an encyclopaedia in the 10-volume *Y Gwyddoniadur Cymreig* (The Welsh Encyclopaedia; 1854–79); this work of nearly 9000 pages, which was edited by Thomas Gee (1815–98) and John Parry (1812–74), is the longest publication ever to have appeared in Welsh. During the same period, Owen Jones (1806–89) edited the 2-volume *Cymru: yn Hanesyddol, Parthedegol a Bywgraphyddol* (Wales: Historical, Topographical and Biographical; 1871–5), a national encyclopaedia of the other kind, which – appearing from the late 19th century onwards – dealt exclusively with a particular nation or region.

Such developments led eventually to the publication of encyclopaedias devoted to individual cities or towns, of which the sole Welsh example to date is W. Alister Williams's *The Encyclopaedia of Wrexham* (2001). Many city encyclopaedias are considerably more expansive than this volume, which has had to squeeze the long and complicated story of an entire nation into little more than 720,000 words. Work began in January 1999, with Nigel Jenkins chiefly responsible for editing the English version, and Menna Baines chiefly responsible for the Welsh; John Davies, engaged initially as editorial consultant, became a full editor in 2002, and Peredur I. Lynch, who had been involved as a consultant from the outset, and who had contributed greatly in an unofficial capacity, joined the editorial team in 2005. The first task was to divide Wales into 36 subject categories, each with its own list of entries – agriculture; transport; food and drink; visual culture; music, and so forth – one of which, human environment, was sub-divided into 29 regional lists of places. With a set number of words allocated to each list, and assisted by our editorial consultants, we began the fiddly, painstaking business of selecting our entries and deciding, one by one, how many words to accord them and who might write them. Occasionally, to the editors' delight, a contributor would take on all or most of the entries in a subject category, but more often the lists were divided between dozens of hands, rendering the commissioning process (and the associated chasing up of our more leisurely contributors) the most protracted aspect of the project. Eventually, the products of these scores of lists were decanted into a single, straightforward A to Z; while this, inevitably, precludes the close grouping of related topics, except by alphabetical accident, we hope that the resulting contiguity on the page of sometimes surprising neighbours may delight both the casual browser and the intent researcher. Although each entry is intended to be self-contained and readable without recourse to other information, our cross-referencing system, explained in the Reader's Guide, alerts the reader to related topics. A degree of overlap is unavoidable in an encyclopaedia of this kind, sometimes with information presented from different viewpoints. Where matters of fact are concerned, we have striven to be clear and unambiguous, although when referring to certain rare or endangered species we have maintained a protective vagueness as to exact locations. Matters of interpretation, however, may be personal to individual authors; while, as editors, we may not necessarily endorse them, we have preferred to allow their expression rather than attempt to impose on a subject a possibly spurious sense of coherence or consistency.

Although the encyclopaedia aims to be as comprehensive as possible, both in its selection of subjects and in its treatment of them, we acknowledge the impossibility of treating them exhaustively. Some subjects have been extensively treated elsewhere: the literary arts, for instance, may be explored at length in *The Companion to the Literature of Wales*, and the biographies of notable individuals and families are available in *The Dictionary of Welsh Biography* and its supplements, and in *The Oxford Dictionary of National Biography* (2004), in far greater detail than is possible here. Other subjects, such as science, which habitually has been overlooked in general accounts of Welsh culture, are accorded, for the first time in a conspectus of this nature, the attention that has long been their due. With reluctance, we have often had to allow constraints of space to rule out an entry, but only rarely, in pursuit of material in the more abstruse subject fields, have we failed to find someone equipped with the necessary expertise to provide an entry, obliging us therefore to omit an item we had considered important.

Mindful of the notorious imbalance in most encyclopaedias between entries for males and females (the sole entry on woman in *Britannica*'s first edition, 'WOMAN, the female of man. See HOMO.', is all too reminiscent of a subsequent *Britannica*'s famously disdainful 'For Wales, see England'), we have tried throughout to redeem women from the condescension of history, while eschewing the dubious inclusiveness effected by 'positive discrimination'. Nevertheless, the proportion of female entries remains lamentably low, and we invite suggestions from those who will judge that we have not tried hard enough, so that in a new edition women may be represented more fully.

The encyclopaedist's fundamental problem is one of selection: what to include, what to exclude, where and how to draw the line? If a subjective element is inevitable, too great a reliance on a sense of the 'numinous' or the 'resonant' is likely to frustrate and confuse the reader more than it enlightens. Therefore, as we made our choices, we devised, and endeavoured to abide by, certain criteria, in an attempt to achieve balance and objectivity, while leaving the door ajar for the expression of opinion and for the occasional flight of selector's fancy. There are three main classes of entry: people, places and topics.

Biographical entries are restricted to the dead, celebrity often proving transitory, but the living may nevertheless gain entry 'by the back door': it would be bizarre, for instance, to treat pop music without mention of Shirley Bassey, or devolution without reference to Ron Davies. Individuals, or families, have been selected on the basis of Welsh provenance or association, so that a Welshman such as Richard Burton who made his career largely outside the country, while making an unmistakeable impression at home, is as entitled to an entry as, say, the English-born railway engineer Isambard Kingdom Brunel, whose activities in Wales made a significant impact. Personages who, though born in Wales, achieved prominence in entirely non-Welsh contexts, and celebrities 'of Welsh descent', such as the American architect Frank Lloyd Wright, may be mentioned in passing but are rarely accorded an entry. In one field – science – there are exceptions to this rule. In order to encourage an appreciation of Wales's significant but generally neglected contribution to science and technology, we have been more hospitable than usual to those of 'Welsh background and English foreground', acknowledging that until comparatively recently Welsh people aspiring to a career in science usually have had to leave the country in order to fulfil their ambitions in what is a notably international pursuit. The production schedule determined that from the mid summer of 2007 there could be no further additions to the text; it is with regret, therefore, that we have been unable to update certain entries and to include entries on distinguished Welsh people such as Roland Mathias (1915–2007), Sir Tasker Watkins (1918–2007) and Ray Gravell (1951–2007) who died after that watershed.

Topographical entries include the more prominent mountains and mountain ranges, and major landmarks and thoroughfares such as Offa's Dyke and the M4. Institutions of national significance, such as the University of Wales or the National Library, have their own entries, but landscape features such as castles, churches, ancient monuments, historic houses, bridges and theatres are generally to be found under the entries for the cities, towns or communities in which they are situated. Space also had to be found for a small selection of places outside Wales – such as *Yr Hen Ogledd* (The Old North), the other Celtic countries, London, North America, Patagonia, the Khasi Hills – which have figured prominently in the Welsh experience, or where the Welsh have played a significant role.

Many patently Welsh topics, from the Eisteddfod to Welsh cakes, selected themselves for inclusion. Greater difficulties attended the selection of those with more widespread application. With subjects such as socialism, for instance, or the Bronze Age, we have made no attempt at the kind of all-embracing histories and definitions that are readily available in general books of reference; rather, we have sought to concentrate on the specifically Welsh dimensions of such topics. The constant need to be selective faced us with some particularly problematic if not uncomfortable choices: a mining accident is no less a disaster for the individuals and families involved if one person is killed than if 150 lose their lives, but the encyclopaedist's perennial obligation 'to draw the line' has meant that with subjects such as colliery disasters, shipwrecks and aviation accidents we have been able to devote solo entries only to the very 'worst', which is to say those which are unusual of their kind, in which the death toll was exceptionally high. A happier task was to devise criteria for the inclusion of subjects such as works of creativity and the imagination: it was decided that books, paintings and buildings, for instance, would normally be referred to under the names of those responsible for them, while a deciding factor for the inclusion of a representative selection of songs, hymns, and radio and television programmes would be their relative popularity. We cannot claim to have devised entirely logical or consistent criteria for inclusion, but we hope that as users of the Encyclopaedia find their way around the book they will develop a feel for the principles of its organization; resort to the index should solve most problems.

In a work of this nature, it is inevitable that as editors we have been obliged to rewrite, in whole or in part, a majority of the entries we commissioned, chiefly to reduce the incidence of repetition or of obvious contradiction, and to ensure clarity of expression. In addition, we have had frequently to update material submitted to us, particularly in view of the years that have elapsed between the commissioning stage and the period in which the entries were given their final shape. We have attempted also to achieve stylistic consistency, although seamless harmonization of style is impossible in a work with nearly 400 contributors.

The English and Welsh editions of this Encyclopaedia are basically parallel texts, differing mainly in the alphabetical arrangement of their content and in the provision, throughout the English edition, of an element of translation – of quotations, place names or song titles, for instance, or of items such as 'Hen Wlad fy Nhadau', the national anthem.

As editors our debts are far and wide. We are grateful to Philip Gwyn Jones, formerly of HarperCollins, who first proposed an encyclopaedia of Wales, and who pursued the development of the project with such enthusiasm, until, on his departure from HarperCollins, the University of Wales Press took on responsibility for publishing the English volume. We wish to thank the Welsh Academy, which instigated and managed the *Encyclopaedia of Wales* project, for the opportunity of editing this book, and the Academy's executive committee and ever-attentive staff for seeing through this challenging project on the managerial, financial and administrative levels. We are deeply indebted to our willing team of editorial consultants and specialist advisers, who in many cases gave freely of their expertise, and to our nearly 400 authors, without whose knowledge and enthusiasm the project would have been inconceivable. Of comparable importance has been Janet Davies who, in the later stages of the project, was engaged as assistant editor.

There are many others who contributed in less obvious but nevertheless vital ways. To acknowledge every one of them is almost as impossible as it would be to repay them, but we could not have compiled this encyclopaedia without the dozens of people who gave generously of their time, suggestions and special knowledge, and we list below the more prominent of them.

M. Wynn Thomas, director of the Centre for Research into the English Literature and Language of Wales, in the Department of English, University of Wales Swansea (Swansea University), who, with his departmental heads, the late Ian Bell and, subsequently, Robert Penhallurick and Neil Reeve, provided the Encyclopaedia with a rent-free office in Swansea, together with considerable help with office expenses. Nigel Jenkins in particular is profoundly grateful to the English Department staff for their warm welcome; to the departmental secretaries Gabriella Wasiniak, Ann Evans, Sandra Beynon and Kathryn Richards for their friendly and unstinting support; and to the Library Information Service's Trevor Evans for his diligent trouble-shooting of technical problems.

Branwen H. Jarvis, formerly of the University of Wales, Bangor, who instigated arrangements for the provision of a rent-free office in the School of Welsh for the Encyclopaedia project. Menna Baines is grateful to the School's secretaries, Gwyneth Williams and Kirsty Haston, and to her neighbours during her stay at the college, the staff of the Social Sciences School's Centre for Applied Community Studies for many a favour, in particular the Centre's administrators, Adrienne Hebenstreit and Lynda Jones. Thanks are also due to the Information Services Department, whose technicians provided assistance on many occasions. During the 2006–7 academic year, Peredur I. Lynch was released from all teaching and administrative duties in the School of Welsh in order to persevere on this project, and he is grateful to Gerwyn Wiliams for facilitating that arrangement.

Einion W. Thomas, Archivist and Welsh Librarian at the University of Wales, Bangor, whose guidance, in relation to Bangor's rich collections of Welsh material, went well beyond the call of duty.

The academic staff of both the University of Wales Swansea and the University of Wales, Bangor, who gave generously of their scholarly advice and expertise. The staff of the National Library of Wales and of the Library of the University of Wales, Aberystwyth, to whom John Davies is particularly indebted. John Davies, who was originally based at Aberystwyth and later in Cardiff, provided his own office space.

The distinguished encyclopaedist David Crystal, who gave us invaluable methodological guidance in the early days of the project.

Roy Morgan of Mertec Evesham Ltd, Swansea, who kindly loaned the project a laptop computer.

Special thanks are due to: Kevin Thomas, our project manager and picture editor in the early years; Tony Bianchi, project monitor for a period; and Brynley F. Roberts, chairman of the encyclopaedia management committee. We thank the directors of the University of Wales Press, Susan Jenkins and her successor Ashley Drake, and the press's editorial staff – Matthew Cory for HarperCollins, initially, and subsequently for the University of Wales Press, Ruth Dennis-Jones, Dafydd Jones, Eira Fenn Gaunt, Nicky Roper and Siân Chapman (production management) and Sue Charles (picture research) among others – for their painstaking attentiveness; we are also grateful to Stuart Booth (project manager at the production stage) and team for their work on the English edition, as well as to Anna Ratcliffe, of the University of Wales Swansea, for drawing most of the original maps which appear in the book, and to Alun Ceri Jones for their meticulous preparation for publication. The final index is the result of painstaking labour on the part of Janet Davies, with the assistance of Hannah Austin and Alwen Lloyd-Wynne at Merrall-Ross.

We acknowledge with gratitude the National Museum Wales (for the Geological Time Scale table), Gwasg Gomer and the estate of Waldo Williams (for permission to reproduce his *englyn*), Emyr Lewis (for permission to quote from his poetry), and Meic Stephens for permission to quote from the poetry of Harri Webb. We also received valuable assistance or suggestions and advice from Amanda Bentley of Weatherbys, Neil ap Jones, Alun Davies (Wrexham), John Davies (Brecon), John Eirug Davies, Jasmine Donahaye, Andrew Dulley, Miranda Aldhouse-Green, Llŷr D. Gruffydd, Clive Hughes, Martyn Jenkins, Emyr Lewis, Evan Lynch, John May, Dai Michael, Myrddin ap Dafydd, the Office of National Statistics, Morgan Parry, Pamela Petro, Patrick Sims-Williams, Dei Tomos, Deri Tomos, Geraint Vaughan (Manchester), Daniel Williams, O. Arthur Williams, Rol Williams, Romilly Witts – and from the many people who wrote in or telephoned their recommendations for entries. We thank them all.

Anyone who has had the misfortune of being in close proximity to an encyclopaedist will know that these unfortunate creatures are fixated obsessives with no apparent interest in anything other than the encyclopaedic task in hand: food is an afterthought, sleep an irrelevance; the headword, the cross-reference, the word-count is all. Our families and friends have been remarkably tolerant of our implacable monomania during the ten years it took us to produce this book, and we thank them warmly for their patience and understanding, which have sustained and encouraged us throughout.

Although every one of the 720,000 or so words of this book has been read and re-read by the editorial team, it is certain to contain errors. The editors accept responsibility for them all, and for any inconsistencies or omissions, and ask that corrections and suggestions for any future edition be sent to them at the Welsh Academy, Mount Stuart House, Mount Stuart Square, Cardiff CF10 5FQ.

JOHN DAVIES
NIGEL JENKINS
MENNA BAINES
PEREDUR I. LYNCH

envolopasade task in hand; food is an afterthought; sleep an irrelevance; the household, the cross-reference, the word-count is all. Our families and friends have been remarkably tolerant of our implacable monomania during the ten years it took us to produce this book, and we thank them warmly for their patience and understanding which have sustained and encouraged us throughout.

Although every one of the 73[...] entries or words of this book has been read and re-read by the editorial team, it is certain to contain errors. The editors accept responsibility for them all, and for any incompleteness or omissions, and ask that corrections and suggestions for any future edition be sent to them at the Welsh Academy, Mount Stuart House, Mount Stuart Square, Cardiff CF10 5FQ.

John Davies
Nigel Jenkins
Menna Baines
Peredur I. Lynch

READER'S GUIDE

Readers unfamiliar with the country and those who would appreciate an orientating résumé of Welsh history are recommended to read the entry for **Wales, The history of** (Wales is a word, incidentally, that occurs so frequently in the text that, after this occasion, it does not appear in bold letters).

The entries are arranged alphabetically, with some 3300 subjects appearing under their own headwords in the main body of the book. To compensate for the artificiality of an alphabetical ordering of subjects, the encyclopaedia is equipped with a comprehensive index and a cross-referencing system, which should enable readers to pursue related topics and to locate references in the text to subjects that are not accorded solo entry status. The index gives page reference to people, places, events and topics; references to individual entries are in bold (note that references are bolded in this Reader's Guide). When, in the body of an entry, a reference is made to a subject dealt with separately in its own right, the first use of the word signifying that subject is printed in bold letters. In the English edition, we have adopted a policy of 'approximate bolding', whereby the word bolded in the text is in some cases similar but not identical to the headword to which it refers: sometimes, for instance, an adjective such as **Norman** might be bolded in order to alert the reader to the headword plural noun, **Normans**, or a word such as **iron**works might be partially bolded in order to direct the reader to the entry for **Iron and Steel**; plural forms of words such as *cantrefi* and **mints** have been fully bolded, although the headwords to which they refer take the singular form. Readers should be alert to the possibility of a bolded phrase referring to more than one entry, as in **Snowdonia National Park**, which contains cross-references to both **Snowdonia** and **National Parks**. Where an approximate bolding is impractical, but an element of cross-referencing is desirable, the relevant connection is indicated in brackets, for example: 'The Welsh **Slate** Museum (*see* **National Museum of Wales**)'.

The names of species of animals and **plants** are usually given in **English** only, unless confusion over vernacular terminology – as, for instance, sometimes occurs with the sewin or migratory sea trout (L. *Salmo trutta*) – calls for **Latin** to arbitrate on an ambiguity. A name in **Welsh** is occasionally given if it adds interest.

For pre-1971 census figures, in entries such as that on **population**, we follow **L. John Williams**'s (1929–2004) *Digest of Welsh Historical Statistics* (2 vols, 1985).

BIOGRAPHICAL ENTRIES

Most of the biographical entries relate to individuals or families, but there are also entries for a small selection of legendary and fictitious characters. Some (usually brief) biographies are grouped together – for instance, **English Monarchs and Wales** (an entry to which readers should refer when they require further information on English monarchs named elsewhere in the book) – and limited biographical information may be found, via the index, in entries on topics other than people. Biographical entries are normally headed by the subject's surname, followed by forename(s), pseudonyms if applicable, years of birth and death, and the subject's profession or primary claim to fame. Patronymic forms of name, especially those using '*ap*' or '*ab*' (meaning 'son of') or '*ferch*' (daughter), as in **Dafydd ap Gwilym** and (the fictitious) **Branwen ferch Ll}r** – which were common prior to the **Tudor** era and which have survived to some extent into modern times – are kept intact as indissoluble wholes, and listed under the initial letter of the first name. The same principle applies to personal names which include descriptive elements, for example **Llywelyn Bren** and **Iorwerth Drwyndwn**, and to the names of all legendary and fictitious characters, such as **Johnny Onions** and **Dic Siôn Dafydd**. Some personal names, such as Gruffudd or Llywelyn, have undergone changes over time, and readers having difficulty finding, say, the Gruffudd they are pursuing are advised to try variant spellings such as Gruffydd or Griffith. Titles, such as Professor, Lord, Sir, Brigadier, Dame, are not used in headwords, although aristocratic families may be further defined as, for instance, **Stuart family, marquesses of Bute** or **Somerset family, dukes of Beaufort**. When several landed families share the same surname, the name of the family estate is added, as in **Vaughan family (Llwydiarth)** and **Vaughan family (Trawsgoed)**.

With the exception of celebrities from the world of entertainment, such as **Ivor Novello** (b. David Ivor Davies) or **Ray Milland** (b. Reginald Truscott-Jones), who are known universally by the names they adopted for professional reasons, birth names are used for the headwords of the many poets, musicians and others who, according to ancient custom, have acquired pseudonyms or bardic titles. Some, such as Iolo Morganwg (**Edward Williams**) or the pirate Barti Ddu (**Bartholomew Roberts**), are undoubtedly better known by their pseudonyms than by their birth names, but more, probably, are not. A 'grading' system, whereby the better known figures were entered under their pseudonyms and the lesser ones under their birth names, would depend to some extent on subjective judgement and would lead to greater confusion than our policy of giving precedence to birth names in almost all headwords and providing an index to help readers find, say, the harpist Pencerdd Gwalia under **John Thomas** (1826–1913). In the case of eminent figures from the world of sport who are usually known by abbreviated forms of their birth names, the abbreviated form is given first in the headword, followed by the full name in brackets, for example **MEREDITH, Billy (William Henry Meredith)** or **MURPHY, Jimmy (James Patrick Murphy)**.

Individuals with distinctive names, such as **Sarah Jacob**, need no additional identification when they are bolded for cross-referencing purposes, but because of Wales's plethora of identical names, we normally distinguish one bolded John Thomas from another by appending birth and death dates. Dates may also be added to bolded names in order to indicate the period under consideration. Headwords relating to persons with identical names appear in order of the persons' birth.

TOPOGRAPHICAL REFERENCES

The most logical, if by no means perfect, solution to the problem of deciding which places deserve entries was to accord an entry to every officially designated **community** in Wales, of which there were 869 in 2007. (Wales's civil **parish**es, traditionally the lowest tier of local **government**, were abolished in 1974.) Although, in most cases, a **place-name** entry is concerned with a single community, readers should bear in mind that the towns of **Pontypool** and **Cwmbran** consist of a group of communities and that the towns themselves have no existence as local government units. Thus the entries for those two places begin with an explanation of the communities that constitute them. A similar policy has been followed with regard to the **Rhondda**, which, since the local government reorganization of 1996, consists of a group of communities within the **county borough** of **Rhondda Cynon Taff**. There are communities called **Aberavon**, **Baglan**, **Bridgend**, **Caerphilly** and **Port Talbot**, but the entries under those names are also concerned with communities which are essentially suburbs of those five centres of population. Furthermore, although there are **counties** called **Newport**, **Swansea** and **Wrexham**, the cities of Newport and Swansea and the town of Wrexham form only a part of those counties; thus, the entries under those headwords are concerned with the group of communities which essentially constituted Newport, Swansea and Wrexham as they were before the local government reorganization of 1974. The communities which make up the county boroughs of **Cardiff** and **Merthyr Tydfil** do not have separate entries, but do have sub-entries within the Cardiff and Merthyr Tydfil entries; this is also the case with all the other entries which concern more than one community. It should be borne in mind that community boundaries, like those of counties, are not set in stone and are subject to change; the county **maps** show the counties and their communities as they were in 2001; the figures for hectarage, the number of inhabitants per community and other relevant statistics are also those for 2001.

The names and shapes of the counties of Wales, some of which date from the late 13th century and others from the **Act of 'Union'** of 1536, were radically altered by local government reorganization in 1974, and again in 1996. Institutions such as the **University of Wales** have undergone comparable changes over the years (although the production schedule prevented us from incorporating changes which occurred in September 2007). Where places and institutions are referred to in a present-day context, we use the present names, but in an historical context we use the names contemporaneous with the period, followed where necessary with the modern equivalent in brackets. Thus, we state that **Richard Price** was born in 1723 in the parish of Llangeinor in the county of **Glamorgan**, although his birthplace is today located within the community of **Garw Valley** in the county borough of Bridgend. By the same token, **Saunders Lewis** taught at University College, Swansea in the 1920s and 1930s, not at the **University of Wales Swansea**, as the institution was later known (it had become Swansea University by September 2007).

The days when signposts and Ordnance Survey maps used spellings such as Llandilo, Aberayron, Dolgelley and Treorky have mercifully passed, but some Anglicized spellings – **Ruthin** (W. Rhuthun), **Crickhowell** (W. Crucywel), **Denbigh** (W. Dinbych) – remain the preferred option for many, and some English place names, such as Mumbles (W. Mwmbwls), are more 'original' than the Welsh. In the Welsh-language edition of this encyclopaedia, we have followed the spellings provided by **Elwyn Davies** in his *Gazetteer of Welsh Place-Names* (3rd edition, 1967). In the English-language edition, we have with a few exceptions followed the current usage of the census and the Ordnance Survey. In headwords, English forms of place name are followed, where appropriate, by the Welsh forms in brackets. The Ordnance Survey has been working, in conjunction with Professor Hywel Wyn Owen of the School of Welsh at the **University of Wales, Bangor**, to standardize place names on Ordnance Survey maps; unfortunately, we have not been able to avail ourselves of the findings of this on-going and invaluable work, although they would, of course, find reflection in any future edition of this encyclopaedia.

STYLISTIC CONVENTIONS, DATES, MEASUREMENTS AND ABBREVIATIONS

The titles of books, plays, **newspapers**, **periodicals**, manuscripts, **films**, radio and television programmes, **paintings**, **sculptures** and long **music**al compositions are given in italics, as are those of **ships**. The titles of songs, **hymns** and poems (apart from long poems) are given in inverted commas. Where there is a straightforward translation of a Welsh term in a headword or in the text of an entry, it is given in parentheses after the term; if it is a literal translation, it is superseded by the abbreviation 'lit.'.

The familiar dating convention of BC and AD, rather than that of BCE and CE, is used where applicable. Where there is uncertainty about a date, we place a question mark before it thus, ?1749. An italicised '*c*.', for the Latin *circa*, before a date – as in *c.*1749 – means 'in about' or 'around' that year. A 'b.' before a date – as in b.1749 – means 'born' and a 'd.' means 'died'. Where a person's exact birth dates and death dates are not known, 'fl.', meaning flourished, is added to the two dates – as in fl.1749–80 – between which it is known with some certainty that a person was active. Dates which appear thus, 800/900, as opposed to the obvious 1926–2007, indicate a period, difficult to date accurately, during which an event is believed to have happened or developments took place.

While distances, heights and measurements are generally given in metric rather than imperial form, we follow the American definition of a billion, i.e. a thousand million. Our few abbreviations, in addition to those used in association with dates, are well-known standard short forms, which may be looked up, if need be, in any dictionary.

FURTHER READING

The inclusion of a comprehensive bibliography, or of bibliographical footnotes to entries, has been deemed impractical, and only occasionally is there space in the body of the text to draw attention to a crucial book or article. Readers are recommended to consult the invaluable bibliographical compendium *Wales* (1991; compiled by Gwilym Huws and D. Hywel Roberts), volume 122 in the World Bibliographical Series, and such on-line catalogues as that of the **National Library of Wales**.

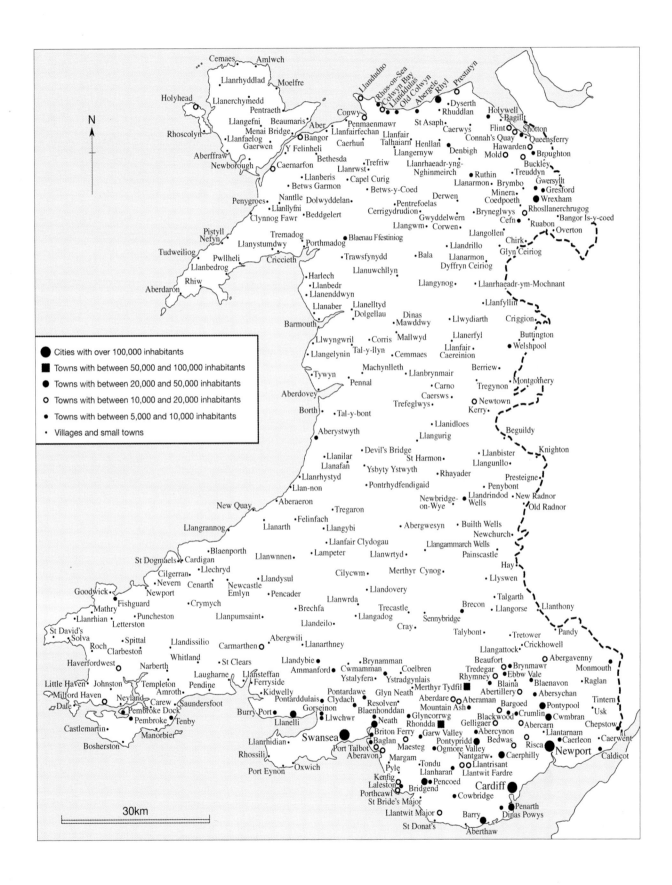

N

Legend:

- ● Cities with over 100,000 inhabitants
- ■ Towns with between 50,000 and 100,000 inhabitants
- ● Towns with between 20,000 and 50,000 inhabitants
- ○ Towns with between 10,000 and 20,000 inhabitants
- • Towns with between 5,000 and 10,000 inhabitants
- · Villages and small towns

30km

A Oes Heddwch? (Is there peace?). Chairing of the bard, Myrddin ap Dafydd, at the National Eisteddfod, 2002

A OES HEDDWCH? (Is there peace?)

A question thrice put to the **eisteddfod** audience during the chief **Gorsedd** ceremonies, including the crowning and chairing. A half-drawn sword is held above the winning poet or author; it is sheathed and the ceremony continues when the response 'Heddwch' (Peace) has been thrice given.

A470, The

The 270-km A470 between **Cardiff** and **Llandudno** is the main arterial **road** linking north and south Wales. With the advent of the **National Assembly** in 1999, it achieved an emblematic status, symbolizing for some the unity or, more accurately, the aspirational unity of the country. North of Cardiff, the A470 links **Merthyr Tydfil**, **Brecon**, **Builth**, **Rhayader**, **Llanidloes**, **Dolgellau**, Blaenau **Ffestiniog** and **Betws-y-Coed**. The allocation of a number to the route was made only in 1972, following a campaign in the *Western Mail*. Until that time, all major roads in Wales ran from east to west. Since its designation, gradual improvements have been made. But, as the entire journey still takes four to five hours, there are constant demands for further improvements to those parts of the road which continue to be narrow and winding.

A5, The

Those numbering the main **roads** of **Britain** visualized them as spokes radiating clockwise from **London**; thus, the A1 led to Edinburgh, A2 to Dover, A3 to Portsmouth, A4 to Bath, A5 to **Holyhead** and A6 to Carlisle. Essentially, the A5 followed the line of the mail-coach road that **Thomas Telford** created early in the 19th century in order to improve communications with **Ireland**. The road was a work of genius; it included the superb **Menai** suspension bridge, and, in its course through **Snowdonia**, its severest gradient is 1:22. The A5 is 445 km in length, 136 km of which is in Wales. Following the completion of a quasi motorway across **Anglesey** in 2001, the chief road across the **island** came to be the **A55** rather than the A5.

A55, The

The A55 is the most important highway in north Wales, being a part of the Euroroute E22 linking Sussnitz on the Baltic coast with **Holyhead** and, via ferry, **Ireland**. The A55 dual-carriage expressway runs 145 km from near Chester to Holyhead, the final section from **Llanfair Pwllgwyngyll** to Holyhead being completed in 2001. Major **engineering** works include the crossing of the **Conwy** estuary by means of **Britain**'s first immersed tube

Aberaeron harbour

road tunnel, further tunnels at Pen y Clip and Penmaenbach, and the **Penmaenmawr** bypass. The Conwy crossing won the British civil engineering award in 1992. The completion of the A55 meant that the **A5** ceased to be the chief road across **Anglesey**. Of the A55's 145-km length, 131 km are in Wales.

AARON, Richard I[thamar] (1901–87) Philosopher
Born at **Seven Sisters** and educated at **Cardiff** and **Oxford**, Aaron published *Hanes Athroniaeth: o Descartes i Hegel* (1932) when he was a lecturer in **philosophy** at **Swansea**. At the age of 32, he was appointed to the philosophy chair at **Aberystwyth**, which he held from 1932 until 1969. Eager to promote the study of philosophy through the medium of **Welsh**, he established in 1931 the philosophy section of the Guild of Graduates of the **University of Wales**; and in 1938 initiated the periodical *Efrydiau Athronyddol*. His chief publications were *John Locke* (1937) and *The Theory of Universals* (1952). In the 1960s, as chairman of the **Council of Wales and Monmouthshire**, he played a key role in the preparation of *The Welsh Language Today* (1963), a pioneering report on the status of the Welsh language. The double 'A' at the beginning of his name ensured that his was the first entry in *Who's Who* – a matter of some pride to him.

ABBEY CWMHIR (Abaty Cwm-hir),
Radnorshire, Powys (5931 ha; 246 inhabitants)
The **community** lies north of **Llandrindod** and consists of an extensive tract of 'muscular country of rounded hills rising over the 1000 feet contour and yet green'. The abbey, a **Cistercian** monastery first founded in 1143, was refounded by monks from **Whitland** in 1176. The nave of its 13th-century church was the longest in Wales (75 m) and its 14-bay colonnades were comparable with those of Canterbury. The church's size may reflect the patronage of **Llywelyn ap Iorwerth**; the headless body of **Llywelyn ap Gruffudd** was

buried within it in 1282. Built for 60 monks, by 1381 it had a mere 8. Little remains of the magnificence which once enhanced this remote and beautiful setting. The abbey, partially destroyed by **Owain Glyndŵr**, was plundered at the time of the **Reformation** (the Fowlers, who received the abbey's lands, became the richest family in **Radnorshire**), was subjected to siege when it was a Royalist fortress in the **Civil Wars** and was extensively cleared between 1822 and 1837. Parts of the nave arcade were transferred to St Idloes, **Llanidloes**, in 1542. St Mary's church (1866) and Abbey Cwmhir Hall (1867) nearby have been described as 'coniferous **architecture** of the purest Victorian conifer age'. Glyndŵr's Way runs through the area.

ABENBURY, Wrexham (693 ha; 718 inhabitants)
Located immediately east of **Wrexham**, the **community** contains Wrexham Industrial Estate developed from the **Marchwiel** Ordnance Factory established during the **Second World War**. Its outstanding building is that of Wessel Pharmaceuticals Ltd (1970), designed by **Colwyn Foulkes**, who was also responsible for the attractive **housing** at Pentre Maelor (1952). Cefn Park and Llwyn Onn are substantial 18th-century country houses.

ABER VALLEY (Cwm Aber),
Caerphilly (1334 ha; 6696 inhabitants)
Located north-west of **Caerphilly** and including the settlements of Senghenydd and Abertridwr, the area was urbanized following the sinking of the Universal and Windsor collieries in the 1890s. On 14 October 1913, the valley suffered the greatest tragedy to befall the south Wales **coalfield** when 439 men and boys were killed by an explosion at Senghenydd's Universal Colliery (*see* **Senghenydd Colliery Disaster**). The **community**'s earthworks are believed to be the boundaries of a **hunting** park of the medieval lords of the *cantref* of **Senghennydd**.

ABER[GWYNGREGYN], Gwynedd
(2970 ha; 222 inhabitants)

Abergwyngregyn on signposts, but Aber to the Ordnance Survey and the census, the **community** is located between **Bangor** and **Llanfairfechan**, and embraces the basin of Afon Aber and its tributaries, Afon Anafon and Afon Rhaeadr-fawr. It was a key point on the main medieval route across northern Wales – which extended from the **Perfeddwlad** over the **Conwy** at Tal-y-cafn and through **Caerhun** to Aber and then across Traeth Lafan to **Anglesey**. Protected from the east by Mynydd **Penmaenmawr**, Aber was the site of one of the favourite courts of the princes of **Gwynedd**. **Joan** (Siwan), wife of **Llywelyn ap Iorwerth**, died there in 1237, as did her son, **Dafydd ap Llywelyn**, in 1246. Aber was also the probable location of the meeting between **Llywelyn ap Gruffudd** and **John Pecham**, archbishop of Canterbury, in November 1282. It is claimed that remains of the court lie beneath Pen-y-bryn Mansion (c.1600, c.1705), now cared for by the Aber Trust.

The Traeth Lafan crossing, which involved a 5-km journey across the sands at low tide and a 0.3-km ferry crossing of the deep channel of the **Menai Strait**, continued in use until the 19th century. Much of the community is owned by the **National Trust**. A delightful footpath leads to the dramatic **waterfall** (35 m) Rhaeadr Mawr. The area is rich in prehistoric cairns, huts and field systems.

ABERAERON, Ceredigion
(159 ha; 1520 inhabitants)

Up until 1807, Aberaeron was merely a geographical expression. In that year, the 'squarson', the Rev. Alban Gwynne of Monachty (see **Dyffryn Arth**) secured an act of parliament to create a new harbour. (The 200th anniversary of the passage of the act was enthusiastically celebrated in 2007.) Aberaeron quickly became a centre of **shipbuilding** and of the importation of **lime**, **coal** and timber. The design of the attractive small town of painted stucco houses is often wrongly attributed to **John Nash**; the influence of the Shrewsbury architect Edward Haycock is more likely. The decline of maritime trade after 1870 was eventually compensated for by growth in local **government** and **tourism**. Aberaeron became the administrative centre for the Aberaeron **urban** and **rural district councils**, established in 1894, and its town hall became the meeting place of the **Cardiganshire** County Council. Following local government reorganization in 1974, Aberaeron was recognized as **Ceredigion** District's main administrative centre, a role that became more important after **county** status was restored in 1996. The **railway** to **Lampeter** (1911) was almost the last public railway to be built in Wales; it ceased to carry passengers in 1951.

ABERAMAN, Rhondda Cynon Taff
(1688 ha; 9833 inhabitants)

Located on the right bank of the Cynon immediately south of **Aberdare**, the **community** contains the villages of Aberaman, Abercwmboi, Blaengwawr, Cwmaman and Godreaman. Evidence of a 16th-century furnace survives at Cwmaman. Major industrial development began in 1845 when Crawshay **Bailey** established the Aberaman

ironworks. As the floor of the Cynon valley is prone to flooding, settlement developed in the valley of the Aman, a tributary of the Cynon. The opening of the Aberdare **Railway** in 1846 led to extensive exploitation of **coal**, and by the 1860s there were five collieries in the area. In 1857, Bailey sold his mines to the **Powell Duffryn Company**, which eventually became the largest coalmining company in Europe.

The Davis family, who initiated the industrialization of Ferndale (see **Rhondda**), was associated with Blaengwawr. Bethesda **Baptist** chapel, Abercwmboi (1864), has a handsome classical façade. The bulky Aberaman public hall and institute (1909) – destroyed by fire in 1994 – once towered over the village; there is a more modest institute at Abercwmboi (1913). With the end of the coal industry, the main source of employment is a large industrial estate. The phurnacite plant, described in the *Observer* as '**Britain**'s dirtiest factory', ceased production in 1990.

ABERAVON (Aberafan), Neath Port Talbot
(563 ha; 18,118 inhabitants)

The town of Aberavon lies within the **communities** of Aberavon, Sandfields East and Sandfields West (see *below*).

Caradog ap Iestyn, Welsh lord of **Afan**, is reputed to have founded a borough on the west bank of the Afan in the early 12th century. It became one of **Glamorgan**'s eight parliamentary **boroughs**, but experienced little growth. The **railway** arrived in 1850, but it was on the river's eastern bank that the most significant industrial development occurred. In the 1950s, the holiday dunes of Aberavon Beach vanished under the Sandfields estate, built to house the employees of **Port Talbot**'s Abbey steelworks (see **Iron and Steel**). In the 1960s, part of the town centre was demolished to make way for the **M4** motorway, and in the 1970s much of the rest of it was replaced by shopping malls.

The communities of Aberavon

ABERAVON (225 ha; 5335 inhabitants)
A narrow strip south of the M4, it contains the main survivor of the original Aberavon – St Mary's church, rebuilt in 1849; the grave of Dic Penderyn (see **Richard Lewis**) is in the churchyard.

SANDFIELDS EAST (Sandfields Dwyreiniol)
(168 ha; 6118 inhabitants)
The eastern wing of the Sandfields estate, the community includes the Afan Lido, a conference and entertainment centre.

SANDFIELDS WEST (Sandfields Gorllewinol)
(170 ha; 6665 inhabitants)
The western wing of the Sandfields estate, the community contains the sprawling Sandfields comprehensive school and several churches of innovative design.

ABERCARN, Caerphilly
(1651 ha; 4793 inhabitants)

The **community** straddles the middle reaches of the **Ebbw** valley. **Iron**working began in the area in the late 16th century. The south Wales **coal**field's earliest surviving intact iron furnace can be seen in Cwm Gwyddon. By the late 19th century, the area was dependent on coalmining, particularly the employment provided by the South Celynen and the Prince of Wales collieries. Abercarn House, now demolished, was the birthplace of Benjamin Hall, Baron **Llanover**. In 1853, Lord and Lady Llanover (*see* **Augusta Hall**) commissioned the building of St Luke's church, on the understanding that services would be in **Welsh**. In 1862, as the result of what they considered to be the bishop of Llandaff's reneging on this, they presented the church to the **Calvinistic Methodists**. Following the closure in the 1980s of Abercarn's impressive parish church (1926), St Luke's came to be shared by the Presbyterian Church of Wales and the **Church in Wales**. The upland parts of the community have been extensively forested and there is a beautiful forest drive through Cwm Carn.

ABERCONWY Constituency and one-time district

Following the abolition of **Caernarfonshire** and **Denbighshire** in 1974, Aberconwy was created as a district of the new **county** of Gwynedd. It consisted of what had been the **borough** of **Conwy**, the **urban districts** of **Betws-y-Coed**, **Llandudno**, **Llanfairfechan** and **Penmaenmawr** and the **rural district** of Nant Conwy, all in the former Caernarfonshire, and the urban district of **Llanrwst** and part of that of Hiraethog in the former Denbighshire. In 1996, Aberconwy, together with most of the district of **Colwyn**, became the **county borough** of Conwy. With the **National Assembly** elections of 2007, the western part of the county borough, most of which had been known as the Conwy constituency since 1950, became – with some boundary changes – known as the Aberconwy constituency.

ABERCONWY, Treaty of (1277)

This treaty, concluded between **Llywelyn ap Gruffudd** and Edward I on 9 November 1277, brought to an end 'the first war of Welsh independence'. Llywelyn lost all his territorial gains and had to cede **Gwynedd** east of the **Conwy** (the **Perfeddwlad**) to the king, being left with Gwynedd west of the Conwy. He also lost the homage of all the other Welsh lords except for five minor ones (four of the house of **Powys Fadog** and one of the house of **Deheubarth**), but was permitted to retain the title of **Prince of Wales** for his lifetime.

ABERCYNON, Rhondda Cynon Taff
(916 ha; 6428 inhabitants)
Located around the confluence of the Rivers Cynon and **Taff**, the **community** contains the villages of Abercynon, Ynysboeth, Carnetown and Tyntetown (the last two places commemorate families owning land in the area – the Carnes of **St Donats** and the Kemeys-Tyntes of Cefn Mably, **Rudry**). One of the original names of the settlement was Y Basin, after the dock on the Glamorganshire **Canal**, which was linked to a network of tramroads. In 1804, that from Penydarren (*see* **Merthyr Tydfil**) carried **Richard Trevithick**'s locomotive, which finished its journey at Abercynon. The canal offices survive as the Navigation public house. Rapid growth began in 1886 with the sinking of Dowlais Cardiff (later Abercynon) Colliery, which at its peak employed nearly 2700 men. The name Abercynon was chosen at a public meeting in 1893.

The site of the colliery has become that of the Valleys Innovation Centre. Abercynon Workmen's Hall, one of the largest buildings in the south Wales **coal**field, was demolished in 1995. The pioneer of oral history **George Ewart Evans** and the flyweight **boxing** champion Dai Dower were natives of Abercynon. The **population** of Abercynon peaked in 1911 at 9109.

ABERDARE (Aberdâr), Rhondda Cynon Taff
(2030 ha; 14,457 inhabitants)
Located on the upper reaches of the Cynon, the **community** consists of the town of Aberdare and its inner suburbs – Abernant, Cwmdare, Gadlys, Robertstown and Trecynon. The place is often considered to be synonymous with the Cynon valley, which is frequently referred to as the Aberdare valley. Until 1974, the Cynon Valley constituency was known as that of Aberdare.

The glaciation which widened the upper end of the Cynon valley enabled Aberdare to develop as a nucleated town. In 1800, however, it consisted of no more than a dozen houses clustered near the minuscule St John's church (12th and 13th centuries). Significant growth began with the establishment in the neighbourhood of three iron-works – **Llwydcoed** (1801), Abernant (1801) and Gadlys (1827). Industrialization led in 1812 to the opening of the Aberdare **Canal**. The **population** of the **parish** of Aberdare (which included the later communities of **Aberaman**, **Cwmbach**, Llwydcoed and **Pen-y-waun**) increased from 1486 (1801) to 6471 (1841). In the 1840s, the area became Wales's chief centre of the mining of steam **coal**, a development much facilitated by the completion of the Aberdare **Railway** in 1846. The parish's population rose to 14,991 in 1851 and to 32,247 in 1861. With Aberdare the most dynamic place in Wales, the saying arose that: 'What Aberdare thinks today, Wales thinks tomorrow.' It was the home of two of Wales's leading religious figures – the **Anglican** clergyman John Griffith (?1818–85) and the **Baptist** minister Thomas Price (1820–88). A major publishing centre (*see* **Printing and Publishing**), Aberdare provided much of the impetus that led in 1868 to the election of **Henry Richard** as MP for the joint constituency of **Merthyr Tydfil** and Aberdare.

It was in the boom years of the 1850s that central Aberdare was laid out. Victoria Square, St Elvan's church with its soaring spire, the large market buildings and several of the town's score and more chapels date from that decade. Aberdare's pre-eminence did not endure. In the 1870s, the meteoric rise of the **Rhondda** robbed it of its role as the centre of Wales's steam coal production; and in the same decade, ironmaking in the town came to an end. (What survives of the Gadlys ironworks represents one of Wales's most significant sites of industrial **archaeology**.) Coalmining did, however, continue to expand, although more modestly than in the 1840s and 1850s. The population of the parish, which in 1894 became the Aberdare **Urban District**, peaked at 55,007 in 1921. Like the rest of the south Wales coalfield, Aberdare suffered gravely during the interwar **depression**, but during the **Second World War** new industries, in particular ordnance factories at

Aberdare public park

Robertstown and **Hirwaun**, helped to alleviate the unemployment problem. After the war, further attempts were made to diversify the **economy** but, at the opening of the 21st century, Aberdare contained some of Wales's most impoverished families.

The **Unitarian** Hen Dŷ Cwrdd, founded at Trecynon in 1751, was the source of much of Aberdare's **radicalism**. Roberstown has the world's earliest dated iron railway bridge (1811). Aberdare public park, laid out in the 1860s, contains **Gorsedd** stones, a reminder that the National **Eisteddfod** was held in the town in 1861, 1885 and 1956. The despoiled mining landscape of Cwmdare has become the Dare Valley Country Park. **Goscombe John**'s statue (1920) of Caradog (**Griffith Rhys Jones**), conductor of the South Wales Choral Union, stands in Victoria Square. **Kate Roberts**, who taught at the grammar school for girls from 1917 to 1928, began her writing career at Aberdare. The Coliseum, Trecynon (1938), and the Little Theatre at Gadlys (an ingeniously converted engine shed), are central to the cultural life of the area. The College of Further Education (*c.*1955) is one of **Glamorgan**'s most distinguished examples of post-war modernist **architecture**.

ABERDARE REPORT, The

In 1880, **Gladstone**'s **Liberal government** appointed Henry Austin **Bruce**, the first Baron Aberdare, as chairman of a committee to examine the state of intermediate and higher **education** in Wales. Its report (1881) revealed that a mere 3827 teenage boys in Wales received any form of intermediate education, mainly in Wales's 27 grammar schools (provision for girls was far less). It also revealed that, while the ratio of university students to the **population** was 1:840 in **Scotland**, it was 1:8200 in Wales. The report – the most significant in the history of Welsh education – paved the way

for the establishment of university colleges at **Cardiff** (1883) and **Bangor** (1884), and the passage of the **Welsh Intermediate Education Act** (1889). Although the historian J. R. Webster argued that 'the committee viewed the educational problems of Wales through essentially English eyes', its members, who included **John Rhŷs**, proved far more sympathetic to Welsh issues than had the authors of the education report of 1847 (*see* **Treason of the Blue Books**).

ABERDARON, Gwynedd
(4764 ha; 1019 inhabitants)

Constituting the westernmost part of the **Llŷn** peninsula, the **community** also contains Bardsey (Ynys Enlli), Ynys Gwylan-fawr and Ynys Gwylan-bach (*see* **Islands**). Before embarking at Porth Meudwy for the short but treacherous voyage to Bardsey, pilgrims would pray at St Hywyn's church, a two-aisled building erected in the 12th and 13th centuries, and maybe eat at 'the big kitchen' (Y Gegin Fawr). Near the church is an attractive group of buildings designed by **Clough Williams-Ellis**. There are **Iron Age** hut circles on Mynydd Mawr, which commands a superb view of Bardsey and the sound. At Braich y Pwll, the drop to the sea – 162 m – is one of the highest in Wales.

Bodwrdda, or Bodwrda, a 16th-century stone house, has an additional wing (*c.*1616) constructed of brick – a highly unusual building material in **Caernarfonshire** at that time. Its owners – a family which included the manuscript copyist Wiliam Bodwrda (1593–1660) – took Bodwrdda as their surname; the name has since died out in Wales, but survives in **North America** as Bodurda. Plas yn Rhiw, owned by the **National Trust**, is a 17th-century house fronted by a 19th-century colonnaded veranda. Near it is the medieval church of St Maelrhys. When walked upon, the beach at Porth Oer emits a curious noise, giving rise to the name

The Aberfan disaster, 1966

Whistling Sands. In 1921, the parish of Bodferin, essentially the northern part of the present community, was unique among the **parishes** of Wales in that it contained no one who could speak **English**.

Aberdaron, the birthplace of the polymath tramp, Dic Aberdaron (**Richard Robert Jones**) has inspired several **Welsh-language** poets, among them Cynan (**Albert Evans-Jones**) and **T. Rowland Hughes**. The place attracted the Bardsey resident **Brenda Chamberlain**, artist and author of *Tide Race*, and the poet **R. S. Thomas**, who was vicar of Aberdaron from 1967 to 1978.

ABERDOVEY (Aberdyfi), Gwynedd
(1128 ha; 781 inhabitants)
Located on the north side of the **Dyfi** estuary, Aberdovey was the place where in 1216 **Llywelyn ap Iorwerth** presided over the apportioning of land between the sons of **Rhys ap Gruffudd** (the Lord Rhys; d.1197). In the 16th century, Aberdovey was a busy **fish**ing **port**; it later exported **woollen** products, **slate** and **lead**, and imported salt, **coal**, **lime** and flour. **Shipbuilding** flourished, especially between 1850 and 1880. By the early 20th century, with Aberdovey becoming an important holiday centre, port activity had given way to **tourism**. The **community**'s seafaring connections are maintained by the maritime museum and by the Outward Bound Sea School, established in 1941. The **golf** course (1892) is one of the finest in Wales; in 1927, a local Sabbatarian took pot shots at those using the course on a Sunday. The poet Ieuan Dyfi (fl.1490–1510) was a native of Aberdovey. In a later age, the place became well known through the song '**The Bells of Aberdovey**'. The novelists Oliver Onions (1873–1961) and Berta Ruck (1878–1978), who married in 1909, lived in Aberdovey from 1939; many of their books have Welsh settings.

ABEREDW, Radnorshire, Powys
(3055 ha; 219 inhabitants)
Extending for 9 km eastwards from the **Wye**, Aberedw was, according to tradition, the last refuge of **Llywelyn ap Gruffudd** – a **cave** there bears his name. The author **Benjamin Heath Malkin**, visiting Aberedw in 1803, was disconcerted to find that the patronal festival of the delightful church of St Cewydd (?14th and 16th centuries) was celebrated by dancing in the graveyard. Much of the castle (c.1284) was destroyed to accommodate the mid Wales **railway**. Aberedw Rocks rise spectacularly above the Wye. There are diminutive medieval churches at Llanbadarn-y-garreg and Rhulen.

ABERFAN DISASTER
Traditionally, colliery waste has been brought to the surface and deposited in tips, sometimes high up on hillsides. The potential hazard that such tips represented for those living in their shadow became manifest in tragic fashion on Friday, 21 October 1966.

At about 9.15 a.m., shortly after registration at Pantglas junior school, the waste tip then being used by the Merthyr Vale Colliery, high on the hillside above Aberfan (*see* **Merthyr Tydfil**: **Merthyr Vale**), began to move. Saturated and made unstable by a hidden underground spring, it slid down the mountainside and, within minutes, a farm, the entire school, part of the neighbouring senior school (where pupils started at 9.30 a.m.) and 20 houses had been engulfed by colliery waste. Of the 144 people who lost their lives, 116 were schoolchildren, mostly aged from 7 to 10. Wales had experienced industrial tragedies with larger death tolls, but the loss of almost an entire generation of children made the Aberfan disaster uniquely poignant.

Scenes of the disaster were broadcast and published all over the world, bringing home to those who had little knowledge of **coal**mining the horrors that could be associated with the industry. In the wake of the disaster, attitudes towards such tips altered, leading to their better management and, in many cases, following the end of mining, to their removal. There was outrage, however, when the **National Coal Board** and the Treasury refused to accept full financial responsibility for the disaster, obliging the Aberfan Disaster Fund – which stood at £1.75 million – to contribute £150,000 for the removal of the remaining Aberfan tips; it was not until 1997 that this money was repaid to the Fund.

ABERFFRAW, Isle of Anglesey
(2955 ha; 608 inhabitants)

Located on the south-west coast of **Anglesey**, the **community** is dominated by the sand dunes of Twyn Aberffraw. The **Law**books described Aberffraw as the *eisteddfa arbennig* (principal seat) of the dynasty of **Gwynedd**. In 1230, in order to emphasize his unique status among Welsh rulers, **Llywelyn ap Iorwerth** adopted the title of prince of Aberffraw and, in 1377, supporters of **Owain ap Thomas** (Owain Lawgoch) stressed his *bonedd o Aberffraw* (his roots in the stock of Aberffraw). Aberffraw (usually pronounced Berffro) almost certainly had a fort, church, court and bond township from the earliest times. The royal court probably shared the hill crowned by St **Beuno**'s church, which contains a Romanesque doorway perhaps dating from the reign of **Gruffudd ap Cynan**.

Barclodiad y Gawres (the giantess's apronful) is a reconstruction of Wales's finest example of a chambered tomb in the Irish Boyne valley tradition. Constructed *c.*3000 BC, the incised designs on some of its stones represent the earliest example of decorative art in Wales. There is a more modest **neolithic** tomb at Din Dryfol. Cable Bay (Porth Trecastell) was the British end of the first transatlantic **telegraph** cable. St Cwyfan church (12th century) is accessible only at low tide. Aberffraw's **manor**ial court, which regulated grazing on the dunes, continued to be held well into the 20th century. There is a motor-racing circuit at Tŷ-croes. The *cantref* of Aberffraw, which constituted most of western Anglesey, contained the **commotes** of **Llifon** and **Malltraeth**.

ABERGAVENNY (Y Fenni), Monmouthshire
(1032 ha; 9628 inhabitants)

The **community** is located at the strategically important point where the River **Usk** leaves its narrow valley to enter the plain of **Gwent**. The importance of the location was recognized by the **Romans** who established there the fort of Gobannium, the *vicus* of which appears to have been a centre for **iron**working.

In *c.*1097, Hamelin de Ballon established a motte-and-bailey castle near the confluence of the Usk and the Gavenny. In 1819, the summit of the motte was crowned by a **hunting** lodge, which now houses the Abergavenny Museum. The castle became the centre of the lordship of Gwent Uwch Coed or Abergavenny. By the late 12th century, it was held by the de **Breos family** and, in 1182, was the scene of the Abergavenny Massacre, when William de Breos murdered his guests, Seisyll ap Dyfnwal and his entourage. By the 15th century, the lordship was held by the **Nevill family**, to whom the marquessate of Abergavenny was granted in 1876. Edward I held a parliament at Abergavenny in 1291.

St Mary's, built as a **Benedictine** priory, was heavily restored in the 1890s. Within it is one of the finest series of

The long replaced Market House at Abergavenny, designed by John Nash and completed in 1795

The Jesse Carving at St Mary's church, Abergavenny

medieval monuments in **Britain**. Among them are a magnificent figure of Jesse and a splendid group of tombs. Thoroughly restored in the 1990s, they include that of Eva de Breos (d.1257) and those of three members of the **Hastings family** and of William ap Thomas of **Raglan** and four of his relations. The enormous Jesse figure, one of the great triumphs of late 15th-century craftsmanship, is carved from a single oak. The stump would have supported other carvings depicting the life of Christ, but only the main figure survived the iconoclasm of the **Reformation**.

The Henry VIII grammar school was founded in 1543. In the 17th century, Abergavenny was a stronghold of **Roman Catholicism**; a secret attic church survives in the Gunter Mansion in Market Street. Abergavenny is one of Wales's most prosperous market towns, and among its imposing landmarks is the Town Hall completed in 1871, with the Market Hall to the rear. **Nevill** Hall, where building began in 1965, is one of Wales's leading hospitals. The Angel Hotel, built in the early 19th century, was a centre of Cymdeithas **Cymreigyddion** y Fenni, a society dedicated to preserving the **Welsh language** and culture, which provided a template for the modern National **Eisteddfod**.

ABERGELE, Conwy (1673 ha; 10,016 inhabitants)

Located in the central part of the resort belt of the north Wales coast, Abergele was the location of a *clas* or Celtic monastery. Its site was later occupied by St Michael's church, among the largest of Wales's Perpendicular double-naved churches. In the south-west corner of the **community** is Dinorben **hill-fort**; totally destroyed by quarrying, it has yielded evidence of continuous occupation from the late **Bronze Age** to the 7th century AD. Parc-y-meirch nearby has also been the source of significant archaeological evidence. Kinmel Park was rebuilt for the Hughes family, whose wealth derived from the **Mynydd Parys copper** mines. (W. T. Hughes was elevated to the barony of Dinorben in 1831.) The mansion (1860s), the work of W. E. Nesfield, was hailed by Nikolaus Pevsner as a milestone in the history of

architecture. It had a room devoted to the ironing of **newspapers**. In 1919, when the park was a barracks, it was the site of **Britain**'s worst post-war mutiny in which 5 Canadian soldiers were killed and 21 were injured. In the 20th century, the Hughes family moved successively to Hendre Gyda (Kinmel Manor) and Coed Bedw (Plas Kinmel). The Kinmel estate village, St George (previously Cegidog), has attractive buildings, including the church and mausoleum of the Hughes family. The champion of the **Welsh language**, **Robert Ambrose Jones** (Emrys ap Iwan), was a native of Abergele; the local secondary school – ironically one of the least Welsh in language in Wales – bears his name. Mynydd Seion chapel (1868) – a rare example of a Gothic Welsh-language chapel – was paid for by David Roberts, a **Liverpool** builder. In front of it is a monument to the Roberts family, which included John Roberts MP, sponsor of the Welsh **Sunday Closing Act** (1881), whose son was ennobled as Baron **Clwyd**.

'ABERGELE MARTYRS, The'

On the morning of the **Prince of Wales**'s investiture at **Caernarfon** (1 July 1969), two men – Alwyn Jones (1947–69) and George Taylor (1933–69) – who were associated with **Mudiad Amddiffyn Cymru**, were killed at **Abergele**. Intending to attack a **government** building, their bomb went off prematurely. Claims were made that they were the first Welshmen to die for Wales since the **Glyndŵr Revolt**.

ABERGELE RAIL DISASTER

Thirty-three lives were lost on 20 August 1868 when the **Holyhead** Mail collided at **Abergele** with some runaway wagons filled with casks of paraffin, making it Wales's worst train disaster. The accident was the result of injudicious shunting by the stationmaster at nearby **Llanddulas**, which sent the wagons along a down gradient towards Abergele. Railwaymen and others tried vainly to douse the conflagration by forming a human chain and filling buckets with seawater. The flaws in **railway** practice revealed by the disaster led to stricter precautions.

ABERGWILI, Carmarthenshire
(3075 ha; 1584 inhabitants)

Located immediately east of **Carmarthen**, the **community** contains the villages of Abergwili, Peniel and Whitemill. A manor of the bishop of **St David's**, Abergwili was one of the residences of the peripatetic medieval bishops. In 1283, its St **David**'s church attained collegiate status. In the 1540s, Bishop **Barlow**, disliking the remoteness of St David's and having alienated his rich manor of **Lamphey**, made Abergwili the chief episcopal residence, a role it still possesses. It was at Abergwili in the 1560s that Bishop **Richard Davies**, **William Salesbury** and **Thomas Huet** prepared the **Welsh** translation of the New Testament (*see* **Bible, The**). In 1974, following the construction of a new episcopal residence, the palace – largely 19th century – became home to the Carmarthenshire Museum and the **Dyfed** Archaeological Trust. Merlin's Hill is reputed to contain the **cave** of the wizard **Merlin**. Merlin's Hill Centre commemorates his alleged associations with the area. The Von Trapp family of *Sound of Music* fame spent some time at

Bryn Myrddin Mansion. The remote church of Llanfihangel Uwch Gwili retains some 16th-century features.

ABERHAFESP (Aberhafesb), Montgomeryshire, Powys (1977 ha; 438 inhabitants)

Located immediately north-west of **Newtown**, the **community** consists of scattered settlements. The name means the mouth of the stream that dries up in summer. St Gwynnog's church, extensively rebuilt *c.*1857, retains its fine early 15th-century roof. **Nonconformists** are represented by Rhydfelin **Baptist** chapel (1791) and Bwlch-y-ffridd **Congregational** chapel (1800). Aberhafesp Hall is a large brick house of *c.*1675. In *c.*1802, the preacher **William Williams** (o'r Wern, 1781–1840) spent some months at Aberhafesp to improve his **English**.

ABERMULE RAIL DISASTER

Seventeen people were killed when two trains collided at Abermule on the single line between **Newtown** and **Montgomery** on 26 January 1921. The trains collided at around 48 kph, the engine of one rearing up and mounting the second carriage of the other. This was the only case in British **railway** history of loss of life as a result of a collision on a single line worked by the 'electric tablet' safety system.

ABERNANT (Aber-nant), Carmarthenshire (2204 ha; 315 inhabitants)

Located north-west of **Carmarthen**, the **community** contains the villages of Abernant and Talog. Its inhabitants played a prominent part in the **Rebecca Riots**. Indeed, it was a disturbance at Talog on 12 June 1843 which convinced the **government** that troops would have to be sent to west Wales. The community contains a delightful stretch of the Cywyn valley.

ABERPORTH (Aber-porth), Ceredigion (1648 ha; 2485 inhabitants)

Located north-east of **Cardigan**, the **community** contains the villages of Aberporth, Blaenannerch, Blaenporth and Parcllyn. The motte at Blaenporth was one of the fortifications built by Gilbert de **Clare** following his invasion of **Ceredigion** *c.*1110. Aberporth was a centre of **shipbuilding**, **fish**ing and coastal trading. The sociologist David Jenkins (b.1921) based his famous classification – *Buchedd A a Buchedd B* (Lifestyle A and Lifestyle B) – on his study of Aberporth; he argued that the difference between regular chapel-goers (*Buchedd A*) and regular tavern frequenters (*Buchedd B*) was more relevant than divisions of **class** and income. The prospects of the area were transformed in 1939 with the coming of the Royal Aircraft Establishment, with its airfield and missile-testing centre. The centre's meteorological work has caused Aberporth to feature in shipping forecasts. Blaenannerch, which played a leading role in the 1904–5 **revival**, is the home of Dic Jones (b.1934), one of the finest modern Welsh poets writing in traditional metres.

ABERSYCHAN, Torfaen (2477 ha; 6826 inhabitants)

Located in the upper reaches of the valley of Afon Lwyd between **Blaenavon** and **Pontypool**, Abersychan consisted of little other than scattered farms until the coming of the **iron** industry. Of the chief companies, that of Varteg opened in *c.*1803, Pentwyn in 1825, British in 1827 and Golynos in 1839. By the 1840s, **Monmouthshire**'s Eastern valley, with Abersychan at its heart, was a close rival to **Merthyr Tydfil** as the chief centre of iron production in south Wales – and indeed in the world. As none of Abersychan's works adopted modern technology, its iron industry was in decline by the 1870s, a decade during which its **population** (which included Pen Tranch; *see* Pontypool) declined from 14,569 to 13,496. Salvation came through the development of **coal**mining. By 1921, the town (it had become an **urban district** in 1894) had 27,087 inhabitants. **Llanerch**, one of its largest collieries, was the scene of a major disaster in 1890, when an explosion killed 176 miners. The interwar **depression** brought heavy unemployment and, apart from opportunities for commuters, the later 20th century brought few new job prospects, as can be seen from the fact that in 2001 the population of the **community**, with that of Pen Tranch, was less than half that of the town of Abersychan as it was constituted in 1921. A compact settlement extending for 2.5 km between Varteg and Snatchwood, Abersychan contains early examples of workers' **housing**, significant industrial remains and some imposing places of worship. The politician Roy Jenkins (*see* **Arthur Jenkins**) was born in Abersychan but, during his upbringing there, he failed to acquire the area's attractive accent.

ABERTILLERY (Abertyleri), Blaenau Gwent (1879 ha; 11,887 inhabitants)

The **community** lies in the lower reaches of the **Ebbw** Fach, an area industrialized later than the **iron**working regions further up the valley. Until about 1840, only a few small **coal** levels existed among the 'numerous farm houses, with small inclosures of corn and pasture' seen by William Coxe in 1801. Change came in the middle of the century; a **tinplate** works was established in 1846 and deep-shaft coalmining began in 1850. By the late 19th century, the **population** was growing dramatically, rising from 6003 in 1891 to 38,805 in 1921, when Abertillery **urban district** also included **Llanhilleth**. Like the rest of **Blaenau Gwent**, the area is now coming to terms with the post-industrial era. The town of Abertillery, its steep streets clinging to the hillside, is dramatically sited above the confluence of the **Ebbw** Fach and the Tyleri Rivers. Cwmtillery, a very narrow valley rising to the heights of Gwastad (551 m), favourably impressed a succession of observers; Coxe considered it 'well peopled, richly wooded, and highly cultivated, almost rivalling the fertile counties of **England**', and John Newman mentions its 'unexpectedly verdant and wooded hills'. The village of Six Bells, further down the valley, developed around the colliery established by John Lancaster in 1890; in 1960, 45 men were killed there in one of the worst colliery accidents of recent times.

ABERWHEELER (Aberchwiler), Denbighshire (1059 ha; 327 inhabitants)

Located north-east of **Denbigh**, the **community** extends from the right bank of the **Clwyd** to the heights of the **Clwydian Hills** at Moel y Parc (398 m). Its **Presbyterian** chapel (1822, 1862) is a handsome building. The theologian

The seafront at Aberystwyth, with the Old College on the right

Edward Williams (1750–1813), one of the founders of the **London Missionary** Society, was born at Glan Clwyd Farm.

ABERYSTWYTH, Ceredigion
(529 ha; 11,607 inhabitants)

The largest urban centre in mid-Wales, Aberystwyth sees itself as the capital of **Welsh**-speaking Wales – although, with 53.52% of its inhabitants having no knowledge at all of Welsh, it is, after **Llanbadarn Fawr** (59.78%), the most linguistically Anglicized of the **communities** of **Ceredigion**. Mesolithic artefacts have been discovered at Tanybwlch Beach. Pendinas is crowned by an extensive **Iron Age hill-fort**. The tower within it (1852) is a monument to the Duke of Wellington. Llanbadarn was a leading *clas* of early Christian Wales, and medieval Aberystwyth was sometimes known as Llanbadarn Gaerog (Walled Llanbadarn).

The first Aberystwyth castle was a ringwork built *c*.1110 overlooking the **Ystwyth** (*see* **Llanfarian**). Following his conquest of northern **Ceredigion** in 1277, Edward I founded a new castle, together with a walled and chartered borough, on a site near the **Rheidol** estuary. **Owain Glyndŵr** captured the castle in 1404, but was obliged to yield it up in 1408. From 1637 to 1643, it was the site of a royal **mint**. Besieged during the first **Civil War**, it was blown up in 1647.

The town was of little importance until seaside holidays became popular towards the end of the 18th century; attractive assembly rooms were built in 1820. Port activity increased slowly from 1700, but the harbour was unsatisfactory until the first quay was built in the 1830s; thereafter, **shipbuilding** and maritime trade flourished until the arrival of the **railway** – from **Machynlleth** in 1864 and from **Carmarthen** in 1867. The main exports were **lead** ore, oak

bark and emigrants; consumer goods were imported from **London**, Bristol and **Liverpool**. As sea trade declined, the railways brought ever more visitors to fill the growing number of hotels and guesthouses. Although a few earlier buildings survive, especially Laura Place (1827), the core of the town is essentially Victorian. A **pier** (later somewhat truncated) was built in 1865 and Aberystwyth's cliff railway – Britain's longest funicular railway – was built in 1896.

In 1790, **John Nash** designed Castle House, around which J. P. Seddon built a hugely ambitious Gothic hotel, but it proved a failure. In 1872, it became the home of Wales's first university college. The **National Library of Wales**, opened in Laura Place in 1909, moved to S. K. Greenslade's attractive building on Penglais Hill in 1916. (Aberystwyth probably contains more books per head of **population** than any other town in the world.) The centrality of Aberystwyth within Wales was recognized as early as 1823, when the confession of faith of the **Calvinistic Methodists** was drawn up in the town. By the early 21st century, it was the location of the headquarters of the **Forestry Commission** in Wales, the **Royal Commission on Ancient and Historic Monuments of Wales, Urdd Gobaith Cymru, Cymdeithas yr Iaith Gymraeg**, the **Farmers' Union** of Wales, **Merched y Wawr, Undeb Cenedlaethol Athrawon Cymru** (the National Union of the Teachers of Wales) and the **Welsh Books Council**.

Home to more than 7000 students, the town is wholly dominated by the **University of Wales, Aberystwyth**. The institution's focus has moved from the promenade to Penglais Hill. While it retains a number of **county** offices, Aberystwyth is yielding the role of county town of Ceredigion to **Aberaeron**. The first protest of Cymdeithas yr Iaith Gymraeg took place at Aberystwyth in 1963.

ABERYSTWYTH NAÏVE ARTIST, The (fl.1840–50)

An unidentified and untrained artist who worked mainly in the **Aberystwyth** area producing small watercolours of local scenes and people. Description and detail dominate the **paintings**, which reveal intriguing aspects of everyday peasant culture – and the presence of tourists. Confident use of light and perspective demonstrate knowledge of formal means, although proportional exaggeration indicates an ignorance of the classical concepts of human scale and landscape. There are several examples of the artist's work in the **Ceredigion** Museum, Aberystwyth.

ABLETT, Noah (1883–1935) Trade unionist and political theorist

The tenth of eleven children, Ablett seemed destined for the ministry but a pit accident and an awareness of the low wages paid to miners working in abnormal places made him an agitator. Educated at Ruskin College, **Oxford**, and subsequently a checkweighman in Maerdy (*see* **Rhondda**), his Marxist and Syndicalist ideas were the inspiration for the Ruskin College strike, the **Plebs' League** and the minimum wage agitation. A main author of *The Miners' Next Step*, it was his writings and cryptic comments that shaped the Welsh phenomenon of **Syndicalism,** which he envisaged as 'scientific' trade unionism. In his later years, he sank into alcoholism.

ABOVE US THE EARTH (1976) Film

This compassionate drama-documentary is central to the canon of the Welsh film-maker Karl Francis. The director casts a caustic eye over **coal**field strife in a **film** less overtly partisan than much of his later work. Centred on the closure of Ogilvie Colliery, **Rhymney Valley**, and its impact on an ailing miner, Windsor Rees (playing himself), Francis's debut feature examines local colliers' conflicting reactions to the expedient policies of both the **National Coal Board** and the **National Union of Mineworkers**.

ABRAHAM, William (Mabon; 1842–1922)
Trade unionist and politician

A native of **Cwmavon**, in 1877 he became the full-time organizer of the **Rhondda**'s Cambrian Miners' Association. A supporter of the sliding scale agreement for determining miners' wages (1875), in 1892 he secured an agreement which gave the miners a holiday on the first Monday of every month – the widely enjoyed 'Mabon's Day'. Elected Lib-Lab MP for the Rhondda in 1885, he formally became a **Labour** MP in 1909; from 1918 to 1922, he represented Rhondda West. In 1898, Mabon became the first president of the **South Wales Miners' Federation**, and was a moderating and conciliating influence in industrial relations. He was a keen advocate of the **eisteddfod** and the **Welsh language**. His willingness to appear on **tea** advertisements made him a relatively wealthy man.

A painting by the Aberystwyth naïve artist depicting the harbour in the 1840s

A

ACLAND, Arthur [Herbert Dyke] (1847–1926)
Politician and promoter of education

A native of Devon and **Liberal** MP for Rotherham, Acland became an adoptive Welshman through his friendship with **T. E. Ellis**. (It is possible that they were lovers.) He lived for a time at **Clynnog** and was elected chairman of the committee planning the operation of the **Welsh Intermediate Education Act** (1889) in **Caernarfonshire**. Although his campaigning for a national education council for Wales came to nothing at the time, it paved the way for the **Central Welsh Board** in 1896. As vice-president of the Council for **Education** (1892–5), he elevated the status of the **Welsh language** in Welsh elementary schools and, working closely with Ellis and **O. M. Edwards**, he facilitated the granting of the charter of the **University of Wales** (1893).

ACT FOR THE BETTER PROPAGATION AND PREACHING OF THE GOSPEL IN WALES, The (1650)

This Act – the most important act relating to Wales passed during the **Commonwealth** era – was designed to invigorate the **Puritan** cause by hook or crook. Commissioners (71 in all) were appointed to examine ministers of **religion** and to replace those who failed to pass muster. Over a period of three years, 278 incumbents were ejected from their livings. Approvers were appointed to seek out godly **preachers** to replace the 'dumb dogs'. Provision was made for **education**, and schools were set up in 63 of Wales's market towns. Committed Puritans believed that this three-year experiment was a great success, but their opponents – and indeed the bulk of the **population** – were convinced that it was run by corrupt **English** firebrands. This 'unexpected experiment of granting Wales religious home rule' (**R. Tudur Jones**) expired at the end of March 1653.

ACTS OF 'UNION', The

This title, misleadingly adopted in the early 20th century, refers to two Acts of Parliament (1536 and 1542–3) whereby Wales was declared 'incorporated, united and annexed' to the English realm. The 1536 Act laid down principles 'for **law** and justice to be administered in Wales in like form as it is in this realm'; the Act of 1542–3, 'for Certain Ordinances in the king's dominion and **Principality** of Wales', contained adjustments and further details. This legislation brought **England** and Wales into a closer political, judicial and administrative relationship, building on social and governmental developments that had been taking place in the Principality, **counties** palatine and **march**er-lordships of Wales since Edward I's reign. The king's authority over Wales had been made more effective from the late 15th century through the development of the **Council of Wales and the March**; steps were taken after the **Glyndŵr Revolt** to treat the king's Welsh and English subjects alike. Many marcher-lordships had come into the king's possession. More immediately, the 'Acts of Union' sprang from the circumstances of Henry VIII's reign, especially the death of Sir **Rhys ap Thomas** (1525), and the unrest caused by Sir Rhys's grandson, Rhys ap Gruffudd (d.1531). Reforms designed to ensure peace and justice were in the air by 1531, though under Bishop **Rowland Lee**

(1534–43) the Council of Wales and the March enforced order in a more traditional and vigorous fashion. More radical reforms were prompted by Henry VIII's divorce and the breach with Rome, the proclamation of royal supremacy over the Church and related issues of order and defence. Preliminary statutes in 1534–5 emphasized the need for effective justice and administration throughout Wales, and justices of the peace from English counties extended their authority to the March. The reforms were also part of an attempt to bring uniformity and control to provincial **government** by attacking independent franchises in England, Wales, **Ireland** and Calais, and there may too have been expectations that such changes would bring financial gain in their wake.

The 1536 Act created five new shires (**Brecon**, **Denbigh**, **Monmouth**, **Montgomery** and **Radnor**) in addition to the six that comprised the old Principality (**Carmarthen**, **Cardigan**, **Anglesey**, **Caernarfon**, **Merioneth** and **Flint**) and two existing counties palatine, **Pembroke** and **Glamorgan**, in the March. The Welsh were formally given equality before the law. English common law, which had made great strides in Wales during the previous two centuries, became official usage. Each Welsh county was given one MP (wealthy Monmouthshire had two), and each county town except poor **Harlech** was given a parliamentary representative, with 'contributory' boroughs providing financial support. In the counties, male freeholders who had land worth 40 shillings a year had the vote, as did all freemen in the **boroughs**. The 1543 Act created JPs in Wales after the English model, thus ending the judicial powers of the marcher-lords; it also granted **Haverfordwest** the status of a county with its own MP, thus raising Wales's parliamentary representatives to 27. In addition, the 1543 Act established the Court of Great Sessions (*see* **Law**), with 12 shires grouped in 4 circuits; Monmouthshire joined the **Oxford** circuit, an anomaly that caused uncertainty and misunderstandings later as to whether or not the county was in Wales. Quarter sessions were established in each county, each with eight JPs. The Council in the March received statutory recognition with supervisory judicial powers. The **English language**, which had made considerable inroads in Wales over the centuries, was to be the language of administration and justice, and this became a source of resentment in later centuries. There was some delay in implementing the Acts fully; the first Welsh MPs were elected in 1542.

The Acts were welcomed by influential Welshmen, some of whom had petitioned for reform, and by English administrators and observers, and Henry VIII was praised for the measures. They were long regarded as of great benefit to Wales, but the growth of Welsh **nationalism** from the late 19th century onwards caused them to be vilified in some quarters. Yet, although the Acts could be seen as legislating that all the inhabitants of Wales were legally English, it would be equally valid to argue that, as there was no longer any advantage in boasting of the condition of being English, henceforth everyone living in Wales was Welsh.

ADAM OF USK (?1352–1430) Cleric and chronicler
Adam's chaotic career forms the basis of the *Chronicon Adae de Usk*. The chronicle contains an important account of the **Glyndŵr Revolt**. The inscription commemorating

him in St Mary's church, **Usk** (*c.*1430), is the oldest surviving such memorial in the **Welsh language**.

ADAMS, David (1845–1923) Theologian

A native of Tal-y-bont, **Ceredigion** (*see* **Ceulanamaesmawr**), Adams was a schoolteacher in **Llanelli** and **Ystradgynlais** before becoming a **Congregational** minister. He was a pioneer of liberal **theology** in Wales. He welcomed the neo-Hegelian emphasis in **philosophy** and applied the theory of evolution to theology, equating the evolution of creation with God's revelation through creation. He stressed the importance of the historical Jesus and of the ethical factor in Christianity. He is believed to have been the minister portrayed in some of the stories of Caradoc Evans (*see* **David Evans**).

ADFER

Adfer (now inactive) broke away from **Cymdeithas yr Iaith Gymraeg** (Welsh Language Society) in 1971. Largely influenced by Emyr Llywelyn (b.1944), it urged Welsh speakers to ensure the survival of **Welsh** by abandoning the Anglicized parts of Wales to build sustainable all-Welsh communities in the west.

AERON River (32 km)

The Aeron rises on the eastern slopes of Mynydd Bach (*see* **Llangwyryfon** and **Lledrod**) and follows a curving course to Cardigan Bay. Llyn Eiddwen and Llyn Fanod, **lakes** protected by the West Wales Wildlife Trust, are two of its headwaters. From Blaenpennal (Lledrod) to Talsarn (**Nantcwnlle**), the Aeron runs parallel to the **Teifi**, both **rivers** following the strike of the folded and faulted Silurian rocks. In the wetland area between Talsarn and **Ciliau Aeron**, the river has been tamed by channel straightening. The Aeron estuary became a **port** following the establishment of **Aberaeron** in 1807. The river has no major tributaries.

AFAN Commote and lordship

Located between the **Rivers** Afan and **Nedd**, Afan continued until the 14th century under the rule of descendants of **Iestyn ap Gwrgant**, the last king of **Morgannwg**. As late as 1365, Thomas, lord of Afan, who was styled de Avene, recalled with bitterness the **Norman** destruction of the kingdom of his ancestors. By 1375, however, the family had been induced to yield Afan to Edward **Despenser**, lord of **Glamorgan**.

AFRICANS

Wales's inhabitants of African descent, originating from **seafaring** in the 19th century, concentrated in the docklands, especially those of **Cardiff**. They expanded in the **First World War** because of demands for merchant seamen. Africans constituted approximately 25% of the black population of Butetown in the 1920s and 1930s – about 600 men (often married to local **women**). They came from many different parts of Africa, and included a strong community of **Somalis**, who comprised almost half the total. Both Africans and **West Indians** suffered in Cardiff's race riots of June 1919. Typical of the racial abuse to which they were subject was the comment of David Williams, chief constable of Cardiff, who deplored the fact that some of

them wore white flannel trousers, thus causing 'young girls to admire these beasts'. Such attacks led to the creation of the Sons of Africa Friendly Society in the 1930s, which survived in shadowy form until the 1990s, promoting a positive image of Africa and its people.

AGNOSTICS and ATHEISTS

While it may be convenient to discuss agnosticism and atheism together, it should be borne in mind that, for agnostics, the certainties of dogmatic atheists can be as unpalatable as the certainties of dogmatic religious believers.

For at least 12 centuries following the Christianization of Wales in the immediate post-**Roman** era, being Welsh was virtually synonymous with being Christian. Baron Herbert of Cherbury (**Edward Herbert**) is generally considered to be **Britain**'s first deist. His belief that religious faith was dependent upon reason rather than revelation was shared by late 18th-century radicals such as **Richard Price** and **David Williams** (1738–1816), but was fiercely rejected by most of the leaders of Welsh society, who claimed that they were speaking for the great mass of their fellow Welsh. They were probably correct for, as Scott Latourette, a leading historian of Christianity, noted, Christianity was more successful in retaining the informed allegiance of the mass of the **population** in Wales than in any other country in Europe.

Some change may be discerned in the second half of the 19th century, when geological discoveries, the theories of Darwin, and the rise of Higher Criticism – the rigorous analysis of biblical texts – all seemed to be undermining belief in the literal truth of the **Bible**. However, the growth of scepticism in Wales was slower than elsewhere, partly because, as the theologian Thomas Lewis put it: 'the **Welsh language** was a solid barrier keeping back the flood.' Among the early **Socialists**, there were those who argued that Christianity was being cynically used to persuade the working **class**es to accept their lot. Yet, for many **Labour** pioneers, the Christian message – especially the Sermon on the Mount – was the bedrock of their beliefs.

By the early 20th century, liberal or modern **theology** had been developed to accommodate the advances in **science** and criticism. To religious fundamentalists, it was a drab compromise; for many sceptics it was so threadbare that it seemed more intellectually honest to reject totally religious dogma. As the century advanced, many leaders of Welsh society acknowledged – in private at least – that they were agnostic. Some – the poet **T. H. Parry-Williams**, for example – were more open about their scepticism.

By the early 21st century, with hardly more than 5% of the inhabitants of Wales regular attendants at a place of worship, Wales had become one of the world's most secular countries. The Welsh did not revolt against religion, showing nothing of the antagonism and anti-clericalism characteristic of many **Roman Catholic** countries. Rather, they slipped away from its grasp, particularly as new diversions, many of which could conveniently be followed on Sunday, became popular. (Attendance at **Sunday school** declined in exact inverse proportion to the rise in private car ownership.) Even the most confirmed Welsh agnostics tend to view Christianity as it is practised in Wales in a benevolent light, and to consider the country's dwindling congregations to be centres of good – or at least to believe that it is unchivalrous to show hostility to such beleaguered groups. Yet, with a growing perception that much of the evil in the world has religious roots and, with the emergence of attitudes reminiscent of the hard religious Right of the United States, Welsh agnostics and atheists may yet become vocal.

AGRICULTURAL COUNCIL FOR WALES, The

An early example of **devolution**, the council was inaugurated in 1912 to oversee educational and livestock improvement schemes; its first commissioner was **C. Bryner Jones**. Nominated members from county councils, the **University of Wales** and the farming industry met twice a year, until its abolition after the **Second World War**.

AGRICULTURAL LABOURERS

Although not specifically paid servants, the *taeogion* (bond men) of medieval Wales were essentially agricultural labourers. With the development of capitalist farming, these labourers became the largest **class** in most Welsh rural communities. As the demand for **food** increased, concurrent with the rapid expansion of the **population** of **Britain** in the first half of the 19th century, so the numbers of agricultural labourers advanced dramatically between 1801 and 1851. Taken on by farmers at hiring fairs, Welsh labourers were either unmarried living-in servants (*gweision*), frequently accommodated in stable lofts (*see* **Stable-Loft Singing**) or married labourers (*gweithwyr*) who had separate accommodation, often in a cottage rented from the employer. Additionally, there were the 'bound tenants', labourers renting a small (1–2 ha) holding attached to a particular farm, and the casual workers who travelled from farm to farm seeking seasonal work. Farm labourers often enjoyed close social contact with employers through joint membership of **Nonconformist** chapels, although there were subtle and carefully orchestrated social divisions between the classes, especially on the larger farms.

As the **railway** system expanded and employment opportunities opened up in the southern valleys and elsewhere, Wales's agricultural labourers declined in number from 73,300 in 1851 to 39,500 in 1911 – a fall of 46%. The numbers continued to decline inexorably, largely as a result of farm rationalization and the mechanization of **agriculture**. From the late 19th century onwards, the social gulf between farmers and labourers deepened, especially during the **First World War** when agricultural wages (still paid partially in kind) failed to keep up with the cost of living. There was a brief period of interest in **trade unionism** between 1917 and 1920, but activists failed to stimulate mass action by labourers, thus giving rise to what David Pretty described as 'the rural revolt that failed'. Fear of eviction, dismissal and unemployment on the part of the workers effectively precluded large-scale unionization. Perhaps for this reason the Agricultural Wages Boards and official bodies later in the 20th century consistently failed to raise the wages of the rural labourers in Wales to those of their urban counterparts. In 2002, Wales had 2954 farm employees working full time, 2691 working part time, and 5173 working seasonally or on a casual basis.

AGRICULTURAL SOCIETIES

The encouragement of improved farming practices through the formation of agricultural societies, which sponsored competitive shows of livestock and prizes for the best **arable crops**, as well as the purchase of superior bulls and stallions for local use, began in the mid-18th century. The first – the **Breconshire** Agricultural Society – was founded in 1755, and by 1817 there was one in every Welsh **county**. Initiated by landowners to ensure their lands were maintained in good heart and their tenants could afford their rents, in the early 20th century they became part of the national agricultural establishment.

In 1904, the Welsh National Agricultural Society held the first national show at **Aberystwyth**. In 1920, it became the Royal Welsh Agricultural Society and continued to expand steadily; since 1963 its show has been held annually at the society's permanent ground at **Llanelwedd** near **Builth**. The **Royal Welsh Agricultural Show** has become the major annual festival of the countryside in Wales, but the society has always been more than simply a show society, as demonstrated by its support of the native breed societies, the holding of conferences and the organizing of demonstrations and open days.

Many local agricultural societies were formed by Welsh farmers during the first half of the 20th century, to purchase farm requisites more cheaply and to market their produce more effectively. Apart from the statutory marketing boards, co-operative purchase generally proved more successful than co-operative marketing. In the last decades of the 20th century, many of these local organizations amalgamated with one another to form much larger buying groups.

AGRICULTURE

Agriculture has a wholly exceptional place among the activities that have absorbed the energies of humanity. As **food** is its primary product, it is the only activity that produces a commodity which human beings cannot live without. Thus, over the many millennia when human endeavours could produce little beyond basic necessities, the bulk of the **population** consisted of agriculturists. In the case of Wales, this meant that from the coming of agriculture 6000 years ago to at least the early decades of the 19th century, the majority of the country's population was directly involved with the land. Over that vast period, the economic and social history of Wales is essentially the history of agriculture.

Compared with much of Europe – Scandinavia, for example, or the arid lands of the Mediterranean littoral – the agriculture of Wales is not particularly disadvantaged. Yet, as most commentators on the subject assume that the norm is that which pertains to lowland **England**, the prevalent view insists that farming in Wales is, and always has been, congenitally backward and impoverished. With heavy rainfall (*see* **Climate**) and with almost half the country situated over 200 m above sea level, few areas are well suited to cereal production – the central consideration in the European Union's declaration that only a third of the agricultural land of Wales rises above the 'less favoured' category. Nevertheless, much of the country provides admirable pasture, the key factor determining that farming

Pig-killing day at Maescar, Breconshire, *c.*1900

in Wales is mainly concerned with stock rather than crops. This would seem to have been the case with the earliest farmers who were primarily **cattle** raisers, although they also kept **goats**, **sheep** and **pigs**, and they hoed patches of land on which they planted beans and emmer wheat (*see* **Neolithic Age**). Their farms were clearings in the woodland that had covered Wales following the end of the last Ice Age. Low population density meant that there was no need to ensure the continued fertility of the land; exhausted fields were abandoned and new clearings made. Field clearing was greatly assisted as stone tools gave way to metal ones – bronze after *c.*2000 BC, and **iron** after *c.*500 BC (*see* **Bronze Age**, **Iron Age**). Denser settlement was also encouraged by the improved climate of the millennium after *c.*2400 BC. Higher temperatures led to the colonization of the uplands, which often proved an easier environment than the valley bottoms with their thick forest, extensive waterlogging, and prevalent ague and liver fluke. Pollen studies have shown that cereals were grown in *c.*2000 BC in the upper Brenig valley (*see* **Cerrigydrudion**), 500 m above sea level.

Increasing population, together with climatic deterioration after *c.*1400 BC, caused major changes in the mid and late Bronze Age. Pressure on land led to the abandonment of the 'slash and burn' tactics of earlier generations, forcing farmers to master manuring techniques; they thus became husbandmen, the essential prerequisite of settled agricultural communities. The same pressures gave rise to the notion that land had its owners, thus ushering in the concept of territoriality, which would become a determining factor in the history of Welsh agriculture. It was not only land which could be owned; so also could those who

worked it, and thus the presumed egalitarianism of Neolithic Wales had, by the last millennium of Welsh prehistory, developed into a far more stratified society. By the last centuries of its prehistory, Wales was **Celt**ic-speaking, and it is reasonable to assume that the classical authors' accounts of the Celtic society of mainland Europe, which portray a warlike aristocracy living on the surplus produced by their dependent serfs, were, at least in part, relevant to the situation in Wales.

During the three centuries and more of **Roman** domination, the agriculture of Wales underwent significant changes. In the south-east, villa owners introduced the heavy plough and practised capitalist farming. The needs of the legionary fortress at **Caerleon** and the Roman town at **Caerwent** made demands upon the surrounding area, where drainage schemes and sea defences were undertaken. The Romans brought new crops, possibly apples and **oats** (*see* **Plants**), and almost certainly carrots, turnips, parsnips, **leeks**, cherries, vines, walnuts and sweet chestnuts.

Following the collapse of the Roman Empire, Wales was probably more profoundly agricultural than it had been before the coming of the legions. In the second half of the first Christian millennium, nothing was created comparable with the quasi-urban settlements of the greater **hillforts**, and a thousand years would go by before Wales again had a town the size of Caerwent. In the immediate post-Roman centuries, the centres of Wales's missionary **saints** were a fundamental factor in the country's pattern of agricultural settlement. It is surely significant that over half the names of Welsh ecclesiastical **parishes** begin with *llan* – primarily the word for an enclosure – but one which came,

Haymaking at Pontrhydyceirt, Cilgerran, Pembrokeshire, *c.*1910

primarily, to mean a sacred enclosure in which Christians buried their dead and, eventually, built their churches. The era of the **Celtic Church** was also the era of the consolidation of the Welsh kingdoms, which were wholly agricultural in their economic underpinnings. The nature of their economic structure can be interpreted from the earliest strata of the **Law** of **Hywel Dda**, which make clear that such stability as the kingdoms possessed rested upon traditions relating to the use and ownership of land. The law recognized two main forms of tenure: that of the *taeog*, broadly equivalent to the English villein, who was tied to the land and whose function was to produce agricultural commodities for his superiors; and that of the *bonheddwr* – the freeman, the owner of a portion of his clan's land which passed, on his death, in equal shares to his sons.

The earliest evidence indicates that the *taeogion* were the majority – overwhelmingly so on fertile land. The **Normans** invaded and established the **March**, where they introduced the **manor**ial system of England with its emphasis on cereal production. Links with the religious orders of mainland Europe, fostered by the Normans, led to the establishment of wealthy **monasteries**. Those of the **Cistercians**, an order favoured by the native princes, gained possession of much of upland Wales – the grazing grounds of their flocks of **sheep** which provided the fleeces for an expanding **wool** trade. The Normans, and later the native princes, fostered the development of towns, the growth of trade and the circulation of coinage, all factors which lessened the previously total dependence of the Welsh **economy** on agriculture. Upheavals caused by conquest and

counter-conquest diminished the ranks of the *taeogion*, causing the *bonheddwyr* to represent the majority of the population of Wales, particularly of those areas conquered by Edward I in the late 13th century.

Economic development from the 11th century onwards and the improved climate of the 250 years after *c.*1050 encouraged population growth. By 1300, Wales had perhaps 300,000 inhabitants, of whom at least 90% were involved in agriculture. The clan lands or *gwelyau* of the *bonheddwyr* expanded; by 1313, the male descendants of Iorwerth ap Cadwgan (d.*c.*1230) numbered 27, and new settlements were created on assarted land (land cleared of forest to make it cultivatable) long distances from the clan's original home.

Favourable conditions ceased in the early 14th century as a result of climatic deterioration, land exhaustion and cattle disease. The crowning disaster was the **Black Death** of 1348–9, which killed perhaps a third of the population. The plague was at its worst in the more densely populated *taeog* settlements, a section of the population whose usefulness was declining as landlords ceased to be involved directly in farming. By 1400, the population of Wales had declined to about 200,000. This demographic crisis halted the subdivision of the lands of the *bonheddwyr* and created a land market in Wales, a phenomenon outside the scope of the *gwely* system. Traditional Welsh tenures were increasingly abandoned, with the larger landowners – the ancestors of **Owain Glyndŵr** among them – adopting primogeniture, renting land for money rents and consolidating into compact farms the strip lands of the *gwely* system.

By the late 15th century, the essentials of the agricultural economy, which would dominate Wales for at least the following three centuries, were already apparent. Also, most of the great estates that would later characterize the Welsh countryside were already in existence, at least in embryonic form, and their owners were honing the skills in land accumulation which their descendants would exercise so effectively. A **class** system emerged, headed by the **gentry**; beneath them were yeomen, small tenant farmers and landless labourers – the latter benefiting, at least temporarily, from the scarcity of labour caused by population decline.

The more stable circumstances of the 16th and early 17th centuries led to renewed demographic growth, with the population of Wales rising to perhaps 360,000 by 1620. Assartment became more intense, and the English poet Thomas Churchyard (c.1520–1604) praised Welsh farmers for ploughing 'where sturdy oaks once stood'. **Enclosure** became fashionable; **John Leland**, the English antiquarian, noted that **Anglesey** farmers were surrounding their fields with walls, and **Rice Merrick** observed that by his time hedges were universal in the **Vale of Glamorgan**. Welsh agriculture produced an increasing surplus. The chief traded commodity was cattle – **droving** was the main source of ready money in the countryside – but the sale of flannel was also significant, as was the export of dairy produce from favoured areas such as south **Pembrokeshire** (*see* **Woollen Industry**). Flannel production was essentially a domestic industry. Thus, with the growth of proto-industrialism among them, many farmers came to be as dependent on the secondary processes of agriculture as on the primary ones, a development which became more marked in subsequent centuries. Economic growth did not lead to general prosperity, since severe inflation, natural disasters and the ability of landlords to cream off the greater part of the profits of their tenants meant that the majority of the population teetered on the brink of destitution.

The growth of industrial centres such as the **copper** works of **Neath**, the **lead** mines of **Cardiganshire** and the varied industries of the north-east meant that an increasing proportion of the population ceased to be directly dependent upon agriculture, although such developments should not be overemphasized, for they were occurring in sectors which were not, as yet, central to the economy. There was also a significant growth of towns, although most of them were little more than trading centres for the surrounding farms, and many townspeople, with their cattle in back-street byres, were themselves semi-agriculturists.

Farming conditions deteriorated in the mid and late 17th century. The 'mini Ice Age' of the 1690s was particularly devastating, when the harvest failed at least every other year, causing widespread shortages. The main feature of the period, however, was the growth and consolidation of the great estates, a process much aided by marriage with heiresses and by the adoption by landowners of strict settlement, a device preventing the profligate from selling ancestral lands. By the mid-18th century, with the growth in population accelerating, markets for Welsh agricultural products expanded, encouraging landowners to make improvements. Progressive farmers came to adopt crop rotation, the planting of turnips and

potatoes, selective stockbreeding and a greater use of lime (*see* **Limestone**). Such developments were fostered by **agricultural societies**, the first of which – the **Breconshire** society – was founded in 1755. By 1818, every **county** in Wales had such a society. Enclosure was seen as the key to improvement. Field creation had been undertaken in Wales since the Neolithic period, but in 1750, a quarter of Wales – mainly upland pastures – was still common land. 'Inclose, inclose, ye swains!' wrote the poet **John Dyer**, '... in fields/ Promiscuous held, all culture vanishes'. Enclosure by act of parliament began in Wales in 1733, and, by 1818, over 100 acts had been passed enclosing over 100,000 ha of land, legislation motivated more by a desire to intensify landlord rights than by concern for agricultural improvement.

The **French Revolutionary and Napoleonic Wars** (1793–1815) had a massive impact upon Welsh agriculture. Food prices soared, leading to corn riots and rent rises. Landowners sought to exert greater control over the activities of their tenants, and thus the traditional three-life or 99-year leases gave way to annual tenancies. Some Welsh landowners – **Thomas Johnes** of Hafod, in particular – won wide acclaim as estate improvers, but much of the wealth produced by the wartime prosperity of agriculture was spent on unproductive extravagance.

The end of the war led to a sharp fall in the price of agricultural products, despite the attempts of the landlord-dominated legislature to maintain cereal prices through the **Corn Laws**. The post-war years were a period of acute poverty in rural Wales. Appalling weather resulted in harvest failure and the collapse of **banks** brought destitution. Demographic growth caused overpopulation in the countryside, a development that led to squatting on marginal land – the *tai unnos* tradition. The **government** reacted to poverty and underemployment through the harsh **Poor Law** Amendment Act of 1834. Distress lasted until the 1840s and found expression in enclosure riots, corn riots, labourers' risings, anti-Poor Law protests and, above all, the **Rebecca Riots** of 1839–43.

The situation improved from mid-century onwards, as the expanding towns and industrial areas absorbed the rural surplus, and as **railways** facilitated the export of agricultural produce. By then, agriculture no longer provided Wales's main source of employment. In 1811, only 9 of the 87 **hundreds** of Wales had a majority of inhabitants not employed in agriculture. The following decades saw the progressive dethronement of agriculture as the dominant occupation, although its should be borne in mind that many listed in the census as quarrymen or **coal**miners were also smallholders, their land engaging their affections and providing them with a second income; such agro-industrial settlements were a feature particularly of **Caernarfonshire** and the northern fringes of the south Wales coalfield. By 1851, the proportion of adult Welsh males primarily employed in agriculture had declined to 35%, and it would slump to 12% by 1911; in that year, however, they were still a majority in **Radnorshire** and **Montgomeryshire**.

A rapidly rising population increasingly divorced from work on the land created unprecedented markets for the products of the minority who continued to be involved in agriculture. In the third quarter of the 19th century, farmers and landowners vigorously sought to meet the challenge. This was the era of 'High Farming' with heavy investment in farm buildings, tile drains, fertilizers and the rationalization of holdings. Prosperity lasted until the late 1870s, when the competition of imports from America and Australasia led to a sharp decline in the price of agricultural products – although the severity of the decline was more marked in the cereal producing areas of eastern England than it was in Wales with its essentially pastoral agriculture. The agricultural depression led to a major migration from the land, particularly by agricultural labourers fleeing the poverty and subservience of their occupation. Few farmers left the land. Despite the depression, a craving for land continued to be a feature of Welsh rural communities, and the number of farm holdings in Wales over 10 ha remained stable at about 30,000 from the 1870s until the 1950s.

The depression coincided with increasing criticism of landlordism, which had its roots in the writings of mid-19th-century radicals. It was linked with the attack on the entrenched political power of landowners, and derived much of its passion from the political evictions of 1859 and 1868. The **Land Question** in Wales, while never as intense as that in **Ireland**, developed its own distinctive character, finding expression in the **Tithe** War of the 1880s and analysis, through the Royal Commission on Land in Wales, in the 1890s. Owner occupation was lower in Wales than in any other part of **Britain**. Land hunger meant that Wales

Mechanization of agriculture: a Fordson tractor with harrows, Y Ddwyryd farm, Corwen, 1956

had no untenanted farms, and therefore Welsh landowners were not obliged markedly to reduce their rents as were their counterparts in eastern England where there was little competition for tenancies. Above all, landlords were viewed by the mass of Welsh rural dwellers as alien beings, different in language, **religion**, and political allegiance from their tenantry. In the late 19th century, they were stripped of their influence over Welsh **parliamentary representation** and of Welsh local government, influence which inspired much of the rhetoric of **David Lloyd George**. Legislation deprived them of their unfettered control of their tenants, and research institutes and university departments replaced them as disseminators of new agricultural techniques. Welsh landowners, sensing the antipathy of the society around them, sold up and moved out on a scale unequalled elsewhere in Britain, for the transfer of farms from landowner to occupier began earlier and was carried out more thoroughly in Wales than in any other part of Britain.

Large-scale sales were very much a feature of the early years of the 20th century and they continued throughout the **First World War**. The war had a profound effect on Welsh farming, with the price of agricultural produce rising by 300% between 1914 and 1920. Government-established county agricultural committees insisted that agricultural labourers should share in the new prosperity; their earnings rose by 200%, but failed to keep pace with inflation. The immediate post-war years were the heyday of **trade unionism** among labourers. They reacted to their failed 'rural revolt' by leaving the land; Wales had 33,400 full-time farm labourers in 1921 and only 2954 in 2002.

The prosperity enjoyed by farmers during the war enabled many of them to buy their holdings in the large-scale sales held by landowners in the immediate post-war years, a period when perhaps a third of the land of Wales changed hands. However, the repeal in 1921 of the Act of 1917 guaranteeing minimum prices for cereals initiated a deterioration in agricultural prices that turned into a wholesale decline with the onset of the world **depression** in 1929. Those who had paid inflated prices during the sales boom were particularly badly hit, for many of the new freeholders became so burdened with debt that they were owners in name only.

Yet the interwar years was not entirely a period of gloom. **The Welsh Department of the Ministry of Agriculture** was founded in 1919 to co-ordinate government policies in Wales. Agricultural university education made significant advances. A department of agriculture was established at **Bangor** in 1889 and at **Aberystwyth** in 1890, and both departments became increasingly involved in extramural work. Developments at Aberystywth were particularly significant, with **A. W. Ashby** establishing Agricultural Economics as an academic discipline, and **George Stapledon** founding the Plant Breeding Station (now the **Institute of Grassland and Environmental Research**) in 1919. Stapledon sought to improve the productivity of upland Wales through fertilizing and introducing appropriate grasses, a programme which enabled the uplands to sustain far larger flocks of sheep than before. Bangor also had a department of forestry, the students of which were in increasing demand following the establishment of the **Forestry Commission** in 1919; the work of the commission caused timber rather than mutton and wool to become the chief product of much of upland Wales. The Land Drainage Act of 1930 initiated a dramatic increase in drainage schemes. Deficiency payments for fatstock were introduced in 1934, as were grants for spreading lime and basic slag in 1937. Above all, the Milk Marketing Board was established in 1933, building on co-operative ventures among farmers fostered by the Welsh Agricultural Organization Society. By 1939, nearly 20,000 Welsh farms were producing milk for the board, a development which meant that the majority of the country's farmers had, for the first time, a secure market and a regular monthly income.

Hardly had the Milk Marketing Board become firmly established than the **Second World War** broke out. It proved a huge stimulus to agriculture. Official statistics indicate that the net income of British farmers rose by 207% between 1938 and 1942 but, as many farmers were involved in the black market, such statistics probably understate the increase. The re-established county committees set ploughing targets for farmers. Arable land in Wales increased from 215,000 ha in 1939 to 500,000 ha in 1944, a year in which the proportion of the country's land under the plough was greater than it had been during the heyday of 19th-century 'High Farming'. The rapid increase in acreage of arable land created a demand for machinery. There were 1932 tractors on the farms of Wales in 1938 and 13,652 in 1946; the age of mechanized farming was dawning.

Unlike previous wars, the Second World War was not followed by a depression in agriculture. This was partly because food shortages in 1945 were greater than they had been in 1918. More significant, however, was the Agriculture Act of 1947 which guaranteed a market and stable prices for most of the products of the farms of Britain. The Act was the starting point of the array of deficiency payments, grants, subsidies and improvement schemes that helped to revolutionize Welsh agriculture. Henceforth, farming – once the most self-reliant of occupations – would become almost as dependent on government decisions as were the nationalized industries; it was not the weather, but the Annual Price Review, which determined its fortunes. Indeed, it was claimed that Cardiganshire farmers were insisting on getting married in **English**, in order to hear the magic word *grant* during the ceremony.

In this agriculture revolution, mechanization was as great a factor as government intervention. Every farmer came to own a tractor and a host of other machines, a development which caused a further contraction in the number of farm labourers. With labour-saving devices, farmers could farm larger areas of land, and such was the cost of the machines that they were obliged to maximize their income. Machines needed larger fields, and thus hedges were ripped out, altering the appearance of the traditional Welsh bocage, with its small fields and thick hedges. The number of farms in Wales halved between 1951 and 1991; by 2001, the total number working full-time on the land had slumped to 26,100, of whom a mere 12.6% were paid employees. Of the employed population of Wales, 8.2% worked in agriculture in 1951 and 1.07% in

2002. There was, however, an increase in part-time farmers, partners and directors from 12,700 in 1992 to 22,100 in 2001. With mechanization, most traditional farm buildings became redundant. Many were converted for tourist use, while farms acquired tall silos and other buildings that gave them a distinctly factory-like appearance.

The decline in the numbers directly involved with the land led to a fundamental change in the nature of rural communities. The countryside traditionally contained three groupings of people: the primary rural population – those who worked the land; the secondary rural population – those who provided services for the primary population; and the adventitious rural dwellers – those who had no economic role in the countryside but who lived there from choice. In the 19th century, the first two groupings were large and the third very small. By the 21st century, the third grouping far outstripped the other two in size. As mechanization and farm amalgamation caused the **housing** stock of the countryside to exceed the needs of the primary and secondary groupings, a fourth grouping emerged, the temporary rural dwellers who bought the excess housing stock as **second homes**.

The decrease in the agricultural workforce was accompanied by a marked increase in agricultural production. Between 1950 and 1980, the number of sheep in Wales rose from 3.8 million to 8.2 million. In 1950, the Milk Marketing Board bought a total of 820 million litres of milk from its 30,000 Welsh suppliers; in 1980, there were only 7959 suppliers, but they produced 1578 million litres of milk. In 1980, the number of hectares planted with grain in Wales was only two-fifths of what it had been in 1950, but the tonnage of grain harvested had increased by 43%.

Productivity was much encouraged when, in 1972, Britain joined the European Common Market with its generous Common Agricultural Policy. The cost of the policy came under attack, especially as surpluses accumulated. In 1984, strict quotas were imposed on milk producers, a severe blow to the prosperity of many rural districts, particularly in the south-west. Dairy farmers were also affected by the abolition of the Milk Marketing Board; essentially a compulsory co-operative, its existence seemed to be at odds with the competition policy of the European Union, and in 1994 it was replaced by a voluntary co-operative, Milk Marque. Restrictions on the right to receive subsidies for sheep and beef breeding cows were introduced, as were 'set-aside' payments for leaving land unused. Economic losses due to animal health problems were substantial: in the dairy herd (267,700 in 2002) the main problems are mastitis, infertility, lameness and diseases that cause abortion; in the sheep flock (10,050,000 in 2002) the main problems are scrapie, sheep scab, foot rot and fluke, together with the escalating costs of anti-worm treatments and vaccines. Intensive farming, with its heavy use of fertilizers, insecticides and weedkillers caused increasing concern to environmentalists. The unnatural conditions under which many animals are kept, fed and marketed have aroused protests – which seemed justified as stock succumbed to bovine spongiform encephalopathy (BSE or 'mad cow disease'), swine fever and foot and mouth disease, and as food came to be contaminated with e-coli and salmonella.

Traditional sheep farming and a modern wind farm at Cefn Croes, Pontarfynach

An anti-farmer sentiment emerged, a development aided by the **fox-hunting** controversy. As farmers became subject to a plethora of increasingly strict animal welfare codes and anti-pollution laws, keeping a record of their activities became ever more burdensome, with skills in form-filling apparently more important than skills in husbandry. Stress-related illnesses became common among farmers, and suicide increased dramatically.

At the beginning of the 21st century, the prospects for Welsh agriculture seemed bleak. The average age of Welsh farmers was in the late 50s, and with sons and daughters reluctant to follow their parents, the agricultural community seemed destined to attenuate further. As spokesmen for the food lobby were increasingly drawn, not from farmers' representatives but from managers of supermarket companies and middle-class city dwellers (many of them nostalgic for a mythical golden age of contented peasants), farmers came to feel powerless. With agriculturists a minority, even in wholly rural areas, their political influence declined – a decline hastened by the abolition of **rural district** councils in 1974. Farmers came to see themselves as a beleaguered species, punished for their enterprise and industry, and expressed their concern through organizations such as the Countryside Alliance.

Some argue that, since agriculture makes only a minimal contribution to the Gross Domestic Product in Wales, and that as subsidies, although less than they were, represent a significant outlay, consideration should be given to the abandonment of farming, at least in the 'less favoured' areas – although most commentators would shrink from the social and cultural devastation which would thereby ensue.

Others have argued that the future of Welsh farming lies in a return to more natural – and more labour-intensive – methods of food production. Such arguments are mainly concerned with organic farming and with the manufacture of farm-produced food for retail sale – the form of farming practised everywhere in Wales until at least the late 19th century. The first modern organic farm in Wales was that of Dinah Williams, started at Dôl-y-bont (**Geneu'r Glyn** near **Borth**) in 1948, an enterprise which later became Rachel's Dairy. In 1999, the **National Assembly for Wales** called for 10% of Welsh agriculture to be organic by 2005, and in 2000 the Organic Centre Wales was established at Aberystwyth. At the opening of the 21st century, registered organic farming was practised on 35,000 ha of the land of Wales, a country consisting of 2,076,000 ha. Farm-produced food for retail sale – added value products – although still a very small-scale activity, has achieved successes, with the farm **cheeses** of the south-west, in particular, winning wide renown.

There are two other blueprints for the future of Welsh agriculture. One maintains that although farmers are undoubtedly food producers, they are also – and in some areas, more importantly – the guardians of the beauty of the landscape and the diversity of wildlife, and that their efforts in that sphere should be adequately recognized. Thus, much of what the 20th century assumed to be progressive activity – such as the draining of wetlands, and the replacement of natural upland swards with more productive grasses – should no longer be pursued and should, if possible, be reversed. Such was the thinking behind the Tir Cymen scheme and its successor, Tir Gofal, which were attempts to replace production subsidies by land-management strategies in what is perceived to be in the interest of society as a whole.

The other blueprint is encapsulated in that much vaunted option: diversification. Farmers – particularly those on 'less favoured' land – should cease solely to be farmers; they could also be teachers, telecottagers or accountants – a reversion to the agro-industrial communities once numerous on the fringes of Welsh industrial areas. Farms should not only be centres of food production; they could also provide bed and breakfast, pony trekking, **bird** watching, sites for wind farms and a myriad other projects. It remains to be seen whether such suggestions – which indicate in the main that the future lies in returning to the past – are the counsels of despair or whether they offer serious hope for the prospects of Welsh agriculture.

AIRPORTS

During the relatively brief history of aviation, around 50 airfields have at some time been operative in Wales. Among the earliest were airship stations located near **Pembroke** and **Bangor** and at Mona (**Bodffordd**). Wales's chief airport is **Cardiff** International, which began as an RAF station in April 1942. Various sites have served the Welsh capital; the current site – at **Rhoose** – is 16 km south-west of the city. It has one of **Britain**'s longest civilian airport runways (2.354 km) and, among British airports, it has the second best weather record. In 2006, it handled a record two million passengers, the majority travelling on charter services. Scheduled flights are limited but increasing; frequent flights to Amsterdam allow passengers from Rhoose to use the services of KLM and other airlines serving Schipol; in 2004, a summer season transatlantic flight to Florida was introduced. **Swansea** Airport has at various times served the needs of club fliers, general aviation, helicopters and parachutists. Commercial services, suspended in the 1970s, were resumed in 2001, with regular flights to Cork, Dublin and, later, Jersey, Amsterdam and **London**, but the venture failed to attract sufficient numbers of passengers and was discontinued in 2004.

Military requirements are served by RAF stations. At **Valley**, there are flight training schools and search and rescue helicopters, while Mona acts as a satellite field for Valley and also handles light aircraft. In 2006, plans were announced for regular north–south civilian flights between Valley and Cardiff; the four flights a day (initially) would take half an hour each, compared with a car journey of four-and-a-half hours. At **St Athan**, in the **Vale of Glamorgan**, all front-line, high performance fighter aircraft were maintained for both the RAF and Royal Navy until 2007; gliders and the **University of Wales** air squadron are resident there. In 2003, the First Battalion **Welsh Guards** moved from Aldershot to take up residence at the base. The factory near **Hawarden** Airport (*see* Broughton and Bretton) is famous for the manufacture of wing structures for the European Airbus consortium, and also has thriving flying clubs and corporate handling services. **Chirk** is a centre for aircraft restoration, while the **Montgomeryshire** Mid-Wales Airport at **Welshpool** is used by light aircraft. Both **Llanbedr**, near **Harlech**, and **Aberporth** have been employed as military establishments, specializing in drogue target and artillery research. **Haverfordwest** serves both light and executive aircraft operations. The former RAF station at **Brawdy** is now used by the army.

Among the indigenous airline operators, Cambrian Airways holds a special place. The company began operations in 1935 and became the first independent British airline to be granted a licence for a scheduled air service – that between Cardiff and Weston-super-Mare. In 1968, the airline joined forces with BKS to form British Air Services. By 1970, the aircraft fleet included jets and served a network of 30 airports in 10 countries. The airline eventually fell victim to the **oil** crisis, and closed in 1976.

ALBION COLLIERY DISASTER, The,
Cilfynydd (Pontypridd)
At 3.50 p.m. on Saturday, 23 June 1894, an explosion killed at least 290 men, the exact toll being uncertain because it proved impossible to determine precisely how many men were underground. Of 16 men found alive by rescue teams, only 5 survived. The explosion was attributed to an underground shot detonation igniting **coal** dust which, because of inadequate dust suppression, led to the explosion spreading throughout the mine.

The House of Commons refused the plea of **Keir Hardie**, then MP for West Ham South, that there should be a vote of sympathy for the victims' families. Instead, it voted to congratulate the Duke and Duchess of York on the birth of a son (later Edward VIII), thus eliciting from Hardie a celebrated anti-royalist diatribe in which he accurately prophesied that the baby would eventually seek a morganatic marriage.

ALERT
A **Liverpool** sailing packet, the *Alert* hit an offshore rock at West Mouse (**Cylch-y-Garn**), **Anglesey**, on 26 March 1823, and quickly sank, drowning most of those on board: an estimated 130 were lost. The incident was witnessed by Rev. James Williams, rector of Llanfair-yng-Nghornwy; he and his wife Frances devoted the rest of their lives to the promotion of **lifeboats**. They formed the Anglesey Association for the Preservation of Life from Shipwreck, and established at Cemlyn, in 1828, the first operational lifeboat station in the north.

ALLCHURCH, Ivor [John] (1929–97) Footballer
Among an extraordinary post-**First World War** generation of **Swansea**-born **football**ers, Ivor Allchurch was the most closely identified with, and cherished by, his home town. An elegant inside-forward who combined creativity with consistent goal-scoring, he was an international in less than a year from his Swansea Town debut at Christmas 1949, and a Wales regular until the mid-1960s. His totals of 68 caps and 23 goals for Wales were records at the time. In the 1958 World Cup, he scored an extraordinary volleyed goal against Hungary, and was declared 'the finest inside-forward in the world' by Santiago Bernabeu, president of Real Madrid.

He spent most of his career – incorporating 694 league games and 251 goals, both Welsh records at the time – in the lower divisions. Any transfer in the early 1950s would have broken the British transfer fee record, but he chose to stay with Swansea until 1958. He moved to Newcastle before returning to play for **Cardiff** City, then Swansea again.

ALLEN, Norman Percy (1903–72) Metallurgist
Born in **Wrexham** and educated at Sheffield, Allen undertook research at **Swansea** and Birmingham into the porosity of **copper** alloys. He then investigated the formation of high-strength nickel alloys at elevated temperatures; without such alloys the development of the Whittle engine and other gas turbines would have been seriously handicapped. As superintendent of the metallurgical division of the National Physical Laboratory, Teddington, he worked on the problem of 'creep' in stressed materials at high temperature, especially in power stations, and on the development of superconducting magnets and the examination of dislocations in metals.

ALMANACS
Printed almanacs in **Welsh** first appeared in **London** in 1681 and their appeal remained undiminished until the late 19th century. The almanac normally contained miscellaneous information, an astronomical and astrological guide, prognostications of the weather, lists of fairs, markets and festivals, a chronology of historical events, a list of **law** terms, selections of poetry and **literature**, and a wide variety of

advertisements. The most successful almanackers, such as **Thomas Jones** (1648–1713) of London and Shrewsbury, constantly introduced fresh ideas and information in order to appeal to new readers, and almanacs, together with **ballads**, were the cheapest and most avidly read publications on the market. The almanac both reflected and sustained the traditional superstitions and magical practices which were an integral part of the popular culture. It also helped to revive the **eisteddfod**ic tradition. Both Thomas Jones and Siôn Rhydderch (the first to publish an almanac in Wales) used the almanac to publicize *eisteddfodau* held in local taverns. Their successors – Evan Davies, John Prys and Cain Jones – made a comfortable living from publishing almanacs and other popular miscellanea, but the most popular and successful 19th-century almanacs were the **Holyhead** almanacs published by John Roberts and his son Robert, both of whom pursued a thriving trade in pirated editions.

ALYN AND DEESIDE (Alun A Glannau Dyfrdwy) Constituency and one-time district

Following the abolition of **Flintshire** in 1974, Alyn and Deeside was created as a district of the new **county** of **Clwyd**. It consisted of what had been the **urban districts** of **Buckley** and **Connah's Quay** and the **rural district** of **Hawarden**. In 1996, the district became part of the reconstituted county of Flint. The name survives as that of a constituency.

AMBLESTON (Treamlod), Pembrokeshire (1558 ha; 367 inhabitants)

Located east of the **Haverfordwest–Fishguard road** (the A40), the **community** gets its name from Amelot, a **Flemish** settler. St Mary's church was largely rebuilt in 1906; its 12th-century tower survives. The communion service held in 1755 in Woodstock chapel (1754, 1808) was the first such service to be held in a Welsh **Wesleyan** chapel. At Scollock West Farm is what may be considered to be Wales's national monument to the concept of owner occupation. Erected in the 1920s, it consists of full-sized marble statues of John and Martha Llewellin who 'by the blessing of God on their joint endeavours and thrift, bought this farm and hand it down without encumbrance to their heirs'. The figures were carved in Italy from plaster models made from a wedding photograph.

AMBROSIUS (Emrys Wledig; fl.5th century) Political and military leader

Ambrosius, usually identified as Ambrosius Aurelianus, was descended, according to **Gildas**, from a noble **Roman** family. The Emrys Wledig of Welsh tradition, he was credited with leading resistance to the **Anglo-Saxon** invasions. Tradition links him with Dinas Emrys (*see* **Beddgelert**).

AMERIK (Ap Meurig or A'Meryke), Richard (fl.1498) Customs official

A wealthy collector of customs at Bristol and originally from **Glamorgan**, Amerik was an intermediary between Henry VII of **England** and John Cabot when the latter explored **North America**'s eastern coastline in 1497–8. Some claim America was named after him.

AMGOED Commote

One of the **commotes** of **Cantref Gwarthaf**, it seems that, originally, it was part of the commote of **Peulinog**. It came to constitute the westernmost part of **Carmarthenshire**; the name survives in that of Henllan Amgoed (**Henllanfallteg**).

AMLWCH, Isle of Anglesey (1819 ha; 2628 inhabitants)

Located on the north coast of **Anglesey**, the **community**'s main feature is **Mynydd Parys**, a **copper** mine consisting of an astonishing series of deep gulches. Indeed, it is remarkable that Wales's largest landscape of industrial dereliction can be found, not in the heavily developed south Wales **coal**field, but here on the country's northern extremity. Amlwch, originally little more than a **fish**ing village, had by 1801 become the sixth in size among the towns of Wales, and a local lawyer, **Thomas Williams** (1737–1802) of **Llanidan**, had come to dominate the world copper industry. In 1793, work began on a harbour to expedite the export of copper ore for smelting elsewhere, but, with the establishment of smelting works at the **port**, shipment of the finished metal began. Along with the growth of mining, other industries developed, particularly brewing, **shipbuilding** and the processing of tobacco – *baco Amlwch* was popular in Anglesey until well into the 20th century. Prosperity did not endure. The ore became more difficult to extract and there was increasing competition from cheaper foreign ore; by 1839, the Parys mines were considered to be 'but a wreck of what they formerly were'. There have been several unsuccessful efforts to revive the industry; mining resumed in 2005, and there were hopes that it would give a major boost to the local **economy**. Amlwch enjoyed temporary prosperity as an **oil**-importing port following the construction in 1973 of the Shell Marine Terminal.

St Elaeth's church was rebuilt in 1800 to accommodate an increasing **population**, which included a substantial number of miners from **Cornwall**. The chunky Dinorben Arms recalls the Hughes family, later Barons Dinorben, the chief proprietors of Mynydd Parys (*see* **Abergele**). The church of Our Lady Star of the Sea (1930s) is designed as an upturned boat. Bull Bay is an attractive seaside settlement. Curiously, the best-known cultivar of the **New Zealand** shrub *Hoheria* is called 'Glory of Amlwch'.

AMMANFORD (Rhydaman), Carmarthenshire (312 ha; 5293 inhabitants)

A **community** located at the confluence of the **Llwchwr** and the Aman, the place – then known as Cross Inn – was described in 1860 as 'a pleasantly situated village in the **parish** of **Llandybïe**'. A campaign to 'cross out Cross Inn' led in 1881 to the adoption of the name Ammanford; the **Welsh** form, Rhydaman, followed a few years later. With the rise of **coal**mining and **tinplate** production, the **population** increased from 3058 in 1901 to 6074 in 1911; the Ammanford **Urban District** was formed in 1903. Ysgol y Gwynfryn (1880–1915), in which ministers and **eisteddfod** performers were trained, belonged to the tradition of the Welsh dissenting or **Nonconformist academies**; it was at its most influential under the headship of **John Gwili Jenkins**. The White House, where **Labour** activists met in the years immediately before the **First World War**, played an important role in the spread of **socialist** ideas in the area. Among its leading figures was the politician **James Griffiths**, who is buried in the graveyard of the Christian Temple, the chief chapel of Ammanford's **Congregationalists**. In its industrial heyday, Ammanford was a major centre of working-**class** Welsh-language culture. From the 1930s onwards, heavy industry went into marked decline. Attempts to establish light industry have had some success, but unemployment remains a problem.

AMPHIBIANS and REPTILES

There are six species of amphibian native to Wales. The common frog, the commonest and most widely distributed, is famous for the clumps of spawn it deposits in ponds, **lakes** and slow-flowing **rivers** in early spring. The adult's dark colouration during a rainy period and yellowish hue during a sunny spell is regarded as a weather sign at harvest time. The common toad, with its dry, warty skin, mates later in the season, leaving long ribbons of spawn in shallow water. The smaller natterjack toad, with a distinctive yellow stripe down its back, disappeared from Wales during the 1960s, but was successfully reintroduced to sand dunes in **Flintshire** in the early 21st century. The smooth newt is the commonest in Wales, especially in the western uplands. The palmate newt and the great crested newt are much scarcer and confined to the lowlands and eastern parts.

There are five species of reptile native to Wales. The harmless and widely distributed grass snake is the larger of Wales's two snake species. Normally 70–150 cm in length, its body is dark green with vertical black bars running along the sides, and there is usually a prominent yellow collar around the neck. In contrast, the adder is Wales's only venomous snake. It is grey-brown with black zigzag markings down its back and a 'V' on top of the head; normally 50–60 cm in length, it is found in a wide range of habitats, particularly coastal situations. It is rare for a healthy adult to die from an adder bite, although it can make some people ill. Wales's three lizard species are the legless slow worm and the common lizard, both widely distributed, and the very rare sand lizard. The sand lizard was temporarily lost from Wales in the late 20th century, but in 1995 it was successfully reintroduced to a secret sand dunes habitat in the north-west.

AMROTH, Pembrokeshire
(1820 ha; 1243 inhabitants)

Located immediately north-east of **Saundersfoot**, the **community** is subject to erosion by the sea; at low tide, ebonized stumps of the submerged forest of Coetrath are visible. St Elidyr's church, which has a 13th-century nave, contains interesting funereal monuments. Nearby is Earwear, a **Norman** motte. Amroth Castle, a castellated mansion of *c.*1800, now offers holiday accommodation. Colby Lodge (1803) has attractive **gardens**, which are administered by the **National Trust**. There is a **bird** park at Stepaside. In August 1943, **Winston Churchill** was present at Wiseman's Bridge at a rehearsal of the Normandy invasion. The **Pembrokeshire Coastal Path**, opened in 1970, begins at Amroth.

ANDREWS, Elizabeth (1882–1960) Social reformer

Of the hundred greatest heroes of Wales chosen by ballot in 2004, only nine were **women**. They included Elizabeth Andrews, the third of the eleven children of a **Rhondda** miner. She first came to prominence as a suffragette, and won wide renown for the eloquent evidence she gave to the Royal Commission on **Coal** (1919). In particular she stressed the burdens suffered by the women of coalmining communities because of the absence of pit-head baths. In 1918, she became the first woman to be appointed a **Labour Party** organizer in Wales and was in the inter-war years the most outstanding Welsh champion of women's interests. While the cleanliness of the home was her first priority, she was also closely involved in children's issues, opening the first nursery school in the Rhondda in 1938. In 2006, her journalistic work was gathered together and published by Honno under the title *A Woman's Work is Never Done*.

ANDREWS, Solomon (1835–1908)
Transport pioneer and property developer

One of the most successful entrepreneurs in late 19th-century Wales, Solomon Andrews progressed from hawking his own home-made sweets on the streets of **Cardiff**, to becoming a transport pioneer and property developer. His were among the first **buses** to operate in Cardiff, and he later started services elsewhere, including **London**, Portsmouth and Plymouth. He sought to turn **Pwllheli** into a fashionable resort, and invested in improvements at **Barmouth**. His name is emblazoned on the clock tower of Cardiff market.

ANEIRIN or NEIRIN (fl. second half of 6th century)
Poet

One of the *Cynfeirdd* who, like his contemporary, **Taliesin**, was said by the author of *Historia Brittonum* (*c.*830) to have flourished in the **Old North**. To him is ascribed the composition of *Y Gododdin*. Traditions about him appear to have arisen in the Middle Ages, but there is no evidence that they developed into a legend as in the case of Taliesin.

ANGLE, Pembrokeshire (1224 ha; 281 inhabitants)

A **community** located at the southern shore at the entrance of the **Milford Haven waterway**. Brightly colour-washed cottages line the road between West Angle Bay and Angle Bay. Devil's Quoit is a **Neolithic** chambered tomb. St Mary's church, heavily restored in the 1850s, contains 17th and 18th-century memorials and a fishermen's chapel erected in 1447. The Old Rectory is a fine example of a medieval tower house. Writing in 1984, Dillwyn Miles recorded that he was shown a culm fire at Point Inn, which had not been extinguished for a century. Two 19th-century forts are interesting examples of **Palmerston's Follies**. That on Thorn Island (1852–4) has been converted into a hotel accessible only by the hotelier's ferry; closed for refurbishment, there are hopes that it will reopen in the foreseeable future. Fort Popton (1859–70) was once a BP control centre, but is now abandoned. In addition, there is Chapel Bay fort (1890), in which shuttered concrete was used in an innovative manner.

ANGLESEY (Môn), Island, county, constituency
and one-time district (74,889 ha; 66,829 inhabitants)

The third in size of **Britain**'s **islands**, Anglesey is a geologist's delight, containing as it does evidence from almost every geological era. Unusually low-lying compared with

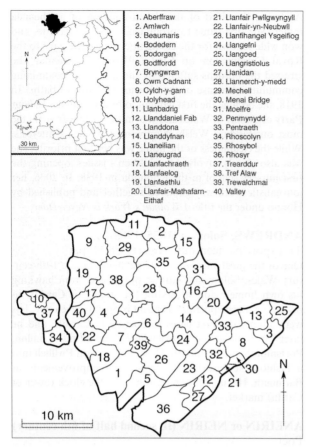

1. Aberffraw
2. Amlwch
3. Beaumaris
4. Bodedern
5. Bodorgan
6. Bodffordd
7. Bryngwran
8. Cwm Cadnant
9. Cylch-y-garn
10. Holyhead
11. Llanbadrig
12. Llanddaniel Fab
13. Llanddona
14. Llanddyfnan
15. Llaneilian
16. Llaneugrad
17. Llanfachraeth
18. Llanfaelog
19. Llanfaethlu
20. Llanfair-Mathafarn-Eithaf

21. Llanfair Pwllgwyngyll
22. Llanfair-yn-Neubwll
23. Llanfihangel Ysgeifiog
24. Llangefni
25. Llangoed
26. Llangristiolus
27. Llanidan
28. Llannerch-y-medd
29. Mechell
30. Menai Bridge
31. Moelfre
32. Penmynydd
33. Pentraeth
34. Rhoscolyn
35. Rhosybol
36. Rhosyr
37. Trearddur
38. Tref Alaw
39. Trewalchmai
40. Valley

The communities of the county of Anglesey

the rest of Wales, its highest point is **Holyhead** Mountain (220 m). It is rich in archaeological remains from the **Neolithic Age** onwards. It was the power base of the **druids**, who were destroyed by the **Romans** in AD 61. In the immediate post-Roman centuries, it was the centre of the power of the kings of **Gwynedd**, who considered **Aberffraw** to be the cradle of their dynasty.

It was the chief Welsh target of the **Vikings**, who probably gave it the Norse name that passed into **English** – *Ongulsey* (*Ongull*, a personal name + *ey*, island). (The **Welsh** name, Môn, is of **Celtic** origin, although written references to the **Latin** form, Mona, predate those to Môn.) The resources of Anglesey – the grain produced by its fertile **soil** in particular – were central to the rise of Gwynedd. **Giraldus Cambrensis** recorded the popular expression, *Môn mam Cymru* (Môn, the mother of Wales). Its fertility explains its profusion of **parishes**, which eventually numbered 76.

Following the **Edwardian conquest**, Anglesey became one of the three **counties** which constituted the **Principality** of north Wales. From the 1890s onwards, the county consisted of the **borough** of **Beaumaris**, the **urban districts** of **Amlwch**, **Holyhead**, **Llangefni** and **Menai Bridge** and the **rural districts** of Aethwy, **Twrcelyn** and **Valley**. In 1974, all these units were abolished, and Anglesey, along with **Aberconwy**, **Arfon**, **Dwyfor** and **Meirionnydd**, became a district of the newly established county of Gwynedd. At the same time, the island's civil parishes were replaced by 39 **communities**, many of which consisted of several of the

former parishes. In 1996, Anglesey regained its county status and the name Isle of Anglesey – or, more commonly, its Welsh equivalent, Ynys Môn – was adopted as the official name of the reborn county.

While a great deal of inland Anglesey is scenically unexciting, in 1967 much of the coast was designated an Area of Outstanding Natural Beauty. The coastal areas have attracted large numbers of incomers from **England**, causing the proportion of inhabitants wholly fluent in **Welsh** to fall below 50% in communities such as **Trearddur** and **Llanfair-Mathafarn-Eithaf**. In 2001, 70.4% of the inhabitants of the county had some knowledge of Welsh, with 50.5% wholly fluent in the language. (*See also* Llangefni and **Llanfair-yn-Neubwll**.) Anglesey was the only constituency in Wales to have been held in the 20th century by four different political parties.

ANGLESEY PENNIES

Some 12 million copper pennies and halfpennies were issued between 1787 and 1791 by **Thomas Williams** (1737–1802) of the Parys Mine Co. (*see* **Mynydd Parys**) to alleviate a shortage of coin and bank notes. The tokens had the company's monogram on one side and the head of a druid on the other; they were made illegal in 1821.

ANGLICANS

Elizabeth I's religious settlement (1558–62) created the Church of **England** as the sole recognized form of **religion** in England and Wales. The practice of referring to the Church's adherents as Anglicans dates from the 17th century. (The **Welsh** form, *Anglicaniaid*, is a 20th-century coinage.) It is an episcopal Church with a **parish** structure. It rejects papal claims and celebrates commemorative communion rather than sacrificial mass. Although often seen as a middle way between the **Roman Catholic** Church and Protestantism, Anglicanism is undoubtedly a Church brought into being as a result of the **Protestant Reformation**.

From the Church's inception until the early 19th century, the Anglican Church was the spiritual home of the vast majority of Wales's inhabitants and was thus, for almost a quarter of a millennium, the most significant organization in Wales. By 1676, Roman Catholicism and Protestant Dissent (*see* **Nonconformists**) had between them the allegiance of less than 4% of the country's inhabitants. Wales did produce **Catholic martyrs** and some **gentry** families remained faithful to Rome, but loyalty to the Church of England – widely seen as the re-creation of Wales's early Church – was long a characteristic of most Welsh patriots. Anglican clerics were responsible for such landmarks in Welsh history as **William Morgan**'s translation of the **Bible** and **Griffith Jones**'s literacy campaign. By the mid-18th century, however, the upper ranks of its clergy were almost wholly English – in the period 1714–1870, no Welsh-speaker was appointed to a Welsh bishopric – thus confirming for many the belief that the Church of England was precisely what its title said it was, and that it had no real relationship with Wales.

The **Methodist Revival** brought new energy to the Nonconformists, whose ranks swelled greatly in 1811 when the **Calvinistic Methodists** abandoned the Church of

Fly-fishing for trout on Tal-y-Llyn Lake, Llanfihangel-y-Penant

England to form their own denomination. By the mid-19th century, of those attending a place of worship, only one in five opted for the parish church. With Anglicans so small a minority, the status of the Church of England as Wales's official Church was increasingly anomalous, thus providing the context of the **disestablishment** campaign. Growing support for High Church (*see* **Oxford Movement**) doctrines and rituals within Anglicanism further alienated Nonconformists, with their deep-seated suspicion of 'popery'.

The Anglican Church faced the challenge of Nonconformity with vigour. It launched a programme of church building, established hundreds of elementary schools, reorganized its structures and sought to project a more Welsh image. However, in its battle against disestablishment, its leaders determined on a strategy of attack, with the result that every aspect of Welsh life was dragged into the conflict. Following disestablishment in 1920, the Anglican Church in Wales was reorganized as the **Church in Wales**. Thus, instead of being merely four **dioceses** of the Province of Canterbury, it became a self-governing province of the Anglican Communion, headed by its own archbishop.

ANGLING

Angling is one of Wales's most popular country and coastal sports, but for much of its history, **fish**ing with a rod and baited hook has been a matter of necessity rather than a pastime. Wales's **rivers** and **lakes**, abundant with trout, salmon, sewin and grayling, have for centuries attracted both native and visiting anglers. In the 1990s, Wales hosted two world fly-fishing championships as well as European and Commonwealth matches.

The earliest reference to angling in Welsh **literature** occurs in a medieval poem, 'Yr Eog', probably wrongly attributed to **Dafydd ap Gwilym**, which addresses the salmon as *cilionwr* (catcher of flies). Early 19th-century books on fishing in Wales, such as George Scotcher's *The Fly Fisher's Legacy* (1820) and George Agar Hansard's *Fishing the Rivers and Lakes of Wales* (1834), reflect the growing interest in the sport. They evoke days of plenty, when anglers could take up to 50 fish a day from the **Teifi** and three men in a boat might take 500 trout from Tal-y-llyn Lake (**Llanfihangel-y-Pennant**).

Hansard's detailed account includes reference to his use of the famous *Coch a bonddu* fly when fishing the Ewenny. Fly dressing is also discussed in the first **Welsh-language** fishing book, William Roberts's *Llawlyfr y Pysgotwr* (1899), which describes the meticulous fly patterns dressed by the natives of **Snowdonia**. Many of those dressed in the **Wye** and **Usk** valleys resemble Scottish patterns, probably resulting from the influence of bailiffs from **Scotland** who were employed in the 19th century to combat poaching.

In the mid-20th century, a new rivers management scheme in Wales enabled angling clubs to purchase fishing rights for rivers that hitherto had been owned by the big estates. This 'democratization' led to wider participation in the sport, but its governing body, the Welsh Salmon and Trout Angling Association, remains concerned about a decline in the number of young people taking up angling.

ANGLO-SAXONS

The Germanic-speaking peoples who established themselves in much of southern and eastern **Britain** from *c.*400 onwards, displacing or assimilating the Romance and **Celtic**-speaking natives. **Gildas**, in the mid-6th century, claimed that the earliest Anglo-Saxons had been brought to Britain as mercenaries to fight against the Picts and **Irish**. By 731, **Bede** was naming **Vortigern** as the native ruler responsible for this, and Hengist and Horsa as the first 'Saxon' leaders. In the early 9th century, *Historia Brittonum* elaborated on this story, suggesting that it was well known to the Welsh by then.

The earliest Anglo-Saxon conflict with Wales proper occurred in the region of **Gwent** in the late 6th century. From *c.*650, two Anglo-Saxon kingdoms bordered Wales; the Magonsaete, between the **Severn** and the **Wye**, and the Mierce (or Mercians), between the Severn and the Mersey. During the 7th century, **Mercia**, having swallowed up the Magonsaete, seems to have enjoyed a period of alliance with **Gwynedd**, and perhaps **Powys**, in the face of a common enemy, Northumbria. Between about 660 and 790, however, Mercia may have pushed into what is now eastern Wales, territory reconquered in the late 8th century by Eliseg, king of Powys, whose grandson Cyngen recorded this achievement in an inscription on an old Mercian cross shaft at **Llantysilio** near **Llangollen**. The response of the Mercian king Offa (757–96) was to construct a defensive dyke. **Offa's Dyke** effectively conceded much territory to Powys along the upper reaches of the **Dee**, Vyrnwy, **Severn** and **Wye**, although the Mercians still controlled the land as far as the **Clwydian Hills**, as Old English names such as Prestatyn (from *prēosta* and *tūn*, the priest's farm) bear witness. In 816, Coenwulf (798–821), one of the greatest Mercian kings, took advantage of civil war in Gwynedd and ravaged **Rhufoniog** and **Eryri**. The following year there was a battle at Llanfaes on **Anglesey** and, in 818, Coenwulf devastated **Dyfed**. It may have been during this raid that the **Llandeilo** Gospels (*see Book of St Chad, The*) were carried off to Lichfield. In 822, Coenwulf's successor Ceolwulf I destroyed Degannwy and annexed Powys. Mercian expansion continued throughout the 9th century, reaching its high point with the capture of Anglesey in 865 and the slaying of **Rhodri Mawr** in 878. Anarawd ap Rhodri reversed the trend and, after defeating Ethelred II (879–911) in 881, restored the eastern boundary of Gwynedd to the Clwyd. In the mid-11th century, **Gruffudd ap Llywelyn** re-established Welsh rule over extensive tracts of land east of **Offa's Dyke**. His activities led to the invasion of Wales by Harold Godwinesson, earl of Wessex, who seems to have annexed **Gwent** Iscoed. From the 890s, the increasingly unified English kingdom seemed more interested in establishing stable relations with Welsh rulers than in annexing territory. From the reign of Aethelstan (924–39), there is increasing evidence of Welsh rulers attending the English court and serving in English armies. From time to time conflict broke out, but increasingly the English tended to support one native dynasty against another rather than engaging in the warfare of an earlier age.

ANGLO-WELSH

A literary term for a writer who is Welsh by birth or association and who writes in **English** rather than in **Welsh**; it also refers to the work of such a writer and, more generally, to the whole genre of such writing. First used with these connotations by **Idris Bell** in 1922, it gained a wider currency towards the end of the 1930s but 'Anglo-Welsh **literature**' began to be replaced by 'Welsh writing in English' during the 1980s.

ANHUNIOG Commote

One of the 10 **commotes** of **Ceredigion**, Anhuniog extended from the lower **Aeron** to the lower Wyre. The name, which is sometimes written as Haminiog, comes from *Annun*, derived from the **Latin** *Antonius*.

ANIAN (Einion; d.1306?) Bishop

Bishop of **Bangor** from 1267, Anian supported Edward I in his wars against **Llywelyn ap Gruffudd** in 1277 and 1282, and was rewarded by the king with grants of estates and rights. Anian promulgated ecclesiastical reforms at a synod in Bangor in 1291.

ANIAN II (fl.1250s–93) Bishop

Anian II, so called to distinguish him from an earlier bishop of **St Asaph**, Anian, held the bishopric from 1268 to 1293. He became an opponent of **Llywelyn ap Gruffudd**, who, in order to raise funds to pay for the terms of the **Treaty of Montgomery** (1267), interfered with episcopal privileges. Anian convened a synod and issued against the prince a *gravamina* (a list of grievances). Llywelyn, already under intense political pressure, backed down. Anian may have been involved in a plot in 1282 to kill Llywelyn. During the war of 1282–3, the cathedral of St Asaph was destroyed by English soldiers, who were excommunicated by Anian. For two years, Edward I considered the bishop *persona non grata*. It appears Anian knew something of Welsh **law**, as his name appears in one of the manuscripts of the *Iorwerth* tradition of native law (*see* **Iorwerth ap Madog**). In his will, the bishop left his cathedral liturgical items and a herd of 300 **cattle**.

ANNWFN or ANNWN

A **Welsh** name for the **Celtic** Otherworld (which may also be perceived as an island or **islands** to the west – *see* **Avalon**). The word is composed of two elements – *an-* (either a negative, or a prefix meaning 'within') and *dwfn* meaning 'world'. *Annwfn* may mean 'not-world', a place that is unlike this world, or 'the world within' (or 'underground'). In either case, it is difficult to locate, but in it there may be supernatural beings and the dead. It is another, magical dimension, and has both a pleasant and a sinister aspect. With the coming of Christianity, Annwfn became a name for Hell.

ANTHONY, Jack (John Randolph Anthony; 1890–1954) Jockey and trainer

A farmer's son from Kilvelgy (Cilfelgi), St Issells, **Saundersfoot**, Anthony began his racing career by riding his father's **horses** in local point-to-points and other events. He went on to win the Grand National in 1911, 1915 and 1920, the year he turned professional. He was champion jockey in 1922 and twice runner-up in the Grand National (1925, 1926). He trained two winners of the Cheltenham Gold Cup (1929 and 1930). His older brothers, Ivor (1883–1959) and Owen (d.1941), were also successful jockeys and trainers; Ivor was a professional rider when he became champion jockey in 1912.

ANWYL, Edward (1866–1914) Scholar

A pupil of **John Rhŷs** at **Oxford**, Chester-born Edward Anwyl was appointed the professor of **Welsh** at **Aberystwyth** (1892) and became in addition professor of comparative philology there (1905). He published extensively on early Church history, **theology** and **philosophy**, but his main contribution was to the history of Welsh **literature**; his pioneering work on the **religion** of the **Celts**,

The Mabinogion and the **Gogynfeirdd** is still worth reading. His attempts, as a grammarian, to bring spoken and written Welsh closer together contrast with the conservative attitudes of **John Morris-Jones**. A leading figure in Welsh cultural life, he was knighted in 1911. In 1913, he was appointed the first principal of **Caerleon** Training College, but he died before he could take up the post. His brother was the lexicographer John Bodfan Anwyl (1875–1949).

APPERLEY, Charles James (Nimrod; 1779–1843)
Racing journalist and author

Born at Plas Gronow, **Esclusham**, near **Wrexham**, Apperley wrote as 'Nimrod' for *The Sporting Magazine* – trebling the magazine's circulation – and published 10 books about **hunting** and **horse**manship, notably *Nimrod's Hunting Tours* (1835), *The Life of a Sportsman* (1842) and *Hunting Reminiscences* (1843). He lived at Llanbeblig (**Caernarfon**) from 1813 until his death.

'AR HYD Y NOS' ('All through the night') Melody
A popular **harp** melody first published by **Edward Jones** (1752–1824) in *Musical and Poetical Relicks of the Welsh Bards* (1784), and frequently sung to the words by **John Ceiriog Hughes**: 'Holl amrantau'r sêr ddywedant.'

ARABLE CROPS
Historically, crop production was integral to all Welsh farms, producing subsistence **food** for the table and feed for farm animals. Redundant **windmills** in **Anglesey** and grain barns on the **Brecon Beacons** testify to the extent of arable production. Of particular importance were wheat for bread, barley for **beer** and animal feed, beans and peas. It is likely that the **Romans** introduced carrots, turnips, parsnips, **leeks** – and **oats**, the staple diet of the Welsh until the 20th century.

In 2002, arable production occupied 12.27% of the agricultural land of Wales, compared with 32.38% of that of the United Kingdom. Mineral leaching and the nature of the **soil** make Wales unsuitable for intensive arable farming; however, a slightly extended growing season and more fertile soils make cropping feasible in south **Pembrokeshire**, **Gower**, the Vale of Glamorgan, parts of east **Powys** and the north-east. Continuous cropping systems are rare.

Modern husbandry techniques permit the extension of the growing season to produce higher yields; but, generally, the **climate** mitigates against this approach in Wales. Rainfall delays sowing in spring, while harvesting and resowing must be complete before autumn rainfall creates adverse soil conditions: rarely can soils in Wales tolerate surface activity beyond late September. Barley is the most common crop, and frost-free springs, together with vigorous marketing, promote successful early potato production in south Pembrokeshire and Gower.

ARAN FAWDDWY and ARAN BENLLYN
Mountains

Aran Fawddwy (907 m; **Mawddwy**), Wales's highest **mountain** apart from **Snowdon** and its immediate neighbours, dominates the watershed between the **Dee** and **Dyfi** valleys. To its north is Aran Benllyn (884 m; **Llanuwchllyn**), which overlooks **Bala** Lake (Llyn Tegid). Both mountains have

been carved by ice into dramatic columnar cliffs, arêtes and cirques with tiny deep glacial **lakes**, such as Llyn Lliwbran and Creiglyn Dyfi, and precipitous streams, such as the Camddwr and the Llaethnant. On a clear day, the view from Aran Fawddwy extends from Snowdon to the **Brecon Beacons**. Indeed, its summit is probably the best place in Wales from which walkers can gain the impression that they can see the country in its entirety. The descent by the cascade-jewelled Camddwr into Cwm Cywarch is one of the glories of the Welsh landscape (*see* **Landforms, Landscape and Topography**).

ARCHAEOLOGY and ANTIQUARIANISM
From the time of *Historia Brittonum* in the 9th century through the figments of the imagination of Iolo Morganwg (**Edward Williams**) in the 18th century to the present, there have been many fanciful attempts to interpret the monuments of Wales. Antiquaries sought to fit them into biblical chronology and to relate them to semi-mythical figures such as **Caradog** and **Arthur**. From the 16th century onwards, such studies were pursued more systematically through the work of Welsh antiquaries such as **Humphrey Lhuyd** of **Denbigh**, **George Owen** of Henllys (**Nevern**) and **Rice Merrick** of Cotrell (**St Nicholas**), and English antiquaries such as **John Leland**. In addition, these antiquaries were fascinated by other aspects of the country's past, in particular **heraldry**, **genealogy** and folklore.

Later antiquarians and topographers were heavily influenced by the work of these earlier scholars. Foremost amongst them was the polymath **Edward Lhuyd**, one of the principal founders of the tradition of recording historical monuments by description and illustration, a tradition that led directly to the itineraries of **Thomas Pennant**, published in 1778 and 1781. Pennant was one of the first antiquaries to commission paintings and plans of Welsh monuments by artists such as **Moses Griffith**. Broadly contemporary with Pennant were antiquarian topographers concerned to record the history of Wales's **counties**, among them **Theophilus Jones** (**Breconshire**), **Samuel Rush Meyrick** (**Cardiganshire**), **David Williams** (**Monmouthshire**), **Benjamin Heath Malkin** (**Glamorgan**) and Jonathan Williams (**Radnorshire**).

In the later 19th century, antiquarian studies came increasingly under the influence of theories relating to natural history and **geology**. Darwin's theory of evolution and Lyell's theory of geological continuity had a profound impact, for they suggested that the origins of the Earth and of human beings were vastly older than the chronology laid out in the **Bible**. Furthermore, the theory of stratigraphical succession is as relevant to archaeology as it is to geology. Classification of material remains led to the recognition of a system based on stone, bronze and **iron** artefacts. Thus, the prehistoric era was divided into the Stone Age (**Palaeolithic and Mesolithic Age; Neolithic Age**), the **Bronze Age** and the **Iron Age**. These chronological periods still retain their relevance in modern archaeological studies, although, with the advent of absolute dating techniques, more refined methods of measurement are available.

Archaeological excavations in Wales made significant contributions to the emerging picture of early man, particularly to an understanding of the Palaeolithic Age. In 1823, William Buckland excavated at Paviland (**Rhossili, Gower**), discovering what modern archaeologists consider to be an Upper Palaeolithic cave burial that has been dated to 24,000 BC. In the 1860s, the geologist **Boyd Dawkins** excavated extensively in **Denbighshire**. At Pontnewydd in the Elwy valley (**Cefnmeiriadog**), he discovered a major Palaeolithic site. His interpretations of his finds not only contributed to the debate on the subdivisions of the Palaeolithic Age, but also to acceptance of the antiquity of humanity.

The antiquaries' excavation techniques were rudimentary in the extreme. Until the late 19th century, it was the **gentry** alone who had the means and the time to excavate monuments, which were often located on their own estates. Among such members of the gentry **class** were **Richard Fenton** in **Pembrokeshire** and W. O. Stanley (1802–84) in **Anglesey**. This unscientific approach to excavation continued well into the 20th century, as the excavations and reports on **Roman** forts such as **Caerhun**, Caer Llugwy (**Capel Curig**), **Gelligaer** and **Caerwent** testify.

Nevertheless, the longstanding antiquarian tradition, so often the preserve of learned clergymen, contributed greatly to the founding of archaeological studies in Wales. Two significant figures were **John Williams** (Ab Ithel; 1811–62) and **H. Longueville Jones**, who, in 1847, established the **Cambrian Archaeological Association**. They epitomized the diverging approaches that were becoming apparent, with Ab Ithel representing the old tradition, in which enthusiasm often triumphed over knowledge, and Jones embracing a more scientific approach. It was the latter approach that would succeed. It was supported by the

numerous excavations funded by the Association and by the reports published in its journal, *Archaeologia Cambrensis* (1846–). Other journals, those of county **historical societies** in particular, also publish reports of excavations; in addition, they help to sustain the enthusiasm of local historians – the heirs to Wales's distinguished antiquarian tradition.

The founding of the **National Museum [of] Wales** in 1907 was an important step in establishing a scholarly understanding of the prehistory of Wales. **Mortimer Wheeler**, the museum's keeper of archaeology (1920–4) and its director (1924–6), published the first academic review of Welsh archaeology. He insisted that archaeological excavations should be conducted to the highest standards and that their results should be promptly published. He developed the box method of excavation, which allowed him to maintain stratigraphical control of a site, a method he used in his masterly excavations at Segontium (**Caernarfon**) and at **Caerleon**. His methods were followed by his successors at the National Museum, notably by **W. F. Grimes**, **V. E. Nash-Williams** and **Cyril Fox**.

Mortimer Wheeler was the first to lecture on archaeology in the **University of Wales**, at **Cardiff**. This led to the establishment of a department of archaeology there, a step followed at **Bangor** and **Lampeter**. Archaeology has come to be recognized not only as an academic discipline in its own right but also as one that contributes invaluably to historical studies. An excellent example of the fruitful marriage between written and archaeological evidence is the work at the castle at Hen Domen (**Montgomery**), undertaken by Philip Barker between 1960 and 1992. Archaeology has become an invaluable adjunct to studies of the **Industrial**

An archaeological treasure – the Bronze Age Caergwrle bowl

Medieval fields on North Hill, Angle, Pembrokeshire

Revolution. Two Welsh sites in which industrial archaeologists have played a prominent role have attracted international attention. They are **Mynydd Parys** (**Amlwch**, Anglesey) – once the world's largest **copper** mine – and the **Blaenavon** Ironworks – a key location in the history of iron-making and designated a World Heritage Site in 2000.

The British state has made a significant contribution to the safeguarding of the archaeological heritage of Wales. **The Royal Commission on the Ancient and Historical Monuments of Wales**, established in 1908, records sites county by county in its published inventories. Until 1984, the Ministry of Works was responsible for protecting archaeological sites; it was then replaced by **Cadw**, which originally undertook the work under the **Welsh Office**, and, since 1999, under the **National Assembly for Wales**. In 1961, the British Council for Archaeology (founded in 1944) established a Wales working group, which acts as a forum for professional and amateur archaeologists and which publishes an annual survey of archaeological work in Wales. In the mid-1970s, archaeological trusts were established for **Gwynedd, Clwyd-Powys, Dyfed** and Glamorgan-**Gwent**. They undertake rescue archaeology and keep records of the sites and monuments within their regions. Some of **Britain**'s most interesting landscapes are in Wales, among them those related to the prehistoric era in upland **Meirionnydd** and the **Conwy** valley, and to the industrial era in the southern and northern **coal**fields and in the Gwynedd **slate** belt. Thus, strategies are needed not only to preserve individual sites but also to safeguard entire archaeological landscapes.

By the beginning of the 21st century, archaeology had become fully established as an academic discipline. New scientific techniques help to interpret the way human beings have adapted to their environment. Radiometric dating has shown that in Wales human endeavour stretches back at least a quarter of a million years. Further research will establish whether there is any link between Wales's earliest people and the country's present inhabitants.

ARCHDRUID

The chief officer and symbolic head of the **Gorsedd** of Bards. Clwydfardd (David Griffith; 1800–94), who considered himself to be the first *Archdderwydd*, was confirmed in his position in 1888; between that year and 2007, 29 Archdruids have been elected. Since 2001, the Archdruid has been elected triennially by all Gorsedd members and not by members of the Gorsedd board alone.

ARCHERY

In the late 18th and early 19th centuries, archery became fashionable among the aristocracy and **gentry**, probably because of a nostalgic taste for the Gothic and medieval. Furthermore, **women** could both compete in the contests and display their 'feminine forms' whilst doing so. Thus archery facilitated introductions, flirtation and romance.

Wales's most famous archery society was the Royal British Bowmen, which served the gentry of **Denbighshire** and **Shropshire**. Its early meetings featured recitals of songs and poems that mixed references to **Boudicca**, ancient Wales, the **longbow** and chivalric notions, and it linked Welsh traditions with patriotism for the modern British state. During the 19th century, there were archery societies named after **Breconshire, Carmarthenshire, Chepstow, Gwent, Glamorgan**, North **Cardiganshire, Radnorshire** and **Raglan**.

Caerphilly Castle is a fine example of medieval military architecture

Although archery passed out of fashion at the end of the 19th century, losing favour to **tennis** and croquet, it made a recovery during the 20th century as a sport for all **class**es. At the beginning of the 21st century, the Welsh Archery Association had about 1000 members, divided between 45 clubs.

ARCHITECTURE

Prehistoric

The earliest structures to have survived in Wales are megalithic chamber-tombs erected more than 5000 years ago during the **Neolithic Age**. The chambers were built with massive stone slabs and covered by enormous earthen mounds, mostly rectangular in shape, but circular in **Anglesey**. The **Bronze Age** that followed is also characterized architecturally by its burial mounds, although these were little more than circular, grass-covered hummocks containing individual graves. During this period, numerous stone circles were erected, possibly for astronomical purposes. Although no upstanding domestic remains have survived from either the Stone Age or the Bronze Age, archaeological evidence suggests that their dwellings started off as roughly rectangular units before becoming predominantly circular in layout (*see* **Housing**). **Iron Age** people, who left no burial structures, appear to have lived, initially at least, mainly in fortified hilltop and clifftop villages. Hundreds of these organically arranged **hill-forts**, some strongly defended by earthen banks and ditches (or stone walls in the north-west), were constructed across Wales. In the later Iron Age, lightly enclosed or open farmsteads became more common. The dwellings themselves were usually circular, often of stone in the north-west (as at Tre'r Ceiri (**Llanaelhaearn**)), with its 150 huts within a protective wall), but timber elsewhere (such as the reconstructed examples at Castell Henllys (**Nevern**), and at the National History Museum; *see* **St Fagans**).

Roman and post-Roman

The **Romans** brought a standardized building technique to Wales in the 1st century, entirely different from anything that had existed hitherto. They built regularly conceived temples, baths and amphitheatres in association with geometrically planned forts and towns, as well as villa-type houses in the countryside. Roman buildings were constructed of timber and cut stone, or brick faced with stucco, and had low roofs covered with clay tiles. Interior decoration included wall **painting**s and mosaics. With the collapse of Roman authority, the forts were abandoned. Without adequate defence, or without a viable urban **economy**, towns and villas fell into disuse, and gradually the Roman building methods were forgotten.

There followed a revival of power centres based on easily defended sites, such as the hill-fort at **Dinas Powys**. Unusually, a crannog (artificial island), retained by timber piles, was built at **Llangorse** Lake during the late 9th century. An important unifying feature during much of the post-Roman period was the early Christian church. **Celt**ic monasteries (*see* **Clas**), comprising a number of small buildings enclosed by a curvilinear *llan* wall, were established in mainly coastal areas (Ynys Seiriol, **Llangoed**; Burry Holms, **Llangennith**). Most buildings were of wood and have thus disappeared. Any monastic stone structures may well have been based on corbelled vaults similar to those found in early Irish oratories.

Medieval: military

Following hard upon their conquest of **England**, the **Normans** attempted to conquer Wales. In the conquered areas, they consolidated their hold by erecting castles. At **Chepstow** (Great Tower, *c.*1071), they built one of the earliest stone castles in **Britain**, on a spectacular site above sheer cliffs to guard the crossing of the **Wye**. Most early castles, however, were motte-and-bailey constructions of earth and timber. When conditions became more settled, many of the earlier castles were rebuilt in stone, as at **Cardiff**, where the original timber keep was replaced in the early 12th century by a splendid stone shell keep. The walls of Norman castles were generally featureless apart from occasional arrow slits and flat, pilaster-like buttresses. Windows were small, round-headed and sparingly used. The main entrance, on the other hand, could be quite showy as in the boldly detailed doorway at Newcastle, **Bridgend**.

By the beginning of the 13th century, Anglo-Norman **march**er-lords dominated the southern coastal strip and the **Usk** and Wye valleys. To maintain control, new castles were built and older castles rebuilt with round keeps. These were superior to rectangular keeps, as they had better all-round fields of fire and were more difficult to damage with battering rams. The stimulus for many such towers seems to have been the majestic keep at **Pembroke**, which was erected soon after 1200 by William **Marshal** and was inspired by the castles built earlier in northern France. The largest and most spectacular of all marcher castles was **Caerphilly**, begun by Gilbert de **Clare** in 1268. It was surrounded by an artificial **lake** and equipped with almost impregnable systems of defence, including five twin-towered gateways and an elaborate defence platform above a water barrage.

Nearly 40 earthwork and stone castles are known to have been built by the Welsh **princes**; all those that are now visible date from the 13th century and were mostly located away from the sea, often on rocky sites which dictated irregular layouts. The design of keeps varied: **Dolwyddelan** (*c.*1210–40), Y Bere (**Llanfihangel-y-Pennant**), Dinas Bran (**Llangollen**) and Dolforwyn (**Llandyssil**) (1273), all in the north, had rectangular keeps; the round keeps at **Dinefwr** (**Llandeilo**) (*c.*1220–33) and Dryslwyn (**Llangathen**), in the **Tywi** valley, were probably influenced by the marcher castles of the south-east; in **Snowdonia**, Dolbadarn's (**Llanberis**) dramatically sited round keep (*c.*1230–40) was a sophisticated design with spiral stairs built within the thickness of the wall; Ewloe (**Hawarden**), in **Flintshire**, had a D-shaped keep (1257) that, overlooking the entrance, gave a better field of fire than a rectangular tower. Strong gatehouses were rare, although **Criccieth** was defended by a massive gatehouse (*c.*1230–40) of paired apsidal towers, possibly influenced by English examples.

Following his campaigns of 1277 and 1282–3, Edward I built a chain of powerful castles, mostly near the coast, from **Flint** (1277–84) in the north-east to **Aberystwyth** in the west. The later castles were designed by **James of St George**, an architect from Savoy and master of the king's works in Wales. Planned as exceptionally strong fortresses, they incorporated the latest developments in military technology. **Conwy** (1283–87) had an elongated layout divided into two wards, each defended by four great round towers. **Beaumaris** (1295– *c.*1306) was a classic example of the concentric plan – an octagonal inner ward with two massive gatehouses, encircled by a similarly shaped outer ward. **Caernarfon** (1283– *c.*1330) was designed as an ostentatious demonstration of imperial power, its horizontally banded stonework and angular towers were probably inspired by the walls of Constantinople. Almost as impressive are some of the castles James of St George designed for **march**er-lords; the three octagonal towers of the Great Gatehouse at **Denbigh** constitute, perhaps, the most impressive structure created in 13th-century Wales.

Medieval: domestic

With the conquest of independent Wales in the late 13th century, the need for military fortifications declined and the castle gradually gave way to the great house. At Tretower (**Llanfihangel Cwmdu**), for example, a new house with a central hall open to the roof was built near the castle in the early 14th century, and later, in the 15th century, it was divided into two floors and a new wing with a new hall was added. The wealthiest landowners built extravagantly. Bishop **Henry de Gower**, for instance, erected splendid palaces at **Lamphey** and **St David's** in the 14th century; in each, the main rooms were on the first floor above vaulted undercrofts, and the buildings themselves were surmounted by decorative, arcaded parapets. The most ambitious work in the 15th century was **Raglan** Castle. Its hexagonal great tower (1435–45) was surrounded by a moat and designed to withstand gunfire. Few true tower-houses were built in Wales. Llancaiach Fawr (**Gelligaer**), however, seems to have links with both the tower-house and the first-floor hall tradition of the south-west. It is remarkable for the number of stairs built into the thickness of the walls, suggesting that even in the early 16th century defence could still be an important aspect of design.

Medieval: ecclesiastical

A spate of church building followed the arrival of the Normans in Wales. At first, most churches were stocky and relatively plain with simple, aisle-less naves and sanctuaries. Walls were thick, with shallow, flat buttresses and few openings. Herringbone masonry, suggestive of earlier Saxon construction, was sometimes used in the south-east where most Norman buildings were located. The Normans employed the Romanesque style, and everywhere the semicircular shape is apparent: in doorways, windows, chancel arches, aisle arcades (St Mary, Chepstow; **Margam** Abbey) and in barrel-vaulted ceilings (**Ewenny** Priory). Interiors appear dark and heavy, with openings seemingly carved out of solid masonry. In later buildings, decorative doorways comprised tiers of receding arches, each embellished with mouldings.

The earliest Norman monasteries in Wales were usually sited in towns and belonged to the **Benedictine** order. The

Cistercians, in contrast, placed great emphasis on austerity and sited their abbeys in isolated places away from 'the concourse of men' (**Tintern**; Strata Florida (**Ystrad Fflur**)). Architecturally, the concept of monasticism was expressed in a complex of communal buildings arranged around an arcaded cloister garth to one side of the church.

A greater understanding of structural principles and better construction during the 13th century led to improvements in church design. Gradually, medieval builders realized that walls need only be thick at the point at which they were required to support the weight, or to sustain the thrust, of arches. This led to the creation of buttresses which were often stepped to provide greater depth and support. The most characteristic feature of Gothic architecture is the use of pointed arches for windows, doorways and vaulting (**Brecon** Cathedral). Windows were at first tall, slim lancets, used either singly on side walls or in groups on gable walls. Later, lancet windows were clustered together, the area between the arches being pierced with smaller openings to create plate tracery. As the **population** increased, the more important churches were enlarged by adding aisles separated from the nave by arcades of slender piers, linked by pointed arches.

Advances in building techniques allowed the 14th-century builders to experiment. Improvements in construction were matched with greater freedom in decoration and **sculpture**. Deeper buttresses allowed thinner walls and this, together with the development of tracery, allowed windows to be wider. Window tracery evolved into light, geometric patterns that were further developed into naturalistic curvilinear forms with sinuous ogee arches and reticulated (intersecting) bars. Doors became wider, and sometimes had graceful ogee arches. Towers were often added to churches and steeply sided spires became more frequent (as at St Nicholas, **Grosmont**).

During the latter part of the 15th and the early 16th century, increasing wealth resulted in more complex church layouts, and many existing churches were extended and partly rebuilt. In the north, splendid new churches, such as St **Beuno**, **Clynnog** and All Saints, **Gresford**, were erected. Walls became skeletal, and windows, which became flatter and more angular, often took up all the space between buttresses. New towers were usually bold and elaborately ornamented with pinnacles and openwork parapets (St Giles, **Wrexham**). Fine, timber-panelled ceilings – embellished with hammer-beam supports or decorative pendants (St David's Cathedral) – were incorporated in some of the larger churches. Stone vaulting was only occasionally used, and fan vaulting, with radiating ribs, was reserved for special situations (St Winefride's chapel, **Holywell**). Intricately carved rood screens were important features, excellent examples having survived in isolated places such as Patrishow (**Vale of Grwyney**) and Llananno (**Llanbadarn Fynydd**).

16th century

Very few churches were built in the two centuries immediately following the **Protestant Reformation**. From the 16th to the 18th century, most new buildings were domestic in character. Tudor architecture, coming between the late Gothic emphasis on verticality and **Renaissance** ideals and formal planning, was essentially transitional in style. The E-shaped plan, with projecting wings and central porch, became fashionable for large houses, allowing symmetrical front elevations irrespective of internal layouts. Pointed windows almost disappeared, being replaced by rectangular, mullioned openings. Inside Tudor houses, there was a greater stress on comfort and privacy: decorated plaster and wooden panelling were used extensively in main rooms, flat ceilings replaced open roofs, and fireplaces became more common (*see* **Housing**). Increasing wealth and easier travel provided the *nouveaux riches* with opportunities for extensive rebuilding in the latest fashion. Thus at **Carew** Castle, Sir John **Perrot** added a magnificent new wing with giant windows and semicircular bays, as well as a piped water supply to the kitchen. At Plas Clough, **Denbigh**, Sir Richard Clough (d.1570) – who had business interests in the Netherlands – incorporated Dutch-style crow-stepped gables, a feature that soon became popular on many houses in the north. Even more remarkable was Clough's other house, Bâch-y-graig (**Tremeirchion**); crowned by a pyramid roof, it had no parallel in 16th century Britain; sadly, it was demolished in 1817.

17th century

Renaissance architecture arrived late in Wales. Its hesitant introduction can be clearly seen at Beaupré Mansion, **Llanfair**, where an extension included a Tudor outer gatehouse (1586) enriched with pilasters and panelling in debased classical form; 14 years later, an extraordinary inner porch was added, with three tiers of confidently sculpted classical columns. Important elements of Renaissance architecture were compact planning and elevations designed to preconceived concepts. Both of these appear in the design of Plas Teg (1610), **Hope**, a four-square building with militaristic corner towers. Great Castle House (1673), **Monmouth**, a compact town house, has a symmetrical and formal front designed to impress. Erddig (1684), **Marchwiel**, was built on a much larger scale, the very simplicity and regularity of its main front, with long rows of sash windows, emphasizing its grandeur. Tredegar House (1670) at **Coedkernew** near **Newport**, was even more elaborate, and, like Erddig, was surrounded by formal **gardens** that complimented the regular lines of the house. Interiors of gentry houses were planned on ordered principles with large entrance halls and prominent staircases. The main rooms were often placed on the first floor and were plastered or finished in wood panelling. Ceilings might also be panelled or decorated with high relief plasterwork.

18th century

After a brief baroque interlude, during which classical architecture was developed in an original and plastic way, architects returned to a more austere style based on Italian designs by Palladio. Rules of proportion and standards of taste were firmly established, gradually percolating down to ordinary builders. Throughout the 18th century, there

Tredegar House at Coedkernew, near Newport, a superb example of 17th-century architecture

was an underlying current of **romanticism**, and it was not long before this lighter spirit emerged in architecture (Margam Orangery, 1787). There was also a growing interest in medievalism, and one rather superficial development of the romantic trend was neo-Gothicism (Clytha Castle, **Llanarth**, 1790). More influential was the **picturesque movement** – its principles formulated by Sir Uvedale Price and put into practice by both **Thomas Johnes** and **John Nash** – which encouraged asymmetrical composition and naturalistic settings for buildings. Towards the end of the century, Nash developed his romantic classical style based on simple, well-mannered elevations. While many new mansions appeared in the countryside, the 18th century was also important for urban building, particularly in regional centres such as **Carmarthen**, Monmouth, **Swansea** and **Welshpool** (*see* **Housing**). From the middle of the century, turnpike trusts were set up to improve communications between towns. This involved much bridge building, including **William Edwards**'s bold example at **Pontypridd** (1756).

19th century

In domestic architecture, both revived Gothic and revived classical styles were used during the 19th century. Initially, Gothic was the favourite mode for the 'castles' of the newly rich entrepreneurs and industrialists, as at Cyfarthfa Castle (1825), **Merthyr Tydfil** and Gwrych Castle (1819–22), **Llanddulas**. More architecturally convincing was the Norman-style Penrhyn Castle (1827–40) (**Llandygai**), with its monumental 'keep' based on the 12th-century tower of Hedingham Castle, Essex. The late 19th-century work at Cardiff Castle, with tall **clock** tower, dramatic skyline and extravagantly ostentatious interiors by **William Burges**,

was the most remarkable reconstruction of the century. Various other styles were tried, such as at Gregynog Hall (*c.*1870), **Tregynon**, which was transformed into a many-gabled structure, faced in concrete with imitation 'Tudorbethan' half-timbering. Pure classical architecture was usually seen as too restrained, and comparatively few great houses were built in this style, although Clytha Park (1820–8), Llanarth, is a worthy exception. The more seductive French Renaissance was tried in a few instances, notably for the entrance front at Kinmel Park (*c.*1870), **Abergele**.

Many of the most interesting works of 19th-century architecture were public and educational buildings erected in the growing urban areas. As with other buildings of the period, they reflected the historic styles of the past. Some of the most architecturally successful belonged to the Greek Revival (Royal Institution of South Wales, **Swansea**, 1841; Brecon Shirehall, 1842; Bridgend Town Hall, 1843 (demolished 1971)), an academically pure style that had been popularized in France and Germany during the late 18th century. After the mid-century, Greek influence gave way to a more ponderous, but still classical, Roman-inspired style. The larger educational buildings were generally built to some form of Gothic or Tudor design (St David's College, **Lampeter**, 1829), although the Dutch-inspired Queen Anne style (Severn Road School, Cardiff, 1882) was also used occasionally. At Aberystwyth, the Old College (*see* **University of Wales, Aberystwyth**), which was started in 1864 as a **railway** hotel, still retains its extraordinary neo-Gothic appearance despite a fire in 1885 and subsequent rebuilding.

The earliest churches of the 19th century (Tremadog, **Porthmadog**, 1806; **Milford Haven**, 1808) were built in Gothic style but tended to be plain and raw, as though

The west front of Llandaff Cathedral

their designers were unsure of the correct details. In the fast-growing industrial towns of the south, Romanesque was often adopted for churches built by the **iron** companies. Romanesque was also the style sometimes used for those churches built in the 1830s and 1840s with the aid of parliamentary grants (St Mary's, Glyn Taff, **Pontypridd**, 1837). Gothic, in all its varieties, remained, however, the most popular style. **John Prichard**, the best-known Welsh architect of the 19th century, favoured early Gothic for his imaginative restoration (1843–67) of Llandaff Cathedral (Cardiff). Decorated Gothic became even more fashionable, and was adopted for some of the more imposing churches of the mid- and late-19th century. (St Margaret, **Bodelwyddan**, 1860; St Mary, **Halkyn**, 1878; St German, Cardiff, 1884). A popular feature of many late Victorian churches was constructive colouration, whereby the natural appearance of materials was used to produce warm and colourful spaces (St Augustine, **Penarth**, 1866; St Catherine, **Baglan**, 1882).

Although **Nonconformist** meeting houses first appeared in Wales during the late 17th century, the vast majority of chapels were built during the 19th century. The earliest were single storey and simple in design. Typically, the main façade was on one of the long walls, while internally the pulpit was placed at the centre of the long wall, symmetrically between two tall windows. In the fast-growing towns, space was at a premium, so chapels were sited at right angles to the road with the entrance at the pine-end. Many chapels were rebuilt once, twice or even three times during the 19th century to accommodate growing congregations; often a first-floor gallery was added to provide additional accommodation. Architects such as **John Humphrey**, **George Morgan**, **Richard Owen** and **Thomas Thomas** (Glandwr; 1817–88) specialized in designing chapels. As more chapels were built or rebuilt, they became larger and more elaborate. Most were built in classical – rather than Gothic – style, and, when funds allowed, full-blown classical features were used to emphasize a chapel's dignity and importance (English Baptist, Carmarthen, 1872).

With the **Industrial Revolution** came new types of buildings and new forms of construction, from **iron**-girdered or stone-arched viaducts, as the **railways** developed from 1840 onwards, to cast iron **piers** in the fast-growing seaside resorts. In the many ironworks in the south and north-east, large blast furnaces were erected with tall, tapered masonry shells echoing the shape of the blast chambers inside. The largest ironworks, such as Cyfarthfa and Dowlais at Merthyr Tydfil, incorporated banks of furnaces dramatically positioned below cliffs excavated out of the hillsides. Although most iron-industry buildings were strictly functional, some were intended to impress, such as the Egyptian-looking blast furnaces at Bute Ironworks (1825), **Rhymney**, the four-storey engine-house in Cyfarthfa Ironworks (1836) at Ynysfach, Merthyr Tydfil, and the grandiose water-balance tower (1839) at **Blaenavon** Ironworks.

For much of the 19th and early 20th centuries, **coal**-mining was the dominant industry of the south and north-east. Tall winding towers, as at Merthyr Lewis Colliery, Porth (now **Rhondda** Heritage Park), became symbolic icons of the mining industry. Originally constructed of timber or cast iron, winding towers were later made of steel or concrete. Storeyed engine houses, accompanied by tall chimneys, housed steam engines to provide power for winding and pumping. After the **First World War**, pithead baths, often of modernist design in brick or concrete, would become characteristic features of many collieries, as at Big Pit, Blaenavon. The buildings of the quarrying industry include the majestic Ynyspandy **slate** mill (1855), near Porthmadog, Gothicized limekilns (1856) at **Llandybie**, and the classically symmetrical Gilfach Ddu workshops (1870), **Llanberis**.

20th century

The early 20th century was both a period of hopeful experimentation and of wistful looking back. The Arts and Crafts movement emphasized craftsmanship and traditional methods but rejected historicism, and was thus a precursor of the modern movement. One of the main exponents of this style-less vernacular was **Herbert North**. Another, transient, influence on non-traditional architecture was the attenuated and flowing lines of Art Nouveau. Both Arts and Crafts and Art Nouveau influences are apparent in the work of **J. C. Carter**. Historicism was not, however, dead and traditional styles continued to be revived well into the century, especially for public buildings such as the University College of North Wales, **Bangor** (1911) (*see* **University of Wales, Bangor**), and the **National Museum of Wales** (1910–93) in Cardiff. In the 1930s, architecture began to evolve in a different direction, marked by a watering down of period details, resulting in austere buildings with a superficial feel of modernism, such as **Percy Thomas**'s Swansea Guildhall.

During the 20th century, industry became more varied and factories built for manufacturing goods became widespread. Although most factories were little more than very large sheds to protect machines and workers, memorable buildings of architectural significance occasionally emerged – such as, at the beginning of the century, the Egyptian-looking boiler factory (1901) in **Queensferry**, and, towards the end of the century, the futuristic and extrovert Inmos microchip factory (1982) at **Newport**.

Functionalism, characterized by unadorned geometrical forms, made brief appearances in Welsh architecture of the 1930s, occasionally in houses, but more strikingly in public buildings such as **Sully** Hospital (1932–6), near **Barry**. Functionalist architecture came to be used increasingly after the **Second World War** for educational and hospital buildings (Bettws High School, Newport, 1972, and the University Hospital of Wales, Heath, Cardiff, 1971) but in practice it proved difficult to apply the aesthetic principles in a pure way. A consequence of this was the ubiquitous office block, where symbols of modern architecture, such as curtain walling, were often used in clichéd ways with little regard to their suitability. Concrete became one of the favourite post-war materials because it allowed large spans to be covered and difficult forms to be constructed. An outstanding example of the use of concrete in a functional, but expressive way was at **Brynmawr** Rubber Factory (1951, demolished 2001). Gradually, however, a purely rationalist approach to design gave way to a more expressionist or allusive attitude, such as in some of the religious buildings constructed during the 1960s and 1970s.

During the late 20th century, architectural **design** continued to develop in different ways. Apart from the so-called 'postmodernist' style, which was concerned with decoration and symbolism, two seemingly opposed trends emerged. In the high technology category, buildings were characterized by their use of advanced materials, highly organized structures and sophisticated service equipment. 'Green technology' buildings, on the other hand, used sustainable 'natural' materials and these, together with the need to minimize **energy** requirements by recycling and using well-insulated walls (and occasionally grass roofs, as at the Castell Henllys Educational Centre (Nevern), 1993) helped to give them their characteristic handmade appearance.

ARDUDWY Commote

Located between the **Mawddach** and **Glaslyn**, **Ardudwy** was, with **Eifionydd**, one of the two **commotes** of the *cantref* of **Dunoding**. The two commotes came to eclipse Dunoding, and the notion arose that Ardudwy was itself a *cantref*, divided into the commotes of Is and Uwch Artro. Some of the stories in *The Mabinogion* are set in Ardudwy.

ARENIG FAWR and ARENIG FACH
(Arennig Fawr ac Arennig Fach) Mountains

Located between **Bala** and **Ffestiniog**, Arenig Fawr (854 m) and its satellite peaks, Moel Llyfnant (750 m) and Arenig Fach (689 m; all in **Llanycil**), rise from high squelchy moorland like ships of the line from a heather ocean. The two Arenig **mountains** are separated by the Tryweryn valley, dammed to form Llyn Celyn (*see* **Tryweryn Valley, The drowning of**). In 1910–11, the area provided the inspiration for a series of paintings by **Augustus John** and **James Dickson Innes**, who shared the remote cottage of Amnoddwen at the foot of Arenig Fawr. Innes is said to have buried love letters in the summit's cairn, but they were probably destroyed in 1943 when an American Flying Fortress crashed into the mountain, with the loss of its eight crew members.

ARFON *Cantref*, constituency and one-time district

A *cantref* of the kingdom and principality of **Gwynedd**, the name means 'opposite **Anglesey**' (ar Fôn). It was divided into the **commotes** of Is **Gwyrfai** and Uwch Gwyrfai. Arfon was considered to be the heartland of Gwynedd, containing as it did the bishop's seat at **Bangor** and the important *maerdref* (administrative centre) of **Caernarfon**. In 1284, it became part of the newly created **Caernarfonshire**, sometimes loosely referred to as Arfon. In 1885, Arfon (or rather Arvon) became the name of the parliamentary constituency embracing the northern part of the **county**, a constituency abolished in 1918. Following the abolition of the county in 1974, Arfon was created as a district of the new **county** of **Gwynedd**. It consisted of what had been the **boroughs** of **Bangor** and Caernarfon, the **urban district** of **Bethesda**, the **rural district** of Gwyrfai and part of that of Arfon. The district was abolished in 1996. With the **National Assembly** elections of 2007, the Caernarfon constituency, shorn of **Dwyfor** and augmented by the addition of a further part of the one-time Arfon district, became known as the Arfon constituency.

ARGOED, Caerphilly (1564 ha; 2515 inhabitants)

The **community** straddles the Sirhowy valley south of **Tredegar**. It contains the settlements of Argoed, Manmoel and Cwmcorrwg, and the substantial township of Markham, a planned **garden** village which grew under the shadow of Markham Colliery. St **Cadog** was reputed to have built a church at Manmoel.

ARGOED, Flintshire (630 ha; 5888 inhabitants)

Also known as Mynydd Isa, the **community** is wedged between **Mold** and **Buckley**. It is crossed by **Wat's Dyke**. **Coal**mining began in the 17th century. **Daniel Owen**'s father and two brothers were among the 20 killed in the Argoed Hall Colliery disaster of 1837. Following the closure of the mines, Mynydd Isa became a dormitory for those commuting to Mold and Chester. There is an attractive early 19th-century tollhouse on the A494.

ARIANISM

The belief – promulgated in Alexandria by the cleric Arius (*c*.250–*c*.336) – that Jesus Christ was not of one substance with the Father. The notion caused widespread consternation in the Christian world, and was condemned by the Council of Constantinople in 381.

Arianism became popular in Wales during the 18th century among a section of the Older Dissent (*see* **Nonconformists**) of **Cardiganshire** and **Glamorgan**. Its practitioners believed that God, because of his absolute transcendence, could not interfere in his creation in any way and that consequently Christ should be interpreted in terms of his humanity alone. Arianism developed into **Unitarianism**.

ARIANRHOD

A fictional figure represented chiefly in the fourth branch of the Mabinogi (*see* **Mabinogion, The**). She is the mother of **Lleu Llawgyffes** and the sister of **Gwydion**, Gilfaethwy and others – the children of the goddess Dôn. Caer Arianrhod, a rock formation off the coast of **Arfon**, commemorates her (*see* **Llandwrog**).

ARLLECHWEDD *Cantref*

A *cantref* of the kingdom and principality of **Gwynedd**, Arllechwedd consisted of the **commotes** of Arllechwedd Isaf, Arllechwedd Uchaf and Nant **Conwy**. It extended from the **Conwy** to the Ogwen and included the summits of the **Carneddau** and the Glyderau (*see* **Glyder Fawr and Glyder Fach**). Its principal court was at **Aber[gwyngregyn]**; there were other courts at **Trefriw** and **Dolwyddelan**. In 1284, the *cantref* became part of the newly created **Caernarfonshire**. Following the **Acts of 'Union'**, its commotes became **hundreds**.

ARMINIANISM

The belief in Protestant **theology** that individuals possess free will and can therefore contribute actively to their own salvation. The Dutch theologian Jacobus Arminius (1560–1609) disagreed with the Calvinist belief in God's absolute sovereignty (*see* **Calvinism**), holding instead that the election of men and **women** to salvation followed rather than preceded grace. It was possible for individuals to fall from grace and forfeit their salvation.

Arminianism was popularized by the Caroline theologians of the **Anglican** Church and subsequently by the revivalist John Wesley. With the growth of Wesleyanism in Wales, Arminianism may have served to moderate the influence of high Calvinism, although **Owen Thomas** (1812–91) believed that 'the coming of the **Wesleyans** … caused some to be driven to extremes on the opposing side'.

ARNOLD, Matthew (1822–88) Poet and critic

Professor of poetry at **Oxford** (1857–67) and an Inspector of Schools, Arnold delivered a series of lectures at Oxford on the **literature**s of the **Celt**ic countries, which were published as a book in 1867. Although he could read none of the Celtic languages, his belief that their literatures were characterized by magic and melancholy influenced the **Celtic Twilight** movement. Arnold was unsympathetic to the survival of **Welsh** and Irish – he was more concerned about philistinism in **England** – but his lectures lent academic prestige to the study of the Celtic languages and led, in 1877, to the establishment of the chair of Celtic at Jesus College, Oxford, of which the first incumbent was Sir **John Rhŷs**.

ART GALLERIES

Although Wales enjoys a lively artistic culture, the provision of public space for the exhibition of art has been consistently inadequate. Castles, mansions and churches displayed art in medieval and post-medieval times. The **Industrial Revolution** created sufficient wealth to give rise to collectors, if not patrons, on a scale large enough to influence developments. In the late 19th and early 20th centuries, private initiatives and civic pride led to the establishment of the first public art galleries.

Although **Cardiff**'s civic leadership promotes the city as a centre of artistic excellence, it lacks an exhibition space commensurate with its status as capital. After its closure as a library in the 1980s, the Cardiff Free Library (1895) became a successful artists-run venture; in 1999, it became the ill-fated Centre for the Visual Arts, which closed in 2001. The **National Museum** has one of the world's finest collections of post-Impressionist art, but has struggled to maintain the confidence of the artistic community. Its immense collection of predominantly French paintings, donated by the Davies sisters (*see* **Davies family (Llandinam)**) as the foundation of the national collection, may have led to an acquisitions and exhibitions policy that has often been perceived as skewed against indigenous art.

The 19th century saw significant efforts by private sponsors to bring art to the urban masses. The **Vivian family of Swansea** financed the establishment of the Glynn Vivian Art Gallery, which opened in 1911 and is now run by the city. The gallery holds the premier collection of work by locally born, early 20th-century artists, as well as important examples of Welsh **pottery and porcelain**. The Mostyn Gallery in **Llandudno** – which has become the gallery most involved with contemporary trends in art – was established in 1901 by Lady Augusta **Mostyn** as a venue for the **Gwynedd** Ladies' Arts Society, whose members were barred from exhibiting with the gentlemen of the **Royal Cambrian Academy**. It is believed to have been the first fine art gallery in the world built specifically to show the work of women artists. (The academy continues to mount exhibitions – irrespective, these days, of sex – in **Conwy**.)

Social changes after the **Second World War** led to the establishment of combined art centres and libraries; for example, the **Llantarnam** Grange Arts Centre at **Cwmbran**. Swansea Guildhall and **Newport** Civic Centre are among the administrative buildings containing impressive collections as well as extensive murals. Centres such as Chapter in Cardiff and Taliesin in Swansea provide exhibiting space, and the colleges of the **University of Wales** and the country's schools of art have publicly accessible galleries. **Aberystwyth** has two galleries used for teaching and research; together with its arts centre, the **Ceredigion** Museum and the **National Library**, it probably has more gallery space pro rata than any other Welsh town. One gallery without a permanent base, and the most representative and influential of them all, is the arts and crafts pavilion at the peripatetic National **Eisteddfod**.

There are independent galleries such as the Museum of Modern Art (MOMA) at Tabernacl, **Machynlleth**, the Albany and the Martin Tinney in Cardiff, the Attic in Swansea, and the West Wales Centre for the Arts in **Fishguard**, while the late 20th-century expansion of **tourism** led to the establishment of commercial and artist-run galleries in the major resorts. The Washington Gallery, which complements the Turner House Gallery at **Penarth**, is an attractive example of a mixed private and public finance initiative.

As old definitions of art fade, **sculpture** and **painting** are joined by new work in **film**, video and installation in an irreverent mixture, and artists often seek a forum for their work outside the traditional gallery. Nevertheless, the provision of an appropriate space for the exhibition of the best of contemporary Welsh art remains a major cultural priority.

ARTHOG, Gwynedd (3776 ha; 1010 inhabitants)

Located south of the **Mawddach** estuary, the **community** contains the villages of Arthog, Fairbourne and Friog. It extends to Llyn y Gadair, below the summit of **Cadair Idris**. Fairbourne was created as a holiday village in 1890, when a **horse**-drawn **tram**way was built – later converted into a narrow gauge **railway**. It carries tourists to Penrhyn Point, which offers an excellent view of **Barmouth** and the Mawddach railway bridge. Llynnau Cregennen are mysterious **lakes**. The Arthog Circle represents the remains of a **Bronze Age** burial monument. Kings youth hostel is superbly situated. In 2001, 57.91% of Arthog's inhabitants had no knowledge at all of **Welsh**, making it the most Anglicized, linguistically, of all the communities of **Gwynedd**.

ARTHUR

A vast body of (mainly) European **literature** from the 9th century to the present is associated with the name of this hero. According to the earliest records, he was an historical character of the 6th century, although it is not certain where in **Britain** he was active – the **Old North** or the south-west.

In *Historia Brittonum* (9th century), he is the leader of the kings of the Britons opposing the attacks of the **Anglo-Saxons** and 12 of his victories are listed. **Gildas** (*c.*540) refers to the last of these, the battle of Badon Hill, as a great victory that halted the progress of the enemy, though without naming Arthur. His victory at Badon Hill is referred to in the *Annales Cambriae* under 516, and the battle of Camlan, 'where Arthur and Medrawd fell' is noted under 537.

Nevertheless, it is difficult to speak with any greater certainty about the 'historical' Arthur other than that he may have been a military leader who succeeded, before his death at the battle of Camlan, in delaying the advance of the conquerors. This probably lay at the root of his appeal as an important figure in later poems and tales. The list of his victories may derive from a **Welsh** praise poem, and *Historia Brittonum* contains two traditional topographic anecdotes about 'the warrior Arthur'. The more important of these relates the story of Carn Cafall in **Builth**, a stone bearing the footprint of Cafall, Arthur's hound, made during the hunting of *porcum troit*, namely the **Twrch Trwyth** (or Trwyd), one of the central episodes of the tale 'Culhwch ac Olwen' (*c.*1100) in *The Mabinogion*. This tale, together with a number of early Welsh poems, some **saints**' lives and *The Triads of the Island of Britain*, are evidence for a body of tales about the leader of a band of wondrous warriors who free the land of dragons, **giants** and oppressions, and who plunder the Otherworld (**Annwfn**) of its treasures as they free a prisoner. 'Preiddiau Annwfn', a poem from *The Book of Taliesin*, is thought to have been composed sometime between 850 and 1150; it contains an account of an expedition by Arthur and his men against Annwfn. **Geoffrey of Monmouth**, in his *Historia Regum Britanniae* (*c.*1138), was responsible for expanding Arthur's 'historical' features and locating his court at **Caerleon**, rather than at the Celliwig of Welsh tradition,

Coetan Arthur, a Neolithic tomb at St David's Head

but it was in the French romances of the 12th century and later that the courtly Arthur and his knights developed as standards of chivalric behaviour – as portrayed in Welsh in the romances of 'Peredur', 'Owain' and 'Geraint ac Enid' (*see* **Mabinogion, The**). This is the picture that seized the imagination of writers and their audiences, especially after the publication of Thomas Malory's *Morte d'Arthur* in 1485. But even in the early texts Arthur is not consistently heroic and he receives a fair measure of criticism in saints' lives. It appears that his character was a mixture of the heroic and comic, and **Breuddwyd Rhonabwy** (*see* **Mabinogion, The**) is an early example in Welsh of Arthurian satire.

One element in the story, however, persisted strongly in popular tradition in Wales, **Brittany** and **Cornwall**. This was the messianic belief that Arthur had not died and would return one day to restore his nation's freedom. The belief is suggested in a line in the 10th-century '**Englynion y beddau**': 'Anoeth bit bedd i Arthur' (A wonder, or difficulty, of the world is [would be] a grave for Arthur). Throughout the Middle Ages and afterwards, there is clear testimony to the belief that Arthur had been carried to the **Isle of Avalon** to be healed of his wounds, or that he is asleep with his soldiers in a **cave**, awaiting the call to return. Arthur, the saviour who will return, 'the once and future king', is the most abiding figure in folklore, more so than the literary chivalric king. The purported discovery of his grave at Glastonbury in 1180 was an attempt to discredit the belief in his return. Thereafter, efforts were made to present him not as the enemy of the English but as a glorious ancestor of the English royal family.

ARTS COUNCIL OF WALES, The

An autonomous body responsible for the distribution of public funds to the arts and practising artists, the Arts Council of Wales was established in its present form in 1994. It had its origins in the Welsh Arts Council (1967–94), which began life as a committee of the British Arts Council. Since 1999, it has received its funds from the **National Assembly**; in 2005/6, the Council received total funding from the National Assembly of £26.9 million, in addition to £11.5 million of Lottery money. The Council never has enough money to satisfy all the demands made upon it, and so attracts its full share of criticism – a perennial complaint being the proportion of its funding that is spent on the **Welsh National Opera** (£3.9 million in 2005/6, or 14.5% of the Council's National Assembly allocation). Dissatisfaction has been expressed about the Council's lack of accountability to the public, and some believe that it was a mistake, in 1997, to disband the specialist departments responsible for the various arts. However, without the Arts Council's work, the cultural life of Wales would be much the poorer, with many arts practitioners and projects unable to operate. The announcement of the Welsh Assembly Government, in 2004, that public patronage of the arts would, from the spring of 2006, be under the direct control of the Assembly aroused strong opposition; the plan was abandoned.

ARWYSTLI *Cantref*

Representing the south-western part of the later **Montgomeryshire**, the *cantref* was divided into the **commotes** of Iscoed and Uwchcoed. Although originally part of **Powys**, it came to be associated with **Gwynedd** and was

Welsh National Opera's production of *Don Carlos*, 2005

a detached part of the **diocese** of **Bangor**. The dispute between **Llywelyn ap Gruffudd** and **Gruffudd ap Gwenwynwyn** over the possession of Arwystli was the Welsh cause célèbre of the years 1277–82. The question of under which **law** the dispute should be settled – that of Wales or **England** – became a central factor in the deteriorating relationship between Llywelyn and Edward I. The post-**Acts of 'Union' hundred** of Arwystli had similar boundaries to those of the medieval *cantref*. The name survives in Pen **Pumlumon** Arwystli (740 m), the second highest of Pumlumon's summits, and in institutions such as the Arwystli Medical Practice and the Arwystli Society.

ASHBY, A[rthur] W[ilfred] (1886–1953)
Agricultural economist
The son of the leading rural activist Joseph Ashby, he attended Ruskin College, **Oxford**, worked for the Board of **Agriculture**, and was appointed lecturer in Agricultural Economics at **Aberystwyth** in 1924. His chair in the subject (1929) was the first in any British university. He wrote the *Agriculture of Wales and Monmouth* (with Ifor J. Evans, 1943), one of his many studies of the Welsh rural **economy**. While at Aberystwyth, he inspired a new generation of scholars, and was concerned with agricultural training, farmers' co-operatives, farm labourers' conditions and the establishment of the Milk Marketing Board.

ASHLEY, Laura (1925–85)
Fashion designer and entrepreneur
A self-taught designer born in Dowlais, **Merthyr Tydfil**, her company had its humble origins in 1953 when she and her husband Bernard started printing tea towels and scarves in their own distinctive style at their **London** flat. The decision, in 1960, to locate at **Carno**, began the expansion of factories and warehouses which saw the company's establishment as a major employer in the region. By the time of the company's public flotation (November 1985), two months after Laura Ashley's sudden death, it had grown into an international group, manufacturing and retailing its own range of clothes, home furnishings and related products through 219 shops worldwide, the first of which was at **Llanidloes**. By the early 1990s, however, the group had run into difficulties; factory closures and job losses ensued, and its Welsh connections all but disappeared with the Carno factory closing in 2005.

ASHTON, Charles (1848–99)
Bibliographer and literary historian
A native of Llawr-y-glyn, **Trefeglwys**, Ashton was a **lead** miner at Dylife, **Llanbrynmair**, at the age of 12 and, from 1869, a **police**man; he spent his last years at Dinas **Mawddwy**, where he committed suicide. Although largely self-taught, several of his publications, notably a history of Welsh **literature**, *Hanes Llenyddiaeth Gymraeg o 1651 hyd 1850* (1893), have stood the test of time.

ASSER (d.909) Counsellor to Alfred the Great
Educated at **St David's**, where he became bishop *c.*873, Asser was, *c.*884, invited to assist Alfred, king of Wessex, to educate his subjects. In 901, he was appointed bishop of Sherborne. He is believed to have written *Annales rerum gestarum Alfredi Magni*, an account of Alfred's reign, which contains valuable evidence concerning the political condition of 9th-century Wales.

ASSHETON SMITH family
Landowners and industrialists
An influential landed family in north-west Wales who, along with the **Pennant family** of Penrhyn, dominated the Welsh **slate** industry. Thomas Assheton Smith (1752–1828) inherited the Vaynol estate (*see* **Pentir**) and started to exploit the slate deposits in **Llanberis** in 1787. The Dinorwic (**Llanddeiniolen**) quarry was established in 1809; by 1826, some 800 men were employed there, and Assheton Smith had developed the requisite infrastructure, including the port of Port Dinorwic (**Y Felinheli**). He was MP for **Caernarfonshire** (1774–80). The estate and quarry were inherited by his son, also Thomas Assheton Smith (1776–1858), who was mostly famous as a foxhunter (*see* **Hunting**). The family were often absent from Vaynol, acquiring a reputation for a colourful social life that included theatrical performances and the development of a menagerie. The contrast with the lives of the quarrymen was stark, and it is significant that the **North Wales Quarrymen's Union** was formed in 1874 following a strike at Dinorwic, by which time ownership had passed to George William Duff (1848–1904), who appropriated the Assheton Smith name. In 1885, when the company employed 2700 men, there was a further and bitter lockout at the quarries. The Prince and Princess of Wales stayed at Vaynol in 1902, and the house, in beautiful surroundings on the **Menai Strait**, maintained its reputation for upper-class socializing and weekend parties well into the 20th century.

ASSOCIATION (*sasiwn*)
A meeting established by the early Welsh **Calvinistic Methodists** to regulate the activities of their **Societies** and exhorters. In 1740, **Howel Harris** suggested establishing a 'society' for the **revival** leaders. Some meetings were held in 1740–1, but it was in January 1742, at Dugoedydd farmhouse (**Llanfair-ar-y-bryn**), that the first Association proper was held, and control of the whole body of Welsh Calvinistic Methodists was assumed by those present. Later, the term was used for regional gatherings of church representatives.

ASSOCIATION OF WELSH CLERGY IN THE WEST RIDING OF YORKSHIRE, The
Founded in 1821, the Association comprised mainly expatriate **Welsh**-speaking clergymen with an interest in their native land and Church. Its published annual reports (1852–6) witnessed to the claim that its members had a freedom to speak about abuses in the Church of England in Wales (*see* **Anglicans**) – a freedom denied to those serving in Wales. It campaigned for Welsh-speaking bishops and clergy and for a Welsh university.

ASTLEY, Dai (David John Astley; 1909–89)
Footballer
A skilful inside-forward who did much to sustain Welsh morale in the 1930s, Dai Astley was born in Dowlais, **Merthyr Tydfil**. He scored regularly for Charlton Athletic,

Lynn Davies, long-jump Olympic gold medallist in 1964

Aston Villa and Derby County, and although restricted to 13 internationals he scored 12 times. He later coached in mainland Europe.

ASTRONOMY

The first astronomers in Wales were the **Neolithic** inhabitants who set up stone alignments to mark the directions of sunrise at midwinter and midsummer, such as the alignment near Llanfair Discoed (**Caerwent**). Other alignments may have been used to record the extreme positions of moonrise and moonset over the 18.6-year lunar cycle.

Throughout ancient and medieval history, there was no clear distinction between astronomy and astrology, as is apparent from the extensive discussion and colourful diagrams in MS Mostyn 88, the work of the poet **Gutun Owain**. **John Dee** could be regarded as the very last Welshman to combine the two traditions. It is therefore significant that in 1609, less than a year after the death of John Dee, two **Carmarthenshire** men, William Lower and John Prydderch, set up an observatory at Treventy (**St Clears**). They used the latest technology – an optical telescope – to observe the surface of the moon, in exactly the same year as Galileo used his first telescope to study sunspots and the moons of Jupiter.

Just over a century later, Joseph Harris (1704–64) from Trefeca (**Talgarth**), brother of **Howel Harris**, was employed by Halley to make two sea journeys (1725, 1730–2) to test astronomical methods of navigation. At about the same time, **John Bevis** from **Tenby** established his observatory in Stoke Newington and compiled a catalogue of stars that was more complete than any other at the time. Later in the 18th century, Lewis Evans (1755–1827) from **Caerleon** established his observatory in Woolwich.

The most significant contribution that Wales made to astronomy worldwide was in the **photography** of astronomical objects. There is some evidence that an early attempt was made at **Penllergaer** (*see* **John Dillwyn-Llewelyn**), but the first successful photograph of an extragalactic object – the Andromeda Nebula – was made in 1888 by **Isaac Roberts** from **Denbigh** at his observatory in Sussex. He is now recognized universally as the pioneer of astronomical photography. Isaac Roberts was, in the truest sense of the word, an amateur. The 19th century saw the rapid growth of amateur astronomy, with enthusiasts such as John Jones (1818–90) of **Bangor**, 'the working-man's astronomer', playing their part.

In the 20th century, astronomy became increasingly professional, extending its range from the traditional optical observations to the use of infrared and radio waves at lower frequencies, and ultraviolet waves and X-rays at higher frequencies. These measurements depended on large optical and radio telescopes, and telescopes mounted on spacecraft. In these new fields, Welsh astronomers have made a major contribution. **Edward Bowen** built the largest radio telescope in the southern hemisphere. There was one moment in the 1990s when, by chance, four of the largest telescopes in the world were making observations under the direction of Welsh scientists. **Cardiff University** has made a major contribution to infrared and sub-millimetre astronomy, and to studies of the **chemistry** of the early universe. **Aberystwyth** uses radio observations of quasars to measure the solar wind at all solar latitudes, work to which **Phil Williams** made a crucial contribution. Bangor studies the complex chemical structures that exist in interstellar space.

Of a long list of distinguished Welsh astronomers alive at present, one deserves special mention: Mike Disney (b.1937) of Cardiff was the first to propose that a new class of galaxy too diffuse to be recorded by conventional observations – the low-intensity galaxies – might make a significant contribution to the 'missing mass' of the universe. It is now widely accepted that up to half of the visible matter in the universe is in the form of low-intensity galaxies as proposed by Disney.

ATHLETICS

Jumping, throwing and running being fundamental human activities, it is not surprising that athletic pursuits in Wales are traceable to ancient times. **Giraldus Cambrensis** refers to climbing **mountains** and running through forests as a means of improving fitness for war. That athletic proficiency was highly regarded down the ages is testified by medieval poetry celebrating sporting prowess, and by the significance allotted to it in '**the twenty-four feats**', first recorded in print *c.*1500, as standard determinants of human competency. The *gwrolgampau* (heroics) section of these feats emphasized the benefits of physical fitness to mental alertness.

Various athletic challenges were included in the traditional sporting calendar, victory in which assured renown. The greatest pre-industrial Welsh runner was the phenomenal Guto Nyth-brân (**Griffith Morgan**; 1700–37), whose long-distance stamina was unsurpassed, and whose legendary achievements included catching **hares** and outpacing a **horse**. His grave at Llanwonno (**Ynysybwl**) is a place of pilgrimage. In contrast with the rather boisterous and unorganized traditional sports, the growth of relatively structured and professional 'pedestrianism' (long-distance, competitive walking or running) during the 19th century anticipated the development of modern athletics. Catering for runners and walkers alike, pedestrianism's set rules reflected the standardization of an increasingly industrial Welsh society from the 1840s onwards. However, pedestrianism's association with rowdiness, gambling and dishonest behaviour eventually forced its replacement by more respectable amateur forms.

Amateur athletics reached Wales from **England** through the public schools and colleges during the mid-1850s and led to the foundation of Welsh athletic clubs, the earliest opening at **Newport** in 1877. By the 1890s, formalized track, field and cross-country contests had commenced: the first amateur championship events – the 100-yard and mile races for men – were held in 1893, and 1896 saw the establishment of the Welsh Cross-Country Association. The first fully integrated athletics championships were contested at Rodney Parade, Newport, in 1907, and by the late 1920s Welsh teams were competing internationally.

The home of professional running was Taff Vale Park, **Pontypridd**, where the Welsh Powderhall, so-named after Edinburgh's famous professional sprint, was keenly contested between 1903 and 1934.

Despite a temporary cessation of competition during the **Second World War**, athletics continued to develop, notably with the first national Schools Championships in 1947, the formation of the Welsh Amateur Athletics Association in 1948 and, from 1952, the inclusion of **women** in the Welsh championships. In 1958, interest in Welsh athletics was enhanced by **Cardiff**'s hosting of the **Commonwealth Games**, an event that inspired the first Welsh Games a year later, catering for top-class indigenous and international athletes. The successes of Welsh athletes on a world stage, such as Lynn Davies's (b.1942) long-jump gold medal at the 1964 Tokyo Olympics, further raised the sport's profile. The construction of synthetic tracks, and other improvements during the 1970s, combined with the jogging boom of

Dame Tanni Grey-Thompson, Paralympic gold medallist in 2004

the 1980s led to increased participation at all levels. The reputation of Welsh athletics has been heightened in recent times by the international victories of figures such as the Olympic hurdler Colin Jackson (b.1967) and the wheelchair athlete Tanni Grey-Thompson (b.1969), both of them Cardiff-born. In 2004, Grey-Thompson, possibly Wales's greatest ever athlete, became **Britain**'s most successful Paralympian after winning her second gold medal of the Athens Paralympic Games and the 11th of her career.

ATKIN, James Richard (Lord Atkin of Aberdovey; 1867–1944) Judge

Possibly the greatest judge of the 20th century, Atkin was born in Brisbane, **Australia**, but, brought up in **Merioneth** and educated at Christ College, **Brecon**, he regarded himself as a Welshman. He established the fundamentals of civil liability for negligence (*Donoghue* v *Stevenson*, 1932), and famously defended the individual's freedom from arbitrary arrest, even in wartime (*Liversidge* v *Anderson*, 1942).

AUBREY, William (c.1529–95)
Civil and canon lawyer

The scion of an old **Brecon** family, Aubrey was professor of civil **law** at **Oxford** before distinguishing himself as an expert in international and constitutional law. Elizabeth I called him 'my little doctor'. He was a judge in and an advocate of reform of the church courts, and as a maritime lawyer was involved in the suppression of Welsh **piracy**. Aubrey was MP for **Carmarthen** (1554) and Brecon (1558), and owned extensive estates in south Wales. He was a kinsman of both Dr **John Dee** and (more distantly) **John Penry**, in whose condemnation (1593) he took part.

Olympic hurdler Colin Jackson in 2002

Welsh immigrants to Australia and their Gwalia Co-operative Store, 1932

AUDLEY family Marcher-lords

The first of the family to be connected with Wales, Nicholas d'Audley (d.1299), married Catherine, heiress of John Giffard, lord of **Llandovery**. Their son, Nicholas (d.1316), married Joan, heiress of William Martin, lord of **Cemais**. The Audleys and their descendants, the Tuchets, held Cemais and Llandovery until the attainder of James Tuchet, Baron Audley, in 1497. Cemais was restored to James's son, who sold it to the father of **George Owen** of Henllys in 1543. Hugh (d.1347), a member of a cadet branch of the family, married Margaret, the co-heiress of Gilbert de **Clare** (d.1314). Her share of the Clare inheritance was the lordship of **Gwynllŵg**, an arrangement which caused the **Rhymney** River to be the eastern border of **Glamorgan**. Through the marriage of Margaret's daughter, Gwynllŵg passed to the **Stafford family**.

AUGUSTINIAN CANONS

Founded in the 11th century to enable clergy to live a monastic form of life, the Order adopted a rule based on the writings of St Augustine of Hippo. The houses in Wales founded under Anglo-**Norman** patronage were Llanthony (**Crucorney**; 1118), **Carmarthen** (*c*.1125) and **Haverfordwest** (*c*.1210). In the 13th century, the ancient *clasau* of **Beddgelert,** Penmon (**Llangoed**) and Bardsey (**Aberdaron**) adopted the Augustinian rule, probably as a result of the desire of the princes of **Gwynedd** to be associated with mainstream European Christianity.

AUSTRALIA, Wales's associations with

The Welsh presence in Australia has comprised both convicts and free settlers, the latter generally arriving *c*.1840–1920 and, especially, after 1945. Between 1788 and 1868, around 1900 men and 300 **women** from Wales were transported to the penal colonies, including the leaders of the Chartist march on **Newport** in 1839 (*see* **Chartism**) and some of the participants in the **Rebecca Riots**. Few Welsh took advantage of early voluntary emigration schemes, but from the 1840s onwards Welsh immigration increased substantially as a result of rich **copper** finds in South Australia and the spectacular **gold** rushes in Victoria and New South Wales after 1851, together with the gold rush of 1893 in Western Australia: the company which owns the Perth Mint is called the Sons of **Gwalia**. Sizeable Welsh communities developed in Victoria, notably in the Ballarat–Sebastopol area; they were sufficiently strong to support 21 **Nonconformist** chapels, numerous eisteddfodau and **Welsh-language** periodicals. From the 1870s onwards, the **coal**mines of the Hunter valley in New South Wales and Blackstone, near Ipswich, Queensland (pioneered by **Lewis Thomas**), emerged as important Welsh communities. Generally, however, Welsh settlement was thinly dispersed.

Australians born in Wales and of Welsh descent have made important contributions to the country's economic development, labour movement and cultural, musical and religious life. Prominent figures range from Chief Justice **Samuel Griffith** and William (Billy) Morris Hughes (1862–1952; prime minister, 1915–23) to Rolf Harris (b.1930) and Kylie Minogue (b.1968). Of particular note is the history of the eisteddfod, which, after evolving into a cosmopolitan, English-language gathering, has become an increasingly important Australian tradition. Scores of *eisteddfodau* are held every year, although most Australians are unaware of the institution's Welsh roots.

Each Australian state has a Welsh society, the Cambrian Society of Victoria having been in existence since 1872; Welsh churches remain at Blackstone, Ballarat and Melbourne – where the Welsh church is a major city landmark. In 1996, some 27,488 natives of Wales were living in Australia.

AVALON, The Isle of

The otherworld island where **Arthur** was taken to be healed after the battle of Camlan. The **Welsh** name, *ynys Afallach*, may mean either the island of its king, Afallach, or 'the isle of apples'. The **Latin** texts that give an account of Arthur's end reflect the second interpretation, *insula Avalloniae/Avallonis*. In **Celt**ic mythology, the otherworld – or **Annwfn** – was a world of continuous feasting, free from all sickness and anxieties and filled with the song of magical **birds**. In a poem in *The Book of Taliesin*, *ynys Afallach*, though un-named, is described as a timeless world of joy and pleasure. In his chair-winning poem 'Ymadawiad Arthur', **T. Gwynn Jones** drew on this poem to describe the isle of Avalon, there called Afallon, a name that soon passed into popular usage.

AVIATION and AERONAUTICS

Although balloonists such as James Sadler ventured into Welsh skies in the 19th century, it was not until the Edwardian era that aviation proper began to develop. Pioneering aircraft constructors, such as the **Pembrokeshire**-born James brothers, **Horace Watkins** and **W. E. Williams**, were followed by the record seekers: Denys Corbett Wilson flew from **Fishguard** to County Wexford

on 22 April 1912, the first flight from **Britain** to **Ireland**; **Rhyl**-based Vivian Hewitt claimed the **Holyhead**–Dublin crossing on 26 April 1912. Exhibition pilots, such as Gustav Hamel and Henry Astley, who toured Wales giving demonstrations, satisfied a growing public interest in aviation. **Ernest T. Willows**, the first to fly across the **Severn** estuary, was hailed as 'the father of British airships'.

During the **First World War**, airship maritime patrol stations were established on **Anglesey**, for Irish Sea patrols, and near **Pembroke**, for patrols in the south-west approaches. In 1917, the War Office developed two airfields side-by-side at **Queensferry** (Shotwick North and Shotwick South), which were used by training squadrons.

The interwar period saw the dawn of commercial aviation. In 1919, ex-military Avro planes were given a new lease of life and used for pleasure flights from Welsh beaches such as **Swansea** and **Rhyl**. The following years saw barnstorming tours by showmen-aviators such as Alan Cobham and company, one of the most celebrated of whom was the young Idwal Jones from Talysarn (**Llanllyfni**), who was later killed in a flying accident. In the 1930s, air links were established between **Cardiff** and Weston-super-Mare, Bristol and Birmingham, and in 1935 Wales's national airline, Cambrian Airways, was founded; it operated until 1976. The RAF opened a seaplane base at **Pembroke Dock** in 1930 and, later, airfields at four other locations. At **Broughton**, **Flintshire**, a factory and an airfield (RAF **Hawarden**) were built in 1938 to produce Vickers Wellington bombers.

The outbreak of war in 1939 heralded a prodigious growth in military aviation. In addition to the existing

Employees watch the new Airbus A380 make its flypast of the wing-manufacturing site at Broughton, 18 May 2006, en route to Heathrow Airport for its first landing in Britain

7 airbases, 27 others were constructed. Among the most important were Broughton, where 5540 Wellingtons were built, RAF **Valley**, which became a transatlantic terminal, and RAF Pembroke Dock, a base for anti-submarine patrols.

Although the end of the war resulted in the closure of half of the airfields, a legacy was created which strongly influenced subsequent development. Flying training was concentrated at RAF's Valley and **Brawdy**. Brawdy was eventually closed, but Valley grew into a leading fast-jet training airfield. Aircraft manufacturing was recommenced at Broughton in 1948 after a three-year break, and in 1971, with the factory in the ownership of Hawker Siddeley, production began of wings for the A300 Airbus. British Aerospace controlled the factory until 30 November 1999, when BAE Systems was created, forming Airbus UK in March 2000; by 2007, Airbus was wholly owned by the European Aeronautic Defence and Space Company (EADS). A major expansion programme was undertaken to construct wings for the new Airbus A380 super-jumbo.

The terrorist attack on the World Trade Center in New York on 11 September 2001 caused a temporary dramatic downturn in the aviation industry worldwide, and there was consequent concern for the Airbus A380 project at Broughton, but the factory's future seems assured in the light of the industry's subsequent recovery. The aerospace industry is further represented in Flintshire by Hawker Beechcraft (formerly Raytheon Aircraft Services), which has provided aircraft servicing facilities at Hawarden since 1993. (*See also* **Airports**.)

Accidents

Wales's worst air accidents were at **Sigingstone** and **Cwm Edno**, but there have been many others. A combination of high ground and low cloud has sent many an aircraft to its doom, especially during the **Second World War** – of the 27 air accidents in the **Brecon Beacons**, 23 occurred during 1939–46. Among the worst of the wartime crashes was that of an American B-17 Fortress near **Barmouth** on 8 June 1945, in which 20 servicemen were killed. One of the most serious post-war crashes was that of a Boeing Washington bomber on 8 January 1953 near **Wrexham**, which killed the crew of 10.

Aeronautics

Discounting the alleged 'first manned flight' in 1896 of the **Saundersfoot** carpenter **William Frost**, Wales has made significant contributions to the field of aerodynamics. Robert Jones (1891–1962) from **Criccieth** and **Bangor**-born Daniel Williams (1894–1963) both studied at Bangor where the head of mathematics, Professor G. H. Bryan (1895–1926), was one of the founders of the **science**. Jones and Williams worked at the aerodynamics division of the National Physical Laboratory (NPL), Teddington, where they used theoretical models and wind-tunnel experiments to study the performance of aircraft. Jones specialized in the stability of aeroplanes, airships, parachutes and torpedoes, while Williams studied the performance of aircraft and the relationship between the circulation of air and the lift it applies to an aerofoil. **Lampeter**-born William Pritchard Jones (1910–86) also joined the aerodynamics division of the NPL, where he studied vibrations in aircraft wings, and the flow of air over vibrating surfaces. He became head of the division and director of the NATO advisory group for aerospace research and development. Further leading Welsh aerodynamicists from Wales include **Lewis Boddington**, who developed the angled flight deck on aircraft carriers, and Sir **Morien Morgan**, who worked on the effect of aircraft controls on the dynamics of the plane, although he is best known for his leadership of the supersonic project which eventually became Concorde (*see also* **Brian Trubshaw**).

AWDL

An *awdl* (lit. 'rhyme') is a poetic form which, among the **Cynfeirdd** and the **Poets of the Princes**, was a mono-rhyming sequence of lines within which different metres were sometimes combined. The chair at the National **Eisteddfod** is awarded for an *awdl*, and the term presently refers to a poem that includes any number of the traditional 24 metres and which contains *cynghanedd*.

The Cyfarthfa Ironworks in 1910, originally founded by Anthony Bacon in 1765

BACON, Anthony (1718–86) Ironmaster

Born in Cumberland, Bacon was one of the first entrepreneurs to recognize the **iron**making potential of **Merthyr Tydfil**. With William Brownrigg, he opened a forge at Cyfarthfa in 1765, where he adapted **John Wilkinson**'s patent for boring cannon from solid bars. Markets generated by the American War of Independence gave Cyfarthfa a significant lead, which was enhanced when Richard **Crawshay** joined the partnership in 1778. Bacon also took out leases of lands and mineral rights for the establishment of the Plymouth Iron Works in 1777, and at **Hirwaun** in 1780.

BADMINTON

Named after the seat of the Duke of Beaufort (*see* **Somerset family**) at Badminton, Gloucestershire, where the game was believed to have evolved *c.*1870, badminton was being played in Wales by the early years of the 20th century. The Welsh Badminton Union was formed in 1928, and came to consist of 150 senior and 120 junior clubs.

Notable Welsh achievements include **Llantrisant**'s Kelly Morgan winning gold in the 1998 **Commonwealth Games**, and Richard Vaughan, of **Llanbradach**, winning bronze in the 2002 Commonwealth Games. Vaughan won the Welsh International (open) men's singles title in 1999 and 2000, the first Welshman to take the title in successive years since Howard Jennings, of **Pencoed**, in 1968 and 1969. Indonesian-born Irwansyah, who qualified for Wales on residence, took the title in 2001 and 2002.

BAGILLT, Flintshire (1001 ha; 3918 inhabitants)

A **community** located on the **Dee** estuary between **Holywell** and **Flint**, Bagillt is listed in Domesday Book as *Bachelie*. Cefn Coleshill Farm recalls the **commote** of **Coleshill**; Basingwerk Castle, fortified by Henry II in 1157, and captured by **Owain Gwynedd** in 1166, was levelled in the 13th century. Bagillt experienced early industrialization, the resulting pollution causing **Thomas Pennant** to demolish his mansion of Bagillt Hall. Gadlys, founded in 1703, was the first of Bagillt's five major **lead**-smelting works. Bettisfield Colliery – which gave employment to the poet George Tattum (1870–1941) – was one of the area's 12 collieries; its engine house and lamp room survive. From the early 18th to the mid-19th centuries, ferries sailed from Bagillt Dock to the Wirral and **Liverpool**. Enoch Robert Gibbon Salisbury (1819–90), the bibliophile who gave his name to the **Welsh** library of Cardiff **University**, was born at Bagillt.

BAGLAN, Neath Port Talbot
(904 ha; 6654 inhabitants)
Baglan is located within the **communities** of Baglan and Baglan Bay (*see below*).

Adjoining the estuary of the **Nedd**, Baglan experienced extensive industrialization in the early 19th century, when **coal**, **tinplate** and **pottery** were exported from Baglan Pill. The trade was killed off by the **railway** and the place returned to its rural calm until 1963, when BP **Chemicals'** Baglan Bay plant opened. The plant spawned the hi-tech Baglan **Energy** Park.

The communities of Baglan

BAGLAN (576 ha; 6654 inhabitants)
The community, a sprawling housing development, contains St Catherine's church (1878–82), **John Prichard**'s masterpiece. Baglan House was one of the seats of the Villiers family, earls of Jersey, part inheritors of the **Mansel** estates. Griffith Llewelyn of Baglan Hall, a major **Rhondda** landowner, founded Llewelyn & Cubitt (1874), Wales's leading manufacturer of colliery equipment. Blaen Baglan is a derelict **gentry** house of *c.*1600.

BAGLAN BAY (Bae Baglan) (328 ha; 0 inhabitants)
The community, which has no inhabitants, is entirely occupied by industrial enterprises. Three distinctive landmarks – two cooling towers and a redundant power station stack – were demolished in 2003. Opened in 2004 in Baglan **Energy** Park was **Britain**'s first gas-fuelled power station; GE Energy's £300 million plant produces 480 MW of electricity – enough to power 500,000 dwellings.

One of Crawshay Bailey's roundhouses, Nantyglo, built *c.*1816 as a refuge for key workers in times of industrial unrest

BAGPIPE, The (*pibgod*, *piba cwd* or *sachbib*)
Although no complete instruments survive, there is evidence that bagpipes were played in Wales from the Middle Ages until the middle of the 19th century. Pipes (of unspecified type) are mentioned in medieval **law** texts and poetry; there are carvings of a bagpipe possibly dating from the 15th century in **Llaneilian** church, **Anglesey**; and a 16th-century manuscript includes illustrations of both single-chanter and double-chanter bagpipes, the former with a single drone, the latter without. What may be the double chanter of a bagpipe (dating from 1701) is in the National History Museum (*see* **St Fagans**). Both 18th- and 19th-century evidence often places the instrument in the context of a wedding celebration or fair. It is unlikely that there was ever a single standardized form of bagpipe in Wales; various types of Welsh bagpipe have been constructed and played in recent years.

BAILEY family Ironmasters
The Yorkshire-born Bailey brothers, Joseph (1783–1858) and Crawshay (1789–1872), followed their uncle, Richard **Crawshay**, into the **iron** industry of south Wales in the early 19th century. By 1820, they ran the **Nantyglo** Ironworks, one of the bigger producers, and in 1833 leased the **Beaufort** works. The brothers opposed any regulation of the industry and ignored the Ironmasters' Association's attempts, between 1802 and 1826, to fix production, prices and wages. An enthusiastic promoter of **railways**, and one of the first to realize the huge potential of the south Wales **coal**field, Crawshay Bailey was MP for **Monmouth Boroughs** (1852–68). He is the subject of a well-known **ballad**. By his death, Crawshay Bailey had settled at Maindiff Court (**Llantilio Pertholey**), the centre of the 4650-ha estate he had acquired in south-east Wales. Joseph Bailey proved even more adept as an accumulator of land. By 1873, the family's Glanusk (*see* **Llangattock**) estate of 11,500 ha represented perhaps the most rapid example of estate building in the history of 19th-century **Britain**. His grandson was elevated to the peerage as Lord Glanusk in 1899.

BAKER, David (Fr Augustine Baker; 1575–1641)
Mystic
Born in **Abergavenny**, Baker was received into the **Roman Catholic** Church in 1603 and joined the **Benedictine** Order in 1613 or 1619. At Cambrai (1624–33) and at Douai (1633–8), he collected material on English Benedictines, produced prolific treatises on spiritual matters and edited the work of medieval mystics. Selections from his writings were published as *Sancta Sophia* (Douai, 1657). In his autobiography, he claimed that so **Welsh** was Abergavenny in his youth, that it was impossible to learn standard **English** there.

BAKER, Stanley (1928–76) Actor
A rugged, brooding actor from Ferndale, **Rhondda**, Baker proved equally adept in **police** and criminal roles in 1950s and 1960s British **films**. He was notably worldweary as a policeman beset by domestic problems in *Hell is a City* (1960), and the lively stylish trucking film *Hell Drivers* (1957) helped to consolidate his 'tough-guy' image. Baker was impressive in *The Cruel Sea* (1953) and the Joseph

Losey features *Blind Date* (1959), *The Criminal* (1960, from an **Alun Owen** script), *Eve* (or *Eva*, 1962) and *Accident* (1967). His enduring legacy for many is the **South Wales Borderers** epic, *Zulu* (1964), which he co-produced. In this tribute to soldiers' bravery at Rorke's Drift (*see* **South African Wars**), Baker starred as a conscientious Royal Engineer. He was outstanding in the BBC Wales **coal**mining drama *The Squeeze* (1960), but was already ill with cancer during his moving portrayal of Gwilym Morgan in the second BBC television version of ***How Green Was My Valley*** (1976).

BALA (Y Bala), Gwynedd
(263 ha; 1980 inhabitants)
Located where the **Dee** flows from **Bala Lake** (Llyn Tegid), the name comes from the **Celt**ic *belago*, meaning the efflux of a **river** from a lake. (There is a Bala in that part of Turkey colonized by the Celtic-speaking Galatians.) The town, founded by Roger **Mortimer** (*c*.1310), was the last to be established of the **boroughs** of medieval Wales. An earlier motte, Tomen y Bala, gave its name to Tŷ-tan-domen, the grammar school founded in 1712. In the 18th century, Bala was an important centre of **woollen** products, its inhabitants knitting up to 200,000 pairs of stockings a year. It also played a part in the revival of the **eisteddfod**, although that activity waned as Bala became a major centre of Methodism. In 1783, **Thomas Charles**, a native of **Carmarthenshire**, married Sally Jones of Bala and settled in the town. An ordained clergyman, his evangelical views precluded his advancement within the **Anglican** Church, and in 1784 he joined the Bala Methodist *seiat* (*see* **Society**). His talents and the fact that he could offer communion caused Bala to be the chief centre of the second phase in the growth of Welsh **Calvinistic Methodism**. Indeed, with its lakeside location and its religious associations, Bala can be considered the Geneva of Wales. Charles's role in the establishment of the **Bible Society** caused the town to loom large in biblical mythology – in particular through the story of **Mary Jones**, a story savoured from **Madagascar** to the **Khasi Hills**. In 1837, Charles's grandson-in-law, **Lewis Edwards**, established a college for the training of Calvinistic Methodist ministers at Bala; it is now a Presbyterian youth centre. In 1842, the town also became home to a training college for **Congregational** ministers; founded by Michael Jones (1787–1853), it became the centre of much controversy during the principalship of his son, **Michael D. Jones**. In the town's wide main street is a statue of **T. E. Ellis**. Bala is an international centre for water sports, especially **sailing**, canoeing and white-water rafting. **George Borrow** much enjoyed the breakfast offered by the White Lion Hotel.

BALLADS
Narrative poems which may be sung, declaimed or read. Ballads in **Welsh** recounting events from the late 16th and early 17th centuries have survived, such as those telling of the Babington Plot to kill Queen Elizabeth and of the Gunpowder Plot; but it was the arrival of the **printing** press in Shrewsbury in 1695, soon to be followed by presses in Wales itself, that led to the great period of Welsh ballads.

Stanley Baker filming *Return to Rhondda* in 1965

This extended from the beginning of the 18th century to the death of the last of the well-known balladeers, Abel Jones (Y Bardd Crwst; 1829–1901). He and his predecessors – figures such as **Elis Roberts**, Twm o'r Nant (**Thomas Edwards**; 1739–1810) and Dic Dywyll (Richard Williams; *c*.1805–*c*.1865) – tramped the country, hawking their ballad sheets in markets, fairs and wherever people gathered. Although most of their ballads were of a religious and moralistic nature, they encompassed the whole gamut of contemporary life – **colliery disasters**, **shipwrecks**, murders, strikes – and were much prized for their news value. **English**-language ballads were few, but near the end of the 19th century bilingual versions increasingly appeared, especially in industrial parts of the south. The modern literary ballads of Cynan (**Albert Evans-Jones**), **I. D. Hooson** and others are not of this tradition, but rather draw their inspiration from the works of English exponents of the form.

BANCROFT, W[illiam] J[ohn] (1871–1959)
Rugby player and cricketer
The first of the great Welsh full-backs, Billy Bancroft was closely associated with **Swansea**'s St Helen's ground. He lived there in his childhood when his father was groundsman, played his club **rugby** there for Swansea, and enjoyed many of his triumphs as full-back for Wales and as a professional **cricket**er for **Glamorgan** on the ground – before becoming groundsman himself. A skilled defender, sidestepping attacker and superb kicker, he was a fixture in the Wales team during the 1890s. His 33 caps were a Welsh record when he retired, and remained so until beaten by J. P. R. Williams three-quarters of a century later. In 1895, he became Glamorgan's first professional cricketer, and he coached the young **Gilbert Parkhouse**. He was succeeded at full-back for club and country by his younger brother, Jack Bancroft (1879–1942).

BANDO

A game with up to 30 players on each side played on level ground, sometimes on a beach. There were no fixed rules: each player had a bando, resembling a **hockey** stick, and the game consisted of hitting the ball between two marks which served as goals at either end of the pitch. The game was played throughout Wales up to the end of the 19th century and was particularly popular in **Glamorgan**, where the '**Margam** Bando Boys' were commemorated in a macaronic **ballad** of that name earlier in the century.

BANGLADESHIS

In 2001, there were 5436 people of Bangladeshi descent in Wales, of whom 38% were born in Wales. The majority live in the **Swansea** Bay area, **Newport** and **Cardiff**, while others live and work, principally in the restaurant business, throughout Wales. Many of the first generation migrated to Wales from the declining textile-producing towns of Lancashire and Yorkshire from the mid-1960s onwards, mainly to work in catering. The vast majority were originally from the Sylhet region of north-eastern Bangladesh. Some 5000 of Bangladeshis in Wales in 2001 identified themselves as believers in **Islam**. It is an overwhelmingly young community, 39% of whom are under 16. It is also one of the most socially deprived. Its rate of economic activity (53%) is the lowest of any ethnic group in Wales, well below the average of 75% for Wales as a whole, although this may be chiefly attributed to an unusually high rate of female unemployment (21%). In contrast, the 83% rate of economic activity among Bangladeshi men is marginally higher than the overall male average (82%). Nevertheless, Bangladeshis in Wales have the lowest rate of single-dwelling occupancy (8%), the highest percentage of multi-family dwellings (22%), and are most likely to live in overcrowded accommodation (26%). 67.7% own their own dwellings, but 36% of Bangladeshi households have no access to a car or van.

BANGOR, Gwynedd (649 ha; 13,725 inhabitants)

In the early 6th century, St **Deiniol** founded a monastery in the narrow valley of the Adda, a valley hidden from the view of marauders sailing the **Menai Strait**. The original meaning of the name, a wattled or interwoven hedge, came to be applied to the land surrounded by the hedge. Other ecclesiastical foundations, including **Bangor Is-y-Coed**, Bangor Teifi (**Llandyfriog**) and Bangor, **Ireland**, came to bear the name, but whether that was in honour of the original Bangor – Bangor Fawr yn **Arfon** – is a matter of dispute. Parts of the foundations of Deiniol's *clas*, which was sacked in 634, were discovered in the 1890s when land was levelled for the construction of **tennis** courts. While Deiniol is frequently referred to as the first bishop of Bangor, indubitable evidence of Bangor's episcopal status is not available until the 11th century. By then, it was apparent that Bangor's clergy were closely associated with the rulers of **Gwynedd**, an association underlined by their insistence in 1170 on burying **Owain Gwynedd** near the cathedral's high altar, despite the fact that Owain had been excommunicated by the archbishop of Canterbury. However, bishop and prince could be at loggerheads; Bishop **Anian** (d.1306) may have had a part

in the plot hatched in the cathedral bell tower in 1282 to kill **Llywelyn ap Gruffudd**. The earliest surviving parts of the cathedral date from *c*.1130; enlarged from the early 13th century onwards, it was devastated during the **Glyndŵr Revolt**. Refurbished between the 1490s and the 1530s, it was extensively restored in the 1870s. Adjoining it is the bishop's palace (16th and 17th centuries), which has been adapted as local **government** offices. The Erastian views of Benjamin Hoadley, bishop of Bangor 1715–21, gave rise to what became known as the Bangorian Controversy.

Until the late 18th century, Bangor had little significance beyond its status as the centre of an impoverished **Anglican diocese**. The development of the Penrhyn **slate** quarry brought new vigour, especially following the creation in the 1790s of Porth Penrhyn near the city's eastern boundary (*see* **Llandygai**). The completion of **Thomas Telford**'s **Holyhead** road (the **A5**) in 1830, and of **Robert Stephenson**'s North Wales Railway in 1850, provided Bangor with excellent **road** and **railway** links.

Hopes that Bangor would become a leading holiday resort – hopes expressed by the 407-m **pier** opened in 1896 – did not materialize. Instead, the city concentrated upon becoming a major **education**al centre, thus building on a role it had performed since 1557, when **Friars** School was established on the site of the dissolved Dominican friary, founded in 1251. In 1858, Bangor acquired the **Normal College**, which rapidly became Wales's leading centre for training teachers for non-denominational schools. Centres for training **Congregational** and **Baptist** ministers were also established at Bangor, as was St Mary's Anglican college, originally founded at **Caernarfon** in 1856. More significant was the choice of Bangor as the seat of the University College intended to serve north Wales. Opened with 58 students in 1884, it had around 7000 students by the early 21st century. Its main building, designed by Henry Hare and completed in 1911, occupies a commanding site above the city.

In the 20th century, Bangor acquired further institutions, including the northern headquarters of the BBC in Wales (*see* **Broadcasting**) and, from 1941 to 1944, the variety department of the BBC as a whole. As well as being the north-west's main commercial and transport centre, Bangor became home to the region's chief hospital (Ysbyty Gwynedd), theatre (Theatr Gwynedd) and museum (Oriel Gwynedd). The city's industrial estates produce a wide variety of goods, ranging from bicycles to **electronic** equipment and plastics. The chief factor in the **community**'s prosperity is, however, the University College; renamed the **University of Wales, Bangor**, it has absorbed all the city's other collegiate institutions.

BANGOR IS-Y-COED (Bangor-on-Dee) (Bangor Is-Coed) Wrexham (851 ha; 1266 inhabitants)

A **community** located on the east bank of the **Dee**, Bangor was the site of a monastery believed to have been founded by St **Deiniol** in *c*.550. Bede states that it had 2000 monks and that its abbot was among the leading Welsh ecclesiastics who met Augustine of Canterbury *c*.602. Bede claimed that, following the **battle of Chester** (*c*.615), 1200 of Bangor's monks were massacred by the army of

Bangor High Street *c.*1910

Aethelfrith, king of Northumbria. The site of the largely 14th-century church of St Dunawd, or Deiniol, was probably that of the monastery, but no evidence survives. An impressive five-arched 17th-century bridge spans the Dee; it is claimed that it was designed by Inigo Jones. Steeplechasing (*see* **Horse Racing**) began at Bangor racecourse in the 1850s, and races continue to be held there. Nearby is Althrey Hall, built in the 15th century and transformed in the 17th. Much of the village of Bangor has conservation status.

BANGOR PONTIFICAL, The
A 14th-century liturgical manuscript kept at the library of the **University of Wales, Bangor**. It is an important source for students of religious and musical life in medieval Wales.

BANK OF WALES, The
The Commercial Bank of Wales was launched in 1972 by the **Cardiff** financier Sir Julian Hodge (1904–2004) to provide local and direct **banking** services to small and medium-sized companies. His proposed title, the Bank of Wales, was vetoed by the Registrar of Companies and the Bank of **England**, who claimed this would imply an official status. With the head office in Cardiff, branches were opened in **Wrexham** and **Swansea**. In 1988, the Bank was acquired by the Bank of Scotland and the title 'Bank of Wales' was finally assumed. With seven regional offices, the bank provided specialist banking services to a wide range of commercial activities, and in 2000 had assets of over £460 million. But, in 2002, it lost its Welsh identity when it was wholly absorbed into the Bank of Scotland.

BANKES, John [Eldon] (1854–1946) Judge
Of distinguished legal ancestry, Bankes – whose family home was Soughton Hall (**Northop**) – became famous as an exceptionally able appeal judge with a strong sense of public duty. Together with Lords **Sankey** and **Atkin**, he drafted a constitution for the **Church in Wales**, prior to its **disestablishment** (1920). He was knighted in 1910.

BANKING and BANKS
A bank performs three main functions: it provides safe custody for funds deposited; it makes loans; and it transfers money from accounts according to depositors' instructions. Businesses undertaking these three activities emerged in Greece by the 5th or 4th century BC, but it seems that some 2000 years elapsed before banks reappeared in Europe. The first banks in **England** were established in the 17th century.

Before 1750, Wales had no banks, but 42 were established between 1771 and 1815, the first of them being opened in **Swansea** by Landeg, du Buisson & Co. Such partnerships were formed by manufacturers, landowners, traders and lawyers. Despite the evocative names, 'Black Sheep Bank' and 'Black Ox Bank', there is no evidence to support the popular myth that early banks in Wales were founded by **cattle** and **sheep drovers**. These small banking partnerships were vulnerable to swings in business confidence and to the misfortunes of their customers: many of them succumbed in the financial crisis of 1825–6, in response to which the Bank of England opened a branch in Swansea. This 'Branch Bank' had some success in introducing its own banknotes into circulation in Wales in place

A bank promissory note of 1814

of the promissory notes of local banks, and it also engaged in the provision of **coinage** and the collection of taxes.

By 1859, when the 'Branch Bank' was closed, a number of joint-stock banks – the National Provincial Bank and the **North and South Wales Bank**, for example – had been established. In the late 19th and 20th centuries, there were amalgamations of these companies. By the 21st century, nearly all banking business in Wales was undertaken by a few large concerns.

BANWY (Banw), Montgomeryshire, Powys (9188 ha; 534 inhabitants)

Located on the north-western border of **Montgomeryshire**, the **community** extends over the upper reaches of the Banwy valley. It contains the villages of Llangadfan and Foel/Garthbeibio. The restorations of the 19th century have obscured the medieval character of St Cadfan's church. Like St Tydecho's, Garthbeibio, it lies within a circular churchyard. Llangadfan was the home of one of the most remarkable figures of 18th-century Wales: **William Jones**, Dolhywel (1726–95), poet, antiquarian, physician, radical and fervent admirer of Voltaire. The area was also the home of the poet Gruffudd Llwyd (*c.*1380–*c.*1420) and the **archdruid** John Cadvan Davies (Cadvan; 1846–1923). The name of the Cann Office Inn refers to the *can* (drinking vessel) which was the one-time symbol of the inn. Abernodwydd, a delightful timber-framed house from Llangadfan, has been re-erected at the National History Museum (*see* **St Fagans**).

BAPTISTS

A movement of Protestant evangelical Christians who baptize their adherents, on a profession of personal faith, through total immersion in water.

The Baptists trace their roots to 17th-century English separatists who broke from the **Anglican** Church in the belief that Christianity, being a personal conviction, could not be compelled by the state. Having emigrated to Holland in order to worship according to their conscience, the Amsterdam congregation – forsaking infant baptism for the baptism of declared believers – consolidated themselves into a specifically Baptist church in 1609.

The first Baptists in Wales were **Arminian** rather than Calvinist (*see* **Calvinism**), the followers of Hugh Evans (d.1656), pioneer of the denomination in **Radnorshire**, although an earlier congregation had been established at Olchon in **Welsh**-speaking **Herefordshire**. But it was the Calvinist Baptists, located at **Ilston** by **John Miles** in 1649,

who would spearhead subsequent Baptist advance in Wales. Between then and the restoration of the monarchy (1660), the movement struck deep roots within a triangle between **Hay**, **Carmarthen** and **Abergavenny**.

Although post-restoration persecution did not dislodge the movement, it was not until the 18th-century **Methodist Revival** that Baptists became numerous. Some of their main leaders such as Enoch Francis (1688/9–1740) and **Joshua Thomas** spanned the period between the older Dissent (*see* **Nonconformists**) and the new revivalism; it was their missionary zeal that spread the movement from beyond its heartlands to other parts of Wales. Following the northern mission of 1776, Baptist presence became a feature within every Welsh **county**.

The key to the Baptists' success was gospel preaching. **Christmas Evans** was the most successful of the **preachers**, although many others – among them **Titus Lewis**, **Joseph Harris** (Gomer) and John Jenkins (1779–1853) of Hengoed (**Gelligaer**) – became well known throughout Wales. By 1835, the Baptists, together with the **Congregationalists**, the **Calvinistic Methodists** and the **Wesleyans**, had turned Wales into 'a nation of Nonconformists'.

But the Baptists, like others, failed to rise to the challenge of modernity, materialism and scientific discovery. Although the 20th-century movement still produced powerful fundamentalist preachers, modernist biblical scholars such as **John Gwili Jenkins** and religious leaders of the calibre of **Lewis Valentine**, its strength and influence declined as the century progressed. At the movement's height, in the early 20th century, the Welsh Baptists had about 190,000 members; by the beginning of the 21st century, membership had declined to fewer than 20,000.

BARA BRITH (lit. 'speckled bread')

A spicy fruit loaf which was traditionally prepared on baking day by adding sugar, fruit and spices to a portion of bread dough. Eventually, a richer mixture was developed, and the cake became a teatime delicacy prepared for special occasions within both farming and industrial communities. In the industrial valleys of the south-east it is generally known as *teisen dorth* (loaf cake).

BARDD COCOS (lit. 'cockles poet')

A term applied to any writer of doggerel. Victorian Wales had several equivalents of the Scottish rhymester William McGonagall (1825–1902), among them the cockle-seller John Evans (?1827–95) from **Menai Bridge**, the original *bardd cocos*. He wrote, for instance, of the monumental lions on the Britannia Bridge:

> *Pedwar llew tew*
> *Heb ddim blew,*
> *Dau 'rochor yma*
> *A dau 'rochor drew.*
> (Four fat lions/ Without any hair/
> Two over here/ And two over there.)

BARDD GWLAD (Country poet)

A poet who celebrates locality and community, recording noteworthy and possibly humorous incidents as well as such occasions as births, marriages and **deaths**. With little or no higher **education**, such poets often use the strict metres, communicating their poems at social events, in *papurau bro* and on gravestones, in the form of commemorative *englynion*. The Blaenannerch (**Aberporth**) farmer, Dic Jones (b.1934), is one of the best-known contemporary *beirdd gwlad*. The **Gower** folk poet Cyril Gwynn (1897–1988), author of *The Gower Yarns of Cyril Gwynn* (1976), is a comparatively rare example of a *bardd gwlad* who wrote in **English**.

BARDD TEULU (Household poet or poet of the retinue)

According to the **Law**s of **Hywel Dda**, the *Bardd Teulu* was an officer in the king's court. His duty was to sing to the king after the *Pencerdd* (chief of song) had done so, and to entertain the queen in her chamber.

BARGOED (Bargod), Caerphilly
(714 ha; 11,864 inhabitants)

The **community** lies on both sides of the middle **Rhymney**, and joins together Bargoed, formerly in **Glamorgan**, and Aberbargoed, formerly in **Monmouthshire**. The area was intensely industrialized in the late 19th century, and was one of the two areas (**Aberdare** was the other) on which the mighty **coal** empire of **Powell Duffryn** was based. Its Britannia Colliery was the world's first pit to be powered wholly by electricity. Bargoed Tip was so large that there were claims that it was visible from the moon. Aberbargoed is the core of the one-time civil **parish** of **Bedwellty** which extended over much of western Monmouthshire and which was once the name of a constituency and an **urban district**. Bedwellty church, with its 13th-century arcade, is one of the largest in south-east Wales.

BARKER family Artists

Benjamin Barker (1720–90) came to **Pontypool** to work as an artist in the **japan ware** industry, his decorative work focusing primarily on animal motifs. His eldest son, Thomas ('of Bath'; 1769–1847), was born at Pontypool and, after settling in Bath, established a reputation as a lithographer and painter, chiefly of landscapes in the manner of Gainsborough. His second son, Benjamin II (also 'of Bath'; 1776–1838), was born at Pontypool and became a landscape painter. Thomas's son, Thomas Jones Barker (1815–82), born in Bath to a Welsh mother, was well established as a painter of portraits and military, historical and sporting subjects (*see* **Painting**).

BARLOW, William (d.1569) Bishop

Essex-born and **Oxford**-educated, Barlow became successively prior of **Haverfordwest** (1534) and Bisham (1535), and bishop of **St Asaph** (1536), **St David's** (1536–48), Bath and Wells (1549–59) and Chichester (1559–69). He founded Christ College, **Brecon** and moved the bishops' residence from St David's to **Abergwili**. The first Protestant bishop of St David's, he conducted a thorough reform of his **diocese**, which he considered to be corrupted by 'heathen idolatry'. His brothers, Roger and Thomas, gained possession of the house of the Dominican **friars** at Haverfordwest. His son, William Barlowe (d.1652), is credited with the invention of the 'hanging compass' for use at sea.

BARMOUTH (Abermaw, Bermo), Gwynedd
(1600 ha; 2437 inhabitants)

Located on the north side of the **Mawddach** estuary, the **community** contains the town of Barmouth and the village of Llanaber. By the late 18th century, Barmouth had become the chief centre for the export of the **woollen** products of mid-Wales and, in 1797, an act was procured to enlarge the harbour. By 1813, Barmouth was said to possess 100 vessels, many of them built by the local **shipbuilding** yard. The round building near the quay (1820s) was used to impound roistering sailors and **gold**miners. In the early and mid-19th century, Barmouth exported **slate**, **lead**, manganese and zinc. Such activity was in rapid decline by 1867 when the **railway** arrived. Barmouth reinvented itself as a seaside resort; the town, cowering below its cliffs, acquired tall Victorian guesthouses and the large St John's church, opened by Queen Victoria's daughter, Beatrice, in 1889. The previous **parish** church, that of St Bodfan at Llanaber, is an admirable structure of *c.*1200; it is surrounded by a large churchyard abounding in the graves of master mariners. Within the church are two inscribed stones of around the 5th or 6th century.

Dinas Oleu was the first property acquired by the **National Trust** (1895). It is traversed by Panorama Walk, which offers magnificent views, as does the footpath along the remarkable railway bridge across the estuary. Barmouth's Ruskin Trust, founded in 1871, commemorates John Ruskin's association with the town. Charles Darwin resided at Plas Caerdeon while revising *On the Origin of Species* (1859). St Philip's church (1850), Caerdeon, was built specifically to provide **English** services; the vicar of Llanaber sued its founder, claiming that parliament had legislated that **Anglican** services in **Welsh**-speaking Wales were to be in Welsh. The upshot was an Act of Parliament (1863) permitting English services if at least 10 parishioners petitioned for them.

An engraving depicting the 'four fat lions' on Britannia Bridge, celebrated by the *bardd cocos* John Evans (?1827–95)

BARRY ISLAND,

GLAMORGANSHIRE,

The future Watering Place of South Wales, situate in the Bristol Channel, possessing naturally-formed Docks, which are much needed in the neighbourhood. Distant from Cardiff about 7 miles, Newport 22 miles, Swansea 35 miles, Ilfracombe 32 miles, Gloucester 80 miles, Bristol 86 miles, Weston-super-mare 15 miles, Birmingham 117 miles, and London 165 miles; also

COLCOT GREAT FARM,

And several Lots of highly valuable FREEHOLD LAND, situate in the Parishes of Merthyr Dovan and Cadoxton.

An 1877 advertisement of the sale of a farm overlooking Barry Island

BARNES, Walley (1920–75) Footballer
The son of an **English** soldier stationed at **Brecon**, Barnes was one of the best full-backs of his era. He played for Arsenal (1943–55) and 22 times for Wales, often as captain. The first Welsh team manager (1954–6), he was subsequently a BBC commentator.

BARRINGTON, Daines (1727–1800) Judge
This Englishman was more highly valued in Wales than in **England**, where one satirist called him 'Daines … a man denied by nature brains'. As a judge of the Courts of Great Session (*see* **Law**) he carried weight in Wales, and, as a patron of cultural activity, he encouraged research in **archaeology**, natural history and **literature**, especially that undertaken by **Edward Lhuyd** and **Evan Evans** (Ieuan Fardd; 1731–88). His reference in 1768 to Dolly Pentreath is the last recorded comment upon the existence of the Cornish language (*see* **Cornwall**).

BARRY (Y Barri), Vale of Glamorgan
(1760 ha; 47,863 inhabitants)
Barry is Wales's most striking example of a town's meteoric rise and the country's most populous **community**. In 1894, the **parishes** of Barry, Cadoxton, Merthyr Dyfan and part of that of **Sully** became the Barry **Urban District**; the district achieved **borough** status in 1939. The area had 484 inhabitants in 1881; it had 13,278 in 1891 and 27,030 in 1901. The cause of the expansion was the 1884 Parliamentary Act authorizing the construction of a dock at Barry and a **railway** linking it to the **coal**field. The dock was completed in 1889 and a further dock was opened in 1898 (*see* **Ports**). In 1922, when the Barry Dock and Railway Company was taken over by the Great Western Railway Company, the concern consisted of the two docks, three dry docks and nearly 105 km of railway.

The chief advocate of the Barry scheme was David Davies (1818–90) (*see* **Davies family (Llandinam)**), whose statue stands outside Barry's handsome Wren-style dock offices (1897–1900). It is generally believed that, in championing the creation of the dock, Davies and his fellow **coal**owners were reacting to the high charges and congestion at **Cardiff**'s Bute Docks. In fact, Cardiff's dock dues

were not exorbitant, and the undoubted congestion there would shortly be relieved by the completion of a new dock sanctioned in 1882. What the coalowners wanted was a dock under their unfettered control, and the result was the creation of two massive systems of docks – at Barry and Cardiff – serving the central part of the south Wales coalfield. The need to justify the investment helped to propel coal output to unsustainable levels, thus causing the eventual **depression** to be more severe than it would otherwise have been.

The Barry Docks had numerous advantages. They were not located at a **river** mouth and were therefore not burdened with the cost of constant estuary scouring. The depth of the entrance waterway made Barry the Severn Sea's sole port accessible to vessels at any state of the tide. Designed for the largest **ships** then afloat, Barry was free from the Bute company's obsolete investments which arose from the need to service debts incurred in the building of earlier, virtually redundant, docks. Above all, the Barry company owned not only the docks but also the railways serving them, a marked contrast with Cardiff where the docks and the railways were owned by different and often mutually antagonistic companies. These advantages had become apparent by 1901 when Barry replaced Cardiff as the world's greatest coal port. In 1913, its most successful year, Barry exported 11.41 million tonnes of coal. However, any other trade was virtually non-existent and thus Barry was particularly vulnerable to any downturn in the demand for coal.

Evidence of the history of Barry before the coming of the dock is slight. The **Romans** may have established a port there. The chapel on Barry Island may have been built by St Barruc (or Barwg). According to the Life of St **Cadog**, it was Barruc who gave his name to the place, although it is more probable that its origins lie in the word *bar* (brow of a hill). Merthyr Dyfan was the *martyrium* or sanctified cemetery of Dyfan. Cadoxton presumably had links with St Cadog, and both places have churches dating back at least to the 13th century. Remnants of the castle of the de Barri family, ancestors of **Giraldus Cambrensis**, survive. (Giraldus maintained that it was from this place that his family acquired their name.) The community's finest medieval feature is the 13th-century **dovecote** at Cadoxton

Court, by far the largest in Wales. The **manor** of Barry was mapped in 1622 when it was part of the Fonmon estate (*see* **Rhoose**). By the 19th century, it was owned by the Romilly family, whose impact upon Barry includes the landscaping of Porthkerry Country Park and the presentation to the town of Romilly Park.

The town which developed to serve the docks consisted of a dense network of working-**class** housing around Holton Road, created almost in its entirety in 1892–3, and a middle-class enclave adjoining Romilly Park. A later addition was the **garden** suburb west of the park designed by **T. Alwyn Lloyd** and built between 1914 and 1925. In addition to the dock offices, its distinguished public buildings include All Saints church with its prominent tower, the Gothic Holy Trinity chapel, the baroque municipal buildings, some fine board schools and the splendidly sited former teacher training college, now the Vale Resource Centre.

The town evoked varied reactions – to **Llewelyn Williams** its people were 'intent on nothing but money-making' – but, nevertheless, it was the first place in Wales where a branch of **Cymru Fydd** was founded and it was the birthplace of the politician **Gwynfor Evans**, 20th-century Wales's greatest patriot. The town played a central role in the establishment of 'new unionism' in Wales (*see* **Trade Unionism**); its citizens were prominent in the foundation of the **Workers' Educational Association** and its railwaymen were second only to the coalminers as pioneers of the **Labour Party** in **Glamorgan**. Yet, to the bulk of that **county**'s inhabitants, the image of Barry was not that of an industrial town. Barry meant day trips and holidays, lounging on the glorious sands of Whitmore Bay, jollifications at Barry **Island** funfair and, for the more sedate, the delights of seaside walks at the Knap and along Bull Cliff. In the early 20th century, when **Sunday school** trips were at their height, a summer Saturday meant an influx into Barry of tens of thousands of people, packed into trains from the coalfield.

The interwar decline in the coal trade meant that by the late 1920s, Barry's coal exports were less than half what they had been in 1913. There was a revival of activity during the **Second World War** when the docks played a highly significant role. For some decades after the war, Barry enjoyed modest prosperity as a major banana importing centre, but by the end of the century, Dock No. 1 had ceased trading and had become the focus for a major regeneration scheme characterized by bland waterside apartments; a trickle of trade continued through Dock No. 2. By then, apart from **tourism**, the town's major source of employment was provided by the chemical plants on Sully Moors, a legacy of the Second World War and a spectacular sight, especially at night. Tourism survived better than the coal trade. Indeed, it was during the 1920s that major improvements were made at The Knap. In the 1960s, Butlin's Camp came to occupy Nell's Point and was thronged with visitors. Changes in holiday habits, however, have led to the camp's demolition.

Today, Barry is largely a commuter town, with some pockets of severe deprivation and social problems. As more and more people are priced out of Cardiff, Barry's considerable stock of sound housing means that the town has a future, even if only as a dormitory for those employed in its one-time rival.

BASEBALL

The traditional sport of baseball or rounders first became organized in the 1860s. The modern game was codified in 1892, when the term 'rounders' was dropped and the South Wales Baseball Association was established. Baseball was popular in **Cardiff** and **Newport**, and there was particular enthusiasm for the regular international against **England**. Each team has 11 players who dress like **football**ers and pitch underarm. The sport peaked in the 1930s when there were school and **women**'s leagues. Teams such as Splott US, Pill Harriers and Grange Albion were pillars of their communities.

BATCHELOR, John (1820–83)
Controversial radical

Mayor of **Cardiff** in 1853, **ship**builder Batchelor's radical views were anathema to many, not least to officials of the Bute estate (*see* **Stuart family**). The decision, after Batchelor's death, to erect a statue to 'The Friend of Freedom' in the Hayes drove a local solicitor, Thomas Henry Ensor, to write a highly defamatory mock epitaph

A baseball game at Roath Park, Cardiff, 1953

in the *Western Mail*. Ensor was tried for criminal libel in Cardiff in 1887 and acquitted, the judge declaring, 'The dead have no rights and can suffer no wrongs'. The verdict established in **law** the principle that one cannot libel the dead.

BATES, Audrey [Glenys] (1924–2001) Sportswoman
One of Welsh sport's great all-rounders, **Cardiff**-born Audrey Bates played for Wales in **tennis**, **table tennis**, **squash** and **lacrosse**, and was offered, but declined, a **hockey** cap. She played at Wimbledon in singles and doubles tournaments, and was a regular member of the Welsh tennis team between 1947 and 1954; she played squash for Wales between 1947 and 1965, and for **Britain** in the 1950 Wolfe-Noël Cup match against the United States. She also played table tennis for Wales in the 1953 **women**'s world team championship.

BATS
Fifteen of **Britain**'s sixteen native bat species have been recorded in Wales, with the Welsh populations of both the rare and endangered greater and lesser horseshoe bats considered to be of European significance. **Slebech** in **Pembrokeshire** is particularly important for horseshoe bats; in 2004, refurbishments at the Slebech Park conference centre included the building of an underground hibernaculum for the several bat species that breed in the park. The pipistrelle and the brown long-eared, roosting mainly in buildings, are Wales's commonest bats; other common bats are Daubenton's, the noctule, Brandt's and Natterer's. They use buildings, **caves** and hollow trees, and all may have separate summer, winter and maternity roosts. The dramatic decline in bat populations during the 20th century led to all bats being protected under the Wildlife and Countryside Act 1981; interest in bats subsequently blossomed and new discoveries were made. Nathusius's pipistrelle, for instance, was found to be a resident Welsh species, not, as previously thought, merely a vagrant from the European mainland.

BAUSLEY WITH CRIGGION (Bausley A Chrugion), Montgomeryshire, Powys
(1660 ha; 623 inhabitants)
Located in the north-eastern corner of **Montgomeryshire**, the **community** contains the villages of Bausley, Criggion and Crew Green (Maes y Crewe in 1599). The area is dominated by Breiddin Hill (365 m). Occupied from the **Neolithic Age** onwards, the hill is crowned by substantial late **Bronze Age** enclosures, begun *c*.1000 BC. Superimposed upon them is an **Iron Age hill-fort** containing clusters of round huts. The fort was destroyed by the **Romans**, but reoccupied in the 6th and 7th centuries. On the summit is Admiral Rodney's Pillar, erected to thank Montgomeryshire for the oak timber used in the **ships** which gave Rodney victory over the French at Dominica in 1782. Criggion church (1774) retains its box pews. Criggion Hall is an intriguing 17th-century house.

BAXTER, William (1650–1723) Scholar
A nephew of Baxter, the **Puritan** divine, William Baxter was born at Llanllugan (**Dwyriw**), became a schoolmaster

in **London**, and is remembered as a **Celt**ic scholar. He published in 1719 a glossary of British antiquities and, after his death, Moses Williams (*see* **Samuel and Moses Williams**) in 1726 edited his *Reliquiae Baxterianae*, a **dictionary** interpreting **place names** of early **Britain**, drawing attention to their Celtic origins.

BAYLY, Lewis (d.1631) Bishop and author
A native of **Carmarthen** and educated at **Oxford**, Bayly published *The Practice of Piety* (1611), which was translated into **Welsh** by **Rowland Vaughan** (1630). He was appointed bishop of **Bangor** (1616) and supported the publication of **John Davies**'s (*c*.1567–1644) **dictionary**.

BBC NATIONAL ORCHESTRA OF WALES, The
The orchestra's beginnings can be traced to the formation, in 1928, of the National Symphony Orchestra of Wales, which was disbanded in 1931 and reformed by the BBC in 1935. Having undergone various changes, in 1946 the orchestra was reconstituted with a playing strength of 31 players and given a wider **broadcasting** and touring brief. It expanded to 66 players in 1976, with further players added subsequently. It adopted its present name in 1992. During the 1990s, the orchestra undertook numerous important foreign tours, and produced several well-received recordings; it also greatly expanded its **education**, community and broadcasting roles.

BBC CARDIFF SINGER OF THE WORLD, The
An international opera singing competition, known until 2003 as Cardiff Singer of the World, held every two years. The contest was founded in 1983 by the BBC (*see* **Broadcasting**), to mark the opening of St David's Hall. It is widely considered to be the most important international event of its kind, and has launched the careers of several opera stars (*see* **Music**). A prize for *lieder* singing was introduced in 1989. Winning that prize launched the international career of baritone Bryn Terfel.

BEALE, Anne (1815–1900) Novelist
Born in Somerset, of farming stock, Anne Beale came to **Llandeilo** in the early 1840s as a governess. In 1844, she published *The Vale of the Towey; or, Sketches in South Wales*, praised at the time, in both Wales and **England**, for its truth to nature, and influential in the development of the Welsh novel in **English** (*see* **Literature**). Her success launched her career as a popular novelist; she produced 12 novels in all, a number of them located in Wales.

BEASLEY, Trefor (1918–94) Language campaigner
The stand taken by Trefor Beasley and his wife Eileen (b.1921), from **Llangennech**, inspired a generation of campaigners for the **Welsh language**. In 1952, in a bid to secure communications in Welsh from their local authority, they refused to pay their rates to **Llanelli Rural District** Council. In reaction, the council employed bailiffs on six occasions to seize goods from their home, but victory came in 1960 when a Welsh form was grudgingly produced. Their determination proved a stimulus to the formation of **Cymdeithas yr Iaith Cymraeg** (the Welsh Language Society), especially as **Saunders Lewis**, in his radio broadcast *Tynged*

Beaumaris Castle

yr Iaith (1962), had urged supporters of the language to emulate the Beasleys' defiant civil disobedience.

BEAUCHAMP family Marcher-lords

William Beauchamp, ninth earl of Warwick (d.1298), was prominent in the campaign against **Llywelyn ap Gruffudd** in 1277 and led the victorious forces at the **battle of Maes Moydog** (1295). His son, Guy (d.1315), became lord of **Elfael** through his marriage with Alice, heiress of Ralph de Tony. Their descendant, Richard, the thirteenth earl (d.1439), acquired **Glamorgan** through his marriage with Isabella, heiress of Thomas **Despenser** (d.1399). (By her first marriage, Isabella had brought Glamorgan and Elfael to another member of the Beauchamp family, Richard, earl of Worcester, lord of **Abergavenny** (d.1422)). Richard (d.1439) was active in suppressing the **Glyndŵr Revolt** and presided at the trial of Joan of Arc. He commissioned the erection of the range of buildings along the western curtain wall of **Cardiff** Castle. Following his death, Glamorgan and Elfael passed to his son, Henry (d.1445). Henry's lands passed to his daughter, Anne (d.1449) and then to his sister Anne, and her husband, Richard Neville, the 'Kingmaker', lord of Glamorgan and Elfael until his death in 1471.

BEAUFORT (Cendl), Blaenau Gwent
(1095 ha; 10,328 inhabitants)

The **community** of Beaufort, at the head of the valley of the **Ebbw Fawr**, lies on the northernmost fringe of the south Wales coalfield and is virtually a suburb of **Ebbw Vale**. It takes its '**English**' name from the lord of the **manor**, the Duke of Beaufort (*see* **Somerset family**), and its '**Welsh**' name from Edward Kendall, who leased a site there for an **iron**works in 1780. The works were subsequently acquired by Crawshay **Bailey** and amalgamated with his works at **Nantyglo**. Nothing remains of the five forges built between

1785 and 1833. The community's most interesting building is Carmel **Congregational** chapel, designed by the Rev. **Thomas Thomas** of **Swansea**, the doyen of Welsh minister-architects.

BEAUMARIS (Biwmares), Isle of Anglesey
(856 ha; 2040 inhabitants)

Located at the north-eastern end of the **Menai Strait**, Beaumaris was the **county** town of **Anglesey** until 1889 and the assize town until 1971. The **borough** was founded by Edward I in 1296 to accompany the castle built after the **Welsh revolt of 1294–5**. Built on a 'fair marsh', the castle and its town were given the name Beau Marais. Although unfinished, Beaumaris Castle is perhaps the most sophisticated example of military **architecture** in **Britain**. Although it does not dominate its surroundings as do **Caernarfon**, **Conwy** and **Harlech** castles, its superb concentric symmetry makes it a structure of the greatest distinction. Beaumaris is alone among Edward I's Welsh castles in having a wet moat; linked to a dock, it enabled **ships** to unload directly into the castle. Captured by the Welsh during the **Glyndŵr Revolt**, the castle was sometimes used as a **prison**, housing at various times Scottish prisoners of war, **Lollard** scholars and Eleanor Cobham, duchess of Gloucester, imprisoned for trying to use magic to kill Henry VI.

The **community** of Beaumaris includes Llanfaes, which under the Welsh princes was the principal commercial centre of **Gwynedd**. A Franciscan friary was established at Llanfaes in 1237; it contained the tomb of **Joan** (Siwan) (d.1237), wife of **Llywelyn ap Iorwerth**. Following the quelling of the revolt of 1294–5, the Welsh **population** of Llanfaes was forcibly removed to Newborough (**Rhosyr**) and the new foundation of Beaumaris took over Llanfaes's markets, fairs and ferry across the Strait. The friary survived, but, following its support for **Owain Glyndŵr**, Henry IV allowed it to continue only on the condition that it housed **English** friars. No remains of the friary are visible above ground. A local benefactor, David Hughes, commissioned an attractive group of almshouses at Llanfaes (1613).

Beaumaris was the leading **port** of the medieval **principality** of north Wales but, unlike Caernarfon and Conwy, it was not originally provided with a wall, although one was built following the Glyndŵr Revolt; little of it survives. In the mid-15th century, William **Bulkeley** from Cheadle, **Cheshire**, settled in the town and established the family which was to dominate the town and county for the next four centuries. The house, Henblas, which he built near the church, was demolished in 1869; the family had moved in 1618 to a new house, Baron Hill. Rebuilt by Samuel Wyatt *c.*1800, Baron Hill remained the Bulkeleys' residence until the **Second World War**; thereafter it fell into ruin. There is a memorial to the family on Twt Hill.

Beaumaris continued to enjoy prosperity in the 16th and 17th centuries; in 1603, David Hughes founded a grammar school which remained in the town until 1962, when Ysgol David Hughes was established at **Menai Bridge**. During the **Civil Wars**, Beaumaris Castle played an important role in the transit of Royalist supporters from **Ireland**. The last skirmish of the war took place on Red Hill, to the west of the town on 2 October 1648.

The rise, first of Chester and then of **Liverpool**, hastened the decline of the port of Beaumaris. The access to Anglesey via the low-tide route across Traeth Lafan sands to Beaumaris – a vital factor in the town's prosperity – lost its importance following the completion of **Telford**'s suspension bridge (1826). The **railway** to **Holyhead**, completed in 1849, passed Beaumaris by. To compensate, the town council sought prosperity through encouraging the growth of a watering place, a development assisted by a visit from the young Princess Victoria in 1832. Unlike Caernarfon, which was overwhelmed by the surrounding Welsh population, Beaumaris never recovered from its English origins. The building in 1830 of Victoria Terrace on the Green – designed by Joseph Hansom of cab fame – was intended to attract a wealthier **class** of visitor. In the 20th century, the town benefited in particular from the rise of **sailing** on the Menai Strait.

St Mary's church (14th century) contains the elaborate carved lid of Joan's coffin, brought from Llanfaes, and memorials to the Bulkeley family. The courthouse (1614) has become an educational centre. The former county gaol (1829) (*see* **Prisons**) houses a fascinating museum.

BEAVER, The

The European beaver (L. *Castor fiber*; W. *llostlydan*: broadtail, or *afanc*) makes its earliest appearance in the British archaeological record in **Neolithic** times, and it survived in Wales into the medieval period. The earliest dependable descriptions of beavers in **Britain** are those found in the Welsh **laws**. They refer to the king's right to the skin of the beaver, the **pine marten** and the ermine, wherever killed, because from them the borders of his raiment were made; a beaver was worth 120 pence and a marten 24 pence, which testifies to the high regard attached to the beaver and possibly to its rarity by that time. By the late 12th century, the beaver was very rare: according to **Giraldus Cambrensis**,

it existed nowhere in southern Britain except on the **River Teifi**. It was almost certainly extinct in Wales by the 18th century. The four **Welsh place names** that appear to refer to the beaver – far fewer than those referring to the **wolf** – are ambiguous because, like the name of a pool on the **Conwy** called Llyn yr Afanc, they employ the indeterminate word *afanc*, which originally referred to various water beasts, including a mythical monster.

BEBB, Dewi [Iorwerth Ellis] (1938–96)
Rugby player

A rare north Wales **rugby** star, **Bangor**-born Dewi Bebb's speed and skill on the wing were so obvious that he played only two senior games before winning the first of his 34 caps. Appropriately for a son of the **nationalist** intellectual **Ambrose Bebb**, he reserved his best for **England**, scoring six tries – still a record for the fixture – in eight games against them. Twice a British Lion, he played his club rugby for **Swansea**.

BEBB, W[illiam] Ambrose (1894–1955)
Historian, writer and politician

A farmer's son from **Tregaron**, Bebb was educated at **Aberystwyth** and became an assistant lecturer in **Celtic** studies at the Sorbonne. In several books he proved himself an enthusiastic interpreter of France, **Brittany** and the life of mainland Europe. From 1925, he was lecturer in history at the **Normal College, Bangor**. An early member of **Plaid [Genedlaethol] Cymru**, he served it as journalist, councillor and parliamentary candidate. He was the only historian in the first half of the 20th century – in a sequence of five books on Welsh history – to identify with the standpoint of modern Welsh **nationalism**. He was the father of the **rugby** player **Dewi Bebb**.

BECA

The Beca group of artists, founded in the 1970s by Mumbles-born Paul Davies (1947–93), brought a new national consciousness to late 20th-century Welsh art. Continued into the 21st century by his brother, Peter Davies – together with Ivor Davies, Iwan Bala, Peter Finnemore and Tim Davies – and finding respectability under postmodern reassessments, the group uses a mixture of installation, **painting**, **sculpture**, performance and book making to engage with language, environmental and land rights issues.

BEDDGELERT, Gwynedd
(8593 ha; 617 inhabitants)

Extending from near Yr Wyddfa (the summit of **Snowdon**) to the boundaries of **Porthmadog** and **Penrhyndeudraeth**, the **community** contains the eastern part of the Snowdon massif, most of the basin of the **Glaslyn**, and Llyn Dinas, Llyn Gwynant and Llyn Llydaw (*see* **Lakes**). Allegedly, the name commemorates the grave of **Gelert**, the hound of **Llywelyn ap Iorwerth**, a fiction believed to have been invented (*c.*1800) by the proprietor of the Royal Goat Hotel. As a ploy to appeal to tourists, the fiction still works, for thousands continue to inspect the 'grave'. Dinas Emrys **hill-fort**, occupied in the immediate post-**Roman** centuries, is linked by tradition with **Vortigern** and with the red dragon. Beddgelert's Celtic *clas*, founded in the 6th century, became an **Augustinian** priory *c*.1200; it was dissolved in 1536. St Mary's church contains parts of the priory church. The poet **Dafydd Nanmor** (fl.15th century), lived in the Nanmor valley.

The area had **lead** and **copper** mines; Sygin copper mine is open to the public. The beautiful Aberglaslyn Pass can be explored via the abandoned track of the Welsh Highland **Railway** (1922). The community contains the Watkin Path to Yr Wyddfa; named after the railway pioneer Edward Watkin, it was opened by **W. E. Gladstone** in 1892, a ceremony performed at Gladstone Rock above Llyn Dinas. In the 1930s, the renowned **Snowdonia Harp** Choir (*Côr Telyn Eryri*) was formed at Beddgelert by Edith Evans (*Telynores Eryri*). At the top of Nant Gwynant is the Penygwryd Hotel, where the climbers who conquered Everest in 1953 stayed while training on Snowdonia's crags.

BEDFORD, Francis (1816–94) Photographer and publisher

The English photographer Francis Bedford is best known for his stereographic views. During the 1860s, he produced many thousands of views of scenes in **Britain**, including series on north Wales, south Wales, **Monmouthshire** and **Welsh costume**. His North Wales Illustrated series alone runs to over 400 views.

BEDWAS, TRETHOMAS AND MACHEN, Caerphilly (1842 ha; 10,428 inhabitants)

The **community** hugs the bend in the **Rhymney**. Industrial development began with a 16th-century forge. The early 19th century saw the establishment of a **tinplate** works and a blast furnace, but, by the late 19th century, the chief source of employment was the Bedwas Colliery. Following the collapse of **coal**mining, the numerous factories on the floor of the Rhymney valley became the mainstay of the local **economy**. The **buses** of the now defunct Bedwas and Machen **Urban District** were once a ubiquitous sight in urban south-east Wales. Machen contains the interestingly named tavern of Ffwrwm Ishta – Gwenhwyseg **Welsh** for a seating bench. (Lower Machen is in the community of Graig, **Newport**.)

BEDWELLTY (Bedwellte) One-time civil parish, urban district, constituency and Poor Law Union

The civil **parish** of Bedwellty extended over a wide swathe of western **Monmouthshire**. Abolished in 1974, it was replaced by the **community** of **Blackwood** and much of the communities of **Argoed** and **Penmaen**. From 1894 to 1974, Bedwellty was an **urban district**. In 1918, it became one of the four constituencies of the Monmouthshire **coalfield** (**Ebbw Vale**, **Abertillery** and **Pontypool** were the others). From 1950 to 1970, its MP was Harold Finch (1898–1976), author of *Memoirs of a Bedwellty MP* (1972). From 1970 to 1995, the constituency (renamed **Islwyn** in 1983) was represented by Neil Kinnock.

By the mid-1920s, the interwar **depression** had caused the Bedwellty **Poor Law** Union to be home to some of the most impoverished communities in **Britain**. The alleged over-generous payments granted to the unemployed by its Board of Guardians led to the suspension of the Board in 1927; its replacement by commissioners sent from **London** led to a marked reduction in payments. (The West Ham and Chester-le-Street Boards suffered the same fate.) The subsequent furore, in which **Aneurin Bevan** played a prominent role, was a major factor in the abolition of the Poor Law in 1929.

BEDWEN HAF (The summer birch)

A birch tree felled early on May Day (**Calan Mai**) and decorated with greenery to celebrate the coming of summer. The custom, which was recorded in **Llanidloes** in the 14th century, was prohibited during the **Commonwealth** but revived after the Restoration especially in the north-east, where a summer branch would be carried from house to house by the **Cadi Haf** and accompanying dancers. In the south-east, the custom was associated with the midsummer celebrations and the *taplas*.

BEER, BREWING and BREWERIES

Beer is the national drink of Wales. Down the centuries, it has lubricated every social occasion – from funerals to **rugby** matches – and refreshed workers from the mines and the harvest fields; yet Welsh beer never gained a reputation to match Irish stout or Burton ales. In part, this was because few Welsh breweries managed to sell their beer beyond Wales, most struggling to keep up with local demand during the industrial boom of the 19th century. Another factor was the strength of the **temperance movement**, which forced most Welsh breweries to maintain a low profile. No nation boasts less about its beer, although Welsh ale was once highly prized in **Britain**. King Ine of Wessex ruled in AD 690 that the food rent for 10 hides of land should include 'twelve ambers of Welsh ale'. This was a heavy brew, laced with spices, often sweetened with honey; known as *bragawd* or bragget, it was almost as famous as that other **Celtic** drink, **mead**.

The considerably milder 'small' or table beer (*cwrw bach*) was the everyday drink of the people, brewed on a domestic scale in many households and every inn. Farms were expected to provide beer for their workers. The only large-scale business involved was malting, producing beer's basic ingredient from barley. In 1822, **Welshpool** had 14 maltsters in 1822, but no commercial breweries.

The **Industrial Revolution** overturned this rural **economy**, the hordes of workers in the **iron**works and **coal**mines needing to quench their thirst. Publican brewers could not cope with the demand, and common brewers sprang up to supply the many new pubs allowed by the Beer House Act of 1830. By 1848, **Merthyr Tydfil** had 12 breweries and 300 pubs.

While the **Rhymney** Iron Company set up its own brewery in 1839, most industrialists were opposed to strong drink, as drunkenness became rife. The churches and chapels were appalled, and temperance **preachers** found a swelling audience. This powerful movement forced through the **Welsh Sunday Closing Act** in 1881, and pressed for local prohibition. It was in this hostile atmosphere that the Welsh brewing industry developed, and most of the beers produced were relatively weak milds – light or dark in colour – to satisfy both the raging thirsts of the workers

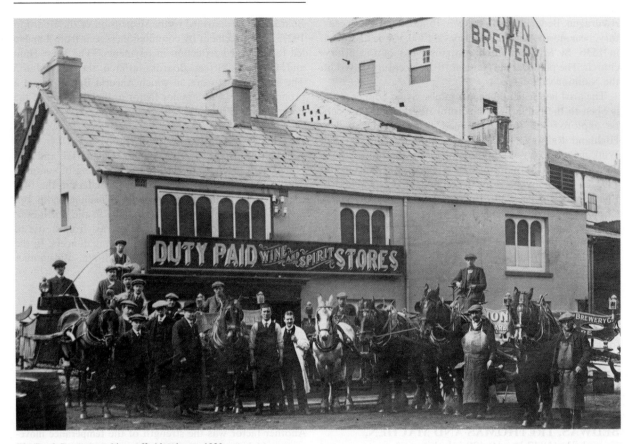

The Rock Brewery and its staff, Aberdare, *c.*1920

and the demands of the temperance movement. Stronger beers tended to come from Burton, though some brewers, such as S. A. Brain and Co. of **Cardiff**, also produced premium pale ales. Even the Welsh brewing capital of **Wrexham**, once famed for the strong ales from its 19 breweries, eased the strength of its brews. When the Wrexham Lager Beer Company was established in 1881, boasting that it was the first lager brewery in Britain, its light Pilsener was promoted as a temperance drink that would 'diminish intoxication'. Other notable developments included the Felinfoel Brewery (*see* **Llanelli Rural**); to help the local **tinplate** industry, it became in 1935 the first brewery in Europe to can beer.

By the end of the 20th century, Felinfoel was one of only two remaining independent breweries in Wales, along with S. A. Brain and Co., which had taken over Crown Buckley of **Llanelli** in 1997. English breweries had swallowed most of the famous names during the 1960s, from Rhymney and Evan Evans Bevan of **Neath** by Whitbread, to Hancock's of Cardiff and **Swansea** by Bass. However, from the 1980s, a new wave of local breweries began producing traditional ales. Many soon disappeared, but a few survived into the new millennium, such as Bullmastiff of Cardiff, Plassey near Wrexham and the ambitious Tomos Watkin of Swansea, taken over in 2002 by the rapidly expanding Hurns Brewing Company which was founded in Swansea in 1888 as The Hurns Mineral Water Company. All these are dwarfed to insignificance by the huge brewery at **Magor** on the **M4**, which makes international brews such as Stella Artois and Heineken.

BEES

For the best part of two millennia, bees and the production of honey and beeswax, have occupied a place in Welsh life and culture. Rhigyfarch, in his *Vita Dauidis* (A Life of St David, *c.*1094), refers to an Irish monk carrying a swarm of bees on the prow of his ship from **St David's** to **Ireland**, purportedly the first bees ever to enter that country.

Beekeeping, or at least the tending of wild honeybees, was undoubtedly practised among speakers of Common **Celt**ic. Before the importation of cane sugar into Western Europe (around the 12th century), honey was the only available sweetener. It was also essential for the production of **mead** and bragget, consumed as a relish in its own right, and valued for its medicinal properties by practitioners of traditional medicine such as the **Physicians of Myddfai** (*c.*13th century). Medieval Welsh **law** contains a short essay concerning bees and the relative values of different swarms: the law set 24 pence – the price of a calf – as the value of a swarm of bees in May, although by the end of August it was worth only 4 pence. Bees were also an exploitable aspect of medieval woodland (*see* **Forestry**), as the monks of Strata Marcella (**Welshpool**) found to their benefit with their wood of Coed-y-Mynach.

Honey and mead are frequently mentioned by the praise poets of the Middle Ages. There are also three extant poems from the 16th century, by **Gruffudd Hiraethog**, Morus Dwyfech and Roger Cyffin, composed on behalf of patrons requesting beehives from friends. However, an early Welsh name for **Britain**, *Y Fêl Ynys* (The Island of Honey), first attested in 14th-century poetry, may be nothing more than a corruption of *Ynys Feli*, the Island of Beli, a legendary ruler of Britain. The belief that Elizabeth I insisted on having her mead fermented with honey from Penmynydd in **Anglesey**, the ancestral home of the **Tudors**, also seems apocryphal.

The first book printed in **Welsh**, **John Price**'s *Yny Lhyvyr hwnn* (1546), instructed gardeners as to the best month in which to move their bees. In the first Welsh scientific book, *Golwg ar y Byd* (1725) by Dafydd Lewys, numerous references are made to bees, while in *The Antient Bee-keeper's Farewell* (1796), John Keys refers to the Welsh custom of making beehives or skeps from rushes or wicker baskets. They were protected from bad weather by being placed during the winter in recesses called bee boles, in walled **gardens**, or in special houses. In 1827, a Welshman, Dr Edward Bevan, published *The Honey Bee*, which offered innovative and sound advice on the art of beekeeping, and 1888 saw the first book in Welsh on the subject, *Y Gwenynydd*, by **Michael D. Jones** and H. P. Jones.

Beekeeping became increasingly popular in Wales during the latter half of the 20th century. The Welsh Beekeepers Association, founded in 1943, continues to promote the art throughout the country. Honey production varies from year to year, owing to the variable **climate**. The early 1990s witnessed incursions by the mite *Varroa jacobi*, which has spread throughout Wales; weaker colonies – particularly those of wild bees – have been destroyed, but the stronger ones have survived.

BEGUILDY (Bugeildy), Radnorshire, Powys
(7333 ha; 704 inhabitants)
The **community** hugs the English **border** in **Radnorshire**'s far north-east. **Ffransis Payne** suggests that the **English** form of the name was adopted to prevent local children being nicknamed 'bugs'. Beguildy church has a fine 15th-century screen. Bryndraenog, praised by **Ieuan ap Hywel Swrdwal**, is one of the best-preserved timber hall-houses in Wales. Heyop was one of the areas where **Welsh** declined early, its churchwardens reporting in 1684 that the **parish**ioners understood English. The castle at Knucklas is in ruins, but Howse considers its 'lofty, isolated hill' among the finest castle sites in **Britain**. The Puritan **Vavasor Powell** was born in an inn at Knucklas in 1617. Knucklas viaduct on the Central Wales **railway** line is an impressive structure.

BEK or BECK, Thomas (d.1293) Bishop
Before becoming bishop of **St David's** (1280–93), Bek was chancellor of **Oxford** and keeper of the king's wardrobe. Bek founded collegiate churches at **Llanddewi Brefi** and **Abergwili**, and two hospitals. **Pecham**'s archiepiscopal visitation of 1284 was not made welcome by Bek.

BELL, David (1915–59) Writer, curator and artist
The son of **Idris Bell**, he was born in **London**, trained at the Royal College of Art and came to **Cardiff** in 1946, on his appointment as regional arts officer for Wales. He became curator of the Glynn Vivian **Gallery**, **Swansea** in 1951, and his book *The Artist in Wales* (1957) created controversy by seeming to deny that Wales had a worthwhile **visual** cultural history. Bell established the 'Pictures for Welsh Schools' scheme to bring contemporary art to the young, and gave significant support to living artists, such as **Ceri Richards**, by buying their work for the Glynn Vivian Gallery.

BELL, [Harold] Idris (1879–1967)
Scholar and translator
Having learned **Welsh**, Lincolnshire-born Idris Bell published, between 1913 and 1942, three pioneer volumes of **English** translations of Welsh poetry, which, although considered rather old-fashioned today, were unrivalled until the 1950s. Among his many critical writings was *The Development of Welsh Poetry* (1936); he also translated **Thomas Parry**'s *Hanes Llenyddiaeth Gymraeg hyd 1900* (1945) as *A History of Welsh Literature* (1955), adding an appendix on the 20th century. In 1946, two years after retiring as keeper of manuscripts at the British Museum, he settled in **Aberystwyth**.

'BELLS OF ABERDOVEY, The'
('Clychau Aberdyfi') Song
Generally considered a folk song, it originated in Charles Dibdin's opera *Liberty Hall* (1785), though it was first published in **Maria Jane Williams**'s collection of *Ancient National Airs of Gwent and Morganwg* (1884). It is variously claimed to refer either to the legend of the drowned cities of **Cantre'r Gwaelod** in Cardigan Bay and their chiming underwater bells, or to be a love song extolling the loveliness of the belles – fine maidens – of **Aberdovey**.

BENDIGEIDFRAN FAB LLŶR or BRÂN
The **giant** Bendigeidfran features as king of **Britain** (or the Isle of the Mighty) and hero of the second branch of the Mabinogi (*see* **Mabinogion, The**). Leading an attack on **Ireland** in order to avenge the abuse of his sister, **Branwen**, he wades through the sea among his ships, and then lies across a **river** to make a bridge so that his men may cross. Injured, he instructs that his head be cut off and buried at the White Hill in **London**, where it will protect the Island.

BENEDICTINES Monastic order
Before the **Norman** penetration of the country in the late 11th century, the Benedictine rule did not exist in Wales. By 1071, **William Fitz Osbern** had founded Wales's first Benedictine priory, at **Chepstow**, and by 1098 Arnulf of **Montgomery** had established a priory at **Pembroke**. A further 15 priories or cells (there were no abbeys) were founded by 1141, all dependent on houses in **England** or mainland Europe. Most Welsh Benedictine houses were associated with Norman castles and **boroughs**, as at **Abergavenny**, **Kidwelly** and **Monmouth**, but a few, such as **Ewenny**, were in open country. Welsh churches were appropriated and given to Norman and Anglo-Norman Benedictine houses, and some of the most venerable native ecclesiastical communities – *clasau* such as **Llantwit Major** and **Llancarfan** – were reduced to the status of mere possessions of abbeys such as Tewkesbury and Gloucester. In the early 15th century, surviving priories dependent on French abbeys became either independent abbeys or were made dependent upon English houses. Eight houses remained at

the time of the **dissolution of the monasteries**: Abergavenny, **Brecon**, **Cardigan**, Chepstow, Ewenny, Kidwelly, Monmouth and Pembroke. In the 19th century, the Benedictines returned to Wales. In 1869, **Joseph Lyne** (Father Ignatius) established an **Anglican** Benedictine monastery at Capel-y-ffin (**Llanigon**). The Benedictine monastery on Caldey **Island**, founded in 1906, was also, originally, an Anglican foundation. It became associated with the **Roman Catholic** Church in 1913 and was taken over by the **Cistercians** in 1928. The Benedictine Abbey at Belmont, **Herefordshire**, was long the spiritual heart of the Roman Catholic **diocese** of **Newport**.

BENNETT, Anna Maria (c.1750–1808) Novelist
Born Anna Maria Evans, to a **Merthyr Tydfil** grocer, Anna Maria Bennett left her husband, a **Brecon** tanner, to work as a housekeeper in **London** for Admiral Sir John Pye, to whom she bore two children. Her first novel *Anna, or Memoirs of a Welch Heiress* (1785) was an instantaneous success; another of her nine novels, *Ellen, Countess of Castle Howel* (1794), is also set in Wales.

BENNETT, Nicholas (1823–99)
Musician and historian
Bennett, who was born and lived at Glanrafon, **Trefeglwys**, collected more than 700 Welsh folk tunes, of which 500, selected and arranged by D. Emlyn Evans, were published in his two-volume work *Alawon Fy Ngwlad* (1896). This work, which drew extensively on the Llywelyn Alaw manuscripts, includes accounts of **harp**ists and *penillion* **singing**, with explanatory notes on the art.

BERNARD (d.1148) Bishop
Former chamberlain to Queen Matilda, wife of Henry I, Bernard was the first **Norman** bishop of **St David's** (1115–48). He is credited with rebuilding or enlarging St David's Cathedral. Bernard promoted the cult of St **David**, making several unsuccessful searches for the **saint**'s body. During his episcopate, St David was allegedly formally canonized by Pope Calixtus II. Bernard's promotion of the cult was no doubt the groundwork for his unsuccessful campaign to elevate St David's to the status of an archbishopric.

BERNARD DE NEUFMARCHÉ (d.c.1125)
Marcher-lord
A **Norman** adventurer and the first ruler of the **lordship of Brecon**, he began to move into **Brycheiniog** following the death of William I. The killing in 1093 of **Rhys ap Tewdwr**, probably at Battle (**Yscir**, in the **Usk** valley), gave him possession of most of that ancient kingdom. His wife was a granddaughter of **Gruffudd ap Llywelyn**. His descendants would be lords of Brecon until 1521.

BERRIEW (Aberriw), Montgomeryshire, Powys
(4722 ha; 1306 inhabitants)
Located immediately south-west of **Welshpool**, the **English** name obscures the fact that the **community** contains the Rhiw's confluence (*aber*) with the **Severn**. Berriew village offers attractive vistas of half-timbered houses. The church (1804, 1876), dedicated to St **Beuno** – reputedly a native of

Berriew – has a striking timber bellcote. Pentre Llifior chapel (1797) is one of Wales's oldest **Wesleyan** buildings. Llifior Mill was the home of **Thomas Jones** (1810–49), founder of the **Calvinistic Methodist** mission to the **Khasi Hills**. Oak timbers of an earthen long barrow at Lower Luggy have been dated to 3700–3300 BC.

Vaynor, home of the Corbet-Winder family responsible for much of Berriew's charm, was originally a medieval house praised by **Guto'r Glyn**. Rebuilt in brick in c.1650, it was remodelled in 1853. The neo-Greek Glansevern (1807), the home of the politician and educationist A. C. Humphreys-Owen (1836–1905), has a fine **garden**; the family also owned what became Garthmyl Hotel (1762).

BERRY family Industrialists and newspapermen
The **Merthyr Tydfil**-born Berry brothers were powerful figures in industry and **newspapers** during the first half of the 20th century. In 1916, the eldest of the three, Henry Seymour Berry (1877–1928), took control of **D. A. Thomas**'s entire business operations, which included the Cambrian Combine **coal** company and an array of south Wales newspapers, among them the *Western Mail*. After his death, the papers passed to his two younger brothers, William Ewart Berry (1879–1954) and James Gomer Berry (1883–1968), a formidable partnership which had acquired its first paper, the *Sunday Times*, in 1915. By the late 1920s, the brothers controlled 26 Sunday newspapers and daily newspapers, including the *Daily Telegraph*; by 1936, they owned 4 newspapers with a **Britain**-wide circulation and 49 with more restricted circulations. The empire was split between the two brothers in 1937, and in 1958 their Kemsley Newspapers, which included all their Welsh papers, was sold to Roy Thomson. The three brothers were awarded peerages: H. S. Berry became Baron Buckland of Bwlch in 1926, W. E. Berry became Baron **Camrose** in 1929, and J. G. Berry became Viscount Kemsley in 1936. Baron Buckland died after suffering a fall from his **horse**; such was his unpopularity among members of the **Cardiff** Stock Exchange that they considered establishing a fund to raise a memorial to the horse.

BERRY, R[obert] G[riffith] (1869–1945)
Dramatist and short-story writer
A native of **Llanrwst**, Berry was a **Congregationalist** minister at Gwaelod-y-garth, **Cardiff**. His collection of stories, *Y Llawr Dyrnu* (1930), shows a cultured mind, with a taste for satire, and an unusual imagination. His plays, *Ar y Groesffordd* (1914), *Asgre Lân* (1916) and *Yr Hen Anian* (1929), were popular in the interwar years. His best play, *Y Ddraenen Wen* (1922), is a tragedy of the conflict between idealism and worldly wisdom.

BERRY, Ron (1920–97) Novelist
Born at Blaencwm, **Rhondda**, where he lived for most of his life, Ron Berry left school at the age of 14 and worked as a miner. He published six novels: *Hunters and Hunted* (1960), *Travelling Loaded* (1963), *The Full-Time Amateur* (1966), *Flame and Slag* (1968), *So Long, Hector Bebb* (1970) and *This Bygone* (1996); a volume of autobiography, *History is What You Live*, appeared posthumously in 1998, and his *Collected Stories* in 2000.

BERSHAM IRONWORKS, Denbighshire (now Wrexham)

The **iron**works were established at Bersham (**Coedpoeth**) c.1670 by the **Lloyd family** of Dolobran (**Llangyniew**), but became famous, from 1753, under the Wilkinson family. The works were closely linked with Abraham Darby at Coalbrookdale, and smelting with coke took place as early as 1721. It reached its peak after **John Wilkinson** invented a machine, in 1774, for boring cannon from solid bars. Subsequently, this technology was applied to cylinders for steam engines, and the works supplied Boulton and Watt in Birmingham. From the later 1790s, the works declined because of quarrels between the Wilkinson brothers and John's development of a rival site at **Brymbo**. The remains of the works are a highly significant site of **industrial archaeology**.

BERWYN MOUNTAINS, The (Mynyddoedd y Berwyn)

Constituting the spine that separates the basins of the **Dee** and the **Severn**, the Berwyn **Mountains** rise to 827 m at Cadair Berwyn and Moel Sych (**Llandrillo**). A rounded mass overlying Ordovician rock, the range extends for some 23 km from **Llangynog** to south of **Llangollen**. Within it rise important tributaries of the **Dee** and the **Severn**, the Ceiriog and the Tanat among them. Pistyll Rhaeadr, Wales's highest sheer-drop **waterfall**, is located on the Disgynfa, a branch of the Rhaeadr. Glacial activity has produced attractive features, such as the exquisite corrie **lake** of Llyn Lluncaws. Less rugged and receiving less rainfall than **Snowdonia**, the Berwyn Mountains support vast flocks of **sheep** and are among the few areas of Wales where grouse are preserved.

The mountains exude a greater sense of remoteness than does Snowdonia, which is crisscrossed by main roads; the Berwyn Mountains, by contrast, are crossed solely by the B4391 road, which links **Bala** with Llangynog. It was on Berwyn that the expedition of Henry II in 1165 – the most ambitious attempt by an **English monarch** in the 12th century to conquer Wales – came to a disastrous conclusion. The Berwyn Mountains have undergone less human interference than any other Welsh mountain range. **Lead** was once extensively mined at Llangynog and **slate** was quarried at Glyndyfrdwy (see **Corwen**), but the mountains are not markedly scarred by industrial waste. Although Lake Vyrnwy (see **Llanwddyn**) is located at the southern edge of the range, the central part of the mountains contains no **reservoirs**. Afforestation has been minimal and Berwyn's summits have not yet been crowned by wind turbines (see **Windmills**). Indeed, the peace of the mountains is disturbed only by mountain-bikers and off-road drivers, whose activities have created wide stretches of quagmire.

BETHESDA, Gwynedd (389 ha; 4515 inhabitants)

Bethesda was the sole **slate**-quarrying settlement in **Caernarfonshire** to attain **urban district** status (1894). There was hardly a dwelling in the area before the development of the Penrhyn quarry (see **Llandygai**) from the 1780s onwards. Called after the **Congregational** chapel at its centre, Bethesda was one of several quarrying settlements bearing biblical names. The chapel, a large, neo-classical building with stucco mouldings, was rebuilt in 1840; it has since been converted into flats. Consisting essentially of ribbon development along the **Holyhead** road (the A5), Bethesda was very much a company town, living under the shadow of the **Pennant family** of Penrhyn Castle (see **Llandygai**). The Pennants saw themselves as benevolent employers, providing Bethesda with a hospital and building St Ann's church (1865) and a **National Society** school in the hope of weaning their workers away from Nonconformity (see **Nonconformists**). The benevolence, however, was autocratic – an autocracy that led to the bitter and protracted **Penrhyn lockouts** (1896–7, 1900–3). The lockouts were a devastating blow, causing considerable out-migration, especially to the south Wales **coalfield**. Bethesda's **population** peaked at 5281 in 1901. The place is superbly evoked in **Caradog Prichard**'s *Un Nos Ola Leuad* (1961; English translations: *Full Moon*, 1973; *One Moonlit Night*, 1995). **W. J. Parry**, an accountant dubbed 'the Quarryman's Champion', was a native of Bethesda, as was the scholar **Idris Foster**.

The area has been famous for its **music** since the lockout period, when choirs of quarrymen travelled the country raising money. The Penrhyn **Male Voice Choir** is among the best in Wales. The **community** has nurtured pop groups such as Maffia Mr Huws, Tynal Tywyll, Celt and, most notably, the Super Furry Animals.

BETTWS (Betws Cedewain), Montgomeryshire, Powys (1856 ha; 425 inhabitants)

Located immediately north of **Newtown**, most of the **community**'s farms were, until 1914, part of the Gregynog estate (see **Tregynon**). Bettws village clusters around St **Beuno**'s church, which has a 16th-century tower and a 19th-century nave; it contains a fine brass memorial to John ap Meredyth (1531). Highgate (c.1670) is a striking half-timbered farmhouse.

BETWS, Carmarthenshire (1116 ha; 1834 inhabitants)

Located immediately east of **Ammanford**, the **community** contains the villages of Betws and Pantyffynnon. The sinking of two pits in the 1890s led to rapid **population** growth. The New Betws Drift Mine, the last of the area's **coal**mines, finally closed in 2003. St **David**'s church (1872) contains a **stained-glass** window (1960) inspired by **William Williams**'s (Pantycelyn; 1717–91) **hymn** 'Guide Me O Thou Great Jehovah'. The politician **James Griffiths** was born at Betws.

BETWS GARMON, Gwynedd (3900 ha; 216 inhabitants)

Located south-east of **Caernarfon** and embracing the upper reaches of the basin of the Gwyrfai, the **community** contains Yr Wyddfa (1085 m), the highest point in the **Snowdon** massif. Snowdon Ranger, now a youth hostel, has catered for Snowdon's walkers for almost 200 years, and is the starting point of the main westerly route up the **mountain**. Llyn Cwellyn, the source of Caernarfon's water supply, is the deepest and stillest of **Snowdonia**'s **lakes**. The community contains the tiny villages of Betws Garmon and Rhyd-Ddu. Rhyd-Ddu was the home of the poet and scholar **T. H. Parry-Williams**, whose locally inspired sonnets, '*Llyn y Gadair*', '*Tŷ'r Ysgol*' and '*Moelni*', are among the best-loved poems in the **Welsh language**. The floating **island** of **peat** on Llyn y Dywarchen amazed **Giraldus Cambrensis**.

BETWS GWERFIL GOCH (Betws Gwerful Goch), Denbighshire (2250 ha; 362 inhabitants)

Located on the banks of the Alwen south-west of **Ruthin**, the name means the bead-house or oratory of red-haired Gwerful – believed to be the granddaughter of **Owain Gwynedd**. St Mary's church contains medieval carved panels. **J. E. Jones**, general secretary of **Plaid [Genedlaethol] Cymru** (1930–60), was brought up at Melin-y-Wig and is buried there.

BETWS-Y-COED (Betws-y-coed), Conwy (1798 ha; 534 inhabitants)

The **community** of Betws-y-Coed (note the very slightly different **English** spelling) is located on the left bank of the **Conwy** and includes the lower part of the Llugwy valley and the left bank of the Lledr valley; the area is famed for its beauty. Waterloo Bridge (1815 – naturally) was one of the earliest cast **iron** bridges ever built. It carries **Telford's London–Holyhead road** (the **A5**), the construction of which opened up the district to tourists (*see* **Tourism**), particularly those in search of the **picturesque**. In the 1840s, regular visits by **David Cox** inspired other English artists to stay and paint in the area, some of whom would later found the **Royal Cambrian Academy**. Apart from the Waterloo Bridge, the community contains attractive bridges over the Llugwy and the Lledr (both probably 17th-century), and the superbly located Pont y Pair (1800) over the Conwy. St Michael church (*c*.1400, 1843) contains a fine effigy (*c*.1370). In the 18th and 19th centuries, the uplands of the community were

Swallow Falls, Betws-y-Coed

intensively mined for **copper** ore. Swallow Falls are a dramatic **waterfall** on the Llugwy. Although known in **Welsh** as Rhaeadr Ewynnol (Foaming Falls), **Thomas Pennant** referred to them as Rhaeadr y Wennol, the name which led to the adoption of the waterfall's **English** name.

BETWS YN RHOS (Betws-yn-Rhos), Conwy (4875 ha; 944 inhabitants)

Extending over a wide area immediately south of **Colwyn Bay**, the **community** represents the core of the medieval *cantref* of **Rhos**. There are 19th-century churches at Betws yn Rhos (1839) and Trofarth (1873); that at Llaneilian-yn-Rhos contains medieval features, including a rood screen. Llan, Llaneilian, is a thatched cruck hall-house. Coed Coch, an imaginative house of *c*.1800, has been adapted as a school. The scholar and poet **T. Gwynn Jones** was born at Gwyndy Uchaf, Betws yn Rhos.

BEULAH, Ceredigion (5062 ha; 1617 inhabitants)

Extending north of the **Teifi** east of **Cardigan**, the **community** contains the villages of Beulah, Betws Ifan, Bryngwyn, Cwmcou, Llandygwydd, Ponthirwaun and that part of **Cenarth** located north of the Teifi. Within the one-time **parish** of Llandygwydd were five significant **gentry** houses: Blaen-pant, Llwyndyrus, Noyadd Drefawr, Pen-y-lan and Penywenallt. Pen-y-lan (18th century and 1830) contains a wealth of detailed work by Italian craftsmen. Penywenallt was the birthplace of the clergyman and historian **Theophilus Evans**.

BEUNO (6th/7th century) Saint

An abbot linked with a cluster of early churches in the north-west. His principal monastery was **Clynnog** Fawr. A **Welsh** version of his life appears in the ***The Book of the Anchorite***. His apparent ability to restore decapitated bodies reflects elements of pre-Christian **religion**. Believed to be a native of **Berriew**, he is reputedly the first Welshman to hear spoken **English**, an experience which led him to flee from the banks of the **Severn** to **Gwynedd**. Beuno's feast day is 21 April.

BEVAN, Aneurin (1897–1960) Politician

A pit-boy at 13, lodge chairman at 19 and leader of **Tredegar Urban District** Council when 26, Bevan was 32 when he became MP for **Ebbw Vale**, a constituency he represented until his death. A left-wing rebel in the 1930s, he supported the Popular Front and was duly expelled from the **Labour Party** in 1939. During the period of wartime consensus, he was concerned to maintain free speech and became a persistent critic of **Churchill**, not least in the pages of *Tribune*, which he edited (1942–5). He was minister of **health** and **housing** in Attlee's cabinet 1945–50 when, following detailed and heated negotiations with doctors, he introduced the National Health Service, generally regarded as Labour's greatest legislative achievement.

   He resigned from the cabinet in April 1950 as a protest against a budget in which Gaitskell imposed prescription charges whilst increasing expenditure on rearmament. In the years of opposition after 1951, Bevan and his supporters, who included his wife Jennie Lee, were referred to as the 'Bevanites' and were involved, often bitterly, in disputes with Gaitskell. Reconciliation came when Bevan became deputy leader in 1959 and accepted the need for a British nuclear deterrent. At the time of his comparatively early death from cancer he was recognized as one of Labour's most significant leaders, and as the foremost exponent of the democratic **socialism** taken by many to be the party's defining characteristic. Trained as a Marxist, the experience of the **General Strike** in 1926 and his years in local **government** converted him to the notion of parliamentary democracy as the path which Labour should follow in its search for a new society.

Bevan's ability to attract support owed much to the warmth of his personality, his love of European **literature**, his familiarity with socialists from mainland Europe, his wit and his oratory in which he effectively deployed his accent and his stammer. John Campbell has argued that for all his charm there were flaws in his politics, whilst Michael Foot, Dai Smith and K. O. Morgan have all sustained the notion that Bevan's career was the high-water mark of Welsh popular politics. His attitude to Wales was ambiguous; on occasion, he argued that Welsh identity should have a political dimension, but he also expressed fears that any concession to 'regionalism' could divide the British working **class**.

BEVAN, Bridget (Madam Bevan; 1698–1779)
Patron of education
The daughter of John Vaughan of Derllys Court (**Newchurch and Merthyr**), an ardent **education**al reformer, Bridget Bevan became acquainted with **Griffith Jones, Llanddowror** through the involvement of Jones and her father in the **Society for the Promotion of Christian Knowledge**. When Griffith Jones established his **circulating schools** in the 1730s, she became one of his chief patrons, and led the schools movement successfully after his death. In her will, she bequeathed £10,000 to the work, but the legacy was challenged. The money was released in 1809, and new Madam Bevan schools were then established; however, the campaign lacked the vigour of earlier years and the last of the schools closed in 1854. Some parents believed Madame Bevan was a queen, who would 'draw their children away to another kingdom'.

'BEVIN BOYS'
In the spring of 1941, desperate to maintain fuel supplies to assist the **Second World War** effort, the **government** began to adopt policies to reverse the downward trend in the number of **coal**miners. First, existing miners were prevented from leaving the industry, then those registering for National Service were given the option of working underground. When the latter policy failed to secure sufficient voluntary recruits, forced conscription into the mines was introduced in November 1943. The individuals chosen were called 'Bevin boys', after Ernest Bevin, the minister of Labour and National Service who played a central role in the new policy.

BEVIS (BEVANS), John (1693–1771) Astronomer
John Bevis from **Tenby** – also known as John Bevans – studied medicine at **Oxford**, but **astronomy** and optics were the passion of his life. He compiled *Uranographia*

Aneurin Bevan and Jennie Lee on their wedding day, 1934

Astronomicae, the most comprehensive star catalogue of his time, and extended Bradley's work on aberration in declination to cover aberration in right ascension. He discovered a comet in 1744.

BEYNON, [William John] Granville (1914–96)
Radio scientist
Sir Granville Beynon, FRS, an international statesman of **science**, was born in **Dunvant**. With a physics degree from Swansea, he worked under Edward Appleton, at the National Physical Laboratory, Teddington, studying the ionosphere – the ionized part of the upper atmosphere (*see* **Physical Sciences**). His most important discovery was the identification of travelling ionospheric disturbances, large-scale waves in the upper atmosphere. As senior lecturer in Swansea and then professor of physics in **Aberystwyth**, he led a distinguished research group. He was president of the organizing committee of the International Year of the Quiet Sun (1964–5). While president of the International Union of Radio Science (1972–5), he took the initiative to establish EISCAT (the European Incoherent-Scatter Scientific Association), the world's most advanced radar facility for studying the upper atmosphere, located in northern Scandinavia. On Sundays, he travelled from Aberystwyth to Dunvant to play the organ at Dunvant **Congregationalist** chapel.

BIBLE, The
The Bible had in some form been available in Wales from the first appearance of Christianity in the country (*see* **Religion**). In the Middle Ages, virtually the only known version was the **Latin** Vulgate, prepared by St Jerome in the 4th century. The availability of the Bible in **English** from the 1530s onwards was the central factor in the development of Protestantism in the English-speaking areas of Wales. At the same time, the belief arose that a **Welsh-language** version had once existed. The basis of the belief was probably the manuscript *Y Bibyl Ynghymraec*, a late medieval Welsh version of a synopsis of the Bible's historical books. The translation of the Bible into **Welsh** was initiated by **William Salesbury** with his version of the lessons read at Communion, *Kynniver llith a ban* (1551). Following the Act for the Translation of the Bible into Welsh (1563),

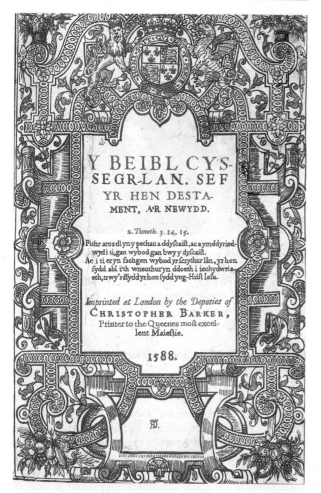

The title page of the first Welsh Bible, 1588

which enjoined that the Bible and **The Book of Common Prayer** be translated by 1567, and be placed side by side with English versions in every **parish** church in Wales, Salesbury, together with **Richard Davies** (?1501–81), bishop of **St David's**, and **Thomas Huet**, precentor of St David's Cathedral, translated the New Testament and Prayer Book (including the Psalms) by the year specified. Although Salesbury, who did most of the translation, was an excellent biblical scholar, the eccentricity of his orthography marred the reception of his work.

It was **William Morgan**, then vicar of **Llanrhaeadr-ym-Mochnant**, who completed Salesbury's work. In 1588 appeared his *Y Beibl Cyssegr-lan* – his own translation of the Old Testament (apart from the Psalms) and Apocrypha – and his revision of Salesbury's New Testament and Psalms. Like Salesbury, Morgan was a fully equipped biblical scholar who was also well-versed in the Welsh literary tradition, especially the work of the professional poets – whom he patronized generously. Unlike Salesbury, he had a sure sense of what was linguistically acceptable, and his translation was immediately acknowledged to be a masterpiece.

In 1611, the English Authorized Version appeared, which impelled Richard Parry, bishop of **St Asaph**, together with his brother-in-law, **John Davies** (*c.*1567–1644), to revise Morgan's Bible in accordance with the readings of the Authorized Version. The fruit of their labours, which appeared in 1620, was for more than 350 years the 'Authorized Version' of Welsh-speaking Wales. There was no need to revise Morgan's translation extensively, but the language and orthography were further regularized, bringing them into stricter conformity with the practices of the poets.

Welsh was the sole non-state language of Europe to become the medium of a published Bible within a century of the **Protestant Reformation**, a fact of central importance in understanding the difference between the fate of Welsh and the fate of other non-state languages – Irish and Scots Gaelic in particular.

The publication, in 1630, of a portable version of the 1620 Bible marks the beginning of the great campaign to provide bibles for the Welsh common reader. Four editions followed in the 17th century (and 3 of the New Testament alone), at least 12 in the 18th (and four of the New Testament), and over 200 in the 19th (and over 150 of the New Testament) – followed by a mere 15 or so in the 20th (together with 18 of the New Testament). It was not until 1988, with the appearance of *Y Beibl Cymraeg Newydd*, that Morgan's version was finally superseded; a new edition of *Y Beibl Cymraeg Newydd*, with 6000 changes, appeared in 2004.

It was Wales's enthusiastic embrace of Protestant Christianity in the 18th and 19th centuries that created the demand for the Bible. By means of **preachers** and catechisms, the **circulating schools** and the **Sunday schools**, vast numbers of people were immersed in the Bible, which became the formative influence in their lives. Towards the end of the 19th century and throughout the 20th, that influence was challenged by theological liberalism and scientific secularism (*see* **Agnostics and Atheists**).

While the prestige of the Bible remained high, Welsh writers – drawing on its vocabulary, its grammatical patterns and its syntactical constructions – found it a rich resource; they also profited from the variety of its literary forms, its rhythms and imagery. Both the prose and verse of the 20th century would have been much the poorer without it. Perhaps it is in the remarkable **hymn**ody of the 18th and 19th centuries that its influence is seen at its most fruitful.

BIBLE SOCIETY, The

Established in **London** in 1804 as the British and Foreign **Bible** Society, its aim was to secure publication and distribution of Bibles. Repeated requests from **Thomas Charles** of **Bala** that the Religious Tract Society should help secure a regular supply of affordable **Welsh** Bibles served to highlight the need, and it is said that he used the story of **Mary Jones** walking barefoot to Bala to seek a Bible as an example. The society, which soon added translation to its aims, is still involved in the same work today.

BIGOD family Marcher-lords

The family became associated with Wales when Roger Bigod I, earl of Norfolk (d.1270), inherited the lordship of **Chepstow** or **Strigoil** from his mother, Maud, co-heiress of William **Marshal** (d.1219). Roger's son, Roger II (d.1306), financed the rebuilding of **Tintern** Abbey church, the erection of Chepstow town walls and the reconstruction of

Chepstow Castle. Impoverished by his activities, Roger bequeathed his estates to the crown in return for an annuity.

BILLIARDS and SNOOKER

Billiards may have evolved from a lawn-based game similar to croquet, becoming a table game in the 15th century. Little is known about the development of the game in Wales, but players such as Horace Coles and Tom Jones reached the amateur world championship final in the late 1920s and early 1930s respectively. From the 1950s to the 1970s, Roy Oriel of **Mountain Ash** was a renowned player; later, Clive Everton became the Welsh team's most familiar name, owing to his high profile as a snooker commentator.

The advent of colour television in the 1970s was a crucial factor in the popularization of snooker. The decade was dominated by **Tredegar**-born Ray Reardon, who was the world snooker champion no fewer than six times. When the first world rankings were introduced in 1976, Reardon was proclaimed the world's number one player. Among Reardon's contemporaries were players such as Gary Owen of Upper Tumble (**Llannon**), who was world amateur champion in 1963 and 1966, and Cliff Wilson, also of Tredegar, who was world amateur champion in 1978.

Another former world amateur champion, Terry Griffiths of **Llanelli**, burst upon the snooker scene in 1979, becoming world professional snooker champion – and a national hero – in his first full season as a professional. Since retiring from snooker in the late 1990s, Griffiths has

had an immense influence on coaching and the organization of the game. During this period, Doug Mountjoy of Tir-y-Berth (**Ebbw Vale**) also made a great impact, becoming runner-up in the 1981 world snooker championship. In recent years, impressive Welsh players have continued to emerge, among them Mark Williams of **Cwm** (near Ebbw Vale), world snooker champion in both 2000 and 2003, and Matthew Stevens of **Carmarthen**, the runner-up in 2000, and the British snooker champion in 2003.

Welsh snooker referees of the calibre of John Williams and Eirian Williams ensure that there is a Welsh feel to many of the major competitions. With the emergence of young players such as David John of Ogmore Vale (*see* **Ogmore Valley**) and Jamie Jones and Michael White of **Neath**, the future looks bright for this highly popular game.

'BILLY PLAYFAIR'

In the steam **coal** trade, miners were paid according to the weight of large coal produced. Initially, the amount of small coal deducted from each dram sent out by a miner was estimated by a colliery official, leading to disputes over payment. During the mid-19th century, a machine to assess accurately the monies due, 'Billy Playfair', was introduced and subsequently became universal. Comprising a set of bars, it enabled the separation of the large coal from the small, providing a more objective measurement. The machine was not always welcomed by the miners; complaints were made as to the accuracy of the scales and about too great a distance between the bars.

World snooker champion in 2000 and 2003, Mark Williams

BIOLOGICAL SCIENCES, The

The collecting of **plants** began with the hunter-gatherers of the **Palaeolithic Age** and was furthered by the development of **agriculture** from *c.*4000 BC onwards. Several classical **Latin** authors discussed the characteristics of plants, and there may well have been knowledge of their works in **Roman Britain**. The value of plants was of interest to the compilers of the **Law** of **Hywel Dda**, and a considerable number of trees and flowers were mentioned by the poets of medieval Wales. As healing agents, plants have a long history and, in Wales, that knowledge was recorded in manuscripts associated with the work of the **Physicians of Myddfai**, the earliest of which date from the 14th century. The properties of herbs were of particular interest to Welsh **Renaissance** scholars, the most prominent of whom, **William Salesbury**, prepared a medicinal herbal – *Llysieulyfr Meddyginiaethol.* (It was not published until 1997.) In the 17th century, plant collecting became a passion for many – no one more so than for the great naturalist **Edward Lhuyd**. The publication of *Systema Naturae* by the Swedish botanist Carolus Linnaeus in 1735 provided a scientific system for the classification of plants and led, in the late 18th and the 19th centuries, to more methodical plant hunting and to the publication of works such as **Hugh Davies**'s *Welsh Botanology: A Systematic Catalogue of the Native Plants of the Island of Anglesey* (1813).

Hunter-gathers had a detailed knowledge of wild animals, knowledge which declined as human beings became increasingly reliant upon domesticated species. Although those who enjoyed **hunting**, or those who felt the need to control what they considered to be vermin, had a detailed understanding of the habits of indigenous creatures, the classification of animals did not attain the popularity enjoyed by the classification of plants. However, the concept that the study of plants and of animals represents a combined discipline is indicated by the coining of the word 'biology' in 1843. (The **Welsh** equivalent, '*bywydeg*', is first recorded in 1852.) The publication in 1859 of Charles Darwin's theory of evolution by natural selection – a theory which owed something to Darwin's boyhood holidays on the coast of **Merioneth**, to his studies of the prehistoric animal remains in the Elwy valley (*see* **Cefnmeiriadog**) and to his correspondence with **Alfred Russel Wallace** – opened up new kinds of investigation, initially into zoology, but shortly also into botany. Hitherto, studies had been devoted largely to revealing the variety of nature; henceforth, they would also be concerned with explaining how and why that variety had come about.

In the 1860s, Thomas Henry Huxley, the leading proponent of Darwin's theories, prepared blueprints for the advancement of teaching and research in the biological sciences, blueprints which would be followed by the colleges which would eventually constitute the **University of Wales**. From its inception (1872), **Aberystwyth** had a chair of natural philosophy, but the college did not establish separate departments for botany and zoology until the 20th century. The two subjects had a professor apiece at **Bangor** by 1895, an arrangement which did not come into existence in **Cardiff** until 1905.

The foundation of the **National Museum [of] Wales** in 1907 initiated major developments. Comprehensive monographs, first issued in the 1930s, on the flowering plants, ferns and timber trees of Wales were compiled from the museum's records. Other studies issued by the museum include the monographs and guides published from the 1920s onwards on Wales's **mammals**, **birds**, **fish**, marine and terrestrial shells and **insects**. Of central importance was the publication of an atlas of distribution **maps** of all British vascular plants (plants containing vessels that circulate liquid) by the Botanical Society of the British Isles in the 1950s; the maps were based on a survey recording the presence of each species of flowering plant in every one of the 10-km squares in which it occurs. Since the 1960s, survey work of this kind has been continued by both statutory and voluntary conservation bodies, as reflected in the quarterly journals – *North Western Naturalist* (1926–55) and *Nature in Wales* (1955–86).

The widening activity of the University of Wales's departments of botany and zoology produced a wealth of knowledge. In Cardiff, the scope of zoology broadened from the 1920s, absorbing techniques and perspectives from other disciplines, such as **chemistry**, biochemistry, physiology and experimental psychology. The teaching of biochemistry began at Cardiff in the 1890s as part of the training of pre-clinical students in chemical physiology; a full department was established in 1956. Degree courses in bacteriology were initiated by Cardiff's botany department in 1946; that led in 1965 to the University of Wales's first department of microbiology – thus adding bacteria and micro-organisms to plants and animals as the three essential elements of biology. Among the major achievements of Cardiff's zoologists is the research of Martin Evans on the modelling of human diseases in rodents, work which will have a major impact in combating cancer and human genetic disorders (*see also* **Science**). He was awarded a Nobel prize in 2007.

At Bangor, the departments of botany and agricultural botany were merged in 1967 to form a school of plant biology. Among the college's achievements in that field is John Harper's *Population Biology of Plants* (1977) and John Farrar's work on the effects of increased atmospheric carbon dioxide and temperature on plant growth, respiration and partitioning. Work on marine science had been initiated in the Bangor area in 1892 when efforts were made to found a marine science station at **Menai Bridge**. Such a station came into existence in 1949, the forerunner of the University of Wales Marine Sciences Laboratory; established in 1962, it joined marine science with the cognate science of physical oceanography.

Distinguished figures among zoologists at Aberystwyth include T. A. Stephenson, an international authority on seashore fauna, and Gwendolen Rees, Wales's first woman academic to be elected to the Royal Society. The college's botanists include Lily Newton, whose almost 30 years as a professor is a record among Wales's **women** academics, and P. F. Waring, the only Fellow of the Royal Society to have spent nine years as an income tax officer. Aberystwyth's best-known contribution to plant studies was made in the field of agricultural botany, in particular by **R. G. Stapledon**, who held the chair in the subject from 1919 to 1942.

The Plant Breeding Station founded by Stapledon at Aberystwyth evolved into Wales's most renowned scientific centre – the **Institute for Grassland and Environmental Research**. Other biological research centres include the **National Botanic Garden** (Middleton) at **Llanarthney** and the National Environment Research Council Centre for Ecology and Hydrology Research at Bangor. Since the 1990s, in response to the revolution in biology, substantial investment has been made in functional geonomics and bioinformatics. In 2002, **Cardiff University** became the focus for the work of the Wales Gene Park, one of six virtual centres established in the United Kingdom to foster expertise in genetic technology, in collaboration with the pharmaceutical and biotechnology industries.

BIRDS

The range of habitats in Wales makes for rich and varied birdlife. Being a peninsular country, Wales supports huge numbers of seabirds on its coasts and **islands**, including important breeding colonies of gannets and Manx shearwaters, which, as a spectacle, can rival African big game. Other seabirds are well represented, including delicate kittiwakes, shags and common cormorants (splendidly named in **Welsh** as *bilidowcar*, *Wil wal waliog* or *llanc Llandudno*), and members of the auk family – puffins, guillemots and razorbills. Maritime heathland – where the vegetation is limited by salt spray and onshore wind – is important for choughs, which also nest at some inland sites. The roseate tern, a few pairs of which nest on **Anglesey**, is one of Europe's rarest nesting seabirds, and there is one colony of little terns which share a stretch of beach at Gronant (**Llanasa**) with hordes of holidaymakers.

With over 60% of the land above the 150 m contour, Wales in its upland habitats supports large numbers of raven, ring ouzel (a summer visitor which has one of the most beautiful songs) and rare birds of prey such as red kite, hen harrier and merlin. The golden eagle had disappeared from **Snowdonia**, its last stronghold in Wales, by about the 18th century, but the common buzzard is an ubiquitous bird of prey; constantly patrolling on wide wings, its mewing cry is one of the wildest sounds of the Welsh countryside. Some birds of prey have only recently colonized. Since the 1960s, the goshawk has found pine plantations – and the plentiful crows and squirrels therein – much to its liking, and the honey buzzard started nesting in upland Wales in 1991. Dwindling populations of two grouse species, the red and the black, are also found.

Oak woodlands draw in many summer visitors, including the pied flycatcher (the males looking as if they are wearing dinner jackets), redstart and wood warbler. In between high and low land is the *ffridd*, a habitat of scattered trees and gorse, which is home to whinchats and white-rumped wheatears. One gorse-loving species, the Dartford warbler, first nested in Wales in 1998, and it seems likely that another species from mainland Europe will follow – the little egret, which **climate** change has helped northwards.

In the winter, vast numbers of starlings visit from Russia and the Baltic states, some flocks numbering as many as the 2 million birds which formed a dark and noisy cloud over **Maenclochog** in 1979.

The estuaries support great numbers of waders and wildfowl. They average almost 80,000 on the **Severn**, which, at Collister Pill (**Magor with Undy**) and Stert Island (on the English side), sustains **Britain**'s largest roost of whimbrel, a diminutive cousin of the curlew. Over 110,000 birds converge on the 20-km length of the **Dee** estuary in winter, including large flocks of elegant pintail ducks, which drift close to shore at high tide. At Traeth Lafan, **Aber[gwyngregyn]**, as many as 500 great crested grebes convene in the autumn to moult, shedding their elegant headdresses – for which, in darker days, they used to be shot. The RSPB has a major reserve at Ynyshir (**Ysgubor-y-coed**) on the **Dyfi** estuary.

Welsh **rivers**, many of them short and fast running, are home to goosanders – tree-nesting sawbill ducks – and kingfishers, which are often little more than a semaphore flash of blue along the river bank. But even this rapid flight cannot compare with the peregrine, Wales's fastest falcon: having spotted its prey, it crumples its wings and becomes a blur, a bird turned into a bullet.

In common with other parts of Europe, Wales has suffered a drastic decline of birds such as swifts and swallows, and songbirds associated with farmland, such as skylarks, song thrushes, linnets, yellow hammers, bullfinches, spotted flycatchers, tree sparrows and reed buntings. Changes in **agriculture** have also contributed to the lapwing's decline, far severer in Wales than in **England**.

Birds of particular significance in Wales

CHOUGH
Britain's rarest crow, formerly widespread, is now confined to the westernmost extremities of Wales, as well as **Scotland**, the **Isle of Man** and **Ireland**. Over 50% of Britain's chough population is found in Wales, with strongholds on the coasts of **Pembrokeshire**, **Ceredigion**, **Gwynedd** and Anglesey, and good numbers inland in Snowdonia. Although chough numbers are generally in decline, they are increasing in coastal Wales, with pairs now breeding in **Gower** for the first time in 100 years.

DIPPER
One of the most distinctive birds of upland rivers and streams, with its prominent white bib, its bobbing motion as it flits among stones and its ability to swim and walk underwater, searching for food.

GANNET
The island of Grassholm, located 14 km off the Pembrokeshire coast, appears to be half black and half white, the white part being composed of thousands of gannets. The second largest gannetry in the world, Grassholm sustains over 32,000 pairs. In flight, gannets are cigar-shaped, with wingspans of 1.8 m. On land, they have to tolerate very near neighbours, cramming their nests, built from seaweed and flotsam, into every available square metre. Gannets can often be seen fishing off the coast: a bird crumples its wings 100 m above the waves, and falls, its dagger-shaped bill turning into a living spearhead as it plunges through the water.

MANX SHEARWATER
Half the world's population – over 200,000 pairs – of this small, albatross-like seabird breeds on the islands of

The red kite, a Welsh conservation success

RAVEN

The low, rasping croak of the raven, the largest member of the crow family, is the most evocative sound of lonely crags and high sheepfolds. Ravens breed in Wales at greater densities than anywhere else in their northern range. The largest winter roost of ravens in Britain, and probably in Europe, is found within the spruce plantations of Newborough Warren (**Rhosyr**, Anglesey), with peak counts of almost 2000 birds. These denizens of wild spaces occasionally nest in cities, the big bill and lozenge-shaped tail marking them out from the more common crows. Pairs, once established, tend to stay in the same area throughout their lives. Known in Welsh as *cigfran* (meat crow), the raven has long been considered a bird of omen, often attendant on death, especially on the corpses of those slain on the battlefield.

RED KITE

Unofficially Wales's national bird, the red kite's survival into the 21st century is a conservation success story. Its history in Wales goes back 125,000 years, and as a scavenger benefiting from unsanitary human settlement it was abundant until the early 19th century. Thereafter, the red kite was persecuted by gamekeepers and suffered the attentions of nest robbers: the population dwindled rapidly. By the beginning of the 20th century, it maintained a precarious hold in the upper **Tywi** valley. Nests were guarded from unscrupulous egg collectors and the human vigilance paid off. By 2003, there were over 300 pairs in Wales, and the kite has been sighted in all Welsh **counties**. With lemon eyes, silvery heads and russet-coloured bodies, these supremely aeronautic creatures are Wales's most elegant birds of prey, scything through the air as they range widely to seek carrion, much of which they obtain from designated feeding sites such as that at Gigrin, **Nantmel**.

BIRDS OF RHIANNON, The

In '**Branwen ferch Llŷr**', the second branch of *Pedair Cainc y Mabinogi* (*see* **Mabinogion, The**), the three Birds of **Rhiannon** sing above the sea at **Harlech** to entertain the seven men who had returned from **Ireland**. In the tale 'Culhwch and Olwen', they are said to 'awaken the dead and put the living to sleep'.

BISHOPSTON (Llandeilo Ferwallt), Swansea
(596 ha; 3341 inhabitants)
Located immediately west of **Swansea**, the **community** contains the delectable **Gower** bays of Caswell and Pwlldu. An early ecclesiastical site, it was dedicated to **Teilo** and the **Welsh** name – Llanferwallt is another form – also refers to Merwallt, possibly a former abbot. Although in the diocese of **St David's** until the creation of the diocese of Swansea and **Brecon** in 1923, it was, by the 17th century, the sole living in **Glamorgan** in the gift of the bishop of Llandaff. The church has some medieval features, and includes a memorial to a one-time incumbent, the **Celt**icist **Edward Davies**. Now a suburb of **Swansea**, developments have not wholly obscured evidence of medieval strip-fields. Bishopston valley is a delightful wooded **limestone** cleft.

Skokholm, Skomer, Ramsey and Bardsey. A transatlantic traveller, the shearwater winters halfway across the world, off the coast of South America: it is the only European bird to migrate there regularly. It nests underground, usually in old **rabbit** burrows. Shearwaters visit land only at night, avoiding predators such as gulls. Before making landfall, huge congregations settle on the sea, forming 'rafts'. The shearwater's night-time cry is extraordinary, described by R. M. Lockley as 'the crow of a throaty rooster whose head is chopped off before the long last note has fairly begun'. In flight, they shear the water in seemingly effortless motion, their wings almost touching the waves. Their homing instinct is remarkable. A bird taken to Massachusetts found its way back to its nesting hole in Pembrokeshire (4880 km away) in 12.5 days.

OWLS

There are five species of owl that breed in Wales: the tawny owl, the barn owl, the little owl, the long-eared owl and the rare short-eared owl, whose best-known habitat is the island of Skomer. As in most other cultures, owls – generally the barn owl and the tawny owl – loom large in myth and folklore, from the famous story in *The Mabinogion* of the magician **Gwydion** turning the beautiful **Blodeuwedd** into an owl, the enemy of all other birds, to conceptions of the owl as a bird of ill omen and an *aderyn corff* (corpse bird; *see* **Death and Funerals**). Owls used to live close to human settlements. A 19th-century owlery in some Pembrokeshire cottages had 50 owls present when they were driven out.

BISHTON (Trefesgob), Newport
(688 ha; 2161 inhabitants)
The **community** contains the eastern wing of the **Llanwern Steelworks**. Its main settlement, the village of Underwood, was built in the 1960s to house steelworkers. The community's name recalls the fact that Bishton (Bishopston) was an episcopal **manor**, which, according to *Liber Landavensis*, was granted to the bishop of Llandaff (*see* **Cardiff**) in the 6th century. The motte north of the village of Bishton represents the remains of the bishop's palace. The church of St Cadwaladr – which gave its name to the original **parish** (Llangadwaladr) – was first built in the 13th century, was remodelled in the 15th and restored in 1887. St Mary's church, Wilcrick, was virtually rebuilt in 1860. It stands beneath Wilcrick Hill, which is crowned by a fine **Iron Age hill-fort**.

BLACK BOOK OF CARMARTHEN, The
A manuscript containing the oldest written collection of Welsh poetry, it was compiled by an unnamed scribe over a period of many years in the mid-13th century. It contains a mixture of religious and secular poetry dating from the 9th to the 12th centuries. At the **dissolution of the monasteries** in the 16th century, the manuscript was rescued from **Carmarthen Augustinian** priory. There is no evidence to show that it was written there, but its compiler's interest in the praise-poetry of the south-west and in poems associated with Myrddin (*see* **Merlin**) suggests that this is likely. It is housed at the **National Library**.

BLACK DEATH, The
Known as 'The Great Mortality' (*Y Farwolaeth Fawr*) and 'The Great Pestilence', this disease blighted communities throughout Europe in the 14th century, killing some 25 million people between 1347 and 1350. The pneumonic form of the disease was caught through breathing in the infection, and the bubonic through being bitten by the fleas of the black rat; fever and vomiting were invariably followed by death within days. In Wales, about a quarter of the inhabitants were wiped out in one year alone (1349–50).

The plague reached south Wales, probably by sea, in March 1349. **Carmarthen**'s **customs** collectors were early victims, as were 36 of the 40 tenants at **Caldicot** manor. During 1349, it spread through the south and along the **Severn** valley and borderland to **Cheshire**. **Pembroke** lordship was 'so devastated by the deadly pestilence which lately raged in those parts' that its annual rent was reduced by a quarter (1350). **Ruthin** and **Denbigh** had high death rates, and **Holywell**'s **lead** miners were decimated. Disruption was also caused by fear and flight, though some returned, such as, in 1354, the Ruthin man who 'left his land during the Pestilence on account of poverty, but now came and was admitted by the lord's favour to hold the said land by the service due'. This and later plagues – in 1361–2 ('The Second Pestilence') and 1369 – threatened landlords' incomes, caused social mobility and cut ties of obligation.

The plague gave rise to millenarian hopes and morbid obsessions, but it introduced opportunities as well as hardships, such as a buoyant land market and thriving **sheep** farming in the middle **March**. Profound social and economic changes in town and countryside included a rise in the standard of living of bondmen, as a result of the demand for their services (the calorific intake of peasants was higher in 1430 than in 1914).

If the inhabitants of Wales numbered about 300,000 at the beginning of the 14th century, it is believed that by the end of the century, mainly because of the plague, they had been reduced by at least 100,000.

BLACK MOUNTAIN, The (Y Mynydd Du)
An extensive tract of land encompassing some 15,000 ha, rising to Fan Brycheiniog (802 m; **Llywel**) and Bannau Sir Gaer (749 m; **Llanddeusant**). The precipitous cliffs of Old Red Sandstone, of which Fan Brycheiniog and Bannau Sir Gaer are part, extend from the western end of **Llyn y Fan Fach** (*see* **Legend of**) to the southern end of Fan Hir. Noteworthy **plants** on the shelves of the cliffs include alpine-arctic species such as roseroot, dwarf willow and cranberry. On clear days, the summits of the Black Mountain offer views of **Mynydd Preseli** to the west, **Pumlumon** and **Cadair Idris** to the north, and the Severn Sea, Lundy Island and Exmoor to the south. The A4069 between **Llangadog** and **Brynamman** rises to the height of 493 m and crosses Ordovician, Silurian, Old Red Sandstone, Carboniferous **Limestone** and Millstone Grit rocks. The novels of Richard Vaughan (**Ernest Lewis Thomas**) portray life on the Black Mountain, which is part of the **Brecon Beacons National Park**.

BLACK MOUNTAINS, The (Y Mynydd Du)
Part of the **Brecon Beacons National Park**, but separated from the Beacons by the **Usk** valley, the Black **Mountains** are a compact sandstone massif, some 16 km from north to south and 13 km from west to east. They consist of three roughly parallel ridges rising to the summit of Pen y Gadair Fawr (800 m; **Vale of Grwyney**). The ridges are separated by the valleys of the Grwyne Fawr, Grwyne Fechan and Honddu, tributaries of the Usk. The **roads** up the two Grwyne valleys eventually peter out, but that up the Honddu valley leads to Gospel Pass linking **Abergavenny** with **Hay**. It follows the course of the delectable Vale of Ewyas, described by **Giraldus Cambrensis** as 'encircled on all sides by lofty mountains, but only an arrowshot broad', and reaches up to Twmpa (Lord Hereford's Knob; 690 m) and Hay Bluff (677 m; both in **Llanigon**), which offer superb views northwards over the **Wye** valley.

The Black Mountains are the epitome of a frontier region, with the lack of central control which that term frequently implies. It was near the Grwyne Fawr that Richard de **Clare** was murdered in 1136. It was the remoteness of the area which in the 12th century attracted William de **Lacy**, founder of Llanthony Priory (*see* **Crucorney**), and in the 19th century attracted another monastic founder, Father Ignatius (*see* **Joseph Lyne** and Llanigon), and in the 20th century attracted the artists Eric Gill and **David Jones**. It was the remoteness too which permitted the survival of Wales's most appealing **parish** church, that of Patrishow (*see* Vale of Grwyney). A refuge for religious rebels, it provided a haven for **Lollards**, a secure place for early **Baptists** and a centre for persecuted Jesuits. Although the entire area had, by the 20th century, fewer than 500 inhabitants, fascination with the mountain people has inspired such

Llanthony Priory in the heart of the Black Mountains

notable works as the posthumously published first two volumes of **Raymond Williams**'s projected trilogy, *People of the Black Mountains* (1989, 1999).

BLACKWELL, John (Alun; 1797–1840) Poet
Born in Ponterwyl (**Mold**), he was apprenticed to a shoemaker and wrote poems and essays. They attracted the attention of local benefactors who enabled him to have an **education**. He eventually entered Jesus College, **Oxford**, was ordained curate at **Holywell** in 1829 and was vicar of **Manordeifi**, **Pembrokeshire**, from 1833 until his death. Alun won **eisteddfod** prizes for strict-metre poems, but he is mainly remembered for a few pre-romantic lyrics such as 'Cathl i'r Eos', 'Cân Gwraig y Pysgotwr' and 'Abaty Tintern'. His works were published posthumously as *Ceinion Alun* (1851).

BLACKWOOD (Coed-duon), Caerphilly
(423 ha; 8162 inhabitants)
Located between the **Rhymney** and Sirhowy Rivers, Blackwood's long High Street follows the line of the Sirhowy tramroad. Substantial settlement began in the 1820s when J. H. Moggridge, in consultation with **Robert Owen**, initiated his 'village system' plan. He cleared sites in the Black Wood and made loans to tenants who agreed to build a cottage and establish a vegetable garden; by 1830, however, Blackwood had the worst sanitation problems in **Monmouthshire**, and little of the early 19th-century development survives. Production of bituminous **coal** grew rapidly, and, by 1839, most of the coal exported from **Newport** originated in Blackwood. By then, its colliers were the most tumultuous of the county's inhabitants and Blackwood was one of the strongest centres of **Chartism**. The fateful decision to embark upon an armed rising seems to have been taken at Blackwood's Coach and Horses Hotel. Later in the 19th century, the mining of bituminous coal gave way to the deep mining of steam coal. Maes Manor Hotel has an elaborate **garden** laid out in 1907. **Gwyn Jones**, one of the most distinguished literary figures of 20th-century Wales, was a native of Blackwood.

BLAENAU GWENT County borough, constituency and one-time district
(10,863 ha; 70,064 inhabitants)
To William Coxe, visiting the area in 1801, Blaenau Gwent was 'the extremity of Gwentland … seldom traversed by the **gentry** except for the purpose of grouse-shooting'. Yet, by 1801, there were major ironworks in the upper reaches of the **Ebbw** and Sirhowy valleys, and **iron** and **coal** production was rapidly placing the region at the forefront of the **Industrial Revolution**. By the end of the 20th century, heavy industry had collapsed, causing much impoverishment. **Welsh**, widely spoken at the beginning of the 19th century – Coxe needed an interpreter – subsequently declined, although educational policies have led to some increase among younger age groups in recent years. In 2001, 13.31% of the inhabitants had some knowledge of Welsh, the percentages varying from 14.8% in **Brynmawr** to 11.79% in **Ebbw Vale**; 6.56% of the **county borough**'s inhabitants were wholly fluent in the language.

Following the abolition of the **counties** of **Monmouth** and **Brecon** in 1974, Blaenau Gwent was created as a district of the new county of **Gwent**. It consisted of what had been the **urban districts** of **Abertillery**, Ebbw Vale, **Nantyglo and Blaina**, and **Tredegar**, in **Monmouthshire**, and the urban district of Brynmawr and the **community** of **Llanelly**, in **Breconshire**. In 1996, the district (bereft of Llanelly) became the county borough of Blaenau Gwent; it includes the entire north-western part of the original Monmouthshire apart from the one-time urban district of **Rhymney**. In 2001, the county borough had Wales's highest proportion of Wales-born inhabitants (92.1%). The constituency of Blaenau Gwent consists essentially of the former constituencies of Ebbw Vale and Abertillery.

BLAENAVON (Blaenafon), Torfaen
(1773 ha; 5763 inhabitants)

The **community** stands near the head of the valley of Afon Lwyd on the north-eastern edge of the south Wales **coal-**field. Easily accessible **iron** ore was exploited from the 1570s onwards for making wire at **Tintern** and iron at **Pontypool**. In 1788, Staffordshire entrepreneurs, led by Thomas Hill, leased 2860 ha of ore-bearing land from Lord Abergavenny (*see* **Nevill family**) and established what was perhaps the world's first multi-furnace coke-fuelled ironworks. By the 1810s, the works were reputed to be the most productive in Wales and possibly in the world. In 1861, a new ironworks came into production 1 km away at Forgeside, where met-alworking continues. It was there in 1879 that **Sidney Gilchrist Thomas** and his cousin Percy Carlyle Gilchrist discovered how to make steel (*see* **Iron and Steel**) using ores containing phosphorus, a discovery which revolutionized steelmaking worldwide. Developments at Forgeside led to the abandonment of the original works. They constitute the world's most complete remains of a late 18th-century iron-works, and include blast furnaces, cast-houses, calcining kilns, a superb water-balance tower and, at Stack Square, rare survivals of 18th-century industrial **housing**. The tram-road tunnel (*c*.1815) leading to Garnddyrys (*see* **Llanfoist Fawr**) was then the longest such structure in the world. Big Pit, sunk in the 1860s and in operation until 1973, survives in its entirety. It became a mining museum in 1983; known since 2005 as Big Pit: The National Coal Museum, it is part of the **National Museum [of] Wales**. In 2005, it won the £100,000 Gulbenkian prize for Museum of the Year, **Britain**'s largest arts award.

Blaenavon town developed on the edge of the iron company's lands. It retains many of its original features and is regarded as Wales's best example of a mid-Victorian iron-making town. St Peter's church (1805) has a unique iron font, and nearby stands the first industrial school in Wales (1816). The massive Workmen's Institute (1894) is used as council

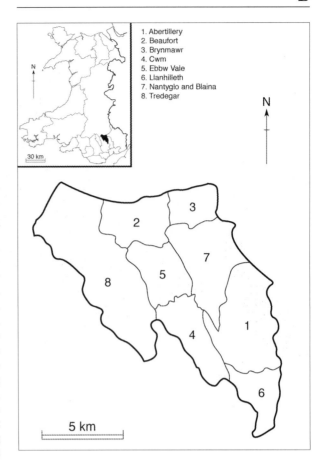

1. Abertillery
2. Beaufort
3. Brynmawr
4. Cwm
5. Ebbw Vale
6. Llanhilleth
7. Nantyglo and Blaina
8. Tredegar

30 km

5 km

The communities of the county borough of Blaenau Gwent

offices. Blaenavon attained World Heritage status in November 2000 on the grounds that its landscape constitutes 'an exceptional illustration in material form of the social and economic structure of 19th-century industry'. (Apart from Blaenavon, Wales's sole other World Heritage Sites are the castles of the north-west, although there is a campaign to grant the status to the Pont Cysyllte aqueduct; *see* **Llangollen Rural**.) There were moves in the early 21st century to turn Blaenavon into a 'booktown', on the lines of **Hay**.

The Big Pit National Coal Museum at Blaenavon

BLAENGWRACH (Blaen-gwrach),
Neath Port Talbot (1466 ha; 1148 inhabitants)
Located north-east of **Resolven** on the left bank of the **Nedd**, the **community** contains remnants of a branch of the Neath **Canal**, built in 1817 to convey **coal** from Blaengwrach collieries. Venallt Ironworks, in operation from 1839 to 1854, was a pioneer venture in the smelting of **iron** using anthracite. A dissenting congregation, established at Blaengwrach in 1662, adopted **Unitarianism** in 1772; it ceased to exist in 1878.

BLAENHONDDAN, Neath Port Talbot
(2129 ha; 11,114 inhabitants)
Located on the right bank of the **Nedd**, the southern part of the **community**, from Bryncoch to Cadoxton, is essentially a suburb of **Neath**. It contains the scanty remains of Nidum, a **Roman** auxiliary fort occupied from the AD 70s until *c*.150. St Cattwg's church has a 13th-century tower. Aberdulais Falls, painted by **Turner** and others and owned by the **National Trust**, provided water power for significant industrial enterprises. Ulrich Frosse established a **copper**works there in 1584; the works were followed by a corn mill, an **iron**works and, from 1830, a **tinplate** works. Adjoining it is the Dulais Rock Hotel (1659), extensively refurbished in 2004. The fine early 18th-century mansions of Cadoxton Lodge and Ynysgerwyn have been demolished. George Tennant of Cadoxton Lodge built the Tennant **Canal** (1824), with its acqueduct and restored Aberdulais Basin. His family included Dorothy, wife of **H. M. Stanley**, and her sister-in-law **Winifred Coombe Tennant**.

BLAENLLYNFI *Cantref* and lordship
The *cantref* of Blaenllynfi – sometimes known as the *cantref* of **Talgarth** – constituted the eastern part of the kingdom of **Brycheiniog**. It consisted of the **commotes** of Crucywel, Talgarth and **Ystrad Yw** (or Tretŵr). In the late 11th century, it became part of the **lordship of Brecon**, but, in 1211, King John, in furtherance of his feud with the de **Breos family**, granted Blaenllynfi to Peter Fitz Herbert, son of **Bernard de Neufmarché**'s youngest granddaughter. It eventually passed to the **Mortimer family** and then to the crown. Its centre was Castell Blaenllynfi (*see* **Llanfihangel Cwmdu**) and it included the sublordships of Tretower and **Crickhowell**.

BLAENRHEIDOL, Ceredigion
(8948 ha; 493 inhabitants)
Constituting the north-easternmost part of **Ceredigion**, the **community** contains the summit of **Pumlumon** (752 m) and the Nant-y-moch and Dinas **reservoirs**. Ponterwyd, the birthplace of the **Celtic** scholar **John Rhŷs**, has a fine 18th-century bridge over the Rheidol. The **George Borrow** Hotel was renamed following Borrow's stay there in 1854. St John's church (1827), Ysbyty Cynfyn, which stands within a prehistoric stone circle, is located above the spectacular Parson's Bridge across the **Rheidol** gorge. Llywernog Museum records the history of **lead and silver** mining. Ystumtuen, once a flourishing miners' village, became a ghost-settlement, but was later reoccupied by incomers. Its **Wesleyan** chapel (1822, 1871) was built to accommodate 430 worshippers.

BLAWTA A BLONEGA
The custom of collecting flour (*blawd*) and fats (*bloneg*) from door to door on Shrove Tuesday for making pancakes. It was customary to sing a verse, and in some areas pancakes, rather than the ingredients, were requested.

BLEDDYN AP CYNFYN (d.1075)
King of Gwynedd and Powys
Acknowledged as king of **Gwynedd** and **Powys** in 1064 following the death of his half-brother **Gruffudd ap Llywelyn**, he submitted to Harold Godwinesson whose campaign had led to Gruffudd's untimely end. Bleddyn supported **Mercia**'s resistance to the **Normans** and resisted the first Norman incursions into north Wales. He was killed in 1075 by the men of Rhys ab Owain of **Deheubarth** during a campaign in **Ystrad Tywi**. Remembered as a generous, just and competent ruler, he was credited with amending Welsh **law**. He is considered to be the founder of one of the seven royal tribes of Wales; all subsequent rulers of Powys were descended from him.

BLEDDYN FARDD (fl.1240–90) Poet
The last of the major **poets of the Princes** of **Gwynedd**, Bleddyn was probably trained by **Dafydd Benfras**, his predecessor in the service of **Llywelyn ap Gruffudd**. Only the poems of his maturity have survived, all but two of them short elegies, notably to Llywelyn ap Gruffudd and his brother **Dafydd ap Gruffudd**. These poems are characterized by an economical style but are unusually personal, with the poet's anguish increasing from poem to poem.

BLEGYWRYD (fl.930–50) Archdeacon of Llandaff
By tradition, the scribe of the commission established by **Hywel Dda** to frame his **law** code. The law book called *Llyfr Blegywryd* (13th century) was long regarded as an account of the law current in south-west Wales, but is now considered to represent a stage intermediate between the more primitive *Llyfr Cyfnerth* (*see* **Cyfnerth ap Morgenau**) and the more advanced *Llyfr Iorwerth* (*see* **Iorwerth ap Madog**).

BLODEUWEDD
When, in the fourth branch of *Pedair Cainc y Mabinogi* (*see* **Mabinogion, The**), **Arianrhod** has placed a fate on her son, **Lleu or Llew Llaw Gyffes**, that he shall never have a human wife, the sorcerers Gwydion and **Math fab Mathonwy** conjure a wife for him, made from the flowers of meadow sweet, oak and broom, and named Blodeuwedd (Flower-face). But Blodeuwedd takes a lover, Gronw Pebr, and together they plot the death of Lleu. Near Bryn Cyfergyr by Cynfael stream in **Ardudwy**, Lleu is struck by Gronw's magic spear, but not killed. He is restored through Gwydion's care. Gronw is executed and Blodeuwedd turned into an owl as punishment.

BLUE SCAR (1949) Film
The committed socialist Jill Craigie and wife of Michael Foot directed this courageously didactic study of a socially aspiring miner (Emrys Jones) in a **coal**mining village (Abergwynfi, **Glyncorrwg**) whose inhabitants are preparing to realize their dream of nationalization of the mines – and

Nant-y-Moch reservoir at the valley head in Blaenrheidol

coming to terms with sometimes unpalatable realities. The tensions within the **film**'s central family are explored perceptively, with **Prysor Williams** as the dogged, resigned patriarch, and **Kenneth Griffith** splendidly sardonic as the left-wing, *Tribune*-reading armchair firebrand. The film is compromised by an unconvincing, romantic subplot, and leaden satire on **London**'s 'arty' scene.

BODDINGTON, Lewis (1907–94)
Aeronautical engineer
Lewis Boddington, who was head of the naval aircraft department at Farnborough, is remembered for the development of the angled flight deck on aircraft carriers, the most important advance in aircraft carrier design since the end of the **Second World War**. The United States navy was the first to use the angled flight deck, followed by the British navy. Born in Brithdir (**Darran Valley**) and educated at **Cardiff**, Boddington was involved in many other developments involving naval aircraft, including the steam catapult and the mirror landing sight.

BODEDERN, Isle of Anglesey
(1932 ha; 1074 inhabitants)
Located immediately east of **Valley**, the **community** contains Presaddfed chambered tomb – a capstone supported by four uprights. It adjoins the shallow Llyn Llywenan. Presaddfed is a handsome mansion (1686, 1821). **John Elias**'s marriage to the widow of Sir John **Bulkeley** of Presaddfed is the theme of **Saunders Lewis**'s play *Dwy Briodas Ann*. St Edern's church has a 14th-century nave. South of the compact village of Bodedern is the **Welsh-medium secondary school serving western Anglesey**.

BODELWYDDAN, Denbighshire
(1673 ha; 2016 inhabitants)
Located south-west of **Rhyl**, the **community**'s chief feature is the 65-m spire of its so-called 'Marble Church' (1856–60). Dedicated to St Margaret and financed by Margaret, daughter of John Williams of Bodelwyddan Castle, as a memorial to her husband, Lord Willoughby de Broke, it is Wales's most lavish estate church. The castle, a neo-classical remodelling (1800–08) of a house of 1600, was heavily castellated in the 1830s. It has been restored to its Victorian splendour and it houses part of the National Portrait Gallery's collection. Glan Clwyd Hospital, which serves mid-north Wales, was opened in 1978. Faenol Bach, Faenol Fawr and Pen Isa'r Glascoed are interesting 16th-century houses; Pengwern (*c.*1770) has massive Ionic pilasters.

BODFARI, Denbighshire (602 ha; 324 inhabitants)
Located north-east of **Denbigh**, the **community** is dominated by the strongly fortified Moel y Gaer **hill-fort**. The church, largely rebuilt in 1865, has a medieval tower. Pontruffydd Hall Farm, with its pointed windows and cupola, was referred to by **Thomas Pennant** as a '*ferme ornée*'. The theologian, **J. E. Daniel**, president of **Plaid Cymru** (1939–43), spent the last years of his life at Tŷ Gwyn.

BODFFORDD, Isle of Anglesey
(2530 ha; 959 inhabitants)
Located immediately north-west of **Llangefni**, the **community**'s main feature is Mona airfield, established for the RAF in 1942 on a site used by naval airships during the **First World War**. The **Anglesey** Agricultural Show (*Primin*

Môn) is held on the airfield. Within the community are Bodwrog church (14th century) and Heneglwys church (1845 but with a fragment of a 6th-century inscribed stone). Llyn Cefni, created in 1951 through the damming of River Cefni, was the first large **reservoir** to be built in Anglesey; it attracts a wide variety of **bird**life.

BODORGAN, Isle of Anglesey
(2607 ha; 900 inhabitants)

Located in south-western **Anglesey**, the **community**'s main feature is Bodorgan Mansion (late 18th century), the seat of the Meyrick family since the early 16th century. The Bodorgan estate (6880 ha in the late 19th century) was one of the best-run estates in Wales, a fact aided by the wealth the family enjoyed as the founders of Bournemouth. The village of Malltraeth overlooks the golden Malltraeth Sands. Nearby is the cob (1788–1812), built to drain the Malltraeth Marsh; the marsh's rich **bird**life inspired the artist **Charles Tunnicliffe**, who lived nearby. The coastal area is rich in **rabbit** warrens.

St **Cadwaladr**'s church (medieval, 1661) contains a 7th-century memorial to Cadfan, king of **Gwynedd** – *sapientissimus opinatissimus omnium regum* (the wisest and most renowned of all kings); the carver of the inscription was aware of the most recent fashion in lettering. Trefdraeth was the subject of a famous 18th-century **law**suit stemming from the appointment of Dr Thomas Bowles, a clergyman lacking a knowledge of **Welsh**, to serve as vicar to parishioners almost all of whom were monoglot Welsh.

BOHUN family Marcher-lords

The Bohun family first became associated with Wales when Humphrey Bohun married Margaret (d.1187), the heiress of **Caldicot**. Their great-great-grandson, Humphrey (d.1265), married Eleanor, co-heiress of William de **Breos** (d.1230), a marriage which brought the family the **lordship of Brecon**. Apart from the years 1265–77, when it was held by **Llywelyn ap Gruffudd**, the Bohuns were lords of Brecon until Mary, co-heiress of Humphrey (d.1373), married Henry Bolingbroke, later Henry IV. Humphrey, lord of Brecon from 1298 to 1321, commissioned much of what is now **Brecon** Cathedral. Caldicot passed to Mary's sister, Eleanor, wife of Thomas of Woodstock, earl of Buckingham (*see* **Stafford family**).

BONAPARTE, Louis-Lucien (1813–91)
Linguist and bibliophile

Prince Louis-Lucien was a nephew of Napoleon, who made his home in **London**. He learnt several European languages and was a pioneer in the study of Basque and of dialectology. Throughout the 1850s, his main interests lay in the **Celt**ic languages, **Welsh** in particular, and he did useful work on the mutations and the classification of dialects. He was primarily responsible for erecting a memorial to Dolly Pentreath, 'the last speaker of Cornish'. Welsh books in his remarkable library included **Gruffydd Robert**'s *Grammar* (1567) and the only extant copy of **Morys Clynnog**'s *Athravaeth Gristnogavl* (1568). The collection was sold to the Newberry Library, Chicago.

BONCATH, Pembrokeshire
(2348 ha; 744 inhabitants)

Located astride the **Cardigan**–**Tenby road** (the A478), 4 km south of the **Teifi**, the **community** is dominated by the hill Y Frenni Fawr (395 m), which is often considered to be the heart of **Welsh**-speaking **Pembrokeshire**. St Michael's, Llanfihangel Penfedw, retains some of its medieval fabric; St Colman's, Capel Colman, does not. Blaenffos was an early **Baptist** centre. Cilrhue farmhouse (17th century), approached by a fine beech avenue, was once the seat of the Lloyd family of Bronwydd (*see* **Troedyraur**). Cilwendeg, originally 18th century, received 19th-century embellishments including conservatories, a grotto and twin lodges, financed by the profits its owner, Morgan Jones, received from the **lighthouse** on the Skerries (**Cylch-y-garn**). Boncath village grew in the wake of the opening of the **Whitland**–Cardigan **railway** in 1885. Within the community are three abandoned churches.

BONTNEWYDD (Y Bontnewydd), Gwynedd
(1005 ha; 1165 inhabitants)

Located immediately south of **Caernarfon** and embracing the lower reaches of the basin of the Gwyrfai, the **community** contains the villages of Bontnewydd and Llanfaglan. Dinas Dinoethwy is an impressive **Iron Age** fort; adjoining it is Plas Dinas, the one-time home of the Armstrong-Jones family. The medieval church of St Faglan, located above Y Foryd, escaped the attentions of Victorian restorers. Y Foryd, the estuary of the Gwyrfai, which at high tide forms an inland sea, is rich in sea**birds**. Cartref Bontnewydd was formerly an orphanage maintained by the Presbyterian Church of Wales. Nearby is the home of opera singer Bryn Terfel.

BOOK OF ANEIRIN, The

A small manuscript dating from the second half of the 13th century, containing the only medieval copy of the poem ascribed to **Aneirin** (fl. 6th century), *Y Gododdin*. The text is incomplete and includes two independent versions written by two contemporary scribes. Hand B's version seems to have been copied from an exemplar in Old **Welsh**, while the orthography and language of Hand A's version is later. The manuscript is kept in **Cardiff** Central Library. (*See also* **Literature**.)

BOOK OF COMMON PRAYER, The

The 1552 version of the **English** Prayer Book was translated into **Welsh** by **William Salesbury** in 1567, in accordance with the Act for the Translation of the **Bible** into Welsh (1563). In 1599, **William Morgan** published a new edition with biblical texts in accordance with his translation of the Bible. Following his revision of the Welsh Bible in 1620, **John Davies** (*c.*1567–1644) published another version of the Welsh Prayer Book in 1621. Use of the Prayer Book was abolished by the Long Parliament in 1645 but was reinstated by the Act of Uniformity (1662). Nineteen editions of the Welsh Prayer Book appeared between 1660 and 1730, including the revised edition (1664) and editions by **Stephen Hughes** (1678) and the **Society for the Promotion of Christian Knowledge** (1709). A revised version of the Prayer Book was adopted by the **Church in Wales** in the 1960s.

BOOK OF ST CHAD, The

Also known as *The Book of St Teilo* and *The Lichfield Gospels*, *The Book of St Chad* is an illuminated **Latin** manuscript containing texts of the Gospels of St Matthew and St Mark and part of that of St Luke. Thought to have been written in the first part of the 8th century, it may have been kept at **Llandeilo Fawr**, but by the end of the 10th century it was in the library of the cathedral of St Mary and St Chad at Lichfield, Staffordshire, where it remains; an exhibition there explains its significance. The manuscript includes a short entry known as the *Surexit Memorandum*; some 64 words in all, written mainly in Old **Welsh** on a legal matter, it is generally considered to be the earliest extant writing in the language.

BOOK OF TALIESIN, The

A manuscript containing a collection of poems attributed to **Taliesin** (fl. 6th century) and also poetry connected with the poet's persona. Most of the poems are the work of anonymous poets, but it is possible that the historical Taliesin was the author of some of them. A copy of a lost original, the manuscript was made by an unnamed scribe early in the 14th century in a scriptorium somewhere in the south-east. It forms part of the Peniarth Collection at the **National Library**.

BOOK OF THE ANCHORITE, The

A manuscript containing the earliest and most extensive collection of religious texts in **Welsh**. Its writer notes that it was compiled in 1346 at the request of Gruffudd ap Llywelyn ap Phylip, a gentleman of Rhydodyn, **Talyllychau**. It appears that the role of the accomplished scribe – of **Llanddewi Brefi** – who gave his name to the manuscript was to transcribe and abbreviate texts which already existed in Welsh. The manuscript is kept in the Bodleian Library, **Oxford**. It includes a life of St **David**.

BOON, Ronnie (Ronald Winston Boon; 1909–98)
Rugby player

A self-confident **rugby** player and track athlete, **Barry**-born Boon scored all Wales's points with a try and drop goal in their first ever win at Twickenham in 1933. A wing-three-quarter, he won 12 caps between 1930 and 1933, and scored a try for **Cardiff** against the 1931 Springboks.

BORDER, The

From almost 1000 years ago, the Welsh–English border was zonal rather than linear, except between **Monmouth** and **Chepstow**, where, by the late 7th century, the **Wye** seems to have been accepted as a fixed boundary. **Offa's Dyke** was presumably intended to mark a distinct line, but that intention was thwarted by **Gruffudd ap Llywelyn** who regained for Wales extensive lands beyond the dyke. The creation of the **March** emphasized the border's zonal nature, particularly as border lords withdrew their lands from the English **county** system and converted them into quasi-independent territories. The **Edwardian conquest** did not give Wales a linear border, except in the north-east where the conquest resulted in the definition of the boundaries of **Flintshire**.

The complete linear border came into being through the **Act of 'Union'** of 1536. Extending from the mouth of the **Dee** to the mouth of the **Wye**, its length as the crow flies is 200 km, although, with its many twists and turns, its actual length is twice that. The principles underlying its delineation are unclear. It did not follow the boundaries of the Welsh **dioceses**; **England** retained a number of **parishes** in the diocese of **St Asaph**; **Presteigne** was to be in Wales, although it was, and still is, in the diocese of Hereford. It did not follow the border of the March, for several marcher-lordships were annexed by **Shropshire** and **Herefordshire**, and others – those of **Ewyas** Lacy and **Montgomery** among them – were divided between England and Wales. It did not follow the linguistic boundary – Wales retained **English**-speaking **Maelor Saesneg** while England retained the areas inhabited by the **Welsh**-speakers of **Erging** and of the vicinity of Oswestry. Perhaps the delineation had no underlying principles, for, as the purpose of the 1536 Act was to incorporate Wales within England, the location of the border was irrelevant to the purposes of its framers.

Even after it had been linearly defined, awareness of the border was slight, at least until the **Welsh Sunday Closing Act** of 1881. In 1961, however, when most border counties voted for Sunday opening, that distinction ceased to be significant. Indeed, in the central borderlands where places in England feel Welsh and where places in Wales feel English, the border still seems to be zonal rather than linear. Nevertheless, as the **National Assembly** implements policies that differ from those in operation in England, a consciousness of where Wales stops and England begins is likely to grow – although there are those who regret that Wales has a border at all. As **Harri Webb** put it: 'What Wales needs, and has always lacked most/ Is, instead of an eastern boundary, an East Coast.'

BOROUGHS

As they were formally constituted urban settlements, the earliest boroughs of Wales can be considered to be the *civitas* capitals of Venta Silurum (*see* **Caerwent**) and Moridunum (*see* **Carmarthen**). Wales's independent kingdoms undoubtedly contained urban settlements, but as there is no evidence they had been formally established, borough creation in early medieval Wales was initiated by the **Norman** invaders. **William Fitz Osbern**, earl of Hereford, founded boroughs at **Monmouth** and **Chepstow**, granting their burgesses the rights of those of Hereford, which were in turn based upon those of Breteuil, Fitz Osbern's original home near Amiens. Indeed, in terms of burgesses' rights, most Welsh boroughs would be daughters of Hereford and granddaughters of Breteuil. With the establishment of **Bala** in 1309 – the last of Wales's medieval towns to be founded – Wales had about 80 urban settlements with claims to borough status. Although the best known of Wales's medieval boroughs are those founded in the wake of the **Edwardian conquest** – in particular **Conwy** and **Caernarfon** – the largest were the **port** boroughs of the south, with **Cardiff** in the 1280s having 421 burgages or urban plots, and **Haverfordwest** 360, compared with 112 in Conwy and 70 in Caernarfon.

Assuming that each burgage housed five people, Cardiff, with over 2000 inhabitants, was 13th-century Wales's largest borough. Its **population**, like that of most other Welsh boroughs, declined sharply in the adverse circumstances of the later Middle Ages. The granting of **parliamentary representation** to Wales in 1536 led to the recognition of 55 of the country's boroughs; they were the towns which elected borough MPs, as single boroughs in the case of **Brecon** and Carmarthen, and as groups of contributory boroughs in the case of the boroughs of the other Welsh **counties** – apart from **Merioneth** which was deemed not to contain a borough worthy of representation. Haverfordwest was singled out, not only by being granted its own MP, but also by being raised to the status of a county.

Between the 16th and 19th centuries, some of the boroughs of Wales grew substantially, with Carmarthen, which had about 4000 inhabitants by 1770, in the lead for most of the period. Others decayed, and those established solely for military reasons became depopulated when their strongholds ceased to be garrisoned; thus Wales contains a number of extinct boroughs, among them Cefnllys (*see* **Penybont**) and Dryslwyn (*see* **Llangathen**). Urban centres with no claims to borough status came into being; of these **Wrexham**, which in the late 17th century briefly overtook Carmarthen as Wales's largest town, was initially the most significant.

The Municipal Corporations Act of 1835 recognized 20 Welsh towns as boroughs, with the right to have a mayor and a corporation elected by the male ratepayers. They all had medieval roots and varied from tiny settlements such as **Llanfyllin** and **Lampeter** to dynamic centres such as Cardiff, **Swansea** and **Newport** – the three Welsh towns which attained **county borough** status following the Local Government Act of 1888. Other urban centres later attained borough status, among them Wrexham, **Rhondda**, **Barry** and **Merthyr Tydfil** (Merthyr became a county borough in 1908). The rest of the towns of Wales had to be content with the status of **urban district**. In 1974, when they were all abolished, Wales had 32 boroughs and 4 county boroughs.

BORROW, George (1803–81) Writer

Norfolk-born George Borrow earned a living from hackwork in which he was able to use his extraordinary talent for languages; he claimed to have learned **Welsh** from a stable-lad in Norwich when still a boy. His book *Wild Wales* (1862), perhaps the most famous of its genre, is an account of an 1854 walking tour. Its unique charm lies in the author's enthusiasm for the language, antiquities and topography of Wales, which sometimes betrays an almost comic reverence, and in his forthright opinions of the people and places he encounters along the way. He was reasonably fluent in Welsh and, although taken for a southerner in the north and a northerner in the south, he insisted on speaking the language at every opportunity. It was the wild scenery and literary associations of north Wales that appealed to him most; the industrial south appalled him. Fond of his **beer**, of robust build and not averse to fisticuffs when in a tight corner, this staunch churchman nevertheless found much to praise in the character of the **Nonconformist** Welsh.

BORTH (Y Borth), Ceredigion
(750 ha; 1523 inhabitants)
Constituting the north-westernmost part of **Ceredigion**, the **community** is squeezed between the sea and the River Leri.

(The Leri's rectilinearity is the result of its canalization in 1863 by the builders of the Cambrian **Railway**.) A former **fish**ing village, its superb beach enabled Borth to become a holiday resort, dependent in the main upon caravanners. It sits precariously on a huge bank of pebbles behind which developed **Cors Fochno**, the largest sea-level **peat** bog in **Britain**. Storms frequently expose the remains of an ancient drowned forest. Ynyslas, part of the Dyfi National Nature Reserve, is a large complex of sand dunes on the **Dyfi** estuary. A ferry formerly carried travellers to **Aberdovey**; in the 1930s, guidebooks informed visitors that 'a loud halloo will bring the boatman'.

BOSWORTH, Battle of

Henry **Tudor**, with an army of some 4000 Frenchmen and Lancastrian supporters, landed at **Dale** on the **Milford Haven Waterway** on 7 August 1485. Supporters gathered slowly as he advanced through Wales, prominent among them **Rhys ap Thomas** and a contingent from **Ystrad Tywi**. On 22 August 1485, Henry – who took the **Red Dragon** of **Cadwaladr** as his banner – defeated the forces of Richard III at Bosworth in Leicestershire. It is estimated that one-third of his soldiers were Welsh. He was crowned on the battlefield and his victory was seen as fulfilment of the prophecy that a Welshman would sit on the throne of **Britain**.

BOTWNNOG, Gwynedd
(3426 ha; 955 inhabitants)
Consisting of a wide swathe of the western part of the **Llŷn** Peninsula, the **community** contains the villages of Botwnnog, Bryncroes, Bryn-mawr, Pen-y-groeslon and Mellteyrn. There was a **Neolithic** axe factory on Mynydd Rhiw. Mellteyrn-born Henry Rowlands (1551–1616), bishop of **Bangor**, bequeathed money to establish a grammar school at Botwnnog. In the 1890s, the school was absorbed into Wales's system of intermediate schools. The schoolroom was drawn in 1774 by **Moses Griffith**, illustrator of **Thomas Pennant**'s *Tours*, who was born at Trygarn, near Bryncroes. The early 19th-century mansion of Nanhoron contains an elegant stair and hall. It featured in Anthony Hopkins's film *August* (1995). St Gwynnin's church, Llanegwning (1840), is a charming toy-like structure; Gruffudd Parry (*see* **Thomas Parry**) delighted in its pepper-pot tower. Safety concerns have caused St Peter ad Vincula (1846), Mellteyrn, a much-praised neo-Gothic church, to be partially demolished. The closure of the primary school at Bryncroes created much controversy in the 1960s.

BOUDICCA (Buddug; fl. 1st century) Heroine

Queen of the Iceni, a tribe living south of the Wash, Boudicca led a rebellion in AD 60 which posed a serious threat to the power of Rome. The rebellion was suppressed, Boudicca committed suicide, and the lands of the Iceni were laid waste. A statue in **Cardiff** City Hall's gallery of Welsh heroes commemorates her – an interesting example of the notion that all pre-**Roman** inhabitants of **Britain** were, somehow, Welsh, or perhaps an admission that no one could conjure up a genuine Welsh heroine. Welsh royalists of the 19th century hailed Queen Victoria as *Buddug* (victorious).

BOWEN, David [Lloyd] (1928–90)
Footballer and manager

Born at Nantyffyllon (**Maesteg**), Dave Bowen played **rugby** for Maesteg Grammar School before the family moved to Northampton. Throughout the 1950s, he was a forceful half-back for Arsenal. On returning to Northampton as player-manager, he needed only six years to take them from the Fourth to the First Division. He won 19 caps, captained Wales in the 1958 World Cup and was part-time manager of Wales from 1964 to 1974.

BOWEN, Edward [George] (1911–91)
Radio scientist

Edward 'Taffy' Bowen, FRS, the inventor of airborne radar, was a native of **Swansea**, and from the age of 12 had an 'obsessive interest in radio'. After graduating at Swansea, he completed his PhD in **London**, supervised by Edward Appleton, and then started work, under Watson Watt, on the development of radar. In 1936, he successfully mounted a radar transmitter and receiver on a Handley Page Heyford aircraft – and this constituted the first airborne radar. In 1940, he was entrusted with taking to the United States one of the earliest resonant magnetrons (the compact radar transmitter that 'won the war in Europe'). After the war, as head of the Council for Scientific and Industrial Research in **Australia**, he was responsible for the construction of the Parkes radio telescope – still the largest radio telescope in the southern hemisphere.

In 1930, when 19, Bowen – a member of **Plaid [Genedlaethol] Cymru** – demolished the BBC's argument that it was technically impossible to secure for Wales a wavelength separate from that for the west of **England**. This led directly to the establishment of the Welsh Home Service (*see* **Broadcasting**). The BBC archives at Caversham contain a file on Bowen, whom John Reith considered to be 'a bumptious young man'.

BOWEN, E[mrys] G[eorge] (1900–1983)
Geographer

'EGB', as he was generally known, was a native of **Carmarthen**. After graduating in **geography** at **Aberystwyth**, he became a lecturer there in 1929 and Gregynog professor of geography and anthropology in 1946. His early work was on physical anthropology, but he turned to the study of rural settlements, especially those that developed around the cells of the **Celtic saints**. His work is epitomized by three books: *The Settlements of the Celtic Saints in Wales* (1954), *Saints, Seaways and Settlements* (1969) and *Britain and the Western Seaways* (1972). Renowned throughout Wales as a superb lecturer and an inspiring teacher, Bowen – wrote his obituarist in *The Times* – 'was quintessentially Welsh. Short and dark, dressed in bible black from shoes to hat, he was as distinctive as he was distinguished.'

BOWEN, Euros (1904–88) Poet

Born at Treorchy, **Rhondda**, Euros Bowen spent much of his life as rector in **Llangywer** and **Llanuwchllyn** in **Merioneth**. He won the crown at the National **Eisteddfod** for 'O'r Dwyrain' in 1948 and again in 1950 for 'Difodiant', but he failed to win the chair in 1963 with his

Boudicca and her daughters, Cardiff City Hall

strict-metre poem 'Genesis', because of its alleged obscurity. From his first volume *Cerddi* (1957) onwards, he was restlessly exploratory, experimenting with *cynghanedd* and the strict metres, and writing free verse, typographic poems and prose poems. He considered poetry a means of conveying thought through imagery rather than as a form of conventional communication. His basic subject was creativity – in nature or in art.

BOWLS

The ancient game of bowls probably came to **Britain** with the **Romans**; in the mid-16th century, the concept of the 'biased' ball was introduced, causing the ball to take a curving path towards its target. It was at the Park Hotel, **Cardiff**, in 1905, that the International Bowling Board was formed. A popular sport for men and **women** of all ages, the modern game takes various forms and has about 20,000 registered players in Wales.

Outdoor flat-green bowling, which is controlled by the Welsh Flat-Green Bowling Association, founded in 1904, has produced two world champions from Wales, Maldwyn Evans from the **Rhondda** (1972) and Janet Ackland from **Penarth** (1988). Indoor flat-green bowling, whose controlling association was formed in 1934, boasts three Welsh world champions: Terry Sullivan of **Swansea** (1985), John Price of **Aberavon** (1990), who has been Welsh indoor champion on eight occasions, and Robert Weale of **Llandrindod** (2000), in addition to one British champion, Betty Phillips of **Colwyn Bay** (2006). The Association has 10 affiliated counties and 290 affiliated clubs throughout Wales.

Outdoor crown green bowling, where the green rises to a 50-cm crown, thereby adding to the unpredictability of the bowl's trajectory, is confined to the north and parts of mid-Wales. Wales has produced three British champions: Cliff Littlehales of **Wrexham** (1958), Eric Ashton of **Abergele** (1959) and Jack Hunt of Soughton (**Northop**) (1975).

Until 1961, indoor bowling in Wales was seriously handicapped by the absence of full-size greens; it also had to contend with the rising popularity of tenpin bowling. Short-mat bowling is still played in small, sub-length halls, where carpets are put down and rolled up after games.

BOXING

The urge of men – especially men – to fight is age-old, and the Welsh experience does not disappoint or edify. While it is rightly identified with the industrial **communities** of the southern **coal**field, fighting was also a common enough pastime in pre-industrial Wales, patronized, as it would be again in a later age, by the **gentry**. In the 18th century, it felt the impact of commercial influences, as gentlemen promoters and publicans organized championship matches that attracted wide support, constant lubrication and heavy betting. The renowned Daniel Mendoza's visit to **Swansea** in the 1790s, and the exhibition bouts staged in south Wales by Tom Cribb and Tom Spring in 1819 stimulated the ambitions of an abundant indigenous talent.

In the industrial settlements of upland **Glamorgan**, bare-knuckle fighting drew large crowds and the laying of wagers. The arrival of the Taff Vale **Railway** in **Merthyr Tydfil** in 1840 was celebrated by a titanic contest between 'Shoni Sguborfawr' (John Jones), emperor of Merthyr's notorious 'China' and later a **Rebecca Riots** activist, and John Nash, champion of Cyfarthfa. The Queensberry Rules (1867), designed as part of the Victorian civilizing project to control and systematize prizefighting, were drafted under the patronage of the Marquess of Queensberry by a Welshman, **J. G. Chambers**, but it took several decades for the insistent urge for direct and physical confrontation to submit entirely to international rules and regulations. Until the early years of the 20th century, all the southern coalfield settlements had their 'bloody spots' on the mountainside above, where early-morning contests took place out of sight of the authorities, eagerly watched by hundreds. A scale of weights and titles evolved, and championship boxing became one of the agencies by which these working-**class** communities found local heroes

Super middleweight Joe Calzaghe

and articulated their collective identity. This was amply demonstrated in the valleys to the north of **Pontypridd**, which produced more champions in the first third of the 20th century than any other area of comparable size in the world: Tom Thomas (Penygraig), Percy Jones (Porth), **Jimmy Wilde** (Tylorstown) – all three from the **Rhondda** – as well as **Freddie Welsh** and 'the fighting Moody brothers' of Pontypridd, fought in the Welsh style of upright stance and sudden flurries of two-fisted attack. All proceeded via the pit, the fairground booths of the notorious 'Black Jack' Scarrott, and the tutorship of fistic 'professors' such as Frank Gess and Harry Cullis, to Welsh, British, European and even world titles. Not that the coalfield had a monopoly: 'Peerless **Jim**' **Driscoll** was the idol of **Cardiff** – of its **Irish** community especially. Boxing was as integral a part of the regional culture as were the other spectator sports of **rugby** and soccer (*see* **Football**). Like them, it attracted by its spontaneity and unpredictability; but it added also the elemental ingredient of danger, and working-class followers particularly appreciated the ornamentation of raw courage by stylistic insolence and the reckless gesture.

Just as an economically buoyant coalfield produced a fistful of champions down to the early 1920s, the subsequent years of slump and **depression** had a reverse effect. The tradition, however, remained as vital as ever, and was upheld in the 1930s by two major heavyweights, **Jack Petersen** of Cardiff and Tonypandy's **Tommy Farr**. In going the full 15 rounds with Joe Louis in New York 1937, Farr became the fighting symbol of his society, buffeted and battered but unyielding, heroic in defeat. In the post-1945 period, Ronnie James (**Pontardawe**), Dai Dower (**Abercynon**), Brian Curvis (Swansea) and Colin Jones (**Gorseinon**) were all worthy but unsuccessful major title contenders, while Cardiff's Steve Robinson briefly held a world featherweight title between 1993 and 1995. A proliferation of governing bodies tended to devalue individual championships, but a return to former glories was signalled when, in 2006, unified titles were triumphantly seized by **Newbridge**'s rugged southpaw Joe Calzaghe (super middleweight) and the formidable Enzo Maccarinelli of Swansea (cruiserweight) to become undisputed world champions.

Though improved material conditions have made for less hungry fighters, boxing continues to exert its appeal to the Welsh, especially in those older industrial areas of limited economic opportunity like the southern **coalfield**. There are still more licensed boxers relative to the population in the former **Glamorgan** than in any other part of **Britain**. Undoubtedly it is Merthyr Tydfil, Wales's first industrial town, that can lay claim to Wales's richest boxing tradition, celebrated in prose, verse and **sculpture**, and personified in the careers of **Eddie Thomas**, world featherweight champion, **Howard Winstone** and fated title contender **Johnny Owen**, proud and supremely skilful exponents of 'the sweet science' who brought to this most elemental, ritualistic and dehumanizing of sporting recreations humility, humanity, courage and tragedy.

BOY SOLDIER (*Milwr Bychan*; 1986) Film

Karl Francis's emotive screen **drama** centres on a **Welsh**-speaking youth from the southern **coal**field serving with the British army in Northern **Ireland**. A teenager, Wil

A hand-tinted photograph of the Cyfarthfa Band, *c.*1855

(Richard Lynch) becomes a political scapegoat after a local man's death during a patrol. Francis suggests that the soldier has greater affinities with the **Celts** in **Ireland** than with his fellow soldiers from **England**, who demean his language and condone the brutality he suffers in military prison. The film's uncompromising treatment of institutionalized violence aroused controversy in the press.

BRACE, William (1865–1947) Trade unionist
Born at **Risca**, he was an early advocate of one union for all British colliers, an issue on which he clashed with **William Abraham** (Mabon). In 1898, he became the first vice-president of the **South Wales Miners' Federation**, taking over as president from 1912 to 1915. Elected in 1906 as a Lib-Lab MP, in essence that was what he remained while representing South **Glamorgan** (1906–18) and **Abertillery** (1918–20). His industrial expertise was reflected in his journalism and in his work as under-secretary at the Home Office (1915–19) and chief labour adviser to the Ministry of Mines (1920).

BRADNEY, Joseph Alfred (1859–1933) Historian
An Englishman who served as a county councillor and a justice of the peace in **Monmouthshire**, Bradney was actively involved with the **National Library**, **National Museum** and **Royal Commission on the Ancient [and Historical] Monuments of Wales**. He learned **Welsh**, wrote widely on local topics, and is best remembered for his multi-volume *History of Monmouthshire* (1904–33, 1998). He was knighted in 1924.

BRANGWYN, Frank (1867–1956) Painter
Born in Bruges, Belgium, of Welsh parents, Brangwyn is best known in Wales for his murals celebrating the British Empire at the Brangwyn Hall in **Swansea**. Commissioned in 1925 and intended for the House of Lords, they were offered to Swansea after their controversial rejection in **London**. Brangwyn, who began his career in the workshops of William Morris, painted with a gusto and bravura that placed his work beyond the approval of modernist arbiters. His work is in a number of British and Welsh collections, including those of the Glynn Vivian and the **National Museum**, and he executed murals in London, mainland Europe and **North America**. There are museums dedicated to his work at Orange in France and in Bruges.

BRANWEN FERCH LLŶR
The story of Branwen, daughter of Llŷr, in the second branch of the Mabinogi (*see Mabinogion, The*), relates that by consent of her brother **Bendigeidfran**, king of the Isle of the Mighty, she is given in marriage to Matholwch, king of **Ireland**. But during the wedding festivities **Efnysien** mutilates Matholwch's **horses** and the **Irish** turn against Branwen. Driven from the royal court to work in the kitchen, she befriends a starling, and sends it across the sea with tidings of her distress. Bendigeidfran and his army cross to Ireland and fierce fighting follows. Many are killed, including Gwern, the young son of Branwen and Matholwch. Branwen dies of a broken heart and is buried at Glan Alaw (*see* **Tref Alaw**) in **Anglesey**.

BRASS BANDS
From the mid-19th century onwards, brass bands became an important feature of **Britain**'s musical culture, partly because of the invention of the piston valve and its use from the 1820s onwards in the manufacture of brass instruments. The bands were at their most popular among members of the working **class** in industrial areas, particularly in those areas where there were paternalistic employers eager to promote **music** making as a constructive activity among the 'lower orders'.

The New Orleans-style opening parade at the Brecon Jazz Festival

There are claims that the first brass band to be established in Britain was that formed in 1832 at 'Pontybederyn' in **Blaenau Gwent**, but as there is no place with such a name, the basis of the claims is flimsy. The best known of Wales's early bands was the **Cyfarthfa Band** (1838), a photograph of whose members (*c.*1855) appears to be the earliest photograph of a brass band. The earliest band in the north-east was almost certainly that at **Buckley**, and, from the late 1830s onwards, bands were established in the **slate-**quarrying areas of **Gwynedd**. The claim that there was one at **Llanrug** by 1834 is contestable, but there is firm evidence that there was a band at Deiniolen (originally Ebenezer; *see* **Llanddeiniolen**) by 1835.

Initially, relations between the bands and the **Nonconformist** chapels were not entirely cordial. Many band members were enthusiastic **beer** drinkers, and *Yr Herald Cymraeg* claimed in 1862 that 'instrumental music is nothing more than a way for men to indulge in their sinful passions'. However, by the late 19th century, bands had become more respectable, with a number of them becoming involved in the promotion of **temperance**. For example, the Tongwynlais Temperance Band (*see* **Cardiff**), which still exists, was founded in 1888, and the **Cory Band**, founded in 1880, began as a temperance band. In addition, bands became closely involved with the processions of the Labour movement. For the bands of Gwynedd, the highlights of the year were the Labour festivals in places such as Bethesda, Blaenau **Ffestiniog** and **Caernarfon**.

One of the most memorable images relating to the recent history of Wales was that of the miners of Maerdy (*see* **Rhondda**) marching behind the village band as they returned to their pit following the miners' strike of 1984–5. Band culture contained a strong competitive element. From its beginnings in the 1860s, the National **Eisteddfod** featured brass bands. The Cyfarthfa Band was successful in the Crystal Palace competitions (1860–3), but in the British Open Championship (1853–) and the National Championship (1900–), Welsh bands had long to wait before they were able successfully to challenge the best of the bands of northern **England**. However, from the 1970s onwards, the Cory Band – called the Buy as You View Band, 2000–7 – won increasing fame; by the early 21st century, it was considered one of the finest bands in the world.

BRAWDY (Breudeth), Pembrokeshire
(3505 ha; 611 inhabitants)

Located at the point where the coast of St Bride's Bay turns westwards, the **community** contains superb cliffs, accessible from the seaside village of Newgale. In St **David**'s church (originally 12th century) there are four 6th-century inscribed stones. Pointz Castle is a late 12th-century motte. Trefgarn Owen has one of Wales's earliest **Congregationalist** causes (1686). The community is dominated by an airfield. The one-time centre of **Pembrokeshire**'s air-sea rescue service, it was the scene of protests during its use as an American spy centre; since 1995, it has served as an army barracks. Llandeloy is the subject of a delightful essay by **R. T. Jenkins**. St Eloi's church was rebuilt in 1927 in the Arts and Crafts tradition.

BRECON, Lordship of (Arglwyddiaeth Brycheiniog)

Brecon, centred on the **Usk** and Llynfi valleys, was one of Wales's **march**er-lordships. Its first **Norman** lord was **Bernard de Neufmarché**, who built his principal castle at **Brecon**. On Bernard's death *c.*1125, the lordship passed to his son-in-law, Milo of Gloucester. Philip de **Breos**, lord of **Builth**, subsequently acquired Brecon by right of his wife Bertha, Milo's daughter. In 1211, the eastern part of Brecon was detached, becoming the lordship of **Blaenllynfi**. In 1230, Brecon passed to Humphrey **de Bohun**, husband of Elinor de Breos. In 1262, **Llywelyn ap Gruffudd** captured the lordship, and his rights were recognized in the **Treaty of Montgomery** (1267). By *c.*1275, however, Humphrey de Bohun had regained possession. In 1373, the lordship passed to the future Henry IV, husband of Mary de Bohun. It later came into the possession of the **Stafford family**, who remained in possession until 1521, when Henry VIII ordered the execution of Thomas Stafford, duke of Buckingham, whereupon the lordship escheated to the crown.

BRECON (Aberhonddu), Breconshire, Powys
(1109 ha; 7901 inhabitants)

When **Bernard de Neufmarché** (commemorated in Newmarch Street, Llanfaes) established himself as lord of **Brycheiniog**, he chose as the strongpoint of his new lordship (*see* **Brecon, Lordship of**) the high ground at the confluence of the Honddu and the **Usk**. A motte-and-bailey castle was built in 1093 and there were later additions – the

Ely Tower in the 12th century and further fortifications in the 13th century; little now remains. Bernard established a **Benedictine** priory, with a church dedicated to St John the Evangelist. Begun in the 1090s, the existing church dates from the 13th and 14th centuries, and the surviving conventual buildings from the 14th and 15th centuries. At the **dissolution of the monasteries**, the priory came into the possession of Sir **John Price**. In 1923, St John's – undeniably the finest church in mid-Wales – became the cathedral of the **Anglican diocese** of **Swansea** and Brecon.

The town of Brecon developed to the south of the castle and the priory. The present layout of the **community** dates from the second half of the 13th century. A relic of Tudor times survives in Buckingham Place, more recently the home of **Gwenllian Morgan**, enthusiast for **Henry Vaughan** and Wales's first woman mayor (1910–11). The town walls, with their five gates, were demolished during the **Civil Wars**. Brecon became a **county** town following the **Act of 'Union'** and was at its most prosperous in the 18th and early 19th centuries. This is reflected in the fact that Brecon has more fine buildings of that period than any other town in Wales. The administrative centre of a flourishing agricultural district, this was the Brecon where **Howel Harris** attended the meetings of the Breconshire **Agricultural Society**, the first such society in Wales. Near the society's meeting-place in Lion Street, lived **Breconshire**'s historian, **Theophilus Jones**. Also in Lion Street is the Memorial church of Thomas Coke (1747–1814), the Wesleyan bishop. Theatrical companies came regularly to perform in the town, and during one such visit (1775) **Sarah Siddons** was born at the Shoulder of Mutton Inn in High Street. In 1823, **Thomas Price** (Carnhuanawc) established Cymdeithas **Cymreigyddion** Aberhonddu. Seventh in size of the towns of Wales in 1821, Brecon was served by the Old Bank, which played a role in financing the development of the south Wales **coal**field. In 1843, the town was endowed with a massive Greek-revival Shire Hall; it is now the Brecknock Museum.

Brecon was a major communications centre, with the Watton the starting point for tramroads and the Brecon and **Abergavenny Canal**. Later, Brecon was to have access to **railways** going in four directions. The railways have gone, but the canal remains, its basin refurbished and now graced by Theatr Brycheiniog. The town has a military tradition; Dering Lines, long the headquarters of the **South Wales Borderers**, is now associated with the **Royal Regiment of Wales**.

A highly successful jazz (*see* **Music**) festival, Brecon Jazz, has been held each August since 1983 and is now the biggest jazz festival in **Britain**, enjoying a worldwide reputation for presenting international stars alongside Welsh talent.

Llanfaes, to the west of the town and the best place to live (*gorau lle i fyw*), according to the poet Ieuan ap Huw Cae Llwyd, has been swallowed up by Brecon. It boasts the attractive buildings of Christ College, founded in 1541 on the site of the former Dominican friary, and Newton, built in 1582 for John Games, high sheriff of Breconshire and descendant of Sir **Dafydd Gam**. In 1975, the Brecon jail in Llanfaes (1858) was adapted as flats by the distinguished architects **Colwyn Foulkes** and Partners, the **Colwyn Bay**-based company.

BRECON BEACONS, The (Bannau Brycheiniog)
Mountains

The Brecon Beacons, Wales's highest **mountain** range south of **Cadair Idris**, rise to 886 m at Pen y Fan (**Glyn Tarell/Llanfrynach**). The upper reaches of the parallel valleys of

The Brecon Beacons

the Tarell, Llwch, Sere, Cynwyn and Oergwm, tributaries of the **Usk**, cut through its Old Red Sandstone escarpments. On the gullies of the north-facing slopes are alpine-arctic **plants** such as purple saxifrage and spring sandwort. At the head of Glyn Tarell lies the one-time Craig y Fro quarry noted for its fossil plants – among them is *cooksonia*, **Britain**'s oldest vascular land-plant.

North-west of Pen y Fan is a fine example of a glacial morraine which holds back the waters of Llyn Cwm Llwch. Pen y Fan and the adjoining Corn Du (873 m) are crowned with **Bronze Age** cairns. The easiest, most popular, but least interesting, route to Pen y Fan starts at Pont ar Daf (Glyn Tarell). It is located on the **A470** immediately north of the Beacons **reservoir**, one of eight reservoirs constructed within the mountain range. The range, which is extensively used for army exercises, is the core of the Brecon Beacons **National Park**, designated in 1957. The Park also includes the **Black Mountain**, Fforest Fawr, **Mynydd Llangatwg** and the **Black Mountains**. Between 1808 and 1814, 15,000 ha of Fforest Fawr were unprofitably enclosed. (*see* **Enclosures**). In 2005, the range was designated – as Fforest Fawr – one of Europe's 24 Geoparks, on the basis of its geological distinction; the designation entitles it to environmental protection from UNESCO.

BRECONSHIRE (Sir Frycheiniog) One-time county

The **Act of 'Union'** of 1536 declared that 'Brecknock, **Crickhowell**, Tretower, Pencelli, English **Talgarth**, Welsh Talgarth, Dinas, Glynbwch, **Cantref Selyf**, **Llanddew**,

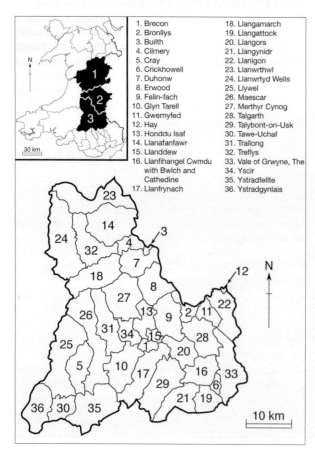

1. Brecon	18. Llangamarch
2. Bronllys	19. Llangattock
3. Builth	20. Llangors
4. Cilmery	21. Llangynidr
5. Cray	22. Llanigon
6. Crickhowell	23. Llanwrthwl
7. Duhonw	24. Llanwrtyd Wells
8. Erwood	25. Llywel
9. Felin-fach	26. Maescar
10. Glyn Tarell	27. Merthyr Cynog
11. Gwernyfed	28. Talgarth
12. Hay	29. Talybont-on-Usk
13. Honddu Isaf	30. Tawe-Uchaf
14. Llanafanfawr	31. Trallong
15. Llanddew	32. Treflys
16. Llanfihangel Cwmdu	33. Vale of Grwyne, The
with Bwlch and	34. Yscir
Cathedine	35. Ystradfellte
17. Llanfrynach	36. Ystradgynlais

The communities of the county of Powys: 3 Breconshire

Blaenllynfi, **Ystrad Yw**, **Builth** and Llangorse ... are all by this law made an integral and *indivisible* part of the **county** of Brecknock'. (The form *Brecknock* had, by the 20th century, become archaic.)

The county was bounded on the east by the **Black Mountains**, with the rounded outline of **Mynydd Epynt** rising to the north. Its heart was the **Usk** valley, but it was the **Brecon Beacons** that gave the county its most striking landmark. 'Imagination', as **Theophilus Jones** put it, 'can scarcely paint objects more sublime and picturesque than the three lofty peaks of these nearly precipitous elevations.' (Jones's *History of the County of Brecknock* (1805,1809) is far and away Wales's best county history.)

The raising of **sheep** and **cattle** was traditionally the principal occupation. The **woollen industry** flourished in some areas in the 17th and 18th centuries, and **iron** was manufactured and **coal** mined in those southern regions which lie within the confines of the coalfield. With the decline of **agriculture**, **tourism** came to play an increasingly important role. At the beginning of the 19th century, **Welsh** was the principal language of the small farmers and what Theophilus Jones called 'the lower rank of people', except in the **hundred** of Talgarth where a 'vile **English** jargon ... has crept into use'. Subsequently, the numbers speaking Welsh declined, a process accelerated by the dispersal of the largely Welsh-speaking inhabitants of Mynydd Epynt in 1940.

The 1536 Act granted Breconshire a county and a **borough** parliamentary representative. In 1885, **Brecon** lost its borough seat, and the county constituency was joined with that of **Radnorshire** in 1918. The county consisted of the borough of Brecon, the **urban districts** of **Brynmawr**, Builth, **Hay** and **Llanwrtyd** and the **rural districts** of Brecon, Builth, Crickhowell, Hay, Vaynor and Penderyn, and **Ystradgynlais**. In 1974, the county was abolished, and Breconshire, minus Brynmawr and **Llanelly** and most of the rural district of Vaynor and Penderyn, became a district of the newly created county of **Powys**. In the further local **government** reorganization of 1996, when former Welsh counties of similar **population** regained county status, Breconshire's failure to liberate itself from Powys was the cause of much regret. Breconshire has only a vestigial autonomy within the county of Powys, but retains vigorous institutions, especially the Brecknock Society. At the time of its abolition in 1974, the county consisted of 189,915 ha and had 53,000 inhabitants.

BREOS, DE family Marcher-lords

Philip (d.*c.*1130), the first of the family to be associated with Wales, was the son of William of Breos, near Falaise, Normandy, a major Essex landowner. From *c.*1095, Philip set about dislodging the native rulers of **Radnor** and **Builth**. His descendant, William (d.1180), married the heiress of **Brecon** and **Abergavenny**. William's son, William (d.1211), acquired **Gower** and the **Three Castles**. His massacre in 1175 of Seisyll ap Dyfnwal and his followers won him infamy as the wicked lord of Abergavenny. His son, Reginald (d.1128), married Gwladus Ddu (d.1251), daughter of **Llywelyn ap Iorwerth**, one of the numerous marriages between the Breoses and members of Welsh princely families. In 1230, William, Reginald's son by an earlier marriage, was hanged by Llywelyn for over-familiarity with **Joan** (Siwan), Llywelyn's wife, the theme of **Saunders Lewis**'s play *Siwan*. As William had no son, his lordships were divided between **Dafydd ap Llywelyn**, **Mortimer**, **Bohun** and Cantilupe, husbands of his daughters. Reginald had yielded Gower to his nephew, John (d.1232), whose male descendants held the lordship until it passed by marriage to the **Mowbray family** in 1326.

BREWER-SPINKS DISPUTE, The

A dispute arose at a factory in Tanygrisiau, Blaenau **Ffestiniog**, in June 1965, after staff were instructed by the company's technical director, W. Brewer-Spinks, to sign an undertaking not to speak **Welsh** at work, since the language was deemed inadequate to discuss the technicalities of modern **engineering**. Two members of staff, Elmer and Neville Jones, were dismissed for refusing to comply, which resulted in furious protests locally and indignant remonstrations across Wales. The director's behaviour was denounced by many leading politicians, including **James Griffiths**, **secretary of state for Wales**, and within a fortnight Brewer-Spinks was forced to climb down. The controversy, along with similar incidents at that time, including the stand taken by the **Beasley**s, the drowning of **Tryweryn** and the campaigning of **Cymdeithas yr Iaith Gymraeg**, made a significant contribution to the linguistic awakening of the 1960s

BRIDGEND, Town of (Pen-y-bont ar Ogwr)
(1148 ha; 25,269 inhabitants)

The town of Bridgend lies within the boundaries of three **communities** (*see below*).

Bridgend had pretensions to be **Glamorgan**'s **county town**. In the early 19th century, those concerned about the rivalry between **Cardiff** and **Swansea** argued that Bridgend should be the county's legal and electoral centre. The massive Greek Doric town hall of 1843 (demolished in 1971) was indicative of the town's ambitions. (Bridgend did eventually become the headquarters of the Glamorgan **Police** and the location of the county's lunatic asylum). From the 16th century onwards, it enjoyed modest prosperity as the market town of the western part of the **Vale of Glamorgan**. Growth accelerated from the early 19th century onwards following the development of industry in the **Ogwr**, Garw and Llynfi valleys and the opening in 1850 of the South Wales **Railway**. The interwar years were not as disastrous for Bridgend as they were elsewhere in Glamorgan, and the establishment during the **Second World War** of a vast munitions factory (*see* **Royal Ordnance Factories**) brought considerable prosperity. The factory subsequently became an industrial estate and the town has benefited from its location alongside the **M4**.

Earlier evidence of the significance of the site is apparent in the impressive and attractively situated castle at Newcastle, probably built in the 1180s. Of the adjoining St Illtyd's church, only the tower survives. The hospice on the road between Newcastle and the River Ogmore is a well-preserved 16th-century structure. The mainly late 19th and early 20th-century town centre has been somewhat mangled by thoughtless modern development. The finest

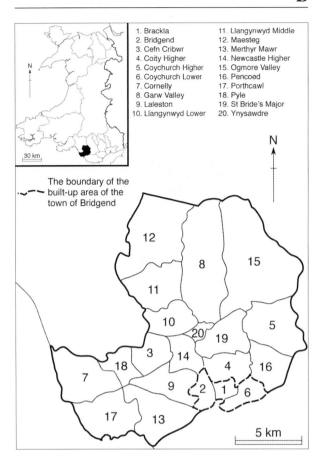

The communities of the county borough of Bridgend

building is St Mary's church (1887), one of **John Prichard**'s greatest achievements. Prichard's Magistrate's Court, the condition of which in 1995 was a matter of concern to John Newman in his *Buildings of Wales*, *Glamorgan*, has recently been skilfully converted into offices. Of the town's numerous chapels, the earliest is the **Unitarian** Meeting House (1795), and the most handsome is Hermon (1862). Much of **Brunel**'s **railway** station (1850) survives.

The communities of Bridgend

BRACKLA (Bracla) (246 ha; 10,113 inhabitants)
The community consists of much of the eastern part of the town of Bridgend.

BRIDGEND (Pen-y-Bont ar Ogwr)
(439 ha; 13,950 inhabitants)
The community consists of the western and most of the central part of the town of Bridgend.

COYCHURCH LOWER (Llangrallo Isaf)
(463 ha; 1206 inhabitants)
Consisting of the south-eastern extension of the town of Bridgend, the community includes the Bridgend Industrial Estate, which occupies the site of what was the world's largest munitions factory. During the Second World War, up to 40,000 people were employed there. St Crallo (13th century) is among Glamorgan's largest churches – a miniature cathedral indeed. It may have been the site of a Celtic

clas or monastery. It contains a monument to the **dictionary** compiler Thomas Richards (1710–90). The crematorium (1970), rich in **stained-glass** windows, is the finest in Wales. Coed-y-mwstwr, a neo-Tudor mansion (1888), is now a hotel. Adjoining the A48 near Brynteg Comprehensive School, a steel fence surrounds the site of the **Island Farm** prisoner-of-war camp, the scene of the Second World War's largest break-out by German prisoners. The escape hut is now a listed building.

BRIDGEND COUNTY BOROUGH
(Bwrdeistref Sirol Pen-y-bont ar Ogwr)
(25,521 ha; 128,645 inhabitants)

In 1974, the **urban districts** of **Bridgend**, **Maesteg** and **Porthcawl**, together with that of Ogmore and Garw (*see* **Ogmore Valley** and **Garw Valley**) and the **rural district** of Bridgend were combined to form the district of **Ogwr** within the **county** of **Mid Glamorgan**. In 1996, with the abolition of Mid Glamorgan, the district, minus three **communities** which were transferred to the **Vale of Glamorgan**, became a **county borough** and was renamed Bridgend. In 2001, 19.92% of its inhabitants had some knowledge of **Welsh**, the percentages varying from 28.12% in **Llangynwyd Middle** to 17.63% in **Ogmore Valley**; 8.09% of the county borough's inhabitants were wholly fluent in the language.

BRIGSTOCKE family Artists

London-born David Brigstocke (1771–*c*.1821) moved to **Carmarthen** to work in house painting, interior decoration, **stained glass** and **architecture**. His family expanded and was active in these trades in the Carmarthen and **St Clears** area for much of the 19th century. His son Thomas (1809–81), attended the Royal Academy Schools in London. He lived in Rome in the 1830s, where he is recorded as being among a group of **Welsh**-speaking artists, including **Penry Williams** and **John Gibson**, whose native language provided a diversion for Roman society at a time of growing interest in matters **Celt**ic. Thomas, the most accomplished of the Brigstockes, was noted for his still-life **painting** and portraits of prominent Welsh families.

BRITAIN Island, state and concept

The **Welsh** name for Britain, *Prydain*, derives from the Brythonic *Prytani* (people of Britain). The name employed by Julius Caesar and other **Roman** authors was *Britannia* and the Romans called the people *Britanni*. The English form is an adaption of the Old French *Bretaigne*.

Throughout the Middle Ages, the Welsh continued to refer to themselves as *Brythoniaid* (from the Brythonic *Britones*) and *Brytaniaid* (from the Middle English *Britan*), with centuries going by before those forms were wholly displaced by *Cymry*. 'British' or 'Cambro-British' were widely used to mean Welsh as late as the 18th century. *Prydeiniwr*, the modern term for a Briton, is first recorded in the 14th century, when it seems to have had the same meaning as Brython. In the 1580s, **John Dee** made familiar the term 'British Empire', which he applied to the reputed empire of King **Arthur**. The term Great Britain was originally used to distinguish the island from **Brittany** – Lesser Britain. The coronation of James I in 1604 gave the name a rather different meaning, a meaning which won increasing currency following the parliamentary union between **England** and **Scotland** in 1707.

The island of Britain, which as a concept corresponded with the Roman province of Britannia (Wales, England and southern Scotland), was for the Welsh an almost mythical country, the setting for many of the events of *The Mabinogion*, and other texts such as *The Triads of the Island of Britain* and the *Thirteen Treasures of the Island of Britain*. The *Brutiau* and other sources present a fairly consistent image of the island, with its Twenty-eight (or Thirty-two) Chief Cities, its Three Chief Rivers, its Three Adjacent Islands, and its two traditional extremities, Pen Blathaon in the **Old North** and Trwyn Pengwaedd (probably Penwith) in **Cornwall**. **Oxford** was considered to be its centre, and it appears that **London–Gwynedd** represented a kind of 'power axis' within the island.

From their earliest beginnings, the Welsh nourished a belief that, because of their sins or their political mistakes (or both), their ancestors, the Britons, had lost Britain to the **English**. As the AD 682 entry in **Brut y Tywysogyon** put it: 'In that year the Britons lost the crown of the kingdom and the English won it.' This belief can be traced through the works of **Gildas**, **Nennius** and **Geoffrey of Monmouth**. Bound up with the *brut*, the history of Britain, is the *brud*, the promise that the Welsh, 'the true Britons', will one day repossess the Island, a theme which came to be proclaimed in the *canu brud*, the medieval vaticinatory verse (*see* **Prophecy**). This created expectations which it was believed were fulfilled by the victory of Henry **Tudor** (Henry VII) at **Bosworth**, which gave rise in Wales to a devotion to the crown and to the strengthening of the age-old idea of the Island of Britain.

There is much discussion about what constitutes British identity. This has a bearing on the predicament and prospects of the Welsh people. It is well to bear in mind the observation made by the historian **Gwyn A. Williams**: 'We Welsh look like being the last of the British. There is some logic in this. We were, after all, the first.'

BRITHDIR AND LLANFACHRETH
(Brithdir A Llanfachreth), Gwynedd
(10,803 ha; 735 inhabitants)

Straddling the Wnion valley immediately east of **Dolgellau**, the **community** contains the villages of Brithdir, Llanfachreth and Rhydymain and the summit of Rhobell Fawr (734 m). There is a **Roman** fortlet at Brithdir. Dolserau and Caerynwch were once centres of substantial estates. The path along the Clywedog has been known since the early 19th century as Torrent Walk. St Mark's, Brithdir (1896), is a replica of St Mark's **Anglican** church, Florence; it contains a **copper** altar and a **lead** font. St Machreth's (1874) replaced a building dating from the 13th century. It contains memorial tablets to Rhys (or Rice) Jones (1713–1801), editor of *Gorchestion Beirdd Cymru* (1773), and to numerous members of the Vaughan family of Nannau. The Vaughans' ancestors, the **Nannau family**, were notable literary patrons, maintaining Wales's last household bard (Siôn Dafydd Laes, d.1695). Of Wales's landowner-mansions, Nannau (1796) occupies the loftiest location (230 m).

The Annunciation, a detail from Henry Wilson's copper altar (1898) of St Mark's church, Brithdir

BRITISH SOCIETY, The

The British Society (or the British and Foreign Schools Society, to give its full name) was founded in 1814 to promote the establishment of non-denominational British schools, as opposed to the denominational **Anglican** schools of the **National Society**. It made little impact in Wales before **Hugh Owen** published his famous letter in *Y Drysorfa* in 1843. In 1847, **John Phillips** was appointed the society's agent in the north, and in 1853, **William Roberts** (Nefydd) in the south. The number of British schools gradually increased and in 1858 the **Normal College, Bangor**, was founded, with John Phillips as principal, to train teachers for them. Following the passage of Forster's Education Act (1870) most of the schools were transferred to the control of school boards and maintained as non-denominational public elementary schools, with support from local rates. Despite religious differences between British and Church schools, their curriculum, dictated by the Revised Code (1862), was more or less identical, with the **Welsh language** practically banished from both.

BRITON FERRY (Llansawel), Neath Port Talbot
(777 ha; 5759 inhabitants)

A **community** located immediately south of **Neath**, the church of St Sawel was rededicated to St Mary by the **Normans**. The name recalls the one-time ferry across the Nedd, which is now crossed by the A483 and **M4** bridges. The area has a history of **coal**mining, and **iron**, steel and tinplate manufacture. Its docks (1861), designed by **Brunel**, provided Neath with its **port**. Bisected by the M4, they fell into disuse. The ship-breaking works at Giant's Grave are a shadow of what once they were. The **hymn**writer Mary Owen (1796–1875) was a native of Briton Ferry.

BRITTANY (Llydaw), Wales's associations with

Between the 5th and 7th centuries, Armorica was colonized by Brythonic speakers from **Britain**, and came to be known as Lesser Britain or Brittany. Although the bulk of the migrants probably came from the south-west of the island, the leaders seem to have had associations with the royal houses of Wales. The lives of the **'saints'** and references to Bretons in the 10th-century poem *Armes Prydein* (*see* **Prophecy**) indicate that in the early Middle Ages, Wales, **Cornwall** and Brittany constituted a single cultural, religious and linguistic entity. From the later 11th century onwards, Breton participation in **Norman** expansion brought many Bretons to Wales. Among them were the ancestors of **Geoffrey of Monmouth**, whose writings initiated the cult of King **Arthur**, in the dissemination of which the Bretons played a leading role.

In the later Middle Ages, there was significant trade between Brittany and Wales, and, when fleeing from Tenby in 1471, it was in Brittany that Henry **Tudor** found refuge. From the 17th century onwards, scholars such as **John Davies** (*c.*1567–1644) and **Edward Lhuyd** explored the linguistic affinities between the Welsh and the Bretons, and the notions of the Breton Paul-Yves Pezron, concerning the origins of the **Celts**, aroused widespread interest in Wales.

By the 19th century, there was a growing interest in pan-Celticism; its leading Welsh exponent, Carnhuanawc (**Thomas Price**), assisted Ar Gonideg in his translation of the New Testament (1827) – which found more buyers in Wales than in Brittany – and Lady Charlotte **Guest** offered patronage to the translator of Breton medieval poetry, Villemarqué, who later plagiarized her work. To the Welsh, however, Brittany was primarily the home of **Johnny Onions** and, to the devoutly Protestant among them, of benighted Catholics. Protestant missions were sent to Brittany, and the compliment was returned with Breton Catholic priests evangelizing in Wales.

In the 20th century, Bretons such as Taldir, Abeozen and Per Denez wrote about Wales, while Welsh writers, such as **Ambrose Bebb**, J. Dyfnallt Owen, and **J. E. Caerwyn Williams**, drew attention to Brittany. The connections between the two countries had practical value at the end of the **Second World War**, when some in Wales helped Bretons accused of collaborating with the German occupation. A society for promoting links between Wales and Brittany was established in 1987. (*See also* **Celtic Associations**.)

BRO GARMON, Conwy (5467 ha; 648 inhabitants)
Located on the right bank of the **Conwy**, across the river from **Betws-y-Coed**, the **community**'s most interesting feature is the Capel Garmon chambered tomb, which has yielded **pottery** dated *c.* 3200 BC. It belongs to the **Severn-Cotswold** group of tombs, suggesting a northern movement of either the people or the ideas associated with that group. The **Iron Age** firedogs found near it is the most

Mostyn Thomas, launching the first public radio broadcast from Wales, 13 February 1923

elaborate artefact of its kind to be discovered in Europe. On the community's southern boundary are the dramatic Conwy Falls; Pont Newydd, nearby, offers fine views of the ravine. Cyffdy (16th century), Soflen (17th century) and Plas Tirion (17th century) are interesting houses.

BRO MACHNO, Conwy (5443 ha; 625 inhabitants)
Constituting the basin of the Machno, a tributary of the **Conwy**, much of the **community** has been forested; great swathes of it, and of its neighbour, **Ysbyty Ifan**, are owned by the **National Trust**. The four 5th- and 6th-century inscribed stones in the churchyard of St Tudclud (1857) are evidence that Penmachno was an important early religious site; one stone refers to the consulate of Justinius (AD 540), indicating contacts between Penmachno and Burgundy. The area contains several substantial houses of the 16th and 17th centuries. Cwm Penmachno was an important **slate**-quarrying area. Gwilym Tilsley lamented its decline in his poem 'Cwm Carnedd'. Tŷ Mawr, Wybrnant, the birthplace of the **Bible** translator **William Morgan,** has been splendidly restored by the National Trust. High above the Machno valley is Llyn Conwy, the source of the Conwy.

BROADCASTING

Public broadcasting began in Wales on 13 February 1923, with the inauguration of the British Broadcasting Company's station at **Cardiff**. The **Swansea** station followed on 12 December 1924. Initially, everything broadcast from Cardiff was produced there, but following the introduction of simultaneous transmission in 1924, around 75% of Cardiff's output, and a higher percentage of that of Swansea, emanated from **London**. By the late 1920s, about 70% of the inhabitants of Wales were able to receive the broadcasts of what became, on 1 January 1927, the British Broadcasting Corporation. With the cheapest valve set costing £6 and with the licence fee a further 10 shillings, it is unsurprising that it was not until 1935 that the proportion of Welsh households in possession of a licence reached 50%. Thus, much early listening to radio broadcasting occurred in public halls, and the enthusiasm of the listeners is proof of their delight in the new worlds which were opening up for them.

In February 1929, Cardiff became the main station for the BBC's West Region, consisting of Wales and southwest **England**. Most of north and mid-Wales was beyond the reach of its transmitter, which was located at Washford on the Somerset coast. Simultaneous transmission meant that only a small proportion of the programmes audible in the new region were produced within it. The need to provide for audiences in both Wales and south-west England meant that Wales could claim a half of that small proportion. As a result, **Welsh-language** programmes were virtually non-existent, much to the satisfaction of the West's director, E. R. Appleton, who argued that when 'His Majesty's **Government** decided to form a corporation for the important function of broadcasting, it was natural that the official language should be used throughout.' He expressed his delight with the West Region, which he argued represented 'the re-creation of the kingdom of King **Arthur**'.

Recording *ITMA* at the BBC studio in Bangor, May 1942, with (left to right) Jack Train, Dorothy Summers and Tommy Handley (1892–1949)

This was the context for the struggle waged from the late 1920s to the mid-1930s by the **University of Wales**, the National Union of Welsh Societies, the Welsh Parliamentary Party and **Plaid [Genedlaethol] Cymru**, a struggle much assisted by the ability of the young physicist **Edward Bowen** to refute the BBC's arguments concerning the scarcity of wavelengths. The upshot was the establishment of a studio at **Bangor** in November 1935, the appointment of a Welsh Regional Director (**Rhys Hopkin Morris**) in September 1936, the erection of a transmitter at Penmon (**Llangoed**) to serve the north in February 1937 and the allocation of a separate wavelength to the Welsh Service in July 1937. The BBC's staff in Wales was expanded and by the late 1930s included such talented individuals as **Alun Llywelyn-Williams**, **Sam Jones**, Dafydd Gruffydd, Elwyn Evans, Nest Jenkins, John Griffiths, Geraint Dyfnallt Owen and Nan Davies. As they were expected to produce programmes in **English** and Welsh, they were all fluent in both languages. Although those lacking a knowledge of Welsh – among them **Mai Jones** and **Philip Burton** – eventually joined the staff, the preponderance of Welsh-speaking producers in the early years of the BBC's Welsh Region was the cause of some resentment among the non-Welsh-speaking Welsh. Perhaps the new region's greatest achievement was the creation of the concept of all-Wales news, an innovation in view of the fact that there was no such thing as an all-Wales **newspaper**. In Welsh, the most popular programme was *Noson Lawen*, produced in Bangor by Sam Jones, the BBC's representative in the north. Broadcasts brought into existence a form of standard spoken Welsh somewhat removed from the staid language of the pulpit, a development of particular interest to Alun Llywelyn-Williams.

With the declaration of war in 1939, the BBC was obliged to transmit a unified service, partly in order to release wavelengths for broadcasts to enemy, allied and occupied countries, partly from the fear that numerous wavelengths, each transmitting its own programme, would provide wireless beams which could be picked up and used by enemy aircraft, but above all because of the urge for centralization inherent in states at war. Some Welsh-language broadcasts survived, transmitted to the whole of the United Kingdom. They included a daily bulletin of world news, which, broadcast at 5 p.m., frequently scooped the English 6 p.m. news. The 1940 National **Eisteddfod** was held on the radio – three hours of transmissions on the British Home Service, which included 15 minutes apiece for the crown and chair adjudications. There was some grumbling in England against what was seen as the imposition of Welsh, but English-language programmes produced in Wales proved very popular – Mai Jones's *Welsh Rarebit* in particular. In addition, the best-loved of all wartime programmes, Tommy Handley's *ITMA*, was produced in Wales; the Corporation's Variety Department moved to Bangor in 1941, causing the *Liverpool Daily Post* to comment that sedate Bangor 'lost its innocence overnight with one trainful of actors'.

On 29 July 1945, 81 days after the surrender of Germany, the BBC's Welsh Home Service was launched. Thus was inaugurated the golden age of sound broadcasting in Wales, an age which lasted until the late 1950s, by which time the majority of Welsh households had acquired television licences. Under the leadership of **Alun Oldfield-Davies**, Welsh director (1945–8) and Controller Wales (1948–67), the service benefited from the talents of such luminaries as **Aneirin Talfan Davies**, **Hywel Davies** and

Alun Williams, and of an increasingly experienced group of sports commentators led by G. V. Wynne-Jones. The BBC annual lecture, originally launched in 1938, was revived, culminating in 1962 with **Saunders Lewis**'s influential *Tynged yr Iaith*. An advisory council for Wales was established in 1947. It was replaced by the **Broadcasting Council for Wales** in 1953, when Wales was recognized as a 'national region'.

The Welsh Broadcasting Council was given responsibility for the policy and content of the Welsh Home Service. It was given advisory powers only in the case of television, which arrived in Wales in August 1952 with the opening of the **Wenvoe** transmitter. By 1952, parts of Wales were already served by transmitters at Sutton Coldfield (1949) and at Holme Moss (1951). Further BBC transmitters followed at Blaenplwyf (**Llanfarian** near **Aberystwyth** (1957)), **Llandrindod** (1961) and **Llanddona** (1962). Initially, the United Kingdom was provided with a single unified service, although Oldfield-Davies did succeed in persuading the Corporation to transmit occasional Welsh-language programmes during closed periods. In England, there were vehement protests against them, although all they replaced was the test card. The first Welsh-language television programme – a religious service from Cardiff – was broadcast on 1 March 1953.

The issues that arose in the efforts to create a national radio service for Wales – the link with south-west England, incomprehension in the London head office, enthusiasm for and opposition to increased provision of Welsh-language programmes – were replicated in the case of television. There were, however, two additional factors. One was the fact that the notion that the Welsh nation had an inalienable right to be a broadcasting unit had been established in 1937 and had been confirmed by the designation of Wales in 1953 as a 'national region'. The other was the beginning in 1955 of commercial television, which from the outset was organized on a regional basis. Wales and south-western England became the responsibility of Television Wales and the West (TWW), whose service was inaugurated in February 1958 from a transmitter at St Hilary (**Llanfair** near **Cowbridge**). However, much of the north-east was served by the Manchester-based Granada company, which began transmitting Welsh-language programmes in 1957 for an hour a week, twice the amount broadcast by the BBC. Most of the south-west and north-west was beyond the range of any ITV transmitter. In September 1962, those areas became the responsibility of Television Wales West and North (also known as *Teledu Cymru*). Its sparsely populated territory failed to generate the income necessary for the company's viability and TWWN merged with TWW in January 1964.

The spur of commercial competition, the urgent pleading of Oldfield-Davies, a less centralist attitude in the BBC's head office and the eloquent arguments of the Pilkington Committee's *Report* (1962) led in 1964 to the inauguration of BBC Wales, a television service unique to Wales. As Wales was also to receive BBC 2, and as there was no commercial television service broadcasting solely to Wales, the notion arose that the BBC should also carry commercially produced programmes aimed at Wales, or at least those in the Welsh language – the kernel of the idea that came to fruition with **S4C** in 1982. It was an idea long resisted by the BBC, largely on the grounds of the difference between the ethos of public service and commercial broadcasting, and the fear that BBC programmes could become contaminated by advertising.

From 1964, while Wales had BBC Wales, answerable to the Broadcasting Council of Wales, **Scotland** had to be content with the basic BBC television service with opt-outs, transmissions over which the Broadcasting Council for Scotland had only advisory powers – a nice example of the way in which broadcasting has fuelled much of the advance in the recognition of Wales as a nation. Further evidence of that recognition came in 1965, when TWW separated the service for Wales from that for the West of England. The existence of separate Welsh services made it possible for Welsh-language programmes to be broadcast at peak hours, a development which led many of those who could not understand them to tune their aerials to receive broadcasts from England. Thus, while it was argued that the paucity of programmes in their language was Anglicizing the Welsh speakers, the fact that such programmes existed at all was causing those with no knowledge of Welsh to turn their backs on anything emanating from Wales. Fears of the BBC losing viewers became more acute in 1968, when TWW lost its franchise to HTV, a company which promised significantly to increase the number and quality of programmes specifically produced for Welsh viewers.

The desire to remove Welsh from mainstream channels coincided with the campaign of **Cymdeithas yr Iaith Gymraeg** (the Welsh Language Society) in favour of a Welsh-language channel, a campaign which led to sit-ins, mast climbing, destruction of property and numerous jail

A BBC camera filming at the Welsh Games in Cardiff, 28 July 1953

The cast of *Pobol y Cwm* in 2007

sentences. The resulting tensions were particularly worrying to John Rowley, Controller Wales 1967–74. His period in office saw significant developments, including the beginning of BBC Wales's colour broadcasts (1970), the establishment of the BBC Welsh Symphony Orchestra (1973; *see* **BBC National Orchestra of Wales**) and the use of VHF and medium wave to provided Welsh-language and English-language radio services on different wavelengths – a development which led to the establishment of Radio Cymru and Radio Wales. Rowley was succeeded by Owen Edwards, son of **Ifan ab Owen Edwards** and grandson of **Owen M. Edwards**, who presided over the launching of the serial *Pobol y Cwm*, the full establishment of Radio Wales and Radio Cymru and the complexities arising from the deliberations of the Annan Committee. In its *Report* (1977), the committee recommended that a Welsh-language fourth channel should be established as soon as the necessary funding was available. The recommendation was attacked by some Welsh-language enthusiasts, among them **Jac L. Williams**, who opposed what he considered to be the banishment of the language to a 'ghetto channel'. In their manifestos for the general election of May 1979, all the major parties pledged that Welsh-language programmes should have priority on the fourth channel. In September 1979, however, the home secretary, William Whitelaw, announced that the government would not proceed with the project. The protests that ensued – the blacking-out of transmitters, mass refusal to pay the licence fee and, above all, the threat of Plaid Cymru's president, **Gwynfor Evans**, to fast to death and the fear of the chronic unrest which would surely have followed his demise – led the government to announce on 17 September 1980 that a Welsh fourth channel would, after all, be established (*see* **S4C**).

The remarkable history of broadcasting in Wales has caused Cardiff to be a major media centre, a significant element in the city's vibrancy. Since the 1980s, the main challenge facing broadcasters in Wales, as everywhere, is the multiplication of both radio and television services. Local radio began in Wales in 1974 with Swansea Sound, the beginning of a proliferation of such services. Radio Wales and Radio Cymru have held their ground, although the latter has been accused of consisting of little beyond pop and prattle. With scores if not hundreds of television stations available to those with satellite or cable services, the fear is that any distinctive Welsh service, whatever its language might be, is in danger of being crowded out. Efforts to prevent this happening are crucial in maintaining and developing a Welsh national consciousness.

BROADCASTING COUNCIL FOR WALES, The

The Broadcasting Council for Wales was established as the result of the recommendation in the *Report* (1951) of the Beveridge Committee that Wales should constitute a 'national region' of the BBC – a notion first mooted by **Megan Lloyd George**. Until 2007, the Council – which replaced the Welsh Advisory Council – had oversight of BBC programming within Wales. The Council was particularly active in the development of television programme making in Wales and during the campaign for a **Welsh** fourth channel (*see* **S4C**). As a result of the BBC's new Royal Charter in 2007, the work of the Council was taken over by the Audience Council Wales. The chairman of the Council is a member of the BBC Trust.

BROMFIELD AND YALE (Brwmffild ac Iâl)
Marcher-lordship
Consisting of the **Powys Fadog commotes** of **Maelor** Gymraeg and **Iâl** and part of that of **Nanheudwy**, the district became a **march**er-lordship in 1283. It was granted to the **Warenne family**, earls of Surrey, from whom it passed in the late 14th century to the **Fitz Alan family**, earls of Arundel. Its centre was the castle of **Holt**. In 1536, it became part of the newly created **Denbighshire**.

B

BRONINGTON, Wrexham
(3482 ha; 1228 inhabitants)
Occupying the easternmost part of **Maelor Saesneg**, the **community** thrusts out towards Whitchurch (**Shropshire**) – Yr Eglwys Wen of Welsh tradition. Edward Hubbard considered Bronington church – converted from a brick barn – to be 'artlessly endearing'. St Mary's church, Whitewell, is also brick-built (1830); it contains a tablet to Philip Henry (d.1696), pioneer of Presbyterianism (*see* **Presbyterians**) and the most saintly of the Welsh **Puritan** leaders. In 1672, his house, Broad Oak, was licensed as Wales's first Presbyterian meeting place. Broad Oak was the birthplace of Philip's son, Matthew (1662–1714), whose biblical commentaries enjoyed a high reputation in Wales. The fine mansion, Iscoyd Park, was built in c.1740 and enlarged in the 19th century. There are moated sites at Wolvesacre Hall and Haulton Ring. The community, which is rich in half-timbered buildings, also contains the extensive raised mire, Fenns Moss, designated a Nature Reserve in 1996.

BRONLLYS, Breconshire, Powys
(1933 ha; 816 inhabitants)
Bronllys, a **community** lying like a hammock below the great bend in the **Wye**, was once the administrative centre of **Cantref Selyf**. The castle has a 13th-century, round, three-storeyed keep, built upon a motte. The church, rebuilt in the 19th century, has a detached tower. Bronllys Hospital was completed in 1920 as a **tuberculosis** sanatorium. Llyswen church was rebuilt in 1863; the *Shell Guide for Mid Wales* remarks regretfully that 'it must have been much nicer before'. In 1265, Simon de Montfort signed a treaty at Pipton recognizing **Llywelyn ap Gruffudd** as **Prince of Wales**. Pipton was a centre for **iron** production, pioneered by the Maybery family in the late 17th century. The 17th-century house built for Herbert Williams survives as the south wing of Llangoed Hall; the rest of the building, completed in 1919 and now a hotel, is the work of **Clough Williams-Ellis**.

BRONWYDD, Carmarthenshire
(881 ha; 572 inhabitants)
Located immediately north of **Carmarthen**, the **community**'s only substantial settlement is the straggling village of Bronwydd Arms. Cwmgwili mansion was home to the prominent Philipps family and contains 17th-century features. Since 1975, a 4-km section of the one-time **railway** between Carmarthen and **Aberystwyth** has been opened as a tourist attraction. Its promoters hope to reconstruct further sections of the Gwili Steam Railway in the future.

BRONZE AGE, The (c.2300–c.700 BC)
The beginnings of metallurgy in Europe – sometime c.2500 BC – coincided with the appearance of a new form of **pottery**. In many parts of Europe, including **Britain**, a range of **copper** weapons and tools, together with examples of the new pottery, have come to light in graves dating from the period 2300–1400 BC. This is the period known as the Early Bronze Age, although the term is somewhat arbitrary. The coming of metal would eventually transform society, but initially the occasional availability of metal objects did not cause revolutionary change. Indeed, the basic characteristics of the **Neolithic Age** would continue to determine the pattern of life during much of the epoch known as the Bronze Age, an indication that the division of prehistory into demarcated 'ages' can be an artificial exercise.

Nevertheless, there was significant change in the period c.2250–2000 BC, change which would accelerate as metal objects became more widely available. Different burial practices came to the fore, with the dead, or at least those of elevated status, being placed in individual graves – a marked contrast with the elaborate collective graves of the Neolithic Age. In this new type of grave, efforts were made to reflect the individuality and status of the deceased, whether male or female, by including personal belongings – pottery beakers in particular – alongside the corpse, which was generally buried in a stone cist covered by an earthen round barrow. Until fairly recently, it was believed that it was migrants from the Rhineland and Iberia – the Beaker folk, as they were known – who introduced the beakers, metalmaking and the new form of burial to wide areas of Europe. However, the present tendency is to suggest that it was the spread of knowledge and ideas, rather than the impact of invasion, which caused the dissemination of technological and cultural change, although there are still supporters of the notion that the Beaker folk were warlike invaders who imposed themselves upon the indigenous inhabitants as a dominant elite.

Evidence from Early Bronze Age sites is slight in Wales compared with other parts of Britain. Burial in a stone cist, with an impoverished range of grave goods – flint knives, jet beads and, very rarely, a copper knife – represents the typical form of Beaker burials – those, for example, at **Brymbo** and **Llanharry**. Numerous beakers have been found in megalithic tombs (*see* **Neolithic Age**), among them Capel Garmon (**Bro Garmon**), Pen-yr-wyrlod and Tŷ Isaf (**Talgarth**) and Tinkinswood (**St Nicholas**). This suggests that the final, closing episodes in the history of these earlier monuments occurred in the Bronze Age – a further reminder of the processes of assimilation that were taking place. A similar association occurs at the henge monuments at **Llandygai**. Beaker pottery also occurs in upland locations, notably at Brenig (**Cerrigydrudion**) on **Mynydd Hiraethog**, suggesting that these remote **mountain** areas were being exploited by agriculturists for the first time.

In the course of the Bronze Age, beaker pottery developed into a series of types of urn that were mainly used as receptacles for the cremated remains of the dead. At burial monuments such as Bedd Branwen (**Tref Alaw**) and **Llanddyfnan** (both in **Anglesey**), paired urns were found, the one containing the cremated ashes and the other empty as if to hold the spirit of the departed. Small cemeteries were common. In Brenig, there is a cemetery consisting of an earlier series of large earthen mounds containing single inhumations or urned cremations, and a later series of stone cairns. Large summit cairns crown many high vantage points, and in the examples excavated on Y Drosgl (**Llanllechid**) and on Corn Du and Pen y Fan (**Brecon Beacons**), the elevated cairns and their contents seem to reflect the high status of the deceased. There appears to be a direct relationship between ceremonial and burial sites and particular places; some that command wide views contain a range of different monument types. There are

The Bronze Age gold cape found in Mold in 1833

fine examples on Mynydd **Penmaenmawr** centred upon the Meini Hirion stone circle, and at the Glandy Cross (**Cilymaenllwyd**) aggregation around the Meini Gŵyr stone circle.

Many of the standing stones, so prominent in the **archaeology** of Wales, belong to the Early and Middle Bronze Age. At the **Pembrokeshire** locations of Devil's Quoit (**Stackpole**) and Langstone Field (**St Ishmael's**), the standing stones represent the only visual reminder of complex ceremonial sites with a long history of development. Other standing stones denote important early trackways. They include those at Bwlch y Ddeufaen (**Caerhun**), the Glandy Cross monuments indicating the route from the **Mynydd Preseli** to the **Cleddau** estuary and, in Gwynedd, the stone-demarcated track from **Talsarnau** to **Trawsfynydd**, and the Ffordd Ddu track above **Arthog**. Mounds of burnt stone are particularly interesting monuments. They often consist of horseshoe-shaped mounds with a central depression, and are generally located near running water. They are deemed to be cooking mounds in which heated stones created boiling water used for cooking meat, although there are those who believe that they might also have been a primitive form of sauna.

The ability to cast artefacts in metal was a major technological advance. Copper was the first metal utilized, its initial use appearing *c.*2300 BC. By *c.*2000 BC, bronze, an alloy formed from tin and copper, had been discovered and it became the premier metal for casting most objects. A range of tools and weapon types developed, starting from simple forms, such as flat axes, knives and daggers, and graduating to more complex types, such as palstaves, socketed axes, rapiers, slashing swords and spear heads.

Recent research has shown that several copper mines in Wales – among them **Mynydd Parys**, the Great Orme (**Llandudno**), Nantyrarian (**Melindwr**, **Ceredigion**) and Gopa Hill in the upper **Ystwyth** valley – all date from *c.*2000–1750 BC, thus making them among the earliest in Britain. Other sites await further investigation. The Great Orme mine is currently considered to be the largest prehistoric mining complex in the world, with its underground levels penetrating 36 m below the surface and extending more that 8 km into the heart of the mountain. Gopa Hill was an open-cast mine in which wooden water launders have been discovered indicating that a distant water source was being tapped. At all the mines, heavy stone mauls were used to pulverize the ore. At the Great Orme, chalcopyritic ore was scraped from an encasing softer deposit by using split bone points, whilst at Gopa Hill an antler pick has been discovered. Contrary to popular belief, these mines seem to belong exclusively to the prehistoric period, since, with the exception of the mine at Llanymynech (**Carreghofa**), a **Roman** phase of exploitation has not been established. The widespread colonization and utilization of upland tracts in Bronze Age Wales may have been partly related to the search for metal ores.

During the Bronze Age, the unique social status of the metalsmith was established. Evidence of the craft comes not only from the artefacts produced but also from the appliances used in their production. Examples include stone moulds for a flat axe (Pont Gethin, **Betws-y-Coed**) and for a socketed axe (Abermad, **Llanilar**), and the two bronze bivalve moulds for casting palstaves (Deansfield, **Bangor**). Early palstave forms may have been developed by Welsh smiths and were part of hoards from **Betws yn Rhos**, and Acton Park (**Wrexham**). By *c.*1400 BC, such palstaves were circulating in northern Germany. By *c.*1000 BC, south-east Wales may have been a production centre of a particular type of socketed axe which had a wide circulation in Wales and central and south-west **England**. It has been claimed that the distribution of axes in Wales by *c.*700 BC may foreshadow the four-part tribal divisions of the Roman era, divisions which anticipate the emergence of the kingdoms of early medieval Wales.

The versatility of the bronzesmith is again observed in sheet metal objects, such as shields, cauldrons and buckets. Shields have been found at **Moel Siabod**, Llanychaiarn (**Llanfarian**) and **Llanbedr**. They are notable for the thinness of their metal cover, which presupposes their use as prestige parade objects rather than as protective devices – an early indication of the mind-set of a heroic society. Equally outstanding are the Arthog bucket and the two bronze cauldrons in the hoard from the Llyn Fawr (**Rhigos**). Once more, their mode of construction, using thin metal plates riveted together, suggests a ceremonial function. They recall the mythical prowess ascribed to vessels of this type in early Welsh **literature**. Many of these status objects were recovered from waterlogged deposits, and they were probably thrown into lakes and rivers as votive offerings.

Throughout its prehistory, Wales absorbed influences from outside, and in the Bronze Age these are best represented by metal objects of mainland European derivation. A bronze arrowhead in the **Pennard** hoard and a knife in the hoard from Ffynhonnau (**Brecon**) are such objects, both having a central European derivation. The Arthog bucket has its ancestry in Hungary and a socketed axe from Trawsfynydd has close analogies with southern Scandinavia. The Parc y Meirch (**Abergele**) hoard contains, among other **horse**-riding accoutrements, a rare north German jangle (an item of horse harness that makes a jangling sound). Razors and harness fittings in the Llyn Fawr hoard bear close comparison with objects from south-east France and southern Germany. The Llyn Fawr hoard contained three early **iron** objects – a sword, spear and sickle – which suggests that precocious native smiths were pioneers in the mastery of iron technology.

The **gold**smith also makes a first appearance in the Bronze Age. The malleability and beauty of gold causes it to be admirable for the making of adornments. Early in the Bronze Age, gold was beaten into paper-thin sheets, such as in the crescent-shaped lunula from the **Dwyfor** at **Dolbenmaen**, but later smiths mastered the technique of drawing and plaiting gold wire. Gold technology appears to be closely linked with **Ireland**, and the gold wire, bar and ribbon torques from **Llanwrthwl**, **Tiers Cross** and Heyop (**Beguildy**) are Welsh examples of Irish-inspired objects. In the cuff bracelets from Capel Isaac (**Manordeilo**), a Breton connection is suggested, but all four objects were probably made from local gold. Later objects are mainly represented by bracelets and lock rings with strong Irish affinities. Their distribution in hoards such as those from Gaerwen (**Llanfihangel Ysgeifiog**) and the Great Orme indicate a trade route along the coast of northern Wales.

Wales can claim two objects that are unique to the European Bronze Age, although both are difficult to date accurately. The first is the astonishing gold mantle, probably from the Middle Bronze Age, discovered in 1833 in the Bryn yr Ellyllon mound in **Mold**, draped around the shoulders of the young man buried in the mound. The mantle weighs 450 g and is decorated with geometric

bosses. The second object was found in boggy ground near Caergwrle Castle (**Hope**) in 1820 and probably dates from the late Bronze Age. It is a boat-shaped bowl carved from shale and is adorned in gold leaf with representations of waves and the oars and shields of the rowers, and it bears a large pair of eyes at each end. In 2006, at St Botolph's (**Milford Haven**), archaeological monitoring of the work on the Milford–Aberdulais (**Blaenhonddan**) gas pipeline found what is believed to be a Bronze Age canoe, weighing 1 tonne, hollowed out of a single trunk of oak.

The craft of the bronzesmith reached its apogee not in the Bronze Age but in the **Iron Age**. Furthermore, the origins of some of the chief features of the Iron Age – **hill-forts** in particular – lie in the Bronze Age. Indeed, seamless development is the outstanding characteristic of the last four millennia of the prehistory of Wales, a fact that is gaining increasing acceptance as the one-time emphasis upon invasion is giving way to the notion of the centrality of indigenous development.

BROUGHTON (Brychdyn), Wrexham (469 ha; 6948 inhabitants)

Wedged between **Gwersyllt** and **Brymbo** north of **Wrexham**, the **community** was industrialized from the mid-19th century onwards, following the opening of **coal**mines. Its most interesting feature is Berse Drelincourt church (1742), built at the expense of Mary Drelincourt in connection with the girls' charity school she founded in 1719.

BROUGHTON AND BRETTON (Brychdyn and Bretton), Flintshire (1231 ha; 5791 inhabitants)

Located on the **border** south-west of Chester, the **community**'s original settlement was Bretton, once part of the Eaton Hall estate of the Grosvenor family, dukes of Westminster. Bretton Hall Farm and other buildings in the vicinity were designed by the distinguished architect **John Douglas**, who was responsible for much of the remarkable building work undertaken by the Eaton Hall estate.

Broughton is essentially a late 20th-century village. Broughton church (1824) has a gallery carried on two pairs of posts apparently from a four-poster bed, reputedly owned by Henry VII. **Hawarden airport** and an aircraft factory dominate the area. The **government**-built factory (1937–9), managed by Vickers Armstrong, was established to construct Wellington and Lancaster bombers. In the immediate post-war years, it produced prefabricated aluminium houses (prefabs). In the 1950s, it returned to the construction of aeroplanes, among them Mosquitoes, Hornets, Doves, Vampires and early Comets. In 1963, it became part of Hawker-Siddeley and subsequently of British Aerospace. The factory was responsible for assembling the HS 125 executive jet, but its main function came to be the building of wings for the European Airbus (*see also* **Airports** and **Aviation and Aeronautics**). There was anxiety about the long-term future of the factory in 2007 when the loss of 800 jobs was announced.

BRUCE family (Barons Aberdare)

The first baron was Henry Austin Bruce (1815–95), son of John Bruce Pryce (b.Knight), owner of the Dyffryn estate, **Aberdare**. As stipendiary magistrate, Pryce played a central role in the **Merthyr Rising** of 1831; in 1837, he was **Conservative** candidate for **Merthyr Tydfil**. In 1852, Henry Austin Bruce succeeded his father's adversary, John **Guest**, as **Liberal** MP for Merthyr, a seat he held until defeated by **Henry Richard** in 1868. Elected for Renfrew in 1869, he was home secretary from 1869 to 1873, one of only three Welshmen to be a member of a 19th-century British cabinet. In 1873, he became Baron Aberdare and Lord President of the Council. He had extensive interests in Africa, and the Aberdare Mountains in Kenya commemorate him. In 1880, he chaired the Aberdare Committee on **education** in Wales (*see* **Aberdare Report**). He was the first president of University College, **Cardiff** (**Cardiff University**) and the first chancellor of the **University of Wales**. His descendants included his second son, William Napier (1858–1936), pro-chancellor of the University of Wales (1927–34), his third son, Charles Granville (1866–1939), the organizer of the first expedition aiming at the ascent of Everest, and the third baron Clarence Napier (1885–1957), an athlete with a worldwide reputation.

BRUNEL, Isambard Kingdom (1806–59)
Railway engineer

An outstanding **railway** engineer, Isambard Kingdom Brunel was the only son of Sir Marc Isambard Brunel, builder of the world's first underwater tunnel. He built the 7ft (2.1336 m) broad gauge South Wales Railway from Gloucester to **Neyland**, which linked with the Great Western Railway from Paddington and completed a vital mail connection with **Ireland**. Among his notable works in Wales were the **Chepstow** bridge across the **Wye**, raised on cast-**iron** piers, and the 37-span Landore (**Swansea**) viaduct over the **Tawe**. Brunel also designed the **Taff** Vale Railway (1841) and the Vale of **Neath** Railway (1851). His statue, crowned by a tall hat, stands at **Neyland**.

BRUNT, David (1886–1965) Meteorologist

Sir David Brunt, FRS, one of the founders of modern meteorology, was born in Staylittle (**Trefeglwys**), but the family moved south to **Llanhilleth**, and he attended secondary school at **Abertillery**. He graduated in **mathematics** at **Aberystwyth** and, subsequently, at **Cambridge**. After a short period teaching at **Caerleon** Training College, and war service in the Royal Engineers, he started work in the Meteorological Office on the diffusion of gases in the lower atmosphere. He is best known for his calculation of the natural period of oscillation of a parcel of air in the atmosphere. A Finnish scientist, Väisälä, calculated the same period independently, so it is known as the Brunt-Väisälä period, one of the key parameters in the theory of atmospheric dynamics. Brunt became professor of meteorology at Imperial College, **London**. He was author of *Physical and Dynamical Meteorology* (1934), a pioneering work that became a standard text.

BRUT, Walter (Gwallter Brut(e); fl.1390–1402)
Heretic

The Welsh **Lollard** Walter Brut was brought before the ecclesiastical courts on several occasions between 1390 and 1393 to defend himself against the accusation of heresy. Priding himself on his Brythonic ancestry, Brut claimed

Brunel's statue at Neyland

that the Welsh had been singled out by God to assist in the overthrow of the Antichrist, whom he identified as the Pope. He also fulminated against **tithe**-gathering, the immorality of priests and the folly of war, and urged his countrymen to take up his heretical views. He refused to recant and eventually the exasperated commission released him. Rebellious to the last, Brut took up arms in support of **Owain Glyndŵr**.

BRUT Y TYWYSOGYON (The Chronicle of the Princes)

A chronicle which relates the history of independent Wales from the death of **Cadwaladr ap Cadwallon** in the late 7th century to the death of **Llywelyn ap Gruffudd** in 1282. It is preserved in two versions which are translations into **Welsh** of a lost **Latin** original believed to have been composed at the **Cistercian** abbey of Strata Florida (**Ystrad Fflur**) at the end of the 13th century. It is based on annals kept at ecclesiastical centres such as **St David's** since the 8th century, three sets of which have survived and have been published under the title *Annales Cambriae*; the *annales* are written in a terse and simple style, unlike that of the original of the chronicle, which was elegant and literary. *Brut y Tywysogyon* was seen as the sequel to **Geoffrey of Monmouth**'s *Historia Regum Britanniae*, the **Welsh** version of which was known as *Brut y Brenhinedd*.

BRUTE family Monumental masons

In a generally non-pictorial society, the art of the monumental mason in Wales has afforded an important means of public visual expression. The Brute family, based at Llanbedr (**Vale of Grwyney**), were active around the **Black Mountains** in the 18th and early 19th centuries. Thomas Brute (1699–1767) and his son Aaron Brute (1731–1801) were the best-known members, the work of Aaron Brute being described as 'Peasant Rococo' because of his inventive use of floral motifs.

BRUTUS Legendary progenitor of the Britons

Brutus or Britto, alleged founder of the kingdom of the Britons, is first mentioned in *Historia Brittonum* attributed to Nennius (fl.9th century). In the 12th century, **Geoffrey of Monmouth** used the name to build up the legend of Brutus the Trojan, great-grandson of Aeneas, who led a remnant of his people from bondage in Greece to their new home, **Britain**, which was named after him. Geoffrey no doubt invented Brutus's friendship with Corineus (alleged founder of **Cornwall**), his marriage to Ignoge (Innogen), and his three sons Locrinus, Camber and Albanactus, the original kings of **England** (*Lloegr*), Wales (*Cymru*) and **Scotland** (*Yr Alban*). Geoffrey's insistence that Locrinus was the eldest son gave **English monarchs** a claim to hegemony over the whole of Britain.

BRYCHAN (5th century) Traditional founder of Brycheiniog

According to *De Situ Brecheniauc* (11th century) and *Cognacio Brychan* (13th century), Brychan was born in **Ireland**, the son of Anlach, son of Coronac, an **Irish** king, and Marchell daughter of Tewdrig, king of Garthmadrun in south-east Wales. The family settled in Wales and on the death of his father Brychan became ruler of Garthmadrun, later known as **Brycheiniog**. Many legends tell of his military deeds, fiery temper and procreative prowess – he is said to have had 11 sons and 25 daughters, many of whom embraced the religious life. Some substance is given to the traditions about him by traces in Brycheiniog of Irish settlements of the 5th century, while the distribution of churches bearing his and his descendants' names suggests a missionary movement of the same period. Brychan's feast day is 6 April.

BRYCHEINIOG Kingdom

Brycheiniog, centred on the valleys of the **Usk** and the Llynfi and extending from **Builth** and **Elfael** in the north to **Gwent** and **Morgannwg** in the south, emerged in the post-Roman centuries as one of the kingdoms of Wales. Originally the kingdom of Garthmadrun, it came to be known as Brycheiniog after the half-Irish **Brychan**, whose rule had strong **Irish** associations. Later kings of Brycheiniog all claimed descent from him. The kingdom was divided into three *cantrefi*: **Cantref Selyf** in the north, **Cantref Mawr** in the south and **Blaenllynfi** or **Talgarth** in the east. The royal residence may have been the crannog on **Llangorse Lake**, the *Brecenan mere* attacked by the Anglo-Saxons in 916. The dynasty seems to have died out by *c.*930 and Brycheiniog was absorbed into the kingdom of **Deheubarth**. **Rhys ap Tewdwr**, king of Deheubarth, was killed in the Usk valley in 1093, his death a prelude to the **Norman** conquest of Brycheiniog.

BRYMBO, Wrexham (1026 ha; 3482 inhabitants)

A **community** located north-west of **Wrexham**, Brymbo was industrialized from the 1790s onwards following **John Wilkinson**'s establishment of the Brymbo **Iron**works. In 1885, the Brymbo Steel Company produced some of **Britain**'s earliest steel manufactured by the **open-hearth** system. In October 1931, following the closure of the steelworks, unemployment among Brymbo's insured males was 81.5%, the highest in Wales. (Ferndale, **Rhondda**, at 73.9%, was the runner-up.) The steelworks reopened in 1934; lavishly refurbished in the late 1970s, they closed in 1990. The site is subject to an extensive reclamation programme, during which, in 2006, an extensive tract of fossilized rain forest was unearthed, providing the most comprehensive record of Carboniferous period plant life ever to have been excavated. Wilkinson's Brymbo Hall, which dated back at least to 1624, was demolished in 1973. A burial cist of the Early **Bronze Age** (*c.*2000 BC), discovered in 1958, contained a partial skeleton. The skull was reconstructed and the resulting wax model of 'Brymbo Man' was unveiled at Wrexham Museum in 2001.

BRYN, Neath Port Talbot
(1313 ha; 913 inhabitants)

Originally Bryntroedgarn, the **community** lies between the Afan valley and **Maesteg**. The monks of **Margam** Abbey mined **coal** there in the 13th century, but significant urbanization did not begin until after 1841, when a tramway was built to carry coal and **iron**stone to the **Cwmavon** works. In the late 19th century, Bryn's fortunes faded with those of the works, but coalmining revived in the early 20th century. By the late 20th century, with the collieries gone, Bryn was being developed for executive **housing**.

BRYN DERWIN, Battle of

In 1255, at Bryn Derwin, on the border between **Arfon** and **Eifionydd**, **Llywelyn ap Gruffudd** defeated his brothers Owain and **Dafydd**, thus establishing himself as sole ruler of **Gwynedd**.

BRYN-CRUG, Gwynedd (3108 ha; 626 inhabitants)

Located immediately north-east of **Tywyn**, the **community** contains an attractive stretch of the Dysynni valley. Castell Cynfael is a motte-and-bailey castle built in 1137 by **Owain Gwynedd**'s brother, Cadwaladr. Ynysmaengwyn (demolished), a handsome mansion built in 1758, was the home of the Corbet family and, after 1884, of the Corbett family, benefactors of Tywyn. Dolau-gwyn is a splendid 17th-century manor house. Bryn-crug has a formidable **football** team. The attractive Dol-goch **waterfalls** are easily accessible from the Talyllyn **Railway**.

BRYNEGLWYS, Denbighshire
(2448 ha; 344 inhabitants)

Located immediately north of **Corwen**, the **community** extends to the summit of **Llantysilio** Mountain. Plas yn Yale was the ancestral home of the **Yale family**. Yale chapel was added to St Tysilio's church (15th century) *c.*1575. The historian **David Powel** (1552–99) was a native of Bryneglwys.

BRYNFORD (Brynffordd), Flintshire
(873 ha; 1098 inhabitants)

Located immediately south-west of **Holywell**, the **community** comprises the **limestone** plateau of Holywell Common. The area was once rich in **Bronze Age** barrows, but many have been destroyed by 18th and 19th-century **lead** mining and by a 20th-century **golf** course. It is now littered with capped shafts and spoil heaps. The monument on Pen-y-Ball Top (1910) was built to commemorate George V's coronation. Henblas (1651) has a symmetrical three-bay front. St Michael's, Brynford (together with St Paul's, Gorsedd), was completed in 1853 to compensate for the loss of the church at Pantasaph (*see* **Whitford**).

BRYNGWRAN, Isle of Anglesey (1692 ha; 781 inhabitants)

Crossed by the **A55** north-west of **Aberffraw**, the **community**'s main settlement is Bryngwran village, which, until the completion of the dual carriageway in 2001, was a major bottleneck. The footings of the medieval church of the Holy Rood survive.

BRYN-JONES, Delme (1935–2001) Opera singer

The baritone Delme Bryn-Jones was born in Brynamman (**Quarter Bach**); originally Delme Jones, he added the first syllable of his birthplace to his name. He abandoned work as a **coal**miner and the prospect of a distinguished **rugby** career (he was an under-21 rugby international) to study singing at the Guildhall School of **Music**, **London**, and in Vienna. His success at major opera houses was almost immediate. Though especially renowned for his performances in Verdi operas, he also won acclaim for performances of Mozart, Gluck, Berlioz and Britten. His celebrated performances as Macbeth and Rigoletto for the **Welsh National Opera** in the 1970s helped propel the company to international status.

BRYNMAWR (Bryn-mawr), Blaenau Gwent
(576 ha; 5599 inhabitants)

Brynmawr, described by Richard Haslam in his volume on **Powys** in the series *The Buildings of Wales* as 'a town of terraced houses, situated improbably at twelve hundred feet', is perched at the eastern entrance to the heads of the valleys road above the remarkable Clydach Gorge (**Llanelly**). Originally in **Breconshire**, but bordering on **Monmouthshire**, Brynmawr, Janus-like, looked two ways: it developed as a dormitory town for **iron**workers, it provided a market for local farmers and it was well placed as a communications centre, once being served by four **railways**. A few scattered cottages in 1801, by the mid-19th century Brynmawr had played its part in **Chartism**, been described as 'degraded and corrupt' by the 1847 Education Commissioners (*see* **Treason of the Blue Books**) and lived through a **cholera** outbreak which led to the establishment of the first Board of **Health** in Wales. It had become a town, its streets laid out in a grid pattern and bearing the names of two very different dynasties – the ancient aristocratic family, the **Somersets**, and the parvenu industrialist family, the **Baileys**. During the interwar **depression**, unemployment among the town's insured males exceeded 90%: it 'presented in miniature a picture of those industrial, social and psychological factors which make up the problems of the Depressed Areas' (Elizabeth Jennings, *Brynmawr: A Study of a Distressed Area*, 1934).

Brynmawr had the unenviable distinction of being the only Welsh **community** whose problems were the subject of a major contemporary study. A group of **Quakers** sought to create employment by setting up a factory which produced the renowned Brynmawr **furniture**. In 1974, the **urban district**, established in 1894, was transferred under protest from the Breconshire district in Powys to the **Blaenau Gwent** district in **Gwent**. In 2001, Brynmawr rubber factory – a masterpiece of the Danish architect Ove Arup – the flagship of the town's post-war prosperity and the first post-war building in Wales to be listed – was demolished in an act of astonishing vandalism (*see* **Architecture**). The town is now dominated by the angular bulk of a computer software factory.

BUAN, Gwynedd (3243 ha; 469 inhabitants)

Extending over much of central **Llŷn**, the **community**'s most prominent feature is Garn Boduan, a hill rich in prehistoric settlements. Garn-Saethon is a striking **Iron Age hill-fort**. Penhyddgan is a well-preserved 17th-century house. St Boduan's church (1894), an impressive neo-Romanesque structure, contains numerous memorials to local families. **John Parry** (*c.*1710–82), the blind **harp**ist, was born near Garn Boduan. Madryn mansion, totally destroyed by fire in the 1960s, was the home of Love Jones-Parry who in 1868 won **Caernarfonshire** for the **Liberals**, defeating the **Conservative**, George Douglas-**Pennant**. Jones-Parry supported the establishment of the Welsh colony in **Patagonia**, where Puerto Madryn commemorates him.

BUCK, Samuel (1696–1779) and Nathaniel
(fl.1727–53) Topographical artists

Active between 1726 and 1753, the English Buck brothers were topographical artists whose drawings of the castles, abbeys and towns of Wales and **England** were published as engravings – in, for example, a three–volume set (1740–2) and *Twelve Views in Aquatinta* (1775). Long, horizontally drawn landscapes in pen and wash became their distinctive style. The originals, from which the prints were made, were noted for their sensitivity; examples can be seen at the **National Library**.

BUCKLEY (Bwcle), Flintshire
(1969 ha; 14,568 inhabitants)

Located east of **Mold**, Buckley was a major centre of earthenware manufacture from at least the 13th century. Initially, high-quality wares were made; domestic ware later predominated, but eventually brick making became more important than the **pottery**. The increasing use of local **coal** enabled the industry to develop rapidly. Buckley attracted numerous immigrants, many from Staffordshire, and elements of their dialect long survived. The works came to specialize in acid-resistant and fire bricks, with the **Shotton Steelworks** a major customer. In the 19th century, the separate settlements of hamlets Bistre (Domesday Book's *Biscopestreu*), Drury, Spon Green and Buckley Mountain coalesced to form Buckley town. With Lane End the sole brickworks still in operation, Buckley's main sources of employment came to be the Padeswood Cement Works (1949), the industrial estates built on the former brickworks sites of Catheralls, Drury and Little Mountain, and the work available to those commuting to Chester and the Wirral. St Matthew's, Buckley (1821), was Wales's sole church financed by parliament's first church-building grant (1818). Old Alltami chapel (1838) is reputedly the earliest Primitive Methodist chapel to be erected in north-east Wales.

BUDDUGRE, SWYDD Commote
One of the **commotes** of the *cantref* of **Maelienydd**, it took its name from Buddugre Hill (**Abbey Cwmhir**); nothing is known of the victory (*buddugoliaeth*) which the hill commemorates.

'BUGEILIO'R GWENITH GWYN'
(Tending the white wheat) Song
The melody of this folk song was first printed by **Maria Jane Williams** in *Ancient National Airs of Gwent and Morganwg* in 1844. The words, attributed to the **Glamorgan** poets Wil Hopcyn and Dafydd Nicolas, and probably modified by Iolo Morganwg (**Edward Williams**), may be a recasting of older folk verses. A tenuous tradition connects the song with the story of Wil Hopcyn's supposed love for Ann Maddocks (1704–27), 'the maid of Cefn Ydfa' (*see* **Llangynwyd Lower**).

BUILDINGS OF WALES, The
A series of volumes by different authors, documenting and describing the **architecture** of Wales. The series, founded by Sir Nikolaus Pevsner (1902–83), complements sister series on the buildings of **England** and of **Scotland**. Each volume describes in detailed, gazetteer form virtually every building of consequence with each locality. By 2007, the volumes on **Powys**, **Clwyd**, **Glamorgan**, **Gwent/Monmouthshire**, **Pembrokeshire** and **Carmarthenshire** and **Ceredigion** had been published.

BUILTH (Buellt or Buallt) *Cantref* and lordship
The *cantref* of Buellt was probably at one time part of southern **Powys**, but along with some adjoining territories, it seems to have become part of an autonomous region sometimes known as Rhwng Gwy a Hafren (between **Wye** and **Severn**). It was reputed to consist of the **commotes** of Treflys, Penbuellt, Dinan and Is Irfon, but information on the commote boundaries is lacking. Buellt was conquered by the **Normans** (*c.*1095), and the de **Breos family** became lords of Builth. Its subsequent fortunes were influenced by its association with that turbulent lineage. It was involved in the disputes between King John and William de Breos, and between John and **Llywelyn ap Iorwerth**. Isabella de Breos brought Builth as a dowry to Llywelyn's son, **Dafydd**, a marriage that took place despite the fact that Llywelyn had hanged her father. The crown refused to recognize the arrangement, and in 1254 the future Edward I was invested with Builth. It was later captured by **Llywelyn ap Gruffudd** but the crown's possession of it was confirmed in 1277 by the **Treaty of Aberconwy**. It was while seeking to support the men of Builth in their revolt against the crown that Llywelyn met his death at **Cilmeri** in 1282.

In 1536, the lordship became the northern part of the newly created **Breconshire**.

BUILTH (Llanfair-ym-Muallt), Breconshire, Powys (304 ha; 2352 inhabitants)
At the end of the 11th century, a motte-and-bailey castle was built in the *cantref* of Buellt to guard the **Wye** crossing. Destroyed by **Llywelyn ap Gruffudd** in 1260, the subsequent refortification, carried out for Edward I, was to a concentric plan which anticipated the castles of **Gwynedd**. The town of Builth was almost totally destroyed by fire in 1691, and **Theophilus Jones** wrote scornfully of the 'one long street ... of shops and public houses' that constituted the rebuilt town. One of the public houses, the Royal Oak, now the Lion, was patronized both by Lady Hester Stanhope (1776–1839), who later left wild Wales for wilder Lebanon, and by the three authors of the Blue Books report of 1847 (*see* **Treason of the Blue Books**), much of which was written there. (The satirical play *Brad y Llyfrau Gleision* by **R. J. Derfel**, is set in Builth.) The oldest surviving Methodist cause in Wales is in Builth; work on Capel Alpha began in 1747 under the direction of **Howel Harris**, and Lewis Morris (1701–65; *see* **Morris Brothers**) recorded sourly that 'most of the People here are drunk with **Religion**'. The **community**'s **economy** rests on **agriculture** and **tourism**, although the prosperous days when workers from south Wales flocked to drink the medicinal waters that added 'Wells' to its name are long past. It is crowded every July when the **Royal Welsh Agricultural Show** is held in nearby **Llanelwedd**.

BULKELEY family Landowners
William Bulkeley (d.1490), a native of **Cheshire**, settled in **Beaumaris** and married Elen, daughter of Gwilym ap Gruffydd of Penrhyn (*see* **Griffith family**). His son, William (d.1516), married Alice, heiress of the Bolde family of **Conwy**, assiduous estate builders in **Caernarfonshire**. The Bulkeleys continued the tradition, amassing estates extending by 1873 to 6680 ha in **Anglesey** and 5400 ha in Caernarfonshire. From their mansion of Baron Hill (**Beaumaris**), they dominated Anglesey's **parliamentary representation** for three centuries. After 140 years as Irish viscounts, they received a British viscountcy in 1784. The recipient, Thomas James Bulkeley, was the last in the direct male line, his estates passing to his half-brother's son, Sir Robert Williams, the ninth baronet of Penrhyn, who assumed the surname Bulkeley. The diary of William Bulkeley of Brynddu (**Mechell**), a member of a cadet branch of the family, provides a fascinating portrait of 18th-century Anglesey. Baron Hill is now a melancholy ruin.

BULKELEY, Arthur (c.1495–1553) Bishop
A member of the landowning **Bulkeley family**, Beaumaris-born Arthur Bulkeley, an **Oxford**-educated clerical lawyer, served as chaplain to the Duke of Suffolk and, in the early 1530s, was in Thomas Cromwell's bureaucratic circle. Appointed Bishop of **Bangor** in 1541, he was a key figure in carrying out Henry VIII's secular and religious policies in the **diocese**. The first Bangor prelate for over a century to have been born in Wales and to reside within his diocese, in 1542 he was also the first bishop in Wales formally to

The bridge over the Wye at Builth, first built in 1779

request clergymen and teachers to use **Welsh**. His zeal for implementing the radical Protestantism promulgated during the reign of Edward VI, including removing altars and abolishing the Mass, elicited a hostile reaction in some contemporary Welsh poetry.

BUNDLING

'Courting on the bed' attracted the attention of English travellers in the 18th and 19th centuries. Maidservants were often visited in their bedrooms at night during courtship. Having taken off their shoes, the couple would lie on (not in) the bed to while away their brief leisure hours in private. As long as they continued to talk, it would be assumed by those downstairs that nothing improper was going on. The possibilities for sexual 'immorality' attracted the criticism of the churches and chapels, especially after the publication of the **Education** Report of 1847 (*see* **Treason of the Blue Books**). The custom of bundling was evidently known to the 19th-century American ethnologist and painter George Catlin: while studying the Mandans – the tribe of 'Welsh Indians' allegedly descended from **Madog ab Owain Gwynedd** and company – Catlin identified several supposedly Welsh practices among the tribe, including an inclination to 'prattle' during sexual intercourse.

BURGES, William (1821–81) Architect and designer

Born in **London**, where his practice was based, Burges was responsible for the refurbishment of **Cardiff** Castle and the reconstruction of nearby Castell Coch for the wealthy third marquess of Bute (*see* **Stuart family**). His work, which included the designing of **furniture** and fittings, is an extravagant mixture of pseudo-medieval, Gothic and pre-Raphaelite styles, although his work at Castell Coch is considered to be among Europe's most learned reconstructions of a medieval castle. A follower of Ruskin, Burges believed in the necessity of ornament, covering almost every surface with a mass of animal, **plant** and historic motifs. The Bute Workshops, where many of the designs were realized, became an important training ground for indigenous craftsmen; the sculptor **Goscombe John** trained there. Burges had a marked influence upon the **architecture** of late 19th-century Cardiff, especially in streets such as Cathedral Road.

BURGESS, Thomas (1756–1837) Bishop

For his first 47 years, Burgess, born in Hampshire, had virtually no connection with Wales. In 1803, the prime minister, Henry Sidmouth, who had been his contemporary at Winchester School, appointed him bishop of **St David's**. During his 22 years in Wales, Burgess founded St David's College, **Lampeter** (**University of Wales, Lampeter**), supported *yr hen bersoniaid llengar* (the old literary clerics), learnt **Welsh** well enough to preach in the language, and involved himself in the **eisteddfod** movement. In 1825, at the age of 68, Burgess moved to the less demanding **diocese** of Salisbury.

BURGH, Hubert de (d.1243) Justiciar of England and Ireland

As justiciar of **England** (1215–32), he was closely involved with Wales, acquiring the **Three Castles**, **Montgomery**, **Cardigan** and **Carmarthen**, and the custody of **Glamorgan** and **Pembroke**. Initially well disposed towards **Llywelyn ap Iorwerth**, he sought, by the late 1220s, to contain the

The young Richard Burton, with his father, in the mining village of Pontrhydyfen, Pelenna, July 1953

prince's power. His activities at Montgomery led to Llywelyn's victory in **Kerry** in 1228. Llywelyn successfully challenged him again in 1231, a factor in Hubert's fall from power. His nephew John, husband of Elizabeth, co-heiress of Gilbert de **Clare** (d.1314), was lord of **Usk**, which passed by marriage to the **Mortimer family** in 1368.

BURTON, Pembrokeshire
(1377 ha; 1041 inhabitants)
Located across the **Milford Haven Waterway** from **Pembroke Dock**, Burton was for centuries the northern terminus of the estuary's chief ferry, which ceased operating following the construction of the **Cleddau** toll bridge in 1975. The Hanging Stone **Neolithic** tomb has a large capstone supported by three uprights. Benton, a miniature 13th-century castle, was rebuilt in the 1930s as an exercise in the **picturesque**. St Mary's church, originally 13th century, contains the altar tomb of Richard Wogan of Boulston (*c*.1541).

BURTON, Philip (1904–95) Theatre director
A native of **Mountain Ash**, Burton taught English and drama at Port Talbot, where Richard Jenkins was among his pupils. The young man later took his teacher's surname and became famous as the actor **Richard Burton**; his teacher described their relationship in his book *Richard and Philip: the Burtons* (1992). In 1954, after working for the BBC (*see* **Broadcasting**) in **Cardiff** as an acclaimed radio producer, Philip Burton emigrated to the United States, where he worked as a director on Broadway.

BURTON, Richard (Richard Walter Jenkins; 1925–84) Actor
Often regarded as merely epitomizing massive unfulfilled potential, both on stage and screen, Burton nevertheless achieved an impressive seven Academy nominations – without gaining the coveted Oscar. For a time, through the 1960s and before the tawdry potboilers and morose binges, he was a worthy member of any pantheon of great screen actors.

He was born at Pontrhydyfen (**Pelenna**), near **Port Talbot**, into a **Welsh**-speaking mining family named Jenkins, later adopting the surname of **Philip Burton**, the teacher who inspired his passion for acting. Richard made his stage debut at the age of 18 in **Emlyn Williams**'s *The Druid's Rest*, and studied English at **Oxford**. A comparable passion for **literature** could have made him a writer, but it was giving expression to the words of others to which he primarily devoted his formidable intelligence – and remarkable, resonant voice.

He established an authoritative stage presence early on, making a huge impact on the Stratford, **London** and Broadway stages. There were lauded performances in Christopher Fry plays in London and New York in 1949–50, and in **Shakespeare**'s *Henry IV* (parts I and II) and *Henry V* at Stratford in 1951. He was Coriolanus and Hamlet in a 1953–4 Old Vic season, and in 1955 played the title role in the same company's *Henry V* and Iago and the title role alternatively in *Othello*. He won the New York Drama Critics' Award as **Arthur** in the Lerner-Loewe musical *Camelot* in New York in 1960–1. Burton was a distinguished narrator in Douglas Cleverdon's celebrated 1954 radio production of **Dylan Thomas's** *Under Milk Wood*, but achieved greatest prominence as a screen actor. He made his **film** debut as a tongue-tied, love-smitten shop assistant in *The Last Days of Dolwyn* (1949). He was rarely seen in Welsh material later, although he was a superb on-screen narrator in the Oscar-winning television documentary *Dylan Thomas* (1962). In Andrew Sinclair's joyless and hopelessly misguided *Under Milk Wood* (1972), he looked woebegone, stumbling through pointless, picaresque adventures.

His Oscar Best Actor near-misses were for the *The Robe* (1953), *Becket* (1962), *The Spy Who Came in From the Cold* (1965), *Who's Afraid of Virginia Woolf?* (1966), *Anne of the Thousand Days* (1969) and *Equus* (1977). He gained a Best Supporting Actor nomination for *My Cousin Rachel* (1952).

Burton, who was married five times, was often criticized, probably justifiably, for surrendering to Mammon after he joined the million-dollars-a-role set as co-star with Elizabeth Taylor in the extravagant but troubled *Cleopatra* (1963). Two marriages to Taylor ensured permanent celebrity status, but after the late 1970s his material deteriorated and he rarely displayed the commitment of earlier screen roles. Popular in his homeland, Burton was a generous supporter of Welsh causes and, despite a luxurious life in America and Switzerland (where, at Celigny, he is buried), he always maintained contact with Pontrhydyfen.

BUSES

The story of bus travel in Wales is one of dominance by a few large companies, with dozens of small operators providing more localized services and some degree of competition.

As early as 1826, **horse**-drawn buses were trundling along Oystermouth Road in **Swansea**, three years before Shillibeer's 'first' horse omnibus in **London**. **Cardiff** was slower off the mark, but horse-drawn buses were certainly operating there by 1845, when those running unlicensed services were prosecuted. Cardiff's first by-laws for the regulation of omnibuses were drawn up in 1863; one of the early operators was **Solomon Andrews**. Passengers on the upper deck of his Patent Bus, built in 1882, sat back-to-back along the length of the vehicle, and access was by ladder.

Motorbus services developed hand-in-hand with tramways and involved civic enterprise as well as the efforts of entrepreneurs such as Edward Phillips of **Holywell**, who in 1921 converted a French-built car into a bus. Earlier operators included the **Clynnog** and Trevor Motor Company, formed in 1912 to serve villages between **Pwllheli** and **Caernarfon**, and Express Motors of Caernarfon, founded *c.*1910. The 1920s saw a huge expansion of bus travel, its popularity providing opportunities for enterprising people such as the postmistress of **Llantwit Fardre**, Mrs S. A. Bebb, who in 1924 bought a Chevrolet 14-seater bus for her sons to run services on the **Pontypridd**–Beddau route. Brewer's Motor Services of Caerau, Cardiff, had its origins in a dairy firm whose roundsmen were not averse to giving people lifts on their carts. The buses in use were generally those made by the major motor manufacturers, but there were interesting variations: ex-miner William George Thomas launched Llynfi Motor Services at **Maesteg** in 1923 by paying £650 in sovereigns for an ex-army Fiat with a Massey body.

Crosville Motor Services (1906), set up in Chester by George Crosland-Taylor and a Frenchman, Georges Ville, penetrated deeply into mid and north Wales after the **First**

One of Wales's earliest buses, at Llanarth, Cardiganshire, *c.*1904

World War. In 1929, a year after mainline **railways** had been given powers to run buses, Crosville was bought by London, Midland and Scottish Railway. Following the nationalization of the railways in 1948, it came into state ownership. With privatization, the Crosville name eventually disappeared and its buses were run under the title Arriva Cymru.

South Wales Transport (SWT), established by the British Electric Traction group in 1914 to service the Swansea tramways system, extended its services to **Carmarthen** and **Port Talbot**, and purchased small independent competitors. Its main competitor was United Welsh, which eventually merged with SWT and became part of the National Bus Company. Western Welsh, synonymous with bus travel in many parts of south Wales in the mid-20th century, had its roots in South Wales Commercial Motors (1920), financed by the Cardiff-based brewery company Hancock's. Its modest beginnings – two vehicles and a Cardiff–**Penarth** service – did scant justice to the enterprise of its first managing director, Albert Gray, who in 1924 patented the forerunner to the sliding roof. After the company's services had been merged with the Great Western Railway's south Wales operations in 1929, it was renamed Western Welsh. Its fortunes were linked with those of Red and White Services (1930), which grew independently of the big groups to cover a wide area of south-east Wales and southern **England**. Western Welsh and Red and White merged in 1978 to form National Welsh. A considerable number of small independent bus companies continue to operate, many of them mainly reliant upon school bus contracts.

Municipal operators played a significant role in the development of motorbus services in Wales. **Caerphilly Urban District** Council was the first local authority in south Wales to launch its own bus service, its inaugural route to **Nelson** starting in April 1920; **Bedwas** and Machen (1922) and **Gelligaer** (1928) quickly followed. The development of motor transport services in Cardiff was left to private firms until December 1920, when the city council began running its own buses. **Newport** Corporation, which had run **trams** since 1901, introduced buses in 1924, the year that **Merthyr Tydfil** launched its first operation. In 1926, the West **Monmouthshire** Omnibus Board took over services previously jointly run by **Bedwellty** and Mynyddislwyn councils. The undertaking became **Islwyn** Borough Transport Ltd in 1986. Taff Ely Transport (1974) grew out of bus operations in and around Pontypridd, where the local council had originally preferred tramways.

Long-distance coach travel became established in the 1930s when, for example, passengers paid 33 shillings and 6 pence (£1.67) return for a seat on Ensign Motors' service from London to **Aberystwyth**, or 30 shillings (£1.50) return on A. T. Morse's South Wales Express between **Llanelli** and London. By the later 20th century, several Welsh bus companies – Regina of Blaenau **Ffestiniog**, for example – offered coach holidays in **Britain** and mainland Europe.

In the 1980s, deregulation encouraged the growth of minibus services, and with them came the return of the lively competition that had characterized earlier decades. Scheduled long-distance services continued to run between Wales and England, and, until 2004, the Traws Cambria route linked Bristol and **Llandudno** via Cardiff, Swansea, Carmarthen, Aberystwyth, **Dolgellau**, Caernarfon and **Bangor**. Widespread car ownership has led to a decline in bus patronage, causing **county** council consortiums and the **National Assembly** to seek more co-ordination of operators and funding.

BUSH, Percy (Frank) (1879–1958) Rugby player

An audacious and occasionally wayward **rugby** union fly-half, Bush could single-handedly lose games as well as win them. A great favourite in his native **Cardiff**, whose team he captained for three seasons, he won the first of his eight international caps in the historic Welsh win over the All Blacks in 1905.

BUTLER, Eleanor (?1745–1829) and PONSONBY, Sarah (1755–1831) 'The Ladies of Llangollen'

This aristocratic couple eloped to escape the conventions of life in **Ireland** and set up home together at Plas Newydd in **Llangollen**. Among numerous visitors to the Plas, which is today a tourist attraction, were Shelley, Byron and Wordsworth; the couple were offended by Wordsworth's description of their abode as a 'low-roofed cott', and the poet was not invited back. Among lesbians, the couple have achieved iconic status (*see* **Homosexuality**).

BUTTON, Thomas (*c.*1575–1634)
Admiral and explorer

Born at St Lythans (**Wenvoe**), Button entered the navy *c.*1589. In 1612, he commanded an expedition to Hudson Bay seeking a north-west passage, and was knighted on his return. He was admiral in charge of the Irish coast (1614–34), and was appointed commissioner inquiring into the state of the navy in 1625. Button Gwinnett, one of the signatories of the American Declaration of Independence (*see* **North America**), received his name because of the close family relationship between the Buttons and the Gwinnetts.

Cadair Idris and the Mawddach estuary

CADAIR IDRIS Mountain

Wales's highest **mountain** south of **Aran Fawddwy**, Cadair Idris enjoys a higher reputation than its height of 893 m might suggest. Arising virtually from the sea, it was considered in the 16th century to be the highest mountain in **Britain**. That masterpiece of 18th-century art **Richard Wilson**'s *Cader Idris, Llyn-y-Cau* (*c.*1765) represents the epitome of the glory of high places. Visitors travelling by **railway** to upland Wales generally took the train from **Wrexham** to **Barmouth**; the line was overlooked by Cadair Idris's looming presence, causing it to be the most familiar of all of Wales's mountains. **Siôn Dafydd Rhys** was the first to record the legend linking the mountain to the **giant** Idris; anyone who slept in Idris's bed, it was claimed, would wake up either mad or a poet. The profile of its 13-km ridge suggests a reclining figure, and **Dewi-Prys Thomas** commented that, seen as such, an art critic would judge it to be 'a work of arcane passion'. A magnificent escarpment of Ordovician rock,

glacial activity has caused it to be graced with Britain's finest cirque – the superb hollow which cradles Llyn Cau. Rich in alpine-arctic **plants**, much of it has been designated a National Nature Reserve. Because of its relative isolation, the summit – Penygadair (**Llanfihangel-y-Pennant**) – offers a superb vista on those rare occasions when there are clear views; the finest part of the vista is the exquisite estuary of the **Mawddach** and the huge sweep of Cardigan Bay.

CADFAN (6th century) Saint

According to tradition, Cadfan was the founder of the important church of **Tywyn** (**Meirionnydd**) and first abbot of Bardsey (**Aberdaron**; *see also* **Islands**). 'Canu Cadfan', a 12th-century poem by Llywelyn Fardd is the main source of information about him. It was claimed that he had led a contingent of **saints** from **Brittany** to Wales, and stories concerning him circulated until the late 19th century. Cadfan's feast day is 1 November.

CADFARCH, Montgomeryshire, Powys
(11,009 ha; 849 inhabitants)

Constituting the south-western corner of **Montgomeryshire**, the **community** – one of the largest in Wales – extends from the outskirts of **Machynlleth** to the Nant-y-moch **Reservoir** (*see* **Blaenrheidol**). Formed in 1974 through the amalgamation of the civil **parishes** of Is-y-garreg, Uwch-y-garreg and Penegoes, it contains the villages of Penegoes, Derwenlas and Aberhosan. Its name was borrowed from St Cadfarch's church, Penegoes. Rebuilt in 1877, the church adjoins the Regency rectory which replaced the house in which the artist **Richard Wilson** was born in 1714. Derwenlas – a one-time **port** – is located at the **Dyfi**'s highest tidal point; it thus gives the **county** of **Powys** at least a vestige of a coastline. In the 19th century, the attractive village of Aberhosan was a centre of the **woollen industry**. The cairns on Bryn y Fedwen and the arrowheads found at Bugeilyn indicate that, in the **Bronze Age**, Cadfarch's uplands had a substantial **population**. In the far south of the community stand Cerrig Cyfamod Glyndŵr, quartz standing stones purporting to mark the site of **Owain Glyndŵr**'s victory in the **battle of Hyddgen** (1401). Glaslyn Lake is a nature reserve.

CADI HAF

A processional **dance** in the north, performed by a male group and including the comically and colourfully dressed Ffŵl and Cadi, the latter with a blackened face and wearing a mixture of male and female attire. The summer birch (*see* **Bedwen Haf**) was carried by the dancers from house to house as part of the May Day (*Calan Mai*) celebrations, the Cadi collecting money in a ladle as they danced.

CADOG (5th/6th century) Saint

One of the foremost religious leaders of his age, Cadog was the founder of a monastic school at **Llancarfan**. Several churches were dedicated to him in Wales, **Cornwall**, **Brittany** and **Scotland**. A Life of Cadog, of questionable historical value, was written by Lifris of Llancarfan at the beginning of the 12th century. Lifris states that Cadog was the son of Gwynllyw ap Glywys, a chieftain of **Gwynllŵg**, and Gwladus ferch **Brychan**. He spent some time in **Ireland**. Cadog's feast day is 24 January.

CADW

Cadw (Welsh Historic Monuments) is a directorate of the **National Assembly** responsible for the protection of the built heritage. This role, formerly performed by the Ministry of Works for **Britain**, was transferred to the **Welsh Office** in 1984. Cadw – Welsh for 'to preserve' – became an executive agency in 1991, charged with scheduling ancient monuments of national importance, listing buildings of special architectural or historic interest, and managing and interpreting historic sites in state care; in 2005, its status was changed from that of agency to directorate of the Assembly **Government**. Cadw is able to help owners of scheduled monuments and listed buildings with financial grants for repairs and conservation work. There are more than 130 sites in state care in Wales that are open to the public, from prehistoric burial chambers to remains from the **Industrial Revolution** to 20th-century prefabs.

The Ancient Monuments Board for Wales is an independent body that advises the Assembly and Cadw on ancient monuments. The Historic Buildings Council for Wales is a similarly independent body advising the Assembly and Cadw on planning matters and grant aid for listed buildings. (*See also* **Royal Commission on the Ancient and Historical Monuments of Wales**.)

CADWALADR AP CADWALLON (d.664/682)
King of Gwynedd

The son of **Cadwallon ap Cadfan**. The Peniarth MS of *Brut y Tywysogyon* opens with an account of his death in 682, commenting: 'And from that time onwards the Britons lost the crown of the kingdom and the Saxons won it.' Cadwaladr figured in later tradition as a *Mab Darogan* (*see* **Prophecy**) and as Cadwaladr Fendigaid, patron **saint** of Llangadwaladr (**Bodorgan**) and other churches. The **Red Dragon** was considered to be Cadwaladr's banner.

CADWALLON AP CADFAN (d.633)
King of Gwynedd

A descendant of **Maelgwn Gwynedd**, his victory, in alliance with **Mercia**, over Northumbria at Meigen (Hatfield, near Doncaster) in 632 became part of the heroic tradition of the Welsh. A poem in his praise contains the earliest reference to '**Cymry**'.

CADWGAN (d.1241) Bishop

A **Cistercian** monk of **Irish** and Welsh parentage, Cadwgan rose to be abbot of **Whitland** before his election as bishop of **Bangor** (1215). As bishop, he was involved with **Llywelyn ap Iorwerth** and in 1234 procured grain from **Ireland** to feed the poor of his **diocese**. Cadwgan's religious sensibilities and commitment to pastoral care are illuminated by his writings, which include advice to priests on hearing their **parish**ioners' confessions.

CADWGAN AP BLEDDYN (d.1111)
King of Powys

Cadwgan, son of **Bleddyn ap Cynfyn**, half-brother of **Gruffudd ap Llywelyn** (d.1063), first appears in 1088 in an attack on **Deheubarth**. He was one of the leaders of the Welsh revolt of 1094. In 1098, he fled to **Ireland** in the wake of the **Norman** invasion of north Wales, but he seems to have been established in **Powys** by 1099. Powys was briefly the dominant power in Wales, but Cadwgan failed to control his family; in 1109, his son **Owain** abducted **Nest**, wife of Gerald of Windsor, precipitating a major crisis. In 1111, Cadwgan was killed by his nephew Madog ap Rhirid. Subsequent rulers of Powys were descended from Cadwgan's brother Maredudd (d.1132).

CAEO Commote

As the most mountainous and remote of the seven **commotes** of **Cantref Mawr**, Caeo frequently proved to be a refuge for the beleaguered rulers of **Deheubarth**. Its administrative centre was at **Cynwyl Gaeo**. The commote was the home of Llywelyn ap Gruffudd Fychan, an ally of **Owain Glyndŵr** who was executed at **Llandovery** in 1401. The name survived as that of the post-**Acts of 'Union' hundred** of Caio.

The Roman amphitheatre at Caerleon

CAEREINION Commote

Located in the centre of **Powys Wenwynwyn**, the **commote** contained **Mathrafal**, reputedly the seat of the rulers of **Powys**. The post-**Acts of 'Union' hundred** of Caereinion had similar boundaries to those of the medieval commote. The identity of Einion is unknown.

CAERHUN, Conwy (5668 ha; 1200 inhabitants)

Located on the left bank of the **Conwy**, the **community** extends to the summit of **Carnedd** Llywelyn (1062 m). It contains the villages of Caerhun, Llanbedr-y-Cennin, Rowen, Tal-y-bont and Ty'n-y-groes. Llanbedr-y-Cennin church (13th–16th century) was heavily restored in 1842. St Mary's church, Caerhun (13th–16th century) stands in the north-east corner of the 2-ha **Roman** fort of Canovium. Established AD *c.*78 and abandoned *c.*180, the fort's layout follows the standard pattern of a Roman auxiliary fort. The **road** leading from the attractive village of Rowen to the standing stones at Bwlch-y-ddeufaen – one of the steepest in Wales – was a highly important prehistoric route. The area is rich in cairns, hut circles and house platforms. The ferry crossing the Conwy at Tal-y-cafn operated for centuries until the construction of the road bridge in 1897.

CAERLEON (Caerllion), Newport
(1421 ha; 8708 inhabitants)

Straddling the **Usk** immediately north of the built-up area of the city of **Newport**, the **community** contains the town of Caerleon and the village of Christchurch. In AD *c.*75, the right bank of the Usk was chosen as the site of one of Roman **Britain**'s three long-term legionary fortresses. (Chester and York were the other two.) The fortress was known to the **Romans** as Isca (from Eisca, reputedly the

Brythonic form of Wysg or Usk), and to the Welsh as Caerllion (the fort of the legions). Motives for choosing the site probably included its location well within the territory of the warlike **Silures**, and its access to the navigable Usk.

Accommodating the Second Legion Augusta, consisting of over 5000 men, the fortress was originally built in timber and turf and was rebuilt in stone AD *c.*100. Its layout followed regular Roman practice. Built astride the **road** crossing Wales's southern coastal plain, it contained the legionary headquarters (the *principia*), the legate's residence, tribunes' houses, a bathhouse, a hospital, granaries, workshops and blocks of barracks. Outside the fortress walls were an amphitheatre, further bathhouses, parade grounds, docks on the Usk and a substantial *vicus* – a township housing those providing services for the legionaries.

By the AD 120s, cohorts of the Second Legion Augusta were involved in the building of Hadrian's Wall, and thereafter – with the Silures accepting Roman rule – it is unlikely that Isca ever subsequently housed a full legion. It seems to have been abandoned in the 330s, partly because by then the main threat came from **Irish** pirates, who could be more conveniently dealt with from the reconstructed fort at **Cardiff**. So impressive were its ruins that Caerleon was woven into the legends of medieval Wales. The site of the deaths of Wales's earliest Christian martyrs (**Julius and Aaron**), it was believed to have been the seat of an archbishop and – according to **Geoffrey of Monmouth** – the location of episodes in the life of King **Arthur**. **Giraldus Cambrensis** waxed lyrical on the significance of the ruins, and in 1405 the French army sent to assist **Owain Glyndŵr** made a detour to see the amphitheatre, which was believed to be **Arthur**'s Round Table.

In the 1080s, the **Normans** built a large motte adjoining the fortress and erected St **Cadog**'s church on the site of the *principia*, and, in both buildings, stone from the ruins were employed. Further depredations occurred as Caerleon grew and as Roman artefacts were looted. In 1847, however, the Caerleon Antiquarian Association was founded, largely through the efforts of John Edward Lee. From 1850 onwards, artefacts were preserved in the handsome Greek Doric museum; enlarged in 1987, and known since 2005 as The National Roman Legion Museum, the museum is part of the **National Museum [of] Wales**. Archaeological exploration began in 1908; it culminated in **Mortimer Wheeler**'s work (financed by the *Daily Mail*) on the amphitheatre in 1926, and **Nash-Williams**'s work from 1927 to 1955. Visible remains include part of the fortress walls, much of the fortress baths (encased in a modern cover building, 1984), the amphitheatre and the Prysg Field barracks – the only Roman legionary barracks visible in Europe.

In 1724, Caerleon acquired a charity school of exceptional size, an indication of the increasing importance of the village, which acquired **urban district** status in 1894. In 1855, St Cadog's church was partly rebuilt; it was considerably enlarged in 1934. In 1912, the Caerleon Training College was established, an institution which became part of the **University of Wales**, **Newport** in the 1990s. Its original neo-baroque range, together with innovative additions in the 1980s, are buildings of distinction.

The village of Christchurch, across the Usk from Caerleon, stands on a ridge overlooking the confluence of the Usk and the Llwyd. Its large Holy Trinity church, originally built in the 12th century, contains features from all subsequent medieval centuries and some fine 20th-century **stained glass**. Further along the ridge looms the vast bulk

of the Celtic Manor Hotel. The Ryder Cup competition will be held on its **golf** courses in 2010.

CAERNARFON, Gwynedd
(937 ha; 9611 inhabitants)

The **community** is located where the River Seiont or Saint joins the **Menai Strait**. The name Saint comes from the Brythonic Segonti; when the **Romans** built a fort on high ground west of the present town in AD *c.*78, they named it Segontium. (The name Seiont, adopted in the 16th century, was a learned adaptation of the **Latin** name.) Extending over 2.3 ha, the fort was largely rebuilt in stone *c.*120; left derelict for several periods of its history, it was finally abandoned in 383. A smaller fort, built *c.*220, is located 200 m to its west. Known as Hen Walia, some of the fort's walls stand 5 m high. Traditions gathered around Segontium, linking it with the emperor **Constantine**, with the usurper **Magnus Maximus** and with **Branwen ferch Llŷr** in *The Mabinogion*. The *maerdref* (administrative centre) of the **commote** of Is **Gwyrfai**, *y gaer yn Arfon* (the fort opposite Môn or **Anglesey**) was one of the residences of the princes of **Gwynedd**. Near the site of the Roman mithraeum stands the church of Peblig or Publicus, allegedly one of the sons of Magnus Maximus. Rich in memorials, the present building dates from the 14th century.

In *c.*1090, **Hugh of Avranches**, earl of Chester, built a castle 1 km east of Segontium at the edge of the Menai Strait, the site chosen by Edward I in 1283 as that of the chief stronghold of conquered Gwynedd. Edward I's castle, 180 m long, was badly damaged during the **Welsh revolt** of 1294. Building work resumed in 1296 and continued until *c.*1327. With its octagonal towers and its horizontal bands of different coloured stone, the castle resembles the

Caernarfon Castle

Theodosian walls of Constantinople – an indication that Edward viewed his conquest in imperial terms. Linked with the castle is the 734-m town wall with its eight towers and two twin-towered gateways. The castle and town walls escaped the demolition intended for them following the 17th-century **Civil Wars**. They underwent extensive restoration in the late 19th century and were granted World Heritage status in 1986. In 1911 and 1969, the castle was the site of investitures of **Princes of Wales**. It contains the museum of the **Royal Welch Fusiliers**.

Following the **Edwardian conquest**, Caernarfon became the seat of **government** of **Caernarfonshire** and of the **Principality** of north Wales. It became the county town of Caernarfonshire in 1889 and of the county of Gwynedd in 1974. Intended as a bastion of Englishness, it eventually became linguistically the most **Welsh** of towns. In 2001, 91.76% of the inhabitants had some knowledge of Welsh – the highest percentage for any community in Wales. (*But see* **Llanuwchllyn**.) The townspeople, nicknamed Cofis, possess a unique dialect immortalized in the radio monologues of Richard Hughes and in William Owen's stories *Chwedlau Pen Deitsh* (1961).

Caernarfon's main period of growth was 1801–41, when the **population** increased from 3626 to 9192, largely because of the employment opportunities provided by the **slate**-exporting activities of its **port**. One of the embarkation points of the Anglesey ferry, the town also became a centre of **railways** (1828, 1852, 1867). It won particular prominence as the centre of **newspaper** publishing, becoming the home of the *Caernarvon and Denbigh Herald*, *Yr Herald Gymraeg*, *Y Genedl Gymreig* and *Papur Pawb*. Media activity continues, for the numerous television companies established in its vicinity have made Caernarfon Wales's main **broadcasting** centre outside **Cardiff**.

Architecturally, while retaining its magnificent medieval heritage, Caernarfon is essentially a mid-19th century town, well endowed with the large chapels that reflect the one-time strength of the **borough**'s **Nonconformists**). However, the splendid Capel Moriah (1827) was destroyed by fire in 1976, and Seilo (1900) was demolished to build Caernarfon's controversial through road. Caernarfon's centre is its square (*Y Maes*) where statutes of **David Lloyd George** and **Hugh Owen** (1804–81) have the castle as their backdrop. Caernarfon's finest 20th-century building is the Gwynedd County Council's modern headquarters. A substantial element in the intramural townscape, it was consciously designed by **Dewi-Prys Thomas**, in the style of Swiss cantonal government buildings, to convey a vision of devolved governmental power – a marked contrast to the castle's message of centralized might.

CAERNARFONSHIRE (Sir Gaernarfon)
One-time county

The **county** was established in 1284 following the **Edwardian conquest**. Initially, the intention was to form two counties, one centred on **Conwy** and the other on **Criccieth**. In the event, only one was created. It consisted of the *cantrefi* of **Llŷn**, **Arfon** and **Arllechwedd**, the **commotes** of **Eifionydd** and **Creuddyn**, and the area around **Llysfaen** – a detached part of the commote of **Rhos**.

The **Act of 'Union'** of 1536 granted Caernarfonshire a county and a **borough** MP and that of 1543 led to the appointment of justices of the peace, meeting in the Court of Quarter Session. Surviving from 1541, the court's records are the earliest in Wales. In 1889, Caernarfonshire County Council came into being. Boundary changes in the early 20th century led to the loss of Llysfaen to **Denbighshire**, and the gain of Nanmor (*see* **Beddgelert**) from **Merioneth**. On the eve of its abolition in 1974, the county consisted of the boroughs of **Bangor**, **Caernarfon**, Conwy and **Pwllheli**, the **urban districts** of Bethesda, Betws-y-Coed, Criccieth, **Llandudno**, **Llanfairfechan**, **Penmaen-mawr** and **Porthmadog**, and the **rural districts** of Gwyrfai, Llŷn, **Nant Conwy** and Ogwen. The one-time county was divided into the districts of **Aberconwy**, Arfon and **Dwyfor** within the new county of **Gwynedd**. In 1996, the districts were abolished. Aberconwy merged with **Colwyn** to form the new county of **Conwy**. Arfon and Dwyfor joined **Meirionnydd** to form a smaller version of the county of Gwynedd. At the time of its abolition in 1974, Caernarfonshire consisted of 147,352 ha and had 123,400 inhabitants. In 1950, Caernarfonshire, which had previously consisted of a county and a borough constituency, was divided into the constituencies of Caernarfon and Conwy. By the time of the **National Assembly** elections of 2007, Caernarfon, shorn of Dwyfor and augmented by the addition of the eastern part of the one-time Arfon district, was known as the Arfon constituency.

CAERPHILLY COUNTY BOROUGH
(Bwrdeistref Sirol Caerffili) (27,758 ha; 169,519 inhabitants)

Established in 1996, the **county borough** embraces the former districts of **Rhymney Valley** (**Mid Glamorgan**) and **Islwyn** (**Gwent**). It includes the whole of the basin of the **Rhymney** and much of that of the Sirhowy. In 2001, 16.67% of the inhabitants of the county borough had some knowledge of **Welsh**, the percentages varying from 22.28% in **Aber Valley** to 11.53% in **New Tredegar**; 8.52% of the county borough's inhabitants were wholly fluent in the language.

CAERPHILLY, Town of (Caerffili), Caerphilly
(1805 ha; 30,388 inhabitants)

The town of Caerphilly lies within the boundaries of the **communities** of Caerphilly, Van, and Penyrheol, Trecenydd and Energlyn. *See below.*

The communities of Caerphilly

CAERPHILLY (954 ha; 13,808 inhabitants)
The strategic significance of the site led the **Romans** to build a fort at Caerphilly AD *c.*75. The town is dominated by its huge castle. It covers 12 ha and incorporates earth and water defences in one of the best examples of medieval concentric castle design. As a fortification, it is at least as significant as the Edwardian castles of **Gwynedd**, all of which it predates. Its size reflects the power of the **Clare family**, the 13th-century lords of **Glamorgan**, and their perceived need to defend their lordship against **Llywelyn ap Gruffudd**, Prince of Wales, who enjoyed extensive support

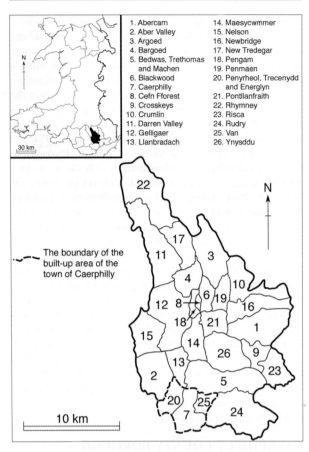

1. Abercarn
2. Aber Valley
3. Argoed
4. Bargoed
5. Bedwas, Trethomas and Machen
6. Blackwood
7. Caerphilly
8. Cefn Fforest
9. Crosskeys
10. Crumlin
11. Darren Valley
12. Gelligaer
13. Llanbradach
14. Maesycwmmer
15. Nelson
16. Newbridge
17. New Tredegar
18. Pengam
19. Penmaen
20. Penyrheol, Trecenydd and Energlyn
21. Pontllanfraith
22. Rhymney
23. Risca
24. Rudry
25. Van
26. Ynysddu

The boundary of the built-up area of the town of Caerphilly

10 km

The communities of the county borough of Caerphilly

among the Welsh of upland Glamorgan. Construction began in 1268 under Gilbert de Clare, the Red Earl; halted in 1270 by Llywelyn's attack, work was rapidly resumed and continued under the Red Earl's son – also Gilbert – and his son-in-law, Hugh le **Despenser**. In 1316, the castle withstood a siege by **Llywelyn Bren** who allegedly surrounded it with a force of 10,000 men. Among its features is the south-west tower, where the departure from the perpendicular is greater than that of the leaning tower of Pisa. Partially reconstructed by the fourth marquess of Bute (*see* **Stuart family**) in the 1920s and 1930s, it passed into state ownership in 1950, when its defensive lakes were reflooded. It is now one of **Cadw**'s most popular sites.

The town of Caerphilly was a small de Clare implantation south of the castle. Evidence of its **borough** status survives in the 14th-century Court House which is now a tavern. Caerphilly developed as the market town of the **Rhymney** valley and as the source of the **cheese** that was the mainstay of the miners' meals underground.

South of the town lies Caerphilly Mountain (or Cefn Cibwr), which marks the boundary between the **commotes** of **Senghenydd** Is Caeach and **Cibwr** (the latter essentially the site of the city of **Cardiff**). On its summit stands Castell Morgraig, often considered to have been built in the 1260s by Gruffudd ap Rhys, lord of Senghenydd. Yet, as much of its stone originated on the coast of Glamorgan where the Clares are unlikely to have allowed a potential enemy to quarry building material, it was probably another Clare castle.

The marriage of the Methodist leader, George Whitefield, took place at Caerphilly in 1741. Two years later, he was at nearby Plas y Watford, where he was elected moderator by the Welsh Methodists and by those of the English Methodists who were **Calvinist** in sympathy (*see* **Calvinistic Methodists**). The election was symptomatic of the division of Methodism between the Calvinists who dominated the movement in Wales and the **Arminian** followers of John Wesley who dominated the movement in **England**.

PENYRHEOL, TRECENYDD AND ENERGLYN
(Penyrheol, Trecenydd ac Ene'rglyn)
(540 ha; 11,530 inhabitants)
Consisting of the western fringes of Caerphilly, the community contains the chapel of Groes-wen, build in 1742 as Wales's first Methodist place of worship. It became a **Congregationalist** chapel in 1745. **William Edwards**, the designer of the bridge at **Pontypridd**, was minister from 1745 until his death in 1789.

VAN (Y Fan) (311 ha; 5050 inhabitants)
Consisting of the eastern edges of Caerphilly, it contains the vast housing estate of Lansbury Park. Castell y Fan, built by Thomas Lewis in the 1580s using stone robbed from the castle, was an innovative building in its day; it was abandoned in the mid-18th century when the Lewis family moved to St Fagans Castle (*see* **Cardiff**). Plans to restore it are afoot. There is a fine example of 12th-century ringwork at Gwern y Domen.

CAERSWS (Caersŵs), Montgomeryshire, Powys (4476 ha; 1526 inhabitants)
Located west of **Newtown**, the **community** extends over the **Carno** valley, which provides a link between the **Severn** and **Dyfi** valleys. It was Caersws's importance as a route centre which caused the **Romans** to choose it as the site of one of their chief mid-Wales forts. Occupied from AD *c.*80 until after 400, little is visible beyond the remains of a turf rampart. From the 1870s to the 1960s, Moat Lane was the **railway** junction for those travelling between south and north Wales. Ministerial students from **Aberystwyth** would spend Monday morning there in the hope of catching the eye of a distinguished **preacher**. In 1959, it was proposed that Caersws should be the centre of a town of 50,000 people, a plan rejected in 1966. From 1871 until his death, the poet **John Ceiriog Hughes** (1832–67), was stationmaster of the branch line from Caersws to the Van **lead** mines (*see* **Llanidloes Without**). He is buried at Llanwnog, 2 km northwest of Caersws village. St Gwynnog's church, partly built from sandstone robbed from the Roman fort, contains a fine screen and rood loft (*c.*1500). Llys Maldwyn Hospital was built in 1840 as the workhouse to serve the Newtown and **Llanidloes Poor Law Union**. Plasau Duon, Clatter (*c.*1640), is a superb half-timbered building. Maesmawr Hall Hotel (*c.*1712, 1874) contains attractive features.

CAERWEDROS Commote
One of the 10 **commotes** of **Ceredigion**, Caerwedros was located on the coast south of the lower **Aeron**. Its caput may have been near the present village of Caerwedros (**Llandysiliogogo**).

CAERWENT (Caer-went), Monmouthshire
(2344 ha; 1719 inhabitants)
Lying between **Newport** and **Chepstow**, Caerwent (Venta
Silurum) was the *civitas* capital of the **Silures**; with
Carmarthen, it was one of two *civitas* capitals established
by the **Romans** in Wales. Caerwent's 18 ha consisted of 20
blocks (*insulae*), divided by one east–west and four
north–south straight streets. The town was probably established in the AD 120s when the departure of soldiers to
Hadrian's Wall created the need for new administrative
arrangements for the Silures. It was initially enclosed by
earthen banks, which were replaced in stone *c.*180. Parts of
the walls still stand up to 5 m high and are the best-preserved Roman city defences in northern Europe. The town
centre contained the forum and the basilica, which housed
the chamber for the ordo, the tribal senate. Caerwent gave
its name to the Welsh kingdom of **Gwent**. King Caradog of
Gwent is reputed to have granted the site to St Tathan,
whose alleged bones were reinterred in the fine 13th century church in 1912. The **Normans** built a motte within the
town walls *c.*1080.

Within the **community** are the manor house at Crick, the
church and castle at Llanvair Discoed, the **Nash**-style villa
of Penheim and the curious underground fernery at
Dewstow. The 10 cottages at Trewent were built in 1937 as
part of a campaign to settle unemployed miners on the
land. A vast weapons store to the west of Caerwent was
operational until 1993.

CAERWYS, Flintshire (1400 ha; 1315 inhabitants)
Located west of **Holywell** and south of the **A55**, Caerwys
was granted **borough** status in 1290. A commercial rather
than a military borough, it had no defences; its rectangular street pattern is still evident. It was perhaps the most
Welsh of all the urban centres of late medieval Wales and
its inhabitants were prominent supporters of **Owain
Glyndŵr**. **Gruffudd ap Cynan** is reputed to have convened
an **eisteddfod** at Caerwys in 1100. The Caerwys eistedd-
dau of 1523 and 1567, held under the patronage of the
Mostyn family, gave authentic poets the opportunity to be
recognized and licensed. St Michael's church, which has
14th-century features, contains an effigy claimed to be
that of Elizabeth, wife of **Dafydd ap Gruffudd**. The Old
Court (17th century) may be on the site of a court of the
Welsh princes. Pendre farmhouse was probably a
medieval hall-house. Pwll Gwyn is a former coaching
inn of *c.*1590. Penucha was birthplace of the Methodist
leader **Thomas Jones** (1756–1820), and the home of his
great-great-nephew, the MP **John Herbert Lewis**. The
antiquary **Angharad Llwyd** (1780–1866) and the poet
William Edwards (Wil Ysgeifiog; 1790–1866) were born in
Caerwys.

CAESAR
The Royal Navy brig *Caesar* was returning to Plymouth
with press-ganged **Swansea** recruits when she hit Pwll-du
Head (**Pennard, Gower**) in fog on 28 November 1760.
Many of those on board were locked below decks when the
vessel filled with water and sank. Sixty-three men and three
women drowned; their bodies were buried in a mass grave
at a place known, consequently, as Graves End.

CAFFLOGION Commote
One of the three **commotes** of the *cantref* of **Llŷn**,
Cafflogion consisted of the southernmost part of the
peninsula. The name is a corruption of that of **Cunedda**'s
alleged son, Afloeg. The commote's *maerdref* (administrative centre) was at **Pwllheli**. In *Cafflogion* (1979), **R. Gerallt
Jones** took a dark view of the future of Llŷn.

CAI, Battle of
In the years following the death of **Cadwallon**, king of
Gwynedd, the Welsh leaders continued his policy of supporting Penda, king of **Mercia** against Oswy of
Northumbria. In 654, Penda and his allies were resound-
ingly defeated (and Penda killed) at Cai (Winwaed), probably near Leeds.

CALAN, Y (New Year's Day)
Omens associated with the appearance of the first person
to come to the house to 'let in' the New Year differed from
district to district. In **Pembrokeshire**, 'New Year's Water'
was carried from house to house to sprinkle on the inhabitants, bringing them good luck in the coming year. The giving of *calennig* (New Year gift) was widespread. After the
change in the calendar in 1752, the old reckoning was
adhered to in some areas; *Yr Hen Galan* (the old New
Year) is still celebrated on 13 January in **Cwm Gwaun**, near
Fishguard, and at **Llandysul**, **Ceredigion**.

CALAN GAEAF (Winter calend)
Winter began in the **Celt**ic calendar on 1 November, a date
associated with the supernatural and the dead. On the previous night – *Nos Calan Gaeaf* – spirits roamed the countryside and various means, including bonfires, were
employed to foretell the future. The medieval Church
established All Saints' Day (1 November) and All Souls'
Day (2 November) as feast days, thus strengthening the
association with the dead. 'Souling' (house-to-house visits
to collect gifts, originally to pay for prayers for souls in
purgatory) was common in the north-east. The British Guy
Fawkes Day (5 November) and an increasingly American-
style Hallowe'en (31 October) have stolen much of the fire
of *Nos Calan Gaeaf*.

CALAN MAI (May calend)
May Day, when summer began in the **Celt**ic calendar, was
associated with outdoor life and above all with **love**, as
reflected, for instance, in the poetry of **Dafydd ap Gwilym**.
Houses were decorated with flowers, and the summer birch
(*Bedwen Haf*) was felled to **dance** around, or a summer
branch would be carried from house to house. As on winter's eve (*Calan Gaeaf*), May Eve was important for divination, and bonfires were lit to foretell the future. The
Church, linking the festival with **Saints** Philip and James,
nevertheless failed to eradicate the pagan elements and in
the 19th century it became a secular occasion associated
with labour.

CALDICOT, Monmouthshire
(465 ha; 9705 inhabitants)
Wedged between the M40 and the M48, Caldicot's chief
feature is its castle, the largest in the **county** apart from

Chepstow and **Raglan**. Built in the 13th century, its gate-house and three of its towers were, until recently, occupied by families. St Mary's church has **Norman**, Decorated and Perpendicular features. A house with the modern name of Llanthony Secunda Priory may have been a grange of the second Llanthony monastery, which was situated near Gloucester (*see* **Crucorney**).

The second **Severn Bridge**, built in 1992–6 and the only bridge directly linking Wales with **England** across the **Severn** estuary, leaves Wales at Caldicot. The Caldicot Levels extend along the shore of the Severn Sea between **Newport** and Chepstow. The most easterly **Welsh**-medium primary school in Wales is located in Caldicot.

CALENNIG

A New Year's gift consisting of a new penny or bread and **cheese** given to children who traditionally carried a deco-rated apple or an orange mounted on three wooden sticks from door to door and sang set verses wishing the house-holder well during the coming year. This had to take place before midday. The custom, which was found throughout Wales, goes back to the medieval period but in its present form was first recorded in the 19th century. A similar cus-tom, involving the sprinkling of 'New Year's Water' in each house, was found in **Pembrokeshire**. *Hel calennig* – going from house to house wishing residents a happy new year and receiving money – continued in much of rural Wales until the later 20th century. For many children, the value of *calennig* greatly exceeded that of Christmas gifts (*see also* **Calan, Y**).

CALLAGHAN, [Leonard] James (1912–2005)
Politician

A native of Portsmouth, Callaghan was elected **Labour** MP for **Cardiff** South in 1945, a constituency (renamed Cardiff South-East in 1950 and Cardiff South and **Penarth** in 1983), which he represented for 42 years. He was the third of the five Welsh MPs to become leader of the Labour Party. In turn chancellor of the exchequer, foreign secre-tary and home secretary, he became prime minister in 1976 – the only Welsh MP, apart from **David Lloyd George** and **Ramsay Macdonald**, to hold that office. Devoted to Cardiff, his interest in Wales as a whole was fitful; he did play a part in establishing the **Kilbrandon Commission**, but, as prime minister, his support for his own **government's devolution** proposals during the referendum campaign of 1979 was lacklustre and he did nothing to curb the strident anti-devolutionists in his own party. His loss of a vote of confidence in his government in 1979 was followed by the election which brought the **Conservative Party** led by Margaret Thatcher to power. Replaced by Michael Foot as Labour leader in 1980, he retired as an MP in 1987, when he was created a life peer, taking the title Lord Callaghan of Cardiff. He is commemorated by Callaghan Square in Cardiff and by the Callaghan Building at the **University of Wales Swansea**, an institution of which he was president.

CALLICE, John (16th century) Pirate

The most notorious of the 16th-century pirates (*see* **Piracy**) who operated in the Severn and Irish Seas. Financed by a number of **gentry** families, from his base on **Sully Island** he attacked and plundered many heavily laden Bristol-bound ships. In 1516, he captured a number of Spanish vessels in **Penarth** Roads and disposed of the goods that he obtained, quite openly, in **Cardiff** and **Swansea**.

'CALON LÂN' (A Pure Heart) Hymn

A **hymn** on the virtues of holy living by Daniel James (Gwyrosydd; 1847–1920), set to music by John Hughes (1872–1914) and first published in 1899.

CALVINISM

The theological system stemming from the thought of the Protestant Reformer John Calvin (1509–64), whose name is inextricably linked with the progress of the **Protestant Reformation** in Geneva, and whose *Institutio Christianae Religionis* (1559) became the key text for those who were to espouse an advanced form of reformed Christianity. Calvin emphasized God's sovereignty in the salvation of humankind, the unique nature of the revelation in Christ, the vital importance of the visible church for living the Christian life, the supreme effectiveness of the sacraments and the call to reform of all aspects of human activity. Although his system includes the concepts of predestina-tion and election, it is held by adherents that they are han-dled not statically but with a dynamism that gives prominence to God's ever-available grace in Christ.

It has been suggested that the 'Five Points' of Calvinism – humanity's total depravity, unconditional election, Christ's vicarious sacrifice for the elect alone, irresistible grace and the impossibility of falling away – which were popularized after Calvin's time and came to characterize advanced Protestant thought (by way of the Westminster Confession of 1647), are guilty of over-rationalizing aspects which Calvin himself had left open.

Lutheranism was the earliest form of Protestant faith to affect Wales – through, for instance, Bishop **Richard Davies** (?1501–81) and the 39 Articles of the **Anglican** Church – but increasingly Wales's advanced Protestants were Calvinist in belief. The Welsh **Puritans** were mostly Calvinist, and Calvinism remained a force within the estab-lished church through the activities of evangelical figures such as **Griffith Jones** and of Methodists like **Daniel Rowland** and **William Williams** (Pantycelyn; 1717–91). Most 18th-century Dissenters and 19th-century **Non-conformists** (apart from the **Unitarians** and **Wesleyans**) held to the same doctrines. When the Welsh Methodists seceded from the Church of **England** in 1811, it was as **Calvinistic Methodists** that they desired to be known.

By the 20th century – because of the rise of secularism and a growing laxity in matters of belief – Calvinism's influence in Wales had declined, although the century wit-nessed a partial revival stimulated by the works of Karl Barth and by the exertions of **J. E. Daniel**, **Martyn Lloyd-Jones**, **R. Tudur Jones** and the poet and scholar Bobi Jones (b.1929).

CALVINISTIC METHODISTS

Calvinistic Methodism has had a profound influence on the shaping of modern Wales. The movement in Wales began in the 1730s within the **Anglican** Church, rooting itself initially in those regions in which Nonconformity

A preaching festival on Mynydd Bach, Ceredigion, 30 July 1915

already had a following (*see* **Nonconformists** and **Methodist Revival**). Young Anglicans, impatient with the perceived lethargy of the established Church, met in impassioned, often open-air gatherings to bear Christian witness and acknowledge sinfulness. A group of converts was organized as a *Seiat* (**Society**), and regulation of the movement as a whole was the responsibility of the *Sasiwn* (**Association**). The goal, initially, was revitalization of the established Church, rather than separation from it, and the early leaders – **Howel Harris** in **Breconshire**, **Daniel Rowland** in **Cardiganshire** and **William Williams** (Pantycelyn; 1717–91) in **Carmarthenshire** – refused to countenance voluntary departure from the Church.

In 1740, the **Calvinist** George Whitefield (1714–70) and the **Arminian** John Wesley (1703–91), the chief leaders of Methodism in **England** – a concurrent movement with, but with origins different from the Methodism of Wales – parted company. The Welsh Methodists supported Whitefield. While **Wesleyan** Methodism had some success in **English**-speaking parts of Wales, the Methodism that won popular appeal in Wales was Calvinistic in its **theology**.

Preaching and **hymn** singing were vital to that appeal, and **revivals** – of which there were about 15 during the next 150 years – were a significant element. The **printing** press was also important. Williams Pantycelyn published his hymns as did **Peter Williams** his Commentary. In 1789, the first of **Thomas Charles**'s catechisms appeared, followed by his scriptural **dictionary** (1805–11). Influential and predominantly Methodist journals included the quarterly *Trysorfa Ysprydol* (1799–1827), the monthly *Y Drysorfa* (1830–1968), the literary quarterly *Y Traethodydd* (1845–) and the connexion's weekly newspaper *Y Goleuad* (1869–).

The Calvinistic Methodists separated from the Church of England in 1811, when they ordained their first ministers. The denomination's Declaration of Faith was published in 1823 and its Constitutional Deed formulated in 1826. Colleges were opened at **Bala** (1836) and Trefeca (**Talgarth**; 1842), and the foreign mission commenced in 1840 when **Thomas Jones** (1810–1849) was sent to the **Khasi Hills** in India.

The Calvinistic Methodists evolved a distinctive form of Church government. Initially, the Association appointed the Societies' officers, but Thomas Charles gave the Societies the right to elect their own elders, the denomination thus taking on an essentially Presbyterian structure. (However, there was no organic connection between the Calvinistic Methodists and earlier Welsh **Presbyterianism**.) The elders and ministers of the churches form the monthly meeting (presbytery), which oversees the local churches. The Association, which supervises the work of the churches and presbyteries, and ordains ministers, meets in three provinces – the North, the South and the East. In 1865, the General Assembly was instituted.

Calvinistic Methodism developed in a distinctively Welsh manner, and offered the Welsh – in a period of great social upheaval and uncertainty – rules for living and structures for the organization of personal, communal and political life that may have been as important to many as the spiritual benefits it conferred. It exerted a profound influence in **education** and public life, and many of Wales's outstanding writers emerged from its ranks, among them **Ann Griffiths**, **Daniel Owen**, Gwenallt (**David James Jones**), **Kate Roberts** and Emyr Humphreys (b.1919).

During the 20th century, Calvinistic Methodism in Wales – in common with other denominations – witnessed a relentless decline in membership, and the closure and demolition of scores of chapels. In 2006, the Calvinistic Methodist connection – formally renamed the Presbyterian Church of Wales in 1928, and popularly known as *Yr Hen Gorff* (The Old Body) – had some 740 churches, 78 ministers and 31,838 members.

CAMBRIA

A **Latin** form of **Cymry** (influenced by the latinized name Cumbria). **Geoffrey of Monmouth** was the first to employ the name to refer specifically to Wales and created as its eponym the suitably named Camber, one of the three purported sons of the mythical **Brutus**. Welsh **Renaissance** scholars gave prestige to Cambria and Cambrian, and although Wales and Welsh have largely superseded them, they still enjoy some currency.

CAMBRIAN ARCHAEOLOGICAL ASSOCIATION, The

The tendency of societies to instigate journals is reversed in the case of the Cambrian Archaeological Association. It was a year after the first publication of the journal *Archaeologia Cambrensis*, by **John Williams** (Ab Ithel; 1811–62) and **H. Longueville Jones** in 1846, that they established the association, chiefly to support the journal. Since their inception, both journal and society have served Welsh antiquarian studies (*see* **Archaeology and Antiquarianism**) with distinction by organizing excavations and associated publications, as well as holding lectures and annual field trips, and promoting the study of many aspects of the history and culture of Wales.

CAMBRIAN INSTITUTE, The

A society founded by **John Williams** (Ab Ithel; 1811–62) in 1853 in opposition to the **Cambrian Archaeological Association**; between 1854 and 1864 it published *The Cambrian Journal*, a quarterly devoted to the **literature** and antiquities of Wales.

CAMBRIDGE, Wales's associations with

In contrast to **Oxford**, Cambridge did not have a significant connection with Wales until the end of the Middle Ages, when several Welshmen, such as the humanist Richard Gwent (d.1534), studied there. Its distance from Wales and the fact that no college had patronage links with Wales made the institution unattractive to Welsh students. This changed during the reign of Henry VII, when the king's mother, Margaret Beaufort, became benefactress to the Queens' College and led to her own foundation, St John's College.

Because Margaret was the wife of Sir William Stanley (*see* **Stanley family**), who had substantial interests in northeast Wales, these colleges came to favour students from those areas. Some scholarships and fellowships were earmarked for the Welsh, and this attracted a number of young men from the north in general. The Welsh association was strengthened following the benefaction left to St John's in 1574 in the will of **John Gwyn** (d.1574), a civil lawyer and native of Trefriw, who had been educated there. Scholarships, which survived until the 19th century, were established for pupils from **Bangor** and **Ruthin** grammar schools, giving an additional advantage to students from the north.

Cambridge played a special part in the progress of the **Renaissance** and the **Protestant Reformation** in Wales. Some of its Welsh graduates contributed greatly to Welsh cultural and religious advancement in the period, notably **Gabriel Goodman**, **Edmwnd Prys** and especially Bishop **William Morgan**. Cambridge was also a nurturing ground for Welsh **Puritans** such as **John Penry** and for some prominent Welsh **Anglicans**, notably **John Williams** (1582–1650), archbishop of York.

In the ensuing centuries, a number of Welsh students continued to attend the university and then occupied livings in Wales. Following university reform in the 1870s, the university became fully accessible to **Nonconformists**, and many college scholarships were extended to able students from whatever background or whichever part of **Britain**. As a result, a number of prominent Welshmen were educated in the university, among them the educationist **R. D. Roberts**, the politician **Ellis Jones Griffith** and the historian **R. T. Jenkins**. Cambridge's **Anglo-Saxon**, Norse and **Celt**ic course continues to be an important nurturing ground of scholars in the field of Celtic studies. Its Welsh society, Cymdeithas y Mabinogi, was founded in the 1930s. The university library holds some of the earliest examples of written **Welsh**.

CAMBRIOL, Newfoundland

Cambriol (New Wales) was a short-lived, early 17th-century Welsh colony on the east side of the Avalon Peninsula, Newfoundland. It was founded by **William Vaughan**, a member of a cadet branch of the **Vaughan family (Golden Grove)**, in an attempt to relieve the poor on his **Llangyndeyrn** estate. Having purchased land for the colony, he financed the settlement there, in 1617, of a group of his tenants, but hostile conditions proved insurmountable. The colony was probably abandoned *c*.1630; farms in **Carmarthenshire** called Newfoundland were given their names by returning settlers.

CAMDEN, William (1551–1623)
Antiquarian and writer

The English writer William Camden published *Britannia* (1586), an account of his tours through the countries of **Britain,** first in **Latin** and subsequently in **English** translation (1610). It presents Wales as the land of three tribes – the **Silures** in the south-east, the **Demetae** in the south-west and the **Ordovices** in the north. Camden drew on the writings of **Giraldus Cambrensis**, William of Malmesbury and **John Leland** among others, for an account of the history and landscape of Wales that remained unparalleled for over 200 years (*see* **Landforms, Landscape and Topography**).

CAMPBELL family (earls of Cawdor) Landowners

The family became associated with Wales through the marriage *c*.1689 of Alexander Campbell and Elizabeth Lort, heiress of the **Stackpole** estate (**Pembrokeshire**). Campbell property in Wales was vastly augmented when, in 1804, John Campbell inherited the estate of John **Vaughan** of Golden Grove (**Llanfihangel Aberbythych**), **Carmarthenshire**. In 1827, John's son, John, received the titles of earl of Cawdor and viscount **Emlyn**. The third earl (1847–1911), a fervent opponent of **David Lloyd George**, was the last **Conservative** MP for Carmarthenshire. By the 1880s, the family owned 20,000 ha of land in Wales, making them second only to the **Williams Wynn family** in the ranks of Welsh landowners. They also owned 20,000 ha in

Telford's Pont Cysyllte aqueduct carrying the Llangollen Canal across the valley of the River Dee

Scotland. Following sales in 1976, the family ceased to be landowners in Wales. In 1988, they sold the titles to their Welsh **manors**.

CAMROSE (Camros), Pembrokeshire
(4592 ha; 1577 inhabitants)
Located immediately north-west of **Haverfordwest**, the **community** contains the villages of Camrose, Keeston, Pelcomb Cross, Simpson Cross, Sutton and Wolfsdale. The rath at Walesland was occupied from the 4th century BC to the **Roman** era; evidence of it was destroyed when an oil refinery was built on the site. Keeston Castle, a large earthwork, is much eroded. The medieval church of St Ishmael has a handsome tower. The family origins of the Berry brothers – Barons Camrose, Buckland and Kemsley – were in Camrose (*see* **Berry family**).

CANALS and WATERWAYS
Before the coming of **railways** and motorized **road** vehicles, travel by water was quicker and more convenient than travel by land. **Rivers** that are navigable for any considerable length are rare in Wales, but the few that are have played a disproportionate part in the country's history. Navigation along the lower **Usk** explains the location of a **Roman** legionary fortress at **Caerleon**, and navigation along the lower **Clwyd** was probably central to **Gruffudd ap Llywelyn**'s choice of **Rhuddlan** as his capital. The scanty urban and industrial growth experienced by Wales before the late 18th century is largely explicable in terms of river transport. **Newport**, Wales's best example of a riverside

urban centre, was dependent upon navigation on the lower Usk, in which **Britain**'s finest extant medieval boat was discovered in 2002. Wales's longest-lived industrial enterprise – the wire works at **Tintern** – relied upon **Wye** shipping. **Carmarthen**, 16th-century Wales's largest town, grew because of its access to the sea via the lower **Tywi**. Of the towns of Wales served by river transport, the furthest inland was **Welshpool**; Pool Quay on the **Severn** enabled it to become in the 18th century the sixth in size among the towns of Wales. Above all, the 5-km navigable section of the **Tawe** linking **coal**-bearing land to the sea was the key to the growth of **Swansea** as the world's chief **copper**-smelting centre. However, the finest inland waterway in Wales, and one of the finest in the world – the **Milford Haven Waterway** – experienced little industrial development until the 1960s.

The earliest evidence of the creation of an artificial waterway in Wales dates from 1277, when Edward I ordered the canalization of the Clwyd between Rhuddlan Castle and the sea. Thereafter, there seem to have been no further ventures until the 1690s, when **Humphrey Mackworth** commissioned a 300-m canal linking the Melincryddan copperworks with the **Nedd**. In the 1750s, some 2 km of the Nedd at Aberdulais were canalized, initiating the array of waterworks undertaken in the south Wales coalfield in the late 18th century. By far the most important of them were those initiated in the 1790s to link the chief **ports** of the coalfield – **Cardiff** (authorized by Act of Parliament in 1790), **Neath** (1791), Newport (1792) and Swansea (1794) – with their hinterlands.

The revolutionary implications of their construction were particularly evident in the case of the **Glamorgan**shire Canal linking Cardiff with **Merthyr Tydfil**. Before its completion in 1798, Cardiff's exports were conveyed to the port on wagons drawn by four **horses** and carrying the equivalent of 2 tonnes of Merthyr's **iron**. A canal barge, drawn by one horse, could convey 25 tonnes. With such a vastly enhanced transport system, it was economical to convey coal – a far less valuable commodity than iron in terms of its bulk – from inland collieries to ports. Until the coming of the canals, the only coal which could be profitably mined for export was that located close to the coast, which explains why Swansea was the only viable coal port of mid-18th century south Wales. With their coming, the vast coal deposits of the south Wales coalfield could be exploited; it was canals therefore which initiated the explosive growth of the coalfield – the central fact of the history of modern Wales. Canal quays were linked to more distant works by tramroads. Those of the two branches of Newport's **Monmouthshire** Canal were particularly numerous; they included Hill's Tramroad (1822), which brought the riches of the **Blaenavon** Ironworks to **Llanfoist** quay, traversing on the way the 2-km Pwll-du Tunnel, the longest in the world when it was opened c.1815.

As the heads of the coalfield valleys could be at an altitude 300 m and more above sea level, canal building involved the construction of numerous locks; there were 51 on the Glamorganshire Canal, 42 on the main line of the Monmouthshire Canal, 36 on the Swansea Canal and 19 on the Neath Canal. The most impressive survivals are on the **Crumlin** branch of the Monmouthshire Canal, where a remarkable group of 14 locks are undergoing restoration. They were designed by Thomas Dadford junior, a member of the family which provided much of the **engineering** skill employed in the construction of the canals of south Wales. Associated with the canals are other engineering triumphs such as the Rhyd-y-car Bridge over the Glamorganshire Canal at Merthyr, the world's first iron girder bridge apart from those built by the ancient **Chinese**.

The coming of railways doomed the canals of the coalfield, for on railways such as the Taff Vale, which linked Merthyr with Cardiff in 1841, a train could carry in an hour what a canal barge could carry in a month. Furthermore, increasing mineral workings caused subsidence, thus frequently causing the flow of water to disappear. Yet, the trade of the canals did not vanish overnight. The Monmouthshire Canal produced a profit until the 1860s and the Neath and Swansea canals until the 1870s; the Glamorganshire Canal continued to pay a dividend until 1887. Thereafter, to the extent that they continued to have a significant role, it was as providers of water to industrial concerns, a role they had played from their beginnings. The **Aberdare** Canal, as a branch of the Glamorganshire Canal, wholly ceased handling commercial traffic in 1900. Sections of the other major canals were closed and drained; all commercial traffic ceased on what was left of the Monmouthshire Canal in 1915, on the Swansea Canal in 1931, the Neath Canal in 1934 and the Glamorganshire Canal in 1945.

In the second half of the 20th century, canals came to be appreciated as an ecological resource and a tourist attraction. In any plans for restoration, however, those of the south Wales coalfield present major problems. These arise partly from subsidence but more particularly from the fact that, as they are confined to individual valleys, they are not connected to the general British canal system and therefore offer no scope for wide-ranging canal cruising. The Swansea Canal survives between **Clydach** and Godre'r Graig, as does most of the Neath Canal and its associated Tennant Canal but, apart from a short stretch in northern Cardiff, the Glamorganshire Canal has disappeared altogether.

Prospects for the Monmouthshire Canal are more promising, for it is linked with the **Brecon** and **Abergavenny** Canal which traverses some of Wales's most beautiful countryside. The latter has a rather different history from that of the other canals of south-east Wales. It was constructed, not to serve major industrial enterprises, but to provide the Usk valley with inexpensive coal and lime (*see* **Limestone**), and to expedite the export of the valley's agricultural produce. The stretch between Brecon and Llanfoist was opened in 1803, but the connection with the Monmouthshire Canal was not completed until 1812. (The intricate discussions involved have been vividly described in Wales's sole 'canal novel': Janet Davies's *Amser i Geisio* (1997).) The entire waterway north of Pontnewydd has been restored and terminates in Brecon's admirably rebuilt canal basin. There are plans to restore the rest of the canal, thus providing a 56-km waterway from Brecon to Newport.

North-western and south-western Wales proved barren ground for canals, although a short stretch was built in 1772 to link Castell Malgwyn (**Manordeifi**) to the **Teifi**. In the north-east, there are the **Llangollen** and **Montgomery**shire canals. Both were extensions of the Ellesmere Canal and were linked to the general British system.

Authorized in 1793 and completed in 1808, the Llangollen Canal was designed by **Thomas Telford**, whose Pont Cysyllte aqueduct is Britain's most splendid canal feature (*see* **Llangollen Rural**). Completed in 1805, it is 305 m in length and carries the canal in a cast-iron trough 39 m above the **Dee**. Almost as impressive is the **Chirk** aqueduct (1801), which crosses the Ceiriog cheek by jowl with Henry Robertson's railway viaduct (1848). Although the canal did carry some industrial traffic, particularly in the neighbourhood of **Cefn** and Chirk, it was primarily a feeder waterway, tapping the Dee by means of Telford's weir – the Horseshoe Falls located on a delectable stretch of the river at **Llantysilio**. By the 1940s, the canal had fallen into disrepair. Subsequently restored, it has become the most popular of all Britain's leisure canals.

By 1797, the Montgomeryshire Canal, authorized in 1794, had reached Garthmyl (**Berriew**, south of Welshpool), a stretch which includes a fine viaduct over the Vyrnwy and which caused Pool Quay to be redundant. It was completed to **Newtown** in 1821, and contributed crucially to the doubling of Newtown's **population** in the 1820s. It was closed to traffic in 1936, but in 2006 a plan was launched to restore the canal in its entirety. The section around Welshpool was well restored in 1973; it is thronged with hire boats, and its banks are graced by the Canal Centre and the **Powys**land Museum.

CANDLEMAS CAROLS

Carols sung on the feast of the purification of the Virgin Mary (2 February), the beginning of spring in the **Celtic** calendar. Pious sentiments were combined with wishing a prosperous year on the land. They were a form of **wassailing** involving a contest in verse between householders and carollers before access was gained to enjoy the hospitality. In **Caernarfonshire**, the 'chair carol', a distinctive form, involved seating a young girl with a baby on her knee to represent Mary and her child; the carol was sung whilst carrying the wassail bowl in procession around the chair.

CANTREF

A territorial and administrative unit, with its court centre and associated demesne, traditionally made up, as the name implies, of 100 townships (although this was more theoretical than actual). Some *cantrefi* (the plural form in **Welsh**) were originally kingdoms in their own right, which had been absorbed by larger neighbours, while others may have been artificial units created later. Although most were superseded by the **commote**, some retained their importance in the later Middle Ages. The antiquity of *cantref* boundaries receives confirmation from the fact that they often mark the boundary between dialects. Many post-**Act of 'Union' hundreds** had boundaries similar to those of *cantrefi*. Some *cantrefi* – **Arfon**, for example, or **Penllyn** – continue to have relevance.

CANTREF BYCHAN *Cantref*

Located south of the **Tywi**, the *cantref* consisted of the **commotes** of **Hirfryn**, **Perfedd** and **Is Cennen**. Despite its name (meaning small *cantref*), it covered a wide area, and was small only in relation to its immediate neighbour, **Cantref Mawr**. A core area of **Deheubarth**, Cantref Bychan had by the 14th century been divided into the **march**er-lordships of **Llandovery** and Is Cennen.

CANTREF GWARTHAF *Cantref*

Constituting most of what later became western **Carmarthenshire** and part of eastern **Pembrokeshire**, the *cantref* contained the **commotes** of **Amgoed**, **Derllys**, **Efelffre**, **Elfed**, **Penrhyn**, **Peulinog**, **Talacharn** and **Ystlwyf**. Gwarthaf (uppermost) refers to the *cantref*'s location on the eastern edge of the kingdom of **Dyfed**. By the early 13th century, the *cantref* had been divided into the **march**er-lordships of **Carmarthen**, **Laugharne**, **Llansteffan**, **St Clears** and **Narberth**. By the 1280s, Carmarthen, Laugharne and Llansteffan and St Clears had become linked with Carmarthenshire. Through the **Act of 'Union'** of 1536, Narberth became part of Pembrokeshire.

CANTREF MAWR *Cantref* (Brycheiniog)

Cantref Mawr was the western portion of that part of **Brycheiniog** lying south of the **Usk**. It included the summits of the **Brecon Beacons**. In its south-west lay the upland region known as Fforest Fawr Brycheiniog. Together with **Cantref Selyf**, it constituted the **march**er-lordship of **Brecon**.

CANTREF MAWR *Cantref* (Ystrad Tywi)

Wales's largest *cantref*, Cantref Mawr (the great *cantref*), consisted of the **commotes** of **Caeo**, **Catheiniog**, **Gwidigada**, **Mabelfyw**, **Mabudrud**, **Maenordeilo** and **Mallaen**. Containing **Dinefwr**, the traditional seat of the rulers of **Deheubarth**, the *cantref* was the chief power base of **Rhys ap Gruffudd** (the Lord Rhys; d.1197). In the late 13th century, it became the core of **Carmarthenshire**.

CANTREF SELYF *Cantref*

Cantref Selyf was the western portion of that part of **Brycheiniog** lying north of the **Usk**. Cwmwd Cantref Selyf, a sub-lordship of the lordship of **Brecon**, was probably seized by Richard Fitz Pons, lord of Clifford, at the time of **Bernard de Neufmarché**'s invasion. His descendants ruled the lordship from their castle at **Bronllys**, retaining it until the early 14th century, when it passed successively to Rhys ap Hywel, the **Bohun family** and Henry Bolingbroke, later Henry IV.

CANTRE'R GWAELOD (The lowland *cantref*)

The best-known version of this legend first appeared in the volume *Cymru Fu* (1862–4), edited by **Isaac Foulkes**. It stated that there was once a kingdom called Cantre'r Gwaelod in Cardigan Bay. Its king was Gwyddno Garanhir, and within it were 16 fine cities. Its land was defended by a series of embankments under the care of Seithennin. Following a night of feasting, Seithennin fell into a drunken stupour. He forgot to close the sluices and the kingdom was inundated. The fact that Gwyddno and Seithennin are referred to in *The Black Book of Carmarthen* shows that this tale has ancient roots. A not dissimilar theme appears in the story, **Branwen ferch Llŷr** in *The Mabinogion*, which refers to the drowning of kingdoms between Wales and **Ireland**. It is claimed that the church bells of Cantre'r Gwaelod may be heard beneath the waters on a calm evening (*see* **'Bells of Aberdovey, The'**.) The legend may preserve a folk memory of the post-Ice Age inundation of the territory that once joined Wales and Ireland.

Evidence that gave rise to the legend includes the layers of **peat**, with stumps of trees, to be seen at low tide on the beaches of Ynyslas (**Borth**) and Clarach (**Tirymynach**). These areas were drowned and the forests growing on them killed as ice sheets of the most recent Ice Age retreated and melted about 8000 years ago, when the sea reached its present level. In addition, undersea so-called causeways such as Sarn Badrig – a ridge which stretches south-westwards for 18 km from Ynys Mochras (**Llanbedr**) – Sarn y Bwch (**Llangelynnin**) and Sarn Cynfelyn (**Llangynfelyn**) bolster the notion of drowned territories. Such *sarnau* are believed to be deposits laid down in front of retreating glaciers.

Drowned forests are found elsewhere around the coast of Wales, such as at Marros beach (**Eglwyscummin**) on Carmarthen Bay and Lleiniog beach near **Beaumaris**. Among the first to describe a drowned forest was **Giraldus Cambrensis** who believed that the biblical flood had brought down the trees which appeared on Newgale beach (**Brawdy**) during the winter of 1171–2. Other legends tell of the drowned lands of Llys Helig (**Penmaenmawr**), and Caer Arianrhod (**Llandwrog**).

CAPEL CURIG, Conwy (7842 ha; 226 inhabitants)

Comprising a wide swathe of the **Snowdonia**n range, the **community** contains the summits of **Glyder** Fach (994 m)

C

Capel Curig's famous 'ugly house'

and Tryfan (917 m) and shares with neighbouring communities the summits of **Carnedd** Llywelyn (1062 m), Carnedd Dafydd (1044 m), Glyder Fawr (999 m) and **Moel Siabod** (872 m). The village of Capel Curig lies on **Telford**'s **London–Holyhead** road (the **A5**), and has a number of old coaching inns (*see* **Stagecoaches**). In 1956, the Royal Hotel became Plas y Brenin, the north Wales headquarters of the Central Council of Physical Recreation. The view across Llynnau Mymbyr to Yr Wyddfa, Snowdonia's highest summit, has achieved iconic status. The Friends of St Julitta's Church were formed in 1995 to save the church of St Curig and St Julitta (13th and 14th century) from decay. Dyffryn Mymbyr is the farm featured in the Canadian author Thomas Firbank's wartime bestseller *I Bought a Mountain* (1940). There is a **Roman** auxiliary fort at Caer Llugwy. Tŷ hyll is a famously 'ugly' small house.

CARADOG OF LANCARFAN (fl.1135)
Hagiographer
The Lives of **Cadog** and **Gildas** are attributed to Caradog, and he may also have been the author of the lives of Cyngar and **Illtud**. Nothing is known of his own life, but the lives he wrote suggest that he was familiar with the traditions of **Llancarfan**. At the end of his *Historia Regum Britanniae*, **Geoffrey of Monmouth** referred to Caradog as his contemporary, and gave him leave to relate the later history of the kings of the Welsh. Some historians have suggested that Caradog was the author of *Brut y Tywysogyon*, which begins where the *Historia* ends, but this is unlikely.

CARATACUS (Caradog, Caradoc; fl. 1st century)
War-leader
Caratacus, son of the Catuvellaunian king Cunobelinus (Cynfelyn of Welsh tradition), opposed the **Roman** invasion in AD 43. Resistance in south-eastern **Britain** collapsed

and he appealed to the **Silures** of south-eastern Wales, who continued the war for a quarter of a century. According to **Tacitus**, the captured Caratacus made a memorable speech in Rome. The name Caradog was revived among the later rulers of **Gwent**.

CARDIFF City and County (Caerdydd)
(14,948 ha; 305,353 inhabitants)
Cardiff, the capital of Wales, is located in the southernmost reaches of the **Taff** valley. It comprises 32 **communities** (*see below*).

Wales's 'chief city has no intrusive/ Dramatic thrust of rock in its flat centre, built/ Mostly on sand and mud' (**Harri Webb**, 1974). Recent expansion has brought some high ground within the city's boundaries – Mynydd y Garth (307 m) is its highest point – but most of its built-up area is less than 50 m above sea level. It stands mainly on marsh and estuarine silt, although its northern suburbs are built on Old Red Sandstone and the city is ringed to the north by Carboniferous **Limestone** hills extending from Pentyrch to **Rudry**. Pen-y-lan consists of Lower Palaeozoic rock, the oldest in **Glamorgan**. Rainfall varies from an average of 97 cm a year in the city centre to 140 cm above Thornhill; while **Swansea** has 222 rain days a year, Cardiff has 186.

The original **borough** consisted of the **parishes** of St John and St Mary and extended over 786 ha. Boundary changes in 1875, 1922, 1938, 1951, 1967, 1974 and 1996 resulted in an almost eighteenfold increase in its area. Cardiff has absorbed 14 neighbouring parishes and has come to occupy the whole of the **commote** of **Cibwr**, the southernmost of the three commotes of the ancient *cantref* of **Senghenydd** – a fact that has given rise to the suggestion that Cardiff's **Welsh-language** dialect should be known as *Cibwreg*.

The early presence of human beings in the district is indicated by the Pen-y-lan handaxe dated earlier than 75,000 BC. Various **Neolithic** and **Bronze Age** objects suggest considerable settlement in and around the ancient borough in later prehistoric eras. There is a megalithic burial chamber near Creigiau, Bronze Age cairns on Mynydd y Garth, and **Iron Age** enclosures at Pentyrch, Caerau and Whitchurch.

The Taff valley lay in the territory of the **Silures** who, until their subjugation in the AD 70s, were a constant threat to the **Roman** invaders. It was probably during the campaigns of the AD 50s that the first Roman fort was built at Cardiff. A large earth and timber construction, it was replaced in about AD 78 by a smaller fort of similar materials, a structure which was further remodelled (*c.*120). Cardiff's fourth Roman fort, built of stone and covering 3.7 ha, was erected *c.*280. It was reconstructed by the **Stuart family**, marquesses of Bute, between 1889 and 1923. Although it is not correct in every detail – the original walls were considerably lower and there is no evidence that they contained a mural gallery – Cardiff is the only place in **Britain** where a convincing reconstruction of a Roman fort can be seen. Outside the fort, a civilian settlement ranged on each side of what later became High Street. It contained rectangular buildings and much evidence of **iron**working. Ironworking was also undertaken at Ely, the site of

Cardiff's only Roman villa, which was occupied between the 2nd and 4th centuries.

The latest Roman coins found in the fort date from the reign of Gratian (367–83), which suggests that it was abandoned when **Magnus Maximus** denuded Britannia of its garrison in 383. Little is known of the Cardiff area over the following six centuries. Its name in Middle Welsh was *Caerdyf* (the fort of the Taff), which gave the anglicized form, Cardiff. The vowel affectation in the last syllable, caused by a lost genitive ending, proves that the name had Brythonic origins. By the 16th century, the *f* had turned to *dd*, giving the modern Welsh form, Caerdydd.

Early medieval Cardiff was part of the Welsh kingdom of **Glywysing**. An expanded Glywysing became known as **Morgannwg** (Glamorgan) in 665, or perhaps in 974. The occurrence in Cardiff of the place name Womanby (from the Norse *Hundemanby*) gave rise to the belief that the **Vikings** had a settlement there, but the lateness of the occurrence and the lack of archaeological evidence makes this doubtful. By the 12th century, the chief ecclesiastical foundation in Glamorgan was at Llandaff. Unlike the name *Caerdyf* (*see above*), the element *daf* (*Taf*) shows that the name belongs to Welsh rather than to Brythonic, and therefore cannot be earlier than the 6th century. A sculptured cross of the late 10th century indicates that Llandaff was an ecclesiastical centre before the coming of the **Normans**, but there is no incontrovertible evidence that it was the seat of a bishop until 1119.

By that time, the area was in the hands of the Normans. William I visited Cardiff in 1081 when a motte may have been raised within the walls of the Roman fort. Nevertheless, Morgannwg remained under Welsh rule until the 1090s when **Robert Fitz Hammo** made Cardiff the base for its conquest. The motte was crowned with a stone keep *c.*1140; its walls were scaled in 1158 by **Ifor Bach** when he kidnapped the Norman lord of **Glamorgan**. The Black Tower in the south wall of the Roman fort was built in the 13th century and apartments were erected along the western wall in the 1430s.

Fitz Hammo's possessions – Cardiff and the lowlands of Glamorgan – passed to his son-in-law, the earl of Gloucester, the patron of **Geoffrey of Monmouth**. (Cardiff is the scene of several of Geoffrey's depictions of King **Arthur**.) Gloucester's descendants held Glamorgan until it went by marriage in turn to King John (1183), the **Clares** (1214), the **Despensers** (1314), the **Beauchamps** (1399) and the Nevilles (1445). It came into possession of the crown in 1483.

The successive lords of Cardiff fostered the borough, which lay to the south of the castle. The burgesses were granted a charter *c.*1125 and further liberties in 1340 and 1421. With its bi-weekly markets, its bi-annual fairs, the trade of its town quay, its role as the centre of the richest of the lordships of the Welsh **March**, and the patronage of some of the most powerful members of the **English** aristocracy, Cardiff came to enjoy considerable prosperity. It acquired walls within which lay, by *c.*1300, 421 burgages, probably occupied by some 2200 people. In that year, it

Cardiff Castle

was almost certainly the largest town in Wales. (**Haverfordwest**, with 360 burgages, was its closest rival.) It had the parish church of St Mary, a number of chapels and, beyond the walls, were the Dominican and Franciscan **friar**ies; Cardiff was the only Welsh town in which both mendicant orders were represented. To the east was the extramural suburb of Crokerton and beyond lay the manor of Roath – essentially the home farm of the castle – and the serf villages of Lisvane, Llanishen and Llanedern. The bishop of Llandaff held extensive lands to the west of the borough, while to the north – just inside Cardiff's modern boundary – Castell Coch, built by the Clares in the late 13th century, commanded the Taff gorge (*see* Tongwynlais *below*). On the boundary of present-day Cardiff there is another medieval castle, that of Morgraig on Caerphilly Mountain, considered either to have been built by the Clares or to be the southernmost stronghold of the Welsh of upland Glamorgan.

The uplanders rose in revolt in 1316, which ended with the execution of **Llywelyn Bren** and his burial at Greyfriars. The later Middle Ages saw a decline in Cardiff's prosperity. Indeed, over 500 years would elapse before the town again attained the **population** level it had had in 1300. The **Black Death** proved devastating, and Cardiff suffered grievously during the revolt of **Owain Glyndŵr**. In 1404, Glyndŵr's forces set it on fire, sparing only the Franciscans, one of whose adherents, John Sperhauke, was executed for asserting that: '*Oweyn Gleyndour est loial Prince de Gales.*' Over the following century, the lords of Cardiff proved to be enthusiastic builders; apart from their work on the castle, they commissioned the north-western tower of Llandaff Cathedral and the superb tower of St John's church (whose 'improved Gothic' crown may be, in part, the late 18th-century stonework of Iolo Morganwg (**Edward Williams**)).

The work at Llandaff was probably commissioned by Jasper **Tudor,** who was granted the lordship of Glamorgan by his nephew, Henry VII, in 1486. The **Act of 'Union'** of 1536 abolished the powers of the marcher-lords; **Glamorgan** became a **county** with Cardiff as its administrative centre. John Speed's **map** of 1610 indicates that by then a shire hall had been built within the outer ward of the castle. The map shows a small T-shaped borough still surrounded by its walls. It was dominated by the castle, one of the residences of the **Herbert earls of Pembroke (of the second creation)**, the first of whom was in 1547 granted the Glamorgan lordships once held by Jasper Tudor. At the time of the grant, the number of occupied burgages at Cardiff had declined to 269. Of their occupants, 35% had Welsh **surnames**, suggesting that migration from the surrounding countryside was changing the ethnic composition of the townspeople.

Preferring their mansion in Wiltshire, the Herberts were absentee landlords and let the castle fall into decay. Taff floods caused much damage; they undermined St Mary's church, which had collapsed by 1678; it was not replaced until the 1840s. By the late 18th century, Cardiff, although the county town, ranked low in Glamorgan's urban hierarchy. Swansea was five times as large; **Neath** was considerably more populous; **Cowbridge** was the capital of the **Vale of Glamorgan**, and the agricultural surplus of the Vale was

exported through Aberthaw (*see* **Rhoose**). To Iolo Morganwg, Cardiff was 'an obscure and inconsiderable place', and a visitor described it in 1770 as 'having more of the furniture of antiquity about it than any town we had seen in Wales'.

In 1704, Cardiff and its associated lordships passed by marriage from the Herberts to the Windsor family. In 1766, it came into the possession of the Stuart family when Charlotte Windsor married Lord Mountstuart, the son of the third earl of Bute. Mountstuart, later the first marquess of Bute (d.1814), did little for the town beyond commissioning Capability Brown to landscape the castle park and to remodel the Beauchamp apartments in a style 'reminiscent of the gaol at Rothesay' (Isle of Bute).

By the late 18th century, Cardiff was on the brink of transformation. The burgeoning iron industry of **Merthyr Tydfil** needed an outlet to the sea. Cardiff, situated on the estuary of the river that drains the richest part of the south Wales **coal**field, was the obvious choice. In 1767, a **road** was built to transport iron to Cardiff by wagon. Such a cumbersome mode of transport ruled out any substantial trade in coal, for coal, in terms of bulk, is a far less valuable commodity than iron. 'We have no coal exported from this port, nor ever shall', wrote a Cardiff customs official in 1782, 'as it would be too expensive to bring it down here from the internal part of the country.'

The situation changed with the completion of the Glamorganshire **Canal** in 1798. Cardiff began exporting coal, although – at least until the 1840s – on a far smaller scale than its rivals. In 1833, the coal exports of both Swansea and **Newport** were three times those of Cardiff. By then, however, Cardiff's pre-eminence as an iron-exporting **port** was evident. The pig iron output of south Wales represented 40% of that of Britain and, of British overseas iron exports, almost half were conveyed on the Glamorganshire Canal and shipped from Cardiff.

The building of the canal gave 'a most notable impulse' to the town. In the 1790s, Cardiff acquired a racecourse (*see* **Horse Racing**), a new bridge over the Taff, and its first **printing** press, **bank**, coffee room and daily **stagecoach** to **London**. Nevertheless, the first official census (1801) showed that Cardiff had a population of merely 1870, causing it to rank twenty-fifth among Wales's centres of population. Its growth over the following 20 years was modest, with the town's population increase keeping pace almost exactly with that of **Bangor**. Indeed, a town plan of 1828 varied little from Speed's map of 1610.

The crucial decade was the 1830s when the second marquess of Bute built, at his own expense, a large masonry dock with access to the Taff estuary. Completed in 1839, it was in 1841 linked to Merthyr by the Taff Vale **Railway**. Further docks followed and, with the completion of the Alexandra Dock in 1907, Cardiff's five docks had a total quayage of almost 11 km, one of the largest dock systems in the world. The railway network was also expanded, and Cardiff became the main export centre for the coal production of the Cynon, Rhondda and **Rhymney** valleys as well as that of the Taff. As the chief landowner in those valleys, the marquess of Bute insisted that his lessees should export their coal at his port, thus markedly expanding Cardiff's hinterland at the expense of its rivals.

Between 1840 and 1870, Cardiff's coal exports increased from the equivalent of 44,350 to 2.219 million tonnes, over one and a half times the combined exports of Swansea and Newport. The boom led to massive population growth, averaging, in those 30 years, 79% per decade. By 1871, Cardiff had outstripped all its Welsh rivals and its inhabitants were beginning to speak of the town as 'the Welsh metropolis'. It was undoubtedly a Welsh town, for the infiltration from the surrounding countryside, already apparent in the 1540s, continued in later centuries. By the early 19th century, perhaps a majority of the inhabitants had a knowledge of the Welsh language; in 1838, the corporation insisted that the clerk of the market should be Welsh-speaking and, in that year, four of Cardiff's seven **Nonconformist** chapels conducted their services in Welsh. Even with the burgeoning of the population from the 1840s onwards, natives of Wales were a high proportion of the migrants. In 1851, 62.5% of Cardiff's inhabitants were born in Wales, 25.2% in **England** and 10.87% in **Ireland**; the figures in 1881 were 60.5%, 30.1% and 5.1%. In the main, the Welsh migrants came from Glamorgan and **Monmouthshire**, the English from the west of England and the **Irish** from Cork, Wexford and Waterford.

Population growth slowed to an average of 50% per decade in the 1870s and 1880s, a period when, as **Gwyn A. Williams** put it, Cardiff changed from 'a counting-house into a community'. It was in those years also that the town was endowed with its most remarkable architectural feature: **William Burges**'s work on the castle, commissioned by the third marquess of Bute, work that encapsulated 'the high Victorian dream'. (Burges was also responsible for the delightful rebuilding of Castell Coch.) Burges-influenced **architecture** became a characteristic of Cardiff, particularly of Cathedral Road. Bute influence was far more pervasive. The layout of the growing town, with its parks and its ambitious **housing** – much of it beyond the reach of the working **class** – was designed by the estate's agents; most of the town's street names commemorate the family and its property, and almost all Cardiff's quarters bear the names of Bute farms. A poorer family would have been tempted to build on the castle park, but the wealth of the Butes ensured that Wales's capital has perhaps the greenest centre of any city in Europe.

Cardiff's status as the chief town of south Wales was affirmed in 1883 when it was chosen as the site of south Wales's university college (*see* **Cardiff University**), a devastating blow to Swansea and a decision celebrated in Cardiff by illuminations and cheering crowds. Nevertheless, the 1880s were worrying years for its townspeople because of the serious challenge represented by the construction of rival docks at **Barry**; indeed, David Davies (*see* **Davies family (Llandinam)**), their main promoter, prophesied that Barry's success would cause grass to grow in the streets of Cardiff. In 1890, the first year of the full operation of Barry Dock, it exported 3.243 million tonnes of coal compared with the 7.538 million tonnes exported from Cardiff. Barry's advantages were apparent. It is the sole Severn Sea port at which vessels can enter or leave at any state of the tide; unlike Cardiff, it was not burdened with redundant investment, and it benefited from the fact that its dock company also owned the railway which served the port. (At Cardiff, at least three railway companies – some of which were antagonistic towards the Bute interest – were responsible for serving the docks.) From 1901 onwards, Barry's coal exports exceeded those of Cardiff. Yet, so great was the world demand for Welsh coal that Cardiff's coal exports continued to grow, although not at the same pace as before. They peaked at 10.736 million tonnes in 1913.

In most statistical tables, Barry's trade figures (and also those of **Penarth**) are included under the heading of the Port of Cardiff, and thus the role of Cardiff itself as a coal port can sometimes be inflated. Yet, in some ways, Barry's remarkable rise was beneficial to Cardiff, for, as no coalowner or **ship**owner relocated to Barry, all the financial, legal and secretarial work created by its trade was carried out at Cardiff. From 1888 onwards, the price of coal on the British – and indeed the international markets – was determined on the trading floor of Cardiff's Coal Exchange, the grandiose building erected in Mountstuart Square in that year. By the 1890s, the Port of Cardiff was not only the world's largest coal-exporting port, it was also the world's largest port, at least in terms of the tonnage of its exports. Its coal kept the British navy afloat; it helped to industrialize France, Spain, Italy, Brazil and Chile. In the late 19th and early 20th centuries, the ports of the Severn Sea played the same role in providing the world with the source of heat and **energy** as would the Persian Gulf in the late 20th century. The world's first million-pound deal was struck at the Coal Exchange in 1907. Eugene O'Neill, when writing the first American **drama** to receive international acclaim, could think of no more stirring a title than *Bound East for Cardiff*. In 1914, Provincetown (Massachusetts) rang to the words: 'You know Fanny, the barmaid at the Red Stork in Cardiff.'

Partly because of competition from Barry, Cardiff's population growth slowed to 28% in the 1890s and to 11% in the 1900s. In those decades the borough made strenuous efforts to enhance its prestige. In 1898, the corporation paid the marquess of Bute £160,000 for 24 ha of **Cathays Park**, which became the site of Britain's most splendid civic centre. The completion of the centre's chief building, the Town Hall (1905), coincided with Cardiff's elevation to city status, a distinction granted not because the town deserved it in terms of population but because no large town in Wales had hitherto been recognized as a city. The city fathers became increasingly adroit at exploiting Cardiff's position as 'the Welsh metropolis'. The home of the southern university college, by 1914 it had also acquired the **National Museum [of] Wales**, the **University of Wales** registry and the embryo of what would become the University of Wales College of Medicine (*see* **Wales College of Medicine, Biology, Life and Health Sciences**). It failed to gain the **National Library** because the library's chief founder, **John Williams** (1840–1926), considered Cardiff to have 'a mongrel and non-Welsh population'.

Cosmopolitan it certainly was. In 1911, with 5000 of its inhabitants foreign-born, it was second only to London in the proportion of its overseas immigrants. They included **West Indians**, **Africans**, **Chinese** and **Indians**, providing the dock area (Butetown or Tiger Bay) with a rich mix of peoples, among whom there was – in British terms – a uniquely high level of intermarriage between male immigrants and local **women**. Members of some 57 nationalities made their home in Butetown where, as Neil Sinclair put it, 'you could see the world in a square mile'. Elsewhere in the city, the Irish had made their mark, particularly in Grangetown and Adamsdown. The Irish influx, and more especially that from England, meant that Cardiff was becoming increasingly **English** in speech. The number of Cardiff's Welsh-speakers, 22,515 in 1891, had halved by 1911, although villages such as Gwaelod-y-garth and Pentyrch, which eventually would become part of the city, remained solidly Welsh in speech. Yet Welsh patriotism was a significant force, with Edward Thomas (Cochfarf) effectively leading Cymrodorion Caerdydd, Cardiff's main society for Welsh speakers. In addition, an **Anglo-Welsh** Cardiff patriotism could be discerned, particularly in the field of sport. The amalgam of peoples produced the Cardiff accent; indebted to Gwenhwyseg (the Welsh-language dialect of south-east Wales), to Ireland and to the west of England, it cuts 'through aural sensibilities like wire through **cheese**' (D. Smith, 1984).

On the eve of the **First World War**, Cardiff was full of confidence. During the war, although its dock trade declined, its industrial base was strengthened, particularly through the expansion of the **East Moors Steelworks** established by the Dowlais Company in 1890. Following the war, with Europe hungry for coal, Cardiff experienced an extraordinary boom, although the boom was not without tensions as the **race riots** of 1919 proved. In 1919, the city had 57 shipping companies with 213 vessels, figures which had risen to 150 and 500 by 1920. Huge fortunes were made, and, with the shipowners lusting after titles, Cardiff became known as 'the city of the dreadful knights'. The boom had collapsed by 1922 and, with the slump in the demand for Welsh coal, the docks went into decline; by 1936, their trade was less than half that of 1913. Nevertheless, Cardiff's role as the de facto capital of Wales strengthened. It became the seat of a **Roman Catholic** metropolitan cathedral in 1916; it acquired the Welsh National **War Memorial** in 1928 and had become the centre for **broadcasting** in Wales by 1937, a development that permitted its later emergence as a media city. It was increasingly the focus for sport in Wales. Although occasional international **rugby** games were played at Swansea (the last was in 1954), Cardiff eventually won total dominance.

During the **Second World War**, the city suffered some bomb damage, including the ruination of Llandaff Cathedral. As in the First World War, its industrial base was strengthened, particularly by the establishment of munitions factories. Following the war, aristocratic lifestyles became almost impossible to maintain; in 1947, the link with the Bute family came to an end when the fifth marquess presented the castle and its park to the city. (The Bute docks had passed to the Great Western Railway Company in 1922 and the Bute **urban leases** to Western Ground Rents in 1938.) In 1955, the city was recognized as the capital of Wales, a decision that had more to do with the fact that it contained marginal **Conservative** constituencies than with any reasoned view of what functions a Welsh capital should have.

Yet, over the following decades, Cardiff's capital status became increasingly meaningful. In 1958, the city was host to the **Commonwealth Games**. In 1964, it became the seat of the **Welsh Office**, a development that caused it to become the headquarters of a large number of national institutions ranging from the **Arts Council of Wales** to the **Wales TUC**, from the Welsh Institute of Sport to the **Welsh Academy**. This was accompanied by a degree of re-Cymricization; by 2001, when the city had a dozen Welsh-medium primary schools, over 10% of all Wales's Welsh-speakers lived within 20 km of Cardiff, compared with less than 5% some 40 years earlier. In that year, 16.31% of the inhabitants of Cardiff had some knowledge of Welsh, the percentages varying from 27.53% in **Pentyrch** to 12.44% in **Old St Mellons**; 8.75% of the county's inhabitants were wholly fluent in the language.

The city's development as an administrative centre coincided with its de-industrialization, symbolized above all by the closure of the East Moors Steelworks in 1978. It also coincided with the rehousing of much of Cardiff's working **class**, a process which began with the building of housing estates at Ely from 1928 onwards. Much of Splott was demolished and Butetown was gutted. ('Who', asked Neil Sinclair, 'was the unknown architect whose dream created our nightmare?') Vast estates came into being at Caerau, Llanrumney and St Mellons, a development not without problems, as the riots at Ely in 1991 demonstrated. With much of the dockland redundant, a major development of Butetown (renamed Cardiff Bay) was launched in the 1980s. It included a barrage, which closed the estuaries of the Taff and the **Ely** thus creating a large freshwater **lake**. Cardiff's most ambitious construction to be erected in the later 20th century was the astonishing Millennium Stadium, built for the Rugby World Cup in 1999. Developments in Cardiff Bay were initially disappointing, with the scheme for an ambitious opera house floundering in 1994. An alternative proposal was eventually accepted, and the indigenously designed Wales Millennium Centre opened in 2004 as an international receiving house for opera, **dance** and **music**als, and as headquarters of a number of national cultural organizations.

In 1997, the voters of Cardiff rejected the **National Assembly** for Wales by 55.63% to 44.37%. As the voters of Swansea had delivered an affirmative vote, that city made a vigorous bid to house the Assembly. After a bitter wrangle, Cardiff was victorious and the Assembly opened at Crickhowell House in Butetown in 1999. The Richard Rogers Partnership's dignified Assembly building – Y Senedd – was opened in Cardiff Bay in 2005. The presence of the Assembly in the city gives a fuller meaning to Cardiff's role as the capital of Wales.

The communities of Cardiff

ADAMSDOWN (Waunadda) (107 ha; 6850 inhabitants)
The area immediately east of the original borough, its densely built-up area represents the earliest expansion of Cardiff beyond the boundaries of the parishes of St John and St Mary. Within it are Cardiff **prison**, the one-time Royal Infirmary and the superb neo-Gothic church of St German (1884).

BUTETOWN (Tre-biwt) (392 ha; 4487 inhabitants)
The dockland area of Cardiff, it includes most of what was the parish of St Mary. West of Bute Street lies cosmopolitan

but gutted Tiger Bay, whose one-time appearance is preserved in the film *Tiger Bay*. From 1886 until 1905, a converted, 46-gun frigate, HMS *Hamadryad*, beached on mud flats at the mouth of the Taff, served as the Royal Hamadryad Hospital for Seamen; it treated over 250,000 sailors and was replaced by a shore-based hospital built nearby and also called the Hamadryad. Cardiff Bay, which hugs the shores of the lake created by the barrage across the Taff and Ely estuaries (2001), is undergoing extensive development. The Wales Millennium Centre and the seat of the National Assembly for Wales stand on the lake shore. The **island** of Flat Holm lies within Butetown's boundaries.

CAERAU (294 ha; 10,189 inhabitants)
A one-time parish whose church is now a melancholy ruin, it is bordered by the River Ely, Cowbridge Road and the A4232. Within it are a 5-ha **Iron Age** fort and the foundations of a Roman villa. It consists in the main of housing estates built in the 1950s and 1960s.

CANTON (Treganna) (308 ha; 13,086 inhabitants)
The name, which dates back to at least 1230, was long applied to an extensive territory west of the Taff straddling the Cardiff–Cowbridge road. Its rapid urbanization from the 1850s onwards gave rise to what Cantonians consider to be Cardiff's premier suburb. The community lies to the west of Llandaff Road, and among its features are the church of St John, Victoria Park and Thompson's Park.

CASTLE (Y Castell) (172 ha; 189 inhabitants)
The heart of Cardiff, it includes most of what was the parish of St John. It extends from Blackweir to the railway embankment south of St Mary's Street. Within it are Cathays Park, the castle, Bute Park, the Millennium Stadium and the commercial core of the city.

CATHAYS (163 ha; 13,751 inhabitants)
The name comes from the Old English *[ge]haeg* (hedge) and came to be applied to land lying north-east of the original borough. Cathays Park, once the **garden** of Cathays House – a mansion built for the first marquess of Bute – gave its name to Cardiff's civic centre, which is located in the Castle community. The community of Cathays is a dense web of streets where students are a high proportion of the population.

CYNCOED (327 ha; 10,310 inhabitants)
A salubrious suburb of middle-class houses built in the 1920s and 1930s, the community includes Roath Lake, excavated in 1889.

ELY (Trelái) (222 ha; 14,751 inhabitants)
Cardiff's first large-scale municipal housing scheme, it was laid out in the late 1920s and 1930s and is centred upon the wide and leafy Grand Avenue. In 1991, Ely suffered a bitter race riot.

FAIRWATER (Tyllgoed) (306 ha; 12,366 inhabitants)
Consisting largely of later 20th-century housing developments, Fairwater also contains Tŷ Bronna, a fine Arts and Crafts style house designed by Charles Voysey.

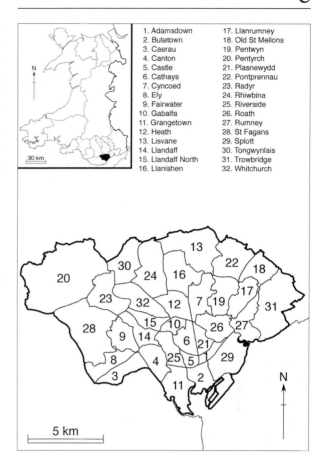

The communities of the city and county of Cardiff

GABALFA (127 ha; 7619 inhabitants)
The name comes from the Welsh *ceubalfa* (the place of the ferry) and recalls the ancient ferry across the Taff. Gabalfa is mainly known for its fearsome road interchange.

GRANGETOWN (Trelluest) (425 ha; 14,367 inhabitants)
A peninsula between the Taff and Ely Rivers, its only building until the 1850s was a farmhouse, the centre of a grange granted to **Margam** Abbey *c.*1200. Developed as a working-class suburb by the **Windsor-Clive family**, it was long the stronghold of Cardiff's citizens of Irish descent and of the city's **baseball** enthusiasts; by the 21st century, however, the community contained a much richer ethnic mix.

HEATH (Y Waun Ddyfal) (315 ha; 11,770 inhabitants)
Once constituting much of Cardiff's **common land** where squatters were forcefully evicted in 1799, Heath's urbanization began in the 1930s. It is dominated by the University Hospital of Wales, completed in 1992.

LISVANE (Llys-faen) (770 ha; 3319 inhabitants)
Cardiff's seriously opulent suburb, Lisvane includes Cefn Onn, a park with a wealth of azaleas.

LLANDAFF (Llandaf) (255 ha; 8988 inhabitants)
The seat of the bishop of the **Anglican diocese** of Llandaff, the place was, until the late 19th century, a small village, although it styled itself a city. The large parish of Llandaff

extended from Grangetown to Caerphilly Mountain, and included most of what became Cardiff west of the Taff. The cathedral, situated in a hollow adjoining the river, was originally a modest church 8.5 m in length. Of the early 12th-century rebuilding, only the sanctuary arch – a fine example of the Romanesque style – survives. The arcade of the nave and the choir dates from the early 13th century, the sanctuary and the Lady chapel from the late 13th century, and the north-west tower from the late 15th century. Thereafter, the building suffered over three centuries of neglect; the roof of the nave fell in, the south-west tower collapsed and the walls of the nave were reduced to mere footings. In 1752, a conventicle based upon the dimensions of Solomon's Temple was erected within the ruins, causing the cathedral to be described as 'a medley of absurdities'. Restoration began in 1841 under the guidance of **John Prichard**, son of one of the cathedral's vicars choral. The work included the erection of a new south-west tower on a scale sufficient to give the building a consequence it had previously lacked. In 1941, a landmine exploded outside the south aisle. All the windows were destroyed and the nave roof again fell in. The rebuilding, carried out by the innovative architect George Pace and completed in 1964, included the **Welch Regiment**'s memorial chapel and a concrete arch bearing Jacob Epstein's *Majestas*.

South of the cathedral is the attractive Green with ecclesiastical residences, the ruins of the 13th-century bell tower and bishop's castle and **Goscombe John**'s superb war memorial. Other features of Llandaff include Prichard's registry, St Michael's Theological College, Howell's School for Girls, the Welsh headquarters of the BBC (*see* **Broadcasting**) and the Cathedral School, which occupies the mansion built for the Mathew family who had gained possession of the manor of Llandaff in 1553.

LLANDAFF NORTH (Ystum Taf)
(199 ha; 8257 inhabitants)
A rectangular block of streets north-west of the Taff, it is approached by a bridge overlooking a fine stretch of the river much used by the Cardiff Rowing Club.

LLANISHEN (Llanisien) (496 ha; 16,019 inhabitants)
This extensive area of middle and lower middle-class housing is enhanced by a large reservoir constructed in 1878 – Cardiff's main source of water until the creation of three lakes in the **Brecon Beacons** between 1892 and 1908.

LLANRUMNEY (Llanrhymni)
(305 ha; 11,226 inhabitants)
Lying north-west of Newport Road, it became part of Cardiff in 1951 and consists of vast housing estates interspersed with playing fields. At its northern end is the handsome late medieval church of St Mellon.

OLD ST MELLONS (Hen Laneirwg)
(339 ha; 2279 inhabitants)
In 1996, the community of St Mellons was divided into Pontprennau and Old St Mellons. The latter is largely open country with some opulent houses along Began Road. Their occupants treasure the adjective 'Old', for it distances them from the housing estates of Llanrumney and Trowbridge – areas frequently known as St Mellons – where, according to John Redwood, **secretary of state for Wales** (1993–5), the residents consist largely of unmarried mothers living on state benefits.

PENTWYN (Pen-twyn) (368 ha; 14,643 inhabitants)
Lying on the west bank of the Rhymney, Pentwyn includes most of the ancient parish of Llanedern. It was rapidly urbanized in the late 20th century.

PENTYRCH (Pen-tyrch) (2029 ha; 6297 inhabitants)
A one-time rural parish in the Border Vale of Glamorgan, it became part of Cardiff in 1996. It is dominated by Mynydd y Garth, once the location of much quarrying and mining. Largely open country, it contains the substantial villages of Gwaelod-y-garth, Creigiau and Pentyrch itself. The Welsh expression, *Rhwng gŵyr Pen-tyrch a'i gilydd* ('Between the men of Pentyrch and each other') suggests that, with their upland location, the inhabitants were considered to be remote from the world.

PLASNEWYDD (163 ha; 16,339 inhabitants)
Lying immediately east of the railway to **Caerphilly**, Plasnewydd is the most densely populated part of Cardiff. Within it lie the dignified streets of Tredegarville, laid out by the **Morgan family** of Tredegar in the 1850s, and Mackintosh Institute, formerly known as Roath Castle, the seat of the Richards family and its successor, the Mackintosh of Mackintosh. The original Cardiff Infirmary, built in the 1830s, stood at the west end of Newport Road. In 1883, the building became the first home of University College, Cardiff (*see* **Cardiff University**) and is now encased in an array of university buildings, an astonishing Gothic concoction of 1915 among them.

PONTPRENNAU (517 ha; 5758 inhabitants)
Straddling the **M4** below Cefn Mably Woods, Pontprennau is Cardiff's most rapidly growing community, and includes the extensive Cardiff Gate Retail Park.

RADYR AND MORGANSTOWN
(Radur a Phentre-poeth) (467 ha; 4658 inhabitants)
Added to Cardiff in 1974, the community includes the salubrious suburbs of Radyr and Morganstown, and the vast sidings where the coal once conveyed by the Taff Vale Railway awaited shipment.

RHIWBINA (Rhiwbeina) (642 ha; 11,249 inhabitants)
Rhiwbina's core is the garden village built in 1912–13 and 1922–3. Until it was wound up in 1976, Rhiwbina Garden Village Limited enjoyed wide powers and employed its own craftsmen and maintenance team. The area north of the M4 – Coed-y-Wenallt – consists of open country offering wide views of the city. South of the motorway is Y Twmpath, a large 12th-century motte.

RIVERSIDE (Glan'rafon) (259 ha; 12,021 inhabitants)
Lying on the west bank of the Taff, Riverside consists of what is often considered to be the eastern part of the suburb of Canton. Cowbridge Road divides it into two distinct

Multicultural modern Cardiff: a Sikh carnival in Riverside

areas. To the north lies Pontcanna, with its extensive open spaces and its leafy streets, the remarkable Cathedral Road among them. To the south lies Riverside 'proper', a dense web of streets and a stronghold of Cardiff's citizens of Afro-Caribbean and south Asian descent.

ROATH (Y Rhath) (335 ha; 11,672 inhabitants)

The ancient parish included the whole of Cibwr outside the borough of Cardiff. In the Middle Ages, it was a manor organized as Cardiff Castle's provisioning centre, with a score of bond tenants working under the supervision of a reeve to supply the castle household with grain, meat and dairy products. Its centre lay at the bottom of the modern Albany Road, where Roath Court – once the mansion of the Crofts Williams family and now a funeral home – perhaps occupies the site of the original *maerdy* of the Welsh rulers of Cibwr. The medieval parish church of St Margaret lay across the road. Rebuilt in superb polychromy by John Prichard in 1870, it contains a mausoleum housing the tombs of seven members of the Bute family.

The present community of Roath, which is less than a fifth of the ancient parish, straddles Eastern Avenue. Its southern part is dominated by industrial estates, warehouses and depots along Newport Road. Its northern part is the prosperous suburb of Pen-y-lan.

RUMNEY (Tredelerch) (346 ha; 8964 inhabitants)

Annexed by Cardiff in 1938, it was the first part of **Monmouthshire** to come within the city's boundary. Its parish church of St Augustine was founded in 1108. The community consists of mid and late 20th-century housing developments, which have obliterated a substantial 12th-century castle.

ST FAGANS (Sain Ffagan) (991 ha; 1480 inhabitants)

Brought within Cardiff's boundaries in 1974, it has 1.5 inhabitants per hectare compared with 100 per hectare in Plasnewydd. Its low population density is likely to continue, for it is a central part of the city's green belt and much of it consists of the park of the National History Museum (*see* **St Fagans**). The castle dates from the 1580s; with its symmetrical layout, it is Glamorgan's most important Tudor house. In 1616, it came into the possession of the Lewis family of Van, Caerphilly. In 1736, it passed through an heiress to the Windsor family, earls of Plymouth, and eventually to the Windsor-Clive family. The castle and its park were donated to the National Museum [of] Wales in 1947.

Under the Windsor-Clive family, St Fagans was a classic example of a 'closed village'. The family owned everything and used its power in a benign way. Evidence of its activity is everywhere – in the superb castle gardens, the restoration of the church, the building of a rectory, a National School and an ambitious inn, the creation of model farms and the maintenance of a picturesque row of thatched cottages.

SPLOTT (Y Sblot) (526 ha; 12,074 inhabitants)

The southern part of the ancient parish of Roath, it lies between the main railway line and the sea. In the Middle Ages, it was ecclesiastical land. The name is popularly derived from God's Plot, but it is more probably a version of the word 'plot', which shows evidence of the dialect of south-western England. Major urbanization began with the establishment of the East Moors Steelworks in 1891. Their closure in 1978 was a heavy blow and marked the culmination of the de-industrialization of Cardiff. Wales's first civil **airport** was opened on Pengam Moors in 1930; it closed in 1954. Splott now consists of a web of late 19th-century streets, water treatment works, an array of business parks and the Welsh National **Tennis** Centre. It is believed that if the East Bay Link Road is built, Splott will experience major economic development.

TONGWYNLAIS (428 ha; 1946 inhabitants)
Wedged into the Taff gorge, the community straddles the **A470**. Greenmeadow (demolished) was the home of Wyndham Lewis, whose widow married Benjamin Disraeli. Above the village stands Castell Coch, Wales's most delightful landmark. The original motte may have come into the ownership of Ifor Bach (fl.1158) but, by the 13th century, it was firmly under the control of the Clares, lords of Glamorgan. They encased the motte in stone and surmounted it with drum towers. A ruin by the mid-19th century, restoration began in 1874, financed by the third marquess of Bute and carried out by William Burges and **William Frame**. Burges's knowledge of 13th-century military architecture ensured that much of the work is authentic. However, the differing heights of the towers and their delightful sloping roofs were the fruit of Burges's search for the **picturesque** – although alpine castles provided him with some precedents. Internally, there are only four decorated rooms, but their decoration, particularly that in Lady Bute's bedroom, is breathtaking. The third marquess planted a **vineyard** below the castle, but the family made little use of the building. It came under the guardianship of the Ministry of Works in 1950, and into that of **Cadw** in 1984.

TROWBRIDGE (921 ha; 14,801 inhabitants)
The community represents the major part of Cardiff's intrusion into the one-time Monmouthshire. Its northern part consists of a web of late 20th-century streets designed as culs-de-sac. It is one of Cardiff's most populous districts. Its southern part includes part of **Wentlooge** Levels, where the landscape is Dutch rather than Welsh and where Cardiff seems remote indeed.

WHITCHURCH (Yr Eglwys Newydd)
(428 ha; 13,628 inhabitants)
Following the establishment of the Melingriffith **Tinplate** Works in 1749, Whitchurch became a substantial village. By the late 19th century, it was becoming one of Cardiff's major suburbs, but it was not brought within the city's boundary until 1962. It is the site of Cardiff's mental hospital, a vast herringbone-plan building completed in 1903. North of the hospital lies Forest Farm Country Park, which contains Cardiff's only surviving section of the Glamorganshire Canal.

CARDIFF (Caerdydd) One-time district
In 1974, the **county borough** of Cardiff was abolished and Cardiff, enlarged by parts of what had been the **rural district** of Cardiff (**Glamorgan**) and that of Magor and St Mellons (**Monmouthshire**) became a district of the new **county** of **South Glamorgan**. On the abolition of that county in 1996, the district, enlarged by the addition of the **community** of Pentyrch, became the city and county of **Cardiff**.

CARDIFF UNIVERSITY (formerly University of Wales, Cardiff)
The decision to establish the University College of South Wales and **Monmouthshire** (as it was known initially) at **Cardiff** was not unexpected, although it created much bitterness in **Swansea**. The college opened its doors to its first 144 students in 1883. Its original home, the one-time infirmary in Newport Road, proved inadequate, but it was not until 1909 that W. D. Caröe's dignified building was opened, splendidly located in **Cathays Park**. Shortly afterwards, members of staff declared that they wished Cardiff to become an independent university similar to the civic universities of **England**, a theme which would regularly surface in later years. Since the college had pioneered medical education in the **University of Wales**, there was resentment when a separate medical school – the Welsh National School of Medicine (*see* **Wales College of Medicine, Biology, Life and Health Sciences**) – was created. There was a crisis in the 1980s when the college's policies caused huge debts. Nevertheless, the college developed strongly and, in 1988, merged with the University of Wales Institute of Science and Technology (UWIST), an institution that traced its origins to 1866. In August 2004, the college merged with the University of Wales College of Medicine and, as Cardiff University, seceded from the federal University of Wales. The new institution has two colleges – an enlarged Wales College of Medicine, Biology, Life and **Health** Sciences, and the College of Humanities and **Sciences**, each headed by a provost. In 2006/7, Cardiff had 22,000 students. Recent independent assessments indicate that Cardiff is one of the most successful academic institutions in **Britain**.

CARDIGAN (Aberteifi), Ceredigion
(2048 ha; 4203 inhabitants)
The first recorded settlement at the mouth of the **Teifi** was the castle of Dingeraint built by Roger de Montgomery (*see* **Montgomery family**), earl of **Shrewsbury**, in 1093. A later castle – that built by Gilbert de **Clare** *c.*1110 – was called Cardigan, a corruption of **Ceredigion**. The lowest convenient bridging point on the Teifi, Cardigan developed into Ceredigion's earliest urban settlement. Seized by **Rhys ap Gruffudd** (Lord Rhys; d.1197) in 1167, it was the location in 1176 of Rhys's famous festival of **music** and poetry. (Considered to be the first recorded **eisteddfod**, the festival's 800th anniversary was commemorated by the holding of the National Eisteddfod at Cardigan in 1976.) In 1200, Rhys's son, Maelgwn, sold Cardigan to the **English**, much to the disgust of the author of the **Brut**, who considered it to be 'the lock and stay of all Wales'. In the 1240s, the town and its immediate vicinity came to form the core of the county of Cardigan (*see* **Cardiganshire**), which was expanded in 1277 and 1284 to include all the ancient kingdom of Ceredigion. From the **Act of 'Union'** of 1536 until 1885, Cardigan was part of the Cardigan **boroughs** constituency. Although originally considered to be the **county** town, it eventually lost all its county functions to **Aberaeron**, **Aberystwyth** and **Lampeter**.

The **Benedictine** priory of St Mary was established *c.*1110. Of the medieval priory church, only the chancel survives. Priory Mansion (converted into a hospital) was for a decade the home of the poet **Katherine Philipps** ('the matchless Orinda', 1631–64). Cardigan Grammar School, established by the **Act for the Propagation of the Gospel in Wales** (1653), surprisingly survived the Restoration and in 1895 evolved into Cardigan County School. Cardigan was an important **shipbuilding** and maritime trading centre. In one of the substantial surviving waterside warehouses is an informative heritage centre. The **port**'s activity, in decline by the 1870s, was further undermined by the arrival of the **railway** (*y Cardi bach*) in 1885; passenger traffic ceased in 1961. With seating for 750 people, Bethania **Baptist** chapel (1847) is one of the largest in rural Wales. Beneath the neo-Gothic Guildhall (1860) is a vaulted market. Mwldan is a lively arts centre. The castle, which deteriorated greatly under private ownership, is undergoing restoration.

CARDIGANSHIRE (Sir Aberteifi)
One-time county

The **county** came into existence in the early 1240s, and consisted originally of the **borough** of Cardigan and the western part of the **commote** of Is Coed. Following Edward I's confiscation of the lands of members of the house of **Deheubarth** in 1277 and 1284, the rest of the ancient kingdom of **Ceredigion** was added to the embryonic county. With **Carmarthenshire**, it constituted the **Principality** of south Wales. The **Acts of 'Union'** gave the county fuller recognition, and granted it and its boroughs an MP apiece. (The borough constituency was merged with the county constituency in 1885.) The first county council was elected in 1889. With its 'legislature' at **Aberaeron**, its 'executive' at **Aberystwyth** and its 'judicature' at **Lampeter**, Cardiganshire vied with **South Africa** as the world's best example of the geographical separation of the powers. In 1974, when it was deprived of county status, Cardiganshire consisted of the boroughs of Aberystwyth, Cardigan and Lampeter, the **urban districts** of **Aberaeron** and **New Quay** and the **rural districts** of Aberaeron, Aberystwyth, **Tregaron** and **Teifi**side. From 1974 to 1996, the former county was the district of Ceredigion within the new county of **Dyfed**. (For its reconstitution in 1996, *see* **Ceredigion, County**)

CAREW (Caeriw), Pembrokeshire
(2255 ha; 1389 inhabitants)

Bisected by the **road** linking **Pembroke** to **Tenby** (the A477 and the B4318), the **community** contains the villages of Carew, Carew Cheriton, Milton, Sageston, Redberth and West Williamston. Park rath is a fortified **Iron Age** farmstead. The Carew cross, carved in memory of Maredudd ab Edwin, king of **Deheubarth** (d.1035), is one of Wales's most elaborate early Christian monuments (*see* **Monuments, Early Christian**). Carew Castle was originally constructed *c*.1100 by Gerald de Windsor, grandfather of **Giraldus Cambrensis**. Rebuilt in stone by Gerald's descendants in the 13th and 14th centuries, it became in 1480 the property of **Rhys ap Thomas**, who built the great hall and a three-storey porch bearing the royal arms. Rhys held a five-day tournament at the castle in 1507. John **Perrot**, granted the castle in 1558, built the magnificent north range with its two rows of large rectangular windows. Attacked during the **Civil War**, thereafter the castle deteriorated for

centuries. In 1983, the **Pembrokeshire National Park** authority leased it from its owners and, with the assistance of **Cadw**, undertook extensive consolidation work.

Carew has Wales's sole working tidal mill (16th century) (*see* **Watermills**). The large late medieval church at Carew Cheriton contains several tombs; that of John Carew (d.1657) includes his effigy and those of his wife, five daughters and three sons. Adjoining the church is Wales's finest charnel house (14th century). The old vicarage retains its 16th-century fortifications. Pisgah **Baptist** chapel (1821, 1877) is a handsome building. There is an oyster farm on the estuary of the Carew **River**.

CARMARTHEN (Caerfyrddin), Carmarthenshire
(2109 ha; 13,130 inhabitants)

Located at the lowest bridgeable point of the **Tywi**, Carmarthen likes to boast that it is Wales's oldest town (*compare* **Caerwent**). A **Roman** fort was established AD *c*.75. Alongside it developed Moridunum, the *civitas* capital of the **Demetae**. (The variant, Maridunum, seems to have originated in the work of Ptolemy.) The town's walls were built in stone AD *c*.220 and adjoining them was an amphitheatre large enough to be the tribe's place of assembly. The defences of Moridunum are still apparent in Carmarthen's street pattern.

Virtually nothing is known of the place in the immediate post-Roman centuries, although the *myrddin* element in the name *Caerfyrddin* gave rise to the legend that it was the birthplace of the wizard Myrddin or **Merlin**. However, the original Brythonic name, *Moridūnon*, contains the elements *môr* (sea) and *din* (fort). Fragments of the so-called Merlin's oak, long a Carmarthen landmark, are preserved in the town's handsome guildhall (1767). By the 12th century, Carmarthen consisted of twin settlements – New Carmarthen around the castle erected by the **Normans** above the Tywi *c*.1109, and Old Carmarthen around St Peter's church and the **Augustinian** priory, established *c*.1125. *The Black Book of Carmarthen* may have been written in the priory *c*.1250. By then, the town was firmly under the control of the English crown and from it royal power was increasingly imposed upon south-west Wales. By 1290, it was the administrative centre of **Carmarthenshire** and of the **Principality** of south Wales, a development that assisted the town's rapid expansion.

In 1284, Carmarthen acquired a Franciscan **friary**. The friary was the burial place of Edmund **Tudor** (d.1456), father of Henry VII, of **Rhys ap Thomas** (d.1525) and of the poet **Tudur Aled** (d.*c*.1526). Following the friary's dissolution in 1538, the tomb of Edmund Tudor was removed to **St David's** Cathedral and that of Rhys ap Thomas to St Peter's. That church, which occupies an island site on the western edge of Moridunum, was largely rebuilt in the 15th century; it also contains the tombs of the essayist Richard Steele and General William Nott, and a memorial to Bishop Ferrar (*see* **Protestant Martyrs**), burnt at the stake in Carmarthen in 1555.

The only substantial visible portion of the castle at New Carmarthen is the twin-towered gatehouse erected in the early 14th century. Most of the rest of the castle has been overtopped by the offices of the Carmarthen County Council, an imposing turreted building completed to the designs of **Percy Thomas** in 1955. In 1451, an **eisteddfod** was held at the castle, which was prised from the control of the eisteddfod's patron, **Gruffudd ap Nicolas**, by Edmund Tudor in 1456.

In 1546, the two towns were amalgamated to form a single **borough**, which became a **county** in its own right in 1604. It acquired its Queen Elizabeth Grammar School in 1576. By then, it had over 2000 inhabitants, making it the largest town in Wales – a position it generally retained until the rise of industrial towns in the late 18th century. It became an important **printing** centre, attracting printers such as John Ross and the **Spurrell family**, and became home to the second weekly **newspaper** to be established in Wales – the *Carmarthen Journal* (1810). In 1819, **Edward Williams** (Iolo Morganwg) held a **Gorsedd** in the **garden** of the Ivy Bush Hotel, thus initiating the association between the Gorsedd and the **eisteddfod**. Carmarthen's **Presbyterian** College (*c.*1704–1963), the seedbed of Wales's **Unitarianism**, was the most distinguished of the country's dissenting or **Nonconformist academies**. Carmarthen acquired **Trinity College** in 1848. Carmarthen School of Art, opened in 1854, now forms part of Carmarthenshire College of Technology and Arts with campuses at Job's Well and Pibwrlwyd.

In the early 19th century, Carmarthen enjoyed considerable prosperity, based upon its markets and quayside trade, its **iron** and **tinplate** works and its rope factory. The centre of the region convulsed by the **Rebecca Riots**, its workhouse was ransacked by protestors in June 1843. In its bibulous heyday, the town had 150 taverns; as they were open all day on market days, and as almost every day was a market day at Carmarthen, it was long the only place in **Britain** with opening hours similar to those of France or Germany.

From the mid-19th century onwards, as more dynamic economic centres developed in the south Wales **coal**field,

the town's **population**, which had increased from 5548 in 1801 to 10,524 in 1851, stagnated. By the late 20th century, new vigour was apparent. The value of its considerable heritage of Georgian houses came to be appreciated, as did the attractiveness of the wide Lammas Street with its fine Baptist chapel (1872). New commercial opportunities arose with the construction of the Greyfriars Centre (1998), and congestion problems were eased with the completion of the eastern bypass in 1999. The capital of southwest Wales, Carmarthen is regaining some of the panache it had in the era when **William Camden** described it as 'the chief citie of the country'.

CARMARTHEN (Caerfyrddin) One-time district

Following the abolition of **Carmarthenshire** in 1974, Carmarthen was created as a district of the new **county** of **Dyfed**. It consisted of what had been the **borough** of Carmarthen, the **urban district** of **Newcastle Emlyn** and the **rural districts** of Carmarthen and Newcastle Emlyn. In 1996, the district became part of the reconstituted Carmarthenshire.

CARMARTHENSHIRE (Sir Gaerfyrddin)
(246,186 ha; 172,842 inhabitants) County

The **county** has its origins in the royal lordship established in **Carmarthen** and its vicinity in 1109. Subsequently, the lordship was frequently under Welsh rule, but, by the 1240s, it had become the centre from which **English** royal power radiated throughout the south-west. By 1290, **Cantref Mawr** and parts of **Cantref Gwarthaf** had become royal territory ruled from Carmarthen, and adjoining **march**er-lordships – **Kidwelly**, **Llandovery**, **Llansteffan**, **Laugharne** and **St Clears** among them – had come to have a degree of dependence upon the royal structures located there. After some confusion in the **Act of 'Union'** of 1536, the Act of 1543 established the boundaries of

Carmarthen and the River Tywi

Carmarthenshire as they exist today. The county consisted of what had been Cantref Mawr, **Cantref Bychan**, most of Cantref Gwarthaf and the **commotes** of **Carnwyllion, Cedweli** and **Emlyn Uwch-Cuch.**

Of Wales's original 13 counties, Carmarthenshire was the largest in area. Its core was the basins of the **Tywi**, Gwendraeth and **Taf** – the rivers which flow into Carmarthen Bay. By the late 19th century, the county had come to consist of two distinct areas: the agricultural district centred upon Carmarthen – Wales's chief dairying area (*see* **Agriculture**) – and the anthracite **coal**field centred upon the important metal production centre of **Llanelli.**

On the eve of its abolition in 1974, the county consisted of the **boroughs** of Carmarthen, Kidwelly, Llandovery and Llanelli, the **urban districts** of **Ammanford**, Burry Port (*see* **Pembrey and Burry Port**), **Cwmamman, Llandeilo** and **Newcastle Emlyn**, and the **rural districts** of Carmarthen, Llandeilo, Llanelli and Newcastle Emlyn. The one-time county was divided into the districts of Carmarthen, **Dinefwr** and Llanelli within the new county of **Dyfed**. In 1996, Dyfed was abolished and Carmarthenshire was recreated as a unitary authority. In 2001, 63.59% of the inhabitants of Carmarthenshire had some knowledge of Welsh, with 48.30% wholly fluent in the language. Carmarthenshire had 84,196 Welsh speakers, the largest number in any of the counties of Wales. (*See also* **Pendine** and **Quarter Bach**.)

CARNE, Edward (*c.*1490–1561) Lawyer and diplomat

Born at Nash Manor (**Llandow**), and a descendant of the princes of **Gwent**, Carne appeared before the papal court (1530–1) concerning Henry VIII's divorce, was commissioner for the **dissolution of the monasteries** (1538–9) and was later ambassador to the Low Countries. He was knighted *c.*1540. Under the **Acts of 'Union'**, he became the first sheriff of **Glamorgan**, and as MP for the **county** he provided the first known example of the committal of a Welsh bill to a Welsh MP. Although a devout Catholic, he gained possession of the buildings and property of the dissolved **Benedictine** priory of **Ewenny**. He became ambassador to Rome under Mary and, under Elizabeth, was held hostage, perhaps willingly, by the Pope until he died.

CARNEDDAU, Y Mountain range

Consisting of six summits exceeding the 3000-ft (914-m) contour, the highest – Carnedd Llywelyn (**Llanllechid/ Caerhun**) – rises to 1062 m, making it only 23 m lower than **Snowdon**'s highest point – Yr Wyddfa. As the Carneddau massif stretches almost to the sea at **Aber[gwyngregyn]**, it is far vaster than Snowdon's massif. With its great bulk and its long northern slopes, the range offers the closest Wales has to an arctic climate. Alpine-arctic **plants** are a feature, particularly of the upper reaches of the Crafnant valley where wood vetch grows on high cliffs. The best access to the high plateau is from Aber[gwyngregyn], past the delectable Rhaeadr Fawr **waterfall** and on to the cirque **lakes** beneath Foel Grach (974 m). The Carneddau were the subject of the earliest published guidebook to a single Welsh **mountain** – Hugh Derfel Hughes's *Llawlyfr Carnedd Llywelyn* (1864).

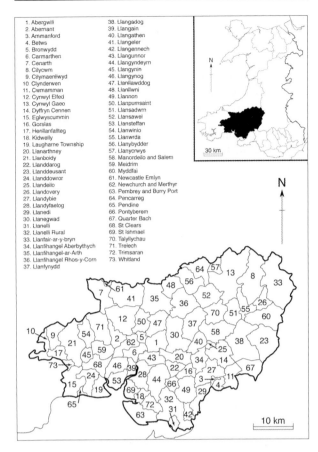

1. Abergwili	38. Llangadog
2. Abernant	39. Llangain
3. Ammanford	40. Llangathen
4. Betws	41. Llangeler
5. Bronwydd	42. Llangennech
6. Carmarthen	43. Llangunnor
7. Cenarth	44. Llangyndeyrn
8. Cilycwm	45. Llangynin
9. Cilymaenllwyd	46. Llangynog
10. Clynderwen	47. Llanllawddog
11. Cwmamman	48. Llanllwni
12. Cynwyl Elfed	49. Llannon
13. Cynwyl Gaeo	50. Llanpumsaint
14. Dyffryn Cennen	51. Llansadwrn
15. Eglwyscummin	52. Llansawel
16. Gorslas	53. Llansteffan
17. Henllanfallteg	54. Llanwinio
18. Kidwelly	55. Llanwrda
19. Laugharne Township	56. Llanybydder
20. Llanarthney	57. Llanycrwys
21. Llanboidy	58. Manordeilo and Salem
22. Llanddarog	59. Meidrim
23. Llanddeusant	60. Myddfai
24. Llanddowror	61. Newcastle Emlyn
25. Llandeilo	62. Newchurch and Merthyr
26. Llandovery	63. Pembrey and Burry Port
27. Llandybie	64. Pencarreg
28. Llandyfaelog	65. Pendine
29. Llanedi	66. Pontyberem
30. Llanegwad	67. Quarter Bach
31. Llanelli	68. St Clears
32. Llanelli Rural	69. St Ishmael
33. Llanfair-ar-y-bryn	70. Talyllychau
34. Llanfihangel Aberbythych	71. Trelech
35. Llanfihangel-ar-Arth	72. Trimsaran
36. Llanfihangel Rhos-y-Corn	73. Whitland
37. Llanfynydd	

30 km

10 km

The communities of the county of Carmarthen

CARNO, Montgomeryshire, Powys (4604 ha; 646 inhabitants)

A **community** occupying the upper reaches of the Carno valley north-west of **Caersws**, the area came to prominence in the 1960s when **Laura Ashley** and her husband Bernard opened a factory in Carno village. The factory office, with its high slit windows, was built in 1973; the factory closed in 2005. The 19th-century church replaced what was probably a medieval structure associated with the Knights of St John and their adjacent grange, Caer Noddfa. The Aleppo Merchant Inn was named after a ship captained by the inn's one-time landlord. The village was the home of Joseph Thomas (1814–89), a popular 19th-century **preacher**. Plasnewydd is a large timber house of *c.*1704. **Bronze Age** finds have been made on Trannon Moor, where 48 wind turbines straddle the Carno-**Llanbrynmair** boundary.

CARNWYLLION Commote

Apparently carved out of the **commote** of **Cedweli**, the western part of the *cantref* of **Eginog**, Carnwyllion's administrative centre was probably at **Llanelli**. It became part of the **march**er-lordship of **Kidwelly**. The name survived as that of the post-**Acts of 'Union'** hundred of Carnwallon.

CARREGHOFA (Carreghwfa), Montgomeryshire, Powys (537 ha; 599 inhabitants)

Located in **Montgomeryshire**'s north-eastern extremity, the **community** includes the western half of the village of Llanymynech (the other half is in **Shropshire**). Until

Sunday closing ended in Montgomeryshire in 1968, Carreghofa had a tavern with one bar closed on Sunday and the other open. The aqueduct carrying the Montgomeryshire **Canal** across the Vyrnwy (c.1796) and Llanymynech Bridge (1826) are structurally interesting. The quintessential artisan-inventor **Richard Roberts** (1789–1864) was a son of Carreghofa's tollkeeper.

CARTER, J[ohn] C[oates] (1859–1927) Architect

Born in Norwich, Carter was articled to J. B. Pearce before becoming assistant and then partner (1884–1904) to John Pollard Seddon (formerly partner of **John Prichard**). Starting from a Gothic base, Carter became steeped in the Arts and Crafts tradition, which he developed in a distinctive way. As Seddon's partner, with an office in **Cardiff**, he was responsible for churches in Cardiff (St Paul, 1887), **Penarth** (All Saints, 1892) and **Chepstow** (St Mary's restoration, 1890), together with houses and other buildings in the Penarth area. Working on his own account, from 1904, he designed some memorable buildings, notably the expressionist All Saints' parish hall (1906) in Penarth, a remarkable Rhenish-style monastery on Caldey (1907–13) (see **Islands**), and a striking stone and concrete church at **Abercarn** (St Luke, 1923).

CARTWRIGHT, Frederick (1907–98)
Engineer and industrialist

Sir Frederick Cartwright was one of the chief architects of the modern British steel industry (see **Iron and Steel**). Born in Norfolk, he joined the **Guest Keen and Nettlefolds** Dowlais Works, **Merthyr Tydfil**, in 1929. Along with S. E. Graff of US Steel, he played a leading role in the establishment of the **Ebbw Vale** strip mill for **Richard Thomas and Co**. In 1940, he became chief engineer at Guest Keen and Baldwins, and from 1943 until 1972 was the managing director of the firm's **Port Talbot** works. He was a central figure in: the creation of the **Steel Company of Wales** (1947); the extension of the Port Talbot works to encompass continuous hot strip and cold reduction mills; the creation, in the late 1960s, of a deep-water harbour for iron-ore carriers in excess of the equivalent of 100,000 tonnes; and in the change from open-hearth steelmaking to the basic oxygen process. In 1967, following the formation of the British Steel Corporation, he became managing director of the South Wales Group, and, in 1970, deputy chairman of the BSC.

CASTLE CAEREINION (Castell Caereinion),
Montgomeryshire, Powys (2733 ha; 509 inhabitants)

Located immediately west of **Welshpool**, the **community** contains several ancient houses, in particular Tŷ Mawr which in 1997–8 was restored to its state as an exemplary Welsh medieval house, dendrologically dated to 1460. Trefnant, a fine mid-18th century mansion approached by an avenue of walnut trees, may occupy the site of the hall granted to Strata Marcella monastery (see **Welshpool**) by **Owain Cyfeiliog** in 1170. Dolarddau, where Henry **Tudor** is said to have lodged on his way to **Bosworth**, has been demolished. Cyfronydd (c.1865) housed a girls' school, closed in the 1990s; the novelist Dyddgu Owen (1906–92), was for many years its headmistress. The compact village contains St **Garmon**'s church (1874) and Twmpath

Garmon – the castle of **Caereinion**, built by **Madog ap Maredudd** in 1156. Much of the community forms part of the Powis Castle estate (see **Welshpool**).

CASTLEMARTIN (Castellmartin),
Pembrokeshire (2434 ha; 147 inhabitants)

Constituting the south-western corner of **Pembrokeshire**, the **community**'s main feature is the extensive duneland of Brownslade Burrows. St Michael's church, largely 13th century, has a 15th-century tower. In 1939, the southern part of the community became an artillery range, and thus public access to the splendid coastline with its Green Bridge and Elegug Rocks is restricted. St Mary's (13th century), Warren, saved from collapse by the British army, contains a pipe organ reputedly once owned by Mendelssohn. Castlemartin gave its name to a breed of long-horned black **cattle**. Linney Head has caused many **shipwrecks**, in particular that of the *Mars* (1862), which resulted in the death of 35 people.

CATHAYS PARK, Cardiff

The splendid civic centre, possibly the finest in **Britain**, stands to the north of **Cardiff**'s commercial centre. It includes more than a dozen civic, governmental and educational buildings – all clad in white Portland stone or what purports to be Portland stone – arranged around central **gardens**. Cardiff Corporation acquired the land in 1897 from John Crichton **Stuart**, third marquess of Bute, with the intention of erecting upon it buildings to fulfil the administrative, legal and **education** needs of Cardiff as a town and as capital of **Glamorgan**. In addition, there was an implicit intention of using the site to enhance Cardiff's position as 'the metropolis of Wales'. The buildings, erected from 1901 onwards, offer a display of varied architectural styles. The centrepiece is the dominating and flamboyantly baroque City Hall (1901–5), with the more restrained **Law Courts** (1901–4) to its right, both designed by Lanchester, Stewart and Rickards. On the left stands the quietly grand **National Museum** (Smith and Brewer, 1913–93). The rococo-style University College (W. D. Caröe, 1905–12) (see **Cardiff University**) occupies the eastern side of the park. The college has also acquired three buildings on the western side – the boldly noble one-time Glamorgan **County** Hall (Harris and Moodie, 1908–12), the restrained one-time Technical Institute (Ivor Jones and **Percy Thomas**, 1913–16), and the modernistic buildings erected for the one-time Welsh College of Advanced Technology (Percy Thomas, 1960–1). Percy Thomas's Temple of Peace and Health (1937–8) is in the streamlined classical style he used for **Swansea**'s Guildhall. The offices of the **Welsh Board of Health** (P. K. Hampton, 1934–8) overlook Wales's National War Memorial (N. Comper, 1924–8).

All the buildings in the park were subject to a height restriction determined by the cornice line of the City Hall. The ruling gave the entire scheme a coherent unity, which was lost when the height restriction was abandoned in the 1960s. The University College built a vast pile in the park's north-eastern corner (Percy Thomas and others, 1958 onwards). The **Welsh Office** (Alex Gordon, 1972–9), described as 'a symbol of closed inaccessible government ... bureaucracy under siege', became the executive offices of

The Welsh National War Memorial in Cathays Park, Cardiff

the **National Assembly for Wales** in 1999. Other buildings in the park include the delightful **University of Wales** Registry (Wills and Anderson, 1903–40) and the Central **Police** Station (John Dryburgh, 1966–8). Harold Carter argued (1965) that the fact that Wales's finest group of 20th-century buildings surrounds a garden rather than a square indicates that the Welsh lack an instinct for urban life.

CATHEINIOG Commote

One of the seven **commotes** of **Cantref Mawr**, the land of Cathen ap Cawdraf, contained some of the most fertile land of the **Tywi** valley. Its chief church was at **Llangathen**. Within it was Dryslwyn Castle. The name survived as that of the post-**Acts of 'Union' hundred** of Cathinog.

CATHOLIC MARTYRS

Records survive of the execution of some 68 **Roman Catholics** of Welsh origin in the 16th and 17th centuries, the majority of them priests. To the authorities – Elizabeth I, in particular – those executed were not punished for their faith, but for their treason. Yet, while there were among the 68 some who were involved in treasonable activities against the English crown, the very fact of being a Roman Catholic priest was considered to be proof of being an emissary of a foreign power. There is substance to the argument that some among those executed suffered martyrdom for their faith; indeed, among the missionary priests there were those who actively sought the glory of martyrdom. The available evidence probably understates the numbers who suffered. The 40 martyrs of Wales and **England** who were canonized in Rome in 1970 were representative of hundreds of causes under consideration. The martyrdom of four Welsh Catholics inspired the **Quaker Waldo Williams** to write his

remarkable poem 'Wedi'r Canrifoedd Mudan'. (*See also* **John Roberts** (1576–1610), **Nicholas Owen**, **Richard Gwyn** and **William Davies** (d.1593).)

CATRIN OF BERAIN (1534/5–91) Matriarch

The granddaughter of an illegitimate son of Henry VII, Catrin (or Katherine) of Berain (**Llannefydd**) was related to many of the leading families of north Wales and had numerous descendants from three of her four marriages, for which reason she was known as 'The Mother of Wales'. Her husbands were John **Salusbury** of Lleweni (**Denbigh**), Richard Clough of Denbigh, Maurice **Wynn** of Gwydir (**Trefriw**) and Edward Thelwall of Plas-y-ward (**Llanynys**); some of her children married her stepchildren. Thomas Salusbury, the eldest son of her first marriage, was executed for his part in the Babington Plot of 1586.

CATS

The wildcat (*Felis sylvestris*), which in **Britain** survives only in **Scotland**, was found in the wildest parts of Wales until the 19th century. Gradually exterminated as guns became common and gamekeepers proliferated, it was confined to **Snowdonia** and remoter areas of mid Wales by 1850. The shooting of a wildcat at Abermule (**Llandyssil**) in 1862 is the last dependable record of the animal in Wales, although several feral domestic cats in mid Wales continued to exhibit some of the wildcat's physical features until the early 20th century.

The domestic cat (*Felis domesticus*) was highly valued in Welsh medieval **law** for defending barns against rodents. The fine for killing a cat was the amount of grain piled to completely cover the cat's body when held by tail-tip with the nose touching the ground. There is much folklore

A herd of Welsh Black cattle, Rhiwlas, Llandderfel, near Bala

concerning cats. For example, **witches** were believed to transform themselves into cats, and cats were used not only to predict the weather but to indicate whether the soul of a recently dead person would go to heaven or hell.

Since the 1970s, there have been regular reports of big cats such as panthers, black leopards and pumas roaming rural Wales and savaging livestock. They may be escapees or deliberately released from private collections following the Dangerous Animals Act, 1976.

CATTLE

Like most European domestic breeds, cattle in **Wales** are descended from the wild aurochs, which became extinct in **Britain** during the **Bronze Age**. Domesticated cattle were used for ploughing (*see* **Agriculture**) as early as the Bronze Age, and by the **Iron Age** several identifiable types had developed, including the small, short-horned **Celtic** cow, the progenitor of most modern dairy breeds. The Welsh medieval **law** books describe plough teams of two, four, six or eight oxen. Cattle ownership meant wealth, and the importance of cattle as units of currency is echoed in the **Welsh** word for capital, *cyfalaf*, which derives from *alaf* (a herd of cattle); the Welsh for good or goods, *da*, also means livestock.

From the Iron Age, if not earlier, cattle, **goats** and **sheep** were moved seasonally between *hafod* and *hendre*, but by the 18th century the practice of transhumance was in decline, and the mountain pastures were grazed almost exclusively by sheep. From the late Middle Ages onwards, rural Wales's main source of income came from the export

of cattle to **England**. Herded by **drovers**, they were described by **John Williams** (1582–1650), archbishop of York, as 'the Spanish fleet of Wales which brings hither the little **gold** and silver we have.' From the 1850s, **railways** took over the transportation of cattle, and village livestock fairs were replaced by marts located near railway stations.

Milk-white oxen having been purportedly the sacred animals of the **druids**, there are various references in **literature** and folklore to the importance attached to white cattle, which were believed to bring luck to their owners. The white cattle traditionally kept at **Dinefwr, Llandeilo**, are a famous old herd, associated both with the royal court of **Deheubarth** and, more fancifully, with the story of the lady of **Llyn y Fan Fach**. Various local breeds developed, such as the **Glamorgan** and the **Montgomery**, both extinct by the late 19th century, and the **Anglesey** and the **Pembroke**. Out of these two developed the Welsh Black, world famous for the quality of its beef. Formal records of the breed go back to the first herd book in June 1874, although it was not until 1905 that the Welsh Black Cattle Society was founded. From the late 1990s, Wales saw a novelty breed, the Asian water buffalo, establish itself on a small number of farms and at the Welsh Wildlife Centre at **Cilgerran**, where these unfussy foragers were introduced to help check the expansion of poor quality land.

The 20th century saw major improvements in the quality of breeds and in production levels, through such measures as bull registration, established in 1914, the creation in 1933 of the Milk Marketing Board, and the introduction of artificial insemination in the 1950s and of embryo transfers in the 1990s. In dairying areas such as **Cardiganshire**, the ownership of a bull used to determine social status, and in some districts almost every bull owner was a chapel elder; artificial insemination thus undermined an age-old hierarchy.

Dairy production, concentrated for climatic reasons in the south-west, is the largest agricultural enterprise in Wales, contributing 25% of agricultural output in 2002. The average milk yield per cow of 3900 litres in 1972 increased to 6528 litres in 2002. While average herd size increased from 25 to 67 cows over the same period, the number of dairy producers declined from 19,944 in 1939 to 4004 in 2002. Modern dairy farming in Wales rarely uses breeds other than the Friesian Holstein, an incomparable animal in terms of yield.

Beef production, always a major activity in Wales, accounted for 23% of total agricultural output in 1998. Beef is produced either from surplus male calves from lowland dairy herds or from purpose-bred beef calves from upland and some lowland suckler herds. Traditional beef breeds used in Wales are the Welsh Black, the Hereford, the Shorthorn and the Aberdeen Angus, but mainland European breeds such as the Charolais, the Limousin, the Belgian blue and the Simmental have come to dominate the sire lines for their high meat yield and rapid rate of growth. Welsh beef enjoys the European Union's coveted Protected Geographical Indicator status, which means that only beef from cattle reared and slaughtered in Wales may be described as Welsh beef.

Two recent animal health crises have seriously affected cattle farming in Wales, as in other parts of Britain. As the industry began to recover from the damage done to beef sales by Bovine Spongiform Encephalopathy (BSE), or 'mad cow disease', which was first identified in the 1980s, it was further undermined, in 2001, by a major outbreak of foot and mouth disease. The worst-affected areas in Wales were **Anglesey**, **Powys** and the south-east. In order to halt the spread of the disease, a total of 286,000 cattle, **pigs** and sheep were destroyed, of which 9% were cattle, and severe restrictions were imposed on the transportation of livestock and on public access to the countryside. The outbreak lasted six months and is estimated to have cost Welsh farming £62 million and the Welsh **economy** £201 million.

CAULDRON OF REBIRTH, The (*Pair Dadeni*)

A magic vessel in the second branch of the Mabinogi (*see* ***Mabinogion, The***) which revives dead warriors but leaves them bereft of speech. It is given by **Bendigeidfran** as a peace offering to Matholwch after **Efnysien** has insulted the **Irish** at the time of **Branwen**'s marriage. Efnysien finally smashes the cauldron, losing his own life in so doing.

CAVE, Jane (*c.*1757–1813) Poet

Jane Cave was born in **Talgarth**, to an English exciseman converted to **Calvinistic Methodism** under the influence of **Howel Harris**. She published *Poems on Various Subjects, Entertaining, Elegiac, and Religious* in 1783; the same year, she married another English exciseman and settled with him in Winchester. Her volume – five editions of which appeared during her lifetime – included an elegy on Howel Harris and a number of poems conveying her Methodist sympathies. She died in **Newport**.

CAVES

With the exception of rock shelters such as Twm Shon Catti's Cave (**Llanfair-ar-y-bryn**), and sea caves, which are formed by the erosive action of the waves, caves are found only in **limestone** rock. A major belt of Carboniferous Limestone surrounds the south Wales **coal**field; there **are** smaller outcrops in the north-east and the north-west.

Cave systems come into existence because of three factors: soluble rock, a flow of water and time. Contact with atmospheric carbon dioxide causes rainwater to become a mild carbonic acid. The water seeps into cracks in limestone, which is slightly soluble in acidic water. When a crack reaches a critical size, it will capture water from the surrounding rock. With increased flow, the process becomes accelerated and slowly a seeping, waterlogged fissure will be transformed to a cave.

At the earliest stage of cave development – the phreatic – underground passages are completely flooded. Substantial sections of Dan-yr-Ogof (**Tawe-Uchaf**) provide classic examples of this type of network. When water levels drop – which happens, for example, as major **rivers** carve ever deeper into their valley floors, or glaciers gouge and over-deepen their channels – some passageways will be partially drained. As a result, a stream runs along the cave floor and airspace appears above – the vadose stage of development. Underground drainage routes often parallel major valleys, into which the water ultimately discharges. The cave systems of the upper **Nedd**, Mellte and Hepste demonstrate this close relationship perfectly. Other

Calcite formations in Dan-yr-Ogof caves

conduits may become completely abandoned by water and are thereafter referred to as fossil passages. The systems located beneath **Mynydd Llangatwg** – a labyrinth of large and very old tunnels dating back many millions of years – contain particularly elaborate examples of such passages.

Other features associated with the erosional sculpting are deep shafts or potholes and large chambers or caverns. Potholes are found at places where water has at some stage found an easy route vertically through rock. Wales's deepest pothole is Pwll Dwfn situated above Dan-yr-Ogof; there, a series of five shafts descend some 93 m to terminate in a water-filled passage. Several factors – the intersection of two major fissures, for example – can lead to the creation of caverns; they are frequently littered with boulders which have collapsed from the roof above. Those beneath Mynydd Llangatwg are among the most spectacular in **Britain**.

While the limestone mass is being eroded, another natural process – deposition – is at work. If water passes through the rock, it carries with it the limestone it has dissolved. It eventually finds its way into the air space of a cave passage, where some of the dissolved rock is precipitated in a white crystalline form known as calcite. The most common outcome is the formation of a delicate, hollow-centred, straw stalactite, hanging from the cave roof. When the water droplet plunges to the cave floor, the calcite laid down forms a stalagmite. When a stalactite and a stalagmite meet, the outcome is a pillar or column. There are remarkable examples of such cave formations at Dan-yr-Ogof, Mynydd Llangatwg and Govan's Cave (**Stackpole**).

Dan-yr-Ogof, the finest showcave complex in Britain, is visited annually by 200,000 people. In 2004, the complex was declared a National Nature Reserve, the first geological phenomenon in Wales to receive that distinction. It consists of three separate caves: Dan-yr-Ogof itself, first explored in 1912 by the fabled Morgan brothers of Abercraf; Cathedral Cave, aptly named after its sheer immensity; and Ogof yr Esgyrn (the bone cave), which contains an archaeological interpretative centre. Beyond the limit of public access, Dan-yr-Ogof penetrates deep beneath the **Black Mountain** and contains a network of passages over 16 km in length. The cave presents experienced speleologists with deep **lakes**, foaming **waterfalls**, long constricted crawl-ways, deep pits and caverns adorned with spectacular displays of rock formations.

More extensive, but less accessible, is the cave complex beneath Mynydd Llangatwg. Consisting of three separate caves with an overall length of 70 km, the complex has been the scene of an epic saga of exploration. Together with much of Mynydd Llangatwg, the caves, which contain important **bat** roosts, have been designated a Site of Special Scientific Interest.

Caves that have yielded important archaeological evidence (*see* **Archaeology and Antiquarianism**) include Pontnewydd (**Cefnmeiriadog**), Ffynnon Beuno (**Tremeirchion**), Hoyle's Mouth (**Penally**), Coygan (**Laugharne**) and Paviland (**Rhossili**).

CAWL (Broth)

A broth regularly served during the winter months in the south-west. Salted bacon or beef was boiled with potatoes,

swedes, carrots and other seasonal vegetables, cut into medium-sized pieces, then thickened with oatmeal or plain flour. The broth itself (without the meat or vegetables) was served as a first course; the vegetables and slices of boiled meat would then be served as a second course. Catwg Ddoeth (Catwg the Wise), an 'authority' fabricated by Iolo Morganwg (**Edward Williams**), noted of *cawl*, in his collection of **proverbs**, 'It is as good to drink the broth as to eat the meat.' *Cawl*, served as a single course, remains a popular dish, as does its equivalent, *lobsgows*, in the north. The meat and vegetables in *lobsgows* were cut into smaller pieces and the stock was not thickened.

CBI WALES

Founded in 1965, the Confederation of British Industry (CBI) has a membership that comprises companies of all sizes from all sectors of business. It is organized into 13 distinct areas, with the CBI Wales office located in **Cardiff**. Viewed as **Britain**'s premier business organization, it exists 'to ensure that the **government** of the day, the European Commission and the wider community understand both the needs of British business and the contribution it makes to the well-being of UK society'.

CECIL family Landowners and officials

Robert Sitsyllt (Seisyll), a follower of Robert **Fitz Hammo**, obtained Alltyrynys (**Herefordshire**) and estates stretching into Wales by marriage. The name 'Cecil' was first used towards the end of the 15th century by Richard Cecil, who married into the Vaughans of Tyleglas, of the lordship of **Brecon**. His grandson, another Richard (d.1552), established himself at Burghley in Lincolnshire and also married into a **Breconshire** family. His son, William Cecil, Lord Burghley (1520–98), Elizabeth I's first secretary of state, took pride in his Welsh ancestry.

CEDEWAIN Commote

Comprising an extensive area of the south-eastern part of what would later be **Montgomeryshire**, the name may mean the 'territory of Cadaw'. Traditionally part of **Powys**, the **commote** was seized in c.1262 by **Llywelyn ap Gruffudd**, who proceeded to fortify it by building Dolforwyn Castle (*see* **Llandyssil**). In 1279, Cedewain was granted to the **Mortimer family**, from whom it passed to the **York family** and thence to the crown. The post-**Acts of 'Union' hundred** of Cydewain had boundaries similar to those of the medieval commote.

CEDWELI Commote

Constituting the western part of **Eginog** – one of the three *cantrefi* of Ystrad Tywi – the **commote** constituted what would later be south-eastern **Carmarthenshire**. At an early date, the commote was divided into two – Cedweli and Carnwyllion. Following the **Norman** invasions, both commotes came to constitute the **marcher**-lordship of **Kidwelly**.

CEFFYL PREN, Y (The wooden horse)

The *ceffyl pren* was a means of reviling an offender by carrying him (or his effigy) on a ladder or pole, often in front of his house in the hours of darkness. This was frequently preceded by a mock trial and a noisy procession of men with darkened faces and wearing **women**'s clothes. It was used in cases of sexual offence or domestic violence and was an unofficial but effective means of social control before the establishment of a **police** force. The attacks of the **Rebecca riot**ers upon the tollgates of the south-west in the 19th century were an extension of this practice, which was also known as the 'cwlstrin' in **Glamorgan** and 'skimmington' in **England**.

CEFN, Wrexham (803 ha; 6699 inhabitants)
Located at the entrance of the Vale of **Llangollen**, the area that would later be the **community** of Cefn, and was earlier the **parish** of Cefn-mawr, was extensively industrialized following the establishment *c.*1800 of blast furnaces at Acrefair. The works, which came into the possession of the British **Iron** Company of **Abersychan** in 1823, much impressed **George Borrow**; they closed in 1888. Extraction of **oil** from **coal** shale led, in 1867, to the establishment of the Monsanto Chemical Works, now the Flexsys plant. Acrefair, Cefn-mawr and Rhosymedre contain some attractive chapels. Plas Madog is an ambitious leisure centre. A large Country Park, Tŷ Mawr, has been opened along the banks of the **Dee**.

CEFN CRIBWR (Cefncribwr), Bridgend
(748 ha; 1546 inhabitants)
Lying north-west of **Bridgend**, the **community** includes the remains of a charcoal-fuelled furnace built in the 1770s for **iron**making. An engine house and kilns of the 1820s also survive. They adjoin vast open-cast **coal** workings. Parc Slip Nature Park is a haven for water**birds**.

CEFN FFOREST, Caerphilly
(64 ha; 3589 inhabitants)
Cefn Fforest is a wholly urbanized **community** forming the western fringes of **Blackwood**. It is the smallest in area of all the communities of Wales.

CEFNMEIRIADOG (Cefn Meiriadog),
Denbighshire (1351 ha; 440 inhabitants)
Located immediately south-west of **St Asaph**, the **community** has yielded the earliest evidence of humanity in Wales – the teeth (250,000 BC) found in the Bontnewydd cave high above the Elwy valley (*see* **Palaeolithic and Mesolithic Ages**). Charles Darwin's visit to the cave in 1829 had an impact upon the development of his theories. In Ffynnon Fair chapel (15th century), the **well** waters flow into a stellar-shaped basin. The Plas-yn-Cefn estate was part of the vast landed property of the **Williams Wynn family**. The mansion is still occupied by the family. Wigfair, remodelled by **John Douglas** in 1884, was the home of the Tudor courtier and poet **Siôn Tudur** (*c.*1522–1602). Dol-belidr was the home of the **dictionary** compiler, Henry Salisbury (1561–?1637). Peter Roberts (fl.1578–1646), author of an interesting chronicle, *Y Cwtta Cyfarwydd*, was a native of Cefnmeiriadog. John Fisher (1862–1930), co-author of *Lives of the British Saints*, and the historian D. R. Thomas (1833–1915) were rectors of St Mary's (1864), a church delightfully situated on an eminence. Maes Robert (1974) is an attractive example of sheltered **housing**.

CEINMEIRCH Commote
The easternmost of the three **commotes** of the *cantref* of **Rhufoniog**, its centre was at Ystrad (**Denbigh**), where there is a farm named Llys (court). The name survives in that of **Llanrhaeadr-yng-Nghinmeirch**.

CEIRIOG UCHA (Ceiriog Uchaf), Wrexham
(5409 ha; 346 inhabitants)
As its name suggests, the **community** embraces the upper reaches of the Ceiriog valley, an area once criss-crossed by **drovers**' roads. It remains a largely agricultural community based around **sheep** farming, **forestry** and the shooting of pheasant and grouse. **Huw Morus** (Eos Ceiriog; 1622–1709) spent most of his life in Pont-y-Meibion, where **George Borrow** heroically sought his legendary chair. **John Ceiriog Hughes** (1822–87), the most popular of all the **Welsh-language** poets of the 19th century, was born at Pen-y-bryn, Llanarmon Dyffryn Ceiriog. The village of Llanarmon contains two attractive inns. The **Iron Age hill-fort** of Cerrig Gwynion surrounds a striking ridge of white quartz. In 2001, 58.21% of the community's inhabitants had some knowledge of **Welsh**, with 40% wholly fluent in the language – the highest percentages for any of the communities of the **Wrexham county borough**.

CELTIC ASSOCIATIONS
The call for a pan-**Cel**tic movement first came in a pamphlet published in 1864 by Charles de Gaulle (1837–80), an uncle of President de Gaulle, in which he advocated a common Celtic language and a federation of self-governing Celtic countries. The first (pan-)Celtic Association emerged in Dublin in 1898, lasting until 1913. It is remembered chiefly for its periodical *Celtia* and its congresses, the most famous of which was held at **Caernarfon** in 1904. Resurrected as the Celtic Congress or Conference by the Welsh MP **E. T. John**, at the 1917 National **Eisteddfod**, it aims to further Celtic co-operation in the fields of language, **literature** and national traditions. It meets in each of the six Celtic countries in turn.

The Celtic League, a body with more specifically political aims, was founded in 1947, under the presidency of the Welsh patriot **Gwynfor Evans**. In the 1960s, it published a series of yearbooks and, in 1971, launched the magazine *Carn*. Other Celtic organizations include the Celtic **Film** Festival, the Congress of Celtic Studies, Celtic Vision and Scrif Celt – the former organizing art exhibitions and the latter publishers' fairs.

CELTIC CHURCH, The
This is a term frequently used uncritically when referring to the Christianity of the first millennium in those areas where **Celtic** languages were spoken. The appeal to the antiquity of the British Church is found in the 13th-century legend of Joseph of Arimathea. The idea of a single Celtic Church appears in a more developed form in the writings of **William Salesbury**, **Richard Davies** (?1501–81) and the Protestants who followed them, writings which stress that the independence and purity of the early Church in **Britain** and **Ireland** contrasted markedly with the situation in the rest of the Christian world. They emphasize the continuity between the early Christian Churches (assumed to have

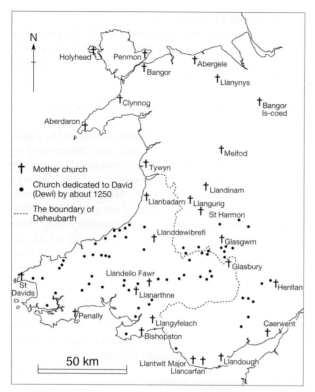

The Celtic Church in Wales (after William Rees 1959)

flourished before the imposition of 'Roman' ecclesiastical authority in these islands) and the new Protestant order, presumably to provide an historical basis and legitimacy for the post-**Protestant Reformation** national Church. It was in effect argued that these Churches constituted a proto-Protestantism. By the 20th century, the term appears, without its denominational agenda, as a convenient catchphrase in the work of such scholars as Nora Chadwick and **Kenneth Jackson**. The concept of a 'Celtic Christianity', and in particular that of a 'Celtic Spirituality', continues to appeal greatly to those who, failing to find what they seek within the traditional denominations, look for alternative and more appealing forms of Christianity. However, as there is no evidence for a monolithic ecclesiastical organization common to all of the Celtic lands, it is anachronistic to believe that there is any analogy between the first millennium Church in Celtic-speaking lands and Christian churches and denominations as they are understood today.

Nevertheless, there is no doubt that the churches of the Celtic lands were in contact with each other. The establishment of Christianity in Ireland was indebted to British **missionaries**, and British influence remained strong until the 7th century. **Scotland** was evangelized from Ireland and the churches of **Cornwall** and Wales played an important role in the story of the growth of Christianity in **Brittany**. Furthermore, the churches of the Celtic lands shared many characteristics, several of them arising from the fact that in all those lands, the Church was operating in a wholly rural environment. They included a lack of a clearly defined ecclesiastical hierarchy, an emphasis upon the abbot rather than the bishop (especially in Ireland), a

delight in asceticism and desolate places, an intimate relationship with nature, **women** with quasi-sacerdotal roles, hereditary ecclesiastical offices and a distinctive method of calculating the date of Easter (*see* **Religion**).

CELTIC TWILIGHT, The

First used as the title of a collection of folktales by W. B. Yeats in 1893, the term was later applied, somewhat sardonically, to a tendency in **English literature** during the 1890s and the early years of the 20th century. Anglo-Irish writers were the main contributors but it also included the work of such Welsh and Scottish poets as **Ernest Rhŷs** and Fiona Macleod (William Sharp). Much influenced by the writings of **Matthew Arnold**, particularly his insistence on magic and melancholy as characteristics of literature in the Celtic countries, the tendency was derided by writers of the next generation such as **Edward Thomas** and James Joyce. A selection of the poetry associated with the Celtic Twilight is to be found in the anthologies *Lyra Celtica* (1896), edited by Elizabeth Sharp, and *A Celtic Anthology* (1927), edited by Grace Rhys.

CELTS

Various names were used by classical writers to describe the **Iron Age** communities to their north and west, including Keltoi, Celtae, Galli, Galatae and Britanni. It is impossible to be sure whether these labels were external impositions or were meaningful to these people themselves. However, the descriptor 'Celts' or 'Celtic' has, since the 18th century, been widely employed to describe people who speak, or historical communities who at one time spoke, a Celtic language – one related to Gaulish and other western European Iron Age languages. Iron Age communities in **Britain** meet this criterion, and the pre-**Roman** tribes of Wales, including the **Cornovii**, **Deceangli**, **Demetae**, **Ordovices** and **Silures** are frequently referred to as Celtic.

Criticism has been levelled at the use of this description as a general label for the later prehistoric European past, with arguments that Celticity, as generally understood, is largely a construct of the early modern period. Nevertheless, authorities such as Barry Cunliffe support the use of Celtic as an archaeological/historical term describing a loosely knit but coherent group of ancient communities. Recurrent elements of a material culture present over large areas of temperate Europe do suggest significant degrees of commonality. Such indicators include imagery on **coins**, the use of torcs as symbols of status, the prominence of the human head in art and ritual activity, the aquatic deposition of ritual objects, and, particularly, common motifs in La Tène art such as triskeles, leaf-crowns and fantastic human and animal imagery. On the basis of place names and other evidence, these common elements in material culture appear to correlate geographically with the distribution of Celtic languages: consequently it seems appropriate to use Celtic as a single identifier.

Early modern attitudes to Celticity and Celtic languages owe much to **Edward Lhuyd** who, in his *Archaeologia Britannica* (1707), argued for the idea of shared Celtic linguistic and ethnic identity among the non-English Britons, the **Irish** and the Bretons. This idea was later romanticized (*see* **Romanticism**) by writers such as Iolo Morganwg (**Edward Williams**) who, in the late 18th and early 19th centuries, created a 'pedigree' of bardic activity stretching from his own time back to the pre-Roman past. A consequence of Iolo's imaginative creativity was the meeting of 'druidical' *gorseddau* on Primrose Hill in **London**. Such trappings were subsequently embraced more widely and became important in shaping the modern **eisteddfod**. Today, 'Celtic' as a linguistic term continues to be a useful way to describe the cognate languages of **Welsh**, Scots Gaelic, Irish, Breton, Cornish and Manx. It is also an important self-identification for many people living in the areas where these languages are spoken, although for many it has become an amorphous term for anarchic lifestyles and 'New Age' **philosophies**.

CEMAES (Cemais) *Cantref*

Along with **Aberffraw** and **Rhosyr**, **Cemaes** was one of the three *cantrefi* of **Anglesey**. Extending over the northern part of the island, it contained the **commotes** of **Talybolion** and **Twrcelyn**.

CEMAIS *Cantref*

The northernmost of the seven *cantrefi* of **Dyfed**, Cemais consisted of the **commotes** of Is Nyfer and Uwch Nyfer. In the early 12th century, it came into the possession of the Fitz Martin family, who organized it as a **march**er-lordship with its caput first at **Nevern** and later at **Newport**. Apart from the occasions when it was recaptured by the Welsh, it remained in the possession of the Fitz Martin family and its descendants, the **Audleys** and the Tuchets, until 1543,

when what remained of the lordship's rights were bought by the father of **George Owen**. The name survived as that of the post-**Act of 'Union' hundred** of Cemais.

CENARTH, Carmarthenshire
(4370 ha; 1022 inhabitants)

Adjoining **Newcastle Emlyn** south of the **Teifi**, the **community** contains the village of Cenarth and the scattered settlement of Capel Iwan. On the west, it is bounded by the delightful valley of the Cych, which features in *The Mabinogion*. St Llawddog's church (1870) has a 13th-century font. The attractive **waterfalls** on the Teifi attract numerous visitors. **Giraldus Cambrensis** reported seeing **beavers** at Cenarth. **Fish**ing for salmon and sewin by **coracle** at Cenarth long enjoyed popularity. In 1935, legislation restricted the right to fish to those already holding a licence; the last of the licence holders died in the 1970s. Coracles from many parts of the world are displayed in the National Coracle Centre. A coracle regatta is held every August. The **Congregational** chapel at Capel Iwan has its origins in 1723.

CENTRAL LABOUR COLLEGE

A **London**-based **Marxist** institution, set up in 1909 and jointly financed by the National Union of **Railway**men and the **South Wales Miners' Federation** to educate working-**class** men for 'their industrial and political tasks'. Its Welsh products included **Aneurin Bevan**, **Ness Edwards**, **James Griffiths** and **George Daggar**. The college established extensive tutorial classes in south Wales, in which **syndicalist** ideas were widely discussed.

The bridge over the Teifi at Cenarth

1. Aberaeron	27. Llangrannog
2. Aberporth	28. Llangwyryfon
3. Aberystwyth	29. Llangybi
4. Beulah	30. Llangynfelyn
5. Blaenrheidol	31. Llanilar
6. Borth	32. Llanllwchaiarn
7. Cardigan	33. Llanrhystyd
8. Ceulanamaesmawr	34. Llansantffraid
9. Ciliau Aeron	35. Llanwenog
10. Dyffryn Arth	36. Llanwnnen
11. Faenor	37. Lledrod
12. Ferwig, Y	38. Melindwr
13. Geneu'r Glyn	39. Nantcwnlle
14. Henfynyw	40. New Quay
15. Lampeter	41. Penbryn
16. Llanarth	42. Pontarfynach
17. Llanbadarn Fawr	43. Tirymynach
18. Llanddewi Brefi	44. Trawsgoed
19. Llandyfriog	45. Trefeurig
20. Llandysiliogogo	46. Tregaron
21. Llandysul	47. Troedyraur
22. Llanfair Clydogau	48. Ysbyty Ystwyth
23. Llanfarian	49. Ysgubor-y-coed
24. Llanfihangel Ystrad	50. Ystrad Fflur
25. Llangeitho	51. Ystrad Meurig
26. Llangoedmor	

The communities of the county of Ceredigion

CENTRAL WELSH BOARD, The

The Central Welsh Board was constituted in 1896 as a body to inspect schools established under the **Welsh Intermediate Education Act, 1889**. Its membership was drawn from representatives of the **University of Wales** and of the **county** and **county borough** councils. It established a set of examinations that tested pupils at four levels, placing the greatest emphasis on academic subjects. Throughout its existence, the Board was accused of hindering the development of technical and vocational **education** and of failing to promote the **Welsh language** in secondary schools. Following a long battle, the Board was replaced after the **Second World War** by the **Welsh Joint Education Committee**.

CENTRE FOR ALTERNATIVE TECHNOLOGY (CAT), Glantwymyn, Powys

The centre, built on the site of a former **slate** quarry north of **Machynlleth**, promotes practical systems in support of more sustainable ways of living and attracts some 65,000 visitors a year. It was established in 1975 as a charity, on the crest of a surge of interest in environmentalism. Its internationally renowned exhibits demonstrate various **energy** themes, including power from renewable sources, especially wind and water, low-energy dwellings and transport systems, and small-scale organic **food** production. Its training and education programmes contribute to a wider international network disseminating information and facilitating the uptake of intermediate technology. In 2004, it

opened Wales's first green college, the £5.2 million Wales Institute for Sustainable Education (WISE).

CEREDIGION, County (Sir Ceredigion)
(181,241 ha; 74,941 inhabitants)

In 1996, Ceredigion, which from 1974 to 1996 had been a district of the **county** of **Dyfed**, regained county status as a unitary authority. It had the same boundaries as the pre-1974 county of **Cardiganshire**, but, on reconstitution, the names Cardiganshire and Sir Aberteifi were replaced in both languages by the name Ceredigion. The county's **population**, which in 1951 had declined to 53,278, had by 2001 exceeded the level at which it had peaked in 1871 (73,441). Its increase between 1991 and 2001 – 13.7%, by far the largest in Wales – is largely explained by the fact that the students at **Aberystwyth** and **Lampeter** were not counted in 1991 and were counted in 2001. (It is remarkable that so thinly populated a county sustains two university colleges.) Ceredigion's natives, known as Cardis, are purportedly tightfisted, but in fact they give generously to philanthropic causes. Ceredigion is also the name of a constituency. In 2001, 68.10% of the inhabitants of Ceredigion had some knowledge of **Welsh**, with 44.11% wholly fluent in the language. (*See also* **Llanbadarn Fawr** and **Tregaron**.)

CEREDIGION Kingdom

Bounded by the **Dyfi** and **Teifi Rivers** and by the Cambrian Mountains (**Elenydd**), Ceredigion, with its distinct boundaries, was, according to **J. E. Lloyd**, 'a kingdom ready made'. Tradition links the name with Ceredig, son of **Cunedda**, although the story may be an example of **Gwynedd**'s expansionist propaganda. The kingdom consisted of four *cantrefi*; only the name of one – **Penweddig** – has survived. In *c*.730, Ceredigion's king, Seisyll, seized **Ystrad Tywi**, thus creating the kingdom of **Seisyllwg**. Following the death of King Gwgon in 872, Seisyllwg came under the authority of his brother-in-law, **Rhodri Mawr**. Rhodri's grandson, **Hywel Dda**, created the kingdom of **Deheubarth**, consisting of Seisyllwg, **Dyfed** and **Brycheiniog**. In 1110, Ceredigion became a **march**er-lordship under the rule of the **Clare** family, but was restored to Welsh rule in the 1130s. From then until the creation of the embryonic **county** of Cardigan (*see* **Cardiganshire**) in the 1240s and the full establishment of the county in 1284, Ceredigion was generally under the rule of the house of Deheubarth, although it became increasingly caught up in the political ambitions of the rulers of Gwynedd (*see also* **Ceredigion, County**).

CERI Commote

The southernmost of the **commotes** of the *cantref* of **Cedewain**, Ceri was more closely linked with places to the south such as **Maelienydd** than with the commotes which were, by the early Middle Ages, considered to be integral parts of **Powys**. While most of Powys was in the **diocese** of **St Asaph**, Ceri was in the diocese of **St David's** (*see* **Kerry**). Its centre was the motte near St Michael's church, Kerry. **Llywelyn ap Iorwerth**'s successful resistance to Henry III during the Kerry campaign of 1228 ensured that, for the rest of his reign, Llywelyn was in an almost impregnable position. In 1279, Ceri, together with the rest of Cedewain, was granted to the **Mortimer family**, from whom it passed to the **York family** and thence to the English crown. Despite its links with the areas which, in 1536, became **Radnorshire**, the **Act of 'Union'** allocated Ceri to **Montgomeryshire**. The post-'Union' **hundred** of Kerry was coterminous with the medieval commote.

CERRIGYDRUDION, Conwy
(6450 ha; 692 inhabitants)
Extending over a vast stretch of **Mynydd Hiraethog**, the **community** includes the highest point of the range – Carnedd y Filiast (669 m). Alwen **reservoir** (1916) was established to supply water to Birkenhead. Before the creation of Llyn Brenig in 1976, the upper Brenig valley was minutely examined. Numerous cairns and ceremonial sites, dating from 1700–1200 BC – a period of mild **climate** – were discovered. An interpretation centre near the dam provides information relating to the prehistoric remains and to evidence concerning 16th-century summer occupation (*see Hafod* and *Hendre*). St Mary Magdalene stands within a circular churchyard. Llaethwryd farmhouse has late medieval origins. Glan-y-gors, overlooking a series of trout pools, was the birthplace of the radical **John Jones** (Jac Glan-y-Gors; 1766–1821). **George Borrow** stayed at the White Lion, where he met a **Welsh**-speaking Italian. Cerrigydrudion was famed for its shepherd poets.

CEULANAMAESMAWR (Ceulan-a-Maesmor),
Ceredigion (6228 ha; 983 inhabitants)
Extending from the **Aberystwyth**–**Machynlleth** road (the A487) eastwards towards **Pumlumon**, the **community** contains the villages of Tal-y-bont and Bont-goch/Elerch. It extends over much of the basin of the Leri and the whole of that of its tributary, the Ceulan. The area was for centuries a major source of **lead** and silver ore. Tal-y-bont was a village of lead miners and weavers; until the 1950s, it had two **woollen** mills. St Peter's church, Elerch (1868), a building inspired by the **Oxford Movement**, once resounded to Gregorian plainsong. The Lolfa publishing and **printing** venture was established at Tal-y-bont in 1967.

CHAMBERLAIN, Brenda (1912–71)
Writer and painter
Born in **Bangor** in 1936 she married **John Petts** and they lived above Rachub (**Llanllechid**). During the **Second World War**, they produced the *Caseg Broadsheets*, which included poems by **Dylan Thomas** and **Alun Lewis**. From 1947 to 1961, she lived alone on Bardsey (**Aberdaron**; *see* **Islands**), an experience vividly described in *Tide-race* (1962), her finest prose work, which also includes poetry and drawings. A strong sense of place informs all her work, even that of her final years, when her **painting** became more abstract.

CHAMBERLAIN, Joseph (1836–1914) Politician
Chamberlain's radical views, put forward in 1885 in his 'Unauthorized Programme', had a strong appeal for Welsh Liberals, **David Lloyd George** among them. However, few members of the **Liberal Party** in Wales followed him in his opposition to **Gladstone** on the issue of Irish Home Rule. Chamberlain's **Liberal Unionist Party** did, however,

capture the **Carmarthen Borough** seat in 1895. His success in persuading the Unionists to advocate Imperial Preference at the expense of free trade was a major factor in their failure to win a single Welsh constituency in the general election of 1906. Chamberlain's policy of limited self-**government** for all the constituent nations of the United Kingdom ('**Home Rule** all Round') strongly appealed to David Lloyd George.

CHAMBERS, J[ohn] G[raham] (1843–83)
Sports organizer
Llanelli-born Chambers, educated at Eton and **Cambridge**, was tireless. Founder of the Amateur Athletic Club (later Association) in 1866, he drafted **boxing**'s Queensberry Rules (1867), staged the first Football Association Cup Final in 1872, and instituted championships for **billiards**, boxing, **cycling**, wrestling and **athletics**. His brother, Charles Campbell Chambers (1850–1906), a prominent figure in **Swansea Cricket** and **Football** Club, was in 1881 first president of the Welsh **Rugby** Union.

CHAPMAN, George (1908–93)
Painter and printmaker
The excitement of discovering the mining valleys of south Wales led **London**-born Chapman to take this industrial landscape as his subject matter. Drawing *in situ*, he developed the work in the studio, focusing on place, rather than people. He won the Gold Medal for Fine Art in the 1957 National **Eisteddfod**.

CHAPPELL, Edgar Leyshon (1879–1949)
Social reformer and historian
Ystalyfera-born Chappell was a pioneer of the socialist movement (*see* **Socialism**) in the **Tawe** valley, coming to prominence as a **housing** reformer and advocate of pithead baths c.1911–20. He was secretary of the Welsh Housing and Development Association, and of the Welsh panel of the Commission on Industrial Unrest (1917), and was editor of the *Welsh Outlook* (1918). Involved in all the reform and planning movements of the day, Chappell was a pioneering urban and industrial historian, writing important works on **Cardiff** as well as on housing, **devolution** and local **government**.

CHARLES, David (1762–1834) Hymnwriter
The brother of **Thomas Charles**, he was born at Llanfihangel Abercywyn (**Llangynog**). A rope maker by trade, he was converted to Methodism at the age of 15, but did not begin to preach until he was 46. Ordained in 1811, he played a leading role in the composition of the **Calvinistic Methodist** Confession of Faith in 1823 and in establishing a firm foundation for the denomination. A number of his sermons were published in **English** and **Welsh**; some of his **hymns** are regarded as among the best in the Welsh language.

CHARLES, Geoff[rey] (1909–2002)
Photographer and journalist
Central to a post-**Second World War** revolution in photojournalism (*see* **Photography**) in Wales was **Liverpool**-born Geoff Charles. After studying journalism in **London** and

working for a variety of **newspapers**, Geoff Charles moved to **Newtown** to take responsibility for the *Montgomeryshire Express*. After the war, he worked for *Y Cymro*, where, under **John Roberts Williams**'s editorship, a standard of photojournalism was reached that surpassed anything previously seen in Wales. Some of his images have become iconic, particularly that taken in 1945 of the poet Carneddog (Richard Griffith; 1861–1947) and his wife Catrin before leaving their home at Carneddi (**Beddgelert**), to live in Hinckley, near Leicester. A large body of Geoff Charles's work remains, as he donated over 120,000 negatives to the **National Library**. The collection is so distinctive that television series have been based on the photographs, and his work is frequently reproduced to illustrate 20th-century life, especially the life of **Welsh-**speaking Wales.

CHARLES, [William] John (1931–2004) Footballer

John Charles was the finest **football**er ever born and bred in Wales, and at his peak he figured among the best in the world. In terms of natural talent, versatility and physical strength he was unique. Admiring journalists likened him to Hercules and Caesar, and the Italians dubbed him 'King John' (*Il Re John*). Since not a single referee ever had cause to caution him, let alone send him off the field, he was known as 'The Gentle Giant'.

A native of Cwmbwrla (**Swansea**), it was obvious from an early age that he was a born footballer. Football scouts soon realized that he possessed all the required skills, but the first to capture his signature was Major Frank Buckley, manager of Leeds United. Buckley was responsible for moving him from his position as centre half to centre forward where, over 308 games, he scored 153 goals for Leeds. By 1957, the eyes of Europe were upon him, and in August Juventus bought him for the then record transfer fee of £65,000. In Italy, in partnership with his fellow striker, the talented Argentinian Omar Sivori, Charles transformed the fortunes of Juventus. Thanks largely to the 93 goals he scored in 155 games, Juventus won the Italian championship three times and the Italian Cup twice. He became an idol among the people of Turin. For Wales, too, he performed brilliantly, either as centre half or centre forward, winning 38 caps and scoring 15 goals. Had he not been injured prior to the crucial game against Brazil in the quarter finals of the 1958 World Cup, Wales might well have progressed to the semi-final.

John Charles was a footballer of genius. At centre half he was the most authoritative of defenders, and as centre forward he scored remarkable goals with head and both feet. He possessed a rare and noble dignity on the football field, and when he died a wave of sadness swept over the whole of Wales.

CHARLES, Thomas (1755–1814) Methodist leader

Leader of the second generation of Welsh **Calvinistic Methodists**, Charles was born at Llanfihangel Abercywyn (**Llangynog**), and educated at **Llanddowror** and the academy at **Carmarthen**. While there, he heard **Daniel Rowland** preach, and was converted.

He graduated from Jesus College, **Oxford**, and, following ordination, served as a curate in Somerset. It was

through his friendship with Simon Lloyd, one of several evangelical Christians he met in Oxford, that he first went to **Bala**. He married there (1783) and made the town his home; although appointed curate at nearby Llanymawddwy (**Mawddwy**), his Methodist sympathies made his services unacceptable there.

He formally joined the Methodists in 1784 and set about consolidating the movement. As **Griffith Jones** had died in 1761, he saw there was again a need for **circulating schools**. He began training teachers, and it was through his efforts that the **Sunday school** became an important element of Welsh Calvinistic Methodism. The magazine published for Sunday school teachers was named *Charles o'r Bala*.

The most important of his literary works were the journal *Trysorfa Ysprydol* (1799–1827), the scriptural **dictionary** *Geiriadur Ysgrythyrol* (4 vols, 1805, 1808, 1810, 1811), and *Hyfforddwr yn Egwyddorion y Grefydd Gristnogol* (1807), a considered statement of his theological stance. Their influence on Welsh culture was immense. Charles was involved in the expulsion of **Peter Williams** from the Calvinistic Methodist movement in 1791, and he presided over the first ordination of Calvinistic Methodist ministers in 1811. He ensured that the denomination's elders were elected by local congregations rather than appointed by the **Association**, an important step towards giving the Calvinistic Methodists a **Presbyterian** structure. He persuaded the **Society for the Promotion of Christian Knowledge** to publish **Welsh Bibles** in 1799, and – perhaps inspired by the heroic walk of **Mary Jones** – played a role in the establishment of the British and Foreign **Bible Society** in 1804. He was the grandfather of **Thomas Charles Edwards**.

CHARLTON, Evan (1904–84)
Painter and educationist

Active in arts and **education** policy, Charlton came to Wales in 1938 as principal of the **Cardiff** School of Art, becoming HM Inspector of Art for Wales in 1945. **London**-born, of Welsh parentage, his dreamlike painting is figurative and classical, often invoking the dockland environments of south Wales in his exploration of metaphysical themes.

CHARTISM

A broad-based reform movement unified by the People's Charter, which called for universal male suffrage, Chartism emerged in the late 1830s under the leadership of such radicals as Feargus O'Connor, Henry Hetherington, William Lovett and Ernest Jones. Following the failure of the first petition to parliament in 1839, protests occurred in **Llanidloes** and **Newport**. Some 5000 men from the industrial valleys marched on Newport's Westgate Hotel, but the **Newport Rising** ended in military defeat and the arrest of **John Frost** and other participants. In 1840, two Chartist newspapers were launched in **Merthyr**, *Udgorn Cymru* and *The Advocate*, to supplement Henry Vincent's *Western Vindicator* (*see* **Morgan Williams**). Hugh Williams, founder of the first Chartist Working Men's Association in **Carmarthen**, and south Wales representative to the first Chartist convention, was closely associated with the

Chartists attacking the Westgate Hotel, Newport, on 4 November 1839; lithograph by James Flewitt Mullock (1818–92)

Rebecca Riots of 1842–3. A second national petition to parliament was rejected in May 1842, after which Chartists organized an abortive general strike. A third and final petition was rejected in April 1848. The last Chartist convention was held in February 1858, by which time much had changed in the Welsh **economy** and society, and many 'moral force' Chartists turned their attention to other pressure groups and to the growing possibilities of **Liberal**ism.

CHEESE

Wales's long tradition of farmhouse cheese making was almost destroyed by the **Second World War**. For three decades, the country's most famous cheese, **Caerphilly**, was made only in **England**, but cheese making has been revived in recent times and is once again a thriving and viable cottage industry. Historically, cheese has long been a staple **food** in Wales – **Welsh rabbit** was already a national dish by **Tudor** times, when it was known as *caws pobi*, or toasted cheese. Caerphilly was not named until 1831, although similar cheeses had been made long before then. When milk rationing was introduced during the Second World War, farmhouse production came to a halt and did not resume until the 1970s. The introduction of milk quotas in 1984 encouraged the revival, and there are now some 25 cheese makers in Wales producing cheeses, from traditional farmhouse Caerphilly, through French-style soft cheeses, to speciality cheeses flavoured with a variety of ingredients. The latter are often frowned on by purists, but the practice does have precedents. Cream cheese flavoured with marigold petals was popular in the 16th century, and in the 18th century a herb cheese was made with sage and spinach juice.

CHEETHAM, Arthur (1864–1936) Film-maker

The first **film**-maker to be based in Wales, Cheetham shot 'actuality' moving pictures in north and mid Wales between 1898 and 1903. Born in Derby, he moved to Wales in the 1880s and operated as a printer, film exhibitor, hygienist – and phrenologist – on the sands at **Rhyl**, where he lived. His 30-plus films include surviving footage of Buffalo Bill Cody in Rhyl in 1903, and the oldest extant British **football** 'short', *Blackburn Rovers v West Bromwich Albion* (1898).

CHEMICALS

Chemical manufacture in Wales covers a wide range of activities, of varying scale and sophistication, providing output for personal, household and industrial use. During the early period of industrialization, the most significant output involved various by-products such as sulphuric acid from zinc works (*see* **Copper, Zinc and Nickel**) and **coal** tar from coke ovens. The sector remained small-scale, with employment amounting to some 2500 in the mid-1930s. Nevertheless, one of the world's largest chemical companies, ICI, owed its origins in part to the chemical industry of west **Glamorgan** (*see* **Mond, Alfred**). During the **Second World War**, the industry experienced a massive, although temporary, expansion related in particular to the operations of several **Royal Ordnance Factories**: when munitions production was at its peak, over 100,000 workers were employed, among them large numbers of **women** filling ammunition.

The second half of the 20th century brought considerable growth in capital investment, although not in employment, reflecting a decline in the output of by-products from coke ovens and other sources, and an emphasis on petro-chemicals. Output grew to encompass the full range of products: pharmaceuticals, synthetic resins, plastics and cosmetics. During the 1960s, a major complex developed at Llandarcy (**Coedffranc**) and **Baglan** Bay (linked with **oil** refining) at the mouth of the **River Nedd**, while amongst the foreign-owned companies which have operated in the sector can be found the names of Nobel at **Pembrey**, Monsanto at **Newport** and **Cefn**, and Dow Corning at **Barry**. After reaching 22,500 in the mid-1960s, chemical industry employment had almost halved by the mid-1990s.

CHEMISTRY

Dr **John Dee** could be considered one of Wales's earliest chemists, but, because his alchemical researches were doomed to failure, it might be more appropriate to look to metallurgy for early evidence of chemical knowledge. The naturalist John Ray, in his *Itinerary of Wales* (1658), noted that the smelters of **Cardiganshire** used 'black and white coal' (charcoal and unburned wood) for the extraction of silver from **lead** ores, a good example of chemical intuition. Much later, **Sidney Gilchrist Thomas** lined the furnaces of **Blaenavon** with magnesian **limestone** and thus transformed the steel (*see* **Iron and Steel**) industry. In **copper**, **zinc and nickel** refining, innovative practices were developed in Wales.

In the field of medical chemistry, **Thomas Henry** of **Wrexham** made his fortune manufacturing and selling magnesia to cure stomach upsets, allowing his son, William Henry (1774–1836), to devote himself to pure chemistry, discovering the laws of solubility of gases in water and, more importantly, supporting John Dalton's development of his atomic theory. Robert Isaac Jones established the 'Cambrian Pill Depot' at Tremadog (**Porthmadog**) in 1838, and **Theophilus Redwood** of Boverton (**Llantwit Major**) became 19th-century **Britain**'s leading pharmacist and public analyst.

The amateur tradition in chemical **science** was not strong in Wales, although it was at the Royal Institution of South Wales in **Swansea** that **William Grove**'s batteries were developed and that **John Dillwyn-Llewelyn**, of **Penllergaer**, and his cousin Henry Fox Talbot experimented with the early chemical processes of **photography**.

It was only with the establishment of the colleges of the **University of Wales** and of secondary schools that chemistry became professionally established in Wales. Graduates went into teaching, as well as into industry, many becoming leading members of the profession and mentors to successive generations of scientists. Following the **Second World War**, departments grew, with increasing emphasis on fundamental research. It is estimated that at the beginning of the 21st century some 2000 people involved in chemistry were employed in Wales – in teaching, public service and industry.

Aberystwyth's most famous chemistry student was probably Frederick Soddy (1877–1956), winner of the Nobel prize in 1921, for his studies of the chemistry of radioactive substances and for the discovery of isotopes. Between the wars, Aberystwyth's most prominent chemist was C. R. Bury, who anticipated Bohr's work on the electronic structure of the atom. Thereafter, **Mansel Davies**'s pioneering work in infrared and dielectric loss spectroscopy

was outstanding, matched only by that of John Meurig Thomas, in the study of catalysts, and of **J. O. Williams** in solid state chemistry. Falling student numbers led to the department's closure in 1987.

Bangor was exceptional in having an unbroken line of professors who were elected FRS, either during their time there or immediately afterwards: J. J. Dobbie (spectroscopy), **K. J. P. Orton**, J. L. Simonsen (terpenes), **E. D. Hughes**, S. Peat (natural products) and C. J. M. Stirling (organosulphur compounds). H. B. Watson (1894–1975) was associated with Orton and Hughes in work on organic reaction mechanisms.

At Swansea, C. W. Shoppee's work on steroids led to an FRS in 1956, and **J. H. Purnell** made gas chromatography a vital quantitative tool for chemists. In 1974, J. H. Beynon, a Swansea graduate from **Ystalyfera**, director of research for ICI at Blackley, brought the Royal Society mass spectrometry research unit to Swansea. His redesigned spectrometer is now in use all over the world. In 2004, the authorities at Swansea took the controversial decision to phase out its chemistry department.

Until the 1950s, the most distinguished chemist at **Cardiff** was S. T. Bowden (1900–59). Thereafter, Cardiff's most notable work has been done by M. Wyn Roberts (of **Ammanford**) on solid state catalysis, and by J. D. R. Thomas (of Gwynfe, **Llangadog**) on ion selective electrodes, bio-sensors and blood electrolyte analysis. Glyn O. Phillips joined Cardiff from Bangor and Harwell, and studied the effects of radiation on natural products and tissues. He continued this work at Salford and later at the **North East Wales Institute of Higher Education**, tackling the problems of setting up tissue banks and treating osteoarthritis.

The number of Welsh people at the heart of the scientific establishment in the last quarter of the 20th century was remarkable. They include Sir John Meurig Thomas, FRS, a Swansea graduate from **Pontyberem**, professor at Aberystwyth and at **Cambridge**, and director of the Royal Institution Laboratories. He is one of Britain's leading scientists and Wales's most distinguished chemist. Other distinguished Welsh chemists include: Sir Ronald Mason of Aberfan (**Merthyr Tydfil**), chief scientific adviser to the Ministry of Defence (1977–83); Sir Dai Rees, of **Hawarden**, chief executive of the Medical Research Council; and Professor Jean Olwen Thomas, of Swansea, one of only 66 female Fellows (in 2007) of the Royal Society.

CHEPSTOW (Cas-gwent), Monmouthshire
(550 ha; 10,821 inhabitants)

Chepstow, for centuries an important **port** on the **Wye**, was established in the late 1060s by **William Fitz Osbern**, earl of Hereford, as part of his campaign to conquer the kingdom of **Gwent**. He initiated the construction of the **community**'s outstanding feature – the castle, splendidly sited above the Wye; the Great Tower (*c.*1075), modelled upon that at Falaise in Normandy, is the earliest datable secular stone building in **Britain**. The castle was the centre of the **march**er-lordship of **Strigoil**. It was twice besieged during the 17th-century **Civil War**. Granted to **Cromwell**, it became a gaol for political prisoners. Linked with the castle were the 13th-century town walls; much of them, along with the Town Gate, survive intact.

Chepstow Castle

St Mary's church was founded by Fitz Osbern as a **Benedictine** priory, the earliest in Wales. Various reconstructions have created an extraordinarily disjointed structure; its earliest work represents Wales's first example of Romanesque **architecture**.

The **road** bridge across the Wye (1816) is an elegant composition. The original **railway** bridge (1852) was one of **Brunel**'s masterpieces. The Wye Viaduct (1966) leads to the first **Severn Bridge**, which – despite **Harri Webb**'s verse – begins and ends in **England**.

CHESHIRE, Wales's associations with

During the **Roman** occupation, Chester (*Deva*), along with **Caerleon** and York, was the site of one of Britain's three legionary fortresses, and the base for Agricola's conquest of the **Ordovices**. The **battle of Chester** (AD 615) opened up the region to **English** settlement, and Chester, with its **port**, **mint** and abbey, became the centre of the extensive and prosperous **county** of Cheshire. In *c.*1071, the county was granted to **Hugh d'Avranches**, a grant that initiated a long conflict over control of northern Wales. By the early 13th century, a degree of equilibrium had been achieved; **Gwynedd** had extended its power almost to the walls of Chester, and the rulers of **Powys Fadog** had annexed the lordship of **Maelor Saesneg**. In 1237, the death, heirless, of John, earl of Chester, the son-in-law of **Llywelyn ap Iorwerth**, brought Cheshire under the direct control of the crown, thus greatly increasing royal power on the eastern borders of Gwynedd. Under Edward I, Chester was the main base for the conquest of the **Principality** of **Llywelyn ap Gruffudd**. Following the conquest, the new county of **Flintshire** was placed under the control of the justiciar of Chester, initiating a legal link between Wales and Cheshire that continued until 2007 (*see* **Law**). When Edward of **Caernarfon** (later Edward II) was invested with the Principality of Wales in 1301, he also received the title of

earl of Chester. In subsequent centuries, Chester was the chief focus for the trade of northern Wales, and attracted many Welsh immigrants. With the development of Merseyside, however, other places in Cheshire – Birkenhead and Wallasey in particular – became more important as centres of Welsh communities.

CHESS

Chess, believed to have originated in India and to have been carried west by the Arabs, was probably introduced to Wales in the 11th century, as a consequence of the **Norman** incursions. The game of *gwyddbwyll* in **The Mabinogion**, which was also a game of skill involving pieces being moved on a chequered board, is thought to bear no relation to chess as it is known, although the modern **Welsh** word for chess is *gwyddbwyll*.

In 1824, Captain **William Davies Evans** invented the Evans gambit – where White gives up a pawn to achieve rapid mobilization of its pieces – while commanding a steam packet plying between **Milford Haven** and Waterford. The second half of the 19th century saw chess clubs forming across Wales. Chess activity increased after the **First World War**, with the British championships taking place at **Swansea** (1951), **Aberystwyth** (1955, 1961) and **Rhyl** (1969). In 1970, the Welsh Chess Union became independent of the British Chess Federation, and from 1972 a Welsh team has competed at the Olympiads. At the beginning of the 21st century, Wales had over 40 chess clubs and some 800 players active at competition level. The Welsh championships celebrated their 50th year in 2004.

CHESTER, Battle of

Fought in *c.*616, this victory of Aethelfrith, first king of Northumbria, over Selyf ap Cynan, king of **Powys**, is chiefly remembered for the slaughter of the monks of **Bangor Is-y-coed**, who had offended Aethelfrith, a pagan, by praying for his defeat. According to Bede, 1200 monks perished.

CHINESE

The nucleus of the Chinese community in Wales was formed by entrepreneurs and sailors from the Sze Yap region of south China, who established boarding houses and laundries in the south Wales **ports** from *c.*1900. There were agitations against their alleged opium smoking, gambling, blacklegging and white slaving, although closer observers found a hardworking, respectable community. The agitations culminated in the riots of 1911 (*see* **Race Riots**) when all 30 laundries in **Cardiff** were damaged. The Chinese were also targets of riots in 1919. A small community continued to exist in interwar Wales, with Cardiff remaining the focus. It was replenished, from the 1950s, by migration from Hong Kong's New Territories, radiating out from its bases in **London**. By the late 1970s, Chinese restaurants and takeaways existed in virtually every Welsh town. Today, the community numbers around 10,000. Since China's opening up to the world in the 1980s, some Chinese local governments have encouraged their 'sons and daughters overseas' to set up ethnic organizations, to further economic opportunities back home. This has revitalized the original Sze Yap community and its contacts with China.

CHIRK (Waun, Y), Wrexham
(1907 ha; 4375 inhabitants)

Located on the **border** south of the **River Dee**, Chirk was the point at which the **Romans** in AD 48 first invaded Wales. (The degree of opposition they expected is suggested by the huge camp at Rhyn Park, just across the border.) In the 13th century, the area was part of the **commote** of **Nanheudwy**, the core of the territories of the lords of **Powys Fadog**. Following the **Edwardian conquest**, Edward I granted **Chirk and Chirkland** to Roger **Mortimer** (d.1326), who may have commissioned **James of St George** to build Chirk Castle. While the shell of the medieval castle survives, the building was progressively transformed by the **Myddelton family** who acquired the castle in 1595. Some of the best work is that of A. W. N. Pugin, decorator of the Houses of Parliament, who worked at Chirk from 1845 to 1848. From 1911 to 1948, the castle's tenant was Lord Howard de Walden (Thomas Evelyn Scott-Ellis; 1880–1946), patron of the arts and champion of **drama** in Wales. Acquired by the **National Trust** in 1981, the castle continued until very recently to be occupied in part by the Myddelton family. The park gates (1712–20) were the work of the Davies brothers of **Esclusham** (*see* **Ironwork** and **Davies family, Ironsmiths**) and are among their finest achievements. William Eames spent 24 years landscaping the park and provided it with Wales's best ha-ha.

Mortimer founded a **borough** at Chirk, but it did not flourish: **Leland** noted in *c.*1537 that '... at Chirk itself be few houses'. St Mary's church has 13th-century origins, but has been much altered; it contains many Myddelton memorials. Lord Howard de Walden commissioned Eric Gill to design the village's distinctive **war memorial**. Halton High Barracks, a terrace of back-to-back-cottages, recall Chirk's past as a **coal**mining village. In the late 20th century, Chirk acquired two large factories, Cadbury and Kronospan; the latter aroused much local opposition on environmental grounds.

Chirk Castle and gardens

The eastern part of the **community** is dominated by Brynkinallt and its park. Built in 1612, it was the home of John **Trevor**, the speaker of James II's sole parliament. Chirk's most memorable sight is the double crossing of the River Ceiriog. **Telford**'s aqueduct (1801) carries the Ellesmere **Canal** and Henry Robertson's viaduct (1848) carries the Shrewsbury to Chester **railway**. Viewed from the **A5**, they present what Edward Hubbard described as a 'spectacle of Roman grandeur'.

CHIRK AND CHIRKLAND (Swydd y Waun), Marcher-lordship

Consisting of the **Powys Fadog commote** of **Cynllaith** and part of those of **Nanheudwy** and **Mochnant**, the district became a **march**er-lordship in 1283. It was granted to Roger **Mortimer** (d.1326), whose grandson, John, was obliged to transfer it to the **Fitz Alan family**, earls of Arundel, in 1359. Its centre was the castle of **Chirk**. In 1536, it became part of the newly created **Denbighshire**.

CHOLERA

Devastating outbreaks of cholera, a diarrhoeal disease caused by the bacterium *Vibrio cholerae*, caused thousands of deaths in urban parts of Wales in the 19th century. The disease, which affects only humans, and is spread by water contaminated by infected faeces, has probably been endemic in Asia since antiquity; however, since 1817 seven major epidemics have occurred. Infection is characterized by massive loss of fluid from the intestinal tract. This results in extreme dehydration, and death may ensue within hours. Untreated, cholera has a mortality rate of 50 to 60%.

Cholera was seen for the first time in **Britain** in 1831 in Sunderland. By 1832 it had spread to Wales, and by that autumn had been responsible for at least 499 deaths, the majority in **Merthyr Tydfil** and **Swansea**. Cholera returned to Wales in 1849 in devastating fashion, the first case being recorded in a sailor at **Cardiff** on 13 May. Over the next few weeks, cases were seen in Merthyr, and by the end of the summer at least 4564 people had died in Wales, including 1682 in Merthyr alone. Merthyr, with its overcrowding, poor **housing** and abysmal sanitation arrangements, had, in 1849, one of Britain's highest cholera mortality rates. The outbreak led to mass prayer meetings, with ministers thanking God for 'this appallingly effective preacher'.

Cholera was again seen in Wales during epidemics in 1854, 1866 and 1893. In the latter half of the 19th century, a series of Public **Health** Acts were introduced which improved sanitation and water supplies, and provided substantial protection for the **population** from water-borne disease.

CHURCH IN WALES, The

The 1914 act that disestablished the **Anglican** Church in Wales was postponed in its operation until the end of the **First World War**. This allowed the four **dioceses** to plan ahead, so that by 1920, the eventual date of **disestablishment**, the necessary structures were in place. These included the representative body, which holds the property of the Church, the governing body – its legislature – and the electoral college, which elects bishops. The new name adopted for the disestablished Church, the Church in Wales, was thought to exclude any sense of superiority. Bishop **A. G. Edwards** of **St Asaph** was elected the first archbishop of Wales in 1920. His chief concern was that disestablishment should not divorce Welsh Anglicans from the mainstream of Anglicanism, a concern partly allayed by the regular Lambeth meetings of the provinces of the Anglican Communion. Of those provinces there would be 35 by 2007; that of Wales has the earliest origins.

Disendowment had deprived the Church in Wales of much of its inherited wealth, and consequently a £1-million fund was organized. Though it did not achieve its target, the fund – and the new provision of a quota on each **parish** – provided the Church with the resources to develop its work, in particular the establishment of two new dioceses, **Monmouth** (1921) and **Swansea** and **Brecon** (1923). In 1924, when the first handbook of the Church was published, the archbishop admitted that disestablishment had some merits, and in the 1930s, when the Church of **England** was in difficulties over **tithe** and the reform of **The Book of Common Prayer**, there were many in England who saw the Church in Wales as an inspiration and a model. By then, Anglicanism, measured by attendance at Easter Communion, was proportionately stronger in Wales than in England.

Significant developments in the history of the Church in Wales include the adoption of new liturgies in the 1960s, and the decision in 1997 to ordain **women** to the priesthood. Following disestablishment, the Church sought to shed its image as an Anglicizing force, but there was considerable disappointment in 1957 when a non-**Welsh**-speaker, Edwin Morris, was elected archbishop of Wales. During the archiepiscopates of **Glyn Simon** (1968–71) and **G. O. Williams** (1971–82), the head of the Church in Wales was increasingly recognized as the leader of the Christians of the country as a whole. Although the Church witnessed a decline in the number of clergy and communicants, it is undoubtedly the strongest of Wales's denominations, and its national role is emphasized by its ownership of nearly all the country's ancient ecclesiastical buildings. In 2003, Rowan Williams, archbishop of Wales from 2000 to 2003, became the 104th archbishop of Canterbury and head of the worldwide Anglican Communion.

CHURCHILL, Winston [Spencer] (1874–1965) Politician

While his role as a great war-leader is assured, Churchill had a chequered relationship with Wales. His admittedly cautious policy as home secretary (1910–11) during the **Tonypandy Riots** led to a military occupation of the **Rhondda** and neighbouring areas. As chancellor of the exchequer, his return to the gold standard in 1925 was a grave blow to the **coal** industry.

Almost deified by the British public in general during and after the **Second World War**, **cinema**goers in Wales continued to hiss him when he appeared on newsreels. However, on returning to power in 1951, he appointed the first minister for Welsh Affairs, a significant step on the road that eventually led to the establishment of the **National Assembly for Wales**.

A scene from the film *Y Chwarelwr* (1935)

CHURCHSTOKE (Yr Ystog), Montgomeryshire, Powys (5430 ha; 1571 inhabitants)

The **community** consists of two parts, the smaller located immediately south of **Montgomery** and the larger constituting **Montgomeryshire**'s south-eastern protuberance. It has a number of half-timbered houses, but the most prominent building, and the chief attraction, is Harry Tuffin's supermarket. There are churches at Churchstoke (1815, but with a massive 13th-century tower), Snead (1870) and Hyssington (1875). Bacheldre is a working 18th-century flour mill. Simon's Castle (12th century) and Hyssington Castle (13th century) were outlying fortifications of the lordship of Montgomery. Roundton Hill, a nature reserve, is crowned by an **Iron Age hill-fort**. The smaller Churchstoke offers a rare example of **Offa's Dyke** actually constituting the **border** between Wales and **England**. Mellington Hall (1876) is an outstandingly ugly neo-medieval pile.

CHWARELWR, Y (*The Quarryman*; 1935) Film

The first **Welsh-language** sound **film** was directed by **Ifan ab Owen Edwards**, shot in Blaenau **Ffestiniog**, and shown in community halls throughout Wales during 1935 and 1936. The film, with its sound emanating from a disk, has a slight storyline grafted on to a documentary style. Made in collaboration with the writer **John Ellis Williams** and his **drama** company, it is more assured than many of Edwards's 'home movie'-style travelogue and actuality films. Striking images of **slate** workers in spectacular surroundings make the film an intriguing document of its place and time.

CIBWR Commote

Lying between the **Rhymney** and **Taff** Rivers, and to the south of the Cefn Cibwr or **Caerphilly** Mountain, Cibwr was the southernmost **commote** of the *cantref* of **Senghenydd**. **Cardiff**, established within it in the late 11th century, came to overwhelm the commote. Cibwreg has been suggested as the name for Cardiff's **Welsh-language** dialect.

CIDER

The fermenting of apple juice is an ancient craft, with a strong association with the **Celtic** peoples. According to tradition, St **Teilo** travelled from Wales to **Brittany** in the 6th century to plant a cider orchard at Dol. The farmhouses of the **Wye** and **Usk** valleys were the heart of Welsh cider making. By 1896, orchards covered nearly 2500 ha, two-thirds of them in **Monmouthshire**, and a **preacher** damned **Breconshire** as a 'cider-besotten county'. But cider was not only a rural drink – miners often preferred it to **beer** during hard times, as it was cheaper and more potent. Some breweries, notably Webbs of Aberbeeg (**Llanhilleth**), expanded into cider production, taking over **Herefordshire** companies. Although large-scale production never developed in Wales, there are still farmhouse presses, and by 2005, when there were nearly 20 professional cider makers in Wales, there were signs of significant growth in both consumption and production.

CILCAIN, Flintshire (2554 ha; 1350 inhabitants)

Located in **Flintshire**'s westernmost bulge, the **community** extends to the summit of the **Clwydian Hills** at Moel

Famau (554 m). The Jubilee Tower (1810) on the summit was erected to commemorate George III's golden jubilee. Only the podium remains of what was the first Egyptian-style monument to be built in **Britain**. St Mary's is a double-naved church; the glorious late Gothic hammer beam roof of the south nave was obviously brought from elsewhere, although there is no evidence to support the tradition that it was once part of Basingwerk Abbey (*see* **Holywell**). Brithdir-mawr and Tŷ Isaf are 16th-century hall-houses; Coed Du (originally 17th century) was visited by Mendelssohn. Hendre is a **limestone** quarrying village. In the **Second World War**, Rhydymwyn's extensive **lead** mines became an underground secret munitions factory. The work done there on isotopes was central to the success of the United States's Manhattan Project. Its surface land, protected by a strong fence, has been officially declared a 'nature reserve'. The village was the home of journalist and editor **Jennie Eirian Davies**.

CILGERRAN, Pembrokeshire
(2624 ha; 1453 inhabitants)

Located on the south bank of the **Teifi** south-east of **Cardigan**, the **community** contains the villages of Cilgerran, Bridell, Llwyncelyn and Pen-y-bryn. At St Llawddog's, Cilgerran (rebuilt 1853–5) and at **St David's**, Bridell (1887), are 6th-century stones inscribed in **Latin** and **ogham**. Cilgerran Castle, splendidly sited above the Teifi, was the caput of Cilgerran **march**er-lordship, which consisted of the **commote** of **Emlyn** Is-Cuch. It may have been a **Norman** foundation and the castle from which Gerald de Windsor, grandfather of **Giraldus Cambrensis**, escaped from **Owain ap Cadwgan** by sliding down the privy. (Owain then seduced Gerald's wife – **Nest**, daughter of **Rhys ap Tewdwr**.) However, the bulk of what survives – the two powerful towers in particular – represents work commissioned in the 1220s by William **Marshal**, earl of **Pembroke**.

As a romantic ruin, the castle attracted artists, **Turner** and **Wilson** in particular, and photographers (*see* **Photography**) such as **John Thomas** (1838–1905). In Pen-y-bryn, a tablet on a cottage marks the birthplace of John Hughes (1872–1914), composer of the **hymn** tune **'Calon Lân'**. Within the Welsh Wildlife Centre – home to buffaloes and other exotic animals – is an ingenious building (1993–4).

CILIAU AERON, Ceredigion
(2661 ha; 936 inhabitants)

Located where the **Aeron** valley narrows, the **community** contains the villages of Ciliau Aeron and Cilcennin. Trichrug (343 m) is crowned by four fine **Bronze Age** burial mounds. There are remains of a medieval **deer** park near Ciliau Aeron village. Plas Cilcennin was an estate in the possession first of the Stedmans of Strata Florida (**Ystrad Fflur**), and then of the **Vaughans** of **Trawsgoed**. Excavation has revealed the remains of a medieval village at Llanerchaeron. Llanerchaeron House, a fine example of a villa designed by **John Nash**, is the property of the **National Trust**. Adjoining it is St Non's church (1798). In the mid-19th century, Cilcennin was one of several places in mid-**Cardiganshire** from which there was substantial **emigration** to **North America**.

CILIE family (Bois y Cilie) Poets

A family descended from the *bardd gwlad* Jeremiah Jones (1855–1902), of Cilie farm (**Llangrannog**). Their published works consist of much light but ingenious material, mostly in the strict metres, but just as often a more profound and classical note is struck. Members of the family include Fred Jones (1877–1948), one of the founders of **Plaid [Genedlaethol] Cymru**, Isfoel (Dafydd Jones; 1881–1968), Simon B. Jones (1894–1964), Alun Cilie (Alun Jeremiah Jones; 1897–1975), Gerallt Jones (1907–84), Jac Alun Jones (1908–82) and Tydfor Jones (1934–83). The

Cilgerran Castle

A cinema queue at the Capitol, Ystalyfera, in the 1950s

latest generation includes the actor Huw Ceredig, the singer and Plaid Cymru president Dafydd Iwan, the **National Assembly** member Alun Ffred Jones and the language campaigner Emyr Llywelyn.

CILMERY (Cilmeri), Breconshire, Powys
(1775 ha; 438 inhabitants)
Located west of **Builth**, the **community** contains the church of Llanganten where, according to tradition, **Llywelyn ap Gruffudd** heard mass before meeting his death on 11 December 1282. In 1902, a commemorative column was raised on the site of his death, Cefn-y-bedd; in 1956, it was replaced by the present monolith, a piece of **Gwynedd** granite 4.6 m high. The anniversary of Llywelyn's death is commemorated at the monument. Pitt's niece, Lady Hester Stanhope (1776–1839), stayed at Glanirfon before leaving for a more exotic lifestyle in Lebanon. On the eastern edge of the community, the **Wye** Valley Walk offers delightful views of the **river**.

CILYBEBYLL, Neath Port Talbot
(2161 ha; 4806 inhabitants)
Located across the **Tawe** from **Pontardawe**, Cilybebyll experienced industrialization following the opening of the **Swansea Canal** in 1796. Rhos, Alltwen and Gellinudd became substantial mining villages. The poet **David James Jones** took his bardic name – Gwenallt – from Alltwen, where he was brought up. The actress **Rachel Thomas** was born there in 1905. The **community** has been extensively forested.

CILYCWM (Cil-y-cwm), Carmarthenshire
(7442 ha; 472 inhabitants)
Hugging the west bank of the **Tywi** immediately north of **Llandovery**, the **community** extends into the **Elenydd** Mountains. Its most prominent feature is Mynydd Mallaen (448 m). St Michael's church (15th century) contains murals, including one of a skeleton holding a spear.

There is an enormous yew tree in the graveyard. The **hymn-writer** Morgan Rhys (1716–79) was a native of Cilycwm. Pont Dolauhirion, which crosses the Tywi at the community's southern extremity, was designed by **William Edwards** (1719–89) and is a copy of his famous bridge at **Pontypridd**.

CILYMAENLLWYD, Carmarthenshire
(2627 ha; 724 inhabitants)
Located on the **Carmarthenshire/Pembrokeshire** border, the **community** contains the villages of Efailwen and Login. The Meini Gwyr stone circle is surrounded by other **Bronze Age** monuments. The attack on the tollgate at Efailwen on 13 May 1839 marked the beginning of the **Rebecca Riots**. There were further attacks on 6 June and 17 July. The July attack was the first occasion the rioters dressed in **women's** clothing and for their leader – believed to be Thomas Rees (Twm Carnabwth) of **Mynachlog-Ddu** – to be addressed as Rebecca. The **Taf** valley around Login is particularly attractive.

CINEMAS
The first public exhibitions of **films** in Wales – apart from those by Birt Acres in **Cathays Park** in 1896 – took place in **music** halls, general halls and fairgrounds. Between 1898 and *c.*1908, for instance, the pioneer **Arthur Cheetham** screened his own films in halls in **Aberystwyth**, Colwyn Bay and **Rhyl**. The Electric Cinema, in Queen Street, **Cardiff**, dating from 1909, was probably the first purpose-built cinema in the city. Many more specially designed buildings opened between 1910 and 1914. By 1910, there were 162 halls showing films in Wales, many of them purpose-built, with 8 venues each in **Swansea** and Cardiff. By 1920, the number of venues had soared to 252. Entry prices varied: in 1919, the Windsor Kinema at **Penarth** charged a mere penny ha'penny, the same as the miners' cinema at **Llanbradach**, but Cardiff's Castle Cinema and the Canton Coliseum charged 2 shillings and 4 pence. By the 1920s,

cinemas presented hugely popular mass entertainment. The first part-sound feature to be shown in Wales, *The Jazz Singer*, starring Al Jolson, appeared at the Queens Cinema, Cardiff in 1928, but in the early days of sound the high cost of equipment combined with the effects of the **Depression** to force the closure of many cinemas. Nevertheless, by 1934 there were 321 cinemas in Wales, a figure eclipsed only by the immediate post-**Second World War** period, an unprecedented boom time for entertainment. During the 1950s and 1960s, many film studios and cinemas closed, owing to the popularity of television. However, a further decline in the late 1980s and early 1990s, attributable mainly to the advent of the video recorder, was reversed by the building of multiplex cinemas and the promotion of audience comfort on a scale not seen since the era of lavish picture palaces in the 1920s and 1930s. By 2003, there were an estimated 173 screens at 57 cinema sites, with 35-mm equipment and showing films from at least once a week to several times a day – almost double the number of screens to be found in Wales as recently as 1994.

CIRCULATING SCHOOLS

A scheme devised and overseen by **Griffith Jones**, **Llanddowror**, from the early 1730s until his death in 1761, to teach the people of Wales to read. It grew from his interest in **education**, from his active support of the **Society for the Promotion of Christian Knowledge** and from his conviction that the best way to enable the populace to achieve salvation was through equipping them to read the **Bible** in their mother tongue, which for the great majority was **Welsh**.

He was guided by two basic principles: that basic literacy could be acquired rapidly and that it was easier for teachers to go to pupils than it was for pupils to go to teachers. Jones would train his prospective tutors at Llanddowror before sending them out to various **parishes** to conduct classes for adults and children. A school would remain in a parish for up to three months before moving on to another location; for the convenience of the pupils, classes were usually held during the autumn and winter, when there was less to do on the farms. The scheme was hugely successful. By 1761, the year of Jones's death, 3325 schools had been held at 1600 places located in all the **counties** of Wales apart from **Flintshire**; about 250,000 people – over half the country's inhabitants – had been taught to read.

The chief patrons, among many, were Sir John Philipps (?1666–1737; *see* **Philipps family**) and **Bridget Bevan**. Following Jones's death, Bevan continued the work with considerable success, and left £10,000 in her will to ensure its survival. The bequest was challenged by her family, and the scheme went into abeyance until 1809. Nevertheless, an enormous amount had been achieved, and the significance of the contribution made by these schools to the life of modern Wales cannot be overstated. In addition to revitalizing **religion**, especially in its **Calvinistic Methodist** guise, the movement was an educational and cultural force among the general populace, a huge stimulus to Welsh **literature**, and profoundly influential in the development of the Welsh press (*see* **Newspapers** and **Printing and Publishing**) and of political **radicalism**. Catherine the Great of Russia commissioned a report on the schools in 1764, and they were suggested as a model by UNESCO in 1955.

CISTERCIANS Monastic order

Named after the mother house, Cîteaux in Burgundy, Wales's 13 Cistercian abbeys played a leading part in medieval Wales. Those in the Welsh heartland – founded directly or indirectly from **Whitland** Abbey (**Llanboidy**) – were staunch allies of the Welsh princes. Welsh nobles, such as **Owain Cyfeiliog** at Strata Marcella (**Welshpool**), found burial within their walls, and Welsh poets such as **Guto'r Glyn** and **Gutun Owain** much appreciated the hospitality of their abbots. The monks of Strata Florida (**Ystrad Fflur**) probably compiled the **Hendregadredd Manuscript** and played a leading role in the compilation of the *Brut y Tywysogyon*. During the **Glyndŵr Revolt**, the abbot of **Llantarnam** was killed whilst encouraging the Welsh forces during the battle of Pwll Melyn (**Usk**). Anglo-**Norman** abbeys of the south coast and the **border**, such as

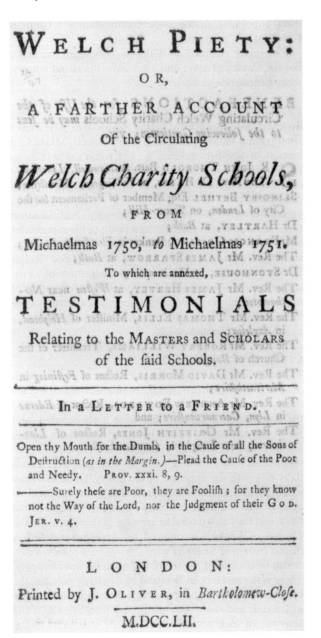

The 1752 edition of Griffith Jones's annual report, *Welsh Piety*

Basingwerk (Holywell), Neath (Dyffryn Clydach), Margam and Tintern, were always closer to the English crown.

There were two small Cistercian nunneries – at Llanllugan (Dwyriw) and Llanllyr, (Llanfihangel Ystrad). At the dissolution of the monasteries in the 1530s, there were only 75 Cistercian monks in Wales. The great church at Tintern, the west doorway of Strata Florida, the chapter houses of Margam and Valle Crucis (Llantysilio), and the dormitory undercroft at Neath, all demonstrate the architectural richness of their former monasteries.

The high quality wool (see Woollen Industry) traded by Tintern, its quay at Woolaston (Gloucestershire), the protective stockade owned by Abbey Cwmhir (at Mynachdy, Llangunllo), a huge granary built by Neath (at Monknash, St Donats), the coalmines of Margam, and the fishery of Cymer (Llanelltyd) on the Mawddach estuary, reflected the Cistercian goal of self-sufficiency. Their lust for land made them unpopular among some commentators – Giraldus Cambrensis in particular.

Cistercians returned to Wales in 1928 when the order bought Caldey (Tenby) and took over the island's previously Benedictine monastery.

CITADEL, The (1938) Film

Together with John Ford's *How Green Was My Valley* (1940), King Vidor's polished, if compromised, MGM film version of Scottish novelist A. J. Cronin's *The Citadel* (1937) helped to establish a stereotype of Welsh mining communities among audiences in England and North America. Cronin (1896–1981) wrote his novel about a young doctor in the imaginary 'Blaenelly', an industrial town in the southern coalfield, as a result of his experiences as a medical inspector of mines during the 1920s. The film, starring Robert Donat, Rosalind Russell and Ralph Richardson, indicts the chicanery and ineptitude of a laissez faire medical profession, but Vidor's condemnation of malingering miners obscures the more radical thrust of the film, which falls short of Cronin's advocacy of an embryonic National Health Service.

CIVIL WARS, The (1642–8)

The wars between Charles I and Parliament arose from a complexity of constitutional, economic and religious issues. Questions of Divine Right, prerogative powers and the sovereignty of common law were hotly debated, and the king's relations with the House of Commons, before and after the 'personal' government (1629–40), led to a constitutional crisis. In Wales, however, Charles's policies initially met with the approval of the gentry. Open as Wales was to possible invasion from Ireland or Spain, they had no quarrel with the raising of Ship Money to strengthen the navy, and they also tended to approve of the reforms to the Church of England introduced by Archbishop Laud, a former bishop of St David's.

But by the end of the 1630s, the situation was changing. There was resistance in Scotland to Charles's policies, the king was believed to be recruiting a Roman Catholic army in Ireland, and there were disturbing rumours about the activities of such noted Welsh Catholic aristocrats as the Somerset family, headed by the earl of Worcester. The Long Parliament, which assembled in 1640, demolished the royal bureaucracy, abolished Laud's Court of High Commission and attacked the bishops and The Book of Common Prayer.

In the early days of the Long Parliament, the only Welsh member who unreservedly supported the king was Herbert Price of Brecon, and members became increasingly hostile following the Irish revolt of 1641, which they feared might be the prelude to an invasion. Nevertheless, when war broke out in August 1642, only five MPs adhered to the Parliamentary cause and only two areas of Wales were sympathetic to the Parliamentarians: southern Pembrokeshire, influenced by the Parliamentary commander, the earl of Essex (see Devereux family), who held land in the area, and by its trade links with Bristol, and Wrexham, where Thomas Myddelton led the Parliamentary forces. But although sympathetic to the king, few of the Welsh gentry were prepared to risk their all in his cause; a notable exception was the earl of Worcester, who is said to have spent £750,000 in support of the king and to whose castle at Raglan Charles retreated after the disaster at Naseby.

Nevertheless, Wales was an important recruiting ground for soldiers for the royal army. It was also strategically important, lying as it did along both the northern and the southern routes to Ireland. Campaigning in Wales was influenced by these strategic considerations. From 1642 onwards, the Parliamentarians endeavoured to gain control of the route that led from Ireland through Pembroke to the king's headquarters at Oxford. Fortunes varied: the Royalist Richard Vaughan (see Vaughan family (Golden Grove)), successful in 1643, was routed in 1644 by the Parliamentarian Rowland Laugharne; Laugharne in his turn was defeated by the Royalist Charles Gerard in 1645, but by 1646, with the fall of Raglan Castle, the Parliamentary forces obtained control of all the southern counties of Wales. The situation in the north was similar, with Thomas Myddelton, after initial reverses, gradually extending Parliament's influence. In March 1647, the First Civil War came to an end with the surrender of Harlech Castle to the Parliamentary forces.

In 1648, events in Pembrokeshire led to the outbreak of the Second Civil War. The preceding months had seen a reaction in favour of the king, caused partly by the heavy taxes levied by the Parliamentarians, partly by their ambiguous relationship with the army and partly by the feeling that moderates should come together to restrain the excesses of extremists who wished to overthrow the established order completely. In Wales, the death of the earl of Essex had weakened Parliamentary influence and John Poyer, castellan of Pembroke, and Rice Powell, castellan of Tenby, declared for the king and marched on Cardiff, where they were joined by the former Parliamentarian Rowland Laugharne. In the north, John Owen (1600–66) of Clenennau (Dolbenmaen) and others followed a similar course. Laugharne assembled an army of 8000 men, but on 8 May 1648 he was decisively defeated at St Fagans (Cardiff) in the most significant Civil War battle to be fought in Wales. Cromwell stormed through the south and resistance ended in July with the capture of Pembroke Castle. In the north, fighting came to an end in Anglesey a few months later.

Among the signatories of Charles I's death warrant were the representatives of two Welsh constituencies: John

Jones (?1597–1660) of Maes-y-garnedd (**Llanbedr**), the member for **Merioneth**, and Thomas Wogan, the member for **Cardigan Boroughs**.

CLARE family Marcher-lords

Richard of Bienfaite (d.*c.*1090) was granted the lordship of Clare in Suffolk by William I. The family's association with Wales came about in 1110 when **Ceredigion** was granted to Richard's son Gilbert (d.1117), following the disgrace of **Owain ap Cadwgan**. Gilbert sprinkled Ceredigion with castles, but following the killing of his son, Richard, by the Welsh of **Gwent** in 1136, Ceredigion returned to Welsh rule.

Gilbert's brother Walter (d.*c.*1138) also became a **march**er-lord with the grant to him in *c.*1115 of Gwent Is-coed (**Chepstow** or **Strigoil**), confiscated from the **Fitz Osbern family**. He was the founder of **Tintern** Abbey. His lands passed to his nephew, Gilbert (d.1148), who in 1138 also received the lordship of **Pembroke**. Gilbert's son Richard (Strongbow; d.1176) initiated the invasion of **Ireland**, where County Clare commemorates the family. The marriage of Richard's daughter, Isabella, to William **Marshal** brought Pembroke and Gwent Is-coed to the Marshal family.

Richard (d.1217), grandson of Richard (d.1136), married Amicia, great-granddaughter of Robert **Fitz Hammo**, a marriage which eventually brought to the Clares the richest prize in the March – the lordship of **Glamorgan**. Over the following three generations, their descendants, Gilbert (d.1230), Richard (d.1262) and Gilbert (d.1295), made Glamorgan into a powerful quasi-kingdom, completing the conquest of the uplands, extending their authority to the **Wye** and establishing a great arsenal at **Trellech**. Gilbert (d.1295) was especially powerful, building **Caerphilly** Castle and greeting his father-in-law Edward I as a fellow sovereign rather than as suzerain. Following the death of his only son, Gilbert, at the battle of Bannockburn (1314), the Clare lands were divided between **Despenser**, **Audley** and de Burgh, the husbands of Gilbert's sisters.

CLARK, G[eorge] T[homas] (1809–98)
Ironmaster and antiquarian

Even for the Victorian age, **London**-born Clark was exceptional as a man of many parts: surgeon, **railway** engineer, public **health** inspector, industrialist, historian and genealogist. At the time of his death, obituaries stressed his studies in **archaeology and antiquarianism**, with only passing reference to his industrial activity. Yet for 40 years, until 1892 when he was in his 83rd year, Clark effectively controlled the Dowlais works at **Merthyr Tydfil**, the greatest of the Welsh ironworks (*see* **Iron and Steel**). The neglect arises partly from his style of control, appointing exceptional managers to whom he left actual operations while insisting on weekly reports and being directly involved in all the main decisions: the post-1850 revival of Dowlais through a vast and risky capital investment; the introduction of the Bessemer process; the move into the sale-**coal** market; the links with Spanish (or rather Basque) iron ore; and the establishment of the steelworks at **East Moors** in **Cardiff**. His home, Talygarn (**Pont-y-clun**), is one of **Glamorgan**'s largest houses.

CLAS Ecclesiastical settlement

The term *clas* (plural *clasau*) is generally used to describe a major native church in early medieval Wales, staffed by a community of clergy, usually headed by a man bearing the title of abbot, and consisting of individual cells rather than of an integrated group of stone buildings – a marked contrast with the **Benedictine** monasteries introduced by the **Normans**. Following the Norman invasions, many of the *clasau* became dependencies of English religious houses; thus, the Benedictine monastery of Gloucester gained possession of **Llancarfan** and that of Tewkesbury of **Llantwit Major**. Others – **Beddgelert** and Bardsey among them – became **Augustinian** priories. The name survives in **Glasbury**.

CLASS

In common with other Western societies, Wales witnessed a transformation from a social and economic structure based on hierarchy, ties of kinship, mutual obligation and tradition to an industrial, class-based society. For centuries, a small number of **gentry** families dominated Welsh political life and the country's economic structure. They were increasingly assimilated into the **English** ruling class, adopting their modes and outlook to a great extent. Although their influence over Welsh life has not totally disappeared, economic, social, religious and political factors gradually diminished their influence.

The expansion of urban communities during the 18th century, combined with a greater mobility among the peasant **population**, provided the impetus for a rapid period of change. The growth of the **iron** industry in concentrated settlements created large working-class communities, distinctive in character, which became the focus for an increasingly determined political class-conscious effort for improved conditions. Continued economic expansion during the 19th century, most notably with the development of the **coal** industry, accelerated the process of social change as a steady flow of immigrants (*see* **Immigration**) was drawn from rural Wales and further afield. Although the social structure of rural Wales saw fewer changes, economic factors and the influence of **Nonconformity** generated tensions in those areas which challenged traditional notions of deference to the established order, manifested notably in protests such as the **Rebecca Riots** and in a changing political outlook. At the same time, Wales witnessed the expansion of a middle class of professional and business leaders, a number of them active in Nonconformist circles, who played a leading role in both economic and political life and who sought to destroy the power of the landed gentry.

Class was the principal determinant of living conditions, aspirations, **health** and family structure. The powerful political events of the first quarter of the 20th century demonstrated the strength of an appeal to class solidarity, especially in the industrial areas. Moreover, in rural areas, traditional relationships between tenant farmers and **agricultural labourers** were influenced by the changing perceptions of those farmers as they became freeholders following the break-up of the great estates. The expansion of **education** provision and the development of the **welfare state** paved the way for greater social mobility, especially after 1945. **Government** policies made a determined effort to ensure that employment opportunities were available in sectors other than the traditional heavy industries; there was an increase in the number of **women** workers, a matter of marked relevance to traditional notions of working-class society in Wales, and more people were employed in non-manual work. By the close of the 20th century, economic change coupled with different social attitudes had eroded the power of class as a basis for political action, but its influence in areas such as health remained pronounced. Social exclusion stemming from prolonged unemployment, poverty, isolation and alienation demonstrated the impact of the rejection of Keynsian economics and the welfare state during the 1980s and early 1990s.

Class alone does not offer a satisfactory basis for an understanding of the experience of Wales: social conscience, religious faith, ethnicity, gender issues, language, **nationalism**, imperialism and obsequiousness have also played their part. Divisions between skilled and unskilled workers, differences between those who subscribed to Nonconformist values and the associated culture of sobriety and respectability and those outside that tradition (*see* **Aberporth**), and rivalry between localities have regularly transcended class loyalty. Nevertheless, class has to be recognized as one of the most important factors in developing an understanding of Welsh society in both a historical and a contemporary context.

CLAY, J[ohn] C[harles] (1898–1973) Cricketer
A remorselessly accurate, probing off-spinner, Johnnie Clay, born in Bonvilston (*see* **St Nicholas and Bonvilston**), played for **Glamorgan** (1921–49) and was one of the club's key figures in the 1930s and 1940s. An on-field contribution of 1317 wickets, including 176 in 1937, six seasons as captain and a comeback at the age of 50 in the run-in to Glamorgan's 1948 championship, was matched off the field by his efforts as treasurer (1933–8). He played for **England** against **South Africa** in 1935.

CLEDDAU Rivers (Western Cleddau, 27 km; Eastern Cleddau, 26 km)
The source of the Western Cleddau (Cleddau Wen) lies at *c.*120 m above sea level on the western flanks of **Mynydd Preseli** in the **community** of **Puncheston**. From **Wolfscastle**, the **river** flows through a narrow gorge to Treffgarne before meandering towards **Haverfordwest**. At Picton Point (**Slebech**), which is 6 km south-east of Haverfordwest, the Western Cleddau joins the Eastern Cleddau (Cleddau Ddu), which has its source at 300 m in the community of **Mynachlog-ddu**. **Reservoirs** have been built on a tributary of the Eastern Cleddau – the Syfanwy – at Rosebush and Llys-y-fran. To the south of the confluence, the river is deep but relatively narrow. The estuary is an excellent example of a lowland river valley submerged by the sea to form a ria. Near the community of **Milford Haven**, the estuary – the **Milford Haven Waterway** – widens to form one of the finest natural harbours in the world. Since the 1970s, the Haven has been **Britain**'s chief **oil**-importing **port**, although traffic has declined since the early 1990s.

CLÊR
A term used in medieval Wales for low-grade bards who composed popular verse involving **satire** and ribaldry. Derided by the higher grades of the bardic order, they also earned the moral censure of clerics. Sometimes the term was used to refer to poets in general. Perhaps the name comes from the Irish *cléir*; it may also have associations with the French *clers*.

CLIMATE
Wales is one of the wettest countries in Europe, a fact reflected in the **Welsh language**'s numerous words for various types of rain. Yet, despite the well-known adage in **Swansea** – Wales's (and **Britain**'s) wettest city – that when **England** is visible across the Severn Sea it is about to rain and when it is not visible it is raining, Welsh weather is anything but consistent. It is marked by considerable local variety and is changeable at all times. A rich diversity of weather is ensured by the contrast between the favoured coastal climates of areas such as the **Vale of Glamorgan**, **Pembrokeshire** and the **Llŷn** peninsula, and the harsh, exposed climates of the uplands that stretch from the **Brecon Beacons** to **Snowdonia**.

After the end of the most recent Ice Age, about 11,500 years ago, the climate gradually warmed up for 3500 years, enabling forests to colonize the land. Between 6500 BC and 3000 BC there followed a stable period of warm, dry conditions, but then began a cooling period that lasted until the later 20th century. The cooling was particularly pronounced during the Later **Bronze Age** (*c.*1000–700 BC), which saw stronger winds, greatly increased rainfall and a drop in mean summer temperatures of at least 2°C. These conditions, which led to the accumulation of **peat** and may have checked the growth of trees (*see* **Forestry** and **Plants**) on coastal plateaux and at higher altitudes, forced Wales's early farmers (*see* **Agriculture**) away from the uplands towards settlements on lower ground – which, although rich with **river** silt, were often subject to devastating flash floods. Such was the influence of rainfall on their lives that the pre-Christian inhabitants of Wales made a god of water, offering placatory gifts at springs, **wells**, rivers and **lakes**, many of which remain sacred in modern times.

Conditions were sufficiently congenial 2000 years ago for the **Romans** to establish **vineyards** in Wales, a tradition maintained by the monasteries in the early Middle Ages, until the climate cooled further. In the late 14th century, severe gales led to several massive inundations of sand, obliterating settlements such as (old) **Rhossili** and the walled town of Kenfig (**Cornelly**) and depositing enormous sand dunes at Newborough Warren (**Rhosyr**) in **Anglesey**.

The milder but often stormy winters of the later 20th century are believed to be symptomatic of global warming. It is forecast that by 2080 temperatures in Wales will have risen 1.1–2.9°C; wetter winters and drier summers are likely, with more frequent storms accompanied by high rainfall and floods. The inundation of Towyn (**Kinmel Bay and Towyn**) in February 1990, when 26 sq km were flooded for nearly a week, was held to be a foretaste of the difficulties likely to confront coastal **communities** as sea levels rise. Only about 30% of the Welsh coastline has some form of tidal defence, yet the larger part of the **population** lives close to the coast and most major industries and power stations have coastal locations.

The contemporary climate

RAINFALL

Welsh rain has no uniform pattern, for precipitation over western Wales is 40% higher than it is over eastern Wales. That is because the Atlantic air streams most frequently experienced by the country meet the upland barrier that stretches unbroken from **Conwy** to **Glamorgan**, a barrier which forces the air flow to rise and shed precipitation. Thus, the summit of **Snowdon** receives around 5000 mm of rain a year compared with 630 mm on the northern tip of **Flintshire**. Of Wales's urban areas, the driest is **Rhyl** (640 mm) and the wettest is Blaenau **Ffestiniog** (3000 mm); indeed, a deluge is sometimes referred to as *glaw 'Stiniog* (Ffestiniog rain).

Little of Wales's rainfall is absorbed into the ground, for the country has few aquifers – stratas of water-retaining rock. Furthermore, the central upland plateaux absorb little rainfall, covered as they are by fairly impermeable blanket peat. A significant proportion of rainfall is lost through evaporation, which is lowest in areas of high rainfall. Of the 2400 mm of rain falling annually on the **Elenydd** Mountains, 400 mm undergoes evaporation; the equivalent figures at **Montgomery** are 700 mm and 500 mm. Thus, discounting other losses, such as water absorbed by vegetation, central Wales has an available annual water surplus of 2000 mm, ten times that available along much of the **border**land. It is this abundance of water in the uplands that makes those areas a prime target for **reservoir** builders.

Although rain is a feature of every period of the year, the country tends to have dry spells in the early summer and the early autumn – key factors in ensuring successful hay and corn harvests. While areas such as south Pembrokeshire, north-west Anglesey and much of Flintshire can have up to 200 rainless days a year, the number of such days in the uplands rarely exceeds 130. In the 20th century, drought – defined as 15 consecutive days with virtually no rain – occurred every four years in the lowlands and every six years in the highlands.

SNOW

Although snow, usually in small amounts, is quite common in upland areas, especially Snowdonia, it is comparatively rare elsewhere. The number of days of snowfall and the amount of snow cover varies enormously from year to year – from none at all in many places, to over 30 days during the winters of 1946–7 and 1962–3. Only occasionally does snow affect everyday life on lower ground. One of the worst snowstorms of the 20th century occurred on 7–8 January 1982, when many areas had more than a metre of level snow; **roads**, including the **M4**, were closed and many rural and even coastal communities were isolated for days. Spring snow, such as occurred in many upland areas in the Aprils of 1950 and 1981, can have a devastating effect on livestock, especially new-born lambs (*see* **Sheep**).

Snow on Moel Bronmiod, Llanaelhaearn, Llŷn

SUNSHINE

The sunniest part of Wales is the south-western coastal strip, with an annual average of over 1700 hours of sunshine, and a daily average of bright sunshine of about 4.5 hours. **Tenby** is Wales's sunniest town. The least sunny areas are the mountain regions, which have fewer than 1100 hours on average, and under 3.5 hours a day. May and June normally have the most sunshine, December the least.

TEMPERATURE

At low altitudes, the mean annual temperature – which decreases by approximately 0.5°C for each 100 m in height – varies from about 9.5 to 10.5°C, with February being the coldest month and July the warmest. In winter, when temperatures are influenced to a considerable extent by those of the surface of the surrounding sea – at its coldest in late February/early March, but still warmed by the Gulf Stream – average maximum temperatures reach about 8°C on both north and south coasts, and 7°C in the borderlands. The lowest temperatures occur away from the moderating influence of the sea, on the floors of inland valleys: the lowest ever recorded in Wales was –23.3°C at **Rhayader** on 21 January 1940. While the micro-climate of Pembrokeshire, like that of Anglesey, usually keeps it a little warmer than the rest of Wales, occasional spells of both day and night-time freezing have occurred, as in January 1987. Conversely, some of the highest winter temperatures in **Britain** (up to 20°C on occasion) have been recorded on the north coast, owing to a local *föhn* effect,

The brass face of a classic, Welsh-made clock

when a moist south to south-westerly airflow warms up downwind of Snowdonia after crossing the mountains. In summer, average maximum temperatures are highest in **Monmouthshire**, at about 21°C, with the lowest on the west coast at about 18°C. In hot spells, temperatures can reach 27–28°C inland, while 33° has been exceeded on the coast between **Newport** and **Port Talbot**. The highest temperature recorded in Wales was 35.2°C at **Hawarden** Bridge on 2 August 1990.

VISIBILITY

Most of Wales enjoys excellent visibility. The country's industrial areas are located near the coast where prevailing breezes normally disperse any smoke that might hamper visibility. Sea fog can plague the coasts, especially in spring and early summer, and hill fog, which can be extensive and frequent, is a potential hazard to walkers in the uplands.

WIND

Wales's prevailing winds come from a south-westerly direction, bringing moist air masses in from the Atlantic and making the coasts of the Irish and Severn Seas the country's windiest regions. In winter, arctic air masses, often accompanied by strong northerly winds, bring cold weather, hail and snow; rarer are polar continental air masses from the east which, accompanied by clear sky conditions, bring bitterly cold weather. Wind on west and north-facing slopes has been an important factor in limiting the growth of vegetation. The lifting and deflection of air masses by the hills and mountains cause wide local variations in wind speed and direction. Gales occur most frequently during the winter and can cause gusts in excess of 180 kph, especially on exposed headlands; the highest gust recorded at a low-level site was 199.5 kph at **Rhoose** on 28 October 1989 (there are no wind recording stations at high altitudes in Wales). In an average year, there are likely to be 15 to 20 days with a gale. Strong winds in the uplands enticed windfarm entrepreneurs from the 1990s onwards to scatter hundreds of highly controversial wind turbines across many of Wales's wilder landscapes (*see* **Windmills**).

CLOCAENOG, Denbighshire
(2414 ha; 232 inhabitants)
Located south-west of **Ruthin**, the **community** has been extensively forested (*see* **Forestry**). A tablet inscribed by Eric Gill records the felling of the forest planted in 1830 and the replanting initiated by the **Forestry Commission** in 1930. The publisher Thomas Salisbury (1567–1620), the **eisteddfod** pioneer Thomas Jones (1740–1810) and the anti-**Methodist** pamphleteer Edward Charles (1757–1828) were natives of Clocaenog. St Foddhyd church (16th century) contains a rood screen.

CLOCKS and CLOCK MAKING
Wales has a long tradition of clock making. None of the earliest-recorded clocks in Wales has survived, but **Dafydd ap Gwilym** (fl.1340–70) describes his sleep being disturbed by a noisy wall clock. This account, written only a few years after the earliest recorded clocks in Italy, is one of the first descriptions of a clock anywhere in **Britain**.

Before the **Industrial Revolution**, every district had its craftsmen working in traditional materials. By 1700, clock makers were recorded at eight locations in Wales – **Caernarfon**, **Denbigh**, **Llanrwst**, **Wrexham**, **Abergavenny**, **Chepstow**, Llandaff (**Cardiff**) and Pont Nedd Fechan (**Glynneath**). **Iorwerth Peate** noted that *c*.1750 Wales had 72 clock makers. He claimed that a further 200 were at work by 1800; they could thus be found in every town. Among the most talented of Welsh clock makers was Samuel Roberts (*c*.1720–1800) of **Llanfair Caereinion**.

The typical Welsh clock was '*cloc un dydd un nos*' ('the thirty-hours movement'), with an engraved multi-piece dial in brass, set up in a long wooden case of oak. There were until recently elderly **Welsh** speakers who used the word *pendil* (pendulum), rather than *cloc*, when referring to any timepiece. Although some clocks were constructed that went for eight days or even for a month on a single winding, these were rare, expensive items, bought by the **gentry** rather than the *gwerin*.

By 1850, most 'clock makers' were merely retailers of clocks made elsewhere (generally in Lancashire or Birmingham), to which they had added their name and town on the painted dial. The long period of distinctively local and 'Welsh' clock making had been eclipsed by the greater availability of factory-made products. A grandfather clock made at **Newtown** stands in the main office of the president of **Ireland**.

CLWYD One-time county

In 1974, the **counties** of **Flint** and **Denbigh** (shorn of the right bank of the **River Conwy**), together with **Edeirnion** (taken from **Merioneth**) were combined to create the county of Clwyd – something of a misnomer, for much of the new county lay within the basin of the **Dee**. Divided into six districts (**Alyn and Deeside**, **Colwyn**, **Delyn**, **Glyndŵr**, **Rhuddlan** and **Wrexham-Maelor**) and with its centre at **Mold**, the county was abolished in 1996. Its western portion was joined with **Aberconwy** to create the county of **Conwy**. Its south-east became the **county borough** of **Wrexham** and the counties of Flint and Denbigh were reconstituted, but with boundaries different from those of their predecessors.

CLWYD River (64 km)

The Clwyd rises on the slopes of **Clocaenog** Forest at 350 m. It flows south before turning north towards **Ruthin**. Carboniferous **Limestone** can be seen at Pwllglas, while Triassic Sandstone can be seen in the walls of Ruthin Castle. Between Ruthin and the sea, the **river** flows along a fairly wide fertile ancient rift valley, which developed between the faults located along the sides of the present valley. The Clywedog, which drains the eastern slopes of **Mynydd Hiraethog**, joins the Clwyd between Ruthin and **Denbigh**, which stands at the foot of the valley's western slopes. Between **St Asaph** and **Rhuddlan**, the Clwyd is joined by its chief tributary, the Elwy, formed by a series of streams that drain the uplands east of **Llanrwst**. The Elwy flows through a deep valley pitted by **caves**, which have yielded the earliest evidence of humankind in Wales (*see* **Palaeolithic and Mesolithic Ages**). The Elwy's tributary, the Aled, drains the northern part of Mynydd

Hiraethog; several **reservoirs** have been created on its upper reaches. Foryd Bridge (**Rhyl**), the lowest bridging point of the Clwyd, overlooks the estuary where the river flows into the sea.

CLWYDIAN HILLS, The Mountain range

The hills (Bryniau Clwyd) straddle the **Denbighshire/ Flintshire** border, and extend for around 28 km southwards from **Prestatyn** to **Llanfair Dyffryn Clwyd**. Generally, they overlie mudstones and Silurian shale, but between **Dyserth** and Prestatyn, their underlying rocks are Carboniferous **Limestone**. Around Halkyn Mountain, the rock contains veins of **lead** ore. The range's highest summit is Moel Famau (**Llangynhafal/Cilcain**; 554 m). The name probably comes from the **Latin** *mamma*; the word means a woman's breast, a fitting description of the summit's profile. It is crowned by the first Egyptian-style monument to be built in **Britain**. Erected in 1810 to celebrate the jubilee of George III's accession to the throne, it collapsed in 1862. Its podium offers a superb vista of the Vale of Clwyd.

The range's thin and generally sour **soil** means that its slopes have a moorland vegetation, although land reclamation schemes have produced extensive pastures grazed by **sheep**. The mixture of habitats sustains a variety of **birds**. The entire area is rich in archaeological remains, with **Bronze Age** cairns on Moel Famau and **Iron Age hill-forts** at Penycloddiau (**Ysgeifiog**), Moel Arthur (**Nannerch**), Moel y Gaer and Foel Fenlli (both in **Llanbedr Dyffryn Clwyd**). The range has been designated an Area of Outstanding Natural Beauty; the **Offa's Dyke Footpath** winds along its ridge.

CLYDACH, Swansea (847 ha; 7320 inhabitants)

There was an **iron** forge in lower Clydach valley by 1755, and the Ynyspenllwch **tinplate** works flourished there from the 1830s to the 1870s. The Nickel Mond Works, now Inco, established in 1902, is the last functioning non-ferrous works in the **Swansea** area. A statue of Ludwig Mond (*see* **Mond, Alfred**) stands outside the works. There was also a patent fuel works, turning the abundant small **coal** into useable blocks – the *pele Mond* (Mond balls) once much appreciated in rural **Carmarthenshire**. The **community** contains much of interest to the industrial archaeologist, and several handsome chapels.

CLYDACH MURDERS, The

The 1999 massacre at **Clydach**, near **Swansea**, of four people – comprising three generations of one family – led to the biggest murder investigation in Welsh history. Mandy Power, aged 34, her 80-year-old mother Doris Dawson and her daughters Katie and Emily, aged 10 and 8, were bludgeoned to death with an **iron** bar, after Power spurned the sexual advances of David George Morris (b.1962), a Craigcefnparc (**Mawr**) builder. It took South Wales **Police** 21 months to arrest the killer, in an investigation that cost £6 million and involved 50 detectives. Morris was sentenced to life imprisonment in 2002 after a trial that lasted 11 weeks. His conviction was subsequently quashed and a retrial was held in 2006, which culminated in confirmation of both the guilty verdict and the life sentence.

CLYDEY (Clydau), Pembrokeshire
(4248 ha; 681 inhabitants)
Located at **Pembrokeshire**'s easternmost point, the **community** contains the villages of Bwlchygroes, Glogue, Star, and Tegryn. Its eastern boundary is the delectable wooded Cych valley. At St Clydai's church (1880s, with a 13th-century tower) are 5th–6th-century memorial stones, one inscribed in **Latin** and the other in both Latin and **ogham**. Llwynyrhwrdd **Congregationalist** chapel (1805, 1874) is an impressive building. **Erasmus Saunders** (1670–1724) was a native of Clydey. The poet Tomi Evans (1905–82) worked at the quarry at Glogue until it closed in 1926.

CLYNDERWEN (Clunderwen),
Carmarthenshire (2340 ha; 656 inhabitants)
Located where **Carmarthenshire** thrusts into **Pembrokeshire**, the **community** contains the village of Clunderwen – a ribbon development on the A478 – and the hamlet of Llandre-Egremont. Rhydwilym **Baptist** chapel dates from 1761, but the congregation was founded 1668, thus making it Wales's oldest surviving Baptist congregation. The chapel stands on the bank of the Eastern **Cleddau** in which its members are baptized. The *cymanfa bwnc* (*see* **Pwnc**), the traditional chanting of the Scriptures, is held in the chapel and in other chapels in the vicinity every Whit Monday. In 2002, the greater part of the community as constituted in 1974 was transferred from Carmarthenshire to Pembrokeshire.

CLYNE AND MELINCOURT (Y Clun a Melin-cwrt), Neath Port Talbot
(935 ha; 815 inhabitants)
Located on the east bank of the **Nedd**, south of **Resolven**, the **community** contains the Carn Caca **Bronze Age** stone circle, two **Roman** camps and the impressive remains of a viaduct, which carried the **Neath Canal** across the **river**. At Melincourt are the remnants of an 18th-century **iron** furnace, an arboretum and a fine **waterfall**, painted by **Turner**.

CLYNNOG, Gwynedd (4551 ha; 860 inhabitants)
The **community** extends from the northern coast of **Gwynedd** to the western outliers of **Snowdonia** at Craig Goch (609 m) and to the northern summit of the **Eifl** range at Bwlch Mawr (509 m). It contains the villages of Clynnog Fawr, Pontllyfni and Aberdesach. **St Beuno**'s church, Clynnog Fawr, was originally a **Celtic** *clas*. It benefited from its location on the route to Bardsey (*see* **Islands**), and was enriched by the offerings made by pilgrims (*see* **Pilgrimage**) to St Beuno's **Well**. It was rebuilt in the early 16th century, probably by the same craftsmen as were then rebuilding **Bangor** Cathedral. They were responsible for one of Wales's finest Perpendicular churches, with hammer-beam roof, screen and misericords. It was the scene of turmoil in 1660, when its **Puritan** rector, Ellis Rowlands (1621–91), was dragged from the pulpit. From 1827 until 1839, the poet **Ebenezer Thomas** (Eben Fardd), kept a school in the church, where an exhibition recounts the history of the area. There are several prehistoric monuments at Graeanog.

CLYNNOG, Morys (1525–80/1)
Recusant and author
Probably a native of **Clynnog**, Morys Clynnog was educated at **Oxford** and later ordained a priest. He received the patronage of Cardinal Reginald Pole, who reconciled the Church of **England** with Rome following the accession of Mary I in 1553. Clynnog held a number of livings in Wales and England. In 1558, he was nominated bishop of **Bangor**, but Mary died before his consecration. Following the accession of Elizabeth I in 1559, he went into exile. He had moved to Rome by 1563. In 1578, he was appointed the first rector of the new recusant seminary (the *Collegium Anglorum*) that was founded in Rome in 1575; opposed by the English seminarians, he resigned in 1579. He was a friend of **Gruffydd Robert**, who printed Clynnog's brief catechism, *Athravaeth Gristnogavl*, in Milan in 1568. The sole surviving copy of the work was found in the library of Prince **Louis-Lucien Bonaparte**. He was apparently drowned in the English Channel in the winter of 1580–1.

CLYRO (Cleirwy), Radnorshire,
Powys (3322 ha; 688 inhabitants)
Adjoining the **Wye** north of **Hay**, the **community** contains two mottes and the 14th-century remains of a grange of **Abbey Cwmhir** at Clyro Court Farm. The diarist **Francis Kilvert** was curate of Clyro from 1865 to 1872. Conan Doyle wrote *The Hound of the Baskervilles* (1902) at Clyro Court, the home of the Baskerville family. The 14th-century black-and-white inn at Rhydspence stands right on the **border**; the **drovers**' herds from **Mynydd Epynt** were shod nearby for the journey to the markets of **England**.

CNAPAN Game
An anarchic form of **football** once popular throughout Wales but played seasonally under this name in north **Pembrokeshire** and south **Cardiganshire**, usually involving one **parish** against another. Teams consisted of any number of men and there were no rules. The aim was to deliver a small, greased, wooden ball (*cnapan*) to a goal, such as a church porch, in one's own territory. The ball was released at a point of equal distance between the two goals and the land in between constituted the pitch. It was generally discouraged in the early 19th century because of associated gambling and violence. Gŵyl y Cnapan, a folk festival originally held at Ffostrasol (**Troedyraur**), enjoyed considerable popularity in the 1980s and 1990s.

CND CYMRU
The British Campaign for Nuclear Disarmament (CND) was founded in 1958 (by the philosopher **Bertrand Russell** among others) to oppose nuclear weapons, nuclear testing and the development, stockpiling and threatened use of weapons of mass destruction.

In the 1970s, opposition to proposals to dump nuclear waste in Wales gave rise to anti-nuclear groups, such as Pandora and Madryn, which combined with CND and 40 other **community**-based organizations to form the Welsh Anti Nuclear Alliance (WANA). This anti-nuclear campaign, stimulated by the 1980 announcement that NATO intended to base nuclear Cruise missiles in Europe, led to a revival of CND in Wales. On 23 February 1982, Wales declared itself, through the authority of its (then) eight **county** councils, a Nuclear Free Zone, the first country in the world to do so.

In 1983, CND Cymru became a national organization. Its campaigns include the issues of nuclear weapons, civil defence, nuclear power, radioactive pollution of the Irish Sea, the militarization of Wales, the arms trade, opposition to multifarious wars and reform of the United Nations. By the early 21st century, the impact of the movement was a shadow of what it had been in the 1960s and 1970s.

CNICHT, MOELWYN MAWR and MOELWYN BACH Mountains

Located west of Blaenau **Ffestiniog**, the three **mountains**, which are composed of **slate** together with a covering of volcanic ash and lava, tower over Traeth Mawr and **Porthmadog**. Cnicht (690 m; **Llanfrothen**), which resembles a miniature Matterhorn, probably gets its name from the **English** word 'knight'. Moelwyn Mawr (770 m; Llanfrothen) and Moelwyn Bach (711 m; Ffestiniog) overlook the Tanygrisiau and Llyn Stwlan **reservoirs**. The mountains have been extensively quarried; the industrial **archaeology** of Rhosydd quarry is particularly interesting.

COAL and COALMINING

Of Wales's two principal coalfields, that of the south is the largest continuous coalfield in **Britain**. Extending some 113 km from **Pontypool** in the east to St Brides Bay in the west, it covers some 2590 sq km, occupying the greater part of the former **county** of **Glamorgan**, much of the former county of **Monmouthshire**, and portions of **Breconshire**, **Carmarthenshire** and **Pembrokeshire**. The coals occur in two detached, basin-shaped or synclinally folded areas, the main portion by far being an oval shape extending between Pontypool and **Carmarthen** Bay, with a maximum north–south breadth of 26 km. The other, outlying, part extends as a narrow belt, rarely more than 6 km in length from north to south, across south Pembrokeshire. The Coal Measures vary from under 1 m to over 3 m thick, and consist of three series: Upper Series, Pennant Grit and Lower Shale Series. In character, the coal falls into three broad categories: anthracite or 'stone coal', mainly found

in the western zone, and estimated in 1904 to account for some 24% of reserves; the world-renowned steam coals (mainly found in the central region, 45%), upon which was based the coalfield's rapid 19th-century growth; and bituminous, or house and gas, coals (concentrated in the eastern and southern outcrops in Glamorgan and Monmouthshire, 31%). Within this range there are coals for almost every purpose for which coal has been used: gas manufacture, low temperature carbonization, malting, domestic heating, fuelling furnaces and kilns, powering **railway** locomotives and **ships**, and the making of metallurgical and foundry coke; among the hundreds of by-products are tar and petrol, dyes and drugs, antiseptics and explosives.

The characteristics of the southern coalfield have influenced the process of mining. For example, in the main sequence of coal-bearing strata (the Lower Steam Coals) mining is especially difficult. An opening made in such ground at once tends to close or 'squeeze' in, with the result that as much labour and material are expended in the maintenance of the mine as are expended in the extraction and raising of the coal. The quantity of pitwood required for the support of roof and sides was, in the early years of development, up to three times as great as in other coalfields, and the quantity of debris to be handled underground, part of which was sent to the surface, may in some cases have equalled the quantity of coal raised. The Welsh tram, as a result, was markedly larger than that used elsewhere, and the pit pony (12–13 hands high) was almost unknown: the Welsh pit **horse** was a short-legged miniature dray horse of 14–15 hands.

The geological conditions of the southern coalfield made it more susceptible to explosion from coal dust than any other field in Britain (*see* **Colliery Disasters**). South Wales accounted for 13 of the 27 principal colliery explosions in Britain between 1890 and 1914. In addition, accidents from other causes, especially roof falls, were an almost daily occurrence. Although the south Wales mines were the most dangerous in Britain, little research was carried out at University College, **Cardiff** (*see* **Cardiff University**) – despite **William Galloway**'s pioneering work in explaining coal-dust explosions – nor anywhere else in Wales.

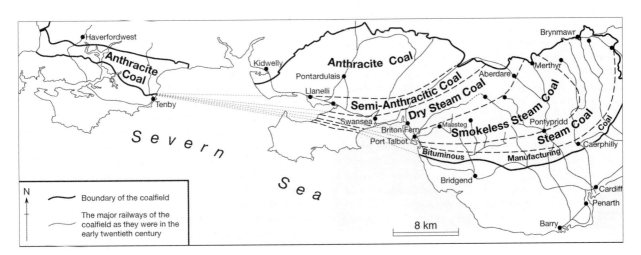

The coals of the south Wales coalfield

The northern coalfield, an extension of that of Lancashire and **Cheshire**, runs along a north–south axis through **Wrexham**, and has a visible area of 267 sq km. Mining has taken place as far south as **Chirk**, and as far north as the **Dee** estuary, at Point of Ayr (**Llanasa**). Its most important seam was the 'Main', whose coal was used for manufacturing purposes, and to fuel locomotives and ships. Anthracite does not occur in the northern coalfield, but 'cannel coal', comparatively rare in south Wales, has in its time been of great importance in the north (the name derives from the candle-like flame with which it burns).

In addition, a small area of Coal Measures extends into **Anglesey**. The seams are very thin and, as they lie beneath the Malltraeth (**Bodorgan**) marshes, workings were subject to severe flooding. In the mid-19th century, Anglesey had five collieries but, by the end of the century, coal extraction in the county had come to an end.

The southern coalfield

Coal has been mined in south Wales for centuries – in the 1530s Leland complained of the 'noxious mineral' burnt on the hearths of **Carmarthen**. Prior to the 18th century, extraction was a small-scale, mainly part-time activity generally centred on bell pits and levels where seams outcropped at the surface. Most of the output was consumed locally, although by the 17th century **Swansea** had a grow-

Sinking the pit at Cefn Coed, with miners and owners in the bucket, 1926

ing export trade, mainly with **Ireland** and south-western **England**. From the late 18th century, the emergence of metal-smelting industries resulted in more extensive enterprises. Development was centred upon the coalfield's north-eastern rim from **Merthyr Tydfil** to **Blaenavon**, in connection with the smelting of **iron** with coke, and in the south-west, around Swansea and **Llanelli**, in connection with the smelting of **copper** and **lead**.

In 1828, the coalfield's annual output has been estimated at 3 million tonnes. By 1840, it had risen to 4.5 million tonnes, of which about 2.25 million was consumed by ironworks, and about 1 million by the other industries and the domestic users of the region. The remaining 1.25 million represented sale coal – that is, the output exported, 95% of which was shipped to **ports** within the United Kingdom. In the first half of the 19th century, the sale-coal trade, a trade which would eventually dominate the Welsh **economy**, was associated in particular with the activities of **Thomas Powell** in Monmouthshire, **Lucy Thomas** in the **Taff** valley and **Walter Coffin** and George Insole in the **Rhondda**. Initially, the trade was almost exclusively in bituminous coal, with **Newport** in 1830 exporting 10 times as much as Cardiff and twice as much as Swansea.

The situation changed in the 1840s with the exploitation of the steam coal of the **Cynon Valley** (*see* **Aberdare**), the building of a large masonry dock at Cardiff and the construction of the Taff Vale Railway. Welsh steam coal came rapidly to be appreciated, particularly by the British Admiralty whose trials in 1845 showed that Welsh steam coal lit more easily, blew steam up more rapidly, and produced less clinker and smoke than did the hitherto preferred coal of Newcastle upon Tyne. From the mid-1840s onwards, the British navy would be primarily dependent for its fuel upon Welsh steam coal. Such was that navy's prestige that other navies followed its example. (In the sea battles of the Russo-Japanese War in 1905, both navies are reputed to have been fuelled by **Bargoed** nuts.) With Welsh steam coal receiving increasing international recognition, foreign coal exports increased markedly and had, by the late 1850s, exceeded those of other United Kingdom ports. Thus arose the outstanding feature of the south Wales coalfield in the decades of its vast expansion – its dependence upon foreign trade.

Cardiff's superior facilities and the fact that the largest deposits of steam coal lay within the basin of the Taff and its tributaries caused it, by the late 1850s, to outstrip its rivals as a coal port. The richest source of steam coal proved to be the Rhondda, where output rose from the equivalent of 2.13 million tonnes in 1874 to 5.8 million tonnes in 1884 and to 9.85 million tonnes in 1913. In the coalfield as a whole, total output was 8.64 million tonnes in 1854, 16.76 million in 1874, 25.9 million in 1884 and 57.7 million in 1913. By the 1890s, south Wales was producing 18% of Britain's coal and 38% of Britain's coal exports. Of the entire global trade in coal in that decade, a quarter emanated from the south Wales ports, and Cardiff had won recognition as the largest port in the world in terms of the tonnage of its exports. This was south Wales at its most imperial, its coal empire extending from Singapore to Valparaiso and its role in fulfilling the world's need for a source of heat and **energy** similar to that of the Middle East a century later. World shipping relied

Coal trucks at Queen Alexandra Dock, Cardiff, when the Port of Cardiff was the world's chief coal exporter

upon supplies of Welsh coal deposited in bunkers at places such as Port Said and Madeira, an enterprise in which **Cory Brothers** of Cardiff was especially prominent.

The **geology** of the coalfield meant that, for long, cutting by hand was the only practical method of extraction; as late as 1924, only 5.4% of the output was cut by machine. So labour-intensive was the industry that the coalfield's ability to attract immigrants (*see* **Immigration**) was second only to that of the United States. In the first decade of the 20th century, Wales was the only country in Europe where more people moved in than moved out. By 1911, 70% of the inhabitants of Wales lived in the southern coalfield and its associated ports, proof that the development of the coalfield is the fundamental fact of modern Welsh history.

Central to that development was the location of the industry in what is Britain's sole mountainous coalfield. Contour determined the shape of the mining communities. The region's previous history – that of a thinly populated pastoral society – meant that it contained no towns dignified by a long tradition of civic life, and thus the process of transforming mining townships into civic communities proved to be protracted. The narrow coal valleys had no industry other than mining; they therefore offered virtually no paid employment for **women** – a key consideration in any assessment of the character of coalfield society. The intense loyalties engendered when an entire community is involved in a single industry found expression in the unique solidarity displayed by the south Wales miners – a marked contrast with coalfields such as Nottingham, where coalminers were outnumbered by those employed in other industries. Where there is total reliance upon a single industry, any faltering in that industry brings calamity – the context of the massive dislocation suffered by Wales's southern coalfield communities following the collapse of the international trade in coal in the 1920s (*see* **Depression of the interwar years**).

As Wales's most heavily populated area was virtually a one-industry region, the entire country's employment profile developed a highly lopsided character. In 1920, when the number of miners in the southern coalfield peaked at 271,516, they represented 31% of Wales's employed males. If those involved in transporting coal by rail and ship, and those providing the services to coalfield communities, are added, the proportion exceeded 50% – a dependence upon a single industry without parallel in the history of any other industrialized country. Furthermore, the dynamism of the coalfield created dependence far beyond its borders – in the holiday resorts of west Wales, for example, or in spa towns such as **Llanwrtyd**, or in the **woollen**-mill villages of the **Teifi** valley. Indeed, it has been argued that, by the end of the 19th century, even in remote areas of rural Wales, the rate of marriage fluctuated in accordance with the price of coal.

The expansion of coal production required massive inputs of investment, in which Welsh businessmen such as **Thomas Powell**, David Davies (*see* **Davies family (Llandinam)**) and David Davis of Ferndale (*see* Rhondda) played a significant role. Landowners, notably the **Stuart family** (marquesses of Bute), made important contributions through their leasing policy, their pioneering of mineral exploitation and their provision of transport infrastructure, docks in particular. English capital was of central importance, particularly in the case of the **Powell Duffryn Steam Coal Company**, formed to take over the collieries of Thomas Powell.

The relationship between capital and labour was often turbulent. The formation of **coalowners' associations** and of **trade unions**, in particular the **South Wales Miners' Federation** (1898), reflected a basic antagonism. Attempts to establish agreed systems of determining wages – through sliding scales from the mid-1870s and conciliation boards in the early 20th century – failed to prevent major strikes such as those of 1898 and 1910. Antagonism towards the coalowners arose, in part, from what was considered to be their callous attitude towards their employees, a matter of widespread concern in the uniquely dangerous coalfield of south Wales. (Between 1880 and 1900, 2328 British miners were killed in disasters where there were more than 25 victims; although south Wales miners constituted only 18% of the miners of Britain, they suffered 48% of the 2328 deaths.) While an earlier generation of miners' leaders – a generation typified by **William Abraham (Mabon)** – believed in gradual improvement through patient negotiation with the coalowners, those rising to prominence on the eve of the **First World War** were, under the influence of **socialist** and **syndicalist** ideas, advocating the abolition of capitalist ownership and control of the industry.

The output of the south Wales coalfield peaked in 1913. The First World War, when the profits of the coalowners soared, and when the British Admiralty became fully aware of its dependence upon Welsh steam coal, deepened antagonism between workers and employers. Hopes that there would be major ownership changes after the war were dashed by **David Lloyd George**'s adroit manipulation of the **Sankey** commission of 1919. The industry was shaken by the coal strike of 1921, but its fortunes revived and Cardiff's coal exports reached their peak in 1923. In the mid-1920s, however, unemployment among south Wales miners increased from 1.8% in April 1924 to 28.5% in August 1925, thus ushering in the interwar **depression** and providing the context for the **General Strike** of 1926. With **oil** becoming the preferred source of energy, the

depression was particularly marked in the steam-coal areas, precisely those which had powered the helter-skelter late 19th-century expansion. The anthracite-producing areas, which had a secure market among Canadian stove owners, fared better; in 1927, when unemployment was 40% in steam-coal-producing Ferndale (Rhondda), it was 10% in anthracite-producing **Ammanford**. The problems of the industry were exacerbated by the cartel system adopted by the leading coalowners. Amalgamation had much reduced their numbers; by 1938, over half the coalfield's production was controlled by three companies: Powell Duffryn – Europe's largest coal company – Partridge, Jones & John Paton, and Amalgamated Anthracite Collieries. The coalowners sought to react to the militancy of the miners by creating **company unions**, financed and controlled by the employers. The struggle to eliminate such unions absorbed much of the energy of the South Wales Miners' Federation in the mid-1930s.

The need to maintain coal production was as essential during the **Second World War** as it had been during the previous war. In May 1941, mining was declared a reserved occupation and, from late 1943, some conscripts (the 'Bevin Boys') were forced to work in the mines. The post-war **Labour** government was determined to fulfil the long-cherished dream of ridding the industry of capitalism. On 1 January 1947, the **National Coal Board** took over Britain's coalmines in the name of the people. During the board's first 10 years, the coal market proved to be buoyant and in the anthracite region, in particular, new pits were sunk, among them Cynheidre (1956), and Abernant

Maurice Barnes, *Industrial Landscape with Red Truck* (1955/65)

The Maerdy Colliery miners proudly return to work in 1985

(1958). By 1957, however, demand was in decline and a programme of pit closures was initiated. By the 1970s, large tracts of the coalfield – the Afan and **Tawe** valleys among them – were bereft of collieries. The 118 pits and 87,000 miners of 1960 had been reduced to 51 pits and 35,000 miners by 1973.

Pit closures were temporarily halted in the 1970s, following a marked increase in the price of oil. Yet, by 1980, south Wales had only 36 collieries, most of which were losing money, and they became victims of the policies introduced by Margaret Thatcher. Their prospects were exacerbated by the bitter **miners' strike** of 1984–5. Of the 28 pits in operation before the strike, half had been closed by 1987, and the total workforce had fallen to 10,200. Following the privatization of the coal industry in 1994, the workers' co-operative at **Tower Colliery**, **Rhigos**, became the sole operating deep mine in south Wales, although some coal continued to be produced through small levels and open-cast sites.

At the opening of the 21st century, the south Wales coalfield had become what was, in essence, a worked-out mining camp. It remained, however, home to half Wales's inhabitants. The challenge implicit in that fact is the central challenge facing the Welsh as a people. For those with roots in the southern coalfield, awareness of its extraordinary history is fundamental to the condition of being Welsh.

The northern coalfield

As its development did not give rise to the scale of change experienced in the south, there is a tendency for the northern coalfield to be marginalized. Yet, its history has features of considerable significance. It underwent early exploitation, it gave rise to a wide range of industries, it was the cradle of trade unionism in Wales, and its labour relations, although not without periods of turbulence, were in marked contrast with those of the southern coalfield.

Coal was being commercially exploited at **Mostyn** as early as the 1340s. By the late 17th century, it was being extensively used for the smelting of lead ore and, in addition, a lively trade with Ireland and the city of Chester was developing along the **Flintshire** coast. A century later, the **Bersham Ironworks**, the copperworks of **Holywell**, the **pottery** and brick works of **Buckley**, the numerous limekilns, and the incipient **chemical** works of Deeside were all substantial consumers of coal. By the late 1820s, average annual output was the equivalent of 0.5 million tonnes, a sixth of that of the south. With the southern coalfield 10 times larger, it could be argued that, in the 1820s, the northern coalfield was being more intensely exploited.

In October 1830, trade unionism came to Wales with the establishment at **Bagillt** of a lodge of the Lancashire-based Friendly Associated Coalminers' Union. The union rapidly won the support of the Flintshire miners; it began recruiting in **Denbighshire** and sent emissaries to the southern coalfield. The severe unrest of 1831 and the hostility of employers undermined the union and drove the miners into sullen acquiescence. Over the following three decades, the output of the northern coalfield continued at around a sixth of that of the south. However, between 1874 and 1913, when the coal output of the north increased by 44%, that of the south increased by 244%. By 1913, Denbighshire and Flintshire were responsible for a mere 6% of Wales's total coal production. Northern townships which were almost totally dependent upon collieries – **Rhosllanerchrugog** is perhaps the best example – had characteristics remarkably similar to those of the south. Such communities were, however, rare, for coal extraction was only one of the varied industries of the north-east – a key factor in explaining the generally moderate attitudes of the region's miners' leaders.

The coal output of Denbighshire and Flintshire peaked in 1913 at 3.55 million tonnes, and the number of miners peaked in 1924 at 19,189. By the late 1930s, the number had halved but – apart from the special case of **Brymbo** – the interwar depression was not as traumatic an experience in the northern coalfield as it was in that of the south. Following the Second World War, output and employment contracted further; by the mid-1970s, it had fallen to below 0.5 million tonnes. The closure of Bersham in 1984 left Point of Ayr as the north's sole operating colliery. Following privatization in 1994, that colliery also closed.

Open-cast mining

Modern open-cast mining began in 1942 when civil engineering firms with spare capacity were brought in to supplement deep-mine output. Although adopted as an emergency wartime system of extraction, it became a long-term feature of the south Wales coalfield, especially in the anthracite districts. (There has been no significant mechanized open-cast coalmining in the north.) In the late 1950s, when demand for coal declined, shortage of smokeless fuels meant that the decision to cease opening new sites did not apply to the anthracite areas. In the 1970s and early 1980s, up to half of anthracite production came from open-cast

sites. There were also significant workings in the bituminous districts, especially near **Llantrisant** and Dowlais (Merthyr Tydfil). The resultant environmental destruction and disruption of communities have been the cause of much protest. Open-cast production peaked at the equivalent of 3.2 million tonnes in 1971. By the mid-1980s, output had decreased to 1.68 million tonnes, representing 18% of total southern production. In 1993, however, south Wales's open-cast output (2.52 million tonnes) exceeded that produced by deep-mine methods (1.98 million) for the first time. Bulldozers had ousted colliers, and the majority of Wales's coal producers had, to quote **Harri Webb**, become 'sunshine miners'. In 2004, there were fewer than 400 miners working underground in Wales, and about 360 working in open-cast mines.

Frederick North's *Coal and the Coalfields of Wales* (1932), in which each section is considered historically, remains the only comprehensive study of its kind. The industry made an important contribution to the development of the industrial novel (*see* **Literature**), and inspired much of the prose and poetry written by Welsh writers, particularly in **English**, in the 20th century. The harsh working and living conditions of the Welsh miner are nowhere more forcefully described than in **B. L. Coombes**'s *These Poor Hands* (1939).

COALOWNERS' ASSOCIATIONS
Coalowners' associations were established in most **coal**fields to provide a unified front against **trade unions**, and to provide mutual aid in times of strikes (*see* **Miners' Strikes**). The first association in south Wales was the **Newport** Coal Association, founded by **Thomas Powell**

C. R. Stock, *Business* (19th century), one of his six cockfighting prints depicting the 18th-century hexagonal cockpit in Welshpool

and Thomas Prothero in 1833. A more ambitious organization, the Aberdare Steam Collieries Association, was formed in 1864. By 1873, a more broadly based association, comprising sale-coal colliery owners and **iron**masters, had been established, subsequently to be called the **Monmouthshire** & South Wales Coal Owners' Association. Members paid levies, calculated on their output, to provide a compensation fund in the event of strikes. In an attempt to reduce the frequency of strikes, the Association played a major role in establishing, in 1875, the 'sliding scale' system for regulating wage rates, and later in the various Conciliation Board agreements for settling disputes. The southern association, and the less prominent association in the northern coalfield, became affiliated to the Mining Association of Great **Britain**, which, in the troubled interwar years, gave expression to the increasingly intransigent attitudes of British coalowners. The nationalization of the coal industry in 1947 led to the disbanding of the mineowners' associations.

COCHRANE, Archibald Leman (1909–88)
Epidemiologist

Born in **Scotland**, and educated at **Cambridge**, Cochrane worked with an ambulance unit during the **Spanish Civil War**, after which he resumed his medical studies at University College Hospital, **London**. During the **Second World War**, he spent several years as a prisoner of war. Long employed at the Medical Research Council's **Pneumoconiosis** and Epidemiological Research Units at **Cardiff**, he was in 1960 appointed professor of chest diseases at the Welsh National School of Medicine (*see* **Wales College of Medicine, Biology, Life and Health Sciences**). He gained worldwide recognition for his work as a researcher in epidemiology, and was responsible for beginning a new phase in the history of the discipline.

COCK FIGHTING

The practice of pitting gamecocks against each other and betting on the outcome, popular among all social **class**es, prevailed from time immemorial until proscribed in Wales and **England** in 1849 (in 1895 in **Scotland**). In towns, circular, purpose-built cockpits were constructed, such as the **Denbigh** cockpit, re-erected at the National History Museum (*see* **St Fagans**), which includes a small central fighting area surrounded by tiers for spectators. In rural areas, farm cockerels might be pitted against each other, using flat pieces of land or even churchyard tombstones as fighting pitches. Some landowners specialized in breeding gamecocks and handlers would be employed to train them. The cock's natural spurs, wattle and comb would be removed and metal spurs placed on the cock's legs. Contests such as the notorious Welsh Main involved 32 gamecocks pitted alternatively against each other until a winner emerged from the final fight.

COEDFFRANC (Coed-ffranc), Neath Port Talbot
(1611 ha; 8308 inhabitants)

Located between the **Nedd** and **Swansea**'s eastern boundary, the **community**'s chief settlement is Skewen, developed to house employees of the Crown **Copper**works, established in the 1790s. It contains Crymlyn Bog, botanically

the richest bog in southern Wales. In the early 20th century, the beach at Jersey Marine (a name recalling the Villiers family, earls of Jersey) was a popular site for **Sunday school** outings. In 1964, the coastlands became the site of the Ford Motor Works, later Visteon, and in 2007, on an adjacent site, the online company Amazon opened the fourth – and largest – of its United Kingdom distribution warehouses, with a promise of 2700 jobs. The vast Llandarcy **oil** refinery – now closed – was established in 1919; it gained its name from William D'Arcy, concessionaire of Iranian oilfields and the only man to achieve what one can call '**Celt**ic' **saint**hood while still alive.

COEDKERNEW (Coedcernyw), Newport
(705 ha; 573 inhabitants)

Located immediately west of **Newport**, the **community** is bisected by the **M4** and contains the junction between the motorway and the **roads** to Newport and **Brynmawr**. A badly damaged **Neolithic** chambered tomb stands in Cleppa Park. Although the city of Newport contains a community called Tredegar Park, Tredegar House, the home of the **Morgan family** from 1660 to 1951, lies within the boundaries of Coedkernew. Originally a modest early 16th-century house, it was transformed by William Morgan (d.1680) who turned it into the finest late 17th-century house in Wales and one of the finest in **Britain**. The building was completed in 1718 with the construction of sumptuous wrought-**iron** railings and gates. Its superbly symmetrical north-western façade, built in warm red brick, leads to a magnificent series of rooms, of which the Brown Room and the Gilt Room are the most memorable. In 1951, the house became a school. It was acquired by the Newport Corporation in 1974 and opened to the public.

COEDPOETH (Coed-poeth), Wrexham
(536 ha; 4721 inhabitants)

Located immediately west of **Wrexham**, the **community** lies in the upper reaches of the Clywedog valley. The valley floor, most of which is **National Trust** land, is traversed by the Clywedog Way, which links significant industrial sites. Chief among them is **Bersham** where, in 1721, Charles Lloyd, of the family that founded Lloyds Bank (*see* **Lloyd family, Dolobran**), was among the first to adopt the innovation introduced by Abraham Darby at Coalbrookdale, **Shropshire**, in 1709 – the smelting of **iron** ore using coke rather than charcoal. In 1753, the ironworks were acquired by **John Wilkinson** who made them a world centre for the production of cannon and steam-engine cylinders. Production ceased in the 1820s, but fascinating evidence of the industry survives. Adjoining the works is St Mary's church, built in 1873 for the Fitzhugh family of Plas Power, a mansion (1757) demolished c.1952. The village of Coedpoeth developed in the late 19th century as a colliery settlement. With the closure of the mines, it became an outlying suburb of Wrexham.

COFFIN, Walter (1784–1867) Coalowner and MP

A pioneer of the **Rhondda coal** trade whose activities helped open up the valleys for subsequent exploitation. In the 1820s, house coal from his Dinas colliery, carried via the Dinas tramroad and **Glamorgan**shire **Canal**, dominated the coal trade of **Cardiff**, much of it being sent to **Ireland**. MP for Cardiff (1852–7), he – a **Unitarian** – was Wales's first **Nonconformist** parliamentary representative. During his five years in the Commons, he never addressed the House.

COINAGE and TOKENS

Wales has never possessed its own coinage. In the early Middle Ages the country was virtually coinless: the few Welsh finds of **Anglo-Saxon** coins were related to **Viking** trading or raiding activities, and a unique penny in **Hywel Dda**'s name was probably an honorific issue struck by Eadred, king of Wessex. Short-lived post-Conquest **mints** at **Rhuddlan**, **Cardiff**, **Pembroke**, **St David's** (possibly) and **Swansea** were intended to meet **Norman** and Plantagenet military needs. As a native monetary **economy** developed, Wales was dependent on English coinage. Although, under Charles I, a temporary mint was established in **Aberystwyth** to coin **Cardiganshire** silver (*see* **Lead and Silver**), its output was not intended for local consumption. In 1972, the British Royal Mint relocated from **London** to **Llantrisant**. Pound coins bear Welsh emblems.

Shortages of small change in the mid-17th, late 18th and early 19th centuries occasioned the local issue of monetary tokens by private tradesmen, town authorities, and – in the latter period – by industrial concerns and banks (*see* **Banking and Banks**). Minted in London in the 17th century, and in the 18th and 19th centuries in Birmingham (mainly), such tokens were not peculiar to Wales, although **Thomas Williams** (1737–1802), the **Anglesey copper** magnate, originated the 18th-century series (*see* **Anglesey pennies**).

COITY HIGHER (Coety Uchaf), Bridgend
(753 ha; 835 inhabitants)

Immediately adjoining **Bridgend**, the **community** contains the town's north-western suburbs. Coity Castle, which began as a late 11th-century ringwork, consists of a late 12th-century keep and curtain wall, a 14th-century domestic range and a 15th-century gatehouse. It was the home of the Turbervilles, a family with a long tradition of arrogance towards the native inhabitants. Payne de Turberville, who advocated the ethnic cleansing of his lordship, was one of the royal administrators of **Glamorgan** following the death of Gilbert de **Clare** in 1314, and his brutality sparked off the revolt of **Llywelyn Bren**. The castle was twice besieged during the revolt of **Owain Glyndŵr**. The Gamage family, who owned the castle in the 16th century, remodelled the living quarters, adding two massive chimney stacks. In 1584, the Gamage heiress, Barbara (d.1621), married Robert Sidney (elevated to the earldom of Leicester in 1618), a marriage which angered Queen Elizabeth's chief minister, William **Cecil**. Barbara's virtues were praised by Ben Jonson. Cadet branches of the Gamages of Coity gave rise to Wales's largest extended family of clergymen.

East of the castle is the large 14th-century church of St Mary. It contains the tomb of Payne de Turberville and also a great rarity – a timber Easter sepulchre of *c.*1500. Tŷ Mawr, Byeastwood, is a fine 16th-century house. Nearby is the chambered tomb of Coed Parc Garw.

COLEG HARLECH, Harlech

An independent residential college for adults established at a beautiful **Merioneth** location in 1927. At a time of **class** tension, the founder, **Thomas Jones** (1870–1955), envisaged an **education** for responsible working-**class** leaders. Financed initially by private donors and subsequently by local authorities, the college established a reputation not for politics but for inspirational teaching, especially in **literature**. Until the 1980s, the college was renowned for summer schools and distinguished visiting speakers, and for producing university students. More recently, changing **government** policies and the general expansion of continuing education have resulted in the college playing a less distinctive role. It merged with North Wales **Workers' Educational Association** in 2001. In 2006/7, Coleg Harlech WEA – as the institution is now called – had about 125 full-time students and some 5000 part-time students in locations across the north.

COLES, Bryan [Randall] (1926–97) Physicist

After graduating in his hometown of **Cardiff**, Coles spent his career at Imperial College, **London**. He became an international authority on the physics of transition, rare-earth and actinide metals and alloys, and on the related interplay of magnetism and superconductivity. His name will always be associated with 'spin glass' – an evocative metaphor to describe alloys where there are random interactions between magnetic impurities.

COLESHILL (Cwnsyllt) Commote

A **commote** of the *cantref* of **Tegeingl** (Englefield), it was the scene of **Owain Gwynedd**'s attempted ambush of Henry II (*see* **Hawarden**). Following the **Acts of 'Union'**, it became one of the **hundreds** of **Flintshire**.

COLION Commote

One of the three **commotes** of the *cantref* of **Dyffryn Clwyd**, its name is sometimes spelled as Coelion. Located southwest of **Ruthin**, it lay within the later **communities** of **Clocaenog** and **Efenechtyd**.

COLLIERY DISASTERS

With the exception of the **Aberfan disaster** of 1966, the major colliery disasters in Wales, particularly before 1914, were caused by underground explosions. Official inquiries into colliery explosions during the 19th century invariably attributed them to outbursts of methane gas (the atmosphere becoming explosive when the percentage of methane in air is about 5–14%), but in the late 19th century, there was a growing realization that **coal dust** alone could form the ignitable medium – the first explosion attributed to this cause being that at the **Albion Colliery**, Cilfynydd (*see* **Pontypridd**) in 1894.

The loss of life caused by an explosion was influenced by the amount of gas and/or coal dust in the workings: the larger the gas outburst and the greater the amount of coal dust, the greater the loss of life. Although many coal seams in south Wales were relatively free from gas, some of the steam coal seams were extremely 'fiery' or gaseous in nature – most notoriously the **Aberdare** Four Foot Seam and the Black Vein Seam of **Monmouthshire** – and most of them,

Some survivors of the Gresford Colliery disaster of 1934

being dry and friable, generated large amounts of dust. This combination made south Wales especially prone to colliery explosions. Thus, while the south Wales coalfield had increased its share of British coal output to 20% by 1914, largely through the expansion of steam coal production, it accounted for 2578, or 37.6%, of the 6853 deaths caused by explosions in British collieries between 1874 and 1914. This total included 439 men killed in the worst ever disaster in British coal mining history, that at the Universal Colliery in 1913 (*see* **Senghenydd Colliery Disaster**).

However, major disasters were responsible for only a small proportion of total deaths: 80% of fatal colliery accidents were the result of individual incidents – what John Benson has called the 'steady drip-drip of death'. In the period before the **First World War**, the replacement of naked lights with safety lamps, the use of mechanical ventilating fans to reduce the methane/air ratio, and watering the coal dust, helped to reduce both the risk of explosions and their consequences. It was the development of stone dusting (the introduction of inert stone dust into the atmosphere underground) and its widespread application in south Wales after the First World War, which played an important role in preventing further major disasters in the coalfield after 1914. Explosions still occurred, however, and the only explosion in the history of the north Wales coalfield ever to kill more than 100 persons occurred in 1934 at the **Gresford** Colliery, near **Wrexham** (*see* **Gresford Colliery Disaster**).

COLWINSTON (Tregolwyn), Vale of Glamorgan
(746 ha; 406 inhabitants)
A **community** located west of **Cowbridge**, its village has been overwhelmed by modern development. Its church has

features from the 12th to the 16th centuries and contains 14th-century wall **paintings**. The churchyard cross retains its original cross head. The Old Parsonage is a fine mid-16th-century house. Pwll-y-wrach, remodelled as a nine-bay mansion *c.*1770, was originally built in the early 17th century. It is the home of Mathew Prichard, grandson and heir of Agatha Christie.

COLWYN One-time district
Following the abolition of **Denbighshire** in 1974, Colwyn was created as a district of the new **county** of **Clwyd**. It consisted of what had been the **borough** of **Colwyn Bay**, the **urban district** of Abergele and the greater part of the **rural districts** of Hiraethog and Aled. In 1996, the district (bereft of the **communities** of **Cefnmeiriadog** and **Trefnant**), together with the district of **Aberconwy**, became the **county borough** of **Conwy**.

COLWYN BAY (Bae Colwyn), Conwy
(778 ha; 9742 inhabitants)
Until the 1860s, the site of what would be Colwyn Bay was a thinly populated bayside area between the villages of Llandrillo and Colwyn. The completion of the **railway** along the north Wales coast in 1849 led to the establishment of the resort of **Llandudno**. The 1865 purchase by entrepreneurs of the Pwllycrochan estate, which included much of the bayside land, was inspired by hopes that another resort could be established 12 km east of Llandudno. By 1921, the **borough** of Colwyn Bay, which was much more extensive than the present **community**, had 21,566 inhabitants, making it Wales's largest borough north of **Merthyr Tydfil**. Although less populous than the built-up area of which **Wrexham** was the centre,

Colwyn Bay came to be the quasi-capital of the north, providing the site of the headquarters of the North Wales **Police**, and the location of significant commercial and **educational** institutions. It is the home of the northern studios of ITV Wales; the offices of the north's main daily **newspaper** – the *Daily Post* – are close by at Llandudno Junction.

Colwyn Bay saw itself as a more genteel resort than **Rhyl**, and also encouraged the development of superior houses aimed particularly at well-heeled retired people from Merseyside and the English Midlands. The result was leafy suburbs, some of them containing houses designed by the distinguished local architect **Colwyn Foulkes**. Indeed, of all the towns of Wales, Colwyn Bay is unique in the degree to which it bears the imprint of a single 20th-century architect. While its role as a holiday resort has declined – the **pier** (1900) is a shadow of its former self, and the promenade lies under the shadow of the **A55** – Colwyn Bay's prospects as a residential and administrative centre seem promising. Among its institutions is Rydal School, the amalgamation of the Penrhos girls' school (1880) and the Rydal boys' school (1890), enhanced by buildings designed by Colwyn Foulkes.

William Davies (d.1593), Catholic priest and martyr (*see* **Roman Catholic Martyrs**), was born at Croes yn Eirias, which stood near the present-day civic centre adjoining Eirias Park. At the southern end of the community is Christchurch, Bryn-y-maen, built in 1899 and enriched with the fine timberwork in which its architect, **John Douglas**, delighted. Colwyn Bay Mountain Zoo is the largest zoo in Wales. In 2001, the built-up area of Colwyn Bay, which includes the communities of **Rhos-on-Sea**, **Mochdre**, **Old Colwyn**, **Llysfaen** and **Llanddulas** as well as the community of Colwyn Bay itself, had a population of 30,564, making it the ninth in size among Wales's urban centres.

COMMISSION FOR LOCAL ADMINISTRATION IN WALES, The

The commission, established in 1974 and based in **Bridgend**, had two roles. The first, under the Local **Government** Act 1974, was to investigate complaints from those who considered that they had suffered injustice as a result of maladministration by local authorities. The second, under the Local Government Act 2000, was to investigate allegations that local authority members had failed to comply with their authority's code of conduct.

In 2005, the office of the local administration commissioner (also known as the local government ombudsman) was amalgamated with three other offices – the **health** service commissioner for Wales, the Welsh administration ombudsman and the social **housing** ombudsman for Wales. The new ombudsman is known as the public services ombudsman for Wales.

COMMON LAND

Land over which more than one party has rights of common, of which grazing is the most important. Such rights also include estovers (collecting firewood), turbary (**peat** digging) and piscary (**fish**ing). In the mid-18th century, almost a quarter of Wales was common land, but the

proportion declined rapidly following a vigorous policy of **enclosure**. Nevertheless, common land is still found throughout Wales, with all rights registered with the local authority. The Commons Registration Act 1965 made a distinction between village greens, which are primarily recreational, and rural commons on which the pastoral **economy** of many upland communities depend. The need to control overgrazing is a serious problem that brings graziers into conflict with conservation interests.

COMMONWEALTH, The (1649–60)

The Commonwealth, established in February 1649, 10 days after the execution of Charles I, lasted until the Restoration of the monarchy (*see* **English Monarchs**) in 1660. Also called the 'Puritan regime' or the 'Interregnum', it was divided into three periods: the Commonwealth proper (1649–53), the first Protectorate (1653–8) and the second Protectorate (1658–9). During this period, the monarchy and the House of Lords were abolished (1649) and the kingdom declared a republic (19 May 1649). Power was given to the House of Commons, **government** was carried out by ordinance rather than by statute, a council of state consisting of 40 members was established, Royalist property was sequestrated and public morals were strictly supervised.

The new order was not welcomed enthusiastically in Wales, where resistance to the Parliamentary cause had been widespread, and the leaders of the new Commonwealth, eager to win support for their ideas and values, determined on an evangelical campaign. In 1650, the **Act for the Better Propagation and Preaching of the Gospel in Wales** was passed. Church income was transferred to two committees of commissioners, which dismissed 278 clergymen, appointed numbers of itinerant **preachers** and set up schools in towns. These developments fostered the growth of the dissenting sects that had been gaining ground in Wales even before 1650. One of the most fervent of the preachers, **Walter Cradock**, had been among the leaders of the **Congregationalists** at **Llanvaches**. Another Puritan, **Morgan Llwyd**, published in 1653 the Welsh Puritan classic, *Llyfr y Tri Aderyn*, while **Vavasor Powell** was one of the fiercest critics of **Cromwell**'s assumption of the title of Lord Protector. Although the 1650 Act ceased to function in 1653 (its work being continued in part by the Commission for the Approbation of Public Preachers of 1654), it sowed in Wales, as Cromwell put it, 'a seed … hardly to be paralleled since primitive times'; numerous congregations of Congregationalists and somewhat fewer congregations of **Baptists** and **Presbyterians** came into existence.

Local administration under the Commonwealth was based on **county** committees. In Wales, with its predominantly Royalist **gentry**, it was difficult to find sufficient suitable candidates for the committees, with the result that men of 'inferior' birth were appointed in their place, and it was reported in 1652 that 'the gentry and people of substance in Wales were sad and downhearted'. The ruling **class**, however, soon adapted to the situation. Some Parliamentary supporters – notably **Philip Jones**, who built up a substantial estate at Fonmon (**Rhoose**) in the **Vale of Glamorgan** – took the opportunity to improve their position, but by the 1650s prominent Royalist families such as the Vaughans of Caergai (**Llanuwchllyn**), the **Salesburys** of Rug (**Corwen**) and even those arch-Royalists the **Somersets** of **Raglan** Castle, were throwing in their lot with the new order. Their enthusiasm cooled, however, during the years of military government (1655–7) under Lieutenant-General James Berry and by 1659 they were eager for a Restoration of the monarchy, Thomas **Myddelton** even going so far as to proclaim Charles II in August of that year, almost a year before the actual Restoration of May 1660.

COMMONWEALTH GAMES, The

Wales was represented at the first British Empire Games in 1930 and is one of only six countries to have competed in every Commonwealth Games since then. The inaugural meeting of the Commonwealth Games Council for Wales was held in City Hall, **Cardiff** in 1933, the Council's aim being to ensure Wales's regular participation in the Games, which are held every four years. In 1958, the Commonwealth Games were held in Wales, mainly in Cardiff.

Wales's first Commonwealth Games medal was won by the swimmer Valerie Davies (*see* **Swimming**) at Hamilton in 1930. The most medals awarded to a Welsh athlete at the Games were won by weightlifter David Morgan (*see* **Weightlifting**), with nine gold and three silver, from a total of six Games.

COMMOTE

A subdivision of a *cantref*. It may have emerged following the increase in **population** from *c.*1050 onwards and the consequent need for more manageable units. Each commote had a royal centre, a maerdref or demesne township and its own court; both commotes and courts survived the loss of Welsh independence. Following the **Act of 'Union'** of 1536, many commotes and some *cantrefi* were given the status of an English **hundred**.

COMMUNIST PARTY, The

The Communist Party of Great **Britain**, formed in 1920, immediately attracted the support of a number of Welsh **Marxists**. Marxist ideas had been circulating in Wales since the 1890s, and the Communist Party was heir to the **Syndicalist** tradition. The party played a prominent role in the political and industrial battles of the 1920s and 1930s. The election in 1936 of **Arthur Horner** as president of the **South Wales Miners' Federation** enormously increased communism's prestige. Communist candidates won several dozen seats on local councils in south Wales, and mining villages such as Maerdy in the **Rhondda** and Bedlinog (**Merthyr Tydfil**) became known as '**Little Moscows**'.

The party remained numerically small in Wales, generally relying on front organizations such as the National Minority Movement and the **National Unemployed Workers' Movement**. Communists were active in organizing hunger marches and protests against the **Means Test**. The party took the lead in denouncing fascism and it was largely communism that inspired 174 Welshmen to fight with the International Brigade in the **Spanish Civil War**.

The party's initial opposition to the **Second World War** was unpopular, but following Germany's attack on the

Harry Pollitt (seated), who nearly won Rhondda East for the Communist Party in the general election of 1945

Soviet Union in 1941, communists became ardent supporters of the Allied war effort. Communist candidates polled consistently well in parliamentary elections in the Rhondda East division; Harry Pollitt came within 972 votes of winning the seat in 1945. Politically, however, the party posed little threat to the **Labour Party**, although it maintained a strong union base and also contributed to a wider Welsh culture by supporting the **Welsh language** and **devolution**. Prominent Welsh communists such as Dai Dan Evans, **Dai Francis** and D. Ivor Rees remained active in Welsh life, and in 1979 **Annie Powell**, elected mayor of the Rhondda Borough, became the sole Communist to hold such a position in Britain. Gradually, however, communism merged into a wider radical tradition, and with the party's demise, many supporters found a home in the Labour Party.

COMMUNITIES

As part of the local **government** reorganization of 1974, the civil **parishes** of Wales (but not those of **England**) were abolished and replaced by communities. Each community can choose to have a community council, but in urban areas in particular the option is frequently not taken up. Communities are among the smallest units of census statistics and their boundaries are shown on the Ordnance Survey's 1:25,000 scale **maps**. They should not be confused with wards – the areas represented by councillors – although many wards have the same name and sometimes the same boundaries as communities. In 2007, Wales had 869 communities, varying in area from **Rhayader** (13,945 ha) to **Cefn Fforest** (64 ha), and in **population** from **Barry** (45,053) to **Baglan** Bay and Margam Moors (*see* **Port Talbot**), which have no inhabitants at all.

COMPANIES HOUSE, Cardiff

Companies House, in Crown Way, **Cardiff**, is an executive agency of the Department of Trade and Industry; it was located in Cardiff in the mid-1970s as part of a fitfully pursued policy of moving **government** offices from **London**. The agency has three main statutory functions: the incorporation, registration and striking off of companies; the registration of documents that must be filed under company **law**; and the provision of company information to the public and enforcement of compliance with legal requirements. It holds public records on over 1.5 million registered companies.

COMPANION TO THE LITERATURE OF WALES, The New (1998)

A revised edition of *The Oxford Companion to the **Literature** of Wales* (1986), this major reference book was compiled and edited by Meic Stephens (b.1938) and published by the **University of Wales** Press in 1998. It contains entries not only on the writers, books and **periodicals** of Wales, but also information about many aspects of Welsh culture and history. A **Welsh** edition, *Cydymaith i Lenyddiaeth Cymru*, was published in 1986, with a revised edition in 1997.

COMPANY UNIONISM

One of the greatest threats to the **South Wales Miners' Federation** was the South Wales Miners' Industrial Union, which grew out of the drift back to work by disillusioned miners towards the end of the 1926 **miners' strike**. It was often called the Spencer Union because of the establishment of the pro-employer Industrial Union by George Spencer in Nottinghamshire. The SWMIU could, at times in the 1930s, claim 6000 members, and as it challenged the hegemony of the Fed, the threat it posed was essentially political. The Fed embarked on a bitterly fought campaign involving stay-down strikes to drive out a rival thought to be supported by employers and **Conservative** politicians. The campaign was successful and in 1938 the SWMIU merged into the Fed.

COMPUTUS FRAGMENT, The

The Computus Fragment, which is held at **Cambridge** University Library, once belonged to a 10th-century miscellany of astrological and calendar material relating to the **science** of the calculation of time, referred to as Computus. One page has two faintly preserved diagrams, one of which is a copy of the so-called circle of Pythagoras; the second consists of a 23-line commentary (the Computus Fragment) on a text that probably derived from Bede's *De ratione temporum*. The commentary, in Old **Welsh**, is written in the question and answer form associated with the early medieval schools, and is concerned with the 18.6-year lunar cycle used to determine the date of Easter.

CONDRY, William (Moreton) (1918–98) Naturalist and author

Although born in Birmingham, William Condry lived most of his adult life in Wales, working as warden of the wild **bird** reserve at Ynys-hir (**Ysgubor-y-coed**). His many books on natural history include *Snowdonia National Park* (1966), *Exploring Wales* (1970), *The World of a Mountain* (1977) and *The Natural History of Wales* (1981). His 'Country Diary' column in the *Guardian* was collected in *A Welsh Country Diary* (1993); his autobiography, *Wildlife, My Life*, appeared in 1995 and *Welsh Country Essays* in 1996.

CONGREGATIONALISTS

Congregationalists – or Independents – are Christian churches that believe themselves responsible before God for the government of their own congregation, independently of any external civil or ecclesiastical authority. Such ideas began to circulate in **England** in the wake of the **Protestant Reformation**, and spread into Wales in the 17th century. Though **John Penry** is regarded as the first Welshman to embrace Independent principles, the first Congregationalist church was not established until 1639 – at **Llanvaches** – by William Wroth, **William Erbury** and **Walter Cradock**. The **Commonwealth government** (1649–60) sought to encourage the formation of independent churches, but, following the Stuart Restoration, Congregationalists suffered persecution. The Toleration Act (1689) brought some relief. With the coming of the **Methodist Revival**, men such as **Edmund Jones** of **Pontypool** and Henry Davies (1696–1766) of **Blaengwrach** attempted to divert some of the new energy towards their own people, but because Congregationalism and Methodism did not share the same temperament, the attempt failed. By the end of the 18th century, however, the Congregationalists had been heavily influenced by the Methodists, and a new vitality informed their activities.

The 19th century was a period of dramatic expansion, with the Congregationalists contributing energetically to the religious, political and social developments of the era. Among their leaders were **William Williams** (1781–1840) of Wern, **Samuel Roberts** and his brothers, **David Rees**, **William Rees** (Gwilym Hiraethog; 1802–83), and **Michael D. Jones**. Unlike the **Calvinistic Methodists**, Congregationalists had no desire to subject their churches to a formal centralized structure, an issue on which Michael D. Jones held particularly strong views. A Congregational Union was established in England in 1832, but it was not until 1872 that the Union of Welsh Independents was established at **Carmarthen**. It is estimated that by then there were over 900 Congregationalist churches in Wales, with a total of 89,000 members.

Expansion continued into the 20th century, with membership reaching some 175,000 in 1933. Then came the decline. Even so, the Congregationalists could still claim to have prominent figures in their ranks: the poet **Pennar Davies** and **R. Tudur Jones** among the theologians, and **Gwynfor Evans** and the folk singer Dafydd Iwan (b.1943) among the political activists.

Many **English**-medium Congregationalist churches joined the United Reformed Church at its creation in 1972. By 2004, there were fewer than 500 churches belonging to the Union of Welsh Independents, with a membership of about 35,000.

CONNAH'S QUAY (Cei Connah), Flintshire (1860 ha; 16,526 inhabitants)

Located on the **River Dee**, which divides the **community** into northern and southern sections, the town's **port** (originally called New Quay) was created in 1793 to provide berths for

15 sailing **ships**. Connected to **Buckley** by **railway** in 1861, the port came to export bricks, earthenware and **coal**. It was also a centre of **shipbuilding**, with Ferguson, McCallum & Baird (1859–1917) building steamers and three-masted schooners, and Crichtons (1910–35) building steel boats.

In 1896, the estuarine mud on the river's northern bank was drained to provide the site of the works of John Summers of Stalybridge (*see* **Shotton Steelworks** and **Summers family**). Originally an **iron**works, steel production began 1902. The company had its own wharf and a fleet of ships ferrying steel to **Liverpool**. By 1969, it employed over 13,000 people. Steel production ceased in 1979, leaving only a steel coating mill employing 2500. Adjoining the site is an extensive rifle range. A new bridge (1998) carries the A548 across the Dee. Nearby is an electricity generating station (1950–8), which has been adapted to burn natural gas. The compact town contains the suburbs of Wepre and Golftyn (*Ulfemiltone*) mentioned in the Domesday Book.

CONSCIENTIOUS OBJECTORS

Military conscription was introduced in **Britain** in January 1916. Unlike most of the other warring states, the legislation permitted conscripts to state their case before a tribunal which could grant them absolute or conditional exemption, force them to serve or imprison them. Between 1916 and 1918, 30% of the 16,500 British objectors suffered imprisonment; the equivalent figures for 1939–45 were 59,192 and 3%. The grounds for objection were Christian, socialist or libertarian, or sometimes a mixture of all three. Of the 16,500 British objectors of the **First World War**, perhaps a thousand were Welsh, this higher proportion being an indication of the strength of radical Christianity and radical **socialism** in Wales. Among the objectors were the absolutists, who refused to conform in any way; **David Lloyd George**'s bitter antagonism towards them helped to erode his radical image. Their case was championed in particular by **Thomas Rees** (1869–1926) and his journal *Y Deyrnas*.

Again in the **Second World War**, conscientious objection was proportionately greater in Wales than it was in Britain as a whole. In that war, there was a new element – Welsh nationalists (*see* **Nationalism**) who denied the right of the 'English' state to conscript them, although no more than a score made their nationality the sole grounds of their objection. Conscientious objection continued to be a feature of Welsh life until the abolition of military conscription in 1959.

CONSERVATIVE PARTY, The

The **Tory Party**, founded in the late 17th century, had the support of the majority of the members of the Welsh **gentry class**. Until the second half of the 19th century, most of the constituencies of Wales were controlled by that class; thus Welsh parliamentary representation was dominated by the Tory Party, which adopted the name Conservative in the 1830s. The general election of 1865 was the first in which Wales elected a non-Conservative majority. Thereafter, with the increasingly democratic nature of elections, the party's role in Welsh politics became marginal. Its members consistently supported causes inimical to the **Nonconformists** of Wales, favouring **Anglican** religious instruction in schools, taking the side of the brewers

Wyn Roberts, Conservative MP for Conwy 1970–97, who became Lord Roberts of Conwy in 1998

against the Welsh **Sunday Closing** Act and, above all, resisting the **disestablishment of the Church**. Their suspicion of free trade alienated industrialists, their belief in land-lordism antagonized tenant farmers and they were reluctant to support any advancement in the national status of Wales. Even the rift in the **Liberal Party** which followed **Gladstone**'s conversion to Irish Home Rule did little initially to increase support for the Conservatives, although by 1895 their position had improved sufficiently for them to win 9 of Wales's 34 seats, a figure not bettered until 1979. Their performance in the first **county** council elections in 1889 proved lacklustre; two Liberals were elected for every one Conservative.

The early years of the 20th century saw further dissatisfaction in Wales over Conservative **education** policies. The Liberals won an overwhelming victory in 1906, an election in which the Conservatives failed to win a single Welsh seat, despite the fact that they had received 33.8% of the Welsh vote. The 1920s and 1930s brought dramatic upheavals in the Liberal Party, but the social exclusiveness of a Conservative leadership largely restricted to the Anglicized gentry class and the poor organization of the party in most of Wales combined to ensure that the Conservatives derived little benefit from them. Only in such areas as **Cardiff**, **Monmouth**, **Newport** and the **Vale of Glamorgan**, where many middle-class Liberals defected to the Conservatives in an attempt to defeat **Labour**, did the party display much improvement on its electoral performance before the **Second World War**. In the seven general elections held between 1918 and 1935, it won fewer seats than either the Liberals or Labour, although it did enjoy some success in local **government** elections. In 1945, with the Conservatives receiving less than a quarter of the Welsh vote, Wales was second only to London's East End as the least Tory area in **Britain**. Thereafter, however, the situation changed significantly; by 1951, the Conservatives,

Conwy Castle overlooking the bridges and estuary

with six Welsh seats, had overtaken the Liberals who, only a few decades previously, had been the dominant party.

One of the features of Welsh politics since the Second World War has been the stability, except in the Labour landslide years of 1945, 1997 and 2001, of the Conservative vote. In 1979, when the overwhelming rejection of **devolution** seemed to indicate that the Conservatives were, for once, in tune with the wishes of the Welsh people, the party won 11 seats in Wales – its best performance since the 1860s. Nevertheless, their share of the poll, 35%, was only 2% higher than it had been in 1959; in terms of the number of seats won, the Conservatives in Wales have usually been ill-served by the electoral system. Support for Conservative policies was, however, undoubtedly increasing, particularly among the agricultural community. In 1983, the party won 14 of the 38 reconstituted Welsh parliamentary divisions, an achievement undoubtedly assisted by the recently formed SDP-Liberal Alliance, which attracted votes from Labour.

The party's advance was not maintained. Many of Margaret Thatcher's policies aroused deep hostility in Wales. In addition, the appointment, from 1987 onwards, of **secretaries of state for Wales** who represented English constituencies caused increased disillusionment with the Conservatives. Conservative-won seats declined from 14 in 1983 to 8 in 1987. In May 1997, and again in June 2001, the party failed to secure any of Wales's Westminster seats. Conservative support fell from 28.6% in 1992 to 19.6% in 1997, but rose slightly to 20.87% in 2001. The party proved even less appealing in the first elections to the **National Assembly** in May 1999, receiving only 15.8% of the constituency vote. It did however win one territorial seat (Monmouth), and the introduction of an element of proportional representation allowed the party to secure, in addition, eight regional seats. In the elections to the European parliament in June 1999, the party's support

increased to 22.8%, with the Conservatives' lead candidate being elected to the third of five possible seats. (In 2004, when the number of Wales's seats in the European parliament was reduced to four, the Conservatives, with 19.37% of the vote, again won one seat.) A slight improvement in the party's appeal was also apparent in the second elections to the National Assembly. It won 19.19% of the constituency, retained Monmouth with 57.52% of the vote and secured 10 regional seats. The general election of 2005 saw the Conservatives return their first Welsh MPs in eight years – in Monmouth, **Preseli Pembrokeshire**, and **Clwyd West** – although their share of the vote remained virtually static in Wales, at 21.4%.

From the mid-1970s onwards, the party sought to shed its 'Anglicized' image, carrying out, under pressure, its election pledge to establish a **Welsh-language** television channel (**S4C**) and passing the **Welsh Language Act of 1993**. In the mid-1980s, it abandoned the practice of regarding Welsh parliamentary constituencies as training-grounds for aspiring English politicians. In 1998, the party was relaunched as the Welsh Conservative Party and an autonomous Welsh board of management was established. It is ironic that, of Wales's four major parties, it is the Conservative Party which has best adapted itself to the new political situation created by **devolution**. In the 2007 Assembly election, the Conservative share of the vote rose to 22.4% and its elected members to 12. With Labour holding only 26 of the Assembly's 60 seats, the creation of a 'rainbow' coalition consisting of **Plaid [Genedlaethol] Cymru**, Conservative and Liberal Democrat Assembly members was widely canvassed. In the event, however, an administration formed from a coalition of Labour and Plaid Cymru members was established. Although the Conservatives are the third party in the Assembly, Plaid Cymru's entry into the coalition resulted in the Conservatives constituting the official opposition.

CONTEMPORARY ART SOCIETY FOR WALES, The

Formed in 1937, under the presidency of **Augustus John**, the society encourages visual artists and gallery visitors, by annually purchasing work for exhibition in public spaces; most of these works then become part of the permanent collections of institutions such as the **National Museum** and the **National Library**. The practice of having a different selector each year has led to a somewhat incoherent purchasing policy; this, combined with a dearth of exhibiting space, has undermined much of the society's original dynamism.

CONWY Conwy (1413 ha; 14,208 inhabitants)

Occupying both sides of the **Conwy** estuary, the **community** contains Conwy itself, Gyffin, Llandudno Junction, Tywyn, Llanrhos and Deganwy. In 1190, a **Cistercian** monastery was founded at Conwy; it became the spiritual heart of **Gwynedd** and the burial place of **Llywelyn ap Iorwerth**. It was at the monastery in 1277 that **Llywelyn ap Gruffudd** was obliged to seal the **Treaty of Aberconwy**, which much diminished his power. Following the **Edwardian conquest**, the monastery was dissolved and refounded 12 km to the south (*see* **Llanddoged and Maenan**).

In its place, Edward I commissioned what J. Goronwy Edwards described as 'incomparably the most magnificent of [the king's] Welsh fortresses'. Designed by **James of St George** and built between 1283 and 1287, it is remarkable for its unity and compactness. It consists of inner and outer wards and eastern and western barbicans. Among its glories are the eight round towers, the great hall, the king's apartments and the chapel royal. The town walls were built simultaneously with the castle. With their 21 towers, 3 battlemented gates and charming group of 12 privies, they extend for 1.3 km and constitute **Britain**'s finest example of a fortified **borough**.

In 1401, the castle was seized by **Owain Glyndŵr**'s cousins, Gwilym and Rhys ap Tudur of **Penmynydd** (*see* **Tudor family**). During the **Civil War**, Archbishop **John Williams** (1582–1650), a native of Conwy, held the castle for Charles I, but, having changed sides, he assisted the Parliamentarians in its capture in 1647. **Telford**'s Conwy bridge (1826), complete with battlemented round towers complementing those of the castle, and **Stephenson**'s tubular bridge (1847) – smaller versions of the bridges the two engineers were to build across the **Menai Strait** – robbed the castle of its almost island-like situation, but also drew attention to Conwy's wonders. The castle came into the care of Conwy borough in 1865 and became the responsibility of **Cadw** in 1984.

St Mary's church includes part of the Cistercian monastery, but dates in the main from the late 13th century. Plas Mawr (1577–80), with its stepped gables, turrets and outstanding plasterwork, was built for Robert Wynn of a cadet branch of the **Wynn family (Gwydir)**. In 1881, the building became the home of the **Royal Cambrian Academy of Art**; the academy moved to Crown Lane, Conwy in 1993. Aberconway House (*c.*1500) was to have been removed to the United States had it not been acquired by the **National Trust** in 1934. As early as the 1920s, Telford's bridge, never intended for motor traffic, was causing road

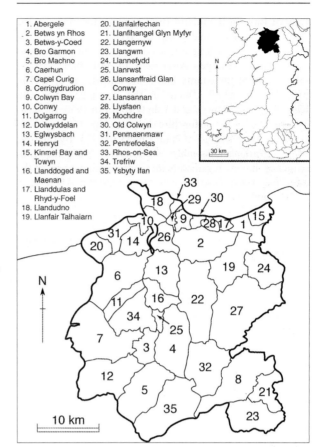

1. Abergele	20. Llanfairfechan
2. Betws yn Rhos	21. Llanfihangel Glyn Myfyr
3. Betws-y-Coed	22. Llangernyw
4. Bro Garmon	23. Llangwm
5. Bro Machno	24. Llannefydd
6. Caerhun	25. Llanrwst
7. Capel Curig	26. Llansanffraid Glan
8. Cerrigydrudion	Conwy
9. Colwyn Bay	27. Llansannan
10. Conwy	28. Llysfaen
11. Dolgarrog	29. Mochdre
12. Dolwyddelan	30. Old Colwyn
13. Eglwysbach	31. Penmaenmawr
14. Henryd	32. Pentrefoelas
15. Kinmel Bay and	33. Rhos-on-Sea
Towyn	34. Trefriw
16. Llanddoged and	35. Ysbyty Ifan
Maenan	
17. Llanddulas and	
Rhyd-y-Foel	
18. Llandudno	
19. Llanfair Talhaiarn	

The communities of the county borough of Conwy

congestion. A new bridge, built in the 1950s, did no more than decant a mass of vehicles into Conwy's narrow streets. A remarkably innovative bypass tunnel, opened in 1991, solved the problem (*see* **A55**). Conwy Mountain is rich in hut circles. Gyffin, on the southern fringes of the built-up area of Conwy, was the birthplace of Bishop **Richard Davies** (?1501–81).

The Conway estuary is a major source of cockles. Across it stands Deganwy **hill-fort**, the 6th-century stronghold of **Maelgwn Gwynedd**. Sherds of **glass** found in the hill-fort testify to trade between Wales and the eastern Mediterranean in the 6th and 7th centuries. The **Norman** castle built there *c.*1080 was destroyed by Llywelyn ap Gruffudd in 1263. A stone head discovered at Deganwy, which may be a portrayal of Llywelyn ap Iorwerth, is the subject of a poem by **Harri Webb**. Bodysgallen Hall, southeast of Llanrhos, a 17th-century mansion once owned by the **Mostyn family**, is perhaps the most luxurious hotel in Wales. Until its closure in the 1990s, the Hotpoint factory at Llandudno Junction was one of the largest employers in north-west Wales. Llandudno Junction is home to the daily **newspaper** of the north, the *Daily Post*.

CONWY COUNTY BOROUGH (Bwrdeistref Sirol Conwy) (115,345 ha; 109,596 inhabitants)

Created in 1996 through the amalgamation of the **Aberconwy** District and most of that of **Colwyn**, the **county** consists essentially of the basin of the **River Conwy**. County administration is divided between Conwy, **Llandudno** and

Colwyn Bay. In the inland rural **communities** most of the inhabitants have some grasp of **Welsh**, but the coastal towns, which have long attracted people from north-western **England**, are largely Anglicized. In 2001, 39.67% of the inhabitants of the county had some knowledge of Welsh, with 23.23% wholly fluent in the language. (*See also* **Kinmel Bay and Towyn** and **Ysbyty Ifan**.) In 1950, the eastern part of **Caernarfonshire** became the Conwy constituency. It was shorn of **Nant Conwy** in 1983. By the time of the **National Assembly** elections of 2007, the constituency, having regained Nant Conwy and lost part of the one-time **Arfon** District, was known as the Aberconwy constituency.

CONWY River (57 km)

The Conwy rises in Llyn Conwy on the Migneint moorland (**Bro Machno**). From its upland tract, the **river** passes through **Betws-y-Coed** before flowing through a fertile valley floor northwards towards **Llanrwst**. Its major tributaries, the Machno, Lledr and Llugwy, drain much of eastern **Snowdonia**. Boats take tourists up the river to **Trefriw**. **Conwy** Castle is superbly located on the estuary. Adjoining it are two innovative bridges – **Thomas Telford**'s **road** bridge (1826) and **Robert Stephenson**'s **railway** bridge (1846). Even more innovative is the tunnel (1991) beneath the river, which carries the **A55**.

CONYBEARE, W(illiam) D(aniel) (1787–1857) Geologist and divine

A practising cleric all his adult life, Conybeare, rector of **Sully** and dean of Llandaff (and lecturer in divinity at **Oxford**, 1839), was a member of the elite of the Geological Society of **London** and elected FRS. Well known for his studies of fossil reptiles and of the **geology** of south Wales, it was he who suggested the name 'Carboniferous' for **coal**-bearing strata. His *Outlines of the Geology of England and Wales* (1822) did much to advance the study of geology in **Britain**.

COOK, Arthur James (1883–1931) Trade unionist

Born in Somerset, A. J. Cook was an **agricultural labourer** and **Baptist** lay-preacher before becoming a **Rhondda** collier active in the **South Wales Miners' Federation**. Educated at the **Central Labour College**, he became a miners' agent and was from 1924 to 1931 general secretary of the **Miners' Federation of Great Britain**. He became a folk hero during the **General Strike** of 1926, when he coined the phrase 'not a penny off the pay, not a second on the day'.

COOMBE TENNANT, Winifred Margaret (Mam o Nedd; 1874–1956) Social reformer

A campaigner for votes for **women**, prominent **Liberal** and **eisteddfod**ic figure, she was born in **Swansea**, married Charles Coombe Tennant and lived at Cadoxton Lodge (**Blaenhonddan**). She stood unsuccessfully as a Liberal candidate in the election of 1922 and was the first British woman to be sent as a delegate to the League of Nations. Under the name of 'Mam o Nedd', she was an enthusiastic and long-serving Mistress of Robes to the **Gorsedd** of Bards. Her patronage of **Evan Walters** was significant in the development of the painter's career.

COOMBES, B[ert] L[ewis] (1894–1974) Author

From the age of 18, B. L. Coombes, who was born in **Herefordshire**, worked as a collier at pits in the **Resolven** area. He wrote extensively about his life as a miner in four books which are among the most authentic accounts of the coal industry in south Wales: *These Poor Hands* (1939), *I Am a Miner* (1939), *Those Clouded Hills* (1944) and the documentary *Miners' Day* (1945); a selection of his other writings appeared as *With Dust Still in His Throat* in 1999.

COOPER, Tommy (1922–84) Comedian

Caerphilly-born Cooper did some **boxing** and military service before developing one of the most original comedy acts of the early television era. In his seemingly shambolic performances, delivered in crumpled suit and trademark fez, nothing appeared to go right, least of all the magic tricks. At first, audiences joined him in laughing at his own self-deprecating jokes, but gradually the realization dawned that he was a master of one-liners and a genius at comedy timing. He died dramatically before a huge television audience during a broadcast from Her Majesty's Theatre, **London** in April 1984.

CO-OPERATIVE MOVEMENT, The

Inspired by **Robert Owen**, established by the Rochdale pioneers in 1844, and encouraged by Dr **William Price**, the movement was legalized in 1852. It expanded rapidly in the 1860s and helped to counteract the pressure exerted by company shops (*see* **Truck System, The**). The first co-operative store in Wales opened at **Cwmbach** in 1860; there were 20,000 members in south Wales by 1892 and 115,000 by 1915. During the interwar **depression** the stores became a source of supplies and ready credit for destitute miners' and steelworkers' families. The Co-operative Party, formed in 1917, became closely allied to the **Labour Party**.

COPPER, ZINC and NICKEL

Copper has been mined in Wales since the **Bronze Age**, as the workings on the Great Orme at **Llandudno** testify. When non-ferrous metalworking became a major industry it was concentrated in the coastal belt between **Kidwelly** and **Port Talbot**, centring on **Swansea**, an area especially favoured for the production of these metals, with about 90% of British production of copper in the 18th and 19th centuries, and 75% of zinc production by *c.*1914.

The smelting of copper started around **Neath** under the Mines Royal Society *c.*1584, and came into its own from the early 18th century onwards, when Swansea displaced Bristol as **Britain**'s copper smelting capital. Swansea's prominence was based on easy access to Cornish ores and the outcropping of **coal** near the surface, which provided cheap fuel, and return cargoes. A ban on smelting (1764) in the **borough** of Swansea – because of municipal aspirations to develop the town as a resort – pushed the copper works to the north and east of the town, generally along the River **Tawe**, but there was no escape from the highly noxious copper fumes, which gave rise to lengthy legal battles over pollution and **health**.

Non-ferrous metal smelting employed small numbers (under 4000 throughout south Wales at its peak in 1911), but the product was of high value and produced notable spin-offs in **chemicals** and other industrial uses. The industry was limited in its scope by the fact that copper was smelted and rolled in the region but not manufactured into finished products. Nevertheless, the Swansea district was, for much of the 19th century, the world's premier metal manufacturing area of non-ferrous metals. Some smelters were of Cornish origin, such as the **Vivian family**, and their concerns were 'vertically integrated', in that they owned and controlled all the processes of production, from mining through to marketing.

In the later 19th century, copper began to be mined in large quantities in **North America**, **Australia**, Chile and the Congo, countries upon which Wales became increasingly dependent for its ores. The growth of smelting in those countries posed a long-term threat to Swansea's dominance – especially as British capital was used to develop rival smelting industries elsewhere.

The copper industry remained prosperous until the 1880s. As it declined, zinc (or spelter), which had been manufactured since the early 18th century, became more prominent, with some works converting to its manufacture. Nickel manufacture was concentrated at **Clydach** where Ludwig Mond, with his three sons as directors (*see* **Mond, Alfred**), established a works that became the largest in the world. Using ores imported from Canada, it commenced production in 1902 and remains in operation, the only metal extraction process still working in the Tawe valley.

For a century, from 1876, the Swansea Vale works of the Imperial Smelting Company was at the forefront of zinc smelting technology. The innovative blast furnace process introduced in 1960 was adopted worldwide: zinc vapour from the furnace was absorbed in a spray of molten lead at 560°C, to prevent oxidation by the atmosphere, and subsequently crystallized out – by cooling to 440°C – with a purity of 97.5%.

A lesser concentration of copper manufacture (from ingots made in Lancashire) was in the Greenfield valley (**Holywell**). The area reached its peak for copper manufacture between 1780 and 1800, when it produced copper bolts for **Thomas Williams** (1737–1802) in accordance with his patents. After his death in 1802, production declined but continued until 1894. Zinc was also manufactured in this area.

The mining of copper was a significant chapter in the industrial history of north-west Wales. In the late 18th century, several workings were established in the heart of **Snowdonia**, some of which lasted for a century and more. Wales's largest copper mine was on **Mynydd Parys** (**Amlwch**), where by 1801 employment in the copper industry had resulted in Amlwch becoming the country's fifth most populated **parish**, with 5000 inhabitants, compared with the 1809 at **Cardiff**; mining resumed on Mynydd Parys in 2005. The vast gulch created by the mining gave rise to one of Wales's most dramatic landscapes.

CORACLE

A small, roundish **river** craft used for transport and **fish**ing and distinguished by its size, fabrication, weight and method of propulsion. Coracles were to be seen at one time throughout **Britain** and **Ireland** (the **Welsh** word cwrwgl is related to the Irish curach: boat) and have been in use since pre-**Roman** times. Traditionally, their frame is made of wicker, usually willow or ash laths covered with animal hide; latterly, hide has been replaced by calico or canvas impregnated with pitch and tar or bitumastic paint. A coracle usually weighs between 11 and 20 kg and can be carried easily on the back

Coracle fishermen on the River Tywi, Carmarthen, in the 1990s

or shoulders, held steady by a strap fitting over the chest. Coracle net fishing, directed towards catching salmon or sewin, is effected by holding a net between two coracles as they drift with the current. The coracle is propelled by one paddle held over the bow by both hands (unless one hand is holding the net) and manipulated in the form of a figure of eight. By the end of the 20th century, coracles were confined to the Rivers **Teifi**, **Tywi** and **Taf**, where a small number of coracle men continue to fish, their livelihoods recognized by the 1975 Salmon and Freshwater Fisheries Act. There is a coracle museum at **Cenarth**.

CORN GWLAD, Y (Horn of the country)
The horn sounded to open a **Gorsedd** ceremony or at an **eisteddfod**ic chairing or crowning ceremony – described by the poet Gwenallt (**David James Jones**) as 'an archaic fart from antiquity'.

CORN HIRLAS, Y (Long blue horn)
In medieval courts, the horn from which mead was drunk had ritual significance, as can be seen from the 12th century poem 'Hirlas Owen' (*see* **Owain Cyfeiliog**). In a later age, that inspired the **Gorsedd** ceremony in which the **Archdruid** is invited to drink from the Corn Hirlas as a token of welcome.

CORN LAWS, The
The price of corn, high during the **French Revolutionary and Napoleonic Wars**, plummeted following the restoration of peace in 1815, and parliament, under pressure from landlords, passed legislation that permitted the import of foreign wheat free of duty only when the domestic price reached 80 shillings per quarter. The Corn Laws were attacked by the working **class** because they increased the price of bread, by employers who believed that the laws obliged them to pay higher wages and by economic liberals who opposed interference with the free movement of goods. A trade depression in 1839 and a succession of bad harvests led to increased support for the Anti-Corn Law League, a predominantly middle-class protest movement founded in 1839. It attracted widespread support from **Nonconformists** in Wales, who saw Free Trade as a moral issue and the League as a useful weapon against the landlords. The Corn Laws were repealed in 1846, following the failure of the potato crop in **Ireland** in 1845 and the resultant mass starvation. The organizational methods of the Anti-Corn Law League were adopted by other movements, such as that seeking the **disestablishment** of the **Anglican** Church in Wales.

CORNELLY (Corneli), Bridgend
(1819 ha; 5982 inhabitants)
Formerly a part – with **Pyle** – of the **community** of Cynffig, the community contains the large villages of North Cornelly and South Cornelly and overlooks the vast sand dunes which extend from **Margam** to Sker Point. The sand conceals the walled town of Kenfig, founded in the 1120s and overwhelmed in the late 14th century. The dunes, visible from the **M4**, conceal a potentially fascinating archaeological site – a Welsh Pompeii, whose topography can be analysed through charter evidence and from the shapes of the dunes themselves. Despite its obliteration, the town was until 1918 a part of **Glamorgan**'s system of **borough** constituencies. St Mary Magdalene, Mawdlam, was enlarged in the 15th century. Sker House stands in a remote location overlooking the dunes. Originally a grange of Neath Abbey (*see* **Dyffryn Clydach**), it was rebuilt by the Turberville family in the late 16th century; long a gaunt ruin, it was recently restored. Elizabeth Williams (d.1776), the '**Maid of Sker**', reputedly suffered a fate similar to that of the 'Maid of Cefn Ydfa' (*see* **Ann Maddocks**).

CORNOVII Tribes
The **Iron Age** tribe occupying what became **Shropshire** and eastern central Wales. The name **Powys** may have been derived from *pagus* – the hinterland of the territory of the Cornovii. The Romano-British *civitas* capital was at Viroconium (Wroxeter). By the 7th century, the territory of the Cornovii was coming under **Anglo-Saxon** control, a process reflected in the **Heledd** poems. By then, the administrative centre of the area was at Pengwern – possibly Baschurch, north-west of Shrewsbury (*see* **Shropshire**). Other tribes called Cornovii lived in Caithness in **Scotland** and in south-western **Britain**; the name is at the root of that of **Cornwall**.

CORNWALL, Wales's associations with
Cornwall survived as a Brythonic kingdom until at least the late 9th century. The name comes from that of the **Cornovii** – the people of the horn/peninsula and *walh* as in **Welsh**. During the 'age of **saints**', its location in relation to the western sea routes made it a pivotal region in the dissemination of Christianity in the **Celtic**-speaking lands. Welsh 'saints' such as **Cadog** and Pedrog were honoured in Cornwall, and Cornish 'saints' such as Piran and Dochau in Wales. Cornwall also shared with Wales the legends of Brythonic peoples, as its role in the story of King **Arthur** testifies.

In the Middle Ages, trade between Cornwall and Wales was significant, but Cornwall's greatest impact upon Wales came with the increasing exploitation of its **copper** and tin ores from the 16th century onwards. By the late 18th century, the link with Cornwall had brought about the most astonishing chapter in the history of the industrialization of Wales – the country's domination of the global production of copper. As 3 tonnes of **coal** were required to smelt 1 tonne of copper, and as coal-less Cornwall needed to import coal to fuel its mine pumps, an efficient sea trade developed with **ships** conveying coal from the **ports** of west **Glamorgan**, returning with Cornish ore. A similar process led to the rise of Wales's flourishing **tinplate** industry. The link with Cornwall brought to Wales some of its leading industrialists, the members of the **Vivian family**, Barons Swansea, in particular.

By the late 19th century, increasing dependence on richer ores from further afield weakened Wales's commercial links with Cornwall. Other links developed through pan-Celticist movements, and through the respect for Welsh cultural and political achievements felt by Cornish patriots. On the occasion of the 1997 **devolution** referendum, Welsh devolutionists celebrated alongside a contingent from Cornwall bearing the flag of St Piran.

The Corona factory in the Rhondda in the 1920s

CORONA

The famous fizzy pop originated in 1897 when **Rhondda** grocers William Thomas and William Evans decided to supply the growing market for soft drinks created by the **temperance movement**. From the first factory in Porth, they rapidly built their business, eventually opening 87 depots. They did so by cutting out the middleman and delivering direct to the door in open-sided lorries, originally bearing the legend 'four large bottles in a case 1 shilling'. The original factory has been converted into The Pop Factory, a pop **music** recording studio.

CORRIS, Gwynedd (4513 ha; 613 inhabitants)

Adjoining the Dulas north of **Machynlleth**, the **community** contains the villages of Corris Isaf, Corris Uchaf, Aberllefenni and Pantperthog – settlements that came into existence in the 19th century to serve the **slate** industry. Quarrying at Aberllefenni ceased in 2003. The **horse**-drawn tramway (1859) linking the quarries to Machynlleth was used by steam engines from 1878; it closed in 1948, but a section of it has been reopened as a tourist attraction. The Corris **Railway** Museum recounts the story. King **Arthur**'s Labyrinth provides access to the tunnels and caverns of one of the former quarries.

CORS CARON (Cors Goch Glan Teifi, Tregaron Bog), Ceredigion

Located in the **communities** of **Tregaron** and **Ystrad Meurig**, this **peat** bog is, with **Cors Fochno**, one of the two largest raised mires in Wales. It developed after the waters of a **lake** – formed at the end of the most recent Ice Age – breached their natural dam, turning the lake into a marsh, with reed beds, woodland and eventually bog mosses

fostering an accumulation of vegetation at a rate of 3 cm a century. It is dominated by three low peat domes, between which the **Teifi** winds along a flood plain scattered with pools. Pollen stored in its layers has provided information about **plant** life in Wales since the bog's formation. The bog was extensively exploited for peat in the past; other ventures include a short-lived scheme to extract **chemicals** from the peat and an attempt to manufacture china from the blue clay beneath the peat. Exceptionally rich in wildlife, it is a National Nature Reserve of around 800 ha.

CORS FOCHNO (Borth Bog), Ceredigion

With **Cors Caron**, Cors Fochno is one of the two largest raised bogs in Wales. Located in the **communities** of **Borth**, **Geneu'r Glyn** and **Llangynfelyn**, it has the raised mire's characteristic domed profile of an upturned saucer, thickening towards the middle, where the **peat** is up to 7 m deep. The Cors Fochno National Nature Reserve, which includes the bog, the **Dyfi** estuary flood plain and the Ynyslas sand dunes, is just over 2000 ha in area; Cors Fochno used to be at least twice its present size. Until the mid-20th century, peat from the bog was the main fuel for local inhabitants. According to legend, an oracular toad and a malaria-inflicting witch were denizens of Cors Fochno. In medieval prophetic verse, Cors Fochno would be the site of the decisive victory of the Welsh over their enemies.

CORWEN, Denbighshire
(6957 ha; 2398 inhabitants)

The most extensive **community** in **Denbighshire**, it embraces a delightful stretch of the **Dee** valley. **Owain Glyndŵr**, lord of Glyndyfrdwy, had a house at Carrog (the mound near its site is a **Norman** motte). It was at Glyndyfrdwy that he was proclaimed **Prince of Wales** on 16 September 1400, and folk memories of him were gathered there in the late 18th century by **Thomas Pennant**. The much-reviled, dwarf-like statue of Glyndŵr, which was raised in the town centre of Corwen in 1995, was removed in 2007 to make room for a new one. The Rug estate, acquired by a branch of the **Salusbury family** in the late 15th century, eventually passed to a member of the Wynn family of Glynllifon (*see* **Llandwrog**). The ardent Royalist William Salusbury (*Yr Hen Hosannau Gleision*: Old Blue Stockings; 1580–1659) commissioned the building of Rug chapel (1637), which reflects the 'high church' liturgical arrangements favoured by Charles I. Its carvings and wall decorations make a visit a great delight. The **eisteddfod** held at Corwen in 1789 was an important step in the evolution of the National Eisteddfod. The almanacker **Thomas Jones** (1648–1713) was born at Tre'r Ddôl. **John Cowper Powys** lived at Corwen from 1935 to 1955; among his friends there was his neighbour, the novelist **Elena Puw Morgan**. A reopened section of the **Wrexham–Barmouth railway** (1865) runs from **Llangollen** to Carrog.

CORY BAND

A **brass band** from Pentre, **Rhondda**. Founded in 1880 as the Ton Pentre **Temperance** Band, it later took the name of the mine-owning **Cory family**, as recognition of the patronage provided by that family. It became the most successful Welsh brass band of the 20th century, a fact routinely disputed by its near neighbours, the Parc and Dare Band from Treorchy. It won the National Championship (1974, 1982, 1983, 1984 and 2000) and the British Open Championship (2000 and 2002). In 2004, it was renamed the Buy as You View Band, as recognition of the patronage provided by the company of that name, but reverted to its original name in 2007.

CORY families Coalowners and shipowners

During the 19th century, two quite separate groups of Corys became involved in shipowning in **Cardiff** (*see* **Ships and Shipowners**). (1) John Cory & Sons was formed by John Cory I (1822–91), of Padstow, **Cornwall**, and his sons John II (1855–1931) and James Herbert (1857–1933). (2) Cory Brothers began as shipowners and colliery agents but, after 1868, also became substantial owners of collieries in the **Rhondda**; it was established by Richard Cory I (1799–1882), of Bideford, Devon, and later run by his sons, John Cory (1828–1910) and Richard Cory II (1830–1914). During the late 19th and early 20th centuries, Cory Brothers became a major colliery and shipping company, operating coaling stations throughout the world. John Cory was responsible for the magnificent Dyffryn **Gardens** (Wenvoe) in the **Vale of Glamorgan**. A major philanthropist, his was the first statue in Wales to be raised to a living person. (That of the **rugby** player Gareth Edwards in Cardiff's St **David**'s Centre is the second.)

COSHESTON, Pembrokeshire
(1306 ha; 713 inhabitants)

Located immediately north-east of **Pembroke**, the **community** lies between Cosheston Pill and the **Carew** estuary. There are rebuilt, originally medieval, churches at Nash

and at Cosheston village – a linear settlement with houses set in long medieval burgages. Upton, a mansion containing parts of a 13th-century castle, is surrounded by attractive **gardens**. The chapel adjoining it contains a large 14th-century monument to a member of the Malefant family, builders of the castle.

COUNCIL OF WALES AND MONMOUTHSHIRE, The

The Council was set up by the Attlee **government** in 1948 as a nominated body of 27 members whose meetings were to be in secret. It was given no powers. **Huw T. Edwards** became the first chairman. Several panels were established, producing a number of detailed reports on Welsh issues and tendering information and advice relating to Wales to successive governments. Edwards sensationally resigned as chairman in 1958 as a protest against governmental inaction in Wales. Thereafter the Council was largely ineffectual, although it survived until 1966.

COUNCIL OF WALES AND THE MARCHES, The

The Council was created by Edward IV in 1471 as a household institution to manage the **Prince of Wales**'s lands and finances. In 1473, it was enlarged and given the additional duty of maintaining **law** and order in Wales and the **borders**. The first lord president was John Alcock, bishop of Rochester. The early history of the Council as an institution for supervising justice is unclear. Its meetings appear to have been intermittent but it was revived by Henry VII for his heir, Prince Arthur. Its seat was at **Ludlow** Castle, once the caput of the **march**er-lordships of the **Mortimer family**. It was not until 1526, however, that it began to increase its power alongside the Council in the North, established in that year. The most famous lord president was **Rowland Lee** (1534–43) who, during a period of significant changes in Welsh administration, governed the country and its borders with an iron hand. His policy was based on fear and he was granted a special dispensation to impose the death penalty. The Council survived his regime, was placed on a statutory basis (1543) and, during the latter half of the 16th century, played a central role in co-ordinating law and administration. Among other notable lord presidents were Sir Henry Sidney (1560–86) and Sir Henry **Herbert**, second earl of **Pembroke** (1586–1602).

The Council declined in the early 17th century because of opposition to its jurisdiction, the rivalry of the **London** courts and its royal connections. Along with the Courts of Star Chamber and High Commission and the Council in the North, it was abolished by Parliament in 1641 but was revived at the Restoration (1660). It was finally abolished in 1689, by which time it had lost much of its power and prestige. **A. H. Dodd** described Ludlow as Wales's 'lost capital'.

COUNTIES

A unit of local **government** originally under the jurisdiction of a sheriff or shire-reeve, the county or shire came into existence in Wessex in the late 8th century. By 1066, the whole of **England** had been divided into shires, but there were none in Wales until the 13th century. The 1240s saw the establishment of the embryonic counties of **Cardigan** and **Carmarthen**. In 1284, the heartland of **Gwynedd** was divided into the counties of **Anglesey**, **Caernarfon** and **Merioneth**, and three non-contiguous areas in the northeast became the county of **Flint**. Thus, by the late 13th century, almost half of Wales consisted of counties directly under the rule of the English crown.

The rest of the country – the **March** – was shired by the **Act of 'Union'** of 1536. The Act established the counties of **Brecon**, **Denbigh**, **Glamorgan**, **Monmouth**, **Montgomery**, **Pembroke** and **Radnor**, enlarged the counties of Cardigan, Carmarthen and Merioneth and added parts of the March to the English counties of **Herefordshire** and **Shropshire**. Thus Wales's 13 counties came into existence, counties which varied in size from **Carmarthenshire** (246,168 ha) to **Flintshire** (65,975 ha). The counties, with their MPs and their administration centred upon the quarter sessions, rapidly became the object of strong loyalty, particularly among members of the **gentry** class. They were **map**ped by John Speed and others, and celebrated by works such as **George Owen**'s *The Description of Penbrokshire* (written in 1603; published 1902–36). The **Poor Law** Amendment Act of 1834 established **poor law unions**; these were grouped to form registration counties which, from 1841 until 1901, were the units to which most census statistics referred. The borders of registration counties often differed markedly from those of administrative counties.

Gentry control of the administrative counties lasted until 1889, when the creation of county councils established representative structures. The **boroughs** of **Cardiff**, **Swansea** and **Newport** were given **county borough** status, thus detaching them from the administration of the counties in which they were located. (A fourth county borough – **Merthyr Tydfil** – was established in 1908.) The Local Government Act of 1894 acknowledged the status of non-county boroughs and divided those areas outside the boundaries of county boroughs and boroughs into **urban districts** and **rural districts**.

Unequal economic development led to marked distinctions between Wales's counties. By 1971, when 27.5% of the inhabitants of Wales lived in Glamorgan (minus its county boroughs; 46.08% with them), a mere 0.6% lived in Radnorshire. In 1974, Wales's 13 counties, 4 county boroughs and 164 boroughs and urban and rural districts were abolished. They were replaced by the counties of **Clwyd**, **Dyfed**, **Gwent**, **Gwynedd**, **Mid Glamorgan**, **Powys**, **South Glamorgan** and **West Glamorgan**. The new counties were divided into districts – 37 in all. In 1996, the 1974 counties and districts were abolished and replaced by 22 unitary authorities:

Blaenau Gwent County Borough
Bridgend County Borough
Caerphilly County Borough
Cardiff City and County
Carmarthenshire County
Ceredigion County
Conwy County Borough
Denbighshire County
Flintshire County
Gwynedd
Isle of Anglesey County
Merthyr Tydfil County Borough
Monmouthshire County
Neath Port Talbot County Borough
Newport City and County
Pembrokeshire County
Powys County
Rhondda Cynon Taff County Borough
Swansea City and County
Torfaen County Borough
Vale of Glamorgan
Wrexham County Borough

COUNTY BOROUGHS

The Local **Government** Act (1888) set up **county** councils in the 13 counties of Wales. It also laid down that large urban centres – generally those in excess of 50,000 in **population** – should be taken out of the counties and treated as counties in themselves. Wales had 5 centres with more than 50,000 inhabitants – **Cardiff** (128,915), **Swansea** (91,034), **Newport** (54,707), **Rhondda** (88,351) and **Merthyr Tydfil** (59,004) (1891 census figures). However, only the first three were granted county borough status. In 1908, that status was granted to Merthyr, despite protests from the southern part of the **borough,** where it was claimed that links with **Pontypridd** were stronger than were those with Merthyr. In 1935, a royal commission on Merthyr argued that the county borough, so heavily burdened by the cost of maintaining the unemployed, should be merged with **Glamorgan** – a responsibility which Glamorgan refused to shoulder. In 1974, county boroughs were abolished. Cardiff became a district of **South Glamorgan**, and Merthyr of **Mid Glamorgan**. Swansea and Newport – both much expanded – became districts of **West Glamorgan** and **Gwent** respectively. In 1996, Wales was divided into 22 unitary authorities; 9 of the new units chose to call themselves county boroughs.

COURTAULDS Textile company

Courtaulds established its first artificial fibres plant in **Flint** in 1917, with the purchase of the former Glanzstoff factory. A second factory was opened in 1922, and further expansion came in 1934, with the opening of a rayon factory at Greenfield, **Holywell**, where annual production capacity was expanded to the equivalent of nearly 51 million tonnes in 1937. Together with **iron and steel**, the artificial fibre sector came to dominate the **Flintshire economy**. By the 1950s, when some 7000 workers were employed in the industry, **Dee**side had established itself as **Britain**'s major rayon-producing centre.

COVE, (William) George (1888–1963)
Politician and educationist

A miner who became a teacher and a National Union of Teachers (NUT) activist, George Cove was born in Treherbert, **Rhondda**. While teaching in the Rhondda in 1919, the local **education** authority attempted to dismiss him because of his **trade union** activities, precipitating a teachers' strike. The support of the miners helped secure his reappointment, and a local salary scale was established in the Rhondda which became the Union's aspiration for the whole of **Britain**. Cove was elected to the NUT executive in 1920, becoming president in 1922. In 1923, he was elected **Labour** MP for Wellingborough, and from 1929 to 1959 was MP for **Aberavon**.

COWBRIDGE WITH LLANBLETHIAN
(Y Bont-faen a Llanfleiddan), Vale of Glamorgan
(859 ha; 4182 inhabitants)
The **borough** of Cowbridge was founded in 1254 by Richard de **Clare**, lord of **Glamorgan**. Located in the heart of the **Vale of Glamorgan** at the point where the Portway (later the A48) crosses the **Thaw**, it was admirably placed to be a commercial borough. The **Romans** had earlier appreciated the advantages of the site. Recent excavations have revealed extensive Roman settlement; indeed, Cowbridge may be the missing *Bovium* of the Antonine Itinerary (written descriptions of the Roman Empire's major **roads**). Unlike most Welsh plantation boroughs, Cowbridge had no castle – that was at Llanblethian, the caput of the lordship within which the borough was established. Early in its history, Cowbridge was surrounded by stone walls pierced by three gateways. The south gate and a fragment of wall survive.

The town expanded rapidly, and may have had over 1000 inhabitants by the early 14th century. Although laid out as a rectangle, it developed as a linear settlement strung along the Portway. It contracted in the latter Middle Ages and over the following centuries its **population** probably never regained its high medieval peak – it had 759 inhabitants in 1801. Nevertheless, its burgesses considered their borough to be the capital of the Vale and the focus of what passed for fashionable life among Glamorgan **gentry** and merchants. Recognized in 1536 as one of Glamorgan's parliamentary boroughs, it proved a difficult place to canvass, for, as it was noted in 1828, the burgesses 'so pique themselves on their respectability and independence ... that it is rather a delicate matter to have any communication with them'.

In the late 20th century, the town expanded considerably to house commuters to **Cardiff**. Southern expansion has been particularly marked, causing Cowbridge almost to adjoin Llanblethian; the linear settlement pattern, however, is still apparent and the pattern of burgage plots remains visible to the rear of High Street's frontages. The town retains a rich legacy of early houses, taverns and shops, with medieval features surviving in The Mason's Arms and The Bear. Façades tend to be 18th or 19th century in style, but they often conceal earlier structures.

Holy Cross church, originally a chapel-of-ease to Llanblethian, was built in the late 13th century, enlarged in the 15th century, and restored by **John Prichard** in 1850–2. It contains a fine monument to William Carne (1616) and a memorial to the travel writer **Benjamin Heath Malkin**; it also once contained the tomb of **Rice Merrick**, historian of **Glamorgan**. Also of note are the United Free church (1828), the neo-classical Town Hall (1830), and Prichard's Grammar School (1849–52, but a 16th-century foundation). Opposite the Town Hall is a plaque commemorating the Cowbridge associations of Iolo Morganwg (**Edward Williams**).

The **community** of Cowbridge includes Llanblethian and Aberthin as well as the great common of Stalling Down or Bryn Owen, the place where, in 1795, Iolo Morganwg conducted the first **Gorsedd** to be held in Wales. St John's, Llanblethian, has a 12th-century chancel and a fine 15th-century tower. Its castle (known as St Quintin's) was refortified by the Clare family; its gatehouse includes work equal in quality to that at **Caerphilly**. Llanblethian was frequently visited by Thomas Carlyle. There are handsome mansions called Great House in both Llanblethian and Aberthin. What is now Aberthin's village hall was originally built in 1749 as Wales's second purpose-built **Calvinistic Methodist** meeting house, and the first in terms of loyalty to Methodism. Other features of the district include the **hill-forts** of Llanquian and Caer Dynnaf, the castle and manorial settlement at Llanquian and the 17th-century farmhouse of Breach.

COX, David (1783–1859) Artist
The water-colourist David Cox was born in Birmingham. After studying **painting** in **London** under John Varley, he travelled widely in Wales, spending long periods painting at **Betws-y-Coed**, where he based himself at the Royal Oak. Interested in both places and people as subject matter, he became a prime influence in establishing the village as an artists' colony. His 1848 painting *The Welsh Funeral* was seminal in developing contemporary views of Welsh culture.

COYCHURCH HIGHER (Llangrallo Uchaf),
Bridgend (1521 ha; 835 inhabitants)
Located north-east of **Bridgend**, the **community** contains the site of Wern Tarw Colliery, the closure of which in 1951 led to the first major post-nationalization **coal**miners' strike.

CRACHACH
A term of abuse applied to those with authority and power in society – the Establishment – who are also considered to be snobs. *Crachach* is a **Welsh** term that has come to be used in conversations in **English**.

CRADOCK, Walter (?1610–59) Puritan minister
A native of **Llangwm, Monmouthshire**, Cradock came to prominence as curate to **William Erbery** at St Mary's, **Cardiff**. He developed such strong **Puritan** leanings that his licence to preach was withdrawn in 1634. He moved to **Wrexham**, began to evangelize in the **border**lands and was among those who established the **Congregational** church at **Llanvaches** in 1639. During the **Civil Wars**, he vigorously endorsed the Parliamentary cause. He served the Propagation movement as an approver and was bitterly critical of the radical millenarianism of some of his Welsh colleagues (especially **Vavasor Powell**) and was even more troubled by the incursions of the **Quakers**. Such was his influence that when the Methodists ventured into the north they were promptly dubbed 'Cradockites'.

CRAFT
There is substance to the argument, advanced by **Iorwerth Peate** in particular, that the visual sensibility of the Welsh resides in a strong craft tradition rather than in the

The Crawshay family seat – Cyfarthfa Castle, Merthyr Tydfil – built in the 1820s

production of high art. While art can be created only out of intention, utile beauty is not bound by this convention, and can be found in many of the crafts. Cultural need and available resources govern their development, although traditional form often manifests itself in new ways. No longer sustained by a rural **economy** in the old sense, the crafts have largely reinvented themselves to cater for the demands of a souvenir-dependent **tourism** industry, in which genuine locally produced crafts are often outnumbered by cheaper imports. Urban escapees to the countryside have led the rebirth of many traditional crafts. **Education**al institutions have played a part in the development of new crafts, on occasion independent of old traditions. Public policy – sometimes favouring grant applications from incomers at the expense of indigenous craftspeople – has encouraged the emergence of crafts and craft centres as a focus for revitalizing the rural economy.

The established and admired **textile**, **furniture** and **pottery** making of rural Wales remain the dominant forms. In addition, there are ceramics, wood, metal, **glass**, **leather** or **slate** objects, often combining with plastics, rubber and synthetic materials in an exotic mixture of ancient and modern. Jewellery making is growing rapidly and traditional musical instruments continue to be made. The tradition of carved stone and slate, in which **R. L. Gapper** made a distinguished contribution, has continued in the work of Ieuan Rees and **Jonah Jones**, which combines the utile and the expressive to complement the strong association between word and image which is a feature of Welsh culture.

Standards in design, materials and manufacture are maintained by craft organizations, official bodies and the curators of **art galleries**, while selection for exhibition at the National **Eisteddfod** is widely considered to confirm excellence.

CRAWSHAY family Ironmasters

Originally Yorkshire farmers, the Crawshay family began their connection with Wales when Richard Crawshay (1739–1810) acquired an interest in **Anthony Bacon**'s works at **Merthyr Tydfil**, becoming sole proprietor by 1794. For a time in the early 19th century, Crawshay's Cyfarthfa was the largest ironworks (*see* **Iron and Steel**) in the world, and he was a prime mover of the **Glamorgan**shire **Canal** (1791–4). The family intermarried with other local dynasties, the **Baileys** and the Halls (*see* **Augusta Hall**). Richard's son, William Crawshay I (1764–1834), having quarrelled with his father (the family was notable for turbulent relations), was chiefly involved in selling iron in **London**. His son, William Crawshay II (1788–1867), dominated the area at the time of the **Merthyr Rising** of 1831, and commissioned the building of Cyfarthfa Castle (subsequently a grammar school and now a museum and art gallery). He was a radical and refused to adopt the **truck system**. He acquired the **Hirwaun** ironworks and established a **tinplate** works at Treforest (**Pontypridd**). His son, Robert Thompson Crawshay (1817–79), initiated the **Cyfarthfa Band** and was notorious for his predatory attitude towards his female workforce. His massive tombstone at Vaynor proclaims 'God forgive me', but his exact sins remain a mystery. His wife, Rose Mary Crawshay (1828–1907), promoted philanthropic, **educa**tional and **women**'s causes. The family ceased to control the works when it was sold to **Guest, Keen and Nettlefolds** in 1902. Later members of the family, especially Geoffrey Crawshay and William Crawshay, were prominent in Welsh cultural and sporting affairs.

CRAY (Crai), Breconshire, Powys
(1775 ha; 264 inhabitants)

Cray lies in the upper reaches of the **Usk** basin. The road traversing the village rises to the open moorland that marks the watershed between the valleys of the Usk and the **Tawe**. The so-called **Llywel** Stone, now in the British Museum, was found in Cwm Crai; 2 m high, it carries inscriptions in **Latin** and **ogham**, an indication of the **Irish** associations of the kingdom of **Brycheiniog**. Crai reservoir provides water for **Swansea**. In its vicinity are several pillow mounds – artificial breeding places for **rabbits**.

CREDIT UNIONS

Credit Unions provide basic lending and borrowing facilities for those members of the public who do not use, or approve of the **banking** system. There are 46 credit unions in Wales. Stemming from the 19th century, credit unions are mutual, self-help co-operatives, registered under the Credit Unions Act 1979 and regulated by the Financial Services Authority. They pool the savings of individual members to provide them with low-cost loans.

CREUDDYN Commote

The southernmost of the three **commotes** of the *cantref* of **Penweddig**, it consisted of the land between the **Rheidol** and the **Ystwyth**. Its centre was probably at Llanfihangel-y-Creuddyn (**Trawsgoed**).

CREUDDYN Commote

One of the three **commotes** of the *cantref* of **Rhos**, Creuddyn constituted the peninsula east of the **Conwy** estuary. In 1284, it was detached from Rhos and included within the newly created **Caernarfonshire**, probably because it commanded the Conwy **River** crossing. The growth of **Llandudno** from the mid-19th century onwards led to the urbanization of much of Creuddyn. In 1974, it became part of the **Aberconwy** district within the new **county** of **Gwynedd**. In 1996, it became part of the unitary county of Conwy.

CRICCIETH (Cricieth), Gwynedd
(673 ha; 1826 inhabitants)

Located halfway between **Porthmadog** and **Pwllheli**, the **community** enjoys a sheltered position overlooking Cardigan Bay. Some of its inhabitants have a curious devotion to double 'c', a usage unknown to modern **Welsh-language** orthography. The place first came to prominence when **Llywelyn ap Iorwerth** transferred the commotal centre of **Eifionydd** from **Dolbenmaen** to a rocky coastal promontory on which a castle was erected. The inner ward, with its entrance passage flanked by two impressive D-shaped towers, had been completed before Llywelyn's death in 1240. The outer ward and its three rectangular towers were built in the later 13th century, when the castle became one of the residences of the itinerant princely court. By late winter 1283, the castle was in the hands of Edward I, who established an English **borough** at Criccieth and gave some consideration to the idea of making it the centre of a new **county**. Attacked and probably captured by **Owain Glyndŵr** in 1404, the castle and borough then fell into decay, although until 1950 Criccieth was one of the contributory boroughs of the **Caernarfon** Boroughs constituency.

By the 16th century, Criccieth was no more than a hamlet, a condition in which it remained until the coming of the Cambrian Coast **Railway** in 1867. Thereafter, it rapidly gained a reputation as a seaside resort. By 1885, when **David Lloyd George** established a **law** firm there, it had grown sufficiently to maintain a small professional **class**. Ever since, Criccieth has been inextricably associated with the Lloyd George family. It continues to find favour as a resort, and is also well known for its annual arts festival. Cwmni **Drama** Criccieth, active under the leadership of W. S. Jones and others in the 1960s and

Glamorgan team members celebrate winning the County Championship at the end of the 1969 cricket season

1970s, played an important role in the reinvigoration of Welsh-language drama. Criccieth-made Cadwalader's ice-cream is considered by many to be the best ice cream in the world.

CRICKET

Cricket was the first of the popular modern team games to be organized and codified. It acquired its first set of rules in 1744 and a de facto ruling body with the creation of the Marylebone Cricket Club in **London** in 1787. By the latter date, the game had reached Wales. The first recorded match in Wales was played at Cross Inn (**Llanegwad**), **Carmarthenshire**, in 1783 and the first mention of a club is at **Swansea** in 1785.

In the later 19th century, aided by the development of the **railways**, cricket spread steadily in Wales; its popularity in schools from the 1850s onwards and its transmission down the social scale, led to working-**class** men playing a game initially associated with the **gentry**. The first regular interclub fixtures started in the 1830s, while grounds later famous for **rugby** – notably **Cardiff** Arms Park and St Helen's, Swansea – were venues for cricket long before they saw the winter game.

In 1859, the visiting All **England** XI was defeated by a South Wales XXII (in the early days of cricket, it was not uncommon for less experienced teams to field 22 players), a result leading to the creation of the South Wales club, the first attempt to develop a first-class team. The first **county** teams were formed around this time, but were short-lived. Welsh cricket's most important 19th-century date was 1888, when the **Glamorgan** club, which was to become synonymous with the first-class game in Wales, was formed. The club joined the Minor Counties championship in 1897 and became joint champions in 1900. It was followed into the competition by **Monmouthshire** (1901–34), Carmarthenshire (1908–11) and **Denbighshire** (1930–1, 1933–5).

In 1921, Glamorgan attained first-class status as the 17th member of the County Championship. The club struggled in its early years, at times coming close to going out of business, and its successes have been occasional and intermittent. In 76 seasons it has finished in the top three of the championship only eight times – five of them between 1962 and 1970.

In spite of this modest record, the club has been accepted as a quasi-national team – an identity underpinned by the subsuming of the Monmouthshire and Denbighshire clubs in the 1930s and recognized by county cricket's rulers, who regard anyone born anywhere in Wales as qualified by birth for Glamorgan.

Its successes – the County Championship victories of 1948, 1969 and 1997, together with Sunday League wins in 1993 and 2002 and two appearances in one-day finals at Lord's – the Gillette Cup in 1975 and the Benson and Hedges in 2000 – have occasioned national enthusiasm. So too have Glamorgan's victories against touring teams – in particular over **South Africa** in 1951 and **Australia** in 1964 and 1968, all achieved at St Helen's, the only British ground on which Australia, South Africa and **New Zealand** have been beaten at both cricket and rugby. St Helen's was also the venue in 1968 for the best-remembered cricket event on Welsh **soil**, when the West Indies all-rounder

Gary Sobers, playing for Nottinghamshire, became the first man to hit six sixes in one over, from the bowling of Malcolm Nash of Glamorgan.

In 1975, St Helen's became the first ground outside normal test venues to stage a one-day international, when England played New Zealand. From Glamorgan's inception, it refused to designate a single county headquarters, mindful of the rivalry between Swansea and Cardiff. This policy persisted until the decision in 1996 to concentrate resources on Sophia Gardens, Cardiff, which staged a World Cup match between New Zealand and Australia in 1999 and a one-day international in 2001. Glamorgan continues to play one game a year in **Colwyn Bay**, a custom initiated in the late 1960s, thanks to **Wilf Wooller**'s associations with the area.

Welsh cricket is inextricably linked to England's, often to the point of invisibility – an identity underlined by the misleading 'ECB' acronym of the game's current ruling body, the England and Wales Cricket Board. Sixteen Glamorgan players, plus the Welsh-born **Cyril Walters** (Worcestershire) and Pat Pocock (Surrey), have played for England. Of these, the off-spinners Pocock (24 matches, 1968–84) and Robert Croft (21 matches, 1996) have had the longest test careers, followed by the pace bowler Jeff Jones (1963–8) and the all-rounder Alan Watkins (1948–52), both of whom played 15 times. Although two Welshmen, Walters (1934) and Tony Lewis (1972–3), have captained England, a strong local conviction that Welshmen have been under-represented in England teams is supported by the fact that the most prolific career run scorer (Alan Jones: 36,049 runs, 1957–83) and wicket taker (Don Shepherd: 2218 wickets, 1950–72) never to play test cricket were both Glamorgan players.

The first-class game in Wales has drawn heavily on vigorous grassroots, notably a club game whose strongest teams were organized into the South Wales and Monmouthshire League in 1926, and the proselytizing work of the Welsh Cricket Association from 1969 onwards. A Wales team has played in the Minor Counties championship since 1988, although with limited success. Perhaps the most successful of all levels of the Welsh game is the villages, with seven titles – won by St Fagans (Cardiff) (three), **Marchwiel** (two), **Gowerton** and Ynystawe (Swansea) – since the British village knock-out was introduced in 1972.

CRICKHOWELL (Crucywel), Breconshire, Powys (809 ha; 2065 inhabitants)

A **community** on the north bank of the **Usk**, Crickhowell has the **Black Mountains** as its backdrop. **Fenton** called it 'the most cheerful looking town I ever saw', but to **Malkin** it was 'old and mean'. The church of St Edmund – an unusual dedication in Wales – was built on land given by Sybil Pauncefoot in the early 14th century, and her monument, together with other Pauncefoot and Herbert tombs, is in the chancel. There are Rumsey tombs in the churchyard and their former home, the Malt House, is in Standard Street. A headstone of 1750 commemorates Samuel Walbeoffe of Llanhamlach, who was obliged to leave the house 'where his ancestors … had lived for six hundred and twenty years … upon the wreck of his fortune'.

Theophilus Jones records that *plygain* was still celebrated in the early 19th century, and he was present at the opening of the **Neolithic** Gwernvale burial chamber, which has since been more thoroughly excavated. Gwernvale Manor, now a hotel, was the home of Sir **George Everest**, after whom the mountain was named. Little remains of the castle, but the 13-arch bridge is the finest of those spanning the Usk. Porth Mawr, on the road to **Brecon**, is an impressive **Tudor** fortified gateway. In the early Middle Ages, Crugywel was a **commote** of the *cantref* of **Blaenllynfi** or **Talgarth**, within the kingdom of **Brycheiniog**.

CRIMEAN WAR, The
Britain and France declared war on Russia, in support of Turkey, in March 1854. In September, an expeditionary force landed on the Crimean peninsula and major battles were fought at Alma (20 October), Balaclava (25 October) and Inkerman (5 November), in which both the **Royal Welch Fusiliers** and the **Welch Regiment** were heavily involved. The siege of Sebastopol lasted until its evacuation by the Russians in 1855. The war ended with the Treaty of Paris of March 1856. Domestically, the war evoked great popular interest (and occasioned a marked rise in **newspaper** circulation), as well as opposition from pacifists (*see* **Pacifism**) and internationalists (*see* **Internationalism**) such as **Henry Richard**. During the war, **Elizabeth Dav[i]es** (Betsi Cadwaladr) played a heroic nursing role. North of Blaenau **Ffestiniog**, the **A470** crosses the Crimea Pass, along a **road** built in the 1850s.

CROES NAID (The Protection Cross)
A jewelled relic which was believed to contain a fragment of the True Cross. From time immemorial, it had been one of the most sacred possessions of the princes of **Gwynedd**, and its presentation to Edward I at **Aberconwy** in June 1283 was an acknowledgement that the dynasty which had cared for it through the ages had been irretrievably destroyed. In 1284, the *croes naid* was paraded through the streets of **London** and displayed for a time at Westminster Abbey. It was among the relics which Edward I took with him on his Scottish campaign of 1307. Exchequer accounts show that the *croes naid* was repaired by a **gold**smith in 1353, but its fate after that is uncertain. English commentators claimed that the relic had been brought to Wales by a Cornish hermit called Neot, a tradition which probably derives from an attempt to explain the Welsh noun *naid* ('protection' or 'fate').

CROMWELL, Oliver (1599–1658) Lord Protector
As he was in direct male descent from Morgan Williams of Llanishen (**Cardiff**), Oliver's **surname** would have been Williams had not his great-grandfather adopted the surname of his brother-in-law, Thomas Cromwell, architect of the **Act of 'Union'** of 1536. Indeed, in his youth Oliver signed himself 'Cromwell alias Williams'. A further connection with Wales came through his sister's marriage with **John Jones** (?1597–1660) of Maesygarnedd (**Llanbedr**). In 1648, he suppressed the rising in south Wales, which had led to the outbreak of the Second **Civil War**. His elevation as Lord Protector was bitterly opposed by **Vavasor Powell** and other Welsh radicals.

CROSSKEYS, Caerphilly
(575 ha; 3092 inhabitants)
A **community** located at the confluence of the **Ebbw** and Sirhowy **Rivers**, Crosskeys gets its name from a one-time public house. The mining of bituminous **coal** began early, but by the late 19th century the area was dependent upon steam coal collieries at Cwmcarn and **Risca**. Crosskeys is the home of the **Gwent** Tertiary College, the successor to the Crumlin School of Mines. Another important local institution, the **rugby** club, was founded in 1885. In the early 1920s, Pontywaun was laid out as an attractive garden suburb. A viaduct (1794) carrying the **Crumlin** branch of the **Monmouthshire Canal** survives there. While buildings fill the valley floor, the entire uplands have been forested.

CRUCORNEY (Crucornau), Monmouthshire
(7156 ha; 1170 inhabitants)
Constituting **Monmouthshire**'s northern projection, the **community** contains the Vale of **Ewias**, the beautiful glen of the Honddu. Llanfihangel Court is a fine house of the late 16th and early 17th centuries. The 17th-century Skirrid Mountain Inn is reputed to have housed a gibbet. The scholar **Raymond Williams** was a native of Pandy. The mansion at Trewyn contains medieval elements. Land movement has caused St Martin's church, Cwmyoy, to lean in all directions; it contains monuments by all three generations of the **Brute family** of sculptors. Llwyncelyn is a splendid intact late-medieval hall-house. Penyclawdd Court is a memorable manor house with splendid chimney stacks. At Forest Coal Pit, charcoal rather than **coal** was produced.

The community's most fascinating feature is Llanthony Priory, which began as the hermitage of William de Lacy, a member of the **Lacy family**, lords of Ewias. In 1118, it became Wales's earliest house of **Augustinian** canons. In 1135, when the region came under Welsh control, some of the non-Welsh canons left to found the priory of Llanthony Secunda near Gloucester. The Lacy family remained faithful to the original foundation and financed the construction of a large priory church. Completed *c.*1217, it is much ruined; the largely intact south transept offers an indication of its original scale and dignity. Following the **dissolution of the monasteries**, the infirmary became the **parish** church of St **David**. In *c.*1800, the western range of the monastic buildings became a shooting lodge; it is now The Abbey Hotel. In 1807, the Llanthony estate was bought by the English poet Walter Savage Landor (1775–1864). He began building the mansion of Siarpal high above the priory ruins, but work was abandoned following Landor's bankruptcy in 1813. The trees he planted greatly enhance the landscape. The surrounding uplands, which include some of the finest parts of the **Black Mountains**, are pockmarked with grouse butts. It was after a visit to Llanthony and the Vale of Ewias in 1967 that the American poet Allen Ginsberg (1926–97) wrote the poem 'Wales Visitation'.

CRUG MAWR, Battle of
In 1136, Owain and Cadwaladr, sons of **Gruffudd ap Cynan**, together with **Gruffudd ap Rhys ap Tewdwr**, annihilated a powerful force of Anglo-**Normans** and **Flemings** in a major battle at Crug Mawr, just north of **Cardigan**, a victory which established Welsh control in **Deheubarth**.

CRUMLIN (Crymlyn), Caerphilly
(1387 ha; 5724 inhabitants)
Crumlin, on the left bank of the **Ebbw**, lies south of the confluence of the Ebbw Fawr and Ebbw Fach, where the landmark tower of Christ church (1909) dominates the scene. A branch of the **Monmouthshire Canal**, completed in 1794, terminated at Crumlin where it linked with tramroads to **Nantyglo** and **Ebbw Vale**. In the early 20th century, settlement expanded rapidly to accommodate workers at the Navigation Colliery; built between 1907 and 1911, some of the colliery's high-quality brick buildings survive. Crumlin's most famous landmark, a lofty **iron railway** viaduct, was demolished in 1985; built between 1853 and 1857, it was 62 m high and 180 m long, and was one of the **engineering** wonders of the age. Two large masonry piers remain as a reminder of the scale of the project.

CRWTH
The crwth was played in Wales from the Middle Ages, when it was one of the instruments of the court, until the end of the 18th century, and since the 1980s it has enjoyed a revival. Its ancient origins are evident both in its lyre-like frame and the tuning of its three double courses. The lowest course does not cross the fingerboard and so may be bowed or plucked with the left thumb. A flat bridge necessitates a chordal performance technique well suited to the accompaniment of declaimed or sung poetry, such as in *cerdd dant* as performed in the Middle Ages (*see* **Penillion Singing**). The crwth was reintroduced to Welsh folk **music** in the mid-1980s by the instrumental trio Aberjaber; its revival has continued in the hands of musicians such as **Ceredigion**-born Bob Evans and **Gwynedd**-based Cass Meurig, both of whom have released notable recordings.

CRYMYCH, Pembrokeshire
(4473 ha; 1596 inhabitants)
Straddling the **Cardigan–Tenby road** (the A478), the **community** contains the substantial village of Crymych and the settlements of Glandŵr, Hermon, Llanfair-Nant-Gwyn, Llanfyrnach, Pentre Galar and Pontyglazier. Foeldrygarn (363 m), the easternmost summit of **Mynydd Preseli**, is crowned by a substantial **Iron Age hill-fort**. Within it are three **Bronze Age** cairns and 140 house platforms. The community's churches are far less interesting than its chapels, especially the **Congregationalist** chapel (1712, 1876) at Glandŵr, and the **Baptist** chapels at Hermon (1808, 1863) and at Pontyglazier (1826, 1873). Pant-y-Deri, Llanfair-Nant-Gwyn, is a handsome 17th-century house. In 1881, the **lead** mines at Llanfyrnach employed around 100 workers. Until the arrival of the **railway** from **Whitland** (1875), the Crymych Arms was the sole building on the site of the later Crymych village. What appears to be an airport control tower is the main building of Crymych Secondary School (1953–7). The decision in the 1980s to designate it a **Welsh**-medium school caused considerable local controversy.

CRYNANT (Creunant, Y), Neath Port Talbot
(2171 ha; 1883 inhabitants)
Located in the Dulais valley, north-east of **Neath**, the local **coal** deposits were exploited following the building of the

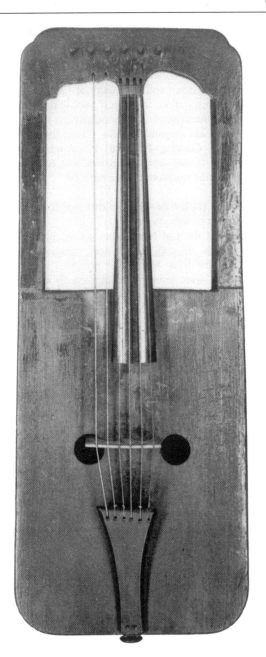

The crwth

Dulais Valley Mineral **Railway** in 1862. When sunk in 1926, the 732-m deep Cefn Coed Colliery was the world's deepest anthracite mine. Closed in 1968, its steam winding gear is the centrepiece of a mining museum. At remote Godre'r-rhos is an intact example of a simple mid-19th-century chapel.

CUDLIPP family Newspapermen
Three brothers from **Cardiff**, who emerged from Welsh journalism (*see* **Newspapers**) to reach the hub of Fleet Street by the 1930s. Percy Cudlipp (1905–62) served his apprenticeship on the *South Wales Echo* before proceeding, via the *Evening Chronicle* in Manchester, to the editorship of the *Evening Standard* (1933–8) and subsequently the *Daily Herald* (1940–1953). In 1956, he was the founding editor of the *New Scientist*. His brother, Reginald Cudlipp (1910–

C

2005), was a sub-editor of the *Western Mail* before joining the *News of the World* in 1938, becoming its editor in 1953. The third brother, Hugh Cudlipp (1913–98), became editor of the *Sunday Pictorial* in 1937. He later became chairman of the Mirror Group and eventually of the International Publishing Corporation, the largest publishing business in the world at the time. Known popularly as 'Prince of the Tabloids', he was knighted in 1974. Of the three brothers, according to **Caradog Prichard**, Percy was the 'most inspired; Reg ... the most industrious and conscientious, and Hugh ... the toughest and the pushiest.'

CUNEDDA (fl.400 or 450) Traditional founder of the kingdom of Gwynedd
A chieftain of the **Old North** who, according to *Historia Brittonum* (9th century), led an army southwards to rid **Gwynedd** of the **Irish**. Many later pedigrees were derived from his eight sons, seven of whom allegedly accompanied him and established in Wales kingdoms bearing their names. The names of the sons probably derived from onomastic lore, Rhufon being invented from **Rhufoniog**, Ceredig from **Ceredigion** and so on, and may represent an attempt to justify the rights of Cunedda's descendants to territories beyond the original kingdom of Gwynedd. Some historians accept that Cunedda himself did migrate to Wales, but debate continues as to the exact date of the migration and the authority for it; some argue for the 380s and others for the 430s.

CURLING
The ice rink at the **Deeside Leisure Centre** in **Queensferry**, where the Welsh Curling Association (WCA) was founded in 1973, is southern **Britain**'s capital of curling, the sport of sliding stones along ice, which may have originated in **Scotland** some 500 years ago. The support given by the Royal Caledonian Curling Club to the WCA at its inception led to regular visits and enduring connections between Welsh and Scottish curlers. A Welsh men's team qualified for the world championships in 1995, and since 1979 both sexes have performed well in the European championships. Television coverage of the 2002 Winter Olympics, when a team from Scotland won gold for Britain, provoked an unprecedented surge of interest in curling and an increase in WCA membership.

CUSTENNIN (Cystennin, Constantine; ?4th century) Purported early ruler(s)
According to **Geoffrey of Monmouth**, Custennin Fendigaid, grandfather of **Arthur**, came to **Britain** from **Brittany** during the period immediately after the **Roman** withdrawal. But Geoffrey also refers to Cystennin mab Constans (Constantine, son of Constantius), the conqueror of **Magnus Maximus**. The confusion probably results from the conflation of two Roman emperors, Constantius I ('Chlorus'), who in AD 296 defeated Carausius's rebel regime in Britain, and his son Constantine I ('the Great') who claimed the imperial throne at York in AD 306. Constantine's mother, Helena, was a Christian and in AD 313 Constantine legalized Christianity within the Empire. Further confusion probably arose because the wife of Magnus Maximus, also Helena, was almost certainly high-born and British, and their son was also called Constantine.

CUSTOMS AND EXCISE
A new tax on **beer**, wine, tobacco and other items was introduced in 1643 as a temporary wartime measure. But, like many short-term measures, it was to continue ever after, and Customs and Excise remain a vital part of state finances.

In Wales, as elsewhere, the excise was particularly unpopular, as were the enforcement officers who operated the system. Southern Wales was administered by three **ports** – **Chepstow**, **Cardiff** and **Milford**; Chester customs house was responsible for the north. There were subsidiary customs houses at **Neath**, **Swansea**, **Carmarthen**, **Pembroke**, **Cardigan**, **Caernarfon**, **Beaumaris** and **Conwy**. There were resident excise officers, all from elsewhere, and many earned a bad reputation. Established in 1698, they were Riding Officers who patrolled a specific section of coast. The letters of William Morris (*see* **Morris Brothers**), deputy customs officer at **Holyhead**, are a rich source of information on the matter (*see also* **Smuggling**).

In 1809, a Preventative Water Guard, patrolling coastal waters in revenue cutters, was added to the force. Inspecting captains were given the task of checking on the boats under their command.

A chief duty of HM Customs and Excise today is to collect and administer duties and VAT; it is also responsible for preventing and detecting the evasion of revenue **laws**. In 2003, there was widespread criticism when Customs and Excise ended a permanent presence at Swansea, **Pembroke Dock** and Chester, delegating coverage at those centres to mobile squads based in **England** and leaving offices only in Cardiff and Holyhead.

CWM (Y Cwm), Blaenau Gwent
(978 ha; 4350 inhabitants)
A **community** in the **Ebbw** Fawr valley, its main settlement – the village of Cwm – consists mainly of one very long street. It came into being to house miners working in the Marine Colliery. The colliery's role as employer has been taken over by the industries based in the Marine Business Park. St **Cadog** is reputed to have built a church on Cefn Manmoel. There is a nature reserve north of the village of Cwm. The Ebbw Valley Walk traverses the area.

CWM (Y Cwm), Denbighshire
(1498 ha; 385 inhabitants)
Located immediately south-east of **Rhuddlan**, the **community** contains several historic houses, among them Plas Is Llan, Pentre Cwm, Terfyn and Pwllhalog. Richard Parry, bishop of **St Asaph** (1604–23), who was involved in the 1620 edition of the Welsh **Bible**, was the son of John ap Harri of Pwllhalog. In the church of St Mael and St Sulien is Wales's most elaborate hooded tomb (1642). The descent into Rhuallt along the **A55** offers splendid views of the vale of **Clwyd** and **Snowdonia**.

CWM CADNANT, Isle of Anglesey
(2312 ha; 2222 inhabitants)
Constituting the area between **Beaumaris** and **Menai Bridge**, the **community** takes its name from the Cadnant **River**. It contains the villages of Llandegfan and Llansadwrn. There is a 6th-century memorial to St Saturninus in St Sadwrn's church. Treffos was one of the

180

medieval residences of the bishop of **Bangor** and the centre of an episcopal manor extending over 4180 ha. Hafoty (home in the 1530s of the constable of Beaumaris Castle), part of which may date from the 14th century, is one of the finest medieval houses in **Anglesey**. There are several standing stones in the area.

CWM EDNO AVIATION DISASTER
On 10 January 1952, a Dakota belonging to Aer Lingus took off from Northolt aerodrome, **London**, bound for Dublin. Flying over **Snowdonia**, where 60-knot winds were blowing, the aircraft was caught in violent downcurrents, which sent it into a terminal dive. It crashed in remote Cwm Edno (**Dolwyddelan**). There were no survivors among the 23 on board.

CWM GWAUN, Pembrokeshire
(3870 ha; 266 inhabitants)
Extending over the delightful **Gwaun** valley south-east of **Fishguard**, the **community** contains nothing resembling a village. The Parc y Meirw row of standing stones at Llanllawer is Wales's longest aligned row of stones. Of Cwm Gwaun's four churches, only St Brynach's, Pontfaen, is of interest; built in the 1860s, it is furnished according to the principles of the **Oxford Movement**, with a stone altar and incense burners. In Llanychaer and Llanllawer churchyards are inscribed stones (7th–9th centuries). Near the latter are the considerable remains (14th century) of a healing and cursing **well**. Cwm Gwaun is famous for celebrating the Old New Year (13 January), its *macsi* (**beer** brewing) and its tradition of reciting or singing the *pwnc* (a chanting delivery of biblical verses). Tŷ Cwrdd Bach (1974) is one of Britain's first modern turf-roofed houses.

'CWM RHONDDA' (The Rhondda Valley)
Hymn tune
Perhaps the most popular and powerful of Welsh hymn tunes, it was composed in 1907 by John Hughes (1873–1932) of **Llantwit Fardre**, near Pontypridd, and associated with the **Welsh** words: 'Wele'n sefyll rhwng y myrtwydd' ('Lo amid the myrtles standing') by **Ann Griffiths**, and the **English**: 'Guide me, O thou great Jehovah' by **William Williams** (Pantycelyn; 1717–91).

CWMAMMAN (Cwmaman), Carmarthenshire
(2745 ha; 4226 inhabitants)
Extending across the middle reaches of the Amman valley east of **Ammanford**, the **community** contains part of the western slopes of the **Black Mountain** and the villages of Glanamman and Garnant, birthplace in 1942 of the musician John Cale (*see* **Music**). From 1912 to 1974, its more densely settled area constituted the Cwmamman **Urban District**. **Coal**mining became a major industry following the arrival of the **railway** in 1842. By the late 19th century, Cwmamman's colliers and **tinplate** workers had created a remarkable example of **Welsh**-medium, working-**class** culture. The district's chief colliery, Gelliceidrim, closed in 1958. By 1985, all the Amman valley mines had gone, although the area continues to be subject to open-cast mining. The advent of small factories has mitigated, but not solved, the unemployment caused by mine closure.

CWMAVON (Cwmafan), Neath Port Talbot
(1003 ha; 5603 inhabitants)
Located immediately north of **Port Talbot**, the area was developed from 1800 onwards through **coal**mines, **iron** and **tinplate** works and, from 1841, **copper** smelting. By 1900, metalworking was moving to the coast and, with the slow decline of mining and the greening of the valley, Cwmavon became part of Port Talbot's commuter belt. Castell Bolan is a 12th-century fortified site built by the Welsh lords of **Afan**. St Michael's church (1851) was one of **John Prichard**'s earliest commissions.

CWMBACH (Cwm-bach), Rhondda Cynon Taff
(608 ha; 4283 inhabitants)
Located immediately south-east of **Aberdare**, the **community** contains the only surviving stretch of the Aberdare **Canal** (1812). In 1837, the Wayne family, owners of Gadlys **iron**works, struck the four-foot seam at Cwmbach, thus initiating the exploitation of the steam **coal** of the **Cynon valley**. Half a dozen other collieries followed in quick succession. The explosion at Lletty Shenkin Colliery in 1849, which killed 52 colliers, was the first recorded **colliery disaster** in Wales to cause more than 50 deaths. The Waynes' enterprise eventually became part of the **Powell Duffryn** empire. The first successful retail co-operative in Wales was founded at Cwmbach in 1860. In the 1960s, the village acquired an innovative **housing** project consisting of curving streets and island groups of houses. The poet **Harri Webb** spent his last years in Cwmbach.

CWMBRAN (Cwmbrân), Torfaen
(2232 ha; 41,725 inhabitants)
The town of Cwmbran lies within the **communities** of Croesyceiliog, Cwmbran Central, Cwmbran Upper, Fairwater, Llanyrafon and Pontnewydd. *See below.*

The only town established in Wales under the New Towns Act of 1946, Cwmbran was, by the opening of the 21st century, the country's sixth largest urban centre. Located on the edge of the south Wales **coal**field, it occupies fairly level land in the Eastern Valley south of **Pontypool**. Until the 1940s, the area was largely open country, although it did have an industrial tradition involving coalmining and the manufacture of **tinplate**, **iron**, wire and vitriol. Originally, the Cwmbran Development Corporation (1949) aimed at a **population** of 35,000, a figure raised to 55,000 in the late 20th century. Its plan envisaged a town centre with open spaces marking out a series of neighbourhoods – 7 initially, 12 eventually. A wholly pedestrianized centre based upon Gwent Square had been built by 1977; its walkways were roofed in 1986. Gwent Square acquired the Congress Theatre, but the proposed civic centre never materialized. Cwmbran's prospects were enhanced by the decision of **Monmouthshire County** Council in 1963 to relocate its headquarters there. In 1974, the county hall became the headquarters of the **Gwent** County Council and of the **Torfaen county borough** in 1996. Hopes that the **University of Wales** Institute of Science and Technology would also relocate to Cwmbran were dashed in the late 1970s. The Development Corporation was wound up in 1988, when Cwmbran's population was approaching 40,000.

C

The communities of Cwmbran

CROESYCEILIOG (218 ha; 5234 inhabitants)
Constituting eastern Cwmbran, Croesyceiliog was already a substantial settlement before the coming of the new town. It contains an admirably designed comprehensive school as well as some of the more visually interesting of the new town's terraces.

CWMBRAN CENTRAL (Cwmbrân Ganol)
(504 ha; 10,469 inhabitants)
Containing Old Cwmbran as well as the centre of the new town, the community's most attractive feature is Taliesin, a superb example of sheltered **housing**. The Tower, Redbrook Way – Cwmbran's 'campanile' – is an ingenious 22-storey block of flats masking the chimney of the boiler which heats the town centre. The centre at St Dials provides **police** cadet training for western **England** as well as for the whole of Wales.

CWMBRAN UPPER (Cwmbrân Uchaf)
(476 ha; 5674 inhabitants)
Constituting north-eastern Cwmbran, the community contains a scenic stretch of the Monmouthshire **Canal**, including a group of five locks. The housing scheme at Gilwern Place is particularly attractive.

FAIRWATER (523 ha; 12,393 inhabitants)
Constituting part of south-eastern Cwmbran, the community contains Wales's best example, apart from that in **Wrexham**, of the Radburn system – the segregation of traffic from pedestrians. Fairwater Square, with its pink walls, is considered by John Newman to be a 'flamboyant gesture'.

LLANYRAFON (302 ha; 3230 inhabitants)
Constituting part of south-eastern Cwmbran, the community contains the Torfaen county offices, the headquarters of the Gwent police, and a hospital built around Llanfrechfa Grange – a mid-19th-century mansion bewildering in its eclecticism.

PONTNEWYDD (209 ha; 4725 inhabitants)
Constituting northern Cwmbran, the area has a long industrial tradition dating back to the establishment of the Pontnewydd tinplate works in 1802. Tynewydd, with its white-rendered terraces (1950–2), represents the first phase of the new town's house-building.

CWMLLYNFELL, Neath Port Talbot
(932 ha; 1123 inhabitants)
The **community** is centred upon a small former **coal**mining village at the foot of the **Black Mountain**. Originally a farming community with poor transport facilities, it was not until the later 19th century that mining became the major occupation. **Welsh-language** culture has always been strong, despite the influx of workers from northern **England**. The local blend of **socialist** debate and chapel-based communal activity has produced a number of notable figures, including the actress Siân Phillips (b.1934), who spent her adolescence in Cwmllynfell.

CWMWD DEUDDWR Commote
Cwmwd Deuddwr lay west of the **Wye**; the 'two waters' (*deuddwr*) were the Wye and the Elan. As a **Mortimer** lordship, it was inherited by the dukes of **York**, thereby becoming a crown possession in 1461. Constituting the north-western part of what would be **Radnorshire**, it was roughly coterminous with the one-time civil **parish** of Llansantffraid Cwmdeuddwr.

CYBI (?6th century) Saint
Founder of a religious community within the remains of a **Roman** fort at **Holyhead** (Caergybi). The story of Cybi's friendship with **Seiriol** and their weekly meetings in the middle of **Anglesey** is recent. The medieval Life of the **saint** (which has no historical value) states that he was a native of **Cornwall**. Cybi's feast day is 5 November.

CYCLING
Male cycling clubs were first formed in Wales during the 1870s and, following the replacement of tricycles and ungainly penny-farthings by the safety bicycle in 1886, **women** also began taking to two wheels. **Road** races were commonplace from the late 1880s, by which time Welsh men's teams were participating in international tournaments. Mixed cycling clubs for both sexes were emerging by the beginning of the 20th century and, with the formation of the Welsh Cycling Association in 1934, further development ensued. The subsequent enthusiasm for cycling was reflected by the foundation, in 1973, of the Welsh Cycling Union, which administers road racing, **mountain** biking and track racing events. From **Arthur Linton**, world champion cyclist in 1895/6, to Nicole Cooke, gold medallist at the 2002 **Commonwealth Games**, Wales has produced cyclists of the highest calibre. In 2003, there were about 60 cycling clubs nationwide.

While Wales's main roads are increasingly dangerous for cyclists, there are many largely traffic-free country roads, and an expanding network of dedicated cycle routes, in both urban and rural situations. Major national cycle routes include the 334-km Lôn Geltaidd from **Chepstow** to **Fishguard**, and the 444-km Lôn Las Cymru running from **Cardiff** or Chepstow through the heart of Wales to **Holyhead**. The latter passes near **Llandrindod**, home of the National Cycle Exhibition.

CYD (lit. 'together')
Founded in 1984 to promote the **Welsh language** by bringing Welsh speakers and learners together through the medium of Welsh, CYD or Cyd – *Cyngor y Dysgwyr* (Council of Learners) – is part of the adult Welsh learning movement that burgeoned after the **Second World War**. Initiated by the poet and scholar Bobi Jones (b.1929), Cyd organizes language courses and social activities, publishes a tri-annual magazine, *Cadwyn Cyd*, and runs the Learner of the Year competition at the National **Eisteddfod**. Cyd has about 100 branches in Wales and several in other countries, but in 2007 its future appeared uncertain after its annual **Welsh Language Board** grant was withdrawn; the Board announced that the work hitherto done by Cyd would become the responsibility of new language centres.

CYFARTHFA BAND

A **brass band** formed by Robert Thompson **Crawshay** of Cyfarthfa Castle, **Merthyr Tydfil** in 1838. It was active until the early 20th century, but its most important period was *c*.1845–78. Its handwritten repertory survives, and is one of the most important manuscript collections of its type. It shows it to have been an ensemble of remarkable virtuosity – perhaps the first truly virtuoso brass band in the world.

CYFARWYDD

A storyteller in medieval Welsh society, *cyfarwydd* meaning 'one who has special skills'. Such storytellers, who would have to have prodigious memories, would entertain the court with tales like those in ***The Mabinogion***. They may also have been poets.

CYFEILIOG Commote

Constituting the north-western part of the later **Montgomeryshire**, the **commote**'s centre was at Tafolwern (**Llanbrynmair**). In 1149, **Madog ap Maredudd** granted it as an appanage to his nephew, the poet (or poets' patron) Owain ap Gruffudd (**Owain Cyfeiliog**). Owain used the commote as his territorial base in his struggle to seize **Powys**, a struggle which eventually led to its division into **Powys Wenwynwyn** and **Powys Fadog**. In the late 13th century, Cyfeiliog, like **Arwystli**, was the subject of litigation between **Llywelyn ap Gruffudd** and **Gruffudd ap Gwenwynwyn**. The post-**Acts of 'Union' hundred** of Cyfeiliog had boundaries similar to those of the medieval commote.

CYFFYLLIOG, Denbighshire
(3159 ha; 484 inhabitants)

Located west of **Ruthin**, the **community** constitutes the upper reaches of the least known of Wales's six Clywedog **rivers**. St Mary's church has a 15th-century wagon ceiling. The area has been extensively forested.

CYFNERTH AP MORGENAU (fl.1190–1230)
Jurist

A famous lawyer's son and one of the distinguished legal family, 'the tribe of Cilmyn Droetddu'. The **law**book that bears his name, Llyfr Cyfnerth (12th century), was long considered to contain the law current in south-east Wales, but is now seen as representing a version of the law more primitive than that contained in Llyfr **Blegywryd** and in Llyfr Iorwerth (*see* **Iorwerth ap Madog**).

CYFRAN

The rule of partible inheritance to land, sometimes incorrectly called gavelkind (the corresponding custom in parts of **England**). Under Welsh **law**, a free man's land was divided equally among all his sons, whether born in wedlock or not. Contrary to the belief of some medieval English kings (and some later commentators), the rule did not apply to kingship; the kingship of each Welsh kingdom was normally indivisible, although suitable provision would be made for other sons. After the death of **Owain Gwynedd** in 1170, for example, the land of **Gwynedd** was divided between his sons **Dafydd** and Rhodri and his grandsons Gruffudd and Maredudd ap Cynan, but

Nicole Cooke, Commonwealth gold medallist in 2002

Dafydd had the kingship and was therefore overlord of his brother and nephews.

The division of land between sons could lead to problems after several generations because individual shares could become too small to be economic; by the later Middle Ages, it was also often seen as an obstacle to the building up of landed estates by ambitious free tenants. Indeed, John **Wynn** of Gwydir (**Trefriw**) described *cyfran* as 'the curse of Wales', but, as he was the owner of an estate which would not have come into existence had his ancestors not abandoned the custom, the only possible comment on his condemnation is to quote the immortal words of Mandy Rice-Davies: 'He would, wouldn't he.' Many whose holdings were no longer viable sold out to their richer and more enterprising neighbours, while those who had accumulated substantial amounts of land adopted the English practice of **primogeniture**. Partible inheritance of land was abolished in Wales by the first **Act of 'Union'** (1536), but it continued to be practised widely and was one of the main causes of the virtual extinction, by the 19th century, of the class of small freeholding farmers. By the 20th century, the equal division of one's property between one's children – female as well as male – was virtually universal.

'CYFRI'R GEIFR' (Counting the goats) Folk song

A song associated particularly with the mountainous regions of **Gwynedd**, but noted in various forms all over Wales. Its origins may lie in the ritual singing of **Candlemas**, when the **wassailing** party would seek entry into the house by challenging those inside to match and develop the sequence of questions and answers beginning: 'Is there another goat?' The goat's colour changes in each verse, and the challenge is to remember the correct sequence and sing the tongue-twisting words progressively faster.

Members of Cymdeithas yr Iaith Gymraeg protesting outside Cardiff Prison in 1966 against the imprisonment of a language activist

CYLCH CATHOLIG, Y (The Catholic Circle)

A society established in the early 1940s to enable **Welsh**-speaking **Roman Catholics** to live a full spiritual life through their native language. Ventures included publications, **pilgrimage**s, youth branches and an annual presence at the National **Eisteddfod**. The Cylch's early leadership included **Saunders Lewis**, who edited the society's journal, *Efrydiau Catholig*, later *Ysgrifau Catholig*. The society ceased its activities in the 1960s but was revived in the 1980s.

CYLCH-Y-GARN, Isle of Anglesey
(2475 ha; 675 inhabitants)

Constituting the north-western corner of **Anglesey** and centred upon Mynydd y Garn, the **community** contains the villages of Llanfairynghornwy, Llanrhyddlad and Rhydwyn. St Mary's church, Llanfairynghornwy, has a 12th-century nave. Caerau and Mynachdy farmhouses have 17th-century origins. Most of the magnificent coast is owned by the **National Trust**. The community includes the Skerries (Ynysoedd y Moelrhoniaid; *see* **Islands**), where a **lighthouse** was built in 1724. It later gave way to a beacon on the isolated rock of West Mouse (Maen y Bugail). James Williams (1790–1872), rector of Llanfairynghornwy, and his wife Frances were among the pioneers of the **lifeboat** movement; the first such boat in Anglesey was stationed at Cemlyn, under their auspices, in 1828. Cemlyn, once a **port**, has been designated a nature reserve. Vivian Hewitt, the aviator who made the first flight across the Irish Sea in 1912, lived at Cemlyn. On Mynydd y Garn is a memorial to the Anglesey shipowner William Thomas, a native of Llanrhyddlad.

CYMANFA GANU (Singing meeting)

Hymn-singing festivals became a feature of **Welsh-language Nonconformist** chapels from the 1830s onwards. As with other choral movements in Wales, the *cymanfa ganu* increased in popularity with the growth of industrialized urban communities and, from the mid-19th century, with the success of the tonic sol-fa movement (*see* **Music**). The *cymanfa ganu* is essentially based on four-part hymn-singing, but its distinguishing feature is the relatively formal music-making framework in which the festival takes place. The hymns are rehearsed and directed – often by an inspirational conductor. The *cymanfa ganu* has become the favoured festival of the **North American** Welsh.

CYMDEITHAS HEDDYCHWYR CYMRU
(The Pacifists' Society of Wales)

A **Welsh-language pacifist** society set up in 1937 to bolster the activities of the energetic Peace Pledge Union established in May 1936 and increasingly active in Wales. The first president was prominent Christian Pacifist **George M. Ll. Davies** (also an executive member of the PPU) and its first secretary was **Gwynfor Evans**. It gave unstinting support to conscientious objectors during the **Second World War**, and published a series of 31 influential pamphlets, *Pamffledi Heddychwyr Cymru*.

CYMDEITHAS YR IAITH GYMRAEG
(The Welsh Language Society)

A pressure group which campaigns on behalf of the **Welsh language**. The society, normally known by its Welsh name, was founded in August 1962 during **Plaid [Genedlaethol**

Cymru's annual conference in **Pontarddulais**. Its formation followed an impassioned radio lecture by **Saunders Lewis** on the BBC's Welsh service (*see* **Broadcasting**) on 13 February 1962. The lecture, *Tynged yr Iaith* (The fate of the language), was an appeal to Plaid Cymru members in the Welsh-speaking districts to abandon what he considered to be their hitherto futile electoral campaigning in order to concentrate on a campaign 'to make it impossible for the business of local and central **government** to continue without using Welsh'. Lewis predicted the death of Welsh unless a determined campaign was fought to restore the language. A small group of young Plaid Cymru supporters consequently decided to establish a language movement – but one independent of the party.

The society's earlier campaigns focused on demanding official forms in Welsh, such as court summonses, **road** tax documents and birth certificates. These campaigns drew attention to the secondary public status of Welsh and to its treatment by officialdom as a second-class language. Over the years, the society's interests have broadened to include radio and television, **education**, **housing** and planning. Initially, the emphasis was chiefly on securing language rights for Welsh speakers, but since the 1970s increasing emphasis has been placed on obtaining an institutional framework to support the language and on creating the conditions necessary for the survival of Welsh-speaking communities.

The society has frequently been associated with direct action, believing that the methods it employs should reflect the seriousness of the crisis facing the language. Its choice of methods mirrors the international popularity of protest as a political instrument; many of its leaders, particularly during the 1960s, were inspired by Martin Luther King's leadership of the black civil rights movement in America. Consequently, the society has placed great emphasis on non-violent methods, and has held protest marches, organized sit-ins, disrupted court cases, refused to pay taxes and licences, and caused damage to public property. For their part in the society's campaigns, thousands of supporters have been hauled before the courts, and nearly 200 members have been imprisoned. Despite being a comparatively small movement, with no more than 2000 members at any time, the society has attracted wide support for its cause.

Although constantly berated by the authorities, the society has played a leading role in the achievement of many important goals. These include the provision of a vast range of bilingual forms and documents, the establishment of bilingual road-signs, a significant increase in bilingual education, a Welsh-medium radio service and television channel (*see* **S4C**), greater use of Welsh in the commercial and public domain, recognition for Welsh in land-use planning policy, and the **Welsh Language Acts** of 1967 and 1993. Undeniably, the public status of Welsh and the official support it receives have increased substantially since 1962.

CYMERAU, Battle of

Fought probably near **Llandeilo** on 2 June 1257, the battle resulted from **Llywelyn ap Gruffudd**'s campaign to establish his authority throughout Wales. His allies, Maredudd ap **Rhys Gryg** and Maredudd ab Owain, overwhelmed an English force acting in support of the dispossessed lord of **Dinefwr**, Rhys Fychan, whose sudden change of allegiance during the fighting proved crucial. Earlier in the day, the English forces had lost much of their supplies at an engagement known as the battle of Coed Llathen (**Llangathen**).

CYMHORTHA

Originally a kind of mutual help among neighbours, it developed into payments that Welsh princes could claim under exceptional circumstances. By the 15th century, it had deteriorated into a means of exacting money illegally by **march**er-lords for their private gain. Legislation in 1534 was intended to abolish the practice, which had contributed to the **law**lessness of the period, especially in the March. The custom survived, purged of its oppressive characteristics, and linked with 'bid ale' to raise money for those who had fallen on hard times. The term also came to mean help during the harvest and other busy periods.

CYMMER COLLIERY DISASTER
Porth, Rhondda

On 15 July 1856, 114 miners were killed in an explosion at this colliery operated by George Insole & Son, the first, but not the last, time that more than 100 people would be killed in a mining disaster in Wales. Managerial shortcomings undoubtedly contributed to the disaster, but its immediate cause was the use of an open safety lamp in the presence of gas.

CYMMRODORION, The Honourable Society of

Founded by Richard Morris (*see* **Morris Brothers**) and others in **London** in 1751, the Cymmrodorion (lit. 'Earliest natives') aspired to promote the literary and philanthropic interests of the London Welsh. Despite the enthusiasm of Richard and his brother Lewis Morris, the society was perceived by many as too ambitious and highbrow, and its early aspirations were not fulfilled. Its first phase lasted until 1787.

Through the work of figures such as **Walter Davies**, W. J. Rees (1772–1855) of Cascob (**Whitton**), and John Jenkins (Ifor Ceri; 1770–1829) of **Kerry** (*see Hen Bersoniaid Llengar, Yr*), the society was resurrected in 1820 to encourage provincial *eisteddfodau* in Wales. Disputes arose between the Cymmrodorion in London and local societies in Wales over money matters and the Anglicizing influence of the London Welsh. Although the society did promote learning and **literature** by donating prizes for poetry and essays, there was more dissension than co-operation and the Cymmrodorion's second phase came to an end in 1843.

In 1873, the society embarked on its third phase – which continues to the present day – when it was restored through the efforts of patriots such as **Hugh Owen** (1804–81) and John Griffith (Y Gohebydd; 1821–77). It concentrated its attention on **education** and social aspects and became the means of establishing the National Eisteddfod as an annual event. It supported the **Welsh Intermediate Education Act (1889)**, encouraged the founding of the **University of Wales** (1893) and recommended increased use of the **Welsh language** in schools. Its historical journal *Y Cymmrodor* was published from 1878 to 1951, and its *Transactions* from 1892–3 to the present day.

The society is responsible for *The Dictionary of Welsh Biography* and its supplements.

CYMREIGYDDION SOCIETY, The

The most democratic in spirit of the **London** Welsh societies. It was established in 1794 with the declared aim of maintaining 'the **Welsh language** pure and undefiled ... by holding debate on substantial and moral topics'; among its founding members were Jac Glan-y-gors (**John Jones**; 1766–1821) and **Thomas Roberts** (Llwyn'rhudol; 1765/6–1841). Like the **Cymmrodorion** and **Gwyneddigion**, the Cymreigyddion (lit. 'persons cultivating Welsh') met in London taverns and, not surprisingly, as the society's own records state, 'cheerfulness would keep breaking in' during its discussions. By the mid-19th century, the conviviality of the early years had been dampened by Victorian respectability, and the society's meetings ceased in 1855. However, in conscious imitation of the original Cymreigyddion, a number of literary societies bearing the same name were established throughout Wales during the 19th century, the most prominent being Cymreigyddion y Fenni (*see* **Abergavenny**, **Augusta Hall** and **Thomas Price (Carnhuanawc)**).

CYMRU FYDD

Cymru Fydd, although it means 'the Wales that will be', is often referred to in **English** as 'Young Wales', thus associating it with other patriotic movements such as Young **Ireland** and Young Italy. The first Cymru Fydd society was formed in **London** in 1886; in 1891, a branch was established in **Barry**, from which the movement spread throughout Wales. It was widely supported in the popular press (*see* **Newspapers**), particularly by **Thomas Gee**.

The movement's bilingual monthly journal *Cymru Fydd* was launched in January 1888. Intended to deepen a sense of national and historical awareness among the Welsh people, it advocated the **disestablishment of the Church of England in Wales**, land and **education**al reform and Welsh **Home Rule**. Although initially it was in the main a cultural organization, repeated efforts were made to transform Cymru Fydd into a national Welsh political organization. In 1888, the South Wales **Liberal** Federation, supported by **D. A. Thomas**, sought to extend the Welsh National Liberal Council to include representatives of Cymru Fydd societies and other Welsh political groups, the object being to form an independent Welsh Party in the House of Commons. Doubts harboured by northern Liberals prevented the creation of such a grouping. **T. E. Ellis**, MP for **Merioneth**, developed a vision of a devolved Wales and communicated it powerfully in a key speech at **Bala** in 1890. Ellis attempted to define Welsh identity in relation to the distinctiveness of the history, language and culture of Wales, laying particular emphasis on the supposed co-operative nature of Welsh notions of community and on the need for a truly national form of Welsh political representation. In the early 1890s, **David Lloyd George** emerged as one of Cymru Fydd's most prominent figures, but in 1895, when the prospect of a successful Welsh Disestablishment Bill offered an opportunity to stress the need for Wales to be treated as a separate national polity, public and parliamentary divisions between David Lloyd George and D. A. Thomas over the distribution of Church property accentuated a rift between north and south, and, indeed, between west and east.

The final conflict took place at the **Newport** conference of the South Wales Liberal Federation in January 1896. **Cardiff** alderman Robert Bird rebuffed Lloyd George's appeal for unity, stating that, 'There are, from **Swansea** to Newport, thousands of Englishmen, as true Liberals as yourselves ... who will never submit to the domination of Welsh ideas.' Lloyd George later noted that representatives of only 7 of the 34 Welsh constituencies were present at the meeting, and that the conference was 'packed with Newport Englishmen'. He claimed, however, that Cymru Fydd had made serious inroads into the southern industrial valleys. 'Wales is with us,' he insisted, 'the **Rhondda** proved that.' But the wealthier leaders of Welsh Liberalism were clearly not 'with' the Cymru Fydd version of Welsh nationality, and political attention quickly turned to other issues. The failure of Cymru Fydd signalled the beginning of the long search for a more sophisticated political programme to unify and represent a diverse and increasingly cosmopolitan nation.

CYMRU: YN HANESYDDOL, PARTHEDEGOL A BYWGRAPHYDDOL (*Wales: Historical, Topographical and Biographical*; 1871–5)

The first **Welsh-language** encyclopaedia and, until 2007, the only one to concentrate on Wales, it was published in 2 volumes – of 22 parts, costing 2 shillings each – by Blackie of Glasgow, between 1871 and 1875. Its editor was Meudwy Môn (Owen Jones; 1806–89), with a large number of Welsh **Nonconformist** ministers as contributors. It contains entries on the main events in the nation's history, its **counties** and towns, as well as biographies. The work contains 13 colour **maps** and 9 illustrated plates.

CYMRY The name

Cymry is the **Welsh** word for the Welsh, while *Cymru* is the word for the country of Wales (*see* **Wales, The name**); the two spellings became differentiated from *c*.16th century onwards. The word originally used for themselves by the Welsh was *Brython*, from their residence in **Britain**, but from the **Anglo-Saxon** settlement onwards they appear gradually to have adopted the word *Cymry*, which is also found in the words Cumbria and Cumberland. *Cymry* first appears in Welsh poetry in the 7th century, and derives from a Brythonic word *combrogos* (plural *combrogi*), meaning fellow countryman.

CYMUNED (Community)

A national pressure group, formed in 2001, to defend traditional **Welsh**-speaking communities from socio-economic forces undermining and threatening to destroy them – and, by extension, the Welsh language. Cymuned campaigns for measures to reverse economic decline in order to stem the exodus of the indigenous **population** and for reforms in **housing** policy incorporating rules such as those in force in the English Lake District and in the Channel Islands, to prevent high levels of inward migration from doing permanent damage to local ways of life. With headquarters in **Pwllheli** and branches throughout Wales, in 2007 it had nearly 2000 members.

CYMYDMAEN Commote

One of the three **commotes** of the *cantref* of **Llŷn**, Cymydmaen consisted of the westernmost part of tlhe Llŷn peninsula and was roughly coterminous with the present communities of **Aberdaron**, **Botwnnog** and **Tudweiliog**. It was named after the yellow rock (*maen melyn*) that forms part of the promontory which faces Bardsey (*see* **Islands**). Its court was probably at Maerdref, which is now a farmhouse near Llandegwning (Botwnnog). In 1252, the commote came into the possession of **Dafydd ap Gruffudd**.

CYNDDELW BRYDYDD MAWR (fl.1155–95) Poet

Among the work of this most prominent of the **Poets of the Princes** are praise poems to some 18 patrons from various parts of Wales, as well as religious and love poetry and humorous verse. Apparently a native of **Powys**, he fought in his youth for **Madog ap Maredudd** of Powys, lamenting the deaths of his fellow warriors and, eventually, giving voice to their grief at the loss of both their prince and his heir, Llywelyn, in 1160. Soon afterwards, Cynddelw moved to **Gwynedd** to seek the patronage of **Owain Gwynedd**. The magnificent elegy composed at the death of Owain in 1170 probably represents the pinnacle of his poetic career. In his old age, he turned for support to the Lord Rhys (**Rhys ap Gruffudd**; d.1197), ruler of **Deheubarth**, and produced for him some splendid poems of reconciliation. It was probably Cynddelw's stature that earned him the title *Prydydd Mawr* (Great Poet), but there is no doubt that before the end of his career the epithet had gained additional significance.

CYNDDYLAN (fl. early 7th century)
Ruler of Powys

Cynddylan defended his kingdom against both the Northumbrians and the **Mercia**ns during the 7th century. Although preserved in late manuscripts only, an elegy to him in *awdl* metre is thought to be genuine. However, there is no historical basis for the portrait of him presented in *Canu Heledd*, a cycle of *englynion* from the 9th or 10th centuries.

CYNFEIRDD, Y (The early poets)

A modern term used for the poets who sang in **Welsh** between the 6th and the 11th centuries; the late medieval term for their poetry was *Yr Hengerdd* (the old poetry). Five of the earliest known *Cynfeirdd*, Talhaearn, **Aneirin**, **Taliesin**, Blwchfardd and Cian, are listed in *Historia Brittonum* and placed in the second half of the 6th century. Poetry is ascribed to only two of these, Aneirin and Taliesin, in manuscripts of a much later date. The work of the others has been lost along with that of Afan Ferddig, Arofan, Dygynnelw and Meigan. A large body of anonymous poetry has been preserved, however, such as the elegy to **Cynddylan** and the eulogy of **Cadwallon ap Cadfan** from the 7th century, the 9th-century 'Edmyg Dinbych' (Praise of **Tenby**), the 10th-century 'Armes Prydein' (The **Prophecy** of **Britain**) and many other narrative, religious and vaticinatory poems which cannot be dated with certainty.

CYNGHANEDD

In the authoritative *Princeton Encyclopedia of Poetry and Poetics* (1993), *cynghanedd* (harmony) is described as 'the most sophisticated system of poetic sound-patterning practised in any poetry in the world'. Based on the complex alliterative patterns and internal rhymes found in the poetry of the *Cynfeirdd* and the **Poets of the Princes**, *cynghanedd* was formalized during the 14th century and is an integral part of the traditional Welsh 24 metres – the most common being the *cywydd* and *englyn* – practised by the **Poets of the Gentry**.

There are four main types of cynghanedd, exemplified below by quotations from poems in both **Welsh** and **English** – although *cynghanedd* is rarely attempted in the latter. In *cynghanedd groes* (cross *cynghanedd*) the consonants in the first part of the line are repeated in the same order in the second part:

> Bara a chaws, / bir a chig (**Goronwy Owen**)

> You silly blue-eyed / whistle-blower (Twm Morys)

Cynghanedd draws (traversing *cynghanedd*) is similar, but at the beginning of the second part there may be one or more unanswered consonants.

> Difyr / yw gwylio defaid (Edward Huws)

> We talked / (reserved) untactile (Emyr Lewis)

In *cynghanedd lusg* (trailing *cynghanedd*) the rhyme at the end of the first part of the line is repeated in the accented penultimate syllable of a polysyllabic word at the end:

> Bedwyr yn drist / a distaw (**T Gwynn Jones**)

> One brief arc / into darkness (Emyr Lewis)

Cynghanedd sain (sonorous *cynghanedd*) contains both rhyme and alliteration and is divided into three parts, with parts one and two rhyming, parts two and three alliterating, and obeying similar rules to *cynghanedd groes* and *cynghanedd draws*:

> Lle bu'r Brython, / Saeson / sydd (anon., 15th century)

> One fleeting / cementing / smile (Emyr Lewis)

The **eisteddfod** movement of the 18th and 19th centuries led to a renewed interest in *cynghanedd*, and in modern-day Wales it is still meticulously employed by a host of poets, especially in poems submitted to the chair competition at the National Eisteddfod (*see* **awdl**). The founding, in 1976, of the Cymdeithas Gerdd Dafod was accompanied by the launching of the society's magazine, *Barddas*, which has enjoyed conspicuous success under the editorship of the poet and prolific critic Alan Llwyd (b.1948).

CYNLLAITH Commote

A **commote** of **Powys Fadog**, it became in 1284 part of the **march**er-lordship of **Chirk and Chirkland**. The senior branch of the house of Powys Fadog retained rights over its eastern part – essentially the **parish** of **Llansilin**. Known as Cynllaith Owain, it was inherited by **Owain Glyndŵr**; it included Sycharth, his chief residence.

CYNON VALLEY (Cwm Cynon)
Constituency and one-time district

Following local **government** reorganization in 1974, Cynon Valley was established as a district of the **county** of **Mid Glamorgan**. It consisted of what had been the **urban districts** of **Aberdare** and **Mountain Ash** and part of the **rural district** of **Neath** in **Glamorgan** and part of the rural district of Vaynor and Penderyn in **Breconshire**. In 1996, the district, together with that of **Rhondda** and most of that of **Taff-Ely**, became the **borough** and county of **Rhondda Cynon Taff**. Cynon Valley is the name of what used to be known as the constituency of Aberdare.

CYNWYD, Denbighshire (3019 ha; 528 inhabitants)

Located immediately south of **Corwen**, the **community** extends from the **Dee** valley to the **Berwyn** range at Moel Fferna (650 m). There are attractive **waterfalls** on Afon Tryston. The area's outstanding feature is All Saints, Llangar, which, unlike the vast majority of Wales's country churches, was left untouched by Victorian restorers. It retains the liturgical arrangements that predated the influence of the **Oxford Movement** – those emphasizing the pulpit rather than the altar. The walls are covered with **paintings**, some dating from the 14th century. The huge skeleton on the north wall is particularly menacing. All Saints escaped the restorers because it was abandoned when St John's church, built 2 km away in the more populous village of Cynwyd, was consecrated in 1856. Following major conservation work, All Saints came into the care of **Cadw**. The poet and translator Edward Samuel (1674–1748) was rector of Llangar from 1721 to 1748. In 2001, 77.04% of Cynwyd's inhabitants, had some knowledge of **Welsh** – the highest percentage for a **Denbighshire** community; however, its percentage of those wholly fluent in the language (60.51%) was exceeded by that for **Gwyddelwern** (61.77%). Ifor Williams's trailer factory is the largest employer in **Edeirnion**.

CYNWYL ELFED, Carmarthenshire
(5957 ha; 953 inhabitants)

Extending over a wide stretch of upland north-west of **Carmarthen**, the **community** contains the villages of Cynwyl Elfed and Cwmduad. St Cynwyl's church contains 14th-century elements and a barrel roof. The area has yielded **Roman** relics, among them silver artefacts and a small statue of the goddess Diana. Y Gangell was the birthplace of the poet **Howell Elvet Lewis** (Elfed; 1860–1953); the house contains a small exhibition to his memory.

CYNWYL GAEO, Carmarthenshire
(10,844 ha; 920 inhabitants)

Located north-west of **Llandovery** and extending to the **Carmarthenshire–Ceredigion** border, the **community** contains the villages of Caio, Crugybar, Cwrt-y-cadno, Ffarmers and Pumsaint. It extends over the upper reaches of the Cothi valley, and constitutes the core of the **commote** of **Caeo**. **Gold** mining at Pumsaint may have begun in the **Iron Age**, and continued intermittently until the mine's closure in 1938. Evidence of the workings of the **Romans** and of their 11.5-km system of leats and aqueducts survive. The mine was protected by a fort, the site of which is bisected by the A482.

St Cynwyl's church has a massive 13th-century tower and a 15th-century nave with aisles. Dolaucothi mansion, partly designed by **John Nash**, was demolished in 1952. It was the home of John Johnes, who was murdered by his butler in 1876. John Harries (d.1839) of Cwrt-y-Cadno and his son Henry (d.1862) claimed to be able to prophesy, counteract spells, call upon spirits and discover thieves; they attracted clients from all over Wales (*see* **Witches and Dynion Hysbys**). There are attractive chapels at Cwrt-y-cadno (1741, 1846) and Crugybar (1765, 1837); Crugybar gave its name to a **hymn** tune.

CYTÛN (Of one accord)

Cytûn: Churches Together in Wales was formed in 1990 to facilitate ecumenical partnerships between the country's main Christian churches. With the **Roman Catholic** Church a full member of the body, it took over from the Council of Churches in Wales, which had been established in 1956 to co-ordinate the activities of Wales's Protestant denominations.

CYWYDD

In the bardic grammars of the Middle Ages, *cywydd* was originally a generic term for a group of poetic metres, but it eventually came usually to refer to the *cywydd deuair hirion* (lit. '*cywydd* with two long lines') which was first popularized in the poetry of **Dafydd ap Gwilym** during the 14th century. A sequence of rhyming couplets, it has no prescribed length. The lines consist of seven syllables, and the end-rhymes in each couplet are formed with the accentuation alternating between the lines' final and penultimate syllables; the *cywydd* also requires *cynghanedd*. Although quintessentially a **Welsh** form, the *cywydd*'s features are demonstrated below by an extract from Emyr Lewis' 'A Once-in-a-lifetime, Never-to-be-repeated Cywydd in English following a chance meeting with the late Allen Ginsberg':

> We talked poetic tactics,
> of form, of the way we fix
> in Welsh, the truculent words
> in crazy little crosswords,
> and wrap them in jagged rhyme,
> our hectic bardic ragtime.

The *cywydd* became the main medium of the **Poets of the Gentry**, and it remains popular among Welsh poets at the beginning of the 21st century.

Daffodils at West Cross, Mumbles, Swansea

DAFFODIL, The

With the **leek** and the **Red Dragon**, the daffodil is a prominent national symbol of Wales. There is evidence of the leek's association with **St David**'s Day from as early as the 16th century; but the daffodil did not become popular until the 19th century, when there were suggestions that it should replace the leek as the emblem of Wales. It was argued that there had been confusion between the **Welsh** for leek (*cenhinen*) and the Welsh for daffodil (*cenhinen Bedr*, Peter's leek), and that the latter, rather than an odorous vegetable, was the emblem intended. Debate on the subject during the early 20th century led to a report in 1916 that found firmly in favour of the leek, which appears on Welsh pound coins.

David Lloyd George, however, appears to have encouraged the claims of the daffodil, which was preferred to the leek at the investiture of the **Prince of Wales** in 1911. The daffodil is now widely worn on St David's Day, and has been used to represent Wales on postage stamps. It appears in a number of coats of arms granted to Welsh people during the 20th century. The **Tenby** daffodil (*see* **Plants**), with its bright yellow petals, is much more attractive than the paler, common wild daffodil.

DAFYDD AB EDMWND (fl.1450–97) Poet

A native of **Hanmer** in **Maelor Saesneg**, Dafydd won the silver chair awarded to the best poet at the **Carmarthen Eisteddfod** in the 1450s. There, he revised the 24 strict bardic metres (*see* **Literature**). This revision, the last of its kind, rendered the poetic art more difficult. He wrote mainly love poems, but his most notable poem was an elegy to Siôn Eos, a **harp**er from **Chirk**land sentenced to death for an accidental killing (*see* **Executions**). Largely English by descent, Dafydd was related to the Hanmers, the family of the wife of **Owain Glyndŵr**.

DAFYDD AB OWAIN GWYNEDD (d.1203)
King of Gwynedd

The son of **Owain Gwynedd**'s marriage to his cousin Cristin. After Owain's death in 1170, he won the kingship, but was obliged to share power with his brother Rhodri. Driven out by his nephew **Llywelyn ap Iorwerth** in 1197, he died in exile in **England**.

DAFYDD AP GRUFFUDD (d.1283) Prince

The third son of **Gruffudd ap Llywelyn ap Iorwerth**, he received the **commote** of **Cymydmaen** in **Llŷn** as his share of the inheritance in 1252. He supported his brother Owain against their brother **Llywelyn ap Gruffudd**; but they were defeated at **Bryn Derwin** and Llywelyn became sole ruler of **Gwynedd** Uwch **Conwy**. He later took part in Llywelyn's reconquest of the **Perfeddwlad**, two *cantrefi* of which, **Rhufoniog** and **Dyffryn Clwyd**, were granted to him.

In 1263, however, he made peace with Henry III and the brothers were not reconciled until 1269. In 1271, Dafydd supported Llywelyn's attack on **Caerphilly** Castle, an incident that marked the high point of Llywelyn's power, but relations subsequently deteriorated. In 1274, Dafydd and **Gruffudd ap Gwenwynwyn** of **Powys** plotted unsuccessfully to assassinate Llywelyn and fled to **England**, where Edward I granted them asylum. The king was encouraged by Dafydd to argue that, according to Welsh **law**, Llywelyn's rights were no greater than those of his brothers, thus challenging the provisions of the **Treaty of Montgomery**.

John Speed described Dafydd as 'the chiefest firebrand in this fatall combustion', which was to lead to the downfall of the house of Gwynedd. Dafydd served with the king's army in the war of 1276–7, but, after the **Treaty of Aberconwy** in 1277, he and other Welsh rulers came under increasing pressure from insensitive royal officials. On 21 March 1282, Dafydd attacked **Hawarden** Castle and, following Llywelyn's death at **Cilmery**, succeeded him as prince. He was captured in June 1283 and on 3 October 1283 was executed with great barbarity at Shrewsbury (*see* **Executions**). He had married Elizabeth Ferrers, a daughter of the earl of Derby; their two sons died in captivity, while their daughters spent the rest of their days as nuns.

DAFYDD AP GWILYM (fl.1315/20–1350/70) Poet

Although the greatest of medieval **Welsh** poets in the eyes of most critics, and certainly the most versatile, no contemporary historical records of Dafydd ap Gwilym appear to have survived. The few historical references in his poetry suggest that he was active around the middle of the 14th century. He belonged to a well-born family from **Cemais**, **Dyfed**, although the poet himself may have been born at Brogynin (**Trefeurig**), then in the **parish** of **Llanbadarn Fawr**. His was an oral art, although it may be that an autograph copy of one of his poems survives in the **Hendregadredd Manuscript**. His poetry has been preserved in manuscripts dating from the 14th to the 18th century, and over 500 poems are attributed to him. **Thomas Parry** included some 150 poems in his magisterial edition of Dafydd's work (1952). However, the question of the authorship of many poems attributed to him remain a matter for debate.

Dafydd was the foremost of the first generation of poets to compose in the *cywydd* metre, but his work also includes examples of almost every genre of poetry known from medieval Wales. He composed *awdlau* and *englynion* in the manner of the **Poets of the Princes**, and *cywyddau* on a range of themes, including nature, **religion** and, above all, love (especially addresses to the unobtainable Dyddgu and the intermittently attainable Morfudd). His poems to his patron Ifor ap Llywelyn (fl.1340–60) – known as Ifor Hael ('Ifor the Generous') – of Basaleg (*see* **Graig**), near **Newport**, broke new ground by combining the techniques of praise poetry with those of love poetry.

Many similarities exist between Dafydd's works and contemporary medieval poetry from **England** and mainland Europe, but identifying the Welshman's sources proves problematic. Contrary to the usual practice of poets like the troubadours of southern France, Dafydd uses the first person to relate his – frequently comic – tales of misfortunes in love. Despite the lively personality at work in the poems, they should not be read as autobiography. Dafydd's fruitful and playful imagination is manifest in his use of the convention of the *llatai*, or love messenger, which is usually an animal, a **bird** or even the wind.

Dafydd's originality was obvious to his contemporaries, as the poet Gruffudd Gryg (fl.1357–70) notes in a famous bardic contention with Dafydd. Deploring Dafydd's emotional exaggerations, Gruffudd declares that King **Arthur** himself would have been long dead had his heart suffered the spear wounds that Dafydd claims daily afflict him. In a famous rebuff, Dafydd defends the use of his imagination by saying that *gwawd* (traditional praise poetry) is no more noble than his '*geuwawd o gywydd*' (*cywydd* of false praise, namely his love poetry).

The work of Dafydd ap Gwilym, which brought Welsh poetry into the European mainstream, retains its vigour and vibrancy to this day, as does the relevance of his favourite themes. Such has been his popularity down the centuries that two places – **Talyllychau** and Strata Florida (**Ystrad Fflur**) – contend for the honour of being his burial place.

DAFYDD AP LLYWELYN (*c.*1215–46) Prince

The son of **Llywelyn ap Iorwerth** and **Joan**. In the 1220s, his father endeavoured to ensure that the English crown, the papacy and the other Welsh rulers would accept Dafydd as his heir, rather than his elder son **Gruffudd ap Llywelyn**. Following Llywelyn's stroke in 1237, Dafydd seems to have become the effective ruler of **Gwynedd**. A year later, the other Welsh rulers were summoned to do homage to him at Strata Florida (**Ystrad Fflur**), probably to mark his formal investiture as prince; but this was forbidden by his uncle, Henry III. On Llywelyn's death in 1240, Dafydd succeeded him; but at Gloucester, a month later, he was forced to accept a treaty which reserved the homage of every Welsh ruler to the crown and obliged him to surrender his father's territorial gains. He tried to procrastinate, but in 1241 had to agree to hand over his brother Gruffudd, who had been imprisoned by Dafydd since 1239.

Gruffudd's death in 1244 made it possible for Dafydd to go to war; and his attempt in the same year to become a papal vassal was a declaration of independence. However, the prince's health was never robust and he died early in 1246. His marriage to Isabella de **Breos** was childless.

DAFYDD BENFRAS (fl.1220–60) Poet

As the most prominent poet in **Gwynedd** in the first half of the 13th century, he appears to have succeeded **Llywarch ap Llywelyn** (Prydydd y Moch) as court poet to **Llywelyn ap Iorwerth**. His poems reflect the troubled history of the princes of Gwynedd in this period. He sang a series of four emotional, but masterly, elegies at the deaths of Llywelyn and his sons during the calamitous decade of 1240–50. However, the pinnacle of his career was his joyful *awdl* celebrating the supremacy (*c*.1260) of **Llywelyn ap Gruffudd**. If Dafydd is indeed the subject of the elegy by his successor, **Bleddyn Fardd**, he was killed in battle in **Deheubarth** and buried at **Llangadog**.

DAFYDD GAM (Dafydd ap Llywelyn ap Hywel Fychan) (d.1415) Soldier

Dafydd belonged to one of the leading families in the **lordship of Brecon**. Loyal to Henry IV throughout the **Glyndŵr Revolt**, he was regarded as one of **Owain Glyndŵr**'s leading Welsh opponents, although the story that he attempted to assassinate Owain at **Machynlleth** in 1404 is apocryphal. He was captured and ransomed in 1412.

In 1415, he fought at Agincourt and was killed there, although he was not, as was traditionally believed, knighted on the battlefield. His daughter, Gwladys, was the mother of William **Herbert** (d.1469), earl of Pembroke, and ancestor of the **Somerset family**, dukes of Beaufort, and of the **Stuart family**, marquesses of Bute.

DAFYDD NANMOR (fl.1450–90) Poet

Dafydd hailed from Nanmor Deudraeth (**Beddgelert**), **Rhys Goch Eryri** probably being his bardic teacher. As a young man, he addressed love poems to the married Gwen o'r Ddôl. Because of this, he was exiled from **Gwynedd** following his conviction by a jury. He afterwards obtained the patronage of the Tywyn family of **Y Ferwig**, **Cardiganshire**. His 10 extant poems to them constitute a notable body of poetry. Among his other poems are those evoking the golden hair of Llio Rhydderch and an elegy to a girl from Gwynedd Is **Conwy**. He also composed learned religious poems.

'DAFYDD Y GARREG WEN'
(Dafydd of the White Rock) Melody

This popular tune, which first appeared in **Edward Jones**'s *Musical and Poetical Relicks of the Welsh Bards* (1784), has been attributed to the **harp**ist Dafydd Owen (1710–39 or 1720–49) of Y Garreg Wen (**Porthmadog**). Reputedly, he played it on his deathbed, but there is no certainty that he composed it. The tunes 'Codiad yr ehedydd' and 'Roslin Castle' are also attributed (undoubtedly wrongly) to him.

DAGGAR, George (1879–1950)
Trade unionist and MP

Born in **Cwmbran**, he began working underground at only 12 years of age. In 1911, he attended the **Central Labour College** and in 1921, he became a miners' agent and a member of the executive council of the **South Wales Miners' Federation**. As MP for **Abertillery** from 1929 until his death, he was unopposed in 1931 and 1935, and in 1945 and 1950 his percentage of the vote (86.6% and 87.1%) was the highest in **Britain**. Of all the Welsh MPs of the 20th century, he was perhaps the most tireless in his concern for his constituents.

DAHL, Roald (1916–90) Author

Born and brought up in **Cardiff**, Dahl was the son of Norwegian parents, his father being a **ships**' chandler in Cardiff. He was the author of many hugely popular books for children, such as *James and the Giant Peach* (1961) and *Charlie and the Chocolate Factory* (1964), which subsequently became a **film**. The element of cruelty and the grotesque in his books that offends certain adults is, often, precisely that which appeals to young readers. He described his childhood in his book *Boy* (1984).

Roald Dahl

DALE, Pembrokeshire (839 ha; 192 inhabitants)
Constituting the peninsula that juts out on the northern side of the opening of the **Milford Haven Waterway**, the **community** includes the **island** of Skokholm. Medieval documents refer to the place as Villa de Vale, and also le Dale – the later from the Old **English** *dæl* or the Old Norse *dalr*. There is a large **Iron Age** fort at Dale Point. Dale Castle was the home of the de Vale family. Apart for its 15th-century tower, St James's church was rebuilt in 1761. On 7 August 1485, Henry **Tudor** launched his successful attempt to seize the English throne at Mill Bay, an episode commemorated in a tapestry in Dale village hall. The area's vulnerability caused Henry VIII *c.*1540 to commission a fort at West Bunkhouse Point; the site was refortified in the 1850s (*see* **Palmerston's Follies**). The same decade saw the building of Dale Fort, which is now a field centre. From the 16th to the 18th century, Dale was a busy **port** with **smuggling** connections. It had 18 inns and a brewery.

Although much shrunk, the village enjoys prosperity as the centre of a thriving **sailing** club. The **lighthouse** at St Ann's Head was built in 1844. Dale Camp, a large **Second World War** complex, lies derelict on the community's boundary.

DANCE

While hundreds of thousands of people in Wales participate in ballroom dancing, disco dancing, tap dancing, line dancing and aerobics, the dance forms that have deep roots in Welsh tradition are folk dancing and clog dancing. In addition, community-based initiatives have led to an appreciation of contemporary dance. Wales does not have a national ballet company, for until recently there was no

A step dancer from Pontypridd performing at Llangollen International Musical Eisteddfod, July 2001

tradition within Wales from which such a company might emerge and promising young dancers have had to go outside Wales for their professional training. In 1999, however, **Swansea**'s Grand Theatre offered a home to Ballet Russe, a group of Russian dancers which has begun to welcome Welsh trainee ballerinas into its ranks. At an amateur level, there are many thousands of young people who enjoy learning ballet to a high standard.

Folk dancing

Although the earliest written record of dancing in Wales is a 12th-century account by **Giraldus Cambrensis** of a curative festival in St Elenud's churchyard near **Brecon**, dance had almost certainly occupied a significant social role from much earlier times. Further references to dance in Welsh **literature** from the 13th century onwards confirm its abiding presence, both among the common folk – who gathered for open-air events – and the upper classes who frequented indoor balls. Country dancing was among the highlights of seasonal festivities, such as May Day (**Calan Mai**) and Midsummer. These, along with *mabsantau* – held in honour of the **parish**'s patron **saint** – provided an opportunity to join in a communal celebration centred upon feasting and revelry. The attendant boisterousness and drunkenness eventually lead to their abandonment. Nonetheless, well into the 18th century, folk dance enjoyed a secure existence in an agricultural society revolving around the seasons and their related rituals.

By the 19th century, attitudes towards folk customs – dance included – began to change. That was in part because of the urbanization resulting from the **Industrial Revolution**, and the advent of the **railways**, which enabled people to experience new leisure activities further afield. Traditionally, however, the decline in folk customs has been attributed to the influence of **Nonconformists**, who described 'worthless' physical diversions as satanic, and who deemed mixed dancing, with its bodily closeness between partners, to be particularly corrupt. Small wonder, therefore, that dancing topped a list of 12 sins compiled by Rhys Prydderch in *Gemmeu Doethineb* (Gems of Wisdom; 1714) – ahead of such depravities as usury and marrying children in their infancy.

With the exception of clog dancing and some morris dancing in the north-east area, dancing had virtually vanished by the early 20th century. There were similar developments in **England**, a fact that inspired a group of concerned individuals, led by Cecil Sharp (founder in 1911 of the English Folk Dance Society), to collect the orally transmitted dances and set them down on paper. In Wales, comparable work was undertaken by Lois Blake (1890–1974), an **English**woman who settled in **Llangwm** (**Conwy**, but in **Denbighshire** until 1974) in the 1930s. Almost single-handedly, she rescued the remaining fragments of a once vigorous tradition and published, in collaboration with the musician and author **W. S. Gwynn Williams**, numerous instructive pamphlets containing both steps and **music**. Long-forgotten dances, such as 'Lord of Caernarvon's Jig' (first published in John Playford's *The Dancing Master* in 1652), the Llangadfan set (transcribed by **William Jones** (1726–95) in 1790) and the '**Llanover** Reel' (popular at Llanover Court until the late 19th century), were rediscovered.

Contemporary dance in Wales: the Diversions Dance Company's *Up Close and Personal* (2006)

By the time of the foundation of the Welsh Folk Dance Society (WFDS) in 1949, considerable progress had been made. The society's cause was helped initially by members of **Urdd Gobaith Cymru**, who, in performing the dances, brought to life an activity that had long been in desuetude. This renewed interest was strengthened by the growing role of folk dance at the National and the Urdd **Eisteddfod**, by the rich variety of folk dances observable at the **Llangollen International Musical Eisteddfod**, by the recalling of the Nantgarw (*see* **Taff's Well**) dances by Catherine Margretta Thomas (1880–1972), and the *twmpath dawns* (barn dance) phenomenon of the mid-20th century. Since the foundation of the WFDS, folk dancing has enjoyed success at home and abroad, with parties travelling to many countries to demonstrate their art.

Clog dancing

Clog or step dancing is an exhibitive form of dance that has continued in Wales in an unbroken tradition – probably because it was performed mainly by soloists indoors, away from disapproving ministers, and avoided the supposedly immoral mixing of the sexes.

The essence of clog dancing is forceful, percussive stepping, amplified by the sound of the thick wooden soles of the clogs hitting the floor. Today, the tradition often takes a competitive form, with dancers in *eisteddfodau* delighting in their strength and athleticism, just as their predecessors did in the taverns of old.

A key figure in the development of clog dancing in the 20th century was Howel Wood (1882–1967) from Parc (**Llanycil** near **Bala**). This member of the **Wood family** of **Romanies** was instrumental in safeguarding the clog dance tradition, by perpetuating the art on local and national stages, and transferring it to younger generations.

Because of its strenuous nature, clog dancing was long male-dominated, but in recent years, a number of female clog dancers have developed their own, unique style.

Contemporary dance

The history of contemporary dance in Wales is brief. Although it is possible to trace work back to the 1970s, there is no formal archive or body of work that documents the growth of the art form.

Early pioneers of contemporary dance in Wales include the company Moving Being, which came from London to **Cardiff** in 1973. This ground-breaking company worked across the art forms, using projected images, sound, voice and dance. Their hybrid approach to performance, in which the boundaries between **drama** and dance were often blurred, would later inform the practice of most of Wales's experimental and 'physical theatre' companies, such as Brith Gof and Volcano.

In 1976, the drama committee of the Welsh Arts Council (**Arts Council of Wales**) proposed the appointment of three community dance specialists (although it would be another six years before the Council instituted a dance department). In the same year, the first worker was appointed, at the Sherman Theatre, and the Cardiff Community Dance Project was born, later to be housed at the Rubicon Dance Centre, which opened in 1982.

Jumpers Dance Theatre was established in 1978, also in Cardiff. At the same time, the **West Glamorgan** Youth Arts Company established the West Glamorgan Dance Fellowship, which, by the late 1990s, developed into the West Glamorgan community dance project, Tân Dance. Footloose Dance Company, established in 1979 in **Llandrindod**, followed a similar path, developing from Theatr **Powys**'s dance work begun in 1976, and later becoming Powys Dance. In 1980, both Jumpers Youth Dance Theatre and the **Clwyd** Dance Project were established; they were followed in 1981 by **Gwynedd** Dance Project (later becoming Dawns i Bawb) and in 1986 by North **Dyfed** Dance Project (later Dawns Dyfed). Community Dance Wales was founded in the late 1990s as a support organization for individual community dance practitioners and projects.

In 1984, Jumpers Dance Theatre Company became Diversions Dance Company, in order to distinguish it from its sister company, Jumpers Youth Dance Theatre. Diversions, The Dance Company of Wales, as it is now known, grew to be recognized as the country's leading contemporary dance company, touring nationally and internationally, employing guest choreographers, and engaging in educational work with schools and communities. Other practitioners and companies of note include Belinda Neave, Carlson Dance Company and Earthfall, whilst Sioned Huws marries contemporary dance with traditional Welsh folk dance.

DANIEL, Glyn [Edmund] (Dilwyn Rees; 1914–86)
Archaeologist and author
An archaeologist of international repute, who did much to popularize archaeology. Born in **Lampeter Velfrey** and brought up in **Llantwit Major**, he spent his entire professional career at St John's College, **Cambridge**. In the 1950s, he became familiar to a wide audience through the television programme *Animal, Vegetable, Mineral?* Among his major publications were *The Prehistoric Chamber Tombs of England and Wales* (1950), *A Hundred Years of Archaeology* (1950) and *The First Civilizations* (1968). Under his pseudonym, Dilwyn Rees, he published two detective novels. In his autobiography, *Some Small Harvest* (1986), he wrote vividly about his Welsh upbringing.

DANIEL, Goronwy [Hopkin] (1914–2003)
Civil servant and college principal
Brought up in the **Tawe** and Aman valleys, Goronwy Daniel studied economics and statistics at **Aberystwyth** and **Oxford**. His articles in the *Statistical Review* on migration from the south Wales **coal**field are particularly valuable.

In 1943, he became a civil servant, and rose to be the first permanent secretary at the **Welsh Office**. Married to the daughter of the second Earl Lloyd-George, in 1969 he was knighted and was appointed principal of his old college at Aberystwyth (*see* **University of Wales, Aberystwyth**). A man of guile and elephantine charm, his deep voice was eminently mimicable and Aberystwyth's students knew of him as Sir Groan. In 1980, with **Cledwyn Hughes** and **Gwilym O. Williams**, he persuaded the home secretary, William Whitelaw, to honour the **Conservative Party**'s pledge that it would establish a Welsh-language television channel. In 1982, he became the first chairman of the **S4C** Authority.

DANIEL, J[ohn] E[dward] (1902–62)
Theologian and political activist
One of the foremost Welsh theologians of his generation, Daniel was born in **Bangor** and educated at **Oxford**. From 1925 to 1946, he lectured at Coleg **Bala**-Bangor, the **Congregationalists'** theological school in his home city, resigning his post in 1946 to become an inspector of schools. He was the chief propagator of the **theology** of Karl Barth in Wales, and he led the backlash against the Protestant liberalism that had entrenched itself among Welsh **Nonconformists** at the turn of the 20th century. His political writings include *Welsh Nationalism: What it Stands For* (1937); he succeeded **Saunders Lewis** as president of **Plaid [Genedlaethol] Cymru** (1939–43).

DANIEL, Ray (William Raymond Daniel; 1928–97)
Footballer
Swansea-born Ray Daniel, whose **football**er brother Bobby was killed whilst on a RAF bombing raid in 1943, signed for Arsenal in 1946. He made his name as a stylish centrehalf before joining Sunderland in 1953. He won 21 caps and later played for **Cardiff** and Swansea.

DANIELS, Jack or Danny (John Dillwyn Daniels; 1916–48) Racing motorcyclist
When Jack Daniels died in an accident near Fairwood, **Swansea**, he was the closest Wales had produced to a world-class racing motorcyclist (*see* **Motor Sports**). Swansea-born, he was a barber in Ben Evans's department store before going into partnership in the motorcycle business. Riding a 1000-cc Vincent-HRD 'Rapide', he won the 1948 Senior Clubman's TT on the Isle of **Man**, and came in fifth in the Junior Manx Grand Prix on a KTT Velocette.

DARBY, H[enry] Clifford (1909–92) Geographer
Born at **Resolven** and educated at **Neath**, Darby graduated in **geography** at **Cambridge**, and was appointed lecturer there in 1931. After professorships at the universities of **Liverpool** and **London**, he returned to the chair at Cambridge in 1966, remaining there until his retirement in 1976. He was a leader in promoting the relationship between geography and other subjects, especially history, and was one of the organizers of the study of the Domesday Book (general editor and contributor, *The Domesday Geography of England*, 1952–77). His many honours include the Daly Medal of the American Geographical Society (1963) and a knighthood (1988).

DARRAN VALLEY (Cwm Darran), Caerphilly
(1968 ha; 2545 inhabitants)
The **community** consists of the valley of the Bargod Rhymni, and contains the villages of Fochriw and Deri, settlements that came into existence to serve the Fochriw, Pencarreg and Groesfaen collieries. It is traversed by the **Rhymney** Valley Ridgeway Footpath.

DARTS
A direct descendant of javelin throwing and **archery**, the game of darts became hugely popular in the 1920s and 1930s, being a relatively cheap hobby that combined quite naturally with the pleasures of **beer** consumption. The game thrived in public houses and workingmen's clubs, with cup competitions and league tables appearing during this period.

The late 1970s and early 1980s are the periods regarded by many as the golden age of darts. This was the era of such names as John Lowe, Eric Bristow, Cliff Lazarenko, Bobby George and Jocky Wilson. Welsh players featured strongly in major competitions, among them Ceri Morgan, **Leighton Rees** and the incomparable Alan Evans. It was Leighton Rees who won the first World Darts Championship in 1978, beating John Lowe of **England** in the final. Wales had to wait until 1995 before another Welshman, Ritchie 'The Welsh Wizard' Burnett, became world champion. Rees led a team comprising himself, Alan Evans and David Jones to the World Darts Federation team event championships in 1977, a feat replicated by Eric Burden, Marshall James, Sean Palfrey and Martin Phillips twenty years later.

DAUGLEDDAU *Cantref*
One of the seven *cantrefi* of **Dyfed** mentioned in the first sentence of Pedair Cainc y Mabinogi (*see* **Mabinogion, The**), Daugleddau constituted the land between the Eastern and the Western **Cleddau**. Following the **Norman** invasions, it became a barony. With its caput at **Wiston**, the barony was part of the **lordship of Pembroke**, although the area centred upon **Llawhaden** was part of the estates of the bishop of **St David's**. The name survived as the post-**Acts of 'Union' hundred** of Dungleddy.

DAVEY, Claude (1908–2001) Rugby player
Capped 23 times at centre between 1930 and 1935, this distinguished **rugby** player was born in Garnant, **Cwmamman**, and was noted for his ferocious tackling. His great double achievement was to captain **Swansea** and Wales to victories over the 1935 All Blacks, and to score in both games. In 1933, he was also in the first Welsh XV ever to win at Twickenham.

DAVID (Dewi; d.?589) Patron saint of Wales
The chief source of knowledge about David is a **Latin** Life written at the end of the 11th century by Rhigyfarch, son of **Sulien**, bishop of **St David's**. According to Rhigyfarch, David was born to a nun called Non (fl. late 5th century), who had been raped by Sant, king of **Ceredigion**. Rhigyfarch's account contains much that is legendary, but there is substance to his emphasis upon David's links with Irish monasticism and upon the asceticism he practised.

St David, a painting by Peter Murphy (1992)

Long known as 'the waterman', David – wrote **Lewys Glyn Cothi** – 'took bread and water cress, or the water from cold **rivers**'. Rhigyfarch describes a visit to Jerusalem made by three Welsh **saints** (David, **Padarn** and **Teilo**). They were consecrated bishops by the patriarch there and David was made archbishop.

The most celebrated episode in David's life was his role in a synod to combat **Pelagianism** held at **Llanddewi Brefi**, when a dove landed on his shoulder as he preached and a hill rose beneath his feet. David's final teaching, which has gripped the Welsh spiritual imagination, comes from the version of the Life in *The Book of the Anchorite* of Llanddewi Brefi (14th century): 'Lords, brothers and sisters, be joyful and keep your faith and your belief, and do the little things that you have heard and seen from me'.

David finally settled at Glyn Rhosyn, the most westerly point of mainland Wales, a place probably chosen because it was a hub of the western sea routes. Acknowledged as 'the leader of all the Britons', David's monastery became the spiritual heart of **Dyfed**. Originally one of Dyfed's seven bishops' houses, St David's had become by the 12th century the seat of a bishop whose **diocese** comprised over half the land area of Wales, including – as it then did – the whole of **Deheubarth** and much of southern **Powys**.

The 10th-century poem 'Armes Prydein' (*see* **Prophecy**) speaks of 'Dewi's holy banner' as the flag of allies united against the **English**. He became the object of **Norman** veneration. Rhigyfarch's reference to him as archbishop inspired the efforts of Bishop **Bernard** and **Giraldus**

Cambrensis to win metropolitan status for St David's, and the Cambro-Norman invaders of **Ireland** had 'Sein Daui' as their battle cry. St David's became a major focus of **pilgrimage**, but the claim that David was formally canonized by Pope Calixtus II c.1120 is doubtful.

March 1 is listed as David's feast day in 9th-century Irish manuscripts. Of Wales's ancient **parish** churches, over 60 were dedicated to David (Teilo, with 25, ranks second). Thus, his patronal festival was celebrated in more Welsh churches than that of any other indigenous saint – the probable explanation for his eventual adoption as Wales's patron saint. The popularity of the name David is the likely explanation for the widespread adoption of the **surname** Davies in south-west Wales.

DAVID (1951) Film

This superbly structured, elegiac **film**, made for the Festival of **Britain**, centres on Dafydd Rhys, a charismatic school caretaker and ex-miner. This is a thinly disguised portrait of the poet and columnist D. R. Griffiths (Amanwy, 1882–1953; brother of the politician **James Griffiths**), who plays himself. **Cardiff**-born director Paul Dickson constructs a detailed mosaic of life around **Ammanford** while telling the caretaker's story as he mourns his son's death, sublimating his grief in a poem written for the National **Eisteddfod**.

DAVID, T[annatt] W[illiam] E[dgeworth] (1858–1934) Geologist and explorer

As professor of **geology** and physical **geography** at the University of Sydney, **Australia** (1891–1924), David, son of the rector of St Fagans (**Cardiff**), was internationally renowned for a range of achievements: leader of the second Royal Society drilling expedition to the coral atoll Funafuti (1897), designed to test Charles Darwin's theory of coral growth; chief scientist on the Shackleton expedition to the Antarctic (1909), when he led the first trek to the South Magnetic Pole; and leader of the Australian mining battalion of tunnellers, and geological adviser to the British Expeditionary Force in France during the **First World War**.

He received international acclaim for his discovery of Permo-Carboniferous glaciation in the southern continents and for his major work *The Geology of the Commonwealth of Australia* (1931). Considered one of Australia's premier scientists, he received many honours and was given a state funeral there.

DAVIES family (Llandinam) Industrialists, politicians and benefactors

David Davies (1818–90), **railway** contractor, colliery owner and philanthropist, was a self-made millionaire who laid the foundations of the family wealth. Born on a poor hillside farm at **Llandinam** to a family of **Cardiganshire** origins, he first worked in his father's sawpit and was nicknamed 'Top Sawyer'. From 1855–67, he played a vital role in the construction of railways in mid and west Wales. His 35-m depth Talerddig cutting, completed in 1861, was the world's deepest rock cutting at the time (*see* **Llanbrynmair**). His Ocean **Coal** Company, consisting of collieries in the **Rhondda** and in **Ogmore Valley**, was one of the biggest exporters of Welsh steam coal. His greatest achievement

was the creation of a new port at **Barry** to rival **Cardiff**'s docks. He was MP for **Cardigan Boroughs** from 1874–85 and for Cardiganshire from 1885 until 1886, when his opposition to **Gladstone**'s Irish policy led to his defeat. A lifelong teetotaller and staunch **Calvinistic Methodist**, he made significant donations to the University College of Wales, **Aberystwyth** (*see* **University of Wales, Aberystwyth**).

His grandson, David Davies (1880–1944), became the first Baron Davies of Llandinam, in 1932. **Liberal** MP for **Montgomeryshire** from 1906 to 1929, he founded the New Commonwealth Society to further good international relations, established at Aberystwyth the world's first chair of international politics, and financed the building of Cardiff's Temple of Peace (*see* **Pacifism**). He and his sisters, Gwendoline (1882–1951) and Margaret (1884–1963), fought the scourge of **tuberculosis** by setting up the King Edward VII Welsh National Memorial Association, which built sanatoria throughout Wales. The sisters are best remembered for their bequest of French Impressionist **paintings** to the **National Museum [of] Wales**. They also set up the Gregynog Press (*see* **Tregynon**), noted for its fine art productions.

DAVIES family Ironsmiths

The family, comprising Hugh Davies (d.1702), his eldest son, Robert (1675–1748), and third son, John (1682–1755), were renowned **iron**smiths with a forge at Croes Foel, (**Esclusham**). They were responsible for many fine examples of ironwork in north-eastern Wales, including the elaborately decorated gates and openwork piers at **Chirk** Castle (1712), the gates of the close of St Peter's church, **Ruthin** (1727), and the gates of the churchyard of St Giles's church, **Wrexham** (1720), as well as chancel screens at **Mold** and Wrexham. Robert appears to have been responsible for the best and most technically assured work; other works attributed to him include splendid screens and gates at **Leeswood** Hall and Erddig (**Marchwiel**).

DAVIES, Alun Talfan (1913–2000) Barrister and public figure

Sir Alun is chiefly remembered as one of the founders of HTV (*see* **Broadcasting**) and as a staunch supporter of **devolution**. A native of **Gorseinon**, he was educated at **Aberystwyth** and **Cambridge**. Called to the bar in 1939, he won public recognition for his legal activity, particularly his work on miners' compensation cases and his chairmanship of the trustees of the **Aberfan Disaster** Fund. With his brother, **Aneirin Talfan Davies**, he founded the publishing house Llyfrau'r Dryw (*see* **Printing and Publishing**) and the **periodical** *Barn* (1962).

DAVIES, Aneirin Talfan (1909–80) Author, critic and broadcaster

Brought up in **Gorseinon**, he was a pharmacist in **London** in the 1930s before settling in **Swansea**. After the destruction of his pharmacy by German bombs during the **Second World War**, he turned to **broadcasting**, becoming head of programmes Wales at the BBC in 1966. He was a poet and the author of the notable travel books *Crwydro Sir Gâr* (1955) and *Crwydro Bro Morgannwg* (2 vols, 1972 and 1976); he published numerous critical studies of the works of both **Welsh** and **English-language** authors; he also wrote on Pushkin. He founded the literary review *Heddiw* (1936–42) and, with his brother **Alun Talfan Davies**, the publishing house Llyfrau'r Dryw (*see* **Printing and Publishing**) and the **periodical** *Barn* (1962). His son, Geraint, was Controller of BBC Wales from 1990 to 1999.

DAVIES, [David] Arthur (1913–90) Meteorologist

Barry-born Arthur Davies graduated in **mathematics** and physics at **Cardiff** and in 1936 became a forecaster at the Meteorological Office. After the **Second World War**, he served as director of the East Africa meteorological department; in 1955, he was appointed secretary general of the World Meteorological Organization (WMO). He held that position until 1979 – the longest period that one person has been an executive head of an organization within the United Nations. In recognition of this distinction, he was awarded the United Nations Peace Prize (1979) and was designated secretary-general emeritus of the WMO for a further 10 years, until his death. He was vice-president of both the **Welsh Centre for International Affairs** and the **Cymmrodorion**.

DAVIES, Ben[jamin Grey] (1858–1943) Tenor

Wales's first truly professional tenor, Davies was born in **Pontardawe**. As a boy alto, he sang in Caradog's (**Griffith Rees Jones**) legendary south Wales choir of 1872–3. After working in a storehouse in **Swansea**, he entered **London**'s Royal Academy of Music in 1878, emerging in 1881 a polished tenor. He sang opera until 1890, after which he concentrated on oratorio and concert performances, singing with distinction in **North America** and mainland Europe during his long career.

DAVIES, Clement [Edward] (1884–1962) Politician

A successful barrister, **Llanfyllin**-born Davies was elected as **Liberal** MP for his native **Montgomeryshire** in 1929, a position he retained until his death in 1962. In 1931, he became a **National Liberal**, but rejoined the Liberal Party in 1945. As Liberal leader between 1945 and 1956, he battled valiantly to keep the party intact at a critical time in its history. A keen advocate of the national rights of Wales, he was also a zealous supporter of liberty and social justice, and was the principal author of a stringent report (1939) on the anti-**tuberculosis** service in Wales.

DAVIES, D[avid] Jacob (1916–74) Unitarian, author, broadcaster and philanthropist

A native of **Llandysul**, who was **Unitarian** minister at **Aberystwyth**, **Aberdare** and Alltyblaca (**Llanwenog**). In his day, he was Wales's best-known Unitarian, partly because of his long service as editor of *Yr Ymofynnydd*, the denomination's journal. He published volumes of poetry and short stories and wrote thousands of radio scripts. As a radio broadcaster, he had few rivals. He was active with the Miners' **Eisteddfod**, and won acclaim for his tireless efforts on behalf of the pensioners of Wales.

DAVIES, D[avid] J[ames] (1893–1956) Economist

A visit to the International People's College in Elsinore, Denmark, in 1924 convinced Davies – a founder member

Alun Talfan Davies, a portrait by David Griffiths

of the **Ammanford Labour Party** – that **internationalism** meant co-operation between free nations, and that a free Wales was necessary for the advancement of the Welsh working **class**. He became a leading member of **Plaid [Genedlaethol] Cymru** and his many publications laid the foundations of the party's economic policies. Influenced by the co-operative principles of the Danish Folk High School Movement, he and his wife Dr Noëlle Davies attempted to establish a folk school at Pantybeiliau, Gilwern (**Llanelly**).

DAVIES, D[avid] T[homas] (1876–1962) Dramatist

A native of Nant-y-moel, **Ogmore Valley**, D. T. Davies was by profession an inspector of schools. Much influenced by Ibsenite social realism, he wrote the pioneering *Ble Mà Fa?* (1913) and *Ephraim Harris* (1914), which concerns the problems that can arise through trying to tell the truth. Other popular, but less challenging, plays include *Y Pwyllgor* (pre-war but published in 1920), *Pelenni Pitar* (1925) and modern morality plays.

DAVIES, Dai (David Davies; 1896–1976) Cricketer

Glamorgan's first home-grown professional **cricket**er after Glamorgan joined the **county** championship in 1921, **Llanelli**-born Dai Davies came off a double steelworks shift for his home debut in 1923. He played until 1939, scoring 15,930 runs and bemusing opponents by calling in **Welsh** when partnered with **Emrys Davies**. Post-war, he umpired 23 tests and famously declared, after giving the final decision when Glamorgan beat Hampshire in 1948: 'That's out, and we've won the championship.'

D

Donald Davies

DAVIES, David (1871–1931)
Colliery official and palaeobotanist
Born at Abercanaid, **Merthyr Tydfil**, Davies ended a life-long career in **coal**mining as colliery manager. He developed a passion for fossil **plants** in the Coal Measures. Collecting on a large scale from individual seams in the southern coalfield, whilst at **Gilfach Goch**, he became a pioneer in fossil **plant** ecology. His extensive collection, housed in the **National Museum**, provided the basis of important research by a number of eminent palaeobotanists.

DAVIES, Dilys (1908–1979) Actress
Sharp-featured and inimitable in Wales as a harridan, Davies, a stalwart of post-**Second World War** BBC radio and television (*see* **Broadcasting**), played two memorable big-screen roles: the mean-spirited doctor's wife in *The Citadel* (1938), and the insufferable postmistress in *The Proud Valley* (1940). Born in Dowlais (**Merthyr Tydfil**), she was Mrs Ogmore-Pritchard in the 1954 radio version of **Dylan Thomas**'s *Under Milk Wood*, and a matron in the Welsh television serial *Pobol y Cwm* during the 1970s.

DAVIES, Donald [Watts] (1924–99)
Computer scientist
The scientist who 'enabled computers to talk to each other' was from Treorchy, **Rhondda**. Davies invented 'packet switching', an essential component of all modern data transmission. After graduating in physics and **mathematics** at Imperial College, **London**, he worked under Alan Turing at the National Physical Laboratory, Teddington. In 1966, he proposed that in transmitting a large file of data along a crowded information channel it would be best to fragment it into short 1024-bit packages that travel independently and are reassembled at the destination.

DAVIES, E[dward] Tegla (1880–1967) Writer
One of the most accomplished **Welsh-language** prose writers of the first half of the 20th century, Tegla Davies was born in **Llandegla**, **Denbighshire**, and spent most of his life as a **Wesleyan** minister. His novel *Gŵr Pen y Bryn* (1923) is a psychological study of 'the awakening of an ordinary soul', with the **Tithe** War as background. He wrote and published several volumes of essays with a sharp satirical edge, and an autobiography, *Gyda'r Blynyddoedd* (1952). The most popular of his works during his own lifetime were his novels for children, beginning with *Hunangofiant Tomi* (1912), all of which demonstrate a gift for humour and fantasy.

DAVIES, E[van] T[homas] (1878–1969) Musician
Born at Dowlais, **Merthyr Tydfil**, E. T. Davies was imbued at an early age with a healthy respect for amateur endeavour, folk **music** and professional excellence. He helped to shape much of the music making in Wales in the interwar years and as organist he performed widely throughout **Britain**. He was director of music at **Bangor** (1920–43), retiring to **Aberdare** in 1950. He left an impressive body of work including arrangements, finely crafted salon music, and the much-loved song 'Ynys y Plant'.

DAVIES, [Herbert] Edmund (1906–92) Judge
Edmund Davies, who was knighted in 1958 and created Lord Edmund-Davies in 1974, was one of the finest judges of his generation. Born and educated in **Mountain Ash**, he achieved the degree of LL.D from the University of **London** when only 22 years old. He was defence barrister to **D. J. Williams** at the trial following the **Penyberth** fire. Successively recorder of **Merthyr Tydfil** (1942–4), **Swansea** (1944–53) and **Cardiff** (1953–8), he became a judge of the High Court (1958), Court of Appeal (1966) and the House of Lords (1974–81). He chaired the tribunal of inquiry into the **Aberfan Disaster** of 1966.

DAVIES, Edward (Celtic Davies; 1756–1831)
Author
A native of Llanfaredd (**Llanelwedd**), Davies was rector of **Bishopston** for quarter of a century. He earned his soubriquet as the author of two books dealing with Welsh and **Celtic** subjects: *Celtic Researches* (1804); and *The Mythology and Rites of the British Druids* (1809). These established him as a leading proponent of belief in a former Golden Age and the idea that the **religion** of the **druids** perpetuated an original patriarchal faith. He was, nevertheless, the first to question the assertions of Iolo Morganwg (**Edward Williams**) concerning the **Gorsedd Beirdd Ynys Prydain**.

DAVIES, Ellis William (1871–1939) Politician
A native of **Bethesda**, he qualified as a solicitor in 1899 and established a practice at **Caernarfon**. He was elected a member of **Caernarfonshire County** Council in 1904 and also acted as solicitor for the **North Wales Quarrymen's Union**. He served as **Liberal** MP for the Eifion division of Caernarfonshire (1906–18). Following the abolition of the seat, he failed to secure nomination

elsewhere in 1918, largely (it would seem) because of opposition from **David Lloyd George**. Elected as Liberal MP for **Denbigh** (1923–9), he later became a member of the **Labour Party**.

DAVIES, Elwyn (1908–96)
Geographer and administrator

Born in **Swansea**, Davies graduated in **geography** from **Aberystwyth** and was appointed lecturer, under **H. J. Fleure**, in Manchester in 1934. After war service, he became secretary to the Council of the **University of Wales** (1945), and permanent secretary in the Welsh Department of the Ministry of **Education** in 1963. He was president of the **National Library of Wales**. Davies edited, with **Alwyn D. Rees**, *Welsh Rural Communities* (1961), and edited *A Gazetteer of Welsh Place-Names: Rhestr o Enwau Lleoedd* (1958), the basic source for the orthography of **place names** in Wales.

His wife Margaret (1914–82), also a student under Fleure, was widely known as a conservationist, geographer and natural historian. He was the brother of the broadcaster **Hywel Davies** and the historian Alun Davies, and was a major benefactor of the **Centre for Advanced Welsh and Celtic Studies**.

DAVIES, [David] Emrys (1904–75) Cricketer

Founder of **Glamorgan**'s long tradition of left-handed opening bowling obduracy, Emrys Davies, who was born at Sandy, **Llanelli**, played for 30 years. His 26,566 runs and 612 first-class games were both **county** records when he retired in 1954, while his slow left-arm bowling saw off 903 batsmen. Although picked for the 1939–40 tour of India, the **Second World War** robbed him of his sole opportunity to play for **England**, but he later umpired nine tests.

DAVIES, George M[aitland] L[loyd] (1880–1949)
Pacifist

In 1914, Davies began to work, without pay, for the Fellowship of Reconciliation. Imprisoned as a **conscientious objector** during the **First World War**, he was elected as Christian Pacifist MP for the **University of Wales** in 1923, subsequently taking the **Labour** whip. Defeated in the general election of 1924, he became a **Calvinistic Methodist** minister in 1926. During the 1930s, he was much involved in work with the unemployed, moving in 1932 to the **Quaker** settlement at Maes-yr-Haf (Trealaw, **Rhondda**); he published extensively, particularly on international peace. Distressed by the onset of the Cold War, he committed suicide. He was the brother of **John Glyn Davies**.

DAVIES, Gwilym (1879–1955) Peace promoter

Born in Bedlinog (*see* **Merthyr Tydfil**), and educated at Nottingham and **Oxford**, Davies was **Baptist** minister at **Carmarthen**, **Abergavenny** and **Llandrindod**. Attracted to social movements, he helped to establish the Welsh School of Social Service. He resigned from the ministry in 1922 to promote world peace and forge links between Wales and the League of Nations (*see* **Pacifism**). His legacy is the goodwill message from the youth of Wales to the children of the world, prepared annually by **Urdd Gobaith Cymru** and broadcast by the BBC.

DAVIES, Haydn [George] (1919–93) Cricketer

Llanelli-born Haydn Davies's volubility behind the stumps was matched by his durability, keeping wicket for **Glamorgan** in every match from 1947 to 1957, and making a total of 784 dismissals. A robust hitter, he was unlucky enough to be around at exactly the same time as Godfrey Evans, who was **England**'s automatic choice as wicket keeper for a decade.

DAVIES, Howel (1716–70) Methodist revivalist

Davies's place of birth is not known, but he worked as a schoolmaster at **Talgarth** in 1737 and underwent religious conversion under the ministry of **Howel Harris**. After a brief period with **Griffith Jones** at **Llanddowror**, he was ordained, but remained curate to him until he moved to Llys-y-frân (**New Moat**) in 1741. A powerful **preacher** and an advocate of itinerant preaching, he increasingly confined himself to **Pembrokeshire** as the years went by, possibly because of ill **health**. He became known as the 'Apostle of Pembrokeshire'.

DAVIES, Hugh (1739–1821) Naturalist

Born in Llandyfrydog (**Rhosybol**) and rector of **Aber[gwyngregyn]**, Davies was the compiler of *Welsh Botanology*, a systematic catalogue, in **Latin**, **English** and **Welsh**, of the native **plants** of **Anglesey**. As the first county flora of any part of Wales, it was a landmark in the history of botany in Wales (*see* **Biological Sciences**). A close friend of **Thomas Pennant**, he edited the second edition (1790) of Pennant's *An Indian Zoology*.

George Maitland Lloyd Davies

DAVIES, Hugh Morriston (1879–1965) Surgeon

Educated at **Cambridge** and **London**, Davies was the author of the first **English** textbook on surgery involving the thorax. He showed that X-rays could be used in the diagnosis of tumours of the lungs, and went on to remove such growths surgically. In 1916, his right hand was infected during a surgical operation, and he almost lost his life, his right hand and arm having become severely malformed. He left his post and bought a small hospital at **Llanbedr Dyffryn Clwyd** in order to treat patients with lung disorders. By his persistence, he was able to resume his surgical work, and gained an international reputation in the field.

DAVIES, Hywel (1919–65) Broadcaster

Born at **Llandysul**, the son of a **Congregationalist** minister, Davies began his career with the BBC in 1942, eventually becoming editor of the wartime **Welsh-language** news, which was then prepared in **London**. In 1946, he moved to **Cardiff**, where he became the outstanding figure in Welsh **broadcasting**. Appointed head of programmes in 1958, he was, at the time of his premature death, Controller-designate of the BBC in Wales.

Highly innovative, he was the first presenter in **Britain** to use a roving microphone in a live broadcast, a practice that terrified head office. He was responsible, either as producer or presenter, for most of the acclaimed radio and television programmes produced in Wales between the late 1940s and the mid-1960s. His brothers were the geographer **Elwyn Davies** and the historian Alun Davies. He was married to the broadcaster Lorraine Davies.

DAVIES, Idris (1905–53) Poet

I was born in **Rhymney**
To a miner and his wife –
On a January morning
I was pulled into this Life.

Leaving school at the age of 14, Idris Davies worked as a miner until the **General Strike** of 1926. He then obtained qualifications in Loughborough, Nottingham and **London** and taught at primary schools in **England** and subsequently in **Llandysul** and in Treherbert (**Rhondda**) before, in 1947, finding a post in his native valley. He published three volumes of verse: *Gwalia Deserta* (1938), *The Angry Summer* (1943) and *Tonypandy and Other Poems* (1945); a volume of his *Selected Poems* appeared shortly before his death, and his *Complete Poems* in 1994. Most of his poems deal with the mining valleys of south Wales during the interwar years, in particular the effects of economic **depression** and from a **socialist** point of view. Despite some moments of banality, his work has a passionate ring to it, a wry humour, a fierce pride in the virtues of the Welsh working **class**, and moral indignation at the hardship they had to suffer.

Some of his poems show the influence of A. E. Housman and **John Ceiriog Hughes** in their verse forms, and of the pulpit (**Welsh** was Davies's mother tongue), while others have the quality of folk song. His best-known poem, 'The Bells of Rhymney', was set to music by the American folk-singer Pete Seeger and recorded by Joan Baez, the Byrds

and many others. A memorial plaque on the wall of the house where he died describes him as 'un o feibion anwylaf ac enwocaf Rhymni' (one of Rhymney's most cherished and most famous sons).

DAVIES, J[ohn] Glyn (1870–1953) Poet and scholar

Born in **Liverpool**, Davies worked for Rathbone Brothers and the Cambrian Line, absorbing many of the shanties sung by Welsh sailors on their **ships**. After a stormy period as librarian at **Aberystwyth** (*see* **University of Wales, Aberystwyth**), he joined the **Celtic** department at Liverpool University. He translated many **English-language** shanties into **Welsh**. His numerous publications include three popular collections of verse for children, the first of which, *Cerddi Huw Puw* (1923), was responsible for popularizing the shanty 'Fflat Huw Puw'. He was the brother of the pacifist **George M. Ll. Davies**.

DAVIES, J[ohn] H[umphreys] (1871–1926)
Bibliophile and public figure

Born in Cwrt Mawr, **Llangeitho**, and educated at **London**, **Aberystwyth** and **Oxford**, J. H. Davies became registrar at Aberystwyth (1905–19) and the college's principal (1919–26) (*see* **University of Wales, Aberystwyth**). He was one of the main supporters of the movement to establish the **National Library of Wales** at Aberystwyth, and through his friendship with **John Williams** (1840–1926), he amassed a large collection of manuscripts and printed books that now forms part of the foundation collection of the Library.

DAVIES, James Conway (1891–1971) Historian

Educated at **Aberystwyth**, **Cardiff** and **Cambridge**, Llanelli-born Davies virtually established the **County** Record Office in **Monmouthshire**, became reader in palaeography and diplomatics at Durham, and was the first editor of the historical *Journal* of the **Church in Wales**. Among other works, many of them on medieval themes, he edited *The Welsh Assize Roll, 1277–82* (1940).

DAVIES, James Kitchener (1902–52) Writer

Brought up on a smallholding at **Llangeitho**, Kitchener Davies spent his working life in the **Rhondda**, where he was an active supporter of **Plaid [Genedlaethol] Cymru**. His controversial play *Cwm Glo* (1934) dealt unflinchingly with the social impact of the **Depression** on the southern **coal**-field. The verse play *Meini Gwagedd* (1944), set in the **Tregaron** area, shows how people can conspire with harsh circumstance to bring about their own destruction. These plays, and the dramatic, autobiographical poem 'Swn y Gwynt sy'n Chwythu' (1953), established him as one of the most perceptive writers of the 20th century.

DAVIES, Jennie Eirian (1925–82) Editor

Llanpumsaint-born Jennie Eirian was an active campaigner with **Plaid [Genedlaethol] Cymru**, standing as parliamentary candidate for **Carmarthen** in both the 1955 general election and the 1957 by-election. She was appointed editor of *Y Faner* in 1979. The journal flourished under her editorship. However, she was frequently at odds with popular opinion, particularly over **Gwynfor Evans**'s threat to starve himself in support of the establishment of a **Welsh-language** television channel (*see* **Broadcasting** and **S4C**). She resigned as editor in May 1982 and died three days later. She was the wife of the poet J. Eirian Davies (1918–98) and mother of the poet and dramatist Siôn Eirian (b.1954).

DAVIES, John (of Mallwyd; *c.*1567–1644) Scholar

A native of **Llanferres**, John Davies held three degrees from the University of **Oxford**. For years, he was in the service of Bishop **William Morgan**, pre-eminent translator of the **Bible** into **Welsh**. In 1604, he became rector of Mallwyd (**Mawddwy**), which has been associated with his name ever since.

Profoundly learned in **Latin**, Greek and Hebrew, he was also steeped in the Welsh literary tradition. He collaborated with William Morgan in the work of translation, and was responsible, together with Bishop Richard Parry (1560–1623), for the revised versions of the Bible (1620) and **The Book of Common Prayer** (1621). His authority as a linguist is evident also in his Welsh grammar, *Antiquae Linguae Britannicae ... Rudimenta* (1621) and his Welsh-Latin and Latin-Welsh **dictionary**, *Antiquae Linguae Britannicae ... Dictionarium Duplex* (1632). The two volumes are based on a life's work of copying Welsh manuscripts and painstakingly studying their contents.

John Davies's influence on the history of Welsh scholarship was immense. He combined wide knowledge of Welsh **literature** with the standards of **Renaissance** learning. The *Dictionarium Duplex* in particular brought the Welsh language to the attention of scholars outside Wales.

DAVIES, John (1772–1855) Missionary

John Davies, Tahiti – as he became known after the island of his mission – spent 55 unbroken years as a missionary in the South Pacific. Born at **Llanfihangel**, he became a schoolteacher at **Llanrhaeadr-ym-Mochnant** and joined the **Calvinistic Methodists**, worshipping at a house called Penllys in the company of John Hughes, Pontrobert (1775–1854), and the **hymn**writer **Ann Griffiths**. In 1800, he was sent by the **London** Missionary Society to Tahiti, where he used his skills as **preacher**, hymnwriter, translator, grammarian and teacher to advance the Christian cause. His voluminous correspondence with John Hughes provided news which captivated home congregations.

DAVIES, John (1882–1937) Educationist

The son of the first to be buried of the 81 victims of the 1885 **colliery disaster** at Maerdy (*see* **Rhondda**), John Davies spent an impoverished childhood at **Llangeitho**. He was apprenticed to a draper at Porth (*see* Rhondda) at the age of 13. His experience of the 1898 lockout led him to become an ardent socialist. Later based at **Swansea**, he became a correspondent of the Labour **newspaper** *Llais Llafur*, and won the admiration of the young **James Griffiths** for his fearless attacks upon the opponents of **socialism**. In 1918, he became the secretary of the **Agricultural Labourers'** Union in **Pembrokeshire**, where he became a close associate of **D. J. Williams**.

In 1919, he was appointed secretary of the south Wales district of the **Workers' Educational Association**, a post he held until his death. Under his leadership, the number of

James Kitchener Davies's 1951 Rhondda West campaign leaflet

classes directly organized by the association rose from nil to 193, and those organized by the WEA in association with the colleges of the **University of Wales** rose from nil to 195. Along with **Robert Roberts** (Silyn), he was closely involved in the educational schemes of **Thomas Jones** (1870–1955), **Coleg Harlech** among them. **W. J. Gruffydd** wrote of him: 'After the death of **John Williams (Brynsiencyn)** and **John Morris-Jones**, there was only one John in Wales'. His nephew is the historian John Davies (b.1938).

DAVIES, John Cecil (1864–1927) Industrialist

A spectacular example of a rags-to-riches story, Davies entered the **tinplate** trade as a mill-boy and ended his life as a knighted magnate of the steel industry (*see* **Iron and Steel**). Born at Waunarlwydd, **Swansea**, he rose to become director of 26 industrial concerns, including Baldwins Ltd. During the **First World War**, his mobilization of Wales's industrial resources for the production of munitions gained him both his knighthood (1922) and the Cross of the French Legion of Honour. At the time of his funeral, some 20,000 steelworkers across all of south Wales stopped work and stood bareheaded in tribute for five minutes. The poet Nigel Jenkins (b.1949) is his great-grandson.

DAVIES, Mansel [Morris] (1913–95) Chemist

Mansel Davies, of **Aberdare**, was an outstanding student at **Aberystwyth** in the 1930s. After research at **Cambridge** and Leeds, he returned to Aberystwyth in 1947 with expertise in infrared spectroscopy and with insights into the importance of the hydrogen bond (the key to DNA). He attracted able research students and established an international reputation. At home, he deserved more recognition than he received, but as a freethinker, **conscientious objector** and supporter of the international peace conference Pugwash, he was not an establishment man. Eventually, he was awarded a personal chair, and in retirement at **Criccieth** devoted himself to history, **philosophy** and his **dogs**. He published a valuable study of the work of Joseph Needham.

DAVIES, Margaret (*c.*1700–85) Poet and copyist
During her early life in Coetgae-du, **Trawsfynydd**, she mastered **Welsh** prosody and thereafter, unmarried and well-off, devoted herself to **literature**. Some 20 of her poems survive and 5 manuscripts entirely in her hand, which reveal her as a significant collector of **women**'s poetry.

DAVIES, Mary (1855–1930) Singer
Born in **London**, she was trained in **music** by her sculptor father **William Davies** (Mynorydd; 1828–1901), and later at the Royal Academy of Music. She became a well-known professional soprano throughout **Britain**, specializing in concerts and oratorios. After the death of her husband, William Cadwaladr Davies, in 1905 she became an official of the **Welsh Folk Song Society**, contributing impressively as collector, lecturer and adjudicator. In 1916, the **University of Wales** honoured her with a doctorate.

DAVIES, [William Thomas] Pennar (1911–96) Writer
Named after his birthplace, Aberpennar (**Mountain Ash**), Davies made his reputation in **Welsh**, although **English** was his mother tongue. After a notable academic career (**Cardiff**, **Oxford** and Yale) he served as a Congregational minister in Cardiff. He later became principal of the **Congregationalists**' Memorial College in **Swansea**, where his theological beliefs, influenced by **Pelagianism**, won considerable respect. His unique modernist voice was heard first in the Cadwgan Circle's anthology *Cerddi Cadwgan* (1953). The other five volumes of his poems are characterized by unconventional spirituality and rich allusiveness. He was also a prolific short-story writer and novelist; his fiction is full of exotic characters and unusual situations.

DAVIES, [Robert] Rees (1938–2005) Historian
A native of **Cynwyd** (**Denbighshire**, but **Merioneth** in 1938), he was educated in **London** and **Oxford**. He joined the history department of University College, **Swansea** (*see* **University of Wales Swansea**), in 1961, and that of University College, London, in 1963. In 1976, he was appointed professor of history at the University College of Wales, **Aberystwyth** (*see* **University of Wales, Aberystwyth**), and in 1995 became Chichele Professor of Medieval History at Oxford. Widely recognized as the finest medieval historian of his generation, his works on Wales include *Lordship and Society in the March of Wales, 1282–1400* (1978), *Conquest, Coexistence and Change: Wales 1063–1415* (1987) and *The Revolt of Owain Glyn Dŵr* (1995). His concern to place the **historiography of Wales** in a wider context is reflected in his *Domination and Conquest: The Experience of Ireland, Scotland and Wales* (1990) and other works.

He served as vice-principal at Aberystwyth, chairman of the National Curriculum History Committee for Wales, chairman of the Ancient Monuments Board for Wales, president of the Royal Historical Society and chairman of the British committee of the International Congress of Historical Sciences. He was knighted shortly before his death.

DAVIES, Rhisiart Morgan (1903–58) Physicist
Corris-born Rhisiart Davies won a scholarship to the physics department at **Aberystwyth**, where he spent most of his career. During the **Second World War**, he was seconded to **Cambridge** where he studied explosions. After the war, he returned to Aberystwyth, succeeding **E. J. Williams** as head of department, and establishing a strong research team to investigate shockwaves in solids. This led to a wider study of explosions and flame-propagation – work that continues, long after his untimely death (*see* **Physical Sciences**).

DAVIES, Rhys (1901–78) Writer
The most prolific of all Welsh prose writers in **English** and a master of the short story, Rhys Davies was born in Blaenclydach (**Rhondda**). He left Wales as a young man to live as a writer in **London**, a profession to which he devoted himself unswervingly. He wrote 20 novels, including the trilogy *Honey and Bread* (1935), *A Time to Laugh* (1937) and *Jubilee Blues* (1938), which deal with the effects of the **interwar depression**, and a dozen collections of short stories, notably *The Trip to London* (1946) and *Boy with a Trumpet* (1949). A volume of autobiography, *Print of a Hare's Foot*, appeared in 1969 and his *Collected Stories*, in three volumes, were published in 1996 and 1998.

DAVIES, Richard (?1501–81) Bishop and translator
Born at Gyffin, **Conwy**, Davies was probably attracted to Protestantism while studying at **Oxford**. He became vicar of two Buckinghamshire parishes in 1549, but, in Mary's reign, he was deprived of both by the Privy Council and fled into exile at Frankfurt-am-Main (1555–8). He was appointed bishop of **St Asaph** in 1559, and in 1561 was translated to **St David's**, where he remained until his death. He was a member of the **Council of Wales and the Marches** and frequently acted for it and the Privy Council as a commissioner. His episcopal register, reports and writings are valuable sources of information. He encountered persistent difficulties on account of the poverty and ignorance of his clergy, the rapacity of the **gentry** and the vestiges of Romanism among all social groups. Severe in his condemnation of contemporary self-seeking, Davies was himself not without similar faults.

An accomplished scholar and author, he was a generous patron of bards and intellectuals at his household in **Abergwili**. He participated in the translation of the **English** 'Bishops' Bible' (1568), but his most important contribution was to the **Welsh** translation of **The Book of Common Prayer** and the New Testament (1567). He and **William Salesbury** were probably responsible for securing the Act of 1563 requiring that translation. Davies contributed translations of five books of the New Testament, written in felicitous Welsh, but did not translate the Prayer Book, although he often gets the credit for doing so.

DAVIES, Richard (Mynyddog; 1833–77) Poet

The author of perhaps the first Welsh pop song, 'Gwnewch bopeth yn Gymraeg' (Do everything in Welsh), and of the lyrics of some of the most famous Welsh songs – 'Myfanwy', 'Cartref', 'Pistyll y Llan' – was born in **Llanbrynmair**. Mynyddog could write in strict metres but he was best known for his singing in *eisteddfodau* and concerts. He wrote the libretto of **Joseph Parry**'s opera *Blodwen* and contributed amusing columns to **newspapers**.

DAVIES, [Thomas] Ryan (1937–77) Entertainer

The most popular Welsh entertainer of the 1960s and 1970s, Ryan Davies was born in Glanaman (**Cwmamman**), and brought up there and in **Llanfyllin**. Having trained as a teacher at **Normal College**, **Bangor**, he taught in Croydon and served an apprenticeship with the **London** Welsh **Drama** Society and with the West Wickham Opera Company before signing a contract with BBC Wales (*see* **Broadcasting**) in 1966.

A thin man with a long, bony face, he was hugely talented as singer, composer, **harp**ist, actor, comedian and mimic; he rapidly became a household name through his extraordinary performances, in both **Welsh** and **English**, in theatre, **film** and television. His best-known television role in Welsh was that of Twm Twm, the **beer**-swilling pigeon-fancier, in the highly popular comedy series *Fo a Fe*. In English, he is best remembered for the equally popular **Ryan and Ronnie** (with Ronnie Williams) and for *Poems and Pints*, with Max Boyce and Philip Madoc. In 1971, he played Second Voice (with **Richard Burton** as First Voice) in a film version of **Dylan Thomas**'s *Under Milk Wood*. He appeared regularly as Dame in pantomimes at the Grand Theatre, **Swansea**. At the New Theatre, **Cardiff**, he featured opposite Bill Owen in *Sunshine Boys*. His most memorable songs include 'Rhy Hwyr' and 'Ti a dy Ddoniau'. His sudden death in America, at the age of 40, robbed Wales of a comic genius at the height of his powers.

DAVIES, S[tephen] O[wen] (1886–1972) Politician

A former miner and miners' agent, Davies was elected as **Labour** MP for **Merthyr Tydfil** at a by-election in 1934. An individualist with a huge popular following in his constituency, he was re-elected with substantial majorities for the rest of his life. A strong advocate of Welsh **Home Rule**, he was rebuked by his party for his part in the Parliament for Wales campaign (*see* **Devolution**). In 1955, he introduced the **Government** of Wales Bill in parliament. Rejected as the official candidate in 1970 on account of his age (84), he stood as independent Labour candidate against the official Labour nominee and won with a majority of 7467. He was a stalwart supporter of the Soviet Union and bitterly attacked American Cold War policies.

DAVIES, T[homas] Glynne (1926–88)
Writer and broadcaster

A son of **Llanrwst**, who followed a career as journalist and broadcaster, Davies won the crown at the Llanrwst

National **Eisteddfod** (1951) for his long poem 'Adfeilion', which observes the disintegration of the old rural way of life, not in a sentimental manner, but through a surrealist lens. A romantic lyricism is wedded to a semi-modernist and impressionist style in his three collections, *Llwybrau Pridd* (1961), *Hedydd yn yr Haul* (1969) and *Cerddi T Glynne Davies* (1987). He also published short stories, *Cân Serch* (1954), and two novels, *Haf Creulon* (1960) and *Marged* (1974), the latter a panoramic novel about the 'slums' of Llanrwst. His son is the composer and broadcaster Gareth Glyn.

DAVIES, Thomas Morris (c.1865–1951) and Walter (c.1870–c.1950) Engineers

The two brothers owned an ironmongery in Stepney Street, **Llanelli**, and, in 1904 – a time in the early days of motoring when spare wheels were not carried – commenced production of their own patented spare wheel. This 'Stepney Spare Wheel', essentially a spokeless wheel with an oversize tyre which was clipped to the damaged wheel, became highly successful and was used throughout Europe.

DAVIES, W[illiam] H[enry] (1871–1940) Writer

Born in **Newport** and brought up by his grandparents in the public house they kept in the town's docklands, W. H. Davies discovered the natural world while walking through **Monmouthshire**, developing an interest in poetry at the same time. In 1893, with a little money left him by his grandmother, he went to **North America**. There, he found sporadic work on farms, wintering in jails, and travelling across the continent. He went again in 1898 and, on his way to the Klondike, fell under the wheels of a train; his leg was amputated. He described his American experiences in his book *The Autobiography of a Super-Tramp* (1908), which proved a great popular success.

Ryan Davies (rear centre) in 1968

Having settled in **England**, and with the encouragement of his friend **Edward Thomas**, he came to prominence as a poet with his book *Nature Poems* (1908), a collection of simple lyrics, and continued to write prolifically in this vein for the rest of his life. Among his most famous poems is 'Leisure', which begins: 'What is this life if, full of care/ We have no time to stand and stare?'

His reputation as a poet was established with the inclusion of some of his poems in all five volumes of the anthology *Georgian Poetry*, which appeared between 1912 and 1922. His *Collected Poems* appeared shortly before his death in 1940.

DAVIES, W[ilfred] Mitford (1895–1966)
Illustrator

A native of **Anglesey**, Davies created many of the characters that peopled the **Welsh-language** children's books and magazines of the early 1920s. A skilled draughtsman, he produced colourful covers and drawings for *Cymru'r Plant* in particular, and was a considerable landscape painter, in both oils and watercolour.

DAVIES, [Henry] Walford (1869–1941) Musician

Born in Oswestry, **Shropshire**, Davies made an important contribution to musical life in Wales. Although the 'RAF March Past' is perhaps his only well-known composition, he was an able composer. From 1919 to 1926 he was professor of **music** at **Aberystwyth**. In 1919, he also became chairman of the Welsh Music Council, a position he retained until his death, even though he took on a number of other posts including organist at St George's chapel, Windsor, and music adviser to the BBC (*see* **Broadcasting**). He was a formidable, if somewhat elitist, force in musical **education**, seeking through his didactic publications and radio broadcasts to educate the public in the wider spheres of Western art music. He was knighted in 1922 and succeeded Edward Elgar as Master of the King's Musick in 1934.

DAVIES, Walter (Gwallter Mechain; 1761–1849)
Cleric and writer

Llanfechain-born Walter Davies spent much of his life as vicar of **Manafon** and was an avid supporter of the provincial *eisteddfodau*. He compiled agricultural and economic surveys of Wales for the Board of **Agriculture** between 1813 and 1815. He assisted Samuel Lewis in the writing of his *Topographical Dictionary of Wales* (1833) and, with **John Jones** (Ioan Tegid; 1792–1852), edited the works of **Lewys Glyn Cothi** (1837).

DAVIES, William (d.1593) Catholic martyr

A native of Llandrillo-yn-Rhos (**Rhos-on-Sea**), Davies was ordained a **Roman Catholic** priest in 1585. He ministered to the Welsh Catholic community and arranged passage for students to seminaries in mainland Europe. He was among those responsible for the secret recusant press at Rhiwledyn (Little Orme's Head, **Llandudno**), where part of *Y Drych Cristianogawl* was printed. Davies was arrested in 1592 and imprisoned at **Beaumaris**. Convicted of treason, he refused to recant, and was executed in 1593 – the only Catholic priest to be put to death (*see* **Catholic Martyrs**) in Wales during the reign of Elizabeth I.

DAVIES, William (Mynorydd; 1828–1901)
Sculptor and musician

Davies was one of many sculptors practising during a significant period of monument making in the later 19th century, a time of increasing national consciousness. Born in **Merthyr Tydfil** and trained in **London**, he reflected in his **sculpture** the idealism of classical form, his best-known work being the statue of **Thomas Charles** at **Bala**. As a young man, he attended the singing classes of **John Thomas** (Ieuan Ddu; 1795–1871) and later became leader of the Welsh Choral Society. He was the father of the singer **Mary Davies**.

DAVIS, David Daniel (1777–1841) Physician

Born in **Llandyfaelog**, Davis graduated in medicine from Glasgow University in 1801. One of his great contributions was that he introduced changes that would decrease the risk of injury to the mother during delivery. He also realized that the feverish condition that often occurred after delivery was infectious, and took steps to minimize the risks involved. He described some disease conditions associated with pregnancy and the post-pregnancy period in his pioneering work *Elements of Operative Midwifery* (1825). In 1827, he was invited to take the first chair in **London** in obstetrics and the diseases of children, at University College Hospital.

DAVI[E]S, Elizabeth (Betsi Cadwaladr; 1789–1860)
Nurse

A **preacher**'s daughter from **Llanycil**, near **Bala**, she led an unsettled life for a considerable time, but eventually was employed by Guy's Hospital, **London**. At the age of 65, she volunteered for nursing service in the **Crimean War**. According to the *Autobiography of Elizabeth Davis*, compiled by **Jane Williams** on the basis of conversations with her (1857; republished in 1987), she had decided beforehand that her relationship with Florence Nightingale might be tempestuous – and so it proved. Her **health** deteriorated there and she had to leave, spending her last years in poverty.

DAVISON, George (1854–1930)
Photographer and anarchist

An exceptionally able pictorialist photographer (*see* **Photography**), George Davison was born in Lowestoft. He became managing director for Eastman Kodak in **Britain**, but was squeezed out of his post after his espousal of anarchism. Moving to Wales, he built Wern Fawr, **Harlech**, using the mansion to host social and political events, including Fabian summer schools. Wern Fawr was sold at a very low price for the establishment of an adult **education** college (*see* **Coleg Harlech**).

DAWKINS, W[illiam] Boyd (1837–1929) Geologist

A native of Buttington (**Trewern**), Boyd Dawkins was the first professor of **geology** at Manchester (1874–1909). His work in **archaeology** and anthropology was summarized in *Cave Hunting* (1874) and *Early Man in Britain and his Place in the Tertiary Period* (1880). His advice to the Channel Tunnel Company in 1882, to extend its borehole near Dover, led to the discovery of **coal** measures and the development of the Kent coalfield. He was elected FRS at the early age of 29, and knighted in 1919.

DAWNS FLODAU (Flower dance)

A ceremonial **dance** devised by the former **Archdruid** Cynan (**Albert Evans-Jones**), and performed by young girls during various **Gorsedd** ceremonies at the National and some lesser *eisteddfodau*. First performed at the **Machynlleth** Eisteddfod proclamation ceremony in 1936, it first appeared on the Eisteddfod stage at **Ystradgynlais** in 1954.

DE LA BECHE, Henry Thomas (1796–1855)
Geologist

Founder and first director of the Ordnance Geological Survey (now British Geological Survey), Sir Henry de la Beche, FRS, was responsible for the first systematic geological survey of Wales (1838–52) and the publication of large-scale **maps** and accompanying memoirs. He also helped in the planning of the sanitation of **Brecon**, **Merthyr Tydfil** and **Swansea** for the **Health** of Towns Commission, advised the Admiralty upon the choice and efficient use of **coal**, and pioneered enquiries into the causes and prevention of explosions in coalmines (*see* **Colliery Disasters**). His daughter married **Lewis Llewelyn Dillwyn**.

DEATH and FUNERALS

According to testimony, mainly from the 19th century, the Welsh believed in many omens of death. The *aderyn corff* (corpse **bird**), whether robin or screech owl with its eerie cry, lurked disturbingly outside the sick person's home or appeared as a supernatural apparition. In some areas, people feared the howling of the *ci corff* (corpse **dog**) and untimely hammerings, *tolaeth*, in the carpenter's workshop. Belief in the corpse candle, a light that travelled from a sick person's mouth to the graveyard, along the exact route of the impending funeral, was particularly strong, especially in the **diocese** of **St David's**, while the dreaded *toili* was a phantom representation of an entire funeral.

Before the advent of professional undertakers, families made their own arrangements by calling a local handywoman to lay out the corpse and a carpenter to make a coffin of oak or elm, according to the deceased's status. Carpenters in **Powys** and the **border**lands made 'fish-tailed coffins'. To purify the corpse, salt – on a sod or a pewter plate – was positioned on the deceased's breast. It was essential to summon the neighbours to pay their last respects, and in the south-west this was the role of the sombrely dressed 'funeral warner'.

Alternatively, the church bell would be tolled, varying the pattern to denote the age and sex of the deceased. Another task was to ensure new, black mourning clothes for the whole family. While the corpse awaited burial, it was feared that evil spirits might snatch the soul of the deceased, and thus candles were kept alight and neighbours came to keep watch. They flocked to view the corpse and to sympathize with the bereaved, bearing gifts of food.

The night before the funeral a *gwylnos* (watch night) was held, a celebration of the life of the departed, with drinking, smoking and playing games, such as *hirwen gwd*, a custom recorded in **Pembrokeshire**, whereby the shrouded

David Cox, *A Welsh Funeral* (1848)

corpse was drawn up the open chimney. Eighteenth-century religious reformers changed the *gwylnos* into a sober prayer meeting.

On the morning of the funeral, mourners might be offered spiced ale and cakes, while the poor would receive charity over the coffin. Then the sin-eater would appear, to repay the family's hospitality by becoming a scapegoat for the sins of the deceased; evidence for this custom is tenuous, but there are references from **Carmarthenshire**, **Breconshire** and **Caernarfonshire**. In the **slate**-quarrying districts, before the commencement of a funeral, everyone present at the home of the deceased would pitch a silver offering on to a table to help defray expenses.

Hundreds attended public funerals, because everyone, rich and poor, desired a princely send-off. Until the 17th century, heralds from the Royal College of Arms organized the funerals of the nobility, and ordinary folk emulated these ceremonials, expressing social solidarity by helping to carry the coffin and singing **hymns** en route. However, in industrial areas towards the end of the 19th century, men-only funerals became popular, the **women** staying at home to grieve and to prepare **food and drink** for the returning mourners; lugubriously decorated horse-drawn hearses were introduced and public cemeteries began to replace overcrowded **parish** graveyards.

The modern way of cremation was pioneered in Wales, when the famous Dr **William Price** caused a furore by cremating his infant son at **Llantrisant** in 1884.

In **Anglican** funerals in the north, the congregation gave an 'offering' for the clergyman's services. This was unpopular with **Nonconformists**, but everyone contributed willingly to the gravedigger's 'spade-offering', collected at the graveside during the singing of the final hymn. The mourners then partook of the funeral feast, contributing by 'paying the shot' if it was held in a tavern. The bereaved were expected to commemorate their dead by remaining in full mourning for a respectable period, attending the end-of-month memorial sermon, sending mourning cards and dressing their family graves every *Sul y Blodau* (Sunday of flowers): cemeteries throughout Wales are still, on Palm Sunday, a moving sight, refulgent with commemorative **daffodils**. It was traditional for the recently bereaved not to take part in hymn singing during chapel services.

By the early 21st century, at least three-quarters of the funerals of Wales were cremations. The mass-attended funerals which had characterized traditional industrial areas belonged to the past, and the notion that the dead should be commemorated by gravestones had been largely abandoned. While funeral services were still generally conducted by clergymen, increasing numbers were opting for secular funerals, with no reference to life after death. Perhaps the most interesting development was the growing popularity of 'green' burials, with mourners invited to bring spades with which to dig a hole into which a biodegradable coffin would be lowered.

DECEANGLI Tribe

The **Iron Age** tribe of the north-eastern **border**land, the Deceangli were the first Welsh tribe to be attacked by **Roman** forces. Ostorius Scapula (governor, AD 47–52)

confronted them, presumably to drive a wedge between the Brigantes of northern **England** and the powerful **Silures** and **Ordovices** in Wales. The name survived in **Tegeingl**, the *cantref* which was the core of the later **Flintshire**.

DECHRAU CANU DECHRAU CANMOL
Television programme

Wales's long-standing tradition of **hymn**-singing festivals (see *Cymanfa Ganu*) and the popularity of *Caniadaeth y Cysegr* on radio prompted BBC Wales, in 1960, to produce its first televised hymn-singing programme – from Trinity **Presbyterian** chapel, **Swansea**. The high audience rating for *Dechrau Canu Dechrau Canmol* (Beginning to sing beginning to praise) encouraged programme planners in **London** to launch a network version in **English**, *Songs of Praise*, a programme frequently introduced by **Harry Secombe**. More recently, *Dechrau Canu Dechrau Canmol* has been produced for **S4C**, not by the BBC, but by independent production companies.

DEE, John (1527–1608) Polymath and magician

Dr John Dee, renowned 'magus of the Elizabethan age', was born in Surrey of Welsh stock. His father was from **Radnorshire** and he claimed descent from **Rhodri Mawr** and cousinship with Blanche Parry. Dee became consultant to Elizabeth I on affairs of state, including matters relating to a British empire (he coined the term) which he believed had once existed in northern Europe and **North America**, a continent which, he claimed, had been conquered by **Arthur** and settled by **Madog ab Owain Gwynedd**. He thus launched a myth that later seized the imagination of **radicals** who sought to establish Welsh communities in North America. His reputation towards the end of his life was marred by his accounts of intercourse with spirits. Among his many treatises, his edition of **Robert Recorde**'s *The Ground of Artes* (1561) and his *Memorials Pertayning to the Perfect Arte of Navigation* (1577) are the most intelligible.

DEE (Dyfrdwy) River (179km, 163 km either in Wales or constituting the Wales/England border)

The Dee rises near Duallt rocks (650 m) in the **community** of **Llanuwchllyn**. It flows through Bala **Lake** (Llyn Tegid) to **Bala**, an ancient **Celtic** word meaning the efflux of a **river** from a lake. At Bala, it is joined by the Tryweryn, which drains the region dominated by the **Arenig Mountains**. Llyn Celyn is the **reservoir** on the Tryweryn (*see* **Tryweryn, Drowning of**). The Tryweryn is popular among white-water rafters.

South of **Corwen**, the Dee is joined by the Alwen, which, with its tributary, the Brenig, drains much of **Mynydd Hiraethog**. Damming them has created major reservoirs. Between Corwen and **Llangollen**, the Dee flows eastwards through Dyffryn **Edeirnion** and Glyndyfrdwy – the glen which gave **Owain Glyndŵr** his name. At Llangollen, the river is crossed by a 16th-century bridge considered to be one of the 'Seven Wonders of Wales'. At Froncysyllte, **Thomas Telford**'s famous aqueduct (Pont Cysyllte) transports the Shropshire Union **Canal** across the Dee (*see* **Llangollen Rural**). Some 5 km east of the aqueduct, the river is joined by the Ceiriog, which drains much of the

Berwyn Mountains. The aqueduct and **railway** bridge which cross the Ceiriog near **Chirk** create a dramatic scene.

North of **Bangor Is-y-Coed**, the Dee is joined by the Clywedog, a river which flows through a valley rich in industrial archaeology (*see* **Coedpoeth**). Two kilometres north of the confluence, the Dee constitutes the Wales–**England** border. North of **Holt**, it is joined by the Alyn, which drains much of **Flintshire**. North-east of Rossett, both banks of the Dee are in **England**, but the river – in a canalized form – returns to Wales west of Chester at **Saltney**.

At **Connah's Quay**, the river enters its wide estuary. On its western, Welsh bank are **Flint**, **Bagillt**, **Holywell** and **Mostyn**. The estuary joins the open sea at Point of Ayr (**Llanasa**), the site, until 1996, of the northern **coal**field's last deep mine.

DEER

Six species of deer have roamed Wales since the end of the latest Ice Age, *c.*11,500 years ago. Reindeer occurred on the post-glacial tundra while the giant Irish elk roamed the blanket bogs of western Europe until it became extinct about 10,000 years ago. The red deer inhabited the early forests but had become extinct in Wales by the later 18th century. A head-and-antler set recovered from shore **peat** near **Barmouth** suggests that members of this Welsh population were bigger than modern animals.

Historically, the most prominent of Welsh deer is the roe. Found throughout Europe, but absent from Wales since the later 18th century, it was first recorded in the 13th century, although it is almost certainly a native species; and *iwrch* (roe) **place names** of unknown antiquity are frequent in Wales. There is reason to believe that the roe is spreading once again into Wales from **England**.

The best-known deer in Wales today is the fallow, introduced to **Britain** by the **Normans** and eventually becoming an ornamental parkland species for the great estates. Escapees from estates such as Nannau (**Brithdir and Llanfachreth**), Golden Grove (**Llanfihangel Aberbythych**) and **Bodorgan**, have established themselves successfully in the wild. During the later 20th century, the exotic Chinese muntjac deer spread to Wales from its points of origin in the animal collections of southern England.

DEHEUBARTH Kingdom

Around AD 920, **Hywel Dda** united **Dyfed** and **Seisyllwg** to create Deheubarth, a kingdom which would later also include **Brycheiniog**. It was the last of the four principal Welsh kingdoms to evolve and consequently never had the sense of identity that existed in **Gwynedd, Powys** and **Morgannwg**. Hywel dominated Wales until his death in 950, as did his grandson, Maredudd ab Owain, during the last decade of the 10th century. In 1081, **Rhys ap Tewdwr** was recognized by William I as ruler of Deheubarth but Rhys was killed in 1093 and most of the kingdom came under **Norman** rule. Its revival was the work of his four grandsons, Anarawd, Cadell, Maredudd and Rhys. The first three died young; but **Rhys ap Gruffydd**, known as the Lord Rhys, emerged after 1170 as the most powerful ruler in Wales. His death in 1197 marked the end of Deheubarth as a significant and united force in Welsh politics. **Dinefwr** was traditionally considered to be its capital.

DEINIOL (d.584) Saint

The grandson of the hero Pabo Post Prydyn and reputed founder of the influential monasteries of **Bangor** in **Arfon** and **Bangor Is-y-Coed**, Deiniol was reputedly the first bishop in **Gwynedd** (consecrated by **Dyfrig**, according to the *Liber Landavensis*). His death was noted in *Annales Cambriae* (*see* **Brut y Tywysogyon**), while **Giraldus Cambrensis** mentions his burial on Bardsey (**Aberdaron**; *see also* **Islands**). The *Legenda*, read on his feast day – 11 September – during the Middle Ages, survives. It describes the **saint** as a hermit miraculously chosen to become bishop of Bangor. It has no historical basis.

DELYN Constituency and one-time district

Following the abolition of **Flintshire** in 1974, Delyn was created as a district of the new **county** of **Clwyd**. It consisted of what had been the **borough** of **Flint**, the **urban districts** of **Holywell** and **Mold** and the **rural district** of Holywell. Delyn was an amalgam of the names of the **Dee** and Alyn **Rivers** and therefore mirrored that of the neighbouring district of **Alyn and Deeside**. In 1996, the district became part of the reconstituted unitary county of Flint. The name survives as that of a constituency.

DEMETAE Tribe

It used to be considered that the Demetae, the **Iron Age** tribe of south-west Wales, were less hostile to **Roman** expansion than their neighbours. This view was called into question by the discovery in 2003 of two Roman forts at **Dinefwr** (*see* **Llandeilo**), one of which was the largest auxiliary fort in Wales. Moridunum (**Carmarthen**) probably became the *civitas* capital of the tribe. Their tribal identity was maintained during the Romano-British period and survived into the emerging kingdom of **Dyfed**.

DENBIGH (Sir Dinbych), Denbighshire
(3136 ha; 8783 inhabitants)

The centre of the *cantref* of **Rhufoniog**, Denbigh's ridge seems to have been first fortified by **Dafydd ap Gruffudd**, lord of Rhufoniog (1277–83). Following Henry de **Lacy**'s acquisition of the **lordship of Denbigh** in 1284, Dafydd's work was replaced by an elaborate castle and a walled town. The castle is evidence of the inventiveness of **James of St George** for, of all the features of the late 13th-century castles of Wales, Denbigh's Great Gatehouse is perhaps the most ingenious. By the late 15th century, the steeply sloping walled town had been abandoned. A new settlement developed at the foot of the hill, where a Carmelite **friar**y had been founded *c.*1290.

In 1536, Denbigh became the **county** town of the newly created **Denbighshire**, and, as the location of the chancery and exchequer of the north-east, it became the capital of one of the four corners of Wales. In 1578, Robert Dudley, earl of Leicester, holder of the lordship of Denbigh from 1563 to 1588, began building a large church near the castle, intended perhaps as a replacement for **St Asaph** Cathedral. A building designed for preaching, it was a unique example in Wales of a large-scale late 16th-century church, and can be seen as the ancestor of the Welsh **Nonconformist** chapel; work on it was abandoned in 1584. The castle, held for the crown during the **Civil War**, was largely dismantled in 1660.

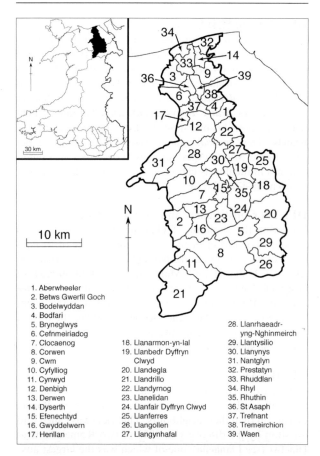

1. Aberwheeler
2. Betws Gwerfil Goch
3. Bodelwyddan
4. Bodfari
5. Bryneglwys
6. Cefnmeiriadog
7. Clocaenog
8. Corwen
9. Cwm
10. Cyfylliog
11. Cynwyd
12. Denbigh
13. Derwen
14. Dyserth
15. Efenechtyd
16. Gwyddelwern
17. Henllan

18. Llanarmon-yn-Ial
19. Llanbedr Dyffryn Clwyd
20. Llandegla
21. Llandrillo
22. Llandyrnog
23. Llanelidan
24. Llanfair Dyffryn Clwyd
25. Llanferres
26. Llangollen
27. Llangynhafal

28. Llanrhaeadr-yng-Nghinmeirch
29. Llantysilio
30. Llanynys
31. Nantglyn
32. Prestatyn
33. Rhuddlan
34. Rhyl
35. Rhuthin
36. St Asaph
37. Trefnant
38. Tremeirchion
39. Waen

The communities of the county of Denbigh

From the 16th to the 19th century, Denbigh was one of Wales's most lively intellectual centres. It was the home of the **map** maker **Humphrey Lhuyd**, the financier Richard Clough (d.1570) and the talented **Salusbury** and **Myddelton** families. **Thomas Edwards** (Twm o'r Nant; 1739–1819) launched his career as a writer of **interludes** at Denbigh. **Thomas Jones** (1756–1820), pastor of the town's Capel Mawr, was the first Methodist layman to give communion to his flock – an act which precipitated the creation of the **Calvinistic Methodist** denomination in 1811.

Thomas Gee made Denbigh one of Wales's chief publishing centres, launching the influential quarterly *Y Traethodydd* (1845; *see* **Periodicals**), *Y Gwyddoniadur Cymreig* (1854–97) and *Baner Cymru* (1857, later *Baner ac Amserau Cymru*; *see* **Newspapers**). Gee's attacks on landowners and the Established Church help to explain Denbigh's central role in the **Tithe** War of the 1880s.

For many in northern Wales, however, Denbigh developed a different connotation. Although the North Wales Hospital for mental disorders, opened in 1848, provided praiseworthy service, it caused Denbigh to become the name of the place to which people dreaded that they might be forced to go. Closed in 1995, the huge complex has yet to find a new function.

Among the interesting features of Denbigh's built-up area are the forlorn friary ruins, Capel Mawr (1829, 1880), the **Congregational** chapel (1838/9, 1875, 1891), two **Anglican** churches (1840, 1874), Howells School (1860) and the Town Hall (1916). Robert Dudley's Town Hall (1572)

was long the centre of Denbighshire county **government**. However, following the establishment of the Denbighshire County Council in 1889, county government was transferred to **Ruthin**.

Denbigh's outer reaches offer a range of interesting places unparalleled by the other market towns of Wales. Chief among them is Denbigh's mother church of St Marcella (Llanfarchell or Whitchurch). A doubled-naved building of the 14th and 15th centuries, it contains a splendid monument to Humphrey Llwyd and an elaborate brass memorial to the Myddelton family. In the churchyard are the graves of Thomas Edwards (Twm o'r Nant), and of the Thomas Jones mentioned above. Lleweni, the home of the Salusbury family, was demolished in 1818. Near it are the ruins of a vast bleach works, established *c.*1785. Richard Clough's Plas Clough (1567) introduced Netherlandish stepped gables to Wales. Galch Hill (16th century) was the birthplace of the Myddelton brothers, Thomas (1550–1631) and Hugh (1560–1631) prominent in the history of **London**. Gwaenynog is another Myddelton house; Beatrix Potter set her Peter Rabbit illustrations in its garden. Near it is a monument commemorating Dr Johnson's visit.

DENBIGH Lordship

Established as a **march**er-lordship in 1284, it consisted of the *cantref* of **Rhufoniog**, most of that of **Rhos** and the **commote** of **Dinmael**. Originally granted to Henry de **Lacy**, earl of Lincoln, it eventually passed to the **Mortimer family** and thence to the crown. In 1536, it became the core of the new **county** of **Denbighshire**. The *Survey of the Honour of Denbigh* (1334), perhaps the most important source on the social history of later medieval Wales, was edited by the Russian historian Paul Vinogradoff (1914).

DENBIGHSHIRE (Sir Ddinbych)
(84,628 ha; 93,065 inhabitants)

The original **county** of **Denbigh** was established in 1536 and consisted of what had been the **march**er-lordships of **Denbigh**, **Dyffryn Clwyd (Ruthin)**, **Bromfield and Yale** and **Chirk and Chirkland**. On the eve of its abolition in 1974, the county consisted of the **boroughs** of **Colwyn Bay**, Denbigh, Ruthin and **Wrexham**, the **urban districts** of **Abergele**, **Llangollen**, **Llanrwst** and the **rural districts** of Aled, Ceiriog, Hiraethog, Ruthin and Wrexham.

Following abolition, **Colwyn** (deprived of the east bank of the **Conwy**), **Glyndŵr** (which included **Edeirnion**, previously in **Merioneth**) and **Wrexham-Maelor** (which included **Maelor Saesneg**, previously in **Flintshire**) came into existence as three of the six districts of the **county of Clwyd**. That county was abolished in 1996, and Denbighshire returned to the map. As the new county consisted of Glyndŵr, **Rhuddlan** and part of Colwyn, it had a markedly different shape from the old Denbighshire. Indeed, the old county's entire coastline became part of the county of Conwy; before 1974, the new county's coastline had been in Flintshire.

The core of the new county is the basin of the **River Clwyd**, although it also includes much of the upper reaches of the **Dee** valley. In 1998, the **community** of Llangollen **Rural** was transferred to the **Wrexham County Borough**, and there were suggestions that the community of

Llangollen should also be transferred. In 2001, 36.04% of the inhabitants of Denbighshire had some knowledge of **Welsh**, with 20.73% wholly fluent in the language (*see also* **Cynwyd**, **Gwyddelwern** and **Rhyl**). At the time of the abolition of the original county in 1974, Denbighshire consisted of 173,201 hectares and had 188,800 inhabitants.

DENIZENSHIP

Following the outbreak of the **Glyndŵr Revolt**, two groups of statutes – later known as Wales's **Penal Code** – were passed (in 1401 and 1402) and which imposed numerous restrictions on Welshmen and on **English**men married to Welsh wives. The revolt over, the legislation was usually ignored, but it could be used against leaders of the native Welsh community by their political opponents. Denizenship was a response to this; it involved granting Welshmen English legal status and consequently exemption from the effects of the penal statutes, sometimes by way of reward and sometimes in response to petitions. The first such grant was in 1413.

DEORHAM (Dyrham), Battle of

One of a number of victories which established the supremacy of the **English** rulers of Wessex in southern **Britain**, the battle was fought in the year 577 in the vicinity of the village of Dyrham, near Bath and Bristol, and gave the victors access to the Severn Sea.

DEPRESSION OF THE INTERWAR YEARS, The

The Depression was the principal happening in the history of 20th-century Wales. It halted and reversed the industrial growth that had characterized the Welsh **economy** for a century and half. Its most obvious consequence was the rise of unemployment, which was 4% among Welsh insured males in 1923 and 42.8% in August 1932. Lack of employment led to **emigration**. Wales had 2,736,000 inhabitants in 1925 and 2,487,000 in 1939. As the **population** experienced natural growth in those years, the total loss through emigration was 390,000.

Every developed Western nation suffered depression in the interwar years, but the experience of Wales was exceptional in its length and severity. That is attributable above all to the dependence of the Welsh economy on the **coal** industry, which employed 291,000 Welsh workers in 1920, and 138,000 in 1939. Collapse in employment in the south Wales coalfield was greater than it was in other British coalfields, because that coalfield had been developed to a unique extent to supply overseas markets. Those markets served it well in 1918–21 and again in 1923 but, in 1924–5, crisis struck, with unemployment among south Wales miners increasing from 1.8% in April 1924 to 28.4% in August 1925.

The crisis was at its worst in the steam-coal areas, precisely those which had expanded most rapidly in the previous 40 years; in 1927, when unemployment was 40%

A soup kitchen for Hirwaun schoolchildren during the 1926 General Strike

among the steam-coal workers of Ferndale (**Rhondda**), it was 10% among the anthracite workers of **Ammanford**. The situation was exacerbated by the **General Strike** and, above all, by the Wall Street crash of 1929, which added cyclical unemployment to the structural unemployment already suffered by the coalfield community.

The massive contraction in the coal industry led to unemployment among dock and **railway** workers, and among those offering services to the coalfield community – shopkeepers, farmers, builders, **textile** workers and holiday resort workers among them. Following the crash of 1929, the entire economy suffered, with employment in such important sectors as steelmaking (*see* **Iron and Steel**) and **slate** quarrying contracting sharply. The closure of the **Brymbo** steelworks near **Wrexham** in 1930 caused unemployment among insured males there to rise to 90%. By the early 1930s, **Brynmawr**, where almost all works had closed, was the most stricken of all Welsh industrial communities.

In the more favoured areas of **Britain**, the worst was over by 1934, but Wales had hardly any such areas. The **government** offered virtually no solutions beyond migration, although the Special Areas Amendment Act of 1937 did mark the beginning of regional employment policies. Some relief also came through the establishment of a new steelworks at **Ebbw Vale** in 1936, and through the employment provided by the government's rearmament programme.

Despite the outflow from Wales, the majority of the unemployed remained at home, for factors such as **housing**, local availability of credit and children's **education** restricted migration. Providing for the unemployed was an enormous task. Those who had exhausted their unemployment benefit had to rely on dole payments, which were subject to a **means test**. Until the abolition of the **Poor Law** in 1929, the dole was the responsibility of the guardians. In 1927, the **Bedwellty** guardians, accused of extravagance, were suspended. In 1929, dole payments became the responsibility of the **counties** and **county boroughs**. Their cost, a huge burden in places such as **Merthyr Tydfil**, caused the downfall of the **Labour** government in 1931. The Unemployed Assistance Board, established in 1934 with the aim of ensuring stricter control of payments, gave rise to the largest demonstrations ever held in Wales. The meagreness of the payments – some 30 shillings (£1.50) a week for a family of four – led to malnutrition, particularly among **women**. Idleness led to despondency, with mass unemployment sapping the vigour of Wales's industrial communities. The assumption that the next generation would relocate to places such as Slough and Dagenham weakened allegiance to the **Welsh language**.

It was widely believed that the Depression was a symptom of the crisis of capitalism. **Marxism** won extensive support, with **Communism** becoming entrenched in the 'Little Moscows' of Maerdy (Rhondda) and elsewhere. Leading members of the Labour Party, **Aneurin Bevan** above all, also had an essentially Marxist view of the Depression. Welsh politics in the years following the end of the **Second World War** were primarily concerned with ensuring that mass unemployment would not recur. By the later 20th century, there were economists who argued that the interwar years were in many ways a period of improvement, and that the Depression was not much more than a blip in a century of unsurpassed economic progress, an interpretation strongly at variance with the views of those who actually experienced Wales's 'age of the locust'.

DERFEL, R[obert] J[ones] (1824–1905) Writer

A native of **Llandderfel**, he adopted the surname Derfel after moving to Manchester, where he was a commercial traveller. He was an eloquent advocate of the cause of **Home Rule** for Wales, and sought to marry **socialism** and **nationalism** in a Christian context. His play *Brad y Llyfrau Gleision* (1854) did much to ignite Welsh opinion against the indictment made by the Blue Books of 1847 (*see* **Treason of the Blue Books**).

DERLLYS Commote

One of the **commote**s of **Cantref Gwarthaf**, Derllys contained **Carmarthen**. The name survived in the post-**Acts of 'Union' hundred** of Derllys. Derllys Court (**Newchurch and Merthyr**) was the birthplace of **Bridget Bevan** (1698–1779).

DERWEN, Denbighshire (1442 ha; 454 inhabitants)

Located north of the **River Clwyd** and south-west of **Ruthin**, the **community**'s **parish** church (St Mary's) contains a rood screen and loft. In the churchyard, there is a fine medieval cross with an ornately carved head. The holy **well**, Ffynnon Sarah, has been attractively restored and landscaped. The **hymn**writer **William Jones** (Ehedydd Iâl; 1815–99) was born at Cefn Deulin, Derwen. In the late 20th century, Clawdd-newydd developed as a commuter village serving Ruthin.

DESIGN

Design in Wales has historically been a matter of utility and functionality, with products only rarely designed for export. Many of the domestic goods produced demonstrate a plain and restrained beauty, which still exerts a strong appeal. **Furniture**, weapons, vehicles, **pottery**, tools, domestic utensils, and **leather**, woollen and sewn goods were the chief material products of pre-industrial life, and they often represented **craft**smanship of a high order.

Growing mechanization from the late 18th century onwards was the dynamo for mass production and the beginning of design, as the term is normally understood. **Japan ware** and ceramic products, particularly **Swansea** porcelain (*see* **Pottery and Porcelain**), were among the first innovatively designed commodities made in Wales. As on the farms and at sea, so in the extractive industries there was a tradition of design by necessity. The miner's lamp, for instance, was augmented by many local refinements, notable examples being designed and made at **Aberdare**.

Opportunities for design became fewer as industries grew and as their headquarters – the usual location of designers – came to be sited outside Wales. The **depression of the interwar years**, however, saw attempts to revitalize regions of industrial decline. Retraining former industrial workers was the aim of the **Brynmawr** project, which produced furniture and leather goods. The design and production of furniture continues after further industrial decline in the late 20th century – and the heads of the southern valleys area is now the sofa manufacturing capital of Europe.

The post-**Second World War** relocation of **textile** and clothing production, assisted by generous grants and low labour costs, created opportunities for Welsh designers. Design **education** expanded and by the 1960s Welsh designers such as Mary Quant and **Laura Ashley** were enjoying international reputations. Laura Ashley moved her production to **Carno**, in an attempt to stem rural de**population**. The factory closed in 2005.

In the new factories of former industrial areas, locally trained designers were employed, particularly in the production of casual wear and lingerie for major retailers such as Marks & Spencer. A short product life and aggressive marketing techniques requires sizeable teams creating a constant flow of design ideas. Small firms design and produce a variety of products, including toys, tableware, furniture, **glass** and Christmas decorations. This sector is suffering major contraction, as much of the production has moved to developing countries.

The establishment of the **Welsh Office**, measures such as the **Welsh Language Act** and the advent of **S4C** and **devolution** have increased design, graphic and print opportunities. Consequently, design and production are located where the requisite skills exist. **Cardiff** in particular, but also the north-west, has seen significant increases in television, animation, **film**, video and **music** production, enabling design students to fulfil their ambitions close to home. A growing sense of national identity has combined with new technology to spawn a host of small, often rurally based, companies involved in the production of T-shirts, posters, magazines, recording covers and related material. The National Centre for Product Design and Development Research at the **University of Wales Institute, Cardiff** is foremost among the university design departments attempting to recharge the **economy** by designing new products and evolving new ways of manufacturing them.

Welsh graduate designers contribute to the design teams of the motor, **aviation**, information technology, electronics and other industries. The furniture designer Angela Giddens, and the fashion designers Dai Rees and Julien Macdonald have won renown, while the designs of Ross Lovegrove – on Apple computers and other sophisticated products – are probably seen by more people than those of almost any designer in history. One of Wales's most famous designs features in major American **films** and soap operas, and is offered by international restaurants and airlines: the shapely, blue, Tŷ Nant bottle, containing spring water from the hills of **Ceredigion**, is among the most widely seen of all Welsh objects; like many things Welsh, it was designed by a committee.

DESPENSER family Marcher-lords

The family became associated with Wales through the marriage of Hugh to Eleanor, co-heiress of Gilbert de **Clare** (d.1314), which brought Hugh the lordship of **Glamorgan**. A favourite of Edward II, he ruthlessly amassed territories extending from the **Wye** to the **Teifi**, activities which sparked off the 'Despenser War' in 1321. In addition, his father, Hugh the elder, was granted the lordship of **Denbigh**. From 1322 to 1326, the kingdom of **England** was ruled by the two Despensers. They were overthrown and hanged in 1326. Their descendants retained a tenuous hold upon Glamorgan until it passed by marriage to the **Beauchamp family**, lords of **Elfael**, in 1399.

DESPERATE POACHING AFFRAY, A (1903)
Film

A pioneering work for Gaumont by the film-maker **William Haggar**. Its violence, iconoclasm and progressive editing have attracted scholarly attention in recent years. The **film**, together with Frank Mottershaw's *Daring Daylight Burglary* and Edwin S. Porter's Edison film, *The Great Train Robbery* (both 1903), is credited with influencing the chase sub-genre of American films that attained its silent-era comic apogee with Mack Sennett's *Keystone Kops*.

DEUDDWR Commote

Located between two waters (*dau ddŵr*) – the **Rivers** Vyrnwy and **Severn** – Deuddwr constituted the north-easternmost part of the later **Montgomeryshire**. Together with **Llannerch Hudol** and **Ystrad Marchell**, it was part of the district known as Teirswydd. The hamlet of Deuddwr (*see* **Llansantffraid**) preserves the name.

DEVAUDEN, Monmouthshire
(3788 ha; 968 inhabitants)

A tract of undulating land north-west of **Chepstow**, the **community** contains the settlements of Devauden, Wolvesnewton, Kilgwrrwg, Newchurch and Itton. Devauden village green was the setting for John Wesley's first sermon in Wales. Itton Court has a medieval gate tower.

DEVELOPMENT AREAS

The 1945 Distribution of Industry Act redefined and renamed pre-war 'Special Areas' of particular need as 'Development Areas'. In the south, the Development Area extended the old Special Area to western parts of the **coal**field, including major towns excluded from the earlier designation, as well as parts of **Pembrokeshire**. In 1946, **Wrexham** also became a Development Area. Over the years, the **government**'s policy instruments relating to Development Areas underwent a number of changes, as did the definitions and boundary delineations of the areas themselves.

DEVELOPMENT BOARD FOR RURAL WALES, The

The Board was established in 1977, charged with the economic and industrial development of mid-Wales (**Powys**, **Meirionnydd** and **Ceredigion**). Central to the Board's policy was the generation and attraction of manufacturing employment by means of advance factories, grants and cheap rents. A strategy based on the selection of specific locations for economic development, focused around **Newtown**, produced a concentration of activity in eastern areas. A change of emphasis in the 1990s encouraged indigenous potential, often at local grassroots level, together with greater geographic diffusion. With the establishment of the **National Assembly**, the Board became part of an enlarged **Welsh Development Agency**.

DEVEREUX family Landowners

The family claimed origins in Evreux, Normandy. Its association with Wales arose when, in 1525, Walter Devereux became steward of Princess Mary's household, a position allowing him to gain possession of much of the property of the attainted Rhys ap Gruffudd (d.1531), the grandson of **Rhys ap Thomas**. Walter's grandson, also Walter, who was granted the earldom of Essex in 1572, belonged to the 'ultra-Protestant party'. (Walter's brother, George, married the widow of **Thomas Jones** (Twm Shon Catti; c.1530–1609).) Walter's son, the second earl, Queen Elizabeth's favourite, was executed in 1601 for an insurrection in which his Welsh tenants, led by **Gelly Meyrick**, were much involved. The third earl (1591–1646) was the leader of the Parliamentary forces, a factor relevant to the role of **Pembrokeshire** in the **Civil War**. He was the last of the earls, but the family's earlier title, viscount Hereford, passed to a cadet line, which was influential in **Breconshire** and **Montgomeryshire** for generations. In 1874, the family, whose chief residence was at Tregoyd (**Gwernyfed**), owned 725 ha in Breconshire.

DEVOLUTION

Political devolution – the transfer of power from the centre to the periphery – became a term of reference widely used in Wales during the 1970s in the context of the British **government**'s proposals for elected assemblies for Wales and **Scotland**. The post-war Attlee governments displayed scant

Devolution campaigners included the singer Cerys Matthews when still a member of the rock band Catatonia

interest in devolution for Wales, grudgingly setting up the **Council for Wales and Monmouthshire**, with a nominated membership, in 1948. A Minister for Welsh Affairs was appointed by the **Conservatives** in 1951, but a petition bearing more than 250,000 signatures presented to parliament by the Parliament for Wales campaigners in 1956 yielded few positive results. A Government of Wales Bill introduced in the House of Commons by **S. O. Davies (Merthyr Tydfil)** in 1955 made no progress. By 1959, however, the **Labour Party**, alarmed by the growth of **Plaid [Genedlaethol] Cymru**, included in its election manifesto a commitment to appoint a **secretary of state for Wales**.

The promise was made good when Labour returned to power in 1964 and **James Griffiths** (MP for **Llanelli**) became the first secretary of state for Wales. The new department's range of responsibilities increased rapidly during subsequent years. The dramatic victory of **Gwynfor Evans** in the **Carmarthen** by-election of July 1966, followed by substantial Plaid Cymru polls at **Rhondda** West in 1967 and **Caerphilly** in 1968, increased the pressure on the Labour Party to consider a far-reaching scheme of devolution for Wales.

Advocates of an elected assembly for Wales depicted its establishment as an admirable complement to a reformed local government structure and membership of the European Community. The long-awaited report of the **Kilbrandon** (formerly Crowther) **Commission**, published in October 1973, proved generally supportive of the idea of an elected assembly for Wales. A long debate ensued within the Labour Party, eventually resulting in the introduction of the Wales and Scotland Bill, which proposed a legislative assembly for Scotland and an executive assembly for Wales. The Wales Act, which advocated a Welsh Assembly with a severely limited range of powers, eventually reached the Statute Book in July 1978.

Debate ensued for months, until the fateful referendum vote of 1 March 1979. Officially, all the political parties in Wales, except the Conservatives, were pledged to support a measure of devolution. However, a number of Welsh MPs, notably Leo Abse (**Pontypool**) and Neil Kinnock (**Bedwellty**), led fierce opposition to their party's proposals, and were supported by Labour councillors in almost every area of Wales. When the vote took place, 243,048 voted in favour and 956,330 against; there was a negative majority in every county in Wales, ranging from 33.1% in **Gwynedd** to 75.8% in **Gwent**.

Within months, the election of a right-wing Conservative government at Westminster under Margaret Thatcher condemned the cause of Welsh and Scottish devolution to oblivion, but the ensuing years of economic crisis and spiralling unemployment eventually led to some reassessment of the political requirements of Wales. The early 1990s saw the emergence of an all-party Campaign for a Welsh Assembly, the appeal of which was strengthened by growing alarm at the dominant position in Welsh life held by **quangos**.

The Labour Party announced new proposals for devolution in May 1995 and formed a government two years later, holding a further referendum on 18 September 1997. The call for a 'Yes' vote was led by Ron Davies, the Secretary of State for Wales (1997–8) and MP for

How Wales voted, by county, in the devolution referendum of 1997

County	Electorate	Turnout	Voters against	Voters in favour	Percentage of voters in favour
Anglesey, Isle of	54,044	56.9%	15,095	15,649	50.9%
Blaenau Gwent	55,089	49.3%	11,928	15,237	56.4%
Bridgend	100,400	50.6%	23,172	27,632	54.4%
Caerphilly	129,060	49.3%	28,841	34,830	54.7%
Cardiff	228,571	46.9%	59,589	47,527	44.4%
Carmarthenshire	133,467	56.4%	26,911	49,115	65.3%
Ceredigion	54,440	56.8%	12,614	18,304	59.2%
Conwy	87,231	51.5%	26,521	18,369	40.9%
Denbighshire	70,410	49.8%	20,732	14,271	40.8%
Flintshire	113,181	41%	28,710	17,746	38.2%
Gwynedd	92,520	59.8%	19,859	35,425	64.1%
Merthyr Tydfil	44,107	49.5%	9,121	12,707	58.2%
Monmouthshire	65,309	50.5%	22,403	10,592	32.1%
Neath Port Talbot	106,333	51.9%	18,463	36,730	66.5%
Newport	94,094	46.1%	27,017	16,172	37.4%
Pembrokeshire	88,720	52.6%	26,712	19,979	42.8%
Powys	96,107	56.2%	30,966	23,038	42.7%
Rhondda Cynon Taff	175,639	49.9%	36,362	51,201	58.5%
Swansea	174,725	47.1%	39,561	42,789	52%
Torfaen	69,505	45.5%	15,854	15,756	49.8%
Vale of Glamorgan	89,111	54.3%	30,613	17,776	36.7%
Wrexham	96,787	42.4%	22,449	18,574	45.3%

Caerphilly. A joint campaign with the **Liberals** and Plaid Cymru yielded a positive outcome, with 559,419 (50.3%) voting in favour, and 552,698 (49.7%) against. Intense wrangling over the location of the new assembly persisted well into the following year.

The first elections to the new 60-seat **National Assembly for Wales**, to be located in **Cardiff** Bay, were held in March 1999. A new chapter in Welsh political and constitutional history had begun.

DIC SIÔN DAFYDD
Comparable with the black American 'Uncle Tom' figure who disdains his origins in order to ingratiate himself with white society, a Dic Siôn Dafydd is a Welshman who pretends to have forgotten his native language and denies his national identity in order to succeed among the **English**. It was originally the name of a character in a poem by **John Jones** (Jac Glan-y-gors; 1766–1821).

DICTIONARIES
One of the earliest printed Welsh books was *A Dictionary in Englyshe and Welshe* (1547) by **William Salesbury**. Despite its title, it is in fact a **Welsh–English** dictionary, where many Welsh words are listed without English equivalents. The most important Welsh dictionary until modern times was *Dictionarium Duplex* (1632) a Welsh–**Latin/** Latin–Welsh Dictionary compiled by **John Davies** (*c.*1567–1644). The Latin–Welsh section is an abridgement of Thomas Wiliems's unpublished adaptation of Thomas

Thomas's standard Latin–English dictionary. The Welsh–Latin section was the basis of a small Welsh–Welsh–English dictionary (listing Welsh words, with synonyms in both Welsh and English), *Y Gymraeg yn ei Disgleirdeb/The British Language in its Lustre* (1688) by **Thomas Jones** the almanacer (1648–1713). It was later translated and published as *Antiquae Linguae Britannicae Thesaurus ... a Welsh–English Dictionary* (1753) by Thomas Richards (1710–90) (*see* **Bridgend**: Coychurch Lower), incorporating additional material from various sources.

The first English–Welsh Dictionary (1725) was a small, poorly produced work by John Roderick (Siôn Rhydderch), the almanacer. The second half of the 18th century saw the publication of an English–Welsh dictionary (1770–94) by John Walters (1721–97) (*see* **Llanfair**), a seminal work in English–Welsh lexicography, which lists in detail the various senses of English words together with their Welsh equivalents, and is based in part on an unpublished work by William Gambold, the author of *A Grammar of the Welsh Language* (1727).

The Welsh of the first half of the 19th century was heavily influenced by *A Welsh and English Dictionary* (1793–1803), by **William Owen Pughe**. Although Pughe was exceptionally knowledgeable about Welsh vocabulary, his work was vitiated by his capricious opinions. The most important lexicographer of the second half of the century was D. Silvan Evans (1818–1903), editor of a compendious English–Welsh dictionary (1847–58), and an unfinished, ambitious, historical Welsh–English dictionary (1887–96).

D

An additional part, up to the word 'ennyd', was published after his death in 1906. A similar fate awaited John Lloyd-Jones's (1885–1956) vocabulary of early Welsh poetry, *Geirfa Barddoniaeth Gynnar Gymraeg* (1931–63), which was far more ambitious than its title would suggest, but reached only the word 'heilic'.

In 1848, William **Spurrell** published a Welsh–English and, in 1850, an English–Welsh dictionary. Several revised editions of these were published, from 1913 onwards, under the editorship of J. Bodvan Anwyl (1875–1949), aided initially by his brother **Edward Anwyl**. These were the standard dictionaries of the first half of the 20th century, as were those of H. Meurig Evans, in particular *Y Geiriadur Mawr* (1958), in the second half.

The 20th century saw a burgeoning of lexicographical activity: dialect glossaries such as *The Welsh Vocabulary of the Bangor District* (1913) by O. H. Fynes-Clinton, and *Geirfa Tafodiaith Nantgarw* (1993) by Ceinwen H. Thomas; bilingual Latin, Breton, German, and **French** dictionaries; dictionaries standardizing technical terms; and electronic spelling-checkers and dictionaries. However, the two most important works are traditional: *The Welsh Academy English–Welsh Dictionary* (1995), compiled by Bruce Griffiths and Dafydd Glyn Jones, undoubtedly the single greatest influence on present-day Welsh vocabulary; and *Geiriadur Prifysgol Cymru* (1950–2002), the multi-volume **University of Wales** standard historical dictionary of the Welsh language (ed. R. J. Thomas, Gareth A. Bevan and Patrick J. Donovan), the equivalent – albeit far more concise – of the *Oxford English Dictionary*.

DICTIONARY OF WELSH BIOGRAPHY DOWN TO 1940, The (1959)

A national biographical dictionary that was published under the auspices of the **Cymmrodorion**, and edited by **J. E. Lloyd**, **R. T. Jenkins** and W. Llewelyn Davies. The original **Welsh** version, *Y Bywgraffiadur Cymreig Hyd 1940*, appeared in 1953. Although most of the entries feature Welsh men and **women** who were born and lived in Wales, there are some entries devoted to people from other countries – of Welsh or other extraction – who made a contribution to the life of Wales, and some on Welsh people who made their contribution in other countries. Ministers of religion are very numerous, and women constitute merely 1.8% of the entries.

Two appendices covering the years 1941–50 and 1951–70, edited by E. D. Jones and Brynley F. Roberts respectively, were published in 1970 and 1997. A one-volume **English** version of both appendices appeared in 2001; and in 2004, the **National Library** launched the free Welsh Biography Online (http://wbo.llgc.org.uk), based on computerized volumes of the Dictionary.

A section of William Salesbury's preface to his *A Dictionary in Englyshe and Welshe* (1547)

DIGITAL COMMUNICATION

In the early 21st century, the technical possibilities for communication in Wales were transformed – blurring the boundaries between information and entertainment, telephony and **broadcasting**, and involving the growth of home computing, two-way (interactive) and other services. Most traffic on the **telephone** network in Wales has come to be data, not voice.

Digital networks and information and communication technologies (ICTs) lie at the heart of contemporary economic development strategies. In 2002, considerable public expenditure – from the **Welsh Development Agency** (WDA), the European Union (EU) and British Telecom (BT) – was devoted to the completion of the fibre-optic network to all exchanges in Wales, the provision of the nodes for high speed data services in **Bangor**, **Aberystwyth** and **Carmarthen**, and the improvement of ISDN2 (Integrated Services Digital Network) and ADSL (Asymmetric Digital Subscriber Line) provision. In the same year, the **National Assembly** announced its £100 million, five-year Broadband Wales programme. This investment in telecommunications infrastructure in Wales is notable in that it has been funded substantially by the public sector, not simply provided in response to demand.

BT has 440 exchanges in Wales, an entirely fibre-optic network running at speeds of up to 2.4 gigabytes/sec. Bandwidth is the volume of data carried in a given time span. Broadband means high bandwidth (normally 128 kilobytes/sec or more), and is necessary for the transmission of large volumes of data, notably moving images. ISDN2 and ADSL are ways of providing broadband access, but can be provided only within 5.5 km of an exchange, and performance degrades as distance from the exchange increases. With so-called local loop unbundling (LLU), many suppliers offer broadband and telephone services to homes and businesses using BT's normal copper cables.

Cardiff was one of the first places in **Britain** in which ADSL was installed. With EU, WDA and BT support, the Llwybr/Pathway Project established ADSL nodes in 10 Welsh towns in 2001 (Aberystwyth, Bangor, **Caernarfon**, Carmarthen, **Denbigh**, **Haverfordwest**, **Holyhead**, **Llandudno**, **Newtown** and **Pembroke**) – a network which provided rural Wales with better high bandwidth provision than comparable areas in Britain. The south Wales Metropolitan Area Network (MAN) connects further and higher **education** institutions to SuperJanet at speeds of up to 155 megabytes/sec. Aberystwyth is connected to this at **Swansea** by a microwave link with the same capacity, and another MAN makes similar provision in the north.

In the south, at the beginning of 2002, Virgin Media's cable network passed 313,104 houses, about 60% of those in its franchise areas in Swansea, **Neath**, Cardiff, **Penarth**, **Newport** and the southern **coal**field. This represents 23% of households in Wales. Some 52% of the residences that might subscribe to Virgin Media do so – which, like satellite television take-up, is a higher figure than the British average. Virgin Media offers cable television as well as telephony and cable modems to the Internet.

Despite the available capacity, the level of demand for high bandwidth is lower in Wales than in Britain generally, because of the lower level of economic activity and lower usage of ICTs and the Internet. ADSL take-up at rural exchanges in Wales is half the rate of urban exchanges, and ISDN2 take-up in Wales is about half that of Britain as a whole. In 2006, 68% of households in Wales had a computer, 59% had access to the Internet, and 42% had broadband connection.

DILLWYN, Amy Elizabeth (1845–1935) Novelist

An early advocate of **women**'s involvement in industrial and public life, cigar-smoking Amy Dillwyn, granddaughter of **Lewis Weston Dillwyn**, was born in **Swansea**. There, after her father's death in 1892, she managed the Dillwyn Spelter Works. The first and best of her six novels was *The Rebecca Rioter* (1880). She was also a literary critic of some renown; her review of *Treasure Island* for the *Spectator* helped enhance the reputation of Robert Louis Stevenson. A feminist society commemorates her.

DILLWYN, Lewis Llewelyn (1814–92)
Industrialist and politician

The son of **Lewis Weston Dillwyn**, he was prominent in the industrial and commercial life of **Swansea**, heading the firm of Dillwyn and Richards at the Landore spelter works and serving as chairman of the Landore-Siemens steel company (*see* **Iron and Steel**). He was mayor of **Swansea** in 1848 and served as Liberal MP for Swansea (1855–85) and for the Swansea Town division (1885–92). A prominent **radical**, he championed the cause of the evicted **Cardiganshire** farmers in 1868, moved almost annual resolutions calling for the **disestablishment of the Church of England in Wales** from 1883 onwards, and affirmed the support of the **Liberal Party** within Wales for **Home Rule** for **Ireland**.

DILLWYN, Lewis Weston (1778–1855)
Industrialist and botanist

Born into the influential **Swansea** family, and owner of the Cambrian **Pottery**, Dillwyn's chief interests were botanical. His main achievement was the co-authorship, with D. Turner, of *The Botanist's Guide through England and Wales* (1805), one of the first books to describe the actual distribution, as opposed to a simple listing, of **plants** throughout southern **Britain**. Elected FRS at the age of 20, he was high sheriff of **Glamorgan** (1818), a **Whig** MP for the **county** (1832–7), mayor of Swansea (1839), and was the first president of the Royal Institution of South Wales.

DILLWYN-LLEWELYN, John (1810–82)
Photographer

This pioneering photographer was the son of **Lewis Weston Dillwyn** and his wife Mary, daughter of John Llewelyn of **Penllergaer**. Inheriting his father's scientific interests, he studied at **Oxford**, and was a keen botanist. Through marriage to Emma Mansel **Talbot** of **Margam**, who was the cousin of William Henry Fox Talbot (1800–77), the English 'inventor' of **photography**, he came into contact with the art, becoming an ardent experimenter in the field, and one of the most influential landscape photographers of the 19th century. Elected FRS in 1836, Dillwyn-Llewelyn collaborated with Charles Wheatstone (1802–75) in his experiments on the electric **telegraph**.

His daughter, Thereza Mary (1834–1926), was also a talented photographer. She was responsible for collecting and annotating a number of her father's photographs, her own and those of her husband, Nevil Story-Maskelyne (1823–1911), another pioneer in the field. She had a great interest in **astronomy**. Her brother, John Talbot Dillwyn-Llewelyn (1836–1927), **Conservative** MP for Swansea (1895–1900), was a member of the Royal Commission on Land in Wales (1896) (*see* **Land Question**).

DINAS CROSS (Dinas), Pembrokeshire
(1443 ha; 798 inhabitants)

Located immediately east of **Fishguard**, the **community** contains spectacular cliffs. Dinas **Island** is a haven for **seals** and sea**birds**. An island no more, it is connected to the mainland by a narrow strip of land with a beach at either end. Dinas's original church was destroyed by the **Vikings**. Its successor – at Cwm-yr-eglwys – was destroyed by a great storm in 1859, an event that has inspired several poets. St Brynach's church (1861) lacks the simple dignity of the chapels of the **Congregationalists** (1830), **Baptists** (1842), and **Calvinistic Methodists** (1842). The area is rich in maritime traditions. In the 1940s, more than 20 master mariners lived in the short main street of Dinas Cross village. The caravan park at Aber Grugog adjoins a 1942 naval battery site.

DINAS POWYS, Vale of Glamorgan
(1232 ha; 7653 inhabitants)

Now a substantial commuter **community** between **Barry** and **Cardiff**, Dinas Powys was transformed from a large agricultural village within the **parish** of St Andrews Major by the building of the **Vale of Glamorgan railway** line and the docks at Barry and **Penarth**. It became, as John Newman put it, 'a haven of villas from workaday Barry'. Some of the villas are of considerable distinction.

There were **Romano**-British settlements at Biglis and on Dinas Powys Common. Other evidence of early settlement includes an **Iron Age** stronghold and an early medieval **hill-fort**, which has yielded evidence of 5th- and 6th-century trade with Mediterranean lands. It may have been the seat of the kings of **Glywysing**, a theory which the name Dinas Powys – the fortress (*dinas*) of the province (*powys*, from the **Latin**, *pagensis*) – may help to confirm. (The Dinas Powys hill-fort is actually within the boundaries of the community of **Michaelston**.)

In the 12th century, the area came into the possession of the de Sumeris family, whose stone castle, once a significant building with a keep and curtain wall, is now crumbling and overgrown. The medieval lordship of Dinas Powys was extensive and included numerous sub-manors. St Andrew's, its parish church, was over a kilometre from the castle. The church was heavily restored in the 1870s but retains some fine late medieval features and a cross-shaft, as well as a tub-shaped **Norman** font. The garage of the rectory has medieval origins. Dinas Powys gave its name to one of **Glamorgan**'s post-**Acts of 'Union' hundreds**; it was bounded by the **Thaw** and **Ely Rivers**. Uniquely among the community councils of the Vale of Glamorgan, that of Dinas Powys is dominated by **Plaid [Genedlaethol] Cymru**.

DINDAETHWY Commote

A **commote** in south-east **Anglesey**, which, with that of **Menai**, formed the *cantref* of **Rhosyr**. The commotal centre was at Llanfaes (*see* **Beaumaris**), where a thriving town developed under the auspices of the 13th-century princes of **Gwynedd**. The name survived as that of a post-**Acts of 'Union' hundred**.

DINEFWR Royal seat and one-time district

Dinefwr (**Llandeilo**), was traditionally considered to be the chief seat of the rulers of **Deheubarth** (*c.f.* **Aberffraw** and **Mathrafal**). In the 13th century, Dinefwr was often in contention between members of the dynasty because of its symbolic importance.

Following the abolition of **Carmarthenshire** in 1974, Dinefwr was created as a district of the new county of **Dyfed**. It consisted of what had been the **borough** of **Llandovery**, the **urban districts** of **Ammanford**, **Cwmamman** and Llandeilo and the **rural district** of Llandeilo. In 1996, it became part of the reconstituted Carmarthenshire. The name survives in that of the constituency of Carmarthen East and Dinefwr.

DINIEITHON, SWYDD Commote

One of the **commotes** of the *cantref* of **Maelienydd**, the name comes from the fortress (*din*) above the **River** Ithon (Ieithon), a tributary of the **Wye**. The fortress was Cefnllys (**Penybont**), believed to have been the stronghold of **Elystan** (or Elstan) **Glodrydd**.

DINLLAEN Commote

One of the three **commotes** of the *cantref* of **Llŷn**, Dinllaen extended from the **Eifl** range to Carn Fadryn. The element *din* (fort) refers to the *dinas*, or fort, which crowns the headland at Porth Dinllaen. Its *maerdref* (administrative centre) was at **Nefyn**.

DINMAEL Commote

One of the four **commotes** of the *cantref* of **Penllyn**, Dinmael was broadly coterminous with the present-day **community** of Llangwm. In 1284, when the rest of Penllyn became part of the new **county** of **Merioneth**, Dinmael became part of the **march**er-**lordship of Denbigh**, which, in 1536, became the core of the newly created **Denbighshire**. The name survives as that of the village of Dinmael.

DINOSAURS

Some of the earliest dinosaur fossils in the world, dating from about 210–220 million years ago, have been found in Triassic rocks in Wales. Trackways of dinosaurs and other reptiles have been found at **Sully**, **Barry** and **Porthcawl**. Bones are rare, but a natural mould of the lower jaw of a large carnivorous dinosaur similar to *Megalosaurus* was found at Stormy Down (**Laleston**) in about 1898 and the skeleton of *Thecodontosaurus*, an early ancestor of the large herbivorous sauropod dinosaurs, was found in sediments filling fissures in older **limestone** near **Cowbridge**. These dinosaurs inhabited a desert plain with hills of limestone, an environment they shared with the earliest **mammals**. Near the end of the Triassic period, this plain was gradually submerged by the sea.

The whole of Wales was probably beneath the sea throughout the Jurassic and Cretaceous periods when dinosaurs were the dominant land-animals. As a result, there are no records of dinosaurs in Wales after the Triassic period (*see* **Geology**).

DIOCESES

The **Church in Wales** is divided into six dioceses, two of which are recent creations. The diocese of **Monmouth**, covering the area of what was then **Monmouthshire**, was created in 1921 out of the diocese of Llandaff (*see* **Cardiff**). **Swansea** and **Brecon**, consisting of **Breconshire**, **Radnorshire** and the ancient **commote** of **Gower**, was formed in 1923 from the vast diocese of **St David's**.

The origins of the four older dioceses are obscure, though they were identified with the cults of various **saints**. Llandaff was associated with the cults of **Dyfrig**, **Teilo** and Euddogwy; St David's with St **David**; **Bangor** with St **Deiniol**. The connection of **St Asaph** with Kentigern is doubtful, and so it is more probable that it was a **Norman** creation.

The Normans took over these mother churches and made them into cathedrals, literally the place which contains the throne (*cathedra*) of a diocesan bishop. Their conception of episcopacy was monarchical, feudal and territorial, with the result that there were frequent disputes over diocesan boundaries. These were defined by the late 12th century, so that Bangor covered the north-west, St Asaph the north-east, Llandaff the south-east, and St David's south-west and central Wales.

Each diocese is presided over by a bishop, elected since 1920 by the electoral college of the **Church in Wales**. The archbishop of Wales is elected from among the existing college of bishops, and retains his individual see as well as serving as archbishop. Each cathedral is presided over by a dean and a chapter, though all but St Asaph Cathedral serve as **parish** churches as well.

The **Roman Catholic** Church in Wales consists of three dioceses: the archdiocese of **Cardiff**, the diocese of **Wrexham** and the diocese of Menevia with its cathedral at **Swansea**. The decision in 1916 to make Cardiff an archdiocese overseeing all the Roman Catholics of Wales (and **Herefordshire**) was a significant recognition by the papacy of the unity and distinctiveness of Wales. It also meant that the Roman Catholics of Wales had an archbishop four years before the **Anglicans** consecrated an archbishop in Wales. Unlike **Scotland**, which has its own hierarchy, Wales's Roman Catholic archbishop and two bishops are part of the hierarchy of **England** and Wales, headed by the archbishop of Westminster.

DISESTABLISHMENT OF THE CHURCH OF ENGLAND IN WALES, The

Disestablishment is the abolition of state **religion**, in order either to remove political influences on a Church or to ensure that all denominations enjoy equality. Implicit in it is the argument that it is inconsistent for a Church, following disestablishment, to continue in possession of the endowments which it had held by virtue of its established status. Thus, disestablishment almost always includes disendowment.

Disestablishment gained credibility from the refusal of the American republic to countenance a state church and from the abolition of the privileges of the **Roman Catholic** Church in France following the revolution of 1789.

From the 1830s onwards, there were advocates of the disestablishment of the **Anglican** Church – the state church in **England**, Wales and **Ireland**. The Anti-State Church Association was founded in 1844 (it changed its name to Liberation Society in 1853) and a **London** Welshman, J. Carvell Williams, was appointed its secretary. Initially, no consideration was given to seeking disestablishment for Wales by itself, for the Anglican Church in Wales was seen as an integral part of the Church of England. However, the realization that the Welsh had become **Nonconformists** on a scale unmatched by the **English**, thus causing the Church of England to be a minority Church in almost all parts of Wales, gave substance to the argument that disestablishment specifically for Wales was a reasonable proposition. The argument gained strength from the belief that in Wales the Church of England was an Anglicizing force, an argument which the very name of that Church seemed to confirm. It also gained strength from **W. E. Gladstone**'s disestablishment and disendowment of the Church of Ireland in 1869.

The **Liberal Party** had inherited sympathy for the rights of Nonconformists from its **Whig** ancestors. Furthermore, the more advanced Liberals had a 'night-watchman' view of the state which rejected the idea that states need to be sanctified through a link with religion. Conversely, members of the **Conservative Party**, with their 'throne and altar' traditions, considered that the defence of establishment was one of the party's primary functions. In order to

An anti-disestablishment demonstration in Swansea on 28 May 1912

Dissolution resulted in abbey ruins such as those at Tintern

justify disestablishment for Wales alone, it was necessary to prove that Wales was an entity which could reasonably demand separate legislation on so delicate a matter – that Wales was a nation and that that fact has political and legal implications. Defenders of the Established Church were obliged to deny such a premise; consequently the Conservatives, who were not in origin more anti-Welsh than the Liberals, were manoeuvred into a position in which they could be portrayed as the anti-Welsh party, a development which was to cast a long shadow over the politics of Wales.

The first Bill to disestablish the Church in Wales was introduced in 1870 by Watkin Williams, MP for **Denbigh Boroughs**. His Bill won little support, but it placed disestablishment on the Welsh political agenda where it stayed until the passage of the Welsh Church Act in 1914. State–Church relations became increasingly controversial as a result of the **Tithe** War of the 1880s. Disestablishment for Wales became official Liberal policy in 1891. The reluctance of the Liberal **government** elected in 1892 to introduce a bill to that end led four Welsh MPs – **David Lloyd George** among them – to refuse the Liberal whip. Bills introduced in 1894 and 1895 failed because of the opposition of the House of Lords and the weakness of the government, which collapsed in 1895.

By the end of the 19th century, the substance of establishment had been much eroded. The Anglican Church no longer had a monopoly of elementary **education**, a stranglehold over universities, or the power to impose church rates and to insist on Anglican services in **parish** churchyards. As a consequence, the demand for disestablishment waned among England's Nonconformists. It did not wane in Wales, much to the dismay of **W. J. Gruffydd** who lamented the energy expended and the denominational bitterness fostered in order to win what was portrayed as a national victory – energy which could have been better directed to activity based upon a shared consciousness of the national heritage. Continuing support for Welsh disestablishment owed much to the '**Welsh Revolt**' over denominational education (1902–5) and to the **revival** of 1904–5, which greatly increased the membership of Nonconformist denominations.

The massive Liberal victory of 1906 led to expectations that the government would move rapidly to secure Welsh disestablishment. Instead, it appointed a royal commission, an act almost universally seen as a delaying tactic. Its chairman proved overly legalistic and the commission became an object of ridicule. It did not publish its recommendations until 1910 and, as there was no unanimity, the entire exercise was widely condemned as futile.

It was evident that Welsh disestablishment would not be achieved as long as the House of Lords retained its veto. That was removed by the Parliament Act (1911), which was followed by the Welsh Church Act, passed in September 1914, 45 days after the beginning of the **First World War**. The implementation of the Act was delayed until 1920 when the **Church in Wales**, a self-governing province of the Anglican Communion, came into existence. That Church was dispossessed of its ancient endowments, a complex process not completed until 1947. By then, £2,466,617 had been transferred to Wales's **county** councils and £989,196 to the **University of Wales**.

The disestablishment story is full of irony. It was passionately resisted by most Anglicans, but by 1924 the leader of the resistance, **A. G. Edwards**, the first archbishop of Wales, expressed satisfaction with the course of events. By the 1930s, when the Church of England was in difficulties over tithe and the reform of **The Book of Common Prayer**, the disestablished Church in Wales was cited as the model to follow. By that decade, commitment to Anglicanism appeared proportionately stronger in Wales than in England. The final irony may yet be the disestablishment of the Church of England itself, under the aegis of a one-time archbishop of Wales – Rowan Williams, consecrated archbishop of Canterbury in 2003.

DISSERTH AND TRECOED (Diserth a Thre-coed), Radnorshire, Powys
(3122 ha; 1036 inhabitants)

A **community** located south-west of **Llandrindod**, it contains the beautifully situated and largely unrestored Disserth church. As Richard Haslam comments, 'the fabric takes one straight into the **parish** life of around 1700'; even the box pews, usually the first casualty, remain. The village of Howey once possessed a full range of services and served the needs of Llandrindod, before the days of the latter's glory. As late as the 1870s, the spa town's postal address was Llandrindod, near Howey.

DISSOLUTION OF THE MONASTERIES, The

Having established himself as supreme head of the English Church in 1534, Henry VIII moved swiftly to extend his hold on its possessions. Two commissions were set up in 1535: one to survey church property, and the other to inquire into the morals and discipline of the monks.

In Wales, there were 32 monasteries (a number of which were cells of larger houses), 10 friaries (*see* **Friars**) and 3 **nunneries**, containing only about 250 inmates in all. Many of the larger and better-known monasteries belonged to the **Cistercian** order, but most of the houses were small and poor. In 1535, **Tintern** alone had the 13 monks considered necessary to carry out the full round of monastic life; the average house had about six to eight, but many smaller ones no more than two or three.

The marked drop in numbers over the 14th and 15th centuries led to a serious decline in the standards of dedication and worship. Some houses were deeply in debt, and the estates of all of them had been leased out for lengthy terms to lay tenants, the most powerful of whom vied with one another for the choice of abbot. Contemporary sources, such as the visitation of 1535–6, tend to reveal that the monks' lifestyle had become secularized and indolent. A number of abbots lived sumptuously in houses built within the abbey walls and had even fathered children.

An Act of Parliament of March 1536 stipulated that all monasteries with less than a clear yearly value of £200 should be dissolved; although all the Welsh houses fell within that category, three were exempted from dissolution – **Neath** (Dyffryn Clydach), Strata Florida (**Ystrad Fflur**) and **Whitland** (Llanboidy) – but by 1539 all were gone. Heads of houses were given pensions, but monks either found benefices or curacies, or re-entered lay life. In 1538, all the Welsh friaries were suppressed, but their inmates received no pensions.

No serious protest was mounted against the dissolution, but it was a sad loss to Wales. Some of the country's finest art and **architecture** was lost, although splendid monastic churches such as **Brecon** or **Ewenny** still stand. Many valuable books and manuscripts disappeared with monastic libraries, and generous patronage of the bards came to an end. Most monastic estates passed first to the crown but were later sold to local **gentry** and formed part of the estates of such leading families as the **Somersets** and the **Mansels**.

DISTRIBUTION OF INDUSTRY ACT, The

The passage of the Distribution of Industry Act in 1945 was a significant milestone in the development of British regional policy, which was given high priority in Wales during the immediate post-**Second World War** period. It encouraged manufacturing industry to locate in problem areas, while restricting its growth in 'congested' areas. Redefining the pre-war Special Areas (renamed **Development Areas**), the Act included measures to influence industrial location.

Firms locating in Development Areas were provided with loans, low rents, tax incentives and preferential treatment in **government** purchasing policy, with a programme of factory provision as an extra incentive. The Town and Country Planning Act of 1947 added a further policy instrument in the form of Industrial Development Certificates, which were necessary for planning permission for any new building exceeding 464.5 sq m. They were awarded only where the development corresponded with 'the proper distribution of industry'.

The passage of the 1960 Local Employment Act reoriented policy away from the encouragement of manufacturing industry in 'problem areas' and towards a broader policy of overall regional development.

DISTRICT LAND REGISTRY FOR WALES, The

Established in 1997 and based in **Swansea**, the Registry is a statutorily created body which records and guarantees the ownership of land in Wales. All transfers of land must be registered with the Registry, from which information concerning land ownership in Wales may be obtained.

DIXEY, Frank (1892–1982) Geologist

A pupil of **T. F. Sibly** at **Cardiff**, Sir Frank Dixey, FRS, of **Barry**, spent the whole of his career as a geologist in **Britain**'s dependent territories in Africa. His major interests were in water supply and in the geomorphology of the rift valleys of East Africa. He was appointed first director of the Commonwealth Geological Survey in 1947.

DODD, A[rthur] H[erbert] (1891–1975) Historian

Wrexham-born A. H. Dodd joined the staff of the history department at **Bangor** in 1919 and succeeded Sir **John Edward Lloyd** as professor in 1930. He wrote extensively on urban and regional history, notably in *The Industrial Revolution in North Wales* (1933) and *A History of Caernarvonshire* (1968). He was interested in Stuart politics and the **Civil War**. *Studies in Stuart Wales* (1952) is his major work on Welsh society in the 17th century. He also published *Life in Elizabethan England* (1961) and, posthumously, *A Short History of Wales* (1977). His brother, Charles Harold Dodd (1884–1973), was the general director of the project to produce the New English **Bible** translation.

DOGFEILING Commote

One of the three **commotes** of the *cantref* of **Dyffryn Clwyd**, it was named after Dogfael, purportedly a son of **Cunedda**. Its centre was at **Ruthin**.

DOGS

Numerous references to dogs in Welsh mythology, folklore, **literature** and **law** testify to the important role they have played in **hunting**, shepherding and guarding. They have also offered companionship and, in more recent times, opportunities for competition in **sheepdog trials** and pedigree dog shows. Hunting dogs feature prominently in the stories of *The Mabinogion*, and the medieval lawbooks contain numerous stipulations about staghounds, greyhounds, terriers, shepherding dogs and guard dogs. Freemen were obliged to maintain the king's hunting dogs and **horses** during his tours, a custom which foreshadowed later farm tenancy agreements, which obliged tenants to keep pack hounds for their landlords.

The main, extant, Welsh breeds

CORGI
There are two breeds of corgi: the long-tailed brown and white, or blue and white, **Cardiganshire** corgi and the short-tailed, sandy-coloured **Pembrokeshire** corgi. Both varieties were freely interbred until the 1930s, after which breeders tried to accentuate their differences. Corgis – the word translates as 'dwarf dog' – were developed for driving livestock by nipping at heels and barking.

SEALYHAM TERRIER
A short-legged, whitish terrier developed in the later 19th century by Captain John Edwardes on his estate at Sealyham (**Wolfscastle**) to hunt badger, **otter** and **fox**, and first exhibited at **Haverfordwest** in 1903. From a Sealyham crossed with a Scottish terrier came the Cesky terrier of the Czech Republic.

WELSH FOXHOUND
A rough-coated, light-coloured breed descended from the Segusii hound, which existed in northern Europe from pre-**Roman** times, and was originally black and tan. Packs were kept for hunting stag and **wild boar** in medieval times, and for otter and fox hunting subsequently. Medieval law valued a trained Welsh hound at 240 pence, whereas a packhorse was valued at only 120 pence. Slightly slower than the English hound, its independence and tenacity make it the ideal hound for Wales's rugged terrain.

WELSH SHEEPDOG
The sheepdog's role in medieval times was to defend as well as to control flocks, as suggested by reference in *The Mabinogion* to 'a herdsman's shaggy mastiff larger than a steed nine winters old'. There were various types of Welsh sheepdog, including the black and tan, and the large, powerful, red (or blue-grey) Welsh hillman, both of them

Pembrokeshire corgi

common in mid-Wales. The long-haired Welsh grey, popular with **drovers** for walking livestock to **England**, accompanied Welsh emigrants to **Patagonia**, where it is known today as the *barboucho*. From the mid-19th century, Welsh sheepdogs were gradually displaced by Scottish collies, and by the late 20th century they had become rare. Interest was revived, however, with the formation of the Welsh Sheepdog Society in 1997. The breed is highly varied in terms of colour, size and length of hair, and its method of working is different from that of the collie.

WELSH SPRINGER SPANIEL
An ancient breed developed to flush out and to retrieve game. With its distinctive red and white coat, the sociable springer has become a popular gundog and pet. The breed was known as the Welsh cocker spaniel until its official recognition by the British Kennel Club in 1902. During the 19th century, another distinctive Welsh gundog was the **Llanidloes** setter, now extinct.

WELSH TERRIER
Black and tan, with a double coat that is wiry on top and woolly underneath, it was bred originally to kill foxes and rats. It has become popular as a pet and is internationally renowned as a show dog.

DOLBENMAEN, Gwynedd (9640 ha; 1300 inhabitants)
Located immediately north of **Porthmadog**, the **community** extends from the summit of Moel Hebog (782 m) almost to the sea east of **Criccieth**, and contains the villages of Bryncir, Garndolbenmaen, Golan, Llanfihangel-y-pennant, Penmorfa, Pentrefelin and Prenteg. Within it is most of the basin of the **Dwyfor**. The beauty of the upper part of the valley – Cwm Pennant – is celebrated in the best known of the poems of Eifion Wyn (**W. Elizeus Williams**), 'Cwm Pennant'.

Dolbenmaen was the original *maerdref* (administrative centre) of the **commote** of **Eifionydd**. Its extensive bond village provides the setting for much of W. O. Roberts's novel *Y Pla* (1987; English translation: *Pestilence*, 1991). Elements of the medieval village's settlement pattern are still apparent. St **Beuno**'s church, Penmorfa, and St Mary's church, Garndolbenmaen, contain medieval elements. Clenennau, now a farm, was the embryo of the estate eventually owned by the **Ormsby-Gore family**, the Barons **Harlech**. Bryncir Old Hall is in ruins; adjoining it is Twr Bryncir, a five-storey folly tower (1821). Bryncir **Woollen** Mill is still in operation. Golan is one of the several **Caernarfonshire** villages named after chapels.

DOLGARROG, Conwy (1534 ha; 414 inhabitants)
Located on the left bank of the **Conwy**, the **community** extends to the outliers of the **Carneddau Mountains**. It contains parts of the **reservoirs** of Llyn Cowlyd and Llyn Eigiau, constructed to provide hydroelectric power (*see* **Energy**) to the Dolgarrog aluminium works. On 2 November 1925, Eigiau Dam burst, releasing a torrent, which gouged a path down the mountainside to the reservoir at Coety. The flood breached Coety Dam, releasing even more water that swept over the cliff onto the village below. Much of the village, including the school, was

Dolgellau, looking south from the town towards Cadair Idris

swept away and 16 people were killed. Following rebuilding, the aluminium industry, with 200 workers, continued to be a major source of employment. The factory faced problems as a result of the attacks on the United States on 11 September 2001. However, through the efforts of the local MP, Elfyn Llwyd, and others, it has continued in production.

DOLGELLAU, Gwynedd
(3501 ha; 2678 inhabitants)
Straddling the Wnion valley and extending to the estuary of the **Mawddach**, the **community** contains the town of Dolgellau and the settlements of Penmaenpool and Tabor. Dolgellau was the administrative centre of the **county** of **Merioneth** and its successor, the district of **Meirionnydd**. The district's subsumption by the unitary county of **Gwynedd** in 1996 left Dolgellau somewhat bereft, although the town continues to house some of the one-time Meirionnydd's institutions – the record office in particular.

Long an important route centre, Dolgellau developed in the early Middle Ages as a *taeogdref* (serf village). St Mary's church, originally 13th century, was rebuilt in the 18th century. The story of Dolgellau's **Quakers** is told in the novels of **Marion Eames** and through the exhibition at Tŷ Meirion. There is a Quaker burial ground at Tabor. The farm of Bryn-mawr gave its name to Bryn Mawr, the **women**'s college in **Pennsylvania**.

In the 18th century, Dolgellau was the centre of Merioneth's **woollen industry**, and in the 19th century the town benefited from the opening of the Mawddach valley **gold** mines, which came to employ up to 500 men. From the late 18th century, climbing **Cadair Idris** grew in popularity, causing Dolgellau to become an important centre for walkers and mountaineers.

The town, much of which is built of **granite** boulders, has more than 200 listed buildings. They include the main bridge (1638) and the building housing Y Sosban restaurant (1606). The buildings of the Dr Williams's School for girls (1875) now house Coleg Meirionnydd. The market hall (1870) in the town centre – known as Neuadd Idris since 1949 – was refurbished in 2007 as Tŷ Siamas, the National Centre for Welsh Folk Music. Dolgellau has Wales's oldest **cricket** club. There is an RSPB Information Centre near the toll bridge at Penmaenpool. Sesiwn Fawr Dolgellau, an international folk **music** festival, draws thousands of visitors to Dolgellau each July.

DOLWYDDELAN, Conwy
(5922 ha; 427 inhabitants)
Located immediately south-west of **Betws-y-Coed**, the **community** comprises the upper reaches of the Lledr valley and rises to the summit of **Moel Siabod** (872 m). Its chief feature is Dolwyddelan Castle, a stronghold of the princes of **Gwynedd**. Although reputedly the birthplace of **Llywelyn ap Iorwerth** (1173–1240), it is unlikely that its sturdy square keep was built until *c*.1220. In the late 15th century, it was occupied by an ancestor of the **Wynn family (Gwydir)**, Maredudd ap Ieuan, whose memorial brass is in St Gwyddelan's, a building financed by him *c*.1510. The castle's dramatic location made it a favourite subject of romantic landscape painters.

At Tanycastell are monuments to the **Calvinistic Methodist** preacher **John Jones**, Talysarn (1796–1857) and his three brothers.

Slate quarrying was an important occupation but declined after the **First World War**.

The **railway** line to Blaenau **Ffestiniog** (1880) runs through the community from the impressive Pont Gethin viaduct to the mouth of the 3.5-km Blaenau tunnel. The **A470** links Dolwyddelan with Ffestiniog via Bwlch y Gorddinan (**Crimea** Pass).

DONALDSON, Jessie (1799–1889)
Slavery abolitionist
The daughter of **Unitarians**, Jessie Donaldson (b. Heineken) founded and taught in a school in her native **Swansea** before marrying, aged 41, her American cousin, Francis Donaldson Jnr, and emigrating to his mother's home, Frandon, in Cincinnati, on the banks of the Ohio River. She became friends with leaders of the Anti-**Slavery** Society and abolitionist movement, and Frandon, situated opposite the slave-holding state of Kentucky, became a safe house for slaves fleeing across the river. So too did a house the couple later bought for themselves, together with a farm owned by her cousin Thomas, which was named Penmaen after his parents' farm at **Rhayader**. At the end of the American Civil War, she returned to Swansea, where she died, aged 90.

DONNELLY, Desmond Louis (1920–74) Politician
Born in India, the son of a tea planter of Irish extraction, Donnelly served in the RAF throughout the **Second World War**. He stood unsuccessfully as the Commonwealth candidate for Evesham in 1945, and entered the House of Commons as **Labour** MP for **Pembrokeshire** in 1950. Initially viewed as a close associate of **Aneurin Bevan**, he then swung to the right, supporting Gaitskell and entry into the Common Market. He launched his own Democratic Party in 1967, was defeated in Pembrokeshire in 1970, and later supported the **Conservative Party**.

DOUGLAS, John (1830–1911) Architect
A native of Northwich, **Cheshire**, Douglas was the most significant architect active in north-east Wales in the late 19th and early 20th centuries. For much of his career, he was architect to the Grosvenor family, dukes of Westminster, whose vast estates included 1350 ha in **Flintshire**. He was inspired by the medieval brick **architecture** of the Low Countries and by the timber-framed buildings of the Cheshire Plain. Fascinated by carpentry, the **woodcarving** in his buildings is of superb quality. His work on the farmhouses and outbuildings of the Grosvenor estate is instantly recognizable (*see* **Broughton and Bretton**). His outstanding buildings include St Mary's church, **Halkyn**, St Michael's church, **Manafon**, St Deiniol's Library at **Hawarden** and country houses such as Wigfair, **Cefnmeiriadog**.

DOVECOTES
Doves or pigeons provided a useful source of food on estates and larger tenant farms in the Middle Ages, and many free-standing dovecotes still survive in lowland or arable farming areas. The earliest dovecotes, dating from the 13th century and often associated with monastic settlements, were massive, circular, stone structures with corbelled domes, such as that at **Barry**. There was a further wave of dovecote building in the 17th century, when pigeon manure was an important source of the potassium used in the manufacture of gunpowder. Later, square, brick structures with timber lanterns became usual. More common, particularly in the 19th century, was the provision of nesting holes in gable or side walls of other buildings.

DOWLAIS SETTLEMENT, The, Merthyr Tydfil
Financed initially by the philanthropist Mary Horsfall, Dowlais was one of several educational settlements established in south Wales during the interwar **Depression**. Attracting influential teachers, some of whom were refugees from mainland Europe (*see* **Refugee Artists**), it made a notable impact on the visual arts. **Cedric Morris** taught there, as did Arthur Giardelli, Heinz Koppel and Esther Grainger. Dowlais became instrumental in the development of local artists such as Charles Burton and **Ernest Zobole**.

DRAMA
The earliest surviving plays in **Welsh** are two medieval miracle plays, *Y Tri Brenin o Gwlen* and *Y Dioddefaint a'r Atgyfodiad*, a Herod and a Passion play, respectively, probably performed by travelling players. The other surviving medieval text, *Ymddiddan y Corff a'r Enaid*, is a morality play celebrating the repentance of sins and the spiritual victory over death. Alongside such text-based theatre there existed the theatricals associated with

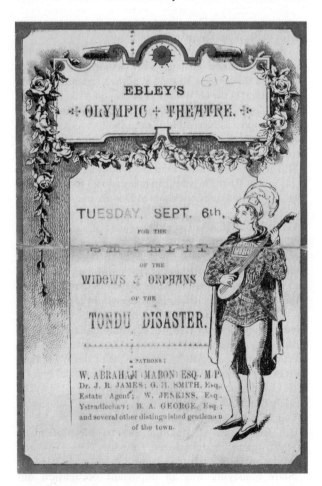

Edward Ebley's Olympic Theatre Company *c.*1905

wassailing and the folk festivals of May Day (*Calan Mai*) and **Mabsant**.

While 16th- and 17th-century **England** witnessed the golden age of theatre, those centuries in Wales were lacking in dramatic output. The only surviving text that bears witness to a possible interest in plays around 1600 is the Welsh-language verse tragedy *Troelus a Chresyd*, a dramatized adaptation, by an anonymous author, of Chaucer's *Troylus and Cryseyde* (*c*.1372–86) and Henryson's *Testament of Cresseid* (1532).

When an indigenous Welsh theatrical tradition finally emerged in the 18th century, it was in the form of the **interlude**, a metrical play performed at fairs and markets. The most accomplished exponent of the interlude was Twm o'r Nant (**Thomas Edwards**; 1739–1810). He and his troupe of players provided entertainment that was a combination of ribaldry and seriousness. Its popular appeal lay in its robust condemnation of social injustices, colourful language and the masterly use of tried and tested comic techniques. No robust, indigenous **English-language** theatre emerged in 18th-century Wales. The semi-professional companies that had existed in the 16th century were superseded in the 17th by a few informal companies that performed at fairs, festivals and markets.

By the 18th century, the town halls in several Welsh market towns had become performance venues for travelling professional companies from **Ireland** and England, among them the renowned Kemble company, which drew crowds in **Monmouth**, **Brecon** and **Carmarthen**. These companies performed plays from their extensive English classical repertoire, and the fashionable audiences attending them were satirized by Twm o'r Nant. While their tenants were enjoying the Welsh-language interludes, the **gentry** were entertained by visiting English companies, some of which performed at private theatres such as that built by the **Williams Wynn family** at Wynnstay, **Ruabon**.

The building of substantial theatres in the larger Welsh towns in the early 19th century drew Edmund Kean, Sheridan Knowles, Andrew Cherry, W. C. Macready and Thomas Barry to Wales. In the second half of the century, the audiences at the Theatre Royal, **Cardiff** saw performances by T. W. Robertson and Sarah Bernhardt. Alongside the new playhouses, there existed in Wales the highly popular portable theatres. The colourful companies that performed in them visited fairs, engaging audiences with entertainments of local appeal, enlivened by songs and striking visual effects. From 1912 onwards, however, most of the owners of the portable theatres settled in one place and purchased theatres, which they later turned into **cinemas**. By the 1930s, most of the 34 portable theatres that had existed at the turn of the century had either been closed down or had become venues for the 'moving pictures'.

While the 19th century had witnessed considerable English-language theatre activity, theatre had not entirely escaped the effect of the **Nonconformists**' prejudice against plays and players, and, between 1854 and 1870, a number of English companies kept away from several Welsh towns. Yet, it was Welsh-language theatre that suffered most from the Nonconformist objection to traditional folk-entertainments and theatrical performances. Although the performance of interludes ceased altogether, some of their basic elements survived, ironically, in the form of the chapel-led *ymddiddanion* (colloquies) and *dadleuon* (debates). These dramatic dialogues, based on biblical tales and extolling the virtuous life, were in essence miniature plays. The verve of theatre manifested itself also in the declamatory style and fiery sermons of leading **preachers**. Despite Nonconformists' disapproval of drama, a prize was awarded at the **Eisteddfod** at **Aberffraw** in 1849 for a translation into Welsh of one of the parts of **Shakespeare**'s *Henry IV*. In 1879, an eisteddfod prize was awarded to **Beriah Gwynfe Evans** for a full-length play on **Owain Glyndŵr**.

The first licensed Welsh-language company was Cwmni **Trefriw**, which, in 1887, toured to full houses with its stage adaptation of **Daniel Owen**'s *Rhys Lewis*. It was the resurgence of interest in the theatre generated by companies such as Trefriw and **Llanberis** that led to a fierce denunciation of play-acting during a **Calvinistic Methodist** gathering at **Corwen** in 1887. An attempt to re-establish drama as a serious art form was made in an address by **O. M. Edwards** at the 1894 National Eisteddfod at **Caernarfon** and again, by **David Lloyd George**, at the 1902 National Eisteddfod at **Bangor**. By 1910, the religious objection to play-acting had been sufficiently eroded to allow the widespread performance of plays to raise money for good causes, including the upkeep of chapels. There then followed a sharp increase in the number of amateur companies and the **First World War** period saw no decline in the popularity of theatre. Indeed, between 1914 and 1918, notable ensembles, such as the **Pontarddulais**-based Dan Matthews Company, were established.

A Llangefni Drama Society playbill, 1963

The post-war period was the golden age of the amateur movement in Wales, and the widespread building of village memorial halls provided the companies with convenient stages for drama competitions and festivals. It has been estimated that in 1931 there existed in Wales up to 500 dramatic societies, and at least 300 published Welsh plays. Amongst the most popular were plays by **W. J. Gruffydd**, **J. O. Francis**, **D. T. Davies**, **Idwal Jones** and **J. Kitchener Davies**.

Amidst the growing popularity of the amateur movement, Lord Howard de Walden (Thomas Evelyn Scott-Ellis; 1880–1946) attempted to establish a Welsh National Theatre Company. In 1914, he and other influential figures met in Cardiff to form a professional touring company, but after the company's tour of the south in that year, the project was abandoned on the outbreak of the First World War. In 1933, Howard de Walden made another attempt at establishing a 'national' company by funding a Welsh National Playhouse at Plas Newydd, **Llangollen**. It had the dual aim of being a bilingual touring company and a resource and training facility. Its exclusivity and a series of unwise artistic decisions meant that it failed to attract Welsh audiences, and the outbreak of the **Second World War** saw its demise. The war also saw the collapse of a substantial number of the amateur companies, only a third of which reformed after it ended.

Some of the new companies that appeared post-war, such as Cwmni **Ceredigion** and Chwaraewyr Garthewin (*see* **Llanfair Talhaiarn**), attracted a more critical audience. The Garthewin Players, at their remarkable 18th-century converted barn theatre on the **Denbighshire** estate of R. O. F. Wynne, staged plays written specifically for the company by **Saunders Lewis**, Wales's leading dramatist. Other small theatres soon followed Garthewin's example

John Ogwen and Maureen Rhys in a 1996 production of *Y Tŵr*

in forging a fruitful relationship between a particular dramatist and a particular local community, such as that between the author/director F. George Fisher and Theatr Fach **Llangefni** and between Theatr y Gegin, **Criccieth**, and the dramatist William Samuel Jones (Wil Sam). In 1965, the important contribution made by the amateur movement to the cultural life of Wales was reflected in the formation of the Drama Association of Wales, a facilitating body serving the needs of amateur companies.

Increasing competition from television saw a growing emphasis in the Wales of the 1950s and 1960s on the need for greater professionalism. During this period, the plays of **Emlyn Williams**, **Gwyn Thomas**, **Alun Richards** and **Alun Owen** were staged, and talented Welsh actors such as **Richard Burton**, **Rachel Roberts**, **Donald Houston**, **Stanley Baker**, Siân Phillips and **Hugh Griffith** were establishing themselves as international stars of stage and screen. In Welsh-language theatre, the plays of **Huw Lloyd Edwards**, **John Gwilym Jones** and **Gwenlyn Parry** commanded loyal audiences. In 1962, the Welsh Arts Council (*see* **Arts Council of Wales**) funded a bilingual touring Welsh Theatre Company under the directorship of Warren Jenkins. When it registered itself as a 'national' company it immediately engendered the wrath of the St David's Theatre Trust, established in 1959 to ensure a custom-built theatre building for a new National Company in Cardiff. An acrimonious battle ensued and the matter was finally resolved by a legal enquiry, which found that the Welsh Theatre Company had no right to the title 'national'. The St David's Theatre Trust faded from view and an enervated Welsh Theatre Company ceased to perform in 1978.

The Welsh-language wing of the doomed Welsh Theatre Company fared better. Formally launched in 1965, Cwmni Theatr Cymru appointed Wilbert Lloyd Roberts as its director in 1968. By 1973, it had become an independent company which, for the first time, provided talented actors with the opportunity to pursue a professional career within the theatre in Wales; among those actors were Gaynor Morgan Rees, John Ogwen, Lisabeth Miles and **Beryl Williams**. It also nurtured the talents of dramatists such as Meic Povey. Internal disagreements led in 1982 to the replacement of Wilbert Lloyd Roberts by Emily Davies who created an ensemble of relatively young actors. The initial exclusion of experienced actors alienated the theatre sector, and despite some notable productions by guest directors such as Ceri Sherlock, the company faltered. Two years later, financial problems led to Cwmni Theatr Cymru's demise, and the idea of a flagship national theatre was temporarily abandoned.

The existence of the mainstream companies had, however, not impeded the development in Wales of innovative ventures such as the Cardiff Laboratory Theatre (subsequently the Centre for Performance Research), established in 1974 by Richard Gough and Mike Pearson. These practitioners had been influenced by the work of Grotowski and Barba's Odin Teatret and, together with Geoff Moore of Moving Being, based then at the Chapter Arts Centre in Cardiff, they looked towards mainland Europe for patterns of experimentation with style and form. In the works of these companies, and in the performances of related companies such as Magdalena, Man Act and Pauper's Carnival, physical, visual and mixed media performances challenged the largely traditional productions of Wales's mainstream theatre. These new, innovative companies also tended to avoid the concrete theatre buildings that had sprung up in towns or on university campuses during the early 1970s, and which acted as receiving venues for visiting companies. One such theatre, with its own producing company, was Theatr **Clwyd** (renamed Clwyd Theatr Cymru in 1996), which provided its English-oriented audiences with classical and popular productions.

In Welsh-language theatre, too, alternative small-scale companies existed alongside the mainstream Cwmni Theatr Cymru. Theatr Ddieithr staged plays by Wil Sam and Meic Povey, and Theatr O sought to provide new perspectives on classical plays. One company in particular, Theatr yr Ymylon, was established in 1972 by a group of actors specifically to create a new theatrical tradition in Wales. This it failed to achieve, but in the first year of its existence the company had performed more plays by promising Welsh dramatists than the Welsh Theatre Company had done in 10 years. In 1979, management difficulties brought the work of the company to an end. Perhaps the most innovative company to emerge in the 1970s was the **Gwynedd**-based Theatr Bara Caws, which first came to prominence in 1977 with its review satirizing the royal jubilee celebrations. This left-wing community theatre company, which continues to flourish, brought its devised performances to pubs, clubs and village halls with the specific aim of 'taking theatre to the people'. In the south, Whare Teg and Theatr Gorllewin Morgannwg served their immediate communities, with the latter developing its own distinct, highly theatrical productions, based on local concerns and on broader Welsh-language issues.

Wales, since the early 1970s, has been served by Theatre in **Education** and Theatre for Young People companies. Some of the companies, notably Spectacle and Arad Goch, have an international outreach, while Theatr na n'Og in the industrial south and Cwmni'r Frân Wen in rural Gwynedd have concentrated on developing loyal local audiences. **Gwent** Theatre, Theatr Iolo and Theatr **Powys** have comparably firm bases in their communities and have nurtured links with dramatists such as Charles Way, Greg Cullen and Dic Edwards. Theatr Clwyd and, in particular, Cardiff's Sherman Theatre also cater for young audiences.

Several of the companies which had an impact on the theatre scene in Wales during the last decades of the 20th century have disappeared – companies such as Hwyl a Fflag, Dalier Sylw, Cwmni Theatr Gwynedd, Made in Wales, Theatrig and Brith Gof, the last of which enjoyed an international reputation. Other companies, however, have survived and continue to expand their repertoire. Volcano's dynamic productions draw audiences at home and abroad, Hijinx tours Wales and England with performances for people with learning disabilities, while Y Cwmni, dramatist Ed Thomas's enterprising company, has widened its remit to include radio, **film** and television. Theatr y Byd and Mappa Mundi present the occasional production, Mega's popular Christmas pantomime plays

Ioan Gruffudd and Nia Roberts in the film *Solomon and Gaynor* (*Solomon a Gaenor*) (1997)

annually to full houses, Clwyd Theatr Cymru (formerly Theatr Clwyd) have kept to their remit to stage the classics, Llwyfan Gogledd Cymru (North Wales Stage) presents work by contemporary dramatists, often working with companies from other countries, and Sgript Cymru, which merged with the Sherman Theatre Company in 2007, works bilingually with authors on script development and production. Despite the lure of journeyman scripting for media entertainments, there has been a resurgence of interest in writing for the stage amongst a new wave of dramatists such as Ian Rowlands, Siân Evans, Christine Watkins, Richard Davies, Frank Vickery, Lucy Gough, Aled Jones Williams, Gary Owen, Sera Moore-Williams and Mark Jenkins.

However, the talent-drain from Wales continues, and young actors such as Daniel Evans, Rhys Ifans, Ioan Gruffudd and Matthew Rhys have become international names in theatre, film and television. The launch in 2004 of the Welsh-medium Theatr Genedlaethol Cymru and the proposed establishment of an English-medium National Theatre Company gave rise to hopes that Welsh audiences would have the opportunity to see these actors perform at home in large-scale productions. The strength of Welsh theatre has traditionally been in the popularity of its vigorous amateur and small-scale professional companies. It remains to be seen whether the advent of a devolved **government** with its own minister of culture will help to guarantee the success of the designated 'national' theatre companies.

DRISCOLL, Jim (James Driscoll; 1880–1925)
Boxer

Born in **Cardiff**'s **Irish** quarter, Jim Driscoll was appearing regularly, by the time he was 17, in Jack Scarrott's fairground **boxing** booths across south Wales, becoming a professional in 1901. Clean-limbed, 1.67-m tall and 57 kg, he adopted an upright stance and a relentless left with which he subdued opponents before finishing them off with a powerful right. He won the British featherweight title in 1906, and during an unbeaten tour of the United States fought a 'no-decision' bout against the world title-holder Abe Attell in 1909. Driscoll could not secure the knockout by which he could claim the title but gave such a consummate performance that former United States marshal turned sports journalist, Bat Masterson, dubbed him 'Peerless Jim'.

Driscoll refused Attell's offer of a return bout for the world title because of a promise to box in Cardiff in aid of Nazareth House Orphanage. He was disqualified during a bitter contest with **Freddie Welsh** in December 1910, won the European featherweight title in 1912 and retired the following year.

After the war, financial difficulties persuaded a by then tubercular Driscoll to revive his boxing career, and in October 1919 he ill-advisedly agreed to fight the much younger European champion, Charles Ledoux. For 14 rounds Driscoll's peerless left jab kept the Frenchman at bay but exhaustion forced his retirement in the 16th. On his death, some 100,000 mourners accompanied his coffin to Cathays cemetery.

DROVERS

Prior to the many 20th-century technological developments that led to improved forage quality on Welsh grasslands, the majority of the **cattle** reared for meat in the north and west of the country were exported to **England**. The export trade was one of the few cash-earning activities within an agricultural **economy** that was, in much of the country until the early 19th century, primarily a semi-subsistence one. This trade, possibly of pre-medieval

Jim Driscoll (right) and Freddie Welsh on 20 December 1910

origins, was conducted by drovers and dealers who drove shod cattle and flocks of **sheep** and geese along time-honoured routes to the fattening pastures of the English Midlands, the stalls and yards of East Anglia, or even directly to the markets of **London**.

While short and medium-distance droving continued to be a feature of rural life in Wales until the beginning of the 20th century, the orientation of drove routes – stretches of which can still be traced – changed with the arrival of the **railways** in the mid-19th century; seasonal fairs, and later weekly marts, came to be relocated to the vicinity of a railhead. Concurrently, the economics of both the cattle and sheep trade ensured that drovers made full use of the expanding rail facilities.

Besides their contribution to the economy of rural Wales, the drovers played a prime role in the social and cultural development of the countryside. Trusted agents of the local **gentry**, for whom they often carried both cash and confidential legal documents to the counting houses of England, they served as the purveyors of news of political and social change, and brought information back to the remote western **counties** concerning novel developments in **agriculture**. There is, however, no evidence to support the popular myth that early banks in Wales (*see* **Banking and Banks**) were founded by cattle and sheep drovers.

Like other travelling people, the drovers were widely distrusted by the inhabitants of settled communities. They were obliged to obtain an annual licence from the Quarter Sessions, without which they could be arrested for vagrancy. Their activities were also limited by a variety of statutes regarding age, marital status and the regulation of market trading. The fact that many drovers rose to become substantial landholders, sturdy pillars of the **Nonconformist** community or, in one or two cases, even High Sheriff of their county, hints at the rewards of the trade for those who evaded the temptations of moral or financial transgression.

DRUIDS

The evidence for **Celt**ic druids derives mainly from the writings of classical authors and the early **literature** of Wales and **Ireland**. Classical authors refer to the druids as one of three learned classes (druids, seers, bards), and their function is described as priestly: they supervised ceremonies of worship and officiated at sacrifices, possibly including human sacrifices; they had legislative and juridical powers; and they were the teachers of the sons of noblemen, offering an entirely oral education. It is likely that they were astronomers (*see* **Astronomy**) and astrologers, had prophetic powers, and were healers. **Anglesey** was regarded as a druidical stronghold.

Little is known of their beliefs, but it appears that they thought of life as a cycle, supposing that the souls of the dead progressed to another life. This has been interpreted as a belief in metempsychosis: the creed that dead souls return to the world in various forms. It appears that the oak tree (*see* **Plants**) was important to them, and attempts have been made to explain various forms of the word 'druid' by associating it with this tree (W. *derw*), but it is more likely that it means something akin to 'very learned' or 'very wise'.

By the Middle Ages, the word had come to mean something akin to prophet and it was believed that the bards had inherited some of their powers. The 18th century saw a romantic revival of interest in the druids, the most important outcome of which is the **Gorsedd** of the Bards, which is still associated with the National **Eisteddfod**.

DRY STONE WALLING

Enclosing fields with walls ensures the penning in of livestock, the protection of crops and the ridding of fields of excess stones. An ancient practice, it gathered momentum with the agricultural changes of the late 18th century. Vast lengths of wall were constructed in rocky uplands such as **Snowdonia**, with some of the lengths the work of French prisoners during the **French Revolutionary and Napoleonic Wars**. The craft enjoyed a revival towards the end of the 20th century as society became more affluent and appreciative of traditional landscapes, and walling competitions were organized. An association was formed, with the co-operation of the Countryside Council of Wales and the **National Parks**, to set standards and provide training. The results can be seen beside **roads** and roundabouts and in the agri-environmental schemes of Tir Cymen and Tir Gofal.

DRYCH CRISTIANOGAWL, Y
(*The Christian Mirror*)

This was first book to be printed in Wales (1587), part of the text being printed on a secret illegal press by a group of **Roman Catholics** in Rhiwledyn **cave** (**Llandudno**). The remainder survives as a manuscript copied in 1600. Its theme is 'the Four Last Things', and it derives broadly from the work of the English Jesuit Robert Persons. The preface ends with the words 'O FWLAN yr eiddoch G. R.' (from Milan yours G. R.), suggesting that it was written by **Gruffydd Robert**, of Milan; but it is more likely that the author was Robert Gwyn (*c*.1540/50–1592/1604), the missionary priest of Penyberth (**Llanbedrog**). The full text, edited by Geraint Bowen, appeared in print in 1996 under the title *Y Drych Kristnogawl*.

DUHONW, Breconshire, Powys
(4375 ha; 300 inhabitants)

Duhonw, a **community** to the south of **Builth**, stretches from the banks of the **Wye** to the northern slopes of **Mynydd Epynt** and embraces the basin of the Duhonw. Aberduhonw, now a farm 2 km east of Builth, is said to have been a grange of Strata Florida (**Ystrad Fflur**). St David's, Maesmynis, is the mother church of St Mary's, Builth. Abercynithon was built by Edward Price, the surveyor responsible for the rebuilding of Builth after the fire of 1691.

DUNODING *Cantref*

Reputedly named after **Cunedda**'s son Dunod (Donatus), Dunoding was located along the northern and northwestern coast of Cardigan Bay. It was divided into the **commotes** of **Eifionydd** and **Ardudwy**, which were separated by the formidable barrier of Y Traeth Mawr (*see* **Porthmadog**). By the 13th century, the name Dunoding had fallen into disuse, and the notion arose that Ardudwy and Eifionydd were themselves *cantrefi*.

A romantic portrayal of druids

DUNVANT (Dynfant), Swansea
(241 ha; 4679 inhabitants)

A village on the Clyne **River**, it came into existence in the 19th century to serve the local **coal** and brick-making industries, and expanded following the arrival of the **railway** in 1866. Industry had faded away long before the closure of the railway in 1964, but the growth of **Swansea**'s outskirts brought the village a new role as a suburb. The village has an internationally recognized **male voice choir** and a remarkably successful **rugby** club. It was the birthplace of the artist **Ceri Richards**, the poet and film-maker **John Ormond** and the physicist **Granville Beynon**.

DUX BRITANNIARUM

A **Roman** military title, *dux* described the general in charge of a newly established area command. In **Britain**, the *dux Britanniarum*, an office established *c*.300, commanded the forces of upper Britain, a mobile army based in York. **Magnus Maximus** may have held the office, while **Arthur** was possibly a commander in the same tradition a century after the title had ceased to exist.

DWYFOR One-time district

As a district of the **county** of **Gwynedd**, Dwyfor came into existence in 1974 and was abolished in 1996. It consisted of what had been the **borough** of Pwllheli, the **urban districts** of **Criccieth** and **Porthmadog**, the **rural district** of **Llŷn** and part of that of **Arfon**. It took its name from the River Dwyfor. With its motto *Angor yr Iaith* (the anchor of the language), it was unique among the 37 districts established in 1974 in that it conducted its internal administration almost exclusively through the medium of **Welsh**. From 1989 until 1996, it was the only part of Wales where **Sunday closing** of public houses was in operation. With the establishment of the unitary **county** of Gwynedd in 1996, the district ceased to exist. By the time of the **National Assembly** elections of 2007, the one-time district, long part of the **Caernarfon** constituency, had become part of the Dwyfor **Meirionnydd** constituency.

DWYNWEN (5th/6th century) Saint

Dwynwen, Wales's patron **saint** of lovers, was a daughter of **Brychan**; her feast day is 25 January. Three **Latin** prayers added to the **Bangor** Missal (1494) claim that Dwynwen walked across the Irish Sea for fear of **Maelgwn Gwynedd**. A different version of her legend is recounted by Iolo Morganwg (**Edward Williams**) who claims that Dwynwen fell in love with Maelon Dafodrill, but was heartbroken when he broke off their engagement. God punished Maelon by turning him into a block of ice and gave Dwynwen three wishes. She requested that Maelon be thawed, that she would be able to hear the prayers of anyone suffering from unrequited love and that she herself would live a solitary existence as a nun on Llanddwyn **Island** (*see* **Rhosyr**). Miraculous healings at her chapel and holy **well** are described by the poet Dafydd Trefor (*c.*1460–*c.*1528) and she is also invoked by **Dafydd ap Gwilym**.

DWYRIW, Montgomeryshire, Powys
(4513 ha; 467 inhabitants)

The name of this **community**, which is located immediately south of **Llanfair Caereinion**, reflects the fact that it extends over the basins of the two Rhiw **Rivers**. A sparsely populated upland area, it contains the hamlets of Llanllugan, Llanwyddelan and Adfa. In *c.*1180, a **Cistercian nunnery** was founded at Llanllugan as a daughter house of Strata Florida (**Ystrad Fflur**); **Dafydd ap Gwilym** expressed a desire to seduce its nuns. It was dissolved in 1536. Its site is unknown, but it was probably on the banks of the southern Rhiw River. St Gwyddelan's church was rebuilt in 1865, but St Mary's Llanllugan remains much as it was in the 15th century. Gezerim, the plain but attractive **Calvinistic Methodist** chapel at Adfa, dates from 1790. Outside it is a memorial column to Lewis Evan (1719–92), **Montgomeryshire**'s first Methodist counsellor and founder in 1742 of the society at Adfa.

DYER, John (1699–1757) Poet and painter

Born at **Llanfynydd**, and brought up from the age of 15 at Aberglasney at nearby **Llangathen**, Dyer was destined for the **law** but became a farmer and then rector of **parishes** in Leicestershire and Lincolnshire. He was better known as a painter until the publication of his poem 'Grongar Hill' (1726), on which he worked while studying **painting** in Rome; the poem celebrates the countryside of childhood home and, in particular, the hill that stands a kilometre to the south-west, overlooking the valley of the **Tywi**; it includes the well-known couplet: 'Ever changing, ever new/ When will the landscape tire the view?'.

As a poet-painter much influenced by Claude, he was a major pioneer of topographical verse in **English**. His long poem about the wool trade, 'The Fleece', begun in 1743 and published in four books in 1757, was admired by Wordsworth, who thought Dyer's style as pure as that of Milton.

Before visiting Rome, Dyer had explored Wales on horseback, drawing and writing his observations along the way. Although few of his paintings survive, he was important in the development of the philosophy of landscape painting, the **picturesque** and an emerging Welsh aesthetic. The beauty of ruins, links with the antique and the softening effect of nature were among his preoccupations.

DYFED Kingdom

One of the kingdoms of early Wales, the name probably came from that of the **Demetae**, the tribe inhabiting southwest Wales during the **Roman** occupation. Its dynasty had **Irish** origins and may have had associations with the migration of the Déisi from **Ireland**, which probably occurred in the late 4th century.

The 20 **ogham**-inscribed stones discovered in Dyfed suggest a sustained relationship with Ireland. According to the first sentence in the first branch of *Pedair Cainc y Mabinogi* (*see* **Mabinogion, The**), the kingdom consisted of seven *cantrefi* – those of **Cantref Gwarthaf**, **Cemais**, **Daugleddau**, **Emlyn**, **Pebidiog**, **Penfro** and **Rhos**.

In the 9th century, the uniting of **Gwynedd**, **Powys**, **Ceredigion** and **Ystrad Tywi** under **Rhodri Mawr** caused the rulers of Dyfed to fear that their kingdom would also be absorbed, and King Hyfaidd ap Bleddri sought protection through the patronage of Alfred of Wessex. However, Llywarch, Hyfaidd's son, seems to have been the last of the kings of Dyfed, for, following his death in 904, the kingdom was annexed by **Hywel Dda**, Llywarch's son-in-law. Dyfed, along with Ceredigion, Ystrad Tywi and **Brycheiniog**, came to constitute the kingdom of **Deheubarth**, which lasted, at least in a truncated form, until the 13th century.

Southern Dyfed was extensively de-Cymricized from the 12th century onwards through an influx of Flemish (*see* **Flemings**) and **English** settlers. Following the **Act of 'Union'** of 1536, western Dyfed became **Pembrokeshire** and its eastern part was allotted to **Carmarthenshire**. Dyfedeg or Demetian is the term used to describe the **Welsh** dialect of the south-west.

DYFED One-time county

Following local **government** reorganization in 1976, Dyfed became the name of one of Wales's eight new **counties**. It consisted of the former counties of **Cardiganshire**, **Carmarthenshire** and **Pembrokeshire**, and was divided into the districts of **Ceredigion**, **Carmarthen**, **Dinefwr**, **Llanelli**, **Preseli-Pembrokeshire** and **South Pembrokeshire**. The county council headquarters was located at Carmarthen. A further reorganization in 1996 reconstituted the former counties and Dyfed, as the name of a local government unit, passed into desuetude.

DYFFRYN ARDUDWY, Gwynedd
(4555 ha; 1667 inhabitants)

Located beteen **Barmouth** and **Harlech**, the **community** contains the villages of Dyffryn Ardudwy, Coed Ystumgwern, Llanenddwyn, Llanddwywe and Tal-y-bont, all of them strung out along the A496. It extends to the summit of Diffwys (750 m) and includes the remote Llyn Bodlyn **reservoir**. On his journey through Wales in 1188, **Giraldus Cambrensis** described the area as 'the

Carreg Cennen Castle, Dyffryn Cennen

rudest and roughest of all Welsh districts'. It contains important groups of **Neolithic** burial chambers – Carneddau Hengwm, in particular – numerous **Bronze Age** cairns and a dramatically sited **Iron Age hill-fort** (Craig y Ddinas). Cors y Gedol has an ornate ceiling (1576), an attractive gatehouse (1630) and a massive barn (1685). It was the home of the **Vaughan family**, one of **Merioneth**'s leading landed families – Llanddwywe church (*c.*1593) contains Vaughan tombs.

In the 19th century, Llanenddwyn was a centre of manganese mining (*see* **Geology**). Egryn featured in the 1904–5 religious **revival**, when a mysterious light appeared in the sky above Dyffryn Ardudwy; Mary Jones, prayer group leader at Egryn chapel, claimed that it had provided her with guidance in choosing people for whom she should pray. Many others witnessed the phenomenon and it was reported widely by the press.

DYFFRYN ARTH, Ceredigion
(4331 ha; 1241 inhabitants)
Located immediately north of **Aberaeron**, the **community** embraces the basin of the Arth and contains the villages of Aberarth, Bethania, Cross Inn and Pennant. Dinerth Castle, in the Arth's deeply incised ravine, was built during **Norman** ascendancy in **Ceredigion** (1110–35). Picturesque Aberarth hugs the estuary; its St **David**'s church, high on a hill above, has a 13th-century tower. On the community's beaches are disused inter-tidal **fish**traps in the form of

banks of stones known as *goredi*. Tŷ Glyn is an attractive 17th-century house. Monachty, on the site of a Strata Florida (**Ystrad Fflur**) grange, was the home of Alban Gwynne (d.1819), founder of Aberaeron. Bethania and Pennant were areas of substantial **emigration** to **North America**. The educationist **Jac L. Williams** was a native of Aberarth.

DYFFRYN CENNEN, Carmarthenshire
(4233 ha; 1206 inhabitants)
Located immediately south of **Llandeilo**, the **community** contains the village of Ffairfach – essentially the southern suburb of Llandeilo – and the hamlets of Dre-fach, Llandyfân and Trapp. Carreg Cennen Castle, Wales's most dramatically sited stronghold, stands on a **limestone** rock 110 m above the River Cennen. Evidence of the original castle of the rulers of **Deheubarth** was obliterated by the building work undertaken between 1283 and 1322, when the castle was held by the Giffard family, lords of **Llandovery**. At the south-eastern corner of the inner ward, steps lead to a vaulted passage which ends in a natural cave, which was in use in the **Neolithic Age**. The castle was captured by **Owain Glyndŵr** in 1402, and was left in ruins following its capture by the **York**ists in 1462.

Cwrtbrynybeirdd is a large 16th-century farmhouse. In the community's southern extremity are Beddau'r Derwyddon, the so called **druids**' graves; but they are, in fact, pillow mounds – artificial **rabbit** burrows.

DYFFRYN CLWYD *Cantref* and marcher-lordship
Together with **Rhos**, **Rhufoniog** and **Tegeingl**, Dyffryn Clwyd was one of the *cantrefi* of the **Perfeddwlad** (the middle country), and contained the **commotes** of **Dogfeiling**, **Llannerch** and **Colion**. In 1284, it became a **march**er-lordship – often called the lordship of **Ruthin** – and was granted to Reginald **Grey**.

DYFFRYN CLYDACH, Neath Port Talbot
(691 ha; 3188 inhabitants)
Located immediately north of **Neath**, the **community** contains Neath Abbey, founded in 1129 as a daughter house of Savigny. (In 1147, the Savignac order merged with that of the **Cistercians**.) The entire complex was rebuilt between *c.*1180 and *c.*1330 on a scale reflecting the monastery's wealth – it owned five fertile granges in **Gower** and the **Vale of Glamorgan**. In 1536, **John Leland** considered Neath to be 'the fairest abbey in all Wales'. When dissolved in 1539, it had an abbot – the distinguished scholar and administrator **Leyshon Thomas** – and seven monks. Following the **dissolution**, a large mansion was built within the monastery; it was abandoned in the 18th century when a **copper**works was built on the site. Of the medieval structures, the outstanding remains are the vaulted undercroft of the dormitory and fragments of the church's west front.

Neath Abbey **Iron**works, 500 m north of the abbey, was founded in 1792 by the Price and Tregelles families. Their most distinguished member was the **Quaker** philanthropist **Joseph Tregelles Price**. Efforts are being made to preserve the ironworks, which include two of the highest masonry blast furnaces ever constructed. Near the abbey is an attractive stretch of the Tennant **Canal**, including a viaduct across the **River** Clydach. Carreg Bica on Mynydd Drumau is a 4.3-m **Bronze Age** standing stone.

DYFI River (60 km)
The Dyfi rises in Creiglyn Dyfi, high on the eastern slopes of **Aran** Fawddwy in the **community** of **Mawddwy**. From Creiglyn Dyfi, the **river** flows towards Llanymawddwy through a steep and narrow upland valley. Several major tributaries, such as the Cerist and the Cywarch, join the

Dyfi before it reaches Dinas Mawddwy, beyond which it flows through the fertile meadows characteristic of a glacial valley. It is joined by the Twymyn at **Glantwymyn** and by the two Rivers Dulas at **Machynlleth**, the river's lowest bridging-point. West of Machynlleth, the Dyfi becomes tidal and often inundates the flood plain. The river flows into the sea in a broad estuary between **Aberdovey** and the sand dunes of Ynyslas and **Borth**. It was long navigable to Derwenlas (**Cadfarch**), once the site of a small **port**.

DYFRIG (5th century) Saint
The pattern of early church dedications suggests that Dyfrig was territorial bishop of **Erging**, the kingdom between the **Rivers Wye** and Monnow – an area long in **Herefordshire**. His influence as a religious leader stretched far beyond the confines of his **diocese**. The Life of **Samson** (7th century) refers to him as 'papa' Dyfrig, emphasizing his special standing amongst his contemporaries. According to the 'Life of Dyfrig' (12th century) in *Liber Landavensis*, he established a successful monastic school at Hennlann (Hentland on Wye). Under Dyfrig's spiritual leadership, Erging became the cradle of Christianity in Wales. His feast day is 14 November.

DYSERTH (Diserth), Denbighshire
(764 ha; 2566 inhabitants)
Located immediately south of **Prestatyn**, the **community** contains a fine **waterfall**. **Limestone** quarrying on Moel Hiraddug has destroyed much of the large **hill-fort** that crowns the ridge. In 1872, excavation there yielded parts of a La Tène shield which may have been used by one of the fort's inhabitants. Dyserth Castle (1250) was destroyed by **Llywelyn ap Gruffudd** in 1263. St Ffraid's church contains an interesting 1533 Jesse **stained-glass** window. In the churchyard is an early medieval wheel-head cross. Talargoch **lead** mine produced royalties for the bishop of **St Asaph**. Bodrhyddan Hall, originally built by Richard Conway in the 15th century, is still occupied by his descendant, Baron Langford. Remodelled in the 1870s by W. E. Nesfield, its gate-piers (1963) were designed by **Clough Williams-Ellis**.

E

An earthquake epicentre in 1984: Llanaelhaearn, Gwynedd

EAMES, Aled (1921–96) Historian

The scholar who taught the Welsh that their history had a highly significant maritime dimension, **Llandudno**-born Eames was educated at **Bangor**, where he became a lecturer in **education**. His numerous works include *Ships and Seamen of Anglesey* (1973), *Porthmadog Ships* (with Emrys Hughes, 1975) and *Venture in Sail* (1987). A founder editor of the journal *Maritime Wales*, he was a prolific television and radio presenter.

EAMES, Marion (1921–2007) Writer

Born in Birkenhead and brought up in **Dolgellau**, Marion Eames was the most prominent **Welsh-language** historical novelist of the 20th century. She studied the piano and **harp** at the Guildhall, **London**, and from 1955 until 1980 was a radio producer with the BBC. Her first two novels, *Y Stafell Ddirgel* (1969) and *Y Rhandir Mwyn* (1972), portrayed the Quaker **Rowland Ellis** who emigrated from Dolgellau to **Pennsylvania**. The books were published in **English** as *The Secret Room* (1975) and *Fair Wilderness* (1976). Her other subjects include **Llywelyn ap Gruffudd** and the Welsh community on Merseyside (*see* **Liverpool**). She also wrote novels for children.

EARTHQUAKES

The biggest recorded onshore earthquake in **Britain** during the 20th century occurred on 19 July 1984, when the **Llŷn** peninsula was shaken by an earthquake measuring 5.4 on the Richter scale. In **Llanaelhaearn**, the earthquake's epicentre, and over north-west Wales in general, a small amount of damage was done to some buildings but the tremor was felt throughout Wales, most of **England**, southern **Scotland** and eastern **Ireland**. Rather than its occurrence, it was the magnitude of the Llanaelhaearn earthquake, which originated at a depth of 20 km, which was unusual. In fact, between 110 and 150 earthquakes are recorded annually in Britain, the majority in Scotland. Most are insignificant seismic events (less than 2.5), of which most people would be unaware; but the strongest could pose a danger to vulnerable structures such as dams. Small movements along old fault lines in the Earth's surface are responsible for Wales's most powerful earthquakes.

It is believed that an enormous undersea landslide, caused by a submarine volcano, led to the greatest environmental disaster in recent British history. It resulted in the (probable) tsunami of 1606 (1607 by modern reckoning), a mass of water that devastated both shores of the Severn Sea, killing

East Moors Steelworks at the height of its production

at least 2000 people. By the time the wave hit the **Monmouthshire** coast, it was nearly 8 m high and travelling at over 60 kph. It reached up to 6 km inland in the **Cardiff–Chepstow** region. Whilst some analysts attribute it not to an earthquake, but to a wind-driven storm surge, the event is recorded on plaques in a number of churches, including those at **Goldcliff, Redwick** and St Bride's **Wentloog**.

In 1986, the British Geological Survey published for the first time a catalogue of earthquakes in Wales and its **borderland**. Between 1727 and 1984, 70 earthquakes measuring 3.5 or more were recorded, 15 of them being over 4.5. Apart from the Llŷn event, the earthquakes in **Pembroke** (1892 and 1893), **Caernarfon** (1903) and **Swansea** (1906) are the most significant. Over the years, clusters of earthquakes have been recorded in these areas, and Caernarfon, in particular, is one of Britain's most seismologically active areas. The Swansea–**Neath** region was shaken by quite powerful shocks in 1727, 1775, 1832, 1868 and 1906, a pattern which, according to the Geological Survey (1999), suggests that the area could suffer another shock in the near future. Between these north and south clusters – and the area beyond **Offa's Dyke** in the vicinity of Bishop's Castle, **Shropshire** – central and west Wales appear to be more or less seismologically quiet.

EAST MOORS STEELWORKS, Cardiff

East Moors Steelworks (*see* **Iron and Steel**), or 'Dowlais by Sea', began production in 1895. Because of the need to import iron ore, the Dowlais Company (*see* **Guest family**) had recognized that the inland location of its works at **Merthyr Tydfil** was commercially disadvantageous.

Thus, the building of four large blast furnaces and eleven open-hearth stoves on a green-field site represented a significant modernization of steelmaking. Its main products were heavy constructional sections and steel plates for **shipbuilding**, although hopes that Cardiff would become a major shipbuilding centre were not realized.

Adverse market conditions forced a closure of the works in 1930, but between 1934 and 1936 it was largely rebuilt, and began to supply steel for the rod mill at the adjacent Castle Works of **Guest, Keen and Nettlefolds**, which was built at the same time. Although East Moors was at the forefront of productive technology, it suffered increasingly from the limitations of its site, and closed in 1978 – a major episode in the de-industrialization of **Cardiff** that occurred in the later 20th century.

EAST WILLIAMSTON, Pembrokeshire
(683 ha; 1787 inhabitants)

Located immediately west of **Saundersfoot**, the **community** contains the villages of East Williamston, Broadmoor, Moreton, Pentlepoir and Redberth. Evidence of **coal**mining survives. St Elidyr's church, largely rebuilt in 1889, retains its 16th-century bell turret. St Mary's church, Redberth, was rebuilt in 1841, but its original box pews survive. At its reopening, **Connop Thirwall**, bishop of **St David's**, preached in **Welsh**, a language he had just learnt. Few of his congregation can have understood him. In 2001, 84.27% of the inhabitants of East Williamston had no knowledge whatsoever of Welsh, making it, linguistically, the most Anglicized of all the communities of **Pembrokeshire.**

EBBW (Ebwy) River (46 km)

The Ebbw Fawr rises at approximately 481 m on Mynydd **Llangynidr** and flows southward through the town of **Ebbw Vale**. At Aberbeeg (**Llanhilleth**), the **river** is joined by the Ebbw Fach, which rises at 500 m on **Mynydd Llangatwg** and flows through **Nantyglo and Blaina** and **Abertillery**. The Ebbw then passes the one-time **coal**mining settlements of **Crumlin**, **Newbridge** and **Abercarn** to join the Sirhowy at **Crosskeys**. The Sirhowy, which also rises on Mynydd Llangynidr, flows through **Tredegar**, **Argoed**, **Blackwood**, **Pontllanfraith** and **Ynysddu**. From the confluence, the Ebbw flows through **Risca** and **Rogerstone** and the western outskirts of **Newport** to join the **Usk** at its estuary.

EBBW VALE (Glynebwy), Blaenau Gwent
(912 ha; 8944 inhabitants)

In 1775, Ebbw Vale, situated at the head of the **Ebbw** Fawr valley, consisted of only a few scattered farms and houses inhabited by some 120 people. In 1801, by which time Harford, Partridge and Co. had established their **iron**works, the **population** had risen to 800; by 1841, it had climbed to 7800; and 80 years later, the Ebbw Vale **Urban District**, which also included **Beaufort** and **Cwm**, had 35,381 inhabitants. This growth stemmed from the activities of the Ebbw Vale Steel, Iron and Coal Co., whose immense works stretched for 5 km down the valley – a conglomeration of Bessemer and **open-hearth furnaces**, coke ovens, strip mills and by-product plants, surrounded by a support network of collieries, brickworks, gasworks and quarries, and overlooked by the bulky Christchurch (1861) on Brierly Hill.

The decision in 1936 to modernize a plant located in an area of high unemployment, but which had ceased to be conveniently located for steel production, was a rare humanitarian attempt to give social considerations precedence over strictly economic criteria. In the 1960s, the works had 14,500 employees, but the later 20th century saw dramatic change. A strike in 1980 was followed by redundancies and closures. The steel mills at Victoria were dismantled and the site used for the 1992 National Garden Festival. By 2002, a mere 450 were employed at what remained of the plant. Total closure came on 5 July 2002. By then, the male unemployment rate was almost twice that of Wales as a whole, and incomes were 78% of the British average.

As the administrative centre of **Blaenau Gwent**, Ebbw Vale has been at the heart of initiatives aimed at creating an industrial base to replace heavy industry. A number of business parks and **industrial estates** have been established, and the Garden Festival site has become a retail park and a leisure facility, offering woodlands, wetlands, ornamental **gardens** and an oriental pavilion. At the height of its prosperity, Ebbw Vale had 21 chapels. As the constituency of **Aneurin Bevan**, and then of Michael Foot, it has an assured place in the history of the British **Labour** movement.

ECCLESIASTICAL SANCTUARY

In medieval Wales, major churches were entitled to grant temporary protection (*nawdd*) within a designated area (*noddfa*) to individuals fleeing their enemies or legal obligations. The entitlement, known as *seintwar*, originated in Welsh legal concepts and was far more extensive than that permitted under canon **law**.

ECONOMY

Historical trends

Since the onset of industrialization some 250 years ago, the Welsh economy has undergone a process of continuous change. During the 19th century, Wales was transformed from a predominantly agricultural society into one of the world's leading industrial economies. The rapid expansion in **coal** production from 1850 onwards was followed, after 1921, by an equally dramatic decline. At its peak in 1920, coalmining employed over 250,000 workers in Wales. By the year 2000, that number had fallen to 1300. There has also been a decrease of over 60,000 in the number employed in **iron and steel** production since the mid-1970s.

The jobs lost in coal and steel during the second half of the 20th century have been replaced mainly by an expansion in service sector employment. However, the replacement jobs have generally been of poorer quality and have been less well paid.

After the **Second World War**, a large number of new manufacturing plants in Wales were established. However, since 1974, there has been a downward trend in manufacturing employment. The sector was particularly badly affected by the post-1979 recession. After 1986,

19th-century terraced houses and 20th-century detached houses at Ebbw Vale

considerable investment in Wales by foreign companies led to a significant restructuring in manufacturing. In particular, the electrical and electronic **engineering** industries became more important, but, by the early 21st century, increased competition from locations with lower costs in eastern Europe and east Asia, a strong pound, and a worldwide recession in electronic engineering, posed a renewed threat to the viability of Wales's manufacturing base. By 2007, employment in manufacturing had fallen to just 13% of total employment, compared with a peak of 34% in 1974.

Growth in the relative importance of the service sector is a feature of all advanced economies. In 1946, the number employed in service sector jobs in Wales was just 239,000. By 2005, it had risen to over a million, and accounted for nearly 80% of the total number of jobs.

Nearly all changes in industrial structure are invariably accompanied by shifts in **population** and by changes in the composition of the labour force. The second half of the 19th century saw a massive exodus from Wales's rural areas. Large numbers of those displaced by the decline in **agriculture** found their way to the south Wales coalfield. After 1921, the collapse of coal exports ushered in a period of prolonged **depression**, and, between 1925 and 1939, nearly 390,000 people left Wales.

The later 20th century saw a surprising reversal in the long decline in the rural population. Somewhat paradoxically, this has been a reflection not of economic resurgence, but of continuing economic debility. A paucity of well-paid job opportunities, coupled with a huge expansion in higher **education**, has meant that outward migration (*see* **Emigration**), especially among the 16–24 age group, has continued. However, since 1970, this has been more than offset by an influx of people (*see* **Immigration**), mostly from outside Wales, seeking a retirement home or a change in lifestyle, and who have been attracted to these areas partly by the relatively low cost of **housing**.

Another major consequence of the changes in Wales's industrial structure has been a dramatic alteration in the position of **women** in society. In the early 20th century, the role of women was largely confined to child rearing and the upkeep of the home. In 1939, there were fewer than 100,000 women in paid employment. By 2007, this number had increased seven-fold, and one half of all employees were women. This increase in female participation in the workforce has been accompanied by an increase in part-time employment. By 2005, over a third of Wales's employees were in part-time jobs.

Gross Domestic Product

Gross Domestic Product (GDP) (or Gross Value Added) is the most widely used indicator of national and regional economic performance. GDP measures the total value of the goods and services produced within a particular geographical area in a given period (usually a year). Table 1 shows that in 2005 Wales had just under 5% of the United Kingdom's population, but less than 4% of the United Kingdom's GDP, a gap of £3870 per person. In 2005, GDP per head in Wales was lower than in any other part of the United Kingdom.

Table 1
The Welsh economy:
Gross Domestic Product in 2005

	Wales	As a % of the United Kingdom
Area (km²)	20,779	8.5
Population (million)	2.95	4.9
GDP (£billion)	40.9	3.8
GDP per head (£)	13,813	78.1

The trend line in Figure 1 below shows that the prosperity gap between Wales and the rest of the United Kingdom has been widening since the mid-1970s.

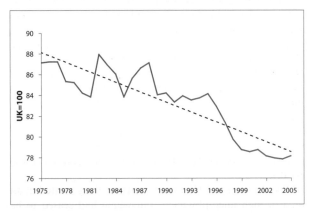

Figure 1 GDP per head in Wales relative to the United Kingdom

There are also large inequalities in wealth within Wales. Figure 2 shows that GDP per head in **Cardiff** and the **Vale of Glamorgan** in 2004 was more than double the level recorded in **Anglesey**.

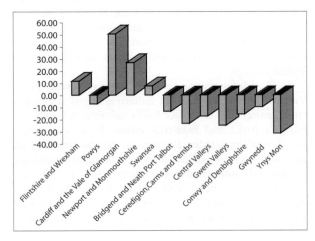

Figure 2 Percentage deviations from the Welsh GDP per head in 2004

Whether GDP per head is the most appropriate indicator of an area's economic health is open to question. GDP is essentially a measure of economic activity rather than economic well-being. Moreover, it encompasses only those activities that form part of the market process. No allowance is made for the value of unpaid work, nor for the enjoyment derived from non-marketed leisure and cultural activities. Factors that detract from well-being, such as pollution and congestion, are disregarded. Nor is any allowance made for differences in the cost of living, which was estimated in 2004 to be 7% lower in Wales than in Britain as a whole. Alternative indicators that incorporate such factors show that, in terms of the overall quality of life, the gap between Wales and Britain as a whole may be considerably smaller than the GDP figures indicate.

Despite this, it is likely that economic policy will continue to focus on GDP per head. In 2000, the **National Assembly** set itself a target of raising GDP per head in Wales as a whole to 90% of the British level by 2010. Its target for the southern coalfield and the west of Wales, areas designated as Objective 1 for the purposes of European Union funding, is lower at 81%.

A leading factor accounting for Wales's relatively low GDP per head is the gap in productivity. In 2005, GDP per worker in Wales was £31,580 – around 9% below the British level. The gap in productivity accounts for the four-fifths of Wales's total prosperity gap. The rest is due to lower levels of employment. Part of the explanation for the productivity gap is that Wales has a higher proportion of part-time workers. In addition, those in full-time employment spend on average nearly an hour less per week at work than their English counterparts. Net out-commuting from Wales, especially to the north-west and south-west of England, is a further contributory factor (the output of workers resident in Wales who work in England is not counted as part of Wales's GDP). However, easily the most important reason for the gap is that output per job is lower in Wales. This is not primarily due to lower productivity in comparable jobs, but rather to differences in industrial and occupational structure.

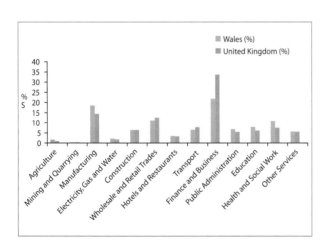

Figure 3 Share of Industry Groups in GDP 2004

In general, the sectors in Figure 3 (such as public sector services) that are more important in Wales than in the rest of Britain, have relatively low levels of productivity. Conversely, Wales is significantly under-represented in high 'value added' sectors such as financial and business services. It is worth noting that in Wales, as in the rest of Britain, the primary sector (mainly agriculture, mining and quarrying) has become relatively insignificant, at least in terms of its contribution to GDP. Differences in occupational structure also partly explain why the level of output per job is lower in Wales. In 2006, the numbers employed in higher managerial and professional occupations accounted for 23.8% of the total number in employment in Wales, compared with 27.8% in Britain as a whole.

Low levels of productivity are reflected in below average levels of weekly earnings. In April 2003, average gross weekly earnings of full-time employees in Wales were £470, which is 87.4% of the figure for Britain, compared with 93.2% in 1984. Among full-time workers, 13% of men and 19% of women were being paid less than the low-pay threshold of £6.50 an hour in 2006 – about 25% higher than the corresponding proportions in England. Nearly one half of all part-time workers in Wales were low paid. There was also a considerable disparity in average weekly earnings across Wales, ranging from £498 in Cardiff, **Newport** and the Vale of Glamorgan to £436 in the west (**Ceredigion, Carmarthenshire** and **Pembrokeshire**), where no less than 30% of all workers were classified as low paid. The gap between male and female earnings, however, has been diminishing, and is narrower in Wales than in any other part of Britain. Even so, men were in 2006 still earning, on average, 23.2% more than women.

The second factor that accounts for the difference in GDP per head between Wales and the rest of Britain is that a lower proportion of the population in Wales is in employment (43.7% in 2005 compared with 46.7% in Britain as a whole).

A higher proportion of pensioners (21.5% of the population compared with the British figure of 18.5%) accounts for part of the gap. The remainder of the gap is mainly due to the high percentage of working-age adults in Wales who are 'economically inactive' (23.3% in the spring of 2007 compared with Britain's 21.2%). These are people who are not in work, but are not officially classified as unemployed because they are not actively seeking employment. The higher figure for Wales is usually attributed to a higher incidence of long-term sickness and disability, but a more fundamental reason may be a concentration, especially in the southern coalfield, of older men with no marketable skills, for whom inactivity has become an established way of life.

For much of the post-war period, attention was focused on the gap in unemployment rates between Wales and Britain generally. However, in the latter part of the last century this gap narrowed considerably. In the spring of 2007, the unemployment rate in Wales was 5.5%, only 0.1 percentage point above the United Kingdom figure. Some groups have continued to experience much higher levels of unemployment. In 2006, the unemployment rate among young adults was above 10%. However, the most striking feature of the overall labour market in the early part of the 21st century is that officially classified unemployment now accounts for only a small proportion of total joblessness.

Household income and expenditure

Lower employment rates, combined with below average earnings, have had an inevitably adverse impact on household living standards. Combined data for the three-year period 2003–6 show household income (before tax) in Wales at £492 a week – 82.5% of the United Kingdom level. This is slightly less than the GDP gap because the latter does not include social security benefits, which account for 17% of household income in Wales compared with 13% in the UK as a whole. The incidence of poverty in the past has also been higher in Wales. However, both child poverty and pensioner poverty have declined since the 1990s. Child poverty (the proportion of children living in households with an income below 60% of median household income for the United Kingdom) in 2006 was 28% compared with 36% in the late nineties. Over the same period there was a fall from 26% to 20% in pensioner poverty. In both cases, the rates in 2006 were close to the United Kingdom average.

Lower levels of household income have led to lower levels of expenditure. Average weekly household expenditure in Wales for the period 2003–6 was £372, which is 86.1% of the British level. This is a smaller gap than that in household income, partly because the amount paid per head in tax is lower in Wales, and partly because Wales has a lower household saving ratio.

Figure 4 shows the allocation of household expenditure in Wales for the period 2003–6. Expenditure patterns in Wales have changed considerably as household incomes have risen in real terms. By the early 21st century, Welsh households were spending more on leisure goods and services (14%) than on **food** (12%), while 40 years earlier the budget share of food was 28% and that of leisure was only 7%.

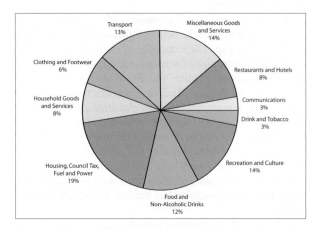

Figure 4 The pattern of weekly household expenditure 2003–6

Government expenditure

British government expenditure in Wales amounted to £24 billion in 2006–7. This represents more than £800 per head of the population, around 11% higher than the British average. This expenditure can be divided into two broad categories: the total budget for expenditure by the National Assembly (the 'block grant'), and government expenditure which is not under the Assembly's control.

Changes in the Assembly's budget are largely determined by the Barnett formula, which operates by allocating a proportion of any increase in planned public spending in England to **Scotland**, Wales and Northern **Ireland**, based on the ratio of each country's population to

the population of England. Although Wales receives the same annual cash increase per head as England, since Wales has a higher baseline level of public spending, this means that the country receives lower percentage increases, resulting in the so-called Barnett 'squeeze'. This has led many to argue that the formula be replaced by one based on a formal assessment of the relative needs of different parts of Britain. A further major source of contention has been the failure on the part of the Treasury to provide the additional money needed to match European Union funding under the Objective 1 scheme. This has meant that the Welsh Assembly has had to divert money from other programmes for this purpose.

Once the total budget for the Assembly has been determined, it is free to determine how to allocate the bulk of the money at its disposal between the different programmes for which it has responsibility. Figure 5 shows how the budget was allocated in 2007–8.

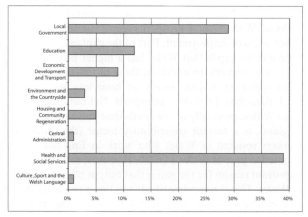

Figure 5 Allocation of National Assembly budget 2007–8 (%)

Key elements in that part of public expenditure not under the control of the Assembly include social security spending (£9600 million) and spending on **law** and order (nearly £1500 million). Social security spending per head in Wales is some 12% higher than the average for Britain generally, and this accounts for one half of the overall differential in identifiable expenditure per head.

Regional policy

The basic aim of regional policy is to reduce economic imbalances between regions. Initial efforts by the British government to tackle regional disparities took the form of encouraging migration from areas of high unemployment to more prosperous areas (*see* **Industrial Transference Board**). However, from 1934 onwards, the main thrust of regional policy was directed at diverting new manufacturing jobs to disadvantaged areas by a series of measures: building **industrial estates**; offering incoming firms financial incentives; improving transport communications; and, after 1945, imposing negative controls on industrial expansion in the south-east of England and the English Midlands.

In the immediate post-war period, this policy was spectacularly successful. By the end of the 1960s, considerable progress had been made towards diversifying Wales's manufacturing base, and many believed that the foundations for stable economic growth had been firmly established. Such views were soon shown to be wildly optimistic. Much of the manufacturing base that had been painstakingly constructed over the post-war period was blown away by the recession of the early 1980s. This led many to question whether Wales's success in attracting branch factories may actually have weakened rather than strengthened the economy. This was not because branch establishments are necessarily more vulnerable in times of recession, but because they offer few opportunities for employees to acquire entrepreneurial skills. Branch factories tend to concentrate on 'back-end' functions, such as assembly work, while the more important 'front-end' functions, such as product innovation and **design**, research and development, and marketing are carried out at the location of the parent factory. Dependence on branch factories has also meant that the financial and business service sector in Wales is relatively underdeveloped, since these services tend to congregate at those locations where there is a concentration of head offices.

After 1979, doubts about the effectiveness of regional policy led to its progressive dismemberment. Regional employment premiums had already been withdrawn in 1976. The Thatcher government responded to the collapse in manufacturing in the early 1980s by removing most of the other instruments of regional policy. Negative controls were abandoned, regional development grants were capped, and subsequently scrapped. The coverage of the areas eligible for assistance was reduced, and eligibility criteria for the receipt of regional selective assistance were tightened. At the same time, changes in the macro-economic environment considerably reduced the effectiveness of those policy instruments that remained. The pace of Britain's economic growth had slackened, and manufacturing employment was in decline. From a practical policy standpoint, therefore, the debate over whether the Welsh economy had benefited from post-war regional policies had become largely academic. The prospect of diverting significant numbers of manufacturing jobs to Wales from other parts of Britain had disappeared, and so it was clear that a new policy direction was required.

The **Welsh Office** and the **Welsh Development Agency** responded by concentrating their efforts in two main areas: the attraction of overseas companies anxious to establish a foothold within the European single market, and the development of Wales's indigenous potential.

Efforts to attract **inward investment** proved highly successful. In the early 1990s, Wales secured one fifth of the projects and jobs attracted to Britain. By 1998, employment in overseas-owned manufacturing plants in Wales had reached 76,000, over one third of total manufacturing employment. As the century drew to its close, however, a number of inward investors began to announce significant job losses, and by 2006 the number employed in overseas-owned plants had fallen to 65,000.

Promoting indigenous growth has proved immensely difficult. Policy makers have had to grapple with a range of problems, many of which are a legacy of Wales's industrial past. Entrepreneurial activity is still viewed in Wales with considerable suspicion. There are proportionately fewer managers in Wales than elsewhere in the United Kingdom.

The percentage of persons with basic functional skills in literacy and numeracy is lower than in England, and Wales has a higher proportion of individuals with no formal qualifications. Wales also has a particularly poor record in product and process innovation, and spends less on research and development. Business use of information and communication technology (ICT) is also lower than in any other part of Britain.

Given these factors, it is not entirely surprising that the rate of business start-ups in Wales in the 1990s was 30% below the British figure. Indeed, more businesses were closed than were opened. Between 1994 and 2006, the stock of VAT-registered firms in Wales increased by only 1.6% compared with a 14.3% increase in Britain as a whole. Part of the explanation for this under-performance is that in poorer areas new businesses tend to cluster in relatively low-entry-cost activities focused on the immediate locality. In this situation, the only way new entrants are likely to succeed is by undercutting existing companies, often leading to their eradication.

Strenuous efforts have been made to improve Wales's economic performance. A concerted attempt has been made, in schools and elsewhere, to create a more positive attitude towards entrepreneurship. Education and training programmes have been revamped, and measures taken to encourage more extensive use of ICT. A range of initiatives has been introduced to improve the competitiveness of small and medium-sized enterprises (SMEs) – for instance, by developing closer links with higher education institutions and by creating clusters of SMEs in industries such as media and communications. Access to finance has been improved, and 2003 saw the establishment of a new body, Business Eye, designed to provide a single, easily accessible point for all business support inquiries. In 2006, the Welsh Development Agency was abolished as a **quango** and its responsibilities transferred to the National Assembly. From a business perspective, one of the advantages of this decision was that firms would no longer have to make separate applications to the National Assembly for regional selective assistance, and to the Welsh Development Agency for finance and other forms of support. However, some maintained that businesses would prefer to deal with an organization that operates at arm's length from government rather than directly with civil servants.

There are signs that the various initiatives outlined above are beginning to bear fruit. Between 2000 and 2007, the total number employed in Wales increased by 128,000, an increase of 10.4%, compared with 5.6% in Britain as a whole. However, much of this increase was in relatively low-productivity public-sector jobs. Moreover, it seemed unlikely that Wales would continue to outperform the rest of Britain in terms of employment growth. Concerns were expressed that given Wales's above-average dependence on public-sector employment, the planned slowdown in the growth of British government public spending from 2008 onwards would be likely to affect Wales disproportionately, in which case a substantial improvement in labour productivity would be needed to narrow the prosperity gap between Wales and the rest of Britain. There was general agreement that this might be very difficult to achieve, and a widespread acceptance that the Welsh Assembly government's original target of raising GDP per head in Wales to 90% of the British level by 2010 would not be met.

It was recognized from the outset that the target of raising GDP per head in the Objective 1 region to 81% of the British level by 2010 would present an even bigger challenge. In 2001, GDP per head in that part of Wales was a mere 67% of the British level. Since 2001, despite £1.2 billion of European Union funding received under the 2001–6 Objective 1 Programme, the economic disparities between different parts of Wales have been increasing. There had been concerns that following the accession of ten new, predominantly low-income member states to the European Union, the level of GDP per head in the west of Wales and the southern coalfield would be above 75% of the EU average, and hence the region would no longer qualify for the highest level of support under the new 2007–13 Convergence Programme. In the event, these concerns proved unfounded. Such was the relative deterioration in their economic circumstances, that those parts of Wales were in 2005 accorded the doubtful distinction of being classified among the least prosperous regions within the newly enlarged Union, and, as such, eligible for a further £1.4 billion of European funding over the period 2007–13.

EDEIRNION Commote

Straddling the upper **Dee** valley, the **commote** was reputedly named after Edern (or Eternus), one of the sons of **Cunedda**. As Edeirnion was traditionally part of **Powys**, the story was probably part of **Gwynedd**'s expansionist propaganda. In 1284, Edeirnion became part of the **county of Merioneth**; the name survived in the post-**Acts of 'Union' hundred** and the post-1894 **rural district**. In 1974, Edeirnion was detached from the district of **Meirionnydd** and added to the district of **Glyndŵr** in the new county of **Clwyd**. In 1996, it became part of the recreated **Denbighshire**.

EDELIGION (Edlogan) Commote

A **commote** of **Gwent**, it extended from the **Usk** to the uplands between the Llwyd and **Ebbw** valleys. Seized by the **Normans** in the late 11th century, it was restored to Welsh rule by Morgan ab Owain, lord of **Caerleon**, in the 12th century. It eventually came into possession of the dukes of **York** and thence of the crown.

EDNYFED FYCHAN (Ednyfed ap Cynwrig ap Iorwerth) (d.1246) Official

Ednyfed Fychan, from the **Abergele** area, became in *c.*1215 *distain* or seneschal to **Llywelyn ap Iorwerth**, prince of **Gwynedd**. For the rest of his life he was the leading counsellor and servant of Llywelyn and of his son and successor **Dafydd ap Llywelyn** and was rewarded with extensive lands and privileges. He was followed in his office by two – possibly three – sons, and his descendants – known as *Wyrion Eden* – were prominent in the **Principality** between the **Edwardian conquest** and the **Glyndŵr Revolt**. The **Tudor** dynasty was descended from him.

EDUCATION

Despite sharing a normally common legislative umbrella with **England**, Wales has developed a distinctive education system. That development arose from different social and

linguistic factors and is now consolidated under the authority of the **National Assembly for Wales**, although Westminster still retains responsibility for primary legislation in the field of education.

The Middle Ages

Education in Wales in the medieval period was essentially the preserve of the Church and the bardic order. In the 6th century, monastic education at **Llantwit Major** drew scholars from most of the places served by the western sea routes. The language used was **Latin**, a legacy of the **Romans**, which dominated clerical and lay education for centuries.

Bardic education was intensive and strictly regulated. Apart from mastering technical matters relating to prosody and language, aspiring poets were also expected to acquire an encyclopaedic knowledge of native lore, learning and **genealogy**. Although instruction was primarily oral, several bardic grammars were produced between the 14th and 16th centuries.

In the later medieval period, the few Welshmen able to proceed to university usually went from household tuition to **Oxford** or, more rarely, to **Cambridge**, aged as young as 14, and to the Inns of Court in **London**. **Owain Glyndŵr** probably studied at the Inns of Court and hoped to set up two universities in Wales. Within the small towns, craft guilds provided apprenticeships, but in an overwhelmingly rural society most skills were learnt from example.

The 16th to the 18th centuries

In the 16th century, formal education continued to be the preserve of an increasingly laicized elite. Grammar schools, for the sons of the 'middling sort', were established in several Welsh towns, such as **Ruthin** and **Brecon**. The grammar schools became more socially exclusive in the 17th century, with some, such as **Cowbridge**, being extended and rebuilt.

Following the **Reformation**, a growing body of **Puritans** bemoaned the lack of literacy that they deemed essential for the saving of souls. Matters were complicated by the fact that the mass of the **population** knew no other language than **Welsh**. In 1588, the **Bible** was published in Welsh and provided a scholarly template for the language. In the following century, it became available in cheaper editions and proved a crucial education textbook until at least the 19th century. Under the **Commonwealth**, Wales was a priority for mission and, under the **Act for the Propagation of the Gospel in Wales** (1650), some 60 schools were established, most of which were abolished following the Stuart Restoration in 1660.

Although legislated against after 1660, ejected ministers and former Commonwealth teachers continued to teach. This provided a link with the work of the **Welsh Trust**, which was founded in 1674 to establish schools and to provide religious **literature**. The trust was short-lived, but the charitable sponsorship of education in order to save souls continued with the work of the **Society for the Promotion of Christian Knowledge**, in whose endeavours Welsh activists were prominent. In Wales, its efforts were handicapped by use of the **English** language. More successful, and involving some outstanding scholars, were the **Nonconformist academies** (*see also* **Nonconformists**).

For the Welsh, the **circulating schools**, started by **Griffith Jones** in the 1730s, were the most successful and original charity school enterprise. It is estimated that these schools taught some 250,000 individuals – about half the population – to read; such remarkable levels of literacy undoubtedly fuelled the radical politics of a later age and made Welsh the most receptive of the **Celt**ic languages to a print-based culture. For the wealthy, however, education meant tuition at home, and attendance at public schools in England, and at Oxford or Cambridge universities, institutions which became, in the 18th century, increasingly elitist in their intake.

The 19th century

The social consequences of the **Industrial Revolution**, and a massive population growth, provide the background to the infamous education report of the commissioners enquiring into the state of Welsh education that was published in 1847 (*see* **Treason of the Blue Books**). Although tendentious in its social commentary, the report proved more accurate on the inadequacies of educational provision. The **Anglican** elementary schools of the **National Society** often provided the only formal education available in an increasingly Nonconformist Wales. **British Society** non-denominational schools were rare in Wales until the 1850s. The more radical Nonconformists – the **voluntaryists** – were against any state involvement in education. The language issue, inadequate teaching and poor accommodation bedevilled effective teaching. **Sunday schools**, held in the mother tongue and open to both children and adults, attracted far more pupils than did day schools. There were some schools attached to industrial works (*see* **Works schools**), but mass education received limited support from landowners and industrialists. Private venture schools were often appalling in every way.

The needs of the Anglican Church received most attention, with the opening in 1827 of a college in **Lampeter** to train clergy (*see* **University of Wales, Lampeter**) and, in 1848, of **Trinity College** in **Carmarthen** to train teachers. In turn, proponents of non-sectarian education established the **Normal College, Bangor**, in 1858, to train teachers for British Society schools.

With the increasing state involvement in education – particularly after the 1870 Education Act, which provided for the establishment of board schools in those places where existing schooling was inadequate – the Welsh story becomes more complex. Welsh society differed from that of England in that Wales was predominantly Nonconformist, the language of the majority was Welsh and economic expansion was largely concentrated in the heavily industrialized south-east. Yet, lacking the power to organize education in accordance with native ideals, the Welsh had to compromise with a state intervention in education that was wholly English in ethos.

Between 1870 and 1914, educational provision was transformed. School Boards came to dominate elementary education and to operate according to curricular patterns dictated after 1862 by the payment by results system. In 1872, the University College of Wales opened at **Aberystwyth** (*see* **University of Wales, Aberystwyth**). The **Aberdare Report** recommended the establishment of two university colleges, one in the south and one in the north, a recommendation that led to the foundation of a college at **Cardiff** (1883) and at Bangor (1884). The three colleges came together in 1893 to form the **University of Wales**.

The Aberdare Report also recommended that the inadequacy of intermediate education in Wales should be rectified. That led to the highly significant **Welsh Intermediate Education Act** (1889), which enabled Wales to have 95 secondary schools by 1902. Partly **government**-funded, the intermediate schools required an examining and inspecting organization, which resulted in the **Central Welsh Board** (1896). Although the intermediate schools were intended to be both academic and vocational, the former aspect soon predominated. A few older schools – mainly boarding schools such as those in Brecon, **Llandovery**, **Monmouth** and Ruthin, as well as the Howell foundations in **Denbigh** and Llandaff (*see* **Cardiff**) – remained outside the intermediate system and came to represent the core of the small independent secondary school sector, which still exists.

The 20th century

The 1902 Education Act replaced school boards with local authority administration. Several of Wales's Nonconformist-dominated **county** councils refused to administer the Act, which provided local authority money for denominational schools (*see* **'Welsh Revolt, The'**). There was an impasse until the advent in 1905 of a **Liberal** government, which introduced a highly significant measure of **devolution**, the **Welsh Department of the Board of Education** (1907), responsible for administering central government policy on schools. **Owen M. Edwards** was its chief inspector from 1907 until 1920.

The curriculum, teaching methods, examinations and attitudes to education in interwar Wales were conditioned chiefly by devastating economic **depression** and British government policy. A Welsh Department attempt to introduce bilateral or multilateral secondary schools was frustrated by the government, and Welsh local authorities in the most depressed areas unsuccessfully attempted to defy government over the means testing of secondary school places. Technical education was largely confined to the very few junior technical schools, while such working-**class** adult education as was available was provided by the **Workers' Educational Association**, Ruskin College, Oxford, the **Central Labour College**, London, and **Coleg Harlech**.

The 1944 Education Act brought an end to the concept of elementary education, which was based on the assumption that the working class should be content with an education up to the age of 13 or 14, which was an end in itself and would not lead to more advanced schooling. The Act stressed the concept of primary schools, which contained the notion that their pupils could go on to secondary and higher education – a revolutionary notion compared with the class-bound ideas that had hitherto been central to educational provision. Class attitudes, however, were not absent from the grammar school/secondary modern

Dowlais central school, Merthyr Tydfil, *c.*1890

division advocated by the Act in the field of secondary education. The **Glamorgan** and **Swansea** local authorities fought for multilateral secondary systems, but initially it was **Anglesey** alone which adopted the comprehensive system. In most of the rest of Wales, teenagers attended either grammar schools or secondary modern schools, at least until the 1970s, a division which perpetuated the widely condemned 11+ examination.

There was some devolution in this period, but within strict 'England and Wales' parameters. In 1964, Wales acquired its **secretary of state** and by 1970 the **Welsh Office** Education Department was responsible for all primary and secondary education. The **Welsh Joint Education Committee**, created in 1949, succeeded the Central Welsh Board. In 1967, the Central Advisory Council for Wales produced the **Gittins** Report. In the 1970s, in compliance with government policy, Welsh secondary schools were transformed into comprehensive schools.

A success story of the post-war period was the growth of Welsh-language schooling. In 1939, the first private Welsh-language primary school was established in Aberystwyth. In 1947, the **Carmarthenshire** County Council established a publicly maintained equivalent at **Llanelli**. In 1956, the first designated bilingual secondary school, Ysgol Glan Clwyd, opened in **Flintshire**. *Ysgolion meithrin*, Welsh-language nursery schools, proliferated and there were already over 60 of them by the time **Mudiad Ysgolion Meithrin** was founded in 1971. Since then, there has been a transformation in attitudes towards Welsh-language education, which came to be seen as successful and economically desirable.

However, there has never been a Welsh-language university college, and Welsh-medium provision in the higher education sector remains seriously underdeveloped: in the University of Wales, for instance, at the beginning of the 21st century, only about 100 of its 5000 academic staff were teaching through the medium of Welsh.

All sectors of higher education expanded dramatically from the 1960s. An abortive attempt in the 1980s to rationalize teaching and research in Welsh higher education, by augmenting the powers of the University of Wales, was replaced in the 1990s by ever-increasing institutional independence. The University expanded far beyond the few colleges of the 1920s. However, in 2004, the largest college – that at Cardiff – seceded from the University of Wales and became **Cardiff University**. Then, in 2007, the University of Wales underwent its biggest change ever by ceasing to be a federal body, its relationship with its original constituent institutions becoming a confederal one.

Another major change, prompted by English priorities in the 1980s, came when the Education Reform Act (1988) promoted the local management of schools and a centralized curriculum. The National Curriculum gave rise to a distinctive programme for schools in Wales – the statutory Cwricwlwm Cymreig. It was initiated by the Curriculum Council for Wales, subsequently mutated into ACCAC (Awdurdod Cymwysterau, Cwricwlwm ac Asesu Cymru – the Qualifications, Curriculum and Assessment Authority for Wales) which was given responsibility for curriculum and assessment. In 2006, ACCAC's responsibilities were brought in-house by the National Assembly.

Such developments, and the fact that the National Assembly has responsibility for the full range of education throughout Wales, make it possible at the beginning of the 21st century to speak of a Welsh education system.

Current provision

In 2006, there were 33 nursery, 1555 primary, 224 secondary comprehensive and 43 special schools in the maintained sector; the small independent sector provided education for 9635 pupils in 56 schools, among them the innovative and international Atlantic College, established at **St Donats** in 1962. In 2004 there were a total of 505,208 pupils in Wales taught by 27,378 teachers.

In 2005–6, there were 25 further education institutions employing 14,695 full-time and part-time staff; 311,145 students enrolled for courses (71% of enrolments were for full-time courses). Wales's 13 higher education institutions included the constituent institutions of the University of Wales, second in size only to London among Britain's universities. In 2005–6, a total of 137,760 enrolments for higher education courses were recorded (62,445 were part-time); 5720 full-time academic staff were employed in higher education, and expenditure was £902 million (the **Open University** in Wales is separately funded). Nearly 43% of the full-time students attending higher education institutions came from outside Wales.

From April 2001, the administration of further and higher education and training changed. The **Higher Education Funding Council for Wales** (HEFCW) continued to disburse funds to that sector; the **National Council for Education and Training for Wales**, funded further, adult and continuing education and, from April 2002, school sixth forms. These two organizations were part of Education and Learning Wales (ELWa; *see* **National Council for Education and Training for Wales**) until 2003, when HEFCW was de-merged.

The National Assembly works with Wales's 22 unitary local authorities, which have increasingly embraced cabinet-style government, with a member responsible for education. Elected councillors are served by a director of education and support staff. In 2006–7, the authorities spent more than £2.3 billion on education, by far the biggest element in their budgets. Each authority receives a block grant from the Assembly and has its own formula for the disbursement of funds to individual schools. The Assembly's decision to cease its earmarking of councils' education budgets within block grants caused disquiet in the schools sector, the resultant discrepancy between funding per pupil across Wales being contentious. Although the relationship between the Assembly and local authorities is closer than that between government and local authorities in England, the potential for confrontation remains, particularly on issues such as the closure of small rural schools.

The control of local authorities over individual schools has been much reduced, although they nominate a proportion of the schools' governing bodies. Governors now exercise the crucial right of appointing and, if necessary, disciplining teachers, including head teachers. Since 2000, teachers in Wales have had their own General Teaching

Council. Local authorities employ advisers who work closely with schools, though they have no formal inspection powers. School inspections are controlled by **Her Majesty's Inspectorate of Education** (Estyn), and are undertaken cyclically by independent inspection teams under a registered inspector. Stressful as inspections can be, they have been carried out in a more enlightened climate than in England, a generalization that may be extended to much of the education system. In particular, the cessation of key stage testing at ages 7, 11 and 14 has been universally welcomed.

EDWARDIAN CONQUEST, The

The **Treaty of Montgomery** (1267) recognized **Llywelyn ap Gruffudd** as **Prince of Wales**, but the next decade saw a sequence of crises in Anglo-Welsh relations that included: a dispute about the position of Welsh lords in **Glamorgan**; an attempt to stop Llywelyn building a castle at Dolforwyn (*see* **Llandyssil**) in 1273; **Edward I**'s reception of **Dafydd ap Gruffudd** and **Gruffudd ap Gwenwynwyn** after their abortive attempt to assassinate the prince in 1274; and the detention of Llywelyn's prospective bride Eleanor de **Montfort** in 1275. In 1272, Llywelyn failed to do homage to Edward after his accession and ceased paying the instalments laid down in the Treaty of Montgomery. Both sides had a case in these disputes, but neither was in a position to display any flexibility. Edward declared war in November 1276 and his three armies advanced, from Chester, **Montgomery** and **Carmarthen**. Llywelyn's territorial gains soon fell to the king. The other Welsh rulers then made their peace and a royal fleet seized **Anglesey**, cutting off the prince's **food** supply, and work was begun on five new castles around the periphery of **Gwynedd**. Llywelyn had to submit, accepting the terms contained in the **Treaty of Aberconwy** on 9 November 1277. Although he retained the title of Prince of Wales for his lifetime and the homage of five lords – four in **Powys Fadog** and one in **Deheubarth** – he lost all his conquests, along with the eastern half of Gwynedd (the **Perfeddwlad**).

Relations improved after Aberconwy, but new disputes included a clash with Gruffudd ap Gwenwynwyn over the *cantref* of **Arwystli** in the upper **Severn** valley, an old bone of contention between Gwynedd and **Powys**. This was not in itself a reason to go to war, but it was overtaken by events. The methods of royal officials in the lands taken from Llywelyn in 1277 were less than sensitive, especially when dealing with those native Welsh lords who had submitted five years earlier. Tension was rising and on the night of 21 March 1282 Llywelyn's brother Dafydd attacked the castle of **Hawarden**. This was followed by further attacks in the north-east and the south-west, which suggests advance planning; all but two of the Welsh lords outside Gwynedd joined the war and Edward was taken completely by surprise. Whether or not Llywelyn was involved from the start, he certainly joined after June, when Eleanor died giving birth to a daughter **Gwenllian**.

Edward followed the same strategy as in 1277, using three armies, seizing Anglesey and advancing carefully through north-east Wales to **Rhuddlan**. A pontoon bridge was built across the **Menai Strait** to enable the Anglesey force to cross and join the main body of Edward's army once it had entered **Snowdonia**. At the beginning of November, the archbishop of Canterbury, **John Pecham**, tried to mediate, but the terms he brought were completely unacceptable to Llywelyn and Dafydd and to their advisers. A truce had been agreed for Pecham's visit and the commander of the troops in Anglesey tried to take advantage of it to move his men to the mainland. During the operation, the bridge collapsed, the tide turned and the result was a Welsh victory.

Llywelyn took advantage of this blow to Edward's strategy and moved south with his army, but on 11 December 1282 he was killed in a skirmish at **Cilmery** near **Builth**. Dafydd carried on the fight in Gwynedd but he was captured in June 1283 and subsequently tried and executed with great barbarity at Shrewsbury. His daughters and Llywelyn's daughter Gwenllian spent the rest of their days as nuns; his sons never emerged from prison. On 9 July 1283 came the formal end to the war, when each community in Gwynedd submitted to the king.

Llywelyn's lands did not become part of the kingdom of **England**. Four new **counties** were created – Anglesey, **Caernarfonshire**, **Merionethshire** and **Flintshire** – and additions were made to the counties of **Cardiganshire** and **Carmarthenshire**, whose origins can be traced back to the first half of the 13th century. The **Statute of Rhuddlan** of 1284 laid down new legal and administrative arrangements, although these were grafted on to existing Welsh institutions in the main. Powys Fadog and much of the Perfeddwlad were divided into **march**er-lordships. In addition to the castles built after 1277, four new ones (**Caernarfon**, **Conwy**, **Harlech** and **Beaumaris**) were constructed within the conquered territories and two existing native castles extended (*see* **Architecture**).

To ensure supplies for the castles, **boroughs** were founded around them, intended as **English** colonies; their charters granted extensive privileges to the burgesses. For most people there was little change; at the local level they attended the same courts, paid the same dues and the officials continued to be the leaders of the local community. Edward realized that his Welsh lands could not be governed without the co-operation of local leaders. They accepted a new order which respected their power and position, although Anglo-Welsh relations over the following two centuries would be a complex combination of sympathy and antipathy.

EDWARDS, A[lfred] G[eorge] (1848–1937)
Archbishop of Wales

A member of a large clerical family from Llanymawddwy (**Mawddwy**), **Merioneth**, Edwards achieved prominence as warden of **Llandovery** College and by his writings resisting the **disestablishment of the Church of England in Wales**. Appointed bishop of **St Asaph** in 1889, he forced the Church into an aggressive but unsuccessful campaign on the issue. **David Lloyd George** described him as 'a second-rate **preacher**, a third-rate theologian and an irate priest'. Elected the first archbishop of the **Church in Wales** in 1920, Edwards successfully led the Church into accepting independence, but his position on the **Welsh language** and **nationhood** was ambivalent, and left an unfortunate legacy. He retired as archbishop in 1934 at the age of 87.

His brother, Henry Thomas Edwards (1837–84), dean of **Bangor** and grandfather of Nicholas Edwards, **secretary of state for Wales** (1979–87), was a passionate Welsh patriot. In his *The Church of the Cymry* (1880), he argued that the Welsh had been driven to be **Nonconformists** because the **Anglican** Church had been used to alienate them from their national traditions.

EDWARDS, Alun R[oderick] (1919–86) Librarian

Alun R. Edwards was born in Llanio (**Llanddewi Brefi**), **Cardiganshire**. As librarian of that county (1950–74) and of the **county** of **Dyfed** (1974–80), he established a network of mobile libraries to serve villages, schools and isolated homesteads. He believed that public libraries in Wales had a responsibility to promote the **Welsh language** and culture and thus developed an annual programme of activities for children, young people and adults. Campaigning incessantly from the early 1950s to promote Welsh book-publishing, Edwards was primarily responsible for establishing Cymdeithas Lyfrau **Ceredigion** (1954), the **Welsh Books Council** (1961) and the College of Librarianship Wales (1964).

EDWARDS, Charles (1628–post-1691) Writer

Llansilin-born Charles Edwards graduated from Jesus College, **Oxford** in 1649, having previously lost his studentship at All Souls following an inquiry by Parliamentary Commissioners into his apparently equivocal attitude towards submitting to the authority of Parliament. Despite this early disagreement, he was drawn increasingly to the **Puritan** cause. He held the living of **Llanrhaeadr-ym-Mochnant** under the **Commonwealth**, and lost it at the Restoration in 1660. He became a licensed **preacher** under the Declaration of Indulgence of 1672, and editor of books for the **Welsh Trust**. His memoir concerning his troubles, *An Afflicted Man's Testimony*, appeared in 1691. His renown as a **Welsh** writer rests upon *Y Ffydd Ddi-ffuant* (1666, 1671, 1677), the second edition containing the important addition on the history of the Christian faith in Wales (*see* **Religion**). Here, for the first time, the Protestant interpretation of Welsh history stands clearly defined.

EDWARDS, D[avid] Miall (1873–1941) Minister and theologian

Born in **Llanfyllin**, Edwards was educated at **Bangor** and **Oxford**. Ordained a **Congregational** minister at Blaenau Ffestiniog in 1900, he moved to **Brecon** in 1904. He was professor of **theology** in the town's Memorial College from 1909 to 1934. A founder of the Welsh School of Social Service, he combined practical with intellectual interests. Alone in the 20th century, Edwards produced a systematic theology in **Welsh** (*Bannau'r Ffydd*, 1939).

EDWARDS, Dorothy (1903–34) Author

A talented singer as well as a writer, Dorothy Edwards was born in **Ogmore Vale** and settled in **Cardiff**. She published only two books: a collection of short stories, *Rhapsody* (1927), and a novel, *Winter Sonata* (1928). Both were highly acclaimed at the time and were republished in 1986. She put an end to her life, for unknown reasons, by throwing herself under a train near **Caerphilly**.

EDWARDS, Huw Lloyd (1916–75) Dramatist

A native of Penisa'r Waun (**Llanddeiniolen**) Edwards was a teacher of **English** before he became a **drama** lecturer at the **Normal College, Bangor**. His early works were pieces of light entertainment. More serious topics were addressed in *Noson o Lety* (1955), and it was his association with the Garthewin Drama Festival (*see* **Llanfair Talhaiarn**) that inspired him to concentrate on ethical, political, religious and social concerns in his later plays: *Cyfyng Gyngor* (1958), *Y Gŵr o Gath Heffer* (1961), *Y Gŵr o Wlad Us* (1961), *Ar Ddu a Gwyn* (1963), *Pros Kairon* (1967), *Y Llyffantod* (1973) and *Y Lefiathan* (1977).

EDWARDS, Huw T[homas] (1892–1970)
Trade unionist

Born at Rowen (**Caerhun**), Edwards, who began work as a quarryman, established branches of the Transport and General Workers' Union and the **Labour Party** in the north. Prominent in public life, he became in 1949 the first chairman of the **Council for Wales and Monmouthshire**, resigning when the council's recommendation that a **secretary of state for Wales** be appointed was disregarded. He was an ardent advocate of **devolution** and in 1959, disillusioned with Labour, joined **Plaid [Genedlaethol] Cymru**, returning to his former allegiance in 1965. He was president of **Cymdeithas yr Iaith Gymraeg** and published two volumes of autobiography, translated as *It Was My Privilege* (1962) and *Hewn from the Rock* (1967).

EDWARDS, Ifan ab Owen (1895–1970) Patriot

Sir Ifan, son of **Owen M. Edwards**, was founder of **Urdd Gobaith Cymru** and of the first **Welsh-language** primary school – a private school established at **Aberystwyth** in 1939. Born at **Llanuwchllyn** and educated at Aberystwyth and **Oxford**, he held several **education**-related posts in Aberystwyth between 1921 and his retirement in 1946, but his life was devoted to the realization of his vision of a national youth organization. He was knighted in 1947.

EDWARDS, J[ohn] Goronwy (1891–1976) Historian

Born in Manchester to Welsh parents, Edwards was educated at **Holywell** and Jesus College, **Oxford**. In 1948, he was appointed director of the Institute of Historical Research and professor of history at the University of **London**. Many of his publications relate to medieval Welsh legal, constitutional and administrative history, and include *Calendar of Ancient Correspondence* (1935) and *Littere Wallie* (1940). In 1969, he published a pioneering study entitled *The Principality of Wales 1267–1967*. He was president of the Royal Historical Society from 1961 to 1964 and editor of the *English Historical Review* and of the *Bulletin* of the Institute of Historical Research.

EDWARDS, John Kelt (1875–1934) Artist

The son of a Blaenau **Ffestiniog** shopkeeper, Edwards was educated at **Llandovery** College and visited Paris and Rome. He exhibited at the Paris Salon and completed portraits of notable Welsh figures, including **David Lloyd George** and **Owen M. Edwards**. After the **First World War**, he designed the banner and badge for the

Meredith Edwards (left) with Hugh Griffith in *A Run For Your Money*, 1949

'Comrades of the Great War' and the roll of honour of the **Royal Welch Fusiliers**. He produced war cartoons and book illustrations.

EDWARDS, Lewis (1803–87)
Theologian, educationist, preacher and writer

Born in Penllwyn (**Melindwr**), Edwards became a schoolteacher and began preaching among the **Calvinistic Methodists**. He attended Edinburgh University, graduating in 1836, the year in which he married Jane Charles, a granddaughter of the Methodist leader **Thomas Charles**. In 1837, along with his brother-in-law, David Charles (1812–78), he established a preparatory school at **Bala**, which soon became a seminary for Calvinistic Methodist ministers. Under Edwards's 50-year principalship, it became the prime theological school in Wales.

Through his work at Bala, Edwards became a means of widening the cultural vision and raising the intellectual standards of the nation as a whole. Through the quarterly magazine *Y Traethodydd*, founded in 1845 on the pattern of the *Edinburgh Review*, he disseminated information on the latest trends in **theology**, **philosophy**, **science** and **literature**. His theological writings were key texts in the development of the Christian mind in Wales. Edwards's work as a religious and intellectual leader was continued by his son, **Thomas Charles Edwards**.

EDWARDS, Meredith (1917–99) Actor

After distinguished stage work, **Rhosllanerchrugog**-born Edwards became a familiar figure on the British screen, mainly in comedies. He was memorable in Ealing Studios' *A Run For Your Money* (1949) as a gullible but forthright miner abroad in **London** with a fellow collier (**Donald Houston**) and a drunken pavement **harp**er (**Hugh Griffith**). Edwards was a London **police** choir's mildly obsessive

Welsh conductor in Ealing's *The Blue Lamp* (1950), humorously pugnacious in the Welsh comedy *Girdle of Gold* (1951) and amusingly self-righteous as a bookworm cleric in **Only Two Can Play** (1962). He narrated the popular cinema documentary *The Conquest of Everest* (1953) and played the Reverend Eli Jenkins in the original television version of **Dylan Thomas**'s *Under Milk Wood* (1957). He adapted for radio and narrated the charming *Wil Six* (1984), about a schoolboy coming of age, and had challenging, dual-lead roles in the intense BBC Wales (*see* **Broadcasting**) television **drama** *Fallen Sons* (1993).

EDWARDS, Ness (1897–1968) Politician

A boy-collier and lodge chairman at the age of 18, Ness Edwards was MP for **Caerphilly** (1939–68) and served as postmaster general in 1951. In 1939, he organized the escape from Germany of 300 anti-Nazi Sudeten miners. Greatly respected by many of his colleagues as a clear thinker on industrial and constitutional issues, he regarded himself as the custodian of an international working-**class** tradition (*see* **Internationalism**) that was completely opposed to **nationalism**, not least Welsh nationalism. He published two histories of the south Wales miners.

EDWARDS, Owen M[organ] (1858–1920)
Educationist, writer and editor

Sir Owen M. Edwards devoted his life, in the words of his motto, to 'restor[ing] the Old Country to its former glory'. He played a crucial role in laying the foundations of Welsh national consciousness in the 20th century. Born at **Llanuwchllyn**, he was educated at **Bala** Theological College and at **Aberystwyth**, Glasgow and **Oxford**, where he was a founder of Cymdeithas Dafydd ap Gwilym. After graduating, he visited mainland Europe, and wrote about his travels in *Tro yn yr Eidal* (1889) and *O'r Bala i Geneva* (1889). In 1889, he was appointed a fellow of Lincoln College, Oxford, where the poet **Edward Thomas** was among his students. Following the death of **T. E. Ellis** in 1899, he was elected MP for **Merioneth** but, having little interest in politics, he did not seek re-election in 1900. On his appointment, in 1907, as Chief Inspector of Schools of the Welsh Board of **Education**, he returned to Llanuwchllyn, where he remained until his death.

His chief ambition was to revitalize Wales's indigenous culture and to broaden the horizons and education of the people of Wales. Exerting a profound and enduring influence in the field of education, he campaigned for teaching through the medium of **Welsh** and for a Wales-oriented syllabus.

In order to reach a wide general readership, he wrote engaging, affordable books in which, as in all his writing, he pioneered a lively and readable prose style. He sought to awaken the interest of his compatriots in Welsh **literature** and history by publishing attractive series such as *Cyfres y Fil* (1901–16) and *Llyfrau ab Owen* (1906–14), and studies such as *Ystraeon o Hanes Cymru* (1894–95), *Hanes Cymru* (1895, 1899), *Wales* (1901) and *A Short History of Wales* (1906). An inspired editor of **periodicals**, he co-edited *Cymru Fydd* (1889–91) before launching several journals of his own, notably the successful monthly *Cymru* (1891–1920), in which he nurtured promising creative talent.

Edwards revolutionized the content and style of Welsh-language children's literature, through his popular monthly magazine *Cymru'r Plant* (1892–1920), and books such as *Llyfr Del* (1906), *Yr Hwiangerddi* (1911) and *Llyfr Nest* (1913). In 1896, he established a society for children, Urdd y Delyn, a precursor of **Urdd Gobaith Cymru**, which was founded in 1920 by his son, **Ifan ab Owen Edwards**.

EDWARDS, Robin James (Robin Jac or Y Fellten Goch, 'Red Lightning'; 1910–79)
Racing motorcyclist

Unique among racing drivers, **Llanuwchllyn**-born Robin Jac was also a poet, being an *englynwr* in the **bardd gwlad** tradition. He raced in the Isle of **Man** from 1934 until 1950, scoring 4th, 6th, 8th and 9th Lightweight Manx Grand Prix placings. Capable of world-class riding, he took 12 fastest laps and came third in the Irish NW 200.

EDWARDS, Roger (1811–86) Author and editor

Born in **Bala** and brought up in **Dolgellau**, Edwards was ordained by the **Calvinistic Methodists** in 1842 and spent his mature years in **Mold**. As editor of his denomination's monthly **periodical** *Y Drysorfa*, he challenged the Methodists' prejudice against novels by inviting **Daniel Owen** to contribute, thus setting Owen on the path to becoming a novelist. He published a **hymn**al, *Y Salmydd Cymreig* (1840), and co-founded the influential journal *Y Traethodydd* (1845–). As a **Liberal**, he was instrumental in steering the Methodists from the conservatism of **John Elias** and towards the Liberalism of **Thomas Gee**.

EDWARDS, Thomas (Twm o'r Nant; 1739–1810)
Poet and dramatist

The most significant figure in Welsh **drama** before the 20th century, Twm o'r Nant was brought up at Nant Isaf, **Nantglyn**, **Denbighshire**. He worked as a stonemason and a haulier, and kept an inn and a tollgate, never with much money to spare. His autobiography (published as a serial in *Y Greal* in 1805) records that he wrote two interludes before he was nine, and that he acted **women**'s parts as a boy of 12. He was hailed by contemporaries as master of the interlude ('our native Garrick' and 'the Cambrian **Shakespeare**'). In works such as *Tri Chryfion Byd* (1789), *Pleser a Gofid* (1787), *Cyfoeth a Thlodi* (1768) and *Tri Chydymaith Dyn* (1769), his characteristic **satire** and criticism may be savoured, along with his catchy lines and skill as a songwriter. He left some 350 poems, of which a small selection was published in *Gardd o Gerddi* (1790). They are poems of advice, exhortation, satire, social comment and personal experience, all in popular measures of the day. He is among the most quotable of **Welsh** authors.

EDWARDS, Thomas Charles (1837–1900)
Educationist and theologian

This great-grandson of **Thomas Charles** was born in **Llanycil**. His father, **Lewis Edwards**, was principal of **Bala** College, which Edwards attended before completing his **education** in **London** and **Oxford**. From 1866, he was a **Calvinistic Methodist** minister in **Liverpool** before becoming the first principal of the University College of Wales in **Aberystwyth** (1872) (*see* **University of Wales, Aberystwyth**).

William Edwards's 'New Bridge' seen under Pontypridd's neon street lights

The new college was plagued by financial difficulties and, in 1885, by fire. Edwards was instrumental in securing its continued existence, working to ensure that Aberystwyth survived the creation of university colleges at **Cardiff** (1883) and **Bangor** (1884). A distinguished **preacher**, teacher and biblical commentator, in 1891 he succeeded his father as principal of Bala College on condition that it became purely a theological college open to all denominations. He remained there until his death.

EDWARDS, [Arthur] Trystan (1884–1973)
Architect and writer
Born in **Merthyr Tydfil**, Edwards studied at **Liverpool** School of **Architecture**, and, after the **First World War**, joined the Ministry of **Health** and **Housing** under Raymond Unwin. He is chiefly remembered for his books on architectural and planning philosophy, including *Good and Bad Manners in Architecture* (1924), *Architectural Style* (1926) and *A Hundred New Towns for Britain* (1933). He also published (1953) a 'homalographic' projection for **map**ping the world, which minimized aerial and shape distortions. On retiring to his hometown, he wrote *Merthyr, Rhondda and the Valleys* (1958), *Towards Tomorrow's Architecture* (1968) and an autobiography, *Second Best Boy* (1970).

EDWARDS, William (1719–89)
Architect, engineer and minister
The son of a farmer, Edwards was born at Groeswen (**Caerphilly**), where he became **Congregationalist** minister in 1746. Starting off as a stonemason, Edwards developed such expertise that he went on to construct numerous forges and bridges. His best-known bridge is the famous 'New Bridge' in **Pontypridd**, where, after three unsuccessful attempts, a graceful, single-arched structure was erected (1756); with a span of 42.6 m, it was the longest in **Britain**, and perhaps in Europe, at the time. Later, Edwards was responsible for designing a new industrial village (1779) at Morriston (*see* **Swansea**).

EDWARDS HEIRS ASSOCIATION, The
The **Pennsylvania**-based Association of Edwards Heirs, formed in 1983, is one of a number of organizations in Wales and **North America** that, since the 1880s, have pursued the claims of the descendants of Robert Edwards (or Edwardes), a **Pontypridd**-born seafarer who died *c*.1780. In 1778, he was granted a 31-ha tract in Manhattan, New York, which he subsequently leased. His 'heirs' believe they are the rightful owners of the land, which includes Wall Street, but this is disputed by the present owners, Trinity Church. The whole issue is the subject of considerable dispute, controversy and litigation.

EFELFFRE Commote
A **commote** of **Cantref Gwarthaf**, Efelffre became, after the **Norman** conquest, part of the **march**er-lordship of **Narberth**. The name survives in those of the **communities** of **Lampeter Velfrey** and **Llanddewi Velfrey**.

EFENECHTYD (Efenechdyd), Denbighshire
(1258 ha; 608 inhabitants)
Located immediately south-west of **Ruthin**, the **community**'s name may be a corruption of the word *mynechdid* (monastery); there is no firm evidence of a monastic

Yr Eifl as seen from the pier at Trefor

institution at Efenechtyd, although there is a tradition that there was once a nunnery in the area. The tiny church of St Michael and All Angels contains a rare wooden font. Simwnt Fychan (*c.*1530–1606) the author of the final version of the poet's grammar, lived at Tŷ Brith. In the late 17th century, the estate of a branch of the **Salusbury family** passed by marriage to Sir Walter Bagot, whose grandson became Baron Bagot in 1798. In the 1820s, the second Baron Bagot built Pool Park, an uninspired neo-Elizabethan pile.

EFNYSIEN

In the second branch of the Mabinogi (*see Mabinogion, The*) the characters Nysien and Efnysien are brothers, and half-brothers to **Bendigeidfran**, **Branwen** and **Manawydan**. Nysien is a peacemaker, but Efnysien stirs up strife. Determined to wreck the marriage of Branwen to the **Irish** king Matholwch, Efnysien disfigures Matholwch's **horses** during the wedding celebrations. He is later to cast Gwern, son of Branwen, headlong into a fire. Finally, his destruction of the **Cauldron of Rebirth** costs him his life.

EGINOG *Cantref*

Together with **Cantref Mawr** and **Cantref Bychan**, Eginog was a *cantref* of Ystrad Tywi. It consisted of the **commotes** of **Carnwyllion**, **Cedweli** and **Gower**, areas which eventually came to constitute south-east **Carmarthenshire** and the westernmost part of **Glamorgan**.

EGLWYSBACH (Eglwys-bach), Conwy
(3384 ha; 928 inhabitants)

Extending from the east bank of the **Conwy** to the uplands of Uwch Dulas, the **community**'s chief feature is Bodnant. The estate was bought by a Salford **chemical** manufacturer, Henry Pochin, in 1874, the house (1876) is substantial if uninspiring, but the **gardens** are one of the wonders of the world. Begun by Pochin, the work continued under his

daughter, Laura, and her husband Charles McLaren (created Baron Aberconway in 1911), and their son, the second baron. The gardens, which were from 1920 to 2004 under the care of three generations of the Puddle family, were given to the **National Trust** in 1949. They contain almost all the **plants** that flourish in a temperate **climate**, many of them representing the earliest examples in **Britain** of specimens gathered by plant hunters. Plants such as *Viburnum bodnantense* have carried the name of Bodnant all over the world. St Martin's church in the attractive village of Eglwysbach was rebuilt in 1782. There are early farmhouses at Plas Llan and Pennant.

EGLWYSCUMMIN (Eglwys Gymyn),
Carmarthenshire (4240 ha; 462 inhabitants)

Located in **Carmarthenshire**'s south-western corner, the **community** contains the villages of Marros and Red Roses. There are four fine **Neolithic** burial chambers at Morfa Bychan. An **Iron Age** fort, Top Castle, stands dramatically above the sea. Eglwys Gymyn was rebuilt in the late 14th century by Margaret Marlos, neice of Guy de Brian, who held the **march**er-lordship of **Laugharne**; it was rededicated to St Margaret, queen of **Scotland**, an ancestress of the family and its patron saint. Its rector from 1730 to 1782 was John Evans, enemy of **Griffith Jones**, **Llanddowror**, and of the **Methodist Revival**, who dismissed his curate, the Methodist **Peter Williams**. The church contains a plaque to Williams and a chained copy of his Bible (1770). St Laurence's church, Marros, has a 13th-century tower. Nearby is a striking **war memorial**.

EGLWYSWRW, Pembrokeshire
(5179 ha; 732 inhabitants)

Extending from the northern flanks of **Mynydd Preseli** almost to the **Ceredigion** border, the **community** contains the villages of Eglwyswrw, Brynberian and Crosswell.

There is a **Neolithic** burial chamber at Bedd yr Afanc and an **Iron Age hill-fort** at Carn Alw. At Brynberian is the earliest **Congregationalist** cause (1690) in north **Pembrokeshire**; the present chapel was built in 1843. John Owen (1836–1915) worked at a local farm when he wrote the much-loved **ballad** 'Y Mochyn Du'. Pistyll Meugan healing **well**, popular with medieval pilgrims, was destroyed in 1592. In 2001, 74.09% of the inhabitants of Eglwyswrw had some knowledge of **Welsh**, with 57% wholly fluent in the language – the highest percentages among any of the communities of Pembrokeshire.

EIFIONYDD Commote
Together with **Ardudwy**, the **commote** formed the *cantref* of **Dunoding**. Allegedly named after Eifion, **Cunedda**'s grandson, it was initially administered from **Dolbenmaen** and, after the 1230s, from **Criccieth**. Eifionydd is one of the few commote names still in popular use. **R. Williams Parry**'s poem, 'Eifionydd', is one of the best-loved **Welsh** poems in praise of a place. Thanks to Colin Gresham's *Eifionydd* (1973), more is known of the landownership of the commote than of any other area of Wales.

EIFL, Yr Mountain
Yr Eifl – sometimes sadly mangled into **English** as 'The Rivals' – is merely 564 m at its highest point. However, as it rises sheer from the sea, it appears to be a substantial range of **mountains**, an impression strengthened by its three shapely conical peaks. It consists essentially of **granite** – igneous rock pushed through the surrounding Ordovician deposits as a result of volcanic action. The granite was long quarried for the production of setts – rectangular paving blocks used in **road** construction. The industry gave rise to the villages of Llithfaen (**Pistyll**) and Trefor (**Llanaelhaearn**), and also to the isolated settlement of Nant Gwrtheyrn (**Pistyll**), which has been adapted as a Welsh-**language** learning centre. On the slopes of Yr Eifl is a bewitching place – Tre'r Ceiri or 'giant's town' – the most striking of all the **Iron Age** sites of Wales.

EISTEDDFOD
The National Eisteddfod is Wales's premier cultural festival. At the beginning of the 21st century, its eclectic array of competitions encompasses such diverse artistic fields as the visual arts, rock **music**, choral singing and the most intricate aspects of **Welsh** poetry. As its location alternates annually between the south and the north, it has no permanent home.

Its highlights, the colourful ceremonies of the **Gorsedd** of the Bards, are among those stereotypical images which have been used for well over a century to project Welsh cultural identity. Although, primarily, a creation of the Victorian era, the eisteddfod (pl. *eisteddfodau*) has its roots

Posters for the National Eisteddfod, 1909 and 1927

in the Welsh cultural renaissance of the 18th century and is a notable example of how patriotism and the reinvention of tradition often go hand in hand.

Emulating the success of the National Eisteddfod, **Urdd Gobaith Cymru** established its own annual youth eisteddfod in 1929 while **Llangollen International Musical Eisteddfod** has, since 1947, provided a multi-national dimension.

A host of smaller *eisteddfodau*, both at a village and regional level, are also held annually throughout the country. However, with the demise of the **coal**mining industry, the annual South Wales Miners' Eisteddfod, staged at **Porthcawl** since 1948, was held for the last time in 2001. *Eisteddfodau* have also played a prominent part in Welsh culture in **England** and in **North America**, **Australia**, **Patagonia** and **South Africa**. Indeed, particularly in Australia and South Africa, the eisteddfod is part of the general cultural scene.

The medieval eisteddfod

Poetic contests were an important feature of the Welsh bardic order throughout the Middle Ages. At the time of the **Poets of the Princes**, a poet acquired the status of *pencerdd* (chief of song) by engaging in a poetic dispute

with his fellow poets, and, according to Welsh **law**, the victorious *pencerdd* was awarded a chair, most probably at the royal court. The festival held by the Lord Rhys (**Rhys ap Gruffudd**; d.1197) at **Cardigan** in 1176 is often referred to as the first recorded eisteddfod, although the earliest record of the word dates from the 14th century, when it meant a dwelling place. According to *Brut y Tywysogyon*: '[Rhys] set two kinds of contest; one between the bards and the poets, and another between the **harp**ists and the crowders (*see* **Crwth**) and the pipers and various classes of string-music and awarded chairs to the victors in both contests.' In arranging such a spectacle, Rhys may well have been emulating the **Norman** *puy*, a guild-festival at which lyric poets competed. The first recorded use of eisteddfod as meaning a formal assembly of poets and musicians dates from 1523.

During the era of the **Poets of the Gentry**, three such assemblies are recorded as having been held: at **Carmarthen** (*c*.1450–1) and **Caerwys** (1523 and 1567). The principal aim of all three was to enhance and safeguard the corporate identity not only of the professional praise poets, but also of the harpists and *datgeiniaid* (professional declaimers of poetry) who were an integral part of the medieval Welsh bardic order. Poetic and musical contests were an important feature of such occasions, and

Tudur Dylan Jones receiving the crown at the National Eisteddfod, Mold, 2007

The National Eisteddfod's pink pavilion, first used here at Swansea in 2006

at the Carmarthen Eisteddfod the prize-winning poet, **Dafydd ab Edmwnd** – who was awarded a small symbolic silver chair – was also entrusted with the task of reformulating the rules of the traditional metres and **cynghanedd**. At the first Caerwys Eisteddfod (1523), the rules governing the training of poets and musicians and those pertaining to their perambulations were refined and formulized in a document called *Statud Gruffudd ap Cynan* (the Statute of **Gruffudd ap Cynan**). According to the *Statud*, card-playing and drunkenness were well beneath the dignity of a poet, and it even stipulated that poets were not to give undue attention to the wives and daughters of their noble patrons.

Reinventing the tradition

The 16th century saw the demise of the bardic order and of the professional poets, but the lowly poets of a later age sought to revive the eisteddfod. During the 18th century, a number of poetic assemblies were held in taverns, mostly in mid and north Wales. They were advertised beforehand in Welsh **almanacs** and called *eisteddfodau*. The poets vigorously competed with each other, but, more often than not, it seems that there was only one victor – Bacchus. John Edwards, a squire from the **Llangollen** area who took a keen interest in such meetings, was, according to his contemporary Gwallter Mechain (**Walter Davies**), 'as fond of *barddoniaeth* (poetry) as of *cwrw* (**beer**) and vice versa'.

In 1789, when only four poets attended an eisteddfod at Llangollen, Thomas Jones, a **Corwen** exciseman, sought the advice and guidance of the **Gwyneddigion Society** in **London**, who agreed to help raise Welsh culture

above the level of the tavern *eisteddfodau*. The year 1789 is therefore a turning-point in the history of the eisteddfod: a movement was launched which would lead in 1861 to the emergence of the National Eisteddfod, and for some 150 years the London Welsh would heavily influence that movement.

The Gwyneddigion provided a blueprint for the modern competitive eisteddfod – subjects set in advance, fit adjudicators appointed to prepare written adjudications, competitors required to use pseudonyms, substantial prizes offered and the public allowed into the meetings. In September 1789, at **Bala**, the revived medieval eisteddfod ceased to be. Instead of closed sessions for poets and minstrels, the eisteddfod began to approximate to a popular festival.

The **French Revolutionary and Napoleonic Wars** retarded its growth, but in 1818 a number of 'literary parsons' (see **hen bersoniaid llengar**) led by Ifor Ceri (John Jenkins; 1770–1829), vicar of **Kerry** near **Newtown**, relaunched the eisteddfod venture. Supported by **Thomas Burgess**, bishop of **St David's**, and sundry patriotic members of the **gentry class**, four provincial societies were established in **Dyfed** (1818), **Gwynedd** (1819), **Powys** (1819), and **Gwent** and **Glamorgan** (1821) which, guided by the **Cymmrodorion** in London, held 10 *eisteddfodau* between 1819 and 1834. These 'Cambrian Olympiads' transformed eisteddfod culture. Prize-winning compositions were published, and in 1819 the Gorsedd of the Bards and the fashionable concert were introduced, thereby starting a linguistic battle between Welsh and **English** that would bedevil the eisteddfod for over a century.

After 1834, further impetus came from **Abergavenny** where another 10 remarkable *eisteddfodau* were held, from 1835 to 1853, by the **Cymreigyddion** Society, inspired by

Carnhuanawc (**Thomas Price**), vicar of **Llanfihangel Cwmdu**, and the redoubtable Lady Llanover (**Augusta Hall**). In the north, *eisteddfodau* at **Aberffraw** (1849) and **Rhuddlan** (1850) caused much excitement and then, in 1858, Ab Ithel (**John Williams**; 1811–62), vicar of Llanymawddwy (**Mawddwy**), organized the Grand Llangollen Eisteddfod, which led directly to the creation of the National Eisteddfod. An unquestioning follower of Iolo Morganwg (**Edward Williams**), Ab Ithel organized a druidical extravaganza which conflicted with the expectations of radicals who aspired to an eisteddfod imbued with the spirit of progress. It was time for a regular National Eisteddfod conducted by an elected body.

The national eisteddfod

'Yr Eisteddfod' was established at **Denbigh** in 1860 and its council organized eight annual National *Eisteddfodau*, in north and south alternately, the first in **Aberdare** (1861) and the last in **Ruthin** (1868), when debts overcame it. In the 1870s, local committees, mainly in the north, tried to emulate 'Yr Eisteddfod' until, in 1880, **Hugh Owen** (1804–81) succeeded in establishing the National Eisteddfod Association which launched the current series of National *Eisteddfodau* at **Merthyr Tydfil** in 1881. Prompted by reformers such as Cynan (**Albert Evans-Jones**), the Association and the Gorsedd united in the revised constitution of 1937 to form the National Eisteddfod Council. In 1952, the constitution was again revised to create the Court of the National Eisteddfod which has been the ruling body ever since.

The National Eisteddfod was to provide a platform on which a small nation, eager to flex itself after the 1847 education report's assault on its character (*see* **Treason of the Blue Books**), could display its talents. Ifor Ceri's programme for a revival of Welsh culture was undermined by costly concerts for the Anglicized gentry. In the 1860s, Hugh Owen's attempt by means of a Social Science Section to project Wales as a progressive country again marginalized the Welsh language, and so things would continue from 1881 onwards, until the 1937 constitution declared Welsh to be the sole official language of the National Eisteddfod. The 'All-Welsh Rule' came into use at **Caerphilly** in 1950, since when it is true to say that the National Eisteddfod has championed the language. For almost a century, it had neglected it.

A major contributing factor to the marginalizing of the language was the fact that the National Eisteddfod from the outset was a showcase for the '**Land of Song**', English being the primary language of the choral competitions and the concerts that attracted the crowds. Welsh was the language of a discounted **literature** and, what was worse, of the Gorsedd which the progressives maintained made Wales a laughing stock. But the Gorsedd survived contempt and continues to demonstrate in a colourful, public way – by chairing and crowning poets, and honouring the winners of the prose medal and of the **Daniel Owen** memorial prize – that a society should celebrate its writers. The choirs no longer dominate the proceedings, but the National Eisteddfod is still a splendid platform for new musicians and singers, as Bryn Terfel's career shows.

Drama, arts and crafts, **architecture**, **dance** and pop culture have long since counted as much as traditional music and literature in the annual fare provided. The alternative 'Maes B' for the young is creating its own mythology, and the national institution that emerged in the 19th century when evolution was first a burning issue, itself continues to evolve. Its survival depends on that – and on the people's appreciation of its part in their story.

ELECTRONICS

The establishment of a significant electronics sector in Wales is a phenomenon of the late 20th century (*see* **Economy**). Driven largely by inward investors, the sector came to employ some 20,000 workers, whose output included televisions, microwave cookers and computers. The first foreign-owned plant was opened by Sony near **Bridgend** in 1973. It was the harbinger of a long list of overseas companies – mainly, though not exclusively, Japanese – including Aiwa, Brother, Hitachi, Matsushita, Orion, Panasonic and Sharp. The few indigenous operations (such as AB Electronics and Race Electronics) were overshadowed by foreign companies, the attracting of which was a central feature of **Welsh Development Agency** policy.

By the mid-1990s, electronic **engineering** accounted for some 30% of total foreign manufacturing employment in Wales. The geographical distribution of these firms, particularly concentrated near the **M4**, reflected the general pattern of foreign **inward investment**. While these operations were at the forefront of the debate regarding the nature and benefits of such investment, there appeared a general consensus that Japanese companies were relatively committed 'stickers', rather than footloose 'snatchers'. Nevertheless, concerns regarding the so-called 'branch factory' syndrome, and the implications of multinational enterprise calculations, were highlighted by the controversial decision by LG (South Korea), in the late 1990s, partly to abort a major investment project near **Newport**, by mothballing its new semiconductor factory (a major part of which was subsequently acquired by the **Irish** company Quinn Radiators). In 2005, Sony, which, in the late 1990s, employed over 4000 people at its Bridgend and **Pencoed** factories, closed the former and downgraded the latter, resulting in 650 job losses and signalling the end of Wales's dependence on large-scale inward investment.

ELENYDD MOUNTAINS, The

Constituting the largest wilderness in southern **Britain**, the Elenydd **Mountains** consist of uplands stretching southwards for 50 km from **Pumlumon** to **Llandovery** and eastwards for 25 km from **Tregaron** to **Llanwrtyd**. This vast region, which covers over 10% of the surface area of Wales, contains no more than a few hundred inhabitants – less than 0.01% of the country's **population**. The name Elenydd features in *The Mabinogion* and in the writings of **Giraldus Cambrensis**. It has not, however, passed into general usage, for Wales's Massif Central is generally known as the Cambrian Mountains. Its highest point is Drygarn Fawr (641 m; **Llanwrthwl**), which, with Gorllwyn (613 m; Llanwrthwl) and Pen y Garn (610 m; **Pontarfynach**) are the only summits between Pumlumon and the **Brecon Beacons** which are over 2000 feet (609 m) above sea level. Elenydd is divided into western and eastern sections by the valley of the upper **Tywi**.

In addition to containing the source of the Tywi, the mountains also contain those of the **Ystwyth**, the **Teifi** and of several of the tributaries of the **Wye**. Among such tributaries are the Elan and the Claerwen, with their major **reservoirs**. An attempt to transform Elenydd into an army training site was thwarted in 1947. Equally unsuccessful was the 1960s proposal to create a 139,000-ha Cambrian Mountains **National Park**.

The mountains won fame as the refuge of the red kite (*see* **Birds**). **Road** access to central Elenydd is provided only by the unnumbered minor road linking Tregaron with Llanwrtyd. Thus, vast areas of the mountains can only be reached on foot or on **horse**back, a matter of much concern during the **Second World War**, when there were fears that German paratroopers would drop into the wilderness and dig themselves in. However, the skills of the 40-strong Mountain Home Guard established at Tregaron to prevent such an eventuality were not put to the test.

ELFAEL *Cantref* and lordship

The *cantref* consisted of the southern part of what would be **Radnorshire**. It was divided by a line of hills into Uwch Mynydd, centred on Colwyn (**Glascwm**), and Is Mynydd, with its caput at **Painscastle**. Its principal church was at Glascwm. The rulers of Elfael claimed descent from **Elystan Glodrydd**, but with the coming of the **Normans** they faced the continuous aggression of the de **Breos** and **Mortimer** families. **Llywelyn ap Gruffudd** held Elfael from 1264 until 1276, when it was acquired by Ralph de Tony. It subsequently passed to the **Beauchamps** and then to the Neville family.

ELFED Commote

One of the **commotes** of **Cantref Gwarthaf**, its administrative centre was probably at **Cynwyl Elfed**. The name survived as that of the post-**Acts of 'Union' hundred** of Elvet. Elfed was the bardic name adopted by the poet **Howell Elvet Lewis**.

ELFODDW (d.809) Cleric

According to *Annales Cambriae*'s entry for 768, Elfoddw was responsible for the adoption by the Welsh of the **Roman** method of calculating Easter. He is referred to as the 'archbishop of the land of **Gwynedd**', which suggests that he might have been an early bishop of **Bangor**. Versions of *Historia Brittonum* attributed to Nennius claim that Elfoddw was his teacher.

ELIAS, John (1774–1841) Minister

The most formidable and influential **preacher** of his generation, John Elias was a fiercely dogmatic and sometime hyper-Calvinist who was known by his enemies as 'the Pope of **Anglesey**'. With his booming voice and physically animated mode of address, he would make oratorical mincemeat of causes such as **Roman Catholic** emancipation and measures such as the 1832 Reform Bill – although in his early career he was sufficiently radical to condemn **slavery**.

Born at Llwyndyrys (**Llannor**), he joined the **Calvinistic Methodists** in 1793 and was ordained in 1811. In 1799, he married and moved to Llanfechell (**Mechell**), Anglesey. He remarried in 1830 and settled in **Llangefni**, where there is a memorial chapel to him.

Successor to **Thomas Charles** as Methodist leader in the north, he took a leading role in drawing up his denomination's Declaration of Faith (1823). He published books and articles on **religion**, and supported several **missionary** societies – although he was implacably opposed to the foundation, in 1840, of his own denomination's missionary society.

ELIAS, Owen (1806–80) Builder

Anglesey-born Elias moved to **Liverpool** at the age of 19 and became one of the famous group of Welsh builders on Merseyside. He was mainly involved in building working-**class** housing, and became known as the 'King of Everton'.

ELIS, Islwyn Ffowc (1924–2004) Novelist

A prolific writer who is considered the father of the modern **Welsh-language** novel, Islwyn Ffowc Elis was born in **Wrexham** and brought up in Dyffryn Ceiriog. A **Presbyterian** minister, first at **Llanfair Caereinion** and then at Newborough (**Rhosyr**), he left the ministry in 1956 in order to become a professional writer, the first in Welsh in recent times. Later, he was employed as a lecturer in **Carmarthen** and **Lampeter**, and also worked for the **Welsh Books Council**.

He first came to prominence in 1951, when he won the National **Eisteddfod** prose medal for a collection of literary essays, *Cyn Oeri'r Gwaed* (1952). But he is chiefly remembered as a pioneering novelist who attracted new readers for Welsh books. When he published *Cysgod y Cryman* in 1953, those readers were charmed by the story of the family of Lleifior. In 1955, he published *Ffenestri Tua'r Gwyll*, a modern psychological novel which was not fully appreciated at the time. Therefore, he returned to the Lleifior family, publishing *Yn Ôl i Leifior* in 1956. Thereafter, he concentrated on writing popular novels, which are nevertheless often innovative and have an underlying political message. They include *Wythnos yng Nghymru Fydd* (1957) – the first prophetic novel in Welsh – *Blas y Cynfyd* (1958), *Tabyrddau'r Babongo* (1961) a *Y Blaned Dirion* (1968). He also published a collection of short stories, *Marwydos* (1974). He played a key role in **Plaid [Genedlaethol] Cymru**'s historical victory in the Carmarthen by-election of 1966.

ELLIS, Rowland (1650–1731) Quaker leader

A prominent Welshman in early 18th-century **Pennsylvania**, Ellis was a religious, political and cultural leader, serving the Society of Friends (*see* **Quakers**), his fellow Welsh and Philadelphia's civic life. Persecuted in Wales for his faith, he bought land in Pennsylvania's Welsh Tract, settling there permanently in 1697. In 1885, his plantation, Bryn Mawr, named after his birthplace (*see* **Dolgellau**), became the site of the renowned **women**'s college of that name. His life is recounted in the historical novels of **Marion Eames**.

E

John Elwyn, *Bore Sul* (Sunday Morning), 1950

ELLIS, Ruth (1926–55) Murderer

The last woman to be hanged in **Britain**, Ruth Ellis was born in **Rhyl**. The manager of a nightclub in **London**, she lived with her playboy lover, the racing driver David Blakely, who left her in 1955 after two stormy years. Ten days after suffering a miscarriage, Ellis shot Blakely as he left a public house in Hampstead. She was executed in Holloway Prison by Albert Pierrepoint.

ELLIS, T[homas] E[dward] (1859–99) Politician

Born at Cefnddwysarn (**Llandderfel**), the son of a tenant farmer, Ellis was educated at **Aberystwyth** and **Oxford**. He was elected as the Gladstonian **Liberal** MP for **Merioneth** in 1886; a staunch advocate of **home rule**, his was the first election manifesto to include self-**government** for Wales. He took a prominent part in the creation of the **Cymru Fydd** movement in 1886; **education**, **disestablishment** and the **land question** were also causes close to his heart. However, his appointment to the office of junior whip six years later and that of chief whip in 1894, while advancing his parliamentary career, undermined his **Radical** appeal and harmed the cause of self-government; it was said of him that he had 'grasped the Saxon gold'.

A cultured man, he maintained the closest links with his roots in rural, **Nonconformist** Wales and charmed the common people with his attractive personality and oratory. He died from typhoid, which he had contracted while on holiday in Egypt. His early death canonized him as the lost leader of Victorian Wales. There are statues to him at **Bala** and at the **University of Wales, Aberystwyth**.

His posthumously born son, Thomas Iorwerth Ellis (1899–1970), wrote a biography of his father along with a range of other books on Welsh themes. He was the long-serving secretary of **Undeb Cymru Fydd**. His widow is the writer Mari Ellis (b.1913) and his daughter Meg Elis won the Prose Medal at the 1985 National **Eisteddfod**.

ELLIS, T[homas] P[eter] (1873–1936) Historian

Born at **Wrexham**, Ellis had a distinguished career in the legal service in India, and retired in 1921 to the **Dolgellau** district, devoting himself to research in the history of **law** and Christianity in Wales, with special attention to **Roman Catholic**ism. His *Welsh Tribal Law and Custom in the Middle Ages* (2 vols, 1926) is a comprehensive discussion of Welsh medieval records, in particular the manuscripts of the Law of **Hywel Dda**.

ELMET (Elfed) One-time kingdom

The southernmost of the chain of post-**Roman** British kingdoms known in medieval Wales as the **Old North**, Elmet was located in what is now west and south Yorkshire. Little is known of its rulers during the two centuries before it was swallowed up by the **English**, but two poems to Gwallog, lord of Elmet at the second half of the 6th century, have been preserved in *The Book of Taliesin*. The English poet Ted Hughes sought in *The Remains of Elmet* (1979) to define an archetypal 'Britishness'.

ELWYN, John (1916–97) Painter

Recollections of rural **Cardiganshire** form the core of John Elwyn's oeuvre. He was born William John Elwyn Davies, the son of the weaver at Elwyn Mill, Adpar (*see* **Llandyfriog**), from which he took his professional name. He studied at **Carmarthen** School of Art and at Bristol, winning a scholarship to the Royal College of Art in **London** in 1938. As a **conscientious objector**, he was engaged in land work during the **Second World War**, completing his studies in 1947. Although he taught in **England**, chiefly at Winchester School of Art, he maintained strong links with Wales, winning the 1956 National **Eisteddfod** Gold Medal. He published many illustrations and prints.

ELY (Elai) River (41 km)

The Ely rises at 365 m near Tonypandy (*see* **Rhondda**). It escapes from the confines of the hills at **Llantrisant** and meanders through gently rolling pastures across Old Red Sandstone and Triassic mudstones to **Peterston-super-Ely**. It has no significant tributaries. Downstream, it is partly confined by **road** and **rail** and by an outcrop of Lower Lias above **Llandough**, before flowing with the **Taff** through the sluices of the **Cardiff** Bay Barrage into the Severn Sea.

ELYSTAN GLODRYDD Patriarch

Little is known of this founder of one of the five 'royal tribes' of Wales. The descendants of Elystan (or Elstan) ruled the land between the Rivers **Wye** and **Severn** until dispossessed, with great ruthlessness, by the **Mortimer** and de **Breos** families.

EMERY, Frank Vivian (1930–87) Geographer

A native of **Gowerton** and a graduate of **Oxford**, Emery was a lecturer at **Swansea** (1956–9) and at Oxford. He wrote extensively on **Edward Lhuyd** and his contemporaries (in Wales and at Oxford), including the bilingual *Edward Lhuyd, F.R.S., 1660–1709* (1971). His book *The World's Landscapes: Wales* (1969) became widely known.

EMIGRATION

As a result of their movement overseas, Welsh people have become a part of the histories of a number of the countries of the world. Emigration has also created small but distinctive Welsh settler communities that broadly, up until the early 20th century, supported a **Welsh-language** religious and cultural life.

Welsh emigration has been relatively small in volume compared with that of other European nationalities, and the overseas movement of the Welsh has never been as prominent as migration to **England**, especially to **London** and **Liverpool**. (Officially, 'emigration' is defined as settlement in another sovereign state. Thus, the Welsh who live in England cannot technically be classed as emigrants.) Nevertheless, the Welsh presence overseas has not been insubstantial. Although historical work on the subject has been largely confined to the Welsh in **North America**, Argentina and, to a lesser extent, **Australia**, a growing

number of studies are now revealing a phenomenon of much complexity and diversity. (For the most intriguing of Welsh overseas ventures, *see* **Patagonia**.)

People have been moving from Wales to settle overseas for centuries. They began emigrating to North America in the early 17th century, and possibly much earlier (*see* **Madog ab Owain Gwynedd**). The settlement of Welsh religious dissenters in the British North American colonies between *c.*1660 and *c.*1720 established the world's first overseas Welsh communities, although there had been a short-lived Welsh colony at **Cambriol** in Newfoundland in the early 17th century. After some 70 years of stagnation, emigration increased again in the 1790s, marking the beginning of an extended and almost unbroken period of movement that was halted only by the worldwide economic **depression** of the interwar years. Since the end of the **Second World War**, emigration from Wales has resumed, although on a smaller scale.

From *c.*1800 onwards, Welsh emigrants expanded their North American presence and also moved to other continents, a trend which accompanied the 19th-century growth of white settlement outside Europe. The primary Welsh contingents were located in Australia, the United States, Canada, **New Zealand**, Patagonia and **South Africa**. At various times, smaller Welsh contingents were located in parts of Africa, Asia, mainland Europe (including **iron**-workers in France's Massif Central in the early 19th century) and parts of South America apart from Patagonia (Welsh **copper** miners were celebrating **St David**'s Day in Coquimbo, Chile, in the mid-1820s). Permanent settlers were accompanied outwards by 'career migrants' who resided abroad for varying lengths of time before returning to Wales. Among them were industrial entrepreneurs and mining surveyors who opened up the **coal**fields of China and Japan, and triggered the industrial development of the Don basin in Ukraine (*see* **John Hughes**; 1814–99). It is not perhaps too frivolous to record that the second motorcar in India, and the first in Calcutta, was the possession of the **Aberystwyth**-born engineer and industrialist David Edward Evans (1859–1951).

Noteworthy, too, are the activities of Welsh **missionaries** in **Brittany**, China, India (*see* **Khasi Hills**), **Madagascar** and Tahiti (*see* **John Davies** (1772–1855)), and those who served overseas as the soldiers and administrators of the British Empire.

In the first two decades of the 20th century, the Chief Justices of both Bengal and Hong Kong were native-born Welshmen, while small communities of military personnel, administrators, businessmen, clergymen and educators and their families sustained Welsh societies such as those in Ceylon and Shanghai. World wars further expanded the range of locations in which Welsh events were held – St David's Day celebrations in Bombay in 1918, and Alexandria, Egypt, in 1919. Between 1943 and 1945, the Welsh Society of Cairo's Welsh-language periodical *Seren y Dwyrain* (The Star of the East) served Welsh armed forces stationed in the Middle East.

Although the number of Welsh emigrants was small, there is disagreement over whether they were proportionately small in terms of Wales's total **population**. Welsh emigrants were often not recorded separately from English

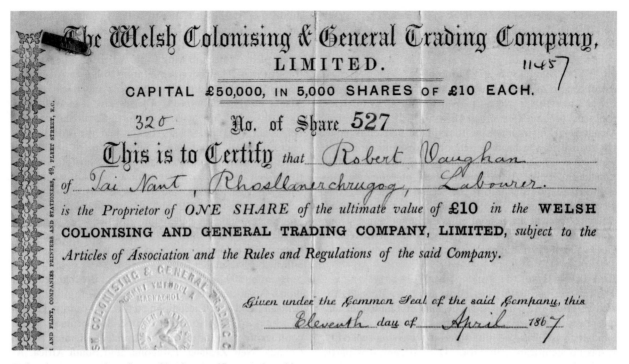

The Welsh Colonising & General Trading Company, LIMITED.

CAPITAL £50,000, IN 5,000 SHARES OF £10 EACH.

No. of Share 527

This is to Certify that Robert Vaughan of Tai Nant, Rhosllanerchrugog, Labourer.

is the Proprietor of ONE SHARE of the ultimate value of £10 in the WELSH COLONISING AND GENERAL TRADING COMPANY, LIMITED, subject to the Articles of Association and the Rules and Regulations of the said Company.

Given under the Common Seal of the said Company, this Eleventh day of April 1867

Emigration was sometimes financed by share certificates such as this

ones. As a result, it is difficult to estimate the total size and direction of the outflow, but the actual numbers of emigrants and Welsh-born persons living overseas are almost certainly higher than the figures recorded by the receiving countries.

It is possible, however, to give a general picture of the relative importance of the primary destinations. Far more Welsh went to the United States than any other country, although by the end of the 19th century, British colonial destinations were proving more popular. In South Africa, for example, although there had been Welsh arrivals since the 1820s, significant Welsh immigration did not occur until after the development of the Kimberley diamond mines and Witwatersrand (Johannesburg) gold industry in the 1860s and 1880s, respectively. The Witwatersrand Cambrian Society first held an **eisteddfod** in 1898, and, in 1926, 4328 inhabitants of South Africa recorded that they had been born in Wales. Canada was the most popular British colonial destination, followed by Australia. The Ottawa home of the Canadian prime minister is known by the Welsh name of Gorffwysfa.

Until the middle of the 19th century, the movement was primarily agrarian in character, but in subsequent decades, key industrial workers such as miners, iron, steel and **tinplate** workers, and **slate** quarrymen, often emigrating with their families, came to predominate. As the Welsh had industrial experience, they, unlike the Irish, were rarely obliged to accept menial jobs in their new home. Welsh emigrant **women** have been less numerous than their male counterparts, but in the 19th century they had a significant occupational presence as domestic servants, dressmakers and agricultural workers. Welsh emigrants moved for a wide variety of reasons, including religious and political ones, but in the 19th century economic considerations – often a combination of difficult conditions at home and the

attractions of land or higher wages overseas – were predominant. Some emigrated for what might be termed nationalistic reasons, such as the various attempts to set up a 'new Wales' in the North American colonies and Brazil, as well as the more permanent *Gwladfa* in Patagonia.

The experiences of the Welsh in the receiving countries were diverse. Some settled as individuals or families in isolation from the more popular areas of Welsh settlement, whilst geographic mobility was a characteristic of many. Wherever they settled in significant numbers, key factors enabled the Welsh to establish visible and distinctive ethnic communities. These include the impact of chain migration; the ties forged by the Welsh language, religious Nonconformity (*see* **Nonconformists**) and culture; and concentration in certain industries – mining in particular – which was crucial not only in determining the location of the Welsh presence but also in bolstering a Welsh identity. Rarely encountering hostility, the overseas Welsh have usually earned recognition and respect as a small but locally influential group. This partly reflects the important contributions made by Welsh emigrants and their descendants to the development of their new homelands, especially in the fields of **education**, industry, **music**, **religion** and the labour movement.

A major issue facing all migrants is that of assimilation versus cultural preservation. Some Welsh migrant leaders urged steadfast attachment to the Welsh cultural and linguistic heritage, and bewailed manifestations of the processes of cultural change, such as a decline in the usage of the Welsh language. Others envisaged the Welsh as patriotic and respectable citizens of their adopted countries. In the case of the Welsh in the British colonies, allegiance to their new homelands often created or reinforced a sense of 'Britishness'. On the other hand, Welsh immigrants to the United States often came to embrace hostility towards the British Empire, hostility expressed in particular in the newspaper *Y Drych*. Indeed, in view of **Michael D. Jones**'s links with the United States, that country played a significant role in the beginning of modern Welsh **nationalism**.

An intriguing feature of Welsh settlement overseas is that in some respects they assimilated deeply yet still retained many vestiges of a Welsh heritage. Indeed, in recent decades, a growing number of Americans, Australians and Canadians are taking an interest in their Welsh heritage and contemporary developments in Wales. More recent emigrants from Wales have taken with them social, cultural and political values, and conceptions of their homeland that differ markedly from those held by earlier migrants and those of Welsh ancestry. This has led to tensions within some overseas Welsh societies, and therefore those societies should not necessarily be regarded as homogenous entities.

At the beginning of the 21st century, the activities of Welsh organizations and societies overseas display a greater vibrancy than has been evident for several decades – a vibrancy assisted by the rapid contact with Wales which the development of electronic mail permits. Numerous Welsh 'exiles' attend the National Eisteddfod, and there was considerable opposition to the decision in 2006 to abolish the Eisteddfod's *Cymru a'r Byd* (Wales and the World) ceremony. There is a renewed interest in the Welsh abroad among the general public, particularly those interested in their ancestry. The subject is developing as a field of academic study, with scholars exploring not only the history of emigration, but also the contemporary Welsh ethnic profile, the Welsh language overseas, and the literary products of the emigrants and their descendants. The global dimension to the Welsh experience is long likely to play a significant part in how Welsh people see themselves and are viewed by others.

EMLYN *Cantref*
Hugging the southern bank of the **Teifi**, Emlyn was one of the seven *cantrefi* of **Dyfed** and consisted of the **commotes** of Is Cuch and Uwch Cuch. Following the **Norman** invasions, Is Cuch became the **march**er-lordship of **Cilgerran** and Uwch Cuch, with its centre at **Newcastle Emlyn**, remained under Welsh rule until the late 13th century, when it became part of **Carmarthenshire**. The **Act of 'Union'** of 1536 granted Cilgerran to **Pembrokeshire**.

EMMANUEL, Ivor (1927–2007) Singer and actor
Best remembered for his stirring rendition of **'Men of Harlech'** in the 1964 **film** *Zulu*, in which he played a private in the **South Wales Borderers**, Ivor Emmanuel was born in Pontrhydyfen (Pelenna), the birthplace also of **Richard Burton**. After his mother, father and sister were killed by a stray German bomb during the **Second World War**, he was taken in by an aunt and began his working life as a coalminer and steelworker. Intent on a singing career, he auditioned unsuccessfully for the D'Oyly Carte Opera Company, but, with encouragement from Richard Burton, he managed to win a part in *Oklahoma!* in **London**'s West End. It launched a distinguished career in stage musicals, radio and television – which included, between 1958 and 1964, the leading role in the popular television series *Gwlad y Gân* (*Land of Song*). In 1982, he retired to a village on Spain's Costa del Sol, where he died.

ENCLOSURES
Although some of the fields of Wales are of great antiquity, much of the land was still unenclosed in the early 16th century. Over the following two centuries, landlords were assiduous creators of hedged fields, the poet **John Dyer** urging in 1757: 'Inclose, inclose, ye swains! … in fields/ Promiscuous held, all culture languishes.'

By the late 18th century, most of the open fields of the lowlands had been enclosed, although some still exist, particularly in **Gower**. While the 18th-century enclosure movement in the English Midlands involved low-lying arable land, in Wales it generally involved the **common lands** of the uplands. Some commons were appropriated by landlords; and others, in the *tai unnos* tradition, were surreptitiously enclosed by squatters. The first Welsh enclosure act was passed in 1733, and between 1793 and 1818 almost 100 acts, authorizing the enclosure of 80,000 ha of Welsh land, were passed, a process which led to the building of the stone walls (*see* **Dry Stone Walling**) which are such a feature of upland Wales. The primary aim of the acts was the intensification of landlord rights, and they were met with rioting by dispossessed squatters and by small farmers deprived of their use of the commons.

ENERGY
The search for energy sources and their development is as old as humanity itself. Pre-industrial Wales experienced a full range of energy forms, from simple human and animal muscle power, through the use of wood and **peat** to generate heat, to the harnessing, via wheel and sail, of water and wind power (*see* **Watermills** and **Windmills**). As the restored 18th-century foundry at Furnace (**Ysgubor-y-coed**) indicates, water power was central to the development of industry in Wales. The Gilfach Ddu site at the National Slate Museum (*see* **National Museum [of] Wales**), contains the largest water wheel in **Britain** – the Laxey wheel on the Isle of **Man** is larger – together with a wide range of machines that were powered by it.

From the dawn of the industrial era until very recently, Wales's principal and dominant energy source was **coal.** Indeed, where the production of energy through steam engines powered by coal is concerned, Wales has had a role of world importance (*see* **Richard Trevithick** and **Railways**). Of the other main fossil fuels, no **oil** has been found in exploitable quantities, despite explorations in the Irish Sea in the 1990s. However, the importation and the refining of oil became key activities during the second half of the 20th century. Indigenous natural gas resources are restricted to a limited offshore discovery near the Point of Ayr (**Llanasa**). As the supply of North Sea gas declined, **Milford Haven** became an important centre for the importation of liquid gas; in 2005, work began on an underground pipe which will convey gas across the south to **England**, provoking protests along much of its route.

As did the rest of Britain, 19th-century Wales came to possess many centres at which gas was made from coal and was stored and delivered through pipelines. The Scot

Modern energy sources typified by a wind turbine and the controversial natural gas pipeline from Milford Haven to Gloucestershire, shown here under construction in 2007

William Murdock (1754–1854) was the pioneer of gaslight. His inventiveness was exploited by a cotton mill built in Manchester in 1806, and, in 1812, gas began to be used to light a cotton mill at **Mold**. From *c.*1818 onwards, **Newtown**'s streets were illuminated by gas lamps, to be followed by **Cardiff** (1821), **Holywell** (1824) and **Wrexham** (1827). With the coming of the gas meter in the 1840s, and of the pre-paid meter in the 1870s, gas came to be increasingly used in dwellings. Virtually every town came to possess a gasholder; that at Grangetown (1881) (*see* **Cardiff**) is a particularly elegant structure. **Borough** and urban authorities played a key role in these developments. When the Wales Gas Board was created following the nationalization of the gas industry in 1948, Wales had 104 gas works. Many of them were demolished in the 1950s and 1960s as oil came to replace coal as a source of gas. From 1971 onwards, gas from the North Sea came to be dominant, and the industry was privatized in 1986. In 2006, 37% of Wales's dwellings were not linked to the gas network, and many families in the remoter parts of the country had reason to be grateful for their cylinders of gas delivered by Calor and other companies.

As with the gas supply, the electricity supply also began in a local, piecemeal fashion. The world's first public supply of electricity was that at Godalming in Sussex (1881). There were a few electric lights in the streets of **Llanelli** by 1882, as there were in The Hayes (Cardiff) by 1885. A generating station opened in **Ogmore Vale** in 1892, **Pontypool** in 1893, Cardiff in 1894, **Llandudno** in 1895, **Bangor** in 1897 and **Colwyn Bay** in 1898. Following the opening of the Dolwen station in 1902, Blaenau **Ffestiniog** became the first place in the United Kingdom to have an electricity supply exclusively produced by water power. As with gas, electricity supplies increasingly became the responsibility of borough and urban authorities. In 1899, Wrexham invested the substantial sum of £36,686 to provide the borough with electricity. Such developments were not exclusively urban. Electricity became available to light **Llanuwchllyn** in 1910, the result of the enterprise of a Llanuwchllyn native, Richard Edwards (1861–1941), who was responsible between 1907 and 1917 for installing 221 small water turbines across the north. (Such a turbine is described by Thomas Firbank in *I Bought a Mountain* (1940).)

The Central Electricity Board was established in 1925, and, when the National Grid was completed in 1933, about half the households of Wales had an electricity supply. When the electricity industry was nationalized in 1947, the decision not to establish a single electricity board for Wales was a disappointment to the members of **Plaid [Genedlaethol] Cymru** and to **devolution**ists such as **James Griffiths**. The north became part of the responsibility of the Merseyside and North Wales Electricity Board (MANWEB), and the south became that of the South Wales Electricity Board (SWEB; later SWALEC). The new boards laboured to ensure that the remoter parts of the country received electricity. (The electricity consumed by the farmers of Wales rose from 17 million khw in 1949 to 278 million khw in 1969.) The industry was privatized in 1990. MANWEB was bought by Scottish Power in 1995, and, after a period of ownership by **Hyder**, SWALEC was acquired by Scottish and Southern Energy in 2000. In 2003, 65.7% of the electricity consumed in Wales was consumed by the industrial and commercial sector, a higher percentage than in England and **Scotland**. Indeed, at the beginning of the 21st century, a single industrial customer – **Anglesey** Aluminium – was responsible for the consumption of 11% of the electricity consumed in Wales, a supply it received directly from the **Wylfa** nuclear power station.

Welsh power stations have encompassed a wide range of types, including coal, gas and oil-fired, and nuclear energy (at **Trawsfynydd** and Wylfa). By the early 21st century, Wales had only two coal-fired power stations – Uskmouth (**Nash**) and Aberthaw (**St Athan**) – a contrast with the heavy dependence upon gas-fired stations. (Plans are afoot to build a 800 MW gas-fired station alongside the coal-fired station at Uskmouth.

Nevertheless, the development of 'clean' methods of burning coal may mean that coal could yet again become a major fuel in Wales's power stations. In the second half of the 20th century, the development of hydropower was particularly noteworthy. The Ffestiniog power station (commissioned in 1963) was Britain's first major pumped-storage power facility, and the Dinorwic power station (opened in 1984), located within tunnels and caverns hollowed out of the Elidir **mountain (Llanddeiniolen)**, is Europe's largest hydroelectric power storage station (*see* **Engineering**). (Although the Dinorwig scheme consumes more electricity than it produces, consumption occurs when demand is low and production occurs when demand is high.) Gravity-fed hydropower schemes operate at **Dolgarrog**, **Maentwrog** and Cwm Dyli in **Snowdonia**, and on the **River Rheidol** (*see* **Blaenrheidol**). Since the inclusion of the Non-fossil Fuel Obligation in the 1989 Electricity Act, various dams, including those at the Elan, Clywedog and Llyn Brianne **reservoirs**, have developed hydropower facilities, and sell to the National Grid at a premium rate.

The power stations of Wales in 2006 with a production capacity exceeding 100 MW

Power Station	Fuel	Production capacity (MW)
Baglan Bay	Gas	575
Barry	Gas	250
Connah's Quay	Gas	1380
Shotton	Gas	180
Deeside	Gas	500
Wylfa	Nuclear	980
Dinorwig	Pumped-storage	1728
Ffestiniog	Pumped-storage	360
Aberthaw B	Coal	1455
Uskmouth	Coal	393

In the late 20th century, Wales came to produce more electricity than it consumed. In the early 1980s, it consumed 6% of the electricity consumed in Britain, while producing 10% of the British production; the figures in 2006 were 6.7 and 8.7.

At the opening of the 21st century, the discovery, exploitation, production, supply and use of energy have become an increasing source of environmental concern with respect to atmospheric pollution and the despoliation of habitats and landscape.

Wales's geography and **geology** means that the country has an array of alternative or renewable energy sources, many yet to be fully developed. In 2000, the Wales Energy Research Centre was established, a cooperative venture between a number of higher **education** institutions which hopes to play a central role in the development of sustainable methods of energy production.

The country's location places it in a zone of high rainfall and strong westerly winds, with frequent cyclonic storms, capable of providing wind and water power (on water *see above*). In 2006, Wales had 24 wind farms with the capability between them of producing 300.60 MW (*see also* **Windmills**). The most productive wind farm on the land of Wales is that at Cefn Groes (**Pontarfynach**), which is capable of producing 58.5 MW. The North Hoyle wind farm located 7.5 km off the coast at **Rhyl**, which opened in 2003, is capable of producing 60 MW. With the British government and the **National Assembly** anxious to ensure that 10% of energy needs will be produced by sustainable methods by 2010, the number and the productivity of wind farms are likely to increase substantially. However, the spread of wind farms has been a source of bitter controversy, with the opinions of environmentalists sharply divided on the proliferation of wind farm sites in upland areas.

Wales could also harness wave power. The long fetch of the Atlantic waves passing through St George's Channel, and the constrictions of the Irish and Severn seas enhance the potential of tidal power. A tidal barrage across the Severn Sea has been proposed; it was estimated in 2006 that such a barrage would cost over £10 billion and that it would produce electricity equivalent to the output of two nuclear power stations. So far, the scheme has been rejected, largely on grounds of cost and environmental impact. Less ambitious, but more environmentally friendly schemes involve the construction of lagoons, schemes for which the Welsh inshore waters are potentially the most productive sites on the planet. The **University of Wales, Swansea** is also pioneering technologies in tidal movement and wave energy.

Another alternative energy source, with more limited potential, is solar power. By displaying the potential of roof-mounted radiators and solar panels, the **Centre for Alternative Technology** has made a valuable contribution in this area, and Wales is in a favourable position to take advantage of photovoltaic technology (the turning of light into electricity). In 2004, Wrexham became the Sharp Company's chief European centre for the production of solar energy panels. Under the leadership of Stuart Irvine, the School of **Chemistry** at the **University of Wales, Bangor**, has produced innovative research in the field. **Bronllys** Hospital was the first National **Health** Service hospital in Britain to rely on solar power for its electricity, following the example of the **Powys** County Council, which installed solar panels in its headquarters at **Llandrindod**.

The development of energy from biomass has had a more chequered history. However, the **Institute of Grassland and Environmental Research** (IGER) has the expertise to develop crops that could be used as fuel to produce electricity. In 2006, plans were announced for **Margam** to become the site of the first biomass power station in Wales; using wood chips as fuel, it should produce 14 MW of electricity worth £33 million – sufficient to supply the electricity needs of 31,000 dwellings. The heating system of Y Senedd, the home of the National Assembly for Wales, is also remarkably progressive. Its main biomass boiler burns wood pellets and chips, and beneath the building there are bore holes drawing heat from rock deep below ground. As pressures intensify to minimize waste landfill, there should also be an increase in the electricity produced through the processing of both domestic and commercial waste.

ENGINEERING

Engineering in Wales comprises a wide diversity of activities, which span the centuries and range from heavy foundry work to the production of intricate electronic components (*see* **Electronics**). The engineering industry has supplied and supported both primary and secondary production, and has provided equipment and infrastructure for transport, communications and utility services.

Richard Trevithick

The operations of Wales's emergent **iron**, **copper** and **slate** industries (*see* **Industrial Revolution**) were based on straightforward extraction and processing, and did not, in general, require a major supporting engineering industry. The same is broadly true of the early years of the **coal** industry, the extraction, transportation and shipping of the coal being sufficiently straightforward and profitable for there to be little stimulus to develop an indigenous engineering industry. With the phenomenal expansion of coalmining in the 1860s and 1870s, the need for mining and ancillary machinery was met largely by long-established companies located elsewhere in **Britain**. There were, nevertheless, some notable companies, such as the renowned Abbey Ironworks (**Neath**), Uskside (**Newport**), Llewellyn and Cubitt (**Rhondda**), Waddle (**Llanelli**) and De Winton (**Caernarfon**). The demands of industry eventually necessitated radical improvements in communications and **energy** supply, many of which called for daring innovation and led to some outstanding engineering achievements.

While the southern **canals**, built largely to serve the iron industry, essentially followed routes straight down the valleys, the **Llangollen** Canal in the north cut across the terrain, requiring aqueducts at **Chirk** (1801) and Pont Cysyllte (1805) (**Llangollen Rural**), designed by **Thomas Telford**. The latter, with its novel, cast iron trough, is the highest aqueduct in Britain.

Barely had the canal era reached maturity, when Telford designed the Shrewsbury to **Holyhead** road, solving the major problem of crossing the **Menai Strait** with the magnificent Menai Suspension Bridge (1826), still in use today. The limitations of the canals were initially overcome by the construction of tramroads. As these were being deployed in the industrial areas, the ironmaster Samuel **Homfray** brought **Richard Trevithick** to the Penydarren Ironworks (**Merthyr Tydfil**) to construct machinery. While there, he built the world's first **railway** locomotive (1804).

As the railway age commenced in earnest, the two routes across Wales to **Ireland** contained notable structures. In the north, **Robert Stephenson**'s railway crossed the **Conwy** (1848) and the Menai Strait (1850) with innovatory tubular iron bridges, making them precursors of today's box-girder bridges. **Brunel**, the engineer for the south Wales railway, crossed the **Wye** at **Chepstow** (1852) with another innovatory design in which the bridge deck was effectively suspended from an iron tube. A few kilometres away from Chepstow is the Welsh portal of the **Severn Tunnel** (*see also* **Portskewett**); with a length of 7 km, it is the longest railway tunnel in Britain. Like the canals, most of the railways built primarily for industrial purposes followed the valleys down to the coast. A notable exception was **Crumlin** viaduct (1857; demolished in 1965), on the line from **Pontypool** to **Aberdare**, which was the tallest railway viaduct in Britain. Alone amongst all the Welsh railway companies, the Taff Vale Railway built a number of its own locomotives in **Cardiff**, one of which has been preserved.

Associated with the south Wales coal trade was the construction of substantial **ports**, from Newport to Burry Port. The first and the last docks to be built in Cardiff, the Bute West (1839) and the Queen Alexandra (1907), were, at the time of their construction, the largest masonry docks in the world.

The damming of river valleys to create **reservoirs** has usually proved controversial, but, considered as feats of engineering, many of Wales's dams, sometimes involving hydroelectric schemes, are impressive – the Llyn Brianne dam (1972), near **Llandovery** (*see* **Llanddewi Brefi**) has a height of 273 m, making it the highest in Britain.

The late 20th century witnessed two major engineering projects. The Dinorwic hydroelectric scheme (opened in 1984) at **Llanddeiniolen** is the largest pumped storage station in Europe. Because virtually all the construction is underground, it is difficult to comprehend the scale of the main machinery hall, which is 180 m long by 60 m high. An ingenious feat of highway engineering is the Conwy road crossing on the **A55**, opened in 1991. Almost as innovative is Newport's new bridge over the **Usk**, completed in 2004. (*See also* **Severn Bridges**.)

The development of academic engineering in Wales is related, in the main, to the growth of new aspects of engineering in the departments of engineering at Cardiff and **Swansea**, initiated respectively in 1890 and 1920. Electrical engineering is taught at **Bangor**, where a chair was created in 1947. At Cardiff, a chair of civil engineering was created in 1950, and mechanics and structural engineering courses were introduced in the 1970s. A chair of electrical engineering was established in 1954 (becoming the chair of electrical engineering and electronics in 1964), followed by a chair of mechanical engineering in 1961; and a solar energy unit was established in 1974. A department for the allied subject of metallurgy was established in 1907, its title changing to metallurgy and fuel technology in 1933 and to mechanical engineering and materials **science** in 1970. At Swansea, the chairs in civil, electrical (and electronics) and mechanical engineering were established in the 1950s, a chair of chemical engineering in 1955 and of industrial engineering in 1965. Engineering is also one of the major subjects taught in the **University of Glamorgan**.

In the later 20th century, the range of engineering activities in Wales was augmented by the growth of **vehicle manufacture** and electronics, which contributed to a more diversified structure and replaced an over-dependence on the traditional, heavier end of engineering. The sector was profoundly affected by the economic recession of the early 1980s which, by *c*.1990, had caused the workforce to be reduced by 30%, to around 75,000: this still accounted for some 9% of total employment in Wales and almost 30% of all industrial production.

ENGLAND, Wales's association with; the Welsh in

It was the expansion of England – more specifically, that of **Mercia** – which determined the eastern **border** of Wales. Despite the construction of **Offa's Dyke**, the border was zonal rather than linear, a situation which lasted until the statutory definition of **county** boundaries through the **Act of 'Union'** of 1536. Throughout the Middle Ages and beyond, there were in **Shropshire** and **Herefordshire** districts wholly **Welsh** in language and social organization. Equally, there were areas almost wholly **English** in speech on the Welsh side of the border, especially in the northeast. The Old English Kingdom achieved a unity and cohesion unique among European monarchies, and the power of that kingdom was a central cause of the inability of

Welsh rulers to attain the regnal solidarity achieved in **Scotland**, a kingdom further removed from the centre of English influence.

From the reign of Alfred (871–99) onwards, Welsh rulers were obliged to recognize the overlordship of **English monarchs**, a recognition that allowed those sovereigns to involve themselves increasingly in the affairs of Wales. Despite the **Edwardian conquest**, completed in the 1280s, Wales – although among the territories of the monarchs of England – did not become an integral part of England itself. Yet, by the 16th century, the economies of the two countries had long been intertwined, especially through the **cattle** and wool trades (*see* **Woollen Industry**), and **London** had become the magnet for Welshmen of ambition. Other parts of England, the border towns and city of Bristol in particular, also attracted numerous Welsh migrants.

From the late 18th-century onwards, with the rise in **population** and the development of industry and transport facilities, movement to England increased dramatically, with Merseyside replacing London as the favoured destination of Welsh migrants. By 1901, there were 265,000 people born in Wales living in England, of whom 35,000 lived in London and 87,000 in **Cheshire** and Lancashire (*see* **Liverpool**). Many of the migrants sought to create microcosms of Wales in their new environments but, with the passing of the generations, these tended to wither away. During the interwar **depression**, Wales lost 390,000 people through migration, the great majority of them settling in England. As late as the 1930s, Welsh-speakers were far and away England's largest linguistic minority. In 1951, England was the home of 649,275 natives of Wales, and by then the London area had been reinstated as the chief focus of Welsh immigrants. In the later 20th century, migration continued, although as a result of personal decisions rather than as a mass reaction to a collapse in employment opportunities at home.

For a thousand years and more, England has been an overwhelming factor in the experience of the Welsh. With the development of the European Union and the growth of foreign travel, other countries are edging into that experience. Yet, with England so close a neighbour, and with a population 17 times that of Wales, any consideration of the future of Wales must take into account that looming presence.

ENGLISH, The

The English, Wales's largest ethnic minority, have been a presence – as colonizers, settlers or migrants – since the time of the Saxons, by which name, *Saeson*, they are still known to **Welsh**-speakers. Historically, their relation to the Welsh has passed through several main stages.

The medieval conquest of Wales by **Norman** barons and **English monarchs** was accompanied by colonization: English governance was consolidated through the creation of fortified **boroughs**, and settled by English incomers. Colonization accelerated the growth of a money **economy**, which would eventually undermine the customary social systems of the Welsh. Before and after the revolt of **Owain Glyndŵr**, the results of that economic dislocation found expression in the ideological and cultural bastions that the Welsh and the English erected against each other. The

Welsh poets articulated a highly conservative defence of Welsh values, while the English parliament passed **laws** discriminating against the Welsh on racial grounds.

The legal unification of **England** and Wales under the **Tudor** dynasty (*see* **Acts of 'Union'**) began that process which, over the next two centuries or so, would see the virtual disappearance of a native Welsh aristocracy, as its members were absorbed – chiefly by marriage alliances – into the English landed **class**. Those who were not so absorbed adopted English manners and English culture through imitation. Thus the Welsh, like the Czechs – possibly their nearest European parallel in this respect – became a nation of peasantry, a term for which the Welsh language, in *y werin* (*see* **Gwerin**), has an especially affectionate name.

The English played a major part in the industrialization of Wales (*see* **Industrial Revolution**), in the process of which the Welsh – uniquely for a 19th-century peasant **population** – repossessed their own country. Both capital and the skills necessary for industrial enterprise came, in the first stage of industrialization, almost exclusively from England – although most coalowners in the second stage were Welsh. In either case, industrialization prompted in-migration – from neighbouring English counties to industrial south and north-east Wales – on a very significant scale. In the communities thus formed, a proletarian consciousness tended to overwhelm any deep sense of ethnic difference.

At the beginning of the 21st century, significant numbers of English people were continuing to move into Wales. In 2001, 20.3% (598,800 people) of the inhabitants of Wales had been born in England. Many, in the 1960s and 1970s, came in pursuit of an alternative lifestyle; others, taking advantage of relatively low house prices, developed a more consumerist relationship with the country, buying cheap rural properties – often in the Welsh-speaking heartlands – and converting them into **second homes**. While many incomers became in time what the historian **Gwyn A. Williams** called 'New Welsh' – informed and active participants in the life of the country – others have tended towards non-engagement with the indigenous culture, contributing significantly to the Anglicization of Wales.

ENGLISH CAUSES

The establishment, in the 19th century, of **English**-medium chapels in largely **Welsh**-speaking towns was motivated by a desire to assimilate non-Welsh-speakers – English incomers in particular – into Welsh Nonconformity (*see* **Nonconformists**). Having no faith in the future of Welsh, religious leaders such as **Lewis Edwards** saw the establishment of English causes as a kind of religious insurance against the decline of the language. Their 'English fever' was vehemently denounced by Emrys ap Iwan (**Robert Ambrose Jones**).

The **Wesleyans** had had English circuits – in **Pembrokeshire**, east **Breconshire** and the **Cardiff** area – since the 18th century. In the early 19th century, the **Calvinistic Methodists** established many small, English-medium chapels in the **border**lands, and, in 1857, the **Baptists** established their 'English Assembly of **Monmouthshire**'. English causes campaigns were launched by the **Congregationalists**

in 1853 and by the Calvinistic Methodists in 1869. By the end of the century, the Calvinistic Methodists had built 43 English-medium chapels.

ENGLISH LANGUAGE, The

Old English – sometimes known as **Anglo-Saxon** – was a descendant of the *Platt-Deutsch* dialects spoken in the eastern coastal regions of the North Sea. It developed as the speech of Germanic settlers in **Britain**. Speakers of the language had reached Wales by *c.*630 when St **Beuno** reputedly heard English being spoken across the **Severn** from **Berriew**. The western spread of Anglo-Saxon settlement caused Old English to be spoken in areas later considered to be part of Wales. This was particularly true of the northeast; there, **Offa's Dyke** demarcated the western **border** of **Mercia**, a kingdom which included parts of the later **Flintshire** and **Denbighshire**. Re-conquest under **Gruffudd ap Llywelyn** is reflected in the Welsh guise acquired by some English settlement names, with *Prēosta-tūn* (farm of the priests) becoming **Prestatyn** rather than Preston as in **England**. Interaction between the Welsh and the **English** led **Welsh** to borrow Old English words. Borrowings which had occurred before the coming of the **Normans** include *llidiart* (gate), *bwrdd* (board, table) and *capan* (cap).

With the Norman conquest of **England**, English was marginalized in the land of its birth, a chronicler lamenting in 1300 that 'there is not a single country that does not hold to its own language save England alone'. But, while Norman French was the language of the knights who carved out lordships in Wales, it was not that of the peasant farmers who settled in the lordships. In its entry for 1105, *Brut y Tywysogyon* records the plantation of a colony of **Flemings** in **Dyfed**. English and Flemish would then have been very similar; joined by English-speaking settlers, the Flemings adopted English, causing Flemish to become extinct in Dyfed.

Other areas settled by English speakers included the **Vale of Glamorgan**, western **Gower** and southern **Gwent**. In addition, the **boroughs** planted in Wales by the Normans came to be bastions of Englishness. Thus, English has a continuous history as a spoken language in both rural and urban Wales for at least 800 years. Further English settlement followed the **Edwardian conquest**, but some of the incoming families were eventually Cymricized. The Landsker – the linguistic boundary in Dyfed – proved remarkably stable, but elsewhere – in the Vale of Glamorgan, for example – English lost ground as demographic change led to the renewal of the domination of Welsh.

But if Welsh was making a comeback, so also was English. In England, **French** and **Latin** were by the 15th century yielding to English in administration and **law**, and as the language of the upper classes. In Wales, as Welsh law gave way to English law and as preparing official documents became the task of professional scribes, documentation in Wales came to follow that of England in language as well as content. Thus, long before the 'language clause' of the **Act of 'Union'** of 1536, English was well on the way to becoming Wales's official language. Welsh **gentry** were increasingly aware of the usefulness of a knowledge of English. John Wynn (1553–1627; *see* **Wynn family (Gwydir)**) noted that his great-grandfather left remote **Eifionydd** – presumably *c.*1470 – to learn English at **Caernarfon**.

The language clause of the Act of 'Union' laid down that: 'all Justices … shall kepe the sessions … in the Englisshe Tonge and … no personne or personnes that use the Welsshe speche … shall have … any … office … within the Realme of Englonde Wales or other the Kinges dominions'.

As the Act placed the administration of Wales in the hands of the Welsh gentry, implicit in it was the creation of a Welsh ruling **class** fluent in English. Two centuries would pass before the vast majority of Welsh gentry families had wholly abandoned Welsh in favour of English and, in that process, factors other than the Act of 'Union' – Welsh heiresses marrying English husbands, for example – were of central importance. The ultimate outcome was a ruling class almost exclusively English in speech, divided from the great mass of **population** who, outside the English-speaking areas, had little or no knowledge of the language.

The dominance of English could well have been further ensured by the **Protestant Reformation** settlement with its emphasis upon the use of the initially English **Bible** and **The Book of Common Prayer**. However, the legislation of 1563 which laid down that Welsh versions of the Bible and The Book of Common Prayer should be available in every **parish** church in Wales, together with the publication of The Book of Common Prayer in Welsh in 1567, and – above all – the 1588 publication of the Bible in Welsh did permit Welsh to have an important role in religious life. This role was strengthened by the foundation of **Nonconformist** denominations worshipping mainly in Welsh. Nevertheless, church records indicate the growing role of English in parish churches from the 18th century onwards, particularly in the borderlands where the encroachment of the English language was gathering pace. This was particularly true of **Radnorshire**, which had become almost wholly English in speech by 1801.

In 1801, Wales had 587,245 inhabitants, around 80% of whom could speak Welsh and 30% of whom could speak English. By 1901, the figures were 2,012,875, 49.9% and 84.9%, respectively. Thus, during the 19th century, Wales's population increased almost fourfold, its Welsh speakers increased twofold and its English speakers increased ninefold. It was probably in the 1870s that those with a knowledge of English first exceeded in number those with a knowledge of Welsh, although, initially at least, many who had gained some knowledge of English probably made little use of their acquired skill. The factors aiding the increasing prevalence of English included migration from England and **Ireland** to **ports** and industrial areas, the rise of holiday resorts, the establishment of a network of elementary schools teaching almost exclusively through the medium of English, the accelerating encroachment of English in the borderlands and the dissemination of utilitarian ideas and notions of social Darwinism hostile to the continuance of minority cultures.

As the 20th century advanced, knowledge of English became virtually universal in Wales. By the 1980s, the process was believed to be complete, for the census of 1981 was the last that sought to discover how many Welsh-speakers were ignorant of English. However, by the opening of the 21st century, increased migration from the third world meant that Wales's cities had considerable populations fluent only in languages such as Bengali and Somali (*see* **Bangladeshis** and **Somalis**).

Forms of English in Wales

There is a widespread assumption that the English spoken in Wales is an undifferentiated form of that language. That is far from being the case. The variations of the English of Wales reflect the different periods and the different ways that the language penetrated the country from the Middle Ages until today. Students of dialects have placed particular emphasis upon the role of the Welsh language in these variations. However, the English of Wales should not be considered solely in this context.

In south **Pembrokeshire**, the Gower peninsula and along the border, regions in which English has been firmly established for many centuries, Welsh was supplanted so thoroughly that it had virtually no influence upon the English of the inhabitants. In the borderlands, words which have or had currency in the western English Midlands – among them *oont* (mole), *sally* (willow), *clem* (starve), *dout* (put out a light or fire) – are in use. The 'r'-colouring on a vowel, which replaces the sequence of vowel followed by a fully articulated 'r', in words such as 'bird' and 'car', common in the borderlands, is probably also derived from neighbouring dialects in England. Although the origins of the dialects of Gower and south Pembrokeshire are a matter of conjecture, the use in Gower of 'z' for 's' in words like *seven* and *silver* follows patterns traditional in southwestern England, while in Pembrokeshire the pronunciation of words like *suck* and *dust* with the same vowel sound as *crook* is a feature common in the speech of the western English Midlands.

There are debates concerning the influence of Welsh upon the accent of the working class of **Cardiff**, an accent which extends from **Newport** to **Barry**. English has been present along the southern coastlands since at least the 12th century and the Cardiff accent shares phonetic elements with the accents of Somerset, Bristol and Gloucester. However, the authors of *Celtic Culture: A Historical Encyclopaedia* (2006) claim that the best-known feature of the dialect – a feature evident in the pronunciation of Cardiff as *keːdif* (*kairdif*)– preserves 'the long open front vowel of the moribund south Glamorgan dialect of Welsh'– a claim not universally accepted.

In much of Wales, English did not strike deep roots until the later 19th century. Although it came to displace Welsh in the communities of the valleys of the south-eastern **coalfield**, in that region the two languages coexisted long enough for Welsh to have an impact. That impact may well be fossilized by now, but in the bilingual areas of the west and the north, Welsh continues to leave its mark upon spoken English. Thus, the major northern and western varieties are rhotic – that is, in words like *car* and *cart*, the postvocalic 'r' is pronounced as a trill, as in Welsh. The retention of 'h' in words like *hat* and *who* – rather than its abandonment as happens in many of the dialects of England – reflects the occurrence of 'h' in Welsh. Another characteristic of the English of the north-west is the absence of the sound 'z', which results in the lack of differential between *seal/zeal* and *sink/zinc*.

Forms taken by the present habitual tense of the verb indicate the influence of both English and Welsh dialects. Thus, sentences such as 'he *do go* to the pub every night' occur in the borderlands and the industrial south-east, and are similar to usage in neighbouring dialects in England. The form 'he*'s going* to the pub every night', prevalent in the south-west, and partly overlapping in distribution with the former structure, is associated with Welsh-language constructions. The one-time tendency in the English dialects of **Gwynedd** to omit the indefinite article in sentences like 'There's (*a*) boat coming in' reflects a similar feature in Welsh, a language lacking an indefinite article.

Wenglish

Although 'Wenglish' is not a term recognized by professional linguists, it enjoys popularity with reference to the English spoken in the southern industrial valleys. It is not inherently unique at any level of structure; rather, it is a mish-mash of forms and pronunciation patterns associated with vernacular usage in parts of England, in other parts of Wales and with forms derived from the Welsh language. It is said to echo the intonation patterns of Welsh, and it has certainly adopted some syntactic patterns from that language. Instances include the use of 'there', as in 'There's tall you are!' (from Welsh '*Dyna dal wyt ti*'), and the word order of an indirect question, as in 'I'm not sure *is it true or not*'. Welsh words in Wenglish include *didoreth* (feckless), *shiggle* (from *siglo*, to shake), *twp* (stupid) and *wuss* (a familiar address between males, from Welsh *gwas*, meaning 'servant or lad'). The English of the industrial south certainly reflects the influence of the intonation of Welsh. In polysyllabic words, Welsh-speakers in the south, raise the pitch of the voice on the last syllable (although stress is placed upon the penultimate syllable). Comments on the 'Welsh lilt' probably refer to this characteristic. Recent research on the English of the **Rhondda** indicates that many influences from Welsh have disappeared from the speech of those under forty, although intonation displaying the impact of Welsh remains a feature of the speech of young and old.

Many natives of the southern **coal**field now in their middle age will remember their bilingual youth –Wenglish for the street and more genteel English with parents. (Those parents who had aspirations for their children abhorred Wenglish.) Now in decline, Wenglish has been granted a modicum of recognition. Collections of idioms are available, as are recordings of speakers of Wenglish. Listening to them can be an almost unbearably poignant experience.

ENGLISH MONARCHS AND WALES

The first evidence of Welsh contact with an English king dates from *c.*616, when Aethelfrith, king of Northumbria defeated Selyf, king of **Powys**, at the **battle of Chester**. There is some evidence that a decade or so later, Tewdrig, king of **Gwent**, won a victory near the **Wye** estuary over an English army, probably led by the king of Wessex. In 633, **Cadwallon**, king of **Gwynedd**, in alliance with Penda, king of **Mercia**, killed the kings of Deira and Bernicia. In 634, Cadwallon was himself killed by Edwin, king of Northumbria. By the mid-7th century, the western expansion of Mercia was defining the Welsh–English **border**, a definition given further substance by the construction of **Offa's Dyke** in the late 8th century.

In the 9th century, the Christian kingdoms of Wales and **England** came under increasing pressure from the pagan **Vikings**, one of the considerations which caused the rulers of **Dyfed**, Gwent, **Glywysing** and **Brycheiniog** to seek the protection of Alfred, king of Wessex (871–99), patron of the scholar **Asser** of **St David's**. This was the beginning of the assumption that English kings had claims to suzerainty over Welsh rulers, a fundamental fact in the political history of Wales over the following four centuries. That assumption gained increasing meaning during the reign of Aethelstan (924–39), who was described by his eulogists as 'Basileus of the English and in like manner the ruler of the whole orb of **Britain**'. He imposed a heavy tax upon Wales, and seems to have expected the leading Welsh ruler, **Hywel Dda**, to attend his court. While the Scots and the Northmen revolted against Aethelstan's suzerainty in 937, the Welsh did not – the context, perhaps, of the writing of the remarkable poem *Armes Prydein* (*see* **Prophecy**).

Relations between Wales and the Old English Kingdom reached crisis point during the career of **Gruffudd ap Llywelyn**, who by *c.*1057 had united all the kingdoms of Wales under his rule. His raids into England and his alliance with Aelfgar, son of the earl of Mercia, led in 1063 to the invasion of Wales by Harold, earl of Wessex. He secured Gruffudd's murder and married Gruffudd's widow, Ealdgyth. Harold's success in Wales was among the factors that enabled him to gain the crown of England in 1066, thus causing Ealdgyth to be, in turn, queen of Wales and queen of England. His accession provided the motivation for the invasion of England by William, duke of Normandy.

Where Wales was concerned, the policy of William I (1066–87) was to stabilize the frontier. To that end, he settled powerful earls at Chester, Shrewsbury and Hereford (*see* **Cheshire**, **Herefordshire** and **Shropshire**) and acquiesced in their campaigns to seize the territories of Welsh rulers, aggression which led to the creation of the **March** of Wales. Evidence of early **Norman** penetration is recorded in the Domesday Book of 1086. In 1081, William led an army to St David's and apparently recognized **Rhys ap Tewdwr** as the ruler of **Deheubarth**. It was an arrangement that did not survive his death for, during the reign of William II (1087–1100), Deheubarth became subject to Norman aggression, as did Brycheiniog and **Morgannwg**. Following the Welsh rising of 1194, William led two campaigns in Wales. As neither was successful, there was still viable kingship in Wales in 1100, when he was succeeded by his brother, Henry I (1100–35).

The growth of the power of the crown in Wales was the outstanding feature of Henry's reign. To the author of *Brut y Tywysogyon*, the king was 'the man against whom none can contend save God himself'. The reign saw the culmination of the first phase of the creation of the

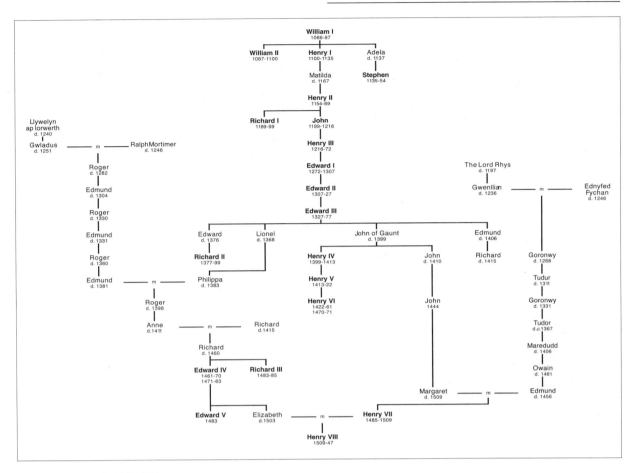

The English monarchs 1066–1547

March. Although the process had begun as the free-booting activity of Norman invaders, Henry gave the *adventi* at least intermittent assistance, establishing Wales's first English royal castle (**Carmarthen**, 1109), settling **Flemings** in southern Dyfed and leading campaigns against **Gruffudd ap Cynan** of Gwynedd and Maredudd ap Bleddyn of Powys. Henry was succeeded by his nephew Stephen (1135–54), an accession contested by Henry's daughter, Matilda, whose main champion was Robert, lord of **Glamorgan**. The consequent 'Anarchy' provided an opportunity for Welsh rulers, especially **Owain ap Gruffudd** in Gwynedd, **Rhys ap Gruffudd** (the Lord Rhys; d.1197) in Deheubarth and **Madog ap Maredudd** in Powys, to recover much of the power lost during the reign of Henry I. The 'Anarchy' also saw the consolidation of the quasi-independence of the marcher-lords, whose freedom of action Henry had sought to curtail.

Stephen was succeeded by Matilda's son, Henry II (1154–89), whose territories extended eventually from the Cheviots to the Pyrenees. The failure of his campaigns in 1157 and 1165 to limit the power of the Welsh rulers led to a change of policy involving the recognition of Rhys ap Gruffudd as the justice of southern Wales. Henry's assumption of the overlordship of **Ireland** had a profound impact on developments in Wales. The crown's acceptance of the role of Rhys ended with the accession of Richard I (1189–99) but, as his kingdom only saw him for six months of his reign, Richard's activities were marginal to events in Wales.

Richard's successor, John (1199–1216), was far more involved; initially as lord of Glamorgan by marriage, and subsequently through his relationship with **Llywelyn ap Iorwerth**, who married his daughter **Joan**. John's campaign of 1211 came close to destroying Llywelyn's power, but his aggression led to the uniting of Welsh rulers and to their alliance with John's baronial opponents. The success of the barons led in 1215 to the sealing of the **Magna Carta**, a document which made important concessions to Llywelyn.

The efforts of John's successor, Henry III (1216–72), to undermine Llywelyn's power proved unavailing. However, following the prince's death in 1240, Henry ensured that **Dafydd ap Llywelyn**'s position was weaker than that of his father. Following Dafydd's death in 1246, Henry was determined to reduce the status of his successors, Owain and **Llywelyn ap Gruffudd**, to that of English barons. Llywelyn, however, succeeded in outmanoeuvring the king. His success was ensured through his alliance with the king's opponents in the English baronial war (1258–65) and culminated in the **Treaty of Montgomery** (1267), which recognized Llywelyn as **Prince of Wales** and as the overlord of the other Welsh rulers.

The reign of Edward I (1272–1307) saw the demise of Llywelyn's **principality**. The king's reluctance to observe fully the provisions of the Treaty of Montgomery caused the prince to delay doing homage to him. The war of 1267–77 ensued, and was followed by the **Treaty of Aberconwy** which drastically curtailed Llywelyn's power.

The revolt of 1282 brought about the prince's death and the king's seizure of his territories, events which caused Edward to be in Wales more often and for longer periods than any other English king. His determination to secure a firm hold upon the country was made manifest by an unprecedented programme of castle building. Edward, a masterful man, also sought to limit the power of the marcher-lords; in 1292, for example, he imprisoned the lords of **Brecon** and Glamorgan for waging war against each other, a course of action rarely practicable for his weaker successors.

Edward I's son, Edward II (1307–27), was born in **Caernarfon** in 1284, the first of England's three Welsh-born kings. In 1301, his father invested him with the principality, thus causing him to be the first English Prince of Wales. Edward seems to have shown considerable sympathy for the Welsh, a chronicler noting 'the remarkable way in which he was revered by [them]'. His reign was dominated by his relationship with leading marcher-lords, especially the **Despensers** and the **Mortimers**. In his final crisis, he fled to Wales; captured near **Llantrisant**, he was put to death at Berkeley Castle. To his successor, Edward III (1327–77), Wales was primarily a source of income and soldiers, with the exploitation of its resources organized by the council of the Prince of Wales (the Black Prince; 1330–76). Richard II (1377–99) sought to build up support in Wales, and in 1398 seized the lands of his cousin, Henry Bolingbroke, the lordships of Brecon, **Monmouth** and **Kidwelly** among them. Captured at **Conwy**, he was obliged to abdicate in favour of Bolingbroke, who ascended the throne as Henry IV (1399–1413).

In Wales, Henry's reign was dominated by the **Glyndŵr Revolt**. The king led several campaigns against the insurgents but, during the later phases of the revolt, that task was undertaken by his son, Henry of Monmouth, England's second Welsh-born king. Henry V (1413–22), eager for Welsh soldiers for his campaigns in France (*see* **Hundred Years' War**), sought to pacify the Welsh, and appointed leaders of the native community as local officials. His widow, Katherine, daughter of Charles VI of France, married Owen **Tudor**. Henry VI (1422–71) inherited the throne at the age of six months. His reign was wracked by baronial struggles which culminated in the **Wars of the Roses**, in which the protagonists made extensive use of the resources of Wales. The weakness of the central **government** led to lawlessness in both the March and the Principality, despite the efforts of the king's half-brothers, Edmund and Jasper Tudor, who were active in Carmarthen and **Pembroke**.

In 1461, Henry VI was dethroned by the **Yorkist** claimant Edward IV, who, apart from Henry's restoration in 1470–1, reigned until his death in 1483. Through the Mortimers, Edward was a descendant of Llywelyn ap Iorwerth and was thus the first English king with Welsh ancestry. With both the **Lancaster** and Mortimer lands in his possession, he held over half the lordships of the March. The caput of the Mortimer lands was **Ludlow**, and there, in 1473, Edward established a council with the aim

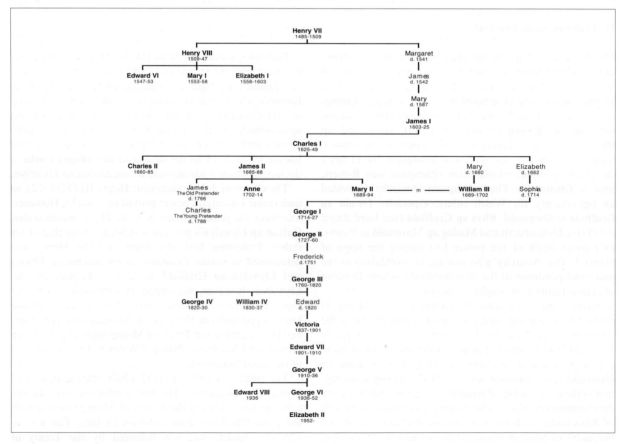

The English monarchs, 1485 to the present

of giving coherence to the government of Wales. His heir, the Prince of Wales, took up residence at Ludlow Castle. On his father's death, Edward V (1483) was seized on his way to **London** by his uncle, Richard, who usurped the crown and probably arranged for the 12-year-old king to be murdered in the Tower.

The usurpation of Richard III (1483–5) opened the way for the Lancastrian claimant, Pembroke-born Henry Tudor (Henry VII; 1485–1509), to land at Mill Bay (*see* **Dale**) near the mouth of the **Milford Haven Waterway**, defeat and kill Richard at the **battle of Bosworth** and seize the throne. The accession of a descendant of the Tudors of **Penmynydd** was hailed in Wales as the fulfilment of Welsh prophetic poetry. Yet, apart from a few symbolic acts – the incorporation of the **red dragon** in the royal arms, for example – Henry showed no particular interest in Wales. No monarch of the house of Tudor set foot in Wales, causing the Tudors to be the sole post-1066 English dynasty no reigning member of which crossed the border.

Henry's son, Henry VIII (1509–47), initiated the changes which eventually caused England and Wales to be Protestant countries, and his secretary, Thomas Cromwell, secured the passage of the **Acts of 'Union'**. Henry VIII's son, Edward VI (1547–53), pushed his father's religious changes in a markedly Protestant direction, a process reversed by his successor, Mary I (1553–8). Under Elizabeth (1558–1603), the moderately Protestant Church of England became Wales's established church (*see* **Anglicans**) – the cause of much contention 400 years later. Her reign also saw a degree of equilibrium in the administration of Wales, as the changes brought about by the Acts of 'Union' took root.

In 1603, James VI of **Scotland** (James I, 1603–25) inherited the English crown. Thus, the kingdom of Great Britain came into existence, a development of importance to the Welsh, who could henceforth consider themselves to be partners in a state representing the union of three nations. The policies of Charles 1 (1625–49) led to the **Civil Wars**, during which Charles visited Wales (1645) – the first monarch to do so since Henry IV in 1402. The Stuart Restoration brought Charles II (1660–85) to the throne, the accession winning a warm welcome from the Welsh. As the king had no legitimate children, his heir was his **Roman Catholic** brother, James, an issue which gave rise to the exclusionist **Whig Party** and the legitimist **Tory Party**, with the Welsh **gentry** – despite their suspicion of Catholicism – strongly in favour of the latter. In 1687, James II (1685–8) visited the shrine at **Holywell** to pray for a son. His prayer was answered and the king's determination to raise the child as a Catholic was among the factors which led to his deposition and to the joint monarchy of his daughter, Mary II (1689–94), and her husband, William III (1689–1702). William, who created a furore in north-east Wales through seeking to make large land grants to a Dutch favourite, was succeeded by his sister-in-law, Anne (1702–14). She endeared herself to the lesser clergy by granting them part of her income – the Queen Anne's Bounty so highly appreciated by impoverished Welsh incumbents.

Hereditary succession had been infringed in 1689, but it was assailed in a far more fundamental way in 1714 with the accession of the Hanoverian dynasty. Many of the Welsh gentry deplored its coming but, as their support for the Stuarts was a nostalgic sentiment rather than a serious commitment, Wales did not experience **Jacobite** risings. Shorn of real political power and unfamiliar with their new kingdom, George I (1714–27) and George II (1727–60) made little impact. George III (1760–1820) proved to be more assertive; his golden jubilee was celebrated by memorials near Devil's Bridge (*see* **Pontarfynach**) and on the **Clwydian Hills**. George IV (1820–30), patron of the Welsh architect **John Nash**, traversed Wales on his visit to Ireland in 1821 – the first monarch to cross the border since James II in 1687 – and an arch at **Holyhead** commemorates the fact. George was succeeded by his brother, William IV (1830–7), who was succeeded in turn by his niece, Victoria (1837–1901).

During her lengthy reign, Victoria spent only seven nights in Wales, compared with seven weeks in Ireland and seven years in Scotland. She had a mainly negative view of the Welsh, whilst they held her in high regard, largely because of her Welsh descent, her Protestantism and her respectability. By the 1880s, however, the money her family received and her role as 'head' of the Church of England were giving rise to some republican sentiment. **Keir Hardie** gave vent to anti-royalist attacks in the context of the lack of sympathy shown by parliament to the victims of the Cilfynydd **Colliery disaster** of 1894. The hostile reaction he received made the **Labour Party** reluctant to express such views; indeed, later Welsh members of the party – **George Thomas** in particular – could be embarrassingly sycophantic towards the royal family.

Edward VII (1901–10) was appointed chancellor of the **University of Wales** in 1895, a sign of a realization in royal circles that some effort needed to be made to ensure the loyalty of the Welsh. His remarks on the need to cure **tuberculosis** sufferers led to the establishment in 1912 of the Edward VII Welsh National Memorial Association to combat the disease. George V (1910–36), pressurized by **David Lloyd George**, presided at Caernarfon in 1911 over the investiture of his heir (later Edward VIII; 1936) as Prince of Wales. During a tour of the south Wales **coal**field in November 1936, Edward expressed sympathy for the plight of the unemployed; he abdicated less than a month later in order to marry the twice-divorced Wallis Simpson. His successor, George VI (1936–52), reasserted the tradition of royal respectability established by Victoria and upheld by George V.

Elizabeth II (1952–) sought to continue that tradition, but the foibles of her offspring dented the image of the royal family. Charles, her heir – invested with the Principality of Wales at Caernarfon in 1969 – has involved himself with Wales to a far greater degree than any of his predecessors. The fatal accident of Diana, his divorced wife, unleashed astonishing emotions and almost derailed the 1997 **devolution** referendum. At the time of her coronation in 1953, Elizabeth II received the adulation of a high proportion of the Welsh. However, by the time of her golden jubilee in 2002, it was apparent that dedicated royalism among them was largely confined to the dwindling generation which remembered the **Second World War**.

ENGLYN

The term *englyn* was originally employed for a group of kindred poetic metres which included the three-line stanzas found in Welsh saga poetry (*see* **Heledd** and **Llywarch Hen**). By now, however, it is synonymous with the four-line *englyn unodl union* (lit. 'direct monorhyme *englyn*') which first became common in the 12th century and which remains immensely popular among Welsh poets.

An *englyn* contains a total of 30 syllables (10–6–7–7) – the last two lines being similar in structure to those of the *cywydd* – and is arranged as in this **English** example by **Waldo Williams**:

> Yes, Idwal, it is oddish; – it is strange;
> It is true outlandish –
> Not a fowl nor yet a fish,
> An englyn writ in **English**.

The *englyn* is employed both individually and in sequences; or in association with other metres within an **awdl**. On account of its concision and tight construction, it has often been compared to the Japanese *haiku*. It is commonly used as an epitaph on gravestones, but it is a versatile form that may also be put to comic or satirical purposes. Unfortunately, as with other Welsh metres containing *cynghanedd*, the *englyn*'s aesthetic appeal is, comprehensively, lost in translation.

ENGLYNION Y BEDDAU
(the *englynion* of the graves)
A series of lyrical stanzas naming the burial places of the heroes of the Welsh people and of which the main collection, preserved in *The Black Book of Carmarthen*, dates from the 9th or 10th century.

ENLIGHTENMENT, The

A period, movement or intellectual tendency with roots in the 17th century. An indication of its attenuated influence on **Welsh**-speaking Wales is the absence of a settled name: *Yr Oleuedigaeth* (The Enlightenment), *Yr Oes Oleuedig* (The Age of Enlightenment) and *Yr Ymoleuo* (Self-enlightenment) all have their advocates.

Familiar factors account for its comparative failure to establish itself in Wales; the absence of towns, universities and libraries, or of a flourishing merchant **class**. Another explanation is suggested by the alternative term 'The Age of Reason', with its reference to the effects of the scientific spirit that arose in the 17th century in the wake of the work of Locke and Newton. Although the emphasis on experiment and questioning authority did not necessarily lead to deism (the chief enlightenment figures in **Scotland**, apart from Hume, were all clergymen), such tendencies were suspect in the eyes both of **Nonconformists** and of most of the leaders of the **Methodist Revival**. **Howel Harris** was notoriously hostile to reason, believing that, after the Fall, it had led humanity to disaster. Admittedly, **William Williams** (Pantycelyn; 1717–91) was more receptive to reason and to scientific investigation, but in general the ground was not welcoming. The **London** Welsh gave a better reception to the new ideas, exemplified by the experiments and hypotheses of Lewis Morris (*see* **Morris Brothers**).

A noteworthy aspect of the enlightened mind was the desire to perfect society by reason and toleration, with an optimistic belief in progress through **education** and equitable political arrangements. Two Welshmen extremely influential in this regard were **Richard Price** and **David Williams** (1738–1816), but their advocacy of freedom in matters of church and state was conducted outside Wales. Alongside them, however, a native **radicalism** arose in the Welsh countryside, as in the case of **William Jones** (1726–95), Llangadfan (**Banwy**), dubbed the Voltaire of Wales. In the same tradition as Richard Price was **Morgan John Rhys**, who championed freedom of thought and individual rights both in Wales and America, and who campaigned against **slavery**.

From being an attitude of mind aiming at gradual reform through reason, enlightenment had become much more radical by the end of the 18th century, partly under the influence of the French Revolution. In London, the raucous assaults on the established order by Jac Glan-y-gors (**John Jones**; 1766–1821), a follower of Tom Paine, contrasted with the relatively moderate attempts at reform of Sir **William Jones** (1746–94), 'the Orientalist'. In Wales, the desire for freedom in **religion** and politics together gave rise to protests against injustice and oppression by Dafis Castellhywel (David Davis; 1745–1827), Tomos Glyn Cothi (Thomas Evans; 1764–1833) and some of the **ballad**eers, although the onslaughts on representatives of authority by Twm o'r Nant (**Thomas Edwards**) were perhaps mainly personal.

EPISTOL AT Y CEMBRU
(An Epistle to the Welsh)
Written by Bishop **Richard Davies** (?1501–81), the letter prefaced the first **Welsh** translation of the New Testament (1567). It sought to provide an outline history of the Christian **religion** in Wales, and claimed that the country was first converted in apostolic times, when its faith was based on the authority of the scriptures. Later, Augustine of Canterbury brought a religion corrupted by papal superstition, which was forced on the Welsh at the point of the sword. The **Protestant Reformation**, Davies claimed, offered them the opportunity to restore Christianity in all its pristine purity.

ERBERY, William (1604–54) Puritan minister
Although he was the son of a **Cardiff** merchant and was educated at **Oxford** and **Cambridge**, Erbery showed more interest in the plight of poor people than any other leading Welsh **Puritan**. In the 1630s, he quarrelled with the bishop of Llandaff (*see* **Cardiff**) and resigned his living as vicar of the **parishes** of St Mary and St John, Cardiff. During the **Civil Wars** he served as a Parliamentary chaplain. He became a bitter foe of orthodox **Calvinists**, and eventually joined the Seekers, whose radical ideas threatened to turn the world upside down. The bulk of his written testimony was published posthumously in 1658.

ERBISTOCK (Erbistog), Wrexham
(1212 ha; 409 inhabitants)
Located on the north bank of the **Dee** south of **Wrexham**, the **community** contains two superb **river** bends and the site of what was for centuries one of the river's few safe ferry-crossing points. The red sandstone Boat Inn and St Hilary's

church (1861) form the attractive nucleus of the village, much of which has conservation status. The village hall was originally a school reputed to have been founded by **Richard Gwyn**, the **Catholic martyr** canonized in 1970. Adjoining Erbistock Hall (1720) is a large **dovecote** (1737). Eyton Manor Hall (*c.*1633) is a delightful timber-framed house.

ERGING Early kingdom

Erging, or Archenfield, was one of the kingdoms of early Wales, comprising the district – in present-day **Herefordshire** – between the Rivers Monnow and **Wye**, and probably named after the **Roman** settlement of Ariconium. In medieval times, it was the centre of the cult of **Dyfrig**, one of the earliest Welsh **saints**, and its communities were known for their skills with the **longbow**. The **Welsh language** was spoken in Erging until at least the 18th century.

ERSKINE, Joe (Joseph William; 1934–90) Boxer

Erskine of Tiger Bay (Butetown, **Cardiff**) was one of **Britain**'s top heavyweights in the 1950s and early 1960s, when that division was well stocked with fighters such as **Dick Richardson**, Henry Cooper and Brian London. Nimble-footed and skilful rather than a slugger, Erskine was British and Empire champion between 1956 and 1958. His lack of a knock-out punch disadvantaged him, not only against physically bigger opponents such as Niño Valdés, Ingemar Johansson and Karl Mildenberger, but also less scientific fighters like London and his constant rival Cooper – whom Erskine beat twice on points but who knocked him out on three other occasions.

ERWOOD (Erwd), Breconshire, Powys
(5070 ha; 401 inhabitants)

It was at Erwood that the **drovers**, coming down from **Mynydd Epynt**, crossed the **Wye** on their way to the fairs of **England**. Today, the Wye Valley Walk crosses the **river** a little further upstream. The hamlets of Crickadarn, Alltmawr, Gwenddwr and Llaneglwys cling to slopes that lead to the **community**'s open **mountain**side. St Mauritius, Alltmawr, is one of the smallest churches in Wales. There is a fine 15th-century porch at Crickadarn church, and near it stands Pool Hall, a mansion built in 1676. Gwenddwr was described by **Theophilus Jones** as 'a vile assemblage of huts'. The area around Llaneglwys has been extensively planted with conifers.

ESCLUSHAM, Wrexham
(1656 ha; 3401 inhabitants)

Located immediately south-west of **Wrexham**, the **community** contains Croes Foel, the site of the smithy of the **Davies family** of ironsmiths (*see also* **Ironwork**). Adjoining Croes Foel is Hafod-y-bwch, an expanded timber-framed hall house. Rhostyllen, a former mining village, is dominated by the large tip of the one-time **Bersham** Colliery. Its village hall (1924) and recreation grounds form an attractive village focal point. A **dovecote** (1721) survives in the grounds of the demolished Pentrebychan Hall, the site of Wrexham Crematorium. Plas Cadwgan, which had 14th-century origins, is a sad example of the demolition of a grade-one listed building. Its aisle truss hall was re-erected in Avoncroft Museum, Worcestershire. Plas Gronw

(demolished) was the home of Elihu **Yale** and of the sporting writer **C. J. Apperley** (Nimrod). The community contains a fine stretch of **Offa's Dyke**. There are numerous grouse butts on Esclusham **Mountain**.

ETIFEDDIAETH, YR (THE HERITAGE), 1949
Film

This documentary **film**, made in both **Welsh** and **English** versions, depicts life in rural Wales (**Llŷn** and **Eifionydd**) after the **Second World War**. Seen through the eyes of Freddie Grant, a black evacuee from **Liverpool**, it represents the finest screen record of a Welsh way of life that was fast disappearing. Premiered at the National **Eisteddfod** in 1949, it was made by the journalist **John Roberts Williams** and **Geoff Charles**, his photographer colleague on *Y Cymro*. Financed on expenses from the **newspaper**, the film took two years to make, shooting and editing at weekends. It owes much to Charles's sharp camerawork and admirable lighting.

EVANGELICAL MOVEMENT OF WALES, The

The movement had its roots in **Bangor** in the late 1940s. It is responsible for two periodicals – *Y Cylchgrawn Efengylaidd* (1948–) and *The Evangelical Magazine of Wales* (1957–) – and its press, Gwasg Bryntirion, publishes Christian **literature**, including *Christian **Hymns*** (1977), which has sold 120,000 copies. The movement also organizes conferences, camps and retreats. Its two centres are at Bryn-y-groes, **Bala**, and Bryntirion, **Bridgend**. The movement, which has no sympathy for ecumenicalism, stresses the final authority of the **Bible**, the need for **revival** and the centrality of personal conversion.

EVANS, Beriah Gwynfe (1848–1927)
Journalist and dramatist

It was as editor of the **periodical** *Cyfaill yr Aelwyd* (1880–91) that Evans, born at **Nantyglo**, came to prominence. Appointed manager of the *Genedl Gymreig* group in **Caernarfon** in 1892, and chief editor of its **newspapers**, he had considerable influence in promoting the career of **David Lloyd George**. He was also editor of *Y Tyst*, the **Congregationalist** weekly (1924–6). A pioneer of **Welsh drama**, his *Owain Glyndŵr* was performed at **Llanberis** in 1880 and at the investiture of the **Prince of Wales** in Caernarfon in 1911. In addition, his *Caradog* was performed at the Caernarfon National **Eisteddfod**, 1906. He was the first secretary of the **Society for the Utilization of the Welsh Language** and was also secretary of **Cymru Fydd**. His *Dafydd Dafis* (1898) is an appealing, political novel.

EVANS, [Richard] Charles (1918–95)
Mountaineer and university principal

Charles Evans came to prominence on the 1953 Everest expedition, as the first to reach the **mountain**'s South Peak, although complications with the oxygen equipment prevented him from reaching the summit. His most memorable climbing achievement was as leader of the successful 1955 expedition to Kanchenjunga – a far more difficult peak than Everest. His earliest climbs were in the **Aran** and **Berwyn** ranges, close to his birthplace at **Derwen**. Having initially embarked upon a career in medicine, in 1958 he became principal at **Bangor** (*see* **University of Wales,**

Bangor). There, his reluctance to further the role of **Welsh** in higher **education** – although Welsh was his mother tongue – led to a bitter confrontation in the 1970s.

EVANS, Christmas (1766–1838) Minister

With **John Elias** (1774–1841) and **William Williams** (1781–1840) of Wern, one-eyed Christmas Evans was a giant of the golden age of Welsh preaching (*see* **Preachers and Sermons**). Born at Esgair-wen, **Llandysul**, on Christmas Day 1766, he became a **farm labourer**. After undergoing conversion during a spiritual awakening at Llwynrhydowen (Llandysul), he became a **Baptist** and moved to the **Llŷn** peninsula, where he was ordained in 1789. It was there that he became the focus for the dynamic revivalism that transformed the older Dissenting Baptist movement.

Evans left to minister in **Anglesey** in 1791, remaining there until 1826, by which time his brand of explicit revivalism had created 'Nonconformist Wales'. He visited each of the Welsh **counties** on an annual and sometimes bi-annual preaching tour. After further periods of ministry at **Caerphilly**, **Cardiff** and finally at **Caernarfon**, he died at **Swansea** during a preaching tour.

EVANS, Clifford (1912–85) Actor

Born in Senghenydd (**Aber Valley**), Evans trained at RADA. Stage performances as Oswald in *Ghosts* (1937), Cassius in *Julius Caesar* (1943) and Ferdinand and Prospero in *The Tempest* (1943, 1951), established his reputation. In **film**, he was particularly impressive as the high-principled union firebrand in *Love on the Dole* (1941), at that time the most radical mainstream British film to have appeared. He made notable appearances in two films produced in Wales, *The Proud Valley* (1940), and the neglected comedy *Valley of Song* (1953), and he scripted Ealing's Welsh comedy *A Run For Your Money* (1949). High-profile

Clifford Evans (right) pictured with Roger Moore in an episode of the television series *The Saint* (1969)

roles included the lead in Cavalcanti's *The Foreman Went to France* (1941) and the title role in *Penn of Pennsylvania* (1941). Evans campaigned tirelessly, but in vain, for a Welsh National Theatre (*see* **Drama**).

EVANS, D[avid] Emlyn (1843–1913) Musician

An amateur musician born at **Newcastle Emlyn**, who contributed extensively to the congregational **hymn** singing and **eisteddfod** tradition, David Emlyn Evans edited hymnals and **music periodicals**, including *Y Cerddor*, and arranged many traditional airs. Celebrated as an adjudicator and for his vocal compositions, particularly in the field of sacred music, he wrote several hymn tunes that have remained popular.

EVANS, D[aniel] Simon (1921–98) Scholar

A native of **Llanfynydd**, **Carmarthenshire**, D. Simon Evans was an authority on medieval **Welsh** and its **literature**. Educated at **Swansea**, **Aberystwyth** and **Oxford**, he was professor of Welsh at Dublin (1952–62), head of **Celtic** Studies at **Liverpool** (1966–74) and professor of Welsh at **Lampeter** (1974–88). His *Gramadeg Cymraeg Canol* (1951) and the **English** version, *A Grammar of Middle Welsh* (1964), are still standard works in the field, and he displayed his usual meticulousness in other publications, such as his editions of two Middle Welsh texts, *Buched Dewi* (1959) (published in English as *The Life of St David* (1988)); and *Historia Gruffud vab Kenan* (1977). His brother, David Ellis Evans (b.1930), is also well-known in the field of Celtic studies; he was professor of Welsh at Swansea (1974–8) and professor of Celtic (1978–96) at Oxford.

EVANS, David (Caradoc Evans; 1878–1945) Author

One of the most controversial Welshmen of his time, Caradoc Evans was born at **Llanfihangel-ar-arth** and brought up at Rhydlewis (**Troedyraur**). At the age of 15, he was apprenticed to a draper in **Carmarthen** and later worked as a shop assistant in **Barry**, **Cardiff** and **London**, drawing on his miserable experience of the drapery trade in *Nothing to Pay* (1930), the first of his five novels.

From 1916 onwards, he worked as a journalist in London, and spent his last years in **Aberystwyth** and the nearby village of New Cross (**Trawsgoed**). It was as a writer of short stories that he won a reputation, which he assiduously cultivated, as 'the most unpopular man in Wales'. He published three collections, namely *My People* (1915), *Capel Sion* (1916) and *My Neighbours* (1919), in which he pilloried many aspects of Welsh rural life, such as Nonconformity (*see* **Nonconformists**), the **eisteddfod** and the **Welsh language** – his mother tongue. They present an unsparing picture of a brutish peasantry, a debased **religion** and a grudging **soil**, in which the characters are motivated by greed, hypocrisy and lust. Their prose style, a unique blend of the biblical and an outlandish **English** idiom of the author's own devising, is deliberately grotesque, and it offended many readers in Wales. His play *Taffy* received a similar response in London in 1923, when it was booed off the stage by an audience consisting mainly of London Welsh, who saw in it a libel of their homeland. Only since the 1970s has Caradoc Evans attracted the attention of

The home of Hedd Wyn (Ellis Humphrey Evans) with bardic chairs arranged outside

more sympathetic critics, who have recognized his perverse genius. He is now regarded by many as 'the father of the **Anglo-Welsh** short story'.

EVANS, [William] David (1912–85) Geologist
Educated at **Cardiff**, David Evans of **Caerphilly** became professor of **geology** at Nottingham University (1949–78). Among the projects of this original and inventive thinker was the mineralogical and geochemical survey of mine dust in the south Wales **coal**field and its relation to **pneumoconiosis**. He was ennobled in 1968 as Lord Energlyn of Caerphilly.

EVANS, David (Gwilym Lloyd) (1933–90) Cricketer
London-born, but **Ammanford**-raised, David Evans was **Glamorgan**'s safe but unobtrusive presence behind the stumps for most of the 1960s. He was later a leading umpire, standing in nine test matches – starting with the so-called 'Botham's Test' at Headingley in 1981.

EVANS, Edgar (1876–1912) Explorer
Born at **Rhossili** in **Gower**, Evans took part in Captain Scott's two expeditions to the Antarctic, the second of which left **Cardiff** on the *Terra Nova* in 1910. The five-man team died on their way back to base camp, having found they had been beaten to the South Pole by the Norwegian Roald Amundsen. Freak weather conditions of –34°C combined with exhaustion and frostbite to cause their deaths. Evans, praised by Scott as 'a giant worker with a really remarkable headpiece', was buried at the foot of Beardmore Glacier, and is commemorated by a tablet in Rhossili church.

EVANS, Elin or Elinor (Elen Egryn; 1807–76)
Poet
Elin Evans learned to compose poetry as a child in **Llanegryn**. She moved to **Liverpool** in 1840, and in 1850, by which time she had returned to her native district, she published *Telyn Egryn*, an important volume of her poems, reflecting the experience of exile. It became a milestone in Welsh **women**'s **literature** and was held by Ieuan Gwynedd (**Evan Jones**) to represent a refutation of the aspersions against Welsh womanhood of the 1847 Education Report (*see* **Treason of the Blue Books**).

EVANS, Ellis Humphrey (Hedd Wyn; 1887–1917)
Poet
A shepherd on his father's farm of Yr Ysgwrn, **Trawsfynydd**, Evans joined the army in 1917 (*see* **First World War**). He had no chance to mature as a poet, but a few lyrics such as 'Dim ond lleuad borffor' and 'Gwae fi fy myw' have caught the imagination of the Welsh people.

Not a willing soldier, he was killed in the battle of Pilkem Ridge, about a month after sailing to France on 31 July 1917. His long, strict-metre poem – ironically entitled 'Yr Arwr' (The Hero) – was declared winner in the Birkenhead National **Eisteddfod** in September of the same year. The chair was draped in black and the event was known ever afterwards as the 'Eisteddfod of the Black Chair'. **R. Williams Parry** wrote a deeply sorrowful elegy for him; and **J. J. Williams** edited the collection of his poems *Cerddi'r Bugail* (1918). His story is told in Paul Turner's **film** *Hedd Wyn* (scripted by Alan Llwyd), which was nominated in 1994 for an Oscar as Best Foreign Film.

EVANS, [David] Emrys (1891–1966)
Scholar and educationist

Sir Emrys Evans, a native of **Clydach**, was educated at **Bangor** and at **Oxford**. He became first professor of classics at **Swansea**. From there, in 1927, he returned to Bangor as principal (*see* **University of Wales, Bangor**). He is chiefly remembered for his dignified translations into **Welsh** of six of Plato's works, including *The Republic* (1956).

As vice chancellor of the **University of Wales**, he was responsible for setting up the 1933 university committee which paved the way for the establishment of the Welsh Region of the BBC (*see* **Broadcasting**). It was probably his direct influence that ensured the choice of Bangor as the centre of the Corporation's northern operations in Wales. His 1941 article in *Y Llenor*, attacking the anti-war policy of **Plaid [Genedlaethol] Cymru**, led to a major controversy.

EVANS, Evan (Ieuan Fardd or Ieuan Brydydd Hir; 1731–88) Poet and scholar

Born in **Lledrod**, Ieuan Evans was set on his way by Lewis Morris (*see* **Morris Brothers**), who had settled in **Cardiganshire** in 1746. He became a skilled poet in the strict metres and the greatest authority of his time on **Welsh** manuscript collections. He won the approbation of both Welsh and English scholars upon the publication of his pioneering work *Some Specimens of the Poetry of the Antient Welsh Bards* (1764). He also campaigned against the practice of appointing monoglot English bishops in Wales and published an **English** poem, *The Love of our Country* (1772), which sought to refute attacks on Welsh history and culture. For this reason, together with his excessive love of drink, he never advanced beyond the status of curate. A more bitter, personal disappointment was his failure to win the essential patronage to publish the contents of the medieval manuscripts, an aim that had been his life-long dream.

EVANS, Evan (Ieuan Glan Geirionydd; 1795–1855)
Poet

The most versatile poet of 19th-century Wales, **Trefriw**-born Evan Evans was a schoolmaster before his ordination in 1826; he held various curacies in **Cheshire** until his retirement in 1852 to Trefriw. He won early fame as a chaired **eisteddfod** poet; but his best-known victory was winning the chair in the controversial **Rhuddlan** Eisteddfod of 1850, with a *pryddest* rather than an *awdl*. He and Alun (**John Blackwell**) were precursors of the lyrical movement in secular Welsh poetry. As a critic, he emphasized the superiority of the free metres. Several of his lyrics and **hymns** have stood the test of time.

EVANS, [Evan] Eynon (1904–89)
Playwright and actor

The homely comedies and **dramas** of the former **Caerphilly** bus driver Eynon Evans were a staple of Welsh **English-language** radio and repertory theatre in the years immediately after the **Second World War**. Born in **Nelson, Glamorgan**, Evans was best known, however, for his contributions as Tommy Trouble on radio's *Welsh Rarebit* in the 1950s. He scripted two feature **film** adaptations of his stage work: *The Happiness of Three Women* (1954) – from his 1946 stage play *Wishing Well* – and *Room in the House* (1955) – from his play *Bless This House* (1954); and he starred in the first of these films. He also played Gwilym Morgan in the first BBC television version of *How Green Was My Valley* (1960).

EVANS, George Ewart (1909–88)
Writer and oral historian

A native of **Abercynon**, George Ewart Evans spent most of his life in East Anglia, where he worked in adult **education**. His many books about country lore – which include *Ask the Fellows who Cut the Hay* (1956), *From Mouths of Men* (1976), *The Pattern under the Plough* (1966) and *Spoken History* (1987) – established him as a key figure in the development of oral history. Although he wrote chiefly about East Anglia, he returned to his roots in industrial Wales in some of his more creative and autobiographical works.

EVANS, Geraint [Llewellyn] (1922–91) Opera singer

Born at Cilfynydd (**Pontypridd**), Geraint Evans came to prominence as a singer in 1948 after joining Covent Garden and making his debut as the character of the Nightwatchman in Wagner's *Die Meistersinger*. He sang Figaro soon afterwards, repeating the role for Herbert von Karajan at La Scala, Milan.

He became a much-loved figure in all the world's major opera houses. Knighted in 1969, he was widely regarded as one of the great singing actors of his era – particularly as Falstaff, a role ideally suited to his theatrical skills. He is commemorated by the Heart Research Institute at **Cardiff** and by the sports centre at **Aberaeron**, where he spent his retirement.

EVANS, Griffith (1835–1935) Bacteriologist

Tywyn-born Griffith Evans was commissioned as a veterinary surgeon in the Royal Artillery in 1860. While a serving officer in 1864, he qualified in medicine at McGill University, Montreal. Soon after, posted to India, in 1880 he demonstrated that *Trypanosoma evansi* was the causative organism of the disease of **horses** called 'surra'. He is now recognized as a pioneer of 'germ theory', which postulated the specific nature of the bacterial cause of disease – a concept hotly disputed in his time and for quite some time later. Sir William Osler felt that Griffith Evans's name should rank among the great pioneers of tropical medicine.

EVANS, Gwynfor [Richard] (1912–2005)
Politician, pacifist, writer and market gardener

The greatest patriot of 20th-century Wales, his dedication to his country did much to transform the national prospects of the Welsh people. The son of the owner of **Barry**'s only department store, he was educated at Barry Grammar School, **Aberystwyth** and **Oxford**. By the late 1930s, he was one of Wales's leading pacifists (*see* **Pacifism**). On the outbreak of the **Second World War**, the Conscientious Objection Tribunal granted him unconditional exemption from military service. He abandoned a career in **law** and became a market **garden**er at **Llangadog** (**Carmarthenshire**).

During his period at Aberystwyth, he fell in love with Wales and learned (or perhaps regained a knowledge of) the **Welsh language.** He joined **Plaid [Genedlaethol] Cymru,** and

during the difficult war years became one of its leading pro-
pagandists. In 1945, he was elected president of the party,
an office he held until 1981. Perhaps his most significant
work was done in the late 1940s and the 1950s, when,
through hugely strenuous efforts and inspired by a passionate vision, he turned Plaid Cymru into a credible electoral
force. Proof of his success in building up the party was its
ability to field candidates in 20 of Wales's 36 constituencies
in the general election of 1959 (an election in which the SNP
was able to field candidates in only 5 of **Scotland**'s 72 constituencies). His leadership on the issue of the drowning of
the **Tryweryn Valley** was particularly tireless, although it
brought his party little immediate electoral advantage.

In 1966, after unsuccessfully fighting six parliamentary
elections, he won the **Carmarthen** by-election gaining a
majority of 2436 over the **Labour** candidate, Gwilym Prys
Davies, who had in the 1940s been prominent in the Welsh
Republican Movement. The by-election was widely seen as
a turning point in Welsh history and proved a major stimulus to a wide variety of national movements. Defeated by
3907 votes in 1970, he stood again in the February election
of 1974, when the majority against him was merely 3.

Re-elected with a majority of 3640 in the October election of 1974, he was defeated in 1979 and again in 1983.
During his first period at Westminster, he asked a host of
parliamentary questions and, on the basis of the answers,
published critical analyses of the **government** of Wales.
During his second period, there were three Plaid Cymru
members at Westminster; in addition, there were 11 SNP
members, all of whom held him in high regard. Indeed, in
some quarters, he was hailed as the leader of the third force
in British politics. The weakness of the Labour government
of 1974 to 1979 gave the Plaid Cymru group considerable
leverage, a situation he skilfully exploited, particularly in
relation to **devolution**. The massive defeat of the Labour
government's policy of a **National Assembly** for Wales in
the devolution referendum of 1979 was an outcome that he
viewed as the nadir of his career.

He was further devastated by the announcement in
September 1979 that the newly elected **Conservative** government had decided not to honour its pledge to establish
a Welsh-language television channel (*see* **Broadcasting** and
S4C). On 5 May 1980, he announced that he would fast
unto death if the decision were not reversed. During the
summer of 1980, he addressed a large number of meetings
which were remarkable for their emotional intensity. The
government yielded on 17 September, the only occasion (it
was widely claimed) that Margaret Thatcher did actually
make a U-turn.

In addition to his services to Plaid Cymru, Gwynfor
Evans wrote prolifically on the history of Wales; served as
president of the Union of Welsh Independents (*see*
Congregationalists); was active in the anti-nuclear movement; visited south-east Asia in the hope of ending the war
in Vietnam; and sought to bridge the divide between Welsh-
speaking communities and non-Welsh-speaking incomers.

The father of seven children, he wished to create the
ideal of a Welsh family. Personable and gentlemanly, he
had a tenacity which some saw as steely resolution and others as wilful obstinacy. His funeral at Aberystwyth is the
nearest Wales has seen to a true state occasion.

Gwynfor Evans

EVANS, J[ohn] Gwenogfryn (1852–1930)
Palaeographer
Born at Ffynnon-felfed, **Llanybydder**, and raised in
Llanwenog, Evans had a short career as a **Unitarian** minister, prior to making a substantial contribution to Welsh
scholarship. Under the influence of **John Rhŷs** at **Oxford**,
he taught himself to read old **Welsh** manuscripts and
established the ambitious *Old Welsh Texts* series.
Appointed an inspector for the Historical Manuscripts
Commission in 1894, he travelled extensively to inspect
private collections of Welsh manuscripts; his detailed
reports on the contents of the collections, issued between
1898 and 1910, provided an important foundation for
modern Welsh scholarship. He was prominent in the
movement to establish the **National Library of Wales**, and
was substantially responsible for ensuring that the most
important Welsh literary manuscripts were entrusted to its
care. His relationship with contemporary Welsh scholars
was often difficult. As a consequence, his contribution was
not fully acknowledged.

EVANS, John (1723–95) Cartographer
John Evans, of Llanymynech (**Carreghofa**), is known for
his published engravings and two major **maps** of north
Wales. His map of 1795, issued in nine sheets, was the best
and largest of the region before the publication of the
1-inch to 1-mile sheets of the Ordnance Survey. It was significant because of its pleasing appearance and the amount
and accuracy of its detail.

EVANS, John [Thomas] (1770–99) Explorer
Evans's life is vivid testimony to the power with which
some Welsh imaginations were captivated during the 1790s
by the legend that **Madog ab Owain Gwynedd** settled in
North America *c.*1170.

Richard Evans, the Moelfre lifeboatman

Born at **Waunfawr**, the impulsive but intrepid Evans became convinced it was God's will that he should search for the supposed 'Welsh Indians'. These were reputedly the descendants of Madog, by then believed to be the Mandan tribe that inhabited the upper reaches of the Missouri **river**. Evans arrived in America in October 1792 and reached the Mandans in September 1796, while in the service of the Spanish **government** (most of the American West was claimed by Spain at that time). Ultimately, his conclusion that the Mandans were not the Welsh Indians broke his health and led to his early death in New Orleans. He was only the second white person to have travelled up the Missouri to nearly 2900 km above its confluence with the Mississippi, and the first to draw a **map** of the area. His sketches, notes and map were of vital importance to subsequent explorers.

EVANS, [Evan] Keri (1860–1941)
Philosopher and minister
A native of **Llandyfriog**, he was initially an apprentice carpenter. He later attended **Carmarthen Presbyterian** College and Glasgow University, where he became assistant to Edward Caird, a pioneer of Philosophical Idealism in **Britain**. Professor of **philosophy** at Bangor (1891–6), he became a **Congregationalist** minister in 1897. A faithful follower of Caird, the burden of his striking religious message, embodied in *Fy Mhererindod Ysbrydol* (My Spiritual Pilgrimage) (1938), was the importance of knowing Christ rather than dogma.

EVANS, Kitty (fl.1920s) Irish revolutionary
Kitty Evans of **Merthyr Tydfil**, a member of a conspiracy in south Wales to send arms to **Irish** republican forces, was imprisoned in April 1922 for possession of explosives. Prominent Irish **republicans** Maud Gonne and Hannah Sheehy Skeffington campaigned for her release.

EVANS, Margaret (Marged uch Ifan; 1695–?1801)
Amazonian
If her date of death is correct, Marged vch Ifan lived in three centuries, but even more awe-inspiring are the tales of her physical exploits as recorded by **Thomas Pennant** and others. She lived at Penllyn (**Llanddeiniolen**), at the lower end of Llyn Padarn (*see* **Lakes**), and was a competent blacksmith, shoemaker and carpenter. According to the **English** verse on her grave, which calls her Peggy Evans, she could also 'wrestle, row, fiddle, and hunt a **fox** too'. There is another tradition that her husband agreed to marry her after she beat him, and that after a second beating he gave up drinking and became prominent with the local Methodists.

EVANS, Rhys (Arise; fl.1607–60) Prognosticator
This bizarre self-styled prophet was born in **Llangelynin**, **Merioneth**. During his apprenticeship with a tailor in **Wrexham**, he began to experience visions. Evans developed an inflated view of his own importance (he came to call himself Arise) and, having moved to **London**, he visited the great and the good to apprise them of his political prognostications. He became a figure of fun in the 1650s for predicting confidently the precise date of the return of the monarchy. Remarkably, he lived to see his prophecy come true; and his regard for the crown knew no bounds when the royal touch, in the person of Charles II, cured a hideously scrofulous growth on Evans' nose.

EVANS, Richard (1905–2001) Lifeboatman
One of only five men to be awarded two gold medals by the Royal National **Lifeboat** Institution – the equivalent of the Victoria Cross for outstanding bravery at sea – Evans was born and lived at **Moelfre**, **Anglesey**. He joined the crew of the Moelfre lifeboat in 1921 at the age of 16, becoming coxswain in 1954; by 1970, when he retired, the lifeboat had been launched 179 times, saving 281 lives.

EVANS, Roy and Nancy (1909–98 and 1903–98)
Table tennis players
Cardiff-born Roy and Nancy Evans, who married in 1933, were world leaders in **table tennis**. He played for Wales at the international level in the early 1930s and she was world ranked number seven in 1938; both held prominent positions, nationally and internationally, in numerous sports organizations, and he was personally responsible, after 10 years of negotiation, for the acceptance of table tennis into the Olympic Games programme in 1988.

He is best remembered as the Welshman behind the 1971 'ping-pong diplomacy' that broke political deadlock between China and the United States. As president of the International Table Tennis Federation, he managed to persuade premier Chou En-Lai to invite Western teams to visit China – including, to his surprise, the American team. This is believed to have paved the way for President Nixon's ground-breaking visit to China the following year.

EVANS, S[amuel] T[homas] (1859–1918) Politician
A fervent and outspoken radical, Evans was elected **Liberal** MP for Mid **Glamorgan** in 1890. *The South Wales Daily News* considered him 'a little too impetuous and militant at times', and prophesied that, in time, 'cool judgement will

restrain impetuous courage.' Evans ended his career on the bench and was one of the foremost architects of British prize **law**.

EVANS, Theophilus (1693–1767) Historian
Born at Penywenallt, Llandygwydd (*see* **Beulah**), Evans spent most of his career as vicar of **Llangamarch**. He is chiefly remembered for his *Drych y Prif Oesoedd* (1716, 1740), a biased but enjoyable account of the early history of Wales which is regarded as a classic of **Welsh** prose style. He is reputed to have discovered the medicinal properties of the **wells** at **Llanwrtyd**. He was a grandfather of **Theophilus Jones**, historian of **Breconshire**, and an ancestor of Sophie, countess of Wessex.

EVANS, Timothy John (1924–50)
Victim of injustice
Merthyr Tydfil-born Timothy Evans is one of the most infamous 20th-century examples of a man hanged for a murder of which he was innocent. In 1949, he was accused of the murder of both his wife and baby with whom he was living in rooms at 10 Rillington Place, **London**, and was convicted of murdering the baby. The chief prosecution witness at Evans's trial was his landlord, John Reginald Halliday Christie, who later confessed to murdering six women. After Christie was executed, Evans was given a royal pardon. Nevertheless, it was not until 2004, after a long campaign by his family, that he was declared by two High Court judges to have been innocent of both crimes.

EVANS, Will (1888–1957) Artist
The painter of **Swansea**'s blitz began his working life as a **tinplate** printer. Born at Waun Wen, Swansea, Evans studied **painting** part-time during his seven-year apprenticeship, winning a free scholarship to Swansea School of Art, where he later taught. His popular, naturalistic work reflected an interest in his home town and its surroundings.

EVANS, William (1895–1988) Cardiologist
One of the most eminent cardiologists of his generation, Evans was born in **Tregaron** and educated at **Aberystwyth** and the **London** Hospital medical school. He became a consulting physician to the cardiac department at the London Hospital, the National Heart Hospital, London, and the Institute of Cardiology, London. He published 100 papers on cardiology and several textbooks.

EVANS, William Charles (1911–88) Biochemist
A stonemason's son from Bethel (**Llanddeiniolen**), Evans graduated in **chemistry** at **Bangor** and in physiology at Manchester, becoming a pioneer biochemist. After working on medical research in **London**, he lectured in

Will Evans, *Temple Street, Swansea, 1941*, portraying the town centre after the Blitz

agricultural chemistry at **Aberystwyth**, returning to Bangor in 1951 as professor in what became the department of biochemistry and **soil science**. His special interests were the biodegradation of toxic chemicals. Assisted by his wife Antice, he worked upon the cause of bracken disease in **cattle**.

EVANS, William Davies (1790–1872)
Seafarer and inventor
Renowned in **chess** circles as inventor of the Evans gambit, this sea captain from St Dogwells, **Wolfscastle**, is celebrated also in the nautical world. For his invention of the system of tri-coloured lighting for **ships**, designed to prevent collisions at night, the British **government** awarded him £1500, and the Tsar of Russia gave him a gold pocket chronometer and £200. He is buried in the Belgian port of Ostende.

EVANS-JONES, Albert (Cynan; 1895–1970)
Poet and dramatist
'The lad from the town of **Pwllheli**', as Cynan styled himself, graduated at **Bangor** and became a **Calvinistic Methodist** minister at **Penmaenmawr**, before being appointed to the department of extra-mural studies at Bangor. His experience as a soldier and chaplain during the **First World War** inspired some of his poems. The long, free-metre poem 'Mab y Bwthyn' – about a young man confronting worldly temptations as he serves in the army abroad – won him the National **Eisteddfod** crown in 1921.

George Everest, geodetic surveyor of the world's highest mountain

He won his second crown in 1923 for 'Yr Ynys Unig', and his third for 'Y Dyrfa' (1931), which concerns John Roberts, the **rugby** player turned **missionary**. A collection of his poems, *Cerddi Cynan*, appeared in 1959. His plays include *Hywel Harris* (1932) and *Absalom fy Mab* (1957), and he published one short novel, *Ffarwel Weledig* (1946). As **Archdruid** of the **Gorsedd** of Bards (1950–4, 1963–6), he cut a striking figure, and did much to streamline the Gorsedd pageantry. He was knighted in 1969.

EVEREST, George (1790–1866) Surveyor
Born in Gwernvale (**Crickhowell**), Everest won such distinction as a geodetic surveyor that the world's highest **mountain** was named after him. Between 1816 and 1843, during which time he became surveyor-general of India, Everest and his team measured the meridional arc of India, from Cape Comorin to the northern border.

EWENNY (Ewenni), Vale of Glamorgan
(1213 hectares; 682 inhabitants)
Located south of **Bridgend**, the **community**'s great glory is the church of its **Benedictine** priory, Wales's finest example of Romanesque **architecture**. The priory was founded before 1126 by William de Londres, lord of **Ogmore**. He granted it to St Peter's Abbey, Gloucester, whose abbot advised Ewenny's monks 'to strengthen the locks of your doors and surround your house with a good ditch and an impregnable wall' – proof of the suspicion of the Welsh harboured by the pioneers of the first phase of **Latin** monasticism in Wales. His advice was taken, although the impressive precinct walls now visible date from the 14th century.

The most memorable part of the church is the vaulted presbytery, modelled upon St Peter's, Gloucester; it is the subject of a painting by **Turner**. Essentially, the nave, which has probably always been the **parish** church, is a separate building and has a particularly fine northern arcade. There are several tombs in the south transept, among them those of members of the Carne family, who – following the **dissolution of the monasteries** – adapted the conventual buildings as a mansion. The mansion was rebuilt in the Regency style in 1805.

The Ewenny ware (*see* **Pottery and Porcelain**) produced in the village potteries provided kitchen utensils for much of **Glamorgan**. Edward Matthews (Matthews Ewenni) was from 1852 to 1864 minister of Ewenny **Calvinistic Methodist** chapel. His dramatic sermons, delivered in his lively **Vale of Glamorgan Welsh**, delighted congregations throughout Wales. The attractive Gothic school at Corntown was designed by **John Prichard**.

EWIAS Commote and lordship
Ewias was the northernmost **commote** of **Gwent** and included much of the **Black Mountains**. In the late 11th century, it came into the possession of the **Lacy family**. It later passed to the **Mortimers** and from them to the dukes of **York** and thus to the crown. The **Acts of 'Union'** divided the lordship between **Monmouthshire** and **Herefordshire**. That part of Ewias which is in Wales is roughly coterminous with the **community** of **Crucorney**, which includes the delectable Vale of Ewias.

J. M. W. Turner, *Ewenny Priory* (*c.*1797)

EXECUTIONS

The notion that it was only after the imposition of English **law** that courts in Wales sentenced criminals to death is mistaken. Although the *galanas* system (*see* **Law**) laid down that a murderer – and his kin – should compensate the kin of the victim, hanging was the punishment for some forms of robbery, considered to be the most heinous of crimes. This is reflected in the hilarious attempt of **Manawydan** in *The Mabinogion* to hang a mouse which had stolen grain.

Llywelyn ap Iorwerth's hanging of William de **Breos** in 1230 for excessive intimacy with **Joan**, Llywelyn's wife, was a particularly defiant act. More savage was the punishment imposed by Edward I upon **Dafydd ap Llywelyn** in 1283. Convicted of treason, Dafydd was dragged by a horse through the streets of Shrewsbury; he was then half hanged and disembowelled before his body was hacked into four pieces for display around the kingdom. The insurgent, **Rhys ap Maredudd**, suffered a similar fate in York in 1292. A further political execution was that of **Llywelyn Bren** in Cardiff in 1317.

Following the **Edwardian conquest** and the **Statute of Rhuddlan** (1284), English criminal law, with its more severe punishments, was enforced in the **Principality**. However, in the **March**, elements of the law of **Hywel Dda** survived. Yet, even there, the Welsh were becoming increasingly subject to English law, as can be seen from **Dafydd ap Edmwnd**'s powerful elegy to Siôn Eos, a **harp**ist from **Chirk**, who was hanged for accidentally killing a man.

There was also the remarkable case of William Grach of **Gower**, a notorious outlaw, who had reputedly murdered 13 men. Although his relations insisted on paying *galanas*, he was hanged in **Swansea** in 1290. Removed from the gibbet, he gradually revived, because, it was claimed, of the miraculous intercession of a deceased bishop of Hereford, Thomas de Cantilupe (d.1282).

Between 1534 and 1543, at the time of the **Acts of 'Union'**, **Rowland Lee**, the president of the **Council of Wales and the Marches,** claimed to have hanged some 5000 people in his campaign to eliminate chronic disorder. Between 1542 and 1679, there were a number of executions for heresy and/or treason (*see* **Catholic Martyrs** and **Protestant Martyrs**).

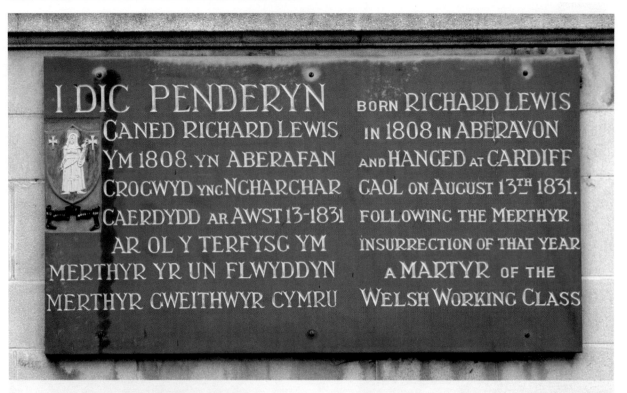

The plaque at Merthyr Tydfil commemorating the hanging of Richard Lewis (Dic Penderyn) at Cardiff in 1831

The Acts of 'Union' brought legal uniformity to Wales. During the heyday of the 'Bloody Code' in the 18th century, there were hundreds of capital offences, although many convicted criminals were transported rather than hanged. The number of executions in Wales was proportionately small compared with that in **England**, and the majority were for murder. Reform of the criminal law in the 19th century restricted capital punishment, and the number of executions fell to one or two a year. The **ballads** of the period are evidence of the public's obsessive interest in them and the most famous hanging in 19th-century Wales was that of Dic Penderyn (**Richard Lewis**) in **Cardiff** in 1831.

The last public execution in Wales took place outside Swansea **prison** in April 1866, when Robert Coe was hanged for murder. A further 48 executions took place inside Welsh prisons between 1868 and 1958.

The last **woman** hanged in Wales was Leslie James, who was convicted of suffocating another woman's baby. She was executed at Cardiff on 24 August 1907. The last man was Vivian Teed, hanged at Swansea for the murder of an elderly sub-postmaster during a burglary on 6 May 1958.

Capital punishment was suspended in Wales and in the rest of **Britain** in 1964, and abolished in 1969.

The Falklands War included the attack on HMS *Sir Galahad* in which 32 Welsh Guards lost their lives

FAENOR (Y Faenor), Ceredigion
(632 ha; 2422 inhabitants)

Located immediately north-east of **Aberystwyth**, the **community** contains the villages of Comins Coch and Waun Fawr, both essentially suburbs of Aberystwyth. Lovesgrove was once the centre of a small estate owned by a branch of the Pugh family.

FAGGOTS

Faggots were a favourite seasonal dish prepared by rural housewives following the slaughter of a **pig**. Minced liver and pork fat were combined with breadcrumbs, sage and seasoning. A tablespoonful of this mixture, wrapped in the stomach lining of the pig, formed a faggot. Placed side-by-side in a large roasting tin, the faggots were cooked in a moderately hot oven. They were traditionally served cold with bread and butter for a dinner or supper snack, or hot with peas and gravy.

FALKLANDS (MALVINAS) WAR, The

The Falkland (or Malvinas in Spanish) Islands in the South Atlantic, initially seized by **Britain** in 1833, were invaded by Argentina on 2 April 1982. A British task force set sail in response.

Following air and sea attacks on Argentine vessels and positions, British forces landed on 21 May and after a succession of land battles, the Argentinian forces surrendered on 14 June.

The **Welsh Guards**, part of the 5th Infantry Brigade, were attacked by Argentine aircraft whilst waiting in the unprotected landing vessel HMS *Sir Galahad* at Fitzroy, en route for Bluff Cove. In the attack, 48 soldiers were killed, 32 of whom were members of the Welsh Guards; a further 150 Welsh Guardsmen were injured. Television footage of the badly burned victims aroused serious consternation and calls (which remained unanswered) for a full-scale inquiry.

The conflict led to a marked revival in the political fortunes of the **Conservative Party** under Margaret Thatcher's leadership (in Wales as much as across Britain), and to the dissemination of often unseemly British nationalist propaganda. The war was opposed by **Plaid [Genedlaethol] Cymru** and by minor left groups, while the **Labour Party** supported the recapture of the islands.

Longstanding Welsh links to **Patagonia** added poignancy to the conflict. Eluned Phillips (b.1915) expresses such feelings in 'Clymau', the poem which won her the crown in the National **Eisteddfod** in 1983. The

'Tonypandy Titan' heavyweight champion Tommy Farr (left) meets ex-cruiserweight world champion Tommy Loughran, 16 January 1936

poet Tony Conran (b.1931) viewed the war with controlled fury in his memorable 'Elegy for the Welsh Dead, in the Falkland Islands, 1982'.

FARMERS' UNIONS and ORGANIZATIONS

From the end of the 19th century, the prosperity of **agriculture** in Wales became increasingly dependent upon political developments beyond the control of individual farmers. As a result, organizations were founded which would safeguard the interests of farmers as a whole, a development much encouraged by the fears aroused by the increasing radicalism of **agricultural workers**. In the early 20th century, such local organizations came into existence in **Cardiganshire**, **Caernarfonshire** and **Flintshire**.

The National Farmers' Union (NFU) of **England** and Wales was founded in 1908, although it was not until 1932 that its first Welsh president was elected. There was an attempt in 1917 to establish a specifically Welsh union with the foundation at **Llanrwst** of the National Union of the Farmers of Wales. That union joined with the local societies in 1919. However, these initiatives proved unsuccessful and the Welsh union was obliged to merge with the NFU in 1921, on the understanding that the NFU would include a Welsh committee.

The NFU became very influential during the **Second World War** and its immediate aftermath, a period of **food** shortages. (Its membership peaked at 200,000 in 1949.) NFU policies at that time tended to favour large-scale arable producers in England and did little for the family farm in Wales. In 1955, the long-running 'corn versus horn' argument came to a head when a group of Welsh farmers – from Carmarthenshire in particular – formed the Farmers' Union of Wales. Within the agricultural community, the coming of the FUW caused divisions and debates worthy of

19th-century denominational conflict at its most fierce. For the rest of the century, the two unions existed in uneasy parallel, with every effort to merge them ending in failure.

By the early 21st century, the impact of the European Union's Common Agricultural Policy and the coming of **devolution** led to the decline in the importance of the British dimension. NFU Wales came to act independently of **London** in its dealings with the **National Assembly for Wales**. In 2007, it became a virtually independent organization, opening up at last the possibility that it would join the Farmers' Union of Wales in a single body.

Apart from the main unions, the Country Landowners Association, founded in 1907, was also active in Wales. By the early 21st century, that organization had been renamed the Country Land and Business Association. The Countryside Alliance, founded in 1997, has won considerable support in rural Wales.

FARR, Tommy (Thomas George Farr; 1914–86)
Boxer

Born into poverty in Tonypandy, **Rhondda**, Tommy Farr was forced to leave school at 12 years of age. His **boxing** career began in the fight booths, and success as a professional was slow in coming. Although he took the Welsh light heavyweight title in 1933, he lost three times to Eddie Phillips in 1934–5. His year of triumph was 1937.

With his crouching style and hard left jabs followed by two-fisted attack, he defeated Ben Foord for the British and Empire heavyweight title in March. A month later, jabbing, crouching and dancing, he out-pointed former world heavyweight champion Max Baer and in June he destroyed Walter Neusel in three rounds. In New York in August, he faced Joe Louis, who was making his first defence of the world heavyweight title he had taken from

James J. Braddock. The thousands listening at home heard the champion being pushed all the way to a hard-earned points victory, as Farr became one of only three ever to go the distance with 'the Brown Bomber'. His plucky fight, in its heroic defeat, can be seen as emblematic of **coal**field society during the **Depression**. His two sons won fame in the pop music business of the late 1960s.

FAWCKNER, J[ames] Follett (1828–98) Architect

A native of Devon, Fawckner was articled to W. G. Habershon, **London**, before being sent to open an office in **Newport**, in 1857, to carry out work for Lord Tredegar (*see* **Morgan family**). On the death of Habershon in 1891, the London office was closed and work was concentrated in **Cardiff** and Newport. In addition to estate **housing** (such as Tredegarville, Cardiff), Fawckner was responsible for many chapels in **Glamorgan** and **Monmouthshire**. His additional commercial work included the Mansion House (1891) and the Park Hotel (1884) in Cardiff.

FELINFACH (Felin-fach), Breconshire, Powys (5492 ha; 585 inhabitants)

An extensive **community** straddling the **A470** north-east of **Brecon**. Llanfilo has a fine church with a sensitively restored early 16th-century rood screen. Tredomen was long the home of the Awbrey family. There is a large church at Llandefalle, but no village. Trebarried, a recently restored mid-17th-century mansion, was once the home of a branch of the Vaughan family and is connected by tradition with **Shakespeare** and *A Midsummer Night's Dream*. The church at Llandefaelog Tre'r Graig contains monuments to the Parry family. Blanch Parry, high sheriff of **Breconshire** in 1619, was the godson of **Blanche Parry**, Elizabeth I's maid of honour.

FELINHELI, Y, Gwynedd (590 ha; 2081 inhabitants)

Located on the **Menai Strait**, midway between **Bangor** and **Caernarfon**, the **community**'s name means a **mill** powered by salt water. It was the **Caernarfonshire** end of the Moel-y-don ferry to **Anglesey**, and may be the place from which the **Romans** crossed to Anglesey in AD 61 to destroy the power of the **druids**. In the 1790s, it acquired a quay from which **slate** from the Dinorwic Quarry (**Llanddeiniolen**) was exported, a development that gave rise to the name Port Dinorwic. In 1825, the quay was linked to the quarry by **railway**, the property – as were the quay, the later dock and the slate-carrying **ships** – of the **Assheton Smith family** of Vaynol (**Pentir**).

The dock has been converted into a marina and Plas Menai is a striking modern building which houses the Welsh National Watersports Centre. Near the centre are the medieval church of Llanfair-is-gaer and Llanfair Hall (originally *c.*1700). The Friction Dynamics (formerly Ferrodo) factory, long the scene of an industrial dispute, closed in 2006.

FELLOWSHIP OF RECONCILIATION, The

A fellowship of Christian pacifists and the main focus for **pacifism** among the Welsh churches during the 20th century. The society was established in **Cambridge** in late 1914, and in Wales almost immediately afterwards. The most active Welsh branches were at **Wrexham** and **Bangor**, where inveterate opponents of the **First World War** – among them **J. Puleston Jones** and **Thomas Rees** (1869–1926) – published the journal *Y Deyrnas* to publicize the Fellowship's ideals. By the 1930s, with another international conflagration looming, the Fellowship attracted such influential new recruits as **Gwynfor Evans**. A **Welsh-language** group associated with it (**Cymdeithas Heddychwyr Cymru**) published 31 pamphlets between 1937 and 1945.

FENCING

Although fencing developed as a sport in the 19th century, it was not until 1947 that the Welsh section of the Amateur Fencing Association came into being. Fencing developed rapidly after a visit to **Cardiff** in 1949 by the Anglo-French fencing master Roger Crosnier. Wales's outstanding fencers include J. Emrys Lloyd, who won the British men's foil championship seven times between 1928 and 1938, and Quentin Berriman, a frequent winner of the British men's epée championship, most recently in 2002. In the 2002 Commonwealth Fencing Championship, the Welsh team won three silver medals and one bronze. At the beginning of the 21st century, some 600 people in Wales were involved in the sport.

FENTON, Richard (1747–1821) Topographical writer

A native of **St David's**, Richard Fenton is chiefly remembered on account of his *Historical Tour through Pembrokeshire* (1810) and his *Tours in Wales 1804–13*, which was not published until 1917. During his years as a lawyer in **London**, he was active with the **Cymmrodorion** and the **Gwyneddigion**.

FENTON, Roger (1819–69) Photographer

Regarded as the first war photographer, for his coverage of the **Crimean War**, in 1857 Lancashire-born Fenton photographed a series of landscapes of well-known beauty

Roger Fenton's 'galvanograph' of Raglan Castle, 1857–8

Blaenau Ffestiniog and the Vale of Ffestiniog

spots around the **Conwy** valley. He was involved in the first electro-photo printing process, which allowed photographs to be published using printers' ink. He published a series of these 'galvanographs' of **Raglan** Castle. Later, he took stereographic views of north Wales, before renouncing **photography** in 1862.

FERNDALE COLLIERY DISASTER Rhondda

On 8 November 1867, at this colliery operated by David Davis & Sons Ltd, 178 men were killed when two separate explosions occurred in the Glo-bach and **Rhondda** districts. The manager was blamed for allowing accumulations of gas to build up, which were ignited (apparently) when some miners opened and removed the gauzes from their safety lamps. On 10 June 1869, a further explosion at the colliery killed 53 men.

FERWIG, Y, Ceredigion
(2828 ha; 1177 inhabitants)

Located immediately north of **Cardigan**, the **community** contains the villages of Ferwig, Gwbert and Penparc. The name is the **Welsh** form of Berwick ('barley grange'). Ferwig church is dedicated to the Cornish saint Pedrog – an indication of the way in which **saints**' cults were spread along the western seaways.

The exquisite isolated church of Mwnt (13th century) stands above a bay where grey **seals** breed and bottle-nosed dolphins may be seen. Gwbert, with its **golf** course and fine views across the **Teifi** estuary, attracts numerous visitors. In the 15th century, Tywyn (Towyn Farm on the Ordnance Survey's **maps**) was an important house visited by the major Welsh poets, such as **Dafydd Nanmor**. The community includes Cardigan **Island**.

FFESTINIOG, Gwynedd
(5699 ha; 4830 inhabitants)

Constituting the northernmost part of the one-time district of **Meirionnydd**, the **community** contains the town of Blaenau Ffestiniog, its chief suburbs – Bethania and Tanygrisiau – and the village of Ffestiniog or Llanffestiniog.

In the late 18th century, the area was entirely rural, but within a century it had became one of the world's most important centres of **slate** production. Output began in 1765 at Diffwys Quarry, but, in the 19th century, production was concentrated in vast caverns. Thus, unlike **Caernarfonshire**'s slate areas with their above-ground slate-quarrying, Ffestiniog was an area of underground slate mining. Again, unlike Caernarfonshire, where the leading entrepreneurs were local landowners, Ffestiniog was heavily dependent upon investment by **English** businessmen such as William Turner, Samuel Holland and W. E. **Oakley**.

Crucial to the success of the industry was the opening in 1836 of the narrow gauge **railway** from Blaenau Ffestiniog to **Porthmadog** harbour. The railway closed in 1946 – although its reopening as a tourist attraction began in 1954.

The **population** of Ffestiniog **parish** increased from 732 in 1801 to 11,274 in 1881, and slate output rose from 45,000 tonnes in 1851 to over 150,000 tonnes in 1881. During its industrial heyday, Ffestiniog was entirely **Welsh** in language and culture; by the late 19th century, it had 25 chapels.

The slate industry peaked before the end of the 19th century and in the 20th century went into inexorable decline. During the **Second World War**, the Manod slate mine provided shelter for many of the **paintings** of **London**'s National Gallery.

Several slate mines have now become tourist attractions, whilst two others – Gloddfa Ganol and Llechwedd – continue to produce slate, but only on a very limited scale. Cwm Stwlan **reservoir** (1963) supplies the Ffestiniog hydro-electric power station (*see* **Energy**).

Although the scars of industry are everywhere and the area is experiencing high unemployment, it offers attractive locations for walkers, mountaineers and anglers. Further, it can be argued that the people of Blaenau Ffestiniog constitute the most remarkable society in Wales, once described by an anonymous observer as consisting of 'individuals, all of whom are bonkers but none of whom are boring'. The author **John Cowper Powys**, who lived there from 1955 until his death in 1963, was enchanted by the place.

FFRAID Saint

A composite – and therefore undatable – saint in Welsh tradition. Ffraid is a conflation of **Saints** Brigid of Kildare, Brigid of Cill-Muine and Birgitta of Sweden; and her legend is recounted in a 15th-century poem by Iorwerth Fynglwyd (fl.1485–1527). There are numerous dedications to Ffraid in Wales; her name is reflected in **place names** beginning with Llansanffraid or St Bride's.

FIDDLE, The

Known in Wales at least since the 17th century, the violin (*ffidil*) became one of the most widely used instruments in the folk tradition, particularly following the demise of the *crwth* around 1800. Extant fiddlers' tune books offer proof of the strength of the fiddle tradition. Two significant sources are the manuscripts of John Thomas of **Powys** and

Morris Edwards of **Anglesey**, together containing more than 600 musical items. The fiddle was widely used to accompany both dancing (*see* **Dance**) and singing, especially in 18th-century **interludes**. Currently, there is an increasing interest among young folk musicians in performing traditional fiddle tunes.

FIFTY-SIX GROUP, The

A group of artists, whose designation normally appears as the 56 Group. It was founded in 1956 – by **Eric Malthouse**, **David Tinker**, Arthur Giardelli and Michael Edmonds – as a pressure group to divert art policy and production in Wales from what they perceived as a national to an international agenda. They were joined by other sympathetic artists, most of whom, like them, had come to Wales as teachers. They became a semi-official avant-garde, exhibiting in Wales and elsewhere in Europe. They never had a coherent philosophy and radical changes in arts policy have reduced their importance and their exhibitions – to the extent that they have become symptomatic of a disparate membership.

FILM

Wales has a long film-making tradition, reaching back to the 1890s. The first film shot in Wales, featuring a royal visit to **Cardiff**, was made in 1896 by the American Birt Acres. Indigenous production began in 1898, when **Rhyl**-based **Arthur Cheetham** made films throughout north and mid-Wales. The first Wales-based film-maker of enduring stature was the travelling showman **William Haggar**, who made over 30 fiction films between 1901 and 1908, many

An early cinematograph at Pwllheli

Brothers Rhys and Llŷr Ifans in *Twin Town* (1997)

of which were circulated around the world (mainly through the Gaumont and Urban companies) (*see Desperate Poaching Affray, A*).

Other extant pre-**First World War** films shot in Wales were made by outsiders. The most impressive are the Charles Urban Company's *Wales, England: Land of Castles and Waterfalls* (1907) and the British Biograph Company's 'phantom train ride' film, *Conway Castle* (1898), which survives in a hand-tinted colour version and contains eye-catching panoramic shots. Footage from the 1906 Wales versus **Ireland** soccer match at **Wrexham**, made by the Blackburn firm of Mitchell and Kenyon, is the oldest surviving footage from a **football** international; while Arthur Cheetham's *Blackburn Rovers v West Bromwich Albion* (1898) is the world's earliest known extant soccer film.

Little sense of early 20th-century Welsh industrial life may be divined from surviving images of the silent era. Nevertheless, rural Wales, from 1912 onwards, was a popular locale for visiting film companies such as Edison and British and Colonial – for instance, Charles Brabin made *The Foreman's Treachery* in north and mid-Wales in 1913. In 1920 alone, nine feature films were set in Wales, all of which are lost. The most celebrated of all Wales's 'lost' silents is *A Welsh Singer* (1915), one of three features adapted from novels by Allen Raine (**Anne Adaliza Puddicombe**) and starring Florence Turner, the one-time leading player of the Vitagraph Company.

In the 1930s, two provocative agitprop documentaries emerged from **London**'s Strand company: the communist director Ralph Bond's *Today We Live* (1937), set among unemployed miners in Pentre, **Rhondda**; and Donald Alexander's *Eastern Valley* (1937), filmed in (then) **Monmouthshire**. The first **Welsh**-language sound film, *Y Chwarelwr* (The Quarryman), was made in 1935 by **Ifan ab Owen Edwards**.

In the early sound era, British mainstream feature films generally offered little more than escapism. However, *The Citadel* (1938), based upon A. J. Cronin's novel and set partly in a south Wales mining community, focused on public **health** problems. An MGM feature made by King Vidor, it did not fully express the novel's political message.

Other films from major British or Hollywood studios and set in Wales were similarly filleted, such as *The Proud Valley* (1940) and *How Green Was My Valley* (1940). The latter, a handsome film by John Ford, won five Oscars but it reflected Ford's predilection for mythology rather than any plausible Welsh industrial life. Jill Craigie's *Blue Scar* (1949), on the other hand, raised serious, radical questions about the nationalization of the **coal** industry. However, it was partly financed by the **National Coal Board** and an awkward, romantic strain was introduced to ensure wider distribution.

Social and political comment disappeared almost entirely from feature films set in Wales after the **Second World War**. The 1950s to the early 1970s were noteworthy for only a few fine genre films, including *Tiger Bay* (1959) and *Only Two Can Play* (1962). However, too many film-makers, particularly from the 1960s to the early 1990s, suffered from a lack of funding, a shortage of talented producers and the absence of an indigenous production infrastructure. The nation's cinema representations have too often reflected the prejudices and preconceptions of 'outside' film-makers content to trade in stereotypes.

More promising was the work produced by Karl Francis from the late 1970s. Chronicling in often graphic, controversial images the contemporary life of the south Wales valleys, he produced several compelling films, including **Above Us the Earth** (1976), *Giro City* (1982), *Ms Rhymney Valley* (1985) and **Boy Soldier** (*Milwr Bychan*; 1986).

By the late 1970s, the film workshop movement was gathering momentum in Wales. Chris Monger and Steve Gough, participants in workshops at the Chapter Arts Centre, Cardiff, went on to make notable features.

The launch of **S4C** in 1982 helped to develop an embryonic film industry. Most of its initial longer dramas lacked contemporary significance or a mature adult perspective, but the company had reassessed its responsibilities by 1986, when *Boy Soldier* and Stephen Bayly's comedy **Rhosyn a Rhith** (*Coming Up Roses*) made history as the first Welsh-language films to gain London West End **cinema** release, albeit in subtitled versions.

The establishment of S4C led to the production of Welsh-language features, complementing the few made from the 1970s onwards by the Bwrdd Ffilmiau Cymraeg (Welsh Film Board), and to the emergence of film-makers of undoubted ability – notably Endaf Emlyn, Marc Evans and Stephen Bayly. In 1995, S4C announced a new policy, allowing one or two feature films a year to play in cinemas before television transmission. Yet film-makers find it difficult to gain entry into a competitive marketplace; even the better Welsh-language films fail to find audiences, because of the reluctance of London-based distributors or agents to handle Welsh-language films.

Hedd Wyn (1992), the first Welsh film to gain a Best Foreign Language Film Oscar nomination (in 1994), won a Royal Television Society Best **Drama** award, but failed to attract a British distributor. Endaf Emlyn's *Un Nos Ola Leuad* (*One Full Moon*; 1991), adapted from **Caradog Prichard**'s novel and among the finest Welsh films ever made, enjoyed only limited exposure; the same fate befell his *Gadael Lenin* (*Leaving Lenin*), voted by audiences at the 1993 London Film Festival as the most popular British film.

Fine **English-language** films such as **House of America** (1996) and *Human Traffic* (1999) have emerged, bearing comparison with the powerful films of social realism made by Karl Francis. Over the past 20 years, Welsh films have reflected Welsh life more accurately and more sensitively than most features previously set in Wales, which were predominantly the work of British studios or units of Hollywood production companies. Yet films such as *House of America* have tended to languish. Its director, Marc Evans, found persuasive visual ways to restructure the original Ed Thomas stage play, but the film received lamentable distribution. Kevin Allen's brash comedy *Twin Town* (1998), satirizing the older Welsh cultural traditions, found a ready British audience but failed to do quite as well as Justin Kerrigan's *Human Traffic*, a stylized comedy set in Cardiff and built around interior monologues, teenage paranoia, drug habits and club culture.

Despite rebuffs and generally low budgets, the nation's film-making standards have risen since the mid-1980s. In 2000, Paul Morrison's *Solomon a Gaenor* became the second Welsh film nominated for a Best Foreign Language Oscar. Since the late 1990s, Sgrin, the Welsh media agency, has encouraged new talent through short-film initiatives, and new projects have received lottery funding. Film-makers have also sought money further afield for their more ambitious co-productions; *House of America* had six sources of funding, including British Screen and Dutch Screen. Multinationals directly funded two other noteworthy Welsh features, Polygram backing *Twin Town* (1997) and Miramax funding Chris Monger's *The Englishman Who Went Up a Hill But Came Down a Mountain* (1995).

The quality of Welsh animation, shown at festivals worldwide, has been the most encouraging development. Prior to the advent of S4C, Wales had produced virtually no animation work since the Cardiff projectionists Sid Griffiths and Bert Bilby created their mischievous canine character Jerry the Tyke, for Pathé cinema news magazines in the 1920s. However, S4C's animation executive, Chris Grace, built successfully on the huge television hit that was the children's series *Superted*, made by the Cardiff-based Siriol company (a company eventually sold to the Disney Channel) – so much so that in 1992, a revamped Siriol made the first Welsh animation main

Swansea-born Catherine Zeta-Jones in *Chicago* (2003)

feature films with an adaptation of **Dylan Thomas**'s *Under Milk Wood* and *The Princess and the Goblin*, a co-production with Hungary.

An influx of talent to Wales, encouraged by opportunities at S4C, included Joanna Quinn, who, with *Girls' Night Out*, took three prizes at the world's leading animation festival at Annécy in 1987. She went on to win numerous international awards, with feisty comedies dealing with sexism and colonialism. In 1999, she gained an Oscar nomination for the Channel Four/S4C production *Famous Fred*. In addition, her *Wife of Bath's Tale* segment was instrumental in S4C gaining a further nomination in 2000 for its *Canterbury Tales*.

Initially, S4C encouraged independents, retrenched, and then expanded animation activities, with co-productions for worldwide consumption and niche markets. These included schools, with their notable series of truncated **Shakespeare** classics, **Bible** stories and operas (*Operavox*). A 1999 animation feature, *Gŵr y Gwyrthiau* (The Miracle Maker), from Cardiff's Cartŵn Cymru and Moscow's Christmas Films, was a by-product of S4C's *Testament* Bible series. Other promising talents included Aaargh Animation (with the *Gogs* television series); and the actress-writer Tracy Spottiswoode, whose witty, literate *Code Name Corgi* won top prize at the 2000 Bradford International Animation Festival.

The post-Second World War documentary tradition in Wales dates from the work of the journalist **John Roberts Williams** and the cameraman **Geoff Charles**, most notably *Yr Etifeddiaeth* (The Heritage; 1949). Cardiff's Paul Dickson made two impressive films, *The Undefeated* (1950) and the Festival of Britain documentary *David* (1951). Significant documentary talents have included **Jack Howells**, who made the Oscar winning *Dylan Thomas* in 1962, and the poet **John Ormond**. Working with the historian, **Gwyn A. Williams**, Colin Thomas produced outstanding drama-documentaries through the 1980s and 1990s for the Cardiff-based Teliesyn company. Fiercely partisan and politically provocative documentaries emerged from the **Tenby**-born actor **Kenneth Griffith** over three decades, notably his attacks on British colonialism such as *Hang Up Your Brightest Colours* (a long-banned portrait of the **Irish** Republican politician Michael Collins; 1973), *Curious Journey* (1977) and *Black As Hell, Thick As Grass* (1979).

Welsh actors have made an impact on screen since **Ivor Novello**, **Gareth Hughes** and **Lyn Harding** thrived in silent cinema. The most significant period for Welsh talent was the 1950s and 1960s, when **Richard Burton**, **Rachel Roberts** and **Stanley Baker** helped inject much needed realism into British films. Since then, the most distinctive Welsh actor on screen has been Anthony Hopkins who gained an Oscar for his portrayal of the cannibalistic killer Hannibal Lecter, in Jonathan Demme's *Silence of the Lambs* (1992). Hopkins's ability to embody stiff and repressed Englishmen is demonstrated in films such as *84 Charing Cross Road* (1986), *Remains of the Day* (1993) and *Shadowlands* (1994).

The 1990s produced a new breed of successful, often abrasive, Welsh actors, including Rhys Ifans and Matthew Rhys, who are among the first generation to enjoy a worthwhile choice of international and indigenous feature roles. **Swansea**-born Catherine Zeta-Jones has established herself as one of Hollywood's highest paid female stars, appearing, notably, opposite Anthony Hopkins in the 1998 box office hit *The Mask of Zorro*. In 2003, she won the Best Supporting Actress Oscar for her part in *Chicago*.

The idea of a Welsh film culture has only slowly taken root, but it has been promoted less self-consciously since the early 1990s, mainly through the International Film Festival, BAFTA Cymru, Sgrin and the Wales Film and Television Archive (now merged into the newly formed National Screen and Sound Archive of Wales). The archive's recent rediscoveries, including the British silent film ***The Life Story of David Lloyd George*** (1918) – lost for 76 years – and the colour version of **Lloyd George**'s visit to Germany and meeting with Hitler (1936), have focused attention on a century-old heritage much richer than many had hitherto suspected.

FIRE SERVICE, The

Before the 20th century, facilities for fire prevention varied widely. All fire brigades were organized on a local basis: some were professional, others voluntary, with no requirement of skills for the job; some had adequate fire-prevention equipment, such as fire engines, while others had none. The piecemeal development of legislation meant that while fire-fighting facilities were generally adequate in Welsh urban areas by *c.*1900, in many rural areas there was little or no provision for fighting fires.

Despite the recommendations of several parliamentary select committees that fire services should be standardized and fully professionalized throughout **Britain**, in practice this did not occur until the formation of the National Fire Service in 1941, which brought all the local fire services in Wales under central command. The Fire Services Act 1947 then transferred all members of the National Fire Service to fire brigades maintained by **county** councils and **county boroughs**.

In April 1996, existing county and borough fire brigades in Wales were amalgamated to create three new fire brigades, which at present provide fire services to the whole country. These are the North Wales Fire and Rescue Service (merging the former **Gwynedd** and **Clwyd** county brigades, with headquarters at **Rhyl**), the Mid and West Wales Fire and Rescue Service (covering **Powys** and what had been the counties of **Dyfed** and **West Glamorgan**, with headquarters at **Carmarthen**), and the South Wales Fire and Rescue Service (merging the former **Mid Glamorgan**, **South Glamorgan** and **Gwent** county brigades, with headquarters at **Pont-y-clun**).

FIRST WORLD WAR, The

A total of 272,924 Welshmen served in the 1914–18 war, representing 21.5% of the male **population** (slightly below the percentages for **England** and **Scotland**). Of these, approximately 35,000 lost their lives. By January 1916, when military conscription was introduced, 122,986 Welshmen had volunteered for the armed forces. Many of them had been persuaded to enlist by the rhetoric of **Nonconformist** ministers – **John Williams** (Brynsiencyn; 1853–1921) in particular – rhetoric which would greatly embarrass later chapel-goers. Conscription brought a further 149,938 men into the British armed forces, although

Mary Jones of Monmouth, waving her three sons off to war, one of whom did not return

conscientious objectors were rather more numerous in Wales than in the kingdom as a whole (*see* **Pacifism**).

All Welsh units were hugely expanded during the conflict, with many infantry battalions having at least nominal local identities. (The 'Pals' battalions, as they were called, were made up of recruits drawn from a particular town.) Welsh troops were to be found in many English regiments, as well as in service and support arms. The contempt to which some of them were subjected fuelled the Welsh **nationalism** of later decades. (Welsh officers were rare; for, on average, Wales contributed fewer officers to the British armed forces than any other part of the United Kingdom.) Nevertheless, as Taffs (*see* **Taffy**) fought and suffered side by side with Brummies, Geordies, Cockneys, Jocks, Scousers, Micks, Kiwis and Aussies, the experience of the war tended on the whole to foster a sense of 'Britishness'.

Major battles involving the **Welsh Army Corps** were those at Mametz Wood on the Somme (July 1916) and Third Ypres (July–August 1917).

Efforts were made to encourage Welsh recruitment through a focus on a supposedly Welsh martial tradition and by the relaxation of minimum height requirements for infantry. Although official hostility to the **Welsh language** became muted, and Nonconformist chaplains and Welsh-language propaganda were provided, Welsh-speaking regions remained the least rewarding recruiting areas and exhibited the strongest strains of pacifistic resistance to the conflict. Elsewhere, there was some socialist internationalist resistance to jingoism and militarism and, as the war

progressed, considerable war-weariness. In Russia, a similar war-weariness led to the Bolshevik Revolution and its impact upon Wales in the 1920s and 1930s would be highly significant (*see* **Communist Party**).

The war ensured the apotheosis of **David Lloyd George**. His elevation to the premiership and his support for conscription split the **Liberal Party**, contributing to its postwar decline. **Trade unionism** was boosted by the need to ensure co-operation in strategic industries. The recruitment of men into the armed forces created increasing opportunities for **women**'s employment.

The British navy's reliance upon the steam **coal** of the south Wales coalfield meant that ensuring the co-operation of Welsh miners was central to the war effort. Nonetheless, industrial relations in the coalfield remained troubled and a major strike in July 1915 hastened full state control over the industry. In fact, the stock of the **Labour Party** rose; its MPs could not be blamed for the war, and the effective use of state power to pursue the conflict gave credence to the party's policies, which advocated the use of state power to defeat poverty and unemployment. Overall, the traumatic experience of the war marked the end of the confidence and prosperity of the Edwardian era.

The peace treaties which followed the war recognized the political rights of many of the nationalities of central and eastern Europe, giving rise to hopes in Wales that the nationality of the Welsh would be similarly recognized; the frustrations of those hopes was a major factor in the foundation in 1925 of **Plaid [Genedlaethol] Cymru**.

FISH and FISHING

The **rivers** and **lakes** of Wales and the **seas** around the country were long rich in fish, and the fishing industry provided a livelihood for many generations of Welsh people. In the past, a wide variety of fish was caught, but the following have been the principal or more notable species.

River and lake fish

CHAR

A colourful member of the trout family found in seven of the lakes of **Snowdonia**, although no longer in Llyn Peris, its former stronghold. Its belly may be red or orange, and its back green or brown, depending on its habitat. Chars grow to 14–27 cm in length.

EEL

Occurring widely throughout western Europe, eel are found in rivers and inland waterways all over **Britain**. Wherever they are found, it is certain that they have travelled from their breeding ground in the Sargasso Sea. Immediately after hatching, the larvae begin their long journey. As they near the European coast in the autumn of their third year, these tiny, transparent leptocephalids change into elvers, about 5–8 cm long. A fully grown eel can be 1.5 metres long.

GWYNIAD (L. Coregonus clupeoides pennantii)

Limited to **Bala** Lake (Llyn Tegid), the gwyniad is a relative of the salmon and char, and is a non-migratory fish caught with rod and line. Bala's annual Gwyniad Festival is a tourist attraction.

LAMPREY

The large sea lamprey, a stone-sucker, enters the rivers of Wales, particularly the **Severn**, early in the year to breed in fresh water, where the young fish remain for from three to five years. They then undergo metamorphosis and develop sharp horny teeth akin to radulae. At this stage, they migrate to the sea and become semi-parasitic, preying on other fish. Two years later, they return to fresh water to spawn. Although lamprey pie was said to be a delicacy in the Middle Ages, the fish is now despised as a parasite. The lampern, or river lamprey, is smaller than the sea lamprey and has a similar life history.

SALMON

Traditionally, almost all the commercial fishing in the estuaries of Wales was associated with the capture of salmon and its close relative, the sewin (see below). The salmon is a large, delicately flavoured fish found in seas and rivers on both sides of the Atlantic. Adult salmon ascend the rivers, mainly in the summer months, to the gravel shallows where breeding takes place between September and February; they do not feed in fresh water and, as a result, by the time they reach the spawning grounds, they are in a poor condition.

A hen salmon lays 800–900 eggs for every half kilo of her weight, and the eggs are fertilized by the cock salmon before the eggs are covered by gravel. In the spring, the eggs are hatched and the tiny salmon or alevins are provided with a yolk sac that is gradually absorbed by the growing fish.

After spawning, the adult salmon return to the sea as kelts; many die before they reach the sea; a few return to the same spawning grounds in later years. Meanwhile, the alevins grow and begin to feed in the river. The alevin becomes a parr, a trout-like fish with a series of dusky mauve marks along its sides. As a parr, it remains in the river for a year or more and gradually changes its colour to silver. The parrs then congregate in considerable numbers, when they are known as smolts, and move towards the sea, where the major part of feeding and growing is done. After a year at sea, they return – sometimes to the river in which they were born – as grilse, as the year-old salmon is termed, and weighing 1.8–4 kg. Many will not return for two or more years, and are consequently much larger and heavier than the grilse.

Climate change, resulting in both reduced feeding opportunities at sea and lower water levels in rivers, has been responsible for a dramatic decline in salmon stocks: rod catches of salmon on the River **Wye**, for instance, declined from 7684 in 1967 to a low, in 2002, of 357.

SEWIN (L. Salmo trutta)

The sewin (or migratory sea trout) has a comparable life cycle to the salmon and its flesh is similar, though lighter in colour. In some rivers, notably the **Tywi**, the **Dyfi** and the **Conwy**, the netting of sewin is as important, if not more important, than fishing for salmon.

SHAD

A migratory and notably bony fish, the shad ascends the larger rivers in shoals in late spring and early summer, to breed in fresh water. It was common practice to net shad in the Severn estuary, although few have been caught since 1900.

SPARLING

Found in the rivers of the north, today the sparling is caught only in the Conwy. Considerable folklore surrounds this cucumber-smelling fish. Local tradition states that sparlings occur in no river but the Conwy; and that they do not appear until all the snow on the **mountain** peaks has disappeared. The fish is connected by legend with St **Ffraid**, who threw a handful of rushes (brwyn) into the Conwy; the rushes turned into sparlings (brwyniaid), which provided **food** for the starving **population**.

OTHER FISH

Coarse river fish such as pike, perch, tench and carp – which may have been esteemed as food in the past – occur in most rivers.

Shellfish and crustaceans

COCKLES

These edible molluscs live close to the surface of the sand on sheltered tidal shores, the most extensive beds occurring in Carmarthen Bay, especially the Burry Inlet.

CRAB

Measuring up to 25 cm across the shell and weighing as much as 5.5 kg, the common crab lives some distance offshore. Like the lobster, it is caught in wickerwork, wire or plastic pots.

CRAWFISH
Also known as the spiny lobster or rock lobster, the crawfish is usually slightly smaller than the true lobster, and has smaller pincers. Like lobster, crawfish are found on rocky grounds off the west coast.

LIMPET
This rock-clinging snail with its conical shell occurs widely on the seashore. Limpets were never gathered commercially but were a survival food among the coastal communities of **Ceredigion** and **Llŷn** in particular.

LOBSTER
Britain's largest crustacean, weighing, on average, about 1.5 kg, and measuring 20–50 cm in length, lives along rocky sections of the Welsh coast; it is blue with brown markings when alive, but turns red when cooked.

MUSSEL
Found all around the Welsh coast wherever there are suitable rocks to which they can attach themselves. Commercial exploitation of the mussel is concentrated in river estuaries. Up until the late 1970s, the most important fishery was in the Conwy estuary where mussels are gathered either on the shore or from the deep water.

OYSTER
The edible oyster, found offshore in shallow water, was of considerable economic importance in Swansea Bay and, to a lesser extent, off the south **Pembrokeshire** coast until the beginning of the 20th century.

PERIWINKLE
A brown-black snail common on rocky shores, the periwinkle was a survival food gathered from September to April, especially along the rocky coast of the Llŷn peninsula.

SCALLOP
Living in deep water offshore on sands or gravel beds, scallops are dredged commercially in Cardigan Bay, traditionally by boats from France or Spain.

SHRIMP and PRAWN
The shrimp is up to 7.5 cm in length and has a single pair of pincers and a flat body which can change colour from yellow to almost black, to match the colour of the sand over which it lives. It occurs widely on many parts of the Welsh coast. The prawn resembles the shrimp, but is larger and has two pairs of pincers.

Sea fish

There are two major classes of sea fish that occur in Welsh waters – pelagic and demersal. Pelagic fish include such species as herring, mackerel and pollack, which live and feed near the surface. Their capture, with drift nets in particular, has been the main occupation of inshore fishermen. Demersal fish live mostly on or near the bottom, and include such species as hake, cod, plaice and haddock. They are normally caught by trawl nets operated by fishing vessels from the more important Welsh **ports** such as **Milford Haven**, **Swansea** and **Cardiff**.

HAKE
Much of the prosperity of Milford Haven as a fishing port was based on the capture of hake off the south-eastern

Lobster pots at St Bride's Bay, Pembrokeshire, 1936

coast of **Ireland**. The over-fishing of those once profitable grounds by Spanish and French fishermen led to the rapid destruction of the hake grounds and the consequent decline of Milford Haven as one of the most important fishing ports of Britain.

HERRING
Herring was once extensively fished round the coast of Wales, and inshore herring fishing was the main occupation of villages along the shore of Cardigan Bay. Fishing usually took place between late August and early December.

MACKEREL
Shoals of mackerel appear along the Welsh coast in the summer months, and although they may be netted, as they often are today, the traditional method of capturing them was with long lines of baited hooks. The mackerel is a migratory fish that comes close inshore in vast shoals for spawning and then returns in smaller shoals to the deep water of the North Atlantic.

OTHER FISH
Other sea fish have been caught by fishermen in the waters around Wales, among them tope, skate, bass, cod, pollack, sole and ling; sand eels were gathered from western beaches in the summer months.

River fishing

Commercial fishing in the estuaries and rivers of Wales has been chiefly concerned with the capture of salmon, 'the King of Fishes', and its close relative, the sewin. Many of the methods of salmon capture that persisted until near the end of the 20th century could be traced back at least to the Middle Ages, a time when Welsh rivers teemed with fish, which were described, in 1603, as 'one of the cheefest world-lie goods wherewith God hath blessed this countrye'. The main methods of salmon fishing adopted in Wales were:

STOP or COMPASS NETTING
A stop net consists of a large bag-like net, suspended from two heavy poles that form a V-shaped frame. Fishing is done against the tide from heavy boats that take up station against mooring poles driven into the bed of the river or attached to a rope fixed to both shores of a river. In Wales, this method of fishing is now limited to two rivers, the Wye at **Chepstow** and the Eastern **Cleddau** in Pembrokeshire.

SEINE NETTING
The shore seine, especially used in river estuaries, is by far the most common means of capturing salmon. The net, usually about 250 m long, is a plain wall of netting attached to a leaded foot rope and a corked head rope. One member of a seine crew of three or four stands on the river bank, while the boat carrying the net proceeds to the deepest part of the river, returning to the shore on a semicircular course; then the net is hauled in with its catch of salmon.

DRIFT NETTING
A drift net consists of a plain wall of netting shot from a boat across the current and allowed to drift freely. One end of the net is fixed to the boat; the other is attached to a floating buoy. In Wales, drift netting is particularly important in the Severn estuary, with boats based in **Newport** and Chepstow.

TRAMMEL NETTING
Limited to the **Dee** estuary, the trammel net is a complex drift net, consisting of a fine wall of netting – the 'lint' – to which are attached two outer walls of large meshes – the 'armouring'. When drifting with the ebb or flow tide, a fish passing through the armouring strikes the lint and, by its impetus, strikes the armouring in front of it. Since at least the 18th century, trammel nets have been operated by members of one family from the town of **Flint**.

CORACLE NETTING
Fishing for salmon with the **coracle** is practised today on only three Welsh rivers – the **Teifi**, the **Taff** and the Tywi. The coracle net, slung between a pair of drifting coracles, is like the Flint trammel net, consisting of coarse-meshed armouring and fine-meshed lint. There are severe restrictions on where coracles may be used; since 1945, they have vanished from such rivers as the Dee, Severn, Cleddau and Conwy.

FISH TRAPS
A method of trapping fish in the Severn estuary is the use of cone-shaped willow baskets ('putchers') that are arranged in ranks of several hundred in three or four tiers to form a weir that is covered at high water. Another method involves large baskets ('putts'), consisting of three large willow baskets dovetailed one into another. A putt rank may contain as many as 120 baskets. There is a strict control of where basket traps may be deployed, and operators have to prove 'immemorial usage' on a particular riverside location. In the past, removable fish traps were located on many Welsh rivers, and the occurrence of the word 'cored' in Welsh **place names** indicates the location of a weir formerly used for the capture of fish.

Sea fishing

When vast stocks of herring used to visit the western seaboard every autumn, fishing for herring with drift nets was a major coastal industry, but an increasing scarcity of the fish, together with restrictive regulations in the second half of the 20th century, has resulted in the virtual disappearance of herring fishing. Mackerel, however, still appear in huge shoals in the summer months; since about 1970, vast quantities of them have been caught in the Irish Sea by large factory ships from many countries. Some are landed at Milford Haven for immediate freezing and export, principally to West African countries.

Conwy and Milford Haven are the principal ports for trawling and drifting for fish such as plaice, cod and sole, although other ports, from Swansea to **Holyhead** and the Dee estuary, are involved with the inshore industry in a minor way. Milford Haven, once the fourth most important fishing port in Britain has witnessed a sharp decline. In 1914, it was a boomtown, landing over 30,000 tonnes of fish. Since 1945, the industry has declined, and today it is

A fishing boat at the port of Holyhead

vessels from other western European ports that use Milford's extensive harbour facilities as a base.

Lobster and crab fishing, involving the use of pots and creels, may be pursued throughout the year, but overfishing in recent times has caused the lobster to become much scarcer.

Mussels are commercially fished in the Conwy estuary and the **Menai Strait**. They are either collected from exposed beds at low tide, or gathered from the river bottom from a boat, using a long-handled mussel rake. By tradition, only four families in **Conwy** have the legal right to gather mussels in the estuary.

Cockles are mainly gathered on Llanrhidian Sands (**Llanrhidian Lower**) in the Burry Inlet of Carmarthen Bay, by licensed cockle gatherers from the north **Gower** villages of Penclawdd, Llanmorlais and Croffty (all **Llanrhidian Higher**). In the past, other villages in Carmarthen Bay, such as **Laugharne**, Llansaint and Ferryside (both called **St Ishmael**), were important centres of the industry. (*See also* **Angling**.)

FISHGUARD AND GOODWICK (Abergwaun ac Wdig), Pembrokeshire (755 ha; 5043 inhabitants)

Curling around Fishguard Bay, the **community** is split into three parts – the Lower Town, the Upper Town on its promontory, and Goodwick, home to Fishguard harbour. The picturesque Lower Town, clustering around the mouth of the **Gwaun**, originated as a herring **fishing** village. It was the setting of the **filming** of **Dylan Thomas**'s *Under Milk Wood* (1971) and of two minutes of *Moby Dick* (1956).

In the Upper Town, the most distinguished building is Hermon **Baptist** Chapel (1776, 1832). On the square, opposite the Town Hall, stands the Royal Oak Inn, where in 1797 the terms of surrender were negotiated following the **last invasion of Britain** (*see also* **Pencaer**). At St Mary's church (1857) is a memorial to Jemima Nicholas (d.1832), who allegedly captured 14 French troops single-handed, armed only with a pitchfork. A tapestry, made by 70 local stitchers, illustrates the invasion. The writer **D. J. Williams** (1885–1970) spent most of his life at Fishguard, where a memorial commemorates him.

Fishguard has a long history as a **port**. In 1827, its hungry inhabitants rioted against the export of corn. The link with the **railway** network (1899) led to ambitious projects, with port-building involving the tearing down of the cliff face at Goodwick and the construction of a 1-km long breakwater. Between 1909 and 1914, the port attracted ships such as the *Mauretania* and the *Lusitania*, but hopes that it would become a major port of call for Atlantic liners were not fulfilled. In 1906, the **Neyland**–Waterford ferry was replaced by the Fishguard–Rosslare ferry, causing Fishguard to become the main port for shipping between **Britain** and southern **Ireland**. By Stena Line's Lynx, the voyage takes 110 minutes.

FITZ ALAN family Marcher lords

This powerful medieval **march**er family was descended from a Breton knight, Alan Fitz Flaad, who settled in **Shropshire** and who was also the ancestor of the Scottish Stuarts. His son, William Fitz Alan, became lord of

Oswestry during the reign of Henry I and subsequently acquired Clun by marriage. In the late 13th century, Richard Fitz Alan became earl of Arundel and in the 14th century the family rose to new heights of wealth and power, obtaining the marcher-lordships of **Chirk and Chirkland** in 1332 and **Bromfield and Yale** in 1347. The direct male line ended in 1415. **Owain Glyndŵr** probably spent his adolescence in the Fitz Alan household at **Chirk**.

FITZ HAMMO, Robert (d.1107) Marcher lord
The **Norman** conqueror of the kingdom of **Morgannwg**, his family had long been in the service of William I. He displayed conspicuous loyalty to William II at the time of Odo of Bayeux's rebellion in 1088 and was rewarded with extensive lands in and around Tewkesbury. In the 1090s, he moved into south-east Wales, eventually seizing the lowlands of Morgannwg. He died early in 1107; his only child and heiress, Mabel was married to Henry I's illegitimate son, Robert of Gloucester (*see* **Cardiff**).

FITZ OSBERN, William (d.1071) Earl of Hereford, marcher lord
Granted the earldom of Hereford by William I in 1067, Fitz Osbern invaded **Gwent** where, to consolidate his territorial gains, he built a number of castles, in particular **Chepstow**. He gave the burgesses of the **boroughs** he established the rights of the burgesses of Breteuil, his birthplace in Normandy. His heir, Roger, rose in revolt in 1075; on his death, childless, in **prison**, the family died out.

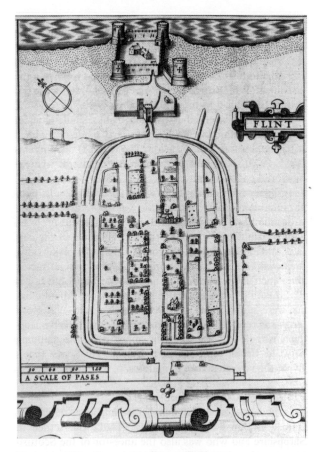

The town of Flint illustrated by John Speed in 1611

FLEMINGS
In 1108, Henry I transferred a body of Flemings from the Scottish borderlands to **Rhos** in **Dyfed**, where they expelled the Welsh inhabitants of the area. The descendants of their leaders, Tancard and Godebert, became hereditary castellans of **Haverfordwest** and barons of **Roch** respectively. About the same time, another band, led by Wizo (who gave his name to **Wiston**), seized western **Daugleddau**, while smaller groups settled at **Angle**, **Tenby**, **Laugharne** and, possibly, **Pembroke**.

Hated by the Welsh, the Flemings were mainly soldiers, **sheep** farmers and traders in wool and woollen cloth. **Giraldus Cambrensis** describes how they used boiled rams' shoulder blades for divination. They maintained their separate identity in the 12th and early 13th centuries, but were gradually swamped numerically as fresh immigrants (*see* **Immigration**), mainly from the west of **England**, settled among them. By the late 14th century, the Flemish language was no longer spoken in these areas, although as late as the 16th century those of Flemish descent were described as *male Anglice loquentes* ('poor speakers of **English**').

FLEURE, H[erbert] J[ohn] (1877–1969) Geographer
A native of Guernsey, Fleure, the first academic geographer to be elected an FRS (1936), graduated from **Aberystwyth** and at the Zoological Institute, Zurich. The first holder of the chair of **geography** and anthropology at Aberystwyth (1918) and of geography at Manchester (1930), he developed, from his early studies in the **sciences**, an estimation of humanity's ever-changing physical environment, and, from his later work in anthropology and **archaeology**, an understanding of humanity's physical and social evolution and inheritance. As the founder of anthropometry, he was noted for his work on cephalic ratios (the relationship between the width and length of the human head); the subject fell under a cloud during the Nazi era, but Fleure's work remains valid.

Fleure's department at Aberystwyth in the 1920s and 1930s became the largest and foremost in **Britain**. As a tenacious fighter for the proper recognition of his subject in schools, his work over 30 years with the Geographical Association rendered remarkable service to teachers of geography at all educational levels.

FLINT (Y Fflint), Flintshire
(1719 ha; 12,804 inhabitants)
Its location along the main road hugging the left bank of the **Dee** estuary has been central to the history of Flint. The **Roman** remains at Pentre Farm are probably those of the residence of the officer in charge of **lead** mining at **Halkyn**. Flint Castle (1277–85) was built under the supervision of **James of St George**. It consists of a rectangular court with round towers at its south-western, north-western and north-eastern corners. At the south-eastern corner, there stands a large detached donjon, a feature unique in **Britain** but paralleled by the Tour de Constance at Aigues Mortes in southern France. The **borough** received its charter in 1284; protected by a ditch and bank rather than by stone walls, its original six parallel streets are still evident in the layout of the modern town. In 1399, Flint Castle was the scene of the seizure of Richard II by Henry Bolingbroke,

soon to be Henry IV. During the **Civil Wars**, the castle was held for the king by Roger **Mostyn**. Captured by the Parliamentarians in 1647, its defences were slighted. The poet John Milton's friend, Edward Young, was drowned near Flint; Milton's *Lycidas* commemorates him.

From the 18th century onwards, the area underwent increasing industrialization, with **coal**mining, lead smelting, **shipbuilding** (1840–59) and alkali manufacture (1840–1910). The Aber Works, the artificial silk works founded in 1908, was taken over by **Courtaulds**, which established the Castle and the Deeside **textile** factories (1920 and 1927). With the demise of the industry, its sites came to be occupied by a 72-ha business park. Paper manufacture, begun at Oakenholt in 1880, still continues.

The neo-Gothic town hall (1840) has a ceiling illustrating the royal tribes of Wales. St Mary's (1848) occupies the site of the medieval town church. Flint has one of the few surviving Italianate **railway** stations designed by Francis Thompson for the Chester–**Holyhead** Railway (1847–8). The National **Eisteddfod** was held at Flint in 1969. The Flint mixed choir, established in 1975, was relaunched in 1976 as a **male voice choir**.

FLINTSHIRE (Sir y Fflint)
(48,948 ha; 148,594 inhabitants)
The **county**, when created in 1284, consisted of three discrete units – **Tegeingl**, **Hope**dale and **Maelor Saesneg** – and was placed under the jurisdiction of the justiciar of Chester. The lordships of **Mold** and **Hawarden** and the enclave of Marford and Horsley (*see* **Gresford**) were added to the county following the **Acts of 'Union'**.

On the eve of its abolition in 1974, the county consisted of the **borough** of **Flint**, the **urban districts** of **Buckley**, **Connah's Quay**, **Holywell**, Mold, **Prestatyn** and **Rhyl** and the **rural districts** of Hawarden, Holywell, **Maelor** and **St Asaph**.

Following abolition, the larger part of the county was divided into the districts of **Rhuddlan**, **Delyn**, and **Alyn and Deeside**; Maelor and Marford together with Horsely became part of the district of **Wrexham-Maelor**. The four districts, together with those of **Colwyn** and **Glyndŵr**, became the county of **Clwyd**. In 1996, that county was abolished. Flintshire reappeared on the map although, as it consisted only of the former districts of Delyn, and Alyn and Deeside, it was considerably smaller than the pre-1974 Flintshire. In 2001, 21.38% of the inhabitants of Flintshire had some knowledge of Welsh, with 10.92% wholly fluent in the language. (*See also* **Saltney** and **Trelawnyd and Gwaenysgor**.) At the time of the abolition of the original Flintshire in 1974, it consisted of 66,391 ha and had 187,000 inhabitants.

FO A FE Television series
This popular 1970s series, written by **Rhydderch Jones** and **Gwenlyn Parry** for BBC Wales (*see* **Broadcasting**), was the first **Welsh-language** situation comedy. It was an astute study of changes in the social and cultural life of Wales at that time. *Fo*, the chapel-going, organ-playing, teetotal northerner, was Ephraim Hughes (Guto Roberts; 1925–99), who spoke pulpit Welsh; *Fe* was Twm Twm (**Ryan Davies**), the beer-swilling, southern pigeon-fancier, who spoke a more earthy form of Welsh.

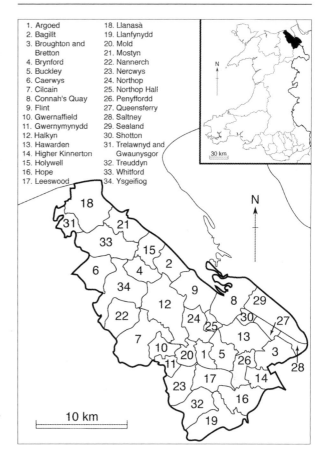

1. Argoed	18. Llanasà
2. Bagillt	19. Llanfynydd
3. Broughton and Bretton	20. Mold
4. Brynford	21. Mostyn
5. Buckley	22. Nannerch
6. Caerwys	23. Nercwys
7. Cilcain	24. Northop
8. Connah's Quay	25. Northop Hall
9. Flint	26. Penyffordd
10. Gwernaffield	27. Queensferry
11. Gwernymynydd	28. Saltney
12. Halkyn	29. Sealand
13. Hawarden	30. Shotton
14. Higher Kinnerton	31. Trelawnyd and Gwaunysgor
15. Holywell	32. Treuddyn
16. Hope	33. Whitford
17. Leeswood	34. Ysgeifiog

The communities of the county of Flint

FOOD and DRINK
The traditional food of a country is inevitably linked to its **agriculture**, which in turn is dictated by its **geography** and **climate**. Archaeological evidence shows that the early Welsh **economy** was based on mixed farming. When journeying through Wales in 1188, **Giraldus Cambrensis** noted that '… almost all the **population** lives on its flocks and on **oats**, milk, **cheese** and butter'. This, generally, was how the Welsh subsisted until well into the 19th century.

Oats and barley were the most commonly grown cereal crops, with wheat confined to the fertile lowlands. Both farmers and cottagers were heavily dependent on their oat crop, the basic ingredient used for preparing cereal-based stews – *siot* (flummery), *uwd* (porridge), *brwes* (brose) and *bwdran* (gruel). In addition, at least one **pig** a year was fattened and slaughtered to provide a supply of salted bacon. On larger farms, a bullock was also butchered and the meat shared between two or three adjoining farms. Keeping **cattle** ensured a plentiful supply of milk to produce butter and cheese; vegetables were grown in the fields and kitchen garden, mainly cabbages, carrots, **leeks**, herbs and, from the 18th century onwards, potatoes.

Wild berries, wild **plants** and fruits in season were harvested throughout the country, and communities living in coastal regions were able to vary their diet by collecting shell**fish** such as cockles and mussels, and seaweed to make **laverbread**. In this way, Welsh rural society was largely self-supporting. Sugar, salt, **tea** and currants were the main products that had to be purchased, with the addition of rice to make rice puddings on Sundays and on special occasions.

The narrow range of available ingredients necessitated great ingenuity to provide a varied day-to-day menu. The preparation of an assortment of dishes from one basic ingredient, oatmeal, required considerable skill. Similar dexterity was required for broths such as *cawl*, *lobsgows* and *potes cig*, using home-cured bacon and beef.

Another factor governing the types of food that could be prepared was the limited cooking facilities. The open fire was central to cooking throughout the 18th and 19th centuries, and in many rural houses well into the 20th century. A cooking pot or cauldron was used for boiling various stews or joints of meat, dumplings and boiled puddings over an open fire. Pot ovens, for roasting meat and baking cakes and fruit tarts, were named according to region – such as *crochan pobi*, *cidl*, *cetel* and *ffwrn fach*. The bakestone, also widely used, was similarly known by different names in different areas – such as *gradell*, *planc*, *llechwan* and *maen*. Oatcakes, drop scones, soda bread, pancakes and griddlecakes (such as **Welsh Cakes**) were baked by this method. Spits, bottle-jacks (for rotating meat over a fire) and Dutch ovens were used for roasting meat.

Before tea became widely available in the early 19th century, it was commonplace for both children and adults to drink ale or **cider** rather than water, which could not be relied upon for its purity. Cider was the traditional drink in east Wales, but **beer** was the favoured tipple elsewhere.

The preparation and consumption of traditional foods were closely integrated with patterns of life in rural Wales. Before labour-saving agricultural machinery, farmers were dependent on the co-operation of their neighbours to complete seasonal work. The main tasks were essentially communal efforts requiring communal meals and celebrations. The *boten ben Fedi* (harvest pie) was a traditional dish associated with the harvest supper; by the late 19th century, it usually consisted of mashed potatoes with minced beef, bacon and onions. Threshing and **sheep**-shearing days were other occasions marked with generous meals. Cold lamb or beef, potatoes and peas would be served followed by a creamy rice pudding for dessert. A favourite in parts of **Gwynedd** was *tatws popty* – beef, onions and potatoes. Afternoon tea consisted simply of home-baked bread, butter, cheese and jam; rich yeasted fruit cake and gooseberry pie were considered as shearing and threshing specialities.

In the industrial towns and villages, it was the common practice to prepare food for sale. Wives would help to support their families in periods of hardship by preparing and selling home-cooked dishes. **Coal**miners' wives or widows prepared **faggots** and peas to sell from their homes. Similarly, pickled herrings were sold in the northern **slate**-quarrying communities; they were cooked in earthenware dishes, flavoured with onions, treacle, pickling spices and vinegar, and were usually consumed with home-made oatcakes.

Breadmaking in the village bakehouse at Llanelidan near Ruthin, *c.*1905

Penderyn single malt, launched on 1 March 2004, the first whisky to be distilled in Wales for over 100 years

Eventually, the Welsh way of eating was transformed by industrialization, urbanization and improved transportation. Town dwellers, divorced from the land, were obliged to rely on shop-bought products. The tradition of living off the land survived until a later period in the rural areas, but change came with improved **roads** and modern shopping facilities, as well as with the arrival of refrigerators and home freezers. Thus, the majority of the dishes eventually termed traditional food disappeared from the tables of rural Wales.

The later 20th century saw a revival of interest in 'Welsh food', although to some commentators the expression appeared to be a contradiction in terms, and the fare presented as such in some of Wales's pricier establishments has little of the 'traditional' about it. In the early 1990s, the restaurant critic of the *Sunday Times* wrote that it was possible to travel the length and breadth of Wales 'without ever stimulating a taste bud'. The comment stung; but the fact remained that the standard of pub and restaurant catering across Wales was decidedly patchy. Although the renaissance of good-quality Welsh produce was already underway in some hotels and restaurants, most eating-places were still serving unimaginative fare, often poorly cooked and presented.

Nowadays, many chefs and restaurateurs are promoting the idea of good-quality Welsh produce. Indigenous ingredients such as lamb, Welsh Black beef, venison, salmon, sewin and cockles (*see* **Fish and Fishing**), cheeses, laverbread and leeks are sourced and cooked, sometimes using foreign culinary techniques, or simply presented to let the quality and flavour speak for themselves. At the same time, however, the ordinary diet of many Welsh people owes more to India, China or America than it does to their own country. Chicken tikka masala is the nation's favourite dish; and burgers and chow mein are now more popular than fish and chips as a takeaway. Pub food (now the most common eating-out experience) is often influenced by Thailand, Italy and Japan, while Welsh food is usually prominent only on St **David**'s Day.

The opportunities to buy Welsh produce are increasing: in the last few years, supermarkets, where the majority of people buy their food, have begun to stock specialities such as laverbread and the new Welsh wines and cheeses. The number of small, speciality food producers has grown over the last two decades, their ranks swollen by farmers seeking to diversify in a declining industry. Confectioners, smokeries, dairies, preservers and so on are turning out high quality and often award-winning produce. As the price of these goods is usually too high for them to compete on the supermarket shelves, many of the companies export their produce to **North America** or **London**. On the other hand, some traditional foods, such as Welsh lamb, which used to be a luxury for Sunday dinners only, are now cheaply available in supermarkets.

A 2001 survey by the Food Standards Agency Wales reported as follows: 'Knowledge of healthy eating is limited, with only a minority of Welsh people aware of the balance of foods they should eat each day.' Wales has the highest fat consumption in Britain, and consequent high levels of obesity. Traditional in their food habits, most people in Wales are meat eaters, and **women** (83%) are the main shoppers of the household.

Concerns for unhealthy eating habits are matched by those for the consumption of alcohol. The bravado attached to drinking copious amounts of alcohol goes back a long way. Ancient warriors used to fire themselves up for battle by quaffing huge quantities of **mead**, as described by **Aneirin** in *Y Gododdin*. The ritual is nowadays translated into **rugby** fans downing numerous pints of beer before a match. Industrialization played a key role in the development of the contemporary drinking culture. Despite the **temperance movement** and, more recently, **government health** campaigns, the conspicuous consumption of alcohol continues, with inevitable consequences for health – the average incidence of drink-related disease in Wales is higher than it is in the United Kingdom as a whole. The practice starts young: 29% of boys between 11 and 16 years old admit to drinking beer on a regular basis.

Recent years have seen a revival in the making of wine, mead and **whisky**. Viniculture, which began under the **Romans** and was continued by the monasteries until their **dissolution**, has now been re-established, with over 20 **vineyards** from **Tintern** to **Anglesey**.

FOOD RIOTS

During the 18th century, **food** riots were the commonest type of disturbance in **Britain**. Occurring in various Welsh towns at different times over the years 1709, 1713, 1728, 1740, 1752, 1757–8, 1765–6, 1778, 1783, 1789, the mid-1790s and 1801. All years of scarcity and high prices, they demonstrated the dependence of the poor upon bread as a staple food. Wedded to the moral **economy** with its notion of a fair or just price as a traditional right, at times of scarcity the lower orders took corn, butter, **cheese** and beans by force from middlemen such as corn factors, millers and large farmers, whom they rightly saw as attempting to rig the market. Such riots – which took place in coastal and riverine **ports** and in market towns that supplied the new manufacturing centres – were angry outbursts over the export of grains and other foodstuffs in times of scarcity. **Merthyr, Swansea, Carmarthen, Haverfordwest, Pembroke, Newport (Pembrokeshire), Aberystwyth, Pwllheli, Caernarfon, Beaumaris, Conwy, Denbigh, Rhuddlan,** and **St Asaph** were all places where disturbances erupted, prominent participants being craftsmen and industrial wage-earners, such as colliers and **lead** miners, who were far more exposed than agricultural workers to price fluctuations in the open markets.

FOOTBALL

At the close of the 20th century, when every nation in the world seemed anxious to appear in the football world rankings, Wales was unable to make it into the top 100. Nevertheless, there was considerable national pride in a history that had seen the establishment of the Football Association of Wales (FAW) as early as 1876, the year in which Wales played its first international: a match against **Scotland** at Glasgow.

Since those Victorian origins, two themes have dominated the game in Wales. Whilst always having to live with the notion that the largely southern game of **rugby** was the national sport, football was played by thousands in local clubs in every part of Wales, and supporters have always taken considerable interest in the fortunes of those Welsh teams which played in the English leagues and in the careers of individual players who played for the major English clubs. Furthermore, it has long been appreciated that the matches played by the Welsh team in the Home International Championship and against the other nations of the world confirms the country's national status. Only in 1958 did Wales appear to be a force in world football, but there was the consolation that individual players such as **John Charles**, Ian Rush and Ryan Giggs were world-class.

In **England**, the modern game of football had been codified at the public schools in the first half of the 19th century, and only in the 1860s and 1870s did it become established in the industrial towns of the north and the Midlands. It was the proximity of industrial north-east Wales to Lancashire and Birmingham that ensured that clubs sprang up in towns such as **Wrexham** and **Ruabon**. It was this local activity that prompted the formation of the FAW, the selection of a national team and the inauguration of the Welsh Cup in 1877. For some 20 years, Welsh football was dominated and controlled by the Wrexham area. Teams began to appear in mid-Wales, but the south, distant not only from Wrexham but also, crucially, from industrial England, was regarded as distinctly unpromising footballing territory, having fallen into the hands of an upper middle **class** who had played rugby at their public schools. There were, nevertheless, missionary ventures, and Wales's 46th international fixture – the first in the south – was played in 1894 at **Swansea**, a town where in 1874 the famous Cricket and Football team based at St Helen's had switched to rugby after a brief flirtation with soccer. The first football international staged in **Cardiff** (1896) was the 53rd match Wales had played, and it was not until their 67th fixture that a southern player was selected.

In the 1890s and the early 20th century, competitive league and cup football proliferated in the south. A crucial development was the admission of Welsh clubs into English leagues. The modern era of the game in Wales began essentially in 1909–10 when Swansea, **Newport**, Ton Pentre (**Rhondda**), **Merthyr Tydfil**, **Aberdare** and a team previously known as Riverside – but by this juncture, at the third time of asking, being allowed to call itself Cardiff City – entered the new English Southern League. Meanwhile, crowds were growing, new middle-class patrons were emerging and teams were winning vital matches. Swansea's stunning FA Cup defeat of the reigning Football League Champions, Blackburn Rovers, in January 1915 was the clearest indication that the south was coming of age as a home for a football culture.

All the promise of the heady Edwardian days came to fruition during the immediate post-war years. Cardiff City joined the Football League in 1920, and was soon joined by Aberdare, Wrexham, Swansea, Merthyr and Newport. Not only did Wales have six league teams but the well-supported and affluent Cardiff City soon proved to be one of the best teams in **Britain**. The team won promotion to the First Division in 1921 and then failed to become champions in 1924 only by a goal average difference of 0.024. It was the FA Cup that had caught the imagination of the public, and the romantic appeal of Welsh football was ensured by Cardiff's appearance in the Wembley final in 1925, by Swansea beating Arsenal to reach the semi-final in 1926 and, most especially, by Cardiff's victory over Arsenal in the Wembley final of 1927. Famously, this was to be the only occasion, so far, that a non-English team won English football's greatest prize, but the essentially British (and Irish) dimension of the sport was reflected in the fact that on that April day in 1927 Cardiff had selected three Welsh players, four players from **Ireland**, three Scots and one Englishman, whilst Arsenal fielded two Welsh players.

The historian Martin Johnes has argued that Cardiff City's finest moment came at a time when Welsh football was past its best, for already the interwar **depression** was plunging the domestic game into mediocrity. The Cardiff team of 'all-stars' broke up and by 1931 the team was playing in the Third Division. Meanwhile, the **coal**field towns of Aberdare and Merthyr lost their league status in 1927 and 1930 respectively, as briefly did Newport (1931–2). The only consolation was that the national side, although always hampered by the refusal of English teams to release star players, won the Home International championship three times in the 1920s and, even more remarkably, on three further occasions in the 1930s as well as a share of it in 1939. In the victories over England in 1933, 1936 and 1938, **Astley** and **Bryn Jones**, both sons of an economically stricken Merthyr, were prominent.

Prosperity returned in the 1950s by which time the four Welsh teams playing in the English League had established solid reputations, the highlights being Cardiff's two sojourns in the First Division (1952–7 and 1960–2). Meanwhile, non-league football flourished in towns such as **Barry**, Merthyr and **Bangor**. More evident was the emergence of individual stars, most of whom were lured away by the big English clubs. Attention focused on the Home Internationals when the heroes came together most memorably for keenly fought contests with England and Scotland. The results did not always reflect it, but the British press willingly conceded that in players such as **Ivor Allchurch**, Ron Burgess, Roy Paul, **Trevor Ford**, Cliff Jones, **Jack Kelsey** and, in particular, John Charles, Wales possessed world-class talent. One remarkable feature of these years was the skill of a generation of players born within a few kilometres of each other in Swansea, a town where even the schoolboy side attracted crowds of 20,000. Just as it seemed that Wales would have difficulty in

The Welsh national football team in 1958 when Wales qualified for the World Cup

replacing older players, the national team enjoyed its finest hour. Wales was extremely fortunate to qualify for the 1958 World Cup Finals in Sweden. Of the five games played in that tournament the team won only one; nevertheless, with a core of six Swansea-born players, they made it to the quarter-finals, at which stage (and without the injured John Charles) they lost to the eventual champions Brazil, for whom the then unknown youngster Pelé scored a fortuitous goal.

In subsequent decades, Welsh football was to offer a bewildering mix of isolated successes, tragedy and farce. There were memorable cup runs by both Swansea and Wrexham, but in league terms the achievement of Swansea in climbing from the Fourth to the First Division was off-set by the side's subsequent return to the depths and by Newport County's exit from the Football League in 1988. The demise of the Home International Championship in 1984 placed a new emphasis on the need to qualify for the World and European Cup Finals. In this respect, there was considerable frustration as a series of unfortunate, trau-matic and untimely defeats in the 1980s made it seem certain that world-class Welsh players such as Ian Rush, Neville Southall and Mark Hughes were destined never to play in the sport's showcase finals. The League of Wales was founded in 1992, although Cardiff, Swansea and Wrexham continued to play in the English League. Newport, **Colwyn Bay** and Merthyr Tydfil also refused to join the League of Wales.

In the early years of the 21st century, there was still a general disappointment that, notwithstanding all the enthusiasm, and the advantage of a magnificent stadium in Cardiff, Wales had failed to secure a niche in the highly lucrative world of televised club and international football. Individual clubs seemed plagued by indebtedness, but there was still sufficient optimism for Swansea to build the new Liberty Stadium and for Sam Hammam's Cardiff City to entertain, momentarily, Premiership ambitions. In 2004, under the management of Mark Hughes, the national team failed to reach the final rounds of the European Championship. It was also unsuccessful in the preliminary rounds of the 2006 World Cup, and Mark Hughes was replaced by John Toshack, his erstwhile critic-in-chief.

FORD, Trevor (1923–2003) Footballer

One of the greatest goal scorers in Welsh **football** history, **Swansea**-born Ford scored 174 goals in 349 Football League appearances for Swansea, Aston Villa, Sunderland, **Cardiff** and **Newport**. He became the most expensive for-ward in **Britain** when Sunderland paid £30,000 for him in 1950. Ford also played in the Netherlands with PSV Eindhoven when he was banned by the Football League after admitting in his autobiography, *I Lead the Attack* (1956), that he had received illegal payments while at Sunderland. A giver and taker of hard knocks, Ford was renowned as the scourge of goalkeepers. His shoulder-charging of them, legal in football at the time, was charac-teristic of the abrasive style that brought him 23 goals in 38 appearances for Wales, a record he held jointly with **Ivor Allchurch** for many years. Concluding his league career with Newport in 1960, he went into the garage business with the entertainer Stan Stennett.

FORDEN WITH LEIGHTON AND TRELYSTAN (Ffordun gyda Thre'r-llai a Threlystan), Montgomeryshire, Powys (3483 ha; 1320 inhabitants)

Located across the **Severn** from **Welshpool**, the **community** is crossed by **Offa's Dyke**. On the summit of Long Mountain (Cefn Digoll; 412 m) is the **Iron Age hill-fort**, Beacon Ring (Caer Digoll); both sites are mentioned in 'Breuddwyd Rhonabwy' (*see Mabinogion, The*). At the community's southern extremity is Forden Gaer, a **Roman** cavalry fort which was probably the Lavobrinta listed in the Ravenna Cosmography. The motte at Nantcribba was built by the Corbet family of Caus *c.*1260 and destroyed by **Gruffudd ap Gwenwynwyn** in 1263. Bryn Hyfryd Hospital was built in 1795 as a house of industry to accommodate 1000 inmates; it was described as 'a splendid receptacle of misery'.

Forden church (1867) has a fine **stained-glass** window based on cartoons by Burne-Jones. Trelystan church, high on Long Mountain, is Wales's sole medieval timber church; it was unsympathetically restored in 1856. Leighton church (1853) is a complete contrast; lavishly high Victorian, its spire is a splendid Severn valley land-mark. It contains the mausoleum of the Naylor family who acquired the Leighton estate in 1849. John Naylor, of **Liverpool**'s Leyland Bank, commissioned the building of Leighton Hall in 1851. As a prodigious neo-Gothic man-sion, its decoration was based on designs by A. W. N. Pugin. Leighton home farm was developed on an astound-ing scale and included a funicular **railway** to convey liquid manure. In the equally ambitious **gardens** is the original of the Leyland cypress (*see Plants*).

FORESTRY

Woodlands occupy some 250,000 ha – 12% of the land area of Wales – mainly as a result of an enormous state-spon-sored programme of afforestation during the 20th century (*see Forestry Commission*), which more than trebled the wooded area of Wales in little more than 60 years, despite the depredations caused by two world wars.

Prior to the major deforestations undertaken by Wales's early farmers, from the **Neolithic Age** onwards (*see Plants*), most of Wales was covered by forest – as distinct from forestry, which may be defined as productive woodland. (The word forest can sometimes mean an un-wooded area designated as a hunting ground; **Radnor Forest** is Wales's best example.) A combination of factors – worsening **cli-mate**, livestock grazing, deliberate military destruction during the **Edwardian conquest**, encroachments and clear-ances for **agriculture**, overcutting for early industry, and sheer neglect and abuse – resulted in the reduction of the area of native woodlands from perhaps 80–90% of the land area in prehistoric times, to some 4% by the 19th century.

Throughout historic times, the native woodlands of Wales have consisted of mixed deciduous broadleaved trees, with oak the principal species, and beech forming a significant element in the south-east. The only coniferous tree species in the lists of trees in the medieval Welsh **laws** was the yew. (There are late medieval references to *mery-wen* – juniper.) An early version of the law illustrates two of the main methods of woodland utilization – coppicing

Modern forestry in Wales

and lopping. For centuries, the native deciduous woodlands provided many of life's necessities for the small, mainly rural, **population**: nuts and berries, fuel, construction timber, bark for tanning, charcoal, wood for a multitude of domestic utensils and farming implements, sheltered grazing for livestock and pannage for **pigs**. A good example of multiple use is Pengelli Forest, near Felindre Farchog (**Nevern**), whose history has been documented since the 14th century.

The decline in native broadleaved woodlands has been paralleled by the introduction of non-native tree species, mainly conifers, at first for ornament and amenity, later for commercial timber production. The first recorded introduction of conifers from **North America** was by Thomas Bowen, a **Pembrokeshire** landowner, c.1596. Subsequently, many Welsh landowners planted conifers as adornments to their estates. By the mid-18th century, the first small plantations of conifers were appearing in the Welsh countryside; then came a period of extensive planting by many Welsh landowners, the most famous of whom was **Thomas Johnes** of Hafod (**Pontarfynach**), who, between 1782 and 1814, planted over 5 million trees – mainly European larch – on his north **Cardiganshire** estate.

Two early Welsh writers on forestry were clergymen: William Watkins, of **Hay**, who published *A Treatise on Forest-Trees* (1753), and Henry Rowlands, of **Llanidan**, whose *Idea Agriculturae* was written in 1704 but not published until 1764. Forestry was heavily influenced during the 19th century by expatriate Scots employed as foresters, agents and gamekeepers on many of Wales's larger estates. The need for higher **education** and professional training in forestry stimulated the establishment in

1904 of a school of forestry at **Bangor**, and in 1907 Bangor became the first place in **Britain** to offer a degree course in forestry.

A critical wood shortage during the **First World War** induced the **Lloyd George government** to establish the Forestry Commission, to create a state-owned forest resource as a strategic reserve of timber against time of war or national emergency, and to promote private forestry. After the heavy felling and disruption caused by the **Second World War**, land acquisition for afforestation was resumed with intensified energy. Investment in **road** building, forest research and mechanization accelerated the rate of development, with extensive forests changing the **map** of Wales. Grant-aid and fiscal incentives greatly increased the amount of planting by private individuals and companies, and improved the standard of management in private woodlands.

The annual cut of wood from state and private forests in Wales is now well over 1 million cubic metres. Major forest-based industries utilizing the produce from Welsh forests include wood-pulp mills at **Shotton** and Sudbrook (**Portskewett**), the BSW (Brownlie, Smiths and Western) sawmill at Newbridge-on-Wye (**Llanyre**) and the medium-density fibreboard factory at **Chirk**.

Changing public attitudes have brought about changes in forestry policy and in the implementation of forestry. Increasing concern for landscape values, recreation, heritage preservation and conservation of natural diversity is being articulated by many bodies, including Coed Cymru and the Woodland Trust. This is effecting a turning away from the old uniformity of coniferous monocultures towards the greater diversity of mixed forests and native broadleaved woodlands. A distinct Woodland Strategy for Wales was adopted by the **National Assembly** in 2001, and in 2005 the Assembly Government launched a £2.3 million scheme to restore some 5400 ha of ancient Welsh woodland, representing nearly a quarter of land which has been continuously wooded since 1600.

FORESTRY COMMISSION, The

Established in 1919, the Commission's aim was to reduce **Britain**'s dependence upon timber imports, dependence which had caused problems during the **First World War**, in particular because cordite – an essential component of explosives – was made from wood alcohol. By 1939, the Commission had acquired 28,000 ha of land in Wales. Timber shortage was even more acute during the **Second World War**, a fact which led the Commission to acquire a further 20,000 ha of Welsh land between 1946 and 1951. Its use of compulsory purchase – particularly of hill land – aroused the hostility of **sheep** farmers. They argued that, deprived of upland pastures, farms became unviable. The vigorous implications of the planting were attacked by Gwenallt (**David James Jones**), who wrote of *coed y trydydd rhyfel* (the saplings of the third war) in his poem 'Rhydcymerau'. The forests, planted with non-native conifers and edged with harsh straight boundaries, were also attacked on ecological and aesthetic grounds.

By the 1970s, by when the Commission owned 134,000 ha in Wales, it had become by far the country's largest landowner. Thereafter, its policies were reconsidered, mainly because it was realized that protracted wars were unlikely in the future. Increasing emphasis was placed on planting native deciduous trees and upon forests as an amenity (*see* **Forestry**). The Commission began selling land; by 1995, Wales's privately owned woodlands (125,000 ha) exceeded the Commission's Welsh holdings (123,000 ha). Among the Commission's largest forests are Coed y Brenin (**Meirionnydd**), **Clocaenog** and Brechfa (**Carmarthenshire**). Particularly landscape-transforming is Coed **Morgannwg**, which covers much of the hill land of the central part of the south Wales **coal**field.

FOSTER, Idris [Llewelyn] (1911–84) Scholar

A man of immense learning, Idris Foster committed surprisingly little to paper. Nevertheless, between 1947 and 1978, during his time as Jesus Professor of **Celtic** Studies at **Oxford**, a generation of young Celtic scholars were enthused by his erudition. He was also deeply admired in his native land on account of his unstinting service to cultural organizations such as the National **Eisteddfod**. A native of Carneddi, **Bethesda**, he was educated at **Bangor** and Dublin; his time as head of the department of Celtic in the University of **Liverpool** (1936–47) was disrupted by wartime service in Naval Intelligence. He was knighted in 1977.

FOSTERAGE

Although the practice of fosterage has been recorded in numerous societies and was especially prevalent in the **Celtic** countries in the medieval period, the evidence for the practice in medieval Wales is scant in comparison with the wealth of detail which emanates from the early Irish **law** texts.

Two main features can be clearly established: giving an unweaned infant (boy or girl) to a wet nurse to suckle, and sending a young child (usually a boy) to a family other than his own for his upbringing. The practice was both approved and condemned in the Middle Ages. It was argued that fostering created permanent bonds between the child and his foster father and also helped to cement cordial relationships between the participating families. However, it was also viewed, especially by **Giraldus Cambrensis**, as a practice that destroyed natural affections between brothers, since loyalty to a foster brother was generally stronger than loyalty to a blood brother, as fratricidal strife in Welsh princely families amply testifies.

FOULKES, [Sydney] Colwyn (1884–1971) Architect

Colwyn Foulkes, who practised in **Colwyn Bay**, was a talented architect who, though inclined to classicism, worked in a variety of styles. He designed a number of neo-Georgian houses in northern Wales as well as commercial and public buildings (including two chapels) in other styles, and some pleasantly conceived housing estates. He is best remembered as a designer of **cinemas** between 1920 and 1938, notably those at **Conwy** and **Rhyl**.

FOULKES, Isaac (Llyfrbryf; 1836–1904)
Publisher and author

Born at Llanfwrog (**Ruthin**), Foulkes was apprenticed to a Ruthin printer. He moved to **Liverpool** in 1854, where he worked as a printer, opening his own press in 1862. He published many popular and inexpensive books in **Welsh**, wrote biographies and novels, and edited the works of some of the foremost Welsh authors and poets. He founded *Y Cymro* (1890–1909), a weekly **newspaper** that had a wide circulation.

FOXES

Like its cousin the **wolf**, the fox (L. *Vulpes vulpes*; W. *cadno* in the south; *llwynog* in the north) was present in Wales during an interglacial period 225,000 years ago. No wolf has been seen in Wales for hundreds of years, but the red fox, surviving centuries of persecution by farmers, fox hunts (*see* **Hunting**) and gamekeepers, flourishes almost everywhere except on the offshore **islands**. Long absent from **Anglesey**, it re-established itself on the island in the early 1960s, at about the same time as it began to adapt to urban environments, becoming, by the late 20th century, a not uncommon sight in cities and towns. After years of controversy, fox hunting with **dogs** in Wales and **England** was made illegal in 2005.

The fox has long featured in Welsh folklore, **literature** and **place names**. It was regarded in some areas as the devil's spy, and to see several foxes together was considered unlucky; but to see one alone in the morning was a good omen. The magic of such an encounter is captured in **R. Williams Parry**'s famous sonnet 'Y Llwynog'.

FOX, Cyril [Fred] (1882–1967) Archaeologist

Fox studied at **Cambridge** and was director of the **National Museum [of] Wales** from 1926 to 1948. He played a key role in the establishment of the Welsh Folk Museum (The National History Museum; *see* **St Fagans**), although the first curator of that museum, **Iorwerth C. Peate**, would not

William Frame's Pierhead Building in Cardiff in 1896

have acknowledged as much – in the history of scholarship in Wales there is nothing to match Peate's loathing of Fox. Fox's most important publications were *The Personality of Britain* (1932), his analysis (1946) of the extraordinary finds from Llyn Cerrig Bach (**Llanfair-yn-neubwll**), and, with Baron Raglan, a survey of the country houses of **Monmouthshire** (1951–4). He was the first to make a complete survey, on scientific principles, of **Offa's Dyke**.

FRAME, William (1848–1906) Architect

After pupilage with **John Prichard**, Frame assisted **William Burges** in restoring Castell Coch (*see* **Cardiff**) (1874–81) for the third marquess of Bute (*see* **Stuart family**). After Burges's death, Frame worked directly for the third and fourth marquesses of Bute, completing restorations of Castell Coch and Cardiff Castle, as well as carrying out work in **Scotland** – at Mountstuart, Canna and Falkland Abbey. In Cardiff, Frame designed the eclectic but powerful Pierhead Building (1896) for the Cardiff **Railway** Company.

FRANCIS, (David) Dai (1911–81) Trade unionist

A lifelong **Communist**, **Onllwyn**-born Dai Francis was general secretary of the south Wales area of the **National Union of Mineworkers** (1963–76) and was particularly prominent in the successful **miners' strikes** of 1972 and 1974. He played a crucial role in the establishment of the **Wales TUC** in 1974, and, as its first chairman, did much to put **devolution** on the political agenda. He was an advocate of a national assembly in the doomed 1979 campaign, when his bilingual speeches and support of Welsh cultural institutions earned him wide popularity. In 2001, his son Hywel was elected **Labour** MP for **Aberavon**.

FRANCIS, J[ohn] O[swald] (1882–1956) Dramatist

The son of a **Merthyr Tydfil** blacksmith, Francis was educated at **Aberystwyth**, where his first plays were produced for the entertainment of fellow graduates at college reunions. His best-known play, *Change* (1913), placed Francis at the forefront of a fermenting if short-lived Welsh theatre movement. Based on the **Llanelli railway**men's strike of 1911 (*see* **Llanelli Riots**), the play – performed in **London** and New York – deals with the period of intense religious and political change in industrialized Wales.

FREE WALES ARMY, The

Set up in 1963 and originally known as the Welsh Freedom Army, this became the best known of the fringe nationalist groups of the 1960s. Led by Julian Cayo Evans (1937–95), it aimed at a revolution designed to culminate in Welsh independence. Its motley membership donned military-style uniforms and engaged in elaborate manoeuvres, claiming responsibility for a succession of explosions that rocked Wales between 1963 and 1969.

Nine activists were rounded up and tried between April and July 1969. Three, including Evans, were sentenced to terms of imprisonment, with the sentences pronounced on the day of the investiture of Prince Charles (*see* **Princes of Wales**) at **Caernarfon** Castle. The FWA had a considerable impact on Welsh politics and public life, although it probably never had as many as a hundred members.

FREEMAN, Kathleen (Mary Fitt; 1897–1959)
Novelist and scholar

Born in **Cardiff**, Kathleen Freeman was a lecturer in Greek at the University College there (*see* **Cardiff University**). Besides works of classical scholarship, she published several books relating to the **Second World War** such as *What They Said at the Time* (1945) and, under her pseudonym, some two dozen detective novels, including *Death and Mary Dazill* (1941), *Clues to Christabel* (1944), *Pity for Pamela* (1950) and *Love from Elizabeth* (1954).

FREEMASONRY

A controversial organization, the Freemasons are still seen by critics as a secret society. Welsh freemasonry is organized into four provinces: South Wales Eastern (covering **Cardiff**, **Swansea** and much of the south Wales **coal**field), South Wales Western, **Monmouthshire**, and North Wales. The oldest extant lodge is the Cardiff-based **Glamorgan**, which dates from 1753. Freemasonry thrived in the 19th century; a St David's lodge was founded in **Milford Haven** (1821) and in **Bangor** (1826), with Loyal Monmouth following in 1838. A revolutionary force in the politics of much of the European mainland, freemasonry came to be profoundly conservative in **Britain**; yet, its ability to absorb democratic reforms allowed its membership to grow rapidly. South Wales Eastern, with 3200 members on the eve of the **First World War**, had 13,000 by the mid-1950s. By the 1970s, however, numbers began to decline, possibly because of the more open nature of society after the **Second World War**, together with attacks on the allegedly pagan characteristics of masonic ritual and the potential corruption of secret membership.

Virtually nothing was written about Welsh freemasonry until the 1980s, when the radical magazine *Rebecca* began a series of exposés, after which mainstream **newspapers** began to take an interest. To some extent, freemasonry responded by adopting a more open policy. There are no official Welsh membership figures but an analysis of yearbooks in the late 1990s suggests there are about 20,000 masons in the four provinces.

FRENCH

French, or rather Anglo-**Norman**, co-existed with **Welsh**, **Latin** and **English** as one of the main languages of medieval Wales. It was the language of administration and justice in Wales's **march**er-lordships and of the culture of the court of the English monarch from the Norman conquest until the 14th century, when it gradually gave way to English. The spread of Anglo-Norman was encouraged by mixed marriages, as in the family of **Giraldus Cambrensis**, but the language remained largely the preserve of the aristocracy. Its literature includes *Fouke le Fitz Waryn* (or Fulk Fitz Warine; d.1256), the semi-mythological account of a Norman ally of **Llywelyn ap Iorwerth**; the story reflects events on the **border** and in the north-east in the 12th and early 13th centuries.

Apart from contact within Wales, French language and culture spread from **England**, as well as through Welsh links with the European mainland in ecclesiastical life, trade, politics and **education**. The borrowings of words into Welsh started early, as revealed by certain stories in *The Mabinogion*. By the 13th century, three French romances by Chrétien de Troyes had their Welsh counterparts in 'Owain', 'Geraint fab Erbin' and 'Peredur fab Efrog', and French **literature** became as fashionable in Wales as in the rest of western Europe. Manuscripts of texts such as verse epics, **Arthur**ian romances and the 'Roman de la Rose' were available, especially in the south and the border region, leading to a number of prose translations into Welsh; the influence of French literary traditions can be traced in the work of poets such as **Dafydd ap Gwilym**. In the 20th century, French literature had a profound effect upon Welsh writers, **Saunders Lewis** in particular.

FRENCH REVOLUTIONARY AND NAPOLEONIC WARS, The

France and **Britain** were at war (with two brief interruptions) from 1793 to 1815. Until Nelson's victory at Trafalgar on 21 October 1805, conflict was mostly a matter of sea warfare. Local militias, volunteer corps and yeomanry were raised, and **Pembrokeshire** was much agitated by the '**last invasion of Britain**' (1797). Most of the British–French military conflict took place in the Peninsular War (1808–14), with Welsh infantry regiments distinguishing themselves at battles in Portugal and Spain. Napoleon was finally defeated on 18 June 1815 at Waterloo, a battle in which General **Thomas Picton** was killed and Henry **Paget**, marquess of **Anglesey**, lost his leg. The war had a profound impact upon **agriculture** in Wales, and boosted the prospects of the nascent Welsh **iron** industry. It is argued that the long conflict with France caused a specifically British national feeling to gain ground in Wales.

FREYSTROP, Pembrokeshire
(649 ha; 474 inhabitants)

Located south of **Haverfordwest**, the **community** hugs a bend in the Western **Cleddau**. St Justinian's church, originally 14th century, was largely rebuilt in 1874. Clareston is a handsome 18th century mansion. South of Freystrop village are traces of the light **railway** built to carry **coal** from New **Hook** anthracite colliery to Hook Quay; the colliery closed in 1948.

FRIARS

All the principal mendicant orders were represented in medieval Wales, with all friaries having an urban setting. Most numerous were the Dominican houses, all five of which benefited from the will of Queen Eleanor (1291), who had toured Wales with Edward I. The friary at **Bangor** was said to possess 'the holiest relic in all north Wales'. The friars of **Rhuddlan** acted as chaplains to the English army during the **Edwardian conquest**. The other Dominican friaries were at **Brecon**, **Cardiff** and **Haverfordwest**.

There were three Franciscan friaries. That at **Llanfaes** was founded by **Llywelyn ap Iorwerth**, close to the burial site of his wife, **Joan** (Siwan; d.1237). The **Carmarthen** friars benefited from a visit by Edward I (1284); a room there long bore the name 'the king's chamber'. The **Cardiff** house was in the suburb of Crockerton. There was one Carmelite friary (at **Denbigh**), and one house of Austin friars (a late foundation of 1377, in **Newport**). References to other supposed friaries have little basis in fact.

Irish prisoners arriving at Frongoch internment camp in 1916

Such evidence as exists suggests that the friaries attracted Welshmen and were in sympathy with national feeling, and that the friars fulfilled preaching and scholarly roles. The Welsh friars were highly praised by Archbishop **Pecham** during his metropolitan visitation (1284) but, being himself a Franciscan scholar, his judgement may have been biased. Gruffudd Bola, who translated the Athanasian Creed into **Welsh**, is commonly (though not certainly) accounted a friar. Welshmen who found vocations in friaries elsewhere included the Franciscan **Johannes Wallensis**, who became regent-master of the order in Paris, and the Dominican Thomas Wallensis (fl.1300–50), imprisoned at Avignon after attacking a papal exposition on the Beatific Vision (1333).

All the Welsh friaries were suppressed during the course of 1538 and 1539. There were then some 60 friars in Wales. Only scant remains of their friaries survive, save for the former Carmelite church at Denbigh, and the choir of the Dominican church at **Brecon** – which now functions as the school chapel of Christ's College. Elsewhere, only street or **place names**, such as Friars Park in Carmarthen, Friars Lane in Haverfordwest and the one-time Friars School, Bangor, bear witness to the religious life there long ago.

FRIENDLY SOCIETIES

In the early 19th century, most villages had at least one friendly society which met in a public house or schoolroom. Members received benefit payments for sickness, old age and funeral expenses, in return for regular contributions. Often an annual dinner would be preceded by a public procession. Some were merely convivial clubs, while others professed higher moral or cultural aims. Separate **women**'s societies were also common in the first half of the 19th century.

After 1850, there was a spectacular expansion in societies with branches having some form of central control over a network of local 'lodges', such as the Manchester Unity of Oddfellows and the **temperance** Rechabites. Wales-based Orders included the True **Ivorites**, the **Merthyr** Unity Philanthropic Institution, the Ancient Britons (Unity of Dowlais and Merthyr) and the Loyal Order of Alfreds. Other societies, such as the **Aberystwyth** Ships' Carpenters, **Gower** Farmers and numerous individual colliery clubs, were based on occupations. Official returns suggest a membership of over 250,000 in 1876.

Thereafter, friendly societies suffered from the growth of commercial **insurance** companies and alternative leisure activities. This decline accelerated in the 20th century with the introduction of state old-age pensions and national **health** insurance.

FRONGOCH INTERNMENT CAMP

From May to December 1916, 1800 **Irish**men were interned at Frongoch (**Llandderfel** near **Bala**), following the Easter Rising of that year. The camp, on the site of a bankrupt **whisky** distillery (*see* **Price family (Rhiwlas)**), was used because of its remote location, and German prisoners of war were relocated to make way for the Irish.

Known as 'the University of Revolution', Frongoch became a symbol of the revolutionary period in the history of **Ireland**. The most famous inmate was Michael Collins, who became commander-in-chief of the Irish Free State army; other inmates held posts in successive Irish governments.

FROST, John (1784–1877) Chartist
Born at the Royal Oak Inn, **Newport**, Frost was a vigorous radical campaigner. Imprisoned for libel in 1823, by 1835 he was a town councillor, subsequently becoming a magistrate and mayor of Newport. He opposed both **Whigs** and **Tories**, being especially critical of the **Morgan family (Tredegar)**. Elected to the **Chartist** convention in **London** in March 1839, the following November he was one of the leaders of the Chartist march on Newport (*see* **Newport Rising**). Condemned to death for treason in 1840, the sentence was commuted to transportation. A convict in Van Diemens Land from 1840 to 1854, he was pardoned in 1856 and died at Bristol.

FROST, William (1848–1935) Aviator
It has been claimed that the credit for the world's first manned flight should go not to the American Wright brothers, who designed and flew their aircraft in 1903, but to a **Saundersfoot** carpenter.

In October 1894, William Frost successfully applied for a patent on what he described as: '[a] flying machine … propelled into the air by two reversible [hand-cranked] fans revolving horizontally.' The craft, which seems to have been a cross between a glider and an airship, was apparently lifted from the ground by a combination of hydrogen 'pouches' and the reversible fans; it would glide forward until it needed a further boost in height. After Frost invested his savings in building the machine, he allegedly flew it over a field in 1896. The undercarriage was caught by the top of a tree and the craft seems then to have been left in the open and destroyed by an overnight storm. Unfortunately, there was no photographic record of the flight, and the **government** refused to give Frost any funding to rebuild his machine.

Whether Frost's machine flew or not, its designer and builder has remained in obscurity. Detractors point either to the impracticality of manual power, or to the likelihood of an earlier precedent; the claim that, in 1872, the Frenchman Dupuy de Lome constructed an airship and – with the combined power of 8 men – achieved a speed of nearly 10 kph.

FURNITURE
Traditional Welsh furniture was highly distinctive. Items such as the *cwpwrdd deuddarn* (two-part cupboard), the *cwpwrdd tridarn* (three-part cupboard) and the *coffor bach* (small chest) are much prized by collectors worldwide, while the reproduction 'Welsh dresser' is a popular product of the modern furniture industry.

An ancient and independent tradition is testified by drawings of officials' chairs in 13th-century **law** manuscripts. Some of the earliest furniture known in **Britain** emanates from Welsh houses, including a 15th-century cradle from **Monmouth** Castle, 16th-century canopied cupboards from Troy (**Trellech**), and Gwydir (**Trefriw**), and armchairs and a four-poster bed of the same period from Newton (**Llandeilo**). Carpenters enjoyed a high status, and the bards ('carpenters of song') often compared the two crafts. The favoured material was native oak (*see* **Plants**). By the 17th century, furniture was being produced in numerous small workshops, with craftsmen combining joinery, turning and **woodcarving** skills. In **England**, these were performed by separate trade guilds; the situation in Wales encouraged greater individuality and a wider variety of styles, leading to the emergence of innovative forms such as the *cwpwrdd tridarn*.

By the 18th century, the **gentry** increasingly sought their furnishings in **London**, but cost and local need meant that the rest of society continued to patronize local carpenters. In towns such as **Carmarthen**, some pieces were produced by cabinet makers using mahogany and other imported woods, but, for most of the **population**, functionality and durability mitigated against the pursuit of urban fashions. Thus the production of traditional items such as the *cwpwrdd deuddarn* long continued. Many furniture craftsmen were part-time wheelwrights and farmers, and the use of local timber, often grown on the customer's land, remained the norm. Their work frequently incorporated decorative flourishes, articulating not only the pride of the maker but also the value attached to the product by the customer, who often acquired items such as the *coffor bach* to celebrate a special event, particularly a marriage (*see* **Love and Marriage**).

Furniture developed according to local conditions; this is epitomized by the wide variety of dressers and **food** cupboards. Forming the focal point of the all-purpose kitchen, frequently with a long-case **clock** alongside, the dresser combined utilitarian and display functions. Imbued with personal associations, such items were handed down the generations, and are frequently still owned by the original families.

Improvements in transport initially boosted the furniture trade by making it easier to obtain materials, but eventually led to its decline, as mass-produced goods were imported. However, the many extant **eisteddfod** chairs show that numerous skilled furniture makers were still at work at the beginning of the 20th century. In the 1930s, the furniture in contemporary style made by the philanthropic venture at **Brynmawr** found a ready market among those sympathetic to the plight of the depressed areas.

By the start of the 21st century, furniture making, often the enterprise of a single craftsman, was undergoing something of a revival in Wales. Mass production of sofas is a significant industry in the northern part of the southern **coal**field.

Rhys T. Gabe (to the left of the captain) in the Welsh rugby team of 1905

GABE, Rhys T. (1880–1967) Rugby player

Llangennech-born Gabe was a powerful, hard-running **rugby** three-quarter. He created an effective partnership with his fellow centre for **Cardiff** and Wales, **Gwyn Nicholls**. He scored 11 tries in 24 international appearances and was a member of the legendary Welsh XV that beat the All Blacks in 1905.

GAFAEL (lit. 'holding')

The holding of a lineage group, the *gafael*, rather than the *gwely*, was the predominant unit of hereditary tenure on which rents and services were assessed in many parts of Wales, for example in much of the **county** of **Merioneth**, the lordship of **Chirk and Chirkland**, the **Conwy** valley and parts of **Powys**. The term was also applied to the holdings of unfree tenants in the *maerdref*, the court or demesne township that existed in each commotal centre in **Gwynedd**, although there were no hereditary rights in these.

The origins of the *gafael* are unclear, as is the nature of its relationship with the *gwely*. In some cases, it may have been the result of a subsequent division of the *gwely*. Indeed, this seems to have been the case in the lordship of **Denbigh**, where the two institutions co-existed, the *gafael* being a subdivision of the *gwely*, but other *gafaelion* may

have emerged in upland areas where arable holdings would have been smaller.

GALLIE, Menna (1920–90) Novelist

Ystradgynlais-born Menna Gallie wrote five novels: *Strike for a Kingdom* (1959), which deals with the **General Strike** of 1926, *Man's Desiring* (1960), *The Small Mine* (1962), *Travels with a Duchess* (1968) and *You're Welcome to Ulster!* (1970). Manifest in them all is a talent for interweaving the serious and the humorous. She also translated **Caradog Prichard**'s novel *Un Nos Ola Leuad* under the title *Full Moon* (1973).

GALLOWAY, William (1840–1927)

Mining engineer

William Galloway, a Scotsman, was appointed an inspector of mines in 1873, serving nearly two years in the west of **Scotland** before moving to south Wales. There, he was an assistant inspector (1874–9) and his insistence, in 1875, that **coal** dust rather than firedamp was the primary cause of coalmine explosions (*see* **Colliery Disasters**) was unpopular with the authorities. As a result, he was, effectively, forced to resign his post. He undertook many experiments that vindicated his views, which at last became widely accepted, together with his advocacy of the use of stone dust as a means of reducing the risk of explosions. As professor of mining at **Cardiff** (1891–1902), he maintained an active consultancy and was knighted in 1924.

GANLLWYD (Y Ganllwyd),
Gwynedd (4483 ha; 178 inhabitants)
Located north of **Dolgellau** and straddling the **A470** and the **Mawddach** and Eden valleys, the **community**'s sole significant settlement is the hamlet of Ganllwyd. Most of it lies within Coed y Brenin (the King's Forest), named in honour of the Silver Jubilee of George V in 1935. The largest of the **Forestry Commission**'s Welsh forests, it contains a well-known **mountain** biking centre. Dolmelynllyn Mansion, now a hotel, was home to W. A. Madocks who built the cob at **Porthmadog**. Near it is the impressive Rhaeadr Ddu **waterfall**. Gwynfynydd was the centre of **Merioneth**'s **gold**-mining industry.

GAPPER, R[obert] L[ambert] (1897–1984) Sculptor
Born at **Llanaelhaearn**, Gapper worked in a range of materials and became a prominent letterer. After service in the **First World War**, he worked as an electrical engineer in Rugby before attending the local art school and, later, the Royal College of Art, **London**. Travelling scholarships took him around Europe, and from around 1928 he worked in the **granite** quarries of his native **Caernarfonshire**.

The Pin Mill at Bodnant Gardens

He lectured at **Aberystwyth** (1934–62) and executed many commissions, notably the portrait bust of the poet **Alun Lewis**, at **Aberdare**.

GARDENS, PARKS and ORCHARDS
There have been gardeners in Wales for at least 6000 years, Indeed, the country's first crop raisers (as hoers of tiny plots) were horticulturists rather than agriculturists. Prehistoric peoples probably also had pleasure gardens; and they would have cared for ornamental **plants**, particularly those used in rituals. The earliest evidence of formal gardens comes from the **Roman** occupation when the legionary legate at **Caerleon** had an enclosed garden with a central pool, and when courtyard gardens adorned the larger houses of **Caerwent**. Plants introduced by the Romans include carrots, turnips and parsnips, and the cherry, vine, walnut, fig, mulberry, medlar and sweet chestnut.

For subsequent centuries, evidence of gardening comes from the **laws** of **Hywel Dda**, the works of the poets, the life of **Gruffudd ap Cynan** and the records of castle building (*see* **Architecture**). The layout of a garden of the bishop of **St David's** survives at **Lamphey**, where in 1326 there were beds of **leeks** and cabbages, and orchards of apples, as well as **fish**ponds and a **dovecot**. As virtually self-sufficient communities, monasteries undoubtedly had extensive gardens; remains of precinct walls have been traced at **Tintern** and Llanthony (**Crucorney**). The fullest evidence of a Welsh medieval garden comes from **Raglan**. There, in the early 15th century, an orchard adjoining the castle produced a wide variety of fruit. **Cadw** has re-created a medieval garden at Tretower Court (**Llanfihangel Cwmdu**).

Although the making of a garden involves some degree of landscape manipulation, more extensive is the work involved in laying out parks. In the Middle Ages, that aspect was concerned particularly with the establishment of **hunting** parks, such as those at Parc le **Breos** (**Ilston**) and around Ysgyryd Fawr (**Llantilio Pertholey**). Although not generally consisting of dense woodland, some such parks were known as forests, **Radnor Forest** being Wales's best example.

In the 16th century, concepts that were developed in Italy had reached Raglan, where a Renaissance garden was created, and featuring terraces, statues, gazebos and water parterres. Elsewhere, gardens continued to be haphazard in their layout, although restoration work at Aberglasney (**Llangathen**) has revealed what may be a symmetrical cloister garden of *c*.1600. As the 17th century advanced, planned gardens were established in increasing numbers; evidence of one of them may be seen at **Chirk** Castle. Of the formal gardens of the 18th century, the most magnificent is that at Powis Castle, **Welshpool**. An engraving of 1742 shows the scale of the vast terraces, which are still a delight today. Glories surviving from the classical phase of Welsh gardening include the gates at **Chirk**, **Leeswood** and Erddig (**Marchwiel**), the work of the **Davies family** of blacksmiths (*see* **Ironwork**).

By the late 18th century, classicism had given way to **romanticism**, with landscape gardening seeking to enhance nature rather than to provide a contrast with it. Thus, meandering drives, bold clumps of trees and sinuous **lakes** found favour at the expense of straight avenues, clipped hedges and formal water features. Among romantic gardens were those at Leeswood, site of Wales's earliest ha-ha (c.1730); Gnoll (**Neath**), rich in follies; Hafod (**Pontarfynach**); and Piercefield, situated dramatically above the **Wye** (**St Arvans**).

The leading landscape designer of this period was the famous 'Capability' Brown, whose work survives at **Cardiff** Castle and Wynnstay (**Ruabon**). With their majestic trees, rich wildlife and **cattle**- or **deer**-grazed pastures, the parks created by the romantic landscape architects were magnificent additions to the landscape.

Romanticism coincided with increasing imports of new plants, a development delighted in by **Thomas Hanmer** of Bettisfield (**Maelor South**), one of Europe's leading tulipomaniacs. Tender plants needed special care, a consideration that led to the erection of 18th-century Wales's finest building – the Orangery at **Margam**. Importations excited the banker John Naylor, owner in the mid-19th century of Leighton Hall (**Forden**) – home of Britain's largest Californian redwoods, and origin of that scourge of modern suburbia, the Leyland cypress. They also excited the Aberconway family who, by the early 20th-century, had created one of the wonders of the world – the gardens at Bodnant (**Eglwysbach**), home to virtually every plant which can survive in a temperate climate.

While landowners were responsible for highly ambitious schemes, the less opulent delighted in more modest horticultural activities, although the cottage garden was never as prominent a feature in Wales as it was in southern **England**. Many viewed gardening primarily as a means of raising vegetables, the landless seeking to do so on allotments, which enjoyed considerable popularity in industrial Wales from the late 19th century until after the **Second World War**. (By the early 21st century, allotments were back in favour.) Most farmers devoted some of their land to orchards, and significant strains of fruit trees – apples in particular – were developed in Wales (*see* **Plants**). However, fruit growing was of little economic importance beyond the eastern fringes of **Monmouthshire** and **Breconshire** and, even there, commercial orchards have generally been abandoned.

By the 20th century, the main creation of large-scale gardens was being undertaken by public authorities. Fine examples can be found in Cardiff, **Swansea**, **Newport** and elsewhere. In 1992, the [British] National Garden Festival was held at **Ebbw Vale**. Wales's greatest recent horticultural event was the opening in 2000 of the **National Botanic Garden** at **Llanarthney**.

GARMON (Germanus; d.437–8) Saint

A bishop of Auxerre in Gaul, whose 'Life' was written by Constantius around 480. At the request of the local clergy, he was sent by the Pope to **Britain** in 429, in order to uproot **Pelagianism**. Reputedly, he led an army of Christian Britons against the Picts and Saxons (*see* **Anglo-Saxons**), bidding them shout 'Hallelujah!' as they defeated the invaders.

Garmon may have made a second visit to Britain in 447 – but it was probably a different Garmon who founded the churches in **Powys** named Llanarmon. The central figure in

Saunders Lewis's play *Buchedd Garmon* combines the two **saints**. The 'Hallelujah Victory' (*c*.447) was alleged to have been fought near **Mold** and is commemorated by the obelisk near Maesgarmon Farm (**Gwernaffield**).

GARW VALLEY (Cwm Garw), Bridgend
(3062 ha; 7570 inhabitants)

Embracing the entire basin of the Garw, a tributary of the **Ogwr**, the **community** includes Werfa (568 m), the highest point in the uplands of mid-**Glamorgan**. Industrialized from the 1880s onwards by the Ocean **Coal** Company and others, Blaengarw and Pontycymer consist of rows of terraced houses interspersed by substantial chapels.

Blaengarw Workmen's Hall (1894) – which once had a theatre, library and reading room – is now a community arts centre. At Blaengarw, the A4064 road simply stops, making Garw one of the few cul-de-sac valleys of the southern coalfield. Bettws, which has expanded of late to accommodate commuters to **Bridgend**, has a much-restored late medieval church. Llangeinor church, with its 15th-century tower and with a tavern as its only neighbour, is sited high above the valley.

Richard Price, perhaps the most original thinker Wales has ever produced, was born at Llangeinor.

GEE, Thomas (1815–98) Publisher, newspaper proprietor and political leader

After serving his apprenticeship in his father's **printing** business in **Denbigh**, Gee spent a short period in **London** before returning to Denbigh as overseer of the press. He broke new ground in Welsh publishing history by starting the quarterly *Y Traethodydd* in 1845 (*see* **Periodicals**). Having invested heavily in the business – the first in Wales, early in 1853, to use steam-powered printing machines – Gee embarked upon a bold publishing programme. As well as commencing *Y Gwyddoniadur Cymreig* in 1854, he published many books, mainly religious and practical works, but also scholarly titles such as the second edition of *The Myvyrian Archaiology* (1870).

Although his parents were **Anglican**, Gee became a **Calvinistic Methodist** in 1830. A **preacher** and zealous supporter of **Sunday schools**, he arranged in his will for medals to be awarded to the most faithful attenders. He was also an ardent proponent of teetotalism (*see* **Temperance Movement**). Although he attacked **Tory**ism and the landlords' hold over their tenants, his main aim was to abolish what he considered to be the unjust privileges of the Established Church (*see* **Disestablishment**). From 1857 onwards, his campaigns enjoyed the support of his **newspaper** *Baner Cymru*, the main voice of the **radicals** among Wales's **Nonconformists**. In 1859, the paper was renamed *Baner ac Amserau Cymru* after Gee bought *Yr Amserau* and amalgamated the two titles. Its influence was particularly prominent during the **Tithe** War. The paper devoted considerable space to Gee's other interests, including non-denominational elementary **education** and the establishment of a university for Wales, with proper provision for the **Welsh language**.

By the 1890s, Gee's era was drawing to a close. His publications began to lose their appeal and, although his political views remained uncompromisingly radical – as a

Gelert's 'Grave' at Beddgelert

supporter of **Cymru Fydd** he argued for **home rule** for Wales – his programme seemed marginal in an increasingly industrial Wales. Nevertheless, Gee continued energetically, becoming the first chairman of **Denbighshire County Council** in 1889. Gee's biography by **T. Gwynn Jones** (1913) is a literary classic which epitomizes the radical-Nonconformist vision of 19th-century Welsh history.

GELERT

The legendary hound of **Llywelyn ap Iorwerth**, after which **Beddgelert** is allegedly named.

The earliest version of the legend, recorded in the late 15th century, mentions Cilhart, Llywelyn's dog, which was respectfully buried at Beddgelert after dying of exhaustion following a hunt. The best-known version, which was popularized in the 18th and 19th centuries, is based on the motif of a faithful animal wrongfully slain. Llywelyn, believing his blood-soaked hound had attacked his son while he slept in his cradle, killed the **dog** only to find that Gelert had saved the child from a marauding **wolf**. The remorseful prince gave Gelert a dignified burial.

Some evidence exists that this story was known in medieval Wales, although its dissemination owed much to the eagerness of the proprietor of Beddgelert's Goat Hotel to further **tourism**. One of six crests – the one representing Wales – borne by Richard III, depicts a golden cradle and a silver greyhound.

GELLIGAER (Gelli-gaer), Caerphilly
(2038 ha; 16,573 inhabitants)
The **community** lies west of the **Rhymney** and includes the settlements of Gelligaer, Penpedairheol, Cefn Hengoed and Ystrad Mynach. The **Roman** fort at Gelligaer was probably constructed AD *c.*120 and abandoned *c.*190. Excavation has revealed revetted defensive banks and ditches as well as a range of barracks, administrative buildings and a bathhouse. On Gelligaer Common are the remains of four Roman practice camps.

The heavily restored church of St Catwg in Gelligaer has a baptistry for total immersion. The adjoining 12th-century motte of Castell Twyn was almost certainly a Welsh construction. Llancaeach Fawr, a well-preserved early 16th-century house, was visited by Charles I in 1645. Taken over by the local authority in 1981, it has become a highly successful museum of 'living history'. A school at Gelligaer was founded under the will of Edward Lewis of Gilfach Fargod who died in 1715; known as the Lewis School **Pengam**, a pile of stone at Glanynant marks the site of the 18th-century building in which the school was originally accommodated.

The community was not industrialized until the late 19th century. By the early 20th century, its chief source of employment was Penallta Colliery, sunk by the **Powell Duffryn** Company in 1909, the most elaborate colliery to be constructed in Wales in that period.

GENEALOGY
As long ago as the 12th century, the Welsh were described by **Giraldus Cambrensis** as being: 'devoted to their pedigrees, and more desirous of marrying into noble than into rich families'.

Under Welsh **law**, a knowledge of one's pedigree was necessary, since a man's rights and responsibilities in society depended on his place in a kindred. For example, land was not held individually, but by kindred. The law texts have words for relationships as far distant as sixth cousin. Even with the decline of Welsh law, and its eventual abolition in 1536, the importance to the Welsh of their pedigrees remained strong. This love of ancient ancestry and pride in descent provoked much scorn from the **English**, as witness a letter from William of Worcester to John Paston in 1457: 'I send a bill of the names indited to my master and you, to see and laugh at their Welsh names descended of old pedigrees.'

Initially, pedigrees were transmitted orally. A knowledge of the pedigrees of the princes and other principal families formed part of the repertoire of the bards, and in addressing their patrons they praised their noble descent, sometimes at great length. Written compilations of the pedigrees of **gentry** families, sometimes made in roll form, became increasingly common from the 15th century onwards. Two traditionally trained bards – **Gruffudd Hiraethog** (d.1564) and Lewys Dwnn (fl.1568–1616) – were appointed deputy heralds for Wales, and visited the gentry all over the country, recording their pedigrees in detail.

In the 17th century, several very large compilations were made of Welsh pedigrees, with strenuous efforts to follow all lines and record all the descendants. The last of these compilations, based largely on the earlier ones, is the *Golden Grove Book* of *c.*1765, now in the **Carmarthenshire County** Record Office. There is very little recorded evidence for the earlier parts of the pedigrees, and the bards, with few exceptions, did not quote dates or sources; but where it is possible to check the traditional pedigrees against record evidence, they are found to be surprisingly accurate. A strong interest in family relationships still remains a feature of Welsh society.

GENERAL STRIKE, The

The most serious industrial dispute in British history lasted for nine days in May 1926. In Wales, however, the predominance of the **coal** industry meant that the far lengthier lockout of the coalminers had a much more devastating impact (*see* **Miners' Strikes**). The origins of the strike lay firstly in labour unrest which pre-dated the **First World War** and secondly in the particular problems of the coal industry. A major clash was only narrowly averted in 1919 by the setting up, by **David Lloyd George**, of the Royal Commission on Coal (the **Sankey** Commission); the chief recommendation of the majority report – the nationalization of the industry – was rejected. In 1921, the coalmines, which had remained under wartime state regulation, were decontrolled and returned to private ownership. This led immediately to a lockout of the miners. The dockers and **railway** workers – the miners' allies in the Triple Alliance – failed to act in support and 21 April 1921 became known as 'Black Friday'; the miners remained in dispute until June.

In 1925, unemployment levels began to rise and battle was re-engaged as the coalowners demanded more wage cuts. This time, the **government** responded on 'Red Friday', conceding a subsidy to the industry and promising an inquiry into the coal industry chaired by Lord Samuel. The commissioners' report, published in April 1926, did not resolve the conflict; the owners demanded district agreements and longer hours and posted lockout notices for 31 April. A special conference of the Trades Union Congress agreed that a general strike in defence of the miners should start at midnight on 3 May. Negotiations failed and, on 4 May, 2 million workers in the transport, **printing**, **iron and steel**, building, electrical and gas industries came out on strike. Desperate attempts to negotiate a return to work, in which Jimmy Thomas, the railway workers' leader from **Newport**, played a pivotal role, resulted in an unconditional and humiliating capitulation by the TUC on 12 May.

In the coalfields the lockout continued. The coalowners' leader was **Evan Williams** of **Pontarddulais**, the president of the Mining Association of Great **Britain**; while the general secretary of the **Miners' Federation of Great Britain** was **A. J. Cook** of the **Rhondda**, 'the man the British middle **class** loved to hate'. The dispute was marked by collective action aimed at alleviating distress; soup kitchens were set up and **male voice choirs** toured to raise funds. There were also many serious disturbances, particularly as men began to return to work, although solidarity was such that as late as November only 14% of the miners of south Wales were working, as opposed to 35% throughout Britain.

In December 1926, severe deprivation brought the strike to an end. Wales's coalfields, that in the south in particular, were devastated; the miners had lost some £15 million in wages and the power and prestige of the **South Wales Miners' Federation** had been greatly diminished. There was a movement towards political rather than industrial action; the southern coalfield became a highly politicized, **socialist** region, a development which also

occurred, to a lesser extent, in that of the north. The memory of the General Strike and its bitter aftermath lived on in Wales for many generations. 'Do you remember 1926?' asked the poet **Idris Davies**. 'Yes, I shall remember 1926 until my blood runs dry.'

GENEU'R GLYN (Genau'r-glyn),
Ceredigion (1806 ha; 735 inhabitants)
Located between **Borth** and **Aberystwyth**, the **community** contains the villages of Llanfihangel-geneu'r-glyn (or Llandre), Dôl-y-Bont and Rhydypennau. Castell Gwallter, built by Walter de Bec during the **Norman** ascendancy in **Ceredigion** (1110–35), is a large motte with a double bailey. Glanfred, once the property of the **Pryses** of Gogerddan, was the home of Bridget Pryse, mother of **Edward Lhuyd**. The **commote** of Geneu'r Glyn was the northernmost commote of the *cantref* of **Penweddig**.

GENTRY and LANDLORDS

In early medieval Wales, land was held either by freemen under the *gwely* system or by bondmen under that of the *taeogdref* (villein township). In addition, **manors** became established in areas under heavy **Norman** influence. During the later Middle Ages, the traditional systems collapsed under the impact of the rise of money rents, the **Black Death** and the abandonment of direct farming by **march**er-lords. By the 15th century, an embryonic Welsh landlord **class** had emerged. Some were descendants of Norman and subsequent invaders; but most were descended from the *bonedd* – native families of pedigree. (The *bon* element is the equivalent of the *gens* element in gentleman.) By the 16th century, intermarriage and similarity of interests had largely eroded the distinction between native and adventitious stocks.

The *boneddigion* were originally those above the *taeog* (villein) class and, by the later Middle Ages, constituted the majority of the **population** of Wales. Most Welshmen considered themselves gentry, a cause of derision in **England**. However, in the 17th century, the word came to be restricted to those with sufficient income to enjoy a life of ease. The Welsh gentry warmed to the **Tudors**, whose legislation favoured them. The extension of Justices of the Peace to Wales in the 1530s delivered local **government** into their hands. The **Acts of 'Union'** granted Wales **parliamentary representation** and, for four centuries, virtually all the country's MPs would be drawn from the Welsh landlord class. Most gentry families accepted Elizabeth's religious settlement, causing them to share the **Anglican**ism of England. They were increasingly assimilated into the English ruling class. They adopted the English practice of having fixed **surnames** and bequeathing their entire property to their eldest sons. They learnt to speak **English**, although the gentry did not wholly abandon the **Welsh language** until the 18th century.

The landowning class used every method of aggrandizement – royal favour, profits of office, commercial ventures, **smuggling**, **piracy**, appropriation of crown and church property, litigation, bullying and, above all, marriage with an heiress. The class included great variations in wealth; in the 1580s, the **Herbert earls of Pembroke**, with £5000 a year, were 10 times richer than the average Welsh squire.

Landed gentry: the Gwynne-Hughes family at Tregib, Dyffryn Cennen, in 1900

Ennobled families holding land in Wales were rare in the 16th century, but they would increase in number as the peerage was enlarged.

In the **Civil Wars**, the Welsh landowning class was largely royalist. However, it survived Parliament's victory remarkably well. The Stuart Restoration in 1660 inaugurated its golden age. Most landed families adopted strict settlement, ensuring that estates passed in their entirety from father to eldest son. Heiresses of families lacking sons were great prizes, and their marriages to heirs of other estates were the chief factor in the concentration of land in the hands of fewer families, a process illustrated in particular by the **Williams Wynn family**. As Welsh landed families became richer, heiresses were targeted by families outside Wales, bringing **Stuarts** to **Cardiff** and **Talbots** to **Margam**.

Many Welsh landed families were essentially parasitic, spending 'their useless lives', as **David Williams** (1900–78) put it, 'in the preservation of game and its wholesale slaughter'. Some, however, had philanthropic interests, and others were involved in Welsh cultural organizations. Many enriched the Welsh landscape with mansions, parks and **gardens**. The more intelligent were interested in agricultural improvements, with **Thomas Johnes** creating a much-admired estate (*see* **Pontarfynach**) and the Yorkes of Erddig (*see* **Marchwiel**) guiding their tenants towards better husbandry.

With the **Industrial Revolution**, landlords found new sources of wealth – profits from the minerals of their estates, ground rents from urban settlements and payments from dock and **railway** companies. Yet, the forces unleashed by industrialization eventually overwhelmed

them. Their disdain for industrialists made the new capitalist class eager to humble them. New radical ideas caused their mainly **Nonconformist** tenants to spurn their leadership. Their paternalism seemed irrelevant as the state groped towards a more equitable **welfare** system. **Socialists** had no respect for power based upon inherited estates.

Yet, in its twilight years, the Welsh landed class reached its apogee in terms of landed possessions. In the 1880s, 89.8% of the land of Wales was owned by landowners who rented their farms to the actual cultivators of the **soil**. In **Gwynedd**, 55% of the land was owned by a mere 33 families. Twenty Welsh estates consisted of at least 8000 ha apiece, with the origins of three-quarters of them dating back to the 15th century or earlier.

The decline in power of the Welsh landed class became apparent in the mid-19th century, when their virtual monopoly of Welsh parliamentary representation was challenged, a challenge almost wholly successful by 1906. In local government, the gentry were virtually swept away in the first **county** council elections in 1889. In the 1890s, sales of estate farms to their tenants began, a process which hugely increased immediately after the **First World War**. Sales were partly caused by **David Lloyd George**'s anti-landlord rhetoric and by rising death duties, but the chief motivation was the realization that landownership, when bereft of unique political power, is less attractive than other forms of investment. Willingness to sell was markedly greater in Wales than in England and **Scotland**. Although other forms of landlordism emerged – that of the **National Trust** and the pension funds, for example – landlords as a class were extinct in Wales by the late 20th century.

GEOFFREY OF MONMOUTH (Galfridus Monemutensis, Sieffre o Fynwy; d.1155) Writer

Of all writers connected with Wales in the Middle Ages, Geoffrey had the greatest appeal and influence. He was probably of Breton descent, and his family may have come to the **Monmouth** area in the wake of the establishment of the **Norman** castle and lordship there. Geoffrey's talents flourished in the context of Anglo-Norman culture. He settled in **Oxford**, where his name occurs, between 1129 and 1151, in documents relating to local religious houses, in which he probably acted as a teacher. Although chosen bishop of **St Asaph** in 1151, there is no record that he visited his **diocese**.

Geoffrey is remembered for his literary work, especially *Historia Regum Britanniae* (History of the Kings of **Britain**), completed *c.*1138, a work which purported to give the history of the kings of Britain from **Brutus** to the death of **Cadwaladr** the Blessed. The author claimed that the work was translated 'from an ancient book in the British tongue'. In fact, the *Historia* is a highly original and deliberate composition. Varied sources were drawn upon to create a pseudo-history where truth and falsehood were skilfully blended. The British were given (through Brutus) a Trojan lineage similar to that of the **Romans** in Virgil's *Aeneid*. Most space was given to **Arthur** and his reign, but the glory departed with his loss. Saxon (*see* **Anglo-Saxons**) hold of Britain became ever tighter and Cadwaladr received angelic warning not to try to regain the kingdom.

Contained in the *Historia* are **prophecies** which, it was claimed, the seer **Merlin** spoke before King **Vortigern**. These *Prophetiae Merlini* were independently available in manuscripts *c.*1135, before being repeated in the *Historia*. Geoffrey wrote, *c.*1148, another work connected with Merlin, *Vita Merlini* (Life of Merlin), in which he displayed considerable awareness of some native Welsh legends; these are combined with wide learning and fruitful imagination to produce a 1529-line **Latin** poem in hexameters.

The purpose of Geoffrey's hugely influential *Historia* was partly political, to present to the Normans an appealing picture of Britain's ancient past. It also inspired a large body of Arthurian **literature**, in Britain and on mainland Europe. In Wales, the *Historia* was translated and adapted, in different versions, under the title *Brut y Brenhinedd* (The Chronicle of the Kings). (**Brut y Tywysogyon** was written as a sequence to it.) The Welsh were especially reluctant to reject Geoffrey's interpretation of British history, and Henry Tudor (*see* **Tudor family** and **English Monarchs**) was seen as fulfilling the prophecy, at the end of the *Historia*, that a day would come when the kingdom would be restored to the British.

GEOGRAPHY, The study of

Geography is one of the oldest studies. Its early Welsh practitioners include: **Giraldus Cambrensis** who wrote a topography of **Ireland** and two books about Wales in the late 12th century; Roger Barlow of **Slebech** whose *Geographie* (*c.*1540) contains the earliest account of the New World in **English**; **Humphrey Lhuyd** who prepared two **maps** of prime importance to British cartography – of Wales, and of **England** and Wales, both published in Antwerp as a supplement to Abraham Ortelius's *Theatrum* (1573); **George Owen** of Henllys, author of *The Description*

of Penbrokshire in 1603; and Lewis Evans (1700–56) of Llangwnadl (**Tudweiliog**), successful geographer, cartographer and protogeologist in colonial **North America**.

Modern geography had emerged by the end of the 19th century, and academic geography achieved its full institutional status towards the end of the **First World War**. In 1918, there were two academic institutions offering degree courses in **Britain** – **Liverpool** and **Aberystwyth**; by 1945, most universities had accepted the subject as part of their core curriculum, and the number of sixth-form pupils studying the subject had increased enormously.

Although geography had been taught at Aberystwyth from the inception of the college, it did not gain separate status until 1908. For the next 10 years, it was taught in the department of **education** to potential teachers. Full departmental status came (largely due to the advocacy of **H. J. Fleure**) with the establishment of the Gregynog chair of geography and anthropology in 1918. In spite of the dual title, the purpose was to study humanity and the environment together, from an evolutionary standpoint. The breadth of Fleure's courses is reflected in the subject matter of further degrees between 1918 and 1930, namely **archaeology** and anthropology – both social and physical – as well as aspects of systematic, regional and physical geography. The changing emphasis introduced by Fleure's successors, C. Daryll Forde and **E. G. Bowen** up to the late 1960s, is detailed in the retrospective *Geography at Aberystwyth* (ed. E. G. Bowen, et al. 1968). In 1989, geography and **geology** were merged under the auspices of the Institute of Earth Science Studies, under the direction of David Q. Bowen.

In the early years, the employment of geography graduates was confined almost exclusively to school teaching. The inauguration of the Land Utilisation Survey of Britain in 1930 marked a change. The complete set of 1-inch to 1-mile maps of Wales and England, together with the complementary **county** reports, clearly demonstrated the importance of a geographical approach. The timing made them fundamental documents in the growing concern for some form of **government** planning of land. The commissioner for the Special Areas, for example, asked the Survey in 1935 to accelerate the preparation of its maps for the designated areas, including industrial south Wales. The need for a new generation of planners with wider spatial skills was in considerable part filled by geographers (some graduates from Aberystwyth and **Swansea**) who were prominent on the staff of the new Ministry of Town and Country Planning (1943) and involved in planning for access to the countryside for the new **National Parks** and for the new towns. Equally important was the emphasis on urban geography, an area of study in which Harold Carter of Aberystwyth made a distinguished contribution.

When the second department of geography – at Swansea – gained its independence from that of geology in 1954, geography was becoming involved in a conceptual revolution. During the 1960s, there was a fundamental reorganization of its methodology of enquiry, involving the realignment of geography within the main stream of modern scholarship, increased contact with other disciplines, and greater mobility of geographers. Initially, one of the specialisms at Swansea was climatology (*see* **Climate**); later, it was social (including urban), political and cultural geography, as well as geomorphology and topographic science. Geomorphology as a research and teaching topic was taught initially in the **University of Wales**'s three geology departments. From the **Second World War** onwards, however, the subject was gradually acquired by the geography departments.

The creation of the third department immediately followed the incorporation of St **David**'s College, **Lampeter** (*see* **University of Wales, Lampeter**) as a constituent institution of the university in 1971. The first professor was David Thomas (who studied rural deprivation in Wales) and the first Welsh geographical journal, *Cambria*, was launched in 1974. The department closed in 2001.

The importance of maps as part of the essence of geography – described as 'the analysis of distribution' or 'the science of aerial differentiation' – is well documented in the variety of maps in *Atlas Cenedlaethol Cymru: National Atlas of Wales* (ed. Harold Carter, 1981–7). Other national atlases compiled by Welsh geographers include *Disease Mortality* by Melvyn Howe (1970) and *Agriculture* by J. T. Coppock (1964, 1976). The latter led to the development of some of the world's earliest forms of computer-based mapping.

GEOLOGY

Mainland geology

The rocks that make up the foundation of Wales, together with their fossils and minerals (*see below*), provide evidence of a complex history of over 700 million years. This history has evolved through both time and space, as this small region of the earth's crust drifted across the globe, following its formation far south of the equator, to its present position at about 52° in the eastern Atlantic Ocean – a journey of some 15,200 km. Only since the 1960s has there been a generally accepted understanding of the physical processes that drive the movements of different segments of the planet, with convection currents deep inside the interior of the molten Earth rising to the thin rocky crust and forcing it into motion; these are the processes of plate tectonics and continental drift. In its drift across different latitudes, Wales has crossed many climatic zones, and the evidence of the different environments is locked up in the geology of the country. The Earth itself is 4600 million years old, so in Wales there is a preserved record of less than 16% of physical and biological history. That history is told by the geological succession that follows.

PRECAMBRIAN ERA (4600–543 million years ago)
Geophysical data suggest that much of Wales is underlain at relatively shallow depths (perhaps 4–20 km) by a 'basement' of crustal rocks between about 600–700 million years old. Fragments of this basement are brought to the surface by folds and faults in regions such as **Pembrokeshire**, **Anglesey**, **Llŷn** and the **border**lands. Everywhere, the rock successions comprise altered (metamorphic) and highly fractured sequences of sediments, volcanic remnants and granitic rocks injected into the crust from originally deeper levels.

At least four structural components may be present in the Anglesey–Llŷn fault zones: the Monian Supergroup (mostly altered sediments and igneous rocks), the Coedana Complex (granites and gneisses), the Anglesey blueschists (highly altered rocks from a sub-sea floor of oceanic origin), and the Sarn Complex. All of these rocks may have been related originally to similar complexes in the Gander region of Newfoundland. Large, chaotically arranged blocks of **limestone** in the upper Monian Supergroup appear to indicate collapse down deep marine slopes; these rocks contain primitive fossil algal structures (stromatolites) and 'bacteria' – possibly some of the oldest evidence of life in Wales.

Some of the most dramatic exposures of Monian rocks are in the South Stack (**Trearddur**) area, where there are visually stunning examples of the intense faulting and folding effected by the huge forces involved in the processes of plate tectonics and continental drift.

The Welsh Borderland and South Wales Precambrian successions suggest close affinity with those of the Avalon Platform of Newfoundland, originally on the opposite side of an ocean from the Gander terrains. Igneous rocks at Stanner-Hanter (**Old Radnor**) are 702 million years old, the oldest reliable date in Wales. Similar volcanic rocks occur in the **St David's**, **Hayscastle** and Roch–Treffgarne (**Nolton and Roch** and **Wolfscastle**) areas of north Pembrokeshire, with intrusive igneous rocks exposed to the south of **Haverfordwest**. There are sediments associated with all these rocks, which, in an isolated exposure near **Carmarthen**, have yielded fossil 'jellyfish' comparable with forms described first from southern **Australia**.

LOWER PALAEOZOIC ERA
(543–417 million years ago)
As southern **Britain** drifted northwards into subtropical–tropical latitudes over a period of 125 million years, Cambrian, Ordovician and Silurian rocks were deposited in a relatively deep sea basin and in surrounding shallow marine shelf areas. The early Cambrian invasion of the sea over the ancient Precambrian surfaces brought influxes of grits, sands and muds across the region, together with newly evolving forms of marine life, including the earliest trilobites and brachiopods that represent distinctive elements of the Welsh fossil faunas. The Welsh Basin was situated along the south-eastern flank of a proto-Atlantic (or Iapetus) Ocean, which separated most of present-day Europe from **North America** and Greenland – although eastern Newfoundland was on the 'European' side and most of **Scotland** was on the 'American' side. Cambrian rocks and fossils from eastern Newfoundland are remarkably similar to those of Wales.

The massive sandstones forming the **Rhinogydd–**Harlech Dome of **Gwynedd** are the most impressive outcrops of Cambrian rocks in Wales. Most of these deposits (Harlech Grits Group) formed as submarine fans, involving currents driven by gravity down slopes from neighbouring regions; these typical sand rocks, known as turbidites, were first interpreted in this part of Wales. There is little evidence here of intermittent shallow marine sedimentation. Similar rocks crop out in eastern Llŷn, notably in the dramatic cliffs of Porth Neigwl and Porth Ceiriad on St Tudwal's peninsula (**Llanengan**).

Rocks of about the same age in the **Llanberis–Bethesda–Bangor** region of the Gwynedd **slate** belt are mostly mudrocks in their upper part, probably deposited in a deeper trough between the Welsh Basin and a rising 'Irish Sea Landmass'. These are the fine-grained rocks now forming the huge outcrops of slate in the Penrhyn-Llanberis quarries and neighbouring areas.

In the south, Cambrian rocks are preserved mostly in the St David's–**Solva**–Newgale–Treffgarne area, forming the Caerfai, Solva and Menevian groups, in almost continuous, spectacular exposure along that stretch of coast. They are mostly shallow marine deposits formed on the southern shelf margin of the Welsh Basin. Outcrops at Solva, Porth-y-Rhaw and Nine Wells are famous for their Cambrian fossils, especially the large trilobite *Paradoxides davidis*, first found in the mid-19th century.

Minor outcrops of Cambrian rocks – which were originally deposited as shallow marine sediments and which contain fossil brachiopods and trilobites – are also preserved in the **Llangynog** area of **Carmarthenshire**, where evidence suggests that the sediments were derived from a nearby landmass to the south.

In the Ordovician Period, Wales continued to form part of a marine basin, accumulating muds, sands and grits, with local lime-rich sediments around the shallower margins. The rock sequences and their enclosed fossil faunas are of international significance in that they form standards for interpreting geological successions throughout the world (*see below*, 'The Study of Geology').

One particular aspect of Ordovician geology in Wales differentiates it from the preceding Cambrian geology, namely the widespread development of volcanic rocks, resulting from the continuing northward drift, which was to lead to collision with the 'North American' continent of Laurentia. Eruptions began in the late Tremadoc period, evidence of which is preserved in the volcanic rocks around Rhobell Fawr (**Brithdir and Llanfachreth**). Then there were successive volcanic episodes in the **Arenig**–Llanvirn and Caradoc intervals. The Arenig Fawr–Migneint and Llŷn areas contain numerous intervals of volcanic rocks and ashes from the earlier period, and there are similar extensive developments in the **Aran mountains** and the **Builth–Llandrindod** area. Most extensive, however, are the coastal successions exposed from Ramsey **Island** to Strumble Head (**Pencaer**) near **Fishguard**. There were major volcanic centres on Ramsey and around Fishguard, with a further minor centre around Abereiddy Bay (**Llanrhian**). Most of this succession was erupted underwater, leading to the formation of basaltic pillow lavas.

The second major Ordovician volcanic episode in the Caradoc period involved particularly intense submarine and terrestrial activity across **Snowdonia**, extending through the Aran mountains and the **Cadair Idris** range, and across to the **Berwyn Mountains**. **Snowdon** itself comprises mostly a succession of basalt lava flows overlain by sub-aqueous volcanic ashes and sediments containing marine fossils.

In uppermost Ordovician times, there was an abrupt cut-off of volcanic activity, signalling an eventual end to collision with the 'North American' continent. At the same

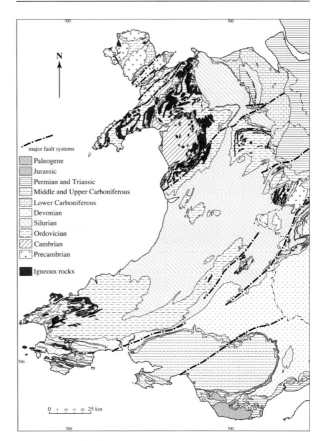

The geology of Wales

time, there is evidence of a period of global cooling and of falling sea levels; this is reflected in sedimentation in the Welsh Basin, when sediments from exposed shelf areas were eroded and slumped off by gravity into the deeper trough. The **Llangranog–Newquay** coastal sections of **Ceredigion** are particularly demonstrative of such features, involving the deformation of 'semi-plastic' rocks in the slumping process.

In the early Silurian period, about 440 million years ago, Wales lay in the southern tropics, and rising sea levels again led to the spread of the sea across the Welsh trough and neighbouring shallow shelf regions. Muds, silts and sands were deposited into the marine areas, derived in part from a land area to the south of the Severn Sea named Pretannia (cf. *Prydain*, Britain), from which **river**/delta systems flowed northwards. Shallower marine areas, as in the **Usk** region of **Monmouthshire** and in the adjacent borderlands, saw the development of reefs similar to those forming in the Caribbean today. Rich faunas of corals, trilobites, brachiopods, together with algae, are present in the reefs and surrounding bedded limestones.

By the end of Silurian times, southern Britain had collided progressively with Scandinavia and the North American continent. The collision resulted in uplift and mountain building to the north (the Caledonian earth movements) leading to the sea becoming shallower and retreating once more. During this interval, the earliest freshwater **fish** appeared in Wales, and the first vascular **plants** colonized the land.

GEOLOGICAL TIME-SCALE

ERA	PERIOD	AGE (Millions of years ago)	SUMMARY OF GEOLOGICAL HISTORY OF WALES
CENOZOIC QUATERNARY	Holocene or Recent	0.01–present	Coastal areas drowned by rising sea level caused by melting ice at the end of the Ice Age. Deposits of alluvium and peat, with further development of present drainage patterns and modern flora and fauna. Modification of landforms by human activity.
	Pleistocene	1.8–0.01	The Ice Age, with repeated glaciations and milder interglacial periods. The most recent major glaciation reached a maximum about 20,000 years ago, and the last local ice left Snowdonia and the Brecon Beacons 11,500 years ago. Modification of landforms by ice scouring and deposition of glacial drift. First evidence of humans (Neanderthals) in Wales from Pontnewydd Cave (Cefnmeiriadog, Denbighshire) about 200,000 years old.
	Neogene	23–1.8	Prolonged, pulsatory uplift and erosion. Late Paleogene and early Neogene terrestrial sediments known only from Mochras (Llanbedr) and locally in Gwynedd and the south-west. Early Paleogene intrusive igneous rocks in north-west Wales. Basic landform and drainage pattern established.
	Paleogene	65–23	
MESOZOIC	Cretaceous	140–65	No rocks of this age known in Wales, but much of the region was probably covered by the chalk sea in warm climates. Any sediments deposited in this period have since been eroded away.
	Jurassic	195–140	Lower Jurassic marine rocks preserved in Vale of Glamorgan and Mochras borehole, with thick, younger sediments in the Severn Sea and Cardigan Bay basins. Warm, shallow sea may have immersed Wales through the period but direct evidence is lacking.
	Triassic	251–195	Arid and semi-arid terrestrial conditions, with evidence of periodic flash floods. Dinosaur footprints and early mammal remains known from Vale of Glamorgan. Marine transgression in the south at the very end of the period.
PALAEOZOIC UPPER	Permian	298–251	Uplift and mountain building (Variscan Orogeny). Erosion across most of Wales, with desert sediments preserved around the margins.
	Carboniferous	354–298	Marine immersion early in the period, leading to spread of warm, subtropical seas with rich coral/brachiopod faunas; extensive deposition of carbonate sediments that now form Carboniferous Limestone. Regression in middle of period, with widespread deltaic deposits. Rich forest vegetation on coastal plains and deltas in late Carboniferous times; peat accumulated to form the coal seams of the Coal Measures.
	Devonian	417–354	Uplift and mountain building (Caledonian Orogeny) continued from Silurian times, resulting in the deposition of the terrestrial Old Red Sandstone across most of Wales in extensive river and floodplain environments. Rapid diversification of land floras and non-marine fish faunas.
LOWER	Silurian	443–417	Marine muds, silts and sands, with local carbonate sediments including subtropical reefs in the borderlands and south-east Wales. Volcanoes in south-west Wales. Land with deltas across southern Wales. Shallowing and retreat of the sea late in the period, with widespread onset of terrestrial conditions. Earliest fish in Wales, and first vascular land plants appeared.
	Ordovician	490–443	Marine muds, sands, grits and local carbonate sediments. Extensive sub-marine and terrestrial volcanicity in north, mid and south-west Wales. Fossil faunas increasingly diverse, including first corals.
	Cambrian	543–490	Transgression of sea into Wales, with deposition of grits, sands and muds. First abundant fossils, including earliest trilobites and brachiopods.
PRECAMBRIAN		4600–543	Oldest rocks in Wales dated at about 700 million years, but are possibly considerably older. Evidence of intermittent marine conditions and volcanicity, with periods of major faulting, folding, uplift and erosion. Earliest fossils from Wales are jellyfish, from Carmarthenshire, of late Precambrian age, and primitive algae from Anglesey.

UPPER PALAEOZOIC ERA
(417–251 million years ago)

Uplift and mountain building continued from Silurian through Devonian times, during which Wales was part of an extensive desert landmass that straddled the equator and stretched from present-day North America across northern Europe to Russia. Until about 350 million years ago, extensive river systems drained from the mountains, carrying the red sands and silts that form much of the **Black Mountain** and the **Brecon Beacons**, together with the rich red **soils** that blanket much of the borderland. The red sandstone cliffs of **Manorbier**, Barafundle (**Stackpole**) and the **Milford Haven Waterway** in Pembrokeshire, and parts of eastern Anglesey are also remnants of this ancient landmass. In these Old Red Sandstone continental environments, there was continuing rapid diversification of land floras and non-marine fish faunas.

In the early Carboniferous period, the warm, subtropical sea invaded yet again, spreading lime-rich sediments with abundant corals around the northern and southern margins of the country. The Great Orme and the Little Orme headlands at **Llandudno**, and the Eglwyseg escarpment (**Llantysilio**) near **Llangollen** are formed of the massive Carboniferous Limestone resulting from these deposits. The rim of the southern **coal**field and the beautiful sea cliffs of **Gower** and the **Castlemartin** coast – with its spectacular blowholes and the Green Bridge of Wales arch – are preserved in the same rocks.

Eventually, the shallow seas silted up, filled with sand and mud carried in rivers from the uplands of central Wales to form large deltas and low coastal plains in both the north and the south. On these swampy plains grew lush subtropical vegetation, not unlike the Florida everglades of today. The dense plant cover was drowned, at intervals, by brief incursions of the sea; the vegetation thereby killed off formed thick deposits of **peat**. This pattern was repeated in numerous cycles and the peat beds were buried and compressed, eventually being transformed into the Coal Measures preserved in the coalfields of the north-east and the south. These rocks are a rich source of delicately preserved fossil plants.

About 300 million years ago, at the beginning of the Permian Period, the great Coal Forests were destroyed, and renewed uplift again turned Wales into a mountainous desert region. Until about 250 million years ago, there was intense erosion across the whole region.

MESOZOIC ERA (251–65 million years ago)

Through most of the Triassic Period, Wales remained largely an upland desert region where erosion was dominant; very few rocks of this age are preserved. In marginal areas, there is evidence of screes and of the deposition of fine silts and muds from river systems. In some cases, coarse debris formed in wadis, indicating periodic flash floods. Leaching from these highly oxidized sediments was probably the source of the **iron** ore deposits (hematite) preserved in Carboniferous rocks in the **Llanharry** area. Upper Triassic rocks in **Glamorgan** contain fossil evidence of a fairly diverse land fauna, including rare finds of **dinosaur** bones, numerous dinosaur footprints and abundant skeletal remains of some of the earliest known **mammals**. At the very end of Triassic times, about 200 million years ago, invasion by the sea began again from the south and there were marine connections from the present Severn Sea area westwards to the Irish Sea. A wide range of vertebrate and invertebrate fossils is known from the marine sediments.

Marine invasion continued through the early Jurassic Period, with rocks preserved on the coast of the **Vale of Glamorgan** and in a borehole at Mochras (**Llanbedr**). The distinctive creamy-coloured limestone cliffs of Glamorgan, extending from **Penarth** through **Rhoose**, **Llantwit Major** and Nash (**St Donats**) to Ogmore, contain rich associations of shallow marine fossils. In part, these sediments were deposited around islands that formed an archipelago across southern Wales. The thick succession of Lower Jurassic rocks at Mochras, discovered in 1968, provides evidence of a deep Mesozoic basin occupying Cardigan Bay, with the coastline closely following the line of a fault which displaces the rocks through a vertical distance of over 1000 m, to bring them adjacent to the nearby Cambrian rocks onshore.

There is no evidence of any younger Jurassic or Cretaceous rocks across Wales. Modern interpretations, however, suggest that warm, shallow seas covered the region for most of that time and that any sediments then deposited have since been eroded away. It is not unlikely that there was a covering of chalk by the end of the Cretaceous period, 65 million years ago, by which time Wales had drifted north from the tropics more or less to its present location. The modern Atlantic ocean began to open during Jurassic times, introducing a temperate maritime **climate**.

CENOZOIC ERA (65 million years ago to the present)

In the Paleogene and Neogene periods, from about 65 million to 1.8 million years ago, Wales finally emerged from the sea as a result of prolonged pulses of earth movements leading to uplift and erosion. Terrestrial sediments of these ages are known only from Gwynedd – including Mochras – and the south-west. The uplift was accompanied by the intrusion of igneous rocks in the north-west. The basic patterns of Wales's **landforms**, and of its river drainage system, were established during this long era. Because of the dominance of erosion, there is little or no preserved evidence of animal or plant evolution in Wales at this time, when elsewhere 'modern' faunas and floras, including mammals and grasslands, were replacing the older, pre-Cenozoic faunas and floras.

From 1.8 million years ago, the earth's climate became cooler, a process which continued until c.11,500 years ago, and which caused the Ice Age – a central factor in the creation of Wales's present landforms. The era was characterized by repeated glaciations and milder interglacial periods. It is believed that the first human beings to settle in Wales (early Neanderthals) reached the north-east in an interglacial period about 200,000 years ago. When the latest glaciation was at its peak c.20,000 years ago, ice covered the entire country apart from the Vale of Glamorgan, south Gower and south Pembrokeshire, and a vast ice sheet occupied the Irish Sea Basin. In the north, large glaciers carved out deep U-shaped valleys such as Nant Ffrancon and Nant Peris, together with the numerous cirques and peaks throughout Snowdonia and neighbouring areas.

Huge amounts of rock eroded by the glaciers were eventually dumped as boulder trails over much of the landscape. Glacial erosion carved the deep basins later occupied by many of Wales's **lakes**.

With so much water locked up in the ice, there was a fall in the sea level by as much as 100 m, turning the Irish and Severn Seas into dry land. As the ice slowly melted over the years 18,000–*c.*11,500 BC, sea levels rose, and Wales's modern coastline began to assume its present form. On land, the retreating ice sheets and glaciers deposited vast amounts of rock and soil debris across the landscape, material which became a significant factor in determining the patterns of vegetation and **agriculture**. Weathering, erosion and deposition continue to shape the landscape (*see* **Landforms, Landscape and Topography**).

Offshore geology

Until the 1960s, little was known of the offshore geology in Wales, or, indeed, of that of any other part of the world; it was generally assumed that the onshore geology extended across the continental shelf without significant change. Most of the earlier geologists would be astounded to learn that the rocks beneath the seas off Wales are commonly very much younger than the old, predominantly Palaeozoic rocks of the mainland. Some enlightened early geologists did however make deductions about the differing age of offshore rocks. In 1919, **Edward Greenly** produced a sketch **map** showing Mesozoic strata in the Irish Sea – based on the distribution of erratics (non-local rock fragments) in glacial deposits on the Anglesey coast – and **O. T. Jones** predicted in 1952 that Triassic rocks are present in Cardigan Bay.

A fundamental change in thinking on continental shelf geology in the 1960s was significantly influenced by research in and around Cardigan Bay. When **Alan Wood**'s borehole drilling at Mochras in the late 1960s proved that the sedimentary rocks were even younger than had been predicted, it was found scarcely credible that such a thickness of Mesozoic rocks could be present just a stone's throw from the classic Cambrian succession of the Harlech Dome.

Maps produced by the British Geological Survey show that the basic outline of Wales is essentially delineated by the boundary of the Mesozoic and Cenozoic rocks occupying the sedimentary basins that surround it; only in south Glamorgan and the Vale of **Clwyd** do these younger rocks crop out on land. The closest correspondence between the Mesozoic–Cenozoic boundary and the present-day coastline is in Tremadog Bay and along the north coast. Around Pembrokeshire, Llŷn and Anglesey the Palaeozoic rocks outcrop well beyond the mainland. The present-day coastline is, of course, temporary and will change as sea level rises and falls; nonetheless, Wales will remain an inlier or 'island' of older, more resistant rocks surrounded by younger, more easily eroded strata.

The discovery of offshore Mesozoic sedimentary basins has led to the search for hydrocarbons in Welsh waters, for it is primarily in rocks of this age that **oil** and gas have been found in the North Sea. In the Irish Sea, large gas fields have been found at the Morecambe Bay Field to the west of Blackpool. Following this major discovery, other fields were found further south; the Douglas oilfield and part of the Hamilton gasfield are located in what could be defined as the Welsh sector of Irish Sea. The Douglas oilfield, with estimated recoverable reserves of 11.69 million tonnes, was discovered in 1990, and began production in 1996. Seismic surveys and drilling operations in Caernarfon Bay, Cardigan Bay and St George's Channel have met with no success to date.

Another difference in the offshore geology is that whereas the Quaternary glacial deposits on land are generally very thin, the offshore deposits are commonly much thicker. Furthermore, during the most recent glaciation, the southern limit of ice lay some way north of the southern coast, but extended much further south in St George's Channel. The sediments are over 100 m thick over a wide area to the west, and locally exceed 400 m in channels where erosion has been particularly severe. In the Severn Sea and Liverpool Bay areas, these Quaternary deposits are being dredged as valuable sources of aggregates.

While the geology of mainland Wales has had a huge influence on the economic and social development of the country, economic exploitation of the sub-marine area has been limited. This may remain the case, although much has still to be learned about the offshore geology of Wales.

Minerals

Wales has a rich and diverse mineral wealth, with over 350 different kinds being recorded to date. Some are renowned worldwide for their aesthetic quality, among them millerite (a rare nickel sulphide) which occurs as spectacular, needle-like crystals in clay ironstone nodules in coal-bearing strata of the south. Equally famous are very fine brookite (titanium oxide) crystals collected from Prenteg, near **Porthmadog**, illustrated as early as 1809 by the famous mineralogist James Sowerby, in the third volume of his *British Mineralogy* treatise. It is likely that crystals from this locality were utilized in the first formal description of the mineral in 1825 by the French mineralogist A. Michel Lévy.

Several other minerals were first reported from Wales, including anglesite (lead sulphate), named after Anglesey, cymrite (a complex barium aluminium silicate hydroxide hydrate), named after Cymru (Wales), bannisterite (barium sodium aluminium silicate), brammallite (a sodium-rich mica) and dickite (a clay mineral), all named after eminent mineralogists, and pennantite, named after **Thomas Pennant**. A more recent discovery is that of namuwite (a zinc copper sulphate hydroxide hydrate), from Aberllyn mine, near **Llanrwst**, and named after the **National Museum [of] Wales**. Other very rare minerals identified from Wales include only the second world occurrence of aleksite (a lead tellurium bismuth sulphide) the presence of which was confirmed in 1990 on a specimen from St David's mine (**Llanelltyd**).

Mineralogically, Wales is perhaps best known for the occurrence of **gold**. It was exploited by the **Romans** at Dolaucothi (**Cynwyl Gaeo**) where it occurs as microscopic grains in arsenopyrite (an arsenic iron sulphide mineral), and is rarely visible to the naked eye. In contrast, gold from the **Dolgellau** area occurs as visible grains, commonly in association with quartz.

However, it was the sulphide ores of **lead** (galena), **copper** (chalcopyrite) and, later, zinc (sphalerite), which were the chief metals exploited in Wales. The major mineral fields were located in the north-east, Snowdonia and mid-Wales. Recent studies in mid-Wales have revealed high cobalt and nickel contents in the veins, resulting from the presence of the rarer minerals ullmannite (nickel antimony sulphide), siegenite (nickel cobalt sulphide) and gersdorffite (nickel arsenic sulphide). Silver was also won from a few mines in this area, owing to the local occurrence of tetrahedrite (a copper iron silver zinc antimony sulphide).

Wales's most remarkable site of copper extraction is **Mynydd Parys**, which, in the late 18th century, briefly became the world's greatest source of copper. In contrast to the copper deposits of Snowdonia or mid-Wales, where the copper occurs in quartz-rich veins, the Mynydd Parys copper occurs as a series of massive deposits of admixed chalcopyrite, galena and sphalerite, generated as a result of the exhalation of hot, mineral-rich fluids into the sea in late Ordovician or early Silurian times. As well as being the locality where anglesite (lead sulphate) was first described, the mineralogy of Mynydd Parys is of considerable importance for the diverse range of other sulphate minerals present, among them jarosite, halotrichite, copiapite and melanterite (all iron sulphates), pickeringite (magnesium sulphate), chalcanthite (copper sulphate), barite (barium sulphate) and anhydrite (calcium sulphate), many of which have precipitated from the extremely acidic mine waters

resulting from decomposition of original iron sulphide minerals in post-mining times.

The various mineral ores across Wales have been subjected to weathering, both before and after mining. A range of complex, and sometimes rare, mainly sulphate, carbonate and phosphate secondary minerals have developed, including lautenthalite, langite, cerussite, hydrocerussite, hydrozincite, elyite, wulfenite, schulenbergite, schmiederite, pyromorphite, brochantite and aurichalcite.

Iron and manganese ores have long been exploited in Wales. Iron ores were worked in the north from bedded chamosite (iron aluminium silicate) ores in strata of Ordovician age, and in the south from ores occurring as massive bodies of hematite and goethite (both iron oxides) in limestones of Carboniferous age. Manganese was worked from the south's sole mine at Tŷ Coch (**Porthcawl**); ores from this locality contain the very rare mineral pyrobelonite (a lead manganese vanadate), this occurrence being only the second recorded in the world. On the Llŷn peninsula, manganese ores extracted at the Rhiw and Nant mines (**Llanbedrog**) were found to contain a range of new and rare minerals including banalsite, celsian (barium aluminium silicate), bannisterite, cymrite, paracelsian (barium aluminium silicate), ganophyllite (potassium manganese aluminium magnesium silicate hydroxide) and pennantite. In the Harlech Dome region, manganese was extracted from red and yellow bedded ore deposits of Cambrian age, composed largely of spessartine (manganese-rich garnet), rhodonite (manganese iron magnesium calcium silicate) and rhodochrosite (manganese carbonate).

Galena, a sulphide ore of lead, mined in north and mid Wales

Not all potentially commercial mineral deposits in Wales have been exploited, however. In the mid-1970s, a major deposit of porphyry copper was discovered at Coed y Brenin, **Meirionnydd**. Exploration revealed an estimated reserve of 200 million tonnes of copper ore at 0.3% copper; but because the copper could be extracted only by open-cast mining methods, and the deposit lay within the Snowdonia **National Park**, its exploitation was not pursued.

The study of geology

Even before geology became accepted as a scientific discipline in the late 18th century, there were acute observations of geological features in Wales as part of wider studies within natural history. In 1595, **George Owen** of Henllys described with remarkable accuracy the disposition of limestones around the southern coalfield, and in 1699 **Edward Lhuyd**, one of the founders of scientific palaeontology in Britain, produced the first systematic catalogue of British fossils; his work included the first illustrations of trilobites from Wales.

Geology established itself as a new kind of **science**. It was the first to be concerned largely with the history of nature and with the age of the earth. The emphasis during much of the 19th century was on establishing, classifying, correlating and interpreting sequences or successions of strata wherever possible on their organic content, and erecting an overall table of systems or chapters that would be acceptable internationally.

Pioneering work from the 1830s onward on some of the older and little known strata underlying the distinctive Old Red Sandstone strata in Wales and the borderland led to the recognition of three geological systems which were given names with distinct Welsh associations. The youngest, the Silurian, was named in 1835 after the **Silures**, by Roderick Impey Murchison (1792–1871); the oldest, the Cambrian (after the **Latin** for Wales; *see* **Cambria**), based on the strata of north-west Wales, by Adam Sedgwick (1785–1873), also in 1835; and the middle, the Ordovician (after the **Ordovices**), suggested by Charles Lapworth (1842–1920) in 1879, incorporated parts of the first two. These three names were eventually accepted worldwide. A fourth system, the Carboniferous, based partly on the strata of the south Wales coalfield, had already been named by **W. D. Conybeare** in 1822. Further Welsh names – the Tremadoc Series, Arenig Series, Llanvirn Series and Llandeilo Series – have gained a 'sort of scientific immortality' by being chosen as defined subdivisions of the Ordovician system.

Contemporaneous with the work of the individual pioneers, the first team of geologists, forming the initial Ordnance Geological Survey (currently the British Geological Survey), carried out a systematic study of the whole of Wales and the borders during the years 1838 to the mid-1850s, with revisions up to 1880. They improved on all previous work and pioneered the preparation of large-scale geological maps with accompanying cross-sections and vertical sections, large enough to illustrate the position of every productive coal seam in Wales's two coalfields. Other examples of pioneering work were the recognition, by Andrew C. Ramsay, of the significance of the

extensive high-level plateaux of central Wales – 'the most remarkable feature of the physical **geography** of Wales' – and of the glacial erosion of the rock basins underlying many of the lakes of the north-west.

With the establishment of chairs of geology at the three constituent colleges of the **University of Wales** in the first two decades of the 20th century, much of the country was restudied in even greater detail, using more sophisticated methods in stratigraphy, palaeontology and petrography.

In the years following the **Second World War**, new disciplines were created: geophysics at **Cardiff** and **Swansea**; geochemistry at Swansea; palaeobotany at Cardiff and Bangor; palaeoecology at Swansea; marine geology at Bangor; micropalaeontology at **Aberystwyth** and Swansea; geomorphology and Quaternary studies at Aberystwyth. In the 1990s, at the **government**'s behest, the Geological Survey resurveyed the south Wales coalfield over a period of 15 years and assessed the economic potential of the ore fields, particularly in mid and north Wales.

The acceptance of the theory of plate tectonics in the 1960s changed the perspective for most research workers. In particular, the unexpected results of the deep borehole on the sea's edge at Mochras in 1968 transformed the understanding of the geological history of southern Britain.

The role of Wales over many decades as one of the chief training grounds for young geologists is the result of the historical significance of so many of its localities, the singular richness and diversity in such small compass of its geology, physiography and mineralogy, and its convenience to most British universities.

The pattern of academic departments has changed materially since the 1980s. In 1989, the departments at Swansea and Cardiff were merged, at Cardiff. At much the same time, the department of mineral exploitation (originally 'mining') and the maritime studies department at Cardiff were incorporated within the geology department. In 1996, geology was discontinued as an honours degree subject in the Institute of Earth Studies at Aberystwyth. At Cardiff, currently with a staff of 40, there are research groups in palaeobiology, crustal processes and geoenvironment, glacial geomorphology, palaeo-oceanography and coalfield research.

The most important institutional developments in applied geology in Wales have been: the formation of the **National Coal Board** in 1946, with its deep mining, open cast and research divisions; the founding at **Llanddulas** (later at **Llandudno**), in 1961, of the Robertson Research Company, which carries out a wide range of applied geology worldwide; and the British Geological Survey's establishment of a Welsh office at **Llanfarian** in 1980 (closed in 1994) partly to provide detailed modern geological maps for Wales.

That Welsh geologists are particularly well represented throughout the profession is due in part to the unusual popularity of geology as a subject in some southern schools – **Caerphilly** and **Llanelli**, in particular – and to the success of Swansea and Aberystwyth in attracting large numbers of students in the 1960s, 1970s and 1980s. The number of amateur geologists, however, has been consistently small.

Most Welsh studies during the last 200 years (as reflected in over 7000 publications) have been on stratigraphy and palaeontology. The bias is reflected in the list of Fellows of the Royal Society – for example, **W. Boyd Dawkins**, **T. W. E. David**, **T. N. George**, O. T. Jones, **T. McK. Hughes**, **W. J. Pugh**, **A. E. Trueman** and **H. H. Thomas**. The contributions of two recent Fellows, Sir Alwyn Williams (1977) and Dianne Edwards (1996) are, respectively, on Lower Palaeozoic biostratigraphy and on the earliest fragmental plant forms well represented in the Silurian and Old Red Sandstone of south Wales.

The main reference collections of fossils, rocks and minerals relating to Wales are housed in the National Museum [of] Wales, the Sedgwick Museum, **Cambridge**, the Manchester (University) Museum and the British Museum.

GEORGE, T[homas] N[eville] (1904–80) Geologist

Born into a family of teachers at Morriston, **Swansea**, Neville George, FRS, was himself a particularly inspiring university teacher, committed to adult **education** and the teaching of **geology** in schools. Graduating at Swansea and at **Cambridge**, he followed his first teacher, **A. E. Trueman**, in the chair of geology at Swansea (1933) and at Glasgow (1947). His major research work was in the stratigraphy of the Lower Carboniferous, theoretical palaeontology and the geomorphological evolution of Welsh **landforms**.

GIANTS

Wales has a wealth of onomastic myths and folk stories relating to giants, many of them dating back to the Middle Ages and earlier. In his *Historia Regum Britanniae*, **Geoffrey of Monmouth** claimed that, before **Brutus** arrived in **Britain** and drove them away, giants were the **island**'s sole inhabitants. Benlli Fawr, who is associated with Foel Fenlli (**Llanbedr Dyffryn Clwyd**), is mentioned in the *Historia Brittonum* (9th century), and *The Mabinogion* has much to say about **Bendigeidfran fab Llŷr** and Ysbaddaden Bencawr. King **Arthur**'s victories against giants feature prominently in traditional stories, and, indeed, judging by the **place names** which purport to celebrate his feats, Arthur himself could be considered to be a giant. In the late 16th century, stories concerning Welsh giants and giantesses were gathered by **Siôn Dafydd Rhys**, who listed and located 72 of them. *The Giants of Wales* (1993), the work of the Texan scholar Chris Grooms, is an admirable study of the entire subject.

GIBSON, John (1790–1866) Sculptor

For much of the 19th century, Gibson was regarded, in **Britain** at least, as the world's greatest carver of marble. Born in humble circumstances at Gyffin, **Conwy**, Gibson was apprenticed first as a cabinet maker and later as a mason, after the family had moved to **Liverpool** in 1799. Having educated and improved himself under the patronage of the historian William Roscoe, he travelled to Rome in 1817, where he worked in Canova's studio.

Gibson was the chief exponent of high Victorian classicism, reintroducing the Greek method of tinting marble. He spent most of his time in Rome, leaving occasionally for **London** for such purposes as modelling a statue of Queen Victoria (1850 and 1851). Some of his works may be seen at **Bodelwyddan** Castle.

John Gibson

GILBERTSON, Francis William (1873–1929)
Steel and tinplate manufacturer

After studying **chemistry** at **Oxford**, Francis ('Frank') Gilbertson became the leader of the third generation of the family to operate a **tinplate** works at **Pontardawe**. By the time he formally assumed control in 1912, the firm had extended into steel production (*see* **Iron and Steel**). Gilbertson's main importance was as the accepted spokesman for the sheet steel industry, signified by his long presidency of the South Wales Siemens Association (1918–29) and of the **Swansea** Royal Metal Exchange (1911–29). He was also, from 1920, the first president of the new University College at Swansea (*see* **University of Wales Swansea**).

GILDAS (*c.*495–*c.*570) Writer

Gildas was famous for his *De Excidio Britanniae* (On the destruction of **Britain**), an open letter denouncing the sins of the leaders of Wales. A difficult text to interpret, it is nevertheless the main source of information on the history of 6th-century Wales. Gildas refers disparagingly to five contemporary kings, among them **Maelgwn Gwynedd**, and alludes to traditions about the coming of the **English** to Britain by invitation of **Vortigern**. A learned monk, Gildas wrote colourful **Latin** in a sophisticated style. In a Life written by a 9th-century Breton monk, it is claimed that he was born on the banks of the Clyde and that he established a monastery at Ruys in **Brittany**. According to another 9th-century tradition, Gildas was educated by **Illtud** at **Llantwit Major** along with **Saints David**, **Samson** and Paul. Church dedications to him in Wales, **Cornwall** and Brittany commemorate the movements of his followers. He was also held in high regard in **Ireland**. A second Life, the work of **Caradog of Llancarfan**, was written in the 12th century.

GILFACH GOCH (Y Gilfach-goch), Rhondda Cynon Taff (603 ha; 3434 inhabitants)

Located south-west of the **Rhondda** in the upper reaches of the valley of the **Ogwr** Fach, Gilfach Goch is an archetypal **coal**field settlement; indeed, it is the setting of the best known of all the writings on the south Wales coalfield, *How Green Was My Valley* by Richard Llewellyn (**Richard Herbert Vivian Lloyd**). Until the advent of industrialization, the area was remote and pastoral. Large-scale coalmining began with the coming of the **railway** in the 1860s and, by 1910, the Britannic Merthyr Steam Coal Company had established three large collieries. Rows of semi-detached houses (1910–14) represent the earliest venture of the Welsh Garden Cities Company.

GILPIN, William (1724–1804) Writer

An English clergyman whose didactic and topographical *Observations on the River Wye* (1782) was highly influential in the development of contemporary attitudes towards landscape and beauty (*see* **Landforms, Landscape and Topography**). For Gilpin and his followers, the countryside and ruins of Wales became a source of developing theories concerning nature, beauty and the picturesque. His frequently republished book sparked a tourist invasion of the **Wye** valley (*see* **Tourism**).

GIRALDUS CAMBRENSIS (Gerald the Welshman, Gerallt Gymro, Gerald of Wales, Giraldus de Barri; c.1146–1223) Writer

Giraldus was born in **Manorbier**, the fourth son of William de Barri and his wife Angharad. He was proud of his mixed ancestry, although he sometimes felt that this had been an obstacle to his career, being under suspicion by both sides; socially and culturally. However, his place is with the Cambro-**Normans**.

He received the best **education** of his day, in Gloucester, Paris, Lincoln and Hereford. In about 1175, he returned to Wales and was appointed archdeacon of **Brecon** in the **diocese** of **St David's**. He was an enthusiastic reformer and was nominated by the canons of St David's to succeed his uncle as bishop in 1176; but the king was not in favour, it was said, because of Giraldus's associations with his kinsman, the Lord Rhys (**Rhys ap Gruffudd**; d.1197). However, he accepted election by the chapter of St David's in 1199 and campaigned vigorously at court and in Rome (three times) to have his election as bishop confirmed and the metropolitan status of St David's recognized, but he was finally obliged to accept defeat in 1203.

Giraldus was more of a writer than a politician. Though he spent many years in the service of Henry II, he had little regard for the life of the court. His two visits to **Ireland** (1183 and 1185) provided him with material for his first two books, *Topographia Hibernica* or *The Topography of Ireland* (1188) and *Expugnatio Hibernica* or *The Conquest of Ireland* (1188). The second of these gives an account of the Norman campaign from the viewpoint of his own family and reveals Giraldus's skill in organizing his material thematically and in creating a lively historical narrative in the classical style. In the *Topography*, he describes the landscape and wildlife of Ireland, together with the customs of the people (though not without a considerable amount of prejudice). In 1188, Giraldus spent six weeks as a member of the party that accompanied Archbishop Baldwin on his tour of Wales to preach the crusade and also, no doubt, to emphasize the authority of Canterbury. *Itinerarium Kambriae* or the *Itinerary through Wales* (1191) contains a description of the country and its people interspersed with frequent digressive anecdotes and personal observations. It was a unique book in its time and remains entertaining. The more formally structured *Descriptio Kambriae* or *Description of Wales* (1194) is an equally exceptional composition. It is an historico-geographical analysis of the development of Wales, followed by a description of the strengths and weaknesses of Welsh society and of the morals and customs of its people, and finally by advice on how the Welsh may be conquered and how they may resist and revolt. These books, Giraldus's best writing, are the most vivid of all contemporary accounts of 12th-century Welsh society.

Giraldus continued to write for the rest of his life – **saints**' lives, moral precepts, discussions on church and court reforms, and the personal story of his battle for St David's: some 20 books in all. Through his writing, his complex personality comes alive – the learned scholar, determined and self-confident but strangely naive and conceited, never able wholly to identify himself with either the one strain or the other in his ancestry.

GITTINS, Charles [Edward] (1908–70) Educationist

Born at Rhostyllen (**Esclusham**) and educated at **Aberystwyth**, Charles Gittins was a teacher and educational administrator in Durham and subsequently Yorkshire, before becoming director of **education** for **Monmouthshire** (1944). In 1956, he became professor of education at **Swansea** during a period of unprecedented expansion in teacher training. The report published in 1967 by the Central Advisory Committee for Education (Wales) takes its name from him: it advocated a child-centred approach to primary education, rather than learning by rote, and recommended the teaching of **Welsh** to all primary school pupils. From 1967 until his death in a **sailing** accident off the **Gower** coast, he was vice-principal at Swansea (*see* **University of Wales Swansea**).

GLADESTRY (Llanfair Llythynwg), Radnorshire, Powys (5365 ha; 419 inhabitants)

The **community** adjoins the **border** with **England** south of **New Radnor**. Gladestry church, of the 13th to 16th centuries, has a sanctus bellcote. The Court of Gladestry, where a later farmhouse stands today, was the home of **Gelli Meyrick**. The **Offa's Dyke Footpath** runs through the village, and also through Newchurch to the south, where Charles I stopped to drink a glass of milk on his march through **Radnorshire**, and where **Kilvert** was astonished to see a clergyman's daughters helping to castrate lambs. The Great House at Newchurch is a cruck hall of *c.*1490, its roof span (8.6 m) the widest in Wales. The little church at Michaelchurch-on-Arrow has early 15th-century ceiling bosses and a pre-**Reformation** rood screen and ciborium.

Because **Welsh** is so well taught in the local primary school, the community has the highest proportion of

Welsh-speakers in **Radnorshire** (12.4%). The community's Welsh name, meaning the St Mary's church in Llythynwg, suggests that Llythynwg or Llwythyfnwg was once a **commote** of the *cantref* of **Elfael**, but the early conquest of the area obliterated ancient administrative boundaries.

The Black Hill (517 m) is considered to be the setting for Bruce Chatwin's novel *On the Black Hill* (1982).

GLADSTONE, William Ewart (1809–98) Politician

Gladstone entered parliament in 1832. In 1839, he married Catherine Glynne of **Hawarden** Castle, which later became his home. He became **Liberal** leader in 1867 and prime minister in 1868, immediately tackling the Irish problem by passing the Irish Church Bill and the Irish Land Bill – measures which aroused considerable interest in Wales, where the demand for **disestablishment** and land reform was gaining support. In 1880, the Liberals were returned with a substantial majority, but the measures they introduced proved disappointing to radical party members. For men such as **Lewis Llewelyn Dillwyn**, **Chamberlain**'s 'Unauthorized Programme' had a powerful appeal. Gladstone's hold over the affections of the Welsh was, however, amply demonstrated when in 1886 he introduced his Irish Home Rule Bill. Despite the fact that Chamberlain, who opposed Gladstone's measure, was a **Nonconformist radical**, despite anti-**Roman Catholic** prejudice and despite the misgivings of such influential figures as **Thomas Gee** and David Davies (*see* **Davies family (Llandinam)**), the majority of Welsh Liberals remained true to their allegiance to 'the grand old man', a staunch **Anglican**. Such was their support that Gladstone, whose position in **England** had been weakened by the schism over **Ireland**, was obliged in 1887 to include Welsh disestablishment in the Liberal programme, while in 1893 he was persuaded by **T. E. Ellis** to set up a royal commission on the **land question** in Wales. The Gladstone Library at Hawarden commemorates him.

With the exception of the biographies of **David Lloyd George**, the **Welsh-language** biography of Gladstone by Griffith Ellis of Bootle is the sole Welsh biography of a British prime minister.

GLAMORGAN (Morgannwg) One-time county

The **county** was established by the **Act of 'Union'** of 1536, through the amalgamation of the lordship of **Glamorgan** with that of **Gower** and Kilvey. From the mid-18th century onwards, its uplands underwent large-scale industrialization and several of its coastal towns – **Cardiff** and **Swansea**, in particular – became major **ports**. As a result, Glamorgan became by far the most populous of Wales's counties, containing 47% of the country's **population** by 1921. The Glamorgan County Council, established in 1889, was responsible for the entire county apart from the **county boroughs** of Cardiff and Swansea. (**Merthyr Tydfil** became a county borough in 1908.) On the eve of abolition in 1974, the administrative county consisted of the **boroughs** of **Barry, Cowbridge, Neath, Port Talbot** and **Rhondda,** the **urban districts** of **Aberdare, Bridgend, Caerphilly, Gelligaer, Glyncorrwg,** Loughor, **Maesteg, Mountain Ash,** Ogmore and Garw, **Penarth, Pontypridd** and **Porthcawl,** and the **rural districts** of Cardiff, Cowbridge, **Gower** and **Llantrisant** and **Llantwit Fardre,** Neath, Pen-y-bont, and **Pontardawe.**

Following abolition, the county was divided into the three counties of **Mid, South** and **West Glamorgan**. Although no local authority unit called Glamorgan now exists, Glamorgan institutions such as its **Cricket** Club and its History Society continue to flourish. At the time of its abolition in 1974, Glamorgan consisted of 211,750 ha. The Census of 1971 recorded that the ancient county had 1,264,800 inhabitants and the administrative county – the area under the administration of the Glamorgan County Council (that is, those regions not included within the county's three county boroughs) – had 751,390 inhabitants.

GLAMORGAN (Morgannwg) Lordship

Established by **Robert Fitz Hammo** following his defeat of **Iestyn ap Gwrgant** in the 1080s, the lordship was held until 1485 by Fitz Hammo's descendants, among them the **Clare** and the **Despenser** families. In 1486, it was granted to Jasper **Tudor**; it passed to the crown following the death of Jasper in 1496. With its caput at **Cardiff**, it extended from the **Tawe** to the **Rhymney** and thus encompassed only part of the ancient kingdom of **Morgannwg**. From the late 11th century onwards, its lowlands were extensively manorialized and settled by **Norman** knights and **English** peasants. Its uplands continued under a degree of Welsh control until the late 13th century. In 1536, the lordship was linked with that of **Gower** and Kilvey to create the **county of Glamorgan**.

GLANTWYMYN, Montgomeryshire, Powys (11,175 ha; 1106 inhabitants)

Extending over a wide tract on both banks of the **Dyfi** east of **Machynlleth**, the **community** contains eight villages: Cemmaes Road (the settlement which grew around the **railway** station and which came to be known in Welsh as Glantwymyn); Cemmaes (Cemais) and Cwm Llinau on the banks of the Dyfi; Abercegir, Darowen and Comins Coch, south of the **river**; and Llanwrin and Ceinws, north of the river.

Nash Point on the Glamorgan coast

There are late medieval churches at Cemais and Llanwrin, the latter containing a **stained-glass** window bearing the arms of Edward IV. From 1876 until 1903, the rector of Llanwrin was the lexicographer D. Silvan Evans (*see* **Dictionaries**), appointed in 1875 as the first professor of **Welsh** at **Aberystwyth**. He held the part-time post until 1884, commuting to Aberystwyth from Llanwrin. There are two 19th-century flannel mills at Abercegir.

According to tradition, Henry Tudor (*see* **Tudor family** and **English Monarchs**) stayed at Mathafarn in 1485 while on his way to **Bosworth**. He perplexed his host, Dafydd Llwyd – a noted prognosticator – by asking him to predict his future. On the sage advice of his wife, Dafydd prophesied success. The house was burned down by the **Cromwellians** in 1644. **The Centre for Alternative Technology** is located south of Ceinws.

GLASBURY (Y Clas-ar-Wy), Radnorshire, Powys (3887 ha; 902 inhabitants)

Glasbury, the southernmost of the **communities** of **Radnorshire**, contains the villages of Boughrood, Cwmbach, Glasbury, Llanstephan and Llowes. There was a **Celtic** monastery or *clas* at Glasbury, and possibly also at Llowes. Glasbury lost its medieval church to **Breconshire** *c.*1660 when the **Wye** changed its course. Unusually for Wales, it has a village green surrounded by houses. The Old Vicarage, dating from *c.*1400, is one of Wales's oldest houses still lived-in. Maesllwch Castle, an extravagant castellated structure, was built in the 19th century for the de Winton family. The Independent (*see* **Congregationalists**)

chapel at Maesyronnen, adapted from a barn in 1697, is a monument to the simple piety of early **Nonconformists**. Boughrood, still a hamlet in 1980, has grown considerably over the last 20 years. Boughrood Castle, begun in 1817, has, according to the *Shell Guide to Mid Wales*, 'a curious colonial flavour'. There is a tollhouse on the bridge over the Wye at Boughrood and a suspension bridge upstream at Llanstephan.

GLASCWM (Glasgwm), Radnorshire, Powys (7030 ha; 479 inhabitants)

The **community** is a wide tract south-east of **Llandrindod**. The motte at Colwyn, the administrative centre of the **commote** of **Elfael** Uwch Mynydd, was crowned with a stone castle in 1240; it was in ruins when **John Leland** visited it in the 1530s. Glascwm village, beautifully and remotely situated, was the site of a **Celtic** monastery or *clas* where the greatest treasure was *Bangu* – St **David**'s portable bell, which was endowed with miraculous powers. Glascwm was still **Welsh**-speaking in 1745, when its parishioners petitioned against the appointment of a monoglot **English** vicar. Bedo Chwith, a patron of **Lewys Glyn Cothi**, lived at Cregrina, where the last **wolf** in Wales was reputedly killed in the reign of Elizabeth I.

GLASLYN River (33 km)

The headwater of the Glaslyn rises as a stream below the summit of **Snowdon** before flowing through Llyn Glaslyn and Llyn Llydaw. Below Pen-y-Gwryd (**Beddgelert**), it turns south-west and flows through Llyn Gwynant and

The Glaslyn estuary with the hills of Meirionnydd in the background

Llyn Dinas in Nant Gwynant, perhaps the most beautiful valley in Wales. A hydroelectric power station (1903) at Cwm Dyli harnesses the **river**'s power (*see* **Energy**). Beyond Beddgelert, the river flows through a narrow gorge at Bwlch Aberglaslyn and under the famous Aberglaslyn bridge. In the early 19th century, William Alexander Madocks built an embankment (the Cob) across Traeth Mawr, the broad estuary of the Glaslyn. **Porthmadog** was developed adjacent to the Cob to export **slates** from the quarries of Blaenau **Ffestiniog**. The narrow-gauge Welsh Highland **Railway** is to be reopened all the way from **Caernarfon** to Porthmadog, providing an added opportunity to enjoy the magnificent views of the Glaslyn.

GLASS

Along with speech, **agriculture** and writing, glass is one of the most significant of human inventions. Windows are central to any concept of **architecture** and domestic comfort; spectacles enable people to pursue intellectual activities into middle age and beyond; microscopes and telescopes are fundamental to scientific advance.

Prehistoric sites in Wales have yielded glass beads, and the **Seven Sisters** hoard (AD *c.*50) provides evidence of the ability to manufacture glass's close associate – enamel. Window glass came to Wales with the **Romans**, who used it extensively in the fortress baths at **Caerleon**. In the post-Roman centuries, imported glassware was in use in settlements such as the fort at **Dinas Powys**, but centuries would go by before glass was again used in Wales for windows. In the later Middle Ages, **stained glass** enjoyed increasing popularity in Welsh churches but, until the 16th century, the domestic use of window glass was restricted to aristocratic residences such as **Raglan** Castle. By the 17th century, houses such as Kennixton (re-erected at the National History Museum; *see* **St Fagans**), the home of a prosperous **Gower** yeoman, had glass windows, but as late as 1820 most of the peasant houses of northern **Glamorgan** had to make do with shutters rather than glass windows.

The availability of sand and **limestone** – the basic ingredients of glass – together with access to **coal**, led to establishment of glass manufacture in Wales's southern coastal towns. There was a bottle factory in **Swansea** Castle by 1678 and, before the building of the West Bute Dock (1839), the sole building on **Cardiff**'s moors was John **Guest**'s glass factory. Glass manufacture as a large-scale industry came to Wales in the second half of the 20th century through the activities of the Pilkington Company founded in St Helens, Lancashire, in 1826. The company's centres in Wales are the electro-optical systems factory at **St Asaph** (1957), the fibreglass factory at **Wrexham** (1971) and the glass insulation products factory at **Pontypool** (1976).

GLYDER FAWR, GLYDER FACH, Y GARN, ELIDIR FAWR and TRYFAN Mountains

One of Wales's three massifs – **Snowdon** and **Y Carneddau** are the other two – rising to over 3000 feet (914 m), the range includes the summits of Glyder Fawr (999 m), Glyder Fach (994 m), Y Garn (946 m), Elidir Fawr (924 m) and Tryfan (917 m). Of these **mountains**, the most impressive is Tryfan; with its three precipitous faces, and crowned by the two upright slabs known as Adam and Eve, it is the only peak in Wales which can be climbed only by those prepared to use their hands. On the summits of Glyder Fawr and Glyder Fach are frost-shattered rocks piled into strange formations such as the Cantilever and the Castle of the Winds. At the core of Elidir Fawr is the remarkable Dinorwic hydroelectric scheme (*see* **Llanddeiniolen**, **Energy** and **Engineering**). The most fascinating feature of the range is the great Devil's Kitchen cleft surrounding the glacial **lake** of Llyn Idwal. Designated Wales's first National Nature Reserve in 1954, Cwm Idwal is renowned not only for its **geology** but also for its **plants**, among them the Snowdon lily. The slabs overlooking Llyn Idwal are important in the history of rock climbing and George Mallory trained on them before being killed whilst on Everest in 1924.

GLYN, William (1504–58) Bishop of Bangor

William Glyn, born at Heneglwys (**Bodffordd**), spent most of his career at **Cambridge**, becoming Lady Margaret Professor of Divinity in 1544. Opposed to the radical Protestantism promulgated during the reign of Edward VI, he believed in transubstantiation (1549), and was one of the stoutest disputants against the Protestants Cranmer, Latimer and Ridley at **Oxford** (1554). In 1555, he was appointed bishop of **Bangor**, where he promoted the aims of the Catholic reforming circle of Reginald Pole by establishing clerical discipline, and insisting on instruction in and conformity to the basic tenets of the **Roman Catholic** faith. **Friars** Grammar School, Bangor, was founded by his brother, Geoffrey Glyn (d.1557).

GLYN TARELL, Breconshire, Powys
(5975 ha; 575 inhabitants)

The **community**, which straddles the **A470** between **Brecon** and **Merthyr Tydfil**, contains the villages of Libanus, Llanilltyd and Llanspyddid. It offers spectacular views of the **Brecon Beacons**; Pen-y-fan (886 m), the highest peak, marks its eastern flank. A **Mountain** Centre, providing information for visitors to the Brecon Beacons **National Park**, is sited on the slopes of Mynydd Illtud, and there is an Outdoor **Education** Centre at Storey Arms. According to **Theophilus Jones**, the circular churchyard at Llanilltyd contains the grave of St **Illtud**, while Anlach, the father of **Brychan**, is said to be buried in the churchyard at Llanspyddid. At the southern end of the community lies Beacons reservoir, the northernmost of **Cardiff**'s three **reservoirs** on the main branch of the **River Taff**.

GLYNCORRWG, Neath Port Talbot
(5595 ha; 5544 inhabitants)

The core of the **community** is the basin of the **River** Corrwg, a tributary of the Afan. It was an area of pastoral farms until the later 19th century, when **railways** linked the new pit villages of Glyncorrwg, Cymmer, Abergwynfi and Blaengwynfi with the coast. This then allowed the local **coal** seams to be exploited effectively. Following the closure of the mines, there are hopes that the community's extensive forests (*see* **Forestry**), the Glyncorrwg Ponds and the Afan Argoed Country Park will offer alternative employment in **tourism**. Where the village of Glyncorrwg stops, the **road** stops, making the Corrwg a classic example of a cul-de-sac valley.

GLYNDŴR One-time district

Following the abolition of the **counties** of **Denbigh** and **Merioneth** in 1974, Glyndŵr was created as a district of the new county of **Clwyd**. It consisted of what had been the **boroughs** of **Denbigh** and **Ruthin**, the **urban district** of **Llangollen** and the **rural districts** of Ceiriog and Ruthin and part of that of **Wrexham**, in Denbighshire, and the rural district of **Edeirnion** in Merioneth. The name was chosen because the district contained Sycharth (**Llansilin**) and Glyndyfrdwy (**Corwen**), the chief estates of **Owain Glyndŵr**. In 1996, the district was divided; five **communities** were attached to **Wrexham County Borough** and three to **Powys**; the rest became the core of the reconstituted Denbighshire.

GLYNDŴR REVOLT, The

The revolt of **Owain Glyndŵr** began on 16 September 1400 when Owain was proclaimed **Prince of Wales** at Glyndyfrdwy (**Corwen**). The initial outbreak in the northeast was soon defeated and Henry IV led a force through the north to restore order. The rising flared up again in 1401 with the capture of **Conwy** Castle and Owain's victory at Mynydd **Hyddgen** (*see* **Cadfarch**); it spread across Wales and successive royal expeditions were unable to suppress or contain it. The crushing of Henry Percy's revolt at Shrewsbury in 1403 had no effect on Owain's progress and 1404 saw the capture of the castles of **Harlech** and **Aberystwyth**, the holding of a parliament at **Machynlleth**, a treaty of alliance with France and the defection to Owain of a number of prominent Welsh clerics, among them the bishop of **St Asaph**, **John Trefor**, and the archdeacon of **Merioneth**, **Gruffudd Young**, who became Owain's chancellor. The high point of the revolt came in 1404. A French force arrived in 1405 but it achieved little, although it is said to have advanced with Owain as far as Woodbury Hill near Worcester before returning to Wales.

Glyndŵr's seal on the Pennal Letter

The year 1405 saw the drawing up of the Tripartite Indenture, an agreement between Owain, Percy, earl of Northumberland, and Edmund **Mortimer** for the division of **England** and a much-expanded Wales, and the holding of a parliament at Harlech, but it was also the year when a royal force from **Ireland** reoccupied **Anglesey**. Both individuals and communities were by then submitting to the English crown, and the French left in November 1405. Despite these reverses, in a letter dated at **Pennal** in Merioneth in the same year (*see* **Pennal Letter**), Owain set out his terms for the transfer of the spiritual allegiance of Wales from the Pope at Rome to his rival at Avignon; the terms included a separate Welsh ecclesiastical province and the foundation of two universities. But the tide had turned; a faction favouring peace with England had come to power in France and Owain's ally Northumberland was defeated and killed at Bramham Moor in 1408; that year also saw the fall of Aberystwyth. In 1409, Harlech fell, and members of Owain's family were captured. The last raid on the **border** was in 1410; Owain disappeared and died, apparently, in 1415 or 1416. In 1421, his son Maredudd's acceptance of a pardon finally marked the end of the revolt.

The revolt is the defining event in the history of late medieval Wales. Traditionally said to have begun as Owain's response to a border dispute with his neighbour Reginald **Grey**, lord of **Ruthin** or **Dyffryn Clwyd**, it has in fact to be seen in the context of the crises and tensions and subsequent revolts which took place all over Europe after the middle of the 14th century. Among the contributory factors were the **Black Death** and the general restlessness and disorientation that followed it. In Wales, there was also a nationalistic dimension, stemming from the disillusion of the leaders of the native Welsh community, both lay and clerical, with the English crown and a feeling that the restoration of the native Principality was possible. These leaders were the men behind a revolt that may well have been planned in advance; the deposition of Richard II in 1399 provided the opportunity and they were able to harness popular social and economic grievances of the kind which were so common after 1350.

The revolt failed because, in the absence of adequate French assistance, superior English resources were bound to triumph in a war of attrition. There were few reprisals, apart from heavy communal fines; many leading figures who had held offices in the 1390s, were in rebellion for the next decade, and back in their offices after 1410. Wales could not be governed without their co-operation. The short-term economic effects were severe, but such well-documented factors as the flight of bondmen and the abandonment of rural communities are more likely to have been the consequence of the plague and its associated crises rather than of the revolt. There were some losers, but most of the political nation emerged with augmented power at the local level. The revolt did strengthen national awareness, since it saw most of the country acting together, but the 15th-century evidence suggests that there was a general agreement to make a fresh start.

GLYNNEATH, (Glyn-nedd), Neath Port Talbot
(2616 ha; 4368 inhabitants)

Located on the right bank of the **River Nedd**, the rural parts of the **community** have been extensively forested (*see*

Forestry). **Coal**mining began in 1793 and expanded rapidly following the arrival of the **Neath Canal** in 1795. Several interesting canal features survive, including the remains of an inclined plane built in 1805 to connect the canal with the **Aberdare iron**works. The sprawling village contains a half-timbered building, a rarity in **Glamorgan**. St **Cadog**'s Church (1809) stands in what were the grounds of Aberpergwm House, home in the 15th century of Rhys ap Siancyn and his descendants, the most prominent of the poets' patrons in Glamorgan during the period. Later, it became the home of the Williams family, one of the few Welsh **gentry** families to remain faithful to the **Welsh language**. Theirs was among the last of the Welsh household bards (Dafydd Nicolas; ?1705–74); the folksong collector **Maria Jane Williams** was a member of the family. The family's motto, *A ddioddefws a orfu* (He who suffers triumphs), became that of the Glamorgan **County** Council. The mansion, remodelled in 1876, is now derelict. Rheola House was extended in 1812 by the architect **John Nash** for his partner, John Edwards-Vaughan. There is a vast open-cast coal site on the community's northern edge.

GLYNRHONDDA Commote

One of the **commotes** of the *cantref* of Penychen. Following the **Norman** seizure of the kingdom of **Morgannwg** in the late 11th century, the commote enjoyed a degree of autonomy under the descendants of **Cadwallon ap Caradog**, the grandson of **Iestyn ap Gwrgant**, the last king of Morgannwg. However, the 'second conquest of **Glamorgan**' in the mid-13th century brought it directly under the rule of the **Clare family**. The commote was broadly coterminous with the **parish** of Ystradyfodwg and with the later **borough** of the **Rhondda**. Those whose ancestors lived in Glynrhondda before the coming of large-scale **coal**mining are known as *Gwŷr y Gloran* (lit. 'men of the tail'), an old name which derives from the fact that Glynrhondda was considered to be Glamorgan's tail (*cloren* or *cloran*).

GLYNTRAIAN (Glyntraean), Wrexham
(2969 ha; 878 inhabitants)

Located south of **Llangollen**, Glyntraian embraces the central stretch of the Ceiriog valley. One of the five **communities** of the former **Glyndŵr** District to be absorbed by the **county borough** of **Wrexham**, its eastern boundary, which is also the **Wales/England border**, follows **Offa's Dyke**. At the Butchers Arms, Pontfadog, **George Borrow** was told that fairies (see **Tylwyth Teg**) very rarely danced in the neighbourhood. Near the village is the 1200-year-old Cilcochwyn oak tree, reputedly the oldest in **Britain**; legend maintains that it was the only tree to survive the forest destruction ordered by Henry II during his invasion of Wales in 1165. According to tradition, his defeat by the forces of **Owain Gwynedd** occurred in Crogen and the slain were buried at Adwy'r Beddau, a gap in Offa's Dyke. However, **J. E. Lloyd** argued that marching via Crogen made no strategic sense.

GLYWYSING Kingdom

The earliest surviving name for the land between the **Rivers Tawe** and **Usk**, Glywysing was probably named after the early 5th-century king named Glywys. He is reputed to have been the father of Gwynllŵg, who gave his name to the land between the Rivers **Rhymney** and Usk, and the grandfather of St **Cadoc**. In the 7th century, Glywysing seems to have merged with **Gwent** to form the kingdom eventually known as **Morgannwg**.

GOATS

Giraldus Cambrensis wrote in the late 12th century that the wooded crags of **Snowdonia** were full of goats and **sheep**. Domesticated earlier than either **cattle** or sheep, and introduced to **Britain** by **Neolithic** farmers, goats may have been more numerous in Wales than sheep until the 16th century, but their numbers declined with the demise of transhumance (see *Hafod* and *Hendre*) and the onset of **enclosures** in the 18th century, when large flocks of sheep replaced goats and cattle in the uplands.

Cheese was made from goats' milk, candles from their tallow and their meat was dried for winter use. Goats grazing on cliffs were thought to keep cattle away from dangerous places. Some farmers continued to keep small numbers of goats with their cattle even into the 1950s. Since the 1970s, Wales's growing cheese industry has stimulated a revival of goat-keeping among smallholders.

Several tribes of feral goats, mostly descendants of domestic escapees, are found in Snowdonia. Kashmir goats, introduced in the 19th century and living feral on the Great Orme (**Llandudno**), provide mascots for the **Royal Welsh Fusiliers**.

GOBLE, Anthony (Barnet) (1943–2007) Painter

Newtown-born Tony Goble, as he was invariably known, left **Wrexham** School of Art in 1964, and for the rest of his life was a practising painter. He exhibited extensively both nationally and internationally, and his pictures are to be found in many public art collections, including that of the **National Museum**. His role in the development and success of the Llanover Hall Arts Centre in **Cardiff** was considerable, and his students found him an inspirational teacher. His **painting**s ('narratives' he called them) abound in wit, dreams, voyages and, above all, imagination. As Goble himself said, 'My work is personal but it is not a secret.'

'GOD BLESS THE PRINCE OF WALES' Song

A once popular, often parodied song composed by **Brinley Richards** in 1862, with words in **English** by George Linley and in **Welsh** by **J. Ceiriog Hughes**. It was included in Richards's *Songs of Wales* (1873).

GODODDIN, The Tribe

A British tribe known to the **Romans** as the Votadini, whose kingdom may have extended from the Firth of Forth to the Tyne. It was centred on Din Eidyn, a fortification which probably stood on the Rock of Edinburgh. It was captured by the Angles in AD 638 and as a result the kingdom came to an end. A battle fought by the Gododdin against the Angles at Catterick (AD c.600), and disastrously lost, is commemorated in the long poem *Y Gododdin*, attributed to **Aneirin**. **Cunedda** is reputed to have migrated to north-west Wales from **Manaw Gododdin**.

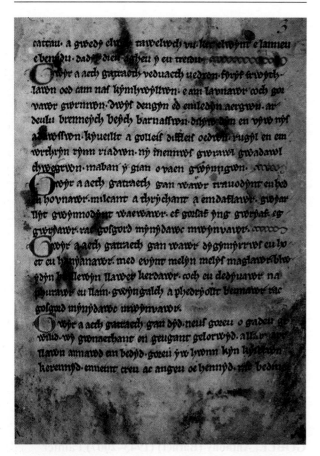

Y Gododdin in the 13th-century manuscript *The Book of Aneirin*

GODODDIN, Y

The name given to a collection of poems or stanzas attributed to the late 6th-century poet **Aneirin**. Transmitted orally before eventually being written down, *Y Gododdin* is preserved in two versions in the same 13th-century manuscript, ***The Book of Aneirin***. Totalling 1257 lines, it is frequently treated as if it were a single poem dealing with a single event – a 6th-century military expedition by the warriors of the **Gododdin** (or Votadini) tribe from their lands in Lothian to engage with overwhelmingly superior numbers of Angles (*see* **Anglo-Saxons**) at Catraeth (identified with Catterick in Yorkshire).

It is likely that written copies of the poem were in existence in the era of Old **Welsh**, but the version in the ***Book of Aneirin*** is in Middle Welsh. What proportion, if any, of the text was genuinely composed by Aneirin and is contemporary with the events it describes is hotly debated by linguists, students of **literature** and historians, and no immediate resolution of the problem seems at hand.

Many of the stanzas commemorate the heroic deaths of individual members of the war-band of the Gododdin, in what was a catastrophic defeat. Their generosity and civility at times of peace is praised, as well as their courage and ferocity on the field of battle. Some sections are devoted to lamenting the war-band as a whole, extolling their supreme loyalty to their lord. The language, metrics and literary devices used in *Y Gododdin* suggest that its author was heir to a long tradition of praise poetry in the (earlier)

Brythonic language. Its imagery, however, although vivid, is surprisingly limited and might reflect a process of editing as the text was transmitted.

GOETRE FAWR, Monmouthshire
(2183 ha; 2335 inhabitants)

Lying between **Pontypool** and the **Usk**, the **community** includes the substantial village of Penperllenni. Goytre Wharf on the **Brecon** and **Abergavenny Canal** has a range of admirably restored 19th-century features, including the wharf itself, an aqueduct, a cottage and a **lime**kiln. Persondy at Mamhilad is an intact 16th-century house with a wealth of excellent oak carpentry.

'GOGS' and 'HWNTWS'

Light-hearted nicknames – with a hint of the sardonic – for people from north and south Wales. The term 'Gogs', from an abbreviation of *gogledd* (north), became current among young people during the late 1960s and early 1970s, as increasing numbers of northerners sought work in **Cardiff**. The originally somewhat disdainful term 'Hwntw' is derived from the south-eastern word *hwnt* (beyond). In the 1970s, an innovative folk group from that region called themselves Yr Hwntws. The Gogs and Hwntws theme featured in the television series *Fo a Fe*.

GOGYNFEIRDD, Y (lit. 'The fairly early poets')

A term for the poets who sang using ***awdl*** and ***englyn*** metres between the first half of the 12th century and the second half of the 14th, including the **Poets of the Princes**.

GOLD

The **Romans**, attracted to **Britain** partly by rumours of precious metals, worked gold at Dolaucothi (**Cynwyl Gaeo**), although the scale of their activities has been exaggerated.

Modern engagement rings made from Welsh gold

Dolaucothi, now a tourist attraction, was developed between the 1880s and the 1940s, apparently on the site of Roman workings. The other concentration of gold is in the **Dolgellau** area. Finds in the **Mawddach** estuary in the 1840s were followed by those in California and **Australia**, which resulted in increased interest in **Merioneth**, though hardly a gold rush there. None of the mines operating in Merioneth from the 1840s to the 1920s was very productive, for the gold, although of good quality, was not abundant. Most mines lost money, although they made significant contributions to employment locally. The most productive mines were Clogau (**Llanelltyd**) and Gwynfynydd (**Ganllwyd**), the source of the gold used since the 19th century for English royal wedding rings. The workings at Gwynfynydd were opened up by William Pritchard Morgan, MP for **Merthyr Tydfil** (1888–1900), who was subsequently prosecuted for mining without a royal warrant.

GOLDCLIFF (Allteuryn), Newport
(1421 ha; 339 inhabitants)
Located on the **Severn** estuary south of the former **Llanwern Steelworks** site, the **community** contains at least two dozen footbridges crossing the reens of the **Gwent Levels**. A sea wall to protect the levels was built by the **Romans**, as testified by an inscribed stone found on the beach and preserved at the National Roman Legion Museum at **Caerleon**. The yellowish mica in the cliffs gave rise to the names Goldcliff and Allteuryn. Little survives of the **Benedictine** priory established *c.*1113 and abandoned

*c.*1467. Hill Farm contains a section of its wall. The priory was partly destroyed by floods *c.*1424, after which a church was built 2 km inland. A tablet in the chancel commemorates the 12 **parish**ioners of Goldcliff drowned by the great flood of 1606 (1607 by modern reckoning), which was probably a tsunami (*see* **Earthquakes**). A walk along the sea wall extending from Goldcliff to **Magor** offers fine views of the estuary.

GOLF
Golf is chiefly associated with **Scotland** where the sport was played during the Middle Ages. Wales's first full golf courses were established during the 1880s (although there was a short course at Pontnewydd, **Cwmbran**, in 1875). Among the earliest courses – developed on coastal **common land**, where the turf was considered suitable – were **Tenby** (1880), **Borth** and Ynyslas (1885), **Conwy** (1890), **Penarth** (1890), **Porthcawl** (1891) and **Aberdovey** (1892). The development of **tourism** gave the new golf clubs the opportunity to attract visitors, and **railway** companies advertised their locations.

From its early days, the sport was played by both men and **women**; the Welsh Ladies' Golf Union was founded in 1904. Members of the middle **class** were primarily responsible for establishing and running the early golf clubs. The sport was considered by many to be essentially English and elitist, with no connection with the native Welsh. In the 1920s, protests were held against the playing of golf on Sundays.

Ian Woosnam playing from a bunker in the Celtic Manor Wales Open, 1 June 2006

Improved standards of living and a diminution in class differences in the later 20th century saw golf become popular among all sections of society. The first Welsh amateur golf championship was held in 1895 at Aberdovey and the first professional championship at Radyr, **Cardiff**, in 1904. Subsequently, golfers such as **Dai Rees** and Ian Woosnam became famous for their exploits in the world's major golf tournaments. Woosnam, with David Llewellyn, won the World Cup in 1987, and in 2005 Stephen Dodd and Bradley Dredge were winners of the Golf Championships World Cup. The pinnacle of Woosnam's career came in 2006, when he captained Europe to its unprecedented third successive Ryder Cup victory over the United States. The 2010 tournament is due to be held at the **Celt**ic Manor's courses (**Caerleon** near **Newport**).

GOODMAN, Gabriel (1528–1601) Cleric
A native of **Ruthin**, where he endowed the grammar school (1574) and founded Christ's Hospital (1590), **Cambridge**-educated Goodman served the **Cecil** household as a chaplain. He survived the pre-1559 religious changes and was appointed dean of Westminster in 1561. He was one of the translators of the Bishops' Bible (1568) and assisted **William Morgan** in publishing the first **Welsh Bible** (1588). Although he was not made a bishop, he became, through his connection with the Cecils, an important link between the Court and Wales.

GOODWIN, Geraint (1903–41) Writer
Newtown-born Geraint Goodwin worked as a journalist in **London** until **tuberculosis** forced him to take a long convalescence abroad; thereafter, he lived mostly in Wales. His four novels include the highly acclaimed *The Heyday in the Blood* (1936) which, as in much of his writing, explores the tensions between Welsh heritage and Anglicized superficiality in Welsh **border** country. His *Collected Stories* were published in 1976.

GORDDWR Commote
Constituting the only part of the later **county** of **Montgomeryshire** located east of the **Severn**, the **commote** reached to the heights of the Long Mountain (408 m). In the mid-13th century, it was the subject of a complex territorial dispute between **Gruffudd ap Gwenwynwyn** and the Corbet family, who succeeded in incorporating it in their **march**er-lordship of Caus. Following the **Acts of 'Union'**, Gorddwr became part of the **hundred** of Ystradmarchell (*see* **Ystrad Marchell**).

GORDON, Alex (1917–99) Architect
Born in **Scotland** and brought up in **Swansea**, Gordon showed early talent by winning a competition, in 1937, for **Cardiff**'s street decorations celebrating the coronation. In 1949, he joined **Alwyn Lloyd** in partnership. On Lloyd's death, the practice became known as Alex Gordon Partnership and developed into one of the largest in Wales. The company's major buildings include the **music** department (1970) of what is now **Cardiff University**, and the **Welsh Office** extension (1972–9), Cardiff. Gordon was knighted in 1987.

GORSEDD BEIRDD YNYS PRYDAIN
(lit. 'The throne of bards of the Isle of Britain')
A society of poets, musicians and representatives of Welsh culture, founded by Iolo Morganwg (**Edward**

The Gorsedd at the National Eisteddfod, Llandeilo, August 1996

Williams) in the late 18th century. He saw the Gorsedd as a bardic system dedicated to promoting the **Welsh** literary tradition. His insistence on its ancient origin has long been rejected, and the Gorsedd today is accepted as a colourful and dignified part of the National **Eisteddfod** ceremonies.

Iolo held his first Gorsedd in 1792 on Primrose Hill in **London**, where he lived at the time, and his first in Wales, on Stalling Down (**Cowbridge**), in 1795. At an eisteddfod held in **Carmarthen**, in 1819, the Gorsedd was associated for the first time with the eisteddfod movement, when, in the garden of the Ivy Bush Hotel, Iolo inducted several persons into the Gorsedd by tying different coloured ribbons on their arms. These same colours today signify the various Gorsedd orders: green for members of the Order of Ovate (who gain admission by examination or special acknowledgement); blue for the Order of Poet, Musician and Author (who gain admission by examination); and white for the Order of Druid (who gain admission by invitation).

During National Eisteddfod week, five Gorsedd ceremonies are held, two in the open air within a Gorsedd circle of stones, and three in the main pavilion, when winning poets are crowned and chaired, and when the prose medal is awarded. The Gorsedd, which has its own regalia, is led by the **Archdruid**, who is elected for a term of three years, and who is supported by a number of officials. In 2005, the Gorsedd was held in association with lightweight portable stones, a change which caused considerable controversy.

GORSEINON, Swansea (630 ha; 7874 inhabitants)

Located immediately north of **Llwchwr** with which it merges, the settlement grew around **coal**mines, and steel (*see* **Iron and Steel**) and **tinplate** works, all of which have closed. Its **railway** station was first named **Pontardulais** [*sic*] South, but the village was later given the more specific name Gorseinon (Einon's moor), from an area of open land 3 km further east. Seion **Baptist** chapel (1902) has polygonal turrets. The church of the Blessed Sacrament (1968) – a rather gimmicky building according to John Newman – contains attractive **stained-glass** windows by **John Petts**.

GORSLAS (Gors-las), Carmarthenshire
(1654 ha; 3724 inhabitants)

Located at the centre of **Carmarthenshire**'s anthracite **coal**field, the **community** contains the villages of Gorslas, Capel Seion, Cefneithin, Drefach and Foelgastell. Llyn Llech Owain, the source of the Gwendraeth Fawr, is linked with legends concerning Owain ap Thomas (**Owain Lawgoch**). Supporters of the **Rebecca Riots** held a large gathering at the lakeside in 1843. Capel Seion **Congregational** chapel, originally built in 1712, is among the district's earliest **Nonconformist** causes.

The area became populous in the late 19th century following the exploitation of its coal; only open-cast mining survives. Former pupils of the Gwendraeth Valley Secondary School include the chemist Sir John Meurig Thomas, and the **rugby** players **Carwyn James**, Barry John, Gareth Davies and Jonathan Davies.

GOUGH, Jethro (1903–79) Pathologist

Abercynon-born Jethro Gough had a distinguished undergraduate career at the Welsh National School of Medicine, **Cardiff** (*see* **Wales College of Medicine, Biology, Life and Health Sciences**). Having spent some time in Manchester, he returned to Cardiff as a lecturer, and in 1948 was appointed professor and head of the Pathology Department. An outstanding research worker, he gained an international reputation following his discovery that it was **coal** dust, rather than silica, which caused **pneumoconiosis** in workers in the coal industry. Cardiff became world-famous for its work in that field.

GOUGH, Mathew (Mathau Goch; d.1450) Soldier

A native of **Flintshire** and a relation of **Owain Glyndŵr**, Gough was one of the outstanding captains in the English armies in France from *c*.1423 until the final defeat of the English in Normandy at Formigny in 1450. In that year, he was killed defending **London** Bridge against Jack Cade and his rebels. His death was lamented in the immortal words: 'Morte Matthei Goghe/ Cambria clamitavit, Oghe' (Matthew Gough is dead/ Cambria mourns, alas!).

GOULD, Arthur [Joseph] (1864–1919) Rugby player

Welsh **rugby**'s first superstar, Arthur Gould was a handsome man with piercing black eyes, whose rugby career began with **Newport** when 16 years of age; he went on to make 27 international appearances between 1885 and 1896, and captained Wales to their first Triple Crown in 1893. A champion track athlete, there was little he could not do on the rugby field: his outstanding attacking and kicking skills drew thousands to see him in action and made him a **music**-hall celebrity.

Such was his reputation that in 1897 a testimonial fund was launched and the proceeds used to present him with the deeds of his house in Newport. The other countries took exception to this apparent breach of the amateur regulations and broke off relations with Wales. To avoid embarrassment, Gould retired from playing and took up refereeing.

GOVERNMENT and ADMINISTRATION

From the post-Roman period until 1830

Following the collapse of the **Roman** Empire in the 5th century, Wales comprised a number of kingdoms, chief among them **Gwynedd**, **Powys**, **Dyfed** and **Glywysing**; various smaller ones were gradually absorbed by their larger neighbours. **Gildas**, in the 6th century, rebuked five kings for their sins, among them **Vortepor** of Dyfed and **Maelgwn** of Gwynedd. These rulers saw themselves as the legitimate heirs of Roman power in **Britain**. It was not until the coming of the **Anglo-Saxons** and the construction of **Offa's Dyke**, which defined Wales's **border** with **England**, that they began to think in terms of Wales. Within the kingdoms were smaller units – the *cantrefi* and later the **commotes**, although several of the *cantrefi* had themselves once been kingdoms in their own right.

The arrival of the **Normans** in the later 11th century brought changes. The process of conquest was based on existing political units, and the Anglo-Norman **march**er-lordships were made up of *cantrefi* or **commotes**, at least in the upland areas. In some lordships, English-style **manors** were established in lowland areas, although something similar to them may have existed in such areas under native rule. Within *Pura Wallia*, or native Wales, government and administration also underwent change, especially under the 13th-century rulers of Gwynedd (*see* **Kings and Princes**). These included specialization in government with more elaborate financial machinery and a more sophisticated military organization. The rulers of Gwynedd were seeking to create a single Welsh Principality in which the other rulers would do homage to them and they would, in turn, do homage to the king of England. This objective was attained through the **Treaty of Montgomery** of 1267, but the **Edwardian conquest** of 1282 brought what by then remained of the **Principality** into the possession of the English crown.

In 1301, Edward I granted the Principality to his heir, later Edward II. For administrative purposes there were two principalities – that of the south, based on **Carmarthen**, and that of the north, based on **Caernarfon**. The **Statute of Rhuddlan** (1284) grafted three new **counties** – **Caernarfonshire**, **Anglesey** and **Merioneth** – on to the existing commotes in the newly conquered northern lands; in the south, **Carmarthenshire** and **Cardiganshire** had been in embryonic existence since 1241. The three non-contiguous territories of **Tegeingl**, Hopedale and **Maelor Saesneg** became **Flintshire**, which was placed under the control of the justiciar of Chester.

Edward I could not legislate for the whole of Wales, for the marcher-lordships were quasi-independent, owing only homage and fealty to the king. A statute of 1354 stated that their lords were in no way subject to the Principality. The *cantrefi* or commotes and their component townships remained as they had been before the conquest, the townships being the basic units for the assessment of dues and services. In the northern and southern principalities and in the marcher-lordships, there were administrative organizations – headed in the former by justiciars and in the latter by stewards.

During the later Middle Ages, many marcher-lordships came – by marriage, inheritance or confiscation – into the possession of the English crown. This did not, however, lead to administrative rationalization. Each crown-lordship retained its own identity, although there were arrangements for co-operation and a mechanism for negotiation between neighbouring lordships, known as the Day of the March, which went back to the time of the native rulers. The 15th century was a period when weak central government often led to a lack of order and efficiency, as much in Wales as in other territories of the king of England. Absentee justiciars and lords led to local power struggles and the emergence of local bosses such as the notorious **Gruffudd ap Nicolas** in the southern principality. Edward IV depended on a trusted servant, William **Herbert** (d.1469), to govern Wales, and his example was followed after 1485 by Henry VII, who left Wales in the care of such men as Sir **Rhys ap Thomas**, although under Henry there was more supervision. Edward IV had set up a council at **Ludlow** to govern Wales in the name of his young son; it was revived by Henry VII when his son Arthur was made **Prince of Wales** in 1489. The council survived Arthur's death in 1502 to become the **Council of Wales and the Marches**, with the task of supervising the Principality and the March.

Under Henry VIII, steps were at last taken to reorganize the government of Wales. Marcher-lordship had long outlived its usefulness. The fall and **execution** of the last marcher magnate, the Duke of Buckingham, in 1521 and the perceived threat from Spain following the king's divorce from Katherine of Aragon were among the factors which persuaded Henry's minister Thomas Cromwell that something had to be done. **Rowland Lee**, bishop of Coventry and Lichfield and president of the Council of Wales and the Marches (1534–43), was given the remit of imposing order.

The Act of 1536, the so-called first **Act of 'Union'**, brought to an end the distinction between Principality and March. Most of the marcher-lordships were amalgamated to form seven new **counties** – **Breconshire**, **Denbighshire**, **Glamorgan**, **Monmouthshire**, **Montgomeryshire**, **Pembrokeshire** and **Radnorshire** – and the rest were added to existing Welsh or English counties. Wales was to be represented in parliament by 27 members (*see* **parliamentary representation**). Henceforth, parliamentary legislation and parliamentary taxation applied in Wales in the same way as it did in England. It could be argued that henceforth, everyone living in Wales was legally English; on the other hand, as there was no longer any advantage of boasting of the condition of being English, it would be equally valid to argue that henceforth everyone living in Wales was Welsh.

The 1536 Act defined the territory of Wales for the first time. The settlement of Wales was completed by a second act in 1542–3, which extended to the rest of the country the system of courts (*see* **Law**) that had existed in the Principality since the 13th century. Wales was divided into four circuits, each of three counties; Monmouthshire was attached to the **Oxford** circuit in England, which gave rise to the mistaken notion that it was an English county. This system of courts, known as the Great Sessions (*see* Law), survived until 1830. The Acts of 1536 and 1542–3 are known as the Acts of 'Union' but in reality they united Wales within itself rather than uniting it to England.

Legislation in the 1530s introduced justices of the peace to Wales. The justices, assembled in Quarter Sessions, became the governing bodies of the counties, as they had long been in England. Members of Parliament and justices of the peace were drawn from the ranks of the **gentry**. At the lowest level, the township was gradually superseded by the **parish** as the unit of administration; it was the parish which was made responsible for such functions as poor relief (*see* **Poor Law**) and highway maintenance (*see* **Roads**). The Council of Wales and the Marches retained its oversight of government in Wales. It was also a court and, like the other prerogative courts, came under attack from parliament in the 1630s and was abolished in 1641. It was revived at the Stuart Restoration (1660), but failed to recover its former prestige and was finally abolished in 1689. Thereafter, the Great Sessions were the only distinctive Welsh institution.

From 1830 until 1884

An act abolishing the Great Sessions was passed in 1830 despite the opposition of Welsh MPs. Wales became part of the English system of assize courts and some of the responsibilities of the Great Sessions were transferred to the higher courts at Westminster. At the county level, administration continued to be the responsibility of the justices of the peace at Quarter Sessions. They also dealt with welfare matters or petty criminal cases in their own localities, normally monthly at the Petty Sessions. By the 1820s, it had become compulsory for each county to create petty sessional administrative divisions, and 97 such divisions, generally based upon the pre-existing **hundreds**, were established in Wales.

The Reform Act of 1832 initiated a period of administrative and social reform. In 1834, the Poor Law Amendment Act, largely a reaction to the unrest of 1829–31, ordained that those in receipt of poor relief were obliged to reside in workhouses. Wales's 48 (later 50) **Poor Law Unions**, composed of groups of parishes, were given the responsibility for building workhouses, and also became administrative units in their own right, especially in relation to the collection of statistics.

The following year saw the passage of the Municipal Corporations Act. In Wales, there were 56 places with some pretension to **borough** status, but only 20 were granted the new-style borough councils. The councils, elected by male ratepayers, were given sweeping powers to provide public services but, since such provision was not mandatory, little was done. Long-established urban areas, such as **Wrexham**, were excluded, as were newly industrialized places such as **Merthyr Tydfil**. Rapid urbanization did, however, give rise to some developments in local government, with the larger urban centres gaining boards of **health** following the passage of the Public Health Act of 1848. Under the Public Health Act of 1875, all urban and municipal districts were made into sanitary districts, while the poor law boards acted as sanitary authorities in the rural areas. Burial boards also came into being to oversee the provision of cemeteries (*see* **Death and Funerals**).

Additional duties were given to the Quarter Sessions. For example, they were obliged to co-operate with the Poor Law guardians in organizing mental health care and to undertake increasing responsibility for the maintenance of order, especially following the legislation of 1839, which permitted counties which felt the need for a professional **police** force to establish one. In the early 1840s, five Welsh counties – Glamorgan, Carmarthenshire, Montgomeryshire, Denbighshire and Cardiganshire – all of which had experienced significant social unrest, acquired constabularies; the other eight counties followed when obliged to do so in 1856. Some municipal boroughs had possessed their own forces since 1835, although all but eight had been absorbed by the county forces by 1888.

Roads had been the responsibility of turnpike trusts, supervised by the Quarter Sessions, but, following the **Rebecca Riots**, six of the seven southern counties (Monmouthshire was excluded) were obliged in 1845 to establish county boards to amalgamate and administer the trusts. In the north and in Monmouthshire, however, the old order survived until the 1870s. Local roads were the responsibility of the parishes, supervised by the magistrates; however, following legislation in 1849 and 1860, they were organized under petty sessional divisions.

The creation of elected school boards under the 1870 **Education** Act was an important step towards local democracy. Denominational quarrels had poisoned the provision of elementary schooling, and the act offered the opportunity to establish non-denominational schools maintained by local rates and administered by elected boards. Ratepayers – including for the first time, **women** ratepayers – were to elect the members of the school boards, elections which gave wide scope for denominational rivalries. Wales had 288 board schools by 1887 and 893 by 1900.

From 1884 to the present

Following the widening of the franchise in 1884, there were increasing calls for the reform of county government, with William Rathbone, **Liberal** MP for Arvon or **Arfon** (North Caernarfonshire), a prominent advocate of such a measure. It was argued that magistrates did not represent a fair political and social cross-section of Wales, an argument borne out by their decisions during the **Tithe** War. However, even after the passing of the County Councils Act of 1888, they retained some responsibility for maintaining public order. Under the terms of that act, 13 Welsh county councils and 3 **county borough** councils – **Cardiff**, **Swansea** and **Newport** – were established, a pattern of county government which, apart from the granting of county borough status to Merthyr Tydfil in 1908, lasted until 1974. In the first elections, held in 1889, there were clear Liberal majorities in 11 of the 13 counties, with 'hung' councils in Breconshire and Radnorshire. Councillors were drawn from a wider spectrum of the **population** than were their English counterparts. The creation in 1894 of **rural** and **urban districts** and of parish councils further strengthened the representative nature of local government, while the field of influence of county councils was extended by the **Welsh Intermediate Education Act** of 1889, which established county joint education committees, most of whose members were councillors. Following the passage of the 1902 Education Act, which abolished school boards, the county education committees also became responsible for elementary education. The needs of an increasingly complex society imposed further duties upon local authorities, among them the provision of pure water, the supply of electricity and gas (*see* **Energy**), the establishment of efficient systems of local transport, and, in the 20th century, the building of working-class **housing**.

These developments coincided with a demand for an elected body for Wales as a whole, but, despite the rhetoric of **T. E. Ellis** and **David Lloyd George**, the efforts of **Cymru Fydd**, legislative attempts such as the National Institutions (Wales) Bill of 1891–2 and the campaigns of **E. T. John**, such demands brought meagre results. Chief among them were the establishment in the immediate pre-war years of the Welsh Department of Education, the Welsh Commission for health **insurance** (the nucleus of the later **Welsh Board of Health**), an agricultural commissioner for

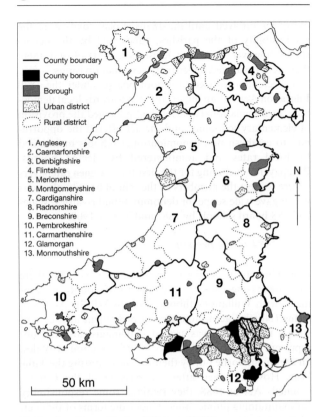

The local government units of Wales until 1974

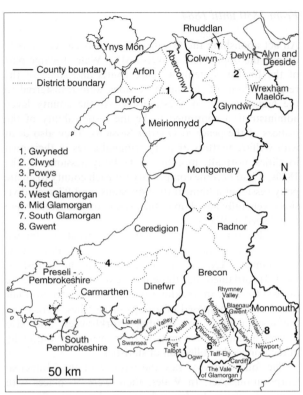

The local government units of Wales, 1974–96

Wales and a Welsh Standing Committee to consider bills relating exclusively to Wales (in fact a very small number).

The immediate post-war years saw a massive recognition of the claims of small nations, thus encouraging demands for a measure of **home rule** for Wales to resurface. Yet, apart from the establishment of the Welsh Board of Health, and the final victory of the **disestablishment** campaign, David Lloyd George's era as prime minister brought no additional recognition of the distinctiveness of Wales, one of the factors which led in 1925 to the establishment of **Plaid [Genedlaethol] Cymru**.

The **depression of the interwar years** placed severe strains upon local administration. The Poor Law Unions, obliged to provide relief at a time of massive unemployment, faced grave difficulties, and in 1927 the **Bedwellty** Board of Guardians was declared in default and was replaced with commissioners. The boards were abolished in 1929, when their duties were transferred to the public assistance committees of the counties and county boroughs. The change brought little relief, as the problems of Merthyr Tydfil, revealed by the royal commission on the town in 1935, amply demonstrated. Despite adversity, the local authorities of industrial Wales proved remarkably adept and compassionate. This was in marked contrast with those in the rural areas, the complacency and inefficiency of which were mercilessly exposed in **Clement Davies**'s report on the anti-**tuberculosis** service in Wales, published in 1939.

Davies and others looked with envy to **Scotland**, which had had its own secretary of state since 1885. Bills proposing the appointment of a **secretary of state for Wales** were introduced but they met with no success. In the 1940s, there was some slight administrative recognition of the

existence of Wales, including the establishment of the Welsh Reconstruction Advisory Council (1942), the annual 'Welsh Day' debate in the House of Commons (from 1944) and the creation of the **Council for Wales and Monmouthshire** (1948), which merely had an advisory role. The wide-ranging nationalization programme of the post-war **Labour** government, however, led to the setting up of no administrative structures specific to Wales, apart from the **Welsh Hospitals Board** and the Wales Gas Board. The frustrations thus caused led in part to the Parliament for Wales campaign, launched in 1950, and to the Government of Wales Bill introduced in the Commons by **S. O. Davies** in 1955.

It was the **Conservative Party**, the most unionist of the parties, which took the initiative in changing the way Wales was administered. In October 1951, David Maxwell Fyfe, the Conservative home secretary, was appointed minister of Welsh affairs, assisted by David Llewellyn (Cardiff North) as an additional minister of state at the Home Office. Fyfe (popularly known as Dai Bananas) was succeeded by **Gwilym Lloyd George** in 1954. The post was attached to the Ministry for Housing and Local Government in 1957; it was held by Henry Brooke from 1957 to 1961 and by Keith Joseph from 1961 to 1964. Brooke's period in office was particularly stormy (*see* **Tryweryn Valley, Drowning of**). The role of the minister was ill-defined, but the 13 years the office lasted were ones in which steps were taken that gave the administration of Wales a modicum of unity and coherence. These included the publication of the *Digest of Welsh Statistics* (1954 onwards), the recognition of Cardiff as capital (1955), and the establishment of the **Welsh Grand Committee** (1960).

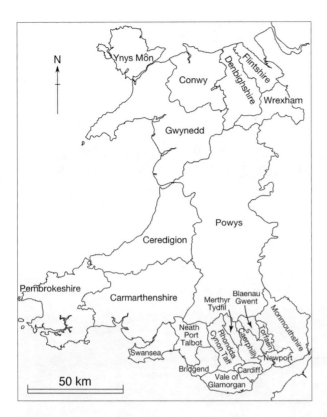

The local government units of Wales since 1996

its division into two districts. Above all, there was confusion concerning the spheres of the counties and the districts. Also, in 1974 the civil parishes of Wales, which had varied wildly in size and population, came to be a thing of the past. Rural Wales was divided into **communities**, most of them embracing several of the defunct parishes. Urban Wales was also divided into communities, the boundaries of many of which coincided with those of wards.

The administration structures created by the legislation of 1974 were a factor in the debate on the government of Wales, which took place during the **devolution** referendum of 1979. Wales, it was argued, already had five layers of administration – the emerging power of Brussels, the governmental structures based on Westminster and Whitehall, the counties, the districts, and the admittedly rapidly attenuating community councils. To add yet another body at the all-Wales level seemed to many to be an indication of perverse bureaucracy, one of the considerations which led to the comprehensive defeat of the devolution scheme on offer in 1979.

In 1996, the 8 counties and the 37 districts created in 1974 were abolished. They were replaced by 22 unitary authorities, known either as counties or as county boroughs, thus removing one of Wales's layers of administration – a factor in the far more positive vote on devolution in the referendum of 1997.

The **National Assembly for Wales**, which came into existence following that referendum, has begun to have an impact upon the day-to-day lives of the people of Wales. Whether it will increasingly do so depends upon the implications of the adage that 'devolution is a process rather than an event'.

The Labour party, in its 1959 manifesto, had committed itself to the appointment of a secretary of state for Wales. When it assumed office in 1964, it honoured its commitment and **James Griffiths** became what he called the 'charter' secretary (*see* **Welsh Office**). One of the major issues facing the new office was the future of local government, which had been the subject of debate at least since Clement Davies's 1939 report. There was a widespread belief that many of the boroughs and rural and urban districts were too small to be efficient and that Glamorgan, the home of almost half the inhabitants of Wales, was too dominant among the counties of Wales.

In 1963, a commission had advocated comprehensive reorganization, but there was among the patriotic elements in the Labour Party a desire not to proceed with change unless it was accompanied by the establishment of an elected body for Wales as a whole. It was an issue on which **Cledwyn Hughes**, secretary of state from 1966 to 1968, was defeated, largely because of opposition from Scotland.

In the event, it was the Conservative government elected in 1970 that carried through the reorganization. In 1974, eight new counties were created – **Gwynedd, Clwyd, Powys, Dyfed, Gwent**, and **Mid, South** and **West Glamorgan**. Of the pre-existing counties, it was only Gwent – essentially a re-branding of Monmouthshire – which in any way resembled a pre-existing county. The reorganization also involved the substitution of 37 districts for the previous 164 boroughs and rural and urban districts. The change had few champions. Impoverished Mid Glamorgan resented being hived off from prosperous South Glamorgan. Powys, which extended almost from **Llangollen** to Merthyr, was considered to be ridiculously elongated. Pembrokeshire resented

The Pierhead Building in Cardiff Bay with Y Senedd, the seat of the National Assembly for Wales, in the background

Three Cliffs Bay, Gower

GOWER (Gŵyr), Commote, lordship, district and constituency

Lying between the **Rivers Llwchwr** and **Tawe**, Gŵyr was a **commote** of **Ystrad Tywi** and became part of the kingdom of **Deheubarth**. It consisted of the peninsula (Gower *Anglicana*), whose southern portion below Cefn Bryn was heavily **manor**ialized following **English** colonization, and the moorland Welshry (Gower *Wallicana*), which extended to the **Black Mountain**.

Henry de Beaumont, earl of Warwick, conquered Gower *c.*1100. Kilvey, on the east bank of the Tawe, became part of the **march**er-lordship, the caput of which was established at **Swansea**. In the early 13th century, Gower and Kilvey came into the possession of the de **Breos family** whose descendants held it until 1480. Its later acquisition by the **Somerset family** explains the prominence of the dukes of Beaufort in the affairs of Gower and Swansea. Through the **Act of 'Union'**, Gower and Kilvey were united with the **lordship of Glamorgan** to form the **county** of **Glamorgan**.

From 1894 until its absorption into the Swansea District in 1974, the peninsula was the Gower **rural district**. The constituency of Gower, which includes most of the ancient commote, was established in 1918.

Much of the Gower Peninsula has been declared an Area of Outstanding Natural Beauty, the first such designation in **Britain**. Much of the charm of the peninsula can be attributed to its **geology**. Consisting essentially of a Carboniferous **Limestone** plateau, the cliff-backed bays of its southern coast are delectable; the cliffs contain **caves** of great archaeological interest (*see* **Rhossili**). The ridge along

the northern coast overlooks the marshes of the **Llwchwr** estuary, which are rich in migratory **birds** and in cockles (*see* **Fish and Fishing**). The Gower Society was established in 1948.

GOWER, Henry de (1278?–1347) Bishop

Bishop of **St David's** from 1328 to 1347, Henry de Gower was described by **Glanmor Williams** as the greatest builder of medieval Wales. He commissioned the building of the bishop's palace at St David's and the east range of the palace at **Lamphey**, both of which have arcaded and battlemented parapets. Such parapets are also a feature of **Swansea** Castle: they may have been built by the bishop's masons, who were employed by him to build the town's Hospital of the Blessed St David (now much altered and, in fact, the Cross Keys tavern) and the choir of St Mary's church.

GOWERTON (Tre-gŵyr), Swansea
(756 ha; 4928 inhabitants)

The settlement came into being in the late 19th century to house **coal**miners, steelworkers (*see* **Iron and Steel**) and **tinplate** workers. On the 1879 Ordnance Survey **map** it was named simply 'Gower' Road' – the more dignified 'ton' came a little later. It soon had two **railway** stations on two main lines, and was the junction for the branch line to Penclawdd and Llanmorlais (*see* **Llanrhidian Higher**). Only one line remains but, with new **roads** built to Llanrhidian, Gowerton can claim to be one of the gateways to Gower. St John's church (1880–2) has an attractive polychromatic interior.

GRABER, George Alexander (Alexander Cordell; 1914–97) Novelist

Alexander Cordell was born in Ceylon, to an English family, but in 1950 he settled in **Abergavenny**. Cordell wrote a bestselling novel, *Rape of the Fair Country* (1959), which, with *The Hosts of Rebecca* (1960) and *Song of the Earth* (1969), forms a trilogy about life in early industrial Wales. These novels present a romanticized view of the struggle for workers' rights in the **iron**works, of the **Chartist** movement and of the **Rebecca Riots**. His novel *The Fire People* (1972) deals with the **Merthyr Rising** and *This Sweet and Bitter Earth* (1977) with the **Tonypandy Riots**.

GRAIG, Newport (1424 ha; 5492 inhabitants)

Located in the north-western corner of the **county** of **Newport**, the **community** contains the villages of Bassaleg, Rhiwderin, Pentre-poeth and Lower **Machen**. Gwernyclepa in Bassaleg was the home of Ifor Hael (Ifor the Generous; fl.1340–60) traditionally believed to have been the chief patron of **Dafydd ap Gwilym**. The verses of **Evan Evans** (Ieuan Brydydd Hir; 1731–88) to the court of Ifor Hael are the finest *englynion* composed in the 18th century. St Basil's church, Bassaleg, was a cell of Glastonbury abbey. It contains the mausoleum of the **Morgan family (Tredegar)**. Nearby is the Pye Corner viaduct; built across the **Ebbw** in 1826 to carry the **Rhymney** Valley tramroad, it is the south Wales **coal**field's earliest surviving viaduct.

The comprehensive school at Bassaleg (1935, 1958), the primary school at Pentre-poeth (1986) and the community centre at Rhiwderin (*c.*1860) are buildings of distinction. Lower Machen, a prosperous village in the Rhymney valley, has its own annual festival. Its St Michael's church

preceded St Basil's as the mausoleum of the Morgan family, who, until they moved to Tredegar House in 1660, lived at Plas Machen, a building which retains some 16th-century features.

GRANITE

A word often used for a range of hard rock, not all of which may be granite. Wales's granite quarrying industry, sited generally near the sea for ease of transport, was concentrated in the north-west, with five quarries between **Llandudno** and the end of **Llŷn**, and two in **Anglesey**. North **Pembrokeshire** was less productive, but has notable remains of a crushing and grading plant at Porthgain (**Llanrhian**), which closed in 1931.

Activity started with a **Neolithic** axe factory at **Penmaenmawr** (where granite is still quarried), the products of which have been found at sites in many parts of **Britain**. Extensive modern working began in 1830. Granite setts were used for street paving, causing the industry to be – like **slate** – a by-product of urbanization. Peak production was in the 1930s, and several quarries have since closed, notably that at Nant Gwrtheyrn (**Pistyll**), which is now a centre for learners of **Welsh**. In 1931, **Caernarfonshire** produced over 1.17 million tonnes, but by the 1970s the county's output had more than halved; the workforce also declined, from 1100 to under 150, and production shifted from setts to crushed stone.

GREENHAM COMMON, Newbury, England

On 27 August 1981, following NATO proposals to site United States Cruise nuclear missiles in Europe, 40 Welsh people walked in protest from **Cardiff** to the United States' base at Greenham Common. A **women**'s peace camp was

Protestors marching from Wales to Greenham Common over the Severn Bridge in 1981

set up, surviving evictions and persecution by the authorities, the 1983 arrival of Cruise missiles and their 1989 departure, and ending in December 1999. It became famous worldwide as both an inspiration to women and a focus for protest against nuclear weapons.

GREENLY, Edward (1861–1951) Geologist
Trained in the north-west Highlands of **Scotland** whilst a member of the Geological Survey, Bristol-born Greenly spent 20 years (1895–1915) unravelling the complicated **geology** of **Anglesey**, producing a **map** and accompanying memoir – both classics of their kind – which the Survey readily incorporated into its national series.

For the remainder of his life, he studied the geology and physiography of the area between the **Menai Strait** and **Snowdonia**. He was joint author, with Howel Williams, of *Methods in Geological Surveying* (1930).

GRENFELL, D[avid] R[hys] (1881–1968) Politician
A miners' agent who became MP for **Gower** (1922–59), Grenfell made the case for nationalization of the **coal** industry whilst minister for mines (1940–2) and in his book *Coal* (1947). In 1946, he led a deputation urging the appointment of a **secretary of state for Wales**.

GRESFORD (Gresffordd), Wrexham
(906 ha; 5334 inhabitants).
Located immediately north-east of **Wrexham**, the **community** contains All Saints' church, incomparably Wales's finest **parish** church. Completed in 1498, it was financed by the income of its miracle-working image and by the patronage of Margaret Beaufort and her husband, Thomas **Stanley**, earl of Derby. Modelled upon the Perpendicular churches of the **Cheshire** Plain, it surpasses all of them in quality. The church contains a wealth of monuments and **stained-glass** windows of the highest quality. Its bells are listed in an 18th-century doggerel as one of 'the **seven wonders of Wales**'.

Gresford village, with its church, school, almshouses, green and duck pond, is highly attractive. Late 20th-century **housing** development has quadrupled its size. Gresford Colliery, opened in 1911, was the scene in 1934 of one of the worst disasters in Welsh mining history (*see* **Gresford Colliery Disaster**). The colliery was closed in 1972 and its architecturally significant pithead baths were demolished.

In 1974, Gresford absorbed Marford and Horsley, which had, since 1284, been an enclave of **Flintshire**. Its main feature is the Trevalyn estate village (1803–15), a notable example of the **picturesque**.

GRESFORD COLLIERY DISASTER,
Denbighshire (now Wrexham)
On Saturday, 22 September 1934, at about 2 a.m., an explosion of gas killed 262 miners. Three members of the rescue brigade also lost their lives and, on the following Tuesday, a surface worker was killed when further underground explosions showered debris onto him. This was the worst ever **colliery disaster** in the north Wales **coal**field, and the fourth worst in Wales. It is the subject of a memorable **ballad**.

GREY family Marcher-lords
The family's association with Wales originated with Reginald (d.1307) who, as Justice of Chester, incurred the wrath of the inhabitants of north-east Wales, a factor in the Welsh rising of 1282. Following the **Edwardian conquest**, he was granted the *cantref* of **Dyffryn Clwyd**. Greys succeeded each other at **Ruthin** until 1508 when Richard, Baron Grey and earl of Kent, sold his rights to the English crown. It has been claimed that it was the antagonism of Reginald (d.1448) that sparked off the **Glyndŵr Revolt**. In 1402, **Owain Glyndŵr** captured Reginald, receiving 10,000 marks for his release.

GREYHOUND RACING
Greyhound racing in **Britain** is controlled by the National Greyhound Racing Club (NGRC), but since the closure of Somerton Park, **Newport**, in 1963 and of the Arms Park, **Cardiff,** in 1977, Wales no longer possesses any licensed tracks affiliated to the NGRC. However, in 2007 there were three privately owned tracks – at **Swansea**, **Bedwellty** (*see also* **Bargoed**) and Hengoed (**Gelligaer**).

Hugh Griffith as King Lear at the Grand Theatre, Swansea, 1949

Introduced into **England** from America in 1925, greyhound racing soon established itself in Wales, and several tracks opened in the late 1920s. Following a cessation of competition during the **Second World War**, the sport then boomed, at a time when greyhound tracks were the only legal betting venues. The first Welsh Derby in 1951 came during a highpoint for greyhound racing across Britain, and the sport flourished until the end of the decade. However, with the opening of betting shops from 1961 onwards, and with rising land values encouraging the lucrative selling of many tracks, greyhound racing suffered markedly and attendances dropped.

Despite something of a revival during the mid-1970s, greyhound racing in Wales has been unable to recapture its former popularity. Whereas miners and steelworkers could once afford a dog, and made good money at the races, the sport is now too expensive to be enjoyed as a hobby. Although the Welsh Derby remains an important annual event in racing circles, crowds are decreasing, many tracks have shut in recent years, and a new generation of supporters is proving difficult to attract.

GRIFFITH family (Penrhyn) Landowners

The leading family in north-west Wales in the later Middle Ages, it owed its rise to a childless **Anglesey** squire who died in 1376, leaving his lands to his nephew, Gruffudd ap Gwilym, husband of Morfudd, a descendant of **Ednyfed Fychan**. Their son, Gwilym (d.1431), built a new house at Penrhyn (**Llandegai**), and was among the first to abandon **Owain Glyndŵr**; strategic marriages and frenetic land purchase made the family a major force. In 1540, the inheritance was divided between three sisters. The later owners of Penrhyn, the **Pennant family**, claimed descent from Angharad, the daughter of Gwilym ap Gruffudd.

GRIFFITH, Ellis Jones (Sir Ellis Jones Ellis-Griffith; 1860–1926) Politician

A brilliant barrister, Griffith was associated with the **Cymru Fydd** campaign and in 1895 was elected **Liberal** MP for **Anglesey**. He was prominent in furthering Welsh **educational** causes and in guiding the 1912 Welsh **Disestablishment** Bill through the House of Commons. He lost his seat to **Labour** in 1918.

GRIFFITH, Hugh [Emrys] (1912–80) Actor

One of the 20th century's great character actors, Hugh Griffith was born at Marianglas (**Llaneugrad**), and worked in a bank before attending RADA (1938–9). His acting career, interrupted by military service, took off after the **Second World War**. Between 1946 and 1972, he won acclaim in **London**, Stratford and New York, with memorable interpretations of Falstaff, Prospero and Lear. A flamboyant character with a famously sonorous voice, he appeared in over 60 films, including *A Run For Your Money* (1949), *The Last Days of Dolwyn* (1949), *Ben Hur* (1959) – for which he gained an Oscar – and *Tom Jones* (1963). His most memorable television role was probably his roistering undertaker and **rugby** fan in *Grand Slam* (1978). His sister, **Elen Roger Jones**, was one of Wales's leading actresses.

Kenneth Griffith (centre) in a 1953 adaptation for television of Dostoyevsky's *Crime and Punishment*

GRIFFITH, James Milo (1843–97) Sculptor

A native of Pontseli (**Pembrokeshire**), Griffith emerged from the artisan tradition of the mason to become an accomplished carver in stone. He worked on the restoration of Llandaff Cathedral (*see* **Cardiff**), before spending a period in San Francisco as a professor of art. His many public commissions include 'The Four Apostles' in Bristol Cathedral and memorial statues in Wales, such as that of **Hugh Owen** (1804–81) in **Caernarfon** and that of John Batchelor in Cardiff.

GRIFFITH, John Edward (1843–1933)
Naturalist and genealogist

The titles of Griffith's two main publications indicate his areas of activity: *Flora of Anglesey and Caernarvonshire* (1894) and the monumental *Pedigrees of Anglesey and Caernarvonshire Families* (1914). In his flora, he used the Welsh **plant** names given by **Hugh Davies**, whose manuscripts were at one time in his possession. A prosperous pharmacist at **Bangor**, Griffith also published a *Portfolio of Photographs of Cromlechs* (1900).

GRIFFITH, Kenneth (1921–2006)
Actor and film-maker

The feisty **Tenby**-born Griffith will be remembered for performances as humorous foil to Peter Sellers in British comedy **films** of the 1950s and 1960s, yet he made an initial impact as a malevolent blackmailer in the *noir* thriller *The Shop at Sly Corner* (1947). He was hilarious as Sellers's lugubrious, henpecked library colleague in the **Swansea**-set *Only Two Can Play* (1962) and persuasive as a fawning trade union nark in *I'm All Right Jack* (1959). A BAFTA Cymru Lifetime Achievement winner, Griffith took most pride later in his passionately polemical **drama-**

documentaries, with their bellicose anti-colonialist stance. *Hang Up Your Brightest Colours* (1973), a sympathetic study of IRA leader Michael Collins, fiercely critical of the British **government**, was banned from television for over twenty years. Long-term television censorship also befell *Curious Journey* (1977), based on interviews with survivors of the Irish Troubles. Griffith gave free rein to his histrionic talents in a robust canon which included the pro-Zulu *Black As Hell, Thick As Grass* (1979) and a vitriolic indictment of Cecil Rhodes, *A Touch of Churchill, A Touch of Hitler* (1971).

GRIFFITH, Moses (1747–1819) Artist

This self-taught topographical artist and occasional portraitist, born in Trygarn, **Botwnnog**, accompanied **Thomas Pennant** on tours of **Scotland** and Wales, providing illustrations for many of Pennant's publications. Most of his work for Pennant was completed between 1769 and 1778; he also worked with Pennant's son, David, between 1805 and 1813. The **National Library** holds many of his works, including volume 2 of his finest achievement, the extra-illustrated *Tours in Wales*, published in **London** in 1783.

GRIFFITH, Samuel [Walker] (1845–1920)
Judge and politician

As premier of Queensland and the pre-eminent lawyer in Australian politics, **Merthyr Tydfil**-born Sir Samuel Griffith was responsible for drafting the constitution that led to the federation of **Australia**'s six states on 1 January 1901. The future prime minister of Australia, Alfred Deakin, wrote of Griffith's work: 'few even in the mother country or the United States could have accomplished such a piece of draftsmanship'. He died at Merthyr, his house in Brisbane; the Welsh library of the Brisbane Cymmrodorion is a memorial to him.

GRIFFITHS, Ann (b. Thomas; 1776–1805)
Hymnwriter

The most famous of all Welsh female poets, she was born Ann Thomas (or Nansi Tomos as she was generally known) at Dolwar Fach farmhouse in the **parish** of Llanfihangel-yng-Ngwynfa, **Montgomeryshire** (now in the **community** of **Llanfihangel**), into a family whose circumstances were fairly comfortable and whose members were prominent in the local community. She spent her whole life at Dolwar Fach. She was notably fond of dancing, but became a **Calvinistic Methodist** in 1796–7 during a period of **revival** in the area. Her spiritual life was characterized by its remarkable intensity. She married Thomas Griffiths, a Montgomeryshire Methodist leader, in October 1804, and died in August 1805 following childbirth.

Around 1802, she began composing verses to crystallize her spiritual experiences. They were composed orally, with no intention of their becoming congregational **hymns**. Just over 70 of these verses have survived, mainly through the efforts of her friend and spiritual mentor, John Hughes (1775–1854) of Pontrobert (**Llangyniew**), and his wife, Ruth Evans, who had been a maid at Dolwar Fach. One *englyn* that she composed as a child has also survived, together with seven letters to John Hughes and one to Elizabeth Evans (Ruth Evans's sister,

by all accounts). The letters, like her hymns, are considered spiritual classics.

There has been a tendency to label Ann Griffiths a mystic, but Calvinistic Methodist is a more appropriate term since it emphasizes the combination of subjective experience and objective **theology** which is to be found in her work – the heat and the light (to echo her biographer, Morris Davies). Her verses are characterized by a wide-ranging and detailed scriptural knowledge. The **Bible** is the main source of her vivid imagery, and in her hands biblical vocabulary becomes the language of her deepest experiences. Her best-known hymn is her ode of love to Christ, 'Wele'n sefyll rhwng y myrtwydd', usually sung to the tune 'Cwm Rhondda'. **Saunders Lewis** described her longest poem, 'Rhyfedd, rhyfedd gan angylion', as 'one of the majestic poems of the religious poetry of Europe'.

GRIFFITHS, E[rnest] H[oward] (1851–1932)
Physicist and educationist

Born in **Brecon**, Griffiths commenced research in **Cambridge** at a time when many believed the only thing left for the **Physical Sciences** was to carry measurements to one more decimal place. He improved the platinum thermometer and determined the freezing point of solutions with unprecedented precision. His most important work was to compare the mechanical and electrical units of energy, concluding that the calorie was equal to 4.192 joules. Elected FRS in 1895, he followed **J. Viriamu Jones** as professor of experimental **philosophy** and as principal of the University College of South Wales and Monmouthshire, **Cardiff** (1902–18; *see* **Cardiff University**) at a critical time in its history. He found time to continue research, determining the heat capacity of metals at low temperatures with singular accuracy – measurements that confirmed the revolutionary predictions of quantum theory. In 1907, he was awarded the Royal Society's Higher Gold Medal.

GRIFFITHS, Ezer (1888–1962) Physicist

Ezer Griffiths, a world authority on the subject of insulation, and the son of an **Aberdare** colliery mechanic, graduated in physics at **Cardiff**. He started research under principal **Ernest Griffiths** before taking a post in the National Physical Laboratory, Teddington. He devoted his life to the physical theory of heat (*see* **Physical Sciences**) and its applications. In addition to work with Griffiths on the specific heat of metals at low temperatures, his research covered the measurement of temperature, including pyrometry, heat transfer, evaporation, cloud formation and the effect of extreme temperatures on human beings. Among his early triumphs was the solution of the problems of transporting fruit and meat by sea from **Australia** and **New Zealand**. Elected FRS in 1926, the youngest ever to be so honoured, he was president of the Institut International du Froid (1951–9) and subsequently honorary president.

GRIFFITHS, J[ohn] Gwyn (1911–2004)
Scholar and poet

Born in Porth (**Rhondda**) and educated at **Cardiff**, **Liverpool** and **Oxford**, J. Gwyn Griffiths spent most of his academic career at **Swansea**, where he became professor of

Classics and Egyptology; he published major scholarly works on Egyptian **religion** and Greek and **Latin** texts. A **Welsh-language** poet who published four collections of verse, he was the founder, during the **Second World War**, of Cylch Cadwgan, an avant-garde literary circle in the Rhondda, whose members included **Pennar Davies** and **Rhydwen Williams**. He fought elections for **Plaid [Genedlaethol] Cymru**, edited the party's **newspaper** *Y Ddraig Goch* (1948–52) and campaigned for a Welsh-medium university college. His wife was the German-born novelist and Egyptologist Kate Bosse-Griffiths (1910–98), who had a distinguished academic and curatorial career in Germany, **England** and Wales, and who wrote – chiefly in Welsh – on a wide range of topics. Their sons are the poet and novelist Robat Gruffudd (b.1943), who, in 1967, founded the Lolfa publishing firm, and the writer, educationist and Welsh-language campaigner Heini Gruffudd (b.1946).

GRIFFITHS, James (1890–1975) Politician

Born at **Betws** near **Ammanford**, the son of a blacksmith, Jim Griffiths joined the **Independent Labour Party** in 1905, was educated at the **Central Labour College** and was a miner for 17 years. A fluent **Welsh** speaker and a fine orator, he was the most representative and popular of Welsh **Labour** leaders. He was an effective president of the **South Wales Miners' Federation** (1934–6) and was MP for **Llanelli** (1936–70). His major achievement was Labour's system of National **Insurance**, which he introduced in the form of three major bills (1946–8). A Labour moderate, he was in the cabinet as colonial secretary (1950–1) and was deputy leader of his party (1956–8). Appropriately for an ardent advocate of **devolution**, he was the first **secretary of state for Wales** (1964–6).

GRIFFITHS, [Benjamin] Mervyn (1909–74)
Football referee

Mervyn Griffiths, a **Newport** schoolteacher, became one of the world's most respected **football** referees in the 1950s. He officiated at three World Cup tournaments (including semi-finals in 1954 and 1958) and in the famous 'Stanley Matthews' Wembley Cup Final of 1953.

GRIMES, W[illiam] F[rancis] (1905–88)
Archaeologist

A native of **Pembrokeshire**, Grimes was recognized as an innovative excavator and a fine draughtsman. He started his career at the **National Museum [of] Wales** and later became curator of the **London** Museum. From 1956 until his retirement in 1973, he was director of the London Institute of **Archaeology**. Grimes published the first authoritative study of the archaeological collections in the National Museum, which was republished in 1951 under the title *The Prehistory of Wales*. His most important Welsh excavations include those at the megalithic tombs of Tyisha (**Talgarth**) and Pentre Ifan (**Nevern**).

GRINDELL-MATTHEWS, Harry (1880–1941)
Radio scientist

Gloucestershire-born Grindell-Matthews, who lived at **Clydach** near **Swansea**, won fame in the 1930s for his attempts, in the hills north of Swansea, to develop a 'death ray' for the Air Ministry. This was a forerunner of the 'Star Wars Programme', but, without a device such as the laser to generate coherent electromagnetic radiation, the experiments were unsuccessful. His earlier achievements include, in 1911, the first radio message to an aeroplane, transmitted from Ely (**Cardiff**), and the first radio **telephone** link, between the Westgate Hotel, **Newport** and *The Western Mail* in Cardiff. His inventions also contributed to the simultaneous recording of vision and sound on the same **film**.

GROSMONT (Y Grysmwnt), Monmouthshire
(4670 ha; 760 inhabitants)

Hugging the English **border** north-west of **Monmouth**, the **community** includes the settlements of Grosmont, Llanvetherine, Llangattock Lingoed and Llangua. Grosmont was a medieval **borough**, as its town hall bears witness. Its early 13th-century castle, the most compact of **Gwent**'s **Three Castles**, was unsuccessfully attacked by **Owain Glyndŵr** in 1405. Grosmont church, originally built in the 13th century and reconstructed in 1870, is impressively spacious. The diminutive Llangua church is a much-loved landmark for travellers on the **Newport**–Shrewsbury **railway** line. Other churches include St **Cadog**, Llangattock Lingoed, with its perpendicular tower and St James, Llanvetherine, with monuments carved by the **Brute family**. The area is rich in fine **gentry** houses and farmhouses of the 16th and 17th centuries, the most interesting of which is Great Pool Hall (1619), with its massive chimney breasts.

GROVE, William Robert (1811–96) Scientist

An outstanding scientist, famous for inventing the fuel cell, Sir William Grove, FRS, was born in **Swansea**. He received a legal **education** and was called to the Bar in 1835. While recuperating from illness, he developed a strong interest in **science**. A founder member of the Royal Institution of South Wales, Swansea, he became a close friend of Michael Faraday at the Royal Institution, **London**.

Grove was first to publish the Law of the Conservation of Energy, in *The Correlation of Physical Forces* (1846), although others are often given the credit. He was also the first to confirm the thermal dissociation of molecules, showing that steam in contact with heated platinum decomposes into hydrogen and oxygen. Grove developed the two-fluid electric battery, and used such a battery to provide electric light for his lectures as professor of experimental **philosophy** (1841–5) at the Royal Institution, London. His most significant achievement was the construction of the first fuel cell. His device produced electric current from hydrogen and oxygen reacting on platinum electrodes. Fuel cells have since been used in spacecraft and they are now used in vehicles in a small way. If manufacturers succeed in finding a safe, economic way to store hydrogen, then Grove's fuel cell could replace the petrol engine as a non-polluting power unit for cars, **buses** and lorries.

Grove became vice-president of the Royal Institution and president of the British Society for the Advancement of Science. While secretary of the Royal Society (*c.*1847),

The Talybont motte, Grovesend

he successfully used his legal skills to campaign for it to become a society for serious professional scientists, rather than for amateurs, of whom Grove was one of the last and most eminent. He became a Lord Chief Justice in the High Court and a member of the Privy Council (1887).

GROVESEND (Pengelli), Swansea
(456 ha; 1181 inhabitants)
Located immediately south of **Pontarddulais**, the **community** contains Talybont Castle (*c.*1106), a prominent motte adjoining the **M4**. Originating as a 19th-century **coal**mining settlement, the village was also a centre of steel (*see* **Iron and Steel**) and **tinplate** manufacture. In the mid-20th century, the Bryn Lliw deep mine was sunk to exploit the area's anthracite deposits. The mine was closed in the 1980s and the extensive surface facilities have been cleared away.

GRUFFUDD AB YR YNAD COCH (fl.1277–83)
Poet
Author of the famous elegy to **Llywelyn ap Gruffudd** and, possibly, a varied collection of religious poems. He was probably a lawyer in the service of the princes of **Gwynedd**, but it is difficult to trace his career with any certainty. The fact that he received a substantial sum of money from the English crown suggests that, like many other Welsh noblemen, he deserted Llywelyn during the conflict of 1277. But his elegy, a howl of cosmic despair without parallel in Welsh **literature**, indicates that he had returned to Llywelyn's side by the rebellion of 1282.

GRUFFUDD AP CYNAN (d.1137)
King of Gwynedd
Son of Cynan ab Iago of the **Gwynedd** dynasty and Ragnhildr, daughter of the **Viking** king of Dublin, Gruffudd was brought up in exile in **Ireland**. In 1075, he tried to recover his patrimony, but was driven out. In 1081, he tried again, together with his fellow exile **Rhys ap Tewdwr** of **Deheubarth** but after their victory at **Mynydd Carn** he was captured by the **Normans** and imprisoned in Chester. Free again by about 1090, he was responsible for the death of Robert of **Rhuddlan**, who had seized power in north Wales. He and **Cadwgan ap Bleddyn** of **Powys** were leaders of the Welsh revolt of 1094, but in 1098 they had to seek refuge in Ireland following the Norman invasion of Gwynedd. Gruffudd's Viking connections may have led to the appearance of a Norwegian fleet off **Anglesey** and the withdrawal of the Normans. For the next few years he kept a low profile but, on his death in 1137, his son, **Owain Gwynedd**, inherited a powerful position. Gruffudd is the only Welsh ruler to be the subject of a contemporary biography, *Historia Gruffud vab Kenan*. All later rulers of Gwynedd were descended from him.

GRUFFUDD AP GWENWYNWYN (d.1286)
Ruler of Powys Wenwynwyn
The son of **Gwenwynwyn** of **Powys**, Gruffudd's early life was spent in exile in **England**. He recovered his patrimony in 1241, but was ejected by **Llywelyn ap Gruffudd** in 1257. In 1263, he did homage to Llywelyn, but in 1274 he was involved with **Dafydd ap Gruffudd** in an unsuccessful plot

to assassinate the prince and fled to England. During the two Welsh wars, he remained loyal to Edward I. He died in 1286, having succeeded in maintaining the identity and integrity of **Powys Wenwynwyn**.

GRUFFUDD AP LLYWELYN (d.1063)
King of Gwynedd and of Wales
The son of Llywelyn ap Seisyll, ruler of **Gwynedd** (1018–23), Gruffudd was ruling Gwynedd and **Powys** by 1039, the year in which he defeated the Mercians. Over the next 16 years, he tried to seize **Deheubarth**, eventually succeeding in 1055. Some two years later he seized **Morgannwg**, thus becoming the sole ruler in the history of Wales to have authority over the entire country. He became the ally of Aelfgar, earl of **Mercia**, twice enabling Aelfgar to recover his lands. Gruffudd was powerful and confident enough to attack **England**, and the Domesday Book records his ravages along the **border**. But his alliance with Aelfgar, coupled with his close relations with the **Viking** kingdom of Dublin, was seen by Harold Godwinesson, the dominant influence in England, as a serious threat to the balance of power and to Harold's hopes of succeeding the childless Edward the Confessor on the throne. In 1062, Harold raided Gruffudd's court at **Rhuddlan** and destroyed his fleet. Gruffudd escaped but, in the summer of 1063, Harold attacked Gwynedd again and Gruffudd was killed, probably by Cynan ap Iago, whose father Gruffudd had put to death in 1037. Gruffudd's widow, Ealdgyth, Aelfgar's daughter, married Harold Godwinesson and thus was in turn queen of Wales and queen of England. Gruffudd's half brother, **Bleddyn ap Cynfyn**, was the ancestor of the later rulers of Powys.

GRUFFUDD AP LLYWELYN AP IORWERTH (d.1244) Father of Llywelyn ap Gruffudd
Son of **Llywelyn ap Iorwerth** and Tangwystl, daughter of Llywarch Goch. Llywelyn's marriage to King John's daughter **Joan** (Siwan) led to Gruffudd's disinheritance in favour of Siwan's son, **Dafydd ap Llywelyn**. Gruffudd was one of the hostages handed over to John in 1211 and released in 1215. During the 1220s, Llywelyn took steps to have Dafydd recognized as his heir, giving Gruffudd's illegitimacy as one reason for this. Gruffudd was granted a substantial appanage, but by 1228 he had been deprived of his lands and imprisoned. Released in 1234, he was by 1238 holding **Llŷn** and **Powys**; not long afterwards he was seized by his brother and incarcerated again. In 1241, he was handed over to Henry III and lodged in the Tower of **London**. In 1244, he fell to his death while attempting to escape. His sons included **Llywelyn ap Gruffudd** and **Dafydd ap Gruffudd**.

GRUFFUDD AP NICOLAS (c.1390–c.1460)
Official
Of **Carmarthenshire** stock, Gruffudd ap Nicolas lived at Newton (see **Llandeilo**), and dominated his **county** socially and politically. He began his career as an official (c.1415) in the lordship of **Kidwelly**, exploiting the absences of royal lieutenants from south-west Wales to exercise personal power there. He and his sons extended their influence into **Cardiganshire** and the **lordship of Pembroke**; during the **Wars of the Roses**, he helped sustain the Lancastrian regime in south Wales, resisting efforts by **York**ists to

dislodge him in the 1450s. He was granted English **denizenship** (1437), yet was admired by Welsh poets, partly for patronizing **Carmarthen**'s **eisteddfod** (c.1450). His grandson was Henry **Tudor**'s supporter **Rhys ap Thomas**.

GRUFFUDD AP RHYS AP GRUFFUDD (fl.1267)
Lord of Senghennydd
The great-grandson of **Ifor Bach**, Gruffudd was the last lord of **Senghennydd**. In 1267, Gilbert de **Clare**, lord of **Glamorgan**, deprived him of his lands and imprisoned him in **Ireland** because of his dealings with **Llywelyn ap Gruffudd**, who claimed his homage.

GRUFFUDD AP RHYS AP TEWDWR (d.1137)
Ruler in Deheubarth
Following his father's death in battle in 1093 and the **Norman** conquest of **Deheubarth**, Gruffudd spent his youth in exile in **Ireland**. By about 1113, he was back in Wales and, in 1116, he rose in revolt, capturing **Carmarthen**. He later came to terms with Henry I and acquired the **commote** of **Caeo**. He was one of the leaders of the revolt that followed Henry's death, taking part in the **battle of Crug Mawr**. He and his wife, **Gwenllian**, the daughter of **Gruffudd ap Cynan**, died in 1137; their youngest son, **Rhys ap Gruffudd** (the Lord Rhys; d.1197), was to be the greatest of all the rulers of Deheubarth.

GRUFFUDD HIRAETHOG (d.1563) Poet
Although his own praise poems are, by modern standards, monotonous and uninspiring, during his own age Gruffudd Hiraethog was a highly respected teacher of poets – both Wiliam Llŷn and **Siôn Tudur** were among his pupils – and the leading authority on Welsh **genealogy**. His friendship with the **Renaissance** scholar **William Salesbury** provided a bridge between the native learning of the bards and Welsh humanism, and it was Gruffudd's collection of **proverbs** which formed the basis of Salesbury's *Oll Synnwyr pen Kembero Ygyd* (1547). Gruffudd was born and buried at **Llangollen**, and Hiraethog (see **Mynydd Hiraethog**) was probably attached to his name because of the prolonged patronage given to him by the family of **Elis Prys** of Plas Iolyn (**Pentrefoelas**), where his bardic school may have been located.

GRUFFUDD LLWYD (Sir Gruffudd ap Rhys; d.1335) Soldier
One of the many important descendants of **Ednyfed Fychan**, Gruffudd held various offices in the north and saw military service in Flanders and **Scotland**. He was one of the leaders of the native Welsh community, especially during the troubles of the reign of Edward II. There are suggestions that he led a Welsh revolt in 1322, but his activity in that year probably represented an attempt to support the king in his struggle with the reform party, which included most of the **march**er-lords of Wales.

GRUFFYDD, Elis ('The Soldier of Calais'; c.1490–c.1552) Soldier and chronicler
Born at Gronant Uchaf (**Llanasa**), Gruffydd was present at the Field of the Cloth of Gold in 1520. In the late 1520s, he made a collection of Welsh poetry and prose. He enlisted in

the Calais garrison in 1530. In *c*.1548–52, he compiled his famous chronicle in which he sought to give an account of the history of the world up to his own time. Although mainly based on a variety of **English**, **French** and **Latin** sources, it also contains important material of Welsh provenance.

GRUFFYDD, W[illiam] J[ohn] (1881–1954) Scholar, poet and commentator

A native of Bethel (**Llanddeiniolen**), Gruffydd studied Classics and **English** at Jesus College, **Oxford** from 1899, and came under the influence of **John Rhŷs**, and more particularly of **Owen M. Edwards**, the first part of whose biography he later wrote (1937). He became lecturer in **Welsh**, later professor, at **Cardiff**. During the **First World War**, he served in the navy. In 1937, he was temporary deputy vice president of **Plaid [Genedlaethol] Cymru**, but, in 1943, he won the **University of Wales** parliamentary seat for the **Liberals**. The contest between him and **Saunders Lewis** in that by-election created a split in Welsh intellectual circles. An inheritor of 19th-century **Nonconformist radicalism**, he was the editor (1922–51) of the quarterly journal *Y Llenor*, which became a platform for his ideas. As a poet, he made an impression at a young age with his volume *Telynegion* (in collaboration with Silyn (**Robert Roberts**; 1900) and with his long poem in free metres, 'Trystan ac Esyllt', which came close to winning the crown at the 1902 National **Eisteddfod**. Then came *Caneuon a Cherddi* (1906), *Ynys yr Hud a Chaneuon Eraill* (1923) and *Caniadau*, published by the Gregynog Press (*see* **Tregynon**) in 1932. He began his poetic career as a romantic, but his style became starker in poems such as 'Gwladys Rhys'. His anthology *Y Flodeugerdd Gymraeg* (1931) had considerable influence in schools, and his memoir *Hen Atgofion* (1936) is regarded as a prose classic. His main scholarly interests involved studies of *The Mabinogion*.

GUEST family Industrialists

In 1767, John Guest (1722–85) moved from Broseley, **Shropshire**, to manage the small **iron**works at Dowlais, **Merthyr Tydfil**. In 1781, he purchased a share of the works, which was inherited by his eldest son Thomas (?1749–1807) and his son-in-law, William Taitt (1748–1815). By 1801,

Lady Charlotte Guest in Dowlais Central School, which she commissioned in 1855

the Dowlais Iron Company was owned by Taitt, Thomas Guest and William Lewis (d.1819). On Thomas's death, his son Josiah John (1785–1852) inherited his interest and, on Taitt's death, assumed managerial control, which he retained for life. His eagerness to apply the latest technology and his sharp commercial acumen raised Dowlais from third position in Merthyr to the largest ironworks in the world in the 1840s. His 5000-strong workforce probably meant that he had more employees than any other individual on earth.

It was chiefly through Guest's influence that the new **borough** constituency of Merthyr was established in 1832, and he was elected unopposed as its first representative, holding the seat as a **Liberal** for 20 years (1832–52). He was the chief instigator and the first chairman of the **Taff** Vale **Railway**, and the first chairman of the Merthyr Board of Guardians (1837) and the Merthyr Board of **Health** (1850). A paternalistic employer, he funded local schools, workmen's libraries and Dowlais church (1827), and in 1834 was a patron of Cymreigyddion y Fenni (*see* **Abergavenny**).

His wife, Lady Charlotte Guest (1812–95), who gave birth to nine children, was also involved in these activities. She is best remembered as a diarist and, above all, for translating into **English** the 11 tales now known as *The Mabinogion*, together with the Tale of **Taliesin**, which were published in three volumes in 1846. In this task she was assisted by several Welsh scholars, among whom **Thomas Price** (Carnhuanawc; 1787–1848) was prominent. This was the only English version of the prose masterpiece until the publication of the far superior translation made by **Gwyn Jones** and **Thomas Jones** and published in 1948. Between 1852 and 1855, Lady Charlotte effectively controlled the works, but when she remarried, trustees – G. T. Clark, in particular – assumed the family's responsibilities.

By the late 1840s, the family's main residence was Canford Manor in Dorset. Nevertheless, the Guests retained links with **Glamorgan**: Alfred Guest was the **Conservative** candidate at **Cardiff** in 1880, and Ifor Guest represented Cardiff as a Liberal from 1906 to 1910.

GUEST, KEEN AND NETTLEFOLDS (GKN)

GKN is one of **Britain**'s major industrial conglomerates, although it no longer has any holdings in Wales. It originated in 1902 as a result of the amalgamation of the Guest Keen Company (itself a year-old combination of Guests, the south Wales steel producer which owed its origins to the activities of the **Guest family** in **Merthyr Tydfil**, and Keens, the English Midlands steel and bolt makers) with Nettlefolds, Britain's leading screw manufacturer. This made GKN Britain's leading steel (*see* **Iron and Steel**) and **engineering** group, with assets in 1905 of £4.5 million. Its Welsh interests included the original Dowlais steelworks at **Merthyr Tydfil**, **East Moors** in **Cardiff** and a steelworks at **Rogerstone**.

In 1930, GKN and Baldwins amalgamated their heavy steelmaking interests to form the British GKB steel company, which led to major capital investments at **Port Talbot** and Cardiff. GKN then independently built the Castle Works in Cardiff – relocated from Rogerstone – to be supplied with steel from the adjacent East Moors and to produce rods, wire and nails.

GUILSFIELD (Cegidfa), Montgomeryshire, Powys (3001 ha; 1640 inhabitants)

Located immediately north-west of **Welshpool**, the **community**'s **Welsh** name means the place of the hemlock. Guilsfield village, much expanded in the late 20th century, is rich in 18th and 19th-century buildings. Indicative of its prosperity is the branch **canal** built to link it with the **Montgomeryshire** Canal. St Aelhaearn's, one of the finest churches in Montgomeryshire, has a sturdy tower (*c*.1300), a well-proportioned nave and chancel (15th and 16th centuries), a splendid early 16th-century roof with intriguing bosses and numerous funerary monuments. The church was sensitively restored in 1879.

The **Lollard** Sir John Oldcastle, the probable model for **Shakespeare**'s Falstaff, was taken prisoner at Guilsfield in 1417. The Netherlandish Maesmawr Hall (1692) and the Georgian Trawscoed Hall (1777) are attractive buildings, but Guilsfield's glory was Garth, built *c*.1809 for Richard Mytton, chaplain to the governor-general of India. Wales's sole neo-Mogul building, it was demolished in 1946. The Guilsfield Hoard, discovered in Crowther's Camp (*see* Welshpool) and consisting of over 100 bronze weapons and tools, is exhibited in the **National Museum**.

GUTO'R GLYN (fl.1440–93) Poet

Possibly a native of **Llansantffraid Glyn Ceiriog** or Glyndyfrdwy (**Corwen**), he was one of Wales's greatest medieval poets. As a young man, he fought in France at the end of the **Hundred Years War**, addressing poems to the Welsh commanders Sir Richard Gethin and **Mathew Gough**. Later, he served in Edward IV's royal guard. He addressed poems to patrons throughout Wales; among the most prominent were members of the **Herbert family**. Guto's personality enlivens his poetry, and he transcended the poetic conventions of his age. He died and was buried at Valle Crucis Abbey (**Llantysilio**).

GUTUN OWAIN (fl.1450–98) Poet

A native of Dudleston near Oswestry (*see* **Shropshire**), Gutun accompanied his bardic teacher, **Dafydd ab Edmwnd**, to the **Carmarthen eisteddfod** (*c*.1450); his copies of the bardic grammar incorporate the metrical changes formulated there by Dafydd. The manuscripts he wrote include *The Black Book of Basingwerk*. His poems were mostly addressed to **gentry** and monastic patrons in the north-east; he excelled in poems requesting gifts and in his metrically intricate *awdlau*.

GUY, Henry Lewis (1887–1956) Engineer

Born in **Penarth**, and intrigued by **railways**, Guy studied **engineering** in **Cardiff** before beginning a career, with various concerns in **England**, studying and designing steam turbines. He realized that the development of the turbine called for major advances in metallurgy and the use of steam at very high pressure. He was elected FRS in 1936 and knighted in 1949.

GWALIA

A name for Wales used alongside *Wallia* (from the Old **English** *Walas* or *Weales*) in medieval **Latin** documents. The initial 'g' was the result of **French** influence. It occurs

Gwaun-Cae-Gurwen-born Gareth Edwards in the winning Wales side against England at Twickenham, 4 February 1978

in **Welsh-language** manuscripts from the 16th century onwards, as in the verse prophesying that the Welsh would lose all their land apart from 'gwyllt Walia'. Like **Cambria**, it was revived during the 19th century and is still sometimes used, although mostly for its quaintness.

GWAUN-CAE-GURWEN (Gwauncaegurwen),
Neath Port Talbot (1366 ha; 4133 inhabitants)
Known colloquially as GCG, the **community** is located in the upper Aman valley, south of the **Black Mountain**. There was a small colliery at Blaengurwen in 1802. Later, in 1887, when the Llanelly [*sic*] Dock **Railway** Company extended its network to the area, major development began. The new settlements – Gwaun-Cae-Gurwen, Cwmgors and Lower Brynamman – were endowed with some of Wales's largest chapels. **Rugby** legend Gareth Edwards and the actress Siân Phillips were born in Gwaun-Cae-Gurwen to a family that included the evangelist Rosina Davies. The area is dominated by vast open-cast mining operations (*see* **Coal**). In 2001, 77.37% of the inhabitants of Gwaun-Cae-Gurwen had some knowledge of **Welsh**, with 53.88% wholly fluent in the language – the highest percentages of all the communities of the **county** of **Neath Port Talbot**.

GWEHELOG FAWR, Monmouthshire
(1739 ha; 461 inhabitants)
Located immediately north of **Usk**, the **community** contains the settlements of Gwehelog, Kemeys Commander, Llancayo and Trostrey. Gwehelog was once the **common land** of Usk. The tiny church at Kemeys Commander stands within a group of farms. There is an extensive **hillfort** at Campswood and a **windmill** at Llancayo. The 2001 census reported that 85.8% of the inhabitants had some

knowledge of **Welsh**, with 71.51% wholly fluent in the language; a rare example of a misprint in published census reports, the Office of National Statistics has confirmed that the correct figures are 12.6 and 7.7.

GWELY (lit. 'bed')
A family group descended from a common ancestor and sharing proprietary rights in land. It may have been of very early origin, but the 14th-century northern extents and surveys seem to indicate that the eponyms of individual *gwelyau* (the word's plural form) lived around 1200. By the early 13th century, the term had come to apply to the land as well as to the group that held it. Rights in land within the *gwely* were shared equally among sons and were inalienable; this regular subdivision meant that after several generations individual shares of arable land might be small, but every member also enjoyed extensive grazing rights.

The size of a *gwely* could vary greatly; a single township might contain several, and in some cases township and *gwely* could be coterminous. Others might extend over more than one township and it was not necessarily a single coherent territorial unit. As a land market developed in the later Middle Ages, outsiders began to move in and the link between land and lineage was diluted. The *gwely* remained but it was increasingly an empty shell, its only significance being as a unit on which customary rents continued to be assessed (*see also* **Gafael**).

GWENLLIAN FERCH GRUFFUDD
AP CYNAN (d.1137) Princess
Gwenllian, daughter of **Gruffudd ap Cynan**, was the wife of **Gruffudd ap Rhys** of **Deheubarth** and mother of **Rhys ap Gruffudd** (The Lord Rhys; d.1197). She was killed leading

her husband's men against the **Normans** near **Kidwelly**, where the name of Maes Gwenllian commemorates her. It has been suggested that the 'four branches of the Mabinogi' (*see **Mabinogion, The***) is her work; the suggestion is almost certainly without foundation.

GWENLLIAN FERCH LLYWELYN AP GRUFFUDD (1282–1337) Princess

Gwenllian was the only daughter of **Llywelyn ap Gruffudd**; her mother Eleanor (*see **Montfort, de family***) died in childbirth. After Llywelyn's death, she fell into the hands of Edward I and was placed in the priory of Sempringham, Lincolnshire, where she became a nun; she died there. There is a society devoted to her memory.

GWENT Kingdom

Deriving its name from **Caerwent**, the kingdom emerged in the immediate post-**Roman** period. Caradoc (*see **Caratacus***), its first recorded king, bore the name of the hero who had led the **Silures** against the Romans in the 1st century. King Tewdrig, whose body is reputed to lie at **Mathern**, defeated the invading Saxons *c.*620 (*see **Anglo-Saxons***). The kingdom seems at times to have been part of that of **Morgannwg**. It was divided into the *cantrefi* of Is Coed and Uwch Coed; the border between them was Wentwood, a ridge rising to 309 m and containing igneous rocks, which are very rare in south-east Wales. Extinguished as a kingdom following the campaigns of **William Fitz Osbern**, a remnant of it was revived by Morgan ab Owain of **Caerleon** in the mid-12th century. Gwent survived as a regional description, as the titles of **newspapers** such as *The Star of Gwent* indicate. (*See also* Gwent, One-time county.)

GWENT One-time county

In 1974, **Monmouthshire**, deprived of the left bank of the **Rhymney** and augmented by the annexing from **Breconshire** of **Brynmawr** and **Llanelly**, became the **county** of Gwent, which was divided into the districts of **Blaenau Gwent**, **Islwyn**, **Monmouth**, **Newport** and **Torfaen**. The county was abolished in 1996 when Blaenau Gwent, Newport and Torfaen became **county boroughs**, Monmouth became a county and Islwyn became part of the county borough of **Caerphilly**. The name Gwent is still in use for combined services such as the **police** force and the County Record Office.

GWENT LEVELS, The

Consisting of low-lying wetlands adjoining the **Severn** estuary, the levels have been embanked by seawalls and drained for **agriculture**. The **Usk** estuary separates the levels' western wing, **Wentlooge**, from its eastern wing, **Caldicot**. The levels are underlain and flanked to the north by Old Red Sandstone, Triassic Mudstone and Carboniferous **Limestone**. Drift deposits include silts and **peats** laid down as the rise of the sea level drowned the mouth of the Severn, thereby creating a very muddy estuary with a tidal range (14.8 m) exceeded in height only by that of the Bay of Fundy in Canada. Submerged forests are widespread. The area is rich in evidence of prehistoric activity, including footprints left by Mesolithic hunter-gatherers and remnants of **Bronze Age** and **Iron Age** settlements. Finds of waterlogged boats include fragments of Bronze Age plank boats, a **Romano**-British boat from Llandevenny (**Magor and Undy**), and medieval boats from Magor Pill (1240) and **Newport** (1466). A stone found at **Goldcliff** records **Roman** work on sea defences.

The area is interlaced with drainage channels known as reens; elaborate local by-laws ensure their effective operation. The drainage has produced one of the few areas of Wales containing land of first-class quality; its fertility is reflected in large churches such as those at **Nash** and Peterstone Wentlooge. In the latter, a mark 168 cm above the chancel floor indicates the level reached by the disastrous flood of 1606 (1607 by modern reckoning), which was probably a tsunami (*see **Earthquakes***). The building of the **Llanwern Steelworks** (*see **Iron and Steel***) subjected the levels to extensive industrial development. The Gwent Levels Wetland Reserve was established in the mid-1990s to compensate for the loss of **bird** habitat resulting from the Cardiff Bay development.

GWENWYNWYN AB OWAIN CYFEILIOG (d.1216) Lord of Powys Wenwynwyn

In 1197, Gwenwynwyn succeeded his father **Owain Cyfeiliog** as ruler of southern **Powys**, which became known as **Powys Wenwynwyn**. An able and ambitious prince, he sought to recover the position Powys had enjoyed before 1160; the failure of his siege of **Painscastle** in 1198, however, was a major setback. He and **Llywelyn ap Iorwerth** of **Gwynedd** competed for supremacy and King John endeavoured to play them off against each other. In 1208, a misjudged attack on a **march**er-neighbour led John to imprison Gwenwynwyn. Llywelyn occupied his lands, which were restored to him two years later. With the other Welsh rulers he joined John's campaign against Llywelyn in 1211 and, like them, joined Llywelyn the following year, taking part in the great sweep through the south in 1215. In 1216, John persuaded him to change sides; Llywelyn expelled him and Gwenwynwyn died in **England** later the same year. His son, **Gruffudd ap Gwenwynwyn**, would play a role similar to that of his father.

GWERFUL MECHAIN (fl. *c.*1460–1502) Poet

A native of **Llanfechain**, Gwerful was one of the very few known female poets of medieval Wales. She was associated with the poet Dafydd Llwyd (*c.*1395–*c.*1486) of Mathafarn, possibly her bardic teacher. Gwerful's poetic voice was distinctly feminine: she defended **women** in a *cywydd* responding to a poetic attack on them by Ieuan Dyfi. Her famous poems 'To the cunt' and 'To jealous women', and the erotic *englynion* she exchanged with Dafydd Llwyd, are notably frank expressions of female sexuality. She also wrote an *englyn* castigating her husband for beating her.

GWERIN

Originally signifying a body of soldiery and later the common folk, by the 18th century the term was used to differentiate the mass of the people from the **gentry**. To the early **radicals**, it meant the struggling working **class**, but by the late 19th century the word carried the notion of the Welsh as a cultured people intent on gaining self-respect and respectability. In the later 20th century, the word was often used as a way of camouflaging class divisions.

GWERIN Political movement
Established at **Bangor** (*see* **University of Wales, Bangor**) in 1935, this group of students, led by **Goronwy O. Roberts** (**Labour** MP for **Caernarfon**, 1945–74), sought to make **Plaid [Genedlaethol] Cymru** more sympathetic to **socialism**, and the Labour Party more sympathetic to Welsh cultural and constitutional issues.

GWERNAFFIELD, Flintshire
(753 ha; 1851 inhabitants)
Located immediately north-west of **Mold**, the **community** is bordered on three sides by the **River** Alyn. Pantymwyn is a former **lead**-mining area. The smelting works at Llyn-y-pandy were developed by **John Wilkinson**. The obelisk (1736) north of Maesgarmon Farm purports to mark the site of the 'Hallelujah Victory' (*c.*447) in which the Britons, led by Germanus (**Garmon**), defeated the Saxons (*see* **Anglo-Saxons**) and the Picts. Rhual (1634) is **Flintshire**'s sole early 17th-century brick-built house. In the late 20th century, the village of Gwernaffield-y-Waun acquired rectangular blocks of commuter dwellings.

GWERNYFED, Breconshire, Powys
(2171 ha; 995 inhabitants)
Gwernyfed stretches from the **Wye** southwards towards **Talgarth**. The fine Jacobean mansion of Old Gwernyfed was reputedly visited by Charles I following his defeat at Naseby in 1645. The later mansion built in Gwernyfed Park is now a secondary school. Tregoed, rebuilt after a fire in 1900, replaced the 17th-century house built for the **Devereux family**, the viscounts Hereford. A change in the course of the Wye means that the ruins of the late 11th-century church built on the north side of the river at **Glasbury** are now on its south side. There is a long barrow of the **Severn**–Cotswold type near Little Lodge. Three Cocks, which local patriots wish to replace with the name Aberllynfi, was once a junction on the **Brecon**–Hereford **railway** line.

GWERNYMYNYDD, Flintshire
(479 ha; 1210 inhabitants)
Located on a **limestone** ridge immediately west of **Mold**, the **community** has become one of Mold's outer suburbs. In the 19th century, it was the scene of extensive **lead** mining and limestone quarrying. The large quarry at Cefn-mawr supplies limestone to Padeswood cement works (*see* **Buckley**). Fron Hall is a five-bay mansion built in 1765.

GWERSYLLT, Wrexham
(788 ha; 10,956 inhabitants)
Located immediately north of **Wrexham**, the area was industrialized from the 1780s onwards following the establishment of wire mills and forges. **Coal**mines were later sunk; with their closure, the **community** became one of Wrexham's outer suburbs. Like many buildings in the neighbourhood, Gwersyllt Hall, which dated from the 16th century, suffered from subsidence; it was demolished *c.*1910. Stansty Park (demolished) was the original site of the splendid railings and gates attributed to the **Davies**

family of **Esclusham** (*see* **Ironwork**) and re-erected in 1908 at Erddig (*see* **Marchwiel**). Gwersyllt is the home of the Marcher Sound local radio station.

GWIDIGADA Commote
One of the seven **commotes** of **Cantref Mawr**, Gwidigada or Widigada was located immediately east of **Carmarthen**. The origin of the unusual name is unknown.

GWLAD Y MENIG GWYNION
(Land of the white gloves)
One of the names for Wales in the late 19th century (the first reference dates from 1861), referring to the custom of presenting judges with white gloves when there were no cases for them to try. It reflected an idealized view of the country, especially the rural areas, and arose in response to the aspersions of the Blue Books of 1847 (*see* **Treason of the Blue Books**).

GWRINYDD *Cantref*
Gwrinydd or (later) Gorfynydd is believed to have been a *cantref* within the kingdom of **Morgannwg**, and probably consisted of the territory between the **rivers Thaw** and Afan. It is likely that its centre was at Llyswrinydd or Llysworney (*see* **Llandow**). A corrupt form of the name survives in Gronedd, a deanery of the **diocese** of Llandaff (*see* **Cardiff**).

GWRTHEYRNION Commote and lordship
Gwrtheyrnion (or Gwerthrynion) lay between the **Wye** and the Ithon. The name derives from Gwrtheyrn (**Vortigern**), traditionally considered the ancestor of its dynasty. In the mid-12th century, it was seized by the **Mortimers** who yielded it to **Llywelyn ap Gruffudd** in 1256. Under the terms of the **Treaty of Montgomery**, Llywelyn retained possession of the lordship, but it subsequently reverted to the Mortimers and later, through their heirs, the dukes of **York**, to the crown.

GWYDDELWERN, Denbighshire
(1765 ha; 508 inhabitants)
Located immediately north of **Corwen**, the **community**'s name is frequently interpreted as indicating an ancient **Irish** (*Gwyddel*) presence in the locality. Here, however, *gwyddel* probably refers to shrubs or bushes. St **Beuno**'s church, although remodelled in the 19th century, retains its medieval wagon roof. Two poets, a father and son, both clergymen, are associated with the church – Robert Wynne (d.1720) and Edward Wynne (1685–1745). The village inn (Tŷ Mawr, formerly the Rose and Crown) has a fine 16th-century timber frame. Although the percentage of the inhabitants with some knowledge of **Welsh** (77.45%) is exceeded by that for **Cynwyd**, Gwyddelwern's percentage of those wholly fluent in the language (61.77%) is the highest in any community in **Denbighshire**.

GWYDDONIADUR CYMREIG, Y
(*The Encyclopaedia Cambrensis*)
This 10-volume work, the longest **Welsh-language** book ever published, resulted from **Thomas Gee**'s reaction to the attacks of the Blue Books of 1847 (*see* **Treason of the Blue Books**). His initial response was to publish, from 1850

onwards, a series of books outlining the rudiments of knowledge for the benefit of the monoglot Welsh. This scheme was soon superseded by a far more ambitious plan to publish a *gwyddoniadur* (encyclopaedia) – a term probably coined by the lexicographer D. Silvan Evans (*see* **Dictionaries**). Gee was inspired by patriotic motives, believing that practically all civilized nations possessed such a work.

John Parry of **Bala** College was appointed editor. On Parry's death in 1874, Gee himself assumed responsibility. The first shilling part, published in 1854, was very favourably received. Initially, 4000 copies were printed, but by the tenth volume, in 1879, Gee was printing 12,000 copies of each part, as well as reprinting earlier parts for new subscribers. Between 1889 and 1896, a second edition appeared, containing over 1800 new articles.

The *Gwyddoniadur* has historical significance as the epitome of the world-view of its period, and many of its biographical articles retain their value, since they contain information not included in *The Dictionary of Welsh Biography*.

GWYDION Sorcerer

A sorcerer and magician who is alluded to in medieval **Welsh** poetry and more especially in the fourth branch of the Mabinogi (*see* **Mabinogion, The**; *also* **Arianrhod**, **Blodeuwedd**, **Lleu Llawgyffes**, **Math fab Mathonwy**).

GWYN, Richard (Richard White; d.1584)
Martyr and poet

Born to a Protestant family in **Llanidloes**, Gwyn was educated at **Oxford** before moving to the **Wrexham** area to teach. It was there that he was received into the **Roman Catholic** Church. Persecuted by the authorities on account of his support for missionary priests, Gwyn was obliged to move frequently to avoid arrest. He was first captured in 1579 but escaped. Arrested again in 1580, he was imprisoned until his **execution** in 1584 – Wales's first **Roman Catholic martyr**. Gwyn composed five **Welsh** carols – free-metre poems promoting the Catholic faith. He was canonized in 1970.

GWYNEDD County
(262,224 ha; 116,843 inhabitants)

The **county** was established in 1974 following the abolition of the ancient counties. It consisted of the counties of **Anglesey** and **Caernarfonshire**, the right bank of the **Conwy** Valley (previously part of **Denbighshire**), and the whole of **Merioneth** apart from **Edeirnion** (which became part of the new county of **Clwyd**). The county was divided into the districts of Anglesey, **Arfon**, **Aberconwy**, **Dwyfor** and **Meirionnydd**.

Further reorganization in 1996 led to a marked contraction in Gwynedd's area. Anglesey became a separate county and Aberconwy became part of the **county borough** of Conwy. Thus, the 1996 county consisted of what had been Arfon, Dwyfor and Meirionnydd, districts which ceased to exist following the establishment of Gwynedd as a unitary county authority. As Wales's strongest **Welsh**-speaking region, the county of Gwynedd, both in its 1974 and its 1996 guise, proved innovative in its use of the

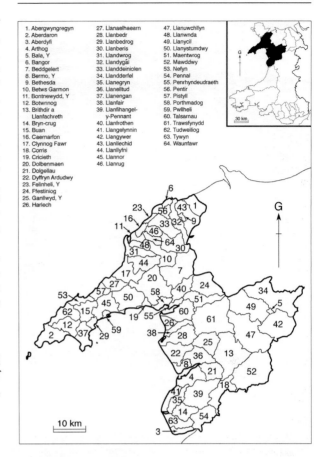

1. Abergwyngregyn
2. Aberdaron
3. Aberdyfi
4. Arthog
5. Bala, Y
6. Bangor
7. Beddgelert
8. Bermo, Y
9. Bethesda
10. Betws Garmon
11. Bontnewydd, Y
12. Botwnnog
13. Brithdir a Llanfachreth
14. Bryn-crug
15. Buan
16. Caernarfon
17. Clynnog Fawr
18. Corris
19. Criccieth
20. Dolbenmaen
21. Dolgellau
22. Dyffryn Ardudwy
23. Felinheli, Y
24. Ffestiniog
25. Ganllwyd, Y
26. Harlech
27. Llanaelhaearn
28. Llanbedr
29. Llanbedrog
30. Llanberis
31. Llandwrog
32. Llandygái
33. Llanddeiniolen
34. Llandderfel
35. Llanegryn
36. Llanelltud
37. Llanengan
38. Llanfair
39. Llanfihangel-y-Pennant
40. Llanfrothen
41. Llangelynnin
42. Llangywer
43. Llanllechid
44. Llanllyfni
45. Llannor
46. Llanrug
47. Llanuwchllyn
48. Llanwnda
49. Llanycil
50. Llanystumdwy
51. Maentwrog
52. Mawddwy
53. Nefyn
54. Pennal
55. Penrhyndeudraeth
56. Pentir
57. Pistyll
58. Porthmadog
59. Pwllheli
60. Talsarnau
61. Trawsfynydd
62. Tudweiliog
63. Tywyn
64. Waunfawr

10 km

30 km

The communities of Gwynedd

language. In 2001, 76.11% of Gwynedd's inhabitants had some knowledge of Welsh, with 60.63% wholly fluent in the language – the highest percentages in Wales. (*See also* **Arthog**, **Caernarfon** and **Llanuwchllyn**.)

GWYNEDD Kingdom and Principality

Gwynedd was usually the most powerful Welsh kingdom, mainly because the natural fortress of **Snowdonia** made it the most easily defendable. **Maelgwn Gwynedd**, in the first half of the 6th century, was the dominant ruler in Wales. The early 7th-century king Cadfan is commemorated at Llangadwaladr (**Bodorgan**) near the royal seat at **Aberffraw**; his memorial describes him as 'the wisest and the most renowned of all kings'. His successor **Cadwallon** struggled with the Northumbrians for the control of what was to become northern **England**, was briefly successful, but was killed in 634.

In 825, **Merfyn Frych** established a new dynasty. His son and successor **Rhodri Mawr** brought **Powys** and **Seisyllwg** under his rule; he was also the first Welsh ruler successfully to resist **Viking** incursions. Rhodri was killed in 878 and Gwynedd may have been subject to some kind of Scandinavian overlordship in the late 10th and early 11th centuries. Revival came under **Gruffudd ap Llywelyn** (d.1063), a warlord who extended his authority over the whole of Wales. The death of his half-brother, **Bleddyn ap Cynfyn**, in 1075 was followed by a bid for power by the **Norman** Robert of **Rhuddlan**. Robert was killed in turn and by the end of the century **Gruffudd ap Cynan,** of the lineage

The memorial at Cwmhir Abbey to Llywelyn ap Gruffudd, ruler of Gwynedd and Prince of Wales

of Rhodri Mawr, had regained his patrimony, having survived a Norman invasion in 1098.

Under Gruffudd, the borders of the kingdom were extended. He was succeeded in 1137 by his son **Owain Gwynedd**, under whom Gwynedd continued to expand. Owain's death in 1170 was followed by a power struggle between his sons; **Dafydd ab Owain Gwynedd** eventually won the kingship, but during the 1190s he and his brother Rhodri were challenged by their nephew **Llywelyn ap Iorwerth** Drwyndwn. By 1200, most of Gwynedd was under Llywelyn's control. His two objectives were to pass on an undivided realm to his son, **Dafydd ap Llywelyn**, and to be recognized by the English crown as overlord of all the other Welsh rulers. He failed to win that recognition, and when he died in 1240 the whole polity, depending as it did on his own personality, proved to be very fragile.

Dafydd was forced to abandon most of his father's achievements. His death in 1246 left Gwynedd divided between two of his nephews, Owain and **Llywelyn ap Gruffudd**. The **Treaty of Woodstock** of 1247 was the nadir of Gwynedd's fortunes before 1282. But under Llywelyn, who won sole control in 1255, there was continued progress, culminating in Llywelyn's recognition by Henry III as Prince of Wales through the **Treaty of Montgomery** (1267). Gwynedd's dominance of native Wales was thus confirmed, but a succession of crises in Anglo-Welsh

relations in the 1270s led to Edward I's two Welsh wars (*see* **Edwardian Conquest**) and to the death of Llywelyn in 1282, the **execution** of his brother Dafydd ap Gruffudd a year later and the end of Welsh independence, which had come to be identified with Gwynedd and its rulers.

GWYNEDDIGION SOCIETY, The

A literary and cultural society founded in **London** in 1770. Although its name (lit. '**Gwynedd** scholars') suggests a geographically limited focus, from the beginning it embraced the whole of the north and soon welcomed natives from all parts of Wales. Its first president and one of its main benefactors was **Owen Jones** (Owain Myfyr); Iolo Morganwg (**Edward Williams**) was also a member. His fascination with the alleged discovery of America by **Madog ab Owain Gwynedd** led to the society raising the funds to send **John Evans** (1770–99) of **Waunfawr** in search of the 'Welsh Indians'. The society had its own library and awarded a silver medal annually as a prize for **literature**. It supported *eisteddfodau* in Wales, and the publication of Welsh literary texts such as *Barddoniaeth Dafydd ab Gwilym* (1789) and *The Myvyrian Archaiology of Wales* (1801–7). The first Gwyneddigion society merged with the Cymreigyddion (lit. 'The Welsh scholars'), but a new Gwyneddigion society was founded in London in 1978.

GWYNIONYDD Commote

One of the 10 **commotes** of **Ceredigion**, Gwynionydd extended along the north bank of the **Teifi**. It contained Rhuddlan Teifi where, according to *The Mabinogion*, **Pryderi** entertained the wizard **Gwydion**.

GWYNLLŴG *Cantref*

Located east of the **Rhymney**, Gwynllŵg was a *cantref* of **Glywysing**, although it seems at times to have been a separate political entity. Seized by the **Normans**, it was successively held by the **Clare**, **Audley** and **Stafford** families. Often known as the **marcher**-lordship of **Newport**, it passed to the crown in 1521, and became part of the **county** of **Monmouth** in 1536. The Gwynllŵg (**Wentlooge**) Levels are the western wing of the **Gwent Levels**.

GWYNN, Eirwen [Meiriona] (1916–2007) Science promoter, and GWYNN, Harri (1913–85) Poet and broadcaster

Born in **Liverpool** and brought up at **Llangefni**, Eirwen Gwynn was the first **woman** student at **Bangor** to be awarded a doctorate in physics (1940). She concluded her varied career as tutor-organizer with the **Workers' Educational Association**. She published extensively on scientific subjects, and also wrote novels and short stories. A prolific broadcaster, she was prominent as a campaigner for the **Welsh language**. Her husband, Harri Gwynn, who was born in **London** and raised in **Penrhyndeudraeth**, enjoyed a varied career as civil servant, farmer, journalist and broadcaster. The period he and his wife spent farming in **Eifionydd** is described with humour in *Y Fuwch a'i Chynffon* (1954). At the **Aberystwyth** National **Eisteddfod** in 1952, the refusal by **W. J. Gruffydd** and fellow adjudicators to award him the crown for his *pryddest* 'Y Creadur' caused considerable controversy. In the late

1930s, Harri Gwynn and his future wife were prominent in the **Gwerin** movement.

GWYNNE, Rowland (*c.*1658–1726) Politician
Sir Rowland Gwynne of **Llanelwedd** was MP for **Radnorshire** from 1679 to 1698. A **Whig** whose praises were sung by Macaulay, he successfully proposed in 1696 that an oath of allegiance should be sworn to William III. Financially incompetent, he died bankrupt in the Fleet prison.

GWYNNE-VAUGHAN, David Thomas (1871–1915) Botanist
Born in **Llandovery**, Gwynne-Vaughan was a member of the Gwynne family of Glanbrân. Educated at **Cambridge**, he undertook research work at the Jodrell Laboratory, Kew, and two expeditions to the Amazon rubber plantations, before his appointment as lecturer in botany at Glasgow. In 1897, he undertook botanical explorations in east Asia, subsequently becoming professor of botany at Belfast (1909) and at Reading (1914). His specialism was **plant** anatomy, particularly the arrangement of the stem cells of ferns and fossil ferns.

GWYRFAI Commotes and rural district
Located to the north and to the south of the **River** Gwyrfai, Is Gwyrfai and Uwch Gwyrfai were the two **commotes** of the *cantref* of **Arfon**. From 1894 until 1974, Gwyrfai was one of the **rural districts** of **Caernarfonshire**.

GYMDEITHAS FEDDYGOL, Y (The Medical Society)
Open to both doctors and medical students, the society was formed in 1975 to allow for the discussion of medical matters through the medium of **Welsh**. It holds two conferences a year, publishes an annual journal, *Cennad*, and co-operates with the **University of Wales** in the coinage of new Welsh-language medical terms. A similar society, Y Gymdeithas Ddeintyddol, exists for dentists.

GYMNASTICS
While the benefits of regular gymnastic activity had long been recognized for building strength, power, flexibility and balance, structured gymnastic competitions in Wales date only from the mid-19th century. The growth of organized sport led to the development of gymnastics at schools and colleges, and displays and contests became increasingly popular. Horizontal bars, ropes and parallel bars events featured in the **Llandudno** Olympic festival of 1866, and in 1874 *The North Wales Chronicle* proclaimed that nothing was 'healthier and more invigorating to the human frame' than gymnastic exercise.

The Welsh Amateur Gymnastic Association (WAGA) was formed in 1902 to promote the sport nationally.

Gymnast David Eaton representing Wales at the Commonwealth Games, Melbourne, 2006

International success was quickly achieved, notably by **Swansea**'s **Arthur Whitford**, who won a remarkable 17 titles between the late 1920s and early 1950s, including Olympic and World Championship gold medals. British gymnastics in this period was dominated by Welsh gymnasts, thanks mainly to high-quality coaches, such as Walter Standish from the Swansea club. The introduction of a concentrated coaching course in 1949 further improved standards, and in 1952 half of the British Olympic gymnastics team came from Wales.

Following a relatively quiet post-war period, the profile of gymnastics was lifted by the captivating performances of the Russian Olga Korbut in the 1972 Munich Olympics, which led to thousands of youngsters taking up the sport in Wales. Such enthusiasm has been sustained; by 2007, over 80 clubs were currently affiliated to WAGA. Amateur championships are held annually, catering for men and **women**'s artistic gymnastics, acrobatics, rhythmic gymnastics, aerobics, trampolining and general gymnastics (including special needs).

H ~ H

A scene from William Haggar's film *The Life of Charles Peace* (1905)

HAFOD* and *HENDRE (lit. 'summer dwelling' and 'old dwelling')

A system of transhumance and of medieval origins, if not earlier, it involved the occupation of two holdings: the upland *hafod* (or *lluest*), where **cattle** were tended between May Day (***Calan Mai***) and All Saints' Day (***Calan Gaeaf***); and the lowland *hendre*.

At the *hendre*, a permanent site with fertile **soil**, **arable crops** were grown undisturbed after the cattle had been moved to the *hafod* in the summer months. By the late 17th and early 18th centuries, when cattle had been superseded by **sheep** as the mainstay of the upland **economy**, the system fell into disuse. By 1800, it had all but disappeared from Wales, as *hafodydd* (the plural of *hafod*) tended to evolve into self-contained upland farms.

HAGGAR, [Arthur] William (1851–1925)
Film-maker and showman

A leading British **film** pioneer and director, the sometime stage actor William Haggar screened his own work in travelling **cinemas** (bioscopes) at fairgrounds, ran and performed in peripatetic theatre shows and later set up permanent cinemas. Born in Dedham, East Anglia, he made all his films in Wales, operating from bases at **Pembroke** and **Aberdare**. Of more than 35 Haggar 'shorts', four are extant and at least seven were circulated in America. *The Salmon Poachers* (1905) sold more copies than any other British Gaumont release of pre-rental days. Of the surviving films, *A Desperate Poaching Affray* (1903) was a crucial influence on early American film-makers and *The Life of Charles Peace* (1905) owes much to Haggar's roots in melodrama. *The Sheepstealer* (1908), lost for decades, was rediscovered in the 1970s, in the collection of a Swiss Jesuit priest.

HALKYN (Helygain), Flintshire
(2860 ha; 2876 inhabitants)

Located immediately south-west of **Flint**, Halkyn was the chief centre of **Flintshire**'s **lead**-mining industry. The impressive Moel y Gaer **hill-fort**, first occupied in *c.*650 BC, contained a village of round houses. The **Romans** mined lead ore at Halkyn as did the Welsh princes and the officers of the Black Prince. Major exploitation occurred in the 18th and 19th centuries. In 1896, work began on a sea-level drainage tunnel, dug to drain the mines. Mining finally ceased in 1977, leaving a landscape pitted with shafts and

349

spoil heaps. Much of Halkyn Mountain belonged to the Grosvenor family, which greatly benefited from the profits of its mines. Halkyn Castle (1827) was reputedly built to provide Lord Grosvenor with accommodation during the **Holywell** Races. St Mary's (1878), designed by **John Douglas**, is one of the north-east's finest 19th-century churches. There are large **limestone** quarries at Pant and at Pant-y-pwll-dwr and a vast sand and gravel pit at Rhosesmor. Gwysaney Hall was the seat of the Davies (later the Davies-Cooke) family, one of the first families to adopt the **surname** Davies. The original house, built in 1603, has been much altered.

HALL, Augusta (Lady Llanover, Gwenynen Gwent; 1802–96) Welsh cultural enthusiast

From her home at **Llanover** Court near **Abergavenny**, Augusta Hall came under the influence of **Thomas Price** (Carnhuanawc; 1787–1848), who helped her to develop in a practical way her love of all things Welsh. She was particularly interested in supporting **dance** and **music** and in winning acceptance for what she conceived to be a **Welsh costume**. Although not a fluent speaker of **Welsh**, she was an enthusiastic promoter of the language, becoming an influential benefactor of **Cymreigyddion** y Fenni and of the Welsh Manuscript Society. An ardent Protestant, she was much aggrieved when her only surviving child married into the old **Roman Catholic** family the Joneses (later the Herberts) of **Llanarth**. Her support for the **temperance movement** led her to close all the taverns on the Llanover estate.

Her husband, Benjamin Hall (Baron Llanover; 1802–67), was MP for **Monmouth Boroughs** and subsequently for Marylebone. When he was commissioner of works, the great **clock** erected at Westminster was named Big Ben after him. He campaigned against the infamous **truck system**

Augusta Hall, Lady Llanover wearing the Welsh costume she designed

and, together with his wife, he established a church at **Abercarn** where the services were to be in Welsh. When the bishop of Llandaff reneged on the agreement, he transferred the church to the **Calvinistic Methodists**. In 1873, the Hall family owned 1461 hectares in **Monmouthshire**.

HALSINGOD (hailsing)

Popular carols, of the 17th and 18th centuries, which were mainly associated with north **Pembrokeshire**, **Carmarthenshire** and south **Cardiganshire**. Scriptural in content and of a rustic idiom, they proclaim the inevitability of death and judgement, the importance of repentance and Sabbath observance, and the rejection of Popery. One author of *halsingod* carols was the **Methodist revival**ist **Daniel Rowland**.

HANBURY family Industrialists

By the 1730s, the Hanburys had created the foundations for the development of **tinplate** manufacture. Having worked a fluting mill in Staffordshire, Capel Hanbury (1625–1704) moved to establish various interests at **Pontypool** and **Tintern**. His son, John Hanbury II (1664–1734), was associated with the birth of tinplate by developing a technique (1728) for 'expanding bars by means of compressing cylinders' at his Pontypool rolling mill. The manufacture of thin, malleable, **iron** plates became technically possible – and increasingly economically viable – as the machinery was improved throughout the 18th century. The Hanburys' associates, the Allgood family, were responsible for the widely appreciated Pontypool **japan ware**. The stables of the family home, Pontypool Park, are now a museum of local history.

HANDBALL

A folk game in which two players strike a ball against a wall using the palm of the hand. A popular game in Welsh churchyards from the medieval period, it became a competitive sport in the southern **coal**field in the 19th century, when open-air courts were constructed. Resembling squash courts, they were built in proximity to public houses, which sponsored matches. In the late 20th century, the sport was standardized, and international matches, played under Welsh handball rules, were organized at the **Nelson** handball court near **Caerphilly**.

HANLEY, James (1901–85) Novelist

Dublin-born James Hanley lived in Wales (which he liked to think of as his homeland) from 1930 to 1964, mainly at **Llanfechain**, where he was buried. Among his many novels, some of which are about life at sea, four have Welsh settings: *Don Quixote Drowned* (1953), *The Welsh Sonata* (1954), *Another World* (1971) and *A Kingdom* (1978); his *Collected Stories* were published in 1953.

HANMER, Wrexham (1822 ha; 726 inhabitants)

Constituting the heart of **Maelor Saesneg**, Hanmer's main feature is Gredington Park, described by **Thomas Pennant** as 'extremely beautiful: varied with a **lake** of fifty acres bounded on all sides with small cultivated eminences, embellished with woods' – a description which still has substance. In 1678, Gredington came into the possession of

Parliamentary Election, 1906.

Borough of Merthyr Tydfil.

Address to the Electors

BY

J. Keir Hardie

. THE .

LABOUR CANDIDATE

Printed (T.U.) by Joseph Williams & Sons, "Tyst" Office, Merthyr, & Published by Frank Smith, Agent for the Labour Candidate, at 97 High st., Merthyr.

A poster used in Keir Hardie's Merthyr Tydfil campaign in the general election of 1906

the Kenyon family, a family later prominent in the history of **education** in Wales. Gredington Hall (1775, 1811, 1916) was demolished amid much controversy in 1982. Hanmer village is dominated by St Chad's church, rebuilt after a fire in 1889. It was probably the church in which **Owain Glyndŵr** married Margaret Hanmer *c.*1383. Halghton Hall, The Bryn and West View are attractive 18th-century houses.

HANMER, Thomas (1612–78) Gardener
Of the Hanmer family, of Halton, **Flintshire**, Thomas was an innovative **garden**er and a correspondent of John Evelyn and John Rea. Respected for his floricultural skills and especially for his success with tulips, Hanmer described vine growing in Wales (*see* **Vineyards**). His *Garden Book*, written in 1659, was published in 1933.

HARDIE, [James] Keir (1856–1915) Politician
Born in Lanarkshire, the descendant of a **Chartist**, Hardie worked in the Ayrshire **coal**field before becoming a miners' leader and a journalist. In 1893, he founded the **Independent Labour Party** (ILP), also editing its paper the *Labour Leader*. He made several visits to Wales during the **miners' strike** of 1898 and wrote a series of articles describing the workers' suffering. In the general election of 1900, the Labour Representation Committee sponsored Hardie as a candidate in the constituency of **Merthyr Tydfil** and **Aberdare**. His appeal as a fellow **Celt**, his apparent support for Welsh **Home Rule**, his Christianity – his pamphlet *Can*

a Man be a Christian on a Pound a Week? was widely read – and the unlikely support of the industrialist **D. A. Thomas**, his fellow candidate in the two-seat constituency, all contributed to his victory – although he never topped the poll.

Hardie organized Labour as a separate party in the House of Commons, along the lines of the Irish Party, and his individualism, coupled with his distinctive appearance and apparel, promoted the notion of Labour's independence. His determination and sincerity provided the basis for the early growth of the **Labour Party** in the south Wales coalfield. He was heartbroken by the outbreak of the **First World War** and deeply hurt when shouted down by warmongers in his own constituency. Following his death, his seat was won by the jingoistic rabble-rouser **C. B. Stanton**.

HARDING, Lyn (David Llewellyn Harding; 1867–1952) Actor
After a distinguished stage career, **Newport**-born Lyn Harding entered **films** in 1920, his screen experience embracing both silent and talking films. As Henry VIII, he appeared with the American star Marion Davies in the 1921 comedy *When Knighthood Was In Flower*, and subsequently partnered her in *Yolanda* (1924). He played Bismarck in *Spy of Napoleon* (1936), and his impressive screen gallery of 'heavies' included the infamous Moriarty in both *The Speckled Band* (1931) and *The Triumph of Sherlock Holmes* (1935). He was also Chips in MGM's *Goodbye Mr Chips* (1939).

HARES

The commoner of Wales's two hare species, the brown hare, with its long, black-tipped ears, was probably introduced to **Britain** by the **Romans**. Hunted for sport and **food**, and capable of fleeing predators at 70 kph, it is found mainly in exposed habitats and on arable farmland. Owing to intensive **agriculture**, particularly silage making, and a rise in the **fox** population, its numbers declined markedly during the 20th century, and are particularly low in western pastoral landscapes. The rare and slightly smaller blue or **mountain** hare, whose coat turns white in winter, was introduced from **Scotland** in the 19th century to some upland areas of **Snowdonia** and mid-Wales.

There are many references to hares in Welsh mythology, **literature** and folklore. According to tradition, the 6th-century princess **Melangell** became the patron **saint** of hares after a hare took sanctuary beneath her robes (*see* **Llangynog**). In the late 12th century, **Giraldus Cambrensis** noted the belief that **witches** could transform themselves into hares in order to suck milk from cows. It was believed that good or ill fortune could be divined from the way a hare ran, and that if a pregnant woman saw a hare her child might be born with a hare-lip.

HARLECH, Gwynedd (1451 ha; 1406 inhabitants)

Located south of the Dwyryd estuary, the **community** consists largely of flat land created by the retreat of the sea. Rearing above the flat land is the rock of Harlech, which features in the second branch of *Pedair Cainc y Mabinogi* (*see* **Mabinogion, The**). Between 1283 and 1289, the rock was crowned by the most dramatically situated of all Edward I's Welsh castles. Designed by the brilliant Savoyard architect **James of St George**, it has been recognized by UNESCO as a world heritage site. With its massive round corner towers and its powerful gatehouse, it is a masterpiece of medieval military **architecture**. **Owain Glyndŵr** captured the castle in 1404; it was his chief centre of power until he was obliged to yield it in 1409. His second parliament was held there in August 1405. During the **Wars of the Roses**, Harlech was the last Lancastrian (*see* **Lancaster family**) castle to fall to the Yorkists, and during the first **Civil War** it was the last royalist stronghold in **Britain** to submit to the Parliamentarians. The **borough** established in association with the castle was acknowledged to be **Merioneth**'s **county** town, but, alone among the county towns of Wales, the framers of the **Act of 'Union'** of 1536 did not consider it significant enough to be granted **parliamentary representation**.

The **railway** reached Harlech in 1867, the central factor in the development of **tourism** along the coast of **Ardudwy**. Harlech won fame as the home of one of Wales's best known **golf** courses – that of the Royal St David's club. Much of the community lies within the Morfa Harlech Nature Reserve. In 1988, an extremely large leatherback turtle was stranded on Morfa Harlech beach; its corpse is preserved in the **National Museum**. **Coleg Harlech**, established in 1927, is a key factor in the local **economy**. Adjoining it is Theatr Ardudwy, a popular centre for artistic performances. Y Lasynys, the home of **Ellis Wynne** (originally 16th-century), has been restored as a memorial to him.

Alan Sorrell's imaginative reconstruction of Harlech Castle

The harpist Catrin Finch

HARP, The

The harp is considered to be Wales's traditional musical instrument. Yet Venantius Fortunatus, the 6th-century poet-priest and bishop of Poitiers, claimed that the Britons of his time played the *crwth*; it was the Teutonic 'barbarian' who played the harp. Early Welsh **literature** is reticent about the harp and the *crwth*, although the **law** of **Hywel Dda** holds musicians in high regard.

Unlike the **Irish**, the Welsh favoured a more delicate, light instrument with strings of horsehair and, later, of gut. Originally, Welsh and Irish harpists used their nails as well as fingertips, resulting in a bright, clear, almost percussive sound. They held the harp on the left shoulder and played the treble with the left hand – contrary to the rest of Europe. **Dafydd ap Gwilym** refers to his small harp, which he presumably played as an accompaniment to his declamation of his *cywyddau*.

It is assumed that medieval **music** was unwritten, but in 1584 **David Powel** stated that music books existed; indeed one manuscript of old Welsh harp music has survived – that of **Robert ap Huw** (*c*.1613), which appears to be the product of an earlier age. A list of music played by harpists and crowthers during Christmas 1595 at Lleweni (**Denbigh**), names 82 melodies, all of them imported from **England**. No wonder that poets of the time complained that their compositions were no longer appreciated; according to Edward ap Raff (fl.1578–1606), they were called upon to provide foolish ditties and silly songs: 'our world and our age-old art are disappearing in riddles'.

The triple harp, with its three rows of strings, originated in Italy *c*.1600, and was introduced into the English court *c*.1629. The two outer ranks of strings would be tuned alike in a diatonic scale, and the centre row would give the accidentals. The court harpist Charles Evans may have been the first Welshman, in 1660, to adopt the triple harp: Charles II paid £15 for Evans's new Italian instrument. It is said that the first triple harp actually made in Wales, some years later, was by Elis Siôn Siamas of Llanfachreth (*see* **Brithdir and Llanfachreth**) – a harpist to Queen Anne.

While most 18th-century Welsh harpists remained loyal to the single-row harp, the more adventurous took to the triple harp; the most illustrious was the blind **John Parry** (Blind Parry; *c*.1710–82), who gave concerts throughout **Britain**. Thomas Jones, another blind harpist, played in Handel's opera *Esther* in 1718, and Handel wrote a harp concerto for William Powell (d.1750) who was harpist to the **Prince of Wales**.

Edward Jones (1752–1824), from **Llandderfel**, went to **London** *c*.1775; he became known as *Bardd y Brenin* – the King's Bard. A second John Parry (1776–1851), known as *Bardd Alaw*, settled in London in 1807; some of his melodies, notably 'Cadair Idris', 'Llanofer' and 'Cainc y Datgeiniaid', are still used in the harp and *penillion* repertoire. There were scores of other harpists who sustained the old traditions, competing at *eisteddfodau* and playing in taverns, while others combined harping with other employments. Griffith Owen (1750–1833) of Penmorfa, for example, was both butler and resident harpist at Ynysmaengwyn Hall (**Bryn-crug**). In addition to the semi-professionals, there were the **Romanies**, of whom the **Wood family** are the most famous.

During the 19th century, the most outstanding harpist was **John Thomas** (Pencerdd Gwalia; 1826–1913), harpist to Queen Victoria, professor and composer. In the 20th century, the colourful **Nansi Richards** handed on her skills with the triple harp to a younger generation of musicians. Among Wales's best known harpists are Osian Ellis (b.1928), Llio Rhydderch (b.1937), Robin Huw Bowen (b.1958) and Catrin Finch (b.1980).

Over the last 100 years, thanks to an abandonment of the 19th-century salon style, the harp has acquired a new repertoire of music from Welsh composers such as **David Vaughan Thomas** and **David Wynne**. An outstanding landmark was the harp concerto by Alun Hoddinott (b.1929), which was first performed at the Cheltenham Festival in 1958, and a month later at the London Proms. **William Mathias** wrote a harp concerto for the Llandaff (*see* **Cardiff**) Festival in 1970, and other harp works followed.

Since 1996, the enterprising music publishers Curiad, of Penygroes (**Llanllyfni**), have produced harp works by a new generation of Welsh composers. Although associated primarily with folk and art music, the harp has featured increasingly in rock and jazz ensembles.

HARRIES, [Thomas] Ronald [Lewis] (1930–54)
Murderer
A married man with a three-month-old daughter, Harries was working at Cadno Farm, **Pendine**, in 1953 when his uncle and aunt, John and Phoebe Harries, suddenly disappeared from their home at nearby **Llangynin**. Harries claimed they had gone on holiday, but their bodies were discovered in a shallow grave on Cadno Farm. He was convicted of their murder and executed at **Swansea**. The name of Cadno Farm was subsequently changed to Bronwydd Farm and the area of the field in which the bodies were found has been left uncultivated.

HARRIS family Artists
Cleopas Harris set out to make portraiture affordable to all **class**es when he established his business in **Merthyr Tydfil** *c.*1866 after leaving Canada, where he had served as a soldier. The economic buoyancy of the town was such that he was able to employ his three sons, Albert, George and Charles, and was soon bringing in painters from **England** to meet the demand. He cut financial corners by **painting** over photographs of his subjects. In addition to portraits, the Harrises produced local views, lithographic prints and religious tracts. The Australian-born television personality Rolf Harris is descended from the family.

HARRIS, Henry C[harles] (1851–85) Architect
Harris lived at **Penarth** and was probably a native of the area. He appears to have designed his first building, a chapel (1869) in St Mellons, **Cardiff**, when only 18. He was responsible for a variety of buildings in **Glamorgan**, the most ambitious being the French Gothic-style Capel Pembroke Terrace, Cardiff (1877) and **Maesteg** Town Hall (1881).

HARRIS, Howel or Howell (1714–73)
Methodist leader
One of the founders of Welsh **Calvinistic Methodism**, Harris was born at Trefeca (**Talgarth**), and educated at the academy at Llwynllwyd (**Llanigon**). His conversion (1735) is generally considered to mark the opening of the **Methodist Revival** in Wales. He began preaching around Talgarth, gathering his converts together into **societies** (or *seiadau*).

Soon after meeting **Griffith Jones** of **Llanddowror** in 1736, Harris met **Howel Davies**, **Daniel Rowland** and **William Williams** (1717–91) of Pantycelyn. In 1739, he met George Whitefield, the leader of the **Calvinist** wing of English Methodism. In Whitefield's company, he travelled to **London** where he met the Wesleys, the countess of Huntingdon and the **Moravians**. Between 1735 and 1743, Harris set about organizing his movement, which was Calvinist in **theology**.

In the late 1740s, differences developed between Rowland and Harris, particularly over Harris's patripassian tendencies (*see* **Sabellianism**) and his relationship with the 'prophetess' Sidney Griffith of Cefnamwlch (**Tudweiliog**). Separation ensued and Harris withdrew from public view to establish a Christian community at his home in Trefeca. The 'Trefeca Family', as it became known, came to have over 100 members, and occupied a remarkable early example of a neo-Gothic building, apparently designed by Harris.

In 1759, during the Seven Years' War, Harris joined the local militia, but military service took him no further than Great Yarmouth. When he returned home in 1762, he was invited back to his former position by Rowland and Williams, but, with his responsibilities within the 'Family', and the countess of Huntingdon establishing a college at Trefeca in 1768, he was unable to resume his one-time gruelling programme of preaching tours (*see* **Preachers**).

Of his brothers, Joseph Harris (1704–64) was a noted astronomer (*see* **Astronomy**), assay-master at the Royal **Mint** and, with Howel, a founder of **Breconshire**'s **Agricultural Society**. The other, Thomas Harris (1705–82), made a fortune selling uniforms to the British army.

HARRIS, James (1810–87) and James (1847–1925)
Marine artists
The 19th century saw the development in **Swansea** of a distinctive school of marine artists, of whom the most prominent were James Harris and his son, also James. Exeter-born Harris Snr began his career as a painter, teacher and artists' colourman in 1828, when his family moved to Swansea. His oils, which found ready patrons among the town's growing number of shipowners (*see* **Ships and Shipowners**), show the busy seaways of Swansea Bay, usually in dramatic weather. Harris Jnr, who painted mainly in watercolours, voyaged out of Swansea and completed studies along the way, his sketchbooks illustrating both life afloat and seaboard views of South America and **South Africa**. Many of the Harrises' works are exhibited at Swansea's Glynn Vivian **Art Gallery**.

HARRIS, Joseph (Gomer; 1773–1825)
Editor, printer and minister
Gomer founded and edited the first **Welsh-language** weekly **newspaper**. The inaugural edition of *Seren Gomer* appeared

in January 1814; although it survived for no more than two years, the paper was revived in 1818 as a fortnightly magazine (a monthly from 1820). Born in St Dogwells (**Wolfscastle**), he began to preach with the **Baptists** in Llangloffan (**Pencaer**) in 1796, and became a minister in **Swansea** in 1801. There he kept a school, a shop and a **printing** office. Swansea's Capel Gomer commemorates him.

HARRY, Miles (1699–1776) Minister
Miles Harry was born at Llyswedog Fach, Sirhowy (**Tredegar**), baptized as a believer at **Abertillery** (1724) and ordained as co-pastor of the **Baptist** church at Penygarn, **Pontypool** (1732). Apart from preaching, he set up a **printing** business in **Abergavenny** and was instrumental in establishing a school for the training of Baptist ministers at Trosnant, Pontypool. One of the few non-**Anglican** colleagues of **Howel Harris** in the work of the evangelical **revival**, he became the foremost Welsh Baptist leader of his generation.

HARTSHORN, Vernon (1872–1931) Politician
A pit-boy from Pontywaun (**Crosskeys**), Hartshorn was a prominent member of the **Independent Labour Party** and a **coal**miners' leader. President of the **South Wales Miners' Federation** (1922–4), he lost the support of the Federation's more militant members. **Labour** MP for **Ogmore** (1918–31), he was in the cabinet as postmaster general (1924) and as lord privy seal (1930–1), the first former miner to achieve cabinet status.

HARVEST MARE, The
The term for the last tuft of corn cut with a reaping hook in a competition between harvesters. The winner brought the mare, or *caseg fedi,* to the house, despite the attempts of the **women**folk to wet him, taking the seat of honour at the table during the harvest feast. The custom probably derives from the belief that the potency of vegetative growth remained in the last tuft. The ornamental corn dolly of the tourist shop is its descendant.

HASTINGS family Marcher-lords
The family became associated with Wales when John Hastings (d.1313) inherited **Abergavenny** and **Cilgerran** from his uncle, George Cantilupe (d.1273). John also acquired the lordship of **Pembroke** through his marriage with Isabella, heiress of William de **Valence** (d.1296). The Hastings family were leading **march**er-lords until the death, childless, of John Hastings, earl of Pembroke, in 1389. St Mary's church, Abergavenny, contains Hastings tombs of high distinction.

HATTON, Ann Julia (Ann of Swansea; 1764–1838) Poet and novelist
A daughter of strolling players Roger Kemble and Sarah Ward, and sister of **Sarah Siddons**, Hatton was of English birth but her name is chiefly associated with **Swansea**. She settled there in 1799, after she and her second husband took the lease of a bathing house. She published two volumes of verse – *Poems on Miscellaneous Subjects* (1783) and *Poetic Trifles* (1811) – and dozens of novels, including *Cambrian Pictures* (3 vols., ?1810) and *Chronicles of an Illustrious House* (5 vols., 1814).

HAVENS, The, Pembrokeshire
(2007 ha; 1024 inhabitants)
Hugging the south-eastern corner of St Bride's Bay, the **community** contains the villages of Broad Haven, Little Haven, Haroldston West, Talbenny and Walton West. On its western extremity are the Mill Haven and Howney Stone **Iron Age** promontory forts. Broad Haven and Little Haven have delightful sandy beaches, which are linked at low tide. Broad Haven has long been popular as a holiday resort and once had bathing machines. Known in the 1930s as '**Haverfordwest**-by-Sea' because of its invasion in summer by the inhabitants of the **county** town, the area subsequently attracted holidaymakers from further afield. St Mary's church, Talbenny, retains its 15th-century bellcote. An abandoned airfield survives at Talbenny.

HAVERFORDWEST (Hwlffordd),
Pembrokeshire (719 ha; 10,808 inhabitants)
Located in the heart of **Pembrokeshire**, the **community** is situated at what was the highest navigable point of the Western **Cleddau**. Its castle, first built *c.*1110 by the **Fleming** Tancred, had been rebuilt as a substantial stone fortification by 1220 when it was besieged by **Llywelyn ap Iorwerth**. Extended in the 1290s, three of its towers survive. It later became a **prison**, a mental hospital and then, until 1962, a **police** station. It houses the Pembrokeshire Record Office.

Haverfordwest was the centre of the area of early 12th-century Flemish settlement. As the **English** and Flemish languages were then very similar, the settlers came to be English speaking, although, as late as the 16th century, the inhabitants of Haverfordwest were described as 'male Anglice loquentes' (poor speakers of English).

Judging by the number of its burgages (urban plots), late 13th-century Haverfordwest was second in size to **Cardiff** among the **boroughs** of Wales. Alone among Welsh medieval towns, it was divided into three **parishes**; the parish churches – those of St Thomas, St Martin and St Mary – all retain some of their medieval fabric, as does St David's church, Prendergast. The ruins of the **Augustinian** priory, founded *c.*1210, were until 1981 obscured by ivy and scrub. Work by **Cadw** has revealed the footings of almost all the monastic buildings.

In the 16th century, Haverfordwest may have been the largest town in Wales. In 1543, it attained the status of a **county** and was granted its own MP; in addition, it became the only town in the territories of the English crown to have its own lord lieutenant. Central to its prosperity was its Cleddau-side **port**. Accessible to **ships** of up to 40 tonnes, the port was the focus of lively trade until the coming of the **railway** in 1853; riverside warehouses survive near the priory. Haverfordwest's role as the market town for much of Pembrokeshire is commemorated by names such as Pig Bank and Horse Fair. Many local gentry families built handsome Georgian town houses in the town, among them Foley House, which was perhaps designed by **John Nash**. Handsome inns and chapels add to what is perhaps Wales's finest example of a well-built country town. Tabernacle is among Wales's finest **Congregationalist** chapels. Haverfordwest's **Moravian** meeting-house, the last to survive in Wales, was demolished in 1961.

In 1885, the Haverfordwest constituency was merged with that of **Pembroke Boroughs**. In 1889, the town became the seat of the Pembrokeshire County Council. On the banks of the Western Cleddau are the vaguely castle-like buildings (1999) housing the offices of the revived Pembrokeshire. Withybush is Pembrokeshire's base hospital.

HAWARDEN (Penarlâg), Flintshire
(1730 ha; 13,539 inhabitants)
Located immediately east of **Buckley** and south of **Connah's Quay**, the **community** contains the villages of Ewloe, Aston, Hawarden and Mancot. The Domesday Book lists Hawarden and Aston as *Haordine* and *Estone*. **Owain Gwynedd**'s attempt to ambush Henry II (1157) probably occurred in the Wepre ravine. Overlooking the ravine is Ewloe Castle, built by **Llywelyn ap Iorwerth** *c.*1210 and enlarged by **Llywelyn ap Gruffudd** in 1257. Hawarden Castle, originally built by Hugh Lupus, earl of Chester *c.*1075, was seized by **Dafydd ap Gruffudd** in 1282, an attack which precipitated the war which led to the destruction of Llywelyn ap Gruffudd's **principality**. Dismantled following the **Civil War**, it is known as Hawarden Old Castle. Hawarden (New) Castle, formerly Broadlane Hall (rebuilt *c.*1756), was the home of the Glynne family. Following the death of the distinguished antiquary Sir Stephen Glynne in 1874, the castle became the property of his sister Catherine and her husband, **W. E. Gladstone**. It was while felling a tree in Hawarden grounds that Gladstone declared, on becoming prime minister in 1868: 'My mission is to pacify **Ireland.**'

Relaxing at the Hay Festival

The house is still occupied by the Gladstone family. Of particular interest is Gladstone's study – his Temple of Peace – with its remarkable collection of axes. St **Deiniol**'s Library, the only major public building designed by **John Douglas**, was founded by Gladstone in 1895. It offers residential facilities, and among its collections are 30,000 books from Gladstone's own library.

The Gladstone statue that was commissioned for Dublin in 1910 was, in fact, rejected by the Dublin City Council when completed in 1923. Subsequently, it was erected in front of the library in 1925. St Deiniol's church, heavily restored by Gilbert Scott following a fire in 1857, contains recumbent effigies of Gladstone and his wife and a superb **stained-glass** window designed by Edward Burne-Jones (1898). The Old Rectory, initially built in the early 18th century, became the **Flintshire** Record Office in 1958. In the 18th and 19th centuries, Mancot and Ewloe were important **coal**mining areas. Remnants of mines and tramways survive. Mancot village originated as a settlement for munition workers (1916–18), and included hostels, a church hall and a hospital.

HAY (Y Gelli [Gandryll]), Breconshire,
Powys (150 ha; 1469 inhabitants)
Hay stands at the point where the **Wye** flows into **England** and is a quintessential **border** town. The **English** name derives from the Old English *(g)haeg*, which originally meant a fence and then part of a forest enclosed by fences (for **hunting**). For 500 years, Hay was a walled town, with the castle and the **parish** church outside the walls. The church – a chapel of **Brecon** priory – collapsed around 1700, leaving only its tower; it was rebuilt, as was the chapel of St John (Eglwys Ifan), Hay's medieval guild church. The castle, built by the de **Breos family**, was destroyed successively by King John, **Llywelyn ap Iorwerth** and **Owain Glyndŵr**. It, and the adjacent 17th-century mansion, were acquired by Richard Booth, who has crowned himself King of Hay. Booth is responsible for the fact that Hay, a pleasant blend of 17th and 19th-century houses, is profusely provided with bookshops. He pioneered the notion of a town of bookshops now evident in many parts of the world.

It is the location of the Hay Festival, held annually since 1988 and now the largest literary event in the world. In 2001, it was found that 88.66% of the inhabitants of Hay had no knowledge at all of **Welsh**, making it, linguistically, the most Anglicized **community** in **Breconshire**.

HAYCRAFT, Anna (Alice Thomas Ellis; 1932–2005)
Writer and publisher
Born in **Liverpool**, brought up at **Penmaenmawr**, and a pupil at **Bangor** before attending Liverpool School of Art, Anna Haycraft was known in the literary world under two names. As Anna Haycraft, she ran the **London** publishing house Duckworth, owned by her late husband, Colin Haycraft, where she nurtured authors such as Beryl Bainbridge. As Alice Thomas Ellis, she wrote about a dozen volumes of fiction, and a similar body of non-fiction, including the autobiographical *A Welsh Childhood* (1990). Several of her novels, among them *The Sin Eater* (1977), have Welsh settings.

HAYSCASTLE (Cas-lai), Pembrokeshire
(2710 ha; 423 inhabitants)

Located inland from the north-east corner of St Bride's Bay, the **community** contains scattered farms and some ribbon development along the **Haverfordwest–Mathry road** (the B4330). Remote St Edren's church has been converted into a house. South of the 12th-century motte near the church, **place names** are **English**; north of it, they are **Welsh**.

HAYWARD, Isaac James (1884–1976)
Local government leader

Born in **Blaenavon**, Hayward was the most distinguished figure to have started his working life as a miner at Big Pit (*see* **National Museum [of] Wales**). **Trade union** work took him to **London**, where in 1928 he became a **Labour** member of the **county** council. Leader of the council from 1947 until 1965, the degree of authority he wielded over London's affairs exceeded that later exercised by Ken Livingstone. His advocacy of the development of the South Bank as a cultural centre caused its Hayward Gallery to bear his name.

HEALTH

The health of the Welsh from post-Roman to modern times

The gravestone of Melus – *medicus* – at Llangian (**Llanengan**), is proof that there were doctors in Wales in the immediate post-**Roman** centuries, an era when the country was afflicted by plague. Despite the legendary efforts of healers such as the **Physicians of Myddfai**, medieval medicine offered few cures. Epidemics such as the **Black Death** of 1349, further attacks of the plague in 1361, 1369, 1593 and 1652, and the sufferings caused by outbreaks of killer diseases such as **smallpox**, typhus and **cholera**, were viewed by the people of Wales as evidence of the wrath of God.

Evidence from the 16th century suggests that life expectancy at birth was around 35, the low figure largely caused by the fact that half the children died during their first year. (Those who did survive that year could go on to enjoy a ripe old age.) The growing towns of the period, although a sign of economic prosperity, were probably less healthy than the countryside where the vast majority still lived. People remained highly vulnerable to dangerous diseases, and poor economic conditions, especially periods of bad harvest, could prove lethal, particularly to those struggling to survive at subsistence levels. Nevertheless, the **population** of Wales, *c.*360,000 in the early 17th century, had increased to *c.*500,000 by 1770.

In the 19th century, hundreds of thousands migrated from the rural **counties** to find work in the south Wales **coalfield**, which became home to the great majority of the Welsh people. There, they suffered industrial pollution, inadequate **housing**, overcrowding, poor sanitation, and the contaminated water which led to periodic epidemics of virulent diseases such as cholera.

Public health did not become a significant policy issue until the publication in 1842 of Edwin Chadwick's *General*

A late 19th-century proprietory 'cure all', the 'Penygroes remedy'

Report on the Sanitary Condition of the Labouring Population of Great Britain. A central Board of Health was established in 1848 and, by 1856, 25 places in Wales had local boards of health charged with responsibility for drainage, paving, street cleaning and the provision of sewerage and piped water.

The rapid expansion of towns such as **Cardiff** and **Merthyr Tydfil** during the 19th century had serious consequences for health. 'The overcrowding [in Cardiff],' reported an official investigator in 1850, 'is fearful beyond anything of the kind I have ever seen'. Merthyr's first officer of health was appointed in 1853 and, by 1885, the death rate there had fallen from 33 to 22 per 1000. In Cardiff, Dr H. J. Paine was similarly successful: it was estimated at the time of his retirement in 1887 that public health measures had saved 15,480 lives in Cardiff alone.

In spite of local improvements, there was little alteration in the death rate in Wales as a whole. Recorded as 20.2 per 1000 in 1841, it took until the end of the century for it to settle at below 20, while infant mortality remained at over 120 per 1000 live births for most of the century, not falling consistently below 100 until the **First World War**. There is some evidence that people were marginally healthier in the countryside than in the towns. Nevertheless, the dwellings of the rural poor were far from salubrious; in the 1860s, doctors could sink into the mud floors of their patients' houses, and, in the 1890s, overflowing cesspools were a serious health hazard in **Pembrokeshire**. Yet, rickets, a childhood illness prevalent in the southern coalfield in the late 19th century, was reported by the British Medical Association to be relatively rare in the rural areas of the north.

The growth of state intervention during the First World War led to some amelioration in hospital and health care provision, and the interwar years, despite severe economic **depression**, saw an undoubted improvement in the health of the Welsh. Infant mortality fell sharply, partly because a significant reduction in the birth rate meant that children could be better looked after. Even so, **women**'s mortality rate at childbirth was much higher in Wales than in **England** (in 1922, 5.43 per 1000 compared with 3.81). Furthermore, although there was a 27% reduction in the death rate from **tuberculosis** in the 1920s in England, this classic disease of poverty and bad housing continued to be identified particularly with Wales, where the decrease over the same period was less than 17%. By the late 1930s, 1% of the Welsh population was still on the TB register; and in 1939 a committee of enquiry chaired by **Clement Davies** reported that the seven counties in southern **Britain** where mortality from the disease was highest were all in Wales. Every one of them was in the rural north and west, partly reflecting the complacency of local authorities. It was only after the **Second World War** that tuberculosis and other infectious diseases were brought under control.

The establishment of the National Health Service (NHS) in 1948, together with substantial improvements in living standards, higher levels of employment, better housing, developments in medical technology and the introduction of new drugs, all played their part in the progressive improvement of the health of the Welsh people (*see* **Welfare State**).

With sustained vaccination and immunization programmes, diseases such as smallpox, diphtheria and polio were eliminated, although a few cases of whooping cough continue to be notified each year. Meningitis Group C was a problem among children and university students until an effective vaccine was developed in 1999. By 2002, a decline in the percentage of children protected against measles, mumps and rubella – from 95% to 80% or less – was a matter for concern, especially in the south-west. Tuberculosis continues to be reported.

The percentage of low birth-weight babies increased from 6.8% in 1994 to 7.7% in 1999, largely because of medical interventions to save pre-term babies and because an increased use of fertility treatment resulted in more multiple births.

A Nuffield Trust study on the health of the Welsh, *Freeing the Dragon* (1999), declared in its opening sentence that 'the state of health in Wales leaves much to be desired', and in 2001 a Welsh Consumer Council survey confirmed that the Welsh, leading increasingly sedentary lives, were among the most unhealthy people in Europe, with nearly a third of the population taking no regular exercise.

In 2004, a report by the Global Initiative for Asthma declared Wales the world's premier asthma blackspot, with almost 30% of adults aged 20–44 and one in three 13–14-year-olds suffering from the disease; poverty and smoking were cited as the main causes. A ban on smoking in public places, introduced by the **National Assembly** in April 2007 (three months before a similar ban in England), significantly reduced the incidence of passive smoking and seemed, according to early indications, to be encouraging some smokers to abandon the habit.

Mortality

The kinds of ill-kept and overcrowded burial grounds, associated in 'miasmatic theory' with evil smells and epidemics, no longer exist, a change assisted by the widespread acceptance of cremation, a practice pioneered by Dr **William Price** of **Llantrisant**. In 1893, Cardiff was the first local authority to build a crematorium, on the **island** of Flatholm, where infected seamen could be isolated in a cholera hospital. The crematorium was used only once, in 1900, to cremate a ship's 'donkey man' who had died of bubonic plague. A second crematorium was opened in **Pontypridd** in 1924, and by the end of 2005 there were 13, carrying out a total of 20,182 cremations, over 60% of all deaths registered in that year.

In 2002, Wales had a standardized mortality ratio (SMR) of 105, higher than England (100) and Northern **Ireland** (99), but lower than **Scotland** (114). Within Wales, there was considerable variation in the SMR of unitary authorities, ranging from 122 in Merthyr Tydfil to 89 in **Ceredigion**. In 2004, the main causes of death were circulatory diseases (38%) and cancers (27%). Over the period 1994–2003, there was a significant increase in life expectancy.

Of particular note is the fact that the number of people aged 85 or over has grown five-fold since the mid-20th century, reaching 59,000 in 2001. Among unitary authority areas, **Conwy** had, in that year, the highest proportion of people of pensionable age (26%) and Cardiff the lowest (17%).

Health care provision

PRE-MODERN MEDICINE
Records of pre-modern medical practice reach back to the time of the **druids** who, in the first century AD, according to Pliny, had a religio-magical ritual for the collection of mistletoe, using it both as a drink to 'impart fecundity to barren animals' and 'as an antidote for all poisons'.

With the Romans came hospitals, such as the substantial one at **Caerleon**, rebuilt in stone in the 2nd century. Dream therapy, as in the cult of Asclepius, the Greek god of healing,

LIFE EXPECTANCY (IN YEARS) AT BIRTH

	1994	1995	1996	1997	1998	1999	2000	2001	2002	2003
Males	73.4	73.7	73.8	74.2	74.4	74.7	74.9	75.4	75.6	76.0
Females	79.0	79.1	79.1	79.3	79.4	79.6	79.8	80.1	80.2	80.4

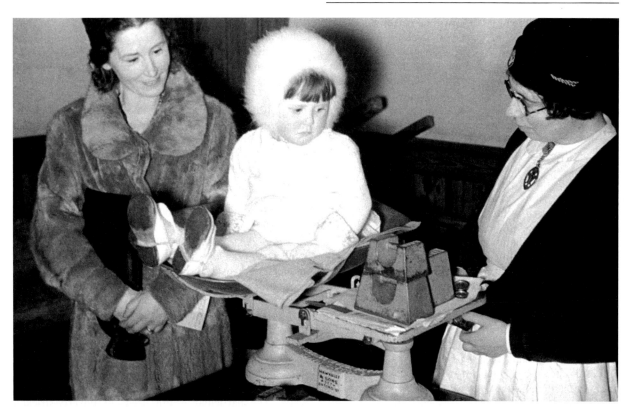

Checking a child's weight, an essential public health measure, in 1941

was practised at the temple of Nodens (*Nudd* in **Welsh**) at Lydney on the **Severn**. An altar from Chester is dedicated in Greek to the 'mighty saviour gods' by Hermogenes, believed to have been a *medicus* in the 20th Legion.

The spread of Christianity fostered native traditions of miracles and religious cures, such as those by St **Samson** described in *Liber Landavensis*. Holy **wells**, often adapting to pre-Christian healing traditions, abounded: St Tegla's Well at **Llandegla**, offered a cure for *clwyf Tegla* (epilepsy).

The **law** of **Hywel Dda** (d.950) describes the court mediciner, his rights and responsibilities, and offers insight into methods of his remuneration, and the treatment and compensation for the injured. In the later Middle Ages, fine Welsh-language manuscripts on medical matters were produced. They include Mostyn Manuscript 88, a medical astrology, with illustrations of Zodiac Man, Bleeding Man and the Circle of Urines, and instructions for their use in diagnosis, and Wellcome Manuscript 417 – *The Welsh Leech Book* – which contains many recipes and treatments.

In the 16th century, forerunners of popular 'home doctor' types of book appeared. Sir Thomas Elyot (?1499–1546) compiled *The Castel of Helth* (1536), translated into Welsh by **Elis Gruffydd**. Humfre Lloyd (fl. 16th century, and almost certainly not **Humphrey Lhuyd**, the **map** maker) translated from the **Latin** two popular works on medical lore, *The Judgement of Urines* (1552) and *The Treasury of Health* (1585). **Robert Recorde** of **Tenby** (*c.*1510–58), better known as a mathematician, wrote the *Urinal of Physic*, an early work on doctor–patient co-operation. **William Salesbury** (*c.*1520–?84) is credited with the compilation of a Welsh herbal, the *Llysieulyfr*, a paraphrase of some of the best-known herbals of the

16th century, in particular *De Historia Stirpium* and *A New Herball*. Although better known as a linguist, **Siôn Dafydd Rhys** was a skilled physician. Thomas Phaer (?1510–60) of **Cilgerran** wrote the first book in **English** on paediatrics in 1545; the second, *On the preservation of Bodie and Soule*, was by another Welshman, John Jones (1645–1709).

Medieval and early modern Wales had several dynasties of healers, of which the most famous was the Physicians of Myddfai. There are many examples of folk medicine of uncertain antiquity. *Clefyd y galon* (disease of the heart) was not a cardiac condition but a depressive illness. It was also known as *Clwyf yr edau wlân* (the woollen yarn disease) because of the method of diagnosis and treatment using a skein of wool. **Carmarthenshire** Museum contains exhibits of the Gilfachwen hydrophobia stone, used as a treatment for rabies, and the mystic adderstone, *maen magl* or *maen glain*, in the form of **glass** rings.

Belief in folk remedies and in the skills of the *dyn hysbys* (*see* **Witches and Dynion Hysbys**) remained a feature of Welsh life until the early 20th century. Indeed, among present-day enthusiasts for alternative medicine, there is a readiness to believe that many of the remedies of the past have qualities absent from modern forms of treatment.

HEALTH SERVICES

Formal medical services began in Wales with those associated with Roman settlements. The monasteries of the **Celtic Church** offered rudimentary health treatment, and this provision became more formalized through the infirmaries of medieval religious houses. The incidence of leprosy created the need for leper hospitals – such as that at Cardiff. Although primarily a military order, the Knights

H

Hospitallers of St John had medical associations; **Ysbyty Ifan** (John's Hospice) in the Conwy valley and **Slebech** were the Knights' two houses in Wales. (St John the Baptist in Cardiff is now the chief church of the order.)

As a professional **class**, physicians did not enjoy high status until at least the 18th century. As advanced medical **education** was not available in Wales, the country came to be heavily dependent upon doctors trained at the universities of Scotland. The 18th century also saw the establishment of a number of dispensaries; they offered 'outdoor' facilities, but several came to provide 'indoor' treatment and thus became an element in the haphazard provision of voluntary hospitals, which developed in the 19th century. The workhouses established under the **Poor Law** Amendment Act of 1834 offered medical treatment, and many became infirmaries for the poor.

Provision of health services improved markedly in the first half of the 20th century. **David Lloyd George**'s Act of 1911 provided health **insurance** for those in employment and, despite its imperfections, the **Welsh Board of Health**, established in 1919, sought to oversee the provision of a coherent health service for the country as a whole. In the 1920s, local authorities became increasingly active in the field of health, and their responsibilities were much enlarged following the abolition of the **Poor Law Unions** in 1929. In many industrial areas, medical aid societies were established. That at **Tredegar** was particularly effective and, in establishing the NHS, **Aneurin Bevan** claimed that his chief aim was to extend to the entire population of Britain the benefits enjoyed by the members of the Tredegar society.

Yet, until Bevan's great innovation, health services remained patchy. Although health insurance paid the basic medical costs of those covered by it, there were those unable to afford any medical treatment at all unless doctors were prepared – as many of them were – to overcharge wealthy patients in order to provide free treatment for the indigent. Hospital provision was particularly inadequate. Some hospitals were privately owned; others were run by voluntary institutions or by local authorities, or had been hastily built to deal with wartime casualties. Most were antiquated, many being mid-19th century workhouses. The best were newly built general hospitals established by enlightened local authorities; they included those at **Llandough** near Cardiff and at Church Village (**Llantwit Fardre**).

With the creation of the NHS, the new state health services in Wales were put under the control of the Welsh Board of Health. The Welsh Regional Hospital Board (later the **Welsh Hospital Board**) assumed responsibility for the administration of state hospitals. Much of its work was delegated to hospital management committees; each committee had its own area, although psychiatric hospitals and the United Cardiff Hospitals (Cardiff Royal Infirmary and Llandough Hospital) were separately managed.

Since 1948, the administrative structure of the NHS has been reorganized several times. Local **government** reorganization in 1974 resulted in the establishment of 8 area health authorities coterminous with the (then) new county councils. Following a further reorganization in 1996, Wales was served, until 2003, by 5 health authorities, and, with the passing of the NHS and Community Care Act

1990, 26 NHS Trusts took over responsibility for the ownership and management of hospitals and other health service facilities that were previously controlled by the district health authorities. Overall responsibility for health, excluding primary legislation, was devolved to the National Assembly in 1999. As a result of reorganization in April 2003, there were 13 hospital trusts and one ambulance trust serving the whole of Wales. At the same time, 22 local health boards were created, coterminous with the unitary local authorities established in 1996; the boards and the authorities are jointly charged with formulating and implementing strategies for the health of the public.

Almost 40% of the total Assembly budget is spent on health care, and about 75,000 people (6.5% of the Welsh workforce) are employed in the NHS. The budget for health of £4.9 billion in 2005–6 was nearly twice the budget adopted by the Assembly at its inauguration in 1999. **Devolution** has produced small but significant differences between Wales and England. Revisiting NHS basic principles, the Assembly, which had already frozen and then reduced prescription charges, voted in 2007 to scrap them altogether – a policy widely divergent with that in England, where prescription charges were increased to £6.85. There are free dental checks for those under 25 and over 60; there are free eye examinations for those in risk groups; there is free nursing care for nursing home residents. The particular health needs of poverty-stricken communities and of those living in remote areas were recognized by a major resource allocation review, which led to the establishment of a Health Inequalities Fund to address health issues, such as the prevention of heart disease, in the most disadvantaged communities: with an annual budget of £5.8 million, the fund was supporting 62 projects in February 2006.

The ratio of general practitioners to population is higher in Wales than elsewhere in the United Kingdom, but they are not evenly distributed, and the workload, especially for those working single-handedly in the more populous areas, is notably stressful. In October 2002, the Assembly government estimated that 175 additional GPs would be needed in the following 8 years. The establishment of the Gwent and the north Wales clinical schools linked to the **Wales College of Medicine, Biology, Life and Health Sciences** and the establishment of a graduate entry scheme based at the **University of Wales Swansea**, has facilitated an expansion of the annual medical school entry in Wales, between 2001 and 2006, from 190 to 360. With dental students also increasing, there were over 1500 medical students and 300 dental students in training in 2006/7. It is planned to increase the number of hospital consultants by 525, of hospital nurses by 4752 and of paramedics by 250 by the year 2010.

With rising expectations of the services provided by the NHS, many hospitals have experienced difficulties in recruiting and retaining staff, particularly nurses. Between 1996/7 and 2005/6, the percentage bed occupancy increased from 78% to 82.9%, with increases in both bed turnover and personnel vacancies presenting challenges to standards of hygiene and intensifying the risk of hospital-acquired infections.

The beginning of the 21st century saw much criticism of the amount of time patients spent on waiting lists, with both numbers of patients and the time-spans involved showing a steady upward trend – although there were improvements by the middle of the decade. The National Assembly's adoption of a series of waiting-list targets for different diagnoses resulted in there being, by the end of October 2006, no patients waiting over 6 months for cardiac surgery, and none waiting more than 4 months for either angiography or cataract surgery.

It is estimated that 5200 children – 1% of the child population – need specialized health services annually, at a cost of at least £20 million. Those in the north have traditionally been treated in **Liverpool**, and those in the south in Bristol. However, in 2006, phase one of the Children's Hospital of Wales at Cardiff was opened on the campus of the University Hospital of Wales, Cardiff, making it possible for all but a handful of serious medical conditions to be treated in Wales. Important reports relating to Welsh children – on child cardiac surgery, retained organs and child abuse – have led to remedial action, including the appointment, in 2001, of a children's commissioner, the first such appointment in Britain. A report by Save the Children in 2002 revealed that Welsh children, a third of whom are living in poverty, are the poorest in Britain.

One of the most controversial contemporary issues is the retention of smaller ('cottage') hospitals, of which there are many. These were largely built as voluntary institutions, and local communities tend to identify strongly with them. As there were fewer treatments available when they were constructed, it was possible to provide a wider range of services at a local level. With the introduction of expensive new diagnostic techniques and treatments, much of the clinical work has been concentrated in the newer, larger district general (or major acute) hospitals, of which Wales had 17 in 2006 (not one of which was sited in Powys). However, the Welsh Assembly government's policy document, *Designed for Life* (2005), heralded a period of further change in the shape of Wales's health services. Plans are well advanced to complete 7 new community hospitals in Wales by the end of the decade – in the **Cynon Valley**, **Ebbw Vale**, **Holywell**, **Monmouth**, **Porthmadog**, the **Rhondda** and **Tenby**.

WALES'S 17 DISTRICT GENERAL HOSPITALS

Bronglais General, Aberystwyth
Llandough
Morriston, Swansea
Neath Port Talbot
Nevill Hall, Abergavenny
Prince Charles, Merthyr Tydfil
Prince Philip, Llanelli
Princess of Wales, Bridgend
Royal Glamorgan, Llantrisant
Royal Gwent, Newport
Singleton, Swansea
University Hospital of Wales, Cardiff
West Wales General, Carmarthen
Withybush General, Haverfordwest
Ysbyty Glan Clwyd, Bodelwyddan
Ysbyty Gwynedd, Bangor
Ysbyty Maelor, Wrexham

One indisputable, but frequently forgotten, change brought about with the introduction of the NHS is that it sought to ensure that a medical service of uniform quality should be provided for all those who relied on it. Considering the accompanying financial constraints, a remarkably high level of efficiency has been maintained, although prosperous places such as Cardiff are able to offer superior services to those available in the rundown industrial areas and the remoter rural districts.

PSYCHIATRIC SERVICES

The statement that psychiatry has a long past but only a short history has particular relevance for Wales, where a lack of facilities meant that few attempts were made to deal with the matter. The different manner of presentation of psychiatric illness, together with centuries of superstition concerning its nature, also served to isolate those affected. With few facilities in Wales, those suffering from psychiatric problems – including those knowing not a word of English – were often sent to English asylums.

Charles Watkin **Williams Wynn** (1775–1850), MP for **Montgomeryshire** (1799–1850), was responsible for establishing a select committee to investigate the conditions under which psychiatric patients were living. There followed an Act of Parliament in 1808, which allowed quarter sessions courts to set up county asylums in Wales and England. The only Welsh county to take advantage of this was **Haverfordwest** (which had the status of a county at that time). The town's jail was made available, thus inaugurating what was probably the bleakest episode in the history of psychiatry in Wales. No structural changes were made to the building, and, although no charges of deliberate cruelty to patients seem to have been made, standards of care were abysmally low, and the magistrates, who were responsible for the asylum's maintenance, took little interest in its management. It was closed in 1866.

Three private asylums were opened in Wales: in Swansea (1815–?20), **Briton Ferry**, (1843–96) and **Amroth** (1851–6). The Swansea asylum seems to have provided a better standard of care than the other two. As well as accepting private patients, the asylums also took paupers, who were paid for by the county authorities. Some patients were also cared for in private houses, while others were sent to the workhouses or **prison**.

Later, other Welsh counties built their own asylums. The North Wales Asylum, **Denbigh**, was opened in 1849, and those at **Abergavenny**, Carmarthen (replacing Haverfordwest), **Bridgend** and **Talgarth** followed in the second half of the 19th century. Whitchurch Hospital, Cardiff, and Cefn Coed Hospital, Swansea, were built in the 20th century. These belonged to a different tradition, with their full-time, properly trained medical superintendents. They were concerned with offering more than imprisonment and ill-treatment to their patients, and laid the foundations for a vastly improved service.

Those buildings served as psychiatric hospitals for much of the 20th century, their structure having been adapted to meet the demands of a new age. Doors were no longer locked, and the whole ethos was vastly altered. New drugs were developed which were to help transform the lives of thousands of patients. By the end of the 20th century, in many cases psychiatric facilities had been transferred to the general hospitals, and more emphasis had been placed on treating patients in the community, although sufficient funds were not made available to make this venture successful.

At the beginning of the 21st century, alcoholism and drug abuse, among young adults in particular, remained major problems in urban communities. During 2005–6, Swansea had the highest rate of those seen for alcohol and drug abuse, followed by Merthyr Tydfil and **Newport**; the lowest rate was in **Anglesey**.

HEDGEROWS

Hedges owe their existence to field creation. Many Welsh fields are surrounded by **dry stone walling**, the building of which increased massively following the **enclosure** of the uplands in the 18th and 19th centuries. Following the rise of quarrying, fields were sometimes enclosed by upright **slate** slabs. In more recent times, wire fences have been widely erected. Nevertheless, hedgerows – banks surmounted by shrubs and trees – are by far the commonest form of field enclosure in Wales; indeed, the country contains almost 50,000 km of them.

Wales's earliest hedges date back to the coming of **agriculture** in the **Neolithic Age**. The importance of clear barriers between fields is stressed in Welsh medieval **law**. Hedge creation gathered momentum during the intensification of rural settlement characteristic of the 12th and 13th centuries – an intensification involving the process of assartment, which created hedges from the trees and shrubs left standing as fields were carved out of the wildwood. **Rice Merrick** commented that in the **Vale of Glamorgan** a century earlier than the year in which he was writing (1578), there were no hedges between the portway (the later A48) and the sea. The comment indicates that assartment was not always accompanied by hedge creation, and in the Vale and elsewhere, hedges were the result of deliberate planting from the early 16th century onwards.

Lowland Wales experienced little of the parliamentary enclosure undertaken on such a large scale in lowland **England** – enclosure that produced large fields with straight hedges. Instead, it experienced slower, more organic development, which led to small fields with meandering hedges – meanders which were believed to offer better shelter for **cattle**. 'Hooper's Rule' – the theory that the age of a hedge can be determined by the number of tree species it contains – is considered to be fairly reliable where eastern England is concerned. It appears that it is less applicable in Wales, and thus, where no documentary evidence exists, dating Welsh hedges can be difficult. However, there can be little doubt that among the oldest are those bordering ancient tracks. The small fields of lowland Wales mean that the country has a superabundance of hedges. In the dairying areas of **Carmarthenshire**, where a 40-ha farm can contain 40 fields, hedges can constitute 10% of a farm's area.

Ancient hedgerows, defined as those in existence before *c.*1800, are estimated to constitute 42% of the hedgerows of **Britain**. They generally support a greater number of **plant** and animal species than do more recent hedgerows. Mostly planted on banks formed from the arisings from boundary or drainage ditches, the most common tree species they contain are hawthorn, blackthorn, hazel and ash, all of which lend themselves to hedge-laying. Species allowed to grow into hedgerow trees include oak, ash, holly and beech. Among unusual hedgerow trees are laburnum in **Ceredigion** and elm on the coastal levels.

Hedgerows can be regarded as miniature woodlands. They offer a habitat to over 500 plant species, among them colourful spring-flowering plants such as greater stitchwort, lesser celandine, primrose and bluebell. Over 60 breeding **bird** species have been recorded in hedgerows and they offer a home to most lowland small **mammals**, several species of reptiles and hundreds of invertebrates. Where the landscape is intensively farmed, hedgerows provide a connection between fragmented habitats, both for mobile species such as birds and mammals and for more sedentary life forms, which may gradually spread along these corridors. The use of expensive farm machinery is profitable only in large fields, and thus in recent years vast stretches of Wales's hedges have been ripped out, an activity which poses a serious threat to wildlife. The Hedgerow Regulations issued in 1997 and the introduction of grant schemes offer some protection.

Good hedge management involves regular laying and trimming, and the leaving of hedgerow trees every 50 m. Local styles of hedge care have evolved, those of **Breconshire** and Carmarthenshire being the most distinctive. By the late 20th century, high maintenance costs and the coming of mechanized hedge cutters threatened the craft with extinction, but training and competitions have revived standards of workmanship.

HELEDD Princess
Protagonist of a cycle of 9th or 10th-century *englynion*, 'Canu Heledd' (The song of Heledd), and the sole remaining member of the royal family of **Powys**, she mourns the deaths of her brothers, especially her lord **Cynddylan**, and laments the loss of her home and country.

HEMANS, Felicia [Dorothea] (1793–1835) Poet
Liverpool-born Felicia Hemans was brought up at **Llanddulas** and later lived in **St Asaph**. Her most famous poem is 'Casabianca', which begins, 'The boy stood on the burning deck'. Her highly popular *Welsh Melodies* appeared in 1821 and her *Collected Poems*, in seven volumes, in 1839. Widely admired by her contemporaries, her florid verse has not stood the test of time. Nevertheless, her affection for the Welsh landscape and her treatment of Welsh subjects contributed in **England** to a renewed interest in Wales.

HEMP, Wilfrid [James] (1882–1962) Archaeologist
An Englishman who had spent many youthful holidays in Wales, Hemp was in 1911 appointed an inspector of ancient monuments in Wales, specializing in the **Neolithic Age**. In 1928, he became secretary of the reformed **Royal Commission on the Ancient [and Historical] Monuments of Wales**. In 1937, he oversaw the publication of the **Anglesey** inventory, which set new standards of scholarship.

HEN BENILLION (lit. 'old stanzas')

These short individual verses, sometimes forming a series of three or four, first appeared in 17th-century manuscripts, but probably existed as spoken or sung poetry long before they were transcribed. They are mostly anonymous, written by the folk for the folk, to be sung to the accompaniment of the **harp** at social gatherings. Simple and lyrical, they reflect the whole gamut of rural, pre-industrial Welsh life.

HEN BERSONIAID LLENGAR, YR
(lit. The old literary clerics)

A group of patriotic (and generally anti-Methodist) **Anglican** clergymen who came together in the early 19th century to defend **Welsh** culture. They established the Cambrian Societies (which held important regional *eisteddfodau*), the periodical *Y Gwyliedydd* (1822–37), the Welsh Manuscripts Society (1837), St David's College, **Lampeter** (1827; *see* **University of Wales, Lampeter**) and **Llandovery** College (1847). Although they made a valuable contribution to Welsh life, their influence was eventually replaced by that of **Nonconformist** ministers. **R. T. Jenkins** coined the phrase.

'HEN WLAD FY NHADAU' ('Old land of my fathers') The Welsh national anthem

A song written in **Pontypridd** in 1856 – the words by Evan James (Ieuan ap Iago; 1809–78) and the melody (known as 'Glanrhondda') by his son James (Iago ap Ieuan; 1833–1902); **John Owen** (Owain Alaw; 1821–83) wrote the harmonies in 1860. By around 1874, its huge popularity in *eisteddfodau* had made it the pre-eminent **music**al expression of Welsh national sentiment. Father and son are commemorated at Ynysangharad Park, Pontypridd, by a splendid monument (1930) designed by **Goscombe John**.

In 1884, the song was the focus of a virulent controversy when it was claimed that the melody was plagiarized from an English folk song. James James sought to refute the claim in a letter to *The South Wales Daily News* describing the song's composition. Further evidence of its authenticity is the manuscript in James James's hand at the **National Library**. It appears that the melody was written first, with the words following shortly after.

Although it has three verses, on most occasions only the first is sung.

Mae hen wlad fy nhadau yn annwyl i mi,
The old land of my fathers is dear to me,
Gwlad beirdd a chantorion, enwogion o fri;
Land of poets and singers, famous and renowned;
Ei gwrol ryfelwyr, gwladgarwyr tra mad,
Her brave warriors, patriots so fine,
Dros ryddid collasant eu gwaed.
For freedom they shed their blood.

Tich Gwilym, who recorded a Hendrix-inspired version of 'Hen Wlad fy Nhadau'

Chorus:
Gwlad, gwlad, pleidiol wyf i'm gwlad;
Land, land, I pledge myself to my land;
Tra môr yn fur i'r bur hoff bau,
While the sea is a wall to the pure loved place,
O bydded i'r hen iaith barhau.
May the old language endure.

Hen Gymru fynyddig, paradwys y bardd,
Old mountainous Wales, paradise of the bard,
Pob dyffryn, pob clogwyn, i'm golwg sy'n hardd;
Every valley, every cliff is lovely to my sight;
Trwy deimlad gwladgarol mor swynol yw si
Through love of country, enchanting is the murmur
Ei nentydd, afonydd i fi.
Of her streams and rivers to me.

Gwlad, gwlad ...

Os treisiodd y gelyn fy ngwlad dan ei droed,
If the enemy has trampled my land underfoot,
Mae hen iaith y Cymry mor fyw ag erioed;
The old language of the Welsh is as alive as ever;
Ni luddiwyd yr awen gan erchyll law brad,
Poetry has not been choked by the foul hand of treason,
Na thelyn berseiniol fy ngwlad.
Nor my country's sweet-sounding harp.

Gwlad, gwlad ...

As 'Bro Goz Ma Zhadou', it was adopted in 1902 as the national anthem of **Brittany**, and a version in Khasi, 'Ri Khasi, Ri Khasi' (lit. 'Khasi land, Khasi land'), written by the **missionary** John Roberts (1842–1908), has been the people's anthem of the **Khasi Hills** in north-east India for over 100 years. In the 1970s, the guitarist Tich Gwilym (Robert Gwilliam; 1950–2005), performing with Geraint Jarman a'r Cynganeddwyr, popularized a Jimi Hendrix-inspired version of the melody. The painful attempts of John Redwood (**secretary of state for Wales**, 1993–5) to pretend he knew the words of the anthem provided a highly popular **film**ed vignette.

HENDREGADREDD MANUSCRIPT, The

An anthology of the work of the **Poets of the Princes**, compiled by one main scribe and many others at the beginning of the 14th century, probably at Strata Florida Abbey (**Ystrad Fflur**). During the 1330s, when the manuscript was in the possession of Ieuan Llwyd of Parcrhydderch, **Llangeitho**, a number of contemporary poems were added, including some by **Dafydd ap Gwilym**. The manuscript came to light in 1910 in a cupboard at Hendregadredd, a mansion near Pentrefelin (**Dolbenmaen**). It is housed at the **National Library**.

HENFYNYW, Ceredigion
(1347 ha; 1067 inhabitants)

Located immediately south of **Aberaeron**, the **community** contains the settlements of Henfynyw, Ffos-y-ffin, Llwyncelyn and Oakford. The name contains the element *Mynyw* (Menevia) associated with St **David**, who allegedly was educated at Henfynyw. Gilfach-yr-Halen is a delightful inlet. The school opened at Neuadd-Lwyd in 1810 by the **Congregational** minister Thomas Phillips (1772–1842) prepared ministers for most denominations and played a particular role in training **missionaries** for **Madagascar**. In 1973, Oakford was the centre of a bitter controversy over the sale of houses as **second homes**.

HENLLAN, Denbighshire (465 ha; 745 inhabitants)

Located immediately north-west of **Denbigh**, the **community** contains several historic houses, among them Foxhall, the family seat of **Humphrey Lhuyd**, Garn, home of the locally prominent Griffith family, and Plas Heaton, with its Doric loggia (*c*.1805). If Foxhall Newydd, begun *c*.1600 for the Panton family, had been completed, it would have been a remarkably ambitious house. St Sadwrn's church has a detached 15th-century tower.

HENLLANFALLTEG (Henllan Fallteg),
Carmarthenshire (1624 ha; 423 inhabitants)

Located on the **Carmarthenshire/Pembrokeshire** boundary immediately north-west of **Whitland**, the **community** contains the villages of Llanfallteg West and Llanfallteg. The congregation at Henllan Amgoed, established in 1697, was among the earliest **Nonconformist** causes in Carmarthenshire. It was frequently rent by theological controversy. The massive, dully modernized chapel is surrounded by an extensive burial ground.

HENLLYS, Torfaen (1075 ha; 2695 inhabitants)

Located north-west of **Newport**, the **community** was, until the 1980s, almost entirely rural. In the Middle Ages, Henllys (the old court) was perhaps one of the seats of the lord of **Gwynllŵg**, a notion which may gain credence from the fact that the farmhouse of Cwrt Henllys contains medieval features. St Peter's church, a simple medieval building, stands in splendid isolation, as does the unspoilt Zoar chapel (1836). Although in a highly Anglicized area, it was claimed by **Joseph Alfred Bradney** that in 1891 all Henllys's 392 inhabitants could speak **Welsh**. With a five-fold **population** increase between 1991 and 2001, Henllys was then Wales's most rapidly growing community. The growth was entirely the consequence of the building of a large compact settlement immediately south of **Cwmbran**.

HENRY, Thomas (1734–1816) Chemist

Thomas Henry was born in **Wrexham** where he was apprenticed to an apothecary and developed an interest in **chemistry**. He became a doctor in Manchester, where he pursued his chemistry experiments, especially on nitrogen fertilizers. His son William Henry (1774–1836) followed in his footsteps, and formulated 'Henry's Law' – the principle that the amount of a gas dissolved at equilibrium in a given quantity of liquid is proportional to the pressure of the gas in contact with the liquid. His grandson William Charles Henry (1804–92) was also a distinguished chemist. All three were elected FRS, a remarkable achievement for one family.

HENRYD, Conwy (1914 ha; 694 inhabitants)

Located immediately south of **Conwy**, the **community** contains the villages of Henryd, Llangelynin and Llechwedd.

St Celynin's church (15th century and later) contains memorials to the **Bulkeley family**. The area is rich in **hill-forts**, hut circles and prehistoric field systems. The standing stones at Maen Pen-ddu mark a significant route to the **Neolithic** axe-making centre of Graiglwyd above **Penmaenmawr**.

HER MAJESTY'S INSPECTORATE OF EDUCATION

Inspectors were first appointed in 1839 to visit elementary schools in Wales and **England** and were given powers to inspect the intermediate schools established following the passage of the 1889 **Welsh Intermediate Education Act**. The situation was complicated in the early 20th century by the conflict between the inspectors of the **Central Welsh Board** (1896) and those of the **Welsh Department of the Board of Education** (1907), a conflict eventually solved by compromise.

By the early 20th century, there was a substantial change in the inspectorate's attitudes to Wales. Most of the inspectors of the Victorian period had been exceedingly reluctant to recognize the special educational needs of Wales. Furthermore, with rare exceptions such as **Harry Longueville Jones**, they were hostile to the **Welsh language**. But by the time of the Welsh Department's foundation and the appointment of **Owen M. Edwards** as chief inspector of schools in Wales, a more enlightened view prevailed and the inspectorate was generally supportive of bilingualism. Following the passage of the 1944 Education Act, the inspectors became responsible for implementing its provisions; their range of activities increased, and they became responsible for an array of Welsh-language schemes, and for publishing a number of influential reports. Since 1999, the inspectorate for education and training in Wales has operated under the name of 'Estyn'.

HERALDRY

Heraldry has been defined as the systematic use of hereditary devices centred on the shield. In Wales, the adoption of coats of arms began among princely families; after about 1350, the practice spread to the **gentry**, initially to those who frequented English knightly society; by the 15th century, it had become widely established.

The earliest arms recorded are those of **Gruffudd ap Llywelyn** (d.1244) of **Gwynedd**, followed by his sons **Llywelyn ap Gruffudd**, prince of Wales, **Dafydd ap Gruffudd** (d.1283), and **Gruffudd ap Gwenwynwyn** (d.1286) of **Powys**.

The bards largely ignored heraldry until the 15th century when some of them, such as **Lewys Glyn Cothi**, introduced it freely into their work, and it became part of the bardic repertoire. Some, known as herald bards, took a particular interest in heraldry, making collections of coats of arms and recording those seen in churches and houses. Among them were **Gruffudd Hiraethog** (d.1564) and Lewys Dwnn (fl.1568–1616), both of whom were appointed deputy heralds for Wales.

Heraldic devices are now most widely seen on inn signs on which names such as 'Dynevor Arms' are accompanied by the coat of arms of the family commemorated in the inn's title. The mottos associated with coats of arms are

The Glamorgan County Council coat of arms

often ancient Welsh proverbs. That of the Williams family of Aberpergwm (**Glynneath**), 'A ddioddefws a orfu' (He who suffers triumphs), was adopted as the motto of **Glamorgan** County Council.

HERBERT family (earls of Pembroke of the first Herbert creation) Landowners

William (d.1469), son of Sir **William ap Thomas** of **Raglan** and Gwladys, daughter of **Dafydd Gam**, was among the first Welshmen to adopt a permanent **surname**. As William Herbert, he became a famous military leader, serving in Normandy with **Mathew Gough**. An enthusiastic builder, he initiated the building of Raglan Castle. Knighted in 1450, he acquired extensive possessions from the confiscated estates of the duke of **York** and earl of Warwick (1460). Despite grants of York land, he became the mainstay of the Yorkist cause in south Wales, where he was granted wide powers and rose high in the favour of Edward IV (*see* **Wars of the Roses**). He was made a privy counsellor and in 1461 was created Baron Herbert of Raglan, the first person of wholly Welsh descent to be promoted to the English peerage. The young Henry **Tudor** was entrusted to his care and, following his capture of **Harlech** Castle, he was created earl of **Pembroke** (1468). The following year, he was defeated by the Lancastrians at the battle of Edgecote and executed. He was a patron of **Guto'r Glyn** who urged him to save the Welsh from the tyranny of English officials, and his death was regarded by the poets as a national disaster. His heir, also William, the second earl (d.1491), left a daughter, Elizabeth, who married Sir Charles **Somerset**, first earl of Worcester; thus did the Raglan estate come into the possession of the Somerset family, later dukes of Beaufort.

HERBERT family (earls of Pembroke of the second Herbert creation) Landowners

William Herbert (*c*.1501–70), son of Richard Herbert of **Ewyas**, illegitimate son of William **Herbert, earl of Pembroke** (d.1469) entered the service of Sir Charles **Somerset** and rose rapidly at court when his sister-in-law, Katherine Parr, became Henry VIII's last wife. He received lands in Wales and in Wiltshire and, as one of the executors of Henry's will, he was one of the governors of the young Edward VI. He became president of the **Council of Wales and the Marches** (1550–3, 1555–8) and in 1551 was created Baron Herbert of **Cardiff** and earl of Pembroke. He succeeded (a difficult task) in retaining the favour of Mary I and of Elizabeth I, and added to his lands and influence during their reigns. His first language was **Welsh**; the **Roman Catholic** scholar **Gruffydd Robert** dedicated his *Gramadeg Cymraeg* (1567) to him and he was a patron of Sir **John Price**. He was succeeded by his son Henry (*c*.1534–1601), the second earl, refurbisher of Cardiff Castle, patron of **literature** and initiator of industrial enterprises.

Henry's son William (1580–1630), the third earl, **Shakespeare**'s patron, wielded substantial electoral influence in **Monmouthshire**, **Glamorgan**, **Radnorshire** and **Montgomeryshire**. Welsh connections weakened after the death of Philip, the fourth earl (1584–1650). In 1703, the family lands in Glamorgan passed to Thomas, first Viscount Windsor, on his marriage to Charlotte Herbert, daughter of Philip, the seventh earl. In 1776, they came to Thomas's granddaughter, Charlotte, and her husband, John **Stuart**, later the first Marquess of Bute.

HERBERT family (earls of Powis) Landowners

In 1587, Edward Herbert (d.1595), son of William **Herbert, earl of Pembroke** (*c*.1501–70), purchased Powis Castle (*see* **Welshpool**). His son, William (1573–1656), became the first Baron Powis in 1629. A staunch royalist, he defended Powis Castle for Charles I, assisted by his son Percy (d.1666), the second baron. The third baron (*c*.1626–96) was elevated to the earldom (1674) and then to the marquessate of Powis (1687). Considered the leader of the **Roman Catholic** aristocracy, his **London** house was burned during the unrest arising from the claims of Titus Oates. James II entrusted his son to the marquess and his wife, who smuggled the baby prince to France in 1688. The marquess shared the exile of the king, who created him duke of Powis in 1689. The second marquess (*c*.1665–1745) was restored to his estates and titles (apart from the dukedom) in 1722. On the death of the third marquess (*c*.1698–1748), the earldom, but not the marquessate, was granted to his neice's husband, Henry Arthur Herbert.

In 1801, the Powis estates passed by marriage to Edward Clive (1754–1839), the son of Clive of India, for whom the earldom of Powis was revived. Edward's son (1785–1875), who was active in suppressing unrest in **Montgomeryshire** in 1839, adopted the surname Herbert. His descendants continue to live in Powis Castle, which is owned by the **National Trust**. In 1873, the earl of Powis owned 13,575 ha in Montgomeryshire and a 10,921 ha estate in **Shropshire**, which included **Ludlow** Castle.

HERBERT, Edward (Baron Herbert of Cherbury; 1583–1648) Writer and philosopher

Born in **Shropshire**, the eldest brother of **George Herbert**, Edward married into the family of William Herbert (*c*.1501–70) (*see* **Herbert family, earls of Pembroke of the second creation**). His *Life*, an eccentric work discovered in manuscript in 1737, describes his adventures in the Low Countries and his service as ambassador to the French court, following which he was created Baron Herbert of Cherbury (1629). In *De Veritate* (1623), he argued that religious faith was dependent upon reason rather than revelation; his position as the originator of deism derives from this work (*see* **Agnosticism and Atheism**). In the **Civil Wars**, he supported first the king and then Parliament, but took no real part in the struggle. His grandson, the fourth baron (d.1691), founded the **Royal Welch Fusiliers**.

HERBERT, George (1593–1633) Poet

Born either in Eutun, **Shropshire**, or in **London**, George was the son of Richard Herbert, whose tomb is the glory of St Nicholas church, **Montgomery**, and who was the great-grandson of Richard Herbert, the brother of William Herbert (d.1469) (*see* **Herbert family, earls of Pembroke of the first Herbert creation**). MP for Montgomery (1624–5), John Donne encouraged him to abandon politics and to take holy orders. In 1630, he became an **Anglican** priest – in Wiltshire – but died three years later.

Very little of his work was published during his lifetime, but manuscript copies of some of his poems had circulated among his friends. Within a few months of his death *The Temple* (1633) appeared, a collection of poems about the conflicts of Christian faith, doubt about his priestly calling, and the love of God for mankind. His influence on other **English-language** poets of the 17th century, especially **Henry Vaughan**, is well attested. Echoes of his work may be found in that of **R. S. Thomas**.

HERBERT, John (*c*.1540–1617) Politician

A grandson of George Herbert, brother of William Herbert (*c*.1501–70) (*see* **Herbert family, earls of Pembroke of the second Herbert creation**), Herbert was born in **Swansea**. A proficient linguist, he was used to interrogate foreign prisoners, and undertook various foreign embassies. Closely allied to the **Cecils** at court, he eventually became a clerk to the privy council (1590), a privy councillor (1600) and the junior of the **government**'s two secretaries of state, which earned him the nickname 'Mr Secondary Herbert'. He was knighted in 1602. Herbert was an ardent advocate of the union of the parliaments of **Scotland** and **England** following the union of the crowns in 1603. He was in turn MP for six constituencies, **Glamorgan** and **Monmouthshire** among them – a record in the history of the English parliament. Like others in his family, he had a fiery temper, and may have died of wounds following a duel. His tomb is in St John the Baptist Church, **Cardiff**.

HERBRANDSTON, Pembrokeshire
(562 ha; 401 inhabitants)

Located immediately west of the town of **Milford Haven**, the **community** is dominated by the Elf-Murco **oil** refinery, which is linked by pipeline to a 715-m jetty in the haven.

St Mary's church contains a worn effigy supposed to be that of a 14th-century knight. South Hook Fort (1850–70), one of **Palmerston's Follies**, was once a country club but is now derelict. Herbrandston is a 'fortunate village', with the happy distinction of having no **war memorial**, since none of its residents was lost in either world war. Off the coast, Stack Rock is a major danger to shipping in the **Milford Haven Waterway**.

HEREFORDSHIRE, Wales's associations with

South-west Herefordshire can plausibly be considered to have been the cradle of the Welsh nation, for it was there, in **Erging** (Archenfield), that one of the defining characteristics of the nation's early history – the activity of the **Celtic Church** – is first apparent. Erging was the setting for the work of Dubricius (**Dyfrig**), the earliest of the leaders of the 'Age of **Saints**'. It was also a region in which St **David** was held in high regard, with dedications such as that at Much Dewchurch.

By c.800, Erging had become part of the **county** and **diocese** of Hereford. Influences emanating from the city of Hereford increasingly Anglicized its northern parts, but southern Erging remained **Welsh** in language and social organization for many centuries, and still has **place names** such as Llangarron and Bagwy Llidiart. On the eve of the **Norman** conquest, much of Herefordshire was devastated by the campaigns of **Gruffudd ap Llywelyn**. Following the conquest, Hereford became the base for Norman attacks upon south-east Wales, attacks which brought about the extinction of the Welsh kingdom of **Gwent** and which bestowed 'the customs of Hereford' upon the towns planted in Wales by the invaders. In subsequent centuries, Hereford became a major centre for the trade of the southern Welsh **border**land, and the landed families of the county played a role in Welsh history, with Kentchurch providing **Owain Glyndŵr** with a son-in-law and Hergest offering patronage to Welsh poets.

The **Act of 'Union'** added most of Ewias – the region between the Monnow and the Dore – to Herefordshire, thus increasing the county's Welsh-speaking **population**. The strength of the Welsh language in the county was recognized by parliament in 1563 when the four Welsh bishops, along with the bishop of Hereford, were commanded to ensure that the **Bible** would be available in Welsh. The Herefordshire borderland played a role in Wales's post-Reformation religious history, with Olchon the home of the earliest Welsh-speaking **Baptists**, and Cwm the location of a Jesuit college serving the **Roman Catholics** of southeast Wales.

Until the 19th century, Hereford remained a major centre for the Welsh; for example, the *Hereford Journal*, founded in 1713, was for long one of the main **newspapers** circulating in **Monmouthshire** and **Glamorgan**. With the urbanization of south-east Wales, the roles were reversed.

HERKOMER, Hubert von (1849–1914) Artist

Hubert von Herkomer, who was born in Waal in Bavaria and made a living as a painter in **London**, came to Wales after meeting **Charles Mansel Lewis** of **Llanelli**. His work was typical of the period: people in romantic or picturesque settings, and subject **painting**s dealing with British

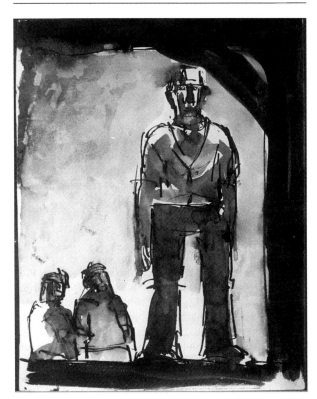

Josef Herman, *Pithead, three miners* (1945)

mythologies; he also painted portraits. He became involved with the **National Eisteddfod**, acting as an adjudicator and designing insignia, costumes and regalia for **Gorsedd Beirdd Ynys Prydain**.

HERMAN, Josef (1911–2000) Artist

Herman exhibited as an expressionist in his native Poland, leaving for Brussels in 1938. Always one step ahead of the tragedies of his times, he left Belgium for France, and then, as the German army swept through mainland Europe, arrived by chance in **Scotland**. He lost his entire family in the Holocaust.

Herman's creative epiphany occurred while on holiday in Wales, where he lived – at **Ystradgynlais** – between 1944 and 1955. He recounts in his autobiography, *Related Twilights* (1975), seeing miners crossing a bridge after work; silhouetted against the sun, their massive forms made an impression that never left him. Everything he created thereafter was charged with this carboniferous magic. His panel for the 'Minerals of the Islands' display at the 1951 Festival of **Britain** depicted Welsh miners, and his influence on the art of Wales was immense. He finished his days in **London** where he continued to paint, his subject matter ranging from flowers to sporting figures.

HEY, Donald Holroyde (1904–87) Chemist

As the scientist who discovered the existence of free radicals in solution, Donald Hey, FRS, made an outstanding contribution to organic **chemistry**. A native of **Swansea**, he completed his first degree there before becoming a lecturer at Manchester. From 1950, he was head of chemistry at King's College, **London**.

In 1934, Hey published his famous paper proposing that the decomposition of benzoyl peroxide gave rise to free phenyl radicals. This was a revolutionary proposal, contradicting the prevailing theory that organic reactions involved intermediate radicals with paired rather than single electrons. It took 20 years for the theory of free radicals to be universally accepted; but free radicals are now recognized as key participants in many chemical reactions, and the basis of numerous processes in the petrochemical and polymer industries. In addition, the role of free radicals in biological processes is now acknowledged: for example, it is the presence of free radicals that gives red wine its valuable medical properties.

HEYCOCK, Llewellyn (1905–90)
Local government leader
Lord Heycock of Tai Bach began his career as an engine driver at the Dyffryn Yard Loco Sheds in his native **Port Talbot**. He was an outspoken member of **Glamorgan** County Council (1937–74), of which he was chairman (1973–5). He was chairman of its **education** committee (1944–74), and showed considerable sympathy for the establishment of **Welsh**-medium schools. He was the first chairman of the new **county** of **West Glamorgan**. Heycock's forceful personality, his influence on education, and his close identification with the **Labour** domination of local **government** in Glamorgan brought him respect and condemnation in equal measure. His speech to the **University of Wales** Court in 1964 was a key factor in ensuring the continued unity of the university.

HICKS, Henry (1837–99) Physician and geologist
A native of **St David's**, Henry Hicks, FRS, was trained at Guy's Hospital, **London** before practising medicine at St David's and then becoming head of a private mental home in Hendon. His interest in **geology** was directed towards the Precambrian and Cambrian rocks of Wales, and the **cave** faunas of the Vale of **Clwyd**. He was the first Welshman to be elected president of both the Geological Society of London and the Geologists' Association.

HIGHER EDUCATION FUNDING COUNCIL FOR WALES, The
Established in 1992, the Council disburses funds to the institutions of higher **education**. Since 1994, HEFCW has also been responsible for funding initial training for schoolteachers and commissioning research to improve standards of teaching and teacher training. Together with the **National Council for Education and Training for Wales**, HEFCW was part of ELWa (Education and Learning Wales) until 2003, when the merger of the two councils was reversed.

HIGHER KINNERTON, Flintshire
(925 ha; 1634 inhabitants)
Separated from Lower Kinnerton (**Cheshire**) by the Wales/**England border**, the **community** is more akin to the Cheshire Plain than to industrial **Flintshire**. Higher Kinnerton village grew substantially in the later 20th century. Its All Saints' church (1893) is an uncharacteristically commonplace example of the work of **John Douglas**.

HILL family Ironmasters
Richard Hill (d.1806) was granted through Chancery the operating rights to the Plymouth Ironworks, Troed-y-rhiw (*see* **Merthyr Tydfil**) in 1788, following the death of his brother-in-law, **Anthony Bacon**. Subsequently, Hill assumed ownership and, on his death, the works were run by his son, Anthony (1784–1862). Like most of the Merthyr **iron**masters, both father and son were actively involved in those transportation improvements, notably the **Glamorgan**shire **Canal** in the 1790s and the **Taff** Vale **Railway** in the 1830s, which made location at the northern rim of the **coal**field commercially viable. On Anthony's death, the works were sold to Fothergill, Hamley and Bateman for £250,000. They closed *c*.1880.

HILL-FORTS
Wales has some 600 hill-forts, varying in size from the small enclosures numerous in the south-west to the large, multi-rampart forts of the uplands of the **border**land. It is difficult to be precise about who built them. There was once a belief that they were the work of invaders, but there is now an increasing tendency to argue that they were an indigenous development, and to emphasize that there was a strong element of continuity between the way of life of the people of the Late **Bronze Age** and of those of the **Iron Age**. Most of them date from the period 500–100 BC, but some, such as the Breiddin (**Bausley and Criggion**), have definite Late Bronze Age antecedents. Others continued to function into the **Roman** period, among them Tre'r Ceiri (**Llanaelhaearn**), Braich y Ddinas (**Penmaenmawr**) and Dinorben (**Abergele**). Some, such as Dinas Emrys (**Beddgelert**) or **Dinas Powys** were still in use well into the early Christian period.

Hill-forts vary in area from 0.5 ha to over 30 ha and, as a generalization, the higher their vantage position the larger their size. As they vary greatly in distribution, size, shape and sophistication of construction, it is likely that hill-forts had a variety of functions; indeed, to use the same term for all of them may impose an artificial unity upon very dissimilar groups of structures. The 200 or so which are less than 0.5 ha in extent were probably individual fortified farms. The middle-sized structures may have been folds for animals, sacred enclosures, centres for seasonal agricultural activities, occasional refuges or the strongholds of petty chieftains. There are a score and more which exceed 6 ha, and some of these offered protection for the houses of a substantial number of people, proof that the **economy** in the last centuries of prehistory, in some parts of Wales at least, was capable of sustaining quasi-urban communities. Some of the houses were of stone, as at Foeldrygarn (**Crymych**), and others of timber, as at Moel y Gaer. Hill-fort interiors clearly received as much thought as did the defences, with demarcated zones for habitation, storage, crop processing, animal penning and ritual practices. Successive enlargements can be identified at Foeldrygarn, Pendinas (**Aberystwyth**) and Carn Ingli (**Newport**).

The larger hill-forts tend to occupy prominent, easily defendable locations made more secure through the construction of encircling univallate (Penycloddiau, **Ysgeifiog**) or multivallate defences (Ffridd Faldwyn, **Montgomery**).

Foeldrygarn, Crymych: Bronze Age cairns within an Iron Age hill-fort

Ramparts were built of earth, stone or combinations of both. Earthen ramparts could be complex structures, as at the Breiddin and at Moel y Gaer (**Halkyn**). Where stone was plentiful, massive dry masonry ramparts were built, admirable examples of which survive at Tre'r Ceiri and Garn Goch (**Llangadog**). Strongly defended gaps in the ramparts provided entrances. Heavy timber gates, vouched for by excavated post sockets, blocked the entrance. In-turned gateway terminals (Moel Fenlli, **Llanbedr Dyffryn Clwyd**), or complex outworks (Gaer Fawr, **Guilsfield**), provided added protection. Stone guard-chambers were also constructed, as at Dinorben. Entrances were straddled by bridge-like constructions (**Conwy** Mountain), affording uninterrupted passage along the rampart walkway as at Tre'r Ceiri. Further defence could be provided by a *chevaux-de-frise* – a construction of closely packed upstanding stonework (Pen y Gaer, **Caerhun**, and Carn Alw, **Eglwyswrw**). The construction of the larger hill-forts is proof of social cohesion and co-operation on a massive scale; it also implies authoritarian planning and implementation.

HIRFRYN Commote

The northernmost of the three **commotes** of **Cantref Bychan**, Hirfryn's administrative centre was **Llandovery**. With **Perfedd**, it came to constitute the **march**er-lordship of Llandovery.

'HIRLAS OWAIN' (lit. 'Owain's drinking-horn')

An unusual praise poem attributed to prince **Owain Cyfeiliog**, but which was possibly the work of his poet, **Cynddelw Brydydd Mawr**. Composed to celebrate Owain's campaign in 1156 to rescue his brother Madog from **prison**, it describes a feast held in honour of Owain and his retinue, where drinks are served in precious vessels to each warrior in turn.

HIRWAUN, Rhondda Cynon Taff
(5910 ha; 4851 inhabitants)

Straddling the heads-of-the-valleys **road** (the A465) north-west of **Merthyr Tydfil**, most of the **community** was until 1974 part of the **parish** of Penderyn, **Breconshire**. Hirwaun (the long moor) was for centuries an expanse of **common land** famous for its breed of small **horses**. There may have been an **iron**making furnace at Hirwaun as early as the 1660s. The more elaborate ironworks established in 1757 were acquired by **Anthony Bacon** in 1780 and by the **Crawshay family** in 1819. Never as successful as the other Crawshay ventures, the works ceased operation in the 1880s; remains of four blast furnaces survive. East of them is a dry-stone causeway (1808), the longest such structure in south Wales, built to carry a tramroad across the Cynon. Although most of the community lies north of the **coal**field, in the later 19th century Hirwaun became home to many of the miners employed at collieries in **Rhigos**. Two 12-storey tower blocks built in the 1960s were demolished in 2004. (For the Hirwaun Trading Estate, *see* Rhigos.)

Penderyn, featured in a well-known folk song, was the source of much of the **limestone** used in the iron industry. St Cynog's church, largely rebuilt in the 19th century, retains its medieval tower. Large and small depressions known as swallow holes or shakeholes characterize the limestone outcrop east and west of the village. The attractive **waterfalls** on the Hepste are known locally as *sgydau*.

HISTORIA BRITTONUM
(The History of the Britons)

Historia Brittonum, the earliest version of which is dated *c*.829/830, is a collection of historical texts ascribed, but without certainty, to Nennius. It gives an account of the history of the Britons (the Welsh in particular) from the end of the **Roman** period to the **Anglo-Saxon** invasions, and draws on such sources as annals, king lists, **saints'** lives, literary traditions, folklore and tales. The *Historia* has been used by historians from the time of **Geoffrey of Monmouth** to the present, since it contains the earliest references to **Arthur** and his battles, the coming of the Anglo-Saxons and the contention between **Vortigern** and Hengist and Horsa. Here, too, is found the earliest reference to some of the *Cynfeirdd* of the **Old North**. Current opinion casts doubt on the author's method of using his sources and *Historia Brittonum* is regarded as more a conscious composition than a bare collection of facts. The collection is not a reliable witness to 6th-century history, though it can reveal something of 9th-century Welsh scholarship.

HISTORICAL SOCIETIES

The longest-lasting of Welsh societies is the **Cymmrodorion** (1751), which began as a society concerned with all aspects of Welsh life but which developed to be essentially concerned with the history of Wales. Other organizations, such as the early 19th-century Cambrian societies, underwent a similar transformation and came to emulate the Cymmrodorion in such matters as the offering of prizes for historical essays. In the 1840s, **Swansea**'s Royal Institution of South Wales established a museum, as did the **Caerleon** Antiquarians. The **Cambrian Archaeological Association** was founded in 1847, and Wales's first county historical society, The **Powys**land Club, with its journal, *The Montgomeryshire Collections*, was established in 1867. By the second half of the 20th century, all the Welsh **counties** then existing had historical societies publishing annual journals and, within the counties, a number of districts had their own societies and publications.

All the major religious denominations have their historical societies and journals, and, in 1993, a more general publication, *The Journal of Welsh Religious History*, was founded. In addition, a society devoted to the history of Welsh chapels publishes the journal *Capel*, and the society studying the history of Welsh **hymn**ology has its regular bulletin.

Other Welsh historical societies include the Society for the Study of Welsh Labour History with its journal *Llafur*, the Welsh Historic **Gardens** Trust with its bulletin, and Cymdeithas Bob Owen (*see* **Robert Owen**; 1885–1962), the society for bibliophiles with its journal *Y Casglwr*.

HISTORIOGRAPHY OF WALES, The

The first published account of the history of Wales was **David Powel**'s *Historie of Cambria* (1584), a revision of which was published by William Wynne in 1697; that was republished in 1702, 1774, 1812 and 1832 and was the standard version of the history of medieval and early modern Wales until the publication of **Jane Williams**'s *A History of Wales from Authentic Sources* in 1869. The interest in local history inspired by **William Camden**'s *Britannia* (1586) bore fruit in **George Owen**'s *Description of Penbrokshire* (1603 and 1994) (*see* **Archaeology and Antiquarianism**). The need to revise Camden's work led to the researches of **Edward Lhuyd**, the first use of scholarly methods in analyzing linguistic evidence and material remains relating to Wales.

A Protestant interpretation of the history of Wales was provided by **Charles Edwards** in his *Y Ffydd ddi-ffuant* (1667, 1671, 1677) and a far more fanciful interpretation by **Theophilus Evans** in his *Drych y Prif Oesoedd* (1716, 1740). The **Morris brothers** contributed substantially to Welsh historiography, but, like most of their predecessors, they were reluctant to abandon that central feature of Welsh identity – the portrayal of early Wales offered by **Geoffrey of Monmouth**. The legendary element in Welsh history was further strengthened by Iolo Morganwg (**Edward Williams**). A more judicious approach was taken by **Theophilus Jones**, a grandson of Theophilus Evans, in his *History of the County of Brecknock* (1804, 1809), incomparably Wales's finest **county** history. His close associate, **Thomas Price** (Carnhuanawc), was rather more romantic, although, in his *Hanes Cymru* (1836–42), he declared that he was 'anxious not to assert anything except upon authority'. However, the basic source materials for the study of Welsh history were difficult of access until the second half of the 19th century, and there were few outlets for learned articles until the launching of the journals of **historical societies** such as the **Cambrian Archaeological Association** and the **Honourable Society of Cymmrodorion**.

Until the establishment of the colleges of the **University of Wales**, Welsh historiography was almost wholly dependent upon the efforts of amateur historians, a dependence which did not disappear with the creation of university departments of history, for the fruitful relationship between the amateur and the professional has been an abiding feature of Welsh historical studies. The greatest of Wales's academic historians is **J. E. Lloyd**, whose *History of Wales from the Earliest Times to the Edwardian Conquest* (1911) created sound foundations for all future work on early medieval Wales. Lloyd was very much heir to 19th-century historiography, which saw the task of the historian as analyzing the rise of political institutions, particularly the governmental structures of so-called nation states. While Wales had a degree of political distinctiveness for a quarter of a millennium after the collapse of the native **Principality** in 1282, it had virtually none following the passage of the **Acts of 'Union'** of 1536 and 1543. Thus, assuming that Wales had any history at all (a notion denied in the infamous note in the 1911 edition of *The Encyclopaedia Britannica* – 'For Wales, *see* **England**'), it certainly did not have a history in the post 16th-century era. To modern historians, the obsession with political history seems highly archaic, but, nevertheless, it was necessary to wait until other forms of history – social, economic, cultural and demographic – won acceptance before any period of the history of Wales since 1282 received the attention it deserved.

While the three decades following the publication of J. E. Lloyd's masterpiece saw major advances in Welsh literary and linguistic studies, they saw less progress in Welsh historical studies, partly because the University colleges appointed few academics whose primary duty lay in that field. **Cardiff** appointed its first professor of Welsh history (**William Rees**) in 1930 and **Aberystwyth** (**E. A. Lewis**) in 1931. Although **R. T. Jenkins** was appointed at **Bangor** in 1930, he did not become a professor until 1946. However, those with no specific duties in the field of Welsh history made distinguished contributions to the subject – **A. H. Dodd** at Bangor in particular. Furthermore, the work of scholars outside the University of Wales – **J. Goronwy Edwards** in **London**, for example – was of seminal importance.

In the years immediately after the **Second World War**, the most significant contributions were those of **David Williams** (*A History of Modern Wales* (1950) and *The Rebecca Riots* (1955)) and **T. Jones Pierce**'s ingenious research on medieval Welsh society. However, it was university expansion, begun in the 1960s, which led to the greatest advances: advances which mean that, of the professional historians of Wales over the past century, the great majority are still alive. The chief architect of the advances was **Glanmor Williams**, who, ironically – or perhaps significantly – was professor at **Swansea**, a college which had eschewed the option of establishing a department of Welsh history. He was the founder of the *Welsh History Review* and the main mover in three multi-volume projects – the **Oxford** *History of Wales*, the history of **Glamorgan** and the 'Studies in Welsh History' series of monographs – in addition to his own massive contributions, particularly to the history of the medieval church and the **Protestant Reformation**. At Swansea, he ensured the appointment of a remarkable group of historians, among them Ieuan Gwynedd Jones, dissector of politicized Nonconformity, Kenneth O. Morgan, chronicler of Wales in British politics, Ralph Griffiths, chief authority on the House of **Lancaster**, Prys Morgan, interpreter of Wales's 18th-century renaissance, David Howell, scholar of Wales's rural history, **D. J. V. Jones**, analyst of radical protest, and Peter Stead, historian of Wales's popular culture. Other one-time colleagues of Glanmor Williams include **Rees Davies**, illuminator of the history of the **March** and of **Owain Glyndŵr**, Dai Smith, the champion of the unique society of industrial south Wales (or South Wales, as he would have it), and John Davies, whose *Hanes Cymru* (1990; **English** version, *A History of Wales*, 1993; new editions 2007) sought to build on the achievement of R. T. Jenkins and others in strengthening the role of **Welsh** as a language of historical scholarship.

However, it was with Aberystwyth that Wales's most exciting and wide-ranging historian was mainly connected. He was **Gwyn A. Williams**, whose many writings include a celebration of the history of **Merthyr Tydfil**, and whose interaction with **Wynford Vaughan Thomas** in the television series *The Dragon has Two Tongues* was a unique exercise in history as dialectic. Aberystwyth was also the base of Beverley Smith, whose biography of **Llywelyn ap Gruffudd** (Welsh version, 1986; English version, 1998) is a magnificent achievement, and of Geraint H. Jenkins, interpreter of early modern Wales and editor of *Cof Cenedl* – an annual volume of historical essays – and of a remarkable series of studies on the social history of the Welsh language. The publication in 2005 of Huw Pryce's *Acts of the Welsh Rulers, 1120–1283* was a major landmark.

Denominational history, the mainstay of Wales's 19th-century historiography, continued to have its practitioners – **R. Tudur Jones** in particular. The most interesting development of the later 20th century was the emergence of a school of feminist historians, Deirdre Beddoe and Angela John in particular. Equally enriching were **Aled Eames**'s affirmation that Wales's history has a significant maritime dimension, Peter Lord's insistence that, throughout their history, the Welsh people have demanded visual art, and **John Williams**'s empowerment of Welsh historians by providing them with exhaustive tables of historical statistics. The most innovative study of recent years is undoubtedly Russell Davies's *Hope and Heartbreak* (2005), an extraordinary work which seeks to analyze the psychological condition of the 19th-century Welsh. It can safely be prophesied that, with its publication, Welsh history will never be the same again.

Yet, despite the major achievements of the present generation of Welsh historians, there are those who argue that, by the 20th century, so diverse were the experiences of the inhabitants of the various regions of Wales that there was no common Welsh experience and therefore to write the history of modern Wales is metaphysically to impose an artificial unity upon an arbitrary extent of land whose history is less than the sum of the history of its parts. So argued M. J. Daunton, author of that excellent volume, *Coal Metropolis, Cardiff, 1870–1914* (1977), in his review of Kenneth O. Morgan's *Rebirth of a Nation, Wales, 1880–1980* (1981). In refutation, it could be argued that a consciousness of Welshness, however defined, is a living reality to a host of people throughout Wales and that that reality has found expression in an ever-increasing number of movements and institutions. The writing of the history of any nation is to some extent a metaphysical act, but the fact that there exists the will to undertake the task indicates that it is a substantive task also.

A more positive development is the rise of what has been called the 'new British history', the fruit, in part, of the rejection of the long-standing notion that the history of England and the history of **Britain** are one and the same. Thus, in 1989, the American historian Hugh Kearney published *The British Isles: A History of Four Nations*, and in 2000 Norman Davies published his hugely fascinating, if eccentric, volume *The Isles*, which contains not only the text of 'Hen Wlad fy Nhadau' but also one of the songs of Dafydd Iwan. Such studies were significantly stimulated by the emergence of political **nationalism** in **Scotland** and Wales, but they also owe much to the appreciation, outside Wales, that Welsh historical studies are flourishing mightily. As Gwyn A. Williams put it in 1990: 'Whatever the twentieth-century Welsh will be remembered for, they will surely be remembered for their historians.'

HOBBES, Thomas (?1757–1820) Psychiatrist

Having lived originally in **Monmouth**, Hobbes moved to **Swansea** *c.*1804. There, as the earliest known Welsh psychiatrist, he took charge of the first private Welsh asylum,

May Hill's House (*see* **Health**). He was also honorary physician to the Swansea Dispensary, and later to the Swansea Infirmary.

HOCKEY

The modern game was born when the Hockey Association (**England**) was established in 1886. The Welsh Hockey Association was formed in 1897, and the Welsh **Women**'s Hockey Association in 1898. The first Welsh club was founded in **Rhyl** in 1885, and it was that club which organized the world's first international match – between Wales and **Ireland** – on Rhyl's Palace **Gardens** in January 1895 (Ireland won 3–0). The men's game was introduced into the Olympic Games in 1908, when Wales won the bronze medal.

The glory years for Welsh hockey were the 1960s and 1970s. In 1963, the Welsh women were the first team to beat England at Wembley, and in 1975 were seeded second in the world. In 1973, the Welsh men won the Triple Crown and beat England for the first time. During this period, they were placed in the top 20 of over 100 playing nations. Both associations were amalgamated into the Welsh Hockey Union in 1995.

These successful years saw Anne Ellis play 138 consecutive matches for Wales; she also captained the Great **Britain** side. Austin Savage was the first to win over 100 caps for Wales; he won a further 20 for Great Britain, including victories at the Munich Olympics of 1972.

HOGG, A[lexander] H[ubert] A[rthur] (1908–89)
Archaeologist

Hogg began his career as a civil engineer, lecturing at Newcastle and **Cambridge** Universities, but **archaeology** had been a passionate hobby from adolescence. In 1949, he was appointed secretary to the **Royal Commission on the Ancient [and Historical] Monuments of Wales**, where he presided over an expansion of staff and activity, and oversaw the publication of the three-volume **Caernarfonshire** inventory (1956, 1960, 1964). He was particularly involved in the classification of hut groups and the survey of **hill-forts**.

HOGGAN, Frances Elizabeth (1843–1927) Doctor

Brecon-born Frances Hoggan (b. Morgan) was the first Welsh woman to qualify as a doctor. Since she was not allowed to do so in **Britain**, she became a student at Zurich University. After graduating MD in 1870, she practised in **London**, but her name did not appear on the *Medical Register* for a further seven years. Later in life, she worked enthusiastically for equal rights in higher **education** for **women**.

HOLT, Wrexham (1802 ha; 1762 inhabitants)

Located immediately east of **Wrexham**, the **community** hugs the **Dee** at a point where it forms the Wales/**England border**. The kilns at Holt provided tiles and pottery for the **Roman** legionary fort at Chester. Soon after being granted the lordship of **Bromfield and Yale** in 1282, the de **Warenne family** built Holt Castle, a regular pentagon perhaps designed by **James of St George**. Associated with the castle was a **borough**, whose bastide plan is still evident in Holt's rectangular layout. Some of the features characteristic of the so-called **Stanley** churches, survive in St Chad's church. A 15th-century eight-arched bridge links – indeed virtually merges – Holt with Farndon in **Cheshire**. The community contains several attractive

Strawberry pickers at Holt in 1953

country houses, including Cornish Hall, Llwyn Onn Hall and Borras Hall. Holt is famous for its fields of strawberries, a crop introduced in 1860. The western part of the community is dominated by a vast gravel pit. South of the pit is Bryn Estyn, a one-time approved school whose residents were subject to sexual abuse. Renamed Erlas House, it became an information technology centre.

HOLYHEAD (Caergybi), Isle of Anglesey
(666 ha; 11,237 inhabitants)

Holyhead shares Holy **Island** (Ynys **Gybi**) with the **communities** of **Trearddur** and **Rhoscolyn**. Since the 14th century, it has been one of the main **ports** linking **Britain** to **Ireland**; mails for Ireland have been carried via Holyhead from at least the 17th century (*see* **Postal Service**). In 1727, Jonathan Swift considered the place to be 'scurvy, ill-provided and comfortless'. William Morris (*see* **Morris Brothers**) was collector and subsequently comptroller of **customs** at the port from 1737 to 1763. The parliamentary union between Ireland and Britain in 1801 increased the traffic to Ireland, traffic greatly expedited by the completion (by 1830) of **Telford**'s improvements to the **London–Holyhead road**. Communication was further facilitated by the completion of the Chester–Holyhead **railway** in 1849. There were extensive improvements to the port as the 19th century progressed, including the massive breakwater designed by James Rendel to provide a harbour of refuge (1847–73). In addition to the Irish traffic, Holyhead had a considerable coastal and foreign trade and a flourishing **shipbuilding** industry. Near the port is a marble arch commemorating George IV's visit in 1821 – the first visit to Wales by an **English monarch** since 1687.

There is much evidence of prehistoric settlement on Holy Island (*see also* **Trearddur**). Within Holyhead's boundaries is the Tŷ Mawr **Bronze Age** standing stone (2.5 m). In the 4th century, the **Romans** constructed a coastal fort as a defence against **Irish** marauders; its stone walls are well preserved. Tradition maintains that, in the 6th century, **Maelgwn Gwynedd** granted the fort to St Cybi. Within it are Eglwys y Bedd – allegedly the grave of Cybi – and St Cybi's church. One of the most important foundations in medieval **Anglesey**, it was a collegiate church served by a chapter of canons; built in the 13th century and later given Perpendicular features, its portrayal of the Trinity (*c.*1520) is a remarkable **sculpture**.

Between 1850 and 1950, Holyhead was dominated economically by the railway companies – successively the LNWR and the LMS – who also operated the mailboats to Ireland. During the economic war between Britain and the Irish Free State in the 1930s, it was one of the worst unemployment blackspots in Britain. Subsequently, there was some industrial development, culminating in the opening of an aluminium smelter in 1971. Following the introduction of Stena Line's Sea Lynx catamarans in 1993, the voyage from Holyhead to Dun Laoghaire was reduced to less than two hours.

The town of Holyhead is dominated by the port offices and by **Nonconformist** chapels, one of which – Disgwylfa – was long served by the Reverend H. D. Hughes, father of **Cledwyn Hughes**, Holyhead's most distinguished son. The town's history is admirably interpreted at the Maritime Museum. The attractive Ucheldre Arts Centre occupies a former **Roman Catholic** convent.

HOLYWELL (Treffynnon), Flintshire
(956 ha; 8715 inhabitants)

Located on the **Dee** estuary, the name commemorates St **Winefride**'s holy **well**. A place of pilgrimage for almost a millennium and a half, its fine Perpendicular chapel was financed by Margaret Beaufort, wife of Thomas **Stanley** and mother of Henry VII. Despite the **Protestant Reformation**, Holywell continued to be a stronghold of Roman Catholicism. In 1687, James II visited the well to pray for a son; his prayer was answered. His determination to raise his son as a **Roman Catholic** was a major factor in his dethronement in 1688. Adjoining the well is St James's church, largely rebuilt in 1770. A **Cistercian** monastery, founded in **Tegeingl** in 1131, was certainly located at Basingwerk by 1157. Footings and parts of the south transept survive.

By 1774, when Dr Johnson counted 19 works within two miles of St Winefride's Well, Greenfield, the valley lying between Holywell and the estuary, had became a major industrial centre. It was involved with **coal**mining, **copper** working (1743–1894), **lead** smelting (1774–1900), cotton spinning (1777–1839), silk ribbon weaving (1795–1850), vitriol manufacture (1790s), papermaking (1820–1982) and wool spinning and weaving (1840s–1987; *see* **Woollen Industry**). Of particular importance were **Thomas Williams**'s copper works (1780–*c.*1810). Its remarkable past makes Greenfield – a heritage park – a veritable open-air museum of industrial **archaeology**. **Courtaulds** established a flagship artificial fibre works at Greenfield in 1936. Its site is now a business park.

Holywell High Street contains some fine 18th-century Georgian fronts. The 19th-century dwellings in Panton Place, which originally contained workshops, have been converted into sheltered **housing**. Rehoboth, a handsome chapel built in 1827, was rebuilt (as Pen Bryn) in 2006. The 18th-century Croesonnen **windmill** at Penymaes is a prominent landmark. Greenfield is the best conserved of the Italianate stations designed by Francis Thompson for the Chester–**Holyhead railway** (1847) (*see also* **Flint**).

HOME RULE

Home Rule All Round (that is, for all the nations of the United Kingdom) was proposed in 1886 by **Joseph Chamberlain**. It was envisaged that in Wales Home Rule would take the modest shape of an elected body under the sovereignty of the Westminster parliament. **Cymru Fydd**, set up, in part, to further the cause, established branches throughout Wales but failed in its main aim of uniting **Liberal Party** organization and had ceased to function by the end of the century. The case for Home Rule was kept to the fore by **E. T. John**, who in March 1914 introduced a Welsh Home Rule Bill in the House of Commons. The measure attracted little attention, and John's efforts were engulfed in the maelstrom of the **First World War**.

By 1918–19, when the principle of self-**government** for small nations was one of the chief issues being considered by the First World War victors, it was confidently expected that the principle would be applied to the United Kingdom.

In May 1918, at a conference held at **Llandrindod**, representatives of 11 of Wales's 17 **county** authorities demanded: 'a Welsh parliament that would be responsible for all functions of government apart from Imperial concerns'.

In July 1918, the **Labour** Party Conference passed a resolution in favour of a federal **Britain**, a policy also supported by many **Conservatives**, partly in the hope of watering down what might be offered to **Ireland**. Thus, with **David Lloyd George**, a former Cymru Fydd stalwart, as British prime minister, Welsh Home Rule seemed imminent. Yet, little attention was paid to the report (1920) of a conference set up to consider the matter and chaired by the speaker of the House of Commons. Both Liberals and Labour lost enthusiasm for the cause and Lloyd George failed to enact the part of a Welsh messiah, leading his people to the promised land of Home Rule. **Plaid [Genedlaethol] Cymru**, established in 1925, refrained from using the term, calling instead for dominion status for Wales (*see also* **Devolution**).

HOMFRAY family Ironmasters

Encouraged by John **Guest** to move to **Merthyr Tydfil**, Francis Homfray (1726–98) left the Calcott Works near Broseley, **Shropshire** to establish the Penydarren **Iron**works in 1784. Francis's eldest son Jeremiah (1759–1833) initiated ironmaking in **Ebbw Vale** and was involved in the ironworks at **Hirwaun** and Abernant (**Aberdare**), but by 1813 he was bankrupt. His second son, Samuel (1762–1822), became the sole manager of Penydarren, founded the **Tredegar** ironworks and was prominent in the construction of the **Glamorgan**shire **Canal**. The Homfrays, commercially aggressive and famously disputatious with neighbouring concerns, claimed credit – dubiously – for the introduction of the refining process. In 1804, the historical significance of the Penydarren works was ensured when **Richard Trevithick** ran the world's first steam-powered engine from the works to **Abercynon**. In 1814, the family sold Penydarren to the Foreman and Thompson Partnership.

HOMOSEXUALITY

Classical authors such as Aristotle, Strabo and Athanaeus referred to male homosexuality among the **Celts** of the European mainland; and there are ancient references to male homosexuality in Wales. But references to female homosexuality are rare – although Lady **Eleanor Butler** and **Sarah Ponsonby**, who took up residence at **Llangollen** in 1779, were recognized (discreetly) as Europe's most renowned lesbian couple.

The stories of *The Mabinogion* open many a window on **Iron Age** beliefs and practices; and there are traces of pre-Christian depictions of homosexuality in the depiction of Gilfaethwy and **Gwydion** in the story of **Math fab Mathonwy**. The 6th-century penitentiaries setting penance for homosexual acts indicate the existence of such acts in Wales and of the Christian condemnation of them. **Gildas** believed that **Maelgwn Gwynedd** had committed homosexual acts and that God had punished him for them. **Giraldus Cambrensis** claimed that the Britons had lost Troy and **Britain** as a punishment for their homosexual practices. Under the influence of Church **law**, some of the Welsh law

texts would not accept the evidence of a man who had committed homosexual acts.

Accusations of homosexual behaviour are to be found in the Welsh court records from the 16th century onwards. However, because Wales had no large urban centres, a homosexual subculture did not develop until the 20th century. The harsh provisions against male homosexual behaviour enshrined in English law led to the imprisonment and the suicide of a number of Welshmen, episodes that the Welsh collective consciousness has chosen to ignore. Those provisions were relaxed in 1967, partly because of the campaigning of Leo Abse, MP for **Pontypool**.

By the late 20th century, Wales had the beginnings of a gay liberation movement. A lively gay scene emerged, especially in **Cardiff**.

The earliest local initiative openly to provide assistance and advice to homosexual people came in the early 1980s with the establishment of the **Bangor** help-line. Cylch, an association for **Welsh**-speaking homosexuals, was active from 1990 to 1996. The Lesbian, Gay and Bisexual Forum, financed in part by the **National Assembly for Wales**, was founded in 2001. It was renamed Stonewall Cymru in 2003.

Cardiff's annual celebration of gay identity, the Mardi Gras, is one of the largest such events in Britain. Since 2005, homosexual people in Wales have taken advantage of legislation that allows them to enter into civil partnerships.

HONDDU ISAF, Breconshire, Powys
(3058 ha; 395 inhabitants)

The road from **Brecon** to **Builth** over **Mynydd Epynt** traverses the **community** via Lower Chapel. Castle Madoc, built in 1588 for the Powel family, was much modified in the 19th century. The site was fortified in the 11th century and vestiges of two castles remain. In the 18th century, it was the home of Charles Powel the antiquary, a friend of **Howel Harris** and one of the founders of **Breconshire**'s **Agricultural Society**. The church at Garthbrengy has a 17th-century tower. That at Llandyfaelog Fach contains a 10th-century inscribed stone and is splendidly sited above the Honddu valley.

HOOD, Archibald (1823–1902) Coalowner

The son of a Scottish colliery official, Hood first came to Wales in 1860 and later became a colliery proprietor at **Gilfach Goch** and at Llwynypia (**Rhondda**). The **Glamorgan** Colliery Company at Llwynypia came to be known both for its Scottish immigrants ('Scotch Colliery') and its high quality coke, declared by **government** analysts in 1900 to be the best in the world. Hood was a promoter of the **Barry Railway** Company.

HOOK, Pembrokeshire (304 ha; 656 inhabitants)

A part of **Llangwm** until 1999, the **community** hugs the southern bank of the Western **Cleddau** where Hook Bight marks a sharp turn in the **river**. The **coal** mined at Hook Colliery – among **Pembrokeshire**'s last working collieries – was shipped at Hook Quay. East Hook Mansion contains 18th-century elements.

HOOSON, I[saac] D[aniel] (1880–1948) Poet
A popular lyricist and **ballad** writer, whose poems were often recited from **eisteddfod** platforms, Hooson hailed from **Rhosllanerchrugog** and was a solicitor in nearby **Wrexham**. Two volumes of his poems were published, *Cerddi a Baledi* (1936) and *Y Gwin a Cherddi Eraill* (1948). He wrote charmingly about nature in his first volume, but a more sombre note is struck in his later poems. His poems for children were particularly popular.

HOPE (Yr Hob), Flintshire
(1397 ha; 4172 inhabitants)
Adjoining the northern boundary of the **county borough** of **Wrexham**, the area was the core of the **commote** of Yr Hob, or Hopedale, one of the commotes of **Powys Fadog**. In 1284, Hopedale became one of the constituent parts of the county of **Flint**. The **Bronze Age** Caergwrle Bowl and the **Iron Age hill-forts** of Caer Estyn and Caergwrle Hill are proof of early settlement. The **community** is crossed by **Wat's Dyke**. Caergwrle Castle, begun by **Dafydd ap Gruffudd** *c.*1278, and refurbished by Edward I in 1282, suffered a fire in 1283. Apparently, it was never repaired.

It was at Caergwrle, in 1863, that the first Khasi (*see* **Khasi Hills**) ever to visit Wales – the evangelist U Larsing Khongwir – died after a gruelling preaching tour. His grave is in Chester public cemetery.

Hope attained **borough** status in 1351. **Lead** mining is recorded from the 14th century. Fferm is a late 16th-century hall house, but Bryn Iorcyn, another hall house, was encased in stone in the 17th century. Plas Teg, Wales's most remarkable early **Renaissance** mansion, was built *c.*1610 for John Trevor (d.1630), who had profited vastly from his position as Surveyor to the Navy. The double-naved St Cyngar's church contains his elaborate tomb. **Thomas Pennant** noted that there were salt springs at Rhydyn, where a spa had a brief existence in the early 20th century.

HOPKINS, Gerard Manley (1844–89) Poet
Although English-born, Hopkins's experience of Wales had a seminal influence on him. After graduating at **Oxford**, he trained for the **Roman Catholic** priesthood, latterly at St Beuno's College (**Tremeirchion**). The three years he spent there were crucial to the development of his ideas about prosody, particularly the 'sprung rhythm' he found in **Welsh** poetry. He learned Welsh and employed some of the rules of *cynghanedd*. Among later poets influenced by Hopkins were W. H. Auden and **Dylan Thomas**.

HORNER, Arthur [Lewis] (1894–1968)
Trade unionist
Born in **Merthyr Tydfil** but subsequently associated with Maerdy (**Rhondda**), Horner was the most popular and effective of Welsh miners' leaders. His autobiography *Incorrigible Rebel* (1960) was aptly named. In 1916, his involvement in the Easter Rising in **Ireland** led to his

Plas Teg, Hope, Flintshire

imprisonment. His brand of **Communism** made him the strongest link between **Syndicalism** and the new industrial realities of the mid-20th century. Horner was president of the **South Wales Miners' Federation** (1936–44) and of the South Wales Area of the **National Union of Mineworkers** (1945–6), and general secretary of the NUM (1946–59).

HORSE RACING

Organized **horse** racing is divided into flat racing, national hunt (steeplechase and hurdle) racing, and harness racing, better known in Wales as 'trotting'.

Flat and steeplechase racing originated with the aristocracy and **gentry**. Among the earliest organized races were 'point-to-point' meetings – still popular today, albeit in more controlled circumstances – in which different hunts competed across open land. By 1833, there were internationally recognized flat races at **Cowbridge**, **Haverfordwest**, **Conwy**, **Aberystwyth**, **Brecon**, **Carmarthen**, **Knighton** and **Wrexham**. Steeplechasing at **Bangor Is-y-Coed** began in the 1850s, and races continue to be held there.

Cowbridge races attracted entries from as far away as Yorkshire. Races were scenes of heavy betting and accompanying entertainments – from exclusive balls to **pig** racing and prostitution. The popular sideshows and the general excitement of a day at the races made for a mingling of social **class**es, but the sport remained very much under the control of the gentry, who used it to demonstrate their

social status and their interest in local affairs. Keen to ingratiate themselves with their **English** – and even mainland European – peers, the Welsh gentry celebrated racing's place in a wider, elite, British culture. However, there was also pressure on the sport from religious quarters, because of the unruly and drunken behaviour that accompanied it. This led to the abandonment of the Wrexham races from 1862 until 1890.

During the 20th century, **newspaper** coverage and off-course betting ensured an interest in racing among the Welsh working class. A major flat racecourse was opened at **St Arvans** near **Chepstow** in 1926, although it remained on the margins of British racing until the opening of the first **Severn Bridge** in 1966. The Welsh Grand National, held at Chepstow between Christmas and the New Year, is a highlight of the Welsh racing calendar. In the face of diversifying leisure opportunities and the expense of keeping and breeding horses, both flat and national hunt racing were in long-term decline in Wales from the late 19th century onwards, and by the mid-20th century many of Wales's racecourses had closed.

Wales has produced a number of jockeys of international note, among them **Jack Anthony** and Hywel Davies (b.1957) of **Cardigan**, who won the Grand National on Last Suspect in 1985. Carl Llewellyn (b.1965) of **Angle** was twice winner of the Grand National (1992, 1998) on Party Politics and Earth Summit, respectively.

Welsh mountain ponies preparing to enter the ring at the Royal Welsh Show

A less familiar but unusually popular form of racing in Wales is trotting, in which horses race at a non-galloping gait while being driven by men or **women** poised on two-wheel 'sulkies'. The sport in Wales began in the late 19th century and involved Welsh cobs competing along **roads**. Towards the end of the century, the races were transferred to grass tracks, and 'standard bred' horses, imported mainly from America, replaced the native Welsh stock. Wales's oldest harness race meeting, the **Llangadog**, has been held every Easter Monday since 1884. One of the most recent ventures is the American-style Tir Prince raceway (**Kinmel Bay and Towyn**), established in 1990; its weekly races are regularly televised.

HORSES, PONIES and COBS

There were domesticated horses in **Britain** as early as the **Neolithic Age**, but there is no archaeological evidence of their use in harness until the **Bronze Age**. By the **Iron Age**, small 'Celtic' horses, forerunners of the Welsh **mountain** pony, were greatly valued, and the horse goddess Epona, source of the modern **Mari Lwyd**, was worshipped.

Welsh medieval **law** distinguishes between the riding horse, the packhorse and the workhorse. **Giraldus Cambrensis**, in the late 12th century, praised the **Powys** horses with Spanish blood. From these, crossed with Arab horses during the Crusades, are descended the Welsh cob. Shire or heavy horses, descended from the large warhorses of the **Normans**, were adapted for agricultural purposes from the 18th century onwards, replacing oxen as plough teams; cobs were also used as workhorses, especially on upland farms. The 19th century saw much development of ponies and cobs for riding and for pulling light vehicles, and there was a substantial demand for pit ponies, a few of which were still to be seen in small, private mines as late as the 1990s.

In 1911, there were 175,000 heavy horses working on Welsh farms. Horses held their ground in **agriculture** until the 1950s, when they were almost completely replaced by tractors. Today, working heavy horses are extremely rare, but they are still to be seen, trimmed and plaited, in agricultural shows and as novelty items at ploughing matches.

Horses and ponies have always been used for sport, recreation and trade, and it is in these capacities, as well as being captivating presences in the wilder landscapes, that they are conspicuous in modern Wales. **Horse racing**, trotting races, showing and show jumping, driving in harness, **hunting**, and equestrian eventing are pursuits that attract large numbers of participants and spectators. Wales is seen by many tourists as Britain's Wild West, with scores of horse- and pony-trekking centres, especially in upland and coastal areas. The breeding of pedigree animals, particularly the indigenous breeds, is a multimillion-pound industry, although over-breeding, towards the end of the 20th century, led to increasing numbers of ponies being slaughtered for **dog** food and for the horsemeat market of mainland Europe.

There are four indigenous breeds, whose pedigrees are documented by the Welsh Pony and Cob Society, the largest of Britain's ten native breed societies. Established in 1901, the society published the first volume of *The Welsh Stud Book* in 1902, containing the breeding details of four 'sections' of Welsh pony or cob, all of which may be any colour except piebald or skewbald.

WELSH MOUNTAIN PONY (SECTION A)
Bred in the mountains and wild regions for many generations, they are hardy, spirited and intelligent, with a kindly disposition that makes them popular all over the world as a child's riding pony. Their height should not exceed 12 hands (121.9 cm).

WELSH PONY (SECTION B)
Similar to the Welsh mountain pony but larger, although not exceeding 13.2 hands (137.2 cm). These were the hill farmer's main means of transport, herding **sheep**, **cattle** and wild ponies over rough and mountainous terrain. Natural jumpers, they have had to be hardy, balanced and fast to survive.

WELSH PONY OF COB TYPE (SECTION C)
A stronger counterpart of the Welsh pony, but with cob blood, these ponies are natural jumpers and excel in harness. Their height should not exceed 13.2 hands (137.2 cm).

WELSH COB (SECTION D)
Often described as 'the best ride and drive animal in the world', Welsh Cobs are known for their courage, tractability, agility and endurance. They make good hunters and perform well in all competitive sports. Most are between 14 hands (142.2 cm) and 15 hands (152.4 cm) high, but there is no height limit.

HOUSE OF AMERICA (1996) Film

A provocative and intense feature **film** set in a southern **coal**mining community, *House of America* focuses on a brother and sister (Steven Mackintosh and Lisa Palfrey) obsessed with the American writer Jack Kerouac. It tackles issues such as Welsh identity, the nation's perceived inferiority complex, its need for indigenous heroes and its 'colonization' by the United States and the **English**. The film was scripted by Ed Thomas from his own stage play and directed by Marc Evans. Matthew Rhys and Siân Phillips also appear.

HOUSING

The available evidence suggests that the dwellings of the **Palaeolithic** inhabitants of Wales were **caves** such as that at Bontnewydd (**Cefnmeiriadog**). Known remains of the **Neolithic** dwellings are few; they include a small defended enclosure at Clegyr Boia (**St David's**) and a three-roomed wooden house at **Llandygai**. Many of the **hill-forts**, which have their origins in the later **Bronze Age**, were fortified villages; they generally consisted of round houses with mud walling, reconstructed examples of which may be seen at the National History Museum (*see* **St Fagans**). In rockier districts, stone was used – as at Tre'r Ceiri (**Llanaelhaearn**), where the houses were occupied well into the **Roman** era.

The Romans built town houses with courtyards and underfloor heating (*see* **Caerwent**) and elaborate country villas, but, during the Roman occupation, the majority of the inhabitants of Wales continued to occupy essentially

Iron Age dwellings. Evidence from the immediate post-Roman centuries is slight, although excavation at **Dinas Powys** yielded evidence of houses built of dry stone rubble. Regulations in Welsh **law** concerning the control of fire indicate that there were rudimentary streets in early medieval Wales, although **Giraldus Cambrensis** maintained that the Welsh led solitary lives in woods 'in small huts made of the boughs of trees twisted together'. The **Normans** introduced castles, the homes of the **march**er-lords and their immediate followers, a practice imitated by the native Welsh rulers. Lesser lords built tower houses such as that at Scethrog (**Talybont-on-Usk**) and the wealth-ier Welsh **gentry** acquired hall houses – that owned by **Owain Glyndŵr** at Sycharth (**Llansilin**), for example. By the 15th century, half-timbered houses proliferated, especially along the **border** and in **boroughs** such as **Ruthin**, but west-ern Wales remained faithful to stone.

By the early 17th century, mansions such as Plas Teg (**Hope**) – centrally planned houses inspired by **Renaissance** ideas – were being built in Wales, but most dwellings con-tinued in the sub-medieval tradition. The **long house** – in which the cowshed and homestead are linked by internal access – was a marked feature of upland Wales. The devel-opment of Wales's vernacular **architecture**, admirably ana-lyzed by **Iorwerth C. Peate** (1940) and Peter Smith (1975), involved the partition of hall houses, the construction of additional storeys and the installation of **glass** windows. Chimneys were built, with distinct regional patterns emerg-ing in the west, the north-east and the south-east. Yet, too much should not be claimed; in William Richards's satiri-cal volume *Wallography* (1682), the houses of the Welsh poor were described as 'dung heaps shaped into cottages'. Little had changed a century later, when a commentator declared that 'the shattered hovels which half the poor … are obliged to put up with is truly affecting to a heart fraught with humanity'.

The so-called 'great rebuilding' of the years 1560 to 1640, much more marked in eastern than in western Wales, was largely a rural phenomenon. By the 18th century, house building was more a feature of urban Wales, with towns such as **Carmarthen**, **Brecon**, **Welshpool** and **Montgomery** acquiring middle-**class** houses featuring scaled-down aspects of the classical idiom.

By the end of the 18th century, Wales was in the throes of its greatest ever house-building boom – the provision of dwellings in its burgeoning industrial areas, provision com-plicated by the fact that most industrial development in Wales occurred in upland locations. The earliest industrial housing in places such as Dowlais (**Merthyr Tydfil**) was very modest indeed, but it much surpassed that built in the **slate**-quarrying areas of **Caernarfonshire** and the **lead**-mining areas of **Cardiganshire**. By the later 19th century, standards had improved and the streets of terraced houses characteristic of places such as the **Rhondda** became home to the majority of the inhabitants of Wales. Often owner-occupied, they were generally built under the leasehold sys-tem (*see* **Urban Leases**), a cause of deep concern when the 99-year leases expired. Some industries gave rise to specific forms of housing. In the **woollen industry** towns of **Llanidloes** and **Newtown**, dwellings were topped by attic workshops, and in raw industrial areas, where the majority

of the workforce consisted of unmarried young men, bar-racks rather than houses were provided.

By the early 20th century, concern about the standards of working-class housing – both urban and rural – was a central issue for social reformers. They advocated the cre-ation of model villages, an advocacy which gave rise to Oakdale (**Penmaen**) and Rhiwbina (**Cardiff**). Above all, they argued that public money should be used to provide subsidized housing for the working class, an argument accepted by the **David Lloyd George government** of 1918–22. The result was extensive council estates such as that at Ely (**Cardiff**), generally consisting of semi-detached houses. In the interwar years, despite the **depression**, some urban councils, **Newport** and **Wrexham** in particular, became enthusiastic house builders – a marked contrast with the **rural district** councils, whose scandalous neglect was roundly condemned by **Clement Davies**'s anti-**tubercu-losis** report of 1939.

Housing shortages after the **Second World War** led to the construction of pre-fabricated houses, a type of dwelling in which Newport is rich. Concern that the build-ing of semi-detached houses involved a profligate use of land led to more concentrated housing, in particular the building of flats – dwellings rare in Wales before the mid-20th century. Some innovative housing schemes, such as that at Penrhys (**Rhondda**) in particular, proved to be socially unsuccessful. The blocks of flats, astonishingly built on the wide expanse of the **Hirwaun** Moor, were blown up in 2004.

However, there were also critics of many house clear-ance schemes, such as that which led to the virtual obliter-ation of the unique community at Butetown (**Cardiff**). There were even more critics of the distortion caused to housing availability in rural areas by the demand for **sec-ond homes**.

By 1976, of Wales's 1,029,000 dwellings, 29% were rented from local authorities, a proportion which declined following the sale of council houses initiated by the **Conservative** government in the 1980s. In 2005, when Wales had 1.3 million dwellings, 74% were owner-occupied; 12% were rented from local authorities; 9% from private landlords; and 5% from registered social landlords. As the Welsh share the very British belief that everyone should seek to be a house-owner, the remarkable boom in house prices that became apparent in the early 21st century gave rise to serious concern.

HOUSTON, Donald (1923–91) Actor

Rhondda-born Donald Houston was the muscular hero of the popular, original screen version of the romance *The Blue Lagoon* (1949), and foil to **Meredith Edwards**'s fellow miner in the Ealing comedy *A Run For Your Money* (1949). He was priggish in the role as the jealous husband in Ealing's impressive *Dance Hall* (1950), and in *Room at the Top* (1959), where he played a restraining influence on Laurence Harvey's odious social climber, Joe Lambton. Possibly Houston's finest screen role – employing his remarkable stage voice to full advantage – was as the lead in D. J. Thomas's BBC television version of **Dylan Thomas**'s *Under Milk Wood* (1957). His brother, Glyn Houston (b.1926), played leads in numerous British 'B' movies, notably *Payroll*

(1960) and *Solo for Sparrow* (1962), and was typically impressive in the two Alan Clayton/Robert Pugh **dramas** for HTV, *Ballroom* (1988) and *Better Days* (1988).

HOW GREEN WAS MY VALLEY (1941) Film

This **film**, which was made by Twentieth Century Fox and won five Oscars, is based on Richard Llewellyn's novel of the same name (*see* **Richard Herbert Vivian Lloyd**). It focuses on the Morgan family, who live in a southern **coal**-field community; but its director John Ford seemed more concerned with exploring potent myths and his own family background than in establishing a reliable reflection of the society under consideration. As a result, the film is bereft of political content and it over-romanticizes the miners.

There is only one Welshman in a significant role, namely Rhys Williams as Dai Bando. Other leading roles are played by the Englishman Roddy McDowall, the Canadian Walter Pigeon and the Scotsman Donald Crisp; the remainder of the cast are mainly **Irish** or Irish-Americans. Although superbly shot by the Academy Award winner Arthur Miller, and with a script by Philip Dunne that is not without merit, the film is laden with elements that betray a woeful ignorance of Wales – such as the siting of a coalmine on top of a **mountain**. The film has, nevertheless, entertained millions – in **North America**, **England** and Wales itself – who have swallowed its sentimental portrayal of the 'Welsh' miners.

HOWARD-JONES, Ray (original first name, Rosemary) (1903–96) Artist

Although Berkshire-born, Rosemary Howard-Jones felt herself to be Welsh. She attended schools in **Penarth** and **London**, before studying fine art at the Slade. She was involved with **archaeology**, theatre, and medical and documentary drawing; as a war artist, she was attached to the Royal Navy. She travelled widely and lived in remote locations, including Skomer (*see* **Islands**), working in mosaics, murals, gouache and watercolour. Her work reflects her enthusiasm for the idea of **Cel**tic spirituality, which she believed resided on the islands and headlands of Wales.

HOWELL, David (Llawdden; 1831–1903) Cleric

Born of **Nonconformist** stock in **Llangan**, **Glamorgan**, Howell was ordained an **Anglican** clergyman in 1855. His preaching gifts were much used during the 1859 **revival**. His outstanding work at **Cardiff** (1864–75) and **Wrexham** (1875–91) was quoted as evidence of the Anglican Church's revival, but his real significance lay in his evangelical witness, his concern for an indigenous Welsh Church, and his desire for religious unity. Howell thus came into conflict with his bishop, **A. G. Edwards**, who managed to marginalize his impact upon the Anglican Church, although he ended his days as dean of **St David's**. He wrote poetry under the pseudonym of 'Llawdden'.

Donald Houston (left), with Alan Ladd, in *The Red Beret* (1953)

Cledwyn Hughes when MP for Anglesey

HOWELL, James (*c.*1593–1666) Writer

Born at **Abernant** (**Carmarthenshire**), and educated at **Oxford**, from 1616 Howell spent four years travelling on the European mainland on behalf of Sir Robert **Mansel**'s **glass**-making company. Employed by Charles I's **government**, perhaps as a spy, he was imprisoned in the Fleet from 1642 to 1650. At the Restoration, he was appointed Historiographer Royal, a post specially created for him. He published more than 40 books on historical and political topics and was perhaps the first Welshman to be a professional writer in the modern sense.

HOWELL, James (1835–1909) Retailer

The man behind one of Wales's best-known brand names, James Howell was born in Cwmcath, near **Fishguard**, the son of a blacksmith and farmer. He worked for various drapers before founding in **Cardiff** (1865) what was to become one of Britain's biggest department stores. It is now owned by the House of Fraser.

Howell also founded the Park Hall and Hotel, and was prominent in civic life, helping to bring the Salesbury collection of Welsh books to Cardiff; he backed the city's bids to house the **National Museum** and **National Library**. He owned several farms, including a stud farm where he bred hackney **horses**.

HOWELLS, Geraint [Wyn] (1925–2004) Politician

Born at Ponterwyd (**Blaenrheidol**), Howells became a wealthy **sheep** farmer while developing a political career in which the **economy** and culture of rural Wales, the **Welsh language** and **devolution** were consistent priorities. He was **Liberal** (**Liberal Democrat** from 1988) MP for **Ceredigion** (Ceredigion and **Pembroke** North from 1983)

from 1974 until 1992, when he lost the seat to Cynog Dafis standing for **Plaid [Genedlaethol] Cymru** and the Green Party. Leader of the Welsh Liberals from 1979 to 1988, in 1992 he was created a life peer as Baron Geraint of Ponterwyd. The deputy speaker of the House of Lords (1994–9), Howells often seemed to be the reincarnation of a late 19th-century Welsh rural **radical**, and represented, as Bruce Anderson commented, 'an archetypal Welsh mixture of charm and cunning'. When Liberal spokesman for **agriculture**, he was asked by a prosperous Suffolk farmer: 'What is the Liberal policy on the burning of stubble?', to which he replied: 'I don't know; in rural Wales, we only burn **second homes**.'

HOWELLS, Jack (1913–90) Film-maker

Jack Howells, of Abertyswg (**Rhymney**), was a schoolteacher before turning to the world of **film** and becoming an accomplished editor and director. He is best known for his impressionistic, lyrical documentaries, but he also wrote screenplays for feature films, such as *Front Page Story* (1953), and narration for documentaries, including *Elstree Story* (1952). With Peter Baylis and the Pathé company, he made *The Peaceful Years* (1947) and *Scrapbook for 1933* (1950). His notable television documentaries include *Dylan Thomas* (TWW/BBC, 1962) and *Nye!* (TWW, 1965). *Dylan Thomas*, the only Welsh film to have won an Oscar (best short documentary, 1963), features **Richard Burton** as narrator, visiting **Dylan Thomas**'s haunts.

HOYLE, W[illiam] Evans (1855–1926) Museum director

Born in Manchester, and educated at Manchester, **Oxford** and **London**, this researcher in invertebrates became director of the Manchester Museum (1899–1909) and was the first director of the **National Museum [of] Wales** (1908–24). He was influential in the planning of the new building at **Cathays Park**.

HUET, Thomas (d.1591) Translator

A native of **Breconshire**, Huet was educated at **Oxford** and held a number of livings. He adopted Protestantism and survived Mary I's religious policies. In 1560, he was appointed precentor of **St David's** and, in 1561, was elected canon of the cathedral. He is best known for translating – in a style which reflected the dialect of south-west Wales – the Book of Revelation in the first **Welsh** New Testament (1567).

HUGH OF AVRANCHES, earl of Chester (Hugh the Fat; d.1101) Marcher-lord

Hugh was granted the earldom of Chester by William I in the 1070s. He, and Robert of **Rhuddlan**, led the **Norman** advance into north Wales in the late 11th century. His descendants held the county palatine of Chester until 1237, when it fell to the English crown – a fact which greatly facilitated the **Edwardian conquest**.

HUGHES, [Emyr] Alun Moelwyn (1905–78) Chemist

A son of the manse, and of a notable Welsh **hymn**ologist, **Cardigan**-born Hughes was educated at **Liverpool** and

Oxford, before being appointed to a post at **Cambridge**. He was a brilliant theoretical chemist who delighted in abstruse topics and **Welsh** poetry. He was as much in his element in the university's Welsh society, Cymdeithas y Mabinogi, as he was around the dining tables of the Cambridge colleges.

HUGHES, Annie Harriet (Gwyneth Vaughan; 1852–1910) Novelist

A miller's daughter from **Talsarnau**, Gwyneth Vaughan became famous throughout Wales as a novelist, public speaker, journalist, nationalist and administrator for the **temperance movement** and the **Liberal Party**. Her chief works are the novels *O Gorlannau y Defaid* (1905) and *Plant y Gorthrwm* (1908).

HUGHES, Arwel (1909–88) Musician

The son of a **coal**miner, Hughes was born at **Rhosllanerchrugog**, and educated at the Royal College of Music, **London** where he studied with Vaughan Williams. In 1935, he joined the **music** department at BBC Wales (*see* **Broadcasting**), and was its head from 1965 until his retirement in 1971. He was closely associated with **Welsh National Opera**, for whom he conducted many performances, as well as composing two operas, *Menna* (performed in 1954) and *Serch yw'r Doctor* (performed in 1960 with a libretto by **Saunders Lewis**). He was a skilful composer with a particular facility for choral works with orchestra, a talent best demonstrated in his oratorios *Dewi Sant* (1950) and *Pantycelyn* (1963). Perhaps his most famous composition is the **hymn 'Tydi a roddaist'** (1938), with words by **T. Rowland Hughes**. His son is the conductor Owain Arwel Hughes.

HUGHES, Cledwyn (Lord Cledwyn of Penrhos; 1916–2001) Politician

A native of **Holyhead** and a son of the manse, Hughes graduated at **Aberystwyth** in 1937, qualified as a solicitor in 1940, served in the RAF during the **Second World War** and worked as a solicitor in **Anglesey** from 1946. After standing twice as the **Labour Party** candidate against Lady **Megan Lloyd George** in 1945 and 1950, he captured Anglesey in 1951, holding the seat until his retirement in 1979.

A fervent **devolution**ist, Hughes was the second **secretary of state for Wales** (1966–8), pressing successfully to extend the powers and authority of the **Welsh Office**. He was minister of **agriculture** (1968–70) and chairman of the Labour Party (1974–9). Following his retirement from the Commons, he became Lord Cledwyn of Penrhos and was opposition leader in the Lords (1982–92). He was an active president of the University College of Wales, Aberystwyth (1975–85; *see* **University of Wales, Aberystwyth**) and subsequently pro-chancellor of the **University of Wales** (1985–94). An erudite, cultured, patriotic Welshman, he was passionately supportive of the National **Eisteddfod**.

HUGHES, Cledwyn (1920–78) Writer

Born in **Llansantffraid**, he abandoned pharmacy in 1947 in order to concentrate on writing at his home in **Arthog**. He wrote 27 books, including the distinguished novel *Civil Strangers* (1949), a sensitive portrayal of an adolescence overshadowed by a ruthless headmaster. He also wrote useful books about the topography of Wales, including *A Wanderer in North Wales* (1949) and *Portrait of Snowdonia* (1967).

HUGHES, David (1820–1904) Builder

Originally from **Anglesey**, Hughes became one of the most prosperous of the Welsh builders on Merseyside, building extensively in Anfield and Bootle, and expanding into warehousing and other ventures. A prominent **Calvinistic Methodist**, he built large houses for himself in **Liverpool**, where he spent the winter, and at Wylfa (**Cylch-y-Garn**). As a teetotaller, he refused to allow public houses to be established in the streets he developed. It was a refusal which proved highly profitable, for it ensured that his sober tenants paid the rent promptly.

HUGHES, David [Edward] (1831–1900) Scientist and inventor

Born into a family of **Merioneth** musicians, Hughes was renowned as a **harp**ist when only six years old. When he was ten, the family emigrated to perform for Welsh communities in **North America**. He is best known as the inventor of the teleprinter (1855), which made him rich and famous, and of the microphone (1878). In 1875, he settled in **London**, but retained his American citizenship.

Hughes's most important achievement was in 1879 when he gave a practical demonstration of electromagnetic radiation, as proposed theoretically by J. C. Maxwell. His transmission of radio signals from one end of Great

David Edward Hughes

Portland Street to the other was the first demonstration of electromagnetic waves, eight years before Heinrich Hertz's acclaimed discovery. It predated Marconi's radio transmission by some 20 years (*see* **Physical Sciences**). However, the panel of referees appointed by the Royal Society, which included **W. H. Preece**, dismissed his results as 'Faraday induction', electing him a fellow as partial consolation. Ironically, Hughes went on to do pioneering work on the use of Faraday induction in the detection of metals. The failure to recognize Hughes's work on electromagnetic radiation remains a major scientific injustice.

HUGHES, E[dward] D[avid] (1906–63) Chemist
The youngest son of a quarryman-farmer from **Criccieth**, E. D. Hughes, FRS, played a pioneering role in developing an explanatory theory for organic reactions in terms of the electronic structure of atoms and molecules. Most of this research was carried out at University College, **London**, but he returned to Wales as head of the **chemistry** department at **Bangor** (1943–8). He and his wife bred and raced greyhounds, reflecting his boyhood love of animals.

HUGHES, Edward (1856–1925) Trade unionist
Born in **Flintshire**, he worked in a number of local collieries and also in the Durham **coal**field. He returned to Wales in 1887 and in 1897 became general secretary of the **North Wales Miners' Association**, a position he held for 27 years. On his death, his son Hugh succeeded him as agent.

John Hughes (1814–99), the industrialist who founded Hughesovka (later Donets'k) in Ukraine

HUGHES, Elizabeth Phillips (1850–1925)
Educationist
Born a doctor's daughter in **Carmarthen**, Elizabeth Phillips Hughes was educated at Cheltenham and at **Cambridge**. In 1885, she became the first headmistress of the Cambridge Training College for **women** teachers. The only woman on the committee that drew up the charter of the **University of Wales**, she campaigned assiduously to promote Welsh women's **education**, publishing *The Education of Welsh Women* (1887) and *The Education of a Nation* (1919).

HUGHES, Ellen (Elen Engan; 1862–1927) Writer
Ellen Hughes of **Llanengan** contributed regularly to the **periodicals** *Y Gymraes* and *Y Frythones*, expressing radical ideas about **women**'s role in society. As an officer of the South Wales Women's **Temperance** Union, she constantly encouraged other women to write. Two volumes of her essays, stories and poems were published: *Sibrwd yr Awel* (1887) and *Murmur y Gragen* (1907).

HUGHES, Gareth (1894–1965) Actor
Although the diminutive **Llanelli**-born Gareth Hughes topped and tailed his screen career with stage appearances, he made over 30 Hollywood **films** between 1918 and 1932. He played a college boy who infects his girlfriend with VD in *And The Children Pay* (1918), but was frequently cast as a youthful charmer or a degenerate reformed by social or peer pressure. He earned superb notices in the long-lost *Sentimental Tommy* (1921), and his performance in *The Chorus Girl's Romance* (1925) earned him a long-term Metro contract. Hughes later became a pastor to the Paiute Indians in Nevada.

HUGHES, Griffith (1707–?60) Naturalist
Tywyn-born Griffith Hughes became clergyman to Welsh settlers in **Pennsylvania**, but he was considered uninspiring in his sermons. Responsible for one of the first **Welsh-language** books to be published in **North America**, he moved to Barbados in 1736, where he developed an interest in natural history. His *Natural History of the Island of Barbados* was published in 1750. Although elected FRS in 1747, defects in his **science** were remarked upon by some of his fellow naturalists.

HUGHES, Hugh (1790–1863) Artist
As the portraitist of central figures in the religious enthusiasms of 19th-century Wales, Hugh Hughes has a seminal position in Welsh visual culture. He was born into a farming family at Pwll-y-Gwichiad, **Llandudno**, and moved with his family to **Liverpool**, where he learned wood engraving and oil **painting**.

In 1819–21 he toured Wales making sketches, and at the family home at Meddiant, **Llansanffraid Glan Conwy**, he engraved the 60 plates of his best-known work, *The Beauties of Cambria* (1821). In **Carmarthen** in the 1820s, he published books and magazines, and married Sarah, the daughter of **David Charles**. While living in **London**, Hughes fell foul of **John Elias** for signing a petition in favour of **Roman Catholic** emancipation; Elias's insistence that the petitioners be expelled turned Hughes into a **radical** campaigner against the **Calvinistic Methodist** authorities.

He subsequently lived in **Caernarfon**, Chester, **Barmouth**, **Aberystwyth** and Malvern, where he died. Hughes produced landscapes, portraits, illustrations and political and religious cartoons. He was an idealist who emphasized the moral, material and intellectual self-improvement attainable through faith and study.

HUGHES, Hugh Price (1840–1902) Minister

Born in **Carmarthen**, Hughes was educated in **London** and ministered to numerous **Wesleyan** congregations before settling in London in 1884. He was moved by the plight of the working **class** and their estrangement from mainstream Christianity. His desire to combine a sense of individual conversion with social concern led him to establish the West London Mission in 1886. Editor of the *Methodist Times*, he was elected president of the Wesleyan Conference in 1898. He is best remembered as a major spokesperson for the **Nonconformist** conscience. His comments about Charles Stewart Parnell's adultery with Kitty O'Shea proved to be damagingly influential.

HUGHES, John (1814–99) Industrialist

Having trained as an engineer at the Cyfarthfa **iron**works in his native **Merthyr Tydfil**, Hughes acquired an international reputation for marine **engineering** and armaments production. Invited by the tsar's **government** to help develop Russia's **railways** and heavy industry, Hughes moved to Ukraine in 1870. The steelworks he subsequently established at Hughesovka (Yuzovka) became the basis of the great Don basin industrial district. Yuzovka was first renamed Stalino and then Donets'k.

HUGHES, John Ceiriog (Ceiriog; 1832–87) Poet

The author of the most celebrated lyrics of 19th-century Wales was born in Llanarmon Dyffryn Ceiriog (**Ceiriog Ucha**). While living in Manchester (1849–65), he worked as a shopkeeper and **railway** clerk; he returned to Wales in 1868, initially as stationmaster at **Llanidloes** and subsequently, from 1871, as supervisor of the newly opened railway linking **Caersws** with the **lead** mines at Fan (**Llanidloes Without**).

Ceiriog's **eisteddfod** poems, 'Myfanwy Fychan' (1858), a love-poem, and 'Alun Mabon' (1861), a pastoral, made him the pre-eminent popular national poet – over 20,000 copies of his *Oriau'r Hwyr* (1860) were sold. There followed *Oriau'r Bore* (1862), *Cant o Ganeuon* (1863), *Y Bardd a'r Cerddor* (1864), *Oriau Eraill* (1868), *Oriau'r Haf* (1876) and, posthumously, *Yr Oriau Olaf* (1888). He also composed **Welsh** words for some 50 traditional airs in **Brinley Richards's** famous collection, *The Songs of Wales* (1873). Ceiriog arose as a poet when the nation was concerned to repair the damage done to its character by the 1847 **Education** Report (*see* **Treason of the Blue Books**); he was celebrated for boosting his compatriots' sense of their worth as both native Welsh people and British subjects. The appeal of his lyrical, reassuring muse lives on in poems such as 'Cân yr Aradr Goch', 'Nant y Mynydd' and 'Aros a Mynd'.

HUGHES, R[ichard] S[amuel] (1855–93) Musician

One of Wales's first professional musicians of the Victorian era, Hughes travelled frequently to **London** from his home

John Ceiriog Hughes

in **Aberystwyth** to perform and to accompany, before being appointed organist of Bethesda chapel, **Bethesda**. He composed some 60 songs, including favourites such as 'Elen Fwyn' and 'Bwthyn bach melyn fy nhad', which are characteristic of both his style and the period.

HUGHES, Richard (Dic Huws; c.1565–1619) Poet

Born at Cefn Llanfair, **Llanbedrog**, to a **gentry** family of bardic patrons, Hughes became footman to Elizabeth I in 1599 and remained in the service of James I until his death. He was buried in Llanbedrog. Several racy *englynion* are attributed to him, but his greatest achievement is his lyrical love poetry in free metres.

HUGHES, Richard (1900–76) Writer

Although born in Surrey, Richard Hughes regarded himself as a Welshman and spent the last decades of his life in **Talsarnau** (1946–76). He wrote his best play, *A Comedy of Good and Evil* (1924), for the Portmadoc Players, the company he founded; it is set in Cylfant, an imaginary village in **Snowdonia**. *Danger* (1924), the first play ever to be broadcast on the radio, takes place in a **coal**mine. His most famous work is the novel *A High Wind in Jamaica* (1929), which was made into a successful **film** and is a modern classic. Of his projected magnum opus, *The Human Predicament*, only two parts were published – *The Fox in the Attic* (1961) and *The Wooden Shepherdess* (1973); but in their broad scope they are among the finest achievements of any Welsh writer in **English**.

HUGHES, Stephen (1622–88) Minister, translator, editor and publisher

As vicar of **Meidrim**, **Carmarthen**-born Hughes preached the gospel so tirelessly in his native **county** that he became known as 'The Apostle of **Carmarthenshire**'. Following the Stuart Restoration (1660), he was ejected from his living but avoided the wrath of the **law** by becoming an occasional conformist. Around 1665, he married an affluent woman from **Swansea**, where he settled and began to further the charitable work of the **Welsh Trust** and to publish and disseminate **Welsh** translations of works by **Puritan** authors. He published editions of the catchy poems of **Rhys Prichard** in 1658, 1659 and 1672, and was responsible for giving the 1681 edition the celebrated title *Canwyll y Cymru* (The Candle of the Welsh). He was responsible for the 1678 edition of the Welsh **Bible**, 8000 copies of which were distributed. The fact that Swansea had more Dissenters (*see* **Nonconformists and Dissenters**) than the whole of the **diocese** of **Bangor** speaks volumes for his influence during the years of the persecution of those who refused to conform to the **Anglican** Church.

HUGHES, T[homas] Mc[Kenny] (1832–1917)
Geologist

Although McKenny Hughes, FRS, a native of **Aberystwyth**, carried out considerable research in Wales, he was best known as the man who built up the **Cambridge** department of **geology** into the first of the large research units in **Britain**, gathering around him a staff of distinction. He was inevitably involved, although less effectively, in defending the work of his predecessor, Adam Sedgwick, during the acrimonious Cambrian–Silurian controversy.

Llewelyn Humphreys: the gangster 'Murray the Hump'

HUGHES, T[homas] Rowland (1903–49)
Writer and broadcaster

A quarryman's son from **Llanberis**, Hughes based several of his novels on his memories of that **slate**-quarrying area. After **education** at **Bangor** and **Oxford**, he had a succession of teaching posts. In 1935, he became a radio producer in **Cardiff**, where he won much acclaim. Worsening multiple sclerosis led him to abandon regular employment and turn to writing novels, five of them appearing in five consecutive years: *O Law i Law* (1943); *William Jones* (1944), whose action moves from the slate-quarrying north to the **coal**mining south; *Yr Ogof* (1945), which tells the story of Joseph of Arimathea; *Chwalfa* (1946), his greatest novel, about the infamous **Penrhyn lockouts**; and *Y Cychwyn* (1947), about a quarryman who became a minister. In their fusion of the sad and the humorous, these novels have been among the most popular of the 20th century. The author had already gained recognition as a poet before he turned to fiction, winning the National **Eisteddfod** chair in 1937 and 1940; his *Cân neu Ddwy* (1948), includes such popular poems as 'Tydi a Roddaist', 'Harddwch' and 'Ras'.

HUMPHREY, John (1819–88) Architect

Born at Morriston (**Swansea**), the son of a collier, Humphrey was self-taught, starting as carpenter and joiner before progressing to builder; he never referred to himself as an architect. Nevertheless, he was responsible for numerous **Congregational** chapels, mainly around Swansea and **Llanelli**, but also in **Cardiganshire** and at **Llanidloes**, as well as for schools in Swansea. His most imaginative chapel designs incorporated massive, linked Italianate arches on their main façades, as in the imposing Tabernacl (1873) in Morriston, the so-called 'cathedral of Welsh Nonconformity' (*see* **Nonconformists**).

HUMPHREYS, E[dward] Morgan (1882–1955)
Editor and author

One of the leading figures of the **Welsh-language** press in the first quarter of the 20th century, Humphreys was born in **Dyffryn Ardudwy**. After an apprenticeship as a reporter with the *Barmouth Advertiser* and employment on the *Liverpool Courier* and the *North Wales Observer*, he was editor of *Y Genedl Gymreig* at **Caernarfon** for nearly 20 years (1908–14 and 1918–30). He edited *Cymru* and *Y Goleuad* for brief periods. He contributed columns to the *Liverpool Daily Post* and the *Manchester Guardian*, and was well known as a broadcaster. He was also a pioneer of the Welsh-language mystery novel, in books such as *Dirgelwch Gallt y Ffrwd* (1938).

HUMPHREYS, Llewelyn Morris or Murray (1899–1965) Gangster

Born in Chicago to **Welsh**-speaking parents from **Carno**, Humphreys became the henchman of Al Capone, and was noted for his business acumen and legal expertise. With the end of prohibition on alcohol, he moved into Las Vegas gambling, the Hollywood **film** industry and American presidential politics, laundering his illegal gains by investing them in legitimate enterprises.

Known as 'The Camel' and 'Murray the Hump', he was believed to have been behind the St Valentine's Day massacre, in which rival gangsters were murdered in a garage. Arrested only once and never brought to justice, Humphreys was the subject of a biography by **John Morgan**, *No Gangster More Proud* (1985). A distant relative of Humphreys is the politician Dafydd Wigley.

HUNDLETON, Pembrokeshire
(3074 ha; 780 inhabitants)

Located immediately west of **Pembroke**, the **community** contains the villages of Hundleton, Maiden Wells, Pwllcrochan and Rhoscrowther. The area is dominated by the Texaco **oil** refinery, the building of which obliterated much of Rhoscrowther. The jetties built to serve it can accommodate vessels of up to 280,000 tonnes. When completed in 1972, Pembroke Power Station was the largest oil-fuelled power station in Europe; it was demolished in 2000.

There is a remarkable group of **Bronze Age** barrows near Lightapipe Farm. St Mary's church, Pwllcrochan, which has some 14th-century features, was converted into a private house in 1994.

Easington is a fine 14th-century tower house. Orielton House (1810) was the home of the Owen family, whose members sat in 76 parliaments; John Owen (1776–1861) was an MP for 51 years. In 1954, Orielton became the home of the naturalist **R. M. Lockley**; his study of **rabbit** life on the estate is said to have inspired Richard Adams's *Watership Down* (1972).

HUNDRED YEARS WAR, The (1337–1453)

A protracted war between **England** and France, it arose from a number of associated matters: French claims to sovereignty over English territories in France; French fears of English commercial power in Flanders; and English claims to the French crown through Isabella, daughter of Philip IV and mother of Edward III.

The first phase of the war, which included the English victories at Crécy (1346) and Poitiers (1356), ended with the Treaty of Bretigny (1360) by which Edward III abandoned his claim to the French throne and gained Calais, Ponthieu and Gascony. Conflict was rekindled in 1369, and in the 1370s, **Owain Lawgoch**, heir to the house of **Gwynedd**, proved a doughty enemy of England. In 1415, Henry V revived the English claim to the French throne, invaded Normandy and won the battle of Agincourt, at which the Welsh **longbow**men excelled themselves. In 1420, Henry was recognized as heir to the kingdom of France, but by 1453 the campaigns initiated by Joan of Arc led to the driving out of English forces from the whole of France, apart from Calais.

The wars had a profound effect upon Wales, offering employment to Welsh mercenaries, creating heroes such as Sir Hywel y Fwyall (**Hywel ap Gruffudd**) and **Matthew Gough**, providing **Owain Glyndŵr** with the opportunity to ally with the French king, and giving rise to large bodies of footloose soldiers. They also destabilized the **Lancaster** dynasty, a major factor in causing the **Wars of the Roses**, in which Wales played a prominent role.

HUNDREDS

Following the **Acts of 'Union'**, Wales was divided into 90 hundreds – a hundred being a unit which had its origins in the Old English Kingdom, and probably originally represented a territory inhabited by a hundred families. The hundred shared many of the characteristics of the Welsh *cantref*, whose boundaries it often inherited. Resident justices of the peace presided over the hundred's petty sessions, and the high constable had control over the hundred's skeleton **police** force. They were virtually obsolete by the late 19th century, but some of the **rural districts** established in 1894 inherited their boundaries.

HUNGER MARCHES

The economic **depression** of the interwar years reduced what were previously well-paid workers to abject poverty through unemployment and the operation of the **means test**. Of the many responses to mass unemployment, the hunger marches were the best reported and are considered to be the most poignant symbols of a whole era. By comparison, many larger demonstrations held in Wales were under-reported. The hunger marches were a brilliant propaganda coup for the **National Unemployed Workers' Movement**, a **Communist**-front organization. The NUWM organized marches from 1921 onwards and the procession of marchers through the southern **counties** of **England** and into central **London** between 1927 and 1936 made a considerable impact. In general, marches were boycotted by the TUC and the **Labour Party**; in Wales, however, where the Communist Party had provided firm leadership in numerous local campaigns, the march of 1936 was supported by many sections of the Labour movement.

HUNTING

Hunting with hounds, a traditional pastime combining country sport with game and vermin control, has been a popular activity in Wales throughout recorded history. The Life of **Illtud** (12th century) records how a stag being chased by the hounds of the king Meirchion Wyllt took refuge in the **saint's** cell. The first branch of the Mabinogi (*see* **Mabinogion, The**) opens with the story of **Pwyll, Pendefig Dyfed**, hunting a stag with hounds; the savage boar hunt of the **Twrch Trwyth** forms the central theme of the tale of 'Culhwch and Olwen'; and hunting imagery and allusions occur in 'Peredur' and other tales. The story of St **Melangell** involves the hunting of **hares**. **Dafydd ap Gwilym**, in the 14th century, composed poems on the **fox** and the roebuck.

The rules, rituals and etiquette of hunting in medieval Wales are laid out in detail in contemporary manuscripts, especially in the **Laws** of Court attributed to **Hywel Dda**. Details include the status, privileges and perquisites of the chief huntsman as a court official, the types and values of the hounds (greyhounds and staghounds), and the value of the principal quarry, the red **deer** stag. Hunting was truly the sport of kings.

The **Normans** established parks (*see* **Gardens, Parks and Orchards**) where red and fallow deer were kept, and selected animals could be coursed by a few hounds within the confines of the park. They also set aside large tracts for hunting, such as **Radnor Forest**. The continuing fascination with hunting ritual is seen in the 16th-century **Welsh** compilation *Y Naw Helwriaeth* (The Nine Huntings), which incorporates material from the Welsh lawbooks and from **French** and **English** hunting manuals, as well as

A meet at Lampeter of the Neuadd Fawr foxhounds on Boxing Day, 1908

a small amount which is unique. However, from the 16th century onwards, as numbers of the main game animals declined – sometimes to the point of extinction – the medieval hunting rituals associated chiefly with stag hunting fell into disuse. Apart from park deer, huntsmen increasingly turned for their sport to the still abundant lesser game – fox, hare and **otter** – and hunting came to be less a royal pastime and more enjoyed by a wider cross section of society. Formal and informal hunts, and private and subscription packs of hounds, co-existed. Some hunts were small, poorly financed and short-lived; although changes of hunt name, amalgamations and dissolutions were frequent by the 20th century, several famous foxhound packs such as the Wynnstay, the Tivyside and the Ynysfor could boast a continuous recorded history extending back well over 200 years.

From the earliest times, hunting has been enjoyed as a convivial pursuit. Prints and **paintings** of hounds, **horses** and hunting scenes were an enormously popular artistic genre. The 19th century saw the appearance of an extensive hunting **literature**, including many hunting songs and some rather rambling poetry, in both Welsh and English. These pieces were uproariously received at hunt balls, dinners and other festive gatherings. The songs extol not only the virtues of the hounds, the countryside that they hunted and the personalities involved, but also the quarry – in Wales the fox and the hare, but in **Patagonia** the *huanaco* and the ostrich.

In 1900, there were nearly 40 formally organized hunts in Wales (mainly foxhounds, but also harriers and otter hounds), each hunt with its own locality and distinctive uniform. By 2000, however, changes in land ownership, agricultural practices, and political and social attitudes had gradually conspired to put hunting on the defensive. In 2005, fox hunting with **dogs** in Wales and **England** was declared illegal.

HUNTING THE WREN

A folk custom associated with Epiphany (6 January). A wren would be caught and its body carried from door to door in an ornamented bier and shown to the inhabitants in return for money or drink. This 'wren house' was carried by four men groaning, as if carrying a heavy burden. In verses sung at the door, they would refer to the wren, the smallest of birds, as the king. The custom is reminiscent of turning the world upside-down and is associated with the Saturnalia of ancient Rome. The custom flourished in **Pembrokeshire**, but folk songs referring to it, such as 'The King' and 'The Cutty Wren', are also found in other **counties**.

HUWS, Richard [Llywelyn] (1902–80) Artist

From his early days in **Anglesey** – at Penysarn (**Llaneilian**) and later at **Llangoed** – Huws exhibited the creative resourcefulness that distinguished all his subsequent work. Training as a naval architect, he discovered a talent for caricature, which paid his way around Europe and enabled him to study art in Vienna, where he was radicalized on experiencing the rise of Nazism. He lived in Paris, **London** and Anglesey, lectured in **architecture** at **Liverpool**, and designed **sculpture** for the Festival of **Britain**. His cartoons appeared in such publications as the *Listener*, the *Radio Times*, *Y Ddraig Goch* and *Heddiw*. An early member of **Plaid [Genedlaethol] Cymru**, he designed the party's familiar 'Triban' symbol. His wife Edrica (b.Tyrwhitt; 1907–99) was a noted poet and **textile** artist. Their son Daniel Huws is the leading authority on Welsh medieval manuscripts and an able **English-language** poet.

HWYL (lit. 'mood' or 'humour')

When used in connection with the preaching of **Nonconformists** during the 19th and early 20th centuries, the word *hwyl* denotes the dramatic and sometimes ecstatic climax of a sermon (*see* **Preachers and Sermons**). Both rhythmic and musical in tone, it signified the divine afflatus or the spirit's anointing of the message.

HYDDGEN, Battle of

In the summer of 1401, **Owain Glyndŵr** won a significant victory at Hyddgen (*see* **Cadfarch**) on the slopes of **Pumlumon** against a numerically superior force. The victory greatly enhanced Owain's prestige in Wales, as well as opening the way to the south.

HYDER Company

Hyder was formed in 1996, following Welsh Water's post-privatization acquisition of the SWALEC electricity company. With the addition of regional gas supply and distribution to its utility portfolio, as well as running non-regulated, worldwide operations that included **engineering** consulting, construction and management activities, the **Cardiff**-based group became Wales's largest indigenous company.

Hailed as a success story, at its peak Hyder – whose name in **Welsh** means 'confidence' – employed over 9000 people, including 1500 overseas, and had a reported turnover in excess of £1 billion. Hyder began to experience financial difficulties as the imposition of the **government**'s windfall tax, and substantial price cuts from two regulatory reviews, were accompanied by a large capital investment programme to meet statutory environmental requirements and a substantial debt burden mainly relating to the SWALEC acquisition.

Following some strategic sell-offs, Hyder was eventually taken over by the American-owned Western Power Distribution company in 2000. The new owners retained the SWALEC electricity distribution business for integration with their own operations in the south-west of **England**, and sold the Welsh Water assets to Glas Cymru. Operating as a debt-financed, not-for-profit company, Glas Cymru is limited by guarantee and owned by members, with operations, maintenance and customer services delegated to third parties.

HYMNS

During the second half of the 19th century, the hymn became an essential part of the **Land of Song** image which Wales was projecting to the world. In whatsoever country or continent the Welsh gathered, the singing of hymns became a collective expression of their identity as a people. Indeed, the *Cymanfa Ganu* (singing festival) is the chief festival of those people in **North America** who are of Welsh descent.

By the end of the 19th century, hymns had become central to the popular culture of a large proportion of the inhabitants of Wales; in 1896 it was estimated that some 12% of them had attended a *cymanfa ganu* over the previous twelve months. (For the musical evolution of the hymn, *see* **Music**).

Among the first examples of Welsh hymns are those in *Gwassanaeth Meir*, a translation of *Officium Parvum Beatae Mariae Virginis* attributed to Dafydd Ddu o Hiraddug (fl. 14th century). In the wake of the **Protestant Reformation**, there were several efforts to produce **Welsh-language** metrical versions of the psalms, with **Edmwnd Prys**'s *Salmau Cân*

(1621) pre-eminent among them. Nevertheless, the true beginnings of the Welsh hymn tradition are associated with the 18th-century **Methodist Revival**. The tradition became rooted first in the south as is evident from the work of **Morgan Rhys**, Dafydd William (1720/21–94), **Dafydd Jones** of Caeo, and, above all, that of **William Williams** (1717–91) of Pantycelyn. By the first half of the 19th century, the heartland of the hymn-writing tradition had moved north, as can be seen from the hymns of **Edward Jones** of Maes-y-plwm (1762–1836), Pedr Fardd (Peter Jones; 1775–1845) and Robert ap Gwilym Ddu (**Robert Williams**; 1766–1850). That shift gave substance to **W. J. Gruffydd**'s thesis that, in the context of Welsh culture, it is the south which initiates, and it is the north that preserves.

In literary terms, the golden age of the hymn was the era up to *c.*1850. Many Welsh hymns – those of William Williams and **Ann Griffiths** in particular, but also some hymns of a later period (the strongly-imaged hymn of Ehedydd Iâl (**William Jones**; 1815–99), for example) – are firmly part of the Welsh literary canon. With the development in the second half of the 19th century of congregational music making, hymns became a social phenomenon significant beyond the walls of places of worship. Hymn singing was central to the religious **revival** of 1904–5, an event which inspired hymnwriters such as J. T. Job (1867–1938), Dyfed (Evan Rees; 1850–1923) and J. J. Williams (1869–1954). The enthusiasm of the revival led to the composition of the tune '**Cwm Rhondda**', a tune which did much to promote the concept of the Land of Song, both within and outside Wales.

The singing of Welsh hymns remained an important cultural phenomenon at least until the mid-20th century. Welsh-speaking students at **Bangor** spent their Saturday mornings singing hymns, a practice which lasted until the early 1960s. It became a feature of jubilation on the terraces of **rugby** fields, while also providing sustenance in

A Richard Huws cartoon in which Wales is saying to Ireland: 'After you with the scissors'

Max Boyce's 'Hymns and Arias' remains an iconic song

situations of crisis and suffering. As Robert Graves noted in *Goodbye to All That* (1929), Welsh soldiers during the **First World War** 'always sang [hymns] when they were a bit frightened and pretending that they were not; it kept them steady'. During the interwar **depression**, hymn-singing by unemployed Welsh miners was heard on the streets of London, and in the **film** *Proud Valley* (1940), **Rachel Thomas** did much to promote the notion that in adversity the Welsh working **class** turn to hymns for support.

Social and economic change, together with increasing secularism, meant that hymn-singing had declined in significance by the early 21st century, although, even then, hymn-singing in taverns was not unknown. Furthermore, two remarkable hymns were composed in the later 20th century – **Lewis Valentine**'s 'Gweddi dros Gymru' (Prayer for Wales), sung to Sibelius's *Finlandia*, and 'Tydi a wnaeth y wyrth, O Grist, Fab Duw' (It is Thou who wrought the miracle, Oh Christ, the Son of God) by W. Rhys Nicholas (1914–96), sung to the tune 'Pantyfedwen', the work of M. Eddie Evans (1890–1984). In addition, the television programme *Dechrau Canu Dechrau Canmol* (the prototype for the **English-language** programme *Songs of Praise*, frequently introduced by **Harry Secombe**) ensured that hymn-singing would continue to be widely heard. (It was following a broadcast of *Dechrau Canu Dechrau Canmol* that the BBC at Llandaff (**Cardiff**) received a letter noting that 'some people gets drunk on **beer**; I gets drunk on hymn-singing.')

'HYMNS AND ARIAS' Song

Perhaps the best known of entertaining singer-songwriter Max Boyce's narrative songs, it was released on Boyce's 1974 album *Live at Treorchy*. Its chorus, 'And we were singing/ hymns and arias/ Land of my Fathers/ *Ar Hyd y Nos*', quickly attained the status of a folk song among **rugby** supporters.

HYWEL AB OWAIN GWYNEDD (fl.1139–70)
Prince and poet

The author of the earliest extant love poetry in **Welsh** was a natural son of **Owain Gwynedd** and an Irishwoman named Ffynnod. It appears that his father placed **Ceredigion** under his authority, and Hywel seems to have won many victories against the **Normans** during the 1140s. By 1153, however, he had lost Ceredigion. For the last 15 years of his life there is no mention of him in the chronicles. He is the subject of a fine praise poem by **Cynddelw Brydydd Mawr**. Hywel may have been appointed successor to his father, but, shortly after Owain's death, he was killed by his half-brother, **Dafydd ab Owain Gwynedd**, in a battle at **Pentraeth**. Six love poems are attributed to him as well as two fragments that refer to Owain's victories in 1157. Striking a personal note that is unusual in the poetry of the **Gogynfeirdd**, Hywel is famous for his praise of the wild landscapes and the **women** of Meirionnydd. He is the hero of Ellis Peters' novel *The Summer of the Danes* (1991) (*see* **Edith Pargeter**).

HYWEL AP GRUFFUDD (Syr Hywel y Fwyall; d.c.1381) Soldier

An **Eifionydd** man descended from **Ednyfed Fychan**, Sir Howel of the Axe, as he became known, won fame during the **Hundred Years War**. He led a contingent of Welshmen at Crécy (1346), and caused so much destruction with his battle-axe at Poitiers (1356) that the Black Prince, according to John Wynn (*see* **Wynn family (Gwydir)**), gave the weapon a place of honour in his hall, ordering **food** to be served before it. He spent his later years as constable of **Criccieth** Castle.

HYWEL DDA (Hywel ap Cadell; d.949/950)
King and lawgiver

Hywel inherited **Seisyllwg**, the southern part of the kingdom of his grandfather, **Rhodri Mawr**, and acquired **Dyfed** *c.*904 after marrying the daughter of its ruler, Llywarch ap Hyfaidd. He seems to have gained possession of **Brycheiniog** around 930 and seized **Gwynedd** and **Powys** when Idwal Foel was killed 12 years later; of the kingdoms of Wales, only **Morgannwg** remained beyond his grasp.

Because of the **Viking** threat, he submitted to **English** overlordship and developed a close relationship with Wessex, his name appearing frequently in Wessex court documents during the period between 928 and 949. There is some evidence that he had **coins** struck bearing his name. In 928, he is believed to have gone on **pilgrimage** to Rome.

According to the tradition recorded in the medieval **law** books, representatives from every *cantref* in Hywel's dominions were summoned to **Whitland** in Dyfed, there to assist in the work of recording the laws and customs of the lands over which he ruled. The tradition that he was a lawgiver presumably gave him the epithet 'Dda' (Good). Although the earliest manuscript of the Law of Wales dates from the 13th century, it is credible that it was by Hywel's authority that the work was put in hand, probably in the 940s. He was thus responsible for giving substance to one of the chief bulwarks of national consciousness in medieval Wales.

I

The Cardiff Devils ice hockey team in action

IÂL Commote

A **commote** of **Powys Fadog**, in 1284 it became part of the **march**er-lordship of **Bromfield and Yale**. In the 16th century, the Anglicized form of the name – Yale – was adopted by a prominent local family, whose members included **Thomas Yale** and also Elihu Yale, who gave his name to Yale University.

ICE HOCKEY

The origins of ice hockey are obscure, but the game has been played in **Britain** since at least the late 19th century. It arrived in Wales as recently as 1974, following the opening of a rink at **Queensferry**. **Dee**side Dragons remained the country's only senior team until the launch of the **Cardiff Devils** in 1986. The teams enjoyed a brief rivalry in the British League and the Welsh Cup, until the Cardiff team won promotion to the top level.

Cardiff's first major achievement was the Heineken British League and Championship double in 1989/90, before going on to further success in the Superleague and in European competitions. Although Cardiff has relied mainly on Canadian and English talent, Welsh players such as Nicky Chinn and Stevie Lyle have enjoyed

international success, with the latter representing Britain in the 1999 World Championship.

ICE SKATING

Ice rinks at **Queensferry** (since 1973) and **Cardiff** (since 1986; the Cardiff rink was demolished in 2006, but plans are afoot to replace it) are the focal points of ice skating in Wales, which consists of speed skating, figure skating and ice dancing; the sport's governing body is the Welsh Ice Skating Association, founded in 1985. Outstanding Welsh skaters, all of whom have competed at world or European level, include Karen Wood, twice British **women**'s champion; Steven Cousins, eight times British men's champion; Marika Humphreys, five times British ice **dance** champion, with three different partners; and Jonathan O'Dougherty, British ice dance champion in 2002, with Pamela O'Connor.

IESTYN AP GWRGANT (fl.1081–1100)
Ruler of Morgannwg

Iestyn ap Gwrgant, a shadowy figure, appears to have won control of **Morgannwg** following the death of Caradog ap Gruffudd at the **battle of Mynydd Carn** in 1081, only to lose it to **Robert Fitz Hammo**, probably in the 1090s. One later account of the conquest says that he sought the aid of Fitz Hammo against his neighbour **Rhys ap Tewdwr** of **Deheubarth**, but there is no firm evidence for this. He was the ancestor of the medieval lords of **Afan**, and many of the leading families of **Glamorgan** claimed descent from him. Iestyn has become a popular name in families of Glamorgan patriots.

IEUAN AP HYWEL SWRDWAL (fl.*c*.1436–70)
Poet

Ieuan, whose ancestors were Anglo-**Norman** settlers in **Brycheiniog**, was the son of the **Newtown** poet Hywel Swrdwal. The poet Hywel Dafi's elegy for Ieuan associated him with Newtown, **Brecon** and **Oxford**. Ieuan's patrons were mostly from mid-Wales – one of his poems describes the newly built Bryndraenog (**Beguildy**), one of Wales's most distinguished hall-houses. He is chiefly remembered for his **English** '**Hymn** to the Virgin', a poem cast in the Welsh *awdl* form, employing *cynghanedd* and written in **Welsh** orthography:

> *O michti ladi, owr leding – tw haf*
> *At hefn owr abeiding:*
> *Yntw ddy ffest efrlesting*
> *I set a braents ws tw bring.*

Ieuan's poem was allegedly composed to counter Oxford Englishmen's taunts that 'there was not one good Welsh scholar'. It has been hailed as marking the beginning of **Anglo-Welsh** or English-language Welsh **literature**.

IEUAN AP RHYDDERCH (fl.1430–70) Poet
Ieuan's family were noted patrons in **Cardiganshire**. His father, Rhydderch ab Ieuan Llwyd, owned *The White Book of Rhydderch*, the writing of which may have been commissioned by him. Ieuan wrote a boasting poem vaunting his university **education** and a poem to St **David**. His other works included a political **prophecy** and a satire.

IFOR BACH (Ifor ap Meurig; fl.*c*.1158)
Welsh lord

Ifor ap Meurig was lord of **Senghennydd** and brother-in-law of **Rhys ap Gruffudd** (the Lord Rhys; d.1197). In 1158, he killed Morgan ab Owain, lord of **Caerleon**, and his poet Gwrgant ap Rhys. In the same year, he carried out an audacious raid on **Cardiff** Castle, capturing his overlord, William, earl of Gloucester, with whom he was in dispute, along with his wife and son. The earl was soon released and Ifor's grievances remedied, but the raid was long remembered (Cardiff's Clwb Ifor Bach is named after him). His descendants perhaps included **Llywelyn Bren**, the leader of the 1316 revolt in **Glamorgan**.

ILLINGWORTH, Leslie Gilbert (1902–79)
Cartoonist

One of the leading political cartoonists of the 20th century, Illingworth was born in **Barry** and attended **Cardiff** Art School before joining the *Western Mail* (*see* **Newspapers**). After a further period of study at the Slade School of Art, he returned to the *Western Mail*. Then, in 1939, he joined the *Daily Mail*, and also became the chief cartoonist for the

satirical **periodical** *Punch* in 1945, but remaining with the *Daily Mail* until his retirement in 1969. Nearly 5000 of his cartoons – which document a pivotal period in Welsh, British and world history – were digitized in 2004 by the **National Library of Wales**, and made available on a free Illingworth website.

ILLTUD (5/6th century) Saint
The 7th-century Life of **Samson** describes Illtud as a pupil of Germanus (**Garmon**) of Auxerre. Probably **Dyfrig**'s successor as leader of the Christians of Wales, Illtud established a monastic school at **Llantwit Major**, a place of pivotal importance in the history of the development of Christianity in **Celt**ic-speaking lands (*see* **Celtic Church, The**). To Samson's biographer, Illtud was 'the renowned master of the Britons, learned in the teachings of the Church, in the culture of the Latins and in the traditions of his own people'. The humane traditions of Llantwit seem to have been rejected by the following generation of Welsh Christian leaders – **David** among them – who opted for a more ascetic way of life. A biography by a 12th-century **Norman** cleric, which has no historical basis, depicts Illtud as a married man who, cruelly, rejects his wife. The Life reflects the Norman campaign against the Welsh tradition of married priests and hereditary ecclesiastical offices. Illtud's feast day is 6 November.

ILSTON (Llanilltud Gŵyr), Swansea
(1901 ha; 538 inhabitants)

Extending inland from the delectable Three Cliffs Bay to **Swansea Airport** on Fairwood Common, the **community** contains the remains of the medieval chapel of St Cennydd. From 1649 to 1660, the chapel was the home of Wales's first **Baptist** congregation. Led by **John Miles**, the congregation migrated to Swansey, Massachusetts, following the Stuart Restoration.

The heavily restored church of St **Illtud** has a 14th-century west window. The old mill at Parkmill is the focus of a visitor centre. Footpaths lead northwards to the Green Cwm or Parc le **Breos** valley, once part of the **hunting** park of the lords of **Gower**, to the impressive Parc Cwm **Neolithic** chambered tomb – which once contained the remains of at least 20 people – and to Cathole **Cave**, where excavation uncovered a range of **Palaeolithic** tools.

Mount Pisgah chapel (1822), Parkmill, is one of Wales's earliest chapels to have the pulpit at the gable end. In Penmaen burrows are the remains of a megalithic tomb, an early **Norman** castle, and a besanded medieval church. The tiny Nicholaston church was lavishly rebuilt in the 1890s through the patronage of Olive **Talbot**.

IMMIGRATION
Wales presents an open **border** to **England** and, in consequence, immigration has been a constant feature, peaking when particular resources offered attraction. Apart from immigration in the prehistoric and immediate post-**Roman** eras, three such periods can be identified.

The first was during the 12th and 13th centuries, when invading **Norman** lords sought the most productive agricultural land, bringing their retainers with them to settle and ensure effective control. The **march**er-lands of east and south were the areas most affected, the most distinctive area being southern **Dyfed** where *c*.1108 Henry I introduced a community of **Flemings**. The castle towns created by the Anglo-Normans, where initially the Welsh were not permitted to hold land, were also aggregations of incomers.

The second period was that of the **Industrial Revolution**, beginning in the mid-18th century. Most early movements, however, were within Wales. In 1851, only 12.1% of the inhabitants of **Merthyr Tydfil** had been born outside Wales, over half of them in **Ireland**. It was not until near the end of the 19th century that immigration from England became dominant. In 1891, of the total immigrants in the **Glamorgan coal**field, 98,569 were Welsh-born and 71,687 non-Welsh. But between 1901 and 1911, some 63% of the migrants into the Glamorgan coalfield came from England, and a further 3.9% from **Scotland** and Ireland. There was an even greater movement into the coastal towns, with **Cardiff** recording the largest number from outside Wales, some of them being the immigrants who created the famous Tiger Bay. In 1891, non-coalfield Glamorgan included 24,396 immigrants from other parts of Wales, and 57,597 from outside Wales. Industrial Wales had communities of **Spaniards**, **Italians** and **Jews**. The northern coalfield also attracted migrants, particularly from Lancashire. Furthermore, migrants from that **county** have consistently constituted a high proportion of the inhabitants of Wales's northern coastal resorts. However, the **slate**-quarrying areas of the north-west experienced only short-distance migration, which perhaps explains the disproportionate contribution made to Welsh **literature** by the inhabitants of those areas.

The third period covers the second half of the 20th century to the present. In the larger towns, there has been the growth of communities whose members have their origins in the Third World: **Chinese**, **Africans**, **West Indians**, **Indians**, **Bangladeshis** and **Somalis** among them. In the countryside, the predominant feature has been 'counter-urbanization' – the distinctive shift of people from the largest cities to rural areas. In 2001, when Wales had 2,903,085 inhabitants, *c*.715,000 had been born outside the country (almost 25%). Of the migrants, 598,000 had been born in England, 45,000 in Scotland or Ireland and 24,000 in other countries within the European Union. Of the remaining 56,000, a significant proportion had been born in south Asia. The percentages of those born outside Wales ranged from 42% in **Flintshire** to 7.9% in **Blaenau Gwent**.

Immigration has contributed substantially to social change in Wales, and has furthered Anglicization, the most controversial aspect of immigration. This is particularly true in most recent times, when migration has been largely directed to rural Wales and the heartlands of the **Welsh language**.

INDEPENDENT LABOUR PARTY (ILP)

The ILP was founded at a conference in Bradford in 1893, when **Keir Hardie** brought together a number of **trade unionists** and socialists willing to accept his notion of independent working-**class** representation. Notoriously, the only Welsh delegate to this conference failed to arrive, having missed his train at **Cardiff**.

Although the party did not attract a large membership in Wales, its branches and publications disseminated

An Illingworth cartoon depicting the reactions of Khrushchev and Eisenhower to the space race, 1959

radical ideas concerning democracy, the empire and **women**'s rights, as well as industrial issues. It was Keir Hardie's visits to Wales during the 1898 **miners' strike** that encouraged the ILP branches in **Merthyr Tydfil** and **Aberdare** to propose his candidature in their constituency in 1900 – the year in which the ILP, in alliance with trade union leaders, succeeded in launching the Labour Representation Committee. Thereafter, the example of Hardie's independence in parliament challenged the whole position of the Lib-Labs and allowed the ILP to play a major part in the ballot that led, in 1909, to the affiliation to the **Labour Party** of the **Miners' Federation of Great Britain**. Between 1904 and 1918, active branches of the party were established in the north-west. The branches were inspired by Silyn (**Robert Roberts**), who sought to further both **socialism** and Welsh national aspirations, an aim also pursued in **Glamorgan** by **John Davies** (1882–1937) and others.

During the Labour Party's early decades, ILP members played a vital role in fighting local elections, setting up local Labour representation committees and urging the rejection of Lib-Labism. A new generation of miners' leaders, including **Vernon Hartshorn**, James Winstone and **James Griffiths**, were largely shaped by the ILP. Its anti-war sentiments were its last significant contribution to the Labour movement. Continuing as a left-wing pressure group, it was disaffiliated from the Labour Party in 1932. In 1934 and 1935, it put up a candidate against the Labour candidate in Merthyr Tydfil. In 1937, the ILP joined with the **Communists** and the Socialist League in the Unity Campaign.

INDIANS

In 2001, there were over 8000 people of Indian descent in Wales, nearly a quarter of whom were born there. The majority live in **Cardiff**, while others are dispersed in smaller-sized groups in places such as **Swansea**. More than 90% of Indian males in the 16–74 age group are economically active. Many are in the professions, working as doctors, academics or in business; almost half are categorized as being in social classes I and II. In fact, 68.6% are property owners and are the least likely of any ethnic group to have no central heating and the most likely of any Asian-based ethnic groups to have access to higher **education** and cars.

INDUSTRIAL and TRADING ESTATES

Among the provisions of the Special Areas (Development and Improvement) Act of 1934 were those for the building of **government**-funded industrial and trading estates. This was part of a policy to persuade industrial enterprises to locate in the severely depressed regions. The estates possessed all the necessary public services, and factories were constructed either as standard units of various dimensions or to meet specific requirements. Financial assistance was available for 'settlers', together with favourable rents and service terms.

Wales's first estate was established at Treforest (*see* **Taff's Well** and **Llantwit Fardre**) in 1936, by the South Wales and **Monmouthshire** Trading Estates Limited. While a range of small, light industries gradually settled on the estate, the most prominent feature of its early years was the arrival of many refugee industrialists who had fled the persecutions in central Europe. The estate company was involved in the development of seven other industrial sites within travelling distance of Treforest (**Cwmbran**; Cyfarthfa, Dowlais (both in **Merthyr Tydfil**); **Llantarnam**; Porth, Treorchy and Ynyswen (all three in **Rhondda**)), leased from the Special Areas commissioner. Initially, however, the number of new jobs created was limited.

During the **Second World War**, the Treforest estate underwent a major transformation: many existing premises were requisitioned by the government to house war production, and extensions and new factories were built. At the end of hostilities, the estate's industrial space had grown to nearly 140,000 square metres, available to house both returning firms that had been evicted and a large influx of newcomers; by 1947, some 11,000 people were employed in miscellaneous enterprises, with total employment eventually increasing to over 20,000.

Under the 1945 **Distribution of Industry Act**, the Board of Trade continued the policy of developing estates, which were regarded as vital to the creation of a more diversified manufacturing base. Conversions of **Royal Ordnance Factories** at **Bridgend**, **Hirwaun** and **Marchwiel** were followed by new estates, such as that at Fforest-fach, **Swansea**. By the 1960s, the 'estate' model of industrial development had become relatively commonplace. The activities of the **Development Board for Rural Wales** and the **Welsh Development Agency** led to the establishment of further industrial estates and parks.

INDUSTRIAL REVOLUTION, The

The Industrial Revolution is a term used to describe the period of rapid industrial development that occurred between *c*.1750 and *c*.1850. The British Industrial Revolution has been characterized as a period when the **iron** and cotton **textiles** industries developed rapidly, generating a 'take-off' into self-sustaining economic growth (*see* **Economy**), and when work on the land ceased to be the occupation of the majority. However, many historians question the validity of the concept of a 'revolution', stressing instead the gradualness of economic development over a much longer period.

In the Welsh context, as **William Rees** and others have shown, industrial activity, albeit scattered, could be found prior to the Industrial Revolution period in activities associated with **agriculture**, such as corn milling and the manufacture of woollen textiles (*see* **Woollen Industry**), as well as mining (both of **coal** and metalliferous ores) and quarrying (of stone and **slate**). Most were carried out in a small, localized manner, relying largely upon natural sources of **energy**, especially water.

Early signs of emerging industrialization commenced with the development of **copper** smelting in the **Swansea** area. Favoured by outcropping coal seams and natural harbour facilities, the region was the most readily accessible source of coal for the copper mines of **Cornwall**. When a major deposit of copper ore was discovered on **Mynydd Parys** in the 1760s, Swansea was able to enhance its advantageous position, becoming, in the 19th century, the world's major centre of non-ferrous metal smelting.

The Industrial Revolution: Swansea's Hafod Copper Works in 1810

Even at its peak, however, copper smelting was never on the same scale of significance as iron smelting. Following Abraham Darby's discovery of a method of manufacturing iron using coke, iron manufacture developed in both the north and the south in locations where ironstone, coal and **limestone** were found in close proximity. In the north, the major location was around **Bersham**, where **John Wilkinson** perfected a method of boring both cannon and the cylinders used in the steam engines produced by Boulton and Watt. There were also significant developments at **Holywell**, where in 1774 Samuel Johnson counted 19 different works within two miles of St Winifred's **Well**. But the major growth was in the south where, following the establishment of the 'Merthir' furnace at Dowlais in 1759 (later associated with the **Guest family**) and the subsequent founding of the Penydarren, Cyfarthfa and Plymouth works, **Merthyr Tydfil** emerged as the most significant centre of iron manufacture in Wales. In the 1820s, south Wales accounted for 40% of the pig iron manufactured in **Britain**.

During the early stages of Welsh industrialization, the role of the coalmining industry was a subservient one, its expansion resulting from the demands made on it by the growth of Wales's metal smelting industries. Only from the 1820s, when markets outside Wales began to be exploited on a regular, large-scale basis, did the coal industry develop as an independent source of economic expansion, a development which was not fully felt until after 1850.

The role of heavy industry is indicative of the fact that the emphasis in Wales was on the production of capital goods rather than of consumer goods, as was the case in the cotton towns of Lancashire. Even where heavy industry was concerned, Wales produced bulk metals rather than objects made of metal, for its workers did not develop the skills evident in the workshops of Birmingham and Sheffield. The factory system producing consumer goods is generally considered to be the central feature of the Industrial Revolution. Nevertheless, there is increasing support for the belief that the revolution's key significance lay in the harnessing of a new form of energy, and in that development Wales's contribution was of central importance.

The establishment of an efficient transport infrastructure was vital to the process of industrialization. Inland transport in mid 18th-century Wales was difficult: tracks were often impassable in winter and few **rivers** were easily navigable for any distance. Some early industrialists constructed tram-roads or short **canals** to link their works and mines to waterborne transport routes, but it was the building of the major canals in south Wales in the 1790s – the **Glamorgan**shire, **Monmouthshire**, **Neath** and Swansea – which provided the basis for a more rapid industrialization. These canals proved effective for moving iron and coal to the emerging **ports** of **Cardiff**, Swansea and **Newport** until the 1820s and 1830s, but growing congestion necessitated the development of an improved method of transportation. **Railways** were to provide the eventual solution, but they made little headway in Wales until the 1840s, despite **Richard Trevithick**'s experiments on the Penydarren tramroad in 1804.

The development of heavy industry needed the input of capital and labour. **England** was the most important source of capital – some key figures being the **Vivians** (copper smelting), the Guests and **Crawshays** (iron smelting) – but there is increasing evidence to suggest that indigenous entrepreneurship also played a role. In addition, England was the source of a significant part of the labour force, as was **Ireland** (*see* **Immigration**); however, the primary source was the rise in the indigenous birth rate. The **population** of Wales rose from *c.*489,000 in 1750 to 587,245 in 1801 and 1,163,134 in 1851. The growth, however, was unevenly spread, being much faster in and around the southern coalfield. In Glamorgan and Monmouthshire, the population more than trebled between 1801 and 1851, those **counties'** combined share of the Welsh population consequently increasing from 19.8% in 1801 to 33.5% in 1851.

While it was by no means obvious in 1800 where the industrial centre of gravity would eventually lie, the increasing reliance upon steam power fuelled by coal meant that, by 1850, the coalfields had become the fulcrum of industrialization. In consequence, parts of north-west and mid-Wales may be said to have experienced an industrial revolution that failed.

INDUSTRIAL SITES and LANDSCAPES

Industrial activity has modified the Welsh landscape since the **Neolithic Age**. Prehistoric activity has left evidence of quarrying at Graiglwyd (**Penmaenmawr**), **copper** mining on the Great Orme (**Llandudno**) and in the **Ystwyth** valley, **lead** mining at **Llangynog** (**Montgomeryshire**) and **iron** smelting at numerous sites. **Gold** mining by the **Romans** at Dolaucothi (**Cynwyl Gaeo**) involved the construction of 11.5 km of leats, and evidence of medieval lead mining in **Flintshire** is readily apparent. The quickening pace of industrial activity from the late 16th century onwards modified the landscape in the lead-bearing areas of **Cardiganshire** and at **Tintern**, Llangynog, **Neath**, **Swansea** and elsewhere. Although careful coppicing can provide a constant supply of charcoal for smelting, inconsiderate exploitation can lead to extensive deforestation, a matter of distress to the 16th-century author of the poem 'Coed Glyn Cynon'.

From the mid-18th until the early 20th century, the Welsh **economy** was dominated by mineral extraction and metal production. In consequence, most parts of Wales bear the scars of industrial development. The most dramatic of them is the huge gulch carved by copper miners on **Mynydd Parys** (**Amlwch**). Landscapes almost as dramatic are found in the **slate**-quarrying areas – the immense hole at Penrhyn (**Llandygai**), the terraces at Dinorwic (**Llanddeiniolen**) and the vast heaps of slate waste at Blaenau **Ffestiniog**.

More numerous, if less dramatic, are the industrial landscapes resulting from the development of the southern **coal**field. The mining of **iron** ore through the scouring action of water left an indelible mark in places such as Pontymoile (**Pontypool**). The slag produced by the industry led to the creation of highly distinctive spoil heaps – the curious landscape at Garn Ddyrys (**Llanfoist Fawr**), for example, and the the Dowlais Great Tip which long dominated the skyline of **Merthyr Tydfil**. Wales is rich in the remains of ironworks – the six furnaces surviving at Cyfarthfa (Merthyr Tydfil), for example, the remarkable remains of **John Wilkinson**'s **Bersham Ironworks** (**Coedpoeth**) and, above all, the remains of the **Blaenavon** ironworks. Copper smelting has an even more profound impact upon the landscape. That was particularly obvious in the Lower **Swansea** Valley, where the industry poisoned 360 ha. It was Europe's most extensive tract of derelict land and the task of reclamation, launched in 1961, is the most remarkable chapter in the history of landscape regeneration in Wales. The area is the subject of a classic study of an industrial landscape – Stephen Hughes's *Copperopolis* (2002).

By the mid-19th century, coalmining had overtaken metalworking as Wales's chief industry. One aspect of its impact upon the landscape was subsidence, as at Erddig

(**Marchwiel**), where the underpinning of the mansion proved to be laborious and expensive. Coalmining led to the creation of hundreds of spoil heaps – tragically so at Aberfan (Merthyr Tydfil). The **Aberfan Disaster** in 1966 led to a campaign of tip clearing and, as a consequence, the scars of industry are far less evident than they were a generation ago.

A concomitant of industrial development was the expansion of transport networks. The construction of **canals**, **railways** and **roads** involved the building of aqueducts and viaducts, the construction of embankments, the excavation of cuttings and the laying out of increasingly elaborate highways.

Wales's remarkable experience of industrialization means that a wide range of industrial landscapes and buildings came into existence in a relatively small area. Indeed, Elizabeth Beazley claimed in 1959 that 'a history of industrial revolution buildings might be written using Welsh examples only'. The impact of industry attracted artists, with **J. M. W. Turner** painting the mill at Aberdulais (**Blaenhonddan**), **Penry Williams** recording the transformation of Merthyr Tydfil and John 'Warwick' Smith delighting in the weird appearance of Mynydd Parys.

Industrial and transport undertakings created habitats that developed their own ecology. Thus, ruined limemortared walls attracted **plants** absent from Wales's generally acidic soil. A specialist flora came into existence around the Dolaucothi goldmines. Quarries – those at Ludchurch (**Lampeter Velfrey**), for example – became havens for rare plant communities. Over time, coal tips become clothed by a mosaic of heath and acid grassland, and even slate quarry waste is eventually colonized by vegetation. With their high toxicity, **soils** affected by lead mining or copper smelting are slow to attract plants, but some sites are home to rare metalophyte lichens. Disturbed land along railways and roads has provided channels for the spread of alien species – pests such as Oxford ragwort and Japanese knotweed among them. Of all human-made habitats, the most attractive are the canals, which generally have a greater diversity of flora and fauna than have **rivers** which have been much impoverished by the effects of intensive farming activities.

The richness of Wales's industrial heritage was not appreciated until the emergence in the 1950s of the new discipline of industrial **archaeology**. That tardiness means that much of great interest has been lost. Even the acclaimed removal of coal tips and other spoil heaps can result in the destruction of rare habitats. A new concern for industrial sites became apparent in 2000 when the Blaenavon industrial landscape was recognized as a world heritage site; throughout the world, only five sites relating to metal industries since the 18th century have been granted that status.

INDUSTRIAL TRANSFERENCE BOARD, The

Established in January 1928, the board produced a report that formed the basis of the **government**'s approach to unemployment until the 1934 Special Areas legislation. The policy of transferring labour from the areas worst hit by the interwar **depression** to relatively prosperous areas meant that the government was abandoning its previous insistence that unemployment would be short-term. In south Wales, the scheme accounted for only part of the heavy out-migration during the period up to the **Second World War**. Throughout its operation, there was considerable opposition to the scheme because of potentially detrimental long-term effects on society and the **economy**.

INFLUENZA

This highly contagious acute respiratory viral disease has the capacity to produce widespread epidemics, with a high attack rate and substantial mortality, particularly among the very young and old. Cases occur every year in most communities, and this maintains a level of immunity in the **population**. But when variants of the virus arise, populations are exposed to a virus against which they have no immunity, and this may herald a new pandemic.

There have been probably 11 of these since *c.*1800. The last 6 occurred in 1889–91, 1900, 1918–20, 1957–8, 1968–9 and 1977–8. The 1918–20 pandemic was the most devastating. It is estimated that it affected 25% of the world's population and may have claimed 40–50 million lives. The epidemic reached its peak in Wales in 1918, a year in which influenza claimed the lives of 112,329 people in Wales and **England**.

In **Cardiff**, with a population of over 200,000 at the time, most cases occurred in October and November of that year. In these two months alone 384 people died in the city, the majority being under 45 years of age, which is an unusual occurrence in most other outbreaks of the disease. In 2006, there was much discussion of the possible impact of avian influenza.

INNES, James Dickson (1887–1914) Painter

The early promise of one of the most prodigious talents of 20th-century Welsh art was cut short by Innes's death from **tuberculosis** at the age of 27. Born in **Llanelli**, Innes trained at **Carmarthen** School of Art before completing his studies at the Slade School in **London**. He travelled to **Ireland**, Spain and France, painting at Collioure, where earlier the 'Fauves' had begun looking at landscape directly and expressively. Innes used their influence to create a distinct and personal pictorial language, imbuing his **painting**s with a sparkling immediacy, clear colour and sharp composition. He became friendly with **Augustus John**, who introduced him to the **mountains** of **Gwynedd**, where his own responses to the landscape were informed by his experiences elsewhere in Europe. Both were represented in the famous 1913 Amory exhibition in New York.

James Innes, *The Heavy Cloud, Arenig* (*c.*1910)

Winifred Coombe Tennant was an important patron of Innes's work.

INSECTS

Of the thousands of insect species recorded in Wales, there are some of particular intrinsic interest (*see also* **Bees**).

BEETLES

Over 4000 species of beetle have been identified in **Britain**, one of which, the beautiful rainbow beetle, may be seen only in the **mountains** of **Snowdonia**, although it has been recorded in central Europe. It is found near its food **plant**, wild thyme, and the adults are visible from June to October. Another rare beetle is the Yellow Sand Beetle, with two black, wavy lines across its wing cases. Found on the southern coast, it spends the day sheltering under seaweed and wreckage before emerging at night to feed on sand hoppers. In 2006, two giant capricorn beetles and a live grub – members of a species considered to be extinct in Britain since 1700 – were found by timber restorers from **Llanelli** in a consignment of oak wood.

BUTTERFLIES and MOTHS

Three common but beautiful butterflies found in Welsh **gardens** are the small tortoiseshell, the red admiral and the peacock, all of which, in the larval stage, feed on nettles. Another butterfly to feed on nettle leaves – as a caterpillar – is the comma. With its scalloped-edged wings and conspicuous white comma mark on the underside, it reappeared in Wales during the 20th century. Yet another to feed on nettles, and also on thistles, is the lovely painted lady. Both the red admiral and the painted lady are migrants from the Mediterranean region.

A rare and striking visitor is the monarch butterfly of **North America**, possibly transported on **ships** but more probably carried by the wind. The first ever to be recorded on the western side of the Atlantic was captured in **Neath** in 1876. Records since then show that the monarch's usual landfall in Europe is on Wales's southern and western coasts.

On **Cors Caron** in **Ceredigion**, the large heath butterfly reaches the southernmost point of its distribution in Britain. It is also found on some bogs in the north, including Cors Goch **Trawsfynydd**. The butterfly's larval food plant, white beak sedge, is found on these bogs.

A handsome butterfly with a striking wing pattern is the marsh fritillary. Its habitat is wet pastures where the caterpillar's food plant, devil's bit scabious, grows. Whilst its numbers are declining in the rest of Europe, Wales, with its strong populations, is an important country for the butterfly's future.

Wales has two species of moth found nowhere else in Britain. One was discovered on moorland near **Usk** in 1972 and named silurist after the **Silures** tribe. Why it is restricted to a small patch of moorland in **Monmouthshire** remains a mystery, since its food plant is common on moorland throughout Wales. The silurist is known scientifically by the disparaging name *Eriopygodes imbecilla*: it was believed, wrongly, that because the female's abdomen was so fat she could not possibly fly. The other is Ashworth's rustic, discovered by Joseph Ashworth at **Llangollen** in 1853. It breeds on the mountain pastures of Snowdonia, the **limestone** hills of the north-east, and the slopes of **Cadair Idris** and **Pumlumon**.

When the draining of the Huntingdonshire fens destroyed the habitat of the rosy marsh moth in 1851, it was assumed that the moth had ceased to exist as a British species. But over a century later, in 1967, it was recorded on **Cors Fochno**, near **Borth**.

The largest of the spectacular hawkmoths is the impressive death's head hawkmoth, which arrives in Wales intermittently from May to September and whose sinister name refers to the prominent skull-and-crossbones mark on its thorax. The adults, if handled, give what sounds like a shrill squeak. Another occasional visitor to Wales is the equally impressive convolvulus hawkmoth. A day-flying hawkmoth, which visits Wales most years, is the hummingbird hawkmoth. A wondrous flyer, it suspends itself before a flower on unseen wings and plunges in its bent proboscis to suck the nectar before moving off at great speed to the next blossom. A resident and common hawkmoth is the lovely elephant hawkmoth, whose larva resembles in form and colour an elephant's trunk. A smaller relation, but equally beautiful with its deep pink body and wings, is the small elephant hawkmoth.

Some moths, to avoid being eaten by predators, mimic aggressive insects. One group of moths, known as the clearwings, differ from other moths in that their wings are clear, mimicking the bees, wasps and flies, and they fly during the day. A fine example is the Welsh clearwing, first noted at Llangollen in about 1854. Sightings of the Welsh clearwing continued until 1881, but there followed over 100 years of absence from the record. Then, news broke that the Welsh clearwing was breeding in Snowdonia. Much commoner is the large red-belted clearwing, whose larva, like that of the Welsh clearwing, feeds on birch bark.

DRAGONFLIES

Among the most conspicuously beautiful and dexterous of insects are Wales's several species of dragonfly. A common dragonfly of the **peaty** moors is the large golden-ringed dragonfly, with distinctive ring-shaped markings along its abdomen. On the slopes of **Mynydd Preseli**, it is accompanied by the rare southern damselfly, which reaches its northernmost location in Britain on Cors Erddreiniog (**Llanddyfnan**) in **Anglesey**.

INSTITUTE OF GRASSLAND AND ENVIRONMENTAL RESEARCH, The (IGER) (The Welsh Plant Breeding Station)

Established in 1919 on the strength of a capital gift to the University College, **Aberystwyth** (*see* **University of Wales, Aberystwyth**), of £10,000 from Laurence **Philipps** (Baron Milford) of the Picton Castle (**Slebech**) family, the Welsh Plant Breeding Station was initially envisaged as a scientific and commercial institution devoted in particular to breeding **plants** adapted to the needs of Wales. Under the direction of **George Stapledon**, a small team of scientists, including **T. J. Jenkin**, William Davies, E. T. Jones and R. D. Williams, elucidated the reproductive biology of the grasses and clovers, and produced and marketed a series of herbage varieties which transformed the pasturelands of Wales and many other parts of the world. By the 1940s, the station had become internationally renowned both for its fundamental scientific work and its extensive activities in the fields of grassland and hill-land improvement.

Post-war directors, among them J. P. Cooper and P. T. Thomas, encouraged increasingly sophisticated study of the cell structure, physiology and metabolism of herbage species, and the expansion of the station's interests to embrace cereal, pulse and brassica crops. A 'rationalization' of **government**-funded research stations in the later 1980s resulted in the Grassland Research Institute at Hurley near Reading merging with the Welsh Plant Breeding Station; this resulted in the creation, in 1990, of the Institute of Grassland and Environmental Research (IGER). While retaining its original remit to breed **oat**, grass and clover varieties, the institute's activities have broadened to embrace environmental issues and the integrated study of herbage/animal relationships. In this and other of the institute's work, molecular biology is playing a major role (*see also* **Biological Sciences**).

Based at Gogerddan (**Trefeurig**), one-time home of the **Pryse family** and now part of the University of Wales, Aberystwyth, IGER is Wales's sole major government-financed research centre.

INSTITUTE OF WELSH AFFAIRS, The (IWA)

Founded in 1987, the IWA is an independent, politically non-aligned think-tank based in **Cardiff**, with branches throughout Wales and an affiliated organization in **London**. It aims to raise the level of information and debate on public policy issues; economic development, **education** and constitutional change are prevailing concerns. Its journal *Agenda* appears three times a year.

INSURANCE

The roots of the insurance industry in present-day **Britain** can be traced back to the second half of the 16th century when **London** merchants began to underwrite marine insurances. Fire insurance also became available in London at the end of the 17th century. The foundations of life insurance in the modern world were laid by three remarkable Welshmen. The foremost was **Richard Price** (1723–91) from Llangeinor (**Garw Valley**), who first calculated actuarial tables of life expectancy and used the tables to calculate life assurance on a proper statistical basis. In this work he was followed by his nephew, William Morgan (1750–1833) from **Bridgend**, a strong **Radical** (like his uncle) who became chief actuary of the Society for Equitable Assurances on Lives and Survivorships (later Equitable Life), a society in which the Gould family (*see* **Morgan family (Tredegar)**) played a prominent role. Morgan also published several important papers on the principles of insurance. He was followed in turn by Griffith Davies (1788–1855) from **Llandwrog**, who developed Morgan's mathematical work to provide a firm scientific basis for the insurance industry (and who lectured publicly in **Welsh** on scientific topics).

During the 19th century, Wales witnessed the rapid growth of **friendly societies**, but the introduction of state old-age pensions (1909) and national **health** insurance (1911) by **David Lloyd George** saw a sharp decline in their fortunes. From c.1850 onwards they also had to compete

with commercial insurance companies. By that time, insurance brokers and the agents of mostly London, **Liverpool** and Scottish-based companies had offices throughout Wales. In 1868, there were 22 such offices in **Bangor** alone and as many as 38 in **Swansea**. Some small Welsh insurance companies, such as the **Cardiff**-based Welsh Insurance Corporation (1909), were formed; other interesting examples of native entrepreneurship were the Welsh **Calvinistic Methodist** Assurance Trust Ltd (1886–2006) and the Welsh **Baptist** Insurance Company (1888–2001), both exclusively concerned with the insurance of the properties of their respective denominations. One of the few large-scale Welsh insurance companies – The Provincial Welsh Insurance Company – was established at **Wrexham** in 1852. It was mostly involved in agricultural insurance, and had branches not only throughout Wales, but also as far away as London and Glasgow; the company's impressive headquarters (1860–1), designed by R. K. **Penson**, still stands on Wrexham's High Street. By the end of the 19th century the Provincial Welsh's operations had been acquired by the Alliance, a development that gave immense satisfaction to Robert Lewis (1835–1919). A native of **Coedpoeth**, Lewis was briefly employed by the Provincial during his youth before being summarily dismissed. However, by the close of the 19th century he had become a leading figure of the British insurance industry, primarily on account of his feat in transforming the insignificant Alliance – a part of the present-day Royal & Sun Alliance – into a major international insurance company.

Wales's strong maritime tradition (*see* **Seafaring** and **Ships**) was the context of strenuous efforts by native shipowners during the second half of the 19th century to create mutual marine-insurance societies in the **ports** of north and west Wales. Such developments are indicative of an increasingly sophisticated Welsh middle **class**, which sought financial independence from the marine insurers of Liverpool and London. During its heyday the Portmadoc Ship Insurance Company (1841–1917) was particularly successful (*see also* **Porthmadog**), and similar endeavours were undertaken at ports such as **Aberystwyth** (1852), Bangor (1853), **Pwllheli/Nefyn** (1843 and 1858) and **Aberaeron** (1880). With the remarkable growth of Cardiff as a port, marine insurance institutions proliferated in the city. However, during the first decade of the 20th century, Cardiff became the focus of great unease and distrust among Britain's leading marine insurance underwriters. At a time when the market value of smaller vessels was often lower than their insured value, Cardiff-registered vessels were lost at sea with suspicious regularity. For example, after unloading **iron** ore at Seriphos in 1907, the *Powis* sank in a crystal calm sea. Suspicions were further aroused by the unsavoury practice of 'gambling policies', speculative insurance policies taken against ships in which the policyholder had no direct financial interest. Such malpractices led **Winston Churchill**, the president of the Board of Trade at the time, to introduce the Marine Insurance (Gambling Policies) Act in 1909.

During the course of the 20th century, through amalgamations and acquisitions, the insurance industry came to be the preserve of increasingly powerful companies. Some small companies were established in Wales, such as the

Cambrian Insurance Company (1934) and Undeb (1952), a venture that enabled its founder, Trefor Morgan (1914–70), to be a noted benefactor in the history of the Welsh-language movement. At the beginning of the 21st century, the financial services sector in Wales employed some 28,000 people, with 21% being employed by insurance and pension companies. Zurich and Legal & General both had significant operations based in Cardiff at that time. Furthermore, by 2007, the car insurance company Admiral, which began trading from Cardiff in 1993 with 57 employees, had a workforce of 1700 in Cardiff and Swansea.

INTERLUDE

A type of verse-play (*see* **Drama**), known in **Welsh** as *anterliwt*, which was popular, chiefly in the north-east, from the 17th to the early 19th centuries. Interludes were presented in the open air on a cart or improvised stage, with a minimum of resources. The actors – all male – would charge a penny for seeing the play, and they would also sell copies. Forty-four interludes have been preserved, in manuscript and/or in print. All interludes comprise a tale of a fool deceiving a miser, with a parallel plot based on biblical, legendary or contemporary material. Some interludes contain social and political satire, some are allegorical, and nearly all of them provide pious and moralistic exhortation, along with bawdy humour.

Twm o'r Nant (**Thomas Edwards**; 1739–1810) was the best of the interlude writers on account of his satire, his lively dialogue and the quality of his songs. But there are other authors whose work repays scrutiny. In the interlude *Y Rhyfel Cartref*, **Huw Morys** gave a short, sharp and entirely one-sided account of the conflict between king and parliament. In *Y Capten Ffactor* and *Histori'r Geiniogwerth Synnwyr*, Huw Jones (d.1782) of **Llangwm** effectively retold popular tales from contemporary chapbooks. With his friend Siôn Cadwaladr (fl.1760), he penned a highly original version of the history of King David. Edward Thomas was comparably enterprising with the story of the Fall of Man. *Ffrewyll y Methodistiaid* is a cruel satire on the early Methodist reformers by William Roberts (fl.1745). Other notable authors were Jonathan Hughes (1721–1805), Richard Parry (d.1746) and **Elis Roberts** (Elis y Cowper).

INTERNATIONALISM

Internationalism as a concept – the belief in and the furtherance of co-operation and understanding between states and nations – became rooted in Wales in the late 18th century. Initially, this was through the activities of the **radicals Richard Price** and **David Williams** (1738–1816); and later through the efforts of men such as **Joseph Tregelles Price** and **Henry Richard**, whose internationalism bordered upon **pacifism**.

Early Welsh **socialists** saw themselves as internationalists, although for some of them the term implied the speedy Anglicization of the world and, therefore, a useful weapon against those seeking to further Welsh national causes. The League of Nations movement of the interwar years was infused with internationalism, which found expression in such activities as the annual goodwill message of **Urdd Gobaith Cymru**. David Davies (*see* **Davies family (Llandinam)**), an enthusiast for the League of Nations, established the world's first department of international politics at **Aberystwyth** in 1919, and financed the building of the Temple of Peace in **Cathays Park**.

The most self-sacrificial internationalist act in the history of Wales was the enlistment of 174 Welshmen – most of them **Communists** – in the International Brigade formed to support the Republican side in the **Spanish Civil War**. The **Labour Party** retained an international strand, as evinced by the career of **S. O. Davies** and others, although the belief could sometimes degenerate into a form of British nationalism. Internationalism has also been an element in the thinking of **Plaid [Genedlaethol] Cymru**, especially in that of **Gwynfor Evans** – although for him, as for others, the concept was hardly distinguishable from pacifism.

The most practical expression of internationalism in Wales is found in the activities of charitable societies, especially those concerned with Third World debt and deprivation. As a cultural phenomenon, it finds its finest expression in the **Llangollen International Musical Eisteddfod**.

INWARD INVESTMENT

Foreign inward investment has been a feature of the Welsh **economy** for over a century. Dominated for the most part by investment from the United States, it was particularly notable during the last quarter of the 20th century, as Wales's more diversified industrial structure exhibited a significant multinational presence in both manufacturing and services. Electrical and **electronics** manufacture featured prominently, together with **vehicle manufacture** and **chemicals**, with a high concentration of Japanese firms in an increasingly cosmopolitan mix.

By 1990, Wales was receiving 20% of the United Kingdom's annual inward investment total; as it has only 5% of the kingdom's **population**, it was clearly outperforming other parts of **Britain**. Its success was variously ascribed to location and cost factors, together with the contribution of the development agencies and the **Welsh Office** in providing attractive packages, including financial inducements. In 2003, *c.*64,000 people were employed by about 340 overseas-owned enterprises, spread across some 540 manufacturing plants. Generally, these factories were larger than those of domestic companies, and were heavily concentrated along the **M4** corridor and in **Flintshire**. Reservations were expressed regarding the degree of integration in the local economy, the footloose nature of the branch factory syndrome, the quality and remuneration of many 'screwdriver' assembly jobs, and the relative lack of technologically advanced functions. Concern was also expressed regarding the cost-effectiveness of attracting inward investment at the expense of promoting indigenous businesses.

Following the establishment of the **National Assembly** and the formation of an enlarged **Welsh Development Agency**, there emerged a reorientation of policy towards the more western areas, and a greater selectivity towards inward investors, balanced by increased emphasis on indigenous business development. The closure, in 2005, of **Bridgend**'s Sony plant, with the loss of 400 jobs, was considered by some economists to mark the end of the era of big inward investment projects into Wales.

IOLO GOCH (*c.*1325–*c.*1403) Poet

Iolo's ancestors held land in Lleweni (**Denbigh**), but Iolo probably lived at Llechryd (**Llannefydd**). He received a church **education**, possibly at **St Asaph**; he addressed a poem to Dafydd ap Bleddyn, bishop of St Asaph, before 1345. Iolo adopted the new *cywydd* metre and was responsible for establishing it as a medium for traditional praise poetry. He addressed *cywyddau* to dignitaries such as Edward III, Sir **Rhys ap Gruffudd** (d.1356), the **Tudor family**, Roger **Mortimer** and **Owain Glyndŵr**, and also to the lowly labourer. He is traditionally remembered as Glyndŵr's bard; his poem describing Sycharth, Owain's dwelling at **Llansilin**, is famous. It was once thought that Iolo died before **Glyndŵr's Revolt**, but it has been shown that a previously rejected *cywydd* is Iolo's authentic work addressed to Owain *c.*1401–3.

IORWERTH AP MADOG (fl.1230–40) Jurist

One of a family of northern Welsh lawyers known as 'the tribe of Cilmin Droetu'. The **law** book which Aneurin Owen (1841) dubbed the *Venedotian Code* is today described as *Llyfr Iorwerth*, and it contains a developed form of the laws that were exercised in **Gwynedd** in the first half of the 13th century, in the time of **Llywelyn ap Iorwerth**.

IORWERTH DRWYNDWN (d.*c.*1174) Prince

According to tradition, Iorwerth, the eldest legitimate son of **Owain Gwynedd**, was excluded from the succession because of a physical defect (his soubriquet 'Trwyndwn' means broken-nosed); he appears to have received the **commote** of **Nantconwy** as his share of the patrimony. He was the father of **Llywelyn ap Iorwerth**.

IRELAND, Wales's associations with

Early Wales was shaped to a high degree by the cultural influences disseminated by those sailing the western sea routes. The impact of Ireland was, therefore, of central importance. In the **Neolithic Age**, the chambered tombs of **Anglesey** were in the tradition of the rich culture of the Boyne valley of Ireland.

The **Romans** integrated Wales into the province of Britannia; but, with the Empire's decline, the western sea routes again became dominant. There was extensive **Irish** migration. The dynasties of **Dyfed** and **Brycheiniog** were of Irish origin, but **Cunedda** was reputed to have driven the Irish from **Gwynedd**.

During the 'Age of **Saints**', Cambro-Irish relations were especially close, and early Welsh **literature**, *The Mabinogion* in particular, has many links with Ireland. Wales was drawn into the **Viking** world largely through the

Internationalism, the guiding principle of the Llangollen International Music Eisteddfod, in action on the streets of the town in July 1957

activities of Viking settlers in Ireland. During the **Norman** invasions, Ireland offered a refuge to beleaguered Welsh rulers, as in the case of **Gruffudd ap Cynan**. The invasion of Ireland in 1169 was essentially a Cambro-Norman venture, and the English king's hold upon Dublin was a factor in the subjugation of Wales.

Following the **Protestant Reformation**, Ireland's adherence to **Roman Catholicism** and fears that the island would be used as a base for the invasion of Wales caused the Welsh **gentry** to be fearful of Ireland. At the same time, they hoped that the assertion of English power there would provide them with lucrative opportunities. In Elizabeth's Irish Wars, the Welsh were disproportionately represented in the royal armies, and a number of Welshmen carved out estates for themselves in Ireland. **Cromwell**'s Irish campaign found approval in Wales, as did that of William III, the occasion of the founding of the **Royal Welch Fusiliers**. Suspicion of Ireland continued for centuries and was intensified in the 19th century as a result of heavy Irish **immigration** to Welsh industrial areas. The opening up of northern Wales by **road** and **railway** was largely motivated by **London**'s need for rapid communication with Ireland.

Welsh suspicion of the Irish declined in the late 19th century as Welsh patriots came to admire their successes on issues such as Church **disestablishment**, land reform, improved higher **education** and – certainly for some patriots – **home rule**.

'Ireland,' declared **David Lloyd George** in 1890, 'is the college of Europe [teaching] how every wronged and oppressed nationality can secure justice and redress'. As Irish nationalism moved towards insurrection and defiant republicanism, Welsh sympathies declined, but the Irish struggle and the Irish literary revival had a major impact upon the founders of **Plaid [Genedlaethol] Cymru**. The introspective Irish Free State with its stagnating **economy** proved a disappointing model for supporters of Welsh **nationalism**, and the violence in the north was universally condemned in Wales. In more recent times, Ireland, with its vibrancy and prosperity and its role as a source of employment for commuters from Gwynedd, has become the object of envy in Wales. The appointment in 1998 of an Irish consul-general in Wales was considered a highly significant development, as was the establishment in 1999 of the British-Irish Council, a body including representation from the **National Assembly for Wales**.

IRISH, The

The proximity of **Ireland** and **Wales** has occasioned sporadic movements of people between the two countries throughout the centuries. The sea that separates them has generally been a highway along which trade and exchange takes place, rather than a barrier to contact. A degree of contact continued despite the **Roman** occupation of **Britain** and, in the 4th century, irrespective of the Romans' reorganization of the sea defences of Wales, Irish colonists settled in considerable numbers in north-west and south-west Wales.

Tradition maintains that **Cunedda** and his men drove the Irish out of **Gwynedd**. In the early post-Roman period further Irish migrants strengthened the Irish presence in the south. **Literature** in Old Irish records the settlement of part of the Déisi tribe in **Dyfed**, and from there Irish influence spread eastwards to **Brycheiniog**. The existence of some 40 **ogham**-inscribed stones in Wales testifies to the strength of Irish culture during the immediate post-Roman centuries, especially in what are now **Pembrokeshire**, **Carmarthenshire** and **Breconshire**.

Despite the longevity of this contact between the two countries, it is the 19th century that has most occupied historians. During that century, industrialization and urbanization in Wales attracted Irish workers to excavate docks, to build **railways** and to labour at the docks, and in the ironworks and coalmines (*see* **Iron and Steel** and **Coal**). A major impetus to **immigration** came with the Great Famine of 1845–50. During these years, the **ports** of south Wales were inundated by thousands of starving refugees fleeing from appalling conditions in Ireland.

The north-east – **Wrexham** in particular – also attracted Irish immigrants, partly as an overflow from **Liverpool**. The incomers lived in poor accommodation and were particularly susceptible to the periodic epidemics that swept urban Wales. Anti-Irish riots (*see* **Race Riots**) intensified during these years: between 1826 and 1882, Irish immigrants in Wales were the targets of serious rioting on 20 separate occasions. However, it would be a mistake to believe that all immigrants were alienated and outcast. Some Irish workers established their own **friendly societies** and embraced the **temperance** movement, participating fully in the cult of respectability so beloved of the **Nonconformist** Welsh. Moreover, there was a small, but important, Irish middle class, composed of businessmen and doctors, such as the Irish **Home Ruler** James Mullin.

Such people occasionally came into conflict with those other leaders of the Irish community, the **Roman Catholic** clergy. Some commentators have overestimated the religious devotion of Irish immigrants in the mid-19th century, but the Catholic Church undoubtedly played a central role in immigrant life, and the advent of the Irish transformed the prospects of Catholicism in Wales. Eager to establish its own schools, the church invested heavily to ensure that the sons and daughters of immigrants were instructed in the faith. Occasionally, there were tensions between the demands of Catholicism and the pull of the home country. The church was inveterately opposed to the revolutionary Fenian movement, which in the 1860s attracted considerable support among the Irish abroad. The beginnings of an armed Fenian conspiracy were discovered at Dowlais, **Merthyr Tydfil** in 1867, and two Irishmen were transported for their part in it.

Despite the alienation of the famine years, signs of Irish integration can be discerned from the late 1880s onwards, partly because of Welsh Liberalism's support for Irish Home Rule, and partly because of the creation of mass **trade unions** at the docks, which drew the Irish into the labour movement.

Irish migration to Wales tailed off from the 1920s as a result of the stagnation of the Welsh **economy**. By then, there were some 150,000 people of Irish extraction in Wales. Among those who came to prominence were the novelist **Joseph Keating** and the republican activist **Kitty Evans**. Another notable 20th-century Irish immigrant was **Michael McGrath**, archbishop of **Cardiff**, eulogized in verse by **Saunders Lewis**. By the early 21st century, migration from Wales to Ireland was becoming more usual than migration from Ireland to Wales.

Irish–Welsh scholarly cooperation has been especially fruitful in **archaeology**, **literature** and **Celtic** linguistics. The career of Proinsias Mac Cana (1926–2004) testifies to this.

IRON AGE, The (*c.*700 BC–AD 50)

Iron is abundant in the earth's crust, constituting at least 5% of igneous rock. Unlike **gold** and **copper**, it hardly ever exists in its free form. As a result, extracting the true metal involves complex processes. The evidence is that these methods were discovered in the Near East at the beginning of the last millennium BC, and had become known in **Britain** by *c.*700 BC.

With iron ore being so plentiful, the ability to extract the metal permitted the output of an almost inexhaustible supply of material for making tools, weapons and equipment. To the distinguished prehistorian Gordon Childe, iron was 'the democratic metal', and so great is its usefulness that the Iron Age has, in effect, lasted until the present time.

In the past, those knowing the secret of ironmaking represented a threat to those ignorant of it. There is an echo of this threat in the story of **Llyn y Fan Fach**, in which the lady, a symbol of the old world with her magic and her white **cattle**, returned to her world upon being struck thrice with iron.

Among the earliest iron artefacts found in Britain are the implements discovered at Llyn Fawr (**Rhigos**), an indication perhaps that Wales had pioneer iron metallurgists.

In much of Europe, the Iron Age is equated with the emergence of **Celt**ic peoples, whose culture and languages spread over vast areas from Iberia to Turkey, and from Italy to Britain and **Ireland**. The concept of a single Celtic civilization is being re-examined, with some scholars denying that it made a fundamental contribution to the late pre-history of Europe.

Evidence of the Iron Age in Wales is patchy. For example, hardly anything is known of burial practices. **Pottery** is also rare, evidence perhaps of a lack of suitable raw materials, or of the era's predilection for wood or **leather** vessels and containers. Thus, it would seem that the Iron Age communities of Wales were materially poorer than those in other parts of Britain. Certainly, they were less sophisticated than those in the kingdoms of south-eastern Britain. By the first century BC, those kingdoms were on the edge of the **Roman** world and therefore had access to material riches which could be used to enhance the prestige of their rulers.

Nevertheless, Wales's numerous large **hill-forts** suggest the existence of powerful, hierarchical communities. There are also large forts on the coast using narrow promontories or rugged cliffs as a natural form of defence, thus requiring ramparts on the landward side only; it is likely that the inhabitants of some of these were involved in sea-borne trade. Many of these forts have been eroded by the sea, among them Porth y Rhaw (**St David's**) and Dinas Dinlle (**Llandwrog**). In addition to hill and promontory forts, the abundance of single and nucleated settlement sites indicates the vitality of Iron Age society.

In the south-west and north-west, in particular, small (often undefended), individual farms were numerous.

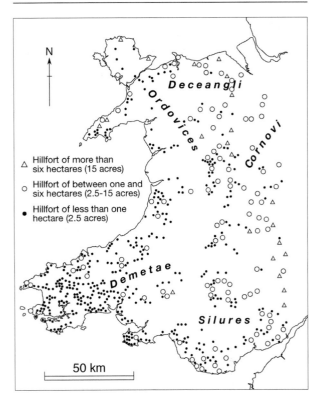

Iron Age hill-fort distribution in Wales (after Ordnance Survey)

Sometimes, the entire layout can be traced, as in marginal upland areas fringing the **Snowdonia** massif, where house structures, enclosures and fields delineated by **dry stone walling** survive. In the richer soils of the lowlands, modern **agriculture** has erased most vestiges of Iron Age settlement patterns, although evidence of turf and timber-built farmsteads has been discovered by chance or through aerial photography. In **Gwynedd** and **Anglesey**, recent excavation at sites such as Moel y Gerddi (**Llanfair**), Graeanog (**Clynnog**), Bryn Eryr (**Pentraeth**) and Tŷ Mawr (**Holyhead**) permits these settlements to be arranged in chronological succession. The earliest pre-date 400 BC, but more complex forms developed thereafter, culminating in polygonal enclosures, as at Graeanog, Din Lligwy (**Moelfre**) and Cae Meta (**Llanddeiniolen**), enclosures that were probably created during the Roman occupation.

A mixed farming **economy** was practised at these settlements. Various types of quern or hand-mill attest to the widespread growing of grain crops. Marks made by an ard or light plough have been discovered at **Stackpole**, and the tip of a wooden ard was found in the ditch at Walesland Rath, **Camrose**. Paleobotanical evidence from Graeanog and elsewhere shows that spelt was the favourite form of wheat, although emmer was also widely grown – for example, at Breiddin (**Bausley and Criggion**) and Tŷ Mawr. Barley and **oats** were the other main cereal crops. Evidence for animal husbandry is rarer, for bone seldom survives in acid **soils**, but **sheep**, **goats**, **pigs** and cattle would have been the mainstays of the economy.

In warfare, small, sturdy ponies were highly prized, for they drew chariots of the type described by Caesar, fragments of such a vehicle having been found at Llyn Cerrig Bach (**Llanfair-yn-Neubwll**).

Many of the large highland hill-forts had attached enclosures, probably used mainly in the summer by communities practising transhumance (see **Hafod** and **Hendre**). In the lowlands, small fields, about 0.5 ha in area, are distinguished by their earthen or stone boundaries or appear as lynchet terraces. To refer to them as 'Celtic' may be a misnomer, for many must pre-date the Iron Age. Equally misleading is the vernacular reference to the round house structures as '*cytiau'r Gwyddelod*' (**Irish**men's huts).

The few artefacts discovered at settlement sites do not fully represent the quality and versatility of the material culture of the age. Pottery is almost absent outside the south-east and the Marches; and iron artefacts rarely survive in the acid soils of Wales. Where they have survived, as in the **lake** hoard from Llyn Cerrig Bach, they are of high quality. The skill of the blacksmith is further attested by the firedog, bearing a bull head at each end, which was recovered from a bog at Capel Garmon (**Bro Garmon**).

That the material culture of Iron Age Wales had its roots in mainland Europe is apparent in the decorative bronze objects of the period. Although such objects are rare, they can be highly significant, for they are often examples of the Celtic insular art inspired by the style known as La Tène, after the remarkable lakeside site in Switzerland. In addition to being beautiful, such objects probably had a deep symbolic meaning, with motifs constantly shifting to conjure images that hover between the natural and the supernatural. Notable examples are the shield bosses from Tal-y-llyn (**Llanfihangel-y-Pennant**) and Llyn Cerrig Bach, and the sublime triskele plaque from the latter site. The fragmentary bronze hanging bowl from **Cerrigydrudion** is one of the earliest examples of continental-inspired artwork in Britain. Indeed, it may have been an import from mainland Europe. The infilling of motifs with coloured enamel represents the final stage in the development of insular Celtic art. This was used to great effect in the feline face on a bowl discovered on the slopes of **Snowdon**, in the anthropomorphic faces on a harness mount from **Seven Sisters**, and in the running frieze on the mount for a harness ring from Pentyrch (**Cardiff**).

Many prestige objects have been recovered from watery locations, among them the **Trawsfynydd** tankard, the Capel Garmon firedog, and the hoards from Llyn Fawr and Llyn Cerrig Bach. Such objects may have been deposited in lakes and **rivers** as votive offerings. Indeed, the richness of the Llyn Cerrig Bach hoard helps to confirm written evidence that Anglesey was a major stronghold of the **druids**. The archaeological evidence also indicates that marshes, lakes or rivers were scenes of human sacrifice. The three bodies recovered from Whixall Moss near the **border** at Wem in **Shropshire** may represent such sacrifices. The human head, to the Celts the font of all the senses, was greatly venerated. Carved stone heads, such as that from Hendy (**Llanfairpwll**), or the later example from **Caerwent**, are evidence of the importance of the cult.

Prehistory is the era before the existence of written records. As the Roman invasion launched in AD 43 gave rise to a modicum of written information about Wales, Wales's prehistory comes to an end in the first century of the Christian era. Indeed, Iron Age and Celtic civilization was brought to its conclusion in Britain by that invasion.

Wales, as a geographical rather than a cultural entity, eventually capitulated to the might of Rome, and by the late first century was being integrated into a classical, imperial order.

IRON and STEEL

Iron ore in Wales occurs at three levels in the geological column (see **Geology**): discontinuous oolitic ores interbedded with Ordovician sedimentary rocks, mined in scattered localities in **Anglesey** and **Gwynedd**; veins of haematite in the Carboniferous **Limestone**, particularly around **Llanharry**; and clay ironstone in the **Coal** Measures, which, in association with the coal and limestone, largely determined the location of the main centres of Wales's iron industry. On the northern rim of the south Wales coalfield and in the area immediately north of **Pontypool**, the abundance and accessibility of ironstone led to its being mined in large open patches at an early date.

The scale of iron production in **Britain** increased from the 16th century onwards with the introduction of the blast furnace. Indeed, in the later 16th century the charcoal furnaces were accused in a celebrated poem, 'Coed Glyn Cynon', of having caused the deforestation of the Cynon valley. However, ironmaking did not become a major industry in Wales until the late 18th century, when industrialists began making widespread use of coke as the smelting fuel, a method pioneered by Abraham Darby at Coalbrookdale in **Shropshire**. In 1840, 36.2% of Britain's pig iron was smelted by the 26 works that stretched from **Hirwaun** to Pontypool. At **Merthyr Tydfil**, the major centre, four works – Dowlais (1759), which became the world's largest, with perhaps 5000 employees in 1850, Plymouth (1763), Cyfarthfa (1765) and Penydarren (1784) – consistently produced over 30% of the region's total. Substantial capital investment in most of the south Wales works enabled the latest methods of production to be employed, and specialization – particularly in heavy bar iron for Britain's and the world's **railways** – saw the region emerge as the world's major iron producer between 1820 and 1850.

Developments in the southern coalfield were characterized by large-scale production of bulk iron, for the region did not acquire the workshops found in places such as Birmingham and Sheffield, in which objects made of iron – machines, tools, utensils and armaments – were manufactured. This was in marked contrast with developments in the north-eastern coalfield, where the industry – admittedly much smaller in scale – was concerned with iron production at a far more sophisticated level. This was particularly true of the **Bersham Ironworks**, where **John Wilkinson** proved very innovative. Bersham became the principal supplier of the large cast cylinders used in Boulton and Watt's beam engines, which were bored out to an accurate circular form by a machine developed by Wilkinson. Bersham, and its sister concern at **Brymbo**, also became major producers of cannon, activity much encouraged by the **French Revolutionary and Napoleonic Wars**.

By the end of the 19th century, steel had largely replaced wrought iron as the main constructional material, as Henry Bessemer's converter (1856) and **Wilhelm Siemens's open-hearth furnace** (developed at Landore, **Swansea** in 1868) made its large-scale manufacture an economic proposition. In 1879, the introduction of the 'basic process' by Gilchrist and Thomas (*see* **Sidney Gilchrist Thomas**) at **Blaenavon** completed the technological transformation. Only six of the ironworks changed to converter-based steelmaking – Dowlais, Cyfarthfa, **Ebbw Vale**, **Rhymney**, **Tredegar** and Blaenavon. The remainder closed. As the new process demanded richer iron ore, ore henceforth had to be imported. Therefore, to be located on the coalfield's northern rim was no longer advantageous. Apart from Dowlais, which continued producing until 1930, and Ebbw Vale, all the inland works had closed by 1914; a movement to the coast, initiated by the completion of the Dowlais works at **East Moors**, **Cardiff** (1895), indicated a new direction for the industry.

The western parts of the coalfield, around **Llanelli**, Swansea, **Neath** and **Aberavon**, witnessed the growth of open-hearth steelmaking, mostly for steel sheets for the **tinplate** industry. By 1914, there were 28 steelworks scattered across the region, almost all with their own tinning facilities. In the north, the main development was the **Summers family**'s establishment of the **Shotton Steelworks** (1896). Specializing in galvanized corrugated sheets, the steelworks had 3500 employees by 1914.

The interwar **depression** was a severe blow to the steel industry. Merthyr Tydfil was badly hit following the closure of Dowlais in 1930, but the greatest sufferer was Brymbo, where closure in 1931 caused unemployment among insured males to approach 90%. Matters improved from the mid-1930s onwards. There was substantial capital investment at Cardiff and **Port Talbot**, but the major development was the construction at Ebbw Vale of Britain's first continuous strip mill. Opened by the **Richard Thomas Company** in 1937, the choice of location was dictated more by social need than by strictly economic considerations. Wales's second continuous strip mill was opened at Shotton in 1940.

Increasingly, steelmakers felt the need for the kind of major reorganization that was transforming the industry in the United States. In 1930, **Guest Keen and Nettlefolds** (GKN) and Baldwins combined their heavy ends to form the British (Guest Keen and Baldwins) Iron and Steel Company. In 1945, the Richard Thomas and the Baldwins companies merged to become **Richard Thomas and Baldwins** (RTB), and in 1947 the **Steel Company of Wales** (SCOW) was created by the region's four main steel and tinplate combines. This spelled the beginning of the end for traditional steelmaking and the sheet mills, and by the mid-1950s virtually all the old tinplate mills had closed.

By the 1960s, SCOW at Port Talbot (1952), and RTB at Ebbw Vale (1938) and **Llanwern** (1962) completely dominated sheet steel production. With their continuous strip mills, they could respond to the growing demand from the manufacturers of cars and consumer durables, and could achieve a level of productivity far beyond the capabilities of traditional methods.

The creation of the British Steel Corporation was the result of the renationalization of the steel industry in 1967. (The industry had been temporarily nationalized between 1949 and 1953.) In 1969, a deep-water harbour was opened at Port Talbot, allowing ore carriers in excess of 100,000 tonnes to exploit the economies of transporting high-grade ores from sources such as **Australia** and Brazil. Increasingly, BSC was forced to improve its international competitiveness, through technological innovation and labour-shedding. The advent of continuous casting at Port Talbot in 1982 and at Llanwern in 1988 was symbolic of a consistent improvement in the technology of steel production, which, between 1979 and 1985, almost doubled the level of labour productivity. The concomitant reduction in employment, which had begun in the mid-1960s, came to a climax between 1980 and 1985, when BSC laid off some

Thomas Hornor's painting of the Penydarren ironworks *c.*1817

Port Talbot steelworks

32,000 workers. In 1970, almost 80,000 were employed in the industry in south Wales. That figure had declined to 22,000 by 1985; and to 8000 by 2004.

When British Steel was privatized in 1988, BSC Ltd benefited commercially from the massive productivity gains it inherited, but rapidly changing global markets imposed increasing pressures during the 1990s. BSC was absorbed into a British-Dutch consortium, Corus, in 1998, and stringent rationalization in 2001 saw substantial redundancies, as steelmaking at Llanwern ceased. A year later, Ebbw Vale closed. In the north, the Shotton Steelworks, which had had 10,000 employees in 1960, closed in 1979, although a steel-coating plant employing some 700 workers survived. In 2007, Corus was taken over by the Indian-based company Tata Steel.

Although large-scale continuous strip mills have dominated the modern Welsh steel industry, there were other, smaller enterprises such as the Orb works at **Newport**, which specialized in electrical steels, Cardiff's East Moors works, which made heavy constructional sections (closed in 1978), and Allied Steel and Wire in Cardiff, which specialized in steel reinforcing rods (closed in 2002).

IRONWORK

The ability to shape **iron**, one of the commonest of the earth's metals and a metal still crucial to contemporary civilization, gave the prehistoric iron-using peoples (*see* **Iron Age**) a revolutionary advantage over the users of **copper** and bronze (*see* **Bronze Age**).

Among the oldest iron artefacts discovered in **Britain** – part of a sword from *c.*600 BC – was found in 1908 at Llyn Fawr above the **Rhondda** valley (*see* **Rhigos**). Other Iron Age finds include the Capel Garmon (**Bro Garmon**)

firedogs, now in the **National Museum**, and the Llyn Cerrig Bach hoard (**Llanfair-yn-Neubwll**), discovered in 1942, which attests to the centrality of **Anglesey** in druidical religion. Welsh **law** emphasized the status of the blacksmith, confirming his right to free land, use of the royal mill and other privileges.

The decorative use of iron was largely a matter of forging: beating hot metal over an anvil to create forms. When later innovations refined the casting of iron, many of the customary patterns and shapes of the forge were adapted to the new decorative mouldings.

In the 18th century, new uses were found for iron in both domestic and industrial **architecture**. It became fashionable to adorn mansions with iron balconies, verandas, gates and fireplaces. Wales's finest workers in iron were the **Davies family** of **Esclusham**. Functional structures were partly constructed from and embellished with iron. For example, the chains for the first Brighton pier (1823) were made at the Brown Lennox Chainworks, **Pontypridd**. Wales found a worldwide market for its iron rails. Indeed, it was probably on a rail bearing the letters GL (**Guest** Lewis, the trademark of Dowlais) that poor Anna Karenina met her end. In the later 19th century, nine largely iron **piers** were built at Welsh resorts, and towns were endowed with fountains, street furniture, bandstands, memorial **clocks**, verandahs and balconies made from iron.

One of the principle 19th-century British designers in iron was the **London**-born Welshman **Owen Jones** (1809–74), superintendent of the Great Exhibition of 1851 and author of the seminal *The Grammar of Ornament* (1856). Historical influences and imperial motifs resulted in a curious amalgam of contrasting forms being brought into novel decorative use. During the **Second World War**, much early street furniture and many gates and railings were lost in the appeal for scrap metal to fuel the war effort – much of which was never used. In the late 20th century, David Petersen (whose father was boxer **Jack Petersen**) and his sons led a revival in Wales in the making of artistic iron-work.

IS CENNEN Commote

The southernmost of the three **commotes** of **Cantref Bychan**, it contained Carreg Cennen Castle (**Dyffryn Cennen**). Is Cennen became a **march**er-lordship and subsequently a **hundred**.

IS COED Commote

One of the 10 **commotes** of **Ceredigion**, Is Coed constituted the south-western corner of the ancient kingdom. It was divided into Is Hirwern and Uwch Hirwern. The former, and the town of **Cardigan**, were under **English** control by the 1240s, when they became the nucleus of **Cardiganshire**. As descendant of the senior line of the house of **Deheubarth**, **Owain Glyndŵr** held land in Uwch Hirwern.

ISAAC, Bert (1923–2006) Artist

Cardiff-born Bert Isaac grew up at Church Village (**Llantwit Fardre**) on the edge of the southern **coal**field. From 1940 to 1944, he studied under **Ceri Richards** at Cardiff and developed a style that fused romantic, abstract and surrealist approaches, articulating a lyricism that was relatively rare in the work of Welsh painters of his generation. A favourite theme was the return to nature of post-**industrial sites and landscapes**. He spent much of his life teaching art in **London**, but in 1986 he returned to Wales, settling in **Abergavenny**, his wife Joan's birthplace. In 1992, he published *The Landscape Within*, a set of woodcuts with an essay on the creative process.

ISLAM

A **religion** founded by the prophet Mohammed, who was born at Mecca in AD 570. He had his first revelation from Allah (God) in the year 610 and this and later visions were compiled into the Muslim holy book, the Koran. A monotheistic religion, with meticulous regulations about living, Islam has over 1200 million followers worldwide. In 2001, there were some 24,000 in Wales, among them native Welsh people who have converted to the religion. Welsh Muslims live mainly in the cities of **Cardiff**, **Newport** and **Swansea**, although most of the towns of Wales are home to at least a few Muslim families, who are generally involved in the restaurant and retail trades. In the main, they are of **Bangladeshi**, **Somali** or **Yemeni** origin. In 2004, there were 33 mosques in Wales, a number of them adaptations of redundant **Nonconformist** chapels.

Bert Isaac, *Blue Landscape*, from *The Landscape Within* (1991)

Island Farm Camp, Bridgend, 1944

ISLAND FARM CAMP

Built at **Bridgend** for munitions workers and subsequently used by American troops, Island Farm camp was redesignated in 1944 for the holding of 2000 prisoners of war. On 10–11 March 1945, 67 escaped, all being eventually recaptured. The **Second World War**'s biggest mass escape of German prisoners, it is the subject of Herbert Williams's *Come Out, Wherever You Are* (1976; 2nd edition, 2004). Thereafter, the camp was used to hold German officers awaiting trial at Nuremberg.

ISLANDS

There is broad substance to the adage that there are as many islands around **Scotland** as there are days in the year; around **England,** as there are weeks in the year; and around Wales, as there are months in the year.

Despite Wales's comparative paucity of islands, its largest – **Anglesey** (71,480 ha) – is third in size among the islands of **Britain**. Yet, as it enjoys **county** status and is linked by **road** and **railway** to mainland Wales, Anglesey does not conform to the traditional concept of an island. (In the medieval text 'Enwau Ynys Prydain', it is listed, along with the Isle of **Man** and the Isle of Wight, as one of the 'Three chief Adjacent Islands of the Isle of Britain'.)

Equally linked to the mainland is Wales's second largest island – Holy Isle (Ynys Gybi) (3489 ha) (*see* **Holyhead, Rhoscolyn** and **Trearddur**) – an offshore island of an offshore island of an offshore island.

Other islands are linked with the mainland, not by road or rail but by spits of land traversable at low tide. They include Llanddwyn (**Rhosyr**), Gateholm (**Marloes and St Brides**) and **Sully**; **Barry** Island was accessible only at low tide until the 1880s, when the construction of the Barry dock and railway firmly linked it to the mainland. Conversely, Wales has stretches of rock which are islands at low tide but are inundated at high tide. Among the largest of them are Tusker Rock (**St Brides Major**) and Creigiau'r Odyn (**Llanfaelog**).

Islands are at their most numerous around the coast of southern **Ceredigion** and **Pembrokeshire**. While **Cardigan** Island (Ynys Aberteifi; **Y Ferwig**), Grassholm (Gwales; Marloes and St Brides) and Ramsey Island (Ynys Dewi; **St David's**), rise to considerable heights, Skomer (Sgomer; Marloes and St Brides), Skokholm (Sgogwm; **Dale**) and Caldey (Ynys Bŷr; **Tenby**) are flat-topped islands some 50 m to 70 m above sea level. The solid **geology** of each island reflects that of the neighbouring mainland – the folded Ordovician sedimentary rocks of Cardigan Island, the sedimentary and Ordovician volcanic and intrusive rocks of Ramsey, the early Silurian volcanic rocks of Skomer and Grassholm, the folded Old Red Sandstone of Skokholm and the Old Red Sandstone and Carboniferous **Limestone** of Caldey.

Flat Holm (Ynys Echni; **Cardiff**) is underlain by limestone deposited on the floor of a shallow tropical sea during the Carboniferous Age. On Sully Island, Triassic sedimentary rocks lie uncomfortably on Carboniferous Limestone. Llanddwyn is an assemblage of ancient rocks which include volcanic pillow lava, and Ynys Seiriol (Puffin Island; **Llangoed**) represents an extension of the Carboniferous Limestone of south-eastern Anglesey.

The flora of the islands of Wales varies from the almost subtropical vegetation of Caldey to the sparse growth on the bleak Skerries (Ynysoedd y Moelrhoniaid; **Cylch-y-Garn**). Among the rare **plants** growing on them are the golden hair lichen of Llanddwyn and the spotted rock rose and spatulate fleawort of Holy Isle. **Mammals** include the bottle-nosed dolphin (*see* **Whales, Dolphins and Porpoises**) frequently visible from Bardsey and the grey **seals** which breed on Pembrokeshire's islands. Isolation can lead to the evolution of sub-species, such as the form of the common bank vole known as the Skomer vole. Cardigan Island is home to a flock of Soay **sheep** brought there from the park of Woburn Abbey, Bedfordshire.

It is, however, the **birds** that are the glory of Wales's islands. Half the world's population of Manx shearwater breed on Skomer, Skokholm, Ramsey and Bardsey. Grassholm, the breeding ground for over 32,000 pairs of gannets, is home to the world's second largest gannetry. Skokholm, with its cormorants, shags, oystercatchers, kittiwakes, fulmars, choughs, puffins, guillemots and razorbills, became in 1933 the site of Britain's first bird observatory. Holy Isle has a few pairs of roseate terns, one of Europe's rarest seabirds. Ynys Gwylan-fawr (**Aberdaron**) has a major colony of puffins, but those which once bred on Ynys Seiriol have been devastated by brown rats, which have also destroyed the puffin colony on St Tudwal's Islands (**Llanengan**) off Abersoch.

Caves on Caldey have yielded human bones dating from c.16,000 BC. Holy Isle, with its **Neolithic** burial chamber, **Bronze Age** standing stones, **Iron Age hill-fort**, prehistoric hut groups and **Roman** fort, offers impressive evidence of continuous human occupation. Skomer provides Wales's finest examples of the layout of Iron Age fields.

Leaders of early Christianity found islands irresistible. Ynys Seiriol (known as Priestholm as well as Puffin Island) was associated with St **Seiriol**, Holy Island with St **Cybi**, Llanddwyn with St **Dwynwen**, Ramsey with St **David**, Caldey with St **Samson**, Barry with St Barruc or Barwg and Flat Holm with St **Cadog**. Above all, there is Bardsey (**Aberdaron**), reputedly the resting place of 20,000 **saints** and one of the most popular **pilgrimage** centres of medieval Wales. The Welsh Chronicle, *Annales Cambriae*, records that **Cadwallon**, king of **Gwynedd**, was besieged on Ynys Glannauc (Ynys Seiriol) in 629, and Gwales (Grassholm) features in the second branch of *Pedair Cainc y Mabinogi* (*see* **Mabinogion, The**). For the **Vikings**, islands provided convenient landfalls. Indeed, many of the **English** forms of the names of Welsh islands have Norse roots.

With the **Reformation**, when the house of the **Augustinian** canons on Bardsey and the Tironian priory on Caldey were suppressed, islands ceased to be centres of sanctity. Over the centuries, other functions were found for them, including **piracy** and **smuggling**. Holy Island's location in relation to **Ireland** led to the establishment of the port of Holyhead, and the shelter offered by Barry Island was a key factor in the creation of the port of Barry.

Lighthouses were built on the Skerries, Llanddwyn, Bardsey and Flat Holm, a light beacon on West Mouse (Maen y Bugail; Cylch-y-Garn), a **telegraph** station on Ynys Seiriol and a fort on Thorn Island (**Angle**). Flat Holm came to be used intensely. Apart from its lighthouse and its major **rabbit** warren, it acquired a barracks as well as Britain's sole insular isolation hospital (1884–1937); in 1897, Guglielmo Marconi made it the first place in the world from which a radio message was transmitted across water.

A usage was found for Caldey more in tune with tradition. In 1906, it was bought by **Anglican** monks, who built a monastery near the site of the medieval priory; the monks joined the **Roman Catholic** Church in 1913, and in 1928 the monastery was acquired by the **Cistercians**. By the 1920s,

of Welsh islands solely accessible by sea, only Caldey, Bardsey and Flat Holm had permanent residents. Bardsey, which had 58 inhabitants as late as 1921, ceased to be the home of a farming and **fish**ing community in 1977. It was acquired by the Bardsey Island Trust, which rents the ex-farmhouses to visitors and concerns itself with wildlife conservation. The conservation of wildlife has also become the main concern of most of the other small islands of Wales. The exceptions are Caldey, which is still the home of Cistercian monks, and Thorn Island (**Angle**), where the hotel adapted from the one-time fort is likely to reopen in the foreseeable future; staying in it will be Wales's ultimate experience in isolationism.

ISLWYN Constituency and one-time district
The name, a shortened version of Mynyddislwyn – the ancient **parish** that embraced much of western **Monmouthshire** – was adopted in 1974 as the name for one of the districts of the new **county** of **Gwent**. It consisted of what had been the **urban districts** of **Abercarn**, **Bedwellty**, Mynyddislwyn and **Risca**. In 1996, the district was merged with that of **Rhymney Valley** to form the **county borough** of **Caerphilly**. **William Thomas** (1832–78), a leading 19th-century **Welsh** poet, took the bardic name of Islwyn. The Bedwellty constituency was renamed Islwyn in 1983. It was represented from 1970 to 1995 by Neil Kinnock.

ISYCOED (Is-y-coed) (1360 ha; 348 inhabitants)
Located east of **Wrexham** and adjoining the **Dee** at its most meandering stage, the **community** contains the eastern wing of the Wrexham Industrial Estate. St Paul's church (1829) is surmounted by an **iron** corona.

Bardsey, off the Llŷn peninsula, a place of pilgrimage

The Italian Cordani family's Market Café, Commercial Street, Tredegar, *c.*1946

ITALIANS

Towards the end of the 19th century, a group of Italian street vendors of ice cream, forced out of **London** by a saturated market, arrived in south Wales seeking fresh opportunities. These pioneers, often accompanied by their wives, established a network of cafés, ice cream parlours and **fish** and chip shops, which soon stretched from the southern **coal**field into mid and north Wales.

Most of them had originated in a part of the Apennine **Mountains** of northern Italy, centred on the little town of Bardi. When they needed fresh labour for their rapidly expanding businesses, they returned to their native villages in search of workers. Many of those they brought to Wales were children who in turn became shop managers and owners.

The Italian cafés, offering snacks and soft drinks as well as tobacco, sweets and ice cream, became focal points for the community – places where people could gather for conversation and a little inexpensive entertainment. However, the fact that they were open on Sundays led to **Nonconformist** comments about 'the Italian menace'. In the **Rhondda** valley, an area in which the cafés proliferated, they were known as 'Bracchis', a name derived, perhaps, from Angelo Bracchi who established the first café in the Rhondda in the early 1890s.

Some of the most successful of the immigrants transformed the cheap and cheerful concept of catering embodied by the cafés and fish and chip shops into something more sophisticated. The brothers Frank and Aldo Berni, for example, who began their business lives in **Merthyr Tydfil,** before moving to the west of **England**, started the Berni Inn chain of steakhouses. With menus limited to a few perennial favourites such prawn cocktail, steak and chips, and Black Forest gateau, the inns brought the middle-**class** concept of an evening out at a restaurant within reach of almost everyone's pocket.

The bleakest period for the community was during the **Second World War** when, following Mussolini's declaration of war on **Britain** in June 1940, Welsh-Italians who had not obtained British citizenship were classed as enemy aliens. Many males were interned in camps on the Isle of **Man**. Others were sent to Canada. When the ship carrying them, the *Arandora Star*, was torpedoed by a German submarine, 50 of the 446 Italians who died were from Wales.

IVORITES, The

The Philanthropic Order of True Ivorites **friendly society** (named after Ifor Hael, 'Ifor the Generous' – patron of **Dafydd ap Gwilym**) was inaugurated in **Wrexham** in 1836. After moving its headquarters to **Carmarthen** in 1838, the order expanded rapidly in west Wales, with lodges established for **women** as well as for men. Besides providing sickness and funeral benefits in return for regular contributions, the Ivorites' main aim was to promote the **Welsh language** and Welsh cultural activities. Lodge and national *eisteddfodau* were held, and attempts were made to publish magazines for members. From the 1850s, the centre of Ivorite activity shifted eastwards into the developing **coal**field communities.

At its height, membership was possibly as much as 20,000. However, towards the end of the 19th century the order shared the fate of the friendly society movement as a whole. A change of rules in the 1920s, removing the emphasis on the Welsh language, failed to halt the decline. By 1955, membership had fallen to little over 1000, and the Order was dissolved on 31 December 1959. The name survives in a number of inn names.

The Carmarthen criminal register, 1870, recording that Evan and Hannah Jacob had been convicted of the manslaughter of their daughter Sarah Jacob

JACKSON, Kenneth (Hurlstone) (1909–91) Scholar
During the **Second World War**, Kenneth Jackson was called upon to serve in the British Imperial Censorship in Bermuda, and he qualified as a censor in no fewer than 23 languages. As a scholar, he specialized in the study of the **Celt**ic languages and in his major work *Language and History in Early Britain* (1953) he sought to date the phonetic changes that occurred as the parent British language evolved into **Welsh**, Cornish and Breton. A native of Surrey, he was educated at **Cambridge**, **Bangor** and Dublin. He became a lecturer at Harvard in 1939, but spent most of his career (1950–79) as professor of Celtic studies at Edinburgh.

JACOB, Sarah (1857–69) 'The Welsh Fasting Girl'
The story of Sarah Jacob, of Llethr-neuadd Uchaf (**Llanfihangel-ar-Arth**), attracted great attention in the press. According to her parents, she did not eat or drink during the two years preceding her death, aged 11, in 1869. Others suspected Hannah and Evan Jacob of secretly feeding her, thus deceiving visitors who came to marvel and leave gifts; and one doctor claimed that the girl was feeding herself. The post-mortem showed that she had starved to death, and her parents were jailed for manslaughter. There were two similar cases in Wales: Gaenor Hughes from Bodelith, **Llandderfel**, a woman who was said to have lived solely on spring water for nearly six years before her death in 1780; and Ann Morgan, from **Borth**, a little girl who reputedly went without **food and drink** for several weeks in the 1870s, before breaking her fast in hospital.

JACOBINISM
The Jacobins were an anti-aristocratic and republican element in the French Revolution who originally met in the one-time Paris monastery of St Jacques. They sought to put into revolutionary practice the ideas of Jean-Jacques Rousseau and others. The Jacobin-inspired slogan 'Liberty, Equality and Fraternity' gave a powerful impetus to radical democrats worldwide. Elements of Jacobinism were popularized in Wales in *Y Cylchgrawn Cynmraeg*, edited by **Morgan John Rhys**, and in the pamphlets of Jac Glan-y-gors (**John Jones**; 1766–1821); but most Welsh radicals, **Richard Price** and **David Williams** (1738–1816) among them, sympathized with the more moderate Girondists.

Alfred Janes, *Salome* (1938)

JACOBITISM

The Jacobites opposed the succession of the Hanoverian dynasty to the throne, supporting instead the claims of the Old Pretender James Edward, the son of James II, and his son, Charles Edward (Bonnie Prince Charlie, the Young Pretender).

In Wales, Jacobitism found support among the lesser clergy – the bishops were Hanoverian appointees – and the **Tory gentry**. The Cycle of the White Rose was established in the north-east in 1710 and received a new impetus in 1723 from the leadership of Sir Watkin **Williams Wynn** of Wynnstay (**Ruabon**). In the south-west, the Society of Sea Serjeants, founded in 1726, upheld the Jacobite cause.

The advisers of the Young Pretender expected powerful support from Wales during the Jacobite Rising of 1745, and the fact that such help was not forthcoming was one of the factors which induced the prince not to advance further south than Derby.

In reality, Jacobitism in Wales was largely an affair of secret societies whose members met to drink the health of 'the king over the water' in specially engraved glasses decorated with the white rose, the Stuart emblem. After the failure of the 1745 rising, the movement gradually faded away.

JAMES OF ST GEORGE (*c.*1230–1309) Architect

The architectural power behind the **Edwardian conquest** of Wales was James of St George, from Savoy in the Alps.

He was a military architect of genius who masterminded the building of almost all the major late 13th-century castles of Wales. He was also the Master of the King's Works in Wales and had gained his experience from his work on various great castles on the European mainland, among them the Savoy fortress of St George d'Esperanche, from which he took his full name. With massive resources at his disposal, he began his work in Wales at **Rhuddlan** and concluded it at **Beaumaris**, the most sophisticated – if unfinished – example of military **architecture** of the Middle Ages. He was directly responsible for at least 12 of the 17 castles that Edward I built, rebuilt or strengthened. He was also responsible for work on the castles of some of the **march**er-lords, in particular at **Denbigh**. His most imposing castles were **Conwy**, **Harlech** and **Caernarfon**, begun in 1283, and Beaumaris, begun in 1296. They represent an artful synthesis of beauty and awesome power; Caernarfon deliberately echoes the walls of Constantinople and established a fresh icon of empire at the western edge of Europe.

JAMES, Carwyn (1929–83) Rugby player and coach

In the masculine and sometimes boorish world of **rugby** football, Carwyn James stood out by virtue of his sensitivity, intellect and wide cultural interests. Born at Cefneithin (**Gorslas**), he enjoyed a school and university (**Aberystwyth**) career of academic and sporting distinction. He also developed an abiding love of **Welsh** and European **literature**, and during his national service he learned Russian.

A willowy but resilient fly-half of poise and prodigious drop-kicking ability, his international career coincided with that of the physically more robust Cliff Morgan, confining him to two caps in 1958. For all his playing achievements, it was as a coach that he won fame. His meticulous preparation, technical expertise and searching analysis of the opposition, allied to soft-spoken man-management, inspired the 1971 British Lions to a first-ever Test series against the All Blacks. He then coached his club, **Llanelli**, to victory over them the following year. In the late 1970s, he coached Rovigo to the Italian championship.

Unfailingly generous, but an essentially private and unclubbable person, James did not endear himself to a Welsh rugby fraternity who remained wary of his anti-apartheid stance, political **nationalism** and cultivated articulacy. A fluent communicator in both Welsh and **English**, he had found his vocation in **newspapers** and **broadcasting** when his premature death robbed Wales and world rugby of one of its foremost thinkers.

JAMES, David [John] (1887–1967) Businessman and philanthropist

Born in **London**, James was brought up in his family's old home of Pantyfedwen (Pontrhydfendigaid, **Ystrad Fflur**). He began to train for the ministry, but returned to London to run the family's milk business. He made a fortune from this and other ventures. He owned 13 **cinemas** and built the first of London's 'super-cinemas' (1920). Through the Pantyfedwen (1952) and other trusts, he disbursed considerable sums of money to religious, **education**al and cultural organizations in Wales, including the **eisteddfod** held annually in Pontrhydfendigaid. He was knighted in 1959.

JAMES, Emrys (1930–89) Actor

A member of the Royal **Shakespeare** Company for over 20 years, Emrys James was possibly the company's finest character actor. Born in **Machynlleth**, he studied at **Aberystwyth** and the Royal College of Dramatic Art. Always a dangerous actor, he accentuated the complex, contradictory natures of the characters he played. The American critic Homer Swander described his acting as 'awesome'. Emrys James appeared in many television **dramas** and occasional feature **films**. He was married to the novelist Siân James (b.1932).

JANES, Alfred (1911–99) Artist

Born above the family fruit shop in **Swansea**, Alfred Janes studied at the local art school before winning a scholarship to the Royal Academy Schools, **London**. His **paintings** and constructions maintain a vigorous, mathematical discipline, although he experimented widely. His interest in **music** and **science** was reflected in his art, which was systematic, structural and occasionally humorous. His intricate portraits of close friends **Dylan Thomas**, **Daniel Jones**, **Vernon Watkins** and **Mervyn Levy** are in the Glynn Vivian **Art Gallery**, Swansea.

JAPAN WARE

The only consciously artistic product of Wales's heavy industries, japan ware was developed at **Pontypool** in the early 18th century after John Allgood and his son Edward developed a method of producing lacquered **tinplate** having the same appearance as Japanese lacquered wood.

Factories at Pontypool, where the Japan Works opened in 1720, and later at **Usk**, produced affordable domestic goods for the burgeoning **population** of industrial Wales.

Decorated by hand, generally using **bird**, animal and **plant** motifs, japanning was applied to **clocks**, trays, tableware, **tea** caddies, snuff boxes and other household items. The industry attracted artists to the area, some of whom, like the **Barker family**, were to have a major influence on the development of art in Wales. The advent of lithography and the mechanization of **printing** methods brought an end to the industry by the mid-19th century. The **National Museum** contains examples of the ware.

JARMAN, A[lfred] O[wen] H[ughes] (1911–98) Scholar

A. O. H. Jarman did more than anyone to unravel the complexities of the legend of Myrddin (**Merlin**). He published studies of the **Cynfeirdd**, *Y Gododdin* and on Arthurian **literature** (*see* **Arthur**) as well as on the **Morris brothers** and 18th-century historiography. After a period as a lecturer under the auspices of the extramural department at **Bangor**, his native city, he spent his career in the **Welsh** department at **Cardiff**, where he was professor (1956–79). With his wife Eldra Jarman (1917–2000), who was proud of her **Romany** descent, he published *Y Sipsiwn Cymreig* (1979) and *The Welsh Gypsies* (1991).

JAZZ or GAZOOKA BANDS

Terms used in the industrial south to describe the competitive marching bands that were ubiquitous in the first half

Junior world championship jazz band winners, the Gelligaer Stewardesses, with their trophy in 1977

of the 20th century. Marching and costume design were more important than the quality of the performance of melodies played on a collection of wind instruments, among them the kazoo – a cigar-shaped instrument containing a diaphragm of thin paper which vibrates when a player hums into it. The rhythmic exhibitionism of percussionists is also a feature of these bands.

JEFFREYS, George (c.1644–89) Judge

Born in Acton (see **Wrexham**), 'Bloody Judge Jeffreys' is notorious for his sentencing to **execution** in 1685 of 320 people in the aftermath of the rebellion of the Duke of Monmouth. The number is probably exaggerated, but there is no doubting that Jeffreys was far from impartial in trying cases where there was a royal interest, especially in cases of high treason. Following his appointment as Chief Justice of the King's Bench (1683), he acquired an unenviable reputation for bias and harshness in his conduct of such cases. As a judge in civil cases, however, he was a model of judicial propriety. He became lord chancellor (1685); but when James II fled abroad, he was forced to resign and seek refuge in the Tower of **London**, where he died.

JEFFREYS, John Gwyn (1809–85) Zoologist

A solicitor in his native **Swansea** and a barrister in **London**, Jeffreys spent most of his spare time collecting molluscs. Involved in many marine expeditions to mainland Europe and America, he recovered molluscs from depths previously regarded as impossible. Retirement from the **law** at the age of 57 enabled him to complete his still definitive *British Conchology* (5 vols, 1862–69). Elected FRS in 1840, Jeffreys's contribution to marine biology has yet properly to be assessed.

JEFFREYSTON, Pembrokeshire
(1967 ha; 540 inhabitants)
Located north-west of **Tenby**, the **community** contains the villages of Jeffreyston, Cresselly, Loveston and Yerbeston. St Leonard's church, Loveston, is an unspoilt medieval building. St Lawrence's church, Yerbeston – minute and abandoned – has an 18th-century belfry turret. St Jeffrey's church, heavily Victorianized, stands in a circular churchyard, suggesting that it may occupy a pre-Christian site. Near it is a 14th-century preaching cross. Cresselly House (1771, 1816) contains fine plasterwork. Jeffreyston was the birthplace of the **hymn**ologists James and John Kelly, who, in the 18th century, established an active and independent sect ('the Kellites') in the locality. Anthracite was mined in the area and shipped from Cresswell Quay. In 1936, seven men were killed in the Loveston pit disaster.

JEHOVAH'S WITNESSES
Founded in the United States in 1870, the first congregation in Wales was established in **Clydach** in 1911. By 1914, a number of the denomination's publications were available in **Welsh**. By the early 21st century, there were over 7000 Jehovah's Witnesses active in Wales, with the congregation at **Caernarfon** worshipping in Welsh. A regional assembly held at **Cardiff** in 2002 attracted over 10,000 people.

JEHU, Thomas John (1871–1941) Geologist
A native of **Llanfair Caereinion**, Jehu graduated in both medicine and **geology** at Edinburgh and **Cambridge** respectively. Appointed to the newly created lectureship at St Andrews in 1903, he was chosen as a member of the Royal Commission on Coast Erosion (1906) and appointed regius professor of geology and mineralogy at Edinburgh (1913). His first important research project was on the bathymetry (measuring the depths) of the **lakes** of **Snowdonia**, followed by that on the glacial deposits of north **Pembrokeshire** and west **Caernarfonshire**. His subsequent work was on the older rocks of the Highlands and islands of **Scotland**.

JENKIN, Thomas James (1885–1965) Botanist
A farmer's son from **Maenclochog**, Jenkin studied at **Aberystwyth** without the benefit of secondary **education**, but with a sharp countryman's eye and a keen scientific curiosity. As senior research officer at the Welsh Plant Breeding Station (WPBS; see **Institute of Grassland and Environmental Research**), his major success was the discovery of a perennial ryegrass in **Pembrokeshire**, which could be cropped to ground level without damage, and the subsequent development of strain S.23, which improved pastures throughout the world. He became director of the WPBS and, in 1942, succeeded Sir **George Stapledon** as professor of agricultural botany at Aberystwyth.

JENKINS, Albert [Edward] (1895–1953)
Rugby player
One star shone brightly throughout the gloomy 1920s, when Welsh international **rugby** was as depressed as the **economy**. Despite his prodigious goal-kicking, tackling and try-scoring feats for **Llanelli** – where he was born and idolized – Jenkins was never properly appreciated by the national selectors, who awarded him only 14 caps between 1920 and 1928.

JENKINS, Arthur (1882–1943)
Trade unionist and MP
Born at Varteg, **Abersychan**, Jenkins started work as a **coal**miner at the age of 12. In 1908, he went to Ruskin College, **Oxford**, where he took part in the strike which resulted in the establishment of the **Central Labour College**. He then spent nine months in Paris, where he developed a lifelong devotion to **French** culture and became acquainted with Laura Lafargue, Karl Marx's daughter.

A miners' agent from 1918, in 1926 he was sentenced to nine months' imprisonment for riotous assembly. A conciliatory figure, his sentence caused consternation, and pressure from the leaders of the **Labour Party** reduced his period in **prison** to four months. In 1934, he was elected vice-president of the **South Wales Miners' Federation** and co-operated with the president, **James Griffiths**, in the struggle against **company unionism**. Elected MP for **Pontypool** in 1935, from 1940 to 1946 he was Clement Attlee's parliamentary private secretary. The bond between the Labour Party and the **trade union** movement was the determining factor of his life.

His son, Roy Jenkins (1920–2003), became British home secretary (1965–67), chancellor of the exchequer (1967–70), leader of the 'yes' campaign in the referendum on **Britain**'s entry into Europe, president of the European Commission, and the chief figure in the establishment of the Social Democratic Party. His urbane and lordly demeanour as president of the European Commission earned him the soubriquet 'le roi Jean Quinze'.

After his upbringing at Abersychan and a year at University College, **Cardiff** (*see* **Cardiff University**), his contacts with Wales were slight. Indeed, following his election as SDP member for Hillhead, Glasgow, he is purported to have expressed his gratification that the Scots were prepared to elect an Englishman. However, he did serve as president of the **University of Wales** Institute of Science and Technology, which he saw as an apprenticeship for his term as chancellor of Oxford University, an office he greatly relished. A ferocious croquet player, Jenkins was an acclaimed biographer – *Churchill* (2002) won particular praise – whose autobiography, *A Life at the Centre* (1991), is both reflective and amusing. His mother, the daughter of a manager of the **Blaenavon Iron**works, made strenuous efforts to ensure that he did not find out that his father had been to prison.

JENKINS, Cyril (1889–1978) Musician

A trenchant critic of progressive views, Jenkins courted notoriety through his scathing attacks on the **music** and influence of **Joseph Parry**. He was born at **Dunvant** and brought up in **Pontypridd**. His lengthy musical career took him to **Australia** and the United States where he became director of the famous **Mormon** Tabernacle Choir in Salt Lake City. He was a prolific composer, from piano music to large-scale choral and orchestral works. His 'Life Divine' and 'Coriolanus' remain staples of the **brass band** repertoire.

JENKINS, David (1582–1663) Judge

The best-known member of a family which held land at Hensol (**Pendoylan**), he was judge of Great Sessions (*see* **Law**) for south-west Wales, but during the **Civil Wars** his relations with Parliament soured: summoned before Parliament in 1650, he is said to have challenged them to hang him, saying that he would go to the scaffold with the **Magna Carta** under one arm and the **Bible** under the other. He published many challenging Royalist declarations and made an innovative collection of eight centuries of law reports, published in 1661.

JENKINS, David (1848–1915) Musician

Born at Trecastle (**Llywel**), Jenkins was apprenticed to a tailor, but chose instead a career in **music**, becoming, in 1874, one of **Joseph Parry**'s first students at **Aberystwyth**. After graduating from **Cambridge**, he returned to Aberystwyth where he was, successively, instructor, lecturer and, in 1910, professor. Jenkins is mainly remembered for some fine **hymn** tunes (such as 'Builth', 'Penlan' and 'Bod Alwyn') and for several large-scale choral works, such as *Job*, which were popular during his lifetime. He was well known throughout **Britain** and the United States as an adjudicator and conductor (often referred to as the 'Kaiser of the *Cymanfa*'). His house, Castell Brychan, high above Cardigan Bay, became the home of the **Welsh Books Council**.

JENKINS, John (Gwili; 1872–1936)
Theologian and poet

Gwili was the author of a pioneering history of **theology** in Wales, *Hanfod Duw a Pherson Crist* (1931). He was born at Hendy (**Llanedi**) and educated at **Bangor**, **Cardiff** and **Oxford**. In 1923, he became professor of New Testament studies at the Bangor **Baptist** College. As a poet, he won the crown at the National **Eisteddfod** of 1901 and served as **archdruid** (1932–6). He was a friend of the poet **Edward Thomas**.

JENKINS, Joseph (1818–98) Diarist

In December 1868, Jenkins, a substantial tenant farmer in **Tregaron**, impulsively moved to Victoria, **Australia**. There he remained for the next 25 years, mainly as an itinerant labourer or 'swagman'. He is most noteworthy for the remarkable **English-language** diaries he kept daily, from 1839 until his death, and their acute observations on Welsh and colonial life. Widely known in Australia, they were published as *The Diary of a Welsh Swagman 1869–1894* (1975).

JENKINS, Leoline (1623–85) Lawyer

Llantrisant-born Leoline Jenkins was probably the leading civil lawyer of his generation. Much employed as a diplomat after the Stuart Restoration (1660), he was principal of Jesus College, **Oxford** (1661/2–73), of which he is considered the second founder. He was responsible, with others, for drafting the important Statute of Frauds (1677).

JENKINS, R[obert] T[homas] (1881–1969) Historian

Liverpool-born R. T. Jenkins, brought up by his grandparents in **Bala**, was educated at **Aberystwyth** and **Cambridge**. After periods of teaching at **Llandysul**, **Brecon** and **Cardiff**, he was appointed lecturer in Welsh history at **Bangor** (1930), becoming a professor in 1946. **Nonconformist** and Methodist history was his specialized field, but he wrote in **periodicals** such as *Y Beirniad* and *Y Llenor* on a wide range of historical and literary subjects, in particular travel and French life and culture. Selections of his essays were published in *Yr Apêl at Hanes* (1930), *Ffrainc a'i Phobl* (1930), *Casglu Ffyrdd* (1956) and *Ymyl y Ddalen* (1973). His textbooks on the history of Wales in the 18th and 19th centuries are written in a notably engaging style, as is his autobiography, *Edrych yn nôl* (1968). A history of **roads** in Wales, *Y Ffordd yng Nghymru* (1933), was written for children but appeals to all ages.

His fiction includes the historical novel *Orinda* (1943), based on the story of **Katherine Philipps**, and *Ffynhonnau Elim* (1945), published under the pseudonym Idris Thomas. He bore the main share in the editing of *Y Bywgraffiadur Cymreig* (1953) and the entire responsibility for editing its counterpart in **English**, *The Dictionary of Welsh Biography* (1959).

JENKINS, Vivian [Gordon James] (1911–2004)
Rugby player

Raised in **Coity** and schooled at **Llandovery**, Jenkins was a double Blue at **Oxford**. He played county **cricket** for **Glamorgan** between 1931 and 1937, but his fame rests on his **rugby** prowess. A British Lion in 1938, he won the first of his 14 caps in the first Welsh win at Twickenham, in 1933. The strong-tackling Jenkins became in 1934 the first Welsh international player to score a try from full-back, a feat not repeated until 1967, and he converted two of the Welsh tries in the pulsating 13–12 win over the 1935 All Blacks. His playing-field qualities of style and enthusiasm characterized his later career as chief rugby correspondent of *The Sunday Times*.

JERNEGAN, William (1751–1836) Architect

Although said to have come from the Channel Islands, little is known of Jernegan's early life. He built up a flourishing practice in **Swansea**, and became the town's principal architect. He was closely involved in the layout of much of Swansea's maritime quarter, and designed the Assembly Rooms (1810–21), a new town hall (1825, unbuilt) and Mumbles **lighthouse** (1793). He was also responsible for a number of **gentry** houses in the area, such as the octagonal Marino (1783, later incorporated into Singleton Abbey) and Stouthall (1787–90) (**Reynoldston**), as well as commissions in **Cardiff** and **Milford Haven**.

JEWS

Some Jewish people already lived in Welsh towns in the 13th century, and there are several references to Jews – often contemptuous – in medieval Welsh poetry. After the readmission of Jews in 1655, following their expulsion from the territories of the English crown in 1290, there were itinerant Jewish peddlers in Wales, but no settled community until *c*.1750, when one was formed in **Swansea**. Others communities followed: in **Cardiff** in 1813 and **Merthyr Tydfil** in 1848. **Colwyn Bay** became a favoured resort of the Jewish community of Merseyside.

By the early 20th century, Jewish settlement in Wales was widespread rather than concentrated and, unusually for **Britain**, Jews had a virtual monopoly on pawnbroking. Although Jewish communities in the eastern **coal**field were attacked in August 1911, and much property was destroyed, many Welsh people saw an affinity between themselves and the Jews – although that Welsh **Liberal** icon **O. M. Edwards** wrote a truly appalling anti-Semitic tirade.

Paul Morrison's Oscar-nominated **film** *Solomon and Gaenor* (1998) tells a romantic tale of uneasy Jewish–Welsh relationships in an industrial southern community in 1911.

In the interwar **depression**, Jewish communities in the coalfield declined, and many moved to Cardiff or **London**. The Cardiff community became focused on Cyncoed, where a new synagogue was erected in 1955. In Wales, Jewish people tended to be newcomers and thus observers of orthodox religion, rather than adherents of the reform tendencies of the more assimilated. Reform currents became more significant after 1945. From the late 1930s, Jewish refugees from mainland Europe made an important contribution to the diversification of the **economy** of south Wales.

The physicist Brian Josephson (b.1940), one of only three Welsh-born Nobel laureates (the others are **Bertrand Russell** and the Swansea-born economist Clive Granger (b.1934)), was brought up as a member of Cardiff's Jewish community, as were two of Wales's best-known **English-language** writers, Dannie Abse (b.1923) and **Bernice Rubens**.

The scholar and **Welsh**-language writer Kate-Bosse Griffiths (*see* **J. Gwyn Griffiths**) was a Jewish refugee from Nazi Germany. The **English**-language writer Jerusalem-born Judith Maro (*see* **Jonah Jones**) ensured that her work

The Jewish cemetery at Cefn-coed-y-cymer, Merthyr Tydfil

was translated into Welsh. The Welsh **Nonconformist** enthusiasm for 'the People of the Book', a tradition in which **David Lloyd George** had been nurtured, was partly responsible for his authorization of the Balfour Declaration (1917), which opened the way for the establishment of the state of Israel.

JOAN (Siwan; d.1237) Princess

An illegitimate daughter of King John of **England**, Joan – or Siwan as she became known in Wales – married **Llywelyn ap Iorwerth**, prince of **Gwynedd**, in about 1205. (In 1226, the Pope declared that Joan was the legitimate daughter of her father.) This was essentially a political alliance; it meant that any children of the marriage would be recognized outside Wales as being of royal blood and that the house of Gwynedd would thereby be set apart from the other Welsh dynasties. Joan was a strong personal and political support to her husband, interceding for him with her father on occasion.

The marriage came under severe strain in 1230 following her affair with William de **Breos**, who was hanged by Llywelyn after they were caught together. However, husband and wife were reconciled; and when Joan died in 1237, the prince founded a Franciscan **friary** at Llanfaes (**Beaumaris**) in her memory and it was there that she was buried. She bore Llywelyn one son, **Dafydd ap Llywelyn**, who succeeded him, and at least three daughters. **Saunders Lewis**'s play *Siwan* (1956) commemorates her.

JOHANNES WALLENSIS (John of Wales, Siôn o Gymru, Johannes Gallensis, John Waleys; fl. *c.*1260–83) Friar

Johannes, who entered the Franciscan order (*see* **Friars**) before 1258, trained at **Oxford** and then at Paris, where he became a regent-master of **theology**. In 1282, he was associated with the negotiations of the archbishop of Canterbury, John **Pecham**.

JOHN, Augustus [Edwin] (1878–1961) Artist

At the time of his sister's death in 1939, posterity seemed to have declared that **Tenby**-born Augustus John would be remembered only as the brother of **Gwen John**. If posterity has, yet, finally to make up its mind, there were signs by the early 21st century that Augustus John's reputation as an artist was indeed being eclipsed by that of his sister. A 2004 exhibition at the National Museum, showing the work of brother and sister side-by-side, was an artistic revelation.

After studying at the Slade School in **London**, he displayed immense skill as both draughtsman and portraitist, with an instinctive bravura in the handling of paint. However, as his life unfolded, talent and character conspired to create a caricature of the artistic bohemian. Moving restlessly with his extended family, he played at being a gypsy (*see* **Romanies**) and revelled in high society. This was often at the expense of his art, with him becoming a figure of the gossip columns. **Dylan Thomas**, whom John introduced to his future wife, Caitlin Macnamara, parodied him as Hercules Jones in *The Death of the King's Canary* (1976).

He exhibited in the famous New York Amory Exhibition of 1913, supported by his patron John Quinn.

Influenced by the post-Impressionists, the Symbolists and Puvis de Chavannes, he was in continuous rebellion against academic conservatism. Nonetheless, he depended on his academic skills, rather than invention, in order to maintain his practice. In his later years, he was aware of his own shortcomings, realizing ultimately that, for all his fame, he had dissipated his talent. His early drawings – rather than his portraits of artists, poets, statesmen and composers – remain his lasting, creative legacy.

JOHN, Bob (Robert Frederick John; 1899–1982) Footballer

Barry-born Bob John, originally an apprentice docks' blacksmith and part-time professional **football**er for Barry Town, went on to become one of **Britain**'s greatest halfbacks. His record 421 games for Arsenal included the 1927 Cup Final against **Cardiff**. He won 15 Welsh caps.

JOHN, [David] Dilwyn (1901–95) Zoologist and museum officer

The Polar Medallist Dilwyn John, of **St Bride's Major**, graduated in zoology and **agriculture** at **Aberystwyth**. He served as leader of the scientific staff on the research ship *Discovery II* (1931–3), during the first circumnavigation of the Antarctic in winter months, and as a taxonomist and curator of echinoderms (creatures such as starfish and sea urchins) at the Natural History Museum, **London**. He was director of the **National Museum [of] Wales** (1948–68), a time when the folk museum (The National History Museum; *see* **St Fagans**), the Museum Schools Service and the department of industry were in their infancy.

JOHN, E[dward] T[homas] (1857–1931) Politician

A native of **Pontypridd** who became an **iron**master at Middlesbrough, John turned to politics in middle age, representing East **Denbighshire** as **Liberal** MP (1910–18). He was an unremitting champion of the cause of **Home Rule** for Wales, diligently assembling statistical data intended to strengthen the economic argument for self-**government**. In 1914, he introduced a Welsh Home Rule Bill in the House of Commons. He joined the **Labour Party** in 1918. John was president of the National Union of Welsh Societies and of the Peace Society.

JOHN, [William] Goscombe (1860–1952) Sculptor

The decades around 1900 saw a marked expansion in monument making (*see* **Sculpture**), as Wales, in a new spirit of patriotism, endeavoured to celebrate the country's prime movers and significant moments. A leading contributor to this remarkable upsurge was Goscombe John; it is probable that more people encounter his work, often unbeknown, than that of any other Welsh artist – from the *Corn hirlas* he designed for the National **Eisteddfod** to his monument to the authors of '**Hen Wlad fy Nhadau**' in Ynysangharad Park, **Pontypridd**.

He was born in **Cardiff** into a strong **craft** tradition. His father and brother both worked for **William Burges** in the Bute (*see* **Stuart family**) workshops, which, after studying at Cardiff School of Art, John himself joined. There he met Thomas Nicholls, for whom he later worked in his **London** studio, undertaking commissions that made him

Gwen John, a self-portrait (c.1902)

internationally famous. Knighted in 1911, Goscombe John was essentially a classicist, and his style suited the public taste of the time. His figure of **Owain Glyndŵr** in Cardiff City Hall is among his most memorable works, as is his superb war memorial at Llandaff (*see* **Cardiff**).

JOHN, Griffith (1831–1912) Missionary
The **Swansea**-born **Congregationalist** Griffith John is, with **Timothy Richard**, one of the two Welsh **missionaries** most prominently associated with China. Having married Jane, the daughter of the **Madagascar** missionary David Griffiths (1792–1863), he was originally intended for that island, but was sent to China in 1855. His centre from 1855 to 1911 was Hankow, but he travelled extensively, preaching and establishing churches, schools, a home for lepers and a theological college. His Wen-li New Testament appeared in 1885 and the Mandarin version in 1889. He returned in 1911, died in **London** and was buried at Sketty, Swansea.

JOHN, Gwen[dolen Mary] (1876–1939) Artist
Gwen John, who was born in **Haverfordwest** and moved with her family to **Tenby** in 1884, followed her famous younger brother **Augustus** to the Slade School, **London**, in 1896. She never returned to Wales after leaving for France in 1903, where she lived alone, first in Paris, where she had previously studied in Whistler's *Académie Carmen*, and later in suburban Meudon. Much has been made of her affair with Rodin, for whom she modelled. It would seem from her correspondence that she was a more resilient character than was once believed.

Gwen John was a quiet, reclusive personality whose **painting**s – contemplative in feeling and restrained in colour and brushwork – reflect these qualities. She adopted a version of 'Intimism', in which a single figure generally dominates the composition. Her subject matter ranged from portraits of the nuns at Meudon, to young girls, cats, interiors, still lives and townscapes. Valued by many more highly than that of her flamboyant brother, her work has an air of pensive autobiography.

JOHN AP JOHN (?1625–97) Missionary
Known as 'the apostle of the **Quakers** in Wales', this **Ruabon** yeoman accompanied George Fox on his famous tour through Wales in 1657 and was clapped into **prison** on several occasions. Undaunted, he worked tirelessly to win supporters. Unlike many of his colleagues, he resisted the temptation to emigrate to **Pennsylvania** and devoted over 40 years to furthering the Quaker cause in his homeland.

JOHNES, Thomas (1748–1816)
Landowner and scholar
Descended from an ancient Welsh family, Thomas Johnes inherited the remote and derelict Hafod property in Cwmystwyth (**Pontarfynach**) in the 1780s. Intent on creating an estate according to the 'picturesque' canon and turning it into a private paradise, he proceeded to invest his – and his family's – resources in Hafod with a profligacy which to many seemed insane. As money poured into the wet and barren acres, so the ancestral properties in **Herefordshire**, **Radnorshire** and **Cardiganshire** were sold; with bankruptcy imminent, Johnes eventually retired to Dawlish in Devon, where he died. By the mid-20th century, Hafod had become a ruin, and was demolished in 1962; its **garden** is being restored.

Johnes's contribution to the **picturesque movement** is widely acknowledged. At the same time, the house at Hafod, the work of Baldwin of Bath and **John Nash**, was celebrated throughout **Britain** and became something of a haven in, what seemed to some, the cultural desert of Cardiganshire. A concerned and caring landlord, his agricultural experiments (including the introduction of merino **sheep** and the manufacture of Parmesan **cheese**) were well-meaning, but were hopelessly impractical and doomed to failure.

He was one of the foremost collectors of books and manuscripts in Wales, although much of the material was destroyed by fire in 1807. His library was visited by scholars, antiquaries and dilettanti from all over Europe. Coleridge may have been inspired by Hafod in the writing of 'Kubla Khan'.

MP for **Cardigan Boroughs** (1775–80), Radnorshire (1780–96) and Cardiganshire (1796–1816), he was also an indefatigable scholar and remains to this day the only person to have translated into **English** the *Chronicles* of Froissart in their entirety. These, and other translations, especially of Joinville and Monstrelet, were printed at the Hafod Press (*see* **Printing and Publishing**) located at Pwllpeiran, not far from the mansion itself. The volumes are among the most memorable achievements of a dreamer of the age of **Romanticism**.

JOHNNY ONIONS (Sioni Wynwns or
Sioni Nionod)
The nickname given to any member of the small army of
onion-sellers who used to cross from **Brittany** during the
second half of the year and who would travel to all parts of
the United Kingdom. Their sales activity began in 1828
and they were still occasionally to be seen at the beginning
of the 21st century. However, the golden age of their trade
was between 1919 and 1930, when as many as 1200 would
arrive annually. A familiar sight in many a Welsh town and
village would be that of 'Johnny' pushing his bicycle along,
with his merchandise hanging in thick strings from the
handlebars. His first language was usually Breton, which
made it comparatively easy for him to pick up a little
Welsh, assuring him of a warm welcome in Welsh-speaking
areas.

JOHNS, Mervyn (1899–1992) Actor
Although **Pembroke**-born Johns often epitomized on screen
the indomitable 'little man' of integrity, he could also create
a chilling ambience. He was unforgettable in Thorold
Dickinson's feature *Next of Kin* (1942), as the phlegmatic
Nazi spy posing as a man from **Cardiff** and teasing indiscre-
tions from gullible Britons. For Ealing Studios, Johns
played a pivotal role in the murder-thriller *Pink String and
Sealing Wax* (1945), and was a Welsh prisoner of war in

The Captive Heart (1946). He was the narrator and a leading player in Basil Dearden's engrossing time-warp fantasy
Halfway House (1944) and the definitive Bob Cratchit to
Alastair Sim's Scrooge in *A Christmas Carol* (1951). The
actress Glynis Johns (b.1923) is his daughter.

JOHNSTON, Pembrokeshire
(546 ha; 1778 inhabitants)
Located south-west of **Haverfordwest**, the **community** has
been extensively urbanized and serves as a commuting area
for both Haverfordwest and **Milford Haven**. St Peter's
church retains much of its medieval fabric. Johnston Hall
was one of the residences of the Edwardes family, Barons
Kensington (*see* **Marloes and St Brides**), whose members
provided most of Haverfordwest's MPs between 1747 and
1885. The tramway from **Hook** on the Western **Cleddau**
terminated at Johnston.

JONES, Alfred Lewis (1845–1909) Entrepreneur
Born in **Carmarthen**, Jones moved to **Liverpool** when two
years old and eventually became a commercial and shipping magnate. A leading figure in the Elder Dempster shipping line, he developed trade with West Africa and was a
founder of the Liverpool School of Tropical Medicine.
Knighted in 1901, he was described by **David Lloyd George**
as 'not a man but a syndicate'.

Mervyn Johns with his daughter Glynis in *Halfway House* (1944)

JONES, Alice Gray (Ceridwen Peris; 1852–1943)
Temperance activist and writer
One of the founders (1892) of Undeb Dirwest Merched Gogledd Cymru (the North Wales **Women's Temperance Union**), **Llanllyfni**-born Alice Gray Jones was a regular contributor to **periodicals** such as *Y Frythones*. After *Y Frythones* ceased publication, she launched a new monthly women's magazine, *Y Gymraes* (1892–1934). She also published a volume of verse (1934).

JONES, [Thomas] Artemus (1871–1943) Judge
A stonemason's son from **Denbigh**, Jones studied **law** while working on **newspapers** in Manchester and **London**, and was called to the bar in 1901. He became a **county** court judge in 1930, and was knighted in 1931. During the **Second World War**, he was chairman of the North Wales **Conscientious Objectors'** Tribunal.

He was the successful plaintiff in the famous libel case of *Hulton* v. *Jones* (1910), after which it became customary for publishers of novels to disclaim any similarity between living persons and fictional characters. His advocacy of the use of **Welsh** in courts of **law** did much to assist the passage of the **Welsh Courts Act 1942**. His wife, Mildred Mary David, was a leading figure in the interwar peace movement (*see* **Pacifism**).

JONES, Arthur (Arthur Machen; 1863–1947)
Author
A master of the macabre, Arthur Machen – who used his Scottish mother's maiden name as a pseudonym – was

Arthur Jones (Arthur Machen)

born in **Caerleon** and lived as a literary journalist and, for a time, an actor in **London**. Profoundly influenced by the landscape of his native **Gwent**, together with Welsh and **Celtic** folk tales, Gothic, occult and Rosicrucian writings, Machen became a prolific writer of supernatural tales. One of the most popular, which he continually recycled, was 'The Bowmen', in which a spectral host of archers joins British soldiers in the trenches of Mons. His many books include two volumes of autobiography, *Far Off Things* (1922) and *Things Near and Far* (1923). By the 1920s, he was a cult figure in **North America**, a status he continues to enjoy.

JONES, Bedwyr Lewis (1933–92) Scholar
Bedwyr Lewis Jones had that rare ability to make academic subjects such as **place-name** studies and etymology comprehensible to non-specialists. Consequently, he was a familiar voice on BBC Radio Cymru (*see* **Broadcasting**) and a polished performer on the stage of the literary pavilion of the National **Eisteddfod**. A native of **Llaneilian**, he was educated at **Bangor** and Jesus College, **Oxford**. He returned to Bangor as a lecturer in 1959 and was appointed professor of **Welsh** there in 1974. His scholarly interests spanned the whole history of Welsh **literature**.

JONES, Bryn[mor] (1912–85) Footballer
This most famous of **Merthyr Tydfil**'s **football**ers became **Britain**'s most expensive player when he transferred from Wolverhampton to Arsenal in 1938 for the (then) record fee of £14,000. Arsenal did not see the best of the short, dynamic player, but he remained a star for Wales, gaining 17 caps. Cliff Jones, the 1960s player, was his nephew.

JONES, C[adwaladr] Bryner (1872–1954)
Agriculturist
Born at **Brithdir**, Jones taught at **Bangor** and at King's College, Newcastle-upon-Tyne, before becoming professor of **agriculture** at **Aberystwyth**, and subsequently chairman of the **Welsh Agricultural Commission**. From 1919 until 1944, he was secretary of the **Welsh Department of the Ministry of Agriculture and Fisheries**. The recipient of many official and academic honours, and popular among farmers, Jones was knighted in 1947 for his services to the agriculture of Wales, which included involvement in the establishment of the Welsh Plant Breeding Station (**Institute of Grassland and Environmental Research**), the foundation of the Department of Agricultural Economics at Aberystwyth (1924), and the launching of the National **Soil** Survey at Bangor.

JONES, Calvert Richard (1802–77)
Pioneer of photography
Swansea-born Calvert Jones, an **Anglican** clergyman who was only briefly responsible for a **parish**, became involved with **photography** through his connection with William Henry Fox Talbot (1800–77). His work – especially his studies of shipping – is important in the early history of photography. He took the first dated Welsh photograph; preserved at the **National Library**, it is a daguerreotype of **Margam** Castle (1841).

Calvert Jones's 1841 daguerreotype of Margam Castle

JONES, Cliff (1914–90) Rugby player and administrator

After a brilliant playing career, **Rhondda**-born Cliff Jones became a notable **rugby** administrator. His speed off the mark, devastating side-step and mastery of the teasing grub-kick brightly illuminated the dark Saturday afternoons of the **Depression**. Capped 13 times between 1934 and 1939, including Wales's 13–12 victory over the 1935 All Blacks, he became a national selector (1956–78) and enthusiastic advocate of the coaching initiatives which underlay Welsh rugby's success in the 1970s.

JONES, D[avid] J[ohn] V[ictor] (1941–94) Historian

One of the most distinguished historians of his time, **Carreghofa**-born D. J. V. Jones joined the staff of the department of history at **Swansea** in 1966. He was awarded a personal chair two years before his death. His main interest was in popular protest in rural and industrial Wales. His chief publications were *Before Rebecca* (1973), *Chartism and the Chartists* (1975), *The Last Rising* (1985), *Rebecca's Children* (1989), *Crime in Nineteenth-Century Wales* (1992) and *Crime and Policing in the Twentieth Century: The South Wales Experience* (1996).

JONES, Dafydd (1711–77) Hymnwriter

As a **drover**, Dafydd Jones o Gaeo (**Cynwyl Gaeo**) learned **English**. After his religious conversion, some dissenting ministers asked Dafydd – who was known as a ***bardd gwlad*** – to translate the **hymns** of Isaac Watts into **Welsh**; these, together with his own hymns and translations of other

English hymnists, appeared between 1753 and 1770. Several of his hymns remain familiar in worship. In his longer poems, he sanctified the idiom of secular love songs.

JONES, Daniel [Jenkyn] (1912–93) Composer

Born in **Pembroke** and brought up in **Swansea**, Jones attended the Royal Academy of **Music, London**, where he won the Mendelssohn Scholarship for works he had written as a schoolboy. A close friend of **Dylan Thomas**, **Vernon Watkins** and **Alfred Janes**, Jones came to prominence after 1945. He wrote 13 symphonies, 8 string quartets, chamber music, orchestral works, choral pieces and operas. His system of complex metres reflects his lifelong concern with pattern, and his largely tonal output is notable for its intellectual vigour. He used to advertise his services in the *Yellow Pages* telephone directory – the sole entry under 'Composers' in the Swansea edition.

JONES, David (Dafydd Jones o Drefriw; (?1708–85) Publisher and writer

A countryman from a poor background, David Jones of **Trefriw** had a strong desire to encourage the ***gwerin*** to read in their mother tongue. A tireless collector of old manuscripts, he published *Blodeu-gerdd Cymry* (1759), a substantial anthology of **Welsh** poetry from the late 17th century onwards, which included some of his own work. He was the author of two chapbooks, *Egluryn Rhyfedd* (1750) and *Cydymaith Diddan* (1766). In 1776, he established a **printing** press in Trefriw and issued scores of **ballads**, many of them his own.

JONES, David (1895–1974) Poet and painter

A major 20th-century modernist, David Jones was born in Brockley, Kent, of a Welsh father and English mother. He attended the Camberwell Art School and, in 1915, joined the **Royal Welch Fusiliers**, serving as a private on the Western Front. During the 1920s, he spent some time in a community led by Eric Gill, latterly at Capel-y-ffin (**Llanigon**) in the **Black Mountains**. There, he developed his view of art as a sacramental act. His experience of trench warfare went into the writing of *In Parenthesis* (1937), a long poem which portrays a group of soldiers – Welshmen and Cockneys – on their way to Mametz Wood, where most are wounded or killed. In its wealth of historical, mythological and literary allusions, notably its many references to Malory, **Shakespeare** and *Y Gododdin*, it sets the war in the context of earlier conflicts involving both the Welsh and **English** who, by fighting alongside one another, recreate the unity of **Britain**.

Received into the **Roman Catholic** Church in 1921, his religious faith was the basis of his epic poem *The Anathémata* (1952); again set in the context of a unified **Roman** Britain, it celebrates the Christian mysteries, particularly the sacrament and its symbols. W. H. Auden referred to it as 'probably the finest long poem in **English** in this century'. Jones also wrote two books of essays, *Epoch and Artist* (1959) and *The Dying Gaul* (1978), both of which discuss the 'Matter of Britain' from a specifically Welsh point of view, as well as the predicament of the artist in the modern world. His later poetic works include *The Tribune's Visitation* (1969), *The Sleeping Lord* (1974) and *The Roman Quarry* (1981).

A David Jones devotional inscription (1956)

As a sickly child, Jones had been encouraged to draw by his mother; he became a master of various forms of visual art, especially watercolour **painting**, **woodcarving** and, later, lettering and the illumination of manuscripts. As in his written work, elements of the antique, the medieval and the contemporary are combined throughout.

An agoraphobic, Jones spent his last years in sheltered accommodation in **London**, but nevertheless corresponded with a wide circle of friends, including **Saunders Lewis**, **Vernon Watkins** and **Aneirin Talfan Davies**; a selection of his letters was published as *Dai Great-Coat* in 1980. Delays by lawyers frustrated David Jones's intention of making a major bequest to **Cymdeithas yr Iaith Gymraeg**.

JONES, David [James] (1886–1947) Philosopher

A native of **Pontarddulais** who excelled as a student at **Cardiff** and **Cambridge**, Jones served as **Calvinistic Methodist** minister at **Brynmawr** and **Swansea**, and with the army (1916–18). He was a tutor at **Coleg Harlech** (1928–38) and professor of **philosophy** at **Bangor** (1938–47). He was a founder of the **philosophy** section of the Guild of Graduates of the **University of Wales** (1931), and its secretary from 1932 until 1947. He made substantial contributions to journals such as *Efrydiau Athronyddol*, *Y Traethodydd* and *Yr Efrydydd*. His most important publication was *Hanes Athroniaeth: Y Cyfnod Groegaidd* (1939) – a history of Greek philosophy.

JONES, David Ivon (1893–1924)
Political activist

Born into a **Unitarian** family at **Aberystwyth**, Jones became a leading **socialist** activist in **South Africa** after his arrival there in 1910. Initially a member of the **Labour Party**, he became a founder of the South African **Communist** Party and pioneered the organization of black workers. He served as 'the delegate for Africa' on the Third International's executive committee in Moscow, and was the first to translate Lenin's works into **English**. He was buried in Nova-Dyevitchi monastery in Moscow.

JONES, David James (Gwenallt; 1899–1968) Poet

Gwenallt took his bardic name from his birthplace – Alltwen (**Cilybebyll**). Brought up in a devoutly **Nonconformist** home in Cwm **Tawe**, his father's death from falling into a vat of molten metal was the major reason why he came to believe that **Marxism** was superior to Christianity. He was imprisoned for his stance as a **conscientious objector** during the **First World War**. Having studied at **Aberystwyth**, it was as a lecturer in **Welsh** in his old college that he spent most of his career. He returned to the Christian fold, and became known as the poet of Christianity and **nationalism**, although he continued to believe that there was 'a place for Karl Marx's fist in His Church'.

Gwenallt won the chair at the National **Eisteddfod** in 1926 and 1931, but the prize was withheld in 1928, the adjudicators finding his long poem *Y Sant* lacking in decorum. He published five collections, including *Ysgubau'r Awen* (1939) and *Eples* (1951). His entire work is full of colourful and dazzling imagery. Despite his industrial background, he was proud of his **Carmarthenshire** roots. His ideal was to fuse 'Tawe and **Tywi**, Canaan and Wales, earth and heaven'. He published two novels – *Plasau'r Brenin* (1934) and *Ffwrneisiau* (1982).

JONES, Dill (Dilwyn Owen Paton Jones; 1923–84) Jazz pianist

Dill Jones, born in **Newcastle Emlyn**, recorded for the British Forces Network during the **Second World War** and, after demobilization, studied at Trinity College of **Music**, **London**, turning professional in 1947. He played with **Harry Parry**'s Band in 1949–50, broadcasting with the BBC. In 1961, he emigrated to New York – 'to explore black *hwyl*' – where he became a highly respected member of that city's jazz community. He eventually died there, leaving a rich legacy of recordings.

JONES, Dyfrig (1940–89) Space scientist

After obtaining PhDs at both **Aberystwyth** and **Cambridge**, **St Dogmaels**-born Dyfrig Jones worked for the European Space Agency in Nordwijk and then for the British Antarctic Survey in Cambridge. In the 1970s, he proposed a theory to explain the radio emissions at kilometre-wavelength from Jupiter and Saturn. This theory made specific predictions concerning the source of the radiation. Ten years later, the Voyager spacecraft passed both planets and confirmed his theory in every detail. The first announcement of this important result was made at the National **Eisteddfod** in **Fishguard** (1986) before its publication in *Nature*. His untimely death was a great loss to **science**.

JONES, Edmund (1702–93) Minister and author

Born in the **parish** of Aberystruth (*see* **Nantyglo and Blaina**), Jones began preaching at the age of 20 and was ordained by the **Congregationalist** church at **Penmaen** in 1734; in 1740, he moved to **Pontypool**. Critical of some aspects of the **Methodist Revival**, he was nevertheless generally supportive of it, although his ideas were a strange blend of orthodox Protestant **theology** and superstition. This led many to be dismissive of him; but it has since been recognized that his *A Relation of Apparitions in Wales* (1780) contains valuable examples of Welsh folklore and customs. His *Historical Account of the Parish of Aberystruth* (1779) is a pioneer work of local history.

JONES, Edward (Bardd y Brenin; 1752–1824) Harpist and antiquary

Born at **Llanddderfel** and trained in **music** by his father, Jones moved to **London** in 1775. He became **harp**ist to the Prince of Wales, later George IV, and used the title 'Bardd y Brenin' (the king's bard). He was a prolific author and collector of books. His own works, particularly *The Musical and Poetical Relicks of the Welsh Bards* (1784), provide a valuable contribution to the understanding of Welsh music.

JONES, Edward (1761–1836) Hymnwriter

Born at **Llanrhaeadr-yng-Nghinmeirch**, but known as Edward Jones, Maes-y-plwm, after the farmhouse near **Denbigh** to which he moved *c.*1796, he wrote mainly alliterative poems in the manner of 18th-century popular poets. He is best remembered, however, as the writer of a handful of enduring **hymns**. They include 'Mae'n llond y nefoedd, llond y byd' and 'Pob seraff, pob sant'.

JONES, Eifionydd (1934–90) Scientist

Among the earliest of many students of **Frank Llewellyn Jones** at **Swansea** to attain distinction at the European Organization for Nuclear Research (CERN) in Geneva, **Clydach**-born Eifionydd Jones is best remembered for his pioneering work in designing, planning and managing huge accelerators. These machines were needed for the study of particles that constitute the very stuff of matter throughout the universe. His passion for the significance of particle physics caused him to lead a vigorous, and ultimately successful, campaign in 1987 against the British **government** when it proposed to withdraw support for CERN. Jones's work was magnanimously acknowledged by Carl Rubbia in an obituary notice in the *Independent* (19 March 1990): 'This proved to be a crucial element in the experiment which led to the Nobel Prize I shared with Simon van der Meer in 1984.'

JONES, Elen Roger (1908–99) Actress

A native of Marianglas (**Llaneugrad**), Elen Roger Jones trained as a teacher and taught periodically. But, being the sister of **Hugh Griffith**, acting was in her blood. Although she had no formal training, she gained valuable experience with Theatr Fach **Llangefni**, and in her middle years she travelled extensively with Cwmni Theatr Cymru. On stage, radio and television, she performed with distinction in both classical **drama** and comedy. One of her last roles was that of Hannah Haleliwia in the television series *Minafon*.

JONES, Elizabeth Mary (Moelona; 1877–1953) Novelist

Elizabeth Mary Jones (b. Owen) was a farmer's daughter from Rhydlewis (**Troedyraur**). After a teaching career, she married John Tywi Jones (1870–1948), **Baptist** minister at Glais (**Clydach**). Of her more than 30 books for children and adults, the most famous was *Teulu Bach Nantoer* (1913), which sold tens of thousands. Her advocacy of **women**'s rights found expression in novels such as *Cwrs y Lili* (1927) and *Ffynnonloyw* (1939). She also wrote textbooks and, in *Y Wers Olaf* (1921), translated into **Welsh** the stories of Alphonse Daudet.

JONES, [Frederick] Elwyn (1909–89) Lawyer

Llanelli-born Elwyn Jones was a leading member of the prosecution team at the Nuremberg trials of Nazi war criminals following the **Second World War**. He was elected **Labour** MP for West Ham (1945) and practised at the bar, becoming recorder of **Merthyr Tydfil** (1949–53), **Swansea** (1953–60) and **Cardiff** (1960–4). He became attorney-general in Harold Wilson's **government** (1964–70) and lord chancellor when Labour returned to power under Wilson and Callaghan (1974–9). Knighted in 1964, and created Lord Elwyn-Jones in 1974, he published an autobiography, *In My Time*, in 1983.

JONES, Elwyn (1923–82) Dramatist

A native of Cwmaman (**Aberaman**), Jones joined the BBC's Television Service in **London** in 1957. His best-known work was the series *Softly, Softly* (1966–70), featuring Inspector Barlow, which developed from the series *Z Cars* (1962–78). He published several books based on Barlow, as well as the documentary studies *The Last Two to Hang* (1966), *The Ripper File (1975)* and *Death Trials* (1981).

JONES, Emyr Wyn (1907–99) Cardiologist and Welsh cultural enthusiast

Waunfawr-born Emyr Wyn Jones graduated in medicine at **Liverpool**, and worked in hospitals there throughout his career. He became chairman of the British Cardiological Society, vice-chairman of the **Welsh Hospital Board**, and chairman of the **Clwyd Health** Authority. Apart from his cardiological research work, he published widely on the history of medicine in Wales. He was elected chairman of the council and president of the court of the National **Eisteddfod**, and was a fellow of the Eisteddfod.

JONES, [Alfred] Ernest (1879–1958) Psychoanalyst and biographer

Born at **Gowerton**, Jones was educated at **Cardiff** and at University College Hospital, **London**, where he qualified as a doctor. It was he, more than anyone else, who introduced Sigmund Freud's written work to the **English**-speaking world, his most significant publication being *Sigmund Freud: Life and Work* (3 vols, 1954–7). It was largely due to his efforts that Freud and his family were released by the Nazis in 1938. A skilled trainer of psychoanalysts, Jones founded the Institute of Psychoanalysis in London, and was the leader of the international psychoanalytical movement for some 30 years. His first wife was the musician **Morfydd Llwyn Owen**. A devoted member of

Plaid [Genedlaethol] Cymru, his lack of fluency in **Welsh** was a matter of much regret to him.

JONES, Evan (Ieuan Gwynedd; 1820–52) Writer

A native of the **Dolgellau** area, Ieuan Gwynedd is remembered chiefly for his defence of the **women** of Wales against the insinuations of the authors of the **education** report of 1847 (*see* **Treason of the Blue Books**). He championed Welsh womanhood forcefully in **newspaper** articles, some of which were republished as short pamphlets. Among them were *A Vindication of the Educational and Moral Condition of Wales* (1848) and *Facts and Statements in Illustration of the Dissent and Morality of Wales* (1849). Educated at the **Congregationalists'** College, **Brecon**, he was a minister at **Tredegar** from 1845 to 1847; in 1848, he moved to **Cardiff** to become editor of the weekly newspaper the *Principality*. He left for **London** the same year, to work on the *Standard of Freedom*. In 1849, he returned to Cardiff, where he edited the literary quarterly *Yr Adolygydd*, and the first **Welsh-language** periodical for women, *Y Gymraes*.

JONES, Ewart [Ray Herbert] (1911–2002) Chemist

One of the most influential scientists of his generation, **Wrexham**-born Ewart Jones studied **chemistry** at **Bangor**. His work on the structure of natural products – terpenes, steroids and vitamins – led to advancement at Imperial College, **London** (1938–45) and chairs at Manchester (1945–55) and **Oxford** (1955–78). Elected FRS in 1950, and knighted in 1963, he led the movement to establish the

Ernest Jones (centre rear) with (clockwise) Sándor Ferenczi, Carl Jung, Granville Stanley Hall, Sigmund Freud and Abraham A. Brill, 1909

unified Royal Society of Chemistry in 1980. He had a keen sense of social responsibility: his commitments after retirement included delivering meals on wheels.

JONES, Frank Llewellyn (1907–97) Physicist

A native of **Penrhiwceiber**, Frank Llewellyn Jones was a student at **Oxford** before his appointment as a physics lecturer at **Swansea**. During the **Second World War**, he was seconded to the Royal Aircraft Establishment, Farnborough, where he studied ignition in aircraft engines. This led to his life's work, a major contribution to the understanding of electrical contact between metal surfaces and electrical discharges in gases. After 20 years as head of the physics department at Swansea, he served as principal of the college from 1965 to 1974.

JONES, G[wyn] O[wain] (1917–2006)
Physicist, museum director and author

Cardiff-born and **Oxford**-educated G. O. Jones made his name, at **London** University, as a low-temperature physicist, having worked on the atomic bomb project during the **Second World War** (an experience which later turned him into an active member of the Pugwash international peace conference). He returned to Wales in 1968 as director of the **National Museum** where his achievements included the establishment in the Cardiff docks area of the Welsh Industrial and Maritime Museum. Retiring from the museum in 1977, he was chairman of the **English-language** section of the **Welsh Academy** from 1978 to 1981, the year in which he published his largely autobiographical *The Conjuring Show*. He also wrote scientific books, novels and short stories.

JONES, Gareth [Richard] Vaughan (1905–35)
Journalist

Barry-born, he was educated at **Aberystwyth** and **Cambridge**, where he became a highly competent linguist. He served as private secretary to **David Lloyd George** (1929–31), before becoming a travelling reporter. He was among the first to report on the famine in Ukraine and was one of the few to interview Lenin's widow. (In 2006, the Ukrainian ambassador to **Britain** unveiled a memorial plaque to him in the old quad of the **University of Wales, Aberystwyth**.)

After a period on the *Western Mail*, he signed an agreement with the *Manchester Guardian* in 1934, prior to departing on a worldwide tour. Kidnapped in Mongolia in August 1935, it is believed that he was killed by Japanese soldiers because he knew too much about Japan's plans to extend its power in northern China.

His father was Edgar Jones, the much-respected Barry headmaster whose appointment in 1931 as Welsh consultant to the BBC was the Corporation's first acknowledgement that **broadcasting** had a Welsh dimension; his mother, Gwen, had lived in Ukraine as tutor to the children of **John Hughes** (1814–99) of Hughesovka.

JONES, Glyn (1905–95) Writer

Merthyr Tydfil-born, Glyn Jones became a teacher in **Cardiff** where the poverty of his pupils profoundly disturbed him. Although not of call-up age, he registered as a

"ME TOO, I WAS BORN HERE AND I WAS NINETEEN BEFORE I COULD PRONOUNCE THE NAME OF THE DAMN PLACE!"

A cartoon by Gren Jones

conscientious objector in 1940; dismissed as a result, he was soon given a post in another school. Jones's Welshness and his Christianity inform all his creative work. His first book was a collection of stories, *The Blue Bed* (1937); a second, *The Water Music*, followed in 1944; his *Collected Stories* appeared in 1999. Of his three novels, *The Island of Apples* (1965) is the most important. He published three volumes of verse (1939, 1954 and 1975); his *Collected Poems*, which includes the enigmatic 'Seven Keys to Shaderdom', were published posthumously in 1996.

He also proved to be an innovative translator of **Welsh** poetry into **English**. His autobiographical book, *The Dragon Has Two Tongues* (1968), is a major critique of Welsh writing in **English** (*see* **Literature**) and a valuable account of his friendship with several writers, including Caradoc Evans (**David Evans**), **Dylan Thomas**, **Idris Davies**, **Jack Jones**, **Keidrych Rhys**, **Gwyn Thomas** and **Gwyn Jones**.

JONES, Gren[fell] (1934–2007) Cartoonist

Gren, as the cartoonist always signed himself, was born in Hengoed (**Gelligaer**). He began drawing caricatures at an early age, and, after working as an **engineering** designer, he turned freelance cartoonist in 1963. Appointed to a staff job on **Cardiff**'s the *South Wales Echo* in 1968, he was given a daily slot on the **newspaper**. Over the following 38 years, he produced thousands of comic drawings of famous creations – such as Ponty an' Pop, Bromide Lil, the knowing sheep Neville and Nigel, and the fictional southern **coal**field town Aberflyarff. His **rugby**-inspired cartoons were among his most popular, and with his annual rugby calendar and his 25 books he won a worldwide audience. Gren was voted **Britain**'s cartoonist of the year on four occasions in the 1980s.

JONES, Griffith (Griffith Jones, Llanddowror; 1683–1761) Founder of circulating schools

Griffith Jones, pre-eminently, was responsible for enabling the Welsh to be a literate people. Born at Penboyr

HYMNS SUNG
BY A
UNITED CHOIR
(Drawn from all parts of Wales) at the Funeral of

GRIFFITH RHYS JONES
"CARADOG"
(Conductor of the South Wales Choral Union),
BORN DECEMBER 21st, 1834;
DIED DECEMBER 4th, 1897;
And Buried at Aberdare Cemetery, Thursday, December 9th, 1897.

Programme for the hymns sung at the funeral of Griffith Rhys Jones in 1897

(**Llangeler**), he was ordained an **Anglican** priest in 1708, and became rector of Llandeilo Abercywyn (**Llangynog, Carmarthenshire**) in 1711. In 1716, he was given the living of **Llanddowror** by Sir John **Philipps**, whose sister he married; it was there that he was to minister for the remainder of his life, so it is with Llanddowror that his name is chiefly associated.

An early supporter of the **Society for the Promotion of Christian Knowledge**, he came to doubt the society's emphasis upon pupils' acquisition of **English**. Realizing that **Welsh** speakers would benefit from being taught through their mother tongue, in 1731 he set about establishing a scheme of **circulating schools**. To promote his endeavours, Jones published over 30 works for use in the schools, most of them catechisms or devotional writings. It is estimated that as many as 250,000 people – over half the country's inhabitants – had attended the circulating schools by 1761, the year of Jones's death.

Though he initially supported the **Methodist Revival**, Jones's fervour cooled somewhat when he realized that some of his patrons disapproved of it. Although many of the revivalists approached him to seek his counsel, he disapproved of preaching by the unordained.

Following the death of his wife Margaret in 1755, Jones was given a home at **Laugharne** by his chief patron, **Bridget Bevan**. He died six years later, having seen the realization of a dream that would have far-reaching consequences in the life of his country. He is buried in Llanddowror.

JONES, Griffith Rhys (Caradog; 1834–97)
Choral conductor

Born at Trecynon, **Aberdare**, Jones was apprenticed as a blacksmith. His precocious musical talent as conductor, organist and violinist brought him prominence by the time he was in his late teens. In 1872 and 1873, he led the South Wales Choral Union, a combined choir of some 400 voices representative of the industrial south, to the championship in contests at the Crystal Palace, **London**. These victories, which earned the choir the soubriquet 'y Côr Mawr' (the Great Choir), made him a national celebrity. Jones was also a successful businessman who amassed a considerable fortune through his brewing companies. A statue of him stands in Aberdare.

JONES, Gwilym R[ichard] (1903–93)
Poet and journalist

Gwilym R. Jones is the only person to have been awarded all three major literary awards of the National **Eisteddfod** of Wales, namely the crown (1935), chair (1938) and prose medal (1941). A native of Talysarn (**Llanllyfni**), he embarked on his journalistic career at **Caernarfon** with *Yr Herald Cymraeg*. Between 1945 and 1977, he edited *Baner ac Amserau Cymru*, a paper which was, during the 1960s, outspoken in its support for the **law**-breaking activities of **Cymdeithas yr Iaith Gymraeg**.

JONES, Gwyn (1907–99)
Scholar, short-story writer and novelist

Born at **Blackwood**, Jones was professor of **English** at **Aberystwyth** (1940–64) and at **Cardiff** (1964–75). In 1939, he launched the *Welsh Review*, which he edited until 1948. He published five novels, including *Richard Savage* (1935) and *Times Like These* (1936), and three volumes of stories; his *Collected Stories* appeared in 1998. Among his scholarly works was the magisterial *A History of the Vikings* (1968), which brought him the highest honour the Icelandic Republic can bestow. The **English** translation of *The Mabinogion* (1948), done in collaboration with **Thomas Jones** (1910–72) (whose widow he later married), won wide acclaim. He edited several anthologies, notably *Welsh Short Stories* (1956) and *The Oxford Book of Welsh Verse in English* (1977).

JONES, H[ugh] R[obert] (1894–1930) Patriot

Born at Ebenezer, a **place name** he succeeded in changing to Deiniolen (*see* **Llanddeiniolen**), a travelling salesman and a passionate advocate of Welsh **Home Rule**, he founded Byddin Ymreolwyr Cymru (the Welsh Army of Home Rulers) in 1924 and became, in 1925, the first secretary of **Plaid [Genedlaethol] Cymru**. An admirer of **Irish** nationalists, he advocated non-violent breaking of the **law,** but was restrained by more moderate and orthodox party leaders. **Saunders Lewis** commented: 'I believe it is correct to say that H. R. Jones established the Welsh Nationalist Party.'

JONES, Harry Longueville (1806–70)
Educationist and antiquary

Born in **London**, Jones had Welsh ancestry, and Wales became his abiding interest following his move to **Anglesey** in 1846. Appointed an inspector of the (**Anglican**) National

Society schools in 1848, he argued in favour of the special educational needs of Wales. His support of the **Welsh language** and culture brought him into conflict with his superiors in London; in 1864, he was forced to resign. He did much to promote Welsh archaeological and historical studies as co-founder of the **Cambrian Archaeological Association** and as editor, for two terms, of the association's journal *Archaeologia Cambrensis*.

JONES, Henry (1852–1922) Philosopher

The son of a **Llangernyw** shoemaker, Jones left school aged 12, but in 1871 went to **Normal College, Bangor**. After a period as a schoolteacher, he entered Glasgow University where he studied **philosophy** under Edward Caird, whose Hegelian Idealism he embraced. He became a lecturer at **Aberystwyth** and held philosophy chairs at Bangor, St Andrews and Glasgow. His most important books are *Browning as a Philosophical and Religious Teacher* (1891), *Idealism as a Practical Creed* (1909), *The Working Faith of the Social Reformer* (1910) and *A Faith that Enquires* (1922). He campaigned for a system of secondary **education** for Wales, and his opinions on higher education were influential during the formative years of the **University of Wales**. He was a fervent supporter of **Britain** in the **First World War**, and a close friend of **David Lloyd George**. His autobiography, *Old Memories*, appeared in 1922. Knighted in 1912, he was made a Companion of Honour in 1922. His son, Elias Henry Jones (1883–1942), was registrar at Bangor, and author of the exciting volume *The Road to Endor* (1920).

JONES, Humphrey Owen (1878–1912) Chemist

The outstanding chemist of his generation, Jones was born at Goginan (**Melindwr**); the family moved to **Ebbw Vale**. In 1897, he was among the first **science** graduates at **Aberystwyth**. He proceeded to **Cambridge** and in 1902 was appointed a demonstrator in the university **chemistry** laboratory, and made a fellow of Clare College. He was a pioneer in studying the deployment of atoms within the molecule, became the recognized authority on the stereochemistry of nitrogen and was elected FRS at the early age of 34. He married Muriel Edwards from **Bangor**, another Welsh chemist. On their honeymoon in the Alps, roped together, they fell to their deaths from Mont Rouge de Peuteret.

JONES, Idwal (1895–1937) Dramatist and humorist

Idwal Jones believed that 'our small country does not take its humour seriously enough', and sought to rectify this by composing a host of popular songs, parodies, limericks and nonsense verse – all comparatively scarce in **Welsh** at the time. He published many of these, in addition to a number of short stories, in three volumes. His best plays are *Pobl yr Ymylon* (1927), an argument against respectability, and *Yr Anfarwol Ifan Harris* (1928). He died in his native **Lampeter**, aged 42, his health having been ruined by service in the **First World War**.

JONES, [James] Ira [Thomas] (1896–1960) Fighter pilot

As a member of the Royal Flying Corps during the **First World War**, **St Clears**-born Ira Jones destroyed 37 enemy aircraft in just three months in 1918. Jones, who was infamous for crashing aircraft when attempting to land, was awarded the DSO, MC, DFC, MM and the Russian Medal of St George.

JONES, Ivor (1901–82) Rugby player

A fast, predatory and constructive wing-forward, **Llwchwr**-born Ivor Jones won 16 **rugby** caps between 1924 and 1930. His dynamic play was widely praised during the British Lions **New Zealand** tour of 1930. A furnace-man by occupation, he was captain of **Llanelli** for seven seasons.

JONES, J[ohn] E[dward] (1905–70) Political activist

'J. E.', as he was known, is remembered for his lifelong commitment to the cause of **Plaid [Genedlaethol] Cymru** and for his involvement in various **nationalist** initiatives in such areas as **agriculture**, **broadcasting** and **education**. A native of Melin-y-Wîg (**Betws Gwerfil Goch**), he was secretary of Plaid Cymru from 1930 until 1962, a period which saw a transformation in the party's prospects. His book *Tros Gymru: J. E. a'r Blaid* (1970), is an invaluable source of information about the party.

JONES, J[ohn] R[obert] (1911–70) Philosopher and patriot

During the 1960s, J. R. Jones became an unexpected cult figure among the young **Welsh-language** campaigners of **Cymdeithas yr Iaith Gymraeg**. Despite his wide philosophical interests, he is best known in Wales for his contribution to the debate on the crisis of Welshness. His writings on the death of God and the crisis of meaningfulness were also controversial, particularly among Welsh Christian denominations. Born in **Pwllheli**, he was educated at **Aberystwyth** and **Oxford**, and lectured at Aberystwyth before holding the chair of **philosophy** at **Swansea** (1952–70), where his views were influenced by those of his colleague **Rush Rhees**. His main works are *Ac Onide* (1970) and *Gwaedd Yng Nghymru* (1970).

JONES, Jack (1884–1970) Novelist

Merthyr Tydfil-born Jack Jones became a **coal**miner at the age of 12, and later served with the army in **South Africa**, India and Flanders. In the 1920s and early 1930s, he was active, in turn, on behalf of the **Communist Party**, the **Labour Party**, the **Liberal Party** and Oswald Mosley's New Party; in the 1940s, he was a popular speaker on the platforms of the Moral Rearmament Movement. The best of his novels are *Black Parade* (1935), *Rhondda Roundabout* (1934), *Bidden to the Feast* (1938), *Off to Philadelphia in the Morning* (1947), *Some Trust in Chariots* (1948) and *River Out of Eden* (1951); among his finest achievements is his three-volume autobiography (1937, 1946, 1950). All his books chronicle life in Wales's southern industrial areas and reflect his generous personality.

JONES, John (?1597–1660) Regicide

A member of the **gentry** family of Maes-y-garnedd (**Llanbedr**), John Jones's second wife was the sister of **Oliver Cromwell**. A staunch **Puritan**, he fought for Parliament in the **Civil Wars**; in 1647, he became MP for **Merioneth**. He was one of the signatories of the death warrant of Charles I and was executed following the Stuart Restoration.

JONES, John (John Jones, Gellilyfdy; pre-1585–1658/9) Collector and copyist of manuscripts

John Jones was born in Gellilyfdy, **Ysgeifiog**, to a family of collectors, copyists and bardic patrons. For years, he was embroiled in litigation with his siblings about family land, and he spent a considerable time in **prisons** – at **Ludlow** and, especially, the Fleet in **London** – mainly because of debt. He spent this time copying and compiling manuscripts, of which over 80, in whole or in part, have survived and are now housed in the **National Library**. They are in beautiful, varied scripts and eccentric orthography, but because of the acidic ink, the paper has been destroyed in many volumes. Several manuscripts contain unique texts. He died intestate in Fleet prison.

JONES, John (1645–1709) Physician, theologian, inventor

Of Pentyrch (*see* **Cardiff**), Jones was the author of medical works including *The Mysteries of Opium Revealed* (1700). His only **Welsh-language** book, *Holl Dd'ledswydd Christion*, was published posthumously in 1716. He invented an extraordinary **clock** 'which moved by the air, equally expressed out of bellows of a cylindrical form, falling into folds in its descent, much after the manner of paper lanterns'. In 1691, he was appointed chancellor of the **diocese** of Llandaff, and is buried near the west door of Llandaff Cathedral (*see* **Cardiff**).

JONES, John (Jac Glan-y-gors; 1766–1821) Radical writer

Born and raised at Glan-y-gors (**Cerrigydrudion**), he lived mostly in **London** where he was an innkeeper, a prominent member of the **Gwyneddigion** and a founder of the **Cymreigyddion** society. A supporter of the views of Tom Paine, he was persecuted for attacking the monarchy, the **government** and the **Anglican** Church. He published his ideas in two pamphlets: *Seren Tan Gwmmwl* (1795) and *Toriad y Dydd* (1797). The Welsh 'Uncle Tom'-type character **Dic Siôn Dafydd** was his invention.

JONES, John (Ioan Tegid, Tegid; 1792–1852) Scholar

Born in **Bala**, Tegid was educated in **Oxford** and became a clergyman there. He is chiefly remembered for championing **William Owen Pughe**'s eccentric system of **Welsh** orthography. The adoption of this system in his edition of *Y Testament Newydd* (1828) involved him in a protracted argument with leading Welsh clergymen. Nevertheless, he adhered to the same system for the edition of **Lewys Glyn Cothi**'s poetry (1837–9) that he co-edited with Gwallter Mechain (**Walter Davies**).

JONES, John (John Jones, Tal-y-sarn; 1796–1857) Preacher

One of Wales's most powerful **preachers**, John Jones was born at **Dolwyddelan**, but is usually associated with Talysarn (**Llanllyfni**), where he worked as a **slate** quarryman. Inspired by the **Beddgelert revival** (1819), he joined the **Calvinistic Methodist** congregation at **Llangernyw**, and in 1821 began to preach; he was ordained in 1829.

The conservatism and autocracy of **John Elias** offended Jones and a younger generation of Methodist leaders, as did the tendency of many talentless preachers to mimic the histrionics of the stars of the pulpit. Strikingly handsome, melodious of voice and rich in vocabulary, Jones introduced a warmer style of preaching which emphasized the practical rather than doctrinal aspects of **religion**. A talented musician, he wrote **hymns** and composed hymn tunes. His biography (1874), by **Owen Thomas** (1812–91), is a major study of 19th-century Welsh religious life.

JONES, John (Talhaiarn; 1810–69) Singer, poet and architect

Talhaiarn, son of the Harp Inn in **Llanfair Talhaiarn**, was one of the most colourful characters of an increasingly dour and respectable Victorian Wales. He coveted the chair of the **eisteddfod** and allegedly leapt on stage in the 1843 **Aberffraw** Eisteddfod to rip to pieces his rejected *awdl*. He found more success writing song lyrics, such as the still-popular 'Mae Robin yn swil'. He was a prominent *penillion* singer, **Gorsedd** member and eisteddfod compère. As an architect, he worked for **Thomas Penson** in Oswestry and for Gilbert Scott and Joseph Paxton in **London**, supervising for the latter the building of the Crystal Palace and the Rothschilds' mansions in **England** and France. Ill **health** brought him back to Wales and to the Harp Inn. There, he shot himself and died a few days later.

JONES, John (Coch Bach y Bala, Jac Llanfor; 1854–1913) Petty thief

Known as 'The Little Welsh Terror' and 'The Little Turpin', on account of his ability to escape from **prison**, Jones won considerable public sympathy for his exploits, particularly after his escape from **Ruthin** jail in 1913. There was outrage when he died from his wounds after being shot by the son of the squire of Euarth, **Llanfair Dyffryn Clwyd**.

JONES, John Gwilym (1904–88) Dramatist

With **Saunders Lewis**, John Gwilym Jones was one of the two major **Welsh-language** dramatists of the 20th century, although their literary outlooks were very different. Born at Groeslon (**Llandwrog**), and educated at **Bangor**, he held various school-teaching posts before joining the BBC in Bangor as producer of radio plays (1949–53). From 1953 until 1971, he lectured in Welsh at Bangor.

The psychological penetration of his realist plays, based mainly on family tensions, caused him to be described as a 'novelistic playwright'. His works are founded on the idea that feeling is a stronger force than intellect. Two of his many plays stand out as masterpieces: *Hanes Rhyw Gymro* (1964), based on the life of the 17th-century **Puritan**, **Morgan Llwyd** – although it is not strictly a historical play, nor is it Puritan in spirit; and *Ac Eto Nid Myfi* (1976), which deals with the complexities of the modern sensibility. He uses Brecht-like techniques to distinctly un-Brechtian ends, and his experimentation is also seen in his volume of short stories, *Y Goeden Eirin* (1946), and in his two novels, *Y Dewis* (1942) and *Tri Diwrnod ac Angladd* (1979). His influence as literary critic and lecturer was profound.

JONES, John Owen (Ap Ffarmwr; 1861–99)
Champion of agricultural labourers

A native of Trefdraeth (**Bodorgan**), 'Ap Ffarmwr' (farmer's son) raised awareness of poor employment conditions among **agricultural labourers**. His three attempts to found an Agricultural Labourers Union in **Anglesey** came to nothing, and in 1894 he moved to **Merthyr Tydfil** where he remained politically active. He chaired the town's first meeting of the **Independent Labour Party**. In 1897, he moved to Nottingham, where he died.

JONES, John Puleston (1862–1925) Minister
and writer

Born at **Llanbedr Dyffryn Clwyd** and brought up in **Bala**, Jones was educated at Glasgow and at **Oxford**, where he was a founder of Cymdeithas **Dafydd ap Gwilym**; in 1888, he was ordained by the **Calvinistic Methodists**. Having been blinded in an accident at the age of 18 months, he devised the Braille system for the **Welsh language** that is still in use. Regarded by Sir **John Morris-Jones** as 'one of the principal benefactors of the culture and **religion** of Wales through its language', Jones published his sermons as *Gair y Deyrnas* (1924); his essays were published in 1926 as *Ysgrifau Puleston*.

JONES, John Tudor (John Eilian; 1904–85)
Editor and poet

Llaneilian-born John Tudor Jones spent some years as a journalist in **London**, Iraq and Ceylon before returning to Wales and establishing *Y Ford Gron*, a popular monthly magazine, in 1930. He later edited the **newspapers** *Y Cymro* and *Yr Herald Cymraeg*. He was head of programmes at the BBC in **Cardiff** (1938–40) and head of the editorial unit of the BBC in general (1940–3) (*see* **Broadcasting**). As a poet, he published, with **E. Prosser Rhys**, *Gwaed Ifanc* (1926) and won the chair at the National **Eisteddfod** in 1947 and the crown in 1949. John Eilian was one of the few **Welsh-language** authors to avow openly his loyalty to the **Conservative Party**: he stood as Conservative parliamentary candidate for **Anglesey** in 1964, 1966 and 1970.

JONES, [Leonard] Jonah (1919–2004)
Sculptor and writer

A miner's son from County Durham, whose Welsh roots became increasingly important to him. During the **Second World War** he served with a field ambulance unit on the European mainland and, later, in Palestine, where, in 1946, he married Judith Maro (b.1927), a native of Jerusalem.

After the war, they came to Wales where Jonah Jones joined the artist **John Petts** at the Caseg Press before establishing his own workshop at Tremadog (**Porthmadog**). Working for several years in Rome and **Ireland**, he regularly returned to Wales where he forged a reputation as a craftsman in the tradition of Eric Gill.

His Welsh works include his memorial to the princes of **Aberffraw**, his bronze **sculptures** of **O. M. Edwards** and his son **Ifan ab Owen Edwards** in **Llanuwchllyn**, and busts of several other eminent Welshmen. Amongst his publications are two novels and a volume of essays.

Judith Maro is also a writer, whose works reflect her deep Zionist sympathies.

JONES, Ken[neth Jeffrey] (1921–2006)
Rugby player and athlete

One of the greatest wings in the history of **rugby** and certainly the fastest, **Blaenavon**-born Ken Jones captained **Newport** and Wales at rugby, and **Great Britain** at **athletics**. The holder of what was for many years a record 44 caps for Wales between 1947 and 1957, he scored the legendary winning try against the 1953 All Blacks from **Clem Thomas**'s cross kick. He allied to his blistering speed a side step, a powerful defence, and a fine ability to read the game, qualities which brought him 145 tries for Newport and 17 for Wales. A member of two 'Grand Slam' Welsh teams (1950, 1952) and of the 1950 British Lions, at the 1948 Olympics he reached the 100-metres semi-final and won silver with the sprint relay team. He captained the British team at the 1954 European Games.

JONES, Lewis (1897–1939) Novelist

Born in Clydach Vale (*see* **Rhondda**), he became at the age of 12 a **coal**miner at the Cambrian Colliery and joined the **Communist Party** in 1923. During the 1930s, he led **hunger marches** to **London** and organized demonstrations against the notorious **means test**. He played a prominent part in the Welsh campaign in support of the Spanish Republic (*see* **Spanish Civil War**): he died of a heart attack in **Cardiff** after addressing some 30 street meetings shortly before Barcelona fell to Franco's forces. He wrote two novels: *Cwmardy* (1937) and its sequel, *We Live* (1939), in which his **Marxist** convictions are clearly apparent.

JONES, Mai (1899–1960) Musician and
broadcaster

Composer of the popular melody **'We'll Keep a Welcome'**, **Newport**-born Mai Jones studied **music** at **Cardiff** and at the Royal Academy of Music, **London**. A member, in London, of various renowned light music groups, she made her first radio broadcast in 1928 with the Jack Payne band. She joined the BBC in **Cardiff** in 1941, making a name as producer of such radio favourites as *Welsh Rarebit*, whose piano theme tune, 'Rhondda Rhapsody', was among her many compositions. Her spirited radio personality combined with an American production style to offer Welsh listeners something entirely novel.

She was married to the composer and musician Davey Davies (d.1964), the uncle of Garnant-born (*see* **Cwmamman**) musician John Cale, co-founder of the Velvet Underground (*see* **Music**). The couple gave the young Cale significant musical encouragement.

JONES, Margaret (Y Gymraes o Ganaan;
?1842–1902) Travel writer

Rhosllanerchrugog-born Margaret Jones's travels began in 1863 when she took a servant's post with a family of **Jews** who had converted to Christianity and who were committed to proselytizing in Jerusalem. The letters she wrote home to her parents were published in a periodical and later as a collected volume, *Llythyrau Cymraes o Wlad Canaan* (1869). They won her instant fame, and were much praised for their capacity to bring distant places vividly to life. After a further period working as a missionary teacher in Mogador (now Essaouira, Morocco), in 1882 she published a second, more conventional, volume on Morocco.

JONES, Mary (1784–1864) Folk heroine
Despite spending her life in poverty and obscurity in **Llanfihangel-y-Pennant** and **Bryn-crug**, Mary Jones is among the best known of Welsh **women**. She became an icon because of her walk in 1800 from her home to **Bala** to buy a **Bible** from **Thomas Charles**. The walk – reputedly a barefoot trek of some 45 km over stony **mountain** paths – is said to have inspired Charles in 1804 to become one of the main founders of the British and Foreign **Bible Society**. The story of her walk, currently available in some 40 languages, has been one of the bestsellers of the Christian book trade ever since its first publication in book form in 1879.

JONES, Michael D[aniel] (1822–98) Patriot
Llanuwchllyn-born Michael D. Jones was ordained a **Congregationalist** minister in Cincinnati, Ohio, in 1847. There, he founded the Brython Association to assist Welsh immigrants. Concerned by the rapid Americanization of the immigrants, he advocated that emigration should be directed at the establishment of viable Welsh communities, but he considered that **North America** was developing too rapidly for such a plan to be feasible there.

A page from Owen Jones's *The Grammar of Ornament*, 1856

On returning to Wales in 1850, he concluded that Welsh immigrants should settle in a remoter part of the world. Although he himself was not one of the colonists, it was his vision, leadership and, in part, financial support, which led to the foundation of a Welsh colony in **Patagonia** (1865). In 1882, he visited Y Wladfa Gymreig (The Welsh Colony), where his son, **Llwyd ap Iwan**, was to be murdered in a notorious ambush in 1906.

Appointed principal of the Independent College at **Bala** in 1853, in succession to his father, he became embroiled in a struggle, known as the 'battle of the two constitutions', against the presbyterianization of the Congregationalist denomination. Hierarchy was anathema to him, and in the same way that he emphasized the value of a community of equal religious congregations, so also did he campaign for a community of equal nations. Although a staunch **Liberal**, he opposed the doctrine of laissez faire and argued that 'there is no consistency in advocating political liberty and denying the liberty of nations'.

Together with Emrys ap Iwan (**Robert Ambrose Jones**), Michael D. Jones is considered to be the father of Welsh **nationalism**. He wrote extensively to the press, arguing in particular that the subjection of the Welsh as a nation was interwoven with their subjection as tenant farmers or industrial workers, and that salvation would not come unless they challenged the political structure that enslaved them. Among later leaders who came under his influence were **T. E. Ellis**, **David Lloyd George** and **O. M. Edwards**.

JONES, Morgan (1885–1939)
Politician and educationist
Bargoed-born Morgan Jones was a teacher at Gilfach School (Bargoed) when, as a **conscientious objector** during the **First World War**, he was dismissed from his post and imprisoned for his views. The first conscientious objector to be elected to parliament, he was **Labour** MP for **Caerphilly** from 1921 until his death, serving in the first two Labour **government**s (1923–4 and 1929–31) as parliamentary secretary to the Board of **Education**.

JONES, O[wen] R[ogers] (1922–2004) Philosopher
A native of **Llanrhaeadr-yng-Nghinmeirch**, he studied at **Bangor** and **Oxford**, and lectured at **Aberystwyth** from 1957. His main philosophical interests were the **philosophy** of **religion**, the philosophy of language and the philosophy of mind. His most important publications were *The Concept of Holiness* (1961) and, with Peter Smith, *The Philosophy of Mind* (1986).

JONES, O[wen] T[homas] (1878–1967) Geologist
Owen ('O. T.') Jones, FRS, regarded for many years as the father figure of British **geology**, was initially an officer of the Geological Survey and successively professor of geology at **Aberystwyth**, Manchester and **Cambridge**. Born in **Beulah** and graduating in physics at Aberystwyth and in geology at **Cambridge**, he was described, on receiving the Royal Medal of the Royal Society in 1956, as 'the most versatile of living British geologists'.

Jones's mastery of the evolution of the Lower Palaeozoic rocks of Wales is evident in his remarkable presidential address to the Geological Society of **London** (GSL) in 1938, his skilful reconstruction (jointly with **W. J. Pugh**) of the shoreline of an Ordovician volcano in the **Builth–Llandrindod** area in 1949, and his grasp of the evolution of the larger **landforms** of Wales in his 1954 GSL lecture. He knew more about and contributed more to the geology of his country than anyone in the history of his **science**. He shared, with **T. W. E. David**, the honour of being the best all-round Welsh-born geologist involved with the period up to the formulation of the Plate Tectonics theory.

JONES, Owen (Owain Myfyr; 1741–1814)
Patron and editor
Born in **Llanfihangel Glyn Myfyr**, Jones moved to **London** as a young man and became rich as a furrier. He was one of the founders, in 1770, of the **Gwyneddigion Society**. He edited, with **William Owen Pughe**, *Barddoniaeth Dafydd ab Gwilym* (1789), and, with Pughe and Iolo Morganwg (**Edward Williams**), *The Myvyrian Archaiology of Wales* (1801–7). He poured a great deal of money into the publication of these volumes. The *Archaiology* was named after him as an acknowledgement of his generosity.

JONES, Owen (1809–74) Architect and designer
A son of Owain Myfyr (**Owain Jones**; 1741–1814), Owen Jones was born in **London** and attended the Royal Academy. He played an important part in the design and ornamentation of the two crystal palaces for the Great Exhibitions of 1851 and 1854. He was also involved in the construction of London's Paddington Station (1849–55). A master of colour **printing**, he produced handsome volumes which are of significance in the history of printing. His ideas on art and **architecture** were influential, especially as they were expressed in his *The Grammar of Ornament* (1856), a study which drew upon the traditions of many cultures. Nearly 200 years after his birth, he became the subject of increasing interest, as can be seen from Gareth Alban Davies's *Y Llaw Broffwydol* (2004) and Carol A. Hrvol Flores's *Owen Jones* (2006).

JONES, Percy Mansell (1889–1968) Scholar
A native of **Carmarthen**, Mansell Jones was professor of **French** at **Bangor**, and subsequently professor of French **literature** at Manchester (1951–6). Among his many books were *Tradition and Barbarism* (1930), *Background to Modern French Poetry* (1951), *The Oxford Book of French Verse* (1957) and *The Assault on French Literature* (1963), as well as studies of Emile Verhaeren, Racine and Baudelaire. He also published a memoir, *How They Educated Jones* (1974), in which he described his meetings with Ezra Pound, André Gide, **Saunders Lewis**, **Morfydd Llwyn Owen** and **Ernest Jones**.

JONES, Philip (1618–74) Parliamentarian
A native of **Llangyfelach**, Colonel Jones became a member of the Council of State and Comptroller of **Oliver Cromwell**'s household, and in the 1650s was virtual ruler of south Wales. He acquired a large fortune and, at the Stuart Restoration (1660), was allowed to retire to his estate, Fonmon Castle (**Rhoose**) in the **Vale of Glamorgan**.

JONES, R[obert] Gerallt (1934–99) Writer
The son of an **Anglican** clergyman in **Llŷn**, he held posts such as the principal of a college of **education** in Jamaica, warden of **Llandovery** College and warden of Gregynog (*see* **Tregynon**). He won the National **Eisteddfod** prose medal for *Triptych* (1977) and *Cafflogion* (1979), and published another three novels. His collection of short stories, *Gwared y Gwirion* (1977), was the basis of the television series *Joni Jones*. His collected poems appeared in 1989, and he published, in addition to criticism, volumes in **English**, such as *Jamaican Landscape* (1969). His writings on India (2003) and the autobiographical *A Place in the Mind: A Boyhood in Llŷn* (2004) were published posthumously.

JONES, R[obert] Tudur (1921–98)
Historian and theologian
The leading Welsh Christian theologian of his generation, R. Tudur Jones was born in Rhoslan (**Llanystumdwy**), and brought up in **Rhyl**. Educated at **Bangor**, **Oxford** and Strasbourg, he was ordained to the Congregational ministry (1948) before being appointed in 1950 to the chair of church history and, subsequently, the principalship of Coleg **Bala**–**Bangor**, the Congregational theological school at Bangor, from which he retired in 1988.

A prolific author, he combined a Welsh nationalist commitment with **Calvinist** doctrine, to create an integrated vision that was significant in the religious life of Wales during the second half of the 20th century. His volumes on the history of Congregationalism in **England**, the **Congregationalists** of Wales, and the religious history of early 20th-century Wales are of the greatest distinction.

JONES, Rhydderch [Thomas] (1935–87) Dramatist
The career of Rhydderch Jones, a native of Aberllefenni (**Corris**), blossomed with the growth of **broadcasting** in Wales from the 1960s onwards. Educated at the **Normal College**, **Bangor**, he joined the BBC in 1965, becoming a producer in the light entertainment department in 1973. He was co-author, with **Gwenlyn Parry**, of the popular series *Fo a Fe*. The best of his single television plays include *Mr Lollipop MA* (1970 in **Welsh**; 1978 in **English**) and *Gwenoliaid* (1986). He published a biography of **Ryan Davies**, *Cofiant Ryan* (1979).

JONES, Rhys (1941–2001) Archaeologist
One of the foremost authorities on the aboriginal history and culture of **Australia**, Rhys Jones was brought up in Blaenau **Ffestiniog** and **Cardiff**. He read **archaeology** at **Cambridge** and then taught at Sydney University, where he began his life's work – completed during three decades at Canberra – the study of the prehistory of Australia. He played a key role in dating the oldest settlements in Arnhem Land, using measurements of luminescent energy to show that the aboriginal population had occupied the continent for at least 60,000 years and that the oldest rock art was of an antiquity comparable to the palaeolithic cave **paintings** of France. These results were crucial in establishing the legal title to land of, among others, the Torres Strait Islanders.

JONES, Richard Robert (Dic Aberdaron; 1780–1843) Polyglot

Described by a contemporary as 'one-quarter idiot, three-quarters genius', this **Aberdaron**-born eccentric spent his life tramping around Wales with a cat, acquiring a reputation as a formidable linguist. His greatest achievement was to compile an unpublished **Welsh–Greek–Hebrew dictionary**, which is preserved in the **National Library**. He is commemorated in a remarkable verse by **T. H. Parry-Williams**. His gravestone in **St Asaph parish** churchyard carries an epitaph which, translated, reads:

> A linguist eight times greater than all the others
> He was truly a dictionary of every province.
> Death removed his fifteen languages.
> Now, below, he has no languages at all.

JONES, Robert (1560–1615) Priest

A native of **Chirk** and probably a pupil of **Richard Gwyn**, Jones entered the Society of Jesus in Rome in 1583. He was professor of **philosophy** at the Roman College (later the Università Gregoriana) from 1590 until 1595, when he returned to Wales as a **missionary**. Based at **Llantarnam**, he organized recusant networks throughout the **border**land and established a Jesuit centre at Y Cwm, Llanrothal, **Herefordshire**. From 1609 until 1613, he was the vice-prefect of the entire Jesuit mission in Wales and **England**.

JONES, Robert (Robert Jones Rhos-lan; 1745–1829) Preacher and author

A key figure in the growth of **Calvinistic Methodism** in the north, Jones was born at Suntur, **Llanystumdwy**; he is normally associated with Rhoslan (Llanystumdwy) where he gathered a Methodist *seiat* (**society**) around him.

Jones began to preach in 1768 but declined ordination in 1811, believing himself to be too old. A former pupil in one of **Griffith Jones**'s **circulating schools**, he persuaded **Bridget Bevan** to reopen circulating schools in the north, and became a tutor in seven of them. His publications include the satirical *Lleferydd yr Asyn* (1770), *Grawnsyppiau Canaan* (1795) (the first **hymn** book used by Methodists in the north) and a majestic if somewhat credulous description of the **Methodist Revival**, *Drych yr Amseroedd* (1820).

JONES, Robert (1809–79) Editor and bibliophile

Although **Llanfyllin**-born Robert Jones spent most of his life as a vicar in **London**, he was actively involved in many aspects of Welsh life, both there and in Wales. He was a founder of the third **Cymmrodorion** society in 1873 and as the first editor of *Y Cymmrodor* he ensured the scholarly basis of that journal from the outset. He was an authority on **Goronwy Owen** and published an edition of his work in 1876. His extensive library of **Welsh** and Breton books was bought after his death by **Swansea public library**. He was among the last of the *hen bersoniaid llengar* (old literary clerics).

JONES, Robert (1857–1933) Surgeon

Born in **Rhyl**, Jones spent much of his childhood in **London**. After completing his medical training at **Liverpool**, he became an apprentice, and then an assistant, to his uncle, **Hugh Owen Thomas**, to whom he was always ready to acknowledge his debt. He became an honorary surgeon to the Royal Southern Hospital, Liverpool and, by around 1900, he turned his attention exclusively to orthopaedic surgery. He had extensive experience of treating wounded soldiers during the **First World War**, and became one of the best-known specialists in his field of work. He received many honours, including a knighthood.

JONES, Robert Ambrose (Emrys ap Iwan; 1848–1906) Minister and writer

A native of **Abergele**, Robert Ambrose Jones studied at **Bala** Theological College, intending to enter the **Calvinistic Methodist** ministry; he also studied and taught in France, Germany and Switzerland. Initially, he was refused ordination because of his opposition, on patriotic grounds, to **English causes**, but he eventually accepted calls from churches at **Ruthin** and Rhewl (**Llanynys**).

The numerous periodical articles of this Welsh European (as he considered himself) testify to his independence of thought. They were chiefly concerned with language and **literature**, in which he defined the character of the **Welsh** prose tradition and re-established standards which had lapsed in the 19th century, and with politics – essays whose pro-European and anti-imperialist bias determined the character of modern Welsh **nationalism**. Two volumes were published posthumously of his *Homiliau* (1906, 1909), sermons which have an elegance of thought and expression. A controversial figure in his lifetime, Emrys ap Iwan was nevertheless revered as preacher, teacher and visionary. His biography (1912) by **T. Gwynn Jones** inspired a new generation of Welsh patriots. Ysgol Emrys ap Iwan, Abergele, commemorates him.

JONES, Rowland (1722–74) Linguist

'Touched in the head' was his contemporary Lewis Morris's (*see* **Morris Brothers**) opinion of **Llanbedrog**-born Rowland Jones, who was also described as a 'linguistic lunatic'. His marriage to a wealthy heiress enabled him to cease working as a lawyer in **London** and concentrate on linguistic studies. The fruits of this labour were five books full of fantastical theories about the origins of language and of the **Welsh language** in particular. He believed, for instance, that **Celtic** was the world's primeval language and that Japheth was a **druid** – ideas he discovered in the writings of the Breton Paul-Yves Pezron. Jones's ideas in turn influenced those of **William Owen Pughe**.

JONES, Sam[uel] (1898–1974) Broadcaster

Sam Jones was the first **Welsh** speaker to be appointed (1932) to a production post with the BBC, to work on Welsh-language radio programmes. Born in **Clydach**, he was a teacher in **Liverpool** (1924–7) and a journalist on the *Western Mail* (1927–32). When the Welsh region of the BBC was formed in 1935, he was appointed the corporation's representative in the north, remaining in **Bangor** until his retirement in 1963 (*see* **Broadcasting**). There, he produced such highly popular programmes as *Noson Lawen* and *Ymryson y Beirdd*, which was later developed as *Talwrn y Beirdd*.

JONES, Samuel (1628–97) Teacher and minister
A native of **Chirk**, Jones was vicar at **Llangynwyd** until he was deprived of his living for failing to comply with the Uniformity Act of 1661. He moved to Brynllywarch, in the same **parish**, where he founded an academy to train ministers – Wales's first **Nonconformist Academy**, and a notably influential one.

JONES, T[homas] G[eorge] (1917–2004) Footballer
Widely acknowledged as 'the prince of centre-halves', **Connah's Quay**-born T. G. Jones bestrode the old First Division of the English league and the Welsh national team in the 1930s and 1940s. In 1936, after six first-team games with **Wrexham**, he was signed by Everton and was instrumental in the **Liverpool** club's renaissance. After the **Second World War**, during which he added 11 appearances for Wales to his 17 pre-war caps, Jones continued to excel for Everton, but there were damaging differences with the management. When he failed to make even the reserves, he would turn out secretly for **Hawarden** Grammar Old Boys. He went on to manage the **Pwllheli** team and in 1962, as manager of **Bangor** City, the Welsh Cup winners, he saw his team beat the Italian giants Napoli 2–0 in the European Cup Winners' Cup.

JONES, T[homas] Gwynn (1871–1949) Writer
The most prolific and multi-talented **Welsh-language** writer of the 20th century, T. Gwynn Jones was born in Y Gwyndy Uchaf, **Betws-yn-Rhos**. When 19, he embarked on a career as a journalist and, in 1909, was appointed to a post at the **National Library**. At the age of 42, he became a lecturer in Welsh at **Aberystwyth**, and was promoted six years later to the Gregynog Chair of Welsh **literature** – despite his having ceased formal **education** when he was 14. His first degree was a D.Litt.

He published four novels in book form, as well as serialized novels and biographies of **Emrys ap Iwan** (1912) and **Thomas Gee** (1913); he also wrote plays, a travel book about Egypt, volumes of literary criticism, a volume of reminiscences, scholarly studies, many songs, and essays and articles on a vast array of subjects. He translated from a number of languages; his **English** translation of **Ellis Wynne**'s *Gweledigaetheu y Bardd Cwsc* was published by the Gregynog Press (*see* **Tregynon**) as *Visions of the Sleeping Bard* (1940).

Jones's strict-metre ode, 'Ymadawiad Arthur', which won the National **Eisteddfod** chair in 1902, was the most important milestone of the early 20th-century literary revival. He won the chair once more with 'Gwlad y Bryniau' (1909). His long poems based on Welsh and **Celtic** myth and legend include 'Tir na n-Óg' (1910), 'Madog' (1917), 'Broseliawnd' (1922), 'Anatiomaros' (1925), 'Argoed' (1927) and 'Cynddilig' (1944). Although he has been described as 'the poet of escape', he was a pessimistic and realistic poet. In the mid-1930s, he changed course and wrote poems on contemporary themes, mainly in *vers libre* fused with **cynghanedd**; they are gathered in *Y Dwymyn* (1944). In 1926, the Gregynog Press published a fine edition of his poems, entitled *Detholiad o Ganiadau*, and, between 1932 and 1937, Hughes and Son published a collection of six uniform volumes of his work.

Sam Jones, the chief pioneer of Welsh language radio broadcasting

JONES, T[homas] H[enry] or Harri (1921–65) Poet
Born at **Llanafan Fawr** (**Radnorshire**), Jones was educated at **Aberystwyth** and taught in **England** before emigrating in 1959 to **Australia** where he became a lecturer in **English** at the University of New South Wales. Prone to bouts of depression and heavy drinking, he met his death by drowning in a rock pool near his home. Possibly Wales's first 'postmodern' English-language poet, Jones was the author, between 1957 and 1966, of four volumes of verse in which his recollections of a Calvinistically straitened Wales often feature, in tension with a turbulent sensuality. His *Collected Poems* appeared in 1977.

JONES, Theophilus (1759–1812) Historian
The grandson of **Theophilus Evans**, he practised as a lawyer and was deputy registrar of the archdeaconry of **Brecon**. His *History of the County of Brecknock* (2 vols; 1805, 1809) is by far the finest of the **county** histories written by a Welsh scholar and antiquarian.

JONES, Thomas (Thomas Johns or **Tomas Siôn Dafydd Madoc** or **Twm Shon Catti;** *c.*1530–1609)
Outlaw, antiquary and herald
Best known since his own day as Twm Shon Catti, Thomas Jones was a member of the minor **gentry**, who lived at Porthyffynnon (**Tregaron**). A man of some culture, he composed occasional verse and won fame as a genealogist. As steward of the lordship of Caron, he became involved in

a bitter dispute with Tregaron's vicar. Described in 1597 as an old, bald, feeble man, nevertheless, in 1607, he took as his second wife the wealthy widow of Thomas Rhys Williams of Ystrad-ffin, the daughter of **John Price** of **Brecon**.

During his youth he allegedly became the leader of a gang of outlaws, and was involved in housebreaking and **cattle**-rustling, before receiving a pardon from Elizabeth I in 1559 for an unknown offence. The fact of the pardon gave rise to the notion that he had been an outlaw. Stories concerning him as a mischievous rogue were related in the Tregaron area during succeeding centuries, and some of them appear in Samuel Rush Meyrick's *The History of the County of Cardigan* (1809) and in **George Borrow**'s *Wild Wales* (1862). He developed into a national figure through the immense popularity of **Thomas Jeffery Llewelyn Prichard**'s novel *The Adventures and Vagaries of Twm Shon Catti* (1828).

JONES, Thomas (1648–1713) Printer

The son of a tailor of Tre'r-ddôl (**Corwen**), Jones went to **London** in 1666 and became a renowned publisher and bookseller. In 1695, he established the first **Welsh** press at Shrewsbury. A cantankerous hypochondriac, he regaled readers of his Welsh **almanacs**, published between 1681 and his death, with graphic accounts of his maladies and nostrums. His almanac was far more readable than any of those produced by his 18th-century successors. Carping scholars dubbed him 'Tom the tailor' and 'Tom-ass', but over a period of 30 years he published a wide range of catechetical and devotional books, a Welsh–**English dictionary** splendidly entitled *Y Gymraeg yn ei Disgleirdeb / The British Language in its Lustre*, and several popular **ballads**.

JONES, Thomas (1742–1803) Painter

Thomas Jones, who had been intended for holy orders, left his home at Pencerrig, **Llanelwedd**, in 1763 to study at the St Martin's Lane Academy, **London**, and later under his compatriot **Richard Wilson**. He was away for more than 20 years, apart from occasional visits to the family home. In Italy, where he lived between 1776 and 1783, he painted his famous study *A Wall in Naples* (1782), which hangs in the National Gallery, London. Its startlingly direct approach, at odds with the **picturesque** mode of the time, created new, naturalistic possibilities for landscape **painting** which were not properly pursued until a century later; he has been hailed as the father of *plein air* painting. In 1786, he visited Hafod, where he made views of the estate and **gardens** for **Thomas Johnes**. The following year, he inherited the property at Pencerrig, where he died. A major exhibition of his work at the **National Museum** in 2003 did much to enhance his reputation.

JONES, Thomas (1756–1820) Theologian and poet

The pre-eminent thinker among the **Calvinistic Methodists** of his time, Jones was born at Plas Penucha, **Caerwys**. He received a classical **education** at Caerwys and **Holywell**, and began to preach in 1783. In 1810, he – a layman – administered the sacraments of communion and baptism in his chapel at **Denbigh**, thus precipitating the ordination in

Thomas Jones, *Buildings in Naples* (1782)

1811 of Calvinistic Methodist ministers. He was among the first to be ordained. Inheriting the property of the first of his three wives, he lived – comfortably – at **Mold** (1795–1804), **Ruthin** (1804–6) and Denbigh (1806–20).

Jones was a close friend of **Thomas Charles**, with whom he edited the quarterly *Y Drysorfa*. His voluminous literary output, in possibly the finest **Welsh** of the period, includes a history of the Church of **England** (1813), an autobiography (1814), a biography of Thomas Charles (1816), several **hymns** and a fine *cywydd* to the thrush. He was a great uncle of the politician **John Herbert Lewis**, who inherited Plas Penucha.

JONES, Thomas (1810–49) Missionary
Little known in Wales, the **Calvinistic Methodists'** first **missionary** to the **Khasi Hills** in north-east India is regarded as a heroic figure in the land of his mission. In 1840, Jones and his wife Anne left **Berriew**, where he had worked as a miller, and laid the foundations for the Christianization of tens of thousands of Khasis. Although his life ended in scandal and tragedy, he is revered as the father of Khasi **literature**, being the first – using **Welsh** orthography – to give the Khasi language a written form, and the first to publish books in the language. His grave in Calcutta bears the inscription 'Father of Khasi Literature'.

JONES, Thomas (1870–1955) Public figure
A native of **Rhymney**, Jones began work as a clerk in the Rhymney **Iron**works at the age of 14. In 1890, he became a student at **Aberystwyth** and then had a distinguished academic career at Glasgow and at Belfast, where in 1909 he was appointed professor of economics. He returned to Wales in 1910 to become secretary of the Welsh National Memorial Association dedicated to the eradication of **tuberculosis**, a post which led to his close association with the **Davies family (Llandinam)**. Appointed secretary of the Welsh **Insurance** Commission in 1912, he was one of the founders and the first editor of the influential monthly *The Welsh Outlook* (1914). In 1916, he became assistant secretary to the cabinet, serving under **David Lloyd George**, Bonar Law, **Ramsay MacDonald** and Baldwin; he wrote some of Baldwin's more memorable speeches. He participated in the negotiations that preceded the Hiberno–British treaty of 1921 and played an important role during the industrial troubles that led to the **General Strike** of 1926. He was the founder, in 1927, of **Coleg Harlech**, one of the wide range of Welsh projects with which he was involved. In 1929, he was made a Companion of Honour; he liked to joke that the initials CH stood for Coleg Harlech.

On resigning his **government**al post in 1930, he became secretary to the Pilgrim Trust, where he developed the ideas that would eventually form the basis of the Arts Council. Chairman (1929–39) of the South Wales **Coal**field Hardship Committee, his credibility as a Fabian **socialist** lost some of its lustre between 1934 and 1940 when he was a member of the Unemployed Assistance Board, which administered a rigid **means test** policy.

From 1944 to 1954, he was president of the University College of Wales, Aberystwyth (*see* **University of Wales, Aberystwyth**), the college which had rejected him as principal in 1919, largely because he was not an orthodox Christian believer. His three volumes of autobiography, four volumes of published diaries and the 300 volumes of his papers at the **National Library** rank among the most important sources relating to the history of 20th-century Wales.

His biographer, E. L. Ellis, considered that the three greatest Welshmen in 20th-century public life were David Lloyd George, **Aneurin Bevan** and Thomas Jones. On being appointed minister of **Health** in 1945, Bevan's first comment was: 'I'll go to see that old bugger from Rhymney.' The **Labour** politician **Eirene White** was his daughter.

JONES, Thomas (1910–72) Scholar
Thomas Jones's main area of interest was medieval **Welsh** prose and he is best known outside Wales for the **English** translation of *The Mabinogion* (1948) which he and **Gwyn Jones** prepared. His creative scholarship contributed greatly to the success of the translation. He also published standard editions of the various versions of the chronicle *Brut y Tywysogyon*, together with detailed studies of the manuscripts. He was a native of Alltwen (**Cilybebyll**) and, apart from a period of military service, he spent the whole of his career in the Welsh department at **Aberystwyth**, where he was professor (1952–70).

JONES, [John] Viriamu (1856–1901)
Physicist and educationist
Viriamu Jones, born in Pentrepoeth, **Swansea**, was named after the celebrated South Sea Islands **missionary** John Williams, 'Viriamu' being the pronunciation of 'Williams' on the island of Erromango. Having won many distinctions in the universities of **London** and **Oxford**, and having laid the foundations for the future development of the University of Sheffield, in 1883 he became the first principal of University College, **Cardiff** (*see* **Cardiff University**) at the age of 27. He played a leading role in framing the charter of the **University of Wales** and became its first vice-chancellor in 1893. In 1894, he was elected FRS for his scientific research, concerned mainly with electrical and physical measurements, which he undertook largely in his leisure time.

No better understanding of the **education**al aims of the national movement may be found than in his eloquent speeches. A personality of rare charm (and an expert **mountain**eer), hitherto no one has equalled him as educational leader in Wales.

His elder brother, David Brynmor Jones (1852–1921), **Liberal** MP for **Swansea** District, was co-author with **John Rhŷs** of *The Welsh People* (1900). His younger brother, the Liberal MP Leifchild Stratten Jones (1862–1939), was elevated to the peerage as Baron **Rhayader** in 1932.

JONES, Walter Idris (1900–71)
Chemist and rugby player
The son of a rollerman in a **Llanelli tinplate** works, Jones was educated at **Aberystwyth** and **Cambridge**. Senior positions in the chemistry of fuel followed, at ICI and at **Powell Duffryn** (where he developed the artificial fuel 'phurnacite'), culminating in his appointment as director-general of research for the embryonic **National Coal Board** (1946), where he remained until his retirement in 1962.

He captained the Welsh **rugby** team in 1924 and 1925. One of his brothers was Lord Elwyn-Jones (**Frederick Elwyn Jones**).

JONES, William (?1675–1749) Mathematician

William Jones was born in Llanfihangel Tre'r Beirdd (**Llanddyfnan**), in the farm next to the home of the **Morris brothers**. His precocious arithmetical ability was noticed by Viscount **Bulkeley**, who sent him to **London**, where he became a tutor in **mathematics** to aristocratic families. Jones was the first to use the Greek letter π (the first letter of *periphereia*, meaning 'periphery') to represent the transcendental number 3.14159 … that is the ratio of the circumference of a circle to its diameter; he also suggested using a dot above a letter as a simple way to represent d/dt in calculus. His son was the distinguished orientalist Sir **William Jones**.

JONES, William (1726–95)
Radical, patriot and antiquary

A native of Llangadfan (**Banwy**), William Jones was admiringly described by one of his contemporaries as 'the hottest arsed Welshman he had ever known'. An avid supporter of the American and French Revolutions, Jones championed the **Jacobin** cause so vigorously that he became known as 'the rural Voltaire'. His manuscripts are peppered with pungent comments about despotic landowners, agents and clergymen. He sought to stiffen the pride of his countrymen in their nationhood by composing a robust Welsh national anthem, and by campaigning on behalf of a **national library** and a national **eisteddfod**.

Not least among his achievements was to record and revive the lively country **dances** associated with the **parish** of Llangadfan and to provide **London**-Welsh scholars with rare literary and musical information. Illness and poverty prevented him from fulfilling his dream of escaping William Pitt's 'reign of terror' by emigrating to America. **Government** spies kept him under close watch until his death.

JONES, William ('Oriental' Jones; 1746–94)
Orientalist and judge

Son of the distinguished mathematician **William Jones** (?1675–1749), Sir William Jones was educated at **Oxford**. There he added Arabic and Persian to his mastery of the classics, Hebrew and modern European languages (although not **Welsh**: a British ambassador once presented him to the king of France as 'a man who knows every language except his own'). A lawyer by profession, he was appointed to the Bengal Supreme Court in 1783. In Bengal, the following year, he founded the Asiatic Society which marked the beginning of Indology – the study of Indian languages, **literature**, **philosophy** and history. In 1786, he was able to affirm (as others had begun to conclude) that the classical languages of India and Europe were descended from a common source, now known as Indo-European, thus laying the foundations for modern linguistics. His book *Hymns to Hindu Deities* (1784–8) was among the works that introduced Europe to the treasure house of south Asian literature. His ambition to prepare a comprehensive digest of Hindu and Moslem law was only partly fulfilled by the publication of *Al Sirájiyyah: or the Mohammedan Law of Inheritance* (1792) and *The Institutes of Hindu Law* (1794), but these works played a crucial role in the process of governing the peoples of India by their own laws.

JONES, William (Ehedydd Iâl; 1815–99) Poet

As his bardic pseudonym suggests (lit. 'skylark of Yale'), **Derwen**-born Jones lived and died in **Denbighshire**, where he was, in turn, a miller, a farmer and a reluctant publican. A productive poet in both strict and free metres, his name lives as the writer of one strongly imaged **hymn**, 'Er nad yw 'nghnawd ond gwellt' (Although my flesh is but straw).

JULIUS and AARON (3rd or 4th century) Martyrs

Two Christians killed in the 'City of the Legions' (**Caerleon**). Their names are included by **Gildas** as probable victims of the emperor Diocletian's persecution (303–5). Modern historians suggest that possibly they were martyred during earlier persecutions, under Decius (250–1) or Valerian (257–9).

JUVENCUS ENGLYNION, The

Two series of stanzas written in Old **Welsh** in the *Juvencus Manuscript* (a 9th-century **Latin** manuscript, held at **Cambridge** University Library). The first is a fragment of a lost saga poem while the second is a religious piece. The provenance of the poems is not known; but they may be the earliest surviving recorded examples of Welsh poetry.

Cardiff City captain Fred Keenor (right) shakes hands with the Arsenal captain before the kick-off of the 1927 FA Cup final

KAPPEN, Joseph William (1941–90)
Suspected murderer

Kappen was a **Margam**-born nightclub bouncer. In 2002, DNA extracted from his exhumed body indicated that he was the killer of three teenage girls from the **Neath** area in 1973, and that he may have murdered others elsewhere. Kappen was the first murder suspect to be exhumed in **Britain** in order to make DNA tests.

KAYLES (W. *Ceilys*)

Similar to skittles or tenpin **bowling**, this folk game involved throwing a wooden ball – or, formerly a wooden stick fringed with metal – at a set of wooden targets, whose size and number depended on local tradition, the object being to knock down with one throw as many targets as possible. Popular for centuries, kayles was constantly under attack from the authorities as a waste of time and for inciting betting, and was therefore subject to banning orders.

KEATING, Joseph (1871–1934) Novelist

A modest pioneer of the novel of the south Wales **coal**field, Joseph Keating, born to **Irish** immigrants at **Mountain Ash**,

began working as a miner at the age of 12. He later moved to **London** where he lived in poverty, but returned to his home town in 1923, when he became active in local politics. The best of his (unexceptional) novels is *Maurice: the Romance of a Welsh Coalmine* (1905).

KEENOR, Fred[erick Charles] (1894–1972)
Footballer

A robust and fearsome half-back and an inspirational captain, Keenor, the son of a **Cardiff** bricklayer, became an iconic figure in Welsh sport in the difficult years of the interwar **depression**. Having been twice wounded on the Western Front during the **First World War**, he returned to Cardiff and became captain of a team entering its glory days. He captained the side in both its Wembley Cup finals (1925, 1927) and he won 32 caps.

KELSEY, Jack (Alfred John Kelsey; 1929–92)
Footballer

Wales's greatest goalkeeper was born at Llansamlet, **Swansea**, and joined Arsenal in 1949 from Winch Wen. He played 351 matches for Arsenal and 41 for Wales, securing

435

a reputation for aerial brilliance and for intimidating aggressive forwards. He played for **Britain** against the Rest of Europe (1955) and in the 1958 World Cup he impressed the Brazilians. An injury sustained against Brazil in 1962 ended his career.

KERRY (Ceri), Montgomeryshire, Powys
(8822 ha; 1922 inhabitants)
Constituting the south-eastern corner of **Montgomeryshire**, the **community**'s boundaries are broadly those of the medieval **commote** of Ceri. It is rich in prehistoric monuments, with **Bronze Age** barrows and standing stones on the Kerry Hills and on the Glog, and two large tumuli north of Kerry village. The motte near the village was probably built *c*.1130 as the caput of the commote. The ringwork south of Sarn was commissioned by **Hubert de Burgh** as part of his abortive attack on the commote in 1228; it came to be known as Hubert's Folly.

In 1176, **Giraldus Cambrensis**, on behalf of the **diocese** of **St David's** had an altercation with the bishop of **St Asaph** during the consecration of the rebuilt St Michael's church. The bishop fled, pursued by a mob. Some of the 1176 work survives, but much of the church was rebuilt in the 14th and 15th centuries, and was extensively restored in 1883. There are attractive churches at Dolfor (1851) and Sarn (1859).

The poet Siôn Ceri settled at Kerry in the early 16th century. **John Jenkins** (Ifor Ceri; 1770–1829), the inaugurator of the provincial *eisteddfodau*, was vicar of Kerry from 1807 until his death. At his neo-Gothic vicarage, The Moat (1811), perhaps designed by **John Nash**, Jenkins held open house for a week a year for poets, singers and **harp**ists. Brynllywarch was the home of William Pugh (1783–1842),

who was instrumental in bringing the Montgomeryshire **canal** to **Newtown**, the major stimulus of the town's **woollen industry**.

KHASI HILLS, north-east India
Between 1841 and 1969, Welsh **Calvinistic Methodist** (or Presbyterian) **missionaries** to this mountainous region north of Bangladesh profoundly influenced the culture of the Khasi Jaintia hill-tribe. Inaugurated by the controversial **Thomas Jones** (1810–49) and supported by money collected from the home congregations, the mission pioneered literacy, publishing, **education** and **health** care, converting thousands of Khasis to Christianity, and extending their work, with Khasi help, into the neighbouring Cachar and Mizo hills, and the plains of Sylhet.

Roughly 500,000 Khasi Jaintia people still adhere to their monotheistic indigenous religion; but of the remainder, 300,000 are Presbyterian and 200,000 **Roman Catholic**. Although no more than 200 Welsh missionaries served in 'Khasia', their legacy endures and is even acknowledged by non-Christians – in spite of the missionaries' hostility to native traditions such as dancing, drinking, animal sacrifice and **archery**. Welsh **hymn** tunes raise the roofs of their overcrowded chapels every Sunday, and a jaunty Khasi version of '**Hen Wlad fy Nhadau**' is their national anthem. Other, incidental, parallels include record-breaking rainfall, **coal**mines, disused **slate** quarries, and a landscape scattered with *cromlechi* and monoliths.

KIDWELLY (Cydweli), Carmarthenshire
(1176 ha; 3289 inhabitants)
Located on the estuaries of the Gwendraeth Fawr and Gwendraeth Fach, the **community** contains the town of

Kidwelly Castle, Carmarthenshire

Kidwelly and the scattered settlement of Mynyddygarreg. In 1106, the **commote** of Cedweli was seized by the **Normans** and fortified by an earth and timber castle on the right bank of the Gwendraeth Fach. By 1115, St Mary's **Benedictine** Priory had been founded on the **river**'s left bank. In the Welsh revolt which followed the death of Henry I in 1135, an army led by **Gwenllian**, wife of **Gruffudd ap Rhys ap Tewdwr** (d.1137) of **Deheubarth** and daughter of **Gruffudd ap Cynan** of **Gwynedd**, attacked Kidwelly, an attack which led to her death in a place known as Maes Gwenllian.

In subsequent years, Kidwelly was intermittently in the hands of the Welsh; but by the 1270s it was firmly under the control of Pain de Chaworth, who commanded Edward I's forces in the war against **Llywelyn ap Gruffudd** in 1277. It was Pain who commissioned the building of the castle's inner ward with its four imposing round towers. By the early 14th century, Kidwelly was held by Henry, earl of **Lancaster**. He was responsible for the splendid curtain wall, the Great Gatehouse and the defences surrounding the town, which adjoined the castle. The south gateway of the town's defences still stands. Following the seizure of the English throne by Henry Bolingbroke, duke of Lancaster, in 1399, Kidwelly became the property of the crown. In 1403, Henry Dwnn, an ally of **Owain Glyndŵr**, seized the town but failed to capture the castle.

A second settlement grew around the Benedictine priory. The priory was dissolved in 1539, but the 14th-century church, with its steeple-capped tower and its spacious nave and chancel, survives. Kidwelly's medieval town became a centre of the **woollen industry**, introduced by **Flemings** in the 12th century. Its **port** enjoyed prosperity until the Gwendraeth Fach estuary silted up. **Tinplate** manufacture began at Kidwelly in the mid-18th century and continued until the 1940s. The works have been restored as the centrepiece of an industrial museum. In 1920, Harold Greenwood, a Kidwelly doctor, was accused of poisoning his wife, a case which added to the legendary reputation of the barrister Marshall Hall, who succeeded in securing a verdict of not guilty. The broadcaster and former **rugby** player Ray Gravell is a native of Mynyddygarreg.

KILBRANDON COMMISSION, The

In the autumn of 1969, a Royal Commission on the Constitution was set up, under the chairmanship of Geoffrey Crowther, to consider in the main the question of **devolution** for Wales and **Scotland**. The **Conservatives** in Wales refused to give evidence to the commission, and it soon became apparent that devolution aroused deep-rooted divisions and tensions in the ranks of the **Labour Party**. Many observers felt that the Wilson **government** was using the commission, with its slow, cumbersome procedures, as a ploy to smother public interest in the question. As the years went by, and Crowther was followed by Lord Kilbrandon, few devolutionists ventured to hope that a positive step towards self-government might result.

When the commission eventually reported in October 1973, its findings were encouraging to devolutionists. Predictably, the 13 commissioners were divided, although all agreed that the existing situation was unsatisfactory. Two advocated regional councils throughout the United Kingdom, two were in favour of increased powers for the Welsh and Scottish Offices, but the remainder recommended an elected assembly for Wales, with six, including the two Welsh members, **Ben Bowen Thomas** and **Alun Talfan Davies**, urging that the assembly should have legislative powers. The commissioners emphasized that deep-rooted fears existed about the growth of centralized power and the remoteness of government, but affirmed their belief in the over-riding unity of the United Kingdom. The complex findings immediately attracted scorn from the Welsh Conservatives and from several Labour MPs; but they did compel the Labour Party to redefine its Welsh and Scottish devolution policies.

KILGETTY (Cilgeti), Pembrokeshire
(1955 ha; 2011 inhabitants)
Located immediately north of **Saundersfoot**, the **community** contains the villages of Kilgetty, Reynalton and Begelly (Begeli), the community's alternative name. Kilgetty was the centre of **Pembrokeshire**'s **coal** industry, which finally came to an end in the 1940s; a museum celebrates the local industrial heritage. St James's church, Reynalton, has a 15th-century tower. The tall tower of St Mary's church, Begelly, was used as a lookout in the **Second World War**. The gipsy camp on King's Moor, where the John children 'ran happily wild', inspired **Augustus John**'s lifelong interest in the **Romany** people. Zion **Calvinistic Methodist** chapel (1828, 1866) is a handsome building. There are remains of an ambitious garden at Kilgetty Farm.

KILVERT, Francis (1840–79) Diarist
The seven years (1865–72) that Wiltshire-born Francis Kilvert spent as curate of **Clyro** were to make his name as a writer. Sometimes over-sentimental, but with a keen eye for detail, he described life in the village and adjacent hills in a simple and vivid prose style which places him among the best **English** diarists. He was particularly fond of children and old people, although with young **women** he was diffident and less successful. In 1872, he took the living of **St Harmon** and subsequently that of Bredwardine, just over the **border** in **Herefordshire**. In 1879, he was at last able to marry, but five weeks later he died suddenly of peritonitis. His diaries remained in the keeping of his widow until her death in 1911 and, with many passages destroyed, were not published until 1938–40.

KINGS and PRINCES

By 1000, **England** and **Scotland** were each ruled by a single king; but in Wales, kingship remained inherent in the individual kingdoms which had emerged since the departure of the **Romans** – there being no such concept as a kingship of Wales.

The main kingdoms were **Gwynedd**, **Powys**, **Morgannwg** (essentially the union of **Glywysing** and **Gwent**) and **Deheubarth**; there were also various lesser kingdoms, which tended to be under the influence of their more powerful neighbours. The king was the leader of his people in peace and war, and the enforcer of **law** and justice; his

Knighton, Powys

powers and perquisites were set out in the lawbooks, as was an elaborate hierarchy of court officials. The king and his court travelled around the kingdom, being maintained by **food** renders from his subjects, both free and unfree; in each of the divisions (either *cantrefi* or **commotes**) of the kingdom there was a court centre and a demesne township or *maerdref* which produced food.

A Welsh king was not succeeded automatically by his eldest son; he could designate as his heir any member of the royal kindred, which consisted of every kinsman who was at least the great-grandson of a king. The institution of kingship in Wales was essentially **Celt**ic and in some ways resembled its Irish counterpart, but from the 10th century onwards, it was much influenced, especially in the leading kingdoms, by West Saxon practice.

By the end of the 12th century, Welsh rulers had abandoned the royal title, replacing it with 'prince' or 'lord'; **Owain Gwynedd** had styled himself both king and prince at different times but his son **Dafydd ab Owain Gwynedd** seems to have been the last to describe himself as a king. The change may have been a consequence of an increasing precision in the vocabulary of political authority in contemporary Europe, and a realization that Welsh kingship did not conform to any new definition. The fact that Welsh rulers were doing homage to the king of England may also have been significant. The title of prince was used by **Rhys ap Gruffudd** (The Lord Rhys; d.1197) of

Deheubarth, but by the early 13th century it was being used only by the prince of Gwynedd, **Llywelyn ap Iorwerth**, the other rulers being described as lords or barons. His objective and that of his grandson, **Llywelyn ap Gruffudd**, was to persuade or force other rulers to do homage to him rather than to the king of England; he would then do homage to the king on behalf of them all.

This would lead to his recognition by the English crown in a formal treaty as Prince of Wales, the princely title being probably considered to be more acceptable than that of king. It was also a title that did not involve the rejection of English overlordship. Llywelyn ap Iorwerth was unsuccessful but his grandson ultimately achieved recognition in the **Treaty of Montgomery** of 1267. The **Principality** of Wales as an institution survived the **Edwardian conquest**.

KINMEL BAY AND TOWYN (Bae Cinmel a Thywyn), Conwy (1040 ha; 7864 inhabitants)

Located across the **Clwyd** from **Rhyl**, the **community** is located on flood-prone **Morfa Rhuddlan**. The protective cob, built to carry the Chester–**Holyhead railway**, proved an inadequate defence in 1990, when the area suffered severe flooding. The church, vicarage and school, designed by G. E. Street in 1873, are a fine example of the 19th-century **Anglican** ideal. Much of the community is occupied by small bungalows, caravan sites and amusement parks, constructed following the break-up of the Kinmel Park estate in the 1930s. Tir Prince trotting racetrack is a prime attraction (*see* **Horse Racing**). In 2001, 62.97% of the community's inhabitants had no knowledge at all of **Welsh**, making it, linguistically, the most Anglicized community in the **county borough** of Conwy.

KNIGHTON (Trefyclo), Radnorshire, Powys (2622 ha; 3043 inhabitants)

Knighton, lying south of the **River** Teme, thrusts eastwards into **England**. Its **Welsh** name, originally Tref-y-clawdd (the town of the dyke), is indicative of its location on **Offa's Dyke**; the Dyke Interpretation Centre was opened there in 1971. The older part of town has a grid of streets reminiscent of an Edwardian plantation. A diminutive market town, Knighton nevertheless has what the *Shell Guide to Mid Wales* describes as 'an air of meaning business ... a municipal look'. Stanage Park was once the property of the Johnes family, and **Thomas Johnes**, later the builder of Hafod (*see* **Pontarfynach**), seems at one time to have thought of settling there. Its house and **gardens** were commissioned by Charles Rogers and carried out by Humphrey and John Adey Repton.

KYFFIN, Morris (*c.*1555–98) Author

Born near Oswestry (**Shropshire**), Kyffin was **Wiliam Llŷn**'s bardic pupil. He served with English armies in the Netherlands, France and **Ireland**. He published *The Blessednes of Brytaine*, a poem praising Elizabeth I (1587), and an **English** translation of Terence's **Latin** comedy *Andria* (1588). His masterpiece was *Deffynniad Ffydd Eglwys Loegr* (1595), a **Welsh** translation of bishop John Jewel's *Apologia Ecclesiae Anglicanae* (1562), which defended the **Anglican** Church against **Puritans** and **Roman Catholics**.

L ～ L

Rhodri Morgan, Leader of the Labour Party in Wales and First Minister in the National Assembly for Wales speaking at a press conference at Llandrillo College, Rhos-on-Sea, 22 February, 2007

LABOUR CAMPS

In August 1932, at the height of the **Depression** of the inter-war years, 42.8% of Wales's insured males were unemployed. The Ministry of Labour was particularly concerned about 'the younger men, who, through prolonged unemployment, have become so soft and temporarily demoralised as to require reconditioning by hardening off ... under canvas and in healthy, open countryside surroundings'.

In Wales, labour camps were established at Brechfa (**Llanfihangel Rhos-y-corn**), and Treglog (**Llansawel**), **Presteigne**, **Ganllwyd** and **Betws-y-Coed**. The unemployed were sent to these camps for 12 weeks, where the work was physically demanding: felling trees, digging ditches and **road** building. Working six 12-hour shifts per week earned them 4 shillings (the equivalent of 20p, but about £16 if inflation is taken into account) and a half-day pass to the nearest town or village. Some 200,000 men attended these camps, over a quarter of whom absconded; only a third of those who remained subsequently found work.

LABOUR PARTY, The

In 1906, the Labour Representation Committee (LRC), which had been formed in 1900, changed its name to the Labour Party. The organization had been established by

Keir Hardie and others to ensure that elected representatives of the working **class** could operate independently of the **Liberals** as members of a House of Commons party in its own right.

In the general election of 1906, Hardie was re-elected at **Merthyr Tydfil** as one of 29 Labour MPs; he was, however, the only one returned in Wales, where the Liberals (including Lib-Labs) won the other 33 seats. In 1908, when the **Miners' Federation of Great Britain** became affiliated to the Labour Party, the four Welsh MPs sponsored by miners became Labour MPs. Local organization was strengthened and there was a steady increase in the number of Labour councillors and Labour JPs. The industrial unrest of the immediate pre-war years and the experience of the **First World War** strengthened the case for independent representation.

The Labour Party assumed a fuller identity, not least in the constituencies, in 1918, when it adopted a **socialist** constitution and made provision for individual membership; 10 Labour MPs were returned from Wales in that year. In 1922, the figure rose to 18, half the total seats, the beginning of a Labour hegemony which would dominate Welsh politics for generations. New career opportunities were opening up for Welsh Labour leaders. During the war,

439

William Brace (MP for South **Glamorgan**) was under-secretary at the Home Office and, when the first Labour **government** was formed in 1924, the prime minister, **Ramsay MacDonald**, himself MP for **Aberavon**, gave **Vernon Hartshorn**, MP for **Ogmore**, a cabinet position as postmaster general.

The problems confronting mining communities in the 1920s strengthened support for Labour in industrial Wales. Even in the election which followed the collapse of the second Labour government in 1931, the party received 44.1% of the vote in Wales, compared with 30.8% in **Britain** as a whole. In the Commons, of the 46 Labour MPs elected in 1931, 16 represented Welsh constituencies, although not one of the 16 was on the party's front bench. At the local government level, Labour hegemony was even more pronounced. By the late 1920s, every local authority in the southern **coal**field was under Labour control. Indeed, some councils consisted exclusively of Labour members, although there were areas where the **Communist** challenge was significant.

It was during the 1930s, and especially at the time of the many parliamentary debates on unemployment and the **means test**, that Labour came to be seen as the natural party to represent industrial Wales, although the complex domestic and international issues of that decade prompted a variety of responses and there was considerable dissatisfaction with Labour's moderate leaders. The various struggles of the **South Wales Miners' Federation** and the demonstrations in support of the unemployed and against fascism often involved working with Communists and supporting the Popular Front. At one stage, the **Rhondda**

Michael Foot, leader of the Labour Party, speaking at the Party Conference in Brighton in 1981

constituency party was disaffiliated; and, in 1939, **Aneurin Bevan** was expelled. However, the participation of so many Labour supporters in local government ensured a degree of party loyalty; Duncan Tanner has rightly summed up the Labour Party of this era as being 'verbally radical but vehemently practical in its policies'. While the southern coalfield and its associated **ports** provided the great majority of Wales's Labour MPs, the northern coalfield eventually became a Labour stronghold, as did, for a period, the **slate**-quarrying areas of the north-west. In the wholly rural areas, support for the Labour Party was also considerable; indeed, **Montgomeryshire** is the only part of Wales never to have been represented by a Labour MP.

The British Labour Party was always to regard its 1945–51 legislative programme as its greatest achievement, and in Wales there was particular pleasure that the most significant measures in that period of reform were introduced by two ministers who had started out as Welsh miners – Aneurin Bevan and **James Griffiths**. The new National **Health** Service, the **Welfare State** and the nationalized industries were all greeted as the desirable outcome of a generation's political struggle, but it was economic growth and full employment that allowed the post-war dispensation to be enjoyed. This was particularly the case in local government, where Labour hegemony benefited from unprecedented Treasury funding, not least for **housing** and **education**.

For a generation, Labour's supremacy in Wales rested on the new prosperity. This led to a degree of consensus in a party increasingly led by the Welsh Regional Council of Labour established in 1947. Much of the bitterness of the Gaitskell versus Bevan feud was avoided in Wales, and in 1956 the five MPs who supported the Parliament for Wales Bill were easily sidelined. Labour's support in Wales peaked in the general election of 1966 when it won 32 of the 36 seats and took 61% of the vote.

With a strong contingent of Welsh MPs in government, the party looked set for an era of total domination, but in reality a new period of anxiety had begun. **Plaid [Genedlaethol] Cymru**'s victory in the **Carmarthen** by-election of 1966, combined with economic stagnation, forced Labour on the defensive. A low point came in 1979, first with the referendum defeat of James Callaghan's **devolution** proposals, which exposed the party's divisions in Wales, and then with Margaret Thatcher's victory in the general election, when the number of Wales's Labour MPs declined to 22.

There was worse to come in 1983, when Labour received only 38% of the vote and won a mere 20 seats. Thereafter the party embarked on a painful process of recovery under Neil Kinnock, MP for **Bedwellty** (later **Islwyn**), who in 1983 succeeded Michael Foot, MP for **Ebbw Vale**, as leader. (Of the 13 leaders of the Labour Party since its foundation, five – Keir Hardie, Ramsay MacDonald, James Callaghan, Neil Kinnock and Michael Foot – represented Welsh constituencies; it would have been six had Tony Blair been successful in his bid to be MP for **Wrexham**.)

In 1997, the electoral victory of Tony Blair's New Labour gave the party a new opportunity. It won 34 of the 40 Welsh seats and 54.7% of the vote; furthermore, its devolution proposals were approved by a narrow majority.

The Welsh women's lacrosse team when European champions in 2004

Thus, as it approached its centenary, Labour seemed secure in its domination of Welsh politics. However, proportional representation combined with rows and scandal ensured a minority position for Labour following the first elections to the **National Assembly for Wales**. With 28 of the 60 assembly seats, in 2000 Labour was forced to enter into partnership with the **Liberal Democrats**. Its loss to Plaid Cymru of three southern **coal**field seats was a traumatic experience for the party. That loss was not repeated in the Westminster elections of 2001, when Labour again won 34 seats in Wales.

In the second Assembly elections in 2003, the party won 30 seats. Following the election, Rhodri Morgan, the Assembly government's chief minister, abandoned the coalition with the Liberal Democrats and formed an exclusively Labour cabinet, with power in the Assembly itself being equally balanced between Labour and the combined opposition (30:30). That balance was lost when Peter Law, Assembly Member (AM) for **Blaenau Gwent**, left the party prior to the Westminster elections of 2005, in protest at the imposition on the local party of an all-**women** shortlist. His subsequent election as an independent MP for Blaenau Gwent, defeating Labour's official candidate by more than 9000 votes, meant the loss to Labour of its safest seat in Wales. Labour lost five Welsh seats altogether in those elections, reducing its total in Wales from 34 to 29; the party's share of the vote in Wales fell to 42.7%. Of the votes cast in the National Assembly election of 2007, the Labour Party won 32.2% at the constituency level and 29.6% at the regional level, but won 43.3% (26) of the seats. The party's attempt to go into a coalition with the Liberal Democrats failed, as did the attempt to create a 'rainbow' coalition led by Plaid Cymru and including the **Conservatives** and the Liberal Democrats, a coalition which would have ousted Labour from power. To the astonishment of many, the

outcome – after much agonizing – was a coalition between Labour and Plaid Cymru, parties which between them held 41 of the Assembly's 60 seats. Intriguingly, the coalition became a reality on 7 July 2007, the 700th anniversary of the death of Edward I.

LACROSSE
The game, devised by native **North America**ns as training for warfare, was championed by Queen Victoria as a decorously 'upright' sport for girls in public schools – where, until the later 20th century, it was largely confined. It is now played all over the world and is one of the fastest growing sports in Wales.

Wales had an international **women**'s side as early as the 1920s, and in the 1930s the Welsh Lacrosse Association was established to administer the game. A Welsh men's team, which had failed to take root in the 1940s, was re-established in 1991. Wales competes as an independent nation in home internationals and in European and world championships. The women's team won the European championship in both 1999 and 2004. A distinguished Welsh player is Vivien Jones, captain for many years of the Wales women's team and the most capped Welsh woman in any team sport.

LACY family Marcher-lords
The Lacy family's origins were in Lassy, Normandy. Walter (d.1085) seized land in the Monnow valley, the nucleus of what would become the lordship of **Ewyas** Lacy. His grandson, Hugh (d.1186), was prominent in the invasion of **Ireland**, his descendants including the earls of Ulster and Meath. The family, patrons of Llanthony Priory (*see* **Crucorney**), held Ewyas Lacy until it passed to the Geneville family by marriage. William Lacy (d.1233) married Gwenllian, daughter of **Llywelyn ap Iorwerth**. John Lacy (d.1240), first earl of Lincoln, belonged to a

Llangorse Lake, with Wales's only known crannog (in foreground)

cadet branch of the family. The third earl (d.1311), a close associate of Edward I, was granted the lordship of **Denbigh** following the **Edwardian conquest** and commissioned Denbigh's magnificent castle. Following his death, Denbigh passed by marriage to the earls of **Lancaster** and eventually to the **Mortimer family**.

LAKES

Outside **Snowdonia**, Wales has few lakes. In **Denbighshire**, **Monmouthshire**, **Montgomeryshire** and **Radnorshire**, there are hardly any natural stretches of water that can be dignified with the name.

Most Welsh lakes are small and even within the Snowdonia **National Park**, where there are at least 250 lakes, well over half of them have a surface area of less than 3.5 ha. Wales's largest lake is **Bala** Lake (Llyn Tegid). At 6 km in length, containing 45,000 megalitres and with a surface area of 454 ha, it is shorter and smaller in capacity and area than several of the country's **reservoirs**.

Outside the uplands of the north and west, the largest lake is **Llangorse** Lake (Llyn Syfaddan), which is 2 km in length and has a surface area of 140 ha. Together, Wales's lakes and reservoirs occupy 130 square km, 0.626% of the country's total surface area.

In mountainous areas, glacial erosion is the primary cause of lake creation. Indeed, the corrie below the summit of **Glyder Fawr** containing Llyn Idwal is one of the prime sites for the study of glaciation. A number of the floors of **Snowdon**'s semi-circular basins or cirques contain lakes, several of which are of considerable depth – Llyn Glaslyn

(39 m), for example, and Llyn Llydaw (57 m). Wales's deepest lake is Llyn Cowlyd (67.7 m), high above the **Conwy** valley. Some cirque lakes formed behind morainic dams – deposits which accumulated around glacier snouts. A combination of rock basin and morainic dam was responsible for lakes such as Llyn Cau, below the summit of **Cadair Idris**, Llyn Llygad Rheidol below the summit of **Pumlumon**, Llyn y Fan Fach (**Black Mountain**) and Llyn Fawr (**Rhigos**).

With the exception of Bala Lake and Tal-y-llyn Lake (Llyn Mwyngil; *see* **Llanfihangel-y-Pennant**), ribbon lakes are confined to Snowdon and its immediate neighbours, where glacial erosion was at its most intense. Several fill deep rock basins on the floors of glacial troughs, among them Cwellyn (37 m), Peris (55 m) and Padarn (27 m). Tal-y-llyn Lake in the Dysynni valley is shallow, dammed behind the debris of a massive landslide that slumped down from the steep slopes below Craig Goch. Llangorse Lake is also shallow. Like many of the lakes of Wales, it occupies a depression in glacial deposits.

Lakes near the coast have different origins, arising as they do from enclosure by spits, bars and sand-dune systems. They include Kenfig Pool (**Cornelly**) and some of the lakes in **Llanfaelog** and **Llanfair-yn-Neubwll**.

In geological terms, lakes are short-lived features. The 3-km lake which occupied the rock basin on the floor of the Nant Ffrancon valley following the retreat of the Ffrancon glacier, has long since been in-filled. **Cors Caron** represents a 10,000-year accumulation of mud and **peat** that filled the lake which had formed behind a moraine on the floor of the

Teifi valley. The **place names** Pwll yr Henllyn and Sychlwch are testimony to the disappearance of two small lakes which once lay between Llyn y Fan Fach and Llyn y Fan Fawr. One lake can become several; thus, Llyn Padarn and Llyn Peris, once a single ribbon lake, became two separate ones because of the sediment load carried by Afon Arddu.

The flora and fauna of Welsh lakes

Most **mountain** lakes, with their acidic, nutrient-poor water, sustain relatively few **plants**, among them shoreweed, water lobelia and bulbous rush. Water stained brown by surrounding peatland may be dominated by growths of sphagnum and other mosses, which often occur in association with carnivorous bladderworts. Warmer, more nutrient-rich lowland lakes can sustain a variety of submerged, floating and emergent plants, including several species of pondweed, water lily, duckweed, spiked water-milfoil and common reed. Wales is considered one of the main strongholds of the increasingly rare floating water plantain.

Of Wales's lake **fish**, the most famous is the *gwyniad* (*coregonus clupeoides pennantii*), unique to Bala Lake; a one-time migratory fish locked into the lake at the end of the last Ice Age, it has evolved into a separate species. Other fish which have undergone a similar experience include the Arctic char of Llyn Cwellyn. While most Welsh lakes are home to the native brown trout, many contain introduced species – mainly the rainbow trout, but also the Loch Leven trout of Llyn Idwal. Llangorse Lake is particularly rich in aquatic species. In 1188, **Giraldus Cambrensis** noted that it 'supplied the country with pike, perch, excellent trout, tench and eels'. The rare glutinous snail has recently been rediscovered in Bala Lake. Most of the species of **mammals**, **birds** and other animals inhabiting Welsh **rivers** also find a habitat in the country's lakes.

Lakes and mythology

Fascination with lakes is a leading feature of Welsh mythology. A favourite story is that of the 'fairy bride', which has associations with at least two dozen Welsh lakes (*see* **Llyn y Fan Fach, Legend of**). Another favourite is that of the drowned city. Bala Lake was reputed to have inundated Tegid's palace, and the bells of the city lying beneath Llangorse Lake were said to be audible when the waters were agitated. There may be substance to such legends, for the town of Kenfig lies beneath Kenfig Pool and its surrounding dunes. It was claimed that King **Arthur** was brought up on the banks of Bala Lake and that his sword, Excalibur, was thrown into Llyn Llydaw across whose water he was borne. According to Giraldus Cambrensis, the birds of Llangorse Lake would sing only to their true prince. As the discoveries in Llyn Fawr and in Llyn Cerrigbach (Llanfair-yn-Neubwll) indicate, the **Celts** considered lakes to be sacred places where the gods were propitiated by casting objects of high value into the waters.

The human use of lakes and its consequences

Archaeological evidence shows that the banks of lowland lakes rich in fish have been places of human settlement since at least the **Neolithic Age**. Fortified artificial islands or crannogs on lakes could offer sites for defensible dwellings. The crannog on Llangorse Lake was probably a seat of the royal house of **Brycheiniog**; the **Anglo-Saxon** Chronicle records that the stronghold on 'Brecenan Mere' was attacked by the **English** in 916. Lakes played a role in industrialization, with **copper** ore conveyed across Llyn Llydaw and **slate** across Llyn Padarn.

The most intense form of lake exploitation has been their enlargement to create reservoirs. The outfalls from many of the lakes of Snowdonia – Llyn Cwellyn, Llyn Cowlyd and Llyn Llydaw among them – have been dammed to make them more effective as water stores, both for domestic and industrial purposes and to power hydroelectric schemes (*see* **Energy**). The most ingenious use of lakes is the Dinorwic scheme (**Llanddeiniolen**) in which difference of altitude between Llyn Marchlyn Mawr (580 m) and Llyn Peris (100 m) is exploited for the production of electricity.

More intrusive is the use of lakes for **tourism**, a development particularly evident around Bala Lake and Llangorse Lake, where the effluent emanating from lakeside camps and activities such as water skiing threaten to upset the delicate ecological balance.

Such upsets have also been caused by other human activities. Copper mining has led to the extinction of trout in Llyn Llydaw and Llyn Glaslyn. Intensive planting of

Bala Lake (Llyn Tegid), home to the *gwyniad*

443

The Great House at Laleston, which has been converted into a hotel

conifers produces water of high acidity. Excess use of fertilizer causes water draining into lakes to be very rich in nutrients, thus encouraging the growth of lush vegetation, which pollutes as it decays. In 1989, when all aspects of water became the responsibility of the National Rivers Authority (later the Environment Agency), such problems have been tackled, although not yet wholly solved.

LALESTON (Trelales), Bridgend
(1026 ha; 8475 inhabitants)
Located immediately west of **Bridgend**, the **community**'s name recalls the **Norman** Lageles family. St **David**'s church in the compact village has 13th and 14th-century features. Great House, built for the Sidney family from the late 16th century onwards, is now a hotel. Cae'rheneglwys was the site of the church of St Cewydd, a **saint** who was the Welsh equivalent of St Swithin. Llangewydd Grange was a grange of **Margam** Abbey. The name Stormy Down recalls not the winds of that exposed ridge but rather a Norman family called Sturmi.

LAMPETER (Llanbedr Pont Steffan),
Ceredigion (1265 ha; 2894 inhabitants)
The third largest of the urban centres of **Ceredigion**, Lampeter is the smallest university town in **Britain**. The name is a corruption of the **Welsh** Llanbedr ('Church of St Peter'); the full Welsh name adds a reference to the bridge which was reputedly guarded by a **Norman** named Stephen. There are several **Iron Age** fortified farms within the **community**. The castle on the large motte in the college grounds,

an early 12th-century Norman fortification, was destroyed by the Welsh in 1137. Lampeter had achieved **borough** status by 1304. From the **Act of 'Union'** of 1536 until 1885, it was part of the **Cardigan** Boroughs constituency.

By the 17th century, local control lay with the Lloyds of Maesyfelin, a large mansion of which nothing remains. In the 18th century, control passed to the Lloyd family of Peterwell, whose members included the despotic and unruly Herbert Lloyd (1719–69). The Peterwell estate passed in 1819 to the Harford family, who built Falcondale (1859), which has been converted into a hotel. J. S. Harford's readiness to sell Castle Field as the site for **Thomas Burgess**'s proposed college was one of the factors which led the bishop to establish St David's College at Lampeter (see **University of Wales, Lampeter**). Another factor was the fame of John Williams (1792–1858) as head of the local grammar school – the school chosen by Sir Walter Scott for his son. Lampeter and Bangor (see **University of Wales, Bangor**) are the only colleges in Wales to have pastiches of an Oxbridge court. The college wholly dominates the town – except on alternate Tuesdays, when the mart brings it into full contact with its rural hinterland. Until their abolition in 1971, Lampeter was the seat of the **Cardiganshire** assizes.

LAMPETER VELFREY (Llanbedr Felffre),
Pembrokeshire (2936 ha; 1097 inhabitants)
Located immediately south-west of **Whitland**, the **community**, together with that of **Llanddewi Velfrey**, constituted the medieval **commote** of **Efelffre**. St Peter's contains

a 13th-century arcade and a 17th-century altar tomb. The **Congregationalist** minister and peace campaigner Nun Morgan Harry (1800–42) was a native of Lampeter Velfrey. Tavernspite was a *hospitium* of **Whitland** Abbey (*see* **Llanboidy**), a resting place for pilgrims to **St David's**. **Limestone** quarrying at Ludchurch has created a curious landscape. St Elidyr's church, Ludchurch, has a handsome 15th-century nave arcade.

LAMPHEY (Llandyfái), Pembrokeshire
(1125 ha; 852 inhabitants)
Located immediately east of **Pembroke**, the **community** reaches the sea at Freshwater East, where the scattering of chalets, caravans and advertisements constitutes perhaps the ugliest place in Wales. Lamphey Palace was the Castel Gandolpho of the **diocese** of **St David's**, where the bishops retreated in their leisure hours. Although the site was probably ecclesiastical land before the coming of the **Normans**, the earliest surviving building – Old Hall – dates from the early 13th century. The finest structure is the hall built for **Henry de Gower**, bishop of St David's (1328–47). With its fine arcaded parapet, it resembles the work undertaken for him at the bishop's palace at St David's, and also work at **Swansea** Castle, probably undertaken by de Gower's architect. In its heyday in the later Middle Ages, the palace was surrounded by **fish**ponds, rich **gardens** and a park containing a herd of 60 **deer**.

Acquired by Walter **Devereux** in 1546, it passed in 1559 to his son, Walter, first earl of Essex, and in 1576 to his grandson, Robert, the second earl, who spent part of his youth at Lamphey. Following Robert's **execution** in 1601, the palace was left to decay. It came into the guardianship of the Ministry of Works in 1925, and into that of **Cadw** in 1984. The tale of a fictitious cantankerous gatekeeper of the 1960s is told by Roland Mathias (1915–2007) in his short story 'The Palace'.

The church of St Tyfái (reputedly a nephew of St **Teilo**) retains its late medieval tower. Lamphey Court (1821), a fine Greek revival house once the centre of an 1850-ha estate, has been converted into a hotel. The church (dedication unknown) in the compact village of Hogeston has a 13th-century tower and a 14th-century chancel. It is cared for by the Friends of Friendless Churches.

LANCASTER family Marcher-lords
The family became associated with Wales in 1267 when Edmund, earl of Lancaster (d.1296), was granted the lordships of **Monmouth** and the **Three Castles** (**Grosmont**, Skenfrith and White Castle) by his father, Henry III. The lordships passed to his son, Thomas, who also acquired **Denbigh** through his marriage to Alice, daughter and heiress of Henry de **Lacy**, earl of Lincoln. Thomas was executed in 1322, but his son, Henry of Grosmont (d.1345), succeeded in recovering Monmouth and the Three Castles. Henry also acquired the lordships of **Kidwelly** and **Ogmore** through his marriage with Maud, heiress of Patrick de Chaworth, and the grant of **Is Cennen**. His granddaughter and heiress, Blanche, married John of Gaunt, duke of Lancaster, son of Edward III. When their son became King Henry IV in 1399, the Lancaster lordships came into the possession of the crown. During the **Wars of the Roses**, the lordships in Wales were of central importance to the Lancastrians. Although part of the crown estates, the Lancaster properties have always been administered as a separate entity. As the records of the properties have been carefully preserved in the royal archives, they are vital to the interpretation of the history of the Welsh **March**.

'LAND OF SONG, The'
The image of Wales as 'The Land of Song' was minted in the 1860s and 1870s. In the 1860s, the tonic sol-fa movement revolutionized **music** making, teaching thousands to read musical notes. Chapel choirs multiplied, the hymn-singing festival (**Cymanfa Ganu**) took hold and, from 1861, the National **Eisteddfod** provided a stage for rousing choral competitions and fashionable concerts. Enthused by ambitious musicians such as Pencerdd Gwalia (**John Thomas**; 1826–1913), **Brinley Richards** and **Joseph Parry**, and thrilled by charismatic singers such as **Edith Wynne** and Eos Morlais (**Robert Rees**; 1841–92), the nation would demonstrate its worth in song. When the *Côr Mawr* (Great Choir) of Caradog (**Griffith Rhys Jones**) triumphed twice in the Crystal Palace festival (1872, 1873), the nation's cup overflowed. The memory of the demeaning **Treason of the Blue Books** of 1847 was erased as Wales excelled on an international stage. Ever since, a flow of splendid singers has ensured that 'The Land of Song' lives on as a popular national image. As the Reverend Eli Jenkins put it in **Dylan Thomas**'s *Under Milk Wood*: 'Praise the Lord! We are a musical nation.'

LAND QUESTION, The
In 1887, 89.8% of the land of Wales was cultivated by tenants and a mere 10.2% by owner-occupiers. Resentment of landlord dominance, which was more marked in Wales than in **England**, found expression in the **enclosure** riots of the late 18th and early 19th centuries and was a factor in the **Rebecca Riots**. From the mid-19th century onwards, through the writings of **Samuel Roberts** and others, issues relating to the land question became part of the programme of the **Radicals**, who demanded legislation on security of tenure, fair rents and assistance to tenants who wished to buy their holdings.

In much of **England**, farming had become imbued with capitalist notions and, with the onset of the late 19th-century agricultural depression, many landlords were unable to obtain tenants for their farms. In Wales, however, craving for land continued throughout the depression, thus giving the land question a prominence it lacked in England. The whole issue was exacerbated by the cultural and religious gulf between the landlords and tenants (*see* **Gentry**) and by the politically motivated evictions which followed the elections of 1859 and 1868. It also became entwined with anti-**tithe** protests and with demands for the **disestablishment** of the **Anglican** Church in Wales. **T. E. Ellis** became the leading advocate of the tenants' cause, which was also a central theme in the early career of **David Lloyd George**. The matter culminated in the Royal Commission on Land in Wales and **Monmouthshire**, which reported in 1896. Unlike the agitation in **Ireland** and the Scottish Highlands, that in Wales did not result in land legislation, partly because rural problems were of declining importance in the face of rapid industrialization. In the 20th century, the break-up of large estates meant that countryside issues ceased to be primarily concerned with landlord–tenant relations.

LANDFORMS, LANDSCAPE and TOPOGRAPHY

The creation of landforms

The high degree of correlation between rocks (*see* **Geology**) and landforms should not obscure the fact that they have separate origins and constitute different areas of study. The rocks of Wales are the materials that have been subsequently fashioned into landforms.

The influence of the rocks and geological structures is particularly evident in the north-east to south-west grain imparted by the Caledonian trend of north and mid Wales. The Caledonian trend is revealed by valley lowlands, which in large measure coincide with lines of geological weakness exploited by agents of erosion; the **Tywi** and the **Teifi** valleys, respectively, follow the course of two anticlines located on either side of the central Wales Syncline, and erosion along the **Bala** Fault has created a near straight-line sequence of valley lowlands traceable from Bala, via Tal-y-llyn, to **Tywyn**. The influence of particular rock types is equally striking, for the rugged summits of **Snowdon**, **Arenig** Fawr and Arenig Fach, **Aran** Fawddwy and Aran Benllyn, and **Cadair Idris** are attributable to the hardness and resistance of the Ordovician igneous outcrops surrounding the **Harlech** Dome. In the south, major scarp slopes such as those above Swansea Bay and overlooking **Rhigos** and **Hirwaun** follow the Variscan trend from east to west. Also of considerable importance is the influence of deep and ancient structures on the orientation of the **Neath** Fault and the **Tawe** Fault, and on the topography of the two valleys. Even in **Gower** and south **Pembrokeshire** where, seemingly, the geological structure is obscured by the coastal plateau, the correlation between rocks and relief persists. Thus, the differential erosion of hard and soft rocks and erosion along geological structures is one key to the explanation for Wales's landforms.

Despite the considerable correlation between rocks and relief, the overall profile of the Welsh landform may be described as a series of dissected plateaux. Illusory according to some, this characteristic of the Welsh landscape is widespread and often spectacular. Those below around a height of 215 m – the Coastal Plateaux – truncate geological structures with spectacular indifference, especially in the **Vale of Glamorgan**, Gower, south Pembrokeshire and **Anglesey**. The higher Dissected Plateaux are characteristic of upland Wales. E. H. Brown subdivided them as the Low Peneplain (215–335 m), the Middle Peneplain (366–488 m), and the High Plateau (520–610 m), with **mountain**ous areas, such as Snowdon, Cadair Idris, **Pumlumon**, the **Brecon Beacons** and the **Black Mountains**, rising above the High Plateau.

The traditional explanation of the origin of the plateaux is that they were fashioned by the sea as wave-cut platforms. As uplift of the land occurred or as sea level fell, the drainage pattern developed by extension seawards across emergent wave-cut platforms. Thus, streams such as the **Ystwyth**, **Rheidol** and lower **Teifi**, long thought to be much younger in age, were in fact part of the original drainage flowing towards the long-extant structural depression of Cardigan Bay.

In contradiction to the marine hypothesis is the notion that the dissected plateaux were fashioned by terrestrial processes. Brown held that the upland plains he recognized had been produced as the result of the removal of deeply weathered rock developed on an early Cenozoic land surface, an origin supported by outliers of presumed Oligocene sediments located at Flimston (**Castlemartin**), Treffynnon (**St David's**) and on **Halkyn** Mountain.

A further theory for the origin of the plateaux deems them to be in 'dynamic equilibrium'. That is, the landforms are always adjusted to the weathering and erosional processes operative over time. Thus, differences in relief are the result of variations in rock resistance. John Challinor argued that the plateaux of **Ceredigion** were illusory, and claimed that they are the logical outcome of long-continued processes of weathering and erosion. Similarly, long-continued erosion of an old Oligocene land surface, by processes operating in 'dynamic equilibrium', could have fashioned the major elements of the Welsh landform.

It appears that the original drainage pattern came into existence either on an emergent chalk sea floor or on an uplifted early Cenozoic land surface tilted and disposed radially away from **Gwynedd**. It was subsequently dismembered by **river** capture that left wind-gaps throughout Wales – for instance, the Derwydd wind-gap near **Llandeilo** through which the Dulais–**Llwchwr** formerly flowed, or the **Cerrigydrudion** wind-gap through which an early River **Conwy** flowed. Relics of the original streams persist, running from north-west to south-east across the geological grain of Wales upon which they had been superimposed. Among such streams are reaches of the **Wye**, Vyrnwy, **Usk**, Cynon and **Taff**.

Although much of the Welsh landform is pre-glacial in origin, there can be little doubt that its details consist of legacies from the Quaternary Period, notably from the Pleistocene ice ages. The last ice age reached its maximum around 20,000 years ago. While its legacies are widespread, its valley glaciers and ice sheets did no more than reoccupy a glaciated landscape formed on previous occasions. The Welsh Ice Sheet ran from the north, east of Arenig Fawr and Rhobell Fawr but west of Aran Fawddwy, thence south to Pumlumon and beyond. A subsidiary ice centre occurred along the high ground of the Brecon Beacons and the **Black Mountain**, while the valleys of the southern **coal**field contained an independent system of glaciers. The Irish Sea Ice Sheet thrust two major lobes southwards, one extending down the **Cheshire–Shropshire** plain, and the other moving down St George's Channel. Glacial deposits in south Pembrokeshire, western **Carmarthenshire** and south-west Gower belong to earlier glaciations.

Three characteristics of glacial erosion – cirques, troughs, and ice-moulded streamlined relief – show that Gwynedd suffered greatest erosion. Cirques may be found amongst Wales's highest mountains and in the uplands of the southern **coal**field. In Gwynedd, watershed breaching

Landforms with a glaciation legacy include Pen-y-Fan in the Brecon Beacons

by ice produced the mountain passes, while several valleys contain ribbon **lakes** in glaciated rock basins. Deep glaciated rock basins occur elsewhere: offshore from the **Mawddach**, **Dyfi** and Teifi estuaries, as well as in the Tawe and **Nedd** valleys.

Landforms of glacial deposition include the in-filling of valley floors and the formation of moraine ridges. Moraines include the Glais at **Clydach**, the **Clynnog Fawr–Bryncir** and the Llanfihangel **Crucorney**. Lying offshore in Cardigan Bay are a number of submerged moraines, among them Sarn Badrig and Sarn Gynfelin. Drumlins (mounds of glacial drift) occur in Anglesey, on **Mynydd Hiraethog** and around Hirwaun.

During de-glaciation, landforms composed of sands and gravels were deposited by meltwater. As the ice thinned, higher ground caused the separation of some ice-masses. Such stagnant ice left legacies of kettle holes, kames, eskers and some forms of meltwater channels. Extensive assemblages of such landforms occur south of **Abergavenny** and south of **Wrexham**. Ice dams, notably in the Teifi valley, impounded proglacial lakes. The margins of proglacial Lake Teifi are indicated by deltas at **Llanybydder**. Anomalous drainage channels, formed by subglacial, submarginal and marginal meltwater streams are found throughout Wales. In some instances, their patterns may be used to infer stages of development as, for example, in the Conwy valley and around **Fishguard**.

Of much importance were the cold, vegetation-scarce periods when periglacial processes on hill slopes and valley floors accomplished prodigious feats of erosion and deposition. For example, during the Younger Dryas stadial, between 13,000 and 11,500 years ago, spectacular moraines formed ahead of the snouts of small glaciers which reoccupied the upland cirques, and a widespread mantle of **soil** and frost-shattered rock waste, including scree slopes, was deposited throughout Wales. Hillsides frequently owe their present profile to such conditions. On valley floors, the mantle of hill-slope waste merges with fluvial periglacial gravels, frequently providing material for contemporary streams.

Landscape

While landforms are the result of natural processes, the landscape owes much to human activity. Traditionally, the countryside has been considered natural, in contrast with the artificiality of the town. Yet, there is nowhere in 21st-century Wales that is in any sense primeval. Even the country's high moorland looks as it does because of human intervention.

Of all landscape-making activities, the most important is field creation. As Oliver Rackham put it in his *History of the Countryside* (1986): 'To convert millions of acres of wildwood into farmland is unquestionably the greatest achievement of our ancestors.' The process began in the **Neolithic Age** and still continues. The generally small size of Wales's fields is a major feature of the country's landscape, as are its **hedges**, some of which may be well be over 1000 years old. The success of the attack upon the wildwood meant that forests (*see* **Forestry**) disappeared from most of

Wales, although, in the 20th century, plantings, particular by the **Forestry Commission**, have led to the re-establishment of forests, generally consisting of non-indigenous species. Other forms of landscape change associated with **agriculture** include the construction of vast stretches of **dry stone walling**, the draining of wetlands, the creation of parklands and the reseeding of hill pastures. Industrialization and urbanization brought even more drastic landscape manipulation (*see* **Industrial Landscapes**).

In writing about the English landscape in 1955, W. G. Hoskins commented that every change it had undergone in the recent past 'has either uglified it or destroyed its meaning or both'. Perhaps the landscape of Wales has escaped such a fate, for it is astonishing that so small a country has such a variety of landscapes of surpassing interest and beauty – from the stately profile of Snowdon to the delectable valleys of the Tywi, the Usk, the **Clwyd** and the **Dee**, from the exhilarating solitudes of the **Elenydd Mountains** to the intimate scenes of the Vale of Glamorgan, from the superb coastlines of Pembrokeshire, Gower, **Llŷn** and Anglesey to the unique landscape of the southern coalfield.

Topography and the appreciation of landscape

In the early 18th century, a rugged landscape was something to avoid. According to Ned Ward, the author of *A Trip to North Wales* (1700), Wales was considered to be 'the fag-end of Creation, the very rubbish of Noah's flood'. Later in the century, with a transformation in sensibility, philosophers, artists and writers came to glorify the wild, the sublime and the **picturesque** – precisely the kind of scenery that Wales had in plenty (*see also* **Tourism**). **William Gilpin**, whose *Observations on the River Wye* (1770) sparked a tourist invasion of the Wye valley, was among the first to suggest that a landscape should be judged by how satisfactorily it could be painted. Indeed, the pioneer of the appreciation of the Welsh landscape was the painter **Richard Wilson**, who began a tradition that was continued by, among others, **Thomas Jones** (1743–1803), **J. M. W. Turner** and David Cox (1783–1859) (*see* **Painting**).

The painters were followed by the topographical writers. Between 1770 and 1815, at least 80 accounts of tours in Wales were published, chief among them the works of **Thomas Pennant** (1778, 1781). Such writers could draw upon earlier writings, such as **Giraldus Cambrensis**'s *Itinerary Through Wales (Itinerarium Kambriae)* (1188), **William Camden**'s *Britannia* (1586), Thomas Churchyard's *The Worthines of Wales* (1587) and Michael Drayton's *Polyolbion* (1613). Many of the travellers produced little beyond Rousseauesque rhapsodies, but others, **Benjamin Heath Malkin** in particular, wrote accounts of abiding value. The tourists included some of the chief figures of English **literature**, among them Wordsworth, Coleridge, Shelley, Southey, Scott, Peacock, Landor and De Quincey.

With mainland Europe again accessible after 1815, published accounts of tours in Wales declined in number. Yet it was the mid-19th century that saw the publication of the classic of the genre – **George Borrow**'s *Wild Wales* (1862). In the 20th century, topographical writing in **English** included work by Thomas Firbank (1910–2000), **Wynford**

Vaughan Thomas, Trevor Fishlock and Jim Perrin. Among those in **Welsh** were the 1950s and 1960s *Crwydro* series and **Ioan Bowen Rees**'s writings on mountains. Publications in other languages include Peter Sager's *Wales*, originally published in German in 1985.

LANGSTONE, Newport
(1482 ha; 2770 inhabitants)
Located immediately north of **Llanwern**, the **community** contains the villages of Langstone, Llandevaud, Llanbeder, Llanmartin and Kemeys. There are medieval churches at Langstone and Llanmartin. The widening of the A449 in 1962 led to the demolition of All Saints' church, Kemeys; its stones were reused in the new choir of St Woolos Cathedral, **Newport**. Llandevaud church (1843) contains a **stained-glass** window illustrating a nuclear explosion. Pen-coed Castle, a medieval house remodelled in the 16th century for a branch of the **Morgan family**, was restored by **D. A. Thomas** (Lord **Rhondda**) in 1914. The house has since been abandoned; fine 16th-century barns survive. Kemeys House has a 13th-century tower and a 16th-century hall range, and is surrounded by remnants of a 17th-century **garden**. Kemeys Folly (17th century), offering a superb view of the **Usk** valley, has been reconstructed as a house.

LAST DAYS OF DOLWYN, THE (1949) Film
The only **film** directed by the Welsh actor and playwright **Emlyn Williams**, who scripted and starred in this evocative study of a 19th-century Welsh village drowned to supply water for **England**. At the film's heart is an evacuated family and its dignified, loving matriarch (played by Edith Evans). Williams, superb as a villainous interloper returning from exile to pay off a long-nurtured grudge, persuaded the producer, Alexander Korda, to use the **Welsh language** in certain scenes. The film marked the screen debut of **Richard Burton**. A beguiling period piece, owing much to Otto Heller's camerawork and the editing skills of assistant director Russell Lloyd, it largely shies away from the political implications of the flooding of valleys and villages in Wales (*see* **Reservoirs**).

'LAST INVASION OF BRITAIN, The'
Having failed to make Bristol, a French force of 600 regulars and 800 ex-convicts landed at Carregwastad (**Pencaer**; *see also* **Fishguard**) on Wednesday, 22 February 1797, under the command of an **Irish**-American, William Tate. The French ransacked nearby farmhouses, well stocked with wine from a recent **shipwreck**, and were soon in no condition to fight. Jemima Nicholas, a cobbler-woman, is said to have captured 12 Frenchmen with a pitchfork, and legend has it that the red-cloaked **women** who had gathered at nearby Fishguard were mistaken for reinforcements. The French surrendered and piled their arms on Goodwick sands on the Friday. The episode is commemorated by a fine tapestry at Fishguard. Following the invasion, some of the **radicals** of the south-west suffered persecution.

LATIN
It was on the lips of the soldiers of the **Roman** conquest that Latin reached Welsh soil, long before Wales was any kind of territorial unit or the **Welsh language** had

developed from its Brythonic mother tongue. Latin inscriptions in **Caerleon** and other centres bear witness to the Roman presence, as do hundreds of Latin words, borrowed by Brythonic, which in time turned into Welsh words.

By the beginning of the 5th century, Roman troops had left Wales. The position of Latin, however, had by then been established as the language of the Christian church. Places such as **Llantwit Major** and **Llancarfan** became centres of Latin learning, and it was in Latin that **Gildas** composed his *De Excidio Britanniae* (The Ruin of **Britain**) in the 6th century. Christian inscriptions, together with the presence in Wales of religious and literary manuscripts (for example, *The Book of St Chad* and the first book of Ovid's *Ars Amatoria*), bear witness to the continuity of Latin learning in Wales between the 7th and 10th centuries. On the threshold of the **Norman** period, some *clas*-churches (as at **Llanbadarn Fawr, Ceredigion**) were important centres for studying and writing the language.

The arrival of the Normans provided opportunity for Latin culture to become further rooted in Wales. Latin is the language of the earliest surviving text of **law of Hywel Dda**. Chronicles such as *Brut y Tywysogyon* were originally in Latin, as were many religious works, including the **saints**' lives. Wales produced two Latin authors of international importance – **Geoffrey of Monmouth** and **Giraldus Cambrensis**. Many medieval Latin writings were translated into Welsh. Latin classical works influenced some Welsh-language writers, notably **Dafydd ap Gwilym**.

During the **Renaissance**, renewed emphasis was placed on classical learning, and on skilled composition in Latin. Among important Latin writers were **John Price, David Powel, Siôn Dafydd Rhys**, Henry **Salusbury** (1561–?1637) and **John Davies** (*c.*1567–1644). An abbreviated version of **Thomas Wiliems**'s Latin–Welsh **dictionary** was included in John Davies's *Dictionarium Duplex* (1632). Among poets from Wales who wrote in Latin were John **Stradling**, **Thomas Vaughan** and John Owen ('the British Martial'; ?1564–?1628). There were also translations from classical works into Welsh. Writing in Latin continued among men of learning until the 18th century, **Goronwy Owen** and **Evan Evans** (1731–88) providing important examples of the practice.

For generations, Welsh grammar schools, together with the **University of Wales**, gave honourable place to the study of Latin. During the 20th century, Welsh translations of several Latin works were published and a Latin–Welsh dictionary was prepared for schools. At the beginning of the 21st century, schools where Latin was taught were few, and at only two of the University's institutions was it possible to pursue degree courses in the language and its **literature**.

LAUGHARNE, Rowland (d.1676?) Soldier

A native of St Brides (**Marloes and St Brides**), Laugharne came to prominence in the **Civil Wars**, defending **Pembroke** against the Royalist Richard Vaughan (*see* **Vaughan family (Golden Grove)**) in 1643. In 1644, Laugharne's forces captured **Haverfordwest** and **Tenby** and occupied **Cardigan** Castle. In 1646, he was appointed commander-in-chief of the Parliamentary forces in south Wales. In 1648, on the outbreak of the Second Civil War, Laugharne, dissatisfied with the policies of Parliament, declared for the king but

was defeated at the **battle of St Fagans**. He was pardoned and, in 1660, became MP for Pembroke **Boroughs**.

LAUGHARNE TOWNSHIP (Treflan Talacharn), Carmarthenshire (2608 ha; 1320 inhabitants)

Located where the **Taf** flows into Carmarthen Bay, the **community** contains the village of Laugharne and the hamlets of Llansadurnen and Llandawke. Coygan **cave**, which has been destroyed by quarrying, is Wales's sole site indubitably occupied in the Middle **Palaeolithic** period. St Martin's church, Laugharne (15th century), contains a sculptured cross of *c.*900. The **commote** of **Talacharn** was seized by the **Normans** *c.*1116. Their control was frequently contested by the Welsh, but by the 1260s the area was firmly held by Guy de Brian, who built a masonry castle on the estuary shore. In 1307, a later Guy de Brian founded Laugharne **borough**; some of the provisions of its charter remain in force. In 1575, John **Perrot** acquired the castle and converted it into a mansion. The structure was slighted following the **Civil Wars**, but the central block survived. It was the home of **Griffith Jones**'s colleague **Bridget Bevan**; Griffith Jones died there in 1761. In the 1930s, it was the home of the novelist **Richard Hughes** (1900–76). In 1949, the poet **Dylan Thomas** settled in the Boathouse; some of the characters of *Under Milk Wood* may be based upon local residents. Thomas is buried in St Martin's graveyard; in the Boathouse is a museum to his memory. Laugharne contains several attractive 18th-century houses. St Oudoceus's church, Llandawke (13th century) contains a **Latin/Ogham**-inscribed stone.

LAVERBREAD

In the 18th and 19th centuries, **women** in the coastal regions of the **Gower** peninsula, **Pembrokeshire** and **Anglesey** gathered the edible seaweed *Porphyra umbilicalis*. At Freshwater West (**Angle**), the seaweed was stored in laver huts built of driftwood boards and thatched with marram grass. Washed, boiled and pulped, the seaweed was then tossed in **oat**meal and fried in bacon fat. Prepared as a commercial product by **Glamorgan** families, most famously those of Penclawdd (**Llanrhidian Higher**), it was sold along with cockles and mussels (*see* **Fish and Fishing**) in southern towns, particularly **Swansea**. Known as *bara lawr* in **Glamorgan**, *llafan* in Pembrokeshire and *menyn y môr* (butter of the sea) in Anglesey, it is recognized today as a Welsh delicacy, and is occasionally referred to as Welsh caviar. In recent years, it has been canned and exported.

LAW

Wales has been governed by a number of different legal systems during the last two millennia. **Roman**, native Welsh, **Norman march**er and English legal influences have all played a part in the country's legal development.

Early history

There is insufficient evidence from the pre-Roman era to support more than speculation as to what the legal arrangements of the native inhabitants would have been. While the Romans probably permitted the native **population** to retain their own customs in matters of private law, especially with regard to their property arrangements and inheritance, the public law would have been that of Rome. Under the provisions of the *constitutio Antoniniana* of AD 212, all free inhabitants of the empire became Roman citizens. Therefore, from that date, the free inhabitants of those parts of Wales firmly under Roman control were subject to Roman law. Rome bequeathed to Wales a rich cultural legacy. In particular, the Welsh successor kingdoms inherited the Christian faith introduced under the empire, a faith shaped by Roman Canon Law. However, those kingdoms seem to have retained little in the way of Roman secular law, for the rich technical vocabulary of Welsh native law includes few words of **Latin** origin.

The law of Hywel Dda

The indigenous law of medieval Wales is traditionally associated with **Hywel Dda** (d.950), king of **Deheubarth**, **Gwynedd** and **Powys**. Some 40 manuscripts of the lawbooks, compiled between *c.*1250 and 1500, survive. They were the workbooks of the lawyers and were in regular use in the courts. Much of what they contain predates the earliest surviving manuscripts and represents either the commitment to writing of oral material or copies from lost earlier compilations. Five manuscripts are in Latin and the rest are in **Welsh**. In them, the compilation of the law is attributed to an assembly held at **Whitland** on the border between **Dyfed** and **Seisyllwg** during the reign of Hywel

A Latin text of the law of Hywel Dda (Peniarth MS 28)

Dda. The assembly was probably held in the 940s, although, as there is no written evidence of it before the mid-13th century, it is impossible to prove that the assembly was ever held. Assuming that it was held, it is reasonable to believe that it was concerned, not with the enactment of a novel code of law, but with the distillation of the legal customs that had developed in Wales over the centuries. Folk law rather than state law, the emphasis of the law of Hywel Dda was upon ensuring reconciliation between kinship groups rather than upon keeping order through punishment.

The law of Hywel Dda is among the most significant cultural achievements of the Welsh, both in terms of the subtlety and vivid imagination of its legal content and the richness of the literary style in which it is expressed. The law was a primary symbol of the unity and identity of the Welsh as a people; it was a conflict of laws that precipitated the final breach between Edward I and **Llywelyn ap Gruffudd**, and it was to the law as the chief marker of Welsh distinctiveness that Llywelyn's advisers appealed in the dire days of 1282. Some historians have argued that the law of Hywel Dda was essentially primitive law and that it would inevitably have become defunct as society became more complex. However, modern scholarship emphasizes its ability to evolve, and stresses that it contained elements of mercy, common sense and respect for **women** and children that would be absent from the law of **England** until very recent times.

It was once believed that the texts fall into three categories relevant to specific regions of Wales – **Gwent** in the case of Llyfr **Cyfnerth**, Dyfed in the case of Llyfr **Blegywryd** and Gwynedd in the case of Llyfr Iorwerth (*see* **Iorwerth ap Madog**). Modern scholarship, however, maintains that the distinctions are chronological rather than geographical, with Llyfr Cyfnerth earlier than Llyfr Blegywryd, which in turn is earlier than Llyfr Iorwerth. Yet, too much can be made of the distinctions, for the law in its essence was the same in all parts of Wales, and every manuscript consists of collections of what is basically the same material.

The manuscripts which survive do not consist of a record of what may have been drawn up at Whitland in *c.*940; neither are they a record of the law as it was administered in the Welsh courts at the time of the compilation of the various law books. Copyists noted innovations but did not necessarily delete clauses that were no longer in force. Thus, manuscripts contain clauses which were current long before the age of Hywel Dda. These, no doubt, had their origins in a common **Celtic** legal tradition. They have links with **Irish** law texts, some of which derive from as early as the 6th century, and they refer to terms which had also once been current in the **Old North**. In addition, the manuscripts contain clauses which were new in the age of the copyist, particularly those reflecting the efforts of the rulers of Gwynedd to strengthen their princely powers and those which represent borrowings from English law and Anglo-Norman practice. Thus, the need to distinguish between the archaic and the novel is one of the major challenges facing students of Welsh medieval law.

Most of the texts begin with a section known as the Laws of the Court, which deals with the regulation of the king's household. It describes the duties of such officers as the *penteulu* (the leader of the king's warband), the *ynad* (who kept order at court), the *distain* (who looked after the king's **food**) and the ***pencerdd*** (the kingdom's chief poet); some texts seem to indicate that such officials were developing wider responsibilities – that they represented, in a sense, the king's 'cabinet'.

The law of Hywel Dda has much to say about status (*braint*), for in no sense do the law books portray a society in which all human beings were equal. The highest status was that of the king and his closest relations, among them the *edling*, a borrowing from the **Anglo-Saxon** *atheling* and an indication of an attempt to ensure that the king had an undisputed heir. Next in status came the freemen, the *bonheddwyr* – those who had *bon* or ancestry (compare *gens* in **gentry**). Then came the unfree (the *taeogion*), a minority by the late 13th century, but almost certainly the great majority in the age of Hywel Dda. Below the *taeog* came the slaves (*y caeth*), a grouping that had become extinct by the 12th century. In addition, the law rather reluctantly recognized the existence of the foreigner (*yr alltud*); it is significant that no freeman with full Welsh lineage on both sides – regardless of which Welsh kingdom he was a native – could be an *alltud* anywhere in Wales.

It was status that determined the nature of a person's position with regard to the law, his right to land and his duties to his superior lord. *Galanas* – the price put upon the life of a person – varied according to status; the amount of a man's *galanas* was largely determined by his ancestry, although holding high office could increase the price. The same variation applied to *sarhad* – the compensation to be paid for insult. The *bonheddwyr* held land as a kindred group, establishing themselves as a ***gwely*** (lit. a bed) around the original settlement of their ancestor. The sons of a *priodor* (a full member of a *gwely*) had equal claims on the arable land, meadows, grazing lands and woodlands of their father, and could create a new *gwely* in the waste. The *taeogion* laboured under the direction of the *maer* (which later came to mean mayor) to supply the needs of their lord. Every adult male *taeog* had a right to a share of the land of the *taeogdref*, but, rather than being an owner of land, he was owed by the land and was barred from the callings which would free him from the bonds of the **soil** – those of the priest, the smith and the poet. In addition to their labours in the fields, *taeogion* housed their lord's officials on their travels, carved paths for him through the forest, fed his **hunting dogs** and erected the buildings of his court. The duties of the *bonheddwyr* were more dignified; they included the paying of *gwestfa* (food render), paid as a recognition of lordship rather than as rent, and the joining of the *cylch* – the campaign of the king's warband.

In addition to emphasizing the unequal, hierarchical nature of the society portrayed in the laws of Hywel Dda, these provisions indicate two other central features of that society – its wholly rural nature and the overwhelming importance of kinship. The law books are much concerned with the value of animals, the renders and fines to be paid in **cattle**, the protection of crops, the measurement of land and the niceties of joint-ploughing contracts. A man's status, role, employment and duties were dependent upon who his father was. Kindred was particularly central to the payment of *galanas*, for that was paid to the kindred of a man killed by the kindred of the man who had killed him, with kindred on both sides extending to third cousins, if not beyond.

A daughter had half the *galanas* of her brother, and a wife a third of that of her husband. In addition, women could not own land nor transfer rights to land to their children. Yet, despite these inequalities, the status of women under the law of Hywel Dda was in some ways higher than it was under other European legal systems. Unlike the position under Roman law, daughters (and sons) were not wholly subject to the arbitrary power of the father. Unlike the position under English law, a husband did not gain unrestricted power over his wife's property on marriage. Furthermore, she could claim compensation and had rights over the children if the marriage should come to an end – for, unlike those countries where Roman Canon Law had wholly triumphed, marriage in early medieval Wales was viewed as a contract rather than a sacrament, and was therefore terminable. The status of children was dependent not on the nature of the union between the parents but on the readiness of the father to acknowledge his offspring. This meant that the distinction between legitimate and illegitimate children was alien to Welsh law, much to the consternation of canon lawyers, who were also appalled by the Welsh propensity for marriage between close relations, such as cousins.

The evidence suggests that on the eve of the Norman invasions, the law of Hywel Dda was intact as the law of the whole of Wales. The Normans brought their own law with them to which they and their followers were subject, but the Common Law of England with its king's writ and its royal courts was not introduced into Wales in the wake of the Norman seizure of Welsh territories. Furthermore, in the marcher-lordships they established, the Normans were content to allow the native inhabitants to continue to live under the law of Hywel Dda. In some areas, a new form of law emerged; first mentioned in the **Magna Carta** (1215), the law of the March – Welsh law as seen through Norman eyes, to quote one definition of it – added to the legal complexities of Wales.

In addition, constitutional, social and economic changes within those regions still under native rule were modifying the law of Hywel Dda. The manslaughter of one of his subjects came to be considered as much a crime against the prince as it was against the kindred of the victim; thus the prince demanded a share of the *galanas*, a key factor in the move from folk to state law. The demands of warfare, in particular the cost of maintaining mounted warriors, led to land grants in return for military service, the essence of the feudal system that held sway in much of England. Payments in money eroded the essentially cattle **economy** described in the earliest sections of the law books, and the growth of towns introduced a factor not catered for in those sections. Thus, by the late 13th century – in Gwynedd, in particular – Welsh law was far from what it had been in the age of Hywel Dda.

Following the **Edwardian conquest**, English law became the law of the **Principality** of Wales in criminal matters, and its introduction is one of the main themes of the **Statute of Rhuddlan**. To an older generation of historians –

admirers of strict order – this was Edward's greatest achievement, but in Wales there were those who condemned the mercilessness of English law. As late as 1470, the poet **Dafydd ab Edmwnd**, whose friend Siôn Eos had been hanged for accidentally killing a man, yearned for the benignity of the law of Hywel Dda. Edward I was prepared to allow the law of Hywel Dda to remain in force in personal and tenurial matters. Indeed, he and the marcherlords could benefit from it, for it permitted them to claim a variety of payments – *ebediw* on the death of a tenant, *amobr* on the marriage of a tenant's daughter, mise when a landowner came into his inheritance, a share in the *galanas* and many a **cymhortha** (obligatory gift).

Thus the law of Hywel Dda became fossilized in the interests of the English authorities, much to the frustration of the wealthier Welsh freemen who were jealous of the ability of the Englishmen living in Wales to use English law to build up landed estates. Some such freemen – **Owain Glyndŵr**'s ancestors among them – abandoned *cyfran* (the practice of dividing land equally among male heirs), the central feature of the *gwely* system. That system did not permit the sale of land, and thus the Welsh mortgage (*tir prid*) was devised – a stratagem whereby land which had been on mortgage for at least 16 years was deemed to have passed into the absolute ownership of the mortgage holder. As the *gwely* system did not allow women to inherit land, the land of a man lacking male heirs escheated to his lord. This process, known as *sied*, became an acute issue following the mass mortality caused by the **Black Death**, and was a further factor in the erosion of the law of Hywel Dda. Yet, in the 14th and 15th centuries, compilations of the law continued to be made, although one compiler expressed his sadness at the futility of writing out the laws of the court, concerned as they were with an institution long defunct.

The law of Hywel Dda continued in fairly vigorous use in Wales up to the early 16th century, especially in **Cardiganshire**, **Carmarthenshire** and parts of the northeastern March. Indeed, although abolished by the **Act of 'Union'** of 1536, elements of it survived in many parts of Wales; this was particularly true of the practice of *cyfran*, a major factor in eroding the number of Wales's small freeholders over subsequent centuries. The gentry class, however, eagerly embraced English law, as it allowed them to accumulate landed estates and to bequeath them intact to the eldest son.

From the Acts of 'Union' until 1830

The Acts of 'Union' of 1536 and 1543 legislated that Wales should be exclusively subject to English law – and that that law should be administered only by those conversant with the **English language**. The Courts of Great Session were established to administer royal justice. These were to be held in each **county** for six days twice a year, and were to exercise the jurisdiction of both the English Court of King's Bench and that of Common Pleas. Following the abolition of the **Council of Wales and the Marches** (1689), the Great Sessions also exercised an equitable jurisdiction similar to that of the English Court of Chancery. The counties were grouped into four circuits: North Wales (**Anglesey**, **Caernarfonshire** and **Merioneth**); **Carmarthen**

(Cardiganshire, **Pembrokeshire** and Carmarthenshire); **Brecon** (Breconshire, **Radnorshire** and **Glamorgan**) and Chester (**Denbighshire**, **Flintshire** and **Montgomeryshire**). The beginnings of the Wales and Chester circuit can thus be discerned (*see* **Cheshire**). The thirteenth county, **Monmouthshire**, being the nearest to **London**, was to send its judicial business to the Westminster courts.

Uncertainty reigned with regard to the question of whether the Westminster courts had concurrent jurisdiction with the Great Sessions over Welsh legal affairs. This issue remained unsettled until 1769, when the King's Bench asserted its concurrent jurisdiction, and this was confirmed by statute in 1773. Given the widespread view that the Great Sessions were inferior to the central courts in terms of efficiency and the ability of the lawyers practising in them, an inevitable decline in their fortunes ensued. From 1817–21, they were investigated and found wanting by a select committee. The spectre of abolition turned them into institutions of national identity, and their shortcomings were ascribed to the second-rate English lawyers who staffed them. They were abolished in 1830, when the administration of justice in Wales became similar in virtually all respects to the system in England.

From 1830 to 1972

The abolition of the Great Sessions meant that all civil litigation in Wales had to be commenced at Westminster. Thereafter, as in England, a date would be set for trial in Westminster Hall unless, before (*nisi prius*) that date, the royal judges arrived in the county from which the case originated, in which case the trial would take place there. In practice, the date set always ensured that the trial would take place locally, but civil actions nevertheless had to commence, and the final verdict had to be given, at Westminster. The royal judges continued to visit each of the Welsh shires on circuit to take such *nisi prius* trials alongside their criminal jurisdiction in the assizes, where the most serious crimes were tried. Lesser offences were dealt with by a bench of legally unqualified justices of the peace in the magistrates' courts or petty sessions, or, in the case of offences which were more serious but not serious enough to merit trial at the assizes, by a bench of magistrates at the county quarter sessions. Several **boroughs** had their own quarter sessions served by a professional judge – the recorder. With the rise of places such as **Merthyr Tydfil**, some industrial towns came to be served in their petty sessions by a legally qualified stipendiary magistrate. From 1846, every county acquired a county court to try civil actions of lesser value.

The modern system

Quarter sessions and Assizes were replaced in 1972 by crown courts held at **Cardiff**, **Caernarfon**, Carmarthen, Merthyr Tydfil, **Mold**, **Newport** and **Swansea**. Trials at *nisi prius* ended, for henceforth the High Court could sit outside **London** to take civil litigation beyond the competence of the county courts. The Court of Appeal may also sit outside London – in Cardiff, for example. Since 1972, the Lord Chief Justice has been described as 'of England and

Wales'. A mercantile court has been established to deal with commercial litigation and, following the inauguration of the **National Assembly for Wales**, certain applications for judicial review may be made in Cardiff. The language clause of the Act of 'Union' has been modified by the **Welsh Courts Act (1942)** and the **Welsh Language Acts** (**1967** and **1993**). In 2005, with the creation of Her Majesty's Court Service, the administration of the Magistrates' Courts was united with those of the Crown Courts and the County Courts, and the Wales and Cheshire Circuit was renamed the Wales and Cheshire Region. In 2007, when Cheshire was attached to the North-Western England Region, Wales became a legal unit in its own right.

Ecclesiastical jurisdiction

The medieval Church sought and eventually generally secured jurisdiction over matrimonial matters and certain forms of inheritance, as well as control over punishment for sins as opposed to crimes. The church's matrimonial and probate jurisdiction was transferred to the state in 1857.

Episcopal churches regulate their government, ministry, doctrine, liturgy, rites and property through canon law. Each church of the Catholic tradition has its own canonical system. The medieval Welsh church was governed by Roman Canon Law, alongside native law. Following the **Reformation**, the Welsh **dioceses** became part of the established **Anglican** Church, and were governed by state law and the Canons Ecclesiastical (1603). The **disestablishment of the Church of England in Wales** in 1920 led to the creation of the **Church in Wales**, considered by state law to be a voluntary association organized on a consensual basis. English ecclesiastical law ceased to exist as law in Wales, but it continues to apply to the Church in Wales if consistent with that institution's constitution and canons.

The Bar in Wales

Although historically based at the Inns of Court in London, in the late 19th century the Bar acquired a permanent presence in Wales. In the 20th century, the original handful of practitioners at Cardiff and Swansea increased to some 350 barristers. The focal point in the north is Chester. The formation of the Wales and Chester Circuit after the **Second World War** was central to the development of a Welsh identity for the Bar, creating a single administrative unit for the profession and the courts in Wales, and recovering some of the distinctiveness existing prior to the abolition of the Courts of Great Session in 1830. Former leading members of the circuit include Lord Edmund-Davies (**Edmund Davies**) and Lord Elwyn-Jones (**Elwyn Jones**).

Legal organizations

The Law Society, the professional body of solicitors, regulates the profession, drafting, monitoring and enforcing rules for the **education** and training of solicitors and how they work. It handles complaints against solicitors and disciplines them if they break its rules. The Society also represents the interests of solicitors and plays a part in law reform. Its Welsh headquarters in Cardiff provides training courses for solicitors and liaises with the National Assembly for Wales to promote the interests of solicitors in Wales. It passes information from the Law Society in London to Welsh practitioners and relays their views to London. In addition, solicitors form local law societies, whose members meet to discuss and respond to issues that affect the profession locally.

The Associated Law Societies of Wales is the oldest legal organization in Wales. It comprises every local law society (except for those in the one-time county of **Gwent**) and every university law department. Its purpose is to promote the interests of solicitors in Wales, by liaising with both the Law Society of England and Wales, and the Law Society in Wales.

The Confederation of South Wales Law Societies was established in January 1997. It was formed by the law societies of Cardiff and district, **Rhymney Valley**, **Bridgend**, **Pontypridd** and **Rhondda**, and **Merthyr Tydfil** and **Aberdare**. It organizes training courses, encourages equal opportunities within the profession and publishes a journal. Unlike the Associated Law Societies, it does not have a campaigning role.

As the practice of law has become more specialized, organizations of lawyers dealing with specialist areas of practice have been formed. Within Wales, these include the Welsh Personal Injuries Lawyers' Association, the Welsh Public Law and Human Rights Association, and the Wales Commercial Law Association.

Legal advice and representation

The Community Legal Service (CLS) consists of two distinct bodies: the Legal Services Commission and the Criminal Defence Service. Both of them, administered nationally from Cardiff, replace what was formerly known as civil and criminal legal aid. CLS funding is available only from recognized providers of legal services. Only solicitors' firms (or the Salaried Defence Service, which has an office in Swansea) may hold a contract with the Criminal Defence Service. In most cases, there is no means test for funding in criminal cases. All other publicly funded work is available from providers of legal services with a relevant contract from the CLS. The work covered by these contracts includes matters such as family, childcare, **welfare**, **housing** and judicial review cases. There is a means test for these services. There are various levels of legal services that may be supplied, ranging from full legal representation to legal help.

Legal education

There are six law schools offering law degrees in Wales's institutions of higher education. The oldest, which has offered the LLB since 1901, is at the **University of Wales, Aberystwyth**; the newest, at the **University of Wales, Bangor**, opened in 2004, offering, initially, the LLB. The others, which, like Aberystwyth, also offer a taught MA and postgraduate research programmes, are **Cardiff**

University (which also trains solicitors and barristers), the **University of Wales Swansea**, **Swansea Institute of Higher Education** and the **University of Glamorgan**. All offer a qualifying law degree for both the Law Society of England and Wales and the Bar Council. The **Welsh Joint Education Committee** offers A-level law.

LEAD and SILVER

Lead has been mined in all the **counties** of Wales at some time; silver, frequently found in the same seams in much smaller quantities, was often a by-product of lead mining. Workings of lead date back to **Roman** times, and **Flintshire**, which **Giraldus Cambrensis** described as 'rich in minerals and silver', was the early centre. **Denbighshire** also has a deeply rooted tradition, as suggested by the place name **Minera** (now in the **Wrexham county borough**), derived from the **Latin** for 'mine' (compare its **Welsh** name, Mwynglawdd). Lead mining was stimulated by the licensing of the Company of Mines Royal (chartered 1568), which had a monopoly over smelting in the Elizabethan period. From 1660, there was continuous production in the north-east, and **Edward Lhuyd** considered that the **Halkyn** area outproduced the rest of Wales combined.

By the 17th century, production was also accelerating in the other main centre – northern **Cardiganshire** – where Sir **Humphrey Mackworth** played an important role. The silver found in conjunction with the lead was sufficient to establish a mint at **Aberystwyth** Castle, which was in operation from 1637 to 1642. A key factor was the challenge by Sir Carbury **Pryse** of Gogerddan (**Trefeurig**) to claims of a royal monopoly over mineral rights; the issue was settled by Act of Parliament in 1693, which reserved only silver and **gold** to the crown.

By the middle of the 19th century, western **Montgomeryshire** had become one of the major British areas of production, with mines such as Dylife (**Llanbrynmair**) and Van (**Llanidloes Without**) in the forefront. Van employed over 500 people in the early 1870s, and did not close until 1921. The settlement it created survives by reason of its proximity to **Llanidloes**; Dylife, 16 km away, was too remote to have an afterlife and is in ruins.

However, the north-east remained pre-eminent, with a total production of over 1 million tonnes between 1845 and 1938 (and perhaps twice this figure before 1845): this represented 13% of British production, and only the North Pennines area produced a higher percentage. Production came to concentrate around the Minera mines near **Wrexham**, which were amalgamated from smaller concerns in 1849 and continued to operate after 1945. From the mid-19th century, a series of elaborate drainage adits was constructed to allow their exploitation. Silver never rivalled lead in the quantities produced; the Van mine, for instance, raised nearly 98,000 tonnes of lead over its lifetime – and around 21 tonnes of silver. The toxic waste from lead mines has contaminated extensive areas of **Ceredigion**, Montgomeryshire and Flintshire. There is a lead and silver museum at Llywernog (**Blaenrheidol**).

LEASES, URBAN

The owner of land being developed for housing has three choices: to build houses himself, to sell the land to those wishing to build houses, or to lease it on building leases. In the mid-19th century, when urban development was proceeding apace in Wales, most landlords opted for leasing, generally for 99 years, a practice which owed much to the leases developed in **London** following the Great Fire of

An abandoned lead mine in the Ystwyth Valley, Ceredigion

1666. The system had its merits; as the history of **Llandudno** illustrates, it could enable a ground landlord to exercise enlightened control over urban development. By the 1850s, landlords were paying for the **roads**, pavements, lighting and drainage of the developed land, costs recovered through ground rents, which in **Cardiff** averaged £3 a year for a modest terraced house.

Of Wales's recipients of ground rents, the most prominent were the **Stuart** family, marquesses of Bute, whose sale of urban land to the Western Ground Rents Company in 1938 included the leases of some 20,000 houses and 1000 shops in Cardiff alone. The disadvantage of the system lay in the fact that, on the expiration of the lease, the landlord became owner, not only of the land, but also of the building standing upon it. Expiration generally led to a new lease, usually at a considerably higher rent. As the 99-year leases granted in the mid-19th century expired in the mid-20th century, the issue won prominence; the **Labour Party**'s victory in **Conwy** in 1966 was attributed to the worries of Llandudno leaseholders. The Leasehold Enfranchisement Act of 1967 permitted leaseholders to buy their freehold but, despite the act, the issue has not been fully resolved.

LEATHER

For centuries, leather was an important element in the **economy** of Wales and a significant item of export. The ready availability of skins of **cattle** and **sheep**, a plenitude of oak bark – essential in the tanning process – and the ubiquity of fresh water supplies meant that most communities, including some of the main monasteries, had their tan yards and currier's shops. Among the most famous tan yards were those at **Dolgellau, Aberystwyth, Newtown, Rhayader** and **Llanidloes**.

The process of preparing hides for tanning was long and complicated, and could take weeks if not months. After washing, the hides were passed through lime pits to loosen hair and skin, preparatory to removal by knife. Then they were taken through a succession of tan pits of progressively increasing concentrations of ground oak bark mixed with water. The hides were then rolled and dried prior to the currier converting the stiff leather into soft and supple material ready for polishing, with cod oil or tallow, and finishing with various hand tools.

The resulting material was available to a wide range of craftsmen, including cobblers, clog makers, saddlers and harness makers, some of whom had permanent workshops, while others were itinerant. One of the best-known footwear-making centres was **Llannerch-y-medd**, where, in the 1880s, there were said to be some 250 cobblers.

By the 1920s, traditional methods of tanning and leather dressing had become largely redundant, and the crafts associated with them gradually disappeared. The last tan yard in Wales, at Rhayader, closed in the 1950s and was reconstructed at the National History Museum (*see* **St Fagans**).

LEE, Rowland (d.1543) Royal official

Rowland Lee, bishop of Lichfield, was lord president of the **Council of Wales and the Marches** from 1534 to 1543. Known for his ruthless suppression of **law**breakers and for his prejudices against the Welsh, Lee's draconian regime emphasized the power of the English crown and the futility of any attempt to rebel against it. He protested against the **Act of 'Union'** of 1536, having more faith in the efficacy of his own sterner methods.

LEEK, The

The earliest certain reference to this vegetable as a Welsh emblem is the giving of a leek to Princess Mary, daughter of Henry VIII, by the yeomen of the guard on St **David**'s Day, 1537. There is a record of Henry VII giving Welshmen money for their feast on St David's Day in 1495, but it does not mention the leek. The exchange in **Shakespeare**'s play *Henry V* (1598), in which the king assures Fluellen that as a Welshman he wears a leek on St David's day, indicates that by the late 16th century it was already considered an 'ancient tradition'.

The colours of the leek – green and white – were associated with the 13th-century Welsh princes. They were worn by the Welsh troops of Edward I in Flanders in 1297 and those of Edward, **Prince of Wales**, in 1346 and 1347, and were the livery colours of the **Tudor** kings. They are the colours of the field of the banner of the **Red Dragon**, flown by Henry VII and now the national flag of Wales.

In the 17th and 18th centuries, the king and the court wore the leek on St David's day. Many 18th-century engravings show Welshmen wearing the leek on their hats. The **Welsh Guards** have a leek as a cap badge, and wear a green and white plume in their bearskin caps. The leek appears on £1 coins. Since the late 19th century, the **daffodil** (*cenhinen Bedr*, Peter's leek) has become an increasingly popular alternative to the leek as a national emblem.

Many earlier writers recorded the partiality of the Welsh to the leek; it formed an important element in their diet, and was prized for its medicinal properties. In the early 17th century, a story appeared recounting that St David had distributed leeks to Welshmen during a battle with the Saxons, to enable them to tell friend from foe, and that they subsequently gained a great victory.

LEESWOOD (Coed-llai), Flintshire
(1169 ha; 2143 inhabitants)

Located south-east of **Mold**, Leeswood was home to an **iron**works (1817–40s) and a works extracting **oil** from the highly volatile local cannel **coal** (1858–77). The glory of the **community** is Leeswood Hall (*c.*1725), built for George Wynne of Leeswood Old Hall (17th century), who acquired sudden wealth from the **Halkyn lead** mines. The 11-bay house once had two additional side wings, each of 13 bays. Its grounds are an early example of landscape **gardening**, and are embellished by Robert Davies's superb White Gates and Black Gates (*see* **Davies family, Ironsmiths**). Leeswood Green Farm is a four-bay cruck house. The delightfully asymmetrical Pentrehobyn (early 17th century) contains a superb carved overmantel. Near it is Llettyau (17th century), a row of eight cells reputedly built to accommodate poor travellers.

LELAND, John (1506–52) Antiquary

The English antiquary John Leland is best remembered for his *Itinerary* (1710–12), which describes his journeys through Wales and **England** between 1536 and 1539. As the king's antiquary, it was his task to search for cathedrals,

455

abbeys, priories and colleges and to record their treasures. His book is a valuable source of information about Wales shortly after the **Act of 'Union'** (1536).

LETTERSTON (Trelelert), Pembrokeshire
(930 ha; 998 inhabitants)

Located south of **Fishguard** and east of **St David's**, the **community** gets its name from a **Fleming**, Letard (d.1137), 'an enemy of God and St **David**', according to *Annales Cambriae* (*see* **Brut y Tywysogyon**). Saron **Baptist** chapel (1828, 1869) is a handsome building. St Silyn's church was rebuilt in 1881. In 1894, a session of the Royal Commission on Land in Wales was held in the substantial village of Letterston.

LEVI, Thomas (1825–1916) Author and editor

Born at Penrhos, **Ystradgynlais**, Levi received little schooling and, at the age of 8, was put to work in Ynyscedwyn **iron**works; but by about 1855, he had become a **Calvinistic Methodist** minister. A noted **hymn**writer, Levi was a prolific author who wrote 30 books on historical and religious subjects and translated 60 books from **English** into **Welsh**. His most significant contribution, however, was his founding and long editorship (1862–1911) of *Trysorfa y Plant*, his denomination's magazine for children, which was of such wide appeal that it achieved a monthly circulation of 44,000, a record for a Welsh **periodical**.

His son, Thomas Arthur Levi (1874–1954), was the **University of Wales**'s first professor of English **law** when the department of law opened at **Aberystwyth** in 1901. During his 40-year tenure of the chair, Levi established a distinguished reputation for the department. His opposition to military conscription led him, an ardent **Liberal**, to

Alun Lewis

oppose **David Lloyd George**, particularly in the famous **Cardiganshire** by-election of 1921. Widely believed to be of **Jew**ish ancestry, his **surname** was, in fact, an example of the adoption by the Welsh of names of biblical origin; compare Isaac, Jeremiah, Moses and Tobias.

LEVY, Mervyn (1914–96) Painter

A childhood friend of **Dylan Thomas** and associated with **Swansea**'s renowned artistic set, Levy studied at the Swansea School of Art under **Grant Murray**, and at the Royal College of Art, **London**. After the **Second World War**, in which he served as a captain in the Royal Army Educational Corps, he held a number of university posts and exhibited his **paintings** widely. Levy's later career focused mainly on writing and **broadcasting**. His many books include his 'fragments of autobiography' *Reflections in a Broken Mirror* (1982).

LEWIS, Alun (1915–44) Writer

Widely considered to be the finest poet of the **Second World War**, Alun Lewis was born in Cwmaman (**Aberaman**). He read history at **Aberystwyth**, and became a teacher at the Lewis Boys' School, **Pengam**. Having joined the army in 1940, despite his **pacifism**, he found the company of his men, most of whom were from industrial south Wales, preferable to that of his fellow commissioned officers. In 1942, he was posted to India with the **South Wales Borderers**, and, while on active service against the Japanese near Chittagong (now in Bangladesh), died from wounds received from his own revolver.

As a writer, he enjoyed just four years of public recognition before his tragic death. Only one collection of his poems appeared during his lifetime, namely *Raiders' Dawn* (1942), and one of his short stories, 'The Last Inspection' (1943); a year after his death another volume of poems, *Ha! Ha! Among the Trumpets* was published, and more stories, *In the Green Tree*, in 1948. His *Collected Stories* and *Collected Poems* appeared in 1990 and 1994 respectively, and the writer's widow, Gweno Lewis, edited his *Letters to my Wife* (1989). Lewis's stories and poems first appealed to their readers on account of their vision of war and suffering and their passionate lyricism. After the boredom of training at camps in **England**, the experience of India forced an early maturity on his work but did nothing to alleviate his depression; nor did his attachment to a woman whom he had met in India release him from his love for his wife. His death, in circumstances that are still not clear, was the single greatest loss to Welsh writing in **English** (*see* **Literature**) during the Second World War.

LEWIS, Charles [Williams] Mansel (1845–1931) Painter

Born in **London**, this painter, patron, collector and sometime teacher of art was brought up and lived in Stradey Castle, **Llanelli**, which he inherited. Many of his paintings and etchings featured the grounds and staff of the estate, his figure **painting** being a romantic version of Victorian social realism. Lewis travelled in the north, painting landscapes – sometimes accompanied by his friend **Hubert von Herkomer** – in a specially built painting-wagon, complete with studio and living accommodation.

LEWIS, David (*c.*1520–84) Lawyer

Born at **Abergavenny**, Lewis was appointed first principal of Jesus College, **Oxford** when it was founded in 1571; he resigned in 1572 to pursue his career as a judge in the Court of Admiralty. A leading maritime lawyer, he examined complaints of **piracy** against Frobisher and Hawkins. He is buried in a magnificent tomb in St Mary's church, Abergavenny.

LEWIS, E[dward] A[rthur] (1880–1942) Historian

Born at **Llangurig**, and educated at **Aberystwyth** and **London**, Lewis was appointed the first professor of Welsh history at Aberystwyth in 1931. His pioneering work on Welsh commercial history has not been superseded. His published works include *Medieval Boroughs of Snowdonia* (1912) and *The Welsh Port Books, 1550–1603* (1927).

LEWIS, Edward Morland (1903–43) Painter

The son of a Ferryside (**St Ishmael**) solicitor, Morland Lewis attended **Carmarthen** School of Art before continuing his studies at the Royal Academy Schools, **London**. Gentle and sensitive, Lewis's predominantly landscape **paintings** seem to belong to an earlier era. He died from malaria while on active service during the **Second World War**.

LEWIS, George Cornewall (1806–63) Politician

By far the most successful Welsh politician of the 19th century, Lewis was in turn chancellor of the exchequer (1855–8), home secretary (1859–61) and secretary for war (1861–3); he was mentioned as a possible prime minister. The son of **Thomas Frankland Lewis** of Harpton Court, **Old Radnor**, he was MP for Hereford (1847–52) and for Radnor **Boroughs** (1855–63). He followed his father as chairman of the **Poor Law** commissioners (1839–47) and was editor of the *Edinburgh Review* (1852–5). Of a melancholy disposition, among his comments was: 'Life would be bearable but for its pleasures.' A 24-m monument to him stands alongside the A44 in **New Radnor**.

LEWIS, Harriet [Mary] (1911–99) Actress

The cheery and chatty woman who played Magi Post in the television serial *Pobol y Cwm* was born at Trebanos (**Pontardawe**). She appeared in the first programme of the serial and continued to portray the meddlesome postmistress of Cwm Deri until her death a quarter of a century later. She was also the bus driver in **Kenneth Griffith**'s documentary **film** *Bus to Bosworth* (1976). Although she left school at the early age of 14, she became headmistress of schools in **Glynneath** and Pontardawe.

LEWIS, Henry (1889–1968) Scholar

A native of Ynystawe, **Swansea**, Lewis was educated at **Cardiff** and **Oxford**. He was a lecturer in the **Welsh** department at Cardiff (1918–21) before becoming the first professor of Welsh at **Swansea** (1921). He appointed **Saunders Lewis** to the department but there was little love between them when the latter was dismissed (*see* **Penyberth Bombing School, The burning of**). Although he edited the religious poetry of the *Gogynfeirdd* as well as the works of some **Poets of the Gentry** and prose texts, his main contribution was in historical linguistics and syntax. He was a notable teacher, able to explicate complex matters effectively, as in his classic *Datblygiad yr Iaith Gymraeg* (1931).

LEWIS, [John] Herbert (1858–1933) Politician

Mostyn-born Herbert Lewis, the great nephew of **Thomas Jones** (1756–1820), was the first chairman of the **Flintshire County** Council (1889), and Liberal MP for **Flint Boroughs** (1892–1906), Flintshire (1906–18) and for the newly created **University of Wales** seat (1918–22). He worked strenuously for the **Liberal Party**, for the cause of **education**, including teachers' superannuation and servicemen's grants, and particularly for the creation and maintenance of the **National Library** and the **National Museum**. While **David Lloyd George** earned both fame and brickbats, Herbert Lewis, knighted in 1922, served Wales and the United Kingdom with quiet devotion and much success. His daughter, Kitty Idwal Jones, was an assiduous collector of folk songs, and his son, Mostyn Lewis, was an authority on the **stained glass** of north Wales.

LEWIS, Howell Elvet (Elfed; 1860–1953) Hymnwriter

Elfed was the author of some of the most popular **hymns** in the **Welsh language**, among them 'Cofia'n Gwlad', 'Rho im yr Hedd' and 'Glanha dy Eglwys'. He also wrote hymns in **English**. With their lyrical style and their social rather than doctrinal emphasis, his hymns are more important than his poetry, although he published volumes in both languages and won the National **Eisteddfod** crown in 1888 and 1891, and the chair in 1894. He was a native of Blaen-y-coed, **Cynwyl Elfed**, and after training at the **Presbyterian** College, **Carmarthen**, he served as a **Congregationalist** minister in Wales and **England**. He was **archdruid** from 1923 until 1927. Although he had lost his sight by 1930, he continued to preach until his death.

LEWIS, Hywel D[avid] (1910–92) Philosopher

One of the most eminent Welsh philosophers of the second half of the 20th century, Hywel D. Lewis made his chief contribution in the field of the **philosophy** of **religion**. Raised in **Waunfawr**, he graduated at **Bangor** and **Oxford**, and was a lecturer in philosophy at Bangor before becoming professor there in 1947. From 1955 until 1977, he was professor of the history and the philosophy of religion at Kings College, **London**. He stressed the importance of reason in religion, and was severely critical of figures such as Barth, Brunner and Niebuhr who represented, in his view, 'anti-rational dogmatism'. His many publications, in both **English** and **Welsh**, include *Gwybod am Dduw* (1952), *Our Experience of God* (1959) and *The Elusive Mind* (1969).

LEWIS, Ivor (1895–1982) Surgeon

Born in **Llanddeusant**, he was educated at **Cardiff** and **London**. After working in London, he became consultant surgeon to the **Rhyl**, **Abergele** and Llangwyfan (**Llandyrnog**) hospitals. A leading authority on the treatment of cancer of the oesophagus, in 1938 he performed the first successful pulmonary embolectomy in **Britain** – an operation to remove a blood clot, or other foreign

Saunders Lewis

material, from one of the blood vessels of the lung. In 1946, he became a Hunterian professor of the Royal College of Surgeons of **England**.

LEWIS, Lewis (Lewsyn yr Heliwr; 1793–1848?)
Agitator

A haulier, who carried **coal** from **Llwydcoed** pits to Penderyn (**Hirwaun**), Lewis took a prominent part in the **Merthyr Rising** (1831), urging on the crowd outside the Castle Inn. Sentenced to death for felony and riotous assembly, he was reprieved and transported for life. It was widely believed that his nickname, *heliwr*, meant hunter rather than haulier, and that he was saved from the gallows by prominent members of **gentry** families who admired his hunting skills. He is the subject of a popular **ballad** by Iorwerth H. Lloyd.

LEWIS, Lewis William (Llew Llwyfo; 1831–1901)
Performer and writer

Born in Penysarn, Llanwenllwyfo (**Llaneilian**), this poet and resonant baritone on **eisteddfod** and concert platforms, editor and columnist for several **newspapers**, was a remarkable embodiment of Victorian energy. He dedicated himself to writing a national epic poem, but he was a slipshod poet, as *Gemau Llwyfo* (1868) proves. In 1855, his **temperance** novel *Llewelyn Parry: neu, Y Meddwyn Diwygiedig* took the prize at the **Merthyr Tydfil** Eisteddfod, but he was more an advocate for the novel than a novelist. Above all else, he was a stage performer hero-worshipped for his considerable theatricality.

LEWIS, Owen (1533–95) Recusant

A native of Llangadwaladr (**Bodorgan**), Lewis was educated at **Oxford**. His adherence to **Roman Catholicism** caused him to go into exile following the accession of Elizabeth I in 1559. In 1568, he played a part in establishing the university at Douai, where he gained doctorates in canon **law** and **theology**. He moved to Rome *c.*1578, where he was among the founders of the English College, and he secured the appointment of **Morys Clynnog** as its rector. Cardinal Charles Borromeo subsequently appointed Lewis as vicar general of the diocese of Milan, but after Borromeo's death in 1584, he returned to Rome where, in spite of his elevation in 1588 to the bishopric of Cassano, Calabria, he remained until his death.

LEWIS, Richard (Dic Penderyn; 1807/8–1831)
Martyr

A native of **Aberavon**, he was, at the time of the **Merthyr Rising** (1831), a miner in **Merthyr Tydfil**. He was charged with feloniously wounding Donald Black of the 93rd (Highland) Regiment, found guilty and sentenced to death. On 13 August 1831, he was hanged at **Cardiff**, despite a petition for his reprieve said to have been signed by 11,000 people. It was reported that his last words on the scaffold were 'O Arglwydd, dyma gamwedd' (Oh Lord, what injustice). Thousands followed his cortège from Cardiff to Aberavon. Later in the century, another man confessed to the crime for which Lewis had been hanged.

LEWIS, [John] Saunders (1893–1985)
Dramatist, poet, novelist, critic and political leader

A major and controversial figure with a self-imposed mission to change the course of Welsh history, Saunders Lewis was born in Wallasey, **Cheshire**, the son of a Welsh **Calvinistic Methodist** minister. He had a **Welsh**-speaking upbringing, but an English **education** at a private school, and **English** was his subject at **Liverpool** University. During the **First World War**, he served as an army officer, reading the work of Maurice Barrés and the biography of Emrys ap Iwan (**Robert Ambrose Jones**) in the trenches. He was a lecturer in Welsh at **Swansea** from 1922 until he was dismissed for his part in the burning of the **Penyberth Bombing School** in 1936. Earlier, in 1925, he and others had founded **Plaid [Genedlaethol] Cymru**, of which he was president from 1926 until 1939. Following his dismissal from Swansea, he worked as a journalist, teacher, inspector of schools and farmer. He returned to the academic world as a lecturer in Welsh at **Cardiff** in 1952, and remained in that post until his retirement in 1957.

His literary output was astonishingly varied. It included critical studies: *A School of Welsh Augustans* (1924), *Williams Pantycelyn* (1927), *Braslun o Hanes Llenyddiaeth Gymraeg* (1932) and *Daniel Owen* (1936); collections of literary and cultural essays: *Ysgrifau Dydd Mercher* (1945), *Meistri'r Canrifoedd* (1973), *Meistri a'u Crefft* (1981) and *Ati, Wŷr Ifainc* (1986); two novels, *Monica* (1930) and *Merch Gwern Hywel* (1964); and his collected poems (1992). However, he saw himself primarily as a **drama**tist, publishing 21 plays, from *The Eve of St John* (1921) to *1938* (1989). He created a cerebral theatre of classical atmosphere, which called for sophisticated acting techniques and an intellectually endowed audience. Verse is the medium of his earlier plays, such as *Blodeuwedd* (1948), which was a reinterpretation of one of the stories of **The Mabinogion**, written in blank verse. He moved tentatively towards *vers libre* (as in *Siwan*; 1956), then towards a prose of tight rhythms and striking poetic imagery (as in *Gymerwch Chi Sigaret?*; 1956). His main themes were taken from legend and history, from the history of 20th-century Europe, and from his own contemporary Wales (as in *Cymru Fydd*; 1967). His plays raise questions of relevance to modern Wales, but they also treat universal themes such as honour, and the clash between *eros* and *agape*. His collected plays were published in two volumes (1996, 2000). English versions, by Joseph Clancy, of 12 of the plays were published in 1985.

Despite the magnitude of his literary achievement, Lewis may perhaps chiefly be remembered as the foremost interpreter of modern Welsh political **nationalism**. He considered that the purpose of politics is the defence of civilization. In his view, civilization is threatened when people are without property, without tradition and without responsibility, and are therefore prey to corrupt influences – economic and political. He yearned above all for a social order which would ensure the well-being of Welsh-speaking communities, and he believed that such communities were at their most vital in the Middle Ages, before they were threatened by the advent of the centralized state and the capitalist system. Strongly opposed to **socialism**, he favoured what he called *perchentyaeth* – a policy of 'distributing property among the mass of the members of the nation'. Received into the **Roman Catholic** Church in 1932, he became increasingly concerned about the threat of 'Godless **Communism**', and was accused of being less concerned with the rise of Fascism. Indeed, his elitist views and his dismissive attitude towards the **Nonconformist**, **radical**, **puritan** and **pacifist** traditions of Wales, led many to argue that he was seeking to lead his country in a direction wholly alien to it. Resigning from the party presidency in 1939, he returned to the fray in 1943 when he received 25.5% of the vote in the celebrated **University of Wales** parliamentary by-election. Thereafter, apart from one intervention, he devoted himself to literary work. That intervention was his radio lecture *Tynged yr Iaith* (The Fate of the Language, 1962), which triggered the formation of the Welsh Language Society (**Cymdeithas yr Iaith Gymraeg**).

LEWIS, Thomas (1881–1945) Cardiologist

Born in **Cardiff**, Lewis was educated at Cardiff and University College Hospital, **London**, where he graduated in medicine; his whole career was spent there, except for a period during the **Second World War**, when he worked in Cardiff. Knighted in 1921, he is largely remembered for his pioneering work on the development of the electrocardiogram. In his obituary in *The Times*, it was said that his 'certainty that clinical medicine was amenable to the discipline of **science** … inspired his whole life's work. [He] was well equipped to lead a revolution in thought.'

LEWIS, Thomas Frankland (1780–1855) Politician

A member of the Lewis family of Harpton Court, **Old Radnor**, Lewis served as MP for **Beaumaris**, Ennis (County Clare), and **Radnorshire**. Given minor **government**al office, Lewis prepared the influential report on the **Poor Law** (1817), and in 1834 became chairman of the new Poor Law Commission, playing an outstanding role until his retirement in favour of his son **George Cornewall Lewis** in 1839.

He chaired the commission of inquiry into the **Rebecca Riots** (1843–4), which he considered to be 'a very creditable portion of Welsh history'.

LEWIS, Timothy Richards (1841–86)
Physician and bacteriologist

Born at Llangan (**Henllanfallteg**), Lewis qualified medically in **London**. A period in India, where he became an adviser to the **government**, produced important publications on **cholera** and leprosy. He specialized in parasitology, describing the presence of *Filaria sanguinis hominis* in the blood, and discovering *Trypanonosoma lewisi*. Lewis also contributed to nutritional **science**, pioneering the comparative study of diets, and publishing quantitative assessments of the diet of prisoners. His early death, a few weeks before he was due to receive his FRS, was caused by one of the microbes he had so sedulously pursued.

LEWIS, Titus (1773–1811) Minister and author

Cilgerran-born Titus Lewis was ordained a **Baptist** minister at **St Dogmaels** (1798) before moving to **Carmarthen** (1801). He published *A Welsh–English Dictionary* (1805), a 624-page history of **Britain** (1810), as well as volumes of **hymns** and biblical commentaries.

LEWIS, W[illiam] T[homas] (1837–1914)
Estate manager and coalowner

As agent of the Bute (*see* **Stuart family**) estate, Lewis was probably the most powerful figure in Welsh industry in the decades before 1914. From a lowly beginning in 1855, he attained the unique position, by 1880, of managing all Bute interests in minerals, docks, **railways**, and urban and agricultural property. He became a major **coal**owner, establishing the Lewis Merthyr Consolidated Collieries Ltd, whose Universal Colliery was the site of the **Senghenydd Colliery Disaster** of 1913. He was a recurring chairman of the **Coalowners' Association** where he ruled uninterrupted (1880–98) over the industry's Joint Sliding Scale Committee, which regulated wage rates; he also represented employers on numerous Royal Commissions. Although hugely industrious, his imperious attitude lent substance to such descriptions as 'the best-hated man in the Principality' (by Sidney and Beatrice Webb) or as 'terrifying' (by an admirer).

A supporter of 'free' labour, he was totally opposed to **trade unions**, displaying an inflexibility that by 1900 had become inappropriate. Thus, his 'triumph' in humiliating the miners in the six-month stoppage in 1898 (*see* **Miners' Strikes**), effectively ended his dominance of labour relations in the industry. That 'triumph' removed the miners' long reluctance to associate with the **Miners' Federation of Great Britain** (the 'English' union); it alienated public opinion and divided the coalowners. Lewis was raised to the peerage as Lord Merthyr in 1911. By then, he had taken up residence at Hean Castle, **Saundersfoot**, where his descendants still live.

LEWIS, William Vaughan (1907–61)
Geomorphologist

Pontypridd-born Lewis was educated at **Cambridge**, becoming a lecturer in **geography**, with research interests in the processes of geomorphology. In the study of coastal **landforms**, he led the way with innovative papers; in glacial studies, he changed the course of research in **Britain** through his detailed work on glacial motion and erosion in Iceland, Norway and Switzerland.

LEWYS GLYN COTHI (or Llywelyn y Glyn; *c.*1420–89) Poet

Lewys took his name from the forest of Glyn Cothi near **Llanybydder**. A follower of Jasper **Tudor**, after the battle of Mortimer's Cross (1461) he was an outlaw in **Gwynedd** and in the hills of **Pumlumon**. His 238 extant poems show him to have travelled Wales extensively, plying his craft in **gentry** houses. His masterpiece is his poignant elegy to his five-year-old son, Siôn y Glyn. He wrote a vituperative *awdl* to the men of Chester for mistreating him, an action possibly encouraged by the racially discriminatory anti-Welsh **penal code**.

LHUYD, Edward (*c.*1660–1709) Naturalist and linguist

Neither the place nor date of birth of Edward Lhuyd is known (he adopted the **Welsh** form of his **surname**, which he frequently spelled Lhwyd, *c.*1688), but he was brought up in **Shropshire**, partly on the decaying estate of his father, Edward Lloyd, at Llanforda, Oswestry. His mother was Bridget Pryse of Glanfred (**Ceulanamaesmawr**). He was probably a pupil at Oswestry school, but of greater importance for his later career was the botanical training he received from the experienced **garden**er and field botanist Edward Morgan in Llanforda and, it appears, through his father's interests in **chemistry** and horticulture.

He went to Jesus College, **Oxford**, in 1682 but left without completing his degree, in order to take up a post in the Ashmolean Museum, Oxford. He was appointed keeper of the museum in 1691, and he spent the remainder of his comparatively short life in that post. He came to prominence first as a member of the university scientific society and subsequently as a well-informed and astute botanist, palaeontologist and naturalist. In 1693, he was invited to prepare descriptions of the Welsh **counties** for a revised **English** version of **William Camden**'s *Britannia*. He travelled through Wales during 1693–4 gathering antiquarian and epigraphic material, and the quality of his contributions to *Britannia* led to a further invitation in 1695 to prepare a book on the natural and human environment of Wales. He planned a series of studies on the natural history, languages, cultures and antiquities of Wales and the **Celt**ic countries, under the general title *Archaeologia Britannica*. He distributed questionnaires to every **parish** in Wales and after spending five years, from 1697, travelling through Wales (mainly) and the other Celtic countries, he succeeded in collecting a wide range of information and specimens. While on his travels, he succeeded in completing his pioneering illustrated catalogue of the fossils of **Britain** (*Lithophylacii Britannici Ichnographia*, 1699) and in writing four essays discussing the origins of these stones. He returned to Oxford and to the Ashmolean Museum in 1702 and began preparing the first volume of the *Archaeologia*, namely *Glossography*, a collection of materials and discussions on the Celtic languages – grammars, **dictionaries**, lists of manuscripts and old texts. This book, which appeared in 1707, is a pioneering study in that Lhuyd attempted to systematize the phonological variations between these languages and revealed the true significance of the term 'Celtic languages' – work which has earned him the description 'the father of comparative philology'.

Edward Lhuyd was elected FRS in 1708. In his day, he was acknowledged 'the best naturalist now in Europe', and a major authority on British alpine flora – his name is commemorated in *Lloydia serotina,* the **Snowdon** lily (*see* **Plants**), which he was the first to describe. He was also a perceptive archaeologist. He is best described as the first Celtic scholar, since his genius is seen most clearly in the field of linguistics.

LHUYD (LLWYD), Humphrey (*c.*1527–68) Antiquary and cartographer

A prominent figure in the history of the **Renaissance** in Wales, and of key importance in the history of **map** making in Wales, Humphrey Lhuyd was born at **Denbigh**, and educated at **Oxford**. He represented Denbigh in parliament (1563–71), and supported the campaign that led to the Act for the Translation of the **Bible** into **Welsh** 1563. He was the author of several publications in both **Latin** and **English**, among them the works which became the basis for **David Powel**'s *Historie of Cambria* (1584).

His finely engraved map, *Cambriae Typus*, was the first printed map of Wales. It was published, together with his map of **England** and Wales, at Antwerp in 1573 as part of the publisher Abraham Ortelius's *Theatrum Orbis Terrarum*, the first modern atlas. A considerable improvement on previous maps, it provides valuable information on the location and names of administrative units, places and physical features; it was reprinted almost 50 times until 1741. He is buried in a tomb surmounted by a globe in the church of St Marcella, Denbigh.

LIBER LANDAVENSIS (The Book of Llandaff)

This manuscript, held at the **National Library**, consists chiefly of 158 charters purporting to confirm grants of land made to the **diocese** of Llandaff (*see* **Cardiff**) from the 6th to the 12th century. Most of it was compiled in the 1120s when the **Norman**-supported Bishop **Urban** was involved in boundary disputes with the bishops of **St David's** and Hereford. The manuscript also contains biographies of **Dyfrig**, **Teilo** and Euddogwy – the alleged founders of the diocese – and it was once considered a forgery compiled to further Urban's ambitions. However, research has shown that the charters are adaptations preserving records of land grants extending over many centuries. They are a source of central importance for the study of the **Welsh language**, society and **economy** in the early Middle Ages.

LIBERAL (LIBERAL DEMOCRAT) PARTY, The

Until the later 19th century, Welsh politics were controlled by members of the **gentry class**, most of whom supported the **Tory Party**. There were, however, some supporters of the **Whig Party**, from which the Liberal Party (a name that was generally adopted in the 1830s) in part developed. Whig sympathy for **Nonconformists** was one reason why the successor party enjoyed the support of the great majority of Wales's chapelgoers. Other reasons include support by industrialists for the Liberal principle of free trade, and the attacks of the **radicals** (another element of the Liberal Party) upon the powers of the landed class and other vested interests.

The Liberals first won a parliamentary majority in Wales in 1865, the beginning of a supremacy which lasted until 1922, when the party was overtaken by the **Labour Party**. In 1868 – and previously in 1859 – **Conservative** landlords sought to stem the rise of Liberalism by evicting tenants who had defied their landlords and voted Liberal, an action which in part brought about the passage of the Ballot Act in 1872 which ended the practice of public voting. In 1880, the Liberals won 29 of Wales's 34 seats. A charter of national demands was drawn up, seeking the **disestablishment** of the church, **education**al reform, **land** reforms, **temperance** legislation and the creation of Welsh national institutions. Liberal Federations of North and South Wales came into being (1886–7), championed by politicians such as **T. E. Ellis**, **Samuel T. Evans**, **David Lloyd George**, **Ellis Jones Griffith**, **J. Herbert Lewis** and **D. A. Thomas**. Their influence came to fruition with the passage of the **Welsh Intermediate Education Act** (1889), the appointment by **Gladstone** of the Royal Commission on Land in Wales (1892), the granting of a charter to the **University of Wales** (1893) and a succession of Welsh disestablishment bills. However, the **Cymru Fydd** movement did not succeed in building a consensus in favour of **devolution** for Wales. Following the first **county** council elections (1889), the Liberals came to control almost all the county councils of Wales, dominance they retained until the 1920s.

Following the general election of 1906, only one non-Liberal MP – **Keir Hardie** at **Merthyr Tydfil** – represented a Welsh constituency at Westminster. At constituency level, the party was sustained by shopkeepers and middle-**class** professional men, by an array of local **newspapers** and **periodicals** and by links with local **government** and Wales's then buoyant staple industries. The spirit of free trade, individual freedom and social equality, strongly backed by Welsh Nonconformity, had penetrated deep into the fabric of Welsh society. Yet, by 1906, industrial dissension and political militancy had already begun to undermine the Liberal consensus in the southern **coal**field. Lloyd George had long broadened his horizons on the wider political stage. The Asquith–Lloyd George split of 1916 reverberated in Welsh constituencies. In the 'Coupon' general election of December 1918, 20 Liberal supporters of David Lloyd George's coalition with the Conservatives were returned, and only one independent Asquithian Liberal. A number of Labour gains followed in a succession of key by-elections in industrial constituencies and, by 1922, the Liberals had suddenly become primarily the party of rural Wales. When David Lloyd George's revitalized Liberal Party attempted a spectacular 'comeback' in 1929, it captured only 10 seats in Wales. The political crisis of 1931 heralded still further dissension and fragmentation, with the Welsh Liberal MPs split into three distinct camps. David Lloyd George's dramatic 'New Deal' proposals, so flamboyantly unveiled at **Bangor** in January 1935, soon proved to be little more than a damp squib.

Geraint Howells, Liberal MP for Ceredigion 1974-92

Even so, in 1945, rural Wales still proved to be the most resilient of the Liberal strongholds, with 7 (of 12) Liberal MPs representing Welsh constituencies – and with a relatively unknown backbencher, **Clement Davies** (**Montgomeryshire**), chosen as leader of the Parliamentary Liberal Party. Thereafter, numbers diminished still further; by 1951, there were only 6 Liberal MPs, including three from Wales – Clement Davies, Roderic Bowen (**Cardiganshire**) and **Rhys Hopkin Morris** (**Carmarthen**), all three lodged firmly on the right wing of their tiny party. Some revival followed in the early 1960s; Emlyn Hooson comfortably retained Montgomeryshire following Clement Davies's death, a chief organizer for Wales was appointed in 1962, and party activity was somewhat rekindled in the industrial south.

In 1966, a Welsh Liberal Party was established. However, only Montgomeryshire and Cardiganshire remained Liberal seats. In local government, the Liberal collapse was even more dramatic, and those Liberals who survived usually sat as Independents. In the **devolution** campaign preceding the 1979 referendum, both Liberal MPs from Wales – Emlyn Hooson (Montgomeryshire) and **Geraint Howells** (Ceredigion) – were prominent in the 'Yes' camp, but their party reaped little popular support as a result. Hooson was defeated in the 1979 general election, although Alex Carlile succeeded in recapturing the seat in 1983. In 1987, the Liberal Party merged with the Social Democratic Party and adopted the Liberal Democratic title. In 1992, Ceredigion fell to **Plaid [Genedlaethol] Cymru**. In 1997 and 2001, Wales's safe Liberal seats were Montgomeryshire constituency and that of **Brecon and Radnor**. These seats were also won by the Liberals in the 1999 elections for the **National Assembly for Wales**, when the party also won Wales's most heavily urbanized seat, **Cardiff** Central. In addition, the Assembly's devolved electoral system enabled the party to secure 3 regional seats, giving the Liberals a total of 6 Assembly members. In 2000, they joined Labour members to form a coalition government. The coalition came to an end following the second

The Moelfre lifeboat

Assembly elections in 2003, when the Liberal Democrats retained their 6 seats. The Liberal Democrats were the chief beneficiaries of the 2005 Westminster elections, when the number of their MPs doubled to four. They regained Ceredigion from Plaid [Genedlaethol] Cymru, won Cardiff Central from Labour and increased their share of the vote in Wales by 4.5% to 18.5%.

In the early 21st century, the Liberal Democrats made marked advances in local government, becoming the largest party in the **Bridgend**, Cardiff, **Swansea** and **Wrexham** county councils.

In the Assembly election of 2007, the Liberal Democrats again won 6 seats, and it was widely assumed that the party would once more enter into coalition with the Labour Party. However, in the post-election discussions, the party proved unwilling to ally with Labour, or, indeed, with any other party.

LIBERAL UNIONIST PARTY, The

In July 1886, **Gladstone**'s Irish Home Rule Bill received its second reading in the House of Commons; 93 **Liberals** voted against the **government**, and subsequently formed their own Liberal Unionist Party, a step which caused many Welsh Liberals to reconsider their attitude towards Gladstone and the party leadership.

The dissident Liberals included seven from Wales; Richard Davies (**Anglesey**) abstained. Prominent figures such as Sir Robert Cunliffe, David Davies (*see* **Davies family (Llandinam)**) and Sir Hussey **Vivian** joined the Loyal and Patriotic Union and won the support of **radical Nonconformists** such as **Thomas Gee**, but many Welsh Liberals decided that they 'would trust only Gladstone in this doubtful business'. This attitude was reflected in the 1886 election; only one avowed Liberal Unionist, William Cornwallis West (West **Denbighshire**), was elected. Waverers such as C. R. M. **Talbot** (Mid **Glamorgan**) and

Sir Hussey Vivian (**Swansea** District) returned to the Liberal fold. Liberal Unionism in Wales went into decline. Sir John Jones Jenkins was elected Liberal Unionist MP for **Carmarthen Boroughs** in 1895, but, shortly afterwards, the remnants of the party joined the **Conservative** and Unionist Party.

LIFE OF CHARLES PEACE, THE (1905) Film

This robust, short **film** by the director and showman **William Haggar** explores the crimes of the burglar and murderer Charles Peace who was executed in 1879. In this very early 'biopic', Haggar fused theatre techniques, melo-**drama** and backdrops with advanced film-editing skills, making resourceful use of west Wales locations. Tilting at the Establishment, the film offers a surprisingly subversive, almost sympathetic, view of Peace.

LIFE STORY OF DAVID LLOYD GEORGE, THE (1918) Film

Lost for 76 years after disappearing in murky circum-stances, this pivotal and impressive British silent **film** was rediscovered in 1994. Made by Maurice Elvey and starring Norman Page as the then prime minister, the film cele-brates **David Lloyd George**'s achievements as social reformer and war leader. Allegedly a victim of political pressure, the film was withdrawn by **London**'s Ideal com-pany before release; on its recovery, the film was restored and given its world premiere in 1996 in **Cardiff**. It boasts fine special effects, with bravura set pieces of violence dur-ing a Lloyd George speech in Birmingham and suffragette riots in London.

LIFEBOATS

Before lifeboats began to be provided around the Welsh coast in the early 19th century, lifesaving at sea was a makeshift, fortuitous affair. In the 1770s, for instance, a

Mrs Williams of **St David's** single-handedly rowed out to rescue Swedish sailors shipwrecked on a remote rock.

The first purpose-built lifeboats were constructed in the 1790s, and there were lifeboats at **Holyhead** in 1808, **Barmouth** in 1813 and **Fishguard** in 1822, partly funded by Lloyds of **London**. The wrecking of the *Alert* in 1823, with an estimated loss of 130 lives, prompted the foundation of the **Anglesey** Association for the Preservation of Life from **Shipwreck**, and subsequently six lifeboats were stationed around the island (*see* **Cylch-y-Garn**). The need for an organization encompassing all the countries of **Britain** was acknowledged in 1824 when the National Institution for the Preservation of Life from Shipwreck was formed, changing its name in 1854 to the Royal National Lifeboat Institution (RNLI). The RNLI relies entirely on voluntary contributions and its boats are manned by local volunteers. There are 31 lifeboat stations in Wales.

LIGHTHOUSES and LIGHTSHIPS

Wales's first lighthouse, at St Ann's Head (**Dale**), marking the entrance to the **Milford Haven Waterway**, was constructed in the 17th century. **Liverpool ship** merchants built private lighthouses around **Anglesey** in the 18th century, and on the Smalls (**Marloes and St Brides**), 30 km off **Pembrokeshire**, in 1774. Prior to 1801, only two keepers maintained the light on the Smalls. When one of them died, his colleague made a shroud and kept the corpse outside, afraid of being accused of murder if he buried the body at sea, and he had to wait three weeks for a relief boat. It then became policy to station three keepers on remote lighthouses, although today all lights are automated and require no permanent presence. The Smalls lighthouse was the most lucrative lighthouse in the world; based on tonnage of cargoes that passed by, tolls were collected when ships arrived at **ports** such as Liverpool and **Swansea**.

Trinity House maintains all the lighthouses and major navigational marks. Principal lighthouses off the Welsh coast (*see also* **Islands**) are Point Lynas, Skerries, **Holyhead** South Stack, Bardsey, St Tudwal's, Strumble Head, South Bishop, Smalls, Skokholm, St Ann's Head, Caldey, Mumbles, Nash, Flat Holm and East Usk. The only remaining lightship is Breaksea, off **Porthcawl**.

LIMESTONE

Thin, discontinuous layers of **limestone** (calcium carbonate) occur in the Precambrian rocks of **Anglesey** and **Llŷn** and in the Ordovician and Silurian strata of central **Pembrokeshire**, parts of **Carmarthenshire** and the **Old Radnor** and **Bala** districts, while impure limestone occurs in the Old Red Sandstone (Devonian) sequence in southeast Wales and northern Anglesey. The main occurrence, however, is in the Carboniferous Limestone series. These varied and highly fossiliferous strata form a practically continuous rim around the southern coalfield, the rim being at its thickest in the striking cliffs of south **Gower** and south Pembrokeshire. Carboniferous Limestone strata also occur in Anglesey, on both sides of the Vale of **Clwyd** and along the eastern flank of the **Clwydian Hills**.

The South Stack lighthouse at Holy Island, Anglesey

Alternating layers of limestone and shale, well illustrated in the coastal cliffs, occur in the Liassic (Jurassic) of the **Vale of Glamorgan**.

Rainwater, falling on the Carboniferous Limestone outcrops, slowly dissolves the rock along the prominent joint systems and bedding planes, creating characteristic fissures or grykes. **River** water makes its way into the strata along these fissures, creating virtually dry riverbeds, underground channels and **caves**. Water is also responsible for the characteristic swallowholes or 'sinks'; a wide range of such phenomena are to be found in the higher reaches of the **Nedd** and **Tawe** valleys. These lime-rich areas add an extra dimension to the varied ecology of Wales, providing the basis for a striking wealth of trees and flowers (*see* **Plants**). The Great Orme (**Llandudno**), the boldest and shapeliest of the limestone headlands, has been called 'the botanical **garden** of **Cambria**'.

Lime, produced by burning limestone at $1000°C$, was by the 16th century in regular use in Welsh **agriculture** as a soil conditioner, rendering inherently acid **soils** workable and potentially fertile. In the north and west, the very practice of arable agriculture would have been difficult without lime, burned in sod kilns on farms or at the many coastal limekilns between Pembrokeshire and Anglesey. Limestone was extracted from the Carboniferous Limestone quarries of Gower and south Pembrokeshire, where individual quarries were reputed to produce limestone of different qualities to serve different purposes. Limestone from quarries to the east of **Welshpool** was carried westward by **canal** and later by **rail**. Slaked lime was used as a component of farmhouse fuel, a disinfectant, a seed dressing and an ant killer. The toll on carts carrying lime was one of the chief causes of the **Rebecca Riots**.

High-grade limestone, occurring in close proximity to deposits of **iron**stone and coal, played a significant role in the rise of the iron-smelting industry in both the southern and northern coalfields. Lime was used as a flux in the ironmaking process, and was central to the basic system of steelmaking devised by **Sidney Gilchrist Thomas** – a process which gave rise to the agriculturally important by-product, basic slag. The principal component of mortar, lime was used extensively in the building of Edward I's castles. It is used in the manufacture of cement, in **road** construction, tanning and as a purifying element in gas and sewage systems. There is a major cement factory at Aberthaw (**Rhoose**).

LINDSAY, Lionel [Arthur] (1861–1945) Policeman
Captain Lionel Lindsay succeeded his father as chief constable of **Glamorgan** in 1891, having previously served with the Egyptian Gendarmerie (1884–9). By the time he retired in 1936, he had become notorious for his vigorous policing of bitter industrial disputes and political demonstrations. Appropriately, he played the Chief Ruffian at the Welsh National Pageant in **Cardiff** in 1909.

LINTON, Arthur (1868–96) Cyclist
Born in **Aberaman** and the leading member of the celebrated **Aberdare** Cycle Club, formed in 1884, in the 1890s Arthur Linton was one of Wales's greatest sportsmen, becoming champion cyclist of the world in 1895–6 (*see*

Cycling). Within weeks of his last and finest achievement, tying for first place in the blue riband Bordeaux to Paris cycle race, he was dead, officially from typhoid fever. However, if the rumours at the time are true, his may be the first modern sporting death induced by the illegal use of drugs, administered by his trainer.

LITERATURE

Wales, like **Ireland**, can lay claim to one of the oldest unbroken literary traditions in Europe. From the 6th century to the present, this varied and rich tradition has contributed immensely to the vitality of the **Welsh language**, and with the coming of age of **English** writing in Wales over the past hundred years or so, it can rightly be claimed at the beginning of the 21st century that the Welsh possess two thriving literatures. In **Geoffrey of Monmouth** and **Giraldus Cambrensis**, the Welsh can also lay claim to two of the finest **Latin** authors of the Middle Ages.

Early and medieval Welsh poetry

The earliest body of Welsh verse – that of **Taliesin** and **Aneirin** (both 6th century), two of the *Cynfeirdd* – survives not in its original state, but in medieval versions which have undergone considerable linguistic change. It consists of panegyrics and elegies extolling the heroic virtues of an aristocratic warrior elite, and relates, almost entirely, to the Brythonic kingdoms of northern **Britain**, the **Old North** of Welsh tradition. At least three other eulogistic poems from the so-called Dark Ages survive. Throughout the 12th and 13th centuries – the era of the **Poets of the Princes** (the *Gogynfeirdd*, the 'not so early poets') – praise poetry remained an integral feature of the Welsh bardic tradition. Despite the loss of native rule in 1282–3, praise poetry was reanimated during the era of the **Poets of the Gentry**. Apart from providing ritual entertainment in the halls of their patrons, the poets were the custodians of native lore and learning. They shaped and upheld the ideology of the ruling elite, and in a society where the notions of shame and honour were of integral importance, the fact that satire was also a weapon at their disposal further enhanced their authority.

Despite the primacy of eulogistic poetry, the Welsh bardic tradition of the Middle Ages was an extremely diverse one. The 9th and 10th centuries saw an outpouring of saga poetry (*see* **Heledd** and **Llywarch Hen**) and much nature and gnomic material. Traditions relating to **Arthur**, **Merlin** and the pseudo-Taliesin appear in verse at about the same time. **Prophecy** of a political nature lies at the heart of much Welsh poetry between the 10th and the 16th centuries, and throughout the Middle Ages a rich and substantial body of religious verse was produced. Although some of the earliest religious poems, such as those in the **Juvencus** manuscript and *The Black Book of Carmarthen*, were possibly composed by ecclesiastics, it seems that most of these *genres* represent different facets of the poetical activities of the official praise poets. This is certainly true in relation to the love poetry of the period. Elements of courtly love are found in praise poems composed by the Poets of the Princes to the wives and the daughters of their patrons. By the 14th century, the treatment of love in such poetry had acquired greater prominence, and in the work of **Dafydd ap Gwilym**, the most innovative of the Poets of the Gentry and the most outstanding Welsh poet of all time, it is fused with a host of sub-literary influences and enlivened by vivid descriptions of the natural world. Dafydd played a pivotal role in two of the great metrical innovations of the 14th century – the creation of the *cywydd* metre and the formalization of *cynghanedd*.

Medieval prose

In Wales, as in Ireland and Iceland, prose, rather than verse, was the medium of narrative literature throughout the medieval period. The story-teller in medieval Wales, the *cyfarwydd*, undoubtedly possessed an immense repertoire of tales, but only fragments have survived. As one of the ultimate sources of European Arthurian romance (the *Matière de Bretagne*), the indirect influence of this extensive body of oral traditions on the course of medieval literature was profound. In Wales itself it was also the direct source of much of the material found in the acclaimed tales of *The Mabinogion* – which are, of course, conscious literary creations rather than faithful reproductions of the oral tales of the *cyfarwyddiaid*. In the 'Four Branches', the semi-divine heroes of **Celtic** oral tradition may well be present, but there are also underlying themes, such as the nature of friendship, marriage and feud, which reflect firm authorial intentions.

No original Welsh narrative texts appear to have been produced during the later Middle Ages, but many were translated from **French** and Latin. Despite *The Mabinogion*'s appeal in modern times, in Wales itself from the 13th century onwards the most influential and widely copied narrative texts were translations of Geoffrey of Monmouth's *Historia Regum Britanniae*. Known in Welsh as *Brut y Brenhinedd*, the *Historia*'s portrayal of a Brythonic golden age made a deep impression on the Welsh psyche and its influence far outweighed that of *Brut y Tywysogyon* which related to the events of a more immediate past. Among other translations of the 13th and 14th centuries were a version of the Grail legend, *Ystoryaeu y Seint Greal*, which was based on two independent French texts, and *Ystorya de Carolo Magno*, a rendering from both Latin and French sources of the Charlemagne romances. Latin was also the source of an extensive body of religious prose, which included the Lives of a host of both native and internationally familiar **saints**, although the 13th-century mystical treatise *Ymborth yr Enaid* (*Nourishment for the Soul*) seems to have been an original Welsh composition. Most of these religious texts were purely practical in aim and they form part of a substantial body of functional prose relating to such matters as **law**, bardic instruction and medicine (*see* **Physicians of Myddfai, The**).

From the Tudor era to the 19th century

The political and religious changes of the Tudor era transformed Welsh literature. Although the 16th century saw extensive patronage of the bards, social and intellectual changes – the gradual Anglicization of the **gentry** class among them – had, by the late 17th century, led to the extinction of the professional poets. However, the integration of the native elite into a wider cultural world was not wholly a negative development. During the 16th century, humanists such as **William Salesbury** and **John Davies** (*c.*1567–1644) returned to Wales from English universities, fired by **Renaissance** ideals. Through the publication of grammars, **dictionaries** and religious works, they ensured that Welsh literature became attuned to the age of print (*see* **Printing and Publishing**). The crowning achievement of their learning, driven as it was by the needs of the **Protestant Reformation**, was the translation of the **Bible** into Welsh, a momentous task accomplished by **William Morgan** in 1588. A tradition of translating and adapting didactic and homiletic tracts was also firmly established at this time. It served the needs of the **Anglican** establishment, and formed an important part of recusant activity in Wales, as exemplified by the output of Robert Gwyn (*c.*1540–50 to 1592–1604), the reputed author of *Y Drych Cristianogawl* (1585). During the 17th century, Dissenters and **Puritans**, most notably **Morgan Llwyd**, put pen to paper, and it is to the same broad tradition of religious and moralistic writing that the satirical and entertaining *Gweledigaetheu y Bardd Cwsc* (1703) of **Ellis Wynne**, a highly opinionated Anglican, also belongs. Two classics of the early modern period, **Charles Edwards**'s *Y Ffydd ddi-ffuant* (1667, 1671, 1677) and **Theophilus Evans**'s *Drych y Prif Oesoedd* (1716 and 1740), stand somewhat apart from this tradition in that they purport to be works of history, but as palpable Protestant interpretations of the history of Wales they undoubtedly belong to the same milieu.

From the 16th century onwards, the most important development in the field of poetry was the proliferation of 'free-metre' verse, a broad category which encompasses moralistic carols, love poetry, eulogies and elegies, as well as the delightful *hen benillion* and several *genres* relating to seasonal folk rituals (*see* **Candlemas Carols**, **Summer Carols** and **Wassailing**). Originally, the only difference between 'free-metre' verse and the classical, syllabic strict-metres was the absence of *cynghanedd* in the former, but from the middle of the 17th century a host of intricate accentual metres based on imported English tunes became popular, and were embellished with *cynghanedd* by poets such as **Huw Morys**. Communal in nature, such poetry had, by the 18th century, come to be composed by a host of unassuming country poets (the predecessors of the *bardd gwlad*), and their work was given wide currency in **ballad** sheets and **almanacs**. A closely allied tradition was that of the **Interlude**, of which the finest practitioner was Twm o'r Nant (**Thomas Edwards**). Poetry, and more especially hymn-writing, played an essential part in the **Methodist Revival** of the 18th century. Although **William Williams** (Pantycelyn; 1717–91) wrote two poems of epic length and several lively prose tracts, his place in the literary canon is assured by his **hymns** and a breathtaking ability – an attribute shared by **Ann Griffiths** more than a generation later – to convey the profound emotional intensity of his spiritual experiences.

William Williams and the Methodists had little interest in the literature of the medieval period, but the antiquarian activities of Ieuan Fardd (**Evan Evans**; 1731–88) and the **Morris brothers** and the establishment of the **Cymmrodorion** and **Gwyneddigion** Societies in **London**, represent a renewed interest in the Welsh literary tradition and form an integral part of the Welsh cultural renaissance of the 18th century. Infused with English neo-classical ideals, this movement found its finest poetical exponent in **Goronwy Owen**. Although Goronwy's grand ambition of writing a Welsh Christian epic-poem remained unfulfilled at his death, that aspiration had a seminal influence on the poetry of the 19th century. Fuelled by the **eisteddfod** and its literary competitions (*see* **awdl** and **pryddest**), the creation of a sublime Welsh epic became a national obsession. However, poets such as Gwallter Mechain (**Walter Davies**), Eben Fardd (**Ebenezer Thomas**) and Gwilym Hiraethog (**William Rees**; 1802–83) toiled for the most part in a creative cul-de-sac. Although the Welsh renaissance of the 18th century was influenced by neo-classicism, the wild Druidic dreams of Iolo Morganwg (**Edward Williams**) demonstrate that is was also influenced by **Romanticism**. The growth of a fine meditative Welsh lyric tradition may be traced from Ieuan Glan Geirionydd (**Evan Evans**; 1795–1855) and Alun (**John Blackwell**) to **John Ceiriog Hughes**. In the case of Islwyn (**William Thomas**; 1832–78) on the other hand, the romantic impulse led to loftier and far more substantial designs, although the Romanticism of his acclaimed *Y Storm* was tempered by **Calvinism**.

Driven by the needs of **Nonconformists**, the Victorian era was a golden age of Welsh printing and publishing. Books of scriptural commentary and weighty biographies of the heroes of the pulpit, such as **Owen Thomas**'s celebrated *Cofiant John Jones, Talsarn* (1874), flowed from the press. Serialized works of fiction by writers such as the **Anglican** Brutus (**David Owen**), and the **radical** Gwilym Hiraethog, were an important feature of Welsh **newspapers** and **periodicals**. From the 1830s onwards, a host of sentimental stories were published to promote the cause of **temperance**. However, with one notable exception, the Welsh novel failed miserably to outgrow such didactic and melodramatic beginnings. That exception was **Daniel Owen**. Although his plots are often cumbersome, such deficiencies are more than compensated for by his rounded characters and their ability to communicate the crude hypocrisies of the age.

The 20th century

The formation of university colleges in Wales between 1872 and 1884 and the growth of Welsh as an academic discipline led to a general broadening of literary horizons at the close of the Victorian era and enabled Welsh literature to reach unparalleled heights during the 20th century (*see* **University of Wales, The**). Paradoxically, from the 1920s onwards, the source of much of this vitality was the angst of writing in an increasingly endangered and marginalized language and the frustrations of living in what had become a fractured national community.

T. Gwynn Jones's 'Ymadawiad Arthur' (The Passing of Arthur) – an **awdl** for which he was awarded the National Eisteddfod chair at **Bangor** in 1902 – is still considered to be the finest example of the aesthetic romanticism which gave new directions to Welsh poetry before the **First World War**. Largely through the endeavours of Emrys ap Iwan (**Robert Ambrose Jones**) and **John Morris-Jones**, the stilted

and long-winded style of Victorian Welsh prose came under attack during the same period. Clarity and simplicity were championed as stylistic aims, especially by **O. M. Edwards**, whose idealized portrayal of the Welsh *gwerin* represents another aspect of the neo-romanticism of the turn of the century.

Although an interesting body of war literature was produced in Welsh, the indirect influences of the First World War on Welsh literature were far more significant. In Wales, as elsewhere, old values and certainties were destroyed by the slaughter of the trenches and, during the interwar years, it was **T. H. Parry-Williams**, both in poetry and prose, who most memorably articulated humanity's tortured predicament in a world of spiritual dislocation. **R. Williams Parry** and T. Gwynn Jones came to realize that the romantic aestheticism of the turn of the century was a thing of the past, and the war's greatest legacy in their poems was pessimism and disillusionment. Changes in the political life of Wales also had a bearing on Welsh literature. **Plaid [Genedlaethol] Cymru**, established in 1925, made little electoral headway until the 1960s, but on the intellectual front – at that point where literature, criticism and political theory converge – the influence of **Saunders Lewis**, its main ideologue, was seminal. In Lewis's plays (*see* **Drama**), poetry, criticism and politics there lurk the same reactionary impulses as may be found in the work of T. S. Eliot; it was with Lewis's contentious poem 'Y Dilyw' (The Deluge) that Welsh poetry came nearest to finding a truly modernist idiom during the interwar period. Much of Lewis's criticism was published on the pages of the literary quarterly *Y Llenor* (1922–55), where his views were increasingly called into question by the editor, **W. J. Gruffydd**, and by the erudite literary essayist **R. T. Jenkins**. The leftist journal *Tir Newydd* (1935–9) voiced similar suspicions, although the cosmopolitan poems of its young editor, **Alun Llywelyn-Williams**, displayed many of Lewis's literary ideals.

After the **Second World War**, Welsh poets were preoccupied by matters pertaining to faith and nationality. In the work of both Gwenallt (**David James Jones**) and **Waldo Williams**, Wales's Christian tradition is viewed as a bulwark against the rampant materialism and militarism of the Western world. In style, their output is indicative of the modernistic temperament of much Welsh poetry at this time. *Vers libre* became the preferred medium of the avant-garde; in the 1950s, the innovative diction of **Euros Bowen** and Bobi Jones (b.1929) provoked heated arguments concerning the function of poetry. From the 1960s onwards, largely under the influence of Gwyn Thomas (b.1936), younger Welsh poets such as Iwan Llwyd (b.1957) have been more at ease with American popular culture and, increasingly, their concerns have been those of Western society in general, a movement complemented at the close of the century by the distinct feminine voice of Menna Elfyn (b.1951). This development has been counterbalanced to a degree by a resurgence of interest in *cynghanedd* inspired by Dic Jones (b.1934), Gerallt Lloyd Owen (b.1944) and Alan Llwyd (b.1948). However, at the beginning of the 21st century, the boundaries have become unclear, with even *cynghanedd* poets such as Emyr Lewis (b.1957) displaying a great deal of postmodern subtlety and irony.

In the field of fiction, the most influential figure between the 1920s and the 1970s was **Kate Roberts**, and her contribution to both the Welsh short story and the novel remains unsurpassed. In relation to the subject matter of her early work – the life which evolved around the **slate** quarries of the north-west – the short-story writer Dic Tryfan (**Richard Hughes Williams**) was an important precursor. Her contemporary, **D. J. Williams**, also contributed, from the 1930s onwards, to steering the short story to new heights, as did **John Gwilym Jones** with his collection *Y Goeden Eirin* (1946). However, the enthusiasm with which the novels of **T. Rowland Hughes** were received between 1943 and 1947 showed that there was an insatiable desire among Welsh readers for the 20th century's quintessential literary form. The novel was given further vitality during the 1950s by **Islwyn Ffowc Elis**, whose tales of youthful rebellion against accepted norms and traditions captured the imagination of an appreciative younger audience. By the 1960s and 1970s, especially in the work of Jane Edwards (b.1938), Eigra Lewis Roberts (b.1939) and John Rowlands (b.1938), the novel had come to reflect an unmistakably modern and secular Wales. Apart from **Caradog Prichard**'s acclaimed *Un Nos Ola Leuad* (1961) and **Dafydd Rowland**'s underestimated *Mae Theomemphus yn Hen* (1977), up to the 1980s Welsh fiction remained, by and large, in a realistic mould. But in Wiliam Owen Roberts's *Bingo!* (1985) and *Y Pla* (1987) and, more especially, in the work of Mihangel Morgan (b.1955) and Robin Llywelyn (b.1958), order and reality have been consciously undermined. The work of the former dwells, with irreverent humour, on a post-Nonconformist Wales where cross-dressers and leather-clad sado-masochists rub shoulders with professors of Welsh and lorry drivers whose one ambition in life is to win the chair at the National Eisteddfod.

Literature in English

'Ei sik, ei sing, ei siak, ei sae': **Ieuan ap Hywel Swrdwal**'s 'A Hymn to the Virgin' (*c.*1470) is reputedly the first Welsh poem in English. Using Welsh spelling and native strict-metre verse forms, this defiant exercise by an **Oxford** student has many of the features of a 'post-colonial' poem – camp mimicry of the colonial language and a contortion of it to accommodate 'foreign' cultural practices. As such, it contrasts with most of the sedulously conventional English literature of Wales of the succeeding four centuries, which may reasonably be designated '**Anglo-Welsh**' to suggest those (qualified) respects in which it resembles the Anglo-Irish literature of a settler, ascendancy class.

While the mass of the **population** remained Welsh speaking well into the 19th century, English steadily established itself as the language of **government**, law, business and **education** from the 1536 **Act of 'Union'** onwards (although there were pockets, such as south **Pembrokeshire** and southern **Gower**, where English had long been the native language of most inhabitants). Works in such fields were accordingly produced by the gentry and the professional classes, as were consciously cultivated poems by parsons and scholars, and, in due course, fashionable fictions by the largely alien bourgeoisie. This modest body of work,

The grave of poet Henry Vaughan at Llansantffraed, Talybont-on-Usk

spanning some four centuries, offers insights into Wales as a zone of cultural instabilities and strange hybridities: the Welsh-speaking **John Davies** (of Hereford; ?1565–1618), addressing his 'Cambria' (1603) to James I; the major metaphysical poet **Henry Vaughan**, 'civilizing' his native region by rendering it as classical landscape; **John Dyer** conforming to the emerging English taste for romantic landscape in 'Grongar Hill' (1716); distinguished Welsh-language writers such as Morgan Llwyd and William Williams (Pantycelyn; 1717–91) turning to a much poorer English for religion's sake. From the late 18th century, these cultural indeterminacies find new forms of expression in novels of romance and sensibility, often written by **women** (whose own social status was changing), several of whom (such as 'Ann of Swansea' (**Ann Julia Hatton**)) were cultural immigrants. At the same time, a Romantic (and later, Victorian) poetry sporadically appeared eulogizing landscapes denuded of people or vaguely hymning the Welsh past. One author of such poetry, **Thomas Jeffrey Llewelyn Prichard**, went on to produce in *The Adventures and Vagaries of Twm Shon Catti* (1828) what is often claimed to be the first distinctively Welsh novel, colourfully picaresque in character.

By the mid-19th century, Welsh-language culture had developed its own educated bourgeoisie, comfortably bilingual but still regarding Welsh as the language of literature and the soul. Thereafter, socio-economic changes, along with the in-migration that accompanied industrialization, transformed Wales into a country where, by the beginning of the 20th century, the majority spoke English only. These transformations found oblique expression in the patriotically unionist poetry of Sir **Lewis Morris**, the reactively nationalist novels of Mallt Williams (**Alice Matilda Langland Williams**) and her sister Gwenffreda Williams, and the self-conscious representation of a preindustrial Wales in the enormously popular romances of Allen Raine (**Anne Adaliza Beynon Puddicombe**). An obscure sense of cultural displacement haunts the work of writers of a 'lost generation' such as **Arthur Machen** and the Georgian pastoralist **W. H. Davies**.

'Welsh Writing in English' (as distinct from 'Anglo-Welsh' literature) is arguably a 20th-century phenomenon and the product of a 'new' Wales, largely anglophone, industrial and urban. It begins around the time of the First World War, with *My People* (1915) by Caradoc Evans (*see* **David Evans**; 1878–1945), a dramatic attempt to portray – or perhaps to denigrate – traditional Welsh-language rural culture – work which aroused in Welsh-language writers a deep and long-lasting suspicion of Welsh literature in English. There were also attempts to map the dynamic configurations of a violently new industrial order (**J. O. Francis**'s *Change* (1912)). By the mid-1930s, a number of striking talents had emerged, some of whom gradually, with the help of such journals as *Wales* and *The Welsh Review*, came to feel part of a common writing culture. Sensitive to the economic crisis of their industrial communities, almost all of them (perhaps excluding **Vernon Watkins**) felt a degree of social obligation, differently expressed in the modernist writings of **Dylan Thomas** and **Glyn Jones** than in the panoramic entertainments of **Jack Jones**, the social realism of **Gwyn Jones**'s fiction or the *engagé* writing of the **Communist Lewis Jones**. As is conspicuously evident in the poetry of **Idris Davies**, their work frequently involves the adaptation of existing forms so as to mediate Welsh experience – a feature that later greatly interested **Raymond Williams**, himself an indirect by-product of this culture. But, their reputation enhanced by the dark glamour of a **Depression** society, these writers, as they came to be regarded as 'definitively' Welsh, tended to obscure other significant aspects of the literature of the time – the brief flare of distinctive talent in the short stories of **Dorothy Edwards**; the important phenomenon of elective Welshness, evidenced by **Richard Hughes**, **David Jones**, **John Cowper Powys**, **Lynette Roberts**, **Margiad Evans** and Richard Llewellyn (**Richard Herbert Vivian Lloyd**) (author of the quintessentially 'Welsh' novel *How Green Was My Valley*); the opening of Wales to the world in **Alun Lewis**'s stories and poems about India; the suave interrogation of traditional gender roles in **Rhys Davies**'s fiction; the disclosure of a 'hidden Wales' beyond the industrial south-east in the fiction of **Geraint Goodwin** and (later) **Brenda Chamberlain**.

With the premature death of many of this generation, and the rapid decline of industrial culture and the ideologies it had produced, writers of the post-Second World War generation found themselves disorientated, an experience variously inscribed in the work of writers such as **T. Harri Jones**, **Gwyn Thomas** and **Ron Berry**, and in the researches of the poet-scholars Raymond Garlick (b.1926) and Roland Mathias (1915–2007). Although a sense of 'non-alignment' became a hallmark of the writings of the likes of Dannie Abse (b.1923), **Leslie Norris** and **John Ormond**, it was politico-cultural nationalism that powered the major work of **R. S. Thomas** and Emyr Humphreys (b.1919), an ideology that helped create a better climate for inter-cultural relations in Wales – a development much encouraged by the work of Tony Conran (b.1931) and M. Wynn Thomas (b.1944). The suspicion of English-language Welsh writing harboured by Welsh-language writers since the time of Caradoc Evans was appeased by the overt patriotism of such English-language poets as **Harri Webb** and **John Tripp**, and was finally laid to rest in 1968 with the establishment of an English-language section of Yr Academi Gymraeg, which had been founded in 1959 to foster Welsh-language writing (*see* **Welsh Academy, The**). Even more significant was the creation in 1967 of the Welsh Arts Council (**Arts Council of Wales**). Public funding was consequently made available for the support of authors and to underwrite publishing ventures (Poetry Wales Press, later Seren Books, began in 1981), so that for the first time Welsh writers in English had the option not only of living and working but of actually publishing in Wales (*see* **Printing and Publishing**). It was the beginning of a new era, marked by the emergence of a new generation of writers, including a number of women poets, the most prominent of whom was Gillian Clarke (b.1937).

Although legatees of the sixties revolution, few of the writers who came to prominence since the late seventies have embraced the politico-cultural values of that period. While some have graphed the decline of industrial Wales and with it the disappearance of traditional markers of anglophone Welsh identity, others have revelled in the physical and cultural mobility, and the pluralism of identity, that characterize the postmodern period. The multiple pun in the word *Shifts* (the title of an important post-industrial novel (1988) by Christopher Meredith (b.1954) would seem to capture the spirit of an ideologically decentred, eclectic body of writing, some of which passingly resembles – in its culturally ambiguous character – that hymn by Ieuan ap Hywel Swrdwal with which it all began, almost six centuries earlier.

'LITTLE MOSCOW'

By the 1930s, several British communities were being referred to, affectionately or disparagingly, as 'Little Moscows', but perhaps only Lumphinnans in **Scotland**'s Vale of Leven deserved the title as much as Maerdy at the top of **Rhondda** Fach. Initially, the tag was meant as an insult, but Maerdy accepted it with pride and thought it entirely appropriate, given the local presence of a glorious banner which had been presented to the British miners during the **General Strike** by the **women** of Krasnaya Presna, Moscow. That initial link with the Soviet Union was to be reflected in the subsequent strength of the **Communist Party** in Maerdy, a **community** closely linked with **Arthur Horner**, who lived there from 1919 to 1934. Above all, the appellation was accepted as reflecting both the degree of local solidarity and the extent to which the miners' lodge dominated local affairs. In 1930, the lodge virtually broke away from the **South Wales Miners' Federation** and, over half a century later, it was the Communist officials of the lodge who led the widely reported march back to work in 1985 at the end of a strike in which the Maerdy miners had again remained wholly united.

LIVERPOOL, Wales's associations with

During much of the 19th and early 20th centuries, the Welsh community on Merseyside was the largest and most influential Welsh community outside Wales. In 1901, some 87,000 Welsh-born people lived in the north-west of **England**, the largest concentration being in Liverpool and neighbouring Birkenhead. Some 20,000 Welsh-born people lived on either side of the Mersey, exerting a strong influence not only on Merseyside's complex ethnic mix, but also on Welsh history and culture. The Liverpool conurbation, easily accessible from the north, was often referred to as the 'capital of north Wales'.

Male Welsh immigrants were concentrated in the building trades, whilst **women** were largely employed in domestic service, Liverpool's many Welsh chapels operating as labour exchanges and marriage bureaux for newly arrived migrants. The building industry allowed a significant number of Welshmen to progress from being craftsmen to becoming small independent builders; a few, such as **Owen Elias**, came to dominate the city's construction trade, and others moved into related industries such as building societies, finance and **banking**. There were also prominent Welshmen in shipping and trading, such as Sir Alfred Lewis Jones (1845–1909), and in retailing, including the hugely successful Owen Owen (1847–1910), who established the first of his first department stores in Liverpool.

The conspicuous wealth of a significant section of the Liverpool Welsh, and the wider community's reputation for thrift and hard work (and also for being clannish), allowed them to make a significant contribution to Welsh life. The National **Eisteddfod** was held on Merseyside in 1884, 1900, 1917 and 1929, and the John Lewis department store held a successful eisteddfod in the 1930s and 1940s. The Liverpool Welsh National Society was established in 1885 and, in 1893, an influential Young Wales (**Cymru Fydd**) Society was founded. Gwilym Hiraethog (**William Rees**; 1802–83) edited his pioneering **newspaper** *Yr Amserau* from Liverpool, and **Isaac Foulkes**, Hugh Evans (1854–1934) and others established Liverpool as the pre-eminent centre of **Welsh**-language **printing and publishing** (*see Papurau Bro*). Princes Road chapel (*c.*1868) was recognized as the grandest of all the chapels of the **Calvinistic Methodists**, and the Liverpool pulpits attracted many of the most famous ministers of their time. The University of Liverpool's department of **Celt**ic studies made a significant contribution to Welsh scholarship until its closure in the 1970s.

Saunders Lewis, born and brought up in Wallasey and educated at Liverpool University, was acutely conscious of the Welsh-speaking community around him. The vitality of the language, however, depended on fresh immigrants arriving from Wales, for second-generation immigrants tended to adopt **English**. But the Welsh language and the Welsh community survive into the 21st century, with an annual eisteddfod and a community newspaper, *Yr Angor*. The decline of Liverpool itself since the **Second World War**, however, allied to the changing patterns of Welsh migration, has led to a decline in the Welsh presence on Merseyside. In the 1950s, the drowning of the **Tryweryn Valley** to provide Liverpool with water soured relations between the city and the people of Wales; in 2005, the Liverpool Corporation formally apologized for the drowning.

Roger Livesey in *A Matter of Life and Death*, 1948

LIVESEY, Roger (1906–76) Actor

Barry-born Livesey, from a notable Welsh acting family, had a powerful screen presence, often leavening a sense of authority with avuncular good humour, and a fruity, nasal delivery of his lines. He established an international screen reputation, starring in three **films** for Michael Powell and Emeric Pressburger: *The Life and Death of Colonel Blimp* (1943), in which he conveyed, movingly, the integrity – beneath the bluster – of an anachronistic soldier; *I Know Where I'm Going* (1945); and *A Matter of Life and Death* (1948), in which he played a surgeon pleading the cause of a pilot, played by David Niven, at a celestial court hearing. He stole more than one scene as Laurence Olivier's ageing father in the screen version of John Osborne's play *The Entertainer* (1960).

LLAN

Originally a word meaning any kind of enclosure (thus *gwinllan* – vineyard; *perllan* – orchard; *ydlan* – rickyard), during the early Middle Ages *llan* came to be applied specifically to an enclosed burial ground and hence to the church built within it. A common element in **place names**, it is generally formed by combining *llan* with the (mutated) name of a **saint**, as in **Llandeilo** (*llan*+Teilo). Of the 1132 names of Welsh **parishes** or part-parishes listed in the **tithe** apportionments of the 1830s and 1840s, 457 (40%) begin with *Llan*. However, some *Llan* names (Llangawsai, for example) represent the corruption of the word *glan* (bank) or *nant* (valley or brook).

LLANAELHAEARN, Gwynedd
(2741 ha; 1067 inhabitants)
Straddled by the **Caernarfon–Pwllheli road** (the A499), the **community**'s most striking feature is **Yr Eifl** (564 m), the highest point of the Eifl range (*see also* **Clynnog, Earthquakes** and **Pistyll**). On its slopes is Tre'r Ceiri, a spectacular **Iron Age hill-fort** consisting of high ramparts enclosing about 150 round stone houses, some of whose walls still stand up to 2 m high. Occupation continued into

the **Roman** period. In St Aelhaearn's church (12th to 16th century) are three early inscribed stones (*see* **Monuments, Early Christian**), one of which commemorates Aliortus, stated to be a native of **Elmet**, a Brythonic kingdom near modern Leeds. The community's main settlement is Trefor, which developed to house those employed at the **granite** quarries of Yr Eifl. Widely exported as paving setts, the granite was considered unequalled for the manufacture of **curling** stones. In the 1970s, a co-operative movement, Antur Aelhaearn, was established to create employment and combat rural de**population**; it attracted international interest. The Trefor silver band enjoys a high reputation.

LLANAFAN FAWR, Breconshire, Powys
(8249 ha; 475 inhabitants)
A vast expanse west of the **Wye**, the **community** extends to the summit of Y Gorllwyn (613 m). Its church holds the tomb of Afan, one of the chief **saints** of mid Wales. Religious dissent (*see* **Nonconformists**) struck early roots in the area. **Walter Cradock** and **Vavasor Powell** both preached at Llanafan Fawr. A **Congregationalist** church was established there between 1640 and 1660. The first chapel was built at Cribarth in 1689, but the congregation moved to Troedrhiwdalar in 1714. Carnhuanawc (**Thomas Price**) was born at Llanfihangel Bryn Pabuan in 1787. Llysdinam, a mansion above the Wye, is the home of the Venables-Llewelyn family, descended from the **Dillwyn** and **Dillwyn-Llewelyn** families prominent in the history of **Swansea**. It contains a bedroom transported intact from **Penllergaer**. The poet **T. Harri Jones** was a native of Llanafan Fawr.

LLANARMON-YN-IAL (Llanarmon-yn-Iâl), Denbighshire (2785 ha; 1069 inhabitants)
Located south-east of **Ruthin**, the **community** contains numerous **caves**, some of which have yielded **Neolithic** human remains. Tomen y Faerdref is the site of a motte, probably constructed in the 11th century. In the double-naved church of St **Garmon** are interesting funereal monuments and a superb pre-**Reformation** brass chandelier. A memorial to the anti-**tithe** activist John Parry (1835–97) stands outside Rhiw Iâl chapel. The area is riddled with the shafts of abandoned **lead** mines.

LLANARTH (Llannarth), Ceredigion
(4591 ha; 1564 inhabitants)
Located between **Aberaeron** and **New Quay**, the **community** contains the villages of Llanarth, Gilfachreda, Mydroilyn and Synod Inn. St **David**'s church (medieval but heavily restored in 1872) occupies a prominent site on a steep hill, the *garth* which gives Llanarth its name. Plas y Wern (17th and 19th centuries) is the successor to the house in which Henry **Tudor** is reputed to have stayed in 1485 on his way to **Bosworth** Field. The village of Llanarth contains some attractive late Georgian houses in the style of the houses at Aberaeron.

LLANARTH (Llan-arth), Monmouthshire
(2855 ha; 878 inhabitants)
Straddling the A40 east of **Abergavenny**, the **community** contains the settlements of Llanarth, Clytha, Bettws Newydd, Bryngwyn and Llanvapley. Llanarth Court, now

a hospital, was the seat of the recusant Jones (later the Herbert) family whose 18th-century chapel is a significant building in the history of the revival of **Roman Catholicism** in Wales. William Jones commissioned the building of the neo-Gothic Clytha Castle (1790), in order to relieve 'a Mind sincerely afflicted by the Loss of a most excellent Wife'. He was also responsible for the remarkable Greek Revival Clytha Park (1797). Bettws Newydd church has a spectacular rood screen and loft. The 13th-century church of St Mable at Llanvapley has survived virtually intact. There is a massive **hill-fort** at Coed y Bwnydd.

LLANARTHNEY (Llanarthne),
Carmarthenshire (2792 ha; 738 inhabitants)
Located south of the **Tywi** halfway between **Carmarthen** and **Llandeilo**, the **community** contains the village of Llanarthney and the hamlet of Capel Dewi. St **David**'s church (1826) retains its medieval tower. The triangular Paxton's Tower, one of Wales's finest landmarks, was commissioned by **William Paxton** (1744–1824) to honour Horatio Nelson. His mansion, Middleton Hall (1790s), was destroyed by fire in 1931. Its fine stables provide offices for the **National Botanical Garden of Wales**, established on 277 ha of the Middleton estate and opened in 2000. Its **glass** dome, the world's largest, was designed by Norman Foster and contains 5000 sq m of glass.

LLANASA, Flintshire (2453 ha; 4820 inhabitants)
Constituting the northernmost tip of **Flintshire**, the **community** contains the villages of Llanasa, Talacre, Gronant, Gwespyr, Trelogan, Glan-yr-afon, Pen-y-ffordd and Ffynnongroyw. The picturesque Llanasa village has received several conservation awards. Its double-naved church, dedicated to St Asaph and St Kentigern, has a six-bay Perpendicular arcade. Near it is Henblas, a fine **limestone** house (1645). Step-gabled Golden Grove may date from 1578. Gyrn Castle, castellated in 1824, has a tall **clock** tower.

The community's best-known location is Point of Ayr, where a **lighthouse** (1777) marks mainland Wales's northernmost tip. Point of Ayr **coal**mine, originally sunk in the 18th century, became the most successful colliery in **Flintshire**, and had workings stretching out under the sea. It was notable for its conciliatory industrial relations – operating throughout the strike of 1926 (*see* **Miners' Strikes**), harbouring a **company union** in the 1930s, and having a majority of working miners during the strike of 1984–5. For a brief period before the reopening in 1995 of the **Tower Colliery**, Point of Ayr was Wales's sole deep mine; it was closed in 1996.

Near the one-time colliery is the village of Talacre. Talacre Hall was the seat of the **Roman Catholic** branch of the **Mostyn family**; among its members was **Francis Mostyn**, bishop of Menevia and second archbishop of **Cardiff**. Since 1920, it has housed an enclosed community of **Benedictine** nuns (*see* **Nunneries**). The dunes between Talacre and Gronant contain a reserve of the Royal Society for the Protection of **Birds** and several caravan parks. Nearby is the BHP natural gas terminal visitor centre. An important **lifeboat** station existed originally at Gronant (1803–74) and then at Talacre (1874–1923). Upper Gronant developed in the 19th century as a lead mining and limestone quarrying centre. Gwespyr, a quarrying village, gave its name to the local sandstone. From the 17th to the 19th centuries, there were productive lead mines at Trelogan. The father of the playwright **Emlyn Williams** was the licensee of the tavern at Glan-yr-afon. Ffynnongroyw developed following the opening of the Chester–**Holyhead Railway** in 1848. From 1870 to 1922, its **Congregational** minister was the author and editor Dr Evan (Pan) Jones.

LLANBADARN FAWR, Ceredigion
(314 ha; 2899 inhabitants)
Located immediately east of **Aberystwyth**, Llanbadarn was the site of a *clas* church, associated with St **Padarn**. In the late 11th century, the work of Rhigyfarch (d.1099) and Ieuan (d.1137), sons of Bishop **Sulien** of **St David's**, ensured that Llanbadarn was then the chief centre of native Welsh ecclesiastical culture. St Padarn's church (13th century and 1869–84), which can seat 700 worshippers, has on occasion been suggested as the cathedral for a mid-Wales **Anglican diocese**. It contains an informative exhibition which includes two inscribed stones of the 9th–11th centuries. The original **parish** of Llanbadarn extended over much of northern **Ceredigion**, and its **tithes** represented considerable wealth; they were for centuries the property of the notorious tithe-mongers, the Chichester family of Arlington, Devon. Llanbadarn's subordinate churches and chapels eventually became separate parishes. The church, in which **Dafydd ap Gwilym** ogled the girls, contains the grave of Lewis Morris (1701–65; *see* **Morris Brothers**) and memorials to the **Pryse family (Gogerddan)** the **Powell family (Nanteos)** and the Pugh family of Abermad and Lovesgrove. One of the most prominent plaques in St Paul's Cathedral, Calcutta, states that the Indian administrators, the Pugh brothers, had been taken back for burial 'to the land of their fathers at Llanbadarn Fawr in Wales'. The **community** contains the Welsh Institute of Rural Studies, Aberystwyth's department of information and library studies, and Coleg Ceredigion. In 2001, 59.76% of the inhabitants of Llanbadarn Fawr had no knowledge at all of **Welsh**, making it, linguistically, the most Anglicized of all the communities of Ceredigion.

LLANBADARN FAWR, Radnorshire,
Powys (1476 ha; 654 inhabitants)
A **community** consisting of a tract of undulating land north-east of **Llandrindod**, its church was restored by S. W. Williams of **Rhayader** who, as the *Shell Guide to Mid Wales* put it, 'built at least five rather ugly churches in this part of **Radnorshire**'. However, the Romanesque tympanum above the south door survives; it is one of only two in Wales and is adorned with two lively animals resembling lions. **Giraldus Cambrensis** sought sanctuary in the church in 1176. A bare-knuckle fight (for a prize of £50) took place in Llanbadarn Fawr as late as 1896.

LLANBADARN FYNYDD, Radnorshire,
Powys (6010 ha; 323 inhabitants)
A tract of hill country astride the **Llandrindod–Newtown road** (the A483), the area was described by Samuel Lewis as 'dreary and wild'. There is a group of **Bronze Age** barrows on Rhiw Porthnant, and a ringwork and the platform sites of four ancient houses at Castell-y-Blaidd. The glory of the

community is the screen of *c.*1500 in the tiny church at Llananno. Both lavish and delicate, it is one of the very few surviving examples of the work of the **Newtown** school of screen-carvers and is among Wales's greatest treasures. Castelltinboeth, located at 410 m above the River Ithon, was among the highest castles in Wales. As it stands, the name may mischievously be translated as 'hot arse castle'. But the standard Welsh form is Castell Dinbawd, which possibly derives from *twmpath* (hillock, mound).

LLANBADOC, Monmouthshire
(2569 ha; 887 inhabitants)
Located immediately west of **Usk**, the **community** is dominated by the arsenal of Glascoed, established during the **Second World War**. Near it is the **Gwent** Tertiary College complex, originally the **Monmouthshire** Institute of **Agriculture**. The toll house by the **Usk** bridge is dated 1837.

LLANBADRIG, Isle of Anglesey
(1371 ha; 1392 inhabitants)
Located immediately west of **Amlwch**, the **community**'s chief feature is the **Wylfa Nuclear Power Station**, opened in 1971. Coming upon the station's vast bulk, set against sea and sky, is an astonishing experience. **Cemaes**, an early Christian site and the centre of a medieval *cantref*, is a substantial village. Clustered around its attractive harbour, it was formerly a centre of brick making and **shipbuilding** and of the importation of timber – a commodity scarce in **Anglesey**. Dinas Gynfor is a substantial **Iron Age** promontory fort. Middle Mouse (Ynys Badrig; *see* **Islands**) is the northernmost part of Wales. St Padrig's church, restored in 1884, contains **Islam**ic-style tiles installed by the Muslim convert Baron Stanley of Alderley (*see* **Trearddur**). In 2007 the **Llangefni**-based cooking oil producer Calon Lân established Wales's first commercial olive grove at Llanbadrig; the planting was inspired by the belief that global warming would ensure the profitability of the plantation, which is believed to be the most northerly olive grove in Europe.

LLANBEBLIG BOOK OF HOURS, The
The only 'Book of Hours' of certain Welsh provenance, this late 14th-century manuscript, preserved in the **National Library**, was written in **England** for a Welsh patron, probably Isobel Godynough of Llanbeblig (*see* **Caernarfon**). Four folios of full-page miniatures were added locally, a rare example of Welsh manuscript art; they include a possible representation of **Magnus Maximus**.

LLANBEDR, Gwynedd (5031 ha; 531 inhabitants)
Located south of **Harlech**, the **community** contains the summits of Rhinog Fawr (720 m) and Rhinog Fach (712 m), the core of the **Harlech** Dome (*see* **Rhinogydd**). In the range are two passes, age-old routes offering access to **Ardudwy**; the northernmost follows a medieval track erroneously known as the **Roman** Steps, and the southernmost leads to Y Crawcwellt (*see* **Trawsfynydd**) via Bwlch Drws Ardudwy. Cwm Nantcol leads to the southern pass; in it is Maes-y-garnedd, the home of the regicide **John Jones** (?1597–1660). Salem **Baptist** chapel was the setting for Curnow Vosper's iconic **painting** *Salem*. The village of Llanbedr stands on the banks of the Artro, which rises in

the delectable Llyn Cwm Bychan. The standing stone near the village is one of the tallest in Wales (3.3 m). Across the **river** from it is the former airfield of the Royal Aerospace Establishment. Shell Island (Ynys Mochras), with its wildlife, camping and **sailing** facilities, is a peninsula popular with visitors. South of it is one of Wales's few official nudist areas.

LLANBEDR DYFFRYN CLWYD, Denbighshire (1649 ha; 866 inhabitants)

Located immediately east of **Ruthin**, the **community** contains the large **hill-forts** of Foel Fenlli and Moel y Gaer. St Peter's church (1863) replaced an earlier church, whose ruins stand nearby. It contains several neo-classical funereal monuments, including one sculpted by **John Gibson** in Rome (1863). St Meugan's church, Llanrhydd, Ruthin's mother church, contains a rood screen and numerous funereal monuments. The sculptor Robert Wynne (c.1655–1731) was a native of Llanbedr. Bathafarn, the home of Edward Jones (1778–1837), a pioneer of Welsh **Wesleyan Methodism**, gave its name to the denomination's historical journal. Llanbedr Hall was the home of Joseph Ablett (1773–1848), philanthropist and friend of Southey and Wordsworth; later it became a sanatorium, which was bought in 1918 by the medical pioneer **Hugh Morriston Davies**. The splendidly sited Castell Gyrn, seemingly a medieval tower, was built in 1977.

LLANBEDROG, Gwynedd (929 ha; 1020 inhabitants)

Located immediately south-west of **Pwllheli**, the **community**'s main settlement, the substantial village of Llanbedrog, overlooks a delightful bay. St Pedrog's church, largely 15th century, contains a minstrels' gallery. In the early 20th century, a **horse tram**way was built connecting Llanbedrog to Pwllheli. It carried visitors to Glynyweddw (the widow's glen), built in 1856 as the dower house of the Love Jones-Parry family of Madryn (see **Buan**). It was later turned into an **art gallery** by Solomon Andrews, Pwllheli's developer. Now once more a gallery, it specializes in modern work; courses are also held there. Near the community's western boundary stands Capel Newydd, built in 1769 for the congregation founded by Richard Edwards of Nanhoron (d.1704; see **Botwnnog**). Believed to be the north's oldest **Nonconformist** chapel, it was restored in 1958 and is safeguarded by a trust. The historic Penyberth farmhouse was demolished in 1936 to make way for an RAF airfield, the scene on 8 September 1936 of an arson attack (see **Penyberth Bombing School, The burning of**). Following the **Second World War**, a home for Polish refugees (see **Poles**) was established there. In 2001, the average age of Llanbedrog's inhabitants was 52.11 years – the highest in Wales.

LLANBERIS, Gwynedd (4614 ha; 2018 inhabitants)

Located at the foot of the **Snowdon** massif, the **community** embraces the upper reaches of the basin of the Seiont (or Saint). Although the highest point of the massif – Yr Wyddfa (1085 m) – lies within the community of **Betws Garmon**, Llanberis is considered to be the place most intimately linked with the **mountain**. The Llanberis Pass has traditionally offered the main route through the heart of **Snowdonia**, a fact recognized by **Llywelyn ap Iorwerth**, who commissioned the building of Dolbadarn Castle (c.230) to guard access to the pass. Strategically sited on a spur between Llyn Peris and Llyn Padarn (see **Lakes**), the castle's round tower served as the prison for Owain, eldest brother of **Llywelyn ap Gruffudd**. It was one of the favourite subjects of the artists of the **Romantic** era, **J. M. W. Turner** foremost among them.

Llanberis owed its growth to the Dinorwic (see **Llanddeiniolen**) and Glynrhonwy **slate** quarries. The quarrying community is admirably portrayed in the novels of the Llanberis native **T. Rowland Hughes**. Quarrying developed alongside **tourism**, for the Llanberis Path offered the least arduous route to Yr Wyddfa. Since 1896, **Britain**'s sole rack-and-pinion **railway** has followed much the same 7-km route to the summit. The area offers superb rock climbing, in particular on Clogwyn Du'r Arddu. With its mountaineering equipment shops and bunkhouses, Llanberis is the closest Wales has to an Alpine climbing village; there are plans to make it Britain's chief open-air adventure centre.

LLANBISTER, Radnorshire, Powys (5819 ha; 414 inhabitants)

A tract of hill land on either side the **Llandrindod–Newtown road** (the A483), the **community** represents the core of the *cantref* of **Maelienydd**. Its chief attraction is the unusual church of St Cynllo with its massive tower at the east end, and a flight of steps leading up from the main door to the floor of the church. The woodwork is particularly noteworthy and includes a 15th-century screen and a musicians' gallery dating from 1716. Another unexpected feature is a baptistery for total immersion.

LLANBOIDY, Carmarthenshire (6246 ha; 988 inhabitants)

Extending from **Whitland** to the **Carmarthenshire–Pembrokeshire** border, the **community** contains the villages of Llanboidy and Llanglydwen. Gwal y Filiast, standing near a fine stretch of the **Taf** valley, is a **Neolithic** burial chamber. The **Cistercian** monastery of Whitland stood on the banks of the Gronw in the community's southern extremity. Founded c.1157 and dissolved in 1539, it was the mother house of Cistercianism in *Pura Wallia*. Nothing survives of its buildings apart from some grassy footings. The Georgian mansion Maesgwynne, once the centre of the 1500-ha estate of the Powell family, is now a farmhouse. In St Brynach's churchyard, a member of the family, W. R. H. Powell (1819–89), is commemorated by a monument carved by **Goscombe John**. St Clydwen's church, Llanglydwen, contains memorials to the Protheroe family of Dolwilym mansion, which has long been derelict. Llanboidy **cheese** enjoys a high reputation.

LLANBRADACH AND PWLLYPANT (Llanbradach a Phwll-y-pant), Caerphilly (622 ha; 4622 inhabitants)

Lying immediately north of **Caerphilly**, the **community**'s streets, which fill the floor of the **Rhymney** valley, were erected to accommodate workers at the Llanbradach

Colliery, which operated from 1894 to 1961. Its focal point is the tower of the abandoned church of All Saints (1897). Llanbradach Fawr, originally built in the 16th century, was the home of the wealthy Thomas family of local squires.

LLANBRYNMAIR (Llanbryn-mair),

Montgomeryshire, Powys (12,954 ha; 958 inhabitants)
Located east of the **Dyfi** valley, this vast **community** is 18 km from north to south. Notable for its craftsmen, peasant poets (*see bardd gwlad*), and **Congregationalists**, Llanbrynmair's original centre (Llan) is 2 km south of the modern village. Richard Haslam notes that the 15th-century hilltop church of St Mary's has benefited from the fact that it 'has never been tidied up by learned architects'. The old Congregational chapel (yr Hen Gapel, founded in 1729) is celebrated in a sonnet by **Iorwerth Peate**, first curator of the Welsh Folk Museum (*see* **St Fagans**). Others raised in the Old Chapel include the encyclopaedist **Abraham Rees** (1743–1825), and the ministers and editors **John Roberts** (J. R.; 1804–84) and his brother **Samuel Roberts** (S. R.; 1800–85). The landlord's treatment of the Roberts family, tenants of Y Diosg, was described in S. R.'s *Diosg Farm* (1854), a notable anti-landlord tract (*see* **Gentry and Landlords**). The **Methodist** historian Richard Bennett (1860–1937) was a native of Llanbrynmair.

Tafolwern, the caput of **Cyfeiliog**, a motte-and-bailey castle probably erected by **Owain Cyfeiliog** *c.*1150, stands near the modern village. The **railway** to Machynlleth runs through the Talerddig cutting, the deepest rock cutting in the world at the time of its completion in 1861 by David

Davies (*see* **Davies family (Llandinam)**). In the **mountains** to the south are the few houses that remain of Dylife, the 19th-century **lead**-mining centre, where 500 workers lived in barracks. There are large wind farms (*see* **Windmills**) on Trannon Moor and Mynydd Cemaes.

LLANCARFAN, Vale of Glamorgan

(2597 ha; 736 inhabitants)
Located south of the A48, east of **Cowbridge**, the **community** contains the settlements of Llancarfan, Llantrithyd, Llancadle, Llanbethery, Tre-Aubrey, Moulton, Walterston and Pen-onn – places in which late 20th-century development is less evident than it is elsewhere in the **Vale of Glamorgan**. Llancarfan (originally Nantcarfan) was the seat of a *clas* associated with St **Cadog**. The extensive churchyard of St Cadog's – a large and airy building of the 13th and 14th centuries – may represent the monastic enclosure. Following the **Norman** invasion, the *clas* was granted to St Peter's **Benedictine** monastery at Gloucester. In its twilight years, it was associated with **Caradog** of Llancarfan and with Lifris, author of a life of St Cadog. Members of the *clas* may have been involved in the compilation of *Liber Landavensis* (*The Book of Llandaff*). The area is rich in historic monuments, among them Castle Ditches **hill-fort**, the **Roman**ized farm at Moulton, the ringwork at Moulton and houses with medieval or early modern features at Garnllwyd, Walterston-fawr, Tregruff, Crosstown and Llanvithyn. The community's most fascinating feature is the ruined Llantrithyd Place, built in the early 16th century and embellished in the early 17th century. The outline of its **garden** survives. St **Illtud**'s church,

Llanberis Pass

Llantrithyd, has a 14th-century chancel arch and fine monuments to the Basset and Aubrey families. Iolo Morganwg (**Edward Williams**) was born at Pennon.

LLANDDANIEL FAB (Llanddaniel-fab),
Isle of Anglesey (1349 ha; 699 inhabitants)
Located immediately south-west of **Llanfair Pwllgwyngyll**, the **community** contains the splendid **Neolithic** henge and chambered tomb, Bryn Celli Ddu. A mound surmounts an 8.2-m passage which leads to a polygonal chamber 2.4 m wide and roofed by two cover stones. Plas Newydd was the centre of the 2500-ha **Anglesey** estate which the **Paget family** (the Bayly family until 1769) acquired through marriage from a branch of the **Griffith family (Penrhyn)**. The house, owned by the **National Trust**, was rebuilt (1795–1806) by James Wyatt for Henry Bayly Paget, co-owner of the **Mynydd Parys copper** mine (*see* **Amlwch**). It contains the artifical leg designed by Henry William Paget, first marquess of Anglesey (1815), to replace the limb he lost at Waterloo, and a famous series of murals by Rex Whistler (1936–7). The **gardens** were designed by Humphrey Repton. Plas Coch, built in 1569 for the local benefactor David Hughes (d.1609), is a good example of the smaller Elizabethan country house. One of the six ferries across the **Menai Strait** operated from Moel-y-don.

LLANDDAROG, Carmarthenshire
(1655 ha; 1095 inhabitants)
Located south-east of **Carmarthen** and bisected by the A48, the **community** contains the villages of Llanddarog and Porthyrhyd. The spire of St Twrog's church (1856) is a prominent landmark. Adjoining it is the White Hart Inn with its thatched roof, by the 20th century an uncommon sight in **Carmarthenshire**. While the Capel Newydd **Calvinistic Methodist** congregation was founded in 1795, the chapel itself dates from 1903. In a poll held in 2002, Llanddarog was declared to be the friendliest place in Wales.

LLANDDEINIOLEN, Gwynedd
(4153 ha; 4885 inhabitants)
The **community** extends from the eastern boundary of **Caernarfon** to Elidir Fawr (924 m). The community contains the villages of Bethel, Brynrefail, Clwt-y-bont, Dinorwic, Rhiwlas, Penisa'r Waun, and – the largest of them – Deiniolen, originally called Ebenezer. Dinas Dinorwig is a circular **Iron Age hill-fort**. Below it is Ffynnon Cegin Arthur, unsuccessfully promoted in the mid-19th century as a spa. Llanddeiniolen church was rebuilt in 1843. **W. J. Gruffydd** is buried in the churchyard, which contains the yew tree he eulogized in the poem 'Ywen Llanddeiniolen'.

At the community's south-eastern corner are the vast galleries of the Dinorwic quarry. Intensive exploitation of its **slate** began in 1809. Following the closure of the quarry in 1969, its workshops became the core of the National Slate Museum, part of the **National Museum [of] Wales**. A section of the **railway** that served the quarry has been reopened as a tourist attraction. It hugs the **lake** shore of Llyn Padarn. The community contains the ingenious Dinorwic hydroelectric power station, opened in 1984. At times when there is little demand for electricity, water is pumped from Llyn Peris (100 m above sea level) to Llyn Marchlyn Mawr (580 m above sea level); at times of high demand, water is released back to Llyn Peris to work the generators. Europe's largest pumped storage scheme, its machine hall could accommodate **London**'s St Paul's Cathedral (*see* **Energy** and **Engineering**). At the lower end

The galleries of the Dinorwic quarry beside Llyn Padarn, Llanddeiniolen, Gwynedd

of Llyn Padarn is Penllyn, home to the Amazonian Marged uch Ifan (**Margaret Evans**).

LLANDDERFEL, Gwynedd
(11,533 ha; 1052 inhabitants)

Located north and east of **Bala**, the **community** consists of the pre-1974 civil **parish** of Llandderfel and part of that of Llanfor. Llanfor was the largest of all Wales's pre-1974 civil parishes (13,280 ha). Within the community are the villages of Llandderfel and Llanfor and the hamlets of Bethel, Cefnddwysarn, Cwmtirmynach, Frongoch, Sarnau and Glan-yr-afon. The church of Derfel Gadarn, heavily restored in the 1870s, was a place of **pilgrimage**. The wooden image of the **saint** was burned in **London** in 1538, but the part of the shrine known as St Derfel's Horse survives. Llanfor is mentioned in the poems of **Llywarch Hen**. St Deiniol's church, Llanfor (1874), adjoins the mausoleum of the **Price family (Rhiwlas)**, financed by the winnings of one of the family's **horses**, Bendigo, in the Kempton Park jubilee race of 1887. In 1873, R. J. Lloyd Price (1843–1923) of Rhiwlas invented **sheepdog trials**, and in 1887 he started a **whisky** distillery at Frongoch; in 1916, it became the **Frongoch Internment Camp**. The community contains part of Llyn Celyn, the **reservoir** created following the controversial drowning of the **Tryweryn Valley**. A memorial chapel to the destroyed village of Capel Celyn stands on the **reservoir** bank – so also does a plaque commemorating **Quakers** from **Penllyn** who emigrated to **Pennsylvania** in the late 17th century. International canoeing competitions take place on the Tryweryn. Crogen, a late medieval house, was enlarged in 1800. Pale Hall (1870), now a hotel, was built by the **railway** magnate Henry Robertson; Queen Victoria stayed at Pale in 1887. **T. E. Ellis** is buried at Cefnddwysarn.

LLANDDEUSANT, Carmarthenshire
(6152 ha; 233 inhabitants)

Located south of **Llandovery** and extending to the **Carmarthenshire–Breconshire** border, the **community** contains **Llyn y Fan Fach**, which features in one of Wales's best-known folk tales. Above the **lake** are the summits of Bannau Sir Gaer, part of the **Black Mountain**. The church of St Simon and St Jude (14th and 15th centuries) has a plastered barrel roof. The writer **Ernest Lewis Thomas** (Richard Vaughan; 1904–83), a native of Llanddeusant, portrayed Black Mountain life in his novels.

LLANDDEW (Llan-ddew), Breconshire, Powys
(918 ha; 246 inhabitants)

A **community** located immediately north of **Brecon**, Llanddew was the site of a **Celtic** monastery or *clas*. The bishop of **St David's** established a residence there in the 12th century. **Giraldus Cambrensis** came to live in it in 1175 on his appointment as archdeacon of Brecon; only ruins now remain of his 'place suited for meditation and work'. The ecclesiastical importance of Llanddew is reflected in the substantial Holy Trinity church which contains a fine 13th-century chancel with two squints. Pytindu (together with Pytingwyn and Pytinglas in **Honddu Isaf**) is one of the three mottes built in the 1090s by Roger Peyton.

LLANDDEWI BREFI (Llanddewibrefi),
Ceredigion (11,343 ha; 723 inhabitants)

The most extensive **community** in **Ceredigion**, Llanddewi Brefi extends from the **Teifi** valley to the upper **Tywi**. St **David**'s church (13–14th and late 19th centuries) stands on an early Christian site attested by 6 inscribed stones of the 6th–9th centuries (*see* **Monuments, Early Christian**). The natural mound on which the church stands is by tradition that which rose under David when preaching. (As the area has such a proliferation of hills, in the history of miracles, can there be anything more uncalled-for than the creation of a hill at Llanddewi?) In 1287, Bishop **Bek** of **St David's** reorganized the church as a college of secular canons, serving 13 of the surrounding churches. In 1346, an anonymous anchorite of Llanddewi copied a valuable collection of **Welsh** religious texts, now preserved in the Bodleian Library at **Oxford** (*see Book of the Anchorite, The*). The **Roman** fort of Bremia at Llanio was occupied from AD *c*.75 to *c*.160. The last interment at the Werndriw **Quaker** burial ground took place in 1790. Soar y Mynydd (1828) is the remotest chapel in Wales. The community contains the dam of Llyn Brianne, a **reservoir** completed in 1973. The notion that there is only one gay man in Llanddewi Brefi has attained mythical status.

LLANDDEWI VELFREY (Llanddewi Felffre),
Pembrokeshire (1630 ha; 348 inhabitants)

Straddling the A40 immediately south-west of **Whitland**, the **community**, with that of Lampeter Velfrey, constitutes the greater part of the medieval **commote** of **Efelffre**. Llanddewi Gaer is a massive **Iron Age** inland promontory fort. St **David**'s church was almost entirely rebuilt in the later 19th century. A far more interesting building is the **Baptist** chapel, built in 1832 for a congregation founded in 1723. In the 17th century, the area was a **Quaker** stronghold and the home of Lewis David who, in 1681, purchased land in **Pennsylvania** for the settlement of **Pembrokeshire** Quakers.

LLANDDEWI YSTRADENNY (Llanddewi
Ystradenni), Radnorshire, Powys
(2503 ha; 301 inhabitants)

Straddling the Ithon north of **Llandrindod**, the **community** contains two **hill-forts** on Cwm Cefn-y-gaer. The remote and picturesquely situated Castell Cymaron was the principal centre of the **Mortimer** family in **Maelienydd**. Built for Hugh Mortimer (d.1181), it was rebuilt in 1195 and captured by **Llywelyn ap Iorwerth** in 1202. Dolydre is a fine 17th-century cruck-framed building. In 2001, 88.28% of the community's inhabitants had no knowledge at all of **Welsh**, making it, linguistically, the most Anglicized community in **Powys**.

LLANDDOGED AND MAENAN (Llanddoged a
Maenan), Conwy (1971 ha; 574 inhabitants)

A **community** located on the east bank of the **Conwy** immediately north of **Llanrwst**, until 1974 the area represented an eastern protuberance of **Caernarfonshire**. The double-naved church of St Doged in the compact village of Llanddoged retains its box pews and unusual triple-decker pulpit. Of the **Cistercian** monastery, moved from **Conwy** to Maenan in 1283, virtually nothing survives. It stood near

Driving sheep across the bridge over the Tywi at Llandeilo in 1903

the present-day Maenan Abbey Hotel. A medieval house called Maenan stood on monastic land. Restored by Lord Aberconway (*see* **Eglwysbach**), it contains noteworthy 16th-century plasterwork.

LLANDDONA, Isle of Anglesey
(1621 ha; 639 inhabitants)
Located immediately north of **Beaumaris**, the **community** hugs the south-eastern side of Red Wharf Bay (Traeth Coch). Bwrdd Arthur is an impressive **Iron Age hill-fort**, but the principal landmark is the mast of a television transmitter. The churches of Llaniestyn (14th century), Llanfihangel Dinsylwy (15th century) and Llanddona (1873) are all on isolated sites.

LLANDDOWROR, Carmarthenshire
(2878 ha; 809 inhabitants)
Located south-west of **Carmarthen** and bisected by the Carmarthen–**Tenby road** (the A477), the **community** contains the villages of Llanddowror and Llanmiloe. St **Teilo**'s church retains its 15th-century tower; its nave and chancel were rebuilt in 1865. Within in it is the tomb of **Griffith Jones**, rector of Llanddowror from 1716 to 1761 and pioneer of literacy in Wales. Llanmiloe is essentially an extension of **Pendine**. Cwmbrwyn is the site of the westernmost known **Roman** villa in Wales.

LLANDDULAS AND RHYD-Y-FOEL (Llanddulas a Rhyd-y-foel), Conwy (512 ha; 1572 inhabitants)
Wedged between **Abergele** and the eastern suburbs of **Colwyn Bay**, the **community** stands under the shadow of

Pen-y-corddyn-mawr **hill-fort** with its impressive guard chambers. The dominant local feature is the astonishing Gwrych Castle (1816–53). With its lodges and curtain walls, the castle extends for almost 2 km, and is as much a folly as a dwelling place. It was built for Lloyd Bamford Hesketh, who also commissioned the attractive church of St Cynbryd (1869) and the fine ecclesiastical grouping at **Kinmel Bay and Tywyn**. In 2007, plans were announced to convert Gwrych Castle into a 5-star hotel. **Lewis Valentine** (1893–1986), first president of **Plaid [Genedlaethol] Cymru**, was a native of Llanddulas.

LLANDDYFNAN, Isle of Anglesey
(4323 ha; 1027 inhabitants)
Located immediately east and north of **Llangefni**, the **community** contains the villages of Talwrn, Llangwyllog and Capel Coch. Mynydd Bodafon (178 m), a place of complex settlement, rises steeply from the surrounding undulating land. Interesting houses include Marian (16th century), Plas Llanddyfnan (16th and 18th centuries) and Plas Tregayan (17th century). The vast Hirdre-faig mansion (18th century and earlier) has been demolished. The four **Morris brothers** were born near Maenaddwyn between 1701 and 1706.

LLANDEGLA, Denbighshire
(4219 ha; 494 inhabitants)
Located south-east of **Ruthin**, the **community** extends to the heights of Cyrn-y-Brain (563 m), and contains the Red Grouse Country Park. St Tegla's **Well** was much resorted to by sufferers from epilepsy (*see* **Wells of the Saints**). Tomen

y Rhodwydd, a fine motte-and-bailey castle, was probably built by **Owain Gwynedd** in 1147. St Tegla's church (1866) contains a late medieval brass candelabra of a quality almost equal to that at **Llanarmon-yn-Ial**. Bodidris Hotel was originally built *c.*1600. The novelist **E. Tegla Davies** (1880–1967) was born at Hen Giât, Llandegla.

LLANDEILO, Carmarthenshire
(515 ha; 1731 inhabitants)
Located in the heart of the **Tywi** valley, the **community** consists of what were, until 1974, the **urban district** of Llandeilo and the civil **parish** of Llandyfeisant. In the 6th century, **Teilo** established a *clas* or **Celt**ic monastery at Llandeilo, which became the greatest of the so-called Teilo churches. Because of Teilo's links with **Llandaff**, that **diocese** sought to gain possession of Llandeilo and much of eastern **Deheubarth**. The present church was rebuilt between 1848 and 1850, although it retains its 13th-century tower. Within it are two stone crosses carved *c.*900 (*see* **Monuments, Early Christian**). *The Book of St Chad* (also known as *The Book of St Teilo*; *c.*750), which contains the earliest examples of written **Welsh**, may have had its origins at Llandeilo.

Dinefwr, traditionally considered to be the chief seat of the rulers of Deheubarth, is located 2 km west of St Teilo's church. Dinefwr Castle, which dates largely from the late 12th and early 13th centuries, was the work of **Rhys ap Gruffudd** (the Lord Rhys; d.1197) and his descendants; adjoining it was a Welsh **borough**, nothing of which survives. Following the seizure of the castle by the English crown in 1277, an English borough – Newton – was founded to its north. In the 1490s, the castle was granted to **Rhys ap Thomas**. He eventually abandoned it in favour of a new mansion at Newton, which became the seat of his descendants, the Rice family, Barons Dynevor. The present house (1660s, 1850s) became the property of the **National Trust** in 1989. In the park, which was praised by Lancelot (Capability) Brown in 1775, are white **cattle** traditionally associated with the legend of **Llyn y Fan Fach**. In 2003, archaeologists discovered the remains of two **Roman** forts in the park, one of which, covering nearly 4 ha, is the largest in Wales apart from the legionary fortress at **Caerleon**. An important agricultural and trading centre for the Tywi valley, Llandeilo was the headquarters of Dinefwr District (1974–96). When it was completed in 1848, the 44-m bridge across the Tywi was one of the longest single-arched bridges in **Britain**. The line of houses climbing the hill rising north of the bridge forms an attractive townscape.

LLANDINAM, Montgomeryshire, Powys
(7070 ha; 942 inhabitants)
Located between **Llanidloes** and **Newtown**, the **community** extends over an attractive stretch of the **Severn** valley. St Llonio's stands on the site of a *clas* or **Celt**ic monastery. The church, remodelled in 1865, retains medieval features. Llandinam village has won several best-kept village awards. David Davies (1818–90; *see* **Davies family (Llandinam)**), **railway** pioneer, **coal**owner, builder of **Barry** Docks and MP, was born at Draintewion. His statue, a replica of that at Barry, stands near Llandinam bridge

(1846), **Montgomeryshire**'s earliest **iron** bridge. In 1864, he built Broneirion, later a Girl Guide study centre. His wealth endowed Llandinam with one of Wales's most elaborate **Calvinistic Methodist** chapels (1873). In 1884, he bought the neo-medieval Plas Dinam (1874), which continues to be occupied by his descendants, the Barons Davies. Plasdinam Hall, first built *c.*1680, contains attractive half-timbered features.

Cefn Carnedd is one of Wales's most impressive **hillforts**. Rhos Ddiarbed, a motte which gave its name to Moat Lane (*see* **Caersŵs**), was probably built (*c.*1082) by Roger de **Montgomery**. **Howel Harris** and **John Wesley** stayed at Tyddyn, a farmhouse on the community's western boundary. Llandinam's wind farm (*see* **Windmills**), with its 104 generators, is the largest in Wales.

LLANDISSILIO WEST (Llandysilio),
Pembrokeshire (707 ha; 475 inhabitants)
Hugging the **Pembrokeshire–Carmarthenshire** boundary north of **Narberth**, the **community** is bisected by the **Tenby–Cardigan** road (the A478). St Tysil's church, largely rebuilt in the 1890s, contains a 5th-century inscribed stone commemorating Clutorix (Clodri), perhaps a king of **Dyfed**.

LLANDOUGH (Llandoche), Vale of Glamorgan
(162 ha; 1920 inhabitants)
A commuter settlement located immediately north of **Penarth**, the **community** is dominated by its 1934 neo-classical hospital, which boasts the longest corridor in Europe. Llandough was an important early medieval ecclesiastical

Llandinam's statue of David Davies, a replica of the statue at Barry

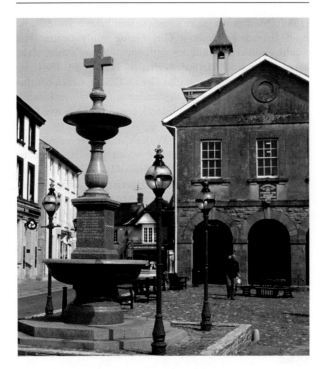

The Town Hall and Market Square, Llandovery

site. As at **Llantwit Major**, the monastery lay near the remains of a **Roman** villa, thus sparking conjecture about the relationship between Roman and post-Roman territorial organization. The present church dates from 1865, and has a dramatic brick interior; in the churchyard is a 3-m high cross bearing the name Irbic, an impressive decorated monument of *c*.1000.

LLANDOVERY (Llanymddyfri), Carmarthenshire
(1914 ha; 2235 inhabitants)

Located where the **Tywi** leaves the uplands and turns south-westwards towards its lush valley, the **community** consists of what were until 1974 the **borough** of Llandovery and the civil **parish** of Llandingad. Seized by the **Normans** (*c*.1116), who built a motte-and-bailey castle there, Llandovery was later recovered by the rulers of **Deheubarth**. In 1277, it came into the possession of Edward I. He granted it to John Giffard who was chiefly responsible for the masonry castle, little of which survives. In October 1401, Henry IV was at Llandovery witnessing the execution of Llywelyn ap Gruffudd Fychan of **Caeo**, one of the allies of **Owain Glyndŵr**. Llywelyn is commemorated by a dignified stainless steel memorial on the castle mound.

Llandovery had two parish churches. St Dingad (1906 with a medieval tower) was from 1602 until his death in 1644 in the care of **Rhys Prichard** (the old vicar) whose religious verse was first published in 1659. The 12th-century St Mary, built on the site of a **Roman** fort, was known as Llanfair-ar-y-bryn. (That church should not be confused with the St Mary's church built within the present community of **Llanfair-ar-y-bryn** in 1883.) The **hymn**writer and evangelist **William Williams** (Pantycelyn; 1717–91) is buried in the churchyard of Llandovery's St Mary's. The English Methodist chapel (1886) in High Street commemorates him.

In the 18th and early 19th centuries, Llandovery was an important centre for the **drovers**. It also became a **banking** centre; the Black Ox Bank (1799) was acquired by Lloyds Bank in 1909. In 1829, William Rees of the nearby small mansion of Tonn established a **printing** press at Llandovery. Responsible for such works as Charlotte **Guest**'s translation of *The Mabinogion*, it became the most distinguished press of 19th-century Wales. The press and some of its publications are exhibited in the Llandovery Heritage Centre. The town's attractive market hall was built in 1840. A monument alongside the A40 commemorates a mail coach which toppled into the Gwydderig River. Llandovery College was founded in 1848 by Thomas Phillips, who had been a physician in India. Phillips had intended it to be a distinctly Welsh institution, but the college eventually came to conform to the norms of the English public school.

LLANDOW (Llandŵ), Vale of Glamorgan
(1594 ha; 754 inhabitants)

Located immediately west of **Cowbridge**, the **community** contains the villages of Llandow, Llysworney, Sigingstone (*see also* **Aviation**) and Llanmihangel. Llandow village, with its **Norman** church, medieval Church Farm and 18th-century Great House, has a strongly historical atmosphere. To its south lies Sutton, one of the seats of the Turberville family and among the finest of **Glamorgan**'s 16th-century houses. Llandow Industrial Estate occupies the site of a former RAF station. Near it is a **motor sports** circuit. North of Llandow lies Stembridge Farm, which, until the abolition of civil **parishes** in 1974, constituted the smallest such parish in Wales; in 1971, it had 5 inhabitants.

Llysworney, as the centre of the **cantref** of **Gwrinydd**, enjoyed territorial significance prior to Norman colonization. The village clusters around St Tydfil's church, and among its attractions are the 16th-century Carne Arms and the 17th-century Moat Farm. Nash Manor to the south was once owned by the bishops of Llandaff, but after the **Reformation** became a seat of the recusant **Carne** family.

The finest building in the community is Llanmihangel Place with its magnificent first-floor hall, splendid chimney pieces and superb panelling. Of early 16th-century origins, its complicated design seems to have been influenced by defensive needs. Adjoining it is a magnificent Elizabethan barn of seven bays. Built by the Thomas family, Llanmihangel Place was bought in *c*.1687 by the **Nonconformist** businessman Humphrey Edwin. Elected lord mayor of **London** in 1697, his attendance at a dissenting chapel in full mayoral livery led the **Tories** to strengthen legislation excluding Nonconformists from public office. There is a memorial to him in Llanmihangel church. In 1950, Sigingstone witnessed Wales's worst **aviation** disaster (*see* **Sigingstone Aviation Disaster**).

LLANDRILLO, Denbighshire
(6231 ha; 587 inhabitants)

Located east of **Bala**, the **community** embraces the Ceidiog basin and extends from the **Dee** valley to the highest point of the **Berwyn Mountains** at Cadair Berwyn (827 m). Together with the communities of **Betws Gwerfil Goch**,

Corwen, Cynwyd and Gwyddelwern, Llandrillo constituted the commote of Edeirnion, which until 1974 was part of Merioneth. The poet Llygad Gŵr (fl.1256–93) was court poet at Hendwr, which was also the home of Dafydd ab Ieuan ab Einion (fl.1440–68) who, during the Wars of the Roses, held Harlech Castle for the house of Lancaster (1460–8). St Trillo's church has an attractive spire.

LLANDRINDOD WELLS (Llandrindod),
Radnorshire, Powys (1268 ha; 5024 inhabitants)

Llandrindod's saline and sulphur springs were discovered in the 17th century. In 1756, their medicinal benefits were publicized in a book by Dr Wessel Linden. Their efficacy was graphically described in a manuscript compiled by an interested but surreptitious observer of the consequences of 'taking the waters'. Llandrindod's virtues were trumpeted in the *Gentleman's Magazine*, and Llandrindod Hall was converted into a hotel offering balls, concerts and billiards, and providing luxury goods in a series of small shops. Visitors to the Race Balls of the 1750s would have found Llandrindod a lively town, but this very liveliness proved its undoing. Undesirable characters were attracted and gaming for large sums became common; £70,000 is said to have changed hands during one session at the hotel, which closed in 1787.

Llandrindod's fortunes began to revive in the early 19th century with the rebuilding of the Pump Room, but it was not until the coming of the railway in 1865 that its most successful phase began. Built largely between 1890 and 1910, the town centre has a coherent and orderly air. The waters can still be sampled, but the numerous hotels now cater mainly for conferences and coach tours. Since 1974,

Llandrindod has been the county town of Powys. Its heyday is commemorated annually in the Victorian Festival, which has been held since 1981. Holy Trinity church has been the location of elections of archbishops of the Church in Wales. Within the community are 18 Roman practice camps, the largest group in the Empire.

LLANDRINIO, Montgomeryshire,
Powys (2750 ha; 1137 inhabitants)

Located immediately north of Welshpool, the community contains the villages of Llandrinio, Sarnau and Arddleen (*Arddlin* – the flax garden). St Trunio's church has Romanesque features. Guto'r Glyn (*c.*1435–*c.*1493) described Llandrinio rectory as a moated house with nine rooms. Holy Trinity church, Penrhos, rebuilt in 1845, contains fine neo-Greek monuments. There is a handsome bridge (1775) over the Severn, the earliest stone bridge between the river's source and Shrewsbury. The area has several distinguished houses, among them Trederwen House (*c.*1616), Llandrinio Hall (*c.*1670) and – on the site of the rectory referred to by Guto'r Glyn – Yr Henblas (17th century).

LLANDUDNO, Conwy
(1931 ha; 20.090 inhabitants)

Occupying most of the one-time commote of Creuddyn, the community is located between the Penrhyn and Conwy Bays, and thus has east and west facing coasts. The town of Llandudno, formed like a cradle swinging between the Great and Little Orme, is the best-planned urban centre in Wales and is among the most elegant seaside resorts in Britain.

The promenade at Llandudno

The resources of the Great Orme were extensively exploited during the **Bronze Age** when it was the site of the largest **copper** mine in the world. In the 6th century, St Tudno is reputed to have established a chapel on the Great Orme's north side; on the south side was a residence belonging to the bishops of **Bangor**, commonly called Gogarth Abbey. South of the Little Orme was Penrhyn Old Hall, the home of the Pugh family, one of whose members, the **Roman Catholic** recusant Robert Pugh, was involved in establishing the first **printing** press in Wales. Secretly located in a **cave** on his land, the press was used to print the first part of *Y Drych Cristianogawl* (1586–7). Until the 1850s, the village of Llandudno was dependent on **agriculture**, **fish**ing and the dwindling copper mines, the last of which closed in 1854.

For centuries, the chief building on the Creuddyn peninsula was Gloddaeth, one of the seats of the **Mostyn family**. It was a member of the family, E. M. L. Mostyn (1830–61), who realized the significance of the completion of the Chester–**Holyhead railway** in 1849, in particular for transporting visitors to Llandudno, a development that would much enrich the family. He sponsored the Llandudno Improvement Act (1854), which was the beginning of the resort of Llandudno. Laid out as a grid by the Mostyn estate architect, Owen Williams, its chief glory is its extremely wide promenade backed by a curving line of stucco hotels in a style described by **Clough Williams-Ellis** as 'Pimlico-Palladian'. In its heyday (1880–1910), Llandudno boasted a host of attractions: theatres, a 427-m **pier** (1875), bathing machines, public **gardens**, **golf** links, open-air entertainment at Happy Valley, boat trips to the Isle of **Man**, carriage journeys along the Marine Drive and **tram**way rides (1903) to the summit of the Great Orme. Among visitors were Queen Elizabeth of Romania, and also the Liddell family whose daughter, Alice, was the model for *Alice in Wonderland* – permitting Llandudno to overexploit its somewhat tenuous connection with Lewis Carroll. **Lewis Valentine**, the first president of **Plaid [Genedlaethol] Cymru**, was minister of Tabernacl **Baptist** chapel from 1921 to 1947.

During the **Second World War**, the headquarters of the Inland Revenue was evacuated to Llandudno. With the decline of the British seaside holiday, Llandudno, which has at least a fifth of Wales's total visitor accommodation, has reinvented itself as a conference and coach-touring centre. However, to the German travel writer Peter Sager, Llandudno is in danger of becoming the 'Old Mother Riley of Costa Geriatrica'.

LLANDWROG, Gwynedd
(2991 ha; 2466 inhabitants)

Extending from Y Foryd – the estuary of the Gwyrfai – to the summit of Mynydd Mawr (698 m), the **community** contains the villages of Llandwrog, Carmel, Groeslon and Y Fron. Dinas Dinlle, an **Iron Age hill-fort**, overlooks the attractive Dinas Dinlle beach. Caer Arianrhod, an offshore rock submerged at high tide, features in *The Mabinogion*. As in neighbouring **Llanwnda**, much of the community consists of smallholdings created through encroachment upon **common land**. In 1827, Thomas John Wynn, second Baron Newborough, sought to enclose the land and evict the smallholders. He was thwarted by Griffith Davies (1788–1855), a local smallholder's son, who, through his brilliance as a mathematician, had won influential friends in **London**.

At Glynllifon, the one-time seat of the Newborough family, four successive mansions were erected; the most recent of which is a massive neo-classical pile (1836, enlarged 1890). Its park – which is in the care of Gwynedd **County** Council – is rich in follies, including a fake cromlech. The family built the attractive neo-Gothic church of St Twrog (1860), the centrepiece of the estate village of Llandwrog. Fort Williamsburg (1761) housed the Newborough family's own militia. Belan Fort (1770s onwards) was built to defend the mouth of the **Menai Strait**. When Glynllifon became a college, the fort became the seat of the Newborough family. Across the dunes from it is **Caernarfon Airport**, birthplace of the RAF **Mountain** Rescue Service. The dramatist **John Gwilym Jones** was a native of Groeslon. The scholar **Thomas Parry** was a native of Carmel. The Sain **recording company** is located at Llandwrog.

LLANDYBIE (Llandybïe), Carmarthenshire
(4165 ha; 9634 inhabitants)

Located immediately north of **Ammanford**, the **community** contains the villages of Llandybie, Blaenau, Capel Hendre, Cwmgwili, Pen-y-groes and Saron. The original **parish** was of great antiquity, for its boundaries are those of the *maenor* (*see* **Manor**) of Meddyfnych described in *The Book of St Chad* (*c.*750). St Tybïe's church (13th and 14th centuries) is rich in memorials. Derwydd, one of the houses of **Rhys ap Thomas**, has fine 17th-century fireplaces and panelling. Glynhir mansion, today a **golf** club, was owned by the Huguenot Du Buisson family. Near it, the **Llwchwr** forms a fine **waterfall**.

The belt of Carboniferous **Limestone** which surrounds the south Wales **coal**field is at its most exploitable at Llandybie. The Cilyrychen Limekilns (1857) were designed by the church architect R. K. **Penson**; a splendid example of industrial Gothick, they are still in at least partial operation. It was, however, **coal**mining which gave rise to the community's numerous industrial settlements. Although all the collieries have closed, open-cast mining continues. The Apostolic Church, which emerged following the religious **revival** of 1904–5, has its headquarters at Pen-y-groes (*see* **Pentecostalism**).

LLANDYFAELOG, Carmarthenshire
(3517 ha; 1273 inhabitants)

Located immediately south-east of **Carmarthen**, the **community** contains the villages of Llandyfaelog, Bancycapel, Croesyceiliog, Cwmffrwd and Idole. Within it is a fine stretch of the left bank of the **Tywi**. Gruffydd Dwnn (*c.*1500–*c.*1570), copyist, collector of manuscripts and patron of the bards, lived at Ystradferthyr. Gellilednais was the home of the **Bible** expositor **Peter Williams** (1723–96). Dr David Daniel Davis (1777–1841), who brought Queen Victoria into the world, was born in Llandyfaelog. Carmarthen's **Welsh**-medium secondary school, Ysgol Bro Myrddin, is located within the community.

LLANDYFRIOG (Llandyfrïog), Ceredigion
(2984 ha; 1821 inhabitants)
Located immediately west of **Llandysul**, the **community** contains the villages of Llandyfriog, Aber-banc, Adpar, Henllan and Penrhiw-Llan. Adpar, essentially a suburb of **Newcastle Emlyn**, was part of the **Cardigan Boroughs** constituency, a status it lost in 1742 and regained in 1832. In 1718, Isaac Carter established at Adpar the first legally sanctioned **printing** press in Wales. Cilgwyn (1870s) was the home of the Fitzwilliam family. During the **Second World War**, Italian prisoners of war built a delightful chapel at Henllan. A 3-km length of the Llandysul–Newcastle Emlyn **railway** (1895) has been reopened as a tourist attraction at Henllan, where the **Teifi** valley is at its most attractive.

LLANDYGAI (Llandygái), Gwynedd
(3382 ha; 2522 inhabitants)
Located immediately east of **Bangor**, the **community** extends from the mouth of the Ogwen and along the **river**'s entire left bank to the summit of **Glyder Fawr** (999 m). It includes the botanically important Llyn Idwal and Cwm Idwal, and the Devil's Kitchen and the Idwal Slabs, challenges much appreciated by climbers. An area of early settlement, its lowland is the site of two **Neolithic** henges – one of the largest such sites in Wales. Within the community are the villages of Llandygai and Tregarth and the curiously named hamlets of Dob and Sling. St Tegai's church (15th century, 1853) contains the tomb of **John Williams** (1582–1650), archbishop of York.

The community's most spectacular feature is the Penrhyn Quarry. **Slate** exploitation began there in 1782, and over 200 years of quarrying has produced an astonishing chasm, widely believed to be the only man-made object in Wales visible from the moon. Penrhyn was the scene of the most protracted labour dispute in the history of Wales (see **Penrhyn Lockouts**). The slate was exported from Port Penrhyn. Located on the eastern side of the estuary of the Cegin – the boundary between Bangor and Llandygai – the **port** was linked to the quarry by **horse** tramway in 1800. Adjoining the port is a 12-seater men's lavatory resembling a **dovecote**.

The Penrhyn Quarry was the property of the Douglas-**Pennant family**, Barons Penrhyn, who created a fine example of an estate village at Llandygai. The family residence, Penrhyn Castle, was completed in 1830 to the design of Thomas Hopper. The castle, 190-m long, is a Romanesque fantasy awash with blind arcading, ribs, bosses, chevrons and billets. It became the property of the **National Trust** in 1951.

LLANDYRNOG, Denbighshire
(1804 ha; 962 inhabitants)
Located immediately east of **Denbigh**, the **community** extends to the heights of the **Clwydian Hills**. The double-naved church of St Tyrnog contains a **stained-glass** window illustrating the seven sacraments (c.1500). Plas Ashpool (18th century) was the home of the **Calvinistic Methodist** activist Robert Llwyd (1716–92). A monument notes the site of Tŷ Modlen, where the locality's first Methodist meetings were held. An early Methodist chapel was built at Cefn Bithel (1776). Llandyrnog Creamery is renowned for its mature cheddar **cheese**. Llangwyfan Hospital (1920), one of Wales's largest **tuberculosis** sanatoria, was closed in 1981. Llandyrnog was the home of Gwen ferch Ellis, who in 1594 became the first Welsh **witch** to be executed.

LLANDYSILIO, Montgomeryshire, Powys
(1350 ha; 962 inhabitants)
Located in the north-east corner of **Montgomeryshire**, the **community** hugs the right bank of the Vyrnwy. St Tysilio's church (1868) lies within a circular churchyard. At Four Crosses is the attractive Golden Lion Inn (c.1750). Pentreheylin New Bridge (c.1773) is a well-proportioned structure. There is an **Iron Age hill-fort** (Bryn Mawr) at Pentreheylin and a motte-and-bailey castle (Rhysnant Domen) at Four Crosses.

LLANDYSILIOGOGO, Ceredigion
(4944 ha; 1167 inhabitants)
Located south of **New Quay**, the **community** contains the villages of Bwlch-y-fadfa, **Caerwedros**, Llwyndafydd, Plwmp and Talgarreg. Cwmtydu, a tiny and attractive haven, was once associated with **smuggling**. The community's name combines those two churches: the isolated church of St Tysilio (1890) and Gogof (**cave**), the ancient name of the neighbouring community of **Llangrannog** (the cave concerned is Ogof Crannog). Banc **Siôn Cwilt** is high bare open land. At a bend on the A487 is Ffynnon Ddewi (St **David**'s **Well**). The vagabond poet David Emrys James (Dewi Emrys; 1881–1952) lived at Talgarreg. Bwlch-y-fadfa has one of **Ceredigion**'s chief **Unitarian** chapels.

LLANDYSSIL (Llandysul), Montgomeryshire, Powys (2896 ha; 1218 inhabitants)
Located immediately east of **Newtown**, the **community** contains the villages of Llandyssil, Abermule, Aberbechan and Llanmerewig (Llamyrewig). In 1273, **Llywelyn ap Gruffudd** began to build Dolforwyn Castle on a high ridge above the **Severn** valley – the last castle to be built by a Welsh prince. Edward I considered the castle to be a challenge to the royal stronghold at **Montgomery**. Llywelyn's answer to the king's objection is a valuable statement of his view of his status as Prince of Wales. **Cadw**'s excavations, completed in 2002, revealed that the castle's remains are more extensive than was previously believed. According to **Geoffrey of Monmouth**, Dolforwyn (maiden's meadow) was the place where the maiden Sabrina (Severn) was drowned in the **river** at the behest of an envious queen, Gwendolen.

In the 1920s, the composer Philip Heseltine (Peter Warlock; 1894–1930) lived at Cefn Bryntalch (1869), a house that initiated the Georgian revival of the 1870s. St Tyssil's church was rebuilt in 1866; the porch of an earlier church survives nearby. At St Llwchaiarn's, Llanmerewig, much of the eccentric work of the rector and watercolourist **John Parker** (1798–1860) has been destroyed, but there is enough left to be notable. Abermule primary school (1951) is an innovative building. In 1921, two Cambrian trains collided head-on near Abermule, killing 17 passengers (see **Abermule Train Disaster**).

481

L

LLANDYSUL, Ceredigion
(6670 ha; 2902 inhabitants)

Extending northwards from the **Teifi**, the **community** contains the quasi-town of Llandysul and the villages of Capel Dewi, Horeb, Pont-Siân, Pren-gwyn, Tregroes and Rhydowen. An 18th-century **map** of its regular plots suggests that Llandysul may have been a failed medieval **borough**. The medieval church of St Tysul, much restored, contains a 6th-century inscribed stone, and memorials to the Lloyd family of Alltyrodyn (mid 19th century). The church holds a special Old New Year service on 13 January (*see* **Calan**). Its tower was a focal point in **cnapan** games. Seion **Congregationalist** chapel (1871) is an innovative building designed by **Thomas Thomas**.

Castell Howell commemorates **Hywel ab Owain Gwynedd** (d.1170), who repaired the castle. It was the site of the school which was run by David Davis (Dafis Castellhywel; 1745–1827), a key figure in the development of south **Cardiganshire Unitarianism**. In 1876, the Unitarian congregation at Llwynrhydowen was deprived of its meeting house by a vengeful landowner because of the radical activities of its minister, William Thomas (Gwilym Marles; 1834–79), a great-uncle of **Dylan Thomas**. Gwasg Gomer, Wales's largest publisher, was founded at Llandysul in 1892. The humorist and story teller Eirwyn Jones (Eirwyn Pontshân; 1922–94) lived at Pont-Siân – his *Hyfryd Iawn* (1966) was a set text for students of **Welsh** at Harvard. The Teifi at Llandysul is popular with anglers and canoeists.

LLANEDI, Carmarthenshire
(2631 ha; 5195 inhabitants)

Located between **Ammanford** and **Llanelli**, the **community** hugs the right bank of the **Llwchwr** and contains the hamlet of Llanedi and the villages of Fforest, Hendy, and Tycroes. St Edi's church, rebuilt in 1860, retains the base of its late-medieval tower. In the second half of the 19th century, the growth of **tinplate** manufacture and anthracite mining led to the establishment of the community's industrial settlements. The lexicographer John Walters (1721–97; *see* **Dictionaries**) was born at Fforest. The poet and scholar **John Jenkins** (Gwili; 1872–1936) was born at Hendy.

LLANEGRYN, Gwynedd
(2352 ha; 303 inhabitants)

Located immediately north of **Tywyn**, the **community**'s outstanding feature is the superb 15th-century rood loft and screen in the church of St Egryn and St Mary. The church also contains tombs of the **Wynne family (Peniarth)**. Peniarth (1700), western **Merioneth**'s earliest brick building, had one of Wales's finest libraries; the Peniarth manuscripts (originally the library of **Robert Vaughan** of Hengwrt) constitute the core of the literary treasures of the **National Library of Wales**. The scholar-landowner, W. W. E. Wynne (1801–80), was influenced by the **Oxford Movement**, a factor which caused him to be strongly opposed by Merioneth's radical **Nonconformists** in the general election of 1859. At Ebenezer chapel is a monument to one of the pioneers of **Congregationalism**, Hugh Owen (1639–1700).

LLANEGWAD, Carmarthenshire
(5383 ha; 1388 inhabitants)

Located north of the **Tywi** between **Llandeilo** and **Carmarthen**, the **community** contains the villages of Llanegwad, Court Henry, Felingwm, Pont-ar-gothi and Nantgaredig. Llanegwad village clusters around St Egwad's church (1849). The Bath family of Alltyferin mansion built the remarkable Holy Trinity church (1878), located above a fine stretch of the lower Cothi valley. Erasmus Lewis (1671–1754), who in 1726 organized the

The village of Llanegryn, *c.*1885

Llanelli defeating New Zealand at Stradey Park in 1972, with captain Delme Thomas being assisted by Derek Quinnell

publication of his friend Jonathan Swift's *Gulliver's Travels*, was born at Abercothi.

LLANEILIAN, Isle of Anglesey
(1668 ha; 1192 inhabitants)

Constituting the north-eastern corner of **Anglesey**, the **community** contains the substantial village at Penysarn. St Eilian's church has a 12th-century tower and a fine 15th-century rood screen and loft. The **lighthouse** at Point Lynas was built in 1835, although there had been a light there since 1781. Llysdulas (demolished) was the seat of the Hughes family, enriched by its share of the **copper** mines on **Mynydd Parys**. Ynys Dulas is a large offshore rock. The journalist and poet **John Tudor Jones** (John Eilian) and the scholar **Bedwyr Lewis Jones** were raised at Llaneilian, as was the versatile actor Glyn Williams (1926–82) of Penysarn.

LLANELIDAN, Denbighshire
(2150 ha; 315 inhabitants)

Located south of **Ruthin**, the **community** contains a monument known as Bwrdd y Tri Arglwydd (Table of the Three Lords), marking the site of the land that was reputedly the cause of the original dispute between **Owain Glyndŵr** and Reginald **Grey**. The double-naved church of St Elidan contains some fine tombs. **John Jones** (Coch Bach y Bala; 1854–1913), a thief shot while on the run from Ruthin Gaol, is buried in the churchyard. In the 1960s and 1970s, **Clough Williams-Ellis** was much involved in the remodelling of Nantclwyd Hall, a rare example in those decades of massive expenditure on a country house. Glan Hesbin (1641, 1698) contains a '**preachers**' door', a relic of 18th-century Nonconformity (*see* **Nonconformists**).

LLANELLI, Carmarthenshire
(938 ha; 23,422 inhabitants)

Located at **Carmarthenshire**'s southernmost point, the town and **community** of Llanelli is the **county**'s largest urban centre. (For Llanelli's outer suburbs, *see* **Llanelli Rural**.) Llanelli, which was probably the administrative centre of the **commote** of **Carnwyllion**, developed around St Elli's church, which was largely rebuilt in 1904–6, although some medieval elements survive. Adjoining the church is Llanelli House (*c*.1700), long the home of the Stepney family, the restoration of which has at last begun.

According to **John Leland**, **coal** was exported from Llanelli in the 1530s. The place became a centre for **copper** and **lead** smelting, but above all it was through **tinplate** that Llanelli won its industrial fame. There were 31 tinplate mills in the town and its environs by the 1870s. (The concept of Llanelli as Tinopolis finds expression in the name of the local television company.) Some of the tinplate was used for the manufacture of saucepans; a saucepan features on Llanelli's coat of arms; saucepans cap the goalposts at Stradey Park, home of the Llanelli **Rugby** Club, whose supporters are enamoured of the jingle '**Sosban Fach**'. There were plans in 2007 to construct a new stadium in the Pemberton area and, controversially, to build houses on the Stradey Park site. From 1840 to 1923, Llanelli was home to a distinguished **pottery**; examples of the porcelain it produced are exhibited in the Parc Howard Gallery and Museum. Almost as famous was Llanelli's role as a centre of brewing. Henry Childe began brewing there *c*.1760; his business passed by marriage to the Reverend James Buckley (d.1839), the only Methodist minister whose portrait appears on a **beer** bottle.

Llanelli early developed a reputation for **radicalism**, with **David Rees** (1801–69), minister of Capel Als, editing *Y Diwygiwr* (the Reformer); Rees's adoption of Daniel O'Connell's slogan, 'Agitate, Agitate, Agitate', caused him to be known as *y Cynhyrfwr* (the Agitator). Llanelli was the scene of the bloodiest industrial conflict in 20th-century **Britain** – the **railway**men's strike of 1911, during which two men were shot dead by soldiers and four others were killed in an explosion (*see* **Llanelli Riots**). In 1945, its **Labour** candidate, **James Griffiths**, had the largest Labour majority in British history (34,117).

Llanelli became an **urban district** in 1894 and a **borough** in 1913. By then, it had acquired 5 docks, 30 chapels – including the elaborate Tabernacl (1873) – an attractive park and a wealth of terraced houses rich in detail. The docks closed in 1952 and, by the end of the 20th century, they were being redeveloped as part of the Millennium Coastal Park. Small-scale tinplate works all closed following the opening of the giant Trostre Works in the 1950s. All that seemed to survive of an earlier era was the townspeople's delight in rugby. Llanelli Rugby Club was founded in 1872; some 150 of the 'Scarlets' have worn the red shirt of Wales since the **Second World War**, 12 of whom have represented the British Lions in trial games.

In the mid-20th century, Llanelli was the largest town in the world over half of whose inhabitants were speakers of a **Celt**ic language. In 2001, however, the proportion of its inhabitants having some knowledge of **Welsh** had declined to 47.87% and the proportion wholly fluent in the language to 19.33%. Its Welsh-medium primary school, Ysgol Dewi Sant (1947), was the first such school to be established by a local authority. Michael Howard (b.1941), leader of the **Conservative Party** from 2003 to 2005, was brought up in Llanelli. The family, of Romanian origin, took its **surname** from Parc Howard.

LLANELLI Constituency and one-time district

Following the abolition of **Carmarthenshire** in 1974, Llanelli was created as a district of the new **county** of **Dyfed**. It consisted of the **boroughs** of **Llanelli** and **Kidwelly**, the **urban district** of Burry Port and the **rural district** of Llanelli. In 1996, the district became part of the revived county of Carmarthenshire. The boundaries of the constituency of Llanelli coincide with those of the defunct district.

LLANELLI RIOTS, The

On 19 August 1911, during the first **Britain**-wide **railway** strike, a confrontation between regular troops of the Worcestershire Regiment and pickets at the strategically important **Llanelli** railway line led to the deaths of two young bystanders. The ensuing wave of violence and looting, which lasted for several hours, resulted in considerable damage to shops and railway sidings; there were four further deaths when a truck which had been set alight exploded. A number of prosecutions followed and questions were asked in parliament. **Keir Hardie** wrote a pamphlet attacking the use of the armed forces in industrial confrontations. The impact on local politics, however, proved to be minimal.

LLANELLI RURAL (Llanelli Wledig),
Carmarthenshire (6214 ha; 21,043 inhabitants)

The **community** contains the **Llanelli** suburbs of Bynea, Cwmcarnhywel, Dafen, Felinfoel, Furnace, Llwynhendy and Pwll, the one-time **coal**mining villages of Pont-Henri and Pontyates and the rural hamlet of Five Roads. The district was an early stronghold of Nonconformity (*see* **Nonconformists**). In the upper reaches of the Lliedi valley are two **reservoirs** created to supply Llanelli with water; scenically attractive, the area is known as Swiss valley. The brewery at Felinfoel was founded *c.*1835; surrounded by **tinplate** works, it was the first brewery in **Britain** to use **beer** cans. It is the only brewery in Wales still owned by the founding family. Cynheidre, the massive anthracite colliery sunk near Pontyates in 1951 at a cost of £10 million, closed in the 1980s. The National Wetlands Centre, Wales, opened in 1991, annually attracts 70,000 migrant **birds**. The creation of the Millennium Coastal Park – a 22-km stretch of highly industrialized coast extending from the **Llwchwr** estuary to **Pembrey**, much of which lies within the boundaries of the Llanelli Rural community – was the biggest land reclamation project in **Britain**.

LLANELLTYD (Llanelltud), Gwynedd
(4305 ha; 495 inhabitants)

Located immediately north of **Dolgellau**, the **community** extends to the summit of Diffwys (750 m), the highest point of the **Harlech** Dome. It contains the confluence of the **Mawddach** and the Wnion. Near the confluence are the ruins of the **Cistercian** abbey of Cymer, founded in 1199 as a daughter house of **Abbey Cwmhir**. Only the abbey church survives to any height. The **National Museum** has the abbey's chalice and paten, which almost miraculously came to light in a foxhole in nearby Cwm Mynach. That there is a church dedicated to St **Illtud** at the head of the Mawddach estuary is an indication of the way **saints**' cults spread along the western sea routes. The present building, which lies within a circular churchyard, was built in 1900. Hengwrt, the home of the manuscript collector **Robert Vaughan** (1592–1667), suffered a disastrous fire in the 1960s. In the late 18th century, there was a flourishing **ship-building** business at Maes-y-garnedd. The village of Bontddu, which overlooks a fine stretch of the Mawddach estuary, long suffered the after-effects of a leak from the petrol station in 1996. To its north is Clogau Mine, the source of 120,000 ounces (3,402,000 grammes) of **gold**, some of which has been used for the wedding rings of members of the English royal family.

LLANELLY (Llanelli), Monmouthshire
(1827 ha; 3810 inhabitants)

Located between **Brynmawr** and **Abergavenny**, the **community** contains the villages of Gilwern, Clydach and Darrenfelen. Until 1974, it was part of **Breconshire**. Llanelly church (largely 13th century) offers magnificent views of the **Usk** valley. The Clydach Gorge, which links the valley to the industrial towns of **Blaenau Gwent**, is virtually an open-air industrial museum. It contains evidence of an 18th-century blast furnace and forge, a series of early tramroads, two **lime**works, the Clydach **Iron**works – enlarged in the 1840s to employ 1350 people – and the viaducts and tunnels of the

Merthyr, Tredegar and Abergavenny Railway (1861). The embankment carrying the Brecon and Abergavenny Canal involved diverting the River Clydach through a tunnel. Clydach House (1693) was the birthplace of the empire builder Bartle Frere (1815–84), whose family had long been associated with the Clydach Ironworks. Thomas Price (Carnhuanawc), curate of Llanelly from 1816 to 1825, founded at Gellifelen what was reputed at the time to be Wales's sole Welsh-medium elementary school. In the 1930s, Noëlle and D. J. Davies sought to establish a folk high-school on the Danish model at Pantybeiliau mansion.

LLANELWEDD, Radnorshire, Powys
(1721 ha; 436 inhabitants)
Lying across the Wye from Builth, Llanelwedd is the home of the Royal Welsh Agricultural Society, whose four-day Royal Welsh Agricultural Show has been held annually at Llanelwedd since 1963. In 1993, the National Eisteddfod was held on the site, the sole occasion for the festival to visit Radnorshire. Cefndyrys was built in 1785 for David Thomas, paymaster-general for the British army in the American War of Independence. Pencerrig was the home of the landscape and portrait painter Thomas Jones (1742–1803), a pupil of Richard Wilson. The tiny, ancient church at Llanfaredd is beautifully situated above the Wye. Its churchyard contains the largest yew in Radnorshire, as well as some attractively lettered gravestones, one of which commemorates 'A virgin in her blossom nipt'. Hendre Einion was the birthplace of the scholar and poet Edward Davies, whose enthusiasm for druids earned him the soubriquet 'Celtic Davies'. Builth Road was formerly the railway junction linking the mid Wales line with the lines to Hereford and to Moat Lane (Caersws).

LLANENGAN, Gwynedd
(3352 ha; 2124 inhabitants)
Located south-west of Pwllheli, the community constitutes the southernmost part of the Llŷn peninsula. It contains the villages of Llanengan, Abersoch, Bwlchtocyn, Llangian and Mynytho. A 6th-century inscribed stone (see Monuments, Early Christian) at Llangian commemorates Melus, medicus (doctor). St Engan's church (14th to 16th century) contains a fine rood screen and loft. St Tudwal's Islands shelter St Tudwal's Roads where sailing ships took refuge in times of storm from the dangers of Porth Neigwl, which the old seafarers had good reason to call Hell's Mouth. The walls of Castellmarch (1630s), Llangian, are adorned with the arms of Wales's princely families; the place is associated with the legend of King March ap Meirchion, a legend which inspired a dramatic ballad by Cynan (Albert Evans-Jones). Mynytho, the centre of a patchwork of small fields carved from common land, was home to quarrymen and manganese miners. The opening of its village hall was commemorated in one of the best known of R. Williams Parry's englynion. Abersoch is a well-known yachting centre.

LLANERCH COLLIERY DISASTER
At this Abersychan colliery, leased by Partridge, Jones & Co. from the Ebbw Vale Steel, Iron and Coal Company, 176 men were killed on 6 February 1890. Unlike other mines suffering an explosion, Llanerch was neither dry nor dusty, and the coal seams did not contain large amounts of gas. Nevertheless, the cause was attributed to a large and unforeseen outburst of gas being ignited by the naked lights still being used in part of the mine.

LLANERFYL, Montgomeryshire, Powys
(6137 ha; 402 inhabitants)
Straddling the Banwy valley west of Llanfair Caereinion, the community includes a wide tract of the moorland of mid-Montgomeryshire. St Erfyl's church, rebuilt in 1870, contains the remnants of a 15th-century shrine. In the circular churchyard, there is an ancient yew, unique in form; beneath it was a Christian gravestone of the 5th or 6th century, commemorating the death of a 13-year-old girl. The southern part of the community includes Cwm Nant yr Eira, which in the 20th century suffered severe depopulation.

LLANEUGRAD, Isle of Anglesey
(1141 ha; 273 inhabitants)
Located north-east of Llangefni, the community contains the village of Marianglas, birthplace of the actor Hugh Griffith. St Eugrad's church was built in the 12th century. In its churchyard are the graves of a number of the victims of the wreck of the Royal Charter. Near Parciau is a 17th-century dovecote. Marble was formerly quarried in the area. Traeth Bychan was the scene of a tragedy in 1939 when the failure of the submarine Thetis to resurface led to the deaths of 99 men.

LLANFACHRAETH (Llanfachreth),
Isle of Anglesey (844 ha; 566 inhabitants)
Located across Holyhead Bay from Holyhead, the community is bisected by the Holyhead–Amlwch road (the A5025). It was the home of the poet Gruffudd ap Maredudd ap Dafydd (fl.1352–82), whose work is preserved in The Red Book of Hergest. The diary kept from 1630 to 1636 by Robert Bulkeley, squire of Dronwy, is a valuable historical source.

LLANFAELOG, Isle of Anglesey
(1216 ha; 1679 inhabitants)
Located immediately north-west of Aberffraw, the community contains the seaside resort of Rhosneigr and the villages of Llanfaelog and Pencarnisiog. There is a fine Neolithic chambered tomb at Tŷ Newydd. Rhosneigr developed following the opening of its railway station (1849). St Maelog's church (19th century) contains a 6th-century memorial stone to Conws or Cunogusus, whose name gave rise to that of Pencarnisog. In the 18th century, the neighbourhood was associated with Lladron Crigyll, who sought to attract ships to be wrecked on the treacherous rocks south of Traeth Crigyll (see Shipwrecks).

LLANFAETHLU, Isle of Anglesey
(1681 ha; 574 inhabitants)
Located on the north-west coast of Anglesey, the community contains the villages of Llanfaethlu and Llanfwrog. The coastal fort at Castell Trefadog may be of Viking origin. Carreglwyd (17th to 18th centuries) was the seat of the Griffiths family, one of Anglesey's leading families. The Renaissance scholar Siôn Dafydd Rhys was born in Llanfaethlu. Along the coast are delightful bays.

LLANFAIR, Gwynedd (1808 ha; 474 inhabitants)
Located immediately south of **Harlech**, the **community** contains the villages of Llanfair and Llandanwg. The area is rich in **Neolithic** burial chambers, **Bronze Age** barrows and standing stones, and **Iron Age** hut circles. St Mary's church has a fine 15th-century roof; its predecessor provided lodging for **Giraldus Cambrensis** and Archbishop Baldwin in 1188. The 13th-century St Tanwg's church, picturesquely situated above the sea, was, until 1841, Harlech's **parish** church. It contains two inscribed stones of the 5th–6th centuries (*see* **Monuments, Early Christian**). Gerddi Bluog is often erroneously stated to be the home of **Edmwnd Prys**. **Ellis Wynne** was rector of Llanfair and Llandanwg. Chwarel Hen offers tours through impressive **slate** caverns.

LLANFAIR (Llan-fair), Vale of Glamorgan
(1127 ha; 619 inhabitants)
Located immediately south of **Cowbridge**, the **community** contains the villages of St Mary Church, Llandough and St Hilary. St Mary Church is a delightfully compact settlement. Its church was heavily restored in 1862 but retains a fine medieval roof. The rectory was built in the early 17th century for Thomas Wilkins (d.1699), the first of a succession of Wilkins rectors of St Mary Church. Thomas Wilkins (d.1799) was a leading bibliophile, and during his incumbency the rectory contained such treasures as *The Red Book of Hergest*. South of the village lies Fishweir, a mid-16th-century house associated with the Bassets of Beaupré. Adjoining it is **Glamorgan**'s tallest barn, a 16th-century structure of eight bays.

Llandough is a rather more scattered settlement. From 1759 to 1797, its rector was the lexicographer John Walters (1721–97) (*see* **Dictionaries**). Its church contains Glamorgan's earliest brass memorial (1427). West of the church are fragments of an early 15th-century tower house incorporated into Llandough Castle, a castellated mansion built *c.*1600 and enlarged *c.*1803. St Hilary is situated on the breast of a hill commanding wide views to the south. It is best known for its ITV transmitting station, which in fact lies in the Cowbridge community. The village contains a significant collection of late 16th and 17th-century cottages and farmhouses and an intriguing 18th-century stone circular pigsty. The church was massively restored in 1862 by George Gilbert Scott – his sole work in Glamorgan. Within it are a 12th-century tomb, an altar tomb of an armoured knight (1423), and a memorial to Daniel Jones (d.1841), founder of **Cardiff** Infirmary.

The community's finest feature is Beaupré, described by John Newman as Glamorgan's 'only really spectacular architectural showpiece'. Its glory is 'the tower of the orders' (1600), an entrance porch with coupled columns in which Doric supports Ionic and Ionic supports Corinthian – a work of astonishing sophistication. Beaupré was owned by the Basset family from the 13th to the 18th centuries. The original house was an L-shaped building of *c.*1300. This was extensively remodelled in the early 16th century, and building culminated in Richard Basset's splendid late 16th-century commission which includes Glamorgan's earliest example of the use of brick. The Basset inheritance eventually passed to the Jones family who settled in the undistinguished mansion of New Beaupré.

LLANFAIR CAEREINION, Montgomeryshire,
Powys (6254 ha; 1616 inhabitants)
Located in the heart of **Montgomeryshire**, the **community** extends over the central part of the basin of the **River** Banwy. The town of Llanfair Caereinion never received a charter of incorporation but, in the 18th and 19th cen-

Llanfair Caereinion post office, *c.*1885

turies, it formed a prosperous enough community, in spite of the great fire of 1758, which destroyed many buildings. It was a centre for craftsmen, among them the gifted **clock** maker Samuel Roberts (*c.*1720–1800); in the 1820s and 1830s, there were also printers, originally in connection with the **Wesleyan** Bookroom, but best known for an encyclopaedia, *Y Geirlyfr Cymraeg*, published between 1830 and 1835.

Within the town are some attractive 18th and 19th-century buildings. St Mary's church, largely rebuilt in 1868, retains some medieval features, including an effigy of a knight in full armour (*c.*1400). It contains the tomb of David Davis (d.1790), who bequeathed sixpence to everyone attending his funeral; 1030 people turned up. Llanfair was one of the early and important centres of **Calvinistic Methodism**. In 1903, it was linked to **Welshpool** by a narrow-gauge railway, one of the last **railways** to be built in Wales. Closed in 1956, the Welshpool and Llanfair Light Railway was reopened as a tourist attraction in 1963. The community contains some ancient farmhouses. **Islwyn Ffowc Elis** wrote his hugely successful novel *Cysgod y Cryman* (1953) while a minister at Llanfair Caereinion.

LLANFAIR CLYDOGAU, Ceredigion
(3232 ha; 770 inhabitants)
Located immediately north-east of **Lampeter**, the **community** embraces the basins of Clywedog-isaf, Clywedog-ganol and Clywedog-uchaf; the meaning of 'clywedog' is 'audible' or 'noisy', a reference to the rivers Clydogau (or Clywedogau originally). It contained the southernmost of **Cardiganshire**'s **lead and silver** mines, which was highly productive in the 1760s. Ebeneser Congregational chapel (1799) was originally a brewery. The scholar **G. J. Williams** (1892–1963), the first president of Yr Academi Gymraeg (*see* **Welsh Academy**), was a native of Cellan.

LLANFAIR DYFFRYN CLWYD, Denbighshire
(2991 ha; 1070 inhabitants)
Located immediately south-east of **Ruthin**, the **community** contains the spectacularly sited **hill-fort** of Craig Adwy Wynt. In the double-naved church of St Cynfarch and St Mary are remnants of a rood screen. Plas Uchaf (*c.*1500) is a three-unit hall house. Jesus chapel (Capel y Gloch, 1619) is an unusual L-shaped **Anglican** church. Roger Morris (fl.1590), a prolific copyist, lived at Coed-y-Talwrn. Llysfasi, a medieval residence owned in turn by the Thelwall, Lloyd (Bodidris), **Myddelton** and West families, is now an agricultural college.

LLANFAIR PWLLGWYNGYLL, Isle of Anglesey
(365 ha; 3040 inhabitants)
Located immediately west of **Menai Bridge**, the **community** enjoys some notoriety on account of the long name (Llanfairpwllgwyngyllgogerychwyrndrobwll-llantysilio-gogogoch) attributed to it. While Llanfairpwllgwyngyll is an ancient name, the longer version is entirely spurious. Apparently, it was invented in 1869, probably by a local tailor eager to attract visitors. It is generally known as Llanfairpwll or Llanfair PG.

Within the column erected there in 1816 in honour of the Waterloo hero, Henry William **Paget**, first Marquess of

Anglesey, 115 steps lead to his statue (1860). One of his sons, Admiral Lord Clarence Paget, was responsible for the statue of Nelson (1873), which stands on the shore. He lived at Plas Llanfair, which became a sea-training establishment, known as *Indefatigable* and which closed in 1995. **Britain**'s first **Women's Institute** was established at Llanfairpwll in 1915.

The construction of **Telford**'s **Holyhead road** encouraged urban development. **Stephenson**'s **railway** bridge (1849), which enters Anglesey at Llanfairpwll, was adapted in the 1970s to carry a road as well. As a result, the main road to Holyhead – now the **A55** – enters Anglesey at Llanfairpwll rather than, as formerly, at Menai Bridge.

LLANFAIR TALHAIARN (Llanfair Talhaearn), Conwy (4252 ha; 979 inhabitants)
Located immediately south of **Abergele**, the **community** straddles the middle stretch of the Elwy valley. The double-naved church of St Mary (15th century, 1876) contains a tank for immersion baptism and monuments to the Wynne family, originally of Melai – an 18th-century house surrounded by extensive farm buildings of *c.*1804. Robert Wynne of Melai (d.1682) married the heiress of the Prices of Garthewin where their descendants would live until the late 20th century. Garthewin, rebuilt in the 18th century but containing earlier portions, received the attention of **Clough Williams-Ellis** in 1930. In 1937, R. O. F. Wynne (1901–93), **Roman Catholic** and nationalist, converted a barn into a theatre, in which five of the plays of his close associate **Saunders Lewis** were first performed. Talhaiarn (**John Jones**; 1810–69) was a native of the village. On the northern boundary of the community is Abergele hospital (1912, 1931), built as a sanatorium for Manchester. Plas Newydd and Faerdre have 16th-century origins.

LLANFAIR-AR-Y-BRYN, Carmarthenshire
(9701 ha; 635 inhabitants)
Constituting the north-eastern corner of **Carmarthenshire**, the **community** extends from **Llandovery** to the Brianne **reservoir**. It contains the hamlets of Cynghordy, Pentre-ty-gwyn and Rhandirmwyn, and is bisected by the Llandovery–**Llanwrtyd** road (the A483), which makes a dramatic detour around the Sugar Loaf **Mountain**. The St Mary's church which gives the community its name is in Llandovery. The community's **Anglican** church, another St Mary's, was built in 1883.

At Ystrad Ffin is a **cave** traditionally associated with Twm Shon Catti (**Thomas Jones**; *c.*1530–1609). Near it is the Dinas Reserve of the Royal Society for the Protection of **Birds**, which, during the 1940s, was Wales's last refuge of the red kite. At a neighbouring cave – that of Craig y Wyddon – Rhys Prydderch (?1620–99) held dissenting services. Cefnarthen, one of Wales's earliest **Nonconformist** chapels, was built shortly after the passing of the Toleration Act of 1689. The **hymn**writer and evangelist **William Williams** (Pantycelyn; 1717–91) was born in Cefn Coed; in 1748, he moved 1 km south to Pantycelyn, which was thereafter inextricably linked with his name. The first *sasiwn* (**association**) of Wales's Methodists was held at Dugoedydd farmhouse in 1742. In the late 18th century, 400 workers were employed at the Nantymwyn lead mine. Cynghordy was long famous for its bricks. Cynghordy viaduct (1868) carries the **Swansea–Shrewsbury railway**.

LLANFAIR-MATHAFARN-EITHAF
(Llanfair Mathafarn Eithaf), Isle of Anglesey
(1512 ha; 3408 inhabitants)
Located in the middle of **Anglesey**'s east coast, the **community** contains the seaside resort of Benllech and the villages of Tynygongl, Brynteg, Llanbedrgoch and Red Wharf Bay. Since 1994, excavations at Glyn, Llanbedrgoch, have revealed the remains of a **Viking** settlement – the first to be found in Anglesey. From the 14th century onwards, several local millstone quarries supplied many Anglesey **windmills**; in addition the stones were exported from the quay at Red Wharf Bay. There were also marble quarries in the neighbourhood. The poet **Goronwy Owen** was born at Rhosfawr and served as curate at Llanfair-Mathafarn-Eithaf.

LLANFAIR-YN-NEUBWLL, Isle of Anglesey
(1602 ha; 1688 inhabitants)
Located opposite Holy **Island**, the **community** contains the villages of Llanfairyneubwll, Llanfihangel yn Nhowyn and Caergeiliog. With eight **lakes**, the area is known as Ardal y Llynnoedd (the Lake District), where W. D. Owen's 1925 novel *Madam Wen* is set. Offshore is the large rock known as Ynys Feirig.

A Royal Air Force station known as RAF **Valley** was established on Tywyn Trewan during the **Second World War** and is still in use. When the airfield was under construction in 1943, **Iron Age** metal artefacts, including weapons, **horse** gear, tools, a trumpet and the remains of chariots, some 144 items in all, were discovered at Llyn Cerrig Bach. Exhibited at the **National Museum**, they were probably votive offerings, suggesting that the lake had religious significance.

Because of the presence of the airfield, Llanfair-yn-Neubwll is linguistically the most Anglicized of the communities of **Anglesey**. Of its inhabitants, 45.6% have some knowledge of **Welsh** and 30.93% are wholly fluent.

LLANFAIRFECHAN, Conwy
(1792 ha; 3755 inhabitants)
Located immediately west of **Penmaenmawr**, but separated from it by a steep promontory, the **community**'s uplands are rich in hut circles, burnt mounds and house platforms. A complex field system, which may have prehistoric origins, is indicative of the dense agricultural settlement which sustained the area's **economy** until the development of quarrying and **tourism** from the mid-19th century onwards. Both have largely disappeared and Llanfairfechan has become a place of retirement or of commuting to **Bangor**. Bolnhurst, designed by **Herbert North** in 1899, is Wales's finest house in the Arts and Crafts tradition.

LLANFARIAN, Ceredigion
(3352 ha; 1442 inhabitants)
Located immediately south of **Aberystwyth**, the **community** contains the villages of Llanfarian, Blaenplwyf, Capel Seion, Chancery, Moriah and Rhydyfelin. Llanfarian is not a genuine *llan* name; it is probably a corruption of *nant*

(stream) plus *marian* (alluvial land). The ringwork above the mouth of the **Ystwyth** was built by Gilbert de **Clare** *c.*1110. It gave its name to Aberystwyth, although the later town and castle would more suitably be known as Aberrheidol.

Nanteos, the centre of a 9000-ha estate, is a fine house in the Palladian style, begun in 1739. It was home to the Jones and then the **Powell family** who played prominent roles in **Cardiganshire**'s history. The Nanteos cup, a battered wooden bowl claimed by some to be the sacred cup used at the Last Supper, and which reputedly inspired Wagner to compose *Parsifal*, is in a vault in a Hereford bank; experts concluded in the 1970s that the bowl, made of wych-elm rather than of olive wood – as once believed – dates from no earlier than the 14th century.

Above the village of Chancery is the Conrah Hotel. Originally the Victorian mansion of Ffosrhydgaled, it was the one-time home of the heiress of the Smiths Crisps fortune. St Llwchaearn's church, largely rebuilt in 1880, contains monuments to local landed families. The community includes Aberystwyth's Glanyrafon Industrial Estate.

LLANFECHAIN, Montgomeryshire, Powys
(1685 ha; 521 inhabitants)
Located immediately east of **Llanfyllin**, the **community** extends over the central part of the basin of the **River** Cain. Llanfechain village clusters around St **Garmon**'s church; the nearest **Montgomeryshire** has to a Romanesque church (late 12th century), it contains distinguished work by **John Douglas**. Among the community's ancient houses are Tŷ Coch (originally 15th century), Pentre (16th century) and Bodynfoel (late 17th century). The writer and antiquarian Gwallter Mechain (**Walter Davies**; 1761–1849) and the educationist **David Thomas** (1880–1967) were born at Llanfechain. The novelist **James Hanley** (1901–85) lived in the village from 1940 to 1964.

LLANFERRES, Denbighshire
(1536 ha; 676 inhabitants)
Located south-west of **Mold**, the **community** contains two large **limestone** quarries. On the **Denbighshire–Flintshire** border is a monument incorporating a stone reputedly bearing the hoof mark of King **Arthur**'s steed. The philologist and biblical translator **John Davies** (1570–1644), later of **Mallwyd**, was a native of Llanferres. The Loggerheads Inn at one time displayed a pub sign reputedly painted by **Richard Wilson**. Colomendy, where Wilson spent his final years, has become an environment studies centre.

LLANFIHANGEL (Llanfihangel-yng-Ngwynfa),
Montgomeryshire, Powys (5365 ha; 516 inhabitants)
Straddling the Vyrnwy valley south of **Llanfyllin**, the **community**'s delectable landscape reflects its full name: St Michael's in Paradise. The district was the subject of **Alwyn D. Rees**'s influential sociological study *Life in a Welsh Countryside* (1950). On the second Sunday of the New Year, Llanfihangel holds *Y Blygain Fawr* (the Great *Plygain*), the most celebrated in Wales. St Michael's church was rebuilt in 1862. From the old church, three 14th-century inscribed stones survive, one bearing the name

Madog ap Celynin, an ancestor of the **Vaughan family (Llwydiarth)**. In 1718, the Llwydiarth estate passed by marriage to the **Williams Wynn family**; the mansion has been demolished. There are 19th-century churches at Pont Llogel and Dolanog. The **hymn**writer **Ann Griffiths** is buried in Llanfihangel churchyard. Her home, Dolwar Fach near Dolanog, is a place of **pilgrimage**. Her memorial chapel at Dolanog (1903) is a delightful building in the Arts and Crafts tradition.

Pendugwm, in the community's south-eastern corner, was the home of **John Davies** (1772–1855), a **missionary** in Tahiti who established the orthography of the island's language. It may be significant that Pendugwm is scarcely 3 km from Tan-y-ffridd, **Llangyniew**, birthplace of **Thomas Jones** (1810–49), who made a similar contribution to the **Khasi** language.

In 2001, 72.51% of the community's inhabitants had some knowledge of **Welsh**, with 56.18% wholly fluent in the language – the highest percentages in any of the communities of **Powys**, and in the former **county** of **Montgomery**.

LLANFIHANGEL ABERBYTHYCH,
Carmarthenshire (2640 ha; 1241 inhabitants)
Hugging the south bank of the **Tywi** immediately southwest of **Llandeilo**, the **community** contains the hamlet of Llanfihangel Aberbythych and the village of Carmel. The area is rich in **Bronze Age** graves. St Michael's church (19th century) is beautifully located. The community's chief feature is Golden Grove, successively the seat of the **Vaughan family (Golden Grove)**, earls of Carbery, and the **Campbell family**, earls of Cawdor. The mansion, a structure built 1826–34 in the Elizabethan style, became an agricultural college in 1952. Its attractive park contains a **deer** herd. Jeremy Taylor (1613–67) wrote his *Holy Living* and *Holy Dying* at Golden Grove when chaplain to the Vaughan family.

LLANFIHANGEL CWMDU with BWLCH and CATHEDINE (Llanfihangel Cwm Du gyda Bwlch a Chathedin), Breconshire, Powys (4497 ha; 918 inhabitants)
Located immediately north-west of **Crickhowell**, the **community** contains the villages of Bwlch, Cwmdu and Tretower. (The hamlet of Cathedine is in the community of **Llangors**.) The **Roman road** from **Abergavenny** to **Brecon** ran along the Rhiangoll valley before turning towards Bwlch; the remains of a Roman fort have been found at Pen-y-gaer.

North of Bwlch are the ruins of Castell **Blaenllynfi**, the centre of a lordship which included Tretower and Crickhowell. Tretower Castle was built for Picard, a follower of **Bernard de Neufmarché**. Tretower Court, which replaced the castle as a dwelling *c*.1300, passed from the Picards via the **Herberts** to the **Vaughan family (Tretower)**. It has now been stripped of later accretions to reveal a superb medieval structure, which is in the care of **Cadw**. Middle Gaer has Elizabethan wall **paintings**.

Between 1825 and 1848, Cwmdu was the home of Carnhuanawc (**Thomas Price**), author of *Hanes Cymru*, polymath, pan-**Celt**icist and enthusiast for the **Welsh** language. A plaque commemorates the Welsh-medium school he established there. He is buried in St Michael's churchyard. The church, consecrated in the 11th century, was largely rebuilt in 1831–2. The bridge over the Rhiangoll at Felindre dates from *c*.1700.

The church at Penmyarth contains a monument to the **iron**master Sir Joseph **Bailey**, who commissioned its building in 1852. Buckland House, once the home of the Games family, came to be associated with the industrialist and financier Seymour **Berry**, Baron Buckland, and was later the British Legion's Crossfield House. The Italianate mansion Gliffaes – now a hotel – offers fine views of the **Usk**. On the community's eastern boundary stands Pen Allt-mawr (719 m), one of the summits of the **Black Mountains**.

LLANFIHANGEL GLYN MYFYR, Conwy
(2352 ha; 195 inhabitants)
Located on the eastern boundary of the **county** of **Conwy** south-east of **Ruthin**, the **community** embraces the middle stretch of the Alwen valley. The **Iron Age hill-forts** of Caer Ddunod and Caer Caradog testify to early habitation in the locality. St Michael's church, probably dating from the 15th century, has been much altered. Bodtegir (17th–19th centuries, with an earlier predecessor) became the home of William **Salusbury** ('Old Blue Stockings'; 1580–1659), after his honourable surrender of **Denbigh** Castle to Parliamentary forces in the **Civil Wars**. Tyddyn Tudur was the birthplace of Owain Myfyr (**Owen Jones**; 1741–1814), the wealthy **London** furrier who financed the publishing of Welsh manuscripts in *The Myvyrian Archaiology of Wales* (1801–7) and was among the founders of the **Gwyneddigion** society for the London Welsh in 1770.

LLANFIHANGEL RHOS-Y-CORN,
Carmarthenshire (5096 ha; 498 inhabitants)
Located in the heart of northern **Carmarthenshire** northwest of **Llandeilo**, the **community** contains the villages of Abergorlech, Brechfa, Gwernogle and Llidiad-Nenog. Bordered to the south by the Cothi, the community consists of high land drained by one of Wales's many **rivers** named Clydach. Within it are three 19th-century churches; near that at Brechfa is Tŷ-mawr, a large house with medieval origins. Fforest, another, contains 16th- and 17th-century features. Much of the area consists of Brechfa Forest (*see* **Forestry**), a vast plantation undertaken by the **Forestry Commission** in the years immediately after the **Second World War**. Abergorlech is a particularly attractive village.

LLANFIHANGEL RHYDITHON
(Llanfihangel Rhydieithon), Radnorshire, Powys
(2418 ha; 243 inhabitants)
The **community** lies to the east of **Llandrindod** and extends to the upper reaches of **Radnor Forest**. The church was entirely rebuilt in 1838, and is one of the 'neat edifices' which, as **Ffransis Payne** feelingly laments, replaced ancient churches. A gravestone commemorates three shepherds lost in a snowstorm in the Forest in 1767. According to *Y Gwyliedydd*, **Welsh** was still spoken by the older inhabitants as late as 1829.

LLANFIHANGEL YSGEIFIOG, Isle of Anglesey
(2086 ha; 1599 inhabitants)

Located immediately south of **Llangefni**, the **community** contains the villages of Pentre Berw and Gaerwen, essentially ribbon developments along the original **Holyhead road**. The café at Gaerwen (now closed) is the subject of a popular song by the duo Tony ac Aloma. Llanfihangel Ysgeifiog church is a ruin. Plas Berw was formerly the seat of the Holland family. From the 15th until the late 19th century, **Anglesey** had a small-scale **coal** industry, with most of the workings situated in Cors Ddyga (**Malltraeth Marsh**) in the area centred upon Llanfihangel Ysgeifiog. Llynnau Gwaith Glo were associated with the workings.

LLANFIHANGEL YSTRAD, Ceredigion
(4647 ha; 1427 inhabitants)

Straddling the Aeron valley at its broadest point, the **community** contains the villages of Cribyn, Dihewyd, Felinfach and Ystrad Aeron. Llanllyr was the site of a small **Cistercian nunnery** founded *c.*1180. No trace of it remains, although there is an 8th-century inscribed stone on the site (*see* **Monuments, Early Christian**). Llanllyr mansion (largely 19th century) was long occupied by the Lewes family. The Vaughan family of Green Grove were descendants of Edward Vaughan (1733–96), son of Dorothy Vaughan, Viscountess Lisburne, but almost certainly not of the Viscount (*see* **Vaughan family (Trawsgoed)**). Edward seems to have been granted Green Grove by his putative father, David Lloyd, of the nearby mansion of Brynog – the whole story providing 18th-century **Cardiganshire** with a delicious scandal.

Theatr Felinfach is mid-**Ceredigion**'s chief cultural centre. The Felinfach Creamery, opened in 1951, closed in the 1990s. A **cheese**-packing centre was opened on the site in 2001, but its viability proved problematic. The bulls kept nearby introduced 'y tarw botel' (bottled bull) to the farms of Ceredigion.

LLANFIHANGEL-AR-ARTH, Carmarthenshire
(6253 ha; 2051 inhabitants)

Located south of the **Teifi** and east of **Llandysul**, the **community** contains the villages of Llanfihangel-ar-Arth, Alltwalis, Gwyddgrug, Pencader, Pont-Tyweli and New Inn. The medieval features of St Michael's church have been rendered undateable by over-zealous restoration in 1873. It contains two inscribed stones (*c.*500 and *c.*700; *see* **Monuments, Early Christian**). In 1041, **Gruffudd ap Llywelyn**, king of **Gwynedd**, defeated Hywel ab Edwin, king of **Deheubarth**, at the battle of Pencader, where Gilbert de **Clare** built a motte-and-bailey castle in 1145; it survives, looking like an upturned pudding. According to **Giraldus Cambrensis**, an **old man of Pencader** told Henry II that until the Day of Judgment the **Welsh language** 'will answer for this corner of the world'; a memorial commemorating the old man was unveiled in the 1950s. Pencader was an important centre of the **woollen industry**. Dissent (*see* **Nonconformists and Dissenters**) struck roots at Pencader in 1650, where Tabernacl chapel (1909) is a particularly attractive building. Llethr-neuadd Uchaf was the home of **Sarah Jacob**, known as 'The Welsh Fasting Girl'.

LLANFIHANGEL-Y-PENNANT, Gwynedd
(7750 ha; 402 inhabitants)

Extending over a wide swathe of central southern **Meirionnydd**, the **community** contains the beautiful **lake** of Tal-y-llyn and the summit of **Cadair Idris** (893 m), second in height only to **Aran** Fawddwy (903 m) among the **mountains**

Llanfyllin on livestock market day, *c.*1885

of Meirionnydd. Craig yr Aderyn (bird rock), a massive rock above the Dysynni valley, is a nesting place of sea**birds**.

Castell y Bere, the southernmost of the stone castles of the princes of **Gwynedd**, was begun by **Llywelyn ap Iorwerth** in 1221 and was the last Welsh stronghold to yield in the war of 1282–3. Its layout, which resembles that of Château Gaillard on the borders of **Norman**dy, was determined by the shape of the rock on which it stands. At its foot is Caerberllan, a perfect 17th-century **manor** house. St Michael's church, built in the 15th century, has a primitive air. Nearby is a memorial to **Mary Jones** of **Bible** fame. St Mary's church on the banks of Tal-y-llyn has a 13th-century roof. The lakeside Ty'n y Cornel Hotel was built in 1844.

Abergynolwyn, a 19th-century **slate**-quarrying village, is the terminus of the Talyllyn **railway** (1865). The bend (*ystum*) in the Dysynni – a fine example of **river** capture – may have given its name to the **commote** of **Ystumanner**.

LLANFOIST FAWR (Llan-ffwyst Fawr),
Monmouthshire (3756 ha; 3017 inhabitants)
Lying astride the **Usk** west of **Abergavenny**, the **community** contains the villages of Govilon, Llanellen and Llanfoist, the summit of the Sugar Loaf (596 m) and the entire rounded bulk of the Blorenge (559 m). East of the Blorenge is Garn Ddyrys, where **iron** slag litters the site of the settlement featured in Alexander Cordell's *Rape of the Fair Country* (*see* **George Alexander Graber**). Llanfoist, where the tramroad from **Blaenavon** brought iron to the **Brecon and Abergavenny Canal**, is now virtually a suburb of Abergavenny. The tramroad from **Nantyglo** connected with the wharf at Govilon where a warehouse built to store iron still stands.

The community has six late 18th-century bridges crossing the canal. A fine example of a 16th-century cruck house survives at Llanellen, where St Helen's church has an attractive spire (1851) designed by **John Prichard**. Llanwenarth House is a remarkable 16th-century **gentry** residence. The now vanished **Baptist** chapel, erected at Llanwenarth in 1695, was one of the very earliest purpose-built **Nonconformist** places of worship in Wales.

LLANFROTHEN, Gwynedd
(3368 ha; 436 inhabitants)
Located immediately north-east of **Penrhyndeudraeth**, the **community** contains the villages of Llanfrothen, Croesor, Garreg and Rhyd. Within it are the summits of **Cnicht** (690 m), Moelwyn Mawr (770 m) and Moelwyn Bach (710 m). St Brothen's church retains 13th-century features. It was the Llanfrothen Burial Case (1886) – against a vicar who had refused to allow a **Nonconformist** service in the churchyard – which first brought **David Lloyd George** to public notice. Plas Brondanw was the home of **Clough Williams-Ellis**. Examples of his work, a mock ruined castle among them, adorn Llanfrothen. The **slate**-quarrying village of Croesor was the home of the remarkable bibliophile Bob Owen (**Robert Owen**; 1885–1962). Ynysfor, once an island in the swamps of Traeth Mawr (*see* **Porthmadog**), is famous for its hounds. In the 1970s, Rhyd consisted almost entirely of **second homes**. The Brondanw Arms in the village of Garreg is very popular.

LLANFRYNACH, Breconshire, Powys
(6706 ha; 577 inhabitants)
The **community**, which contains the villages of Llanfrynach, Llanhamlach, Cantref and Llechfaen, sweeps from the **Usk** valley to Pen-y-fan (886 m), the summit of the **Brecon Beacons**. In 1775, the remains of a **Roman** bathhouse (now in the **National Museum**) were found in Llanfrynach, where, as **Theophilus Jones** put it, 'the British youth were first taught the luxuries of the warm bath, and other effeminacies'. Ty-mawr, adjoining St Brynach's church, contains woodcarvings by Carnhuanawc (**Thomas Price**). Abercynrig was the home of William Aubrey, the prominent Elizabethan lawyer. Nearby, the **Brecon** and **Abergavenny Canal** crosses the Usk by an attractive viaduct. Peterstone Court, Llanhamlach, is a handsome Georgian house built in 1741. There are attractive **waterfalls** in the upper reaches of Cwm Oergwm.

LLANFYLLIN, Montgomeryshire, Powys
(4175 ha; 1407 inhabitants)
The **community** extends over the upper reaches of the basin of the **River** Cain. The town of Llanfyllin, the largest settlement in northern **Montgomeryshire**, received its charter in 1294. Built in the main of local brick, its streets have a wealth of undisturbed 18th- and 19th-century detail. Although the demolition of the Georgian town hall and the Queen Anne rectory have impoverished the townscape, some amends were made in the mid-1990s when grants made possible the refurbishment of the town centre. The brick church of St Myllin is one of Wales's few large 18th-century churches. Opposite, above a chemist's shop, is a room decorated with 13 romantic murals painted *c.*1812 by a French prisoner-of-war, Captain Augeraud. Pendref, one of Wales's oldest **Congregationalist** chapels, was built in 1701. Burned down by **Jacobites** in 1715, it was rebuilt at **government** expense in 1717. It was at the chapel that the **hymn**writer **Ann Griffiths**, who had come to Llanfyllin to **dance**, experienced religious conversion. The five-bay Manor House (1737) is Llanfyllin's finest building. Llanfyllin's large workhouse (1838) dominates the southern access to the town. Northwest of the town is Bodfach Hotel (1767, 1870); once home of the Kyffin family, it has extensive rhododendron **gardens**. There are several ancient farmhouses in the vicinity.

LLANFYNYDD, Carmarthenshire
(4394 ha; 538 inhabitants)
Located north-west of **Llandeilo**, the **community** hugs the left bank of the Cothi. Its only settlement of any size is the village of Llanfynydd in its 'cobweb of narrow lanes' to quote the *Shell Guide to South-West Wales*. St Egwad's church (13th and 15th centuries) has a handsome west tower. The **hymn**writer **Morgan Rhys** (1716–79) is buried in the churchyard, where there is a memorial to him. Pant Glas Hall was the home of David Jones, founder of the Black Ox Bank, **Llandovery** (*see* **Banking and Banks**). Damaged by fire in the 1970s, the hall became a holiday and leisure centre. Llanfynydd was the birthplace of the scholars **D. Simon Evans** and his brother D. Ellis Evans.

LLANFYNYDD, Flintshire
(1947 ha; 1752 inhabitants)

Constituting **Flintshire**'s south-western corner, the **community** once contained **coal** and **iron** mines at Coed Talon and Pontybodkin; by the 20th century, however, it was almost wholly rural. Llanfynydd village lies in the Cegidog valley where the B5101 overlies **Offa's Dyke**. Nant y Ffrith is a narrow ravine with picturesque **waterfalls**. A **Roman** hypocausted building excavated at Ffrith was probably linked to **lead** mining at **Minera**. Trinley Hall (1653) is a vernacular attempt to interpret **Renaissance** architectural principles.

LLANGADOG, Carmarthenshire
(7660 ha; 1303 inhabitants)

Located between **Llandeilo** and **Llandovery**, the **community** contains the villages of Llangadog, Bethlehem and Capel-Gwynfe. It extends from the **Tywi** to the heart of the **Black Mountain** and is bisected by the dramatic **road** (the A4069) that links Llangadog with Brynamman (**Quarter Bach**). Its outstanding feature is Garn Goch – two **Iron Age hill-forts**, Garn Fawr (11 ha) and Garn Fach (1.5 ha), which have massive stone-built ramparts and splendid views over the Tywi valley.

Llangadog was the administrative centre of the **commote** of **Perfedd** and had a castle (destroyed in 1204). In 1326, the *villa* (**borough**) of Llangadog – the property of the bishops of **St David's** – had 33 burgesses. Although the borough declined into oblivion, Llangadog remained an important centre of trade; a commentator in 1842 complained that the **drovers** frequenting its market 'were such savages that they would not listen to **law** or reason'. St **Cadog**'s church was largely rebuilt in 1898 but retains its medieval tower. The prosperity of the area suffered a severe blow in 2005, when the Llangadog creamery closed, with the loss of some 200 jobs. A year later, however, Cambrian Pet Foods opened a canning plant on the site.

The village of Bethlehem, named after its **Congregational** chapel (1800, 1834, 1872), has long been popular with those posting their Christmas cards. The closure of the original post office led to the opening of a restricted service in the old school, which has been converted into a community centre. Near it is Newfoundland Farm, probably named by those associated with the attempt by **William Vaughan** to establish a Welsh colony – **Cambriol** – in Newfoundland between 1616 and *c*.1630. **John Williams** (1840–1926), the main benefactor of the **National Library**, was born in Gwynfe. Y Dalar Wen, a superbly located house designed by **Dewi-Prys Thomas**, was long the home of **Gwynfor Evans**; there is a monument to him at Garn Goch.

LLANGAIN (Llan-gain), Carmarthenshire
(1175 ha; 574 inhabitants)

Located immediately south-west of **Carmarthen**, the **community** hugs the right bank of the **Tywi**. Within it are three standing stones and two much-ruined chambered tombs. Castell Moel (Green Castle), a ruined 15th-century house overlooking the Tywi, was the home of the Reed family, whose praises were sung by **Lewys Glyn Cothi**.

LLANGAMARCH, Breconshire, Powys
(6933 ha; 505 inhabitants)

Stretching from the Irfon valley to the heights of **Mynydd Epynt**, over half the **community** lies within the 'Danger Areas' of Epynt's artillery range. The *Shell Guide to Mid Wales* calls Llangamarch 'the smallest and dreariest of spas', although admitting that its waters were found efficacious in cases of heart disease.

Theophilus Evans, vicar of the **parish** from 1738 to 1763, is buried in the churchyard, as is his grandson, **Theophilus Jones**, **Breconshire**'s historian. **John Penry**, the **Puritan** martyr and pamphleteer, was born at Cefn-brith. Parc Farm, at 44 m in length, is among Wales's longest **longhouses**. Tirabad, a hamlet inhabited by **forestry** workers, is surrounded by vast conifer plantations.

LLANGAN (Llan-gan), Vale of Glamorgan
(1126 ha; 764 inhabitants)

Located south-east of **Bridgend**, the **community** contains the settlements of Llangan, St Mary Hill and Treoes. Llangan church is dedicated to Canna, which may indicate associations with Treganna (Canton) and Pontcanna in **Cardiff**. From 1767 until his death in 1810, its rector was David Jones whose sympathy for Methodism caused Llangan to be thronged on Communion Sundays. His death was one of the factors which led the **Calvinistic Methodists** to ordain their own ministers in 1811. **John Prichard**, Wales's most prolific 19th-century architect, was the son of a later rector. The church of St Mary Hill stands alone in a large circular churchyard. Tradition links the place with King **Arthur**. The **place name** Ruthin recalls one of the medieval lordships of **Glamorgan**.

LLANGATHEN, Carmarthenshire
(2311 ha; 475 inhabitants)

Located north of the **Tywi** immediately west of **Llandeilo**, the **community** contains the villages of Llangathen, Broad Oak and Felindre. The battle of Coed Llathen (*see* **Cymerau, Battle of**), fought near Broad Oak in 1257, was a notable Welsh victory. Cadfan is a remarkable 16th-century farmhouse. Dryslwyn Castle, perched on a rocky crag in the heart of the Tywi valley, was one of the strongholds of the rulers of **Deheubarth**. In 1287, its lord, **Rhys ap Maredudd**, rose in revolt against Edward I. The royal attack on the castle, which involved an army of 11,000 men, a siege engine and the sapping of its foundations, is a remarkably well-documented siege. Subsequently repaired, the castle was adjoined by a **borough**, which in 1359 had 48 urban plots. After being attacked by **Owain Glyndŵr**, the castle and borough went into rapid decline. Excavation in the 1990s proved that both were more elaborate than had previously been realized.

St Cathen's church has a 13th-century tower and contains the elaborate tomb of Anthony Rudd, bishop of **St David's** from 1594 to 1615. Aberglasney, Rudd's residence, was acquired by the Dyer family in 1710. The house stands beneath Grongar Hill, the view from which was described by **John Dyer** in 1726 in a poem which anticipates the spirit of **Romanticism**.

Georgian Aberglasney encloses the remains of Rudd's house. In an advanced state of decay by the 1990s, it has been renovated by the Aberglasney Trust. The trust's work on the **garden** is particularly noteworthy. Hailed as 'the garden lost in time', it contains what may be a rare 16th-century cloister garden and a remarkable yew tunnel. Court Henry (15th and 18th centuries) was the home of Henry ap Gwilym, eulogized by **Lewys Glyn Cothi**. In 1833, its later owners built the dramatically sited St Mary's church on an adjoining hill.

LLANGATTOCK (Llangatwg), Breconshire, Powys (3142 ha; 1006 inhabitants)

Located across the **Usk** from **Crickhowell**, the **community** contains the village of Llangattock and the hamlets of Dardy and Ffawyddog. Llangattock once had several tramroads connecting the **Brecon** and **Abergavenny Canal** with the **iron**-producing areas and **limestone** quarries to the south. The church contains stocks, a whipping post and a striking group of late-18th-century monuments, including one to a midwife, Anne Lewis, who delivered 716 children during her career. Glanusk (demolished) was the mansion of the ironmaster Joseph **Bailey**, ancestor of the Barons Glanusk. Dan-y-parc (also demolished) was built by the Kendalls, the **Beaufort** industrialists. Llangattock Court dates from the late 17th century. Llangattock Park (1838) was the **Breconshire** seat of the **Somerset family**, dukes of Beaufort. Glanwysc was designed by **John Nash**. Craig y Cilau, a National Nature Reserve, is **Britain**'s sole habitat of *Sorbus minima*, the lesser whitebeam (*see* **Plants**). It contains several extensive **cave** systems, particularly Agen Allwedd and Eglwys Faen. Mynydd Llangatwg is riddled with shakeholes.

LLANGATTOCK-VIBON-AVEL (Llangatwg Feibion Afel), Monmouthshire (5395 ha; 955 inhabitants)

Located immediately north-west of **Monmouth**, the **community**'s name has baffled historians. Its northern part is dominated by Skenfrith Castle, one of the **Three Castles** of northern **Gwent**. Built in the 1220s, it has an early example of a round keep. Skenfrith church is an ambitious building of the 13th and 14th centuries. There are attractive restored medieval churches at Llangattock, St Maughans and Rockfield. The Hendre, **Monmouthshire**'s sole full-scale Victorian country house, was built for J. A. Rolls, who was elevated to the peerage as Baron Llangattock in 1892. His third son was **Charles Stewart Rolls**, the aviator and co-founder of Rolls-Royce Ltd. Rockfield's attractive almshouses were commissioned by Baron Llangattock in 1906. The world's first residential recording studios were established at Rockfield in the 1960s. Many Welsh and international rock stars have recorded there.

LLANGEDWYN, Montgomeryshire, Powys (2523 ha; 380 inhabitants)

Located immediately north-east of **Llanfyllin**, the **community** was, until 1996, part of the **Glyndŵr** district of the **county** of **Clwyd**. St Cedwyn's church, rebuilt in 1870, contains a memorial to Edward **Vaughan (Llwydiarth)** and Llangedwyn, whose estates passed on his death in 1718 to the **Williams Wynn family**. Llangedwyn Hall, the centre of what remains of that family's estates, is an interesting example of a 17th and 18th-century mansion adapted in the 1950s to the realities of 20th-century country-house life. Its 17th-century terraced **gardens** are still well maintained. Southey wrote sections of his *Madoc* (1805) at Llangedwyn Hall. The artist J. H. M. Bonnor (1875–1916) was a member of the Bonnor family of Bryn-y-Gwalia. Llangedwyn's striking **war memorial** was executed to his designs. Henblas (originally 15th century) and Plas Uchaf (18th century) are interesting houses. Antur Tanat Cain was established in the village in 1987 as

The village of Llangadog, showing the post office and Castle Hotel, *c.*1885

Wales's first telecottage; there is a crafts centre in the same group of buildings.

LLANGEFNI, Isle of Anglesey
(1111 ha; 4662 inhabitants)

Located in the middle of **Anglesey**, Llangefni was recognized in 1889 as **county** town. It was already a major trading centre, having replaced **Llannerch-y-medd** as the county's principal market in the late 18th century. Tregarnedd is a site associated with **Ednyfed Fychan**; the moated site nearby may date from the 13th century. In the early 19th century, Llangefni was the home of Wales's leading **Baptist** minister, **Christmas Evans**, and its leading **Calvinistic Methodist** minister, **John Elias**. The **community**'s **architecture** is dominated by the chapels in which they ministered, and by the county hall. Llangefni has grown substantially since the **Second World War**, partly because of its industrial estate. Theatr Fach, founded in 1953 by a local schoolmaster, George Fisher (1909–70), was a pioneering venture. Oriel Ynys Môn illustrates the history of Anglesey and has a large collection of the **bird paintings** of **Charles Tunnicliffe**. In 2001, 89.24% of the inhabitants of the community had some knowledge of **Welsh**, with 69.72% wholly fluent in the language – the highest percentages in Anglesey.

LLANGEITHO, Ceredigion
(3829 ha; 874 inhabitants)

Straddling the middle reaches of the **Aeron** valley, the **community** extends to Llyn Fanod on Mynydd Bach; it contains the village of Llangeitho and the settlements of Capel Betws Lleucu, Llanbadarn Odwyn, Llwynpiod and Penuwch. Parcrhydderch was the home of Rhydderch ap Ieuan (d.1400), whose name is associated with *The White Book of Rhydderch*.

    Daniel Rowland, curate of Llangeitho from 1735, made the village the chief centre of the **Methodist Revival**, with thousands coming from all parts of Wales to receive communion at his hands. Deprived of his curacy *c*.1763, Llangeitho chapel was built for him. A statue was erected to him in 1883, despite the protest of the bishop of **St David's** who deplored 'the immense amount of mischief [Rowland had caused] to the church in which he had received his commission'. The evangelist **Martyn Lloyd-Jones** was brought up at Llangeitho. Llyn Fanod is one of the sources of the Aeron. Cwrt Mawr (*c*.1845) was the home of **J. H. Davies**, a major benefactor of the **National Library of Wales**.

LLANGELER, Carmarthenshire
(6032 ha; 3222 inhabitants)

Hugging the **Carmarthenshire–Ceredigion** border immediately south-east of **Newcastle Emlyn**, the **community** contains the hamlets of Llangeler, Penboyr, Pentrecagal and Rhos, and the villages of Drefach-Felindre, Pentre-cwrt and Saron. It is rich in **Bronze Age** graves. Llysnewydd mansion, designed by **John Nash** *c*.1800, was demolished in 1971. In the late 19th and early 20th centuries, the area was an important centre of the **woollen industry**, with 23 woollen factories in Drefach-Felindre alone. Since 1976, its Cambrian Mill (1902) has housed the National Wool Museum, a branch of the **National Museum**. **Griffith Jones**, **Llanddowror**, was born at Penboyr.

LLANGELYNIN (Llangelynnin), Gwynedd
(2154 ha; 708 inhabitants)

Located immediately north of **Tywyn**, the **community** contains the village of Llwyngwril and the hamlets of Llangelynin and Rhoslefain. Within it are excellent examples of **dry stone walling**. The 13th-century St Celynnin's church stands high above the sea. Adjoining it is the Cambrian Coast **railway** at its most scenic. The churchyard contains the grave of Abram **Wood** (1799), patriarch of the famous family of Welsh **Romanies**. Castell y Gaer near Llwyngwril is an **Iron Age hill-fort**. The gate to the **Quaker** cemetery bears the date 1646, which predates the foundation of the Society of Friends. From the 1940s to the 1960s, Tonfanau was a large army camp.

LLANGENNECH, Carmarthenshire
(1222 ha; 4510 inhabitants)

The **community** is located immediately north-east of **Llanelli**, of which the two main settlements – the villages of Llangennech and Bryn – are essentially suburbs. St Cennych's church, largely rebuilt in 1900, retains its medieval tower. From the mid-19th century onwards, **coal**mining and **tinplate** manufacture led to considerable **population** growth. During the **Second World War**, Llangennech's Royal Naval Stores employed over 1000 workers. The stores closed in 1988, exacerbating the problems already caused by the closure of coalmines and tinplate works. Light industries have been established, but the bulk of the community's workers commute to Llanelli or **Swansea**. **Trefor Beasley** and his wife, Eileen, whose **Welsh-language** protest provided a model for **Cymdeithas yr Iaith Gymraeg**, lived at Llangennech.

LLANGENNITH, LLANMADOC AND CHERITON (Llangynydd, Llanmadog a Cheriton), Swansea (2722 ha; 822 inhabitants)

Occupying the north-west corner of the **Gower** peninsula, the **community** contains the tidal islet of Burry Holms – the location of an **Iron Age** fort and of St Cennydd's hermitage. St Cattwg's, Cheriton, is the peninsula's finest church. From the early 12th century until 1414, St Cennydd's church was a dependent cell of Evreux Abbey. St Madoc's church contains a 5th-century inscribed stone (*see* **Monuments, Early Christian**).

    The area is rich in prehistoric monuments. The cast-**iron lighthouse** at Whiteford Point, built in 1865 to guide **ships** into **Llanelli** harbour, is a rare survival. The 15th-century fortified manor house at Landimore overlooks Landimore Marsh, an area riddled with root-shaped waterways.

LLANGERNYW, Conwy
(7005 ha; 982 inhabitants)

Located in hilly country east of the **Conwy** valley, the **community** contains the villages of Llangernyw, Pandy Tudur and Gwytherin. Inscribed stones (6th–9th centuries; *see* **Monuments, Early Christian**) in the churchyards of Gwytherin and Llangernyw testify to an early Christian presence, traditionally associated with St **Winefride**. Llangernyw churchyard has a 4000-year-old yew tree (*see* **Plants**), the oldest living in Wales. St Winifred's church (1869), Gwytherin, contains two 14th-century sepulchral slabs. The cruciform church of St Digain, Llangernyw, largely rebuilt in the 19th century, contains memorials to the Sandbach family, **Liverpool ship**owners who also built Llanddewi church (1875), which has since been converted into a dwelling.

The Sandbach mansion, Hafodunos (1866), perhaps the most influential of the country houses designed by George Gilbert Scott, suffered massive fire damage in 2004. Its **gardens**, in former times, contained a wealth of **plants**. Y Cwm, the shoemaker's cottage home of the philosopher **Henry Jones**, is a museum. The philologist **Robert Roberts** (Y Sgolor Mawr) was born at Pandy Tudur.

LLANGOED, Isle of Anglesey
(902 ha; 1275 inhabitants)
Constituting the easternmost corner of **Anglesey**, the **community** includes Ynys Seiriol (Puffin **Island** or Priestholm). Penmon was the site of a 6th-century *clas* or **Celtic** monastery associated with St **Seiriol** – the cell and holy **well** survive. Two 10th-century stones bearing interlacing patterns stand in St Seiriol's church, which has a nave of *c.*1140 and transepts of the 1160s. A large chancel was added to it *c.*1220, when the monastery became an **Augustinian** canonry. Ruins of the three-storeyed monastic buildings adjoin the church. Following the **dissolution**, the site became the property of the **Bulkeley family**, and *c.*1600 Richard Bulkeley built a fine **dovecote** nearby, containing 1000 nestholes. Castell Aberlleiniog is a late 11th-century motte, possibly built by Hugh the Fat (**Hugh of Avranches**), earl of Chester, and surmounted by a stone structure, perhaps built at the time of the **Civil Wars**.

Along the shore are the remains of several quarries, which provided stone for the building of **Beaumaris** Castle, Penrhyn Castle and the **Menai** and Britannia bridges. The **lighthouse** at Trwyn Du was first built in 1834.

LLANGOEDMOR, Ceredigion
(1942 ha; 1174 inhabitants)
Located immediately east of **Cardigan**, the **community** contains a delectable stretch of the **Teifi** offering superb views of **Cilgerran** Castle. Plas Llangoedmor (1760, 1830) was acquired in 1801 by Benjamin Millichamp (1756–1829), chaplain in Madras and collector of oriental manuscripts. The mansion eventually passed to his great-grandson, H. M. Vaughan (1870–1948), benefactor of the **National Library** and author of *The South Wales Squires* (1926). The substantial village of Llechryd once had one of Wales's few Swedenborgian chapels, erected in 1881. Llechryd bridge is the most picturesque of all the bridges crossing the Teifi.

LLANGOLLEN, Denbighshire
(2532 ha; 3412 inhabitants)
Beautifully situated on the banks of the **Dee**, the **community**'s name commemorates Collen, a figure of great obscurity. St Collen's church has a superb 15th-century roof. The poet **Gruffudd Hiraethog** (d.1546) is buried in its churchyard, which also contains the neo-Gothic tomb of **Eleanor Butler and Sarah Ponsonby**, the Ladies of Llangollen. Llangollen bridge (*c.*1500), one of the '**seven wonders of Wales**', was originally built in the 1280s. The Llangollen **Canal** (1808), much used for boating trips, was

Llangollen: the 16th-century bridge over the River Dee

designed by **Thomas Telford**, who, in 1819, drove the **Holyhead road** (the **A5**) though the town.

In 1780, the Ladies of Llangollen settled at Plas Newydd; the house's best-known feature, its half-timbered front, was added by a later resident, General Yorke. The ladies attracted well-known figures to Llangollen, thus boosting its appeal to visitors. **George Borrow** began the walk he described in *Wild Wales* at Llangollen, where he spent three months in 1854.

In 1858, the first truly national **eisteddfod** was held in the town, which since 1947 has hosted the **Llangollen International Musical Eisteddfod**. In 1992, the eisteddfod acquired a permanent pavilion. Much of the early vision and artistic quality of the eisteddfod flowed from the activity of **W. S. Gwynn Williams**, a Llangollen **music** publisher. The European Centre for Training and Regional Cooperation (ECTARC) has its headquarters at Llangollen.

High above the town stands the castle of Dinas Bran; the name perhaps recalls the **Celtic** deity **Bendigeidfran**. The present remains are those of the castle built by Gruffudd ap Madog (d.1269), ruler of **Powys Fadog**. Pengwern (17th century) was the home of the poet Jonathan Hughes (1721–1805). The chain bridge at Berwyn is a delightful feature. Nearby are two innovative 19th-century houses – Vivod and Plas Berwyn.

LLANGOLLEN INTERNATIONAL MUSICAL EISTEDDFOD

Founded at **Llangollen** in 1947 by **W. S. Gwynn Williams**, this annual festival of **music** and **dance** is renowned for its special emphasis on national cultures and international co-operation. Choirs from Germany were heard there soon after the **Second World War**, and the young Pavarotti appeared in the festival as a member of his father's choir. Llangollen has done much to introduce into Wales new repertoire and new standards of choral singing from (particularly) eastern Europe, Scandinavia and **North America**.

LLANGOLLEN RURAL (Llangollen Wledig), Wrexham (122 ha; 1999 inhabitants)

In 1996, the **communities** of **Llangollen** and Llangollen Rural became part of the reconstituted **Denbighshire**, but Llangollen Rural was transferred to the **county borough** of **Wrexham** in 1998. The community – essentially an extension of **Cefn** – contains Trevor Hall, a fine 18th-century brick mansion, and **Telford**'s astonishing Pont Cysyllte aqueduct (1805). Carrying the unfinished Ellesmere **Canal** in a cast-**iron** trough across the Vale of Llangollen, 'the stream in the sky' stands 39 m above the **Dee**. The aqueduct is a candidate for recognition as a World Heritage site. Argoed Hall was built for R. F. Graesser, founder of the Monsanto Chemical Works and the Wrexham Lager Brewery (*see* **Beer, Brewing and Breweries**).

LLANGORS (Llan-gors), Breconshire, Powys (3694 ha; 1045 inhabitants)

Located east of **Brecon**, the **community** contains the villages of Llanfihangel Tal-y-llyn, Llangasty Tal-y-llyn and Llangors, and the hamlets of Cathedine and Llanywern. Llangorse **Lake** (Llyn Syfaddan) – confusingly given a

A colourful scene at the Llangollen International Musical Eisteddfod

different spelling on Ordnance Survey **maps** from that of the community – is the largest natural stretch of water in southern Wales. According to a tradition recorded by **Giraldus Cambrensis**, its **birds** sing only for a truly Welsh prince. The fortified dwelling in the lake – a seat of the royal house of **Brycheiniog** – is Wales's only known crannog. It offers evidence of Brycheiniog's links with **Ireland**, where crannogs abound. *The Anglo-Saxon Chronicle* records the capture of the queen of Brycheiniog at 'Brecenan Mere' in 916.

The church, vicarage and school at Llangasty Tal-y-llyn, designed by J. L. Pearson, are a remarkable group of buildings inspired by the Tractarian ideals (*see* **Oxford Movement**) of Robert Raikes who lived in the impressive mansion of Treberfedd (1852). The junction between the **Hay** and the **Merthyr–Brecon railways** was at Tal-y-llyn. In the 19th century, the graveyard at Llanywern was so marshy that **Theophilus Jones** recommended the cutting of drainage trenches, so that those interred there 'might all moulder dryly, snugly and comfortably together'.

LLANGRANNOG, Ceredigion
(1966 ha; 796 inhabitants)

Located on the coast halfway between **Aberaeron** and **Cardigan**, the **community** contains the villages of Llangrannog, Pontgarreg and Pentregat. Llangrannog, squeezed into its tiny valley and the most picturesque of all **Ceredigion**'s seaside villages, bred generations of skilled seamen (*see* **Seafaring**). **Sarah Jane Rees** (Cranogwen), writer and proto-feminist, conducted a school at Llangrannog at which she taught basic navigation skills. Pigeonsford Mansion (Rhydycolomennod; basically 1755) was owned by the Jordan family. The first permanent camp of **Urdd Gobaith Cymru** was established at Llangrannog in 1932. **Cilie** was home to the best known of recent **Welsh** bardic families. Pendinaslochtyn is a dramatically located **Iron Age** coastal **hill-fort**. It is owned by the **National Trust**, as is the delectable Ynys-Lochtyn.

LLANGRISTIOLUS, Isle of Anglesey
(2543 ha; 1217 inhabitants)

Located immediately south-west of **Llangefni**, the **community** contains the villages of Llangristiolus, Cerrigceinwen and Rhostrehwfa. There were once **coal** workings in the vicinity. The important medieval township of Lledwigan lay within Llangristiolus **parish** and this may explain the impressive 13th-century chancel arch in St Cristiolus church. Paradwys (Paradise) was originally a house, the name being derived from the Persian word for the walled **garden** it once had; the name later came to be applied to the neighbourhood, which was the home of Ifan Gruffydd (1896–1971), author of *Gŵr o Baradwys* (1963). Henblas (17th century) has become the centre of a country park.

LLANGUNLLO (Llangynllo), Radnorshire,
Powys (4825 ha; 377 inhabitants)

A tract of **mountain**ous land west of **Knighton**, the **community** contains the hamlets of Llangunllo and Bleddfa. When **Edward Lhuyd** was collecting material for his *Parochialia* in 1696, the area was predominantly **Welsh**-speaking, but by the 1730s, **English** was gaining ground rapidly. St Mary Magdalene's church, Bleddfa, has a fine medieval roof. Since the 1970s, all its internal fittings are moveable, allowing performances to be held in an unencumbered space. Monaughty, the largest late 16th-century house in **Radnorshire**, was a grange of **Abbey Cwmhir**.

LLANGUNNOR (Llangynnwr), Carmarthenshire
(2342 ha; 2282 inhabitants)

Located immediately south-east of **Carmarthen**, the **community** contains the hamlets of Llangunnor and Nantycaws, the Carmarthen suburbs of Pen-sarn and Tre-gynor, and the industrial estate around Carmarthen **railway** station. The isolated church of St Ceinwr (14th century) contains a memorial to the **English** essayist Richard Steele (1671–1729), who acquired the mansion of Tygwyn through marriage in 1707. Tygwyn is now a farmhouse. The **hymn**writer **David Charles** and the poet **Lewis Morris** are buried in the churchyard. Pibwrlwyd, once owned by the Dwnn family, is the site of **Carmarthenshire** College.

LLANGURIG, Montgomeryshire, Powys
(12,769 ha; 670 inhabitants)

Located immediately west of **Llanidloes**, this vast **community** contains the source of the **Wye** and the uppermost part of the basin of the **river**. It mostly consists of **sheep** farms and **Forestry Commission** land. The public convenience on the cycle track at Nantybenwch must be the remotest in Wales. Near the A44, which links Llangurig with **Aberystwyth**, is the **Roman** fort of Cae Gaer. The Welsh-built motte, Rhyd-yr-onnen, lies west of Cwmbelan, which was once a centre of the **woollen industry**. St Curig's church stands on the site of a *clas* or **Celtic** monastery. The church's 12th-century tower is crowned by an embattled turret, part of the restoration of 1878 that largely obliterated the 15th-century nave and chancel.

LLANGWM, Conwy (4114 ha; 516 inhabitants)

Constituting the south-eastern corner of the **county** of **Conwy**, the **community** is one of three in Wales called Llangwm, all of which have churches dedicated to St Jerome. That in this Llangwm was remodelled in 1747 and restored in 1874. St Catherine's church, Dinmael (1878), was designed by the amateur architect William Kerr, who lived at neo-Tudor Maesmor (*c.*1830), an ancient site that has yielded significant prehistoric evidence. Dinmael, which bears the name of a medieval **commote** of **Dinmael**, contains a fine example of **Thomas Telford**'s skill as a **road** engineer. In 1887, Llangwm witnessed some of the most turbulent scenes of the **Tithe** War, which led to the court appearance of 31 so-called 'Tithe Martyrs'.

LLANGWM (Llan-gwm), Monmouthshire
(1785 ha; 400 inhabitants)

The **community** consists of undulating land east of the town of **Usk**. Its chief attraction is the magnificent rood screen (*c.*1500) in St Jerome's church. There is another medieval church in the delightfully named village of Llanfihangel Torymynydd. Gaer Fawr is the largest **hill-fort** in **Monmouthshire**; there is another hill-fort at Llansoy. **Walter Cradock**, the pioneer of Welsh **Puritanism**, was born at Llangwm.

LLANGWM, Pembrokeshire
(643 ha; 854 inhabitants)

The **community** overlooks the confluence of the Eastern and the Western **Cleddau**. St Jerome's church contains canopied niche tombs and remnants of a rood screen and loft. Llangwm village was long-famed for the proud exclusiveness of its inhabitants. For centuries, its chief industry was the gathering of cockles, mussels and oysters; Llangwm cocklewomen, with their baskets of shell**fish**, were a regular sight at markets in **Haverfordwest**, **Pembroke** and **Tenby** well into the 20th century.

Peregrine Phillips, expelled from the living of Llangwm in 1662, became pastor of a group of dissenters at Haverfordwest. In 1999, the northern part of the community became the community of **Hook**.

LLANGWYRYFON, Ceredigion
(3190 ha; 625 inhabitants)

The **community** occupies the western slopes of Mynydd Bach and contains the **mountain**'s highest point – Hafod Ithel (361 m). The village of Llangwyryfon lies in the upper reaches of the Wyre valley. St Ursula's church was one of the many livings acquired by the notorious **tithe**-mongers, the Chichester family. Trefenter, a scattered settlement, was originally composed of *tai unnos*; the squatters fiercely defended their houses against the would-be encloser Augustus Brackenbury in **Rhyfel y Sais Bach** (The War of the Little Englishman; 1820–6). Trefenter was the ancestral home of the poet and scholar **Gwyn Williams** (1904–90).

LLANGYBI, Ceredigion (2852 ha; 779 inhabitants)

Located immediately north of **Lampeter**, the **community** contains the villages of Llangybi, Betws Bledrws and Silian. St Sulien's church, Silian, contains two early inscribed stones, one of them (*c.*9th century) bearing superb knotwork patterns (*see* **Monuments, Early Christian**). Derry Ormond (1824, but demolished) was the home of the Inglis-Jones family. The family built a folly – Twr y Dderi – in order to create local employment. The cause founded at Cilgwyn in 1654 became the mother church of **Congregationalism** in **Cardiganshire**. Glan-Denys was the home of Julian Cayo Evans (1937–95), founder of the **Free Wales Army**. Ysgol y Dderi is a notable example of a primary school serving a cluster of villages.

LLANGYBI, Monmouthshire
(2666 ha; 865 inhabitants)

Located south of the town of **Usk**, the **community** extends from the Usk's flat valley floor to the Llandegfedd **reservoir**, completed in 1966 to supply water to **Cwmbran**. The almost wholly ruined Llangybi Castle was a massive structure, probably built by the **Clare** family in the early 14th century. The fine avenue leading to Llangybi House survives, although the house has been demolished. St **Cybi**'s church is an impressive building with elaborate monuments and medieval wall **paintings**.

LLANGYFELACH, Swansea
(1169 ha; 2351 inhabitants)

Once a huge **parish** that covered much of the ancient Welshry of the lordship of **Gower**, the present **community**

straddles the **M4**. The church of St Cyfelach and St David was rebuilt in the 1830s on a new site within the churchyard, leaving the original tower to stand alone. The church contains W. D. Caröe's rood screen (1916), modelled on the medieval screens of **Powys** and **Gwent**. The vast **Velindre Tinplate Works** (1952–6), designed by **Percy Thomas**, were closed in 1995 and demolished. The site of the works was the location of the National **Eisteddfod** of 2006. Llangyfelach features in a well-known folk song lamenting the cruelties of the **press gang**, and it was the birthplace of the painter **Evan Walters**. Suburban **Swansea** has reached even this ancient settlement, but the views to the hills are still superb.

LLANGYNDEYRN, Carmarthenshire
(4720 ha; 2953 inhabitants)

Embracing the central stretch of the basin of the Gwendraeth Fach immediately north-east of **Kidwelly**, the **community** contains the villages of Llangyndeyrn, Carway, Crwbin, Four Roads, Meinciau and Pontantwn. Mynydd Llangyndeyrn is rich in prehistoric monuments. The church of St Cyndeyrn or Kentigern (13th century, 1888) has a slender tower. Within it is a memorial to **William Vaughan** (1575–1641) who attempted to establish a Welsh colony – **Cambriol** – in Newfoundland.

Located on the edge of the south Wales **coalfield**, the exploitation of the area's **limestone** and coal led, in the second half of the 19th century, to considerable **population** expansion. In 1963, the **Swansea** Corporation sought to dam the Gwendraeth Fach valley, but when engineers came to survey the area, local residents prevented them by locking the gates of every field. In 1983, a plaque commemorating the resistance was unveiled near the church hall of Llangyndeyrn village.

LLANGYNFELYN, Ceredigion
(2314 ha; 641 inhabitants)

Located immediately east of **Borth** and hugging the southern bank of the **Dyfi** estuary, the **community** contains the villages of Llangynfelyn, Tre'r-ddôl and Tre Taliesin. The name of the latter was a Victorian invention inspired by the belief that a nearby **Bronze Age** cairn was the grave of the poet **Taliesin**. The American architect Frank Lloyd Wright, who claimed that his ancestors came from the area, called his house Taliesin. At Lodge Park, once the property of the **Pryses** of Gogerddan, are the remains of a **deer** park. The religious **revival** of 1859 began at Tre'r-ddôl under the leadership of Humphrey Jones (1832–95), a native of Llangynfelyn. The success of the revival led to the building of a new **Wesleyan** chapel at Tre'r-ddôl, where, in the 1980s, the original chapel (1835) became a museum.

Glasfryn was the home of W. Basil Jones, bishop of **St David's** (1874–97). According to tradition, it was at Traeth Maelgwn that **Maelgwn Gwynedd**'s pre-eminence among the rulers of Wales was acknowledged.

LLANGYNHAFAL, Denbighshire
(1191 ha; 673 inhabitants)

Located south-east of **Denbigh**, the **community** contains Moel Famau Country Park, which extends to Moel Famau (554 m), the highest point of the **Clwydian Hills**. St

Cynhafal's church contains a carving (1690) of a pelican feeding its chicks – a symbol of Christ in the Eucharist. In 1791 and 1793, Wordsworth stayed with his friend Robert Jones at Plas-yn-Llan, a timber-framed house near the church. The antiquarian Ab Ithel (**John Williams**; 1811–62) was born at Tŷ Nant, Llangynhafal. In 1964, the 15th-century cruck house Hendre'r-ywydd Uchaf was rebuilt at the National History Museum (*see* **St Fagans**).

LLANGYNIDR, Breconshire, Powys
(4949 ha; 1005 inhabitants)

Extending from the **Usk** to **Blaenau Gwent**, the **community** contains a fine stretch of the **Brecon** and **Monmouthshire Canal**. The village has greatly expanded in recent years. The six-arch bridge (*c.*1600) is one of the oldest and finest spanning the Usk. The **road** over Mynydd Llangynidr to **Beaufort** is among the highest in Wales. The mountain's **limestone** was once extensively used in the **iron**works of Blaenau Gwent. The area abounds in shakeholes. Ogof Fawr (the **Chartists' cave**) features in Chartist folklore.

LLANGYNIEW (Llangynyw), Montgomeryshire,
Powys (2157 ha; 539 inhabitants)

Located immediately north of **Llanfair Caereinion**, the **community** contains the confluence of the Banwy and Vyrnwy **Rivers**. The hilltop church of St Cynyw has a fine rood screen and a splendid 15th-century timber porch. The 8-m high motte at **Mathrafal**, standing above the Banwy, was reputedly the chief seat of the rulers of **Powys**, but excavation there has yielded disappointing results. Dolobran Hall – of which a mere fragment of the 18th-century mansion survives – was the home of the **Lloyd family**, **Quaker** industrialists and bankers. The fittings of the Dolobran Quaker Meeting House have been taken to **Pennsylvania**, where Thomas Lloyd of Dolobran served as William Penn's lieutenant-governor.

The community's largest settlement is Pontrobert, where John Hughes (1775–1854), biographer of **Ann Griffiths**, was **Calvinistic Methodist** minister from 1814 until his death; his wife Ruth, Ann's servant, recorded her employer's **hymns** from memory.

LLANGYNIN, Carmarthenshire
(1313 ha; 270 inhabitants)

Located immediately north-west of **St Clears**, the **community**'s only settlement of any size is the village of Llangynin. The isolated St Cynin's church has three rough medieval arches. Castell Gorfod, home to a number of **gentry** families since the 16th century, was acquired by the Buckley family of **Llanelli** in 1871. The family's library, now in the **National Library**, includes the only known copies of the *Cambrian Magazine* (1773), the first **English periodical** to be published in Wales.

LLANGYNOG, Carmarthenshire
(2690 ha; 559 inhabitants)

Located south-west of **Carmarthen** and extending to the estuary of the **Taf**, the **community**'s only settlement of any size is the village of Llangynog. The capstone of the **Neolithic** chambered tomb of Twlc y Filiast has been displaced and rests partly on the ground. St **Teilo**'s church,

Llandeilo Abercywyn, is in ruin. While he was rector there (1711–16), **Griffith Jones, Llanddowror**, won his reputation as a **preacher**. The isolated church of St Cynog was built *c.*1879. Coomb, a large 19th-century mansion that was home to a branch of the **Philipps family**, became the first Cheshire Home to be established in Wales. Fernhill was the home of **Dylan Thomas**'s aunt; the poet spent his childhood holidays there and made it the subject of his best-known poem.

LLANGYNOG, Montgomeryshire, Powys
(4353 ha; 321 inhabitants)

Located at **Montgomeryshire**'s north-western corner, the **community** comprises the upper reaches of the Tanat basin. It extends almost to the summit of the **Berwyn Mountains**, which are crossed by the B4391, the **road** which links Llangynog with **Bala**. Craig Rhiwarth is crowned by a spectacularly sited **hill-fort** and offers evidence of prehistoric **lead** mining. Mining resumed in the late 17th century. From the 1690s to the 1740s, Llangynog was Europe's most important lead-mining area, with a **population** rising on occasion to over 2000. From *c.*1850, **slate** and **granite** quarrying enjoyed prosperity sufficient to cause Llangynog in 1904 to be linked to Oswestry by **railway**; the line closed in 1960.

To the west of Llangynog village lies the delectable Cwm Pennant, the location of St **Melangell**'s church. Tradition maintains that, while **hunting**, Brochfael Ysgithrog, a 6th-century ruler of **Powys**, came upon the cell of Melangell, daughter of an **Irish** king. She protected a **hare** from his hounds and he gave her land to found a **nunnery**. The enchanting little church dates originally from the 12th century. It contains Melangell's reconstructed shrine (*c.*1165; restored 1959), a delicate Romanesque structure unique in **Britain**.

LLANGYNWYD LOWER (Llangynwyd Isaf),
Bridgend (889 ha; 467 inhabitants)

The southern part of the old **parish** of Llangynwyd, the **community** contains the once-elegant 18th-century Coytrehen House, several medieval house platforms and part of the **Ogwr** Ridgeway Walk. Near its northern boundary is the farm of Cefn Ydfa, the home of Ann Maddocks (b.Thomas; 1704–27), who was, according to tradition, forced to marry the wealthy Anthony Maddocks rather than her lover, the poet Wil Hopcyn. She is said to have died of a broken heart and is commemorated in the song 'Bugeilio'r Gwenith Gwyn' in an opera by **Joseph Parry** and in a novel by Isaac Hughes (Craigfryn; 1852–1928).

LLANGYNWYD MIDDLE (Llangynwyd Ganol),
Bridgend (1352 ha; 2843 inhabitants)

The **community** is the core of the old **parish** of Llangynwyd, traditionally known as yr Hen Blwyf (the old parish). It was one of the first areas of upland **Glamorgan** to be subject to the direct rule of the **Norman** invaders, and came to be known as **Tir Iarll** (the earl's land). In 1257, its castle was destroyed, probably by **Llywelyn ap Gruffudd**. Rebuilt by Gilbert de **Clare** in the 1260s, the remains of the gatehouse have similarities with Gilbert's concurrent work at

Caerphilly. Despite the early date of its conquest, Welsh traditions remained rooted in the area. It has been central to the Welsh literary activity of upland Glamorgan, and the community is notable for its persistence in maintaining the Christmas **Mari Lwyd** ritual.

By the 21st century, most of the inhabitants were living on the banks of the Llynfi in the townships of Cwmfelin and Pont Rhyd-y-cyff. However, the community's historic centre is located on a ridge above the valley, an unusual example of an upland parish with a nucleated village at its centre. St Cynwyd's church, built in the 14th century and including an impressive tower, was much altered during its 19th-century restoration. Ann Maddocks (b.Thomas; 1704–27; *see* **'Bugeilio'r Gwenith Gwyn'** and **Llangynwyd Lower**), is buried in the churchyard. Adjoining the church is the Old House tavern, which claims to offer Wales's widest choice of malt **whisky**.

LLANGYWER, Gwynedd
(7778 ha; 212 inhabitants)

Located immediately south of **Bala**, the **community** extends from Bala Lake (Llyn Tegid) to the **Berwyn Mountains** at Foel Cwm-Sian Llwyd (648 m). St Cywair's church, originally 13th century, was largely rebuilt in 1871. In the churchyard is one of Wales's oldest yew trees (*see* **Plants**). The Lloyd family of Plas Rhiwaedog (1664) claimed descent from **Owain Gwynedd**; its members were generous patrons of the bards. Along the shores of Bala Lake, 6 km of the Bala–**Dolgellau railway** (1868) have been reopened as a tourist attraction. The community, which has been extensively forested, contains Bala **Sailing** Club. 'Ffarwel i blwyf Llangywer' (Farewell to the parish of Llangywer) is a well-known folk song. The poet **Euros Bowen** spent most of his career as rector of Llangywer.

LLANHARAN, Rhondda Cynon Taff
(2346 ha; 7104 inhabitants)

Located immediately west of **Llantrisant**, the **community** contains the villages of Llanharan, Bryncae, Brynna, Llanilid, Peterston-super-Montem and Ynysmaerdy. The area is overlooked by Mynydd Garthmaelwg, on which is a once much-frequented sulphurous **well**. St Ilid's church has a 12th-century tower; adjoining it is a 12th-century ringwork. Of the medieval church of St Peter, footings and tombs survive. The Jenkins family, owners of a 2500-ha estate, lived at Llanharan House (*c*.1750) and provided it with a superb staircase (*c*.1806). In 1857, the family financed the rebuilding of the church of Sts **Julius and Aaron**, an attractive structure designed by **John Prichard** and J. P. Seddon.

The employment provided by the Meiros and Brynna collieries, first sunk the 1870s, led to much in-migration, especially from the Forest of Dean. Impressive colliery buildings survive at Ynysmaerdy. The collieries have long gone, but Mynydd Hywel Deio, one of Wales's largest manmade holes, proved to be a productive open-cast mine. There are plans by the actor and director Richard Attenborough to build a **film** studio on this site, thereby creating a thousand permanent jobs; in 2007, work began on the projected Dragon International Film Studios – or Valleywood, as the venture has been dubbed.

LLANHARRY (Llanhari), Rhondda Cynon Taff
(737 ha; 2919 inhabitants)

Located immediately south-west of **Llantrisant**, the **community** offers a good example of the landscape of the Border **Vale [of Glamorgan]**. With **coal** near the surface and with a band of haematite **iron** ore, Llanharry was a centre of industrial activity from at least the 16th century. It had Wales's last iron ore mine, which closed in 1976. At St **Illtud**'s church (1868) is a cast iron slab bearing the arms of the Gibbon family. Llanharry is home to the second **Welsh**-medium secondary school to be established in **Glamorgan** (1974).

LLANHENNOCK (Llanhenwg), Monmouthshire
(1538 ha; 454 inhabitants)

Located immediately north-east of **Newport**, the **community**'s finest feature is the bridge over the **Usk**, believed to have been built in 1779 by a member of the Edwards family of bridge builders (*see* **William Edwards**). There are attractive churches at Llanhennock and Tredunnock. Glen Usk (*c*.1820) is a superb neo-classical villa. Colomendy Wood (1914) represents the Arts and Crafts tradition at its best.

LLANHILLETH (Llanhiledd), Blaenau Gwent
(742 ha; 4776 inhabitants)

The southernmost part of **Blaenau Gwent County Borough**, the **community** contains the confluence of the **Ebbw** Fawr and Ebbw Fach. **Coal** was worked in small levels from the late 17th century onwards. By the late 19th century, a major settlement had arisen, dependent upon the Llanhilleth Colliery of Partridge, Jones and Co. Rows of terraced houses line the valley bottom and form serried ranks on the hillside. High above them stands the church of St **Illtud**, a foundation of the **Cistercians** of **Llantarnam**, on what tradition claims was originally a 5th-century site. The medieval church is the oldest building in north-west **Gwent**. It was deconsecrated in 1957 and subsequently restored by Blaenau Gwent District Council.

North of the church is the curiously named Castell Taliorum, where excavations revealed the remains of a medieval tower and of another structure resembling a keep. At Upper Hafodarthen, there is an example of the 'unit system' – two farmhouses served by a single farmyard.

LLANIDAN, Isle of Anglesey
(1399 ha; 979 inhabitants)

Located across the **Menai Strait** from **Y Felinheli**, the **community** contains the substantial village of Brynsiencyn, associated with the **preacher John Williams** (1854–1921). The medieval **parish** church was demolished in 1844; a larger church was built in the hope of competing with the the proliferation of **Nonconformist** chapels. There is a **Neolithic** chambered tomb at Bodowyr. Castell Bryn-gwyn is an enclosure occupied from Neolithic to **Roman** times. The rectangular enclosure at Caer Lêb was probably built by the Romans. Llanidan may have been the site of the massacre of the **druids** (AD 61) reported by **Tacitus**. The Oceanarium is an imaginative modern aquarium that displays the marine life around **Anglesey**.

Llanidloes: the Market Hall, built *c.*1600

LLANIDLOES, Montgomeryshire, Powys
(540 ha; 2807 inhabitants)

The **community** consists of the town of Llanidloes and its immediate environs. (For the area beyond the town's boundaries, *see* **Llanidloes Without**.) Llanidloes, which had earthen defences, received its charter in 1280. The Old Market Hall (*c.*1600) at its centre is the only one of its kind extant in Wales. John Wesley preached from a stone by its side, and **Howel Harris** under a nearby oak. The splendid church of St Idloes has a 13th-century arcade transported from **Abbey Cwmhir** in 1542; the magnificent roof may also have come from the abbey. Llanidloes was the birthplace of **Richard Gwyn**, the first Welsh **Catholic martyr**.

In the first half of the 19th century, Llanidloes, with a **population** approaching 4000, was an important centre of the **woollen industry**. Following unrest in April 1839, three **London police**men were sent to the town; they were besieged in the Trewythen Hotel, and for a week Llanidloes was under the control of the protestors. Generally seen as an episode of **Chartism**, the butt of the protest was more likely to have been the new **Poor Law**. The streets of Llanidloes repay inspection, for they contain a wealth of interesting buildings, among them the handsome Sion chapel (1878).

LLANIDLOES WITHOUT (Llanidloes Allanol),
Montgomeryshire, Powys (5843 ha; 593 inhabitants)

The **community** consists of the countryside west, north and east of the town of **Llanidloes**. In its north-western corner is the source of the **Severn**. The Van **lead** mines were at their most productive between 1869 and 1881, when they employed over 500 workers. In 1871, they were linked by **railway** to **Caersws**. Chimneys and ruins of terraced houses survive. Clywedog Dam (1967), the tallest mass of concrete in **Britain**, contains hollow buttresses with vaults higher than those of any cathedral. Nearly 10 km of the valley was flooded, not only to provide water but also to control the flow of the Severn (*see* **Reservoirs**). Bryn Tail lead mine, at the foot of the dam, is cared for by **Cadw**.

LLANIGON, Breconshire, Powys
(4832 ha; 525 inhabitants)

Hugging the English **border** south of **Hay**, the **community** contains several **Neolithic** tombs. The area was an early centre of **Nonconformist** activity. In 1672, Henry Maurice began ministering to the congregation at Llanigon, his labours earning him the title of 'Apostle of **Breconshire**'. A barn at Pen-yr-wyrlod was adapted as a dissenting chapel in 1707. David Price established a school at Llwynllwyd, and **Howel Harris** and **William Williams** (Pantycelyn; 1717–91), were among the pupils.

Further south, on the other side of the Gospel Pass, a different religious tradition manifests itself. In 1869, Father Ignatius (the Rev. **Joseph Lyne**) established an **Anglican Benedictine** monastery at Capel-y-ffin in the Ewias valley, thereby shocking **Francis Kilvert**; Ignatius is buried there. To Lyne, the monastery was intended to be Llanthony Tertia (*see* **Crucorney**). The monastery church has become a dangerous ruin; there are plans afoot to restore it. In 1924, the monastery came into the possession of Eric Gill, who established a small community and built a chapel. There is a **painting**, *Crucifixion* by **David Jones** (1895–1974), on the refectory wall. There are spectacular views from Lord Hereford's Knob (696 m) and Hay Bluff (677 m).

501

LLANILAR, Ceredigion
(2828 ha; 1055 inhabitants)

Situated on the southern bank of the **Ystwyth**, the **community**'s sole centre of **population**, the village of Llanilar, is one of **Aberystwyth**'s chief commuting areas. St Hilary's church has a sturdy 14th-century tower. Above it rises Castle Hill, the site of what may be an **Iron Age** fort altered by the **Normans**. The hill's ancient **Welsh** name – Garth Grugyn – is mentioned in the story 'Culhwch ac Olwen' (see **Mabinogion, The**). Castle Hill mansion (1777) passed by marriage to the Loxdale family, which still owns it. Abermad (1872), once the home of the Pugh family, is an old people's home. Llidiardau, a 17th-century mansion rebuilt in the 19th century, was, until the mid-20th century, the home of the Parry family. The **English** novelist Rose Macaulay (1881–1958) spent part of her youth at Tŷ Isaf.

LLANLLAWDDOG, Carmarthenshire
(3207 ha; 687 inhabitants)

Straddled by the A485 north-east of **Carmarthen**, the **community** contains the villages of Pontarsais and Rhydargaeau. The isolated church of St Llawddog was rebuilt in 1849. Only part of a tower (1838) survives of Glangwili, which was the centre of the Lloyd family's 1600-ha estate.

LLANLLECHID, Gwynedd
(4609 ha; 885 inhabitants)

Located between **Bangor** and **Llanfairfechan**, the **community** extends from the mouth of the Ogwen to the summits of **Carnedd** Llywelyn (1064 m) and Carnedd Dafydd (1044 m). Well over half of it is owned by the **National Trust**. Ysgolion Duon (the black ladders), at the upper end of Cwm Llafar, offer extreme challenges to the climber and delights to the student of alpine-arctic **plants**. Llanllechid shares with **Llandygai** the remarkable Nant Ffrancon section of the Ogwen valley and Rhaeadr Ogwen, the **waterfall** which debouches from Llyn Ogwen. The **Holyhead road** (the A5), which follows the right bank of the **river**, provides impressive evidence of **Thomas Telford**'s **engineering** skills. Cochwillan, a superb 15th-century hall house, has been restored and is still occupied; it was the home of **John Williams** (1582–1650), archbishop of York, a leading figure in the 17th-century **Civil Wars**.

LLANLLWCHAIARN (Llanllwchaearn),
Ceredigion (1729 ha; 786 inhabitants)

Originally the **parish** out of which the **urban district** of **New Quay** was carved in 1894, the **community** contains the village of Cross Inn, the hamlet of Llanina and the delightful bay of Cei Bach. Llanina House, elaborately rebuilt in the mid-18th century, is undergoing restoration.

LLANLLWNI, Carmarthenshire
(2672 ha; 676 inhabitants)

Hugging the **Teifi** south-east of **Llandysul**, the **community** extends to the summit of Mynydd **Llanybydder** (408 m). The scattered ribbon development along 4 km of the A485 constitutes the village of Llanllwni. The area is rich in **Bronze Age** graves. St Luke's or St Llwni's church, which stands in isolation above the Teifi, retains some 16th-century elements.

Within it is the one-time private pew of the Mansel family, who lived in the large mansion of Maesycrugiau (1903).

LLANLLYFNI, Gwynedd
(4276 ha; 3919 inhabitants)

Straddling the **Caernarfon–Porthmadog road** (the A487), the **community** extends to Trum y Ddysgl (710 m) and embraces most of the basin of the Llyfni; the Llyfni valley is generally known as Dyffryn Nantlle. Within it are the villages of Llanllyfni, Drws-y-coed, Nantlle, Nasareth, Nebo, Penygroes and Talysarn, villages which developed in the 19th century to house the workforce of the Pen-yr-orsedd and Dorothea **slate** quarries. (The latter was named after the wife of Richard Garnons, a local landowner.)

Because of the run of the vein, the slate of Dyffryn Nantlle was extracted from huge holes rather than by the more usual method of opening galleries in the hillside. Among the Dorothea Quarry's owners was **John Jones** (Talysarn; 1796–1857), one of the best-known **preachers** of the age. The poet **R. Williams Parry** was a native of Talysarn. In the fourth branch of *Pedair Cainc y Mabinogi* (see **Mabinogion, The**), Lleu Llawgyffes is discovered in Nantlle transformed into an eagle. *Lleu* is the title of the local community **newspaper** (see **Papurau Bro**).

LLANMAES (Llan-faes), Vale of Glamorgan
(447 ha; 418 inhabitants)

A **community** located immediately north of **Llantwit Major**. Llanmaes is one of the prettiest villages of the **Vale of Glamorgan**. St Catwg's church has a late medieval rood loft and screen. The village is dominated by Great House, redesigned in the early 18th century for the rector, Illtyd Nicholl, but retaining extensive earlier fabric. Near the church are the remains of a medieval tower house.

LLANNEFYDD (Llanefydd), Conwy
(3075 ha; 562 inhabitants)

Located north-west of **Denbigh**, the **community** is bordered by the Elwy valley, where **caves** have yielded evidence central to the early prehistory of Wales (see **Palaeolithic Age** and **Cefnmeiriadog**). The two-naved 15th-century church of St Nefydd is light and spacious. Berain was a medieval hall and the ancestral home of **Catrin of Berain**; it was extended in the 16th century. Although it has been much altered over the centuries, there are still traces of the early building to be seen. Penporchell Isaf was the birthplace of Twm o'r Nant (**Thomas Edwards**; 1739–1810). In 1888, anti-**tithe** agitation at Llannefydd led to the deployment of the 9th Lancers. The site of Mynydd y Gaer **hill-fort** offers magnificent views.

LLANNERCH Commote
One of the three **commotes** of the *cantref* of **Dyffryn Clwyd**, Llannerch lay within the later **communities** of **Llanfair Dyffryn Clwyd** and **Llanelidan**. Most of the commote was the property of the bishop of **Bangor** – the central reason why Dyffryn Clwyd was an enclave of the **diocese** of Bangor within that of **St Asaph**.

LLANNERCH HUDOL Commote
Hugging the west bank of the **Severn** between **Welshpool** and **Berriew**, the **commote**, together with those of **Deuddwr**

and **Ystrad Marchell**, was part of a district known as Teirswydd. Following the **Acts of 'Union'**, Llannerch Hudol became part of the **hundred** of Ystradmarchell. The mansion of Llanerchydol (*see* **Welshpool**) preserves the name, which means 'enchanting glade'.

LLANNERCH-Y-MEDD, Isle of Anglesey
(2986 ha; 1185 inhabitants)
Occupying a wide swathe of north central **Anglesey**, the **community**'s sole substantial settlement is the large village of Llannerch-y-medd, whose inhabitants once considered themselves to be town dwellers. Regular fairs were held as early as the 14th century. The wide main street testifies to the one-time importance of the place as a market, a role it yielded to **Llangefni** in the late 18th century. In the 19th century, the making of boots and clogs was an important activity (*see* **Leather**). By 1833, there were 250 cobblers working at Llannerch-y-medd, but output declined *c*.1870 in the face of Northampton's mass production. Snuff was also manufactured there. In the northern part of the community lies part of Llyn Alaw (*see* **Reservoirs**).

LLANNON (Llan-non), Carmarthenshire
(3846 ha; 4999 inhabitants)
Located immediately north-east of **Llanelli**, the **community** contains the villages of Llannon, Cross Hands and Tumble and the Pont Abraham service station at the western terminus of the **M4**. The area is rich in **Bronze Age** monuments, including Maen Hir (4.6 m), the tallest standing stone in **Carmarthenshire**. St Non's church, originally 15th century, was drastically altered in 1841 but still has its imposing tower. Tumble and Cross Hands developed to house the anthracite miners employed by the Dynant and Great **Mountain** Collieries. With the demise of the **coal** industry, new ventures such as the Cross Hands Business Park have been established. The area has nurtured a number of **rugby** players, among them Archie Skym, who played for Wales 21 times, and Gareth Davies.

LLANNOR, Gwynedd (4817 ha; 2244 inhabitants)
Located immediately north of **Pwllheli**, the **community** contains the villages of Llannor, Abererch, Efailnewydd and Y Ffôr (formerly Four Crosses). Holy Cross church (13th century), Llannor, has a 15th-century tower. The late medieval church of St Cawrdaf, Abererch, has a handsome roof. In the area are several small mansions, among them Bodfel, the birthplace of Dr Johnson's friend **Hester Lynch Piozzi**; it is now an adventure playground. The South Caernarfonshire Creamery at Rhydygwystl is well known for its *Caws Llŷn* (Llŷn **cheese**).

LLANOVER (Llanofer), Monmouthshire
(4903 ha; 1373 inhabitants)
Located south-east of **Abergavenny**, the **community** represents the amalgamation of six **parishes**. At its centre is the Llanover estate, created in the 1820s following the marriage of Augusta Waddington (**Augusta Hall**) of the Ty Uchaf estate, with Benjamin Hall, owner of the Llanover House estate. In 1859, they became Lord and Lady Llanover. Llanover House was demolished in 1935. Ty Uchaf, a neo-classical building erected in the 1790s and

surrounded by fine **gardens** and a large park, is still inhabited by the family. Lady Llanover financed a chapel (1898) for **Welsh**-medium **Calvinistic Methodist** services at Rhydy-meirch. Tre Elidyr (1920s) is a planned hamlet in the Arts and Crafts style.

St Bartholomew's church has a fine 15th-century tower and is adjoined by the enormous tomb of Lord Llanover. There are also attractive churches at Llangattock-juxta-Usk, Llanvihangel Gobion, Llanddewi Rhydderch, Llanfair Kilgeddin and Llansantffraed. The area is rich in interesting farmhouses and country houses. The charming hill of Ysgyryd Fach is located at the northernmost part of the community.

LLANPUMSAINT, Carmarthenshire
(2610 ha; 595 inhabitants)
Located north of **Carmarthen**, the **community** contains a delightful stretch of the Gwili valley. The *pumsaint* (five **saints**) to whom the church (1882) is dedicated are Ceitho, Celynnin, Gwyn, Gwynno and Gwynoro. Brutus (**David Owen**; 1795–1866), editor and satirist, was born in Llanpumsaint, as was William Williams (1788–1865), MP for Coventry, whose question in the House of Commons in 1846 led to the report on **education** in Wales (*see* **Treason of the Blue Books**). The community was crossed by the Carmarthen–**Lampeter railway**, part of which has been reopened. Skanda Vale is a Hindu monastic centre which attracts 70,000 devotees annually.

LLANRHAEADR-YM-MOCHNANT,
Montgomeryshire, Powys
(7456 ha; 1223 inhabitants)
With the division of **Powys** in the late 12th century, **Mochnant** Is Rhaeadr became part of **Powys Fadog**, and Uwch Rhaeadr part of **Powys Wenwynwyn**; the division survived the creation of **Denbighshire** and **Montgomeryshire** and of the **counties** of **Clwyd** and Powys. However, in 1996 the whole of Mochnant became part of Montgomeryshire and Llanrhaeadr's two civil **parishes** were amalgamated to create a single **community**. The much-restored St Dogfan's church contains fragments of a Romanesque shrine comparable with that at Pennant **Melangell** (*see* **Llangynog**, Montgomeryshire). From 1578 to 1595, its vicar was **William Morgan**; thus, it was in Llanrhaeadr vicarage that he prepared his translation of the **Bible** (1588).

Eight km north-west of Llanrhaeadr village is Pistyll Rhaeadr, where the Disgynfa plunges 75 m to a pool, from which it plunges a further 25 m; it is the country's highest **waterfall**, and one of the '**seven wonders of Wales**'. The two great boulders below the fall – the Giant's Burden and the Maiden's Apronful – testify to the legend of the giant Berwyn and his family.

Tegla Davies's fantasy *Tir y Dyneddon* (The Land of the Little People, 1921) is set at the frozen waterfall. He was **Wesleyan** minister in the village, the denomination being, unusually, the strongest, with an Arts and Crafts style chapel (1904). The **film** *The Englishman Who Went Up a Hill But Came Down a Mountain* (1995) was shot at Llanrhaeadr. The uplands of the community are rich in **Bronze Age** cairns and standing stones.

LLANRHAEADR-YNG-NGHINMEIRCH,
Denbighshire (4479 ha; 1080 inhabitants)

Located immediately south of **Denbigh**, the **community** extends from the confluence of the Clywedog with the **Clwyd** to the Brenig **reservoir**, high on the Denbigh Moors (*see* **Mynydd Hiraethog**). St Dyfnog's church contains a magnificent Jesse window (1533) and the sumptuous tomb of Maurice Jones of Llanrhaeadr Hall (1702). In the churchyard are the graves of members of a branch of the **Wynn family (Gwydir)** together with those of the MP Sir Henry Morris-Jones (1885–1972) and the **hymn**writer **Edward Jones** (Maes-y-Plwm; 1761–1836). The remarkable gravestone of John ap Robert (d.1642, aged 95) displays his pedigree back to Cadell, king of **Powys**. The handsome Llanrhaeadr Hall contains 16th-, 18th- and 19th-century features and a fine **garden**. In the community's far west corner is Hen Ddinbych, a square earthwork which may be **Roman**. Nearby are ruins of *hafotai* (*see* **Hafod** and **Hendre**) and a trail linking the **Bronze Age** remains discovered prior to the creation of the Brenig reservoir (*see* **Cerrigydrudion**).

LLANRHIAN, Pembrokeshire
(2301 ha; 897 inhabitants)

Located immediately north-east of **St David's**, the **community** contains the villages of Llanrhian, Croes-goch, Porthgain and Tre-fin. St Rhian's church retains its 13th-century tower. The **Baptist** chapel (1816, 1858) at Croes-goch is a handsome building. **Slate** quarried at Abereiddi and Porthgain was exported from Porthgain dock which could receive 20 **ships** a day; the dock closed in 1931. Quarrying produced the so-called 'blue lagoon'. The ruined mill at Tre-fin is the subject of a well-known poem by Crwys (**William Williams**; 1875–1968). The campaign of **Cymdeithas yr Iaith Gymraeg** to ensure that signposts carried correctly spelt **Welsh place names** began in 1964 at Tre-fin – then spelled Trevine. Llanrhian has a distinguished **cricket** team.

LLANRHIDIAN HIGHER (Llanrhidian Uchaf),
Swansea (2251 ha; 5138 inhabitants)

The **community**, which stretches inland from the southern bank of the estuary of the **River Llwchwr**, is the area where **Welsh Gower** met **English** Gower. **Coal**mining began in the 16th century, and a **copper** works was established at Penclawdd in 1788. John **Vivian** began copper smelting there in 1800 – the family's first venture in Wales. The **railway** reached Penclawdd in 1867 and was extended to Llanmorlais in the 1870s. The furthest railway penetration of the Gower peninsula, it was a venture that assisted the development of cockle gathering (*see* **Fish and Fishing**) in the Llwchwr estuary, an activity that proved to be of enduring importance. The settlements of the community are dominated by chapels, particularly Bethel and Tabernacl in Penclawdd, and Capel y Crwys in Three Crosses.

LLANRHIDIAN LOWER (Llanrhidian Isaf),
Swansea (2391 ha; 537 inhabitants)

Located immediately south-west of **Llanrhidian Higher**, the community illustrates the marked contrast between the **Gower** peninsula's northern and southern coasts. While both are **limestone** escarpments, the southern cliffs have the lively **Severn** Sea at their foot, while the northern cliffs gaze down upon wide grazing marshland, favoured by wildfowl (*see* **Birds**). Llanrhidian village, the sole significant centre of **population**, straddles the escarpment and overlooks the Llanrhidian marsh and, at low tide, the vast Llanrhidian Sands. The church, the largest in the peninsula, contains a 9th-century inscribed stone (*see* **Monuments, Early Christian**).

Llanrwst: the bridge over the Conwy, originally built *c.*1636

Weobley Castle, high above the marshes, is a well-preserved fortified manor house built by the de la Bere family in the 14th century, and enlarged by **Rhys ap Thomas** in the late 15th. At the southern end of the community stands Arthur's Stone, a **Neolithic** chambered tomb crowned by a 40-tonne capstone.

LLANRHYSTYD (Llanrhystud), Ceredigion
(2776 ha; 865 inhabitants)
Located on the coast south of **Aberystwyth**, the **community** contains the village of Llanrhystyd and the hamlets of Joppa and Llanddeiniol. St Rhystud's (R. K. **Penson**, 1857), a remarkably confident neo-Gothic building, is proof of the strength of **Anglicanism** in Llanrhystyd – a rare example of a Welsh village devoid of chapels. St Deiniol's church, largely rebuilt in 1883, retains its medieval tower. Mabws was once the centre of an estate substantial enough to permit its owners to be high sheriffs and MPs. The narrow gorge of the Wyre offers delightful walks. There is an attractive **garden** at Carrog.

LLANRUG, Gwynedd (1571 ha; 2755 inhabitants)
Located immediately east of **Caernarfon**, the **community** embraces much of the basin of the Seiont (or Saint). Its uplands are rich in prehistoric monuments. St Michael's church retains its 15th-century roof. Bryn Bras Castle is an eccentric house built *c.*1835. The village of Llanrug grew as a result of the development of the Dinorwic **slate** quarry (*see* **Llanddeiniolen**); its later development resulted from its role as a dormitory area for Caernarfon and **Bangor**. 'Mrs Jones, Llanrug' is the Welsh equivalent of the person on the Clapham omnibus.

LLANRWST, Conwy (524 ha; 3037 inhabitants)
Until the building of **Telford**'s bridge at **Conwy** (1826), Llanrwst was the lowest point on the **river** with a bridge – that traditionally and probably erroneously attributed to Inigo Jones. Built in 1634, it is an elegant structure, with a rise so steep that a driver on one side cannot see a vehicle on the other. St Grwst has a fine rood screen (*c.*1500); the adjoining Gwydir chapel (1634) contains tombs of members of the **Wynn family** of **Gwydir** and a stone coffin reputed to be that of **Llywelyn ap Iorwerth**, brought from Maenan Abbey following its **dissolution**. Near the church are almshouses (*c.*1612), built by John Wynn to provide for 'eleven aged men and an old woman bedmaker'. Cae'r Berllan, originally 17th century, contains 20th-century additions and a **garden** in the Arts and Crafts style. In the 18th century, Llanrwst was home to several prolific **clock** makers. Seion chapel (1883) is an imposing building. The poet, broadcaster and novelist **T. Glynne Davies** was a native of Llanrwst. Until 1974, the **community** was an **urban district**.

LLANSADWRN, Carmarthenshire
(2990 ha; 461 inhabitants)
Situated on the right bank of the **Tywi** between **Llandeilo** and **Llandovery**, the **community** contains the hamlets of Llansadwrn and Felindre. Carreg Fawr, a massive **Bronze Age** standing stone, was allegedly re-erected by **Rhys ap Thomas** (1449–1525) in the grounds of his mansion, Abermarlais (demolished 1970), to commemorate the battle of **Bosworth**. St Sadwrn's church, standing in the centre of a compact village, was largely rebuilt in 1884. Libanus Baptist chapel (1841) is an attractive building. In 2006, it became the first chapel to be preserved by the Welsh Religious Buildings Trust. Aberdeunant, a remarkable example of vernacular farm buildings, is owned and has been restored by the **National Trust**. The farm of Brownhill was the birthplace of the writer and MP **W. Llewelyn Williams**.

LLANSANFFRAID GLAN CONWY, Conwy
(1745 ha; 2290 inhabitants)
Located south-east of **Conwy** on the right bank of the **river**, the **community** centres upon the substantial village of the same name. It contains the church of St Ffraed (1839) and its more interesting church hall, designed by **Colwyn Foulkes** (1932). To the south is the splendidly named Allor Moloch (Moloch's altar) **Neolithic** chambered tomb. At Felin Isaf are a clover mill, a grain mill and a rare **oat** kiln, with much of their machinery still intact. Plas Isaf and Plas Uchaf are interesting early houses.

LLANSANNAN, Conwy
(9537 ha; 1291 inhabitants)
Extending from the Aled valley to the heights of **Mynydd Hiraethog**, the **community** has a special place in the history of Welsh culture. A monument (1899) designed by **Goscombe John** commemorates five men of letters associated with the locality: the poet **Tudur Aled**, the New Testament translator **William Salesbury**, the **Calvinistic Methodist** minister Henry Rees (1798–1869), his brother the **Congregationalist** minister and journalist Gwilym Hiraethog (**William Rees**; 1802–83), and the **Baptist** minister and poet Edward Roberts (Iorwerth Glan Aled; 1819–67). The **Liberal** MP Watkin Williams (1828–84), who introduced the first Welsh **Disestablishment** Bill, was the son of the rector of Llansannan.

There are interesting country houses at Plas Isaf and Eriviat Hall. St Sannan's church, remodelled in 1778, was Victorianized in 1879. The austere St Thomas's church (1857), Bylchau, was designed by George Gilbert Scott. Gwylfa Hiraethog shooting lodge (1913), 500 m above sea level, offers extensive views of Mynydd Hiraethog. The nearby Sportsman's Arms is the remotest, and, at 450 m above sea level, the highest tavern in Wales. Llansannan lies at the centre of the area served by *Y Gadlas*, perhaps the most successful of the *papurau bro* (community **newspapers**).

LLANSANTFFRAID (Llansanffraid), Ceredigion
(1703 ha; 1241 inhabitants)
Located on the coast north of **Aberaeron**, the **community** extends over the basins of the Cledan and the Peris. St Ffraid's church has a 15th-century tower and a chapel-like interior; its graveyard contains many memorials to those who died at sea. In Capel Mawr, Llan-non, there is a sign, 'Cofiwch y Morwyr' (Remember the Seamen). Llansantffraid has been subsumed by the substantial village of Llan-non. Morfa Esgob, the land between Llan-non and the sea, was once owned by the bishop of **St David's**. Over 100 of its medieval furlongs or strips (*lleiniau*) remain in multiple ownership, causing it to be a landscape that is

unique in Wales. The mansion of Brynawelon was built for the Alban-Davies family, the most prominent **London-Welsh** dairying family.

LLANSANTFFRAID (Llansanffraid),
Montgomeryshire, Powys
(2502 ha; 1215 inhabitants)
Located in **Montgomeryshire**'s north-eastern corner, the **community** contains parts of the **commotes** of **Mechain** and **Deuddwr**. The village of Llansantffraid-ym-Mechain clusters around St Bride's church, originally 12th century but much altered. One of its windows was unveiled by William Morris Hughes, prime minister of **Australia** (1915–23), whose mother was a member of a local farming family. The handsome late 18th-century bridge across the Vyrnwy leads to the village of Deuddwr. The Plas yn Dinas moraine is crowned by a 12th-century castle.

LLANSANTFFRAID GLYN CEIRIOG
(Llansanffraid Glynceiriog), Wrexham
(2959 ha; 1086 inhabitants)
Located south-west of **Llangollen**, the **community** extends from the Ceiriog to the grouse butts on the **Berwyn Mountains**. The locality seems to be an idyllic rural retreat but, from the 16th century to the early 20th, it was a centre of quarrying for **slate**, dolerite **granite**, china stone and silica. Tomen y Meirw is a large **Bronze Age** barrow whose rifling led to wild rumours of what was found when it was dug into. St **Ffraid**'s church in its circular graveyard high above the village of Glynceiriog was rebuilt c.1790. **Owain Glyndŵr**'s sister Lowri is reputed to have lived at Blaen Nantyr. The Ceiriog Memorial Institute (1911, 1929) commemorates the Ceiriog valley poets **Huw Morys** (1662–1709), Cynddelw (Robert Ellis; 1812–75) and Ceiriog (**John Ceiriog Hughes**).

LLANSAWEL, Carmarthenshire
(4080 ha; 413 inhabitants)
Located north of **Llandeilo**, the **community**'s only settlement of any size is the village of Llansawel. St Sawel's church, much restored in the 1880s, retains its 14th-century lancet windows. Edwinsford (17th century but now a ruin) was the seat of the Williams-Drummond family, which produced eight High Sheriffs and three MPs. Beili Ficer (16th century) has a massive chimney stack. Most of Pen y Dinas hill has been removed through quarrying. The community contains a fine stretch of the Cothi valley.

LLANSILIN, Montgomeryshire, Powys
(4744 ha; 648 inhabitants)
The **community** was in **Denbighshire** from 1536 until 1974, when it became part of the **Glyndŵr District** of the **county** of **Clwyd**. It was transferred to **Montgomeryshire** in 1996. The attractive Llansilin village clusters around St Silin's church, which stands on the site of what may have been a *clas* or **Celt**ic monastery. Remodelled in the 15th century as a double-aisled church, the much-altered building retains vestiges of a 13th-century cruciform structure. Llangadwaladr church, largely rebuilt in 1883, stands in splendid isolation, as does Christ Church, Rhydycroesau (1838). Llansilin is rich in houses of the 15th to the 18th centuries,

the most interesting of which is Pen-y-bryn, a 15th-century hall house restored in 1972.

Huw Morys (Eos Ceiriog), a fervent **Royalist** and the most skilful of the 17th-century Welsh poets, is buried at Llansilin. A call to apprentice poets to meet at his grave was the occasion for the founding of the Powys **Eisteddfod** in 1819. Other natives of Llansilin include **Charles Edwards**, author of one of the classics of Welsh prose, *Y Ffydd ddi-ffuant* (The Sincere Faith, 1667, 1671, 1677), and William Maurice (d.1680), antiquarian and collector of manuscripts. A pamphlet published in **London** in 1677, *Wonderful News from Wales, a True Narrative of an Old Woman Living Near Lanselin in Wales*, claimed that she was 130 years old.

Sycharth, **Owain Glyndŵr**'s chief dwelling, was located about 2 km south of Llansilin village. It was eulogized in a poem by **Iolo Goch** c.1390; excavation has shown that the eulogy was partially accurate. Glyndŵr's English enemies burned Sycharth to the ground in May 1403.

LLANSTADWELL (Llanstadwel), Pembrokeshire
(1029 ha; 904 inhabitants)
Located between **Milford Haven** and **Neyland**, the **community**'s chief feature is Scoveston Fort (1861–8), the most massive of **Pembrokeshire**'s **Palmerston's Follies**; tree growth has much obscured it. The Gulf **oil** refinery, established near Waterston village in 1968, closed in 1997.

LLANSTEFFAN, Carmarthenshire
(2120 ha; 1076 inhabitants)
Constituting the peninsula between the estuaries of the **Tywi** and the **Taf**, the **community** contains the villages of Llansteffan, Llanybri and Morfa Bach. In the early 12th century, the area was seized by the **Normans**, who built a ringwork castle on the site of an **Iron Age hill-fort**. The **march**er-lordship of Llansteffan became the property of the de Camville family, who built the masonry castle (*c.*1220–*c.*1280) with its imposing twin-towered gatehouse. St Stephen's church (13th century) contains a wealth of memorials. Llansteffan's one-time **borough** status is remembered in the continuing ceremony of electing a mayor. **John Williams** (1840–1926), a royal physician, lived at Plas Llansteffan (late 18th century) from 1903 to 1909, gathering there the books and manuscripts which became the core collection of the **National Library of Wales**.

The village, with its superb location and its tranquil Victorian air, has proved attractive to writers, among them **Glyn Jones**, **Keidrych Rhys** and his wife **Lynette Roberts**, Raymond Garlick (b.1926) and the Welsh-American poet Jon Dressel (b.1934). Osi Rhys Osmond and Julia Jones are among the artists who live there. In the 17th century, the medieval church at Llanybri became a dissenting chapel; closed in 1960, it fell into ruin.

LLANTARNAM (Llanfihangel Llantarnam),
Torfaen (656 ha; 3299 inhabitants)
The southernmost **community** of **Torfaen**, its northern parts have been extensively urbanized and are essentially a suburb of **Cwmbran**. In 1179, Hywel ap Iorwerth, lord of **Caerleon**, founded a **Cistercian** monastery as a daughter house of that of Strata Florida (*see* **Ystrad Fflur**). Its original location may have been Caerleon, but it was certainly

in Llantarnam by the 13th century. Of its buildings, only an 11-bay stone barn survives. The monastery had strong Welsh sympathies. Its early 15th-century abbot, John ap Hywel, a close associate of **Owain Glyndŵr**, was killed at the battle of Pwllmelyn (**Usk**) in 1405. On the eve of its **dissolution** in 1536, the monastery had six monks and an annual income of £71. Its buildings came into the possession of William Morgan (d.1582), who also owned the abbey grange of Pentrebach, where the family's 16th- and 17th-century building work still survives.

The Morgans of Llantarnam, a branch of the **Morgan family (Tredegar)**, were devoted **Roman Catholics** and, along with their relations, the **Somerset family** of **Raglan**, were central to the survival of the old faith in **Monmouthshire**. In the mid-1830s, T. H. Wyatt rebuilt the abbey as a neo-Elizabethan mansion, which since 1946 has been occupied by the Sisters of St Joseph. Llantarnam church contains arches that may have been salvaged from the abbey. The Green House Inn has a sign (1719) advertising good **beer** and good **cider** in **Welsh**. The community contains a delightful stretch of the Monmouthshire **Canal**.

LLANTILIO CROSSENNY (Llandeilo Gresynni), Monmouthshire (4201 ha; 680 inhabitants)

Located east of **Abergavenny**, the **community**'s chief feature is White Castle, the largest of the **Three Castles** of northern **Gwent**. Originally built in the 1180s, it was vastly strengthened in the 1250s to protect the region from **Llywelyn ap Gruffudd**. A royal garrison rather than the residence of a **march**er-lord, it was kept in repair until c.1450. The bishop of Llandaff had a manor house at Hen Gwrt. St **Teilo**'s church is an ambitious building of the 13th and 14th centuries. There are smaller churches at Llanvihangel Ystern Llewern and Llanfair Cilgoed. Great Cil-llwch is a rare example of a medieval open hall. Great Tre-rhiw is an impressively complete 17th-century farmstead. Talycoed Court (1882) was the home of **Joseph Bradney**, the historian of **Monmouthshire**.

LLANTILIO PERTHOLEY (Llandeilo Bertholau), Monmouthshire (1909 ha; 3965 inhabitants)

Located immediately north of **Abergavenny**, the **community**'s main feature is the delectable eminence of Ysgyryd Fawr (486 m), where in the 17th century **Roman Catholics** gathered at the ruined church of St Michael to celebrate secret masses. St Teilo's church is an impressive church of the 13th and 14th centuries. The restaurant of the Walnut Tree Inn at Llanddewi Skirrid, under the ownership of the Italian Franco Taruschio, was for many years among Wales's finest. Triley Court is an exceptionally attractive early 19th-century mansion. Maindiff Court was used as Rudolf Hess's place of detention. It was built to be the seat of the Crawshay **Bailey family** but was demolished in 2006.

LLANTRISANT, Rhondda Cynon Taff (1782 ha; 14,915 inhabitants)

Located immediately south-west of **Pontypridd**, the **community** contains the villages of Llantrisant, Beddau, Cross Inn, Gwaun Miskin, Talbot Green and Pen-y-coedcae. Llantrisant is perhaps Wales's best example of a hilltop settlement. Probably the caput of the **commote** of **Miskin**, it was seized c.1246 by Richard de **Clare**, who built Llantrisant

Castle, little of which survives. He seems also to have established the borough of Llantrisant, although the first extant charter is that of 1346. Following the **Act of 'Union'** of 1536, the **borough** was one of the eight constituting the **Glamorgan** borough constituency, a status it retained until 1918. The church of 'y tri sant' (the three **saints** – **Illtud**, Gwynno and Tyfodwg) retains its massive 15th-century tower. The interior (1874) – the work of **John Prichard** – contains an effigy of a 13th-century warrior, who may be Cadwgan, lord of Miskin. Penuel chapel (1826) is an attractive building.

The focal point of Llantrisant is the Bull Ring (or Bull Square), dominated by the Model House craft centre (c.1989). The square contains a statue (1981) of **William Price**, whose pioneer cremation was held in 1893 on Cae'r-lan Fields, west of Llantrisant. Caerau is a massive circular **Iron Age hill-fort**. Edward II's capture in 1326 is reputed to have taken place near Llantrisant. Castellau (c.1807) is a handsome Regency villa.

The Royal **Mint** transferred to Llantrisant in 1967, is housed in long low blocks completed in 1968. The mint and other enterprises in the Llantrisant Business Park have created new employment opportunities, which have led to the development of a virtually continuous urban area linking **Pont-y-clun** with Talbot Green and Beddau. Talbot Green was the home of the Gilbern car, the only car ever to be manufactured in Wales (*see* **Vehicle Manufacture**). Beddau came into existence following the opening of Cwm Colliery in 1914; the colliery closed in 1986. The Royal Glamorgan Hospital (*see* **Health**) was opened in 1999 on the site of the one-time **lead**-working site of Ynys-y-plwm.

LLANTRISANT FAWR (Llantrisaint Fawr), Monmouthshire (2283 ha; 369 inhabitants)

Located immediately south-east of **Usk**, the **community** contains the settlements of Llantrisant, Llanllowell, Llangeview and Gwernesey, all of which have restored medieval churches; that at Llangeview retains its 18th-century fittings. The 'tri sant' (three saints) of Llantrisant are John, Paul and Peter. The area is rich in 16th and 17th-century farmhouses. There is a grass ski slope at Llanllowell.

LLANTWIT FARDRE (Llanilltud Faerdref), Rhondda Cynon Taff (1762 ha; 13,993 inhabitants)

Located immediately south of **Pontypridd**, the **community** contains the villages of Llantwit Fardre, Church Village, Efael-isaf and Ton-teg. At its centre is a well-preserved 12th-century motte with an intact moat. Industrialization began in the late 17th century with the mining of **coal** and the quarrying of stone for roof tiles, but the key to more recent **population** growth is the area's role as part of **Cardiff**'s commuter belt. The massive East Glamorgan Hospital (1939–99) was replaced by the Royal Glamorgan Hospital at **Llantrisant**. A major contributor to the local economy and population is the Treforest Industrial Estate, established in the late 1930s.

LLANTWIT MAJOR (Llanilltud Fawr), Vale of Glamorgan (1737 ha; 9687 inhabitants)

Llantwit Major was, from the late 5th century onwards, the seat of the *clas* or **Celtic** monastery founded by St **Illtud**. (The *twit* in Llantwit is not an 'English' corruption,

Llantwit Major: the Samson Stone (10th century) and the Houelt Stone (late 9th century) in St Illtud's church

large village – indeed, almost a small town – with a quasi-urban pattern of occupations and trades, though it did not attain **borough** status. Its growing prosperity is reflected in many good examples of 16th- and 17th-century houses and cottages. Local **gentry** families resided in Llantwit, in houses such as Great House, Plymouth House and Old Place. The Old Rectory has late medieval origins, although it now looks more like the school it became in 1878. The over-restored 16th-century town hall – originally the courthouse – stands on the square adjoining fine examples of 16th-century yeoman houses, notably the White Hart and the Old Swan. One of the features of the **community** is the large royal arms of Sweden, fixed to the house of the Swedish consul in Wales.

As a result of the establishment of RAF **St Athan**, Llantwit expanded greatly, making it a nightmare for motorists. Following more recent development, it has overwhelmed the hamlet of Boverton, the site of the substantial remains of the late 16th-century mansion Boverton Place. Nearby, there is a group of houses designed by **T. Alwyn Lloyd** in 1936 as an agricultural settlement for unemployed miners. On the coast are two large **Iron Age** promontory forts. Near the community's northern fringes stands the **Congregational** chapel of Bethesda'r Fro; from 1806 until 1844, its minister was the **hymn**writer **Thomas William**.

LLANTYSILIO (Llandysilio-yn-Iâl), Denbighshire (2796 ha; 472 inhabitants)

Located immediately north of **Llangollen**, the **community** contains the Eglwyseg Rocks and the Horseshoe Pass, crossed by the A452 on its way to one of the most delectable parts of the **Dee** valley. Alongside the **road** is the Pillar of Eliseg, the remnant of a high cross erected by Cyngen, king of **Powys** (d.854) in memory of his great-grandfather Eliseg. The original inscription, now illegible, celebrates the royal house of Powys and claims that **Magnus Maximus** and **Vortigern** were among its ancestors.

Near the pillar are the ruins of Valle Crucis Abbey, founded in 1201 by Madog ap Gruffudd (d.1236), ruler of **Powys Fadog**. Established by a colony of monks from Strata Marcella (*see* **Welshpool**) – the abbey serving **Powys Wenwynwyn** – it was the last **Cistercian** monastery to be founded in Wales. Built in the early 13th century, with a few later additions, a considerable amount of its masonry survives, including the west front, the presbytery, the transepts, the chapter house and the monks' dormitory. Among its many sepulchral slabs is the superb carving commemorating Madog ap Gruffudd (d.*c*.1306), grandson of the founder and grandfather of **Owain Glyndŵr**. Adjoining the ruins is Wales's only surviving monastic **fish**pond. Leading poets, among them **Gutun Owain**, **Tudur Aled** and **Guto'r Glyn**, delighted in the hospitality of the abbey. It is claimed that numerous important texts were copied at the abbey, a claim that is difficult to substantiate.

St Tysilio's church contains good Pre-Raphaelite **stained glass**. The **Liberal** MP **George Osborne Morgan** is buried in the churchyard. The Llangollen **Canal** has its origins near the church, where the Horseshoe Falls, a weir designed by **Thomas Telford**, supplies the canal with water. The neo-Elizabethan Llantysilio Hall (1874) is a remarkable

but a contraction of an Irish form of Illtud's name.) The *clas* was the axis of early Christianity among Celtic-speaking peoples. Located in a hollow 2 km from the sea, its site, like those of other *clasau*, was probably chosen because it offered convenient sea access, along with concealment from coastal raiders. The fact that it was less than 1 km from a **Roman** villa is also surely significant. An indication of the continuing importance of the *clas* is the existence in St Illtud's church of a collection of 9th and 10th-century inscribed stones (*see* **Monuments, Early Christian**), among them a memorial to Hywel ap Rhys, king of **Glywysing** (d.886). Following the **Norman** invasion, the *clas* was dissolved and the church given to St Mary's Abbey, Tewkesbury.

St Illtud's is the largest medieval **parish** church in **Glamorgan**. It consists of a chancel, a four-bay nave surmounted by a tower, a rectangular space known as the Western Church and a ruined chantry chapel. It represents several building phases extending from the 12th to the 15th century. Among the numerous monuments are a fine 13th-century niche surrounded by a carved Jesse Tree and some late medieval wall **paintings**. The churchyard contains a chantry priest's house, and beyond it are the remains of Tewkesbury Abbey's grange, including a gatehouse, barn and **dovecote**.

The medieval manor of Llantwit with Boverton contained excellent arable land and was kept in demesne by the lords of Glamorgan. Within it, Llantwit developed as a

example of a little-altered Victorian country house. Bryn Tysilio was the home of Theodore Martin, biographer of the Prince Consort. Queen Victoria visited the house to see the desk on which the life of her beloved Albert had been written.

LLANUWCHLLYN, Gwynedd
(11,712 ha; 622 inhabitants)

Extending over the entire basin of the upper **Dee** and of its tributaries, the Lliw and the Twrch, the **community** contains the summits of **Aran** Benllyn (885 m) and Moel Llyfnant (751 m). The **Roman** auxiliary fort at Caergai was occupied from AD *c*.75 to *c*.120. By the 16th century, Caergai was the home of the Vaughan family, the most distinguished of whom was the Royalist and writer **Rowland Vaughan**. Burnt by the Parliamentarians, the house was rebuilt in the 1650s. **Llywelyn ap Iorwerth** was probably responsible for the building of Castell Carndochan as part of his campaign to annex Penllyn, traditionally considered to be part of **Powys**.

The **gold** mine nearby operated until the early 20th century. **Michael D. Jones** was born in the chapel house of Yr Hen Gapel, the **Congregational** chapel of which his father was minister during a period of bitter theological debate. Coed-y-pry was the home of **O. M. Edwards**, who built Neuadd Wen in Llanuwchllyn village. He and his son, **Ifan ab Owen Edwards**, founder of **Urdd Gobaith Cymru**, are commemorated by a roadside memorial. Appositely, Glanllyn, one of the former homes of the **Williams Wynn family**, is an Urdd centre. Tom Jones of Llanuwchllyn (Thomas Jones; 1910–85) was a shrewd politician at local **government** level, and was the first conductor of the renowned Côr Godre'r Aran. The **road** up Cwm Cynllwyd crosses Bwlch y Groes (545 m) on its way to Llany**mawddwy**.

Llanuwchllyn is considered to be **Welsh**-speaking rural Wales at its most cultured, an image of the place which owes much to **W. J. Gruffydd**'s biography of O. M. Edwards (1937). Although beaten by **Caernarfon** (91.76%) in terms of the percentage having some knowledge of Welsh (86.88%), it leads all Wales's communities in terms of the percentage of the inhabitants wholly fluent in the language (81.06%).

LLANVACHES (Llanfaches), Newport
(763 ha; 365 inhabitants)

Constituting the north-eastern corner of the **Newport county borough**, the **community**'s claim to fame is that it was the location of Wales's earliest dissenting congregation. In 1638, William Wroth (1576–1641) abandoned the rectorship of Llanvaches and, in the following year, became Wales's first **Congregationalist** minister. The gathered church at Llanvaches attracted the support of other **Puritans**, among them **William Erbery** and **Walter Cradock**. With the outbreak of the **Civil War** in 1642, the congregation was forced to flee. Tabernacle United Reformed church (1924) stands on the site of its meeting house. St Dyfrig's church (13th and 14th centuries) contains a tablet carved by Eric Gill. Wentwood **reservoir** was constructed in the 1840s to supply water to **Newport**; Wentwood Lodge offers fine views over **Wentwood**. The Andrac **Vineyard** produces Llanvaches – a sparkling white wine.

LLANWDDYN, Montgomeryshire, Powys
(10,040 ha; 310 inhabitants)

Embracing the upper reaches of the Vyrnwy valley in the north-western corner of **Montgomeryshire**, the **community** is dominated by Lake Vyrnwy (Llyn Efyrnwy or Llyn Llanwddyn), created in 1888 to supply **Liverpool** with water. The city built a new village nearby, to replace the village it had drowned. The **reservoir**, Europe's largest when it was completed, has a beauty of its own; the straining tower, disguised as a stone fortress, is reminiscent of Bavaria's Neuschwanstein. In 1974, the reservoir came into the possession of **Severn** Trent Water.

The church inundated by the reservoir once belonged to the Knights of St John; on the hill south of the reservoir are the remains of a *hospitium*. In the 17th century, Llanwddyn had a **Quaker** congregation.

LLANWENOG, Ceredigion
(4505 ha; 1391 inhabitants)

Located immediately west of **Llandysul**, the **community** contains the villages of Llanwenog, Cwrtnewydd, Gorsgoch and Rhuddlan Teifi. The **National Museum** has a stone from Llanwenog inscribed, in the 5th century, in **Latin** and **ogham** in memory of Trenacatus, son of Maglagnus. St Gwenog's is perhaps the most attractive medieval church in **Ceredigion**; it contains a remarkable font bearing 12 identical carved faces. Llanwenog was the birthplace of one of Wales's most distinguished physicists, **Evan Williams** (1903–45). Rhuddlan Teifi figures in the first branch of *Pedair Cainc y Mabinogi* (*see* **Mabinogion, The**). Highmead was once the seat of the Davies-Evans family. Of the community's six chapels, the best known is that of the **Unitarians** at Alltyblaca, where the writer and broadcaster **D. Jacob Davies** was minister. Llanwenog is the name of a well-known breed of **sheep**.

LLANWERN (Llan-wern), Newport
(684 ha; 333 inhabitants)

In 1962, adjoining the eastern boundary of the built-up area of the city of **Newport**, Llanwern became the location of a massive steelworks which extended for 4.8 km, well into the community of **Bishton**. Steel manufacture ceased in 2001 (see **Llanwern Steelworks**). W. H. Davies felt nostalgia for the green village of Llanwern. Rusticity survives in the upper part of the community, north of the **railway** line. Llanwern House, the seat of **D. A. Thomas** (Lord **Rhondda**), has been demolished, but the institute in the Arts and Crafts style he financed (*c*.1906) still graces the village. The 15th-century St Mary's church contains fine **stained glass** made by Celtic Studios.

LLANWERN STEELWORKS, Newport

To ensure sufficient supplies of sheet steel (*see* **Iron and Steel**) for a burgeoning consumer-durables boom, the nationalized **Richard Thomas and Baldwins** built the Spencer Works at Llanwern, which commenced production in 1962 as the first wholly oxygen-blown integrated steel plant in **Britain**. Although constructed on a greenfield site with a modern layout, Llanwern suffered persistent production and labour difficulties, culminating in the ending of steelmaking in 2001, with the loss of 1300 jobs. The works became a finishing plant and by 2004 was employing nearly 2000 workers and rolling over 50,000 tonnes of steel a week. In 2004, plans were announced for a £200-million redevelopment of some 240 ha of the site, involving a mixture of housing, industry and business.

LLANWINIO, Carmarthenshire
(2930 ha; 432 inhabitants)
Located north of **St Clears** and extending to the **Carmarthenshire–Pembrokeshire** border, the **community** contains the villages of Blaenwaun, Cwmbach and Cwmfelin Mynach. The isolated church of St Gwynio was rebuilt in 1846. Cilsant was the cradle of the **Philipps family** of Picton Castle.

LLANWNDA, Gwynedd
(1573 ha; 1893 inhabitants)
Located south of **Caernarfon**, the **community** contains the villages of Llanwnda, Rhosgadfan and Rhostryfan. The former is a ribbon development along the A487; its church, St Gwyndaf (1847), contains interesting memorials. Rhosgadfan and Rhostryfan developed to house **slate** quarrymen; they are surrounded by the small fields typical of the agro-industrial settlements of the quarrying districts. The author **Kate Roberts** was a native of Rhosgadfan. Her birthplace, Cae'r Gors, has been restored and in 2007 was opened as a heritage centre. The area is rich in prehistoric hut circles.

LLANWNNEN, Ceredigion
(2339 ha; 1391 inhabitants)
Located immediately west of **Lampeter**, the **community** extends over the basin of the Grannell, a tributary of the **Teifi**. St Gwnnen's church has a 15th-century tower. The **Unitarian** cause (1802) at Capel-y-Groes is one of the dozen and more Unitarian congregations in southern **Ceredigion** – a concentration of rural Unitarianism unique in **Britain**. To devout Trinitarians, the district constitutes *y spotyn du* (the black spot), a name which local Unitarians have accepted with pride.

LLANWRDA, Carmarthenshire
(2316 ha; 513 inhabitants)
Hugging the north bank of the **Tywi** immediately west of **Llandovery**, the **community** contains the villages of Llanwrda and Porthyrhyd. St Cawrdaf's church retains some medieval features. Pentre Meurig and Neuadd Lwyd were seats of the Powell family. The former **Drovers** tavern in Porthyrhyd was once a focal point of the **cattle** trade.

LLANWRTHWL, Breconshire, Powys
(7953 ha; 201 inhabitants)
The village of Llanwrthwl stands on the banks of the **Wye**, but the **community** extends across the whole of northern **Breconshire**, embracing a vast tract of **mountain**ous country. It rises to 641 m at Drygarn Fawr, the highest point between **Pumlumon** and the **Black Mountains**. The dams creating the **reservoirs** on the Claerwen and Elan **Rivers** have inundated parts of the community's northern reaches. The site of Llanwrthwl church is probably pre-Christian. There are numerous **Bronze Age** burial cairns and standing stones on the moorlands of Gamriw, Cefn-y-ffordd and Drum-ddu. Llannerch-y-Cawr is a fine cruck-built **longhouse**.

LLANWRTYD WELLS (Llanwrtyd),
Breconshire, Powys (10,874 ha; 762 inhabitants)
Llanwrtyd, which claims to be the smallest town in **Britain**, was once a centre of the **woollen industry**; the woollen factory from Esgairmoel has been re-erected at the National History Museum (*see* **St Fagans**). The town's fame is the result of the discovery of the medicinal properties of its springs. In 1732, the vicar, **Theophilus Evans**, observed a frog swimming unharmed in the waters of Ffynnon Ddrewllyd (stinking spring – the water contained sulphur); he resolved to try them himself and was cured of scurvy. Other **wells** were discovered, and Llanwrtyd became an important spa, a process encouraged by the arrival of the **railway** in 1886. The largely **Welsh**-speaking visitors organized **eisteddfod**au, concerts and summer schools. Present-day tourist events revolve around **beer** festivals, **man versus horse events** and the World Bog Snorkelling Championship. The **community**, which extends to the source of the **Tywi**, includes part of the Brianne **reservoir** and some of Wales's remotest **sheep** farms. The **road** to **Tregaron** via Abergwesyn involves the ascent of the Devil's Staircase. David Jones, who in 1796 rebuilt the remote Llwynderw mansion, was reputed to own 10,000 sheep.

LLANYBYDDER, Carmarthenshire
(3670 ha; 1420 inhabitants)
Hugging the south bank of the **Teifi** south-west of **Lampeter**, the **community** contains the large village of Llanybydder and the hamlet of Rhydcymerau. St Peter's church, largely dully Victorian, retains its squat medieval tower. Llanybydder has one of **Britain**'s largest **horse** sales, held on the last Thursday of every month. The poet **Lewys Glyn Cothi** is reputed to have been born at Pwllcynbyd. Rhydcymerau, the *milltir sgwâr* (the square mile) of the writer **D. J. Williams**, was the inspiration of much of his work.

LLANYCIL, Gwynedd (8727 ha, 426 inhabitants)
Located immediately west of **Bala**, the **community** extends from Bala **Lake** (Llyn Tegid) to Llyn Celyn (*see* **Tryweryn valley, drowning of**) and contains the summits of **Arenig** Fawr (854 m) and Arenig Fach (689 m), together with Llyn Arenig Fawr, Llyn Arenig Fach and part of Llyn Tryweryn. Llyn Arenig Fawr attracted the painters **Augustus John** and **J. D. Innes**. Until 1868, St Beuno's (rebuilt 1881) was Bala's **parish** church; its churchyard contains the graves of many of the town's dignitaries, **Thomas Charles** among them. The community's largest settlement is the village of Parc, where **Merched y Wawr** was founded in 1967.

LLANYCRWYS (Llan-crwys), Carmarthenshire
(1363 ha; 221 inhabitants)
Located south-east of **Lampeter**, the **community**'s only settlement of any size is the hamlet of Ffaldybrenin, whose **Congregational** chapel (1873) is a handsome building. Ffaldybrenin was the birthplace of **Timothy Richard**, a **Baptist missionary** in China; on occasion, he was ruler of large parts of that country, probably causing him to have exercised more power than any other native of Wales. *Cerddi Ysgol Llanycrwys* (1934) is an interesting collection of local lore.

LLANYNYS, Denbighshire
(1738 ha; 784 inhabitants)

A **community** located immediately north-west of **Ruthin**, in the 6th century Llanynys was the centre of an ecclesiastical community or *clas*. Its site is occupied by the double-naved church of St Saeran in which a 15th-century St Christopher mural was rediscovered in 1967. A branch of the **Salusbury family** owned Bachymbyd (rebuilt 1666). Plas-y-ward was the chief seat of the Thelwall family. Rhyd-y-Cilgwyn is associated with the poet Edward ap Raff (fl.1578–1606). Emrys ap Iwan (**Robert Ambrose Jones**), author and nationalist, is buried at Rhewl.

LLANYRE (Llanllŷr-yn-Rhos), Radnorshire, Powys (2987 ha; 1061 inhabitants)

The **community** lies west of **Llandrindod** between the Ithon and **Wye**. Its two chief settlements – Llanyre and Newbridge-on-Wye – are examples of ribbon development. Newbridge – one of the mid-Wales centres of the **Rebecca riot**ers – enjoyed a brief reputation as a spa. Newbridge's substantial All Saints' church was completed in 1883. The community's chief monument is the **Roman** fort at Castle Collen. Built in AD *c.*78 to accommodate 500 soldiers, it commanded the main north–south Roman **road** through Wales. Between 1811 and 1813 Carnhuanawc (**Thomas Price**) was curate of Llanfihangel Helygen. The permanent traffic lights on Pont ar Ithon are a reminder of the inadequacy of the **A470**.

LLANYSTUMDWY, Gwynedd
(6013 ha; 1919 inhabitants)

Located immediately north-west of **Criccieth**, the **community** embraces the lower reaches of the basins of the Dwyfor and the Dwyfach. It contains the villages of Llanystumdwy, Afon Wen, Chwilog, Llanarmon, Llangybi, Pencaenewydd and Rhoslan. Llanystumdwy is indelibly linked with **David Lloyd George** who arrived there in 1864 at the age of 19 months. He left in 1878 and returned in 1939, following his acquisition of Tŷ Newydd (mid-18th century), where he died in 1945. His childhood home, Highgate, is open to the public. His grave, designed by **Clough Williams-Ellis**, stands above the Dwyfor; linked with it is the Lloyd George Museum. Tŷ Newydd has become a centre for writing courses.

The medieval church of St **Cybi**, Llangybi, adjoins St Cybi's **Well** and attractive almshouses (1760). The 15th-century church of St **Garmon**, Llanarmon, contains a fine rood screen. Penarth Fawr, near Chwilog, is an attractive late medieval hall house. Gwynfryn, the seat of Ellis Nanney, Lloyd George's **Conservative** opponent in 1890, became a hotel; engulfed by fire in the 1980s, it is now a ruin. Shelley lived in the house in 1813, following an attack on his life at Tremadog (*see* **Porthmadog**). The community is bisected by an old avenue known as Y Lôn Goed (the tree **road**); it was immortalized by the poet **R. Williams Parry**. An army camp near Chwilog was adapted in 1946 as the **Pwllheli** Butlins Holiday Camp; it closed in 1998 and the site became a caravan park.

Among the other distinguished figures associated with the area are the artist Elis Gwyn (1918–99), his brother the dramatist Wil Sam Jones (Wil Sam; b.1920), the author

Jan Morris (b.1926) and the actor Guto Roberts (1925–99). Earlier writers from the area include **Robert Jones** (1745–1829), historian of the **Methodist Revival**, and the poets Robert ap Gwilym Ddu (**Robert Williams**), Siôn Wyn o Eifion (John Thomas; 1786–1859) and Eben Fardd (**Ebenezer Thomas**).

LLAWHADEN (Llanhuadain), Pembrokeshire
(1630 ha; 634 inhabitants)

Located immediately west of **Narberth**, the **community** contains the villages of Llawhaden and Robeston Wathen. In the Middle Ages, the barony of Llawhaden was the richest of the properties of the **diocese** of St **David's**. In about 1120, **Bernard**, the first **Norman** bishop of St David's, built a ringwork at Llawhaden which became part of the belt of fortifications created to defend the lands conquered by the invaders. Seized by **Rhys ap Gruffudd** (The Lord Rhys; d.1197) in 1192, it was recovered by the bishops in the early 13th century, who reconstructed it in stone. **Thomas Bek**, bishop 1280–93, remodelled it as a fortified mansion and established Llawhaden **borough** and hospital. Following the **Protestant Reformation**, the castle fell into decay; its ruins were much appreciated by 18th-century romantic painters. It came into the guardianship of the Ministry of Works in 1931 and into that of **Cadw** in 1984.

Llawhaden House, originally 16th century, was destroyed by fire in 2000. St Aidan's church has two towers. Bethesda **Congregational** chapel, first erected in 1797, is a handsome building. According to the *Shell Guide to South-West Wales*, the church (dedication unknown) in the compact village of Robeston Wathen was 'decently victorianized'.

David Lloyd George's grave at Llanystumdwy

Harry Llewellyn on *Foxhunter*

LLAY (Llai), Wrexham (909 ha; 4905 inhabitants)
Located immediately north of **Wrexham**, the **community**
was wholly rural until 1873 when the Llay Hall Colliery
was opened. A far more ambitious scheme was launched in
1914 with the sinking of the Llay Main Colliery. It became
Wales's largest colliery and, at 730 m, the deepest pit in
Europe. The village, the work of the **Garden** City enthusiast Barry Parker, was laid out from 1920 onwards; it has
been described as a low-budget version of Port Sunlight or
Bourneville. The colliery was closed in 1966. The wealth it
once generated is reflected in the village's focal point, the
Miners' Institute (1929–31). Edward Hubbard described it
as 'not so much Neo-Georgian as Edwardian Baroque
Survival'. The **county** of Wrexham's largest country park,
Alyn Waters, borders the village.

LLEDROD, Ceredigion (3795 ha; 736 inhabitants)
Located south-east of **Aberystwyth**, the **community** contains the villages of Lledrod, Blaenpennal and Bronnant.
It includes the eastern part of Mynydd Bach, an outlier of
the **Elenydd** or Cambrian **mountains**, and cradles its own
lake, Llyn Eiddwen, a winter haunt of migrating wild
geese. A memorial to four of the poets of the area stands
above the lake. Ieuan Brydydd Hir (**Evan Evans**; 1731–88)
is commemorated in St Michael's church, Lledrod. The
area was involved in **Rhyfel y Sais Bach** (*see also*
Llangwyryfon).

LLEU or LLEW LLAWGYFFES
(lit. the Bright One of the Skilful Hand)
A character in the fourth branch of the Mabinogi (*see*
Mabinogion, The). His mother, **Arianrhod**, places three

fates upon him: that he shall have neither a name nor
weapons nor a human wife. His uncle, **Gwydion**, over-
comes by magic means the first two fates; to counter the
third, Gwydion and **Math fab Mathonwy** create for Lleu a
wife made from flowers, **Blodeuwedd**. After Blodeuwedd's
lover, Gronw Pebr, strikes Lleu with a spear, he is found by
Gwydion in the form of a wounded eagle perched on an
oak tree at Nant Lleu (Nantlle; *see* **Llanllyfni**). The Irish
god Lugh (*Lugus* in Gaulish) is a cognate of Lleu.

LLEWELLYN, David (1879–1940) Coalowner
After training as a mining engineer at **Cardiff** and in
America, Llewellyn acquired a series of small drift mines
around **Aberdare**. The significant stage of his industrial
career began when, *c.*1916, he joined Seymour **Berry** in the
project of extending, through mergers and acquisitions,
D. A. Thomas's dominance of the **coal** industry. Like
Berry, Llewellyn's flair was in finance and marketing; this
group effectively introduced south Wales to 20th-century
management styles. In 1930, the amalgamations were consolidated in Welsh Associated Collieries Ltd, which, in
1935, merged with **Powell Duffryn** to control 90 pits, producing over 20 million tonnes of coal. Knighted in 1922,
Llewellyn was a keen huntsman (*see* **Hunting**); one of his
sons was the showjumper **Harry Llewellyn**. Although for
long he lived at The Court, St Fagans, Cardiff, he was born
and he died in Aberdare.

LLEWELLYN, Harry (Henry Morton Llewellyn;
1911–99) Showjumper
Aberdare-born Sir Harry Llewellyn, who settled near
Abergavenny, made a central contribution during the 1950s
to raising British showjumping from mediocrity to international acclaim. A son of the colliery owner **David (Richard)**
Llewellyn, initially he was a steeplechaser (*see* **Horse**
Racing) and finished second in the 1936 Grand National. A
bronze medallist at the 1948 **London** Olympics, he won a
showjumping gold medal with the British team at the 1952
Helsinki Olympics, riding his famous bay gelding
Foxhunter. Over his career, Llewellyn won 78 international competitions. He was also recognized for his military achievements during the **Second World War**. The
remains of Foxhunter are buried on the Blorenge **Mountain**
(**Llanfoist Fawr**), where there is a memorial to the **horse**;
Llewellyn's ashes were scattered nearby.

LLEWELLYN, Willie (1878–1973) Rugby player
Rhondda-born Llewellyn, a pharmacist, was one of four
former pupils of Christ College, **Brecon** in the Welsh **rugby**
team that defeated the All Blacks in 1905. On his début in
1899, he tore the English defence apart to score four tries.
He scored 18 tries in 20 international appearances between
1899 and 1905. Such was his sporting celebrity that the
rioters who sacked Tonypandy High Street in 1910 (*see*
Tonypandy Riots) left his chemist's shop unscathed.

LLEWELYN, Desmond [Wilkinson] (1914–99)
Actor
Newport-born Desmond Llewelyn played many small roles
in British **films** from 1935 onwards. Appearing in 19 consecutive James Bond films, starting with the second, *From*

Russia With Love (1963), he became identified, almost exclusively, with the eccentric boffin Major Boothroyd or 'Q', who devised weird and wonderful devices for Bond.

LLIFON Commote

A **commote** in western **Anglesey**, which, with that of **Malltraeth**, constituted the *cantref* of **Aberffraw**. The site of the commotal centre is uncertain but it may have been at **Bodedern**. The name survived as that of a post-**Acts of 'Union' hundred**.

LLIW VALLEY (Dyffryn Lliw) One-time district

Following local **government** reorganization in 1974, Lliw Valley was established as one of the four districts of the newly established **county** of **West Glamorgan**. It consisted of what had been the **urban district** of **Llwchwr** and the **rural district** of **Pontardawe**. Named after the Lliw **River**, a tributary of the **Llwchwr**, its council offices were at **Penllergaer**. The district was abolished in 1996 when it was divided between the counties of **Swansea** and **Neath Port Talbot**.

LLOYD family (Dolobran)

Industrialists and bankers

The Lloyd family of Dolobran (**Llangynyw**), who claimed descent from Aleth, king of the **Demetae**, made distinguished contributions, from the 17th century onwards, as industrialists, bankers and public administrators. The family's significance for the industrial development of Wales began with the establishment by Charles Lloyd (1613–57) of **Mathrafal** forge in 1651–2. His son Charles II, (1637–98), built the separate New Forge at Dolobran (*c.*1720) and a new blast furnace at **Bersham**, which, thanks to **Quaker** connections with Darby of Coalbrookdale, used pit-**coal** for smelting as early as 1721.

The family's broader importance also arose from Quakerism, which led to Charles's long term of house arrest after 1660 and to his brother Thomas (1640–94) emigrating to **Pennsylvania**, where he became deputy to William Penn. Charles Lloyd II's son, Sampson (1664–1724), became involved in industrial activities around Birmingham, leading into **banking** and the formation of Lloyds Bank. His descendant George Ambrose Lloyd (1879–1941) was raised to the peerage in 1925 as Baron Lloyd of Dolobran.

LLOYD, [Thomas] Alwyn (1881–1960)

Architect and town planner

Born in **Liverpool**, Lloyd worked under Raymond Unwin at Hampstead Garden Suburb, **London** (1907–12), before becoming architect to the Welsh Town Planning and **Housing** Trust. He established a practice in **Cardiff**, and was responsible (in conjunction with Unwin) for planning **Barry** Garden Suburb (1915), garden village housing schemes at **Machynlleth** and **Wrexham** (both 1914), and embryonic villages for ex-miners at **Penllyn**, near **Cowbridge**, and Boverton (**Llantwit Major**) (both 1936), all of which showed Arts and Crafts influences. Lloyd was co-author, with Herbert Jackson, of the *South Wales Outline Plan* (1949) for the Ministry of Town and Country Planning.

LLOYD, D[avid] Tecwyn (E. H. Francis Thomas; 1914–92) Writer

D. Tecwyn Lloyd is remembered as an accomplished essayist of exceptionally wide interests, a perceptive literary critic and a literary spoofer. Born in Glan-yr-afon (**Llandderfel**), he was educated at **Bangor**. He worked in adult **education**, journalism and publishing. The first volume of his biography of **Saunders Lewis** was published in 1988, but he died before completing the second.

LLOYD, David [George] (1912–69) Singer

After an apprenticeship as a carpenter, this miner's son from Trelogan (**Llanasa**) won a scholarship to the Guildhall School of **Music**, **London** in 1933, winning the Gold Medal in 1937. Following appearances at Glyndebourne and Sadler's Wells, he resumed his career after the **Second World War**. His career was again interrupted because of an accident in 1954, but he was able to enjoy a final period after 1960 when he became well-known for his interpretations of the Welsh **music** repertoire.

LLOYD, J[ohn] E[dward] (1861–1947) Historian

Liverpool-born J. E. Lloyd was educated at **Aberystwyth** and **Oxford**. He began his academic career in 1885 as a lecturer in **Welsh** and history at Aberystwyth but, in 1892, was appointed registrar and lecturer in Welsh history at **Bangor**, and professor of history there seven years later. His two masterpieces are *A History of Wales from the Earliest Times to the Edwardian Conquest* (2 vols. 1911) and *Owen Glendower* (1931). The former, written with immaculate style, was the first reliable comprehensive survey of the history of early medieval Wales. Among Lloyd's many contributions to Welsh life was his work as consultant editor to *The Dictionary of Welsh Biography* (1953). In an elegy for him, **Saunders Lewis** referred to Lloyd as 'llusernwr y canrifoedd coll' (the lamplighter of the lost centuries).

LLOYD, John Ambrose (1815–74) Composer

A major figure in 19th-century Welsh musical life, **Mold**-born Lloyd was a teacher in **Liverpool**'s Mechanics' Institute, but he gave up his post because of ill **health**, and embarked on various business ventures. Lloyd contributed enormously to religious **music** in Wales, with **hymn** tunes such as 'Wynnstay', 'Wyddgrug' and 'Eifionydd' (the finest Welsh hymn tune, according to **Walford Davies**), the cantata *Gweddi Habacuc* (the first of its kind in **Welsh**) and the anthem 'Teyrnasoedd y Ddaear', one of the most popular settings of religious texts in Welsh.

LLOYD, Richard Herbert Vivian (Richard Llewellyn; 1906–83) Novelist

The author of the most famous novel ever written about Wales appears to have been born to parents of Welsh descent in **London**. At the age of 20, he joined the army, serving in India and Hong Kong. The fame of his first novel, *How Green Was My Valley* (1939), is attributable partly to John Ford's 1940 Hollywood **film** of the book; it made its author so much money that he was able to live on the royalties for the rest of his life. Set in a southern mining village, generally assumed to be **Gilfach Goch**, in the late 19th century, it tells the story of the Morgan family

David Lloyd George

1908 chancellor of the exchequer, in which position he spearheaded an array of social reforms, notably the introduction of old age pensions in 1908 and of national **insurance** in 1911. His introduction of the 1909 'People's Budget' – the most controversial budget in British history – brought about a constitutional crisis over the role of the House of Lords which led to two general elections in 1910. The resultant curtailment of the Lords' veto opened the way to disestablishment. In 1913, he launched a radical land campaign, inspired in part by his memories of the landlord-ridden society of **Caernarfonshire**.

When the **First World War** broke out in August 1914, Lloyd George reluctantly came to support British involvement. Appointed minister of munitions in May 1915, he soon displayed the dynamism and tact required in industrial negotiations. He came to advocate military conscription, a stand which brought him close to the **Conservatives**. In July 1916, he became secretary of state for war, and in December succeeded Asquith as prime minister, heading a small war cabinet. His boldness and resourcefulness brought him the popular accolade of 'the man who won the war'. In 1916, he played a key role in the settlement of the strike in the south Wales **coal**field. In 1917, he authorized the release of the Balfour Declaration, the foundation document in the history of the establishment of the state of Israel, an authorization much influenced by the bibliolatry of the Welsh Nonconformity in which he had been bred.

In December 1918, Lloyd George was re-elected at the head of a Conservative-dominated coalition **government**, which remained in office until October 1922. He was one of the primary forces behind the signing of the Peace of Versailles in 1919. His devious handling of the coalminers' strike of 1919 (*see* **Sankey Commission**) went far to destroy support for the Liberal Party in the south Wales coalfield. In his discussions with **Irish** Republicans in 1921 – discussions which led to the establishment of the Irish Free State – he constantly referred to his Welsh origins, but he did little to sustain the groundswell of support for '**Home Rule All Round**' which occurred during his premiership. The withdrawal of Conservative support in the autumn of 1922 led to the collapse of the coalition and Lloyd George's fall from power.

He never returned to the hub of British politics, although he succeeded Asquith as leader of the reunited Liberal Party in 1926. During the mid-1920s, he used his political fund, somewhat dubiously amassed during the post-war coalition, to finance major policy studies. His campaign to return to power in the general election of May 1929, with the pamphlet *We Can Conquer Unemployment* as its centrepiece, proved unsuccessful.

Thereafter, Lloyd George became an increasingly peripheral figure in British political life. Laid low by ill **health** in August 1931, the time of the formation of the so-called national government (to which he was vehemently opposed), he subsequently headed a tiny Lloyd George party of six MPs in the new House of Commons. His political swansong came with the launching of his radical 'New Deal' proposals to his **Bangor** constituents in January 1935, and the subsequent setting up of the Council of Action for Peace and Reconstruction. In 1940, he made his last major speech in the Commons, calling forcefully for

and is narrated by the lyrically gifted Huw, their youngest child. It describes an idealized community and is less concerned with historical accuracy than with the creation of a myth in which the hard work and solidarity of the valley's inhabitants are spoiled by greed on the part of both owners and workers, and by confrontation between the old **Liberal**ism and the new militancy of the **Labour** movement.

For all its sentimentality, the novel has many powerful scenes and some memorable characters; it also contributed to the stereotype of Wales as a land of singing miners that still survives in **England** and elsewhere. Although Richard Llewellyn wrote another 21 novels, including *Up, Into the Singing Mountain* (1963), which is set among the **Patagonia** Welsh, none had the undeniable charm and emotional charge of his first novel, and most are insubstantial.

LLOYD GEORGE, David (1863–1945) Politician
Born at Manchester, Lloyd George was brought up at **Llanystumdwy** by his widowed mother and her brother Richard Lloyd, a pervasive influence in his nephew's life. The young Lloyd George made his mark locally as a solicitor and, in 1888, was adopted as **Liberal** candidate for **Caernarfon Boroughs**, a seat he won in 1890 by 18 votes and held until 1945.

Welsh issues, particularly the **disestablishment of the Church of England in Wales** and issues relating to the **Land Question**, preoccupied Lloyd George during his first years in parliament; he was also among the leaders of the **Cymru Fydd** movement. He was a vocal opponent of the **South African War** (1899–1902) and led **Nonconformist** and **radical** opposition to Balfour's **Education** Act (1902). In 1905, he was appointed president of the board of trade and in

the resignation of Chamberlain. In January 1945, less than three months before his death, the 'Great Commoner' caused widespread amazement by becoming Earl Lloyd-George of Dwyfor. He returned to die at Llanystumdwy; his grave on the banks of the **Dwyfor** was designed by **Clough Williams-Ellis**.

Lloyd George's political career was controversial in his own lifetime and beyond. He was accused by some of abandoning the Welsh causes of his early years, yet, for many, his career gave Wales heightened recognition and a new lustre.

His brother William George (1865–1967) did much to finance David Lloyd George's early political career. A leading enthusiast for the **Welsh language** and prominent in local government, he was the oldest practising solicitor in the history of **Britain**. His son William Richard Philip George (1912–2006) won the crown at the National **Eisteddfod** of 1974 and also served as **Archdruid** from 1990 to 1993. W. R. P. George wrote extensively about his uncle's career and served as vice-president of **Plaid [Genedlaethol] Cymru**.

LLOYD GEORGE, Gwilym (1894–1967) Politician

The son of Margaret and **David Lloyd George**, he saw active service during the **First World War**. He was **Liberal** MP for **Pembrokeshire** (1922–4, 1929–50); following his defeat at Pembrokeshire in 1950, he became **National Liberal** and **Conservative** MP for Newcastle-upon-Tyne North in 1951. While home secretary and minister for Welsh affairs (1954–7), he announced on behalf of the **government** that **Cardiff** was to be the capital of Wales. He was the first chairman of the Pantyfedwen Trust (*see* **David James**). Gwilym Lloyd George was created Viscount **Tenby** of Bulford (*see* **Tiers Cross**) in 1957. From 1955 to 1965, he was president of University College, **Swansea** (*see* **University of Wales Swansea**).

LLOYD GEORGE, Megan (1902–66) Politician

The daughter of Margaret and **David Lloyd George**, she was brought up at 11 and 10 Downing Street, and accompanied her father to the 1919 Paris Peace Conference. Widely regarded by the mid-1920s as **David** Lloyd George's natural political heir, she was elected **Liberal** MP for **Anglesey** in 1929, the first woman MP in the history of Wales. In 1931, she became one of the tiny band of Lloyd George Liberals and during the 1930s spoke regularly in the House of Commons on **agriculture**, unemployment and Welsh affairs.

During the **Second World War**, Megan Lloyd George became increasingly well known as an advocate of **women**'s rights and Welsh aspirations. She was clearly moving leftwards in the political spectrum, and there were persistent rumours that she was likely to join the **Labour Party**. In 1949, **Clement Davies** appointed Lady Megan (a title she acquired in 1945 when her father became an earl) deputy leader of the Parliamentary Liberal Party, but in 1951 she lost her seat in Anglesey to **Cledwyn Hughes**; in 1955, she joined the Labour Party. She was president of the Parliament for Wales campaign (1950–6) and in 1957 was elected Labour MP for **Carmarthen**, serving until her death in 1966. She remained a backbencher. A brilliant

broadcaster, it was she who invented the concept of a 'national region', the concept which gave rise to the **Broadcasting Council for Wales**.

LLOYD-JONES, [David] Martyn (1899–1981)
Preacher and writer

Born in **Cardiff**, Lloyd-Jones spent his youth in **Llangeitho** and **London**. After a year, he left what promised to be a distinguished medical career to become a **Calvinistic Methodist** minister. He ministered at Sandfields, **Aberavon** (1927–38), and at Westminster, London (1938–68). According to the theologian Emil Brunner, Lloyd-Jones was one of the great **preachers** of the 20th century. A prolific author, his publications include commentaries, theological works and historical studies. His writings are probably more widely read than those of any other Welsh author. He deeply influenced the **Evangelical Movement of Wales**.

LLWCHWR, Swansea (729 ha; 9080 inhabitants)

The **Romans** established a fort – Leucarum –at the lowest fordable place on the **River Llwchwr** *c.*70 AD. In the 12th century, the **Normans** built a ringwork within the fort; it was captured by the Welsh in 1115, 1136 and 1213. In *c.*1300, the ringwork was crowned by a stone tower, part of which survives. Llwchwr, the second **borough** in the lordship of **Gower**, withered whilst **Swansea** flourished. The viaduct (1852) carrying the **railway** across the Llwchwr is the last to survive of the timber viaducts designed by **Brunel**. **Evan Roberts**, the chief figure in the religious **revival** of 1904–5, was born in Llwchwr. He is commemorated by a plaque on Moriah chapel, where he initiated the revival's most intense phase. The college (*c.*1955) on

Megan Lloyd George

Belgrave Road is among **Glamorgan**'s earliest examples of Modernist **architecture**. In 1974, the **community** of Llwchwr replaced the civil **parish** of Loughor Borough.

LLWCHWR River (45 km)

The Llwchwr rises on the western slopes of the **Black Mountain** in the **community** of **Dyffryn Cennen**. Initially, it flows through Carboniferous **Limestone**, Millstone Grit and **Coal** Measures. South of **Ammanford**, it is joined by the Aman, which rises on the Black Mountain's southern slopes. Tidal from **Pontarddulais** southwards, it is crossed near **Llwchwr** Castle by **road** and **rail** bridges. The sands of its wide estuary contain Wales's richest cockle beds (*see* **Fish and Fishing**).

LLWYD, Angharad (1780–1866)
Antiquarian and author

One of the most important collectors and scribes of her day, Angharad Llwyd was born in **Caerwys**, where her father was rector. She inherited her father's library and greatly extended his collection of manuscripts and documents. She regularly visited **gentry** houses in **Denbighshire**, **Flintshire** and **Merioneth**, seeking out materials for her research on Welsh history and pedigrees. The **National Library** has many of her transcripts and original manuscripts. She was a supporter of regional *eisteddfodau*, and, on the strength of her eisteddfodic essays and publications on Welsh history, was made an ovate in the **Gorsedd** (1821).

LLWYD, Morgan (1619–59) Puritan author

Born in Cynfal Fawr, **Maentwrog**, Llwyd attended school in **Wrexham**, where, aged 16, he was converted by listening to **Walter Cradock**. At **Llanvaches**, in 1639, he was involved with Cradock setting up the first Independent or 'gathered' church (*see* **Congregationalists**); it was there that he married Ann Herbert, who bore him at least 11 children. In 1643, he followed the church to Bristol and then to **London**, where he enlisted as chaplain in the Parliamentary army and saw action in southern **England**. After the **Civil Wars**, he returned to Wrexham, where he was appointed an approver under the **Act for the Better Propagation and Preaching of the Gospel in Wales (1650)** and a minister (1656); he died there.

Although he wrote poetry in both **Welsh** and **English**, including an astrological text, Llwyd is pre-eminent as a writer of prose, producing five works in Welsh and three in English. In 1653, he published three volumes intended to prepare the Welsh for the second coming of Christ – *Llythur ir Cymru cariadus*, *Gwaedd ynghymru yn wyneb pob Cydwybod* and *Llyfr y Tri Aderyn* – in which Llwyd's millenarianism and the influence on his thinking of the German mystic Jakob Böehme are apparent, but the sinewy, metaphorical prose is Llwyd's alone.

LLWYD AP IWAN (1862–1909) Pioneer

Llwyd ap Iwan, son of **Michael D. Jones**, played a significant role in realizing his father's vision of a Welsh colony in **Patagonia**. Brought up in **Bala** and trained as an engineer and land surveyor in **England** and Germany, he emigrated to the colony in 1886. He supervised the creation of a **railway** and **canal** network, and led expeditions to the Andes in search of minerals and new land. In 1909, he was killed by bandits – none other than Butch Cassidy and the Sundance Kid, according to popular myth, although it is more likely that two of their acquaintances, William Wilson and Bob Evans, were responsible.

LLWYDCOED (Llwytgoed), Rhondda Cynon Taff (820 ha; 1382 inhabitants)

Essentially a north-eastern suburb of **Aberdare**, the **community** extends to the summit of Mynydd Aberdâr (457 m). It was the site of the earliest major **iron**works in the Aberdare area (1801–66). Much of the community bears evidence of the patching system used in the mining of ironstone. An attractive bridge (1834), which carried a tramroad over the Cynon, survives. In the later 19th century, Llwydcoed was dependent upon the Dyllas Colliery. Scale Houses (1912–14) is an attractive group of houses inspired by **garden** city principles. Llwydcoed Crematorium (1971) offers the dead an elegant place of exit.

LLŶN Peninsula, *cantref* and one-time rural district

The western part of Llŷn consists of Precambrian rocks, which are a continuation of those of **Anglesey**; most of the rest of the peninsula overlies Ordovician rock pierced by igneous material, which has given rise to hills such as Garn Boduan (**Nefyn**). The medieval divisions of the peninsula consisted, on the eastern side, of part of the *cantref* of **Arfon** and of the **commote** of **Eifionydd**, and, on the western side, of the *cantref* of Llŷn comprising the commotes of **Dinllaen**, **Cymydmaen** and **Cafflogion** – names which survived as those of post-**Acts of 'Union' hundreds**. Llŷn **rural district**, established in 1894, was absorbed into the district of **Dwyfor** in 1974.

LLYN Y FAN FACH, The legend of

The legend is associated with Llyn y Fan Fach (**Llanddeusant**), a **lake** beautifully situated on the eastern side of the **Black Mountain** beneath the Old Red Sandstone heights of Bannau Sir Gaer. It relates how one of the sons of Blaen Sawdde farm married a beautiful maiden who appeared from the waters of the lake. They lived happily at Esgair Llaethdy, **Myddfai**, raising three sons. After her husband inadvertently struck her with **iron** on three occasions, thus breaking a pledge given before marriage, she fled back to the lake followed by the animals given to her as a dowry. She later appeared to her sons at Llidiard y Meddygon and revealed to her eldest son, Rhiwallon, the virtues of **plants** and their medicinal uses. The three sons became distinguished doctors, thus initiating the long line of **physicians of Myddfai**.

LLYSFAEN, Conwy (562 ha; 2652 inhabitants)

Essentially an eastern suburb of **Colwyn Bay**, the **community** has long been a centre of **limestone** quarrying. In 1399, Richard II was ambushed at Penmaen Head, sparking off a train of events which led to his deposition. Until 1923, when it was transferred to **Denbighshire**, Llysfaen was an enclave of **Caernarfonshire**. The two-naved church of St Cynfran was drastically restored in 1870. On a hill above it is a **telegraph** station built it 1841 to send semaphore messages to **ships** sailing to **Liverpool**.

LLYWARCH AP LLYWELYN (Prydydd y Moch; fl.1175–1225) Poet

One of the **Poets of the Princes** of **Gwynedd** for over half a century, Llywarch sang during his early years to at least five of the descendants of **Owain Gwynedd** who were fighting for supremacy: Owain's sons Rhodri and **Dafydd ab Owain Gwynedd**, their nephews, Maredudd and Gruffudd ap Cynan, and Owain's grandson, **Llywelyn ap Iorwerth**. When Llywelyn managed to gain the upper hand around 1200, Llywarch became his poet and served him for the rest of his life, composing powerful poems of support for his policy of uniting the whole of Wales under his authority. Most of his work consists of eulogies and elegies to princes, but a religious poem, a **love** poem and an enigmatic verse addressed to 'the Hot Iron' have also survived. The significance of his strange nickname, 'The Poet of Pigs', remains a mystery.

LLYWARCH HEN Legendary figure

Protagonist in a cycle of *englynion* from the 9th or 10th centuries, *Canu Llywarch Hen* (The poetry of Llywarch the Old). He is depicted as a cantankerous, lonely old man who, through his boasting and taunting, drove each of his 24 sons to death in battle.

LLYWEL, Breconshire, Powys (10,770 ha; 524 inhabitants)

Extending from the upper **Tawe** to the upper **Usk**, the **community** includes Fan Brycheiniog (802 m), the highest point of the **Black Mountain**, and also Llyn y Fan Fawr and part of the Usk **reservoir**. St **David**'s church, a fine example of Perpendicular Gothic **architecture**, stands in splendid isolation on the bank of the Gwydderig; within it are a pillar stone inscribed in **ogham**, a set of stocks and a plaster cast of the so-called Llywel Stone found at **Crai**, the original of which is in the British Museum. The church also contains a memorial to the satirist Brutus (**David Owen**). The village of Trecastle was once part of the **Brecon borough** constituency, and its tendency to differ in its political loyalties from the burgesses in the **county** town occasionally gave rise to skirmishes. On Mynydd Bach Trecastell stands a group of **Bronze Age** stone circles and the two **Roman** marching camps of Y Pigwn – overnight stages on the Roman **road** from Brecon to **Llandovery**.

LLYWELYN AP GRUFFUDD Prince of Wales

The second son of **Gruffudd ap Llywelyn ap Iorwerth**, Llywelyn's activities were first recorded in 1243. When his uncle **Dafydd ap Llywelyn** died in 1246, he seemed the obvious successor, but the return from England of his elder brother Owain led to the division of **Gwynedd** between them, an arrangement confirmed by the **Treaty of Woodstock** (1247), which imposed humiliating conditions upon them. A third brother, **Dafydd ap Gruffudd**, received a share of the inheritance in 1252. In 1255, Llywelyn defeated his two brothers and made himself sole ruler of Gwynedd Uwch **Conwy**. In 1256, Llywelyn added the **Perfeddwlad** to his territories and, in the following two years, he brought most of *Pura Wallia* under his control. The majority of the other Welsh rulers may have done homage to him in 1258, the year in which he called himself Prince of Wales for the first time. In the early 1260s, there were further gains in the **March**, and when civil war broke out in **England** in 1264, he allied himself with the baronial leader Simon de **Montfort**. At Pipton (*see* **Bronllys**) in 1265, Llywelyn set out the terms he had been seeking from the

Aberdaron on the Llŷn peninsula and the Gwylan Islands

1. Aberffraw
2. Aber
3. Dinas Brân
4. Mathrafal
5. Dolforwyn
6. Dinefwr
7. Caerfili

Gwynedd

Territories of Welsh Lords, vassals of Llywelyn ap Gruffudd

Territories conquered by Llywelyn

Lordships of the king of England

Territories of the lords of the March

Llywelyn's pressure on upland Glamorgan

50 km

Wales in 1267: the Treaty of Montgomery (after William Rees, 1959)

king since 1259: recognition as Prince of Wales and as overlord of the other Welsh rulers.

The end of the civil war led to the **Treaty of Montgomery** (1267). Henry III recognized Llywelyn as Prince of Wales and overlord of the other native Welsh rulers; the same recognition was to be extended to his successors. Llywelyn undertook to pay 25,000 marks (£16,667) over 10 years and did homage to the king. But there was a succession of crises in the 1270s, with disputes in **Glamorgan** and over the building of a **castle** at Dolforwyn (**Llandyssil**) in the **Severn** valley. Henry III died in 1272; Llywelyn failed to do homage to his successor, Edward I, to attend Edward's coronation or to continue the payments due under the Treaty of Montgomery. In 1274, his brother and heir, Dafydd, plotted with **Gruffudd ap Gwenwynwyn** to assassinate him. This was not Dafydd's first change of allegiance; the plot was aborted by bad weather, and by the end of the year the conspirators had fled to England. Llywelyn refused to do homage to Edward until they had been handed over. Since he no longer had an heir, a longstanding plan to marry Simon de Montfort's daughter Eleanor was revived and, in 1275, Eleanor set out from France. She was captured by English sailors, thus adding to Llywelyn's grievances. Both sides appealed to the pope, but, in November 1276, Edward declared war. Llywelyn's **principality** melted away as the Welsh lords made their peace with the king. **Anglesey**, with its substantial corn lands, was seized by the royal fleet, depriving the prince of his main **food** supply. The **Treaty of Aberconwy** of November 1277 stripped him of most of what he had gained at Montgomery; he retained the title of Prince of Wales but was limited to his original patrimony of Gwynedd Uwch Conwy. Relations improved

after Aberconwy; Llywelyn did homage to Edward and married Eleanor. But there were new disputes and the behaviour of royal officials in the north-east aroused bitterness. Matters came to a head on 21 March 1282 when Dafydd began the final war by attacking **Hawarden** Castle. Llywelyn may not have joined in until Eleanor died giving birth to a daughter, **Gwenllian** (1282–1337), in June. Edward employed the same strategy as in 1276–7. An attempt at mediation by **John Pecham**, archbishop of Canterbury, failed. On 11 December 1282, Llywelyn was killed in a skirmish at **Cilmery**.

Llywelyn ap Gruffudd achieved more than any other Welsh ruler before him, but to lay foundations for his new principality he needed time and money; he did not have enough of either. The firm rule that was required to hold the principality together created enemies, and the concept did not have time to take root. He was faced with a sequence of crises in his relations with the crown in the 1270s, when neither he nor Edward I could afford to be flexible. But he succeeded, if only for a time, in uniting much of Wales under a single ruler and in doing so contributed to the emergence of Welsh national consciousness.

LLYWELYN AP IORWERTH (Llywelyn the Great; *c.*1173–1240) Prince

The son of **Iorwerth Drwyndwn** and the grandson of **Owain Gwynedd**, Llywelyn was challenging his uncles, Rhodri and **Dafydd ab Owain Gwynedd**, from an early age. Between 1194 and 1197, he ejected both from their lands and, by 1201, he controlled all **Gwynedd**. In 1201, he and King John made the first formal treaty between a Welsh ruler and the English crown. Llywelyn married John's illegitimate daughter **Joan** (Siwan), possibly in 1205; an earlier partner, Tangwystl, daughter of Llywarch Goch, had borne him at least two children, but, by 1205, he was seeking a more advantageous match and this alliance presented obvious dynastic benefits.

In 1208, Llywelyn occupied **Powys**; in 1209, he joined his father-in-law on campaign in **Scotland**, but his dealings with William de **Breos** (d.1211) angered the king, who was able to take advantage of an increasing fear and resentment among the other Welsh rulers. John's invasion of Gwynedd in 1211 forced the prince to a rapid and humiliating submission. However, war broke out again in 1212, when John's struggle with France and the papacy induced Philip Augustus, king of France, to offer Llywelyn an alliance. In 1213, Llywelyn recovered the lands he had surrendered two years earlier, and another successful campaign in the south in 1215 was followed by an assembly at **Aberdovey** of the Welsh rulers, who may have done homage to him; he was to all intents and purposes Prince of Wales.

The Peace of Worcester (1218) was a cessation of hostilities rather than a formal treaty. Llywelyn aimed at ensuring the succession of his son, **Dafydd ap Llywelyn**, whose position as the prince's heir was recognized by the English crown (1220), the papacy (1222) and the other Welsh rulers (1226). Dafydd was Joan's son; Tangwystl's son, Gruffudd ap Llywelyn (d.1244), was older but his legitimacy was questionable, while Dafydd, as nephew of King Henry III, had better family connections. The 1220s saw the rise to power in **England** of the ambitious **Hubert de Burgh** and

Llywelyn responded to the threat which Hubert posed. He was powerful and confident enough in 1230 to hang a leading **march**er-lord, William de Breos (the grandson of William de Breos, d.1211), who had had an affair with Joan while a prisoner at the prince's court. At about the same time he adopted a new title; formerly prince of north Wales, he now restyled himself prince of **Aberffraw** and lord of **Snowdon**. The new title indicated the basis of his power; he may have refrained from calling himself Prince of Wales until he was able to secure recognition by treaty. The quest for such a treaty was the object of much of his diplomacy during the 1230s – but the king, Henry III, would not negotiate.

The struggle with Hubert de Burgh ended with the justiciar's fall in 1232, and the **Pact of Middle** (1234) meant that there were no further hostilities for the rest of Llywelyn's life. In 1237, Joan died and the prince suffered a stroke; in the same year his son-in-law, the earl of Chester, died without an heir and Chester escheated to the crown, leaving Llywelyn's eastern border exposed. He seems to have transferred power to Dafydd; in 1238, the other rulers were summoned to Strata Florida (**Ystrad Fflur**) to do homage to his son. The assembly may have been intended to mark Llywelyn's formal abdication, but this was forbidden by the king. Dafydd's problems were aggravated by the existence of an elder brother whom many felt had been unjustly disinherited; although Llywelyn had given him extensive lands, Gruffudd seems never to have been reconciled to his exclusion. Llywelyn died at the **Cistercian** abbey of Aberconwy on 11 April 1240 and was buried there.

He was one of the greatest rulers of independent Wales; he aimed to create a single Welsh **principality**, based on the homage of the other Welsh rulers, he married his daughters to Anglo-**Norman** marcher-lords, seeking perhaps to create ties of dependence, he encouraged changes in Gwynedd and was generous to the church. His principality did not survive him; everything he had achieved had depended on his personality and it proved impossible to sustain his achievement after his death. Although, in that respect, his career might be described as a failure, it demonstrated that the creation of a Welsh principality was feasible, and provided the agenda for the career of Llywelyn's grandson, **Llywelyn ap Gruffudd**.

LLYWELYN BREN (d.1318) Insurrectionist

Llywelyn Bren may have been a son of Gruffudd ap Rhys and therefore the great-great-grandson of **Ifor Bach**. Described as 'a great man and powerful in his country', he was clearly of a family which had long enjoyed power in upland **Glamorgan**. On the death of Gilbert de **Clare**, earl of Gloucester (1314), Glamorgan came for a time into the hands of the English crown. The harshness of Edward II's officials alienated Llywelyn; summoned before parliament, he refused to attend. On 28 January 1316, he attacked the castle at **Caerphilly** and burnt the town. His forces devastated the **Vale of Glamorgan** and several towns, including **Cardiff**. Confronted by an army led by Humphrey de **Bohun**, earl of Hereford, Llywelyn and two of his sons surrendered at **Ystradfellte** rather than endanger their followers. They were imprisoned in the Tower of **London** and

Castell Dolwyddelan, presumed to be the birthplace of Llywelyn ap Iorwerth

Llywelyn's possessions, including documents and books in **Welsh** and **French**, were seized. In 1318, Llywelyn was moved to Cardiff Castle and hanged on the orders of the new lord of Glamorgan, Hugh **Despenser** the younger. Llywelyn's sons were restored to their property after Despenser's death (1327). Llywelyn's insurrection was more than a revolt by a Welsh lord against English rule: it was an episode in the internecine warfare between **march**er-lords and in their resistance to royal rule in the March.

LLYWELYN GOCH AP MEURIG HEN (fl.1346–90) Poet

A member of the **Nannau family** of **Meirionnydd**, Llywelyn addressed *awdlau* to patrons such as Goronwy ap Tudur (*see* **Tudor family**) of **Penmynydd**, Rhydderch ab Ieuan Llwyd of **Cardiganshire** and Hopcyn ap Tomas of Ynystawe (**Swansea**), but he is more famous as an early exponent of the *cywydd*. He addressed **love** poems to Lleucu Llwyd, a married woman from **Pennal**. His poignant elegy for her in serenade form is a masterpiece.

LLYWELYN-WILLIAMS, Alun (1913–88) Poet and critic

A poet of a notably urbane sensibility, Alun Llywelyn-Williams was brought up in **Cardiff**. Under the influence of **R. T. Jenkins** at Cardiff High School, he began to take an interest in the history and **literature** of Wales, and eventually graduated in **Welsh** and history at Cardiff. His employment at the BBC (*see* **Broadcasting**) was interrupted by the **Second World War** and active service with the then **Royal Welch Fusiliers**. From 1948 until 1979, he was director of extramural studies at **Bangor**. He edited the magazine *Tir Newydd* between 1935 and 1939, and felt that literature needed to widen its horizons and to break down barriers if it were to grapple with contemporary issues. His most important poems, in which a civilized and sympathetic voice is clearly audible, were collected in *Y Golau yn y Gwyll* (1979). He published an important study of Welsh **Romanticism** (1960), an account of his youth and early career (1975), volumes of critical essays (1968, 1988), travel books about **Arfon** and **Breconshire** (1959, 1964), and a monograph on R. T. Jenkins (1977).

LOCKLEY, R[onald] M[athias] (1903–2000) Naturalist

A native of **Cardiff**, R. M. Lockley was a pioneer of sea**bird** studies and of nature conservation. He travelled widely, had a passion for **islands** and chronicled his life and work in over 40 books, the best known of which is *The Private Life of the Rabbit* (1965). His name will always be associated with **Pembrokeshire**: he established the first British bird observatory, on Skokholm; persuaded Julian Huxley and Alexander Korda to film the private life of the gannet on Grassholm; helped form the Pembrokeshire Bird Protection Society (now Wildlife Trust West Wales) and established the **Pembrokeshire Coast Path**.

LOGAN, William Edmond (1798–1875) Geologist

A Canadian by birth, Logan spent 10 years in **Swansea** as manager of a family **copper**-smelting and **coal**mining venture. The accuracy and 'excessive detail' of his large-scale geological **maps** of part of the south Wales coalfield led to their being incorporated in the published work of the Geological Survey, and to his being appointed director of the newly created Canadian Geological Survey. Mount Logan (6050 m), Canada's highest **mountain**, is named after him, as is Mont Logan (1135 m), Quebec. In 1974, the Geological Association of Canada placed a plaque on his grave at **Cilgerran**, where he spent the last six years of his life.

LOLLARDS

Lollardism was a movement launched in **England** by John Wycliffe (d.1384). The name came from a Dutch word meaning the mumbling (of prayers). Wycliffe believed that the Church was at odds with the teachings of Christ and the apostles. The most vocal Welsh heretic was **Walter Brut**, who vigorously denounced the Church for its ritualism, greed and persecution, and who claimed that the Welsh had been chosen by God to overthrow the Anti-Christ, the Pope. Perhaps because of the many gaps in the records of Welsh **dioceses**, evidence of Lollard activity in Wales – Brut apart – is slight. There is no historical basis to the belief that the poet **Siôn Cent** was inspired by Lollardism.

LONDON (Llundain), Wales's associations with

In the Middle Ages, the Welsh were attracted to London as soldiers, traders and lawyers. Since the 16th century at least, there has been a considerable Welsh community there, mainly because it was the only metropolitan centre within reach of a society which, until the 19th century, had few towns of consequence. Perceived as the source of political power, **education** and advancement, London attracted the squirearchy, administrators, entrepreneurs and, in particular, the poor. **Drovers** walked their livestock there, the rich sent their sons to the Inns of Court, the ambitious sought high office – and impoverished girls came to weed the market **gardens**.

In the 18th century, new institutions and societies gave the London Welsh community a stronger identity and structure. A Welsh school was opened in 1717 and, in 1751, the **Cymmrodorion** Society was founded, followed by the **Gwyneddigion** and **Cymreigyddion**. Meeting in taverns, these societies reflected a lively interest in preserving Welsh **literature** and promoting knowledge of the past. They also influenced the reorganization of *eisteddfodau*, and the first **Gorsedd** was held on Primrose Hill in north London in 1792.

Rural poverty in the 19th century compelled thousands to leave Wales, feeding the needs of a booming city. The Welsh were particularly successful producers and sellers of milk – a development, perhaps, from droving – and were also known for their skill as drapers – a link with the age-old **woollen industry**. The Cardis (a common nickname for people from **Cardiganshire**) were prominent in the milk trade, and some of the drapery businesses became great department stores, whose names still echo their Welsh origin, such as John Lewis, and Dickens and Jones.

The community came to be organized around the numerous chapels, which were attractive oases of Welshness to new migrants. Prominent figures among the

London Welsh were eager to serve their homeland, and, through the Cymmrodorion in particular, contributed greatly to the establishment of the **University of Wales**, the **National Library of Wales** and the **National Museum [of] Wales**.

The London Welsh increased in number during the interwar **depression**, and a Welsh surplus of teachers infused the community with a new energy; there was barely a school in London without two or three teachers from Wales. But this strong social life diminished rapidly after the 1970s, and many chapels closed as congregations shrank dramatically. By the end of the 20th century, **Cardiff** was absorbing much of the 'elite' which once gave London its significance to Wales. The Welsh community is widely dispersed (it never was concentrated); although there are still flourishing societies, such as the London Welsh Association, the Cymmrodorion, the London Welsh **rugby** team and the fashionable SWS club for socialists (Social, Welsh and Sexy), many people now rely on Internet contacts to satisfy their desire to maintain a Welsh identity in the English capital.

Until the establishment of the National Museum, most treasures discovered in Welsh **soil** came into the ownership of the British Museum, among them the astonishing **gold** cape of **Mold**, and a coin believed to have been minted for **Hywel Dda**. Material at the British Library and the National Archives (Kew) are essential in the study of the history of Wales.

LONGBOW, The

One of the most effective weapons in late medieval warfare, the longbow was usually made of yew (*see* **Plants**), although **Giraldus Cambrensis** stated that in Wales, where it may have originated, it was made of dwarf elm trees. Longbows were lighter and more adaptable than crossbows, and Welsh longbowmen, especially from **Glamorgan** and **Gwent**, played a significant role in the defeat of William Wallace at the battle of Falkirk (1298), for they protected the army by shooting high, thus dispersing the ranks of advancing enemy forces. Longbowmen were also prominent in the battles of Crécy (1346), Poitiers (1356), Agincourt (1415) and other encounters in mainland Europe (*see* **Hundred Years War**).

LONGHOUSE, The

The longhouse – a farmhouse where people and animals lived under the same roof – can be traced back to the Middle Ages and probably earlier. The main door opened onto a cross-passage, which divided the building into two parts and gave access to the dwelling as well as serving as a feed passage to the byre. Some believed that cows gave more milk if they could see the fire burning in the hearth. Longhouses were normally sited down-slope, with the animal quarters at the lower end for better drainage. Surviving examples are found mostly in upland west and south-east Wales.

LORAINE, Robert (1876–1935) Aviation pioneer

An English actor with a thirst for adventure, Loraine learnt to fly in 1910 and, on 4 August of the same year, he flew from Blackpool along the north Wales coast, intending to make the first flight across the Irish Sea, from **Holyhead** to Dublin. Although his record-breaking attempt failed, he nevertheless became one of the first aviators to fly in Wales – the first, if the claims of **William Frost** and **Horace Watkins** are discounted.

Morgan-ap-Shones's and Unafred Shones's journey to London, 1747

A marriage certificate from Llanelly, Breconshire, of 1839 (note that both the bride and a witness signed it 'X')

LOVE, Christopher (1618–51) Minister

This **Cardiff**-born, **Oxford**-trained **Presbyterian** minister served as chaplain to Colonel John Venn's regiment in the **Civil Wars** before becoming a zealous pastor of various **London** churches. In May 1651, he was accused of conducting treasonable correspondence with the exiled Charles Stuart, and in August he was executed on Tower Hill.

A selection of lovespoons

LOVE and MARRIAGE

According to descriptions from the 18th and 19th centuries, aspiring lovers would attempt on any of the three 'spirit nights' – May Eve (**Calan Mai**), Midsummer's Eve and Hallowe'en (**Calan Gaeaf**) – to foresee their fate in dreams or through divination, using nuts or **tea** leaves. At other times, they entreated **Dwynwen**, patron **saint** of lovers, to help them, and would make **pilgrimages** to the centre of her cult in Llanddwyn (**Rhosyr**).

Since the round of agricultural work was so restrictive, and since lovers were not to be seen courting in public, formal occasions – weddings, communal knitting evenings and shearings – were valued as opportunities to socialize. Hiring fairs, with their rituals of 'fetching and pulling' girls, buying fairings, drinking and sleeping rough, were among the highlights of the courting calendar. In the countryside, especially in the hayfields of the south-west, the custom of 'foxing' – throwing a maidservant into a haycock and cuddling her – was reminiscent of old fertility rites. With the growth of Nonconformity (*see* **Nonconformists**), the 'monkey parade' after the evening service gave chapelgoers a chance to socialize.

As a relationship matured, a lover might present his girlfriend with a homemade gift, such as a **lovespoon**, a carved stay-busk or a Valentine card. Giving a birch twig signified true love, a hazel twig symbolized rejection; sending a *llatai* (love messenger) was a convention between lovers from the Middle Ages onwards. To continue the courtship, a lover would visit his girlfriend at her lodging, drawing her attention by throwing gravel at the loft window or by serenading under the eaves. If he was acceptable, he would be allowed to climb the 'courting ladder' into the bedroom and the couple would then 'court on the bed' (*see* **Bundling**), a custom common in other countries. Censured by Victorian moralists and religious reformers, the custom did not survive migration from the countryside to the new industrial districts.

The arrangements for marriage began with a meeting between the two parties to decide on their contributions to the new home of **furniture** and, in the case of smallholders, livestock. At this meeting (known as *rhetyddia* in the south-west), the guest list was drawn up and a bidder chosen to solicit financial assistance for the couple. On his rounds he wore a white apron adorned with ribbons and carried a staff identifying his function and his right to enter every house unannounced to deliver his formal invitation for all bidding debts to be repaid. Sometimes a bidding letter would be circulated naming creditors who wished debts to be repaid not to them but to the young couple. It was the bidder's job to persuade as many as possible to attend the wedding and to bring with them their financial contributions in the form of gifts, loans and repayments.

On the wedding day, the 'seek-outs' would come on **horse**back to fetch the bride, but obstacles, such as a 'quintain' (a rope held across the **road**), were placed in their way. Before gaining admittance to the house, they had to best those inside in a contest in extempore verse (*pwnco*). Once inside, they would seize the bride, who would have concealed herself, and carry her in a wild race on horseback to the church, hotly pursued by members of her family. In some districts, the furniture would be ceremonially brought to the new home the previous night, and **food** would be received for the wedding feast. If the families were popular, hundreds might attend a bidding, and detailed accounts were kept of the numerous small sums contributed. Although the total might often be considerable – between £10 and £70 (at a time when farm servants received about £10 a year) – the contributions that were not debts made good would eventually have to be repaid. By the early 21st century, such traditions had passed into oblivion. While love, in the sense of *eros* and of *agape*, was alive and well, marriage seemed to be in terminal decline. In 2003, Wales became the first country in the United Kingdom in which the majority of babies – 50.3% – were born outside marriage; in 1976, the figure was 8.6%.

LOVESPOON, The

A wooden spoon decoratively carved as a love symbol to be presented by the carver to his sweetheart. The practice predates the year 1667, which is inscribed on the earliest known dated example. Wooden spoons for everyday use were carved during the long winter evenings and the various symbols of love, such as hearts, anchors, chains, **birds** and **plants**, were added to emphasize their purpose as love tokens. The spoons were intended to reflect the skill of the carver by incorporating such intricate elements as a broad perforated panel (sometimes with twin bowls) in place of the usual thin stem, making them impractical to use. Other types – carved from a single piece of wood – consisted of a chain of balls within open pillars.

Lovespoons were usually presented when courtship began, but there was no definite rule. Because of the craftsmanship involved, competitions in the carving of lovespoons were held in local *eisteddfodau*. In the 20th century, partly machine-tooled lovespoons were produced commercially for the tourist market or as wedding presents.

LUDLOW, Wales's associations with

Now a tranquil **Shropshire** town of some 7500 inhabitants, Ludlow traces its origins to *c*.1085 when the castle and **borough** were established. In *c*.1306, Ludlow came through marriage into the possession of Roger **Mortimer** (d.1330), owner of extensive lordships in the Welsh **March**. In 1425,

Ludlow Castle

Anne, the last of the Mortimers, brought the family's lands to her husband, Richard, Duke of York, and then to their son, Edward IV, causing the **Yorkist** king to be the greatest of the marcher-lords. Long the administrative centre of the Mortimer lordships, in 1471 Ludlow became the seat of royal **government** in Wales, with the **Prince of Wales** and his council taking up residence in the castle. From 1471 to 1689 (apart from the years 1483–9 and 1642–61), Ludlow, as the home of the **Council of Wales and the Marches**, was the quasi-capital of Wales. Wholly English in atmosphere, the town benefited from its status, as testified by its handsome inns, the superb monuments in its church and the fine hall of 1561 erected within the castle.

LYNE, Joseph [Leycester] (Father Ignatius; 1837–1908) Monk

Ignatius' great ambition was to graft the **Benedictine** religious order upon the **Anglican** Church. Ordained into the Church of **England**, his enthusiastic espousal of the ideas of the **Oxford Movement** gained him notoriety. After many abortive attempts, he finally established a religious community at Capel-y-ffin (**Llanigon**) in the **Black Mountains.** He built a monastery there, which he considered to be Llanthony Tertia (*see* **Crucorney**), but the community barely survived his lifetime. He wrote several popular works about monasticism, and is commemorated by a number of biographies.

A woodcarving of tales from *The Mabinogion* at Cwmcarn Forest Drive, Abercarn

M4, The

The M4 motorway is the main **road** to south Wales from **London**, running 309 km from Chiswick flyover to Pont Abraham service station (**Llannon**), 118 km of this distance being in Wales. The Chiswick flyover opened in 1959; and the first section in Wales, from the **Severn** estuary to Coldra, **Newport**, in 1967. Major works include the Brynglas tunnels in Newport and the **Severn bridges**. In 2004, when 112,000 vehicles a day were using the M4 through Newport, plans were announced for a £350 million, 22-km M4 relief road to the south of the city; scheduled to open in 2012, it would be Wales's first and **Britain**'s second toll motorway.

MABELFYW Commote

One of the seven **commotes** of **Cantref Mawr (Ystrad Tywi)**, its administrative centre may have been at **Llanybydder**.

MABINOGION, The

A collection of 11 **Welsh** prose tales, by various unknown authors, preserved in *The White Book of Rhydderch* and *The Red Book of Hergest*. Although conserved in a literary form, they embody certain stylistic features which prove that their raw material originated in the oral tradition of

the storytellers (*see **Cyfarwydd***) of the Middle Ages. The four tales known as *Pedair Cainc y Mabinogi* (the four branches of the Mabinogi) are closely connected. At the end of one of these branches, the incorrect form *mabynnogyon* found its way into the text, and this was the form adopted by Charlotte **Guest** as the general term for all the indigenous tales when she published her **English** version of them between 1838 and 1849. The translation published by **Gwyn Jones** and **Thomas Jones** (1910–72) in 1948 gave yet wider currency to the name, which has continued to be applied to all 11 stories, with the *Pedair Cainc* only being distinguished as *mabinogi* (meaning 'childhood', 'childhood story' or simply 'story').

The *Pedair Cainc* were composed, possibly in **Gwynedd**, between 1050 and 1120. The first branch, 'Pwyll, Pendefig Dyfed', tells the story of Pwyll's visit to **Annwfn**, followed by the story of his meeting and marriage with **Rhiannon**. The tragic story of the marriage of **Branwen** to the Irish king **Matholwch** is the subject of the second branch, 'Branwen ferch Llŷr', whilst '**Manawydan** fab Llŷr' concerns the enchantment that falls on **Dyfed** and Manawydan's perseverance in rescuing **Rhiannon** and **Pryderi**. Central to the fourth branch, 'Math fab Mathonwy', are the sorceries of **Gwydion** (*see also* **Blodeuwedd** and **Lleu**). Although these tales contain mythic elements of **Celt**ic origin, they are infused with the moral voice of their author. In an era when the heroic ethos remained a powerful force in the land, the virtues he emphasized were compassion, justice and the ability to compromise.

In terms of spirit and style, 'Culhwch ac Olwen', which took its final form in south-west Wales *c.*1100, differs considerably from the *Pedair Cainc*. This colourful story, the first written tale in any language with **Arthur** as its hero, tells how Arthur's men help Culhwch to win the hand of Olwen, daughter of Ysbaddaden Bencawr (*see also* **Twrch Trwyth**).

Although Arthur's men also feature in 'Owain' (or 'Iarlles y Ffynnon', The Lady of the Fountain), 'Geraint fab Erbin' and 'Peredur fab Efrog', the chivalric influence predominates, with Arthur's court being situated in **Caerleon** rather than in Celli-wig in **Cornwall**. The first of these relates the story of Owain fab **Urien**, in the guise of an Arthurian knight, happening upon a magic fountain and becoming the husband of the lady who owns it. The second tells of the meeting and marriage of Geraint and Enid, and of how, following a misunderstanding, the relationship is restored after a long period of trial.

'Peredur fab Efrog' follows the development of Peredur, from being a rustic lad sheltered from the world by his mother, to becoming the best knight in Arthur's court. These tales correspond in some features to the romances of the **French** author Chrétien de Troyes (fl.*c.*1160–82). This reflects the fact that they all draw on common Celtic traditions, and that the French influence on the Welsh texts is attributable not to direct borrowings from the work of Chrétien, but to the fact that they evolved during the 12th century in a shared cultural environment.

'Breuddwyd Rhonabwy' (Rhonabwy's Dream) presents an altogether different view of the Arthurian tales' chivalric world. Rhonabwy is a man of **Powys**, who, in a dream, has a comic-satiric vision of the Arthurian golden age. It is possible that there is a political point to this tale, which reflects the vulnerability of Powys, either at the end of the 12th century, or during the early decades of the 13th when **Llywelyn ap Iorwerth** of Gwynedd was extending his power.

The two remaining stories are a Middle Ages fusion of fiction and pseudo-history. In 'Breuddwyd Macsen Wledig' (Macsen Wledig's Dream), which also belongs to the era of Llywelyn ap Iorwerth, Macsen, emperor of Rome (*see* **Magnus Maximus**), sees in a dream a beautiful lady who lives in a far country. She is Elen daughter of Eudaf from **Arfon**, and Macsen comes to seek her hand. He forfeits the crown of Rome for her sake, but regains it through the effective intervention of Elen's brothers. In 'Cyfranc Lludd a Llefelys' (The Tale of Lludd and Llefelys), the two heroes are brothers, kings of **Britain** and of France, who successfully collaborate to remove three 'oppressions' from the Island of Britain. This tale embodies an old Welsh tradition that had reached its present form by 1200, when a version of it was included in a Welsh translation of **Geoffrey of Monmouth**'s *Historia Regum Britanniae*.

MABSANT

A celebration – often week-long – associated with the feast-day of the patron **saint** of the **parish** church. Although the religious element declined after the **Protestant Reformation**, the festivals retained their popularity as occasions for games, feasting, singing and fighting (often between youths from adjoining parishes). Outdoor social dancing (*see* **Dance**) was frequently a part of *mabsant* celebrations and was accompanied by itinerant musicians who travelled from one festival to the next. Fairs came to be held during the patronal festivals and survived them as important social occasions.

The *mabsantau* declined in the 18th and 19th centuries, as their excesses were attacked by religious reformers. As over 60 of Wales's ancient parish churches were dedicated to St **David**, his mabsant festival (*gwylmabsant*), the first of March, eventually became Wales's national day. In the later 20th century, a folk group took Mabsant as its name.

MABUDRUD Commote

One of the seven **commotes** of **Cantref Mawr** (Ystrad Tywi), its administrative centre was probably at Pencader (*see* **Llanfihangel-ar-Arth**).

McBEAN, Angus (1904–90) Photographer

Self-described as 'stage struck and camera mad', **Newbridge**-born Angus McBean was, from 1934 to 1963, a freelance portrait and theatrical photographer (*see* **Photography**). He is also remembered for his painstakingly created surrealist portraits. He was much in demand for record album-cover images, his successes having included *Please Please Me* for the Beatles.

One of Angus McBean's surrealist self-portraits, 1947

MACDONALD, [James] Ramsay (1866–1937)
Politician

Leader of the **Labour Party** in 1911, MacDonald expressed his support for **home rule** and **disestablishment** for Wales. Opposing the **First World War**, he resigned the leadership in 1914. In 1922, he was re-elected leader and elected MP for **Aberavon**. He became **Britain**'s first Labour prime minister on 22 January 1924. In 1929, he abandoned Aberavon for a seat in County Durham. His decision in 1931 to form a coalition with the **Conservatives** caused great bitterness among Labour activists, especially in Wales, where support for MacDonald's National Labour Party was minimal. Macdonald, **David Lloyd George** and **James Callaghan** were the three Welsh MPs to become British prime minister. **Keir Hardie**, Macdonald, James Callaghan, Michael Foot and Neil Kinnock were the five Welsh MPs to lead the British Labour Party.

McGRATH, Michael [Joseph] (1882–1961)
Archbishop

A native of Kilkenny, **Ireland**, McGrath trained for the **Roman Catholic** priesthood and began his ministry at Bristol. In 1919, he was transferred to the Welsh **diocese** of Menevia and, in 1935, after serving at **Flint**, **Aberystwyth** and **Bangor**, was appointed bishop of Menevia. He succeeded **Francis Mostyn** as archbishop of **Cardiff** in 1940. His archiepiscopate was characterized by a dedication to the **Welsh language**, his enthusiasm for maintaining the **Welsh Sunday** and his unabashed Welsh **nationalist** sympathies. McGrath counted among his friends such figures as **T. Gwynn Jones** and **Saunders Lewis**, whom he visited at Wormwood Scrubs in full episcopal vestments. An outspoken criticism of mixed marriages, an emphasis on Catholic education and a strict defence of Catholic moral and doctrinal teaching also marked his period in office.

McKINLEY TARIFF, The

Given the dependence of south Wales's **tinplate** manufacturers on exports to the United States – between 1881 and 1891 averaging over 60% of total output – it was feared that the tariff sponsored through Congress in 1891 by William McKinley, congressman for the steelmaking state of Ohio, would sound the death knell of the industry. The tariff imposed a 2.2 cents/lb (0.45 kg) duty on imported tinplate, representing a swingeing 70% levy on its monetary value. The tariff led in Wales to a sharp, temporary fall in prices, output and – especially – exports, resulting in the shaking out of marginal firms, and causing widespread unemployment and **emigration** to **Pennsylvania**. By the **First World War**, the industry had recovered its productive position through new export markets and increasingly varied uses for tinplate. McKinley became the 25th president of the United States in 1897, and was assassinated in 1901 at the beginning of his second term.

MACHYNLLETH, Montgomeryshire, Powys
(506 ha; 2147 inhabitants)

This most westerly **Montgomeryshire** town is one of Wales's chief route centres. A charter granted in 1291 authorized a weekly street market, which is still held.

Owain Glyndŵr held a parliament in the town in 1404, an event commemorated in Jan Morris's *Machynlleth Trilogy* (1994), in which the author also fantasizes about a future independent Wales ruled from Machynlleth.

The broad Maengwyn Street contains several interesting buildings, among them the so-called Parliament House, purporting to be the location of the 1404 parliament; however, although basically a 15th-century building, it is later than 1404. Adjoining it is the Glyndŵr Institute (1911). In it, a mural of Glyndŵr has the face of David Davies (*see* **Davies family (Llandinam)**), who financed its building.

Plas Machynlleth, a former mansion of the Vane-Tempest family, marquesses of Londonderry, is a mainly 19th-century building. Between 1995 and 2006, it housed Celtica, an ambitious centre established by the then Montgomery District Council to illustrate the history and culture of the **Celts** – but its failure to attract sufficient visitors forced its closure.

The town **clock** tower, an imposing landmark, was built in 1873 to celebrate the coming of age of the Londonderry heir Lord Castlereagh. St Peter's church, largely rebuilt in 1827, has a 15th-century tower. The former **Wesleyan** Methodist chapel, Y Tabernacl, has been adapted as the Museum of Modern Art, Wales (*see* **Art Galleries**); the Machynlleth Festival is held there annually. The workhouse (1834) became a chest hospital. **T. Alwyn Lloyd**'s garden village (1913) is an attractive group of gabled houses. Machynlleth's **Roman Catholic** church, designed by **Percy Thomas** (1965), is an austere building, full of light. The **community**'s several 'green' shops are indicative of Machynlleth's role as the starting point for the **Centre for Alternative Technology**.

MACKWORTH, Humphrey (1657–1727)
Industrialist and politician

Born in **Shropshire**, called to the Bar in 1682, and knighted in 1683, Mackworth married Mary Evans of Gnoll, **Neath**, in 1686, subsequently inheriting the estate. He developed **coal**mining and **copper** and **lead** smelting there and acquired lead mines in **Cardiganshire**. His Company of Mine Adventurers became bankrupt in 1709, amidst financial scandal, but he formed the Company of Mineral Manufacturers in 1713, which survived until 1719. He was MP for Cardiganshire (1701; 1702–5, 1710–13) and for Totnes (1705–7). A high church **Tory**, Mackworth was a founder of the **Society for the Promotion of Christian Knowledge**.

MADAGASCAR, Wales's associations with

Welsh **missionaries** from the **London** Missionary Society sustained a relationship with the people of Madagascar, east of Africa in the Indian Ocean, throughout the period 1818–1977. The **Congregationalist** pioneers David Jones (1797–1841), David Griffiths (1792–1863) and David Johns (1796–1843) set down the language of the country in Roman script for the first time, promoted literacy and translated the **Bible** into Malagasy. With the **printing** of the Bible barely complete in 1835, Madagascar's queen started a persecution of Christians, which lasted 26 years. The missionaries were expelled, some hundred Malagasy were martyred, and many more suffered savage punishments.

When the missionaries were able to return, they found that, strengthened by persecution, Malagasy Christianity had taken deep root. Thus, from its earliest days, the Protestant faith in Madagascar has been strongly associated with the indigenous culture. Of the present population of 15 million, 41% are Christian, just under half of whom are Protestant. The most enduring testimony to the Welsh connection is the fact that written Malagasy is entirely phonetic (*see also* **Man, Isle of** and **Khasi Hills**).

MADDOCK, Ieuan (1917–88) Physicist

A scientist who made a major contribution to the development of Britain's atomic bomb, Sir Ieuan Maddock, FRS, came from **Gorseinon** and graduated at **Swansea**. He started research on optical measurements and then went on to work on the detonation mechanism of the atomic bomb; he was in overall charge of the first six British tests. Later, he became involved in the Test Ban Treaty, working on sensitive seismographic arrays that could detect underground nuclear explosions. In 1964, he joined the newly created Ministry of Technology and later became **government** chief scientist. In this position, he criticized excessive expenditure on defence, and emphasized the importance to manufacturing industry of investment in high technology.

MADDOX, G[eorge] V[aughan] (1802–64) Architect

Monmouth-born Maddox established a practice in Monmouth as architect and builder. His principal work was the development (1837) of Priory Street, Monmouth, including its Greek Doric-style Market House, all partly elevated above an arcaded Shambles. He was also responsible for a chapel and other houses in the town, some country houses, and shops in **Pontypool**.

MADDOCKS, William Alexander (1773–1828) Entrepreneur

A **Radical** MP for Boston (1802–18) and Chippenham (1820–6), **London**-born Madocks bought the Tan-yr-allt Estate, Penmorfa (**Dolbenmaen**) in 1798. He used his wealth to enclose and reclaim Traeth Mawr, and to build the planned village of Tremadog (**Porthmadog**). His visionary scheme included promoting **woollen** manufacture and capturing the Dublin mail route for Porth Dinllaen (**Nefyn**), but the wider projects failed. In 1821, he obtained an Act of Parliament for the construction of Porthmadog harbour. Although his enthusiasms often led him into financial trouble, many were of long-term benefit to the area.

Madocks's radical opinions attracted Shelley to Tan-yr-allt, where the poet's views on animal welfare led local shepherds to plan his murder. Diana, Princess of Wales, was among Madocks's descendants.

MADOG AB OWAIN GWYNEDD (fl.1170) Legendary figure

The belief that America was discovered by Prince Madog ab Owain Gwynedd c.1170, some three centuries before Christopher Columbus, is one of the most powerful and enduring legends in the history of the Welsh. Although modern scholarship, from the time of **Thomas Stephens**

onwards, has shown that there is no sound evidence for the story, a memorial to Madog was erected as late as 1953 near Fort Morgan on Mobile Bay, Alabama, by the Daughters of the American Revolution, on the basis of the belief that it was there that he had landed.

There is no evidence that **Owain Gwynedd** had a son named Madog. However, a reference in the work of the poet Maredudd ap Rhys (fl.c.1450–c.1483) shows that, by the 15th century, there were traditions in Wales concerning a figure called Madog, who sailed the high seas and who was associated with Owain Gwynedd. It was **Humphrey Lhuyd** in his *Cronica Wallia* (a work completed in 1559, but not published at the time) who first provided a fairly detailed account of the story. This was elaborated upon by **David Powel** in his *Historie of Cambria* (1584), a work heavily dependent upon Lhuyd's chronicle. Powel related that, following the death of Owain Gwynedd in 1170, Madog, distressed by the fratricidal struggle for the succession, left **Gwynedd**. He sailed beyond **Ireland** and discovered an abode of bliss. He returned to Gwynedd before sailing again to the land beyond the ocean, this time accompanied by compatriots fleeing the violence at home.

As the works of historian **Gwyn Alfred Williams** have shown, the true significance of Madog's adventures should be assessed not in terms of their literal truth, but in the context of the use made of them by the Welsh themselves – and of the remarkable way in which they were used to further the imperialist geo-political ambitions of **Britain**, Spain and the United States. The story was used by **John Dee** to justify Elizabeth I's claim to territories in the north Atlantic and to give currency to the notion of a Brythonic or British Empire. The heyday of the legend was the 18th century, when it inspired **John Evans** (1770–99) to undertake his futile quest to find the Madogwys, the 'Welsh Indians' who were believed to be the descendants of Madog and his followers.

MADOG AP GRUFFUDD MAELOR (d.1236) Prince

Madog became prince of northern **Powys** (**Powys Fadog**, which took its name from him) in 1191. He was one of **Llywelyn ap Iorwerth**'s most dependable supporters, although his loyalty was not absolute. He founded the **Cistercian** abbey of Valle Crucis (**Llantysilio**).

MADOG AP GWALLTER (fl.1250–1300) Poet

Possibly a native of **Llanfihangel Glyn Myfyr**, in what is now **Conwy**, he wrote a poem on the Nativity, 'Geni Crist', which may be the first Christmas carol extant in **Welsh**. He also wrote a prayer for deliverance and stanzas to Michael, the patron saint of his **parish**.

MADOG AP LLYWELYN (fl.1278–1312) Welsh lord

Madog was a member of a cadet line of the **Gwynedd** dynasty. He was a son of the last lord of **Meirionnydd**, who was ejected from power by **Llywelyn ap Gruffudd** in 1256. Madog may have served Edward I in the first Welsh war of 1276–7. In 1278, he attempted unsuccessfully to recover his inheritance by litigation. He led the northern rebels in the

Welsh revolt (1294) and was styled Prince of Wales in at least one document. By the summer of 1295, he was in **prison** and records show that his incarceration continued until at least 1312, but the date of his death is unknown. His son served the English crown.

MADOG AP MAREDUDD (d.1160)
King of Powys

Grandson of **Bleddyn ap Cynfyn**, Madog, who became ruler of **Powys** in 1132, was the greatest of its kings and rebuilt its strength and prestige after the bloody struggles of the early 12th century. According to *Breuddwyd Rhonabwy* (*see* **Mabinogion, The**), his kingdom extended from Pulford near Chester to **Arwystli**. Aware of the vulnerability of Powys, situated between **Gwynedd** and **England**, he maintained good relations with the English crown. The powerful kingdom he had built up did not survive his death; his son and designated successor, Llywelyn, also died in 1160 and the kingdom was permanently divided. Madog won renown as a patron of the bards, among them Gwalchmai ap Meilyr (*see* **Meilyr Brydydd**) and **Cynddelw Brydydd Mawr**.

MAELGWN AP RHYS FYCHAN (d.1295) Rebel

The son of **Rhys Fychan ap Rhys ap Maelgwn**, Maelgwn led the **Welsh revolt** (1294–5) in **Cardiganshire**, although his father was in the service of the English crown. He was killed near **Carmarthen** in the summer of 1295. His brothers Rhys and Gruffudd spent the rest of their lives in **prison**.

MAELGWN GWYNEDD (d.c.547)
King of Gwynedd

The son of Cadwallon Lawhir and the great-grandson of **Cunedda**, Maelgwn ruled over **Gwynedd** in the second quarter of the 6th century. In **Gildas**'s work, Maglocunus or Maelgwn, the *insularis draco* (the Island Dragon), is one of the five kings condemned for their transgressions. Gildas asserts that Maelgwn murdered his wife and nephew, and then took his nephew's widow as his wife. Gildas also portrays him as an enemy of monasticism and mocks the court poets who addressed the king in sycophantic verse. Although Gildas associates Maelgwn with the Isle of **Anglesey**, the legend *Hanes Taliesin* locates his court at Deganwy (*see* **Conwy**). According to a tradition recorded in some of the **law** texts, he claimed the homage of other Welsh rulers in a ceremony on Traeth Maelgwn (*see* **Llangynfelyn**) on the **Dyfi** estuary. He reputedly died of the 'yellow plague' and was buried on Ynys Seiriol (**Llangoed**; *see* **Islands**).

MAELIENYDD *Cantref* and lordship

The *cantref* embraced what would be northern and central **Radnorshire**. It was divided into three **commotes** – **Rhiwlallt**, **Buddugre** and **Dinieithon**. Its ecclesiastical centre was the church of St Cynllo at **Llanbister**, the richest church in the archdeaconry of **Brecon**. From the late 11th century, the *cantref*, ruled by descendants of **Elystan Glodrydd**, came under **Norman** pressure. It became a lordship of the **Mortimers**, although their possession of it was disputed by both **Llywelyn ap Iorwerth** and **Llywelyn ap Gruffudd**. In the 15th century, it passed into the hands of

The construction of William Alexander Madocks's embankment (the Cob) across Traeth Mawr

the dukes of **York**, descendants of the Mortimers, and through them to the English crown. Its main strongholds were Cymaran (**Llanddewi Ystradenny**) and Castelltinboeth (**Llanbadarn Fynydd**).

MAELOR *Cantref*, hundred and rural district

Constituting the easternmost part of **Powys Fadog**, Maelor consisted of two **commotes**: **Maelor Gymraeg** and **Maelor Saesneg**. It became the name of a **hundred** and a **rural district**; from 1974 to 1996, **Wrexham Maelor** was a district of the **county** of **Clwyd**. In 1996, Wrexham Maelor, together with part of the former district of **Glyndŵr**, became the **Wrexham County Borough**.

MAELOR GYMRAEG Commote

With **Maelor Saesneg**, the commote constituted the *cantref* of **Maelor**. Following the **Edwardian conquest**, **Maelor Gymraeg** – called Bromfield in **English** – became part of the **march**er-lordship of **Bromfield and Yale**. In 1536, the lordship became the easternmost part of **Denbighshire**. **Wrexham Maelor**, established as a district of the **county** of **Clwyd** in 1974, essentially represented the union of the commotes of Maelor Gymraeg and Maelor Saesneg.

MAELOR SAESNEG Commote

Constituting the eastern bulge of north-east Wales, the area underwent extensive Saxon settlement from the 7th century onwards and came to be considered part of **Mercia**. The Domesday Book included it in the **Cheshire** hundred of Dudestan; but, by the 13th century, it was part of **Powys Fadog**. In 1284, it became part of the new **county** of **Flint**. In 1894, it became the **rural district** of **Overton**. In 1974, that rural district – by then called Maelor – joined with those of **Wrexham** and Ceiriog and with the **borough** of Wrexham to form **Wrexham Maelor**, one of the six districts of the county of **Clwyd**.

MAELOR SOUTH (De Maelor), Wrexham
(1867 ha; 1137 inhabitants)

The southernmost part of **Maelor Saesneg**, the **commun**ity's largest settlement is Penley, the scene of considerable late 20th-century expansion. Its Madras School, still operating in the original thatched building, was founded in 1811. It was the first National School (*see* **National Society**) in Wales, and the name reflects the fact that the school's monitorial system was based upon that developed in India by Andrew Bell. Penley Court was demolished in the 1960s. In its grounds is a Polish hospital, founded in 1946 as a refuge for members of the Free Polish Army who were unable to return to their homeland (*see* **Poles**). It still accommodates a few elderly residents in another building on the site. Llannerch Panna (1874), now called Tudor Court, is perhaps Wales's best example of the revival in the construction of half-timbered houses. A barn from Stryd Lydan has been re-erected at the National History Museum (*see* **St Fagans**).

At the south-eastern corner of the community is Bettisfield (Llys Bedydd) with its attractive St John's church (1874) and Bettisfield Old Hall. The Hanmer family, kinsmen of **Owain Glyndŵr**, were originally associated with **Hanmer**, but by the 17th century their main seat was at Bettisfield Park. There, the tulipomaniac **Thomas Hanmer** created a remarkable **garden**. The mansion, originally built in the 17th century, was transformed over the following centuries and partly demolished *c.*1950. What remained was sold by the Hanmer family in 1989 and has been extensively restored.

MAEN LLOG, Y (lit. 'the logan-stone')

The central stone in the bardic **Gorsedd** circle, on which the **archdruid** stands to conduct open-air ceremonies. An invention of Iolo Morganwg (**Edward Williams**), its name may mean 'rocking' or 'sacrifice' stone.

MAENCLOCHOG, Pembrokeshire
(3128 ha; 679 inhabitants)

Extending from the highest point of **Mynydd Preseli** (Foel Cwmcerwyn, 536 m) to the middle reaches of the Eastern **Cleddau**, the **community** contains the villages of Maenclochog, Llanycefn and Rosebush. Foel Cwmcerwyn is crowned with cairns, which were excavated by **Richard Fenton** in 1806. St Mary's Church (1806, 1881) in the village of Maenclochog contains two 6th-century inscribed stones apparently commemorating two brothers; one bears a **Latin** inscription and the other inscriptions in Latin and **ogham**. They were brought from the ruined church of St Teilo, whose **well** near the ruin was venerated for its healing powers until very recently. Yr Hen Capel (1790, 1870, 1904), Maenclochog, a striking building, closed in 1999.

The **slate** quarries at Rosebush were the largest in **Pembrokeshire** in the 1870s, when they were linked by **railway** to **Clynderwen**. Their owner, Edward Cropper, sought to develop Rosebush as a spa and built Tafarn Sinc, a zinc-clad tavern which holds an annual **eisteddfod**. Penrhos is an example of a *tŷ unnos* (one-night house; *see* **tai unnos**), which has been preserved as a museum. Llanycefn school (1876) was adapted (1982, 1989) to create a remarkable series of buildings for Nant-y-cwm Steiner school.

MAENORDEILO Commote

One of the seven **commotes** of **Cantref Mawr** (**Ystrad Tywi**), it contained **Dinefwr**, traditionally considered to be the chief seat of the rulers of **Deheubarth**.

MAENTWROG, Gwynedd
(3958 ha, 585 inhabitants)

Located immediately south of **Ffestiniog**, the **community** contains the villages of Maentwrog and Gellilydan and the decommissioned **Trawsfynydd Nuclear Power Station**. The standing stone (*maen*) in St Twrog's Church, which gives the place its name, is mentioned in the fourth branch of *Pedair Cainc y Mabinogi* (*see* **Mabinogion, The**). Tomen-y-mur **Roman** auxiliary fort was occupied from AD *c.*78 to *c.*140; the oval enclosure adjoining it was probably a training ground. William II was at Tomen-y-mur in 1095 when a motte was built there. Cynfal Fawr (17th century) was the birthplace of **Morgan Llwyd**.

Maentwrog village was laid out in a Swiss style by W. E. **Oakeley**, a leading figure in the development of the **slate** industry of Blaenau Ffestiniog. He built the neo-Gothic Plas Tanybwlch, now a **Snowdonia National Park** study centre. Opposite the mansion, the trees of Coed Camlyn pick out Oakeley's initials. The village of Gellilydan has an interesting **Roman Catholic** church. The community contains a dramatic stretch of the Ffestiniog **Railway**. Maentwrog Power Station (*see* **Energy**) (1930) is operated by water from Llyn **Trawsfynydd**.

MAES MOYDOG, Battle of

The **Welsh revolt** of 1294–5, sparked by the refusal of Welsh soldiers to fight in France and fuelled by high taxation, presented a serious challenge to English royal authority in Wales. Edward I led a 35,000-strong army to subdue the Welsh, who were defeated at Maes Moydog in **Caereinion** on 5 March 1295.

MAESCAR (Maes-car), Breconshire, Powys (9900 ha; 998 inhabitants)

A one-time civil **parish** in the upper Senni valley, Maescar is now a **community** centred upon Sennybridge and Defynnog. Sennybridge is dominated by a camp accommodating soldiers training on **Mynydd Epynt**. St Cynog's church, Defynnog, is one of **Breconshire**'s largest parish churches. From 1716 to 1732, its vicar was the scholar Moses Williams (1685–1742; *see* **Samuel Williams**). The first meeting between **Howel Harris** and **Daniel Rowland** took place in the church in 1737. The church of Llandeilo'r Fan has a fine 16th-century roof. Maen Llia, a standing stone 4 m high and 2.5 m wide, dominates the pass leading to **Ystradfellte**.

MAESTEG, Bridgend (2721 ha; 17,859 inhabitants)

The **community** embraces the upper basin of the Llynfi, its built-up area stretching for 6 km along the **river**. The growth of the settlement dates from the opening of the Maesteg **Iron**works in 1826 and its linkage in 1828 to **Porthcawl** by a tramroad for **horse**-drawn vehicles. The Llynfi Ironworks were established in 1837 and their blast-engine house, a blast furnace and rows of ironworkers' houses still survive. In addition, there were **tinplate** works at Llwydarth. The district came to depend upon the pits of North's Navigation Collieries, a company founded in 1889.

The town has an air of civic pride, with a dignified town hall (1881), market (1881) and elaborate council offices (1914). A local architect, **W. Beddoe Rees**, who developed a national reputation as a chapel specialist, designed several of the chapels, the 1000-seat Bethania (1908) in particular. The most notable **Anglican** church is St Michael's (G. E. Halliday, 1895). The community's uplands have been extensively forested. It was as the representative of the Maesteg miners that **Vernon Hartshorn**, Wales's first **Labour** cabinet minister, came to prominence. The inter-war **depression** hit Maesteg severely, its **population** declining by 24% between 1921 and 1931. By the early 1980s, Maesteg had a mere 250 **coal**miners; then, following the miners' strike of 1984–5, there were none.

MAESYCWMMER (Maesycwmer), Caerphilly (751 ha; 2141 inhabitants)

Lying along the east bank of the **Rhymney**, the **community** includes a 260-m **railway** viaduct across the **river**. Tabor (1876) was a handsome classical-style chapel designed by the minister-architect **Thomas Thomas** of **Swansea**. The community is crossed by the Rhymney Valley Ridgeway Path.

MAGNA CARTA

The Great Charter granted by King John at Runnymede on 15 June 1215 has been seen as the foundation of English liberties, a belief which played a part in the 17th-century **Civil Wars**. Because of **Llywelyn ap Iorwerth**'s alliance with the baronial party in **England**, four clauses relating to Wales were included. They concern the restitution of lands to Welshmen who had been dispossessed, the spheres of Welsh, English and **march**er law (the first extant reference to that interesting hybrid), the return of Welsh hostages and the cancellation of undertakings made by Welsh rulers after John's successful campaign in Wales in 1211.

MAGNUS MAXIMUS (Macsen Wledig; d.388) Usurper

A Spanish soldier who visited **Britain** in the AD 360s and returned as **Roman** commander-in-chief in 379, Magnus Maximus achieved more in legend than in life. He led a revolt against Emperor Gratian in 383 and ruled much of western Europe from Trier, before being slain by his former patron, Theodosius, at Aquileia. **Gildas** regarded Maximus as the last legitimate Roman emperor to rule in Britain and this seems to have been the beginning of his career as the legendary Macsen Wledig (*see* the discussion of *Breuddwyd Macsen Wledig* in **The Mabinogion**). According to Welsh tradition, Macsen married Elen, the daughter of Eudaf Hen of **Gwynedd** and was the ancestor of many of the medieval royal dynasties of Britain. There are parallels in the legend of Míl Espáine – the soldier from Spain – who was considered to be the ancestor of the major **Irish** dynasties. These curious traditions may reflect some achievement of Maximus in Britain that went unnoticed by contemporary chroniclers. On leaving for the European mainland in 383, he may have confirmed the powers of native British rulers, a belief that gave rise to the notion that he was the father of the Welsh nation.

MAGOR WITH UNDY (Magwyr gyda Gwndy), Monmouthshire (1530 ha; 6070 inhabitants)

Located east of **Newport**, the **community**'s best-known feature is the Magor Service Station on the **M4** (1991). St Mary's, Magor, built in the 13th and 14th centuries, is an impressive church. Near it is a substantial ruin, which was probably a late medieval priest's house. St Mary's, Undy, is a modest building with a fine 13th-century font. Ebenezer, Magor, is a good example of an early 19th-century chapel. The war memorial bears a tribute to **D. A. Thomas**, Viscount Rhondda. The community includes part of **Gwent Levels**. Magor Brewery (1979), which brews international lagers such as Carlsberg, is by far the largest in Wales (*see* **Beer, Brewing and Breweries**).

'MAID OF SKER, The'

Two versions of the song 'The Maid of Sker' are recorded in one of Iolo Morganwg's (**Edward Williams**) manuscripts attributed to Thomas Evans, a **harp**ist. Elizabeth Williams (*c*.1746–76), of Sker House, **Cornelly**, purportedly fell in love with Evans, the supposed composer of the song, but she died of a broken heart after being forced by her father to marry another man. Her story is recounted in *Y Ferch o'r*

Scer by Isaac Hughes (Craigfryn; 1892; **English** translation, 1902). However, R. D. Blackmore's *The Maid of Sker* (1872) has no bearing whatsoever upon her life.

MALE VOICE CHOIRS

The male voice choir is widely regarded as a characteristically Welsh institution. It found congenial soil in the country's populous mining valleys, metallurgical centres and quarrying districts. The choirs, which emerged in the 1870s, were preceded by monastic and cathedral choirs, English catch and glee clubs, and, in the mid-19th century, by pseudo-African-American touring entertainers such as the Christy Minstrels.

Welsh male voice choirs began as the tenors and basses of existing mixed choirs performing independently of their parent body. A form of recreation and fellowship for a predominantly male industrial workforce, the typical Welsh male voice choir was attracted less by the jollity of English glees than by the robust militaristic style of the Franco-Prussian tradition. Composers such as de Rille ('Martyrs of the Arena'), Adam ('Comrades in Arms') and Gounod ('Soldier's Chorus') inspired Welsh imitators such as **Joseph Parry** ('Pilgrim's Chorus'), **Daniel Protheroe** ('Nidaros') and T. Maldwyn Price ('Crossing the Plain'), catering for the fondness of Welsh choristers and audiences for dramatic narratives, wide dynamic contrasts and thrilling climaxes.

The communities of the southern **coal**field were the heartland of male choral singing. The **Rhondda** Glee Society visited **North America** in 1888-9 and again in 1893,

when they won a famous victory at the Chicago World's Fair. The famous **Treorchy** Male Voice Choir, founded in 1885, sang at Windsor Castle in 1895 and undertook an 80,000-km world tour in 1908-9.

Products of the convergence of Nonconformity (*see* **Nonconformists**), industrialization and the competitive culture of the **eisteddfod**, male voice choirs fulfilled similar roles to **football** teams in providing a focus for local identity and opportunities for disciplined collective expression. Choirs were also products of industrial **depression**. The renowned choirs of Pendyrus (Rhondda) and **Cwmbach** were formed during the strife-torn 1920s. In the 1930s, 60% of Pendyrus's 150 choristers were unemployed. The clash between these and their rivals to the east (**Tredegar, Beaufort**), west (Morriston, Manselton (both in **Swansea**) and **Pontarddulais**) and north (Rhos (**Rhosllanerchrugog**) and y Brythoniaid (Blaenau **Ffestiniog**) held National Eisteddfod audiences of 10,000 and more enthralled as late as the 1960s, but since then the more celebrated choirs have spurned the competitive stage for the concert hall and recording studio, broadening their repertoire to include songs from **music**al shows and other popular works. The reluctance of younger men to join choirs means that the tradition is under threat.

MALKIN, Benjamin Heath (1769–1842) Author

London-born Malkin's interest in Wales sprang from his marriage to Charlotte Williams, daughter of the headmaster of **Cowbridge** Grammar School, bringing him into contact with Iolo Morganwg (**Edward Williams**). Malkin's

The Rhondda male voice choir on tour in Pittsburgh, 1913

continuing reputation is based on his book *The Scenery, Antiquities and Biography of South Wales* (1804), which draws on two journeys undertaken in 1803. In the pre-industrial **Rhondda** valleys, he noted the **picturesque** 'contrast of the meadows, rich and verdant, with **mountains** the most wild and romantic, surrounding them on every side'.

MALLAEN Commote
One of the seven **commotes** of **Cantref Mawr (Ystrad Tywi)**, its administrative centre was probably at **Cilycwm**. At its core was Mynydd Mallaen (448 m).

MALLTRAETH Commote
A **commote** in western **Anglesey**, which, with that of **Llifon**, formed the *cantref* of **Aberffraw**. The commotal centre was at Aberffraw. The name survived as that of a post-**Acts of 'Union' hundred**.

MALTHOUSE, Eric (1914–97) Artist
Birmingham-born Malthouse taught at **Cardiff** School of Art and was instrumental in the establishment of the modernizing 56 Group (*see* **Fifty-six Group**). His colourful **painting** – initially figurative, though eventually abstract – was influenced by mainland European styles and features working-**class** people and, famously, homing pigeons.

MAMMALS
Some of the earliest evidence of mammals in the world has been found in Wales, particularly in quarries of a region to the south of **Bridgend** in the **Vale of Glamorgan**. For instance, *Morganucodon watsoni*, a shrew-like mammal that lived some 200 million years ago, was first discovered in 1947 in sediments filling fissures in the older Carboniferous **Limestone** of the **Ewenny** area. A primitive mammal, close to its reptilian ancestry, it shared what would become **Glamorgan** with small reptiles of various sorts and the newly evolved **dinosaurs**.

Many of the species that were present 225,000 years ago have long disappeared from Wales but archaeological investigations of their remains, augmented by written records from the **Roman** period onwards, provide information about mammals past and present – and about their relationships with that most meddlesome of mammals *Homo sapiens*.

An early reference to mammals in Welsh **literature** occurs in the lullaby 'Pais Dinogad' which may have been composed in the 7th century and which was incorporated in *Y Gododdin*. It refers to the **pine marten**, the **wild boar**, the **fox**, the wildcat (*see* **Cats**) and the roe **deer**. Other sources of information about mammals include **place names**, the Welsh **laws**, the stories of *The Mabinogion*, **parish** registers and the observations of writers such as **Giraldus Cambrensis**, **John Leland**, **George Owen** and **Thomas Pennant**.

The remains of mammals spanning both interglacial and post-glacial periods have been found in Cefn and Bontnewydd (**Cefnmeiriadog**) **caves** in **Denbighshire**. There is evidence from the protracted **Paleolithic Age** of the presence in Wales of long-extinct mammals such as the mammoth and the woolly rhinoceros, but more familiar mammals such as the **horse,** the **wolf**, the fox, the **hare** and the reindeer were also present, as were the bison and the hyena. In warmer, interglacial periods, the lion, the straight-tusked elephant and the narrow-nosed rhinoceros would have been seen in Wales. Rodents from the Paleolithic Age included various species of vole and lemming.

The melting of the ice, from around 9500 BC onwards, led to a transformation of the steppe grasslands into thick forest (*see* **Forestry**) and the isolation of a much altered fauna as **Britain** became an **island**. Common mammals included the aurochs (a type of **cattle** which would die out in Britain in the **Bronze Age**), the wild boar and the wolf, which would survive in Wales until *c.*1600, the red and the roe deer, both absent from Wales after the 18th century, and the **beaver**, recorded on the **Teifi** in the late 12th century, but almost certainly extinct by the 18th century.

The spread of **agriculture** in the **Neolithic Age** had a revolutionary impact on animal life. By then, **dogs** and horses had already been domesticated. **Goats**, domesticated earlier than cattle, **sheep** and **pigs**, were introduced from mainland Europe, and would outnumber sheep in Wales until the early medieval period. To secure grazing for their animals and land for growing crops, Wales's early farmers massively extended the wildwood clearances that had begun in Mesolithic times. Deforestation, which inevitably destroyed the habitats of many **birds** and of such animals as bears, wolves, deer, foxes, squirrels and badgers, was pursued with renewed vigour in the 12th and 13th centuries, and again from the 16th century onwards. Reforestation in the 20th century, often with a monoculture of sitka spruce, cannot generally be accounted a restoration of faunal habitats.

By the Bronze Age, cattle were being used for ploughing, and by the **Iron Age**, if not earlier, cattle, goats and sheep were being moved seasonally between lowland settlements and mountain pastures (*see* **Hafod and Hendre**). Pigs were generally given the run of the forest, and domestic chickens and geese were introduced from mainland Europe (*see* **Poultry**).

As the domain of domesticated animals expanded, so the province of wild animals contracted, and the large beasts of prey began to disappear – the brown bear before the **Norman** conquest, followed by the wolf and, in the 19th century, the wildcat. Badgers were baited from early times, as testified to in *The Mabinogion*, and the practice of badger digging, outlawed since 1973, continues illicitly to the present day. **Otters**, foxes, pine martens and even hedgehogs were hunted for sport or persecuted as vermin. The development of the breech-loading gun led to the systematic destruction of large numbers of animals in the name of game rearing. Both estate logbooks and parish 'bounty' records show that the onslaught was the work of all sections of society.

Several wild and feral mammal species have been introduced from outside Britain, usually deliberately but in some cases by accident. Both the black rat, which arrived about the 12th century, and the brown rat, which arrived in the 18th century, were escapees from ships. The black rat, whose fleas were implicated in the spread of the **Black Death** of the 14th century, has by the 21st century been dispossessed by the larger brown rat. A more recent interloper is the mink, an escapee from fur farms, which competes ecologically with native species such as the otter; it has had a severe impact on the rapidly declining water vole.

Mammals introduced to Wales deliberately, for utilitarian or aesthetic reasons, include the fallow deer and the **rabbit**, imported by the Normans, and the mountain hare, introduced to **Snowdonia** in the 20th century for sport. The **North American** grey squirrel was imported as a novelty in the 19th century, with devastating consequences for the native red squirrel.

Some mammals make their first recorded appearance in the modern period despite being native species. The 15 species of **bat** occurring in Wales today were not distinguished until the Linnaean method of classification, combined with scientific advances, allowed the more obscure species to be systematically described. The various species of mouse (4), shrew (3) and vole (3) were likewise not distinguished until recent times. No genetic work has yet been carried out to trace the origins of the so-called Skomer vole, a form of the common bank vole which, isolated on its island home, has evolved distinctive characteristics, being larger, tamer and redder than its mainland cousin. Two species of small rodent, namely the yellow-necked mouse and the dormouse, are of particular Welsh note, having an interesting distribution restricted to – in British terms – the historically less disturbed countryside of the **border** area. The mole and the hedgehog, both large relatives of the shrew, are as ubiquitous today as probably they ever were, in both woodland and farmland. Also well represented in such habitats are stoats and weasels, although, being largely nocturnal, they are not commonly seen.

MAN, ISLE OF (Ynys Manaw), Wales's associations with

Visible from Wales, **Scotland**, **Ireland** and Cumbria, the **island** is the pearl at the heart of what might be described as 'the Mediterranean Sea' of the **Celts**. At the dawn of the Christian era, it may have been inhabited mainly by Brythonic speakers, although the lack of Brythonic elements in the island's **place names** may cast doubt on this theory. From the 5th century onwards, migration from Ireland caused Old Irish to be the island's chief language. By the 13th century, the island's language, together with that of Gaelic Scotland, had become distinct from Irish, and by the 15th century Manx and Scottish Gaelic had also become distinct languages. The island's inhabitants shared in the Celtic Christianity of the 'Age of **Saints**'; indeed, the island's 180 and more *keeills* or oratories represent a unique concentration of early Christian monuments.

It can be claimed that the chief dynasty of medieval Wales was Manx in origin. In 1896, a cross was discovered on the island bearing the words *CRUX GURIAT* (the cross of Gwriad). The Gwriad of the cross may well have been the Gwriad who in the late 8th century married Esyllt, daughter of Cynan ap Rhodri of the royal house of **Gwynedd**. In 825, on the death of the last of the direct male line of that royal house, their son, **Merfyn Frych**, seized the throne of Gwynedd. In the poem 'Cyfoesi Myrddin a Gwenddydd' (12th to 13th century; The Conversation of Myrddin and Gwenddydd), Merfyn Frych is described as from 'the land of Manaw', although that Manaw may perhaps have been **Manaw Gododdin** in the **Old North**. Merfyn

married Nest, daughter of Cadell ap Brochfael, king of **Powys**, and their son, **Rhodri ap Merfyn** (Rhodri Mawr), became king of the greater part of Wales.

From *c.*800 onwards, Man was extensively colonized by **Vikings** and became a base for their attacks upon Wales. They created the kingdom of Sodor (the south isles) whose king, Reginald, involved himself in the politics of Gwynedd in 1193. Seized in 1263 by Alexander III of Scotland, in the 14th century the island became a possession of the crown of **England**. In 1406, Henry IV granted it to John **Stanley**, whose descendants held it until 1765. The Stanleys, major landowners in north-east Wales, were leading church builders; their badge – the Legs of Man – can be seen in several of the region's churches (*see* **Gresford** and **Wrexham**).

As a result of the island's close association with Scotland, the Manx language came to be closer to Scots Gaelic than to Irish. It became a written language *c.*1610, when John Phillips, a Welshman and the bishop of Sodor and Man, translated the **Book of Common Prayer** into Manx. Phillips failed to find a publisher for his translation. Apparently, this was because John Ireland, the governor of Man, believed that any work by a Welshman 'could never do any good'; it was not published until 1894. In creating the orthography, Phillips made use of Welsh conventions, but in the 18th century, when publication of works in Manx began, its orthography was based upon the conventions of Early Modern **English**, thus giving rise to a marked distinction between written Manx on the one hand and written Irish and Scots Gaelic on the other.

In 1900, the Isle of Man, which then had 4657 Manx-speakers, joined with Wales, Scotland, Ireland and **Brittany** to form the Celtic Congress (*see* **Celtic Associations**). (**Cornwall**, which had no native speakers of a Celtic language, was not admitted until 1904.) On 27 September 1974, Ned Maddrell, the last native speaker of Manx, died, causing Manx to be the sole European language to become extinct in the 20th century. In the later 20th century, there was a marked rise in interest in Manx and efforts were made to introduce it into the school curriculum, especially following the appointment of Alun Davies, a **Welsh**-speaking Welshman, as the island's director of **education** in 1974. In 2006, Welsh-speakers on the island established a society which they called Cymdeithas Gwriad.

MAN VERSUS HORSE EVENTS

According to legend, one of the impressive achievements of the champion 18th-century runner Guto Nyth-brân (**Griffith Morgan**) was to outpace a **horse**. This was a feat unmatched until the mid-1980s, when the Welsh international athlete Dic Evans outpaced his equine rival on an eight-mile (12.9-km) circuit at Ponterwyd (**Blaenrheidol**). Since 1980, a marathon event over 22 miles (35.4 km) has been held annually at **Llanwrtyd**, in memory of Guto's win. Despite a 15-minute head start for the runners, only one – Huw Lobb of **London**, in 2004 – has so far been victorious. With a financial reward of several thousand pounds on offer to anyone who beats the best horse, what began as an amateur challenge on a local level is now a money-spinning competition attracting widespread interest and publicity.

MANAFON, Montgomeryshire, Powys
(1593 ha; 336 inhabitants)
Located immediately south-east of **Llanfair Caereinion**, the **community** extends over the central part of the Rhiw valley. St Michael's church, originally 14th century, was much restored in 1859 and again in 1898, when **John Douglas** enriched it with excellent woodwork. The church has been served by several literary figures, among them **Evan Evans** (Ieuan Brydydd Hir; 1754–6), **Walter Davies** (Gwallter Mechain; 1807–37) and **R. S. Thomas** (1942–54), many of whose best-known poems are located in the area. In the 18th and 19th centuries, the hamlet of New Mills, with its corn and **woollen** mills powered by the **River** Rhiw, enjoyed considerable prosperity.

MANAW GODODDIN

A sub-kingdom of the **Gododdin** located in the area of Clackmannan and Falkirk in present-day **Scotland**. It was from this region, it is said, that **Cunedda** and his sons set off in the 5th century to expel the **Irish** from **Gwynedd**.

MANAWYDAN FAB LLŶR

In the third branch of the Mabinogi (*see Mabinogion, The*), which bears his name, Manawydan accepts possession of the seven *cantrefi* of **Dyfed** through marriage to **Rhiannon**, mother of his friend **Pryderi**. An enchantment falls on Dyfed, and, in the story, Rhiannon and Pryderi are abducted by unknown powers. In a dramatic encounter with the sorcerer Llwyd fab Cilcoed, Manawydan obtains their release and the lifting of the enchantment. His name corresponds to that of the Irish sea-god Manannán mhac Lir.

MANORBIER (Maenorbŷr), Pembrokeshire
(1481 ha; 1288 inhabitants)
Located between **Pembroke** and **Tenby**, the **community** contains King's Quoit, a **Neolithic** burial chamber splendidly sited above the sands of Manorbier Bay, sands used by **Giraldus Cambrensis** to make churches, and by his brothers to make castles. Manorbier Castle, first built by Giraldus's grandfather, Odo de Barri, was reconstructed in stone in the 1140s, probably in time for Giraldus to be born within its stone walls (1147). Further building was undertaken in the 13th, 14th and 15th centuries. With its hilltop position and its impressive towers and curtain walls, Manorbier makes as fine an impression as any castle in Wales. It was acquired in 1670 by the **Philipps family (Picton Castle)**, which still owns it. St James's church consists of a rambling series of medieval buildings and contains a 14th-century effigy of a member of the de Barri family. To Giraldus, Manorbier was 'the pleasantest spot in Wales'. Virginia Woolf spent her childhood holidays there; Quentin Bell, in his biography of her, describing it as 'a wild and desolate place'.

MANORDEIFI (Maenordeifi), Pembrokeshire
(1811 ha; 478 inhabitants)
The most north-eastern of the **communities** of **Pembrokeshire**, Manordeifi contains the hamlets of Abercych, Newchapel and Pontrhydyceirt. The delightful Cych valley features in *The Mabinogion*. St **David**'s church, endangered by **Teifi** floods, retains its 18th-century fittings; it contains a memorial to **John Blackwell**, vicar of

Manordeifi (1833–40). In the early 18th century, one of Wales's earliest **canals** was built to serve **iron**works at Castell Malgwyn, where the one-time ironmaster's house is a country hotel. Ffynone, designed by **John Nash** in 1793, had a Greek Doric front added to it in the early 19th century. It is the home of Earl Lloyd-George. Its **gardens** contain some of the largest examples of *Gunnera* in Wales.

**MANORDEILO AND SALEM
(Maenordeilo a Salem),** Carmarthenshire
(4691 ha; 1587 inhabitants)
Hugging the **Tywi** immediately north-east of **Llandeilo**, the **community** contains the villages of Manordeilo, Salem, Capel Isaac, Cwmifor, Maesteilo and Rhosmaen. Taliaris mansion (17th and 18th centuries) has been converted into flats, but in front of it are the remains of an octagonal cockpit. Hermon (1812, 1848, 1868), north of Manordeilo, and the **Baptist** chapel in Cwmifor (1789, 1836, 1864) are handsome buildings.

MANORS and *MAENORAU*

The Welsh *maenor* or *maenol* was a territorial unit within the *cantref* or **commote**. These *maenorau* could be of great antiquity. The boundaries of the *maenor* of Meddyfnych – which was broadly coterminous with the **parish** of **Llandybie** – are described in an entry in *The Book of St Chad* (*c*.730). By the end of the age of the native princes, such units had become defunct, although the forms *maenor* (in the south) and *maenol* (in the north) survived in some **place names**.

The first mention of the English manor in Wales dates from the reign of Edward I (1272–1307). Parts of the country, particularly the **Vale of Glamorgan** and south **Pembrokeshire**, were extensively manorialized, but the manor does not loom as large in Wales as it does in the lowland areas of **England**. Following the demise of the old Welsh *maenor*, it was the *tref* (township) or *maerdref* (administrative centre) which most closely resembled the English manor.

The manor was an area of land held by a lay or ecclesiastical lord, who enjoyed rights of jurisdiction over the inhabitants of the manor and who received a wide range of payments and services from his tenants. These could include fines on entry and alienation, labour dues, heriots, deodands, rights of wreck, control of fairs and markets and powers over wastes and **common land**. The records of manorial courts are a major historical source. By the 19th century, most of the rights of manor owners had been eroded, although powers over common land greatly enriched the major landowners of Wales's industrial areas. In the original **Principality**, most of the manors were owned by the crown. Following **disestablishment**, the 41 manors owned by the **Anglican** Church became the property of the **University of Wales**. The university's manors, and those of other owners such as Earl Cawdor (*see* **Campbell family**), have been sold. Their purchasers acquired little beyond the right to style themselves lords or ladies of manors.

MANSEL family Landowners
The founder of the family is reputed to be Henry Mansel who settled in **Gower** in the 13th century. His descendant, Hugh, married the heiress of the **Penrice** estate, which became the family's chief seat until Rice Mansel (d.1559)

bought **Margam** Abbey, following the **dissolution of the monasteries**. The Penrice–Margam property became the largest landed estate in **Glamorgan**, consisting by the 1880s of 13,600 ha. Rice's great-grandson, Thomas (d.1733), was created Baron Mansel. For seven years the controller of Queen Anne's household, Mansel was a friend of **Edward Lhuyd**, who dedicated his *Glossography* to him, and also of Jonathan Swift. After three successive barons Mansel died without heirs, the estate passed to the first baron's daughter, Mary. Her marriage to John **Talbot** of Lacock Abbey, Wiltshire, caused the Talbots to become Glamorgan's leading landed family. Other members of the Mansel family include Robert Mansel (1573–1656), vice-admiral of **England** and a pioneer of **glass** production, Francis Mansell (1579–1665), master of Jesus College, **Oxford**, 'by far the most picturesque figure in the College's history', and Bussy Mansel (1623–99), the leader of Parliamentary forces in Glamorgan during the **Civil Wars** and MP for Glamorgan (1679–99).

MAP (MAHAP or MAPES), Walter (*c.*1140–*c.*1209) Author

Perhaps a Welshman and probably a native of **Erging**, the **Welsh**-speaking part of **Herefordshire**, Walter Map referred in his semi-satirical *De Nugis Curialium* (Court Gleanings), a collection of anecdotes composed between 1180 and 1193, to 'compatriotae nostre Walensis', but this may have meant 'our Welsh neighbours' rather than 'our Welsh compatriots'. The work, preserved in a manuscript from the 14th century, was described by its editor as 'the untidy product of an untidy mind'. Nevertheless, the anecdotes remain highly entertaining, and offer valuable sidelights on the history of Wales, in particular the career of **Gruffudd ap Llywelyn**.

MAPS

Maps are historical documents, contemporary reports, research tools, documents in the history of a technical **craft** and, commonly, objects of art. They are a vital form of communication, and the term 'graphicacy' has been coined – by W. G. V. Balchin, of the **University of Wales Swansea** – to take its place alongside literacy, numeracy and articulacy as a basic skill.

Wales featured very imperfectly in a number of medieval maps, including Matthew Paris's map of **Britain** and **Ireland** (*c.*1250) and the large-scale manuscript wall map of the world, the *Mappa Mundi* (*c.*1290), a notable version of which is housed at Hereford Cathedral. A map of Wales dating from even earlier was drawn by **Giraldus Cambrensis** to accompany his volume *Descriptio*

Sir Thomas Mansel and his wife Jane by an unknown artist, *c.*1625

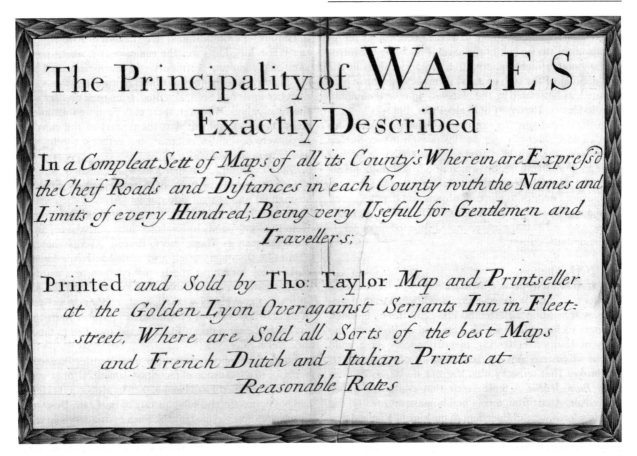

The Principality of **WALES** Exactly Described

In a Compleat Sett of Maps of all its County's Wherein are Express'd the Cheif Roads and Distances in each County with the Names and Limits of every Hundred; Being very Usefull for Gentlemen and Travellers;

Printed and Sold by Tho: Taylor Map and Printseller at the Golden Lyon Overagainst Serjants Inn in Fleet-street. Where are Sold all Sorts of the best Maps and French Dutch and Italian Prints at Reasonable Rates

An announcement of the publication of the first atlas wholly devoted to Wales – that of Thomas Taylor, 1718

Kambriae (*c.*1194); it was described shortly before its destruction by fire in 1694.

The earliest printed map of Wales is **Humphrey Lhuyd**'s *Cambriae Typus* (1573), published in Antwerp in a supplement to Abraham Ortelius's *Theatrum*, in which the traditional Welsh kingdoms are presented in **Latin**, **Welsh** and **English**. Christopher Saxton's atlas, including maps of the 13 shires of Wales, was published in 1579. There followed the 'proof' map of Wales (*c.*1580), in which the depiction of the country's outline was a considerable improvement on that shown on earlier maps.

The 1607 edition of **William Camden**'s *Britannia* contained **George Owen**'s map of **Pembrokeshire** (1602), together with Saxton's maps of the other Welsh **counties**. John Speed's *Theatre of the Empire of Great Britain* (1611), directly influenced by Lhuyd and Saxton, included a map of Wales, and maps of the 13 shires, each one with accompanying town plans, representing a most significant innovation.

Among the most intriguing 17th-century maps are the strip **road** maps prepared by John Ogilby; published in 1675, they give considerable prominence to Wales. The first atlas of Wales was Thomas Taylor's *The Principality of Wales Exactly Described* (1718). Regional maps were compiled – of the south (1729) by Emanuel Bowen and of the north (1795) by John Evans (1723–95). Lewis Morris (1701–65; *see* **Morris Brothers**) prepared a survey of the Welsh coast from **Llandudno** to the **Milford Haven Waterway**. Published in 1748, a revised version including the entire Welsh coast appeared in 1801.

By then, plans for the scientific mapping of Wales were already afoot. The Trigonometrical (later Ordnance) Survey of Wales and **England** was founded in 1791, and involved marking out the two countries in a series of triangles. Typical of the work was that undertaken in the **Swansea** area, which included the setting up of a trigonometrical station on Cefn Bryn in **Gower**, and lengthy discussions on matters such as whether 'a handsome gentleman's seat' should appear on maps as Cilfrwch or Kilvrough (*see* **Pennard**).

The Swansea inch-to-a-mile map (number 37 in the series) was published in 1830, and maps for the whole of Wales had appeared by 1870. Thus was launched what is incomparably the best record of the Welsh landscape. The work of the Ordnance Survey reached its apogee in the 1:25,000 Explorer series of the 1990s, masterpieces of the cartographer's art and maps which go a long way to make amends for the mangling of Welsh **place names** which had characterized the Survey's early work. Despite ongoing revisions, many imperfections and inconsistencies remain.

Manuscript maps, held at the **National Library**, county record offices, the National Archives (Kew) and elsewhere, include a survey of the **manor** of **Crickhowell** (1587) – Wales's earliest estate atlas – **tithe** apportionment maps, **enclosure** maps and **railway**, public utility, mining and quarry maps. Maps of Wales – in printed, microfilm and digital data format – are produced by **government** agencies other than the Ordnance Survey, as well as by commercial firms.

One remarkable aspect of maps is their adaptability to purposes more or less remote from their function as representations of the surface of the earth. Following the introduction of the highly interpretive geological map in the first decades of the 19th century, thematic maps have proliferated, as illustrated in *The National Atlas of Wales* (ed., Harold Carter, **University of Wales** Press, 1980–7).

In the digital age, the word 'map' signifies much more than a folded sheet of paper. In 1995, the Ordnance Survey completed the world's first computerized National Topographic Database, on which about 400 million features of the British landscape are digitally stored. The database, using satellites to pinpoint objects and detailing even the shapes of buildings and the precise alignments of roads, replaces some 230,000 maps previously printed on paper. It can be updated daily.

MARCH, The

The word 'March', related to 'mark', means a frontier or a frontier region. In Wales, the term was applied to the lordships established in the 11th and 12th centuries by **Norman** invaders such as **Mortimer**, de **Lacy** and de **Breos**. By the reign of Henry I (1100–35), they extended over a wide swathe of eastern and southern Wales from **Tegeingl** to **Pembroke**. That territory was *Marchia Wallie*, as distinct from *Pura Wallia* – those lands that continued under native rule. Apart from owing him homage and fealty, the marcher-lords were independent of the king of **England**, for the March was not part of the English kingdom (*see* **English Monarchs and Wales**). The royal writ had no force in the March, where marcher-lords could wage war, erect castles and hold courts without reference to the crown. **J. Goronwy Edwards** argued that the unit of sovereignty in the Welsh kingdoms was the **commote**. By taking possession of commotes, Norman lords became invested with sovereignty over them; thus, the exceptional powers of the marcher-lords had been 'inherited' from their predecessors, the Welsh kings. However, there may be more substance in **Rees Davies**'s argument that the powers of the marcher-lords were not an 'inheritance', but rather a condition of existence in the March itself.

Marcher conquest is particularly associated with the castle. This was the symbol of marcher power, being both stronghold and seat of **government**. Around the castle, a town usually developed, its first inhabitants often coming from the lord's lands in England; such were the origins of **boroughs** such as **Montgomery**, **Brecon**, **Abergavenny** and Pembroke. Incomers often also settled in fertile lowland parts of the lordship – the Englishry – where a manorial structure was frequently introduced. The rest of the lordship was the Welshry where tenants continued to live by Welsh **law** and custom administered in Welsh courts, and to render the same dues and services as they had to the former Welsh rulers.

Lack of male heirs meant that most lordships passed by marriage to a succession of families; **Glamorgan**, for example, was held by **Robert Fitz Hammo**, then by Robert Fitz Henry, earl of Gloucester, and subsequently by the **Clare**, **Despenser**, **Beauchamp** and Neville families. Such marriages could cause marcher-lordships to be part of much larger complexes of estates. For example, the **Bohuns**, in addition to being lords of Brecon, were also earls of Hereford and Essex.

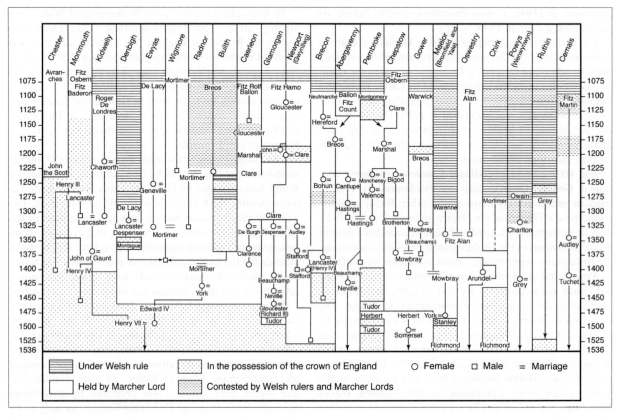

The holdings of the principal Marcher lords (after John Davies, 1990)

With the destruction of the **Principality** of **Llywelyn ap Gruffudd** in 1282, the March lost its *raison d'être*, for there was no longer any need for a *cordon sanitaire* between England and the henceforth defunct *Pura Wallia*. Yet, although the **Edwardian conquest** coincided with the king's efforts to restrict the power of the marcher-lords, Edward I lacked the resources to abolish that power. Indeed, in the north-east, he created the new marcher-lordships of **Denbigh**, **Ruthin**, **Chirk and Chirkland**, and **Bromfield and Yale**.

The chief features of the late medieval history of the March were the turbulent contribution to English history made by the marcher-lords, the growing perception of the lawlessness of the March, and the progressive acquisition of marcher-lordships by the English crown. This turbulent contribution was particularly prominent during the reign of Edward II, but it was also evident during the **Wars of the Roses**. The perception of lawlessness was not always well grounded. Although the malfunctioning of the courts and the lack of supervision of local officials did feed the notion that the March was a hotbed of disorder, there was, in fact, considerable co-operation between lordships, especially on such matters as the extradition of fugitives.

The crown became a major holder of marcher-lordships in 1399, with the accession of Henry IV, duke of **Lancaster** and lord of Brecon, **Monmouth**, the **Three Castles** and **Kidwelly**. The largest accretion of marcher-lordships was that of the Mortimer family, who in 1328 received the title of earl of March. Its lordships – a broken chain extending from Denbigh to **Caerleon** – became crown property in 1461 following the accession of Edward IV, duke of **York**. In 1473, Edward established a council at **Ludlow** charged with the duty of maintaining order in both the March and the Principality (*see* **Council of Wales and the Marches**).

Long an anomaly, the powers of the marcher-lords were abolished by the first **Act of 'Union'** (1536), a process vastly aided by the fact that most of the lordships were by then in the hands of the English crown. The Act lists the lordships, but the list provides no real guide to their number, for it contains sub-lordships and manors as well as fully fledged quasi-independent territories. Some of the lordships were added to pre-existing **counties** in both Wales and England. The rest became **Breconshire**, **Denbighshire**, Glamorgan, **Monmouthshire**, **Montgomeryshire**, Pembrokeshire and **Radnorshire**. The abolition of the March – and the rise of the assumption that the Principality embraced the whole of Wales – led J. Goronwy Edwards to argue that the real union effected in 1536 was not that between Wales and England, but that between the Principality and the March.

MARCHWIEL (Marchwiail), Wrexham
(1488 ha; 1418 inhabitants)

Located immediately south of **Wrexham**, the **community** is largely rural, although its western parts are riddled with abandoned underground workings, which cause serious subsidence problems. Marchwiel village is rapidly expanding as one of Wrexham's outer suburbs. The church of St Marcellus was rebuilt in 1778 and contains several monuments to the Yorke family. Marchwiel Hall (now an open-air activity centre), Bryn-y-grog and Old Sontley are attractive country houses, but the glory of the community

is Erddig. The house (*c.*1687, 1720) was owned by the Yorke family from 1733 until 1973, when it was donated to the **National Trust**. Its 19-bay front overlooks the **garden**; one of the most important early 18th-century gardens surviving in **Britain**, it is enclosed by the splendid railings originally erected at Stansty Park, **Gwersyllt**, and perhaps the work of Robert Davies (*see* **Ironwork** and **Davies family, Ironsmiths**). The Yorkes were renowned for their philanthropic attitude to their servants, whose portraits are a major feature of the house. Indeed, unlike many National Trust properties, which were stripped of their valuables before the Trust acquired them, Erddig was handed over intact. This was in accordance with the wishes of the donor, Philip Yorke, who remained in residence and acted as a guide until his death in 1978. His residence at Erddig (1966–78) has been eulogized in local mythology, which portrays him as the priceless and penniless wanderer with a penchant for the performing arts.

In the 1970s, subsidence was threatening to topple the house; its lengthy and costly restoration brought eminently satisfactory results, for Erddig is one of the best-loved of all the Trust's properties. The grounds, which contain an ingeniously landscaped **waterfall** and a delightful stretch of the Clywedog valley, are also the site of the castle of Wristlesham or Wrexham, mentioned in the Pipe Roll of 1161. Pickhill Hall (1720s), a fine example of provincial baroque, is being restored after a fire in 1985. (For the Marchwiel Ordnance Factory, *see* **Abenbury**.)

MARGAM, Neath Port Talbot
(3754 ha; 2389 inhabitants)

Located at the sole point where **Glamorgan**'s uplands reach the sea, the **community** has long been of strategic importance. Mynydd Margam has a wealth of prehistoric monuments, and the rich collection of inscriptions in the Stones Museum is proof that Margam was the one of the chief religious centres of early Christian Wales (*see* **Monuments, Early Christian**). Margam village grew up around the **Cistercian** abbey founded in 1147 by Robert of Gloucester. Although a **Norman** foundation, the abbey became closely involved in Welsh culture and *The White Book of Hergest* may have been copied there. It was dissolved *c.*1540 and its church's 12th-century nave became Margam's **parish** church. The church, which contains fine funereal **sculpture**, is Wales's sole surviving Cistercian church. The rest of the complex came into the possession of Rice **Mansel**, who converted the buildings into a mansion. It was demolished in the 1770s, and Margam became a pleasure **garden** dominated by a 100-m long orangery (1790), the finest building to be erected in late 18th-century Wales.

In 1824, the 13,600-ha Margam-**Penrice** estate – Glamorgan's largest – was inherited by C. R. M. **Talbot**, the length of whose membership of the House of Commons (1830–90) is unsurpassed. He built Margam Castle, a vast pile whose construction led to the relocation of Margam village to Y Groes, 1 km to the west, where Talbot erected Beulah, a rare example of an octagonal chapel. (Following the construction of the **M4**, the chapel was rebuilt near junction 39.) The castle, the orangery, the abbey ruins and a remarkable late 17th-century temple are now part of Margam Country Park, administered by the **Neath Port**

Talbot county borough; the park contains open-air displays of sculpture. In 2006, work began on a £9.5 million refurbishment of the castle, which will include the establishment of the National Centre for **Photography** in Wales. (For the Margam Works, *see* **Port Talbot**.)

MARI LWYD (lit. 'Holy Mary')

A form of **wassailing** found formerly across the south, involving a **horse**'s skull – the Mari (possibly originally from the **English** 'mare' rather than from the Virgin Mary)

A Mari Lwyd

– carried on a pole and partially covered by a long white sheet to conceal the bearer. Accompanied by Sergeant, Merryman, Punch and Judy, the Mari was led from house to house after dark during the Christmas season. Verses were sung to request admittance, but the family would initially refuse, engaging in a battle of wits in extempore verses until the singers were finally let in. The Mari was adorned with ribbons, and the bearer could operate the jaws to make the teeth click, augmenting the fear induced when he entered the house. The Mari would chase the young **women** present, neighing as he tried to kiss them. The singing was occasionally accompanied by dancing, which was spontaneous and had no set steps (*see* **Dance**). After partaking of **food and drink**, the Mari party would move on to another house. By the 21st century, the custom survived in only a few districts, notably **Llangynwyd** and **Maesteg**.

MARLOES AND ST BRIDES (Marloes a Sain Ffraid), Pembrokeshire (2155 ha; 323 inhabitants)

Constituting the northern part of the **Dale** peninsula, which juts out into the mouth of the **Milford Haven Waterway**, the **community** includes the **islands** of Skomer, Grassholm and the Smalls. The Smalls had one of Wales's earliest **lighthouses**; first built in 1774, it was long the most profitable in **Britain**. Nab Head is one of the most important Mesolithic sites in Wales (*see* **Paleolithic and Mesolithic Ages**). It has yielded a range of stone objects of *c.*7000 BC, among them the 'Nab Head Venus', said to be Britain's sole known Mesolithic carving in the round (*see* **Sculpture**), although experts are not unanimous on the matter.

At the community's western extremity is an extensive promontory fort. Gateholm, an island at low tide, contains evidence of early medieval settlement. Stack Rocks are striking offshore reefs. The churches of St Bride and of St Peter, Marloes, retain medieval features; the former contains a baptistry sunk into the floor. Philbeach farmhouse has a large 'Flemish' chimney. St Brides was the home of the Laugharne family whose members included **Rowland Laugharne**, the chief leader of Parliamentary forces in south Wales during the first **Civil War**, and a major figure in the second. St Brides later came into the ownership of the Edwardes family (*see* **Johnston**). William Edwardes (1711–1801) inherited land in west **London** and in 1779 received the title of Baron Kensington in the peerage of **Ireland**. St Bride's House (1833, 1905), a vast pile renamed Kensington Castle, became a hospital and then a timeshare holiday centre. Streets in Kensington and Earls Court bearing names such as **Pembroke**, Marloes, Philbeach and Penywern recall associations with the Edwardes family. Marloes has a **clock** tower (1904) built in memory of Baron Kensington. St Brides gave its name to St Brides Bay.

MARS

Ferrying passengers and livestock from Waterford to Bristol on 1 April 1862, the paddle steamer *Mars* hit a rock in thick fog at Linney Head (**Castlemartin**), a headland notorious for **shipwrecks**. She quickly sank, and although the **ship**'s boats were launched, they were smashed into the cliffs. Thirty-five people lost their lives.

MARSHAL family Marcher-lords

William Marshal (d.1219), *rector* of **England**, married Isabella, heiress of Richard de **Clare** (Strongbow), lord of **Pembroke** and **Chepstow**. (Marshal became the earl of Pembroke following the death of Strongbow in 1176.) He proved a doughty opponent of the Welsh rulers, seizing **Cilgerran** and **Caerleon** and seeking to thwart the ambitions of **Llywelyn ap Iorwerth**. His five sons, all childless, succeeded to his lands in turn and were closely involved in the politics of Wales. With the death of the last of them, Anselm (1245), the family's lands were divided between Munchensey, **Bigod** and **Breos**, husbands of his sisters and nieces.

MARSHALL, Walter Charles (1932–96)
Physicist

Lord Marshall of Goring, FRS, an outstanding theoretical physicist, is widely remembered for his advocacy of nuclear power. Born in Rumney, **Cardiff**, he completed a PhD at the early age of 22 before joining the Atomic Energy Research Establishment, Harwell. His work on the scattering of thermal neutrons remained a standard for many years, especially his use of neutron scattering in the study of magnetism. As director of Harwell, he pioneered the use of **government** laboratories to provide industrial services on a commercial basis. He became increasingly interested in **energy** policy, and chaired the UK Atomic Energy Authority (1981) and then the Central Electricity Generating Board (1983). He planned a major contribution to generating capacity from pressurized water reactors, but the Chernobyl disaster in Ukraine (*see* **Nuclear Fallout**) and the financial implications of privatization led to the abandonment of the programme.

MARSHFIELD (Maerun), Newport
(584 ha; 2636 inhabitants)

Wedged between the M48 and the **railway**, and hugging **Cardiff**'s eastern boundary, the **community** contains the sprawling developments of Marshfield and Castleton, which may be considered suburbs of **Newport**, or perhaps of Cardiff. St Mary's church – originally 13th century, but extensively rebuilt in the 15th century – is one of the finest churches of lowland **Gwent**.

During the great flood of 1606 (*see* **Earthquakes**), Jane Morgan of Gelli-ber – which is still a farmhouse – was drowned as the waters engulfed her house. Castleton **Baptist** chapel (1858) is an exercise in neo-Romanesque polychromy; the adjoining **Wesleyan** chapel (1854) is almost as florid.

MARTIN, Edward (d.1818) Mineral surveyor

Born in Cumberland, Martin settled in Morriston, **Swansea**, in the 1770s as a mineral surveyor. He became the chief mining agent of the duke of Beaufort (*see* **Somerset family**), built up a private practice as a civil and mining engineer, and was considered the greatest authority on **coal** and coalmining in south Wales. His knowledge was summarized in a paper to the Royal Society of **London** (1808) containing the first geological sketch **map** of the southern coalfield.

A centenary Welsh translation of the Communist Manifesto

MARTLETWY, Pembrokeshire
(3786 ha; 523 inhabitants)

Located on the east bank of the **Cleddau**, the **community** contains the villages of Martletwy, Lawrenny and Landshipping. St Marcellus's church, Martletwy (largely rebuilt 1848–50), contains a carved head of a tonsured priest; St Caradoc's church, Lawrenny (13th century), contains an effigy of a knight. The community contains substantial **Baptist**, **Congregationalist** and **Calvinistic Methodist** chapels. The quays at both Lawrenny and Landshipping once exported **coal**, **limestone**, corn and oysters. A mining disaster at Landshipping in 1844 killed 40 workers. Lawrenny Hall (demolished 1950) was the home of the Lort-Phillips family. Oakwood is a popular entertainment centre, replete with roller-coasters, white-knuckle rides and other attractions.

MARXISM

A materialist **philosophy** of history that originated with the critical analysis of capitalism that was expounded in the writings of Karl Marx and Friedrich Engels, in which they proposed that human societies are riven by internal contradictions that transform them into their opposites. The capitalism of the 19th century would thus make way for a society dominated not by capitalists but by their workers – just as feudal forms of lordship had given way to

Thomas Jones, *The Bard* (1774), inspired by the legend of the massacre of the bards

mercantile and entrepreneurial society. Marxism claimed that the major fault line running through modern societies was defined by **class**, and that class struggle was the major engine of historical change.

Marxist ideas of change strongly influenced revolutionary movements in early 20th-century Europe, particularly Russian Bolshevism. The **Communist Party** of Great **Britain** was established in 1920–1, with workers in the south Wales **coal**field among its strongest supporters. Marxist ideas had been circulating in Wales since the 1890s and they formed an inspiration for the **Syndicalism** which underlay the industrial unrest after 1910, and which subsequently fuelled the **Plebs' League**, the Unofficial Reform Committee and the **Rhondda** (later the South Wales) Socialist Society.

The resilience of capitalism after the **Second World War**, the Cold War and the collapse of the Soviet Union in the late 1980s, severely weakened 'official' Soviet-style Marxism. From the 1960s, however, ideas derived from Marxism continued to exert strong influence, especially in protest movements, anti-colonial struggles and in academic circles. Studies of culture and social relations by writers in the Marxist tradition, including **Raymond Williams** and **Gwyn Alfred Williams**, strongly influenced literary, historical and political writing in Wales. That tradition continues to have its champions, although support for specifically Marxist parties has become minimal.

MARY

Taking passengers from Dublin to Chester on 25 March 1675, the *Mary* – which was Charles II's royal yacht – hit the Skerries (**Cylch-y-Garn**; *see also* **Islands**) off **Anglesey** in a fog and sank. Of the 75 people on board, 36 were lost.

Indiscriminate salvage of the site in 1971 prompted the 1973 Protection of Wrecks Act. The wreck is designated an Historic Wreck Site.

MASSACRE OF THE BARDS, The

The alleged massacre of the Welsh bards by Edward I is not only the subject of Thomas Gray's Pindaric ode 'The Bard' (1757), but also of a hugely popular dramatic **ballad** by the Magyar poet János Árány (1817–82). Gray based his poem on a legendary tale found in Thomas Carte's *History of England* (1747–55); Carte, in turn, is believed to have drawn on an account of the massacre discovered in a manuscript version of Sir John **Wynn**'s *History of the Gwydir Family*, which was published in 1770. The story appealed to the growing **Romanticism** of the age, and inspired such painters as Fuseli, John Martin and **Thomas Jones** (1742–1803) of Pencerrig (**Llanelwedd**).

The myth was particularly influential in Hungary. There is a statue to the author of *A Walesi Bárdok* (The Welsh Bards) outside the National Museum in Budapest. János Árány rose from a peasant background to become secretary-general to the Hungarian Academy of Sciences. During the 1848 Revolution, Hungarians rebelled against the Austrian Empire that ruled them. Árány supported the nationalist Kossuth. Published in 1867, after the rebellion was put down, Árány's poem, in which the silenced bards are avenged on the murderous king, was a protest against censorship imposed on Hungarians by the Austrian Empire.

An English translation, by Neville Masterman, may be found in 'The Massacre of the Bards: The Migration of a Myth' (*Welsh Review*, vol. 7, no. 1, 1948), and a Welsh version, by John Henry Jones, in *Cardi o Fôn* (ed. Gareth Alban Davies, 1991).

MATH FAB MATHONWY

In the story of 'Math fab Mathonwy' in the fourth branch of *Pedair Cainc y Mabinogi* (*see* **Mabinogion, The**), Math is king of **Gwynedd** and has magical powers. Yet, there is a strange condition on his life: he must always rest with his feet in the lap of a virgin, except in time of war. When his nephews **Gwydion** and Gilfaethwy rape the royal footholder Goewin, he punishes them severely. Later, he seems to have become reconciled with Gwydion when together they conjure up **Blodeuwedd**, the lady made from flowers.

MATHEMATICS

Wales's first distinguished mathematician was **Robert Recorde** (d.1558) of **Tenby**, who published the first book in **English** on algebra and introduced the equals sign (=) into everyday mathematical notation. **Anglesey**-born **William Jones** (?1675–1749) also wrote books on mathematics and edited some of the works of his friend Isaac Newton. It was William Jones who first used the Greek letter pi (π) to represent the ratio of the circumference of a circle to its diameter (3.14159...) and who suggested using a dot above a letter as a simple way to represent d/dt in calculus. This was the notation used by John Harries, a **London** Welshman, who published the first book in English on calculus (or 'fluxions' as he called the subject, in loyalty to Newton).

Welsh mathematicians have also made a major contribution to various branches of applied mathematics. In the 18th and 19th centuries, the statistical foundations of the **insurance** industry were established by three remarkable Welshmen, the foremost of whom was **Richard Price** of Llangeinor (**Garw Valley**). It was also Richard Price, acting as executor for the estate of the Rev. Thomas Bayes, who recognized the significance of some notes written by his deceased friend, and published them in the *Proceedings of the Royal Society* as Bayes's Theorem, the basis of all modern statistics. In **health** statistics, **Britain**'s greatest expert is Treorchy (**Rhondda**) born Brian T. Williams, FRS (b.1938).

Other branches of applied mathematics where there has been a strong Welsh input include theoretical aerodynamics (*see* **Aviation and Aeronautics**) and computer **science**. In the latter, **Donald Davies** from Treorchy invented 'packet switching' whereby large data files are separated into smaller packages of 1024 bits, for storage on a computer memory or for transmission along a shared communication channel. By the beginning of the 21st century, Samuel Braunstein's work on quantum transportation had made **Bangor** renowned worldwide.

MATHERN (Matharn), Monmouthshire
(1447 ha; 990 inhabitants)

A **community** located immediately south-west of **Chepstow**, Mathern is reputed to have been a **manor** of the bishop of Llandaff (*see* **Cardiff**) as early as 600. Its palace was long the bishop's sole residence. Moynes Court (early 17th century) was another episcopal residence. John Marshall, bishop of Llandaff (from 1475 to 1496), greatly enlarged the church of St Tewdrig. (The **parish**'s original name was Merthyr Tewdrig.) It contains a 17th-century memorial to King Tewdrig of **Gwent** who, according to

The Book of Llandaff (*Liber Landavensis*), defeated the invading Saxons *c*.620. St Peter's church contains memorials to the Lewis family whose seat, St Pierre, is now a luxury hotel. Mounton House (1914), now a school, was the last full-scale country house to be built in **Monmouthshire**; it was built for **H. Avray Tipping**, who commissioned the restoration of the bishop's palace. Runston, which in the 13th century was a settlement of at least 25 houses, was finally abandoned *c*.1785 – although the ruins of the church survive and the earthworks indicating the site of the deserted village are perceptible. Runston is in the care of **Cadw**.

MATHESON, Colin (1898–1977) Zoologist

Born and educated in Aberdeen, Matheson spent 45 years at the **National Museum [of] Wales**, where he specialized in the relationship of animals to humanity, with particular reference to Wales's southern ports. He was among the first to record the outstanding changes in the composition of the **mammal**ian and **bird** faunas of Wales within the historic period.

MATHIAS, William [James] (1934–92) Composer

Born in **Whitland** and employed at **Bangor** between 1959 and 1988 as lecturer and subsequently professor of **music**, Mathias came to prominence early in his career. His output is wide-ranging and catholic, with a large body of orchestral works, chamber pieces, incidental music and choral music in which his eclectic but highly original voice, forged from a diverse range of influences – from Britten, Copland, Tippett and Messiaen to Latin American jazz rhythms and poetry from the **Celt**ic countries – comes into its own. Works such as *Ave Rex*, *Lux Aeterna* and *Elegy for a Prince* display an interest in his Welsh roots and in the ritual or celebratory nature of music, as well as a sense of repose, and are likely to remain popular, particularly in America where Mathias's breezy rhythms and jazz-inflected scores won him a large following. For many years, he was artistic director of the North Wales Music Festival at **St Asaph**, and chose to be buried there.

MATHRAFAL

Tradition portrays Mathrafal as the principal seat of **Powys**. Located in **Llangyniew** near **Meifod**, the burial place of the early rulers of Powys, it gave its name to the ruling house descending from **Bleddyn ap Cynfyn**. However, Mathrafal's status is not as well attested as are those of the other royal residences of Wales – **Aberffraw** and **Dinefwr** – and excavation has produced disappointing results. By the 13th century, when the caput of southern Powys was at Powis Castle (*see* **Welshpool**), Mathrafal's status was no more than that of the *maerdref* of the **commote** of **Caereinion**.

MATHRY (Mathri), Pembrokeshire
(2972 ha; 564 inhabitants)

Located halfway between **Fishguard** and **St David's**, the **community**'s main settlement – the village of Mathry – has an attractive hilltop site. Carreg Samson near Abercastle is an impressive **Neolithic** burial chamber with a huge capstone. In Holy Martyrs' church (rebuilt in 1867) is a bilingual (**Latin–ogham**) inscribed stone (5th century). The creek at Abercastle is coastal **Pembrokeshire** at its best. One of the characteristics of Mathry's **Welsh** dialect is to greet others using the third rather than the second person.

MATTAN, Mahmood Hussein (1923–52)
Victim of injustice

Record damages of £1.4 million were paid to the family of the **Cardiff Somali** Mahmood Mattan in 2001, in recognition of his wrongful **execution** in 1952, having been charged with slitting the throat of a woman shopkeeper for just £100. Mattan's arrest was based on a **police** informer saying he had seen a Somali seaman in the area minutes before the murder. A jury in **Swansea** returned a guilty verdict, but they were not aware of certain facts: that the informer was paid for giving evidence; that information about another Somali was not disclosed; and that four witnesses had failed to identify Mattan. The last person to be hanged in Cardiff **prison**, Mattan was pardoned 45 years later. The ensuing compensation was the first award to a family of a person hanged for a crime he or she had not committed.

MAWDDACH River (35 km)

The Mawddach rises at 450 m in the uplands of the **community** of Llanuwchllyn, south-west of **Bala**. Within the forest of Coed y Brenin (**Ganllwyd**), it is joined by the Cain and the Eden, which drain much of northern **Meirionnydd**. Ordovician and Cambrian rocks underlie the catchment area; veins in the Cambrian rock have been mined for **gold**. There are striking **waterfalls**, such as the Mawddach and Rhaeadr Ddu falls. The Wnion, which flows through **Dolgellau**, joins the Mawddach near **Llanelltyd**, where the

Mawddach becomes tidal. Thereafter, the Mawddach enters its floodplain; the extensive open estuary includes alluvial deposits, where gold has been discovered through panning. Ro Wen is a classic example of a sand and gravel spit, extending from the Fairbourne (**Arthog**) north across the estuary towards **Barmouth**. Between Morfa Mawddach and Barmouth the Cambrian Coast **Railway** crosses the estuary by a spectacular bridge.

MAWDDWY, Gwynedd
(11,596 ha; 603 inhabitants)

Constituting the upper reaches of the basin of the **Dyfi**, the **community**'s most prominent features are the spectacular rock face at the head of Cwm Cywarch and the summit of **Aran** Fawddwy (905 m), Wales's highest **mountain** outside the **Snowdonia** range. The community contains the villages of Aberangell, Dinas Mawddwy, Llanymawddwy and Mallwyd. In the two last-named villages there are churches dedicated to the Breton **saint** Tŷdecho. That at Mallwyd contains a memorial to Wales's leading **Renaissance** scholar **John Davies** (*c*.1567–1644), rector from 1604 to 1644. **A. G. Edwards** (1848–1937), the first archbishop of Wales, was the son of the rector of Llanymawddwy. Dinas Mawddwy, the community's main settlement, owed its origins to **lead** mining and **slate** quarrying, and later became a centre of the **woollen industry**. Pont Minllyn, a 17th-century bridge – said to have been designed by John Davies – is in the care of **Cadw**. The Brigands Inn recalls the '**red bandits**' of the **commote** of **Mawddwy**. The indigenous inhabitants of Aberangell have bravely defended their shopkeeper – a **Welsh**-speaking Asian – against the attacks of incoming racists.

Looking south across the Mawddach estuary and the Cambrian Coast Railway bridge

MAWDDWY Commote
Constituting the upper reaches of the basin of the **Dyfi**, Mawddwy was a **commote** in western **Powys**. The **Act of 'Union'** of 1536 allocated it not to **Montgomeryshire** but to **Merioneth**, presumably because the Act's framers believed that it would be better to attach so **law**less a district to long-established Merioneth rather than to newly established Montgomeryshire. The anarchic nature of its inhabitants was made manifest in 1555 when Judge Lewis Owen was murdered by 'the red bandits of Mawddwy'. The **community** of Mawddwy, formed in 1974, is broadly coterminous with the commote.

MAWR, Swansea (5781 ha; 1800 inhabitants)
Located in rolling hill country north of **Llangyfelach**, the **community** includes much of the old Welshry of the lordship of **Gower**. Its name – meaning 'large' – arose from the fact that it was the most extensive parcel of land within the old **parish** of Llangyfelach. Its unfenced hilltops are excellent walking country. Between the ridges are deep fertile valleys containing the numerous scattered farms that have been a feature of the area since early times. Penlle'rcastell, a stronghold of the lords of Gower and remotely situated at 370 m above sea level, was burnt by the Welsh in 1252 and subsequently reconstructed in stone. The intact corn mill at Felindre dates from the 18th century. Craig-cefn-parc, located high above the lower Clydach valley, owed its growth to local **coal**mining. In 2001, 56.27% of the inhabitants of Mawr had some knowledge of **Welsh**, with 35.78% wholly fluent in the language – the highest percentages for any of the communities of the **county** of **Swansea**.

MEAD and METHEGLIN
An alcoholic beverage made by the fermentation of honey and water, mead was widely enjoyed throughout Europe, and classical sources attest to its early popularity among the **Celts**. In the 6th–7th century poem *Y Gododdin*, the expression *talu medd* (paying for one's mead) refers to the warrior's willingness to face death on behalf of his lord and patron. Throughout the medieval period, mead – together with **beer** and bragget (a liquor made of ale and honey) – remained an essential feature of the Welsh diet; and in native Welsh **law** the mead-brewer is listed among the king's officers.

The Welsh also spiced their mead with herbs and spices. It appears that they called it *meddyglyn,* which also meant a medicinal draught. The word was adopted by the **English** in the 1530s, hence 'metheglin' which was used for both plain and spiced mead. As honey was displaced by less expensive sugars in the late Middle Ages, mead was gradually displaced by less costly beer and ale.

MEANS TEST, The
The Means Test was a response to the dramatic increase in unemployment and in the sums spent on relief. Some Public Assistance Committees had attempted to apply the regulations generously, but the Unemployment Act (1934) set up a statutory commission, the Unemployed Assistance Board, to ensure uniform practice throughout the United Kingdom and to insist that the able-bodied unemployed would rely initially on the joint means of the household, without any relief from the state. The board's members included **Thomas Jones** (1870–1955).

Opposed in the House of Commons by **Aneurin Bevan** among others, the Act triggered off the largest protests ever seen in Wales. On 3 February 1935, some 300,000 people demonstrated in the **Rhondda**, **Aberdare**, **Pontypool** and elsewhere. The following day, the Assistance Board's offices in **Merthyr Tydfil** were attacked and there were violent scenes in **Abertillery** and Blaina (**Nantyglo and Blaina**). The introduction of the new measure was suspended until November and even then was not enforced in its full rigour. The Means Test helped to shape the **Welfare State**, with its emphasis on flat-rate benefits.

MEBWYNION Commote
One of the 10 **commotes** of **Ceredigion**, Mebwynion extended from the southern bank of the **Aeron** to the middle reaches of the **Teifi**. Mebwynion probably derives from a male personal name.

MECHAIN *Cantref*
Occupying much of the north-eastern part of later **Montgomeryshire**, the *cantref* extended over the valley of the River Cain – the origin of its name. It was divided into the **commotes** of Is Coed and Uwch Coed, and contained **Meifod**, **Powys**'s premier church. The post-**Acts of 'Union' hundred** of Mechain consisted of the *cantref*, along with the commote of **Mochnant** Uwch Rhaeadr. The **community** of **Llanfechain** and the village of **Llansantffraid**-ym-Mechain preserve the name.

MECHANICS' INSTITUTES
These educational institutions, pioneered by George Birkbeck in **London** in 1823, were aimed at grounding skilled workers in areas of scientific knowledge. They spread rapidly, the first of 30 in Wales being opened at **Swansea** in 1826. Many were short-lived, but those at **Cardigan**, **Carmarthen**, **Neath** and **Llanelli** all lasted for at least 40 years. They were promoted by industrialists, professional men and philanthropists, and provided basic scientific **education**, as well as libraries and museums. By the later 19th century, local authorities were beginning to offer such services.

MECHELL, Isle of Anglesey
(2352 ha; 1282 inhabitants)
Located immediately south-west of **Amlwch**, the **community** contains the nucleated village of Llanfechell and stone-strewn Mynydd Mechell. St Mechell's church contains 12th-century features. Brynddu was the home of William **Bulkeley** (1691–1760), whose detailed diary is an important source for the social history of 18th-century **Anglesey**. In the 18th century, Llanfechell had three fairs a year and a weekly market. Plas Boderwyd (15th to 18th centuries) is a picturesque grouping.

MEFENYDD Commote
One of the 10 **commotes** of **Ceredigion**, the commote extended from the coast south of the mouth of the **Ystwyth** to the ancient kingdom's eastern boundary. Its name possibly derives from a lost personal name, Mafan.

M

MEGÁNE, Leila (Margaret Hughes, b. Jones; 1891–1961) Singer

Leila Megáne was Wales's most celebrated singer during the 1920s and 1930s, performing in operas and concerts on the world's most famous stages and recording extensively. Born in **Bethesda**, she grew up in **Pwllheli** and received voice training in **London** and Paris. While in France, the contralto entertained soldiers wounded in the **First World War**. She inspired her first husband, the composer and pianist Thomas Osborne Roberts, to compose solos such as 'Y Nefoedd', 'Y Gwanwyn Du' and 'Cymru Annwyl'.

MEIBION GLYDŴR (Sons of Glyndŵr)

A clandestine **nationalist** group which, during the 1980s, initiated an arson campaign against holiday and **second homes** in rural north and west Wales. Its activities intensified in the face of the **Conservative government**'s refusal to introduce legislation giving priority in the property market to local people. Many of its communiqués were signed by Rhys Gethin, the name of one of the captains of **Owain Glyndŵr**.

MEIDRIM, Carmarthenshire
(2651 ha; 601 inhabitants)

Located immediately north of **St Clears**, the **community**'s only settlement of any size is the village of Meidrim. Bethel **Calvinistic Methodist** chapel (1904) is an impressive building. The Puritan **Stephen Hughes**, known as the Apostle of **Carmarthenshire**, held the living of Meidrim until ejected in 1661.

MEIFOD, Montgomeryshire, Powys
(6840 ha; 1323 inhabitants)

Located north-west of **Welshpool**, the **community** extends over the Vyrnwy valley at its most delectable. Meifod may have been the seat of **Powys**'s early bishops. Its churchyard, extending over 4 ha, was the site of a *clas* or **Celtic** monastery and became the necropolis of the rulers of **Powys**. On the site, St Gwyddfarch's chapel (*c.*550) was succeeded by St Tysilio's church (7th century) and then by St Mary's, which was consecrated in 1156, much altered in the 14th and 15th century, and then extensively restored in 1872.

A cross slab in the church, bearing Celtic and **Viking** motifs, may be the tomb of **Madog ap Maredudd** (d.1160). Madog was the patron of **Cynddelw Brydydd Mawr**, who celebrated Meifod's beauty and worldly and spiritual treasures.

Christ Church (1864) at Bwlchycibau is an attractive church designed by George Gilbert Scott. Meifod has several interesting country houses, including Glascoed (*c.*1600), Bryngwyn (*c.*1776) and Penylan (*c.*1810). In 2003, the National **Eisteddfod** was held at Meifod, the fourth time for the festival to visit **Montgomeryshire**.

MEILYR BRYDYDD and DESCENDANTS Poets

Meilyr (fl.1100–37), author of an elegy to **Gruffudd ap Cynan**, is the earliest known of the **Poets of the Princes**. There is no evidence that any of his forebears were poets, but the work of three, if not four, of his descendants – his son, Gwalchmai (fl.1130–80), his grandsons, Einion (fl.1203–23) and Meilyr ap Gwalchmai (fl. second half of the 12th century), and possibly Elidir Sais (fl.1195–1246) –

has been preserved. During his long and eventful career, Gwalchmai served **Madog ap Maredudd** of **Powys** as well as **Owain Gwynedd** and his sons, Rhodri and **Dafydd ab Owain Gwynedd**. **Llywelyn ap Iorwerth** was probably the chief patron of Elidir and Einion. Little is known about Meilyr since only his religious poems have survived. It is possible that Trefeilyr and **Trewalchmai** in **Anglesey** were named after members of this family, and that they were lands granted them by royal patronage.

MEIRIONNYDD *Cantref*

Constituting the area between the **Dyfi** and the **Mawddach**, the *cantref* consisted of the **commotes** of **Talybont** and **Ystumanner**. The name allegedly came from that of Marianus or Meirion, grandson of **Cunedda**. Meirionnydd long had its own dynasty, but by the early 12th century it had come within the orbit of **Gwynedd**. Its beauty inspired the prince-poet **Hywel ab Owain Gwynedd**. In 1284, the name **Merioneth** was applied to the newly created **county**, which consisted of the *cantrefi* of Meirionnydd and **Penllyn** and the commotes of **Ardudwy** and **Edeirnion**.

MEIRIONNYDD One-time district

In 1974, the **county** of **Merioneth** was abolished and replaced by the district of Meirionnydd. Part of the newly formed county of **Gwynedd**, it was called Meirionnydd in both **English** and **Welsh**. Apart from the loss of the **Edeirnion rural district**, which became part of the **Glyndŵr district** in the new county of **Clwyd**, the new district had the same boundaries as the old county. In 1996, a shrunken Gwynedd became a unitary county, consisting of the former districts of **Arfon**, **Dwyfor** and Meirionnydd.

Thus, Meirionnydd has ceased to be a unit of local **government**, although the name survives as that of several institutions, among them the record office and the history society.

MELANGELL (6th–7th century) Saint

Melangell, the patron **saint** of **hares**, is supposed to have fled from **Ireland** to Wales in order to avoid an arranged marriage. According to her **Latin** Life, *Historia Divae Monacellae*, she established a **nunnery** and sanctuary at Pennant Melangell (**Llangynog**) on land given to her by Brochfael Ysgithrog, prince of **Powys**. One day, Brochfael came across the saint while he was **hunting** a hare. The hare hid under Melangell's skirt and the hounds refused to approach the holy virgin. In her church at Pennant Melangell, there is a remarkable Romanesque shrine, and her legend is depicted on a carved 15th-century rood screen. Her feast day is 27 May.

MELINDWR, Ceredigion
(4083 ha; 1189 inhabitants)

Located east of **Aberystwyth**, the **community** straddles the middle reaches of the **Rheidol** valley and contains the villages of Aber-ffrwd, Capel Bangor, Goginan, Penllwyn and Pisgah. Goginan was a significant **lead**-mining centre. The greater part of the Vale of Rheidol **Railway** lies within Melindwr's boundaries. The Cwmrheidol Power Station is part of the hydroelectric scheme that includes the Nant-y-moch and Dinas **reservoirs** (*see* **Energy**). Lewis Morris (1701–65) (*see* **Morris Brothers**) married the heiress of

Penbryn. **Lewis Edwards** (1809–87) was born at Pwllcenawon; his bust stands on a plinth outside Penllwyn chapel. The Rheidol Falls are a striking **waterfall**.

'MEN OF HARLECH'
('Rhyfelgyrch Gwŷr Harlech')
One of the best known of all Welsh songs. A traditional melody, it was published for the first time in *Musical and Poetical Relicks of the Welsh Bards* (1784) by **Edward Jones** (Bardd y Brenin; 1752–1824). By the end of the 18th century, it was beginning to appear in the arrangements of **London** publishers. It was included in **Brinley Richards**'s *Songs of Wales* (1873), with **Welsh** words by Ceiriog (**John Ceiriog Hughes**) and **English** words by John Oxenford. An arrangement by **D. Emlyn Evans** included words by Talhaiarn (**John Jones**; 1810–69). In the **film** *Zulu* (1964), it was sung by **Ivor Emmanuel**, a performance which gave it worldwide exposure. Kaiser Wilhelm II considered it to be the world's finest marching tune.

MENAI Commote
A **commote** in south-west **Anglesey**, which, with that of **Dindaethwy**, formed the *cantref* of Rhosyr. The remains of the commotal centre have been discovered in the **community** of **Rhosyr** and have been extensively excavated. The name survived as that of a post-**Acts of 'Union' hundred**.

MENAI BRIDGE (Porthaethwy), Isle of Anglesey
(343 ha; 3146 inhabitants)
A **community** located on the **Menai Strait**, the small town of Menai Bridge overlooks the dangerous currents of the Swellies. Before the construction of **Thomas Telford**'s suspension bridge (1826), it was the landing place of the most important of the six ferries across the Strait. Menai Bridge Fair or Ffair y Borth (24 October) was one of the bishop of **Bangor**'s fairs; originally held on the other side of the Strait, it was moved to the **Anglesey** side in the late 17th century. The community contains the four main **islands** of the Strait. Of these, Church Island, the site of St **Tysilio**'s church (15th century), can be considered to be Anglesey's pantheon, for on it are the graves of **Henry Rees**, **John Edward Lloyd** and **Albert Evans-Jones** (Cynan). Pili Palas is a butterfly farm.

Ysgol David Hughes, established at **Beaumaris** in 1603, was relocated at Menai Bridge in 1962. The town's growth was the result of its role as the gateway to Anglesey, but, with the Britannia Bridge (*see* **Pentir**) adapted in the 1970s to carry a **road**, the main route (the **A55**) into Anglesey now skirts **Llanfair Pwllgwyngyll**. The Welsh name comes from *porth* ('ferry' or 'crossing place') and *Daethwy*, the name of a **Celt**ic tribe associated with the area.

MENAI STRAIT, The
A narrow stretch of sea dividing **Anglesey** from mainland Wales, the Menai Strait marks the boundary between the Precambrian rocks making up much of Anglesey and the largely Cambrian and Ordovician rock of the neighbouring mainland. Deepened by the action of ice and meltwater during geologically recent Ice Ages, it attained its present form *c.*5000 BC, several thousand years after the end of the latest Ice Age, when the sea flooded in and Anglesey became an **island**.

The Menai Strait with the Menai Bridge

The Strait is about 20 km long and as narrow as 230 m in places; it has the appearance, therefore, of a broad **river**, which is reflected in its Welsh name, Afon Menai (River Menai). The tidal range is considerable – up to 8 m at **Beaumaris** – and the resulting currents are at their strongest between the Menai Bridge (opened 1826) and the Britannia Bridge (opened 1850), where they can reach speeds above 14 kph. But there are many sheltered places, above and below water, contributing to rich and internationally important habitats that support over 1000 species of marine animals and **plants** and are protected by an array of conservation designations.

The Strait has long had strategic importance. Segontium (**Caernarfon**) was built in part to ensure **Roman** control of its waters. Edward I commissioned the building of Caernarfon Castle at its western end, and Beaumaris Castle at its eastern end. In the 1770s, Belan fort (**Llandwrog**) was constructed to defend it. The Strait has provided **food** and a livelihood for local people for centuries, and **fish**ing still plays a part, particularly near **Bangor**, where there are substantial mussel beds. Tourist attractions along its shores include a sea zoo at Brynsiencyn (**Llanidan**) and boat cruises.

MENELAUS, William (1818–82) Engineer

Soon after Menelaus, a Scotsman, arrived as an engineer at the Dowlais Iron Company, **Merthyr Tydfil**, in 1851, he was put in charge of forges and mills, becoming works manager in 1856. The following year, he presented his influential Works Report, which laid down the conditions for the development of Dowlais, entailing the transference

Billy Meredith, football's first superstar

from wrought iron to steel production, supported by unstinting investment in the latest technology. He quickly became a major voice in the district's ironmaking fraternity, giving significant practical credence to Bessemer's steelmaking discoveries. In 1857, Menelaus helped to establish the South Wales Institute of Engineers, and was elected its first president. He was also prominent in the establishment of the **Iron and Steel** Institute, becoming its fourth president and succeeding such notables as the duke of Devonshire, Henry Bessemer and Isaac Lowthian Bell.

MERCHED Y WAWR (Daughters of the Dawn)

When head office of the **Women's Institutes** (WI) movement insisted on **English** as the official language of the WI in Wales, the members of Parc (**Llanycil**) WI broke away, in 1967, and began a new movement, Merched y Wawr, which would operate solely through the medium of **Welsh**. A voluntary, non-party-political organization, Merched y Wawr aims to promote **women**'s issues and to support culture, **education** and the arts in Wales. Merched y Wawr grew rapidly, gaining 10,000 members in some 275 branches within its first 20 years. Its magazine, *Y Wawr*, was launched in 1968 and an anthem, 'Fy Iaith, Fy Ngwlad' (My Language, My Land), was composed for the movement – by two men, **D. Jacob Davies** and Elfed Owen (1907–77). The creeping Christianization of the supposedly non-denominational movement caused some distress to its founder, Zonia Bowen (b.1926), an atheist who resigned in 1975 rather than face expulsion.

Over the years, members have campaigned on behalf of women's **health** issues, the disabled and women in the Third World (which has involved twinning with women in Lesotho); their promotion of the Welsh language has included support for learners and nursery schools. In 1994, a young members' section was launched and, in 2000, a national centre was opened at **Aberystwyth**. In 2007, the movement had about 6500 members.

MERCIA, Wales's associations with

Mercia was founded *c.*610 in the upper Trent valley in what would later be Staffordshire. Situated on the **border** between English and Welsh settlement, the name means **march**land. In 633, its pagan king, Penda, in alliance with **Cadwallon** of **Gwynedd**, killed Edwin, king of Northumbria. Christianized in the late 7th century, its religious centre was at Lichfield and its capital at Tamworth. In the 8th century, its kings won overlordship of all **England** south of the Humber, and King Offa (757–96) demarcated the border of Wales through commissioning the building of **Offa's Dyke**. Weakened in the 9th century by Danish invasions, by 920 Mercia had been annexed by Wessex and demoted to the status of an earldom. In the mid-11th century, its western parts were laid waste by **Gruffudd ap Llywelyn**, who allied with the outlawed Aelfgar, son of Leofric, earl of Mercia, and his wife Godiva. With the **Norman conquest**, Mercia ceased to be a political unit.

MEREDITH, Billy (William Henry Meredith; 1874–1958) Footballer

Voted the most popular player in football in 1904, Billy Meredith has been called the game's first superstar. He won a Welsh Cup medal with his hometown club, **Chirk**, but spent his entire professional career in Manchester, with City (1894–1905, 1921–4) and United (1907–21). Stanley Matthews is the only outfield player to exceed his 30-year career span, incorporating 670 league games – a record at the time. He appeared in an FA Cup semi-final when just short of 50, making him the competition's oldest player. A winger famed for the quality of his crossing, he was also a prolific goal scorer in the early part of his career. His 48 caps – all in the Home Championship – and 11 goals for Wales were both records at the time. A strong-minded individualist, Meredith was banned for 18 months from mid-1905 for offering bribes to an opponent.

MERFYN FRYCH (Merfyn ap Gwriad; d.844)
King of Gwynedd

Merfyn's mother, Esyllt, was descended from **Maelgwn Gwynedd**, and his father, Gwriad, probably of the royal lineage of the kings of **Man**, was said to be a descendant of **Llywarch Hen**. On the extinction of the male line of the descendants of Maelgwn in 825, Merfyn seized the throne of **Gwynedd**. He married Nest, of the royal house of **Powys**, and **Rhodri Mawr** was their son. Merfyn's court appears to have been a centre of culture.

MERIONETH (Sir Feirionnydd)
One-time county

Established as a **county** in 1284, Merioneth consisted of the *cantrefi* of **Meirionnydd** and **Penllyn** and the **commotes** of **Ardudwy** and **Edeirnion**. With **Caernarfonshire** and **Anglesey**, it constituted the **Principality** of north Wales. The **Act of 'Union'** of 1536 added the commote of **Mawddwy** and granted the county **parliamentary representation**; however, Merioneth was the sole Welsh county not to be granted a **borough** MP. Although both **Harlech** and **Bala** were medieval boroughs, no town in Merioneth gained borough status under the Municipal Corporations Act of 1835. Harlech was considered to be the county town, but following the establishment of county councils in 1889, the more centrally located **Dolgellau** became the seat of the council and of county administration. The county consisted of the **urban districts** of Bala, **Barmouth**, **Dolgellau**, **Ffestiniog** and **Tywyn**, and the **rural districts** of Deudraeth, Dolgellau, Edeirnion and Penllyn.

In 1974, Merioneth ceased to be. While most of it became the district of **Meirionnydd** in the new county of **Gwynedd**, Edeirnion became part of the **Glyndŵr** District in the new county of **Clwyd**. At the time of its loss of county status in 1974, Merioneth consisted of 170,931 ha and had 34,400 inhabitants.

The parliamentary constituency of Merioneth survived until 1983, at which time Edeirnion became part of the new constituency of Clwyd South, and the remainder of the former county, corresponding to the district of Meirionnydd, was combined with **Nant Conwy** to create the constituency of Meirionnydd Nant Conwy. In 2007, Nant Conwy was transferred to the newly created **Aberconwy** constituency, and Meirionnydd, together with the area covered by the former **Dwyfor** district, became the constituency of Dwyfor Meirionnydd.

Merlin the prophet dictating his predictions to a scribe, as depicted in a 15th-century woodcut

MERLIN (Myrddin) Legendary poet and prophet

Legendary material about Merlin, or rather, Myrddin, has been preserved in a series of vaticinatory, or prophetic, poems attributed to him in *The Black Book of Carmarthen* and *The Red Book of Hergest*, including the 'Afallennau', the 'Hoianau', 'Cyfoesi Myrddin a Gwenddydd ei Chwaer' and 'Gwasgargerdd Fyrddin yn y bedd'.

It appears from these difficult texts that Myrddin was a member of the court of Gwenddolau fab Ceido, who was killed at the Battle of Arfderydd in 573. Myrddin lost his reason as a result of a terrifying vision seen during the battle and fled to Celyddon Wood where he lived as a wild man in fear of Rhydderch, Gwenddolau's enemy. In his madness, he received the gift of **prophecy**. Scholars believe that the wild man theme of the Myrddin story is connected with the Irish poem about Suibne Gelt and with the tale of Lailoken preserved in the Life of St Kentigern. It is thought that the story originated in the **Old North** and that it was relocated in Wales, its protagonist being named Myrddin after the **place name** Caerfyrddin (**Carmarthen**). Myrddin adopted the role of a prophetic poet and was linked with **Taliesin** in the early poem 'Ymddiddan Myrddin a Thaliesin'.

Geoffrey of Monmouth, in *Historia Regum Britanniae*, created another Myrddin, a fatherless young boy with special powers, based on the figure of Ambrosius in *Historia Brittonum*. In his later poem, 'Vita Merlini', Geoffrey attempted to connect this character with the prophet of the Welsh tradition, which he had apparently learned about in the meantime. References by poets to Myrddin from the

10th century onwards reflect the popularity of the many tales about him which were current in medieval Wales. Under the name Merlinus (Merlin), created by Geoffrey of Monmouth, and by means of his association with **Arthur**, he became a mainstay of the Arthurian legend in mainland Europe.

MERLIN'S BRIDGE, Pembrokeshire
(674 ha; 2184 inhabitants)

Located immediately south of **Haverfordwest**, of which the **community**'s main settlement – the village of Merlin's Bridge – is essentially a suburb. The long-ruined St Magdalen's chapel may have been a late medieval leper sanctuary. The village's original name was from the chapel, recorded in 1564 as 'Mawdyn's Bridge' or Mawdlyn's Brydge', before being corrupted to its present form. Fragmentary Haroldston, one of the houses of the **Perrot** family, has 13th-century origins.

MERRICK, Rice (Rhys Meurug or Rhys Amheurug; c.1520–87) Historian
Owner of the Cottrell estate (**St Nicholas and Bonvilston**), his principal work is *A Booke of Glamorganshire Antiquities*, written between 1578 and 1584, but not published until 1825. The most important of the older accounts of the **county**, its portrayal of **Glamorgan**'s conquest by the **Normans**, and the description of Glamorgan society in the 16th century, are particularly valuable.

MERRIFIELD, Leonard (1880–1943) Sculptor
Although born in **England**, Leonard Merrifield, who studied with **Goscombe John**, played a large part in the monument-making process in Wales (*see* **Sculpture**). He created the figure of **William Williams** (Pantycelyn; 1717–91) for the National Hall of Fame in **Cardiff** City Hall and a number of monuments in **Merthyr Tydfil**. He is best remembered for his statue of the poet Hedd Wyn (**Ellis Humphrey Evans**) at **Trawsfynydd**.

MERTHYR CYNOG, Breconshire, Powys
(7202 ha; 257 inhabitants)

A **community** occupying much of **Mynydd Epynt** and extending to the **mountain**'s second highest point at Drwm Ddu (474 m). Much of it lies within the Epynt artillery range. The church is traditionally held to be the burial place of St Cynog, and the arms of Roger Vaughan of Ysgyr Fechan (mainly *c.*1670), the area's most substantial house, are engraved on a tombstone in the chancel. The churchyard is round, indicating a pre-Christian religious site. The orientalist David Price (1762–1835) was born in Merthyr Cynog.

MERTHYR MAWR, Bridgend
(1467 ha; 256 inhabitants)

The **community**, located immediately east of **Porthcawl**, is dominated by the vast dunes adjoining the estuary of the **Ogwr**. They were used in the **filming** of David Lean's 1962 epic *Lawrence of Arabia*, based on the life of Tremadog-born (**Porthmadog**) T. E. Lawrence. Sand has inundated much of the area, engulfing sites dating from the Mesolithic (*see* **Palaeolithic and Mesolithic Ages**) to the Bronze Age and threatening to envelop Candleston Castle, the 14th-century fortified manor house of the de Cantilupe family.

The village of Merthyr Mawr has picturesque vernacular houses and cottages, several of which are thatched. Unlike most of the villages of the **Vale of Glamorgan**, it has no recent intrusions. The attractive St **Teilo**'s church was rebuilt in 1851. Its churchyard contains a collection of 11th–12th-century headstones and a 5th-century inscribed stone pillar. Merthyr Mawr House, built in 1806 for the Nicholl family, is surrounded by an extensive park. Near it is the 15th-century chapel of St Roch. New Inn bridge is a medieval structure; New Bridge is a tower-like farmhouse of *c.*1600.

The compact village of Tythegston lies to the west of Merthyr Mawr. Its small church – of nave and chancel only – was restored by **John Prichard** in 1876. The village is notable for its fine grouping of 16th- and 17th-century houses and the uniformity with which these stand gable-end to the street. Tythegston Court was remodelled for the Knight family in the late 18th century.

MERTHYR RISING, The
The Merthyr Rising of June 1831 is one of the pivotal examples of workers' rebellion during the early **Industrial Revolution** and has an iconic significance in Welsh industrial history.

The background to the Rising was the tension arising from the attempt in 1831–2 to reform **parliamentary representation**. The mass of **Merthyr Tydfil**'s 22,000 inhabitants were enthusiastic reformers, and their demand for political rights and an improved standard of living was heightened by the distress resulting from the depression of 1829. In May 1831, William **Crawshay**, the owner of the Cyfarthfa **Iron**works, himself an ardent reformer, reduced wages and dismissed some of his employees. Following a mass meeting advocating parliamentary reform at Twyn y Waun above the town on 30 May, a large crowd assembled in the streets of Merthyr. Over the following days, houses and shops were ransacked, the Court of Requests (which was responsible for collecting small debts) was attacked and the red flag was raised aloft, the first time for the red flag to be raised in **Britain** – on one occasion the flag was a sheet soaked in the blood of a sacrificed calf. With magistrates, businessmen and ironmasters under siege in the Castle Hotel, the town was in the hands of the protesters – between 7000 and 10,000 of them – for six days. On 3 June, 68 soldiers were sent to Merthyr, and in the ensuing agitation at least 24 members of the public were shot dead and 16 soldiers were wounded. The protesters succeeded in disarming the yeomanry, which was sent from **Swansea**; but further soldiers, from the Argyll and Sutherland Highlanders, were sent to Merthyr, and by 7 June the authorities had restored control.

The Rising endures in popular memory because of the **execution** of Dic Penderyn (**Richard Lewis**) for wounding a soldier. Dic was innocent but despite a campaign to pardon him he was hanged in **Cardiff** on 13 August 1831, becoming a working-**class** martyr. The real leader of the revolt, Lewsyn yr Heliwr (**Lewis Lewis**; 1793–?1848), was also condemned to death, but his sentence was commuted to transportation for life.

MERTHYR TYDFIL (Merthyr Tudful)

County borough (11,102 ha; 55,981 inhabitants)

The **county borough** consists of twelve **communities**; *see below*.

Merthyr Tydfil was the *martyrium* or holy place of St Tydfil, reputedly the daughter of **Brychan**; the notion that she was martyred appears to have been invented by Iolo Morganwg (**Edward Williams**).

The town is better known in Wales and beyond as the **iron** manufacturing capital of the **Industrial Revolution**, some 13 centuries later than the time of Tydfil. Occupying the upper reaches of the **Taff** valley, its elevation varies from 100 m above sea level at its lowest southern point to over 400 m in the foothills of the **Brecon Beacons**. Its **geology** has been central to its modern history, for its rocks offered the **coal**, iron ore and **limestone** essential to the iron industry. Heavy rainfall (*see* **Climate**) fed the streams, which provided water power. Furthermore, the high water levels and the thin **soils** on the higher ground were factors in moving the area towards an industrial rather than a rural role.

Barrows, cairns, stone circles and mounds on the adjacent hillsides are evidence of human settlement dating back to at least the **Bronze Age**. The **Romans**, when building their **roads** through Wales, established a fort at Penydarren. In the immediate post-Roman centuries, the shrine of Tydfil probably became the centre for a small settlement. Situated in the *cantref* of **Senghennydd**, Merthyr was part of the early medieval kingdom of **Morgannwg**. Following the **Norman** invasion of the kingdom, Senghennydd remained under native Welsh rule until the late 13th century, when Gilbert de **Clare** made it subject to his castle at **Cardiff**. The elaborate but largely ruined Morlais Castle is proof of Clare power in the district.

Until the late 18th century, the large **parish** of Merthyr consisted of thinly populated agricultural land. Many of its inhabitants were attracted to religious dissent, with **Congregationalists** and **Quakers** establishing congregations by the late 17th century. The Methodist leaders John Wesley and **Howel Harris** both visited the parish. In 1749, Ynysgau became the first chapel to be built in Merthyr village. In the late 18th century, **Unitarian**ism attracted a number of adherents, a crucial factor in the **radical**ism of the district.

Small-scale industrial activities were carried on in the area from at least the 16th century. Iron was manufactured for local use, the woodlands providing the charcoal for the smelting process. Limestone and coal were raised from surface outcrops and **woollen** mills were established on the banks of the Taff and its tributaries. There were regular markets and fairs, dating from medieval times, notably the Waun Fair on the hillside above Dowlais.

Revolutionary change began in the mid-18th century. In 1748, Viscount Windsor, owner of the Cardiff Castle estate and lord of the **manor** of Senghennydd, agreed to lease out all the minerals of the commons of Senghennydd Uwch Caeach for 99 years at £23 a year. This was the foundation lease of the Dowlais Ironworks, which, after coming under the management of John **Guest** in 1760, rapidly expanded production, using coal rather than charcoal in the smelting

process. The cheap lease, the superabundance of coal and the availability of limestone and iron ore provided the ideal conditions for large-scale iron production. Similar factors aided the rise of the Cyfarthfa Iron Company, which, by the 1790s, had come into the possession of Richard **Crawshay**. He proved even more innovative than John Guest, adopting the **puddling** process of ironmaking, which enabled cast iron to be converted into wrought iron. While Dowlais and Cyfarthfa were the giants, there were also successful ironworks at Abercanaid – the Plymouth works on land leased from the earl of Plymouth of St Fagans Castle (*see also* Cardiff) – and at Penydarren.

The availability of raw materials and the resourcefulness of ironmasters were essential ingredients for success, but equally necessary were a skilled labour force and convenient access to markets. Workers poured into Merthyr, initially from neighbouring parishes and then from further afield. By 1801, Merthyr had a **population** of 7705, making it the most heavily populated parish in Wales. (In that same year, the built-up area of **Swansea**, which consisted of several parishes, had a population in excess of 10,000.) Convenient access to markets presented greater problems. Initially, the iron was carried to the **port** of Cardiff in panniers borne by **horses** and donkeys. A **road** for use by wagons was built in the 1770s, but the real breakthrough came with the building, in the 1790s, of the **Glamorgan**shire **Canal**, linking Merthyr with Cardiff. Although the canal's 52 locks caused the 38-km journey to be a lengthy one, a canal barge drawn by one horse

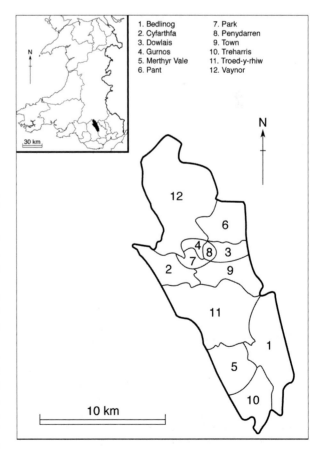

1. Bedlinog
2. Cyfarthfa
3. Dowlais
4. Gurnos
5. Merthyr Vale
6. Pant
7. Park
8. Penydarren
9. Town
10. Treharris
11. Troed-y-rhiw
12. Vaynor

The communities of the county borough of Merthyr Tydfil

The Dowlais Iron Company's locomotive *Fochriw*, 1896

could convey 25 tonnes, whereas a wagon drawn by four horses conveyed merely 2 tonnes.

The vastly enhanced ease of transport, together with the demand for iron created by the **French Revolutionary and Napoleonic Wars**, ensured the success of Merthyr's ironworks. On his death in 1810, Richard Crawshay was among the earliest of **Britain**'s industrialist millionaires. Although the market for iron declined with the coming of peace in 1815, new uses were found, particularly in construction work – the **Menai** Bridge chains, for example, were made at Penydarren. What would, in the 1840s, be Merthyr's chief product – iron rails – was presaged in 1804 with **Richard Trevithick**'s experiments in locomotion on the Penydarren tramroad. The opening in 1841 of the Taff Vale **Railway** linking Merthyr to Cardiff created even more of a revolution in transport than had the canal, for a train could convey to Cardiff in an hour more than a canal barge could convey in a month. These factors caused Merthyr to become the world's chief centre of ironmaking. Visitors considered the flames from its furnaces offered a vision of hell.

By 1851, Merthyr had 46,378 inhabitants (compared with 31,461 at Swansea, 19,323 at **Newport** and 18,351 at Cardiff) causing it to be by far the largest town in Wales. It proved a magnet to **Irish** immigrants, who comprised 10% of the population by the 1850s. Later immigrants included **Spaniards** and **Italians**. The number of inhabitants born in **England** was also significant, particularly among the wealthier townspeople, although Merthyr consistently had a majority of inhabitants born in Wales.

The town was urban rather than civic, for it did not have even a rudimentary administrative structure and it lacked the amenities associated with civic status. An almost exclusively working-**class** community, its overcrowded tiny terraced houses and the absence of efficient sewerage and of pure drinking water threatened its inhabitants with a variety of diseases. In the 1820s, 49.7% of the children born in Merthyr did not survive to the age of five, and there was a death toll of 1682 in the **cholera** epidemic of 1848–9.

The ironworks and their associated coalmines and levels could be lethal places, and Merthyr's problems were exacerbated by the fact that a high proportion of the townspeople were young unmarried men who had nowhere apart from the tavern to spend their leisure hours. Those problems were at their worst in the infamous China – a den of thieves and prostitutes along the Taff near the town centre. Yet, despite its drawbacks, migrants flocked to Merthyr, a comment upon the even worse living conditions in the countryside. Wages in the town were at least three times those of farm servants – even an ordinary labourer in Merthyr owned a watch. Houses were warm, for coal was cheap. The town offered the camaraderie of a mass society – a new experience for the Welsh. There was pride too – pride in understanding the ways of the furnace and the vagaries of the seam.

This mixture of deprivation and pride was at the root of the most dramatic episode in the town's history – the **Merthyr Rising** of 1831. The rising was shortly followed by the Reform Act of 1832, which – partly because of the unrest – granted Merthyr (along with **Aberdare**) a parliamentary seat, which from 1832 to 1852 was held by the **Whig** John Guest of Dowlais.

Despite its drawbacks, Merthyr developed a rich cultural life. Two milestone publications in the history of

Welsh culture – Charlotte Guest's **English** translation of *The Mabinogion* (1838–49) and **Thomas Stephens**'s *The Literature of the Kymry* (1849) – were the work of Merthyr residents. The process of 'civilizing the urban' was proceeding apace, with Merthyr's many **Nonconformist** chapels in particular greatly enriching the town's social and cultural life. Choirs proliferated, and Merthyr produced Wales's favourite composer, **Joseph Parry** (1847–1903).

There were attempts to cure Merthyr's ills. A report on the sanitary condition of the town, packed with nauseating detail, was published in 1850. A campaign to provide adequate sewerage and clean water ensued, marked in particular by the completion in 1858 of the Pentwyn **reservoir** on the Taf Fechan **River**. The sense of working-class solidarity, a central feature of the rising of 1831, found expression in *Y Gweithiwr/The Worker* (1834), Wales's first working-class **newspaper**, in the **Chartist** movement and in the growing support for **trade unionism** (*see* **Morgan Williams**). The Reform Act of 1867, which granted Merthyr an additional MP, increased the number of its voters from 1387 to 14,577, making it the most 'democratic' constituency in Britain. This dramatic enlargement led in 1868 to the victory of **Henry Richard**, whose success was the result of the support of his working-class, Nonconformist supporters.

As the 19th century advanced, Merthyr began losing its advantages as an ironmaking centre. Pig iron gave way to steel, which needed richer ores than those available locally, so Merthyr's works were burdened with the expense of conveying ore 38 km inland from Cardiff Docks. Dowlais was alone among the four great works in investing in steelmaking techniques. Although Cyfarthfa struggled on until 1910, Penydarren closed in 1859 and Plymouth had ceased production by 1880. Merthyr's population – 51,949 in 1861 – had declined to 48,861 in 1871. Many of Merthyr's skilled ironworkers migrated to the United States, where they were much in demand. Some left for Ukraine, where **John Hughes** (1814–99) of Merthyr established an ironworks in 1869.

In the mid-1870s, Merthyr achieved renewed prosperity following the sinking of deep shafts to veins of steam coal in areas south of the town, where the new coalmining communities of Merthyr Vale, Treharris and Bedlinog came into being. The increase in the number of coalminers strengthened trade unionism, especially following the establishment of the **South Wales Miners' Federation** in 1898. Working-class solidarity found expression in the election of 1900 when **Keir Hardie**, Wales's first **socialist** MP, gained 5745 votes at Merthyr, thus becoming the constituency's junior member. (The senior member, the **Liberal D. A. Thomas**, gained 8598 votes.) The buoyancy of the coal industry led to a further increase in population, which peaked at 80,990 in 1911. The town's size made it eligible to become a county borough, a status it achieved, after some controversy, in 1908.

The **First World War** saw some revival in the metalmaking industries of Merthyr, but the **depression of the interwar years** was a traumatic experience for the town. The Dowlais Company, which had established the **East Moors** Works at Cardiff in 1891, concentrated its investment there, and the greater part of the Dowlais works

closed in 1930. By 1932, unemployment among adult insured males at Dowlais was in excess of 80%, and the county borough as a whole had 13,000 families with no income from employment. The cost of employment benefit pushed up the rate levied to 27s 6d (137 pence today) in the pound, and the problems of taxing the employed to maintain the unemployed virtually bankrupted the corporation.

In 1935, a Royal Commission report recommended that Merthyr's county borough status should be abolished. No action was taken, however, for the Glamorgan **County** Council shuddered at the thought of being responsible for Merthyr. Those able to leave left, with Merthyr experiencing an out-migration of 27,000 between 1921 and 1939. The belief that employment could be obtained only through **emigration** to England was a severe blow to the **Welsh language**. Spoken by 50% of Merthyr's inhabitants in 1921, the proportion had declined to 25% in 1951. By then, knowledge of it was concentrated among the elderly, and, as their ranks were depleted, percentages plummeted. By the early 21st century, however, Welsh-medium schools had brought about some improvement in the language's fortunes.

The onset of the **Second World War** temporarily solved the unemployment problem. The post-war **Labour government** was determined to maintain full employment and it encouraged the establishment of the American-owned Hoover washing-machine plant at Abercanaid. The factory was taken over in 1995 by the Italian company Candy and by the early 21st century it provided far fewer jobs than it had in the 1970s. In the later 20th century, Merthyr came to rely increasingly upon light manufacturing firms, generally located on purpose-built trading estates and often providing more work for **women** than for men – a stark contrast with the iron and coal industries.

The town's geographical location makes it a convenient commuting centre for those taking advantage of the greater employment opportunities available in Cardiff and along the **M4**. Sited as it is on the edge of the Brecon Beacons **National Park**, Merthyr also has the potential to become a lucrative centre of **tourism**. However, following the completion of the by-pass in the 1990s, those approaching the park from the south could be forgiven for being scarcely aware that Merthyr exists at all.

Despite the blows suffered by Merthyr, its people have shown great resilience. Two of Wales's most distinguished novelists, **Jack Jones** and **Glyn Jones**, were natives of Merthyr. The Merthyr **rugby** team, a founder member of the Welsh Rugby Union, has had periods of success, and its **football** team was supreme in Wales in the 1950s. The sport in which Merthyr natives have excelled, however, has been **boxing**, with the successes of **Howard Winstone** and Dai Dower, and the sad fate of **Johnny Owen**, the 'matchstick man'.

Keir Hardie's victory in 1900 presaged the dominance that the Labour Party would achieve in Merthyr. Yet, other political views found expression, particularly in the 1930s when the town had advocates of the extremes of Left and Right. In 1974, the county borough ceased to exist and Merthyr, expanded by the addition of part of the former rural district of Vaynor and Penderyn, became a district of the county of **Mid Glamorgan**. In 1976, control of the district temporarily fell to **Plaid [Genedlaethol] Cymru**, the first such success for the party anywhere in Wales. In 1996, Mid Glamorgan was abolished and Merthyr once again became a county borough.

In 2001, 17.74% of the inhabitants of Merthyr Tydfil had some knowledge of Welsh, the percentages varying from 21.28% in Vaynor to 12.19% in Gurnos; 10.15% of the county borough's inhabitants were wholly fluent in the language.

Of all Wales's counties, Merthyr Tydfil has the smallest population – so small indeed that it has to be combined with **Rhymney** in order to create a viable parliamentary constituency.

The communities of Merthyr Tydfil

BEDLINOG (1521 ha; 3399 inhabitants)
The community embraces the basin of the Bargod Taf River. Its settlements came into existence to accommodate the employees of the Bedlinog and Taff-Merthyr collieries. During the struggle against **company unionism** in the 1930s, Bedlinog was the scene of much strife. The local primary school (1911) is, according to John Newman, 'a piece of abnormal fantasy'.

CYFARTHFA (705 ha; 6141 inhabitants)
Containing the settlements of Heolgerrig and Gellideg, the community reaches up to the summit of Mynydd Aberdâr (457 m). The engine-house of Cyfarthfa Ironworks at Ynysfach has been restored as a museum. Houses from Rhyd-y-car are now the favourite exhibit at the National History Museum (*see* St Fagans). (Cyfarthfa Castle is in the community of Park.)

DOWLAIS (331 ha; 3990 inhabitants)
Dowlais is the quintessential settlement of the heroic era of ironmaking. In the 1840s, when the Dowlais Iron Company had perhaps 5000 employees, its works were the largest in the world. Apart from an engine-house, which became a chocolate factory, the site of the works has been buried. The stable block (1820), built for the company's horses and now adapted as sheltered housing, is a monumental building. Dowlais House, where Charlotte Guest translated *The Mabinogion*, has been demolished, as has the neo-Gothic school she commissioned in 1855. However, the splendid Guest Memorial Library (1863), designed, like the school, by Charles Barry, survives. The Dowlais Great Tip once dominated the Merthyr scene.

GURNOS (153 ha; 5034 inhabitants)
Consisting of an extensive post-war housing estate, Gurnos is dominated by Prince Charles Hospital, begun in 1965.

MERTHYR VALE (Ynysowen)
(829 ha; 3925 inhabitants)
Straddling the Taff in the south of the county borough, the community contains the site of the appalling **Aberfan disaster**. Aberfan cemetery, where the victims of the disaster are buried, is the most poignant place in Wales.

PANT (749 ha; 2656 inhabitants)
Located north of the Heads of the Valleys road, the community contains the main station of the Brecon **Mountain** Railway, a reopened stretch of the **Brecon** to Merthyr Railway. Morlais Castle, erected in the 1280s by Gilbert de Clare, and the cause of a bitter dispute between him and Humphrey de **Bohun**, lord of Brecon, offers extensive views. A fine vaulted undercroft survives.

PARK (Y Parc) (206 ha; 4307 inhabitants)
Extending north of Pontmorlais Circle, the community is dominated by Cyfarthfa Castle, the castellated mansion built for William Crawshay in the 1820s. Latterly a school, now a museum, it contains fascinating material relating to the history of Merthyr. The castle provided a dramatic view of the Cyfarthfa Ironworks, located in the valley below. The vast furnace bank of the works survives. The iron aqueduct of Pont y Cafnau at Georgetown (1793) has been described as 'an innovation of international technological significance'. Almost as innovative was the Rhyd-y-car iron bridge, which has been re-erected near the aqueduct. Chapel Row has examples of Merthyr's early 19th-century ironworkers' houses, among them the birthplace of Joseph Parry. Georgetown was an early centre of the **Mormons** and is the location of Wales's largest Mormon church (1969).

PENYDARREN (113 ha; 5253 inhabitants)
Wedged between Cyfarthfa and Dowlais, its recreation ground is the site of the 2-ha auxiliary Roman fort built AD *c*.75 and occupied for about 50 years. The Penydarren Ironworks, the third in size of Merthyr's four great works, was founded by the **Homfray** family in 1784; the bases of its blast furnaces are still visible. Penydarren was the starting point of the tramroad used by Richard Trevithick for his 1804 experiment in locomotion.

TOWN (Y Dref) (764 ha; 6554 inhabitants)
The Town community lies east of the Taff and south of the road to Dowlais. It is rich in 19th-century chapel **architecture** and contains Wales's earliest purpose-built synagogue (1875). St Tydfil's church, reputedly located on the site of Tydfil's *martyrium*, has an attractive neo-Romanesque interior. Near it is a splendid cast-iron fountain canopy. Thomastown offered the closest that 19th-century Merthyr had to a middle-class enclave. The Castle Cinema, which closed in 2003, was built on the site of the Castle Hotel, opposite the old town hall and overlooking what was the focal point for the Merthyr Rising of 1831. The demolished mansion of Gwaelod-y-garth was the birthplace of the **Berry** brothers – Barons Camrose, Kemsley and Buckland.

TREHARRIS (806 ha; 6252 inhabitants)
The southernmost community of the county borough, it contains the burial ground that gave its name to **Quakers** Yard. The steepness and narrowness of the Taff valley at Treharris led to the construction there of a remarkable number of bridges and viaducts.

TROED-Y-RHIW (2116 ha; 5005 inhabitants)
Located immediately south of the town of Merthyr, the community contains Abercanaid, the site of the Plymouth

Ironworks, the smallest of Merthyr's four great works. The Triangle, a remarkable exercise in workers' housing built *c.*1800, was demolished in the 1970s. The Hoover Factory was built there in 1948, when it was hailed as the answer to Merthyr's unemployment problem. In 1804, the Penydarren tramway tunnel near Abercanaid became, on the occasion of Richard Trevithick's experiment, the world's first tunnel to be used by a locomotive. A mosaic plaque commemorates the occasion.

VAYNOR (Y Faenor) (2808 ha; 3465 inhabitants)

The northern thrust of the county borough, its settlements include Trefechan, built in 1947 as an integrated community. Yr Hen Dŷ Cwrdd, Cefn-coed-y-cymer, first built in 1747, was the centre of one of Wales's most influential Unitarian congregations. The Cefn railway viaduct (1866) is one of the finest in Wales. The massive gravestone of Robert Thompson Crawshay (*see* Crawshay family) in Vaynor churchyard bears the inscription 'God forgive Me'. The **Jew**ish burial ground adjoining the **A470** is the largest such burial ground in Wales.

METHODIST REVIVAL, The

An 18th-century evangelical revival that revitalized Christianity in several countries. It is impossible to say where it began. A revival broke out among the **Moravians** in Germany in 1727, and another under the ministry of Jonathan Edwards (1703–58) in Massachusetts in 1734.

In **Britain**, the conversion of **Howel Harris**, on Palm Sunday 1735, heralded its beginning, but George Whitefield (1714–70) and **Daniel Rowland** underwent similar spiritual experiences at about the same time, with **Howel Davies** and **William Williams** (Pantycelyn; 1717–91) following a few months later. However, it was not until May 1738 that John (1703–91) and Charles (1707–88) Wesley underwent their evangelical conversions, although many have argued that they had been under spiritual conviction long before that. As they were so devout and disciplined during their days at **Oxford**, they were dubbed 'Methodists' as early as 1732. Before long, the name was being used to describe anyone who appeared to be in sympathy with their beliefs.

The main characteristics of the Revival were powerful **preaching**, conversions, the gathering of converts in **society** meetings, and a distinct organization created from fear of ejection from the Church of **England** (*see* **Anglicans**). The leaders opposed any suggestion that they should leave voluntarily, the most zealous in their opposition being Howel Harris in Wales and Charles Wesley in England.

Though the leaders co-operated during the early years, it was not long before differences surfaced. George Whitefield and all the Welsh revivalists embraced **Calvinism**, while the Wesleys adopted an **Arminian** stance. John Wesley insisted that Calvinism led to antinomianism (the belief that by the dispensation of grace a Christian is

George Childs, *The Dowlais Works, Merthyr Tydfil* (1840)

released from the obligations of moral **law**), and therefore opposed it vigorously. This led to Wesley's separation from Whitefield in 1741(*see* **Wesleyans**).

The deaths of Rowland, William Williams and John Wesley in the early 1790s marked the end of the Methodist Revival. Its influence on Wales was immense, as it led to the establishment of a new **Nonconformist** denomination – the **Calvinistic Methodists** – and to the revitalization of the old dissenting churches.

MEYRICK, Gelly (*c.*1556–1601) Soldier

A **Pembrokeshire** man, he acquired estates in **Radnorshire** by marriage, making his home in **Gladestry**. He served as a soldier under the second earl of Essex (*see* **Devereux family**) and was executed for the active and prominent part he took in the Essex revolt of 1601.

MICHAELSTON-LE-PIT (Llanfihangel-y-pwll), Vale of Glamorgan (859 ha; 306 inhabitants)

Located immediately west of **Cardiff**, the **community** consists of the former civil **parishes** of Michaelston-le-pit and Leckwith. Its extensive woodlands are part of Cardiff's green belt. Of the two parish churches, only St Michael's (largely 14th century) is worth a visit. The mansion of Cwrtyrala, a neo-Georgian concoction (1939) by **Percy Thomas**, occupies a dramatic site. Its name comes from the Raleigh family, the late medieval owners of the site. The **Dinas Powys hill-fort** lies within the community's boundaries, as does part of the medieval Leckwith bridge.

MICHAELSTONE-Y-FEDW (Llanfihangel-y-fedw), Newport (664 ha; 316 inhabitants)

Located on the western boundary of the **county** of **Newport**, the **community** contains the junction between the M4 and **Cardiff**'s eastern approach **road**, but remains remarkably rural. In the substantial 13th-century church of St Michael is the burial chapel of the Kemeys-Tynte family of Cefn Mably (*see* **Rudry**). A sonnet by **W. J. Gruffydd** lamented that all that remained of the family was *ychydig lwch yn Llanfihangel draw* (a little dust yonder in Michaelstone). In the churchyard is the grave of a native of Michaelstone, Elizabeth Mackie. The grave was erected by her husband, Carl Hess. By a subsequent marriage, Hess became the father of Hitler's deputy, Rudolf Hess. The **Bronze Age** standing stone at Druidstone House is 2.7 m high.

MID GLAMORGAN (Morgannwg Ganol) One-time county

The county of Mid Glamorgan was established in 1974 following the abolition of the ancient **counties**. It consisted of what had been the **county borough** of **Merthyr Tydfil**, the **borough** of **Rhondda**, the **urban districts** of **Aberdare**, **Bridgend**, **Caerphilly**, **Gelligaer**, **Maesteg**, **Mountain Ash**, Ogmore and Garw (*see* **Ogmore Valley** and **Garw Valley**), **Pontypridd** and **Porthcawl**, the **rural districts** of **Llantrisant and Llantwit Fardre** together with Penybont and parts of the rural district of **Cardiff** (all in the one-time **Glamorgan**), the urban district of **Rhymney**, parts of the urban districts of Bedwas and Machen (*see* **Bedwas, Trethomas and Machen**) and **Bedwellty** and part

of the rural district of Magor and St Mellons (all in the one-time **Monmouthshire**) and part of the rural district of Vaynor and Penderyn (in the one-time **Breconshire**). It was divided into the districts of **Cynon Valley**, Merthyr Tydfil, **Ogwr**, Rhondda, **Rhymney Valley** and **Taff-Ely**. Abolished in 1996, it was replaced by the county boroughs of Bridgend, Merthyr Tydfil and **Rhondda Cynon Taff** and the western part of the county borough of **Caerphilly**.

MIDDLE, Pact of (1234)

A two-year truce agreed at Middle in **Shropshire** on 21 June 1234 between **Llywelyn ap Iorwerth** and Henry III. It involved the cessation of hostilities and a return to the pre-war state of affairs and it remained in force for the rest of the prince's life.

MILES, John (1621–83) Baptist pioneer

Born in **Erging**, **Herefordshire**, and educated at **Oxford**, Miles came to profess **Baptist** views during the 1640s and established his first church at **Ilston** in 1649. He created a network of fellowships at **Carmarthen**, **Llantrisant**, **Llanigon** and **Abergavenny**, becoming – with **Walter Cradock**, **Vavasor Powell** and **Morgan Llwyd** – a leader among the Welsh **Puritans**. He played a key part in the **Commonwealth**'s political settlement in Wales. Then, on the restoration of the monarchy in 1660, he emigrated to **North America**. By that time, the foundation for the later growth of the Baptist movement had been laid, principally by Miles. In Massachusetts, he founded the settlement of Swanzey (now Swansea), where he died. He belonged to the 'Particular' or **Calvinist** wing of the Baptists.

MILFORD HAVEN (Aberdaugleddau or Milffwrd), Pembrokeshire (1540 ha; 13,086 inhabitants)

Located on the north shore of the Haven whose name it shares (*see* **Milford Haven Waterway**), the **community** contains the town of Milford and the villages of Hakin, Hubberston, Liddeston, Steynton and Thornton. There is a large **Iron Age** fortified farmstead near Thornton. Pill priory was established *c.*1200 as a cell of the Abbey of **St Dogmaels**; the church's lofty chancel arch and a barrel vault in the adjoining house survive. Until the 1790s, the main settlements were the villages of Hubberston and Steynton, where there are heavily restored medieval churches.

The town of Milford was founded in 1790, when an Act of Parliament authorized Sir William Hamilton – husband of Lord Nelson's Emma – to build 'Quays, Docks, Piers and other erections'. The original plan, overseen by Hamilton's nephew, Charles Greville, was to develop a major whaling **port** manned by **Quaker** whalers from Nantucket, Massachusetts. A visit to the Quaker burial ground, where the graves are inscribed solely with initials, is a moving experience. (It is paradoxical that so pacific a people followed so bloody an occupation.)

Despite the boost given to Hamilton's plans by Horatio Nelson's visit in 1802, the ambitious scheme for a port to rival **Liverpool** never fully materialized. The coming of the **railway** in 1863 led to grandiose plans for a Manchester to Milford railway, but they came to very little. The Milford

Docks Company was formed in 1874 and the docks (completed in 1889) were adapted to the **fish**ing industry. Milford thrived as a fishing port until the 1950s, landing 60,000 tonnes of fish in 1946. The £1.5 million Milford Fish Auction, established in 1998, suffered huge financial losses and closed down in 2003. The town's grid pattern, with its three parallel streets, was probably designed by the **Swansea** architect **William Jernegan**. St Katherine's church (1802–8) seems from the outside to be the dullest church in Wales; inside, it is a remarkable example of Georgian Gothic. A **granite** memorial commemorates the 700 Belgian trawlermen who found refuge in the town during the **First World War**. The one-time Custom House (*c.*1794) – probably the work of Jernegan – houses the town museum.

In 1960, as the fishing industry declined, Esso built an **oil** refinery to the west of the town. Over the following 13 years, BP, Texaco, Gulf and Amoco also built oil installations in the neighbourhood. Only the refinery of Texaco refinery at **Hundleton** and that of Elf-Murco on the former Amoco site at **Walwyn's Castle** are still operative. Nevertheless, Milford Haven remains the busiest port in Wales, and the sixth busiest in **Britain**, handling 33.8 million tonnes of cargo in 2001. The Cutty Sark Tall Ships Race was held at Milford in 1991. The Torch Theatre (1970) is one of Wales's liveliest centres of **drama**.

MILFORD HAVEN WATERWAY, The (Aberdaugleddau), Pembrokeshire

No less a person than King **Arthur** visited Milford Haven, according to the legend of 'Culhwch ac Olwen' in *The Mabinogion*. The haven is a ria or drowned valley, formed as the sea level rose gradually following the retreat of ice sheets of the most recent Ice Age. Its present form dates from *c.*7000 years ago when the lower reaches of the **Cleddau** Wen and Cleddau Ddu, and tributaries below their confluence, were drowned by the sea. As a result, the tide extends as far as **Haverfordwest**, 36 km from the mouth of the estuary. The estuary has a tidal range of 7.5 m, and the channel in its western part is over 18 m deep.

The Haven's naval and commercial possibilities were not exploited until the 1790s, when William Hamilton established the town of **Milford Haven** on its shores. Horatio Nelson, on a visit in 1802, considered the Haven to be second only to Trincomalee in Ceylon among the world's great waterways. His comment was an encouragement to those who established the **Pembroke Dock** Royal Dockyard in 1814. In the 1860s, fear of invasion led to the fortification of the Haven (*see* **Palmerston's Follies**). More extensive commercial utilization came in the 1960s with the implementation of plans to develop the Haven as **Britain**'s chief **oil** port.

MILITARY BASES

The advent of the **Second World War** saw the establishment of a number of military bases in Wales. Military airfields were constructed at **St Athan** and around the coast at **Tenby** (actually in **Carew**), **Brawdy**, **St David's** (actually in **Solva**), **Tywyn**, **Llanbedr**, Penrhos (**Llanbedrog**), **Llandwrog** and **Valley** (actually in **Llanfair-yn-neubwll**), while a

research institution was established by the air force at **Aberporth**. Because of the high rate of accidents among wartime trainees, the first **Mountain** Rescue Service Unit was formed at RAF Llandwrog in 1942, but was later transferred to RAF Valley. Although some of the smaller airfields were closed after the war, stations such as RAF Valley, RAF Brawdy and RAF St Athan remained in operation as flight training schools and aircraft maintenance units. Wartime demands led to the construction of armaments depots in Wales, several of which remained in operation in peacetime. Munitions were stored at the Royal Naval Armaments Depots at **Trecŵn**, **Milford Haven** and **Johnston**, while a Royal Naval Stores Depot was established at **Llangennech**.

The Ministry of Defence requisitioned thousands of hectares of land in Wales for military training – an act which was strongly opposed by many Welsh patriots. In 1940, over 200 people were evicted from their homes on **Mynydd Epynt**, in order to establish a firing range at Sennybridge (**Maescar**), while land at **Castlemartin** was designated a training site for live firing. Between 1961 and 1996, Castlemartin was used as a training ground by German 'Panzer' tank battalions. Since the 1990s, there has been a drastic curtailment in **government** spending on defence, and several military bases in Wales, notably in **Pembrokeshire**, have been closed, resulting in the loss of hundreds of civilian jobs. The RAF base at **Penyberth** proved to be short-lived; it was the location of the best-known protest against a military installation in Wales.

MILLAND, Ray (Reginald Truscott-Jones; 1907–86) Actor

The most prolific and consistent of all Welsh screen stars and second-leads, **Neath**-born Milland was the first Welshman to win the Oscar for best actor, for Billy Wilder's *The Lost Weekend* (1945), in which he gave the performance of his career as a writer ravaged by alcoholism. Milland made his **film** debut in 1929 and played minor roles in British films before arriving in Hollywood, where he performed in serviceable, lightweight comedies, his good looks and hauteur making him a popular male support for numerous female stars. He played in *Three Smart Girls* (1937), a Deanna Durbin vehicle that helped rescue the financially ailing Universal studios, and in the same year appeared as Sapper's hero in *Bulldog Drummond Escapes*. From the 1940s, he played more challenging roles – notably the amnesiac enmeshed in espionage in Fritz Lang's *Ministry of Fear* (1944), and a charmer mixed up with a flighty, underage girl (Ginger Rogers) in *The Major and the Minor* (1942). Milland starred in two other significant 1940s films, the ghost story *The Uninvited* (1944) and the thriller *The Big Clock* (1948). He was typically urbane but persuasively sinister in Hitchcock's only 3-D film, *Dial M for Murder* (1954). Milland filmed in Wales just once – in Jacques Tourneur's substandard thriller *Circle of Danger* (1951).

As Milland's patrician good looks faded, he turned to directing, making four features, including *The Safecracker* (1958), from a **Rhys Davies** short story, and the praised but reactionary **drama** of nuclear menace *Panic in the Year Zero* (1962). Milland later excelled in roles for Roger

Ray Milland

construction of the new standards in 1843 and subsequently to the new Royal Commission. Elected FRS in 1838, Miller was the Society's foreign secretary (1856–73) and was awarded the Royal Medal in 1870, the year that he was appointed to the Commission Internationale du Metre.

MILLS, Robert Scourfield (Arthur Owen Vaughan, Owen Rhoscomyl; 1863–1919) Adventurer and writer

Owen Rhoscomyl was born in Southport and brought up at **Tremeirchion**. He ran away to sea at the age of 15 and, following his adventures in the American Wild West, he distinguished himself as commander of a troop of cavalry in the Boer War (*see* **South African Wars**). His chief mission as an author was to demonstrate Wales's contribution to the formation of the British Empire; his most famous book is *Flamebearers of Welsh History* (1905), one of the earliest modern histories of Wales to be written from a forthrightly patriotic viewpoint. The same fervour inspired his scripting of the National Pageant of Wales, held at **Cardiff** Castle in 1909.

MINERA (Mwynglawdd), Wrexham
(1177 ha; 1608 inhabitants)

Located west of **Wrexham**, the **community** embraces the upper reaches of the Clywedog valley. The earliest surviving record of the name Minera (Low **Latin** for 'mine') dates from 1343; the name Mwynglawdd (a mine) dates from 1700. Both names indicate the exploitation of the area's mineral wealth, its **lead** ore in particular. Minera is the starting point of the Clywedog Trail, which takes walkers on a tour through the industrial heritage of the valley and terminates at King's Mills (*see* **Wrexham**). The visitor centre at Minera Country Park provides access to restored 18th- and 19th-century buildings associated with lead mining. The **cave** system, discovered in 1964 in the upper part of the community, has been declared a site of special scientific interest.

MINERS' FEDERATION OF GREAT BRITAIN (MFGB), The

Founded at **Newport** in 1889, its aims were the eight-hour day and the abolition of the sliding scale, which controlled wages. The north Wales miners affiliated to the new union, as did around 6000 **Monmouthshire** miners led by **William Brace**. The majority of miners in south Wales, led by **William Abraham** (Mabon), did not join immediately because they supported the sliding scale. With the formation of the **South Wales Miners' Federation** in 1898, the stage was set for Mabon to take his followers into the MFGB, a union that they were soon controlling. The federation became the **National Union of Mineworkers** in 1945.

MINERS' INSTITUTES

Miners began to contribute towards the building and running of their own institutes from the 1890s onwards. By c.1910, almost every town and large mining village had its own institute, complete with reading room and library, in some cases financially assisted by the local **coal**owner.

Corman, the producer-director of horror exploitation films, appearing in *Premature Burial* (1962) and *The Man With X-Ray Eyes* (1963).

MILLER, W[illiam] H[allowes] (1801–80)
Crystallographer

The founder of modern crystallography, Miller was born at Felindre (**Llangadog**). He graduated in **mathematics** at **Cambridge**, and soon became concerned with the application of mathematics to the various **sciences.**

Appointed to the Cambridge chair of mineralogy in 1832, his name is connected with two branches of scientific work. Firstly, his *Treatise on Crystallography* (1839) formulated crystallographic theory in a way which, though based on the work of others, including his predecessor William Whewell, was particularly his own; what came to be known as 'Miller's system' dominated 19th-century crystallography, and even today it is a major influence. Miller's system permitted the working out of all the problems that a crystal can present, in a form that appealed at once to the sense of symmetry of the mathematician.

Secondly, he was the main force in the re-establishment of the parliamentary standards of measurement and weight, following the fire that destroyed the Houses of Parliament in 1834 and ruined the existing standards. He was appointed to the **government** committee overseeing the

Aneurin Bevan attributed his intellectual training to the **Tredegar** miners' library. Following the recommendation of the Royal Commission on Coal (1919), a Miners' Welfare Fund was established to provide amenities for the miners – baths, welfare halls and scholarships. The interwar years saw the construction of welfare halls in those areas which had no institute, especially in the anthracite coalfield.

By the eve of the **Second World War**, there were over 100 miners' institutes in Wales, among the most attractive of which was that at **Rhosllanerchrugog** (Y Stiwt, 1926). The biggest was that at **Abercynon** (1904, demolished 1995), and the most impressive is the Park and Dare (1905, 1913) in Treorchy (*see* **Rhondda**).

The institutes and halls survived into the 1970s, run jointly by management and miners, with representation from members of the general public. Many miners' libraries are preserved at the South Wales Miners' Library, **Swansea**. The Oakdale Institute, complete with library, has been re-erected at the National History Museum (*see* **St Fagans**).

MINERS' MEDICAL AID SOCIETIES

From the 1890s, workers in many parts of industrial Wales clubbed together to employ a doctor. By the 1920s, most of the clubs' members made a weekly contribution and, in some cases, the general public was eligible to join. Members could call on the services of a number of doctors,

specialists and free facilities in the hospitals. It was an embryonic national **health** service, a working-**class** initiative, sometimes aided by colliery companies, aiming at making sickness a communal burden. Disputes often arose over the running of the societies and over the rights of members who had become unemployed.

Among the best known of the societies was that at **Tredegar**, which **Aneurin Bevan** stated was his inspiration when he created the National Health Service (*see* **Welfare State**).

MINERS' NEXT STEP, The

The Miners' Next Step, published in Tonypandy (**Rhondda**) in 1912, is the most famous of all Welsh pamphlets. It was written mainly by **Noah Ablett**, assisted by a small group who had been involved in the **Plebs' League** and the Cambrian Combine strike of 1910–11 and who were active in the Unofficial Reform Committee. A sustained critique of the cautious leadership of **William Abraham** (Mabon), it made immediate demands with regard to wages and hours, but more spectacularly went on to offer a new concept of 'scientific' **trade unionism** and a vision of a union-controlled industry in which the employers would be 'eliminated'.

Although the so-called **Syndicalists** were never to control their own union, the anger and confidence they generated ensured that the miners of south Wales dominated British industrial relations in the turbulent era down to

Oakdale Miners' Institute library in 1945

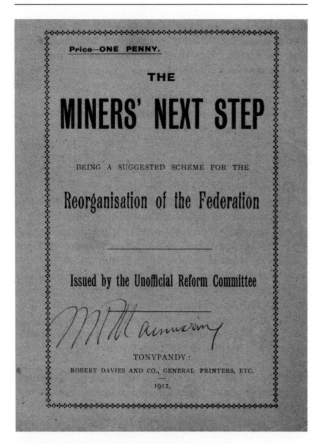

The title page of *The Miners' Next Step*

1926. *The Miners' Next Step* was unrivalled as a statement of the potential of trade unions to become instruments of political revolution.

MINERS' STRIKES

The reputation for being strike-prone that Welsh miners were to earn in the early 20th century was not undeserved. Strikes and lockouts had been endemic in Wales since the inception of the **Industrial Revolution**, with the miners following a tradition established initially by the **iron**workers. The south Wales **coal**field was adjudged to be at a standstill at various times in 1816, 1822, 1830, 1832 and then again in 1847, 1853, 1857 and 1867. The greatest strikes were organized under the auspices of the Amalgamated Association of Mineworkers in 1871, 1873 and, finally, in 1875, when a lockout ended in victory for the employers. Strikes could also be bitter in the northern coalfield, where there were severe troubles in 1830–1 and 1869, and again in the 1870s and 1880s.

The **South Wales Miners' Federation** (SWMF) was founded during a six-month lockout in 1898; it joined the **Miners' Federation of Great Britain** in 1899. A conciliation board was established in 1902 and it was opposition to the decisions of that board which led to the emergence of a new generation of agitators in the south and to their tactic of direct action. Although the **North Wales Miners' Union** had joined the British federation in 1889, its members proved to be less militant. The Cambrian Combine dispute of 1910–11 (*see* **Tonypandy Riots**) began a new era in which Welsh miners' leaders set the agenda for miners

throughout **Britain**. There followed the Minimum Wage strike of 1912, the Welsh wartime strike of July 1915 and the strike of 1920.

Up to that point, Welsh-inspired militancy had seemed to pay off. The miners had preserved their standard of living, created the possibility of changing the nature of the industry (by converting wartime state control into some system of joint control) and sustained the threat of union solidarity – in the shape of the Triple Alliance of miners, **railway**men and dockers. The militant position, however, was totally undermined by the collapse of the boom that followed the **First World War**. The **government** resolved to return the pits to the owners, who were determined to drive down wages. The miners' partners in the Triple Alliance decided to err on the side of caution, leaving the miners isolated. The failure of the 1921 lockout was followed by the disaster of the 1926 **General Strike**, after which the miners were locked out for eight months. The prosperity and confidence of mining communities collapsed.

The miners, not least in Wales, began a long period of rethinking tactics and, although stay-down and short local strikes were used throughout the ensuing decades, it was not until the 1970s that coal strikes again appeared in the news headlines. By that time, there were only 36,000 miners in south Wales, and some 2000 in the north; but there was enthusiastic support for the strikes of 1972 and 1974, which brought about higher wages as well as the downfall of a **Conservative** government – and there was even talk of 1926 having been revenged.

The story, however, was to turn to tears, for by the time of the strike against pit closures in 1984–5 several new realities were evident. The miners were then led from Yorkshire and the decision to call a strike reflected the influence of Arthur Scargill, the president of the **National Union of Mineworkers**. A majority of Welsh miners voted against striking – there was no Britain-wide vote – but a strike ensued and lasted for a year. It was a traumatic experience which helped to shape a new Welsh politics in which **women**'s groups were remarkably prominent, and in which there was a coming together of trade unionists and a number of Welsh radical and **nationalist** groups.

The widely reported march back to work by the men at Maerdy (**Rhondda**) – with their band playing and banners flying – marked the end of an era in Wales. The pit at Maerdy was soon to be closed, as indeed were almost all the remaining collieries (*see also* **Tower Colliery**).

MINERS' UNIONS

The earliest evidence of a **trade union** among **coal**miners in Wales comes from **Bagillt** (**Flintshire**), where a branch of the Friendly Associated Coal Miners' Union was established in 1830. Further branches were founded in and around **Merthyr Tydfil** in 1831 but, within a few months, unionism had been killed by employer hostility, a fate that also befell the unions established in the mid-1830s under the inspiration of **Robert Owen** (1771–1858). The Amalgamated Association of Mineworkers, founded in Lancashire in 1869, had attracted a Welsh membership of 45,000 by 1873, but the association collapsed following the employers' lockout of 1875. It was succeeded by district unions; the most important of these was the **Rhondda**'s

Cambrian Miners' Association, which appointed **William Abraham** (Mabon) in 1877 as its full-time organizer. In 1875, a system was adopted whereby wages in the southern coalfield rose and fell in accordance with the price of coal. This was the sliding scale system, which – as it precluded bargaining over wages – offered little scope for union development. Thus, the unions of south Wales, unlike the **North Wales Miners' Association** founded in 1886, kept aloof from the **Miners' Federation of Great Britain**, founded in 1889 – an organization opposed to sliding scale agreements.

In 1898, seven district associations joined together to form the **South Wales Miners' Federation** (the Fed). As its aims included the abolition of the sliding scale – an aim achieved in 1903 – the Fed became affiliated to the British federation in 1899. The Fed dominated Welsh trade unionism until it was absorbed by the **National Union of Mineworkers** in 1945. In addition to the Fed, there were also **company unions** and smaller unions, most of which reflected the variety of distinct craft and supervisory jobs in the coal industry. The South Wales and **Monmouthshire** Colliery Enginemen, Stokers' and Craftsmen's Association, founded in 1889, merged with the Fed in 1921. In 1895, the South Wales and Monmouthshire Colliery Enginemen's Association was founded, an organization which did not join the South Wales Area of the NUM until 1948. At various times, there were in south Wales a Colliery Examiners' Association, a Master Hauliers' Association, a National Association of Colliery Managers, a National Union of Clerks, a South Wales Colliery Officials Union and, as has been already noted, a South Wales and Monmouthshire Colliery Enginemen,

Boilermen and Craftsmen's Association. In the north, there was also a range of organizations, some of which were part of the unionism of the Lancashire coalfield.

Issues arising from differences of craft and grade within the industry were illustrated by the role of the National Association of Colliery Overseers, Deputies and Shotfirers (NACODS) during the **Coal Strike** of 1984–5. The traditional enmity between the NUM and the 'gaffers' union' was exacerbated by the refusal of NACODS to join the strike, although the majority of its members, who had grievances of their own, did not cross picket lines. By the beginning of the 21st century, the virtual disappearance of the coal industry meant that miners' unions, once a fundamental factor in the life of Wales, were of minimal significance.

MINT, The Royal

Established by Alfred, king of **England**, in 886, the Mint was located in the Tower of **London** for 500 years from the end of the 13th century before moving to Tower Hill in 1810. Preparatory to the adoption of decimal currency in 1972, a new building housing the Mint was opened at **Llantrisant** in 1968; minting was progressively moved to Llantrisant from Tower Hill, which minted its last coins in 1975. The Mint produces circulating **coins** for some 100 countries, as well as official medals, **seals** and commemorative coins. Despite the existence of the so-called **Hywel Dda** penny, there is no evidence that Welsh rulers minted coins.

MISKIN (Meisgyn) Commote

A subdivision of **Penychen**, the **commote** extended from the Cynon valley to that of the **Ely**. The name survives in the village of Miskin (**Pont-y-clun**). Following the **Acts of**

Mounted police confronting striking miners at Tonypandy, 12 November 1910

'Union', Miskin became one of the **hundreds** of **Glamorgan**. In the early years of the **Industrial Revolution**, the **manor** of Miskin provided the **Aberdare** area with a rudimentary form of local **government**.

MISSIONARIES

Wales's first evangelists were the 5th- and 6th-century missionary **saints** of the dawn of **Cel**tic Christianity. They evangelized in their homeland and also in **Ireland**, **Brittany**, **Cornwall** and Galicia (*see* **Celtic Church**). Following the **Protestant Reformation**, a number of **Roman Catholic** priests saw themselves as missionaries. During the **Methodist Revival**, the work of **Howel Harris**, **Daniel Rowland** and **William Williams** (Pantycelyn; 1717–91) was characterized by missionary zeal. Having revitalized Christianity in Wales, Welsh **Nonconformists** began to focus their attention on the spiritual condition of 'the perishing heathen' elsewhere. Although, to quote the English missionary Jacob Tomlin, it was perceived among Protestant missions that 'the great foes to Christ and his gospel [were] the Pope, Mahomed and Brahma', it was axiomatic that missionary endeavour was generally more fruitful among adherents of minority faiths than among subscribers to major **religions** such as **Islam** and Hinduism.

The first Welsh evangelist of the new missionary age was probably Thomas Coke (1747–1814), a **Brecon**-born

Wesleyan Methodist who went to the West Indies in 1786; he later set sail for India, but died on the voyage. Missionary life was fraught with danger, and missionaries, to many, were heroes; accounts of their exploits were eagerly anticipated by the home readership of such **periodicals** as *Y Drysorfa Ysbrydol* and congregations were encouraged to make regular donations to the missionary cause.

Initially, it was through missionary societies founded outside Wales that Welsh missionaries were deployed, among them the non-denominational London Missionary Society (LMS), launched in 1795. The leading Welsh supporter of the LMS was **Thomas Charles** of **Bala**, who was made a director in 1797. The LMS's first missionary was **John Davies** (1772–1855), who left for Tahiti in 1800. But the 'brethren in distant lands' who initially most concerned the Welsh were the presumed descendants of **Madog ab Owain Gwynedd** in **North America** and their Celtic cousins 'lost' to Roman Catholicism, in Brittany and Ireland. The Madog enthusiasm waned, but a small number of missionaries were sent to Brittany and Ireland, and also to the **Jews** in **London**; few converts were made.

It was in Africa, Asia and the South Seas that the Welsh made their biggest mark, increasingly through their own mission societies. The main fields for the **Congregationalists** were the South Sea Islands, India, China and

A gathering of Welsh missionaries at Shillong in the Khasi Hills, India, 1935

Madagascar. Two Welshmen with enormous influence in China were **Griffith John** and **Timothy Richard**, a missionary statesman who effectively ruled the country for a time. In the **Khasi Hills** in north-east India the **Calvinistic Methodists** developed a model mission field. India was also an important field for the **Baptists**. Notable Welsh missionaries in Africa include William Davies (1784–1851), a prominent early Wesleyan in Sierra Leone; and Thomas Lewis (1859–1929), who was active for the Baptists in the Cameroons and Congo.

By the mid-20th century, with both the British Empire and the chapels in rapid decline, most of Wales's classic missionary activity had ceased. But in little more than 150 years, Welsh missionaries had succeeded in converting hundreds of thousands of people to Christianity, far beyond the confines of their own land. If, in the process, they sometimes did damage to other people's cultures, they also made valuable contributions by, for instance, committing languages to writing, building schools and hospitals, and equipping their host communities with the political means to make their way in the modern world.

In the late 19th century, as allegiance to institutional **religion** declined, there was renewed emphasis upon the home mission with organizations such as the Salvation Army, the Church Army and the Forward Movement of the Calvinistic Methodists. In addition, Breton Roman Catholics sent a mission to Wales and many of the **Irish** priests in Wales saw themselves as missionaries. **Mormon** missionaries have been active in Wales since 1845.

MITCHEL TROY (Llanfihangel Troddi), Monmouthshire (4464 ha; 1159 inhabitants)

Lying immediately south-west of **Monmouth**, the **community** constitutes the basin of the **River** Trothy. There are attractive restored medieval churches at Mitchel Troy, Dingestow, Cwmcarvan and Wonastow. Dingestow Court, the seat of the Huguenot Bosanquet family, was one of the **county's** major **gentry** houses. Its library contained a fine **Welsh** version of **Geoffrey of Monmouth's** *Historia*; it was published as *Brut Dingestow* (ed. **Henry Lewis**) in 1942. The area is rich in 16th- and 17th-century houses. Treowen is **Monmouthshire's** most important early 17th-century mansion. Troy House, built for the dukes of Beaufort (*see* **Somerset family**), is a massive 17th-century pile. There is an elaborate 20th-century **garden** at High Glanau near Cwmcarvan.

MOCHDRE, Conwy (282 ha; 1862 inhabitants)

Located on **limestone** ridges south of the **A55**, the **community** contains the westernmost suburbs of **Colwyn Bay**.

MOCHDRE, Montgomeryshire, Powys (2605 ha; 482 inhabitants)

A **community** located immediately south-west of **Newtown**, the name ('place of **pigs**') first occurs in 1200. It is not too fanciful to suggest that it was at Mochdre, 'between **Ceri** and Arwystli' (*see* **Arwystli**), that **Pryderi** and **Gwydion** spent the night with their swine on their journey through Wales (*see* **Mabinogion, The**). All **Saints'** church, extensively renovated in 1867, retains its fine early 16th-century roof. Two medieval wooden figures of Christ and the Virgin from the church are in the **National Museum**.

MOCHNANT Commote

Comprising the basin of the **River** Mochnant, the **commote** was divided in the late 12th century between Uwch Rhaeadr in **Powys Wenwynwyn** and Is Rhaeadr in **Powys Fadog**, a division that survived the creation of **Montgomeryshire** and **Denbighshire** in 1536 and of the **counties** of **Powys** and **Clwyd** in 1974. In 1996, the two civil **parishes** called Llanrhaeadr-ym-Mochnant were united to form the single **community** of **Llanrhaeadr-ym-Mochnant**. The ancient commote consisted of that community and those of **Llangynog**, **Llanwddyn** and **Pen-y-Bont-Fawr**.

MOEL SIABOD Mountain

The easternmost of **Snowdon's** neighbours, Moel Siabod (872 m) rises like a great beast from **Capel Curig**. Its summit and rugged spurs are carved out of a mass of dolerite – a dark igneous rock mined for hone (whetstone used for sharpening tools). The **mountain's** narrow north-eastern ridge is a fine example of an arête. The lack of high mountains in its immediate vicinity means that the summit offers an unrivalled vista of the peaks of Snowdon, **Y Carneddau** and **Glyder Fawr, Glyder Fach, Y Garn, Elidir Fawr and Tryfan**.

MOELFRE, Isle of Anglesey (1390 ha; 1129 inhabitants)

Located on **Anglesey's** east coast, the **community** contains the seaside resort of Moelfre and the village of City Dulas, where there is a monument to the **Morris brothers**. There is a long history of human settlement in the area. Lligwy **Neolithic** tomb has a massive capstone; the Din Lligwy hut group dates from AD *c.*300; the ruined Hen Gapel Lligwy was probably built *c.*1120; Penrhoslligwy was the administrative centre of the medieval **commote** of Twrcelyn.

In October 1859, Moelfre was the scene of one of 19th-century **Britain's** worst **shipwrecks** – that of the *Royal Charter*. Many of the 452 victims were buried in Llanallgo churchyard, where there is a memorial to them. Moelfre has a strong **seafaring** tradition and local men have found their way all over the world. Its **lifeboat** has a long and distinguished record of saving lives; a local coxswain, **Richard Evans**, was twice awarded the gold medal of the Royal National Lifeboat Institution (*see* **Lifeboats**).

MOLD (Wyddgrug, Yr), Flintshire (642 ha; 9568 inhabitants)

Mold was recognized as **Flintshire's county** town in 1833, the year in which a **Bronze Age** cairn near the **River** Alyn yielded the Mold Cape, the most astonishing **gold**work ever discovered in **Britain**. (Held by the British Museum, its repatriation to Wales may yet become a political issue.)

Located within the **commote** of Ystrad Alun, part of the territories of the rulers of **Powys**, Mold was seized *c.*1090 by Robert de Montalt. The **Normans'** attempt to translate Gwyddgrug (*gŵydd* 'cairn', *crug* 'hillock') may have eventually given rise to the name Mold (from medieval **French** *mont-hault* 'high hill'), although the name may recall a place in Normandy. De Montalt's motte-and-bailey castle, the mound of which survives, was frequently seized by the princes of **Gwynedd**. By the late 15th century, Mold had come into the possession of Thomas **Stanley**, whose wife,

Alfred Mond

Margaret Beaufort, financed the rebuilding of St Mary's church. Like other 'Stanley churches', it features the arms of the Isle of **Man**. One of the church's **stained glass** windows commemorates the artist **Richard Wilson**, whose grave is in the churchyard.

From the late 17th century, Mold enjoyed increasing prosperity as a result of the exploitation of the **coal** and **lead** ore in the vicinity. In 1869, two miners at the **Leeswood** Green Colliery were imprisoned at Mold after they had attacked the colliery manager, an Englishman who had reduced wages and had refused to allow them to speak **Welsh** underground. The sentence led to the Mold Riots of 1869, in which four protesters were shot dead by soldiers.

The **community**'s wide high street, constructed to accommodate a street market, contains some interesting buildings, including an attractive Georgian house, the Italianate market hall (1850) and the town hall (1912). Bethesda (1863) is perhaps the most handsome of all the chapels built by the **Calvinistic Methodists**. The neo-Elizabethan county hall (1834) was replaced in 1968 by the shire hall, which, in 1974, became the headquarters of the county of **Clwyd**. Following the restitution of Flintshire in 1996, it became the headquarters of that county. The hall is part of Mold's civic centre, which occupies the grounds of Llwynegryn (1830), once a dower house of the Davies-Cooke family (*see* **Halkyn**). Offering a delightful vista of the **Clwydian Hills**, the civic centre also contains **law** courts, the county library, and the highly innovative Theatr Clwyd (*see* **Drama**). The poets Jane Brereton (1685–1740) and **John Blackwell** (Alun) and the musician **John Ambrose Lloyd** were born in Mold. The town's most distinguished native was the novelist

Daniel Owen, author of the most successful of the Welsh-language novels of the 19th-century. He set most of his work in Mold; his *Rhys Lewis* (1885) has the 1869 riots as its background. He is commemorated by a statue, cultural centre and shopping precinct.

MOND, Alfred [Moritz] (1868–1930)
Industrialist and politician
Born in Lancashire of German-Jewish extraction, in 1895 he joined the board of Brunner-Mond, the **chemical** business of his father, Ludwig (1839–1909). With his father and brother Robert (1867–1938), he founded the Mond Nickel Company (*see* **Copper, Zinc and Nickel**) at **Clydach** in 1900, becoming managing director in 1902 and chairman in 1923. It became the largest nickel works in the world. He was also chairman of the Amalgamated Anthracite Company on its formation in 1923, and of ICI when it was established in 1926 (Brunner-Mond was one of the merged companies). A prominent advocate of industrial rationalization and of industrial co-operation, he facilitated the conference between employers and the TUC (the Mond–Turner talks) in 1927, in the aftermath of the **General Strike**. Mond was **Liberal** MP for Chester (1906–10), **Swansea** (1910–18), Swansea West (1918–23) and **Carmarthen** (1924–8) and minister of **health** (1921–2). He became Baron Melchett in 1928. *Pele mond*, fuel made from mixing small **coal** with cement, was widely used in west Wales households.

MONMOUTH (Trefynwy),
Monmouthshire (2782 ha; 8877 inhabitants)
Located at the confluence of the **Wye** and the Monnow, the **community** includes the only part of **Monmouthshire** lying east of the Wye. It was the site of a **Roman** fort, and it may have been an urban centre when part of the kingdom of **Gwent**. Seized by **William Fitz Osbern** in the 1060s, it eventually became one of the lordships of the duchy of **Lancaster**. **Geoffrey of Monmouth** is believed to have been born there *c.*1090.

The 13th-century castle, the birthplace in 1387 of Henry V, fell into ruin. In 1673, the duke of Beaufort (*see* **Somerset family**) built the remarkable Great Castle House on its site; the mansion is now the headquarters of the Royal Monmouthshire Royal Engineers (Territorial Army). Monmouth's **Benedictine** priory, founded *c.*1075 and much reconstructed, is now St Mary's **parish** church. Of the late 13th-century town walls, only the gate tower on Monnow Bridge – a structure unique in **Britain** – survives.

Following the **Act of 'Union'**, Monmouth became the **county** town of Monmouthshire. Its Shire Hall (1724), built in the style of Wren, stands in Agincourt Square where there are statues of Henry V and **Charles Stewart Rolls**. The courtroom was the scene of a number of important trials, including that of the leaders of the **Newport Rising** of 1839. Monmouth's importance as a regional centre endowed it with many fine buildings, among them those of the 18th century in Monnow Street and those of the early 19th century in Priory Street (*see* **G. V. Maddox**). The town has several distinguished **Nonconformist** chapels. In the 1890s, the Haberdashers Company endowed two schools in Monmouth; the boys' school dominates the scene adjoining Wye Bridge and the girls' school looms above the town. The most notable feature of the area across the Wye is the Kymin, a handsome eminence crowned in 1800 by a temple devoted to **Britain**'s naval triumphs. Nelson, who visited it in 1802, is commemorated at the Nelson Museum, Priory Street.

MONMOUTHSHIRE (Sir Fynwy)
(88,562 ha; 84,885 inhabitants)

Following the abolition of the original **Monmouthshire** (*see below*) in 1974, Monmouth District was created as one of the five districts of the new **county** of **Gwent**. It consisted of what had been the **boroughs** of **Abergavenny** and **Monmouth**, the **urban districts** of **Chepstow** and **Usk** and the **rural districts** of Abergavenny, Chepstow and Monmouth and parts of that of Magor and St Mellons and of **Pontypool**.

Following the abolition of Gwent in 1996, Monmouth District, enlarged by the addition of the **community** of **Llanelly**, became the reconstituted Monmouthshire. Its 88,562 ha represents a marked shrinkage compared with the 140,338 ha of the pre-1974 county. In 2001, 15.31% of the inhabitants of Monmouthshire had some knowledge of **Welsh**, the percentages varying from 15.48% in **St Arvans** to 8.99% in **Magor with Undy** – the lowest percentage in Wales; 6.82% of the county's inhabitants were wholly fluent in the language (*see also* **Gwehelog Fawr**).

MONMOUTHSHIRE (Sir Fynwy)
One-time county

In 1536, through the first **Act of 'Union'**, the lordships of **Newport**, **Abergavenny**, **Monmouth**, **Three Castles**, **Caerleon**, **Chepstow**, **Usk** and part of **Ewias** were joined together to form Monmouthshire. In 1543, the second Act of 'Union' made the county subject to the **Oxford** judicial circuit rather than to the Welsh Courts of Great Session (*see* **Law**). Furthermore, while the other **counties** of Wales were granted one county MP apiece, Monmouthshire was granted two. These differences gave rise to the notion that Monmouthshire had ceased to be part of Wales and led to the popularity of the phrase 'Wales and Monmouthshire'.

As late as the 1960s, Ordnance Survey **maps** portrayed Monmouthshire as an English county, although by then all legislation specifically relating to Wales was automatically applicable to the county. On the eve of its abolition in 1974, the administrative county consisted of the **boroughs** of Abergavenny and Monmouth, the **urban districts** of **Abercarn**, **Abertillery**, Bedwas and Machen (*see* **Bedwas, Trethomas and Machen**), **Bedwellty**, **Blaenavon**, Caerleon, Chepstow, **Cwmbran**, **Ebbw Vale**, Mynyddislwyn, **Nantyglo and Blaina**, **Pontypool**, **Risca**, **Rhymney**, **Tredegar** and Usk and the **rural districts** of Abergavenny, Chepstow, Magor and St Mellons, Monmouth and Pontypool.

Following abolition, Monmouthshire, plus **Brynmawr** and **Llanelly** but excluding the east bank of the **Rhymney**, became the county of **Gwent**. Among Gwent's districts was Monmouth – essentially the rural area of the old county (*see above*). Following further reorganization in 1996, the Monmouth district became the reconstituted **Monmouthshire**. Confusingly, it embraces only about two-thirds of the old Monmouthshire, the rest of which – together with parts of the one-time counties of **Breconshire** and **Glamorgan** – became the **county boroughs** of **Blaenau Gwent**, **Caerphilly**, **Newport** and **Torfaen**. The original Monmouthshire consisted of 140,338 ha.

The Monnow Bridge, Monmouth, with its 13th-century gate tower

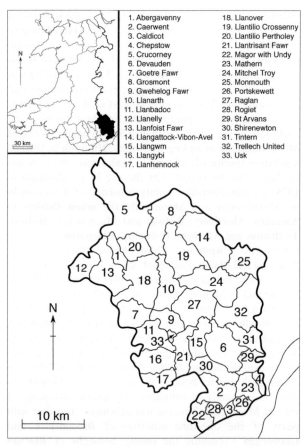

1. Abergavenny	18. Llanover
2. Caerwent	19. Llantilio Crossenny
3. Caldicot	20. Llantilio Pertholey
4. Chepstow	21. Llantrisant Fawr
5. Crucorney	22. Magor with Undy
6. Devauden	23. Mathern
7. Goetre Fawr	24. Mitchel Troy
8. Grosmont	25. Monmouth
9. Gwehelog Fawr	26. Portskewett
10. Llanarth	27. Raglan
11. Llanbadoc	28. Rogiet
12. Llanelly	29. St Arvans
13. Llanfoist Fawr	30. Shirenewton
14. Llangattock-Vibon-Avel	31. Tintern
15. Llangwm	32. Trellech United
16. Llangybi	33. Usk
17. Llanhennock	

The communities of the county of Monmouth

The Census of 1971 recorded that the ancient county had 461,700 inhabitants, and that the administrative county – the area administered by the Monmouthshire County Council (that is, those parts of the county outside the county borough of Newport) – had 348,880 inhabitants.

MONTFORT, DE family Magnates

Simon de Montfort, earl of Leicester (c.1200–65), was the son of the Simon de Montfort who led the crusade against the Albigensians, destroying in the process the Provençal culture of southern France. The younger Simon married Eleanor, sister of Henry III, became the leader of the baronial opposition to the king in the civil war of the 1260s and played a significant part in the establishment of the first English parliament. The treaty agreed at Pipton (*see* **Bronllys**) in 1265 between Simon and his ally **Llywelyn ap Gruffudd** foreshadowed the **Treaty of Montgomery**. A marriage may have been arranged between the prince and Simon's daughter, Eleanor. However, the marriage arrangements were aborted by Simon's death at Evesham in 1265 and his daughter's exile in France; but the project was revived after the defection of Llywelyn's brother and heir **Dafydd ap Gruffudd** in 1274. Eleanor was captured by English sailors on her way to join Llywelyn, but they were eventually married at Worcester in 1278. Eleanor died in June 1282, giving birth to a daughter, **Gwenllian** (1282–1337).

MONTGOMERY (Trefaldwyn), Montgomeryshire, Powys (1359 ha; 1256 inhabitants)

Commanding the route into mid Wales, Montgomery's site has long been of strategic importance, as the vast Ffridd Faldwyn **hill-fort** crowning Montgomery Hill testifies. The **English** name derives from Roger of the **Montgomery family**, appointed earl of Shrewsbury in 1071. It was first applied to Roger's motte-and-bailey castle (Hen Domen), built to guard the ford of Rhyd Chwima (Rhydwhyman on Ordnance Survey **maps**) across the **Severn**. In about 1102, that castle came into the possession of Baldwin de Bollers, who provided the town's **Welsh** name: Trefaldwyn (Baldwin's town).

The town lies below another castle, begun by Henry III in 1223. In the mid and late 13th century, the castle was the English crown's main stronghold on the **borders** of mid-Wales, and Rhyd Chwima – the ford of Montgomery – became the chief meeting place for envoys of Welsh and English rulers. It was there, in 1267, that the **Treaty of Montgomery** was sealed, the agreement that created the **Principality** of Wales. The castle passed to the **Mortimer** family, and then the **Herbert** family, who built a fine **Renaissance** mansion in its middle ward. In 1649, the castle was levelled on the orders of Parliament; late 20th-century excavations have provided evidence of its merits, in particular the twin-towered gatehouse and the innovative high curtain walls; the castle surely owes much to Chateau-Gaillard in eastern **Norman**dy.

The poet **George Herbert** was born in Montgomery. He and his elder brother, the philosopher **Edward Herbert** (Baron Herbert of Cherbury), are sculpted as children on the remarkable tomb (1600) of Richard Herbert in the church of St Nicholas. Originally built in the 13th century, the church has a magnificent hammer beam roof of c.1500.

Montgomery received its charter in 1227 but, with the growth of **Welshpool**, it lost its importance. The **community** therefore remains attractively antiquated in appearance with its town hall (1748) and a number of half-timbered houses. Indeed, so rich is it in cornices, doorcases, fanlights, gables and other undisturbed delights that it has claims to be considered the most delectable town in Wales.

MONTGOMERY family Marcher-lords

In about 1071, Roger (d.1094) of Montgomery in **Norman**dy, was granted the earldom of Shrewsbury (*see* **Shropshire**), which he used as his base for invading Wales. His castle at Rhyd Chwima (Rhydwhyman on Ordnance Survey **maps**) on the **Severn** came to be known as **Montgomery**. Roger invaded **Ceredigion**, building a castle at **Cardigan**. He had three sons. Arnulf invaded **Dyfed**, establishing a castle at **Pembroke**; Hugh was killed by Magnus, king of Norway, while invading **Gwynedd**; Robert rose in revolt against William II in 1102; his defeat brought the family's role in Wales to an end.

MONTGOMERY, TREATY OF (1267)

Concluded at Rhyd Chwima or Rhydwhyman ford (*see* **Montgomery**) on 29 September 1267 between **Llywelyn ap Gruffudd** and Henry III, this treaty recognized Llywelyn as Prince of Wales and overlord of all native Welsh rulers apart from Maredudd ap Rhys of Dryslwyn (**Llangathen**). (He acquired Maredudd's homage in 1270.) These rulers would do homage to him, and he alone would do homage to the king for the **Principality** of Wales. His successors would also be recognized as princes of Wales, which meant that the treaty recognized the Principality of Wales as a constitutional entity distinct from the person of an individual prince. Llywelyn's territorial gains were confirmed and he was to be reconciled with his brother **Dafydd ap Gruffudd**. In exchange, Llywelyn agreed to pay 25,000 marks (£16,667) in 10 annual instalments. The significance of the Treaty of Montgomery was that for the first time there was a stable relationship between the English crown and the new Principality of Wales, based on a treaty agreed by both sides. **Llywelyn ap Iorwerth** had unsuccessfully sought such a settlement, and it had been the principal objective of Llywelyn ap Gruffudd's diplomacy since 1258. The treaty can be seen as the high point of independent Wales, but the vagueness of its territorial terms were a fatal flaw. (*See also* **English monarchs and Wales**.)

MONTGOMERYSHIRE (Sir Drefaldwyn)
One-time county

Montgomeryshire was one of the seven Welsh **counties** created by the **Act of 'Union'** of 1536. Its boundaries broadly corresponded to those of **Powys Wenwynwyn**, although the unruly **commote** of **Mawddwy** was attached to the long-established county of **Merioneth**. Except for the transfer of Clun to **Shropshire** in 1546, there was very little change until 1974 when Montgomeryshire became a district of the new county of **Powys**. Up to 1974, the county had consisted of the **boroughs** of **Llanfyllin**, **Montgomery** and **Welshpool**, the **urban districts** of **Llanidloes**, **Machynlleth** and **Newtown** and the **rural districts** of Forden, Llanfyllin, Machynlleth, and Newtown and Llanidloes.

Following further reorganization in 1996, its district status was abolished, although some Montgomeryshire institutions – its federation of **Young Farmers' Clubs**, for example – continued in existence. Although named after the town of Montgomery, the assizes came to be held alternately at **Welshpool** and Newtown. The chief county offices were established at Welshpool, although other institutions – the county library, for example – were in Newtown. With the establishment of the county of Powys in 1974, Montgomeryshire's county **government** came to be located at **Llandrindod** (**Radnorshire**).

Geographically, the county consisted of the fertile land of the valleys – **Severn** and its major tributaries, Vyrnwy, Banwy and Tanat, to the east, and **Dyfi** to the west – the hill country between Severn and Tanat, and the high moorland covering almost all the western part. Its highest points were Moel Sych and Cadair **Berwyn** (both 827 m in height).

Although the county once had major **lead** mines, it was always primarily agricultural. In the 18th and 19th centuries, **wool** and flannel manufacture were major industries. In the late 20th century, developments at Newtown gave Montgomeryshire a broader economic base. Granted a county and a borough MP by the Act of 'Union', the borough seat was abolished in 1918. Of all the constituencies of **Britain**, Montgomery county has been the most

Attractive old houses in Montgomery

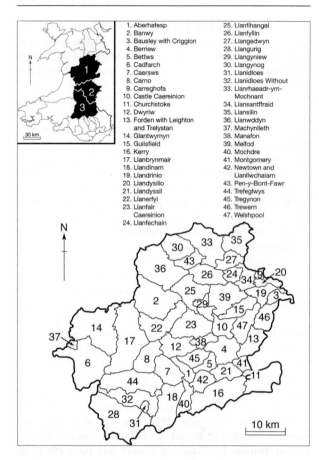

1. Aberhafesp	25. Llanfihangel
2. Banwy	26. Llanfyllin
3. Bausley with Criggion	27. Llangedwyn
4. Berriew	28. Llangurig
5. Bettws	29. Llangyniew
6. Cadfarch	30. Llangynog
7. Caersws	31. Llanidloes
8. Carno	32. Llanidloes Without
9. Carreghofa	33. Llanrhaeadr-ym-
10. Castle Caereinion	Mochnant
11. Churchstoke	34. Llansantffraid
12. Dwyriw	35. Llansilin
13. Forden with Leighton	36. Llanwddyn
and Trelystan	37. Machynlleth
14. Glantwymyn	38. Manafon
15. Guilsfield	39. Meifod
16. Kerry	40. Mochdre
17. Llanbrynmair	41. Montgomery
18. Llandinam	42. Newtown and
19. Llandrinio	Llanllwchaiarn
20. Llandysilio	43. Pen-y-Bont-Fawr
21. Llandyssil	44. Trefeglwys
22. Llanerfyl	45. Tregynon
23. Llanfair	46. Trewern
Caereinion	47. Welshpool
24. Llanfechain	

The communities of Powys: 1 Montgomeryshire

consistently **Liberal**, having for a century and more elected a Liberal at every election except at that of 1979. It is the only part of Wales never to have been represented by a **Labour** MP. Montgomeryshire's **historical society**, the Powysland Club, founded in 1867, is the oldest in Wales. The club's journal, the *Montgomeryshire Collections*, has been published since 1868.

The phrase 'Powys paradise of Wales' comes from the **Llywarch Hen** poems (9th or 10th century) and references to '*mwynder Maldwyn*' (the gentleness of Maldwyn) are proverbial. Indeed, perhaps there is something in the landscape that soothes – or tranquillizers. At the time of its loss of county status in 1974, Montgomeryshire consisted of 206,439 ha and had 43,900 inhabitants.

MONUMENTS, EARLY CHRISTIAN
The inscribed stones and crosses of the early Christian period constitute the most important material evidence relating to the Wales of the half a millennium following the fall of the **Roman** Empire. Other forms of evidence include **hill-forts**, boundary lines (**Offa's Dyke** and **Wat's Dyke**) and religious foundations (*see* **Celtic Church, The**). There are almost 450 stones and stone crosses in Wales bearing inscriptions carved between the 5th and 11th centuries. **V. E. Nash-Williams** divided them into three categories: simple inscribed stones (5th to 7th century); stones bearing some form of cross (7th to 9th century); and carved stone crosses (9th to 11th century). (For stone carvings later than the 11th century, *see* **Sculpture**.)

Almost all the stones mark graves. They were usually located in hallowed burial grounds, many of which were, or later became, the sites of churches. Not all of the stones remain in their original locations, for many of those vulnerable to weather damage have been moved into churches or museums; indeed at **Margam**, a special stones museum has been established. Some stones bear the name of the deceased, a few of whom are known from documentary evidence; the vast majority, however, are unknown, although many of them were probably rulers of the petty kingdoms which came into existence in the wake of the collapse of the Empire.

The stones of the 5th to the 7th centuries throw valuable light on a period of crucial change, for they provide evidence concerning the social, linguistic, cultural and political condition of Wales precisely in the era when the Welsh nation was born and when the Christian **religion** was striking deep roots in the country. The legacy of the Roman Empire and the imperial context of the spread of Christianity are apparent in the fact that the great majority of the inscriptions are in **Latin**.

However, there are in Wales some 40 stones bearing **Irish** names, carved in the **ogham** script. Almost all of them are in the south-west and confirm other evidence indicating that that region was the scene of considerable Irish colonization and that early **Dyfed** was ruled by an Irish dynasty. Most of the ogham-inscribed stones also bear inscriptions in Latin, among them that removed from Castelldwyran (**Clynderwen**) to the **Carmarthenshire**

The 11th-century Carew Cross, on which the Cadw logo is based

museum at **Abergwili**. It commemorates Vorteporix (*see* **Vortiporius**). The stone states that Vorteporix bore the Roman-style title of *Protector*, one of the several examples of nostalgia for the Empire apparent in the Wales of the immediate post-Roman era. Thus, a stone at Llangian (**Llanengan**) commemorates Melus, the *medicus*, and that to Cantiorix at Penmachno (**Bro Machno**) notes that he was the cousin of Maglos, the *magistratus*. Another stone at Penmachno states that the monument was erected during the consulate of Justinus, a man who is known to have been appointed consul in 540 by a remnant of Roman power surviving around Lyon. Contact with the Lyon area is also apparent in the most attractive of the early inscribed stones – that to King Cadfan of Gwynedd (d.*c*.625) at Llangadwaladr (**Bodorgan**) – in which the lettering followed the style then popular in the Rhône valley. The most important of Wales's earliest inscribed stones is that to Ceinrwy at St Cadfan's Church, **Tywyn**; dating from sometime between the 7th and 9th centuries, it commemorates Cyngen and bears the earliest surviving inscription in **Welsh**.

The stones of the second period (7th to 9th century) bear a rich variety of incised crosses but few names. However, it is to that period that the lengthiest inscription belongs. It was carved on Eliseg's Pillar, which stands at **Llantysilio** near **Llangollen** and was erected by King Cyngen of **Powys** (d.854) in honour of his great-grandfather Eliseg (fl.*c*.750). Now undecipherable, the inscription, copied by **Edward Lhuyd** in 1696, consisted of at least a hundred words commemorating the glories of the house of Powys.

The carved crosses of the 9th to the 11th centuries include memorials to leading rulers, among them those to Ithel, king of **Gwent** (d.848) and Hywel, king of **Glywysing** (d.886), both at **Llantwit Major**, and that to Maredudd, king of **Deheubarth** (d.1035) at **Carew**. These, and other crosses of the period, bear a rich variety of interlacing and provide evidence of influences from **Ireland**, northern **England** and Scandinavia. Scandinavian influence is particularly apparent in Maen Achwyfan, a monolithic slab at **Whitford**. The finest stone cross in Wales is that at **Penally**; the largest is the Cynfelyn Stone at Margam, which bears carvings of St Mary and St John.

By the late 11th century, Romanesque influences from mainland Europe were introducing new forms of stone carving. Wales came to be endowed with fine sculptures in the Romanesque style – above all, the 12th-century shrine at Pennant Melangell (**Llangynog, Montgomeryshire**). By then, however, with documentary evidence becoming more plentiful, inscribed stones were ceasing to be the major source of information that they had been over the previous 600 years.

MORAVIANS

A pietistic Protestant sect that may be traced to 15th-century Moravia, in what is the modern-day Czech Republic, its members developed a conviction that they were to evangelize to the world. Their tradition had a significant influence on Welsh religious life, as testified by the activities of figures such as **Morgan Llwyd**, **Griffith Jones** and, above all, **Howel Harris**, whose 'Holy Family' at Trefeca (**Talgarth**) was partly inspired by Moravian example.

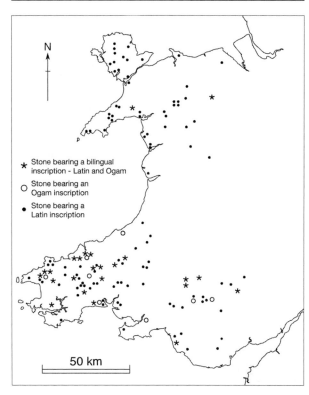

The distribution of inscribed stones of the period 400 to 700 (based on V. E. Nash-Williams, 1950)

Moravians are associated primarily with two places in Wales: Drws-y-Coed (**Llanllyfni**) and **Haverfordwest**. Wales's last Moravian chapel, in Haverfordwest, was demolished in 1961.

MORFA RHUDDLAN, Battle of

At Morfa Rhuddlan (**Kinmel Bay and Towyn**) in 796, the Welsh, led by Caradog, king of **Gwynedd**, were heavily defeated by the forces of Offa of **Mercia** – although Offa himself was killed in the fighting. The English poet Robert Graves (1895–1985) called Morfa Rhuddlan the 'Flodden of Wales'.

MORGAN family (Tredegar) Landowners

Of **Carmarthenshire** origins, by the 15th century the family had gained possession of a substantial estate centred upon Tredegar (**Coedkernew**, near **Newport**). (The town of **Tredegar**, 28 km distant, owes its name to the Tredegar **Iron**works, established in 1799 on land in the upper Sirhowy valley leased from the Tredegar estate.) Other branches of the family established themselves at Machen (**Graig**), Gwern-y-Clepa (Coedkernew), **Langstone**, **Llantarnam**, Llanrhymney (Cardiff), Ruperra (**Rudry**), Bassaleg (Graig) and elsewhere. William Morgan (d.1680), who acquired Y Dderw (**Bronllys**) estate in **Breconshire** by marriage, initiated the rebuilding of Tredegar House (*c*.1664). Completed by 1718, it is incomparably the finest building erected in Wales in that period. Throughout the 18th century, the Morgans were the south-east's most politically active family, producing 13 MPs for the **county** and **borough** constituencies of **Monmouthshire** and Breconshire.

On the extinction of the direct male line in 1771, the estate passed to Jane Morgan. She married Charles Gould, who took her **surname**. In 1859, their grandson, Charles Morgan (1792–1875), was elevated to the peerage as Baron Tredegar. His son, Godfrey (1831–1913), took part in the Charge of the Light Brigade during the **Crimean War**. A generous benefactor of Newport and **Cardiff**, he is commemorated by a statue in **Cathays Park**. He was promoted to a viscountcy in 1905; in 1911, he published his speeches under the title *The Wit and Wisdom of Lord Tredegar*, a volume which proved that he was not over-endowed with either. He was succeeded by his nephew, Courtenay Morgan (1867–1934), for whom the viscountcy was revived in 1926; it died out with Courtenay's son, Evan Frederic (1893–1949) – artist, poet, ardent **Roman Catholic**, and resident on the island of Bali.

The family benefited greatly from the development of Newport and the south Wales **coal**field. The wayleave payment it received from the 'golden mile' – a stretch of railway crossing Tredegar Park – was among the factors that radicalized **John Frost**. Courtenay Morgan's appearance before the **Sankey** Commission on the Coal Industry in 1919, when he sought to defend the royalties he received from his 7500 ha of mineral-bearing land, caused him to be portrayed, not wholly fairly, as the epitome of a greedy landlord. (His son and successor was wholly opposed to mineral royalties.) In 1873, the family owned 10,300 ha in Monmouthshire, 2950 ha in Breconshire and 2490 ha in **Glamorgan**.

MORGAN, David (1833–1919) Retailer

A native of **Breconshire**, Morgan, aged 14, was apprenticed to a draper in **Newport**, before starting his own business in **Rhymney**. Aged 46, he moved to **Cardiff** where he began the process of acquiring properties in The Hayes that would become the city's second largest department store. The store remained under family ownership until its closure in 2005.

MORGAN, Diana (1910–86) Screenwriter

An Ealing Studios stalwart, **Cardiff**-born Diana Morgan made significant script contributions to the Welsh comedy *A Run For Your Money* (1949), *Dance Hall* (1950), Cavalcanti's *Went The Day Well?* (1943) and Robert Hamer's *Pink String and Sealing Wax* (1945), a *film* noir featuring Googie Withers as the most unsympathetic female in Ealing's *oeuvre*. A former actress and chorus girl, she also scripted Philip Leacock's *Hand in Hand* (1960), about friendship across racial barriers.

MORGAN, Dyfnallt (1917–94) Poet and writer

A native of Dowlais (**Merthyr Tydfil**), Dyfnallt Morgan is remembered as a distinguished broadcaster and author of one of the best poems to be submitted to the National **Eisteddfod** crown competition, although it failed to win the crown at the 1953 festival. 'Y Llen', written in dialect, depicts the end of a way of life centred on the **Welsh language** and culture in an industrial valley in **Glamorgan**. During the **Second World War**, Morgan's stance as a **conscientious objector** eventually led him to Italy, Austria and China with the **Quakers'** Ambulance Unit. Having spent

several years as a BBC producer, he became a lecturer in the extramural department at **Bangor**. As well as poetry, he published literary criticism and translations of plays and songs. A selection of his works was published posthumously in 2003, edited by his son, Tomos Morgan.

MORGAN, Elena Puw (1900–73) Novelist

Elena Puw Morgan lived in **Corwen** all her life. Among her stories for children are *Kitty Cordelia*, which appeared in *Cymru'r Plant* in 1930, *Angel y Llongau Hedd* (1931) and *Tan y Castell* (1939). She exploited her knowledge of the life of **Romanies** when writing her novel *Nansi Lovell* (1933). Her most mature novels, *Y Wisg Sidan* (1939) and *Y Graith* (1943), were successfully dramatized for television. *Y Graith* won the National **Eisteddfod** prose medal in 1938. Both convey the harshness and cruelty of 19th-century rural communities.

MORGAN, Eluned (1870–1938) Author

The daughter of Lewis Jones (1836–1904), a founder of *Y Wladfa*, the Welsh colony in **Patagonia**, Eluned was **surnamed** Morgan (sea-born) because she was born at sea. She lived intermittently in Wales and Patagonia, before settling permanently in Patagonia in 1918. As a teacher and as editor of the **newspaper** *Y Drafod*, she bore a large share of the responsibility for maintaining the **Welsh** life of *Y Wladfa*. Her publications include three books descriptive of the Patagonian adventure, notably *Dringo'r Andes* (1904), and two volumes of correspondence, *Gyfaill Hoff* (1972) and *Tyred Drosodd* (1977).

MORGAN, George (1834–1915) Architect

Born near **Laugharne**, and brought up in **Pembrokeshire**, Morgan was a farmer's son who, around 1855, left home to join a building firm in **Carmarthen**. By 1871, Morgan was practising on his own, first as a builder and surveyor and later as an architect, carrying out work in much of southern and mid-Wales. Best known for his chapels, including the splendid **English Baptist** chapel (1872) in Carmarthen, he also designed many schools and large houses in the area.

MORGAN, George Osborne (1826–97) Politician

In 1868, Morgan, a son of a vicar of **Conwy**, won one of the two **Denbighshire** seats for the **Liberal Party**. In 1885, the constituency was divided, and the following year he was elected for the eastern division, defeating Sir Watkin **Williams Wynn** and ending more than 180 years of the Wynnstay family's domination over Denbighshire politics. Morgan was the prime mover in placing the Burials Act (1880) on the statute book. He took an interest in **education** in Wales and in the Welsh settlement in **Patagonia**, was an advocate of **disestablishment** and supported the Welsh **Sunday Closing** Act (1881).

MORGAN, Griffith (Guto Nyth-Brân; 1700–37) Runner

One of a number of popular runners of the 18th and 19th centuries on whose exploits bets were laid by an enthusiastic public, Guto was brought up at Nyth-brân, a smallholding near Porth, **Rhondda**. Various legends have grown around him, one of which is recorded in **I. D. Hooson's** popular **ballad** 'Guto Nyth Brân'. He took part in **man versus horse** races, but his most famous race was his last, when he took 53 minutes to run the 19 km from **Newport** to **Bedwas**, defeating Prince, his English rival. He is reputed then to have dropped dead when a supporter slapped him too vigorously on the back. His grave is in Llanwonno (**Ynysybwl and Coed-y-cwm**) churchyard. His feat is commemorated in **Aberdare**'s New Year race, which actually takes place in **Mountain Ash**.

MORGAN, Gwenllian Elizabeth Fanny (1852–1939)
Public figure and antiquary
Born at Defynnog (**Maescar**), 'Miss Philip Morgan' – as she was known, after her father – was a prominent figure in the public life of **Brecon**, where she lived from 1868; she became the first woman in Wales to serve on a **borough** council and to become mayor (1910–11). Her chief interests were **education**, the history of her native **county** – on which she wrote for antiquarian journals – and the poet **Henry Vaughan**, on whom she did important pioneering research. In 1894, she gave valuable testimony, particularly on the circumstances of **women**, to the Land Commission in Wales. A **housing** development in Brecon commemorates her.

MORGAN, Henry (c.1635–88) Pirate
Reputedly the son of a yeoman farmer from the Llanrhymney area (*see* **Cardiff**), Henry Morgan was related to the **Morgan family (Tredegar)**. He emigrated to the West Indies and attained considerable fame as one of the foremost pirates of the 17th century (*see* **Piracy**). Based at Port Royal, Jamaica, one of the most iniquitous **ports** in the world, he undertook many bloody expeditions against Spanish ships, trading ports and property in the Caribbean. Despite his history as a particularly cruel buccaneer, he was knighted in 1674 and appointed deputy governor of Jamaica. Captain Morgan's name lives on as a brand of dark rum.

MORGAN, Mary (1788–1805) Murderer
Mary Morgan, an under-cook in the household of the **Radnorshire** MP Walter Wilkins, killed her illegitimate daughter almost immediately after the baby's birth. Found guilty of murder, she was hanged in April 1805 (having just turned 17) at Gallows Lane, **Presteigne**, the last **woman** in Wales to be publicly executed (*see* **Executions**). Her grave in Presteigne churchyard is marked by two headstones. One epitaph is charitable; the other, erected by the earl of Ailesbury, a friend of the judge, is more censorious.

MORGAN, Morien (1912–78) Aviation engineer
Sir Morien Morgan, FRS, who led the project to develop Concorde (*see also* **Brian Trubshaw**), was born at **Bridgend** and educated at **Cambridge**. He developed a passion for **aviation and aeronautics**. In 1935, he started work at the Royal Aircraft Establishment (RAE), Farnborough – and, in his own words, 'lived happily ever after'. Although short-sighted, he overcame official barriers to the test flying of aircraft. His academic skill, combined with his experience as a pilot, led to work on the aerodynamic stability and manoeuvrability of aircraft. He studied how the distorting effect of aileron adjustments on the fuselage and wings were important ingredients in the dynamics of a plane, work leading to design improvements in the wings of the famous **Second World War** fighter, the Spitfire.

Eventually, he became director of RAE, where his best-known achievement was his leadership of the project for the supersonic transport aircraft that eventually became Concorde. He was largely responsible for the initial **engineering** assessment and for providing the sustained enthusiasm for the venture, which overcame all objections.

MORGAN, T[homas] J[ohn] (1907–86)
Scholar and writer
As a scholar, T. J. Morgan's most notable contribution – on mutations in **Welsh** – was *Y Treigladau a'u Cystrawen* (1952), an immensely readable book on the most uninspiring of subjects. He was also a prolific writer of literary essays. His survey of the **Nonconformist** culture of industrial Wales, *Diwylliant Gwerin* (1972), relates, in part, to his own humble upbringing in Glais (**Clydach**). Educated at **Swansea**, he was appointed a lecturer in Welsh at **Cardiff** (1930) and transferred to the civil service during the **Second World War**. He became registrar of the **University of Wales** (1951), before returning to Swansea as professor of Welsh (1962). With his son, the writer and historian Prys Morgan (b.1937), he published the important volume *Welsh Surnames* (1985). His other son is the **Labour** politician Rhodri Morgan (b.1939), first minister of the **National Assembly for Wales** (2000–).

Henry Morgan, pirate, knight and governor

MORGAN, Teddy (Edward Morgan; 1880–1949)
Rugby player
Aberdare-born Teddy Morgan acquired **rugby** immortality as the scorer of the try that enabled Wales to beat the otherwise undefeated All Blacks in 1905. Small and speedy, an expert cross-kicker and resolute tackler, 'Dr Teddy', of Guy's Hospital, **London**, was a fixture in the Welsh sides of the first golden era, scoring 14 tries in 16 internationals. On his last appearance in 1908, he captained Wales in their first-ever game against France, and scored two tries.

MORGAN, Thomas (Y Cor/The Dwarf; 1604–79)
Soldier
Born at Llangattock Lingoed (**Grosmont**), probably into the same family as **Henry Morgan** the buccaneer, he was a small man with a European reputation as one of the greatest soldiers of his age. He fought in the Thirty Years War until 1643, and for the forces of Parliament upon his return to **Britain**, with his mining operations at **Raglan** Castle sealing the fate of that major Royalist stronghold. Although barely literate, he proved an able administrator, spending his last 14 years as Governor of Jersey.

MORGAN, William (c.1545–1604)
Bishop and translator
Born at Tŷ-mawr, Wybrnant, Penmachno (**Bro Machno**) to parents who were relatively prosperous tenant farmers on the estate of the **Wynn family (Gwydir)**, William Morgan was educated at **Cambridge**. Ordained in 1568, he was appointed to the vicarages of **Llanbadarn Fawr** (1572–5), **Welshpool** (1575–8) and **Llanrhaeadr-ym-Mochnant** (1578–95), among other appointments. In 1595, he was made bishop of Llandaff (*see* **Cardiff**) and was translated to **St Asaph** in 1601. He died in 1604, a relatively poor man, and was buried in his cathedral, although the precise spot is unknown.

Morgan's masterpiece was his translation of the **Bible** (1588), the most important book ever published in **Welsh**. The work of translation was carried out in Llanrhaeadr, in spite of the fact that some of Morgan's powerful parishioners did their best to hinder him, possibly from religious motives. His task was to revise the translation by **William Salesbury** and his colleagues of the New Testament and Psalms, and then to translate the Old Testament (apart from the Psalms) and the Apocrypha. He was able to exploit the latest advances in biblical scholarship, especially the Antwerp Polyglot Bible (1572), John Immanuel Tremellius's **Latin** version (1579), the **English** Geneva Bible (1560) and Theodore Beza's Greek and Latin New Testament (1582). Crucially, Morgan was a good Welsh scholar, well versed in Welsh **literature**, especially the work of the professional poets.

Salesbury's use of language, particularly in the matter of orthography, was deliberately archaic. In revising Salesbury, Morgan consistently modernized and regularized the language – in general, according to the practice of the poets. Naturally, he also applied the same principles to his own original translations. His Bible is regarded as a classic, which became a model for later writers. It greatly enhanced the scope of Welsh as a literary medium, and vindicated its claim to be regarded as a learned language.

Morgan's version of **The Book of Common Prayer** (1599) was also important.

MORGANNWG Kingdom
The name derives eponymously from that of an early medieval ruler of south-east Wales – either Morgan ab Athrwys (d.*c.*700) or Morgan ab Owain (d.974). **Glamorgan** represents a version of this (*gwlad* + Morgan). The core of the kingdom of Morgannwg was **Glywysing**, but it seems to have also encompassed **Gwent** and, at times, two of the *cantrefi* of **Ystrad Tywi**. The main source of the kingdom's history is *Liber Landavensis* (*The Book of Llandaff*). Extinguished as a kingdom in the 1080s, following the invasion of **Robert Fitz Hammo**, its last king was **Iestyn ap Gwrgant**, some of whose descendants retained a degree of authority in upland Glamorgan until the early 14th century.

MORMONS
The popular name for adherents of The Church of Jesus Christ of Latter Day Saints, founded by Joseph Smith (1805–44) at Manchester, New York State, in 1830. The Church's beliefs are based upon the contents of *The Book of Mormon*, a document Smith claimed had been revealed to him by an angel named Moroni. Having sanctioned polygamy, Smith was murdered in a riot in Illinois in 1844 when in the company of Captain Dan Jones (1810–61) of **Halkyn**. Brigham Young, who established the headquarters of the Church at Salt Lake City, Utah, in 1847, succeeded Smith as leader. In 1845, Daniel Jones began a missionary campaign in Wales and, in 1849, led 249 Welsh Mormons to Utah, the first of several such migrations.

In 1851, when Wales had a mere 20 **Roman Catholic** churches, it had 28 Mormon places of worship. The movement published two **Welsh** periodicals: *Prophwyd y Jubili* (1846–49) and *Udgorn Seion* (1849–62). A Welsh translation of *The Book of Mormon* was published by John Davis at **Merthyr Tydfil** in 1852. Among the Welsh members of the Church was Evan Stephens of Pencader (**Llanfihangel-ar-Arth**), who was appointed conductor of the Tabernacle Choir in Salt Lake City in 1890. Young Mormon **missionaries** continue to be active in Wales, where there are a number of successful branches of the Church. Because Mormons rebaptize their ancestors, Salt Lake City has a wealth of genealogical material relating to Wales.

MORRIS BROTHERS Antiquaries
One of the richest sources for the cultural and social history of the 18th century is the extensive correspondence of the four Morris brothers from Pentre-eiriannell, Penrhoslligwy (**Moelfre**). The eldest, Lewis Morris (1701–65), was a surveyor and cartographer (*see* **Maps**) who published charts of the Welsh coastline. From *c.*1742, he lived in **Cardiganshire** where he was deputy steward of the crown **manors**. Although his time there was beset with problems, he was able to pursue his studies in the language, **literature** and history of Wales. His dream was to bring the treasures of **Welsh** literature within reach of the common reader. He published *Tlysau yr Hen Oesoedd* (1735) on his own press in **Holyhead**, but he lacked the resources to produce a projected standard **dictionary** and a dictionary of

place names. He inspired a circle of poets and scholars, including **Goronwy Owen**, Ieuan Fardd (**Evan Evans**; 1731–88) and **Edward Richard**.

Richard Morris (1703–79) spent much of his life in **London** where he was a clerk in the Navy Office. A founder, in 1751, of the **Cymmrodorion** Society, he was editor of new editions of the **Bible** and **The Book of Common Prayer** for the **Society for the Promotion of Christian Knowledge**.

The most scientifically oriented of the brothers was William Morris (1705–63). An excise officer in Holyhead by occupation but a **garden**er and botanist by inclination, he had a wide knowledge of the **plants** of **Snowdon**. His important gardening manuscript was published in *Transactions of the Cymmrodorion* (1979). He also had a keen interest in **music**.

Less is known about John Morris (1706–40), although he shared his brothers' cultured interests to some extent. He went to sea and died in an attack on Cartagena in Spain.

MORRIS, Cedric (1889–1982) Painter
A descendant of the founder of Morriston, **Swansea**, Cedric Morris painted carefully crafted observations of still lifes, people, flowers, **birds** and landscapes. He studied art in Paris, lived in East Anglia, where he opened his own art school, and travelled extensively. Visiting Wales as a landscape painter in the late 1920s, his conscience was stirred by the poverty he witnessed, leading him to the

Dowlais Settlement, where he began to teach art, influencing a generation of Welsh painters. In the 1930s, he was involved with the National **Eisteddfod**.

MORRIS, John William (1896–1979) Judge
Born and brought up in **Liverpool**, of Welsh parents, he became – as Lord Morris of Borth-y-Gest – a distinguished **law** lord in a period of judicial activism, serving in the High Court (1945), Court of Appeal (1951) and House of Lords (1960–75). He won the MC in the **First World War**, supported **devolution** in retirement, was a pillar of **London** Welsh society, and was pro-chancellor of the **University of Wales**.

MORRIS, Johnny (1916–99) Broadcaster
One of the most famous faces on television, he was born Ernest John Morris, the son of a **Newport** postmaster. He joined the local repertory company before moving to **London**, aged 17, to try to make the theatre his profession. Nothing came of this ambition until 1946, when a BBC radio producer overheard him telling an anecdote in a Wiltshire pub. A string of radio and children's television successes followed, including appearances as a storytelling hot-chestnut man, and as a zookeeper in the famously anthropomorphic *Animal Magic*, which ran for 23 years.

MORRIS, Lewis (1833–1907) Poet
A **Carmarthen** man, Lewis Morris was a lawyer by profession. He played a part in the establishment of the

Cedric Morris, *Pontypridd* (1945)

University of Wales. Knighted in 1895, he had an ambition to be Poet Laureate after the death of Tennyson, but it is alleged that his hopes were dashed when Queen Victoria was told that he had a common-law wife and three children. His best-known poem is *The Epic of Hades* (1876–7), but most of his work is insipid in both style and content.

MORRIS, Rhys Hopkin (1888–1956) Politician

Born at **Maesteg** and educated at **Bangor**, Morris became an officer in the **Royal Welch Fusiliers** during the **First World War**. He took an active part in the **Cardiganshire** by-election of 1921 and, in 1923, was elected Independent **Liberal** MP for the **county**, resigning in 1932 on his appointment as a **London** magistrate. Throughout these years he was vehemently opposed to **David Lloyd George**. In October 1936, he was appointed the first director of the BBC's new Welsh Region, lending unfailing support to **Welsh-language broadcasting**. In 1945, he was elected MP for **Carmarthen**, the only Liberal gain from **Labour** in the election; he retained the seat until his death. Knighted in 1954, he was notable for his independence of outlook.

MORRIS-JONES, Huw (1912–89)
Academic and public servant

A native of **Mold**, Morris-Jones was educated at **Bangor** and **Oxford**. After a period of social work, he was appointed lecturer in **philosophy** at Bangor (1942). In 1945, he was **Labour** candidate for **Merioneth**. He served on several public bodies. This, combined with his academic specialism in social philosophy and sociology, led to his appointment to the new chair of social theory and institutions at Bangor (1966). For a period he was a member of the **Broadcasting Council for Wales**. Both he and **Gwynfor Evans** resigned in 1960 when Rachel Jones, a non-**Welsh**-speaker who had spent most of her life outside Wales, was appointed to the chair of the Council. Later, he was a member of the Independent **Broadcasting** Authority and of the first board of **S4C**. A somewhat dour man, new acquaintances were surprised to hear that he was known as 'Humorous Jones'.

MORRIS-JONES, John (1864–1929)
Scholar, critic and poet

A native of **Anglesey**, he graduated in **mathematics** at **Oxford**, but began to study **Welsh** under the influence of **John Rhŷs**. After a period as lecturer in **Bangor**, he was appointed first professor of Welsh there in 1895. With John Rhŷs, he published an edition of *Llyfr yr Ancr* (1894) and, in 1896, he edited a new edition of **Ellis Wynne**'s *Gweledigaetheu y Bardd Cwsc*.

His most important work was *A Welsh Grammar* (1913). His *Cerdd Dafod* (1925) analyses **cynghanedd** and the strict metres. He raised doubts about the authenticity of Iolo Morganwg's (**Edward Williams**) Gorsedd of Bards, published a study of the work of **Taliesin**, and edited *Y Beirniad* (1911–19). His *Welsh Syntax* (1931) appeared posthumously. He created strong foundations for the 'correctness' of literary Welsh and purged it of what he considered to be 19th-century errors. His influence is evident in *Welsh Orthography* (1893) and *Orgraff yr Iaith Cymraeg* (1928).

He made an impact as an adjudicator at *eisteddfodau* and was one of the most important poets of the literary revival at the beginning of the 20th century. His volume *Caniadau* (1907) includes his long poems in the strict metres, 'Cymru Fu: Cymru Fydd' and 'Salm i Famon', as well as lyrics, poems in the *cywydd* metre and translations – particularly selections from Heine and Omar Khayyám.

MORTIMER family Marcher-lords

The family became associated with Wales *c.*1075, when Ralph Mortimer was granted lands around Wigmore (**Herefordshire**). He initiated attacks upon the Welsh rulers of **Maelienydd**, **Elfael** and **Radnor**. In 1230, his descendant, another Ralph Mortimer, married Gwladus Ddu, daughter of **Llywelyn ap Iorwerth**. **Llywelyn ap Gruffudd** may have been lured to his death at **Cilmery** by their grandson, Edmund Mortimer. Edmund's son, Roger (d.1330), was the greatest of the lords of the **March**, a fact underlined in 1327 when he was elevated to the earldom of March. The lover of Edward II's queen, Isabella, he was from 1326 to 1330 the virtual ruler of the English realm and encompassed the murder of Edward II (1327). In 1330, however, he was beheaded for treason. His uncle, another Roger (d.1326), was granted the lordship of **Chirk** in 1282.

Roger, the second earl of March (d.1360), was restored to royal favour. His son, Edmund (1351–81), married Philippa, who inherited the claim to the throne of her father, Lionel, second son of Edward III. Their son, Edmund, was captured by **Owain Glyndŵr** in 1402 and married Owain's daughter, Catrin. Under the Tripartite Indenture (*see* **Glyndŵr Revolt**), Edmund's nephew, another Edmund, was to become ruler of southern **England**. His niece, Anne, inherited the vast Mortimer lands, which included **Denbigh**, **Cedewain**, **Kerry**, Maelienydd, Radnor, **Builth**, **Blaenllynfi**, **Ewias** and **Narberth**, with their *caput* at **Ludlow**. She married Richard (d.1415), heir to the rights of Edmund, fourth son of Edward III, their joint ancestry representing the **York**ist claim to the throne. With the accession of their grandson as Edward IV in 1461, the Mortimer property passed to the crown. Much was made of Edward's descent, through Gwladus Ddu and the Mortimers, from Llywelyn ap Iorwerth. Indeed, **David Powel** argued that whereas Henry VII had inherited England from his father, heir to the house of **Lancaster**, he had inherited Wales from his mother, Elizabeth, daughter of Edward IV and heiress to the house of York, the Mortimers and Llywelyn ap Iorwerth.

MORYS (MORUS), Huw (Eos Ceiriog; 1622–1709)
Poet

The most talented and productive poet of the 17th century, Huw Morys was probably born near **Llangollen**, but for most of his life he lived with his brother's family in Pontymeibion, **Llansilin**. A bachelor, he had the leisure to visit the **gentry** houses of the north. He used the traditional strict metres but excelled in his use of free metres, which he embellished with *cynghanedd* and rhymes; several poems have tunes associated with them. He was a staunch royalist and **Anglican** who, after the Restoration, excoriated **Cromwell** and the **Puritans**.

MOSTYN, Flintshire (1170 ha; 2012 inhabitants)
Located on the **Dee** estuary immediately north-west of
Holywell, Mostyn was the home of Ithel Fychan
(fl.*c*.1350), whose descendant Thomas ap Richard (d.1558)
adopted the surname Mostyn. The **Mostyn family** still
occupies Mostyn Hall; remodelled in 1847, it is **Flintshire**'s
largest house. Its drive tunnels beneath Drybridge Lodge
(1849). **Coal**mining began in the 17th century, and Mostyn
also became a **lead**-smelting centre. Llannerch-y-mor, the
chief lead works, had its own dock and was in operation
from the 1680s to 1898. Its mill buildings have been conserved. Although it has long lost its role as the chief **port**
for the export of Flintshire coal to **Ireland**, Mostyn Docks
had, by the end of the 20th century, diversified its trade
and found new prosperity. The **community**'s Italianate **railway** station (*see* **Flint** and Holywell) is now a mere shell.

MOSTYN family Landowners
Still one of the leading landowning families in northern
Wales, the Mostyns stemmed from a series of marriages in
the 14th and 15th centuries which brought together the
'Five Courts': Pengwern (**Llangollen**), **Mostyn** in **Flintshire**,
Gloddaith (**Llandudno**), Trecastell and Tregarnedd (both
in **Anglesey**). In 1540, Thomas ap Richard (Thomas
Mostyn I) inherited all five estates and adopted the **surname** Mostyn. The family had a special relationship with
the bardic order and played a part in the **Caerwys**
eisteddfodau of 1523 and 1567. The Mostyn library was
famous; most of its **Welsh** manuscripts are now in the
National Library or in the library of the **University of
Wales, Bangor**. The direct male line ended in 1831 and the
estate passed to a nephew who was created Baron Mostyn.
The town of Llandudno was developed on the Gloddaith
estate following the arrival of the Chester–**Holyhead railway** in 1849. **Francis Mostyn**, of the **Roman Catholic**
Talacre (*see* **Llanasa**) branch of the family, was the second
archbishop of **Cardiff** (1921–39). In 1873, the family owned
2210 ha in Flintshire and 620 ha in **Caernarfonshire**.

MOSTYN, Francis [Joseph] (1860–1939)
Archbishop
Born at Talacre (**Llanasa**), into the Talacre, **Roman
Catholic**, branch of the **Mostyn family**, he trained for the
priesthood at Durham. In 1884, he was ordained for the
diocese of Shrewsbury, which then included Wales's six
northern **counties**. In 1895, he became vicar apostolic of the
new vicariate of Wales, which became the diocese of
Menevia in 1898. As bishop of Menevia, Mostyn's sympathy for the **Welsh language** and culture began a trend
among Welsh Catholic bishops. In 1921, he was consecrated the second Roman Catholic archbishop of **Cardiff**.
His time in office was characterized by a crusade against
'immorality' in **films**, and tireless efforts to provide
Catholic churches and schools.

MOTOR SPORTS
Motor racing grew out of **horse** and cycle racing (*see*
Cycling) in the early years of the 20th century. A
Demonstration Motorcycle Race at **Carmarthen** Park on
Whit Monday, 1905, is one of the earliest recorded races,
followed by a race for motorcycles on **Pendine** Sands as

part of the annual August bank holiday Sports and Races.
The Motor Union's 1909 speed tests on Pendine constituted Wales's first motor rally.

Speed trials on public **roads** before 1925, such as those at
Caerphilly and Arnold's Hill, **Haverfordwest**, took the form
of hill climbs or sprints, at the discretion of chief constables
and the RAC. Motorcycle grass-track trials and scrambles
were organized by local clubs under Auto Cycle Union
rules. From the early 1920s, **Llandrindod** was the focus of
the International Six Day Trial (ISDT) for motorcycles, an
important event in the sporting calendar. The Welsh TT,
staged from 1922 over three days at Pendine, attracted star
Isle of **Man** and Brooklands riders on works machines,
watched by crowds estimated at 40,000.

The rugged, forest-road terrain of mid and north Wales
provides the arena for special stages in motor rallies, both
on local club and international levels. Welsh stages always
prove among the most challenging to competitors in the
RAC (latterly Network Q) Rally. Wales lacks an internationally accredited Grand Prix circuit. Road races have
been run on tarmac since the **Second World War** on **military bases**, such as the **Mynydd Epynt** gunnery range, and
disused airfields – including **Llandow**, **Pembrey** and
Fairwood Common (**Ilston**).

MOUNTAIN ASH (Aberpennar), Rhondda
Cynon Taff (1202 ha; 7039 inhabitants)
Constituting the central part of the Cynon valley, the **community** contains the town of Mountain Ash and the villages
of Cwmpennar, Darranlas, Glenboi and Newtown. The
urban district of Mountain Ash (1894–1974) included the
later communities of **Abercynon**, **Penrhiwceiber** and
Ynysybwl as well as that of Mountain Ash, and was
broadly coterminous with the old **parish** of Llanwonno.
Aberpennar, first recorded in 1570 with reference to the
confluence of the Pennar with the Cynon, was adopted as
the **Welsh** name of the town in 1905. The town's **English**
name was originally that of a tavern.

A 16th-century poem lamenting the felling of 'Coed
Glyn Cynon' may reflect the anger directed at a local
English **iron**master whose demands for charcoal were
believed to be devastating the forests. Duffryn House
(demolished) was one of the seats of the **Bruce** (originally
Pryce) family, Barons Aberdare. Major development in
the area began in the 1850s through the efforts of John
Nixon, who pioneered the export of Welsh steam **coal** to
France. Nixon's Navigation Company came to own four
large pits around Mountain Ash, and the Nixon
Workmen's Institute (1899), now demolished, was for a
considerable period the handsomest building in the town.
The community contains a wealth of ecclesiastical **architecture**. The unusual **gorsedd** circle in Duffryn Woods is a
reminder that the National **Eisteddfod** visited Mountain
Ash in 1905 and 1946.

The Pavilion, once Wales's largest auditorium and, in
the 1930s, the home of the Three Valleys Festival, has been
converted to industrial use. In the main street, the statue of
the runner Guto Nyth Brân (**Griffith Morgan**) is the focal
point of the annual *Nos Galan* (New Year's Eve) races. The
popular Welsh **hymn** 'Calon Lân' was written in Mountain
Ash. The pioneer Cambro-Hibernian author **Joseph**

Keating was a native of Mountain Ash, as was the poet and theologian **Pennar Davies**. A plaque in the public library commemorates **Harri Webb**'s service as librarian (1964–74). The **population** of Mountain Ash urban district peaked at 43,287 in 1921.

MOUNTAINS

O. M. Edwards famously began his book *Wales* (1900) with the statement: 'Wales is a land of mountains'. In view of the fact that in a number of European countries there are mountains three and four times higher than Wales's highest – Yr Wyddfa, the summit of the **Snowdon** massif (1085 m) – the statement is debatable. As a native of Switzerland commented, viewing Wales's mountains in the late 19th century: 'The good Lord has forgotten to put tops on them.' Nevertheless, the riposte 'Ours start lower down' has substance. A 4000-m mountain rising from a 3500-m plateau can look less impressive than a 1000-m mountain rising from a 100-m valley. Snowdon looks 'every inch a complete mountain', a comment that can also be applied to the **Brecon Beacons**, the **Carneddau** and **Cadair Idris**, together with Glyder Fawr, Glyder Fach and Tryfan (*see* **Glyder Fawr** for all three).

Even if Wales is not a mountainous country in the Norwegian or Swiss sense, the fact that more than half its surface lies over 200 m means that it is certainly dominated by uplands. Of the 13 ancient **counties**, all but **Anglesey**, **Flintshire** and **Pembrokeshire** contain land over 600 m. In terms of their underlying rock, Wales's oldest mountains are those of the **Harlech** Dome (*see* **Rhinogydd**), with their thick succession of Cambrian strata (*see* **Geology**).

Surrounding the Dome is a wide expanse of more recent Ordovician rock. That rock, which offers much evidence of volcanic activity, is associated with the precipitousness of the slopes of the mountains of **Snowdonia** and constitutes the material from which **Arenig**, **Aran** and Cadair Idris were carved. To the east is a further group of Ordovician rock containing little igneous material – that which underlies the gentler outlines of the **Berwyn Mountains**. Then to the north, south and west stretches a wide tract of plateau country carved across sedimentary rocks of the Ordovician and Silurian eras, a tract which includes **Mynydd Hiraethog**, the **Kerry** Hills, **Radnor Forest**, **Pumlumon** and the **Elenydd Mountains**. More recent again is the Old Red Sandstone underlying **Mynydd Epynt**, the Brecon Beacons and the **Black Mountains**. Even more recent are the **Coal** Measures of the uplands of the south Wales coalfield. Then, in the south-west is the band of Ordovician rock, rich in intrusive igneous material, which constitutes **Mynydd Preseli**.

Wales has experienced glaciation on at least five occasions, with each successive ice age obliterating much of the evidence of the previous one. Cumulatively, they have played a key role in the creation of the present profile of the country's mountains – the cirques of Snowdonia and the Brecon Beacons, for example, or the drumlins of Mynydd Hiraethog. The end of the most recent Ice Age, some 11,500 years ago, presaged the subjection of the mountains to the impact of human activity. By *c.*5500 BC, Wales's uplands were covered on the lower slopes by a thick canopy of trees, which gave way, as the altitude rose, to scrub and eventually to grassland and alpine heath.

Richard Wilson, *Cader Idris, Llyn-y-Cau* (1765–6)

Tree felling, together with the domestic animals introduced from the **Neolithic Age** onwards, led to deforestation and the creation of blanket **peat** bogs. Thus, the mountains of Wales, often considered to be the acme of unspoilt beauty, in fact represent a relict landscape with its natural condition destroyed. Such landscape transformation was a particularly marked feature of the climatically favourable early **Bronze Age**, the era when many Welsh hills were crowned with cairns and when cereals were grown high on Mynydd Hiraethog.

Its mountains have played a major role in the history of Wales. **Cyril Fox**'s theory that in the lowlands new cultures tend to be imposed, whereas in the highlands old cultures tend to be retained, has considerable relevance in the Welsh context. It is the country's geographical relief that obliged the **Romans** to spend decades conquering it, and which insured that, throughout the Roman occupation, Wales was a frontier rather than a civil zone. The advance of the **Anglo-Saxons**, a lowland people, ceased when they reached the Welsh uplands, and it was altitude that was the key to **Norman** settlement in Wales, with its lowland Englishries and its upland Welshries.

Mountains are usually cited as the main cause of the failure of medieval Wales to become a united polity with regnal solidarity. Yet, bearing in mind that **Scotland** – a more mountainous country – achieved that condition, it may be more relevant to consider that a major factor in Wales's failure was the absence of a single dominant lowland comparable with Scotland's linked basins of the Tay, Forth and Clyde, the heartland of the kingdom of the Scots. Indeed, the portrayal of the Welsh mountains as impenetrable barriers can be misleading, for they are permeated everywhere by valleys generally linked by traversable passes, causing Wales to be perhaps more a country of valleys than it is of mountains.

It was the uplands that caused Wales to be a land of pastoral rather than arable **agriculture**. It was the resources of the mountains – **slate** and **iron**, **copper** and **lead** ores and the falling waters that powered early machinery (*see* **Watermills** and **Energy**) – which enabled Wales to partake in the **Industrial Revolution**. Southern Wales has **Britain**'s sole mountainous coalfield, a major factor in the development of coalfield society and the dominant one in the emergence of the coalfield's townscape.

Following the decline in upland settlement caused by the deteriorating **climate** of the late Bronze Age and the **Iron Age**, occupation of the higher uplands tended to be restricted to the summer months (*see* *Hafod* and *Hendre*). By the later Middle Ages, however, as **sheep** replaced **cattle** and **goats** as the chief grazers of high pastures, transhumance declined. In subsequent centuries, **population** pressures caused the *hafotai* (summer dwellings) to become independent farms, a development which led to the **enclosure** of the uplands and to the most striking man-made feature of the mountains of Wales – the hundreds of kilometres of **dry stone walling**. Much of the enclosure was surreptitious; it was the work of squatters who built *tai unnos* (houses built in one night) on **common land**, causing a commentator to describe the southern slopes of the Brecon Beacons as a district to which 'an Irish estate had been transferred and filled in as a patchwork amongst the Welsh mountains'.

The era of the culmination of the reoccupation of the mountains – the late 18th century – coincided with an emerging appreciation of their beauty. Before the rise of the **Romantic** Movement, sensitive travellers on mountain **roads** pulled down the blinds of their coach lest they should be pained by the barbarity around them. A revolution in sensibility led to a glorification of the wild, the sublime and the **picturesque**, thus initiating a tourist invasion of the mountains – a major factor in their history over the last 250 years. The pioneers were the painters, with **Richard Wilson**'s *Cader Idris, Llyn-y-Cau* (1765–6) magnificently capturing the spirit of high places. Walkers followed and, by 1831, it was stated that 'there is no place more public than the higher ground of Snowdon during the summer'. The rugged slopes of Snowdonia became one of the chief nurseries of the art of **rock climbing**, but there were those who preferred the more rounded – and less crowded – slopes of the uplands east and south of Snowdonia; **George Borrow** found Pumlumon particularly appealing.

Prominent among mountain lovers are the botanists, for whom the northern slopes of Snowdonia are especially significant. Although far lower than the Alps, their more northerly latitude means that they provide habitats for alpine **plants**; although far more southerly than the Arctic, their cold sunless windswept slopes also provide habitats for arctic plants. Chief among their Alpine-Arctic flora is the Snowdon lily, named *Lloydia serotina* in honour of the great Welsh scholar **Edward Lhuyd**. Others include the Alpine mouse-ear, the Alpine hawkweed and the mountain avens. Other mountain ranges are also home to rare plants, among them the cloudberry of the Berwyn, the purple saxifrage of the Brecon Beacons and the lesser whitebeam of **Mynydd Llangatwg**. In the 20th century, however, the activity of the **Forestry Commission** caused much of upland Wales to be dominated an alien species – the sikta spruce imported from **North America**.

Afforestation is only one aspect of the transformation undergone by the Welsh mountains over recent centuries. Waste from slate quarrying abounds in Snowdonia, and the more toxic waste from lead mines is a feature of the Elenydd Mountains. **Rivers** have been dammed to create mountain **reservoirs**. Mynydd Epynt and much of the Brecon Beacons have become army training grounds (*see* **Military Bases**). Eminences have been crowned with wind farms (*see* **Windmills**). Almost as intrusive is the impact of pounding feet, an impact particularly visible on the tracks leading to Yr Wyddfa, a summit reached annually by at least a million walkers. Yet, the degree to which Wales's mountains are swarming with visitors can be exaggerated; in the Elenydd Mountains – southern Britain's largest wilderness – a wanderer can walk all day without seeing anyone at all.

MOWBRAY family Marcher-lords

The family became associated with Wales through the marriage of John Mowbray (d.1322) and Aline, heiress of William de **Breos** (d.1326), lord of **Gower**. Their grandson, John (d.1368) married Elizabeth, granddaughter and heiress of Thomas, earl of Norfolk, half-brother of Edward II and lord of **Chepstow**. Their son, Thomas (d.1399), created duke of Norfolk in 1397, married Elizabeth, co-heiress of Richard **Fitz Alan**, lord of **Bromfield and Yale**. The Mowbrays failed in the male line in 1476, and their Welsh lordships passed to the English crown; Gower was later granted to the **Herbert** family. The dukedom was revived in 1483 in favour of John Howard, grandson of the first Mowbray duke.

MOXHAM, Glendinning (*c.*1860–*c.*1935) Architect
A native of **Swansea**, Moxham studied at Nottingham and entered into partnership with James Buckley Wilson of Bath in 1888. Together they were responsible for many houses in a picturesque style in the Swansea area, as well as general works, including Swansea Market (1889). Moxham designed Swansea's Glynn Vivian Gallery (1911) and wrote *Country Houses and Cottages* (1914).

MUDIAD AMDDIFFYN CYMRU (Movement for the Defence of Wales)
Rumours of the existence of Mudiad Amddiffyn Cymru (MAC), a secret, **nationalist** organization, became widespread in 1963 following a bomb attack on the site of the **Tryweryn** dam. Between 1966 and 1969, the organization was responsible for a succession of explosions, including an audacious attack upon the Clywedog dam (*see* **Llanidloes Without**). Its supporters were fiercely opposed to the investiture of the **Prince of Wales** at **Caernarfon** in 1969. The **'Abergele Martyrs'**, killed on the morning of the investiture, were linked to the organization. Attacks came to an end in 1970 with the imprisonment of John Barnard Jenkins (b.1933), the organization's charismatic leader.

MUDIAD YSGOLION MEITHRIN
Meaning, literally, the nursery schools movement, it is a voluntary organization established in 1971 to provide a national structure for developments in **Welsh**-medium nursery **education**. An open-door policy was adopted, for children from both Welsh and non-Welsh-speaking homes, with the aim of immersing the latter in the language. Financial backing was received from the departments of social services and education at the **Welsh Office** and subsequently from the **Welsh Language Board**.

The movement's head office is in **Aberystwyth** and development officers in the field are staff employees, but volunteers and *cylch meithrin* (playgroup) leaders remain the backbone of the organization. Increasingly, provision has been made for children with special needs and for supporting parents and child-minders in *cylchoedd Ti a Fi* (parent and toddler groups). The movement has grown phenomenally, from 65 groups in 1971 to over 500 *cylchoedd meithrin* and over 400 *cylchoedd Ti a Fi* in 2007. It is credited with having contributed significantly to the revival of the language and to the future of Welsh-medium education, and it has inspired those wishing to restore lesser-used languages worldwide.

MURPHY, Jimmy (James Patrick; 1910–89)
Footballer and manager
Rhondda-born Murphy played for West Bromwich and won 15 caps as an attacking half-back. In 1946, he joined Manchester United as a coach, becoming assistant manager (1955–71). He managed Wales (1956–64), his glory

Children of Ysgol Feithrin Llandegfan, Anglesey, with the entertainer Dewi 'Pws' Morris in 1971

year being 1958. Following the Munich disaster (1958), he stood in for Matt Busby and took United to the Cup Final before leaving for Sweden and an impressive performance with Wales in the World Cup, in which the team reached the quarter-finals.

MURRAY, [William] Grant (1877–1950)
Educationist and painter

While Scottish-born Grant Murray's **painting** was skilled in a wide range of observational genres, it was as a visionary and influential teacher that he made his mark in Wales. By 1909, when he was appointed principal of **Swansea** School of Art, the scholarship system had begun to give the industrial working **class** an opportunity to study art, and Grant Murray became the mentor of an important group of emerging Welsh artists, widening the art school curriculum and appointing inspirational teachers. Influential as the first director of the Glynn Vivian **Art Gallery**, he organized the art and **craft** section of the 1926 National **Eisteddfod** at Swansea. Under Grant Murray's direction, Swansea School of Art made the most significant single scholastic contribution to 20th-century Welsh art.

MUSIC
Modern ideas that link Wales with music derive largely from 19th-century conceptions of Wales as a **'land of song'**. Much of this was based on developments from **Nonconformist** choral music and musical manifestations of *eisteddfodau*. It obscured the fact that the Welsh have long regarded music making as one of their primary means of expression and communication, and that the modes and media of that expression have always been extensive and diverse. The music of Wales is especially rich in its vernacular traditions, and it is possible to detect distinctive indigenous elements in Welsh art music and commercial popular music of the recent period. These later developments must be seen in the light of the emergence of new forums for Welsh music making in which institutions such as the BBC (*see* **Broadcasting**), **Welsh National Opera**, **record companies** such as Sain, the **Arts Council of Wales** and various initiatives in **education** have been prominent.

Traditional music

The country's oldest traditional songs are probably those connected with seasonal customs. The period around the winter solstice saw the performance of the **Mari Lwyd horse** ceremony and **Hunting the Wren**, both of which included processional songs in which repetition is a marked musical feature. New Year's Day *Calennig* songs (*see also Calan, Y*) requested gifts and wished good fortune to the giver. The coming of spring was celebrated in the **Candlemas** ceremony, held on 2 February, in which a solemn **wassail** ritual was followed by dancing (*see* **Dance**) and feast songs, such as 'Un o fy mrodyr i'. Children celebrated Shrove Tuesday by singing 'pancake' songs from house to house. On the first day of May (*Calan Mai*) came **summer carols** and dancing to the **Cadi ha** song.

Winter solstice rituals and May Day dancing carried pagan overtones, but the Christian element was also strong. Christmas *plygain* carols and Welsh summer carols were doctrinal rather than hedonistic. In the 17th and 18th centuries, these carols featured complex poetry based on *cynghanedd*. Some were sung to English tunes such as 'Crimson Velvet', but Welsh melodies such as 'Ffarwel Ned Puw' were also used. These carol tunes might have been employed for **ballads** and songs in the **interlude** (*anterliwt*).

The most common type of Welsh folk song is the **love** song. Frequent themes include praise of the girl, sorrow at parting, *chansons d'aventure* and night visits. **Birds** sometimes feature as love messengers and counsellors. A few songs refer to **bundling**, and may employ sexual metaphor. Some songs are macaronic, with **Welsh** and **English** alternating.

Next in popularity were ballads. Until the 19th century, these tended to employ complex melodies and texts, but this complexity was replaced subsequently by simpler poetic forms with a strong narrative function. Common themes have always been murder, thwarted love, **emigration**, **colliery disasters**, humorous topics with easily memorable melodies, sometimes from **Ireland** or **North America**. The oldest work songs are probably the oxen-ploughing songs mentioned by **Giraldus Cambrensis**, which were still sung in the late 19th century. Some 20 survive, simple in character and distinguished by a 'call' to the oxen at the end of each verse. Iolo Morganwg (**Edward Williams**) noted one in the 18th century, as well as a milkmaid's song. An Irish tune, 'St Patrick's Day in the Morning', popular in Wales, was used in one smithy to accompany the striking of the anvil. But most Welsh work songs described actual labour such as **fish**ing, **sheep** shearing and ploughing.

Humour, satire and exaggeration are common in Welsh song, including the *penillion telyn* (**harp** verses), which are detached stanzas sung to simple tunes, some with boisterous, collaborative refrains, others quiet and reflective. Some of these refrains were originally instrumental. 'Triban Gwŷr Morgannwg' was noted by **William Jones** (Llangadfan, **Banwy**; 1726–95) as being sung in the 18th-century manner, with short instrumental 'symphonies' between the lines of verse. When a version of the same tune was printed about half a century later in **Maria James Williams**'s *Ancient National Airs of Gwent and Morganwg*, the instrumental symphonies had been replaced by vocal refrains of nonsense syllables ('fa-la-la', and so on).

The relatively narrow melodic compass, the descant-like quality of some tunes, and the comparative lack of ornamentation, signal the association between the harp and the voice that is often evident in the musical characteristics of Welsh songs. Declamation of poetry may have led to another characteristic, the opening of a song by chanting on the fifth of the scale; and declamation is a prominent feature of *canu pwnc* (lit. 'singing text'). The influence of the harp may also be responsible in part for the preponderance of major and minor scale patterns, and the stepwise movement found in many melodies. Of the other scale patterns, the dorian ('re') mode is the most common in Wales; other songs are based on the mixolydian ('sol') mode, but many of these are foreign in origin. Some rhythmic characteristics derive from the rhythmic patterns of the Welsh language, which generally puts the accent on the penultimate syllable. If the syllable is 'snapped' at a fast tempo it creates syncopation; at a slow tempo it suggests an *appoggiatura*. These characteristics, taken together, help to differentiate the Welsh musical tradition from other European traditional music.

Although most traditional songs of Wales are in Welsh, there is also a considerable stock of English-language material. English-language songs were most prevalent in those areas that were traditionally English-speaking, such as south **Pembrokeshire** and west **Gower**, but they have also been found in other parts of Wales. Songs can cross the language barrier. '**Llangollen** Market', for example, was collected in English as part of an entry to the 1858 National Eisteddfod, but is now best known in its translated Welsh form, while 'Y Saith Rhyfeddod' (The **Seven Wonders**) was found in an English form in the **Tawe** valley.

The English-language songs can be divided into social, ceremonial and industrial categories. Social songs are strongest in west Gower, where **Phil Tanner** of **Llangennith** was the best known of a large number of singers. Gower also had ceremonial songs such as 'Get Up a New Year's Morning', 'The Gower Wassail' and 'Poor Old Horse', while ceremonial songs found in Pembrokeshire included the wren custom songs, 'The King' and 'The Cutty Wren'.

Broadside ballads came in with the industrial era. Many printers, including Ebenezer Rees of **Ystalyfera**, J. T. Morgan of **Merthyr Tydfil**, and Davies and Thomas of Treorchy (**Rhondda**) produced thousands of broadsheets marking notable events, sometimes in English, sometimes in Welsh, and frequently back-to-back in both languages. The **coal**field, with large numbers of English-speaking immigrants arriving to join the Welsh-speaking natives, generated a number of macaronic songs.

John Roberts (Ieuan Gwyllt; 1822–77)

Welsh seamen developed distinctively local styles of work song. The 50 shanties and sea songs collected in 1928 from Rees Baldwin, William Fender and other **Cardiff**, **Barry** and **Swansea** sailors by the American collector James Madison Carpenter, show a greater familiarity with the complexities of music and singing than was common among sailors. Many English-language shanties collected by **J. Glyn Davies** from the men of the Cambrian Line and the other **Liverpool**-based Welsh-owned companies in the last years of the 19th century showed that Welsh crews and black American sailors shared a talent unknown among the seamen of other maritime nations – the ability to sing naturally in harmony.

While traditional songs have long been a staple of the eisteddfodic stage, performed in a somewhat operatic style, the 1970s saw the beginnings of a folk song revival influenced at least in part by rock music and the formidable international success of Irish folk acts. Groups such as Ar Log, Plethyn, Yr Hwntws and the instrumentally experimental Aberjaber found new audiences for the music – in folk clubs, festivals and on international tours – establishing a foundation for the scores of Welsh folk groups that currently flourish. The development of folk music was given a fresh impetus in 2007 with the opening in **Dolgellau** of Tŷ Siamas, the National Centre for Welsh Folk Music.

Hymns and music of the chapel

The earliest **hymns** for congregational use were published by **Edmwnd Prys** in 1621 and set to psalm tunes derived from Scottish and other sources. Although hymns were written by Dissenters in the 17th and 18th centuries, it was the **Methodist Revival**, especially in its second phase from 1762, that provided the impetus for the development of hymn singing. Hymns composed by **William Williams** (Pantycelyn; 1717–91) and others were set to popular secular tunes like 'Lovely Peggy' and 'God Save the King' and by the late 18th century congregations were adopting native Welsh ballad tunes for chapel use, and composing their own melodies. These were later noted down in collections such as John Roberts's (1807–76) *Caniadau y Cysegr* (1839) and Richard Mills's (Rhydderch Hael; 1809–44) *Caniadau Seion* (1840).

The appointment of Henry Mills (1757–1820) of **Llanidloes** as a musical overseer to the Methodist congregations of central Wales in the 1780s heralded a drive to improve the standard of singing. In the 1820s and 1830s, local musical societies were formed throughout Wales – at **Bala**, **Aberystwyth** and **Bethesda** among others – to encourage singing in parts and to foster an understanding of the rudiments of music. Musical primers and collections of tunes appeared. The first collection was John Ellis's (1760–1839) *Mawl yr Arglwydd* (1816), and the publication of primers reached a climax with the appearance in 1838 of John Mills's (Ieuan Glan Alarch; 1812–73) *Gramadeg Cerddoriaeth* (The Grammar of Music), which established itself as a fundamental work of musical education.

Congregational singing was given further impetus by the **temperance movement**. From its inception in 1854, the Temperance Choral Union of **Gwent** and **Glamorgan** organized annual festivals for the singing of choruses and hymn tunes by combined choirs. In 1859, the publication of *Llyfr Tonau Cynulleidfaol* (Congregational Tune Book) by **John Roberts** (Ieuan Gwyllt; 1822–77) provided congregations with a body of standard tunes that were less florid than those of a previous generation, and with unadorned harmonies. The collection was widely disseminated, and the practice of combining together to sing tunes from the book laid a firm foundation for the development of the *cymanfa ganu* (hymn-singing festival).

From the 1860s onwards, the growing availability of music in the tonic sol-fa notation, promoted by **Eleazar Roberts** and Ieuan Gwyllt, enabled congregations to learn to read music more fluently, strengthening the practice of singing in parts. Chapel singing was still mainly unaccompanied. The growing popularity of the *cymanfa ganu* from the 1870s onwards encouraged the composition of hymn tunes by local composers for use in festivals that became increasingly denominational; by the end of the 19th century, each denomination had its own hymnal reflecting its traditions and practices. The larger and more enterprising congregations would incorporate anthems and psalms in the service to supplement the staple fare of hymns, and organs became more common in chapels from the 1890s onwards.

Developments in the 20th century confirmed the pattern established in previous generations. Denominational hymnals were revised and supplemented by other collections. The *cymanfa ganu* acquired iconic status as a symbol of Welshness, particularly at national events and outside Wales (it is the chief festival among the Welsh of North America). Hymn singing was viewed as a characteristically Welsh practice whenever Welsh people were gathered together, in clubs, pubs and **rugby** stadiums, as much as in chapel. New hymns and tunes composed during the later 20th century have tended to follow established patterns, with only limited experimentation, and the decline in chapel attendances has undermined the tradition of four-part singing. Nevertheless, the tradition remained sufficiently strong at the beginning of the 21st century for an interdenominational hymnal, *Caneuon Ffydd* (Songs of Faith), to be published in 2001.

Secular choral music (see also **Male Voice Choirs**)

Although the greater volume of choral music by Welsh composers in the 19th century was religious, Welsh composers after **Joseph Parry** have added considerably to the secular choral music repertoire. Parry himself is perhaps best known for his 'Myfanwy', a beautifully crafted part-song. Many of the other secular choral works by Parry and his contemporaries, among them Gwilym Gwent (William Aubrey Williams; 1838–91), **David Jenkins** and **D. Emlyn Evans**, were tailored for the Victorian music market. A later generation of composers tended to show greater ambition in the texts they chose to set. **David Vaughan Thomas** was drawn in several of his choral works to George Meredith, and he also produced a fine setting of Thomas Gray's 'The Bard' (*see* **Massacre of the Bards**), probably the most advanced work of its kind composed by a Welsh composer before 1914. In the field of male voice composition, T. Maldwyn Price (1861–1934) (and later **Daniel Protheroe**)

reflected popular concerns in colourful works such as 'Crossing the Plain'. Many composers followed the lead given by mainland European composers such as de Rille, whose 'Martyrs of the Arena' probably influenced a wide range of similar works by Welsh composers, including D. C. Williams's (1871–1926) 'Charge of the Light Brigade', **Cyril Jenkins**'s 'Fallen Heroes' and David Jenkins's 'The War Horse', which have their origins in eisteddfod competition. Composers such as D. Afan Thomas (1881–1928) also made an important contribution with, for instance, his 'Battle of the Baltic'. Arrangements of Welsh folk tunes have been very common in the work of virtually every Welsh composer since Joseph Parry. Large-scale works of a secular nature, such as the folk-influenced 'Llyn y Fan' of David Vaughan Thomas, inspired by the legend of **Llyn y Fan Fach**, and later the ***Mabinogion***-based 'Culhwch ac Olwen' of **William Mathias**, had their first performances at the National Eisteddfod.

Since 1945, with the advent of the orchestras of BBC Wales and the Welsh National Opera, most Welsh composers have been increasingly drawn to instrumental and orchestral composition. Nevertheless, they have continued to show an interest in the setting of religious texts. Mathias in particular made a significant contribution to church music, while his contemporary Alun Hoddinott has also added to this field. One feature of post-war Welsh secular music has been the willingness of composers to explore the widest possible influences in **literature**: **Daniel Jones** in settings of Blake, for example, Mathias in settings of **Dylan Thomas** and **Gerard Manley Hopkins**, and David Harries in settings of the poets of his native Pembrokeshire. Both Gareth Glyn and Brian Hughes have been drawn to the poems of Gwyn Thomas (b.1936), while composers such as Mervyn Burtch, Ian Parrott, Hoddinott and **David Wynne** have all been drawn at various times to the poetic and mythical past of Wales.

Music education

Alhough concern for music education is apparent from the 1830s onwards in publications such as John Mills's *Gramadeg Cerddoriaeth*, formal music education did not take root in Wales until the mid-19th century, when the tonic sol-fa movement became especially influential. The gifted leader of the Welsh movement was Ieuan Gwyllt who initiated, as hymnodist and teacher, a process of popular music education; his *Blodau Cerdd* (1852) contained specimen hymn tunes and a programme of basic music lessons. This work was continued by his pupil, D. Emlyn Evans, and they set standards of taste in the writing and performance of congregational music for *cymanfaoedd canu*.

In 1919, the creation of the National (or University) Council of Music established a critical forum for choral singing in Wales. **Walford Davies**, its first director, played an important part in musical education in Wales through his BBC broadcasts. He succeeded in drawing people away from over-dependence upon the choral tradition, encouraging a public interest in instrumental music and in the classical European tradition. Music departments were established at the **University of Wales** early in the history of

Dafydd Iwan, singer, record company owner and politician, photographed in the late 1960s

its constituent colleges – at Aberystwyth in 1873, where Joseph Parry was the first professor of music (the department closed in 1992), at Cardiff in 1883, and at **Bangor** in 1920. The **Royal Welsh College of Music and Drama** was founded in Cardiff in 1949.

The cultivation of diverse music skills in Wales gathered pace after 1945, when a widely based, publicly funded infrastructure was added to private and informal music education provision. Local authorities appointed music advisers to promote instrumental and vocal teaching in schools, and the **National Youth Orchestra of Wales** began its celebrated history in 1946. The orchestra's influence on young music makers was later augmented by the foundation of four specialist ensembles: the National Youth **Brass Band** of Wales (1982), the National Youth Choir of Wales (1984), the National Youth Jazz Orchestra of Wales (2001) and the National Youth Wind Orchestra of Wales (2002). The culmination of these developments came with the implementation of a distinctively Welsh music curriculum following the passage of the Education Act of 1988.

Art music

The term 'art music' refers to notated instrumental and vocal music, both sacred and secular, encompassing that which is normally termed classical music as well as modern and contemporary styles, in contrast with folk music and pop or jazz music, which mostly belong to the aural and recording traditions respectively. From the earliest recorded times Wales has sustained traditions of sacred and secular music. Musical activity before the 6th century is described in myth and folklore, and evidence for it can be found in archaeological discoveries. Welsh poetry from the 13th century frequently mentions military horns and trumpets, and a vivid picture emerges of bards and their aristocratic patrons. **Gildas** described the beauty of young voices praising God in song, and the *crwth* is mentioned in medieval sources.

Giraldus Cambrensis famously described the Welsh people's liking for singing in parts. When he toured Wales in 1182, he was impressed by the tradition of harp playing. After the **Edwardian conquest** of 1282, the arts were affected by changing social conditions, and new rules were set for the bardic profession, with *eisteddfodau*, particularly those held at **Carmarthen** (*c.*1451) and **Caerwys** (1523 and 1567), becoming central to the tradition. From the 13th century onwards, the *crwth* was increasingly played with a bow, and the continuing popularity of the harp is attested to in the poetry of **Dafydd ap Gwilym**.

The earliest source for Welsh sacred music is the 14th-century **Penpont Antiphonal**, which contains settings for St **David**'s Day services. The early 17th-century **Robert ap Huw** manuscript is the earliest source for harp music, and one of the most important sources of its type, in a European as well as in a Welsh context; it offers evidence that the bardic tradition incorporated music as a fundamental element of performed poetry.

From the 12th century onwards, Welsh musicians appear in the English court's account books. Composers such as Siôn Gwynedd, Philip ap Rhys, John Lloyd, Elway Bevin and **Thomas Tomkins** contributed to the English church tradition. The shift towards **England** as the cultural centre weakened the bardic tradition, and traditional Welsh instruments were gradually displaced. The *crwth* was eventually replaced by the **fiddle**, and the triple harp was imported from Italy during the later 17th century. Published collections of Welsh harp music and Welsh airs date from the middle of the 18th century, when the eisteddfod became an increasingly national festival, the **Corwen** Eisteddfod of 1789 marking an important turning point. Both choral singing, which was sustained in the industrial heartlands in particular, and *penillion* singing were actively promoted by the eisteddfod.

Social and demographic changes in Wales in the 19th century contributed to a growth in amateur performance groups, both vocal and instrumental. The ready availability of modestly priced, printed editions provided opportunities for the performance of art music. Such activity proliferated, especially in the southern industrial belt. Joseph Parry, who composed the most enduring vocal music of the period, also wrote competent instrumental works, including the 'Tydfil Overture', which is probably the first original work for brass band.

By 1900, the National Eisteddfod was well established, and increasingly provided a platform for performances of works not only by home-grown talents such as Cyril Jenkins, but also of the great choral works – often for the first time in Wales: for example, Stravinsky's *Firebird* was performed in Barry in 1921 and Bach's *Mass in B Minor* in **Ammanford** in 1922. Various non-competitive festivals were established, and those held at **Harlech** (1869–1934) and Cardiff (1892–1910), and the Three Valleys Festival (1930–9) held at **Mountain Ash** did much to raise awareness of wider trends. While choral music flourished around the turn of the century, Welsh composers also emerged with a clearer view of what might constitute a national 'school'. David Vaughan Thomas, **Morfydd Llwyn Owen** and David de Lloyd (1883–1948) did much to create a new awareness of the musical potential of early Welsh poetry in their works, and were often influenced by folk sources, benefiting from the systematic collation of folk music undertaken by the **Welsh Folk-Song Society** from 1906, and from the work of individuals such as **J. Lloyd Williams** and **W. S. Gwyn Williams**. In addition to Walford Davies's championing of instrumental and classical music, a substantial contribution was made by the sisters Gwendoline and Margaret Davies (*see* **Davies family (Llandinam)**) who established the annual Music Festival at their home of Gregynog (**Tregynon**).

The period after 1945 was one of impressive growth, aided by the patronage of institutions such as the BBC, the Welsh National Opera, the University music departments, the Welsh Arts Council (Arts Council of Wales), the National Eisteddfod and the **Llangollen International Musical Eisteddfod**, together with the proliferation of music festivals, the formation of the National Youth Orchestra of Wales and, from 1955 onwards, the pioneering work of the Guild for the Promotion of Welsh Music (now known as the Welsh Music Guild) from 1955 onwards. Several composers whose careers had been disrupted by the war – **Mansel Thomas**, **Arwel Hughes**, Daniel Jones, David Wynne and **Grace Williams** – were followed by a younger generation who rose rapidly to prominence: among these were Alun Hoddinott and William Mathias, both of whom quickly became known internationally, and

David Harries, Mervyn Burtch and Brian Hughes. They, in turn, were followed by composers such as John Metcalf, Jeffrey Lewis, Richard Elfyn Jones, Richard Roderick Jones, Gareth Glyn and Martin Davies. By the early 21st century, Wales had a wide range of composers whose styles reflected the musical pluralism of the wider world. Karl Jenkins, whose early career was as a jazz composer and performer, and John Cale, best known in rock music, have made notable contributions in the field of art music. Others, such as Dilys Elwyn-Edwards, Enid Luff, Lynne Plowman, Rhian Samuel and Hilary Tann were gaining significant reputations by the end of the 20th century.

Despite the achievement of Wales's composers, the country's chief contribution to the world of 20th-century music was that of its singers, particularly its opera singers. **Leila Megáne** sang with the Opéra Comique in Paris between 1912 and 1916, and also performed at Monte Carlo, Milan, Moscow and New York. In a later era, **Geraint Evans**, Gwyneth Jones and **Delme Bryn-Jones** graced the world's greatest opera houses, as did Stuart Burrows, Margaret Price, Dennis O'Neill, and Rebecca Evans. By the opening of the 21st century, Bryn Terfel enjoyed massive international recognition. Katherine Jenkins and Charlotte Church gained popularity, and Aled Jones, who had won acclaim as a boy soprano, succeeded in reinventing himself as a tenor.

Since the mid-20th century, Wales has also made its mark in instrumental music – Osian Ellis on the harp, for example, and, in later decades, Llŷr Williams (piano) and Catrin Finch (harp). In addition, Owain Arwel Hughes has won a reputation as an orchestra conductor of international importance.

Ystradgynlais Prize Band, 1905

Popular music

Three features are prominent in the story of popular music in Wales between 1830 and the end of the **Second World War**: the continuation of the rurally based Welsh-language popular tradition; the absorption of that tradition into newly urbanized areas (sometimes with a synthesis of traditional and newer forms of communal music making); and the adoption of the commercialized popular music culture that was prevalent elsewhere – the products of which were sometimes invested with a particularly Welsh flavour.

The new industrial communities, lacking the benefit of wealthy patrons or centres of sophisticated taste, literally found their voice and their identity in collective musical expression. This took the forms of *cymanfaoedd canu*, oratorio concerts, choral competitions, flute and **brass bands** and, for the talented individual, solo vocal and (to a lesser extent, for these were working-**class** communities) instrumental expression. Choirs became the focus of community loyalty, and up to the early 20th century their competitive rivalries fired powerful collective passions that often spilled over into disorder and mayhem.

The surge in amateur instrumental ensemble performance evident in **Britain** by *c*.1850 made its mark in Welsh industrialized communities somewhat later, but by the late

Tom Jones on stage

1870s amateur orchestras and brass bands were a common feature of the cultural landscape. Brass bands long continued to be a popular element in the working-class culture of Wales. Choral and amateur instrumental music in which musical literacy (through staff notation or tonic sol-fa) was common, created a strong amateur music infrastructure that was further developed in the later 19th century in the wake of the mass purchase of pianos and harmoniums, aided by the growth of deferred payment facilities.

Amateur light opera companies became established in the 1890s and, drawing on local talent, they established a foothold especially in the industrial villages of the southern coalfield. These, like instrumental and orchestral formations, were better able to adjust to declining chapel attendance and increasing secularization which, along with the changing social patterns of leisure and entertainment symbolized by the arrival of the **cinema** (*see* **Film**), gramophone and wireless, contributed to the ebbing of once-fierce communal musical passions. From the 1890s, the male voice choir established itself as the emblematic Welsh musical institution, and by the mid-20th century it had displaced the mixed choir as the most distinctive expression of a collective Welsh popular music culture. At the same time, other forms of musical activity, such as the uniquely Welsh art of *penillion* singing, retained (and still retain) their popularity among the more scattered population of rural Welsh-speaking Wales.

In the 20th century, many products of Welsh popular music culture have been built on the 'land of song' notion. Such stereotyping has been propagated by male voice choirs, which have toured abroad since the late 19th century, and through popular media presentations such as BBC Wales's **Welsh Rarebit** and cinema representations of Welsh life. This imaging of the place of music in Welsh popular life was greatly exaggerated and caricatured, but it has its origins in fact. Along with sport, music making is the most prominent ingredient of Welsh popular culture.

While popular choralism and its by-products have sustained a place in Welsh cultural life, the period after 1945 has been marked by the success of Welsh artists who exploited new styles of popular music. Rock and pop music has a rich history in both languages, the two linguistic strands seeming initially to develop independently, but later converging to some (occasionally controversial) extent in the 1990s. It could be argued that the country's pop and rock artists have made a bigger impression internationally than performers in any other genre of music. **Donald Peers** enjoyed massive popularity in the 1940s and 1950s; and Tom Jones and Shirley Bassey became world-famous singing stars in the 1960s. International fame was also enjoyed by a later generation, including rock groups such as the Manic Street Preachers and the Stereophonics, and individuals such as Cerys Matthews, who came to prominence as the lead singer of Catatonia and who sometimes, in her subsequent solo career, sings in Welsh.

Welsh-medium popular music developed in parallel with English, its history mapping the evolution from light entertainment to rock, and from local to international stages. The BBC radio programme *Noson Lawen* created a truly national audience for Welsh-language popular music in the

1940s, and introduced such groups as Triawd y Coleg, Adar Tregaron and Bois y Frenni. While swing was the rage in Anglo-American culture, *Noson Lawen* offered Wales the opportunity to develop its own folk-based pop sound. As well as performing on the radio, these groups performed in a wide range of live concerts, preparing the way for the pioneering groups of the 1950s, such as Hogia **Bryngwran**, Criw Sgiffl Llandegai (who became Hogia Llandegai; *see* **Llandygai**), and the most enduring of all the 'hogia' (lads), Hogia'r Wyddfa.

The 1960s saw many important developments in Welsh-language popular music, with BBC television programmes such as *Hob y Deri Dando* and *Disc a Dawn* providing a weekly stage for young musicians, and launching the careers of many bands. The most important influence on Welsh-language popular culture in the 1960s was **Cymdeithas yr Iaith Gymraeg** (the Welsh Language Society). Dafydd Iwan (b.1943), a prominent member of Cymdeithas yr Iaith, brought protest music to Wales through his appearances on the TWW programme *Y Dydd*, promoting the language movement and creating in the process a new Welsh folk music much influenced by American country styles.

Many Welsh artists in the 1960s were attracted to the Anglo-American cultural marketplace and joined the English-language pop music boom; others, such as the singer-songwriter Meic Stevens and the folk singer Heather Jones continue to perform in Welsh. The influence of the Beatles was apparent in the crossover from folk to pop of Welsh singer Mary Hopkin, and the Apple Records career of the band Badfinger. This was also the era of internationally acclaimed acts such as Man, Spencer Davis, Dave Edmunds, Budgie and Racing Cars. Although they infrequently addressed Welsh issues, they owed much to their Welsh background: they were mainly working-class, politically astute, intelligent, witty and subversive, with interests in a wide range of music. The Welsh musician with the most far-reaching and influential career was probably John Cale (b.1942, Garnant, **Cwmamman**). A classically trained musician, Cale was a member of the seminal New York band, the Velvet Underground, and his career as composer, solo artist, producer and collaborator remains in the forefront of musical culture.

Electric rock came to Welsh-language Wales rather later than elsewhere, when Y Blew performed at the Bala National Eisteddfod in 1967. The next electric band was Edward H. Dafis, formed in 1973. The most fundamental catalyst for change to popular music in Wales was the establishment of the Sain record label in 1969 (*see* **Llandwrog** and **Record Companies**), which raised the standards of the Welsh recording industry from an amateur to a professional level. Welsh pop went through a period of expansion during the 1970s, as two musical paths were forged, rock and folk. Overseas, Shakin' Stevens and Bonnie Tyler were among Wales's contributions to Anglo-American rock and roll culture. Although for some bands in Wales, musical enjoyment was more important than musical accomplishment, the 1970s saw some productive experimentation. Geraint Jarman began fusing reggae with his experiences of life in Cardiff; and punk came to the attention of the Welsh-language audience with Trwynau

John Cale at London's Royal Festival Hall

Coch. A Welsh 'New Wave' followed in their wake, as did the Welsh label Fflach Records. With punk in decline by the early 1980s, the Welsh musical revolution was reignited by Anhrefn, whose campaign to shake the foundations of Welsh-language pop inspired a further fragmentation within the scene. 'Underground' bands such as Anhrefn and Datblygu soon caught the attention of the BBC Radio One disc jockey John Peel (1939–2004), and many bands began looking beyond the confines of the Welsh radio audience in the hope of succeeding in the English market and further afield, while The Alarm reinvented themselves as a Welsh-language band.

At the end of the 1980s the Welsh pop scene was flourishing, although the Welsh-language aspect of it could be considered to be lacking in confidence. Although it was possible for bands to be heard singing in Welsh on Radio One, many young bands began turning to English. Some bands whose members had little knowledge of Welsh, such as the Stereophonics and the Manic Street Preachers, managed to draw attention to their Welshness through the medium of English, while bands with largely Welsh-speaking members, such as Super Furry Animals, Gorky's Zygotic Mynci, and Catatonia tended to perform bilingually, with English predominating.

Jazz

Early jazz forms came to Wales in 1874 through the 'strange weird Slave Songs, Prayer Songs, Plantation Melodies and Jubilee Choruses' that were performed by the Fisk Jubilee Singers from Fisk University, Nashville, on a tour to raise funds for their first University for the Education of the Children of Freed Slaves (*see* **Slavery**). Minstrelsy gave way to ragtime music during the early 20th century. Making inroads in the southern coalfield during

The Super Furry Animals

the 1920s, jazz also included African rhythms in Joe Slade's Ystrad Zulus Carnival Band. The first blues band in Wales appeared in Swansea in 1924; rhythm clubs were established in **Newport**, Cardiff and Swansea in the early 1930s; swing orchestras burgeoned during the Second World War, followed in the 1950s by jazz clubs and societies offering traditional, mainstream and modern jazz.

The post-war bebop era fired the talent of **Newcastle Emlyn**-born pianist **Dill Jones**, who became a stalwart of the New York jazz scene. Notable contemporary jazz musicians include composer/saxophonist Karl Jenkins, of Soft Machine fame, who made early appearances at Swansea Jazz Society during the 1960s, the saxophonist Lee Goodall, the bassist and composer Paula Gardiner and Swansea's remarkable multi-instrumentalist Cottle brothers – Laurence, Dave and Richard. Two illustrious pianists are Huw Warren, who also plays accordion, and Gareth Williams, who has recorded both with Claire Martin and his own trio.

A focus for Welsh jazz in recent years has been the **Brecon** Jazz Festival, Britain's largest. Another has been the **Women**'s Jazz Archive, established in Swansea in 1992 by the pianist and cultural historian Jen Wilson, in order to highlight the socio-cultural heritage of African-American music in Wales since the mid-19th century.

MYDDELTON family Entrepreneurs and landowners

Around 1394, Rhirid ap David of **Penllyn** married the daughter of Sir Alexander Myddelton of Myddelton, **Shropshire**, and adopted his wife's **surname**. His descendants held crown offices in **Denbigh**. Three of the nine sons of Richard Myddelton (*c.*1508–75) migrated to **London**. Sir Thomas Myddelton (1550–1631) became a leading businessman, was lord mayor of London (1613) and helped finance the first popular **Welsh-language Bible** (1630). Sir Hugh Myddelton (1560–1631), a goldsmith, constructed and partly financed a channel, the remarkable 64-km 'New Cut', to solve London's dire water supply problem; he later leased **lead and silver** mines in **Cardiganshire**. Their cousin William Midleton or Myddelton (*c.*1550–*c.*1600), soldier, sailor and poet, published a bardic grammar (1593) and a strict-metre Welsh translation of the Psalms (1603). Sir Thomas Myddelton (1586–1666) of **Chirk**, son of the London lord mayor, led the Parliamentary forces in north-east Wales with some success in the second **Civil War**, but opposed the trial of Charles I, was purged from parliament and retired to Chirk. A loyal **Anglican**, he welcomed the Restoration of Charles II. His son Thomas (*c.*1624–63) was made a baronet in 1660 for services to the monarchy. After

Myddeltons had represented the Denbigh county or borough constituency for more than 150 years, the family died out in the male line in 1796. Its estates passed through the marriages of heiresses to the Cornwallis West family at **Ruthin** and the (Myddelton)-Biddulph family at Chirk. In the 1870s, the former family owned 2200 ha in **Denbighshire** and the latter family 2230 ha.

MYDDFAI, Carmarthenshire
(5500 ha; 415 inhabitants)
Located immediately south of **Llandovery**, the **community**'s only settlement of any size is the hamlet of Myddfai. Within it is Mynydd Myddfai (440 m). On Y Pigyn at the community's eastern extremity are two **Roman** marching camps superimposed upon each other; they probably date from AD *c.*75. St Michael's church (14th and 15th centuries) was somewhat mauled by 19th-century restorers. The **Physicians of Myddfai**, believed to be descendants of Rhiwallon, reputedly the son of the legendary lady of **Llyn y Fan Fach**, practised at Myddfai until the death of Dr Rhys Williams in 1842. John Thomas (1730–?1804), author of *Rhad Ras*, one of the earliest **Welsh** autobiographies, and **Congregational** minister at **Rhayader** (1767–94), was born in Myddfai. The old mansion of Cilgwyn has become a nursing home. In 2006, the Duchy of **Cornwall** bought the 80-ha Llwynywormwood (lit. Wormwood Scrubs) estate with the intention of providing there a place at which Prince Charles could stay on his visits to Wales.

'MYFANWY' Song
A part song (*c.*1880) for male voices by **Joseph Parry**, the melody and lyrics are among the most famous of **Welsh** compositions. The Welsh words are by **Richard Davies** (Mynyddog; 1833–77), who also collaborated with Parry on his opera *Blodwen*.

MYNACHLOG-DDU, Pembrokeshire
(3387 ha; 489 inhabitants)
Constituting most of the southern flanks of **Mynydd Preseli**, the **community** may have been the source of the Stonehenge blue stones. The Gors Fawr circle of 16 stones dates from the **Bronze Age**. In the cemetery of Bethel **Baptist** chapel (rebuilt in 1877) is the tombstone of Thomas Rees (Twm Carnabwth; ?1806–76), leader of the first episode in the **Rebecca Riots**; the laconic inscription states that he died while harvesting cabbage. From the age of seven to eleven, the poet **Waldo Williams** lived in Mynachlog-ddu, years which were central to his concept of the world; a huge boulder starkly inscribed *Waldo* commemorates him.

In the late 1940s, when there were plans to establish an artillery range on Mynydd Preseli, the people of Mynachlog-ddu mounted successful resistance, led by the local minister, R. Parry Roberts; hailed as the 'Gandhi of the Preseli', he vowed that if the range were established, he would make his home in the centre of it. The community's name – meaning 'black monastery' – recalls a grange owned by the monks of **St Dogmaels**; the 'black' refers to the bleak landscape. St Dogmael's church retains medieval features.

MYNYDD CARN, Battle of
This battle, which took place in 1081 at an unidentified location in south-west Wales, had enduring consequences. **Gruffudd ap Cynan** and **Rhys ap Tewdwr** joined together to defeat Trahaearn ap Caradog, ruler of **Gwynedd**, and Caradog ap Gruffudd, ruler of **Gwynllŵg**, thus establishing the dynasties which thereafter ruled Gwynedd and **Deheubarth**.

MYNYDD EPYNT Mountain
Located between **Brecon** and **Builth**, the **mountain** rises to 475 m in the **community** of Llangamarch and – 13 km to the east – to 472 m in the community of **Erwood**. Sandstones and mudstones, chiefly of Old Red Sandstone, form its geological foundations. Its steep ice-eroded north-western escarpment contrasts with its gentle south-eastern slopes. Drained by the Bran, the Yscir and the Honddu (tributaries of the **Usk**), and by the Duhonw and the Dulas (tributaries of the **Wye**), Epynt overlies **limestone** and Old Red Sandstone. Along its ridge – at one time a route of **drovers** driving **cattle** from west Wales to **England** – is a line of old quarry pits, the source of the stone tiles once locally used for roofing. Until 1940, the mountain was the heart of **Welsh**-speaking rural **Breconshire**. In that year, its inhabitants – some 400 in all – were driven out. Their houses were destroyed, and a 16,000-ha army firing range was established (*see* **Military Bases**), a process which pushed the boundary of Welsh-speaking Wales 15 km westwards. The army remains in possession; its unexploded shells provide a lethal deterrent to anyone who might wish to enjoy Epynt's delectable uplands.

MYNYDD HIRAETHOG Mountain
Extending 21 km eastwards from **Bro Garmon** to Clocaenog, and 24 km southwards from **Llanfair Talhaiarn** to **Llangwm (Conwy)**, the **mountain** – sometimes known as the **Denbighshire** Moors – rises to 519 m at Foel Goch in **Llanrhaeadr-yng-Nghinmeirch**. Silurian sandstones and shales underlie the plateau which is drained by tributaries of the **Clwyd**, the **Conwy** and the **Dee**, several of which have been dammed to create the **reservoirs** of Llyn Aled, Llyn Aled Isaf, Llyn Alwen, Llyn Brân and Llyn Brenig. The construction of Llyn Brenig was preceded by a minute examination of the valley's **archaeology**; as a result, the area provides the fullest available evidence of the **Bronze Age** occupation of upland Wales. If left undisturbed Mynydd Hiraethog would be dominated by heather, cottongrass, rushes and mountain grasses. Reseeding, however, has produced extensive grazing lands for **sheep**, and conifer plantations (*see* **Forestry**) have proliferated, especially around Clocaenog. The villages nestling in the mountain's valleys – **Llansannan** and Llangwm in particular – have traditionally enjoyed a rich cultural life. Much of the moorland was once devoted to grouse shooting; Gwylfa Hiraethog (Llansannan), a ruined shooting lodge, stands at 496 m above Llyn Brân. From 1894 to 1964, Hiraethog was the name of one of Denbighshire's **rural districts**.

MYNYDD LLANGATWG Mountain
Located between **Brynmawr** and **Crickhowell**, the **mountain**, consisting of **limestones** and sandstones of the Carboniferous age, rises to 529 m. Its spectacular cliffs have

been designated a National Nature Reserve. Craig y Cilau is home to a rich variety of **plants**, including the rare lesser whitebeam (*sorbus minima*). Beneath the mountain is one of the longest **cave** systems in **Britain**. A complex which extends for more than 70 km, it consists in the main of three caves: Ogof Agen Allwedd (34 km), Ogof Darren Cilau (27 km) and Ogof Craig a Ffynnon (9 km). The caves provide important roosts for **bats**, among them the rare lesser horseshoe bat. The mountain, which dominates the **community** of **Llangattock**, is riddled with swallowholes and shakeholes.

MYNYDD PARYS Mountain

According to local tradition, the **Romans** mined **copper** at **Amlwch**, but attempts to locate the lode failed until 1768. The deposit was large, though of low quality. However, it could be worked cheaply in great open-cast pits. Developed by **Thomas Williams** (1737–1802), it made the **parish** of Amlwch one of the most populous in Wales by 1801, although much of the ore had been by then extracted from the two open pits, and it became necessary to sink shafts. This lost Parys its advantage, and it fell into decline, although sporadic efforts to revive it have been made ever since. In 2005, when rising metal prices made viable once more the prospect of mining for **gold**, zinc, copper and lead on Mynydd Parys, the **Anglesey** Mining Company embarked on a project to extract ore from the vast site – which conjures up visions of the surface of the moon.

MYNYDD PRESELI Mountain

Extending for 20 km eastwards from Mynydd Carn Ingli (347 m; **Newport**) to Frenni Fawr (395 m; **Boncath**), the **mountain**'s highest point is Foel Cwmcerwyn (536 m; **Maenclochog**). The rugged tors so characteristic of Preseli are the result of the sheets of intrusive igneous rock which were injected into the mountain's main constituent – the mudstones which originated in the Ordovician era as layers of mud on the sea floor. Among those igneous rocks are the blocks of spotted dolerite believed to have been transported from Carn Meini to Stonehenge in the early **Bronze Age**. Other evidence of prehistoric human activity comes from the superb Pentre Ifan **Neolithic** chambered tomb (**Nevern**), numerous Bronze Age cairns and standing stones, and splendidly sited **Iron Age hill-forts** such as that crowning Foeldrygarn (**Crymych**). Later exploitation of Preseli stone came in the 19th century when **slate** was quarried, especially at Glogue (**Clydau**) and Rosebush (**Maenclochog**). An attempt to establish an army training ground (*see* **Military Bases**) on Preseli in the late 1940s was attacked in one of the best known of the poems of **Waldo Williams**, a monument to whom stands at **Mynachlog-ddu**. Debate rages over the correct spelling of the mountain's name; the Ordnance Survey uses Preseli, but many competent authorities argue in favour of Presely. The name probably comes from *pres* (a variant of *prys* 'thicket') and *Seleu*, (a variant of *Selyf*, the Welsh form of Solomon).

MYVYRIAN ARCHAIOLOGY OF WALES, The

A collection of **Welsh** texts (3 vols., 1801–7) edited by Owain Myfyr (**Owen Jones**; 1741–1814), Iolo Morganwg (**Edward Williams**) and **William Owen Pughe**. Named after Owain Myfyr, who paid for its publication, it contains a selection from the earliest poetry, the *Brutiau* and other texts, but the work as a whole was corrupted by texts forged by Iolo Morganwg.

Mynydd Parys, Amlwch, Anglesey

Dinas Bran Castle, centre of the commote of Nanheudwy, as depicted in 1794

NANHEUDWY Commote

A **commote** occupying the area between the **Dee** and Ceiriog valleys, its centre was Dinas Bran Castle above **Llangollen**. In 1283, Nanheudwy north of the Dee became part of the **march**er-lordship of **Bromfield and Yale**, and Nanheudwy south of the Dee became part of that of **Chirk and Chirkland**.

NANNAU family Landowners

Claiming descent from the rulers of **Powys**, by the late 16th century the family held a substantial estate at Nannau (**Brithdir and Llanfachreth**). They were patrons of the poets, and the death *c.*1695 of their household poet, Siôn Dafydd Laes (or Las), marked the end of the age-old tradition of professional praise poets in the north. In 1719, Nannau passed by marriage to the Vaughans of Hengwrt (**Llanelltyd**); and in 1874 to John Vaughan of Dolmelynllyn (**Ganllwyd**). His son, Major-General John Vaughan (1871–1956), wrote *Cavalry and Sporting Memories* (1955), a wry look at a dying world.

NANNERCH, Flintshire (1435 ha; 531 inhabitants)

Located north-west of **Mold**, the **community** extends to a crest of the **Clwydian Hills**, which is crowned by the strongly fortified 5-ha **hill-fort** of Moel Arthur. St Mary's church contains a monument by Grinling Gibbons (1652).

Walgoch and Penbedw Uchaf have fine mullioned windows. Nannerch village was a mere hamlet until 1969 when the purchase of the Penbedw estate by a property development company heralded major expansion.

NANT CONWY Commote and one-time rural district

One of the **commotes** of the *cantref* of **Arllechwedd**, Nant Conwy, bounded by the west bank of the upper **Conwy**, extended into the heart of **Snowdonia**. Its original chief stronghold was at **Dolwyddelan**, and its *maerdref* (administrative centre) was at **Trefriw**. The name survived as that of a post **Acts of 'Union' hundred**. The **rural district** of Nant Conwy, which was in existence from the 1930s to 1974, included most of the former rural districts of Conway, Geirionydd and Glaslyn. Following constituency reorganization in 1983, the name was revived as part of the constituency of **Meirionnydd** Nant Conwy. By the time of the **National Assembly** elections of 2007, Nant Conwy was part of the **Aberconwy** constituency.

NANTCWNLLE (Nancwnlle), Ceredigion (3961 ha; 819 inhabitants)

Straddling the **Aeron** valley west of **Tregaron**, the **community** contains the villages of Abermeurig, Bwlch-llan,

Gartheli, Llundain-fach, Llwyn-y-groes, Tal-sarn and Trefilan. Trefilan, with its large motte, had claims to urban status and sought recognition as part of the **Cardigan Boroughs** constituency. Pantybeudy, Bwlch-llan, was the birthplace of **Daniel Rowland**. The last woman in **Cardiganshire** formally accused of **witch**craft (1693) was a native of Nantcwnlle.

NANTGLYN, Denbighshire
(3458 ha; 331 inhabitants)
Constituting the western bulge of **Denbighshire**, the **community** contains the Llyn Brân **reservoir** and the upper part of the Brenig reservoir. St James's churchyard contains the grave of the philologist **William Owen Pughe**, which bears an inscription in the **druid**ic alphabet devised by Iolo Morganwg (**Edward Williams**), and that of the poet Robert Davies (Bardd Nantglyn; 1769–1835). The poet and naval surgeon **David Samwell** (Dafydd Ddu Feddyg), who witnessed the death of Captain Cook (1797), was the son of a vicar of Nantglyn.

NANTMEL, Radnorshire, Powys
(5598 ha; 686 inhabitants)
Nantmel is a **community** of **mountain**ous land south-east of **Rhayader**. The village has an attractively sited but dull church. Within the community is Doldowlod, where James Watt (1736–1819), the inventor of the steam engine, acquired an estate which eventually extended over 2445 ha. His descendants, who still live at Doldowlod, built an interesting example of a neo-Elizabethan mansion and surrounded it with trees. A visit to the kite-feeding centre at Gigrin is an awe-inspiring experience (*see* **Birds**).

NANTYGLO AND BLAINA (Nant-y-glo a Blaenau), Blaenau Gwent (1533 ha; 9123 inhabitants)
The **community**, located in the upper reaches of the **Ebbw Fach** valley, was part of Aberystruth, a **parish** whose history was chronicled in 1779 by **Edmund Jones**. A rebuilt version of the medieval parish church of Aberystruth (1856), which stood in the middle of Blaina, was demolished in the 1960s. In the mid-1790s, Hill, Harford and Co. established an **iron**works in Nantyglo. In 1813, it was bought by Joseph and Crawshay **Bailey**, who made it one of the world's largest ironworks. The footings of Joseph Bailey's mansion, Tŷ Mawr, are still visible. More impressive are the Roundhouses, sturdy cylindrical towers probably built during the industrial troubles of 1816 to provide a refuge for trusted ironworkers. A humanist society, Cymdeithas Dynolwyr Nant-y-glo, founded in 1829, advocated a radical form of Welsh **nationalism**.

The area contributed a substantial contingent to the 1839 **Chartist** march on **Newport**; it was led by **Zephaniah Williams**, the licencee of the Royal Oak, who was exiled to Van Diemen's Land (Tasmania). Blaina developed following the establishment of the Cwmcelyn Ironworks in the mid-19th century. By the early 20th century, the main source of employment was the Lancaster Company's collieries at Rose Heyworth, South Griffin, Henwaun and North Blaina. As the result of the collapse of the **coal** industry, the community is one of the most depressed in western Europe.

NARBERTH (Arberth), Pembrokeshire
(1286 ha; 2358 inhabitants)
Located 16 km north of **Tenby**, the **community** adjoins the **Pembrokeshire–Carmarthenshire** boundary. Narberth (or rather Arberth) is mentioned in the second sentence of the first branch of *Pedair Cainc y Mabinogi* (*see* **Mabinogion, The**) as one of the chief courts of **Pwyll**, lord of the seven *cantrefi* of **Dyfed**. Narberth Castle is first mentioned in 1116 when it was attacked by **Gruffudd ap Rhys ap Tewdwr**. The **march**er-lordship of Narberth included the **commote** of **Efelffre** as well as the eastern part of the *cantref* of **Penfro**. In the 13th century, it came into the possession of the **Mortimer family**, from whom it passed to the **York family** and thence to the crown. **Cadw**'s recent work on the castle has shown that it is a more significant building than was previously thought. St Andrew's church (largely 1881) retains its late medieval tower. The town has some attractive Georgian houses, several large chapels (Tabernacle, 1858, and Bethesda, 1889, in particular), a handsome town hall (*c.*1835, 1880) and the Landsker Visitor Centre. Narberth was the name of a post **Acts of 'Union' hundred** and of a **rural district**. The town was part of the **Haverfordwest Borough** constituency from 1832 to 1885 and of the **Pembroke** Borough constituency from 1885 to 1918.

NASH (Trefonnen), Newport
(1034 ha; 281 inhabitants)
Located on the eastern bank of the **Usk** estuary immediately south of **Newport**, the **community** lies on the **Gwent Levels**. It contains the East Usk **Lighthouse** (1893), several of Newport's outlying factories, the sludge beds of the city's sewerage system, and the Uskmouth Power Station. Eton College, which held the rectory of Nash, financed the building of St Mary's church, with its remarkable Perpendicular steeple and its Georgian nave with gallery, pulpits and box pews still intact.

NASH, John (1752–1835) Architect
Of Welsh descent, Nash was born in either **Cardigan** or **London**. He moved to **Carmarthen** and established an office there after he had been declared bankrupt in 1783. As well as designing numerous houses, such as Ffynone (**Manordeifi**; 1792), and Llanerchaeron (**Ciliau Aeron**; *c.*1794), for the local **gentry**, he designed **prisons** at Carmarthen (1789), Cardigan (1791) and Hereford (1792), and a number of bridges, and he rebuilt the west front of **St David's** Cathedral (1790–3). As a result of contacts with **Thomas Johnes** and Sir Uvedale Price, for whom he designed an octagonal library at Hafod Uchdryd (**Pontarfynach**) and a castellated villa at **Aberystwyth**, respectively, Nash developed a taste for the **picturesque** and became its leading architect. He settled in London in 1796, where he developed a fashionable practice and, enjoying royal patronage, was responsible for laying out Regent's Park and Regent Street, and remodelling the Royal Pavilion, Brighton.

NASH-WILLIAMS, V[ictor] E[rle] (1897–1955) Archaeologist
A native of Fleur-de-lys (**Pengam**), Nash-Williams became keeper of **archaeology** at the **National Museum [of] Wales** in

1926, and did pioneering work on the **Roman** and Early Christian periods. He excavated extensively at sites in Wales, particularly those at **Caerleon** and **Caerwent**. His most important publications were the definitive *The Early Christian Monuments of Wales* (1950) and *The Roman Frontier in Wales* (1954).

NATIONAL ASSEMBLY FOR WALES, The

Following the affirmative vote in the 1997 **devolution** referendum, the first National Assembly election was held on 6 May 1999, and the Assembly was opened by Elizabeth II on 26 May 1999. Following much debate about its location – a debate in which **Swansea** made a determined effort to secure it – it was temporarily housed in Crickhowell House in Cardiff Bay. In 2006, it moved to a magnificent new building nearby, designed by Richard Rogers and known as Y Senedd. The executive arm of the Welsh Assembly Government is housed in the one-time **Welsh Office** in **Cardiff**'s **Cathays Park**.

The Assembly's 60 members are elected by universal suffrage and elections are held every four years. The method of election combines the traditional first-past-the-post system with the additional member form of proportional representation. Each voter has two votes – the first for one of the 40 constituency members (based upon the Westminster parliamentary constituencies) and the second for regional members (four for each of what had been until 2002 Wales's five European parliamentary constituencies). This is designed to ensure that each party's representation reflects its overall share of the vote. Members meet under the chairmanship of the presiding officer or *llywydd*, whose role approximates to that of the speaker of the House of Commons.

The Assembly decides on priorities and allocates funds in a large number of policy areas in relation to Wales, among them **agriculture**, economic development, **education**, **health**, **housing**, industry, local **government**, social services, **tourism**, transport and the **Welsh language**. Other aspects of government remain the responsibility of Westminster, among them **broadcasting**, defence, foreign affairs, the justice system, the **police** service, **prisons**, social security benefits and taxation. Unlike the Parliament of **Scotland**, the Assembly lacks the authority to vary taxation, and until 2007 it lacked the power to enact legislation, although it took over the powers of the **secretary of state for Wales** with regard to secondary legislation – the right to fill in the detail of Westminster acts – from the outset.

The Assembly members nominate a first minister (the **Welsh** form, *y prif weinidog*, translates into **English** as 'prime minister'), who is appointed by the Queen. The Queen also gives approval to all ministerial appointments and to the appointment of a counsel general. Following the Government of Wales Act (2006), the Assembly is able to legislate within its policy areas. However, such powers are conferred upon it by the Westminster parliament through the granting of Legislative Competence Orders relating to specific legislative fields. Until 2007, the Assembly's procedures were a bewildering hybrid of those of Westminster

The National Assembly in session in Y Senedd

and those of a **county** council. But following the Act of 2006, the National Assembly for Wales (the legislature) and the Welsh Assembly Government (the executive) became distinct legal entities.

In the election of 1999, when the turnout was 46%, the first-past-the-post constituencies were contested by 199 candidates. In all, the **Labour Party** won 28 seats, **Plaid [Genedlaethol] Cymru** 17, the **Conservatives** 9 and the **Liberal Democrats** 6. Of the 60 elected, 24 were **women**, a remarkable advance in view of Wales's previously appalling record in electing female representatives.

The Assembly's first four-year term was beset by problems. Three of the party leaders – Alun Michael (Labour), Dafydd Wigley (Plaid Cymru) and Rod Richards (Conservative) – resigned, and were replaced by Rhodri Morgan, Ieuan Wyn Jones and Nicholas Bourne. The difficulties experienced by Rhodri Morgan's minority Labour administration led in October 2000 to a coalition with the Liberal Democrats. Although the Welsh Assembly government adopted several popular policies on matters such as prescription charges, school tests and university fees, many in Wales felt that it had made no difference to their lives and that it was no more than an expensive talking-shop. Nevertheless, there were others for whom the mere establishment of the Assembly was little short of miraculous. In the second Assembly elections (2003), the turnout declined to 38.16%. Of the Assembly seats, 30 were won by the Labour Party, 12 by Plaid Cymru, 11 by the Conservatives, 6 by the Liberal Democrats and 1 (**Wrexham**) by an Independent. With Labour winning half the seats, Rhodri Morgan decided to form an exclusively Labour administration. In the 2003 election, 30 men and 30 women won seats, making the National Assembly the first national elected body in the world to consist of equal numbers of men and women. The Labour cabinet was also unprecedented, for the majority of its members were women. There were increasing demands that the Assembly should receive the same powers as the Scottish parliament, particularly following the British government reshuffle of 2003, which changed the secretaryship of state into a part-time office. The Richard Commission (2004) came to the conclusion that the Assembly should progressively acquire legislative powers; it believed that the process could be completed by 2011, by which time the Assembly should have 80 members elected by the single transferable vote system. Labour's Government of Wales Act (2006) fell short of that aim, but it foresaw the gaining of full legislative powers were that development to be approved by referendum.

In the third election (2007), the most interesting development was the increase in the readiness to vote, with 44.4% of the electorate going to the polls – compared with 38.16% in 2003. The Labour Party won 26 seats. Plaid Cymru 15, the Conservatives 12 and the Liberal Democrats 6. The Labour Party had lost the ability to govern alone and its attempts to establish a coalition with the Liberal Democrats proved unsuccessful. Efforts by Plaid Cymru, the Conservatives and the Liberal Democrats to create a 'rainbow' coalition also failed. The surprising outcome was the establishment of a coalition between Labour and Plaid Cymru, parties that, between them, held 41 of the Assembly's 60 seats. Intriguingly, the coalition became a fact on 7 July 2007, exactly 700 years after the death of Edward I.

NATIONAL BOTANIC GARDEN OF WALES, The

Situated in a restored 18th-century park at **Llanarthney**, and opened in 2000, the **garden** – known as Middleton – aims to conserve threatened **plant** species, study plant diversity, and educate and entertain visitors. Its focal point is the Norman Foster-designed great **glass**house, the largest single-span glasshouse in the world. It houses a unique collection of 1000 plant species that flourish in a Mediterranean-type climate, many of which are facing extinction in their natural habitats. Beyond the main visitor area is a 162-ha estate with a diversity of habitats and wildlife. Among the garden's rare and threatened Welsh plants is the whitebeam *Sorbus leyana*, **Britain**'s rarest tree, of which there are only 16 specimens growing wild.

In 2002, the garden opened a bio**science** incubator. Then, in 2003, the garden ran into serious financial difficulties, as the private trust which runs it hovered on the brink of bankruptcy. It was widely argued that it should become a public body under the authority of the **National Assembly**. In 2004, its trustees accepted a financial package from the National Assembly, the **Carmarthenshire County** Council and the Millennium Commission, which was intended to secure its future.

NATIONAL COAL BOARD, The

On 12 July 1946, the **Coal** Industry Nationalisation Act established the National Coal Board (NCB) whose first chairman (1946–51) was Lord Hyndley, formerly a managing director of the **Powell Duffryn Steam Coal Co. Ltd**. On 1 January 1947, the NCB found itself in charge of over 1500 collieries, a workforce of over 700,000, and assets worth £394 million. Charged with promoting efficient mining and the safety, **health** and welfare of the workforce, the NCB had to ensure that the industry's revenue covered current outgoings on an average of good and bad years.

Wales's southern coalfield formed the bulk of the NCB's South Western Division, while the northern coalfield was included in the North Western Division. Benefiting from excess demand during the first 10 years of its existence, from 1957, the NCB found customers increasingly moving over to other fuels, especially **oil**. The actions of the Organisation of Petroleum Exporting Countries in raising prices during 1973–4 provided a temporary respite, but the industry proved to be in terminal decline. The privatization campaign of Thatcher's **Conservative governments** led, in 1986, to the NCB being renamed British Coal, prior to the remnants of the industry being privatized in 1994.

NATIONAL COLLIERY DISASTER Wattstown, Rhondda

At 11.45 a.m. on 11 July 1905, all but one of the 120 men of the underground day shift were killed when gelignite was used to blow out an underground barrier to allow the water and sludge behind it to run off. Numerous lapses in relation to this incident were highlighted, not least the illegal use of gelignite, which was not an explosive permitted for use underground at the colliery.

NATIONAL COUNCIL FOR EDUCATION AND TRAINING FOR WALES, The

Founded in April 2001, the council was responsible for funding, planning and promoting all **education** and training for those 16 years and upwards, with the exception of the higher education sector. Formed from the merger of the four TECs (Training and Enterprise Councils), the Council of Welsh TECs and the Further Education Council for Wales, it operated under the name of ELWa (Education and Learning Wales) and was the largest public body sponsored by the **National Assembly**. In a long-anticipated, post-**devolution** 'bonfire of the **quangos**', ELWa was abolished in 2006 and its functions were brought in-house by the Assembly.

NATIONAL LIBERALS, The

In June 1931, a group of 28 right-wing **Liberal** MPs, led by Sir John Simon, relinquished the party whip and to some extent joined forces with the **Conservative Party**. In the October general election, four National (or Simonite) Liberals were returned in Wales: Fred Llewellyn Jones (**Flintshire**), Henry Morris-Jones (**Denbigh**), **Clement Davies** (**Montgomeryshire**) and Lewis Jones (**Swansea West**). Most National Liberals were eventually absorbed into the Conservative Party, but Clement Davies returned to the mainstream party fold in 1941 and became Liberal Party leader (1945–56). In 1950, E. H. Garner-Evans, Morris-Jones's successor in Denbigh, adopted the label National Liberal and Conservative, a practice continued by his successor, W. Geraint Morgan until 1964 when the defunct title was rejected in favour of Conservative.

NATIONAL LIBRARY OF WALES, The

The creation of a comprehensive collection of **Welsh** written materials was one of the chief ambitions of the **Cymmrodorion** in the mid-18th century, but it was not realized. In the 1850s, the English bibliophile Thomas Phillipps (1792–1872), looking for a home for his substantial collection of Welsh books and manuscripts, considered several locations, among them **Swansea**, **Llandovery** and **Manorbier** Castle, but his plans came to nothing at the time. At the National **Eisteddfod** at **Mold** in 1873, a campaign was launched to secure for Wales a national copyright library and a repository for the nation's cultural treasures. In the 1890s, **Herbert Lewis** campaigned vigorously for a Library and **National Museum** for Wales. In 1896, following the death of Thomas Phillipps, **Cardiff** library bought the greater part of his Welsh material, including *The Book of Aneirin*, in the hope that the National Library would be located there. In 1905, however, a committee of the Privy Council recommended that the Library should be established at **Aberystwyth** and the Museum at Cardiff. Royal charters were granted to the institutions in 1907.

The Library's home, when it opened in January 1909, was the Old Assembly Rooms, Aberystwyth, but in 1916 it moved to its present purpose-built home, designed by Sidney Kyffin Greenslade, overlooking the town. Further extensions have been added to the building over the years, the latest of which opened in 2004. Following the granting of a Supplementary Charter in 2006, the Library's Court and Council were replaced by the Board of Trustees, which has 15 members. The Treasury had sole responsibility for

The National Botanic Garden of Wales with the dome of its Norman Foster-designed glasshouse

The National Library of Wales, Aberystwyth

financing the institution until 1965, when it was superseded by the **Welsh Office** and, later, by the **National Assembly**.

The University College of Wales (*see* **University of Wales, Aberystwyth**) took an active part in the Library's development, transferring its Welsh Library and other collections to its care. Significantly, **John Williams** (1840–1926) of Plas **Llansteffan**, who owned the greatest library ever assembled in Wales, promised to present his collection to the Library on condition that it was established at Aberystwyth. The Library's charter ordains that its main responsibility is to preserve and accumulate manuscripts, books and pictures of all kinds in Welsh, or any other **Celt**ic language, relating to Wales and the Celtic peoples, as well as works in other languages. A supplemental charter in 1978 extended this objective to include audiovisual material. Currently, the Library consists of three main departments: Collection Services, Public Services and Corporate Services. It is estimated that the collections include some 4 million printed items, 40,000 manuscripts, 4 million deeds and documents, and a substantial collection of pictures, **maps**, sound recordings and videotapes.

The Library's most important collection is John Williams's library of some 25,000 volumes. It includes the Shirburn Castle collection assembled by Moses Williams (*see* **Samuel and Moses Williams**), and contains copies of the majority of the earliest Welsh books. The libraries of Edward Owen (1850–1904) and **J. H. Davies** also form part of the foundation collection, and a number of important libraries have been presented to the Library over the years, such as those assembled by F. W. Bourdillon, A. R. Llewellin-Taylor and **G. J. Williams**. The Library has been enabled to assemble a comprehensive collection of modern British publications under the Copyright Act of 1911, which empowers it to claim a free copy of every book and **periodical** published in the United Kingdom and the Irish Republic.

The Hengwrt-Peniarth collection, presented by John Williams, is the Library's greatest treasure. It contains over 500 volumes which belonged to **Robert Vaughan**, Hengwrt (**Llanelltyd**). In 1926, the Master of the Rolls approved the Library as a repository of **manor**ial records and, in 1944, the diocesan records of the **Church in Wales** were transferred to the Library by the Church's Representative Body. The Welsh Political Archive includes the papers of Welsh political parties and politicians.

The Library contains a range of graphic material, including pictures and topographic prints, portraits and photographs such as the **John Thomas** (1838–1905) and **Geoff Charles** collections, **paintings** in oils and watercolour, cartoons, ephemera such as posters and postcards, and **tithe** and Ordnance Survey maps. There has been a huge increase in holdings of audiovisual material in recent years including sound, videotapes and **film**. In 2001, the National Screen and Sound Archive of Wales was established by the Library, along with Sgrîn, the media agency for Wales. The archive brings together all the sound and moving images collections of both organizations.

The Library has been responsible for compiling and publishing various catalogues and bibliographies, including *Bibliotheca Celtica* (1909–84) and a *Subject Index to Welsh Periodicals* (1968–84). *The Bibliography of Wales* (1985–) is a combination of these two publications. Eiluned Rees's *Libri Walliae*, a bibliography of Welsh books and of books printed in Wales between 1546 and 1820, appeared in 1987. Manuscripts are listed in *Handlist of Manuscripts in the National Library of Wales* (1940–), and the *National Library of Wales Journal* appears twice a year. Developments in computer technology have enabled the Library to extend its services to users and scholars worldwide.

The first national Librarian was John Ballinger (1909–30). He was succeeded by William Llewelyn Davies (1930–52), **Thomas Parry** (1953–8), Evan David Jones (1958–69), David Jenkins (1969–79), R. Geraint Gruffydd (1980–5), Brynley F. Roberts (1985–94), Lionel Madden (1994–8) and Andrew Green (1998–).

NATIONAL MILK BARS

The fashionable haunt of teenagers in the 1950s and 1960s was originally conceived as a means for one Welsh dairy farmer to market his produce. R. W. Griffiths opened the first National Milk Bar in 1933 in **Colwyn Bay**, with the idea of selling the milk and cream from his farm at **Forden** directly to the public. The venture proved popular, and Griffiths went on to open a total of 17 bars in Wales and north-west **England** – with their signature black-and-white chequered floors, bar stools, juke boxes and gleaming chrome fixtures.

NATIONAL MUSEUM [OF] WALES, The

The National Museum [of] Wales owes its inception to the actions of a few enthusiasts who, in the 1880s, brought the absence of such an institution to the attention of parliament. Their efforts came to fruition in 1903 when a resolution approving such a project was accepted by the House of Commons. A committee of the Privy Council decided that the museum should be at **Cardiff**, and the royal charter was granted in 1907. Cardiff Corporation reacted enthusiastically, allocating a site in **Cathays Park** next to the City Hall, and handing over the entire collections of the municipal museum as well as the annual produce of a halfpenny rate.

The museum's development has differed in a number of ways from the other British state-funded museums and galleries. The three differences implicit in the original charter are: the size and the representativeness of the Court of Governors (and its executive arm, the Museum Council), particularly up to the granting of a new charter in 1991; the emphasis on strong links with **education**al bodies; and the range of the collections, reflecting aspects of the visual arts, humanities, **sciences** and technology. The public title was changed, in 1995, from The National Museum of Wales to the National Museums & Galleries of Wales in order better to reflect this diversity; the name was changed again in 2005 to The National Museum Wales; its **Welsh** title was changed from Amgueddfa Genedlaethol Cymru to Amgueddfa Cymru. Other differences include: the acquisition, from 1921, of specialist branch museums; the establishment in 1923 of an affiliation scheme with local museums; the creation of the first national Museum Schools Service in 1948; and the gradual adoption of a bilingual policy.

The design of the main building was that of the **London** architects Smith and Brewer, who were selected from 130 competitors. The resulting structure has been described both as architecturally 'the most completely satisfying

The National Museum of Wales in Cathays Park, Cardiff, with Gorsedd stones in the foreground

building of the whole group in Cathays Park' and as standing 'almost alone among great museums as an example of intelligent planning'. Among its distinctive features are the large, impressive entrance hall and the allocation of almost as much space for the collections as for the exhibition galleries. Because of financial difficulties, the impact of two World Wars and the need to finance developments on other sites, progress was very slow. The first contract was signed in 1911, but the central court galleries were not completed until 1993. This, the main museum, has been known since 2005 as The National Museum Cardiff.

The first curatorial departments – **archaeology**, art, botany, **geology** and zoology – created between 1914 and 1918, represent the traditional museum disciplines. They encompass such other museum subjects as numismatics, palaeobotany, mineralogy and entomology. For the greater part of the museum's history, the materially different nature of their collections meant that the departments were, in effect, run as four separate museums and an art gallery, each with a specialist library in addition to the general museum library. The collections of the department of art, dealing with both fine and applied art, are complemented by those of the department of prints and drawings at the **National Library**.

The first two outstations were Turner House, **Penarth** (established by **J. Pyke Thompson** in 1888 for the public

exhibition of his private art collection), handed over to the museum in 1921, and the Museum of Antiquities (now The National **Roman** Legion Museum) on the site of the legionary fortress of Isca, at **Caerleon**, presented by the **Monmouthshire** and Caerleon Antiquarian Association in 1930. The collections of the third, in the small museum within the grounds of the auxiliary fort at Segontium, **Caernarfon**, became the responsibility of the museum in 1937. Both site museums were in effect by-products of **Mortimer Wheeler**'s innovative excavations, initiated at Segontium.

The next two curatorial departments at Cathays Park represented new museum disciplines. The first, Folk Culture and [related] Industries, was formed in 1936, and was the first of its kind in **Britain**; the second, Industry, representing the 'Special industries of Wales' of the original charter, was established in 1959. The two were to provide the basis for the major developments at **St Fagans** (Cardiff), from 1946, and West Bute Dock, Cardiff, from 1977.

Provisional plans for an annexe to the main building to illustrate aspects of Welsh life had been considered since the 1910s, and study visits to the open-air folk museums of Scandinavia from 1909 onwards had provided the blueprint. The museum's acceptance, in 1946, of St Fagans Castle, its formal **gardens** and grounds as a gift from the third Earl of Plymouth (*see* **Windsor-Clive family**), together

The National Slate Museum, Llanberis (the museum is actually in the community of Llanddeiniolen)

with its purchase of 32 ha of adjacent parkland, enabled the museum to create an open-air folk museum, as well as to interpret aspects of the life of the Welsh landed **gentry** in the 16th-century manor house. The Welsh Folk Museum, renamed in 1995 the Museum of Welsh Life, and renamed The National History Museum in 2005, opened in 1948 (*see* **St Fagans**).

The department of industry, initiated in 1959 and accommodated in the new west wing in 1966, became the nucleus of the Welsh Industrial and Maritime Museum in 1977. Designed to illustrate how the various Welsh industries, over some 200 years, obtained power to drive the machines necessary for production, the first phase of development was housed in a brick structure adjacent to Cardiff's West Bute Dock. It was the first new building in a dockland that had been decaying since before the **Second World War**. In 1997, following the earmarking of the site by the Cardiff Bay Development Corporation for retail development, it was sold and some of the money used to create a museum collection centre at Nantgarw Business Park (**Taff's Well**). A partnership to create a major successor museum was entered into with the city and county of **Swansea**, with a new building added to the Swansea Industrial and Maritime Museum; the resulting National Waterfront Museum opened in 2005.

Two other outstations of the 1970s are: the North Wales Quarrying Museum (now The National **Slate** Museum), established in the scheduled central repair and maintenance workshop of the mammoth Dinorwic quarry (**Llanddeiniolen**), which ceased production in 1969; and The National Wool Museum (*see* **Woollen Industry**) which opened in the buildings of the Cambrian Mills at Drefach Felindre (**Llangeler**) in 1976. The former, created by a joint initiative of **Caernarfonshire County** Council, the Ancient Monuments Board (**Cadw** since 1984) and the museum, reflects aspects of the history of the 'most Welsh of Welsh industries' in Britain's main slate producing area; the latter does the same for what was the most widespread rural industry in an area where it was of particular importance. Three other outstations – the **Graham Sutherland** Gallery at Picton Castle (**Slebech**; 1976–95), Yr Hen Gapel, Tre'r-ddôl (**Llangynfelin**; 1978–92) and Oriel Eryri (later Amgueddfa'r Gogledd; **Llanberis**; 1981–96) are no longer the responsibility of the museum.

The museum's latest outstation is at **Blaenavon**, within the World Heritage Site designated in 2000. Formal discussions from 1975 onwards between the **National Coal Board** (NCB), the National Museum, the Wales Tourist Board and local authorities led to the establishment in 1981 of the Big Pit Mining Museum (subsequently Big Pit: The National **Coal** Museum), as a commercial venture that received a major endowment from the NCB and was run by a board of trustees. The venture was handed over to the National Museum in February 2001. Big Pit, which closed in 1980 when there were 250 men working there, is a typical Welsh deep mine. A shaft was sunk at the site in 1860 by the Blaenavon **Iron** and Coal Company, but amidst earlier workings, giving the mine a history of over 200 years. In 2005, the Blaenavon museum won the Gulbenkian Prize, the prize most coveted by the museums of the United Kingdom.

Central to the museum's role in the cultural fabric of Wales is the array of collections that it conserves for the nation. They are the basis of its contribution to scholarship and of its distinctive contribution to education, as well as a source of public enjoyment and enlightenment. The museum organizes lectures, demonstrations and field excursions, provides advice and information, issues publications and mounts permanent and temporary exhibitions. Much of this work is done outside the museum sites, and the staff work with other museums, as well as with universities, colleges, schools and amateur, professional and specialist societies.

Individual donations of objects have ranged in size from the unusually large collection of around a million mollusc shells from J. R. le B. Tomlin, to individual items. The record of thousands of small donations chronicled in the annual reports emphasizes the importance of the part played by the public in the creation of comprehensive collections. Among them are those presented by the Friends of the Museum, established in 1954 to raise money to purchase objects of particular interest. A number of the donations are of international significance. They include the Tomlin collection; the French Impressionist **paintings** from the bequests of the sisters Gwendoline and Margaret Davies (*see* **Davies family (Llandinam)**), which materially changed the stature of the museum's art collection; and the very early photographs (1840–55) of the **John Dillwyn-Llewelyn** collection (*see* **Photography**).

The gradually expanding size and range of the collections, coupled with the many developments at the eight sites, means that the National Museum is progressively becoming a microcosm of Wales, reflecting the considerable variety that exists in a relatively small geographical compass.

The museum's first director was **W. Evans Hoyle** (1908–24), who was followed by Mortimer Wheeler (1924–6), Sir **Cyril F. Fox** (1926–48), **D. Dilwyn John** (1948–68), **Gwyn O. Jones** (1968–77), Douglas A. Bassett (1977–85), David W. Dykes (1985–9), Alistair Wilson (1989–93), Colin Ford (1993–8), Anna Southall (1998–2003) and Michael Houlihan (2003–).

In 2001–2, the total number of visitors to the various branches of the museum increased by 87.8% to 1,430,428 as a result of the reintroduction – by the **National Assembly** – in April 2001, of free entry. In 2005–6, the number of visitors was 1,343,685.

NATIONAL PARKS

The three National Parks of Wales, brought into being through the National Parks Act 1949 and covering a total of 412,900 ha – some 20% of the surface area of Wales – are the **Snowdonia** National Park (1951; 218,850 ha), the **Pembrokeshire** Coast National Park (1952; 59,373 ha) and the **Brecon Beacons** National Park (1957; 134,677 ha). Proposals in the early 1970s for a fourth, the Cambrian Mountains National Park (*see* **Elenydd Mountains**) were rejected, but in terms of landscape protection the case for it remains urgent. National Park designation – as with Wales's five designated Areas of Outstanding Natural Beauty: the **Gower** and **Llŷn** peninsulas, the **Clwydian Hills**, the **Anglesey** coastline and the **Wye** valley – affords only a theoretical degree of environmental protection through planning controls. In practice, subservience to **governmental** needs often causes the protection to be compromised – as demonstrated by the extensive military training areas (*see* **Military Bases**) in the Pembrokeshire and Brecon Beacons Parks. The major determining forces in the modern Welsh landscape – **agriculture**, **forestry** and **tourism** – were released further from already inadequate planning control by **Conservative** countryside legislation of the 1980s and have caused immense damage to much of the landscape of the Welsh Parks.

The term 'National Park' is itself misleading, for the land within the parks is mainly privately owned, and before the passage of the Countryside and Rights of Way Act 2000, access agreements to it were both unreliable and limited. Nevertheless, designation has afforded a measure of protection to some of Wales's prime landscapes, from the wild elegance of Snowdonia's **mountains** in the north, to the whaleback moorland ridges of the south, and across to the west, where the fretted white sea-cliffs of **Castlemartin** contrast perfectly with the bluff headlands of Strumble (**Pencaer**) and **St David's**. In 2006, it was estimated that the National Parks provide 12,000 jobs and boost the Welsh **economy** by £177 million annually.

Elugig Stacks (Castlemartin) in the Pembrokeshire Coast National Park

NATIONAL SOCIETY, The, [for the education of the poor]

The National Society was founded in 1811 to establish and maintain elementary schools for working-**class** children. Its aim was to provide **education** that included instruction in **religion** according to the principles of the **Anglican** Church. Supported by endowments and substantial patronage, the society established schools throughout Wales and **England**; by 1870, there were over 1000 in Wales, in comparison with the 300 non-denominational schools of the **British Society**. The Society played the central role in the establishment of **Trinity College, Carmarthen** (1848) which continues to have links with it. The Education Act of 1870 provided the means to establish non-denominational elementary schools controlled by elected School Boards; such schools were not established in areas where schools established by the National Society already existed – a matter of acrimony in those places in which the majority of those attending National schools came from **Nonconformist** families. The position of the National schools was strengthened by the Education Act of 1902, which gave them assistance from the rates, but many of them were unable to meet increasingly rigorous **government** standards regulating the fabric and design of school buildings; this, together with the hostility of some local education authorities towards them, led to the closure of many schools. Some, however, became the basis for **voluntary** schools, established by the Education Act of 1944.

NATIONAL TRUST, The

Established in 1895 as a non-profit-making company devoted to the preservation of buildings and land of beauty or historic interest, the National Trust was incorporated by act of parliament in 1907. Its founders were a curious alliance of right-to-roam **radicals** and Gothic-loving conservatives. The first property it acquired was Dinas Oleu, a high point above **Barmouth**, which offers superb views over Cardigan Bay. The Trust came to be perceived as an organization enabling aristocratic families hit by death duties to remain in their ancestral homes. In Wales, however, the Trust has only two such properties – Plas Newydd (**Llanddaniel Fab**) and Powis Castle (**Welshpool**). Other historic buildings it owns include Erddig (**Marchwiel**) and Penrhyn Castle (**Llandygai**). Powis Castle and Erddig include superb **gardens**, but of all the Trust's gardens the finest is that at Bodnant (**Eglwysbach**). It has also acquired historic sites such as Segontium Fort (**Caernarfon**) and Skenfrith (**Llangattock-Vibon-Avel**) and **Cilgerran** castles. Among its coastal properties are **St David's** Head and **Rhossili** Downs. It also owns Ysgyryd Fawr (**Llantilio Pertholey**) and the summits of **Snowdon** and the **Carneddau**. Owner of 44,575 ha of Welsh land, the Trust is second only to the **Forestry Commission** among Wales's landowners; its largest property is the 10,500-ha **Ysbyty Ifan** estate. The Trust operates in Wales, **England** and Northern **Ireland**. In Wales, the Trust has a rudimentary degree of **devolution**, but there have been accusations that it has shown less concern for buildings of specific Welsh interest than the Scottish National Trust – a separate organization founded in 1931 – has shown for buildings of specific Scottish interest. However, it has superbly restored Tŷ Mawr (**Bro Machno**), the home of the **Bible** translator **William Morgan**.

NATIONAL UNEMPLOYED WORKERS' MOVEMENT, The

Established in 1921, the NUWM led the campaign against unemployment in interwar **Britain**. Much influenced by the **Communist Party**, the movement advocated a policy of demonstrations and direct action, including the **hunger marches** from distressed areas. Leaders such as **Will Paynter** organized the resistance of the unemployed and attracted much public sympathy. In 1935, the NUWM was involved in one of the high points of the campaign against the **means test**, when over 300,000 people protested on the streets of south Wales. The movement also conducted countless individual appeal cases on behalf of the unemployed.

NATIONAL UNION OF MINEWORKERS, The

In 1944, the members of the **Miners' Federation of Great Britain** voted overwhelmingly in favour of the creation of a union which would give them a more united voice, and on 1 January 1945 the National Union of Mineworkers (the NUM) came into existence. Individual **coal**fields retained a considerable degree of autonomy and financial independence within the NUM. The **South Wales Miners' Federation** (the Fed) became the South Wales Area of the new union. (The area also contained the Forest of Dean; the coalminers of Somerset became part of it in 1960.) The miners of the northern coalfield became part of the North West area. Under presidents such as **Will Paynter** and **Emlyn Williams** and general secretaries such as Dai Dan Evans (1898–1947) and **Dai Francis**, the South Wales area played a leading role in the NUM from its foundation until the fateful **miners' strike** of 1984–5, and during that period was also central to the **trade union** movement in Wales. In particular, it was pivotal in the campaign to establish the **Wales Trade Union Congress**.

From the outset, the NUM, under the leadership of **Arthur Horner**, sought to work with the newly elected **Labour government** to achieve nationalization. The industry passed into the hands of the people, or at least the state, on 1 January 1947, and Vesting Day witnessed flag-hoisting ceremonies at many pits.

In 1946, Horner's Miners' Charter, which included a five-day week and wage increases, was largely accepted by the **National Coal Board**. There followed a golden era in which high wages were accompanied by an excellent training scheme. This new confidence found cultural expression. The Miners' **Eisteddfod**, launched under the auspices of the NUM at **Porthcawl** in 1948, went from strength to strength and in 1953 the Miners' Gala was launched at **Cardiff**, a colourful occasion which rapidly became an important feature in the calendar of trade unionists.

But disillusionment was to set in. There were many small disputes, especially in the anthracite coalfield, occasions when National Coal Board officials, sometimes with a degree of arrogance, sought to undermine traditional work practices, an issue which erupted in bitter contention at **Gwaun-Cae-Gurwen** in 1956. However, the chief cause of conflict was the Board's pit closure programme; conflict could give rise to a lodge's readiness to act locally and unofficially, the cause of occasional tension within the union.

In the 1960s, pit closures accelerated and miners' wages went into relative decline. In 1972, the NUM organized the first **Britain**-wide strike by coalminers since 1926; it resulted in significant wage increases, not least because of the union's highly effective picketing tactics. The erosion of those gains led to a further strike in February 1974, and this time the result was the overthrow of a **Conservative** government (*see* Miners' Strikes).

Meanwhile, the contraction of the industry continued apace; between 1947 and 1974 the number of miners in the southern coalfield declined from 115,000 to 31,000 and in the northern coalfield from 9000 to fewer than 2000. In 1984, the NUM, under the leadership of Arthur Scargill, embarked on a Britain-wide strike in opposition to a programme of pit closures, a strike launched without seeking the vote of the whole body of British coalminers. Originally, 18 of the 28 southern lodges were opposed to the strike, but, when it began, their members were, with few exceptions, wholly loyal to the union. After a year's confrontation with the Board, 94% of the NUM's members in the South Wales area were still on strike. It is that astonishing solidarity which gave the miners of the south Wales coalfield the moral authority to call upon the union centrally to bring the strike to an end. With the failure of the strike, the virtual demise of Wales's coalfields was inevitable. At the time of privatization in 1994, Point of Ayr (**Llanasa**) was Wales's sole deep coalmine. That closed in 1996 and by then the country's sole deep coalmine was **Tower Colliery (Rhigos)**, reopened as a co-operative venture in 1995. By early 2006, the NUM had a mere 1813 members in the whole of Britain. The South Wales area survived in name, but the main role of its officials was modified to that of safeguarding the interests of retired miners.

NATIONAL YOUTH ORCHESTRA OF WALES, The

The first national youth orchestra in the world, it was founded in 1946, chiefly through the efforts of Irwyn Walters who was schools inspector for **music** in Wales. Since then, the orchestra has played a key role in the development of Wales's best orchestral musicians. Players are selected by audition to take part in short residential schools and concert tours, and are coached by leading professional musicians. This method of providing an advanced musical experience for the most talented young musicians has been replicated in many other countries.

NATIONALISM

While a sense of **nationhood** has existed in Wales for up to 1500 years, nationalism – the belief that each nation should achieve statehood and that a viable national community is an essential precondition for the fulfilment of individual aspirations – in Wales is hardly 150 years old. (The word was first used in English in 1844; its Welsh equivalent, *cenedlaetholdeb* dates from 1858.) The phenomenon found its first expression among Welsh migrants in **England** and **North America** (*see* **Emigration**). **Michael D. Jones**, generally considered as the father of Welsh nationalism and the inspirer of that archetypal nationalist venture, the establishment of the **Patagonian** colony, developed his theories between 1847 and 1850, the years he ministered to a Welsh congregation in Cincinnati.

The nationalism of Wales was much encouraged by developments in **Ireland** and mainland Europe, by the advance of democracy, by the struggle against Anglicized landlords and by the campaign for the **disestablishment of the Church of England in Wales**. In the late 19th century, the notion that Wales should enjoy parity with other nations seized the imagination of intellectuals such as **O. M. Edwards**, **T. E. Ellis** and **John Morris-Jones** and was the basis of much of the rhetoric of the young **David Lloyd George**. Nationalism found expression through the creation of institutions such as the **University of Wales** (1893), and the **National Library** (1907) and the **National Museum** (1907). The demand for self-**government**, however, was muted and won virtually no success. The **Cymru Fydd** (Young Wales) movement, formed in 1886 and extinct by 1899, advocated **home rule**, but opposed any suggestion that it could be achieved otherwise than through the agency of the British **Liberal Party**.

The declining interest in the issue shown after the **First World War** by both the Liberal Party and the **Labour Party** led in 1925 to the formation of **Plaid [Genedlaethol] Cymru**. (While in the late 19th and early 20th centuries, the word 'nationalist' was widely used to describe any Welsh patriot, it tended, after 1925, to be used solely to denote those who were members of Plaid Cymru.) Although the party failed to achieve any major break-through until **Gwynfor Evans**'s victory in the **Carmarthen** by-election of 1966, its nationalism found expression in its demand for adequate radio services for Wales (*see*

Broadcasting), in the **Penyberth bombing school** episode (1936), and in its demand that Wales had a right to be neutral in what it saw as England's wars.

Nationalism was also a factor in the establishment of **Urdd Gobaith Cymru** in 1922, in the demand for the greater use of the **Welsh language** in **education** and in the Parliament for Wales campaign (1950–6). A new nationalist impetus in the 1960s saw the formation of **Cymdeithas yr Iaith Gymraeg** (the Welsh Language Society) in 1962. The formation of other bodies such as the Welsh Arts Council (**Arts Council of Wales**) and the **Welsh Development Agency** also owed something to the growth of nationalism from the 1960s onwards, a growth measurable by the increase in the vote for Plaid Cymru. Yet, the rejection by 956,330 votes to 243,048 of a Welsh assembly in 1979 suggested that the vast majority of the inhabitants of Wales had no desire to see their country having a national future. With Wales denied constitutional expression, some elements within Welsh nationalism turned to violence, in particular by setting fire to **second homes**, which were seen as threats to Welsh-speaking communities and as a factor in pushing house prices beyond the means of local inhabitants. The situation was transformed in 1997 when, by a very narrow majority, the Welsh electorate endorsed the establishment of a **National Assembly for Wales**. Although it would be wrong to claim that the vote was a victory for nationalism, it did indicate that the notion of a national future for Wales was a far more acceptable concept in 1997 than it had been in 1979.

Celebrating the outcome of the devolution referendum of 1997: Dafydd Wigley, Peter Hain, Ron Davies, Win Griffith and Roger Livsey

NATIONHOOD

The Welsh trace their origins as a nation to the centuries following the end of the **Roman** occupation, when they formed part of Brythonic **Britain**. The adoption of the name *Cymry* (from the Brythonic *combrogos*: 'fellow-countryman'; plural *combrogi*), probably in the late 6th century, indicates an early sense of group solidarity. **Celt**ic Christianity (*see* **Celtic Church**), kindred social and economic structures, the development of the **Welsh language** and the growth of a body of Welsh **law** strengthened that sense of solidarity. **Anglo-Saxon** invasions led to the severing of connections between the Welsh and their compatriots elsewhere in Britain, and the construction of **Offa's Dyke** in the late 8th century deepened the perception that *Cymru* (Wales) was uniquely the homeland of the *Cymry* (the Welsh). In *c.*930, an anonymous poem 'Armes Prydein' (*see* **Prophecy**), called on the Welsh and their allies to join in a common alliance against the Saxons.

Following the consolidation of Anglo-Saxon power to the east and, later, the **Norman** invasions of Wales, the Welsh were again forced to defend their nationhood. In the campaign to elevate **St David's** to archiepiscopal status, **Giraldus Cambrensis** offered a remarkable definition of the essentials of a nation. The attempt of the princes of **Gwynedd** to establish an autonomous **principality** was infused with a sense of nationhood. In the 14th century, following Edward I's conquest and the plantation of English castles, **boroughs** and officials, an enhanced sense of nationhood emerged, often reflected in prophetic poetry linked to the bardic order patronized by the emerging **gentry**. Among the most popular literary works were versions of **Geoffrey of Monmouth**'s *Historia Regum Britanniae,* works which deepened the belief that the Welsh were the true possessors of Britain. That belief fuelled the **Glyndŵr Revolt** (1400–10) and was increasingly identified with the desire for a 'national deliverer' to emancipate the nation from foreign control. For many, Henry **Tudor** was viewed as that deliverer (*see* **English Monarchs and Wales**).

Henry VIII's political settlement (1536–43) established firmer ties with **England** (*see* **Acts of 'Union'**), which led eventually to a weakening of the links between the Welsh gentry and Welsh culture, and to a perception that it was the lower **class**es who were the true guardians of Welsh nationhood. Concepts of nationhood proved useful to **Protestant reform**ers who argued that rejecting **Roman Catholicism** meant a return to the pristine doctrines of the Celtic Church. Welsh humanists delighted in all aspects of Welsh tradition, and the publication of the **Bible** in Welsh in 1588 vastly improved the prospects of the language.

In the 17th and early 18th centuries, however, it seemed as if the sense of Welsh nationhood was ebbing. Although the country remained largely Welsh-speaking, fears were expressed that the Welsh would be expunged from history. The bardic schools were in advanced decay, native **music**al tradition was being abandoned and parents were ceasing to give Welsh names to their children. Out of enfeeblement came renewal, not so much through the restoration of the old but through the creation of new traditions, a development particularly associated with the **Morris brothers** and with Iolo Morganwg (**Edward Williams**). Their activities coincided with the literacy campaign of **Griffith Jones** and

with the **Methodist Revival**, movements which, although inspired by evangelical rather than patriotic motives, served to deepen the awareness of Welsh nationhood.

While the **Industrial Revolution** attracted a substantial non-Welsh **population** which was not fully assimilated, it greatly increased employment opportunities in Wales, allowing the country, during a period of marked population increase, to retain within its **border**s the greater part of that increase – a stark contrast with **Ireland**. The wealth engendered by industrialization was central to manifestations of nationhood, such as the **eisteddfod** and the remarkable flowering of the Welsh press (*see* **Newspapers** and **Printing and Publishing**).

Yet, although by the 19th-century Welsh nationhood seemed buoyant, the country had no unifying political organization and virtually no national institutions. By the mid-19th century, there were demands for such institutions, proof that a new phenomenon, Welsh **nationalism**, had come into existence. In the main, however, Welsh patriotism remained apolitical, expressing itself through musical and literary tradition (*see* **Literature**), and through bodies such as the **Cambrian Archaeological Association**, founded in 1847. Nevertheless, the offensive comments of the commissioners responsible for the 1847 **education** report (*see* **Treason of the Blue Books**) and the growth of a distinctive Welsh **radical**ism fostered by deep-rooted agrarian and religious grievances aided the development of a more politically conscious patriotism.

The years around 1900 saw Welsh nationhood winning major victories, including the establishment of a national university (*see* **University of Wales**), a **national library** and a **national museum** and the bringing of the **disestablishment of the Church of England in Wales** into the realm of practical politics. Despite such advances, there was cause for concern. The 1911 census revealed that the proportion of the inhabitants of Wales speaking Welsh had fallen below 50%. There was an awareness that Nonconformity (*see* **Nonconformists**), to many a central marker of Welsh nationality, was in decline. There were fears that the advance of **socialism** would prove inimical to Welsh identity. The **First World War**, allegedly fought for the little 'five foot five' nations, did nothing to advance the cause of Wales, and the country gained no benefit from the emphasis on national self-determination apparent in the post-war treaties. The interwar years, although they saw the establishment of **Urdd Gobaith Cymru** and **Plaid [Genedlaethol] Cymru**, were dominated by economic **depression**, and were virtually devoid of any increased institutional recognition of the existence of Wales.

In the decades after the **Second World War**, however, institutional recognition gathered pace. A host of organizations, such as the **Welsh National Opera Company**, the Welsh Arts Council (**Arts Council of Wales**) and the **Sports Council for Wales**, came into existence, a process which culminated in the establishment of the **National Assembly for Wales** in 1999. Yet, it could seem as if institutional recognition was occurring hand in hand with the erosion of the substance of Welsh nationhood. During the 20th century, the proportion of the inhabitants of Wales able to speak Welsh declined from 50% to 20%, and incomers had changed the character of many **communities**, particularly in the rural areas. But perhaps the referendum result of 1997 was indicative of a more subtle shift – that awareness of Welsh nationhood was ceasing to be primarily a cultural phenomenon, becoming instead a civic and territorial one.

NATURE CONSERVATION

The richness of wildlife in Wales is reflected in the high proportion of the country's land surface (2,075,899 ha) – well over a quarter – which has been designated as protected land. Since the mid-20th century, a succession of statutes and international obligations and a proliferation of organizations have sought to protect Wales's habitat and richness of species from such dangers as pollution, building development, and changes in land management practices, including **agriculture** and **forestry**. Land that is not covered by such designation may nevertheless be protected through planning policy, regulations and licensing systems or through ownership by local authorities and voluntary organizations. Increasingly, through agri-environment schemes, individual landowners are being encouraged to manage and restore landscapes and habitats sympathetically.

The national wildlife conservation authority for Wales and its inland waters is the Countryside Council for Wales (CCW), which came into being when the Nature Conservancy Council (1973–91) was dissolved. The CCW's work includes advising **government** and local authorities on matters affecting the environment, monitoring change in habitats, species and the landscape, and co-ordinating the activities of land users, countryside visitors and the various conservationist bodies. It co-operates with the Campaign for the Protection of Rural Wales.

Chief among the CCW's partner organizations are Wales's three major **National Parks**, designated in the 1950s, which cover 412,900 ha. The five Areas of Outstanding Natural Beauty – the **Anglesey** coastline, the **Clwydian Hills**, the **Gower** and **Llŷn** peninsulas and the **Wye** valley – account for 83,200 ha. A total of 496 km of coastline, comprising sections in Anglesey, **Ceredigion**, Llŷn, **Pembrokeshire**, Gower and the Vale of **Glamorgan**, have been accorded Heritage Coast status.

The **National Trust**, Wales's second biggest landowner after the **Forestry Commission**, has a significant conservationist role in relation to the 44,515 ha it holds. A further 19,714 ha are in the ownership of the Royal Society for the Protection of **Birds**, and the Wildlife Trusts, with their 224 reserves, own a total of 5400 ha.

About 70 sites in Wales are classified as being of international importance, with a further 1064 as important in a United Kingdom context and 79 as important nationally. All sites in the first two categories are designated as Sites of Special Scientific Interest (SSSI). Of Wales's approximately 1000 SSSIs – covering 224,790 ha – many are located in the National Parks. They are also well represented elsewhere in Wales. They include the best examples of the different kinds of terrestrial and inter-tidal habitats found in Wales, and range from small, individual fields to enormous sites such as the **Dee** and **Severn** estuaries, **Laugharne** Burrows, Traeth Lafan (**Aber|gwyngregyn|**) and Malltraeth Marsh (**Bodorgan**). Wales's National Nature Reserves – around

Wetlands at Burry Port on the Burry Inlet, one of ten 'Ramsar' sites in Wales

70 in number – are scattered throughout the country, and range from coast to **mountain** summit. Some of the more dramatic reserves occur in the uplands of the north-west, but they also include **Cors Caron** and locations in Gower, Pembrokeshire, the **Berwyn** range, the **Pumlumon** massif and the **Brecon Beacons**. There are 10 'Ramsar' sites – named after an agreement signed in 1971 at Ramsar in Iran to protect wetlands of international importance; they extend over 30,861 ha and include the **Dyfi** estuary along with **Cors Fochno**. The Dee estuary and the **islands** of Skomer and Grassholm are among Wales's Special Protection Areas, which exist to safeguard birdlife and consist of 85,982 ha. Wales has 90 (candidate) Special Areas of Conservation, 5 of which are cross-**border** sites; the purpose of this designation is to conserve the best representative examples of Europe's rarest **plant** and animal species and habitat types, both on land and at sea (*see also* **Amphibians and Reptiles, Insects, Fish and Fishing, Mammals**).

Other sites enjoying degrees of protection include Local Nature Reserves (non-statutory reserves managed by private and public organizations), Sites of Nature Conservation Importance, Regionally Important Geological and Geomorphological Sites, and Country Parks – of which there are 38 in Wales. Changes in the European Union's Common Agricultural Policy, announced in 2003, are likely to cause grants to farmers to be linked more to nature conservancy than to the production of agricultural surpluses.

NAVAL COLLIERY DISASTER
Penygraig, Rhondda

This steam coal colliery, belonging to Messrs Rowlands and Morgan, suffered an explosion on 10 December 1880 in which 100 lives were lost. The mine had a history of large outbursts of gas, and had previously experienced explosions, though with less serious loss of life. The report of the official inquiry pointed to managerial failings.

NEATH (Castell-nedd), Neath Port Talbot (1020 ha; 18,604 inhabitants)

The **Romans** realized the importance of having a fortified crossing of the **Nedd**, establishing the fort of Nidum in the AD 70s (*see* **Blaenhonddan**.) Their example was followed by the **Normans**, who founded a **borough** and built a castle near the **river** (*c.*1114); footings, a ruined tower and a 14th-century gatehouse survive. The navigable river and the availability of **coal** led in the 1690s to the establishment of a **copper**works, an industry which had been introduced to nearby Aberdulais in 1584 (*see* Blaenhonddan). The pioneer of Neath's copperworks was **Humphrey Mackworth**, whose family's mansion, Gnoll, was demolished in 1957. Its restored **gardens** contain cascades, **lakes** and follies. **Canal** and **railway** development aided the town's 19th-century growth, to which the local benefactor, Howel Gwyn of Duffryn Clydach, greatly contributed. However, the attempt in 1878 to endow the town with a floating harbour had little success, and thus local exports continued to be shipped at **Briton Ferry**.

The largely pedestrianized town centre, dominated by the massive church of St **David** (1869), and containing several impressive chapels, an indoor market, the **Mechanics Institute** (1847; designed by **Alfred Russel Wallace**), and the

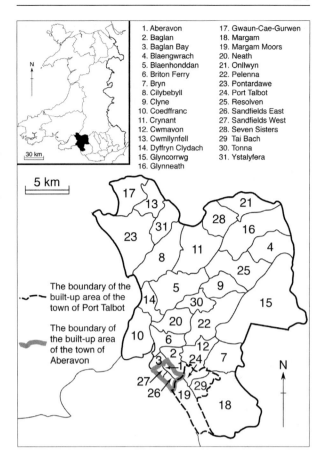

1. Aberavon	17. Gwaun-Cae-Gurwen
2. Baglan	18. Margam
3. Baglan Bay	19. Margam Moors
4. Blaengwrach	20. Neath
5. Blaenhonddan	21. Onllwyn
6. Briton Ferry	22. Pelenna
7. Bryn	23. Pontardawe
8. Cilybebyll	24. Port Talbot
9. Clyne	25. Resolven
10. Coedffranc	26. Sandfields East
11. Crynant	27. Sandfields West
12. Cwmavon	28. Seven Sisters
13. Cwmllynfell	29. Tai Bach
14. Dyffryn Clydach	30. Tonna
15. Glyncorrwg	31. Ystalyfera
16. Glynneath	

The communities of the county borough of Neath Port Talbot

Gwyn Hall (1887; home of the Neath Museum), provides the **community** with an attractive townscape. The light industry area of Millands gave **Ray Milland**, the Neath-born actor, his stage name. The Welsh **Rugby** Union was established at the Castle Hotel in 1881; the room where the meeting took place is preserved as a memorial. For Neath Abbey, *see* **Dyffryn Clydach**.

NEATH (Castell-nedd) Constituency and one-time district

Following the abolition of the **county** of **Glamorgan** in 1974, Neath was created as a district of the new county of **West Glamorgan**. It consisted of the **borough** of **Neath** and most of the **rural district** of Neath. In 1996, the district, together with that of **Port Talbot** and part of that of **Lliw Valley**, became the **county borough** of **Neath Port Talbot**. The boundaries of the Neath constituency are broadly coterminous with those of the defunct district.

NEATH PORT TALBOT (Castell-nedd Port Talbot) County borough (45,192 ha; 134,468 inhabitants)

In 1974, **Neath**, **Port Talbot**, **Lliw Valley** and **Swansea** became the four districts of the new **county** of **West Glamorgan**. Neath consisted of the **borough** and most of the **rural district** of Neath, and Port Talbot of the borough of Port Talbot and the **urban district** of **Glyncorrwg**. At reorganization in 1996, it was expected that both districts would become **county boroughs**, and there were protests when the two districts were combined with five **communities** previously in Lliw Valley to form the county borough of Neath Port Talbot. In 2001, 28.82% of the county borough's inhabitants had some knowledge of **Welsh**, with 12.83% wholly fluent in the language. (*See also* **Gwaun-Cae-Gurwen** and Port Talbot: Tai Bach.)

NEDD Commote

A **commote** of the kingdom of **Morgannwg**, it constituted the basin of the **River Nedd** and part of the east bank of the **Tawe**. Following the **Norman** conquest, it became the westernmost part of the lordship of **Glamorgan**. Following the establishment of the **county** of Glamorgan, it became a **hundred**.

NEDD River (47 km)

The **River** Nedd comes into being at Pontneddfechan (**Ystradfellte**), where the rivers which drain Fforest Fawr in the **Brecon Beacons** – the Nedd Fechan, Mellte and Hepste – come together. These rivers form a series of spectacular **waterfalls** in narrow, wooded valleys. On occasion, they flow underground through the channels they have formed in the **limestone**. Porth yr Ogof on the Mellte is a particularly spectacular example. From Pontneddfechan to **Tonna**, the river, flanked by one-time **coal**mining villages, flows through a thickly wooded valley, which follows the Neath Fault which runs from the north-east to the south-west. The Dulais joins the Nedd at Aberdulais, where an attractive waterfall once powered one of **Glamorgan**'s earliest **copper** works (1584). The lower Nedd flows through a heavily industrialized area; the fact that the river was navigable for 7 km is the key to the rise of the ports of **Neath** and **Briton Ferry**. The river flows into the sea in Baglan Bay.

NEFYN, Gwynedd (1523 ha; 2619 inhabitants)

Located halfway along the northern coast of the **Llŷn** Peninsula, the **community** contains the villages of Nefyn, Edern and Morfa Nefyn. Porth Dinllaen Bay swings like a hammock between the rocky outcrops of Penrhyn Nefyn and Trwyn Porth Dinllaen.

Nefyn was the *maerdref* (administrative centre) of the **commote** of **Dinllaen** and one of the seats of the princes of **Gwynedd**. Edward I was there on Midsummer Day 1284, celebrating his conquest of Gwynedd by holding an **Arthur**ian round table; the floor collapsed under the festivities. The Welsh princes had fostered Nefyn as a **port** and urban settlement. Edward I granted it **borough** status and, until 1950, it was one of the contributory boroughs of the **Caernarfon** borough constituency. In the rebuilding of St Edern's church (1868), the timbers of its fine medieval roof were reused. Until the advent of **tourism**, the local **economy** depended upon **seafaring**; indeed, it was said that some streets had a master mariner living in every house. Nefyn's herring harvest (*see* **Fish and Fishing**) was an important seasonal activity. Porth Dinllaen is famous for its **lifeboat**. Attempts in the 1770s, the 1820s and the 1830s to make Porth Dinllaen the chief packet station for **Ireland** floundered on the inability to raise capital to built a **road** (or later a **railway**) via **Newtown** and **Dolgellau** to the Llŷn Peninsula.

NELSON, Caerphilly (1098 ha; 4577 inhabitants)

Carved out of the ancient **parish** of Llanfabon, Nelson consists of undulating land between the **Taff** and **Rhymney** valleys. A hotel commemorating Horatio Nelson gave the **community** its name. There is a rare **handball** court at the Royal Oak Hotel.

Sunset over Nefyn, Llŷn, with Morfa Nefyn, Porth Dinllaen and Carreg Ddu in the further distance

NEOLITHIC AGE, The (The New Stone Age; *c.*4400–2300 BC)

The chief feature of the Neolithic Age was the development of **agriculture** as the activity of almost the entire **population**. The people of the age had no knowledge of metal production. As a result, the belief arose that there was a chasm between them and the people of subsequent periods – the **Bronze** and **Iron Ages**. More recently, it has become customary to stress continuity rather than cataclysmic change. Although the term Neolithic Age is still current, it has come to be used as a convenient way of referring to a period that was, above all, part of a continuum. Agriculture provided an economic base that ensured the production of a managed and more constant **food** supply. Its dissemination throughout Europe during the 6th and 5th millennium BC coincided with a period of climatic maxima that has not been subsequently surpassed in the most recent geological period – that of the Holocene (*see* **Geology**). Farming was introduced to **Britain** during the 5th millennium, presumably by settlers from the European mainland, rather than through the inherent agricultural activities of the native Mesolithic inhabitants (*see* **Palaeolithic and Mesolithic Age**).

The distribution of Neolithic artefacts, such as stone axes and **pottery**, offers the best indicator of the rapid spread of farming. Such artefacts are generally found in the more fertile and easily cultivated soils – those sustaining a lighter forest cover or those overlaying well-drained gravels or **limestone**. With a rudimentary technology based on stone implements, the forest cover was progressively removed, to be replaced by a patchwork of small, enclosed fields. In the fields, there developed mixed farming based upon the breeding of **sheep**, **goats**, **pigs** and **cattle**, and the growing of crops such as emmer wheat and primitive forms of barley. The identification of fields as specifically Neolithic is difficult since many have been incorporated into later agricultural enclosures and are erroneously referred to as 'Celtic' fields. Likewise, it is difficult to identify settlements, although an early house structure has been excavated at **Llandygai**, and others are known from Moel y Gaer (**Halkyn**), Nottage (**Porthcawl**) and from within the small defended enclosure of Clegyr Boia (**St David**'s).

The polished stone axe is one of the hallmarks of the Neolithic Age. Production of such axes was undertaken in a number of upland localities in Wales. The most important was at Graig Lwyd (**Penmaenmawr**), with lesser centres at Rhiw (**Aberdaron**) and Carn Meini (**Mynachlog-Ddu**). Axes from Welsh production sites are widely distributed in southern, central and eastern **England**. This, combined with the fact that stone axes from Cumbria, **Cornwall**, and Northern **Ireland**, and flint axes from south-eastern England, have been found in Wales indicates the existence of trade routes and exchange mechanisms. Carn Meini may also have been the source of the bluestones that many believe were transported to Stonehenge in Wiltshire at the beginning of the Bronze Age. In the late Neolithic Age, shaft-hole implements such as battleaxes, axe hammers and mace heads became common artefacts, their use denoting rank and prestige in a society that was increasingly showing signs of social stratification. Source rocks for the production of some of these

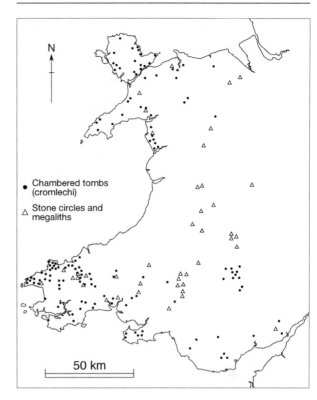

Chambered tombs, stone circles and megaliths (after Ordnance Survey)

Map legend:
● Chambered tombs (cromlechi)
△ Stone circles and megaliths
50 km

artefacts are known from Carn Meini and Cwm Mawr (**Churchstoke**). One of the most sophisticated stone objects of the period is the flint mace head from Maesmor (**Llangwm, Denbighshire**) on which 170 lozenge facets have been carved with great care and precision. The Neolithic Age also saw the production of the first pottery; sherds of simple vessels have been found in **Anglesey** and **Pembrokeshire**.

The principal monuments of the Neolithic Age are megalithic tombs – the earliest surviving examples of **architecture** in Britain. Massive stone chambers within stone or earth mounds, they contain evidence of collective interment. The earliest monuments were built *c.*3600–3000 BC. There are in Wales the remains of some 150 megalithic tombs. They are mainly distributed along the coastal lowlands, with some inland clusters in areas such as the **Wye** and the **Conwy** valleys. The building of such massive constructions involved the labour of large numbers of men – as many as 200 in the case of some of the tombs. Clearly, therefore, there were populous communities in some parts of Wales by *c.*3000 BC, communities with the ability to cooperate effectively. The monuments combined social and ceremonial purposes with reverence for departed ancestors. The remains of at least 40 people – adults, children and babies – were found in the Parc le Breos tomb (**Ilston**). Many tombs were enlarged sequentially to include more than one burial chamber, as at Trefignath (**Trearddur**), **Dyffryn Ardudwy** and Tyisha (**Talgarth**).

Generally, it is only the megalithic chambers that survive. One of the few exceptions is Pen-yr-wyrlod (Talgarth), where both tomb and mound survive in a relatively intact monument. Pen-yr-wyrlod has yielded a man's skull; the face has been reconstructed as a computer image and provides an insight into the remarkably modern appearance of an inhabitant of the Neolithic Age. Mounds up to 75 m long are visible in reconstituted tombs such as Parc le Breos, Dyffryn Ardudwy, Trefignath, Tinkinswood (**St Nicholas**), Gwernvale (**Crickhowell**), Capel Garmon (**Bro Garmon**) and Llety'r Filiast (**Llandudno**).

The architectural form of the chambers and their positioning in the mound allow regional groups to be identified. In the **Severn**-Cotswold group, the position of the chamber varies from a simple end siting (Tinkinswood) to side chambers (Gwernvale, Pen-yr-wyrlod and Capel Garmon). The chamber itself may be a single rectangular cist (Tinkinswood) or a complex cruciform or transeptal type (Parc le Breos and Ty Isaf). These monuments show close affinities with Cotswolds tombs, and have more distant analogies with the megalithic graves of **Brittany**. Another megalithic form, this time with close analogies in **Ireland**, is the portal dolmen. This form is characterized by a massive capstone that is supported at an inclined angle on tall portal stones that front a small burial chamber. Pentre Ifan (**Nevern**), standing 3.12 m high, is the best-known Welsh example; smaller versions include Carreg Coetan Arthur (**Newport**, Pembrokeshire) and the six tombs in Dyffryn Ardudwy. A different, and chronologically later, megalithic tradition is represented by the passage grave, of which Anglesey's Barclodiad y Gawres (**Aberffraw**) and Bryn Celli Ddu (**Llanddaniel Fab**) are the outstanding examples. These tombs consist of a chamber – cruciform at Barclodiad y Gawres and polygonal in Bryn Celli Ddu – connected to a long passage, the structures

were covered by a round mound. At Barclodiad y Gawres, five stones bear incised geometric or spiral decoration, indicating direct links with the tombs of the Boyne valley culture in Ireland, and connections with Brittany and, ultimately, with the Iberian peninsula.

There are notable gaps in the distribution of megalithic tombs, particularly in the **Ceredigion** coastal belt, in the north-east and in the upland core. It is likely that other forms of burial were practised in those areas. In the north-eastern limestone belt, for example, multiple inhumations in **caves** are known in the Gop (**Trelawnyd and Gwaenysgor**), Perthichwareu (**Llanarmon-yn Ial**) and Rhos-ddigre (**Llandegla**).

Large ceremonial henge monuments are also characteristic of the late Neolithic Age. These sites are circular earthen enclosures with an internal ditch and entered by single or double entrances. They appear to define sacred areas and are sometimes accompanied by parallel-sided cursus monuments and smaller ditched circular enclosures. Such a group of monuments was excavated at Llandygai. The group may be aligned with two Anglesey henges at Bryn Celli Ddu and Castell Bryngwyn (**Llanidan**) and a more enigmatic monument at Bryn Celli Wen (Llanddaniel Fab), thus emphasizing the sanctity of both shores of the **Menai Strait**. A similar complex may have existed in the Severn valley near **Welshpool**. The building of such large structures probably involved the co-operative endeavours of many communities, and their existence suggests the presence of a sacred priesthood. One of the largest man-made monuments in Britain – a timber palisade enclosure

The Neolithic burial chamber of Pentre Ifan, Nevern, Pembrokeshire

with an estimated area of 35 ha – has recently been discovered at Walton (**Old Radnor**), and nearby there may be another enclosure, almost as large.

If the essence of the Neolithic Age was communities of farmers lacking metals, then it did not come to an end in Wales until *c.*1400 BC, when metal tools were probably within the reach of everyone. However, the coming of metal in *c.*2300 BC was the harbinger of eventual profound economic and cultural change, and thus that date is generally considered to denote the end of the Neolithic Age and the beginning of the Bronze Age.

NERCWYS, Flintshire (1296 ha; 566 inhabitants)

Located immediately south of **Mold**, the **community** has one of Wales's rare tower houses – that built in the mid-15th century for Rheinallt ap Gruffydd, one of the many members of the **gentry** praised by **Lewys Glyn Cothi**. St Mary's church contains Romanesque and Perpendicular features and the remnants of a rood screen. Nercwys Hall (1638) has fine rococo chimneypieces. Other historic houses include Plas Onn (a 15th-century hall house), Glan Terrig (1629), Hendre Ucha (1635) and Hendre Isa (mid-17th century).

NEST FERCH RHYS AP TEWDWR
(fl.*c.*1090–1130) Princess

Sometimes described as 'the Helen of Wales', Nest the daughter of **Rhys ap Tewdwr**, the last king of **Deheubarth**, is remembered as one of the most colourful and romantic figures in Welsh history. Her marriage to Gerald of Windsor, the constable of **Pembroke**, was probably a political alliance intended to give Gerald a foothold in the aristocratic society of south-west Wales; one of their grandchildren was **Giraldus Cambrensis** and the family played a prominent part in the **Norman** invasion of **Ireland**. Indeed, Nest has been described as 'the queen bee of the Cambro-Norman swarm'. Her abduction by **Owain ap Cadwgan** in 1109 precipitated a succession of political crises; she also bore children to at least three other men, among them Henry I.

NEVERN (Nyfer), Pembrokeshire
(6132 ha; 822 inhabitants)

Located south-west of **Cardigan**, the **community** contains a fine stretch of the north **Pembrokeshire** coast and includes the westernmost flanks of **Mynydd Preseli**. Pentre Ifan is the most recognizable of Wales's **Neolithic** chambered tombs. There are more modest tombs at Trellyffaint and Llech y Drybedd. There is a group of **Bronze Age** cairns at Crugiau Cemmaes. West of Moylgrove (Trewyddel) are two dramatically sited **Iron Age** coastal promontory forts. At Castell Henllys, Iron Age houses have been reconstructed on the foundations of the original dwellings. In the 1st century BC, it was home to perhaps 100 people. The adjoining visitors' centre is a sensitively designed building. The historian **George Owen** was born at nearby Henllys.

In the churchyard of St Brynach's church (14th century, 1864) is a superb cross, carved *c.*1030 with complex interlacings; 147 different species of **plants**, including a 'bleeding' yew, have been recorded in the churchyard. Nevern Castle was the original caput of the **march**er-lordship of **Cemais**; it

was destroyed by the sons of **Rhys ap Gruffudd** in 1195. Llwyngwair, the centre of a caravan park, contains elements from the 16th to the 19th century. **Saunders Lewis** claimed that Ioan Siencyn's late 18th-century poem to the squire of Cwmgloyne (17th-century) was proof of the vitality of the **Taliesin** tradition. In Ceibwr Bay there is a memorial to **Wynford Vaughan Thomas**, who bought the land around the bay and presented it to the **National Trust**. Fachongle was the home of John Seymour (1914–2004), guru of the self-sufficiency movement of the 1960s, a movement which did much to Anglicize rural Wales's **Welsh**-speaking areas.

NEVILL family (marquesses of Abergavenny)
Marcher-lords

The family became associated with Wales through the marriage of Elizabeth (d.1448), heiress of the **Beauchamp** lords of the **march**er-lordship of **Abergavenny**, to Edward Nevill, son of Ralph, earl of Westmorland. The title Baron Abergavenny (or Bergavenny) dates from the 14th century, the earldom from 1784 and the marquessate from 1876. Nevill landholdings included the site of the **Blaenavon iron**works. Abergavenny's hospital, Nevill Hall, commemorates the family. In the mid-15th century, the related Neville family briefly held the lordship of **Glamorgan**.

NEVIN, Edward Thomas (Ted Nevin; 1925–92)
Economist

An economist of international repute, and the leading authority on the Welsh **economy** for nearly 40 years, Ted Nevin was born in **Pembroke Dock**. Professor of economics at **Aberystwyth** (1963–8) and at **Swansea** (1968–85), and a prolific author, he made important contributions in many areas, including monetary policy and European integration. In *The Social Accounts of the Welsh Economy* (1956, 1957), he demonstrated that, contrary to assumptions, Wales paid more in tax than it received in **government** spending – an observation which gave a significant boost to the arguments of **Plaid [Genedlaethol] Cymru**.

NEW MOAT (Y Mot), Pembrokeshire
(2840 ha; 426 inhabitants)

Extending from the southern edges of **Mynydd Preseli** to the **Pembrokeshire–Carmarthenshire** boundary, the **community** contains the villages of New Moat, Bletherston, Llys-y-frân and Pen-ffordd. **Place names** indicate that the northern half of New Moat belongs to **Welsh** Pembrokeshire and the southern half to **English** Pembrokeshire. The motte which gives the community its name has a classic inverted pudding-basin shape. St Nicholas's church, largely rebuilt in the 1880s, retains its medieval tower and a 17th-century altar tomb. The Mote, the seat of the Scourfield family, has been demolished. Llys-y-frân **reservoir** (1968–72) is a nature reserve; 75 ha in extent, it is well stocked with trout (*see* **Fish and Fishing**).

NEW QUAY (Ceinewydd), Ceredigion
(321 ha; 1115 inhabitants)

Located on a rising shelf overlooking one of the most attractive beaches of Cardigan Bay, the 'new quay' was originally constructed before 1700 to give protection to vessels seeking shelter. The quay is itself sheltered by the

The monument to George Cornewall Lewis, New Radnor

rebuilt in 1845, in what Richard Haslam described as 'an extreme example of unsuitable rebuilding'. The castle, probably first commissioned by Philip de **Breos** *c.* 1096, was destroyed by **Owain Glyndŵr**. A roadside monument, 24 m high, commemorates **George Cornewall Lewis**, the most successful politician of 19th-century Wales. Castell Crug Eryr, to the north, was the seat of Llywelyn Crug Eryr, whose descendants were noted patrons of Welsh poetry and learning.

NEW RISCA COLLIERY DISASTER
Risca, Monmouthshire (now Caerphilly)
This colliery, which had begun working only two years previously, and which was considered well managed, with an adequate system of ventilation, suffered an explosion on 15 July 1880, killing all 120 men working on the repairing shift. The explosion was attributed to an outburst of gas, following a rock fall, being ignited by a Clanny safety lamp – raising doubts about the safety of such lamps.

NEW TREDEGAR (Tredegar Newydd),
Caerphilly (965 ha; 4945 inhabitants)
The **community** extends across the **Rhymney** valley north of **Bargoed**. The name derives from the new pit sunk in 1858 by the **Tredegar Iron** and **Coal** Company near Troedrhiw-fuwch, a settlement threatened by landslides. The view of New Tredegar from the A469 offers a memorable panorama of the rows of terraced houses typical of the south Wales coalfield (*see* **Housing**).

NEW ZEALAND, Wales's associations with
Welsh people have emigrated (*see* **Emigration**) to New Zealand since the early 19th century, either directly from Wales or from **Australia**, but they have been comparatively few in number and constituted only a small fraction of the country's immigrants. Several Welsh **missionaries** were active in the 19th century, and the Otago **gold** rushes of the 1860s significantly expanded the Welsh presence. There was also notable **immigration** in the years immediately following the **First World War**, including that of Welsh mining families attracted to the Canterbury **coal**mines. In 1921, some 2575 natives of Wales lived in New Zealand, and a further 1760 had Welsh-born fathers. In the 1996 census, 9966 included 'Welsh' among their ethnic origins. Given the size of the Welsh element, the number of Welsh cultural and religious organizations in New Zealand has inevitably been small. The oldest still in existence is the Cambrian Society of Christchurch, founded in 1890. Because of the obsession with **rugby** football, New Zealand is one of the few countries where everyone knows of Wales.

NEWBRIDGE (Trecelyn), Caerphilly
(1034 ha; 6000 inhabitants)
Straddling the **Ebbw** between **Blackwood** and **Cwmbran**, the **community** developed to accommodate workers at the North Celynen Colliery. The Celynen Workmen's Institute, opened in 1924, was one of the last institutes to be built in the south Wales **coal**field. Cwmdows, on the west bank of the Ebbw, is the best preserved 16th-century building in upland **Gwent**. Newbridge **rugby** club, founded in 1888, has a distinguished history.

newer stone pier built as a result of the New Quay Harbour Act of 1835. The place became a **shipbuilding** centre; over 200 **sailing** vessels of up to 300 tonnes were constructed, the last in 1882. There was a New Quay Mutual **Ship Insurance** Society, and the carrying trade flourished for much of the 19th century. By the end of the century, however, the sailing-ship trade was in rapid decline, and hopes that a link with the **railway** network would offer new opportunities were not realized. Early 20th-century New Quay was a place in crisis, the reason perhaps for its central role in the religious **revival** of 1904–5. Eventually, **tourism** offered a degree of salvation, although the industry's seasonal nature means that the **community** has periods of high unemployment. Lobster and crab **fish**ing continue. **Dylan Thomas** was a resident in 1944–5, a fact that found partial expression in *Under Milk Wood*.

NEW RADNOR (Maesyfed), Radnorshire,
Powys (5101 ha; 410 inhabitants)
The **community** embraces much of **Radnor Forest**, including the summit at Great Rhos (660 m) and the picturesquely named **waterfall** Water-break-its-neck. The village, once the **borough** of the lordship of **Radnor**, has a grid layout and is a classic example of a planned town that failed to achieve its potential. Archbishop Baldwin, accompanied by **Giraldus Cambrensis**, visited New Radnor in 1188 to raise recruits for the Third Crusade. It was the **county** town of **Radnorshire** until supplanted by **Presteigne** in the 17th century. Its once attractive town church was

NEWCASTLE EMLYN (Castellnewydd Emlyn), Carmarthenshire (291 ha; 973 inhabitants)

Located on the **Teifi**, the **community** consists in the main of the town of Newcastle Emlyn, which extends across the river to Adpar in **Ceredigion** (*see* **Llandyfriog**). The place was the administrative centre of the **commote** of **Emlyn Uwch Cuch**. The new castle in Emlyn was first mentioned in *Brut y Tywysogyon* in 1215, when it was seized by **Llywelyn ap Iorwerth**. By *c.*1240 it was in the possession of Maredudd ap Rhys (d.1271) of the house of **Deheubarth**. (Emlyn's earlier castle was that at **Cilgerran** in Emlyn Is Cuch.) It fell to the English crown in 1288. The ruined, twin-towered gatehouse dates from the 1340s when the castle's constable was Llywelyn ap Gwilym, an uncle of the poet **Dafydd ap Gwilym**. Destroyed during the **Glyndŵr Revolt**, it was rebuilt by **Rhys ap Thomas** *c.*1500. It was blown up following the 17th-century **Civil Wars**.

Holy Trinity church (1840s, 1920s) has a fine tower and is floored with Cilgerran **slate**. Its **sheep** and **cattle** market serves a wide area. Of the three Jones brothers brought up at Parc-nest, a farm on the edge of the town, one has won the National **Eisteddfod** chair once and the crown twice, one the chair and one the crown.

NEWCASTLE HIGHER (Y Castellnewydd ar Ogwr), Bridgend (661 ha; 3695 inhabitants)

Located immediately north-west of **Bridgend**, the **community** contains the townships of Pen-y-fai, Cwrt Colman and Abercynffig. The hospital at Pen-y-fai was built in the 1860s as the **Glamorgan** Lunatic Asylum. Cwrt Colman, built for the Llewellyn family in the 1830s, is now a hotel. Near its gates are the church, parsonage and school commissioned by the family in 1903. St John's, Abercynffig, is yet another church designed by **John Prichard**.

NEWCHURCH AND MERTHYR (Llannewydd a Merthyr), Carmarthenshire (2507 ha; 623 inhabitants)

Located immediately north-west of **Carmarthen**, the **community** contains the hamlets of Newchurch, Merthyr and Bwlchnewydd, and some of Carmarthen's outer suburbs. The new church (St Michael) was built in 1829. The handsome Cana Congregational chapel (1821, 1862) stands alongside the A40. **Bridget Bevan**, patron and colleague of **Griffith Jones**, **Llanddowror**, was brought up at **Derllys Court**.

NEWPORT (Trefdraeth), Pembrokeshire (1768 ha; 1122 inhabitants)

Located halfway between **Cardigan** and **Fishguard**, the **community**'s main features are the striking Carn Ingli crag (337 m) and the fine views across Parrog beach. There are **Neolithic** burial chambers at Carreg Coetan Arthur and Cerrig y Gof, and **Iron Age hill-forts** on Carn Ingli and Carn Ffoi. In 1204, the Fitz Martin family, **march**er-lords of **Cemais**, established the caput of the lordship at Newport, which they laid out as a planned town. In 1859, the castle's gatehouse was incorporated into a house. Granted a charter *c.*1215, Newport had its own mayor – an office that still exists. St Mary's, largely rebuilt in 1879, retains its medieval tower. Capel yr Eglwys (1799) is one of the **Calvinistic Methodist** chapels in north **Pembrokeshire** that remained within the **Anglican** Church following the split of 1811. The chapels of the **Baptists** (1855) and of the

The New Zealand All Blacks rugby team performing their haka war dance

Peter Fink's *Steel Wave* sculpture on Newport's Baltic Quay

Congregationalists (1845) are substantial buildings. Newport's Eco Centre contains **Britain**'s smallest solar-electric generating station.

NEWPORT (Casnewydd), City
(3740 ha; 97,773 inhabitants)

This entry is concerned with 14 of the 29 **communities** of the Newport County Borough (*see below*). Those 14 communities constitute the built-up area of the city of Newport and essentially represent what was the pre-1976 county borough of Newport. In 1996, the present Newport county borough replaced Newport District (*see* Newport **County Borough** and one-time district), which was, from 1974 to 1996, one of the five districts of the **county** of **Gwent**.

Wales's third largest urban centre, Newport is located in the lower reaches of the **Usk** valley and extends from land hardly above sea level to land rising to 100 m and more. Indeed, perhaps the chief feature of Newport is that it is a hilly place – within it is the only tunnel on the **M4**. Another feature is its status as Wales's premier riverside urban centre. As that **river** is the tidal Usk, which has one of the world's largest differences between high and low tide, yet another feature of Newport is its superabundance of riverside mud.

The original **borough** of Newport consisted of about a third of the 1450-ha **parish** of St Woolos. As the result of boundary changes in 1874, 1922, 1938, 1951, 1967 and 1974, it absorbed the parishes of Bettws and Malpas, and much of those of **Bassaleg**, Christchurch and **Nash**, causing urban Newport to consist of 3740 ha.

Early presence of human beings in the area is indicated by **Palaeolithic** footprints preserved in the mud of the Usk estuary, the **Neolithic** chambered tomb at Cleppa Park (*see* **Coedkernew**), the **Bronze Age** palstave discovered at Liswerry and the **Iron Age hill-fort** at Gaer. The **Romans** concentrated their activity 4.5 km to the north-east at **Caerleon**, and left little evidence to suggest that they impinged upon the site of what would later be the borough of Newport. In the 6th century, the Welsh chieftain, Gwynllyw (a name anglicized as Woolos), lord of the land between the Usk and the **Rhymney** which came to bear his name (Gwynllŵg or **Wentlooge**), was reputedly converted to Christianity by his son, St **Cadog**. Gwynllyw established a church on Stow Hill, eventually the site of St Woolos Cathedral. Gwynllŵg became part of the kingdom of **Seisyllwg**, which later joined with that of Gwent to form the kingdom of **Morgannwg**. The navigable Usk meant that the ecclesiastical settlement on Stow Hill and a likely embryonic quay on the river were vulnerable to **Viking** attacks, such as the devastating raid of 896. A 22-m long Viking ship, which may have taken part in that raid, was discovered during the excavation of the North Dock in the 1870s.

The Vikings' descendants, the **Normans**, reached the estuary of the Usk in the 1090s, when **Robert Fitz Hammo** seized the lowlands of Morgannwg. He built a castle on Stow Hill, the remains of which were destroyed during the building of **railways** in the 1840s. Robert's son-in-law, Robert, earl of Gloucester (d.1141), established the borough of Newport – the *novo burgus* (new borough, or new **port**) first mentioned in 1126. (To the Welsh, the significant innovation was the castle – the *castell newydd* contracted into the name Casnewydd.) The earl probably also commissioned the rebuilding of St Woolos, thus endowing Newport with a fine Romanesque church, the superb doorway and the nave bays of which survive. The **march**er-lordship of Gwynllŵg or Newport remained part of the lordship of **Glamorgan** until the failure of the **Clare family** in the male line in 1314. The Clare successors, the **Audley** and **Stafford** families, built a stone castle on the banks of the Usk to control the river crossing. They may have enclosed the borough with walls, pierced by two gates – the east gate near the crossing and the west gate at the foot of Stow Hill where the Westgate Hotel would later stand.

Newport acquired a house of Austin **friars** in 1377, the last of the religious houses of medieval Wales to be founded. The burgesses were granted a new charter in 1385; its clauses relating to trade indicate the growing prosperity of the borough and its port. **Owain Glyndŵr** attacked Newport in 1402, causing such devastation that its lord received no income from the borough in the following year. Recovery, however, was rapid, with Newport benefiting from its proximity to the rising port of Bristol. The scale of its trade is reflected in the 25-m long mid-15th-century armed merchantman discovered in the mud banks of the Usk in July 2002. It is a discovery of international significance, for the merchantman is the only surviving example of such a boat. Further proof of Newport's late medieval prosperity was the work undertaken at St Woolos's church where a tower and widened nave aisles were built.

With the establishment of **Monmouthshire** in 1536, Newport became subject to the county town of **Monmouth**. A feature of its history in the 16th and 17th centuries was the growing power of local **gentry** families, initially that of the Herberts of St Julians, and subsequently that of the **Morgan family (Tredegar)**. Also of significance was the growth of the export from Newport of charcoal-smelted **iron** produced at **Pontypool**, **Abercarn** and elsewhere, a trade apparent by the early 17th century. In the later 18th, with the introduction of smelting with coke, the iron reaching Newport's Uskside quays increased rapidly, a development vastly aided by the opening in 1799 of the Monmouthshire **Canal** linking Newport with Pontypool and **Crumlin**, and connected by tramroads to the burgeoning ironworks of northern Monmouthshire.

The cheapness of canal transport made the export of **coal** as well as iron an economic proposition. By 1830, Newport had emerged as south Wales's leading coal port, with coal exports four times larger than those of **Cardiff**. Newport's **population** rose from 1135 in 1801 to 7062 in 1831, when the town was larger than Cardiff, a lead it maintained until the 1850s when the great riches of the **Cynon Valley**, and later the **Rhondda**, gave Cardiff a decisive advantage. With Newport in the 1830s the largest town in south-east Wales, it was the natural target of the **Chartist** rising of 1839. The **Newport Rising** was the most memorable happening in Newport's history and is commemorated by **John Frost** Square. Frost, mayor of Newport (1836–7), had been radicalized by his fight against the Morgan family of Tredegar, in particular by the family's imposition of a toll of £3000 on goods crossing

1.6 km of Tredegar Park – the notorious 'golden mile'. In the story of the rise of Newport, the impact of that family is inescapable. The estate architects, the Habershon family, were responsible for much building work, including the restoration of St Woolos, the Havelock Street Presbyterian church, much of Commercial Street and the almshouses built as a memorial to Queen Victoria. Several of Newport's open spaces were saved from development by the Morgans, and the castle, badly mauled by railway construction, was saved from collapse after becoming part of the Tredegar estate.

Although primarily a working-**class** town, Newport did acquire streets of distinction, including Habershon's Italianate villas in Gold Tops, and Victoria Place, Stow Hill – a group of stuccoed houses much filmed by television companies. Its poorer areas tended to be occupied by **Irish** immigrants. Newport's role as Wales's chief centre of **Roman Catholicism** was recognized in 1850 when, on the occasion of the re-creation of the Catholic hierarchy in Wales and **England**, Newport became the seat of the bishop of Newport and Menevia, who had care of the Catholics of Wales's seven southernmost counties together with **Herefordshire**. Newport retained its bishop until the establishment of the archbishopric of Cardiff in 1916.

With the Irish influx, and with a far greater influx from England, Newport, which probably had had a **Welsh**-speaking majority in the 1830s, came to be seen as a thoroughly un-Welsh town, a belief compounded by the ambiguity about the status of Monmouthshire. In the late 19th century, the St George Society of Newport vehemently insisted that Newport was in England; in Newport,

The transporter bridge over the Usk at Newport, opened in 1906

Cymru Fydd received its death blow, when David Lloyd George was told in 1896 that 'there are from Swansea to Newport, thousands upon thousands of Englishmen, as true Liberals as yourself ... who will never submit to the domination of Welsh ideas'. Lloyd George returned to Newport the following year to attend the National Eisteddfod and to be accepted as a member of the Gorsedd of Bards.

With the completion of the dock system in 1892, Newport expanded southwards as the Pillgwenlly area became intensely urbanized. Growth also occurred on the left bank of the Usk with the expansion of Liswerry. The sole bridge crossing the river was that built near the castle in 1800 by David Edwards, son of William Edwards, designer of the famous bridge at Pontypridd. It was 4 km from the growth areas south of the town centre, but suggestions that Pillgwenlly and Liswerry should be linked by a bridge were opposed on the grounds that such a structure would seriously impede the continuingly significant navigation on the Usk. The solution to the problem was what was to become Newport's greatest treasure – the transporter bridge, opened in 1906. Designed by the French engineer Ferdinand Arnodin, its construction was much delayed by the fact that its builders worked in feet while its designer worked in metres. The bridge is a suspended ferry or 'gondola', consisting of a platform carrying passengers and vehicles, which is propelled across the river by cables moving along a deck supported by two piers of a height sufficient to ensure uninterrupted navigation for the tallest shipping. It was based on bridges previously built at Rouen and Marseilles. Newport's transporter bridge is believed to be one of only seven such structures in the world still functioning. Newport has other remarkable bridges: George Street Bridge (1964), the earliest cable-stayed cantilever bridge to be built in Britain, provided the model for the second Severn Bridge; equally innovative is the latest bridge over the Usk (2004).

The late 19th and early 20th centuries were the most flourishing years in the history of Newport, with its population rising from 38,469 in 1881 to 83,691 in 1911. It was the place of the founding of the Miners' Federation of Great Britain (1889). It attained county borough status in 1891. Its South Dock, when opened in 1892, was the largest masonry dock in the world. Although Newport's coal exports were, in the boom year of 1913, only 6.242 million tonnes compared with the 24.97 million tonnes exported by the Port of Cardiff (Cardiff with Penarth and Barry), its international trade was sufficiently large for 8 consuls and 14 vice-consuls to be based in the town. Its economy had a broader base than that of other major Welsh towns. Its foundries and engineering works produced a wide range of products, including Newport's finest gift to the world – the 'self-grip' Mole wrench, invented by a Newport resident, Mr Mole. Its large cattle market served much of Monmouthshire, and the town provided the main shopping centre for the inhabitants of the county, most of whom had ready access to Newport, the hub of Monmouthshire's dense network of railways. During the First World War, Newport's dock trade declined, but its industrial base was strengthened as the demand for the products of its foundries and engineering works soared.

In the general election of 1918, Newport had, for the first time, an MP to itself. (It had previously joined with Monmouth and Usk in electing the Monmouth Boroughs member.) The death in 1922 of the town's first MP, the Lloyd George Liberal, Lewis Haslam, led to the most politically significant by-election in British history. It occurred on 18 October and coincided with the Carlton Club meeting held to discuss whether the Conservatives should continue to remain in coalition with Lloyd George. The capture of Newport by an anti-coalition Conservative encouraged the Conservatives to vote to abandon the coalition, a vote that sealed Lloyd George's fate. (He was never fortunate in his dealings with Newport.)

By the time of the by-election, the post-war boom in Newport's coal exports was coming to an end. From the early 1920s onwards, the Depression set in, with the town's total seaborne trade declining from 5.53 million tonnes in 1919 to 3.12 million in 1936. Although Newport did not suffer the appalling unemployment levels experienced by the mining towns of northern Monmouthshire, unemployment among the town's insured males reached 34.7% in 1930. Despite its economic difficulties, the Newport of the 1920s and 1930s was probably the most progressive place in Wales, the corporation in those years succeeding in rehousing over half the town's population.

The Second World War temporarily solved the unemployment problem, but by the late 1940s there were fears that the scourge would return. The opening of the Llanwern Steelworks in 1962 ushered in an era of prosperity, a development assisted by the building of the M4, whose links to Newport make it the best-connected place in Wales. In 1975, however, iron ore importation was transferred to the huge new terminal at Port Talbot, thus markedly reducing the trade of Newport's docks. Employment at Llanwern declined in the 1980s, and its steel production plants closed in 2003. Nevertheless, other sources of employment emerged. Newport acquired a passport issuing office, the Patent Office and the Central Statistical Office. The Inmos microchip factory (1982) proved to be highly innovative, but the hopes aroused by the £2.55 billion invested in new enterprises in Newport between 1990 and 2002 – by the Korean Company, LG, in particular – were not wholly fulfilled, although in 2005 the Irish company Quinn Radiators acquired a major part of the largely abandoned LG site, turning it into a domestic radiator plant.

The late 1990s and early 2000s were an auspicious time for Newport. Its popular music scene was flourishing and there were suggestions that Newport was becoming the new Seattle. The transporter bridge, splendidly refurbished, was reopened in 1995 and was granted Grade One listed status. The role of Newport (and that of the Celtic Manor Hotel, see Caerleon) in the world of golf was recognized with the announcement that it would be the location of the 2010 Ryder Cup competition. The 15th-century boat found in the Usk was declared to be a far more significant discovery than the Mary Rose. In 2002, the bishop of Monmouth and archbishop of Wales, Rowan Williams, left Newport to become archbishop of Canterbury and leader of the worldwide Anglican Communion. And, to crown it all, in the same year the town of Newport became a city.

The communities of Newport

ALLT-YR-YN (Allt-yr-ynn) (384 ha; 8583 inhabitants)
Located north-west of central Newport, the community contains the Ridgeway, which offers fine views of the city. Allt-yr-yn (ash tree hill) is locally pronounced Altar-een. The community contains the junction of the two branches of the Monmouthshire Canal. Raglan Barracks, built in 1845 to ensure that there would be no repeat of the Newport Rising of 1839, is an impressive 39-bay building. The buildings of the one-time Newport Technical College (1958) constitute the main site of the **University of Wales, Newport**. Much of the southern part of the community is occupied by the vast and fascinating St Woolos cemetery. Clytha Square (1850s) has some of Newport's earliest middle-class villas, as does the splendidly named Gold Tops. On the lower slopes of Allt-yr-yn stands the shire hall (1902, 1913), which ceased to be the administrative centre of Monmouthshire in 1963 when a new county hall was built at **Cwmbran**. Adjoining it is the civic centre, built following the decision in 1936 to make Newport rather than Monmouth the judicial centre of the county. The City Hall (1939, 1964), whose clock tower dominates central Newport, is a pale version of Swansea's superb Guildhall; it contains excellent murals by Hans Feibusch (1964) illustrating the history of Gwent.

ALWAY (177 ha; 8492 inhabitants)
Located east of the city centre, the community is bisected by the A48. Apart from Ladyhill and Liswerry Parks, it consists of a network of streets mainly built from the 1930s onwards, many of them named after musicians.

BEECHWOOD (152 ha; 7594 inhabitants)
Located east of the city centre, the community gets its name from Beechwood House, a mansion built by the Habershons for George Fothergill, a mayor of Newport. The community consists of a dense network of late 19th and early 20th-century streets. St John's church, Kensington Place (1860), with its 55-m spire, is an impressive building designed by **John Prichard** and J. P. Seddon.

BETTWS (Betws) (513 ha; 8287 inhabitants)
Constituting the north-western corner of the built-up area of Newport, the community contains the interpretation centre (1976) of the 14 locks of the Crumlin branch of the Monmouthshire Canal, which Bettws shares with the community of **Rogerstone**. Built by 1799 and designed by Thomas Dadford, the locks enabled the canal to rise 51 m in 0.8 km. The Ynysfro reservoirs are known as Little Switzerland. John Frost married at St Mary's church in 1812. Bettws High School (1972) is a remarkable building.

GAER (Y Gaer) (282 ha; 8586 inhabitants)
Constituting the westernmost part of the built-up area of Newport, the community gets its name from the impressive Iron Age hill-fort which dominates it. Stow Park contains a wealth of late 19th-century villas. The Modernist **housing** erected at Stelvio (c.1946–51) has been highly praised.

LISWERRY (486 ha; 10,335 inhabitants)
Constituting the south-eastern part of the built-up area of Newport, the community is dominated by industrial estates. It contains Newport's **cricket** and **football** grounds.

MALPAS (193 ha; 8148 inhabitants)
The central part of the northern built-up area of Newport, the name comes from the Old French *mal* and *pas* – difficult passage. A cell of the Cluniac abbey of Montacute, Somerset, was established at Malpas *c.*1110. Its church was rebuilt by John Prichard in 1850 as a neo-Romanesque copy of the original. The churchyard contains the grave of Thomas Prothero, bitter enemy of John Frost and agent of the Tredegar estate, who lived at Malpas Court. A handsome neo-Tudor house (1838), the court is the social club of the progressive estate built in the 1950s by Newport Corporation; its streets all bear the names of distinguished scientists.

PILLGWENLLY (Pillgwenlli) (546 ha; 5333 inhabitants)
Constituting Newport's docklands, the community contained the junction between the Monmouthshire Canal and the Usk. Most of the Town Dock (1842, 1858) has been filled in, but part of its entrance lock survives. The North Dock (1875) and the South Dock (1893) – jointly known as the Alexandra Docks – provide 50 ha of enclosed water. Plans in the 1990s to build a barrage across the Usk, which would have ensured that Newport's superabundance of riverside mud would be constantly covered by water, were abandoned following protests by ecologists, who are also hostile to the proposed M4 relief road, which, if built, would bisect Pillgwenlly. Newport's importance as a centre of the livestock trade is indicated by the large cattle market in Ruperra Street.

RINGLAND (243 ha; 8470 inhabitants)
Constituting the easternmost part of the built-up area of Newport, the community contains the Bishpool and Treberth estates, consisting of a concentration of well-maintained prefabricated houses of the late 1940s, a type of housing in which Newport is bountifully supplied. Two later estates have streets named after **Labour** leaders and naval heroes. Newport's Welsh-medium primary school is located on the community's eastern edge.

ST JULIANS (196 ha; 8729 inhabitants)
Located on the left bank of the Usk and hugging the great loop in the river, the community's name probably commemorates St Julius, martyred at Caerleon (*see* **Julius and Aaron**). St Julians contains Newport Yacht Club and a Snooker School of Excellence. The demolished 16th-century seat of the Herbert family of St Julians was located in St Julian's Park, which lies within the community of Caerleon. Newport's **war memorial** stands at the junction of Clarence Place and Chepstow Road. Adjoining it is Wales's showiest Art Deco **cinema** (1938), which has become the Al Capone Pool Hall.

SHAFTESBURY (162 ha; 5488 inhabitants)
Located between the Usk and the Monmouthshire Canal, the community is named after Shaftesbury Park, which

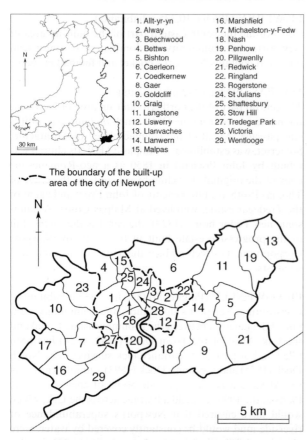

1. Allt-yr-yn	16. Marshfield
2. Alway	17. Michaelston-y-Fedw
3. Beechwood	18. Nash
4. Bettws	19. Penhow
5. Bishton	20. Pillgwenlly
6. Caerleon	21. Redwick
7. Coedkernew	22. Ringland
8. Gaer	23. Rogerstone
9. Goldcliff	24. St Julians
10. Graig	25. Shaftesbury
11. Langstone	26. Stow Hill
12. Liswerry	27. Tredegar Park
13. Llanvaches	28. Victoria
14. Llanwern	29. Wentlooge
15. Malpas	

The communities of the city and county of Newport

commemorates the philanthropist, the seventh earl of Shaftesbury. Its chief feature is Newport Castle, only the eastern range of which survives. Built in the late 14th century, the range acquired an elaborate suite of rooms in the 1440s when it was the administrative centre of the Welsh lands of the Stafford family. It subsequently became a tannery and then a brewery. Squeezed between the railway and road bridges, it was bought by the Morgan family in 1899 and came into the guardianship of the Office of Works in 1935. As its impressive east front rises directly from the Usk's mud banks, it can be viewed only from the road bridge or from the river's left bank.

STOW HILL (131 ha; 4453 inhabitants)
Embracing the centre of Newport, the community's spine is the pedestrianized Commercial Street, which is enhanced by attractive modern **sculptures**. At its northern end stands the former Westgate Hotel, scene of the climax of the Newport Rising of 1839, where bullet holes are carefully preserved. Austin Friars and Friars Street mark the site of the medieval friary. Olde Murenger House in High Street is an early 17th-century half-timbered building. John Frost Square, created by mid-1970s redevelopment, contains Newport's library, museum and **art gallery** and the fascinating Automaton Clock (1992). On the Baltic Quay stands the Steel Wave sculpture by Peter Fink which promises to become as powerful a symbol of Newport as the transporter bridge. It was during the digging of the foundations of the Riverfront Arts Centre (opened in 2004) on the quay that the remarkable 15th-century boat was discovered; it is

displayed in the Riverfront's basement. A nightclub on Stow Hill contains Wales's largest metal dragon, constructed in the 1990s by David Petersen (*see* **Ironwork**). Stow Hill leads to St Woolos, the cathedral of the Anglican diocese of Monmouth; the diocese was founded in 1921, but the church was not fully recognized as a cathedral until 1949. Nearby is St Mary's church (1840), which from 1850 to 1916 was the seat of the Roman Catholic bishop of Newport. There are elegant **garden** features in Bellevue Park; adjoining it is St Woolos Hospital, originally built as a workhouse in 1838 and incorporating The Friars (1840), one of the mansions of the Morgan family.

TREDEGAR PARK (Parc Tredegyr) (180 ha; 3387 inhabitants)
Constituting the south-western corner of the built-up area of Newport, the community constitutes the park of Tredegar House (*see* **Coedkernew**). It contains the Duffryn housing estate, described by John Newman as 'the largest experiment in "perimeter planning" ever attempted'. Consisting of wriggling terraces of houses surrounding a triangular woodland, it adjoins Richard Rogers's astonishing Inmos microchip factory, the two groupings representing what Newman considers to be 'the most remarkable concentration of late 20th-century **architecture** in Wales'. Tredegar Park was the site of the National Eisteddfod in 1988 and in 2004; they were widely considered to be among the most successful National *Eisteddfodau* ever held.

VICTORIA (95 ha; 6688 inhabitants)
Located across the Usk from the city centre, the community constitutes Newport's densest network of streets. At Rodney Parade stands Newport's rugby ground. The Fairoak estate was laid out in the 1850s as terraces of Italianate villas.

NEWPORT (Casnewydd) County Borough and one-time district (21,835 ha; 137,011 inhabitants)
In 1974, the **county borough** of Newport ceased to exist. Along with the **urban district** of **Caerleon** and most of the **rural district** of Magor and St Mellons, it became the Newport district of the **county** of Gwent. In 1996, that county was abolished and the district, consisting of 29 **communities**, became the reconstituted county borough of Newport. (For 14 of those communities, see under their names. For the 14 which constitute the built-up area of the city of Newport, *see* **Newport, city of.**) In 2001, 13.37% of the inhabitants of the county had some knowledge of **Welsh**, the percentages varying from 17.65% in **Michaelstone-y-Fedw** to 10.67% in **Llanvaches**; 7.18% of the inhabitants of the county were wholly fluent in the language.

NEWPORT RISING, The
At 9.20 a.m. on 4 November 1839, 5000 men armed with muskets and pikes entered **Newport**, massing before the Westgate Hotel; supporters of the People's Charter (*see* **Chartism**) from industrial **Monmouthshire**, they were for the most part **coal**miners and **iron** workers. A detachment of the 45th Foot, some special constables and the mayor, **Thomas Phillips**, confronted them. The Chartists attacked and were repulsed in a 25-minute battle. Their casualties

numbered between 22 and 28 killed and over 50 wounded; of their opponents, two soldiers and Thomas Phillips were seriously wounded. The Chartist leaders, **John Frost**, the **radical** campaigner and former mayor of Newport, **Nantyglo** publican Zephaniah Williams and William Jones, an actor and watchmaker from **Pontypool**, were arrested, tried, found guilty of high treason and sentenced to death; the sentences were subsequently commuted to transportation for life. Thomas Phillips was knighted.

Chartism had begun to establish itself in Monmouthshire in the summer of 1838, when a Working Men's Association was founded in Newport and rapidly gathered members. In November 1838, Frost was appointed local delegate to the Chartist National Convention. By the spring of 1839, when Chartist missionary Henry Vincent toured the area, there were possibly 25,000 Chartists in Monmouthshire. Among the factors which precipitated the rising was the rejection by the House of Commons of the first Chartist petition (12 July) and the conviction of Vincent for illegal assembly and conspiracy (2 August).

The aims and plan of campaign of the Monmouthshire Chartists have remained a matter of debate, although there is agreement that a violent insurrection was intended. It was probably part of a wider revolutionary design, which involved the Welsh Chartists holding their territory while other risings took place elsewhere in **Britain**. As far as the assault on Newport was concerned, the Chartists were unduly optimistic, expecting that their appearance would overawe the troops (whom they also believed, wrongly, to be sympathetic) and remove the necessity for armed confrontation. The military tactics they adopted were wholly unsuited to the battle that followed, and poor leadership, bad weather and general confusion combined to bring the episode to a conclusion both farcical and tragic. Chartism continued to attract support in Wales, **Merthyr Tydfil** being the main centre in the 1840s, but its subsequent history produced nothing as dramatic as the Newport Rising.

NEWSPAPERS

Compared with urban **England**, the growth of newspaper publishing in Wales was slow. Before the advent of the **railways**, it was difficult to distribute newspapers, and taxes on paper, advertisements and newspapers themselves further hindered their growth. But during the first half of the 19th century, Wales experienced sweeping social change. The **population** grew rapidly, industrial development transformed the **economy**, **Nonconformists** became the majority of the country's worshippers and **radicalism** became part of the nation's political awareness. The developments of newspaper publishing were a response to these social changes.

In 1804, Wales's first weekly newspaper appeared when the *Cambrian* was published in **Swansea**. Its circulation was restricted to the minority in the principal southern towns who were able to read **English**, but the venture proved successful and was followed by other weeklies such as the *North Wales Gazette* (**Bangor**, 1808), and the *Carmarthen Journal* (**Carmarthen**, 1810). In 1814, the first **Welsh-language** weekly newspaper was published when *Seren Gomer* was founded in Swansea by Gomer (**Joseph Harris**). It aimed to publish home and foreign news, and political, religious and literary contributions, which would safeguard and spread the language. Although its circulation was considerable, *Seren Gomer* ended after 85 issues, because the tax on paper made it too expensive and the income it derived from advertisements was too small. It was relaunched as a fortnightly in 1818, and became a monthly in 1820 (*see* **Periodicals**).

Few newspapers were established in Wales in the 1820s and 1830s. The *Cardiff Weekly Reporter* (**Cardiff**, 1822), the *Newport Review* (Cardiff, 1822), *Cronicl yr Oes* (**Mold**, 1836–9) and the *Cambrian Gazette: Y Freinlen Gymroaidd* (**Aberystwyth**, 1836) were short-lived, but others such as the *Monmouthshire Merlin* (**Newport**, 1829–91) and the *Welshman* (Carmarthen, 1832–1984) were more successful. *Yr Amserau*, established in **Liverpool** by Gwilym Hiraethog

Welsh newspaper circulations (2006 figures)

Title	Frequency	Established	Circulation
Western Mail (6 editions; Trinity Mirror)	Daily	1869	42,578
Daily Post (Welsh edition; Trinity Mirror)	Daily	1955	39,651
South Wales Argus (4 editions, South Wales Argus Ltd)	Evening	1892	30,282
South Wales Echo (2 editions, Trinity Mirror)	Evening	1889	53,780
South Wales Evening Post (1 edition, South West Wales Publications Ltd)	Daily	1932	56,104
Wales on Sunday (5 editions: Trinity Mirror)	Weekly	1989	44,591
Y Cymro (Cambrian News)	Weekly	1932	6000

(**William Rees**; 1802–53) in 1843, was the first successful Welsh-language newspaper. It was bought by **Thomas Gee** of **Denbigh** in 1859 and amalgamated with *Baner Cymru*, which had been established two years previously. *Baner ac Amserau Cymru* became a powerful influence on Welsh life, mainly through the journalistic work of John Griffith (Y Gohebydd), the paper's **London** correspondent; it gave constant support to radical causes, including the defence of the concerns of Nonconformists.

The number of newspapers increased when the tax on advertisements and the stamp duty on newspapers were abolished in 1853 and 1855, and most of the denominational papers originated in this period: the **Baptists'** *Seren Cymru* (1851), the **Congregationalists'** *Y Tyst Cymreig* (1867), the **Calvinistic Methodists'** *Y Goleuad* (1869), the **Wesleyans'** *Y Gwyliedydd* (1877) and the **Anglican** Church's *Y Llan a'r Dywysogaeth* (1881). These were national newspapers which published home and national news, and gave leadership on political and social issues. **Aberdare** and **Merthyr Tydfil** developed as important centres for newspaper publishing. In Aberdare, *Y Gwron Cymreig* (1854–60) and the *Aberdare Times* (1861–1902) were published by Josiah Thomas Jones, and *Y Gwladgarwr* (1858–82), which supported the cause of the worker, was launched by David Williams (Alaw Goch). The most important of these newspapers was *Tarian y Gweithiwr* (1875–1934) which, as a **Liberal–Labour** publication, had wide appeal among southern miners and **tinplate** workers. The *Cardiff and Merthyr Guardian* (1832–74), the *Merthyr Star* (1859–81) and *Y Fellten* (1868–76) were published nearby at Merthyr Tydfil. The *Workman's Advocate: Amddiffynydd y Gweithiwr*, a bilingual newspaper, was established there in 1873, continuing the tradition begun by *Y Gweithiwr: The Workman* and *Udgorn Cymru: The Trumpet of Wales*, two publications allied to **Chartism**, which were published in the town in 1834 and 1842.

In the north, Bangor and **Caernarfon** developed as centres of newspaper publishing. The *North Wales Gazette* was established in Bangor in 1808 by the Broster family of Chester; its title changed to the *North Wales Chronicle* in 1827. The *Caernarvon Herald* was published by William Potter at Caernarfon in 1831, and by 1836 it appeared as the *Caernarvon and Denbigh Herald*. The conflict between these newspapers was considerable, since their viewpoints were diametrically opposed – the *Chronicle* stood for **Tory**ism and the Established Church, while the *Herald* was Liberal and Nonconformist. Both newspapers continue to be published. *Y Cymro* (1848–51), *Cronicl Cymru* (1866–72), *Llais y Wlad* (1874–84), *Gwalia* (1886–1921) and *Y Chwarelwr Cymreig* (1893–1902) were also published in Bangor.

An attempt was made to establish a Welsh newspaper in Caernarfon in the 1830s when *Y Papyr Newydd Cymraeg* was published between 1836 and 1837. The town's most important newspaper publisher was James Rees, who established *Yr Herald Cymraeg* as a Liberal paper in 1855; **literature** featured in its columns, and Llew Llwyfo (**Lewis William Lewis**), **Richard Hughes Williams**, **T. Gwynn Jones**, Meuryn (Robert John Rowlands) and John Eilian (**John Tudor Jones**) served on its staff. Caernarfon was also the birthplace, in 1877, of *Y Genedl Gymreig*, which was

bought by a number of prominent politicians, including **David Lloyd George**, in 1892, when **Beriah Gwynfe Evans** was appointed editor. Ap Ffarmwr (**John Owen Jones**), Eifionydd (John Thomas; 1848–1922) and **E. Morgan Humphreys** were among its editors. *Yr Herald Cymraeg* and *Y Genedl* were amalgamated under the former title in 1937. It came to an end as a distinct publication in 2004, but continued as a supplement of the *Daily Post*. Other papers published at Caernarfon include *Yr Amseroedd* (1882–5), *Briwsion i Bawb* (1885–6), *Y Werin* (1889–1914), *Y Gadlef* (1887–92), *Papur Pawb* (1893–1916) and *Yr Eco Cymraeg* (1889–1914).

By the later 19th century, when all main Welsh towns had their own newspapers, some smaller towns – **Newcastle Emlyn**, **Pwllheli** and **Ystalyfera**, among them – also published newspapers. The weekly *Llais Llafur* (1898–1915), published at Ystalyfera, contributed to the growth of the Labour movement in the **coal**mining areas of west **Glamorgan** and east **Carmarthenshire**. *Y Cymro* (1890–1909) was published in Liverpool by **Edward Foulkes** (Llyfrbryf), and although it was founded for the Welsh inhabitants of that city it had a wide circulation in Wales. *Y Brython* (1906–39) was also published in Liverpool, by Hugh Evans, and, under the editorship of John Herbert Jones (Je Aitsh), it too was extensively read in Wales. A second paper to be entitled *Y Cymro* was founded as a national newspaper by Rowland Thomas of Woodall, Minshall, Thomas and Co. in Oswestry in 1932, under the editorship of John Eilian. Slow in establishing itself, it became particularly popular under the editorship of **John Roberts Williams**, who recruited several lively professional correspondents and photojournalists, particularly **Geoff Charles**. Today it is published by the Cambrian News Company.

The *Cambria Daily Leader* (1861–1930), founded at Swansea as a Liberal paper, was Wales's first daily newspaper. It was followed in Cardiff by the *Western Mail* in 1869, a **Conservative** paper established to promote the political aspirations of the marquess of Bute (*see* **Stuart family**). It was sold to Henry Lascelles Carr in 1879, and under his editorship, and later that of William Davies, it became an influential newspaper. Bought by the Thomson Company in 1959, it favoured **devolution** in 1979 and 1997, and it has developed a more pro-Welsh stance in recent years. It is now published by Trinity Mirror, owners also of the *Daily Post* (Llandudno Junction, **Conwy**), which has a wide circulation in the north. The evening newspaper the *South Wales Echo* and the weekly *Wales on Sunday*, established in 1889 and 1989 respectively, belong to the same company, as does the Celtic Press Group which is responsible for publishing several weekly newspapers in the south. Daily newspapers based in England – the *Manchester Guardian* and the *Daily Herald* among them – long published editions for Wales, a practice briefly followed in the late 1990s by the *Daily Mirror*.

By the early 20th century, *Baner ac Amserau Cymru* had lost its earlier influence, but it revived under the editorship of **E. Prosser Rhys** between 1923 and 1945, when **Saunders Lewis** was among its most regular correspondents. In 1935, it was bought by **Kate Roberts** and Morris T. Williams and, in 1958, it became the property of Gwasg y Sir, **Bala**. Gwilym R. Jones was its editor from 1945 until 1977, when it became a weekly magazine edited, successively, by Geraint Bowen, **Jennie Eirian Davies**, Emyr Price and Hafina Clwyd. *Y Faner* folded in 1992 when the Welsh Arts Council (**Arts Council of Wales**) withdrew its grant.

An attempt was made to establish a Welsh-language Sunday paper in 1982 when *Sulyn* appeared, under the editorship of Dylan Iorwerth and Eifion Glyn. It aimed to serve **Gwynedd** in particular, making use of dialect and colloquial language. Its circulation reached a peak of 9000 copies a month, but lack of capital caused it to cease publication after a few months. Welsh-language community newspapers (*see Papurau Bro*) have enjoyed more continuous success, and they have become increasingly widespread in the Welsh-speaking districts since the early 1970s. For decades there have been aspirations to establish a Welsh-language daily – an aspiration which will become a reality in 2008 with the launching of *Y Byd*.

The Welsh newspaper press also flourished abroad, especially in **North America**, where *Y Drych* was established in 1851; in 2003, *Y Drych* merged with *Ninnau*, which was founded in 1975. *Y Drafod*, founded in 1891 to serve the Welsh in **Patagonia**, is still published as a quarterly, although most of its articles today are in Spanish rather than in Welsh.

NEWTOWN AND LLANLLWCHAIARN (Drenewydd, Y, a Llanllwchaearn), Montgomeryshire, Powys (2709 ha; 10,783 inhabitants)

In 2001, Newtown overtook **Welshpool** as the largest town in **Montgomeryshire**. The **Latin** form of its name – *nova villa* – is first recorded in 1295; **English** and **Welsh** forms appear in the 14th century, replacing the earlier name, Llanfair-yng-Nghedewain. The new name probably arose following the granting of a charter in 1279. For 400 years and more, the town's history was undistinguished, but there was a notable awakening in the 19th century through the development of the **woollen industry**. The **population** increased from 1665 in 1801 to 6842 in 1841, an increase greatly aided by the arrival of the Montgomeryshire **Canal** in 1821. By the 1830s, 1200 looms were operative, justifying the sobriquet, 'the Leeds of Wales'. Newtown's substantial industrial population gave vent to the discontents of the time; the first large **Chartist** meeting in Wales was held in the town in 1838. Industry was concentrated at Penycloddfa, Llanllwchaiarn, across the **Severn** from the town centre. In 1967, a group of weavers' houses at Penycloddfa – their upper floors accommodating the looms – became the Newtown **Textile** Museum.

From the 1850s onwards, competition from the mechanized mills of northern **England** was strangling Newtown's industry and, by 1901, the town's population was less than it had been in 1841. A search for new customers led Pryce Jones in 1859 to launch the first mail-order business in the world; it was conducted from his Royal Welsh Warehouse (1872), the bulkiest building in mid-Wales. His clients included the Prussian army, which bought vast numbers of the sleeping bag he had devised. Pryce Jones financed the re-erection in Newtown of **Dolgellau**'s Cwrt Plas-y-Dre, a 15th-century aisled hall. He was not related to the Pryce family of Newtown Hall, one of whom, Sir John, the fifth baronet (d.1761), kept the embalmed bodies of his first two wives on either side of his bed until his third wife insisted on their removal.

The restored ruins of St Mary's church, abandoned in the 1840s because of flooding – a persistent threat to the

Newtown, with the frozen River Severn in the winter of 1940–1

town until the building of Clywedog Dam (*see* **Llanidloes Without**) – contains the grave of **Robert Owen**. Owen was born in Newtown in 1771 and died there in 1858, but had little connection with the town during the years of his fame. His memorial museum attracts visitors from far and wide. The replacement church, St **David**'s (1847), contains the remnants of a rood screen (*c.*1500) of exceptional quality. Newtown has some attractive 17th- and 18th-century houses and 19th-century shop fronts. Zion **Baptist** Tabernacle (1881) is an imposing building.

Following the abandonment in 1966 of the plan to establish a large new town in the upper Severn valley, Newtown was designated as the Mid Wales Development Corporation's chief centre of expansion. Factories and **housing** estates were to be built with the intention – subsequently almost realized – of doubling the population of 5500 by the end of the 20th century. The plan involved the construction of satellite settlements, two of which – Trehafren and Treowen – contain buildings of some distinction. The cultural life of the **community** is enriched by the Davies Memorial Gallery and Theatr Hafren.

NEYLAND, Pembrokeshire
(195 ha; 3276 inhabitants)
Located 5 km east of **Milford Haven**, the area was until the 1850s a thinly inhabited part of the **parish** of **Llanstadwell**. In 1856, it became the western terminus of the South Wales **Railway**, and **Isambard Kingdom Brunel**'s choice as the **port** for the **postal service** to southern **Ireland**. Brunel's 19,216-tonne *Great Eastern* berthed in Neyland in 1860. Briefly known as Milford Haven and then as New Milford, the name Neyland was adopted in 1906, six years after the place had achieved **urban district**

status. With the building of railways to Milford Haven (1863), **Pembroke Dock** (1864) and **Fishguard** (1899), Neyland ceased to be the sole **Pembrokeshire** port linked to the railway system and Brunel's hopes were not fulfilled; the railway link was closed in 1964. A splendid statue of Brunel, complete with his tall hat, graces the esplanade. Central to the **community**'s **economy** is the marina on Brunel Quay (1999).

NICHOLAS, T[homas] E[van] (Niclas y Glais; 1878–1971) Poet
Born in Llanfyrnach (**Crymych**), but more usually associated with Glais (**Clydach**) in the **Tawe** valley, where he lived for a time (1904–14), Nicholas was a **Congregationalist** minister until his espousal of Communism (*see* **Communist Party**), after the 1917 Russian Revolution. He was forced from the ministry, whereupon he took up dentistry. He stood as **Labour** candidate in **Aberdare** in 1918 when he lost disastrously to **C. B. Stanton**. During the **Second World War**, he and his son Islwyn were imprisoned for four months on a spurious charge of espionage.

Considered a better poet than a dentist, he published 10 collections of verse in which the war between Capital and Labour is his main theme. An impassioned and eloquent champion of the working **class**, both as a poet and as a **newspaper** columnist, he was acclaimed by the Communist leader Harry Pollitt, in 1949, as 'Wales's greatest man'.

NICHOLLS, [Erith] Gwyn (1874–1939)
Rugby player
Born in Flaxley, Gloucestershire, but Welsh by location and adoption, Gwyn Nicholls was a key figure in the first golden age of Welsh **rugby** (1900–11), and captain of its

Neyland, where Brunel's statue overlooks the place where his *Great Eastern* berthed in 1860

Nolton Haven, Pembrokeshire

greatest single triumph, against **New Zealand** in 1905. A tall, thrusting centre with a gift for putting those outside him into space, his unquestioned place in the team, tactical sense and social assurance – he was a successful business-man – made him a natural choice as captain. He was twice persuaded out of retirement to lead Wales, which he did in 10 of his 24 appearances. He was the first Welsh British Lion (going to **South Africa** in 1899), played 417 games for **Cardiff** and, in 1908, published *The Modern Rugby Game*, the first Welsh coaching book. Later a Welsh Rugby Union committeeman and selector, he is commemorated by the Gwyn Nicholls Gates of the Millennium Stadium, Cardiff.

NIMROD

Whilst taking passengers and general goods from **Liverpool** to Cork on 28 February 1860, this paddle steamer's engine broke down. She set sail for **Milford Haven** but a gale blew her into cliffs at **St David's** Head where the *Nimrod* was smashed into three pieces. All 20 crew and 25 passengers were lost.

NOD CYFRIN, Y or NOD PELYDR GOLEUNI

('the mystic mark' or 'the mark of the shaft of light') The symbol / | \ devised by Iolo Morganwg (**Edward Williams**) to represent Love, Justice and Truth for the regalia and ceremonies of **Gorsedd Beirdd Ynys Prydain**. Although also held to signify three sunrays or 'the light's eye', the poet Talhaiarn (**John Jones**; 1810–69) saw it as 'a crow's foot-print'.

NOLTON AND ROCH (Nolton a'r Garn), Pembrokeshire (2447 ha; 746 inhabitants)

Overlooking St Bride's Bay, the **community** contains the villages of Nolton, Nolton Haven, Roch, Druidston, Cuffern and Simpson. Roch Castle (13th century) is the westernmost of the fortifications marking the line between Anglicized south **Pembrokeshire** and the **Welsh** north. In 1601, the castle was purchased by William Walter, whose daughter **Lucy Walter** was a mistress of Charles II and mother of the Duke of **Monmouth**. The castle was skilfully converted into a private house *c.*1910. St Madoc's church, Nolton, and **St David**'s church, Roch, retain medieval features. South of Newgale Sands are the remains of what was Trefran, the westernmost colliery of the south Wales **coal**field. Nolton Haven is a delightful creek. The turf roof of Malator (1998) allows the house to merge into the landscape.

NONCONFORMIST ACADEMIES

Educational institutions established by the **Non-conformists**, chiefly to train young men for the Non-conformist ministry. As their religious beliefs prevented Nonconformists from attending **Oxford** or from graduating at **Cambridge**, their educational needs were provided for through the setting up of academies, which were at the height of their influence in both Wales and **England** during the late 17th and 18th centuries.

The first to be established in Wales was at the home of **Samuel Jones** (1628–97) at Brynllywarch, **Llangynwyd**: it opened soon after he was deprived of his living in 1662.

Others appeared afterwards at places including **Abergavenny**, Llwynllwyd (**Llanigon**), **Carmarthen**, **Brecon**, Trosnant (**Pontypool**) and **Haverfordwest**. One of the reasons why so many were established was that it was customary to move the academy to the tutor; the death of a tutor would therefore result in the academy moving to a new location. The academies represented the various traditions that had developed in Wales, being **Presbyterian**, **Congregationalist** or **Baptist**: some received patronage from the Presbyterian and Congregational Boards in **London**. In scholarly terms, Wales's finest academy was that at Carmarthen, the seedbed of Welsh **Unitarianism**. The standard of the **education** was high, and by the mid-19th century some of the academies had evolved into denominational theological colleges.

NONCONFORMISTS and DISSENTERS

Initially, Dissenters were small groups of stubborn worshippers who dissented from the doctrines and practices of the established **Anglican Church**. They included **Presbyterians**, who sought to replace the Anglicans as the established Church, and Separatists who believed in the sovereignty of the individual congregation and who therefore rejected the concept of an established Church. The earliest Welsh separatist of note, **John Penry**, was executed in 1593. He left no disciples, but in the early 17th century small groups of **Congregationalists** and **Baptists** began to emerge. **Llanvaches** became the mother church of Congregationalism in 1639 and, 10 years later, **Ilston** became Wales's first Baptist church. In the 1650s, Presbyterianism gained a foothold, especially in **Flintshire**. The **Commonwealth government** encouraged the growth of such **Puritan** movements, but legislation passed in the 1660s persecuted Dissenters. They were not allowed to have their own chapels or preach their doctrines openly until the Toleration Act of 1689. The passage of the Toleration Act meant that refusal to conform to the Established Church was no longer an offence. However, Nonconformists, as they would henceforth be called, were – officially at least – not allowed to hold public office until the repeal of the Test and Corporation Acts in 1828.

In the 18th century, under the influence of the **Methodist Revival**, many Dissenting chapels acquired an evangelical hue and their fortunes improved. The foundation of the **Calvinistic Methodist** denomination in 1811 greatly increased the numbers of Nonconformists in Wales. By the early 19th century, a strong Nonconformist conscience was evident, especially on issues such as **temperance**. By the time of the religious census in 1851, nearly 80% of worshippers in Wales were Nonconformists – a name which also included the Calvinistic Methodists and the **Wesleyans**, who were not heirs to the older Dissent. Awareness of their numerical superiority led to demands for the **disestablishment of the Church of England in Wales**. This was achieved in 1920. Thereafter, as there was no established Church to dissent from – nor not to conform to – the words Dissenter and Nonconformist, in their religious sense, lost their meaning. Denominations which had belonged to the Nonconformist tradition came to call themselves Free Churches. Their membership declined sharply in the 20th century.

NORMAL COLLEGE, Bangor

The Normal College opened in 1858 to train male teachers for the non-denominational British schools (*see* **British Society**). Its first principal was **John Phillips**, and its curriculum was soon geared to the Revised Code of 1862. The **Welsh language**, excluded as a subject in 1865, was restored

Women students at Bangor Normal College

in 1907. **Women** were admitted in 1910. Three-year diploma courses in handicraft and domestic **science** were introduced in the 1930s, and segregation of the college into men's and women's departments was abolished. Major changes in the 1950s saw the introduction of Welsh as a medium of instruction, and in 1965 the BEd degree was instituted. Always a victim of outside pressures and barely escaping closure in the 1970s, the College was merged with the **University of Wales, Bangor**, in 1996.

NORMANS, The

Knights from Normandy in northern France arrived in Wales in 1051, when Edward the Confessor's nephew Ralph of Mantes became earl of Hereford and some of his followers established themselves on the **border**. After William I seized the English throne, he established earldoms at Chester, Shrewsbury and Hereford (see **Cheshire**, **Shropshire**, **Herefordshire**) and entrusted them to **Hugh of Avranches**, Roger of **Montgomery** and **William Fitz Osbern**. These border earldoms have often been seen as springboards for Norman advances into Wales, but their purpose was as much defensive as offensive. William's main concern was a secure frontier; he did not seek to conquer Wales, seeing himself as the legitimate successor of the West Saxon kings and the inheritor of their relationship with the Welsh and Scottish rulers. In the interests of stability, he was prepared to reach agreements with native rulers, as he seems to have done with **Rhys ap Tewdwr** following his visit to **St David's** in 1081. Such agreements protected the Welsh rulers from the depredations of Norman adventurers.

The first reference to them in a Welsh source dates from 1072, when Maredudd ab Owain of **Deheubarth** was killed by Normans who were assisting Caradog ap Gruffudd of **Gwynllŵg**. Their territorial gains in the early period were not usually at the expense of native rulers, but when there was a disputed succession or a power vacuum an individual might make a bid for power and territory; the evidence of Domesday Book in 1086 bears this out. Southern Wales was recorded as being in the hands of a certain Riset, almost certainly Rhys ap Tewdwr of Deheubarth, who paid an annual tribute of £40 to the king, while the north was held by the Norman adventurer Robert of **Rhuddlan** who paid the same sum. Robert had moved into the north following the death of the king of **Gwynedd**, **Bleddyn ap Cynfyn**, in 1075, and he appears to have been recognized by William as ruler of Gwynedd by right of conquest.

The death of William I in 1087 was followed by further advances, since his son and successor William II was not bound by his father's agreements; he also needed the support of Norman lords on the border against his brother, Robert of Normandy. **Bernard de Neufmarché** began to advance into **Brycheiniog**. Rhys ap Tewdwr saw this as a threat and responded; he was killed near **Brecon** in 1093, leaving Deheubarth open to the Normans. It was overrun by Arnulf of Montgomery; he built a castle at **Pembroke** and appointed Gerald of Windsor, the grandfather of **Giraldus Cambrensis**, as its constable. In mid-Wales, Philip de **Breos** founded the family which was to dominate the **March** in the 12th century, while **Glamorgan**, one of the four main kingdoms, fell to **Robert Fitz Hammo**. These Norman conquests formed the March, best described as a

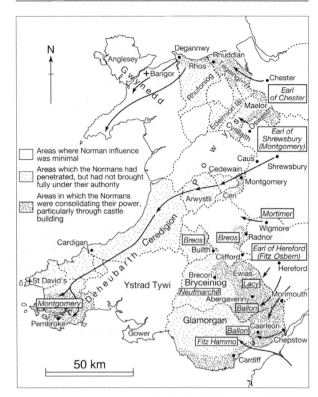

Norman assaults upon Wales, 1067–99 (after William Rees, 1959)

number of independent Welsh lordships ruled by Anglo-Norman lords, which were not part of the English kingdom. They were the work of individuals; no royal campaign in Wales in the 11th and 12th centuries was aimed at conquest. By the death of Henry I in 1135, most of south Wales was under Norman rule but the next few years saw a Welsh recovery.

The Norman impact on Wales was substantial. In political terms, it was responsible for the division between the March and *Pura Wallia*, which lasted until 1536. Native rulers soon learned military lessons, building and besieging castles and using armoured knights. In the 12th century, the Welsh church saw far-reaching changes, owing much to Norman influence, with the development of territorial **dioceses** and **parishes,** and the coming of mainstream European monasticism in the shape of the **Benedictines** and later the **Cistercians** – an order which caught the Welsh imagination; it also saw the subjection of the church to the authority of the archbishop of Canterbury. There were cultural influences; the **eisteddfod** held by the Lord Rhys (**Rhys ap Gruffudd**; d.1197) at **Cardigan** in 1176 may have been influenced by gatherings of poets and minstrels in southern France, while professional interpreters in the March may have been the channel through which the **Arthur**ian legend reached mainland Europe.

Relations between the Welsh and the Normans were not invariably hostile; there was a good deal of mutual respect between two warrior aristocracies, and in the south-west the marriage of Gerald of Windsor and **Nest**, daughter of Rhys ap Tewdwr, was the origin of that Cambro-Norman aristocracy which was to play such a significant part in the invasion of **Ireland**, and which produced Giraldus Cambrensis.

ninnau

The North American Welsh Newspaper®
Papur Bro Cymry Gogledd America™
Incorporating Y DRYCH™

Periodicals Postage
PAID
at Basking Ridge, NJ

© 2007 NINNAU Publications, 11 Post Terrace, Basking Ridge, NJ 07920-2498   Vol. 32, No. 7   May 1, 2007

Cambria's Editor Retires

Mr. Henry Jones-Davies, founder and editor of CAMBRIA - The National Magazine of Wales, announced his retirement as editor in his last editorial in the latest issue of the publication.

Mr. Jones-Davies, who is well known among the Welsh in North America, founded CAMBRIA magazine in 1997. "The magazine," he said, "has grown in tandem with the new Wales, the Wales of devolution." Since

A close observer of the political life of Wales for a number of decades, he continued, "Devolution at least offers the country the mechanisms it needs for change. Given the right circumstances, and the will, the future is indeed bright. But first we must see a fundamental change in our political climate. Without it, Wales is destined to limp painfully on into the future, a sad appendage of a shrinking United Kingdom.

A 2007 edition of *Ninnau & Y Drych*, the newspaper of the North American Welsh

With the accession of the Angevin Henry II in 1154, and particularly following the loss of Normandy by the English crown in 1204, the notion that there was a specifically Norman presence in Wales was undermined. However, the **French** language and culture the Normans brought with them would continue for centuries to be a major influence in both Wales and **England**.

NORRIS, Leslie (1921–2006)
Poet and short-story writer

Although he spent most of his life in **England** and the United States, **Merthyr Tydfil**-born Leslie Norris was influenced in much of his work by his upbringing in the southern **coal**field; an influence on his later work, in addition to his experience of America, was the natural environment of the **Llandysul** area, where he owned a **second home**. After serving with the RAF in the **Second World War**, he moved to England in 1948, working as a teacher and college lecturer; from 1973 onwards, he lived chiefly in America, earning his living as a writer-in-residence at various academic institutions.

He came to prominence as a poet in the 1960s, thanks largely to exposure in the magazine *Poetry Wales*, and he soon established himself as a major figure in the 'second flowering' of Welsh **literature** in **English**, publishing over 20 books of poetry, short stories, translations and criticism. Significant themes in his writing include childhood, the past, exile, nature and the dark machinations of instinct in apparently everyday situations.

NORTH, Frederick John (1889–1968)
Geologist and museum curator

Born and educated in **London**, North was head of the **geology** department at the **National Museum of Wales** for 45 years and a founder of its department of industry. He was prominent in pioneering the role of museums in formal and informal **education**. He also demonstrated the relevance of geological knowledge and techniques to **archaeology**, **architecture** and landscape history as well as to folk history.

NORTH, Herbert [Luck] (1871–1941) Architect

Born in Leicester, educated at **Cambridge** and articled in **London**, North was an assistant to Sir Edwin Lutyens before settling in **Llanfairfechan** in 1900 to set up his own practice. He was an exponent of the Arts and Crafts style, making sensitive use of local materials in his buildings. North carried out much domestic work, including developing a private estate (1910) at Llanfairfechan, church work, a hospital (**Dolgellau**, 1928) and **Bangor** Church Hostel (1930s). He was co-author (with Harold Hughes) of *The Old Cottages of Snowdonia* (1908) and *The Old Churches of Snowdonia* (1924).

NORTH AMERICA, Wales's associations with

North America has been by far the most popular overseas destination of Welsh migrants (*see* **Emigration**). Welsh people have settled there since at least the 17th century (and earlier, according to the legend of **Madog ab Owain Gwynedd**). Apart from miners and **iron**workers active in Mexico in the 19th century, the Welsh presence in North America is concentrated in what became the United States (after 1783) and Canada (after 1867). In both countries, the Welsh have integrated and assimilated easily, yet from the 1970s onwards, among the younger generation especially, there has been a growth of Welsh ethnic awareness and a greater interest in Wales. Although links between the Welsh in Canada and the United States have always existed, there now appears to be a more unified North American Welsh community. It supports a monthly **newspaper**, *Ninnau & Y Drych*, the result of a merger in 2003 between *Ninnau* (established 1975) and *Y Drych* (first published in New York in 1851). Since 1959, the premier Welsh-American gathering, the annual National **Cymanfa Ganu** (inaugurated Niagara Falls, United States in 1929), has been held on nine occasions at Canadian venues.

Canada

Apart from the **Cambriol** colony in the 17th century and the Campobello Island settlement in the 18th century, the first Welsh settlements in Canada were those established at New Cambria (Nova Scotia) and Cardigan (New Brunswick) by emigrants from west Wales in 1818–19. Immigrants from Wales during the 19th century included those attracted by the Cariboo **gold**fields rush in British Columbia after 1858. But the greatest growth in the Welsh presence occurred during the 20th century. Between 1901 and 1961, the number of people claiming Welsh origin rose from 13,421 to 143,962. Nevertheless, the Welsh have always been a minor element in Canada, never more than 0.8% of the total **population**. The residence of the Canadian prime minister, Gorffwysfa, was originally that of a **Montgomeryshire**-born timber merchant.

As the Canadian Welsh generally settled throughout the country rather than in concentrated areas, their dispersal has been regarded as a key factor in explaining their rapid assimilation. Among the few locations to acquire a significant Welsh presence were the prairie settlements of Wood River (near Ponoka, Alberta) and Bangor (Saskatchewan), established by Welsh migrants from **Patagonia** in 1902. Canada currently boasts a number of important Welsh societies and cultural events, notably Capel Dewi Sant, Toronto, and the Ontario Cymanfa Ganu Association, founded in 1909 and 1957, respectively. Prominent Canadians of Welsh ancestry include the explorer David Thompson (1770–1857) and the novelist Robertson Davies (1913–95).

United States of America

Apart from **England**, the United States has attracted more Welsh than any other country. They form a diverse group, and have emigrated for a variety of reasons: political, religious and economic. In the first phase of Welsh emigration, 1660–*c.*1720, Welsh religious dissenters predominated, establishing communities in New England and **Pennsylvania**. Until the mid-19th century, the immigrants were mainly farmers who settled, initially, in New York, Pennsylvania and Ohio, and, later, in the mid-Western states, notably Wisconsin. After the 1850s, the dominant influx was one of industrial workers and families from the **coal**, iron and **tinplate** districts of the south and the **slate** quarrying areas of the north. They settled in increasing numbers in the large cities and industrial regions, notably those in the Pennsylvania and Ohio coalfields. Utah attracted Welsh **Mormons**, who played a leading role in establishing the renowned Tabernacle Choir. By 1890, there were 100,079 natives of Wales (excluding **Monmouthshire**) resident in the United States. The late 19th century was the highpoint of **Welsh-language** cultural life in America, reflected in national and local *eisteddfodau*, well-attended chapels, numerous choirs and the publication of **Welsh** and **English-language** books and **periodicals**. The first Welsh-language book in America was published as early as 1721 (*see* **Ellis Pugh**).

In the 20th century, Welsh emigration to the United States declined. The death of older Welsh speakers and the end of mass immigration led to the virtual disappearance of

Welsh Patagonians on board the steamship *Numidian* en route to Canada, 1902

Yale University, Connecticut. Its Wrexham Tower is based on that of St Giles's church, Wrexham, where Yale's benefactor Elihu Yale is buried

the language in those areas which had been Welsh speaking, such as Utica, in the state of New York, and some rural mid-Western communities. Welsh urban and industrial communities experienced more rapid language shift and cultural change somewhat earlier. Institutionally, however, early 21st-century Welsh America appears to be vibrant. As well as state, regional or local Welsh societies, national organizations include the Welsh National Cymanfa Ganu Association and the National Welsh American Foundation; since 1977, Cymdeithas Madog has held annual Welsh-language crash courses. In 1995, the North American Association for the Study of Welsh Culture and History was founded at Rio Grande, Ohio. Recent censuses have recorded a growth in the number of Americans claiming Welsh ancestry – over two million in 1990.

Many people of Welsh descent have become prominent in American life. It has been claimed by some that 18 of the 55 signatories of the Declaration of Independence (1776) were of Welsh ancestry, although others put the figure at five; only one of the signatories was born in Wales – the New York merchant Francis Lewis (1713–1802). Other distinguished Welsh Americans include the benefactors Elihu Yale (1649–1721; *see* **Thomas Yale**) and Morgan Edwards (1722–95; one of the founders of Brown University), the film mogul D. W. Griffith (1875–1948), the presidential candidate Charles Evans Hughes (1862–1948), the vice-president Hubert Horatio Humphrey (1911–78), the architect Frank Lloyd Wright (1869–1959), the educationist Margaret Evans Huntington (1842–1926), the miners' leader John L. Lewis (1880–1969) and the poet Denise Levertov (1923–97).

NORTH AND SOUTH WALES BANK, The

The aim of the 'Wales Bank', established in 1836 in **Liverpool**, was to provide **banking** services throughout Wales via a network of branches. Its offices were acquired mainly by taking over local banks – eight in north and mid-Wales – between 1836 and 1877. From 1845 to 1898, it grew steadily under the direction of the eminent banker George Rae, who advocated a strong balance sheet and cautious lending. The Bank collected deposits from rural areas and found profitable outlets in the growing commercial activity in Liverpool. In 1908, the 'Wales Bank' was taken over by the Midland Bank, which was later subsumed by HSBC.

NORTH EAST WALES INSTITUTE OF HIGHER EDUCATION (NEWI), Wrexham

The North East Wales Institute of Higher and Further **Education** formed in 1975, incorporating three local colleges: Cartrefle College, **Wrexham**, established in 1946 as an Emergency Training College; William Aston Technical College, Wrexham, originally the **Denbighshire** Technical Institute (1927); and Kelsterton College of Technology, **Connah's Quay**, opened in 1956 as the **Flintshire** Technical College. In 1993, NEWI became an independent education corporation financed by the **Higher Education Funding Council for Wales**. It relinquished its further education role – a role retained by Kelsterton, which opted out of NEWI on becoming Deeside College – and provided a broad programme of undergraduate and postgraduate studies. Until 2004, it was an associated institution of the **University of Wales**, awarding the University's degrees, but in that year it became a constituent member of the University. In 2006/7, NEWI had over 7000 students.

NORTH WALES MINERS' ASSOCIATION, The

Founded in 1886 at a time of industrial unrest, initially the association was led by Edward Hughes (1856–1925). It was among the first district unions to become affiliated to the

Miners' Federation of Great Britain, established in 1889. From the outset, organization was weak, the **coal**owners intransigent and solidarity difficult to achieve. The situation improved in the early 20th century, with membership increasing from 2732 in 1898 to 15,229 in 1925. Close links were formed with the local **Labour Party**, and headquarters were opened in **Wrexham**. However, in the 1930s, when the association faced the threat of **company unionism** and the anguish of the **Gresford Disaster** (1934), non-unionism remained a problem. The northern miners seldom showed the militancy characteristic of the miners of the south, and the association proved largely ineffective during the **miners' strike** of 1984–5. The Wrexham headquarters closed in 1988. Following the closure in 1996 of the north's last surviving deep colliery, Point of Ayr (**Llanasa**), miner-unionism in northern Wales became virtually extinct.

NORTH WALES QUARRYMEN'S UNION, The

There was an abortive attempt in 1865 to establish a union for the **slate** quarrymen of northern Wales, but success came in 1874 and the union was active until it merged with the Transport and General Workers' Union in 1923. It faced consistent hostility from most quarry owners; indeed, within a few weeks of its foundation, George William Duff (*see* **Assheton Smith family**), sought to force the quarrymen of Dinorwic (**Llanddeiniolen**) to choose between employment and the union. Duff was defeated and the new union went on to seek better conditions for the quarrymen of Penrhyn (**Llandygai**). Support for the union varied from area to area. In the first 20 years of its existence – apart from a brief period in 1878, when membership rose to 8000, a little more than half the total workforce – **trade union**ism among the quarrymen of the north-west was a minority pursuit.

The union was notable for the fact that for the first 25 years of its existence its leaders were middle-class **Liberals** such as **W. J. Parry** – men who had no personal experience of the industry. This situation arose largely because quarrymen feared victimization. The union was involved in bitter conflicts at Dinorwic in 1885–6 and at Llechwedd (**Ffestiniog**) in 1893, as well as in a number of minor disputes. Its major challenge came through the **Penrhyn lockouts** of 1896–7 and 1900–3, which brought the union prominence throughout **Britain**. In the early 20th century, under the leadership of R. T. Jones, briefly **Labour** MP for **Caernarfonshire** (1922–3) and the first quarryman to undertake the leadership of the quarrymen, the union became better organized and by the early 1920s it represented almost the entire workforce. Even after the merger with the TGWU, it retained a great deal of autonomy, including the practice of keeping all its minutes and other documentation in **Welsh**. By the end of the 20th century, the decimation of the Welsh slate industry meant that, despite a bitter conflict in 1985–6 at Blaenau Ffestiniog, quarry-worker unionism in Wales had become virtually non-existent.

NORTHOP (Llaneurgain), Flintshire
(1136 ha; 2983 inhabitants)

Located immediately north of **Mold**, the **community** is dominated by the fine 16th-century tower of the church of St Eurgain and St Peter. In the churchyard is a building erected *c.*1608 as a grammar school. Llys Edwin was a moated house, reputedly the refuge to which Edwin, earl of **Mercia**, fled following the **Norman** conquest. Adjoining it is the Welsh College of Horticulture, founded in 1955. Northop village developed as a Welsh settlement between the plantation towns of **Flint** and Mold. Among its residents was the wealthy cleric Hywel ap Dai, patron of **Guto'r Glyn**, **Dafydd ab Edmwnd** and **Gutun Owain**. Soughton Hall, originally an early 17th-century Baroque mansion, was remodelled by Charles Barry in 1835. Soughton was a **coal**mining area developed initially in 1796 by **John Wilkinson** to supply his **lead** smelter at Llyn-y-pandy. One of Soughton's residents, the distinguished labour leader **Huw T. Edwards**, removed the sign, Soughton, and replaced it with one bearing the **Welsh** name Sychdyn (which is actually a Cymricization of Soughton).

NORTHOP HALL (Neuadd Llaneurgain),
Flintshire (353 ha; 1685 inhabitants)

Located between **Northop** and **Connah's Quay**, the name derives from the raised hall house built in the 15th century for Dafydd ab Ithel Fychan. The eastern part of the **community** was once known as Pentre Moch (the **pigs'** village). The Dublin & Irish **Coal** Company began mining in the area in 1790. The rows of colliers' houses it built were called Dublin, Cork and Vinegar. Most of the output of the Dublin Main (1873–86), Galchog (1876–1913) and Elm (1876–1934) collieries was exported to **Ireland** from Connah's Quay.

NOSON LAWEN (lit. 'Merry evening')

Traditionally, an evening of informal entertainment including singing, storytelling and dancing held in winter in rural parts of Wales. The term is first attested in 1856, but the tradition is older and may originally have formed part of such customs as wakes and welcoming-home parties. The tradition has survived, albeit in a more formal guise, the present event being more of a concert, and it has provided a stage for talents such as those of the folksinger Bob Roberts Tai'r Felin (**Robert Roberts**; 1870–1951), the renowned compère Llwyd o'r Bryn (Robert Lloyd; 1886–1961) and the comic trio Triawd y Coleg. *Noson Lawen* was the title of a popular radio series in the 1940s, which in turn inspired a short **film** of the same name (with an **English** version entitled *The Fruitful Year*) made in 1949 for the National Savings Committee. **S4C** transmits a television series based on the same idea.

NOTT, William (1782–1845) Soldier

William Nott, who was born near **Neath**, joined a volunteer corps at **Carmarthen**. During the Afghan War he became commander of troops in Afghanistan, and he was appointed resident at the court at Lucknow. Sir William's statue, made from bronze guns captured at Maharanjpur, stands on Nott Square, Carmarthen, where he spent his retirement.

NOVELLO, Ivor (Davies, David Ivor; 1893–1951)
Musician, playwright and actor

Ivor Novello was born into a musical family in **Cardiff**, taking his name from the professional name of his mother, Clara Novello Davies, who was one of the leading Welsh singers and singing teachers of the Victorian era. He published his first song when just 17 years old. His fame was

Ivor Novello

assured at the outbreak of the **First World War** when his 'Keep the Home Fires Burning' (1914) captured the public imagination.

Novello's contribution, as actor and sometime writer, to 22 **cinema** features between 1919 and 1934, has been undervalued by both the actor and numerous biographers, but in the late 1920s he was the most popular British male star in domestic **films**. His ambivalent presence as a Jack the Ripper suspect added frissons to Hitchcock's *The Lodger* (1926), and he delivered a charismatic performance as a Paris club gigolo in *The Rat* (1925); this Gainsborough Studios melodrama, based on a stage success by Novello and Constance Collier, kept Gainsborough afloat. He reprised the Rat role in two further films, and also appeared in Hitchcock's *Downhill* (1927) as an expelled schoolboy living a debauched life in Marseilles. An early visit to Hollywood at the invitation of the silent screen's most venerated director, D. W. Griffith – for Griffith's *The White Rose* (1923) – proved unsatisfactory, as did a later spell as an MGM writer. However, he was unforgettable as an incorrigibly mischievous Russian exile in Maurice Elvey's British feature *I Lived With You* (1933), scripting the film from his own stage play.

Novello's screen career was curtailed – a casualty of his extensive theatre commitments. He is best remembered for his stage **music**als, especially *Glamorous Night* (1935), *The Dancing Years* (1939) and *King's Rhapsody* (1949), which broke **London** box-office records. Novello is considered one of 20th-century Britain's most successful writers of musicals, many of which transferred successfully to cinema, making him an international celebrity. He won notoriety in the **Second World War** when convicted of using black market petrol, an incident commemorated in the satirical song 'Keep the Home Tyres Turning'.

NUCLEAR FALLOUT

The first nuclear fallout – of the artificial element strontium-90 – followed the initiation of nuclear-bomb testing in 1952. The material was distributed worldwide, with concentrations in certain areas of Wales. Because of heavy rainfall and calcium-deficient **soils**, the radioactive element (being chemically very similar to calcium) stayed in the soil and thus passed into milk and into the bones of young children. By 1964, with the continuation of nuclear testing, 48 units of strontium, on average, were recorded in milk in Wales, with 224 units in **Merioneth** and 375 in **Caernarfonshire**. In 1958, the Medical Research Council had announced that when the level of Sr-90 reached 10 units it would be a matter of serious concern.

A week after the explosion on 26 April 1986 at the Chernobyl nuclear power station in northern Ukraine, the plume (or cloud) of radiocarbon fallout expelled into the atmosphere moved northwards across **Britain**. Heavy rains on May 2 and 3 resulted in the deposition of radio-caesium on around 4.1 million ha of **Gwynedd** and **Powys**. Because of the nature of the soil over much of this area, the pollutant passed quickly into the grasses. As a result, restrictions were imposed immediately on the sale, movement and slaughter of some 2 million **sheep** on 5000 farms in the north-west. Despite predictions that the effects and restrictions would be short-lived, 53,000 ha and 359 farms were still affected in 2004, when it was said that restrictions could last a further 50 years. It was not until 2004 that research began into the effects on human **health**, Gwynedd having notably higher rates of cancer than other parts of Wales.

NUNNERIES

There were only three long-standing nunneries in medieval Wales: two **Cistercian** houses for **women**, at Llanllyr (**Llanfihangel Ystrad**) and Llanllugan (**Dwyriw**); and a **Benedictine** priory at **Usk**. The convent at Llanllyr was founded before 1197 by the Lord Rhys (**Rhys ap Gruffudd**; d.1197), serving as a daughter-house of Strata Florida abbey (**Ystrad Fflur**). Llanllugan, founded probably between 1170 and 1190 by Maredudd ap Rhobert, was placed under the jurisdiction of Strata Marcella (**Welshpool**). Richard de **Clare** (d.1136) was probably responsible for the Benedictine nunnery at Usk, where its fine, mainly 12th-century, church survives. **Giraldus Cambrensis** claimed that there was another nunnery at Llansanffraed-in-Elwel (**Glascwm**), and that one of the nuns eloped with Enoc, abbot of Strata Marcella. At the **Dissolution**, there were about 17 nuns in Wales.

A number of religious communities for women, belonging to a variety of different orders, have appeared in the modern period, including the Cistercian nunnery at **Whitland**, the Poor Clares at **Neath**, the Carmelites at **Dolgellau** and **Hawarden**, and the Ursuline sisters at **Llanelli**, **Swansea** and **Brecon**.

Samuel Walters, *Burning of the Ocean Monarch off the Great Orme, 24 August 1848* (1848)

OAKELEY family Industrialists

A land-owning, **Conservative** family of Plas Tanybwlch (**Maentwrog**). They took possession of **slate** mines in Blaenau **Ffestiniog**, including the Holland and Rhiwbryfdir mines in 1878, and expanded them to create the Oakeley slate mine, the largest slate mine (as opposed to open quarry) in the world, employing 1600 men in 1891. The family mansion, Plas Tanybwlch, is now the **Snowdonia National Park** Study Centre.

OATS

Climate and **soil** conditions determined that oats was the cereal crop that thrived throughout Wales. Farmers and cottagers alike were dependent on their crop of oats, described by the historian **R. T. Jenkins** as 'the old bearded one, our forefathers' staff of life'. Once harvested and thrashed, the cereal was taken to the mill to be dried, ground and sifted. The oatmeal was stored in special oak chests housed in a warm, dry room, usually above the kitchen.

Uwd (porridge), *llymru* (flummery), *sucan* (sowans) or *bwdram* (thin flummery) and *griwel blawd ceirch* (oatmeal gruel) were among the day-to-day foods served in most rural areas until the early 20th century. The dishes named *sucan* in the south and *llymru* in the north are substantially

the same: a quantity of oatmeal was steeped in cold water and buttermilk, then boiled and stirred until it thickened. It was usually served cool, in cold milk or water sweetened with treacle.

The bread consumed most regularly throughout Wales was oat-bread. Oatmeal and water were mixed to create a dough, which was formed into wafer-thin, circular loaves that were baked on a bakestone or griddle held over an open fire. In the north, oat-bread was used as a basic ingredient in cereal pottages. *Siot* (shot) or *picws mali* (a form of shot), consisting of crushed oat-bread steeped in buttermilk, was a popular light meal. A common breakfast for farm workers in the north was *brwes* (brose): crushed oat-bread steeped in meat stock, with a second layer of crushed oat-bread sprinkled on top. By the early 20th century, oat-bread was served more as a delicacy, side by side with a wheaten loaf, rather than as a daily bread.

OCEAN MONARCH

The American **ship** *Ocean Monarch*, transporting emigrants, was outward bound on 24 August 1848 when she caught fire off Great Orme's Head, **Llandudno**. Totally engulfed in flames, she had insufficient ship's boats to help the 354 passengers. Two ships came to help, but 175 people lost their lives, and the ship burnt to the waterline and sank.

O

OFFA'S DYKE

The separateness of Wales is signified in the **border** landscape by the presence of this monumental earthwork, the biggest **engineering** project in Europe at the time of its construction in the 8th century. It was built as a frontier line between **Mercia**, the powerful kingdom of middle **England**, and the smaller Welsh kingdoms to the west, particularly **Powys**, which were resistant to Saxon incursions. Even today, some lengths of the earthwork correspond with the national boundary between Wales and England. It was **Asser**, the Welsh monk and biographer of King Alfred, who attributed its construction to the powerful Mercian king, Offa, who reigned from 757 to 796. Writing within 100 years of Offa's death, Asser famously declared that it was built 'from sea to sea' – a misleading reference that has resulted in much fruitless exploration for missing sections, both north and south. Indeed, late 20th-century excavations and surveys suggest that the earthworks, particularly in the south-east, cannot be considered integral sections of what is generally considered to be Offa's Dyke.

The frontier territory defined by the Dyke may have extended from the **Severn** estuary near **Chepstow** in the south, to the **Dee** estuary at Basingwerk (**Holywell**), a distance of 226 km, though the line traceable on the ground is much shorter. The major section runs as a continuous alignment from Rushton Hill, near **Knighton (Radnorshire)** to **Llanfynydd (Flintshire)**, in which region the Mercian engineers seem to have used the earlier earthwork, **Wat's Dyke**, for part of its northern alignment to the Dee estuary. Running alongside each other, the two dykes are never more than 6 km apart, suggesting that the relationship between them was an important, if complex, one.

The aim of Offa's Dyke was to regulate access to and from Wales and to check border raids from the west. It retains an impressive profile in many areas, striking boldly across the countryside and following a powerful line through mountainous zones of between 350 and 426 m in altitude. It stands up to 3 m high and its west-facing ditch is still visible, despite centuries of erosion.

The significance of the Dyke as a frontier boundary continued beyond its Mercian beginnings. In 1233, the men of Chirbury Hundred (**Shropshire**) 'this side of Offediche' were distinguished in the Patent Rolls from those who dwelt west of the Dyke. Another 'Offediche' reference occurs in a 13th-century English deed dealing with land crossed by the Dyke at Rhiston. These references clearly reflect the persisting tradition of the original purpose of the earthwork.

The present-day consensus is that Offa's Dyke was not, as once suggested, a symbolic or an agreed boundary, but a defensive barrier – possibly patrolled and backed up by an early-warning beacon system. It was, in effect, Offa's 'Western Front'. There is a Dyke Interpretation Centre at Knighton.

OFFA'S DYKE PATH

Following in part the late 8th-century earthwork **Offa's Dyke**, this most pastorally beautiful of **Britain**'s long-distance trails stretches for 290 km through the **border**land, from **Prestatyn** in the north to the Severn Sea at Slimeroad Pill (Beachley, Gloucestershire) in the south. It was officially opened in 1971. The scenery throughout is extraordinarily attractive and varied, and the walking for the most part amiable and straightforward, though rougher, higher sections cross the moors south-west of **Wrexham** and traverse a high ridge of the **Black Mountains** further south. The numerous attractive old towns – **Llangollen**, **Montgomery**, **Knighton**, **Presteigne**, **Hay**, **Monmouth**, **Chepstow** – along or close by its route, add to the convenience, enjoyment and historical atmosphere. It is also – main holiday periods aside – remarkably unfrequented.

OGHAM or OGAM

The **Irish** name for an Irish-language script devised in **Ireland** but also found inscribed on commemorative stones in areas – south-west Wales in particular – that were subject to raiding, trading and settlement from Ireland in the late **Roman** and post-Roman periods (*see* **Monuments, Early Christian**). Some 40 ogham-inscribed stones have survived in Wales.

The ogham alphabet consists of 20 letters, to which a further five were later added. The letters consist of between one and five straight or diagonal strokes meeting or crossing a centre line, usually represented by the stone's edge. The inscriptions, which record the commemorated

The Offa's Dyke Path at Llanfair Hill, north of Knighton

individual's name, along with customary formulae, are usually read from the bottom upwards; most are accompanied by a **Latin** translation in the Roman alphabet – Wales's first bilingual signs. The stone commemorating Voteporix (*see* **Vortiporius**), a 6th-century ruler of **Dyfed**, is the only ogham-inscribed stone anywhere which bears the name of an identifiable individual; found at Castelldwyran (**Clynderwen**), it is now at the **Carmarthenshire** Museum (**Abergwili**).

Ogham is believed to have been derived from the Roman alphabet and originated in the 4th century AD (or possibly earlier), perhaps as a result of Irish contact with literate Romanized Britons from Wales. When elements of the Déisi tribe from south-east Ireland began to settle in south-west Wales in the 4th century, they brought with them the tradition of carving ogham on wood and stone. Most of Wales's ogham stones were carved between the 5th and the 7th centuries.

OGMORE Lordship, hundred and constituency

A sub lordship of the **march**er-lordship of **Glamorgan**, Ogmore consisted of an Englishry on the left bank of the **River Ogwr** and a detached Welshry in Glynogwr. It was acquired *c.*1116 by the de Londres family, founders of the **Benedictine** priory at **Ewenny** and builders of Ogmore Castle (**St Brides Major**). Like **Kidwelly**, which was also held by the de Londres family, the lordship passed by marriage to the Chaworth family. In 1296, through the marriage of Maud Chaworth, it became the property of Henry of **Lancaster**, and, in 1399, it passed to the English crown. As the duchy of Lancaster was and is a separately administered part of the crown lands, material relating to the Lancaster family's properties has been carefully preserved in the state archives. In consequence, Ogmore is the best documented territorial unit of late medieval Wales. Following the **Acts of 'Union'**, Ogmore became a **hundred**; it has been a constituency since 1918. *See also* **Ogwr**.

OGMORE VALLEY (Cwm Ogwr),
Bridgend (3875 ha; 7800 inhabitants)

Embracing most of the basins of the **Ogwr** Fawr and Ogwr Fach, the **community** extends to Bwlch-y-clawdd, where dramatic **roads** with hairpin bends lead to the **Rhondda** and Afan valleys. Originally a thinly populated pastoral region, industry began with the **coal**mining undertaken by the Tondu **Iron**works in the 1850s. The two valleys were extensively settled from the 1860s onwards, with the establishment of the pits of what became the Ocean, **Cory**, Lewis Merthyr and Glenavon coal companies. The most thickly populated places are the townships of Nant-y-moel, Price Town and Ogmore Vale. The dominant buildings are **miners' institutes** and chapels; Bethlehem chapel (1876) has been adapted as a **male voice choir** centre. The colliery buildings have been demolished, and the inhabitants now look towards **Bridgend**'s factories and shops for employment.

St Tyfodwg, sited high above the Ogwr Fach, and largely rebuilt by **John Prichard** in the 1870s, was the church of the **parish** of Llandyfodwg, which embraced a wide tract extending from **Llantrisant** to the Rhondda. Bryn-chwith is a fine 17th-century farmhouse.

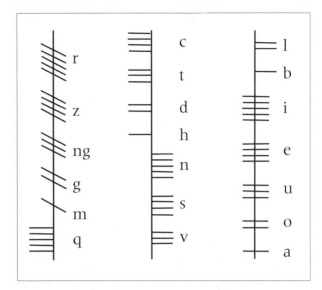

The Ogham script

OGWR One-time district

Following the abolition of the **county of Glamorgan** in 1974, Ogwr was created as a district of the new county of **Mid Glamorgan**. It consisted of what had been the **urban districts** of **Bridgend, Maesteg, Porthcawl** and Ogmore and Garw (*see* **Ogmore Valley** and **Garw Valley**) and the **rural district** of Bridgend. In 1996, the district (bereft of three **communities** which were transferred to the **Vale of Glamorgan**) became the **Bridgend County Borough**.

OGWR River (25 km)

The Ogwr Fawr, which rises at Craig Ogwr (527 m) in the **community** of **Ogmore Valley**, is joined by the Ogwr Fach at **Blackmill**. At **Ynysawdre**, north of **Bridgend**, they are joined by the Garw and Llynfi; the former rises north of Blaengarw (**Garw Valley**) and the latter at Blaencaerau (**Maesteg**). South of Bridgend, the **river** is joined by the Ewenny, which is crossed by picturesque stepping stones at Ogmore Castle (**St Brides Major**). The estuary of the Ogwr adjoins the extensive **Merthyr Mawr** Warren.

OIL

Despite explorations in the Irish Sea in the 1990s, particularly in Cardigan Bay, no exploitable quantities of oil have been found in Wales. Imported oil has been the basis of the oil refining industry that developed in Wales in the second half of the 20th century.

Wales's first oil refinery was opened in 1919 at Llandarcy (**Coedffranc**, between **Neath** and **Swansea**). This was the earliest major refinery based on imported oil to be built in **Britain**, with oil shipped through Swansea docks and transported to Llandarcy by **road** and **railway**. The logistical shortcomings associated with the site became increasingly apparent during the 1930s, when the plant's operations tended to languish. However, the **Second World War** brought a considerable expansion in activities, which continued over the following decades. (The severe German bombing of Swansea in 1941 was aimed at crippling Swansea as an oil importing **port**.) By the early 1970s, the refinery had a capacity of over 8 million tonnes a year, with

The Texaco oil refinery on the south shore of the Milford Haven Waterway, 2001

a significant share of its output piped to the petrochemical plants (*see* **Chemicals**) that were being developed, across the mouth of the **River Nedd**, at Baglan Bay. This locality was also the site for a gas-from-oil plant, built primarily to augment supply for the Wales Gas Board – both to meet increasing demand, and to supplement gas supplies formerly provided by the coke ovens of the **Steel Company of Wales** works at **Margam** (*see* **Energy**). The various activities of the Llandarcy/Baglan Bay complex made it one of the most important concentrations of its kind in Britain.

The problem of supplying the Llandarcy refinery through Swansea docks led to an alternative development which involved importing crude oil via the **Milford Haven Waterway**, and sending it by pipeline 97 km eastward to Llandarcy. While **Milford Haven** became the dominant import gateway for Llandarcy, the docks at Swansea provided the export and coastal trade facility for refined products.

Milford Haven itself was the location for significant developments in oil refining during the 1960s. The Haven's naturally deep waters can provide berthage for even the largest supertankers, and the clear advantages of its location brought a concentration of refineries owned by the major companies. The first refinery was that commissioned by Esso in 1960, and this was followed by the BP Ocean terminal in 1961, Texaco in 1964, Gulf in 1966, and Elf in 1973. A 450-MW capacity oil-fired power station was built at **Pembroke Dock**. Although the 1960s and 1970s were periods of intensive oil-related activity, this began to decline in the early 1980s, as the closure of the Esso refinery (1983) was followed by that of BP in 1986. During the late 1990s, the Gulf refinery also closed, although it was retained for reduced capacity use by Petroplus. Llandarcy refinery closed in the 1990s.

There had been earlier oil spills, but environmental concerns regarding the dangers of large-scale oil transportation were highlighted to devastating effect in February 1996, when some 72,000 tonnes of crude oil were discharged from the grounded tanker *Sea Empress*. The spillage severely affected wildlife and polluted the beaches of south **Pembrokeshire**, with serious implications for local **tourism**.

In the north, the only oil-related activity of note involved the establishment of a tanker docking facility at **Amlwch**, with oil pumped ashore to a storage depot at nearby Rhosgoch (**Rhosybol**). These facilities were operated by Shell from 1972 until 1990, with the oil pumped along an inland pipeline to the Stanlow refinery near Ellesmere Port in **Cheshire**.

OLD COLWYN (Hen Golwyn),
Conwy (392 ha; 7626 inhabitants)
In the 1870s, Colwyn provided the adjoining growing resort to its west with its name – **Colwyn Bay**; thereafter, Colwyn was known as Old Colwyn and was eventually swallowed up by the upstart. The **community** contains several interesting buildings designed by the distinguished architect **Colwyn Foulkes**.

OLD MAN OF PENCADER, The
Henry II, while invading **Deheubarth** in 1163, is said to have asked an old man at Pencader (**Llanfihangel-ar-arth**) how he saw the future. The old man replied that, though Wales might be attacked and defeated by its neighbours, it could be destroyed only by divine anger; at the last judgement the Welsh themselves, in their own language, would answer for their country. The story, told by **Giraldus Cambrensis** at the end of his *Description of Wales*, is often

cited as a symbol of the Welsh instinct for survival. A plaque in Pencader commemorates the old man.

OLD NORTH, The (Yr Hen Ogledd)
The name given by the Welsh to the post-**Roman** British kingdoms which covered much of southern **Scotland** and northern **England**. **Rheged**, Al Clud (Dumbarton), **Gododdin** and smaller kingdoms such as **Elmet** and Aeron (Ayr) had been carved out of what had been, during the Roman occupation, the territories of the British tribes, the Novantae, Selgovae, Votadini and Brigantes. The ruling families of these kingdoms, known in Wales as *Gwŷr y Gogledd* (Men of the North), claimed descent from either Coel Hen or Dyfnwal Hen. Their **genealogies**, histories, tales and poems were probably preserved in the kingdom of **Strathclyde** which retained its independence long after the other kingdoms were lost in the 7th century. These materials were transmitted to Wales from the 9th century onwards and were kept as part of the learned tradition of the Welsh long after any Brythonic language was spoken in the north.

OLD RADNOR (Pencraig),
Radnorshire, Powys (5101 ha; 741 inhabitants)
Old Radnor, lying between **Presteigne** and **New Radnor**, offers a delectable landscape with excellent views of **Radnor Forest**. Its 15th-century church is among the finest in **Radnorshire**; it has a wealth of interesting features, including the oldest organ case in **Britain**. Other churches in the **community** are less attractive. Richard Haslam considered Evenjobb church, rebuilt in the mid-19th century, to be 'solid and ugly', and quotes Goodhart-Rendel's remark that it 'shews a dreadful knowledge of what generous church builders required at that date'. The timber palisade enclosure recently discovered at Walton is one of the largest **Neolithic** monuments in Britain. The moated motte at Womaston dates from the mid-11th century. It was built before 1066, and can be considered the earliest motte in Wales. That at Kinnerton was built in the 12th century. Ednol church was demolished *c.*1910. Stanner Rocks is a site particularly rich in **plant** species.

Harpton Court, the seat of the Lewis family, was demolished in 1956. Its most distinguished resident, **George Cornewall Lewis**, who held most of the great British offices of state and almost became prime minister, is remembered for his comment that 'life would be bearable but for its pleasures'.

OLDFIELD-DAVIES, Alun (1905–88) Broadcaster
The son of a **Congregationalist** minister from **Clydach**, Oldfield-Davies joined the BBC as schools assistant in 1937 (*see* **Broadcasting**). He held a number of posts with the Corporation before being appointed director of the Welsh Region in 1945, a post renamed Controller Wales in 1948. Throughout his long stewardship (1945–67) of the BBC in Wales, he sought to maintain high standards and to increase the resources available to Welsh broadcasters to make programmes for radio and, later, for television. Although considered by some to be too puritanical and unadventurous, his devotion to the BBC and to Wales was absolute. Part of the BBC's head office in **Cardiff** is called Tŷ Oldfield in memory of him.

ON THE BLACK HILL (1988) Film
A moving feature **film** based on Bruce Chatwin's novel of the same name, which is located on the Black Hill (in the **community** of **Gladestry**). Spanning the passage of 80 years, the film focuses on twin brothers, symbiotically and emotionally linked, and the **class** differences that drive a wedge between their parents. The ensemble playing is exemplary, especially from the lead actors, Mike Gwilym and Robert Gwilym, and Gemma Jones as their mother. The film was directed by **Cardiff**-born Andrew Grieve.

ONLLWYN, Neath Port Talbot
(1087 ha; 1214 inhabitants)
Located on the watershed between the upper **Tawe** and the upper **Nedd**, the **community** contains a 2-ha **Roman** fort, built in turf and timber in the AD 70s and abandoned *c.*150. Banwen **iron**works, which operated briefly in the 1840s, is the most complete to survive in the anthracite **coal**field. Large-scale coalmining in the area began in 1862, following the opening of the **Neath** and **Brecon Railway**. The unique Banwen Miners' Hunt (*see* **Hunting**) enjoyed the patronage of the duchess of Beaufort (*see* **Somerset family**). The miners' leader **Dai Francis** was a native of Onllwyn, where his son, Hywel, established the Community University of the Valleys.

ONLY TWO CAN PLAY (1962) Film
Peter Sellers plays a feckless librarian and woefully ineffectual lecher in Frank Launder and Sidney Gilliat's popular and humorous examination of male sexual peccadilloes. Adapted from the novel *That Uncertain Feeling* (1955) by Kingsley Amis (1922–95), the **film** is set in **Swansea**, where Amis lectured from 1949 to 1959. It teams Sellers with **Kenneth Griffith**, at his best as a work colleague and an emotionally constipated, henpecked husband. Two other Amis novels with Swansea associations, both of which were filmed, are *Lucky Jim* (1954) and *The Old Devils* (1986) – although Amis claimed that the former was based chiefly on his friend Philip Larkin's experiences of Leicester University.

ONUFREJCZYK, Michael (1895–1967) Murderer
Onufrejczyk, a **Pole**, who farmed Cefnhendre, Cwmdu (**Talyllychau**), was in partnership with a fellow countryman, Stanislaw Sykut. In December 1953, Sykut disappeared, Onufrejczyk claiming he had been kidnapped. Onufrejczyk forged a document showing the sale of Sykut's share of the farm to him. Despite the absence of a body, Onufrejczyk was convicted and sentenced to life imprisonment. He was released in 1966 and was killed in a **road** accident in Bradford.

OPEN UNIVERSITY IN WALES, The
The Open University in Wales, founded in 1970, constitutes a 'National Region' of the **Britain**-wide Open University, serving students registered in Wales. Its headquarters in **Cardiff** supports some 20 study centres, 350 associate lecturers and 6000 undergraduate students. All its courses are delivered by distance-teaching techniques, supported by local tutorials, **telephone** and computer-network contacts, and by residential weekend and summer schools.

631

Requiring no formal entrance qualifications, many students begin with a foundation course before proceeding to higher-level studies for their degree. A programme of postgraduate work includes research degrees. The overwhelming majority study in their spare time while continuing in employment. The six faculties are headed by academics in Cardiff who contribute to course production as well as to the University's programme of research and publication, particularly on themes relating to Wales. The *gradd allanol* (external degree) initiated by the **University of Wales, Aberystwyth**, offers a similar service through the medium of **Welsh**.

OPEN-HEARTH FURNACE, The

Along with the Bessemer converter, the open-hearth furnace revolutionized steelmaking (*see* **Iron and Steel**) during the second half of the 19th century. Perfected in 1868 by **Wilhelm Siemens** at his newly constructed works at Landore, **Swansea**, in collaboration with Daniel Edwards at the nearby Duffryn works, Morriston, the open-hearth furnace became the basis of the Welsh sheet steel and **tinplate** industry. Known as the Siemens–Martin furnace, because of related experiments by the Martin brothers in France, it was essentially based on the regenerational principle to recover waste heat and apply it usefully in the furnace. It was much slower than the Bessemer process, but with the significant compensating advantage that this gave much greater quality control. It was also an advantage that the open-hearth method allowed the use of scrap metal in the furnace charge. Open-hearth furnaces increased in average size from just over 15 tonnes in the 1880s to just over 60 in the 1930s, the ultimate being the nearly 410-tonne **oil**-fired furnaces installed at the Abbey Works, **Margam** in 1960.

ORDOVICES

The principal **Iron Age** tribe of north-west Wales, the Ordovices were attacked by **Suetonius Paulinus** in AD 59, his two-year campaign culminating in an assault on the **druid**ical centre on **Anglesey**. Hostilities were interrupted by the revolt of **Boudicca**, and it was not until AD 78, following the annihilation of a **Roman** cavalry unit in their territory, that the Ordovices were finally defeated, with much slaughter. There are some doubts about the claim that the **place name** Dinorwic derives from the *din* (fort) of the Ordovices (*see* **Llanddeiniolen**).

ORMOND, John (1923–90) Poet and film-maker

One of the finest poets of his generation, John Ormond was born at **Dunvant**. After graduating at **Swansea**, he joined the staff of *Picture Post* in **London** in 1945. His early poems (under the name Ormond Thomas) appeared in the book *Indications* (1943) with those of James Kirkup and John Bayliss, and he was represented in **Keidrych Rhys**'s anthology *Modern Welsh Poetry* (1944). He returned to Wales in 1949 and began a distinguished career with the BBC as a director and producer of documentary **films**.

Having been advised by **Vernon Watkins** to publish no more poetry until he was 30, he became so self-critical that he destroyed all his unpublished work. He resumed the writing of poetry in the mid-1960s; his first collection, *Requiem and Celebration* (1969), was followed by *Definition of a Waterfall* (1973), which established his reputation. Many of his poems are elegiac and explore his background as a Welshman and as the son of the village shoemaker, while others celebrate the natural world, often in philosophical terms; all are meticulously crafted and complex in their imagery. His *Selected Poems* appeared in 1987.

Wilhelm Siemens's steelworks at Landore, Swansea *c.*1880

As a film-maker, Ormond is remembered in particular for his sensitive portrayals of writers and artists such as **Dylan Thomas**, **Ceri Richards**, **Graham Sutherland**, **Daniel Jones** and **Alfred Janes**, and for documentaries concerned with the working **class** and with refugees, in particular *Borrowed Pastures* (1960), which explores the lives of two Polish ex-soldiers scratching a living on a **Carmarthenshire** smallholding.

ORMSBY-GORE family (Barons Harlech)
Landowners

The family became associated with Wales in 1777, when Owen Ormsby married Margaret, daughter and heiress of William Owen (d.1768), grandson of Owen Wynn (d.1682) of Glyncywarch (**Talsarnau**) and great-grandson of **John Owen** (1600–66) of Clenennau (**Dolbenmaen**) and Brogyntyn (**Shropshire**). Margaret's daughter, Mary Ormsby, married William Gore. In 1876, their son, Ralph Ormsby-Gore (1816–76), was elevated to the peerage as Baron Harlech. David, the fifth baron (1918–85), British ambassador to Washington, was the initiator and first chairman of the Harlech Television Company (subsequently HTV; *see* **Broadcasting**). In 1873, the family owned 3470 ha in **Caernarfonshire** and 2800 ha in **Merioneth** as well as extensive lands in **England** and **Ireland**.

ORTHODOX CHURCH, The
Christianity had its roots in the eastern Mediterranean, and many of the features of the **Celtic Church** were importations from that region. They include the delight in desolate places, the central role of monasticism and much of the iconography of illuminated manuscripts. Respect for the Eastern hierarchy is indicated in the story of the episcopal consecration of **Saints David**, **Padarn** and **Teilo** by the patriarch of Jerusalem. The growing rift between the Western Church, headed by the Pope, and the Eastern hierarchy, led by the patriarch of Constantinople, culminated in schism in 1054. However, following the **Protestant Reformation**, the **Anglican** Church maintained cordial, if distant relations with the Orthodox Church, with which it was and is in communion.

In more recent times, the churches in Wales have begun to develop new contacts with the Eastern Orthodox Church. The Greek **parish** in **Cardiff** is the oldest Orthodox congregation in Wales, and some of Wales's indigenous inhabitants – those worshipping in **Welsh** at the Orthodox church at Blaenau **Ffestiniog**, for example – have converted to Orthodoxy.

ORTON, Kennedy (Joseph Previté) (1872–1930)
Chemist and educator

Orton came to **Bangor** in 1903 from **Cambridge** and Heidelberg, and held the chair of **chemistry** there until his death. He was elected FRS in 1921 for his pioneering studies of how organic chemical reactions take place, work which was later developed by one of his students, **E. D. Hughes**. He also helped **Edward Greenly** to elucidate the **geology** of **Anglesey** with detailed chemical analyses of the **island**'s rocks. An enthusiastic musician and ornithologist, the Orton Lecture, delivered annually by an eminent naturalist, commemorates his name.

John Ormond, *c.*1960

O'SHEA, Tessie (1913–95) Entertainer
The slim, **Cardiff**-born actress and singer broke into British **films** during the 1940s. In a later, buxom guise, she made the most of her 'Two Ton Tessie From Tennessee' image, describing her role in *The Blue Lamp* (1949) as providing 'a pretty substantial alibi'. She became a highly paid transatlantic cult figure, known for full-blooded, ukulele-accompanied renditions and for a stream of character roles in major films.

OTTERS
Wales is a stronghold of the native otter (L. *Lutra lutra*; W. Welsh *dwrgi*, 'water dog'), which was once widespread along the **rivers** and coasts of **Britain** but which came close to extinction in the 1960s. A semi-aquatic member of the weasel family, it has brown fur, a streamlined body (up to 120 cm long), a long thick tail and webbed feet. It has been hunted for its pelt (medieval Welsh **law** assigned a value of 12 pence to an otter as compared with 24 pence for a **pine marten** and 120 pence for a **beaver**) and, as a presumed pest, for sport. Otter packs came into being in the 1790s and were kept specifically for this purpose until as recently as the 1970s.

Ironically, it is the records of these hunts that document most fully the decline of the otter over the 20th century. The decline was attributable mainly to drainage schemes and pollution – particularly from **sheep** dips. However, a survey in 2004 found that, following improvements in water quality, otters were to be found in over seven out of ten riverbanks and wetland sites in Wales, including areas such as the **Conwy** and **Clwyd** valleys and the industrial south, where otters were almost totally absent in the 1970s. A protected but, in Wales, no longer a threatened species, the otter may even succeed in displacing the alien mink – rather than the reverse, which was once feared.

OVERTON (Owrtyn), Wrexham
(1832 ha; 1276 inhabitants)

Located on the east bank of the **Dee**, the **community** constitutes the westernmost part of **Maelor Saesneg**. Overton's **borough** status, granted by Edward I in 1292, has long lapsed, but the growing village, with its rectangular layout and broad High Street, has an urban air. St Mary's church has a 15th-century nave and is rich in funereal monuments. An 18th-century doggerel claims that its graveyard yews are one of the 'seven wonders of Wales'. Of Bryn-y-pys, a large mansion remodelled by Alfred Waterhouse in 1883, only the stables and entrance lodges survive. Overton bridge is a stylish structure of *c*.1815.

OWAIN AP CADWGAN (d.1116) Prince

Son of **Cadwgan ap Bleddyn**, he precipitated a major crisis in Anglo-Welsh relations in 1109 when he abducted **Nest**, daughter of **Rhys ap Tewdwr** and wife of Gerald of Windsor, constable of **Pembroke**. This was an affront to the king, Henry I, as well as to Gerald; Owain was forced to flee to **Ireland** and his father was deprived of his lands. The ensuing instability in **Powys** and on the **border** eventually forced the king to reinstate Cadwgan but he was murdered in 1111 and Owain emerged as his successor. In 1114, the king took Owain with him to Normandy; he was knighted – probably the first Welshman to receive that honour. In 1116, while campaigning against **Gruffudd ap Rhys ap Tewdwr** of **Deheubarth**, he was attacked and killed by a band of **Flemings**, possibly at the instigation of Gerald of Windsor whom he had cuckolded seven years previously.

OWAIN CYFEILIOG (Owain ap Gruffudd ap Maredudd; d.1197) Prince

Son of Gruffudd (d.1128), the eldest son of Maredudd ap **Bleddyn ap Cynfyn** of **Powys**, Owain may have been too young to succeed on his grandfather's death in 1132, when Maredudd's second son, **Madog** (d.1160), became ruler of Powys. In 1149, Madog granted the **commote** of **Cyfeiliog** to Owain and his brother Meurig as an appanage; Owain was subsequently known as Owain Cyfeiliog to distinguish him from his contemporary and namesake **Owain Gwynedd**. Following the death of Madog and his son Llywelyn in 1160, Owain used his base in Cyfeiliog to gain authority over southern Powys, later known as **Powys Wenwynwyn**. In 1165, he joined the other Welsh rulers in resisting Henry II's abortive invasion. He is said to have founded the **Cistercian** abbey of Strata Marcella *(see* **Welshpool**), where he was buried. **Giraldus Cambrensis** praised his intelligence and ability as a ruler. He was long considered to have been a poet of some distinction, but recent research suggests that the poetry attributed to him is in fact the work of the Powys court poet **Cynddelw Brydydd Mawr**.

OWAIN GLYNDŴR (Owain ap Gruffudd Fychan; d.*c*.1415/16) Prince and insurgent

In the Welsh historical imagination, Owain Glyndŵr enjoys unique prominence. Furthermore, no other Welshmen has so successfully stepped from the world of history to the world of myth. During the Welsh national revival of the late 19th century, Owain won recognition as

The bridge over the Dee at Overton, in an aquatint by Paul Sandby (1776)

the nation's greatest hero, and in **J. E. Lloyd**'s distinguished study *Owen Glendower* (1931), he was hailed as the father of Welsh **nationalism**.

Owain was the senior descendant of the rulers of **Powys Fadog** and held estates as a Welsh baron at Glyndyfrdwy (**Corwen**) and at **Cynllaith**. Through Elen, his mother, he also held land at **Is Coed** Uwch Hirwern and **Gwynionydd** Is Cerdyn near **Cardigan**. The 14th-century history of his ancestors was typical of that of other native Welsh leaders in their willingness to come to terms with English rule (*see* **Gentry**), and, until 1400, that was equally true of Owain himself. In about 1383, he married Margaret, daughter of Sir David Hanmer (d.*c.*1388) of **Maelor Saesneg**, one of the leading judges of the age, and Owain may well have studied at the Inns of Court in **London**. In the 1380s, he served as a soldier on more than one occasion, and in 1387 took part in a naval expedition against the French led by his neighbour, the earl of Arundel (*see* **Fitz Alan family**). Although his income could not compare with that of members of the English aristocracy, it is evident from **Iolo Goch**'s famous *cywydd* to his chief seat at Sycharth (**Llansilin**) that the comfortable sufficiency Owain enjoyed enabled him to be generous in his hospitality.

In the light of his ancestor's history, Owain's decision to raise the banner of revolt at Glyndyfrdwy on 16 September 1400 was a dramatic break with a century of family loyalty to the English crown. At the national level, the causes of the revolt were complex (*see* **Glyndŵr Revolt**). In the case of Owain himself, the immediate cause is believed to have been a dispute between him and Reginald **Grey**, lord of **Ruthin** (**Dyffryn Clwyd**). But following the murder of **Owain Lawgoch** in 1378, it was inevitable that Owain would be considered to be the central figure in any attempt to restore native rule in Wales. He was heir to Powys Fadog and was a descendant of the house of Deheubarth, and, although his links with the house of **Aberffraw** were more distant, his great seal came to bear the coat of arms of the princes of **Gwynedd**. It is evident too that Owain was well aware of the national myths promulgated by **Geoffrey of Monmouth** and in the **prophecies** of the poets, and it is likely that it was his belief that the signs of the times were in his favour that gave him the confidence to rise in revolt in 1400.

Although the Revolt had numerous local leaders, contemporary commentators had no doubt that it was the Glyndŵr Revolt. The available sources concerning the Revolt provide only occasional glimpses of Owain himself. The fullest evidence is that provided by letters of English officials relating to his march through the **Tywi** valley in July 1403. The letters provide evidence of the terror felt by his opponents and refer to his implacable methods of warfare – his refusal, for example, to provide a safe conduct to the **women** under siege in Carreg Cennen Castle (**Dyffryn Cennen**). The Revolt became more sophisticated in 1403–6, but it is impossible to decide whether the evidence for that – the **Pennal Letter** in particular – can be ascribed to Owain himself or to advisers such as **John Trefor** and **Gruffydd Young**. However, there can be no doubt that Owain had an astonishing ability to win and keep the loyalty of his followers. That is evident from the longevity of the Revolt and from the fact that – despite the offer of lucrative

The statue of Owain Glyndŵr at Cardiff's City Hall

rewards – not one of his followers sought to betray him. Following the storms which laid low the army of Henry IV in September 1402, a belief arose in **England** that Owain had supernatural powers, an aspect of his character to which **Shakespeare** gave memorable expression in *Henry IV, Part One*.

The English capture of **Harlech** Castle in 1409 essentially marked the end of the Revolt. Thereafter, Owain, in the company of his son Maredudd, was a fugitive outlaw. He had paid a heavy price for his Revolt. His houses at Sycharth and Glyndyfrdwy had been burnt; his brother, Tudur, had been killed at the battle of Pwllmelyn (*see* **Usk**) in 1405, a battle which led to the capture of his son, Gruffudd. Gruffudd died in the Tower of **London** in 1411, and it was in the Tower, too, that Owain's wife, Margaret, and their two daughters died, after their capture at Harlech in 1409. Owain was offered a pardon in 1415, and again in 1416, but he remained obdurate. It is possible that he spent his last days in the home of one of his daughters, Alis, who had married John Scudamore of Kentchurch and Monnington Straddel in **Herefordshire**. He died *c.*1415/16, but his place of burial is unknown.

With his death, Owain acquired what **Rees Davies** called his 'second career'. To those involved in prophecy, he had not died; he had vanished, as had **Cadwaladr**, Cynan and **Arthur**, to await the call to return to liberate his people. Although much of the evidence is fairly recent, it would appear that a wealth of traditions concerning him survived. Tudor historians and antiquarians were contemptuous towards him. In his *Historie of Cambria* (1584), David Powel described him as a man seduced by empty prophecies and foolish dreams. It was the warm portrayal of him, provided by **Thomas Pennant** in his *Tours in Wales* (1778), which initiated the cult of Owain Glyndŵr, a cult that shows no sign of ebbing.

OWAIN GWYNEDD (Owain ap Gruffudd ap Cynan; d.1170) King of Gwynedd

Owain Gwynedd succeeded his father, **Gruffudd ap Cynan**, in 1137, having already played an active part in extending the frontiers of **Gwynedd**. By 1157, he had reoccupied and resettled the north-east and was threatening Chester, causing Henry II to invade north Wales. Although Henry's army came near to disaster (*see* **Hawarden**), Owain was forced to withdraw to the **Clwyd** and to do homage, the first occasion on which a ruler of Gwynedd did so. In 1160, he took advantage of the death of **Madog ap Maredudd** of **Powys** by moving into some of the border areas of that kingdom. Owain was usually careful not to provoke Henry, but in 1165, when the king planned a massive campaign to deal with the Welsh, the native rulers all placed themselves under Owain's command and prepared to face the royal army at **Corwen**; however, Henry was driven back by storms and there were no further attacks. During the last decade of his reign, Owain defied both the Archbishop of Canterbury and the pope over the appointment and consecration of a new bishop of **Bangor** and also over his refusal to divorce his cousin Cristin; he was excommunicated but was nevertheless buried in Bangor Cathedral. He offered military assistance to Louis VII of France against Henry, the first example of a Welsh ruler seeking an alliance with a ruler on the European mainland. His death in 1170 was followed by a power struggle between his descendants, which eventually led to the seizure of power by his grandson, **Llywelyn ap Iorwerth**. Owain Gwynedd was an outstanding ruler and statesman who built up the strength of his kingdom and who laid the foundations on which the 13th-century princes were able to build. He was the first to be styled Prince of Wales.

OWAIN LAWGOCH (Owain ap Thomas ap Rhodri; Owen of Wales; Yvain de Galles; d.1378) Mercenary captain

As the grandson of Rhodri, youngest brother of **Llywelyn ap Gruffudd**, Owain was the last heir of **Gwynedd** in the direct male line. He was abroad when his father died in 1363 and returned to claim his inheritance – lands in **England** and in **Mechain** and **Llŷn**. By 1369, he had transferred his allegiance to the French and his lands were confiscated. For the rest of his life he commanded a free company, made up largely of Welshmen, in French service. In 1369, he tried, with French support, to recover his patrimony but his **ships** were driven back by winter

Alun Owen wrote the screenplay for *A Hard Day's Night*, 1964

storms. Another attempt, in the summer of 1372, was aborted when Owain was recalled for a diplomatic mission to Castile. In 1375, he was employed to overthrow the Duke of Austria, but his company was defeated by the Swiss. In 1378, while besieging Mortagne-sur-Gironde, he was assassinated by John Lamb, a Scot in the pay of the English.

There is evidence of official concern about the level of support for Owain in Wales, which probably explains Lamb's mission. Owain was not forgotten; stories circulated in which he was said to be sleeping in a **cave**, awaiting the call to return and redeem his people. His grave at St Leger, on the banks of the Garonne, was destroyed during the **French Revolution**. In 2003, the Owain Lawgoch Society and the **National Assembly** combined with the commune of Mortagne to erect a monument where he died.

OWEN, Alun (1925–95) Dramatist

Born in **Liverpool** of **Welsh**-speaking parents, Owen served as a **'Bevin Boy'** in collieries in south Wales during the **Second World War**, before resuming a career as actor and director. He wrote numerous plays for the stage, radio and television, many of them set in Liverpool or in north Wales; they include the television plays *No Trams to Lime Street* (1959), *Lena, Oh my Lena* (1960), *After the Funeral* (1960) and *Maggie May* (1964). His screenplays for the cinema include the Beatles' feature film *A Hard Day's Night* (1964).

OWEN, Daniel (1836–95) Novelist

The foremost **Welsh-language** novelist of the 19th century was born in **Mold**. His father and two of his brothers were killed in a **coal**mining accident in 1837, a tragedy that cast a long shadow over the poverty-stricken family. Owen received little formal **education** but he acknowledged his debt to the **Sunday school**.

His apprenticeship as a tailor with Angel Jones, an elder with the **Calvinistic Methodists**, was a significant step. He described the workshop as 'a kind of college', and under the influence of one of his colleagues he began to write poetry, using the nom-de-plume *Glaslwyn* when competing in eisteddfodau and publishing his poems. After discarding the nom-de-plume in 1866, Owen published occasional poetry throughout his life. In 1859, he translated a popular American **temperance** novelette – Timothy Shay Arthur's *Ten Nights in a Bar Room* (1854) – and in 1860 he began to preach. Intending to enter the Calvinistic Methodist ministry, he enrolled at **Bala** Theological College, but he left without finishing his course. From 1867 to 1876, he worked as a tailor in Mold, preached on Sundays, and threw himself into the public life of the town.

The serious illness that struck him in 1876 was a turning point. It was then that he began to write in earnest, using the vehicle offered to him by his minister, **Roger Edwards**, editor of the Methodist monthly *Y Drysorfa*. He first published sermons, then ventured into fiction with tales of chapel life. As his confidence grew he went on to write the novels that would make him a national hero. Between 1877 and 1884, he wrote *Offrymau Neilltuaeth* (1879), *Y Dreflan* (1881) and *Rhys Lewis* (1885), all of which were first serialized in *Y Drysorfa*. Combining social comment with

A badge issued in 1936 to mark the centenary of the birth of Daniel Owen

reminiscence, and the portrayal of a variety of characters and their manner of speech, Owen conveyed the movements and tensions of his times. The religious context was the focal point, but there are also – in *Rhys Lewis*, for example – vivid sketches of elementary education and of industrial unrest. *Y Siswrn*, a collection of poetry and short prose, appeared in 1886, when Daniel Owen was planning his next work, *Profedigaethau Enoc Huws* (1891). In this fine novel, he exposed the hypocrisy which he saw everywhere in his society. Towards the end of his life, at a time of failing **health**, the historical impulse grew stronger, as exemplified in *Gwen Tomos* (1894), his novel about the beginnings of Calvinistic Methodism in rural **Flintshire**, and in the stories of *Straeon y Pentan* (1895).

Daniel Owen sought to provide edification and entertainment, and his work displays a strong moral impulse as well as elements of wit and comedy. **Goscombe John**'s bronze statue to his memory, unveiled in Mold in 1902, bears an inscription in the novelist's own words: '*Nid i'r doeth a'r deallus yr ysgrifenais, ond i'r dyn cyffredin*' (I wrote not for the wise and the learned, but for the common man). In Mold, he is commemorated by a statue, a cultural centre and a shopping precinct.

OWEN, David (Brutus; 1795–1866) Journalist and preacher

In the religious sparring of the 19th century, Brutus was one of the most scathing of satirists. Born in **Llanpumsaint**, he was raised among the **Congregationalists** before he joined the **Baptists** and later the Established Church. He edited *Lleuad yr Oes* (1827–30), *Yr Efangylydd* (1831–5) and the Church monthly *Yr Haul* (1835–66). After joining the **Anglicans**, he viciously attacked **Nonconformists** in *Yr Haul*, and was involved in several battles with **David Rees**, editor of the Congregationalists' journal *Y Diwygiwr*.

OWEN, Dickie (Richard Morgan Owen; 1876–1932)
Rugby player

The brilliant **Swansea** scrum-half Dickie Owen was little more than 1.5 m high and 60 kg in weight, and in the course of 35 international appearances between 1901 and 1911 withstood relentless pummelling at the hands of forwards twice his size. Known variously as 'the Bullet' and 'the Pocket Oracle', it was Owen who devised and played the key role in the move that led to **Teddy Morgan**'s winning try against the All Blacks in 1905.

OWEN, George (c.1552–1613) Antiquary

The squire of Henllys (**Nevern**) in northern **Pembrokeshire**, George Owen is remembered chiefly on account of *The Description of Penbrokshire* (1603). The work did much to kindle public interest in Welsh antiquities. It was first published in the *Cambrian Register* in 1795–6; further editions were published in 1892–1936 and 1994.

Owen had a particular interest in the rocks and minerals of Pembrokeshire. By establishing that beds of various limestones could be traced across the county, and by following and describing the **limestone** (now known as Carboniferous Limestone) which outcrops around the entire south Wales **coal**field, he was the first to 'map', if only in words, a British geological formation. He produced a **map** of Pembrokeshire which was published in the sixth edition of **William Camden**'s *Britannia*.

OWEN, Goronwy (1723–69) Poet

Goronwy Owen was born into a family of tinkers and rural craftsmen in the **parish** of **Llanfair-Mathafarn-Eithaf**. He acquired some knowledge of traditional **Welsh** metres from

Johnny Owen

his father who was familiar with what remained of the bardic tradition. He learned **Latin** at Friars School, **Bangor**. Ordained deacon in 1746, he failed to find a permanent living in Wales and eventually accepted a teaching post in Virginia. He sailed in 1757, but his wife and the youngest of their three children died on the voyage. He remarried in America, but following the death of his second wife, he turned to alcohol and lost his job. He spent his last nine years as a vicar and tobacco planter in Brunswick County, Virginia, marrying for the third time in 1763. He was buried on his plantation.

As part of the **Morris brothers**' antiquarian circle, Owen devoted himself to the study of traditional Welsh poetry, especially that of the **Poets of the Princes**, convincing himself that the creation of epic poetry, embodying a vision of 'the good life', should be the goal of every poet. His own poetry did not succeed in this, but he produced a number of fine strict-metre poems, some of which deal with his long exile from **Anglesey** and Wales and the painful circumstances of his life. His poems remain an important link in the long chain of Welsh traditional poetry, but his influential ideas on epic poetry frequently had a detrimental effect on the poets of succeeding generations.

OWEN, Hugh (c.1575–1642) Recusant scholar

Hugh Owen was born into the **gentry** family of Gwenynog, Llanfflewin (**Mechell**). He became a **Roman Catholic** c.1620 and, after going into exile to escape persecution, he settled at **Raglan** under the patronage of the **Somerset family**. Owen was the pre-eminent **Welsh-language** recusant writer of the 17th century. An accomplished linguist, he translated several devotional works, among them Thomas à Kempis's *De Imitatione Christi*. That translation, *Dilyniad Crist*, was published in 1684 by his youngest son, Hugh Owen (1615–86), a Jesuit priest known as Father John Hughes. The younger Owen, who spent most of his adulthood at **Holywell**, wrote a work of Catholic apologetics; entitled *Allwydd neu Agoriad Paradwys i'r Cymry*, it was published in Liège in 1670.

OWEN, Hugh (1804–81) Promoter of education

From Llangeinwen (**Rhosyr**), Hugh Owen went to **London** where, in 1853, he was appointed chief clerk of the **Poor Law** Commission; in 1871, the commission became subject to the Local **Government** Board, of which Owen became, in effect, the permanent secretary. To his compatriots, his chief service was his promotion of **education** in Wales. In 1843, he urged the Welsh to establish British schools (*see* **British Society**) for **Nonconformists**. A shortage of teachers prompted him to campaign vigorously to found the **Normal College, Bangor** (1858). He deplored the absence of a university in Wales and it was largely through his exceptional persistence that the University College at Aberystwyth (*see* **University of Wales, Aberystwyth**) opened in 1872. He travelled extensively to raise funds and he rejoiced at the appointment of the Aberdare committee, to which he presented valuable testimony (*see* **Aberdare Report**). His aims were not always fulfilled. Owen was something of a philistine and saw no reason for making university provision for the **Welsh language**. Typical of his interests was his furtherance of the social **science** section of the National **Eisteddfod**. His statue stands in Castle Square, **Caernarfon**, where Ysgol Hugh Owen also commemorates him. The Hugh Owen Library at the University of Wales, Aberystwyth is named after him.

OWEN, [Herbert] Isambard (1850–1927)
Physician and educationist

Chepstow-born Isambard Owen graduated at **Cambridge** and became dean of St George's medical school, **London**. He enthusiastically supported use of the **Welsh language** and the establishment of intermediate schools in Wales. His proposals formed the basis of the charter of the **University of Wales** (1893). His wise leadership, as senior deputy chancellor to the first three chancellors of the University, was indispensable during the early, tumultuous years. He was knighted in 1902; in 1904, he became principal of Armstrong College, Newcastle upon Tyne, and from 1909 to 1921 was vice-chancellor of Bristol University. He was the first chairman of the **Society for the Utilization of the Welsh Language**.

OWEN, John (1600–66) Soldier and landowner
Sir John Owen, a descendant of the Maurice family of Clenennau (**Dolbenmaen**) and Brogyntyn (**Shropshire**), was among the most successful estate builders of 17th-century Wales. In 1642, he became leader of the royalist forces in north-west Wales. As governor of **Conwy** Castle, he came into conflict with **John Williams** (1582–1650), archbishop of York. In the Second **Civil War**, he roused **Merioneth** for the king. Condemned to death for treason in 1649, he was quickly reprieved. He spent his last years avenging himself upon his parliamentary enemies. Eventually, his estates passed to the **Ormsby-Gore** family, Barons **Harlech**.

OWEN, John (1698–1755) Clergyman
Llanidloes-born Owen was appointed vicar of **Llannor** and Deneio (**Pwllheli**) in 1723, canon at **Bangor** in 1742 and chancellor in 1743. When the **Methodist Revival** spread to the north in the 1740s, he reacted to it by persecuting its supporters. An effective **preacher**, he was also litigious and quarrelsome. He experienced some persecution himself – from Dorothy Ellis, known as Dorti Ddu, of Llannor, who so hated Owen that, following his death, she walked to Llanidloes to desecrate his grave.

OWEN, John (Owain Alaw; 1821–83) Musician
In 1844, Chester-born Owain Alaw ceased work as a cutler to become a professional singer, composer and organist in several Chester churches. By the early 1850s, he was prominent in Welsh **music**al life, and was highly influential in the development of the Welsh concert. A prolific composer, teacher, adjudicator, soloist, accompanist and impresario, he was author of *Gems of Welsh Melody* (1860–64), one of the most popular volumes of the period. His tunes 'Mae Robin yn Swil' and 'Myfi sy'n Magu'r Baban' are still sung. The oratorio *Jeremiah* (1878) long enjoyed popularity.

OWEN, John (1854–1926) Bishop
Born into a **Welsh**-speaking, **Nonconformist** home in **Llŷn**, Owen entered Jesus College, **Oxford**, in 1872. There, he joined the **Anglican** Church. In 1879, he was appointed

Morfydd Llwyn Owen

professor of Welsh at St David's College, **Lampeter** (*see* **University of Wales, Lampeter**). In 1885, he became warden of **Llandovery** College, and, as a protégé of Bishop **A. G. Edwards**, served as dean of **St Asaph** (1889), principal of Lampeter (1892) and bishop of **St David's** (1897–1926). Owen was one of the leading defenders of the Anglican Church during the **disestablishment** campaign, and was able to bring to that Church his sympathetic understanding of Nonconformity and his concern for the Welsh language. He and A. G. Edwards were the chief architects of the **Church in Wales**.

OWEN, Johnny (1956–80) Boxer
The fourth of a working-**class Merthyr Tydfil** family of eight children, Owen began **boxing** at eight years of age. By the time he was 24, and facing the hard-hitting Lupe Pintor of Mexico for the world bantamweight title, he was Welsh, British, Commonwealth and European champion. In character shy, kind and unassuming, he was articulate only in the ring, where the skeletal frame of 'the Matchstick Man' concealed amazing reserves of stamina. They availed him little on a September night in Los Angeles when, in the 12th round, Pintor knocked him into a coma from which he died six weeks later.

OWEN, Morfydd Llwyn (1891–1918) Composer
Born in Treforest (**Pontypridd**) and educated at **Cardiff** and the Royal Academy of Music, **London**, she quickly emerged as a talented composer. Her varied output includes **hymn** tunes, chamber **music**, choral and orchestral works, piano solos and songs, many of them inspired by

Welsh literary and folk song sources. A woman of great beauty, she led a colourful life, particularly in London where she moved in a wide range of circles. In 1917, she married the psychoanalyst **Ernest Jones**. Her death the following year, at the age of 26, robbed Wales of a composer of precocious achievement and exceptional promise.

OWEN, Nicholas (?1550–1606) Martyr

Born in **Oxford** of a strongly recusant Welsh family, Owen joined the Society of Jesus *c.*1577. Because of his lack of height, he was known as 'little John' – hence **Waldo Williams**'s reference to 'John' Owen in his poem 'Wedi'r Canrifoedd Mudan'. A carpenter and mason by profession, Owen's skill in devising hiding places saved the lives of many **Roman Catholic** laymen and priests and furthered the Church's covert work. He suffered imprisonment on three occasions; in 1605, he was captured and repeatedly tortured. He died of his injuries in March 1606. Owen was canonized in 1970 (*see* **Catholic Martyrs**).

OWEN, Owen (1847–1910) Retailer

One of the most dramatically successful Welsh entrepreneurs of the Victorian age, and born in **Machynlleth**, Owen was first apprenticed as a draper at Bath before moving to **Liverpool**. There he was one of the pioneers of department store retailing, with the shop that bore his name. He later moved to **London**, but owned a holiday home in **Penmaenmawr**.

Robert Owen (1771–1858)

OWEN, R[obert] Llugwy (1836–1906)
Minister and author

Born in **Betws-y-Coed**, Llugwy Owen worked as a quarryman before training – at **Bala** College and the Universities of **London** and Tübingen – for ministry in the **Calvinistic Methodist** Church. He published volumes of sermons and poetry, but his most important book is *Hanes Athroniaeth y Groegiaid* (1899), a substantial – and, in **Welsh**, pioneering – volume on the history of Greek **philosophy** from its beginnings to the Christian era.

OWEN[S], Richard (1831–91) Architect

Born at Four Crosses (now Y Ffôr, **Llannor**), Owen was apprenticed to his father as a joiner before moving to **Liverpool** where he was employed by a building firm. After studying drawing at evening classes, he opened an office in 1862, and within two years was given his first chapel contract. Thereafter, he ran a prolific practice, specializing in designing chapels (mostly **Calvinistic Methodist**) in northern Wales and Merseyside, with a few in mid Wales and **Carmarthenshire**. Owen is reputed to have designed over 250 chapels. He was also responsible for many secular works, including **Caernarfon** Free Library (1888).

OWEN, Robert (1771–1858)
Industrialist and socialist

Newtown-born Robert Owen founded a cotton-spinning business and, in 1799, bought the New Lanark Mills in **Scotland**. For the next 24 years, Owen's cotton-spinning business grew to become the largest in **Britain** and the most innovative in terms of production methods and industrial relations. From *c.*1812, and particularly in the aftermath of the **French Revolutionary and Napoleonic Wars**, Owen began to argue that his **education**al and **welfare** programmes at New Lanark were applicable to British society generally. There he had restricted working hours, provided medical care and established a school for his employees' children. His schemes for social reconstruction (which he termed **socialism**) drew favourable responses from many, until his criticisms of the institutions of family and **religion** became too pronounced. Abandoning Britain for **North America** in 1824, he invested his fortune in an estate in Indiana. There, he established the community of New Harmony, run along Owenite socialist lines, but which ended in acrimony in 1827. Returning to Britain, Owen became a leading figure in the **trade union** movement (1829–34), and a focus for Owenite ideals, communities and publications (1835–45).

He continued to write prolifically, visited Paris during the revolution of 1848 and became a spiritualist. In 1858, he returned to Newtown, where he died. In 1902, the **Co-operative Movement** raised a monument in his honour in the cemetery of St Mary's church, Newtown, his burial place. Newtown's confined but informative Robert Owen memorial museum was opened in 1983.

OWEN, Robert (Bob Owen Croesor; 1885–1962)
Antiquary and bibliophile

A former farm labourer and **slate** quarry clerk, Bob Owen Croesor became an immensely popular lecturer with the **Workers' Educational Association**. He was a native of

Llanfrothen and settled in the village of Croesor (Llanfrothen), where he worked as a quarry clerk. There, he amassed a huge library of 47,000 books. He and his wife shared their bedroom with classics by **Charles Edwards** and precious old **periodicals**. His services as a genealogist were in great demand, especially amongst Welsh Americans (*see* **Genealogy**). After his death, his books were dispersed to various locations, including the **National Library of Wales** and the library of University College, Swansea (**University of Wales Swansea**). Cymdeithas Bob Owen, a society for bibliophiles which publishes the periodical *Y Casglwr*, was named after him.

OWEN PUGHE, William (Idrison; 1759–1835)
Lexicographer and antiquarian

Born William Owen in **Llanfihangel-y-Pennant**, he adopted the surname Pughe out of respect for a distant relative who left him an estate in **Nantglyn**. He spent a large part of his life in **London**, where he was prominent in the **Gwyneddigion** and other Welsh societies. Pughe was one of the staunchest supporters of the prophetess Joanna Southcott.

With Owain Myfyr (**Owen Jones**), he edited *Barddoniaeth Dafydd ab Gwilym* (1789), and Iolo Morganwg (**Edward Williams**) joined them to edit *The Myvyrian Archaiology of Wales* (1801–7). His most famous effort at poetry was *Coll Gwynfa* (1819), his translation of Milton's *Paradise Lost*. His *Dictionary* and *Grammar* (1793–1803) had a detrimental effect on a generation of Welsh writers because of his erroneous theories about orthography and etymology. However, the illustrative quotations show Pughe's vast knowledge of the old **Welsh** texts. Among the 100,000 words in his dictionary are many weird coinages, but some – *pwyllgor* (committee), for example – have won their place in the Welsh language.

OWENS, Arthur George (1899–1976) Double agent
In the annals of 20th-century espionage, the case of Arthur Owens is considered to have been the cornerstone of the 'double-cross system', which enabled MI5 to fool the Germans with false intelligence throughout the **Second World War**.

Born in **Swansea**, Owens emigrated to Canada at an early age, but moved to **London** in 1933 and formed the Owens Battery Company. He became entangled in the murky world of espionage through his frequent business trips to German shipyards during the 1930s. To his credulous German handlers, he was a virulent Welsh patriot, and during the early years of the war they actively encouraged him to recruit fifth-columnists from among the ranks of **Plaid [Genedlaethol] Cymru**. However, Owens was also in the pay of MI5, and his 'Welsh' saboteurs were either fictitious or MI5 nominees, such as the retired Swansea **police** inspector Gwilym Williams (1886–1949). Owens's avarice and erratic behaviour caused MI5 increasing consternation. He was interned in 1941 and remained in captivity until the end of the war.

OXFORD, Wales's associations with
Welsh connections with Oxford can be traced to the earliest days of the university in the 12th century, when **Geoffrey of Monmouth** lectured there. There is evidence

Oxford, The Bodleian Library: a page from the *Red Book of Hergest*

later for Welsh academics such as the two men called Thomas Wallensis (fl.1230–55 and fl.1300–50) and **Giraldus Cambrensis** studying at Oxford. Although records are not full until the reign of Henry VIII, many Welshmen were recorded studying the arts and canon **law**. Welsh scholars are recorded as departing Oxford in 1400–1 to join the **Glyndŵr Revolt**; Oxford graduates were among **Owain Glyndŵr**'s closest advisers.

By the 16th century, there were close ties between Wales and colleges and halls such as Oriel, Brazenose, All Souls and Gloucester Hall. Sons of Welsh **gentry** and yeomen attended the university and there were many others among the townsfolk. Ties were strengthened when Jesus College, Oxford's first post-**Protestant Reformation** foundation, was established in 1571. Elizabeth I was the college's official founder but it was its chief benefactor, Hugh Price (or Aprice; ?1495–1574) of **Brecon**, treasurer of the **diocese** of **St David's**, who was its real creator. Through the efforts of Price and others, the college came to be regarded as an institution largely (but not exclusively) serving Wales. Many Welsh gentlemen and clergy were educated there and, until the 19th century, there was an almost unbroken line of Welsh principals who secured for it lands and endowments; **Leoline Jenkins** (1661–73) of Llanblethian

(Cowbridge) was effectively its second founder. Although the Welsh links survive to this day, its direct contribution to Welsh **education** diminished from the late 19th century onwards. Nevertheless, in 1877 Jesus College became the seat of the professorship of **Celt**ic, a post often occupied by Welsh scholars, among them **John Rhŷs**, **Idris Foster** and D. Ellis Evans (b.1930). John Rhŷs was also principal of the college (1895–1915) and first president of Cymdeithas **Dafydd ap Gwilym** (the Dafydd ap Gwilym Society), which was established in 1886 by Welsh students at Oxford.

Jesus College was not the only one to attract the Welsh. The association with many of the colleges noted above continued, and colleges such as Christ Church became popular with the sons of the higher Welsh gentry. In the 1870s, the university was reformed so that its doors were opened to **Nonconformists**. T. E. Ellis went to Lincoln College, for example, and **O. M. Edwards** attended Balliol. With the establishment of Ruskin College in 1899, higher education for members of the working **class** began to be provided. Several Welshmen who attended Ruskin became pioneers of **socialism** in Wales, among them W. J. Edwards, author of *From the Valley I Came* (1956), Noah Rees, a prominent leader of the miners of the south, and **Noah Ablett**, chief author of the *The Miners' Next Step* and instigator of the strike at Ruskin that led to the establishment of the **Central Labour College** in **London**. In the 1920s and the 1930s, Oxford became a focal point for unemployed emigrants from Wales; their history is recounted in **Raymond Williams**'s novel *Second Generation* (1964). A number of notable Welsh and **Welsh-language** manuscripts are held in Oxford libraries, the most important of which is *The Red Book of Hergest* in the Bodleian Library.

OXFORD MOVEMENT, The

The first phase of the **Oxford** Movement (1833–45) was essentially a debate within the University of Oxford. The Movement's aim was to renew the life of the **Anglican** Church through reaffirmation of its Catholic nature in matters of faith, ritual and church order. It drew upon the 17th-century High Church tradition best represented by William Laud, bishop of **St David's** (1621–6) and archbishop of Canterbury (1633–45). Among the movement's most ardent supporters was Isaac Williams of Llangorwen (**Tirymynach**). The High Church views of W. W. E. Wynne of Peniarth (**Llanegryn**) were a factor in the 1859 general election in **Merioneth**.

In Wales, the spread of the Movement sharpened differences between Anglicans and **Nonconformists** and encouraged the **Calvinistic Methodists** to make common cause with the denominations originating in 17th-century Dissent. In the 20th century, the High Church beliefs which sprang from the Oxford Movement influenced writers such as **Aneirin Talfan Davies** and church leaders such as **Timothy Rees**, **Glyn Simon** and Rowan Williams, archbishop of Wales (2000–3) and archbishop of Canterbury (2003–). High Church beliefs are especially strong among the clergy of Llandaff, the largest of the **dioceses** of the **Church in Wales**, one of the reasons why that Church lagged behind the Church of England on the issue of the ordination of **women**.

The Temple of Peace and Health in Cathays Park, Cardiff

PACIFISM

Pacifism – the belief that it is immoral to take part in war – should be distinguished from the term 'pacificism', which is the belief that, while all effort should be made to avoid war, the use of armed force can be justified. From its beginnings, Christianity contained a pacifist element; but pacifism as a political creed is essentially a 20th-century development. **Quakers** were consistently advocates of peace, and the Welsh Quaker ironmaster **Joseph Tregelles Price** of **Neath** was one of the founders of the **London** Peace Society in 1816. As the 19th century advanced, anti-war sentiments won increasing support among Welsh **Nonconformists** and **Liberals**. **Samuel Roberts** was vocal on the issue, and **Henry Richard**, 'the Apostle of Peace', was secretary of the Peace Society, 1848–85.

Modern pacifism was the product of the **First World War**. A minority of Christians and Socialists opposed the war, joining organizations such as the **Fellowship of Reconciliation**, the No Conscription Fellowship and **Urdd y Deyrnas**. As post-war euphoria ebbed away, anti-war sentiment found expression in the election of the **conscientious objector Morgan Jones** as MP for **Caerphilly** in 1921 and of **George M. Ll. Davies** as Christian Pacifist MP for the **University of Wales** in 1923.

Plaid [Genedlaethol] Cymru, established in 1925, contained a significant pacifist element, and pacifism was one factor in the **Penyberth Bombing School** episode (1936). The **Welsh Council of the League of Nations Union**, founded in 1922 under the patronage of David Davies (*see* **Davies family (Llandinam)**), won wide support, with **Gwilym Davies**, the creator of the Goodwill Message of the Children of Wales, as its secretary. The Peace Ballot of 1935 – a pacificist rather than a pacifist ballot – attracted the votes of 62% of the adults of Wales, compared with 38% in **Britain** as a whole. Welsh pacifists were active in the Peace Pledge Union, and **Cymdeithas Heddychwyr Cymru** was founded in 1936, with **Gwynfor Evans** as its secretary. In 1938, the Temple of Peace and Health, in **Cathays Park**, **Cardiff**, was opened as a gift from David Davies to the Welsh people. He wanted it to be a memorial to all – of whatever nationality – who had lost their lives in the First World War.

With the coming of the **Second World War** in 1939, pacifism lost much of its appeal. Nevertheless, Cymdeithas Heddychwyr Cymru continued its campaigns, and resistance to military conscription was more widespread in Wales than it was in Britain as a whole. Following the war, there were protests, particularly by the members of Plaid Cymru, against the imposition of conscription in peacetime and the acquisition of Welsh land by the War Office.

Welsh pacifists and pacificists were active in the anti-nuclear movement (*see* **CND Cymru**), and the **Greenham Common women**'s movement opposing nuclear missiles owed its origins to a march from Cardiff.

PADARN (6th century) 'Saint'

The Welsh Triads (**Trioedd Ynys Prydain**) list Padarn, **Teilo** and **David** as the 'Three Blessed Visitors of the Island of **Britain**'. Rhigyfarch (*see* **Sulien**) describes their visit to Jerusalem. The tradition reflects the importance of the **clas** established by Padarn at **Llanbadarn Fawr** (**Ceredigion**) in the 6th century, a community still in existence in 1188 when **Giraldus Cambrensis** visited the area. Padarn's influence extended from Ceredigion to **Maelienydd**. A Life of Padarn, not dependable historically, was written at Llanbadarn Fawr *c.*1120. The author confused his subject's life with stories about other **saints**. Padarn's feast day is 15 April.

PAGET family (Marquesses of Anglesey)
Landowners

The family was descended from **Lewis Bayly** (d.1631). He married Ann, heiress of Henry Bagenal, who had inherited property from his mother, Eleanor, co-heiress of Edward Griffith of Penrhyn. Lewis's grandson Nicholas married Caroline, heiress of the Paget family, major landowners in Staffordshire. Their son, Henry (1744–1812), assumed the surname Paget, was created earl of Uxbridge (1784) and was a pioneer of the **Anglesey copper** industry. His son, Henry (1768–1854), commanded the British cavalry at Waterloo, where he lost a leg. Created Marquess of Anglesey, the Marquess of Anglesey Column (1816) at **Llanfairpwll** was erected in his honour and is a major landmark.

The Pagets, close associates of the young Queen Victoria and owners of Plasnewydd (**Llanddaniel Fab**), splendidly sited on the **Menai Strait**, were prominent in the politics of Anglesey and **Caernarfonshire**. In 1873, the family owned 3435 ha in Anglesey, but the fifth marquess (1875–1905) underwent a spectacular bankruptcy in 1904. The seventh (b.1922) is a distinguished military historian.

PAINSCASTLE (Llanbedr Castell-paen),
Radnorshire, Powys (5488 ha; 483 inhabitants)

A wide stretch of southern **Radnorshire**, the **community**'s chief feature is the nucleated village of Painscastle, which is dominated by the huge mound and very large moats of the castle, once the chief strongpoint of the **commote** of **Elfael** Is Mynydd. The name is believed to be derived from Payn Fitz John (d.1136), although after William de **Breos** had seized Elfael, he renamed it Castrum Matilidis in honour of his wife. The castle was enlarged by Henry III during his campaigns against **Llywelyn ap Iorwerth**. There are 14th-century churches at Llanbedr and Llandeilo Graban. Bryngwyn church, originally 13th century, was rebuilt in the 1870s; its chancel contains a columnar pillar stone incised with a cross *c.*700.

Plasnewydd (Llanddaniel Fab) on the Menai Strait, home of the Paget family

Ceri Richards, *The Cycle of Nature* (1944)

PAINTING

If painting is the non-utile application of colour to impart a sense of the numinous, then it might be said that painting in Wales began 26,000 years ago, with the staining with red ochre of the bones of the 'Red Lady of Paviland' (*see* **Rhossili** and **Palaeolithic and Mesolithic Ages**). Much later, **Celt**ic and indeed pre-Celtic peoples produced colours to adorn their **pottery**, and dye from woad with which they decorated themselves and their artefacts.

Painted murals and mosaic pictures have been discovered on **Roman** sites, particularly at **Caerleon** and **Caerwent**. There were undoubtedly painters in the Wales of the age of the princes, exercising their art in courts and churches, although nothing of their work has survived. Among the earliest extant wall paintings are those of the 15th century at St Teilo's church (**Pontarddulais**), which has been re-erected at the National History Museum at **St Fagans**, and at All Saints' church, Llangar (**Cynwyd**). The exquisite *Llanbeblig Book of Hours* is one of Wales's few surviving examples of a medieval illuminated book. The **dissolution of the monasteries** curtailed patronage of the visual arts and led to the loss of many wall paintings; later iconoclasm during the **Commonwealth** era led to the disappearance of many more.

Hans Memling's portrait of the Dwnn family (*see* **St Ishmael**), in a triptych of the 1470s, is the earliest of any Welsh family. A late 15th-century painting at Kentchurch (**Herefordshire**) – long believed, most certainly wrongly, to be that of either **Siôn Cent** or of **Owain Glyndŵr** – may be Wales's earliest surviving movable portrait. By the 16th century, portraits were becoming increasingly important as representations of the powerful and wealthy. Lists of portraits in Welsh mansions provide evidence of increasing collections from the mid-16th century onwards, although few were the work of indigenous painters. They include those of the **Goodman** family of **Ruthin**, and the **Vaughan family (Tretower)**. The 1590 painting of Sir Edward and Lady Agnes **Stradling** at **St Donats** is an interesting combination of image, text and heraldic device. Portraits of Sir Thomas Mansel of **Margam** and his wife Jane, painted in the early 17th century, demonstrate the **Mansel family**'s power and influence.

In the 17th and 18th centuries, improving technology and increasing patronage led to a huge expansion in picture making, allowing a multiplicity of Welsh images to be produced, not only as single works of art, but also as engravings. While the needs of the **gentry** were generally met by visiting artists – many of them by the late 18th century inspired by **William Gilpin**'s writings and the **picturesque movement** – there was also patronage of native artists, whose work was rooted in the artisan tradition. The self-taught **Moses Griffith** accompanied **Thomas Pennant** on his 1770 tour of Wales.

Of Wales's academically trained painters, **Richard Wilson** is widely considered to be the father of British landscape painting, while his pupil, **Thomas Jones** (1742–1803), although a frequent exponent of the picturesque, brought a naturalistic freshness to his studies that anticipated later developments.

English artists – **J. M. W. Turner** pre-eminent among them – resorted to Wales for the 'exotic'. With the Romantic Movement (*see* **Romanticism**) and the extravagant

Ivor Davies, *Sweet Captivity* (1991)

fancies of **Celt**icism, 'wild' Wales became the backdrop for melodramatic fantasies. The urge to record beautiful landscapes gave rise to the **Betws-y-Coed** artists' colony and to enthusiasm for the scenery of **Snowdonia**, the impetus that led in 1881 to the establishment of the **Royal Cambrian Academy of Art**.

The post **Protestant Reformation Anglican** Church proved a less enthusiastic patron of painting than had its medieval predecessor, although 17th-century paintings at Llangar and elsewhere offer evidence of what escaped the attention of over-enthusiastic 19th-century restorers. Although Nonconformity (*see* **Nonconformists**) has traditionally been seen as inimical to image making, the need to commemorate its heroes provided livelihoods for portrait painters such as **Hugh Hughes** and **William Roos**. In addition, the press which had developed in the wake of increased literacy provided an expanding market for engravings of the work of painters (*see* **Printing and Publishing**; **Periodicals**; **Newspapers**).

With industrialization and urbanization came new wealth, with **Swansea** in particular giving rise to a school of painters with a marked interest in maritime scenes. **Merthyr Tydfil** provided the launching pad for the career of **Penry Williams**, who later distinguished himself in Rome. The success of the **Harris family** of Merthyr illustrates the important link between economic and cultural production, with the owners of the new **iron**works,

collieries and estates becoming both patrons and subjects of art. His income from the south Wales **coal**field allowed the third marquess of Bute (*see* **Stuart family**) to commission **William Burges** to decorate **Cardiff** Castle and Castell Coch, a venture which had a significant impact upon the artistic history of Cardiff. The requirements of industrialized society gave rise to art and technical schools; established from the mid-19th century onwards, primarily to train skilled artisans, they came also to be centres of expressive creative activity.

The early 20th century produced an iconic image of Wales when the Englishman Sidney Curnow Vosper's painting of Siân Owen, Ty'n y Fawnog, in Salem chapel (*see* **Salem**), Cefncymerau (**Llanbedr**), was distributed as a print with Sunlight soap; it rapidly became the most popular image the Welsh had of themselves. The **mountains** of Wales also provided inspiration, with **Augustus John** and his friend **James Dickson Innes** interpreting Snowdonia through a mild form of Fauvism. The **First World War** produced painters concerned to record its horrors, with **Christopher Williams** painting a mural commemorating the battle of Mametz Wood, and **David Jones** (1895–1974), who had fought in that battle, producing work, both artistic and literary, which was imbued with memories of the trenches.

The imagery of industrial life attracted other artists, many of whom, such as **Evan Walters** and Vincent Evans (1896–1976), were working-**class** painters who trained at Swansea School of Art and who contributed to the emergence of Swansea as a centre of native artistic excellence. The **depression of the interwar years** had a profound effect on much subsequent art. The depression had lifted by 1943, when **Josef Herman**, the most prominent Wales's **refugee artists**, began applying a highly dramatic version of expressionism to the mining theme. **Ceri Richards**, however, was inspired by a lyrical spirit that soared above the predictable, and what was becoming the somewhat morose theme of much Welsh painting. **Graham Sutherland** and **John Piper**, both romantic modernists, lived and worked in Wales for long periods, while **Will Roberts** pursued a singular path, painting portraits, agricultural workers and the customers of his **Neath** jeweller's shop.

By the 1960s, abstraction and theories of modernity began to advance through the restrictions of the art school system. With official patronage from the **Arts Council**, Welsh painting moved through various phases, never consistently and always driven by the independent will of key practitioners. The works of John Selway (b.1937) and **Ernest Zobole** – locally observed, but international in vision – have the narrative energy of the novel and the lyricism of the poem, reinforcing a constant theme in Welsh painting, which is even more explicit in the landscapes of Mary Lloyd Jones (b.1934) – namely the relationship between the image and the word.

The American-influenced 1960s produced painting that included local versions of almost every international style, although landscape continued to exercise **Kyffin Williams**, whose slabs of paint seem to bear a geological relationship with their mountain subject matter, and **Peter Prendergast** who forged his expressionistic visions from an intense study of his Welsh surroundings.

A late 20th-century explosion of interest in Welsh art, accompanied by television programmes and the publication of books and CDs, was due, in part, to National Curriculum requirements for art education but, pre-eminently, to the pioneering work of the artist and academic Peter Lord (b.1948). His radical reassessment of Welsh art history, articulated through numerous articles, books and, latterly, the Visual Culture of Wales project at the **University of Wales Centre for Advanced Welsh and Celtic Studies**, has transformed attitudes towards Welsh art at both the academic and popular levels. Another transformation worthy of note has been the number of **women** involved in art. There are regrettably few entries on women artists in this *Encyclopaedia*, chiefly because until the later 20th century their contribution was constrained by social protocols; but by the beginning of the 21st century women were active and successful as artists in equal numbers to men.

As the visual arts become an amalgam of **photography**, **film**, installation, interception, sound and whatever means come to hand, the old genre divisions are being exploded. Art is no longer simply painting and **sculpture**; indeed, some considered painting to be exhausted by the end of the 20th century. Yet, groups were formed to advance its cause, aware that only paint can express certain sensations. Late 20th-century postmodern theory conferred respectability on the local, and painting, like other artistic endeavours, came to address questions of identity, language, mythology and **nationhood**, alongside international contemporary issues. In a recent work, Ivor Davies (b.1935) takes the earth pigments of upland Wales, mixes them with his paint, and paints in red ochre the continuing story of Wales.

PALAEOLITHIC and MESOLITHIC AGES, The (Old and Middle Stone Ages; *c.*250,000–4000 BC)

Homo erectus, or its hominid descendants, is believed to have colonized **Britain** between 750,000 and 500,000 BC. In Wales, the earliest evidence for man's presence comes from Pontnewydd **cave** in the Elwy valley (**Cefnmeiriadog**) and has been dated to *c.*250,000 BC.

Pontnewydd is one of the few sites in upland Britain to have yielded evidence of the Lower Palaeolithic Age (the earliest period of the Old Stone Age). The evidence was discovered in the 19th century, but the site's importance was not fully appreciated until the last quarter of the 20th. The remains indicate that groups of hunters and gatherers used the high vantage point of the cave to hunt in the narrow valley below. The environment of the period is considered to have been a cold, open steppe in which large herbivore herds and their carnivore predators roamed in plenty. A burnt flint nodule from the cave suggests the presence of a domestic hearth around which the group's social and domestic activities were organized. Their artefacts included hand axes, knives, points, scrapers and flakes made of stone or flint. Most of the raw materials could have been obtained locally, although some of them came from further afield, possibly from **Snowdonia**. This suggests either the existence of a rudimentary exchange system or that the **hunting** territories of the group were very extensive. Animal bones, particularly of large herbivores, attest to the group's hunting prowess. Human finds include the remains of between three and six individuals, one of them a child. They are probably the remains of early Neanderthal people, who are considered to be an archaic lineage descended from late *Homo erectus* human forms.

The entrance to the important Palaeolithic site of Pontnewydd Cave, Cefnmeiriadog

The cave at Paviland where 'The Red Lady of Paviland' was found

Neanderthal humans disappeared from Europe with the advent of the first *Homo sapiens*, who appear to have first settled in Wales *c*.30,000 BC, during the period of intense cold and climatic oscillation that characterized the later phases of the Pleistocene Ice Age. Britain may not have been populated at all at the height of the glacial advances, but these new hunting communities showed great adaptability to the changing environment. Several of Wales's **limestone** caves have yielded evidence of their artefacts. Foremost amongst them are early Upper Palaeolithic assemblages from Paviland (**Rhossili**), Hoyle's Mouth (**Penally**) and Ffynnon Beuno and Cae Gwyn (**Tremeirchion**), and later Upper Palaeolithic finds from a number of **Pembrokeshire** coastal caves and from caves on the Great Orme (**Llandudno**) and in the Vale of **Clwyd**.

Some of the artefacts – keel-shaped scrapers, for example – show close affinities with the Aurignacian material of south-western France. Decorative pieces – among them an engraved **horse** jawbone and a series of incised **deer** teeth from the Great Orme, and the bone spatulae and ivory rods from Paviland – recall more widely distributed Upper Palaeolithic objects. Paviland has yielded the only known formal burial of the period in Britain. Originally believed to be the remains of a woman of the **Roman** era, the bones were stained with red ochre, giving rise to the name 'The Red Lady of Paviland'. The body is now known to be that of a young man, and has been dated to 26,000 years ago, at a time prior to the glacial maximum. It is also likely that a later Upper Palaeolithic burial of great significance – that associated with the horse jawbone and decorated teeth mentioned above – was destroyed in a cave on the Great Orme.

The end of the last Ice Age, *c*.11,500 BC, was followed by a series of changes in the **climate** that mark postglacial periods. As the ice retreated, temperatures rose worldwide, resulting in rising sea levels and causing major changes to both vegetation and fauna. In western Europe, by *c*.7000 BC, the steppe grasslands of the Pleistocene era had been transformed into thick forest (*see* **Forestry**), causing the hunter-gatherer **populations** of the Mesolithic era (the Middle Stone Age) to adopt more specialized hunting techniques based largely on the bow and arrow. By *c*.8500 BC, Britain had become an **island**, leading to the progressive development of more insular social groups lacking intimate contact with their mainland neighbours.

In Wales, Mesolithic settlement was mainly located near the coast and in those **river** valleys where the tree cover was less dense. Hunting would have chiefly involved herds of red and roe deer, wild **cattle** and **wild boar**, although **birds**, **fish** and shellfish would have provided additional sustenance. Seasonal migration between lowland and upland sites is attested, particularly in the later stages of the Mesolithic Age (*see* **Hafod** and **Hendre**). In summer, hunters followed their quarry from their winter lowland quarters to open upland grazing areas. Evidence of such migrations has been found in lowland sites such as Ogmore (**St Bride's Major**), **Prestatyn** and **Rhuddlan**, and in upland sites such as Waun Fignen Felen (**Llywel**), Brenig (**Llanrhaeadr-yng Nghinmeirch**) and Llyn Aled Isaf (**Llansannan**). At the latter two sites, beach pebble flint and black chert from Gronant (**Llanasa**) were the principal raw materials used. At Waun Fignen Felen, the nearest source of one particular lithic raw material is located 80 km from the site.

The principal artefacts of the Mesolithic Age were microlithic points – small flakes used as arrowheads and knives – but there were also scrapers, awls and heavy stone axes with a characteristic oblique cutting edge. Barbed antler and bone spear points were widely employed, as were antler mattock heads, such as the example from the foreshore at **Rhyl**. Rhuddlan has yielded a number of engraved pebbles, decorated with geometric patterns. These objects, so far unique in the British Mesolithic Age, must have played a part in some kind of ritual. The distribution of sites suggests that no more than four tribal groups occupied the whole of Wales at any particular time, each exploiting to its maximum the fauna and flora of its own particular domain.

The Palaeolithic Age was by far the longest chronological phase in the history of mankind. The Mesolithic Age, in comparison, was but a short interlude. Yet, it is during that age of crucial environmental change that migratory hunting communities in the Near East slowly adapted to become settled farmers, thus starting a process that would establish **agriculture** as the bedrock upon which all subsequent civilizations would be based (*see* **Neolithic Age, The**).

PALMER, Alfred Neobard (1847–1915) Historian
A native of Suffolk, Palmer moved to **Wrexham** in 1880. An analytical chemist by training, he was employed for a while at **Brymbo** Steel Works. Palmer developed a deep interest in local history, and learnt the **Welsh language**, publishing original work on **John Wilkinson** and the

Bersham Iron Works, ancient land tenures, the origins of Nonconformity (*see* Nonconformists) in Wrexham, and the history of Wrexham and Gresford parish churches. Several of his books were reissued in the 1980s.

PALMERSTON'S FOLLIES

A series of massive coastal and island fortifications erected in southern Wales and southern England during the mid-19th century as defences against possible French attacks. They were named after Lord Palmerston, the British Prime Minister (1855–8, 1859–65). In Wales, they include a group of 12 forts and Martello towers around the mouth of the Milford Haven Waterway, built to protect Pembroke Dockyard and prevent the Haven being used as an anchorage by enemy ships; the largest of them was Scoveston Fort (Llanstadwell). In addition, there was the fort on St Catherine's Island (Tenby), fortified batteries at Mumbles Head (Swansea), and at Lavernock Point (Sully), and a fort and three batteries on Flat Holm (*see* Islands) in the Severn Sea.

PAPURAU BRO (Neighbourhood newspapers)

A remarkable phenomenon in the history of the Welsh-language press during the last quarter of the 20th century was the growth of the *papurau bro*. Between 1973 and 1983, 50 of these Welsh-language community newspapers were founded to serve communities throughout Wales, and there were 52 in circulation by the beginning of the 21st century. They were established out of concern for the future of the language and in the belief that they could play an important role in giving prominence to Welsh cultural activities within communities. Each of these monthly papers depends on a team of volunteers to collect and edit the news, take photographs, arrange advertisements and distribute the paper. Although the communities served by them differ greatly, the core content is basically similar – items of news, reports by local institutions and societies, photographs, advertisements by local businesses, and regular feature columns. More remarkable than the growth of these newspapers is the fact that such a high percentage of them have survived for over 25 years, and have become a vital part of the cultural and community life of their areas.

PARC SLIP COLLIERY DISASTER,
Newcastle Higher, near Bridgend

An explosion at this colliery at 8.30 a.m. on 26 August 1892 killed 112 men. The mine, situated on the southern outcrop of the south Wales coalfield, was operated by North's Navigation Collieries (1889) Ltd. The explosion was attributed to an ignition of firedamp, probably caused by a broken or unsafe lamp, but because only the dry, dusty parts of the mine were affected, coal dust was seen as a major contributory factor.

PARGETER, Edith (Ellis Peters; 1913–95) Novelist

Under the name of Ellis Peters, this Shropshire-born novelist wrote 19 detective novels, set in the reign of King Stephen, in which the central character is Brother Cadfael, a Welsh crusader who becomes a monk. His erudition, native wit and understanding of Welsh society help to solve a number of murder mysteries in and around Shrewsbury Abbey. The public's interest in Cadfael and his world led to the publication of *Cadfael Country* (1990), a tourist guide, and *The Cadfael Companion* (1994). Under her own name, the author published a series of four novels about Llywelyn ap Gruffudd and his brother Dafydd ap Gruffudd, and three novels about life on the border in the Middle Ages.

PARISHES

A parish, in its original, religious, sense, is a subdivision of a diocese and has its own church and priest. As Christianity in Wales was organized around mother churches or *clasau* – often serving an entire *cantref* – the country, on the eve of the Norman invasions, lacked a network of parishes similar to that which had been established in most of England by the 10th century. By the early 11th century, parish creation was proceeding apace in regions such as the Vale of Glamorgan. The *Historia* of Gruffudd ap Cynan states that, during his reign (*c.*1100–37), Anglesey came to shine as if with stars, as a result of the whitewashed churches built on the island. It is likely that the building of a church involved the demarcation of the territory – the parish – for which its priest was responsible.

By the later Middle Ages, parish creation in Wales was more or less complete. The entire country, apart from areas of extensive common land such as Cefn Bryn in Gower, had been divided into parishes, each one served, at least theor–etically, by a church and a priest maintained by church land (glebe) and tithe payments. The more fertile the land, the smaller the parish; indeed, the parishes of Wales varied in size from 15 ha (Stembridge; *see* Llandow) to 13,280 ha (Llanfor; *see* Llandderfel). It is estimated that 15th-century Wales had 850 parish clergy and, presumably, 850 parishes, although later subdivisions would increase that number.

From 1538, parishes were obliged to keep a register of births, marriages and deaths. Wales's earliest surviving parish register is that of Conwy (1541). While 16th-century Welsh registers are rare, those surviving from the 17th century are numerous and a valuable source for the study of population history. In the 16th century, parishes became secular as well as religious units, receiving responsibilities with regard to such matters as roads and the Poor Law, and the parish vestry became the basic form of local government. Thus emerged the civil parish, whose boundaries would over the years come to differ from those of ecclesiastical parishes. From the first official census (1801), the civil parish was used as the fundamental statistical unit. By then, there were 1132 in Wales, their boundaries frequently bearing no relationship to demographic realities. With the establishment of parish councils in 1894, it was recognized that civil parishes were meaningful only in a rural context. In the 1930s, several Welsh counties reorganized their civil parishes; in Monmouthshire, for example, the number was reduced from 145 to 58.

In 1974, the civil parishes of Wales (but not of England) were abolished and replaced by communities. Ecclesiastical parishes continued in existence, many of them consisting of clusters of ancient parishes, with names such as Llanfaes and Penmon, and Llangoed with Llanfihangel Dinsylwy.

P

Roman Catholic parishes, some of them very large, were established following the restoration of the hierarchy in 1850.

PARKER, John (1798–1860) Painter
Rector of Llanmerewig (**Llandyssil**), 1827–44, Parker was inspired by an interest in Gothic **architecture**, making watercolours and drawings. He painted pictures of all the rood screens in Wales and recorded varieties of font, as well as completing many views, notably of **Snowdon**. Of his artistic work in Llanmerewig church little survives.

PARKHOUSE, Gilbert (William Gilbert Anthony Parkhouse; 1925–2000) Cricketer
Perhaps the most elegant of Welsh batsmen, **Swansea**-born Parkhouse's emergence with **Glamorgan** coincided with the championship triumph of 1948. Picked for **England** within two years, in 1950–1 he became the first Welshman chosen for a tour of **Australia**, but in an era of great batting strength he would play only seven tests. His stylish right-handed stroke play remained Glamorgan's most attractive feature until 1964, producing 23,508 runs. He also played **rugby** for Swansea.

PARLIAMENTARY REPRESENTATION
Wales had sent representatives to the English parliament in 1323 and 1329, but a regular pattern of representation was not established until the 16th-century **Act of 'Union'**. Following that act, Wales consisted of 13 **counties**; **Monmouthshire** was granted 2 county members and the other 12 counties one apiece. The county towns of 12 counties were each granted a **borough** member, with 'contributory' boroughs providing financial support. **Harlech, Merioneth**'s county town, was considered too impoverished to be represented. In 1543, **Haverfordwest** was granted its own member, bringing Wales's total to 27 out of a House of Commons of 349 members. As the **population** of Wales was then about 7% of that of **England**, the arrangement was broadly equitable. In the counties, 40-shilling freeholders had the vote, as did all freemen in the boroughs. Welsh members were first summoned to parliament in 1542.

In the first decades of representation, Welsh members seem to have been somewhat taciturn, but from the late 16th century they won increasing prominence at Westminster. Between 1571 and 1603, thirty Welsh members gained experience of committee work in the House of Commons, and during James I's first parliament (1604–11) four out of five contributed to the business of the House. In the 16th and early 17th centuries, members were drawn from a considerable number of generally **gentry** families but, with the consolidation of large estates, representation came to be dominated by a tight caste of about two dozen families, including such leviathans as the **Williams Wynns (Wynnstay)**, the **Morgans (Tredegar)** and the **Bulkeleys (Baron Hill)**. The struggle for a seat rarely led to an electoral contest. Of Wales's 432 election returns between 1660 and 1714, only about 40 were decided through the casting of votes. The rest were settled through private deals between landowners, thus avoiding the vast cost of an electoral contest.

The rise of the **Tory** and **Whig** parties in the late 17th century did introduce an ideological element into politics, but by the 18th century such labels had become almost meaningless. Nevertheless, contests could be bitter and expensive; in 1741, Watkin Williams Wynn spent £20,000 to thwart the ambitions of the **Myddelton family** in **Denbighshire**, and in 1802 **William Paxton** spent over £15,000 in **Carmarthenshire**, only to lose by 45 votes. When such rare contests occurred, landowners were able to manufacture voters in the counties by granting life leases and in the boroughs by controlling the enrolment of freemen.

From the 1790s onwards, there were calls for parliamentary reform, made more pressing by the increasing difference between the populations of rural and industrial counties. **Radnorshire**, for example, had the same representation as **Glamorgan**, although the latter had 10 times the inhabitants of the former – and by industrialists' resentment of landlord power. The First Reform Act (1832) gave Wales five additional members: Glamorgan, Carmarthenshire and Denbighshire were each given an extra member, **Merthyr Tydfil** became a borough constituency, and the Glamorgan boroughs were divided, with one group centred on **Cardiff** and the other on **Swansea**. The borough franchise was extended to men whose estate exceeded £10 a year and the county franchise to male tenants paying an annual rent of £50 or more. Although about 20% of adult males were enfranchised, hardly any of them belonged to the working **class**, a fact that led to widespread popular discontent, powerfully manifested in the activities of the **Scotch Cattle**, the **Chartists** and the **Rebecca Riot**ers.

The Second Reform Act (1867) enfranchised all male householders in the boroughs and all those occupying premises rated at £12 or more in the counties. As a result, the Welsh electorate increased by 263%. The growth of borough electorates was particularly marked, with that of Merthyr (which gained an additional MP) rising from 1387 to 14,577. The Reform Act of 1867 was followed in 1872 by the Ballot Act which brought an end to open voting, an act which was partly motivated by the political evictions in **Cardiganshire** and Carmarthenshire following the election of 1868.

The Third Reform Act (1884) gave the vote to all male householders, thus enfranchising about 60% of Wales's adult males. The Redistribution Act (1885), which significantly enhanced the representation of the growing industrial areas, brought the number of Welsh constituencies to 34. By the 1880s, with business and professional men capturing seats, landowners had become rare among Welsh representatives. **Conservatives** were even rarer. The **Liberal Party** had captured a majority of Welsh seats in 1865 and, in 1906, the Conservatives failed to win a single Welsh constituency. Following the Third Reform Act, the majority of the electorate was working class. Yet, in 1885, the **Rhondda** was the sole constituency to elect a working-class member. He was **William Abraham** (Mabon) who, as a representative of the Lib-Lab tradition, fitted comfortably into the progressive wing of the Liberal Party. In 1900, however, **Keir Hardie** captured the second Merthyr seat – the sole Labour Representation Committee candidate to be elected in Wales. In 1909, when the **South Wales Miners' Federation** affiliated to the **Labour Party**, the four MPs from Wales who received the Federation's endorsement became Labour members. However, the Liberals remained the dominant political party in Wales at the beginning of the **First World War**.

The Representation of the People Act (1918) gave the vote to all men over 21 and to all **women** over 30 (women between 21 and 30 were enfranchised in 1928), increasing the Welsh electorate from 430,000 to 1,172,000. An attempt was made to create broadly equal parliamentary constituencies, each with about 70,000 electors. The Act laid down that there were to be 36 Welsh constituencies, 22 of them in Glamorgan and Monmouthshire, 5 in the other southern counties and 8 in the north; the **University of Wales** was also given a seat. In 1948, the business vote and the University seats were abolished, causing the 1950 election to be the first general election in which virtually all adults had a vote, but only one vote. The following years saw some changes. By 2002, Wales had 40 MPs, with redistribution reflecting population decline in rural areas and in the south Wales **coal**field and population increase in places such as Cardiff and **Newport**.

There were changes too in the pattern of political representation. In 1918, Labour captured 10 Welsh seats and 30% of the popular vote. There were 25 Welsh Labour MPs by 1929 (a total repeated in the landslide Labour victory of 1945), 27 in 1950 and 32 out of 36 in 1966. In 1983, a bad year for Labour, its share of seats fell to 20, a figure that rose to 34 out of 40 in 1997 and 2001. The number declined to 29 in 2005. Support for the Liberals plunged as the party retreated to the rural north and west, capturing 7 Welsh seats in 1945, 3 in 1951 and only 1 (**Montgomeryshire**) in 1966. Thereafter the party usually held 2 seats, but the number rose to 3 in 1983 and to 4 in 2005. **Conservative** fortunes in Wales reached their peak in 1983, when the party won 14 seats. However, in 1997 and in 2001, it failed to win any; the party revived somewhat in 2005 when it won three seats. **Plaid [Genedlaethol] Cymru** won its first seat in the **Carmarthen** by-election of 1966; it won 4 in the general election of 2001, and 3 in the election of 2005.

PARRI, Dafydd (1926–2001) Author

A native of Rowen (**Caerhun**), Dafydd Parri and his wife Arianwen established at **Llanrwst** in 1955 one of the earliest **Welsh-language** bookshops. A teacher by profession, he published his first work – a novel for children – in 1961. He became a full-time author in 1975. By 1991, he had published over 36 books, among them the highly successful *Llewod* series, novels which, while in the *Famous Five* tradition, had locations and characters that were wholly Welsh. His sons include the poet Myrddin ap Dafydd (b.1956) and the journalist Iolo ap Dafydd (b.1964).

PARRY, David Hughes (1893–1973) Academic

A son of **Llanaelhaearn**, Hughes Parry chaired the Committee on the Legal Status of the **Welsh Language**, whose report led to the **Welsh Language Act 1967**, which failed to implement its main recommendations. He was professor of English **law** at the University of **London** (1930–59), founder director of its Institute of Advanced

Gwenlyn Parry

Legal Studies and the University's vice-chancellor (1945–8). Knighted in 1951, he was the author of leading legal works on property and succession; his Hamlyn lectures on the Sanctity of Contracts in English Law, in particular, are justly admired.

PARRY, [William] Gwenlyn (1932–91) Dramatist

Born in Deiniolen (**Llanddeiniolen**), Gwenlyn Parry discovered an interest in **drama** while teaching in **London**, where he enjoyed friendships with **Rhydderch Jones** and **Ryan Davies**. He joined the BBC in **Cardiff** in 1966, eventually becoming chief script editor. He established himself as a stage dramatist with *Saer Doliau* (1966), a Pinteresque drama about conflict between **religion** and **science**. He continued to experiment, exploring the territory between comedy and tragedy, in plays such as *Tŷ ar y Tywod* (1968), *Y Ffin* (1973) and *Y Twr* (1978). He made his most distinctive contribution in television, as producer, editor and scriptwriter of such programmes as *Fo a Fe*, *Pobol y Cwm* and the play *Grand Slam* (1978).

PARRY, Harry (1912–56) Jazz musician

Bangor-born Harry Parry was an internationally renowned composer and bandleader, who played the clarinet and saxophone. From his base in **London**, where he played in clubs and **dance** halls, and broadcast frequently with the BBC, he led bands touring mainland Europe, the Middle East and India into the 1950s. One of the best known of his many combos was the Radio Rhythm Club Sextet, whose pianist for a time was **Dill Jones**. *Harry Parry and His Radio Rhythm Club Sextet* (1984) is a retrospective anthology of some of his most popular recordings.

PARRY, John (Y Telynor Dall or Blind Parry; c.1710–82) Harpist

Born at **Nefyn**, and residing at **Ruabon**, Parry was the most famous of 18th-century Wales's **harp**ists. Family harpist to the **Williams Wynn family (Wynnstay)**, by the age of 23 he was playing Vivaldi and Corelli at Drury Lane Theatre, **London**. Between 1742 and 1781, he published three important collections of harp **music**. Parry's playing was universally admired, his virtuosity inspiring the poet Thomas Gray to complete his poem 'The Bard' (*see* **Massacre of the Bards, The**).

His son, John William Parry (1742–91), was a painter and portraitist who trained with Shipley and Reynolds, and at the Royal Academy Schools before taking up a position at Wynnstay in 1770. During the early 1770s, he lived in Rome and on his return was elected Associate of the Royal Academy. His celebrated portrait of his father is probably his most evocative work.

PARRY, John (Bardd Alaw; 1776–1851) Musician

Parry, whose father was a **Denbigh** stonemason, was taught to play the clarinet by a dancing master; he also played the **harp**. He joined the **Denbighshire** militia band in 1793, becoming bandmaster two years later. In 1807, he moved to **London**, and began working as a composer and arranger for theatre and opera in 1809, when he first wrote music for Vauxhall Gardens. One of the most popular of his many

Joseph Parry

ballads was 'Jenny Jones'. He also collected and arranged Welsh melodies, and wrote about **music**. Parry conducted and adjudicated at *eisteddfodau*, and was named Bardd Alaw (bard of melody) at the **Powys** Eisteddfod of 1820.

PARRY, Joseph (Pencerdd America; 1841–1903) Composer

As a child, **Merthyr Tydfil**-born Joseph Parry worked in a **coal**mine and then at the Cyfarthfa **iron**works. In 1854, he emigrated with his family to Danville, **Pennsylvania**, where he worked in an iron mill. He learned **music** there, and began to compete in *eisteddfodau*. At the **Aberystwyth** Eisteddfod of 1865 he was inducted into the **Gorsedd** and given the bardic title 'Pencerdd America' (Chief Musician of America). In 1868, he went to the Royal Academy of Music, **London** on the strength of a public subscription fund, and in 1871 became the first Welsh person to be awarded a MusB from **Cambridge** University. In 1874, he became the first professor of music at **Aberystwyth**. He resigned in 1880 and later became head of music at the new University College at **Cardiff** (*see* **Cardiff University**).

He is best known for his **hymn** tunes, especially 'Aberystwyth', and for the part-song **'Myfanwy'**, but his output was considerable, and included six operas, one of which, *Blodwen* (1878), was the first **Welsh-language** opera; the duet 'Hywel a Blodwen' from that opera has been immensely popular on the eisteddfodic and concert stage. He wrote the *Tydfil Overture* (*c.*1879) for the **Cyfarthfa Band**, claiming that it was this band that first stimulated his interest in music.

PARRY, Sarah Winifred (Winnie Parry; 1870–1953) Author

Winnie Parry was born in **Welshpool** and brought up in **Y Felinheli**. Her best-known work, *Sioned* (1906), depicts a young girl's life in late 19th-century **Caernarfonshire**. This novel, which first appeared in instalments in the magazine *Cymru* in 1895, broke new ground in Welsh fiction, especially in its use of dialect. Most of Winnie Parry's other works also made their first appearance in **periodicals**, including the children's stories *Y Ddau Hogyn Rheiny*, published as a volume in 1928. She spent most of her life in **England** and edited *Cymru'r Plant* from Croydon (1907–12).

PARRY, Thomas (1904–85) Scholar

A quarryman's son from Carmel (**Llandwrog**), Thomas Parry filled a series of important posts in Welsh cultural life: professor of **Welsh** at **Bangor** (1947), national librarian at the **National Library of Wales** (1953) and principal at **Aberystwyth** (1958–69). As author of a history of Welsh **literature**, *Hanes Llenyddiaeth Gymraeg* (1945), and editor of *Gwaith Dafydd ap Gwilym* (1952) and *The Oxford Book of Welsh Verse* (1962), he completed some of the most basic tasks in the world of Welsh literature. He wrote a historical play, *Llywelyn Fawr* (1954), and translated T. S. Eliot's *Murder in the Cathedral* as *Lladd wrth yr Allor* (1949). *Amryw Bethau* (1996) is a selection of his literary essays.

Less prominent, but possibly a more gifted and fluid prose-writer, was his brother Gruffudd Parry (1916–2002); among his best works is the travel book *Crwydro Llŷn ac Eifionydd* (1960).

T. H. Parry-Williams and his motorcycle KC 16, the title of one of his best-known essays

PARRY, W[illiam] J[ohn] (1842–1927) Businessman, author and local leader

A native of **Bethesda**, Parry was a leading figure in a range of activities – business, **trade unionism**, **religion**, politics, journalism, publishing and **gold** prospecting in **Patagonia**. He was the first general secretary of the **North Wales Quarrymen's Union** in 1874 and later its president. A **Liberal** member of **Caernarfonshire County** Council, he was its chairman in 1892–3. A prolific writer, he published many religious works, as well as volumes on the predicaments of the **slate** industry, such as *Chwareli a Chwarelwyr* (1897) and *Cry of the People* (1906). In 1901, he was successfully sued for libel by Baron Penrhyn (*see* **Pennant family**).

PARRY-JONES, Daniel (1891–1981) Author

Llangeler-born Daniel Parry-Jones spent his career as a clergyman, mainly at **Llanelly**. He is remembered for his books about the rural traditions of Wales; they include four autobiographies, which were written partly to counter the negative portrayal of Welsh life found in the work of Caradoc Evans (**David Evans**; 1878–1945) and others.

PARRY-WILLIAMS, T[homas] H[erbert] (1887–1975) Poet and essayist

The son of the schoolmaster of Rhyd-ddu (**Betws Garmon**), Parry-Williams wrote a well-known sonnet to the schoolhouse where he was brought up. He had a brilliant academic career, graduating in **Welsh** and **Latin** at **Aberystwyth**, and studying at **Oxford**, Freiburg and the

Sorbonne. His early works of scholarship were linguistic (he published *The English Element in Welsh* in 1923), but he made a pioneering contribution in the field of early free verse (including *Canu Rhydd Cynnar*, 1932), and his book *Elfennau Barddoniaeth* (1935) was very popular. His first post was as lecturer in Welsh at Aberystwyth, but, in 1919, because he was not appointed professor (owing to his stance as a **conscientious objector**), he decided to become a **science** student. Welcomed back to the Welsh department as professor in 1920, he remained there until his retirement in 1952. A prominent figure in Welsh public life, he was knighted in 1958.

He won the chair and crown in both the 1912 and the 1915 National *Eisteddfodau*, a unique feat at the time. In its portrayal of the seamier side of Parisian life, his long poem in the free metres, 'Y Ddinas' (1915), went against the grain of **John Morris-Jones**'s romantic aesthetics. Parry-Williams's rejection of poetic diction, Bobi Jones has remarked, caused his voice to sound like that of a 'big black raven'.

In his so-called *rhigymau* (rhymes) – such as 'Hon', 'Dic Aberdaron', 'Yr Esgyrn Hyn', 'Carol Nadolig' and 'Bro' – he employs a misleadingly lackadaisical style, but under the humorous façade there is irony and philosophical depth. In contrast, the sonnets are smooth and controlled, and they too meditate on the basic questions of human existence. Although the most consistent subject of Parry-Williams's creative work is his own native district of **Snowdonia**, both his poems and essays are ultimately concerned with the meaning – or lack of meaning – of life.

P

PASK, Alun [Islwyn Edward] (1937–95)
Rugby player

Though he never left his unfashionable club of **Abertillery**, Alun Pask won 26 consecutive caps for Wales between 1961 and 1967, and toured twice with the British Lions. His mobility, intelligent anticipation and tireless cover-tackling, allied to his height at the back of the line-out and his fondness for the ball in (generally one) hand, made him the prototype modern back-row forward. He demonstrated his versatility by deputizing confidently at full-back during the Triple Crown decider against **Ireland** in 1965. He died tragically in a fire at his home in **Blackwood**.

PATAGONIA, Wales's associations with

During the 19th century, when many Europeans emigrated (*see* **Emigration**) in search of a better life, the Welsh favoured **North America**, but once there, they tended to lose their national identity. The same was true of a small number who, in 1850, settled in Rio Grande do Sul in Brazil, in the colony that became known as Nova Cambria. This is why the leaders of the movement to establish a Welsh colony overseas, **Michael D. Jones**, Lewis Jones, Hugh Hughes (Cadfan Gwynedd), Edwin Cynrig Roberts and others, sought land where there would be no outside influences, and this they believed they had found in Argentina.

The first settlers, a group of 160, sailed from **Liverpool** on the *Mimosa* on 25 May 1865, and landed in New Bay on 28 July. They then travelled south to the **River** Chubut (Camwy, to the Welsh settlers), their primary need being a source of fresh water. They settled initially in what is now Rawson (named after the Argentinian minister of the interior, who had given the settlers vague promises), and from

there established their farms to the west along the river valley. Their main problem, at first, was drought, often followed by floods, which washed away their houses and all their belongings. The drought was relieved by the building of canals; later, the floods were checked by building a dam.

In 1886, a **railway** was built connecting the Chubut valley with Porth Madryn (now Puerto Madryn), the name given to the place where the first settlers landed and called after Madryn (**Buan**), home of Love Jones-Parry, a supporter of the venture. The railway encouraged the growth of the town of Trelew, named after Lewis Jones. Today, the **Welsh language** is most prevalent in Trelew, Gaiman and Dolavon. The settlement expanded to include Cwm Hyfryd at the foot of the Andes, where, from 1885 onwards, many members of the original families carved out farms at Trevelin and Esquel. This area, together with the Chubut valley, constitutes Y Wladfa, the Welsh colony. Welsh-language writers associated with Y Wladfa include **Eluned Morgan**, R. Bryn Williams and Irma Hughes de Jones.

For a time, the dream of a colony conducting its affairs exclusively in Welsh was realized. But other immigrants arrived, and the government in Buenos Aires intruded increasingly in the life of the colony, which failed to gain the status of a province; in particular, the colonists opposed the government's demand that they should undertake military training on Sundays. Consequently, the speaking of Welsh declined, although some Welsh traditions survived. The **eisteddfod** has been a part of the life of the colony from the outset. With the coming of the **Second World War**, contact with Wales more or less lapsed, but it was re-established in 1965, the year of the centenary

Puerto Madryn, Patagonia, showing the caves in which the newly-arrived Welsh immigrants sheltered

celebrations. The eisteddfod, the **noson lawen**, the chapels, the Welsh **teas** and the celebration of Gŵyl y Glaniad (the festival of disembarkation) were, by the early 21st century, the visible signs of Welshness.

During the 1990s, there was renewed interest in learning Welsh, and classes were held throughout the Chubut valley, in Cwm Hyfryd, and in Comodoro Rivadavia to the south, where many went from the valley to work in the **oil** field. In the late 1990s, the British Council established a Welsh project and engaged teachers to build on the previously voluntary work. Visitors from Wales – particularly young people – are now numerous in Patagonia, and in 2001, the **archdruid** of Wales went to Y Wladfa to establish a **Gorsedd** there.

PATENT OFFICE, The

An executive agency of the Department of Trade and Industry, with statutory responsibility for the registration of patents (in relation to inventions), trademarks and industrial designs. Based at Concept House, **Newport**, and with a staff of 1000, it processes annually some 20,000 applications from the United Kingdom and 10,000 applications from abroad for those who wish to extend their rights to the United Kingdom; it also advises businesses, individuals and the **government** on intellectual property policy. The decision in the 1970s to locate the office at Newport was motivated by an interest in moving institutions out of south-eastern **England**, which found occasional expression during that decade.

PATRICK (Padrig; d.461?) Patron saint of Ireland

Born on the west coast of **Britain**, Patrick spent his youth as a slave in **Ireland**. Around 432 or perhaps later, he returned there voluntarily as a **missionary** to the **Irish**. Some scholars suggest that his mother tongue was a form of Early **Welsh** and that he is the earliest identifiable Welsh speaker. His feast day is 17 March.

PATTI, Adelina (1843–1919) Opera singer

Born in Madrid, of Italian parents, and brought up in New York, the world-famous soprano died at her home in Wales, Craig-y-nos Castle (**Tawe Uchaf**). Her remarkable career, during which she was the highest paid entertainer in the world, took her to all the major opera houses. She bought Craig-y-nos to escape from the pressures of fame, and returned there by special train after each international tour. In retirement at Craig-y-nos, Dame Adelina contributed widely in the area and built a theatre – a miniature version of that at Bayreuth. She eventually donated her winter garden to the people of **Swansea**, where it is known as the Patti Pavilion. Her pure voice, regarded by Verdi as the greatest of her time, was recorded at Craig-y-nos towards the end of her life. She is buried in Paris.

PAXTON, William (c.1744–1824)

Landlord and politician

A wealthy Bengal merchant, Paxton bought the Middleton estate (**Llanarthney**; see **National Botanic Garden of Wales**), where he was resented as an 'upstart nabob'. In the **Carmarthenshire** election of 1802, his supporters drank 200,000 bottles of **beer** and 11,000 bottles of liquor, but his

Adelina Patti

vast expenditure did not bring success. Elected unopposed for **Carmarthen Borough** in 1803 and for Carmarthenshire in 1806, he lost his seat in 1807 and his candidature in the borough in 1821 was unsuccessful. His folly, Paxton's Tower, is a delightful landmark, and his **gardens** at Middleton became the basis for the National Botanic Garden of Wales. He was much involved in the development of **Tenby**.

PAYNE, Ffransis [George] (1900–92) Historian

Born at Kington (**Herefordshire**), Ffransis (originally Francis) Payne was educated at **Cardiff**. He worked for some years on the land and subsequently as curator and librarian before joining, in 1936, the **National Museum [of] Wales**; in 1962, he became head of the department of material culture at the Welsh Folk Museum (now the National History Museum; see **St Fagans**). His published works include *Yr Aradr Gymreig* (1954), an important study of early Welsh **agriculture**, two delightful volumes on **Radnorshire** – *Crwydro Sir Faesyfed* (1966, 1968), the first books on that **county** to be written in **Welsh** – and two collections of essays.

PAYNTER, Will[iam] (1903–84) Trade unionist

Born in Whitchurch, **Cardiff**, Will Paynter moved to the **Rhondda** when he was 11 and was working underground when 14. He joined the **Communist Party** in 1929, was imprisoned for assaulting the **police** in 1930, took part in **hunger marches** and organized support for the International Brigade during the **Spanish Civil War**. He was president of the **South Wales Miners' Federation** (1951–9) and general secretary of the **National Union of Mineworkers** (1959–68). Much concerned with the issue of **trade union** reform, he was briefly a member of the Commission on Industrial Relations.

PEARSON, James Denning (1908–92) Engineer

From **Cardiff** Technical School, Pearson obtained a scholarship and graduated in **engineering** before joining **Rolls-Royce**, eventually becoming chairman and chief executive in 1963. During his career, he saw the transition from piston engine to jet engine, and had the long-term vision and confidence to promote the innovatory RB211 family of engines, which helped Rolls-Royce to lead the world. He was knighted in 1963.

PEAT and PEATLANDS

Peat consists of partially decomposed vegetable matter accumulated under wet, acidic conditions. Peatlands fed more or less exclusively by rainfall (ombrogenous peatlands) occur throughout Wales in two main types – lowland raised bog and blanket bog. Lowland raised bog usually succeeds an earlier fen or swamp phase, as the gradual accrual of rain-fed peat raises the surface of the mire to a level above groundwater. The peat may attain a thickness of 10 m or more, laying down a multi-millennial record of vegetation and **climate** change in the form of preserved biogenic and inorganic deposits. Such bogs occur in several different landscape contexts, among them **river** floodplains, estuary margins and valley bottoms. They vary considerably in form and size, from the impressive raised bog landscapes of **Cors Caron** and **Cors Fochno** to small basin raised bogs less than 5 ha in area.

By far the most extensive peatland type in Wales is blanket bog, which covers around 70,000 ha of the uplands. Much of it came into existence through human activity – the tree felling which began in the **Bronze Age** and which precipitated waterlogging and the acidification of land. Blanket peat is the source of most of the rivers that rise in central Wales. Such peatlands generally have a restricted range of vegetation, although some of them have been extensively colonized by *Rhododendron ponticum*, which dominates many parts of the uplands.

Much rarer than ombrogenous peatlands are minerotrophic peatlands – those influenced by water that has become enriched with minerals as a result of passage through or over the ground. This heterogeneous category encompasses a wide variety of fen habitats occurring in depressions, river floodplains and seepage zones on sloping ground. Fens fed by water rich in base nutrients support many species and **plant** communities of particular nature conservation interest; key sites include Crymlyn Bog (**Swansea/Coedffranc**) and Cors Goch (**Anglesey**).

Traditionally, peat – much of it located on **common land** – was cut for fuel, roofing material and livestock bedding. Turbary, a commoners' right to cut peat, was widely exercised until the mid-20th century; indeed, it was only then that peat ceased to be the main source of heating on many upland farms. The exploitation of peatland to provide peat for horticultural purposes and for the production of fuel on a commercial scale – industries extensively practised in

Ireland – has not taken root in Wales. Indeed, peatlands have come to be regarded as fragile environments worthy of conservation, both for their characteristic flora and fauna, and for the archaeological material hidden within them.

PEATE, Iorwerth [Cyfeiliog] (1901–82)
Poet and scholar

Founder, with **Cyril Fox**, and first curator (1948–71) of the Welsh Folk Museum (now the National History Museum; *see* **St Fagans**), Peate was born in **Llanbrynmair**. His interest in folk studies was kindled at **Aberystwyth**, where he studied under the anthropologist **H. J. Fleure** and the poet **T. Gwynn Jones**. The vision he realized at St Fagans, in the face of considerable discouragement, even from within the **National Museum**, was inspired by the open-air museums of Scandinavia. He published innovative works on folk culture, in **Welsh** and **English**, and was a pioneer in establishing the study of folk life as a respected academic discipline in **Britain**. He was a strong believer in **pacifism** and in a monoglot Welsh-speaking Wales. A selection of his poetry – romantic and stylistically conservative – was published in *Canu Chwarter Canrif* (1957).

PEBIDIOG *Cantref*

One of the seven *cantrefi* of **Dyfed**, Pebidiog (or Dewisland) extended from **Fishguard** to **St David's**. One version of the Welsh **Laws** states that Pebidiog was to render nothing to the lord of **Dyfed**, and **J. E. Lloyd** maintained that it had 'no other lord in early times save the successor of St **David**'. By the 12th century, the *cantref* was an episcopal barony held directly of the English crown by the bishop of St David's. Considerable parts of it were subinfeudated, causing 10 mesne **manors** to be established within the barony. Following the **disestablishment of the Church of England in Wales** in 1920, the manorial titles became the property of the **University of Wales**. At auctions held in 1987, 1988 and 2000, they were acquired by the type of buyers who relish the right to be called lords and ladies of the manor.

PECHAM or PECKHAM, John (d.1292)
Archbishop of Canterbury

As head (1279–92) of the archdiocese of which Wales was a part, Pecham was involved in the **Edwardian conquest**. The self-appointed mediator between **Llywelyn ap Gruffudd** and Edward I (*see* **English monarchs and Wales**), his visit to Llywelyn in November 1282 produced from Llywelyn's vassals a declaration that they would not yield to a king whose language and **laws** were unfamiliar to them. Pecham viewed the Welsh with condescension and described their laws as the work of the devil. In 1284, he visited the four Welsh **dioceses**, showing concern for discipline, and support for the rights of the Welsh Church.

PEERS, Donald (1909–73) Singer

An exceptionally popular singer in the late 1940s and early 1950s, inducing screaming and swooning among female audiences throughout **Britain**, Peers was the son of an **Ammanford** colliery worker. Intended for a teaching career, he ran away from his Plymouth Brethren family background and eventually made his **broadcasting** debut in 1927. His first major success was 'In a Shady Nook (By a Babbling Brook)' (1944), which became his theme tune. Many other hits followed; he made his last Top Ten entry in 1968.

PELAGIANISM

This doctrine, first formulated by the Brythonic Christian Pelagius (*c.*360–*c.*420), rejects the concept of original sin and maintains that individuals take the initial steps towards salvation by their own efforts and not by the sole virtue of divine grace. This optimistic creed was rejected decisively by the Council of Carthage (AD 418), from which time Pelagianism was deemed heretical by the Christian Church. To challenge its influence, Bishop Germanus (**Garmon**) of Auxerre was sent to **Britain** in 429 and probably again in 447.

Pelagianism resurfaced in Wales in the late 18th century with the growing influence of **Arminianism** and **Arianism**, and again in the 20th century with the widespread acceptance of theological liberalism among **Nonconformists**. It found a scholarly champion in the theologian and author **Pennar Davies**.

PELENNA, Neath Port Talbot
(2001 ha; 1173 inhabitants)
Occupying the basin of the Pelenna, a tributary of the Afan, the **community** contains the settlements of Pontrhydyfen, Efail-fach and Tonmawr. **Coal**mining began in earnest following the linking of Tonmawr with the main line via **Brunel**'s South Wales Mineral **Railway**. The community has been extensively forested. Pontrhydyfen, the birthplace of **Richard Burton**, has an impressive viaduct (1827). Near the Gyfylchi railway tunnel to **Glyncorrwg** is Pelenna **Mountain** Centre.

PEMBREY and BURRY PORT
(Pen-bre a Phorth Tywyn), Carmarthenshire
(4266 ha; 7957 inhabitants)
Located west of **Llanelli**, the **community** – known until 2000 as Cefn Sidan – contains the large villages of Burry Port and Pembrey. Cefn Sidan (silken bank) is the name of the wide expanse of sand that extends from the estuary of the **Llwchwr** to that of the Gwendraeth. In 2005, spikes embedded in the sands during the **Second World War**, to forestall an enemy landfall, were removed, and the RAF began using the beach to test the landing and take-off of Hercules transport planes 'in desert conditions'. **Shipwrecks** on the sands were frequent, some of them caused by local residents who used lights to lure **ships** to their fate. Cargoes were then seized by smashing open holds with hatchets – a practice which led to the epithet, 'the hatchet men of Pembrey'. Among the ships lost was *La Jeune Emma* (1828), commemorated by a plaque in St **Illtud**'s church; a niece of Empress Josephine was among those drowned. The church (13th and 14th centuries) contains numerous memorials to local **gentry** families. Cwrt Farm is a ruined medieval-to-17th-century house.

While the ancient **parish** was Pembrey, **population** growth was concentrated to the east at Burry Port, which was an **urban district** from 1903 until 1974. From the mid-19th century onwards, Burry Port developed as a centre of **copper** and **tinplate** works and acquired a dock capable of

Amelia Earhart, who landed at Burry Port in 1928

handling ships up to the equivalent of 1860 tonnes. The explosives industry, initiated in 1881, reached its climax during the **Second World War** when over 2000 were employed in their manufacture. By the late 20th century, virtually all the industries that had led to the urbanization of the area had closed. The community contains a firing range, an extensive **Forestry Commission** plantation, a coastal park and a county park with a dry ski slope and miniature **railway**. Adjoining the park was an airfield, which has been converted into the Welsh **Motor Sports** Centre. In 1928, Amelia Earhart ended her trans-Atlantic flight – the first such flight by a **woman** – at Burry Port.

PEMBROKE Marcher-lordship
Established in 1093 following the invasion of **Dyfed** by Roger de **Montgomery**, earl of Shrewsbury, its castle was entrusted to Gerald de Windsor, grandfather of **Giraldus Cambrensis**. The Welsh never succeeded in capturing **Pembroke** Castle and its impregnability became the key factor in the consolidation of the lordship. Its lords claimed royal jurisdiction over the lordship itself – essentially the ancient *cantref* of **Penfro** – and also the lordships of **Daugleddau**, **Rhos**, **Walwyn's Castle** and **Narberth**. Pembroke was second in size only to **Glamorgan** among the **march**er-lordships of Wales, and attained the status of a county palatine. It came into the possession of the **Clare** family in 1138, from whom it passed in turn to the **Marshal**, Munchensey, **Valence** and **Hastings** families. Granted to Jasper **Tudor** in 1452 and to William **Herbert** in 1458, the lordship passed to the crown in 1495. In 1536, the lordship, with some additions, became **Pembrokeshire**.

PEMBROKE (Penfro), Pembrokeshire
(1169 ha; 7241 inhabitants)
Located on a southern inlet of the **Milford Haven Waterway**, the area was populated in the Mesolithic era, as the flint tools discovered in Wogan **cave** indicate (*see* **Palaeolithic and Mesolithic Ages**). In 1093, the ridge above the cave became the site of a castle, which came to be

657

known as Pembroke – an Anglicized version of **Penfro**, the southernmost *cantref* of **Dyfed**. Originally built by Arnulf de **Montgomery**, the castle was never captured by the Welsh and was central to the destruction of Welsh power in south-west Dyfed. It was the administrative centre of the extensive **march**er-lordship of **Pembroke** and the launching pad of the Anglo-**Norman** (or rather Cambro-Norman) invasion of **Ireland** in 1169. The castle's finest feature is its 22-m high round tower (*c.*1204), built under William **Marshal**. In the 13th century, Pembroke, with a **population** of up to 2000, was one of the largest towns in Wales; parts of the town walls survive as does much of the 14th-century fabric of St Mary's church. Devastated by the **Black Death**, the town also suffered from the temporary extinction of the earldom of Pembroke in 1399. The earldom was granted to Jasper **Tudor** in 1452, and in 1457 the castle was the birthplace of his nephew, Henry Tudor (Henry VII).

Pembroke supported the Parliamentarians in the first **Civil War**, and the Royalists in the second; in 1648, **Oliver Cromwell** subjected the town to a seven-week siege and then ordered the blowing-up of much of the castle. From the late 17th century to the mid-19th century, the town enjoyed modest prosperity; according to Daniel Defoe, it was in 1727 'the largest and richest and … most flourishing town of all south Wales'. From the 18th and 19th centuries date the pleasant houses in its long, aptly named, Main Street, its several chapels and the churches of St Michael, Pembroke, and St Daniel, Windmill Hill. From the **Act of 'Union'** until 1918, Pembroke was the chief constituent part of the Pembroke **Boroughs** constituency.

In the **community**'s western suburb, Monkton, is St Nicholas's Church, established *c.*1098 as a cell of the **Benedictine** monastery of Seez in Normandy. It contains memorials to the Meyrick and Owen families. Monkton Old Hall, originally the guesthouse of the priory, contains a fine 14th-century vaulted undercroft.

PEMBROKE DOCK (Doc Penfro),
Pembrokeshire (627 ha; 8676 inhabitants)

Until 1974, when it became a separate **community**, Pembroke Dock was a ward of the **borough** of **Pembroke**. The place owes its origins to the Admiralty's decision *c.*1810 to locate a dockyard there, a decision commemorated by an obelisk in Albion Square. A 4-m wall surrounds the dockyard, beyond which the town was laid out as a grid. Originally, the Royal Marines were housed in the woodenwall, the *Dragon*; the Defensible Barracks, built of fine stonework, were completed in 1845, the Lanion Barracks in the 1850s and the Pennar Barracks in 1875. Other buildings include the chapel (1831), the captain superintendent's house (1835) and the guards' house (1840).

The dockyard's first two **ships** – the *Valorous* and the *Ariadne* – were launched in 1816, and over the following 110 years more than 260 ships were built, including the *Royal William* (1833), the first ship to carry over 100 guns, and the *Duke of Wellington* (1852), briefly the most powerful warship in the world. The small warships built at Pembroke Dock became obsolete following the launching of the *Dreadnought* in 1906. The dockyard closed in 1926 and thereafter, until 1939, unemployment among the town's insured males rarely

Pembroke Castle

fell below 50%. An RAF flying boat base established at the dockyard site in 1930 brought some relief; but in 1935 Pembroke Dock was the only place outside the south Wales **coal**field to be included in Wales's unemployment-blighted 'special area'. The town suffered severe bombing during the **Second World War**, notably during a raid in 1940, which caused an 18-day conflagration, the worst in **Britain** since the Great Fire of **London** in 1666. The departure of the RAF in 1959 and the closure of Lanion Barracks were further serious losses. **Irish** Ferries sail twice daily from Pembroke Dock to Rosslare. The **population** of Pembroke Dock peaked in 1911, when it had 11,336 inhabitants compared with the 4337 in Pembroke itself. The literary journal *Dock Leaves* (from 1957, the *Anglo-Welsh Review*; *see* **Periodicals**), was founded in Pembroke Dock in 1949 by Raymond Garlick (b.1926) and Roland Mathias (1915–2007).

PEMBROKESHIRE (Sir Benfro)
(162,063 ha; 114,131 inhabitants)
The **Act of 'Union'** of 1536 declared that 'the lordships ... of Haverforde West, Kilgarran, Lansteffan, Laugeharne ... Walwynscastle, Dewysland, Lannchadeyrn, Lanfey, Nerberth, Slebeyche, Rosemarkett, Castellan and Llandofleure ... shall be united ... to the county of Pembroke'. (**Llansteffan**, **Laugharne** and **Llanddowror** were transferred to **Carmarthenshire** in 1543.) The **county** mentioned in the Act was a county palatine – the area directly administered from **Pembroke** Castle. Yet, as the earls of Pembroke had long claimed that their court had jurisdiction over most of the lordships listed in the 1536 Act, the new county was to a high degree the old county palatine writ large. In the main, it represented the re-creation of the kingdom of **Dyfed**, for, of Dyfed's seven *cantrefi*, all but eastern **Emlyn** and eastern **Cantref Gwarthaf** were within the new county's boundaries.

The county's most distinctive feature is its **Welsh**-speaking north and **English**-speaking south, the result of **Flemish** and English migration into the areas south of **Mynydd Preseli** from the early 11th century onwards. The linguistic boundary – the Landsker – traditionally ran from **Amroth** in the east to Newgale (**Brawdy**) in the west. Linguistic change could be very abrupt. In 1921, 97% of the inhabitants of the **parish** of Llandeloy spoke Welsh; the figure for the parish of **Nolton**, less than 10 km away, was 3%. Subsequently, the contrast became less abrupt as Anglicization reduced the Welsh-speaking proportion in the north and as migration and Welsh-language learning increased the proportion in the south. In 2001, 29.35% of the inhabitants of Pembrokeshire had some knowledge of Welsh, with 16.35% wholly fluent in the language. (*See also* **East Williamston** and **Eglwyswrw**.)

Agriculture has traditionally been the mainstay of the county's **economy**, with south Pembrokeshire having some of Wales's most fertile **soil** and its most favourable **climate**. The mining of anthracite in what is the western end of the south Wales **coal**field was significant from the 18th to the early 20th century. **Fish**ing was a major industry at **Milford Haven**, but was replaced in the 1960s by a short-lived boom in **oil** importation. By the early 21th century, **tourism** had become a leading source of revenue, especially within the Pembrokeshire Coast **National Park**, established in 1952.

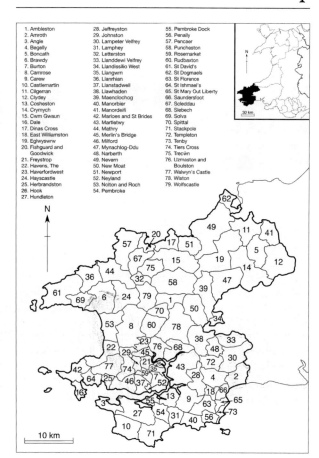

1. Ambleston	28. Jeffreyston	55. Pembroke Dock
2. Amroth	29. Johnston	56. Penally
3. Angle	30. Lampeter Velfrey	57. Pencaer
4. Begelly	31. Lamphey	58. Puncheston
5. Boncath	32. Letterston	59. Rosemarket
6. Brawdy	33. Llanddewi Velfrey	60. Rudbaxton
7. Burton	34. Llandissilio West	61. St David's
8. Camrose	35. Llangwm	62. St Dogmaels
9. Carew	36. Llanrhian	63. St Florence
10. Castlemartin	37. Llanstadwell	64. St Ishmael's
11. Cilgerran	38. Llawhaden	65. St Mary Out Liberty
12. Clydey	39. Maenclochog	66. Saundersfoot
13. Cosheston	40. Manorbier	67. Scleddau
14. Crymych	41. Manordeifi	68. Slebech
15. Cwm Gwaun	42. Marloes and St Brides	69. Spittal
16. Dale	43. Martletwy	70. Solva
17. Dinas Cross	44. Mathry	71. Stackpole
18. East Williamston	45. Merlin's Bridge	72. Templeton
19. Eglwyswrw	46. Milford	73. Tenby
20. Fishguard and Goodwick	47. Mynachlog-Ddu	74. Tiers Cross
21. Freystrop	48. Narberth	75. Trecŵn
22. Havens, The	49. Nevern	76. Uzmaston and Boulston
23. Haverfordwest	50. New Moat	77. Walwyn's Castle
24. Hayscastle	51. Newport	78. Wiston
25. Herbrandston	52. Neyland	79. Wolfscastle
26. Hook	53. Nolton and Roch	
27. Hundleton	54. Pembroke	

N

10 km

30 km

The communities of the county of Pembrokeshire

Of Wales's counties, Pembrokeshire has the longest coastline (230 km). Almost half the surface area of Pembrokeshire lies within the basin of the Eastern and Western **Cleddau**, **rivers** which form the Daugleddau estuary or the **Milford Haven Waterway**. The Cleddau rivers have their source in Mynydd Preseli; rich in prehistoric monuments and legends, the **mountains** have perhaps inspired more affection than any other place in Wales.

On the eve of the abolition of the county in 1974, it consisted of the **boroughs** of **Haverfordwest**, Pembroke and **Tenby**, the **urban districts** of **Fishguard**, Milford Haven, **Narberth** and **Neyland** and the **rural districts** of **Cemais**, Haverfordwest, Narberth and Pembroke.

Following abolition, **South Pembrokeshire** and **Preseli Pembrokeshire** came into existence as two of the six districts of the county of **Dyfed**. That county was abolished in 1996, when Pembrokeshire was re-established as a unitary authority.

PEMBROKESHIRE COAST PATH, The
Opened in 1970, this 295-km path extends from **Amroth** in the south to **St Dogmaels** in the north. It traverses the finest cliff scenery in Wales, particularly around Strumble Head (**Pencaer**), **St David's**, the Elegug Stacks and the Green Bridge of Wales (**Castlemartin**). To walk it in May, with **seals** calving in the inaccessible bays of the north and the spring **plants** and **bird**life at their best, is one of the outdoor delights of the nation. But the path has substantial demerits. There are oppressively large caravan parks in the

Penarth pier

south, and military prohibitions and quixotic exclusions along much of the Castlemartin peninsula – the most impressive stretch of **limestone** coast in **Britain** – cause the path to divert through **oil** refineries and industrial complexes. The **National Park** authority in **Pembrokeshire** has been accused of being disinclined to extend and regularize access to this coast – but one can sample the delights of the south, and walk only the northern portion in its entirety.

PENAL CODE, The

On the outbreak of the **Glyndŵr Revolt**, the English parliament imposed penal statutes on Wales. The first series (1401) was intended to threaten the Welsh **gentry** into submission. Welshmen were not allowed to purchase lands in or near English **border** towns or to settle in them. Those who had already settled in towns were to give surety for their loyalty but were not to hold office. Englishmen who were accused of crime by Welshmen could be convicted only by English justices. The second series (1402) repeated these restrictions and added that Welshmen were not to gather together without licence, bear arms in public or guard castles. The same restrictions applied to Englishmen married to Welsh wives. Although these statutes were not revoked until 1624, they lost much of their impact during the 15th century.

PENALLY (Penalun), Pembrokeshire
(881 ha; 856 inhabitants)

Located immediately west of **Tenby**, the **community** contains a section of the **Pembrokeshire Coast Footpath**. Hoyle's Mouth **Cave** has yielded stone tools of the Upper **Palaeolithic** era. Penally, which may have been the site of a

clas or **Celt**ic monastery, was reputedly the birthplace of St **Teilo**. The superb Penally cross with its triple-beaded knotwork (probably *c.*930) stands in the south transept of St Nicholas's church (13th and 14th century); in the vestry is a fragment of another early cross (*see* **Monuments, Early Christian**). Near the boundary with **St Florence** are the medieval houses of Carswell and West Tarr. During the **Civil Wars**, Trefloyne was the headquarters of the Royalist leader Richard Vaughan, earl of Carbery (*see* **Vaughan family (Golden Grove)**). Members of the Trefloyne family have been generous benefactors of the **University of Wales, Aberystwyth**. Lydstep Haven is a delightful sandy bay dominated by a caravan park. Near it is Lydstep Palace, a medieval hall house.

PENARTH, Vale of Glamorgan
(714 ha; 20,396 inhabitants)

Among the citizens of Penarth, there are those who see themselves as the inhabitants of Wales's most salubrious, opulent and exclusive **community** – a notion at odds with conditions in much of the town. The name means the head (*pen*) of a promontory (*garth*), inspired no doubt by the headland rising above the estuaries of the **Taff** and **Ely Rivers**. Until the mid-19th century, the area's only significant buildings were St Augustine's church on the headland – its saddleback tower a landmark for sailors – the **Norman** church of St Peter's, Cogan, and Cogan Pill, a substantial 16th-century house.

Change began in 1859 when the Taff Vale **Railway** Company sponsored the building of a tidal harbour on the Ely. A masonry dock followed in 1865 and that was enlarged in 1884. Activity reached its peak in 1913 when

Penarth Docks exported the equivalent of 4.5 million tonnes of **coal**, 17% of the total coal exports of the **Port** of **Cardiff** (Cardiff's Bute Docks, together with Penarth and **Barry**). Dock building meant that urban Penarth began as a working-**class** community, a fact still evident in the terraced houses of Cogan. However, the leading local landowner, the **Windsor-Clive family**, was eager to ensure that Penarth became a seaside resort and a place of residence for Cardiff's elite. The resort ambitions are evident in the Railway Hotel (c.1860), the public baths (1885), the **pier** (1894) and the Paget Rooms (1906). Even more evident are the commodious villas; most of them were designed by Harry Snell, architect to the Windsor-Clive estate, although the more idiosyncratic are the work of the Arts and Crafts architect **J. C. Carter**, who also designed the exuberant **parish** hall. The town's crowning glory is William Butterfield's St Augustine's church (1866) with its breathtaking polychromatic interior. Other public buildings include Turner House, built in 1888 to house the collection of a local art lover, **James Pyke Thompson**, which became an outstation of the **National Museum** in 1921.

Penarth's role as Cardiff's premier satellite town increased as the port declined. The dock was closed in 1963 and its environs rapidly deteriorated. From 1984 onwards, it experienced rebirth as a marina and was surrounded by attractive housing developments. The very fine baroque **Custom** House and Marine Buildings with a French pavilion roof (both 1865) survive. Near them is the southern end of Cardiff Bay Barrage, completed in 2001. Within Penarth's boundaries is Cosmeston **Lakes** Country Park, established within a disused quarry. The adjoining medieval village lies within the boundaries of **Sully**.

PENBRYN, Ceredigion (3358 ha; 1283 inhabitants)
Extending inland from the coast between **Llangrannog** and **Aberporth**, the **community** contains the seaside village of Tresaith, the clifftop settlement of Penbryn and the inland villages of Brynhoffnant, Glynarthen, Sarnau and Tan-y-groes. The 6th-century inscribed stone (*see* **Monuments, Early Christian**) at Penbryn commemorating Corbalengus notes that he was an 'Ordovician', suggesting that he was proud of his northern origins (*see* **Ordovices**). At Tresaith, a **waterfall** gushes over a cliff into a delightful bay. The place was the home of the novelist Allen Raine (**Anne Puddicombe**).

PENCAER (Pen-caer), Pembrokeshire
(3588 ha; 424 inhabitants)
Constituting a magnificent peninsula west of **Fishguard**, the **community** contains the villages of Granston, Llangloffan, Llanwnda and St Nicholas. There are **Neolithic** burial chambers at Llanwnda and St Nicholas, a **Bronze Age** standing stone at St Nicholas and two **Iron Age hill-forts** above Pwll Deri. The churches of St Gwyndaf and St Nicholas retain their medieval simplicity; in the latter is a bilingual (**Latin** and **ogham**) stone. The French force of 1400 men that landed at Carregwastad Point in 1797 is known as the **last invasion of Britain**. The dramatically sited **lighthouse** (1908) on Strumble Head is Wales's nearest point to **Ireland**. The **Baptist** chapel at Llangloffan (1862) is a handsome building. Above Pwll Deri's exquisite cove is a memorial to Dewi Emrys (David Emrys James; 1881–1952), whose poem 'Pwllderi' is perhaps the most appealing poem to a place in the whole of Welsh **literature**. Tregwynt is one of Wales's few surviving **woollen** mills.

PENCARREG, Carmarthenshire
(3461 ha; 1123 inhabitants)
Located across the **Teifi** from **Lampeter**, the **community** contains the village of Pencarreg, the Lampeter suburb of Cwmann and the hamlet of Esgairdawe. St Patrick's church (1878) there contains a 12th-century font. **Congregationalists** first gathered at Esgairdawe in 1690. In 1979, three distinguished Welsh people attacked the television mast on Mynydd Pencarreg (415 m) as part of the campaign to secure a **Welsh-language** television channel (*see* **S4C**). Pencarreg **cheese** enjoys a high reputation.

PENCERDD, Y (Chief of Song)
A medieval term for a poet who was an officer of the king's domain and who, perhaps, later became an officer of the court. He had his own chair at court and his duty, according to the **Law**s of **Hywel Dda**, was to sing before the king, firstly to God and secondly to the king.

PENCOED (Pen-coed), Bridgend
(877 ha; 8623 inhabitants)
This heavily urbanized **community** straddles the **M4** northeast of **Bridgend**. The Sony **Electronics** plant, once a major source of local employment, shed thousands of its workforce in 2005. Dyffryn is an interesting 16th-century house.

PENDINE (Pentywyn), Carmarthenshire
(410 ha; 351 inhabitants)
Located on the coast south-west of **St Clears**, the **community**'s chief feature is its sands, part of the 10-km stretch that extends along the coast of Carmarthen Bay. In 1927, Malcolm Campbell and **Parry Thomas** attempted to break the world speed record on the sands. Parry Thomas was killed when his car *Babs* veered off course and somersaulted. *Babs* remained buried in the sand until 1969; now refurbished, the car is occasionally exhibited in the nearby Museum of Speed. The Ministry of Defence uses the sands as an experimental weapons site. Its camp adjoins a large caravan park. In 2001, 71.47% of the inhabitants of Pendine had no knowledge at all of Welsh, making it, linguistically, the most Anglicized of the communities of **Carmarthenshire**.

PENDOYLAN (Pendeulwyn), Vale of Glamorgan
(1490 ha; 508 inhabitants)
Situated on the west bank of the **Ely**, the **community**'s chief feature is Hensol Castle. The building began as the modest residence of the ardent Royalist judge **David Jenkins** (1582–1663). It was eventually inherited by William Talbot who in 1735 added two wings – among the earliest examples of neo-Gothic in **Britain**. There were further extensions in the 1790s, 1840s, 1880s and 1900s, leading to the creation of a vast mansion. In the 1950s, it became a settlement for those with mental health difficulties, then later a conference centre and part of a plan for a hotel and spa. To the north is Llanerch, Wales's most successful **vineyard**.

St Cadoc's, Pendoylan, has a large west tower of *c*.1500. Near it are cottages built as almshouses in 1817 and attractive examples of 1950s council housing.

PENFRO *Cantref*
Penfro – the land south of the **Milford Haven Waterway** – was the southernmost of the seven *cantrefi* of the kingdom of **Dyfed**. Following **Norman** incursions, it became the core of the **marcher**-lordship of **Pembroke**.

PENGAM, Caerphilly (239 ha; 3842 inhabitants)
The **community** adjoins the **Rhymney** west of **Blackwood**. The well-known school Lewis Pengam is in fact in the community of **Gelligaer**. Pengam includes the settlement of Fleur de Lys. Originally, the name was probably that of a tavern; its local pronunciation is illustrated by **Harri Webb**'s limerick:

There was a young fellow from Fleur-de-Lys
Whose motorbike was of great peur-de-lys.
Sometimes, just for fun,
He'd knock up a ton,
That's a hundred miles an heure-de-lys.

PENHOW (Pen-hŵ), Newport
(796 ha; 770 inhabitants)
A **community** located on the eastern boundary of the **county** of **Newport**. Its chief settlement is the village of Parc-Seymour (a name derived from St Maur in **Norman**dy), named after the Seymour family which held Penhow Castle from the 12th century to the 14th, and from which Henry VIII's third wife, Jane Seymour, was descended.

The castle, with its 12th-century rectangular tower and its 14th-century hall range, was remodelled as a mansion *c*.1700. It contains handsome panelled rooms and fine fireplaces. Purchased by a **film** director, Stephen Weeks, in 1973, the castle has been extensively restored and opened to the public. The 4-m long elm table in the great hall was built in situ – following medieval practice – in 1977. The castle and the adjoining church and rectory form an attractive group. Medieval peasant houses have been excavated near the church, the possible site of a **Roman** villa. When **George Borrow** walked through Penhow in 1854, he found that there were among its inhabitants many people who knew no language apart from **Welsh**.

PENILLION SINGING (*Canu penillion*)
The uniquely Welsh art of singing poetry (*penillion*: verses) to **harp** accompaniment is also referred to as *cerdd dant* (string craft) or *canu gyda'r tannau* (singing with the strings). There are those who believe that it has its origins in medieval *cerdd dant* – the instrumental **music** that enjoyed comparable status with *cerdd dafod* (tongue craft), the art of the poet. However, it is generally considered that *penillion* singing represents a much more recent tradition, established in the 18th century. The essence of the craft is that the poetry is sung to one melody while the harp accompaniment follows another, so that the stressed syllables of the poem coincide with the accented beats of the harp melody.

Traditionally, *canu penillion* was the impromptu craft of the individual singer, often in a competitive context, but during the 20th century much of this extemporaneous expertise was lost. Settings began to be prepared in advance, leading to more polished musical arrangements, and the development of group or choral presentations. In 1934, the society Cymdeithas Cerdd Dant Cymru was founded to promote the craft; it holds a national festival annually.

PENLLERGAER (Penlle'r-gaer), Swansea
(602 ha; 2434 inhabitants)
Once a scatter of cottages on the edge of **Gorseinon** common, the **community** has been extensively urbanized and industrialized, developments encouraged by convenient access to the **M4**. The former **Lliw Valley** District Council headquarters stood on the site of Penllergare, a large mansion built in the mid-1830s. It was the home of **Lewis Weston Dillwyn** (1777–1855) and of his son, **John Dillwyn-Llewelyn** (1810–82), who landscaped the valley running south from the mansion, thus creating one of the great **gardens** of Wales. A pioneer of **photography**, Llewelyn's fine views of the estate in the 1850s have been preserved. The mansion became derelict and, in 1961, was blown up as an army training exercise. A lodge and Dillwyn's observatory survive. One of the mansion's bedrooms was reconstructed at Llysdinam, **Powys** (*see* **Llanafan Fawr**). Despite many years of disuse and neglect and the draining of the 8-ha **lake**, many of the principal landscape features remain and are undergoing restoration.

PENLLYN *Cantref* and rural district
Meaning the head of the **lake** (**Bala** Lake or Llyn Tegid), the *cantref* originally contained the **commotes** of **Dinmael**, **Edeirnion**, Penllyn Is **Tryweryn** and Penllyn Uwch Tryweryn, although, by the High Middle Ages, Dinmael and Edeirnion had ceased to be part of Penllyn. Although traditionally part of **Powys**, **Llywelyn ap Iorwerth** brought it within the orbit of **Gwynedd**. In 1284, Penllyn became part of the newly created **county** of **Merioneth**. Considered the heartland of **Welsh**-speaking rural Wales, Penllyn has made a wholly disproportionate contribution to Welsh life. Although its **population** has never exceeded 4000, it produced three of the first six wardens of the **University of Wales** guild of graduates. From 1894 to 1974, Penllyn was one of Merioneth's **rural districts**.

PENLLYN (Pen-llin), Vale of Glamorgan
(2312 ha; 1516 inhabitants)
Located north of **Cowbridge**, the **community** contains the villages of Penllyn, Llansannor, Pentre Meyrick, Trerhingyll and Ystradowen. The area's original centre was probably Llanfrynach, now the site of a deserted village. Uniquely among the medieval churches of the **Vale of Glamorgan**, St Brynach's church was left virtually untouched by Victorian restorers and still stands in splendid isolation. Penllyn Castle was probably built for Robert le Norris, sheriff of **Glamorgan** in 1126. Adjoining it is a castellated mansion, originally built for the Turbervilles in the late 16th century and rebuilt for the Gwinnetts between 1789 and 1804. To the north lies

Fferm Goch, 24 houses designed by **T. Alwyn Lloyd** and built c.1936 as an agricultural settlement for unemployed miners.

To the east lies the growing village of Ystradowen, where the church, built by **John Prichard** in 1868 as a replica of its medieval predecessor, is overlooked by Glamorgan's second largest motte. At the centre of the community is the village of Llansannor where the restored 13th-century church contains a fine stone **sculpture** of an armoured knight, carved c.1400. Llansannor Court, a late 16th-century mansion, offers a striking contrast with Court Drive, eight 1970s houses built in a starkly modernistic style.

PENMAEN (Pen-maen), Caerphilly
(482 ha; 4478 inhabitants)

Located west of the Sirhowy, the **community** includes the township of Oakdale, a garden city designed by A. F. Webb for the **Tredegar Iron** and **Coal** Company, whose Oakdale Colliery was opened in 1907. Consisting of 660 houses in a complex symmetrical arrangement, it has been described by John Newman as 'by far the most ambitious attempt by any mining company in south Wales to provide planned **housing** for its workforce'. The Oakdale Workmen's Institute has been removed and re-erected at the National History Museum at **St Fagans**. The congregation gathered by Henry Walter at Penmaen c.1640 was one of Wales's earliest groups of Dissenters (*see* **Nonconformists and Dissenters**).

PENMAENMAWR (Penmaen-mawr),
Conwy (1524 ha; 3857 inhabitants)

Located immediately west of **Conwy**, the **community** contains the village of Penmaenmawr and the hamlets of Dwygyfylchi and Capelulo. Craiglwyd was an important **Neolithic** centre of stone axe manufacture. Large-scale quarrying of **granite** for **road** setts has destroyed Braich y Ddinas **hill-fort**. The **trade union**ist **Huw T. Edwards** came from a Penmaenmawr quarrying family. By the 1860s, the place was promoting itself as a resort for summer visitors. It found favour with **William Ewart Gladstone**, whose bust adorns the village centre; he found bathing in the sea there later than May to be too enervating an experience. The promontories of Penmaen-mawr and Penmaen-bach prevented the emergence of a convenient coastal route into the heartland of **Gwynedd**. Indeed, it was not until the completion of the first tunnels on the **A55** in 1935 that those travelling west of Conwy were spared the hazardous journey over Pen y Clip. Horeb Independent chapel (1813) is a handsome building.

PENMYNYDD, Isle of Anglesey
(1300 ha; 422 inhabitants)

Located immediately north of **Llanfair Pwllgwyngyll**, the **community**'s sole settlement of any size is Star. Penmynydd was among the lands granted by **Llywelyn ap Iorwerth** to his seneschal, **Ednyfed Fychan**, ancestor of the **Tudor family**. As the residence of the family's senior line, it is considered to be the cradle of the Tudor dynasty. The present Plas Penmynydd (1576, 17th century) is on the site of the medieval house; but the **Anglesey** family was of little account after 1485 and made no attempt to profit from its royal connections. The direct male line died out in the late 17th century. St Gredifael's church contains the tomb of Goronwy ap Tudur (d.1382). Near the church are attractive almshouses (1620). The ridge overlooking the Cefni valley is considered to be the boundary between Sir Fôn Fach (Little Anglesey) and Sir Fôn Fawr (Great Anglesey).

PENNAL, Gwynedd (4171 ha; 355 inhabitants)

Located between **Machynlleth** and **Aberdovey**, the **community** contains the head of the **Dyfi** estuary. The remains of the Pennal **Roman** auxiliary fort have been almost wholly obliterated by cultivation. Domen Las motte was probably the administrative centre of the **commote** of **Ystumanner**. It was from Pennal that **Owain Glyndŵr** in 1406 sent his famous letter to Charles VI of France (*see* **Pennal Letter, The**); the event is commemorated in an impressive **painting** in St Peter's church (1769), which contains much of the building material of the medieval church. One of the best **love** poems in the **Welsh language**, **Llywelyn Goch**'s elegy for Lleucu Llwyd, is dedicated to the fair lady of Pennal. Plas Talgarth, a holiday complex, was for generations associated with the Thurston family. The community contains the Tarren series of hills.

PENNAL LETTER, The

A document sent from **Pennal** by **Owain Glyndŵr** to Charles VI of France on 31 March 1406. Owain agreed to transfer the spiritual allegiance of Wales from the Pope resident in Rome to the one resident in Avignon. His terms included two universities for Wales – one in the north and one in the south – an independent Welsh church and priests conversant with the **Welsh language**. The letter, preserved in the French national archives, was exhibited on loan at the **National Library of Wales** in 2000.

PENNANT family Landowners and industrialists

This was one of the most powerful families in 19th-century Wales, and the pre-eminent force in the development of the **slate** industry. The **Liverpool** merchant and MP Richard Pennant (?1737–1808), with widespread interests in Jamaica (*see* **Slavery**), acquired the Penrhyn estate through marriage in 1765. He developed the slate deposits on his land into the Penrhyn Quarries, and the town of **Bethesda** was established nearby. Elevated to the Irish peerage as Baron Penrhyn in 1783, he invested in infrastructure such as **roads** and a harbour at Port Penrhyn (**Llandygai**) to export the slate, and by the early 1790s he was employing 400 men. The quarries were to become the most important producer of slate in the world. The Penrhyn estates were inherited by his cousin George Hay Dawkins (1764–1840). He adopted the name Dawkins-Pennant in 1816 and was responsible for building the enormous Norman-revivalist Penrhyn Castle (Llandygai) (architect, Thomas Hopper). On his death, the estate passed to Edward Gordon Douglas (1800–86), who assumed the name Douglas-Pennant and was MP for **Caernarfonshire** from 1841 until elevated to the British peerage as Baron Penrhyn in 1866. He was succeeded in 1886 by George Sholto Douglas-Pennant (1836–1907), who was involved in a number of bitter strikes and lockouts with the quarrymen of Bethesda (*see* **Penrhyn Lockouts**).

The family, with its massive landholdings, vast castle, estates in Northampton and house in Belgravia, and its allegiance to the **Conservative Party** and the **Anglican** Church, symbolized all that was detested by 19th-century Welsh **radicals**. In 1949, the estate and the title were separated, and in 1951 the castle and much of the estate were transferred to the **National Trust**. In 1873, the family owned 17,795 ha in Caernarfonshire and **Denbighshire**.

PENNANT, Thomas (1726–98)
Naturalist and antiquary

Thomas Pennant was born and died at Downing, **Whitford**; the house was destroyed by fire in 1922. He is remembered chiefly on account of his *Tours in Wales*, which were published originally in two volumes (1778 and 1781; a three-volume edition was prepared by **John Rhŷs** in 1883). Although they cover only the northern **counties**, they provided the model for the numerous accounts of Welsh tours published in the following decades, and were central to the development of the idea among **English** travellers that Wales was intellectually interesting. His servant **Moses Griffith** made the drawings. Pennant's *The History of the Parishes of Whiteford and Holywell* (1796) is a pioneering work on Welsh local history. He was also a successful zoologist, being the first in **Britain** to use Linnaeus's binomial nomenclature (the naming of **plants** and animals using two **Latin** names). According to Sir Gavin de Beer, Pennant was the leading zoologist after John Ray and before Charles Darwin.

A plate from Thomas Pennant's *Genera of Birds* (1773)

PENNARD, Swansea (1164 ha; 2648 inhabitants)

Extending from **Swansea Airport** to Pwlldu Head, the **community** has been extensively urbanized at Kittle and Southgate. Most of it, however, is still agricultural, with evidence of the strip cultivation characteristic of medieval open-field farming still discernible. Pennard Castle stands high above the valley leading to Three Cliffs Bay. It was built *c.*1300 on the site of a simpler fortress erected *c.*1150. Nearby are the remains of Pennard's original church, overwhelmed by sand in the 14th century. Remnants of it were used to build a replacement church 2 km to the east; the poet **Harri Webb** is buried there and a plaque inside the church commemorates the poet **Vernon Watkins**. Kilvrough Manor, built for the Penrice family in the 1770s, but incorporating earlier work, has a five-bay front entered through a porch of cast-**iron** Tuscan columns.

PENNARDD Commote

One of the 10 **commotes** of **Ceredigion**, the commote constituted a wide swathe of the ancient kingdom. It contained the early religious site of **Llanddewi Brefi** and the later monastery of Strata Florida (**Ystrad Fflur**). The name survived in the post-**Acts of 'Union' hundred** of Penarth.

PENNSYLVANIA, Wales's associations with

Given the close ties that have existed between the Welsh and Pennsylvania from the late 17th-century onwards, it would have been fitting if William Penn, its founder, had been permitted to call his colony New Wales, as he had wished. More Welsh people have settled in Pennsylvania than in any other state in the USA (*see* **North America**), and they have played a significant part in its history. Some of the first Welsh communities in colonial North America were established in the 1680s in Meirion and Gwynedd townships in the so-called 'Welsh Tract' on the outskirts of Philadelphia.

It was here that the first **Welsh-language** book printed in America (written by **Ellis Pugh**) was published. In 1890, when the Welsh immigrant presence in the United States was at its strongest, a remarkable 37% were living in Pennsylvania. Among them were America's three largest concentrations of Welsh, located in the counties of Luzerne and Lackawanna (and their respective centres of Wilkes-Barre and Scranton) on the north-east Pennsylvania anthracite **coal**field, and Allegheny County (Pittsburgh). In the first two, especially, the Welsh formed a much larger proportion of the total **population** than was the case in the United States in general.

Pennsylvania's appeal to the Welsh can be attributed to the same factors that made it attractive to immigrants of other nationalities. The state's early establishment as a colony was founded on religious toleration, and the potential of its agricultural land were key factors in stimulating Welsh **Quakers** and other religious dissenters to settle *c.*1680–1720 (*see* **Nonconformists and Dissenters**). In the 19th century, the key impetus to Welsh in-migration was the state's rich mineral resources. From the 1820s onwards, Welsh industrial expertise and skills were crucial in establishing and sustaining Pennsylvania's important coal, **iron**, **slate** and **tinplate** industries. In the period 1850–1920, many of these new Welsh-American industrial communities were important centres of Welsh-language cultural activity

Portmeirion, Penrhyndeudraeth

based on the **eisteddfod**, choral singing and religious Nonconformity. The state was also the home of a number of Welsh-oriented **English newspapers** and **periodicals** in both Welsh and English.

The economic **depression of the interwar years** undermined Pennsylvania's appeal to Welsh immigrants, but, since 1945, Welsh people have continued to settle in the state although not in such large numbers as during the 19th century. In 1990, some 221,964 people in Pennsylvania claimed Welsh ancestry, 2% of the state's population. In the early 21st century, a number of active Welsh societies continue to play an important part in Welsh-American life, and between 1929 and 2002 the Welsh National *Cymanfa Ganu* has been held in the state no fewer than 12 times. The Welsh Society of Philadelphia (established in 1729) is the world's oldest extant Welsh society.

PENPONT ANTIPHONAL, The

A 14th-century church **music** manuscript, believed to be the earliest music manuscript written in Wales by a Welsh person. It was discovered in Penpont mansion (**Trallong**).

PENRHIWCEIBER (Penrhiw-ceibr), Rhondda
Cynon Taff (213 ha; 6265 inhabitants)
Located on the right bank of the Cynon, Penrhiwceiber is essentially a southern extension of **Mountain Ash**. The word *ceibr* means a rafter, and the name probably means a hilltop bearing trees suitable for use as roof timbers. Major development began with the opening of Penrikyber Colliery in 1878. At its peak in 1913, it employed almost 2000 men; it closed in 1985. The Workmen's Institute (1888), now a **community** centre, is the sole surviving institute in the lower Cynon valley. The **clock** tower was built as a memorial to those killed in the **First World War**.

PENRHYN Commote

One of the **commotes** of **Cantref Gwarthaf**, it constituted the promontory (*penrhyn*) that lies between the estuaries of the **Tywi** and the **Taf**. Its administrative centre was at **Llansteffan**. It came to be the **march**er-lordship of Llansteffan.

PENRHYN LOCKOUTS, The

The dispute, a series of bitter industrial struggles in the Penrhyn **slate** quarries, **Bethesda** (1896–7, 1900–3), was one of the longest in British history. It contributed to the decline of the slate industry in **Gwynedd**; the workforce of 18,801 in 1898 had shrunk to 11,658 by 1914. Many people migrated from the area, particularly to the south Wales **coal**field. The lockouts created deep divisions, lasting for generations, between those who remained on strike, displaying signs proclaiming *Nid oes bradwr yn y tŷ hwn* (No traitors in this house), and those who returned to work. Arising from conflict between an owner bent on managing his quarry as he saw fit and a workforce insisting on its right to form a union, the main protagonists were the **North Wales Quarrymen's Union** on the one hand, and the manager, E. A. Young, and the owner, Baron Penrhyn (*see* **Pennant family**), on the other. Both sides were intransigent, reflecting the social and cultural divide between a **Liberal**, **Welsh**-speaking, **Nonconformist** workforce increasingly sympathetic to the

labour movement, and an **English**, **Conservative**, **Anglican** employer. The strikers were maintained by contributions collected throughout **Britain**, especially from **trade unionists**; three choirs toured, collecting funds, and the dispute attracted considerable press attention. Within Wales, the lockouts assumed an abiding symbolic significance as an expression of struggle against oppression.

PENRHYNDEUDRAETH, Gwynedd
(774 ha; 2031 inhabitants)
Located immediately east of Porthmadog, the **community** occupies the headland (*penrhyn*) between the estuaries of the **Rivers** Dwyryd and **Glaslyn**. Penrhyndeudraeth grew following the building in 1810 of the embankment or cob across the mouth of the Glaslyn (*see* **Porthmadog**). The development of **slate** quarries at **Ffestiniog** aided the expansion of the village, as did the construction of the Ffestiniog **Railway** (1836), which is carried by the cob. The community's outstanding feature is Portmeirion, the unique Italianate village created between 1925 and 1972 by the architect **Clough Williams-Ellis**. He acquired the mansion of Aber Iâ on a headland on the Dwyryd estuary and on the slopes above it erected over 40 buildings, some of them containing parts that had been rescued from demolished buildings elsewhere.

Around the village are the extensive Gwyllt **Gardens**, rich in rhododendrons. Portmeirion was the setting of the cult television series *The Prisoner*. Adjoining Portmeirion is Castell Deudraeth, now a luxurious hotel and restaurant, which perhaps occupies the site of a castle noted by **Giraldus Cambrensis** in 1188. It was the home of David Williams

(1800–69), **Merioneth**'s first **Liberal** MP. The philosopher **Bertrand Russell**, who had been born at **Trellech**, spent the last years of his life at Plas Penrhyn. A toll bridge links Penrhyndeudraeth to the A496 coastal **road**.

PENRICE (Pen-rhys), Swansea
(1422 ha; 454 inhabitants)

The **community** extends from the seaside village of Horton to the glorious expanse of Oxwich Bay. St **Illtud**'s church, Oxwich, has a fine 14th-century tower; it stands almost on the beach to the south of Oxwich village – a long ribbon of cottages backed by chalets and caravans. Oxwich Castle, begun by Rice **Mansel** in the 1530s and completed by Edward Mansel in the 1590s, has, according to John Newman, a 'flaunting recklessness' which makes it **Glamorgan**'s sole example of an Elizabethan prodigy house. The large but inaccessible medieval castle at Penrice was built in the late 13th century. Nearby is the five-bay mansion built by Thomas Mansel **Talbot** in the 1770s. It is surrounded by an 18th-century landscaped park, which contains an orangery – a smaller version of that built by Talbot at **Margam**. St Andrew's church, Penrice, has a 12th-century chancel and wide 14th-century transepts. To its west is a large 12th-century ringwork, the predecessor of the medieval castle.

PENRY, John (1563–93) Puritan martyr

This Welsh **Puritan** martyr was born at Cefn-brith farmhouse (**Llangamarch**). He moved in Puritan circles at **Oxford** and **Cambridge**, and became so troubled by the lack of 'saving knowledge' in his native land that he published a trilogy of treatises (1587–8) in which he urged Elizabeth I and parliament to establish an effective preaching ministry in Wales. He pulled few punches, describing bishops as 'murderers and stranglers of men's souls' and clergymen as 'dumb and greedy **dogs**'. He became heavily involved in the clandestine production of the Marprelate tracts – a series of satirical works that poked fun at bishops. Incurring the wrath of the authorities, he fled to **Scotland** in 1589. Later, upon his return to **England** in 1592, he joined the separatist cause. In March 1593, he was arrested. Although he claimed that his single ambition had been to save the souls of Welsh people, he was executed in **London**. He left a widow, Eleanor, and four young daughters, whose names – Comfort, Deliverance, Safety and Sure Hope – provide a rare example of the use of 'virtue-names' by a 16th-century Welsh Puritan.

PENSON family Architects

Thomas Penson the elder (*c.*1760–1824), founder of a dynasty of architects, lived in **Wrexham** and became **county** surveyor of **Flintshire**. His eldest son, Thomas (1791–1859), established practices in Wrexham and Oswestry, and became county surveyor of **Denbighshire** and **Montgomeryshire**. His works included many **road** bridges and a number of churches in the area. His elder son, Richard Kyrke Penson (1815–85), was born in **Overton**. He established a practice in Ferryside (**St Ishmael**), where he specialized in restoring mansions (including **Dinefwr** (*see* **Llandeilo**) and Bronwydd (**Troedyraur**)) and churches, and designed schools. He became county surveyor of **Carmarthenshire**

and **Cardiganshire**. The younger son, Thomas Mainwaring Penson (1818–64), was also born in Overton; he practised in Chester, built the stations on the Chester–Shrewsbury **railway** and became county surveyor of Flintshire.

PENTECOSTALISM

A version of Christianity which emphasizes the charismatic aspects of the **religion** and adopts a fundamentalist attitude to the **Bible**. Although revivalism has long been part of the Welsh religious tradition, it was not until the 20th century that Pentecostalism developed as a specific tradition. Dramatic spiritual phenomena were experienced under the ministry of **Evan Roberts** during the 1904–5 **Revival**, and many believed that spiritual gifts such as speaking in tongues (glossolalia), **prophecy** and the gift of healing were being restored to the Church. **Coal**miner Daniel P. Williams (1883–1927) established the headquarters of the Apostolic Church at his home village – Pen-y-groes (**Llandybie**). By the interwar years, other Pentecostal bodies such as the Elim Four Square Gospel movement and the Assemblies of God had arrived in Wales. In the 1970s, Pentecostalism – often known as the charismatic movement – began affecting mainstream churches, making a more informal style of worship widely acceptable.

PENTIR, Gwynedd (1887 ha; 2403 inhabitants)

Comprising that part of the one-time civil **parish** of **Bangor** which lay beyond the city limits, the **community**'s major feature is Vaynol, one-time seat of the **Assheton Smith family**, owners of the Dinorwic **slate** quarry (*see* **Llanddeiniolen**). The complex of buildings at Vaynol includes a 16th-century mansion, another built in the 19th century, a 16th-century chapel, a vast 17th-century barn and an apparently endless wall around the park. The place has become a centre for the training of restorers of old buildings. The opera singer Bryn Terfel holds annual concerts in the park, which was the site of the 2005 National **Eisteddfod**.

Near Vaynol is the mainland end of the Britannia Bridge, the innovative tubular bridge designed by **Robert Stephenson** and opened in 1850 to carry the **railway** across the **Menai Strait**. It was named, not after Britannia, but after the Brydan Rock on which its central pillar was built. Opened in 1850, it was redesigned, after a fire in 1970, to carry a **road** as well as a railway. Treborth was the seat of Richard Davies, **ship**owner, MP and patron of **Nonconformist** causes. At Penrhos-garnedd, a suburb of Bangor extending into Pentir, stands Ysbyty Gwynedd, the main hospital serving north-west Wales. At Tŷ'n Llwyn, near the village of Pentir, there are fine examples of farm buildings from the 'High Farming' era of the mid-19th century.

PENTRAETH, Isle of Anglesey
(1469 ha; 1148 inhabitants)

A **community** located in south-eastern **Anglesey**, Pentraeth was the site of a battle in 1170 over the succession in **Gwynedd** in which the poet-prince **Hywel ab Owain Gwynedd** was killed. The large 18th-century brick house Plas Gwyn was the home of the antiquaries Paul Panton, father (1727–97) and son (1758–1822). There are several hut-groups on Mynydd Llwydiarth. Traeth Coch, or Red Wharf Bay, gets its name from the colour of the sand.

PENTREFOELAS, Conwy
(5,386 ha; 339 inhabitants)

Extending over a vast expanse of the **Mynydd Hiraethog** east of **Betws-y-Coed**, the **community** contains Llyn Alwen and the upper reaches of the Alwen **reservoir**. Foelas motte (*c.*1164) was probably built by **Owain Gwynedd**; a replica of a stone inscribed in honour of **Llywelyn ap Iorwerth** stands nearby; the original is in the **National Museum**. From 1545 until its demolition in 1819, Old Voelas House was the home of the Wynne, later the Wynne-Finch, family. Avenues of beech and lime and the outline of a walled **garden** survive. The family moved to Voelas, 2 km to the west, where the house (1961), designed by **Clough Williams-Ellis**, is the third on the site. Voelas Arms was rebuilt in 1839, when the licence was transferred from Cernioge, a one-time posting house on the **A5**, which features on several milestones. Plas Iolyn, rebuilt in the 18th century, was the home of **Elis Prys** and **Tomos Prys**. Near it is y Giler, which dates from the 16th century. It was the home of the poet Rhys Wyn (fl.*c.*1600); it is now a tavern. There are remarkable cairns at Hafod y Dre and Maes Myrddin. The A543 linking Pentrefoelas to Bylchau (**Llansannan**) is one of the remotest **roads** in Wales.

PENWEDDIG *Cantref*

Ceredigion was described as a land of four *cantrefi*, but Penweddig is the only one for which there is documentary evidence. Consisting of the territory north of the Ystwyth, it was divided into the **commotes** of **Genau'r-glyn**, **Perfedd** and **Creuddyn**. The name was revived as that of **Aberystwyth**'s **Welsh**-medium secondary school, Ysgol Penweddig.

PENYBERTH BOMBING SCHOOL, The burning of

In August 1935, the Air Ministry announced that a base specializing in bombing techniques was to be established at Penyberth (**Llannor**) on the **Llŷn** peninsula. The announcement brought condemnation from **pacifists** and also from those who considered that the **Welsh**-speaking communities of Llŷn represented Welsh Christian culture at its best. Protest proved fruitless, the **government** refusing to receive a deputation from Wales.

On 8 September 1936, three prominent members of **Plaid [Genedlaethol] Cymru** – **Saunders Lewis** (its president), **Lewis Valentine** and **D. J. Williams** – set fire to some of the buildings of the bombing school, and immediately reported their action to the **Pwllheli police**. At the trial at the **Caernarfon** assizes, the jury failed to agree on a verdict and the case was transferred to the Old Bailey in **London**, where the defendants were sentenced to nine months' imprisonment. Before the holding of the second trial, Saunders Lewis was dismissed from his lectureship at **Swansea** (*see* **University of Wales Swansea**). When the three were released in September 1937, they were welcomed by 12,000 supporters at the Pavilion at Caernarfon.

However, the fire did not result in a marked upsurge in the support for Plaid Cymru. The Caernarfon judge's contemptuous attitude to the **Welsh language** gave rise to the campaign which led to the **Welsh Courts Act (1942)**. The episode had a marked impact upon Welsh **literature**. The burning was frequently cited during protests against the flooding of the **Tryweryn Valley**.

'The Penyberth Three': Lewis Valentine, Saunders Lewis and D. J. Williams

PENYBONT (Pen-y-bont), Radnorshire, Powys
(3698 ha; 403 inhabitants)
A tract of undulating land immediately east of **Llandrindod**, the **community**'s chief feature is the much-ruined **hill-fort** of Cefnllys Castle situated on a hill encircled on three sides by the **River** Ithon. **Elystan Glodrydd**, progenitor of one of the five royal tribes of Wales, is said to have had a stronghold there. The **Mortimer** family seized it in the 12th century and rebuilt it in stone. A **borough** developed around the castle, which was praised by **Lewys Glyn Cothi**. Under the **Act of 'Union'**, Cefnllys became one of the five boroughs of the **Radnorshire** borough constituency. It eventually became a classic example of a failed town. The chalybeate and sulphur springs of Llandegley, popular in the 18th and early 19th centuries, were supplanted by the superior attractions of **Llandrindod**. Thomas Phillips, the founder of **Llandovery** College, was born at Llandegley. The **Quaker** meeting-house at The Pales is movingly austere.

PEN-Y-BONT-FAWR, Montgomeryshire, Powys
(2349 ha; 361 inhabitants)
Located immediately north-west of **Llanfyllin**, the **community** extends over the middle stretch of the Tanat basin. There are several ancient farmhouses within its boundaries. Hirnant was the main original settlement. Its St Illog's church, largely rebuilt in 1892, retains some medieval features. It contains woodwork from **Llanwddyn**'s submerged church. In the 1680s, a number of **Quakers** left Hirnant for **Pennsylvania** to escape persecution. Pen-y-Bont-Fawr was home to **Nansi Richards** (Telynores Maldwyn; 1888–1979), in her day the leading exponent of the triple **harp**. Another native of Pen-y-Bont-Fawr was Robert Ellis (Cynddelw; 1810–75), a poet and influential critic.

PENYCAE (Pen-y-cae), Wrexham
(1912 ha; 3463 inhabitants)
Adjoining **Rhosllanerchrugog** south of **Wrexham**, the **community** extends to the summit of **Ruabon** Mountain. Situated below two **reservoirs** on Nant Trefechan, Penycae village developed to house colliers and brick makers. Its older parts are a conservation area. The 17th-century Wynn Hall has been embellished with carved oak in the style of Plas Newydd, **Llangollen**.

PENYCHEN Cantref
A *cantref* of the kingdom of **Morgannwg**, Penychen lay between Gwrinydd and **Senghennydd**. It contained what is now the **county borough** of **Rhondda Cynon Taff**, most of that of the **Vale of Glamorgan** and the western part of **Cardiff**.

PENYFFORDD (Pen-y-ffordd), Flintshire
(888 ha; 3715 inhabitants)
Located immediately south-east of **Buckley**, the area developed in the 19th century as a **coal**mining centre. St John's church (1843) is decorated with the wall **paintings** of its first curate, John Troughton. In 1891, **J. E. Southall** was informed that everyone who was respectable in Penyffordd could speak **Welsh**.

PEN-Y-WAUN, Rhondda Cynon Taff
(372 ha; 3322 inhabitants)
Essentially a north-western suburb of **Aberdare**, the **community**'s main feature is Rhydywaun **Welsh**-medium Comprehensive School, completed in 2002.

PERCHENTYAETH (lit. 'houseownership')
In the work of the **Poets of the Gentry**, *perchentyaeth* was associated with the obligation of the members of the **gentry** towards their tenants and their community. This interpretation of medieval **Welsh literature** was a concept taken up by **Saunders Lewis**. He adapted it with relation to the kind of society he wished to see in Wales, a society in which ownership of property would be spread among 'the mass of the members of the nation'. Despite the Welsh associations of the word, Lewis's use of it was essentially in the context of his reworking of the distributivist ideas of G. K. Chesterton and Hilaire Belloc, ideas supported by the encyclicals of the **Roman Catholic** Church.

PERFEDD Commote (Cantref Bychan)
The middle (*perfedd* can mean 'gut') **commote** of **Cantref Bychan**, its administrative centre was **Llangadog**. With **Hirfryn**, it came to constitute the **march**er-lordship of **Llandovery**. The name survived as that of a post-**Acts of 'Union' hundred**.

PERFEDD Commote (Penweddig)
The middle **commote** of the *cantref* of **Penweddig**, **Ceredigion**, it extended from the mouth of the **Rheidol** to the summit of **Pumlumon**. Within it was **Llanbadarn**, the mother church of the whole of Penweddig, and the second **Aberystwyth** Castle.

PERFEDDWLAD
Constituting what would later be most of **Flintshire** and much of **Denbighshire**, the Perfeddwlad (the middle country) – or Y Berfeddwlad – was the land between the **Conwy** and the lower **Dee**. Consisting of the *cantrefi* of **Dyffryn Clwyd**, **Rhos**, **Rhufoniog** and **Tegeingl**, it was sometimes known as the Four Cantreds. The rulers of **Gwynedd** considered the Perfeddwlad to be that part of their territory lying east of the Conwy (Gwynedd Is Conwy), although its southern regions may originally have been more closely associated with **Powys**. Early overrun by the **Normans**, it came firmly under the rule of Gwynedd during the reign of **Owain Gwynedd**. Following his death in 1170, it became a central feature of the Welsh policy of the English crown to detach the four *cantrefi* from Gwynedd. That policy achieved permanent success with the **Treaty of Aberconwy** (1277). Following the **Edwardian conquest**, Tegeingl became the core of the **county** of **Flint**, Dyffryn Clwyd became the **march**er-lordship of **Ruthin**, and Rhos and Rhufoniog (bereft of **Creuddyn** which became part of the county of **Caernarfon**) became the marcher-lordship of **Denbigh**.

PERIODICALS
The first periodical in **Welsh**, *Tlysau yr Hen Oesoedd*, was published and printed by Lewis Morris (*see* **Morris Brothers**) on his own press at **Holyhead** in 1735. Its purpose

was to arouse the interest of the Welsh people in their language and **literature**, but only one issue appeared. It was not until 1770 that the next attempt was made to establish a Welsh periodical, with the appearance of *Trysorfa Gwybodaeth, neu Eurgrawn Cymraeg*, edited by Josiah Rees, a **Unitarian** minister from **Llanfair-ar-y-bryn**. It was followed by three periodicals of a **radical** nature, namely *Y Cylch-grawn Cynmraeg*, established by **Morgan John Rhys** in 1793, *The Miscellaneous Repository, neu y Drysorfa Gymmysgedig*, edited by Thomas Evans (Tomos Glyn Cothi) in 1795, and *Y Geirgrawn* under the editorship of David Davies of **Holywell**, in 1796. A fruit of the **Methodist Revival** was *Trysorfa Ysprydol*, founded by **Thomas Charles** of **Bala** and **Thomas Jones** (1756–1820) of **Denbigh** in 1799; it was the first denominational magazine to provide reading material for itinerant **preachers** and the teachers and pupils of the **Sunday schools**. These periodicals were short-lived, for difficulties of distribution and sale, and the prohibitive price of paper as well as the tax on periodicals, made publication a considerable risk for both editor and publisher.

In the early 19th century, the religious denominations enthusiastically established their own periodicals, such as the **Wesleyans'** *Yr Eurgrawn Wesleyaidd* (the longest lasting of all Welsh periodicals; 1809–1983), the **Baptists'** *Seren Gomer*, the **Congregationalists'** *Y Dysgedydd* and *Y Diwygiwr*, the **Calvinistic Methodists'** *Goleuad Cymru* and *Y Drysorfa*, the **Anglicans'** *Yr Haul* and the **Unitarians'** *Yr Ymofynydd*. The multiplicity of these titles is in itself a clear indicator of the literary activity of the time; but the contents of several of them were often contentious and quarrelsome – as exemplified, for instance, by Brutus (**David Owen**), editor of *Yr Haul*, and **David Rees**, editor of *Y Diwygiwr*. The religious denominations also supported the **temperance** periodical press, which reached its zenith in the 1840s, as well as the several magazines for children established mid-century. The most notable of these was *Trysorfa y Plant*, edited by **Thomas Levi,** which sold 40,000 copies a month in 1881.

Wales's first **English-language** periodical, the *Cambrian Magazine*, was published in **Llandovery** in 1773. It was followed by the *Cambrian Register* (edited by **William Owen Pughe**, and published in **London** in 1795, 1796 and 1818); and by the *Cambrian Visitor* in **Swansea** in 1813. The founding of *Archaeologia Cambrensis* in 1846 led a year later to the establishment of the **Cambrian Archaeological Association**; the journal is still published today, and contains a wealth of material on the antiquities and **archaeology** of Wales. Most of these English periodicals were antiquarian, but in 1882 **Charles Wilkins** founded the *Red Dragon* as a popular monthly that published a variety of material.

A new chapter opened in the history of the Welsh periodical press in 1845 when **Thomas Gee** published *Y Traethodydd* as a quarterly, with **Lewis Edwards** as its editor. This was based on English-language periodicals such as the *Edinburgh Review*, but with its main emphasis on **theology**, **philosophy** and **education**. *Yr Adolygydd* and *Y Beirniad* were similar publications, but were short-lived compared with *Y Traethodydd*, which still continues to appear. The magazines of the second half of the 19th century were of a lighter nature, and the number of popular publications increased. *Y Gymraes*, the first magazine for **women**, was founded by Ieuan Gwynedd (**Evan Jones**) in

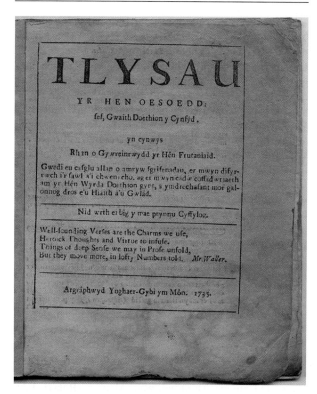

Tlysau yr Hen Oesoedd, the earliest Welsh-language periodical

1850, and lasted for a year. It was followed by *Y Frythones* (1879–91), edited by Cranogwen (**Sarah Jane Rees**), and by another periodical called *Y Gymraes* (1896–1934), edited by Ceridwen Peris (**Alice Gray Jones**).

Over 50 periodicals were published to serve the Welsh communities in **North America** in the 19th century. The majority of these were denominational publications, the most prominent of which were the Calvinistic Methodists' *Y Cyfaill o'r Hen Wlad yn America* (1838–1933), the Congregationalists' *Y Cenhadwr Americanaidd* (1840–1901) and the Baptists' *Y Seren Orllewinol* (1844–69). Two Welsh periodicals were published in **Australia** – *Yr Australydd* (1866–72) and *Yr Ymwelydd* (1874–6).

Y Brython (1858–63), edited by Daniel Silvan Evans, though chiefly of a literary and antiquarian stance, also contained much folk literature, including stories and fables, sayings, common beliefs and verses – material hitherto ignored by the denominational periodicals. *Golud yr Oes*, a popular magazine published by Hugh Humphreys at **Caernarfon**, and *Y Punch Cymraeg* (1858–64), which was based on the English *Punch*, belong to the same period. *Y Geninen* (1883–1928) was more serious in content, providing an opportunity for writers to express their opinions on current affairs. *Cyfaill yr Aelwyd* (1881–94) was founded by **Beriah Gwynfe Evans** as a popular monthly; it contained a variety of material upon which **O. M. Edwards** based his *Cymru* (1891–1927), one of the most successful magazines in Welsh. Edwards's intention was to immerse the Welsh in their history and culture, and other publications established by him include *Cymru'r Plant* (1892; incorporated into *Cip*, the magazine of **Urdd Gobaith Cymru**, in 1987), *Y Llenor* (1895–8), *Heddyw* (1897), and *Wales* (1894–7) for non-Welsh-speakers.

A friend of Edwards, **John Morris-Jones**, was editor of *Y Beirniad* (1911–17), a quarterly which was published by the Welsh societies of the three constituent colleges of the **University of Wales**; it included articles on the Welsh language and its literature by many of the editor's former students. It was followed by *Y Llenor* (1922–55), one of the most important quarterlies of the 20th century, edited by **W. J. Gruffydd** and his successor **T. J. Morgan**. Its main aim was 'to provide and promote literature of the highest standard', and the foremost Welsh poets and writers contributed to its pages. The **University of Wales Board of Celtic Studies** has published several scholarly periodicals over the years, such as the *Bulletin* (1921–93), *Llên Cymru* (1950–), the *Welsh History Review* (1960–), *Studia Celtica* (1966–) and *Contemporary Wales* (1987–), an annual review of economic and social research. The majority of the historical societies of the Welsh **counties** also publish their own journals, as do the various family history societies.

Heddiw (1936–42), edited by **Aneirin Talfan Davies** and Dafydd Jenkins, was an influential literary periodical that published articles on politics, **pacifism** and the **Spanish Civil War**. More radical was **Alun Llywelyn-Williams**'s *Tir Newydd* (1935–9). Another literary periodical was *Y Fflam* (1946–52), edited by **Euros Bowen** and others. *Y Genhinen* (1951–80) was a popular quarterly published by Gomer Press, and among its editors were Meuryn (**Robert John Rowlands**), Simon B. Jones (*see* **Cilie family**) and W. Rhys Nicholas. The literary periodical of the **Welsh Academy**, *Taliesin*, was founded in 1961, and its editors have included Gwenallt (**David James Jones**), **D. Tecwyn Lloyd** and **Bedwyr Lewis Jones**. One of the main literary periodicals in Welsh, it publishes creative and critical works as well as book reviews. *Barn* was established in 1962 by the **Llandybie** imprint Llyfrau'r Dryw as a monthly current affairs publication. Under the editorship of **Alwyn D. Rees**, it had a far-reaching influence on Welsh thought during the late 1960s and early 1970s. Having undergone several changes of emphasis over the years, it has reassumed its political inclination. In 1965, *Lol* was founded as an annual satirical magazine, mocking the Welsh media and the establishment; it was replaced by *Dim Lol* in 2004. *Tu Chwith*, established by a number of young people in 1993 with the intention of investigating postmodernism, appears twice a year.

The only weekly magazine in Welsh is *Golwg*, established by Dylan Iorwerth in 1988 as a lively current affairs publication. The most popular magazines are those devoted to specific subjects, such as *Barddas* (poetry) and *Y Casglwr* (book collecting), both founded in 1976, and *Llafar Gwlad* (folklore and customs) founded in 1983. Pop **music** has been the focus of several Welsh-language magazines, such as *Asbri* (1969–89), *Curiad* (1978–85) and *Sgrech* (1979–82), and since the 1980s various fanzines have appeared, in both Welsh and English, dealing not only with rock music but also with sports such as **rugby** and **football** – although the majority have been short-lived. Since 1963, **Cymdeithas yr Iaith Cymraeg** has published its own magazine, *Tafod y Ddraig*, which now appears only intermittently.

A large number of **Anglo-Welsh** or English-language magazines were founded in the 20th century. *The Welsh Outlook* (1914–33) was an influential monthly which published articles on politics, industry, education and social topics, reflecting the interests of **Thomas Jones** (1870–1955), its first editor. **Keidrych Rhys** was the founder-editor of *Wales*, a literary magazine of which three series appeared (1937–40, 1943–9, 1958–60) providing a platform for young creative writers. The *Welsh Review*, edited by **Gwyn Jones**, appeared as a monthly in 1939 and as a quarterly after the **Second World War** (1944–8). It provided an opportunity for young creative writers, and it also included articles on history, education and politics. A literary group in **Pembroke Dock** was chiefly responsible for establishing *Dock Leaves* in 1949. Its title was changed to the *Anglo-Welsh Review* in 1957, and it continued to appear until 1988. It was followed in that year by the *New Welsh Review*, a quarterly of varying interests with particular emphasis on creative writing. Poetry, literary criticism and book reviews are published in *Poetry Wales*, a quarterly founded by Meic Stephens in 1965, with the aim of promoting Welsh poetry in English. *Planet* first appeared as a bi-monthly in 1970 and was edited by Ned Thomas until 1979. Relaunched in 1985, it includes articles on social issues, the arts and Welsh politics, and supports national and other minority movements in Europe.

PERRI or PARRY, Henry (1560/1–1617) Scholar

A native of Greenfield (**Holywell**), Perri was educated at **Oxford** and subsequently held several livings in **Anglesey**. He had an informed interest in the **Welsh** language and **literature**, and wrote – on the basis of earlier work by **William Salesbury** – *Eglvryn Phraethineb sebh Dosparth ar Retoreg* (1595), a book in which **Renaissance** emphases on the art of rhetoric are applied to the work of Welsh poets.

PERROT family Landowners

Sir John Perrot (1530–92) was reputedly the illegitimate son of Henry VIII and Mary Berkeley, a lady-in-waiting who married Sir Thomas Perrot of Haroldston (**Merlin's Bridge**). A robust, litigious and famously ill-tempered person, he was vice-admiral of the coasts of south Wales, MP for **Pembrokeshire** (1562) and twice mayor of **Haverfordwest**. He was active in suppressing (and profiting from) **piracy**. His period as lord deputy of **Ireland** (1584–8) led to apparently trumped up accusations of treason against him; he died in the Tower of **London**. He was responsible for the building of the magnificent north wing of **Carew** Castle. His illegitimate son, Sir James Perrot (1571–1636), MP for Haverfordwest and for Pembrokeshire, was a prominent Parliamentarian who attacked William Laud's religious policies. Appointed vice-admiral of Pembrokeshire (1626), he urged that measures should be taken against wreckers and that the defences of the **Milford Haven Waterway** should be strengthened. He was a member of the Virginia Company and the author of such works as *Meditations and Prayers on the Lord's Prayer and Ten Commandments* (1630).

PETERSEN, Jack (John Charles Petersen; 1911–90) Boxer

Having won the British Amateur light-heavyweight championship in 1931, **Cardiff**-born Petersen turned professional. Trained by his father and financed by a syndicate, he became one of the most popular and well-supported fighters of the 1930s. Of partially Danish descent, he was tall and lithe. He had difficulty making the weight (he would weigh-in in his suit); nevertheless, this lightweight champion moved up to become British and Empire heavyweight champion (1932–6), his fights with Len Harvey and Walter Neusel being highlights of the decade in the world of **boxing**. One of his sons is the distinguished artist-blacksmith and **Plaid [Genedlaethol] Cymru** activist David Petersen (*see* **Ironwork**).

PETERSTON-SUPER-ELY (Llanbedr-y-fro), Vale of Glamorgan (960 ha; 865 inhabitants)

A **community** located on the east bank of the **Ely**, south of the **M4**, its largest settlement, the village of Peterston has greatly expanded of late and is now home to some of **Cardiff**'s leading figures. Late 20th-century building has overwhelmed Wyndham Park garden village, established by the **Cory family** in 1909. Of the 1000 houses envisaged by the original plan, only 22 had been built by 1914. These include 10 flat-roofed houses which are startlingly modern for their time. The village tavern – the Sportsman's Rest – features in the BBC serial *Pobol y Cwm*. St Peter's church has a fine late-medieval nave. Croes-y-parc **Baptist** chapel (1843) is an attractive symbol of early Victorian Nonconformity. The area is prone to flooding; water levels are recorded in the bar of the Sportsman's Rest.

PETTS, John (1914–91) Artist and printmaker

John Petts was born in **London**, studied at the Royal Academy Schools and came to Wales after marrying **Brenda Chamberlain** in 1936. At **Llanllechid**, they established the Caseg Press, publishing broadsheets and postcards illustrated by their own hand-coloured wood engravings. The marriage ended in 1946. In 1951, Petts joined the newly formed Welsh Committee of the Arts Council of Great **Britain** (*see* **Arts Council of Wales**), leaving in 1956 to concentrate on his own work, which increasingly focused on **stained glass** and mosaic.

PEULINOG Commote

One of the **commotes** of **Cantref Gwarthaf**, **Dyfed**, it seems to have contained within it the emerging commote of **Amgoed**. Its administrative centre was **Whitland**. It came to constitute the **march**er-lordship of **St Clears**.

PHILIPPS family Landowners

In *c*.1490, Thomas Philipps of Cilsant married Joan, heiress of a branch of the Dwnns of **Kidwelly** and of the Wogans of **Wiston**. Energetic estate builders, the family benefited in particular from the fall of Rhys ap Gruffydd (*see* **Rhys ap Thomas**). From their seat at Picton Castle (*see* **Slebech**), the family played a central role in the politics of **Haverfordwest** and **Pembrokeshire**, receiving a baronetcy in 1621. John Philipps (d.1737), the fourth baronet, and patron of **Griffith Jones**, **Llanddowror**, was prominent in Welsh religious and **educational** life. The sixth baronet (d.1764) was a leading **Jacobite**; the seventh died childless in 1823, and the estate passed in turn to the Grant, Gwyther and Fisher families, all of whom assumed the

John Petts and Brenda Chamberlain, *The Sower* (1941–2)

surname Philipps. Other members of the family include the husband of **Katherine Philipps** and the brothers Viscount St Davids, the **Lloyd George Liberal**, and Baron Milford, the agricultural expert (*see* **The Institute of Grassland and Environmental Research**). By 1873, the family owned 5176 ha in Pembrokeshire.

PHILIPPS, Katherine (The Matchless Orinda; 1631–64) Poet

An **English** woman, she married James **Philipps** of **Cardigan** Priory and shared her time between Wales and her native **London**, maintaining by correspondence a coterie of literary and philosophical friends; she was known among them as Orinda, while 'the Matchless' was bestowed by her many admirers. Her verse was first collected in 1664; the standard edition is *The Collected Works of Katherine Philips* (*sic*) (3 vols., 1990–3). **R. T. Jenkins**'s novel *Orinda* (1943) is a delightful evocation of her life.

PHILLIMORE, Egerton [Grenville Bagot] (1856–1937) Scholar

This **English**man's lifelong absorption in the **Welsh language** and culture survived severe personal problems. He edited *Y Cymmrodor* (1889–91) and co-edited *Bye-gones* (1891–3), which were among the **periodicals** in which he published many penetrating articles on Wales, its language, **literature**, history and culture. He also compiled valuable notes on Welsh history and **place names** for an edition of **George Owen**'s *Penbrokshire* (4 vols.,

1892–1936). But perhaps his most interesting work is a collection of bawdy Welsh words that he published in a German **periodical** in 1884. He settled at **Corris** in 1902, and spent the rest of his life there.

PHILLIPS, Dewi Z[ephaniah] (1934–2006)
Philosopher

Dewi Z. Phillips was the most productive philosopher ever to be born in Wales. He published over 20 books and over a hundred articles in both **Welsh** and **English** and was editor of the influential journal *Philosophical Investigations*. He was born in Morriston (**Swansea**) and was educated at Swansea and **Oxford**. After a period as a **Congregational** minister at Swansea, he became in turn a lecturer at Dundee, **Bangor** and Swansea; he succeeded **J. R. Jones** as professor of **Philosophy** at Swansea, a chair he held from 1971 until his retirement in 1996. From 1992 onwards, he was also a professor at the Claremont Graduate School in California. He specialized in the philosophy of **religion** and morals, and played a leading role in ensuring that Swansea became a major centre of Wittgensteinian studies. His interest in **literature** led him to write philosophically based studies of the work of **R. S. Thomas** and **Gwenlyn Parry**. A colourful figure, he was an excellent mimic and raconteur. Seeing philosophy withering in the universities of Wales was a bitter experience for him.

PHILLIPS, John (1810–67) Educationist

Born into a poor family in Pontrhydfendigaid (**Ystrad Fflur**), John Phillips entered Edinburgh University in 1833 with a minimum of formal **education**. He left in 1835 for a **Calvinistic Methodist** pastorate in **Holywell**. In 1847, he became a minister in **Bangor**, but an alternative mission was calling him. Having accepted additional responsibility, in 1843, as representative of the **British Society** in the north, he soon resigned his ministry to concentrate on opening schools. He travelled on foot and on horseback to find sites for schools and the money to build them. The success of this venture led to a shortage of teachers. Phillips enthusiastically co-operated with **Hugh Owen** in the founding of the **Normal College, Bangor** (1858), of which he became the first principal.

PHILLIPS, Thomas (1801–67) Mayor

Born in the **parish** of **Llanelly** (**Breconshire**, now **Monmouthshire**), and raised at Trosnant, **Pontypool**, Phillips was mayor of **Newport** at the time of the **Chartists'** attack on the town in 1839 (*see* **Newport Rising**). Although honoured with a knighthood for his part in repelling the Chartists, he was not at all times an establishment figure, being one of the chief defenders of the Welsh against the calumnies of the authors of the 1847 report on **education** in Wales (*see* **Treason of the Blue Books**).

He attacked their aspersions in his important book *Wales: the Language, Social Condition, Moral Character, and Religious Opinions of the People Considered in Relation to Education* (1849). A staunch **Anglican**, he was an enthusiastic supporter of the **National Society** and its church schools, and of St **David**'s College, **Lampeter** (now the **University of Wales, Lampeter**), where he promoted Welsh studies.

PHILOSOPHY

Very many more Welshmen have left their mark as religious thinkers than as philosophers (*see* **Theology**). Nevertheless, over the centuries, theology and philosophy have intertwined. There were philosophers among medieval Welsh ecclesiastics and **Renaissance** scholars, but most of them were primarily theologians. **Edward Herbert** (Lord Herbert of Cherbury; 1538–1648), however, was primarily a philosopher. He claimed in his *De Veritate* (1623) that all universal truths ('common truths' as he called them) – including the truth that there is one God – are ideas that are innate and God-given to all at birth. Hence 'special revelation' has but a limited role. This led to Herbert being called the father of Deism in **Britain**. The **Puritan** writer **Morgan Llwyd** (1619–59) has been described as a philosopher, but, although he presented an analysis of the self, he did so from within his own religious perspective; therefore, he was not a metaphysician in the philosophical sense.

After Edward Herbert, the second Welsh thinker to gain an international reputation was **Richard Price** (1723–91). He was partly educated in Wales, in two of the numerous **Nonconformist academies**, in which philosophy was an integral part of the curriculum. Price became a minister of religion but his fame in philosophy rests primarily on his ethical treatise *A Review of the Principal Questions and Difficulties in Morals* (1758), a work of considerable originality that anticipates the Kantian emphasis on the centrality of the concept of duty in the analysis of the concept of moral rightness. Price supported the revolution in France and the developments in America. He defended the demand for rights in both countries and wrote extensively on these matters, as did another, younger, contemporary Welshman, **David Williams** (1738–1816) – although this pamphleteer never achieved the same intellectual heights as Price. Writing in **Welsh**, pamphleteers like Jac Glan-y-Gors (**John Jones**; 1766–1821) and **Thomas Roberts** (of Llwyn'rhudol; 1765/6–1841), among others, promoted the same ideals.

Anglicanism in Wales continued to produce fine scholars, such as Isaac Williams (1802–65) from **Llanrhystud**, who became dean of Trinity College, **Oxford**, an able theologian, and a leading light in the **Oxford Movement**. But it was the flourishing academies that produced the men for the pulpits, and from the academies flowed articles on philosophers and philosophical issues in denominational and other journals. One such **periodical** was *Y Traethodydd,* in which **Lewis Edwards** (1809–87), who was deeply influenced by Kant, published extensively. Edwards's theological work *Athrawiaeth yr Iawn* (1860), which echoes much of Anselm's *Cur Deus Homo*, was by far the most influential Welsh theological work of the 19th century.

But without a university, philosophy could not flourish as an independent discipline and could not be pursued freely without its being entangled with theology. In 1872, the first university college was established at **Aberystwyth** and this was soon followed by others. **Thomas Charles Edwards** became the first principal and first professor of philosophy at Aberystwyth. At **Bangor**, a greater Welsh philosopher held the chair from 1884 to 1891. He was **Henry Jones**, who later occupied the chair of philosophy at

Glasgow for several decades. He espoused Absolute Idealism, a development of the philosophy of Hegel. This belief in the total unity of reality was also the philosophy of **David Adams**, one of the first to graduate from Aberystwyth. A modified form of Hegelianism known as Personal Idealism was embraced by Andrew Seth Pringle-Pattison, the first to hold the chair of philosophy at **Cardiff**.

A renaissance in traditional British empiricism at the beginning of the 20th century, largely due to the influence of the **Cambridge** philosophers G. E. Moore (1873–1958) and **Bertrand Russell**, saw the gradual eclipse of Idealism as a dominant force in the universities. By the middle of the century, philosophy chairs at the **University of Wales** were occupied by empiricists: **Richard I. Aaron** at Aberystwyth (1932–69) was a leading Lockeian scholar; **Hywel D. Lewis** at Bangor (1947–55) and subsequently at Kings College, **London**, was widely known as an empiricist philosopher of religion, while remaining a stout defender of Cartesian dualism; **J. R. Jones** at **Swansea** (1952–70), was an empiricist with a Logical Positivist slant (although he moved closer to a Wittgensteinian position later).

In 1931, the Guild of Graduates of the University of Wales established a philosophy section with a view to discussing philosophy through the medium of Welsh. This continues into the 21st century, through conferences and the publication of a journal, *Efrydiau Athronyddol*, which first appeared in 1938. Between 1936 and 1956, principal **D. Emrys Evans** of Bangor produced fine Welsh translations of the dialogues of Plato. Welsh translations of Aristotle appeared subsequently – *Barddoneg* (*Poetics*), by **J. Gwyn Griffiths** of Swansea (1978), and *Moeseg Nicomachaidd* (*Nicomachean Ethics*) by John FitzGerald of Aberystwyth (1998).

During the **Second World War**, Ludwig Wittgenstein visited Swansea regularly to conduct discussions with a former student of his, **Rush Rhees**, who had immense influence as a teacher of philosophy, transforming the department at Swansea into a leading centre of Wittgensteinian studies. A 'Swansea School of Philosophy' became recognized internationally; among the most illustrious philosophers produced by this school was **Dewi Z. Phillips**, who had edited the journal *Philosophical Investigations*. In 2004, the university authorities decided, controversially, to close Swansea's philosophy department.

Until the closure in 1988 of Aberystwyth's philosophy department, political philosophy was taught with great distinction there. A notable contribution was made to the study of the political philosophies of Kant, Hegel and Marx by a member of Aberystwyth's Department of Politics, Howard Williams, joint editor of the *Kantian Review*, published by the University of Wales Press.

PHOTOGRAPHY

Although the earliest dated Welsh photograph was taken in 1841, two years after the invention of the daguerreotype, photography was already the subject of great enthusiasm for a select group of **Glamorgan gentry**. At the centre of this '**Swansea** Circle' was **John Dillwyn-Llewelyn** who was related by marriage to the **English**man William Henry Fox Talbot (1800–77), inventor of the calotype. Another of the

Geoff Charles's iconic photograph of the poet Richard Griffith (Carneddog) and his wife, Catrin, leaving their Snowdonia home in 1945

'Swansea Circle' was the Rev. **Calvert Richard Jones**, who experimented with both daguerreotype and calotype, and who took that earliest of Welsh photographs – the daguerreotype of **Margam** Castle, held by the **National Library**.

The photographic processes used by these pioneers were relatively primitive. The situation was transformed in 1851 by the invention of the wet-plate process. A number of leading photographers – notably Francis Frith (1822–98), **Roger Fenton** and **Francis Bedford** – visited Wales from the 1850s onwards, taking photographs of beauty spots for sale to tourists. In Wales, several talented and well-to-do amateurs took up photography, among them Thomas **Crawshay** and Lady Llanover (**Augusta Hall**). One of the few native Welsh photographers was **John Thomas** (1838–1905): the National Library has some 3000 of his negatives – the pre-eminent photographic record of late 19th-century rural Wales.

By the 1880s, the more convenient dry-plate process had come into being, which, together with improved **printing** papers, launched another major phase in photography, as large numbers of professional photographers set up business. These were local craftsmen, and they came to be found in almost every town. The collection of D. C. Harries and Sons, **Llandeilo**, housed at the National Library, is an excellent illustration of the work undertaken by a typical local studio.

From 1912, when Kodak brought cheap and innovative equipment and services to the market, photography was within the grasp of millions of people. Kodak's British managing director at this time was the intriguing **George Davison**; he moved to Wales to live, and drew many influential people to his bohemian circle in **Harlech**, including the distinguished photographer Alvin Langdon Coburn. Davison was a leading proponent of pictorialist photography, a style notable for its use of focus to replicate a scene as it might appear to the human eye. One of the few Welsh pictorialists was John Wilkes Poundley of **Kerry**, who photographed a series of 'Kerry Characters' in 1918.

In the later 20th century, leading photographers who visited Wales included Robert Frank, Eugene Smith and Bill Brandt. One native photographer who could stand shoulder to shoulder with these major figures was **Angus McBean**, a pioneer in theatre photography. The second half of the century saw a growth in photojournalism: on the international stage, Phillip Jones Griffiths stands out for his bravery and vision, while, in Wales, **Geoff Charles** contributed a massive body of work depicting the life of the nation. Another influential figure was David Hurn, whose pioneering course at **Newport** School of Art inspired a generation of new photojournalists and photographers.

A striking feature of the end of the century was the degree of **government** sponsorship of photography, and the development by Welsh institutions of photography collection policies. Collections of importance to the history of photography in relation to Wales are to be found at the National Library, the **National Museum**, the Glynn Vivian **Art Gallery** (Swansea), the Royal Photographic Society (Bath), the National Museum of Photography, **Film** and Television (Bradford), and the Birmingham Central

The Vietnam War photographed dramatically by Philip Jones Griffiths

Library. In 2006, work began at Margam Castle on the establishment of the National Centre for Photography in Wales.

PHYSICAL SCIENCES, The

Until about the mid-19th century, what is now termed physical **science** was known as natural **philosophy**, a subject taught only in the older universities and practised by a small number of individual experimentalists. This was still the position when a chair of natural philosophy was established at **Aberystwyth** in 1877. Physics, like **chemistry**, was rarely taught in schools at that time; although chairs of physics were established at **Cardiff** (1883) and at **Bangor** (1884), the number of students remained small. It took many years for the consequences of the **Welsh Intermediate Education Act** of 1889 to be reflected in a significant increase in the number of students at these institutions, and the subsequent evolution of the physical sciences in Wales is largely a reflection of the way in which they developed within the university colleges.

Until 1914, physics departments were primarily concerned with teaching. In the early days, it was common for a professor to undertake all the teaching while his one or two lecturers would be responsible for the laboratory classes. What little research was undertaken lay in the realm of classical physics. A prime example of this was at Cardiff, where **John Viriamu Jones** was the first principal of the college and the first holder of the chair of physics in 1883. Not only did he teach but, in his spare time, he undertook research on the standardization of the measurement of the electrical units of resistance and current. Remarkably, his successor as principal was another physicist, **E. H. Griffiths**, who, in collaboration with the Cardiff graduate **Ezer Griffiths**, pursued research on very high precision measurements of the thermal capacities of metals at low temperatures.

The first professor of physics at Bangor, Andrew Gray, held the post from 1884 until 1899 when he was appointed to the chair of natural philosophy at Glasgow. In an unusual sequel, his successor at Bangor, Edward Taylor Jones, was in turn appointed to the same chair in 1925. The electrical bias at Bangor was evident in Taylor Jones's advocacy of a department of hydroelectricity to contribute to the development of hydroelectric power (*see* **Energy**) in north-west Wales. The school of **electronics** would survive the closure of Bangor's physics department in the early 1980s.

When University College, **Swansea** (**University of Wales Swansea**) opened in 1920 with a strong physical science and technology presence, the first professor of physics was E. J. Evans, who initiated a spectroscopic group, which went from strength to strength over the next 20 years.

After the **First World War**, there was phenomenal growth in the new subjects of quantum physics, wave mechanics and atomic structure. Together with their associated concepts, they were of a spectacular nature but were difficult to communicate to a lay public, and this may partly explain why student numbers in the four colleges changed little in the interwar period. There was, however, an outstanding development in 1938 when **Evan Williams** was appointed to the chair of physics at Aberystwyth at the age of 35. In 1940, he made the first identification of the decay of the muon, what was then one of the most enigmatic fundamental particles of physics; after making a crucial contribution to the war effort, he died prematurely in 1945.

Awareness of the pivotal role played by applied physics during the **Second World War** led to expansion of university physics in the post-war period. A major long-term school of ionization physics developed under **Frank Llewellyn Jones** at Swansea; one of his protégés, **Granville Beynon**, established a research team to study the ionosphere and magnetosphere, first at Swansea and then at Aberystwyth. Staff and students from these two departments have made a notable impact internationally, especially in the field of solar-terrestrial physics, a field in which **Phil Williams** made a distinguished contribution.

An emphasis at Cardiff on X-ray crystallography was followed by the establishment of an enlarged school of semi-conductor physics, under Robin Williams, which had numerous ramifications in industry. Throughout physics groups, there was a phenomenal rate of expansion of knowledge, largely the result of increasingly powerful computing facilities.

The later 20th century saw the emergence of hitherto unknown subjects such as opto-electronics, semi-conductor and solid-state physics, micro-electronics and material physics. Topics of this nature, together with other specialisms within the colleges of the **University of Wales**, and more recently at the **University of Glamorgan** and the **North East Wales Institute of Higher Education**, represent a vast pool of knowledge with enormous potential applications. To capitalize on this knowledge, a number of 'Centres of Excellence' were established in 2001 to provide industries with access to the world-class expertise in Welsh universities.

Dyserth-born John Houghton, a leading climate scientist

675

The plaque at Lavernock commemorating the first radio message sent across water

The field of semi-conductor physics saw an outstanding theoretical prediction by Cardiff-born Brian D. Josephson (b.1940), which was subsequently verified experimentally. He was awarded a Nobel Prize (1973) for this work, and the resulting device, known as a Josephson Junction, achieved worldwide usage. (Josephson is one of only three Welsh-born Nobel laureates; the others are the philosopher **Bertrand Russell**, and the Swansea-born economist Clive Granger (b.1934), who won the Nobel Prize for economics in 2003.)

Until the later 19th century, **astronomy** as a science was largely the pursuit of amateurs, but during the 20th century it became increasingly professional. Cardiff established an astronomy department in 1951 and a chair of theoretical astronomy was created in 1976. Major contributions have been made in two principal fields: the enigmatic question of 'dark matter' in the universe and spectroscopic studies relating to the early history of the universe.

Given the small number of people involved in meteorology, a subject that straddles the boundaries of physics and **mathematics**, it is remarkable that three Welshmen should have become directors of the British Meteorological Office. **David Brunt** is widely regarded as the father of modern weather forecasting, through his advocacy of the use of the laws of physics rather than the study of past weather patterns. He was ahead of his time, because it required the development of fast computers to complete predictions in a short enough time to be useful. During his term of office, **Graham Sutton** pioneered the study of atmospheric turbulence and he also advanced the use of high-speed computing facilities when they became available. **Dyserth**-born John Houghton (b.1931) was appointed director in 1983 and he brought with him an international reputation in

spectroscopic atmospheric physics. He later became chairman of the scientific committee of the UN Intergovernmental Panel on Climate Change; it has been claimed that Houghton, as one of the leading scientists behind the Rio and Kyoto conferences on **climate** change, is the most influential Welshman of all time.

The existence of electromagnetic waves – the medium of radio communication – was predicted by James Clerk Maxwell in 1864 and verified experimentally by Heinrich Hertz in 1887; but eight years earlier a Welshman, **David Edward Hughes**, was the first person in the world to transmit and receive radio signals.

It was, pre-eminently, the vision, technical knowledge and business acumen of the Irish-Italian Guglielmo Marconi (1874–1937), building on the Hughes/Hertz discovery, which drove the development of radio. The wireless **telegraph** system patented by Marconi proved its potential in May 1897 when Marconi, working closely with **William Preece**, chief engineer of the Post Office, successfully transmitted radio signals across water, from Lavernock Point (**Sully**) to Flat Holm (*see* **Islands**) and to Bream Down in Somerset. Later, Marconi built the high-power **Waunfawr** wireless station (1914–38), which played an important role in the development of international radio communication. The most significant Welsh contribution to information transmission in the later 20th century was that of **Donald Davies**, who invented packet switching, which is the basis of all high-speed data transmission.

There has been relatively little manifestation of the physical sciences in Wales outside the formal realm of the University of Wales, but the *Proceedings of the South Wales Institute of Engineers* contain significant material on the application of physical science in industry and **engineering**. Two organizations that help bring the physical sciences into direct contact with the general public are the Cardiff Scientific Society, (founded 1926) and the popular interactive science centre Techniquest, which opened in Cardiff in 1986 (*see* **Science**).

PHYSICIANS OF MYDDFAI, The

The earliest reference to the most famous doctors of medieval Wales, who were associated with **Myddfai** in **Cantref Bychan**, dates back to the 13th century. (Evidence of another medical dynasty, the family of Bened Feddyg of **Dyffryn Clwyd**, dates from the end of the Middle Ages.)

A number of **Welsh** medical texts of the 14th and 15th century have survived, and several of them – that in *The Red Book of Hergest*, for example – begin with references to the Physicians of Myddfai. The earliest of the physicians, it was claimed, was Rhiwallon Feddyg, who, with his three sons, was the doctor of **Rhys Gryg**, son of the Lord Rhys (**Rhys ap Gruffudd**, d.1197). The family's link with Myddfai continued for centuries. It was claimed that two local farms, Llwyn Ifan Feddyg and Llwyn Maredudd Feddyg, were named after them, and the **parish** church contains memorials to the last of them – David Jones (d.1719) and his son John Jones (d.1739). In *The Physicians of Myddfai* (1861), edited by John Williams (Ab Ithel; 1811–62), traditions relating to the family are linked with the Legend of **Llyn y Fan Fach**.

The methods followed by the doctors associated with Myddfai, as described in *The Red Book of Hergest* and other sources, were common to much of medieval Europe. The medical issues discussed varied from toothache to anal warts, and remedies included the extensive use of herbs (*see* **Plants**), together with surgery, bleeding, urinoscopy and the use of the cautery and plasters. The emphasis placed upon balancing the body's humours (blood, phlegm, yellow bile and black bile) shows that the physicians were heirs to Hippocrates (d.377 BC) and Galen (d.AD 200). Astrology had a role, as did the importance of choosing the right time to administer treatment.

PIBGORN, The

A mouth-blown reed instrument widespread in Wales for centuries, the pibgorn has a deceptively simple construction: a wooden or bone pipe with a cylindrical bore, six finger-holes and a thumb-hole, and a single reed (originally elder, latterly typically cane), with a reed cap and bell, fashioned from cow horn. It was widely played by **Anglesey farm labourers** until the end of the 18th century, and apparently survived in **Pembrokeshire** well into the 19th century. Three surviving examples are preserved at the National History Museum (*see* **St Fagans**). Successful modern copies have been made by Jonathan Shorland of **Cardiff**.

PICTON, Thomas (1758–1815) Soldier

The fifth son of Thomas Picton of Poyston Hall (**Rudbaxton**), Picton was commissioned in the 12th Regiment of Foot in 1771. As governor of Trinidad in the 1790s, his cruelty reached legendary proportions. He distinguished himself in the Peninsular War, commanding the 3rd Division, but was bitterly disappointed to be denied the peerage granted to the other generals at the conclusion of the campaign. Knighted in 1815, he commanded the 5th Division at Quatre Bras and, though wounded, he led the charge at Waterloo, and was killed. His remains lie in St Paul's Cathedral, **London** where there is a monument to him, as there are at **Carmarthen** and in the City Hall, **Cardiff**.

PICTURESQUE MOVEMENT, The

A phase of taste, especially in landscape **garden**ing and related **architecture**, which enjoyed early application in Wales. The movement was stimulated by the publication of **William Gilpin**'s *Observations on the River Wye* (1782) and Sir Uvedale Price's *An Essay on the Picturesque* (1794, with additional volumes in 1798 and 1810). In a long controversy between Price and his **Herefordshire** neighbour, Richard Payne Knight, the 'picturesque' was defined as an aesthetic quality between the 'sublime' and the 'beautiful', and characterized by rugged wildness in the landscape and asymmetrical irregularity in buildings. As a friend of **Thomas Johnes** and a frequent visitor to Hafod (**Pontarfynach**), Price was influential in Johnes's early use of picturesque principles in his experimental landscaping there (1786 onwards). **John Nash** also came under Price's influence when Price commissioned him to design Castle House, **Aberystwyth** (*c.*1791), as a castellated summer villa based on a triangular plan; later it was

Paul Peter Piech's portrayal of Harri Webb's poem 'Colli Iaith'

incorporated into the hotel which eventually became home to the University College of Wales (*see* **University of Wales, Aberystwyth**).

PIECH, Paul Peter (1920–96)
Artist and printmaker

Piech came to **Cardiff** as a United States serviceman during the **Second World War**, married a local woman and, after a career in advertising and teaching in **Britain** and America, made his home in **Porthcawl**. His deceptively simple wood and lino prints came into vogue as posters from the 1960s onwards, when the iconography of contemporary protest movements reached an international audience. He later produced work that reflected culture and dissent in Wales.

PIERCE, T[homas] Jones (1905–64) Historian

Born and educated in **Liverpool**, Pierce became tutor in the extramural department and assistant lecturer in the history department at **Bangor** (1930), where he worked on the social structure of medieval Wales. Appointed a special lecturer in Welsh medieval history at **Aberystwyth** in 1945, he was given a personal chair in 1948. He was the founder-editor of the **Caernarfonshire** Historical Society Transactions, and was elected president of the **Cambrian Archaeological Association** (1964). His main historical contributions – which include studies of remarkable acumen – were published in *Medieval Welsh Society* (1972), edited by J. Beverley Smith.

PIERCY, Benjamin (1827–88) Railway engineer Trefeglwys-born Benjamin Piercy built much of the **railway** track linking the English **border** with the Welsh coast in association with the contractors David Davies (*see* **Davies family of Llandinam**) and **Thomas Savin**, and engineered the Welsh Coast Railway, with its 731.5-m viaduct at **Barmouth**. One of his triumphs was the 35-m Talerddig rock cutting (1861), then the deepest in the world. He built railways in north-east Wales with **Henry Robertson** and engineered track through difficult terrain in Sardinia.

PIERS

The earliest piers were developed as landing places for coastal steamers. Later, they became popular places along which tourists could promenade. Following the growth of **railway tourism** from the middle of the 19th century, piers were built for pleasure and became important features of many fast-growing seaside resorts around Wales. The earliest of Wales's nine pleasure piers was erected at **Aberystwyth** in 1865; a storm washed part of it away the following year, and later it was further reduced in length by a fire. At 717.5 m, the pier at **Rhyl** (1867) was the longest in Wales, before being demolished in 1972. The longest surviving piers are at **Llandudno** (699 m, erected 1876–8) and **Bangor** (457 m, erected 1896). There are also substantial piers at **Penarth** (1892–4), Mumbles, **Swansea** (1897–8) and **Colwyn Bay** (1898–1900). The pier at **Rhos-on-Sea**, originally erected in 1869 at Douglas, Isle of **Man**, and imported to Rhos in 1895, was demolished in 1954, a year after the demolition of that at **Tenby** (built 1899).

PIGEON RACING

A breed of pigeon, descended from the rock dove and having little relationship with the wood pigeon, was domesticated by the ancient Egyptians and used by most armies to carry messages, from the **Roman** era to the mid-20th century. In the early 19th century, pigeon breeders in Belgium and **Britain** began to race their birds. The establishment of the Royal National Homing Association (1896) was followed by the founding of the Welsh Homing Union and the Royal Pigeon Racing Association (based in **Welshpool**). The sport was a passion in Wales, especially between the 1930s and the 1950s, when racing birds in their crates were a familiar sight at **railway** stations. The image of pigeons circling the terraced **housing** of Wales was memorably captured by the poet **Idris Davies**'s exhortation 'Send Out Your Homing Pigeons, Dai'. Gwenallt (**David James Jones**) offered similar images.

PIGS

Pigs are lowland animals not ideally suited to the damp **climate** of Wales. Although no longer a significant contributor to the Welsh agricultural **economy**, the pig and its

Eric Malthouse, *A Flurry of Pigeons* (1954)

Pilgrimage: a stamp featuring St David's Cathedral issued by the Spanish Post Office in the 1960s

relative the **wild boar** have long featured in Welsh myth, **literature**, folklore and **place names**.

Medieval pigs exhibited many primitive features owing to frequent crossing with wild boar. Pigs were let loose for forest pasturage from mid summer to mid winter, but as woodlands were cleared they became beasts of field and sty. By the 18th century, several Welsh forms of pig were recognized: some were black, brown or spotted, but most were light coloured; all were long in snout, thin backed and slow to mature. The pig's ability to produce a good yield of meat from low quality feed was a godsend to poor, self-sufficient farmers. Pig-killing day was one of the most important in the farm calendar, when the meat would be prepared for salting for the winter. Those parts which could not be salted were consumed in an orgy of meat eating – a practice which came to an end with the coming of refrigeration.

Demand for pork increased during the **Industrial Revolution**. Pigs would be walked by **drovers** to **England** or shipped, for example, from **Llŷn** to **Liverpool**. Breeds improved considerably during the 19th century, and until the mid-20th century the pigsty remained an essential feature not only of every farm and smallholding, but of many a terraced home in the industrial areas.

The Welsh white breed, improved through the 20th century, has little fat and can be reared easily indoors or out. Two main production systems are found: intensive, where large white, Welsh or Landrace pigs are kept indoors; or extensive, where mainly saddleback, Welsh or crossbred pigs are kept outdoors. However, the reliance of modern systems on hybrid lines and processed cereal has seen pig production concentrate in the grain-growing areas away from Wales.

PILGRIMAGE

In AD 326, Helena, mother of Constantine, the first Christian Emperor, went to Jerusalem to discover the holy places connected with the life of Jesus. Many pilgrims, including some from Wales, followed in her footsteps. An old tradition tells of a visit to Jerusalem by the three **saints**: **David**, **Padarn** and **Teilo**. Rome, burial place of Peter, keeper of the keys of heaven, drew Welsh pilgrims, reputedly among them **Hywel Dda**.

By the 8th century, pilgrimage had become part of the penitential system of the Church. Throughout the Middle Ages, Welsh pilgrims visited Santiago de Compostela in Spain. (In the 1960s, the Spanish Post Office issued stamps illustrating departure points of the pilgrimage, one of them bearing a picture of **St David's** Cathedral.) The papacy allegedly declared that two visits to St David's equalled one to Rome and three visits equalled a pilgrimage to Jerusalem. The tradition that 20,000 saints were buried on Bardsey (*see* **Islands**) attracted many visitors there. The **wells of the saints** were attractive to pilgrims, particularly those at St **Winefride**'s well at **Holywell** and St Mary's well at Penrhys (**Rhondda**).

The impact of pilgrimage on Welsh culture is reflected in medieval religious **literature**. Pilgrimage was attacked by exponents of the **Protestant Reformation**, but pilgrimage continued, especially to Holywell, which was visited by James II in 1687. In the 19th century, places associated with the origins of Nonconformity (*see* **Nonconformists**) attracted pilgrimages and, by the opening of the 21st century, the appeal of ancient sites such as St David's and Bardsey was increasingly evident.

PILLETH, Battle of

On 22 June 1402, **Owain Glyndŵr** won a famous victory at Bryn Glas, a hill near the village of Pilleth (**Whitton**). His soldiers overwhelmed a **county** levy from **Herefordshire** led by Edmund **Mortimer**. Hundreds of **English**men were slain and Welsh **women** reputedly mutilated their corpses.

PINE MARTEN

Once found throughout much of **Britain**, this elusive member of the weasel family may be on the verge of extinction in Wales. An early literary reference to the pine marten comes in the lullaby 'Pais Dinogad' (Dinogad's coat) found interpolated in *Y Gododdin*: 'Pais Dinogad fraith fraith/ O grwyn balaod ban wraith.' (Dinogad's shift is speckled, speckled/ It was made from the pelts of martens.) The marten has dark-brown fur with a yellow throat patch and a long, bushy tail, and can grow up to 54 cm long. Prized for its fur by medieval princes (its pelt, according to Welsh **law**, was variously worth 24 or 28 pence); despised as a pest by Victorian gamekeepers, the marten was hunted relentlessly. It favours well-established coniferous plantations and remote, wooded, rocky areas, mostly in **Snowdonia** and the north-east.

PIOZZI, Hester Lynch (Mrs Thrale; 1741–1821) Author

She was born in the mansion of Bodfel (**Llannor**), to a family descended from the Lleweni (**Denbigh**) branch of the **Salusbury family**, and when she was 22 she married Henry Thrale, a rich **London** brewer. She is remembered chiefly on account of her friendship with Samuel Johnson, about whom she published a collection of anecdotes (1786); she also published the first edition of his letters (1788). In 1784, after the death of her husband, she married – to the Doctor's considerable disapproval – Gabriel Piozzi, an Italian musician, and they made their home at Brynbella (**Tremeirchion**). An attractive, mercurial woman, she corresponded with a wide circle of eminent people; a collection of her letters is kept at the **National Library**.

PIPER, John (1903–92) Artist and writer

John Piper, an English-born modernist, married the artist and writer Myfanwy Evans (1911–97), visited Wales and became a romantic. He illustrated, painted, made collages, tapestries and **stained glass**, and designed for the theatre. His eye always found the drama in a landscape, expressing the atmospheric rather than the scenic in his **paintings**.

John Piper, *Coast of Pembroke* (1938–40)

While engaged in the 'Recording **Britain**' scheme during the **Second World War**, he worked in **Cardiff** and **Swansea**. Between 1949 and the early 1960s he lived in Nant Ffrancon (**Llanllechid**), and later moved to **Pembrokeshire**.

PIRACY

As maritime trade developed around the coast of Wales and beyond in the 16th and 17th centuries, so did the activity of those less scrupulous mariners who sought to make a quick and often substantial profit by plundering **ships** engaged on legitimate trade. In Wales, the problem of piracy was especially acute in **Pembrokeshire** in the late 16th century, and it was compounded by the fact that the whole spectrum of society, from aristocrat to **fish**erman, was involved in various aspects of illegal trade. In 1563, for instance, the merchants of **Tenby** financed the ship *Thesus* on what was ostensibly a fishing expedition to the Grand Banks off Newfoundland. The expedition went no further than the Western Isles of **Scotland**, and plundered German and Scottish vessels returning from the rich fishing waters of the North Atlantic. Pirates operating from south Pembrokeshire also raided vessels involved in trade in the Severn Sea. Attempts to suppress these activities were largely doomed to failure, because of the involvement in piracy of officials such as George Clark of **Pembroke**; he kept an alehouse at **Angle**, a recognized rendezvous of pirates such as **John Callice**.

The exploits of pirates who operated around the coasts of **Britain** pale into insignificance when compared with those of the 'Brothers of the Coast', concerned with the plunder of Spanish ships and property. **Welsh** buccaneers such as **Henry Morgan** and **Bartholomew Roberts** (Barti Ddu or Black Bart) were notable members of that notorious fraternity.

PISTYLL, Gwynedd (2069 ha; 492 inhabitants)

Adjoining **Nefyn** halfway along the northern coast of the **Llŷn** Peninsula, the **community**'s only settlement of any size is Llithfaen, a village which developed in the 19th century to house employees of the **granite** quarries of the **Eifl** range. To prevent its closure, Llithfaen's Victoria Hotel has been acquired by a co-operative of local residents. The medieval church of St **Beuno**, Pistyll, contains a 12th-century font. Nant Gwrtheyrn, a hamlet on the coast built to house quarrymen and approached by a vertiginous track, was abandoned in 1959. In 1978, the hamlet became a centre where intensive **Welsh-language** courses could be held in an area where Welsh remains dominant.

PLACE NAMES

Place names are a living record of an area's past. Knowledge about the derivation, meaning and development of a place name is of considerable significance to scholars, particularly as a means of interpreting language and landscape. The inhabitants of an area, local historians and the wider public also take an interest in place names. In Wales, the onomastic element in ancient Welsh legends – that is, the use of place names to infer 'historical' narratives – demonstrates a long-standing fascination with place names. In recent times, that interest is reflected in academic projects that record and analyse place names – the work of

Melville Richards in particular – and in scholarly and popular publications and in radio programmes.

One key purpose of place names is to describe the landscape. For instance, **Rhuddlan** was *rhudd* (red); in **Waunfawr** there was a *gwaun* (pasture, moorland); in Gellilydan a *celli* (grove); **Aberporth** had a *porth* (landing, bay); **Trallwng** was very *llwng* (wet, miry). Occasionally, a word or element developed a further meaning, such as *blaen*, meaning '**river** source' in Blaenaman and then 'highland' in **Blaenau Gwent**, or *nant*, meaning 'valley' in Nantlle and then 'stream' in Oernant.

Place names frequently contain river names, some of the oldest names in Wales. Some refer to a **Celt**ic god or goddess (Alun); others mark a boundary (Bargod); others refer to a person (**Teifi**), an animal (Twrch), a weapon (**Cleddau**, 'sword') or to a characteristic of the water (**Dyfi**, 'black'; **Tawe**, 'dark').

Land was frequently associated with people, as indicated by territorial suffixes such as *-iog* in **Tudweiliog** (Tudwal's land), *-ydd* in **Meirionnydd**, and *-i* in Cydweli (Cadwal; E. **Kidwelly**). Later, especially with reference to industry, a place was associated with a landowner or employer, as with **Porthmadog (W. A. Madocks)**, **Beaufort** (duke of Beaufort), Morriston (Sir John Morris) and Treharris (F. W. Harries).

Place names are a record of Wales's history. *Crug* and *gorsedd* denote a 'tumulus' or 'cairn' (Crugybar (**Cynwyl Gaeo**); Gorsedd (**Whitford**)), and *din* a 'fort' or 'castle' (Dinbych; E. **Denbigh**). A number of Brythonic or Early **Welsh** words survived in a Latinized form, since the **Romans** occasionally adopted native names for their forts. For example, the Roman name for the fort at **Caerhun** was Canovium, a reference to the river (**Conwy**) based on a Brythonic word which is possibly the root of *cawn* (reed) or the word *con-* (excellent, full). It is likely that the Brythonic words corresponding to *môr* (sea) and *din* are in both the Roman Maridunum and Myrddin (*see* **Merlin**) of Caerfyrddin (**Carmarthen**). Frequently, there is a link between a place name and the language of settlers in a specific period. Many of the **English** names of Wales go back to the **Mercian** advance from the 8th century onwards. Some refer to the English as a group (Englefield) or as individuals (Coleshill). The commonest element is the *-ton* (farm) suffix seen so frequently in **England**. It was often Cymricized to *-twn* in the south (Brychdwn) and to *-tyn* in the north-east (**Prestatyn**). In time, for various reasons, dual names emerged, some referring broadly to the same feature (Caergybi/**Holyhead**), others to different features within the same locality (Abertawe/**Swansea**), while others were translations (Glyn Ebwy/**Ebbw Vale**).

A number of places are associated with **Viking** raids. **Anglesey** is *-ey* (island) combined with a Viking personal name to signify 'the isle of Ongul', while Swansea may be 'the isle of Sveinn'. **Fishguard** derives from *fiskr* (**fish**) and *garthr* (fish yard), and **Milford (Haven)** from *melr* (sand bank) and *fjorthr* (fiord). From the 11th century, the **French**-speakers left their mark, as in **Beaumaris** (*beau* 'fine', *marais* 'marsh') and Trefaldwyn (**Montgomery**), 'Baldwyn's settlement'. Montgomery, indeed, is among those names transferred from places in northern France.

There are links with **religion** too. The original meaning of *llan* was enclosure (as in *corlan*, '**sheep**fold') and then

Plaid Cymru, 1927: Lewis Valentine, Ambrose Bebb, D. J. Williams, Mai Roberts, Saunders Lewis, Kate Roberts, H. R. Jones, E. Prosser Rhys

land or a cemetery or ecclesiastical building which is enclosed. Usually *llan* is added to a **saint**'s name (**Llanbadarn**) or to a feature of the landscape (**Llangoed**, in which *coed* means 'wood'). The origin of *betws* (prayer house) is the two Old English words which correspond to bead-house, while a number of place names have developed from Latin and Greek, such as **Merthyr** (martyrium, 'saint's grave') and Basaleg (basilica, 'church'). Several places were named after chapels, among them **Bethesda** and Bethlehem (**Llangadog**). Signposts in Wales long mangled Welsh place names; changing them was a major feature of the 1960s campaigns of **Cymdeithas yr Iaith Cymraeg** (The Welsh Language Society).

PLAID [GENEDLAETHOL] CYMRU
(The [National] Party of Wales)

Plaid Genedlaethol Cymru was founded in 1925 through the amalgamation of two groups convinced that Welsh national claims could no longer be advanced through the traditional **Liberal Party** or the newer **Labour Party**. One was a **home rule** association established by **H. R. Jones** in **Caernarfon**, and the other a clandestine **group** led by academics **Saunders Lewis** and **Ambrose Bebb**.

Originally overwhelmingly a movement of **Welsh** speakers, Plaid Genedlaethol Cymru (the National Party of Wales – the name was changed to Plaid Cymru in 1945), with the conservative **Roman Catholic** convert Saunders Lewis as its president (1926–39), made little political headway. Its objectives, formulated in 1931, mirrored Lewis's concerns; they included dominion status for Wales with membership of the League of Nations, the creation of a distributivist **economy** (*see* **Perchentyaeth**), and official status for the Welsh language. The party contested its first parliamentary election in 1929, when **Lewis Valentine** won 609 votes (1.6%) in **Caernarfonshire**. It fought Caernarfonshire again in 1931 and 1935 with some minimal advance in support. The party did, however, achieve some success in the field of **broadcasting**

and was the mainstay of the petition to secure official status for the Welsh language (*see* **Welsh Courts Act (1942)**).

In 1936, the 400th anniversary of the **Act of 'Union'**, Saunders Lewis, **D. J. Williams** and Lewis Valentine burnt workmen's huts at a new Royal Air Force base (*see* **Penyberth Bombing School, The burning of**). All three were imprisoned, but Lewis's hopes that the action would draw sustained support to the party proved unfounded. Lewis was frustrated by the lack of growth and disappointed by a 1938 conference decision rejecting both violent methods and his views on *perchentyaeth*. Also angered by internal **socialist** criticism of his social and economic views – which, though critical of Fascism, focused on **communism** as Europe's major threat – he resigned as president in 1939.

Lewis hoped a wartime policy of Welsh neutrality would see scores of young Welsh men and **women** refusing to fight in '**England**'s army', but there were only 12 imprisonments for **conscientious objection** solely on **nationalist** grounds. However, Saunders Lewis's substantial vote (22.5%) in the **University of Wales** parliamentary by-election of 1943 provided an unexpected boost. In 1945, the party fought 7 parliamentary election campaigns, compared with only 5 over the previous 20 years.

With such increased activism, and the election of **Gwynfor Evans** as president, Plaid Cymru embarked on a new era. A religious **Nonconformist**, a political liberal and a **pacifist**, Evans was a more familiar figure for Welsh voters, and his leadership brought continuing though slow growth for the party. In 1959, the party contested 20 of Wales's 36 seats; it was then a far stronger party than the Scottish National Party, which contested only 5 of **Scotland**'s 72 constituencies in that election. An intake of more politicized members from the south-east began pressing for party modernization, while concerns about the decline of the Welsh language led to the establishment of **Cymdeithas yr Iaith Gymraeg** (the Welsh Language Society) at the party's 1962 summer school.

In 1964, Labour fulfilled its pledge to appoint a **secretary of state for Wales**. The general elections of October 1964 and March 1966 proved disappointing for Plaid Cymru but, on 14 July 1966, Gwynfor Evans secured the party's first parliamentary victory in the remarkable **Carmarthen** by-election. During a period of heightened expectations, Plaid Cymru candidates came close to winning by-elections in the Labour heartland constituencies of **Rhondda** West (1967) and **Caerphilly** (1968). In the 1970 general election, the party fought all the Welsh seats for the first time; it has done so in every subsequent general election. Its vote increased from 61,071 in 1966 to 175,016 in 1970, but Gwynfor Evans lost his seat and the votes in the south-east failed to reach by-election levels. In February 1974, Dafydd Wigley (b.1943) captured Caernarfon and Dafydd Elis Thomas (b.1946) won **Merioneth**, seats they retained in October 1974, when Gwynfor Evans regained Carmarthen. Nevertheless, the party's overall vote was in decline, a feature of its history until the 1990s. Despite some local **government** gains in the southern **coal**field, the party seemed incapable of breaking out of the Welsh-speaking areas.

The defeat of the Labour government's **devolution** proposals in 1979, followed by Gwynfor Evans's retirement in 1981 after 36 years as president, forced a period of major reassessment, which saw 'decentralist socialism' adopted as party policy. During Dafydd Elis Thomas's radical presidency (1984–91), particular efforts were made to attract non-traditional supporters. Improving local effectiveness was reflected in further parliamentary gains in **Anglesey** (1987) and **Ceredigion** (1992).

During Dafydd Wigley's second period as president (1991–2000), Plaid Cymru made remarkable progress. In May 1999, using a new bilingual name – Plaid Cymru/The Party of Wales – it gained 28.4% of the constituency vote and won 17 of the 60 seats in the first **National Assembly** elections. Of the 17, 8 were regional seats and 9 were constituencies, among them the coalfield seats of **Islwyn**, **Llanelli** and Rhondda. Plaid Cymru became the official opposition in the Assembly. Its role was strengthened by its control of the **Gwynedd**, Caerphilly and **Rhondda Cynon Taff county** councils and by its success in capturing two of Wales's five European parliamentary seats. The successful 1999 breakthrough into the southern coalfield was not repeated in the general election of 2001, when the party lost one seat (**Anglesey**) but gained another (Carmarthen East and **Dinefwr**). Nor was the breakthrough maintained in the second Assembly elections (2003). By losing **Conwy**, Islwyn, Llanelli and Rhondda and one regional seat, its presence in the Assembly was reduced to 12. Its overall constituency vote declined to 21.2%. Ieuan Wyn Jones (b.1949), the president since 2000, immediately resigned and the task of leading the chastened party fell to the folk singer and political activist Dafydd Iwan (b.1943); Ieuan Wyn Jones surprised many by offering himself, and being elected, as party leader in the National Assembly. In addition, Elfyn Llwyd (b.1951) the MP for **Meirionnydd**, was the leader of the party at Westminster. In the 2005 election for the British parliament, the party failed to win back Anglesey and saw the Liberal Democrats regain Ceredigion, reducing to three its total of MPs. In 2007, in the third election for the National Assembly, the party secured 15 seats. Labour's 26 seats did not give that party a majority. Attempts to create a Plaid Cymru-led 'rainbow' coalition including the **Conservatives** and Liberal Democrats failed, and Plaid Cymru went into coalition with Labour. Ieuan Wyn Jones entered the cabinet as deputy first minister and was joined in government by Elin Jones (Ceredigion), Rhodri Glyn Thomas (Carmarthen East and **Dinefwr**) and Jocelyn Davies (Wales South-East).

PLANTS

There are some 1500 plant species in Wales, which represent about 70% of the species found in **Britain**. Very few are survivors of the last Ice Age, for most of the plants of Wales are immigrants.

At the peak of the most recent Ice Age, about 21,000 years ago, most of Wales was covered by a sheet of ice 800 m thick. There was plant life only along a strip of land just south of the ice, and possibly on the highest **mountains** protruding above it, known as nunataks. When the ice began melting, from c.18,000 BC onwards, plants from the periglacial areas and the nunataks gradually recolonized the land, among them various kinds of birch, willow, juniper, grass and sedge, and several arctic-alpine species (plants that grow above the tree line in both the Arctic and the Alps). The **soil** formed by glacial debris was rich in nutrients, and plants could expand into an open environment free from competition. There was time, before Britain became an **island**, for plants to migrate to and from the European mainland. Among the immigrants were the aquatic plants, which came to occupy the **lakes** such as those dammed behind glacial moraines, and various kinds of tree. By c.6000 BC, Britain had become an island, and by then the steppe grasslands of western Europe, Wales included, had been transformed into thick forest (*see* **Forestry**). Extensive woodlands growing on coastal plains were drowned: at **Borth**, for instance, the stumps of ancient alder, birch, oak and pine may be seen sticking through the mud at low tide.

Information about the plants that survived the last glaciation and about those that immigrated during the postglacial period has been obtained from their remains in bogs, levels of **peat** and mud in lakes. Focused initially on macrofossils, such as trees, bark, leaves, seeds, fruit and conifer cones, attention turned to palynology (pollen analysis), a term coined by Harold Augustus Hyde, former keeper of botany at the **National Museum [of] Wales**. The palynologists identified two shrubs from the end of the glaciation period – the dwarf birch and the trailing azalea – which are now extinct in Wales. The analysis of deposits from **Cors Caron**, now a raised bog, enabled them to identify flora from the time c.11,000 years ago when it was a **lake**. They found remains of the common reed, birch, pine, hazel and juniper. Some 8000 years ago, elm and oak had arrived. But, by about 4000 BC, the numbers of pine started to fall and eventually the pine became extinct as a native tree. The oak (*see below*), elm and hazel spread rapidly across the country, since the pioneering birch trees offered no competition. Although the beech and the hornbeam arrived in Britain long before it became an island, their advance was hampered by the established mixed oak

P

The Snowdon lily

woods; they are native, therefore, only to south-east Wales. The tree felling that began in the Mesolithic Age (*see* **Palaeolithic and Mesolithic Ages**) and was pursued relentlessly by farmers of the **Neolithic** and later ages contributed to a decline in the number of elms.

Almost no primary woodland now survives. The vast tracts of wind-bleached moorland that today are considered typical Welsh mountain wildernesses are anything but natural landscapes, being relict sites on a scale that dwarfs even the despoliation wrought by the **coal** and **slate** industries. The open oak and birch woodland of the higher ground – rather than the tangled, swampy forest of the valley bottoms – was the first to be felled. The story of 'Culhwch ac Olwen' in *The Mabinogion*, although first written down in the 11th century, may embody a memory of those early deforestations: the giant Ysbaddaden instructs Culhwch to uproot a great thicket and burn it, 'so that the cinders and ashes thereof be its manure, and that it be ploughed and sown ...' The deterioration in the **climate** during the late **Bronze Age** led to waterlogging, acidification of soil and the stifling by peat of the upland pastures. These moorland conditions favoured the spread of heather, cowberry, bilberry, gorse, fescue, rush, cottongrass (*see below*) and moor-grass, the last two of which turn a fiery red in the autumn.

Although periods of intense deforestation would ensue intermittently until the early decades of the 20th century, Welsh medieval **law** suggests that by about the 10th century there had evolved a greater sense of equilibrium between society and its woodland surroundings. The beech was valued at 60 pence and the oak at 120 pence, a sum equivalent to the value of a king's barn; the various kinds of woodland were differentiated and a woodman's functions carefully regulated. It was less easy to legislate for the impact of domesticated animals. By the Middle Ages, **goats** and **sheep** grazing the uplands had radically reduced the variety of flora, and the constant nibbling of modern flocks

continues to deny sway to plants such as rowan and aspen that might otherwise flourish.

Less attractive to sheep are the screes and rocky slabs of the mountain tops, where heavy rainfall, relentless winds and harsh frosts lead to a much reduced plant life of ferns (*see below*), mosses, clubmosses, lichens, dwarf willow, meadow grasses, rushes, sedges, starveling bilberry and heather. Botanists have found the mountains of Wales, and of **Snowdonia** in particular, rewarding territory. An early visitor was Thomas Johnson (*c.*1600–44) who recorded moss campion, mountain sorrel, alpine saw-wort, dwarf willow and three saxifrages – along with two maritime interlopers, sea campion and thrift, which seem to find the lack of competition to their liking, as they do on the bare, **lead** waste at Rhandirmwyn (**Llanfair-ar-y-bryn**) and elsewhere. After four visits to **Snowdon**, the English botanist John Ray (1627–1705) recorded only one plant, the parsley fern, but his published work, detailing all the British plants known to him, included many from Wales, information about which he had received from the records of **Edward Lhuyd**. Other arctic-alpine plants found in Snowdonia include the Snowdon lily (*see below*), spring sandwort, mountain avens, chickweed willow herb, alpine cinquefoil, roseroot and alpine meadow rue.

In the south, on the **Brecon Beacons**, the **Black Mountain** and Craig y Llyn (**Rhigos**), the arctic-alpine presence includes spring sandwort, dwarf willow, purple saxifrage, roseroot and cowberry. They are joined on Old Red Sandstone cliffs by such plants as green spleenwort, mossy saxifrage, northern bedstraw, cowslip, rock stonecrop and stone bramble.

Another apparently inhospitable environment is the salt marsh, formed by the deposition of mud in estuaries. An early colonizer of this mud is glasswort, a salad plant which was, when reduced to ash, used in **glass** manufacture. Some salt-marsh plants can withstand longer inundation in salt water than others, with the result that they occupy different distances from the shoreline, forming distinct plant zones. Two attractive plants at the halfway stage in the plant succession are the sea aster and sea lavender. At the uppermost level of the marsh can be found the salt-marsh rush and the sea rush.

Near the salt marsh there may be sand dunes, a fairly common habitat in Wales and one dependent for stability on the long, binding rhizomes of marram grass. The surface of dunes is dry and poor in nutrients, but species such as the sand sedge and red fescue grass will colonize and assist in the process of stabilization. In the hollows between dunes, which may be covered in water throughout the winter, may be found creeping willow, round-leaved wintergreen, autumn gentian and dune gentian; dune gentian, found nowhere else in Britain, occurs only in Wales's southern **counties**. The dunes are home also to three rare orchids (*see below*): the fen orchid, found only in the south; the Welsh marsh orchid, found in **Ceredigion**, **Anglesey** and **Gwynedd**; and the dune helleborine, found on the dune slacks of Newborough Warren (**Rhosyr**), Anglesey, its only habitat in Wales.

The 20th century witnessed a reduction in the diversity of plant life. Following a shortage of timber during the **First World War**, vast swathes of upland Wales were planted with angular, regimented plots of – predominantly – **North American** sitka spruce, a monoculture that saps nutrients from the soil and acidifies water courses. Tree canopies in many parts of Wales have been severely thinned by acid rain. **Hedgerow** and meadow plants have been drastically reduced by regular ploughing and resowing, hedge removal, the use of fertilizers, herbicides and pesticides and the grazing of sheep on meadowland. Cornfields red with poppies and meadows white and golden with ox-eye daisies and marigolds exist, for the most part, only as a memory. The once common cowslip is now a rarity, as are bird's-foot trefoil, lady's mantle, yellow rattle, marsh valerian, devil's bit scabious, wood horsetail, saw-wort, moonwort, various orchids and many vetches and sedges. In 2005, *The Vascular Plant Red Data List* for Great Britain warned that one in five of Wales's wildflower species was faced with extinction, prominent among them the Welsh cotoneaster (*see below*), the corn buttercup (found on only one site, in the **Vale of Glamorgan**), the western juniper (of seven plants left in Britain, four are on Ramsey Island, **Pembrokeshire**), the spreading bellflower and the Deptford pink.

Certain plants introduced deliberately or by accident proliferate at the expense of less robust species and are difficult to control or eradicate. *Rhododendron ponticum*, imported as game cover during the 19th century, now empurples many slopes, especially in the north-west, with its thick and rampant jungles. Japanese knotweed has advanced from **railways**, **canal** sides and stream margins to overrun wastelands and many a cemetery. Spartina grass, introduced in the early 20th century to stabilize estuary mud, has become an aggressive colonizer all around the coast, stifling other mud-growing plants such as glassworts, sea-blite and sea spurrey.

Plants of particular significance in Wales

APPLE
The rarest apples in the world in 2000 were found growing on a single tree on windswept Bardsey (*see* **Islands**). Boldly striped in pink over cream, *Afal Enlli* (the Bardsey apple), the hardy survivor from a monastic orchard species, was discovered in that year. *Afal Enlli* is now available commercially. Other Welsh apple varieties include the **Monmouthshire** green, *cawr y berllan* (orchard giant), *bysedd Mair* (Mary's finger), Marged Nicholas, Glory of the West, *pig yr ŵydd* (goose's beak) and *twll tin gŵydd* (goose's arse or Lord Grosvenor).

CLOUDBERRY
Known in **Welsh** as *mwyaren y Berwyn* (the Berwyn blackberry), it was first recorded on the **Berwyn Mountains** by Edward Lhuyd (1660–1709), and noted in 1998 in **Shropshire** and in 2000 on **Pumlumon**. Its flowers are white, solitary and dioecious (having male and female sexual organs on different plants), and its fruit orange; it grows to a height of 20 cm.

COMMON COTTONGRASS
The white, cotton-like head of this perennial plant, growing to a height of 20–75 cm and known in Welsh as *plu'r gweunydd* (feather of the moorlands) or *sidan y waun* (moor silk), is conspicuous in bog land when the plant is in fruit. It used to pain **O. M. Edwards** to travel by train across the desolate landscape of Cors Caron, until one fine July day when he saw it in its glory, lit up by the cottongrass.

FERNS AND THEIR ALLIES
The giant clubmosses (up to 45 m tall), ferns and horsetails that grew in Wales 300 million years ago are now fossils in the coal measures; but their smaller relations grow in profusion today. Wales's damp woodlands and rocky gorges combine with an Atlantic climate to provide them with ideal conditions. Bracken (up to 3 m tall), the bane of farmers (although it invariably indicates productive ground below), is the most familiar fern; the rarest, found in wet fissures and on screes in Snowdonia, include alpine woodsia and oblong woodsia, and the holly fern. First recorded by Edward Lhuyd in 1690, the holly fern was nearly wiped out by over-collecting in the 19th century. More widespread on moorland and mountain habitats throughout Wales are evergreen, perennial clubmosses such as the stag's horn clubmoss; the rarest of these plants is the marsh clubmoss, found on wet moorlands in the north-west and in Pembrokeshire. The horsetails are perennial plants with jointed stems, and spores in cones on the heads of some stems. A common one, cursed by **garden**ers, is the field horsetail. A rarity is rough horsetail, once used as a polisher of metal, wood and bone. Two of Britain's three native quillworts – quillwort and spring quillwort – are widespread in Wales; they form rosettes of narrow leaves on the beds of lakes, to a depth of 6 m and more.

The spreading bellflower

GRASSES

As they occupy around 80% of the land devoted to **agriculture**, grasses are, commercially, far and away Wales's most important plants. Of Wales's grassland, 42% is permanent pasture, 13% is devoted to the production of hay and the rest consists of rough grazing and **common land**. The grasslands came into existence through a process begun in the Neolithic Age – the clearing of the wildwood and the creation of fields. With its mild climate and high rainfall, Wales is one of the best countries in the world for the growth of grasses.

Grasslands are generally divided into three classes. In Wales, acidic grasslands – those deficient in lime – predominate; they include the rough grazing areas of the uplands as well as much of the permanent pasture and hay meadows of more favoured areas. Basic grasslands – those with adequate lime – are much rarer, although there are fine examples on the Great Orme (**Llandudno**) and on the **Gower** peninsula. Also rare are neutral grasslands overlying soils that are only slightly acidic; they include some of the country's most productive pastures. The rich variety of plant species traditionally associated with grasslands – basic and neutral grasslands, in particular – has suffered through the adoption of intensive agriculture, but efforts are being made to re-establish species-rich habitats.

Wales has been in the front line of grasslands research, in particular through the work of the Welsh Plant Breeding Station founded at **Aberystwyth** by **George Stapledon** in 1919, and renamed the **Institute of Grassland and Environmental Research** (IGER); its famous S23 variety of perennial ryegrass has won worldwide fame.

The Radnor lily

LEYLAND CYPRESS

A cross between the genera *Cupressus* and *Chamaecyparis*, this coniferous tree originated at Leighton Park (**Forden**), purchased in 1848 by John Naylor, whose wealth derived from the Leyland Bank, **Liverpool**. Growing 30 m in 50 years, a hedge of Leylandia can cause trouble between neighbours.

MISTLETOE

Magical powers have been attributed to this plant – much reverenced by the **druids** – and its medicinal properties have been applied to both people and animals. Semi-parasitic on a large variety of trees, this evergreen shrub flowers from February to April and its white, viscous berries appear from November to December. Outside eastern **Breconshire** and the **Gwent Levels**, mistletoe is rare in Wales.

OAK

Sacred to the druids and a staple of folklore and fairytales, the oak was Wales's dominant tree for 7000 years, until the extensive planting of conifers in the 19th and 20th centuries. Sessile oaks are associated more with upland areas, and pedunculate oaks with lowland and eastern habitats. A significant shaper of the landscape, and the most valuable tree listed in medieval Welsh law, oak provided acorns for fattening **pigs**, tanbark for making **leather** and wood for a multitude of products.

ORCHIDS

One of Wales's most beautiful orchids, the bee orchid, is found across much of the country in calcareous pastures. Similarly widespread – on verges, in pastures and in woodland – is the early purple orchid. The dune slacks of the southern coast are home to the rare fen orchid. Also uncommon, although it has been recorded across Wales in damp situations under the shade of beech trees, is the pale brown bird's-nest orchid; lacking green leaves, it is dependent entirely on root-associated fungi to manufacture its food.

RADNOR LILY

When it was collected inadvertently in 1965 on Stanner Rocks (**Old Radnor**) – a site exceptionally rich in plant life – it was mistaken for the Snowdon lily. But in 1978 it was confirmed that the plant was *Gagea bohemica*, the Radnor lily, or, in Welsh, *seren-Fethlehem gynnar* (early star of Bethlehem). This plant has been recorded at no other site in Britain.

SERVICE TREE

When a single service tree (*Sorbus domestica*; as distinct from the wild service tree, *Sorbus torminalis*) in Wyre Forest, Worcestershire, was burnt down in 1862, it was accepted that that was the end of the tree as a native British species. But in May 1983, 'on the south **Glamorgan** coast' (the location being kept vague for security reasons), a group of trees was found that looked like the rowan (*Sorbus aucuparia*), but in one of the most exciting discoveries in the history of Welsh botany, they turned out to be examples of *Sorbus domestica*. Ten years later, another population of the tree was found, 4 km to the east of the first site. Both sites are south-facing maritime rocks of Lias **limestone**. The stunted trees, in the teeth of the wind, are between 3 and 5 m high.

SNOWDON LILY
Confined in Britain to Snowdonia, this perennial arctic-alpine plant was first recorded in Wales by Edward Lhuyd, in honour of whom, in 1812, it was named *Lloydia serotina*; the first publication of his plant appeared in Gibson's edition of **Camden**'s *Britannia* (1695). Unique in Britain as a bulbous plant confined to high altitudes, it flowers in the second and third weeks of June and grows to a height of 15 cm. Its narrow leaves resemble grass and its six-segmented flower is white with reddish veins. Although the lily can multiply by vegetative reproduction, there was concern about its future, since there was evidence neither of it being pollinated nor of it setting seed in Wales. In 2000, however, it was reported that it does multiply through sexual reproduction and that it sets viable seeds.

SNOWDONIA HAWKWEED
Thought to have become extinct soon after the mid-20th century, this small perennial – *Hieracium snowdoniense* – with brilliant yellow flowers was rediscovered in 2002 on a mountain slope at Cwm Idwal (**Llandygai**); it was first discovered there in 1887 by the botanist **J. E. Griffith**, and last seen in 1953. Classified as a species in 1955, it is one of the rarest plants in the world.

TENBY DAFFODIL
Introduced to but long naturalized in Pembrokeshire and **Carmarthenshire**, the **Tenby** daffodil flowers in April. Unlike the common wild daffodil, its petals and sepals are of the same deep yellow as the corona (or trumpet) and the leaves are flat without twists.

WELSH COTONEASTER
One of the world's rarest plants, there are only six bushes left in the wild, and they are all on the Great Orme (Llandudno), where grazing by goats could render the plant extinct.

WELSH POPPY
A yellow poppy native to Wales, south-west **England** and western **Ireland**, it favours wet, shady places under trees or on rocks and grows to a height of 61 cm. In 2006, it was chosen as the emblem of **Plaid [Genedlaethol] Cymru**.

WHITEBEAM
Two species of whitebeam are found only in Wales and were first recorded in the late 19th century by Augustine Ley, vicar of Sellack, **Herefordshire**. The lesser whitebeam (*Sorbus minima*) grows on the limestone cliffs of Craig y Cilau, the National Nature Reserve on **Mynydd Llangatwg**. The shrub won renown in 1947 when Tudor Watkins, MP for **Brecon** and **Radnor**, alerted parliament to the threat to *Sorbus minima* from military exercises in the vicinity of Craig y Cilau; the troops were ordered back to barracks. Ley's whitebeam (*Sorbus leyana*), named after its recorder, grows on the Darren Fach (Vaynor, **Merthyr**

Tydfil) and Penmoelallt (**Hirwaun**). Both species reach a height of 3 m, flowering during May and June, and fruiting in September.

YEW
Apart from the juniper, the yew is the sole conifer native to Wales. Capable of living for many hundreds of years, it may have been a sacred tree in pre-Christian times and is often found in churchyards; the anomalous 'bleeding yew' of **Nevern** is a famous example. Wales's oldest living tree is a 4000-year-old yew in **Llangernyw** churchyard. Yew was normally the wood used in late medieval times for **longbows**.

PLEBS' LEAGUE, The
A splendidly named educational and political organization, the Plebs' League was set up following the 1909 Ruskin College, **Oxford** strike, which had arisen over the place of **Marxist** ideas in the curriculum. Such was the enthusiasm of the rebels (and the inspiration of **Noah Ablett**) that they founded the **Central Labour College** and began publishing the Plebs' Magazine. A network of classes was set up, run by the Plebs' League, in which miners were educated in Marxist and, after 1910, **Syndicalist** ideas. The classes eventually became part of the wider tradition of adult **education**.

PLYGAIN Song style
The tradition of *plygain* singing dates back to the 18th century. One of the original meanings of *plygain* (from the **Latin** *pullicantio*, 'cock's crow') was a religious service held at a certain time in the morning, but by the second half of the 18th century it appeared to apply to any hour of the day, sometime between Christmas and the old **New Year**, for the singing of carols. The carols would be a mixture of native and imported melodies, with texts drawn from the work of local poets, or from **ballad** sheets and the oral tradition. Originally, the singers were usually men who would perform unaccompanied as soloists – or in duos, trios, quartets or groups. The tradition still continues in **Montgomeryshire**.

PNEUMOCONIOSIS and SILICOSIS
Pneumoconiosis, a generic term for lung disease resulting from the inhalation of dust, has been, in the form of **Coal Workers' Pneumoconiosis (CWP)**, a scourge of Welsh mining communities. Of the 22,000 British coalminers who, between 1931 and 1948, were forced to give up working in collieries because of the disease, 85% had worked in the south Wales coalfield. As haematite pneumoconiosis, the disease also affected miners of **iron** ore.

Silicosis, a distinct entity, is rare among coalminers, although it is grimly ironic that in the early days of 'stone dusting' (*see* **Colliery Disasters**) – the introduction underground of unreactive stone dust in order to minimize the risk of coal-dust explosions – the stone dust sometimes included shale or **slate**, thereby subjecting miners to the potential hazards of silicosis in addition to the possibility of pneumoconiosis. It is among slate workers that silicosis is prevalent, especially where, as in the Blaenau **Ffestiniog** mines, the quartz (silica) content is unusually high. While coal dust is relatively inert, silica is an active scar producer.

Both diseases cause small areas of scarring and occasional large nodules. **Tuberculosis** frequently complicates silicosis but is less common in CWP. The incidence of lung cancer is lower than normal in CWP, and in silicosis generally higher.

Symptoms are common to both, the lung scarring leading to increasing shortness of breath and, ultimately, heart failure. From 1929 onwards, sufferers from pneumoconiosis have been able to claim compensation, but claiming was a complicated business at least until the adoption of the Coal Workers' Pneumoconiosis Scheme in 1974. In 1979, following the passage of the Dust Disease (Workers' Compensation) Act, ex-quarry workers suffering from silicosis have been able to claim compensation from the **government**, but in the case of both diseases, the scale of the compensation is dependent upon the extent of the lung nodules. Although the related diseases of bronchitis and emphysema (dilated air space) have been long recognized as industrial diseases, it is only as a result of a case in the High Court in 1999 that they have been accepted as eligible for compensation. Protracted arbitration procedures have resulted too often in the affected workers' widows, rather than the workers themselves, receiving the pension.

Although slow to accept the enormity of the problems caused by pneumoconiosis, in 1945 the **government** funded the Medical Research Council's Pneumoconiosis Unit in **Cardiff**. Notable research was carried out by **Archibald Cochrane**, who tracked the fate of 3000 **Rhondda** Fach miners over a period of 30 years.

Asbestos, formerly widely used in the building and construction industry, continues to be a pneumoconiosis risk. It causes extensive lung scarring, and is a potent cause of both lung cancer and mesothelioma, a rare tumour of the lung's lining.

POBOL Y CWM Television serial

BBC Wales's long-running **Welsh-language** serial about the imaginary village of Cwm Deri. Shown since 1982 on **S4C**, it was first broadcast in October 1974 on a weekly basis. In September 1988, it became a daily offering, shown Monday to Friday. For a short period in 1991, with subtitles in Dutch, it was transmitted in the Netherlands, and it was the model for the Scots Gaelic-language serial *Machair*, once produced by BBC **Scotland**. With an omnibus edition broadcast on Sundays, which is subtitled in **English** (subtitles are available as an option on the weekday version), it consistently attracts the highest number of viewers of any Welsh-language programme – about 89,000 in 2007 (including repeat viewings). (*See also* **Broadcasting**.)

POETS OF THE GENTRY

This school of poets, which flourished *c.*1350–1650, favoured the *cywydd* metre and members of the school are often known as *cywyddwyr*. **Iolo Goch** was their prototype, being the first to use the *cywydd* for traditional eulogy addressed to **gentry** patrons. They were generally itinerant poets, visiting gentry houses to present their poems. Their staple products were eulogies and elegies; they also produced request poems and religious, amatory and satirical verse. Though mostly professional poets who had won bardic degrees, some were gentleman amateurs. From the late 16th century onwards, the Anglicization of the gentry, together with other social changes, caused the tradition to decline.

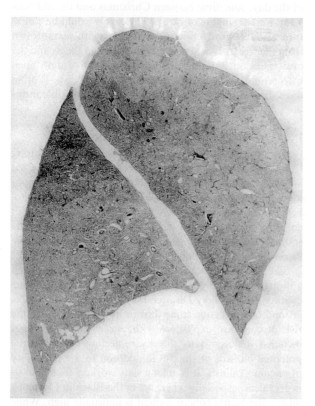
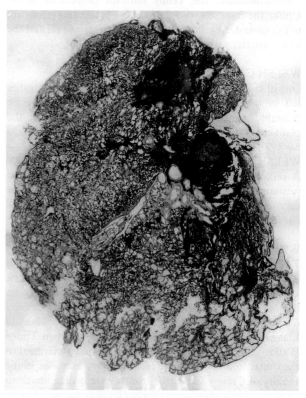

Pneumoconiosis, showing a normal lung on the left and that of a coal-worker with the disease on the right

POETS OF THE PRINCES

The poets (*see also* ***Gogynfeirdd***) who sang in the courts of the Welsh princes during the two centuries before the **Edwardian conquest**. Most of them were professional poets whose main duty was to compose learned and intricate eulogies and elegies for their royal patrons. They also sang religious poetry and would entertain the court with light-hearted compositions.

POLECATS

Widely perceived as the **mammal** equivalent of the quintessentially Welsh red kite (*see* **Birds**), this formerly endangered member of the weasel family, confined to **Snowdonia** and western mid Wales by the late 19th century, began a remarkable comeback in the 20th. Once common throughout **Britain**, this shy, nocturnal ancestor of the domestic ferret can grow up to 65 cm long; it has dark fur with a pale yellow underbody, and a distinctive black and white facial mask. A strong swimmer able to catch **fish**, it eats mainly small mammals, reptiles and birds.

The decline of gamekeeping from the 1920s, along with that of **rabbit** trapping (which killed many polecats) from the 1950s, led to a rapid increase in the polecat population. Polecats are now common in most parts of Wales, although they are not yet fully re-established in the southern **coal**field, possibly because many are killed on the region's busy **roads**. At the beginning of the 21st century, there were over 17,000 polecats in Wales and, as the colonizers surged relentlessly eastward, many thousands more in the English Midlands.

POLES

Polish migration to Wales was a by-product of the relationship established between **Britain** and Poland during the **Second World War**. Both Polish service personnel and displaced persons were left stranded by the tides of Fascism and Communism that swept over Poland. After the war, 80,000 Polish displaced persons were taken into Britain as European Voluntary Workers, with **Glamorgan** and **Flintshire** taking 1700 each, reflecting the fact that many of the Poles had been engaged in mining. Initially, there was some opposition to their employment in mining, and there were brief strikes in the **Rhondda** in 1949. The **National Union of Mineworkers** wanted local labour to have the first call on jobs, and **Communists** seem to have resented the Poles as enemies of the Soviet Union. However, ultimately they were accepted as good workers and **trade unionists**. Branches of the Union of Polish Craftsmen and Workers began to be formed in south Wales in 1948, of which there were 10 by 1950. Poles settled amicably into both mining and farming communities. There are settlements of Polish families at **Maelor South** and at **Llannor** near **Pwllheli** – on the site of the **Penyberth Bombing School**. Both have now become retirement and nursing homes. After Poland joined the European Union in 2004, many Poles migrated to Wales, particularly to work in the catering and building industries.

POLICE

Evidence of a system of policing in Wales dates back to 1284 (*see* **Edwardian conquest**), when the English sheriff system was introduced. The sheriffs' duties included holding inquiries into murders and thefts committed in their **counties**, the arrest of wrongdoers so that they could be brought before the king's justices, and the organization of courts for travelling judges. The sheriffs' policing and judicial roles were later eroded by the emergence of justices of the peace (magistrates), who became responsible for **law** enforcement in each area.

In 1285, the Statute of Winchester founded the 'watch' system in towns in Wales. Under this system, watchmen had to be posted at each gate of a town, and the watch kept from sunset to sunrise. All freemen also had to respond to the 'hue and cry' when the sheriff issued it, and pursue any suspected criminals in the area. The 16th-century **Acts of 'Union'** cemented the dominance of the 'watch' system, which by then was operated by local watchmen and unpaid constables (one of whom was chosen each year by the inhabitants of each **parish**); the system persisted virtually unchanged until the 19th century.

In 1835, parliament passed legislation allowing **boroughs** in Wales and **England** to establish full-time paid police forces, and in 1838 legislation was passed allowing magistrates to do the same in counties. Centralization of these local forces under Home Office supervision was a gradual process. In the 1840s, five Welsh counties with experience of social unrest – **Cardiganshire**, **Carmarthenshire**, **Denbighshire**, **Glamorgan** and **Montgomeryshire** – acquired constabularies. **Swansea** established a force of seven officers, **Cardiff** had five, and **Neath** just one. In Carmarthenshire, the twelve 'coppers' were known as **Carmarthen**'s shilling.

It was not until 1856 that the County and Borough Police Act made the organization of full-time, paid police forces, headed by a chief constable, mandatory in each county and borough. Gradually, constabularies were centralized and amalgamated to form the police forces that exist today. In the south, for example, it was not until 1969, following the reforms of the 1964 Police Act, that the police forces of Glamorgan, Cardiff, Swansea and **Merthyr Tydfil** were amalgamated to form the South Wales Constabulary, which changed its name to South Wales Police in 1996.

Today, there are four police forces covering Wales: North Wales Police, South Wales Police, **Dyfed Powys** Police and the **Gwent** Constabulary. On 31 March 2002, there were 6632 police officers on ordinary duty in Wales, 1.0% of whom were from what were classed as 'ethnic minorities', and 16.8% of whom were female. At that date, there were in Wales an average of 417 people per police officer. A far-reaching plan to reorganize police forces collapsed in 2006. During discussions of the plan there was increasing evidence of support for the notion that Wales should have a police service or police services supervised from Cardiff rather than from **London**.

PONTARDAWE, Neath Port Talbot
(3095 ha; 6440 inhabitants)

The **community** represents the core of the ancient **parish** of Llangiwg, which once embraced much of north-west **Glamorgan**. The medieval church of St Ciwg stands in glorious isolation. Pontardawe itself is dominated by the 60-m spire of St Peter's church (1860). From 1860 until their closure in 1962, the local **economy** was dominated by

Pontarfynach: the three bridges at Devil's Bridge

the steel (*see* **Iron and Steel**) and **tinplate** works eventually owned by the **Gilbertson** family, a dominance which made Pontardawe a classic example of a one-company town. Apart from one building, which contains a rare example of tinning bays, the site of the works is now occupied by the Leisure Centre/Theatr Cwmtawe complex and by Parc Ynysderw, home of the Pontardawe International **Music** Festival, founded in 1977. A loading dock and dry dock of the **Swansea Canal** survive at Ynysmeudwy. On the **mountain** to the west stands Carn Llechart, a **Neolithic** burial chamber. Gellionnen, a **Unitarian** chapel founded in 1692, bears a stone memorial carved by Iolo Morganwg (**Edward Williams**). The poet **Dafydd Rowlands** was born in Pontardawe.

PONTARDDULAIS, Swansea
(1562 ha; 5293 inhabitants)
Located north of the **M4**, the **community** extends for 5 km along the east bank of the **River Llwchwr**. There was a bridge across the river from at least medieval times. The **Llanelli**–Pontarddulais **railway** (1839) – Wales's earliest railway line built for locomotion – aided the establishment of brickworks, **tinplate** works, **iron** foundries and **chemical** works. In the 20th century, these industries largely disappeared, a loss partly offset by convenient motorway links to wider employment opportunities. In the Middle Ages, local settlement was scattered, but the focus was the **parish** church of Llandeilo Tal-y-bont, located on a bend in the river. Replaced in 1851 by a church in Pontarddulais itself, the old 'church on the marsh' has been re-erected at the National History Museum (*see* **St Fagans**). The fine medieval wall **paintings**, revealed during the operation, have been preserved at the museum.

PONTARFYNACH, Ceredigion
(6938 ha; 491 inhabitants)
Extending from the **Rivers** Rheidol and Mynach to the **Ystwyth**, the **community**'s best-known features are the Mynach **waterfalls** and the Devil's Bridge. The bridge is a remarkable triple structure (*c.*1188, 1753, 1901) across the Mynach; the tale associated with it is a typical example of the use of a folk story to enhance the appeal of a tourist centre (compare **Beddgelert**). The Hafod Arms Hotel (1830) overlooking the falls was commissioned by the duke of Newcastle, owner of the Hafod estate. The estate's best-known owner was **Thomas Johnes**. He sought to make Hafod a major cultural and publishing centre and to create an ideal romantic landscape in the upper Ystwyth valley. Hafod mansion has been demolished but efforts are being made to restore the **gardens**.

Eglwys-newydd church, originally built in 1620, contained Francis Chantry's elaborate memorial (1815) to Thomas Johnes's daughter, Mariamne. Following a fire in 1932, all that remains of it are charred lumps of marble. The Pontarfynach–Cwmystwyth **road** is spanned by an arch, built to commemorate the jubilee of George III's accession to the throne (1810). The Ystwyth Valley offers evidence of **Bronze Age copper** mining. From the late 18th century onwards, Cwmystwyth developed as a **lead**-mining centre and contains ruins of early industrial **housing**. It was the mineral wealth of the area which led to the construction of the **Aberystwyth**–Devil's Bridge **Railway** (1902), although any success the railway had was dependent upon **tourism** rather than the carrying of ore. The Cefn Croes wind farm, located on the community's north-eastern boundary, was completed in 2005. It contains 39 1.5 MW turbines, and is the most productive of all the wind farms of Wales (*see* **Energy** and **Windmills**). The manipulation of the landscape involved in its construction led to intense controversy.

PONTHIR (Pont-hir), Torfaen
(343 ha; 1455 inhabitants)
The **community**, located immediately north of **Caerleon**, essentially represents the one-time civil **parish** of Llanfrechfa. All **Saints**' church, most of which was rebuilt in 1874, retains its Perpendicular tower; there are fine **stained-glass** windows in the chancel. The handsome, polychromatic vicarage was designed by **John Prichard** and John Pollard Seddon (1827–1906). Most of the community's inhabitants dwell in the compact settlement of Ponthir, which expanded greatly in the late 20th century.

PONTLLANFRAITH (Pontllan-fraith),
Caerphilly (576 ha; 7773 inhabitants)
Straddling the Sirhowy valley south of **Blackwood**, the **community** includes the township of Penllwyn. Designed by A. F. Webb, Penllwyn is an inferior version of his garden village at Oakdale (**Penmaen**). In its centre is the early 17th-century one-time mansion of Penllwyn. In the 1950s, the building belonged to the Franciscan Sisters of the Atonement; it is now a public house. Siloh (1813) is among the best preserved of the early 19th-century chapels of **Gwent**. The working water-driven corn mill at Gelligroes was originally built *c.*1625.

PONTLLIW (Pont-lliw), Swansea
(543 ha; 2075 inhabitants)
Straddling the Lliw valley, which from 1974 to 1996 gave its name to **Lliw Valley**, a district of the one-time **county** of **West Glamorgan**, the village grew up along the A48 when it was the main **road** to **Carmarthen**. The diversion of through traffic to the nearby **M4** has given the **community** a quieter life. Slight traces remain of the once busy Lliw Forge, which made much of the machinery for 19th and early 20th-century local industries. There is also a former **watermill**, itself on the site of a medieval mill.

PONTYBEREM, Carmarthenshire
(1337 ha; 2829 inhabitants)
Located in the Gwendraeth Fawr valley on the edge of the southern **coal**field, the **community** contains the villages of Pontyberem and Bancffosfelen. Coalmining began in the 17th century, but intense exploitation did not occur until the late 19th century. By 1921, the area, originally part of the civil **parish** of **Llannon**, had 3025 inhabitants. The coal industry came to an end following the strike of 1984–5. New ventures and businesses have been established on the sites of the old coalmines. It is generally believed that the creators of the BBC's long-running serial *Pobol y Cwm* had Pontyberem in mind as its setting.

PONT-Y-CLUN, Rhondda Cynon Taff
(1167 ha; 5794 inhabitants)
Located immediately south of **Llantrisant**, the **community** contains the villages of Pont-y-clun, Brynsadler, Groesfaen and Miskin. Industrialization began with **lead** and **iron** mining in the 16th century. **Tinplate** works followed, and there was marked **population** expansion in the wake of the late 19th-century **coal**mining boom. By the late 20th century, however, the area was part of **Cardiff**'s commuter belt. The name of the medieval **commote**, **Miskin**, was given in the 1870s to the village of New Mill. The renaming was the work of the Welsh patriot Judge Gwilym Williams (1839–1906), whose statue stands outside Cardiff City Hall. He lived at Miskin Manor, a neo-Tudor mansion house (1864), later converted into a hotel. St **David**'s church, Miskin (1907), financed by his widow, contains many **Welsh** inscriptions. Far grander than the manor is Talygarn House, built to his own design for the remarkable scholar-**iron**master **G. T. Clark**. Building began in 1865; it continued until Clark's death in 1898 and involved work by some of the most distinguished Italian decorators of the age; the mansion has been converted into luxury apartments. Clark also designed St Anne's church, Talygarn (1887).

PONTYPOOL (Pont-y-pŵl), Torfaen
(3433 ha; 29,186 inhabitants)
The town of Pontypool lies within the **communities** of New Inn, Panteg, Pen Tranch, Pontymoile and Trevethin (*see below*).

Pontypool was one of Wales's pioneering industrial centres; it had significant **iron**works by 1425, and its blast furnaces, erected in the 1570s, were among the earliest in the country. The leading early ironmaster was Richard **Hanbury**, who came to Pontypool in the 1560s. His descendants would dominate the district until they sold their mansion, Pontypool Park, in 1914. In 1697, **Edward Lhuyd** observed: 'One Major John Hanbury of this Pontypool shew'd us an excellent invention of his own, for driving hot iron … into as thin plates as tin.' Hanbury's invention

Pontypool's famous front row, December 1976: Graham Price, Bobby Windsor and Charlie Faulkner

Japanning, a technique invented at Pontypool

would be central to the world's production of **tinplate** until the first continuous hot strip mill opened in Kentucky in 1924. **Japan ware**, the lacquering of iron plates from which trays and other domestic utensils were made, was invented at Pontypool by Thomas Allgood *c.*1705. Lacquering under the supervision of members of the Allgood family continued at Pontypool and elsewhere in **Monmouthshire** until the 1820s. In 1730, Pontypool acquired a market house (much of it, including its original bilingual plaque, survives) and, in 1740, a **printing** press. Nonconformity (*see* **Nonconformists**) struck deep roots, with the **Quakers** enjoying the patronage of the Allgood family. The **Baptists** built a chapel at Penygarn in 1727 and at Trosnant in 1779. The Baptist Academy moved to Pontypool from **Abergavenny** in 1836. Ebenezer **Congregational** chapel opened in Pontymoile in 1742; its first minister was the author **Edmund Jones**.

In 1799, the Monmouthshire **Canal** linked Pontypool with **Newport**, a major factor in subsequent economic expansion. **Chartism** found wide support in Pontypool, although William Jones, the local Chartist leader, failed to ensure that his men participated in the **Newport Rising** of 1839. In the early 19th century, the area was largely **Welsh**-speaking – in 1815, Welsh was the sole language of the services at Trevethin church. In 1846, however, the commissioners reporting on **education** in Wales (*see* **Treason of the Blue Books**) were told that 'the **English language** is gaining ground rapidly', although Welsh continued to be used in Trevethin's services until 1890. The National **Eisteddfod** was held at Pontypool in 1924, and Ysgol Gwynllŵg, Wales's most easterly Welsh-medium secondary school, established originally at **Abercarn** (1988), was moved to Pontypool in the early 1990s. In Welsh **rugby** mythology, the 'Pontypool front row' represents the epitome of disciplined and muscular manhood. By the end of the 20th century, Pontypool had lost most of its heavy industry. However, with its good **road** communications and its easy

access to the glories of the Monmouthshire countryside, its prospect as a centre of services and light industries seemed promising.

The communities of Pontypool

NEW INN (1197 ha; 6349 inhabitants)
Constituting eastern Pontypool, the community extends to the Llandegfedd **reservoir**. There are attractive medieval churches at Panteg (a village distinct from the community of that name) and at Llanvihangel Pontymoel, the latter adjoining the thatched Horse and Jockey Inn. The **Gwent** Crematorium (1960) was designed by **Percy Thomas**, as were the massive Dupont Factory and the Parke-Davis Pharmaceutical Research Centre. Tŷ-mawr is a fascinating farmhouse of *c.*1600.

PANTEG (Pant-Teg) (322 ha; 6882 inhabitants)
Constituting southern Pontypool, the community contains Griffithstown, laid out in the 1860s for the Great Western **Railway** Company by its supervisor, Henry Griffiths. Panteg Steelworks, opened in 1873, was closed in 2004.

PEN TRANCH (1207 ha; 5872 inhabitants)
The community includes western Pontypool and the town centre. Its chief feature is Pontypool Park, an extensive open space that gives the town a green heart surpassed in Wales only by that of **Cardiff**. The mansion, home of the Hanbury family until 1914, contains 17th, 18th and 19th-century elements and is something of a jumble. Housing a **Roman Catholic** secondary school, its stables contain an admirable local history museum. Within the park is a hermitage (1830–44), floored with the vertebrae of oxen.

PONTYMOILE (Llanfihangel Pont-y-moel)
(209ha; 4794 inhabitants)
Constituting south-western Pontypool, Pantymoile, with western Pen Tranch, are the only parts of the town lying within the **coal**field. Upper Race offers rare evidence of the primitive method of mining surface coal through scouring the land with water. The engine house in Coed Golynos is unique in Wales. West **Monmouth** School (1898), founded by the Haberdashers' Company, stands on Blaendare Road.

TREVETHIN (Trefddyn Catwg)
(498 ha; 5289 inhabitants)
Constituting northern Pontypool, Trevethin's church, St **Cadog**'s, contains the tombs of the Hanbury family. The folly tower, built by the Hanburys in 1762, was demolished in 1939, lest it should serve as a marker to German bombers. It was rebuilt in 1994 and offers superb views. The American **Garden,** an extension of Pontypool Park, contains an astonishing rustic lodge of 1841.

PONTYPRIDD, Rhondda Cynon Taff
(3288 ha; 33,233 inhabitants)
Centred upon the confluence of the **Taff** and the Rhondda, Pontypridd is second only to **Barry** among Wales's most populous **communities**. It consists of the town of Pontypridd and its suburbs, and the outlying settlements of

Cilfynydd, Glyntaff, Glyncoed, Hawthorn, Rhydyfelin, Treforest and Upper Boat. Until the late 18th century, the area's only significance lay in the fact that it offered a convenient place to cross the Taff. As wooden bridges were washed away and new ones built, the place came to be known as Y Bontnewydd or Newbridge, although the name Pont-y-tŷ-pridd (the bridge of the earth-built house) – contracted into Pontypridd – was also in use. A permanent bridge was built in 1756. Designed by **William Edwards** (1719–89), it represented his fourth attempt to bridge the **river**. His three previous attempts had produced too heavy a structure, a problem he solved by inserting three large cylindrical apertures at each abutment. With its elegant slimness and its single span of 42.3 m – perhaps the longest in Europe at the time – the bridge is a memorable sight. As it was too steep for any traffic other than pedestrians and packhorses, a three-span bridge was built alongside it in 1857, thus much diminishing its visual appeal. Newbridge remained the preferred name until 1856, when the name Pontypridd was adopted in order to avoid confusion with **Newbridge, Monmouthshire**.

The development of the area began in 1794 with the coming of the Glamorganshire **Canal**. Pontypridd's main industrial enterprise – the Brown Lenox Chainworks – was established in 1816, but rapid growth did not come about until the opening up of the **Rhondda**. That enabled Pontypridd to become the commercial pivot of the central part of the south Wales **coal**field, with 'Ponty' market enjoying a popularity it still retains. Indicative of its growth was the construction of the large St Catherine's church (1870), the spire of which dominates the scene. In 1894, Pontypridd became an **urban district**, and in 1904 acquired its distinguished district council offices. The town contains a number of handsome chapels, one of which – Tabernacl (1861) – is home to the Pontypridd Historical Centre.

The area played a significant role in **Welsh-language** culture. Iolo Morganwg (**Edward Williams**) held a **Gorsedd** at the so-called Rocking Stone in 1815, a site which came to have mystical significance for the numerous local enthusiasts of **druid**ism. While walking along the banks of the Rhondda in 1856, James James composed the tune of '**Hen Wlad fy Nhadau**', for which his father, Evan James wrote the verses. A memorial (1930) by **Goscombe John** commemorating father and son stands in Ynysangharad Park. Although rapidly Anglicized in the later 19th century, Pontypridd was host to the National **Eisteddfod** in 1893. In 1962, Rhydyfelin (more correctly Rhydfelen) became home to the first Welsh-medium secondary school in southern Wales and, in the late 20th century, Pont Siôn-Norton Primary School played a significant role in the demand for the expansion of Welsh-medium **education**, an education experienced by a quarter of Pontypridd's pupils by the early 21st century.

Of the outlying settlements, the most significant is Treforest where the **Crawshay family** established a major **tinplate** works in 1835. Nowhere else in **Glamorgan** is there so extensive a series of buildings associated with region's **iron** industry. The School of Mines at Treforest (1911) progressed through several stages to become, in 1992, the **University of Glamorgan**. The Treforest Industrial Estate, founded in 1937, actually lies within the boundaries of the communities of **Taff's Well** and **Llantwit Fardre**. Across the river at Glyntaff is Wales's earliest crematorium, appropriately enough cheek by jowl with the Round Houses, built in 1839 by the cremation pioneer **William**

Pontypridd *c.*1910. Tabernacl chapel (left) is now the Pontypridd Historical Centre

The bridge over the Taff at Pontypridd, portrayed on a dish produced by the Nantgarw Pottery

Price (1800–93), as a druidic museum. Of the deep coalmines around Pontypridd, the largest was the Albion, the colliery that gave rise to the village of Cilfynydd, birthplace of the opera singers **Geraint Evans** and Stuart Burrows (b.1933).

POOR LAW, The

The growing **population** and the severe inflation of the later 16th century gave rise to a perception that there was a dangerous increase in the numbers of 'sturdy beggars' – wanderers capable of work but who apparently preferred to survive by begging and petty crime. The perception led to acts in 1597 and 1601 permitting **parishes** to raise rates to maintain the poor, to apprentice orphan children and to punish the workshy. Not all parishes made use of the legislation. Indeed, the evidence suggests that, in the early 18th century, **Wrexham** was alone among the parishes of the **diocese** of **St Asaph** to levy a poor rate. Recipients of parish relief were expected to acknowledge their abject status; in 18th-century **Cowbridge**, for example, the indigent were obliged to wear a badge announcing that they were dependent upon handouts.

In the late 18th century, population pressures, the dislocation caused by war and the suffering resulting from bad harvests obliged most parishes to levy poor rates, and between 1785 and 1819 the total poor rate collected in Wales and **England** increased from £2 million to £7 million. However, the Speenhamland system (the supplementation of low earnings by Poor Law payments), adopted in many parts of England from 1795 onwards, found little favour in Wales. Some attempts were made to solve unemployment through the establishment of workhouses. There was one within the walls of **Caernarfon** Castle in the 1790s, but such schemes were rarely successful. The responsibility of the parish was limited to those who had dwelt within its boundaries for a year or more. Those who had not were obliged to return to their places of birth, and in 1829 a magistrate in **Blackwood** – a place which was experiencing the shifting population characteristic of growing industrial areas – complained that the task of sending them home was absorbing all his energies.

Change came through the Poor **Law** Amendment Act of 1834, which abolished outdoor relief and insisted that all beneficiaries of the Poor Law had to receive indoor relief as inmates of workhouses. The workhouses were to be built by groups of parishes or **poor law unions** administered by boards of elected guardians. The system was supervised by the Poor Law Commissioners, based in **London**'s Somerset House. The first chairman of the commissioners was **Thomas Frankland Lewis**, and the second his son, **George Cornewall Lewis**.

By the mid-19th century, Wales had 42 workhouses. They were hated institutions – and were intended to be so. Within them, families were generally separated, and the conditions and **food** were often appalling; the **Rebecca Riots** commissioners noted that the meals in **Carmarthen** gaol were better than those in the town's workhouse. A Poor Law officer was attacked by a crowd in **Llanfair Caereinion** in 1837, there was an attempt to burn down **Narberth** workhouse in 1839, and Carmarthen workhouse was ransacked in 1843. In **Merthyr Tydfil**, the guardians delayed erecting a workhouse until 1853, and several rural unions, **Tregaron** and **Rhayader** in particular, did not build workhouses until the late 19th century. There were some virtues in the system: there were boards of guardians – that of **Cardiff**, for example – which continued to provide outdoor relief; paupers had better **health** care than they had received under outdoor relief; and some of the buildings were so well built that they survived as hospitals or old people's homes into the 20th century and beyond. In some cases, guardians could show compassion: those of Merthyr were prosecuted in 1900 for giving relief to strikers, and the **Bedwellty** guardians, accused of overspending on destitute families, were replaced by **government** officials in 1927. The misery of prolonged mass unemployment in the 1920s finally prompted the abolition of poor law unions in 1929, when their responsibilities were transferred to the **counties** and the **county boroughs**.

POOR LAW UNIONS

In accordance with the 1834 **Poor Law** Amendment Act, the **parishes** of Wales and its **border**land were grouped into 48 (later 50) poor **law** unions. Each union was obliged to build a workhouse. They were administered by boards of guardians answerable to commissioners at **London**'s Somerset House, a system that represents a key development in the rise of a centralized bureaucracy. In 1837, the unions became the basis for the districts concerned with the registration of births, marriages and deaths. The registration districts were grouped into registration **counties**, whose boundaries differed markedly from those of the ancient counties. From 1841 until 1901, most census information referred to these curious entities, much to the confusion of those studying the statistics of those years.

POPULATION and DEMOGRAPHY

Wales, having no independent census authority, comes under the aegis of the Office of National Statistics. In 2001, the population was 2,903,085 compared with 2,835,073 in 1991, an increase of 2.39%.

The recording of the population falls into two periods. Before 1801, all figures are estimates, based on taxation returns, **parish** registers and other inexact sources. After 1801, the figures are those of the decennial censuses. Some doubt has been cast on the accuracy of the censuses of 1801, 1811, 1821 and 1831. An increasingly mobile population means that the census of 2001 may well be unreliable, especially in **communities** where there is extensive multi-occupancy.

Pre-census estimates are necessarily tentative. For **Roman** times, estimates vary from 100,000 to 250,000. Climatic disasters in the immediate post-Roman era may have led to a catastrophic demographic decline. Comments by **Giraldus Cambrensis** suggest that by the 1190s, Wales had about 160,000 inhabitants. The favourable **climate** of the 13th century may have led to a marked increase, and a figure of 300,000 has been suggested for the time of **Llywelyn ap Gruffudd**. Deteriorating climate, possible **soil** exhaustion and, above all, the **Black Death** caused the 14th century to be an era of demographic collapse, with the population declining to perhaps as low as 150,000. Numbers gradually recovered to an estimated 278,000 in 1536. There followed a period of low, though variant, growth. Birth rates were high, but so were **death** rates; infant mortality was especially high. By the 17th century, a figure of about 400,000 had been reached, and an estimate of 489,000 has been made for 1750. At the first census (1801), the population was 587,245. During this period, the population was essentially rural, the towns being small and undeveloped.

From the mid-18th century onwards, the development of population may be divided into four phases. The first covers the period 1750–1851, and is marked by the rapid expansion of the metallurgical industries in both the north-east and the south-east (*see* **Iron and Steel**). The first five censuses show population increases for all the **counties** but, by 1821, the rate of increase in the rural counties was falling and, by 1851, **Montgomeryshire** and **Radnorshire** both recorded decline; the mid-century, therefore, marks a turning point, when some rural counties began to show losses. All were to do so by 1881, and the long phase of rural depopulation that was to characterize Wales for the next century had set in. The causes are complex, but central to this development was the transition from subsistence to capitalized farming, together with the pull exerted by the burgeoning industrial areas. The corollary of rural decline was industrial growth: the population of **Glamorgan**, 70,879 in 1801, had risen to 231,849 by 1851. In 1801, the most populous civil parish in Wales was **Merthyr Tydfil**, with 7705 inhabitants. However, the built-up area of **Swansea**, which spread over several parishes, contained 10,117 inhabitants, making Swansea the largest urban centre in the country. **Holywell** parish, with 5567 inhabitants, was third on the list. These epitomized growing urbanization and the transformation of distribution, with a movement towards concentration in the south-east and north-east.

The second phase, marked by the dominance of **coal**mining, covers the period from 1851 to 1921. It is best

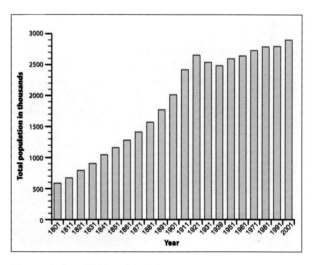

The population of Wales, 1801–2001

represented by the **Rhondda** valley, where the population in 1851 was 1998; by 1921, it was 162,717. During the same period, the population of Glamorgan increased from 231,849 to 1,252,418, that of **Monmouthshire** from 157.418 to 450,794 and that of **Denbighshire** from 92,583 to 154,842. The coal-exporting **ports** gained greatly, and, by 1881, **Cardiff** had become the largest urban centre in Wales with 82,761 inhabitants. Thus, by 1914, population had amassed in the coalfields and the coal-exporting ports. There were minor densely populated pockets in the **slate** areas of **Caernarfonshire** and **Merioneth**, and along the north coast. By 1914, the population of Wales had reached 2.5 million. The industrial areas of Wales imported males and the rural areas exported them. Thus by 1891, when the Rhondda had 1314 males for every 1000 females, the ratio in **Cardiganshire** was 776:1000.

The third phase is the interwar period, when the industrial **Depression** led to unemployment which, associated with continuing rural depopulation, led to significant out-migration. After 1921, Caernarfonshire, Glamorgan and Monmouthshire all declined from a peak in that year. **Carmarthenshire** followed after 1931 when, for the first time, Wales showed a decrease in recorded population. **Emigration** left an increasingly elderly population. That was one of the factors which caused birth rates to decline from about 35 per 1000 in the 1870s to below 20 by 1925. Thus, between 1921 and 1931, Cardiganshire's population fell by 1.58% by natural loss (the number of deaths exceeding births), and by 7.78% by out-migration,

The memorial to lifeboatmen in Port Eynon churchyard

the total population falling by 5697 or 9.36%. For Wales as a whole, the estimated population fell from 2,736,800 in 1925 to 2,487,000 in 1939. As the Welsh population experienced a natural growth of 140,171 during these years, the net loss through emigration was 389,971. In spite of some amelioration occasioned by the economic demands of the **Second World War**, these conditions remained until the 1950s.

Between 1951 and 1961, the Welsh population once more began to increase, and this pattern has continued. However, the overall figures conceal considerable variation. The older industrial areas are still losing people. Between 1971 and 2001, the population of the Rhondda declined from 88,994 to 72,435. Likewise, rural depopulation was taking place, but it was concealed by another significant trend. During this period, many people moved out of the largest cities generating the process of counter-urbanization. Rural Wales became the recipient of a stream of in-migration that has radically transformed its demographic history. Thus, between 1971 and 2001, the population of the three south-western counties increased by 45,802; as the death rate of those counties exceeded their birthrate during that period, the increase was wholly caused by in-migration.

Changes in employment patterns have also generated a redistribution of population. The older heavy industries have been replaced by lighter **electronic** and assembly industries, and there has been major growth in services. These have concentrated along the main transport arteries, especially the **M4** and the **A55,** which traverse the regions with the greatest population increases. Despite a population rise in rural areas, the population of Wales is overwhelmingly urban. In 2001, Cardiff, the largest city, had 305,353 inhabitants, followed by the built-up area of Swansea with 158,139. The distribution is markedly skewed to a concentration in the south-east and in **Dee**side and along the northern coast.

PORT EYNON (Port Einon), Swansea
(1472 ha; 574 inhabitants)

Now a focus of **Gower**'s self-catering holiday trade, the **community** once earned its living from the sea and from several unusual industries. In the 16th century, a sophisticated salt-making operation was conducted in a large building beside the beach, which has been excavated and conserved. **Limestone** quarrying was an active industry until the end of the 19th century, as was paint manufacture. This used local mineral earth, and customers included the Great Western **Railway** Company, seeking the chocolate-brown colour used on its coaches. A memorial in the churchyard commemorates the heroic role of Port Eynon **lifeboat**men in a 1916 **shipwreck**.

Until *c.*1950, Scurlage was just a few scattered farms; it is now a sizeable village. Llanddewi, where there is no village, has a church with a 12th-century nave and a 16th-century mansion, perhaps incorporating parts of a 14th-century palace built by **Henry de Gower**, bishop of **St David's**. As its **Welsh** name (Llan-y-tair-mair) indicates, Knelston church (now ruined) was dedicated to the three Marys, a reference to the belief that Anna, mother of the Virgin Mary, had three daughters called Mary.

PORT TALBOT, Neath Port Talbot
(2204 ha; 9860 inhabitants)

The town of Port Talbot occupies the **communities** of Margam Moors, Port Talbot and Tai Bach (*see below*).

That area of the ancient **parish** of **Margam** lying on the west bank of the lower Afan first experienced industrialization with the establishment in 1770 of a **copper**works. The Morfa pit was sunk in 1848; it would suffer several disasters, including that of 1890 in which 87 **coal**miners were killed. The dock was opened in 1839. Designated Port Talbot in honour of the **Talbot family** of Margam Castle, the name also came to be applied to the adjoining settlement. Indeed, with the establishment of Port Talbot **borough** in 1921, Port Talbot became the name for an extensive area including Margam, **Aberavon** and **Cwmavon**.

The Margam Steelworks (*see* **Iron and Steel**) were opened near the docks in 1916, but the great innovation came in 1952 with the completion of the Abbey Works of the **Steel Company of Wales**. With a labour force of 18,000 (a figure which has subsequently declined drastically), it was Europe's largest steelworks and by far the largest employer in Wales. In 1967, the company came to be known as the British Steel Corporation. Following the denationalization of the steel industry in 1988, the works came to be owned by British Steel plc, a company bought by Corus in 1999. In 2006, the Tata Company of India made a successful bid for the Corus Company. The Port Talbot plant, which looks particularly dramatic at night, dominates the landscape and deposits fine dust upon the whole locality. The scholar and poet **Gwyn Williams** (1904–90) and the actor Anthony Hopkins (b.1937) were born in Port Talbot.

The communities of Port Talbot

MARGAM MOORS (Morfa Margam)
(1260 ha; 0 inhabitants)

The community, which has no inhabitants, is wholly occupied by the former Corus, now Tata-owned, steelworks. The works, originally designed by **Percy Thomas**, have been much altered. The vast deep-water tidal harbour, designed for unloading large iron-ore carriers, was constructed in 1972.

PORT TALBOT (394 ha; 5277 inhabitants)

Wedged into the Afan valley, the community consists of a dense network of streets. The **M4** is carried above the community on cantilevers. Its chief feature is St Theodore's church, completed in 1897 as a memorial to Theodore Talbot.

TAI BACH (Tai-bach) (550 ha; 4583 inhabitants)

Consisting of the southern end of Port Talbot, the community confusingly includes an area called Margam. The location of the 1770 copperworks, the community gets its name (meaning 'little houses') from its original row of small cottages. **Richard Burton** was brought up in the village of Taibach, as was the leading local **government** figure Lord **Heycock** of Taibach. In 2001, 84.72% of Tai Bach's inhabitants had no knowledge at all of **Welsh**, making it, linguistically, the most Anglicized of all the communities of the **county borough** of **Neath Port Talbot**.

Port Talbot: Margam steelworks and the Eglwys Nunydd Reservoir

PORT TALBOT One-time district

Following the abolition of the **county** of **Glamorgan** in 1974, Port Talbot was established as one of the four districts of the new county of **West Glamorgan**. It consisted of the **borough** of **Port Talbot** and the **urban district** of **Glyncorrwg**. In 1996, the district, together with that of **Neath** and part of that of **Lliw Valley**, became the **county borough** of **Neath Port Talbot**.

PORTHCAWL (Porth-cawl), Bridgend
(1337 ha; 15,669 inhabitants)

The **community**'s original chief settlement was Newton, a **port** exporting part of the agricultural surplus of the **Vale of Glamorgan**. By 1800, it was developing ambitions as a watering place. In the 1820s, Pwll or Porthcawl Point became the terminus of a **horse**-drawn tramroad conveying **iron** and, later, **coal** from the Llynfi valley. In 1865, a 3-ha dock was built, but the difficulty of entering it in rough weather led to its closure in 1907. Of Porthcawl's history as a port, a tidal basin, breakwater, warehouse and **lighthouse** survive.

By 1907, Porthcawl had developed a new role as a seaside resort. It became an **urban district** in 1893; its **population**, 1872 in 1901, had risen to 6642 by 1921. The Rest, a grim building erected as a convalescent house for miners (1878), gave its name to Rest Bay. The Grand Pavilion (1932) on the Esplanade was, from 1948 to 2001, the home of the South Wales Miners' **Eisteddfod**. The Royal

Porthcawl is one of Wales's leading **golf** clubs. The fun fair at Coney Island on Sandy Bay was for long one of **Glamorgan**'s favourite attractions. The caravan park at Trecco Bay is among the largest in Europe. Changes in holidaymaking have led to Porthcawl's decline as a resort, although it retains aspirations to attract visitors. By now, however, it is primarily a dormitory for commuters and a favoured place for retirement.

All Saints' church, Porthcawl, is an ambitious building completed in 1914. St John's church, Newton (*c.*1500), has a massive tower. It retains a pulpit that predates the **Protestant Reformation** and is carved with a depiction of the flagellation of Christ. There are good examples of vernacular **housing** at Nottage. Nottage Court (*c.*1608) has a handsome five-bay front. The Gordianus stone, bearing several **Roman** inscriptions, is located in its **garden**; it was rescued from Aberavon during the 19th century, having been used as ballast on a local ship. The English novelist R. D. Blackmore (1825–1900), author of *Lorna Doone* (1869) and several novels with Welsh settings or characters, such as *The Maid of Sker* (1872), spent much of his childhood at Nottage Court, where he had family connections. The hymn writer W. Rhys Nicholas (1914–96) was a minister of **religion** in Porthcawl between 1965 and 1983.

PORTHMADOG, Gwynedd
(1630 ha; 4187 inhabitants)

Porthmadog stands at the north-eastern corner of Cardigan Bay. The town is less than 200 years old, having been built on land reclaimed from the sea by **William Alexander Madocks**'s embankment – the Cob (1808–12) – across the mouth of the **Glaslyn**. The Cob led to the draining of Y Traeth Mawr, much to the distress of the English novelist Thomas Love Peacock (1785–1866), who lamented that '**Snowdon** had lost its liquid mirror'. Those crossing the Cob were obliged to pay a toll, an obligation which lasted until 2003. The town's name is fortuitously ambiguous: its original name, Portmadoc, undoubtedly commemorated Madocks, but the present preferred form, Porthmadog, reflects the legend that **Madog ab Owain Gwynedd** embarked from hereabouts on his voyage to **North America** *c.*1170. The **port** became the chief centre for the export of **Ffestiniog slate**. In 1836, the quarries were linked to the quayside by the pioneering Ffestiniog **Railway**. Closed in 1946, the railway was reopened in stages as a tourist attraction between 1955 and 1982. Porthmadog became an important **shipbuilding** centre. Its Western Ocean Yachts, the construction of which was at its height between 1860 and 1890, are among the most beautiful wooden ships ever built. The quayside maritime museum tells the story.

Near Porthmadog is Madocks's original town, Tremadog, a fine example of 19th-century town planning, with square, town hall, small church and classically fronted chapel. Attacked by the bishop of **Bangor** for giving more prominence to the **Nonconformists** than to the **Anglicans**, Madocks pointed out that while the church was built on rock, the chapel was built on sand. Madocks lived at Tan-yr-allt (1800), which is just over the boundary in the **community** of **Beddgelert**. Shelley stayed in the house from September 1812 to February 1813; following an attempt on his life, he fled to **Llanystumdwy**. T. E. Lawrence (Lawrence of Arabia; 1888–1935) was

The Cob across the mouth of the Glaslyn, with Porthmadog and Moel-y-Gest

born at Tremadog. The rock face behind the village is popular among climbers.

The western part of the community is dominated by Moel-y-Gest (282 m), a rugged eminence. At its foot are the select seaside village of Borth-y-gest and the more populist resort of Morfa Bychan, which adjoins the superb Black Rock Sands. Garreg Wen was the home of the **harp**ist Dafydd Owen (1710–39 or 1720–49), disputed composer of the popular tune **'Dafydd y Garreg Wen'**.

PORTS

From the first discovery in the **Palaeolithic Age** of the ability of human beings to sail, there must have been places in Wales where sea-borne goods could be loaded and unloaded and where passengers could embark and disembark – although such early ports would not have been more than beaches where boats could be dragged beyond the water-line. The **Romans** established a port on the **Usk** at **Caerleon**, and the presence of luxury goods from the Mediterranean lands at places such as **Dinas Powys** and Deganwy (**Conwy**) in the immediate post-Roman centuries indicates the existence of ports, as does the arrival of sea-borne pilgrims at **St David's**, **Llantwit Major** and elsewhere. The location of most of the major castles built by the **Normans** and their successors – **Chepstow, Newport, Cardiff, Swansea, Kidwelly, Carmarthen, Tenby, Pembroke, Aberystwyth, Caernarfon, Beaumaris, Conwy** and **Flint** among them – were chosen because their sites were accessible from the sea. Indeed, it was the English king's control of Wales's sea-borne trade which ultimately led to the defeat of the **Glyndŵr Revolt**.

By the later Middle Ages, a number of the ports of Wales were developing a lively trade, both coastal and international. Carmarthen, recognized as a staple port in 1326, was probably the most important of them, but others, especially Newport, Swansea, Tenby, Caernarfon and Beaumaris, enjoyed considerable prosperity. Some – Carmarthen and Newport among them – were estuary ports where ships could moor at quaysides, but others were served by anchored ships which were loaded and unloaded by small boats. Although the bulk of the trade emanating from pre-industrial Wales consisted of the **woollen** products and the **cattle** conveyed overland to **England**, it was the country's maritime trade that represented the growth sectors of the **economy**. The heyday of the small ports of Wales was the 18th and the first half of the 19th century, a fact recognized by Lewis Morris (*see* **Morris Brothers**), who in 1748 published a chart of the Welsh coast from **Llandudno** to the **Milford Haven Waterway**. **Barmouth** exported woollen goods, Aberystwyth **lead** ore and **Amlwch copper** ore. Caernarfon became a **slate**-exporting port, an activity in which it was joined by the newly established ports of Porth Penrhyn (**Llandygai**), **Y Felinheli** and **Porthmadog**. Long before becoming a tourist resort, **Rhyl** was important in the importation of timber to the wharves at Y Foryd. The **Dee**, long a major navigable waterway, acquired a series of ports exporting the industrial products of **Flintshire** and **Denbighshire**. Most consisted of little more than a quayside wharf or a row of jetties, but others – **Mostyn**, for example – came to have a small masonry dock.

Some Welsh ports did not depend on their hinterlands for trade, for they were designed as passenger terminals, principally for routes between **Britain** and **Ireland**. **Holyhead**, the centre for mail to Dublin since at least the 17th century, became increasingly busy following the British–Irish parliamentary union in 1801 – a role which Porth Dinllaen (**Nefyn**) unsuccessfully sought to usurp. **Neyland** was specifically established as the centre for the packet service to Cork and Waterford, a role eventually acquired by **Fishguard**. Other activities centred at ports included whaling, **fish**ing and **shipbuilding**. The town of **Milford Haven** was founded in the 1790s as a whaling centre; that enterprise failed but Milford eventually became Wales's chief fishing port. Herring fishing, once virtually an Irish monopoly, became an important feature of the activity of the ports of Cardigan Bay and those of the north coast of the **Llŷn** Peninsula – Nefyn, in particular. Almost all the ports of Wales had long been involved in building wooden sailing ships, an activity which reached its apogee at Porthmadog in the 1870s and 1880s.

Apart from those involved with Ireland, the small ports of Wales largely catered for the coastal trade around Britain. It was a trade which received a deathblow with the coming of the **railway**, for locomotion meant that, for the first time in human history, goods and people could be transported more quickly by land than by sea. The demise of **Aberdovey** as a port followed the coming of the Cambrian Coast Railway in 1867, and **Cardigan**'s seaborne trade withered following the arrival of the railway in 1885.

In marked contrast, Wales's leading ports – Cardiff, Swansea, Newport, and, later, **Barry** – became increasing reliant on international trade, and they therefore expanded rather than contracted as more and more railways were built. Swansea had been a major **coal** port since the 16th century, as had Newport since the early 19th century. Cardiff, originally a port trading in the agricultural surpluses of the **Vale of Glamorgan**, had, by the late 18th century, become the port for the **iron** produced by **Merthyr Tydfil**. By the 1880s, it had become the greatest coal port in the world, a position it had to yield to Barry in 1901. With their masonry docks and their kilometres of quayside, Swansea, Barry, Cardiff and Newport (together with smaller centres such as **Llanelli**, **Briton Ferry**, **Port Talbot** and **Penarth**) represented by the early 20th century one of the world's greatest concentrations of ports.

The **depression of the interwar years** brought an end to the prosperity of that formidable phalanx of docks. By the second half of the 20th century, the only place where there was expansion was Milford Haven. There, the importation of **oil** meant that, by 1974, Milford's trade (58 million tonnes) was three times that of the combined trade of all the other ports of Wales. Admittedly, trade on that scale was not destined to endure, but at the dawn of the 21st century, Milford's sole rival in Welsh sea-borne trade was Port Talbot, where vast quantities of iron ore were imported annually. Holyhead, Fishguard, **Pembroke Dock** and Mostyn still operate as ports for Ireland, but Wales's tradition of having a coastline studded with ports has all but died. Indeed, Cardiff, which owed its emergence as Wales's premier city almost entirely to its port facilities, and which

A three-master in the port of Milford Haven in the early 1800s

was once the largest port in the world in terms of the tonnage of its exports, has turned its back on the sea, for its new barrage means that the city no longer has direct contact with salt water.

PORTSKEWETT (Porth Sgiwed), Monmouthshire (740 ha; 2041 inhabitants)

Located south-west of **Chepstow**, the **community** contains the western entrance to the **Severn Tunnel** which, following its completion in 1886, was for the best part of a century the world's longest undersea tunnel. There is a **Neolithic** tomb at Heston Brake, an **Iron Age** fort at Sudbrook Camp and the remains of a **Roman** villa on Portskewett Hill. Earthworks in the centre of Portskewett are reputed to be a structure erected by Harold Godwinesson following his invasion of Wales in 1065. According to **Giraldus Cambrensis**, Wales extended from Porth Wygyr in **Anglesey** to Porth Ysgewin (Portskewett) in **Gwent**. St Mary's church has a fine 12th-century chancel arch. Sudbrook is dominated by the engine hall that houses pumps installed to prevent the flooding of the Severn Tunnel.

POSTAL SERVICE, The

The postal service was established by the appointment of Henry VIII, in 1516, of a 'Master of the Posts'. He organized his own mail system – literally, the Royal Mail – which was not opened to the public until 1635. Each of five post routes radiated from **London**, one of which carried the royal mail to Dublin once a week, via Chester and then to **Rhuddlan**, **Beaumaris** and **Holyhead**.

In the late 16th century, a second route to **Ireland** was launched, via Bristol to the **Milford Haven Waterway** for the packet to Waterford. This service, with stages at **Chepstow**, **Newport**, **Cardiff**, **Bridgend**, **Swansea**, **Carmarthen**, **Haverfordwest** and **Dale**, was notably capricious, because of unreliable postmasters. Roger Whitley, the deputy postmaster-general (and himself from north Wales) wrote in the 1670s that 'Noe letters are so Uncertaine and Irregular as those from South Wales'. By 1675, a third route across Wales, via Leominster to **Aberystwyth**, had been established.

A single letter conveyed from Wales to London cost sixpence, a sum equal to a labourer's daily wage. Before 1700, a letter from north to south Wales would go (by **horse**) to London on the Chester route, and return on the Bristol or Gloucester route. In 1700, as a result of petitioning by the inhabitants of Shrewsbury, a north–south **border** route, through Gloucester, Hereford, Shrewsbury and Chester, was established.

Improvements to the toll **roads** heralded a transformation in the means of transport, with **stagecoach** services being established, in 1785, between London and Holyhead and from London to the Milford Haven Waterway. **Telford**'s virtually new road through the north, only part of which opened in 1808, made for speedier journeys: by the 1830s, most mail coaches were reaching double the speeds of the 1780s.

The advent of the **railways** presaged the demise of the mail coach. The London–Birmingham section of the Holyhead route was transferred to the railway in 1838, and from 1848 the mail travelled all the way by train. The southern route saw comparable changes. The London–Milford Haven–Waterford passage was rerouted, in 1674, from Cardiff and Swansea to **Brecon** and Carmarthen, with a bye-post linking **Monmouth**, Swansea and Cardiff. At the end of the 18th century, the mail route again shifted, using Bristol rather than Gloucester for crossing the **Severn**. Until 1822, delays at the Severn crossing caused the journey from London to Swansea to take a much-criticized 32 hours; in 1835, therefore, the crossing was moved upstream, to run from Chepstow to Aust. In 1851, however, the railway eclipsed the Aust mail passage.

From 1797 to 1848, there was only one postal delivery worker in Swansea; until 1822, it was Mary John, who charged a halfpenny for the service, and was reported to be 'an old and decrepid woman who occupied the whole day in the performance of her duty'. Her place was taken by 'an active man' who made the delivery in just three hours. The delivery charge was dropped, a collection service was introduced (with the new worker touring the town with a bell in the evening), and the houses in the main streets were numbered. By 1838, some 2000 letters a week were being delivered in Swansea.

Rowland Hill's uniform and pre-paid penny post was introduced in 1840, a reform ardently advocated by Welsh **radicals**, and by **Samuel Roberts** in particular. Such radicals were also anxious that collection and delivery should be available everywhere, rather than merely in those areas where influential figures had succeeded in securing local letter carriers. Such a service was provided in the 1850s, when the novelist Anthony Trollope, surveyor for the Post Office, rode around the south determining the site of post boxes and measuring the distances a postman would need to walk. In addition, at least 1000 sub-post offices were established, offices which undertook new duties with the setting up of the Post Office Savings Bank in 1861 and the provision of state pensions in 1909. The number of postal workers in Wales rose from a few hundred in 1839 to some 15,000 by 1910. For the bulk of the inhabitants of early 20th-century Wales, **police**men and postmen were virtually the only evidence of the existence of the British state.

The number of letters posted in Wales increased from some 4 million in 1840 to over 50 million in 1910, an increase which underpinned many of the social changes of the period – the spread of radical ideas, for example, and the impetus given to **emigration** by the letters of those who had already emigrated. The postal service continues to grow; 380 million letters were posted in Wales in 1950, and 491 million in 2000/1. By 2007, however, carriers other than the Royal Mail and Parcelforce were taking an increasing share of the market, and the number of sub-post offices, already much reduced, seemed destined to contract further. With the coming of the **telephone**, the writing of letters, particularly personal ones, declined dramatically, a decline more than compensated for by the rise

of junk mail. Letter writing revived with the coming of e-mail, and entered a semi-literate form with the spread of text-messaging.

POTTERY and PORCELAIN

The earliest shards of pottery discovered in Wales are fragments of coarse earthenware excavated from **Neolithic** sites such as the Tinkinswood burial chamber (**St Nicholas**). The burial sites of the early **Bronze Age** Beaker folk have yielded more elaborate pottery, often ornamented with zigzag designs, such as the vessels discovered at **Merthyr Mawr** and **Clynnog**. There were further developments in the **Iron Age**, although pre-**Roman** Wales did not produce the wheel-made pottery common among the Belgae of south-eastern **Britain**.

Requiring pottery for trade, transportation and storage, the Romans introduced a number of pottery types to Wales, including Samian ware, examples of which may be seen at the **National Museum**. With the **Normans** came influential earthenware and pottery, and monasteries later expanded production and application; the floor tiles from **Neath** Abbey (**Dyffryn Clydach**), now at the National Museum, are a good example. In the Middle Ages and later, pottery was often imported from mainland Europe and from **England**, Bristol being a major source.

By the onset of the **Industrial Revolution**, Welsh pottery had a recognizable appearance. Although the agricultural market demanded a constant supply of pots and vessels, mainly to service the growing dairy industry – met in the south by the **Tintern** and **Rhymney** potteries – the increase in locally based production was the result of the burgeoning **population** of the industrial areas. **Ewenny** Pottery, near **Bridgend**, which had been producing earthenware since the 17th century, and was conveniently close to **coal** supplies, used red and yellow local clay for its distinctive product. In **Flintshire**, **Buckley** created instantly recognizable ware using a base of dark red local earthenware and an elegant slip decoration of pale cream. Like many other potteries, Buckley also provided firebricks for the rapidly expanding metallurgical industries.

The growth of the ceramics industry ran parallel with developments in **science**, technology and society. This was notably exemplified by **Swansea**, where, in 1764, William

A cream-ware teapot made in Swansea in 1788

Rhondda communist Annie Powell receiving her honorary law degree at Cardiff in 1982

which Swansea became famous. Later, Swansea created its own moulds, producing mainly tea and dinner services. Billingsley, a brilliant teacher, joined the Swansea firm, where David Evans and Henry Morris were among his best-known pupils. Thomas Baxter (1782–1821) painted scenes, vignettes and botanical subjects, but is best known for the **garden** scenery dessert service he created for Dillwyn.

The porcelain enterprise, although artistically successful and productive of highly desirable objects, was commercially unrewarding, and Nantgarw gradually merged with Swansea, which itself ceased production in 1870. Several small commercial potteries, including the **Glamorgan** Pottery (1813–39), the Llanelly (**Llanelli**) Pottery (1839–1922) as well as the Ynysmeudwy Pottery (1845–75) (**Pontardawe**) met domestic and some industrial needs. Mass production and cheap imports led to the demise of local pottery manufacture, while the best of the earlier pottery was – and still is – displayed in pride of place on many a family dresser (*see* **Furniture**).

Production since that era has centred on low-volume craftware to meet a new market, largely created by the growing **tourism** industry. There was an influx of craft potters, generally from England, during the 1960s, a period when pottery and ceramics became part of school and adult **education** art activities. Although the highly popular Portmeirion pottery is made in England, it owes its name to the village of Portmeirion (**Penrhyndeudraeth**), founded by the architect **Clough Williams-Ellis**, whose daughter is the potter Susan Williams-Ellis. Clay has become a language of expression, and the craft has become an art in the hands of inventive contemporary makers such as Christine Jones (b.1955). The importance of ceramics in Welsh cultural production is demonstrated annually at the National **Eisteddfod**, where the gold medal for craft is occasionally won by work in fired clay.

POULTRY

Domestic chickens and geese came to **Britain** in the **Iron Age**, ducks in the **Norman** period and turkeys in the 16th century. Chickens were originally bred not only for meat and eggs, but also for **cock fighting**, a sport that retained its popularity until made illegal in 1849. Laying birds were kept by every farmer and smallholder, and in many village back-**gardens** and miners' backyards until the mid-20th century, when intensive battery systems holding tens of thousands of birds became the norm.

Reference is made in medieval Welsh **law** to chickens and geese and the compensation due when they trespassed in corn. The goose had many uses: wings for dusting; feathers for writing quills and arrow flights; quills for **musical** instruments and as teats for feeding orphan lambs; feathers and down for cushions and beds; goose grease for softening **leather**, lubricating machinery and numerous medicinal purposes. Flocks of geese were kept on **common land** and were walked to English markets by goose **drovers**, who applied pitch and sand to protect the **birds**' feet. Many geese were fattened for the Christmas market, and plucking day was an important social event. The **Brecon** Buff, with its distinctive pink legs and beak, was officially recognized in 1934, and is one of the few breeds of geese to evolve in **Britain**.

Cole, an English entrepreneur inspired by the success of Josiah Wedgwood, opened the Cambrian Pottery, using clay imported from England. The original earth 'body' gave way to the famous 'cream-ware', which appealed to the luxury market. Thomas Rothwell joined the pottery and began using transfer-printing techniques to decorate the ware with local views, in blue, black, brown and manganese red. Thomas Pardoe (1770–1823), who worked at the Cambrian Pottery from about 1795, is one of the best-known hand painters, creating a variety of motifs – animal, **bird** and landscape – as well as **craft** objects.

Porcelain manufacture began in Wales in 1813, when William Billingsley of Worcester, knowing the essential secret recipes, opened a factory at Nantgarw (**Taff's Well**) with his son-in-law, Samuel Walker. During its brief history, Nantgarw became inextricably bound up with the older Swansea works – which outlasted it – as entrepreneurs and practitioners moved busily between them. Expensive to make and requiring extremely high temperatures, porcelain was the most desirable consumer item of its time. Billingsley produced a soft paste porcelain with an iridescence that is still highly prized by collectors.

In 1814, on the encouragement of **Lewis Weston Dillwyn**, whose family had bought into the Cambrian Pottery in 1802, moulds were moved from Nantgarw, and porcelain production began in Swansea. Walker had developed a new body, which produced the translucent 'duck egg' quality for

Other traditional farmyard birds were ducks, guinea fowl and black turkeys. From the mid-20th century, white turkeys, being most adaptable to intensive production, became the main Christmas table bird. A few farms kept one or two peacocks, not only for show but also because they killed snakes. By the early 21st century, some Welsh farmers were rearing ostriches for their meat and feathers.

POWEL, David (1552–98) Historian
A **Denbighshire** man, he is said to have been the first student to graduate at Jesus College, **Oxford**, in 1572/3. He spent his life in holy orders and held various livings. His principal literary work, *Historie of Cambria, Now Called Wales* (1584), which owed much to the work of **Humphrey Lhuyd**, reflects the Tudor interpretation of history. It was long considered the standard work on Welsh history, and was reprinted as late as 1811. Powel was the first to publish the works of **Giraldus Cambrensis** on Wales, but he omitted all remarks which could be considered derogatory about the country.

POWEL, Thomas (1845–1922) Scholar
Appointed in 1884 to the chair of **Celt**ic at **Cardiff** (the first such chair to be established in Wales), Powel, a native of **Llanwrtyd**, held the post until 1918. He edited *Y Cymmrodor* (1879–86) and published editions of **Welsh** texts, including *Ystorya de Carolo Magno* (1883). He secured the Salisbury Library for the college in 1886 and was involved in the acquisition by Cardiff Central Library of its fine collection of Welsh books and manuscripts, *The Book of Aneirin* among them.

POWELL family (Nanteos) Landowners
The family originated with Phylip ap Hywel of Ysbyty Cynfyn (**Blaenrheidol**), who died in 1589 a wealthy man, having bought farms in the **Ystwyth** and Paith valleys. For three generations his heirs lived at Llechwedd Dyrys, opposite Nanteos (**Llanfarian**). Thomas Powell (1631–1705) became a judge of the King's Bench and was knighted. His son, William (1658–1738), married the Nanteos heiress Avarina le Brun. The estate continued to increase; William's son Thomas (d.1752), who acquired the Strata Florida (**Ystrad Fflur**) estate of the Stedman family by marriage, built the splendid Palladian mansion of Nanteos. Three Powells became MPs, including W. E. Powell (1788–1854), under whom the estate became burdened with debt. His grandson was the poet, scholar and antiquarian George Powell (Miölnir Nanteos; 1842–82), who collaborated with the scholar Eirikr Magnusson in translating *The Legends of Iceland* (1864–6); he donated his vast collection of printed books and his internationally important **music** manuscripts to the University College of Wales, **Aberystwyth** (*see* **University of Wales, Aberystwyth**). The last squire, E. A. Powell, died in 1930 having outlived his only son, who had been killed in the **First World War**. In 1873, the family owned 8876 ha in **Cardiganshire**.

POWELL, Annie (1906–86) Councillor
Annie Powell, a teacher by profession, was active in relieving the plight of the unemployed during the **depression of the interwar years**. She was elected to represent the Penygraig ward on the **Rhondda** Borough Council in 1955 and, in 1979, became the first and, to date, only **Communist** to serve as mayor of a British **borough**. She stood as the Communist candidate for Rhondda East in the general elections of 1955, 1959 and 1964, when her percentage of the vote was 15.1, 14.5 and 11.8, the highest vote of any Communist candidate in **Britain** in those elections.

POWELL, Thomas (1779–1863) Coalowner
A timber merchant of **Newport**, Thomas Powell began his connection with the **coal** trade *c.*1810, and by *c.*1860 was probably the world's largest coal exporter. His initial activities were concentrated in **Monmouthshire**, particularly in the **Rhymney** valley, where, over the next 30 years, he became the greatest single figure in the trade in bituminous coal. He then turned his attention to the **Aberdare** area, where, beginning with the Duffryn pit in 1840, he sank several pits to the steam coal seams. Success there was followed by an expansion in the Rhymney valley. After his death, his steam coal collieries passed to his three sons, but were sold in 1864 to the **Powell Duffryn Steam Coal Co. Ltd**, formed specifically by George Elliot to take them over.

POWELL, Vavasor (1617–70)
Preacher and millenarian
A native of Knucklas (**Beguildy**), this fiery divine was converted to the **Puritan** cause while a schoolmaster at Clun, **Shropshire**. He came to prominence during the **Civil Wars**, both as a militant **preacher** and a brave soldier, and he subsequently served as an approver under the **Act for the Better Propagation and Preaching of the Gospel in Wales (1650)**. His enemies accused him of gross peculation and intimidation, but no hard evidence was produced. Powell

Nanteos, built by Thomas Powell (b.1752)

John Cowper Powys, a portrait by Augustus John (1895)

developed strong millenarian views and joined the radical separatist group known as the Fifth Monarchists, who believed in the imminence of the personal reign of Christ upon Earth. A staunch supporter of the Barebones or Saints' Parliament of 1653, he launched a thunderous attack against **Cromwell** when he dissolved it. His attack was so vituperative that for a brief period he was committed to prison in **London**. On his release, he began organizing anti-Cromwellian propaganda in the form of a petition entitled *A Word for God* (1655). Estranged from moderate Puritans, he continued to cry 'A Roundhead I will be'. He suffered greatly during the persecutions of the 1660s and died in Fleet Prison.

POWELL DUFFRYN STEAM COAL CO. LTD, The

The company was formed in 1864 to take over collieries previously operated by **Thomas Powell**. Mainly located around **Aberdare**, they produced the equivalent of *c*.412,000 tonnes of **coal** per annum (4% of south Wales's output). Dominated initially by George Elliot, the company expanded rapidly from the late 1880s under the influence of the firm's general colliery manager, E. M. Hann. New sinkings, such as **Bargoed**, Penallta and Britannia, shifted the company's operations increasingly into the **Rhymney** valley. By 1913, Powell Duffryn employed 14,779 miners and produced the equivalent of 4 million tonnes of coal (6.9% of south Wales's output). After the **First World War**, the company continued to expand, mainly through mergers and acquisitions. In 1946, on the eve of the nationalization of the coal industry, the company was the largest coalmining company in Europe, employing some 27,000 miners, and

producing over 9 million tonnes of coal (37% of south Wales's output). It has since diversified into other activities, with, by the 21st century, engineering and **ports** among its main interests.

POWYS County (519,617 ha; 126,345 inhabitants)

Following the local **government** reorganization of 1974, Powys became the name of one of Wales's eight new **counties**. It consists of the former **Montgomeryshire** and **Radnorshire** and most of **Breconshire**. (Those parts of Breconshire adjoining **Merthyr Tydfil** became part of **Mid Glamorgan**; **Brynmawr** and **Llanelly** became part of **Gwent**.) In the run-up to the further reorganization of 1996, there was a vigorous campaign in favour of reconstituting Powys's former counties, as occurred in the case of **Dyfed**. The campaign failed, and the county of Powys, augmented by the addition of part of the one-time county of **Clwyd** (the **communities** of Llangedwyn, Llansilin and the northern part of that of **Llanrhaeadr-ym-Mochnant**) continued in existence. The 1974 county was divided into the districts of Breconshire, Montgomeryshire and Radnorshire, but following the establishment of Powys as a unitary authority in 1996, the one-time districts retained only a vestigial role. Powys is by far the most extensive of Wales's 22 post-1996 counties. In 2001, 30.09% of the inhabitants of Powys had some knowledge of **Welsh**, with 12.94% wholly fluent in the language. (*See also* **Llanfihangel** and **Llanddewi Ystradenny**.)

POWYS Kingdom and lordship

The kingdom of Powys traced its origins back to the last years of the **Roman** occupation. It is probable that the name derives ultimately from the **Latin** *pagus* (district, province), indicating that Powys was seen as a hinterland of the territory of the **Cornovii**. Its position made it vulnerable; in the 7th and 8th centuries it bore the brunt of the **Mercia**n advance remembered in the **Llywarch Hen** cycle and the **Heledd** poems. The military exploits of the 8th-century King Eliseg were commemorated on the Eliseg Pillar at **Llantysilio**. The death of King Cyngen in 856 brought Powys under the rule of **Rhodri Mawr**; little is known of its subsequent history until the fall of **Gruffudd ap Llywelyn** in 1064. Gruffudd's half-brother Rhiwallon ap Cynfyn then became king of Powys; later rulers were descended from Rhiwallon's brother **Bleddyn ap Cynfyn**.

Powys was the dominant power in Wales in the early 12th century. The fall of Robert, earl of Shrewsbury (*see* **Montgomery family**), in 1102 left a vacuum on the **border** and Henry I saw Powys under **Cadwgan ap Bleddyn** as a force for stability. But the kingdom was riven by dynastic quarrels; **Owain ap Cadwgan**'s abduction of **Nest**, the wife of Gerald of Windsor, in 1109 was an affront to the king and led to the removal of Cadwgan, although the resulting disorder soon brought about his reinstatement. Cadwgan was assassinated in 1111 and Owain killed in 1116. Cadwgan's brother Maredudd ap Bleddyn ruled until his death in 1132 when he was succeeded by his son **Madog ap Maredudd**. He built up the kingdom and pursued a policy of friendship with the English crown, but his death in 1160 was followed immediately by that of his son and designated successor, Llywelyn, and the result was a permanent division. The south (**Powys Wenwynwyn**) passed to Madog's nephew **Owain Cyfeiliog**, while the north (**Powys Fadog**) went to his son Gruffudd Maelor. Thus, 1160 marked the end of a united Powys as a factor in the politics and history of Wales.

POWYS FADOG Lordship
Named after **Madog ap Gruffudd** (d.1236), the lordship came into existence as a result of the partition of **Powys** following the death of Madog's grandfather, **Madog ap Maredudd**, in 1160. It consisted of **Maelor Gymraeg**, **Maelor Saesneg**, **Iâl**, **Edeirnion**, **Nanheudwy**, **Cynllaith** and part of **Mochnant**. Its chief stronghold was the castle of Dinas Bran (**Llangollen**) and its spiritual centre the **Cistercian** monastery of Valle Crucis (**Llantysilio**). Its rulers were usually allied with **Gwynedd** and the dynasty collapsed with the death of **Llywelyn ap Gruffudd** in 1282. Parts of Powys Fadog were attached to the **counties** of **Merioneth** and **Flint**, and the rest became the **march**er-lordships of **Chirk and Chirkland** and **Bromfield and Yale**. By the late 14th century, the senior line of the one-time ruling family was represented by **Owain Glyndŵr**. Cadet branches survived as Welsh barons, particularly in Edeirnion.

POWYS WENWYNWYN Lordship
Following the death of **Madog ap Maredudd** in 1160, southern **Powys** was lost by the main line of the house of Powys through the efforts of Madog's nephew **Owain Cyfeiliog** (d.1197). It received its name from Owain's son **Gwenwynwyn**. Its *cantrefi* included **Arwystli**, **Caereinion**, **Cedewain** and **Cyfeiliog**, and its chief stronghold came to be Powis Castle (**Welshpool**). As is evident from the activities of **Gwenwynwyn ab Owain** and **Gruffudd ap Gwenwynwyn**, the Powys Wenwynwyn dynasty tended to side with the English crown in its attempts to thwart the ambitions of the princes of **Gwynedd**, a fact which explains why it was the sole major Welsh dynasty to survive the **Edwardian conquest**. In 1311, Powys Wenwynwyn passed by marriage to the Charlton family and was transformed from a Welsh territory into a **march**er-lordship. In 1536, it became the core of **Montgomeryshire**.

POWYS, John Cowper (1872–1963) Novelist
Because his father claimed Welsh descent, Powys considered himself to be a Welshman, although he was born in Derbyshire and spent his childhood in Dorset and Somerset. Two of his brothers were also writers: T. F. Powys (1875–1953) and Llywelyn Powys (1884–1939). Following a period of teaching in **England**, and after several lecturing tours in America, he settled at **Corwen** in 1935, and in 1955 moved to Blaenau **Ffestiniog**. There he learned to read **Welsh**, and immersed himself in the study of Welsh history and mythology. His novels include *Wolf Solent* (1929), *A Glastonbury Romance* (1932) and *Maiden Castle* (1936), long romances set in Wessex and written under the influence of Thomas Hardy. Two of his novels have Welsh settings, namely *Owen Glendower* (1940) and *Porius* (1951). The first of these is a vivid recreation of the rising of **Owain Glyndŵr** (*see also* **Glyndŵr Revolt, The**), but much of the narrative and the characterization was the product of the author's fertile imagination. While

living in Wales he also wrote some of his most notable literary criticism, including *The Pleasures of Literature* (1938); a selection of his essays was published as *Obstinate Cymric* (1947).

PREACHERS and SERMONS
Little is known about the earliest Welsh preaching. The first of the **saints**' lives, the Life of **Samson**, describes monastic life, but there is no reference to preaching as such. Rhigyfarch's (1056–99; *see* **Sulien**) Life of St **David** mentions David preaching at the synod of **Llanddewi Brefi**, but little can be gleaned concerning the nature of preaching during the Age of the Saints.

Evidence from the later medieval period affords a clearer picture. The ecclesiastical reformation which stemmed from the Fourth Lateran Council (1215) and the spiritual renewal which brought the preaching orders – the **Friars** – to Wales a few years later, improved the standard of parochial preaching; at the same time, Welshmen such as **Johannes Wallensis**, Roger of Conwy (d.1360) and, especially, the Dominican Thomas Wallensis (fl.1300–50) gained a reputation in the universities as experts in the art of preaching. An earlier Thomas Wallensis (fl.1230–55), the Franciscan who became bishop of **St David's** (1248–55), was author of the influential treatise on preparing sermons *De modo componendi sermonis*. In 1281, **John Pecham**, archbishop of Canterbury, issued statutes aimed at raising the standard of preaching among the clergy. The various homiletic aids and other pulpit materials available in **Welsh** by the beginning of the 15th century show that at least some among the **parish** clergy were eager to provide adequate pulpit instruction for their flocks.

The preacher Christmas Evans

The **Protestant Reformation** brought about a revolution in the theory and practice of preaching. The Welsh translation of Archbishop Cranmer's *Book of Homilies* appeared in 1606, by which time a distinctly Protestant preaching tradition had been established. The **Puritans** placed particular emphasis on preaching, while **Anglicans** such as **Rhys Prichard** and **Griffith Jones, Llanddowror** were equally committed to preaching as the chief means of the conversion of souls. Despite the exceptional effectiveness of Methodist preachers like **Daniel Rowland**, it was in the 19th century that Welsh preaching really came into its own. **John Elias, Christmas Evans, William Williams** (Wern; 1781–1840), **John Jones** (Talysarn; 1796–1857) and **Henry Rees** were among the most powerful preachers that Wales had ever seen. By the 20th century, the tradition had waned, but there remained those such as **Martyn Lloyd-Jones** who showed that, even in a secular age, preaching could still be a powerful means of commending Christian faith.

PREECE, William Henry (1834–1913)
Radio scientist

A native of **Waunfawr**, Preece was an electrical engineer who played a major part in the introduction of wireless **telegraphy** and the **telephone** to **Britain**. His graduate studies at the Royal Institution, **London**, under Michael Faraday, aroused his interest in applied electricity and telegraphic **engineering**. For 29 years, from 1870, he was an engineer with the Post Office telegraphic system, and contributed many inventions and improvements, including a signalling system that increased **railway** safety. In 1892, when he had become chief engineer at the Post Office, Preece originated his own system of wireless telegraphy, but his most important contribution to the field was his encouragement, through the Post Office, of Guglielmo Marconi (*see* **Physical Sciences**). He introduced the first telephones into Britain, patented by Alexander Graham Bell. Preece was elected FRS in 1881 and knighted in 1899. However, he was one of the panel of referees who rejected **David Hughes**'s (1831–1900) first ever demonstration of electromagnetic waves.

PREMONSTRATENSIANS Order of canons

The Premonstratensians, or White Canons, also known as Norbertines, were founded by St Norbert in 1120 at Prémontré, near Laon. **Talyllychau** Abbey was the only Premonstratensian house in Wales, founded (1184–9) by **Rhys ap Gruffudd** (The Lord Rhys; d.1197) as a daughter house of St Jean, Amiens. In the late 13th century, the canons of Talyllychau fell into disrepute, and the house was reformed, becoming subject to Welbeck in 1291, and later to Halesowen.

PRENDERGAST, Peter (1946–2007) Painter

One of Wales's pre-eminent landscape painters, Peter Prendergast was born at Abertridwr (**Aber Valley**) where his father was a **coal**miner. It was an industrial environment that was crucial in the development of a landscape vision which, by the early age of fourteen, was unmistakably his own. He studied at **Cardiff** School of Art, the Slade School of Art (where Frank Auerbach was his mentor) and Reading University, before becoming an art teacher, first at Ysgol Dyffryn Ogwen, **Bethesda**, in 1974, and then, from 1980 onwards, at Coleg Menai, **Bangor**. Living at Deiniolen (**Llanddeiniolen**), he was captivated by the **slate**-quarrying landscapes of **Gwynedd**, which he 'reinvented' in his robust, energetic **painting**s, with their surging colours and internal luminosity.

Peter Prendergast, *Approaching Storm* (1996)

PRESBYTERIANS

Presbyterians are advocates of a system of church government by presbyters or lay elders who, originally at least, adhered to **Calvinism**. Unlike the **Congregationalists** and **Baptists**, they have traditionally favoured centralized established churches, such as that of **Scotland**. Virtually unknown in Wales before the 1640s, Presbyterianism was imposed on Wales and **England** by Parliament in 1646. However, during the **Civil War** and under the **Commonwealth**, those advocating the sovereignty of the individual congregation enjoyed greater success in Wales than did Presbyterians.

In the later 17th century, Wales's leading Presbyterian was Philip Henry (1631–96) of **Flintshire**, but he and his fellow campaigners won few followers, the religious census of 1676 revealing that Presbyterians were a poor third behind Congregationalists and Baptists. In the 18th century, most Welsh Presbyterians abandoned Calvinism. They moved from **Arminianism** to **Arianism** and on to **Unitarianism**, a progression in which a key role was played by the **Nonconformist** academy at **Carmarthen**. By the end of the 18th century, the old Presbyterianism was virtually extinct in Wales. There was some revival in the 19th century when immigrants from England and Scotland founded churches in Wales. In 1962, most of those churches joined the United Reformed Church.

When the **Calvinistic Methodists** seceded from the **Anglican** Church in 1811, they adopted a Presbyterian form of government. Their Confession of Faith (1823) was essentially Presbyterian. In 1928, the denomination formally adopted 'The Presbyterian Church of Wales' as its title. However, the Church could not claim any lineal descent from 17th-century Presbyterianism.

PRESELI PEMBROKESHIRE (Preseli Penfro)
Constituency and one-time district

Following the abolition of **Pembrokeshire** in 1976, Preseli Pembrokeshire was created as a district of the new **county** of **Dyfed**. It consisted of what had been the **borough** of **Haverfordwest**, the **urban districts** of **Fishguard**, **Milford Haven** and **Neyland**, and the **rural districts** of Haverfordwest and **Cemais**. It later acquired five **communities** previously part of **South Pembrokeshire**. In 1996, the district, together with that of South Pembrokeshire, became the reconstituted Pembrokeshire. The name survives as that of a constituency.

PRESS GANGS

It was the recruitment problem occasioned by the **French Revolutionary and Napoleonic Wars** that initiated an official press gang policy, although freelance mercenaries had long been engaged in the practice. With the breakdown of the Peace of Amiens in May 1803, the uneasy peace between **Britain** and France was at an end, and a decade and more of all-out war ensued. Press gangs were sent to all parts of Wales forcefully to recruit young men for naval service. Although inexperienced men were caught in the net, it was serving seamen from merchant ships that were preferred. A regular feature in a **ship**'s account was the payment of protection money against the impressment of members of a crew. This fee could vary from 2s 6d to 11s

6d, depending on the status of a sailor. The practice ended in 1815, although the state's right to impress men for service in the navy still exists. However, the adoption of the long service system in 1853 meant that, thereafter, the British navy had an adequate number of volunteers.

PRESTATYN, Denbighshire
(1188 ha; 18,496 inhabitants)

Prestatyn was developed as a seaside resort from *c.*1880 onwards by H. D. Pochin of Bodnant (*see* **Eglwysbach**). An area of early settlement, it had a small **Roman** fort, perhaps built to safeguard the **ship**ment of **lead** ore. The town, part of **Flintshire** until 1974, is the northern terminus of the **Offa's Dyke Path**, although there is no evidence of the Dyke north of **Treuddyn**. A castle, built by Henry II in 1157, was destroyed by **Owain Gwynedd** in 1166. Prestatyn has one of the earliest purpose-built holiday camps. Changes in **tourism** have made it a place of retirement rather than of holidays. The **commote** of Prestatyn was one of the three commotes of the *cantref* of **Tegeingl**.

PRESTEIGNE (Llanandras), Radnorshire, Powys
(2494 ha; 2463 inhabitants)

Located south of the **River** Lugg, the **community** thrusts towards **England**. Saxton, writing in 1575, approved of Presteigne: 'For beauteous building it is the best in the shire.' Richard Haslam considered it 'a lucky town, lying … on an isthmus of land which links it with the wealthier and mellower east.' It has, nevertheless, had its share of disasters; it was destroyed by **Llywelyn ap Gruffudd** in 1262 and by **Owain Glyndŵr** in 1402, ravaged by plague in the 14th, 16th and 17th centuries, and consumed by fire in 1681. Despite these vicissitudes, it remains a pleasing and remarkably unspoiled town. The houses date mainly from the 17th and 18th centuries; the Radnorshire Arms, built in 1616, is particularly attractive. St Andrew's church, dating mainly from the 14th and 15th centuries, with some traces of Saxon origins, is architecturally pre-eminent among **Radnorshire** churches. Presteigne's claims were ignored by the **Acts of 'Union'**. It did not become one of the towns of the Radnor **Boroughs** constituency until 1832. **New Radnor** became the **county** town, and the shire court was to be held alternately at New Radnor and **Rhayader**. However, one of the first judges to visit Rhayader was murdered, and the court was transferred to Presteigne.

By the mid-17th century, the Great Sessions (see **Law**) and, after 1830, the assizes, were also held there. Presteigne's position as the legal centre of Radnorshire is commemorated in the Judge's Lodging, a fascinating re-creation of the accommodation provided for a Victorian justice of assize situated in the old Shire Hall. In 1889, Presteigne was supplanted by **Llandrindod** as the administrative centre of Radnorshire. The village of Norton has a Victorian air; its church was rebuilt by George Gilbert Scott.

PRICE family (Rhiwlas) Landowners

The family traced its descent from Rhys Fawr, Henry **Tudor**'s standard-bearer at **Bosworth**. Rhys's son, the cleric Robert ap Rhys (d.*c.*1534), protégé of Wolsey, acquired extensive monastic estates. His 12 sons included two abbots, together with **Elis Prys** (The Red Doctor) of Plas Iolyn (**Pentrefoelas**), and Cadwaladr, founder of the Price family of Rhiwlas (**Llandderfel**). Cadwaladr's distant descendant, Richard Lloyd (1780–1860), evicted tenants for voting for the **Liberal** candidate in the general election of 1859. Richard Lloyd's grandson, R. J. Lloyd Price (1843–1923), owner of 7170 ha of **Merioneth**, aroused the hostility of **T. E. Ellis**, largely because of his preservation of game. He is reputed to have put up half his estate as a wager on the **horse** Bendigo, spending his winnings on a family mausoleum at Llanfor (Llandderfel). He established a **whisky** distillery at **Frongoch** (Llandderfel) which housed **Irish** insurrectionists in 1916. His great-grandson Kenrick (1912–82), owner of much of the **Tryweryn Valley**, connived in the drowning of Capel Celyn. The family, one of the few Welsh **gentry** families still to reside in the ancestral seat, are again **Welsh**-speaking and were generous patrons of the National *Eisteddfodau* at **Bala** in 1967 and 1997.

PRICE (PRYS), John (?1502–55)
Scholar and administrator

Of a family with deep roots in the lordship of **Brecon**, John Price had a successful career as a royal official, becoming secretary of royal affairs in Wales (1540) and a member of the **Council of Wales and the Marches** (1551). He was involved in the administrative measures that brought about the breach with Rome and the **dissolution of the monasteries**, following which he acquired **Brecon** Priory as well as lands in **Herefordshire**. Sheriff of **Breconshire** in 1543, he was knighted in 1546/7. A collector of old manuscripts, he was responsible for the survival of such important **Welsh** manuscripts as *The Black Book of Carmarthen*. He was a defender of **Geoffrey of Monmouth** against the attacks of Polydore Vergil. In 1546, he published what is believed to be the first printed book in Welsh, *Yny lhyvyr hwnn*. His **Latin** description of Wales, translated by **Humphrey Lhuyd**, was used by **David Powel** in his *Historie of Cambria*. One of his daughters married **Thomas Jones** (Twm Shon Catti; *c.*1530–1609).

PRICE, Joseph Tregelles (1784–1854)
Quaker, ironmaster and philanthropist

A native of **Cornwall**, in 1818 he became managing director of the **Neath** Abbey **Iron**works (**Dyffryn Clydach**), an undertaking in which several **Quaker** families had an interest. Price adhered strictly to Quaker principles, insisting that no cannon, shot or gun should be manufactured at the works. He was one of the founders of the first Peace Society, set up in **London** in 1816, and a prominent patron of the Anti-**Slavery** Movement. Price was one of the foremost defenders of Dic Penderyn (**Richard Lewis**), of whose innocence he remained convinced.

PRICE, Richard (1723–91)
Dissenting minister, philosopher and statistician

Wales's most distinguished philosopher, renowned for his ideological contributions to both American Independence and the French Revolution, was born at Tynton Farm, Llangeinor (**Garw Valley**). He was a cousin of Ann Maddocks (1704–27), the maid of Cefn Ydfa (*see* **Llangynwyd Lower** and '**Bugeilio'r Gwenith Gwyn**'). A

Presbyterian minister, he came to embrace **Arianism**, then Deism and eventually a form of religion based upon reason and nature. He spent most of his life in ministries in **London**.

In *A Review of the Principal Questions and Difficulties in Morals* (1758), Price set out his moral theory according to which (contrary to philosophers such as Hume and Hutcheson) he held moral judgement to be primarily rational in character and not a matter of moral sense or feeling. He also held that right actions have characteristics, independent of their consequences, which make them right. With these views, he anticipated Kant. In *Observations on the Nature of Civil Liberty* (1776), he declared that 'all civil **government** … is the creature of the people'. His political **philosophy**, like that of Locke, is based on a social contract theory, but is more radical in that he held that the people retain the right to change their governors or form of government regardless of whether their governors have transgressed or not. In keeping with his moral philosophy, he believed that the theoretical basis for representative and accountable government lay not so much in the beneficial consequences of such a system as in the inherent dignity of persons. This view led to the notion that every civil society had a right to self-government.

It is as a champion of liberty, therefore, that Price is best remembered. An advocate of the cause of the American colonists, he published *Observations on the Importance of the American Revolution* in 1784. In *A Discourse on the Love of our Country* (1789), he expressed admiration for the principles of the French Revolution. Edmund Burke countered Price's views with a classic expression of political conservatism entitled *Reflections on the Revolution in France* (1790), which in turn stimulated Tom Paine to write his radical classic *The Rights of Man* (1791).

As a keen mathematician, Price made a crucially important contribution to the development of actuarial **science**; he was elected FRS (1765) in recognition of his early work on probability theory, which he had first encountered in the papers of Thomas Bayes, whose executor he was. Price was the first to draw up actuarial tables of life expectancy as the basis of life **insurance**. His skills as a mathematician encouraged Pitt to seek his advice on the national debt, to which Price had drawn attention, in *An Appeal to the Public on the Subject of the National Debt* (1772), as a great evil. Price's arguments resulted in the Sinking Fund Act of 1786.

For his contribution to raising the debate about the colonies from the level of resentment and vituperation to that of philosophical principle, Price was awarded an honorary degree from the University of **Yale** in 1781 – an honour conferred on him and George Washington together. But he felt unable to accept the invitation to become an American citizen and, indeed, never crossed the Atlantic, despite his being invited by the first Congress of the United States to take charge of its financial affairs. On his death, Price was officially mourned in Paris. Tynton has become a tourist attraction.

The Reign of Terror in revolutionary France reduced the appeal of Price's ideas. By the 20th century, however, it was widely appreciated that his works crystallized many of the ideas that are central to Western liberal democracy.

PRICE, Thomas (Carnhuanawc; 1787–1848) Patriot
The greatest Welsh patriot of the first half of the 19th century, Carnhuanawc was born at Llanfihangel Bryn Pabuan (**Llanafanfawr, Breconshire**) and spent his life as an **Anglican** clergyman in his native **county**. Between 1836 and 1842, he published in instalments his *Hanes Cymru*, a work suffused with his warm, and sometimes uncritical, enthusiasm for Wales. He was the leading figure at the *eisteddfodau* of the **Abergavenny** Cymreigyddion (*see* **Cymreigyddion Society**), and was much involved in Lady Charlotte **Guest**'s translation of *The Mabinogion*. The father of pan-Celticism, he assisted Ar Gonideg with his Breton translation of the New Testament. An ardent advocate of the use of the **Welsh language** in worship and **education**, his Welsh-medium school at Gellifelen (**Llanelly, Monmouthshire**; at that time in Breconshire) drew a contemptuous response from the authors of the education report of 1847 (*see* **Treason of the Blue Books**). An artist, a naturalist, a woodcarver and a musician, he was buried at **Llanfihangel Cwmdu** where his grave, until the **Second World War**, was a place of annual **pilgrimage**. Pilgrimages were revived in the 1990s by Cymdeithas Carnhuanawc.

PRICE, W[illiam] C[harles] (1909–93) Physicist
W. C. Price, FRS, made a major contribution to understanding the electronic structure of molecules. Born and educated at **Swansea**, he undertook research at Baltimore, **Cambridge**, Chicago and King's College, **London** where he became Wheatstone professor of physics. Many consider that his pioneering work, spanning ultraviolet, infrared and photoelectron spectroscopy, merited a Nobel Prize. Through discovering that the ultraviolet spectra of molecules formed series similar to those observed in atoms, he established the orbital properties of the outermost electrons in a molecule. Later, he used photoelectron spectroscopy to study the inner orbits of valency electrons. He also studied the vibrational states of molecules and hydrogen bonding – work basic to the understanding of molecules such as DNA.

PRICE, William (1800–93)
Doctor, Chartist and cremationist
Dr William Price, one of the great eccentrics of the 19th century, was born in **Rudry** and lived at **Llantrisant**. Like his father, he suffered from schizophrenia, which, together with the collapse of many a revolutionary but impractical dream, may offer an explanation for his unusual behaviour.

An inventive physician, he was notorious for his advocacy of free **love**, vegetarianism and cremation, and his hostility to the church, the **law** and **iron**masters. In 1823, he was elected works doctor at the **Pontypridd** Chainworks, the first instance in **Britain** of a workforce electing and paying its own physician in return for free medical treatment – an arrangement anticipating by many decades the **miners' medical aid societies**. In 1839, he built a pair of round towers at Glyntaff (Pontypridd) which he intended as a **druid**ic museum. In 1840, as leader of the Pontypridd **Chartists**, Price was instrumental in establishing the Pontypridd Provision Company, the first example in Wales of a cooperative formed for explicitly political purposes.

Price styled himself **archdruid**, and strode the industrial valleys dressed in green trousers, scarlet waistcoat and a **fox**-skin hat. Despite his advocacy of armed insurrection, he was mysteriously absent from the Chartist **Newport Rising**; in its aftermath, he fled to France, disguised as a woman. Gleefully litigious, Price indulged in many lawsuits, the most famous being his trial in 1884 for attempting to burn the corpse of his baby son, Iesu Grist (Jesus Christ). He was found not guilty of having committed an offence, which proved to be a turning point in the history of the movement to legalize cremation. Aged 83, Price began a relationship with Gwenllian Llewelyn, who bore him two children, Iesu Grist yr Ail (Jesus Christ the Second) and Penelopen. Thousands attended Price's own cremation at Cae'r-lan Fields, Llantrisant.

PRICE-THOMAS, Clement (1893–1973)
Surgeon
Abercarn-born Price-Thomas began his medical training in **Cardiff** and completed it at Westminster Hospital where he came under the influence of Arthur Tudor Edwards, a pioneering surgeon of the thorax. Price-Thomas himself became a leader in that field, developing new ways of treating **tuberculosis** and lung cancer, and becoming the first in

Dr William Price depicted in ceremonial regalia

Britain, in 1946, to correct the narrowing of the main artery from the heart. His treatment of a pulmonary condition of George VI led to a knighthood in 1951. During his last years, he was president of the Welsh National School of Medicine (*see* **Wales College of Medicine, Biology, Life and Health Sciences**).

PRICHARD, Caradog (1904–80)
Novelist, poet and journalist

Caradog Prichard first came to prominence as the very young winner of the National **Eisteddfod**'s crown in three successive years, in 1927, 1928 and 1929, a feat which prompted the festival's authorities to change the rules so that no one could emulate his success. But he is chiefly remembered as the author of what many regard as the finest **Welsh-language** novel, *Un Nos Ola Leuad* (1961), a thinly disguised account of his childhood in **Bethesda**. At the core of the novel – and of much of his earlier poetry – is his mother's mental breakdown during his youth and his own response to it. Despite having launched his writing career through the Eisteddfod, and although he won its chair in 1962, Prichard, a **Tory** and a royalist who spent more than half his life outside Wales, living in **London** and working mainly for the *Daily Telegraph*, never quite belonged to the Welsh literary establishment.

PRICHARD, John (1817–86) Architect

The son of the rector of **Llangan**, Prichard developed into one of the most imaginative neo-Gothic architects of his age. After training with A. C. Pugin, Prichard established a practice in Llandaff (**Cardiff**), where he was appointed diocesan architect. Between 1852 and 1863, he was in partnership with John Pollard Seddon. Prichard's greatest work was the extensive restoration of Llandaff Cathedral (1843–69); the best of his new churches was St Catherine, **Baglan** (1875–82). He was also responsible for **Cowbridge** Grammar School (1849–52), the Probate Registry, Llandaff (1860–3), a miners' convalescent home in **Porthcawl** known as The Rest (1874–8), and the Magistrates Court (1880–1) in **Bridgend**.

PRICHARD, Rhys (Rice Prichard or Vicar Prichard or Yr Hen Ficer – the Old Vicar; ?1579–1644/5)
Clergyman and poet

Born at **Llandovery** and educated at **Oxford**, Prichard was vicar of Llandingad church, Llandovery, from 1602 until his death. In 1617, he published two works, *The Catechism ...* and a poem to his son, *A Bishop's Advice to each soul ...* which show the determination of the vicar to educate his **parish**ioners in the Christian faith. This zeal stimulated him to compose his popular verses, which also had a practical purpose, for they discussed the minutiae of rural life, from the treatment of illnesses to the benefits of eating vegetables, and from choosing a wife to avoiding drunkenness. They were published, from 1658, by **Stephen Hughes**, and were collected under the title *Canwyll y Cymru* (The candle of the Welsh) in 1681; a bestseller for nearly 200 years, and also translated into **English**, the volume was as popular among the common people as *Taith y Pererin*, the **Welsh** translation of Bunyan's *The Pilgrim's Progress*.

PRICHARD, Thomas Jeffery Llewelyn (1790–1862) Writer

A native of **Builth**, Prichard was a bookseller in his home town and, after 1839, a strolling player, until he had his nose cut off in a **fencing** accident (thereafter, he wore a wax nose held in place by his spectacles). He is remembered as the author of *The Adventures and Vagaries of Twm Shon Catti* (1828), the book that was chiefly responsible for spreading the myth of Twm Shon Catti (*see* **Thomas Jones**; *c.*1530–1609) as a 'Welsh Robin Hood'; it is sometimes called 'the first Welsh novel in **English**'. Despite the novel's success, Prichard ended his life in penury in a poor quarter of **Swansea**, and died of burns received after falling into his own fire.

PRIMOGENITURE

Primogeniture, the principle of land inheritance at the core of the feudal system, gave precedence to the eldest son, to whom the property passed undivided. It formed an essential part of the family infrastructure and preserved the unity of estates. If there were no sons, the inheritance was divided among the daughters; if there were no heirs, it escheated to the crown. In Welsh **law**, a free man's land was divided equally among all his sons, whether born in wedlock or not (*see* **Cyfran**). The Welsh **gentry** of the 14th and 15th centuries, seeking to consolidate their estates by passing them in their entirety to one heir, sought to abandon this custom, considering it to be, as John Wynn (*see* **Wynn family (Gwydir)**) put it, 'the destruction of Wales ... [and] not a matter to be stood upon'. However, it was not until the second **Act of 'Union'** (1543) that primogeniture was officially imposed upon Wales. However, many Welsh landholders – small farmers in particular – continued to divide their property among their offspring, a practice which had become almost universal by the late 20th century.

PRIMROSE HILL

Sailing for Canada on Christmas Eve 1900, this large barque was being towed when the tow parted off Bardsey (*see* **Islands**). A storm blew her onto the coast near South Stack, **Holyhead** where, on 28 December, the **iron** sailing ship broke up, and 33 of those aboard lost their lives.

PRINCE OF WALES COLLIERY DISASTER,
Abercarn, Monmouthshire (now Caerphilly)

On 11 September 1878, an explosion occurred at the Prince of Wales Colliery (**Abercarn**), killing 268 men. The precise cause was never determined, but it was attributed to a sudden outburst of gas. The practice at the mine of 'bashing' – only partly filling the spaces from which the coal had been extracted – was criticized by the official inquiry report, together with certain newly introduced mining practices, including longwall working and the use of mechanical traction.

PRINCES OF WALES

The **Principality** of Wales came into existence in 1267 when **Llywelyn ap Gruffudd** was recognized as Prince of Wales. Following his death, the title was assumed by his brother **Dafydd ap Gruffudd**, who was executed in 1283. It was revived in 1301 when Prince Edward (later Edward II), heir to Edward I, was invested as Prince of Wales at Lincoln. The motive for the revival was probably the perceived need to create a focus for the loyalty of the emerging Welsh **gentry class**. Twenty-one heirs apparent of the English crown have held the title. It is not, however, their birthright; the title (linked with that of the earldom of Chester) is the gift of the monarch, and it was not granted to Edward III nor to Edward VI.

During its early centuries, the title was no mere label. The prince received the revenues of the Principality, which was considered his sphere of activity. While the Black Prince held the title (1343–76), his council administered the Principality and sought to extend its authority to the **March**. During the Black Prince's principate, the prince's emblem was a single feather; the **Three Feathers** belong to a later era. As Prince of Wales, Henry V was much involved in defeating the ambitions of the rival Prince of Wales, **Owain Glyndŵr**. The Council of Prince Edward (later Edward V) developed into the **Council of Wales and the Marches**.

As the **Acts of 'Union'** united the March with the Principality, the whole of Wales came to be considered the territory of the prince. Yet the decay in revenue and the lack of a holder of the title between 1509 and 1608 led to the virtual severing of links between the prince and Wales. George IV, prince from 1762 to 1820, made one fleeting Welsh visit, and Edward VII, prince from 1841 to 1901, made three. Subsequent princes, Charles (b.1948) in particular, have been more assiduous. The first 19 princes were invested in **England**. In 1911, the investiture of Edward VIII was held at **Caernarfon**, as was that of Charles in 1969.

PRINCIPALITY, The

The concept of a single Welsh principality was a chief element in the policy of the 13th-century princes of **Gwynedd**. The object was to persuade the other Welsh rulers to do homage to the prince and to accept him as their feudal overlord; he would do homage to the king of **England** on behalf of them all. Although the other rulers probably did homage to **Llywelyn ap Iorwerth**, he did not succeed in securing a treaty which would have recognized him as prince and overlord of a Welsh principality.

The question arose again as Llywelyn's grandson **Llywelyn ap Gruffudd** brought most of native Wales under his control; Llywelyn used the title of **Prince of Wales** regularly from 1262 onwards and the Treaty of Pipton (*see* **Bronllys**) in 1265, agreed with Simon de **Montfort** in the name of the king, conceded all he sought. For Llywelyn, Pipton was merely a statement of his demands. It was the **Treaty of Montgomery**, two years later, that recognized Llywelyn and his successors as Princes of Wales and overlords of the other Welsh rulers; the treaty also involved the recognition of the principality of Wales as an institution.

The **Edwardian conquest** did not mean the end of the principality. The institution recognized in 1267 survived the deaths of Llywelyn ap Gruffudd and his brother **Dafydd ap Gruffudd**, and had passed into the possession of the English crown. Llywelyn's lands did not become part of the English kingdom and the principality granted to Edward I's son, Edward of **Caernarfon**, in 1301 was the principality of 1267

and not a new creation. Until the **Act of 'Union'** (1536), Wales was divided between Principality and **March**. Thereafter, insofar as the name 'Principality' had any meaning (apart from its adoption by a building society and by local **government**'s Council of the Principality), it was believed to embrace the whole of Wales.

PRINTING and PUBLISHING

Printing and publishing in Welsh

Welsh was the only **Celtic** language to respond positively to the challenge of print. The earliest printed books in Welsh, *Yny lhyvyr hwnn* (1546) and **William Salesbury**'s publications from 1547 onwards, displayed the two main incentives for publishing in Welsh: **religion** and humanistic learning. Both were united in **William Morgan**'s translation of the **Bible** (1588), the most important of all Welsh books. As humanism ebbed in the early 17th century, religion became the main reason for publishing in Welsh. **Anglicans** could print their books in **London** or **Oxford**, but **Roman Catholics** had to resort either to printing Welsh works in Italy or France or to using clandestine presses such as the one in Rhiwledyn **cave** (**Llandudno**), the first printing office in Wales, which produced part of *Y Drych Cristianogawl* (1587).

The title page of *Yny lhyvyr hwnn* (1546)

Between 1546 and 1600, there were published on average 15 **Welsh-language** books per decade (a total of 173). Although a paltry figure in comparison with the thousands published during this period in German, Italian and **English**, it compares favourably with the 4 published in Gaelic in **Scotland** and the 11 published in the Irish language. Between 1661 and 1700, the average increased to 29 per decade (a total of 112), chiefly because of the efforts of the **Welsh Trust,** which produced subsidized texts such as 8000 copies of a cheap Welsh Bible, and a Welsh translation of *The Pilgrim's Progress*. Equally important was the emergence of a genuinely commercial trade in small books such as the **almanacs** published in London by **Thomas Jones** (1648–1713) from 1681. As soon as the Act restricting the location of presses lapsed in 1695, Jones set up in Shrewsbury, a town which became the major centre for Welsh book publication during the early decades of the 18th century.

The first legitimate press in Wales was set up by Isaac Carter at Trerhedyn (Adpar, **Llandyfriog**) in 1718. In 1721, Nicholas Thomas began to print in **Carmarthen**, the chief centre for Welsh publishing for the remainder of the 18th century. As regularly apprenticed printers replaced self-taught amateurs, production standards improved. Printer-publishers were able to reduce their capital outlay – and poor readers were able to buy their books – by publishing by subscription (from the early 1720s onwards) and by part-publication (from the 1760s onwards).

Presses were set up in a number of Welsh towns during the 18th century but all too often there was insufficient trade to sustain them. It was not until the later 1780s that increasing vernacular literacy and religious **revivals** led to a rapidly growing demand for more Welsh books in larger editions. Printers responded enthusiastically to these new opportunities and, by 1820, there were over 50 printing offices in Wales, mostly small jobbing concerns that might print the occasional book at its author's risk or produce a **periodical** or **newspaper**.

Since Welsh printers concentrated on religious and practical works, dissemination of older literary texts such as the poems of the *cywyddwyr* had to rely on scribal transmission until the last decades of the 18th century. A group of London Welsh then embarked upon an ambitious programme of publishing medieval Welsh texts, commencing with the works of **Dafydd ap Gwilym** in 1789 and culminating in the *Myvyrian Archaiology* (1801, 1807). Increasing literacy and prosperity made the mid-19th century a prosperous period for many publishers – indeed, in the 1860s and 1870s, Scottish and English publishers profited from the demand for Welsh books. Although many Welsh books were still printed for their authors in small jobbing offices, a few large printer-publishers emerged, notably **Gee** of **Denbigh**, Rees in **Llandovery**, Hughes of **Wrexham**, Humphreys of **Caernarfon**, and **Spurrell** of Carmarthen. The large Welsh community in **Liverpool** led to its becoming a significant Welsh publishing centre, a tradition continued by Gwasg y Brython (founded in 1897) up to the mid-20th century. But despite the success of ambitious ventures such as Gee's *Gwyddoniadur Cymreig* and the extensive sales of **Daniel Owen**'s novels and volumes of verse by poets such as Ceiriog (**John Ceiriog Hughes**), the range of material available in Welsh remained comparatively narrow and was dominated by religious works. The production standards of many Welsh books left much to be desired, and there was a general feeling that they were too expensive. A further source of weakness was the reliance of Welsh publishers on a captive monoglot Welsh readership.

The growth of literacy in English following the 1870 **Education** Act put Welsh-language publishing under considerable pressure. The crisis of the **First World War** and the **depression of the interwar years** meant that few new titles appeared each year. Scholarly publishing was placed on a firmer footing in 1922 with the establishment of the **University of Wales** Press. Publishing material for schools received an impetus following the publication in 1927 of the report *Welsh in Education and Life*; a beneficiary of this demand was the Hughes company, which published a number of substantial works between the wars. Gwasg **Aberystwyth**, founded by **E. Prosser Rhys** in 1928, published works by the rising generation of Welsh writers such as Gwenallt (**David James Jones**) and **T. H. Parry-Williams**. Rhys built on its success by launching Y Clwb Llyfrau Cymreig (Welsh Books Club) in 1937. In 1945, Gwasg Aberystwyth was bought by Gwasg Gomer, which had been established as a printing business in 1892 and which would become the most productive of Welsh presses by the time of its centenary in 1992. Between 1920 and 1940, the Gregynog Press at **Tregynon**, the private press of the Davies sisters (*see* **Davies family (Llandinam)**), specialized in the publication of fine editions, some of them in Welsh; it was revived in 1974 by the University of Wales.

The **Second World War** led to paper shortages but also to a few positive developments, notably the launch in 1940 of Llyfrau'r Dryw – Welsh paperbacks modelled on Penguin books. As the impetus given to reading by wartime conditions faded, the grave problems threatening Welsh-language publishing became increasingly apparent. In 1952, the Ready Report laid the foundations for the system of state subsidy that now underpins Welsh-language publishing. A key development was the founding in 1962 of the **Welsh Books Council**. The language revival of the 1960s and 1970s encouraged the establishment of several lively publishers, notably Y Lolfa (1967), Gwasg Gwynedd (1972) and Gwasg Carreg Gwalch (1980). A number of books based on television programmes were published, and the Hughes company was bought by **S4C**. In recent decades, much of the emphasis has been on providing Welsh books for schools and younger readers by publishers such as Cymdeithas Lyfrau Ceredigion (founded 1954), Gwasg y Dref Wen (founded 1970) and Dalen (founded 2005), but providing attractive material for adults is more of a challenge. Although authorship in Welsh remains almost exclusively a part-time occupation, areas such as popular fiction and the humanities have been quite well served, but in others, such as the **sciences**, few Welsh titles appear. The Welsh humanists' aspiration of making Welsh a language in which all branches of knowledge are discussed have yet to be fully realized.

Printing and publishing in English

The first printed book in English by a Welshman was *Historie of Italie* by William Thomas (d.1554), which was published in London in 1550. The first book in English to

Beaumaris goal, originally built in 1829, became a museum in 1974

be published in Wales was *Choice Collections: a devotional anthology* (Carmarthen, 1726). Although, from the 18th century onwards, increasing numbers of Welsh-language books were published in Wales, the bulk of the more ambitious books in English by Welsh authors were published in England, which remains the situation today. There were exceptions, such as the Hafod Press, the private press of **Thomas Johnes** in Cwmystwyth (**Pontarfynach**), which printed a number of fine books between 1802 and 1810, in particular Johnes's English translations of French chroniclers.

Later, excellent work was done by W. J. Rees in Llandovery, which published Charlotte **Guest**'s translation of *The Mabinogion* and **Maria Jane Williams**'s *Ancient National Airs of Gwent and Morganwg* (1844). An abundance of more ephemeral English material has also been produced by Welsh presses, which print far more material in English than in Welsh. Furthermore, some of the presses that concentrated traditionally on Welsh-language books – such as Gomer – are publishing increasing numbers of books in English. English is also the medium of the greater proportion of books emanating from the University of Wales Press. Some presses were established specifically to concentrate on Welsh **literature** in English; the Druid Press, for instance, published **R. S. Thomas**'s first collection, *The Stones of the Field* (1946). This press, and others such as the Penmark Press, succumbed to financial difficulties. However, the system of grant support from the 1960s onwards enabled Poetry Wales Press to develop into Seren Books, which became the chief publisher of English-language literature in Wales. By the early 21st century, the **Cardigan**-based Parthian

Company was becoming a major book producer, with publications including The Library of Wales – a series of reprints of the classics of Welsh literature in English. Honno, which specializes in **women**'s writing, was also highly productive.

PRISONS

In Wales, as elsewhere, the concept of exacting punishment upon wrongdoers through incarceration did not exist in the medieval period. In the dungeons of their castles the native Welsh rulers and the **march**er-lords did have prisons of sorts, primarily for the confinement of hostages and political prisoners – Owain ap Gruffudd (d.*c.*1282) was imprisoned for 22 years by his brother **Llywelyn ap Gruffudd**. Following the **Edwardian conquest** English **law** was introduced in the **Principality** of Wales in criminal matters, but up to the 17th century the most common forms of punishment were fines, corporal punishments and **execution**. At the beginning of the early modern period the sole purpose of prisons was to house debtors and those awaiting trial. However, from the Tudor period onwards, magistrates were empowered by the state to establish correction houses in order to amend the ways of vagrants, those committing petty crimes and the unruly poor. By the 18th century, in places such as **Beaumaris**, **Bangor**, **Dolgellau** and **Aberystwyth**, such institutions were increasingly acquiring the function of modern-day prisons as the courts began to sentence wrongdoers to fixed periods under lock and key.

In his book *State of the Prisons* (1777), John Howard mentions two Welsh prisons – the county jail at **Caernarfon** and **Swansea** town jail. Caernarfon jail is portrayed as practically derelict, with neither drainage facilities nor fresh water supply, housing its inmates – debtors and criminals alike – in tiny, often windowless rooms. The nature of that era's privately owned prisons is shown in Howard's account of the fees of entry and discharge which debtors had to pay, and the deduction by the gaoler of 6d a week from the criminals' weekly allowance, for costs he incurred on their behalf.

Prisons were often built on the sites of existing (and frequently derelict) buildings, making conditions worse. The prison at **Haverfordwest**, for example, was originally built into the inner ward of the ruined castle in 1778, and was considered unfit for prisoners as early as 1819. Another prison, built in the outer ward of the castle, opened in 1820. In 1878, when Welsh prisons came under centralized **government** control, again the prison was deemed unfit for prisoners and was closed. Prisoners were then sent to the prison at **Carmarthen**. Nationalization led to better prison conditions and to the construction of fewer, larger prisons.

Today, there are only four prisons of any size in Wales – Swansea, **Cardiff**, **Usk** and Parc (**Bridgend**; Wales's only privatized prison). All except Parc have been in use for over 100 years, and house only adult male offenders; Wales has no prison for **women** offenders, who are sent to jails in **England**. Usk is a training prison. There are no prisons in northern Wales, where most of those convicted are sent to **Liverpool**, the cause of some concern.

PROPHECY

Darogan (prophecy) refers to the medieval Welsh tradition of political poetry. It foretold the defeat and expulsion of the **Anglo-Saxons** from **Britain** by the Welsh, usually led by a 'son of prophecy' (*mab darogan*), such as Cynan Meiriadog, **Cadwaladr** or Owain, the last name sometimes referring to **Owain Gwynedd**, **Owain Lawgoch** or **Owain Glyndŵr**. An early example of such poetry is 'Armes Prydein' ('The Prophecy of Britain'; *c*.930–42) which prophesied an English defeat by an alliance of the Welsh, fellow-**Celts** and **Vikings**, led by Cynan and Cadwaladr. *The Black Book of Carmarthen* and *The Book of Taliesin* attributed prophecies to **Merlin** and **Taliesin**, famed as bard-seers. 'Merlin's Prophecies' in **Geoffrey of Monmouth**'s 12th-century *Historia Regum Britanniae* inspired a later prophetic vogue for animal symbolism. During the **Glyndŵr Revolt**, legislation proscribed the bards and their prophecies. During the **Wars of the Roses**, poets such as Dafydd Llwyd of Mathafarn and Robin Ddu featured Jasper and Henry **Tudor** as sons of prophecy.

PROTESTANT MARTYRS

Between 1555 and 1558, in the reign of Mary I, three Protestants in Wales were burnt at the stake for their beliefs. The first was Robert Ferrar, a Yorkshireman educated at **Oxford**, who became bishop of **St David's** in 1548. He was a protégé of the duke of Somerset and, on his fall, was accused of heresy by canons at St David's. He was deprived of his see, but refused to retract his Protestant beliefs and was publicly burnt at **Carmarthen** on 31 March 1555. There is a monument to him at Halifax, his birthplace. The second martyr was Rawlins White, a **Cardiff** **fish**erman (*c*.1485–1555/6). Although illiterate, aided by his

son he learnt parts of the **Bible** and became a Protestant. He was imprisoned but refused to recant and was burnt at Cardiff in 1555 (or 1556). A memorial to him was placed on the outside wall of Cardiff's Bethany chapel in 1829. In the 1960s, the chapel was incorporated into Howells department store – the memorial may be seen in the store's menswear department. The third martyr, of whom little is known, was William Nichol of **Haverfordwest**, who was burnt there on 9 April 1558.

PROTESTANT REFORMATION, The

The Church in medieval Wales formed part of the papal Church of Western Christendom. The call for a thorough-going reformation, first heard in Germany in 1517, soon spread elsewhere. Its principal doctrines were justification by faith, the priesthood of all believers and the authority of the scriptures in the vernacular.

Conditions in Wales were unfavourable for its reception. The country had no university, royal court, capital city or **printing** press of its own; many of its clergy were indifferently educated, and its people were mostly poor and illiterate. Some Protestant changes were imposed on Wales from 1529 to 1540 by Henry VIII, who displaced the Pope and set himself up as supreme head of the Church within his realm. The organization of the Church and its sacraments remained unchanged, its clergy were still celibate and the language of worship continued to be **Latin**. However, religious houses were dissolved, and shrines and **pilgrimages** extinguished. The **Bible** was translated into **English**, but no provision was made for a **Welsh** version.

Henry's successor, Edward VI (1547–53), and his advisers brought in rapid and extensive Protestant changes. Clergy were allowed to marry; an English **Book of Common Prayer**, enforced by an Act of Uniformity, introduced Protestant services into all **parishes**, which celebrated the commemorative communion service rather than the sacrificial mass; altars, images and ceremonies were removed. Such alterations were welcomed in Wales only by some of the country's English-speaking minority, and there was widespread opposition to Protestant teaching and English-language services. A handful of Welsh intellectuals argued that reform, if it were to succeed in Wales, should be introduced in Welsh. Their leader was **William Salesbury**, who translated large parts of the Prayer Book into Welsh and published them as *Kynniver Llith a Ban* (1551).

Edward VI was followed by his half-sister, Mary (1553–8), a devout papist. She reconciled the lands of the English crown to Rome, restored Latin services and Catholic belief, and separated priests from their wives. Determined Protestants were burnt at the stake, although Wales saw only three **Protestant martyr**doms. Attempts were made to bring about Catholic reforms, including instructional **literature** in Welsh. Had Mary's reign lasted longer, much might have been achieved in that respect.

Elizabeth I (1558–1603) introduced a moderate Protestant settlement in 1559. She became supreme governor of the Church and brought back the English Prayer Book and Bible. A stronger demand emerged for a Welsh Prayer Book and Bible, and, in 1563, an Act of Parliament required the translation of both. A Welsh New Testament and Prayer Book were published in 1567 and their use was authorized in all parish churches attended by Welsh-speaking worshippers. Richard Davies's (?1501–81) introduction to the New Testament, 'Epistol at y Cembru', commended Protestantism as the return to the pure **religion** which he claimed had existed before Welsh Christianity had been 'polluted' by 'Romish' influences. The first complete Welsh Bible, translated by **William Morgan**, which appeared in 1588, did more than anything else to make the Welsh a Protestant people. Originally, that Protestantism was the moderate form adopted by the **Anglican** Church, but with the rise of Nonconformity (*see* **Nonconformists**), more thoroughgoing forms of Protestantism came to prevail among the Welsh.

PROTHEROE, Daniel (1866–1934) Composer

This prolific composer was born at **Ystradgynlais**, emigrated to America in 1886, and lived successively at Scranton, Milwaukee and Chicago. He edited the **hymn**al *Cân a Mawl* (1918) for the **Calvinistic Methodists** of **North America**, and was a popular conductor and adjudicator. His **hymn** tunes, 'Price' and 'Cwmgiedd', and his male voice part-songs, 'Milwyr y Groes' and 'Nidaros' are still frequently heard.

PROUD VALLEY, The (1940) Film

This Ealing Studios melodrama, set mainly in a **coal**mining south Wales community, featured the distinguished black American singer and political activist **Paul Robeson**, who had forged close links with the miners from the late 1920s and had sung in southern coalfield venues during the 1930s. In his role as David Goliath, Robeson becomes protector of the **drama**'s central family and eventually a sacrificial victim. The politics and sense of social realism in scenes depicting families living 'on tick' were vitiated by an apparent need to allow full rein to Robeson's singing talent. Nevertheless, the **film**'s treatment of racism was progressive for its time, and the **colliery disasters** at its core, though filmed in **London** studios, were well choreographed. The film was based on a story by the left-wing documentary film-maker Herbert Marshall and involved the (sometime) **communist** novelist **Jack Jones** in the scriptwriting, but its producer, Michael Balcon, vetoed a proposed more 'socialist' ending. The film also featured **Rachel Thomas**, making her screen debut.

PROVERBS

A large body of **Welsh-language** proverbs has survived. They are often considered to be a distillation of the wisdom of the common people, although they are, in fact, the fruit of a learned tradition. The earliest known collections date from the 13th century, and the most substantial medieval collection is preserved in *The Red Book of Hergest* (*c.*1400) – two series of which are attributed to Cyrys the Old of Yale. Some of the proverbs are lines from the works of the *Cynfeirdd* and the *Gogynfeirdd*, and others are synopses of legal principles (*see* **Law**). Others of them were drawn from an international tradition and a number were translations from the **French**. **The Poets of the Gentry** often versified proverbs. Following the example of Erasmus, **Renaissance** scholars delighted in

A scene from *The Proud Valley*, with Paul Robeson (centre) and novelist and scriptwriter Jack Jones (right)

proverbs. **William Salesbury** published a collection in his *Oll Synnwyr Pen Kembero Ygyd* (1547). In the **dictionary** he published in 1632, **John Davies** (*c.*1567–1644) included a collection of proverbs which owed much to the work of **Thomas Wiliems**. In his *Originum Gallicarum Liber* (1654), the Dutch linguist Marcus Zuerius Boxhornius claimed that Welsh proverbs represented the remnants of the wisdom of the **druids**, a notion which was given wide circulation by **antiquarians** such as Ieuan Fardd (**Evan Evans**; 1731–88).

The **English** dialects of the south Wales **coal**field feature many pithy sayings, which can perhaps be considered the proverbs of a more recent age.

PRYCE, Tom (Maldwyn Thomas Pryce; 1949–77)
Racing driver

A **police**man's son and agricultural engineer from **Ruthin**, Tom Pryce became a Formula 1 hopeful when he won a Formula Ford 1600 in a driving competition. He made his debut in the Dutch Grand Prix at Zandvoort in 1974, going on to win the 1975 Race of Champions at Brands Hatch, take pole position at the British Grand Prix and accumulate eight Formula 1 championship points. In the 1977 **South Africa**n Grand Prix at Kylami, as Pryce approached, at 257 kph, the scene of his Shadow teammate's car fire, an extinguisher borne by an inexperienced marshal struck his head, killing him instantly.

PRYDDEST

A long poem (from *prydu* – to compose verse) in one or more of the free metres, and not, therefore, in one of the traditional 24 strict metres. It came into its own in the controversial **eisteddfod** at **Rhuddlan** (1850) when a *pryddest* poet – Ieuan Glan Geirionydd (**Evan Evans**; 1795–1855) – was chaired. In 1867, it was decided to award the crown for a *pryddest* and the chair for an *awdl*.

PRYDERI

A character who appears in all four branches of the Mabinogi (*see* **Mabinogion, The**), Pryderi is the son of **Pwyll, Prince of Dyfed** and **Rhiannon**. In the first branch of the Mabinogi, he is abducted from his mother on the night of his birth; he is discovered in **Gwent** by Teyrnon and his wife, who restore him to his parents. In the second branch, he features as one of the seven men who returned from **Bendigeidfran**'s expedition to **Ireland**. In the third branch, Pryderi, together with his mother, is abducted a second time by unknown powers; they are rescued by **Manawydan**, who had married Rhiannon. In the fourth branch, Pryderi is killed by **Gwydion**.

PRYS, Edmwnd (1543–1623) Poet and humanist

A native of **Llanrwst** and related to **William Salesbury**, Edmwnd Prys was educated at **Cambridge**, which familiarized him with humanist ideals. Appointed archdeacon of **Merioneth** in 1576, he lived at Y Tyddyn Du, **Maentwrog**. In his long bardic dispute (1581–7) with **Wiliam Cynwal**, he urged Welsh professional poets to replace mendacious eulogies with poems based on **Renaissance** learning and on the **Bible**. His *Salmau Cân* (metrical psalms; 1621), the main medium for Welsh congregational singing until the **Methodist Revival**, was a masterpiece. Prys published the psalms as a supplement to the **Welsh** version of **The Book of Common Prayer**, and included 12 tunes, the first

Tom Pryce

recorded use of musical notation in a printed Welsh-language text. Some of his psalms continue to feature in Welsh-language worship.

PRYS, Elis (Y Doctor Coch; ?1512–?95)
Administrator and MP
Elis Prys of Plas Iolyn, **Pentrefoelas**, was popularly known as 'Y Doctor Coch' (the Red Doctor), the epithet deriving from the colour of his gown. Zealous in promoting the **dissolution of the monasteries**, he took a prominent part in public life; three times MP for **Merioneth**, he was its sheriff seven times, sheriff of **Denbighshire** four times, of **Anglesey** twice and of **Caernarfonshire** once, as well as being *custos rotulorum* of Merioneth for most of Elizabeth's reign. A close ally of the earl of Leicester, he was described by **Thomas Pennant** as the earl's 'creature … devoted to all his bad designs'. A patron of the bards, he was among the promoters of the **Caerwys eisteddfod** (1567). His brother Cadwaladr was the ancestor of the **Price family** (**Rhiwlas**), and the poet **Tomos Prys** was his son.

PRYS, Tomos (c.1564–1634)
Poet, soldier and privateer
The son of **Elis Prys** of Plas Iolyn (**Pentrefoelas**), he fought on the European mainland, and sailed as a privateer around the Spanish coast. A number of his poems are conventional, but others – as he did not need to receive patronage from the nobility – chronicle his own experiences in **London**, as a soldier and privateer. One of his best-known poems revisits his exploits as a privateer in language full of characteristic **satire** and wit. Although not, perhaps, an outstanding poet, Prys left an indelible mark on the bardic tradition.

PRYS-JONES, A[rthur] G[lyn] (1888–1987) Poet
Brought up in **Denbigh** and **Pontypridd**, A. G. Prys-Jones was for many years an inspector of schools. He edited the first anthology of verse by Welsh writers in English, *Welsh Poets* (1917). His own poetry is traditional in form and patriotic in content; he published six volumes of poetry. His *Collected Poems* appeared in 1988.

PRYSE family (Gogerddan) Landowners
Sir John Pryse (d.1584) was the first member of the Gogerddan (**Trefeurig**) family to use the Pryse surname, after his father Richard ap Rhys. The family had hitherto been comparatively insignificant, although addressed by many leading poets of the 15th and 16th centuries, but Sir John had a successful career as MP and member of the **Council of Wales and the Marches**. His great-niece Bridget Pryse was mother, out of wedlock, of **Edward Lhuyd**. Marriages with a succession of heiresses brought the family extensive properties. The direct male line failed with Sir Carbery Pryse (d.1694), who broke the monopoly of the Society of Mines Royal over **Cardiganshire lead** mines. The succession passed to a **Jacobite** cousin, Lewis Pryse (d.1720), then through more cousins to Lewis Pryse (d.1779) of Woodstock, **Oxford**shire. His heiress married Edward Loveden of Buscot; their son Pryse Loveden took the **surname** Pryse. The last of the line, Sir Pryse Loveden

Saunders Pryse, died childless in 1962. Although no member of the family (other than Edward Lhuyd) achieved any individual distinction, the Pryses were the leading political family in Cardiganshire from 1550 until the late 19th-century eclipse of the **gentry**. In 1873, the family owned 11,608 ha in Cardiganshire.

PRYSE, R[obert] J[ohn] (Gweirydd ap Rhys; 1807–89) Writer and historian
In an industrious age, **Llanbadrig**-born Pryse's industry as a professional writer was phenomenal. Orphaned at the age of 11 and largely self-educated, he worked unceasingly as an editor and contributor to various publications, including *Y Gwyddoniadur Cymreig*. Among his publications were *Hanes y Brytaniaid a'r Cymry* (1872, 1874) and *Hanes Llenyddiaeth Gymreig, 1300–1650* (1883). The poets John Robert Pryse (Golyddan; 1840–62) and Catherine Jane Prichard (Buddug; 1842–1909) were his children.

PUBLIC LIBRARIES
Under the Public Libraries Acts of 1850 and 1855, municipal authorities (in the form of **boroughs** and **parishes**) were empowered to establish rate-supported public libraries but, by 1886, only six Welsh authorities had adopted the Acts. The first of these was **Cardiff** in 1862, soon to be followed by **Newport**, **Swansea** and **Wrexham**, and then by smaller towns including **Bangor** and **Aberystwyth**. Some of these libraries acquired assets from earlier institutions such as literary societies and workers' institutes. Local philanthropists – usually landowners and industrialists – were prominent in encouraging authorities to establish public libraries. A number of these earlier libraries established notable reference collections of Welsh interest. Progress, however, was slow and provision patchy; in 1913, more than half the **population** of Wales (54%) had no access to a public library, although a number of authorities had received assistance from Andrew Carnegie from 1897 onwards and from the Carnegie United Kingdom Trust (CUKT) from 1913 onwards. **County** councils, though established in 1889, were not granted library powers until the passing of the Public Libraries Act, 1919, but parish councils were entitled to establish libraries, the first instance occurring at **Llanuwchllyn** in 1895. Following the 1919 Act, **Caernarfonshire** became the first Welsh county library authority; by 1932, all other counties had followed suit. However, it was not until the Public Libraries and Museums Act of 1964 became **law** that local authorities were legally obliged to provide a 'comprehensive and efficient' service.

The structure of Welsh public libraries was profoundly affected by two major local **government** reorganizations, in 1974 and 1996, and some services have suffered from inadequate resources. In 2007, public libraries were being provided by Wales's 22 unitary authorities, with overall responsibility for standards resting with the **National Assembly**. Library vans supplying books to rural areas, an activity in which **Cardiganshire** was a pioneer, were launched in the 1950s. By the early 21st century, public libraries were providing a wider range of services, including the use of computers and other electronic material.

717

PUDDICOMBE, Anne Adaliza Beynon
(Allen Raine; 1836–1908) Novelist

Born at **Newcastle Emlyn**, she married Beynon Puddicombe, a banker, in 1872; they lived in **London** until 1900, when they moved to Tresaith (**Penbryn**). She published her first novel, *A Welsh Singer*, in 1897, after winning a prize for a story in the 1894 National **Eisteddfod**. She wrote a further 10 romantic novels which brought her fame and fortune; they include *By Berwyn Banks* (1899), *On the Wings of the Wind* (1903), *Hearts of Wales* (1905) and *Queen of the Rushes* (1906), in addition to a volume of short stories, *All in a Month* (1908). Certain later writers, notably **Emlyn Williams**, were influenced by the melodrama of her work.

PUDDLING PROCESS, The

The emergence of south Wales, in the 1820s, as the world's foremost wrought-**iron**-making region is attributable largely to the adoption of puddling, which became widely known as 'the Welsh method' – although it was an Englishman, Henry Cort (1740–1800), who invented the process in 1783. It transformed the technology of ironmaking, but it did not begin to prove its productive and economic worth until its improved implementation by Richard **Crawshay** when he took control of Cyfarthfa Ironworks, **Merthyr Tydfil**, in 1791.

The conversion of cast iron to wrought iron requires the removal of carbon. Early attempts to use **coal** in this process failed because impurities, especially sulphur, were introduced when the coal was in contact with the metal. Cort's furnace obviated the need for this contact. Part of the process then involved the molten iron being stirred to ensure that the carbon was exposed to, and combined with, the oxygen in the air blast. It was this feature that gave to the whole process the name of 'puddling'. Cort himself did not profit greatly from his discovery, and died in relative poverty.

PUGH, Ellis (1656–1718)
Quaker minister and writer

Ellis Pugh, of Tyddyn-y-garreg, **Dolgellau**, settled in the Welsh Tract, **Pennsylvania**, in 1686. He has the distinction of writing the first **Welsh-language** book published in America, *Annerch i'r Cymry*, which appeared posthumously in 1721. Its first **English** translation was published in 1727 as *A Salutation to the Britains*.

PUGH, W[illiam] J[ohn] (1892–1974) Geologist

Born at Westbury, **Shropshire**, W. J. Pugh was educated at **Aberystwyth**. Appointed to succeed **O. T. Jones** in the chair of **geology** at Aberystwyth and at Manchester, Pugh was closely associated with his teacher and friend, successfully

Pumlumon

playing the **Roman** to Jones's Greek flow of ideas. The importance of their work is recognized in a joint Festschrift (1969). Highly praised for his administrative ability, Pugh was appointed director of the Geological Survey of Great **Britain** (now the British Geological Survey) in 1950.

PUMLUMON Mountain

The highest uplands between **Cadair Idris** and the **Brecon Beacons**, the name refers to Pumlumon's five (*pump*) alleged peaks, a meaning obscured when the spelling Plynlimon is employed. The highest of the peaks is Pen Pumlumon Fawr (752 m; **Blaenrheidol**). Consisting of Ordovician rock, Pumlumon is more a rounded mass of moorland than a **mountain**. It is the source of the **Severn**, the **Wye** and the **Rheidol**, all of which begin as oozings out of blanket **peat**. North of Llyn Llygad Rheidol, which nestles below Pen Pumlumon Fawr, are Cerrig Cyfamod Glyndŵr (**Cadfarch**), standing stones believed to denote the location of **Owain Glyndŵr**'s victory in 1401. In the 19th century, the area's **lead**-ore resources were extensively exploited. In the 1970s, the damming of the upper Rheidol led to the creation of Nant-y-moch **reservoir**; constructed as part of a major hydroelectric scheme, the reservoir dominates what **George Borrow** described as 'this waste of russet-coloured hills'.

PUNCHESTON (Cas-mael), Pembrokeshire
(4728 ha; 472 inhabitants)

Located south of the Gwaun valley, the **community** contains the villages of Puncheston, Castlebythe, Henry's Moat, Little Newcastle and – extraordinarily – Poll Tax. The community's **English** name, Puncheston, may be a borrowing from Pontchardon, Normandy. There are 12th-century mottes in Puncheston, Castlebythe and Henry's Moat. The pirate **Bartholomew Roberts** (Barti Ddu or Black Bart) was born in Little Newcastle, where he is commemorated (*see* **Piracy**). The **Moravian** bishop John Gambold (1711–71) was born at Puncheston, where his father, the grammarian William Gambold (1672–1728), was rector. In the square is a memorial to another native – the poet Evan Rees (Dyfed; 1850–1923) who was archdruid from 1905 to 1923. **Waldo Williams** wrote 'Ar Weun Cas' Mael' while teaching at Puncheston during the **Second World War**. The enclosure known as Castle Flemish has nothing to do with the **Flemings**; it is in fact a **Roman** fortification – one of the very few in **Pembrokeshire**.

PURA WALLIA

A term often applied to those parts of Wales which, before 1282, remained under native Welsh rule, as opposed to *Marchie Wallie* (*see* **March**), the territories conquered by the Anglo-**Norman** invaders. Although the boundary between the two fluctuated, *Pura Wallia* generally consisted of (to use the pre-1974 **county** names) **Anglesey**, **Caernarfonshire**, **Merioneth**, **Denbighshire**, much of **Flintshire**, **Montgomeryshire**, **Cardiganshire** and central and northern **Carmarthenshire**. Following the **Edwardian conquest**, most of *Pura Wallia* became the **counties** of the principalities of north and south Wales; however, lands conquered from native Welsh rulers in much of the northeast were converted into marcher-lordships.

PURITANS

H. L. Mencken, the American critic and humorist, described Puritanism as 'the haunting fear that someone somewhere may be happy'. Although a harsh verdict, it gives some insight into the mindset of the 'hotter sort of Protestants' known as Puritans. Puritanism first emerged in the mid-16th century and its most celebrated champion in Wales was **John Penry**, whose career mirrors the choices facing those who sought to reform the established Church. Those who stayed within the **Anglican** Church called for reform, usually in the direction of **Presbyterian**ism; but many, like Penry, abandoned the Church and joined the separatists. Both groups were known as Puritans and both wanted to be rid of **Roman Catholic** vestiges, establish a strong preaching tradition, encourage people to read the scriptures, and nurture a pious, industrious, thrifty and God-fearing society. In the early 17th century, Puritanism was the ideology of the middling sort and it spread along the trade routes in southern Wales and the **border counties**.

The **Civil Wars** and the **Commonwealth** era gave it a new lease of life, with '**saints**' such as **Walter Cradock**, **Morgan Llwyd** and **Vavasor Powell** vigorously propagating the Puritan faith. During the period of the **Act for the Better Propagation and Preaching of the Gospel in Wales (1650–3)** considerable ground was gained – sometimes by militant means – and sectarianism flourished in the 1650s in the form of the **Baptists**, **Congregationalists** and **Quakers**. But the bulk of the populace remained either indifferent or hostile to Puritanism, and were especially aggrieved by efforts to outlaw dancing (*see* **Dance**), bear baiting, **cock fighting**, swearing and cursing. When the monarchy was restored in 1660, many Puritan ministers were deprived of their livings and, following the passage of the Act of Uniformity (1662), people were forced to decide whether to stay within the established Church or join the separatists. After 1662, those who abandoned the Church would henceforth be known as Dissenters and, later, **Nonconformists**. However, a strong Puritan element continued to be present within the Anglican Church, as the moralistic verses of **Rhys Prichard** testify.

PURNELL, [John] Howard (1925–96) Chemist

Purnell's scientific brilliance was such that, from school in the **Rhondda**, he became a university lecturer in **Cardiff** at the age of 21. He moved to **Cambridge** and in little more than a decade had used his knowledge of gas kinetics to develop quantitative gas chromatography. This rapidly became a standard analytical technique that transformed environmental and industrial monitoring. He held a chair at **Swansea** (1965–92), where he became vice-principal. An exuberant personality, he was a jazz pianist and an expert communicator.

PWLLHELI, Gwynedd (533 ha; 3861 inhabitants)

Located halfway along the southern coast of **Llŷn**, the **community** is the peninsula's main commercial centre. It was already a proto-urban centre under the princes of **Gwynedd**. Granted **borough** status in 1355, until 1950 it was one of the contributory boroughs of the **Caernarfon** Boroughs constituency. It enjoyed some success as a **port**, but shipping dwindled rapidly following the arrival of the

Cambrian **Railway** in 1867. The visitors carried by the line brought new prosperity, especially after the **Cardiff** entrepreneur **Solomon Andrews** came on a day's visit in 1893; realizing Pwllheli's potential for family holidays, he invested heavily, particularly in the construction of a promenade. The opening of a marina in the former port has attracted several international **sailing** races to Pwllheli. The small chapel (1859) in Deneio cemetery contains a wealth of monuments from the demolished church of St **Beuno**, which stood on the same site. In his evidence to the education inquiry of 1846–7, the vicar of St Peter's church (1834, 1887) was a leading calumniator of the morals of the Welsh people (*see* **Treason of the Blue Books**). The poet and archdruid **Albert Evans-Jones** (Cynan) was born at Pwllheli, as was the singer **Leila Megáne**. A plaque commemorates the founding of **Plaid [Genedlaethol] Cymru** at a **temperance** hotel in the square (Y Maes) in 1925.

PWNC

In a specialized context, *Pwnc* (subject) is used to denote passages of the Scriptures recited or intoned by adult classes at **Sunday school** or *Pwnc* festivals. The practice itself is referred to as *adrodd Pwnc* (Pwnc recitation) or, later, *canu Pwnc* (Pwnc chanting). From the early 19th century onwards, *Pwnc* festivals were held – on Whit Monday or around Easter – by both small groups of **Anglican parish** churches and of **Nonconformist** chapels. By the 20th century, the south-west was the tradition's remaining

stronghold, but its geographical spread was once wider. It seems possible that *Pwnc* chanting has archaic roots, and might echo an earlier way of intoning the catechism.

PWYLL, PENDEFIG DYFED
(Pwyll, chieftain of Dyfed)

The story of Pwyll, Pendefig Dyfed in the first branch of the Mabinogi (*see* **Mabinogion, The**) relates how Pwyll (wisdom, understanding) changes places with Arawn, king of **Annwfn**, and reigns in his stead for a year. There follows the meeting and marriage of Pwyll and **Rhiannon**. Inadvertently, Pwyll yields his claim on Rhiannon to another suitor, Gwawl fab Clud, but, after a year, Gwawl is tricked into relinquishing his claim. A son is born to Pwyll and Rhiannon, but he disappears in strange circumstances on the night of his birth. He is eventually restored to his parents and then named **Pryderi**.

PYLE (Y Pîl), Bridgend (323 ha; 7205 inhabitants)

Formerly a part – with **Cornelly** – of the **community** of Cynffig, the substantial village of Pyle developed along the A48. St James's church (15th century) was built to compensate for the loss of Kenfig church, which had been overwhelmed by sand dunes. Llanmihangel is an attractive farmhouse of *c*.1600. What was Cynffig secondary school (1957–61) is among **Glamorgan**'s most impressive Modernist buildings. There are remains of a deserted village near the community's eastern boundary.

Pales, the Quaker meeting house at Llandegley, near Llandrindod Wells

QUAKERS

Quakers were the disciples of George Fox, a weaver's son from Leicestershire, whose belief in the inner light became the guiding force behind the Religious Society of Friends, a movement which spread into Wales from 1653 onwards. Its chief spokesman in the early days was **John ap John**, a disciple of **Morgan Llwyd**, though the teachings of the Friends were also zealously propagated by the likes of Richard Davies (1635–1708) of Cloddiau Cochion (**Welshpool**) and Thomas Wynne of **Caerwys**. Their radical programme, exemplified by their refusal to pay **tithes**, doff their hats, swear oaths or bear arms, meant that they were heavily persecuted under the Clarendon Code (1660–89). Therefore, many hundreds of them chose to emigrate to **North America** from the 1680s onwards to assist William Penn in his plans to establish a peace-loving utopia in the state of **Pennsylvania**. Robbed of its best people, the Quaker cause in Wales fared so poorly in the 18th century that even its supporters referred to themselves as the 'remnant'. The more resourceful Quakers prospered in the fields of **banking** and industry, the most prominent among them being the **Lloyd family (Dolobran) (Llangyniew)**, ironmasters and founders of Lloyds Bank.

Following the horrors of the **First World War**, the **pacifism** of the Quakers won new respect, and their ideas much influenced the peace campaigner **George M. Ll. Davies** and the poet **Waldo Williams**. During the interwar **depression**, Quakers were prominent in relieving the distress of the unemployed, especially at **Brynmawr**. Among Wales's surviving Quaker graveyards are those at **Dolgellau** and Quaker's Yard (Treharris, **Merthyr Tydfil**). Of the older Quaker meeting houses, the most moving is that at The Pales (**Penybont**).

QUANGOS (Quasi-autonomous nongovernmental organizations)

Many of the responsibilities of central and local **government** in Wales were entrusted to quangos by the **Conservative** administrations of the 1980s and early 1990s. They became very powerful, setting objectives, formulating policies and allocating funding. They included the **Welsh Language Board,** the Curriculum and Assessment Authority for Wales (ACCAC), the **housing** authority Tai Cymru and – a particular bone of contention – the **Welsh Development Agency** (WDA).

By 1993, Wales had 80 quangos and they had a combined annual expenditure of £1.8 billion, over a third of

Q

Queensferry Bridge, which opened in 1962

Welsh Office spending. There were allegations that **Conservative governments** were packing quangos with Conservative sympathizers, and **Cymdeithas yr Iaith Gymraeg** (the Welsh Language Society) initiated an intensive campaign against them. Concern over the 'democratic deficit' – the delegating of substantial power to unelected bodies – helped to muster support for a **National Assembly**, elected by the Welsh people and providing democratic, open government.

The 'bonfire of the quangos' championed by proponents of **devolution** did not begin until 2004 when it was announced that three bodies representing two-thirds of Wales's 'quangocracy' – the WDA, the Wales Tourist Board (*see* **Tourism**) and ELWa (*see* **National Council for Education and Training for Wales**) – would be abolished as quangos. By the spring of 2006, their functions had been brought in-house by the Assembly.

QUARTER BACH (Cwarter Bach),
Carmarthenshire (3207 ha; 2933 inhabitants)
Located on the slopes of the **Black Mountain** on **Carmarthenshire**'s eastern boundary, the **community** contains the villages of Brynamman, Cefn-bryn-brain,

Rhosaman and Ystradowen. **Coal**mining and **iron**making began in the area in the first half of the 19th century. Coalmining gathered pace over the following decades and, by 1921, Quarter Bach, which had been carved out of the civil **parish** of **Llanddeusant**, had 3027 inhabitants. Originally known as Y Gwter Fawr (the great gutter), the name Brynamman was chosen on the arrival of the **railway**. On his visit in 1854, **George Borrow** was told: 'No Sais [Englishman] understands **Welsh**, and this is a Sais'.

In its industrial heyday, the area developed a lively culture rooted in its vibrant chapels. Those born at Brynamman include the poet Bryan Martin Davies (b.1933) and the folk singer, language activist and **Plaid [Genedlaethol] Cymru** president (2003–), Dafydd Iwan (b.1943). In 2001, 83.29% of the inhabitants of Quarter Bach had some knowledge of Welsh, with 61.73% wholly fluent in the language – the highest percentages for any of the communities of Carmarthenshire.

QUEENSFERRY, Flintshire
(431 ha; 1923 inhabitants)
Located south of the **Dee**'s 'new cut' (*c.*1734–7), the **community** consists of a series of factories flanked by the settlements of Pentre and Sandycroft. First called Lower Ferry, then King's Ferry, the name was changed to Queensferry in 1837 in honour of Queen Victoria. The swing bridge, which replaced the ferry in 1897, was itself replaced in 1926; a more elaborate bridge carrying the A494 was completed in 1962. In the 19th century, the area attracted a variety of industries including **coal**mining, tar extraction, and the making of wire ropes and mining machinery. **Shipbuilding** was particularly important, with the yard of John Rigby (later Cram of Chester), founded in 1820, and that of Abdella & Mitchell (1908–38). The ill-fated *Royal Charter*, Deeside's largest **ship**, was launched at Queensferry in 1855. A factory (*c.*1901–5), designed by H. B. Cresswell for Williams and Robinson, was described by Nikolaus Pevsner as 'the most advanced British building of its date'. A large munitions factory (1916–18) led to the building of Mancot village (*see* **Hawarden**). Deeside Leisure Centre (1970–4) contains an ice rink of international standard.

QUOITS
A popular open-air folk game played from time immemorial. The aim is to throw a quoit, a circular metal disk, from a prescribed distance, at a target located in a square of clay soil. By the middle of the 20th century, the game had been standardized by the Welsh Quoiting Board. Since the Middle Ages, the authorities have sought, unsuccessfully, to discourage the pastime through statutes and by-laws. This was done because quoits was perceived as diverting able-bodied prospective soldiers from the more beneficial military exercises promoted by the **government**.

The Pen-rhiw rabbit warren pillow mounds at Machen, near Caerphilly

RABBITS

The rabbit was introduced to **Britain** by the **Normans**, as is suggested by the lack of a native word for rabbit in either **Welsh** or **English**. The Welsh name *cwningen* comes from the Middle English *konyng* (that is, *cony*), which has its origins in Norman **French**; rabbit comes from the French *rabette*.

Rabbits were bred for their skins and meat, often on **islands** and in warrens on coastal dunes, as at **Bodorgan**; special pillow mounds were constructed for them, but they eventually acquired the ability to dig their own burrows. In the 18th century, many inland estates kept warrens but, despite frequent escapes, rabbits did not become numerous while the wildcat (*see* **Cats**), **polecat**, **pine marten** and **birds** of prey remained common. As these predators were exterminated by gamekeepers in the 19th century, rabbits increased to plague proportions by the early 20th century. Professional rabbiters hunted them and, in the 1940s, some 3 million rabbits a year were exported by train from southwest Wales to **London** and other cities. In the 1950s, the lethal disease myxomatosis, which had spread from France where it had been deliberately introduced to eradicate this costly pest, wiped out 99% of the Welsh rabbit population. Despite gradual recovery, it is unlikely that previous population levels will be achieved.

RABY, Alexander (1747–1835) Industrialist

London-born Raby built the world's first **railway** funded by public subscription – the **Carmarthenshire** Rail Road at **Llanelli** in 1803. Previously a Surrey **iron**master, he gambled his entire fortune on transforming the then small **fishing village of Llanelli into a major industrial town. His ironworks at Furnace (founded 1796), to which the **horse**-drawn wagons of the railway brought **limestone** and iron ore from Mynydd Mawr, produced guns and cannon for the **French Revolutionary and Napoleonic Wars**. Financial difficulties after Napoleon's defeat at Waterloo ruined him. The remains of Furnace ironworks and Llanelli's Stryd Raby are his only memorials.

RACE RIOTS

While it is often claimed that Wales is relatively free from racial prejudice, it has experienced a number of racial disturbances. There were about 20 major assaults on the **Irish** in the 19th century. **Jews** were attacked in 1911 and, in the same year, there were attacks on the **Chinese** in **Cardiff**. The major racial affrays in Wales were the riots in Cardiff, **Barry** and **Newport** in June 1919. Part of an outbreak which affected most British **ports**, they took the form of attacks by large white crowds on settlements of black and Arab sailors. The grievances of the rioters were the high wages

723

earned by black sailors in the **First World War**, compared with servicemen's wages, their relationships with white **women** and the **housing** shortage. The Cardiff outbreak was the most serious of all the British riots; two white men and one Arab died, together with another white man in Barry.

Several subsequent Cardiff riots with a racial element – attacks by black youths on the **police** in Butetown in 1982 and 1986, for example – were ghetto rebellions. A riot at Ely in 1991 started as an attack on an Asian-owned shop.

RADICALISM

The word 'radical', meaning literally 'going to the root', was first used in a political sense in 1802 in **English**, and in 1836 in **Welsh**, to denote an advocate of advanced political reform on democratic lines. In Wales, the first radicals were religious dissenters associated with the Deist and **Unitarian** traditions, but by the 1830s the battle for parliamentary reform and opposition to Church rates were attracting members of other **Nonconformist** denominations to the radical cause. Radicalism was not a wholly consistent concept; within it there was often a reactionary agrarian strand, a romantic and Byronic strand, and a respectable and calculating Benthamite strand. These differing traditions struck varying chords in Wales. In the mid-19th century, **Samuel Roberts** emphasized the importance of the individual conscience and advocated peace, free trade and the limitation of the powers of the state. By the end of the 19th century, **Michael D. Jones** inclined to collective concepts, which embraced **socialism** and **nationalism**.

Although early radicals had been associated with both **Whig** and **Tory** parties, by the mid-19th century they had been drawn into the left wing of the **Liberal Party**. In Wales, that party came to incorporate elements of radicalism into a political programme which included not only the **disestablishment of the Church of England in Wales** and the abolition of the **tithe**, but also demands for **temperance**, free trade, the **land question** and, especially in the work of **Henry Richard**, world peace. Radicalism's most outspoken proponent in Wales between 1890 and the **First World War** was **David Lloyd George**, who, as his **welfare** legislation indicates, held a positive view of the state's role. In the early 20th century, however, the term became increasingly associated with the socialism of the **Labour** and **Communist** Parties, and the social and **trade union** movements that supported them. After 1945, **Plaid [Genedlaethol] Cymru** also adopted a more radical, left-of-centre position. The term, suggesting militancy without dogma, survives as a useful rallying cry for both the Labour Party and Plaid Cymru. Between 1983 and 1991, Plaid Cymru published a journal entitled *Radical Wales*.

The fact that radicalism is not necessarily located in a particular part of the political spectrum is indicated by the rise in the 1970s of the term 'Radicals of the Right', applied to the supporters of Margaret Thatcher.

RADMILOVIC, Paul (1886–1968) Swimmer

Cardiff-born Radmilovic's illustrious 30-year **swimming** career included 15 Welsh 100-yard (91.44 m) freestyle titles between 1901 and 1922, and five Olympic Games appearances from 1908 to 1928, in which he won three gold medals. Also a fine water-polo player, he captained the British team to Olympic victory in 1912 and 1920.

Crowds at Tregaron in 1893 at the unveiling of the statue of the radical politician Henry Richard

RADNOR (Maesyfed) Lordship

The lordship of Radnor (broadly coterminous with the **commote** of Llwythyfnwg; *see* **Gladestry**) contained **Radnor Forest** and most of the easternmost regions of the later **county** of Radnor. By *c.*1095, Philip de **Breos** had established himself as lord of Radnor. In 1230, the lordship passed to Roger **Mortimer** through his marriage to Maud de Breos. In the 15th century, it passed to the dukes of **York**, and thence to the English crown.

RADNOR FOREST (Fforest Clud), Powys

Constituting the central part of **Radnorshire**, the Forest reaches its highest point (660 m) above Harley Dingle (**New Radnor**). It consists of a dome of Silurian rock, with igneous material on the south-east and south-west, and is drained by the Arrow (Afon Arwy), the Lugg (Afon Llugwy) and the Ithon (Afon Ieithon), tributaries of the **Wye**. It is crossed by the A44, which provides access to Wales's most picturesquely named **waterfall** – Water-break-its-neck (New Radnor). The name Forest originated, not from any tree cover, but from the fact that the medieval holders of the lordship of **Radnor** designated the uplands of their **March**er-lordship as a **hunting** ground.

RADNORSHIRE (Sir Faesyfed) One-time county

The **county** of Radnor was created by the **Act of 'Union'** of 1536, combining **Cwmwd Deuddwr**, **Gwrtheyrnion**, **Maelienydd** and **Elfael**, the lordship of **Radnor** and smaller lordships on the eastern border in one administrative unit. **New Radnor** was declared the shire town, and the county court was initially held alternately there and at **Rhayader**. Rhayader was replaced by **Presteigne** following the murder of a judge at Rhayader. There were two MPs, one for the county and one for the combined **boroughs** of New Radnor, Cefnllys (**Penybont**), **Knighton**, Knucklas (**Beguildy**) and Rhayader. Presteigne, although it replaced New Radnor as county town in the 17th century, did not become one of the electoral boroughs until 1832. Radnorshire lies between the **Wye** and the **Severn**; it is a hilly county, with more than half its area lying above 300 m. It is also a poor county, with 'Never a park and never a deer/ Never a squire of five hundred a year' as the verse puts it (making an exception, among the impoverished squires, of the wealthy Fowlers of **Abbey Cwmhir**). The raising of **sheep** and **cattle** has traditionally been the principal occupation, with **tourism** becoming increasingly important as **agriculture** declines. In 1885, Radnorshire lost its borough seat; the county constituency was joined with that of **Breconshire** in 1918. In 1889, following the first county council elections, **Llandrindod** replaced Presteigne as Radnorshire's administrative centre. In 1974, the county became the Radnorshire district within the county of **Powys**. On the eve of the county's abolition in 1974, it consisted of the **urban districts** of Knighton, Llandrindod and Presteigne and the **rural districts** of Colwyn, Knighton, **Painscastle**, New Radnor and Rhayader.

Following the recognition of the county of Powys as a unitary authority in 1996, Radnorshire retained a vestigial autonomy within the county. The **Welsh language** collapsed in Radnorshire in the 18th century, the census of 1891 recording that only 6% of the **population** spoke the

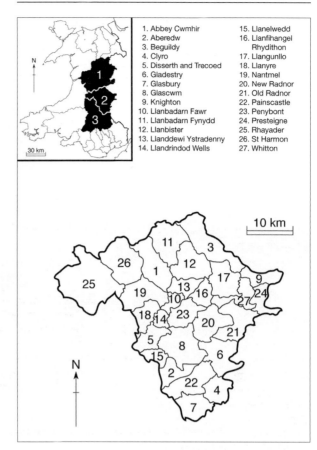

1. Abbey Cwmhir	15. Llanelwedd
2. Aberedw	16. Llanfihangel
3. Beguildy	Rhydithon
4. Clyro	17. Llangunllo
5. Disserth and Trecoed	18. Llanyre
6. Gladestry	19. Nantmel
7. Glasbury	20. New Radnor
8. Glascwm	21. Old Radnor
9. Knighton	22. Painscastle
10. Llanbadarn Fawr	23. Penybont
11. Llanbadarn Fynydd	24. Presteigne
12. Llanbister	25. Rhayader
13. Llanddewi Ystradenny	26. St Harmon
14. Llandrindod Wells	27. Whitton

The communities of the county of Powys: 2 Radnorshire

language. In recent years, however, language teaching has led to a rise in the number of Welsh speakers among younger age groups. At the time of its loss of county status in 1974, Radnorshire consisted of 121,880 ha and had 19,000 inhabitants.

RAGLAN (Rhaglan), Monmouthshire
(3725 ha; 1706 inhabitants)

Straddling the A40 between **Abergavenny** and **Monmouth**, the **community** is dominated by Raglan Castle, among **Britain**'s most imposing 15th-century buildings. **William ap Thomas**, who had acquired the Raglan lordship by the 1430s, built the Yellow Tower of **Gwent**. His son, William **Herbert**, earl of **Pembroke**, commissioned a vast range of buildings adjoining the tower. In the late 16th century, his descendant, William **Somerset**, earl of Worcester, added elaborate apartments. Henry VII spent his childhood at the castle. In 1645, Charles I paid three visits to his ardent supporters, the Somersets of Raglan. Following a Parliamentary siege in 1646, the castle was ruined and never occupied thereafter. Nevertheless, an astonishing amount of superb masonry survives.

St Cadoc's (**Cadog**) Church has an impressive range of medieval features, together with three mutilated alabaster effigies which – following Parliamentarian vandalism – are all that remains of the tombs of the Herberts and the Somersets. The raglan coat – with sleeves that continue to the collar – was named after a member of the Somerset family, the **Crimean War** general, Baron Raglan, who

725

Penygroes railway station *c.*1875, on the Caernarfon–Afon Wen line

ordered the charge of the Light Brigade. His admirers bought Cefntilla (originally Cefntyle) for his son, the second baron. It has a fine Jacobean hall. It was the home of the fourth baron, the authority on the houses of **Monmouthshire** and the *bête noire* of devotees of the **Welsh language**.

There are attractive churches at Penyclawdd and Llandenny. Penyclawdd farmhouse is a well-preserved building of the 16th and 17th centuries. The farmhouse called The Cayo includes a 17th-century **Quaker** meeting house.

RAILWAYS

Although railways are generally considered to be parallel tracks traversed by locomotives – that is, self-propelled engines – they are, in fact, any kind of parallel tracks traversed by any kind of vehicle, self-propelled or otherwise. They existed centuries before the invention of locomotion, and the vehicles traversing them were generally drawn by **horses** – although human muscle or gradients sometimes provided the motive power. There is some evidence that vehicles borne on wooden tracks were in use in **Cardiganshire lead** mines in the 1660s, and **coal** was certainly conveyed along wooden tracks at **Hawarden** in the 1770s. With the late 18th-century growth of the **iron** industry, iron rails came into general use. While modern rails designed for flanged wheels are flat, the rails of the pre-locomotive age usually had a raised outer edge to ensure that the flangeless wheel would stay on track.

Pre-locomotive railways are generally known as tramways. The vast majority of them served industrial undertakings; the Mumbles Railway (1807) (**Swansea**), which was inaugurated as a mineral line in 1804 and began carrying passengers in 1807, is generally considered to be the world's first horse-drawn passenger railway. The heyday of tramways coincided with the **Canal** Age, for it was the use of tramways to convey the output of ironworks and collieries to quaysides which ensured the success of the canals of the south Wales coalfield. While that coalfield had around 240 km of canals, built at a cost of £800,000, it had around 560 km of tramways, built at a cost of £700,000. The most remarkable of them was Hill's Tramway, which slithered down the Blorenge between **Blaenavon** and **Llanfoist**, passing through what was, when built (*c.*1815), the world's longest tunnel (Pwll-du; 2 km) on the way. Tramways were also significant in the **slate** quarrying areas of the north-west, where **Bethesda** was linked with Port Penrhyn (**Llandygai**; 1800), **Llanberis** with Port Dinorwic (**Y Felinheli**; 1825) and Blaenau **Ffestiniog** with **Porthmadog** (1836). In the north-east, the **Ruabon**, **Flint** and **Holywell** districts came to be covered with a network of mineral lines, and the Ellesmere Canal Company constructed tramways linking quaysides to the collieries and **limestone** quarries of **Denbighshire**.

Of all the tramways of Wales, the most significant historically was that linking the Penydarren Ironworks (*see* **Merthyr Tydfil**) with the **Glamorgan**shire Canal at

Abercynon. **Richard Trevithick** built a steam locomotive at the ironworks, and tested it on the tramway in February 1804 – the world's first experiment in rail-borne locomotion. Although not successful commercially, Trevithick's work inaugurated the age of railway locomotion, with milestones such as the opening of the Darlington –Stockton mineral line (1825) and of the **Liverpool**–Manchester passenger line (1830). Wales's earliest railway constructed specifically for locomotion was the **Llanelli** Dock–**Pontarddulais** line, opened in 1839.

Far more significant was the **Taff** Vale Railway (the TVR) linking **Cardiff** with Merthyr Tydfil (1841). The TVR, with branches to **Aberdare** (1846) and the **Rhondda** (1854, 1862), would, by the 1870s, be the most profitable railway company in **Britain**. It was primarily a mineral railway; indeed, the line to Rhondda Fach, completed in 1862, did not carry passengers until 1876. A similar primacy of minerals over people prevailed in the railways constructed in the other valleys of the south Wales coalfield; chief among them were those serving the **Nedd** (1851), Llwyd (1854), **Ebbw** (1855), **Rhymney** (1858), **Tawe** (1860) and Llynfi (1861) valleys. Elsewhere in Wales, railways built primarily to convey minerals included the lines from **Minera** to **Wrexham** (1855), Blaenau Ffestiniog to Llanffestiniog (1866), **Caersws** to Van (**Llanidloes Without**) (1871), **Aberystwyth** to Devil's Bridge (**Pontarfynach**) (1902) and Llanymynech (**Carreghofa**) to **Llangynog** (1904). Some of Wales's railways never carried passengers, built as they were for use within industrial complexes; such was the case with the railways of the Dinorwic slate quarry (*see* **Llanddeiniolen**), those of the **Shotton Steelworks** and those of many colliery concerns. Tracks bearing wagons sometimes drawn by horses survived in private drift mines until the end of the 20th century.

Of the railways built primarily for passengers, the most important were those from Chester to **Holyhead** (1849) and from Gloucester through **Newport** and Cardiff to Swansea (1850). The former line, built specifically to expedite communication between **London** and Dublin, included two engineering marvels – **Robert Stephenson**'s Britannia Bridge across the **Menai Strait** and his miniature version of it across the **Conwy**. The latter line, which was extended to **Carmarthen** in 1852 and to **Neyland** in 1856, was built by the South Wales Railway Company, which amalgamated with the Great Western Railway Company in 1863. Designed by **Isambard Kingdom Brunel**, it employed the 2053-mm broad gauge favoured by Brunel and the GWR; it was narrowed to the 1435-mm standard gauge in 1872. Like the northern railway, that in the south was built with **Ireland** in mind, for Brunel intended Neyland to be the chief **port** of embarkation to southern Ireland. (Neyland was eventually obliged to yield its position to **Fishguard**.)

Other lengthy, but less widely used, railways included those completed between Newport and Hereford (1854), Swansea and **Brecon** (1856), Shrewsbury and Aberystwyth (1864), Merthyr and Brecon (1866), Carmarthen and Aberystwyth (1867), **Dyfi** Junction (**Cadfarch**) and **Pwllheli** (1867), and Ruabon and **Barmouth** (1869). The Shrewsbury–Aberystwyth line, in which David Davies (*see* **Davies family (Llandinam)**) was closely involved, included the 35-m Talerddig cutting (**Llanbrynmair**), the deepest of

its kind in the world when completed in 1861. The Brecon–Merthyr line included impressive viaducts at Cefn-coed-y-cymmer and Pont-sarn, and, at Pontsticill (all in Merthyr Tydfil), southern Britain's highest standard-gauge railway station. The Carmarthen–Aberystwyth line included a 65-km stretch, oddly named the Manchester & Milford Railway – all that remained of a grandiose plan to construct a railway from Manchester to **Milford Haven**, once seen as having the potential to rival Liverpool as a transatlantic port. The Dyfi Junction–Pwllheli line crosses the **Mawddach** over a remarkable wooden viaduct, which provides superb views of Cardigan Bay.

Between 1839 and 1870, about 2300 km of railway track had been constructed in Wales, representing an investment, in mid-19th-century terms, of around £20 million. Some rural railways were built after 1870, among them the much loved *Cardi Bach* between **Crymych** and **Cardigan** (1885), and the **Vale of Glamorgan** line (1897), with its superb viaduct at Porthkerry (**Rhoose**). One of the last railways to be built in Wales was the **Lampeter–Aberaeron** line, completed in 1911.

Although railway construction had slowed down by the 1880s, that decade saw two of the most remarkable developments in Welsh railway history. One was the opening of the **Severn Tunnel**, which reduced journey times from London to south Wales by providing a more direct route than that via Gloucester. Its Welsh mouth was at **Portskewett** and, at 7.078 km in length, it was the world's longest undersea tunnel when it was opened in 1885.

The other major development of the 1880s was the opening in 1888 of the **Barry** Railway, part of David Davies of Llandinam's plan to create the sole integrated rail and

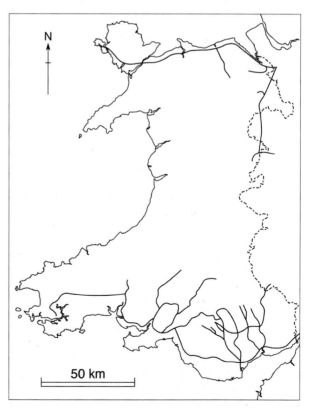

N

50 km

Railways built in Wales 1839–60 (John Davies, 1990)

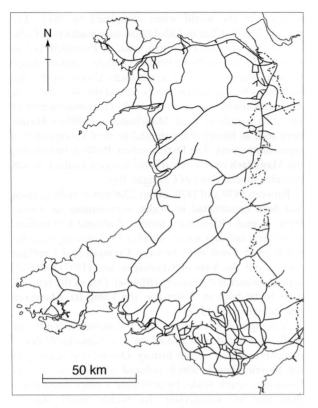

Railways in Wales by 1914

Almost every railway company in Britain bought rails from ironworks such as Dowlais, Cyfarthfa and **Ebbw Vale**. Overseas demand – from the United States, Russia, India and the Austrian Empire in particular – proved buoyant, causing the needs of railway companies to be central to the prosperity of industrial Wales in the mid-19th century.

The coming of the railway to places such as **Llandudno**, Aberystwyth, Barmouth, **Tenby**, **Porthcawl** and **Llandrindod** gave birth to **tourism** as a major factor in the Welsh **economy**. At the same time, the linking of the small ports of west Wales with the railway network brought about the demise of their maritime trade. Locomotion had almost as much of an impact upon **agriculture** as it had upon industry. It brought an end to the ancient practice of droving (*see* **Drovers**), enabled the agrarian south-west to find markets in the industrial south-east, and greatly aided the distribution of lime and fertilizer.

There were those who believed that the railways would destroy the cultural distinctiveness of Wales. Since there was no intention of creating an overall plan that would give unity to Wales, its railway development was a matter of connecting different regions of the country with populous areas of **England**. As the editor of *The Welsh Outlook* put it in 1920: 'From a national point of view, our railway system is the worst in the world.' Yet, the coming of the railway proved to be a constructive factor in the cultural history of Wales. The growing popularity of the National **Eisteddfod**, the vastly increased distribution of books and **periodicals**, and the elevation of many **preachers** to the status of national heroes can all be attributed to the development of the railway network. In addition, national consciousness became more intense as railways undermined the age-old isolation of the communities of Wales.

With the outbreak of the **First World War**, the **government** took control of practically all the railways in Britain. After the end of hostilities, nationalization was rejected in favour of compulsory amalgamation under the Railways Act, 1921. The mass of independent companies was regrouped into the so-called Big Four – Great Western (GWR), London Midland and Scottish (LMS), London and North Eastern (LNER) and the Southern. Thereafter, journeys by rail in Wales – except on some narrow-gauge lines – meant travelling by GWR or LMS. The LMS had the Holyhead and Central Wales lines, but the GWR was predominant. Its castle class locomotives first appeared in 1923, the *Caerphilly Castle* being hailed as 'the most powerful locomotive in Britain'. By 1938, the Cardiff–London journey time had been reduced to 152 minutes, compared with 170 minutes in 1914. Buffet cars and sleeping cars were by then commonplace.

Stringent government control during the **Second World War** was followed by nationalization of the railways in 1948. Responsibility for Welsh railways was divided between the London Midland and the Western Regions of British Railways, the former generally inheriting the old LMS lines and the latter the GWR. Some individuality was preserved in the livery, Western Region chocolate contrasting with London Midland maroon. Two-car diesel sets on some local services in the north in 1956 presaged the future, for by the 1960s main line services throughout Wales were switching to diesel. (No lines in Wales have

dock system in the south Wales coalfield. Bitterly opposed by Cardiff's Bute Docks Company and the TVR, more parliamentary time was spent on the Barry bill than on any other railway bill in British history. With its control of an access to the coalfield as well as of docks, the Barry company had, by 1901, succeeded in making Barry the largest coal port in the world, success which greatly slowed Cardiff's growth. The Bute authorities sought to retaliate by constructing the Cardiff Railway, a vastly expensive 15-km track, and one of the most ill-advised investments in Welsh railway history. The Barry episode was a chapter in the saga of the rivalries between the transport undertakings serving the south Wales coalfield, which had by 1914 one of the densest railway networks anywhere in the world. The TVR played a central role in the history of **trade unionism**. The **Taff Vale Railway Strike** (1900) led to a decision by the House of Lords that a company could sue a trade union for losses resulting from strikes, a legal ruling which virtually deprived workers of the strike weapon. The need to reverse the decision was a central factor in the rise of the **Labour Party**.

It is difficult to discover any aspect of the life of Wales that was not transformed by the coming of locomotion. Nowhere was the impact greater than in the south Wales coalfield. A train could convey in an hour what a canal barge could convey in a month. It was this astonishing advance in the ease of transportation which caused the mining of coal for export to replace ironmaking as the chief activity of the southern industrial valleys. Yet, before ironmaking was dethroned as Wales's leading industry, it enjoyed a huge boom as the result of the demand for rails.

been electrified.) Financial losses led to the Beeching Report of 1963, which was followed by the closure of many lines and stations. Indeed, by the 1970s, Wales had only 1381 km of railway track compared with 3500 km in 1914. Emphasis was placed upon improving services on heavily used lines. The introduction of the high speed Inter-City 125 in 1976 reduced the journey time from Cardiff to London to 105 minutes.

British Rail was privatized in April 1994, when Railtrack took over the ownership of railway infrastructure. Responsibility for the railway lines of Wales was divided between Railtrack Great Western, run from Swindon, Railtrack Midland, run from Birmingham, and Railtrack North West, run from Manchester. Responsibility for running trains in Wales was divided between a number of companies: First Great Western, Wales & West Passenger Trains, Valley Lines (Cardiff Railway Co. Ltd), Central Trains, North Western Trains and EWS (English, Welsh and Scottish). In 2004, however, reorganization meant that the London–Swansea trains were the responsibility of First Great Western, and the Holyhead trains of Virgin Trains; the other trains of Wales and the border were run by Arriva.

Great little trains

A notable feature of the railway system in Wales is the existence of a number of narrow-gauge lines which, having originally served slate quarrying, lead mining and other

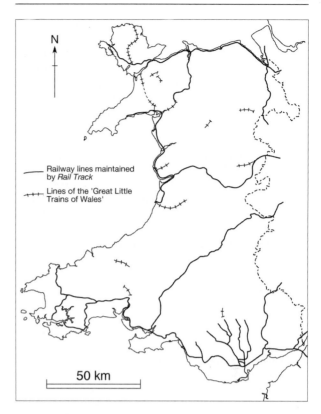

N

—— Railway lines maintained by *Rail Track*

+++ Lines of the 'Great Little Trains of Wales'

50 km

Railways in Wales by 2002

A train approaching Tanygrisiau station on the Ffestiniog Railway

interests, are now sustained by the tourist industry and are marketed as 'The Great Little Trains of Wales'. The movement began with the purchase of the ailing Talyllyn Railway by the Talyllyn Railway Preservation Society in 1951. This was followed by the reopening, in 1955, of the Festiniog (now Ffestiniog) Railway (which had closed in 1946) by the Festiniog Railway Society Ltd. A huge amount of voluntary labour has gone into running these and other narrow-gauge lines.

The Vale of **Rheidol** Railway between Aberystwyth and Devil's Bridge (Pontarfynach) was the last steam railway owned by British Rail until privatized in 1989. The Fairbourne Railway (*see* **Arthog**), with its tiny 38-mm gauge, was originally a 61-mm gauge horse-drawn tramway.

The **Snowdon Mountain** Railway (opened 1896) is the only rack-and-pinion railway in Britain. Modelled on the Swiss system of Dr Roman Abt, it had a disastrous beginning, a passenger on its inaugural journey dying after leaping from the train in panic.

Other 'Great Little Trains' include the **Bala** Lake Railway, the Brecon Mountain Railway, the **Llanberis** Lake Railway, the Welsh Highland Railway, the **Welshpool & Llanfair Caereinion** Railway and the **Teifi** Valley Railway on the former **Llandysul–Newcastle Emlyn** line. Reopened standard gauge railways include the Gwili Railway, opened in 1978 along 1.6 km of the old Carmarthen–Aberystwyth line, and the **Llangollen** Railway to Carrog (**Corwen**) on the one-time GWR line linking Ruabon and Barmouth.

The Rebecca Riots: a print *c.*1842 from *The Illustrated London News*

Accidents

The worst train disasters in Wales were the **Abergele Rail Disaster** (1868; 33 dead) and the **Abermule Rail Disaster** (1921; 17 dead). Other major disasters include those at **Pontypridd** (1878; 12 dead), **Llantrisant** (1893; 13 dead) Hopkinstown, Pontypridd (1911; 11 dead) and **Penmaenmawr** (1950; 6 dead).

RAMSAY, Andrew [Crombie] (1814–91)
Geologist and cartographer
This Glaswegian geologist was responsible, as an officer of the Geological Survey, for the preparation of many of the first 1 inch–1 mile **maps** of Wales, and for the classic memoir *The Geology of North Wales* (1866; 1881). Another major contribution was his recognition of the significance of the extensive upland plains of Wales – 'the most remarkable feature of the physical geography of Wales'. He retired to **Anglesey**, his wife's home, and is buried at Llansadwrn (**Cwm Cadnant**).

REBECCA RIOTS, The
Such was the distress of the small farmers of south-west Wales in the second quarter of the 19th century that, in an unprecedented outburst of rage, they rose up against their oppressors, seeking to right wrongs and to institute popular justice for the poor and despised peasantry. In the 18th century, road trusts had established tollgates on turnpike **roads**, and the frequent tolls – vexatious to struggling farmers forced to use the roads to market their produce and to cart lime (*see* **Limestone**) to counteract the acidity of the region's **soils** – became the focus of their discontent.

On 13 May 1839, a tollgate was attacked at Efailwen (**Cilymaenllwyd**), on the borders of **Carmarthenshire** and **Pembrokeshire**; 13 days later, the first phase of the Rebecca Riots ended when the Water Street gate in **Carmarthen** was destroyed. The winter of 1842 saw further, more severe, rioting, and by the autumn of 1843 tollgates had been destroyed in **Breconshire, Cardiganshire**, Carmarthenshire, **Glamorgan**, Pembrokeshire and **Radnorshire**. The rioters took their name from a Biblical text, Genesis 24: 60: 'And they blessed Rebekah and said unto her, Let thy seed possess the gates of those which hate thee.' Each attack had its 'Rebecca', the leader for the occasion, frequently a man disguised as a woman. No leader has ever been identified, though Thomas Rees (Twm Carnabwth; ?1806–76; *see* **Mynachlog-Ddu**), a pugilist, was popularly believed to have taken part in the attack at Efailwen.

The discontent which gave rise to the riots sprang from the ills of a traditional community, increasingly overpopulated and confronted with the necessity of adjusting to the advent of a money **economy**, while at the same time struggling with the demands of an outmoded system of **government and administration**. Despite a drastic fall in agricultural prices, there was no easing of the farmers' traditional disbursements. Few reductions were made in rents, while **tithes** and poor rates had actually increased, following what was, insofar as the semi-subsistent farmers of south-west Wales were concerned, inappropriate parliamentary legislation during the 1830s. Tollgates were only the most common objects of popular hatred and resentment; workhouses (*see* **Poor Law**) were also attacked, as were weirs that restricted **fish**ing. Farmers perceived a range of oppressors who, collectively, denied them justice: their unsympathetic, culturally alien landlords (*see* **Gentry** and **Landlords**) who failed to grant them rent reductions; local magistrates, who treated the poor 'like dogs' when they came before the bench; masters of workhouses wherein the poor were locked up; tithe agents, bailiffs and **Anglican** clergymen who levied heavy tithes on a largely chapel-going **population**; and toll collectors. The riots were essentially an expression of the discontent of small farmers, and when riot fever spread to **agricultural labourers** they soon came to an end.

Public support for Rebecca was such that, although some of the rioters were arrested, there was rarely evidence available to convict them. Following a Commission of Inquiry, headed by **Thomas Frankland Lewis**, the turnpike trusts were taken over by road boards in six of Wales's southern counties and the tolls reduced and simplified. The Rebecca Riots were a major social disturbance; they were also remarkably successful.

RECORDE, Robert (d.1558) Mathematician

A native of **Tenby**, Recorde settled in **London** as a physician, where Edward VI and Mary I are said to have been among his patients. In 1549, he became comptroller of the **mint** at Bristol and, two years later, surveyor of the mines and monies of **Ireland**, but was removed on suspicion of incompetence or dishonesty; he died in the King's Bench **Prison**. His earliest work, *The Grounde of Artes* (1540), was the first arithmetic textbook in **English**, the first to use Arabic numbers, and the first intended for the unlearned reader. The 'equals' sign (=) was Recorde's invention; he described this device as 'A paire of parallels or gemowe [twin] lines of one lengthe, thus: =, bicause noe 2. things can be moare equale.' His *The Pathway to Knowledge* (1551), a textbook of geometry and **astronomy**, proved useful to navigators, and his *The Whetstone of Witte* (1557) was a textbook of algebra.

RECORDING COMPANIES

Although many recordings of Welsh **music** were released in the 1950s and 1960s on labels such as Qualiton, Teldisc, Cambrian and Dryw, it was not until the later 1960s that a recording industry was established in Wales. While the interests of, predominantly, international rock music were served by Rockfield Studios (**Llangattock Vibon Avel**), those of indigenous music came to be nurtured by the Sain record company. With the older labels ceasing, or their catalogues being bought by major labels, Sain, founded in 1969 by musician-activists Dafydd Iwan and Huw Jones, grew steadily over its first decade, and by 1980 had built a 24-track studio at **Llandwrog**. Sain soon became the mainstream outlet for Welsh music; as a result, the 1980s saw a number of independent labels emerge to accommodate more adventurous musical tastes. The three most prominent labels were Recordiau Fflach (1981), Ankst (1988) and Recordiau R-Bennig (1990). This healthy competition for the youth market prompted Sain to launch its sister-label, Crai, in 1989.

The Arte

as their workes doe extende) to diftincte it onely into twoo partes. Whereof the firfte is, *when one number is equalle vnto one other. And the feconde is, when one nomber is compared as equalle vnto. 2.other nombers.*

Alwaies willyng you to remeber, that you reduce your nombers , to their leafte denominations, and fmalleite fo2mes,befo2e you p2ocede any farther.

And again,if your *equation* be foche, that the greateffe denomination *Coßike*, be ioined to any parte of a compounde nomber , you fhall tourne it fo , that the nomber of the greateffe figne alone , maie ftande as equalle to the refte.

And this is all that neadeth to be taughte , concernyng this woo2ke.

Howbeit,fo2 eafie alteratio of *equations*.I will p2opounde a fewe eraples,bicaufe the extraction of their rootes,maie the mo2e aptly bee w2oughte. And to auoide the tedioufe repetition of thefe woo2des : is equalle to : I will fette as I doe often in woo2ke vfe,a paire of paralleles,o2 Gemowe lines of one lengthe, thus:======,bicaufe noe.2. thynges,can be moare equalle. And now marke thefe nombers.

$$14.\not z. \quad ---- \quad .15.9. \quad ====71.9.$$
$$20.\not z. \quad ---- \quad .18.9. \quad ==.102.9.$$
$$26.3. \quad --+--10\not z \quad ====9.3. \quad --10\not z \quad --+--213.9.$$
$$19.\not z --+--192.9. \quad ===10.3. \quad --+--108.9--19\not z$$
$$18.\not z \quad --+--24.9. \quad ====8.3. \quad --+--2.\not z.$$
$$34.3 \quad ----12\not z \quad ====40\not z \quad --+--480.9----9.3.$$

In the firfte there appeareth. 2. nombers , that is 14.$\not z$.

Robert Recorde's explanation of the equals sign in *The Whetstone of Wit* (1557)

RED BANDITS OF MAWDDWY, The

The **commote** of **Mawddwy** was considered the most **law**less place in Wales, the reason, no doubt, why the **Act of 'Union'** attached it to the long-established **Merioneth** rather than to the newly created **Montgomeryshire**. Evidence of Mawddwy's lawlessness comes from the activities of its red-haired outlaws, who created unrest by plundering and robbing. On 12 October 1555, Judge Lewis Owen of Plas-yn-dre, **Dolgellau**, was murdered by eight of them at Dugoed Mawddwy on his way home from **Welshpool** assizes; the murderers were subsequently sentenced to death at the Court of Great Sessions (*see* **Law**). Many traditions grew around that event and **I. D. Hooson** wrote what has become a popular poem to commemorate the occasion. Plas-yn-dre was re-erected in **Newtown** in 1885.

RED BOOK OF HERGEST, The

A major collection of almost every kind of **literature** written in **Welsh** during the Middle Ages, including prose and poetry, native works and translations. It was copied around

1400 mainly by Hywel Fychan ap Hywel Goch, a professional scribe from **Builth**, for the nobleman Hopcyn ap Tomas ab Einion of Ynysforgan near Ynystawe, in the **Tawe** valley. The manuscript probably passed to the **Vaughan family (Tretower)** and thence to the **Vaughan family (Hergest)**. It is kept in the Bodleian Library, **Oxford**. *The White Book of Hergest*, parts of which, at least, were in the hand of **Lewys Glyn Cothi**, was destroyed by fire in 1810.

RED DRAGON, The

The dragon has been a potent symbol since antiquity, when the **Romans** borrowed it from the Dacians and used it as a military emblem. It was widely used; a wyvern (two-legged dragon) was borne by Harold's army at the battle of Hastings and Henry III had a dragon flag, which was borne against the Welsh.

The *Historia Brittonum*, composed *c.*830, describes a struggle between a red dragon (representing the Britons) and a white dragon (representing the Saxons) at Dinas Emrys (**Beddgelert**), where **Vortigern** was trying to build a fortress. It was foretold that, although the white dragon would long oppress the red one, the final victory would go to the red dragon. This tale was retold by **Geoffrey of Monmouth**, who included it in the prophecies of **Merlin** (Myrddin), and it also appears in the legend 'Cyfranc Lludd a Llefelys' in *The Mabinogion*. **Arthur** is said to have borne a dragon as his crest. The dragon was often used in poetry as a heroic epithet for Welsh princes, **Llywelyn ap**

Iorwerth among them. **Owain Glyndŵr**'s banner was white with a golden dragon, and Owen **Tudor**'s sons Edmund and Jasper used dragons as crests.

The **York**ist Edward IV, descended from the princes of **Gwynedd** through the **Mortimers**, claimed to represent the red dragon, while Henry VI of the house of **Lancaster** represented the white. It was, however, Henry Tudor who gave the fullest recognition to the red dragon, in order to emphasize his claim to descent from **Cadwaladr ap Cadwallon**, 'the last king of the Britons'. He presented a standard of the 'Red Dragon of Cadwaladr' to St Paul's Cathedral after his victory at **Bosworth**. The Tudors displayed the red dragon on standards and as a supporter of the royal arms, and it was one of the beasts set up by Henry VIII in the Hampton Court **gardens**. The Tudor dragon was usually red with a golden belly.

A red dragon on a green mount was adopted as the badge of Wales in 1807, and to this was added in 1953 the motto 'Y Ddraig goch ddyry cychwyn' ('The red dragon gives impetus'), a line taken from a poem, by Deio ab Ieuan Du (fl.1450–80), which refers metaphorically to a bull copulating. A red dragon on a white and green field was declared the national flag of Wales in 1959.

REDWICK, Newport (1199 ha; 194 inhabitants)

Constituting the south-eastern corner of the **county** of **Newport**, the **community** overlooks the Welsh Grounds – vast sandbanks in the **Severn** estuary uncovered at low tide.

The Welsh of the future and the Red Dragon

Redwick lies on the western edge of **Caldicot** Levels and is interlaced with reens or drainage channels with names such as Ynys Mead and Newcut. St Thomas's church, a pinkish-grey **limestone** building with a remarkable Decorated east window, is one of the finest churches of the **Gwent Levels**. Redwick village contains a curious **cider** press cum bus shelter, built (*c.*1975) by a local craftsman, Hubert Jones. Brick House Farm (early 19th century) has seven bays and massive chimney stacks.

REDWOOD, Theophilus (1806–92) Pharmacist
Redwood, who was born and died at Boverton (**Llantwit Major**), was the son of a tanner and schoolmaster. Apprenticed to an apothecary in **London**, he attended **chemistry** lectures at the Royal Institution. A founder of the Pharmaceutical Society of Great **Britain** (1841), he was its professor of chemistry and pharmacy until the age of 79. He was the first president of the Society of Public Analysts (1874). One of his sons, the chemist and petroleum engineer Thomas Boverton Redwood FRS (1846–1919), received a knighthood (1901) and a baronetcy (1911). **Cardiff University**'s Redwood building commemorates the family.

REES, Abraham (1743–1825) Encyclopaedist
Llanbrynmair-born Abraham Rees was the son of the **Congregationalist** minister Lewis Rees (1710–1800). Also a minister, he spent most of his life in **London**. Ephraim Chambers's pioneering two-volume *Cyclopaedia* (1728), which had been the inspiration for the great *Encyclopédie* (1751–76) of d'Alembert and Diderot, was re-edited by Rees in 1778. The success of a subsequent four-volume edition (1781–6), for which Rees was elected FRS, led to the production of a vastly more ambitious work, *The New Cyclopaedia*, much of which he wrote himself. It appeared in 45 volumes between 1802 and 1820, influenced the development of encyclopaedias, and was for long the only serious rival to the *Encyclopaedia Britannica*.

REES, Alwyn D[avid] (1911–74)
Editor and sociologist
Alwyn D. Rees is best remembered for his editorship of the **periodical** *Barn*, where he gave unstinting support to the campaigns of **Cymdeithas yr Iaith**, providing the movement with an intellectual context. Born in **Gorseinon**, he spent most of his career in the extra-mural department at **Aberystwyth** (*see* **University of Wales, Aberystwyth**), where he had been a student. His research into the **parish** of **Llanfihangel**-yng-Ngwynfa, published as *Life in a Welsh Countryside* (1950), was a pioneering work. He co-edited *Welsh Rural Communities* (1961) with **Elwyn Davies**, and wrote *Celtic Heritage* (1961) with his brother, Brinley Rees (1916–2001).

REES, [William] Beddoe (1877–1931) Architect
The son of a **Maesteg** businessman, Beddoe Rees had an office in **Cardiff** from *c.*1900. He published *Chapel Building: Hints and Suggestions* (1903), and is best known for designing chapels, mostly in the south, for various denominations, and for the circular Ebeneser chapel (1909) in **Llandudno**. He designed a garden village (1913–16) at

Abercwmboi (**Aberaman**) and was managing director of Welsh Garden Cities Ltd. His later business interests were in **coal**mining and **ship**ping. Knighted in 1917, he became **Liberal** MP for Bristol South (1922–9).

REES, Dai (1913–83) Golfer
Born at Font-y-gary (**Rhoose**), the son of the **golf** professional at **Aberdare**, Dai Rees was the best-known British golfer of his era. He narrowly missed the coveted Open title on several occasions. He became particularly associated with the Ryder Cup, in which he first played in 1937. **Britain** failed to win the Cup between 1933 and 1985 – except in 1957 when Rees captained the team that triumphed at Lindrick in Yorkshire.

REES, David (1801–69) Editor and minister
A native of **Trelech**, David Rees was one of the architects of Welsh **radicalism**. He was educated at the academy of the **Congregationalists** at **Newtown** and, in 1829, was ordained minister of Capel Als, **Llanelli**, where he remained for the rest of his life, becoming a popular **preacher**. In 1835, he founded the monthly *Y Diwygiwr*, which served the Congregationalists of the south, and through which, for 30 years, he exerted considerable influence, defending the interests of **Nonconformists** and advocating religious, political, social and economic freedom (*see* **Periodicals**).

REES, Dorothy (b. Jones; 1898–1987) Politician
Dorothy Rees dedicated her working life to **education** and **welfare** issues in her hometown of **Barry**, where her father was a dock worker, and within the **county** of **Glamorgan**. She was first elected to Glamorgan County Council in 1934 (subsequently becoming an alderman) and to Barry **Urban District** Council in 1936. She was MP for Barry (1950–1) – Wales's second **woman** MP and the first from a non-privileged background. She served as parliamentary private secretary to Edith Summerskill, the minister of National **Insurance**.

REES, Goronwy (1909–79) Author and academic
Born in **Aberystwyth** and brought up in **Cardiff**, Goronwy Rees was a journalist in **London** and worked in industry before becoming estates bursar of All Souls College, **Oxford**. From 1953 to 1957, he was principal at Aberystwyth, but resigned in acrimonious circumstances. After his death, it was rumoured that he may have been 'the fifth man' associated with the names of the Soviet spies Philby, Burgess, Maclean and Blunt. Vasili Mitrokhin, the KGB colonel who spied for the West, confirmed in *The Mitrokhin Archive* (2000) that Rees had been recruited by the Soviet Union, although he later turned his back on Moscow. Besides three novels, Rees published two volumes of autobiography and a selection of essays.

REES, [Florence] Gwendolen (1906–94) Zoologist
Born in Llandaff, **Cardiff**, Rees graduated in zoology at **Aberystwyth**, remaining there for the rest of her career. Her work in the two principal fields of parasitic worms and the life cycle of endoparasitic flukes brought international recognition for herself and also for Aberystwyth as a

centre for helminthology (the study of parasitic worms). The first **woman** in Wales to be elected FRS, she held a personal chair from 1970 to 1973. A notably elegant woman, she featured in the pages of the magazine *Vogue*.

REES, Henry (1798–1869) Minister
Regarded as the greatest **preacher** of his age, Rees was born in **Llansannan**; he was the elder brother of the **Congregationalist William Rees** (Gwilym Hiraethog; 1802–83). A **Calvinistic Methodist** preacher, it was he, in 1818, who inspired **John Jones** (Talysarn; 1796–1857) to enter the ministry. He trained in Shrewsbury as a bookbinder, was ordained in 1827 and in 1836 moved to **Liverpool**, where he became a powerful influence in the Welsh churches. In 1864, he became the first moderator of the Calvinistic Methodists' General Assembly.

REES, Ioan Bowen (1929–99)
Administrator and author
A native of **Dolgellau**, Ioan Bowen Rees was the chief executive officer of **Gwynedd County** Council from its inception in 1974, and was central to Gwynedd's pioneering role in the use of the **Welsh language** in local **government**. He stood as a **Plaid [Genedlaethol] Cymru** candidate in the general elections of 1959 and 1964. His *Government by Community* (1971), analysing local government in Switzerland, made an important contribution to the **devolution** debate. An ardent **mountain** lover, he wrote four books in Welsh on the subject and edited the anthology *The Mountains of Wales* (1992).

Sarah Jane Rees

REES, J[ames] F[rederick] (1883–1967) Historian
Born in **Milford Haven**, he was educated at **Cardiff** and **Oxford**. After academic appointments at **Bangor**, Belfast, Edinburgh and Birmingham, he was, from 1929 to 1949, principal of University College, Cardiff (*see* **Cardiff University**), where his energy and wisdom were highly regarded. He was chairman of the Consultative Committee on the Problems of Reconstruction in Wales and president of the **Cambrian Archaeological Society**. His publications include *Studies in Welsh History* (1947), *The Story of Milford* (1954), *The Problem of Wales and other essays* (1963) and *The Cardiff Region* (ed. 1960).

REES, Leighton (1940–2003) Darts player
A factory storeman who became the world's first professional **darts** champion and who won a record 77 Wales caps, Rees was born in **Ynysybwl**. When he left school, aged 15, one of his teachers declared he would be 'good only for reading the sports pages of the *South Wales Echo*'. In 1976, he became a professional darts player. The following year, his team won the first World Darts' Federation World Cup and he was acknowledged the World Cup singles champion. The highlight of his career came in 1978, when he won the inaugural Embassy World Darts Championship, which gained darts a mass television audience.

REES, [William] Linford [Llewelyn] (1914–2004) Psychiatrist
A world authority on the use of drugs in treating mental illness, and a prime mover, after the **Second World War**, in establishing psychiatry as a **science**-based discipline, Rees was born at Burry Port (**Pembrey and Burry Port**) and educated at the Welsh National School of Medicine (*see* **Wales College of Medicine, Biology, Life and Health Sciences**). He trained in psychological medicine at **London**'s Maudsley Hospital and was a pioneer of NHS psychiatric services in Wales before being recruited, in 1954, to the Maudsley. In 1966, he took the foundation chair in psychiatry at St Bartholomew's Hospital, whence he retired in 1980 to establish himself in private practice. A prolific author on mental illness and the recipient of innumerable honours, he was president of the British Medical Association from 1978 to 1979.

REES, Robert (Eos Morlais; 1841–92) Musician
Wales's first nationally recognized tenor was born in Dowlais (**Merthyr Tydfil**), and began his working life, aged nine, as a miner. He developed as a musician in Bethania chapel and in 1867 he won the tenor competition in the National **Eisteddfod**. Subsequently, he sang throughout Wales, in **England** and, in 1879, in **North America**. When he died in **Swansea**, a nation mourned the loss of an incomparable, charismatic singer.

REES, Sarah Jane (Cranogwen; 1839–1916)
Writer and temperance activist
Born in **Llangrannog** and a schoolteacher by profession, her *Caniadau Cranogwen* appeared in 1870. From 1879 to 1891, she edited the **women**'s magazine *Y Frythones* (1879–91). A busy **preacher** and lecturer, in 1901 she founded the South Wales Women's **Temperance** Union,

which she ran until her death. She spent years at sea with her father, a **ship**'s captain, and founded a school at Llangrannog at which basic navigation skills and literacy were taught. She was a pioneer of tonic sol-fa (*see* **Music**).

REES, Thomas (1815–85) Minister and historian

Born at **Llanfynydd** (**Carmarthenshire**), Thomas Rees served as a **Congregationalist** minister in Craig-y-fargod (Bedlinog), **Aberdare**, **Llanelli**, **Beaufort** and **Swansea**. Though a notable **preacher**, biblical expositor, author and **hymn** writer, it is as a historian that he is best remembered. *A History of Protestant Nonconformity in Wales* (1861; fuller edition, 1883) is still in use, as are the four volumes he wrote with John Thomas (1821–92) of **Liverpool**, *Hanes Eglwysi Annibynol Cymru*, which chronicle the history of every Congregational church in Wales.

REES, Thomas (1869–1926) Minister and theologian

Born in Llanfyrnach (**Crymych**), Rees worked initially as a farmhand and a **coal**miner. Following a distinguished student career in **Carmarthen**, **Cardiff** and **Oxford**, he was appointed professor of **theology** at the Memorial College, **Brecon**, in 1899, the year in which he was ordained a **Congregationalist** minister. In 1909, he became principal of the Congregationalist college at **Bangor** (Coleg **Bala**-Bangor). There he led the successful campaign to amend the charter of the **University of Wales** to permit the university to teach theology and effectively became the founder of Bangor's distinguished school of theology. He supported movements for social reform and **pacifism**, famously suffering expulsion from the Bangor **Golf** Club for his opposition to the **First World War**. From 1916 to 1919, he was editor of *Y Deyrnas*, the pacifist monthly described by **W. J. Gruffydd** as 'one of the strongest reasons why Wales did not completely lose its soul at the time of the great madness'. He, more than anyone, was responsible for the publication of the biblical **dictionary**, *Y Geiriadur Beiblaidd* (1924–6).

REES, Timothy (1874–1939) Bishop

A native of Llanbadarn Trefeglwys (**Dyffryn Arth**), Rees – influenced by the 1904–5 **Revival** – acted as missioner to the churches in the **diocese** of **St David's**. In 1906, he entered the Community of the Resurrection, Mirfield, an **Anglican** religious order, becoming known as a powerful **preacher** and missioner. As bishop of Llandaff (*see* **Cardiff**) (1931–9), Rees brought new heart to a diocese facing the ravages of the **Depression**. He established a team of missioner priests, and actively worked towards economic solutions.

REES, William (Gwilym Hiraethog; 1802–83) Editor, poet and novelist

A man of astonishing industry, Rees, the brother of **Henry Rees**, was born at **Llansannan** and was a minister with the **Congregationalists** in **Liverpool**. He was editor or co-editor of various **periodicals** and **newspapers**: he is remembered particularly as the radical editor of *Yr Amserau* (1843–59). His published poetry includes a collection of poems (1855) and the epic *Emmanuel* (1862, 1867). In his prose works, he pioneered the novel, broke new ground by using colloquial **Welsh**, and produced an original adaptation of Stowe's

Uncle Tom's Cabin (1851). He popularized the public lecture, wrote **hymns** (including 'Dyma gariad fel y moroedd'), religious and theological works and a religious **drama**.

REES, William (1887–1978) Historian

A native of Aberyscir (**Yscir**), Rees was appointed lecturer in the department of history at **Cardiff** in 1920. In 1930, the college appointed him to the first ever chair of Welsh history; from 1935 to his retirement in 1953, he combined this with the chair of history. His first major publication was *South Wales and the March, 1284–1415* (1924). He was a superb cartographer: his **map**, *South Wales and the Border in the Fourteenth Century* (1933), is of seminal importance, as is his *Historical Atlas of Wales* (1951). Among his other publications are *Cardiff, A History of the City* (1962), *Industry Before the Industrial Revolution* (2 vols., 1968) and *A Calendar of Ancient Petitions relating to Wales* (1975), a volume dedicated to his wife on the occasion of their diamond wedding.

REES, William James (Bill; 1914–95) Philosopher

Political philosophy was the chief interest of Bill Rees, a native of **St David's**. He was educated at **Aberystwyth**, **Oxford** and **London** and, after a brief period lecturing at Aberystwyth and Bristol, he spent the remainder of his career at Leeds University. He made an extensive study of the works of A. N. Raishchev, the Russian liberal thinker of the 18th century. In **Welsh**, he published a volume on Lenin (1981) in the series *Y Meddwl Modern*, translations of Marx's work, including the **Communist** Manifesto (1948), and numerous articles. His most important contribution is his work, in Welsh and in **English**, on the concept of political sovereignty.

REFUGEE ARTISTS

Political upheavals associated with both the **First World War** and the **Second World War** led to a number of mainland European refugee artists finding their way to Wales. Many of those who came as a result of the First World War were Belgians, some of them encouraged by the Davies sisters (*see* **Davies family (Llandinam)**). Before, during and after the Second World War, other artists, many of them **Jews**, came to escape persecution. Martin Bloch (1883–1954), Fred Uhlman (1901–85) and George Mayer-Marton (1897–1960) made short visits to Wales, while **Josef Herman**, Heinz Koppel (1919–80), Ernest Neuschul (1895–1995) and Freidrich Könekamp (1892–1967) settled or stayed for longer periods. They mostly favoured an expressionistic style, which brought a new vitality to Welsh **painting**, and some were influential teachers – notably Koppel at the **Dowlais Settlement**. As political refugees, they felt a kinship with the struggles of working-**class** people, which is strongly reflected in their subject matter.

REICHEL, Henry Rudolf (Harry Reichel; 1856–1931) One of the founders of the University of Wales

Following a brilliant career at **Oxford**, in 1884 Belfast-born Reichel was appointed first principal of the University College of North Wales, **Bangor** (*see* **University of Wales,**

Bangor) at the age of 28; he retired from the post in 1927, at the age of 71. He early identified himself with the national movement that gave birth to the federal **University of Wales**, of which he was vice-chancellor for six terms. He enthusiastically supported many cultural developments, among them intermediate **education** and the study of folk song (*see* **Music**). He was knighted in 1907. Although a somewhat distant personality, when he died, many tributes were paid to him, especially in his adopted land.

RELICS

In medieval Europe, the relics of **saints** played a central role in religious devotion and Wales was no exception. However, unlike many other peoples in the early Middle Ages, the Welsh seem to have been reluctant to disturb the bodies of their own saints. It was only from the 12th century, probably under Anglo-**Norman** influence, that shrines were built to accommodate bones that had been removed from their graves – such as those of St **Melangell** at Pennant Melangell (**Llangynog**) and St Barruc (or Barwg) on **Barry Island**. According to **Giraldus Cambrensis**, the Welsh, like the **Irish**, showed particular veneration for non-bodily relics – gospel books, bells and croziers – which were used in oath-taking. Relics of all types attracted pilgrims seeking the aid of saints, especially in order to cure illnesses (*see* **Pilgrimage**). Although Protestant reformers condemned the cult of relics, it long continued to be an important element in popular **religion** in Wales. In the 19th century, at Gwytherin (**Llangernyw**), pieces of the early medieval wooden reliquary of St **Winefride** (some of which have since come to light) were sold to Catholic pilgrims; at

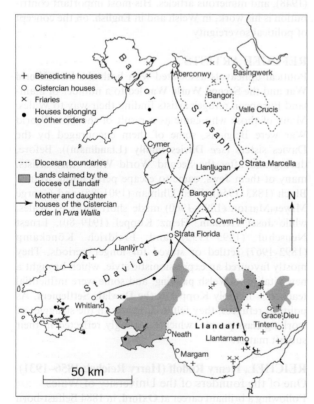

The dioceses and monasteries of medieval Wales (after William Rees, 1959)

Llandeilo Llwydarth (**Maenclochog**), a skull, believed to be that of St **Teilo,** was kept by the Melchior family for drinking water from the saint's **well**; it is now in Llandaff Cathedral. Relics continue to attract devotion today, especially among members of the **Roman Catholic** and **Orthodox Church**es.

RELIGION

The pre-Christian millennia

The earliest known site of religious observance in Wales is Goat's Hole Cave, Paviland (**Rhossili**), where, about 26,000 years ago (*see* **Palaeolithic and Mesolithic Ages**), the remains of a young man were ritually interred – although the religious beliefs of the hunter-gatherers performing the ceremony may only be guessed at. Archaeological evidence from the agricultural settlements of the **Neolithic Age**, at chambered tombs such as Pentre Ifan (**Nevern**) and Bryn Celli Ddu (**Llanddaniel Fab**), is more plentiful, but again nothing is known about specific beliefs. There is little doubt, however, that such sites possessed a definite religious significance, as did sites of the **Bronze Age** and the **Iron Age**.

By the Iron Age, Celtic-speaking peoples inhabited much of central and western Europe. As the **Celts** did not commit their doctrines to writing, the sources concerning their religion are the archaeological record and the works of classical writers. The names of several hundred Celtic gods and goddesses survive, most of them presumably having only a local following. Although he did not name them, Julius Caesar stated that the chief gods of the Celts were equivalent to **Roman** deities such as Mercury and Apollo (**Lleu** and Mabon, perhaps), but it is impossible to equate the Celtic pantheon with the Roman gods in any neat and unambiguous way. The role of the Celtic priesthood – the **druids** – is equally problematic. They were certainly bearers of wisdom and teachers of youth, who also fulfilled a priestly and sacrificial function. The most that can be said with any degree of certainty about the creed of the Brythonic ancestors of the Welsh is that it had to do with nature, wisdom and fertility, and that it was sensitive to the mystery of creation and to the powers which rule the destiny of humankind.

Although the druidic tradition languished following **Suetonius Paulinus**'s destruction of their sacred groves in **Anglesey** in AD 61, it is believed that the Celtic deities left their mark on the people's consciousness, and that legends of their exploits were perpetuated in much later creative **literature**. Although the context had been highly Christianized, there is little doubt that such characters as Lleu, **Gwydion**, **Bendigeidfran**, **Manawydan**, **Pwyll** and **Rhiannon** in the stories of *The Mabinogion* were originally pre-Christian deities.

Early medieval Christianity and the 'Age of the Saints'

The fact that pagan motifs are visible in what was the ostensibly Christianized literature of *The Mabinogion* illustrates the fusion which occurred, by the early Christian centuries, between the old religion and the new. By the

5th century, Celtic paganism was yielding to a new creed centred on the life, death and resurrection of Jesus of Nazareth. Little is known of the way in which Christianity came to Wales, though references by Tertullian (AD *c.*160–*c.*225) and Origen (*c.*185–254) to the gospel's extension even to the distant 'barbarian' **island** of **Britain** suggest that there were Christians there by the 3rd century. Three British bishops were present at the Council of Arles (314) and British Christianity was potent enough to produce such a seminal Christian thinker as Pelagius (*c.*360–420; *see* **Pelagianism**).

The Christianity which spread so remarkably in Wales between the 5th and the 7th centuries is generally believed to have developed in part from that inherited from the Roman Empire, and in part from the work of **missionaries** sailing the western sea routes, and that it was in the southeast – **Erging**, **Gwent** and **Morgannwg** – that these influences coalesced. That era was the 'Age of the **Saints**', when the early leaders, such as **Dyfrig** and **Illtud**, fused native Celtic emphases with the intellectual traditions of the wider European church. Later leaders – **Teilo**, **David**, **Deiniol**, **Cybi** and **Seiriol** among them – represented a more ascetic form of monasticism, which drew upon traditions emanating from the eastern Mediterranean. Parallel developments were occurring in **Brittany**, **Cornwall**, **Ireland** and **Scotland**. As a result, the notion later arose that there had been a **Celtic Church** distinct from the rest of Christendom – a notion which no longer commands credibility. Nevertheless, the lives of the 'saints' are rich in tales of inter-Celtic links, and there are common features in the Celtic-speaking lands in their religious art and monuments – inscribed stones in particular (*see* **Monuments, Early Christian**). In the 8th century, the Welsh Church finally accepted Roman customs on matters such as determining the date of Easter, but Rome's assertion of supremacy, via Canterbury, not only over the **Anglo-Saxons**, who had established kingdoms in southern and eastern Britain, but over the entire island, was staunchly resisted.

The **Norman** conquest of **England** in 1066 and the subsequent conquest of much of Wales by Norman barons reopened Wales to influences from mainland western Europe. A **parish** system was imposed on the older monastic structure and the four territorial **dioceses** of **St David's**, Llandaff (**Cardiff**), **Bangor** and **St Asaph** were established. By the 12th century, **Latin** monasticism had superseded the older *clas* system, first with the introduction of **Benedictine** houses and later with the coming of the **Cistercians**. Between 1131 and 1226, some 13 Cistercian houses were established in Wales. The majority of them enjoyed the patronage of native Welsh rulers and became centres of spiritual and cultural renewal. This close link between religion, politics and culture survived the loss of Welsh independence in 1282 and lasted, in a curtailed way, until the **dissolution of the monasteries** in the 16th century.

The Reformation and beyond

The **Protestant Reformation** was more a political process than a spiritual movement, although its implementation by **Tudor** sovereigns (whose Welsh ancestry made them acceptable to the Welsh) meant that it found a greater welcome

St Iestyn depicted in a *c.*1380 carving at St Iestyn's church, Llaniestyn, Llanddona

among the Welsh than would otherwise have been the case. Its real impact was in Elizabeth I's appointment of resident, **Welsh**-speaking bishops, who combined a commitment to traditional cultural mores with a zeal for reform centred on 'the Word of God'. The Welsh **Book of Common Prayer** and New Testament of 1567, translated chiefly by Bishop **Richard Davies** (?1510–81) and the **Renaissance** scholar **William Salesbury**, and the Welsh **Bible** of 1588, the work of Bishop **William Morgan** (?1541–1604), were of the utmost significance for the later development of the nation's life. Although a powerful group of **Roman Catholic** exiles kept alive the hope of reconverting Wales to the old faith, by the third quarter of the 16th century Reformation values had generally triumphed.

It was not until the 1630s that **Puritan**ism began to manifest itself as a rejection of the rituals and discipline of the established **Anglican** Church. Wales's first **Congregational** church was founded in **Llanvaches**, in 1639, and its first **Baptist** congregation was convened at **Ilston,** in 1649. By the **Commonwealth** period (1642–60), when the Anglican Church was replaced by a non-episcopal religious structure, Puritanism in its Congregationalist, Baptist, **Quaker** and **Presbyterian** guises, rooted itself in different parts of Wales, although it did not become widely influential. The strength of the Puritan movement was in the calibre of its leaders, **Walter Cradock**, **Vavasor Powell**, **Morgan Llwyd** and **John Miles**, whose legacy was abiding – although, at the time, their impact was restricted. The Restoration of the monarchy in 1660 and consequent re-establishment of the episcopal system brought the Puritan ascendancy to an abrupt end. Constrained, until 1689, by harsh legal restrictions, dissent (*see* **Nonconformists**) contracted, with many Baptists and virtually all the mid-Wales Quakers forsaking their land for a more propitious religious future in **Pennsylvania** and other parts of **North America**.

The age of revivals

Although the post-Restoration Anglican Church did not look favourably on Dissent, a certain amount of co-operation between Anglicans and Nonconformists did occur, especially in the field of Christian literature. Conciliation-minded Congregationalists such as **Stephen Hughes** and the Anglican **Society for the Promotion of Christian Knowledge** disseminated Welsh bibles and established schools. **Education**al work and a more vibrant evangelistic mission was undertaken by the remarkable **Griffith Jones** (1683–1761), rector of **Llanddowror**. A more pronounced spiritual renewal began in 1735 with the dawning of the **Methodist Revival** led by **Daniel Rowland**, **Howel Harris** and **William Williams** (Pantycelyn; 1717–91). Ostensibly a movement within Anglicanism, Methodism had an ambiguous relationship with the established church. Unlike its **Arminian** sister movement in England, Welsh Methodism embraced **Calvinism** (*see* **Calvinistic Methodists**). Shunned by the bishops and obliged to create its own structures outside the parish system, it existed in parallel with the state church for nearly three generations. Under the somewhat reluctant leadership of **Thomas Charles**, **Bala**, the body finally seceded from the establishment in 1811, and, as the Welsh Calvinistic Methodist Connexion, it became officially a Nonconformist denomination.

By then, Nonconformity, which since the 1780s had been radically renewed by the evangelical **revival**, had been transformed into a widely popular religious movement. Its success in winning the allegiance of the working **class** was spectacular. What had been a minority, somewhat elitist, movement, confined to the largest towns and **border** regions, became the vibrant activity of Methodists (Calvinistic and **Wesleyan**), Congregationalists and Baptists, who together comprised the principal manifestation of Christianity in Wales. The established church, for its part, languished. Those dissenting traditions which were impervious to the revival – the Presbyterians and the Arminian Baptists – passed into **Unitarianism** and atrophied. Popular Nonconformity produced a generation of **preachers** of unequalled power, of whom the Baptist **Christmas Evans**, the Calvinistic Methodist **John Elias** and the Congregationalist **William Williams** (Wern; 1781–1840) were the most celebrated. 'Perhaps there never has been such a nation as the Welsh who have been won over so widely to the hearing of the gospel,' wrote Christmas Evans. 'Meeting houses have been erected in each corner of the land and the majority of the common people crowd in to listen.' It has been estimated that, between 1800 and 1850, one Nonconformist meeting house or chapel was completed every week. As a result, in parts of Wales the resident **population** was less than the accommodation available in places of worship. As Horace Mann, the organizer of the religious census of 1851, put it: '[the Welsh are] basking in an excess of religious privilege'. The statistics emanating from that census are difficult to interpret, but they suggest that of those in Wales attending a service on Sunday, 30 March 1851, four attended a Nonconformist chapel for every one attending a parish church.

Evan Roberts surrounded by women revivalists

*Radical dissent, Anglican renewal and
Roman Catholic gains*

Literacy and increasing social influence led
Nonconformists to flex their political muscle and, by the
1860s, evangelical Christianity had been combined with
radical politics, initially in order to repeal the civil disabilities under which Nonconformists had laboured since 1660,
but also to abolish more general activities of which they
disapproved. Although spearheaded by such leaders as the
Congregationalists **David Rees** (1801–69) and **William Rees**
(Gwilym Hiraethog; 1802–83), even the previously quietist
Methodists were drawn into the political sphere. The major
intellectual force within Nonconformity was **Lewis
Edwards**, principal of the Calvinistic Methodist college at
Bala. Having convinced his fellow Methodists of the
importance of a learned ministry, he became a means of
widening the cultural vision and raising the intellectual
standards of the nation as a whole. Through the quarterly
magazine *Y Traethodydd*, founded in 1845, he disseminated information on the latest trends in **theology**, **philosophy**, **science** and literature. Although popular preaching
was still highly prized, with such superb practitioners as
John Jones (Talysarn; 1796–1857) and **Henry Rees** retaining the allegiance of the masses, by the mid-Victorian era a
consensus had been created wherein evangelical piety,
social involvement and intellectual endeavour cohered.

Roman Catholicism, which had been virtually extinct
since the late 17th century, was reinvigorated by the **Irish**
influx of the 1840s and subsequent decades. With the
establishment of a Roman Catholic hierarchy in 1850,
there were hopes for the 'reconversion of Wales' and
efforts were made to attract the indigenous Welsh to
Rome. Some success in this direction was achieved, but the
bulk of Welsh Catholics continued to be descendants of
immigrants, not only from Ireland, but also from England,
Italy, Poland and elsewhere. By the mid-20th century,
when the membership of all Wales's other mainstream
churches was in decline, the Roman Catholic Church was
enjoying considerable success and had become the
strongest denomination in many Welsh urban areas. By the
later 20th century, however, Roman Catholicism had
joined the other churches in suffering decline.

Side-by-side with the 19th-century re-emergence of
Roman Catholicism was the reinvigoration of the established church, initiated by – among others – **Thomas
Burgess**, who in 1822 founded St David's College,
Lampeter (*see* **University of Wales, Lampeter**). Structural
change had been initiated in the mid-19th century by such
figures as Alfred Ollivant (1798–1882), bishop of Llandaff,
and Thomas Vowler Short (1790–1872), bishop of St
Asaph. The twin engines of spiritual renewal were 'low
church' evangelicalism and the 'high church' **Oxford
Movement** – the one providing effective gospel preaching
and the other a sense of dignity in worship. Evangelicals
such as David Howell (1831–1903), dean of St David's, and
catholic Anglicans such as Evan Lewis (1818–1901), dean
of Bangor, exemplified and popularized both trends. By
the end of the 19th century, Welsh Anglicanism was perceived to have created a valid spiritual alternative to
Protestant Dissent.

William Rees (Gwilym Hiraethog)

The Nonconformist crisis

Although still outwardly flourishing, Nonconformity was
beginning to show signs of serious strain. The tradition of
popular preaching was continued by such men as **John
Williams** (Brynsiencyn; 1854–1921) and Thomas Charles
Williams (1868–1927), but the chapels were finding it
increasingly difficult to contend with the twin challenges of
modernity and Anglicization. The undermining of belief in
the literal truth of the Bible, together with geological discoveries and the theories of Charles Darwin, proved particularly unsettling. The widespread religious revival of
1904–5, led by **Evan Roberts**, proved more significant in the
development of international **Pentecostalism** than in the
renewal of Welsh Nonconformity. The crisis was exacerbated by the political struggle for the **disestablishment of
the Church of England in Wales**, which pitched Nonconformist against Anglican. Between 1889 (when the controversy effectively began) and 1914 (when parliament
passed the Welsh Church Act, cutting the link between the
Anglican Church in Wales and the state), Christian
integrity on both sides suffered grievously. Disenchanted
by religious disputes, many people came to feel that the
values of the future would be more secular in nature. As
the 20th century progressed, the incipient labour movement would provide an ideological – indeed a spiritual –
home for an increasing number of the people of Wales.

As elsewhere, the **First World War** had a profound effect
on religious practice. The loss of a generation of young
men raised questions about the meaning of life and divine
purpose, while post-war economic dislocation brought
widespread suffering and hardship. The newly disestablished **Church in Wales**, under its first archbishop,
A. G. Edwards, spent its early years adjusting to its independent status. Yet, although it remained weaker numerically than the denominations of the Nonconformist

tradition taken together, it had become, by the 1930s, the strongest single denomination in Wales.

By the 1920s, doctrinal liberalism threatened to eclipse orthodoxy, with such accomplished theologians as **Thomas Rees** (1869–1926), John Morgan Jones (1873–1946) and **D. Miall Edwards** convincing many that, in order to survive, Christianity would have to adapt to the values of the **Enlightenment**. Not all were convinced and, by the 1940s, a spirited Calvinistic renewal had occurred, deeply indebted to the work of Karl Barth. Theologians such as **J. E. Daniel** and preachers like **Lewis Valentine** combined a Barthian emphasis with a commitment to the doctrinal standards of classical Welsh Nonconformity. Evangelicalism of a more conservative character was championed in Wales by the influential **London**-based preacher **Martyn Lloyd-Jones**.

The age of secularization

By the mid-20th century, the Church in Wales, by then confident in its independent status, had gained considerable popular support, its most dynamic personality being **Glyn Simon**, sometime bishop of both Llandaff and the new diocese of **Swansea** and **Brecon**, and, between 1968 and 1971, archbishop of Wales. Roman Catholicism, especially under Archbishop **Michael McGrath**, had also experienced unprecedented expansion and a growing acceptance among the Welsh people at large. Yet, by the late 1960s, secularization was taking its toll on all the main denominations. The agnostic humanism which had characterized some of the Welsh intelligentsia since the early years of the century increasingly became the norm, while the working class, which had previously been notable for its religious commitment, turned away from organized religion.

Rowan Williams, the first Welsh-born archbishop of Canterbury

The final quarter of the 20th century witnessed steep statistical decline across the board. The vitality of the charismatic movement and the establishment of newer evangelical or 'house' churches among Christians did little to stem the secular tide. Secularization appeared more pronounced in Wales, due to the exceptionally high religious profession that had previously characterized the nation's history. If the majority of the Welsh claimed that they believed in God, it was obvious that most of those who saw themselves as Christians had far less commitment to their religion than the Hindus, Sikhs and Muslims (*see* **Islam**) who were settling in Wales had to theirs. Although alternative lifestyles were sometimes characterized by adherence to newer non-Christian religious movements, by the new millennium religion had ceased to be a dynamic element in the lives of the great majority of the people of Wales (*see also* **Agnostics and Atheists**).

RENAISSANCE, The

A word coined in 1869 to describe the developments, evident in Italy from the 14th century onwards, which offered a wider perspective on life than that provided by the feudal system and the medieval Church. (The **Welsh** equivalent, *Dadeni Dysg*, first appeared in the early 20th century.) Delighting in the **literature**, **philosophy** and art of ancient Greece and Rome, the humanists of the Renaissance sought to invest their own languages with the dignity of those of classical times, to satisfy their curiosity about the world and humanity's place in it and to further the notion of the accomplished and educated layman. As Wales had no centres comparable with the prosperous, capitalist cities in which the Renaissance had originated, it is hardly surprising that the humanist ideas that first reached the country in the 16th century had a greater impact upon literature than upon arts which need more elaborate forms of patronage.

Wales's leading Renaissance figure was **William Salesbury**, the preface to whose **proverb** collection, *Oll Synnwyr pen Kembero ygyd* (1547), was the earliest Welsh declaration of Renaissance ideals. Salesbury urged his compatriots to demand learning in the Welsh language. As a fervent Protestant, he wanted learning to be the handmaiden of **religion** and considered a Welsh **Bible** to be an urgent priority. His translation of the New Testament (1567) provided the foundation for **William Morgan**'s Welsh Bible of 1588, which combined biblical scholarship rooted in Renaissance learning with a scholarly command of Welsh. Another leading Welsh Renaissance scholar, **John Davies** (*c.*1567–1644), was chiefly responsible for the Bible of 1620, which further refined Morgan's translation.

The humanists sought to pioneer in Welsh the type of varied literature then being developed in the main European vernacular languages. This desire was evident in **Gruffydd Robert**'s prefaces to his *Dosparth Byrr* (1567), the first part of a Welsh grammar published in Milan, where Robert was a **Roman Catholic** exile. He hoped that his grammar would facilitate the translation of learned works from other languages – especially **Latin**, the main vehicle of Renaissance learning – into Welsh. He urged Welsh poets to compose epic poems – a much-esteemed Renaissance genre – and to abandon the restrictive traditional strict metres of Welsh poetry. Another humanist who wished to

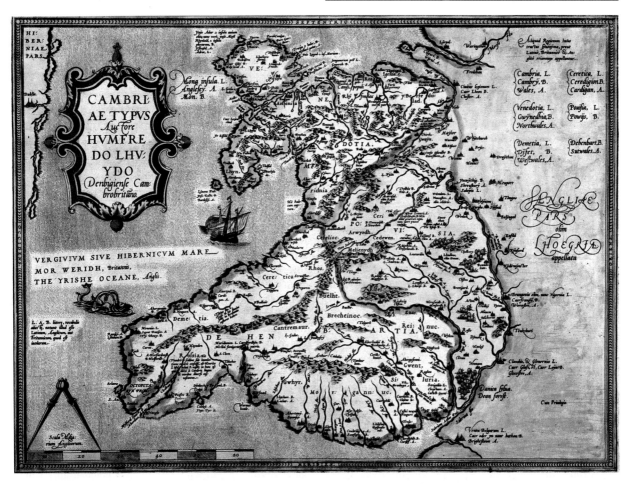

Humphrey Lhuyd's *Cambriae Typus*, the earliest published map of Wales, 1573

transform Welsh poetry was **Edmwnd Prys**, archdeacon of **Merioneth**. In his bardic dispute (1580–7) with the professional poet **Wiliam Cynwal**, he criticized mendacious bardic eulogies; like Robert, the Protestant Prys championed both divine poetry and scientific poetry of the kind then popular in Renaissance Europe. Scientific poetry was also championed by the Siena-educated humanist **Siôn Dafydd Rhys** in his *Letter to the Bards* (1597). In the field of prose, significant historical works were written by humanists such as **Humphrey Lhuyd**, **George Owen**, **David Powel**, **John Price** and Edward **Stradling**.

The study of language characterized humanism everywhere. Grammars were published by Gruffydd Robert (1567–?84), Siôn Dafydd Rhys (1592), Henry **Salusbury** (1593) and John Davies (1621). **Dictionaries** were published by William Salesbury (1547) and John Davies (1632), and **Thomas Wiliems** compiled an extensive manuscript dictionary. Of these, John Davies's works – which reflected bardic linguistic usage – were the most accomplished and influential.

Although achievement in arts other than literature was slight, it did exist, as testified by Richard Clough's remarkable Renaissance mansion of 1567 (Bach-y-graig, **Tremeirchion**; demolished by 1817) and by the **Herbert** tomb of 1600 at St Nicholas, **Montgomery**. Scientific curiosity led to the invention of the equals sign (=) by **Robert Recorde** of **Tenby** and to the remarkable career of that Renaissance

genius **John Dee**. Dee was fascinated by the opening up of the Atlantic sea routes, activity in which Robert **Mansel** of **Margam**, **Thomas Button** of St Lythan's (**Wenvoe**) and **William Vaughan** of **Llangyndeyrn** were involved. Indeed, Wales may have had a stake in the greatest of all adventures – the opening up of America – for there are those who believe that the continent was named after the **Glamorgan** merchant **Richard Amerik** (Ap Meurig), one of the patrons of John Cabot's second voyage. Exploration led to a delight in **maps**, a characteristic feature of the Renaissance. Humphrey Lhuyd's map, published in Antwerp in 1573, was the first recognizable map of Wales – the beginning of a cartographical tradition which took a major step forward with the publication of John Speed's splendid map in 1611.

There were also those in Wales who were inspired by the Renaissance ideal of the accomplished gentleman, among them the soldier-poets **Morris Kyffin**, William Midleton (fl.1550–1600) and **Tomos Prys**, and the scholarly administrator William Herbert (d.1593), who sought to establish a college for Wales in the ruins of **Tintern** abbey. The Renaissance concern for **education** also found expression in the establishment of Jesus College, **Oxford**, and the foundation of almost a score of grammar schools in Welsh market towns.

The achievements of the Welsh humanists fell far below their aspirations. This may not be surprising as they were inhabitants of a country bereft of control over its own fate and lacking any significant centres of wealth. What is surprising is the scale of their achievements and the fact that such aspirations existed at all.

RENDEL, Stuart (1834–1913) Politician

Rendel, a native of Plymouth who amassed a substantial fortune in the family armaments firm, was elected **Liberal** MP for **Montgomeryshire** in 1880, ending the **Williams Wynn family**'s 80-year **Conservative** domination of the seat, domination which had its roots in the victory of an ancestor of the family, Richard Vaughan (*see* **Vaughan family (Llwydiarth)**) in 1647. In 1889, he became leader of the Welsh Liberal MPs. He was influential in promoting the **Welsh Intermediate Education Act (1889)** and, although an **Anglican**, the measures were designed to bring about the **disestablishment of the Church**. A close friend of **Gladstone**, he was created a baron in 1894. A leading advocate of the provision of university **education** in Wales (*see* **University of Wales**), he was a generous patron of the university college at **Aberystwyth** (*see* **University of Wales, Aberystwyth**), serving as its president from 1895 and endowing a chair in **English**, which still bears his name. In 1897, he donated land for the building of the **National Library of Wales**.

REPUBLICANISM

In the 18th century, republican ideas were advanced by **Richard Price** and **David Williams** (1738–1816), supporters of the French Revolution and of American independence. In the 1880s and 1890s, **Thomas Gee** came close to advocating a republic. In the 20th century, **Keir Hardie** attacked the crown on republican grounds, boycotting the investiture of the **Prince of Wales** in 1911. In the interwar years **T. E. Nicholas** and other left-wingers consistently opposed the monarchy. The Welsh Republican Movement of the 1950s, although it fought only one election (**Ogmore**, 1950), published a spirited **newspaper**, the *Welsh Republican* (1950–7), edited by **Harri Webb**. Republican protests resurfaced at the time of the 1969 investiture, and again in the 1980s, with two newspapers, *Y Faner Goch* and *Welsh Republic*, urging the establishment of a Welsh republic.

RESERVOIRS

Until the 19th century, the towns of Wales relied for their water supplies on wells, springs and **rivers**. Wales's first town reservoir seems to have been that built at Brynmill, **Swansea** in 1837. With the devastating impact of waterborne diseases in the mid-19th century – the ravages of **cholera** above all – urban authorities set about establishing ambitious reservoirs to supply clean drinking water. Between 1858 and 1927, 10 reservoirs were created in the **Brecon Beacons** and Fforest Fawr primarily to supply **Cardiff**, **Merthyr Tydfil**, **Neath**, **Newport** and Swansea.

Towns outside Wales also sought their water supplies in the Welsh uplands, where high rainfall (*see* **Climate**) and low evaporation rates produce 10 times as much water run-off as is produced in the English lowlands. **Liverpool** started reservoir construction on the Vyrnwy in 1881 (**Llanwddyn**), and Birkenhead on the Alwen in 1911 (**Cerrigydrudion**). The greatest scheme was that of Birmingham, which between 1893 and 1904 built a series of reservoirs – Caban-coch, Garreg-ddu, Penygarreg and

Craig Goch – in the Elan valley (**Rhayader**). Birmingham's intended concurrent drowning of the adjoining Claerwen valley was not carried out until 1952. There may yet be an even more ambitious scheme in the Elan valley if the plan to enlarge Craig Goch is implemented.

Of Wales's ten largest reservoirs, six were completed between 1952 and 1975. They include Llyn Celyn (1965; **Llandderfel**), the largest by capacity (71,200 megalitres); Llyn Clywedog (1968; **Llanidloes Without**), the longest in length (7 km); and Llyn Brianne (1972; **Llanddewi Brefi/ Llanfair-ar-y-bryn**).

While the earlier reservoirs were linked by pipelines to the towns that had promoted them, those established after the mid-20th century released their water into rivers under controlled conditions. This meant that reservoirs became not only a source of water for households and industry but also a means of raising river levels during periods of drought and lowering them when there was a danger of flooding. Thus, Llyn Clywedog was intended in part to prevent flooding in the **Severn** valley, a role which Llyn Brianne has in relation to the **Tywi** valley. Rivers rather than pipes became the conduits for reservoir water; for example, water from Llyn Celyn is released to flow into the **Dee**, from which it is extracted near Chester. The new policy meant that reservoirs, once somewhat autonomous units under the control of the towns promoting them, became integrated into a wider policy of water management, a change reflected the establishment in 1989 of the National Rivers Authority (the Environment Agency by 1996).

Although artificial **lakes** form the majority of Wales's 150 reservoirs, some natural lakes have undergone enlargement, among them Llyn y Fan Fach (**Llanddeusant**), which supplies **Llanelli**, Llyn Cowlyd (**Dolgarrog**), which supplies **Conwy**, **Colwyn Bay** and the Dolgarrog power station, and Llyn Llydaw (**Beddgelert**), which supplies the Cwm Dyli power station. A number of reservoirs have been specifically created to supply hydroelectric power schemes (*see* **Energy**). Among them are Llyn **Trawsfynydd**, established in 1924–8 to supply the **Maentwrog** power station. (The lake was enlarged in the 1960s to meet the demands of the **Trawsfynydd Nuclear Power Station**.) The Cwm Rheidol (**Blaenrheidol**) and the Tanygrisiau (**Ffestiniog**) hydroelectric power schemes, opened in the 1960s, led to the creation of two reservoirs – Nant-y-moch and Tanygrisiau – as well as to the enlargement of Llyn Stwlan. On the other hand, two natural lakes form the basis of the remarkable Dinorwic scheme (**Llanddeiniolen**), completed in 1984.

Reservoir schemes involving the drowning of land generally arouse opposition, although, remarkably, some major schemes – that at Llandegfedd (1966; **Llangybi**, **Monmouthshire**), for example – did not lead to the inundation of any significant settlements. Where reservoir construction involves the dispersal of a community, feelings can run high, as in the case of Llyn Celyn (*see* **Tryweryn valley, The drowning of**).

RESOLVEN (Resolfen), Neath Port Talbot
(2038 ha; 2313 inhabitants)
Rhos-soflen – stubble moor – was probably the original name of Resolven, which is located north-east of **Neath**. The **community**, which has been heavily forested, contains

Clywedog reservoir

three aqueducts associated with the Neath **Canal**. In the late 19th century, the **economy** of the area was dominated by the collieries of the **Cory** brothers. During the **Second World War**, one of **Britain**'s largest aluminium factories was established at Resolven.

RESURGAM II

The wreck of the world's first self-powered submarine, the cigar-shaped *Resurgam II*, lies 8 km off **Rhyl** where it sank in 1880. The 14-m, 31-tonne craft was designed by the Rev. George Garrett and built for £1538. She sank in a gale while being towed to Portsmouth for sea trials, and was not rediscovered until 1995.

REVIVALS

In the context of **religion**, and especially Christianity, the word 'revival' is used to describe periods of rapid growth. During revivals, the proclamation of the gospel, especially through preaching, becomes particularly effective, often leading to conversions. Some revivals may be local, others national or international – sometimes a combination of all three. For example, in 18th-century Wales, while there were local examples of the **Methodist Revival**, it was also a national phenomenon, and, as similar revivals were concurrently occurring in several other countries, it can also be considered to be an international phenomenon.

Some revivals are regarded in Wales as milestones in its history. This is especially true of the Methodist Revival, the Revival of 1859 and the remarkable Revival of 1904–5 (*see* **Roberts, Evan**). In addition, 19th-century Wales abounded with examples of smaller revivals confined to individual churches, villages or towns.

REYNOLDSTON, Swansea
(431 ha; 430 inhabitants)

Located in the centre of the **Gower** peninsula, Reynoldston remains very much an 'English' Gower village, set around its church, pub and two village greens. The heavily restored St George's church contains a 9th-century pillar stone. Stouthall, a mansion built in the 1780s and now a field study centre, was designed by **William Jernegan** for the Lucas family.

RHAYADER (Rhaeadr Gwy), Radnorshire,
Powys (13,945 ha; 2075 inhabitants)

Rhayader, on the east bank of the **Wye**, was one of the five contributory **boroughs** of the Radnor Boroughs constituency. Old stone cottages stand cheek by jowl with later Victorian accretions. The place where the town's four streets meet is marked by a **clock** tower (1924). The toll houses are still in position, but the tannery has been removed to the National History Museum (*see* **St Fagans**). The remainder of the **community** of Rhayader lies across the Wye, a tract of wild, **mountain** country that was the one-time **commote** of **Cwmwd Deuddwr**. Thomas Evans, writing in 1801, called the area 'an absolute desert' but, later in the 19th century, Jonathan Williams praised the fertility of its **soil** and the high standard of its livestock. Since they wrote, it has been transformed into what the *Shell Guide to Mid Wales* calls a 'new **lake** district'. In 1892, the Birmingham Corporation secured legislation permitting the construction of a series of **reservoirs**. Four dams were built on the Elan (1894–1904), and one on the Claerwen (1946–52). In the process, the church, chapel, mill, farms, cottages and fields of the Elan valley were inundated and the **Welsh**-speaking community dispersed. Two mansions, Nant Gwyllt and Cwm Elan, were also submerged; Shelley, who stayed in both, recorded his impressions of the beauty of the area in his poem 'Cwm Elan', while the untimely end of the two houses was the inspiration for Francis Brett Young's *The House under the Water* (1932). In 1903, a new church replaced the submerged one, and a new village, to house the reservoirs' maintenance staff, was built between 1906 and 1909. Cilewent, a cruck-framed, probably 15th-century farmhouse, has been removed from the Claerwen valley to the National History Museum.

On Rhos y Gelynen, there are five stones in a mysterious **Bronze Age** alignment. The village of Llansantffraed Cwmdeuddwr was the home of Francis Morgan, a famous 18th-century wizard mentioned in the letters of **John Wesley**. In 2001, 22.46% of the inhabitants of Rhayader had some knowledge of Welsh, with 11.60% wholly fluent in the language – the highest percentages for any of the communities of the one-time **county** of **Radnorshire**.

RHEES, Rush (1905–89) Philosopher

A Welsh American and a descendant of **Morgan John Rhys**, Rush Rhees had an enormous influence on **philosophy** in Wales. Having been expelled from a philosophy class at Rochester University, New York, he graduated at Edinburgh. He met Wittgenstein at **Cambridge** and became his close friend and literary executor. When Rhees was a

lecturer in **Swansea** (1940–66), Wittgenstein visited him regularly, and the 'Swansea School of Philosophy', under Rhees's influence, became renowned internationally (*see also* **Phillips, Dewi Z.**). His most important works include *Discussions of Wittgenstein* (1970), *Without Answers* (1970) and, posthumously, *On Religion and Philosophy* (1997) and *Moral Questions* (1999).

RHEGED Kingdom

One of the post-**Roman** British kingdoms which formed what was known in medieval Wales as the **Old North**. At its greatest extent, it probably comprised the whole of modern Cumbria, an extensive area east of the Pennines (including Catterick; *see* **Gododdin, Y**), as well as Dumfriesshire, Galloway and possibly Ayrshire. Its most famous rulers were **Urien** and his son Owain, who are commemorated in Welsh **literature** and legend. The kingdom came to an end *c.*635, when Urien's great-granddaughter married the Northumbrian prince Oswiu. The kingdom is commemorated by the Rheged Centre at Penrith, Cumbria.

RHEIDOL River (45 km)

The headwaters of the Rheidol, which include a stream that flows from Llyn Llygad Rheidol, drain the southern and western slopes of **Pumlumon**. They are collected in the Nant-y-moch **reservoir**, created in the 1960s as part of the Rheidol hydroelectric power scheme (*see* **Energy**). From

The River Rheidol

the reservoir dam, the river flows through the **community** of **Blaenrheidol** to Ponterwyd. South of Ponterwyd, the Rheidol flows over the Gyfarllwyd **waterfalls** in a 'valley within a valley' landscape formed as a result of changes in sea levels during the Pleistocene Ice Age. At **Pontarfynach**, the dramatic fall of the Mynach – the Rheidol's sole significant tributary – into the Rheidol is an excellent example of **river** capture. Lower down the valley, artificial **lakes** adjoin the main power station. **Lead** was extensively mined within the Rheidol basin. In its lower reaches, the Rheidol flows across a level floodplain before reaching the sea at **Aberystwyth**, which is in fact located on the Rheidol rather than the **Ystwyth**. One of the 'great little trains of Wales' (*see* **Railways**) follows the course of the Rheidol valley between Aberystwyth and Pontarfynach.

RHIANNON

A character in the first and third branches of the Mabinogi (*see* **Mabinogion, The**) whose name derives from the **Celtic** *Rīgantōna* (Divine Queen). In the first branch, Rhiannon becomes the wife of **Pwyll**, prince of **Dyfed**. A child is born to them, but on the night of his birth he is abducted by unseen powers, and his mother is accused of having killed him. The child is restored and is named by his mother **Pryderi**. In the third branch of the Mabinogi, Rhiannon becomes the wife of **Manawydan**.

RHIGOS (Y Rhigos), Rhondda Cynon Taff
(1901 ha; 865 inhabitants)
Constituting the north-western corner of **Rhondda Cynon Taff**, the **community** is bisected by the A4061, which swings its way to the **Rhondda** via two dramatic hairpin bends. In 1908, Llyn Fawr yielded a remarkable collection of metalwork including part of a sword of *c.*600 BC – among the earliest **iron** artefacts to be found in **Britain**. **Coal** extraction from shallow pits was long practised at Rhigos, but the first colliery was that established by John Crichton **Stuart**, second marquess of Bute, in the 1830s. By the early 20th century, the area had been leased to the Duffryn **Aberdare** Coal Company, owners of the Coronation and **Tower** collieries. Closed by the **National Coal Board** in 1994, Tower was bought by its own workforce and reopened in 1995 as a co-operative venture profitably employing over 300 workers. The **Hirwaun** Trading Estate, which developed from a **Second World War royal ordnance factory**, is located within the boundaries of Rhigos.

RHINOGYDD, Y Mountains

A range of **mountains** extending 13 km eastwards from **Harlech** to **Trawsfynydd** and 20 km southwards from **Talsarnau** to **Barmouth**. They constitute the Harlech Dome, Wales's largest example of uplifted and eroded Cambrian age sediments. Rhinog Fawr (720 m) and Rhinog Fach (712 m; both in **Llanbedr**) are located on the western limb of the ice-sculptured dome. Glacial erratic boulders of Cambrian grit are a feature of this hard angular terrain. Sheltered by the mountains are a number of **lakes**; several of them – Llyn Eiddew Mawr (Talsarnau) and Gloywlyn (Llanbedr), for example – occupy glacially scoured rock basins. The thin **peaty soils** support a luxuriant growth of heather, which grows with bilberry in a near-natural

habitat. The area is rich in prehistoric monuments, among them **Neolithic** chambered tombs, **Bronze Age** standing stones and cairns, and **Iron Age hill-forts**. Looking west from Moelfre (583 m; **Dyffryn Ardudwy**), it is sometimes possible to see Sarn Badrig, an under-sea glacial moraine which helped to give rise to the notion of the mythical kingdom of **Cantre'r Gwaelod**. Walkers who venture along the old **drovers**' path misleadingly known as the **Roman** Steps are usually unaware of the feral **goats** that graze indifferently on the exposed cliff ledges above their heads.

RHIWLALLT, SWYDD Commote
One of the **commotes** of the *cantref* of **Maelienydd**, its centre was at Weston (Rhiwlallt), south of **Llangunllo**.

RHODD MAM (Mother's gift)
A manual in the form of a series of questions and answers based on the scriptures, first published in **Welsh** in 1811; it owed much to the *Shorter Catechism* of the Church of **Scotland**. Used to examine children in the **Sunday school** classes of the **Calvinistic Methodists**, it became well known for its simplistic classification of children as 'good children and wicked children', which is often quoted in a satirical context. The booklet was reprinted several times in the 19th century; it was translated into **English** in 1813 and into Khasi (*see* **Khasi Hills**) in 1842. A new version was published in 1925. The author of the original version was John Parry (1775–1846), who published *Rhodd Tad i'w Blant* (*A Father's Gift to His Children*; 1837).

RHODRI MAWR (Rhodri ap Merfyn; d.878)
King of Gwynedd
Rhodri's father **Merfyn Frych** seized power in **Gwynedd** in 825. Merfyn was the son of Gwriad (probably a native of the Isle of **Man**) and of Esyllt, a member of the original royal house of Gwynedd, which traced its origins to **Maelgwn Gwynedd** and **Cunedda**. Merfyn married Nest, a member of the royal house of **Powys**. Rhodri succeeded his father as king of Gwynedd in 844 and asserted his claim to Powys *c.*856. Married to Angharad, a member of the ruling house of **Seisyllwg**, he seized that kingdom *c.*871. He thus ruled the whole of Wales apart from **Dyfed**, **Brycheiniog** and **Morgannwg**. He was probably able to take advantage of English weakness in the face of **Viking** attack, although he himself seems usually to have held his own against them in Wales and to have been a capable ruler and military commander; news of his victory over the Norsemen reached the court of the Frankish king, Charles the Bald. In 877, however, they defeated him and he was forced to flee to **Ireland**. He returned the following year and recovered his kingdom, only to be killed in battle against the **English**. He left several sons; Anarawd inherited the kingship of Gwynedd and Powys, and Cadell that of Seisyllwg. Anarawd seems to have sought to continue his father's domination of much of Wales, and other Welsh rulers sought the aid of Alfred of Wessex against him; he also had a short-lived alliance with the Norse kingdom of York. The royal house of Gwynedd in the 12th and 13th centuries was descended from Anarawd, and that of **Deheubarth** in the same era was descended from Cadell, who was the father of **Hywel Dda**.

RHONDDA (Rhondda Cynon Taff) Constituency and one-time borough and district

This entry concerns the 16 **communities** which, until 1996, constituted the **Rhondda district** of the **county of Mid Glamorgan**. (For the communities, *see below*.)

Although **coal** from beneath Rhondda land continues to be extracted via the **Tower Colliery**, with the closure of the Maerdy Colliery in 1990, the Rhondda Valley ceased to have coalmines. That closure ended an era, for, over the previous hundred years and more, the very name Rhondda had been synonymous with the industry. The transformative effect of industrialization is most vividly depicted by the growth in **population**. In 1841, the **parish** of Ystradyfodwg – which constituted most of what would later be the Rhondda **Borough** – had fewer than a thousand inhabitants. When the population peaked in 1924, the borough had 167,900 inhabitants – more than the combined populations of **Cardiganshire**, **Breconshire** and **Radnorshire**.

In the early Middle Ages, **Glynrhondda** was one of the **commotes** of the *cantref* of **Penychen** in the kingdom of **Morgannwg**. By the early 13th century, it appears that it was under the rule of Hywel ap Maredudd, a descendant of the royal house of Morgannwg. Later in that century, however, it became integrated into the **Clare** lordship of **Glamorgan**. Thinly populated, its only well-known site was the shrine of the Virgin at Penrhys, a popular place of **pilgrimage** and the subject of a considerable body of poetry. Until the 19th century, the twin valleys of Rhondda Fawr and Rhondda Fach were remote glens whose beauty drew rhapsodical comments from the few sightseers who visited them.

The earliest evidence of the commercial exploitation of the Rhondda's coal resources dates from the first decade of the 19th century, when the **Bridgend** businessman **Walter Coffin** initiated at Dinas the small-scale mining of coal seams near to the surface. The coal mined – known as 'sale coal' as opposed to 'works coal' mined for the **iron** industry – was taken by pack**horse** to **Pontypridd**, and thence to the **port** of **Cardiff** via the Glamorganshire **Canal**. Over the following decades, Coffin's example was followed by other entrepreneurs, in particular at Cymmer by George Insole of Cardiff.

The increasing exploitation of seams near the surface left untouched the rich steam coal deposits that were widely thought to be too deep to be mined. In the 1850s, the administrators of the Bute estate (*see* **Stuart family**), eager to earn mineral royalties from the 3000 ha of Bute land in the Rhondda, sank a pit at Cwmsaerbren farm. Bute Merthyr, the Rhondda's first steam coal colliery, began producing coal in 1855. Its colliers were accommodated at the newly established township of Treherbert, named after the Bute family's ancestors, the **Herbert** earls of **Pembroke**.

The high quality of the steam coal of south Wales had already been appreciated by consumers of **Aberdare**'s output, the British Admiralty in particular. From the mid-1850s onwards, the likely availability of rich deposits of similar coal in the Rhondda sparked off pell-mell development. Crucial to future growth was the extension in 1854 of the **Taff** Vale **Railway** to Treherbert in Rhondda Fawr and Ferndale in Rhondda Fach. In Rhondda Fach, the leading coalowner was initially David Davis of Aberdare who opened collieries at Ferndale and Tylorstown. Among the many entrepreneurs in Rhondda Fawr, the name of David Davies (*see* **Davies family (Llandinam)**), who sank the Parc and Dare mines at Cwmparc and Treorchy, is especially prominent. In contrast to the **iron**masters who pioneered south Wales's first period of industrialization a century earlier, these were Welsh-born capitalists. It is unlikely, however, that this made them any more loved by their workforce, particularly as individual owners eventually came to be replaced by industrial combines such as the Ocean Coal Company, controlled by the Llandinam family, and the Cambrian Combine, led by the Aberdare industrialist and politician **D. A. Thomas** (Lord Rhondda). By 1914, there were no fewer than 53 large mines in the Rhondda, 21 of which employed more than 1000 men apiece.

As the shafts became deeper, the dangers from gas, flooding and roof-falls became ever greater. The grim roll-call of major **colliery disasters** in the two valleys includes: 114 miners killed at the **Cymmer Colliery Disaster** in 1856; 178 killed at the **Ferndale Colliery Disaster** in 1867; 100 killed at the **Naval** Colliery, Penygraig, in 1880; and 81 men killed by the Maerdy explosion of 1885. Apart from the spoil tips that still scar the landscape in some places, the only significant surviving physical evidence of the industry is the Rhondda Heritage Park built on the site of the Lewis Merthyr Colliery in Cymmer. The Park offers eloquent testimony of the immense **engineering** and craft skills that were deployed by Rhondda miners under circumstances of constant danger.

A fundamental feature of an **economy** wholly dependent upon coalmining is the scarcity of paid employment for **women**. The notion of the wife and mother constantly at home and hailed as the queen of the household – the notion which gave birth to the image of the **Welsh mam** – was very much a Rhondda creation. Unpaid women's labour was, however, abundant: it was an arduous task ensuring a clean house, clean clothes for the men and – before the coming of pithead baths – the cleanliness of the men themselves (*see* **Elizabeth Andrews**). Furthermore, as miners reached their maximum earning power early in their working lives, families tended to be large, thus adding to the burdens of the women. The high birth rate was partly the cause of the Rhondda's rapid population growth, but more important was the influx of people ready to meet the needs of the labour-intensive coal industry. During the era of the dominance of ironmaking, the south Wales coalfield had been largely dependent upon migrants from rural Wales. Initially, this was true of the Rhondda, but, by the end of the 19th century, there was an increasing reliance upon workers migrating from the English **border** counties and south-western **England**. Along with the smaller numbers of **Irish** and **Italian** incomers, this created the heterogeneous mix that became a hallmark of the Rhondda's society. It was claimed in the 1880s that the Rhondda's pits were the best **Welsh-language** schools in the world, but changing patterns in immigration eventually proved to have a baneful effect upon the fortunes of the language. Nevertheless, on the eve of the **First World War**, the Rhondda still had a Welsh-speaking majority, a situation that would continue in places such as Treorchy and Maerdy well into the 20th century. (The marked decline in knowledge of the language in the Rhondda has, in recent decades, been countered by the development of Welsh-medium schools.)

The rapidly growing population created the need for a massive programme of house-building. The programme was carried out with remarkable speed; it provided houses of a far higher standard than those of the early ironmaking towns, and houses, too, which were generally owned by their occupiers. The terraces of the south Wales coalfield represent a unique townscape, and it is in the Rhondda that that townscape can be appreciated in its most developed form. In such a mountainous area, sites suitable for house-building were rare, and thus the density of **housing** in the built-up areas was high; by the early 20th century, it was as high as 450 people per ha in Tylorstown and Ferndale.

That almost the entire housing stock of the Rhondda consisted of modest terraced houses is visual evidence of the fact that its inhabitants belonged to what were essentially one-**class** communities. Virtually the sole buildings with any claim to be **architecture** were the places of worship, with **Nonconformist** chapels – of which, by 1911, the Rhondda had 151 such – overwhelmingly predominant. In them, attendants found not only their spiritual solace but also the cultural life provided by choirs, orchestras, *cymanfaoedd canu* and *eisteddfodau*. A large number of them have been demolished, others have been adapted to other uses, and many of those that remain are probably doomed.

At least as commodious, though less numerous, were the workmen's halls, among which the Parc and Dare in Treorchy is pre-eminent. Although their **billiard** halls and other entertainments offered what might be considered a less exalted form of culture than that of the chapels, their libraries – that of the Cymmer Colliery Workmen's Institute in Porth, for example – were the centres of intense self-improvement and were the base for choirs and **brass bands** (*see also* **Miners' Institutes**).

The chapels and the workmen's institutes, together with organizations such as **friendly societies**, offer evidence of the strong tradition of communal activity rooted in places such as the Rhondda. Another aspect of communal activity – **trade unionism** – was slower to develop. In the early 1870s, the Amalgamated Association of Miners won support, but employer hostility destroyed the movement. The Cambrian Miners' Association, a locally based union, proved more successful and provided the context for the career of **William Abraham** (Mabon). The establishment in 1898 of the **South Wales Miners' Federation** (the Fed) proved a major turning point. Within a decade of its establishment, the south Wales miners had won a reputation for trade union militancy, a development in which Rhondda miners played a central role.

Working-class **radical**ism also found expression in electoral politics. By the general election of 1885, the Rhondda had been granted its own MP, and the seat was won by William Abraham, who trounced the Liberal coalowner Lewis Davis. Abraham was the first 'Labour' MP to represent a Welsh constituency although, as an upholder of the Lib-Lab tradition, he took his place without difficulty on the left wing of the **Liberal Party**. Dependent for his support upon the miners, he was obliged to become a **Labour Party** MP in 1908 when the Fed affiliated to that party. Thus was launched the Rhondda's so far unbroken succession of Labour MPs.

Ton Pentre in the Rhondda in 1905, with the Jerusalem chapel on the right

Abraham's moderation was not reflected in the views of the most articulate of the leaders of the Rhondda's miners. By the early 20th century, **socialist** and, increasingly, **syndicalist**, ideas were winning support as W. H. Mainwaring, Noah Rees, **A. J. Cook**, Will Hay and **Noah Ablett** argued their case at the Aberystwyth Café in Tonypandy. Industrial struggle and class conflict reached a crescendo in the **Tonypandy Riots** of 1911, and the ideas of the syndicalists found expression in *The Miners' Next Step*, published in Tonypandy in 1912. In that year, the Rhondda miners – the largest single unit within the Fed, which was in turn the largest single unit within the **Miners' Federation of Great Britain** – were the motivators of a strike held in all the coalfields of **Britain**, the first occasion for British miners jointly to withhold their labour. The issue was the minimum wage, and the miners were victorious, for the Miners' Minimum Wage Bill became law without delay. The events of 1911–12 were central to the growth of the Rhondda's reputation as one of Britain's greatest strongholds of working-class militancy.

With the onset of the First World War, there were among the Rhondda syndicalists those who argued that what they considered to be an imperialist war should be turned into a class war. In the event, most Rhondda miners proved obedient to the **government**'s demand that they should increase production, in particular to ensure that the British Navy – heavily dependent upon Welsh steam coal – would remain operative; this perhaps indicates that syndicalist beliefs were not as widespread as later legend suggests. Rhondda miners were, however, in the forefront of the strike of 1915, essentially a protest against the exorbitant profits received by coalowners as the price of coal soared. They also showed enthusiasm for the Bolshevik Revolution in Russia, with the Rhondda Socialist Society forming a key element in the coalition that founded the **Communist Party** of Great Britain in 1921. Bitterness over the failure at the time of the **Sankey** Commission in 1919 to wrest the collieries from capitalist control was a further factor in the leftward movement of Rhondda opinion, as were the events leading up to the **miners' strike** of 1921 and the **General Strike** of 1926.

The number of miners resident in the Rhondda peaked at 41,508 in 1921. Central to the ebullience of the Rhondda's radicals was the belief that there was a permanent and expanding demand for coal, a belief shattered by the **Depression**, which set in from the mid-1920s onwards. By 1932, when unemployment among insured adult males was 72.85% in Ferndale and 62.8% in Tonypandy, the vaunted power of the miners had been undermined. As elsewhere in the south Wales coalfield, **emigration** seemed to be the only solution; up to 50,000 people left the Rhondda between 1924 and 1939. To many, the Depression was seen as the result of the failure of capitalism, and in the Rhondda, more than in any other part of the south Wales coalfield, the answer seemed to be Communism – although the majority remained faithful to the Labour Party. (Support for Communism long survived the Depression. In 1979, **Annie Powell** of Llwynypia became the sole British Communist ever to be elected a mayor.)

The **Second World War** temporarily solved the unemployment problem. After the war, salvation seemed to lie in the nationalization of the coalmines, carried out on Vesting Day, 1 January 1947. Over the following decades, such hopes turned out to be false. In 1947, the Rhondda had over 15,000 miners. By 1984, there were miners only at Maerdy, where they played a heroic role in the strike of 1984–5. Indeed, perhaps the most memorable image of the Rhondda is that of the Maerdy miners on 5 March 1985 marching in procession to their doomed mine with their banners flying and their bands playing before the break of day. Now, the Rhondda has no miners at all. Efforts to create alternative sources of employment have had a degree of success, and commuting to Cardiff and elsewhere has offered new opportunities. Yet, the marked decrease in the population – from 167,900 in 1924 to 72,443 in 2001 – suggests that the Rhondda, once Wales's most dynamic economy, encapsulates the problems which have come in the wake of the collapse of Wales's one-time staple industry.

The Rhondda's administrative history reflects its demographic history. Initially, its sole body was the Ystradyfodwg parish vestry meeting. In 1870, most of its built-up area became the responsibility of the Ystradyfodwg Sanitary Board. In 1894, when parts of the parishes of **Llantrisant** and Llanwonno (*see* **Ynysybwl**) were added to that of Ystradyfodwg, the Rhondda **Urban District** Council was established. As the district had a population in excess of 100,000, the council was granted powers not dissimilar to those of a **county borough** – it had its own director of **education**, for example. The Rhondda's growing population led in 1918 to the division of the Rhondda constituency into the two constituencies of Rhondda West and Rhondda East. In 1955, when there was still optimism concerning the future of the coal industry, the urban district attained borough status. In 1974, population decline led to the reversion to being a single-member constituency. In the same year, Rhondda lost its borough status and became one of the six districts of the newly established county of **Mid Glamorgan**. Further demotion came in 1996 when the Rhondda became part of the county borough of **Rhondda Cynon Taff**, a change which meant that the Rhondda ceased to have any local government structure specific to itself. At the local government election of 1999, **Plaid [Genedlaethol] Cymru**, which had scored a spectacular vote in a by-election in Rhondda West in 1968, became the largest party on the Rhondda Cynon Taff Council, thus causing a break in the Labour Party's almost 100-year dominance of the Rhondda's politics. Also in 1999 there were the first elections to the **National Assembly for Wales**, the establishment of which had been endorsed by Rhondda voters in the referendum of 1997. At the election, victory went to the Plaid Cymru candidate, Geraint Davies. However, that party's hopes that it would have a similar victory in the British general election of 2001 proved to be illusory; Labour recaptured the Assembly seat in 2003, and retained it in the 2007 elections.

The readiness of the inhabitants of the Rhondda to vote for **devolution** and to support Plaid Cymru, together with their growing support for Welsh-medium schools, may be a reflection of the fact that the proportion of its inhabitants born in Wales is among the highest in Wales. Once famed

Terraced housing in the Rhondda Valley

for its ability to attract immigrants, many of whom came from outside Wales, the Rhondda's inhabitants have succeeded in weaving together the descendants of those immigrants, thereby creating what is the quintessence of a Welsh community. In the census of 1991, the last before the abolition of the district, the Rhondda consisted of 10,784 ha and had 78,346 inhabitants.

The communities of the Rhondda

CWM CLYDACH (487 ha; 3164 inhabitants)
Embracing the basin of the Clydach, a tributary of the Rhondda Fawr, the community contains the site of the Cambrian Colliery, where an industrial dispute sparked off the Tonypandy riots. **Rhys Davies**, the most prolific of Wales's English-language writers, and **Lewis Jones**, the Marxist novelist, were natives of Cwm Clydach. So also was the boxer **Tommy Farr**.

CYMMER (Cymer) (355 ha; 5109 inhabitants)
Located south of the confluence of the Rhondda Fawr and the Rhondda Fach, Cymmer, like Trehafod, was part of the coal empire of **W. T. Lewis** (Lord Merthyr). The Lewis Merthyr Colliery, where there are rare examples of the pithead gear once ubiquitous in the south Wales coalfield, is now the site of the Rhondda Heritage Park, widely but erroneously considered to be located in the community of Trehafod.

FERNDALE (Glyn Rhedynog) (380 ha; 4419 inhabitants)
Ferndale, where sinking shafts to the steam coal began in 1857, was the first place in Rhondda Fach to be intensively industrialized. Its workmen's hall (1907), one of the largest in the coalfield, is now in a parlous state. Ferndale was the birthplace of the actor **Stanley Baker**.

LLWYNYPIA (258 ha; 2253 inhabitants)
Described in 1803 as 'a region of beautiful fields', Llwynypia was intensively industrialized from 1862 onwards following the development of the collieries of the Scotsman **Archibald Hood**. The fact that Llwynypia was for long the location of the Rhondda's sole maternity hospital meant that for half a century and more, most of the natives of the Rhondda were born there.

MAERDY (1064 ha; 3441 inhabitants)
Maerdy is the archetypal pit village. Following the reaching of the Abergorci seam in 1876, its streets were laid out in a grid. In 1885, the Maerdy Colliery explosion killed 81 men. The colliery was associated with some of the most radical miners' leaders, A. J. Cook and **Arthur Horner** in particular. By the 1930s, so extensive was the support for Communism at Maerdy that it was known as **Little Moscow**. Photographs of the return of its miners to the pit following the conclusion of the miners' strike of 1984–5 provided the most poignant image of that tragic conflict. The closure of the pit in 1990 meant the end of the Rhondda as a coal-producing area.

PENTRE (581 ha; 5424 inhabitants)
Straddling the Rhondda Fawr south of Treorchy, Pentre contains the site of the original Ystradyfodwg parish church. St Peter's church (1890) is by far the largest of the Rhondda's **Anglican** churches. Pentre's Rhondda Engineering Works was the source of most of the colliery equipment used in the pits of south Wales. **Rhydwen Williams**, whose novels offer a portrayal of Rhondda society, was born at Pentre.

PEN-Y-GRAIG (481 ha; 5877 inhabitants)
Located at the Rhondda's south-west corner, Pen-y-graig's Naval Colliery was established by the Rowlands family, the sole natives of the Rhondda to become major coalowners. The community contains the offices of the Rhondda Cynon Taff County Borough, where the buildings are a far cry from the majestic Glamorgan County Hall in Cardiff's **Cathays Park**, the seat, until 1996, of the Rhondda's highest layer of local government.

PORTH (370 ha; 5944 inhabitants)
Located at the confluence of the Rhondda Fawr and Rhondda Fach, Porth sees itself as the capital of the Rhondda. Dinas was the site of the earliest commercial exploitation of Rhondda coal. The firm of Thomas and Evans, owner of a chain of grocery shops and manufacturer of **Corona** soft drinks, had its offices at Porth. The building in which the drinks were produced is now The Pop Factory, dedicated to pop **music**.

TONYPANDY (337 ha; 3495 inhabitants)
The chief settlement in the lower Rhondda Fawr, Tonypandy, as the site of the 1911 riots and the place of publication of *The Miners' Next Step*, was the fulcrum of Rhondda radicalism. The actor **Donald Houston** was born in Tonypandy.

TREALAW (286 ha; 3908 inhabitants)
Located across the Rhondda Fawr from Tonypandy, Trealaw was the home of **J. Kitchener Davies**, whose play *Cwm Glo* (1935) sought to explore the moral degradation brought about by the **Depression**.

TREHAFOD (164 ha; 816 inhabitants)
The southernmost of the Rhondda communities, Trehafod was part of the coal empire of **W. T. Lewis** (Lord Merthyr).

TREHERBERT (2156 ha; 6011 inhabitants)
Located at the head of the Rhondda Fawr valley where the road climbs to an elevation of 489 m on its way to **Rhigos**, the community contains Cwmsaerbren, the site of the earliest exploitation of Rhondda steam coal. Tynewydd House (1652) is the Rhondda's oldest dwelling.

TREORCHY (Treorci) (1330 ha; 8105 inhabitants)
Located where the valley of the Rhondda Fawr is at its widest, Treorchy has a spaciousness absent from other Rhondda townships. Deep mining began there in the 1860s under the aegis of David Davies of Llandinam, whose

The Rhondda: Blaenrhondda at the foot of Pen-pych

Ocean Coal Company, founded in 1887, came to dominate the district. Treorchy's **male voice choir** is among the best known in Wales. Following the demolition of the Workmen's Hall at **Abercynon**, the Parc and Dare Workmen's Hall is the largest in the south Wales coalfield. There is an imposing **hill-fort** on Mynydd Maendy.

TYLORSTOWN (Pendyrus) (590 ha; 4715 inhabitants)
Straddling the central part of the Rhondda Fach valley, the community contains the pilgrimage site of Penrhys, where an estate built to accommodate a thousand families was completed in 1969. Located at an elevation of 350 m, difficulty of access and the lack of amenities there have given rise to major social problems. Stanleytown offers a remarkable view of Rhondda terraced housing. Tylorstown **Conservative** Club is a very handsome building. The boxer **Jimmy Wilde** was a native of Tylorstown.

YNYSHIR (Ynys-hir) (441 ha; 3442 inhabitants)
Located in the lower Rhondda Fach valley, Ynyshir, like Cymmer and Trehafod, was part of the coal empire of W. T. Lewis (Lord Merthyr). Lady Lewis Colliery was opened in 1904.

YSTRAD (714 ha; 6320 inhabitants)
Straddling the central Rhondda Fawr valley, Ystrad contained the most profitable of the collieries of the **Cory** brothers. Tyntyle is a fine 17th-century **longhouse**.

RHONDDA CYNON TAFF (Rhondda Cynon Taf)
County borough (44,497 ha; 231,946 inhabitants)
Following the abolition of the county of Mid Glamorgan in 1996, two of the districts of the defunct county – **Cynon Valley** and the Rhondda – together with most of a third – **Taff-Ely** – were combined to form the **county borough** of Rhondda Cynon Taff. The county borough, which constitutes the heart of the south Wales coalfield, is, after Cardiff, the most populous of the county boroughs of Wales. In 2001, 21.08% of the county borough's inhabitants had some knowledge of **Welsh**, the percentages varying from 31.52% in **Rhigos** to 15.54% in **Gilfach Goch**; 10.26% of the inhabitants of the county borough were wholly fluent in the language.

RHOOSE (Y Rhws), Vale of Glamorgan
(1717 ha; 4875 inhabitants)
Located immediately west of Barry, the **community** contains the settlements of Rhoose, Font-y-gary, Porthkerry, Penmark, Fonmon and East Aberthaw. It is dominated by Cardiff International **Airport**, which developed from Rhoose military airport, a satellite of that at **St Athan**. Adjoining the terminal buildings is the huge British Airways Maintenance Complex; visible from almost every part of the **Vale of Glamorgan**, it is Wales's most obtrusive structure. Almost as dominating are the community's cement works and vast **limestone** quarries and the enormous **Iron Age** coastal earthwork of Bulwarks.

Rhoose with Font-y-gary has become a large and expanding dormitory village settlement, but East Aberthaw, Penmark, Fonmon and Porthkerry remain attractive hamlets with good examples of vernacular

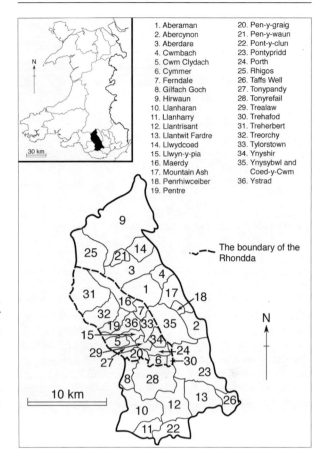

1. Aberaman
2. Abercynon
3. Aberdare
4. Cwmbach
5. Cwm Clydach
6. Cymmer
7. Ferndale
8. Gilfach Goch
9. Hirwaun
10. Llanharan
11. Llanharry
12. Llantrisant
13. Llantwit Fardre
14. Llwydcoed
15. Llwyn-y-pia
16. Maerdy
17. Mountain Ash
18. Penrhiwceiber
19. Pentre
20. Pen-y-graig
21. Pen-y-waun
22. Pont-y-clun
23. Pontypridd
24. Porth
25. Rhigos
26. Taffs Well
27. Tonypandy
28. Tonyrefail
29. Trealaw
30. Trehafod
31. Treherbert
32. Treorchy
33. Tylorstown
34. Ynyshir
35. Ynysybwl and Coed-y-Cwm
36. Ystrad

The communities of the county borough of Rhondda Cynon Taff

architecture. St Mary's church, Penmark is a substantial medieval church with a **Norman** chancel arch. Penmark Castle, a 13th-century stone replacement of a Norman ringwork, fell into ruin in the 15th century. St Curig's Church, Porthkerry is a delightful miniature building. Porthkerry House was the modest 19th-century home of the Romilly family, prominent in the history of Barry. Near it is the handsome viaduct completed in 1897 to carry the Vale of Glamorgan **Railway**.

The most interesting building within the community is Fonmon Castle, reputed to be Wales's oldest continuously inhabited house. It was acquired in 1664 by **Philip Jones**, **Cromwell**'s right-hand man in Wales, and remodelled in the 1760s for Robert Jones, an ardent supporter of Methodism. The remodelling included the construction of superb rococo ceilings. A later Robert Jones of Fonmon showed his disgust of titles by knighting all his **horses** and **dogs**.

RHOS *Cantref* (Dyfed)
The westernmost of the seven *cantrefi* of **Dyfed**, Rhos constituted the area between the Western **Cleddau** and St Bride's Bay. Following the **Norman** invasions, it became a marcher-lordship with its caput at **Haverfordwest**. During the existence of the **March**, Rhos (or Haverford), together with the associated lordship of **Walwyn's Castle**, was generally held by the owners of the lordship of **Pembroke**, although there were periods when its ruling family differed from that of Pembroke. The name survived as that of a post-**Acts of 'Union' hundred**.

751

The Knave hill-fort above the cliffs at Rhossili

RHOS *Cantref* (Gwynedd is Conwy)

With **Rhufoniog**, **Dyffryn Clwyd** and **Tegeingl**, Rhos was one of the four *cantrefi* of the **Perfeddwlad** (the middle country) or **Gwynedd Is Conwy**. Its **commotes** were **Creuddyn**, Uwch Dulas and Is Dulas. In 1284, Uwch Dulas and Is Dulas became part of the **march**er-lordship of **Denbigh**, and Creuddyn became part of **Caernarfonshire**. The **communities** of **Betws yn Rhos** and **Rhos-on-Sea** recall the name.

RHOSCOLYN, Isle of Anglesey
(925 ha; 484 inhabitants)

Occupying the southern part of Holy Island (Ynys Gybi; *see* **Islands**), the **community**'s sole centre of **population** is Four Mile Bridge, formerly the site of a ford, which, until the building of **Telford**'s **Holyhead road**, was the main crossing to the island. As in so many parts of **Anglesey**, the coast presents a hazard to **ship**ping; one of Anglesey's earliest **lifeboats** was established at Rhoscolyn c.1830.

RHOS-ON-SEA (Llandrillo-yn-Rhos),
Conwy (309 ha; 7110 inhabitants)

Comprising the western suburbs of **Colwyn Bay**, the **community** is dominated by Bryn Euryn, crowned by a much eroded **hill-fort**. The 16th-century ruins of Llys Euryn occupy the site of the seat of **Ednyfed Fychan** who was granted the *vill* in 1230. Capel Trillo on the foreshore may have 6th-century origins. The double-naved church of St Trillo contains 13th-century features which may be associated with Ednyfed Fychan. Rhos had one of Wales's nine **piers**; brought from Douglas, Isle of **Man**, in 1895, it was demolished in 1954.

RHOSLLANERCHRUGOG (Rhosllannerchrugog),
Wrexham (608 ha; 9439 inhabitants)

Located south-west of **Wrexham**, until the 19th century the area was a township of the **parish** of **Ruabon**. Its **coal** is first mentioned in the **Holt** Charter of 1563. Mining developed rapidly from the 1840s onwards. Houses constructed from locally made red bricks rose haphazardly on Rhos common, and also in the smaller adjoining settlements of Ponciau and Johnstown. By the early 20th century, Rhos's residents liked to boast (incorrectly) that they lived in the largest village in Wales. The **community** seems to have experienced selective migration, attracting a far higher proportion of **Welsh**-speaking migrants than did the other mining communities around Wrexham. Alone among those communities, it had until the 1970s a Welsh-speaking majority. With its choirs, bands, and its score and more chapels, Rhos developed a social and cultural life remarkably similar to that of the colliery settlements of the south. The interwar **depression** was a grievous experience, with unemployment among Rhos's insured males rising to 78.5% in November 1932. However, by the 21st century, the growth of service industries and general manufacturing was ensuring a degree of prosperity. The one-time centrality of coal is symbolized by the Miners' Institute (Y Stiwt), opened in the fateful year of 1926, the year of the **General Strike**. In the 1990s, local affection and hard work rescued the building from near dereliction.

Although its proportion of those wholly fluent in Welsh had fallen to 23.47% by 2001, Rhos maintains a youth **drama** company, which produces acclaimed productions through the medium of Welsh. The village has nurtured numerous cultural figures including the poet **I. D. Hooson** and the musician **Arwel Hughes**.

RHOSSILI (Rhosili), Swansea
(1020 ha; 299 inhabitants)

Even in a peninsula noted for its natural beauty, the **community**, situated at **Gower**'s south-west corner, has outstanding views, from the sculpted menace of the promontory of Worm's Head to the high open moorland of Rhossili Down, falling steeply to the long sands curving away to distant Burry Holms. A well-preserved medieval-style open field system lies near the village. Parts of the sheer and spectacular **limestone** coastal cliffs are owned by the **National Trust**. Goat's Hole is famous for the 1823 discovery of the skeleton of the 'Red Lady of Paviland', the remains of a young man who lived c.24,000 BC; he was a member of a sparse **hunting** community dwelling on the edges of the habitable world during a temporary retreat of the ice cover (*see* **Palaeolithic and Mesolithic Ages**). The community is rich in **Neolithic**, **Bronze Age** and **Iron Age** remains. The original church and village were overwhelmed by sand dunes c.1300. A replacement church was built above the cliffs; it contains a memorial to the Rhossili native **Edgar Evans**, who died in 1912 when participating in Scott's Antarctic expedition.

RHOSYBOL (Rhos-y-bol), Isle of Anglesey
(3018 ha; 1056 inhabitants)

Located immediately south of **Amlwch**, the **community** includes the upper reaches of Llyn Alaw. The development of Rhosybol village on the **Llanerch-y-medd**–Amlwch **road** (the B511) led in 1896 to the creation of the Rhosybol civil **parish**. Clorach, at the community's southern end, was the legendary meeting place of the two **Anglesey saints, Seiriol** and **Cybi**. According to **Giraldus Cambrensis**, Hugh the Fat (**Hugh of Avranches**), earl of Chester, met his death after desecrating Llandyfrydog church. The **Celtic** scholar **John Rhŷs** was a schoolmaster at Rhosybol from *c.*1860 to 1865. From 1972 until 1990, Rhosgoch was the site of a large **oil** storage depot connected with the Amlwch–Stanlow pipeline.

'RHOSYMEDRE' Hymn tune

A **hymn** tune by John David Edwards (1805–85). Published in the **periodical** *Y Drysorfa* in 1838 under the name 'Lovely', and subsequently included in most Welsh hymnals, it forms the basis of a prelude for organ by Ralph Vaughan Williams. Rhosymedre is a village in the **community** of **Cefn**.

RHOSYN A RHITH (*Coming Up Roses*; 1986) Film

Stephen Bayly's genial, politically salient **Welsh-language** comedy, with a screenplay by Ruth Carter, uses the battle to save a **cinema** in the south Wales **coal**field as a metaphor for de-industrialization in the Thatcher years. The **film** features Dafydd Hywel as a timorous projectionist shedding inhibitions alongside Iola Gregory's feisty cinema usherette. The film confirmed the promise of Bayly and Carter, a promise made clear by **S4C**'s series, *Joni Jones* (1982) and the **drama** *And Pigs Might Fly* (1984).

RHOSYR, Isle of Anglesey
(4440 ha; 2169 inhabitants)

Constituting the south-western corner of **Anglesey**, the **community** – the largest in the **county** – contains the villages of Newborough, Dwyran and Llangaffo. Together with **Aberffraw** and **Cemaes**, Rhosyr was one of the three *cantrefi* of **Anglesey** and consisted of the **commotes** of **Dindaethwy** and **Menai**. In 1974, the name was revived as that of a community. Near Newborough lies the commotal centre, the only court of the princes of **Gwynedd** to have undergone excavation (1990s). Newborough, incorporated as a **borough** in 1303, was established as a home for the Welsh driven from Llanfaes (*see* **Beaumaris**) by Edward I. Llanddwyn, a delectable headland cut off by high tide, contains a ruined 16th-century church, allegedly built on the site of the shrine of **Dwynwen**, patron **saint** of Welsh lovers; a **lighthouse** was erected there in 1846.

The sand dunes of Newborough Warren owe their origins to a great storm in 1330. In 1948, the planting of the 800-ha Newborough Forest began, with the aim of restricting the spread of the dunes. St Peter's church, Newborough (14th century) contains several medieval inscribed stones. Llangaffo church is a local landmark. The area was for long famous for the weaving of marram grass into ropes and mats (*see* **Straw and Marram**). The ferry across the **Menai Strait** from Tal-y-foel to **Caernarfon** continued into the second half of the 20th century.

RHUDDLAN, Denbighshire
(1385 ha; 4296 inhabitants)

Located immediately south of **Rhyl**, Rhuddlan seems to have been the main seat of **Gruffudd ap Llywelyn** (d.1063).

Rhuddlan Castle

In 1073, Robert of Rhuddlan, cousin of **Hugh of Avranches**, the **Norman** earl of Chester, built a motte-and-bailey and established a **borough** on the banks of the **Clwyd**. Evidence of them survives at Twthill. In 1277, Edward I accepted the submission of **Llywelyn ap Gruffudd** at Rhuddlan. Rhuddlan Castle, one of the first wave of Wales's Edwardian castles, was linked to the sea by a wide navigable **canal**. A concentric castle with six round towers, much of it survived the slighting it underwent following its capture by the Parliamentarians in 1646. At Rhuddlan in 1284, Edward promulgated the Statute of Rhuddlan (*see* **Rhuddlan, The Statute of**) , but there is no evidence linking the promulgation with Rhuddlan's so-called Parliament House (late 13th century). Of the Dominican friary (*see* **Friars**), established *c.*1258, some 14th-century fragments survive. St Mary's, built *c.*1300, became a double-naved church in the 15th century. It contains the tomb (*c.*1290), originally located in the friary, of an exiled Syrian bishop. Pengwern is a Palladian-style mansion built in the 1770s. Rhuddlan contains some imposing chapels. (For Morfa Rhuddlan, *see* **Kinmel Bay and Towyn**.) The **commote** of Rhuddlan was one of the three commotes of the *cantref* of **Tegeingl**. Rhuddlan was the name of one of **Flintshire**'s five post-**Act of 'Union'** hundreds (*see below*).

RHUDDLAN District

Following the abolition of **Flintshire** in 1974, Rhuddlan was created as one of the six districts of the new **county** of **Clwyd**. It consisted of what had been the **urban districts** of **Prestatyn** and **Rhyl** and the **rural district** of **St Asaph**. In 1996, the district became part of the reconstituted **Denbighshire**. It was broadly coterminous with the medieval **commote** of Rhuddlan.

RHUDDLAN, The Statute of (1284)

Also known as the Statute of Wales and enacted by Edward I on 19 March 1284, the Statute divided the **Principality** of north Wales, the core of the lands of **Llywelyn ap Gruffudd**, into three **counties**, **Anglesey**, **Caernarfonshire** and **Merioneth**. The king's representative was the justiciar of north Wales or **Snowdon**, who was both governor and judge; such an office had existed in the Principality of south Wales (comprising **Carmarthenshire** and **Cardiganshire**) since 1280. A fourth county, **Flintshire**, created in the north-east out of the lands left over from the creation of four new **march**er-lordships, came under the authority of the justiciar of Chester. The English office of sheriff was introduced in each county and a hierarchy of courts established, with the Welsh **commote** court retained at the local level. Under the statute, English criminal **law** was introduced, while Welsh law remained in civil actions; much of the text of the Statute is concerned with details of English legal procedure. The Statute has been described as 'the first colonial constitution'.

RHUFONIOG *Cantref*

With **Rhos**, **Dyffryn Clwyd** and **Tegeingl**, Rhufoniog was one of the four *cantrefi* of the **Perfeddwlad** (the middle country). Its **commotes** were Uwch Aled, Is Aled and **Ceinmeirch**. In 1282, it became part of the **march**er-lordship of **Denbigh**.

RHYFEL Y SAIS BACH (The war of the little Englishman)

Opposition to **enclosures** of **common land** was widespread in early 19th-century Wales. One of the most celebrated confrontations occurred in 1820–6 when Augustus

The Jovial Jesters, Rhyl, 1911

Brackenbury, an affluent native of Lincolnshire, bought 345 ha of land on Mynydd Bach in mid-**Cardiganshire** (*see* **Lledrod** and **Llangwyryfon**). Poor people and squatters, many of them disguised in **women**'s clothes and with blackened faces, assembled at night to scupper his plan to erect buildings on his land. Each time Brackenbury built a house, it was razed to the ground. The climax occurred on 24 May 1826 when nearly 600 rioters destroyed his third house with pickaxes. As a result, Brackenbury sold his land and took flight.

RHYL (Y Rhyl), Denbighshire
(734 ha; 24,889 inhabitants)
The largest town in **Denbighshire** (although in **Flintshire** until 1974), the name may be from an old form of the **English** 'hill', although there is no obvious hill in the vicinity. Until the **Rhuddlan** Marsh Embankment Trust Act (1794), the area had few inhabitants. Its oldest house is reputedly Tŷ'n y Rhyl, home of the antiquarian **Angharad Llwyd**. Visitors began to arrive in the early 19th century, travelling by paddle steamer from **Liverpool** and landing at Foryd – the estuary of the **Clwyd**. With the opening of the coastal **railway** in 1848, there was a rapid increase in the number of visitors, not only from Merseyside but also from all over northern Wales, where Rhyl came to be considered the ideal destination of **Sunday school** trips. In 1894, when the Rhyl **urban district** was established, the town had a settled **population** of 6500; its summer population could be 50,000 and more, creating a boom in the building of hotels and boarding houses. As a holiday resort, Rhyl, with its broad 3-km promenade, developed a markedly populist character, in distinct contrast with the more genteel resorts of **Llandudno** and **Colwyn Bay**. Of its 19th-century buildings, the most distinguished are St Thomas's, an ambitious church (1869) designed by George Gilbert Scott, and the Town Hall (1876) with its lively **clock** tower.

Among the many entrepreneurs who built a **pier**, baths, theatres and amusements of all kinds, **Arthur Cheetham** (1864–1936) is important as a pioneer of **film**. Rhyl **cinemas** provided the architect **Colwyn Foulkes** with opportunities to excel. Rhyl pier (1867) was demolished in 1972. The Sun Centre (1976–80) covers 1.3 ha and contains bathing pools, an overhead monorail and tropical vegetation. With the changes in holiday habits, Rhyl has ceased to attract its traditional clientele – families seeking an annual holiday. As a consequence, its renowned Ocean Beach funfair, established in 1911, was closed in 2007. Many of its boarding houses have been turned into apartments for those living on social security payments, causing parts of the town to be among the most impoverished places in Wales. In 2001, 22.59% of the inhabitants of Rhyl had some grasp of the **Welsh language**, the lowest percentage for any of Denbighshire's **communities**.

RHYMNEY (Rhymni), Caerphilly
(2172 ha; 8757 inhabitants)
Located in the upper reaches of the valley of the **Rhymney**, the **community** includes the town of Rhymney and the settlements of Pontlottyn, Abertysswg, Twyncarno and Butetown. **Iron**making began at Rhymney in 1800; the role of the metal in the area is commemorated by a monument at the town's entrance. Parts of the Upper Furnace works survive. Butetown, named after the chief local landlord, the marquess of Bute (*see* **Stuart family**), was intended as a model industrial village. Built *c.*1804, it consists of three parallel rows of houses enhanced by Palladian touches. Nothing remains of the Bute Ironworks, erected in a neo-Egyptian style in 1828. The **truck system** lasted longer in Rhymney than in any other part of the south Wales coalfield. The civil servant **Thomas Jones** (1870–1955) delighted in his Rhymney roots, as did **Idris Davies**, the pre-eminent **English-language** poet of the **depression of the interwar years**. Twyncarno was the last place in the former **Monmouthshire** where Welsh survived as the community language. St David's, Rhymney, was for long the sole **Anglican** church in the **diocese** of **Monmouth** where services were conducted in Welsh.

RHYMNEY (Rhymni) River (58 km)
The Rhymney rises at *c.*570 m on the western slopes of Mynydd **Llangynidr** in the **community** of **Talybont-on-Usk**. The town of **Rhymney**, a one-time **iron**making centre, stands on the banks of the infant **river**. The Rhymney flows southwards past the former **coal**mining settlements of **New Tredegar**, **Bargoed**, **Pengam** and **Maesycwmmer** to **Caerphilly**, where it turns eastwards towards **Newport**. It then swings back south-westwards to flow into the sea in eastern **Cardiff**. The river's sole substantial tributary is the Bargod Rhymni (*see* **Darran Valley**).

RHYMNEY VALLEY (Cwm Rhymni)
One-time district
Following the abolition of the **counties** of **Glamorgan** and **Monmouthshire** in 1974, Rhymney Valley was created as one of the six districts of the new county of **Mid Glamorgan**. It consisted of what had been the **urban districts** of **Caerphilly** and **Gelligaer** and part of the **rural district** of **Cardiff**, in Glamorgan, and the urban districts of **Rhymney** and **Bedwas and Machen**, and part of that of **Bedwellty**, in Monmouthshire. In 1996, the district, together with that of **Islwyn**, became the **borough** and county of Caerphilly. For electoral purposes, the upper part of the one-time district is in the constituency of **Merthyr** and Rhymney, and its lower part in that of Caerphilly.

RHYS AP GRUFFUDD (The Lord Rhys; d.1197)
Prince of Deheubarth
The youngest son of **Gruffudd ap Rhys ap Tewdwr** (d.1137) of **Deheubarth**, Rhys came to power in 1155. His attacks on his Anglo-**Norman** neighbours provoked four royal campaigns (1158–63). In 1163, he was briefly imprisoned and in the same year did homage to the king at Woodstock, along with **Owain Gwynedd** and Malcolm IV of **Scotland**. His alliance with Owain in 1164 led to Henry II's abortive Welsh campaign a year later (*see* **English monarchs and Wales**).

The failure of this campaign – along with other pressures, including the rise of Cambro-Norman power in **Ireland** following the invasion of the island by Richard de **Clare** in 1170 – led to Henry reconsidering his Welsh policy. For the rest of his reign, it was based on a friendly personal relationship with Rhys, the most powerful ruler in Wales after the death of Owain Gwynedd in 1170. In 1172, at **Laugharne**, Rhys was appointed justiciar of south Wales, which meant that he was the royal representative there as well as a Welsh prince. Friendship with the king meant that Anglo-Welsh crises could be defused and when Henry's sons rebelled in 1173, Rhys sent one of his sons and a military force to France to assist him. He led the Welsh rulers who met the king at Gloucester in 1175 and at **Oxford** in 1177. But this stability, based on a personal relationship, did not survive Henry's death in 1189. Richard I was less than tactful in his dealings with Rhys, who also had to contend with the restlessness of his own sons. In 1195, he was briefly imprisoned by two of them; he was soon released but the episode foreshadowed the impending power struggle among his heirs. A successful campaign in the middle **March** in 1196 was followed by his death in April 1197 and his burial in **St David's** Cathedral.

The Lord Rhys was one of the greatest native Welsh rulers. As one of the great lords of the Angevin empire, he was part of a cosmopolitan feudal world and that world's influence may have been behind the **eisteddfod** which he held at **Cardigan** in 1176; at the same time, he was a Welsh prince who used the marriages of his children to buttress his position as the dominant native ruler. Among his religious benefactions were the endowing of the **Cistercian** monasteries of **Whitland** (*see* **Llanboidy**) and Strata Florida (*see* **Ystrad Fflur**) and the foundation of the **Premonstratensian** abbey of **Talyllychau**.

The alleged tomb of Rhys ap Gruffudd (The Lord Rhys) at St David's Cathedral

RHYS AP GRUFFUDD (d.1356)
Soldier and administrator

A descendant of **Ednyfed Fychan** and a kinsman of **Dafydd ap Gwilym**, Sir Rhys ap Gruffudd was effectively the viceroy of the **Principality** of south Wales for much of the first half of the 14th century. He may have been the patron of Einion Offeiriad (d.1349), considered to have been the author of a highly influential bardic grammar. He held numerous offices under Edward II and Edward III, to both of whom he showed conspicuous loyalty, and he was often called on for military service in **Scotland** or France, taking part in the battle of Crécy in 1346. In 1327, he attempted to rescue the deposed Edward II from Berkeley Castle, but his indispensability was such that he was soon restored to favour.

RHYS AP MAREDUDD (d.1292) Insurrectionist
The son of Maredudd ap Rhys of Dryslwyn (*see* **Llangathen**), who had opposed **Llywelyn ap Gruffudd**, Rhys was loyal to Edward I during the final Welsh war of 1282; after the **Edwardian conquest**, he was rewarded with the forfeited lands of some of his kinsmen (*see* **Rhys Wyndod**). However, he found the pressure of the royal administration increasingly irksome and, in 1287, he rose in revolt. He received little support; many probably remembered who he had supported in 1282. The revolt was put down with extensive Welsh support; Rhys was captured in 1292 and executed at York.

RHYS AP TEWDWR (d.1093) King of Deheubarth
A member of the royal line of **Deheubarth**, Rhys seized power there in 1078 but was driven into exile in **Ireland** three years later. He returned the same year with **Gruffudd ap Cynan** of Gwynedd and won back his kingdom at the battle of **Mynydd Carn**. It may have been the presence in the battle of Hiberno-Norse mercenaries from Dublin that led to William I's invasion of south Wales and advance to **St David's** in 1081. William seems to have reached an agreement with Rhys, recognizing him as ruler of Deheubarth, and Rhys undertook to pay the king an annual tribute (*see* **English Monarchs and Wales**). While William lived, Rhys was secure, but after the king's death in 1087, Norman incursions intensified. **Brycheiniog** was invaded by **Bernard de Neufmarché**, and Rhys, forced to respond, was killed at Battle (**Yscir**) near **Brecon** in 1093. The revival of the power of Deheubarth was the work of his son, **Gruffudd ap Rhys ap Tewdwr** (d.1137), and his grandson, **Rhys ap Gruffudd** (The Lord Rhys; d.1197).

RHYS AP THOMAS (1449–1525)
Soldier and administrator

The grandson of **Gruffudd ap Nicolas** and a descendant, through his mother, of **Ednyfed Fychan**, his support of Henry **Tudor** in 1485 may have been instrumental in bringing others in Wales to Henry's side. He fought at **Bosworth** and was knighted by the new king. He was rewarded with various offices, including that of chamberlain of south Wales. In 1505, he was made a Knight of the Garter and, in 1507, he organized a tournament at **Carew** as a symbol of the Anglo-Welsh reconciliation symbolized by Henry VII. Both Henry VII and Henry VIII depended on him to manage and govern south Wales. His tomb is in St Peter's church, **Carmarthen**. His grandson and heir, Rhys ap Gruffudd, was executed for alleged treason in 1531. In 1730, Rhys's descendants, the Rice family, were granted the title of Baron Dynevor (*see* **Llandeilo**).

RHYS FYCHAN AP RHYS AP MAELGWN (d.1302) Welsh lord

A descendant of **Rhys ap Gruffudd** (The Lord Rhys; d.1197), he supported **Llywelyn ap Gruffudd** in the war of 1276–7 and was one of the five barons whose homage the prince was allowed to retain under the terms of the **Treaty of Aberconwy**. After the war of 1282–3, he made his peace with the king, serving him until his death.

RHYS GOCH ERYRI (fl.1386/7–c.1440) Poet

According to tradition, Rhys, who lived at **Beddgelert**, was a supporter of **Owain Glyndŵr**. After the **Glynwdŵr Revolt**, his chief patron was Gwilym ap Gruffudd of Penrhyn (*see* **Llandygai**). Rhys satirized a **fox** that had killed his peacock, and the poem allegedly caused the death of the fox. He debated with Llywelyn ab y Moel and **Siôn Cent**, countering Siôn's charge of bardic mendacity by claiming that the muse derived from the Holy Spirit.

RHYS GRYG (d.1234) Welsh lord

The fourth son of **Rhys ap Gruffudd** (The Lord Rhys; d.1197) of **Deheubarth** and a leading figure in Welsh politics after the death of his father, he inherited **Cantref Mawr** and was usually a supporter of **Llywelyn ap Iorwerth**. He died of wounds sustained in the abortive siege of **Carmarthen** in 1234.

RHYS WYNDOD (d.1302) Welsh lord

The great-grandson of **Rhys Gryg** and lord of **Dinefwr** and **Llandovery**, he was one of the lords who remained with **Dafydd ap Gruffudd** until the end of the war of 1282–3. His confiscated lands were granted to **Rhys ap Maredudd** and he spent the rest of his life in **prison**.

RHYS, E[dward] Prosser (1901–45)
Poet, editor and publisher

A native of Mynydd Bach (*see* **Llangwyryfon**), he followed a career in journalism, editing *Baner ac Amserau Cymru* from 1923 until his death. His sonnet sequence 'Atgof', which won the National **Eisteddfod** crown in 1924, touched on the subject of youthful **homosexuality**, and created a furore. As an editor and publisher with Gwasg Aberystwyth and the Clwb Llyfrau Cymreig (Welsh Books Club), Prosser Rhys was an influential literary figure. His collected poems, published posthumously in 1950, include the patriotic poem 'Cymru'.

RHYS, Ernest (1899–1946) Editor and writer

Ernest Rhys, whose father was from **Carmarthen**, was born in **London**, and spent six years of his childhood in his father's hometown. He is remembered chiefly as editor of Everyman's Library, a series of inexpensive editions published by Dent, of which 983 titles appeared before his death. Besides poetry and novels, he published two volumes of autobiography: *Everyman Remembers* (1931) and *Wales England Wed* (1940). He was a leading figure in the **Celtic Twilight** movement, and much of his work has a Welsh or **Cel**tic background.

RHŶS, John (1840–1915) Scholar

Born near Ponterwyd (**Blaenrheidol**), Rhŷs became the first professor of **Cel**tic at **Oxford** in 1877 and principal of Jesus College in 1895. His first and perhaps most important book was *Lectures on Welsh Philology* (1877), which used the methods of comparative philology to study the development of **Welsh**. He also edited, with **J. Gwenogfryn Evans**, the text of *The Mabinogion* from *The Red Book of Hergest* and other medieval works. Among his other books were *Celtic Britain* (1882), *Studies in the Arthurian Legend* (1891) and *Celtic Folklore, Welsh and Manx* (2 vols., 1901), which was the first study to identify significant differences between the Welsh literary folk tradition and the Gaelic tradition of **Ireland** and **Scotland**. He was knighted in 1907. When principal of Jesus College, he resisted the suggestion that the college should provide bathrooms on the grounds that 'the young men are only up for eight weeks'.

RHYS, Keidrych (1915–87) Editor and poet

Born William Ronald Rees Jones at Bethlehem (**Llangadog**), he changed his name on becoming a journalist in **London** (the Keidrych or Geidrych is a stream which joins the **Tywi** at Bethlehem). In 1939, he married **Lynette Roberts**. They settled in Llanybri (**Llansteffan**), but divorced 10 years later. A selection of his poems appeared as *The Van Pool* in 1942, but he is remembered particularly as the editor of the anthology *Modern Welsh Poetry* (1944) and of the influential **periodical** *Wales* (1937–40; 1943–9; 1958–60).

RHYS, Morgan (1716–79) Hymnwriter

Born in **Cilycwm**, a district where early Methodists were active, Rhys was a teacher in **circulating schools** (1757–75). He spent his last years at Cwm Gwaun Hendy, a farm in **Llanfynydd**, **Carmarthenshire**. Between 1755 and 1775, he published some dozen collections of **hymns** and elegies. Every Welsh hymnal contains examples of his work, which is the muscular expression of a deep spiritual experience; it has won him a safe place in the front rank of the Welsh hymnists of the **Methodist Revival**.

RHYS, Morgan John (1760–1804)
Radical activist and pioneer

Llanbradach-born Morgan John Rhys was among the most active of those Welsh **radicals** who were inspired by American Independence (1776–83) and the French Revolution of 1789. He campaigned throughout his relatively short life for peace, the abolition of **slavery**, the rights of Native Americans, and religious and political freedom, writing numerous pamphlets in support of these principles. After serving as a **Baptist** minister in **Pontypool** (1787–91) and following a period of residence in Paris, in 1793 he launched *Y Cylch-grawn Cynmraeg* [*sic*], the first **Welsh-language** political **periodical**. In 1794, he emigrated to the United States and changed his **surname** to Rhees. After travelling widely and establishing a school and church for blacks in Savannah, Georgia, in 1795 he bought land in

Cambria County, **Pennsylvania**, on which to establish a Welsh colony. Though the Beulah colony was short-lived, nearby Ebensburg became an important Welsh settlement. The philosopher **Rush Rhees** was a descendant of his.

RHYS, Siôn Dafydd (John Davies of Brecon; 1534–c.1619) Scholar

Llanfaethlu-born Siôn Dafydd Rhys was the nephew of Bishop **Richard Davies** (?1501–81), and like him studied in **Oxford**. From there he went to Italy, and graduated in medicine at Siena. He was a schoolmaster in Pistoia before returning to Wales and being appointed (1574) headmaster of **Friars** School, **Bangor**. He later moved south, living first in the **Cardiff** area, then near **Brecon**, where he worked as a doctor and devoted himself to his humanist interests.

Siôn Dafydd Rhys is one of the most versatile products of the **Renaissance** period in Wales. While in Italy, he composed works on Greek and **Latin** grammar, together with an important book on the pronunciation of Italian (1569). Back in Wales, he published his weightiest work – on **Welsh** grammar, *Cambrobrytannicae Cymraecaeve Linguae Institutiones* (1592), written in Latin in order to inform foreign scholars about the language and literature of Wales. He is thought to have collaborated with Richard Davies on translating the Old Testament into Welsh. He was, however, a reluctant Protestant and he may have played a part in some of the activities of the Counter-Reformation, especially the secret **printing** of books.

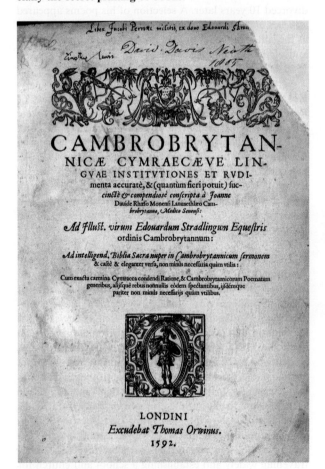

The title page of Siôn Dafydd Rhys's Welsh grammar, 1592

RICHARD, Edward (1714–77) Scholar and poet

Educated at **Carmarthen** Grammar School, Richard spent his whole career as schoolmaster in his native **Ystrad Meurig**, gaining renown as a teacher of Greek and **Latin**. His best-known pupil was **Evan Evans** (Ieuan Fardd; 1731–88). Edward Richard's claim to poetic distinction rests almost entirely on two poems, 'Bugeilgerdd Gruffudd a Meurig', a pastoral in dialogue form published in 1767, and his other, lesser-known pastoral 'Hywel ac Iwan'.

RICHARD, Henry (1812–88) Politician

In 1848, Henry Richard, a native of **Tregaron** and a **Congregational** minister, was appointed secretary of the International Peace Society, a movement that advocated the resolution of international conflict by negotiation and arbitration; he figured prominently in the society's conferences and publications. His *Letters on the Social and Political Condition of Wales* (1866) had a profound impact, especially on **Gladstone**. In 1868, he was elected as one of the two **Liberal** MPs for **Merthyr Tydfil**. Once in parliament, he continued to advocate **pacificist** measures, succeeding in July 1873 in carrying a motion on international arbitration. He also advocated the removal of denominational religious instruction from schools, and was a keen critic of Forster's **Education** Act of 1870. However, he was more reluctant than some of his fellow Welsh Liberal MPs to press for **disestablishment** specifically for Wales. He was closely involved with efforts to acquire state funding for the University College at **Aberystwyth** (*see* **University of Wales, Aberystwyth**), and in 1880 served on the committee of enquiry into Welsh intermediate and higher education (*see* **Aberdare Report**). He is commemorated by a statue in Tregaron (*see* **Radicalism**).

RICHARD, Timothy (1845–1919) Missionary

The **missionaries** sent out into the world from Wales in the 19th and early 20th centuries were often among the most able men and **women** of their time. Perhaps the most gifted of them all was Timothy Richard, who was born at Ffaldybrenin (**Llanycrwys**). In 1869, the **Baptist** Missionary Society sent him to China, where, until 1915, he laboured first in Chafoo, then in Shantung and Shansi and finally in Shanghai. His accomplishments as a scholar, teacher, author, philanthropist, missionary statesman, mandarin and adviser to the court (he more or less governed China for a time) made his name – 'Li T'i-mo-tai' – a household word throughout the land. Indeed, he enjoyed greater power than any Welshman in history, apart from **David Lloyd George**. He was honoured by the Chinese with membership of the Order of the Double Dragon.

RICHARD THOMAS AND BALDWINS LTD

At the end of the **Second World War**, which had disrupted plans for the development of the steel (*see* **Iron and Steel**) and **tinplate** industries, **Richard Thomas and Company**, the dominant force in sheet and tinplate manufacture in south Wales, combined with Baldwins, the English Midlands steel firm (partly owned by the family of the politician Stanley Baldwin), whose substantial Welsh interests included the **Briton Ferry**, **Port Talbot** and **Margam** steelworks. Expediency determined a further amalgamation, and, within two years, what was generally referred to as RTB made a significant contribution to the establishment of the **Steel Company of Wales**.

RTB continued to develop independently with **Ebbw Vale**, the Redbourne Works in Lincolnshire, and smaller steel and tinplate works in Wales. The bulk of British steelmaking capacity was privatized after the nationalization of 1949–51, but RTB remained in public hands and was used to ensure the supply of sheet steel when it built the **Llanwern Steelworks** (1962). Upon renationalization in 1967, RTB was absorbed into the British Steel Corporation.

RICHARD THOMAS AND COMPANY

Richard Thomas and Company, which dominated the **tinplate** industry during the first half of the 20th century, was founded by the **London**-born metal-merchant Richard Thomas (1838–1916) who, in 1865, entered the tinplate trade at **Margam** by borrowing funds to acquire **iron** and tinplate works. With his five sons, he formed, in 1884, the private company of Richard Thomas and Sons, which initially grew through the ploughing back of profits, and later by absorbing smaller competitors such as the Grovesend Company and its 12 works (1923), and the Melingriffith works (1934). By the 1930s, the company controlled nearly 70% of **Britain**'s sheet steel and tinplate capacity, absorbing the **Ebbw Vale** Company in 1934 and transforming it into Britain's first continuous strip mill. In 1945, the company combined with the English Midlands steel firm, Baldwins, to form **Richard Thomas and Baldwins Ltd**.

RICHARDS, Alun [Morgan] (1929–2004) Writer

Among the most prolific Welsh writers of the 20th century, Alun Richards was born in **Pontypridd** and educated at **Swansea** where – in the Mumbles area – he eventually settled after a varied career as a probation officer, teacher and seaman. He is probably best remembered for his writing about the sea – scripts for the popular 1970s television series *The Onedin Line*, for instance, and his novel based on the Mumbles **lifeboat**, *Ennal's Point* (1977), which was also adapted for television. But it is as a trenchant and comic chronicler of post-**Second World War**, de-industrializing Wales that he deserves lasting recognition. Although most of his finest writings – among them the novel *Home to an Empty House* (1973) and the short-story collections *Dai Country* (1973) and *The Former Miss Merthyr Tydfil* (1979) – appear to focus on what he characterized as 'the immensely unattractive world of men', it is the **women** of his fiction who emerge as the defining truth-tellers. Other significant works include *The Penguin Book of Welsh Short Stories* (1976), which he edited, and a biography of the **rugby** player **Carwyn James** (1984).

RICHARDS, Aubrey (1920–2000) Actor

Lugubrious, wraith-like Aubrey Richards was equally persuasive in comic roles or as the incarnation of avarice and evil. **Swansea**-born Richards was Mog Edwards in the 1950s **London** stage version of **Dylan Thomas**'s radio play *Under Milk Wood*, and in the first 'live' television version (1957). He was an amusingly intense Rev. Eli Jenkins in the 1971 **film** of *Under Milk Wood*, and a poisonous deacon in the 1960 television rendition of *How Green Was My Valley*.

Ceri Richards, *Costerwoman*, 1939

RICHARDS, [Henry] Brinley (1819–85) Musician

The son of an organist and **music** shop proprietor in **Carmarthen**, Richards gained the patronage of the Duke of Newcastle and entered the Royal Academy of Music, **London** in 1835. He became a distinguished pianist and choral adjudicator. He was a prominent member of the **Cymmrodorion**, and his *Songs of Wales* (1873), which contained his '**God Bless the Prince of Wales**', did much to propagate a particular vision of Welshness – from outside Wales – in the Victorian period.

RICHARDS, Ceri (1903–71) Artist

Acknowledged internationally as one of the most significant British painters of the 20th century, Ceri Richards was born in **Dunvant**, the son of a **tinplate** worker and musician. The musical background of his home life echoes through his work. Richards studied at **Swansea** School of Art and at the Royal College in **London**, where he lived for most of his life, although he taught at **Cardiff** during the **Second World War**. Superb draughtsmanship underpinned his work, and the ease with which he absorbed all manner of influences from mainland Europe, stamping his own considerable artistic identity upon them, was a mark of his exceptional creativity. He applied his skills to theatre, **stained glass**, **architecture** and illustration. His designs for the poetry of **Dylan Thomas** and **Vernon Watkins** are especially memorable.

Richards's work developed a Surrealist tendency during the 1930s, under the influence of Max Ernst and Jean Arp in particular, and there were times when it became almost abstract. In London, he produced striking pictures of the city's 'pearly kings and queens', and contributed to the 'Objective Abstractions' exhibition in the Zwemmer Gallery in 1934. Briefly a war artist, his drawings of tin-plate workers elegantly express the assured choreography of practised routine. His interpretation of the relationship of the visual arts to **music** took many forms. In his responses to Debussy's *La Cathédrale Engloutie*, he created some of the most sumptuous images of his time.

RICHARDS, Elfyn (1914–95)
Aeronautical and vibration engineer
Born in **Barry** and educated at **Aberystwyth** and **Cambridge**, Richards spent many years in the British **aviation** industry, where he achieved a high reputation as an aeronautical engineer. In 1950, he became professor of aeronautical **engineering** at Southampton University, where he established the Institute of Vibration Research and became recognized as a world authority in the fields of vibrations, acoustics and noise. He was vice-chancellor of Loughborough University from 1967 to 1973.

RICHARDS, [Grafton] Melville (1910–73) Scholar
In the field of Welsh **place name** studies, Melville Richards's contribution remains unsurpassed, and his

Norman Riches

remarkable collection of Welsh place names (containing more than 300,000 research slips) is now deposited at the **University of Wales, Bangor** where he was professor of **Welsh** (1965–73). Born at Ffairfach (**Dyffryn Cennen**), he graduated at **Swansea**, and was appointed lecturer there in 1936. The widely held belief that he filled **Saunders Lewis**'s vacant post is a misconception, as plans to create a post for him were well afoot before the fire at **Penyberth**. He was subsequently a lecturer in **Celt**ic at **Liverpool** (1948–65).

RICHARDS (Jones), Nansi (Telynores Maldwyn; 1888–1979) Harpist
Born at **Pen-y-Bont-Fawr**, Nansi Richards (Jones was her married name) won with the triple **harp** at the National *Eisteddfodau* of 1908, 1909 and 1910. After switching to the modern pedal-harp at the Guildhall School of **Music**, **London**, her independent disposition took her to the stage, music halls and variety theatres; she toured America in 1923–5. A much-loved figure in eisteddfodic circles and the *noson lawen*, she became known as 'Queen of the Harp'. During her last years, she returned to her first love, the triple harp, and her unique style of playing won her widespread popularity.

RICHARDS, Paul [Westmacott] (1908–95) Botanist
Born in Surrey but raised in **Cardiff**, Richards developed an early interest in botany, and graduated at **Cambridge**. Following numerous overseas expeditions, and passionately committed to the significance and survival of rainforests, he wrote the definitive *Tropical Rain Forest: an ecological study* (1952; completely revised, 1996). Winner of the Linnaean Society's Gold Medal for botany, he was professor of botany at **Bangor** (1949–76).

RICHARDS, Thomas (1878–1962)
Librarian and historian
Richards was appointed librarian of University College, **Bangor** (*see* **University of Wales, Bangor**) in 1926, and his catalogues of the library's archives make fascinating reading. His eight books include *Religious Developments in Wales, 1654–62* (1923), *Wales under the Penal Code, 1662–87* (1925) and *Cymru a'r Uchel Gomisiwn* (1929); he also published two volumes of autobiography, which splendidly evoke his childhood at Tal-y-bont (**Ceulana-maesmawr**).

RICHARDSON, Dick (Richard Alexander; 1934–99) Boxer
Newport's 'Dynamite Dick' became **Britain**'s top heavyweight in 1960, when he won the European championship and retained it for two years. A fearless fighter with a fine jab and a powerful right, the 'Maesglas Marciano' often found himself involved in controversial scenes like the notorious brawl following his title defence against Brian London at **Porthcawl** in 1960.

RICHES, Norman [Vaughan Hurry] (1883–1975)
Cricketer
An outstanding batsman for more than 30 years, following his **Glamorgan** debut as a schoolboy, **Cardiff**-born Riches's

appearances were limited by his work as a dentist. At 45, he was still good enough to score 140 against a Lancashire attack spearheaded by the fearsome Australian, Ted McDonald.

RISCA (Rhisga), Caerphilly
(790 ha; 11,455 inhabitants)
Straddling the **Ebbw** north-west of **Newport**, Risca's built-up area fills the valley floor. When the medieval church of St Mary was demolished in 1852, a tile floor was discovered indicating **Roman** occupation on the site. Twmbarlwm (419 m), the **community**'s highest point, is crowned by an **Iron Age** enclosure and a medieval motte. Risca contains the longest surviving stretch of the **Crumlin** branch of the **Monmouthshire Canal**. The working of bituminous **coal** in the area began in the late 18th century, activity succeeded in the mid-19th century by deep-shaft mining of steam coal. There were also brick and **tinplate** works. In the late 19th century, tinplate gave way to steel production (*see* **Iron and Steel**). In 1897, the Risca works and the Britannia Foundry at Pontymister combined to create the Monmouthshire Steel and Tinplate Works. Oxford House has a distinguished history as a centre of adult **education**.

RISCA COLLIERY DISASTER,
Monmouthshire (now Caerphilly)
The 'Black Vein' coal seam in the **Risca** area was notorious for the amount of gas it contained and the frequent occurrence of outbursts of methane. Explosions were a regular hazard, and that on 1 December 1860 at the (Old) Risca colliery killed 142 men. The explosion was attributed to a faulty safety lamp igniting a sudden outburst of gas.

RISMAN, Gus (Augustus Risman; 1911–94)
Rugby player
Only his fellow-**Cardiff**ian **Jim Sullivan** can match Gus Risman's combination of longevity and outstanding achievement in the game of **rugby league**, which he played for 25 seasons (1929–54). He played 18 times for Wales (1931–45) and toured Australasia with the British team three times (1932, 1936 and 1946), the last time as captain. At club level, he captained both Salford and Workington Town to Challenge Cup wins at Wembley and the RL Championship. Big and strong, subtle and skilful, his exemplary demeanour made him one of the sport's most respected figures.

RIVERS
Any tract of land that receives more rain than is lost by evaporation, absorbed by vegetation or stored in water-retaining rock must be permeated by a network of watercourses. With its central core producing a rain run-off exceeding 2000 mm of water a year – 10 times that in lowland **England** – Wales's network of watercourses is one of the densest in Europe. With the exception of the southern coastal dunes, no part of the country is more than a few metres from some form of moving water, be it a drain, ditch, brook or river. Not only are Wales's uplands the source of all the country's rivers, they are also the source of the **Severn** and the **Wye**, the dominant rivers of the western midlands of England.

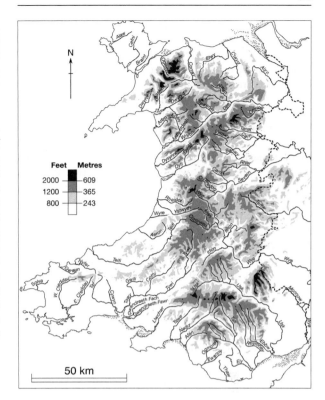

The contours and rivers of Wales

Wales has 24 catchment areas in which the main river is over 25 km in length. Some rivers – among them the **Aeron**, the **Cleddau** and the **Taff** – rise in uplands which are outliers of the country's central **mountain**ous spine, but it is the spine which is the source of the great majority. Among them are the rivers that rise in the blanket **peat** cover on **Pumlumon**; they begin, not in a surface channel created by erosion, but as pipes within the peat which create tunnel springs from which watercourses emerge. With the exception of the **Dee**, which flows into Liverpool Bay, all the rivers flowing east from the central upland core find their way to the Severn Sea. The larger land mass east of Wales's central core means that eastern flowing rivers are longer that those flowing west into Cardigan Bay. Rivers having their source in and around **Snowdon** have steeper gradients than rivers rising in less elevated parts of the uplands, and, as the water run-off from Snowdon is greater, they have a more torrential flow – a particular feature of the western tributaries of the **Conwy**. The rivers flowing southwards from the **Brecon Beacons** and from the Beacons' western and eastern wings – the **Black Mountain** and Fforest Fawr, Mynydd **Llangynidr** and **Mynydd Llangatwg** – drain the south Wales **coal**field, and their narrow valleys have determined the shape of the coalfield's settlements.

The story of the evolution of Wales's river system is a complex one. Some rivers – the Dysynni south-west of Tal-y-llyn **Lake**, for example – follow a fault in the earth's crust. The Clwyd flows through a lowland trough or rift valley created through the forcing down of rock between two parallel faults. The Aeron, the **Teifi** and part of the **Tywi** follow zones of weakness in the underlying rock structure. On the other hand, the rivers of the south Wales coalfield cut across the structural grain of the land, indicating that the courses of those rivers came into being on a cover of later strata which concealed the older structure beneath. In the original drainage pattern as it existed in the Cretaceous era, almost all Welsh rivers flowed in a south-easterly direction, with the upper Conwy joining the Dee and the upper Tywi joining the Cynon and eventually the Taff. The pattern was modified by river capture – the process whereby one river 'beheads' another, as at **Pontarfynach**, where the Mynach, once part of the head-waters of the Teifi, was captured by the **Rheidol**. Modification was also caused by the glaciation brought about in the ice ages. Thus, glacial diversion has caused the Teifi to leave the river's original valley and flow through a series of rock gorges. It is glaciation also which created the U-shaped valleys characteristic of **Snowdonia**.

Rivers generally have three stages – upland, vale and lowland. The upland stage is characterized by a stone-strewn watercourse often flowing through a gorge and sometimes containing pot holes – cylindrical hollows created by pebbles forced to rotate by the current, such as those of the Devil's Punchbowl in the Mynach. Where an upland course cuts alternately through soft and hard rock, irregularities of gradient occur, thus producing **waterfalls**, as on the Hepste, a tributary of the **Nedd**. In its vale stage, a river flows at a lower gradient through a fairly level valley floor often bounded by steep slopes, a

The riverside plant, Wilson's filmy fern

The triple-drop Horseshoe Falls on the Nedd Fechan, Ystradfellte

stage admirably illustrated by the Tywi between **Llandeilo** and **Carmarthen**. The chief characteristic of the lowland stage is a sluggish flow with many bends across a wide flood plain with little drop in altitude, the best example of which in Wales is the lower Dee. Everything in a river's course contributes to change. Thus, waterfalls are in the process of obliterating themselves, and rivers on flood plains carve out new courses as they meander. Such meanders can be recent. South of **Holt**, the Wales/England **border** generally follows the present course of the Dee, but, on occasion, it follows meanders which were in existence a century or two ago. **Maps** of the course of the Severn near **Newtown** dating from 1847, 1886, 1948 and 1975 illustrate marked changes over a period of a mere 128 years.

The volume of water carried by rivers can vary greatly. In the late 20th century, the mean monthly discharge of the Wye at **Erwood** varied from 12 cubic metres per second in June to 68 in January. Sudden rises in river levels following heavy rainfall are a frequent occurrence – so much so that the Clywedog and Brianne **reservoirs** were constructed in part to prevent the flooding of the Severn and Tywi valleys. Rapid melting of snow can also be a cause of floods, as on the Severn in 1947. Global warming may become a cause of more extensive winter flooding; it may also result in drier summers with river flows declining by as much as 25%.

Most of Wales's rivers flow over rocks low in neutralizing bases such as calcium and are therefore vulnerable to acidification. Some, however, flow through Carboniferous **Limestone**, especially on the borders of the coalfields of the south and the north-east. There, rivers can erode the rock to form channels into which they disappear to flow underground – a feature of the Alyn, a tributary of the Dee, and of the Mellte, a tributary of the Nedd.

The flora and fauna of Welsh rivers

Plants are rare in the steepest rivers, for fast flows scour the riverbed. Shaded gorges in west Wales are home to rarities such as the moss *Cruphaea lamyama* and the filmy fern *Hymenophyllum*. In sunnier, less steep, locations, a wide range of plants flourish, among them water starworts, water milfoils, water crowfoots and the scarce floating water plantain. Flag irises are common on the margins of many lowland rivers, but watercress, a cultivated plant in parts of southern England, is less widely distributed in Wales. Quiet sections of several Welsh rivers contain beds of water lilies, spectacularly so at Bosherston in **Stackpole**.

Of Wales's river-dwelling invertebrates, some are in marked decline. An introduced plague has greatly decreased the number of white-clawed crayfish; only one viable population of freshwater pearl mussel survives, and the use of synthetic pyrethroid **sheep** dip has wreaked havoc. Nevertheless, the country contains some species found nowhere else in **Britain**, among them the stonefly *Isogenus nubecula* on the Dee, the mayfly *Potomanthus luteus* on the **Usk** and the Wye, and rare beetles and flies on exposed gravel beds.

Most of Wales's freshwater **fish** are migratory species, among them salmon, trout, eel, stickleback and lamphrey. The shad populations in the Wye, the Usk and the Tywi are the largest in Britain, and the Conwy has a rare population of smelt. Estuarine species such as mullet and flounder regularly venture up river. The larger rivers of eastern Wales have a wider variety of freshwater fish, including cyprinids such as rudd, chub and dace.

Wales's fish-eating **birds** include kingfishers, mergansers, goosanders and herons. Dippers are widely distributed and have been used to study the effects of acidation. Yellow wagtails and sand martins are common, and the gravel beds of the Tywi provide a nesting place for 5% of Britain's population of little ringed plovers.

Among the **mammals** associated with Welsh rivers are **otters**, water voles and **bats**. **Giraldus Cambrensis** claimed that the Teifi was the sole river in southern Britain that was home to the **beaver**, although other sources suggest that several rivers – the Ogwen among them – had beaver populations. Beavers were certainly extinct in Wales by the 18th century, although efforts are being made to reintroduce them. A recent addition to riverbank mammals is the mink, an escapee from fur farms.

The human use of rivers and its consequences

The consequences of human activity on rivers has been evident since the **Neolithic Age**, for the forest clearance which accompanied the spread of **agriculture** increased **soil** erosion, sediment loads and light levels. Mining for metals, which began in the **Bronze Age**, led to the pollution of river water, a problem which can occur naturally, particularly in Snowdonia where water erosion of metalliferous rocks can cause the toxification of rivers.

River navigation was central to the **Roman** occupation of Wales, as the location of **Caerleon** on the Usk indicates. The location of castles was much influenced by proximity to navigable rivers. Edward I ordered the canalization of the lower

River mammals: an otter at Pembroke's millpond

Clwyd in order to allow **ships** to reach the royal castle at **Rhuddlan**. Navigable rivers were a key factor in the trading patterns that developed from the late Middle Ages onwards. **Welshpool** emerged as one of Wales's largest towns because it was situated at the highest navigable point of the Severn. **Canal** construction led to the decline of river navigation, and the coming of the **railways** seemed to herald its extinction. However, river travel found favour among tourists – on the Cleddau, the Conwy and the Wye in particular – and in the early 21st century **Cardiff** acquired waterbuses.

Even more important were navigable estuaries, the key factor in the rise of the **ports** of Carmarthen, **Cardigan** and **Barmouth**. It was to the navigable sections of the **Tawe**, the Taff and the Usk that the ports of **Swansea**, Cardiff and **Newport** owe their origins. The 5-km navigable stretch of the Tawe was particularly important, for it linked coal-bearing land with the sea and came to be lined by the metal works which enabled Swansea to become the world's largest centre of **copper** production. Interference with the course of rivers, initiated by Edward I, was practised in more recent times. In the 1840s, the course of the Taff at Cardiff was straightened, partly to facilitate railway building and partly to drain land near the town centre, land which eventually became Wales's prime piece of real estate – Cardiff Arms Park and the site of the Millennium Stadium. Other examples of river canalization include the Dee west of Chester, the lower Aeron and the Leri at **Borth**.

Originally, water supplies were pumped from **reservoirs** through pipes, but, from the 1950s onwards, a new policy was adopted – that of controlled releases of water from reservoirs into rivers. Thus, water from Llyn Celyn (*see* **Tryweryn**) flows into the Dee to be extracted from the river near Chester, and water from the Elan valley reservoirs is released to flow down the Wye to be extracted near the one-time drought-ridden town of **Monmouth**.

This new policy and other factors made it necessary for all issues relating to river basins to be considered together. This led in 1989 to the establishment of the National Rivers Authority. The Authority took account of river-basin boundaries; thus, although a Welsh Region was established, much of mid Wales became part of the Severn-Trent Region. The Authority was given responsibility for all aspects of rivers and water, including resource management, fisheries management, flood prevention, land drainage and pollution control. Pollution was a serious matter, for, since the onset of the **Industrial Revolution**, many of the rivers of Wales had come to be grossly polluted. They included most of those draining the south Wales coalfield, together with the Dee tributaries – the Alyn and the Clywedog – and the **lead**-polluted Rheidol and **Ystwyth**. The campaign for improved water quality has yielded results; for example, the number of migratory sewin entering the **Ogwr** rose from fewer than 100 in 1957 to *c.*650 in 1999. But industrial pollution remains a problem; a chemical spill on the Dee in 2001 resulted in the death of over 100,000 fish, a telling comment on the fragility of the ecology of the rivers of Wales. In 1996, the duties of the Authority became those of the Environment Agency.

ROADS

Before the arrival of **Britain**'s first great road builders, the **Romans**, the indigenous inhabitants – no strangers to transporting goods over long distances – travelled predominantly

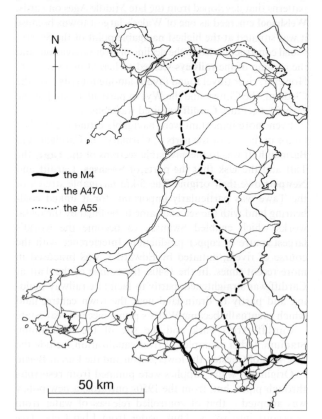

the M4
the A470
the A55

50 km

The M4 motorway and A roads of Wales, 2007

along ridgeway tracks, using **mountain** tops, forest margins, cairns and stone circles as their landmarks. By nature a people of the circle and the contour-conforming curve, they travelled with the land rather than against it, whereas the Romans were, by logic and military might, a people of the straight line. The topography of Wales meant that the rectangular grid of roads they constructed to link their strongholds of Deva (Chester), Viroconium (Wroxeter), Isca (**Caerleon**), Moridunum (**Carmarthen**) and Segontium (**Caernarfon**) suffered more deviations than might such a network in a less mountainous country.

The Romans created a network of metalled surfaced roads with milestones, sections of which form the basis of some of today's routes. The Antonine Itinerary (a 3rd-century route book) shows the similarity of the 'Dolaucothi **gold** route' – from **Llandovery** via **Brecon** to **Abergavenny** – to the present A40, while the route from Carmarthen to **Cardiff** and Caerleon is similar to the A48, and the A55 Chester to Caernarfon road follows the Roman route. Some roads connected with docks and navigable waterways, as at Caerleon where the River **Usk** was a major transport route.

After the collapse of the Roman Empire, 1300 years would go by before any further major development of Wales's roads. The memory of the Roman achievement survived, as can be seen from the traditions concerning **Sarn Helen**. The Roman network catered for most of Wales's overland travel for almost 1700 years, but deteriorating surfaces made for slow and forbidding journeys, while, as late as the 19th century, the risk of robbery was high.

From the 15th to the late 19th century, roads established by **drovers** were used to herd shod livestock to the fattening pastures and markets of **England**. The drovers' legacy remains not only in stretches of the present road system, but also in small bridges and wayside inns – several still called the Drovers' Arms – and the numerous farms that offered accommodation, **food** and grazing. These roads were frequently little more than mud tracks, and many of them survive simply as tracks or public footpaths, often identifiable only in aerial photographs.

An Act of Parliament in 1555 made the **parishes** responsible for roads, and unpaid supervisors were given the power to compel residents to devote six days a year to the repair of the roads within their parish. A day on roadwork came to be known as *diwrnod i'r brenin* (a day for the king); as the phrase was synonymous with a holiday, it is evident that few parishioners took their duties seriously. That recognized highways did exist is proved by John Ogilby's atlas of 1675; consisting of strip road **maps**, it portrayed the routes linking most of the chief towns of Wales. The **government** had little motive to involve itself in road building in Wales for, unlike the Highlands of **Scotland** where Jacobite sentiment led to rebellion and where state funds were spent on military roads, Welsh **Jacobitism** was too feeble to frighten the government into action.

As long as traffic consisted chiefly of driven **cattle** and of goods carried by pack**horse**, pressures for major improvement were slight. The industrial growth of the later 18th century provided a cause for, and was in part the consequence of, road improvement. The improvement was

Men and women tar-spreaders surfacing a road at Ystrad Mynach, Gelligaer, in 1914

financed by turnpike trusts, which levied tolls on road users to pay for their work. The first Act of Parliament establishing a turnpike trust in Wales was passed in 1749; of the earliest 12 such acts, 8 related to the north-east, the first part of Wales to be integrated into the British road system. (It is surely significant that, of the **'seven wonders of Wales'**, all, apart from **Snowdon**, were located either in **Denbighshire** or in **Flintshire**.) The primary routes established by the trusts in Wales ran east–west; they broadly followed the chief Roman roads and, essentially, represented the later A55, A40 and A48.

The only 19th-century road building in Wales to receive significant government funding was that created to expedite the carriage of mail from **London** to Dublin – 'the second city of the empire'. Its route – that of the later **A5** – was adopted in 1815, and the work was completed in 1830. Designed by **Thomas Telford**, it included his masterpiece, the **Menai** suspension bridge. The road opened up the heart of **Snowdonia** and reduced the journey time from London to **Holyhead** from 48 to 27 hours.

The Welsh section of the Irish mail road was the responsibility of the specially constituted Shrewsbury-Holyhead Trust. Other trusts were leased to individuals, with Thomas Bullin taking over the tollgates of seven of the trusts of the south-west. His activities were among the factors that provoked the **Rebecca Riots**. Following the riots, roads boards were established for six of the **counties** of south Wales (**Monmouthshire** was omitted). All trusts within a shire were consolidated, tolls made uniform and investment increased, causing the general system of roads in south Wales to be the best in Britain.

The spread of **railways** led to the neglect of roads and the eventual demise of the turnpike trusts. With the establishment of county councils in 1889, roads became part of their responsibility, although central government accepted some financial obligations where chief or trunk roads were concerned. Demands for road improvement became vocal as car ownership expanded. Wales had 29,291 private car owners in 1926, some 104,800 in 1950 and well over a million by the early 21st century. By then, almost all the substantial towns of Wales had bypasses. The country contained parts of two motorways – the **M4** and the **M48** – with their magnificent **Severn bridges**; in addition, the A55 linking Chester to Holyhead was a dual carriageway approaching motorway standards. Equally significant was the construction of the Heads of the Valleys Road (the A465). Hugging the northern boundary of the south Wales **coal**field between **Brynmawr** and **Glynneath**, it was completed in 1966. Linked with the M4 at Skewen (**Coedffranc**) in 1995, it has a total length of 70 km; plans to make a fully dual carriageway are afoot. Although some improvements have been made to it, the **A470**, which links north and south, remains inadequate – lamentably so in view of its status as the route of 'national unity'. All the roads of Wales are toll-less, except for the Severn bridges, the **Cleddau** bridge (*see* **Burton**), Pont Briwet at **Penrhyndeudraeth** and the Penmaenpool Bridge west of **Dolgellau**. In 2007, analysts reporting to the **National Assembly** revealed that in the 1989–2004 period road traffic in Wales had increased by 33%, and that the full cost to the Welsh **economy** of traffic congestion was £500 million a year.

R

ROBERT AP HUW (*c*.1580–1665)
Harpist and copyist

A grandson of the poet Siôn Brwynog, Robert ap Huw was related to the **Tudors** of **Penmynydd**. He grew up in Llanddeusant (**Tref Alaw**) and eventually settled as a gentleman farmer at Llandegfan (**Cwm Cadnant**). He was an able poet and accomplished **harp**ist, had graduated *pencerdd* (chief musician) by *c*.1615, and probably played for the household of James I on occasion. He is primarily remembered as the copyist of a unique retrospective manuscript of harp **music** (*c*.1613), the only reliable source of traditional *cerdd dant* (string music) to survive (*see* **Penillion Singing**). Of these, 31 compositions in tablature notation are supplemented by a series of exercises on the 24 measures of *cerdd dant*, a table of ornaments, and various lists. All of the pieces were apparently conceived between *c*.1340 and *c*.1500, and have clear associations with the **eisteddfod** repertory mentioned in the 16th-century statute of **Gruffudd ap Cynan**.

ROBERT AP RHYS (d.*c*.1534)
Priest and administrator

The grandson of Rhys ap Maredudd, who reputedly raised the **red dragon** standard at **Bosworth**, Robert enjoyed the patronage of Thomas Wolsey, to whom he was chaplain. In the years immediately preceding the **Protestant Reformation**, he was perhaps Wales's best example of an almost wholly secularized priest. Lessee of much of the monastic land of north-east Wales, he was accused by his enemies of acquiring 18 benefices. At Plas Iolyn (**Pentrefoelas**), he provided lavish hospitality for the bards. Although made vulnerable by the fall of Wolsey in 1529, he was highly successful in advancing the prospects of his 16 children. Among them were **Elis Prys**, the abbots of the **Cistercian** monasteries of **Conwy** and Strata Marcella (**Welshpool**), and the founders of several of the **gentry** families of **Denbighshire** and **Merioneth**, including the **Price family (Rhiwlas)**.

ROBERT, Gruffydd (pre-1532–post-1598)
Priest and grammarian

Probably a native of **Llŷn**, Gruffydd Robert was educated at **Oxford** and appointed, during Queen Mary's reign, archdeacon of **Anglesey**. Following Elizabeth's accession, he went as a **Roman Catholic** exile to mainland Europe. After a period in Rome, he was made canon theologian at Milan Cathedral and confessor to Cardinal Carlo Borromeo. As far as is known, he spent the rest of his life in Milan, often longing for Wales.

In Italy, he composed *Gramadeg Cymraeg* (Welsh Grammar), the work for which he is best remembered. The first part was published in Milan in 1567, and other parts were written from 1584 onwards. Much influenced by the Italian **Renaissance**, Gruffydd Robert wished to release the **Welsh language** from the shackles of the Middle Ages and enable it to stand shoulder to shoulder with the modern languages of Europe.

ROBERTS, Bartholomew (Barti Ddu or Black Bart; *c*.1682–1722) Pirate

So successful was this **Pembrokeshire**-born pirate that he disrupted **ship**ping in the Atlantic and the Caribbean during the years 1719–21. The Royal Navy sent two warships to capture him and, in 1722, he was killed in the ensuing battle off the African coast. Of the 169 of his men who were charged with **piracy**, 52 were hanged for their crimes. Barti Ddu flew the Jolly Roger and had his own Jack Flag made, portraying himself standing on two skulls; in action, he always wore a crimson damask waistcoat and breeches, a red feather in his hat and a diamond cross hanging from a gold chain round his neck. Generally considered the last of the great pirates, he was quoted as saying: 'a merry life and a short one shall be my motto'.

ROBERTS, [John] Bryn (1848–1931) Politician

Bryn Roberts was **Liberal** MP for the Eifion or southern division of **Caernarfonshire** from 1885 until 1906, when he was appointed a **county** court judge. An old school, highly individualistic Liberal, he was strongly opposed to **socialism** and Welsh **nationalism**, as well as to the Boer War and the **First World War**. Roberts was distrustful of **David Lloyd George**, whose activities, he felt, threatened the unity of British Liberalism, and a harsh critic of Lloyd George's coalition **government**. An unimpressive public speaker, he made little political impact at Westminster. As a judge, he was considered hostile to working-**class** interests.

ROBERTS, Caradog (1878–1935) Musician

Born at **Rhosllanerchrugog** and trained as a carpenter, Roberts displayed early talent as a pianist and organist, and studied **music** at **Oxford**. He was director of music at **Bangor** from 1914 until 1920, and edited the **Congregational** hymnals *Y Caniedydd Cynulleidfaol Newydd* (1921) and *Caniedydd Newydd yr Ysgol Sul* (1930). Several of his **hymn** tunes have become well known, notably 'In Memoriam' and 'Rachie', which is set to a temperance hymn, 'I bob un sydd ffyddlon' ('To everyone who is faithful') by Henry Lloyd (Ap Hefin; 1870–1946).

ROBERTS, Eleazar (1825–1912)
Musician and author

Pwllheli-born Eleazar Roberts spent most of his life in **Liverpool**, where he became chief clerk to the stipendiary magistrate. He published a biography of the peace advocate and politician **Henry Richard** (1907) and a novel, *Owen Rees* (1894), depicting Welsh life in Liverpool. Roberts pioneered the use of the tonic sol-fa notation as a means of teaching **music** by adapting the works of John Curwen and translating them into **Welsh**.

ROBERTS, Elis (Elis y Cowper; *c*.1712–89) Writer

Elis Roberts the cooper, the most productive of the **interlude** writers, lived at **Llanddoged**. He claimed to have written 69, of which 8 have survived, including *Y Ddau Gyfamod* (1777; the first interlude to be printed in Wales), *Gras a Natur* (1769) and *Cristion a Drygddyn* (1788). He published many **ballads** and a series of pious letters.

ROBERTS, Evan (1878–1951) Religious revivalist

Born in Loughor (*see* **Llwchwr**), Roberts worked as a **coal**miner before training for the **Calvinistic Methodist** ministry. He abandoned his studies in **Newcastle Emlyn** in some spiritual turmoil, feeling that he was called to be an itinerary evangelist. He returned to Loughor and found himself leader of a religious **revival**, which had spread from south **Cardiganshire**. Between November 1904 and January 1906, he led eight evangelistic missions throughout Wales, which provoked scenes of considerable excitement. Although criticized harshly by some for an overemphasis on experience and feeling, many found his ministry an inspiration. By 1909, he had receded from public view; 42 years later, he died in obscurity in **Cardiff**.

ROBERTS, Evan (Ifan Gelli; 1906–91)
Quarryman and botanist
Widely known in **Snowdonia** and a lifelong resident in **Capel Curig**, Evan Roberts worked in Rhos **slate** quarry from the age of 14 until its closure in 1953. As a young man, chance observation of the rare purple saxifrage on **Moel Siabod** turned his attention to the **mountain** flowers of Snowdonia. Appointed first warden of Cwm Idwal National Nature Reserve in 1954, he travelled widely in pursuit of his botanical passion. Roberts was accepted as a world authority on arctic-alpine flora.

ROBERTS, Glyn (1904–62) Historian
Bangor-born Glyn Roberts was appointed registrar at Bangor in 1946, and professor of Welsh history there in 1949. He wrote mainly about Welsh society in the late medieval period, and his writings were collected in the volume *Aspects of Welsh History* (1969). Among his main contributions were his studies of the origins of the **Tudor family** and his article 'Wales and England: Sympathy and Antipathy' (1963).

ROBERTS, Goronwy [Owen] (1913–81) Politician
While a student at **Bangor**, Goronwy Roberts, a native of **Bethesda**, was leader of the **Gwerin** movement. He was MP for **Caernarfon** from 1945 to 1974. A member of the patriotic Welsh wing of the **Labour Party**, he presented a petition to the House of Commons in 1956 requesting a Welsh parliament (*see* **Devolution**). He was minister of state at the **Welsh Office** (1964–6) and was created Lord Goronwy-Roberts in 1974.

ROBERTS, Isaac (1829–1904) Astronomer
The 'father of astrophotometry' was born in **Nantglyn**. He made his fortune as a builder in **Liverpool**, but his consuming passions were **geology** and **astronomy**, and he twice moved home to find a more suitable site for his observatory. He pioneered the use of **photography** in astronomy; his famous photograph of the Andromeda nebula, demonstrating its spiral form, was the first photograph ever taken of an object outside our own galaxy. He was elected FRS in 1890 and received the Gold Medal of the Royal Astronomical Society.

ROBERTS, John (1576–1610) Martyr
Born in **Trawsfynydd**, Roberts was raised a Protestant, but after graduation from **Oxford** in 1598, he went to Paris where he was received into the **Roman Catholic** Church. At Valladolid, he joined the **Benedictine** order. Ordained priest in 1602, Roberts became in 1607 the first prior of St Gregory's College, Douai. In 1610, while undertaking **missionary** activities in **England**, he was caught and convicted of high treason, for which he was executed. **Britain**'s first Benedictine martyr, he was canonized in 1970.

Isaac Roberts's photograph of the Andromeda nebula, December 1888

Kate Roberts

ROBERTS, John (Ieuan Gwyllt; 1822–77) Musician
Roberts, who was born near **Aberystwyth**, became **Calvinistic Methodist** minister of Pant-tywyll, **Merthyr Tydfil**, in 1859 and, in 1865, of Capel Coch, **Llanberis**. His **hymn**books, including *Llyfr Tonau Cynulleidfaol* (1859), were highly popular and played a major role in the development of congregational hymn singing. A famous hymn tune of his own composition is 'Moab'. From 1861 to 1873, he published *Y Cerddor Cymreig*, one of the most important **music periodicals** in **Welsh**.

ROBERTS, John (Telynor Cymru; 1816–94) Harpist
Born at **Llanrhaeadr-yng-Nghinmeirch**, and descended, through his mother, from the famous **Wood family** of **Romanies**, Roberts learned to play the **harp** after spending nine years in the army. He was taught by his uncle, Archelaus Wood. His nine sons also played the harp, and played as a choir of harps for Queen Victoria at Palé Hall, **Llandderfel**, in 1889. A fluent speaker of Romany, and a handsome figure, he roamed the land with his triple harp on his back. It was at a bardic assembly on the shores of Llyn Geirionydd (**Trefriw**) in 1886 that he was invested with the title of 'Telynor Cymru' (The Harpist of Wales).

ROBERTS, Kate (1891–1985)
Short-story writer and novelist
'The queen of Welsh **literature**', as she has been styled, was the daughter of a quarryman and smallholder from Rhosgadfan (**Llanwnda**). Her autobiography, *Y Lôn Wen* (1960), portrays the rich folk culture of the **slate**-quarrying villages of **Caernarfonshire** during her childhood. Kate Roberts studied **Welsh** at **Bangor**, and then taught at schools in **Llanberis**, **Ystalyfera** and **Aberdare**. She married Morris T. Williams in 1928, and they bought the Gwasg **Gee printing** press in 1935, making their home in **Denbigh**. Her husband died in 1946, and responsibility for the press fell on her shoulders for the next 10 years.

Critics generally talk about two periods in Kate Roberts's literary career: the first, from *Deian a Loli* (1925) to *Ffair Gaeaf* (1937), known as the 'Rhosgadfan period', and the second, from *Stryd y Glep* (1949) to *Haul a Drycin* (1981), known as the 'Denbigh period'. It was the death of her younger brother in the **First World War** that triggered her writing, and the short story was her preferred form. The powerful novel *Traed Mewn Cyffion* (1936; published in **English** as *Feet in Chains*, 1977) belongs to the Rhosgadfan period. She portrays the harsh life of slate-quarrying society, the grinding poverty and the brave stoicism of the people. Poverty is not the bugbear in the second period, which was inaugurated by her husband's illness and death, and her consequent loneliness. In the three novels *Stryd y Glep* (1949), *Y Byw Sy'n Cysgu* (1956; published in English as *The Living Sleep*, 1976) and *Tywyll Heno* (1962), the focus is on the emotional experiences of three **women** in a crisis. The treatment had become far more psychological and self-analytical. Although the storytelling technique of *Tegwch y Bore* (1967) is reminiscent of *Traed Mewn Cyffion*, there is a more modernist slant to this novel. Some stories from the second period evoke Rhosgadfan, such as *Te yn y Grug* (1959; published in English as *Tea in the Heather*, 1968), but in most of the work of this period it is the ennui of middle age that is the fundamental subject. While the early stoicism has not entirely disappeared, there is a greater restlessness beneath the surface – and indeed Kate Roberts has been described as an embryonic feminist.

ROBERTS, Lynette (1909–95) Poet
A late modernist and early magical realist, Lynette Roberts was born in Buenos Aires of Welsh parents. She married **Keidrych Rhys** in 1939 and settled in Llanybri (**Llansteffan**), but they divorced 10 years later and she moved to **England**. She published two collections of verse, *Poems* (1944) and *Gods with Stainless Ears* (1951), and a study of the speech of Llanybri, *Village Dialect* (1944). After suffering a breakdown, she returned to Wales in 1969, devoting herself to evangelizing for the **Jehovah's Witnesses**. The early 21st century saw a revival of interest in her work, with a *Collected Poems*, edited by Patrick McGuinness, appearing in 2005.

ROBERTS, Owen Elias (1908–2000) Science writer
A pioneer of the interpretation of **science** in the **Welsh language**, Roberts was born in **Llanystumdwy**, and later worked in a hospital laboratory in **Liverpool**, before retiring to **Criccieth** and, subsequently, to **Cardiff**. His books on microbiology and atomic physics were followed by *Cyfrinachau Natur* (1952) and *Y Gŵr o Ystradgynlais ac Erthyglau Eraill* (1954), both of which won the National **Eisteddfod**'s prose medal (1952 and 1954). He then turned his attention to Welsh scientists, in *Gwyddonwyr o Gymru* (1956), *Rhai o Wyddonwyr Cymru* (1980) and a biography of Dr **John Dee** (1980).

ROBERTS, R[obert] Alun (1894–1969)
Agricultural botanist

A native of Dyffryn Nantlle (**Llanllyfni**), Roberts became a student, lecturer and professor of agricultural botany at **Bangor**. An ecologist, naturalist and historian of agricultural practice, he was known as 'Doctor Alun' both to his students and to listeners to the radio programme *Byd Natur*. Roberts wrote extensively, in **Welsh** and in **English**, being, in **Saunders Lewis**'s words, 'a master writer with a poet's vision and a prose poet's rhythm and memories'. He did much to reorganize **agriculture** in **Caernarfonshire** during the **Second World War**, and had an unparalleled knowledge of the scientific coupled with the historical and ecological aspects of land use.

ROBERTS, R[obert] D[avies] (1851–1911)
Educationist and geologist

Born in **Aberystwyth** and educated in **London** and **Cambridge**, Roberts began his career as lecturer in **geology** and published *Earth's History: an Introduction to Geology* (1893). He then turned his attention to adult **education** and did pioneering work as secretary of the Cambridge Syndicate for extension lecturers (1894–1902) and as registrar of the external programme of London University (1902–11). His conviction that universities should prepare degree courses for adults without requiring them to attend internal lectures, as in London, was not acceptable to the founders of the **University of Wales** (1893). Nevertheless, he faithfully served the University and, by 1903, was its junior deputy-chancellor.

ROBERTS, Rachel (1927–80) Actress

Llanelli-born Rachel Roberts was at her most impressive playing lusty or sexually repressed, troubled **women**. She made an eye-catching **film** debut as an ebullient gossip-monger 'Bessie the Milk' in the Welsh comedy *Valley of Song* (1953), but her screen reputation was forged in Karel Reisz's *Saturday Night and Sunday Morning* (1962) and Lindsay Anderson's *This Sporting Life* (1963) and *O Lucky Man!* (1973). The first two won her British Film Academy Best Actress Awards. In the 1972 screen version of *Alpha Beta*, she repeated the role she had played in the stage version of that drama. She played three parts in *O Lucky Man!*, but one role – a homebody whose keen sense of inadequacy led to suicide – was excised from the American print after Roberts's death, following drink problems, in California. Formerly married to the actor Rex Harrison, she won a best supporting actress BAFTA prize for *Yanks* (1979).

ROBERTS, Richard (1789–1864) Inventor

Hailed as a 'gigantic mechanical genius' by the president of the Manchester Engineers, Roberts was born at Llanymynech (**Carreghofa**), the son of a tollgate keeper and shoemaker. At the age of 10, he constructed a spinning wheel for his mother, and later became an important inventor in the cotton industry, devising the 'self-acting mule' in 1825. Involved in numerous enterprises in **Liverpool**, **London** and, predominantly, Manchester, Roberts was a 'pure' inventor, for whom financial considerations were secondary. He took out a patent almost every year for 28 years,

Rachel Roberts with Richard Harris in *This Sporting Life* (1963)

devising improvements in **textile** machinery, steam engines, **railways**, **ships**, **lighthouses** and **clocks** – he even invented an (unprofitable) steam-driven motorcar.

ROBERTS, Robert (Bob Tai'r Felin; 1870–1951)
Folk singer

A farmer and miller at Cwm Tirmynach (**Llandderfel**), Bob Tai'r Felin was a masterful singer whose homely delivery made him a popular figure at many a *noson lawen* and **eisteddfod**. From 1944 onwards, he became well known nationally, appearing on radio programmes such as *Noson Lawen* and, later, on **film** and television – publicity that contributed to the perpetuation of songs such as 'Mari fach fy nghariad', 'Moliannwn' and 'Yr Asyn a Fu Farw'.

ROBERTS, Robert (Y Sgolor Mawr; 1834–85)
Clergyman and scholar

The 'Sgolor Mawr' (Great Scholar), whose potential was frustrated by personal difficulties, was born in Llanddewi (**Llangernyw**), and educated at **Bala** College. Following his conversion to **Anglicanism** and his training as a teacher at **Caernarfon**, he served as schoolmaster in several places before he became a clergyman. His appointment to the living of Rug (**Corwen**) enabled him to pursue his scholarly interests, but he fell victim to drink and fled to **Australia**. There he wrote his classic autobiography with its vivid portrayal of 19th-century Welsh social life; it was published in 1923 as *The Life and Opinions of Robert Roberts, a*

SAVE CWM TRYWERYN FOR WALES
BY GWYNFOR EVANS
ONE SHILLING

Robert Roberts (Bob Tai'r Felin) on the cover of a pamphlet published by Plaid [Genedlaethol] Cymru

Wandering Scholar, as told by himself. Unable to rehabilitate himself on his return, he died in poverty. He is also remembered as a lexicographer; some maintain that D. Silvan Evans took unfair advantage of his work (*see* **Dictionaries**).

ROBERTS, Robert (Silyn; 1871–1930) and ROBERTS, Mary (1877–1972) Educationists

Born at **Llanllyfni** at the foot of Craig Cwmsilyn, from which he derived his pseudonym, Silyn was educated at **Bangor** and **Bala**. He came to prominence in 1900 when, with **W. J. Gruffydd**, he published *Telynegion* – a volume of lyric poetry which ushered in a new era in Welsh **literature**. He won the crown at the National **Eisteddfod** in 1902. He was a **Calvinistic Methodist** minister (1901–12), appointments secretary of the **University of Wales** (1912–18), civil servant (1918–22) and extra-mural lecturer at Bangor (1922–5). A convinced **socialist**, he was among north-west Wales's earliest **Labour** councillors. His visit to the Soviet Union caused him to 'long to live for another forty years to see the outcome of the stupendous revolution in Russia'. He was closely involved in the philanthropic activities of **Thomas Jones** (1870–1955). On the formation of the north Wales division of the **Workers' Educational Association** (WEA) in 1925, he was appointed its organizer. His death from a fatal insect bite invoked one of the best known of the poems of **R. Williams Parry**.

In 1905, he married **London**-born Mary Parry, who succeeded him as WEA secretary; she was the first **woman** in **Britain** to be appointed to such a post, which she held until 1951. Under her leadership, the ratio in north Wales between class attendants and the **population** was thrice that in Britain as a whole, making her district the most successful WEA district in Britain. **R. T. Jenkins** declared that no lecturer dared to disobey her commands.

ROBERTS, Samuel (S.R.; 1800–85) Writer

Born at **Llanbrynmair**, S.R. wielded great influence among Welsh **Nonconformists** through his **periodical** *Y Cronicl*, launched in 1843. He was opposed to **slavery**, English imperialism, the **Crimean War**, landlordism, unionism, capital punishment and state intervention in **education**; he supported **temperance**, the penny post, the building of **railways**, and universal suffrage, including votes for **women**. A staunch **Congregationalist**, he advocated the freedom of congregations from centralized authority. He protested vehemently against the 1847 education report (*see* **Treason of the Blue Books**). In 1857, in a bid to escape the hostility of the **Williams Wynn** estate, of which his farm was a part, he emigrated to the United States, where he bought a tract of land in Tennessee. The venture failed and, caught up in the American Civil War, he was obliged to return to Wales in 1867. S.R.'s most important publications were *Diosg Farm* (1854) and *Crynodeb o Helyntion ei Fywyd* (1875).

ROBERTS, Thomas (Thomas Roberts Llwyn'rhudol; 1765/6–1841) Pamphleteer

Although born at Abererch, **Llannor**, in his youth Roberts left for **London**, where he became a **gold**smith. With others, he established the **Cymreigyddion Society** in 1796, and was prominent with the **Gwyneddigion**. In 1798, he wrote *Cwyn yn erbyn Gorthrymder*, a pamphlet attacking bishops,

R

The painter Will Roberts in his studio

attorneys, physicians and excisemen as oppressors of the poor, and expressed opposition to the **tithe**. Roberts supported freedom of conscience in the United States and opposed war against Republican France. He satirized Methodists (*see* **Calvinistic Methodists**), but became their defender in 1806.

ROBERTS, Tom [Aerwyn] (1924–99) Philosopher
Llanbedr-born Tom Roberts was educated at **Bangor** and **Oxford**. During his time as lecturer in historical **theology** at Keele, he published *History and Christian Apologetic* (1960). He became a lecturer in the department of **philosophy** at **Aberystwyth**, and was appointed professor in 1969. Roberts's chief interests were theology and morals, and the philosophy of Kant; his most important works were *Butler's Fifteen Sermons* (1970) and *The Concept of Benevolence* (1973).

ROBERTS, Will (1907–2000) Painter
Will Roberts spent his early life in rural **Flintshire**, before moving south to Cimla, **Neath**, where, apart from RAF service during the **Second World War**, he remained for the rest of his long life. A full-time jeweller, he studied art part-time. **Josef Herman**, who lived at nearby **Ystradgynlais** between 1944 and 1955, was an influential and encouraging friend. Roberts's quiet observations of life reflect his faith in community, family, **religion**, place and purpose. **Music** complemented his art: he played the violin, and while his work was generally sombre in hue, he could, when necessary, make the earth tones sing. Roberts enjoyed commercial, if not perhaps critical success, exhibiting in **London** and in most major Welsh **art galleries** and institutions.

ROBERTS, William (Nefydd; 1813–72)
Educationist and collector of manuscripts
Llannefydd-born William Roberts trained as a shoemaker before being ordained minister of the Welsh **Baptist** church at Stanhope Street, **Liverpool**, in 1837. He moved to Salem chapel, **Abertillery** (1845), where he remained for the rest of his life. As the representative of the **British Society** in south Wales (1853–64), he was responsible for creating a network of nondenominational elementary schools in much of the south. His extensive collection of books and manuscripts, housed at the **National Library**, is a rich quarry of information about the **religion** and culture of 19th-century Wales.

ROBERTS, William (1830–99) Physician
Anglesey-born William Roberts qualified as a doctor at University College Hospital, **London**. A distinguished teacher of clinical medicine, he was the first professor of medicine at Victoria University, Manchester. His most noteworthy contribution was the observation, recorded in the *Philosophical Transactions* (1874), that the fungus called *penicillium glaucum* 'held in check the growth of Bacteria'. He was knighted in 1885.

ROBERTS, William [John] (Gwilym Cowlyd; 1828–1904) Eisteddfod enthusiast
Trefriw-born Gwilym Cowlyd was a mixture of eccentricity and genius, and is chiefly remembered for setting up his own festival to rival the official National **Eisteddfod**, whose increasing use of **English** he resented, also regarding it as having betrayed the original vision of Iolo Morganwg (**Edward Williams**). From 1863, his alternative all-**Welsh**

771

Jim Perrin and Martin Hogge, 1970, about to make the first ever ascent of the larger of the two Elegug Stacks at Castlemartin, Pembrokeshire

festival, or 'Arwest', was held annually on the shores of Llyn Geirionydd (Trefriw); it ran for 40 years and had its own **Gorsedd** which, in 1901, accepted the Emperor of Japan as a member – *in absentia*. An often-scorned figure who lived amongst piles of dust-covered books and manuscripts, he eventually went bankrupt.

ROBERTSON, Henry (1816–88) Railway engineer
Born in Banff, **Scotland**, Henry Robertson studied mining **engineering** before turning to **railways**. He came to Wales in 1842 and promoted the North Wales Mineral Railway. As engineer of the Chester–Shrewsbury railway, he created two outstanding works: the 460-m long, 45-m high viaduct over the **Dee** at **Cefn**, and the 30-m high viaduct over the Ceiriog at **Chirk**. He founded **Brymbo** steelworks (*see* **Iron and Steel**) in 1882 and was a **Liberal** MP, first for Shrewsbury and then for **Merioneth** (1885–6). In 1889, Queen Victoria stayed at his mansion, Palé, **Llandderfel**.

ROBESON, Paul (1898–1976) Actor and singer
Barely a handful of Welsh actors have achieved the iconic status within Wales of Robeson, the black American screen and stage performer, and charismatic bass baritone. For over 40 years, a special bond existed between this humane, dignified giant and Welsh miners. Forged in the depressed 1920s, when he encountered jobless miners singing on the streets of **London**, the connection was particularly strong in the 1950s, after the American government confiscated his passport for eight years. Outlawed for his **Communist** views and vigorous civil rights campaigning, Robeson broadcast over a radio link to the Miners' **Eisteddfod** at **Porthcawl** in 1957. The following year, introduced by **Aneurin Bevan**, he sang at **Ebbw Vale** on the eve of the National Eisteddfod. Emotional symbiosis between Robeson and the Welsh was recreated in the British **film** *The Proud Valley* (1940). He earned ecstatic reviews for his stage Othello, but – ironically – it was as an evil, ersatz **preacher** that he delivered his finest screen performance, in his debut film *Body and Soul* (1925).

ROBIN CLIDRO (fl.1547–53) Poet
This *clerwr* (*see* **Clêr**) or low-grade poet lived in the **Ruthin** area. In metre and content, his poems represented a tradition of 'unofficial' poetry, of which little has survived that is earlier than the 16th century. His work includes an elegy to his tomcat and a self-mocking poem describing a circuit of would-be patrons.

ROCK-CLIMBING and MOUNTAINEERING
Whilst rock-climbing and mountaineering as organized and recorded sporting activities can be accepted as the invention of **English** visitors from the mid-19th century onwards, there was indigenous knowledge of the more rocky and inaccessible places among the Welsh hills from well before that date. Herbalists from time immemorial collected the **plants** that were deemed to partake of the virtues of the most powerful places; local guides sold specimens from the crags to the fern enthusiasts of the Victorian era; shepherds, quarrymen and **copper**-miners faced everyday the environments to which the English sportsmen came later and far more timorously. There is, for example, substantial evidence to confirm that miners from Nant Gwynant (**Beddgelert**) climbed the severe 300-m Slanting Gully on Y Lliwedd 40 years before its supposed first ascent, recorded in 1898 by a party from the English Lake District. The miners' ascent – in search of copper lodes, or the King Arthur's **gold** of legend – is by far the most significant in early climbing history, and is a rebuff to colonialist attitudes.

As a sport, rock-climbing and mountaineering in Wales – and more particularly among the **mountains** of **Snowdonia** – were at first indivisible, the one being regarded as no more than training for the other. Favoured inns of the region would be patronized each Easter by the alpinists of **London** and Oxbridge, as gentlemen prepared for their summer seasons in the Oberland or the Haute Savoie, and they would sally forth to disport themselves upon the more amiable rock faces offered by the Welsh hills. A very few local enthusiasts – **Archer Thomson** most prominently – might consider difficulty a sufficient end in itself, and develop what was termed 'the balance technique', but native climbers have always been distinctly in the minority.

With the arrival in Snowdonia in the late 1920s of a new generation of climbers trained on the northern English outcrops – notably Jack Longland, Menlove Edwards and Colin Kirkus – standards soared. The great natural lines on Clogwyn Du'r Arddu (on the north flank of the **Snowdon** massif and the finest of Welsh cliffs) were ascended, and the region attained a place at the forefront of climbing development that it has never subsequently lost. The influence of Menlove Edwards in particular was profound. In place of a focus on attaining summits by straightforward routes, his was a search for gymnastic difficulty and a facing up to the psychology of fear. The genesis of the modern sport, with its remarkable athleticism and astonishing levels of achieved difficulty, is largely traceable to Edwards, who made over 100 new climbs on the cliffs of Snowdonia.

After the **Second World War**, greater leisure time and the ready availability of military surplus equipment led to a further increase in activity and a rise in standards. The Manchester climbers Joe Brown and Don Whillans, both of whom settled in **Caernarfonshire**, made ascents on Clogwyn Du'r Arddu and along the **Llanberis** Pass which are now regarded as **Britain**'s classic difficult rock-climbs. The most significant revolution in rock-climbing, however, took place in the 1970s, when the combination of the introduction of serious athletic training regimes, and the arrival of new and sophisticated technical aids from America and mainland Europe, resulted in the attainment of standards of difficulty unimaginable even 20 years earlier. That trend has continued and intensified since the 1970s, and Snowdonia has become an international Mecca of rock-climbing. At the same time, new venues for the sport have been explored, from the sea cliffs of **Castlemartin** and **Holyhead** to the disused **slate** quarries of Dinorwic (**Llanddeiniolen**) and the **limestone** faces of Llanymynech (**Carreghofa**); specially created indoor climbing walls have been built throughout the country. The provision of climbing courses and the manufacture and retailing of climbing equipment have become important economic factors, particularly in the north-west, and year-round outdoor **tourism**, of which climbing is a part, is now vital to many formerly depressed communities.

ROGERSTONE (Tŷ-du), Newport
(864 ha; 8807 inhabitants)
Located in the north-western corner of the **county** of **Newport**, the **community** is dominated by factories filling the floor of the **Ebbw** valley. Until 1991, they included the Rogerstone Power Station, the demolition of which caused mixed feelings. Rogerstone contains several interesting places of worship, including an impressive polygon **Baptist** chapel (1996). (For the Fourteen Locks, *see* **Newport**: Bettws.)

ROGIET, Monmouthshire
(847 ha; 1620 inhabitants)
Adjoining the Severn Sea at the junction of the **M4** and the **M48**, the **community** once had three **parish** churches hardly 500 m apart – St Mary's, Rogiet (14th century and 1963), St Michael's, Llanfihangel Rogiet (medieval; now disused) and Ifton (demolished *c*.1755). The village grew following the establishment of the **railway** junction serving the **Severn Tunnel**, completed in 1885.

ROLLS, Charles Stewart (1877–1910)
Engineer and aviator
Although Charles Rolls was born in **London**, the family home was The Hendre, **Llangattock Vibon Avel**, where his father, Lord Llangattock, owned a large estate. Unusually for a son of the aristocracy, he took a **Cambridge** degree in **engineering** and became a pioneer of both the automobile and **aviation** industries. In 1904, he formed a partnership with F. H. Royce and Rolls-Royce was born. In 1910, he was one of the first to receive a certificate as an aviator, and soon afterwards he was the first person to cross from **England** to France and back non-stop. In the same year, he was killed when his biplane crashed – **Britain**'s first aircraft fatality. A statue at Agincourt Square, **Monmouth**, commemorates him.

Charles Rolls, pioneer aviator and motorist

ROMAN CATHOLICS

Although the medieval Welsh Church recognized the role of the Pope and was part of the Catholic (in the sense of universal) Church (*see* **Religion**), the notion that it was Roman Catholic would have been incomprehensible, for the term is not recorded until 1605. (The Welsh *Catholig Rhufeinaidd* is not recorded until 1658.) By the early 17th century, Welsh Protestants viewed Roman Catholics as those who rejected the truths which had emerged from the **Protestant Reformation**, while Roman Catholics viewed themselves as the sole upholders of the true faith.

There was little welcome in Wales for the religious changes brought about by Henry VIII and even less for the more radical ones introduced during the reign of Edward VI. During the reign of Mary I (1553–8), when a determined attempt was made to reverse those changes, no more than a dozen Welshmen felt the need to go into exile. Indeed, had Mary lived longer, she might have succeeded in making Wales a stronghold of renewed Catholicism. However, Elizabeth I's moderate church settlement (*see* **Anglicans**) eventually won the acceptance of the great majority of the Welsh. This was partly because the coercive power of the state was a reality everywhere in Wales by the late 16th century – in marked contrast with **Ireland**, where the officials of the English crown failed to prevent the activities of those determined to ensure that the **Irish** retained their allegiance to the Old Faith. There were those in Wales equally determined, and among the 40 Welsh and **English** martyrs canonized by the Pope in 1970 were figures such as the schoolmaster **Richard Gwyn** (executed, 1584) and the priest **William Davies** (executed, 1593) (*see* **Catholic Martyrs**). Welshmen were prominent in the efforts to train **missionary** priests at Rome, Douai and elsewhere, and recusant writings represent a significant element in Welsh **literature**.

However, the activities of the Welsh Catholic exiles proved largely unproductive, although Roman Catholicism survived in some parts of Wales, especially in **Monmouthshire** where the recusant **Somerset family** of **Raglan** was powerful, and in **Flintshire**, where **Holywell** continued to be a centre of **pilgrimage**. As the 17th century advanced, stories of the Spanish Inquisition and of Louis XIV's persecution of the Huguenots, and fears of invasion by Irish Catholic armies gave rise to hatred of Catholicism among the mass of the people of Wales. The Popish Plot (1678–9) gave vent to that hatred, and from the 1670s, until the 19th-century migration from Ireland the Old Faith in Wales languished almost unto extinction.

The religion census of 1851 revealed that there were only 20 Catholic churches in Wales, almost half of them in rural Monmouthshire. By then, however, Wales had 20,000 Irish-born inhabitants, the vast majority of whom were Roman Catholic, and over the following half century determined efforts were made to cater for their religious and **education**al needs. Those efforts were helped by the re-establishment of the Catholic hierarchy in 1850. The **diocese** of **Newport** and Menevia was founded, consisting of Wales's seven southern **counties** and **Herefordshire**; the six northern counties became part of the diocese of Shrewsbury. The diocese of Newport and Menevia was

Romany children at Brynmawr *c.*1920 on the site later occupied by the Dunlop–Semtex factory

something of an anomaly, for its most distinguished bishop, John Cuthbert Hedley (bishop, 1881–1915), lived in **Cardiff** and the diocese's spiritual centre was at Belmont in Herefordshire. In 1895, the six northern counties, together with all the southern counties apart from **Glamorgan** and Monmouthshire became the vicariate of Wales, a mission field whose needs were considered to be different from those of the two heavily industrialized south-eastern counties. In 1898, the vicariate became the diocese of Menevia. The archdiocese of Cardiff was established in 1916. In 1987, Menevia was divided into the diocese of **Wrexham** (the six pre-1974 northern counties) and the diocese of Menevia (five of the pre-1974 southern counties, along with **West Glamorgan**). That diocese had almost the same boundaries as the medieval diocese of **St David's** – fittingly so, for the medieval diocese was known as Menevia or Maenor Fynyw (*see* **Dioceses**).

While people of Irish descent continued to be the dominant element in Welsh Catholicism, migrants from other countries – Italy and Poland among them – had become a significant element by the middle of the 20th century. So also had converts from indigenous Welsh families, a development encouraged by the appointment of **Francis Mostyn** (of the ancient **Mostyn family** of Flintshire) as archbishop of Cardiff in 1920 and by the strong Welsh sympathies of his successor, **Michael McGrath** (archbishop, 1939–61). Some of the conversions were high profile, particularly that of **Saunders Lewis**, president of **Plaid [Genedlaethol] Cymru** from 1926 to 1939. Welsh anti-Catholicism proved persistent and found expression in attacks upon Lewis and in the reluctance of some local authorities to fund Catholic schools adequately. Catholic participation in ecumenical activities from the 1960s onwards helped to change attitudes, and the Pope's visit to Wales in 1982 proved highly popular. By then, however, the confidence of the preceding century had begun to wane, as the Roman Catholic Church, faced with increasing secularism in Wales, began to encounter a decline in regular worshippers.

ROMANIES

George Borrow depicted the lifestyle of the Romany gypsies of 19th-century Wales as one of nomadic freedom and cultural richness, well suited to the perceived romantic and primitive wildness of the country itself. Today, the increasingly contentious term 'Gypsy' – based upon the assumption that Romanies had their origin in Egypt – is applied to both Romany and other (more numerous) travelling groups. Most have a settled existence, although they remain somewhat marginalized. The organization of Romany-Gypsy society was based traditionally on close-knit extended families with distinct customs and a distinct language. Early ethnography concentrated on their language and customs as reflections of an ancient origin in India, and presented Welsh Romanies as preserving a purer strain of an exotic culture. Current scholarship places more emphasis on the adaptations of different groups to different environments, and less on reconstructing ancient cultural forms.

Accounts of Gypsies perceived by themselves – and by others – as Romany, appeared in Wales in the late 16th century. Early literary references and civil records suggest

John Roberts, the Romany harpist

a mobile **population** of several families, and characterize them, none too sympathetically, as fortune-tellers and vagabonds. However, one of these groups, the **Wood family**, who traced their descent from Abram Wood (?1699–1799), adopted Wales as their home and became an important feature in the cultural life of the north, largely because of their **music**al abilities as **fiddler**s and **harp**ists, and their skill in storytelling. Sarah, Abram Wood's only daughter, was the grandmother of **John Roberts** ('Telynor Cymru'; 1816–94), thus establishing a second branch of the Wood family as a prominent focus for Welsh Romany culture. Knowledge of late 19th-century Romany life depends largely on members of the Wood family having transmitted material to the scholar and collector **John Sampson**, whose work was supplemented by other scholars, such as Dora Yates and Francis Groome. *The Welsh Gypsies* (1991) was jointly written by **A. O. H. Jarman** and his wife, Eldra, who was proud of her Romany roots.

The growing tendency of families such as the Woods and Robertses to identify with Welsh rather than Romany culture is not mirrored in the general Romany population living in Wales today, which still experiences the difficulties and tensions of groups living at the margins of more settled society. Few Welsh Romanies speak **Welsh**, and it is generally asserted that the Romany language is extinct. However, Tim Coughlan, in *Now Shoon the Romano Gillie* (2001), argues that the older, inflected Romany has been replaced by a reduced form of the language, which is regarded by some experts as a dialect of Romany and by others as a very specialized register of **English**.

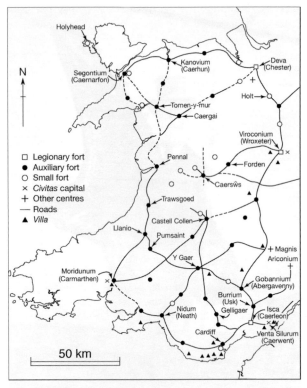

Roman Wales (after Ordnance Survey)

Legend:
□ Legionary fort
● Auxiliary fort
○ Small fort
× *Civitas* capital
+ Other centres
— Roads
▲ *Villa*

50 km

ROMANS, The

In AD 43, the Emperor Claudius ordered the invasion of **Britain**. Roman control was established relatively rapidly in the south-east, but the Catuvellaunian leader **Caratacus** turned for assistance to the war-like **Silures** of south-east Wales, and the western tribes generally remained hostile. Incursions into Wales were initiated by Ostorius Scapula late in 47, when the Romans struck into the territory of the **Deceangli** of north-east Wales, probably in an effort to divide the Silures and the **Ordovices** from the Brigantes. The Roman military effort was soon concentrated against the Silures, who, despite the capture of Caratacus, conducted a successful 25-year guerrilla war – the Silurian War. A legion was defeated, an event described by **Tacitus**, who credited Julius Frontinus with the defeat of the Silures in 74–5. The Ordovices of the north were attacked by **Suetonius Paulinus,** who destroyed the **druids**' centre on **Anglesey** in 61. The tribe was not finally defeated, however, until the genocidal campaign of Agricola in 79.

In the aftermath of conquest, a large military presence was required; it has been estimated that some 30,000 Roman troops occupied Wales in the late 70s. Of the three legionary fortresses in Roman Britain, two – **Caerleon** and Chester – were within Wales or on its **borders**. The fortresses became the administrative centres for Roman forces, and a network of forts garrisoned by auxiliaries and connected by a new **road** system was established throughout Wales. Archaeological investigations, particularly at sites such as Caerleon, have provided a wealth of evidence relating to this military occupation. Caerleon (Isca to the Romans) not only provided living accommodation for the Second Augustan Legion but also large fortress baths and

an impressive amphitheatre. A sprawling civil settlement grew up around Caerleon, which became the largest **population** centre in Roman Wales. Eventually, stability produced increasing interaction and cultural conflation as Romano-British culture developed. This process was accelerated by the implementation of *civitas* administration – limited devolution based on tribal units. Two *civitates* were established in Wales, one in Silurian territory and the other in the territory of the **Demetae** in the south-west. **Caerwent** (Venta Silurum) was the capital of the former and **Carmarthen** (Moridunum Demetarum) of the latter. Excavation has confirmed that the basilica at Caerwent dates from the time of Hadrian, suggesting that *civitas* administration was established there in the 120s, when significant numbers of the legion were transferred north to assist in construction of Hadrian's Wall. Other civil settlements, such the *vicus* adjoining the fort at **Cowbridge** (Bovium), also developed, as did villas in areas like the **Vale of Glamorgan**, including good examples at Ely (**Cardiff**), **Llantwit Major** and **Llandough**. Villa owners practised capitalist **agriculture**, which led to the introduction of new crops such as apples, **oats**, carrots and leeks (*see* **Plants**). Industry also developed, the extractive industries being particularly important in the early years; sophisticated hydraulic features were employed at the Dolaucothi **gold**mine (*see* **Cynwyl Gaeo**).

Archaeological evidence confirms that, as the **economy** matured, a synthesis culture developed, with native and Roman influences mingling, at least in the most Romanized areas. There was, for example, a temple to the conflated deity Mars-Oculus at Caerwent. By the 4th century, there is evidence of Christian worship (*see* **Religion**); two of Roman Britain's three known Christian martyrs, **Julius and Aaron**, died in Caerleon. However, while there is evidence for partial acceptance of *romanitas*, particularly in the south-east, there is also evidence for the survival of native tradition even in such places as Caerwent. Artefacts recovered from 3rd-century contexts in the *civitas* capital, including a seated mother goddess and a stylized carved stone head, seem wholly native in their inspiration. Similarly, interesting excavations at Thornwell Farm near Caerwent demonstrate roundhouse occupation into the 4th century.

Later Roman Britain was increasingly shaped by external threats and internal upheavals. The concentration of military forces shifted to the coasts, and sites such as Cardiff and Segontium (**Caernarfon**) became increasingly important. The army administrative structures changed with the creation of new military titles such as *Dux Britanniarum*. Troops were also periodically removed to support coups and counter-coups in mainland Europe; troop withdrawal by **Magnus Maximus** in 383 was particularly significant. It seems increasingly likely that by 410, when the 'rescript' of Honorius purportedly instructed British authorities to look after their own affairs, many had already been doing so for some time. By this date, which conventionally marks the end of Roman Britain, Roman legacies and native traditions had merged and were to shape early medieval Welsh society. Roman legacies included **Latin**, the language of the church and of scholarship in Wales for 1000 years and more after the fall of the empire, and the source of many **Welsh** words. The dying years of the empire saw the creation of the foundations of the kingdoms of early medieval Wales. Roman success in bringing most of Britain under a single governance provided the Welsh with a tantalising and influential image (*see* Britain, **Geoffrey of Monmouth** and **Prophecy**).

ROMANTICISM

Although Romanticism appeared in Wales at the end of the 18th century, its roots are to be found in the work of antiquarians at the end of the 17th, with their enthusiasm for the remote **Celt**ic and druidic past (*see* **Archaeology and Antiquarianism**).

Romanticism helped to raise the prestige of **Welsh**, with its emphasis on the primeval origins of the language, possibly among the Patriarchs, its word particles supposedly having the potential to explain the origins of words in all other languages. These fanciful theories drove scholars to recover words from old Welsh texts and motivated them to invent a vast new vocabulary. Romanticism's emphasis on seeking out and publishing early and medieval texts transformed **literature** in **Welsh**. The **eisteddfod** movement encouraged the revival of medieval verse forms.

It was Romanticism that created the image of Wales as the **'land of song'**, the harpist 'Blind' **John Parry** (1710–82) claiming that Welsh **harp** music could be traced back to the ancient **druids**. Interest in the wisdom of the common folk led to a revival of *penillion* (folk verses) and of the art of singing to the harp known as *cerdd dant* or ***penillion singing***.

There was a rebirth of interest in early Welsh history. **Owain Glyndŵr** reappeared as a national hero, and the Welsh were fascinated by such myths as the discovery of America *c.*1170 by **Madog ab Owain Gwynedd**, the **massacre of the bards** by Edward I, and the seizure of **Britain** by the **Anglo-Saxons** in the **Treason of the Long Knives**.

The movement also taught people to admire the wild **mountains** of Wales. Travellers came to study ruins and megaliths (then considered to be druidic remains), painters such as **Richard Wilson** and **Thomas Jones** (1742–1803) portrayed wild landscapes attractively, and by 1800 Welsh landscape was the fashion (*see* **Painting** and **Tourism**). By the 1840s and 1850s, the Welsh were persuaded to turn their mountains into a national symbol.

Romanticism in Wales idealized the individual personality. This can be seen in Methodism, especially in the lyric **hymns** of **William Williams** (Pantycelyn; 1717–91). Welsh also developed a language of sensibility, to express all aspects of human character – in, for example, the coining in this period of numerous words beginning with *hunan-* (self-). This was also the period when portraits of Welsh individuals began to appear in large numbers, as did a fair number of autobiographies.

The coming of democratic politics, industrialism and Nonconformity (*see* **Nonconformists**) meant a challenge to Romanticism. There were to be several rearguard actions fought by Romantic writers in such institutions as the eisteddfod, so that in the period from about 1890 to 1914 it was possible for a powerful neo-Romantic literary school to emerge in Welsh, dominated by such figures as **T. Gwynn Jones**.

ROOS, William (Gwilym Rosa; 1808–78) Artist

After nautical training, William Roos taught himself to paint. In 1834, he moved to **Caernarfon**, from Bodgadfa (**Amlwch**), his birthplace, joining the town's growing band of professional artists. He spent time among the expatriate community in **London**, where many of the best-known contemporary figures – Talhaiarn (John Jones: 1810–69) among them – sat for him. He painted animals, histories, portraits and miniatures. The mezzotint he engraved from his portrait of **John Elias** was one of the most popular images of the period.

ROSEMARKET (Rhosfarced),
Pembrokeshire (672 ha; 454 inhabitants)

Located immediately north-east of **Milford Haven**, the name originated with the market established in the 12th century by the Knights Hospitallers of **Slebech**. The **community**'s chief feature is a late medieval **dovecote**, which contained over 200 nesting boxes. Great Westfield is an attractive 18th-century house. The **Congregational** chapel (1883) dwarfs St Ismael's church (largely 1890). Zachariah Williams (1683–1755), an ill-starred inventor admired by Samuel Johnson, was born at Rosemarket.

ROSSER, Melvyn (1926–2001)
Accountant and public figure

A native of **Swansea**, Melvyn Rosser joined the Swansea office of the accountancy company Deloitte's in 1950. By the time he retired in 1985, he was one of the five chief partners at the company's **London** office. From the 1960s onwards, he became prominent in a remarkably wide range of organizations. His public offices included the chairmanship of the Welsh Economic Council, the chairmanship of the HTV Wales Group and presidency of the **University of Wales, Aberystwyth**. He was a fine tenor and his musical talents were inherited by his son, the imaginative composer and singer Neil Rosser.

ROSSETT (Orsedd, Yr), Wrexham
(2555 ha; 3336 inhabitants)

Located north-east of **Wrexham** and bisected by the Wrexham–Chester highway (the A483), Rossett is the northernmost of the **communities** of the **county** of **Wrexham**. The fertility of its land accounts for its numerous **gentry** houses and its two large cornmills. The glory of the community is Trevalyn Hall. Wales's finest Elizabethan mansion, it was built for John **Trevor** in 1576. With its splendid symmetry and its pedimented windows, Trevalyn (together with Plas Clough, **Denbigh**) is proof of the arrival in Wales of **Renaissance** concepts of **architecture**.

ROTHSAY CASTLE

This **ship**, which was sometimes called the *Rothesay Castle*, was one of the first paddle steamers to be built. She was in a poor state of repair when, on 18 August 1831, she was taking day-trippers from **Liverpool** to **Beaumaris**. A storm blew up and, with the drunken captain refusing to turn back, the vessel broke up on a sandbank off Beaumaris. There was no lifesaving equipment and 127 people lost their lives.

ROWENA (Rhonwen or Alys or Alice; fl. mid-5th century) Legendary figure

Daughter of the Saxon (*see* **Anglo-Saxons**) leader Hengist, and wife of the British chieftain **Vortigern**, Rowena is referred to (without being named) in *Historia Brittonum*, where she figures in the story of the **Treason of the Long Knives**. She became well known through the writings of **Geoffrey of Monmouth**. Expressions for the **English** such as 'cyff Rhonwen' (the stock of Rhonwen) and 'plant Alys' (the children of Alys), which originated in the work of the late medieval poets, were used until the 19th century.

ROWLAND, Daniel (1711–90) Methodist leader

Born at Bwlch-llan (**Nantcwnlle**), Rowland was ordained priest in 1735, but owing to his Methodist tendencies served – at Nantcwnlle and **Llangeitho** – only as a curate. Following his conversion under the ministry of **Griffith Jones, Llanddowror**, he met **Howel Harris**, and co-operation followed for a number of years. The two were later joined by **William Williams** (Pantycelyn; 1717–91), who became Rowland's assistant in 1743. Because of differences between Rowland and Harris, the two separated in 1750, thereby dividing the Welsh **Calvinistic Methodists** into two camps. Following Harris's retirement from public life in 1752, Rowland became sole leader of the movement.

In 1762, Harris was invited back to his former position, and his return coincided with the outbreak of a new awakening at Llangeitho. The Church's response to this second wave of **revival** activity was to deprive Rowland of his curacy in 1763, but a chapel was built for his use by his followers at Llangeitho and he ministered there, with considerable success, until his death; people would come from all directions to listen to his preaching. Some of his sermons, **hymns** and translations survive. Rowland's son, Nathaniel Rowland (1749–1831), led the attack in 1791 upon **Peter Williams**'s alleged **Sabellianism**.

ROWLAND, John Cambrian (1819–90) Artist

A self-taught artist who became a renowned portraitist, John Rowland was born in **Lledrod**, beginning his artistic career in **Aberystwyth** before settling in the north. He taught at **Caernarfon** and painted portraits, landscapes and popular subjects (*see* **Painting**). His prints of **Welsh costumes** and customs were published in large numbers; some of these images were appropriated by the ceramic industry (*see* **Pottery**), appearing on tableware.

ROWLANDS, Dafydd (1931–2001) Writer and archdruid

Born in **Pontardawe**, Dafydd Rowlands was educated at **Swansea** and at the Presbyterian College, **Carmarthen**. He was a **Congregationalist** minister and a schoolteacher before becoming a lecturer in **Welsh** at **Trinity College**, Carmarthen in 1968; in 1983, he became a full-time writer. He won the crown at the National **Eisteddfod** in 1969 and again in 1972, the year in which he also won the prose medal for his volume of essays *Ysgrifau yr Hanner Bardd* (1972). A penetrating exploration of his relationship with his father, *Mae Theomemphus yn Hen*, followed in 1977. He published three collections of poetry and scripted numerous television programmes, including the popular comedy series *Licrys Olsorts*. With his sonorous voice and natural dignity, he made a memorable **archdruid** (1996–8).

ROWLANDS, Henry (1655–1723) Antiquary and naturalist

Henry Rowlands was the **parish** priest of Llanedwen (**Llanddaniel Fab**). His knowledge may indeed have been greater than his scholarship but, nevertheless, **Edward Lhuyd** was ready to consult him about the language and antiquities of **Anglesey**. His *Idea Agriculturae*, a treatise on practical **agriculture**, and his essay on the origin of fossils reveal genuine familiarity with these **science**s, but his best-known work is *Mona Antiqua Restaurata* (1723, but written before 1710) which attempts to prove that Anglesey was the chief centre of the **druids**. The work has no historical value but it is of particular significance in the historiography of ideas about the druids. Rowlands is seen at his most astute in *Antiquitates Parochiales*, an essay on the **parishes** of **Menai commote**, which remained unpublished until 1846–8, and in which his obsession with the druids is not so apparent.

ROWLANDS, Robert John (Meuryn; 1880–1967) Poet and journalist

A native of **Aber[gwyngregyn]**, R. J. Rowlands was a journalist at **Liverpool** and **Caernarfon**. He became editor of *Yr Herald Cymraeg* in 1921, the year he won the chair at the National **Eisteddfod**. He wrote children's adventure stories as well as a volume of poetry. He became so well known as adjudicator in the BBC's radio programme *Ymryson y Beirdd* (*see* **Talwrn y Beirdd**) that his bardic name, Meuryn, was adopted as the recognized term for the adjudicator at bardic contests. Eurys I. Rowlands (1926–2006), a highly original interpreter of medieval **Welsh** poetry, was his son.

ROYAL CAMBRIAN ACADEMY OF ART, The

There were numerous attempts during the 19th century to establish an academy for Wales comparable with those in **England**, **Scotland** and **Ireland**. Eventually, a group of largely English-born painters, who worked predominantly in the **Conwy** valley, led by **H. Clarence Whaite**, established the Cambrian Academy at **Llandudno** in 1881, gaining royal patronage in 1882.

Their first exhibition was held in Llandudno, where there were already a number of commercial **art galleries** in the town catering for the growing tourist trade, but from 1884 the Academy was based at Plas Mawr, **Conwy**, where regular exhibitions were held; in 1993, the Academy moved to premises in Crown Lane, Conwy. Among the participants, as among the founders, there remain strong links with north-west England.

ROYAL CHARTER

Hit by a storm when returning from **Australia**, this **Queensferry**-built **Liverpool** clipper was driven onto the **Anglesey** coast near **Moelfre** on 26 October 1859. Waves reported as high as 18 m broke up the **ship**, washing hundreds of passengers and crew into the sea. Of the 110 crew and 388 passengers on board, 459 lost their lives. The same gale was responsible for a further 110 shipwrecks around the Welsh coast. Charles Dickens, who visited the site

10 weeks later, and watched divers searching for bullion, wrote about the wreck in *The Uncommercial Traveller* (1861). Later accounts include Alexander McKee's *The Golden Wreck* (1961) and T. Llew Jones's *Ofnadwy Nos* (1971) and the American singer-songwriter Tom Russell's ballad 'Isaac Lewis'.

ROYAL COMMISSION ON THE ANCIENT AND HISTORICAL MONUMENTS OF WALES, The

Established in 1908, with headquarters at **Aberystwyth**, the RCAHMW was set up to make an inventory of ancient and historic monuments in Wales. Later, its powers were widened to embrace all archaeological, architectural and historical landscapes, including maritime sites. Early publications (1911–25) included surveys of the archaeological and architectural monuments of seven of Wales's **counties**. Standards improved vastly with the publication of the **Anglesey** volume (1937). Since 1975, county surveys have been supplemented by volumes based on specific themes. The RCAHMW is also responsible for co-ordinating archaeological aerial **photography** in Wales. In 1963, the National Monuments Record of Wales was established as the public archive of the RCAHMW.

ROYAL ORDNANCE FACTORIES

As part of the **government**'s rearmament campaign of the late 1930s, eight royal ordnance factories were established in Wales before and during the **Second World War**. Seven new factories were constructed – at **Bridgend**, **Hirwaun**, Llanishen (**Cardiff**), Glascoed (**Llanbadoc**), **Newport**, **Marchwiel** and Rhydymwyn (**Cilcain**) – while the ordnance

factory at **Pembrey** was sited at the works originally owned by the Nobel company. The **engineering** works at Newport and Llanishen specialized in the manufacture of guns, Bridgend and Glascoed filled shells with high explosives, and Pembrey concentrated on the manufacture of TNT. During the war, the factories employed large numbers of **women**. Bridgend ROF, reputedly the largest British factory of its kind, employed some 35,000 workers at its peak, over 70% of whom were women. Following the war, several of the factories were converted to trading estates (*see* **Industrial and Trading Estates**).

ROYAL REGIMENT OF WALES, The

Formed in 1969 from the 1st Battalions of the 24th Foot (**South Wales Borderers**) and of the 41st Foot (**Welch Regiment**), the Royal Regiment of Wales has served in many parts of the world, including Belize, Germany, Hong Kong, Northern **Ireland** and Zimbabwe. In 2004, it was decided to merge the regiment with the **Royal Welch Fusiliers** and on 1 March 2006, a new regiment, the Royal Welsh, came into being. The third battalion of this regiment is the only infantry unit of the Territorial Army to recruit throughout the whole of Wales.

ROYAL SOCIETY OF ARCHITECTS IN WALES, The

A national body, with headquarters in **Cardiff**, which represents the architectural profession; it is affiliated to the Royal Institute of British Architects. The society was established in 1973, following the amalgamation of the South Wales Institute of Architects (founded in 1890 as the Cardiff, South Wales and **Monmouthshire** Society of

John Josiah Dodd, *The Wreck of the Royal Charter* (1859)

Architects) and the North Wales Society of Architects (founded in 1928). It received its 'Royal' prefix in 1995. The society has four regional branches and publishes a half-yearly journal, *Touchstone*. (*See also* **Architecture**.)

ROYAL WELCH FUSILIERS, The

Established by Edward Herbert (the fourth Baron Herbert of Cherbury) in 1689, the 23rd Foot fought at the battle of the Boyne (1690) and throughout the War of the Spanish Succession. In 1702, the Duke of Marlborough converted the regiment into one of three fusilier regiments armed with the flintlock fusil. (The earliest evidence of the **goat** mascot dates from 1775.) Battalions fought in the American Wars, throughout the **French Revolutionary and Napoleonic Wars**), and in the **Crimean War**. Long associated with Wales (with a depot at **Wrexham**), the title the Royal Welch (later Welsh) Fusiliers was adopted in 1881. The 1st Battalion served in the **South African Wars**, and the 2nd during the Boxer Rebellion. During the **First World War**, 42 battalions of fusiliers fought in all major theatres; among their officers were authors Robert Graves and Siegfried Sassoon. During the **Second World War**, the fusiliers fought in mainland Europe, Burma and **Madagascar**, and since 1945 the regiment has served in Germany, Malaya, Cyprus, Singapore, Kenya, Belize and Northern **Ireland**. The 2nd Battalion was disbanded in 1958. In 2004, it was decided to merge the fusiliers with the **Royal Regiment of Wales**, to create the Regiment of the Royal Welsh; it was designated the 1st Battalion alongside the 2nd Battalion (The Royal Regiment of Wales).

ROYAL WELSH AGRICULTURAL SHOW, The

The Royal Welsh Agricultural Show, the premier countryside festival of Wales, is staged annually by the Royal Welsh Agricultural Society, which was founded at **Aberystwyth** in 1904 as the Welsh National Agricultural Society (it adopted its current name in 1920). Despite facing initial jealousy from local **agricultural societies**, it successfully held its first six two-day shows in Aberystwyth between 1904 and 1909. By the latter year, however, it was felt that the society could only achieve a national character if its show became migratory, like the National **Eisteddfod**. Accordingly, between 1910 and 1962, it was staged at centres in north and south Wales in alternate years; it became a three-day event from 1914 onwards. Faced with the mounting costs of erecting a showground at different centres year upon year, the society decided in 1960 to settle at a permanent site. The venue chosen was **Llanelwedd**, near **Builth**; the first show was held there in 1963. Pressure on facilities necessitated the show becoming a four-day event in 1981.

Despite problems such as low membership during the 1970s and the remorseless rise in the cost of running the show – even after moving to Llanelwedd – the society kept afloat and its show expanded enormously. Whereas average attendance between 1922 (when the show was resuscitated after the **First World War**) and 1939 was 35,000, by the 1990s it had risen spectacularly to 219,000. The move to a permanent site proved unpopular for the first 10 years or so, and many people stayed away. Only when the site, from the mid-1970s, began to boast permanent, impressive buildings, did confidence in the Llanelwedd project materialize.

Attracting extensive media coverage and serving as a shop window for Welsh **agriculture**, the show has always been primarily a livestock one, with native breeds like Welsh Blacks (*see* **Cattle**), Welsh Mountain **sheep**, and Welsh ponies and cobs (*see* **Horses**) to the fore. Other attractions for the increasingly non-agricultural visitors are the wide variety of trade stands, the flower show, the **dog** show, the **forestry** section, country pursuits and rural **crafts**, farriery competitions, the fur and feather sections, sheep shearing competitions and **sheepdog trials**. The showground is now used for many other activities, from sheep sales and horse trials to *eisteddfodau* and **bible** weeks. A winter fair has been held there since 1990.

ROYAL WELSH COLLEGE OF MUSIC AND DRAMA, The, Cardiff

This college, which opened in **Cardiff** Castle in 1949 as a small conservatoire and became a corporate body in 1992, is Wales's only specialist centre for professional training in **music** and **drama**. Its first principal was Raymond Edwards (1919–99) whose influence on drama in Wales extended beyond the college, to involvement in such institutions as Theatr Garthewin (**Llanfair Talhaiarn**) and the campaign for a national theatre. In 1974, it moved into purpose-built premises in the castle grounds. A six-figure donation by the actor and one-time student Anthony Hopkins (b.1937) and a National Lottery award of £1.1 million in 1995 enabled the refurbishment of the college's **William Burges**-designed Castle Mews building and its opening, in 1998, as a new centre for rehearsal and performance. In 2006/7, about 600 students were being educated there.

RUABON (Rhiwabon), Wrexham
(2315 ha; 3515 inhabitants)

Located on the north bank of the **Dee** opposite **Chirk**, Ruabon was the core of the Wynnstay estate, which, at over 57,000 ha, was by far the largest of the landed estates of 19th-century Wales. It had been amassed by the **Williams Wynn family** who, in 1740, acquired by marriage a house and estate on **Wat's Dyke**. Originally called Watstay, its new owners renamed it Wynnstay. The fourth baronet laid out a vast park and planned an enormous palace high above the Dee, plans which were not fully realized. After a fire in 1859, the house was rebuilt in a coarse Victorian interpretation of a French chateau. Sold in 1949, Wynnstay became a school and subsequently a block of flats. The park is rich in **lakes** and avenues and contains an ornamental dairy, a Doric column, a tower, lodges and – for the hounds of the Wynnstay Hunt – the kennels in which Sir Watkin Williams Wynn (1693–1749) incarcerated the Methodist evangelist **Peter Williams**.

Originally little more than an estate village at the baronet's gate, Ruabon became a substantial settlement housing **coal**miners and brickmakers as well as estate workers. The Ruabon brickworks, established in 1860, supplied the material for most of the buildings of **Wrexham** and also secured an international market. The works eventually came to specialize in the production of high-quality quarry tiles. St Mary's church has a 14th-century tower and a 15th-century wall **painting**. It contains many funereal monuments especially those of the Wynnstay family. Since

1980, it has been jointly used by the **Anglicans** and the **Roman Catholics**. To the west, above **Offa's Dyke**, is the fine **Iron Age** Gardden Fort.

RUBENS, Bernice (1928–2004)
Writer and film-maker
Bernice Rubens's father was a Lithuanian **Jew** who, fleeing anti-semitism, believed he was heading for America when he boarded ship in about 1900; but he was cast ashore at **Cardiff**, and it was a fortnight before he realized he was not in New York. He raised in Cardiff a notably **music**al family. Bernice, who left it too late to pursue a career as a musician, read **English** at University College, Cardiff (*see* **Cardiff University**), taught English in Birmingham and became an award-winning documentary **film**-maker. She wrote 25 novels, the fourth of which, *The Elected Member* (1969), won the 1970 Booker prize; two of her books, *Madame Souzatzka* (1962) and *I Sent a Letter To My Love* (1975), were made into critically acclaimed films. Although she spent most of her life in **London**, some of her novels – such as her own favourite, *Brothers* (1983) – have Welsh settings, and many involve explorations of Jewish identity; survival and inherited guilt are important themes. Her only work of non-fiction was an autobiography, which she completed shortly before her death.

RUDBAXTON, Pembrokeshire
(2036 ha; 1062 inhabitants)
Located immediately north-east of **Haverfordwest**, the **community** contains the villages of Rudbaxton, Crundale and Poyston Cross. The rath near Crundale is in the form of an impressive **Iron Age** fortified farmstead. St Michael's church, Rudbaxton, originally 11th century, contains a remarkable rustic Baroque monument (1668) consisting of almost life-sized figures of four members of the Howard family of Fletherhill. It also contains a plaque noting that William Laud, when bishop of **St David's** (1621–6), was pluralist rector of Rudbaxton. Poyston Hall (late 18th century) was the early home of the Waterloo hero **Thomas Picton**. Adjoining it is Haverfordwest's Withybush **airport**.

RUDRY (Rhydri), Caerphilly
(2344 ha; 862 inhabitants)
A **community** immediately north-east of **Cardiff**, it contains the villages of Rudry, Draethen, Garth and Waterloo. Ruperra Castle (*c.*1626), a rectangular block with cylindrical angle towers, was a curiously anachronistic building for its date. Built for Thomas Morgan, steward of the earl of Pembroke, it became a melancholy ruin; there are plans afoot to ensure that is not a danger. Cefn Mably, the seat of the Kemeys-Tynte family, contained elements of every period from the 16th to the 19th centuries. It was used as a hospital from 1923 to 1980, but was damaged by a fire in 1994. It is the subject of a wistful sonnet by **W. J. Gruffydd**. A Roman **lead** mine at Draethen extending 120 m underground offers evidence of a 3rd-century counterfeiting operation.

RUGBY LEAGUE
Rugby league has never established itself permanently in Wales, yet it has had a profound impact. Begun in 1895, when leading north of **England** clubs seceded from the Rugby Football Union after being refused the right to compensate players for loss of earnings, it rapidly evolved into a separate game, permitting open professionalism and, in 1907, reducing teams from 15 players to 13.

The Royal Welch Fusiliers parading with their goat mascots

Rugby league legend Billy Boston

League's existence turned **rugby union**'s amateurism from regulation into ideology, but one interpreted with greater flexibility in Wales than in England. Welsh Union's first golden age (1900–11) was in part aided by England's post-1895 weakness, while league provided an opportunity for players to cash in on their skills.

Nine Welsh clubs – **Ebbw Vale** (1907–12), **Merthyr Tydfil** (1907–11), **Aberdare** (1908–9), **Barry** (1908–9), Treherbert (**Rhondda**) (1908–10), **Pontypridd** (1926–8), **Cardiff** (1951–2), Cardiff/**Bridgend** Blue Dragons (1981–5) and South Wales (1996) – have played in the Rugby League. They have been handicapped by travelling costs, the disinclination of union supporters to pay to watch second-rate league, and the fact that the very best Welsh talent continued to opt for the top north of England clubs.

More than 150 Welsh internationals have 'Gone North', making the league scout a pantomime villain figure, the thief of local heroes. The flow began pre-1895, with players such as the James brothers of **Swansea**, and it peaked between the wars. This went into reverse after rugby union went professional in 1995, with the return of players like Jonathan Davies and Scott Gibbs and the signing by the WRU of Oldham-born league star Iestyn Harris in 2001. Several of the greatest Welsh league players went north before becoming union stars. The three Welshmen – Billy Boston, **Gus Risman** and **Jim Sullivan** – among the eight charter members of the Rugby League Hall of Fame all went as teenagers, as did **Clive Sullivan**.

Wales staged the first ever league international, beating **New Zealand** 9–8 at Aberdare in 1908. The Wales team has since oscillated between success (winning three European championships in the late 1930s) and inactivity (not playing at all between 1954 and 1967). Although the team

reached the semi-final of the 1995 and 1999 World Cups, it is increasingly reliant on players of Welsh descent rather than birth.

Only at amateur student level has league made good its ambition to be truly national. The outstanding success here has been the **University of Wales Institute, Cardiff**, who were British Universities Sports Association champions four times between 1998 and 2002.

RUGBY UNION

For over 100 years, rugby **football** has attracted strong passions, a large popular following and close media interest in Wales. It is seen by many as a symbol of Welsh identity and an expression of national consciousness.

Ball games of an informal kind had been played in Wales for many centuries, but rugby acquired its modern form when the Rugby Football Union (of **England**) was founded (1871), drawing up a set of rules based on those already in use in some public schools and at **Cambridge**. A hybrid football was already being played at the colleges of **Lampeter** and **Llandovery** from the 1850s, and the first Welsh clubs, like **Neath** (1871), **Llanelli** (1872), **Swansea** (1874), **Newport** (1875) and **Cardiff** (1876), were all founded by solicitors, businessmen, surveyors, teachers and industrialists, generally products of the rugby-playing schools and colleges. But the game was soon taken up by the working **class**. Crucial to this growth was the industrial development of Wales in the second half of the 19th century and the immense **population** growth that accompanied it. The game provided an opportunity for physical recreation and the expression of local pride and communal identity. Aided by shorter hours of work, especially the new Saturday half-holiday, rising real wages, and an often dense **railway** network, the conditions were ripe for the emergence of a dramatic, robust spectator sport.

A challenge cup competition was instituted in 1877 under the auspices of the South Wales Football Union, the precursor of the Welsh Rugby Union (WRU), which was established in Neath in March 1881 and was the creation of the ambitious Richard Mullock of the Newport club, who the previous month had organized the first ever Welsh national side to meet England.

Throughout the next decade, the game spread rapidly in the heavily populated **counties** of the industrial south. After an inauspicious international beginning, the game developed sufficiently for Wales to win the Triple Crown for the first time in 1893. By adopting Cardiff's four three-quarter system – an innovation symbolic of the confident, enterprising south Wales of the late 19th century – allied to the muscularity of colliers and **tinplate** workers in the pack, the platform was laid for the first golden era (1900–11), when a further six Triple Crowns were won. Recognizing that the only way to defeat their socially superior, better-fed and bigger (but less imaginative) **English** and Scottish opponents, was to think and act faster, Welsh rugby developed a tradition of producing nippy, elusive backs; given the ball by powerful forwards skilled at ripping the ball out of mauls, the backs proceeded to bring an aesthetic and scientific dimension to the game that was widely admired. Less admired by outsiders was the perceived Welsh flouting of the amateur regulations, but canny administrators of the game within Wales tolerated an accepted level of remuneration in the interests of keeping it socially inclusive. At the Cardiff Arms Park on 16 December 1905, the **New Zealand** All Blacks suffered their only defeat in a 32-match tour at the hands of a rampant Wales. It was an event of national significance. **Teddy Morgan**, who scored the winning try, **Dickie Owen** who devised the stratagem that led up to it, and team captain **Gwyn Nicholls** became household names, and Welsh rugby success joined **education**al, cultural, economic and political advance as symbols of an Edwardian high noon of national optimism and prosperity.

When the economic indicators fell back during the inter-war **depression**, Welsh rugby felt the chill. The crisis in the **coal**field affected the **ports** as well, and the gears of pre-war in-migration were reversed, as 390,000 people left Wales, a high proportion of them young men in the 15–29 age group. Where once rugby clubs had opened – almost, it seemed, with the frequency of Victorian collieries and chapels – now they closed, especially in the hard-hit valleys of east **Glamorgan** and **Monmouthshire**, as spending power and spectators dwindled, financial and playing resources diminished, and Welsh international fortunes plummeted. The Triple Crown, last won in 1911, remained hopelessly elusive. The WRU, struggling to keep afloat, became increasingly unconfident in all its dealings. International selection became ever more erratic, with Llanelli's **Albert Jenkins**, the finest player of his era, a notable victim of selectorial whim.

The decision of over 700 players, including 70 internationals, to join the professional ranks of **rugby league** in the north of England between 1919 and 1939 further undermined Welsh fortunes. In the 1930s, the selectors turned for salvation to the grammar schools and universities, and were fortunate in the outstanding abilities of Oxbridge Blues such as **Vivian Jenkins**, **Cliff Jones** and **Wilfred Wooller**, and Welsh university products such as **Claude Davey**, **Watcyn Thomas** and Haydn Tanner. These, in alliance with tough manual workers up front, secured historic wins at Twickenham for the first time ever in 1933 and, in a brilliant display of attacking rugby, over the 1935 All Blacks. The satisfying on-field social mix was hailed, in the words of the *Western Mail*, as 'a victory for Wales … that probably is impossible in any other sphere'. Once again, rugby's significance extended far beyond the field itself.

The post-1945 return to full employment was soon reflected in consistently better results. Under the head-masterly eye of the strict disciplinarian John Gwilliam, who played his rugby in England and **Scotland**, Wales recaptured the Triple Crown in 1950 and 1952. Gwilliam's detachment from the intensity of the Welsh club game, allied to a generally shrewd tactical appreciation, brought the best out of outstanding players such as Lewis Jones, Bleddyn Williams, Cliff Morgan and Roy John. Club rugby enjoyed immense popularity too, but by the late 1950s the game had sunk into a dour pattern of low-scoring battles of attrition. New inspiration and new ideas were

Rugby union's home in Cardiff, the Millennium Stadium, opened in 1999

The 2005 Grand Slam: Gareth Thomas with the ball, in action against England

needed to break the deadlock, and the 1960s provided them. The irrepressible Clive Rowlands nagged and kicked his forwards up the touchline to a Triple Crown in 1965. Thanks to the foresight of shrewd administrators like Kenneth Harris, Hermas Evans and Cliff Jones, the key appointment in 1967 of Ray Williams to the new position of coaching organizer meant that the concurrent transformation of the historic Cardiff Arms Park into the National Ground would provide a stage worthy of the cluster of breathtaking talent that announced its arrival with another Triple Crown in 1969.

The 1970s saw Welsh rugby's second golden era, whose play was much indebted at club and British (though regrettably not Welsh national) level to the innovative coaching skills of **Carwyn James**. Inspiring captain John Dawes, like Watcyn Thomas and Gwilliam before him, was an exile. At **London** Welsh, he captained a team of enormous ability and even greater potential. When confident, well-educated young men like Gerald Davies, Mervyn Davies and J. P. R. Williams (also an outstanding **tennis** player), combined their talents with the stunning gifts of those at home such as Gareth Edwards, Barry John and Phil Bennett, their achievements brought the Welsh sides of the 1970s a collective renown that extended far beyond Wales itself. Three Grand Slams and six Triple Crowns were won between 1969 and 1979, four of them in succession (1976–9). Wales also provided the Lions team's share of the victorious British tours of New Zealand (1971) and **South Africa** (1974); the former was captained by Dawes and coached by Carwyn James.

The last two decades of the 20th century were grimly reminiscent of an earlier period of economic dislocation and social crisis. The end of the second golden era in 1979 coincided with the rejection of **devolution** and the inauguration of two decades of Thatcherite Conservatism. The miners were finally defeated in 1984–5, the traditional heavy industries were dismantled, and unemployment rates soared. In that decade, the Rugby League was able to recruit 13 Welsh internationals; the chance to play rugby at a higher skill level than was current in Wales was not lost on the most gifted player of his generation, Jonathan Davies, whose move north in 1989 relieved him of having to be part of the near-collapse of the Welsh game in the early 1990s. Administratively, it was saved by the barrister Vernon Pugh (1945–2003) who brought legal acumen and intellectual muscle to reforming the structure of the WRU before becoming, via the chairmanship of the International Board, the most decisive voice in world rugby. It was Pugh who masterminded and drove through the game's embrace of professionalism, a revolutionary move for which the game was ready and which signalled the return of prodigal sons like Davies, but otherwise did the game in Wales few favours, the densely concentrated club structure sitting uneasily with the demands of the new professional era. A clean break with the past was symbolized by the demolition of the National Stadium and the building of the 72,000-seater Millennium Stadium; the brainchild of WRU chairman and treasurer Glanmor Griffiths, it was completed on the same site just in time for the fourth Rugby World Cup, which Wales hosted in 1999.

Favoured by an obsessive media, rugby remained at the start of the 21st century a key component of Welsh popular culture, though less enthusiastically celebrated in song, cartoon, verse and even **sculpture** than it once was. What Welsh rugby lacked was a national team worthy of its fine new stadium. Two decades of demoralizing results led to the expensive appointments of New Zealanders Graham Henry (national coach, 1998–2002) and Steve Hansen (2002–4) to arrest the decline, but Welsh rugby had fallen too far behind for overnight recovery, even after a Welshman, to general relief, eventually took the coaching helm again in 2004 in the person of Mike Ruddock. The drastic attempts by a new corporate administration headed (2002–5) by yet another Antipodean import, Group Chief Executive David Moffet, to revitalize the game, or more accurately its finances, by imposing a regional organization onto the time-hallowed club structure saw historic first-class clubs rebadged (like **Gwent**, essentially Newport, Dragons), forced into shotgun marriages under unfamiliar names (such as the Swansea-Neath Ospreys) or, most criminally, abandoned (like **Pontypridd** and **Bridgend**).

The enforced demise of first-class rugby north of the **M4** threatened to disenfranchise a million people in an area that had once been as much the heartland of the Welsh game as of its **economy**. Any hopes that the winning in 2005 of the first Grand Slam since 1978 – in a style worthy of the Welsh game at its exuberant best – would reconcile the disaffected were promptly deflated by Ruddock's abrupt departure halfway through the 2006 season (succeeded by Gareth Jenkins). Here was further proof that Welsh rugby, despite – indeed because of – its enormous grass-roots support was struggling to survive in the post-industrial era, without traditional community roots that had sustained it, and as ever a barometer of the national condition.

RURAL DISTRICTS

Under the Local **Government** Act of 1894, all those parts of Wales not constituting **boroughs** or **urban districts** were divided into rural districts. The title was something of a misnomer: although some rural districts – **Penllyn** in **Merioneth**, for example – were wholly rural, others such as **Neath**, **Cardiff** and **Wrexham**, were heavily urbanized. Rural district councils had responsibility for matters such as **housing**, sanitation and public **health**, and the record of some of them – such as **Tregaron** – gave rise to much criticism, especially in **Clement Davies's** anti-**tuberculosis** report (1939). By the mid-20th century, Wales had 57 rural districts, varying in **population** from Wrexham (60,000) to **Painscastle** (1500). The local government reorganization of 1974 abolished them all and transferred their powers to districts – the sub-divisions of the new **counties**. The more rural the council, the more likely it was to be dominated by farmers, and thus abolition weakened the political voice of **agriculture**.

RUSSELL, [Arthur William] Bertrand (1872–1970)
Philosopher and mathematician
Although he was born and died in Wales, one of the greatest thinkers of the 20th century can hardly be considered a 'Welsh philosopher', having made his career in an entirely non-Welsh context. He was born at Ravenscroft, **Trellech**,

the son of John, Lord Amberley and the grandson of Lord John Russell who was twice **Liberal** prime minister of **Britain**. Orphaned before he was four, he was brought up by his grandmother and educated at **Cambridge**. He achieved prominence with *The Principles of Mathematics* (1903), and, with A. N. Whitehead, *Principia Mathematica* (1910–13). These were the first major works of a vast output that included *A History of Western Philosophy* (1945). In 1950, he won the Nobel prize for **literature**. (The only other Welsh-born Nobel laureates are the **Swansea**-born economist Clive Granger (b.1934) and the **Cardiff**-born physicist Brian D. Josephson (b.1940).) Imprisoned twice for anti-war activities, in 1958 he became the founding president of the Campaign for Nuclear Disarmament (**CND**). His last years were spent at Plas Penrhyn, **Penrhyndeudraeth**. It was from Penrhyndeudraeth post office that he dispatched telegrams to Krushchev and Kennedy during the Cuban missile crisis of 1962, and it was at Plas Penrhyn that he wrote *The Autobiography of Bertrand Russell* (3 vols., 1967–9). In its prologue, he declared: 'Three passions … have governed my life: the longing for love, the search for knowledge, and unbearable pity for the suffering of humanity.'

RUTHIN (Rhuthun), Denbighshire
(818 ha; 5218 inhabitants)
The chief centre of the upper **Clwyd** valley, Ruthin seems to have been first fortified by **Dafydd ap Gruffudd**, lord of **Dyffryn Clwyd** from 1277 to 1282. Following Reginald de **Grey**'s acquisition of the **march**er-lordship of Dyffryn

Bertrand Russell

Ryan and Ronnie: Ryan Davies (left) and Ronnie Williams

attractive townscape, with the three tiers of dormers of Myddelton Arms ('the seven eyes of Ruthin') and the one-time courthouse (1401), housing the NatWest Bank. In 1827, Ruthin's medieval court rolls were found there, a discovery which made Ruthin one of the best-documented of all Wales's marcher-lordships.

Until the 18th century, most of the towns of Wales sparkled with black-and-white houses. 'Now', as Peter Smith observed, 'only Ruthin remains. It should be scrupulously preserved as a national monument, as our last reminder of a departed urban gaiety before it was effaced by the dull reign of stone and stucco.' Outstanding among the town's sparkling buildings is Nantclwyd House, perhaps the birthplace of Gabriel Goodman. The Old County Gaol, rebuilt in 1775, has been adapted as a museum; it wonderfully evokes penitentiary history (*see* **Prisons**). With the completion of the **county** council offices in 1908, Ruthin became the centre of the former **Denbighshire**'s county **government**, a role it regained in the reconstituted county.

Attractive, timber-framed, Cae'r Afallen farm is located in the northern part of the **community**. To the west is the village of Llanfwrog, dominated by the massive tower of St Mwrog's church.

Clwyd – generally called the lordship of Ruthin – in 1284, a castle was built and a **borough** was established. On 18 September 1400, **Owain Glyndŵr** launched his revolt (*see* **Glyndŵr Revolt**) with an attack on the town and castle. Destroyed in the **Civil Wars**, in 1826 the castle's ruins became the site of a mansion built for the West family, who inherited the Ruthin part of the estates of the **Myddelton family**. Sold in 1920, the castle became a private clinic and subsequently a hotel.

St Peter's, originally a chapel of St Meugan's church (*see* **Llanbedr Dyffryn Clwyd**), may have housed a college of **Augustinian** canons, suppressed in 1536. Built largely in the 14th century, the church has a fine nave roof and a wealth of funereal monuments.

The buildings of the canonry came into the possession of **Gabriel Goodman** (1528–1601) and became the location of Christ's Hospital, the almshouse he endowed. It was he also who endowed the grammar school, which was originally located nearby. St Peter's Square constitutes an

RYAN AND RONNIE Television series

Ryan and Ronnie, broadcast on the BBC network between 1971 and 1973, was adapted into **English** from BBC Wales's hugely popular **Welsh-language** *Ryan a Ronnie*, first shown in 1967. The brainchild of Meredydd Evans (b.1919), the innovative head of BBC Wales's light entertainment department, the programme brought together **Ryan Davies** and Ronnie Williams (Ronald Clive Williams; 1939–97), an announcer and actor from Cefneithin (**Gorslas**), in a programme which featured sketches, songs and **dance**. Among the highlights was a sketch called 'Our House', with Ryan as a **Welsh Mam**, Ronnie as her husband, Derek Boote and the late Bryn Williams and **Myfanwy Talog** as their children; Ryan's line 'Don't call Will on your father' (a deliberate echo of Welsh syntax in English) is often quoted in jest. Equally successful on stage, the partnership ended in 1974 because of Ronnie's health problems. Unlike Ryan, and despite his talents as an actor and scriptwriter, Ronnie failed to establish himself in a solo career. Ravaged by alcoholism, depression and financial problems, he committed suicide in 1997.

The master control room at S4C Digital

S4C

S4C (Sianel Pedwar Cymru: Channel Four Wales) was launched on 1 November 1982 after a long and often bitter struggle (*see* **Broadcasting**). The following day saw the launching of the equivalent service for **England**, **Scotland** and Northern **Ireland** – Channel Four, a service which was also available to those inhabitants of Wales (the great majority) who could receive programmes broadcast from transmitters in England. S4C was the first channel in western Europe with the primary duty of broadcasting in a 'lesser-used' language. Headed by Owen Edwards, Controller of the BBC in Wales (1974–81), S4C brought together the BBC, HTV and a number of independent producers to provide an initial service of 22 hours of **Welsh**-language programmes each week. The venture was a pioneering example of co-operation between the public service broadcasting service and the commercial sector and required complex arrangements concerning, for example, to what extent advertisements could be included during programmes produced by the BBC.

Although many of the **English**-language programmes which appear on Channel Four are broadcast on S4C, peak hours are reserved for those in Welsh. The launch of the new channel gave rise to one of the few growth industries in the Wales of the 1980s, not least because of the impetus that was given to the development of independent production companies. Several of the companies were located around **Caernarfon**, providing much needed employment in that depressed area. The establishment of Barcud (later Barcud Derwen), a Caernarfon-based technical resources consortium, greatly eased the task of setting up such companies. S4C itself launched an enterprise company promoting its programmes abroad. The initiative has enjoyed some success, for Welsh programmes have been sold to over 50 countries, with animated programmes proving especially popular. The use of subtitles means that Welsh programmes are watched by many who do not understand the language. S4C Digidol, a digital service providing 12 hours of Welsh-language programmes each day, was launched in 1998. Following the establishment of the **National Assembly**, S4C became responsible for a channel broadcasting the Assembly's debates.

S4C has become an accepted feature of the broadcasting scene. It has, however, been subject to criticism, both from those non-Welsh-speakers who are resentful of the money spent on it and from those Welsh-speakers who consider that many of its programmes follow formats which are pale imitations of English and American prototypes. Its greatest successes have been its daily broadcast of *Pobol y Cwm* and its coverage of sport. Like all television services, its greatest challenge is to attract viewers in an era of massive proliferation of channels.

SABELLIANISM

The unorthodox belief, promulgated by the 3rd-century theologian Sabellius, that Father, Son and Holy Spirit are different aspects of the divine unity rather than three separate persons within the godhead. The biblical expositor **Peter Williams** was expelled by the **Calvinistic Methodists** in 1791 for interpreting the prologue of the Gospel of John, in his Welsh edition of John Canne's **Bible** (1790), in a Sabellian fashion. Sabellianism is often known as Patripassionism – the belief that God the Father died on the cross. The quarrel between **Daniel Rowland** and **Howel Harris** sprang from Rowland's belief that Harris had embraced Patripassionism.

SAGE, Lorna (1943–2001) Writer and academic

Born in **Hanmer**, Lorna Sage was powerfully influenced in her early years by her eccentric, bookish grandfather, who was vicar of Hanmer (and to whom **R. S. Thomas** was curate for two years). During annual holidays with relatives in the **Rhondda**, she noted the esteem given to **education** there, in contrast with her own **border** area, which she perceived as a backwater. She spent almost her entire working life teaching **literature** at the University of East Anglia. Her autobiography, *Bad Blood*, published shortly before her early death, won the 2001 Whitbread prize and became a bestseller. Her selected journalism, *Good As Her Word*, was published posthumously in 2003.

SAILING

The sport of sailing, popular in most coastal towns and an important factor in **tourism**, has its origins in the **seafaring** traditions of Wales. In the early 19th century, if not earlier, **fish**ermen and sea pilots would compete in regattas to test their seamanship, and soon the **gentry** were commissioning yachts for pleasure. Wales's first yacht club was the Royal Welsh at **Caernarfon** (1847).

By the 1930s, the sport was becoming more accessible. Thus, in 1937, a **Beaumaris** sea captain, Ben Williams, commissioned a new boat, so that he could sail with his children on the **Menai Strait**; others followed his example, and soon the racing fleet of Menai Strait One Designs was born. These boats can still be seen racing at Beaumaris.

After the **Second World War**, the availability of new construction materials made it possible for anyone to build a sailing dinghy; this led to a dramatic increase in sailing clubs and dinghy racing – on **lakes** and **reservoirs** as well as at sea. By the early 21st century, around 30,000 people in Wales were participating in the sport, only 15% of whom were members of the country's 115 sailing clubs. A notable Welsh achiever at European and world championship levels is Ian Barker, an Olympic silver medallist in 2000.

ST ARVANS, Monmouthshire
(1281 ha; 710 inhabitants)

Located immediately north of **Chepstow**, the **community** offers spectacular views of the **Wye** valley. In the late 18th century, the owners of the Piercefield estate, seeking to satisfy the contemporary taste for the sublime, laid out walks from Alcove to Wyndcliff past Piercefield Cliffs and the Apostle Rocks, thus providing a panorama of Lancaut (Llancewydd) – virtually the only place in Gloucestershire with a name of **Welsh** origin. His realization of the similarities between the lushness of St Arvans and the lushness of Botany Bay caused Joseph Banks, the naturalist on Captain Cook's voyages, to suggest that eastern **Australia** should be called New South Wales. Piercefield House, an exquisite neo-classical villa (1790s), is in a lamentable condition. St Arvan's church contains **Norman** elements.

Sᵗ ASAPH, FLINTSHIRE.

The cathedral and the bridge over the River Elwy at St Asaph

St Athan in its heyday as a centre servicing fighter aircraft

Wyndcliffe Court (1922) is a charming example of the Arts and Crafts tradition. Adjoining Piercefield is Chepstow racecourse; laid out in 1923, it is the home of the Welsh Grand National Race (*see* **Horse Racing**).

ST ASAPH (Llanelwy), Denbighshire
(645 ha; 3491 inhabitants)
Tradition claims that St Asaph has been the seat of a bishop since the time of St Kentigern or St Mungo in the late 6th century. It is more likely, however, that the **diocese** of St Asaph was founded under **Norman** auspices in 1143. St Asaph Cathedral, the smallest **Anglican** cathedral in **Britain**, was rebuilt after being burnt by Edward I's troops in 1282. Although burnt again by **Owain Glyndŵr** in 1402, the 14th-century masonry of the nave and transepts largely survived. The tower dates from 1391. The building underwent a major restoration by George Gilbert Scott in the 1870s. It contains Wales's sole extant medieval canopied stalls. **William Morgan**, bishop of St Asaph (1601–4), is buried in the cathedral. He and his fellow biblical translators are commemorated in the churchyard by the Translators' Memorial (1892). On 1 June 1920, **A. G. Edwards** was enthroned at St Asaph as the first archbishop of the **Church in Wales**. The cathedral is the venue for the annual North Wales **Music** Festival. Its first director, composer **William Mathias** (1934–92), is buried in the churchyard.

The mainly 14th-century **parish** church is dedicated to St Kentigern and St Asaph; its churchyard contains the grave of the itinerant linguist **Richard Robert Jones** (Dic Aberdaron; 1780–1843). **H. M. Stanley** Hospital, built in 1837 as the St Asaph workhouse, was named after the

explorer who spent some of his childhood years within its confines. Ysgol Glan Clwyd, the first **Welsh**-medium secondary school, originally established at **Rhyl** (1956), was moved to the St Asaph **community** in 1969. The attractive Pilkington Factory (1977) manufactures electro-optical systems (*see* **Glass**). The **Roman Catholic** exile and author Roger Smyth (1541–1625) was born at St Asaph.

ST ATHAN (Sain Tathan), Vale of Glamorgan
(1161 ha; 3836 inhabitants)
Located on the west bank of the **River Thaw**, St Athan is the site of **Britain**'s largest military airfield. Its building inspired **Iorwerth Peate**'s famous sonnet, which makes skilful use of the **Welsh place names** of the **Vale of Glamorgan**. Its future was called into question in 2005, when it was announced that the RAF would be pulling its fighter-servicing operations out of St Athan by mid-2007. The anticipated loss of over 500 jobs was partially compensated for by the announcement in 2006 that St Athan would be the base for the newly formed 'counter-terror' Special Forces Support Group, and by its winning, in 2007, of two defence training contracts worth £14 billion, involving the establishment of a military academy to train all of Britain's army, navy and air-force recruits; some 5500 jobs were promised, in addition to 1000 construction jobs. The **community** contains the settlements of St Athan, Flemingston, Gileston, Eglwys Brewis and West **Aberthaw**.

The substantial village of St Athan clusters around its large 14th-century church which contains the tombs of members of the de Berkerolles family, owners of a **manor** house whose romantic ruins stand in the deserted village of

East Orchard – one of the numerous late medieval sites in the locality. Flemingston, a village favoured by the more opulent of the residents of the Vale, was the home of **Edward Williams** (Iolo Morganwg). The church contains a monument to him and also a fine effigy of Joan de Fleming, whose family gave the place its name. Flemingston Court is a well-preserved early 16th-century manor house. There are attractive churches at Gileston and Eglwys Brewis – the latter enmeshed within the RAF station. Gileston Court, while 18th century in appearance, contains late medieval features. The entire area is dominated by the Aberthaw power station, the construction of which involved damming the estuary of the **Thaw**, once the location of the Vale of Glamorgan's chief **port**.

ST BRIDES MAJOR (Saint-y-brid),
Vale of Glamorgan (2010 ha; 2009 inhabitants)
Located south-east of **Bridgend** and extending to the estuary of the **River Ogwr**, the **community** includes the offshore 1-km wide Tusker Rock, the seaside settlements of Ogmore-by-Sea and Southerndown, and the exhausted quarry of Sutton stone, medieval **Glamorgan**'s favourite building material. The large, multivallate promontory fort at Dunraven is one of Wales's most dramatically sited **hillforts**. Ogmore Down was the site of a remarkable **Iron Age** warrior burial. The community's outstanding monument is Ogmore Castle, built by the de Londres family in the 12th century; it has one of **Britain**'s earliest surviving chimneypieces. In 1296, the lordship of **Ogmore** became part of the lands of the **Lancaster family**; in the 1450s, a courthouse

Ogmore Castle and stepping stones across the River Ewenny, St Brides

was built in the castle's outer bailey. Stepping stones across the Ewenny link the castle to the picturesque hamlet of **Merthyr Mawr**.

St Bride's church, first built in the 12th century, was poorly restored in 1851. It contains important monuments, including a life-size effigy of John le Botiler (*c.*1335), and the tomb of John Butler of Dunraven and his wife (*c.*1540). Dunraven Castle (1806), the seat of the Wyndham-Quinn family, earls of Dunraven, owners in 1873 of 9594 ha in Glamorgan, was demolished in the 1950s; a remarkable walled **garden** survives.

ST BRIDES MINOR (Llansanffraid-ar-Ogwr),
Bridgend (1034 ha; 5575 inhabitants)
Lying north-east of **Bridgend**, the **community** is dominated by the large **housing** development of Sarn, the location of a sprawling service station on the **M4**.

ST CLEARS (Sanclêr), Carmarthenshire
(3075 ha; 2820 inhabitants)
Located in the heart of west **Carmarthenshire**, the **community** lies between the **Taf** and the Cywyn and contains the villages of St Clears, Bancyfelin and Pwll-trap. The **Normans** had penetrated the area by *c.*1100, but the **march**er-lordship they established frequently fell to the Welsh. Remains of a substantial motte-and-bailey castle survive. A Cluniac priory eventually dependent upon St-Martin-des-Champs in Paris was established *c.*1100; it ceased to exist following Henry V's seizure of alien priories in 1414. St Mary Magdalen church, built on the priory site, contains the priory church's fine Romanesque arch. There are some attractive Georgian and Victorian façades in St Clears village. The second phase of the **Rebecca Riots** began at St Clears, with Pwll-trap the centre of considerable disturbances. The one-time **parish** church of Llanfihangel Abercywyn stands in ruins above the confluence of the Taf and the Cywyn. Dating from the 13th century and with six medieval grave slabs in its churchyard, it was abandoned in 1848 when a new St Michael's church was built alongside the A40. Treventy nearby was the home of a branch of the **Perrot family**. The amateur scientist William Lower married Penelope Perrot *c.*1601. In 1609, he and a neighbour, John Prydderch, set up one of **Britain**'s earliest telescopes at Treventy, where they studied the craters of the moon and the movement of Halley's Comet (*see* **Astronomy**).

ST DAVID'S and THE CATHEDRAL CLOSE
(Tyddewi), Pembrokeshire
(2036 ha; 1797 inhabitants)
Located at Wales's westernmost point, St David's is the holiest of Welsh holy places. The **community** was a centre of ritual and settlement long before the time of St **David**. Coetan Arthur and Carn Llidi are **Neolithic** burial chambers. Clegyr Boia is a fortified farmstead occupied from the Neolithic to the **Iron Age**. Around St David's are at least five promontory forts, including those of Caerau, perilously poised above vertiginous cliffs.

In the 6th century, the peninsula, with its accessible bays, was not the remote place it seems today. It was closely linked with the western sea routes, a factor, no

St David's Cathedral, with the ruins of the bishop's palace in the foreground

doubt, in its choice *c.*550 as the site of the monastery headed by David, prince of the royal house of **Ceredigion**, and the cause of David's fame in **Ireland**, **Cornwall** and **Brittany**. Nothing survives of the buildings of pre-**Norman** St David's, although inscribed stones are proof of its importance (*see* **Monuments, Early Christian**).

Pope Calixtus II (1119–24) blessed St David's as a place of **pilgrimage**, giving rise to the belief that two pilgrimages to St David's were equal to one to Rome. Under Bishop Peter de Leia (1176–98), a new church in the late Romanesque style was completed, but the collapse of the tower in 1220 led to the rebuilding of the choir and the transepts in the early Gothic style. Further construction – the Lady chapel, the heightening of the tower and a stone screen – resulted in a building over 92 m long, by far the largest church in Wales. Its finest feature is the richly carved oak nave ceiling (*c.*1500). The west front was rebuilt by **John Nash** in 1789 and by George Gilbert Scott in 1863, work necessitated by the waterlogged foundations which have caused the nave arcade to lean disconcertingly. The cathedral's numerous tombs include that of Edmund **Tudor** (d.1456) and what may be that of **Rhys ap Gruffudd** (The Lord Rhys; d.1197). A statue of **Giraldus Cambrensis** has at its feet the mitre he was never granted. By the 14th century, the cathedral close had been surrounded by walls with four gateways, and contained a college, archdeacons' residences and the bishop's palace erected by Bishop **Henry de Gower**. The palace, with its superb arcaded parapet (*compare* **Lamphey** and **Swansea**), was stripped of its lead in 1536 by Bishop **William Barlow**, who sold the metal in order to provide his five daughters with dowries large enough to ensure that they all married bishops. To come across a cathedral in so remote a place – the Octopitarum

Promontorium (the Cape of the Eight Perils), as Ptolemy called it in AD *c.*150 – is an astonishing experience. Equally astonishing is the fact that the cathedral offers no evidence of its existence until the visitor gazes directly down upon it, nestling in the delightful Vallis Rosina.

In the square is the City Cross (14th century). In neighbouring bays are the medieval chapels of St Non and St Justinian. According to the tale 'Culhwch ac Olwen' in *The Mabinogion*, the **Twrch Trwyth** landed at Porth Clais, as did **Gruffudd ap Cynan** in 1081 when campaigning to regain the throne of **Gwynedd**. The community contains Ramsey **Island** and the Bishops and Clerks rocks. Whitesands Bay is popular with surfers. The sport of coasteering – following cliffs by **swimming** and **rock climbing** – was invented at St David's. The Tourist Information Centre (2001) is a remarkable exercise in post-modernism; Oriel Albion is an attractive **art gallery**. The heart of Welsh episcopalianism, St David's has, nevertheless, several impressive **Nonconformist** chapels. Although long considered a city, St David's was not formally so designated until 1994.

ST DOGMAELS (Llandudoch), Pembrokeshire (1113 ha; 1318 inhabitants)

Constituting the northernmost part of **Pembrokeshire**, the **community** abuts upon that part of **Cardigan** lying south of the **Teifi**, where there were major boundary changes in 2002. The **English** form of the name commemorates St Dogmael; the origin of the **Welsh** form is less clear. The community's main feature is a ruined abbey located on the site of a **Celtic** *clas*. Seven inscribed stones dating from the 5th to the 11th century (*see* **Monuments, Early Christian**) provide evidence of the importance of the *clas*, which was attacked by the **Vikings** in 988. In 1120, Robert Fitz

Martin, **march**er-lord of **Cemais**, replaced the *clas* with Wales's sole monastery of the order of Tiron, a reformed branch of the **Benedictine** order founded at Tiron, near Chartres. The monastery spawned three dependent priories – at Caldey (*see* **Islands**), Pill (*see* **Milford Haven**) and Glascarreg in **Ireland**. As drinkers and womanizers, the monks disturbed the peace in Cardigan. Of the monastic buildings, the most substantial survivals are parts of the north transept, the chapter house and the infirmary. Adjoining the ruins is St Dogmael's church (1850), which houses the inscribed stones.

St Dogmaels has a long **seafaring** tradition as a **port** and as a **fish**ing and **shipbuilding** centre. Little survives, apart from fishing with nets in the Teifi estuary. Albro Castle, now flats, is a skilful adaptation of the Cardigan workhouse. The village of St Dogmaels suffers from landslides. The beach at Poppit Sands marks the northern terminus of the **Pembrokeshire Coast Path**.

ST DONATS (Sain Dunwyd), Vale of Glamorgan (1276 ha; 686 inhabitants)

Located at the point where the coast of **Glamorgan** turns north-westwards, the **community** contains the settlements of St Donats, Marcross and Monknash. Its outstanding feature is St Donats Castle, dramatically perched above the sea. Originally built in the late 11th century by the de Hawey family, it passed in 1298 to the **Stradling family**, in whose possession it remained until 1738 when the last of the Stradlings was killed in a duel at Montpellier. The Stradlings massively enlarged the castle, but its interior is largely attributable to the American **newspaper** baron, William Hearst, who bought it in 1925. Hearst brought in fragments of medieval and **Renaissance** buildings to create

his own confection, notably his Bradenstoke Hall, with its early 14th-century roof secretly removed from Bradenstoke priory in Gloucestershire. In 1962, the castle became the home of Atlantic College, the first of the United World Colleges. The presence of the college causes the inhabitants of St Donats to have the lowest average age of any community in Wales (29.51 years).

In the *cwm* to the west of the castle is the **parish** church, 12th century in origin and containing 17th and 18th-century monuments to the Stradlings. The churchyard contains a complete 15th-century preaching cross. There are churches of 12th-century origin at Marcross and Monknash where there are also granges established by **Neath** Abbey (*see* **Dyffryn Clydach**); that at Monknash includes a circular **dovecote** and a 13th-century barn of 11 bays. Near the **Iron Age** promontory fort at Nash Point, are two **lighthouses** built in 1832.

ST FAGANS: THE NATIONAL HISTORY MUSEUM

The museum, an outstation of the **National Museum [of] Wales**, opened in 1948 as the Welsh Folk Museum, at St Fagans Castle (**Cardiff**), a building which, with its **gardens** and grounds, was a gift from the Earl of Plymouth (*see* **Windsor-Clive family**). Inspired by the open-air museums of Scandinavia, and the first of its kind in **Britain**, the museum was the fulfilment of the long-held aspiration of **Cyril Fox**, director of the National Museum, to display materials reflecting the folk culture of Wales.

Initially, under **Iorwerth Peate** (with a largely **Welsh**-speaking staff), the museum's main emphasis was on the gathering of a representative collection of traditional buildings from rural Wales, their orderly dismantling and

Heraldic beasts in the garden of St Donats Castle

The woollen mill (1760) from Esgair Moel, Llanwrtyd, re-erected (1952) at the National History Museum, St Fagans

re-erection, with the introduction of demonstrating crafts-men in the workshops. The hub of the museum was created in 1968 when purpose-built facilities (designed by the **Percy Thomas** Partnership) were provided to accommodate exhibition galleries, reference collections, a library, archives, conservation laboratories and staff. In the late 1980s, the remit was broadened to include the urban and industrial communities, with the re-erection of a terrace of **iron**workers' cottages from **Merthyr Tydfil** as the first obvious reflection of the change. At the beginning of the 21st century, over 30 buildings had been re-erected, allowing visitors to walk around a representation of Wales that extends from prehistoric **Celt**ic times to the present. The buildings include farmhouses and outbuildings, a school, a chapel, a medieval church, a workmen's institute, a cockpit (*see* **Cockfighting**), a tannery (*see* **Leather**), a **watermill**, commercial premises and a house of the future. Complementing the public activity of the museum is a programme of research into Welsh dialects, folk **music**, customs and crafts; the institution became a pioneer in recording oral traditions. In 1995, the museum's name was changed from The National Folk Museum to The Museum of Welsh Life; in 2005, the title The National History Museum was adopted.

ST FAGANS, Battle of
This battle, fought on 8 May 1648, was the most significant engagement of the **Civil Wars** in Wales. A Royalist army of 8000 under **Rowland Laugharne** was defeated by a much smaller force; following the Parliamentary victory, **Cromwell** swept through the south, putting an end to all resistance.

ST FLORENCE, Pembrokeshire
(1657 ha; 751 inhabitants)
Located immediately west of **Tenby**, the **community** contains the villages of St Florence and Gumfreston. The spacious St Florence's church retains much of its medieval fabric. St Lawrence's church, Gumfreston, has a tall, 14th-century tower; its churchyard contains three medicinal springs. There are several round 'Flemish' chimneys in the area.

ST GEORGES-SUPER-ELY (Sain Siorys),
Vale of Glamorgan (772 ha; 391 inhabitants)
Located immediately west of **Cardiff**, the **community** contains the settlements of St George's, St Bride's, Drope and St y-Nyll. The church of St George is a fine cruciform building with a crossing tower; that of St Bride contains a **Norman** arch brought from **Margam**. St y-Nyll has one of **Glamorgan**'s few surviving **windmills**. Castle Farm contains a fascinating 15th-century first-floor hall. Coedriglan (frequently, but incorrectly, known as Coedarhydyglyn), a delightful villa completed in 1820, was the home of the distinguished patriot Sir Cennydd Traherne (1910–95), the first Welshman since the earl of Powis (1844) to be appointed a Knight of the Garter.

ST HARMON (Saint Harmon), Radnorshire,
Powys (7354 ha; 535 inhabitants)
A tract of hill country immediately north of **Rhayader**, the **community** contains a number of **Bronze Age** monuments, the barrows at Grugyn and Bangelli being particularly fine. The church of St Garmon, originally a *clas*, was the

ecclesiastical centre of the **commote** of **Gwrtheyrnion**. In Dyrysgol, two early medieval platform houses perch at 400 m. **Welsh** survived in the area for much of the 19th century; it was the language of the **parish** church until 1853, of Nant-gwyn chapel until 1860 and of Sychnant chapel until 1870. **Francis Kilvert** was briefly vicar of St Harmon (1876–7). A dramatically sited wind farm stands above the **Wye**.

ST ISHMAEL (Llanismel), Carmarthenshire
(1857 ha; 1319 inhabitants)
Located immediately west of **Kidwelly** and constituting the promontory between the **Tywi** and Gwendraeth estuaries, the **community** contains the villages of Ferryside and Llansaint. The village of St Ishmael was inundated by sand in 1606; the size of the fine 14th-century church of St Ishmael is an indication that it had been a substantial settlement. Hugh Williams (1796–1874), widely believed to be the leader of the **Rebecca Riots**, is buried in the churchyard. Llansaint is an attractive compact village. Penallt is a ruin. In the late 15th century, it was the home of John Dwnn; Memling's portrait of the Dwnn family is the earliest of any Welsh family. A ferry long plied across the Tywi estuary from Ferryside to **Llansteffan**. The community's beaches were once renowned for their cockles (*see* **Fish and Fishing**).

ST ISHMAEL'S (Llanisan-yn-Rhos),
Pembrokeshire (1107 ha; 490 inhabitants)
Located west of **Milford Haven** just east of the point where the coast swings southwards to **Dale**, the **community** contains the **Bronze Age** Langstone Field standing stone. The *Shell Guide to South-West Wales* considers that St Ishmael's church represents the 'Victorian *beau-ideal*'. Mullock is reputed to be the place where **Rhys ap Thomas**, in fulfilment of a vow, lay below the bridge while Henry **Tudor** rode over it. Sandyhaven House originated as a medieval tower house.

ST MARY OUT LIBERTY (Llanfair Dinbych-y-pysgod), Pembrokeshire (509 ha; 630 inhabitants)
That part of the ecclesiastical **parish** of **Tenby** which lay outside the **borough**, the **community** constitutes the area between Tenby and **Saundersfoot**, and consists largely of caravan parks. Scotsborough House, originally 15th century, was one of the seats of the **Perrot family**.

ST NICHOLAS AND BONVILSTON
(Sain Nicolas a Thresimwn), Vale of Glamorgan
(1339 ha; 793 inhabitants)
St Nicholas and Bonvilston, the **community**'s highly appealing villages, are strung out along the A48, the former Portway. Among St Nicholas's attractions are its 14th-century church tower, the 17th-century Blacksmiths' Row and Llanewydd House, **Percy Thomas**'s 1940 interpretation of the Arts and Crafts tradition. Cottrell, lying north of the village, was the home of **Rice Merrick** (d.1586 or 1587), the historian of **Glamorgan**. Button Close commemorates the voyager **Thomas Button**, who resided at Doghill; Button Island, Hudson Bay, is named after him. His property later passed to his relations, the Gwinnett family, an association that explains the name of Button Gwinnett, one of the signatories of the American Declaration of Independence.

Simon de Bonville (fl. mid-13th century) gave his names to Bonvilston – the first to the **Welsh** form and the second to the **English**. Its late medieval church tower dominates **John Prichard**'s nave and chancel (1864).

The surrounding area is rich in early monuments, chief among them the **Neolithic** chambered tomb at Tinkinswood, where excavations in 1914 revealed the remains of at least 50 individuals. Its capstone, weighing over 40 tonnes, is among the largest in **Britain**. Other monuments include Y Gaer – an **Iron Age** fort – two **Norman** ringworks and moats and – near Doghill – the best preserved moated site in Glamorgan.

SAINTS
The early history of Christianity in Wales abounds with stories of saints, although none of them can indubitably be shown to have been formally canonized – the usual defining feature of a saint according to the **Roman Catholic** tradition. The period *c.*450–700 in Wales is known as the 'Age of Saints', but both written and archaeological evidence concerning the saints is slight. **Patrick**'s Confession (5th century) casts light on the mind of a Brythonic Christian, and **Gildas** describes the condition of the Welsh church in the 6th century, but the only example of hagiography possibly written within living memory of its subject is the Life of **Samson** (7th century). Attempts have been made to interpret the range of the activities of the saints on the basis of the churches dedicated to them, but, as it is generally not known whether the dedications were contemporary or whether they reflect a later cult, such studies are fraught with difficulties.

The earliest of the saints is believed to have been **Dyfrig** (fl.475), who was probably a territorial bishop in **Erging**. The chief figure of the following generation was **Illtud** (d.*c.*525), whose monastery at **Llantwit Major** was of pivotal importance in the development of Christianity in the Celtic-speaking lands. The saints of the later 6th century – among them **David**, **Teilo**, **Padarn** and **Deiniol** – seem to have embraced a more ascetic form of **religion** than that represented by the learned Illtud. They are portrayed as abbots heading monastic communities or *clasau*, which developed into the mother churches that came to dominate the religious life of wide areas. Many of them were reputed to have had links with **Ireland**, **Cornwall** and **Brittany**, and sometimes with **Scotland** and the Isle of **Man**, thus giving rise to the later erroneous belief that the saints were members of a **Celtic Church** detached from the rest of Christendom.

A list of those to whom the **parish** churches of Wales had been dedicated by the Later Middle Ages contains hundreds of names. Some totally obscure figures were locally honoured as saints, although they may have been no more than the donors of the land (*see* **Llan**) on which the church had been built. Some churches – **Dwynwen** and **Melangell** among them – were dedicated to **women**, and others were dedicated to more than one saint, as at **Llanddeusant**, **Llantrisant** and **Llanpumsaint**. With the demarcation of borders of **dioceses** from the 11th century onwards, saintly dedications became a matter of territorial importance, an issue which led to the writing of a number of saints' lives and the compiling of much dubious documentation (*see* ***Liber Landavensis***). Under **Norman** influence, some dedications were changed from indigenous saints to the leading saints of the Christian tradition, such as Mary, Peter and Michael.

In the 17th century, the practice of describing devout **Puritans** as saints became widespread. In 1919, the **oil** tycoon William D'Arcy attained 'sainthood', in the Celtic manner, when the Llandarcy Oil Refinery (**Coedffranc**) was named after him.

SALEM Picture

This picture of Siân Owen, Ty'n y Fawnog, and the small congregation at Salem Chapel, Cefncymerau (**Llanbedr**) is one of the most influential icons of Wales ever created. It was painted by Sydney Curnow Vosper (1866–1942) in 1908 and was exhibited at the Royal Academy in **London** in 1909. Seven of the eight characters portrayed were real people (the exception is a tailor's dummy), but only one of them, Robert Williams, who is seen beneath the clock, was a member of Salem. Siân Owen's hat and her famous shawl were borrowed for the sittings. In 1909, the watercolour was bought by the industrialist William Hesketh Lever, Lord Leverhulme, for a 100 guineas (£105). It won popularity when its owner used it to promote the sale of the Lever Brothers' Sunlight soap; purchasers of the soap could claim a coloured print of the picture in return for collecting tokens. It is now exhibited at the Lady Lever Art Gallery at Port Sunlight on the Wirral (**Cheshire**).

The picture aroused interest particularly because it seemed that the face of the devil can be seen in the folds of Siân Owen's shawl, although the artist denied that that was intentional. The painting's iconic status among the Welsh probably owes much to the notion that it offered them – very much as did the writings of **O. M. Edwards** – a comforting image which identified Welshness with **Nonconformity** and rural life. By the early 21st century, Vosper had become a forgotten figure in the history of art in **England**. A native of Stonehouse, Devon, where his father was a brewer, Vosper abandoned his intention of becoming an architect and went to Paris to study **painting**.

He visited Wales regularly, marrying Constance James of **Merthyr Tydfil** in 1902. In his day, he was immensely successful as an artist, a popular character of great energy and a swimmer and cyclist of renown. Siân Owen (1837–1927) appears in another of Vosper's paintings – *Market Day in Old Wales* (*c*.1910).

SALESBURY, William (*c*.1520–?99)
Scholar and translator

A central figure in Welsh religious and cultural history, Salesbury, a member of a cadet branch of the **Salusbury family**, is remembered especially as the principal translator of the New Testament into **Welsh**. Born in **Llansannan**, he also lived in **Llanrwst**. He was educated at **Oxford**, and perhaps at the Inns of Court in **London**. He learnt much about the Welsh literary tradition in his native area, especially through friendship with the poet **Gruffudd Hiraethog**. He came under the twofold influence of the **Renaissance** and the **Protestant Reformation**, and was inspired by the ability of the **printing** press to spread that influence.

Between 1547 and 1552, he was vastly productive, and his works display the breadth of his humanist interests. In 1547, he published *A Dictionary in Englyshe and Welshe* (*see* **Dictionaries**), to help his compatriots to learn **English**, and *Oll Synnwyr pen Kembero ygyd*, Gruffudd Hiraethog's collection of Welsh **proverbs**. In 1550, four publications appeared, including *A briefe and a playne introduction, teachyng how to pronounce the letters in the British tong.*

The most important of Salesbury's early works – *Kynniver llith a ban* (1551) – was a Welsh translation of the gospels and epistles in the 1549 **Book of Common Prayer**. This marked the beginning of Salesbury's campaign to secure for his people a Welsh version of the scriptures. During Mary I's reign, he had to lie low, but after Elizabeth's accession he resumed his efforts, supported by Bishop **Richard Davies** and **Humphrey Lhuyd**. After the passing (1563) of legislation ordering the translation of the **Bible** and Book of Common Prayer into Welsh, Salesbury was invited to undertake the task, in co-operation with Richard Davies, and was chiefly responsible for the major literary achievement of the two volumes that appeared in 1567 – the Prayer Book and the New Testament. Despite some orthographical quirks, the two books immediately conferred special status on Welsh as a language of learning and of **religion**. Salesbury and Richard Davies intended, after 1567, to proceed with the translation of the Old Testament, but there was disagreement between them and they parted company. Between 1568 and 1574, Salesbury worked on a medicinal herbal, but it was not printed during his lifetime.

In his day, Salesbury's was the clearest vision concerning the possibility of harnessing the forces of the Renaissance and Reformation to meet the needs of Wales. By pioneering use of the press for the purposes of publishing in Welsh, he initiated the **literature** of the modern period in Wales.

Sydney Curnow Vosper, *Salem* (1908)

SALMON, [Harry] Morrey (1890–1985)
Soldier and ornithologist

Born in **Cardiff**, Morrey Salmon was Wales's leading 20th-century ornithologist, and the father of British **bird photography**. He was responsible for the definitive but confidential report (1971) on the conservation of the red kite in central Wales, based on over 40 years' work. He was awarded the Military Cross and Bar while serving with the **Welch Regiment** in the **First World War**. In 1940, he was seconded to the Royal Air Force to set up the Royal Airforce Regiment, which was active in the entire Mediterranean arena.

SALTNEY, Flintshire
(373 ha; 4769 inhabitants)

Located immediately south-east of **Queensferry**, the **community** is essentially a suburb of Chester. In the 19th century, its industries included candle and cable making, **oil** distilling and **shipbuilding**. They have been replaced by business parks and light industry. In the late 20th century, Saltney experienced a great expansion of **housing** estates built to meet commuter demands. In 2001, 86.9% of Saltney's inhabitants had no knowledge whatsoever of **Welsh**, when making it, linguistically, the most Anglicized community in **Flintshire**.

The *Samtampa* memorial window at Oystermouth church

SALUSBURY family Landowners

Sir John (d.1289), founder of the Carmelite friary at **Denbigh**, was probably the first of the family – variously known as Salusbury, Salisbury and Salesbury – to settle in Wales. His descendants became wholly Cymricized and founded several landed families including those of Lleweni (Denbigh) and Rug (**Corwen**). John Salusbury of Lleweni (d.1566) was the first husband of **Catrin of Berain**. One of their sons, Thomas (1564–86), was executed for his part in the Babington Plot to replace Elizabeth I by the Roman Catholic Mary, Queen of Scots. Another, John (1567–1612), a member of an intellectual circle that included Walter Raleigh, was a prolific **English**-language poet, as was John's grandson, Thomas (1612–43). The scholar **William Salesbury**, was a member of a cadet branch of the family, as was the grammarian Henry Salusbury (1561–?1637). The Lleweni family died out in the male line in 1684; among its descendants was **Hester Lynch Piozzi**. One of the Salusburys of Rug, Owen, was killed while participating in the Earl of Essex's revolt (1601). His brother, William (1580–1660), held Denbigh for Charles I, at his own expense, in 1643. Known as *Hen Hosanau Gleision* (old blue stockings), he built the private chapel at Rug. Thomas Salusbury (1575–1625), founder in 1622 of the Jesuit College at Cwm (*see* **Roman Catholics**), was a member of a cadet branch of the Salusburys of Rug. The Rug branch of the family died out in the male line in 1658; its estate eventually passed to the Wynns of Glynllifon (**Llandwrog**).

SAMPSON, John (1862–1931) Investigator of Welsh Romanies

This self-taught scholar of the **Romanies**, who was born in Cork, became librarian of **Liverpool** University in 1892. He produced a comprehensive *Dialect of the Welsh Gypsies* (1926) and published numerous articles, mainly in the *Journal of the Gypsy Lore Society*. His work was based on his association with the prominent Welsh Romanies, the **Wood family**. His substantial *Welsh Gypsy Folktales* (1968), edited by Dora Yates, was published after his death. His ideas about the Romany diaspora and the purity of the Romany dialect, founded almost exclusively upon the testimony of the Romanies themselves, are controversial. The interest in Romanies was inherited by his grandson, Anthony Sampson, author of *Who Runs This Place?: The Anatomy of Britain in the 21st Century* (2004).

SAMSON OF DOL (c.485–565) Saint

The 7th-century Life of Samson portrays him as a native of south Wales, a disciple of St **Illtud**, and a founder of monasteries in **Ireland** and **Cornwall**. He died in **Brittany** at his monastery of Dol. The historical bishop attended a Council of Paris in the mid-6th century. Samson's feast day is 28 July.

SAMTAMPA and MUMBLES LIFEBOAT

A double tragedy occurred on 23 February 1947 when the large ship *Samtampa* was hit by a storm; driven from her anchors, she struck the **Glamorgan** coast at Sker Point (**Cornelly**). Rockets fired from the shore were ineffective in the hurricane-force winds, and all 39 crew were lost. The

Mumbles (**Swansea**) **lifeboat** went out to assist, but she failed to return and was found upside down further along the beach, all eight lifeboatmen having drowned. Tim Lewis's **stained-glass** window in Oystermouth (Swansea) **parish** church commemorate the incident.

SAMWELL, David (Dafydd Ddu Feddyg; 1751–98)
Doctor and author

Nantglyn-born Samwell travelled as **ship**'s surgeon with Captain James Cook on some of his expeditions. Having witnessed Cook's death in Hawaii in 1779, he recorded his impressions of the event in *A Narrative of the Death of Captain James Cook* (1786). His unpublished journal, 'Some Account of a Voyage to South Seas 1776–1777–1778', is an innovative work of social anthropology. He wrote poetry in **English** and **Welsh**, and was a prominent member of the **Gwyneddigion Society**.

SANKEY, John (1866–1948) Lawyer
Born in **England**, but having family ties with **Cardiff**, he began his political career as a **Conservative**, but converted to the **Labour Party** after chairing the **Coal** Commission (1919), the majority of whose members recommended nationalization of the collieries. He was appointed lord chancellor (1929) by **Ramsay MacDonald**, and retained the office during the National **Government** (1931–5). He established the Law Revision Committee (1934) and, with Lord **Atkin** and Lord Justice **Bankes**, drafted the constitution of the disestablished **Church in Wales** (*see* **Disestablishment**). He became a baron in 1929 and a viscount in 1932.

SARN HELEN
Sarn Helen (Helen's Causeway) is the name used for the **Roman road**, running south from **Caernarfon** to **Ceredigion** and then back east to **Brecon** Gaer (**Yscir**), traces of which survive in Ceredigion, **Gwynedd** and **Powys**. It is likely that the road was maintained to facilitate Romano-British extractive industries. The name perhaps commemorates Elen Luyddog (Elen of the Hosts), traditionally the wife of **Magnus Maximus**, although there is much confusion between her and Helena, mother of Constantine the Great.

SAUNDERS, Erasmus (1670–1724)
Cleric and author

Clydey-born and **Oxford**-educated, Saunders held livings in **England**. His main work was *A View of the State of Religion in the Diocese of St Davids* (1721), in which he harshly criticized the condition of **religion** in the **diocese**.

SAUNDERSFOOT, Pembrokeshire
(675 ha; 2784 inhabitants)

Located north of **Tenby**, the **community**'s liveliness as a seaside resort makes it difficult to appreciate that it was once a significant industrial centre. In the 18th century, anthracite collieries with galleries extending beneath Saundersfoot's sands were thriving concerns. The **Pembrokeshire Iron** and **Coal** Company was established in 1846, and the Stepaside Ironworks in 1849. In the mid-19th century, **horse**-drawn trams conveyed coal, iron and **limestone** to the newly built harbour. Iron production ended in 1877, but coal production continued until 1939. Of these

An aerial photograph of Sarn Helen at Trefeglwys, Montgomeryshire

enterprises, little beyond examples of 19th-century industrial **housing** survives. St Issell's church has a 13th-century tower and a Victorianized interior. The coal-owning Vickerman family built Hean Castle (1871). It was acquired in 1898 by **W. T. Lewis**, later Baron Merthyr, whose descendants continue to occupy it. Saundersfoot has won fame as a **sailing** centre.

William Frost, a Saundersfoot carpenter, claimed in 1896 that he had been airborne. Details of his vehicle were registered at the **Patent Office** and are providing the basis for a reconstruction. If the reconstruction is found to be airworthy, Saundersfoot may have been the first place in the world where humanity experienced controllable flight.

SAVIN, Thomas (1826–89) Railway contractor
Savin, born in Oswestry, **Shropshire**, first worked in partnership with David Davies (*see* **Davies family (Llandinam)**) but later operated on his own. He and Davies constructed the Vale of **Clwyd Railway** (1858) before completing lines linking Oswestry with **Aberystwyth**. Davies dissolved the partnership because he thought Savin's scheme for a Welsh coast railway to **Pwllheli** too reckless. Savin anticipated package holidays by building a seafront hotel in Aberystwyth and offering rail fares inclusive of accommodation. The failure of a clearing bank in 1866 bankrupted

him and the hotel building became the 'College by the Sea' – the first constituent college of the **University of Wales** (1872) (*see* **University of Wales, Aberystwyth**).

SAVORY, H[ubert] N[ewman] (1911–2001)
Archaeologist

Brought up in **Oxford**, Savory spent most of his career at the **National Museum [of] Wales**, as assistant keeper of **archaeology** initially and later as the department's keeper (1955–76). He was an authority on the prehistory of Wales, **Britain** and the Iberian peninsula. Savory's excavations at sites such as the Dinorben **hill-fort** (**Abergele**) and the Pen-yr-wyrlod megalithic tomb (**Talgarth**) led to an enrichment of the museum's collections. His publications included *Guide Catalogue of the Early Iron Age Collections* (1976) and *Guide Catalogue of the Bronze Age Collections* (1980).

SCHOTT, George Augustus (1868–1937)
Mathematician

George Augustus Schott, FRS, developed the full theory of radiation from electrons travelling at close to the speed of light. Born in Bradford and educated at **Cambridge**, he was appointed assistant lecturer in the physics department at **Aberystwyth**, where he spent the rest of his life, becoming head of the applied **mathematics** department and vice-principal of the college. It was during his early years in Aberystwyth that Schott published his classical work on electromagnetic radiation. Many years later, it was realized that the blue light observed near synchrotron particle accelerators, called 'synchrotron radiation', was the radiation predicted by Schott. Later, it was recognized that the radiation from distant radio galaxies and quasars was also synchrotron radiation. Synchrotron radiation is now used as a powerful tool in the study of the atomic structure of matter.

Alfred Russel Wallace

SCIENCE

Over the past 300 years, Wales has made a substantial contribution to the development of science. Welsh-born scientists and/or those working in Wales include an impressive number who pioneered entirely new branches of science. Prominent examples are the mathematician **Robert Recorde**, the statistician **Richard Price**, the crystallographer **W. H. Miller**, the biologist **Alfred Russel Wallace**, the astronomer **Isaac Roberts**, the meteorologist **David Brunt**, the orthopaedic surgeon **Robert Jones** (1857–1933) and the chemist **Donald Hey**. It is appropriate that the second of Wales's three Nobel laureates, Brian D. Josephson (b.1940), is a physicist. (The other Welsh-born laureates are **Bertrand Russell**, and the **Swansea**-born economist Clive Granger (b.1934), who won the Nobel Prize for economics in 2003.) The roll-call of scientists is matched by the list of inventors: **William Grove** invented the fuel cell; **David Hughes** the microphone and teleprinter; **Sydney Gilchrist Thomas** developed the Basic Method for manufacturing steel (*see* **Iron and Steel**) from phosphate ores; **E. G. Bowen** (1911–91) produced the first airborne radar; **Lewis Boddington** designed the angled flight deck for aircraft carriers; and **Donald Davies** invented 'packet switching' for the electronic transmission of data. Wales's achievements in science, disproportionate to its **population** and size, prompted the physicist **Phil Williams**'s wry suggestion that the national anthem's (*see* **'Hen Wlad fy Nhadau'**) description of Wales as 'a land of poets and singers' should be changed to 'a land of scientists and inventors'.

However, in the absence of an equivalent of the Royal Society of Edinburgh (est. 1783), of a companion to the former **University of Wales Board of Celtic Studies** or of a journal of international standing, there is no Welsh scientific body to help co-ordinate and promote work being carried out by scientists in Wales. The scientists are largely members of societies based in **London** or elsewhere.

Central to the development of the sciences are the disciplinary societies, the first of which was the Royal Society of London (est. 1660). By the late 18th century, there was fragmentation, with the formation of specialist societies, the first six (all still active) being the Linnaean (1788), Geological (1807), Astronomical (1820), Zoological (1826), Entomological (1833) and Chemical (1841). Although all are based in London, they embrace **Britain** as a whole, each stressing the importance of enquiry, peer assessment and the sharing of ideas and experience at the societies' meetings. Initially made up of amateurs and gentlemanly scientists, the societies progressively became more professional.

A significant number of Welsh scientists have been rewarded for the quality of their contribution to these societies. A small number have been elected to the Royal Society which, from the 1860s and 1870s, evolved into an exclusive body for eminent professional scientists with Fellowship (FRS) signifying a level of distinction in their fields of research.

In the 19th century, voluntary adult **education** was being provided concurrently by two kinds of society: the literary and philosophical societies from the 1780s (the term 'philosophical' including scientific matter) and the **Mechanics' Institutes** from 1824. The former were designed to serve the intellectual needs of the middle **class**es and **gentry**, and the

The stem-cell scientist and Nobel laureate Sir Martin Evans

latter (providing the first initiative in technical as well as scientific study) served the artisans and mechanics. Alumni of **Nonconformist academies**, particularly **Unitarians**, played significant roles in both bodies. The only example of the former in Wales was the Literary and Philosophical Society of Swansea (1835), soon renamed the Royal Institution of South Wales. Although established by a remarkable group of scientists and industrialists, the active scientific role of the body was brief. At their height, there were 30 Mechanics' Institutes in Wales, but only 4 were functional in the final quarter of the 19th century – at **Cardigan**, **Ebbw Vale**, **Neath** and **Llanelli**. These were helped, from 1859 onwards, by the newly created Department of Art and Science and, from 1879, by the City and Guilds of the London Institute.

The South Wales Institute of Engineers, established at **Merthyr Tydfil** in 1857, later relocated in **Cardiff**; its voluminous *Transactions* provided the only local medium for a diversity of scientific and technical papers. Another group, the Cardiff Naturalists' Society (est. 1867), was initially concerned in the main with biological and geological themes. The two bodies, the largest such institutions in Wales, reached their peak membership – around 1000 and 850 respectively – in the 1930s.

Until the 20th century, there was little **government**-sponsored scientific research. The decision of the government in 1915 to involve itself systematically in the administration of science was of fundamental importance. The establishment of the Council for Scientific and Industrial Research led almost immediately to the creation of a Department of Scientific and Industrial Research (DSIR). The DSIR, with the Medical Research Council (1929) and the Agricultural Research Council (1931), were the forerunners of today's research councils. Redistribution of the responsibilities of the DSIR, following the Science and Technology Act 1965, led to the establishment of the Department of Technology and to the setting up of the Natural Environmental Research Council (NERC) and the Science Research Council (SRC). The former was concerned with research in the earth sciences and ecology, the latter with the 'whole field of fundamental science'. Spectacular improvements in scientific techniques have arisen from advances in nuclear physics (*see* **Physical Sciences**) and from the revolution in **electronics**.

The prominence of science in Wales owes much to the **Welsh Intermediate Education Act** (1889) which led to the establishment of a network of secondary schools. **Ezer Griffiths**, who became a world authority on the measurement of heat, stated that had it not been for the opening of an intermediate school in **Aberdare**, he would have become a **coal**miner like his father. Many secondary schools in Wales established an enviable tradition in the sciences. **Ammanford** Grammar School produced a remarkable number of professors, including Fred Nash (physics, Nottingham), Wyn Roberts (chemistry, Cardiff), Colin Grey-Morgan (physics, Swansea) and Eric Sunderland (anthropology, Durham). This record was matched by Bishop Gore School in Swansea, with Sir Sam Edwards (head of the Cavendish Laboratory), Lord Flowers (physics), Sir John Cadogan (chemistry, St Andrews) and **Edward Bowen** among its famous alumni; and by **Gowerton** Grammar School which boasted Sir **Ieuan Maddock** (physics), Sir John Maddox and Sir **Granville Beynon** (radio) among five former pupils who were elected FRS.

The establishment of the colleges of the **University of Wales** was of central importance. The first three colleges were intended to be general centres of higher education, with the science departments a part of the fabric, but Cardiff, because of its associations with the southern **coal**-field, was conceived as a potential 'flagship' of higher technical education. Plans for a school of mines and metallurgy as part of the institution were not realized, but in 1912 leading coal companies established a school of mines at Treforest (**Pontypridd**; later the **University of Glamorgan**), with the emphasis on practical mining. Similarly, the direct inspiration for the college at Swansea in 1920 had come from its own region and the need to produce a technological centre to serve the major industries of the district.

Until the **First World War**, Wales's science departments were small, with few students and inadequate facilities. As a result of developments during that war, there were a large number of changes in scientific research and teaching – some of them revolutionary. Since the **Second World War**, the number of science graduates has increased markedly and the quantity of published material has grown exponentially. The increase in the number of societies, many concerned with the borderlands of the traditional disciplines, reflects the creation of new university departments, among them marine biology (**Bangor**, 1951), chemical engineering (Swansea, 1954), biochemistry (**Aberystwyth**, 1959) and microbiology (Cardiff, 1964).

The tradition continues. One of the most ambitious and exciting scientific projects of all time is the Large Hadron Collider (LHC), at CERN (*Conseil Européen pour la Recherche Nucléaire*), Geneva, the most powerful particle accelerator yet conceived. When complete, it will be used to search for the Higgs boson – the particle that is believed may hold a key to the history of the universe. In charge of the LHC is Lyn Evans (b.1945) from Aberdare.

The only journal to be concerned specifically with material of a scientific, technological and medical nature from a Welsh standpoint has been the **Welsh**-language *Y Gwyddonydd* (The Scientist; 1963–96), edited by the chemist and promoter of science Glyn O. Phillips. The publication of *Y Gwyddonydd* led indirectly to the establishment, in 1971, of Y Gymdeithas Wyddonol Genedlaethol (The National Science Society).

Important work in the popularization of science has been undertaken by Techniquest since its foundation in 1986 as a hands-on science education venture. Techniquest's third home, a distinctive metal and glass structure in Cardiff Bay, is Britain's first purpose-built science discovery centre. Techniquest receives over 500,000 visitors a year, both to its dockside premises and its Europe-wide travelling exhibitions; its educational work is supported financially by the **National Assembly**.

The Techniquest science discovery centre, Cardiff

SCLEDDAU, Pembrokeshire

(1859 ha; 586 inhabitants)
Located immediately south-west of **Fishguard**, the **community** contains the villages of Scleddau, Jordanston and Manorowen. Jordanston Hall (17th century) and Llangwarren (19th century) are interesting houses. St Bwrda's church, Jordanston (1797), contains fine **Celtic** Studios **stained glass**; St Mary's church, Manorowen, (rebuilt 1872) is in a pleasantly wooded setting.

SCOTCH BAPTISTS

Despite their name, the Scotch Baptists derived not from **Scotland** but from Wales, **Merioneth** and Dyffryn **Maelor** especially. In 1798, J. R. Jones (1765–1822), minister at Capel Ramoth, **Llanfrothen**, announced that he and his followers were seceding from the **Baptists** to form a new connection of anti-revivalist fellowships. Intent on restoring the pristine faith of the apostolic age, and in accordance with the tenets of the Scots Dissenters John Glas and Archibald McLean, they rejected a salaried ministry, monthly communion and inter-church co-operation. By the late 1830s, these churches themselves split under the influence of the Scots-American Alexander Campbell, with Campbellite or 'Disciples of Christ' churches being formed in, among other places, **Rhosllanerchrugog**, **Harlech** and **Criccieth**. It was in the Campbellite church of Berea, Criccieth, that **David Lloyd George** was both raised and baptized.

SCOTCH CATTLE, The

The Scotch Cattle was a secret society of workers in the eastern part of the south Wales **coal**field. It was active mainly in the 1820s and 1830s, although isolated examples occurred as late as the 1850s. Indeed, the term was used during the miners' lockout of 1926 (*see* **Miners' Strikes**). The activity had no apparent links with **Scotland**; the aim of the protestors was to scotch – or put an end to – subservience to employers. The society's object was to impose solidarity on workers by intimidation, thereby reinforcing community discipline. Its victims were 'enemies of the community', including **Irish** and **English** immigrants, bailiffs and grasping employers. Disguised members of the society visited their victims at night and conducted a ritual mock trial before breaking windows and **furniture** and manhandling their victims. Visits were preceded by letters containing bloodcurdling threats. These fearsome activities and the authorities' inability to break through the community's silence led to the eastern part of the south Wales coalfield being dubbed the Cattle's 'Black Domain'.

SCOTLAND, Wales's associations with

For much of the first Christian millennium, the inhabitants of Wales and southern Scotland belonged essentially to the same ethnic group, with western Brythonic and its descendant, **Welsh**, being spoken from Fife to the Severn Sea. The most renowned of the early Welsh poets, **Aneirin** and **Taliesin**, were court poets of kingdoms in southern Scotland. According to tradition, the dynasty of **Gwynedd** was founded by **Cunedda**, a native of **Manaw Gododdin** in the Forth valley. In the 'Age of **Saints**', there was extensive contact between Scotland and Wales; St Kentigern

Jacob Epstein, *Christ in Majesty* (1955), Llandaff Cathedral

(Mungo), for example, was commemorated in **St Asaph** and in Glasgow. The Welsh participated in the Scottish wars of the English kings, and Welsh **longbow**men were prominent in the battles of Falkirk (1298) and Bannockburn (1314). Nevertheless, Robert Bruce hoped for assistance from Wales in reasserting Scottish sovereignty; in turn, there were hopes during the **Glyndŵr Revolt** that Wales would receive assistance from Scotland. The accession of James VI of Scotland to the English throne in 1603 led to expectations in Wales that the English polity would become a British polity. Welsh dissenters found inspiration in Scottish **Presbyterian**ism, with Welsh **Calvinistic Methodists** owing much to the Free Church of Scotland. In the later 19th century, Welsh and Scottish patriots found increasing common cause and, from the later 20th century, **Plaid [Genedlaethol] Cymru** and the Scottish National Party evolved in tandem. The move towards **devolution** in Wales is only fully intelligible in the context of parallel developments in Scotland.

SCULPTURE

Wales's lack of suitable stone for carving has meant that most examples of early native sculpture tend to be simple in form, and often incised rather than three-dimensional. Limitations of means led to the development of an aesthetic that considered the intrinsic quality of the stone, something that appeals strongly to modern sensibilities and was surely not lost on the makers of prehistoric monoliths and early Christian stone crosses.

Goscombe John's 1930 memorial at Ynysangharad Parc, Pontypridd, to Evan and James James, author and composer of 'Hen Wlad fy Nhadau'

Wales's earliest known sculpture – as distinct from arte-facts such as tools – is the tiny 'Venus' figurine or phallus from Nab Head, **Marloes**, which is believed to be (although experts are not unanimous on the matter) the only carving in the round from a Mesolithic site in **Britain** (*see* **Palaeolithic and Mesolithic Ages**). Now in the **Carmarthenshire** Museum (**Abergwili**), it was carved in shale, and was discovered surrounded by hundreds of per-forated shale beads. The middle **Bronze Age** Caergwrle (**Hope**) Bowl in the **National Museum** is among Wales's finest ancient objects. **Coracle** shaped, inscribed, inlaid with **gold** leaf and describing schematically the oars and the waves through which it might pass, it is made not of oak, as originally thought, but of shale.

The large **Celtic** sandstone head, discovered at Hendy, **Llanfair Pwllgwyngyll**, and displayed at Oriel Ynys Môn, **Llangefni**, is one of Wales's few examples of pre-**Roman** stone sculptures. The Roman occupation saw the importa-tion of new materials and styles, such as the 10-cm bronze Mercury figure found at **Caerleon**. The admixture of indigenous and Roman forms is demonstrated in a goddess figure (*c.*200) from **Caerwent**.

Of the sculptured stones of early medieval Wales (*see* **Monuments, Early Christian**), among the finest are the cross at **Llantwit Major** commemorating Hywel, king of **Glywysing** (d.886) and that at **Carew** commemorating Maredudd, king of **Deheubarth** (d.1035). The most intri-guing is the Eliseg Pillar (**Llantysilio**), carved in memory of a mid-8th-century king of **Powys**. The use of interlacing was a prominent feature of such sculptures, as is evident in the exhibits at the Stones Museum at **Margam**.

The influence of the Romanesque tradition of stone carv-ing is best exemplified by the superb shrine of St **Melangell** (**Llangynog**), and the curious tympanum at St Padarn's church, **Llanbadarn Fawr** (**Powys**). In later centuries, the more refined stone carvings made for churches and monas-teries often involved the use of imported stone. While some sculptures were concerned with Christian iconography, many were memorials to the dead; St Mary's church, **Abergavenny**, contains Wales's richest collection of medieval stone tombs. It also contains the country's finest **woodcarving** – the late 15th-century Sleeping Jesse carved from a single, huge oak.

The more settled **Tudor** era enabled the relatively pros-perous **gentry** to embellish churches and private property with memorial sculpture in a complex and ambitious style, an art exemplified by the Herbert memorial (1600) in St Nicholas's church, **Montgomery** (*see* **George Herbert**). By the early 18th century, Baroque influence was apparent, as can be seen in the flamboyant memorial to Maurice Jones at **Llanrhaeadr-yng-Nghinmeirch**.

In the 19th century, Welsh-born **John Gibson** was widely hailed as the world's finest carver of marble; however, he undertook virtually no commissions for locations in Wales. By then, civic, national and denominational pride was lead-ing to an upsurge in the commissioning of open-air statuary. Monumental public sculpture became the mostly widely seen and appreciated art form. It remains influential; for example, the pantheon of historic figures in **Cardiff**'s City Hall (1913–19) furnishes many a Welsh imagination with its pri-mary image of national heroes. The sculptor of St **David** in that pantheon was Cardiff-born **Goscombe John**, who was early 20th-century Wales's leading commemorative sculptor.

War memorials and the commemoration of cultural figures kept many sculptors busy, notable exponents being **James Milo Griffith** and **Leonard Merrifield**, whose statue of Hedd Wynn (**Ellis Humphrey Evans**) at **Trawsfynydd** is a moving tribute. While most work continued in an Edwardian, narrative, tradition, Eric Gill's war memorial at **Chirk** (1919) represented a more innovative style.

In the mid-20th century, most commissions came from churches – Jacob Epstein's Christ at Llandaff Cathedral, for example – but, from the 1950s onwards, the development of new towns and new institutions stimulated greater activity, such as Anthony Stevens's commission at **Cwmbran** and **David Tinker**'s panels for various public buildings. In the later 20th century, support from the **Arts Council of Wales**, augmented by the work of the Welsh Sculpture Trust, played an increasingly important role in the development of sculpture. Formed in 1981, the trust became Cywaith Cymru/Artworks Wales in 1991 and took over from the Arts Council as commissioning agency for all the visual arts.

The nature of art changed profoundly during the 20th century, and sculpture became increasingly concerned with form. Towards the end of the century, however, postmodern theories permitted a re-engagement with the local, allowing national issues to become legitimate concerns for artists. Post-industrial rehabilitation and 'green politics' inspired work that engaged directly with places, sometimes cosmetically, often exploring meaning in a narrative way. Sculptors such as David Nash (b.1945) and Lois Williams (b.1953) have gone beyond the old, confining boundaries, exploiting materials and practices which link sculpture more closely with other art forms.

SEAFARING

Despite the romance associated with **sailing ships**, life on the ocean wave was never anything but dangerous. In square-riggers at the mercy of wind and current, voyages were often long and hazardous; **food** was poor and monotonous, and living accommodation as bad as in the worst slums of a Victorian city. The crew of a sailing ship slept in the fo'c'sle, which often contained the windlass attached to the chains that worked the anchors. Wooden bunk beds or swinging hammocks were crowded into a small space, and the mattress was usually a straw-filled 'donkey's breakfast'. The agility to climb the rigging in raging storms, trim sails and undertake other dangerous tasks, was essential.

Yet, despite such hazards, the sea long attracted the men of many a Welsh coastal village. Although commercial coastal activity had declined significantly by the last quarter of the 19th century, seafaring remained a staple occupation of seaside villages, causing them to be essentially outward looking. Coastal communities became increasingly isolated from landward living communities, developing a society and personality that was unique. Most of the male inhabitants of such villages as **Llangrannog** and **Aberporth** in **Cardiganshire**, **Nefyn** and **Aberdaron** in **Llŷn**, and **Moelfre** and **Amlwch** in **Anglesey** were seafarers or were dependent on sea-going trade.

The seafaring traditions of coastal Wales survived the arrival of the steamship, with the great **ports** such as **Liverpool** and **Cardiff**, Newcastle and Glasgow becoming the home ports of the steamers on which Welshmen sailed. It was quite common for a Cardiff-owned tramp steamer of the early 20th century to be manned almost entirely by sailors from a Cardiganshire village. The custom was to

Brian Fell's merchant seafarers war memorial (1996), at the Pierhead, Cardiff

sign on with a local ship's master rather than on a particular vessel, and very often, when a captain changed ship, a whole crew would follow him. With employment provided by the steamship companies, families remained in the coastal villages at a time when inland villages were depleted by **emigration**.

Conditions for the sailors on steamships were little better than they had been in the days of sail. Crews still occupied space in the fo'c'sle; few vessels had refrigerators; and seldom were there sheltered bridges – open bridges remained the norm until at least 1939, especially on the extensive fleets of south Wales **coal**-carrying tramp steamers. One master mariner who served an apprenticeship on a Cardiff steamer in the 1930s said, 'We were paid fifteen shillings to a pound a month, overtime was often worked but never paid for. We were on a starvation diet, and as soon as the contents of the communal sea chest on deck thawed in the tropics, we had no fresh meat, and we depended on salted beef and pork.' As recently as 1955, one Cardiff shipping company allocated as little as 1s 4d (approximately 7 pence) per person per day to feed a ship's crew.

By the last quarter of the 20th century, the British merchant fleet had been drastically reduced, and by the 21st century seafaring was no longer a significant attraction to the men of the Welsh coast. Sailors are almost completely absent from villages that once regarded the sea as providing the principal employment of the male inhabitants. Ships are manned by seamen from all quarters of the globe, and the Welsh sailor has become a rarity. In addition, the location of many a port has changed to cope with larger vessels, and few major ports are located in the heart of urban centres, as in the past. As a result, many a dockside community, such as Tiger Bay in Cardiff and Port Tennant in **Swansea**, has lost its character as a 'sailor town', and a tradition has ended.

SEALAND, Flintshire (2046 ha; 2746 inhabitants)
Located on the right bank of the canalized **Dee**, Sealand is what its name suggests – land reclaimed from the estuary. The **community**'s rich **soil** sustains horticultural nurseries and substantial farms. Sealand Garden City was founded in 1910 to house the employees of the John **Summers** steelworks (*see* **Connah's Quay** and **Shotton Steelworks**). The Deeside Industrial Park was founded by the British Steel Corporation following the cessation of steelmaking in 1979 (*see* **Iron and Steel**). Sealand aerodrome, established in 1917 by the Royal Flying Corps, was closed to aircraft in 1957, although gliders continue to use it. St Bartholomew's church (1867) was designed by **John Douglas**.

SEALS (authenticating devices)
The earliest known seals of Welsh provenance date from the late 12th century; thereafter seals reflected many aspects of Welsh history and society. They possess nothing specifically Welsh to mark them out from those in use elsewhere in **Britain**. The **Welsh language** only rarely appears upon them; the great seal used by **Owain Glyndŵr** (1404), to attest the famous **Pennal Letter**, is markedly similar to contemporaneous royal seals in **England** and mainland Europe – as it had to be, because Owain was making a statement about his status as a European leader.

The more notable medieval seals include those of **Llywelyn ap Iorwerth** (1208; on **horse**back), Lleision ap Morgan, lord of **Afan** (*c.*1220; showing the dress of a Welsh gentleman), the unfinished corporate seal of the burgesses of **Denbigh** (1285; the castle portrayed as a reminder of the **Edwardian conquest**); the first common seal of Llandaff (**Cardiff**) Cathedral (*c.*1200; exhibiting the church as built by Bishop **Urban**); and the common seal of Llanthony Priory (**Crucorney**) (1316; depicting the Baptism of Christ in the Jordan).

Welsh seals of more modern times are illustrative of **education** (a birch-carrying master: Friars School, **Bangor**; 1568); industry (an **iron**works: the **Blaenavon** Iron and Steel Company; 1876); and communications (**coal**-bearing trucks: the Sirhowy Tram Road Company; 1802).

SEALS (mammals)
The long-standing presence of the Atlantic grey seal (*Halichoerus grypus*), a species native to **Britain**, dates back at least to Mesolithic times. Although the north-east Atlantic population of grey seals is the largest of three discrete populations worldwide, the Welsh population is relatively small: around 2000 animals, or 2% of Britain's population. They occur in greatest numbers along the **Pembrokeshire** coast and the **Llŷn** peninsula. Requiring undisturbed beaches for dropping their pups in autumn, they favour secluded, cliff-bound bays, **caves** and sparsely populated **islands** such as Skomer and Bardsey.

The misleadingly named common seal (*Phoca vitulina*), rare in Wales, is found mostly in the Severn Sea. The body of a walrus (*Odobenus rosmarus*) – which, like the seal, belongs to the pinniped order of aquatic **mammals** – was washed up on Cefn Sidan (**Pembrey and Burry Port**) in 1986, and a hooded seal (*Cystophora cristata*) visited the **Milford Haven Waterway** in 2001.

SEAS, COASTS and ESTUARIES
The coastline of Wales is 1562 km in length; in contrast, the land **border** with **England**, with all its twists and turns, is a mere 400 km. Furthermore, no part of Wales is more than 75 km from salt water. It is curious, therefore, that the sea is not as important to the Welsh psyche as it is to the psyche of peoples such as the Bretons or the Norwegians. However, without the sea and its Gulf Stream, Wales – located as it is on the same latitude as Labrador – would be virtually uninhabitable. During the most recent millennium, the influences that have been central to the experience of the Welsh have largely come from the east, across the land border with England. In previous millennia, however, seaborne influences were frequently paramount. **Neolithic** chambered tombs were clearly linked with the western sea routes, as was the culture of **Bronze Age** Wales, with its strong contacts with **Ireland**. The Christianity of the 'Age of **Saints**' was spread by **missionaries** sailing those routes, and the civilization they created was enfeebled by the seafaring **Vikings**. In more recent centuries, the sea has played a leading role – through 18th-century coastal **ship**ping, for example, and above all during the boom years of the **coal** industry, when at least a quarter of the world's trade in the sources of heat and **energy** originated at Welsh **ports**.

The overall structure or morphology of Wales's coastline – the shape of its major bays in particular – was laid down in the Permo-Triassic era 290–206 million years ago. However, its detail was fashioned in the Quaternary era – the last 1.75 million years (*see* **Geology**). About 20,000 years ago, at the peak of the most recent Ice Age, the sea level was about 135 m lower than it is now. Thereafter, with the melting of the ice sheets, the sea level rose. It reached its present level *c.*7000 years ago, a process which created such remarkable features as the **Milford Haven Waterway**, the **Dyfi** and **Mawddach** estuaries and **Rhossili** beach, and which led to the inundation of Cardigan Bay – the possible origin of the legend of **Cantre'r Gwaelod**.

The marine environment extends from the high-water mark through the inter-tidal zone to the sub-tidal seabed, which reaches out to the limit of territorial waters. Wales's marine environment covers an area equivalent to three-quarters of the country's land surface. Most of that environment consists of the shallow, enclosed waters of the Irish Sea with its large embayments in Liverpool and Cardigan Bays. The Severn Sea, where gales may be as few as three a year, is even more shallow and sheltered. Far more exposed are the waters of the south-west; they are part of an open ocean stretching to Newfoundland, which produces the high wave energy that pounds the exposed rocky shores.

As a habitat, the sub-tidal seabed is subject to a number of factors, including the nature of the seabed, oceanic currents, tidal rise and fall, the strength of wave action and the quality and **chemistry** of the water. It provides a home for animals and **plants** adapted to living in, on or near the seabed (benthic), or in or on the upper waters (pelagic). Among them are **fish**, **whales, dolphins and porpoises**, turtles, **seals** and sea**birds**. Less visible are the single-celled phytoplankton and bacteria that have fundamental roles at opposite ends of the **food** chain – in capturing energy from the sun and in releasing it through the decomposition of dead animals. Sub-tidal areas near rocky coastlines and **islands** can provide particularly diverse habitats, offering a home to sponges, sea anemones, starfish and sea urchins. Wales's sea plants are far less various; they consist in the main of a rich array of seaweeds, some lichen and a few marine flowering plants, among them the eel grass which flourishes in the sandy areas of the Milford Haven Waterway.

Intertidal areas – those in estuaries such as the **Severn**, **Dee**, **Llwchwr**, **Dyfi** and **Mawddach**, in particular – are home to creatures such as ragworms, lugworms and small crustaceans, creatures that attract migrant and over-wintering wildfowl. The vegetation of such areas often forms colourful zonation patterns, with each zone containing its own assemblage of plant species. The pioneer plants on the seaward fringes include species such as glasswort and annual sea-blite that are able to tolerate long periods of inundation in seawater, whereas the more landward zones contain species with an ever-decreasing tolerance of such inundation. In the mid-marsh zones, colourful sea aster and sea lavender may be found with salt-marsh grass, whilst in the upper-marsh zones sea couch usually becomes commonplace.

The Carboniferous Limestone cliffs of St Govan's Head, Pembrokeshire

Harry Secombe

Distinct zones are also a feature of the ecology of rocky shores. On sheltered shores, such those of the **Menai Strait**, seaweeds are usually the dominant species. A typical pattern would be channelled wrack on the upper shore, bladder wrack in the mid shore, and knotted wrack on the lower shore. In contrast, exposed shores, such as St Govan's Head (**Stackpole**), are mainly the domains of marine animals such as barnacles and limpets.

Other coastal habitats include dunes and cliffs. Wales has some 50 sand-dune systems, the largest of which are Newborough Warren (**Rhosyr**) and Kenfig Burrows (**Cornelly**). Dunes can be mobile, semi-fixed or fixed. What causes them to cease to be mobile are specially adapted plants such as marram grass and lime grass, which are able to colonize and stabilize the sand. Older, acidic dunes can develop into heather-covered dune heath, as at Crumlin Burrows (**Swansea/Coedffranc**). Among Wales's rare dune plants are Kenfig's fen orchid and Newborough's dune helleborine.

Sea cliffs are home to a wide variety of plants and animals. In very exposed situations, such as Trwyn Cilan (**Llanengan**), maritime vegetation can extend for up to 500 m inland, and can dominate entire islands or headlands. The most maritime community, often restricted to exposed cliff ledges, usually includes rock samphire and thrift, but on **limestone** cliffs, such as the Great Orme (**Llandudno**), wild cabbage – the ancestor of several vegetables – may dominate. Maritime grasslands on the clifftops, where red fescue is generally the main species, can also provide a habitat for wild carrot, golden samphire, buck's-horn plantain and sea campion. Above all, the cliffs of coastal Wales are home to an astonishing number of seabirds; **Pembrokeshire**'s islands, in particular, provide nesting sites of international importance.

SECOMBE, Harry [Donald] (1921–2001)
Entertainer

Swansea's celebrated ambassador Harry Secombe grew up near the docks in St Thomas, sang in the church choir and worked as a steelworks clerk. In the **Second World War**, he saw active service as a lance bombardier in North Africa and Italy. The army allowed him to develop as an entertainer, and after 1946 he worked as a comedian at the Windmill Theatre, **London**; he also toured extensively and broadcast on radio. His great breakthrough came with the anarchic radio series *The Goon Show* that ran throughout the 1950s. It made him into an international figure, performing regularly at the London Palladium and at Royal Command performances. His tenor voice was adjudged to be of operatic standard and he put it to good effect in his **broadcasting**, in the **film** *Davy* (1957), and in the West End and Broadway show *Pickwick* (from 1963), in which he sang what became his signature tune, 'If I Ruled The World'. He published several books, including a novel, and in later life his Christian faith made him an effective and popular presenter of BBC television's *Songs of Praise* (*see* **Dechrau Canu Dechrau Canmol**). A genuine and natural entertainer, he was knighted in 1981.

SECOND HOMES

While the very wealthy had long owned summer homes in some of Wales's most scenic areas, numbers were low until the second half of the 20th century when spiralling personal wealth enabled many urban dwellers to buy second or holiday homes in rural Wales. The 1991 census statistics revealed that the incidence of holiday homes was highest in the **Llŷn** peninsula, with second homes accounting for 37% of the **housing** stock of **Llanengan**. The demand for second homes was seen as a major cause of rising house prices, which in low-income areas could mean that house ownership was beyond the reach of the indigenous inhabitants. An array of social problems resulted: many young couples were compelled to migrate, local schools were closed because of falling pupil numbers and, without all-the-year-round patronage, local amenities – **bus** services and village pubs, shops and post offices – often ceased to exist. The Anglicization of **Welsh**-speaking rural areas came to be seen as wholly bound up with the spread of second homes, although the process of Anglicization was, in fact, the consequence of a complex array of economic, demographic and social factors. From the 1970s onwards, the issue became an important theme in Welsh politics. **Cymdeithas yr Iaith Gymraeg** (the Welsh Language Society) campaigned for legislation that would give priority to local people in the property market. Such schemes existed in some of the scenic but impoverished areas of **England**, but there were those who argued that to demand such legislation in Wales was tantamount to raising racist objections to buyers from England, the place of origin of the great majority of Wales's second home owners. In 1979, a group called **Meibion Glyndŵr** began to set fire to holiday homes, an activity which continued intermittently for almost a decade. The ownership of second homes and holiday homes declined during the housing depression of the early 1990s – from about 20,000 in 1991 to 15,516 (1.2% of the total housing stock) in 2001; it accelerated in the wake of the remarkable housing boom of the early 21st century, when new growth areas for second homes began to emerge in the **Vale of Glamorgan** and eastern **Carmarthenshire**.

SECOND WORLD WAR, The

In the 1939–45 war, Welsh servicemen and **women** fought in all the major theatres of war: some 15,000 of them were killed. The war was also fought on the 'home front', German bombing raids bringing major loss of life to **Swansea**, **Cardiff** and **Pembroke Dock**. The threat of German invasion, the need for rationing and the imposition of a night-time 'blackout' to thwart air attack, contributed to a widespread sense of popular involvement in the conflict. Men too elderly or infirm to serve overseas could join the Local Defence Volunteers (the 'Home Guard'); from 1943 onwards, one-tenth of those conscripted aged 18 became '**Bevin Boys**', rectifying labour shortages in the **coal**mines. Women might join the Land Army or other volunteer forces; many thousands worked in the **Royal Ordnance Factories** and other armaments plants established across Wales. The war provided a temporary solution to the unemployment which had plagued Wales during the **Depression** years, and also enabled Welsh workers to acquire the new skills essential to the post-war reconstruction of the Welsh **economy**. Domestic mobilization was not without its problems: the coal industry remained troubled by serious industrial disputes, notwithstanding it being state-controlled from 1943; and the arrival of thousands of evacuees and other temporary migrants from **England** was seen as threatening the **Welsh language** and culture.

Politically, Wales was almost united in support of the 'people's war' – a struggle for democracy against the threat of fascism. **Pacifists** were relatively small in number and, despite the tortuous progress of the **Communist Party**'s official response to the conflict, Welsh Communist leaders came to be committed to the war effort. Only **Plaid [Genedlaethol] Cymru** advocated a neutral stance, on the grounds that it was an 'imperialist war'. The landslide victory of the **Labour Party** at the 1945 general election symbolized the leftward shift encouraged by collectivist experiences of wartime, which also strengthened existing identifications with Britishness at the expense of Welshness.

SECRETARY OF STATE FOR WALES, The

The National Institutions (Wales) Bill introduced by **Alfred Thomas** in 1892 had sought to establish a secretary of state for Wales; there was renewed support in the years 1918–22, a period which saw the emergence of a Welsh bureaucracy; in 1946, **D. R. Grenfell** led a deputation to the **government** advocating the creation of such an office. It was not until 1959, however, that the **Labour Party**, made uneasy by the **Conservative government**'s appointment of a minister for Welsh Affairs and urged on by **Huw T. Edwards** and **James Griffiths**, abandoned its opposition (**Aneurin Bevan** had been one of the most vocal opponents). A pledge to appoint a secretary of state was included in its 1959 election manifesto – a pledge ultimately redeemed on 17 October 1964 with the appointment of James Griffiths and the creation of the **Welsh Office**. The following have held the office of secretary of state for Wales:

Evacuees, with identification tags, arriving at Newtown station in 1939

James Griffiths, 1964–6
Cledwyn Hughes, 1966–8
George Thomas, 1968–70
Peter Thomas, 1970–4
John Morris, 1974–9
Nicholas Edwards, 1979–87
Peter Walker, 1987–90
David Hunt, 1990–3
John Redwood, 1993–5
William Hague, 1995–7
Ron Davies, 1997–8
Alun Michael, 1998–9
Paul Murphy, 1999–2002
Peter Hain 2002–

The establishment of the **National Assembly for Wales** in 1999 meant that many of the duties of the secretary of state passed to the Assembly. The appointment in 2003 of Peter Hain as leader of the House of Commons was a recognition that Wales no longer needed a full-time secretary of state. The role of the office was curtailed further by the establishment in 2003 of the Department for Constitutional Affairs.

SEIRIOL (6th century) 'Saint'
The founder of a Christian community at Penmon (**Llangoed, Anglesey**), who later became a hermit on Ynys Seiriol (Puffin **Island**). There were still hermits there in **Giraldus Cambrensis**'s day. Seiriol is also linked with **Penmaenmawr**. The story about his regular meetings with **Cybi** is comparatively recent.

SEISYLLWG Kingdom
Seisyll ap Clydog, king of **Ceredigion**, acquired *c.*730 the three *cantrefi* of **Ystrad Tywi**, his extended kingdom being subsequently known as Seisyllwg. On the death of his descendant Gwgon ap Meurig (871), Seisyllwg fell into the hands of **Rhodri Mawr**, whose wife was Gwgon's sister, Angharad, and was united with **Gwynedd** and **Powys**. Rhodri's son Cadell inherited Seisyllwg. Cadell's son, **Hywel Dda**, united Seisyllwg with **Dyfed** and **Brycheiniog** to form the kingdom of **Deheubarth**.

SELECT COMMITTEE ON WELSH AFFAIRS, The
The committee was established in 1979 to scrutinize the work of the **Welsh Office**. Its membership of 11 MPs replicates the balance of parties in the House of Commons. Because of the paucity of Welsh **Conservative** MPs – indeed, their total absence between 1997 and 2005 – MPs representing constituencies outside Wales have sat on the committee. Since its establishment, its chairmen – Leo Abse, Donald Anderson, Gareth Wardell, Martyn Jones and Hywel Francis – have all been **Labour** MPs. The committee generally meets in **London**, but it has held sessions in Wales and has also undertaken overseas visits. It was in part set up to compensate for the failure to secure a Welsh Assembly in 1979. With the establishment of the **National Assembly for Wales** in 1999, most of the committee's work passed to the Assembly's members.

SENGHENNYDD *Cantref*
Occupying the land between the **Rivers Taff** and **Rhymney**, Senghennydd (*y cantref breiniol* – the privileged *cantref*) was divided into the **commotes** of Uwch Caeach, Is Caeach and **Cibwr**. Following the **Norman** invasion of the kingdom of **Morgannwg**, Cibwr, which contained **Cardiff**, became the core of the march**er**-lordship of **Glamorgan**. The northern commotes remained under native Welsh

The Great Universal Colliery Disaster at Senghenydd in 1913

The 16th-century tower of St Giles church, Wrexham, one of 'the seven wonders of Wales'

lords, **Ifor Bach** among them. The close alliance between those lords and the rulers of **Deheubarth** and **Gwynedd** was of concern to the marcher lords, particularly in the mid-13th century, when **Llywelyn ap Gruffudd** was expanding his power. The concern found expression in Gilbert de **Clare**'s massive castle at **Caerphilly**. The 'second conquest of Glamorgan', carried out in the early 1270s, dispossessed the Welsh rulers and made Senghennydd an integral part of the Clare lordship of Glamorgan. In 1894, it became (as Senghenydd) the name of the village (*see* **Aber Valley**) serving the Great Universal Colliery, the site of Wales's worst **colliery disaster**.

SENGHENYDD COLLIERY DISASTER

A total of 439 men and boys, the largest number in a single British **colliery disaster**, died at the Great Universal Colliery, Senghenydd (*see* **Aber Valley**) at about 8.10 a.m. on Tuesday 14 October 1913. The west side of the mine was devastated by an explosion, the location and cause of which were never clearly determined. Some experts considered that the explosion may have been caused by an unlocked lamp, others by sparks from the bell signalling system, with the effects being magnified by **coal** dust.

SESSWICK, Wrexham (1069 ha; 591 inhabitants)

Situated across the **Dee** from **Bangor Is-y-Coed**, the **community** is the location of the confluence of the Dee and the Clywedog and contains some of the flattest meadows in Wales. Bedwell Hall, Gerwyn Hall, Pickhill Hall and Pickhill Old Hall are all attractive 18th-century houses.

SEVEN SISTERS (Blaendulais), Neath Port Talbot (1165 ha; 2032 inhabitants)

As its **Welsh** name indicates, the **community** is located in the upper reaches of the valley of the Dulais, a tributary of the **Nedd**. Its **English** name recalls the venture of David Bevan, who named the **coal** pit he sunk in 1875 after his seven daughters. The Seven Sisters Hoard, discovered in 1902 at Nant-y-cafn-isaf, is a collection of 1st-century **Celtic** and **Roman** metalwork. The community contains a stretch of tramroad constructed in 1834; it is a rare example of a 'hybrid' line, intermediate between the **horse**-worked tramroad and the locomotive-hauled **railway**.

'SEVEN WONDERS OF WALES, The'

An anonymous rhyme written in the late 18th or early 19th century, in which all but one of the wonders – **Snowdon** – is situated in **Denbighshire** or **Flintshire**, the first areas of Wales to be opened to **tourism** through the construction of turnpike **roads**:

> Pistyll Rhaeadr and **Wrexham** steeple,
> Snowdon's **mountain** without its people,
> **Overton** yew trees, St **Winefride**'s **wells**,
> **Llangollen**'s bridge and **Gresford** bells.

Pistyll Rhaeadr refers to Wales's highest **waterfall** at **Llanrhaeadr-ym-Mochnant** and Winefride's well refers to **Holywell**. If the verse reflects the growing fashionability of tours in north Wales, its second line would seem to imply a modicum of impatience with aspects of tourism.

SEVERN (Hafren) River
(354 km, 73 km wholly in Wales)

Rising at 752 m in the **community** of **Trefeglwys**, the Severn – the Sabrina of the Brythons and the **Romans** – flows eastwards from the eastern slopes of **Pumlumon**. The frequent floods which afflicted the upper Severn valley ceased in the 1960s following the construction of a **reservoir** on the Clywedog (**Llanidloes Without**), which joins the Severn at **Llanidloes**. The Rhiw, which drains much of the uplands of mid-**Montgomeryshire**, joins the **river** between **Newtown** and **Welshpool**. The Severn was navigable up to Welshpool, a key factor enabling that town to become the sixth largest in 18th-century Wales. At **Bausley**, where the Severn flows into **England**, it is joined by the Vyrnwy (Afon Efyrnwy), which, with its tributaries, the Tanat, the Banwy and the Cain, drains most of northern Montgomeryshire. Near Worcester, the Severn is joined by the Teme (Afon Tefeidiad), which drains much of northern **Radnorshire**. From **Chepstow** westwards, the north bank of the Severn estuary is in Wales. The estuary crossing – by ferry, the **Severn Tunnel** and the **Severn bridges** – has played an important role in Welsh history.

SEVERN BRIDGES, The

The two toll bridges across the **Severn** estuary are vital parts of the motorway network linking south Wales with the west of **England** and **London**. The first Severn **road** bridge opened in 1966, replacing the slow and cumbersome Beachley–Aust car ferry. A suspension bridge with two 123-m towers, a main span of 997 m and two side spans each of 307 m, it cost £8 million and was then the most advanced engineering project of its kind in the world. The poet **Harri Webb** greeted this award-winning bridge – which is actually in England at both ends – with a four-line verse noting that all the tolls were collected 'on the English side'. By the 1980s, traffic along the **M4** had increased so much that a second bridge was deemed necessary. The second Severn crossing, opened in 1996, runs close to the line of the **Severn Tunnel** and is in Wales at its western end (*see* **Caldicot**). It stretches more than 5 km across the estuary at the English Stones by means of viaducts and the 947-m cable-stayed Shoots Bridge. Special construction techniques were required to cross the soft estuarine sedimentary plains and to avoid damage to the Severn **railway** tunnel. The bridges solved problems that had taxed British engineers for over a century, **Thomas Telford** having first proposed a suspension bridge in 1824. Following the opening of the second bridge which carried the M4, the original bridge came to carry the M48.

SEVERN TUNNEL, The

The **Severn** Tunnel was an outstanding piece of Victorian **railway engineering**. At 7 km long and 7.92 m wide, for nearly a century it was the longest undersea tunnel in the world. Built by the Great Western Railway, it cut journey times appreciably between south Wales and **London**. Work began in 1873 but little headway was made until Thomas Andrew Walker (1828–89), who had built railways in Canada and the Sudan, took over as contractor in 1879. He was an autocrat who lengthened the working day from

The second Severn Bridge, opened in 1996

eight hours to ten and summarily dismissed men he deemed 'troublemakers'. He provided **housing** for his workers and their families and built a hospital and mission hall at Sudbrook (**Portskewett**) at the Welsh end. At their busiest, the works employed 3600 men, the best-paid averaging £1 18s per week (£1.90). Walker claimed that 'considering the magnitude of the enterprise, we were very free from accidents', but men died from falling into shafts or from ladders, while the hot, damp conditions led to deaths from pneumonia and rheumatic fever. Some 76,400 million bricks were used in the construction of the tunnel. The first train ran through in September 1885 and passenger services began in December 1886.

SEWARD, Edwin (1853–1924) Architect

Somerset-born Edwin Seward came to **Cardiff** in 1870 and became principle assistant to G. E. Robinson before joining the practice of W. P. James in 1875. In 1880, Seward won the competition for Cardiff's Free Library (1882), and this was followed by many significant commissions, including Cardiff's Royal Infirmary (1883) and **Coal** Exchange (1885), the Turner Gallery (1887) in **Penarth** and the **Port** Office (1903; subsequently Morgan's Hotel) in **Swansea**. Seward was president of the South Wales Institute of Architects (1894–5). He was an early protagonist for a **National Museum**. Seward became interested in **Celt**ic art and designed a 'Celtic Corridor' shopping arcade (1905) in Newport Road, Cardiff.

SHAKESPEARE and WALES

Since several Welsh names (for instance, Hugh ap Shon and Howard ap Howell) appear in late 16th-century Stratford records, William Shakespeare (1564–1616) may have made early acquaintance with the Welsh. Traditionally, one of his teachers was said to be Welsh, but the claim is doubtful. Hugh Evans, the Welsh schoolmaster in *The Merry Wives of Windsor* 'makes fritters of English'; although cowardly, he is essentially good-natured. Shakespeare's Welsh characters – Owen Glendower (**Owain Glyndŵr**), 'Lady' **Mortimer**, Fluellen (*see* **Roger Williams**) and the Welsh captain in *Richard III* – are, to varying degrees, figures of fun, but the 'mockery' is always affectionate. In *Henry IV, Part I*, Glendower and his daughter, 'Lady' Mortimer, converse in **Welsh**, though their words are not recorded. 'Lady' Mortimer also sings in Welsh. In *Cymbeline* – in scenes set near the **Milford Haven Waterway** – Wales provides the setting for a vision of native 'British' nobility of character. Lear has his origins in Llŷr, who was father of **Manawydan**, **Bendigeidfran** and **Branwen**. Various Welsh-language authors have adopted Shakespeare as a literary exemplar. National **Eisteddfod** competitions for Shakespearean translation produced one outstanding work in J. T. Jones's (1894–1975) *Nos Ystwyll* (Twelfth Night, 1952). **Thomas Parry**'s verse-**drama** *Llywelyn Fawr* (1954) is an impressive imitation of the Shakespearean model.

SHEEP

For thousands of years, sheep have been a major factor in the **economy** of rural Wales, providing milk in former times as well as meat, skins and, pre-eminently, wool (*see*

Sheep on the Brecon Beacons

Woollen Industry). As foragers of vast tracts of **common land**, they have also had a major impact on the appearance of the Welsh landscape.

The best adapted of all agricultural animals to the Welsh **climate** and topography, sheep were established in Wales during the **Neolithic Age**, when forests were cleared to make way for livestock and arable farming (*see* **Forestry**). Large-scale sheep farming, introduced to Wales by **Cistercian** monks, gave rise to an important domestic weaving industry. However, sheep rearing remained secondary to that of **cattle** until the land **enclosures** of the 18th and 19th centuries, when large flocks of sheep were established on **mountain** sheep walks. When synthetic fibres superseded wool in the 20th century, meat became the main product of sheep, Welsh lamb being famous for its quality and flavour. Following **Britain**'s entry into the European Common Market in 1973, generous subsidies and increased farm specialization saw the Welsh sheep flock grow to a total of over 11 million; by 2002, when it was responsible for about a quarter of agricultural output, the flock had declined by nearly a million. The market for Welsh sheep extends far beyond Britain. In 2003, the European Commission awarded Protected Geographical Indicator status to Welsh lamb, meaning that only lamb reared and slaughtered in Wales may be described as such.

From the 18th century onwards, there has been much improvement of Welsh sheep breeds through selective breeding, and several new types have been developed in an effort to find the best inter-breed crosses to suit various conditions. Noted for its hardiness and ability to graze the most difficult of land, the Welsh mountain sheep is the main breed in Wales. Mountain breeds, which also include the south Wales mountain, the black Welsh mountain, the Beulah speckled face, the **Radnor** and the badger face, are small and well adapted to severe conditions. Hill or 'intermediate' breeds, such as the **Kerry** Hill and the Clun Forest, are found in the **border** region, while the **Llŷn** and the **Llanwenog** are raised in the western areas. Lowland breeds popular in Wales include the blue-faced Leicester, the border Leicester, the Suffolk and the Dorset Down. In the mid-20th century, the Welsh half-bred (Welsh mountain crossed with border Leicester) and the Welsh mule (Welsh mountain crossed with blue-faced Leicester) were developed as new breeds. Combining the good quality meat of the mountain breeds with the greater size and faster growth rate of the lowlanders, they are useful for further crossing with a lowland ram – frequently Suffolk, Texel or Charollais – to produce quarter-bred lambs for slaughter.

Wales is a world leader in involving farmers in the genetic improvement of sheep. Welsh farmers have long used traditional methods to improve the quality of their flocks, but since the later 20th century they have enjoyed increasing access to the latest tools of **science**, from artificial insemination and embryo transfer, to the ultrasound scanning of eye muscle and fat depth. In 1976, Britain's first group breeding scheme was inaugurated at **Pentrefoelas**, its purpose being to pursue genetic improvements not so much within isolated flocks, which had been the traditional approach, but across a range of flocks, bringing the best of their ewes and rams together to form a central nucleus flock. Genetic selection was practised only within the nucleus flock, and the best rams within each generation were returned to individual contributor flocks to promote genetic improvement within them. A further eight schemes have since been established, giving Wales the highest number of sheep genetic improvement programmes in the northern hemisphere.

The shepherding calendar follows a distinct annual cycle, with weather determining that activities in the mountainous regions occur a month or two later than in the lowlands. Mating takes place in the autumn, its timing controlled to ensure that lambs are not born too early in harsh weather. Mountain sheep usually rear one lamb, while lowland sheep rear at least two. Lambing, which involves intense activity for about a month, takes place between January and April in the lowlands, with single lambs being sold from May onwards, and the majority being sold between July and September. Pure breeding is characteristic of the hill farms, where lambing starts at the end of March. In late spring, identifying earmarks are cut, male lambs are castrated, and in early summer shearing, followed by dipping for parasites, takes place.

Sheep shearing was originally undertaken by a large workforce using hand shears. Traditionally, each farm in an extensive neighbourhood would settle on a date for shearing, and whatever the circumstances – with the exception of the weather – it was impossible to change that day, for shearing depended on co-operation and the exchange of labour between a group of farmers. With shearing gangs numbering up to 100 in some cases, shearing day was regarded as the most important in a farmer's calendar and a great social occasion. The best **food** was produced, and often storytellers and singers would attend to entertain the workers. Hand shearing has been replaced by a machine-shearing style, pioneered in **New Zealand** in the 1950s. Shearing has developed into a competitive sporting event with local, national and international championships, often involving itinerant shearers from the southern hemisphere who visit Wales each summer.

SHEEPDOG TRIALS

The first recorded **sheep**dog trials in **Britain** took place at Garth Goch (**Llangywer**) in 1873. They were organized by the local landowner, R. J. Lloyd Price (*see* **Price family (Rhiwlas)**), and the winner, with his dog Tweed, was James Thomson, a sheep farmer from **Scotland**, who had settled in Wales. Enthusiasm for trials developed quickly, and they have become one of the most popular country pastimes in sheep farming areas worldwide. The International Sheepdog Society organizes annual competitions between the countries of Britain, and there is an extensive network of local trials affiliated to the Welsh sheepdog associations. In 2002, the first ever World Sheepdog Trials were held near **Bala**; a local farmer, Aled Owen of **Llangwm** (**Conwy**), was the winner, with a dog called Bob.

SHERWOOD, Alf[red Thomas] (1923–90)
Footballer

Aberaman-born Alf Sherwood, a schoolboy international in **football** and **cricket**, left the pits to join **Cardiff** City, making 353 appearances (1941–56). Master of the sliding tackle, he was a full-back much respected by Stanley Matthews. In 1956, in his last international, he saved a penalty as an emergency goalkeeper. The winner of 41 caps, he played for **Newport** County, coached in New York and managed **Barry** Town.

SHIPBUILDING

Most of the **ships** that were owned and traded from Welsh **ports** until the outbreak of the **First World War** were wooden **sailing** vessels, a large proportion of which were built in Wales, many on isolated beaches and in obscure creeks where it is difficult today to imagine any kind of maritime activity. Cei-bach (**Llanllwchaiarn**), Penmaenpool (**Dolgellau**), **Pwllheli** and **Porthmadog** were hives of activity, as large ocean-going vessels were built in considerable numbers. Shipbuilding could be carried out wherever there was a level piece of ground in proximity to deep water. Oak (*see* **Plants**), the staple shipbuilding timber, does not grow well in areas exposed to salty winds, and much of the timber had to be obtained from inland woodlands. As the supply of native oak dwindled, an active trade between Wales and Scandinavia, the Baltic and Canada developed. Equipped with a sawpit and a few simple tools – saws, adzes, hatchets, chisels and wooden mallets – the shipbuilders of Wales were capable of highly skilled work.

Typical of the Welsh shipbuilder of this era was Thomas Richards (fl.1855–80) of **Aberdovey**, who built 14 superb sailing ships during his 22 years of active work, all capable of sailing across the Atlantic in 17 days. With the disappearance of wooden sailing vessels, shipowners became dependent on **iron** steamships from the shipyards of the Clyde, Tyne and Wear. Early 20th-century hopes that **Cardiff** would become a major shipbuilding centre, using the special ships' steel manufactured at **East Moors**, were not realized. A yard at **Chepstow** constructed **iron** merchant vessels until 1920, and the naval shipyard at **Pembroke Dock** was operative until 1926; thereafter, apart from a few builders of small boats, the ship construction industry in Wales became defunct.

Aberystwyth harbour in the 1860s, its shipping heyday

SHIPS and SHIPOWNERS

Until about the last quarter of the 19th century, ships provided the lifeblood of most coastal communities in Wales. Many, in **Cardiganshire**, **Llŷn** and **Anglesey**, for instance, were owned by their masters, while others were owned by non-sailors. Farmers, in particular, were heavily involved in shipowning, for it was to their advantage to control the means of importing fuel for their fires and lime to fertilize their land, and to have vessels available to export their produce. Merchants, groups of relatives, companies of local people, **craft**smen and **Nonconformist** ministers were all involved in the trade, contributing to a complex pattern of ownership.

The shipowners of the most rural parts of the west and north were owners of **sailing** vessels, and as soon as sailing vessels were replaced by steamships, there began a decline in the fortunes of the once prosperous shipowning families. Of the 37 shipowners operating 89 vessels from their offices in the Cardiganshire village of **New Quay** in 1865, virtually all had disappeared by 1900. Nevertheless, during the death throes of the sailing ship in the last quarter of the 19th century, many invested in larger vessels, frequently built in **North America** to operate on a worldwide basis. Large ocean-going barques and full-rigged ships were operated from such **ports** as **Pwllheli**, **Menai Bridge**, **Amlwch**, **Aberystwyth**, New Quay and **Milford Haven** – although they hardly ever visited their home ports. Many vessels that traded from the great ports of **Britain** – **Liverpool, Cardiff**, Newcastle-upon-Tyne and Glasgow, among them – were commanded and crewed by men from a ship's port of registration. It was only a matter of time before some of the shipowners, like the sailors, moved their centre of operation to one of those great ports.

Until at least the outbreak of the **First World War**, many shipowners were still using wooden-hulled sailing ships. **Slate** continued to be transported under sail until well after the turn of the century, and the shipowners of **Swansea**, heavily engaged in the South American **copper** trade, preferred wooden vessels, which were cheaply built from softwood, usually in shipyards on Prince Edward Island in Canada. Badly built ships, negligent crews and greedy owners took a heavy toll on Swansea ships: between 1873 and 1895, no fewer than 200 vessels were lost at sea.

While, with the advent of **iron** steamships, Swansea rapidly declined as a shipowning port, Cardiff was to flourish as one of the principal ports of Britain. It attracted not only those shipowners who hitherto had operated from the isolated coastal settlements of **Pembrokeshire** and Cardiganshire, but businessmen from all parts of Europe and beyond. From the Channel Islands came the Morel Brothers, J. B. Hacquoil and H. B. Marquand; from the west of **England** came John Cory and his distant cousins the Cory brothers (*see* **Cory families**), Edward Nicholl, John Angel Gibbs, W. J. Tatem and William Reardon Smith. Rural Wales supplied many shipowners, ranging from John Mathias, a grocer and merchant from Aberystwyth, to the brothers Owen and Watkin Williams from Pwllparc, a farm at Edern (**Nefyn**) in Llŷn. The Cardiganshire village of **Aberporth** provided a number of successful Cardiff companies; that established by Captain Evan Thomas of Dolwen, in association with Henry Radcliffe of **Merthyr Tydfil**, was by far the largest and most prosperous; manned largely by crews from Cardiganshire, the company owned as many as 35 tramp steamers in 1914. Immediately after the First World War, Cardiff experienced a remarkable boom, with the number of shipping companies located there increasing from 57 in 1919 to 150 in 1920. By then, when 500 vessels with a total capacity of 2 million tonnes were registered there, Cardiff was the greatest centre for the ownership of tramp steamers in the world. The crash, when it came in 1921, was spectacular.

In the north, Liverpool was the main attraction for both the seamen and shipowners of **Gwynedd** and Anglesey. The Davies family of **Menai Bridge**, Robert Thomas of **Criccieth** and others that originated in Wales were highly successful, but again, by the 1920s, the one-time prosperity had vanished.

SHIPWRECKS

Through extreme weather conditions, navigational blunders and wartime activity, **ships** have been lost on the Welsh seaboard throughout the ages. The earliest known finds include a 4th-century flat-bottomed boat at **Magor** (1994) and a **Viking** longboat in the dock mud at **Newport** (1878). **Sailing** ship losses reached a peak during the mid-19th century, when over 100 shipwrecks occurred each year around Wales, with an annual loss of life of about 78 sailors. One gale, in 1859, caused no fewer than 111 shipwrecks around Wales (*see* **Royal Charter**).

From 1852, the Board of Trade has kept a register of shipwrecks, prior to which Lloyds List, from 1760, gave details of losses. Few records remain of shipwrecks before these dates, but the lords of **manors** had rights of wreck, which caused bitter disputes and occasionally led to deliberate wrecking. In 1773, a ship from Dublin was wrecked near **Holyhead**, owing to false lights being shown from the shore, and one man was duly hanged for plundering the wreck. Such too was the fate of wreckers from Crigyll (**Llanfaelog**), also in **Anglesey**, in 1741 – an event vividly described by Lewis Morris (*see* **Morris Brothers**) in his poem 'Lladron Grigyll'. There are stories of wrecking practices at **Marloes** in **Pembrokeshire**, **Pembrey** in **Carmarthenshire**, and **Gower** and Nash (**St Donats**) in **Glamorgan**.

Wartime action caused losses near Holyhead, **Milford Haven** and **Swansea**. Anglesey and Pembrokeshire, with many offshore rocks and unlit **islands**, are notorious for shipwrecks, and disasters still occur in these areas – in 1991, the *Kimya*, a Maltese coaster, sank off Anglesey, with the loss of 10 crewmen; and in 1996, the *Sea Empress* oil tanker was holed, dispersing over 73,000 tonnes of North Sea **oil** on the Pembrokeshire coast.

Shipwrecks have become a fascination for recreational divers. Innovations in detection and location equipment allow previously unknown wreck sites to be discovered.

SHIRENEWTON (Drenewydd Gelli-farch), Monmouthshire (2307 ha; 1014 inhabitants)

Located north-west of **Chepstow**, the **community** contains the villages of Shirenewton and Mynydd Bach, which are growing rapidly as commuter centres. The Japanese **Gardens** at Shirenewton Hall, laid out around 1900, are delightful. Earlswood (1754) is one of the **county**'s earliest **Nonconformist** chapels. The community includes much of Wentwood, the forest which divided **Gwent** into Uwch-coed and Is-coed.

The oil tanker *Sea Empress*, aground off the Pembrokeshire coast in 1996

SHOTTON, Flintshire (247 ha; 6265 inhabitants)
Squeezed between **Connah's Quay** and **Queensferry**, the **community** was a **coal**mining area from the 17th to the 19th century. It grew rapidly following the opening in 1896 of the John **Summers** steelworks (*see* **Iron and Steel**), which were often known as the **Shotton Steelworks**, although they were actually located within the community of Queensferry. **William Ewart Gladstone** paid for the building of St Ethelwold's church; completed in 1902, it was designed by **John Douglas**.

SHOTTON STEELWORKS

In 1896, Henry and James **Summers** established **iron and steel** works on **Dee**side, a branch of the company – John Summers and Sons – which their father had founded at Stalybridge, **Cheshire**. Although located within the present **community** of **Queensferry**, the employees of the works were mainly residents of the adjoining settlement of **Shotton**, which gave the concern its popular name. By 1914, the works, with its 30 rolling mills and 9 **open-hearth furnaces**, employed 3500 workers, and output – mainly of galvanized corrugated sheets – averaged about 4500 tonnes per week. The **First World War** saw annual output double to 500,000 tonnes, with a commensurate growth in the labour force. In the later 1930s, Shotton, as **Britain**'s leading galvanized steelmaker, began to adopt the technological revolutions that had transformed the American industry, by installing Britain's second continuous strip mill, which commenced production in 1940.

Expansion to a fully integrated works began in 1948, and a new open-hearth plant was added in 1953. By 1960, when some 10,000 were employed, Shotton was at the forefront of new coatings technology, having pioneered the first organic agent, Stelvetite, in 1957, and commissioning coil-to-coil lines for electrozinc plating and plastic film laminating in 1972. Steelmaking ceased in 1979; further closures in 2001 meant that by the early 21st century the works employed a mere 700 people, engaged in an advanced steel coating plant.

SHROPSHIRE, Wales's associations with

During the **Roman** occupation, the mid **Severn** valley was the home of the **Cornovii**, a tribe whose territory extended to the hill country between the upper **Dee** and the upper **Wye**. That upland territory, together with much of the present **county** of Shropshire constituted the early kingdom of **Powys** – a name derived perhaps from *pagus*, a **Latin** word for hinterland – and the kingdom may have represented the continuation of the tribal structure of the Cornovii. In about 650, lowland Powys was overwhelmed by Saxon invaders (*see* **Anglo-Saxons**), events commemorated in *Canu Heledd*, verses that mention the destruction of Pengwern, a place located perhaps at Y Berth near Baschurch north-west of Shrewsbury.

The Saxon advance led to the defining of Shropshire's western boundary, which was confirmed *c.*780 by the construction of **Offa's Dyke**. Although that **border** proved not to be wholly stable, Shropshire did not become the launching pad for a sustained attack upon Wales until the 1070s when Roger **Montgomery** – granted the lordship of Shrewsbury by William I – initiated his incursions into

Wales. **Norman** aggression led, not to the expansion of Shropshire at the expense of Wales, but to the expansion of Wales at the expense of Shropshire. By the 13th century, wide swathes of western Shropshire had been withdrawn from the English shire system and had become a series of quasi-independent lordships in the **March**. That situation lasted until the **Act of 'Union'**, when the western boundary of Shropshire was defined by statute. The definition involved including in **England** districts wholly **Welsh** in language and social organization. Indeed, well into the 20th century, there were Welsh-speaking families around Oswestry with no ancestral connection with Wales itself.

Wales's involvement with the towns of Shropshire has deep roots. Oswestry was long considered to be a Welsh town. It was the favourite town of **Guto'r Glyn**, and in 1932 the weekly **newspaper** *Y Cymro* was founded there. For centuries, **Ludlow** was the quasi-capital of Wales. Shrewsbury was and is the chief commercial centre of the middle borderland and, until it lost its monopoly in 1624, the town's Drapers' Company had an iron grip upon the Welsh **woollen industry**. Shrewsbury played an important part in the development of **printing and publishing** in Welsh, as the career of **Thomas Jones** (1648–1713) testifies. With the creation of the **railway** network, Shrewsbury became the only place with direct train services from north, mid, south-west and south-east Wales, a factor which made it the favoured venue for the meetings of Welsh institutions – the **University of Wales** in particular. Indeed, so significant was its role that there were demands that it should be annexed by Wales and declared the country's capital. By the 21st century, however, the situation had been reversed – Shrewsbury's postcode, SY, is that of most of mid Wales, suggesting that the postal authorities believe that the core of an ancient nation is no more than the backyard of a border town. Shrewsbury's newspaper, the *Shropshire Star*, publishes a coastal edition aimed at the inhabitants of the shores of Cardigan Bay.

SIBLY, T[homas] F[ranklin] (1883–1948)
Geologist and administrator

A Bristol graduate in experimental physics, Sibly became professor of **geology** at **Cardiff** (1913–18) and then at Newcastle upon Tyne. Although a fine geologist, his main reputation rests on his exceptional gifts as an administrator. Chosen as the first principal of University College, Swansea (*see* **University of Wales Swansea**) in 1920, partly because he was the main architect of a scheme for the co-ordination of higher technical **education** in Wales, he set the new college on secure foundations and established effective working relations with the three older sister colleges. He was knighted in 1938.

SIDDONS, Sarah (1755–1851) Actress

The great tragedienne of the English stage was born at the Shoulder of Mutton Inn in **Brecon**, to the travelling players Sarah Ward and Roger Kemble. As a child-actor, she toured extensively. She married the actor William Siddons despite her parents' objection to him: he was thrown out of the family company for making an appeal for her in verse to the Brecon audience. In 1775, she was invited by David

Sarah Siddons

Garrick to the **London** stage; by 1782, she had become famous, her most notable role being that of Lady Macbeth. The poet **Ann Julia Hatton** was Sarah Siddons's sister.

SIDNEY, Henry (1529–86) Administrator
President of the **Council of Wales and the Marches** (1559–86), he was also lord deputy of **Ireland** (1566–71, 1575–8). During his presidency, the Council was at its most active, and he considered that 'a better country to govern [than Wales] Europe holdeth not'. He fostered Welsh culture and mineral exploitation in **Glamorgan** and **Anglesey**. He was father of the poet Philip Sidney (1554–86) and father-in-law of Henry **Herbert**, earl of Pembroke (1534–1601).

SIEMENS, Wilhelm (1823–83)
Inventor and industrialist
Siemens came from a family in Lethe, Hanover. For their application to industry of scientific discoveries, the family has been called the most innovative in history. His major invention (1856), made jointly with his brother Friederich, was the regenerative furnace, which applied the principle of the condenser. Its application to steelmaking (*see* **Iron and Steel**) owed much to the contribution of Pierre Martin of Sireuil in 1864, and it is generally known as the Siemens-Martin or **open-hearth furnace**. The revolutionary process was developed and tested at Landore, **Swansea**, from 1869 to 1888, although this works was not itself commercially successful.

SIGINGSTONE AVIATION DISASTER
Wales's worst **aviation** disaster, and the worst in the world at the time, occurred on 12 March 1950. An Avro Tudor airliner, with 78 passengers and 5 crew, was on a flight from Dublin to **Llandow airport** west of **Cowbridge**. The passengers were **rugby** supporters, returning from an international game in **Ireland**. The aircraft, about to land, stalled and crashed near Sigingstone village, just 750 m from the runway. Only three people survived. Temporary alterations to the plane's seating layout had moved its centre of gravity too far aft, causing instability and loss of control during the critical landing phase.

SILURES
The **Iron Age** tribe of south-east Wales, the Silures provided the most implacable resistance to **Roman** expansion of any of the British tribes. Even after the capture of the war leader **Caratacus**, the Silures conducted a successful guerrilla war for over a quarter of a century, defeating a Roman legion in the process. They were not overcome until AD *c.*75, when the fortress of Isca (**Caerleon**) was built in their territory. **Caerwent** (Venta Silurum) was established as their *civitas* capital. Their territory was essentially the later **Glamorgan**, **Monmouthshire** and southern **Breconshire**; the poet **Henry Vaughan**, a native of the **Usk** valley, styled himself 'the Silurist'. To **Harri Webb**, the **Newport Rising** of 1839 was an attempt to establish 'the republic of Siluria'.

SIMON, [William] Glyn [Hughes] (1903–72)
Archbishop
Glyn Simon, born in **Swansea**, was successively dean of Llandaff (**Cardiff**), bishop of Swansea and **Brecon**, bishop of Llandaff and, from 1968 to 1971, archbishop of Wales. The first archbishop of Wales generally to be regarded as the leader of all Christians in Wales, Glyn Simon raised the profile of the **Church in Wales** within the **Anglican** Communion. He was a zealous defender of the **Welsh language**, although he did not acquire real fluency in it.

SIÔN CENT (fl.1400–30/45) Poet
The history of late medieval Wales's greatest religious poet is unknown, but his poem praising **Brycheiniog** may indicate an association with that area. **Saunders Lewis**'s contention that he was educated at **Oxford** and influenced by the **philosophy** of William Ockham and his school is debatable, but his poems do refer to authors whose works were university texts. Apart from his Brycheiniog poem and a political **prophecy** which may reflect the disillusion and despair which followed the failure of the **Glyndŵr Revolt**, his poetry is didactic and fervently moral. A favourite theme is the transience of worldly success and power. His trenchant descriptions of the body's corruption in the grave – a dead nobleman features 'with eight hundred worms tasting him' – contrasts sharply with his delirious portrayal of the joys of the righteous soul in heaven. He disputed with **Rhys Goch Eryri**, castigating the mendacity of professional poets of his era.

SIÔN CWILT (fl.18th century) Smuggler
A character associated with the high moor between Post Bach and Capel Cynon in **Ceredigion**, a district still known

as Banc Siôn Cwilt (**Llandysiliogogo**). Traditions dating from the later 19th century allege that he kept his contraband in **caves** and sold the goods to local **gentry** at exorbitant prices. *Cwilt w*as reputedly a reference to the multi-coloured patches on his clothes, although it is more likely that his original name was John Gwilt or Quilt, from the **Welsh** *gwyllt* (wild); such a **surname** probably originated in the **border**lands.

SIÔN PHYLIP (*c.*1543–1620) Poet

The most important and prolific of the Phylip family of poets from **Ardudwy**, he was regarded as the particular poet of the **Vaughan family (Corsygedol)**, although, as an itinerant poet, he travelled throughout the north. Taught by **Gruffudd Hiraethog** and **Wiliam Llŷn**, he graduated at the second **Caerwys Eisteddfod** (1567). He copied a version of the bardic grammar and was an enthusiastic flyter (one who engages in versified disputations). He drowned on a bardic tour; an *englyn* by his son Gruffydd (d.1666) describes the voyage with the corpse from **Pwllheli** to Mochras (**Llanbedr**).

SIÔN TUDUR (*c.*1522–1602) Poet

The poetry of Siôn Tudur displays a degree of liveliness rarely found in the work of other 16th-century praise poets. He was born at Wigfair (**Cefnmeiriadog**) and most of his praise poems relate to **gentry** families from the north-east. He served as a Yeoman of the Guard both before and after Edward VI's ascension to the throne (1547), and during the early years of Elizabeth I's reign he further served as a Yeoman of the Crown. Such positions entailed periods of residence in **London**, and Siôn Tudur's satirical poems show the influence of contemporary English literary fashions.

SIÔN Y GOF (d.1719) (John the blacksmith)
Murderer

A **Cardiganshire** man who was employed in the **lead** mines at Dylife (**Llanbrynmair**), he was hanged for killing his wife and two children by throwing them down a mineshaft, in the belief that the end of the world was imminent. His skull may be seen at the National History Museum (*see* **St Fagans**).

SLATE

The older rocks of Wales (*see* **Geology**) have been quarried for slate from at least **Roman** times, although written records do not go back further than the late 14th century. Initially, quarrying was no more technically advanced than was the digging of **peat**. However, from the late 18th century onwards, the growth in the commercial market led to more sophisticated methods of extraction. While slate was also produced in Cumbria, **Cornwall**, **Scotland**, **Ireland**, France and **North America**, Wales became the world's main supplier. Some of Wales's slate came from **Pembrokeshire** (*see* **Clydey** and **Llanrhian**), but by far the greatest proportion was produced in the north-west, where the chief centres of extraction were in central **Caernarfonshire** – the so-called Great Slate Belt, worked in

Hand quarrying slate at the Penrhyn Quarry

beds of early Cambrian age – and in the area around Blaenau **Ffestiniog**, in strata of early Ordovician age. Although a much smaller industry than **coal**, slate-working represents a highly significant chapter in Welsh history; certainly, no extractive industry has made a more enduring impression on the landscape.

The siting of the major quarries was largely determined by the availability of water power and by access to **railways**. Quarrying methods are governed by a combination of geological and geomorphological factors. At the mammoth Penrhyn (**Llandygai**) and Dinorwic (**Llanddeiniolen**) quarries, the slate was extracted on large terraces or galleries, connected by inclines and excavated at 18-m intervals up to some 550 m. The Dorothea and Pen-yr-orsedd quarries in Dyffryn Nantlle (**Llanllyfni**) were worked in chasm-like quarries, characterized by aerial cableways (*blondins*) spanning the workings in all directions. At Oakeley and Llechwedd (Blaenau Ffestiniog) – the source of slate that was less tough but finer and smoother than that from Caernarfonshire – production occurred in enormous underground chambers. Most of the output was roofing slates, but some quarries – **Corris**, Aberllefenni (Corris) and Abergynolwyn (**Llanfihangel-y-Pennant**) among them – have specialized in slate slabs.

Slate's usefulness as a roofing material depends on the ease with which it splits along the natural planes of rock cleavage, and on its impervious nature, durability and resistance to atmospheric agents. It has also been used for other purposes, such as fencing, **dry stone walling**, laboratory work surfaces, writing slates and pencils, gravestones, flooring and enamelled domestic products. Because of the ease with which it can be sawn into large slabs of uniform grain and because it has no tendency to shrink, it is useful for **billiard** tables and school blackboards. As it is stable under almost all conditions, cannot burn and is a poor conductor of electricity, slate is especially suitable for electrical switchboards.

The role of the **railways** was threefold: linking the quarries to the harbours by narrow gauge tracks – for example, Penrhyn to Porth Penrhyn (Llandygai), Dinorwic to Port Dinorwic (**Y Felinheli**) and Blaenau Ffestiniog to **Porthmadog**; linking the quarries with the standard gauge network; and transporting slate within the quarries and to the railheads.

Large-scale slate production began in Wales at Penrhyn in 1782; by the 1790s, 400 men were employed there, rising to 3000 by the 1890s. At its height in the late 19th century, when there were dozens of quarries, the industry employed some 15,000 men. Slate found its largest market in the burgeoning towns of northern **England**, but was also exported worldwide. Germany, where the merits of Welsh slate were discovered following the destruction of Hamburg by fire in 1842, was a particularly important market. The industry suffered the problems associated with the boom-and-bust nature of the construction industry: during depressions, there was over-production and prices fell; during booms, production could not be increased to meet demand, and foreign competitors and other materials took advantage of the market. During the **First World War**, production virtually ceased. There was some recovery in the interwar period, when Wales was the source of between 75% and 80% of total British production. Serious problems arose

Slate workers preparing roofing slates

after the **Second World War**, because of the increased use of manufactured tiles, and the rapidly rising cost of slate; the need to split and dress every slate by hand was a crucial factor. The closure of Dinorwic in 1969 was a severe blow. However, Penrhyn, acquired by McAlpine, continued in production; by the early 21st century, it had become a flourishing concern.

Because of the remoteness of the quarry areas, the entrepreneurs were usually local landowners, such as the **Pennant** and **Assheton Smith families**. However, at Blaenau Ffestiniog, businessmen of English origins, such as the **Oakeley family**, were prominent. Unlike the largely **Nonconformist** and **Liberal** workforce, the owners were mostly **Conservative** and **Anglican**.

One of the most characteristic features of the working relationship was the *bargen* (bargain) system, whereby a group of five or six men representing a variety of skills negotiated with the management on a monthly basis regarding the wages for working a particular area of quarry face. The determination to maintain this system – in which the quarryman was more like a contractor than a paid employee – was the major cause of the bitter and protracted **Penrhyn lockouts** (1896–7, 1900–3).

Working conditions were generally poor, and accidents were frequent. Inhaling slate dust caused silicosis (*see* **Pneumoconiosis and Silicosis**), and in the 1920s the quarry villages had southern **Britain**'s highest rates of mortality from **tuberculosis**. In 1979, a scheme to compensate quarrymen suffering from silicosis was introduced, but by then the industry and those who had worked in it were rapidly disappearing.

The composition of the workforce, drawn almost entirely from nearby rural areas, meant that the communities were almost wholly **Welsh**-speaking, making slate quarrying, in the words of the historian **A. H. Dodd**, 'the most Welsh of Welsh industries'. Indeed, there was a widespread belief that the rock could not understand **English**. The quarrying communities made a wholly disproportionate contribution to Wales's cultural life, for the majority of the leading Welsh-language writers of the 20th century were the products of such communities. They include **T. Rowland Hughes** (**Llanberis**), **R. Williams Parry** (Talysarn, Llanllyfni), **T. H. Parry-Williams** (Rhyd-ddu, **Betws Garmon**), **Thomas Parry** (Carmel, **Llandwrog**), **W. J. Gruffydd** (Bethel, Llanddeiniolen), **Kate Roberts** (Rhosgadfan, **Llanwnda**), **John Gwilym Jones** (Y Groeslon, Llandwrog), **Caradog Prichard** (**Bethesda**), Gwyn Thomas (b.1936) and Eigra Lewis Roberts (b.1939) (the last two from Blaenau Ffestiniog).

Aspects of the traditional industry are interpreted at the Welsh Slate Museum (part of the **National Museum [of] Wales**), at Llanberis (1972), which has the workshops of Dinorwic Quarry (1809–1969) as its centrepiece, and at Llechwedd Slate Caverns (the first commercial venture of its kind in Britain, 1972), located in Llechwedd (or Greaves) Quarry, Blaenau Ffestiniog (1846 to the present).

SLAVERY

The estimation that 15% of Americans of African descent have Welsh-sounding names, and that half of the most popular names among them are of Welsh origin, suggests – because slaves had their names imposed on them – that many slave owners were themselves Welsh. Several Welsh **gentry** families benefited from slave owning; the **Pennant family** of Penrhyn Castle (**Llandygai**), for instance, made a fortune from Jamaican sugar plantations worked by slaves. Surprisingly, many Dissenters (*see* **Nonconformists and Dissenters**), fleeing religious persecution in Wales, were enthusiastic slave owners in America. The allocation of land according to the size of families (including slaves) encouraged slave owning, and the Dissenters' brand of **Calvinism** allowed some of them to justify the practice theologically.

The proximity of Wales to the slaving **ports** of **Liverpool** and Bristol permitted a number of Welsh people to exploit the trade. For example, Philip Protheroe (1781–1846) from **Pembrokeshire** became a successful slave trader in Bristol and was rewarded with the mayoralty of the city in 1810.

It was in Bristol that **Morgan John Rhys** (1760–1804), a Welsh **Baptist** minister, first encountered the abolitionist movement. He translated one of their pamphlets into **Welsh**, pursued the subject in his political magazine *Y Cylch-grawn Cynmraeg* [sic], and, after emigrating to America in 1794, published in the *American Universal Magazine* a series of essays attacking John Lawrence's pamphlet *Negro Slavery Defended by the Word of God*. Published in 1798 as *Letters on Liberty and Slavery*, Rhys's essays became influential in the abolition movement. Other notable Welsh abolitionists include Iolo Morganwg (**Edward Williams**), **Samuel Roberts** and **Jessie Donaldson**.

The publication of *Uncle Tom's Cabin* (1852) provided emancipationists with powerful propaganda. (Its author, Harriet Beecher Stowe, was descended from migrants from **Llanddewi Brefi**.) Within a year, there were three Welsh versions circulating, by Hugh Williams (Cadfan; ?1807–70), William Williams (Y Lefiad; fl.1853) and Gwilym Hiraethog (**William Rees**; 1802–83). An edited version for Welsh-Americans was published by Robert Everett (1791–1875) in 1854.

In the American Civil War (1861–5), essentially a conflict between the non-slave-owning northern states and the slave-owning southern states, the Welsh were generally supportive of the North, although Jefferson Davis, president of the Confederate States, was of Welsh descent.

SLEBECH (Slebets), Pembrokeshire
(1817 ha; 172 inhabitants)
Located east of **Haverfordwest** on the north bank of the Eastern **Cleddau**, the **community** contains the country houses of Slebech Hall and Picton Castle. Slebech was the site of Wales's sole commandery of the Knights of St John. Founded in the mid-12th century by the lords of **Wiston**, the commandery won fame for its hospitality. On the **dissolution of the monasteries**, the church – the only part of the commandery to survive – became the **parish** church. Within it is the grave of William Hamilton (1730–1803), one of the founders of **Milford Haven** and husband of Lord Nelson's Emma. In the 1840s, the de Rutzen family of Slebech Hall deliberately ruined the church in order to ensure that the congregation would attend the new, large neo-Gothic church erected alongside the A40; that church was abandoned in 1990. Slebech Hall (1770s) is a substantial building with rounded projections at each corner.

Picton Castle came into the possession of the **Philipps family** in the 15th century, through Thomas Philipps's marriage to the heiress of the Dwnn and Wogan families. The castle, which dates from 1300, is one of Wales's most splendid country houses and is still occupied by Philipp's descendants. Between 1976 and 1995, the castle contained an **art gallery** devoted to the work of **Graham Sutherland**. Picton Home Farm (1827) is an excellent example of a model farm.

In 2006, work began on the £110 million Bluestone holiday park, which had been resisted by many conservationists because of its situation within the **Pembrokeshire Coast National Park**. Its supporters claim that the project, which will include 300 timber cabins, a Waterworld and a Snowdome, will inject £32 million into the local **economy** and create 900 jobs in an area of high unemployment.

SMALLPOX

An acute, highly contagious, viral disease characterized by high fever and a pinkish, pustular rash, which leaves a pitted skin if the disease is survived. Occurring in Wales in epidemics and sporadically, its effects were devastating, particularly in the 18th century. In 1774, Sir Watkin **Williams Wynn** arranged for the poor of **Ruabon** to be inoculated by an apothecary, using fluid from the patients' pocks; 150 were inoculated in 1779.

The last outbreaks in Wales occurred in 1962 after a Pakistani man who had travelled to **Cardiff** was diagnosed with the disease, 25 cases occurred in the **Rhondda**, and 6 people died. Later that year, a second outbreak occurred at Glan-rhyd Psychiatric Hospital, **Bridgend**. In 20 cases, the diagnosis was confirmed and 12 died. Approximately 880,000 Welsh people were vaccinated. In December 1979, it was announced that the world was free of the disease, although the virus, stored in the United States and Russia, could yet give rise to further attacks.

SMITH, Ray (1936–91) Actor

Born in Trealaw, **Rhondda**, Ray Smith was compelling in proletarian television roles, notably as the avuncular George Barraclough in the Granada series *Sam* (1973). He played the bitter thespian in Richard Lewis's **drama** *Babylon Bypassed* (1988), Dai Bando in BBC television's *How Green Was My Valley* (1976) and one of the boozy coterie in the BBC's adaptation of Kingsley Amis's *The Old Devils* (1992). For much of the 1960s, he was employed by **Plaid [Genedlaethol] Cymru**.

SMUGGLING

Smuggling around the coasts of **Britain** was at its height in the 18th century, largely because of the high tolls on imports such as **tea**, tobacco, liquor, candles, soap and salt (*see* **Customs and Excise**).

With its lengthy coastline and its many remote beaches, smuggling was practised everywhere along coastal Wales. Some of the leading smugglers, such as John Connor (the leader of the Rush Gang), Thomas Field and Stephen and Thomas Richards had armed ships operating from **Ireland** or the Isle of **Man**, and in the Severn Sea Thomas Knight was a constant affront to the authorities. Burdened as they

were by high tolls, the bulk of the **population** warmed to the smugglers, and the **gentry** in particular were eager purchasers of contraband goods. In 1786, four chests containing 399 pounds of tea were discovered in the attic of G. Francis-Lloyd, a one-time sheriff of **Anglesey**. So bold were the smugglers that, at **Pwllheli**, they carried out their activities in full daylight, and **Bangor** in 1757 was described as 'a great thoroughfare for smugglers'. **Howel Harris**, the Methodist leader, felt constrained to castigate congregations on the **Cardiganshire** coast for their 'wickedness in stealing wreck and cheating the King of all things excised'.

The customs officers who were responsible for suppressing smuggling had few resources; when eight **Aberdovey** officers sought to seize a load of salt at **New Quay** in 1704, they were attacked by a crowd of 150. An act of 1736 laying down that such attacks should carry the death penalty had little effect. Four of the officers boarding one of the **ships** of the smuggler William Owen at **Cardigan** in 1744 were killed in the resulting turmoil. In 1788, when officers visited a farm at Pwlldu (**Pennard**) on the **Gower** peninsula, they were faced by 50 people armed with knives, pokers and **iron** bars.

With a marked reduction in the tolls on commodities such as tea, and with coastguards better organized, the golden age of the smugglers had, by the 1830s, come to an end, and their activities had become a romantic memory (*see* **Siôn Cwilt**).

In the 20th century, drug smugglers sought to make use of Wales's remote beaches. In 1983, Operation Seal Bay caught a gang who had invested heavily in the creation of an underground drug storehouse on a beach at **Dinas Cross** in **Pembrokeshire**. In addition, the continuing demand for cheaper commodities is reflected in the fact that up to a quarter of the cigarettes smoked in Wales in the early 21st century had been smuggled into the country.

SNELL, D[avid] J[ohn] (1880–1957)
Music publisher

Having established a **music** retail business in his native **Swansea** in 1900, Snell bought the stock and copyrights of Benjamin Parry in 1910 and embarked on a publishing career. Adding the stock of other publishers to his catalogue, he became Wales's principal music publisher. In addition to reissuing popular works such as **Joseph Parry**'s 'Blodwen' and '**Myfanwy**', he published new compositions by **David Vaughan Thomas**, **Meirion Williams**, Idris Lewis and W. Bradwen Jones. Snell offered prizes for the choice of **eisteddfod** test pieces from his catalogue.

SNOWDON Mountain range

Snowdon is a massif with four major peaks, chief among them Yr Wyddfa (1085 m; **Betws Garmon**), the highest peak in Wales, and the highest in **Britain** south of Ben More, north-east of Loch Lomond. The other peaks of the massif are Crib-y-ddysgl (1065 m), Crib Goch (921 m) and Y Lliwedd (898 m; all in **Beddgelert**). The massif is widely considered to be the handsomest **mountain** in Britain: Jan Morris has claimed that the view of it from **Porthmadog** 'is like an ideal landscape, its central feature exquisitely framed, its balance exact, its horizontals and perpendiculars in splendid counterpoint'. So great is its fame that Jawaharlal Nehru, whose ancestral roots were among the far higher mountains of Kashmir, felt compelled in 1911 to send a postcard to his mother in Allahabad to express his delight that he had seen Snowdon.

The massif is essentially the product of intense heat and intense cold, for the volcanic tuff and lava which constitute its basis bear the imprint of the primeval force of ice (*see* **Geology**). The most spectacular part of the mountain is the Snowdon Horseshoe high above Llyn Glaslyn and Llyn Llydaw (*see* **Lakes**); the path along it follows the razor-sharp edge of Crib Goch and the almost equally precipitous cliffs that lead to Y Lliwedd. Scoured rock is particularly evident on Clogwyn Du'r Arddu, a paradise for rock climbers and **plant** hunters.

The name Wyddfa, first recorded *c.*1284, meant a summit cairn, although the word *gwyddfa* could also mean a high place or a burial place; indeed a tradition arose that Yr Wyddfa's summit cairn was the grave of Rhita Gawr, who, according to **Geoffrey of Monmouth**, was killed by King **Arthur**. A reference to *Snawdune* (from the Old **English** *snāw* (snow) and *dūn* (hill)) occurs as early as 1095, and, from the 16th century onwards, there are frequent references to Snowdon Hill. (Global warming may well mean that in the future there will rarely be snow on Snowdon.) The first occurrence of the name simply as Snowdon is found in the work of the botanist Thomas Johnson, where it is used as a synonym for Yr Wyddfa. (The Latinized form **Snowdonia** continued to be used to refer to a much wider area.)

Although the first ascent of Yr Wyddfa to be recorded in print was that undertaken by Thomas Johnson in 1639, native Snowdonians had undoubtedly possessed for centuries, if not for millennia, an intimate knowledge of its slopes. It is fitting that the first recorded ascent should have been by a botanist, for it was the mountain's **plants** which were initially the primary attraction. Chief among visiting botanists was **Edward Lhuyd**, one of whose discoveries – the Snowdon lily – was named *Lloydia serotina* in his honour. With the Romantic movement (*see* **Romanticism**), tourists came in search of the sublime, visits encouraged by the work of the painters; one **painting**, **Richard Wilson**'s *Snowdon from Llyn Nantlle* (two versions, *c.*1765–6 and *c.*1756–7), magnificently encapsulates the mountain's appeal. It was claimed in 1831 that 'there is no place more public than the higher ground of [Snowdon] during the summer', but it was the coming of the **railways** that opened up the mountain to mass **tourism**. Yr Wyddfa itself became subject to locomotion with the opening in 1896 of its rack-and-pinion railway. The 7-km journey, following an average gradient of 1:7.8, takes an hour; in contrast, some of the contestants in the annual Snowdon Mountain Race run to the summit and back in little more than an hour. (The record is that of Kenny Stuart in 1985: 1 hour 2.29 minutes.) The summit cafe, described by Prince Charles as 'the highest slum in Europe', will be replaced in 2008 by a new building to be known as Hafod Eryri. Snowdon features in the Three Peaks Race, which involves climbing yr Wyddfa, together with **Scotland**'s highest mountain (Ben Nevis; 1344 m) and **England**'s (Scafell Pike; 978 m).

Snowdon, Yr Wyddfa

SNOWDONIA (Eryri) Region

Snowdonia is generally considered to consist of the **mountain** core of north-west Wales and therefore includes the **Snowdon** massif and its immediate neighbours, among them **Y Carneddau**, **Gluder Fawr**, **Gluder Fawr and Tryfan** and **Moel Siabod**. In the 13th century, however, it clearly had a wider meaning, for both **Llywelyn ap Iorwerth** and **Llywelyn ap Gruffudd** styled themselves *Dominus Snowdonie*, which suggests that Snowdonia was then considered to include all the ancestral territories of the house of **Gwynedd**, from **Llŷn** to the lower **Dee** and from **Anglesey** to **Meirionnydd**. The post-conquest Royal Forest of Snowdonia was more restricted in its boundaries; **John Leland** claimed in 1533 that it lay exclusively within **Caernarfonshire**. With the designation of the Snowdonia **National Park** in 1951, yet another set of boundaries was decided upon, for the park, while including most of upland Caernarfonshire, is located in the main in **Merioneth**. **William Camden** believed that the **Welsh** form of Snowdonia – Eryri – had its origin in the word *eira* (snow). **Edward Lhuyd** traced it to *eryr* (eagles) and translated Eryri as the haunt of eagles. However, **Ifor Williams** showed that, while *eryr* and *eryri* had the same root, the original word could mean 'rising ground'; thus Eryri originally meant a mountainous region.

SOCIALISM

The decades following the French Revolution were a seed-time for new political philosophies. The terms 'socialist' (1827) and 'socialism' (1837) were first used by **Robert Owen**, although they occurred in France at much the same time. (In **Welsh**, **R. J. Derfel** used the word *cymdeithasiaeth*, but *sosialaeth* was the form that ultimately triumphed.) Initially, socialism was less influential than the contemporary doctrine of **Liberalism**, but, in time, industrial society presented Liberals with the growing dilemma of reconciling the rights they held dear with the dynamic realities of economic power. The essence of socialism, which had drawn its original inspiration from the French Revolution and subsequent utopian thinking, was the advocacy of an alternative social order in which privilege and crude economic power would be negated. By the end of the 19th century, socialism was winning increased support, for its ideas appealed not only to intellectuals, who responded in particular to the historical determinism of Karl Marx (*see* **Marxism**), but also to the increasingly organized working **class**.

The Wales of the early 20th century provided a classic example of how growing class tension could erode Liberalism's political base. When **Keir Hardie** and the **Independent Labour Party** brought their socialist ideas to Wales, much was made of Robert Owen, R. J. Derfel and a **Celt**ic legacy of co-operation, but it was only with the industrial struggle from 1910 onwards that the weaknesses of Liberalism were exposed. The infant **Labour Party** advocated specific reforms, but nevertheless owed many of its values and much of its ethos to Liberalism and Nonconformity (*see* **Nonconformists**). **Syndicalism**, which was as much a challenge to the socialism of Labour as it was to the Liberals, enjoyed some support. As Syndicalism gave

Snowdonia (Eryri), showing Llyn Gwynant in Nant Gwynant

way to **Communism**, Wales was characterized by two strands of socialism; though often clashing over details, they had much in common, co-existing as they did within a Labour movement that was on the defensive throughout the 1930s.

Eventually, socialism in Wales became identified with the legislative achievements of the 1945–51 **government**, ironically a programme inspired to a large extent by the writings of the Liberals J. M. Keynes and William Beveridge. Apart from **Aneurin Bevan**'s *In Place of Fear* (1952), there was little indigenous socialist thought and the doctrine was largely associated with a defence of the **welfare state** and the mixed **economy**. Nevertheless, the rhetoric of socialism remains a potent means of expressing democratic and egalitarian values.

SOCIETY (*Seiat*)

The formation of societies was one of the main features of the **Methodist Revival**. Their purpose was to deepen spirituality through simple acts of worship, and through personal guidance offered by an exhorter. Initially, the *Sasiwn* (**Association**) appointed the societies' officers, but the societies were later given the right to elect their own elders, a crucial step in the **Presbyterian** structure which came to characterize the **Calvinistic Methodist** denomination.

SOCIETY FOR THE PROMOTION OF CHRISTIAN KNOWLEDGE, The (SPCK)

The SPCK was established in **London** in 1698 by Thomas Bray (1656–1730) and four other laymen, to combat vice which – to their minds – was rooted in ignorance of Christian principles. The society established charity schools and produced and distributed Christian **literature**. Because it enjoyed the patronage of figures such as Sir John **Philipps** and Sir **Humphrey Mackworth**, the SPCK was active in Wales from its early days. By 1715, 68 schools had been established in houses, churches and vestries, usually with curates teaching the pupils to read and write. A period of unease followed the accession of the Hanoverians, with Dissenters (*see* **Nonconformists and Dissenters**) withholding their support and the schools being suspected of promoting **Jacobitism**. Between 1715 and 1727, only 28 new schools were established, after which development ceased completely and the movement contributed no further to the development of **education** in Wales. However, it was his letter to the society in 1731 that was the starting point of the literacy campaign of **Griffith Jones, Llanddowror**. Today, the SPCK still produces Christian literature for distribution worldwide.

SOCIETY FOR THE UTILIZATION OF THE WELSH LANGUAGE, The

Also known as Cymdeithas yr Iaith Gymraeg (the **Welsh Language** Society, but as distinct from **Cymdeithas yr Iaith Gymraeg** of the second creation, 1962), the society was established at a meeting held – entirely in **English** – under the auspices of the Honourable Society of **Cymmrodorion** at the **Aberdare** National **Eisteddfod** in 1885. Its leading figure was Dan Isaac Davies (1839–87) who published a book in 1885 outlining his dream of 3 million bilingual people living in Wales by 1985. **Isambard Owen** was the society's first chairman, with **Beriah Gwynfe Evans** its secretary.

Socialism, still an article of faith to many in Wales

Although Davies's long-term ambition was 'to strengthen our national backbone' and 'to secure a more respected place for our nation among other nations', the society's initial aim was to use Welsh as an instrument of **education** in Wales by pressing the **government** to recognize Welsh as a grant-aided school subject and as a medium of instruction. The aim was to facilitate the teaching of English to monoglot Welsh-speaking pupils, and to allow Welsh to be taught as a subject and used as a medium of instruction in elementary schools. The society persuaded the commission inquiring into the working of the Elementary Education Act (1888) to provide such grants from 1889 onwards, but few schools took advantage of this concession. Davies's untimely death in 1887 dealt the society a severe blow, and it failed to develop into the influential organization envisaged by its creator.

SOILS

Soils are a country's most neglected basic resource. They are the foundation of all terrestrial ecosystems, including **agriculture** and **forestry**, providing a vital link between physical environment and living world. Formed at the surface of the earth, soils are natural entities resulting from the interaction of **climate** and vegetation with weathered geological materials. The pattern of soils on the landscape is complex. Wales experiences the mild temperatures of north-western Europe, but its **mountain**ous nature causes cold, cloudy conditions and heavy rainfall at higher elevations. The rocks of Wales vary in age from Pre-Cambrian to Recent (*see* **Geology**), but in the context of soil formation their mineralogical character is more important than their age. Weathering breaks down the solid rocks into smaller and smaller fragments, eventually forming the sand, silt and clay particles that make up the inorganic part of the soil. The decay of plant material provides its organic constituent. Rainfall can leach soils and this results in strongly acidic, infertile materials composed of silica sand, silt and low activity clays. Under extremely wet conditions, organic matter may accumulate to form **peat**.

Wales has played a significant role in the development of soil **science**, largely through the influence of Gilbert Wooding Robinson (1889–1950), professor of agricultural **chemistry** at **Bangor** (1926–50). He initiated soil surveys in **Anglesey**, **Gower** and elsewhere and was president of the International Society of Soil Science. His surveys established the methodology for soil surveys in **Britain**.

It is the climate and the nature of soils that determine the quality of land. Wales has little land in the first class category – none at all in the 1A and 2A groups, which represent soils abundant in the corn-growing areas of eastern **England**. However, good quality land in the 2AG, 3G and 4G groups – soils particularly suited for the growing of grass and, in restricted places, for the growing of **arable crops** – exists in considerable qualities in **Flintshire**, Anglesey, **Pembrokeshire**, the **Tywi** valley and the **Vale of Glamorgan**. Most of the low-lying land of the south-west and north-east is considered to be of medium quality, generally in the 6AG group of general-purpose soils. Most of upland Wales consists of land in the 8H poor quality group; such land constitutes almost half the country's surface area and consists of soils capable of sustaining little beyond rough grazing.

Types of soil

Soils are recognized by their profile – the vertical sequence of layers or soil horizons down to the parent materials from which the soil is derived. At the surface is the topsoil, enriched with organic matter. The subsoil may simply be weathered rock material, or it may have an enrichment of clay, **iron**, aluminium or organic matter. Using the terminology of the Soil Survey of England and Wales, the soils of Wales are as follows:

BROWN SOILS
Freely or moderately well-drained soils with a clearly differentiated subsoil horizon – reflecting observable change from the parent material – are widespread on sloping ground throughout central and west Wales. They are more than 30 cm deep, may overlie any type of rock and are relatively fertile. Some brown soils survived the most recent Ice Age, because they were lying outside the limits of glaciation. Although they suffered erosion, remnants of these brown soils, with clay-enriched lower horizons, still exist in Gower and the Vale of Glamorgan.

HUMAN-AFFECTED SOILS
Virtually all the soils of Wales have been influenced by the actions of human beings – through, for example, the addition of lime, peat and fertilizers. However, some soils have been profoundly modified by human action, such as those destroyed by excavation, by burial or by being changed through the addition of other materials.

LITHOMORPHIC SOILS
Limited by continuous hard rock within 25 cm of the soil surface, or very gravelly throughout, these soils are characteristic of steep slopes and high mountain regions. There are two sub-groups. The first, rendzinas, are shallow soils on hard **limestone**s or screes, developed over Carboniferous Limestone on the Great Orme (**Llandudno**), or over Mesozoic limestones in the Vale of Glamorgan. The second, rankers, are shallow soils on non-calcareous rocks or scree and are characteristic of higher mountain areas such as **Snowdonia**.

PEAT SOILS
Unlike mineral soils, these develop from peats laid down in conditions of low temperature and waterlogging that retard the decomposition of plant material. To qualify as a peat soil, there must be more than 40-cm depth of organic material. On high plateaux, extremely acidic raw peat soils develop in blanket peat, and on lowlands examples occur of raised bogs with similar soils.

PODZOLIC SOILS
The high rainfall, and parent materials lacking in calcium carbonate – conditions occurring throughout upland Wales – means soils undergo strong leaching, especially where drainage is not impeded; they thereby develop as podzolic soils. The surface horizon becomes enriched with black, partially decomposed organic material; acids strip iron and aluminium from the surface soil horizons and carry these elements downwards to form a strong brown lower horizon. In the south-west, a brown podzolic soil is extensively developed, but occasionally a full podzol is encountered on sandy materials with a grey, sandy horizon above a black or very dark-brown lower horizon.

RAW SOILS
These soil materials are limited in depth or lack horizons. They cannot support agriculture or forestry; sparsely vegetated, they are typical of dune and outer estuarine areas.

SURFACE-WATER AND GROUND-WATER GLEY SOILS
When water occupies all the pores in the soil, air is driven out, causing the soil to be anaerobic. This results in the development of the features of 'gleying'. In this process, iron minerals are chemically reduced to give dull grey colours. Mottling develops where alternately dry and saturated conditions occur. Soils that are temporarily saturated by rainwater are referred to as surface-water gley soils. Soils influenced by a permanently high ground-water table are termed ground-water gley soils. In most cases, these gley soils have organic-rich surface horizons, as on the uplands of the southern **coal**field.

Uses and misuses

The soils of upland Wales are pre-eminently suited to the production of grass and fodder crops in a predominantly pastoral system of agriculture. There is only a short period during the winter when grass growth is restricted. The more fertile soils of the lowlands of the south and west are also largely devoted to grass production although some arable crops are grown, especially vegetables and early potatoes. Drainage is often necessary. Forestry is equally dependent on the nature of soil present, with sitka spruce planted extensively upon wet plateau sites, and lodgepole pine, Corsican pine and hardwoods on the better-drained soils of slopes.

Soil erosion is not usually a problem in Wales, but where overgrazing occurs, or where cultivated soils on sloping land are left unprotected, its impact can be dramatic. Cultivation of steep hillsides can only be achieved by working up and down slopes, otherwise the tractor may overturn. Consequently, even pasture fields may be exposed to serious erosion if heavy rain occurs before reseeded grass has taken hold. In a few places, operations for upland forestry have been equally damaging where erosion has taken place along planting furrows.

Intense industrialization in many parts of Wales has left its mark upon the soils. Mining by the **Romans** led to localized heavy metal contamination by **copper**, **lead** or zinc. Further contamination ensued, from the mid-18th century onwards, in places where ores were concentrated or smelted. In the lower **Swansea** valley, above all, two centuries of metalliferous smelting gave rise to derelict land and intensive soil contamination.

Following open-cast mining in large areas of the southern coalfield, soils placed to one side while the coal was extracted have been returned to a new landscape. Re-establishing the soil as an organic, living surface to the land has not always been easy. The process has been successful where there was reasonable depth of soil to begin with, but at higher elevations, the establishment of grass on strongly acidic, shallow soils has been slow and some erosion has occurred.

SOLVA (Solfach), Pembrokeshire
(1859 ha; 809 inhabitants)
Located immediately east of **St David's**, the **community**'s main feature is its ria (submerged valley), which makes Solva perhaps the most delectable place in coastal **Pembrokeshire**. In the 18th and 19th centuries, the tiny harbour, now the delight of leisure sailors, was a **shipbuilding** centre and a **port** of embarkation to **North America**. Outside the harbour mouth are three tiny **islands**. There is a **Neolithic** burial chamber at St Elvis and an **Iron Age** promontory fort at Solva Head. St **David**'s church, Whitchurch, retains medieval elements. St Aidan's church, Solva (1878), contains a medieval font from the ruined church of St Elvis. The strength of Nonconformity (*see* **Nonconformists**) is indicated by the large **Baptist** chapel (18th–20th century) at Middle Hill, and by the attractive **Congregationalist** chapel at Solva (1896). The troubadour Meic Stevens (b.1942) is a native of Solva. Within Solva's boundaries is St David's **airport**, site of the National **Eisteddfod** of 2002.

SOMALIS
Somalis first came to Wales as sailors, as a result of the sea-trade in **coal**, and because the two World Wars boosted demand for their nautical skills. Later, the **population** was swollen by refugees from the 1980s civil war. In the early 21st century, they numbered about 6500, and lived mainly in the old docklands areas of Butetown and Grangetown in **Cardiff** and Pillgwenlly in **Newport**. The early settlers were chiefly from the Dir and Darod tribes.

The Somalis, distinguished from many of the other **African** peoples by their strict adherence to **Islam** – they are all Sunni Muslims – acquired their own mosque in 1947, after conflicts with Arab groups. The new incomers, from the north of the country – the old British Somaliland – are from the Ishaq tribe. In their homeland, the refugees had been nomadic **goat** and camel herders, and they were entirely perplexed in an urban environment. The Somali language was written down for the first time as recently as 1973: the Welsh Somalis still maintain an oral **literature**, one generation handing on the *heeloy* (poetry) and the *sheekoxariirooyin* (folk tales) to the next. The Somali presence in Wales is celebrated in Glenn Jordan's *Somali Elders: Portraits from Wales* (2004).

SOMERSET family (dukes of Beaufort)
Landowners
Charles Somerset (1460–1526), illegitimate son of Henry Beaufort, third duke of Somerset, married Elizabeth, daughter and heiress of William **Herbert, earl of Pembroke** (d.1491) and received the title of Baron Herbert of **Raglan** in 1504. As chief steward of the crown lordships in the **March** and high sheriff of **Glamorgan**, he wielded substantial power in Wales. In 1513, he was created earl of Worcester. Henry, the fifth earl (*c*.1577–1646), an ardent supporter of the crown in the **Civil Wars**, was created a marquess in 1642. His chief seat, Raglan Castle, was

The ria at Solva

rendered unusable by Parliamentary forces and, after 1660, the family settled at Badminton House, Gloucestershire. Until the late 17th century, the family were faithful to **Roman Catholicism**, the main reason why **Monmouthshire** was, for at least two centuries, Catholicism's greatest stronghold in Wales.

Edward, the second marquess (1601–67), invented a device that harnessed the pressure of the atmosphere so as to raise water, preceding Newcomen's steam engine by nearly 50 years. In 1672, Henry, the third marquess (1629–1700), became president of the **Council of Wales and the Marches** but rarely visited **Ludlow**; in 1682, he was created first duke of Beaufort. Lord Fitzroy Somerset (1788–1855), youngest son of the fifth duke, served under the Duke of Wellington; created Baron Raglan, he was commander-in-chief in the **Crimean War** and died on the battlefield. In 1873, the family owned 11,048 ha in Monmouthshire, 1626 ha in **Breconshire** and 492 ha in Glamorgan. As lords of **Gower**, they enjoyed considerable influence in **Swansea**. The town of **Beaufort** was built on land leased from the duke whose name it bears. The political influence of the Somersets was considerable. Lords-lieutenant of Monmouthshire and sometimes of Breconshire, they were also MPs, Monmouthshire being represented by family members for 69 unbroken years (1805–74). Henry, the ninth duke (1874–1924), began disposing of his Welsh properties, **Tintern** Abbey among them; Raglan Castle was placed under the guardianship of the Ministry of Works in 1938 (*see* **Cadw**).

'SOSBAN FACH' (Little Saucepan) Song

A nonsense song associated with the **tinplate**-making town of **Llanelli**. Consisting of a verse and chorus, the tune is of uncertain origin. Sung to a dirge-like beat, the first verse was written by **Richard Davies** (Mynyddog; 1833–77) in 1873, while the words of the far livelier chorus are attributed to Talog Williams of Dowlais (*see* **Merthyr Tydfil**), who dreamed it up while on holiday in **Llanwrtyd**, and published a version in 1896. The baffling references to Mary Ann's sore finger, Dafydd the poorly servant, the baby crying in its cot, and the **cat** that scratched little Johnny have done nothing to diminish its popularity among **rugby** crowds.

SOUTH AFRICA, Wales's associations with

In 1820, 42 families, mainly from **Pembrokeshire**, migrated to South Africa, the first recorded such migration (*see* **Emigration**). The earliest migrants became farmers, but with the discovery of **gold** and diamonds, most Welsh migrants were miners, presumably on the grounds that, if there is a hole anywhere in the world, there must be a Welshman at the bottom of it. By the 1890s, there were Cambrian Societies in six South African towns and a Welsh chapel in Johannesburg. In 1892, the annual South African **eisteddfod** was founded, an institution which came to be absorbed into the general cultural scene. Gilwern-born (*see* **Llanelly**) Bartle Frere (1815–84), appointed governor of the Cape in 1877, was recalled in 1880 because of his treatment of the Zulus. The role of the **South Wales Borderers** in the battle of Rorke's Drift (1879; *see* **South African Wars**) is commemorated in the **film** *Zulu*.

T. E. Ellis, who spent lengthy periods convalescing in South Africa, was mesmerized by Cecil Rhodes's imperialist plans. The Second Boer War (1899–1902) was a factor of considerable prominence in Welsh politics. The 4328 natives of Wales resident in South Africa recorded in 1926 was probably an underestimate. Welsh immigrants included **Aberystwyth**-born **David Ivon Jones**, one of the founders of the country's **Communist** Party. The willingness of the Welsh **Rugby Union** to play in South Africa during the apartheid years led to much controversy.

SOUTH AFRICAN WARS, The

During the 1879 Zulu War, over 600 men of the 1st and 2nd battalions of the 24th Foot (later the **South Wales Borderers**) were killed, the vast majority at the battle of Isandhlwana (22 January). Later that day and throughout the night, the 24th Battalion's B Company successfully defended Rorke's Drift mission station against Zulu attacks; 11 Victoria Crosses were awarded for this action, 7 to members of the 24th (the highest number of awards for a single action). (The battle is portrayed in the **film** *Zulu*.) All three Welsh infantry regiments were involved in the Second Boer War (1899–1902), the domestic impact of which has generated controversy. There was sympathy, particularly among **Nonconformist Liberals** (headed by **David Lloyd George**), for the strongly Protestant Boers, but this should not be exaggerated. Public enthusiasm at the relief of British garrisons at Ladysmith (28 February 1900) and Mafeking (17 May 1900) was marked and, although the Liberals made gains at the October 1900 general election, many of their victorious candidates were enthusiastic imperialists. Only in the later stages of the war, which degenerated into a guerrilla struggle involving the controversial British use of concentration camps to house captured Boer populations, did public opinion in Wales become more united in distaste for the continuing conflict.

SOUTH GLAMORGAN (De Morgannwg)
One-time county

The county was established in 1974 following the abolition of the ancient **counties**. It consisted of what had been the **county borough** of **Cardiff**, the **boroughs** of **Barry** and **Cowbridge**, the **urban district** of **Penarth**, the **rural district** of Cowbridge and parts of the rural districts of Cardiff and of Magor and St Mellons. It was divided into the districts of Cardiff and the **Vale of Glamorgan**. Abolished in 1996, it was replaced by the city and county of Cardiff and the county of the Vale of Glamorgan.

SOUTH PEMBROKESHIRE (De Sir Benfro)
One-time district

Following the abolition of **Pembrokeshire** in 1974, South Pembrokeshire was created as one of the six districts of the new **county** of **Dyfed**. It consisted of what had been the **borough** of **Pembroke**, the **urban districts** of **Milford Haven**, **Narberth**, **Neyland** and **Tenby** and the **rural districts** of Narberth and Pembroke. Five of its northern **communities** were later transferred to the district of **Preseli Pembrokeshire**. In 1996, the district, together with that of Preseli Pembrokeshire, became the reconstituted Pembrokeshire.

SOUTH WALES BORDERERS, The Regiment
Established in 1689 as Sir Edward Dering's Regiment of
Foot, and commanded in 1702 by the Duke of
Marlborough, the 24th (2nd Warwickshire) Regiment
fought in the Egyptian campaign of 1801, being awarded
the insignia of the Sphinx, and in the Peninsular War. In
1873, the 24th was allotted a permanent depot at **Brecon**,
recruiting from the **border counties** of south and mid
Wales. After serving in the 1879 Zulu War (including the
battles of Isandhlwana and Rorke's Drift; *see* **South
African Wars**), the regiment was retitled the South Wales
Borderers in 1881. Expanded to 18 battalions during the
First World War, its soldiers – **Saunders Lewis** among them
– fought in theatres of war from France to China. In the
Second World War, the 2nd Battalion was the only Welsh
battalion to land in Normandy on D-Day. The 1967
Defence Review forced the amalgamation of the South
Wales Borderers with the **Welch Regiment** to form the
Royal Regiment of Wales. In 2004, that regiment was amal-
gamated with the **Royal Welch Fusiliers**.

**SOUTH WALES MINERS' FEDERATION
(SWMF), The**
The Fed, as its members invariably called it, was formed in
1898 in the immediate aftermath of a disastrous lockout
(*see* **Miners' Strikes**) during which the miners had failed to
bring about the abolition of the sliding scale, which determined their wages. **Trade unionism**, which had come slowly
to the south Wales **coal**field, burgeoned following the

establishment of the new organization. The union affiliated
to the **Miners' Federation of Great Britain** in 1899 and to
the **Labour Party** in 1908.

The Fed was led at first by the Lib-Labs **William
Abraham** (Mabon) and **William Brace**, but control soon
passed into the hands of younger and more militant leaders; by the time of the minimum wage agitation of 1912, it
was clear that south Wales was setting the agenda for miners throughout **Britain**. The period 1920–6 was a crucial
turning point for the Fed, as the collapse of the coal trade
and unsuccessful strikes and lockouts forced the union to
abandon radical demands and concentrate rather on the
rearguard defence of living standards.

It was in the **Depression** of the 1930s, however, that the
Fed earned its special niche in the affections of its members
and in Welsh **Labour** mythology generally. The union often
had to struggle to maintain its membership, and its worst
crisis came in the early 1930s, when it could claim the loyalty of less than half of those miners in employment.
Perhaps the Fed's finest hour was its fight-back under the
presidency of **James Griffiths** (1934–6) and **Arthur Horner**
(1936–46). The tactic of stay-down strikes was used to
combat both **company unionism** and non-unionism, and the
Fed itself was thoroughly streamlined and given a new
democratic constitution which allowed for a rank-and-file
executive and more centralized decision-making.
Particular features of the Fed were its dogged work on
compensation issues, a pattern of leadership in which officers were judged according to their ability rather than by

Soldiers of the South Wales Borderers following their successful defence of the Rorke's Drift mission station in 1879

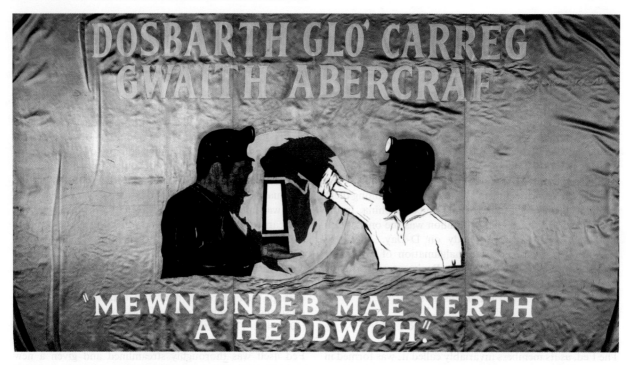

DOSBARTH GLO' CARREG GWAITH ABERCRAF

"MEWN UNDEB MAE NERTH A HEDDWCH."

The banner of the Abercraf lodge of the South Wales Miners' Federation

their **Communist** or Labour affiliation, and a unique arrangement that allowed unemployed miners to participate in union affairs. In 1945, when the Fed became the South Wales Area of the **National Union of Mineworkers**, it was poised to play an influential and decisive role in the new post-war industrial dispensation.

SOUTHALL, J[ohn] E[dward] (1855–1928)
Printer and author

A Quaker from Leominster, **Herefordshire**, Southall lived in **Newport** as a printer from 1879 until his retirement in 1924. He published school textbooks, books about **Quakers** and – having learned **Welsh** as a young man – important books on the language. They include *Wales and her language considered from a historical, educational, and social standpoint* (1892), which affords useful information about the status of the language in the **border**lands, and *Preserving and Teaching the Welsh Language in English Speaking Districts* (1899).

SPANIARDS

Spanish settlements in Wales were a by-product of the ore trade from Bilbao to south Wales of the late 19th century. Many of the migrants were ethnically Basque. The immediate cause of the formation of these communities was labour shortages during the Boer War (1899–1902; *see* **South African Wars, The**) and possibly a desire for cheap labour – immigrant labour was a minor theme in the 1906 election in **Cardiff** and **Merthyr Tydfil**. The first community was at Dowlais in Merthyr, of which that at Abercraf (**Tawe Uchaf**) was a later offshoot, formed during a lockout in the **iron** industry, and attracted by the French ownership and especially cosmopolitan workforce of the International Colliery at Abercraf. The settlements were small, numbering only hundreds each, largely confined to

particular streets, and variously seen as adding to the colourful nature of cosmopolitan south Wales or as a challenge to **Nonconformist** values. There were minor conflicts, notably a campaign to remove foreigners from pits in Abercrave in 1913–14. Eventually, the newcomers became better accepted, especially after their **trade union** and political credentials were understood, and they helped shape the miners' response to the **Spanish Civil War**. Three of the Welsh volunteers for the International Brigades were drawn from these communities, and all three were killed.

SPANISH CIVIL WAR, The

The military rising against the democratically elected Spanish Popular Front Republican Government, which led to the Spanish Civil War (1936–9), evoked a significant response in Wales, led by the **South Wales Miners' Federation** and the **Communist Party**.

The 174 Welshmen who volunteered to fight in Spain represented the largest regional industrial grouping within the British Battalion of the International Brigades; only one Welshman fought for Franco's forces. The political and **class** profile of the volunteers was distinctive. They were Communist or **Labour** in sympathy, largely from the central valleys of the **Rhondda**, Cynon and **Taff**, although there were volunteers from the north-eastern **coal**field and from rural Wales. They were hardened 'class warriors', having had over a decade of bitter experience since the **General Strike** of 1926. Of the Welsh volunteers, 33 were killed in the war.

Following the fall of the Basque Country in 1938, support in Wales broadened beyond the largely working-class Spanish Aid Committees to wider, more humanitarian Basque Children's Refugee Committees, with **David Lloyd George** and university academics and teachers taking the lead.

The response in Wales, unlike that in **England,** was not characterized by any great intellectual political awakening. An exception, however, was **Lewis Jones**, the Communist leader of the Rhondda unemployed, whose novels *Cwmardy* (1937) and *We Live* (1939) conclude with a powerful evocation of the Welsh miners' response to Spain. The **Welsh-language** writers who supported the Republican cause did so through the magazine *Heddiw* which was established in response to the Francoist sympathies of **Saunders Lewis**, the president of **Plaid [Genedlaethol] Cymru**.

SPEEDWAY

Motorcycle dirt-track racing, or speedway as it soon became known, was introduced to **Britain** from **Australia** in 1928. The first meeting in Wales was at **Cardiff** on Boxing Day of that year, in front of 25,000 spectators. The new **motor sport** soon spread to **Pontypridd**, **Tredegar** and **Caerphilly**, and Cardiff became home to a successful Wales team, which won at Wembley in 1929, but in less than a decade the sport had died out in Wales. It returned with short-lived teams at Cardiff (1951–3) and at **Neath** (1962), before **Newport** (1964–77 and 1997–) became the sport's most stable home in Wales. A further track opened at **Carmarthen** in 2002, and, since 2001, Cardiff's Millennium Stadium has hosted Britain's world championship round.

Although he never rode for a Welsh team, Wales's most famous speedway son remains **Port Talbot**-born Freddie Williams (b.1926), who won the world title in 1950 and 1953.

SPITTAL, Pembrokeshire (1135 ha; 501 inhabitants) Located north of **Haverfordwest**, the **community** is bisected by the **Cardigan**–Haverfordwest **road** (the B4329). It was named after a *hospitium* associated with **St David's** Cathedral; the first reference to it dates from 1259. St Mary's church, largely rebuilt in the 19th century, contains a 5th–6th-century inscribed stone. The visitors' centre (1993) adjoining Scolton Manor (1842) is the earliest structure in **Pembrokeshire** to be built to reflect environmental concerns.

SPORTS COUNCIL FOR WALES, The

Established by royal charter in 1972, the SCFW exists to promote sports and recreational activities on a national level, and is designed to increase participation and raise performance standards. The primary adviser to the **National Assembly** regarding **athletic** matters, the SCFW holds ultimate responsibility for allocating lottery funds to all areas of sport and leisure. Its headquarters are at the Welsh Institute of Sport in **Cardiff**, which, together with the Plas **Menai** National Watersports Centre (**Y Felinheli**), also acts as a national centre.

SPRING, Howard (1889–1965) Novelist

This **Cardiff**-born journalist worked his way to Fleet Street before becoming a full-time – and hugely popular – author, eventually settling in **Cornwall**. His childhood in Cardiff was described in *Heaven Lies About Us* (1939), and his play *Jinny Morgan* (1952) was set in the **Rhondda**, but there is little that is Welsh in any of his other books, all of which are written in a solidly traditional style. The best of them

Speedway in Cardiff: the B final of the British Speedway Grand Prix at the Millennium Stadium, 9 June 2001

Stackpole

are *O Absalom!* (1938), *Fame is the Spur* (1940) and *These Lovers Fled Away* (1955).

SPURRELL family Printers

Originally from Bath, the family settled in **Carmarthenshire** in the late 18th century. In 1840, a second-generation descendant, William Spurrell (1813–89), an able grammarian, historian and engineer, founded a significant printing house at **Carmarthen**. The proprietor contributed to the success of the business by compiling his highly acclaimed **Welsh** dictionaries and local topographical works. After his death, he was succeeded by his son, Walter Spurrell (1858–1934), who further enhanced the reputation of the business by engaging J. Bodvan Anwyl to revise his father's **dictionaries**. In addition to continuing the family tradition of meeting the **printing and publishing** needs of the **Anglican** Church, Walter penetrated new markets with, for example, the fine facsimiles of early Welsh texts produced for the **University of Wales** Press. Following his death, the business was sold by the family; it struggled in the hands of several owners until its demise in 1969.

Copyright of the dictionaries was acquired by Collins in 1957, and revised editions continue to be published by HarperCollins. The *Collins Spurrell Welsh Dictionary* and the *Collins Gem Welsh Dictionary*, remain consistent bestsellers in the Welsh book market.

SQUASH RACKETS

The men's Professional Squash Association (PSA), the sport's international governing body, has been based in **Cardiff** since 1984. In 2006, the PSA had over 250 playing members from about 30 countries, and was responsible for over 100 tour events. The national governing body, Squash Wales, had over 100 clubs playing at venues throughout the country.

Alex Gough, the **Newport**-born Welsh international with a highest world ranking of 5 in July 1998, was appointed to the PSA board in December 2002. He was then ranked 16, with David Evans, of **Pontypool**, at 23. By February 2001, Evans, the 2000 British Open champion, was world number 3, which remains the best rating ever obtained by a Welshman. The 1989 European champion, Adrian Davies of **Llanelli**, was in the world top 10 for much of the 1987–95 period, and earned 99 caps for Wales, over 60 of them as captain. Davies had only seven hours coaching in his life – aged 12, from the **Glamorgan** cricketer **Haydn Davies**. Leading **women** players have included Cardiff's **Audrey Bates**, **Swansea**'s Tegwen Malik, Welsh closed champion in 2002 for the sixth time, and Siân Johnson, of Cardiff and formerly of Llanelli, with well over 100 Welsh caps.

SQUIRE, William (1917–89) Actor

A notable **Shakespeare**an stage player, **Neath**-born William Squire also boasted distinguished performances on television – most memorably as the notorious Dr **William Price** of **Llantrisant**, and as Hunter, the hero's boss, in the 1980s television series *Callan*. He was Captain Cat in the television version (1960) of **Dylan Thomas**'s *Under Milk Wood*, Mr Gruffydd in the BBC's 1960 adaptation of *How Green Was My Valley*, and **Arthur** in the American stage **music**al *Camelot* (1961).

SQUIRES, Dorothy (1915–98) Singer

Born in a vehicle in **Pontyberem**, Dorothy Squires provided one of the most dramatic and cautionary riches-to-rags careers. She went from the **Llanelli** Ritz to the glamorous nightclubs of wartime **London** and then on to a dazzling transatlantic recording career. In 1953, she married the actor Roger Moore (b.1927), but their divorce in 1969 preceded a sad decline featuring bankruptcy and constant litigation. Dependent on charity and obsessed with Moore, she died in poverty.

STABLE-LOFT SONGS

These songs were part of the informal entertainment associated with the traditional stable-loft dormitory accommodation of unmarried farm servants, mainly in the north and west, in the 18th and 19th centuries. Despite the lack of heating (except for warmth from the **horses** beneath), servants enjoyed the independence afforded by this means of accommodation and frequently visited the lofts of neighbouring farms after supper, to sing and to amuse themselves. Folk songs, often picked up in the hiring fairs or from **ballad** sheets, and sung to the accompaniment of the jew's harp, flourished as part of a vigorous social life centred on the stable loft. **Scotland**'s bothy ballads belong to a similar tradition.

STACKPOLE, Pembrokeshire
(2850 ha; 443 inhabitants)

Located at **Pembrokeshire**'s southernmost point, the **community** contains the villages of Stackpole, Bosherston, Cheriton, St Petrox and St Twynnells. Natural arches, stacks, **caves**, blowholes and the fearsome Huntsman's Leap are features of its magnificent coastline. Within the community are several significant **Bronze Age** standing stones. Bosherston and Flimston are dramatically sited **Iron Age** promontory forts. A narrow fissure in precipitous cliffs was probably the location of the cell of the **Irish** hermit St Govan; the chapel there dates from the 13th or 14th century. There are medieval churches at Bosherston, Cheriton, St Petrox and St Twynnells. St Elidyr's church, Cheriton (or Stackpole Elidor), contains fascinating tombs of the Stackpole, Lort and **Campbell** families. The Campbell family acquired the Stackpole estate through marriage (1689) with the heiress of the Lorts. By the 19th century, the Campbells – earls of Cawdor from 1827 – were owners of 20,849 ha in Pembrokeshire and **Carmarthenshire**, and were second only to the **Williams Wynn family (Wynnstay)** among the landowners of Wales. Stackpole Court (1735) was demolished in 1963. A series of dams, the building of which began in the 1790s, caused the flooding of the valley of the Bosherton brook. The resultant sweet-water **lakes** are famous for their lily ponds and pike. The lakes were presented to the **National Trust** in 1978.

STAFFORD family Marcher-lords

The family became associated with Wales when Ralph, first earl of Stafford (d.1372), became lord of **Gwynllwg** following his marriage to Margaret **Audley**, great niece and co-heiress of Gilbert de **Clare** (d.1314). Their grandson, Edmund (d.1403), married Anne, daughter of Thomas, duke of Buckingham, the youngest son of Edward III, and

of Eleanor, who inherited **Caldicot** from her father, Humphrey de **Bohun** (d.1373). **Brecon** and **Hay**, the other Welsh lordships of the Bohuns, passed to Eleanor's sister Mary and her husband, Henry Bolingbroke (Henry IV), but eventually they became the property of Humphrey, duke of Buckingham (d.1460), son of Edmund and Anne. Humphrey's grandson, Henry, encouraged Richard III in his usurpation of the throne in June 1483 and became virtually viceroy of Wales. Four months later, however, he rose in revolt and was executed. Henry's son, Edward, was restored to his family's properties by Henry VII. As the most prominent of the **march**er-lords, and as a descendant of Edward III, he won the hostility of Henry VIII, who engineered his **execution** in 1521. With the removal of the last of the great marcher-lords, the March was almost totally under royal control, a fact which greatly facilitated the **Act of 'Union'**. The Staffords commissioned significant building work at Brecon, **Newport** and Caldicot.

STAGECOACHES

Until the coming of **railways**, stagecoach travel was the fastest form of land transport. It involved teams of **horses** hauling four-wheel coaches, with fresh teams of horses taking over at set intervals (stages), to ensure maximum speed. Four-horse teams were most common, although three-horse (unicorn) teams were not unusual.

THE PROPRIETORS
OF THE
Cardiff & Merthyr Mail Coach

BEG most respectfully to inform the Public that ON and AFTER SATURDAY, the 14th day of NOVEMBER next, Passengers will be conveyed by the above Coach to and from Cardiff and Merthyr, and the intermediate Stage, at the following fares, viz:—

	In.	Out.
From Cardiff to Newbridge	3s	2s
———————— Merthyr	6s	4s

PARCELS under 28lb delivered at One Shilling.
Cardiff, 11th Nov., 1840.

It will be perceived from an advertisement in our paper that the coach proprietors have lowered the fares to passengers by the mail to Cardiff, in order to meet the charges of the railway company, so that those who prefer this mode of conveyance may do so without incurring greater expense than by travelling on the railway.

THE Public are respectfully informed that the MERTHYR and SWANSEA MAIL COACH will during the Winter Months, RUN only THREE DAYS in the Week, to and from the former and latter place; viz, MONDAYS, WEDNESDAYS, and FRIDAYS, commencing MONDAY, the 16th instant.
Castle Hotel, Merthyr, November 5th, 1840.

A stagecoach company poster of 1840

"Onward. Christian. Soldiers."

Joseph M. Staniford's cartoon attacking the Nonconformists' readiness to use children in their protest against the Education Act of 1902

The system was greatly advanced by a **government** decision in 1784 to send Post Office mail (*see* **Postal Service**) by special coaches run to strict schedules. This led to improvements in coach design and in **roads**, and to the development of a network of services with inns and post houses providing horses and passenger comforts.

Wales was important for the connection it provided with **Ireland** via **Holyhead** and the **Milford Haven Waterway**. Both the Holyhead Mail and the Milford Haven Mail services began running from **London** in 1785. By 1836, the Holyhead Mail was completing the 418-km journey in 26 hours and 55 minutes, fully 12 hours quicker than in 1817. Its route – through Shrewsbury, Oswestry, **Llangollen**, **Corwen**, **Capel Curig**, **Bangor** and **Menai Bridge** – was engineered by **Thomas Telford**; it included the Menai Suspension Bridge, opened in 1826 (*see* **A5**). The Milford Mail took one of two routes – the 'upper' road via **Oxford**, Gloucester and **Brecon** or the 'lower' road via Bristol, **Cardiff** and **Swansea**, the latter involving crossing the **Severn** estuary by ferry.

Mail coaches, manned by coachman and guard, were the most sophisticated form of travel at the time, but other stagecoaches competed for custom. They were generally much slower than the mail: in 1827, for instance, the 'Imperial stage carriage' took nine hours to travel from Swansea to Brecon. They did, however, facilitate trade and enhance social life by linking towns that had hitherto had

little regular contact with each other. Travel was not cheap, but moneyed people found the cash – and the endurance – to journey from **England** to seaside resorts such as **Aberystwyth**, **Barmouth** and **Tenby**.

Stagecoach travel was often hazardous, especially in winter, when passengers were imperilled by floods and snowfalls. The dangers were sometimes of human agency. Mail Coach Pillar, in a lay-by above the **River** Gwydderig (**Llandovery**), marks the spot where, in 1835, a drunken coachman plunged the mail nearly 37 m down a sharp descent, fortunately without loss of life. Guards were provided not only with horns to warn tollgate keepers of their approach, but also with pistols or blunderbusses for protection against highwaymen.

The development of railways, from the 1840s onwards in Wales, brought a swift decline in stagecoach travel and a resultant loss of trade in country inns, which was not compensated for until the growth of motoring in the 20th century.

STAINED GLASS

Thanks largely to the innovative courses offered by the **Swansea** School of Art (now part of the **Swansea Institute of Higher Education**), which trains artists from all over the world, Wales enjoys an international reputation in an art form which may be considered inimical to the country's once dominant puritan aesthetic.

The **Cistercians** were among Europe's first major glass painters, although no medieval Cistercian glass survives in Wales. In common with the later builders of **Nonconformist** chapels, they had a suspicion of strong colour and figurative designs, tending to deplore material revelry as an indulgent distraction from that supreme entity, light. Among the earliest examples of stained glass surviving in Wales are the famous Jesse window at **Llanrhaeadr-yng-Nghinmeirch** (1533), **Gresford**'s remarkable 15th-century display, which includes images of the martyred Apollonia, patron **saint** of toothache sufferers, and the extraordinary windows at Llangadwaladr (**Bodorgan**), where the skeleton of Christ looms eerily through his flesh.

Glass produced in Wales between the 15th and 18th centuries had stylistic affinities with glass elsewhere. It was not until the end of the 18th century, when it had fallen out of fashion throughout **Britain**, that David Evans (1793–1862) of **Newtown** appeared as the first thoroughgoing Welsh designer of stained glass. The Victorian period saw an upsurge in stained glass, much of it imported and often unremarkable. Notable exceptions to the mass productions of the time include the works of [William] Morris and Co. and of artists such as Edward Burne-Jones (1833–98), as testified by windows in the churches of St Mary, **Coity** (1863), St Catherine, **Baglan** (*c.*1880) and St Deiniol, **Hawarden** (1898).

Wales's first course in glass design, inspired from the outset by mainland European rather than English design and practice, was established in 1935 at the Swansea School of Art; it was taught by the innovative artist-craftsman Howard Martin (1907–72). Martin, at his studio in Morriston and, later, at his Celtic Studios, welcomed secular as well as ecclesiastical commissions, and began exporting glass all over the world. Notable practitioners of Martin's generation, including **John Piper** and **John Petts**, have been succeeded by Swansea-trained artists such as Tim Lewis, Amber Hiscott, David Pearl, Alex Beleschenko and Catrin Jones – several of whom enjoy international acclaim.

STANIFORTH, Joseph M. (1863–1921) Cartoonist
Published usually in the *Western Mail*, Staniforth's drawings and cartoons describe political and social unrest in Wales between 1890 and the **First World War**. In his cartoons, attitudes towards the working **class** generally followed the editorial line. He was born in **Cardiff** and trained as a lithographic printer with the **newspaper**, for which he later wrote art reviews. His most famous image was that of Dame Wales.

STANLEY family Landowners
Gwilym ap Gruffudd, founder of the **Griffith family (Penrhyn)**, married Joan Stanley, daughter of Sir William Stanley of Hooton. William Stanley's brother, Sir John Stanley, was the grandfather of Thomas, Lord Stanley (created first earl of Derby in 1485, who married Margaret Beaufort, mother of Henry **Tudor**) and his brother William, whose support ensured Henry VII's victory at **Bosworth**. The Stanleys extended their properties into north-east Wales, where a number of 'Stanley churches' bear witness to their zeal for church renovation (*see*, for example, **Gresford**). A descendant, Edward Stanley, became constable of

Harlech Castle in 1551. Further Welsh links were established in 1763 when Sir John Thomas Stanley, of Alderley Park, **Cheshire**, married Margaret Owen, heiress of Penrhos (**Trearddur** near **Holyhead**). Among the descendants of this marriage were the third baron Stanley (d.1903; the barony was established in 1839), who converted to **Islam** and built a mosque at Penrhos, Arthur Penrhyn Stanley, the famous dean of Westminster (1864–81), and the philosopher **Bertrand Russell**.

STANLEY, Henry Morton (1841–1904)
Journalist and explorer
He was born John Rowlands at **Denbigh** and, illegitimate, spent most of his childhood in the **St Asaph** workhouse. While on his way to the United States, he was befriended by one Henry Stanley, and took his name. He is famous for having found the **missionary** David Livingstone at Ujiji in 1871, when he is reputed to have uttered the words, 'Dr Livingstone, I presume?' As agent of King Leopold of the Belgians, he was a founder of the Congo Free State, a regime of infamous rapacity. The H. M. Stanley Hospital at St Asaph – essentially the old workhouse – commemorates him.

STANTON, C[harles] B[utt] (1873–1946)
Trade unionist
C. B. Stanton came to prominence after 1908 as a militant miners' agent at **Aberdare** and as an outspoken advocate of direct action on the executive of the **South Wales Miners' Federation**. Always a showman, Stanton was an avowed **Marxist**, but the outbreak of war in 1914 transformed his

Henry Morton Stanley

outlook. He became a jingoistic British nationalist and fervently opposed the anti-war policy of the **Independent Labour Party**. In 1915, he won the by-election at **Merthyr Tydfil** that followed the death of **Keir Hardie**. He was MP for Merthyr (including Aberdare) from 1915 to 1918. In 1918, standing as the candidate for the National Democratic Labour Party, he won the Aberdare constituency by 22,824 votes to 6,229 against the **Labour** candidate **T. E. Nicholas**. He was defeated by Labour in 1922 when he stood as a **Lloyd George Liberal**.

STAPLEDON, [Reginald] George (1882–1960)
Agronomist
A founder of the **science** of grassland agronomy, Stapledon was born in Devon and educated at **Cambridge**. He worked for the **food** production department of the Board of **Agriculture** and **Fish**eries during the **First World War**, before beginning his long association with Welsh agriculture at **Aberystwyth**, where he was appointed first director of the Welsh Plant Breeding Station (**Institute of Grassland and Environmental Research**), following its establishment in 1919. With his colleagues at the station, he pioneered studies of the botany and ecology of the *graminae*, developed a wide range of grass and clover varieties, and ensured the station's position as world leader in the science and technology of hill land improvement. He encouraged the employment of local people, at all levels, in the work of the station.

Stapledon's pioneering role in developing the unrealized potential of British grassland was recognized in 1937, when research workers from 38 countries appointed him president of the Fourth International Grassland Conference held at Aberystwyth. The event marked a revolution in British agricultural thought and was a landmark in focusing attention on the potential of grass throughout the world. Stapledon's 'Plough-up' campaign for the **government**, from 1938, was of crucial importance during the **Second World War**, Sir Reginald Dorman Smith, minister of agriculture in 1937, later maintaining that 'without [Stapledon's] victories we most certainly would have been starved of food and there would have been no military victories about which our generals now may argue.'

STEEL COMPANY OF WALES, The
The Steel Company of Wales was established in 1947 to embrace the modernization that had already revolutionized production in the United States. **Richard Thomas and Baldwins**, Guest Keen and Baldwins (GKBs), John Lysaght and the Llanelly Associated Tinplate Companies pooled the bulk of their resources in order to construct a fully integrated steelworks with modern **tinplate** capacity. The steelworks, with a new 80-inch continuous hot stripmill and cold reduction facilities, was constructed on a site that also incorporated GKBs' existing **Port Talbot** and **Margam iron-and steel**making plant; it opened in 1952. Social considerations, however, dictated that tinplate manufacture should remain in its traditional heartland further west, and, after much political manoeuvring, two new tinplate works with electrolytic capacity began full production at **Trostre** (**Llanelli**; 1953) and **Velindre** (**Swansea**; 1956).

All three plants, together with Lysaght's Orb Works at **Newport**, transformed Welsh steel and tinplate manufacture.

Workers from the many handmills that closed during the 1950s found re-employment in the massive new works, the early 1960s witnessing an employment peak: Port Talbot, 18,000; Trostre, 2700; Velindre, 2500. In 1967, at the time of its absorption into the British Steel Corporation, the company employed a total of 21,000 people.

STEPHEN, Edward [Jones] (Tanymarian; 1822–85)
Musician
Tanymarian was born at **Maentwrog** and spent a lifetime preaching, lecturing, singing, conducting and composing. He was the first to popularize in **Welsh** the Victorian parlour **ballads**, but he is chiefly remembered as the composer of *Ystorm Tiberias* (1851–2), the first Welsh oratorio, which enjoyed great popularity.

STEPHENS, Thomas (1821–75) Scholar
Born in Pontneddfechan (**Ystradfellte**), Stephens became a chemist in **Merthyr Tydfil** and an influential figure in public life. A distinguished scholar and literary critic, he won fame and some notoriety as an objective researcher – an unusual figure in that period – for works such as *The Literature of the Kymry* (1849, 1876) and his essay *Madoc* (1893). The latter was commended as the outstanding entry at the **Eisteddfod** held at **Llangollen** in 1858, but the adjudicators refused Stephens the prize, unwilling to accept his debunking of the notion that the Welsh had reached America centuries before Columbus (*see* **Madog ab Owain Gwynedd**).

STEPHENSON, Robert (1803–59)
Railway engineer
Stephenson, son of George Stephenson – designer of *The Rocket* locomotive – is chiefly remembered in Wales for his tubular bridges over the **River Conwy** and the **Menai Strait**, which were part of the Chester and **Holyhead Railway**. The Britannia Bridge (*see* **Pentir**), completed in 1850, was regarded as an **engineering** marvel. Stephenson was elected **Conservative** MP for Whitby in 1847. He refused a knighthood because, in his view, 'it would be no honour to be ranked with some titled people'.

STOCK EXCHANGES
Twelve brokers formed the **Cardiff** Stock Exchange in 1892, following dissatisfaction with the prices of south Wales shares in **London** – although dealing had begun earlier, in the 1870s, when two brokers dealt in **railway**, **iron** and **coal** company shares. In **Swansea**, share broking started in the 1890s; the Exchange was set up in 1903, brokers meeting in the Metropole Hotel. The **Newport** Stock Exchange was formed in 1916. Stock exchanges lost a large number of the companies quoted on them following the implementation of the post-Second World War **Labour government**'s nationalization programme. Following the Jenkins Report in 1962, they merged with the Midland & Western Stock Exchange, which was later absorbed into the London Stock Exchange.

STRADLING family Landowners
The first of the Stradlings of **Glamorgan** was Peter, who married the heiress of **St Donats** Castle in 1298. By the later Middle Ages, the Stradlings had become a prime example of a Cymricized family of *adventi*, marrying into native

gentry families and offering patronage to the bards. Thomas (d.1573) suffered for his adherence to **Roman Catholic**ism. His son, Edward (1539–1609), was responsible for improvements to the **port** at Aberthaw (*see* **St Athan**). He amassed a distinguished library at St Donats, was the patron of **Siôn Dafydd Rhys** and wrote an essay on the **Norman** conquest of Glamorgan, which was incorporated in **David Powel**'s *Historie of Cambria* (1584). John, his successor (d.1637), a prolific author, founded the **Cowbridge** Grammar School; John's successor, Edward (1601–44), fought for Charles I at Edgehill. Edward's widow gave refuge to Archbishop Ussher. The senior line died out in 1738 when Thomas Stradling was killed in a duel in Montpellier. Among the numerous descendants of the family was the distinguished physicist **Phil [Stradling] Williams**, member of the **National Assembly** (1999–2003).

STRATHCLYDE Kingdom

The British kingdom of Strathclyde is a phenomenon of the 10th and early 11th centuries. Based at Govan (now in Glasgow), it reached south as far as Cumberland. Its predecessor was the kingdom of Dumbarton (Al Clud), a post-**Roman** British kingdom centred on the Clyde. This was destroyed by **Vikings** in about 870, and Dumbarton was abandoned in favour of Govan. It was probably from Strathclyde that records and **literature** of the **Old North** were transmitted to Wales.

STRAW AND MARRAM, The plaiting of

Plaiting wheat straw was formerly one of Wales's most important rural crafts. Although some made a living from the work, it was predominantly an amateur, part-time **craft**, with farmers, smallholders, **farm labourers**, **women** and children working in the evenings or between other tasks to produce a variety of goods, including baskets, **bee**hives, straw hats, and even easy chairs and cradles. In coastal areas, plaiting with marram grass was also possible. In the village of Newborough (**Rhosyr**), this activity developed into a highly prosperous small industry; at the beginning of the 20th century, baskets and mats were being sent to all parts of **Britain**.

STRIGOIL Marcher-lordship

Strigoil was the **march**er-lordship centred upon **Chepstow**, an alternative name for the lordship. Seized by **William Fitz Osbern** in the 1060s, it passed in turn to the **Clare**, **Marshal** and **Bigod** families, and then to the dukes of Norfolk who were in possession at the time of the **Act of 'Union'**.

STUART family (marquesses of Bute) Landowners

The Stuarts of Bute, descendants of John, illegitimate son of King Robert II of **Scotland**, became associated with Wales through the marriage, in 1766, of John, Baron Mountstuart (the son of George III's prime minister, the third earl of Bute) to Charlotte, daughter of Viscount Windsor. The Windsors had inherited the **Cardiff** Castle estate from the **Herbert earls of Pembroke** (of the second Herbert creation), the first of whom had been granted extensive lands in **Glamorgan** by Henry VIII and Edward VI.

Baron Mountstuart (1744–1814), created first marquess of Bute in 1796, had only a tenuous association with his

Castell Coch, the reconstruction of which was commissioned by John Crichton Stuart, third marquess of Bute

Welsh estates, but his grandson, John Crichton Stuart, the second marquess (1793–1848), was among the central figures in the history of Wales in the first half of the 19th century. By commissioning an elaborate dock at Cardiff, he laid the foundations for the town to become the world's greatest **coal port**. As the landlord of the Dowlais **Iron** Company, he played a key role in what was the world's largest iron company. By initiating the search for the **Rhondda**'s steam coal, he ensured its growth as the world's most renowned coal valley. In addition, his agents planned the expansion of Cardiff – Butetown in particular – and upheld the marquess's influence over politics, administration and philanthropy in Glamorgan.

The second marquess was succeeded by his son who did not come of age until 1868. The agents of the third marquess (1847–1900) expanded the Bute docks until they were one of the world's greatest dock complexes. They established the *Western Mail* (*see* **Newspapers**) and presided over the growth of Cardiff, relying in the main on 99-year **urban leases**. So successful were they in leasing Bute mineral land that the Butes came to receive more in mineral royalties than any other British landed family. The marquess, a convert to **Roman Catholicism**, was a medieval enthusiast, refurbishing Cardiff Castle and rebuilding nearby Castell Coch in accordance with the designs of **William Burgess**.

During the marquessate of the fourth marquess (1900–47), the docks became the property of the Great Western **Railway** Company, the mineral reserves were nationalized and the urban leaseholds were sold to the Western Ground Rents Company. In 1947, the fifth marquess presented the castle and its park to the city of Cardiff.

SUETONIUS PAULINUS (fl.*c*.58–61)
Roman governor

In AD 60, Suetonius launched an assault on **Anglesey**, an important centre of druidism. The resistance of 'ferocious warriors, wild **women** and praying **druids**' is graphically described by **Tacitus**. In AD 61, the campaign in Wales was broken off in response to **Boudicca**'s revolt and, later in that year, Suetonius was recalled to Rome.

SULIEN AND HIS DESCENDANTS
(11th–12th centuries) Family of learned clerics

It was probably Sulien (*c*.1010–91) who established the centre of learning at **Llanbadarn Fawr** which was continued by his four sons, Rhigyfarch (?1056–99), Ieuan (d.1137), Daniel and Arthen, and by their sons, Sulien, Cydifor and Henry. Amongst the manuscripts associated with Llanbadarn is a copy of St Augustine's *De Trinitate* in the accomplished hand of Ieuan, and a **Latin** manuscript containing Rhigyfarch's translation of the Hebrew Psalter and some of his own verse, copied by a scribe called Ithael and illuminated by Ieuan. Among Ieuan's other works to have survived is a Latin poem to his father, the main source of information concerning Sulien, twice bishop of **St David's** (1073–8, 1080–5), who spent 13 years studying in **Ireland**. Rhigyfarch was responsible for a lamentation that describes the suffering wrought upon the inhabitants of **Ceredigion** by attacks by the **Normans**, and for a Latin Life of St **David** written (*c*.1094) as part of the campaign to defend the independent status of the bishopric of St David's. Ieuan's verse is of inferior quality, but Rhigyfarch's mastery of Latin metres is outstanding. Although no works in **Welsh** are associated with the family except for a stanza on the crozier of St **Padarn** found at the top of one of the manuscripts, it has been suggested that the story of **Branwen ferch Llŷr** in *The Mabinogion* was written by either Sulien or Rhigyfarch.

SULLIVAN, Clive (1943–85) Rugby league player

The first black captain of a British national team in a major spectator sport, **Cardiff**-born Clive Sullivan's captaincy of Great **Britain** was highlighted by lifting the World Cup in 1972 after scoring a typical 80-yard (73.15 m) try in the final. A wing who combined a sprinter's pace with watertight defence, Sullivan scored 406 tries in all, including 250 for Hull. His status as a rare hero uniting both sides of Hull – he also played for Hull Kingston Rovers – was underlined by the massive attendance at his memorial service following his premature death from cancer.

SULLIVAN, Jim (James Sullivan; 1903–77)
Rugby league player and coach

A Barbarian and a Welsh **rugby union** trialist before he signed for Wigan aged 17, **Cardiff**-born Jim Sullivan was one of the dominant figures of interwar **rugby league**. Capped 26 times for Wales and 25 for Great **Britain**, he played in 5 series against **Australia** – all victorious – and was the first Welshman to lead a British tour there in 1932, his third visit. He was a highly successful coach of Wigan and St Helens.

SULLY (Sili), Vale of Glamorgan
(699 ha; 4239 inhabitants)

Located between **Penarth** and **Barry**, the **community** includes Sully **Island**, accessible by foot at low tide. The origin of the name is in doubt. The Life of **Cadog** (early 12th century) refers to the church of *Silid*, but more likely the de Sully

Sully Island and the Glamorgan coast

family, its lords in the 12th and 13th centuries, probably influenced the name's later development. The once attractive village has recently been overwhelmed by commuter dwellings. The community contains Lavernock Point, where the coast of **Glamorgan** turns north and from where, in 1897, Marconi transmitted the world's first radio message across water. The deserted village at Cosmeston was excavated in 1981; the reconstructed buildings there seek to illustrate peasant life before the onset of the **Black Death**. Sully Hospital, built for **tuberculosis** patients in 1932, is a remarkable example of functional **architecture**. The third marquess of Bute (*see* **Stuart family**) had a **vineyard** at Swanbridge. Cog Farm is a model farm dating from *c.*1817.

SUMMER CAROLS

Religious carols sung outside houses early in the morning throughout May. They frequently referred to God's bountiful kindness and to the fruitfulness to be expected in the coming months, describing in intricate metres the beauty of nature. They became popular in the 17th and 18th centuries, under the influence of the Church, and were intended to counteract pagan elements in the age-old May Day (**Calan Mai**) celebrations.

SUMMERS family Industrialists

John Summers (1822–76) established an **iron and steel** company – John Summers and Sons – at Stalybridge in **Cheshire**, where his four sons gained experience of the industry. In 1896, two of them, Henry and James, established a steelworks on **Dee**side (*see* **Shotton Steelworks** and **Queensferry**). The company long remained in family control, with Geoffrey, Henry's son, in charge in the 1940s. Nationalized in 1951, the works returned to the ownership of John Summers and Sons in 1954.

SUNDAY CLOSING OF PUBLIC HOUSES

The campaign to close Wales's public houses on Sunday sprang from evangelical respect for the Sabbath, the activity of **temperance** and teetotal movements such as the United Kingdom Alliance, and the desire for Wales to have legislation that was already in force in **Scotland** and **Ireland**. Under the leadership of John Roberts, MP for **Flint Boroughs**, legislation curtailing the sale of alcohol on Sundays in Wales (excluding **Monmouthshire**) was passed in 1881, a **law** hailed as a landmark recognition of the status of Wales. In 1890, a Royal Commission report declared that the Act was working effectively in rural areas but stressed that it was widely flouted or circumvented in the larger urban areas. Teetotal campaigners hoped, in vain, that the Act would be a springboard for total prohibition. During the **First World War**, extensive controls on drink were imposed and, in 1921, the 1881 Act was confirmed and extended to Monmouthshire.

As the middle **classes** drank at home, the Act was essentially an attack upon the public drinking of the working classes. It associated Welshness with negativity and – in view of the readiness of many apparently respectable people to make Sunday visits to public houses via the back door – with hypocrisy. From 1961 onwards, local referendums were held every seven years, with each successive vote adding to the number of **counties** or districts opting

for Sunday opening. Following the 1989 referendum, the only 'dry' area was **Dwyfor**. As the district was home to less than 1% of Wales's inhabitants, claims that Sunday closing was an important marker of Welsh distinctiveness had clearly become untenable. In 1996, Dwyfor joined the rest of Wales as a 'wet' area. In 2003, when the next referendum was due to be held, it was decided that the issue should no longer be subject to a vote. (*See also* **Welsh Sunday**.)

SUNDAY SCHOOL

Classes held by churches on Sundays to teach adults and children the rudiments of the Christian faith. Although the Sunday school became an important aspect of Christian activity in Wales in the 19th century, it was not a Welsh invention. A network of schools had been established in Italy in the 16th century, and the idea captured the imagination of many in **England** through the work of Robert Raikes (1736–1811) of Gloucester. The foundation of the Welsh Sunday school movement was laid by the **circulating schools** of **Griffith Jones** (1683–1761); following their collapse in the 1780s, and the establishment of the Sunday School Society in **London** in 1785, the late 18th century saw a revival of interest in providing Christian **education** for the mass of the people. Under the skilful leadership of the **Calvinistic Methodist**, **Thomas Charles** (1755–1814) of **Bala**, the idea of conducting classes on Sundays gained acceptance, although there was some resistance. The work developed quickly, and, following the adoption of similar strategies by the **Nonconformist** denominations, Sunday schools were soon established in every part of the country.

Their success can be attributed to the fact that people of all ages were taught within them, and that they were flexible in their organization. While the **Bible** was used as a teaching tool to disseminate information and enrich understanding, the teaching methods ensured the development of skills such as clear reasoning, debating and public speaking. The schools therefore became influential in Welsh public life: many of the nation's 19th and early 20th century leaders were nurtured in Sunday school classes.

The golden age of the Welsh Sunday school was 1870 to 1920; thereafter, serious decline eventually led in 1966 to the establishment of the interdenominational Cyngor Ysgolion Sul (the Sunday School Council), mainly concerned with promoting Sunday school activities through the medium of **Welsh**. By the early 21st century, that organization was in difficulties and there were calls for a new body which would take responsibility for all aspects of Christian endeavour aimed at children and young people.

SURFING

Popular with both natives and visitors, surfing came relatively late to Wales (*c.*1963). Its Welsh founders – John Goss, Viv Ganz, Howard Davies, Rob Hansen and Pete Jones (senior) – pioneered wave riding at the **Gower** beaches of Langland, Caswell (both Mumbles, **Swansea**) and **Llangennith**.

A visit to Langland in 1967 by reigning Australian champion Keith Paul was a defining moment in Welsh surfing. Watching that day was another Pete Jones ('PJ'), from Langland, who was soon to become the dominant

Swansea-born surfing champion Carwyn Williams

force in Welsh and European surfing. At the 1977 European championships at Freshwater West (**Angle**) in **Pembrokeshire**, Jones emerged triumphant.

The 1980s saw the emergence of one of Wales's finest talents, Carwyn Williams, of **Swansea**. Although Williams's promising professional career was cut short by injuries sustained in a car accident, he remains a dominant figure in the sport. Another British and European champion of the 1990s was long-boarder Chris 'Guts' Griffith, also from Langland.

SURNAMES

The **English** adopted their present system of fixed surnames during the later Middle Ages, but the Welsh had a patronymic naming system, the holder's baptismal name being linked by the particle '*ap*' or '*ab*' (son of) or '*ferch*' (daughter of) to the father's baptismal name, and so forth to perhaps the seventh generation. Presumably the system arose from the Welsh **laws**, whose tenets made it essential for all to know how people were descended from an ancestor and their exact relationship to cousins. These laws were in decay by the later Middle Ages, and gradually, from the 15th to the 17th century, the patronymic naming system was replaced by fixed surnames. The commonest method was to take the father's baptismal name, and, having Anglicized the spelling, to make it the fixed surname for the future. If, for instance, a Welshman called Rhys ap Gruffudd were told to take a surname, he would probably find himself turned into Rees Griffiths – an end-of-name 's' generally denoting 'son of' in **English** patronymic surnames. The patronymic particles '*ap*' or '*ab*' were sometimes absorbed into the new surnames, Bowen coming from Ab Owain, and Price from Ap Rhys. Occasionally, descriptive names were turned into

surnames, so that Lloyd came from Llwyd (brown or grey), and Gwynne or Wynn from Gwyn (white). In other instances, **place names** were adopted as surnames, Trevor coming from Trefor, Nanney from Nannau, and Lougher from Loughor.

The stock of Welsh surnames is remarkably small. Before the 16th century, the Welsh had used a great variety of baptismal names, but the **Protestant Reformation** introduced a more limited conventional stock of names based upon biblical names such as John, Thomas, Simon, Moses or Tobias, or royal names such as William or Edward, or well-known English names such as Robert or Hugh. This process of conventionalizing names occurred at the same time as the process of taking fixed surnames. In most parts of Wales the stock of names of the fathers had been pared down to a few conventional ones such as John, David, Thomas, William, and so on, so that their children took on the surnames Jones, Davies, Thomas, Williams in very large numbers. In the late 20th century, many Welsh patriots abandoned surnames such as Jones (a surname first recorded in **England** in 1279, centuries before surnames existed in Wales) in favour of more authentically Welsh names. The world record for the biggest gathering of people with the same surname was broken in 2006, when a total of 1224 Joneses assembled at the Wales Millennium Centre, **Cardiff**.

SUTHERLAND, Graham [Vivian] (1903–80) Artist

Having begun as an engineer, Sutherland took up etching and engraving, the discipline required for these informing almost all his subsequent development as an artist. Born in **England**, he became a war artist in 1941 and produced drawings of industrial south Wales. He was commissioned after the war to create tapestries for Coventry Cathedral and images for other religious sites.

Visiting **Pembrokeshire** in 1934 was a seminal experience; the light, tides, nature and **geology** of the **Cleddau** estuary caught his imagination and he returned for extensive periods, alternately living there and in the south of France. He painted, designed books, made prints, and completed many portraits, notably one of **Churchill**, which was not well received. In 1976, he acknowledged his creative debt to Wales by donating a representative body of work to form a gallery at Picton Castle (**Slebech**); the gallery was closed in 1995.

SUTTON, [Oliver] Graham (1903–77)
Meteorologist and mathematician

Sir Graham Sutton, FRS – one of a family of mathematicians – was born in Cwmcarn (**Abercarn**), where **David Brunt** inspired his interest in **meteorology**. He graduated at **Aberystwyth** and taught in the **mathematics** department there before joining the Meteorological Office, where, on secondment to the Chemical Defence Experimental Station, Porton Down, he carried out his major scientific research on the diffusion of gases. This was originally motivated by the need to understand the dispersion of poisonous gases, but it led to a fundamental study of diffusion in turbulent atmosphere. This work could not be published during the **Second World War** but, when it eventually became publicly available, it was recognized as an important contribution to the study of the physics of turbulence. Sutton became head of the Meteorological Office and, after his retirement, was appointed first chair of the Natural Environment Research Council. He received the World Meteorological Organization's international medal and prize (1968).

SWANSEA (Abertawe) City
(8587 ha; 158,139 inhabitants)

This entry is concerned with 16 of the 38 **communities** of the **county** of Swansea (*see* **Swansea County**) which constitute the built-up area of the city of Swansea and broadly represent the pre-1974 Swansea **county borough**. (For Swansea's communities, *see below*.)

Swansea, Wales's second city, owes its origins to the seizure of the **commote** of Gŵyr or **Gower** by Henry de Beaumont, earl of Warwick *c*.1100, a seizure encouraged by Henry I. Evidence of earlier settlement is meagre. There was probably a **Roman** villa at Oystermouth, and it is widely believed that the name Swansea derives from the Old Norse *Sveinn* (a proper name) and *ey* (**island**). While there is no archaeological proof that there was ever a **Viking** settlement on the **Tawe** estuary or *aber* (the source of the **Welsh** name *Abertawe*), the extensive activities of the Northmen along the western sea routes give plausibility to the belief.

The castle erected by de Beaumont near the estuary became the caput of the **march**er-lordship of Gower, and the adjacent settlement became Swansea. The site was well chosen for, in addition to the protection of the strongly sited castle, the estuary provided a sheltered natural harbour. The castle occupied a convenient knoll but its immediate surroundings were generally level, and this, seven centuries later, gave room for the town to expand. A wide belt of grass-covered sand dunes lined the bay and to the north the land rose gently to the foot of the steep, sheltering escarpment of Townhill (170 m).

The settlement was vulnerable, for the **Norman** intrusion was deeply resented by the native Welsh. It was captured

Graham Sutherland, *Solva Hills* (1935)

by **Llywelyn ap Iorwerth** in 1217, burnt by **Rhys ap Maredudd** in 1284 and threatened by **Owain Glyndŵr** in 1403. In the late 12th century, the castle was rebuilt in stone and, following the attack of 1284, was further strengthened by the de **Breos family**, lords of Gower from 1203 to 1326. However, it was the **Mowbrays**, lords of Gower from 1326 to 1480, who were responsible for the castle's finest feature – the arcaded parapet, probably built in the 1330s. Its similarity to arcades erected at **St David's** and **Lamphey** during the episcopate of **Henry de Gower**, bishop of St David's from 1328 to 1347, makes it likely that it was the work of builders previously employed by the bishop, whose Hospital of the Blessed David was founded at Swansea in 1332. Part of the hospital's fabric survives as the back wall of the Cross Keys Inn. It is Swansea's only remnant of medieval ecclesiastical **architecture**, for the town church – St Mary's – and the church of the Order of St John (which occupied the site of the present church of St Matthew in the High Street) were later wholly rebuilt.

The **borough** received its earliest charter some time between 1158 and 1184, and a more elaborate charter in 1306. By then, it had probably been surrounded by a stone wall which enclosed a semicircular area extending from High Street to Wind Street. By this time it had established its fourfold role as the capital of Gower, as the focus of markets and fairs, as the centre of a wide range of **crafts** and as a **port**, dealing in wine, hides, wool, cloth and, increasingly, **coal**. It is only in the westernmost part of the south Wales coalfield that coal deposits reach the coastline, a crucial factor in an era when transporting so bulky a material as coal was practicable only by water. Along that coastline, the Tawe was the most navigable **river**; admittedly, it was navigable for only 5 km, but that was enough to enable coal to be brought to the port from as far away as Llansamlet. Indeed, its possession of a navigable river flowing through coal-bearing land was to become the decisive factor in Swansea's history. Coalmining at Swansea is first recorded in 1306. No evidence is available for the port's medieval coal trade, but by the 1590s it was exporting the equivalent of 3000 tonnes a year, a figure which rose to the equivalent of 12,000 tonnes in the 1630s, when Swansea was probably **Britain**'s third largest coal port after Newcastle and Sunderland.

By the 1630s, the marcher-lordship of Gower had been defunct for a century, although the lordship's erstwhile lords, the **Somerset family**, later the dukes of Beaufort, were to retain significant **manor**ial powers in both Swansea and Gower. The **Act of 'Union'** of 1536 abolished marcher privileges and united the lordship of Gower with the lordship of **Glamorgan** to create the county of **Glamorgan**, with **Cardiff** as its county town. This demotion of Swansea was long resented there, although for a century and more after 1536, Cardiff was probably the larger of the two; in 1670, Cardiff had 341 hearths and Swansea 337, which perhaps suggests that the former had about 1705 inhabitants and the latter 1685.

Cardiff's slight advantage was not destined to endure. The first official census (1801) showed that Cardiff's **population** was 1870 and Swansea's 6099. As a figure of 7705 was recorded for **Merthyr Tydfil**, Swansea is generally considered to have been the second largest town in Wales in 1801. In fact, the census understated Swansea's size, for the borough included only part of the town's built-up area. The true figure was 10,117, thus in 1801 Swansea was rightfully Wales's largest urban centre. (Swansea was overtaken by Merthyr in 1821, a lead Merthyr retained until 1881. Swansea's lead over Cardiff remained massive until the 1850s, but the parvenu had won by 1881.)

The key to Swansea's 500% population growth between 1670 and 1801 lies in the development of its industries and port. Signs of that development are apparent in Francis Place's **painting** of 1678, the earliest known picture of Swansea. It shows **ship**ping in the river, **shipbuilding** in progress along its banks and, within the decrepit remains of the castle, the existence of a **glass** bottle manufactory, an example of the innovative industries being established in the town.

A far more significant industry arrived in 1717 with the opening of a **copper**-smelting works at Landore. With the Tawe the nearest navigable coalfield river to the copper ore mines of **Cornwall** and, as the refining process needed three times more coal than ore, shipping the ore to the coal made sound sense, especially as the ore-carrying ships could return to Cornwall with cargoes of coal. By 1724, the Landore venture had come under the control of Robert Morris of Bishop's Castle, the first of a line of Morrises prominent in the history of Swansea. In 1748, he established a second copperworks north of Landore, where Morriston would eventually be founded. In the 1770s, the Morrises settled at Clasemont, a large Palladian mansion overlooking the works but, by 1806, noxious fumes had driven them to Sketty Park, built by **William Jernegan**, whose work looms large in the architectural history of Swansea.

Eventually, the fumes emitted by the copperworks caused the industry, which had secured a foothold near High Street in 1720, to be ejected from the borough itself. Ejection was motivated both by the burgesses' concern for their own comfort and by their desire to develop Swansea as a fashionable watering place. In the late 18th and early 19th centuries, there was much talk of 'the Welsh Weymouth' and 'the Brighton of Wales', and Swansea was provided with assembly rooms, public **gardens** and bathing machines. A theatre was opened in Wind Street in 1785, and another in Temple Street in 1807; there were hopes that the healing springs of Uplands would vie with those of Bath. Swansea did experience some success as a holiday resort, aided by the opening of the Oystermouth (subsequently Mumbles) **Railway** in 1804. Intended as a mineral railway to exploit the coal of the Clyne valley and the **limestone** of Mumbles, it began in 1807 to carry **horse**-drawn passenger coaches. It was thus the world's first passenger-carrying railway, and it enabled visitors to enjoy the beauty of Swansea Bay – beauty much praised by Walter Savage Landor (1775–1864), whose friendship with Rose Aylmer began on its sands – and to explore the coast beyond. (Its closure in 1960 gave rise to much recrimination and nostalgia.)

Swansea's future, however, lay not with **tourism** but with heavy industry, a fact accepted by the burgesses on the understanding that the industries should be located east of the borough enabling the prevailing winds to waft the fumes towards **Neath**. Morris's works were followed by those of a group of Bristol financiers who established the White Rock copperworks below Kilvey Hill in 1737. By 1810, there were eight such works along the banks of the lower Tawe, the most recent of which – that at Hafod – was founded in 1809 by John **Vivian**, a Cornishman whose family would come to dominate copper production, not only in Swansea but globally. Among the coppermasters' best customers were the **slave** traders, who wanted trinkets to barter in West Africa, and the British Admiralty, which used the metal to give its wooden ships their 'copper bottoms'. In 1810, 71% of the world's copper was produced in Britain, with 85% of British output emanating from Swansea. Thus, Swansea was responsible for 60% of the metal's global production. It was indeed Copperopolis. Manufacture demanded a high level of proficiency, with over a quarter of copperworkers belonging to the highly skilled category – a proportion far higher than in the coal, **iron** and **textile** industries. The 'Welsh method' of copper smelting developed at Swansea, consisting of repeated roastings of ore in a succession of specially designed reverberating furnaces, was considered to be 'one of the finest examples of the metallurgist's art'.

Other concerns were established on the banks of the lower Tawe valley, among them enterprises producing **lead and silver**, zinc, nickel, cobalt and arsenic. Within the borough itself, there was the Cambrian **Pottery**, founded in the 1760s, which initially produced rough earthenware. Output improved in the 1790s, but it was the exquisite porcelain produced from 1814 to 1817 – a wholly unviable venture commercially – which made Swansea's name in the world of ceramics. The area's reputation for industrial innovation received a further boost in the 1860s with the establishment of the Siemens **open-hearth** steel works (*see* **Wilhelm**

Siemens and **Iron and Steel**) at Landore. Not content with having attained world dominance in the copper industry, Swansea went on to attain an almost equal dominance in **tinplate** production. By the late 19th century, there were 11 tinplate works in the lower Tawe valley and, in 1887, the Swansea Metal Exchange, Wind Street, became the international centre for trade dealings in tinplate, a task previously performed by the **Liverpool** Exchange.

Swansea's extensive and varied industrial base created an increasing demand for coal, the resource that underpinned the entire industrial **economy**. By the mid-19th century, deposits in the lower Tawe were near depletion and mining moved to Cockett and, later, to **Dunvant** and **Gorseinon**, with most of the production undertaken by the Glasbrook and Vivian Companies. Local demand and the fact that the deposits of western Glamorgan were meagre compared with those in the east of the county meant that Swansea's coal exports were far smaller than those of Cardiff. In the peak year of 1913, when Swansea exported what would be today 4.5 million tonnes of coal, the Port of Cardiff (the Bute Docks, **Barry** and **Penarth**) exported nearly 25 million tonnes.

Despite its relatively limited coal trade, Swansea had a long history as an export centre. Initially, quays along the navigable Tawe had been adequate, but from 1798 the river was supplemented by the Swansea **Canal**, which linked the harbour with enterprises as far north as **Ystradgynlais**, and which was connected to individual works and mines by an intricate network of tramroads. At the same time, the river channel was deepened and piers were built to concentrate the flow of the river, thus increasing its self-scouring ability. In 1824, a tidal harbour was established at Port Tennant as a terminus for the Tennant Canal which

A view of Swansea from Mount Pleasant, 1850

Swansea Bay, looking south-west towards Mumbles Head

provided access to the industries of the **Nedd** valley. In 1845, the lowest course of the Tawe was diverted to the 'New Cut' and, in 1852, the North Dock, occupying the river's former course, was opened. Two years previously, the South Wales **Railway** reached Swansea, a development that coincided with the building of the first **road** bridge across the lower Tawe, where hitherto only a ferry service had been available. In 1859, the South Dock was opened, sited on the Burrows. More ambitious docks followed – the Prince of Wales (1881), the King's (1909) and the Queen's (1920) – all of them built on the seabed, east of the Tawe at Fabian's Bay.

The vibrancy of Swansea during its industrial heyday was reflected in its intellectual life, which far outclassed that of any other place in Wales. It was the home of Wales's first **English** weekly **newspaper** (the *Cambrian*, 1804), and its first Welsh weekly newspaper (*Seren Gomer*, 1814). It acquired fine Regency houses such as those in Prospect Place, the attractive assembly rooms (1821) and a grand Guildhall (1848–52), now the **Dylan Thomas** Centre. It was the setting for the pioneering work on **photography** of **Calvert Richard Jones** and **John Dillwyn-Llewelyn**. In 1835, its citizens founded the Swansea Philosophical and Literary Society – later the Royal Institution of South Wales – and provided for it the splendid Greek Revival building (1839–41) that became Swansea Museum. Prominent among the institution's founders were **Lewis Weston Dillwyn**, polymath and owner of the Cambrian Pottery in its fine-porcelain period, and George Grant Francis, who was proprietor of the local coach-building works, who produced sumptuous publications on the history of Swansea and Gower. Swansea was widely seen as Wales's chief urban centre; it provided the headquarters

for the Welsh **Congregationalists** and the Welsh **Baptists**, and it delighted in the fact that, in the mid-19th century, it had 32,000 inhabitants compared with Cardiff's mere 18,000. By 1881, however, Cardiff's population had risen to 82,761, while Swansea's lagged behind at 76,430, a vital factor in the decision in 1883 to locate Wales's southern university college at Cardiff (*see* **Cardiff University**), a blow to Swansea's self-esteem from which it took a long time to recover; indeed, in view of Swansea's continuing animus towards Cardiff, it probably never did recover. However, Swansea was considered large enough to be a county borough, a status it attained in 1889.

By the late 19th century, Swansea's hitherto buoyant economy was experiencing chill winds. The available copper ore was declining in quality, and major copper smelting centres were developing in Canada and elsewhere. The United States's **McKinley Tariff** on tinplate imports (1891) was a severe blow; although tinplate production had recovered by 1900, the industry ceased to be the focus of soaring growth. The **First World War** brought some relief, particularly to the steel industry, and the interwar **Depression** proved to be less traumatic in Swansea than it was in other parts of industrial Wales. Indeed, the 1920s and 1930s can be seen as a period of equilibrium in Swansea's history. While most Welsh towns saw a sharp decline in population, that of Swansea remained static. There were investments in its economic future, especially the completion of the Queen's Dock in 1920. Constructed specifically for **oil** tankers, it was proof that Swansea sought to become a major centre of the petro**chemical** industry.

In the same year, Swansea became the home of the fourth college of the **University of Wales** (*see* **University of Wales Swansea**). In 1923, it became a titular Anglican diocese, although the bishop resided at **Brecon**. (Swansea would not become the home of a bishop until 1987 when St Joseph's, located near the old centre of **Irish** settlement at Greenhill, became the cathedral of the reorganized **Roman Catholic** diocese of Menevia.) In 1924, the town became the home of a BBC **broadcasting** station, which proved to be more innovative than Wales's far better financed BBC station at Cardiff. The National **Eisteddfod** held at Swansea in 1926 – an occasion when full use was made of the talents of the distinguished Swansea musician **David Vaughan Thomas** – was hailed as the best eisteddfod ever. In 1935, Swansea **rugby** team won a victory over **New Zealand**, the first such victory by any British club. The corporation proved to be progressive, undertaking **housing** schemes such as that in Townhill. Symptomatic of the town's continuing confidence was the completion in 1936 of Wales's finest interwar building – the new Guildhall, **Percy Thomas**'s splendid exercise in 'stripped classicism'. As in the early 19th century, the Swansea of the 1930s was home to Wales's most distinguished group of intellectuals, among them the poets Dylan Thomas and **Vernon Watkins**, the composer **Daniel Jones** and the artist **Alfred Janes**.

Central Swansea was wiped out by the bombing raid of 19–21 February 1941, much of it remaining an area of devastation for at least a decade. (**Waldo Williams** referred memorably to the raids in his poem 'Y Tangnefeddwyr'.) The initial phases of the rebuilding were grossly unimaginative, the writer Kingsley Amis (1922–95) – a colourful resident of 1950s Swansea – noting that a 'bunch of architects/ Named this the worst town centre they could find'. Yet, some of the town's finest buildings escaped the bombing. Ironically, they were those in the vicinity of the docks, precisely that part of Swansea at which the German bombers were aiming. They included the old Guildhall, the Royal Institution, the offices of the harbour trust (subsequently Morgan's, Swansea's only five-star hotel), a group of Georgian terraces and the massive banks of Wind Street, all of which eventually underwent sensitive restoration. The bombed St Mary's, the fine neo-Gothic church built in the 1890s, was meticulously reconstructed. However, one remarkable building that had escaped the bombing – Weaver's flourmills (1898), perhaps the earliest reinforced concrete building in Europe – was demolished in 1984.

While the immediate post-war reconstruction was banal, the later 20th century endowed Swansea with more interesting buildings, among them the massive and vibrant market (1961), the British Telecom Building (1970, 1992), the controversial extension of the Glynn Vivian **Art Gallery** (1974), and the botanical complex Plantasia (c.1987). In 1969, Swansea became a city, giving it parity with Cardiff. In 1974, it lost its county borough status; combined with the **rural district** of Gower, it became one of the four districts of the new county of **West Glamorgan**. Further reorganization in 1996 led to the establishment of the county of Swansea, consisting of Swansea District and most of **Lliw Valley** District. The census of 1971, the last before the abolition of the old county borough, revealed that Swansea had 173,413 inhabitants.

In 1997, unlike the county of Cardiff, the county of Swansea recorded an affirmative vote in favour of the **National Assembly for Wales**, a vote that led to a campaign to locate the Assembly at Swansea. The campaign was unsuccessful but, as a result of a trade-off with Cardiff, Swansea was endowed with further significant buildings – Wales's national **swimming** complex, which opened in 2003, and the National Waterfront Museum (2005).

The latter forms part of central Swansea's most imaginative project – the redevelopment of the South Dock (the North Dock has been filled in). The work began in 1976, and it has resulted in the creation of a delightful marina, surrounded by attractive waterside **housing**, and giving access to the boldly postmodern Ferrara Quay and the remarkable Sea Gate, Wales's first estuary barrage. A short distance upstream is the architecturally exuberant Sail Bridge (2003) for pedestrians, the central mast of which is a landmark visible for miles. To the west, virtually on the shore, is the prominent West Glamorgan County Hall (1984), subsequently home to the county of Swansea's chief offices, which, in 2007, also came to be the site of the relocated central library.

The local council's reconstruction of the maritime quarter was a minor project compared with that undertaken by the council in Copperopolis's industrial heartland, where large-scale copper production came to an end in the mid-1920s. In that heartland, the fumes produced by smelting had destroyed the vegetation over a wide swathe of land between Llansamlet and St Thomas. The ruined works and waste tips, some of them containing highly toxic material, covered an area of 360 ha – Europe's largest tract of derelict land. There were doubts whether anything could be done to reclaim the area, which lay astride the principal rail and road approaches to Swansea. In 1961, Swansea University College launched the Lower Swansea Valley Project, a major interdisciplinary study of the valley, with particular emphasis on the toxicity of materials there and the prospects for clearing and replanting the barren areas. The local council implemented a programme of land acquisition, which enabled it to undertake the huge task of clearance and reclamation proposed by the academic study. The end result is a classic of its kind, the former 'moonscape' having been transformed into a modern industrial, retail and leisure park, set amidst dense tree planting and large grassed areas, all centred around a fine **lake**. So great was the transformation that even those directly involved had difficulty in believing that it had actually been achieved. Unfortunately, although some evidence of the industrial past has survived, the reclamation scheme made no systematic attempt to preserve significant elements of what was Wales's most significant early industrial landscape.

At the opening of the 21st century, Swansea feels itself to be somewhat out on a limb – located virtually at the end of the **M4** and envious of the perceived benefits bestowed on more favoured places to the east. None of the developments it has experienced in the recent past are comparable with those during its industrial heyday. Even its once proud boast that it was the capital of Welsh-speaking Wales – a snub to what it considered to be Anglicized Cardiff – is less convincing now that the percentages of Welsh-speakers in the two cities are converging. Nevertheless, Swansea still retains a strong sense of identity, and sensitive restoration, together with innovative planning – for instance, the £30-million Liberty Stadium (*see* Landore *below*) or the £250-million SA1 waterfront development around the Prince of Wales Dock – have added to the attractions bestowed upon it by its beautiful setting and by its nearness to the glories of the Gower peninsula. Its history as a port and an industrial centre – in a sense, the history of Cardiff and Merthyr combined – gives substance to the belief of its citizens that Swansea is not Wales's second city, but its first.

The communities of the city of Swansea

BIRCHGROVE (906 ha; 5807 inhabitants)

Located at the north-eastern corner of the old county borough, the community, which is largely rural, contains Birchgrove, Lon-las and part of Glais, settlements which developed to house the employees of the Birchgrove Colliery Company.

BONYMAEN (Bôn-y-maen*)* (847 ha; 6304 inhabitants)

Located east of the Tawe, Bonymaen contains the sites of what were significant industrial enterprises, among them the Middle Bank and Upper Bank Works, the Swansea Hematite Works and the Mannesman Tube Works. Grenfelltown, three terraces of working-class housing, was erected by the Grenfell family in 1803–13. The community extends to the nature reserve of Crymlyn Bog (*see* **Peat**).

CASTLE (Y Castell) (303 ha; 11,933 inhabitants)

The community extends from Mount Pleasant to the marina and embraces most of central Swansea. The Swansea Jack pub near the **prison** commemorates Jack, the

black retriever that lived in the docklands in the 1930s. The dog is believed to have saved 27 people from drowning. It is commonly assumed that the dog gave Swansea people their familiar nickname; but the expression 'Swansea Jack' came before the dog, 'Jack' being a common word for sailor in many British ports. Thus, Swansea's renowned Cape Hornermen came to be categorized universally, from the 19th century onwards, as 'Swansea Jacks'.

COCKETT (Y Cocyd*)* (858 ha; 12,586 inhabitants)

Located at the north-western corner of the old county borough, the community contains the settlements of Cockett, Waunarlwydd, Fforest-fach and Gendros. In the mid-19th century, Cockett was Swansea's most highly developed coal-producing area. The remnants of a garden village, begun in 1910, survive west of Carmarthen Road. In the late 1940s, the Fforest-fach industrial estate became Swansea's main focus of new sources of employment.

CWMBWRLA (150 ha; 8217 inhabitants)

The smallest of Swansea's communities, Cwmbwrla consists of a dense network of neat terraces centred upon Manselton and Brynhyfryd.

KILLAY (Cilâ) (324 ha; 5733 inhabitants)

The westernmost community of the old county borough, Killay consists of late 20th-century housing developments overlooking the country park established in the Clyne valley. Hendrefoilan, now part of the University of Wales Swansea, was built in 1860 for the prominent industrialist and politician Lewis Llewelyn Dillwyn.

The National Waterfront Museum, Swansea

LANDORE (Glandŵr) (223 ha; 6121 inhabitants)
A sad example of the mangling of a Welsh **place name**, Landore was the place where Copperopolis began, with the opening in 1717 of the first copper works to be established on the banks of the Tawe. Other works followed at Morfa and Hafod and the sulphuric stench thus produced gave rise to the doggerel: 'It came to pass in days of yore/ the Devil chanced upon Landore./ Quoth he: "By all this fume and stink/ I can't be far from home, I think."' In the 1860s, Landore became the location of yet another industrial development of worldwide significance when Wilhelm Siemens perfected there his open-hearth system of steel production. Such was his success that, by 1873, Landore was one of the world's four largest steelworks. Engine houses at Hafod, the Landore river quay and viaduct and part of the Morfa works – intended as the Lower Swansea Valley exhibition centre – survive, albeit in a parlous condition. Opposite, on the western bank of the Tawe, is the dazzling white Liberty Stadium, home to the Swansea City **Football** Club and to the Osprey Rugby Team. What also survive are two turrets, part of Morris Castle, Wales's first block of flats, built for John Morris in 1774 to house 24 families. Additional evidence of house-building activities by industrialists may be seen at Trevivian, built by J. H. Vivian for his employees at the Hafod Copperworks; their construction involved the use of copper slag blocks, a favourite building material in industrial Swansea. Landore has several churches and chapels of distinction.

LLANSAMLET (649 ha; 6196 inhabitants)
The one-time **parish** included virtually the whole of Kilvey – that part of the lordship of Gower lying east of the Tawe. In the 18th century, the area was the chief source of the coal exported from Swansea, and its collieries were linked to the port in 1784 through the construction of the Llansamlet Canal. Among Llansamlet's important industrial enterprises were the Upper and Lower Forest Works and the Duffryn and Worcester Works. Interesting remains of engine houses and part of a pumping house survive. Such were the emissions of its works, and the pollution blown there from Landore and Morriston, that Llansamlet came to be the centre of the wasteland created by the industries of the lower Tawe valley. In 1981, following the reclamation scheme (*see above*), Llansamlet became the site of Britain's first enterprise zone.

MORRISTON (Treforys) (733 ha; 16,781 inhabitants)
Morriston owes its origins to John Morris, who decided in 1768 to construct a settlement to house his employees. Laid out by **William Edwards** as a grid surrounding the church of St John, it is Wales's earliest planned industrial village. The original buildings have been replaced, but the layout survives. The entire scheme was upstaged in 1873 following the completion of the Congregational chapel, Tabernacl, frequently referred to as the 'cathedral of Welsh Nonconformity'. Designed by John Humphreys and financed by the tinplate entrepreneur Daniel Edwards, it has a seating capacity of 1450. With its soaring spire and its three arches supported by eight Corinthian pillars, it dominates the townscape of northern Swansea. The community is the home of the Morriston Orpheus Choir. In 2001,

25.46% of the inhabitants of Morriston had some knowledge of Welsh, with 10.23% wholly fluent in the language – the highest percentages for any of the communities of the city of Swansea.

MUMBLES (Y Mwmbwls) (1140 ha; 16,774 inhabitants)
Mumbles has always been considered a place apart. As the verse puts it: 'Mumbles is a funny place,/ A church without a steeple,/ Houses made of old ships wrecked,/ And most peculiar people.' With its coastline sweeping round to the southernmost point of Swansea Bay, it offers fine vistas, in particular from the pier (1898) and from the **lighthouse**, erected in 1793 on the outer of the two tidal islands of Mumbles Head. The community's southern coastline contains the attractive bays of Caswell, Langland and Limeslade. Rising steeply from the promenade – the location of a renowned series of pubs, known as the 'Mumbles Mile' – the place has the air of a fishing village; indeed, its oysters once enjoyed a high reputation.

Oystermouth Castle contains elements dating from the 12th, 13th and 14th centuries, the later work being the most impressive. It was for long the chief stronghold of the lords of Gower. Fragments of a mosaic pavement in All Saints' church suggest that the church was built on the site of a Roman villa. Its churchyard contains the grave of Thomas Bowdler (1784–1825), the English physician notorious for 'bowdlerizing' the works of **Shakespeare** – that is, expunging everything 'which cannot with propriety be read aloud in a family'; Bowdler spent the last 15 years of his life at Rhyddings House in Swansea's Brynmill area. Recent housing developments between Oystermouth and Black Pill have obscured some interesting early 19th-century villas. Clyne Castle, originally built in 1791, was acquired in 1860 by one of the Vivians, who extended it vastly. Surrounded by fine **gardens**, from 1956 until 2003 it was one of the halls of residence of the University of Wales Swansea; by 2007, it had been converted into apartments. Near it are the remains of a copper and arsenic works, the sole such works in the Swansea region to preserve remains of its long defunct productive plant. Within the boundaries of Mumbles is The Mayals – with Langland, Swansea's seriously affluent suburb.

MYNYDDBACH (Mynydd-Bach)
(357 ha; 8756 inhabitants)
Located between Morriston and **Llangyfelach**, Mynyddbach was the centre of the Swansea district's earliest Congregationalist church. Established in the late 17th century, its members worshipped in Cilfwnwr farmhouse until the building of a meeting house in 1762. The present building dates from 1866; its extensive cemetery is an indication of the importance of the cause. Within the community are Swansea's crematorium and the offices (1974) of that much-maligned institution, the Driver Vehicle Licensing Agency – Swansea's largest employer apart from the county council.

PENDERRY (Penderi) (405 ha; 10,961 inhabitants)
Located between Landore and Cockett, Penderry is one of Swansea's most impoverished communities, with owner-occupying families representing hardly one in five of the

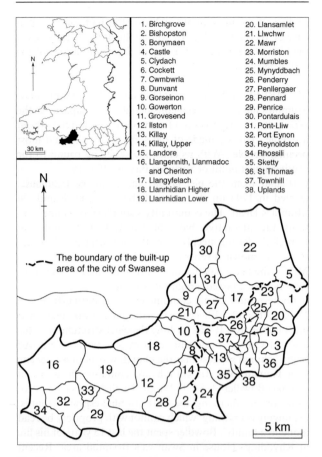

1. Birchgrove
2. Bishopston
3. Bonymaen
4. Castle
5. Clydach
6. Cockett
7. Cwmbwrla
8. Dunvant
9. Gorseinon
10. Gowerton
11. Grovesend
12. Ilston
13. Killay
14. Killay, Upper
15. Landore
16. Llangennith, Llanmadoc and Cheriton
17. Llangyfelach
18. Llanrhidian Higher
19. Llanrhidian Lower
20. Llansamlet
21. Llwchwr
22. Mawr
23. Morriston
24. Mumbles
25. Mynyddbach
26. Penderry
27. Penllergaer
28. Pennard
29. Penrice
30. Pontardulais
31. Pont-Lliw
32. Port Eynon
33. Reynoldston
34. Rhossili
35. Sketty
36. St Thomas
37. Townhill
38. Uplands

The communities of the city and county of Swansea

inhabitants. Its most prominent building is the former Penlan Comprehensive School, erected in 1956 and enlarged in 1994; in 2003, it reopened as Ysgol Gyfun Gymraeg Bryn Tawe, the county of Swansea's second Welsh-medium secondary school.

ST THOMAS (591 ha; 6373 inhabitants)
Located east of the Tawe, the community extends from Kilvey Hill to the coast. It developed following the creation in 1824 of Port Tennant, and includes the Prince of Wales, the King's and the Queen's Docks. Its most charming building is the Norwegian church, which, in 1910, was moved from **Newport** to a site at the entrance to the docks; it was dismantled and rebuilt in 2004 on a site at the heart of the eastside's SA1 development. The community's most prominent building is St Thomas Primary School, built in 1897 to educate 1200 children. Stone-built coaling stages dating from the 1780s survive at Foxhole. The community includes the White Rock Industrial Archaeology Park, the site of the White Rock Copperworks, established in 1737. In 2001, 87.07% of the inhabitants of St Thomas had no knowledge at all of Welsh, making it, linguistically, the most Anglicized of the communities of the county of Swansea.

SKETTY (Sgeti) (688 ha; 13,799 inhabitants)
Sketty has claims to be Swansea's premier suburb. Attractively situated on Swansea Bay and screened by prevailing winds from the pollution of the Tawe valley, by

the mid-19th century it had come to consist largely of the parks and mansions of the lords of Copperopolis, branches of the Vivian family in particular. Chief among them was Singleton Park, now occupied by Swansea's main public park, Singleton Hospital and the University of Wales Swansea. Singleton Abbey, originally built in 1784 as an octagonal neoclassical villa, was acquired by the Vivians in 1817; enlargements in 1818, 1827 and 1837 transformed the building which in 1920 became the nucleus of what was then called University College, Swansea. Adjoining it is a remarkably compact campus consisting largely of buildings designed by the firm of **Percy Thomas**. St Paul's church, with its attractive broach spire, contains tombs of the Vivian family. Other features of the community include the late 18th-century Sketty Hall, a Gothic belvedere – the sole remnant of Sketty House – several interesting late 19th and early 20th-century villas and the massive Cefn Coed Hospital (1912–29).

TOWNHILL (181 ha; 8443 inhabitants)
Until the 20th century, Townhill was virtually uninhabited; now, with 57 residents per ha, it is Swansea's most densely populated community. Development began at Mayhill in 1909 and continued on Townhill itself in the early 1920s – evidence of Swansea corporation's enlightened policy on working-class housing. Most of the houses have the advantage of fine views but the disadvantage of steep gradients. As John Newman notes: 'The switchback ascent of Ceiriog Road is positively Alpine.' An attractive feature of Mayhill is its primary school, a spectacularly sited D-shaped building visible from most of central Swansea.

UPLANDS (232 ha; 13,355 inhabitants)
Located between Townhill and the sea, Uplands represents the earliest westward thrust of middle-class Swansea, its attractions including the town planning around St James's church and the impressive houses of Ffynone Road – once the centre of Swansea's now defunct spa. The community includes Cwmdonkin Drive, where number 5 is the childhood home of Dylan Thomas. It also includes St Helen's, where **cricket** matches began in the 1840s, and where Swansea's rugby team (originally a soccer team) took up residence in the 1870s. Adjoining St Helen's is the **Patti** Pavilion; the one-time winter garden of Craig-y-nos (*see* **Tawe-uchaf**), it was re-erected in Victoria Park in 1920, serving as a hall for conferences and concerts, among other roles. In 2007, there were plans for a major refurbishment of the building.

SWANSEA (Abertawe) County (42,123 ha; 223,301 inhabitants)
The **county** came into existence following the local **government** reorganization of 1996. As it consists of most of that part of the old county of **Glamorgan** lying west of the **Tawe** (together with four **communities** lying east of the **river**), it essentially represents the old **commote** of Gŵyr (**Gower**). The reorganization was the latest in a lengthy process of expanding the territory bearing the name Swansea. Originally a small **parish** and **borough**, the town of Swansea underwent progressive enlargement to become in 1889 the 2105-ha **county borough** of Swansea. By 1974, it consisted of

10,114 ha and ranked fifth in area among the county boroughs of **Britain**. In that year, Swansea, together with the former **rural district** of Gower became Swansea District, one of the four districts of the newly created county of **West Glamorgan**. In 1996, that district, together with **Lliw Valley** (but minus the communities of **Cilybebyll**, **Cwmllynfell**, **Gwaun-cae-gurwen**, **Pontardawe** and **Ystalyfera**) became the city and county of Swansea (*see also* **Swansea, City**). In 2001, 22.47% of the county's inhabitants had some knowledge of **Welsh**, with 9.38% wholly fluent in the language. (*See also* **Mawr** and **Swansea, City: St Thomas**.)

SWANSEA INSTITUTE OF HIGHER EDUCATION

Swansea Institute of Higher Education took its present name in 1992 when it became an independent **education** corporation financed by the **Higher Education Funding Council for Wales**. Previously called the **West Glamorgan** Institute, its constituent elements were the Swansea College of Education, founded in 1872 as a training college for **women**, the Swansea School of Art (1853) and the Swansea Technical College. Until 2004, it was an associated institution of the **University of Wales**, awarding degrees; but in that year it became a constituent member of the University. It has two faculties – humanities, which

oversees a number of schools – and applied **design** and **engineering**, whose school of architectural **stained glass** enjoys an international reputation. In the academic year 2006/7, it had almost 6000 students.

SWIMMING

Swimming has been practised in Wales since ancient times, for it was an essential skill for crossing the country's many **rivers**. Medieval poetry refers to swimming as one of the **'twenty-four feats'** and an accomplished swimmer was regarded as a fully rounded individual.

A sea-bathing craze at the end of the 18th century anticipated the rise of competitive swimming, which flourished with the opening of indoor baths from the late 19th century onwards. Organized swimming at schools and colleges increased its popularity, and, with the affiliation of several Welsh clubs to English associations, the scene was set for further development. The Welsh Amateur Swimming Association (WASA) was formed in **Cardiff** in 1897 to control and promote all aspects of the sport; the first Welsh Championship (men's 100-yards freestyle), was held in that year. Cardiff-born **Paul Radmilovic** dominated this freestyle event throughout this period, winning the title some 15 times between 1901 and 1922. Although a female freestyle race was not introduced until 1905, **women** had

Cardiff-born watersports champion Paul Radmilovic diving into the Taff

competed in the water since the 1890s, having been involved, like the men, in regular water-polo matches.

Until the early 1930s, most competitive swimming took place at Cardiff, **Newport**, **Penarth** and **Swansea**. Highpoints included Radmilovic's three Olympic gold medals, and a string of titles won by Cardiffians Irene Steer and Valerie Davies. Steer was one of the victorious 4x100-yard freestyle relay team which set a world record while taking Olympic gold in Stockholm in 1912. Davies won gold in the 4x100-yard relay at the 1927 European Championships, and was the sole Welsh swimming representative at the 1932 Los Angeles Olympics, when she gained a backstroke bronze. Such success came to a halt with the outbreak of the **Second World War**, when most competitions stopped and many pools were closed. Matters improved during the 1950s, with the reopening of pools, a surge of interest in school swimming, and the establishment of a structured coaching system.

Welsh swimming was further boosted by the building of the 50-m Empire Pool at Cardiff for the 1958 **Commonwealth Games**. New clubs were formed as a result, and the sport's profile steadily increased as more swimming pools were constructed during the 1960s and 1970s. Interest in swimming has continued; in 2007, there were more than 9000 members of WASA, in more than 90 clubs. The absence of 50-m training facilities following the demolition of the Empire Pool in 1997, which seriously affected Welsh performances at international level, was rectified in 2003 by the opening of a national pool in Swansea. Cardiff's David Davies has made a strong impression at the international level, winning medals at European, Commonwealth and world championships, and the Paralympic swimmer David Roberts of **Pontypridd** dominates the sport, winning numerous gold medals.

SYNDICALISM

A political doctrine taking its name from *syndicat*, the French term for a **trade union**, syndicalism advocated that trade unions, as free associations of workers, should take control of the means of production, thereby eliminating employers and bypassing the state. It was much in vogue between 1890 and 1920, both in France, where it remained a potent tradition, and in America. In Wales, the term was used by the contemporary press to describe those associated with *The Miners' Next Step* and subsequently with the Unofficial Reform Committee. Some have argued that, in the Welsh context, syndicalism was a misnomer and amounted to nothing more than a predilection for direct action, but it remains a useful term to describe the extent to which pre-**Communist** trade unionists were committed to the idea of strikes being used to achieve workers' control.

The Llandaff weir on the River Taff

TABLE TENNIS

Wales was a founder member of the International Table Tennis Federation in 1926 and later had two world leaders in the sport, **Roy and Nancy Evans** of **Cardiff**. By 2004, the Table Tennis Association of Wales (founded in 1921) had some 1500 members; it has been estimated that in Wales the sport attracts well over 40,000 casual players. Among outstanding players of recent times is Alan Griffiths, Wales's coach since 1985, who won the Welsh Closed title a record 10 times. Outstanding **women** players have included Betty Gray of **Swansea** and **Audrey Bates** of Cardiff.

TACITUS, Cornelius (c.56–c.120) Roman historian

An orator and public official, Tacitus served as both consul and proconsul. He is best remembered for his literary works including the *Historiae* and the *Annales*. In these, he provides the most complete account of **Roman** military activity in Wales, including descriptions of the war against the **Silures**, the attack upon the **druids** of **Anglesey** and the campaigns against the **Ordovices**.

TAF River (48 km)

The Taf rises at around 209 m at the eastern end of **Mynydd Preseli** within the **community** of **Crymych** and runs south parallel to the **Cleddau rivers**, crossing narrow bands of igneous rocks intruded in the Ordovician sediments. It rapidly becomes incised in a narrow valley, 100 m deep with partly wooded sides. The river turns east at **Henllanfallteg**; from there to **St Clears**, the valley provides a route for the **Fishguard Railway**. The Taf is joined by the Cynin at St Clears and by the Cywyn at the head of its estuary, two rivers that drain much of western **Carmarthenshire**. The Taf flows into Carmarthen Bay at **Laugharne**. The river was once famous for its **coracle fishermen**.

TAFF (Taf) River (67 km)

The Taf Fechan and the Taf Fawr rise on the southern slopes of the **Brecon Beacons** in the **community** of **Glyn Tarell**. The headwaters of Taf Fechan drain the southern slopes of Pen y Fan before flowing southwards through the Upper Neuadd, Pentwyn and Pontsticill **reservoirs**. The Taf Fawr drains the western slopes of Corn Du before flowing southwards through the Beacons, Cantref and Llwyn-on reservoirs. In the community of Vaynor the two tributaries come together and flow southwards. **Housing**, industry and **road** and **railway** links have all been built close together within the narrow sinuous valley. The **river** skirts the western edge of the town of Merthyr Tydfil. The Cynon, whose valley contains the pioneer industrial town of **Aberdare**, joins the Taff at **Abercynon**. The world-renowned **Rhondda**, whose tributaries, Rhondda Fawr and Rhondda Fach, come together at Porth, joins the Taff at **Pontypridd**. Before reaching **Cardiff**, the Taff flows through the narrow **Taff's Well** gorge. The **Ely** joins the Taff at its estuary, which has been transformed by the building of a barrage across the estuary mouth to form the focal point of the Cardiff Bay redevelopment. The waters of the Taff are now released into the Severn Sea through sluice gates. The Taff's 3 km of navigable water was crucial to the rise of the **port** of Cardiff.

TAFF VALE RAILWAY STRIKE, The

In 1900, workmen on the **Taff** Vale **Railway** embarked on an unofficial strike over wages. They were supported by their union, the Amalgamated Society of Railway Servants (ASRS), which had sought to persuade railway companies to accept collective bargaining and workers' rights. The Taff Vale Company, which employed blackleg labour and experienced difficulty in maintaining services, took the union to court. After a number of hearings, the House of Lords fined the ASRS £23,000 (and £25,000 costs) for being 'in restraint of trade', a judgement which caused **trade unions** to rush to affiliate to the new **Labour Party**. As G. D. H. Cole put it: 'The TVR case created the Labour Party'. The Trades Dispute Act (1906), introduced by the **Liberal** government following its electoral victory in 1906, restored the ability of unions to organize strikes free from the fear of being driven into bankruptcy.

STRIKE !

ON THE

Taff Vale Railway.

Men's Headquarters,
Cobourn Street.
Cathays.

There has been a strike on the Taff Vale Railway since Monday last. The Management are using every means to decoy men here who they employ for the purpose of black-legging the men on strike.

Drivers, Firemen, Guards, Brakesmen. and SIGNALMEN, are all out.

Are you willing to be known as a

Blackleg ?

If you accept employment on the Taff Vale. that is what you will be known by. On arriving at Cardiff, call at the above address. where you can get information and assistance.

RICHARD BELL,

General Secretary.

The Taff Vale Railway strike

TAFF-ELY (Taf-Elái) One-time district

Following the abolition of the **county** of **Glamorgan** in 1974, Taff-Ely was created as one of the six districts of the new county of **Mid Glamorgan**. It consisted of what had been the **urban district** of **Pontypridd**, the **rural district** of **Llantrisant** and **Llantwit Fardre** and part of that of **Cardiff**. In 1996, the district (bereft of the **community** of Pentyrch) became part of the **county borough** of **Rhondda Cynon Taff**.

TAFFIA

'Taffia' is a successor to the 17th-century epithet 'Taphydom', which referred generally to Wales and the Welsh. Taffia is used in a derogative sense to refer to the alleged influence, perhaps corruption, of Welsh people in high places in public life, its similarity to 'mafia' underlining the point. (*See also* **Taffy**.)

TAFF'S WELL (Ffynnon Taf), Rhondda Cynon Taff (673 ha; 3464 inhabitants)

Located on the eastern side of the **Taff** gorge north-west of **Cardiff**, the **community** contains the villages of Taff's Well and Nantgarw and the southern part of the Treforest Industrial Estate. Taff's Well long rejoiced in the title 'the world's smallest spa', and its waters won fame as a cure for rheumatism. Although disused since the 1950s, the **well** survives near the Taff's Well Inn.

Iron ore was mined at Taff's Well from at least the 16th century, causing the sides of the gorge to be riddled with workings. However, substantial **population** growth in the area began in the 1860s following the opening of major **coal**mines and a chainworks. The superb Walnut Tree viaduct carried the **Barry Railway** across the gorge; one of its piers survives as a monument. Nantgarw had **canal** warehouses and cottages for boatmen. Its **pottery** produced superb porcelain from 1813 to 1822, and earthenware from 1833 until the 1920s. The works have been refurbished and are open to the public. The memories of Mrs Margretta Thomas, of Nantgarw, recorded by her daughter, Ceinwen Thomas, are a prime source on the vocabulary and traditions of **Welsh**-speaking south-east **Glamorgan**.

TAFFY

The common **English** nickname for a Welshman, Taffy is derived from the supposed Welsh pronunciation of Dafydd (David). Taffy is the name of the **goat** mascot of regiments associated with Wales, and the nickname survives most commonly in the British armed forces. The nursery rhyme beginning 'Taffy was a Welshman, Taffy was a thief ...' appeared in print late in the 18th century, and its ultimate derivation is uncertain. (*See also* **Taffia**.)

TAI UNNOS (One-night houses)

The landless poor in Wales, as elsewhere in **Britain**, were often forced to settle on **common land**, which, by the 18th and early 19th centuries, was frequently subject to **enclosure**. According to traditional belief, if a house of turf could be built overnight, and a fire lit in the hearth, then the builder could claim ownership of both the house and as much surrounding land as could be encompassed by the distance an axe could be thrown. (The first known reference to a *tŷ unnos* – the term's singular form – dates from

1818.) Such unauthorized constructions frequently led to conflict between squatters and those with rights of common, the latter intent on their destruction. If they survived, however, the householders generally set about erecting more permanent dwellings in their place. Penrhos (**Maenclochog**), an example of such a house, has been preserved as a museum.

TALACHARN Commote

One of the **commotes** of **Cantref Gwarthaf**, it came to constitute the **march**er-lordship of **Laugharne**.

TALBOT family Landowners

This **gentry** family, whose name is commemorated in **Port Talbot**, originated in Wiltshire and became connected with **Glamorgan** through the marriage of Mary **Mansel** to John Talbot, a marriage which led, in 1750, to their son, Thomas, inheriting the Mansel estates. Thomas's grandson, Christopher Rice Mansel Talbot (1803–90) served as MP for Glamorgan from 1830 to 1885 and for Mid Glamorgan from 1885 until his death; he was father of the House of Commons for over 15 years. Reputedly worth £6 million, he was said to be the wealthiest commoner in **Britain**. His wealth derived almost entirely from his ownership of 13,760 ha of Glamorgan land, as well as **railway** and industrial concerns. He was highly cultivated, with interests in both the arts and **sciences**. As his sole male heir, Theodore Talbot (1839–76), predeceased him, his estates eventually passed to his daughter Emily and her husband John Fletcher. The family connection with William Henry Fox Talbot explains why the most significant early Welsh photograph is a daguerreotype of **Margam** Castle (*see* **Photography**).

TALGARTH, Breconshire, Powys
(5528 ha; 1645 inhabitants)

The **community** extends from the Llynfi to the highest point of the **Black Mountains** at Waun Fach (818 m). The village of Talgarth contains a tower house, one of two in **Breconshire**. **Howel Harris** is buried in Talgarth church, where both he and **William Williams** (Pantycelyn; 1717–91) experienced conversion. In 1900, Talgarth was chosen as the site of the Mid Wales Hospital, a decision that brought the village a measure of prosperity. To the south is Trefeca, where in 1752 Howel Harris established his religious community or 'Family'. On the site of his old home, he commissioned the erection of a building which pioneered the use of the 'Gothick' style and which may have been designed by Harris himself. Nearby, in 1765, the Countess of Huntingdon established a college to train Methodist evangelists (*see* **Calvinistic Methodists**). Great Porthaml, the home of a branch of the **Vaughan family (Tretower)**, has a fine 15th-century hall and a Tudor tower gate. Castell Dinas, at 455 m, is the highest castle in Wales; its **Iron Age** ramparts are extensive, but little remains of the medieval castle built within them – **Leland** described it as 'now ruinous almost to the hard ground'. The church at Llanelieu has a fine 14th-century screen. There are cairns of the Severn-Cotswold type at Ffostill, Ty Isaf, Mynydd Troed and Pen-yr-wyrlod. A computer image derived from a 5500-year-old skull found at Pen-yr-wyrlod produced a

The face of a Neolithic man, created by computer on the basis of a skull of *c*.3500 BC discovered in a chambered tomb at Pen-yr-wyrlod, Talgarth

face of astonishing modernity. Talgarth **commote** was the northernmost commote of the *cantref* of **Blaenllynfi**, which itself was sometimes known as the *cantref* of Talgarth.

TALIESIN (fl. late 6th century) Poet

One of the *Cynfeirdd* who, like his contemporary, **Aneirin**, was placed in the **Old North** by the author of *Historia Brittonum*. During the Middle Ages, he was remembered as court poet to some of the chieftains of the Old North, while some 20th-century scholars have argued that he was a native of **Powys**. Twelve praise poems to **Urien Rheged** and others have been preserved which might belong to the 6th century and are thought to represent his authentic work.

From the 9th century, he was incorporated in a legend on the origin of poetic inspiration. *Hanes Taliesin* (The story of Taliesin) is extant in its full form only in the chronicle of the 16th-century antiquarian **Elis Gruffydd**, but court poets of the 12th century also refer to it, and it was argued in the 20th century that the story developed in north Wales in the 9th or 10th century. *Hanes Taliesin* recounts how the goddess Ceridwen brews a magic potion intended for her son, Morfran, so that he will imbibe the gift of poetry. But her servant, Gwion Bach, swallows some drops of the potion and, when pursued by Ceridwen, both of them undergo a series of transformations, until he is ultimately swallowed as a grain of wheat by Ceridwen in the form of a hen. When he is reborn from her womb, she casts him adrift on the sea, where he is discovered by Elffin ap Gwyddno Garanhir.

He is renamed Taliesin and introduced eventually to the court of **Maelgwn Gwynedd**, where he silences the household poets with his superior bardic skills.

The work of the historical Taliesin, and later work attributed to the legendary Taliesin (largely religious, narrative and prophetic poetry), are found mingled together in *The Book of Taliesin*. He figures also in semi-legendary tales, as a follower of **Bendigeidfran** in the story of **Branwen** in the second branch of 'Pedair Cainc y Mabinogi' (*see* **Mabinogion, The**) and as one of **Arthur**'s men in the poem 'Preiddiau Annwfn'. His reputation as a prophet grew between the 11th and 13th centuries and his name is frequently coupled with that of Myrddin (**Merlin**) in order to give authority to the vaticinatory poetry of the period (*see* **Prophecy**). In the literary criticism of **Saunders Lewis**, Taliesin is identified with the praise tradition of **literature** in **Welsh**, a theme elaborated upon by the novelist Emyr Humphreys (b.1919) in his *The Taliesin Tradition* (1983).

TALOG, Myfanwy (Myfanwy Talog Williams) (1945–95) Actor

A talented actor in both **Welsh** and **English**, Myfanwy Talog won acclaim for her roles in television comedy programmes, particularly as the chaotic Phyllis Doris in the series *Ryan and Ronnie*. She appeared in many children's programmes and her melodious contribution to the cartoon series *Wil Cwac Cwac* was central to the success of those programmes. A different aspect of her talent became apparent in her role in **Rhydderch Jones**'s television drama *Gwenoliaid* (1986). She was long the partner of the actor David Jason. There is a plaque to her on the house at **Caerwys** where she was born.

TALSARNAU, Gwynedd
(4403 ha; 525 inhabitants)
Located immediately north of **Harlech**, the **community** extends from the salt marshes at Traeth Bach on the Dwyryd estuary to the **mountains** west of **Trawsfynydd**. Bryn Cader is a beautiful **Bronze Age** cairn. The village of Talsarnau developed following the construction in 1810 of a turf embankment to drain the marshes. Until then, St Michael's church, Llanfihangel y Traethau (12th century, but largely rebuilt in 1871), stood on what was virtually an **island**. St Tecwyn's church, Llandecwyn, was rebuilt in 1879. Glyn Cywarch (1616) is one of the mansions of the **Ormsby-Gore family**, Barons Harlech. The 17th-century Maes y Neuadd is a hotel.

TALWRN Y BEIRDD Radio series
The popular Radio Cymru programme *Talwrn y Beirdd* (The poets' cockpit) developed from *Ymryson y Beirdd* (The poets' contest), which was first transmitted in 1937 on

Talyllychau Abbey ruins

the BBC Welsh Home Service. Devised by **Sam Jones**, *Ymryson y Beirdd* took the form of a bardic competition based on the intricacies of *cynghanedd* and involving, eventually, teams of poets from all over Wales. When Radio Cymru was launched in 1979, the programme returned as *Talwrn y Beirdd*, with the poet Gerallt Lloyd Owen (b.1944) as 'meuryn', as the adjudicator is called, after Meuryn (**Robert John Rowlands**) who was the original adjudicator.

TALYBOLION Commote

A **commote** in the north-west of **Anglesey** which, with that of **Twrcelyn**, formed the *cantref* of **Cemaes**. The commotal centre was at Cemaes. In the story of **Branwen Ferch Llŷr** in the second branch of '*Pedair Cainc y Mabinogi*' (*see* **Mabinogion, The**), the name is onomastically explained as *tâl [am] ebolion* (payment for colts) – but in reality it refers to the place's location at the end (*tal*) of an undulating landscape (*bolion* means bellies). The name survived as that of a post-**Acts of 'Union' hundred**.

TALYBONT Commote

The northernmost of the two **commotes** of the *cantref* of **Meirionnydd**, it contained the **Cistercian** monastery of Cymer (**Llanelltyd**). Its original centre seems to have been Talybont (**Llanegryn**), but was later at **Dolgellau**.

TALYBONT-ON-USK (Tal-y-bont ar Wysg), Breconshire, Powys (7827 ha; 743 inhabitants)

The **community** extends from the border with **Blaenau Gwent** to within sight of **Llangorse Lake**. The village, once engaged in the **woollen industry** and now a tourist centre, lies astride the **Brecon** and **Abergavenny Canal**, which passes over an aqueduct to the north of Talybont and through the Ashford Tunnel to the south. A steel drawbridge carries the road to Talybont **reservoir**, built by **Newport** Corporation. To its south-east are the Pentwyn and Pontsticill reservoirs, near which are the vast **limestone** quarries that served **Merthyr Tydfil**'s **iron**works. The former **railway** station at Pontsticill was **Britain**'s highest standard-gauge station south of the Scottish border. Of Pencelli Castle, once owned by Ralph **Mortimer**, a rectangular tower and part of the bailey wall survive. Mortimer was also responsible for the building of the 13th-century church at Llanfigan. Across the **Usk**, at Scethrog, stands one of **Breconshire**'s two tower-houses (the other is in **Talgarth**). Built by the Picard family, it was once the home of George Melly (1926–2007), founder of the Brecon Jazz Festival. The poet **Henry Vaughan** is buried at Llansantffraed, where his brother, the alchemist **Thomas Vaughan**, was rector until expelled during the **Commonwealth**. Newton, their home, is nearby, but the present house dates from later than the 17th century. To the south lies the hamlet of Llanddeti, home of Jenkin Jones, a fervent Parliamentarian who expressed his disgust at the Restoration by discharging his pistol at the church door.

TALYLLYCHAU, Carmarthenshire
(3326 ha; 534 inhabitants)
Widely but unacceptably known as Talley (admittedly a name first recorded in 1382), the **community** is located north of **Llandeilo** and contains the village of Talyllychau

Phil Tanner, the 'Gower Nightingale'

and the hamlets of Halfway and Cwmdu. In the 1180s, **Rhys ap Gruffudd** (The Lord Rhys; d.1197) established Wales's sole **Premonstratensian** abbey south of Talyllychau's two small **lakes**. A church with an eight-bay nave had been laid out before 1200, but in the following decades only four bays were built, an indication that the canons secured a smaller endowment than they had hoped, perhaps because they suffered from the enmity of the abbot of **Whitland**. A 26-m high section of the church tower is the only substantial part of the abbey still standing. St Michael's church (1772) retains its box pews. Providence **Baptist** chapel (1789, 1839, 1883), Cwmdu, is an attractive building.

In the 1950s, Cwmdu was the scene of a gruesome murder (*see* **Michal Onufrejczyk**). The hamlet later became famous for its tepee village. Cwmdu's Georgian street with inn and shop was acquired by the **National Trust** in 1991. Newfoundland is one of the farm names recalling the early 17th-century attempt by **William Vaughan** to establish a Welsh colony in Newfoundland.

TANNER, Phil (1862–1950) Folk singer
The youngest son of a family of **Gower** weavers famous in **Llangennith** for singing and dancing, Phil Tanner was recorded by the BBC in 1937 and 1949, and was the subject of a celebrated 1949 *Picture Post* feature. Although only a fraction of his huge repertoire of songs was ever preserved, he is recognized by scholars as one of the most accomplished traditional singers in the **English language**. A CD compilation of his recordings, *The Gower Nightingale*, was released in 2003.

TAPLAS

A meeting usually held on a Saturday night between Easter and Winter's Eve, to sing, **dance**, play ball and engage in various feats, prizes sometimes being given to the winners by local publicans. In **Glamorgan**, it was associated with the summer birch (**Bedwen Haf**) and midsummer day, and under the name '**mabsant**' was often confused with 'Gwylmabsant' (patronal festival). In the north, the name 'twmpath chwarae' or 'chwareufa gampau' was given to a similar meeting held during the summer months after the day's work had been completed. By the early 19th century, these meetings had declined in importance. The word was later adopted as the name for a Welsh folk music magazine.

TAWE River (48 km)

The Tawe rises in the uplands of the **Black Mountain** near Llyn y Fan Fawr, on the eastern slopes of Fan Brycheiniog in the **community** of **Llywel**. Its headwaters drain south towards the Dan-yr-Ogof **caves** – caves typical of the outcrop of the Carboniferous **Limestone** that forms the rim of the southern **coal**field – and the Craig-y-nos Country Park (**Tawe-Uchaf**). The Tawe valley follows the north-east to south-west Tawe fault. Between Abercraf and **Ystradgynlais**, the river flows through a narrow valley in which the scarcity of flat land has given rise to a ribbon settlement pattern. The Tawe is joined by the Twrch at **Ystalyfera**. At **Pontardawe**, the valley's narrowness continues to restrict development. The valley widens where the Clydach joins the Tawe, the beginning of the flat valley floor that was

long the location of the world's chief **copper**-producing centre. The industry's use of the Tawe's water was particularly ingenious. The river's 5 km of navigable water, linking the **coal**field with the sea, was the key to the rise of the **port** of Swansea.

TAWE-UCHAF, Breconshire, Powys
(2968 ha; 1516 inhabitants)

Within the **community**, the red sandstone characteristic of **Breconshire** gives way to a carboniferous rock, and the landscape offers **caves**, gorges, vanishing streams and the Henryd **waterfall**. The Dan-yr-Ogof caves are among the largest underground system in western Europe. **Pottery** and metalwork were found in Ogof yr Esgyrn, a rare instance of a known **Bronze Age** occupation site. Craig-y-Nos, a Gothic folly built in the early 1840s, was enlarged following its purchase in 1878 by the opera singer **Adelina Patti**. Her winter **garden**, the Patti Pavilion, has been moved to **Swansea**, but her lavishly decorated theatre, a miniature version of that at Bayreuth, still exists. The group of Bronze Age ritual monuments at Cerrig Duon is one of the finest in Wales. **Coal**mining in the area began in 1758 at Abercraf, where there was once a significant Spanish community (*see* **Spaniards**) and where there are now vast open-cast workings. The circular **cattle**-house at Waun-lwyd is believed to be the sole such structure in the United Kingdom.

TAYLOR, A[rnold] J[oseph] (1911–2002)
Archaeologist

On becoming inspector of ancient monuments for Wales in 1946, **London**-born Taylor applied his knowledge of medieval accounting and documentary research and his penetrating architectural analysis to the great Edwardian castles of north Wales (*see* **Architecture**). Through lectures and publications, he raised international appreciation of the importance of the castles, revealing much about the history of their design and construction. He undertook fascinating research on the architect **James of St George**. His masterpiece is the section on Wales in H. M. Colvin (ed.), *The History of the King's Works*, which was published separately in 1973 as *The History of the King's Works in Wales, 1277–1330*.

TEA

Eighteenth-century **ballads** and **interludes** show that the custom of meeting to drink tea and chat was already well established among Welsh **women**, although tea remained expensive. The profit made from selling tea enabled **William Williams** (Pantycelyn; 1717–91) to finance his preaching tours. The loquacious 'tea club' was satirized by 19th-century poets, but, as the price dropped, they began to write amusing eulogies to the refreshing cup that was becoming a daily drink for all. Teetotallers (*see* **Temperance Movement**) seized the opportunity to urge the drinking of tea rather than alcoholic beverages, and the holding of tea festivals became a popular method of raising money to repay the debt on **Nonconformist** chapels. The similarity in colour of milk-less tea to whisky allowed many of those believed to be teetotallers to enjoy a cup of their favourite tipple undetected.

A traditonal cup of tea

TEGEINGL *Cantref*
Together with **Rhos**, **Rhufoniog** and **Dyffryn Clwyd**, Tegeingl was one of the *cantrefi* of the **Perfeddwlad** (the middle country). The name probably derives from **Deceangli**, the Brythonic tribe inhabiting north-east Wales at the time of the **Roman** invasion. Known to the **Mercia**ns as Englefield, it became an area of contention between the earls of Chester and the princes of **Gwynedd**. It consisted of the **commotes** of **Rhuddlan**, **Prestatyn** and **Coleshill**. In 1284, it became the core of **Flintshire**.

TEIFI River (117 km)
The Teifi rises in Llynnoedd Teifi in the southern part of the **Elenydd** or Cambrian **Mountains** in the **community** of **Ystrad Fflur**. The more recent and less resistant rocks of the late Ordovician and early Silurian eras form the geological foundation of the catchment area. The Teifi follows the geological trend or alignment of the rocks from north-west to south-west. It flows past the site of the **Cistercian** monastery of Strata Florida (Ystrad Fflur) and through the remarkable **Cors Caron** before reaching **Tregaron**. Beyond Tregaron, the **river** meanders across fertile lowlands to **Lampeter**. Between Lampeter and **Cardigan**, the Teifi denotes the **Ceredigion/Carmarthenshire** boundary. It forms a striking **waterfall** at Cenarth. Of the Teifi's numerous small tributaries, the most attractive is the Cych (Afon Cuch), which for most of its course forms the Carmarthenshire/ **Pembrokeshire** boundary. The Teifi flows into Cardigan Bay between Cemaes Head (**St Dogmaels**) and Carreg Lydan (**Y Ferwig**). Cardigan **Island** is located off the estuary's northern shore.

TEILO (Eliud; 6th century) 'Saint'
Founder of the church of **Llandeilo** Fawr and one of the three **saints** (with **David** and **Padarn**) who were reputedly consecrated bishops by the patriarch of Jerusalem. An 8th-century note in the margins of ***The Book of St Chad*** records that the manuscript was given 'to God and St Teilo on his altar'. Another note refers to the brothers of the monastery founded by him as 'all Teilo's family'. The book is proof of Llandeilo's importance as a Christian centre. A Life of Teilo was written in the 12th century by Geoffrey who, as brother of **Urban**, bishop of Llandaff (*see* **Cardiff**), wished to link the saint with Urban's **diocese**. The Life contains references to Teilo's visit to **Brittany**. Several Breton churches were dedicated to the 'saint' and he is regarded there as the patron saint of **horses** and apple trees. The squabble between churches over his **relics** was evidence of his fame. It is said that a miracle provided the solution. The Welsh Triads (***Trioedd Ynys Prydain***) refer to the 'three bodies' that God made for Teilo. One was kept at Llandaff, another at Llandeilo Fawr and the third at **Penally**, his reputed birthplace. Teilo's feast day is 9 February.

TELEGRAPH, The
The best-known telegraph in Wales was that between **Holyhead** and **Liverpool**, the first private and commercial telegraph in **Britain**, operated by the Liverpool Docks Trustees from 1827 until 1907. It was a semaphore telegraph, with mechanically operated arms which could

The River Teifi near Cilgerran, Pembrokeshire

be adjusted, rather like old **railway** signals, to communicate one of 10,000 possible numbers, each of which corresponded to a word or phrase, according to the system's code.

The signal was read by telescope from the next of the system's 11 stations, which then sent its signal onwards; messages were transmitted the entire length of the telegraph in five minutes. It did not work in fog, therefore the semaphore stations were sited above the sea mist and below the hill mist. Electric telegraphy largely superseded the Holyhead telegraph in 1860, but traces of what was the last semaphore telegraph to operate in Britain are still visible.

The development of the electric telegraph paralleled that of the railways, and was closely linked with **ship**ping. Wales's second electric telegraph was established between **Milford Haven** and the royal dockyards at **Pembroke Dock** in 1861, to provide information about incoming vessels. The telegraph was important for **lighthouses**, ship rescue, weather forecasting and, later, the **fire** and **police** services.

Unusually for the 19th century, the state was heavily implicated in the telegraph, nationalizing it in 1870, in order both to facilitate trade and to control a medium with significant security implications. Indeed, the telegraph was used by the **government** to undermine **Chartism**.

Experiments in telegraphy in Wales included those of Charles Wheatstone (1802–75) who used Swansea Bay in 1844 and 1845 to investigate underwater currents. But the era of the telegraph was short-lived, as it was overtaken by the **telephone**.

TELEPHONE, The

The British telephone system was developed in the 1880s by the United Telephone Company, the Post Office and others as a series of local networks that were later connected – an arrangement notably different from the **London**-centred **postal service**. By 1882, there were telephone exchanges in **Cardiff**, **Newport** and **Swansea**, by 1886 in **Carmarthen**, **Holyhead**, **Bangor** and **Caernarfon**, and, by 1887, many more.

The 1897 telephone directory lists 'Cardiff' as an area of the 'Western Province' of the National Telephone Company (NTC) – which also included Evesham and **Cornwall**. The number of telephones in towns in the 'Cardiff Area' in 1897 ranged from 767 in Cardiff and 231 in Swansea, to 6 in **Abergavenny** and 5 in Porth (**Rhondda**). Subscribers included hotels, the **police**, local **government**, shipping companies (*see* **Ships and Shipowners**) and major industrial concerns.

A brief period of competition between telephone companies ensued. The NTC was formed from a series of amalgamations and take-overs of private telephone companies, one of which was the Western Counties and South Wales Company. By 1890, the NTC and the Post Office were the sole providers; by 1899, the Post Office had about 1000 subscribers against the NTC's 100,000.

Municipal involvement was at its height *c.*1900. The 1899 Telegraph Act authorized municipalities to operate telephone systems. Swansea was one of six local authorities in the United Kingdom to be granted a licence (1902),

opening an exchange in 1903. In 1907, when it had 1215 subscribers' lines, Swansea's system was sold to the NTC, which, in turn, was acquired by the Post Office in 1912. In 1969, the telephone system was separated from the Post Office and made into a nationalized industry; it was privatized as British Telecom (BT) in 1984.

By the early 21st century, BT was competing with numerous other providers, notably Virgin Media. Traffic grew enormously; having peaked at 91% in 2003, 89% of Welsh households had a landline telephone in 2006. About three-quarters of people in Wales had a mobile telephone in 2006, although there were indications that this was a market that may be reaching saturation. Reception problems in west and mid Wales were one reason for non-ownership.

TELFORD, Thomas (1757–1834) Civil engineer

Born in Dumfriesshire, the son of a shepherd, Telford engineered the 175-km Shrewsbury–**Holyhead stagecoach** route, later the **A5**, which was part of the 418-km Irish mail route from **London**. The **road**'s finest feature was the suspension bridge over the **Menai Strait**, opened in 1826. Telford's engineering skill ensured that the steepest gradient through **Snowdonia** was the 1:22 at Nant Ffrancon Pass, compared with 1:6 along parts of the old road. Telford also designed the **Chirk** and Pont Cysyllte (**Llangollen Rural**) aqueducts for the Ellesmere **Canal** Company.

TEMPERANCE

The consumption of alcohol has always been a feature of Welsh life. In the early 19th century, it reached epidemic proportions in the new industrial areas, with their high proportion of young unmarried men who had few meeting places apart from public houses. Over-indulgence was a cause of concern to many: to the employer because it undermined his efforts to create a disciplined workforce; to working-**class** wives who were jealous of the public house (the 'masculine republic') and who were bitter when the household's meagre resources were spent on drink; to the more serious of the working class who were saddened by the sodden condition of their fellow-workers; and to the respectable members of every class who were disgusted by public drunkenness.

Temperance societies were first established in the 1820s in **North America**. The first such societies among the Welsh were those established by migrants to English industrial cities, but by 1835 there were 25 temperance societies in Wales itself. The emphasis of the earliest societies was upon moderation. Thus, members of the **Ebbw Vale** Temperance Society were allowed to drink two pints of beer a day. Its leaders were distressed to find that some members saved up their pints to enable them to drink 14 on Saturdays. Such obfuscation encouraged the advocacy of total abstinence, and Wales's first teetotal society was founded at Llanfechell (**Mechell**) in 1835. A vigorous temperance subculture came into existence, with **periodicals**, meetings, songs, orders, ceremonies, hotels and pledges, and, by 1850, teetotalism had been absorbed into the moralistic system of the **Nonconformists**. Originally, temperance advocates sought to create a sober society through example and persuasion, but rapidly the demand arose for legislation to restrict or prohibit the liquor trade. Thus, the

A temperance poster of 1862

Tenby as depicted by Moses Griffith (1812)

temperance movement was transformed from a moral crusade into a political campaign and it became another element in the Nonconformists' legislative programme.

In Wales, the movement's greatest success was the **Sunday closing of public houses**, achieved in 1881. Proponents of the legislation hoped, in vain, that it would be the first step towards total prohibition, an issue absorbing much of the energy of some Welsh politicians until at least the 1920s. Thereafter, secularization, the increasing popularity of other forms of socializing and the rise of more sophisticated analyses of the causes of working-class poverty led to a decline in the interest in temperance. However, with binge drinking increasingly prevalent, temperance may yet return to the political agenda.

TEMPLETON (Tredeml), Pembrokeshire
(1424 ha; 808 inhabitants)

Located immediately south of **Narberth**, the **community**'s name recalls a hospice established in 1282 by the Knights Templar. Templeton Fair, held on the day after Michaelmas, was famous for its **cat**'s pies – made of mutton. St John's church (19th century) is on the site of a building once used as a **Unitarian** meeting house. Mounton chapel is an abandoned medieval church. The houses along the A478 have long burgage plots, the remnants of medieval linear planning.

TENBY (Dinbych-y-pysgod), Pembrokeshire
(437 ha; 4934 inhabitants)

Located on **Pembrokeshire**'s south-eastern coast, Tenby (Dinbych – the little fort) is the subject of the first surviving **Welsh-language** poem in praise of a place – the 9th-century 'Edmyg Dinbych' (Praise of Tenby). Preserved in *The Book of Taliesin*, the poem, in *awdl* metres, praises the fort at Tenby and mentions the old manuscripts – 'the writings of **Britain**' – kept in its cell. The fort probably stood on the rocky headland later occupied by a 12th-century motte, one of the fortifications of the lordship of **Pembroke**. The castle was rebuilt in the 13th century, perhaps following the sacking of Tenby by **Llywelyn ap Gruffudd**'s forces in 1260. Of the considerable stretches of the town walls to survive, the most impressive is the 14th-century barbican defending the south gate. Known as the Five Arches, it was described by **Augustus John** – Tenby's most celebrated son – as 'a piece of **cheese** gnawed by rats'.

St Mary's church has an elegant nave arcade (14th century) and a tower and wagon roof (15th century). It contains the effigy of the merchant, Thomas White (d.1482), who assisted the flight of Henry and Jasper **Tudor** to France in 1471. An underground passage beneath Boots the Chemists is purported to be the place in which he concealed them. The church also contains a memorial to the Tenby-born scientist **Robert Recorde**, deviser of the equals sign (=).

From the 14th to 18th centuries, Tenby enjoyed success as a **port**. The Merchant's House is a well-restored 15th-century building. In the late 18th century, the town won increasing fame as a watering place; **Richard Fenton** described it in 1800 as being 'unrivalled by any in the principality'. **William Paxton** arrived in 1805, determined to make Tenby a prime saltwater-therapy spa, a task assisted by the town's position above the superb south and north beaches and by the views across the water to Caldey **Island**. He commissioned the building of public baths and the laying out of attractive promenades and terraces. Tenby's ability to attract visitors was much improved by the arrival of the **railway** in 1866. The town acquired assembly rooms, a **pier** (1899; demolished in 1953), an archaeological and geological museum, an annual regatta and the Welsh national memorial to Prince Albert (1865). On St Catherine's Rock is a fort built in 1868, a belated example of **Palmerston's Follies**. From the **Act of 'Union'** until 1918, Tenby was part of the **Pembroke Boroughs** constituency.

Changes in holiday habits have not hit Tenby to the extent they have other Welsh resorts. The **community**'s charms have insured a faithful clientele, although those charms are less evident on those occasions when the town lives up to its reputation of being Britain's hen-party capital.

TENNIS

There are various claims that lawn tennis – as distinct from real or royal tennis, the indoor game of European aristocracy since at least the 13th century – originated in Wales. In 1804, **Benjamin Heath Malkin** referred to 'Young men play[ing] at fives and tennis against the wall of the church' in many parts of Wales, and in 1887 a Welsh game called *Cerrig y Drudion* was cited as the precursor of lawn tennis. However, histories of tennis tend to accord greater credence to the claims of 'Sphairistiké', a game invented by Major Walter Clopton Wingfield of Rhysnant Hall, **Brymbo** in 1873. His hourglass-shaped court and 'unsatisfactory' rules failed to gain acceptance, but they seem to have been a decisive catalyst for the modern game. By the 1880s, lawn tennis tournaments were being held in Wales, and the game quickly became popular with **women**, for whom the sport signalled the emergence of more energetic activities, with clothing to match.

The game in Wales is governed by Tennis Wales, which has 95 affiliated clubs and co-ordinates approximately 200 tournaments and competitions annually; it has over 11,000 player members. Leading players have included Elizabeth James of **Penarth**, at her peak in the 1960s; Mike Davies of **Swansea** and Gerald Battrick of **Bridgend**, British hard court champions in 1960 and 1971 respectively; John (J. P. R.) Williams, British junior champion in 1966 (*see also* **Rugby**); Ellinore Lightbody, of Swansea, Welsh number one in 1977; and Sarah Loosemore, of **Cardiff**, British champion in 1988.

TENOVUS

This cancer charity with fund-raising shops throughout Wales and **England** was founded in 1943 by a group of 10 **Cardiff** businessmen. By 2007, it was raising over £6 million a year for cancer research, **education**, patient care and counselling. It began when one of the group, haulier Eddie Price (1910–2001), was given a radio during a long hospital stay, but was unable to use it as it disturbed the other patients. His friends decided that they would launch an appeal, under the name 'Ten-of-us', to equip all the hospital beds with radio headsets. It was the first of many **health**care projects, although, since 1964, Tenovus has concentrated on cancer.

TEXTILES

By the 16th century, woollen manufacture (*see* **Woollen Industry**), the main textile industry in Wales, was moving away from towns, with their guild restrictions, to the

An embroidered wall hanging, part of a set at Brynkinallt, Chirk *c.*1710–20

countryside, and from south to north and mid Wales. However, cloth manufacture for local use was pursued in most parts of Wales, as indicated by the frequency of the word *pandy* (fulling mill) in **place names.**

By the 18th century, there were three major cloth-making areas, centred on **Dolgellau**, **Newtown** and Glyn Ceiriog (*see* **Llansantffraid Glyn Ceiriog**). From the late 18th century onwards, **Liverpool** merchants began to penetrate north and mid Wales, seeking woollen goods particularly at the cloth markets established at **Welshpool** (1782), Newtown (1832) and **Llanidloes** (1836). The early 19th century saw a cloth-making boom in the upper **Severn** valley. By the 1880s, however, the area was in decline. The **Teifi** valley emerged as a significant centre, but, by the 1920s, that area too was experiencing decline. Woollen manufacture continues at a number of mills, largely as a tourist attraction.

Flax was grown in Wales until the early 19th century, and linen was woven on a domestic scale, but the industry was killed by Lancashire cotton imports. The manufacture of linen was especially important in the Severn valley, where Arddleen (*gardd lin* – flax **garden**) is a village in the **community** of Llandrinio.

In the late 18th century, there was some manufacture of cotton and, more exotically, of silk, at **Holywell** – an overspill from the industries of Lancashire and **Cheshire**. Rayon manufacture began in **Flintshire** in the 1930s (*see* **Courtaulds**), and a major British Nylon Spinners factory was built at New Inn (**Pontypool**) in 1948. Both became victims of subsequent de-industrialization. In 1973, **Laura Ashley**'s substantial centre of textile manufacture was opened at **Carno**. It was associated with extensive outworking for the making up of clothes, but the work came to an end in 2005.

A wide range of products – cloth, flannel, tweed, shawls, blankets and bedcovers – has been made from wool. Patterns in flannel are predominantly stripes, although by 1850 checks had been introduced. *Carthenni* are twill woven blankets with birdseye or linear patterns, most surviving examples dating from 1850 to 1940. These geometric double-cloth coverlets were woven on handlooms initially, but became much more common when mechanical looms were introduced. Although referred to as 'Welsh tapestry', similar patterns are also found in **England** and **North America**.

Some of the earliest embellished textiles known in Wales were embroideries. Medieval Welsh poems describe clothing embroidered with silks and gold threads, with motifs of **birds**, animals and **plants**. Survivals include raised-work pictures, gloves, and bed hangings, mainly from 1650–1800. Later, samplers were popular. Quilts and patchwork, made from the 18th century onwards, continued as a domestic craft until the **First World War**. Although there was a revival during the 1920s and 1930s, quilting as an industry did not survive the rationing of the **Second World War**. Welsh quilts consist of an upper and lower cover, with a layer of filling held in place by stitching, using patterns which became traditional. Patchwork, using large rectangular and triangular pieces of fabric, had its roots in Wales, and was exported to America by 19th-century emigrants.

THATCHING

Before the widespread availability of Welsh **slate** or terracotta tiles in the mid-19th century, wheat thatch (often underlain with gorse, rushes or heather) was a common roofing material. Ricks also had to be protected against rain, the wheat thatch being weighted down in windy coastal areas with a network of anchored straw ropes. Norfolk Reed was grown in many parts for thatching and, if carefully applied to a roof, would last for a century or more. On both stacks and buildings, a roof pitch of at least 50 degrees was essential if the thatch were to deflect water effectively. A number of thatched cottages survive, especially in the **Vale of Glamorgan**, and there are modern examples in opulent suburbia, such as **Cardiff**'s Lisvane.

THAW (Ddawan) River (32 km)

The Thaw rises at an altitude of 60 m in the **community** of **Llanharry** and flows through gently undulating pastureland towards **Cowbridge**. Shifting meanders have created a broad floodplain encased by wooded bluffs 30–40 m high; south of Cowbridge, resistant Lias **Limestone** confines the **river** in a narrow valley which in places is a 25-m deep ravine. The limestone has been quarried to supply the cement works at Aberthaw (**St Athan**) on the river's estuary. The construction of a power station involved the damming of the estuary, long the site of the harbour from which much of the agricultural produce of the **Vale of Glamorgan** was exported.

THEOLOGY

Although the Greek term *theologia* (*theos* = God, *logia* = word) was originally used of the pagan gods of antiquity, by the early Christian centuries it had come to describe God's particular revelation to Israel and its fulfilment in Jesus Christ.

Because of Christianity's central place within the Welsh experience, theology has played a significant role in the creation of the national psyche. During the 'Age of the **Saints**' and the Middle Ages, Christian theology became the basic discourse. Eminent Welsh theologians of the late Middle Ages included the four known as the 'Wallensis Brothers'. The first of these, Johannes Wallensis (fl.1214–20), taught canon **law** at Bologna University, while the first Thomas Wallensis (fl.1230–55), who became bishop of **St David's**, was admired by the English philosopher Roger Bacon (*c.*1214–*c.*1294) and, more importantly, by the Platonist Robert Grosseteste (?1175–1253). The second **Johannes Wallensis** (fl.*c.*1260–83) became the head of the Franciscans (*see* **Friars**) at **Oxford** and Paris. In the following century, another Thomas Wallensis (fl.1300–50), who also taught at both Oxford and Bologna, was a theologian of considerable influence.

Most of Wales's **Renaissance** scholars were primarily theologians. During the centuries following the **Protestant Reformation**, **Calvinism** won widespread acceptance, with **Puritan** writers such as **Morgan Llwyd** (1619–59) playing an influential role. By the early 20th century, Protestant liberalism became popular among Welsh **Nonconformists**, although there were some who reacted against it, generally under the influence of evangelicalism and the writings of Karl Barth.

The golden age of theology in Wales was the period from *c.*1760 to *c.*1930. The enormous strength of Nonconformity and popularity of the **Sunday school** ensured that the common people (*gwerin*) became uncommonly well versed in both biblical knowledge and the minutiae of Christian doctrine. If such well-known leaders as **Thomas Charles**, **Thomas Jones** (1756–1820), **Lewis Edwards**, **D. Miall Edwards**, **J. E. Daniel** and others had become the public interpreters of the discipline, it was the tens of thousands of ordinary folk in the chapels and churches who provided the nation with an impressive intellectual energy. By the early 21st century, however, that energy had much abated.

THIRLWALL, Connop (1797–1875) Bishop

Chosen by a **Whig government** as bishop of **St David's** in 1840, in order to obtain an effective voice in the House of Lords, Thirwall held the **diocese** until 1874. An outstanding thinker, he had little understanding of his diocese and little sympathy with his clergy. Although he learnt to speak **Welsh**, few claimed he was intelligible in it. His *Charges*, in which he dealt with the Church issues of his day, was extremely influential.

THODAY, David (1883–1964) Botanist

Born in Devonshire and a graduate of **Cambridge**, Thoday was professor of botany at **Bangor** from 1923 until his retirement in 1949. Although specializing in physiological botany and the interpretation of **plant** structures, his main contribution was his immense and international influence on botanical thought and teaching. He was elected FRS in 1942. As a skilful deviser of scientific equipment, he is remembered for the 'Thoday potometer' and the 'Thoday respirometer'. After retirement, he taught at the University of Alexandria, but returned to Bangor in 1955. He died at **Llanfairfechan**. His son, John Thoday (b.1916), is a well-known geneticist.

THOMAS, Alfred (Baron Pontypridd; 1840–1927) Politician

Cardiff-born Alfred Thomas was a member of the Cardiff **Borough** Council (1875–86) and mayor (1881–2). In 1885, he was returned as **Liberal** MP for the newly created division of East **Glamorgan**, holding the seat for 25 years. He was chairman of the Welsh Parliamentary Liberal Party (1888), president of the Welsh **Baptist** Union, one of the founders of University College, Cardiff (*see* **Cardiff University**), and the first president of the **National Museum [of] Wales**. In 1892, he introduced the National Institutions (Wales) Bill, the first attempt to achieve a degree of Welsh **Home Rule**. He was raised to the peerage in 1912.

THOMAS, Ben Bowen (1899–1977) Educationist and public figure

A native of the **Rhondda**, Ben Bowen Thomas became warden of **Coleg Harlech** in 1927, and director of extra-mural studies at **Aberystwyth** in 1940. As permanent secretary to the Welsh Department of the Ministry of Education (formerly the **Welsh Department of the Board of Education**) from 1945 to 1963, he played a key role in the development of **Welsh**-medium schools, and as a member of the **Kilbrandon Commission** he advocated a parliament for Wales. He was chairman of the executive board of

UNESCO (1958–60). A historian, his published works include *Hanes Economaidd Cymru* (1941) and *Drych y Baledwr* (1958).

THOMAS, Brinley (1906–94) Economist

Born in Pontrhydyfen (**Pelenna**), Brinley Thomas was head of the economics department at **Cardiff** (1946–73) and chair of the **Council of Wales** (1968–71). He published his first book in 1936 and his last in 1993 at the age of 87. His major work was *Migration and Economic Growth* (1954). In *Wales and the Atlantic Economy* (1959), he advanced the controversial thesis that the **Industrial Revolution** had been a blessing to the **Welsh language**. One of the world's leading authorities on the movement of **population** and capital, he is considered to be among the most brilliant scholars Wales has produced.

THOMAS, Clem (Richard Clement Charles Thomas; 1929–96) Rugby player and journalist

A native of Brynamman (**Quarter Bach**), Clem Thomas played **rugby** for **Cambridge** University, **Swansea**, Wales and the 1955 British Lions. A robust wing-forward, it was he who, in 1953, 'hoofed' the ball crossfield to **Ken Jones** who scored the try that enabled Wales to beat **New Zealand**. He later combined business interests in both Wales and France with journalism and **Liberal Party** politics.

THOMAS, D[avid] A[lfred] (Viscount Rhondda; 1856–1918) Industrialist and politician

The fifteenth of 17 children, D. A. Thomas was born at Ysgubor-wen, **Aberdare**, the son of Samuel Thomas, a **Rhondda** coalowner. As **Liberal** MP for **Merthyr Tydfil** (1885–1910), he courted the miners' vote with criticism of the **Coalowners' Association** and, especially, of the autocratic **W. T. Lewis**. In the 1890s, he emerged as **David Lloyd George**'s arch-enemy in the **Cymru Fydd** controversy. In 1900, he proved sympathetic to **Keir Hardie**, who defeated Thomas's fellow Liberal MP, Pritchard Morgan, in the two-seat Merthyr constituency. From 1906 to 1910, he was MP for **Cardiff**.

At Westminster, his political talents were largely unrecognized and, after 1906, he channelled his energies into changing the structure of the coal industry. Starting from the modest base of his family's Cambrian Collieries in Clydach Vale (Cwm Clydach, **Rhondda**), he amassed a vast fortune and established the mighty Cambrian Combine, which was at the centre of the year-long coal stoppage of 1910–11 (*see* **Miners' Strikes**), during which the **Tonypandy Riots** took place. The former would-be champion of the colliers had come to be seen as their chief scourge.

His political fortunes changed during the **First World War**. In 1915, Lloyd George sent him on a mission to the United States; on his return, he was raised to the peerage as Viscount Rhondda. President of the local **government** board (1915–17), he was appointed **food** controller in 1917; he was notably successful in introducing food rationing, his most enduring claim to fame. A prolific author on economic and industrial matters, D. A. Thomas was a striking embodiment of Victorian individualism. His wife, **Sybil Margaret Thomas**, was a prominent feminist, as was his daughter, **Margaret Haig Thomas**.

THOMAS, Daniel Lleufer (1863–1940)
Magistrate and social reformer

One of the most distinguished Welshmen of his age, Daniel Lleufer Thomas was born at Cwmdu (**Talyllychau**). While at **Oxford**, he was a founder of Cymdeithas **Dafydd ap Gwilym**. From 1909 to 1933, he was stipendiary magistrate for **Pontypridd** and **Rhondda**, a position which brought him into prominence, especially following the **Tonypandy Riots** of 1910. He conducted an inquiry into the living conditions of **agricultural labourers** (1893), was secretary to the Royal Commission on Land in Wales (1893–6) and chaired the Welsh panel of the Commission on Industrial Unrest (1917). A member of the departmental committee on *Welsh in Education and Life* (1923–27), he played a significant role in ensuring that it went beyond its strict remit by recommending the repeal of the language clause of the **Act of 'Union'** and the enhancement of the status of **Welsh** in the courts. Thomas was involved with many Welsh **education**al and social reform causes, such as the **Workers' Educational Association**, the **University of Wales** (inaugurating the **law** faculty at **Aberystwyth** in 1901), the **National Museum** and the **National Library**. He was knighted in 1931.

THOMAS, David (1794–1882) Industrial pioneer
Originally from Cadoxton (**Blaenhonddan**), David Thomas was a crucial figure in American industrialization. In the 1830s, at Ynysgedwyn **iron**works (**Ystradgynlais**), he was the first in the world to cast iron using anthracite. In 1840, he successfully produced iron at Catasaqua, **Pennsylvania**, earning himself the title 'the father of the American anthracite coal industry'.

THOMAS, David (1880–1967)
Socialist pioneer and educator

Born in **Llanfechain**, **Montgomeryshire**, David Thomas became a primary school teacher. From 1908, he was prominent in organizing the **Independent Labour Party** (ILP) and the **trade union** movement in the north. In 1911, he, together with **John Davies** (1882–1937), sought to provide the ILP in Wales with a more autonomous structure (a move interpreted in some quarters as an attempt to create a wholly independent Welsh **Labour Party**). In 1914, he was a central figure in the creation of the North Wales Council of Labour. For more than 30 years (1928–59), he was a tutor for the **Workers' Educational Association** and in 1944 he was appointed editor of the WEA's influential magazine *Lleufer*. He published books on political theory, poetry and history, including *Y Werin a'i Theyrnas* (1909), *Y Ddinasyddiaeth Fawr* (1934), *Llafur a Senedd i Gymru* (1954) and *Silyn* (1956). The author and **Welsh-language** activist Angharad Tomos (b.1958) is his granddaughter.

THOMAS, David Vaughan (1873–1934) Composer
Ystalyfera-born David Vaughan Thomas was educated at **Oxford**, where he graduated in **mathematics** before turning to **music**. After working as a schoolmaster in **England**, he returned to Wales and became a freelance musician, developing a fastidious and cultivated style of composing. His study of early **Welsh** poetry inspired the composition of some fine songs, notably 'Saith o Ganeuon' and 'Berwyn'.

He also composed some large-scale choral works, of which *The Bard* is a notably advanced work of its kind by a Welsh composer. He was the father of **Wynford Vaughan Thomas**.

THOMAS, Dewi-Prys (1916–86) Architect
Born in **Liverpool**, of Welsh parents, Dewi-Prys Thomas studied **architecture** and town planning in that city, before joining **T. Alwyn Lloyd**'s office in **Cardiff**. He became a lecturer at the Liverpool School of Architecture in 1947. In 1960, he was appointed head of the **Welsh School of Architecture**; a superb lecturer, he was first professor of architecture in the **University of Wales**. He won the *Women's Journal* House of the Year Award in 1960, and was responsible (in conjunction with **Gwynedd County** Council architects) for the design of Pencadlys Gwynedd (1980–3) in **Caernarfon**. He was a brother-in-law of **Gwynfor Evans**, for whom he designed a house at **Llangadog**.

THOMAS, Dylan [Marlais] (1914–53)
Poet and prose-writer

One of the most innovative of 20th-century poets in the **English language**, Dylan Thomas was born in **Swansea** to a mother with roots in rural, **Welsh**-speaking **Carmarthenshire** and a disappointed schoolmaster father, with roots in **Cardiganshire**, who read **Shakespeare** and the **Bible** to him in his cradle, initiating, he said, his biblical tone and his lifelong obsession with words. He achieved early fame with the publication of *18 Poems* (1934) when he was only 20, followed by *Twenty-five Poems* (1936), which made his reputation and began the legend – which he encouraged – of the roistering, drunken and doomed poet. He was a

Dylan Thomas

performer all of his life, whether at his many readings in **Britain** and **North America**, or in pubs and bars.

He married Caitlin Macnamara in 1937 when he was 23, and though they remained together until his death, their relationship was alcoholic and mutually destructive. They and their two children lived hand-to-mouth in a number of places, finally settling in **Laugharne**, where a third child was born. Laugharne was the setting for many of his later poems such as 'Poem On his Birthday' and 'Over Sir John's Hill'. The popular favourite *Under Milk Wood* – a mould-breaking 'play for voices' comically depicting a day in the life of a quirky village – may have Laugharne as its background, although claims have been made that **New Quay** is Llaregyb. (Llareggub, a name to be read back to front, was the original spelling, but the spelling was sanitized following the death of the author.)

His early poems, influenced by **Gerard Manley Hopkins** and Hardy, were characterized by verbal density, sprung rhythms, internal rhyme, alliteration, unusual points of view and an obsession with the processes of birth and death, with his own body as microcosm; they are seen by many as a resumption of the Welsh bardic tradition in English. Other volumes, such as *The Map of Love* (1939) and *Deaths and Entrances* (1946), extended his poetic reputation; prose collections such as *Portrait of the Artist as a Young Dog* (1940) and *Quite Early One Morning* (1954) showed him capable of writing accomplished and moving short stories, such as 'The Peaches', and essays, such as 'A Child's Christmas in Wales'. Although immensely popular for a poet of his time, Thomas had to scramble for a living, writing few poems; two of his later ones, 'Fern Hill' and 'Do Not Go Gentle Into That Good Night', are among his most famous. These later, more accessible, poems substitute for a

The Boathouse, Dylan Thomas's home at Laugharne

youthful bravado in the face of death, an elegiac tone for loss of life and innocence. In the latter part of his life, he concentrated on readings and broadcasts; money problems and an unhappy home-life spurred Thomas to try to change his fortunes through four trips, touring and reading in America. He was a huge success with American audiences, but his erratic behaviour and his drinking worsened during these four journeys. In New York on 4 November 1954, when he was weak in body and confused in mind, morphine was administered to him. Thomas slipped into a coma and died five days later. He was buried in the churchyard in Laugharne, where his home, the Boat House, and the shed in which he wrote, are much visited by literary tourists.

THOMAS, Ebenezer (Eben Fardd; 1802–63) Poet

Born at Llanarmon (**Llanystumdwy**), Eben had little formal **education** and lived a troubled, drunken life before settling in **Clynnog** Fawr as a schoolmaster and later as a grocer. He learned his craft from the poets of his native **Eifionydd** and enjoyed early fame when his dramatic *awdl* 'Dinystr Jerusalem' won the chair at the **Powys Eisteddfod** at **Welshpool** in 1824. He won two further chairs (1840, 1858) but was unsuccessful with a religious epic, 'Yr Atgyfodiad', at **Rhuddlan** in 1850. Nevertheless, this rejected poem opened the floodgates to a remarkable deluge of religious and historical epics in the second half of the 19th century.

THOMAS, Eddie (1925–97) Boxer and manager

One of the most popular and successful personalities in the history of Welsh **boxing**, this **Merthyr Tydfil**-born miner won the Amateur Boxing Association lightweight title in 1946 and then, as a professional, became the British, European and Empire welterweight champion (1949–51). A classic boxer with perfect technique, his weight difficulties and damaged hands led to his retirement in 1952, and to new careers as a brilliant corner man and then as a manager. Two of his fighters, **Howard Winstone** (featherweight, 1968) and Ken Buchanan (lightweight, 1970–2), became world champions, and he almost succeeded with Colin Jones (welterweight, 1983). In Merthyr, he was a folk hero; Eddie Thomas, who might have become a **football**er, singer or dancer, ran an open-cast mine and became mayor in 1994. In 2000, a statue was erected in Merthyr in his honour.

THOMAS, Edward (1878–1917) Writer

Edward Thomas was born in **London** but he had family roots in Wales, to which he paid many visits in his childhood and youth. Those visits are reflected in his letters and in books such as *Beautiful Wales* (1905) and the semi-fictitious *The Happy-Go-Lucky Morgans* (1913). He was educated at **Oxford**, where he came under the influence of **O. M. Edwards**. In 1913, after some weeks of discussion with the American poet Robert Frost, and after a long walking tour in Wales, he turned to poetry and began writing poems. Enlisting in June 1915, he was killed near Arras in April 1917, just as his poems, published in **periodicals** under the name Edward Eastaway, were beginning to attract critical attention. The fullest collection of his poems was published in 1978. In many ways a quintessentially English poet in his love of landscape and pastoral scenes, Edward Thomas is now highly regarded for his accurate observation and his bleak but scrupulous honesty. Welsh poets influenced by him include **Alun Lewis**, **R. S. Thomas** and **Leslie Norris**.

THOMAS, Ernest Lewis (Richard Vaughan; 1904–83) Novelist

Born in **Llanddeusant**, he worked as a bank clerk, journalist and teacher in **London**, before retiring to **Talyllychau** in 1961. He is remembered mainly for the novels which became known as the 'Black Mountain Trilogy': *Moulded in Earth* (1951), *Who Rideth So Wild* (1952) and *Son of Justin* (1955), all of which are set on the border between **Carmarthenshire** and **Breconshire**, the setting also of possibly his best novel, *All Through the Night* (1957).

THOMAS, George (Viscount Tonypandy; 1909–97) Politician

Rhondda-born George Thomas represented constituencies in **Cardiff** from 1945 to 1983. He was s**ecretary of state for Wales** (1968–70) and speaker of the House of Commons (1976–83). In 1983, he was created Viscount Tonypandy. A determined campaigner for the reform of **urban leases** and a virulent opponent of Welsh **nationalism** and the principle of **devolution**, he was detested and revered in about equal measure by the people of Wales. He published a ghosted autobiography, *George Thomas, Mr Speaker* (1985).

THOMAS, Gwyn (1913–81) Writer

Born in Porth (**Rhondda**), Gwyn Thomas was educated at **Oxford**. He taught **French** at **Cardigan** and Spanish at **Barry**, and became a full-time writer in 1962. He published four collections of stories, nine novels, six stage plays, two volumes of essays and an autobiography, *A Few Selected Exits* (1968).

The focus of his writing is working-**class** life in the industrial valleys of **Glamorgan**, especially during the inter-war **Depression**, which he treats humorously, despite its fundamentally grim nature. All his characters speak the same colourful idiom, which relies on wit and hyperbole, and his writing is reminiscent of American writers such as Damon Runyon, whom he admired. After his death, his biographer, Michael Parnell, edited and published a further five volumes of his work.

THOMAS, H[ugh] H[amshaw] (1885–1962) Palaeobotanist

Chosen, during the Darwin-**Wallace** Centenary Year (1958), as one of the 20 biologists of the world who had made the most outstanding contributions to the understanding of evolution, **Wrexham**-born Hamshaw Thomas, FRS, was distinguished in two unrelated subjects. Educated at **Cambridge**, where he spent the remainder of his life, it was his work on the fossil **plants** of the Jurassic era of northern **England** that resulted in the Darwin-Wallace citation. He helped establish palaeobotany as a separate subject, rather than as a handmaiden to **geology**.

His pioneering work in geographical reconnaissance in Egypt, using aerial **photography**, proved of outstanding value during Allenby's campaign in 1918. During the **Second World War**, he was in charge of all RAF special photographic interpretation.

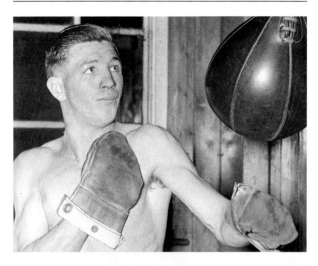

Eddie Thomas practising with a punchbag

THOMAS, Hugh Owen (1834–91) Orthopaedic surgeon

A member of a family of **Anglesey** bonesetters, he qualified in medicine and worked in **Liverpool**, where his small, private hospital, at which he treated impoverished patients, became world-famous. He emphasized the importance of resting fractured bones, and devised a splint that bears his name. His views were thought by many to be unorthodox, but eventually they became accepted. However, he never obtained a post at a general hospital. Sir **Robert Jones** (1857–1933), who originally worked with him, was his nephew.

THOMAS, Isaac (1911–2004) Scholar

Born in Tumble (**Llannon**) and educated at **Cardiff** and **Brecon**, Isaac Thomas was ordained into the **Congregational** ministry at Treorchy (*see* **Rhondda**) in 1935. He taught at his old college, the Memorial College, Brecon, from 1943 to 1958. From 1958 to 1978, he was a lecturer in Biblical studies at **Bangor**. The foremost expert on the history of the Welsh **Bible**, his academic publications displayed a mastery of the texts and of their translation into **Welsh**.

THOMAS, J[ohn] B[rinley] G[eorge] (1917–97) Rugby writer

A prolific writer on **rugby** football, **Pontypridd**-born J. B. G. Thomas was chief rugby writer of the *Western Mail* for 36 years from 1946. He was one of only two British journalists to cover the 1955 Lions tour, the first of eight successive tours that he followed up each time with a book. He wrote 28 books on rugby between 1954 and 1980, some of which, like *Great Rugger Players* (1955) and *Great Rugger Matches* (1959), attained classic status. Although he was often seen as too uncritical, too close to the Welsh Rugby Union and biased towards **Cardiff**, he was held in affection by generations of players.

THOMAS, John (Ieuan Ddu; 1795–1871) Musician and writer

Born at Pibyrlwyd (**Llangunnor**), John Thomas worked as schoolmaster in **Carmarthen**, **Merthyr Tydfil** and **Pontypridd**. A **Unitarian**, he co-edited *Y Gweithiwr/The*

John Thomas (*Pencerdd Gwalia*) with his triple harp

Workman, a **newspaper** which espoused **Robert Owen**'s **socialism**, Thomas pioneered choral singing, adjudicated, taught and composed **music**, and wrote **eisteddfod**ic essays. In 1845, he published *Y Caniedydd Cymreig*, the first inexpensive volume written to fill the need for Welsh song texts for eisteddfod and concert stages.

THOMAS, John (Pencerdd Gwalia; 1826–1913) Musician

John Thomas, designated *Pencerdd Gwalia* (chief musician of **Gwalia**) at the **Aberdare** National **Eisteddfod** in 1861, was born in **Bridgend**. The winner of a triple **harp** at the **Abergavenny** eisteddfod when he was 12, he was noticed by Ada, countess of Lovelace, the daughter of the poet Byron, whose patronage enabled him to spend six years at the Royal Academy of Music, **London**. In 1871, he was appointed harpist to Queen Victoria, and became professor of the harp at the Academy.

THOMAS, John (1838–1905) Photographer

Born in Cellan (**Llanfair Clydogau**), John Thomas spent most of his life in **Liverpool**. From his studio there, the Cambrian Gallery, and a later branch in **Llangollen**, he toured rural Wales photographing people and views, winning a reputation for his portraits of Welsh personalities (*see* **Photography**). He contributed articles and photographs to the magazine *Cymru*; **O. M. Edwards**'s collection of Thomas's negatives, acquired by the **National Library** in the 1920s, is the most important body of 19th-century Welsh photographs.

THOMAS, John Evan (1810–73) Sculptor

Born in **Brecon**, he was trained by Francis Chantrey in **London**. His bronze **sculpture** portraying the death of Tewdrig, king of **Gwent**, won a competition at the **eisteddfod** at **Abergavenny** in 1848. He was responsible for memorials to, among others, members of the **Morgan (Tredegar)**, **Stuart** and **Vivian** families. Among his most highly praised works was his sculpture of Prince Albert at **Tenby**. His brother, William Meredyth Thomas (1819–77), was also a sculptor. Many of his works have been lost, but he may have been responsible for the *Death of Tewdrig*, although it was signed by his brother. William's bust of **Thomas Price** (Carnhuanawc) won considerable acclaim.

THOMAS, Joshua (1719–97) Minister and historian

Born at Caio (**Cynwyl Gaeo**), Joshua Thomas joined the **Baptists** at Leominster while working as a mercer in **Herefordshire**. Ordained in 1746, he served in **Breconshire** until 1753 when he moved to Leominster where he was pastor for 43 years. He retained his links with Wales and was the author of a history of the Baptists, *Hanes y Bedyddwyr* (1778), which has been praised as much for the elegance of its prose as for its value as a work of ecclesiastical history.

THOMAS, Leyshon (Lleision ap Tomas; fl.1513–41) Abbot

The most prominent **Cistercian** abbot in Wales and the last at **Neath** Abbey (**Dyffryn Clydach**), he was educated at **Oxford** and graduated as a doctor of canon **law**. He was appointed a visitor to religious houses in Wales and **England**. On the abbey's **dissolution** (1539) he became rector of Cadoxton Juxta Neath (**Blaenhonddan**). Lewys Morgannwg (fl.1523–55) composed a grandiloquent *awdl* in his honour, praising Neath Abbey as the stronghold of **Welsh** culture.

THOMAS, Lucy (1781–1847) Coalowner

Lucy Thomas is traditionally considered the 'Mother of the Welsh Steam **Coal** Trade', because it was coal from the Waun Wyllt Colliery (Troed-y-rhiw, **Merthyr Tydfil**), opened by her husband Robert in 1824, that helped establish the reputation of Welsh coal in the **London** market in the early 1830s. Although Lucy Thomas, together with her son, took over the business after the death of her husband in 1835, it is probably more correct to credit George Insole, the **Cardiff** agent for the Waun Wyllt coal, as the architect of this success. Her granddaughter became the wife of **W. T. Lewis**.

THOMAS, Mansel (Treharne; 1909–86) Musician

Born at Pontygwaith (Tylorstown, **Rhondda**) and educated at the Royal Academy of **Music**, **London**, Mansel Thomas freelanced until he joined the music staff of the BBC Welsh Region in 1936. After war service, he was principal conductor of the BBC Welsh Orchestra (**BBC National Orchestra of Wales**) and then head of music, BBC Wales (1950–65). Although he was a fine pianist and conductor, composition was his chief love. His numerous and varied works, mainly songs and choral pieces, are accessible and attractive.

THOMAS, Margaret Haig (Viscountess Rhondda; 1883–1958) Feminist and businesswoman

The only child of **D. A. Thomas**, viscount Rhondda, and his wife **Sybil Margaret Thomas**, she inherited her father's title by special remainder following his death in 1918. A militant feminist, she founded the **Newport** branch of the **Women**'s Social and Political Union and was imprisoned for setting fire to the contents of a pillar box in the town. She vigorously, but unsuccessfully, claimed a seat in the House of Lords on her father's death; although life peeresses were allowed into the Lords in 1958, hereditary peeresses were excluded until 1963, five years after her death. She acted as her father's private secretary, assisting him in the running of the business empire she inherited on his death. In 1926, she became the first woman president of the Institute of Directors. In 1920, she founded the weekly journal *Time and Tide*, which she edited until 1926. Among her other publications were a biography of her father (1921) and the autobiographical *This Was My World* (1933).

THOMAS, [William] Miles [Webster] (1897–1980) Industrialist

Hailed as 'the world's most visionary airline executive', Miles Thomas was born in **Cefn**. His early career was in the automobile industry where he rose through the ranks to become managing director (1940–7) of Morris Motors. In 1948, he joined the British Overseas Airways Corporation, and served as chairman between 1949 and 1956, the period that saw the establishment of the comprehensive set of overseas routes that remain the greatest asset of British Airways, and which enabled Heathrow to become the world's busiest international **airport**. From 1956 to 1963, he was head of Monsanto **Chemicals**, a post which allowed him to re-establish links with his boyhood home (the company had established a chemical works at Cefn in 1867). From 1958 to 1967, he chaired the Development Corporation for Wales – the forerunner of the **Welsh Development Agency**. He was knighted in 1943 and made a life peer in 1971.

THOMAS, Owen (1812–91) Minister and author

Considered one of the greatest **preachers** of his age, Owen Thomas was born in **Holyhead** and reared in **Bangor**. He was ordained by the **Calvinistic Methodists** in 1844; he served at **Pwllheli**, **Newtown**, **London** and **Liverpool**. His biographies of the eminent preachers **John Jones** (Talysarn; 1796–1857) (1874) and **Henry Rees** (1890) vividly portray the theological debates of the period. He was the grandfather of **Saunders Lewis**.

THOMAS, Owen (1858–1923) Soldier and politician

Of archetypal **Nonconformist Anglesey** farming stock, Owen Thomas came to prominence as a progressive agriculturist and public figure aligned to the **Liberal Party**. Less conventional was his love of the army, first as captain of local militia, then in volunteering to fight in the Boer War (*see* **South African Wars**). Employed to survey the agricultural prospects of southern Africa, he later became managing director of a land development company in Kenya.

In 1914, **David Lloyd George** recognized his potential as a **Welsh**-speaking recruiter for the new **Welsh Army Corps**. Elevated to brigadier-general, Thomas addressed some 150 meetings, raising over 10,000 men. Too old for active service, in 1916 he was relieved of his training command in dubious circumstances. A knighthood restored his good name, but nothing could compensate for the loss of three sons in the **First World War**.

Rural **trade unionism** had raised working-**class** consciousness in Anglesey. Perhaps to get even with the 'establishment', Thomas stood as **Labour** parliamentary candidate in 1918, winning by 140 votes. Although a lacklustre politician, his enduring personal popularity secured his return as Independent Labour MP in 1922.

In the by-election that followed his death, Anglesey was regained by the Liberal Party.

THOMAS, Parry (John Godfrey Parry Thomas; 1885–1927) Engineer and racing driver

Thomas was the pre-eminent racing driver of his generation, and Wales's best to date. Remembered more for the sensational circumstances of his death than for his genius as a development engineer, he was born in **Wrexham**, and brought up in the vicarage at Bwlch-y-cibau (**Meifod**). He designed and built electrical transmissions for **London buses** and, as Leyland's chief engineer during the **First World War**, an advanced aero engine. His Leyland Eight car was considered superior to a Rolls-Royce, and his 1.5- and 7.2-litre Leyland-Thomas racing cars conquered Brooklands.

Parry Thomas became 'the fastest man on earth' with *Babs* on **Pendine** Sands in April 1926, when he averaged

John Evan Thomas, *The Death of Tewdrig* (1848)

Parry Thomas's restored *Babs*

171.624 mph (276.194 kph) over the measured mile (1.6093 km). Malcolm Campbell raised this record to 174.8 mph (281.3 kph) in February 1927. On 4 March 1927, Thomas took up the challenge. For an unknown reason, *Babs* veered off course at 180 mph (290 kph) and somersaulted, killing the driver. The car was buried in the sand, but it was exhumed by Owen Wyn-Jones in 1969, and gradually restored. It is an occasional exhibit at Pendine's Museum of Speed.

THOMAS, Percy [Edward] (1883–1969) Architect

Born in South Shields, Northumberland, the son of a sea captain from **Narberth**, Percy Thomas was articled to E. H. Bruton, **Cardiff**, before working in various offices in Bath and Lancashire. He won a competition for Cardiff's Technical College (1912), and on the basis of this he opened an office in Cardiff, with Ivor Jones. A number of competition successes followed, the chief being **Swansea**'s Guildhall, completed in 1936. In 1937, the partnership with Jones was ended, and Thomas developed his office to become the largest in Wales. He was knighted in 1946, and the practice, henceforth Sir Percy Thomas and Son, expanded to include **education**al, hospital and factory commissions, and opened an office in Swansea. The vast number of buildings for which he and his practice was responsible include the Temple of Peace in Cardiff, much of the college campuses at **Aberystwyth** and Swansea, and the Abbey works of the **Steel Company of Wales** (*see also* **Port Talbot**). Percy Thomas, in 1935, was the first Welshman to be elected president of the Royal Institute of British Architects.

THOMAS, R[onald] S[tuart] (1913–2000) Poet

Born in **Cardiff** and raised in **Holyhead**, R. S. Thomas was a year older than **Dylan Thomas**, but died 47 years later than the younger man; his substantial body of poetry made him the rival in reputation of his more famous namesake, whose antithesis as a person he was. Gaunt, austere and forbidding, he despised the garrulous, sociable and Anglicized culture of Dylan's industrialized south Wales. A committed **nationalist** (as well as a crusading **pacifist** and conservationist), he identified Welshness solely with the **Welsh-language** culture upon whose ancient tradition of epigrammatically terse *cynghanedd* poetry he partly modelled his own minimalist writing. Having learnt Welsh as an adult, Thomas would write only prose in his acquired 'native' language. He resented having to write his poetry in **English** – which, in his eyes, made him automatically an English poet – yet relished the richness of that language.

In this way, as in many another, he lived in a Yeatsian state of chronic internal division, out of which his highly charged poetry was fashioned.

Thomas was a turbulent priest in the **Church in Wales** and his poetry, crudely divisible into two periods, reflected his experiences. In the first, from *The Stones of the Field* (1946) to *Not that He Brought Flowers* (1968), his attention was obsessively fixed on the enigmatic figure of his imaginary Welsh upland farmer, Iago Prytherch, the product of Thomas's shocked exposure to rural life in the raw in **Manafon**, a **Montgomeryshire parish** not far from the **border** with **England**. Through his protracted and one-sided colloquy with the mute Prytherch, Thomas was able to call into question all the usual explanations of life's ultimate purpose

– including his own Christian beliefs. Such soul-scouring questioning was continued in the poetry of the second period, which opened with *H'm* (1972) and concluded with *No Truce with the Furies* (1995), the final collection whose defiant title suggests the continuing, Lear-like torment of his ageing mind. It was an inscrutable God who haunted his baffled imagination in this period, during which he wrote an existential poetry of religious quest, experimentally modern in idiom and verging on the mystical in experience, which may be looked upon as his greatest achievement.

For much of the second period, he lived at the furthermost tip of the **Llŷn** peninsula, where – at **Aberdaron** village and later at Rhiw (Aberdaron) – the ancient rocks attuned his mind to the eternal, but whose threatened Welsh-language culture made him urgently aware of the politics of the present and moved him to active campaigning on behalf of the causes in which he believed. Allergic to most aspects of modern life, in which he saw the malign narcissism of the human ego writ large, Thomas chose to speak of himself disparagingly in the third person in his dissenting autobiography, *Neb* (No one) (1985). Yet his had been a commanding and controversial presence on the Welsh scene, and his international reputation was reflected in his (unsuccessful) nomination for a Nobel Prize. A volume of uncollected poems, *Residues*, was published posthumously in 2003 (ed. M. Wynn Thomas).

His first wife, whom he married in 1940 (they were together until her death), was the **London**-born painter and illustrator Elsie Mildred Eldridge (1909–91).

THOMAS, Rachel (1905–95) Actress

Rachel Thomas was frequently cast in '**Welsh Mam**' roles, but also played numerous unsympathetic characters, such as Bella in BBC Wales's *Pobol y Cwm* (from 1974 to 1992). Born in Alltwen (**Cilybebyll**), she made her **film** debut in *The Proud Valley* (1940), and was a splendidly vengeful amateur contralto in Gilbert Gunn's comedy *Valley of Song* (1953). Her most significant role was that of Mrs Morgan in the BBC television version of *How Green Was My Valley* (1960).

THOMAS, Robert (1926–99) Sculptor

A strong belief in human dignity distinguishes the work of **Rhondda**-born Robert Thomas, who started his working life as an apprentice electrician before training at **Cardiff** School of Art and the Royal College of Art, **London**. He taught in **England**, returning to Wales in 1972. Among his many commissions were *Captain Cat* in **Swansea**'s maritime quarter, *Aneurin Bevan* in Cardiff and the *Rhondda Mining Family* at Llwynypia (Rhondda).

THOMAS, Robert David (Iorthryn Gwynedd; 1817–88) Minister and writer

A radical **Nonconformist**, who wrote widely on **religion**, **emigration** and **education**. Born in **Llanrwst**, and a minister at Penarth (**Llanfair Caereinion**), Thomas emigrated to the United States in 1855, and became a much respected figure there. He served Welsh churches in New York, Ohio, **Pennsylvania** and Tennessee, and regularly contributed prose and poetry to the Welsh-American press. His most important publication is *Hanes Cymry America* (1872), a valuable survey of Welsh settlements largely based on information gathered during his extensive travels in the United States.

THOMAS, Robert Jermain (1840–66) Missionary

Early death from tropical diseases was often the fate of 19th-century **missionaries**, but Robert Jermain Thomas suffered a grimmer end. Sent by the **London** Missionary Society to China in 1863, the **Rhayader**-born **Congregationalist** made a foray into Korea in 1865, to acquaint himself with the language. The first **Protestant** missionary to visit Korea, he tried to enter the country a second time in 1866, but everyone aboard his ship was captured and killed by the Koreans. In 1931, a memorial church was built near the spot in Pyongyang where he died.

THOMAS, Sidney Gilchrist (1850–85) Industrial chemist

Only a small proportion of the **iron** ore of western Europe was suitable for steelmaking in the early days (*c.*1860–80) of the Bessemer and Siemens-Martin inventions (*see* **Open Hearth Furnace**). Thomas, a **London** legal clerk of **Cardiganshire** stock, an enthusiastic amateur chemist, and his cousin Percy Gilchrist (1851–1935), the works chemist at **Blaenavon**, perfected at Blaenavon the 'basic process' in the late 1870s, which involved lining the furnace with dolomitic **limestone** and a fireproof tar mixture. The resulting basic steel was increasingly to dominate the industry, as acid steelmaking declined in significance. Because steelmaking would depend no longer upon the limited reserves of low phosphoric haematite ore, the basic process greatly widened the potential of steel as the world's major construction material. In particular, it led to the vast expansion of the Ruhr; indeed, without Blaenavon, Germany would have been unable to wage the **First World War**.

R. S. Thomas, experimenting with a smile

William Thomas (Islwyn)

'Basic slag', a major by-product of the process, was to find its own market as an important source of agricultural fertilizer. There is a monument commemorating the cousins' discovery at Blaenavon. Thomas had conducted his early experiments in his bedroom; the fumes he inhaled led to his death at the age of 35.

THOMAS, Sybil Margaret (Viscountess Rhondda; 1857–1941) Liberal and feminist

Born Sybil Margaret Haig at Pen Ithon (**Llanbadarn Fynydd**), in 1882 she married the industrialist and politician **D. A. Thomas**. She made a significant contribution to the Welsh Union of **Women Liberal** Associations, founded in 1891; during her presidency, the union pursued a strongly feminist and pro-suffrage agenda. She was associated both with the moderate and militant wings of the suffrage movement. In 1914, she deliberately sought imprisonment by holding a public meeting outside the Houses of Parliament and was sentenced to one day's imprisonment. Her daughter was the feminist **Margaret Haig Thomas**.

THOMAS, T[homas] H[enry] (Arlunydd Penygarn; 1839–1915) Artist

As well as **painting**, lecturing and writing, T. H. Thomas was a dynamic campaigner on Welsh cultural issues. Born in **Pontypool**, where his father, Thomas Thomas (1805–81), was principal of the **Baptist** College, he received his art **education** at Bristol and **London**, and through travelling to Paris and Rome.

Returning to London in 1861, he devoted himself chiefly to portraiture, **design** and book illustration, but he maintained his Welsh links, exhibiting at the **Cardiff** Art and Industry Exhibition of 1870. Settling in Cardiff in the 1880s, he became involved in the campaign for a **National Museum**. He designed medals and insignia for a number of National *Eisteddfodau* and advocated a reappraisal of **Celt**ic art, particularly of the stone carvings of the 5th to the 11th centuries (*see* **Monuments, Early Christian**).

THOMAS, Thomas (Glandwr; 1817–88)
Architect and minister

Llandeilo-born Thomas Thomas was ordained in 1846 and became minister of Hebron, **Clydach**. He also worked as a building inspector and rebuilt his own chapel in 1848; he went on to design other chapels (mostly **Congregationalist**) in the **Swansea** area. His influence spread to the point that he became one of the most prolific chapel architects in Wales, with at least 119 chapels to his credit, and designed chapels as far afield as **Liverpool**, **London**, Shrewsbury and Durham. Thomas popularized the so-called 'halo' arch based on the broken pediment of San Andrea in Mantua, Italy.

THOMAS, [James William] Tudor (1893–1976)
Ophthalmic surgeon

Born in Cwmgiedd (**Ystradgynlais**), Tudor Thomas was educated at the Welsh National School of Medicine (*see* **Wales College of Medicine, Biology, Life and Health Sciences**) in **Cardiff**, and the Middlesex Hospital, **London**. He took up eye surgery early in his career, and moved to Cardiff as a consultant and lecturer in ophthalmology at the medical school. There, he undertook his outstanding pioneering work in corneal grafting. This technique is now widely used as a means of treatment for blindness caused by diseases of the cornea. He was knighted in 1956.

THOMAS, Watcyn [Gwyn] (1906–77) Rugby player

Capped 14 times between 1927 and 1933, in 1933 **Llanelli**-born Watcyn Thomas captained the first Welsh side ever to win at Twickenham. A mobile and robust forward, he played most of the game against **Scotland** in 1931 with a broken collar bone – and scored a try. A schoolteacher, he played for **Swansea**, Llanelli, and Waterloo (Lancashire) and wrote a colourful autobiography, *Rugby-Playing Man* (1977).

THOMAS, William (Islwyn; 1832–78) Poet

Born at the foot of Mynydd Islwyn in **Ynysddu**, **Monmouthshire**, Islwyn's home language was **English**, but he wrote the greater part of his poetry in **Welsh**. His father intended him to become a surveyor but, in 1859, he was ordained as a **Calvinistic Methodist** minister, although he never accepted a pastorate. In 1853, his fiancée Ann Bowen died, aged 20, a traumatic shock that overshadowed the rest of his life and was the stimulus for his major, free-metre, two-poem work, 'Y Storm' (1854–6), a discursive, comprehensive epic of the soul, asserting eternal providence and, like Milton, intending to 'justify the ways of God to men'. Its multi-layered meditation on the storm metaphor stands unique in 19th-century Welsh **literature**. Islwyn then returned to his earlier role as an **eisteddfod** poet and adjudicator (without winning a prize in the National Eisteddfod), together with preaching and editing poetry columns in the press. On his deathbed, he is reported to have said to his wife, 'Thank you, Martha, for all you did for me. You have been very kind. I am going to Ann now.' Babell chapel, Ynysddu, houses an Islwyn museum.

THOMAS, William (1890–1974)
Chemist and educationist
Maenclochog-born William Thomas's academic record at **Aberystwyth**, Groningen, **Cambridge** and Aberdeen, together with his research publications and *Complex Salts* (1924) marked him as an outstanding young teacher and scholar. With an abiding conviction that if Welsh life were to flourish it urgently needed more applied scientists, he turned to **education**, first as principal of the new Technical College at **Wrexham**. He then joined the inspectorate of the **Welsh Department of the Board of Education**, pioneering two advisory councils for further education – for north and south Wales – and thus laying the foundation of a comprehensive structure of technical education.

THOMAS, Wynford Vaughan (1908–87)
Broadcaster and writer
A son of the composer **David Vaughan Thomas**, Swansea-born Wynford joined the staff of the BBC in 1937. As a war correspondent, he witnessed from the air the bombing of German cities and was one of the first journalists to reach Belsen. Among his books are *Anzio* (1962), *Madly in All Directions* (1967), *Portrait of Gower* (1975), *The Countryside Companion* (1979) and *Wales: a History* (1985). The television series *The Dragon Has Two Tongues*, which he presented with **Gwyn Alfred Williams**, was a remarkable exercise in history as dialectic. He is commemorated at Ceibwr Bay, **Nevern** and near Dylife (**Llanbrynmair**), on the **mountain road** between **Machynlleth** and **Llanidloes**.

THOMPSON, James Pyke (1846–97)
Corn merchant, art collector and philanthropist
Of a family described as having done more 'in the way of generous benefactions than probably any other family in south Wales', Pyke Thompson was born in Bridgwater, Somerset. He joined his father as director and later chairman of Spiller & Co., **Cardiff**, one of the largest milling companies in **Britain**. A philanthropist who was committed to the artistic life of Cardiff, he built the Turner House gallery near his home in **Penarth** in order to make his collection of **paintings** available to the public. Among his many benefactions were £3000 to Cardiff's Municipal Museum and £6000 towards the cost of erecting the **National Museum** building in **Cathays Park**. The Turner House gallery was handed over to the Museum in 1921. In 1924, members of the Thompson family presented the land around their house, Preswylfa in Canton, to the city of Cardiff; it became Thompson's Park.

THOMSON, Archer (James Merriman Archer Thomson; 1863–1912) Rock-climber
A teacher at Friars School, in his native **Bangor**, Archer Thomson began exploring Welsh cliffs in 1894 when the standards achieved there were far behind those reached in the English Lake District. Thomson's climbs ventured out on to the great open rock faces of **Snowdonia** and were of a severity that caused him to be ranked foremost among the climbers of his day. Appointed headmaster of **Llandudno County** School in 1896, he was famously taciturn in character. In 1912 – a year in which many of his friends died in **mountain** accidents – he committed suicide.

THREE CASTLES (Teirtref) Lordship
The territories of the three castles of northern **Gwent** – White (**Llantilio Crossenny**), **Grosmont** and Skenfrith (**Llangattock-Vibon-Avel**) – although established for differing reasons, were welded into a single lordship. Along with the neighbouring lordship of **Monmouth**, Three Castles became part of the duchy of Lancaster (*see* **Lancaster family**).

THREE FEATHERS, The
The badge of three ostrich feathers within a coronet, with the motto *Ich Dien*, appears first with certainty as the badge of Edward VI (1537–53) when heir apparent to the English throne. Edward, who became king aged nine, was not created **Prince of Wales**, and the badge should perhaps be called that of the heir apparent, but since the latter is usually created Prince of Wales it is generally referred to as the 'Prince of Wales's feathers'. It is often seen as an emblem of Wales – it is used by the Welsh **Rugby Union**, for example.

Wynford Vaughan Thomas

A single feather with the same motto was used by earlier princes, especially Edward the Black Prince (1312–77). Although it has sometimes been claimed that the motto comes from the Welsh *Eich Dyn* (Your man), it is in fact German and means 'I serve'.

THREE WALES MODEL, The

The 'Three Wales Model' describes what are purported to be three distinct political areas. 'Y Fro Gymraeg', which has a high proportion of **Welsh**-speakers, is the region in which **Plaid Cymru** enjoys its greatest support. 'Welsh Wales' – the south Wales **coal**field – is **Labour**'s electoral heartland. 'British Wales' consists of the south-eastern and north-eastern coastal belts, **Pembrokeshire** and the regions of mid Wales **border**ing **England**; it is the area in which the **Conservative Party** has a considerable following and where it was dominant for much of the 1980s and 1990s. The source of the model is a 1979 survey on identity conducted under the leadership of Denis Balsom and carried out at the **University of Wales**, **Aberystwyth**. Overall, 57% of the electorate believed itself to be Welsh, 34% British and 8% **English**. Identification with Wales was broadly similar in 'Y Fro Gymraeg' and in 'Welsh Wales' (62.1% and 63%); it was markedly lower in 'British Wales' (50.5%). In 'Y Fro Gymraeg', the prevalence of the Welsh language strengthened identification with Wales; in 'Welsh Wales', that identification was strengthened by the fact that the vast majority of the inhabitants of that region had been born in Wales.

A flyer advertising the film *Tiger Bay*, 1959

This distinctive regionality was reflected in the **devolution** referendum (1997), when support for a 'yes' vote was significantly stronger in 'Y Fro Gymraeg' and 'Welsh Wales' than in 'British Wales'. By 2002, however, when 57% of the electors of 'Y Fro Gymraeg', 58% of those of 'Welsh Wales' and 54% of those of 'British Wales' supported enhanced powers for the **National Assembly**, it appeared that the differences between the three regions were declining.

TIERS CROSS, Pembrokeshire
(1955 ha; 471 inhabitants)

Located immediately south-west of **Haverfordwest**, the **community** contains the villages of Tiers Cross, Dreenhill and Thornton and constitutes the least interesting part of **Pembrokeshire**. From the age of 2–16 months, **David Lloyd George** lived at Bulford Farm. He was taken to **Llanystumdwy** following his father's death in June 1864. His son, **Gwilym Lloyd George** (1894–1967), took the title of Viscount **Tenby** of Bulford.

TIGER BAY (1959) Film

This superbly filmed thriller was set partly in **Cardiff**'s dockland and shot in various Welsh locations, including Cardiff, **Newport** and **Talybont-on-Usk**. Hayley Mills, in her prizewinning screen debut, plays a tomboy who witnesses a killing and protects the culprit (a Polish seaman played by Horst Buchholz), despite the earnest efforts of a **police** detective (John Mills). The **film** was directed by J. Lee Thompson who also, with the producer John Hawkesworth, wrote the script. There are memorable cameos from Welsh members of the cast, **Meredith Edwards**, **Rachel Thomas** and **Kenneth Griffith**, and from Megs Jenkins and Yvonne Mitchell. Photographed in rich black and white by Eric Cross, the film is a valuable record of the capital city's Loudoun Square in its more prosperous days when it was the hub of the docks community.

TINKER, David (1924–2000)
Artist and educationist

David Tinker was born in **London** and moved to **Cardiff** in 1949 to teach at the Art School. Although chiefly a painter, his work included printmaking, stage design and **sculpture**. An active polemicist, organizer and co-founder of the 56 Group (*see* **Fifty-six Group**), Tinker was eager to bring modern ideas into teaching and practice. He advocated the public application of art and completed murals for the Great Hall at **Aberystwyth**, where he lectured, and for the exterior of the **public library** at **Haverfordwest**.

TINPLATE

Tinplate, or tinned plate, developed as a significant industry in the western part of the south Wales **coal**field during the later 19th century, although it had its beginning in the early 18th century when John **Hanbury** patented the rolling process at **Pontypool**. It was not until steel (*see* **Iron and Steel**) superseded iron as the base metal plate, and markets emerged in the later 19th century for utensils to preserve **foods**, that the industry began to realize its potential. Although works such as the Upper Forest, Dafen, **Briton Ferry**, Morfa, and Cwmfelin were established in the **Llanelli** to **Aberavon** belt, it was not until **Wilhelm Siemens**

The Trostre tinplate works, Llanelli

had introduced his **open-hearth furnace** at Landore, **Swansea**, in 1868 that the industry began to manufacture an acceptable product.

By 1891, when the **McKinley Tariff** threatened to deal the industry a mortal blow, there were 71 works manufacturing tinplate in south Wales, mainly around Llanelli ('Tinopolis'), Swansea, **Neath** and Aberavon. By 1914, production had more than recovered from the damaging effects of the tariff. As some works closed, others emerged as market leaders, through absorption and merger. By 1939, the industry was dominated by nine firms, all of which also made their own steel sheets: **Richard Thomas**; Baldwins; **Grovesend**; Gilbertsons; Briton Ferry; Llanelli Associated; Partridge, Jones and Paton; Bynea (**Llanelli Rural**); Upper Forest and Worcester; and Elba. In 1936, Richard Thomas, by far the leading producer, reopened the **Ebbw Vale** works with **Britain**'s first continuous strip mill. There were also 29 independent tinplate concerns.

At the end of the **Second World War**, the companies **Richard Thomas** and Baldwins amalgamated (*see* **Richard Thomas and Baldwins Ltd**) with a view to establishing a continuous strip mill with cold reduction and tinplating facilities – a process which had already revolutionized the industry in the United States. It was the **Steel Company of Wales**, created in 1947, that saw the plan through, establishing continuous strip mills at **Trostre** (Llanelli; 1953) and **Velindre** (Llangyfelach; 1956) – although electrolytic tinplating had already begun at Ebbw Vale in 1948.

These developments marked the beginning of the end of hot-dip tinplating and the old handmills, most of which had closed by 1961, and signalled major improvements in productivity. The labour force fell from an average of 29,000 in the 1930s, to 7500 in the mid-1960s and 2200 in

1998. After the closure of Velindre in 1989, Trostre and Ebbw Vale (until 2002, when Ebbw Vale closed) were able to provide all of Britain's annual average output of around 700,000 tonnes.

TINTERN (Tyndyrn), Monmouthshire
(1737 ha; 732 inhabitants)

A **community** located in a delectable part of the lower **Wye** valley. Tintern Abbey was the earliest **Cistercian** foundation in Wales; it kept its distance from sister foundations in the lands under native Welsh rule. Founded in 1131 by Walter de **Clare**, lord of **Strigoil**, or **Chepstow**, its original 12th-century church was replaced in the late 13th century by the glorious building erected under the patronage of Roger **Bigod** III, a later lord of Strigoil. The monastery gave rise to daughter houses in Gloucestershire and Wexford.

With an annual income of £192, which in 1535 sustained merely 13 monks, Tintern was the wealthiest Welsh monastery. At the **dissolution**, the abbey passed to the earl of Worcester (*see* **Somerset family**). In the 1540s, the **lead** was stripped from the roofs and sold, and the buildings were left as a spectacular ruin. From the mid-18th century onwards, the site attracted large numbers of visitors, its 'picturesque' appeal contributing to the increasingly popular Wye valley tour. William Wordsworth's visits in 1793 and 1798 gave rise to one of the best-known poems in the **English language**.

The availability of waterpower, charcoal, **iron** ore and transportation on the Wye allowed Tintern to become an important early industrial site. The **Tintern Brass Foundry**, founded in 1568, lasted in some form until 1900, making it by far the longest-lived of all Welsh industrial undertakings. Other enterprises include the Tintern Abbey Blast Furnace,

Tintern Abbey

the Middle and Upper Wireworks and the Pont y Saeson Forge. Several sites are now well displayed, making a visit to industrial Tintern as stimulating as a visit to monastic Tintern.

TINTERN BRASS FOUNDRY, Monmouthshire

A scheme for making brass was initiated in 1565 by William Humphrey, the assay master of the Royal **Mint** and, by 1568, a foundry – which would make brass in a new way – had been built near the unlikely setting of the ruined **Tintern** Abbey. To provide the expertise to teach the complexities of brass making, Christopher Schutz of Saxony was recruited. Although brass making was gradually displaced on this site by the easier production of **iron** wire, Tintern's significance was recognized in 1957 when the National Brass Founders Association erected a plaque recording that 'near this place in the year 1568 brass was first made by alloying **copper** and zinc'.

TIPPING, H. Avray (1855–1933)
Architect and landscape designer

Although best known for his architectural articles in *Country Life*, English-born Tipping made a significant contribution to houses and **gardens** in Wales. He was assisted, on the architectural side, by the young **Chepstow** architect Eric Francis (1887–1976). Tipping lived in **Monmouthshire**, initially at **Mathern** Palace, which he restored and enlarged from 1894, and subsequently at Mounton (Mathern; 1912) and High Glanau (**Mitchel Troy**; 1923), both of which he built, surrounding them with delightful gardens. Tipping also advised on **housing** at Bulwark (1919), Chepstow, and, together with Francis, designed houses at Rhiwbina Garden Village, **Cardiff**.

TIR IARLL Lordship

A demesne lordship within the lordship of **Glamorgan**, Tir Iarll ('the earl's land') lay between the Afan and Garw **rivers** and was centred upon **Llangynwyd**. The territory

was probably annexed by Robert, earl of Gloucester (d.1147).

TIR RALPH Lordship

Tir Ralph, named after its lord, Ralph **Mortimer**, was the eastern part of **Cantref Mawr**. Centred on the castle at Pencelli (**Talybont-on-Usk**), it was divided into English Pencelli, in the valley of the **Usk**, and Welsh Pencelli, a **mountain**ous region extending south to the boundary between the lordships of **Brecon** and **Glamorgan**.

TIRYMYNACH, Ceredigion
(1452 ha; 1888 inhabitants)

Located immediately north of **Aberystwyth**, the **community** contains the villages of Bow Street, Clarach, Dole, Llangorwen and Pen-y-garn. Tirymynach (the monks' land) was a one-time grange of Strata Florida Abbey (*see* **Ystrad Fflur**). Bow Street is an example of the use of **London** names in **Ceredigion** (*compare* Chancery, Constitution Hill, Temple Bar and Llundain-fach). All Saints, Llangorwen (1841), the first church to be designed by William Butterfield, was commissioned by the Williams family of Cwmcynfelyn, one of whose members, the poet Isaac Williams (1802–65), was a leading figure in the **Oxford Movement**. The church was the first in rural Wales to reflect the movement's beliefs. The building of a holiday village at Clarach has not improved what was a charming bay. To the north is Sarn Gynfelyn, a ridge of glacial deposits which runs out to sea for several kilometres from Wallog.

TITHE and THE TITHE WAR

Tithe, the one-tenth of agricultural produce payable to the church, has deep biblical roots. Originally paid in kind, there was an increasing tendency to commute tithe into money payments. The process was made universal by the Commutation of Tithe Act (1836), which led to the production of **maps** and apportionments providing an unrivalled source of information concerning the countryside of Wales in the 1830s and 1840s. As the majority of the farmers were, by then, **Nonconformists** who paid from their own pockets to maintain their own denominations, they increasingly resented the obligation to contribute to the maintenance of a denomination – the **Anglican** Church – to which they did not belong. Furthermore, the tithes of many **parishes** had come into the possession of lay people; for example, the Chichester family of Devon was the hereditary owner of the tithe of nine **Cardiganshire** parishes, parishes which provided the family with almost £5500 a year in the mid-19th century. The issue was exacerbated by the agricultural depression that began in the 1870s.

In the 1880s, widespread refusal to pay tithe led to the enforced auction of the goods of anti-tithe debtors – occasions that could lead to violence. 'Tithe Wars' occurred in many parts of Wales, but they were most widespread in the neighbourhood of **Denbigh**, an area where farmers were much influenced by **Thomas Gee** of Denbigh and his **newspaper** *Baner ac Amserau Cymru*. Among the most celebrated riots were those at **Llangwm** in May 1887, **Mochdre** in June 1887 and **Llannefydd** (all in the original **Denbighshire**) in May 1888. Following the Llangwm riots, 31 protestors were summoned to court. At Mochdre, 84 people were injured, 35 **police**men among them. The protestors were supported by the young **David Lloyd George** and by **T. E. Ellis**, who saw a chance to bring Wales on to a wider political stage. To the authorities, Gee's Welsh Land League seemed frighteningly similar to the land agitation then being led in **Ireland** by Michael Davitt, and the **Conservative** press made much of the sufferings of the Welsh clergy, impoverished by the unwillingness of tithe payers to maintain them. The skirmishes diminished as the depression temporarily lifted, and the protestors' tactics

were frustrated by the Tithe Act 1891, which transferred the responsibility for paying tithes from the tenant to the landowner. It thus became part of the rent, the withholding of which could lead to eviction. Tithe in Wales was essentially abolished following the **disestablishment** of the Anglican Church in 1920.

TOMKINS, Thomas (1572–1656) Musician
Born in **St David's**, Tomkins held positions at Worcester Cathedral and the Chapel Royal, **London**. He wrote church, keyboard and consort **music**, and his best work is considered of European stature. A large number of his anthems and services for the **Anglican** liturgy were published posthumously in *Musica Deo Sacra* (1668). His only collection of madrigals, *Songs of 3, 4, 5 and 6 parts* (1622), includes his masterpiece, 'When David heard that Absalom was slain'.

TONNA, Neath Port Talbot
(754 ha; 2465 inhabitants)
Located immediately north-east of **Neath**, the **community**'s uplands contain a **Roman** marching camp and a wealth of prehistoric monuments. A picturesque hamlet until the later 19th century, when it acquired **coal**mines and **tinplate** works, Tonna was in many ways the twin of Aberdulais (**Blaenhonddan**), on the other bank of the **Nedd**. Its elegant neo-Gothic St Anne's church (1893) contains memorials to inhabitants of both villages. The Ivy Tower, a summerhouse built *c.*1780, was one of the Gnoll Estate follies (*see* **Neath**).

TONYPANDY RIOTS, The
The rioting in the main street of Tonypandy (**Rhondda**) on 8 November 1910 led to the destruction of over 60 shops, one death (that of Samuel Rays) and extensive fighting

Cambrian Combine strikers before the Tonypandy Riots

T

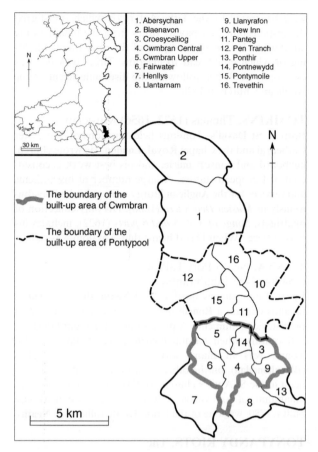

The boundary of the built-up area of Cwmbran

The boundary of the built-up area of Pontypool

1. Abersychan
2. Blaenavon
3. Croesyceiliog
4. Cwmbran Central
5. Cwmbran Upper
6. Fairwater
7. Henllys
8. Llantarnam
9. Llanyrafon
10. New Inn
11. Panteg
12. Pen Tranch
13. Ponthir
14. Pontnewydd
15. Pontymoile
16. Trevethin

5 km

The communities of the borough and county of Torfaen

with the **police**. The rioting happened in the wake of a strike over payment for work in abnormal places at the **coal**mines of the Cambrian Combine (*see* **D. A. Thomas**). A large contingent of police was already defending strike-breakers and colliery property, and, when many more came from **London**, the anger of the strikers boiled over. The home secretary, **Winston Churchill**, was reluctant to answer the call from local magistrates, coalowners and **Glamorgan**'s chief constable for troops, but eventually consented, and, in consequence, much of the southern coalfield experienced several months of military occupation. Although the strike ended in October 1911, without the strikers having achieved their aims, the dispute, and the violence, encouraged miners throughout **Britain** – in what became a new era of militancy – to fight first for a minimum wage, which was partially achieved in 1912, and then for further improvements. The riots at Tonypandy were widely reported and came to have a mythical status in Wales as a manifestation of militancy among industrial workers and of the expression of working-**class** solidarity. The suspicion of Winston Churchill in industrial Wales, aroused by the riots, proved long-standing.

TONYREFAIL, Rhondda Cynon Taff
(2454 ha; 11,035 inhabitants)
Located immediately south of the **Rhondda**, the **community** occupies the upper reaches of the valley of the **Ely**. Once a dairy-farming and livestock-rearing area, many early farmhouses survive. Industrialization began in the late

18th century, around a corn mill and a **woollen** factory. Deep **coal**mining came late but on a large scale. At its peak, Coedely Colliery (1910–85) employed nearly 1800 men, and led to the expansion of Tonyrefail village and the establishment of the colliery settlements of Coedely, Thomastown and Bryngolau. Capel y Ton (1863), which closed in 2002, is a distinctive building, as are the secondary school (1933) and the Community Resource Centre (1993). Choirs led by Richard Williams have given Tonyrefail a distinguished **music**al reputation.

TORFAEN County borough, constituency and one-time district (12,618 ha; 90,949 inhabitants)
In 1974, Torfaen – an alternative name for Afon Lwyd – became the name of one of the five districts of the new **county** of **Gwent**. It represented the merging of the **urban districts** of **Pontypool** (including **Abersychan**), **Cwmbran** and **Blaenavon** and parts of adjoining **rural districts**, and brought the whole of Gwent's Eastern valley under a single authority. With the abolition of the county of Gwent in 1996, the district became the Torfaen **county borough**. The name is also that of a constituency. In 2001, 14.4% of the inhabitants of Torfaen had some knowledge of **Welsh**, the percentages varying from 16.93% in Fairwater (*see* Cwmbran) to 11.77% in Pontymoile (*see* **Pontypool**); 6.68% of the county borough's inhabitants were wholly fluent in the language.

TORY PARTY, The
From 1689 until the mid-19th century, the Tories were one of the two great parliamentary and political parties in Wales and **England**, the other being the **Whigs**. Oddly, the word comes from the Irish *toraidhe*, meaning 'outlaw'. The party had its origins amongst the Royalists of the 17th century and, until the accession of George III in 1760, it was closely associated with the exiled Stuarts. The true Tory believed that royal authority was God-given and rebellion against the crown sinful. The party spoke for the interests of the **gentry**, staunchly supported the authority of Church and State, and impeded all attempts to extend political and religious liberty. By the 1830s, the term 'Tory' had been superseded by '**Conservative**', although the more traditionalist right-wingers still relish the word.

TOURISM
In 2007, it was claimed that the tourist industry contributed over £3 billion annually to the Welsh **economy** – 3.7% of the country's Gross Domestic Product (GDP) – and provided employment for 76,000 tourism workers. It may thus be considered to be one of Wales's largest industries.

While medieval pilgrims (*see* **Pilgrimage**) were tourists of a sort, modern tourism in Wales began in the late 18th century when **English** gentlefolk, denied their Grand Tour because of conflict in mainland Europe, were obliged to seek out oases of the exotic within **Britain**. Inspired by **Romanticism**, these well-heeled travellers, often with an artist in tow, made the 'Tour into Wales' fashionable and left a legacy of landscape **paintings** together with a canon of tourism **literature** (*see also* **Landforms, Landscape and Topography**), advertising to a wider world the charms of a hitherto little-known **mountain**ous realm. Most of these travel journals expatiate lyrically upon the breathtaking rugged scenery and the primitive virtues of the quaint, if somewhat backward, natives. Some travellers, however, found it impossible to hide their disdain for the Welsh, and they poured scorn on the natives' awkward appearance, uncouth behaviour and vulgar language. Joseph Hucks, travelling with his friend Samuel Taylor Coleridge, offered in 1795 the following unflattering description of the **Welsh language**: 'To my ear, I must confess, it is not very harmonious but resembles rather the ravishing sound of a cat-call, or the musical clack of a flock of geese when highly irritated.' Even so, there were English travellers who showed genuine appreciation of the people as well as of the country, most notably **George Borrow**.

With the **Industrial Revolution** giving rise to a prosperous middle class and to improved communications, tourism burgeoned. The early 19th century saw the emergence of the seaside resort, based upon the salubrious properties of Welsh coastal waters and breezes. In 1804, **Swansea** faced the dilemma of choosing between a future as an industrial **port** or as 'the Brighton of Wales'. (The modern city's attempt to regenerate itself as a post-industrial tourist destination reflects the cyclical nature of economic development.) In the later 19th century, the spread of **railways** led to a marked expansion of coastal resorts such as **Tenby**, **Llandudno** and **Aberystwyth**, and to the rise of the inland spas of **Llandrindod** and **Llanwrtyd**. The resorts of the southern coast, notably **Barry** Island, **Porthcawl**, **Aberavon** and Mumbles (Swansea), owed their existence to the industrial development of the south Wales **coal**field and to the introduction of workers' annual holidays. The 'miners' fortnight' was a fixed holiday in August, when thousands of colliers and their families sought sand, sea and cheap accommodation. By the mid-20th century, such accommodation generally meant caravans or chalets in large complexes, particularly those at Porthcawl's Trecco Bay.

The advent in the 1960s of cheap holidays in sunnier places dealt tourism in Wales a severe blow. Resorts with a tradition of offering boarding-house holidays to the less affluent went into decline, as the dilapidated condition of much of the promenade at **Rhyl** testifies. The industry was forced to re-evaluate its dependence on the traditional bucket-and-spade market. By the early 21st century, the growth market was in short breaks (less than four nights) involving business and conference travel, and special-interest tourism undertaken by people interested in cultural and outdoor activities. Sport tourism, including **golf**, **cycling** and **angling**, as well as spectator sports, represents a major growth sector. The ability to host large-scale events at the Millennium Stadium, **Cardiff**, has provided Wales with a significant competitive edge. Marketing campaigns to attract tourists to Wales still rely heavily on promoting the image of a green and pleasant land. However, specifically Welsh cultural tourism is beginning to win recognition, and by the early 21st century, the Wales Tourist Board (WTB) was belatedly acknowledging the potential of Welsh history and culture to attract holidaymakers, especially those from overseas. This was an important development, for the WTB had long been criticized for its perceived reluctance to promote a confident Welsh identity.

In 2006, there were over 10.7 million overnight tourist trips to Wales. Although overseas visitors accounted for around 16% (1.1 million) of these trips and spent around £358 million (17.5% of the gross tourist income), the British domestic market – which includes Welsh tourists within their own country – has always been the biggest source of tourists in Wales. In 2006, that market was the source of 36.4 million nights and an expenditure of around £1.6 billion. The income generated by tourism has become increasingly vital to the economy of a large number of Welsh communities, particularly following the decline of traditional industries and the slump in **agriculture**.

Penarth beach and pier *c.*1905

If the industry's figures are to be believed, and tourism really does contribute over £8 million a day to the Welsh economy, it is little wonder that so much emphasis is placed on it as an answer to many of the country's economic problems. However, the jobs tourism offers are frequently badly paid, menial and seasonal. Investment in tourism enterprises often comes from outside the host communities themselves (a feature of tourist development in many countries), prompting the criticism that the industry is the modern-day equivalent of colonialism. Certainly, a higher than average percentage of privately owned tourist establishments in Wales are owned by incomers. The very limited use of the Welsh language in tourism feeds the notion that it is an industry which has been grafted on to Wales.

The first national organization for tourism in Wales, the Welsh Tourist and Holiday Board, was established in 1948. Comprising a consortium of local authority members and **government** officials, in 1964 it became known as the Wales Tourism and Hotels Association. Answerable to the British Travel and Holidays Board, in 1966 the name was changed to the Wales Tourist Board (WTB), a title that survived the Development of Tourism Act of 1969, which gave the board statutory recognition. Under the Act, the board was given the duty of encouraging people from other parts of Britain, as well as those from Wales, to take their holidays there, and of ensuring the provision and an improvement of tourist facilities. The Tourism (Overseas Promotion) (Wales) Act of 1992 subsequently gave the WTB a degree of independence to market Wales overseas, a task previously undertaken exclusively by the British Tourist Authority.

The WTB's grading scheme for accommodation, introduced in 1982, was extended in 1992 to include outdoor activity providers as well as visitor attractions, caravan parks and self-catering establishments. In 1991, tourism companies were established for north, mid and south Wales, a pattern modified in 2001 when four new tourism partnerships – for south-east, south-west, mid and north Wales – were created. The increasing need for the tourism trade to exert an influence on the government resulted in 2000 in the formation of the Wales Tourism Alliance. In the same year, the WTB launched a 10-year national tourism strategy for Wales, which emphasized the themes of quality, competitiveness, partnership and sustainability. By 2003, the **National Assembly**'s grant-in-aid to the WTB exceeded £22 million – a far cry from the £30,000 that was the board's income in 1966. In 2006, the WTB was abolished as a **quango** and its functions, under the title Visit Wales, were brought in-house by the Assembly.

A key factor in successful tourism development is accessibility, particularly with respect to international air travel. International tourists use **London** Heathrow, Manchester, Birmingham and Cardiff International **airports** as their gateway to Wales. Between 1996 and 2004, the number of people using Cardiff airport increased by over 50% to more than 1.9 million passengers, and in 2007 a twice-daily, north–south airlink was introduced between Cardiff and RAF **Valley** on **Anglesey**. **Road** and rail communications with the main British domestic markets in south-east, central and north-west **England**, are also essential arteries feeding the industry.

The Wales Millennium Centre, Cardiff, opened in 2004

Caravans at Trecco Bay, Porthcawl

In 2006, there were over 4800 serviced establishments (hotels, inns, guesthouses and bed-and-breakfast accommodation) offering almost 40,000 bedrooms, representing some 83,000 bed spaces. Small-scale accommodation predominated, with over 80% of all serviced establishments having no more than 10 bedrooms, but the provision also included large hotels belonging to international chains, such as the Hilton and the Marriott, as well as the five-star golf resort and spa complex at Celtic Manor near **Newport** (*see* **Caerleon**), and the five-star St David's Hotel and Spa – part of the Cardiff Bay regeneration scheme. A recent phenomenon has been the growth of budget hotels (such as the Travel Inn and Travelodge) along the main roads.

Chalets, caravans, camping and **second homes** – the non-serviced sector – loom large. In 2006, there were more than 6500 self-catering units and 1900 caravan parks containing 90,000 pitches, accounting for almost 419,000 bed spaces; there were, in addition, around 140 graded hostels. These figures demonstrate that tourism in Wales caters disproportionately for the least prosperous segment of society and thus produces less income than would be generated if the industry were more concerned with wealthier clients. Furthermore, caravans and chalets raise serious environmental issues. Because of the attraction of inexpensive holidays, huge tracts of land, especially along the northern and Cardigan Bay coasts, were developed in the years after the **Second World War** for static caravan parks. Among them are the 82 parks, providing over 7000 pitches, which occupy an unbroken 6-km stretch of coastline between Rhyl and **Abergele**. By the late 1960s, such proliferation had become so unsightly that many local authorities were prohibiting new developments.

Another contentious issue related to tourism is second and holiday homes (*see* Second Homes). By the beginning of the 21st century, there were over 15,500 in Wales, with the result that in some communities second houses constituted nearly 40% of the total **housing** stock. The social effects of second home ownership include the pricing out of local people from the housing market, and the curtailment of community services caused by a diminishing all-year-round resident **population**. There is a close link between second home ownership and the permanent **immigration** of outsiders to the host community, and second homes have been perceived as a serious threat to the indigenous language and culture.

Tourist attractions include ancient monuments, historic houses, museums and **art galleries**, farms, zoos, aquariums, visitor and heritage centres, **piers**, craft centres, historic steam railways, and country parks. Among the parks, of which there are 25 in Wales, is that at **Margam**. The parks are tracts of countryside, generally close to urban areas, whose purpose (as set out in the Countryside Act 1968) is to provide managed recreational space to help protect more fragile areas (such as **National Parks**, Areas of Outstanding Natural Beauty and nature reserves) from visitor pressures.

In 1950, there were only 50 tourist attractions in Wales; by 2006, there were over 500. Wales has a dependence on small attractions, with over two thirds of those participating in the Annual Attraction Wales survey recording fewer than 50,000 visitors. Many of the small-scale attractions had fewer than 20,000 visitors a year, causing some of them to be non-viable businesses. However, the top 20 attractions collectively received around 4.4 million visitors. Those attractions are regarded as being in a 'must see' category and are of national or international interest. They include the castles at **Caernarfon**, **Conwy**, **Harlech** and Cardiff, the National History Museum (*see* **St Fagans**), the **National Museum** and the Oakwood Family Leisure Park at **Martletwy**.

Since 1997, the availability of lottery money, together with European regional development funds, has prompted major investment in large-scale attractions – most notably the £50 million **National Botanic Garden of Wales**, the £20 million Millennium Coastal Park linking **Llanelli** with **Pembrey**, the £106 million Millennium Centre in Cardiff Bay, the £25 million Welsh Highland Railway restoration scheme in **Gwynedd** and the £110 million project to establish the Bluestone holiday village near the Oakwood leisure park (*see* **Slebech**).

The future of tourism in Wales is likely to depend on extending the visitor season to spread the volume and the value of tourism throughout the year, on disseminating the benefits of tourism more widely – both geographically and socially – and on minimizing the industry's adverse impacts. These include the erosion of the environment, the undermining of indigenous culture, and – through the demand for second houses – the pricing of the local population out of their own localities.

TOWER COLLIERY, Hirwaun, Rhondda Cynon Taff

Records of mining at this site stretch back to 1759, but the pit is named after a tower erected by the **Crawshay family**, following the **Merthyr Rising**, in order to defend both the pit and the nearby **iron**works. It was variously owned by leading south Wales families – the Crawshays, the Butes (*see* **Stuart family**) – and by **Powell Dyffryn**, but, following its closure by British **Coal** in April 1994, it was bought by the workforce, under the leadership of Tyrone O'Sullivan, and since 1995 has operated successfully as a co-operative. The struggle to save the pit was the subject of Alun Hoddinott's opera *Tower* which toured Wales in 1999–2000. In 2007, the colliery, with a workforce of 300, was expected to close early in 2008. Although generally linked with **Hirwaun**, the colliery is in fact in the community of **Rhigos**.

TOWNSHIP

The township or *tref* was the basic unit of settlement and of assessment in medieval Wales, corresponding to the English -vill. It varied in area, unfree communities tending to be smaller. Its origins also varied; some may have gone back to **Roman** times or earlier, while others were the result of the expansion of settlement in the 12th and 13th centuries. From the 16th century onwards, the **parish** replaced it as the unit of local administration. One hundred *trefi* theoretically constituted a **cantref**. There are exhaustive lists of Wales's townships in **Melville Richards**'s *Welsh Administrative and Territorial Units* (1969).

Tyrone O'Sullivan, chairman of Tower Colliery

The banner of the Werntarw lodge of the NUM

TRADE UNIONISM

The prominence of the Labour movement in Wales in the 20th century has rather obscured the troubled early history of trade unionism, when permanent organizations and loyal membership were established only with difficulty. The formation of a branch of the Friendly Associated **Coal** Miners' Union at **Bagillt** in **Flintshire** in 1830 is usually taken to be the first formal evidence of trade unionism in Wales. Following the **Merthyr Rising** (1831), trade union-ism appeared in the **iron** towns on the northern edge of the south Wales coalfield, but within a few months this activ-ity had collapsed. For almost half a century thereafter, such unions as were formed tended to be short-lived *ad hoc* affairs, rarely surviving a particular dispute. The collapse of the Amalgamated Association of Mineworkers in 1875 spectacularly illustrated the difficulties confronting unions in the later 19th century.

The turning point came in the 1890s. Unions were better protected both legally and financially, while industrial workers were better educated and more affluent. Inspired by the **London** dock strike (1889), the so-called 'new unions' and the rail unions recruited in the Welsh **ports**. Of all the unionized workers of Wales, the most heroic were the members of the **North Wales Quarrymen's Union**, who sustained, during the **Penrhyn lockout**, one of the longest protests in the industrial history of **Britain**. In terms of numbers, however, developments among the miners of the south Wales coalfield were far more significant. They remained under-organized and divided until the formation of the **South Wales Miners' Federation** in 1898. From that year onwards, **miners' strikes** were rarely out of the news and Wales became associated with industrial militancy.

The Triple Alliance of 1913 was a high watermark for the miners; the **railway**men and the transport workers were both under the influence of militant Welsh branches and leaders. Yet recruitment was always a problem, with even the south Wales miners having difficulty in sustaining membership. This was particularly the case following the **General Strike** (1926), when the miners felt that they had been abandoned by other unions; in addition, they had to combat both unemployment and **company unionism**. Furthermore, unions representing **agricultural workers** had only temporary success, although in 1920, the year of their apogee, at least a third of Wales's agricultural labourers were union members.

The post-1945 **welfare state** and the accompanying full employment ushered in decades of consensus, when unions such as the TGWU, the GMWU and the ISTC were prominent in Welsh life. White-collar unions – those of administrators, teachers and medical workers in particular – also expanded. After 1979, de-industrialization, marked by bitter strikes in the mines and steelworks, greatly reduced the significance of unions, although the **Wales TUC** played an important role in supporting the principle of **devolution**. In a new era of realism, the flexibility of unions played a part in encouraging overseas investment in Wales. By the early 21st century, there were signs of a revival of militancy among trade unionists.

TRALLONG (Y Trallwng), Breconshire,
Powys (5906 ha; 364 inhabitants)

The **community** straddles the **Usk** and extends up to the artillery ranges on **Mynydd Epynt**. Trallwng Cynfyn is referred to by the 12th-century poet Gwynfardd

Brycheiniog. Philip Powell, hanged at Tyburn for his **Roman Catholic** faith, came from Trallong. The Brân stream passes through the isolated village of Llanfihangel Nant Brân to join the Usk near Aberbrân Fawr, the home of the Games family before its move to Newton (**Brecon**). On the banks of the Usk, 1 km apart, stand Penpont and Abercamlais, two impressive mansions built for different branches of the Williams family. Betws Penpont church was designed by George Gilbert Scott. Abercamlais has a fireplace from Fonthill and its own bridge over the Usk. At the other end of the Camlais valley stand the remains of the castle of Blaencamlais, the shortest-lived of any Welsh castle; built by **Llywelyn ap Gruffudd** in 1262, it was destroyed by the future Edward I in 1265.

TRAMS

While wagons transporting minerals along tramroads were ubiquitous in industrial Wales before the **railway** age, trams are generally considered to be passenger-carrying conveyances. By the 1870s, **horse**-drawn trams running on rails in the middle of streets were a familiar sight in **Cardiff**, **Swansea**, **Newport** and **Wrexham**. Originally in private hands, the trams generally came under the control of the local authorities in the early 20th and underwent electrification. In the history of Cardiff's trams, a leading figure was **Solomon Andrews**, a pioneer of tram operation in Wales and also in English cities, Manchester among them. His company began services in Cardiff in 1872 and, by the

end of the 19th century, it was running trams in **Llanelli**, Newport, **Pontypridd** and **Pwllheli**. Trolleybuses, which had no track but obtained power from overhead wires were, from the 1920s, introduced in Pontypridd, Llanelli, **Aberdare** and Cardiff. Cardiff, which introduced its well-loved trolleybuses in 1942, was among the last cities to remain loyal to them; they ceased operation in 1970.

In Swansea, the Oystermouth Tramroad Company was incorporated in 1804. As trams run on rails along a highway, and as the Oystermouth – or Mumbles – line followed its own dedicated track, it can be considered to have been a railway rather than a tramway; indeed, it is sometimes referred to as the world's earliest passenger railway. Its horse-drawn carriages were replaced by trams drawn by steam-operated locomotives in 1877. The line closed in 1960. The Oystermouth line was only one aspect of pioneering at Swansea, for the town was the first in Wales to have electric tramways (1900).

The **Merthyr** Electric Traction Company operated electric trams from 1901; they were replaced by council-run buses in 1939. The **Rhondda** had trams from 1902 to 1933. Pontypridd was so proud of its trams that it was the last southern local authority to introduce **buses**. Electric trams ran in Wrexham from 1903 to 1927. In the 1930s, the trams of the **Llandudno** and **Colwyn Bay** Electric Railway Company competed with Crosville buses along the shoreline. One of the great successes of tramway operation in Wales is the Great Orme tramway at Llandudno;

Publicizing a Harold Lloyd film on a tramcar in Aberdare *c.* 1930

pioneered by a private company in 1902, it has been munic-
ipally owned since 1949. A two-stage funicular cable railway, partly sharing the **road**way, it carried nearly 4 million
passengers in its first 30 years of operation. It is Wales's
sole surviving tramway.

TRAWSFYNYDD, Gwynedd
(12,380 ha; 949 inhabitants)
Extending over a wide swathe of northern **Meirionnydd**,
the **community** contains Y Crawcwellt, an extensive stretch
of swampy land reaching up to the heights of the **Harlech**
Dome. The **Roman** practice camps near the community's
northern border were used by the garrison at Tomen-y-
Mur (**Maentwrog**). Castell Prysor, the administrative centre of the **commote** of **Ardudwy** Uwch Artro, was a Welsh
castle probably built in the early 13th century. St Madryn's
church has a medieval roof. Trawsfynydd Lake was created in 1930 to serve the Maentwrog hydroelectric scheme
(*see* **Energy**). From 1965 to 1991, it had a role in the operation of the **Trawsfynydd Nuclear Power Station**. The
British army had firing ranges in the district from 1906
onwards; the camp at Bronaber was closed in 1958 and
became the site of a holiday village. In 1951, **Gwynfor
Evans** led a sit-down protest against the expansion of military land at Trawsfynydd. In the centre of Trawsfynydd
village stands **L. S. Merrifield**'s statue of Hedd Wyn (**Ellis
Humphrey Evans**), who was killed on the Western Front
two months before he was to be chaired at the 1917
National **Eisteddfod** at Birkenhead. The community
extends to Llyn **Tryweryn**, the source of the Tryweryn
River.

TRAWSFYNYDD NUCLEAR POWER
STATION, Gwynedd
Trawsfynydd nuclear power station is situated on the shore
of Llyn Trawsfynydd, an artificial reservoir formed in 1930
as headwater for the **Maentwrog** hydroelectric power station. Trawsfynydd began generating electricity in 1965, as
the fourth member of a family of Magnox power stations
built by the Central Electricity Generating Board to supply
electricity to the 'national' grid. Operational until decom-
missioning began in 1991, the station had twin reactors
supplying some 390 megawatts of electricity. Peak employment levels at the plant amounted to some 400 permanent
staff.

TRAWSGOED, Ceredigion
(4286 ha; 977 inhabitants)
Occupying a wide swathe of land extending northwards
from the middle **Ystwyth** valley, the **community** contains
the villages of Abermagwr, Cnwch Coch, Llanafan,
Llanfihangel-y-Creuddyn and New Cross. Its main feature
is the mansion of Trawsgoed, seat of the **Vaughan family**
from the 14th century until 1947. By 1873, the Trawsgoed
estate extended over 17,266 ha of **Cardiganshire** – the
largest landed estate in the **county**. The mansion, the 16th
and 17th-century elements of which were overwhelmed by
a new wing erected in 1891, is surrounded by fine **gardens**.
It has been converted into luxury apartments. Near the
mansion is a **Roman** auxiliary fort, discovered in 1959 and
occupied *c.*AD 80–120. Llanafan developed as the home of

Trawsgoed estate workers and of **lead** miners. St Afan's,
largely rebuilt *c.*1860, was one of the many Cardiganshire
livings acquired by the Chichester family, notorious appro-
priators of **tithes**. Llanfihangel-y-Creuddyn is a nucleated
village with an impressive 14th-century church containing
fine timber beams. Caradoc Evans (**David Evans**) is buried
at New Cross.

TREARDDUR, Isle of Anglesey
(1898 ha; 1858 inhabitants)
Occupying the central and north-western parts of Holy
Island (Ynys Gybi), the **community**'s main settlement is
Trearddur Bay, a water-sports centre and a residential suburb of **Holyhead**. At Penrhos (18th century), once the residence of Barons **Stanley** of Alderley, are Muslim features
installed by the third baron (d.1898) following his conversion to **Islam**. It is now the site of a nature reserve.
Trefignath is a fine **Neolithic** chambered tomb. There are
Bronze Age standing stones at Penrhosfeilw. Hut groups at
the foot of Holyhead **Mountain** – wrongly known as
Cytiau'r Gwyddelod (the **Irish**men's huts) – were occupied
from Neolithic to **Roman** times. Caer y Tŵr **Iron Age hill-
fort** has impressive stone ramparts. There is a Roman
watchtower within it. The dramatically sited South Stack
lighthouse was built in 1809. The **Anglesey** Aluminium (formerly Rio Tinto) plant was established in 1971.

TREASON OF THE BLUE BOOKS, The
Brad y Llyfrau Gleision (The Treason of the Blue Books)
was the title of a play (1854) by **R. J. Derfel**, satirizing the
government's 1847 report on **education** in Wales. The title
refers to the report's blue covers and it also evokes the
Welsh myth of '**The Treason of the Long Knives**'. It took
hold of the public imagination to such an extent that ever
since the report has been known by that name.

In March 1846, **Llanpumsaint**-born William Williams
(1788–1865), one of the MPs for Coventry and later for
Lambeth, and a prominent **radical** backbencher, induced
the **government** to appoint a commission 'to enquire into
the state of education … in Wales, especially into the
means afforded to the labouring **class**es of acquiring a
knowledge of the **English language**'. The government
responded with a three-man commission appointed by the
Privy Council's committee on education. The commissioners, Lingen, Symons and Johnson, had no knowledge of
Welsh, of Nonconformity (*see* **Nonconformists**) or of elementary education. Yet, they worked with immense energy
and efficiency to produce three hefty tomes, giving a devastating and immensely detailed picture of schools in
Wales, attacking the **gentry**, clergy and capitalists for their
indifference to the task of founding schools, but also etching a sharply critical picture of the Welsh as a people.

The racial theories of the period probably encouraged
them to denounce the Welsh as backward and barbaric.
The Welsh took particular offence at being portrayed as
dirty, lazy, feckless and mendacious, with their wives and
mothers depicted as slatterns. They resented the commissioners' insistence that the survival of Welsh and the concomitant strength of Nonconformity were the cause of
Welsh barbarity. The implication of the report was that
the government should at once intervene by providing

The Treason of the Blue Books, a satirical portrayal by Hugh Hughes, *c.*1848, of J. C. Symons, one of the commissioners

Wales with a complete network of English-medium elementary schools.

Several patriotic Welsh **Anglicans** began the attack on the Blue Books, the most effective demolition job being done by **Thomas Phillips**, a former mayor of **Newport**; but the Nonconformists, under the leadership of journalists such as **Evan Jones** (Ieuan Gwynedd), gradually moved into the vanguard of the attack. After this came R. J. Derfel's play with its incisive title. The notion of 'treason' arose from the fact that much of the unfavourable material had been contributed by Welsh Anglican clerics, men who came to be seen, in many quarters, as an internal enemy.

Welsh opinion eventually came round to the view of the commissioners that, in order to participate in the progress of the Empire, the Welsh must learn English and English ways, a factor which helps to explain the partial Anglicization of Wales later in the 19th century. Even more significant was the urge to prove that the Welsh were as respectable and virtuous as any people on Earth, the key perhaps to what has been seen as their pusillanimous attitudes to their native traditions. Yet, the 'Blue Books' also had the effect of creating a more self-aware and defensive **nationalism**, inspiring a growing number of Welsh people to create national institutions to defend and strengthen the nation against criticism.

TREASON OF THE LONG KNIVES, The

A mythical event in early Welsh history connected with the coming of the **Anglo-Saxons** to **Britain** *c.*440. The story, found first in *Historia Brittonum* and based on a vague suggestion by **Gildas** in *De Excidio Britanniae*, is that the British leader **Vortigern** fell in love with the daughter of the Saxon leader Hengist – she was later given the name Rhonwen or **Rowena** – and Hengist invited Vortigern and 300 British chiefs to a great banquet. At a given signal, '*Nemet eour saxes!*' (Grab your knives!), each Saxon took out his long knife, hitherto concealed, and stabbed the British guest sitting nearest him, leaving alive only Eidol, ruler of Gloucester, and Vortigern himself, who was then forced to yield enough land in southern Britain for the Saxons to establish their first permanent settlements. **Geoffrey of Monmouth** elaborated the story, details of which formed part of the stock of references of the Welsh medieval bards. The 18th-century historian **Theophilus Evans** gave the tale a fresh lease of life, and poems and books popularized it again during the era of **Romanticism** – so much so that when, in 1854, **R. J. Derfel** decided to satirize the Blue Books on Welsh **Education** (1847) in his play *Brad y Llyfrau Gleision* (**The Treason of the Blue Books**), the public made immediate associations with the mythic meaning.

There is a parallel story of the Saxons in Germany, and it is this, rather than the Welsh story, that formed the basis of 'The Night of the Long Knives' by which Hitler's 'Roehm Purge' in 1934 is generally known. The term was also used to refer to Harold Macmillan's sacking of seven members of his cabinet in 1962.

TRECŴN, Pembrokeshire (1660 ha; 359 inhabitants) Located south of **Fishguard**, the **community** extends over what were (pre-1974) the civil **parishes** of Llanstinan and Llanfair Nant-y-gof. The church of St Justinian retains medieval features; that of St Mary was rebuilt in 1855. John Wesley was an occasional guest at Trecŵn mansion (demolished). The house was sold to the Admiralty in the 1930s following the deaths of all members of the Barham family, its owners, in a motoring accident. From 1939 to

1994, its site was occupied by a military camp and armaments factory, with 58 storage tunnels stretching deep into the hillsides. Closure in the 1990s led to considerable local unemployment.

TREDEGAR, Blaenau Gwent
(3157 ha; 15,057 inhabitants)

The **community** lies at the head of the valley of the Sirhowy, a tributary of the **Ebbw**. The town takes its name from Tredegar House, the home of the **Morgan family** who leased the site in 1799 on which the Tredegar Ironworks (*see* **Iron and Steel**) were built (*see* **Coedkernew near Newport**). The centrality of iron to Tredegar is symbolized by the cast-iron **clock** tower (1858) in the Circle, a rare example of a central space in a town in the south Wales **coal**field. Remains of the area's first coke-fired furnace can be seen at the Sirhowy Ironworks. The tramroad connecting Tredegar with Newport, which opened in 1811, was the earliest major tramroad in south Wales. In 1818, the Sirhowy works were bought by the Harfords, and in 1832 a 2-km tunnel was constructed to take pig iron from Sirhowy to their rolling mills at **Ebbw Vale**. By the late 19th century, Harford's successor concern, the Tredegar Iron and Coal Company, was mainly concerned with the mining of steam coal. By the mid 20th century, the chief source of employment was the steelworks at Ebbw Vale; their decline and eventual closure were a severe blow.

Tredegar Park, once the **garden** of the Morgan family's **Bedwellty** House, contains an ice house, a grotto, an arboretum and a 15-tonne block of coal – the largest single block ever cut. On Bryn-serth stand the massive boulders commemorating the town's most famous son, **Aneurin Bevan**. Trefil, the one-time **limestone**-quarrying village north of Tredegar, is the remotest community in industrial south Wales. There is an attractive country park at Bryn Bach and an impressive **railway** viaduct at Dukestown. The father of Charles Evans Hughes, whose bid in 1916 to be president of the United States was defeated by 4000 votes, was a native of Tredegar.

TREF ALAW, Isle of Anglesey
(3644 ha; 606 inhabitants)

Located south-west of **Amlwch**, the **community**'s main feature is Llyn Alaw; a **reservoir** created in 1966 by the damming of the **River** Alaw, it is the largest stretch of water in **Anglesey**. Melin Llynon is Anglesey's sole working example of the type of **windmill** once common on the **island**. Melin Hywel is Anglesey's sole surviving **watermill**. The windfarm on the northern edge of the community has 34 turbines. Llanbabo church contains a 14th-century effigy of Pabo, the church's patron **saint**. Bedd Branwen is a **Bronze Age** tumulus (*c.*1500 BC) (*see* **Branwen ferch Llŷr**).

TREFEGLWYS, Montgomeryshire, Powys
(8290 ha; 868 inhabitants)

Embracing the basin of the **River** Trannon, a tributary of the **Severn**, north of **Llanidloes**, the **community** contains the villages of Trefeglwys, Llawryglyn and Staylittle, and the northern bank of the Clywedog **reservoir**. The area is rich in timber-framed houses. The folk song collector **Nicholas Bennett** (1823–99) was a native of Trefeglwys, and the

bibliographer **Charles Ashton** (1848–99) of Llawryglyn. The **Quakers** had a meeting house and burial ground in Staylittle (Penffordd-las in **Welsh**, but commonly known as Y Stae or the Stay). The district was celebrated for its powerful preaching festivals, mainly among the **Baptists**; there was a local **revival** in the Stay in 1851.

TREFEURIG, Ceredigion
(2615 ha; 1675 inhabitants)

Located north-east of **Aberystwyth**, the **community** contains the village of Penrhyn-coch – essentially one of Aberystwyth's suburbs – and the former **lead**-mining settlements of Cwmerfyn, Cwmsymlog and Pen-bont Rhydybeddau. Gogerddan, the one-time mansion of the **Pryse family**, is the headquarters of the **Institute for Grassland and Environmental Research**. The institute's experimental crops occupy much of the community's lowlands. **Dafydd ap Gwilym** reputedly lived at Brogynin, although the ruins referred to on the commemorative plaque there date from the 17th or 18th century; a number of the district's **place names** can be recognized in his poetry. Alltfadog was for long the home of Lewis Morris (1701–65; *see* **Morris Brothers**), who described the mining area around Cwmsymlog as 'the richest country I have ever seen'.

Tredegar's cast-iron clock tower, erected in 1858

TREFLYS, Breconshire, Powys
(6162 ha; 460 inhabitants)
A wide expanse of hill country east of **Llanwrtyd**, the **community** contains the villages of Garth and Beulah. Garth Hall was the home of the Gwynne family whose memorials are in Llanlleonfel church, where John Wesley officiated in 1749 at the marriage of his brother Charles Wesley to Sarah Gwynne, the daughter of Marmaduke Gwynne (?1694–1769), one of the leading patrons of **Howel Harris**. Beulah was described by the *Shell Guide to Mid Wales* as 'rather a grim little village'. Eglwys Oen Duw, with its lavish Victorian interior, was commissioned by the Thomas family of Llwyn Madoc, a mansion built in 1747 and, in 1873, the centre of a 5192-ha estate. Caerau farm is sited on a **Roman** fort.

TREFNANT, Denbighshire
(1200 ha; 1409 inhabitants)
Located between **Denbigh** and **St Asaph**, the **community**'s main feature is Llannerch Hall, rebuilt in the early 17th century and remodelled in 1772 and 1864. Of its prodigious **gardens** (1660s), nothing remains. They were laid out for the soldier-adventurer Mutton Davies, whose son, the antiquary Robert Davies (1658–1710), amassed a remarkable library. In the 16th century, the hall was the home of Gruffudd ap Ieuan (c.1485–c.1550), one of the two poets who assisted the commissioners of the first **Caerwys Eisteddfod** (1523). Among the community's other historic houses are Perthewig (1594), Tŷ Coch (1683) and Galltfaenan Hall, remodelled for the sugar-refining Tate family. Holy Trinity church (1855) was designed by George Gilbert Scott.

TREFOR, John (fl.1360–1410) Bishop
John or Siôn Trefor, probably a native of Trevor (**Llangollen Rural**), was a doctor in **law** who started his career as precentor of Wells Cathedral. He was resident in Rome in the early 1390s, before returning to Wales as bishop of **St Asaph** (1395).

Details of his early episcopal career may be traced in the poems of **Iolo Goch**. Trefor was present at the parliament that deposed Richard II and read the deposition order at that assembly. He decided, however, to support **Owain Glyndŵr**. On two occasions he went to France on diplomatic missions for Glyndŵr and was probably among the *prelatos principatus nostri* who helped to compose Glyndŵr's letter to the French king in 1406 (*see* **Pennal Letter**). Another John Trefor was bishop of St Asaph from 1346 to 1357.

TREFRIW, Conwy (3742 ha; 924 inhabitants)
Located on the left bank of the **Conwy** north of **Betws-y-Coed**, the **community** includes the ancient **parish** of Llanrhychwyn. Llanrhychwyn church (late 12th century) may have been commissioned by **Llywelyn ap Iorwerth**, who had a court at Trefriw.

Boatbuilding took place at Trefriw Quay, which also exported **slate**, as well as **lead** and **copper** ore extracted from the hills to the west. Trefriw has a thriving **woollen industry** and cloth is woven in the century-old mill. The waterwheel has been dismantled but the hydroelectric turbines can be seen. The healing properties of the chalybeate waters of

Trefriw Spa were known to the **Romans**. It became a fashionable attraction for Victorian visitors, who could travel to the spa by steamer from Conwy. On the banks of Llyn Geirionydd is a monument purporting to mark the grave of **Taliesin**. It was the site where the rites of the alternative **Gorsedd** founded by **William John Roberts** (Gwilym Cowlyd) were held. Among the distinguished natives of Trefriw were the **dictionary** compiler **Thomas Wiliems** (d.1622), the printer **David Jones** (Dafydd Jones o Drefriw; fl.1750s) and the poet **Evan Evans** (Ieuan Glan Geirionydd; 1795–1855). However, by far the best known native of Trefriw is the fictitious Brother Cadfael, hero of 19 novels by Ellis Peters (*see* **Edith Pargeter**).

Across the 17th-century **Llanrwst** bridge is Tu Hwnt i'r Bont (early 17th century). The **road** continues to Gwydir Castle, a place of importance since the 14th century. The present house dates from *c*.1500, and was the home of the **Wynn family**. After two disastrous fires, recent owners have restored it to its former splendour, reconstructing within it the original panelling which William Randolph Hearst had carried off to New York. A second Wynn residence, Gwydir Uchaf (1604), has been much altered and contains offices of the **Forestry Commission**. Adjoining it is Gwydir Uchaf chapel, which retains its painted ceiling and the liturgical arrangements favoured by the early 17th-century High Church.

TREGARON, Ceredigion
(8639 ha; 1217 inhabitants)
Extending from the **Teifi** to the **Tywi**, the **community** contains some of the remotest places in Wales. The town of Tregaron was originally part of the **Cardigan Boroughs** constituency, a status it lost in 1730. Located on the banks of the Brennig, a tributary of the Teifi, its buildings cluster around St Caron's church, heavily restored in 1879, but retaining a 14th-century tower. On the square is a statue to **Henry Richard**, whose birthplace, Prospect House, bears a plaque. Twm Shon Catti (**Thomas Jones**; *c*.1560–1609) was born at Porthyffynnon, a now-vanished mansion. **Joseph Jenkins**, 'the Welsh Swagman', was born at Trecefel. Tregaron Secondary School, established in 1897, maintained and increased its intake while the **population** of its catchment area declined drastically; consequently, by the 1940s, over 50% of the district's 11-year-old pupils were able to have grammar-school **education** – the highest proportion in Wales, and probably in **Britain**. In the later 20th century, **horse** and pony trekking became a significant element in the local **economy**. The Tregaron Trotting Club, founded in 1980, holds popular harness races annually in August (*see* **Horse Racing**). The Tregaron Kite Centre celebrates the resurgence of the red kite (*see* **Birds**). Within the community is the southern part of **Cors Caron**. In 2001, 76.62% of the inhabitants of Tregaron had some knowledge of **Welsh**, with 61.01% wholly fluent in the language – the highest percentages for any of the communities of **Ceredigion**.

TREGYNON, Montgomeryshire, Powys
(2838 ha; 616 inhabitants)
Located north of **Newtown**, most of the **community**'s farms were, until 1914, part of the Gregynog estate. Gregynog was first mentioned in a poem by **Cynddelw Brydydd Mawr**

(12th century), and was later celebrated in poetry by **Lewys Glyn Cothi** and others. From the 15th to the 18th century, the estate was owned by the Blayney (Blaenau) family, whose praises were sung by Lewys Glyn Cothi and other poets. The mansion was transformed (*c.*1860) by the Hanbury-Tracy family, who encased it in concrete, painted black and white; the sumptuous carved parlour of 1636 remained. In 1920, the estate was bought by the Davies sisters (*see* **Davies family (Llandinam)**), who intended it to be an arts centre for Wales. Their great art collection, dominated by the French Impressionists, was bequeathed to the **National Museum**. In 1960, the hall and 300 ha of land surrounding it were donated to the **University of Wales** as a study and conference centre. The Gregynog Press, one of the world's leading private presses in the 1920s and 1930s, was revived in 1974 as Gwasg Gregynog (*see* **Printing and Publishing**). The tradition of **music** festivals continues, as does the care of Gregynog's **gardens** with their superb arboretum.

As at Gregynog, concrete was the material used in building Tregynon's old school (1872) and several houses in the village. They represent perhaps the earliest examples in the world of casting, roof and all, on site. St Cynon's church, largely rebuilt in 1892, retains its timber bell-turret. The genealogist (*see* **Genealogy**) Lewys Dwnn (*c.*1550–*c.*1616) and the **Wesleyan hymn** writer Thomas Olivers (1725–99) were natives of Tregynon.

TRELAWNYD AND GWAENYSGOR (Trelawnyd a Gwaunysgor), Flintshire (752 ha; 886 inhabitants)

Located south-east of **Prestatyn**, the **community** is dominated by Gop Hill, which is surmounted by Wales's largest man-made cairn, one of the many prehistoric monuments in the area. Among the **caves** in the **limestone** plateau is one on Gop Hill where a late **Neolithic** grave containing the bones of eleven human beings was excavated in the late 19th century. Trelawnyd and Gwaenysgor are listed in Domesday Book as *Rivelenoit* and *Wenescol*. St Michael's church, Trelawnyd, was remodelled by **John Douglas** in 1897. St Mary's church, Gwaenysgor, has a fine late medieval timber roof. Near it, a viewpoint offers a wide vista of the north Wales coast. John Wynne (1650–1714) of Copa'rleni, reputedly Wales's richest **Nonconformist**, established a **Congregational** chapel at Trelawnyd in 1701. He exploited the district's **lead** ore and founded a weekly market at Trelawnyd which he renamed Newmarket. The original name was restored in the 20th century. The Trelawnyd **Male Voice Choir** was established in 1933. In 2001, 38.70% of the community's inhabitants had some knowledge of **Welsh**, with 22.60% wholly fluent in the language – the highest percentages for any of **Flintshire's** communities.

TRELECH (Tre-lech), Carmarthenshire (4689 ha; 744 inhabitants)

Located north-west of **Carmarthen**, the **community** contains the village of Trelech and the hamlet of Bettws. Rock **Congregational** chapel (1827) is an attractive building. Mari Fawr Trelech was a woman of legendary strength. **David Rees**, editor of the **radical newspaper** *Y Diwygiwr*, was a native of Trelech, as was Michael Bowen, the leader

of the attack on the Carmarthen workhouse in 1843 (*see* **Rebecca Riots**).

TRELLECH UNITED (Tryleg), Monmouthshire (4374 ha; 2428 inhabitants)

Located immediately south of **Monmouth**, the **community's** name – probably meaning the three slabs – may have its origins in the group of three **Bronze Age** standing stones – known as Harold's Stones. In the 13th century, Trellech, now a small village, may have been the most populous town in Wales. Archaeological evidence of large-scale **iron**working suggests that it was the chief arsenal of the **Clare family**, whose military activities reached their peak in the late 13th century. It appears that decline set in following the death of Gilbert de Clare at the battle of Bannockburn in 1314. **Bertrand Russell** was born at Trellech, the reason, no doubt, why the *Chambers Biographical Dictionary* describes him as a Welsh philosopher, a description with which he would undoubtedly have disagreed.

There are five churches of medieval origin within the community. St Nicholas, Trellech, with its splendid spire, is one of the finest churches in the **county**; its spaciousness is further proof of the scale of the 13th-century settlement. The valley of the White Brook near Llandogo contains extensive remains of the iron and wireworks begun *c.*1606, and of the papermaking mills that operated in the valley between *c.*1760 and 1880 (*see also* **Tintern**). The importance of the Llandogo quay as a trading centre on the **Wye** is recalled by the Llandogo Trow Inn on the Welsh Back at Bristol. The 17th-century house of The Argoed, south of Penallt, was the home of Richard Potter, father of Beatrice Webb.

TREMEIRCHION, Denbighshire (739 ha; 636 inhabitants)

Located south-east of **St Asaph**, the **community** contains the caves of Ffynnon Beuno and Cae Gwyn, which have yielded evidence of human beings of the **Palaeolithic** era. In Corpus Christi church is an effigy of a 13th-century knight and an elaborate late 14th-century canopied tomb, which was once believed to be that of the bardic grammarian Dafydd Ddu Hiraddug. The church is reputed to be the first in Wales to hold a harvest thanksgiving service. Bâch-y-graig (1569), built for the Antwerp financial agent Richard Clough (d.1570), a native of **Denbigh**, was largely demolished in 1817; Netherlandish in its inspiration, it was one of Wales's earliest examples of a brick-built house. With its pyramid roof, crowned with a cupola, it had no parallel among the buildings of 16th-century **Britain**. Dr Johnson's friend **Hester Lynch Piozzi** (b. **Salusbury**) lived at Bryn Bella (1795). St **Beuno's** College (1840s) is the Jesuit foundation in which **Gerard Manley Hopkins** studied (1874–7). Our Lady of Sorrows, a chapel on a rocky eminence (1866), has been obscured by tree growth.

TREUDDYN, Flintshire (1465 ha; 1567 inhabitants)

Located south of **Mold**, the **community** contains the villages of Treuddyn and Coed-talon. On a ridge above Treuddyn village stands a line of **Bronze Age** barrows. There is a standing stone, Carreg y Llech, in St Mary's churchyard.

Plas-y-Brain is a former hall-house. Pen-y-stryt and Plas-ym-Mhowys are 17th-century farmhouses. During the 19th century, **coal**, **iron** and **lead** were mined at Treuddyn, and a distillery was built to extract **oil** from its cannel coal. Treuddyn blast furnace operated from 1817 to 1865.

TREVITHICK, Richard (1771–1833) Inventor

In 1804, Cornish-born Trevithick constructed the world's first steam locomotive to pull a load along rails, at Samuel **Homfray**'s Penydarren **iron**works at **Merthyr Tydfil**. Travelling at a maximum of 8 km per hour, the engine hauled the equivalent of 10 tonnes of iron, together with some 70 passengers, 14 km along the tramroad from Merthyr to the **Glamorganshire Canal** at Navigation (**Abercynon**). The journey took just over four hours, as there were stops for the removal of boulders and overhanging branches. The locomotive never ran again on the tramroad, and was converted for use in the Penydarren works. A replica of the locomotive, which was constructed by the staff of the former Welsh Industrial and Maritime Museum in **Cardiff**, is on display at the National Waterfront Museum, **Swansea** (*see* **National Museum of Wales**).

TREVOR family Landowners

The family, which, by the 15th century, had been established near **Chirk**, claimed descent from **Hywel Dda**. The most prominent members of the senior branch, the Trevors of Brynkinallt (Chirk), were the leading Royalist Arthur (d.*c.*1666), and his nephew John (1637–1717), the speaker of James II's sole parliament. Descendants of the Trevors continue to live at Brynkinallt.

A cadet branch of the family settled at Allington, north of **Wrexham**. In the early 16th century, John Trevor (d.1589) rebuilt Trevalyn Hall (**Rossett**). His tomb and that of his eldest son, Richard (1558–1638), are among the glories of **Gresford** church. Richard's brother, John Trevor I (d.1630), who prospered as surveyor to the navy, built Plas Teg (**Hope**), Wales's finest early **Renaissance** mansion. His brother, Sackville (d.*c.*1633), a privateer, saved the future Charles I from drowning in 1623. John's son, John Trevor II (d.1673), a member of the Long Parliament and a commissioner under the **Act for the Propagation of the Gospel in Wales** (1650), sat in **Cromwell**'s second parliament. In 1672, he licensed Plas Teg as a conventicle (a meeting house for dissenters; *see* **Nonconformists and Dissenters**). The senior branch of the Trevors of Trevalyn died out in the male line in 1743. Members of younger branches included Richard Trevor, bishop of **St David's** (1744–52).

TREW, Billy (William James Trew; 1878–1926) Rugby player

Vital to a golden age for both Wales and his native **Swansea**, Billy Trew was held by **Rhys Gabe** to be 'the most complete footballer who ever played for Wales'. Frail, but quick and ingenious, he was capped at outside-half, centre and wing, and his tactical sense made him the natural successor to **Gwyn Nicholls** as captain of Wales. He was captain in 14 of his 29 internationals, which included four Triple Crowns and only four defeats, and led Swansea for six seasons between 1906 and 1913, including victories over **South Africa** and **Australia**.

A replica of Richard Trevithick's 'Penydarren' locomotive

TREWALCHMAI, Isle of Anglesey
(675 ha; 898 inhabitants)

Located west of **Llangefni**, the **community** takes its name from the 12th-century court poet Gwalchmai (*see* **Meilyr Brydydd**), who was granted land in the area by **Owain Gwynedd**. Gwalchmai village, which developed along **Telford**'s **Holyhead road**, is the only centre of **population**. The annual **Anglesey** agricultural show (Primin Môn) has its permanent site near the village.

TREWERN (Tre-wern), Montgomeryshire, Powys
(3211 ha; 1167 inhabitants)

Located immediately east of **Welshpool**, the **community** is dominated by the heights of Long **Mountain** and Moel y Golfa. The name is pronounced locally as 'Truhwun' – but any recorded **English** forms of the name, such as Alretone, which like the **Welsh** name refers to a settlement near alder trees, did not survive. Trewern Hall is one of **Montgomeryshire**'s finest half-timbered houses. All **Saints'** church, Middletown (1871), has a curiously carved door brought from Alberbury, **Shropshire**. All Saints' church, Buttington, contains a capital believed to have been brought from the abbey of Strata Marcella (*see* **Welshpool**). Rhyd-y-groes, mentioned in 'Breuddwyd Rhonabwy' (*see* **Mabinogion, The**) was the ford located where Buttington bridge was built in 1872. In 1039, **Gruffudd ap Llywelyn** defeated the **Mercia**ns at the battle of Rhyd-y-groes. Buttington bricks are famous for their hardness and redness.

TRIATHLON

Triathlon, the sport that combines **swimming**, running and **cycling**, was established in Wales in the 1980s and has been administered since 1985 by the Welsh Triathlon Association. There are 30 annual races held in Wales between March and October, including the Excalibur triathlon in **Gower** and the **Brecon** event. In 2001, **Llanberis** became **Britain**'s first ever venue for an official Ironman race, which, in its fullest form, amounts to swimming 3.8 km, cycling 180 km and running 42 km. Wales has produced some of the world's best triathletes. When Annaleise Heard took the junior world championship in 2000 for the second year running, she was the first to do so in triathlon history. In 2002, Leanda Cave won a silver medal in both the **Commonwealth Games** and the senior world championship. Also in 2002, Wales's Richard Jones took the world Ironman championship from Luc Van Lierde.

TRIMSARAN, Carmarthenshire
(1989 ha; 2533 inhabitants)

Located immediately east of **Kidwelly**, the **community**'s most attractive feature is Pont Spwdwr, a six-arch medieval bridge across the Gwendraeth Fawr. The Trimsaran **Iron** Works, established in 1843, attracted numerous migrants from Staffordshire. The local brickworks, opened in 1874, supplied bricks for the building of **Milford Haven** harbour. The vast Ffos Las open-cast site has obliterated the area's numerous small **coal**mines. The **rugby** players Derek Quinnell and Jonathan Davies are natives of Trimsaran.

TRINITY COLLEGE, Carmarthen

The oldest extant teacher-training institution in Wales, Trinity College was founded in 1848 by the (**Anglican**) **National Society** to address the shortage of qualified elementary school teachers at a time when teaching was described as 'a thankless career leading to premature old age and, probably, destitution'. Non-Anglican students were soon admitted, although the college remained male-only until 1957. In recent decades, the college has diversified its course provision, while seeking to retain its historic threefold mission of promoting teacher-training, Welsh culture and the interests of the **Church in Wales**. The college is still owned by the National Society. In 2004, the college became a member of the **University of Wales**. In 2006/7, Trinity had about 3000 students.

TRIOEDD YNYS PRYDAIN (The triads of the Isle of Britain)

The collection of significant events, practices and personages in groups of three was an important mnemonic device in **Celtic Britain** and **Ireland**, whose societies relied on oral instruction for the transmission of vernacular traditions. *Trioedd Ynys Prydain* is the most extensive medieval collection of triads, recording the names of heroes and heroines mainly from the narrative tradition of Wales, as well as the short outlines of some stories. The earliest manuscript copies belong to the 13th century, but it is likely that the triads they contain were collected during the preceding century. Some individual triads are evidently much older, being referred to in both *Y Gododdin* and *The Book of Taliesin*. The practice of **Nonconformist** ministers of organizing their sermons under three headings bears some resemblance to the *Trioedd*.

TRIPP, John (1927–86) Poet

John Tripp was born in **Bargoed**, but the family moved in 1933 to Whitchurch (**Cardiff**). He worked as a journalist in **London**, and returned to live in Whitchurch in 1969, where he made a meagre living as a freelance writer and distinguished himself as a fine performer of poetry. He published eight volumes of poetry, and a selection of his work appeared in *Penguin Modern Poets 27* (1979); his *Selected Poems* appeared posthumously in 1989.

A self-confessed 'modern who reeks of the museum', he was a mordantly witty poet whose work kept a close watch on his country's social and political life. Love, transience and death were themes that came to haunt his later years, characterizing him finally as an ironic chronicler of loss. However, he resisted the comforts of despair, pitting against time's depredations a robust compassion, restorative anger and companionable humour.

TROEDYRAUR (Troed-yr-aur), Ceredigion
(3259 ha; 1408 inhabitants)

Occupying a wide swathe of southern **Ceredigion**, the **community** contains the villages of Brongest, Capel Cynon, Coed-y-bryn, Croes-lan, Ffostrasol, Llangynllo, Penrhiwpâl and Rhydlewis. Dinas Cerdin is a fine **Iron Age hill-fort**. Bronwydd, the centre of the 3202-ha estate of the Lloyd family, was rebuilt as an elaborate Gothic mansion (*c.*1855); abandoned in the 1930s, it is irrecoverably ruined. Rhydlewis was the childhood home of Caradoc Evans

Brian Trubshaw (left), with fellow test pilot John Cochrane, at the controls of Concorde

(**David Evans**; 1878–1945) and the setting for some of the most vicious of his stories. The area is the focus of that masterpiece of rural sociology, David Jenkins's *The agricultural community in southwest Wales at the turn of the twentieth century* (1971). Ffostrasol was the original site of the *Cnapan* folk festival.

TROSTRE TINPLATE WORKS, Llanelli
In 1953, the **Steel Company of Wales** commissioned the Trostre works on a green-field site at **Llanelli**, as part of its modernization strategy. The plant included a cold reduction mill and two electrolytic tinning lines which not only substantially increased productivity but also saw a saving of approximately 50% in the amount required of the increasingly expensive tin. Absorbing the workers released by the closing of hand mills, in 1970 Trostre had 2700 employees and its annual average output was the equivalent of about 550,000 tonnes. Thereafter, changes in technology led to a marked decline in Trostre's labour force. In 2002, following the closure of **Ebbw Vale**, Trostre became **Britain**'s sole **tinplate** manufacturer, producing an average output of around 700,000 tonnes.

TRUBSHAW, Brian (1924–2001) Test pilot
Llanelli-born Brian Trubshaw, whose family owned a local **tinplate** company, won international fame as chief test pilot on the Franco-British Concorde supersonic airliner (*see also* **Morien Morgan**), taking the aircraft on its maiden flight from Filton, Bristol, on 9 April 1969, and carrying out its global tests. Profoundly influenced, at the age of 10, by the landing of the **Prince of Wales**'s aircraft on the beach at **Pembrey**, Trubshaw devoted his life to aeronautics, as a wartime bomber pilot, test pilot and **aviation** consultant.

The second of his two books, *Concorde: The Inside Story*, was published only days before the loss of the Air France Concorde near Paris in July 2000, and the subsequent withdrawal of the Concorde from service.

TRUCK SYSTEM, The
The truck system was introduced in the industrialized areas by employers such as the **Guest family**. Workers were paid vouchers or tokens exchangeable only in company shops, an arrangement that could be considered a useful service in areas lacking retail outlets. By the 1830s, however, the system (also known as the Tommy shop) had come to be regarded as a significant element in the total control exercised by employers. Following the **Merthyr Rising** (1831), truck was made illegal, but the pre-1831 protests and subsequent anti-truck movements, often supported by shopkeepers, showed that the system lived on, with many workers sinking deeper and deeper into debt. The situation began to change only in 1860, with the opening of Wales's first **Co-operative** store at **Cwmbach** near **Aberdare**.

TRUEMAN, A[rthur] E[lijah] (1894–1956)
Geologist and administrator
A graduate in **geology** at Nottingham, Sir Arthur Trueman, FRS, under **T. F. Sibly**'s influence, joined the academic staff at **Cardiff** and then at **Swansea**. Acclaimed as an outstanding geologist, with a wide range of interests, he initiated the departments of geology and **geography** at Swansea. His most distinguished geological work, much of it of direct economic importance, was in theoretical palaeontology and the stratigraphy of the **Coal** Measures and the Lias formation. He later became chair of the University Grants Committee at a critical juncture in its history.

TRYWERYN VALLEY, The drowning of

On 20 December 1955, the water committee of the **Liverpool** Corporation decided that the Tryweryn valley (**Llandderfel/Llanycil**) was the ideal site for its proposed **reservoir**. The city's scheme involved the uprooting of the 48 inhabitants of the village of Capel Celyn and its surrounding farms. In carrying out its plans, Liverpool adopted the procedures it had followed in the 1880s when it created a reservoir in the Vyrnwy valley (**Llanwddyn**) in **Montgomeryshire**. Without consulting any authorities in Wales, it brought forward a parliamentary bill, which received royal assent on 1 August 1957. No Welsh MP voted in favour of the bill in the House of Commons. However, 12 of the country's 36 MPs were absent at the second reading and 16 at the third.

Strenuous efforts were made to oppose the scheme, particularly by **Plaid [Genedlaethol] Cymru**. The perceived high-handed actions of Liverpool were especially resented. To many, the crux of the matter was the dispersal of a wholly **Welsh**-speaking community at a time when such communities were declining rapidly in number. To others, the main issue was the usurpation of Welsh resources by an authority beyond the boundaries of Wales, a point of view that stressed what was, to some, the novel concept of the territorial integrity of Wales. The fact that the drowning had not been endorsed by any of Wales's parliamentary representatives indicated that, as a national entity, Wales was powerless. After the passage of the bill, efforts were made to modify it, culminating in the conference convened by the lord mayor of **Cardiff** in October 1957. Within Plaid Cymru, there were calls for direct action but, largely because of opposition from leading party members in **Merioneth**, no action officially endorsed by the party occurred. However, in 1962 and again in 1963, party supporters committed acts of sabotage in the valley. For the 1963 actions, Emyr Llywelyn and Owain Williams received **prison** sentences.

The Capel Celyn issue had a significant impact upon Welsh politics. It enhanced the role of Plaid Cymru as defender of Welsh rights, although that enhancement was not immediately translated into votes. The readiness of Henry Brooke, the minister of Welsh Affairs (and also the British minister of Local **Government**) to support Liverpool, fuelled the demand for a **secretary of state for Wales**.

TUBERCULOSIS

This ancient affliction, predominantly of the lungs, was traditionally associated with overcrowding and poor hygiene, and became known as 'the white plague'. By the early 21st century, its incidence was comparatively rare, but so devastating were its effects that it was generally considered to have been responsible for more deaths in Wales in the early 20th century than any other disease.

The invention of the stethoscope by the Breton doctor René Laënnec proved a useful tool in the accurate diagnosis of tuberculosis of the lungs. His colleague, Thomas Davies (1792–1839) of **Carmarthen**, is credited with having brought the instrument to **Britain**, but it is not known how widely this new technique was used in Wales at that time.

As there were no known treatments, making an early diagnosis was of less value than would later be the case.

Tryweryn valley residents protesting in Liverpool, 21 November 1956

Eventually, it became apparent that, even though the condition seemed incurable, attempts should be made to prevent it from spreading. Robert Koch, working in Germany, isolated the tubercle bacillus as early as 1882. In spite of the importance of that discovery, the first major advance in dealing with the problem in Wales was not made until 1910. A meeting was called to discuss the most fitting form of memorial for King Edward VII. David Davies (*see* **Davies family (Llandinam)**) suggested that an organization be formed whose aim would be to eliminate the disease, and so the Welsh National King Edward VII Memorial Association was formed. Initially, voluntary contributors, of whom David Davies was the most generous, maintained the work of the association; then, in 1911, the National Insurance Act was passed, allowing local authorities to contribute.

The Temple of Peace and **Health**, **Cardiff**, financed by David Davies, was the organization's headquarters, and medical specialists and their teams of staff were employed to serve every district in Wales. Sanatoria were established so that in-patient treatment could be undertaken. With the coming of the surgical treatment of the disease, the most modern of the sanatoria, and the last to be built by the association, **Sully** Hospital, with its 300 beds, was opened in 1936. This became a specialist centre of great importance. Ultimately, the association became the most active body of its kind in Britain, and possibly in the world. A further impetus, both to research work concerning the problem and to the teaching of doctors, occurred in 1921. This was when the David Davies Professorship of Tuberculosis was established at University College, Cardiff (*see* **Cardiff University**). With the formation of the Welsh National School of Medicine (*see* **Wales College of Medicine, Biology, Life and Health Sciences**), it was transferred there in 1931.

Nevertheless, the scale of the problem continued to cause concern. By 1938, there were nearly 2000 hospital beds for the treatment of the condition, and the death rate from the disease still exceeded that for **England**. An inquiry into the anti-tuberculosis service in Wales, chaired by **Clement Davies**, reported in 1939 that fatalistic attitudes and neglectful local authorities caused tuberculosis to continue to be an intractable problem. It was at its most intractable in rural areas and in the quarrying districts.

In 1944, the first mobile miniature mass radiography unit in the United Kingdom, which could X-ray over 100 individuals an hour, came into use in Wales. Within two years, more than 100,000 people had taken advantage of those facilities. The dramatic fall in the prevalence of the condition during the last century was mainly brought about by an improvement in living conditions and diet. A new era started with the introduction of anti-tuberculous drugs in the 1940s, leading to a further decline in the incidence of the disease.

In the early 21st century, there has been a slight increase in diagnoses in parts of the United Kingdom; they have occurred mostly in large cities and are attributable to homelessness and 'sleeping rough', higher rates of HIV infection, and increased immigration from war-torn and famine-stricken countries. In Wales, however, tuberculosis does not as yet present the major problems that it did in the past.

The Llangefni TB Hospital band, Christmas, 1958

TUDOR family Officials, landowners and monarchs
The sole family of Welsh descent to provide **England** with
a royal dynasty, the Tudors were descended from **Ednyfed
Fychan**, seneschal to **Llywelyn ap Iorwerth**. Following the
Edwardian conquest (1282), Ednyfed's descendants
accepted the new order. In the 14th century, the descendants of his sons, Goronwy, Tudur and Gruffudd, were
prominent in the affairs of the **Principality**. Goronwy's
descendants – the senior line – established the family
known as the Tudors of **Penmynydd** (**Anglesey**). Among
them were the brothers Gwilym and Rhys ap Tudur ap
Goronwy, who served Richard II. Cousins of **Owain
Glyndŵr**, they joined the **Glyndŵr Rising** and captured
Conwy Castle in 1401. Rhys was executed in 1412, and
most of the lands of the Penmynydd family were forfeited,
causing the senior line, which died out in the 17th century,
to be little more than minor squires. A cadet line, descendants of Tudur ab Ednyfed Fychan, won greater prominence as the **Griffith family** of Penrhyn. Another cadet line,
descended from Gruffudd ab Ednyfed, included among its
members Sir **Gruffudd Llwyd** and Sir **Rhys ap Gruffudd**
(d.1356).

It was, however, the largely unknown Maredudd, yet
another son of Tudur ap Goronwy, who was the ancestor of
the royal Tudor line. Maredudd's son, Owain ap Maredudd
ap Tudur (c.1400–61), adopted a fixed **surname**: Tudor. Had
he chosen his father's name rather than his grandfather's,
England, for a century and more, would have been ruled by
the Maredudd dynasty. Owain married Katherine, daughter
of Charles VI of France and widow of Henry V of England,
a dazzling and somewhat inexplicable match for an obscure
Anglesey gentleman. A supporter of the House of **Lancaster**,
he was executed following the **York**ist victory at Mortimer's
Cross (1461) (see **Wars of the Roses**).

Edmund (c.1430–56), Owain's eldest son and Henry VI's
half brother, was created earl of Richmond in 1452/3. He
married the Lancastrian heiress, Margaret Beaufort. In
1457, two months after her husband's death, she gave birth
at **Pembroke** Castle to a son, later Henry VII. Young
Henry was placed under the care of William **Herbert, earl
of Pembroke**, at **Raglan** Castle and then under that of his
uncle Jasper Tudor (c.1431–95). Jasper, created earl of
Pembroke c.1455, became the champion of the power of
his half-brother, Henry VI, in Wales. After the Lancastrian
defeat at Tewkesbury in 1471 and the deaths of Henry VI
and his son, Jasper took his nephew into exile in **Brittany**,
for Henry had become, as the Yorkist Edward IV put it,
'the only imp now left of Henry VI's brood'. Richard III's
seizure of the crown in 1483 changed Henry's fortunes dramatically and Jasper used his Welsh connections to build
up support in Wales; the Welsh tradition of prophetic
poetry was harnessed to Henry's cause. An attempted invasion in 1483 was unsuccessful but, in August 1485, Henry
landed at **Dale**, on the **Milford Haven Waterway**. He
advanced through Wales, gathering support on the way.
Richard was killed at **Bosworth** and Henry became king of
England. The Welsh saw Bosworth as a Welsh victory and
the fulfilment of **prophecy**, and Henry was well aware of his
Welsh roots. Jasper, elevated to the dukedom of Bedford,
was granted the marcher-lordship of **Glamorgan** and given
the chief offices in the **Principality** and the **March**. His

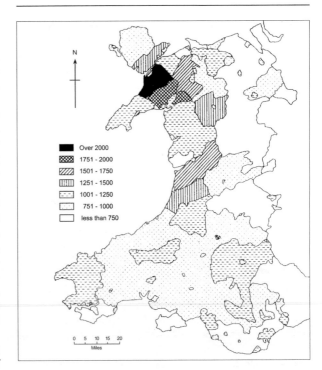

Tuberculosis: average annual death toll per million of the population,
1930–6

praises were sung by **Lewys Glyn Cothi** and **Dafydd
Nanmor**. (For the impact of Henry VII's reign upon Wales,
see **English Monarchs and Wales**.)

TUDUR ALED (c.1470–1525) Poet

Traditionally associated with **Llansannan**, where his family
roots were, Tudur may have been a native of the **commote**
of **Iâl**. He was taught by **Dafydd ab Edmwnd**, whom he
described as 'My uncle by blood'. He was an adviser to the
commissioners of the **Caerwys eisteddfod** of 1523, where he
was the chaired bard. He travelled widely in Wales; however, his chief patrons – the **Salusbury family** of Lleweni
(**Denbigh**) among them – were in the north-east. His poetry
is renowned for its complex *cynghanedd* and its many polished epigrammatic couplets. A poem requesting the gift of
a **horse** is justifiably famous; his well-known poem to
Hwmffre ap Hywel of Tywyn (a farm near **Cardigan**), urging reconciliation with his kinsmen, criticized the querulousness of the **gentry** and their fondness for litigation.
Having donned the Franciscan habit, he died and was
buried at **Carmarthen Friary**.

TUDWEILIOG, Gwynedd
(3553 ha; 810 inhabitants)

Located on the north coast of the **Llŷn peninsula** between
Nefyn and **Aberdaron**, the **community** extends to Carn
Fadryn (371 m), a hill rich in prehistoric remains. The area
has been dominated for centuries by the Griffith family of
Cefnamwlch and their descendants the Wynne-Finches. In
the 17th century, the squire – William Griffith of Llŷn, as
he styled himself – was the richest man in **Caernarfonshire**.
Sidney Griffith (Madam Griffith; d.1752) of Cefnamwlch
was a fervent supporter of the Methodist **Howel Harris** –
a relationship that led to much malicious gossip. The

Carn Fadryn, Tudweiliog

mansion of Cefnamwlch (late 17th century) is adjoined by a gatehouse (1607). Nearby is the fine Coetan Arthur **Neolithic** chambered tomb. St Gwynhoedl's church, Llangwnnadl, completed *c.*1520, consists of three aisles. The small mansion of Bryn Nodol was visited by Samuel Johnson in 1774.

TUNNICLIFFE, Charles (1901–79)
Illustrator and ornithologist
Tunnicliffe's extraordinary studies of the wildlife and **birds** of **Anglesey** were begun after the **Cheshire**-born artist moved to Malltraeth (**Bodorgan**) in 1947. Having trained at Macclesfield School of Art and the Royal College of Art in **London**, he taught illustration and graphic **design**, illustrating Henry Williamson's *Tarka the Otter* (1932) and, later, books for the Ladybird natural history series; he was one of the illustrators employed in the **Second World War** 'Dig for Victory' campaign. His measured drawings were exact in observation and meticulously drawn. His responses to weather, landscape and local society demonstrate his great sensitivity to subject and materials. The largest collection of his work is exhibited at Oriel Ynys Môn (**Llangefni**).

TURNBULL, Maurice [Joseph Lawson] (1906–44)
Cricketer and rugby player
An extraordinarily gifted sportsman, **Cardiff**-born Maurice Turnbull played **hockey**, **squash** and **rugby** for Wales, winning one of his two caps at scrum-half in the first ever win at Twickenham in 1933. But he is most remembered for his contribution to **Glamorgan cricket**, as a benevolent autocrat who worked with **J. C. Clay** to rescue the club during his period as captain (1930–9) and secretary (1932–9). A **county** debutant while still at Downside School, he was the first Welshman to play for **England**, winning nine caps between 1929 and 1936. He scored a total of 17,544 runs, including an innings of 205 against Nottinghamshire in 1932 when fast bowlers Harold Larwood and Bill Voce were experimenting with the 'bodyline' attack that would destroy **Australia** the following winter. Had he survived the war – he died in Normandy – he might have captained England.

TURNER, J[oseph] M[allord] W[illiam] (1775–1851) Painter
The English artist J. M. W. Turner visited Wales several times in the formative years of his career. His famous images of **Snowdon** and **Tintern** Abbey were among those that fuelled the imaginations of the romantic poets, contributing significantly to the idea of landscape as a source of mystery and inspiration (*see* **Romanticism** and **Landforms, Landscape and Topography**). On various tours between 1790–7, he was as moved by the new industrial landscape of the south as he was by the romantic vistas and castles of the north, the journeys preparing him for his epic adventures in mainland Europe, as he searched for the subject matter to match his pictorial ambitions.

TURNER, Joseph (*c.*1729–1807) Architect

One of a family of architects from the **Flintshire/Shropshire border**, Joseph Turner was living in **Hawarden** in the 1760s, but from about 1774 was in Chester; he was buried in Hawarden. His buildings include Pengwern (1770; **Rhuddlan**), **Ruthin** Gaol (1775), Ruthin **County** Hall (1785–90) and **Flint** Gaol (1785). His nephew, John Turner (d.1827), of Whitchurch (Shropshire), furnished the choir of **St Asaph** Cathedral, made alterations to **Llandygai** church, and became Flintshire county surveyor.

TWENTY-FOUR FEATS OF SKILL, The

A series of exercises and feats are mentioned by several poets from the 15th century onwards and described by antiquarians, especially **Edward Jones** (Bardd y Brenin; 1752–1824) in particular, who claimed that in the Middle Ages they were standard practices which all gentlemen worthy of their status and of the chivalric code were bound to accomplish. Poets alluded to their patrons' excellence in individual feats, proof that they should be esteemed as gentlemen. The skills comprised a range of domestic and literary tasks, rural sports such as **fish**ing and falconry, weaponry exercises and rigorous **athletic** pursuits such as throwing, **horse** riding, running, jumping, **swimming** and wrestling.

TWMPATH DAWNS

Organized by **Urdd Gobaith Cymru**, *twmpathau dawns* (loosely translated as 'barn **dances**', essentially a form of folk dancing) flourished in Wales during the late 1950s and 1960s when they were prominent in the evening entertainment of young **Welsh**-speakers, particularly in rural areas. With enjoyment the main objective, dances were simple to learn and required no special dress. Their popularity continued until the early 1970s when they were overtaken by pop **music** concerts and the discotheque, although they continue to be held on occasion.

TWRCELYN Commote

A **commote** in north-east **Anglesey**, which, with that of **Talybolion**, formed the *cantref* of **Cemaes**. The commotal centre was at Penrhoslligwy (*see* **Moelfre**). The name survived as that of a post-**Acts of 'Union' hundred** and, from 1894 to 1974, a **rural district**.

TWRCH TRWYTH, The

A king metamorphosed into a **wild boar** for his sins, this legendary monster is referred to in both *Y Gododdin* and *Historia Brittonum*, but is more fully represented in the tale of 'Culhwch ac Olwen' in *The Mabinogion*. It tells how **Arthur** and his men hunt the ferocious beast in order to snatch from between his ears the scissors and comb that are required to trim the beard and hair of Ysbaddaden Bencawr for the marriage of his daughter.

'TYDI A RODDAIST' (Thou Who Gavest) Hymn

A **hymn** written in 1938 as the conclusion to a St **David**'s Day verse play for radio, *Wales*, by **T. Rowland Hughes** (words) and **Arwel Hughes**, to whom the melody came in a waiting room at Shrewsbury **railway** station. The composer's own arrangement for **male voice choirs** has

Charles Tunnicliffe, *The Rivals* (*c.*1951)

Arwel Hughes

achieved lasting popularity, not least because of its triumphant fourfold 'Amen'.

TYLWYTH TEG, Y (The fair tribe)

In the 19th century, many tales of the *tylwyth teg* were recorded by antiquarians such as **Isaac Foulkes** and Elias Owen (1833–99), author of *Welsh Folk-lore* (1888), and in **periodicals** of the time. These indicate that the tales were current in all parts of Wales and that the motifs were similar to those in circulation in other countries. An early **Welsh dictionary** equates *tylwyth teg* with the **English** word 'fairy', and Welsh narratives use both terms, as well as more local terms, such as *plant Rhys Ddyfyn* (the children of Rhys the Deep) (current in the Teifi Valley), *bendith y mamau* (the mothers' blessing) (**Glamorgan**) and *dynion bach teg* (the small fair men) (**Pembrokeshire**).

The term exploits the ambiguities of physical beauty, moral behaviour and supernatural otherness. **Giraldus Cambrensis** (*c.*1146–1223) describes the abstemious and honest inhabitants of a mysterious realm in **Gower**, but **Walter Map** (*c.*1140–1209) depicts a darker side, when King Herla follows a sinister, Pan-like creature to a sunless underground world. Gwyn ap Nudd represents a link between the *tylwyth teg* and Welsh mythology. Gwyn is named in a poem in *The Black Book of Carmarthen* and in 'Culhwch ac Olwen' (*see* **Mabinogion, The**). However, too much should not be made of the similarities between fairy narratives and episodes containing mythological characters in *The Mabinogion*. Shared themes and motifs need not indicate a shared source; *tylwyth teg* narratives in Welsh have stronger connections with fairy-lore throughout Europe (and beyond) than with mythology. Important narrative types include Walter Map's 12th-century tale of the fairy bride, and stories associated with **lakes**, such as **Llyn y Fan Fach** in **Carmarthenshire**. In addition, there are tales of changelings, fairy gifts, visits to and rescues from fairy realms, human midwives and fairy mothers, domestic implements borrowed by fairies, and visits from fairy **dogs**

and children, as well as numerous sightings and **place name** legends. Such narratives were common in Wales at least until the early 20th century.

TYSILIO (7th century) 'Saint'

Traditionally known as the son of Brochfael Ysgithrog, king of **Powys**, and pupil and successor of Gwyddfarch, first abbot of **Meifod**. Under Tysilio's leadership Meifod became the religious centre of Powys. The reputation of the **saint** and his community is reflected in a poem by **Cynddelw Brydydd Mawr** (12th century). Tysilio's feast day is 8 November.

TYWI River (120 km)

The Tywi rises at 450 m in the **community** of **Ystrad Fflur** in the **Elenydd Mountains**. It then flows due south for 13 km to its confluence with the Camddwr, which drains the least inhabited part of Wales; Soar y Mynydd (**Llanddewi Brefi**), Wales's remotest chapel, stands on the banks of the Camddwr. The confluence between the Camddwr and the Tywi lies beneath Llyn Brianne, a **reservoir** created in the 1970s to supply **Swansea** with water. South of the reservoir, the Tywi is joined by the Doethie and then flows through an ever-widening valley to **Llandovery**, where it turns south-westwards. The Tywi valley between Llandovery and **Carmarthen** is the heart of Wales's dairying country. At its centre is **Llandeilo**, where the Cennen, which washes the foot of the crag crowned by Castell Carreg Cennen (**Dyffryn Cennen**), joins the Tywi. At **Llanegwad**, the Tywi is joined by the Cothi; although a tributary, its 54 km makes it longer than most of the 'real' **rivers** of Wales. The widening Tywi below Carmarthen was once a busy **shipping** lane, a key factor in enabling Carmarthen to be, for centuries, the largest town in Wales.

TYWYN, Gwynedd (2788 ha; 3227 inhabitants)

Located immediately north of **Aberdovey**, the **community** contains Broad Water, the extensive tidal **lake** at the mouth of the Dysynni. St Cadfan's church (12th century and 1885) was the mother church of most of the *cantref* of **Meirionnydd**. Within it is the most important of Wales's early inscribed stones (*see* **Monuments, Early Christian**). **Ifor Williams**'s reading of the inscription is as follows:

+ TENGRUI CIMALTE[D] GU | ADGAN | |
ANT ERUNC DU BUT MARCIAU | | + CUN BEN
CELEN | | TRICET NITANAM.

(Ceinrwy, the wife of Addian [lies here] alongside
Bud [and] Meirchiaw,
Cun, the wife of Celyn: grief and loss remain.)

Experts disagree about the date of the inscription, offering dates varying from the 7th to the 9th century, but all agree that the inscription provides the earliest record of the **Welsh language**. The church also contains two early 14th-century effigies, and tombs of members of the Corbet family of Ynysmaengwyn (**Bryn-crug**). Tywyn is the terminus of the Talyllyn **Railway** (1865). Tywyn as a holiday resort came into existence in the late 19th century. Cwm Maethlon (tourist-speak: Happy Valley) is a picturesque glen.

Rhydygwin Unitarian Chapel, Ystrad Aeron, Ceredigion

UNDEB CENEDLAETHOL ATHRAWON CYMRU (UCAC) (The National Union of the Teachers of Wales)

UCAC is the only trade union working solely through the medium of **Welsh**. It was established in **Cardiff** in 1940 and its head office was moved to **Aberystwyth** in 1983. The union, which in 2006 had 4065 members, has been particularly active in promoting **education** through the medium of Welsh. When education became the responsibility of the **Welsh Office**, other unions involved in education – the National Union of Teachers (NUT), the National Association of Headteachers (NAHT) and the National Association of Schoolmasters/Union of **Women** Teachers (NASUWT) strengthened their presence in Wales, a development even more marked after the establishment of the **National Assembly**.

UNDEB CYMRU FYDD (The Union of the Wales to be)

The result of the merger, in 1941, of Undeb Cenedlaethol y Cymdeithasau Cymreig (The National Union of Welsh Associations) with Pwyllgor Amddiffyn Diwylliant Cymru (The Committee for the Defence of the Culture of Wales), Undeb Cymru Fydd became a forum for all those concerned for the well-being of the **Welsh language** and culture. It acted as a pressure group, lobbying for increased provision for Welsh in **broadcasting** and **education** and against the acquisition of Welsh land for military purposes (*see* **Military Bases**). It was instrumental in the launch of the Parliament for Wales Campaign (1950). Largely eclipsed by **Cymdeithas yr Iaith Gymraeg** (The Welsh Language Society) in the early 1960s, it became an educational charity in 1966, but had ceased to exist by 1969.

UNITARIANS

Unitarianism is the belief that salvation comes, not through faith in the divinity of Christ, but through following his precepts and example; it rejects the concept of original sin and maintains that human reason is the key to understanding the **Bible**. While Unitarian elements may be found in the early history of the Christian Church, in the thinking of the Italian reformer Socinus (1539–1604) and in the writings of the deist Lord Herbert of Cherbury (**Edward Herbert**), Unitarianism in Wales owes its origin to the reaction against the High **Calvinism** that was prevalent among early 18th-century Dissenters (*see* **Nonconformists and Dissenters**). Owing much to the liberal atmosphere of the **Nonconformist Academy** at **Carmarthen**, the reaction

895

developed from **Arminianism** (the belief that God weaves man's response into the work of salvation) into **Arianism** (the belief that the Son is not of the same substance as the Father) and on to full Unitarianism.

The first Unitarian congregation in Wales was that founded in 1733 by the Carmarthen ex-student John Jenkins at Llwynrhydowen (**Llandysul**). By 1851, 17 of Wales's 27 Unitarian chapels were located in southern **Cardiganshire** and northern **Carmarthenshire**, causing that area to be the denomination's sole rural stronghold in **Britain**. Denying the Trinity remained a criminal offence until 1813, and the loathing which that denial inspired caused the area around Llandysul to be known as the 'Black Spot'. Other congregations came into being around **Merthyr Tydfil**, **Aberdare**, **Swansea** and **Wrexham** – congregations to which early industrial **radicalism** would be greatly indebted. Wales's first Nonconformist MP was the Unitarian **Walter Coffin**, who represented **Cardiff** (1852–7).

Leading Welsh Unitarians include Iolo Morganwg (**Edward Williams**), Gwilym Marles (William Thomas; 1834–79), who was driven from Llwynrhydowen by a vengeful landlord, **David Ivon Jones**, a founder of the **South African Communist Party**, and the broadcaster and pensioners' champion **D. Jacob Davies**.

UNIVERSITY OF GLAMORGAN, The

The University of **Glamorgan** began life in 1913 as a School of Mines. Established by a group of leading **coal**owners in Treforest House (**Pontypridd**), former home of the **iron**master Francis **Crawshay**, it was funded through a levy of one tenth of a penny on each ton of coal produced by the companies involved. During the **depression of the interwar years**, the school was taken over by Glamorgan **County** Council. In 1949, it was renamed the Glamorgan Technical College and later the Glamorgan College of Technology, before becoming the Glamorgan Polytechnic (1969). Following a merger with the Glamorgan and **Monmouthshire** College of **Education** at **Barry**, it was renamed the Polytechnic of Wales. In 1992, the Polytechnic became the University of Glamorgan, with powers to grant its own degrees. The University has 11 faculties, which include arts and humanities, social **science**s and **law**, in addition to a range of business, scientific and technological faculties. Mining is no longer part of the curriculum, reflecting the radical change in the post-war **economy** of Wales. The institution has played a significant role in teaching **Welsh** to adults, setting up, in 1967, the first ever course for this purpose. In 2006/7, the university had about 21,000 students, 10,000 of whom were part-time.

UNIVERSITY OF WALES, The

Had **Owain Glyndŵr** succeeded in his ambition to create two universities, higher **education** in Wales would no doubt have developed in a very different way. Thereafter, over four centuries elapsed before national enthusiasm was fired to secure a university. One of its leading advocates was Thomas Nicholas (1816–79), whose eloquence won the attention of **Hugh Owen** (1804–81), who became the key figure in the educational life of Wales. That many of the people of Wales had a reverence for education

found remarkable manifestation in the fund-raising collections made on 'University Sunday', namely the last Sundays in October 1875, 1876 and 1877. After a heroic struggle, a university college was opened at **Aberystwyth** (1872; *see* **University of Wales, Aberystwyth**) and, by 1884, another two – at **Cardiff** and **Bangor** – were preparing students for the University of **London** degree (*see* **Cardiff University** and **University of Wales, Bangor**). The unsatisfactory division between teaching (in the colleges) and examining (by London) continued until 1893, when the University of Wales received its foundation charter. Henceforth, students were taught in their own colleges and examined by the University of Wales. Among the growing pains was contention over the location of the University Registry, which was opened at **Cathays Park**, Cardiff, in 1904. The university's financial privation and other defects prompted the **government**, in 1916, to appoint Lord Haldane to chair a royal commission to examine university education in Wales. The ensuing Haldane Report (1918) is the most influential and valuable document in the history of the university. It firmly stated that one federal, national university was the ideal, but proposed strengthening the autonomy of the constituent colleges. A central executive council was created, and an academic board replaced the laborious procedures of the senate. The path was prepared to receive a new college, the University College of **Swansea**, into the university (1920; *see* **University of Wales Swansea**). After much debate, the Welsh National School of Medicine (*see* **Wales College of Medicine, Biology, Life and Health Sciences**) opened in 1931. Mindful of their roots, it was natural for the colleges to provide extramural classes; in 1920, an extension board was formed to co-ordinate their activities. There were significant developments in this field, especially during the **Depression**.

From 1945 onwards, the number of students increased, with the rise in the number of students from **England** causing tension on occasion. There was a campaign, led mainly by members of staff, to de-federalize the university, but in 1964, after sharp exchanges, the court declared in favour of the status quo. The supplemental charter of 1967 increased the number of court and council members. The University of Wales Institute of Science and Technology (UWIST) became a constituent college in 1967 (uniting with Cardiff in 1988), as did St **David**'s College, **Lampeter** in 1971 (*see* **University of Wales, Lampeter**) and the **University of Wales, Newport**, in 2004.

During the 1980s, University College, Cardiff fell into severe financial difficulties, which caused concern in universities throughout the United Kingdom. The university was powerless to interfere and a committee under the chairmanship of **Goronwy Daniel** was asked to consider its structure and effectiveness. The committee's recommendations were accepted, and subsequently **Melvyn Rosser** chaired a committee (which reported in 1993) to consider recent developments, such as the creation of the **Higher Education Funding Council for Wales** and of the **University of Glamorgan**. It was resolved to form a powerful board, consisting of the six vice-chancellors, which would appoint a senior vice-chancellor and a secretary general, and give special emphasis to a federal partnership between the university's constituent institutions and the colleges.

De-federalization resurfaced in more virulent form in 2004, when the University of Wales College of Medicine merged with the University of Wales, Cardiff, and the new institution – as Cardiff University – seceded from the University of Wales. However, at the same time, four other institutions became members of the University of Wales – the **North East Wales Institute of Higher Education (Wrexham)**; the **Swansea Institute of Higher Education, Trinity College (Carmarthen)** and the **Royal Welsh College of Music and Drama** (Cardiff). The number of constituent institutions separately incorporated and directly funded thereby rose from six to ten, the other member colleges being the University of Wales, Aberystwyth; the University of Wales, Bangor; the **University of Wales Institute, Cardiff**; the University of Wales Swansea; the University of Wales, Lampeter; and the University of Wales, Newport.

By the 21st century, the university was the degree-awarding authority not only for its member institutions, but also for around 50 other higher education institutions both within the United Kingdom and overseas. Annually, it awarded almost 15,000 initial degrees and more than 4000 higher degrees, making it the second largest degree-awarding body in the United Kingdom after the University of London. The member institutions of the University of Wales and its validated schemes of study accounted for a student population of nearly 90,000 located all over the world. Nevertheless, in 2007, the University of Wales underwent a radical change, when it ceased being a federal body and from its central services, a separate higher education institute was created (a vice-chancellor was appointed

in the same year). Its original constituent members became a confederation of institutions of higher education accredited with awarding its degrees. But, with Swansea, Aberystwyth and Bangor all securing the right, by 2007, to award their own degrees, there was increasing uncertainty about their long-term commitment to a University of Wales degree. Swansea, from the beginning of the 2007/8 academic year, became, as Swansea University, an institution independent of the University of Wales (*see below*).

In its new form, the University of Wales continues to have a special responsibility for the promotion of Welsh studies, particularly through the University of Wales Press (*see* **Printing and Publishing**) and the **University of Wales Centre for Advanced Welsh and Celtic Studies**; the **Board of Celtic Studies** was subsumed by the Centre in 2007. A munificent gift to the university from Margaret Davies (*see* **Davies family (Llandinam)**) in 1960 was Gregynog (**Tregynon**), a beautiful centre in **Montgomeryshire** where residential courses are held.

UNIVERSITY OF WALES BOARD OF CELTIC STUDIES, The

Established in 1920, and subsumed by the Centre for Advanced Welsh and Celtic Studies in 2007, the Board of Celtic Studies aimed to promote Celtic studies in Wales, to employ researchers to undertake short-term projects, to publish the fruits of that research and to support the publication of four scholarly journals: *Studia Celtica*, *Welsh History Review*, *Llên Cymru* and *Contemporary Wales*. One of the principal projects of the Board was *Geiriadur Prifysgol Cymru*, the first standard historical **dictionary** of the **Welsh language**.

Cardiff University

UNIVERSITY OF WALES CENTRE FOR ADVANCED WELSH AND CELTIC STUDIES, The

The **University of Wales** Centre for Advanced Welsh and **Celtic** Studies was established at **Aberystwyth** in 1985. It is housed in a building adjoining the National **Library** which also contains the unit producing *Geiriadur Prifysgol Cymru* (*see* **Dictionaries**). Its aim is to undertake research of high quality in the language, **literature** and history of Wales and the other Celtic countries. Among the most notable of its pioneering projects are The **Poets of the Princes**, The Social History of the **Welsh Language**, The Poetry of the Poets of the **Gentry**, The Visual Culture of Wales and The Celtic Languages and Cultural Identity. It merged with the Board of Celtic Studies in 2007.

UNIVERSITY OF WALES INSTITUTE CARDIFF (UWIC), The

In 1996, UWIC became part of the **University of Wales**. Established in that year as the **Cardiff** Institute of Higher **Education**, it had previously been the South **Glamorgan** Institute of Higher Education. That institution, administered by the local education authority, had resulted from a merger (1976) of the Cardiff College of Education, the Llandaff College of Technology, the Cardiff College of **Food** Technology and Commerce, and the Cardiff School of Art. Specializing in vocational degrees and applied research, UWIC is particularly well-known for its teacher-training and sports-related courses. In 2006/7, UWIC had over 9000 students.

UNIVERSITY OF WALES SWANSEA, The (SWANSEA UNIVERSITY)

There was bitter disappointment in **Swansea** in 1882 when it was decided to locate the southern university college in **Cardiff** (*see* **Cardiff University**). In 1916, however, an opportunity came to present the Haldane Commission with Swansea's claims as the centre of a large and flourishing industrial region (*see* **University of Wales**). It was a great advantage that a technical college had been founded

The Shankland Reading Room at the library of the University of Wales, Bangor

there in 1903. Having met the commission's conditions, the University College, Swansea received its charter in 1920. The original site, in Mount Pleasant, proved unsatisfactory; a gift from Swansea's corporation allowed the whole college to be brought together in Singleton Park. At first, the college concentrated on the **sciences**, but the arts were soon nurtured. Apart from the unhappy episode relating to **Saunders Lewis** in 1936–7 (*see* **Penyberth Bombing School, The burning of**), the college developed smoothly. In the 1960s, new buildings were erected and the college, splendidly located overlooking the Severn Sea, became Wales's finest example of a compact university campus. Swansea has five faculties: arts and social studies; business, economics and **law**; **engineering**; science; **education** and **health** studies. In the early 21st century, considerable controversy was caused by the decision to close several departments, some of which – **philosophy** and **chemistry** in particular – had a very distinguished history.

In 2005, Swansea was given Privy Council approval to award its own – as distinct from University of Wales – degrees, thereby threatening the University of Wales with further fragmentation. In addition, for publicity purposes, the college adopted the title Swansea University.

It was announced in May 2007 that from the beginning of the academic year 2007/8, the institution would complete its detachment from the University of Wales by becoming the independent University of Swansea.

Important recent developments include the School of European Languages, the School of Health Science, with its strong emphasis on nursing, and the £50 million Institute of Life Science, the largest research investment ever made at Swansea, which opened in 2007. In 2006/7, the University of Wales Swansea had about 12,000 students.

UNIVERSITY OF WALES, ABERYSTWYTH, The

It was a strong national movement that led to the founding of Wales's first university college in 1872. Earlier hopes of establishing a university awarding its own degrees had come to nothing. Thus, it was a college, not a university, which opened at **Aberystwyth**, with its students studying for the degrees of the University of **London**. For more than a century, it rejoiced in the title University College of Wales. Its all-Wales profile was strengthened by the fact that its catchment area of Welsh students was wider than that of the other Welsh colleges. More than one site had been considered until an unexpected opportunity came to buy a grand hotel on the Aberystwyth seafront – a venture of the bankrupted **Thomas Savin**. Contributions came from all over Wales and beyond. As stressed by its main founder, **Hugh Owen**, the remarkable sacrifice of the poor was a reproach to the wealthy. Yet privation continued: much of the college was consumed by fire in 1885, and it was the exemplary loyalty of former students that sustained the institution, especially after the establishment of grant-aided colleges at **Cardiff** and **Bangor**. In 1893, Aberystwyth joined with the other two colleges to form the **University of Wales**. It was long called 'the College by the sea' because of the seafront site of the Old College, where the departments of **education** and **Welsh** and the registry remain. In 1929, the college received 36 ha at Penglais,

above the town, and in the second half of the 20th century most of the academic departments came to be located there. As at Bangor, special attention has been paid to **agriculture** and rural affairs. The college's proximity to the **National Library** and to the **Centre for Advanced Welsh and Celtic Studies** helps to enhance its role. Its Arts Centre includes a Great Hall, Theatr y Werin, an **art gallery** and a **film** theatre. The college has made a disproportionate contribution to Welsh life, especially in **literature**, **historiography**, **geography** and **law**. Its Welsh-medium hall of residence, Pantycelyn, contains the world's largest Welsh-speaking community under one roof. The present title is the University of Wales, Aberystwyth. In the academic year 2006/7, Aberystwyth had over 7000 students, ensuring that the town has a remarkably modern and thriving ambience, in spite of its geographical isolation.

UNIVERSITY OF WALES, BANGOR, The

After keen competition, and much influenced by the enthusiasm of **slate** quarrymen, the University College of North Wales (as it was called initially) was founded at **Bangor** in 1844. Its first home was the Penrhyn Arms, an old coaching house. The need for additional accommodation prompted the city of Bangor to present the college with the admirable Penrallt site above the city in 1903. A noble building, designed by H. T. Hare – 'the College on the Hill' – was opened in 1911. Suitable **science** buildings were not provided until 1926. From the 1950s onwards, the rise in the number of students, with the majority of them coming from **England**, created the need for a firm bilingual policy. St Mary's College joined the college in 1976, followed by the **Normal College** in 1996. Pioneering courses in nursing **education** began in the 1990s, and, in 1998, building on a long tradition of adult education, a concordat linked eight further education colleges and two higher education colleges to form the Community University of North Wales. Close relations with local industry are fostered. Apart from the **National Library**, Bangor houses the richest manuscript collection in Wales. In 2006/7, Bangor had about 12,000 students.

UNIVERSITY OF WALES, LAMPETER, The

Thomas Burgess, bishop of **St David's**, diligently collected funds to establish a college for ordinands in his **diocese**. Founded in 1822 and opened in 1827, St David's College (currently known as the University of Wales, **Lampeter**) is the oldest higher **education** institution in Wales and **England**, apart from **Oxford** and **Cambridge**. It received the right to award the degree of Bachelor of Divinity in 1852 and of Bachelor of Arts in 1865. Denominational differences precluded its inclusion in the federal **University of Wales** in 1893. For decades, the great majority of students were **Anglicans** preparing for holy orders. State grants were not received and financial stringency in the 1950s seemed to presage a dark future. In 1960, the University College, **Cardiff** (**Cardiff University**) sponsored the college, which, as St David's University College, was incorporated as a constituent institution of the University of Wales in 1971. It renounced the right to award its own degree so that its students might receive the degree of the University of Wales. New subjects were introduced and there were additions to the original buildings, which are the closest Wales

The University of Wales, Lampeter, as it appeared when it opened as St David's College in 1827

has to a pastiche of an Oxbridge court. The library has a notable collection of books and manuscripts. Lampeter is considered to be Europe's smallest university institution. In 2006/7, it had around 1000 resident students, although there were thousands more following its part-time and long-distance teaching.

UNIVERSITY OF WALES, NEWPORT, The

Newport Technical Institute, founded in 1910, became two institutions in 1958: a College of Art and a College of Technology. **Caerleon** College, as the **Monmouthshire** Training College was known, opened in 1914 and, by the 1960s, it was one of the chief teacher-training centres in Wales. The **Gwent** College of Higher **Education** (1975) was formed by the union of Caerleon College of Education, Newport School of Art and **Design**, and Gwent College of Technology. It was given corporate status and, as one of the main providers of higher education in Wales, it won the right to grant degrees in 1995; it became an associated college of the **University of Wales** in 1996 with the title of University of Wales College, Newport; it adopted its present title in 2004 when it became a constituent college of the University. In 2006/7, the institution had about 9000 students.

UPPER KILLAY (Cilâ Uchaf), Swansea
(526 ha; 1308 inhabitants)
The **community**'s main settlement is a straggling village, which originated as a 19th-century **railway** and **coal**mining settlement. Located on the western slope of Clyne valley, it was crossed by the Central Wales Railway, the bed of

which forms part of the **Swansea** Bike Path. **William Jernegan**'s Fairwood Lodge (1830s) is the residence of visiting justices.

URBAN (d.1134) Bishop
Urban, a priest from Worcester, succeeded Herewald in 1107 as the first **Norman** bishop of **Morgannwg**. The first Welsh bishop recorded as having professed obedience to Canterbury, Urban's most significant achievement was the transformation of a **diocese** of nebulous origins and boundaries into the see of Llandaff (*see* **Cardiff**). He organized the building of a cathedral in the Romanesque style at Llandaff and may have commissioned the *Liber Landavensis* (Book of Llandaff), whose suspicious charters and other texts purport to document the history of Urban's predecessors over seven centuries – from St **Dyfrig**, the supposed founder of Llandaff, to Urban himself. His principal preoccupations were disputes over diocesan boundaries and episcopal estates with his neighbouring bishops, **Bernard** of **St David's** and Robert de Bethune of Hereford; this involved a pioneering series of legal suits at the papal courts for over 15 years. Urban died at Pisa in October 1134, arguing his case before Pope Innocent II.

URBAN DISTRICTS
Under the Local **Government** Act of 1894, urban settlements which were not **boroughs** – and these included many of the most heavily populated industrial areas of Wales – could claim the status of urban district. An urban district council, headed by a chairman rather than a mayor, had responsibility for matters such as **housing**, sanitation and

public **health**, and was financed by retention of part of the county rate. By the mid 20th century, Wales had 73 urban districts, varying in **population** from **Pontypool** (42,000) to **Hay** (500). The local government reorganization of 1974 abolished them all and transferred their powers to districts – subdivisions of the new **counties**.

URBAN PLANNING

The **Roman** occupation of Wales was essentially military in character and, in order to maintain control, numerous geometrically planned forts were erected across the country at regular intervals. The Romans also built towns at **Caerwent** (Venta Silurum) and **Carmarthen** (Moridunum). Both towns were roughly rectangular in plan and each was divided by a main street. At Caerwent, the town was divided by shorter streets into 20 uniformly square blocks with a large market place (*forum*) and an aisled assembly hall (*basilica*) at the centre; nearby were public baths and a temple. The layout at Carmarthen was probably similar. By the early 5th century, the Roman towns and forts had been largely abandoned.

An urban **economy** did not develop again in Wales until after the **Norman** invasions. Even then, it was largely a matter of creating artificial **boroughs**, many of them protected by fortified walls, for new settlers introduced under the protective wing of their **English** masters. These towns, often founded in the shadow of castles, were created as much for political as for economic reasons. In planning the new towns, provision was made for standard-sized plots of land for the burgesses and centrally placed plots for churches and a market.

The most outstanding example of medieval urban planning was the chain of *bastide* towns that were established by Edward I alongside his castles at **Conwy** (1283) and **Caernarfon** (1284). Each new town was defended by strong walls and powerful gateways, and was laid out, wherever possible, on a gridiron system of straight streets and rectilinear plots. Unlike Roman forts and towns, Edwardian towns varied greatly, depending on site and topography for their shape and layout.

A lack of significant urban development in Wales during the following centuries meant that the new planning ideas that had been introduced into **England** in the 17th century had little opportunity of gaining acceptance in Welsh towns until the late 18th and early 19th centuries. Among the earliest manifestations of urban planning according to **Renaissance** principles of formality were the planned town adjoining the naval dockyard at **Pembroke Dock** (1809 onwards), the **ports** of **Milford Haven** (1797 onwards), Tremadog (**Porthmadog**; 1800 onwards) and **Aberaeron** (1807 onwards). Apart from Pembroke Dock, the towns were established by landowners keen to develop their estates. In rural areas, early 19th-century model estate villages – such as **Llandygai** and **Llanfachreth**, with their 'rustic' cottages; Marford (**Rossett**), with its fanciful 'Gothic' cottages; and **Merthyr Mawr**, with its low, thatched cottages – were treated in a picturesque manner.

Planned development in industrial areas was mostly limited to small housing estates, such as the Triangle (built in the 1820s, demolished 1973) at Pentrebach (**Merthyr Tydfil**), and Y Drenewydd – or Butetown (**Rhymney**). A

The Triangle at Pentrebach, Merthyr Tydfil: working class housing, built in the 1820s and demolished in 1973

notable exception was Morriston (**Swansea**; 1779), where **William Edwards** designed a new village for employees of Sir John Morris's **copper** works. A more radical solution was adopted at **Tredegar** where a new town was built (*c.*1810–20) with a formally planned centre comprising a circular piazza with streets radiating off it – one leading to the **iron**works, another to the manager's house and park, another to a chapel and a fourth to the turnpike **road**.

The latter part of the 19th century produced a new type of town – the planned seaside resort. **Llandudno**, with its grid of streets carefully adjusted to follow the long, crescent-shaped curve of the beach, is the prime example. Like nearby **Colwyn Bay**, it was made popular and brought within easy reach of the industrial parts of north-western England by the building of the **railway** in 1849.

At the beginning of the 20th century, civic pride led to the creation of **Cardiff**'s splendid civic centre, **Cathays Park**, planned in simple but formal style around a central rectangular park. Various attempts were made to establish model villages in accordance with the theories of the garden city movement. Oakdale (**Penmaen**), the most ambitious of these, was built (1911 onwards) to house mining families and was designed as a symmetrical layout around a central boulevard. Rhiwbina (Cardiff; 1912–23) is Wales's best example of a planned suburb. Apart from the model villages, there were few other examples of planning until the *South Wales Outline Plan* (1949), which envisaged locating overspill from the **coal**field communities and the expansion of existing built-up areas further south. It also

recommended the establishment of a new town at Mynyddislwyn (**Ynysddu**). This was not to be, however, and it was not until the setting up of the **Cwmbran** Development Corporation two years later that Wales's sole 20th-century new town was created. A linear town planned for the **Severn** valley did not materialize; it was replaced by the planned expansion of **Newtown** (1967 onwards).

URDD GOBAITH CYMRU (The Wales Order of Hope)

This youth movement – known in **English** as the Welsh League of Youth – has been of central importance for three-quarters of a century in the history of **Welsh-language** culture. It was founded in 1922 by **Ifan ab Owen Edwards** as Urdd Gobaith Cymru Fach (lit. 'The League of the Hope of Little Wales') in reaction to the perceived militarism of English youth organizations such as the Boy Scouts and the Girl Guides. Originally, members had to pledge that they would speak Welsh, buy and read Welsh books, sing Welsh songs and play in Welsh, never deny their nationality, treat every Welsh person as a friend, and wear the Urdd badge. The children's magazine *Cymru'r Plant*, edited by the founder, became the mouthpiece of the movement, which established its headquarters in **Aberystwyth**. In 1932, the organization adopted its motto, which declares allegiance *i Gymru, i Gyd-ddyn ac i Grist* (to Wales, to Fellow-man and to Christ). In the same year, the rank of *Dysgwr* (Learner) was created in order to welcome

Urdd members staying at the Llangrannog camp enjoying a swim in 1947

A performance of *Dagrau'r Coed* (Tears of the Woods) at the 2007 Urdd National Eisteddfod held at Carmarthen

children who did not speak Welsh as their native language. The movement played a key role in the campaign to establish the first Welsh-medium primary school, a private school opened at Aberystwyth in 1939.

From the outset, the emphasis was on extending the realm of Welsh beyond the world of the chapel and the hearth. In 1928, the Urdd began holding annual camps, which developed into permanent camps at **Llangrannog** and Glan-llyn (**Llanuwchllyn**); both offer round-the-year accommodation and language courses, as well as outdoor pursuits. As early as the 1930s, the rules of **football**, **rugby** and **tennis** were explained in *Cymru'r Plant*, a novelty in the Welsh language. Important interwar activities included the annual *mabolgampau* (national mass sports competitions and displays), a national football competition and various cruises.

During the **Second World War**, a period during which the state compelled every child to be a member of a youth movement or of the cadets, membership increased rapidly from 24,454 to a peak of 57,548. After 1945, when youth organizations declined throughout **Britain**, the Urdd held its ground relatively well. By the early 21st century, the Urdd had over 50,000 members in 1500 branches, many of which were in schools. The movement publishes various magazines. With the opening of the Millennium Centre in **Cardiff** Bay in 2005, the Urdd acquired a hostel which provides accommodation in the capital for young people from all parts of Wales and beyond.

From its foundation, the Urdd has focused on sustaining traditional Welsh-language culture within the younger generation (it is open to those aged from 8 to 25) while developing use of the language in more contemporary domains. In 1929, at **Corwen**, the Urdd National **Eisteddfod** was held for the first time. The event, held alternately in the north and the south, has grown into a week of competing and socializing, and is considered the largest annual youth festival in Europe. More than 40,000 members compete and over 100,000 people attend each year. The Urdd's decision to give a public platform to Charles, the **Prince of Wales**, at the Aberystwyth Eisteddfod, in 1969, angered many of its members and led to a memorable protest at the Eisteddfod itself.

URDD Y DEYRNAS (The Order of the Kingdom)
A movement founded at the end of the **First World War** with the aim of fostering **pacifism** and Christian principles, appealing to young Welsh people to create a new Wales within a new world. Its journal *Yr Efrydydd*, published under the joint auspices of the Student Christian Movement and Urdd y Deyrnas, was published in four series between 1920 and 1955. It sought to promote improved relations between the **Church in Wales** and the **Nonconformist** denominations, and sponsored research into the causes and social effects of the interwar **depression**.

URIEN RHEGED (6th century) King of Rheged
Ruler of one of the kingdoms of the **Old North**, Urien is named in *Historia Brittonum* as one of four native chieftains who resisted the incursions of the Angles (*see* **Anglo-Saxons, The**); his death, at the hands of another Briton on

The bridge over the River Usk in the town of Usk

the island of Lindisfarne, is also reported. It is generally accepted that the nine praise poems to him attributed to **Taliesin** are genuine. In them, Urien is portrayed as an ideal warrior, ruler and patron. Later traditions about his death and its consequences have survived in *Canu Urien*, a 9th or 10th-century cycle of *englynion*.

USK (Brynbuga), Monmouthshire
(266 ha; 2318 inhabitants)

Usk is the most appealing of the towns of **Monmouthshire**. In about AD 55, it became the site of a **Roman** legionary fortress, which gave way to that at **Caerleon** *c.*75. The **march**er-lordship of Usk was held by the **Clare**, **Marshal** and **Mortimer** families and eventually passed to the English crown. In the mid-12th century, however, it was in the possession of the Welsh lords of Caerleon. Parts of the castle date back to the 1170s; its towers offer fine views of the surrounding countryside. St Mary's church was founded in the 1130s as a **Benedictine nunnery**.

The battle of Pwllmelyn, fought north of the town in 1405, was a major factor in the decline in the prospects of the **Glyndŵr Revolt**. **Adam of Usk**, whose chronicle is an important source on the revolt, is commemorated by a brass inscription in St Mary's – the earliest surviving such inscription in the **Welsh language**.

Despite the **community**'s considerable development since the 1950s, Usk remains a well-defined town in open countryside, with its medieval – and even its Roman – plan still discernible. **Alfred Russel Wallace**, who, independently of Darwin, arrived at the theory of natural selection, was born at Usk.

USK (Wysg) River (137 km)

The Usk – the longest **river** wholly in Wales – starts as a series of streams draining the northern slopes of the **Black Mountain**. It flows through the Usk **reservoir**, constructed in 1955 to provide water for **Swansea**. At Sennybridge (**Maescar**), it is joined by the Senni, which drains the northern slopes of Fforest Fawr. As its **Welsh** name (Aberhonddu) indicates, **Brecon** is located at the confluence of the Usk and the Honddu, which, with the Ysgir, Nant Brân and Cilieni, drains much of **Mynydd Epynt**. The Tarell, Cynrig, Menasgin and Caerfanell rivers, draining the northern slopes of the **Brecon Beacons**, join the Usk between Brecon and **Talybont-on-Usk**. The Rhiangoll and the Grwyne, which drain much of the **Black Mountains**, join the Usk between **Llangynidr** and **Abergavenny**. The Clydach flows through its remarkable gorge to join the Usk at Gilwern (**Llanelly**). From Abergavenny, the river flows southwards towards the town of **Usk** and then to **Caerleon**. Just north of Caerleon, the Usk is joined by Afon Lwyd or **Torfaen**, which rises above **Blaenavon**, and which flows through **Abersychan**, **Pontypool** and **Cwmbran**. **Newport**, Wales's best example of a riverside urban centre, stands on the Usk's lower reaches, where the river is spanned by a remarkable transporter bridge. The bridge, which opened in 1906, was built to avoid disrupting navigation on the Usk, the key factor in the development of the **port** of Newport. South of Newport, the Usk, joined by the **Ebbw**, flows into the **Severn** Sea, past the Uskmouth power station.

UZMASTON AND BOULSTON (Uzmaston a Boulston), Pembrokeshire (1466 ha; 571 inhabitants)

Located immediately east of **Haverfordwest**, the **community** hugs a bend in the Western **Cleddau**. Boulston **Manor** (1798) was the seat of a branch of the Wogan family; the ruined Boulston church (dedication unknown) contains Wogan memorials. St Ismael's church (largely rebuilt in 1871–3) retains part of its medieval saddleback tower. Higgon's **Well** (14th century) is remarkably intact.

Vale of Glamorgan: Dunraven Bay

VALE OF GLAMORGAN (Bro Morgannwg)
County, constituency and one-time district
(33,975; 119,292 inhabitants)
Following the abolition of the **county** of **Glamorgan** in
1974, the Vale of Glamorgan became one of the two districts of the new county of **South Glamorgan**. It consisted
of the **boroughs** of **Barry** and **Cowbridge**, the **urban district**
of **Penarth**, and the **rural district** of Cowbridge and part of
that of **Cardiff**. In 1996, the district, augmented by three
communities of the one-time district of **Ogwr**, became the
county of the Vale of Glamorgan. In 2001, 16.90% of the
inhabitants of the county had some knowledge of **Welsh**,
the percentages varying from 24.55% in **Llandow** to 13.4%
in **Llandough**; 8.81% of the county's inhabitants were
wholly fluent in the language.

The Vale, a region of quiet beauty, is a broad coastal
plateau gently decreasing in elevation from around 120 m
on its northern edge to some 40 m along the coastal cliffs.
The plateau is dissected by the **Ely**, the **Thaw**, the Ogwr
and the Ogwr's tributary, the Ewenny. Much of the area's
appeal can be attributed to buildings constructed of Liassic
Limestone, quarried from the rock that underlies much of
the Vale.

VALE OF GRWYNEY, The (Dyffryn Grwyne),
Breconshire, Powys (6871 ha; 702 inhabitants)
The **community** stretches from the slopes of the **Black
Mountains** to the valley of the **Usk** and is still recognizably
the place described by **Theophilus Jones**. 'The surface of the
country,' he wrote, 'is ... extremely uneven, [but] the
painter will be *enraptured* with the view.' Llanbedr **Ystrad
Yw** was the home of the **Brute family**, whose rustically elegant calligraphy is to be found on tombstones in the area;
Thomas Brute is buried in the churchyard. The consecration of St Peter's church in 1060 is recorded in *Liber
Landavensis* (The Book of Llandaff); much of the present
nave probably dates from that year. Moor Park, a small
baroque villa built in 1790, stands just south of the village.
Further down the Grwyne valley lies the village of
Llangenny with its single-arch – probably late 18th-century
– bridge. St Cenau's church contains a wealth of medieval
features. The village of Glangrwyney, now wholly rural in
appearance, played its part in the **Industrial Revolution**. A
forge, established there *c.*1720, continued to operate until
1845, and a tramroad was built to connect it with the **coal-**
producing areas to the south. Near Glangrwyney is Cwrt y
Gollen, which was, until the 1990s, the depot of the Welsh

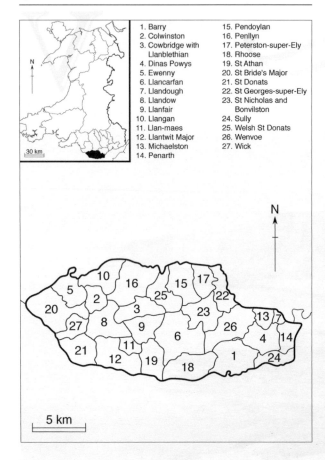

1. Barry	15. Pendoylan
2. Colwinston	16. Penllyn
3. Cowbridge with	17. Peterston-super-Ely
Llanblethian	18. Rhoose
4. Dinas Powys	19. St Athan
5. Ewenny	20. St Bride's Major
6. Llancarfan	21. St Donats
7. Llandough	22. St Georges-super-Ely
8. Llandow	23. St Nicholas and
9. Llanfair	Bonvilston
10. Llangan	24. Sully
11. Llan-maes	25. Welsh St Donats
12. Llantwit Major	26. Wenvoe
13. Michaelston	27. Wick
14. Penarth	

The communities of the Vale of Glamorgan

Brigade. Around the depot is a wealth of mistletoe, a **plant** rare in Wales. The jewel of the community is situated in a lonely valley on its eastern border: the church at Patrishow, with its magnificent 15th-century screen and rood loft, its pre-**Norman** font and its 17th-century altar rails and pulpit.

VALENCE family Marcher-lords

The family became associated with Wales when William de Valence (d.1296) acquired the lordship of **Pembroke** through his marriage with Joan, daughter of Warin de Munchensey (d.1247). In the war of 1282–3, William, an uncle of Edward I, broke the power of the native rulers of **Deheubarth**, and it was his capture of Castell y Bere (**Llanfihangel-y-Pennant**) on 25 April 1283 that brought the war to an end. He sought to enhance the influence of the lordship of Pembroke, browbeating the burgesses of **Haverfordwest** and imposing his overlordship upon **Narberth** and **Ystlwyf**. As part of his policy of curtailing the powers of the **march**er-lords, Edward I insisted that Ystlwyf should be subject to royal officials at **Carmarthen**. William was succeeded by his son, Aymer, who died childless in 1324. Pembroke passed to John **Hastings**, lord of **Abergavenny** and **Cilgerran**, through his marriage with Aymer's sister, Isabella.

VALENTINE, Lewis (1893–1986)
Patriot and author

A **Baptist** minister born at **Llanddulas**, he was the first president of **Plaid [Genedlaethol] Cymru** and, in 1929, stood in

Caernarfonshire as the party's first parliamentary candidate, polling 609 votes. In 1936, with **Saunders Lewis** and **D. J. Williams**, he took part in the act of arson at the **Penyberth bombing school** and was imprisoned for nine months; he recounted his experiences in Wormwood Scrubs in *Beddau'r Byw*, a series of essays – an important contribution to **prison literature** – first published in *Y Ddraig Goch* (1937–9). A learned Hebraist, he had a highly developed interest in new trends in **theology**. He was editor of the Baptist quarterly *Seren Gomer* (1951–75) and wrote a number of **hymns**; the most famous, 'Gweddi dros Gymru', usually sung to the accompaniment of Sibelius's patriotic *Finlandia*, has achieved the status of a second national anthem. His finest prose work, *Dyddiadur Milwr*, first published in *Seren Gomer* (1969–72), is a chronicle of his experiences during the **First World War**, when he served with the Medical Corps. In 2006, a biography by Arwel Vittle was published.

VALLEY (Y Fali), Isle of Anglesey
(866 ha; 2413 inhabitants)

The community, which is coterminous with the one-time civil **parish** of Llanynghenedl, is located at the eastern end of the Stanley Embankment, which was completed in 1823 by **Thomas Telford** in order to carry the mail-coach **road** from **London** (*see also* **A5**) to the end of its journey at **Holyhead**. A parallel embankment was opened in 2001, in order to complete the route of the **A55**. The name, the origin of which has often been disputed, probably comes from the depression left after digging out rubble for the embankment. Valley gave its name to the RAF air base (*see* **Llanfair-yn-Neubwll**) and to one of **Anglesey**'s pre-1974 **rural districts**.

VAUGHAN family (Cors y Gedol) Landowners

For generations the first family of **Merioneth**, the Vaughans were loyal Lancastrians in the **Wars of the Roses** and equally loyal supporters of Henry **Tudor**. They provided numerous sheriffs and MPs for their **county**, and were patrons of Welsh poetry. The oldest surviving part of Cors y Gedol (**Dyffryn Ardudwy**) was built in 1592 by Griffith Vaughan, as was the family chapel at Llanddwywe church. William Vaughan (d.1630) was a friend of the dramatist Ben Jonson. William Vaughan (1707–75) was a noted patron of Welsh **literature** and culture; he was president of the first Society of **Cymmrodorion** and a regular correspondent of Lewis Morris (*see* **Morris brothers**). After the death in 1791 of Evan Lloyd Vaughan, the estate passed to the **Mostyn family**.

VAUGHAN family (Golden Grove) Landowners

Hugh Vaughan began building an estate in **Carmarthenshire** in the early 16th century, benefiting in particular from the fall of his kinsman, Sir Rhys ap Gruffydd (d.1531) of **Dinefwr**. His son, John (d.1575), who settled at Golden Grove (**Llanfihangel Aberbythych**), initiated the Vaughan dominance of Carmarthenshire politics, which lasted for 200 years. John's son, Walter (d.1598), had 15 children, and they were so successful in founding landed families that, by the 17th century, half Carmarthenshire was owned by Vaughans. Walter's eldest son, John

(1575–1634), was created Baron Vaughan and earl of Carbery in the peerage of **Ireland**. John's son, Richard (d.1683), leader of Royalist forces in west Wales during the **Civil Wars**, was the patron of Jeremy Taylor. While lord president of the **Council of Wales and the Marches** (1661–72), his secretary at **Ludlow** was Samuel Butler. Richard's son, John (1640–1713), 'the lewdest man of his age', was president of the Royal Society and a friend of Pope, Evelyn and Aubrey. On John's death, his estates passed to his sister, Anne (d.1751), and then to John (d.1765), a distant cousin. John's grandson, who died childless in 1804, bequeathed his estates to John **Campbell** of **Stackpole**.

VAUGHAN family (Hergest)
Landowners and patrons of Welsh literature
The first of the Vaughans of Hergest (**Herefordshire**) was Thomas ap Rhosier Fychan, son of Gwladys, daughter of **Dafydd Gam** and her first husband, Rhosier Fychan of Bretwardine (Herefordshire). Roger Vaughan (*see* **Vaughan family (Tretower)**) was Thomas's brother and William **Herbert, Earl of Pembroke** (d.1469) his half-brother. Having originally served the Lancastrians, by the 1460s Roger was a supporter of the Yorkists, in whose cause he was killed in 1469 (*see* **Wars of the Roses, The**). Thomas and his descendants, for at least two generations, were generous patrons of Welsh poets, particularly **Lewys Glyn Cothi** and **Guto'r Glyn**. It is believed that the family commissioned the compiling of *The White Book of Hergest*, lost in a fire in 1808. *The Red Book of Hergest*, one of Wales's most important medieval manuscripts, was long kept at Hergest.

VAUGHAN family (Llwydiarth) Landowners
The founder of the family is reputed to have been Celynin, who, in the early 14th century, fled **Carmarthen** after committing murder. He married Gwladus, a descendant of the royal house of **Powys**. In the 16th century, their descendants settled at Llwydiarth (**Llanfihangel, Montgomeryshire**) and acquired the **Llangedwyn** and the Glanllyn (**Llanuwchllyn**) estates through marriage. Edward, the last of the Vaughans, was MP for Montgomeryshire, 1679–1718. His father, also Edward Vaughan, had represented the county in 1647–8, 1659–60 and 1661. Through the marriage of the second Edward Vaughan's daughter, Anne, the entire Vaughan estate passed to Sir Watkin **Williams Wynn** (the third baronet) of Wynnstay, **Ruabon**.

VAUGHAN family (Trawsgoed) Landowners
Established at **Trawsgoed** since the 14th century, the Vaughans came to prominence with the career of the judge Sir **John Vaughan** (1603–74). He bought 8 granges once owned by Strata Florida Abbey (**Ystrad Fflur**), making the estate the largest in **Cardiganshire**; in 1873, the family owned 17,267 ha in the county. In 1695, his grandson, John (d.1721), was ennobled as Viscount Lisburne in the peerage of **Ireland**. John's grandson, Wilmot (d.1800), served in **government** ministries and was created earl of Lisburne, again in the peerage of Ireland, in 1776. Although the family benefited from its **lead** mines, by the late 19th century the Vaughans were burdened with debt. Most of the estate

had been sold by 1947, when the mansion became the Welsh headquarters of the Agricultural Advisory Service. In the late 1990s, it was acquired by a consortium headed by a son of the eighth earl of Lisburne and was converted into luxury residences.

VAUGHAN family (Tretower) Landowners
Roger Vaughan (Rhosier Fychan; d.1471) was the son of Gwladys, daughter of **Dafydd Gam**, and her first husband, Rhosier Fychan of Bretwardine (**Herefordshire**), brother of Thomas Vaughan (*see* **Vaughan family (Hergest)**) and half-brother of William **Herbert, earl of Pembroke** (d.1469). It was Herbert, apparently, who gave Tretower to his half-brother. Tretower Court (**Llanfihangel Cwmdu**), Wales's finest 15th-century house, was built by Roger and his son Thomas. A Yorkist, Roger fought at Mortimer's Cross (1469), after which he led Owen **Tudor** to **execution** (*see* **Wars of the Roses, The**). In 1471, he, in turn, was executed by Owen's son, Jasper Tudor. Roger was a patron of poets, and was eulogized by **Lewys Glyn Cothi**. His illegitimate son, another Thomas (d.1483), was the Vaughan whose ghost, according to **Shakespeare**, haunted Richard III on the eve of the battle of **Bosworth**. Many Vaughan families were descended from Roger, among them the Vaughans of Newton (**Talybont-on-Usk**), one of whose members was the poet **Henry Vaughan**.

VAUGHAN, E[dwin] M[ontgomery] Bruce (1856–1919) Architect
Vaughan joined W. D. Blessley as partner in 1881, with an office in **Cardiff**. The practice concentrated on public buildings throughout Wales, including designs for 25 churches,

Lewis Valentine

An aerial view of Cors y Gedol, Dyffryn Ardudwy, long the home of the Vaughan family

hospitals at **Aberystwyth** and **Llanelli** and various schools. His most remarkable building is the tower entrance (1915) of Cardiff's University College (*see* **Cardiff University**) in Newport Road, the last fling of the neo-Gothic style in Wales.

VAUGHAN, Henry (1621–95) Poet

Henry Vaughan, a descendant of the **Vaughan family (Tretower)**, was born at Newton (**Talybont-on-Usk**). He enrolled at Jesus College, **Oxford**, but left without graduating. He saw action on the Royalist side during the **Civil Wars**. He began as a love-poet and translator of Juvenal with the publication of *Poems* in 1646, some of which are addressed to Catherine Wise, to whom he had become engaged in the Priory Grove at **Brecon**. His most important works are *Silex Scintillans* (1650; 1655) and *Olor Iscanus* (1651), in which he referred to himself as 'Silurist', although what he meant is unclear. He was a **Welsh**-speaker but considered himself an **English** poet. Both books contain poems of great religious fervour, perhaps heightened by the death of his brother William in the **Civil War** in 1648, and possibly by his reading of **George Herbert**'s *The Temple*.

Although the poems express despair at the defeat of the Royalist cause, the most recent commentator on his work considers that Vaughan's attitude to the conflict was one of 'epicurean unconcern'. The second edition of *Silex Scintillans* includes a number of his best-known poems

such as 'They are all gone into the world of light!'; another, entitled 'Peace', has the well-known lines beginning, 'My soul, there is a countrie ...' From about 1655, he practised as a physician and it appears that thereafter he wrote no more verse.

The poet is buried outside the eastern wall of the church at Llansantffraed in his native **parish**. His gravestone bears the inscription: *Henricus Vaughan Siluris servus inutilis peccator maximus gloria miserere* (Henry Vaughan, Silurist, worthless servant, greatest of sinners, Glory, Mercy.)

His twin brother, the alchemist Thomas Vaughan (1621–66), was appointed rector of Llansantffraed *c.*1645, but was discharged under the **Act for the Propagation of the Gospel in Wales**. He wrote treatises under the name Eugenius Philalethes and 24 of his poems were included in Henry Vaughan's *Thalia Rediviva* (1678). He is reputed to have died from inhaling mercury when conducting one of his experiments.

VAUGHAN, Hilda (1892–1985) Novelist

Although born at **Builth** in **Breconshire**, Hilda Vaughan is usually associated with **Radnorshire**, where most of her books are located. In 1923, she married the novelist Charles Morgan. Her novels include *The Battle to the Weak* (1925), *The Invader* (1928), *Her Father's House* (1930), *The Soldier and the Gentlewoman* (1932) and *The Candle and the Light* (1954). Perhaps her finest book is the novella *A Thing of Nought* (1934), a story of star-crossed love set in the hills of **Elfael**. Her daughter, Shirley, married the marquess of **Anglesey** (*see* **Paget family**) and chaired the Welsh Arts Council (*see* **Arts Council of Wales**).

VAUGHAN, John (1603–74) Judge

A member of the **Vaughan family (Trawsgoed)**, he, more than anyone, was responsible for the expansion of the Trawsgoed estate. As a judge, he is famous for establishing, in Bushell's Case (1670), the immunity of jurors from punishment for refusing to bow to the dictates of a judge. Also, his influential opinion that the Westminster courts could not issue final process into Wales, irrespective of the **Acts of 'Union'**, carried sufficient authority to ensure the continuance of Wales's Courts of Great Session (*see* **Law**) until 1830. A Royalist, who retired from legal practice during the **Commonwealth** era, he was involved after the Restoration in the prosecution of the earl of Clarendon (1667).

VAUGHAN, Robert (*c.*1592–1667)

Antiquary and collector of manuscripts

Robert Vaughan of Hengwrt (**Llanelltyd**), more than anyone, secured the survival of medieval **Welsh literature**. He collected over half the extant medieval manuscripts, including most of the critically important ones, and copied others, creating a truly national collection. But his real interest was history, not literature; in **religion** he tended towards **Puritanism**. He wrote several learned historical studies, but only one was published. His manuscript collection, after a period of neglect during the 18th century, came to W. W. E. **Wynne** of Peniarth (**Llanegryn**) in 1859, and, in 1909, to the **National Library**.

VAUGHAN, Rowland (*c.*1590–1667)

Poet and translator

Born into a lesser **gentry** family at Caergai (**Llanuwchllyn**), Vaughan was a zealous **Anglican** and staunch Royalist, probably serving in the king's army during the **Civil Wars**. Caergai was burnt by the Parliamentarians; after the wars, he went to **law** to repossess it, and built a new house there. A gentleman-poet who composed in both the strict and free metres, he is more famous as a translator of religious works. His best-known work is *Yr Ymarfer o Dduwioldeb* (1630), a translation in masterful prose of **Lewis Bayly**'s *The Practice of Piety*.

VAUGHAN, William (1575–1641)

Writer and colonial pioneer

A member of the **Vaughan family (Golden Grove)**, he was appointed **Carmarthenshire county** sheriff in 1616 and knighted in 1628. He published poetry and numerous works on economic, political, religious and **health** matters. He is best remembered for funding the short-lived Welsh settlement at **Cambriol**, Newfoundland. Despite its failure, he remained a strong advocate of colonization as a cure for economic distress.

VEHICLE MANUFACTURE

Vehicle component manufacturing has been a long-established activity in Wales, concentrated along the **M4** corridor and as far west as **Llanelli**, and (to a lesser extent) around **Flint** and **Wrexham**.

The first major factory making motor vehicle parts was established at Felinfoel (**Llanelli Rural**) during the **Second World War**, a **government**-owned plant transferred to Morris Motors Ltd in 1946. In the late 1950s and early 1960s, the government's success in persuading many motor-car manufacturers to locate part of their investment programmes in **Development Areas** resulted in the establishment of several new factories. At Felinfoel, a works was built adjacent to the existing one, and the combined production of the two factories, then owned by the British Leyland Motor Company, included seat frames and radiators. During the same period, the Rover Company opened a factory at **Pengam** (gear boxes), the Ford Motor Company located at Jersey Marine (**Coedffranc**; subframes and axles), and Borg-Warner settled on the Kenfig Industrial Estate (**Pyle**; valves and automatic gear components); the Ferrodo plant at **Y Felinheli** made brake linings.

Two of the Gilbern's 6 main models

The Tintern Parva vineyard in the Wye Valley

Alongside these major developments were a variety of smaller, ancillary suppliers to the car industry such as Cam Gears (**Resolven**), Fram Filters (Treforest (**Pontypridd**) and **Llantrisant**), and Girling Brakes (**Cwmbran**). The sector featured significantly in the **Welsh Development Agency**'s **inward investment** policy; the agency had a role in the establishment of Ford's engine plant at **Bridgend**, Toyota's engine plant on **Deeside** and the Bosch alternators factory at Miskin (**Pont-y-clun**).

An intriguingly indigenous Welsh car manufacturer was the small-scale, specialist Gilbern Cars Ltd. Founded by the unlikely combination of a master butcher, Giles Smith, and a German engineer, Bernard Friese – the initial syllables of their first names forming 'Gilbern' – the company produced limited edition models at its **Llantwit Fardre** factory between 1959 and 1973.

By the mid 1990s, about 25,000 workers were employed in 150 automotive component firms, accounting for more than 8% of total manufacturing output in Wales. By the early 21st century, however, the components manufacturing sector in Wales had undergone some reshaping as a result of global economic forces. The established big manufacturers of vehicles were turning increasingly to cheaper sources of supply in eastern Europe, Asia and elsewhere, and many of the component manufacturers were relocating to countries offering access to cheaper labour.

Some less technologically advanced processes have as a result left Wales but the country still retains a strong stake in automotive components, and especially in engine manufacture. (*See also* **Aviation and Aeronautics**.)

VELINDRE TINPLATE WORKS, Llangyfelach

The **Steel Company of Wales** opened its Velindre works (**Llangyfelach**), in 1956 to complement **Trostre** and to complete the modernization of **tinplate** manufacture. Equipped with cold reduction facilities and two electrolytic tinning lines, Velindre absorbed the redundant labour force created by the closure of the inefficient small handmills in the area. By 1970, Velindre had expanded its employment and production to 2500 people and the equivalent of nearly 490,000 tonnes per annum, but it declined during the 1980s and closed in 1989. The **Swansea** National **Eisteddfod** of 2006 was held on its cleared site.

VIKINGS

Known as *Gynt* (from 'gentiles', and thereby meaning 'pagans') in **Welsh**, the Vikings were first recorded as marauders on the Welsh coast in the mid-9th century. Settlement seems to have taken place in two regions. **Place name** evidence (but no contemporary records) suggest that a territory around **Swansea** ('Sveinn's ey') was colonized. **Anglesey** may have been ruled continuously or intermittently by the Hiberno-Norse dynasty that controlled Dublin from *c.*902 until the time of **Gruffudd ap Cynan** (d.1137), who himself was a grandson of the Norse king of Dublin. Recent archaeological finds from Llanbedr-goch

(**Llanfair-Mathafarn-Eithaf**) seem to support this belief, and the name Anglesey derives from the Norse personal name Ongull + *ey* (island). Other place names in Wales whose **English** forms have Norse origins include **Fishguard**, and **islands** such as Bardsey, Caldey and Skomer.

In 853, the Vikings raided Anglesey, but in 856 Rhodri ap Merfyn (**Rhodri Mawr**) defeated and killed their leader, Horm, much to the delight of the court of the Frankish empire. Indeed, it is probably Rhodri's success against the Vikings which won for him the epithet 'Mawr' (Great). Anarawd ap Rhodri's conquest of much of the north was achieved with help from the Vikings occupying Northumbria. His son, Idwal Foel, seems to have sided frequently with the Hiberno-Norse against the English, particularly in 937 and 940–2. The readiness of Hywel ap Cadell (**Hywel Dda**) to ally with – and perhaps to accept the overlordship of – the kings of Wessex was probably the result of the desire of Christian kingdoms to co-operate against the pagan aggressors. The south-east, which was under English protection from the 880s, suffered attacks by the Vikings operating in western **England** and, in 914, Cyfeiliog, bishop of **Morgannwg**, was kidnapped by them and was ransomed by Edward the Elder (899–924). In the late 10th century, Maccus and Gofraid, based in the Hebrides, raided a number of Welsh monasteries, including **Holyhead**, **Tywyn**, **Llanbadarn Fawr**, **Llancarfan** and **St David's**. In 989, Maredudd ab Owain paid a penny a head to the 'Black Gentiles' (probably Danes), a payment best interpreted as a bribe to get rid of them. The ancestry of Gruffudd ap Cynan indicates that, over the generations,

Viking dynasties ruling in **Britain** and **Ireland** intermarried extensively with native royal kindred. Thus, by the 11th century, political relationships may have ceased to reflect ethnic origins. The invasions of Wales by the **Normans**, descendants of Northmen who had settled in the lower Seine valley, may be considered to be the final phase of Viking aggression.

VINEYARDS

In all probability, the **Romans** introduced vines to Wales. A warmer **climate** saw trellised vines for the table and ground-trailed vines for wine growing in the vicinity of villas and forts, as part of a tradition of viniculture continued by the monasteries of the Middle Ages. A change to a more temperate climate heralded the virtual disappearance of grapes as a crop. Some small-scale planting in the 20th century of select varieties, initially as a hobby but latterly on a commercial basis, has reintroduced wine production; by 2005, there were over 20 commercial vineyards in Wales, producing about 100,000 bottles of wine a year.

VIVIAN family Industrialists

Under the influence of the Vivians, **Swansea** became the metallurgical centre of the world. John Henry Vivian (1779–1855) was trained in the mining schools of Germany, where he was sent by his father, John. John came to Swansea from **Cornwall** (*c.*1800) to investigate using Welsh **coal** for **copper** smelting. The father acquired a small works at Penclawdd (**Llanrhidian Higher**); the son

The Vivian family's dining room in Singleton Abbey *c.*1894

built the more ambitious Hafod (*see* **Swansea**; **Landore**) works (*c.*1810). Hafod, with its advanced processes, rapidly became a showpiece, drawing observers from many countries. But Vivian, despite offering a prize of £1000, failed to solve the appalling pollution from the noxious copper smoke. A leading spirit over many years in promoting improved dock and **railway** facilities for Swansea, he was MP for Swansea from 1832 to 1855.

The **education** of his son, Henry Hussey Vivian (1821–94), was doubly exceptional for 19th-century Welsh industrialists: Eton and **Cambridge**, supplemented by metallurgical study in Germany and France. From *c.*1850, he used his technical knowledge to extend activities at the Hafod works – from copper to other metals (zinc, nickel, cobalt, **lead and silver**) – thus establishing Swansea's metallurgical pre-eminence. He also played a key role – as MP (**Glamorgan**, 1857–85; Swansea District, 1885–93) – in successfully pressing the claims of Welsh coal for use by the British Admiralty. Elevated to the peerage as Baron Swansea in 1893, he was born and died at Singleton Abbey, which later formed the core of University College, Swansea (**University of Wales Swansea**). Later Barons Swansea settled at Caer Beris, **Cilmery**, which was converted into a hotel in the late 1980s.

VOLUNTARYIST SCHOOLS MOVEMENT, The

In April 1845, those Welsh **Nonconformists,** with **Congregationalists** and **Baptists** to the fore, who were opposed to the **government**'s **education** policy, gathered at **Llandovery**. Concerned that a state education meant an **Anglican** education, they agreed to set up schools run on the voluntaryist principle; in 1846, a Normal College was established in **Brecon** (1846), which moved to **Swansea** in 1849. The movement was neither methodical nor unanimous. Anger aroused by the government's education report of 1847 (*see* **Treason of the Blue Books**) postponed its demise but, as the majority of the movement's supporters realized that accepting government education grants did not necessarily infringe religious liberty, the movement had disintegrated by the early 1860s.

VORTIGERN (Gwrtheyrn) Brythonic leader

An ancestor of the kings of **Powys**, Vortigern was one of the leaders of 5th-century **Britain**. According to tradition, some time between 420 and 450 he invited German mercenaries into Britain, giving them land in exchange for military support. By the 9th century, he was regarded as the arch traitor who had caused the Britons to lose their inheritance to the **Anglo-Saxons**. The **commote** of **Gwrtheyrnion** probably commemorates him.

VORTIPORIUS (Gwrthefyr) King of Dyfed

A 6th-century ruler described by **Gildas** as *tyrannus Demetarum*, his name appears in the Harleian **genealogy** of the kings of **Dyfed**. A stone discovered at Castelldwyran (**Clynderwen**), inscribed in **Latin** and ogham, commemorates Vorteporix, who is described as *Protector*, a title of **Roman** derivation (*see* **Monuments, Early Christian**). It has generally been assumed that Gildas and the stone refer to the same person, but the names may refer to different members of the same lineage.

Beach graffiti by a Welsh patriot?

WADE-EVANS, A[rthur] W[ade] (1875–1964)
Historian

Fishguard-born A. W. Wade-Evans, who spent most of his life as vicar of **parishes** in **England**, is remembered as the author of books about Wales in the early medieval period. They include *The Life of St David* (1923), *Welsh Christian Origins* (1934), *Coll Prydain* (1950) and *The Emergence of England and Wales* (1956, 1959). He believed that the Welsh were not Britons who had been forced to flee into what later became Wales, but that, following the collapse of the **Roman** Empire, Roman culture, or *Romanitas*, had been maintained in the culture of Wales while *Barbaritas* had triumphed in what was to become England.

WAEN (Y Waun), Denbighshire
(739 ha; 245 inhabitants)

Located immediately west of **St Asaph**, the **community**'s most interesting feature is Bodeugan, a 17th-century house flanked by a gabled brick **dovecote**. Abbie Williams, president of **Plaid [Genedlaethol] Cymru** (1943–5), lived in Waen.

WALES, the name
The **English** name of the country of the Welsh derives from the **Anglo-Saxon** word *wealas* or *walas*, used for the natives

they found as they conquered parts of **Britain**. Generally believed to mean strangers or foreigners, it was, in fact, a Germanic word referring to people who had been Romanized (compare Walloon and Vlach). It was perhaps derived from a **Celt**ic tribe, the Volcae, familiar to Germanic peoples.

WALES, The history of
The earliest evidence of the presence of human beings in Wales (*see* **Palaeolithic and Mesolithic Ages**) are 250,000-year-old teeth, found in Pontnewydd **cave** in the Elwy valley (**Cefnmeiriadog**). The owner of the teeth – a member of the species *homo sapiens neanderthalensis* – should not be considered to be among the ancestors of the present inhabitants of Wales for, as a result of successive Ice Ages, it is likely that Wales was wholly lacking in inhabitants for tens of thousands of years. There were probably later occasions in the Lower Palaeolithic Era (Old Stone Age) when there was human settlement in Wales, in particular at Coygan Cave (**Laugharne**) and Ffynnon Beuno cave (**Tremeirchion**). The Upper Palaeolithic Era began *c.*35,000 BC when the tools devized by human beings were improving markedly, a development associated with the spread of the Cro-Magnon people – those with the essential characteristics of modern

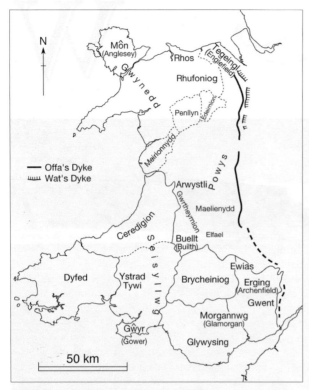

The early kingdoms (after William Rees, 1959)

humankind. The most famous Upper Palaeolithic site in Wales is Goat's Hole Cave at Paviland (**Rhossili**) where a skeleton was discovered in 1823. Carbon 14 dating subsequently established that they are the bones of a young man who lived *c.*24,000 BC.

The ice began to retreat *c.*10,000 BC. The melting of the ice cap caused the sea level to rise; **Britain** became an **island** and, by *c.*8000 BC, Wales had attained roughly the shape it has today. As the temperature rose, the country became covered by a thick canopy of trees (*see* **Plants** and **Forestry**). With the disappearance of vast herds and great open spaces, the palaeolithic way of life was no longer viable. During the Mesolithic Era (the Middle Stone Age), the inhabitants of Wales adapted themselves to their new environment, using **dogs** to hunt the small animals of the forest, and nets and boats to harvest the riches of the warmer waters.

Until the 1960s, it was believed that Mesolithic society, based on **hunting** and gathering, lasted in Wales until *c.*2000 BC when it gave way to **Neolithic** (New Stone Age) society, based upon **agriculture**. However, carbon dating has shown that the country had farming communities as early as 4000 BC. The building of stone-chambered tombs (*cromlechi*), which are particularly numerous near western sea routes, indicates that Neolithic Wales had a fairly populous society with a considerable degree of organization and strong cultural contacts with **Ireland**, **Brittany** and Spain, as well as with other parts of Britain. Perhaps the most magnificent cromlech in Wales is Barclodiad y Gawres (the apron of the giantess) (**Aberffraw**). Major building work occurred there *c.*3200 BC.

If the Neolithic Age is defined as the age of farming communities using stone tools, then it did not finally come to an end in Wales until *c.*1400 BC, by which time metal tools had become widely available, although there were metal objects in Wales – first **copper**, then bronze – as early as *c.*2500 BC. The Early **Bronze Age** (*c.*2300–1400 BC) saw an improvement in **climate**; it became practical to farm the high lands where numerous stone circles and burial chambers indicate the existence of a considerable **population**. Most of the construction work at Stonehenge dates from the early Bronze Age, including the erection of the blue stones believed to have been carried there from **Mynydd Preseli**. A beaker of distinctive design is frequently found in Early Bronze Age graves, and the people associated with these artefacts came to be known as the Beaker folk. Until recently, their presence was seen as evidence of one of a great series of migrations, and the prehistory of Britain was portrayed in terms of wave after wave of invaders. The present tendency is to stress continuity rather than disruption, and to maintain that Wales had received the greater part of its original stock of peoples by *c.*2000 BC.

In the later Bronze Age (*c.*1400–600 BC), metal objects of considerable distinction were produced. The hoards that have been discovered were probably hidden by itinerant merchants, giving rise to the assumption that the years following *c.*1000 BC were increasingly warlike and unstable. The same assumption may be drawn from the existence of **hill-forts**, of which there are some 600 in Wales. The largest of them were tribal capitals, and the smallest were probably agricultural enclosures or fortified homesteads. It was once assumed that the hill-forts were an **Iron Age** development, but as the earliest iron object found in Wales – a sword discovered at Llyn Fawr (**Rhigos**, north of **Rhondda**) – dates from *c.*600 BC and the earliest hill-fort dates from *c.*1000 BC, this assumption is no longer accepted.

The Llyn Fawr sword is in the Hallstatt style (named after a village in Austria); the Hallstatt style developed into the La Tène style (named after a village in Switzerland). These styles are considered to be characteristic of the **Celts**. A large number of La Tène objects has been found in Wales, especially at Llyn Cerrig Bach (**Llanfair-yn-Neubwll**), where metalwork dating from 150 BC to AD 50 has been discovered. By then, Wales was tiptoeing from prehistory into history, for there is some written evidence about Britain and Wales in the century before the **Roman** invasion of AD 43. That evidence indicates that the inhabitants of Britain – or at least the ruling **class** – spoke a Celtic language or languages, and that Celtic culture was dominant in the island. It is generally accepted that Celtic influence became widespread in Britain in the centuries after 600 BC, although there is growing support for the view that some at least of what were traditionally considered to be elements of Celticism were in fact indigenous British developments.

When the Roman legions reached the borders of Wales in AD 48, it would appear that the country was inhabited by the **Silures** in the south-east, the **Demetae** in the south-west, the **Ordovices** in the north-west and the **Deceangli** in the north-east, while the **Cornovii** held the middle reaches of the **Severn** valley. While the Romans quickly overran south-eastern Britain, it was not until 84 that Wales was fully subjugated and the frontier system established. Based upon the two legionary fortresses at **Caerleon** and Chester (*see* **Cheshire**), Wales had a further 30 smaller fortresses all linked by the straight **roads** characteristic of the Romans. The Romans gave the Silures a measure of self-**government** and **Caerwent** became the capital of their *civitas*. **Carmarthen** may have received the same status among the Demetae. Despite the conquest, many areas of Wales were only slightly influenced by the Empire. Although **Latin** was its official language, the Celtic language, Brythonic – while it absorbed a number of Latin words – continued to be spoken by the inhabitants of Wales. Yet, while Romanization was by no means complete, the upper classes in Wales came to consider themselves Romans, particularly after 212 when all free men throughout the Empire were granted Roman citizenship. Further Roman influence came through Christianity (*see* **Religion**), which gained many adherents after Christians were allowed to worship freely in 313.

The Roman Empire, although it appeared strong, was faced with many challenges. The Roman province of Britannia was threatened by the Saxons from across the North Sea, the Picts from beyond Hadrian's Wall and the Goedelic Celts of Ireland. The empire was also weakened by the attempts of ambitious generals to seize the throne. One of them was **Magnus Maximus** (Macsen Wledig), whose attempt in 383 drained Britannia of much of its garrison. Rome itself fell to the Goths in 410, when the emperor advised the British to undertake their own defence. Although it was not until 476 that the western Roman Empire finally came to an end, Britain had long since ceased to be part of it.

The 400 years following the collapse of Roman rule are the most difficult to interpret in the whole history of Wales.

By 500, most of Britain seems to have been divided into a number of kingdoms. While the majority of them were Brythonic in language and culture, **Anglo-Saxon** invaders had established small kingdoms in the east and south-east of the island. The expansion of Anglo-Saxon kingdoms may have been halted by the victory, *c.*496, of the British leader **Arthur**, but that expansion was renewed after *c.*550. By *c.*700, the whole of southern Britain, apart from Wales and **Cornwall**, had become Anglo-Saxon or **English** kingdoms, and the boundary of Wales was defined *c.*790 by **Offa's Dyke**. The Brythonic-speaking inhabitants of **England** were absorbed into the English kingdoms, for there is no evidence to support the old belief that they fled to Wales.

The Brythonic language, which had once been spoken in the whole of southern Britain, disappeared in the areas colonized by the English. The **Welsh language** (*Cymraeg*) is a daughter language of Brythonic, as are Cornish, Cumbric and Breton. It may well have emerged by *c.*500, and it is customary to ascribe its earliest literature to **Taliesin** and **Aneirin**, court poets who flourished in the kingdoms of the **Old North**. The word *Cymry* (*Combrogi*: fellow countrymen) was adopted as the name of the speakers of *Cymraeg*. The word 'Welsh' (*see* **Wales, the name**) comes from an Anglo-Saxon word which is usually considered to mean foreigner, although it was specifically applied to peoples who had been influenced by Rome.

The *Cymry* were Christians from the beginning. Part of their Christian tradition stemmed from the Christianity of Roman Britain, but it was also influenced by **missionaries** who sailed the western sea routes. The Christianity of Wales was linked with that of Ireland, **Scotland**, Cornwall

Maen Llia in Maescar, Brecon Beacons, one of Wales's finest Bronze Age standing stones

and Brittany, and the so-called **Celtic Church** developed its own characteristics. Among them was the central role of its monasteries. The 'saints' of the Celtic Church were usually monastic leaders. **David** (*c.*530–89) is considered the most prominent of them, and his monastery at **St David's** became the centre of a **diocese** which would extend over almost half the surface area of Wales. Under the leadership of the 'saints', large numbers of sacred enclosures were established within which churches were eventually built. The enclosure was called a *llan*, which explains why so many Welsh **place names** begin with *llan*. The early Anglo-Saxon kingdoms were pagan. Augustine's mission to Christianize them began at Canterbury in 597. His attempt to control the Welsh Church was resisted, and ill-feeling between Wales and Canterbury was to last for many centuries.

The small kingdoms of the early Cymry were eventually consolidated into four – **Gwynedd** in the north-west, **Powys** in the centre, **Deheubarth** in the south-west and **Morgannwg** in the south-east. The most powerful royal house was that of Gwynedd, which claimed descent from **Cunedda**. **Rhodri Mawr**, king of Gwynedd (d.877), united most of Wales under his rule and also succeeded in defending Wales against the **Vikings**. His grandson, **Hywel Dda** (Hywel the Good; d.949) is believed to have codified the **law** of Wales and he recognized the overlordship of Alfred, king of Wessex (*see* **English Monarchs and Wales**). Hywel's great-great-grandson, **Gruffudd ap Llywelyn** (d.1063), brought Wales in its entirety under his rule.

The success of Gruffudd ap Llywelyn, particularly his conquests east of Offa's Dyke, brought a hostile reaction from England. Harold, earl of Wessex, invaded Wales in 1063 and Gruffudd's kingdom collapsed. At the time when William of Normandy won the throne of England in 1066, Wales was again divided into at least four kingdoms. William established three earldoms – Chester, Shrewsbury and Hereford (*see* **Cheshire**, **Shropshire**, **Herefordshire**) – on the **border** with England and encouraged the earls to seize the territories of the Welsh. A chain of lordships along the border and the south coast – lordships ruled from the castles of the **Norman** invaders – came to be known as *Marchia Wallie* (the **March** of Wales). In the rest of the country – *Pura Wallia* – the Welsh rulers sought to build up their power. Among them were **Madog ap Maredudd** of Powys (d.1160), Owain ap Gruffudd of Gwynedd (**Owain Gwynedd**; d.1170) and **Rhys ap Gruffydd** of Deheubarth (The Lord Rhys; d.1197).

The Normans were determined to control the Welsh Church and, by 1143, the four Welsh bishoprics had been made subject to the authority of the archbishop of Canterbury. The Welsh reacted by seeking to win recognition for St David's as an archbishopric, a campaign in which **Giraldus Cambrensis** was prominent. Monasteries of orders founded in the European heartland were established in Wales and some of them, those of the **Cistercians** in particular, became important centres of Welsh culture. The Welsh rulers were also patrons of culture, with the Lord Rhys holding an **eisteddfod** at **Cardigan** in 1176.

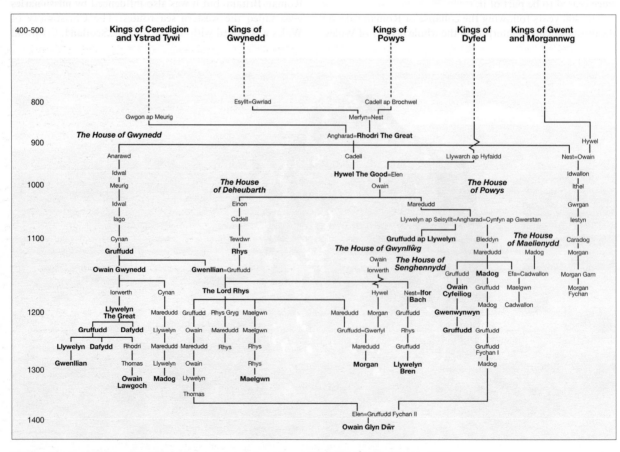

The royal houses of Wales, 400–1400 (with the most prominent figures in bold) (after John Davies, 1990)

The English kings sought to weaken the power of the Welsh rulers. The princes of Gwynedd reacted by seeking to bring the whole of *Pura Wallia* under their authority, an aim partly achieved by **Llywelyn ap Iorwerth** (Llywelyn the Great; d.1240). His grandson, **Llywelyn ap Gruffudd** (Llywelyn the Last; d.1282), succeeded in 1267 in winning recognition as **Prince of Wales** with authority over the other Welsh rulers. He was slow to recognize the overlordship of Edward I, who invaded Wales in 1277. Llywelyn was killed and his **Principality** was overthrown in 1282. To ensure control over the former *Pura Wallia*, the king built powerful castles of which **Caernarfon** is the most magnificent.

Wales did not become part of England following the **Edwardian conquest**. *Marchia Wallie* remained in existence as a series of lordships. Most of the territories whose rulers had recognized the overlordship of Llywelyn – the Principality – were divided into six **counties** – **Anglesey**, **Caernarfonshire**, **Merioneth**, **Flintshire**, **Cardiganshire** and **Carmarthenshire**; most of **Powys Fadog** and the **Perfeddwlad** were, however, converted into marcher lordships. The Principality was given to Edward's son, Edward of Caernarfon (later Edward II), who in 1301 became the first English Prince of Wales.

The two centuries after the conquest were a period of contradictory developments. Although there were no longer princely patrons, the poets flourished, with **Dafydd ap Gwilym** (d.*c.*1370) pre-eminent among them. Towns and trade developed, but the population was cruelly reduced by the **Black Death** of 1349. Although most Welsh customs were unaffected by the conquest, the Welsh system of landholding (*see Cyfran*) was gradually undermined, and the estates of the **gentry** began to emerge. Many Welshmen came to accept the conquest, and large numbers of them fought in the armies of the English kings. At the same time, there was resentment of English rule, which found expression in revolts in 1287, 1294 and 1316, and serious disturbances in the 1340s and 1370s. Above all, there was the **Glyndŵr Revolt** (1400–10), which almost led to the re-establishment of Welsh rule.

The defeat of **Owain Glyndŵr** caused great bitterness which found expression in the works of the poets. During the **Wars of the Roses** (1455–85), the Welsh sought a deliverer among the leaders of the Yorkists and the Lancastrians (*see* **York family** and **Lancaster family**). The most convincing was Henry **Tudor**, of an old Anglesey family, a descendant through his mother of the House of Lancaster. Landing in Wales in 1485, he received considerable support, and Welshmen constituted about a third of the army which won the crown of England for Henry VII at the battle of **Bosworth**.

By the reign of Henry's son, Henry VIII, most of the lordships of the March had come into the hands of the king. In 1536 and 1543, through legislation that came to be known as the **Acts of 'Union'**, the March was divided into seven counties: **Denbighshire**, **Montgomeryshire**, **Radnorshire**, **Breconshire**, **Monmouthshire**, **Glamorgan** and **Pembrokeshire**. The Welsh were granted 27 Members of Parliament (*see* **Parliamentary Representation**). Welsh Law was abolished and the use of the Welsh language for official purposes was prohibited.

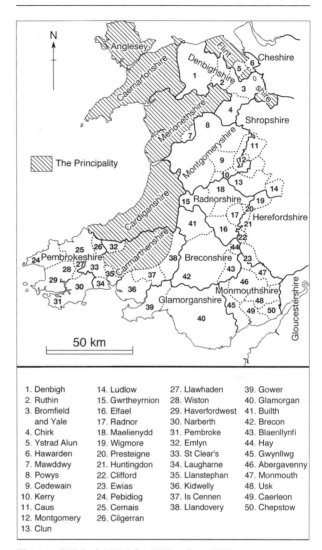

1. Denbigh	14. Ludlow	27. Llawhaden	39. Gower
2. Ruthin	15. Gwrtheyrnion	28. Wiston	40. Glamorgan
3. Bromfield	16. Elfael	29. Haverfordwest	41. Builth
and Yale	17. Radnor	30. Narberth	42. Brecon
4. Chirk	18. Maelienydd	31. Pembroke	43. Blaenllynfi
5. Ystrad Alun	19. Wigmore	32. Emlyn	44. Hay
6. Hawarden	20. Presteigne	33. St Clear's	45. Gwynllwg
7. Mawddwy	21. Huntingdon	34. Laugharne	46. Abergavenny
8. Powys	22. Clifford	35. Llanstephan	47. Monmouth
9. Cedewain	23. Ewias	36. Kidwelly	48. Usk
10. Kerry	24. Pebidiog	37. Is Cennen	49. Caerleon
11. Caus	25. Cemais	38. Llandovery	50. Chepstow
12. Montgomery	26. Cilgerran		
13. Clun			

The Act of 'Union', 1536 (after William Rees, 1959)

At the same time, the king threw off the authority of the Pope, beginning the process which would cause England and Wales to embrace the **Protestant Reformation**. By 1539, the monasteries of Wales had been suppressed and many sacred images destroyed. To encourage worship in the mother tongue, in 1546 **John Price (Prys)** of **Brecon** published his translation of the Creed and the Lord's Prayer – as part of the first book to be published in the Welsh language, *Yny Lhyvyr Hwnn*. The New Testament in Welsh appeared in 1567 and the entire **Bible** in 1588. The Bible, a magnificent translation, was the work of **William Morgan**. As the Welsh language was losing ground in public life and in the homes of the gentry, the existence of the Welsh Bible was central to its continuance as a language of dignity and learning.

The gentry, the dominant force in Wales from the 16th to the early 19th century, were staunchly loyal to the political and religious settlement established by the Tudor monarchs. That became apparent during the **Civil Wars** between King and Parliament (1642–9), when almost the whole of Wales was Royalist. With the victory of Parliament, the **Puritans**, who had hitherto won little support among the Welsh, received encouragement. The

Restoration of the Stuarts in 1660 led to the persecution of **Nonconformists** (those who refused to be members of the **Anglican** Church), but, following the Revolution of 1688, Nonconformists did gain limited legal rights.

With the tightening of the grip of the gentry, Wales became a land of extensive estates, and the estate owners controlled local government and monopolized parliamentary representation. The gentry became increasingly **English** in speech, and thus Welsh-language culture came to be led by the middling sort of people. The **economy** remained largely rural – Carmarthen and **Wrexham**, which in 1700 had some 3000 inhabitants apiece, were the largest towns. The smallholders – perhaps half the population – lived very frugal lives, and those below them – the cottagers and labourers – were often close to destitution. Most of Wales is not primarily cereal-growing country, and thus the raising of **cattle** and **sheep** was the backbone of the economy. The cattle trade was the main source of ready money, and therefore the **drovers** were of central importance. The production of flannel was the chief activity of the **woollen industry**; it was essentially a cottage industry which represented a form of proto-industrialization.

Following the Toleration Act of 1689, the Nonconformists began to build chapels. Nevertheless, the great majority of the population remained members of the Established Anglican Church. Among them were dedicated laymen such as Sir John **Philipps** (1662–1737), a devoted member of the **Society for the Promotion of Christian Knowledge** and the patron of **Griffith Jones** (**Llanddowror**; 1683–1771). Jones's **Circulating Schools** provided a crash course in literacy. By the time of his death, about half the population of Wales had attended his schools, most of which were conducted in the Welsh language. His success prepared the ground for the **Methodist Revival** which began in the 1730s with the missionary work of **Howel Harris** in Breconshire. Other first-generation leaders included both **Daniel Rowland** of **Llangeitho** and **William Williams** (Pantycelyn; 1717–91). Welsh Methodism was **Calvinist** in **theology** and followed a different path from that of the **Wesleyan** Methodism of England. Methodism began as a movement within the Church of England; it was not until 1811 that the Welsh **Calvinistic Methodists**, under the leadership of **Thomas Charles** of **Bala**, ordained their own ministers. Under the impact of the revival, the denominations which had sprung from the Puritans – the **Congregationalists** and **Baptists** – experienced new growth.

The Methodist Revival coincided with the 'Welsh **Renaissance**' of the 18th century. While the Methodists scorned old traditions, others, particularly those associated with the **Cymmrodorion** (founded 1751), were eager to build upon the achievements of the past. As literacy increased, the publication of Welsh books expanded greatly (*see* **Printing and Publishing**). The eisteddfod was revived, the classics of the past were studied and interest in history was stimulated. In this field, the most remarkable figure was Iolo Morganwg (**Edward Williams**; 1747–1826), whose enthusiasm led him to forge a large body of **literature** and to invent the ceremonies of the **Gorsedd Beirdd Ynys Prydain**.

The later 18th century saw a major shift in the history of Wales. The population began to grow rapidly. In 1770, the country had around 489,000 inhabitants; the number rose to 587,000 in 1801 and to 1,163,000 in 1851. In 1770, the vast majority of the Welsh population was in some way involved with agriculture; by 1851, the proportion had declined to one-third, a drift away from the land made possible by the growth of industry. Wales was well blessed with minerals – **coal** and iron ore in the south-east and north-east, **lead** in the centre and the north-east, and **slate** and copper ore in the north-west. These were the raw materials which allowed the Welsh to experience the **Industrial Revolution**, which in Wales took the form of the production of capital goods rather than factory-made consumer goods.

Although the north-east was the pioneer, the most massive developments occurred in the south-east. The northern rim of the southern coalfield contained all the resources necessary for the production of iron and, by the 1820s, the area was responsible for 40% of British production of pig iron. By the 1840s, the Dowlais Ironworks (*see* **Merthyr Tydfil**), with some 5000 employees, was the largest manufacturing concern in the world. Merthyr Tydfil, a tiny village in 1770, had a population of 46,000 by 1841. The south Wales coalfield is the only **mountainous** coalfield in Britain, and the landscape went far to determine the shape of the settlements and the nature of the life of their inhabitants. In the 1790s, the upland works were connected to the coast by a series of **canals**, but the real revolution in transport occurred in the 1840s with the coming of **railways**, a development which enabled coalmining to overtake ironmaking as the chief industrial activity in Wales.

The new communities of the coalfield were frontier communities. The pits and furnaces were dangerous places and the lack of clean water, sewerage and adequate **housing** meant that disease was rife (*see* **Health**). As the towns contained a high proportion of footloose young men, violence often erupted. The **Scotch Cattle** movement of the 1820s was an attempt to create working-class unity through terror. The **Merthyr Rising** occurred in 1831, and the Chartist march on **Newport** in 1839 was an attempt at revolution (*see* **Newport Rising** and **Chartism**). Yet despite the dangers and discontents, the number of inhabitants of the coalfield continued to rise. In the period 1801–41, the population of Monmouthshire increased more rapidly than that of any other county in Britain.

The population of the industrial areas grew largely because of movement from the overpopulated countryside. Agriculture flourished during the **French Revolutionary and Napoleonic Wars** (1793–1815), but in subsequent decades there was a serious depression. Discontent was expressed in many an **enclosure** riot and above all in the **Rebecca Riots** of 1839–43.

Discontent led to an interest in politics. The Reform Act of 1832 had increased the number of Welsh MPs from 27 to 32, but the expansion in the number of voters was small, and the landowners continued to dominate representation. The Chartist movement, which demanded a vote for all adult men, won a large following. Nonconformists, resentful of the privileges of the members of the Church of

An ironmaking furnace (1793) built near the site of Neath Abbey (Dyffryn Clydach)

England, were increasingly involved in politics as it became apparent in the religious census of 1851 that, of those in Wales who attended a place of worship, four out of five chose the chapel rather than the church.

Church–chapel conflict was particularly acute in the field of **education**, with the government report on education in Wales published in 1847 (*see* **Treason of the Blue Books**) creating much denominational bitterness. Until the 1870s, schooling was largely provided by denominational societies, and the Board Schools set up in that decade were bedevilled by the issue of religious instruction. Nevertheless, the later 19th century was a period of much educational advance. The University College of Wales was opened at **Aberystwyth** in 1872 (*see* **University of Wales, Aberystwyth**), the result of a nationwide voluntary effort. Colleges were opened in **Cardiff** (1884; *see* **Cardiff University**) and **Bangor** (1885; *see* **University of Wales, Bangor**), and the three were federated as the **University of Wales** in 1893. The **Welsh Intermediate Education Act** of 1889 led to the establishment of county secondary schools and, by the early 20th century, the opportunity to advance through education was considerably greater in Wales than it was in England.

At the same time, there were exciting developments in politics. Following Reform Acts in 1867 and 1884, the majority of adult males obtained the vote. Partly because of its sympathy for Nonconformists, the **Liberal Party** was the leading choice of Welsh voters; in 1885, it won 30 of the 34 seats in Wales, and in 1889 its candidates triumphed in the elections for the newly established county councils. Welsh Liberals advocated the **disestablishment of the Church of England in Wales**, but this was not achieved until 1920, when the **Church in Wales** became an autonomous province of the Anglican Communion. There were those who advocated the political rights of the Welsh as a nation. Chief among them was **Michael D. Jones**, who was prominent in the establishment of a Welsh colony in **Patagonia**. Under the influence of developments in Ireland, the nationalist movement **Cymru Fydd** (Young Wales) was active between 1885 and 1897. One of its leaders was **David Lloyd George**, who was elected MP for Caernarfon **Boroughs** in 1890. The linguistic rights of Welsh-speakers were stressed by Emrys ap Iwan (**Robert Ambrose Jones**) and there were campaigns over the language's lack of status in schools, particularly over the use of the **Welsh Not(e)**. Welsh was included in the curriculum after 1889, although decades were to pass before there was any movement from lessons *on* the mother tongue to lessons *in* the mother tongue.

The linguistic and demographic make-up of Wales changed markedly in the wake of the phenomenal growth of the south Wales coalfield. Of the country's 2,420,000 inhabitants in 1911, two-thirds lived in Glamorgan and Monmouthshire. The growth of the **Rhondda** was especially spectacular; its population increased from 951 in 1851 to 167,000 in 1924. The number of coalminers in Wales reached a peak of 271,000 in 1920 when they, with their families, represented nearly a third of the entire Welsh population. The main **port** for the export of coal was Cardiff, which grew in population from 1870 in 1801 to 219,000 in 1921; Cardiff became a city in 1905, but it was not formally recognized as the capital of Wales until 1955.

The industrial working class made strenuous efforts to organize itself. This could lead to lengthy conflicts such as the three-year strike at the **Pennant family**'s Penrhyn Quarry in **Llandygai** (*see* **Penrhyn Lockouts**). The most significant union in Wales was the **South Wales Miners' Federation**, established in 1898. The southern coalfield developed a reputation for militancy, particularly as a result of the **Tonypandy Riots** of 1910 and of the rise of radical leaders such as **Noah Ablett**, who sought to overthrow capitalism and replace it with workers' democracy. There was dissatisfaction with the middle-**class** dominated Liberal Party. The **socialist Keir Hardie** became MP for Merthyr Tydfil in 1900, and the **Labour Party**, whose origins can be dated to that year, held five Welsh seats by 1910.

Nevertheless, at least until the **First World War**, the Liberal Party remained the dominant force in Welsh politics, and the Welsh followed with pride the career of David Lloyd George, prime minister from 1916 to 1922. The war, in which at least 35,000 Welshmen were killed, had a profound effect upon Wales. It weakened allegiance to Liberalism and, by 1922, the Labour Party had won half the Welsh constituencies. It led to the overexpansion of the coalfield, making a recession almost inevitable. Between 1920 and 1939, 133,000 jobs disappeared in the coalmines of south Wales. Unemployment soared, reaching a peak of 42.8% among insured Welshmen in 1932 (*see* **Depression of the Interwar Years, The**).

For the first time in centuries, the population of Wales was in decline; 390,000 people moved out of the country between 1925 and 1939. The Depression was made worse by the bitterness between employers and employed, a bitterness that came to a climax in the **General Strike** and the miners' lockout of 1926. The apparent collapse of capitalism encouraged left-wing views, and the

Communist Party, founded in 1920, won considerable support in parts of the coalfield.

The rural areas also suffered depression as the wartime boom in agricultural prices collapsed. Indeed, there was a feeling that the whole basis of Welsh society was being shattered and the characteristics which had made the Welsh a nation seemed to be in peril. The proportion able to speak Welsh, 55% in 1891, had fallen to 37% by 1931. Concern over language was the chief factor which led to the establishment of **Plaid [Genedlaethol] Cymru** in 1925. Its outstanding figure was **Saunders Lewis** who created a body of ideas which put the concept of Wales in a new perspective, and who led the arson attack on the **Penyberth Bombing School** in 1936. Despite concern over the language, the interwar years were a period of great distinction in Welsh literature. Those years also saw the emergence of a distinctive **Anglo-Welsh** literature, the work of **Dylan Thomas**, in particular, winning wide acclaim.

During the **Second World War**, the scourge of unemployment was solved, at least temporarily, by the demands of the armed forces and the war industries – the latter providing vast numbers of jobs for Welsh **women**. Some 15,000 Welsh combatants were killed during the war, less than half the number killed in the First World War. Civilian casualties, however, were considerable, for several Welsh towns, **Swansea** in particular, suffered grievously from aerial bombardment. The war greatly strengthened the power of the central government and, when it was over, there was a determination to use those powers to rid society of poverty and inequality – a determination expressed by the overwhelming support given by the Welsh electorate to the Labour Party in the general election of 1945. Through the nationalization and welfare legislation of the Labour governments of 1945–51, some 60% of the Welsh labour force

The Maerdy Colliery, the last operating colliery in the Rhondda Valley. It closed in 1990

came to be employed in industries and services directly controlled by government decisions. The state ownership of the coal industry was particularly welcomed, although nationalization was to be accompanied by a continuing decline in the employment offered by the collieries. The aims of the post-war Labour government – a mixed economy, the **welfare state** and a determination to ensure full employment – were also the policies of successive governments, both Labour and **Conservative**, at least until the challenge of Thatcherism in 1979.

By the early 1960s, with unemployment at less than 3%, and with a marked rise in the activity rate because of enhanced employment opportunities for women, Wales seemed to have been purged of the horrors of the 1930s. Prosperity was particularly marked in steelmaking centres such as **Port Talbot** (*see* **Iron and Steel**), although technological advance would eventually cause a massive contraction in steelmaking jobs. Contraction was even more marked in coalmining, with the numbers employed in the south Wales collieries declining from 105,000 in 1957 to 40,000 in 1969, and to fewer than 1000 by the early 21st century. Yet, despite the deprivation suffered by many of the older industrial communities, by the end of the 20th century the Welsh economy had undergone a remarkable transformation, partly as the result of the success of the **Welsh Development Agency** in attracting **inward investment**.

Economic transformation was accompanied by social and cultural transformation. By the late 20th century, Nonconformity was in a parlous state, and **rugby**, rather than the chapels, had become the premier symbol of the nation – if not, for many, a substitute for religion. A widespread hedonism developed, which some considered to be at odds with Welsh values. **Sunday closing** of public houses, once a marker of Welsh identity, was voted to extinction through a series of referendums held between 1961 and 1996. The wide swathe of majority Welsh-speaking areas that had, until the 1960s, existed over much of western Wales, was broken up as a result of a complexity of factors, migration from England among them (*see* **Immigration**). **Trade union** membership, another marker of Welshness, slumped with the decline of heavy industry.

Yet, the erosion of older Welsh traditions was accompanied by a reassertion of Welsh distinctiveness. Welsh-language advocates proved to be particularly active. A network of Welsh-medium schools was created and, as a result, knowledge of the language was, by the 1990s, more widespread among the young than among the old. With the foundation of **Cymdeithas yr Iaith Gymraeg** (the Welsh Language Society) in 1962, language campaigners became more militant; among their triumphs were a growing acceptance of bilingualism, the setting up of the **Welsh Language Board** (1993) and, above all, the establishment of **S4C**, the Welsh-language television channel, in 1982. A new assertiveness could be seen in Welsh popular culture, in particular in the widely acclaimed pop and rock groups (*see* **Music**).

Institutional identity was vastly enhanced in 1964 with the appointment of a **secretary of state for Wales** and the creation of the **Welsh Office**. Two years later, Plaid Cymru won its first parliamentary constituency with **Gwynfor Evans**'s victory in the Carmarthen by-election. The rise of

political **nationalism** and the creation of Welsh administrative structures gave salience to the issue of democratic accountability. The Labour government of 1974–9 offered Wales an elected assembly, but that was massively rejected in the referendum of 1979. In the 1980s, with the Conservatives making significant advances, **devolution** seemed to be a defunct issue. Although Plaid Cymru won four parliamentary seats in 1992, its support in the more populous areas of Wales was minimal. With the massive victory of the Labour Party in 1997, devolution returned to the agenda. The referendum of that year endorsed the government's plans for a Welsh assembly by a majority of 0.6% per cent. The opening of the **National Assembly for Wales** in June 1999 was widely believed to inaugurate a new era in the history of Wales.

WALES COLLEGE OF MEDICINE, BIOLOGY, LIFE AND HEALTH SCIENCES, The

Established in 1931 within the **University of Wales**, the Welsh National School of Medicine – as it was initially called – was born of compromise, with pre-clinical medical **education** continuing at what was until 2004 the University of Wales, **Cardiff** (*see* **Cardiff University**), and the clinical component being the responsibility of the school. Using Cardiff Royal Infirmary as its main teaching hospital, the school endured deteriorating academic facilities until 1971 when the University Hospital of Wales opened as a pioneering integrated academic and clinical complex at Heath (*see* Cardiff), joining the dental school and hospital and the **Tenovus** Institute for Cancer Research.

By 1984, the school had become sufficiently self-confident to revise its charter and change its name to the University of Wales College of Medicine, achieving full constitutional parity with the other colleges of the University in 1988. During the 1990s, which saw the opening of the Sir **Geraint Evans** Wales Heart Research Institute, the college greatly enhanced its standing as one of the leading centres for medical research in the United Kingdom. By increasing its range of academic disciplines in 1995 to include several professions allied to medicine, and with a major expansion in nursing and midwifery education, the college became a broadly based 'health' care university' with over 3000 students. The college was the first higher education institution in Wales to have its **Welsh language** policy officially approved by the **Welsh Language Board**.

In 2004, the college merged with the University of Wales, Cardiff, which, as Cardiff University, seceded from the federal University of Wales. Changing its name for the third time, it became an enlarged Wales College of Medicine, Biology, Life and Health Sciences, one of two colleges making up the new Cardiff University (the other being the College of Humanities and Sciences), each headed by a provost.

WALES INTERNATIONAL (Undeb Cymru a'r Byd)

An organization linking Wales with expatriates throughout the world. It was founded as a result of the experiences of a small group of Welsh servicemen in the eastern Mediterranean during the **Second World War**, who discussed the possibility of such an organization in *Seren y*

Dwyrain (Star of the East), a **periodical** published by the Welsh in Cairo for the armed forces serving throughout the eastern Mediterranean and North Africa.

Post-war meetings in **Aberystwyth** led in 1948 to the foundation of what would become Wales International (Undeb Cymru a'r Byd), although its original name was Undeb y Cymry ar Wasgar (The Union of the Welsh in Dispersion). Founder members included **Ifan ab Owen Edwards** and T. Elwyn Griffiths, who became its long-serving secretary and editor of its journal *Yr Enfys*. The organization was responsible for the annual welcoming ceremony to the overseas Welsh at the National **Eisteddfod**; the Eisteddfod's decision in 2006 to abolish the ceremony was a grave disappointment to the members of Wales International.

WALES TUC

The inaugural conference of the Wales Trades Union Council was held at **Aberystwyth** in April 1974, following a year and a half of campaigning by a number of Welsh trade unionists, notably Tom Jones (Transport and General Workers' Union) and **Dai Francis** (**National Union of Mineworkers**). The British TUC, which was reorganizing its regional structure throughout Wales and **England** in line with proposed changes in local **government** boundaries, did not allow Wales an independent congress comparable with the Scottish TUC. Despite recognizing Wales as an entity, it was prepared to concede only a regional council; 'Welsh unions get council without teeth', as the *Western Mail* reported on 5 September 1973. The new organization had a fairly elaborate structure: a chairman (the first to be elected was Dai Francis), a secretary, a treasurer and trustees, a general council of 45 members who held quarterly meetings and an executive committee with five sub-committees. The structure has been amended considerably over the years to meet the increasing demands placed upon it.

Until the mid-1980s, the key figure in the organization was its secretary, George Wright, who was also regional secretary of the Transport and General Workers' Union. It was he who ensured that the Wales TUC gave firm backing to an affirmative vote in the **devolution** referendum of 1979. The first full-time secretary was David Jenkins, who took up the post in 1984. In the same year, a joint office was established at Transport House, **Cardiff**, for the Wales TUC and the TUC Regional **Education** Service, which moved from its former headquarters at **Pontypridd**. During the 1980s, the Wales TUC, appalled by the enactments of the Thatcher administrations, co-operated with the **Labour Party** in drafting policies on regional and local government, economic development, **housing** and **health**. It spared no effort in attempting to ensure the election of a Labour government in 1987 and 1992. From 1997, it expressed reservations about some of the policies of the 'New' Labour government led, until June 2007, by Tony Blair. (*See also* **Trade Unionism**.)

WALLACE, Alfred Russel (1823–1913)
Naturalist and author

The Welshman who formulated a theory of natural selection independently of Charles Darwin was born at **Usk**. After basic schooling in **England**, he returned to Wales in 1839 to work as a land surveyor, first in **Radnorshire** and then at **Neath**. The period at Neath was seminal in Wallace's development as a naturalist. He became acquainted with **L. W. Dillwyn** and other local naturalists, started lecturing on scientific topics at the **Mechanics' Institute** and, in 1847, published his first scientific communication (in the *Zoologist*). He acquired a knowledge of **Welsh** and was in favour of teaching **science** through the medium of that language.

In 1848, he embarked on a collecting expedition to the Amazon, believing that such a venture could provide evidence about the origin of living organisms. A second trip followed (1854–62) to the Malayan archipelago. From there, he sent his ideas on evolution by natural selection to Charles Darwin – who, unknown to Wallace, had already formulated, but not published, a more or less identical theory. Darwin, dismayed by this turn of events, contacted powerful friends, who moved quickly to ensure that Wallace did not receive sole credit for his idea. At a Linnaean Society meeting on 1 July 1858, Wallace's letter (entitled 'On the Tendency of Varieties to Depart indefinitely from the Original Type') was read together with an abstract of Darwin's own views, as a joint paper, thus saving Darwin's good name. Wallace's findings were published as *Contributions to the Theory of Natural Selection* (1870). Later, Wallace became better known for his biogeographical studies and for the identification of a dividing line between the Oriental and the Australasian types of fauna, known today as 'Wallace's line'.

In later life, Wallace embraced a number of 'unorthodox' beliefs, writing prolifically on a wide range of controversial topics. He never succeeded in obtaining permanent employment, and life was at times difficult. Darwin, T. H. Huxley and others petitioned **Gladstone** to award Wallace a **government** pension and, in 1881, an annual award of £200 was agreed. Despite financial and legal difficulties, and personal attacks, he remained intellectually active until the end, publishing over 800 books, pamphlets and papers, including an autobiography, *My Life* (1905). He received the first Darwin Medal of the Royal Society (1890) and the Order of Merit (1910).

WALTER, Lucy (?1630–58) Mistress of Charles II

A **Pembrokeshire** woman, she joined the exiled English court at The Hague at the age of 18 and bore Charles Stuart (later Charles II) a son, James (later duke of **Monmouth**) in 1649, and a daughter, Mary, in 1651. She is the subject of the novel *Liwsi Regina* (1988) by **Rhydwen Williams**. Following the duke of Monmouth's rebellion in 1685, 320 of his supporters were condemned to death at the 'Bloody Assizes' presided over by **George Jeffreys**.

WALTERS, Cyril [Frederick] (1905–92) Cricketer

Born at Bedlinog (*see* **Merthyr Tydfil**), Walters played for **Glamorgan** while still at **Neath** Grammar School, and was the first Welshman to captain **England** at **cricket**. His career blossomed after he moved in 1928 to become club secretary at Worcestershire, where he was captain from 1931 to 1935. His quality as a stylish opening batsman was confirmed by a batting average of more than 50 from his 11 Tests, including one as captain against **Australia** in 1934. He also played **rugby** for **Swansea**.

WALTERS, D[avid] Gwynne (1928–88)
Rugby referee

Gowerton-born Walters captained the local **cricket** team during the years that he became the world's most respected **rugby** referee. Between 1959 and 1966, he refereed 23 international matches. His diminutive stature, his sweater or striped blazer, and his high-pitched voice were as distinctive as his commitment to open and flowing rugby.

WALTERS, Evan (1893–1951) Painter
Born into a family of **craftsmen** in **Llangyfelach**, Walters became an apprentice decorator before studying **painting** at **Swansea** School of Art. Between 1916–19 he lived in New York, then **London**, where he remained for the next 20 years.

Determined to make his living as an artist, Walters poured his enormous talent and energy into his paintings, largely of people such as Welsh miners, later developing his 'binocular vision' technique of vivid, broken colour and mechanistic brush strokes. His early promise did not bring him the rewards he deserved, and his later work lost its vibrancy; his last painting was a portrait of his patron, **Winifred Coombe Tennant**.

WALWYN'S CASTLE (Castell Gwalchmai),
Pembrokeshire (2214 ha; 304 inhabitants)

Located immediately north-west of **Milford Haven**, the **community** contains the villages of Walwyn's Castle, Hasguard and Robeston West, all of which have churches with medieval features; that at Hasguard is being preserved as a ruin. The so-called castle may be an **Iron Age** fort, or perhaps a **Viking** earthwork. Walwyn's Castle was a major medieval barony dependent upon the lordship of **Pembroke**. In the late 14th century, its lords, the Brian family, had a flock of over 2000 **sheep**. There is an **oil** refinery at Robeston West.

WAR MEMORIALS

Until the 20th century, commemoration of men killed in battle was primarily defined by personal wealth, position and influence – the memorial to General **Picton** at **Carmarthen**, for example. The death in battle of the private soldier was largely unmarked. The deaths of an estimated 3500 volunteers in the Boer War (*see* **South African Wars**) led to changes in commemoration, as it became necessary to remember those who had died not only as soldiers but also as citizens.

Of the 700,000 British servicemen who died in the **First World War**, 35,000 are listed in the Welsh Book of Remembrance. The decision taken in 1915 to ban the repatriation of bodies from the battlefield had far-reaching consequences in the commemoration process. The many thousands of local war memorials reflected the desire for an immediate and permanent reminder of the dead, as communities sought public acknowledgement of their loss. The national focus of remembrance in Wales is the Welsh National War Memorial in **Cathays Park**, **Cardiff**, erected in 1928 after a public subscription campaign organized by the *Western Mail*. (Other Welsh towns resented what they saw as Cardiff's attempt to present itself as the capital of Wales.) Questions of site, size, cost and form stimulated

Lucy Walter

debate, but the ultimate choice of memorial was usually governed by financial considerations. Inscriptions on memorials invoke ideals of honour, sacrifice and loyalty, and they are often expressed in **Welsh** and **English**, or, as at **Swansea**, in **Latin**. The **Second World War** prompted a new era of commemoration.

WARENNE family Marcher-lords

John de Warenne, earl of Surrey (d.1304), a close associate of Edward I, led one of the royal armies which invaded Wales in 1282. He was rewarded with an extensive tract of the territory of the princes of **Powys Fadog**, which became known as the lordship of **Bromfield and Yale**. Warenne commissioned the building of **Holt** Castle as the caput of the lordship. On his death, the lordship passed to his grandson, John. John died childless in 1347, and the lordship became the property of his sister's son, Richard **Fitz Alan**, lord of **Chirk**.

WARS OF THE ROSES, The

Wales was involved throughout the civil wars between the Lancastrian and Yorkist factions, which began in 1455 (*see* **Lancaster family** and **York family**). The **Principality** was mainly Lancastrian and the former **Mortimer** lordships Yorkist; some leading protagonists were **march**er-lords, among them the earl of Warwick (**Glamorgan**) and the **Stafford family**, dukes of Buckingham (**Brecon**). The allegiances of the leaders of the Welsh community were often dictated by local power struggles or even by which side their ancestors had taken in the **Glynd ŵr Revolt**. For some, such as **Gruffudd ap Nicolas** at **Carmarthen**, loyalty to

Lancaster or York was a convenient cover for the pursuit of personal ambition.

The war reached the Wales/**England border** in 1459 with a victory for the Yorkists at Blore Heath and for the Lancastrians at Ludford Bridge. The Yorkist victory at Mortimer's Cross near Leominster, a battle fought between two largely Welsh armies on 3 February 1461, led to the coronation of the duke of York as Edward IV. **Harlech** Castle remained in Lancastrian hands until it surrendered in 1468.

The Yorkist party in Wales was led by William **Herbert, earl of Pembroke**, one of Edward IV's closest allies and seen by many in Wales as a potential national leader. The Lancastrian leader was Jasper **Tudor**. Edward IV entrusted Herbert with the oversight of Wales, but his rise caused resentment and contributed to the earl of Warwick's revolt in 1469. Herbert's execution following his defeat by Warwick at Banbury was seen in Wales as a national disaster. Warwick's revolt was followed by the restoration of Henry VI, but Henry was finally defeated in 1471 by Edward IV at Tewkesbury. Jasper Tudor and his young nephew Henry – the Lancastrian heir following the death of Henry VI's son Edward at Tewkesbury – fled to **Brittany**. In 1483, Edward IV died; the subsequent disappearance of Edward V and his brother gave rise to mistrust of their uncle, Richard III. Early in August 1485, Henry Tudor landed at **Dale** on the **Milford Haven Waterway** and marched through Wales, gathering support on the way.

Pistyll Rhaeadr

His victory at **Bosworth** marked the last phase of the Wars of the Roses. The final battle was fought at Stoke in 1487, when the pretender, Lambert Simnel, was defeated; in 1497 another pretender, Perkin Warbeck, was captured and executed.

WASSAILING

The custom of carrying a wassail cup from door to door in expectation of gaining admittance and receiving hospitality and a small sum of money. A fertility rite in origin, it was an occasion to wish good **health** to the householder, his family, crops and animals during the coming year. Wassailing was especially linked with Christmastide (notably the **Mari Lwyd**) and **Candlemas**, and often involved a contest in verse before the wassailers were admitted. The terms *canu yn drws* (singing at the door) and *canu gwirod* (wassail singing) refer to this aspect of the custom.

WATERFALLS

English visitors and occasional Welshmen – **Thomas Pennant**, for example – delighted in such wonders of nature as waterfalls. In terms of sheer drop, the highest in Wales is Pistyll Rhaeadr (**Llanrhaeadr-ym-Mochnant**), where the Disgynfa plunges 75 m to a pool, from which it plunges a further 25 m. It is among the **'seven wonders of Wales'**.

In his *Waterfalls of Wales* (1986), John Llewelyn Jones maps the location of 121 waterfalls, but, if all the falls characteristic of headwater streams of steep glacial valleys are included, the total would be far higher. In their creation, ice was the central factor, for glaciers were responsible not only for creating steep slopes but also for making valleys deeper. Thus, in glacial valleys, tributaries emerge high above the main floor to which they descend by means of long waterfalls. Such hanging valleys are characteristic of the upper reaches of Nant Gwynant in **Snowdonia**, and on the slopes of **Cadair Idris**.

The upper basin of the **Conwy** contains some of the most famous falls and rapids in Wales, among them the Swallow, Machno and Conwy falls and the Fairy Glen rapids. Again, glacial over-deepening was primarily responsible for their formation, although 'steps' or knick-points may have been formed during an earlier period, when the Conwy captured the Llugwy, Lledr and Machno. Similarly, the Twymyn, a tributary of the **Dyfi**, was rejuvenated when it captured the headwaters of the Clywedog, giving rise to a knick-point near the present position of Ffrwd Fawr. Later, that part of the Twymyn valley below the knick-point was deepened by glacial erosion, which created the 50-m sheer drop over which Ffrwd Fawr plunges.

The Ogwen waterfall can also be attributed to glacial erosion. Before ice breached the watershed between the summits of Pen yr Ole Wen and Y Garn, the streams east of the watershed were part of the headwaters of the Llugwy, which flows eastwards. Following the breach and the disappearance of ice, its headwaters were diverted. Although Llyn Ogwen lies on the floor of the upper section of the Llugwy valley, the Ogwen flows westwards from the **lake**, descending 90 m before reaching the flat floor of Nant Ffrancon, one of Snowdonia's most striking glacial troughs.

The waterwheel at Aberdulais, Blaenhonddan

The general consensus is that the **Rheidol**'s capture of the headwaters of the **Teifi** was responsible for the formation of the famous Mynach falls, a series of six falls dropping 120 m (*see* **Pontarfynach**). Similarly, the **Nedd**, by capturing the Cynon's headwaters, created a series of knick-points on the Pyrddin, Nedd Fechan, Mellte, Hepste and Sychryd. Erosion by Pleistocene glaciers further deepened the floor of the main valley. This increased the steepness of the tributaries' longitudinal profiles causing the Mellte to fall 140 m over a distance of only 4 km. In addition, the attractive falls in deep gorges on the Nedd's headwater streams – the first area in Wales to be considered for **National Park** status – owe much to the **river**'s action on hard sandstone and soft mudstone. The sandstone can withstand the scouring force of the river but the mudstones are eroded and washed away. In the case of Sgwd Gwladys on the Pyrddin and Sgwd yr Eira on the Hepste, layers of mudstone occur between the layers of near horizontal sandstones which form both the ledge over which the water plunges and the floor of the river valley below. As the flow's force wears away the soft rocks, blocks of the hard sandstone capstone fall away from time to time, causing these and similar falls to retreat up the valley.

Structurally, Sgwd Henryd, near Coelbren (**Tawe-Uchaf**) is very similar to Sgwd yr Eira. Nant Llech hurls itself over a ledge composed of beds of hard sandstone overlying layers of friable mudstones, and descends 27 m into a relatively deep plunge pool at the foot of the fall in the upper reaches of a wooded gorge.

The steeper a river's channel, the greater the work accomplished by its flow and the processes of erosion are most effective wherever falls and rapids occur. Waterfalls are temporary features in the history of a river, for the continued operation of the processes that create them ultimately results in their obliteration.

Waterfalls were among the favourite subjects of 18th and 19th-century artists. In the mid-19th century, **David Cox** made almost annual visits to paint the waterfalls in and around **Betws-y-Coed**. **J. M. W. Turner** painted Aberdulais Falls (**Blaenhonddan**), one of the few waterfalls whose power was harnessed for industrial purposes, and there were artistic devotees of the most picturesquely named of all Welsh waterfalls – Water-break-its-neck (**New Radnor**).

WATERMILLS

Geography and **climate** make Wales an ideal country for watermills, the streams and **rivers** radiating out from the central uplands providing a ready, generally reliable, source of motive power. Simple watermills were probably in existence in Wales by the 10th century; they were certainly well-established by the end of the 11th century. Most were driven by an 'overshot' waterwheel fed by a leat from a millpond or by water channelled from a river; if there was insufficient fall, 'under-driven' waterwheels, having paddles turned by the flow of the water, were employed.

During the Middle Ages, water power revolutionized the **woollen industry** through the use of fulling stocks, which removed grease from wool and compacted the

Horace Watkins (right) and his *Robin Goch* monoplane, *c.*1914–18

fabric. Water power was also used to operate carding, spinning and weaving machines in woollen factories. It also had a range of industrial and craft applications, including paper production, operating bellows in furnaces and foundries, water pumps in **coal**, **copper** and **lead** mines, and the powering of timber and masonry saws. Imported French burrstones were commonly used for milling wheat, with Welsh conglomerate millstones – from **Anglesey**, Penallt (**Trellech**), **St David's** and the slopes of the **Black Mountain** – being used for barley, **oats** and maize. Because of the moist climate, most mills had an oats drying kiln.

By the 20th century, large industrial mills dominated flour production and traditional mills had gone into almost total decline. Several mills have been restored but are mostly worked as tourist attractions. An example may be seen at the National History Museum (*see* **St Fagans**).

WATERS, [William] Alex[ander] (1903–85) Chemist

It was the lifelong quest of **Cardiff**-born Alex Waters to understand – rather than describe – organic reactions. His first appointment, after graduation and research at **Cambridge**, was to a tiny **chemistry** department at Durham, but through contact with **Donald Hey** he began a historic collaboration, by correspondence, on chemical reactions in solution involving free radicals. He moved to **Oxford** in 1944 when chemists at large were beginning to realize that the work of Hey and Waters on free-radical chemistry was of fundamental importance in several fields, including industrial and biological processes.

WATKINS, [Charles] Horace (1884–1976) Aviation pioneer

Designer and constructor of a tiny, red monoplane named *Robin Goch* (Robin Redbreast), built during 1907–9 at Maindy, **Cardiff**. Watkins claimed to have made brief hops early in 1910, followed by longer flights, but these claims are unverified. If Watkins's assertions are true, then he

could have been the first person to achieve heavier-than-air flight in Wales – although **William Frost**'s alleged flight at **Saundersfoot** in 1896, if it took place, would negate such a claim. The *Robin Goch* is preserved at the National Waterfront Museum, **Swansea** (*see* **The National Museum [of] Wales**).

WATKINS, VERNON (1906–67) Poet

Born in **Maesteg** and brought up in **Swansea** and **Gower**, he spent a year at Magdalene College, **Cambridge**, but found it uncongenial. At his father's insistence, he joined the staff of Lloyds Bank in **Cardiff**, only to suffer a nervous breakdown, after which he was moved to the bank's branch in St Helen's Road, Swansea. Except for military service during the **Second World War**, he was to remain a bank clerk until his retirement. He died after a game of **tennis** in Seattle where he was professor of poetry at the University of Washington.

Although in his early years he was associated with the poets of the New Apocalypse, his poetry was influenced more by the French and German Symbolists; he translated the work of Heine, Hölderlin, Rilke and others. Christian in its themes, although sometimes unorthodoxly so, his work shows little change over the 30 years of its composition and seems to be primarily concerned with 'the conquest of time', a matter which had been the cause of his breakdown as a young man. Many of his poems, when they are not obscure and over-complex, reflect the landscape of Gower, while the later work lays emphasis on the role of the poet in interpreting the natural world.

His most important books are *Ballad of the Mari Lwyd* (1941), *The Lamp and the Veil* (1945), *The Lady with the Unicorn* (1948) and *The Death Bell* (1954); his *Collected Poems* appeared in 1986. His close relationship with **Dylan Thomas** is described by his widow Gwen Watkins in her book *Portrait of a Friend* (1983) and in *Dylan Thomas: The Collected Letters* (ed. Paul Ferris, 1986).

WAT'S DYKE

This linear earthwork is an archaeological and historical enigma. With its high bank and west-facing ditch, the Dyke extends for 61 km through the northern **border**lands, from the confluence of the Vyrnwy and the **Severn** (in **Shropshire**) to Basingwerk (**Holywell**). Like **Offa's Dyke**, its counterpart to the west, Wat's Dyke marked a boundary, yet one evidently designed to deal with a problem confined to the Welsh foothills north of the Severn.

The conventional view has been that it was part of the military strategy behind the great earthwork bearing the name of Offa, king of **Mercia** from 757 to 796 – though dating from somewhat earlier in the 8th century. It has been argued that Offa's engineers used part of its line for the defensive approach to the **Dee** estuary. But carbon-dating evidence, from an archaeological site at Maes-y-Clawdd, Oswestry, has raised the possibility that it may have been built 300 years earlier, by the post-**Roman** rulers of Wroxeter (Viroconium) – once the fourth largest urban centre in the Roman province of Britannia – 8 km southeast of present-day Shrewsbury. Long after the borderland earthworks had lost their primary military function, Wat's Dyke marked the western limits of Mercian control and became fossilized in fiscal arrangements – relating to renders due from an estate – that remained in force until the era of the Domesday Book.

WAUNFAWR, Gwynedd
(1422 ha; 1366 inhabitants)

Located immediately east of **Caernarfon**, the **community** once had several **slate** quarries. Waunfawr village is now part of Caernarfon's commuter belt. The first radio message from **Britain** to **Australia** was sent from Marconi's transmitter above the village on 22 September 1918. (The transmitter was in operation from 1914 to 1938.) David Thomas (Dafydd Ddu Eryri; 1759–1822), teacher of poets, was a native of Waunfawr, as was **John Evans** (1770–99), **map**maker and explorer, who searched the headwaters of the Missouri for the reputedly **Welsh**-speaking Mandan tribe, allegedly the descendants of **Madog ab Owain Gwynedd**. A memorial to him by sculptor Meic Watts stands outside Antur Waunfawr's small museum, which tells the story. Antur Waunfawr, established in 1983 to provide employment and support to those with mental handicaps, employs over 40 people.

WAWR (Workers' Army of the Welsh Republic)

An underground **republican** group formed in March 1980, in reaction to Wales's rejection of **devolution** in the 1979 referendum and the de-industrialization which followed the **Conservative** victory of that year. In 1980–1, it was involved in the bombing of numerous targets in Wales and **England**. The trial of its alleged members, held at **Cardiff** Crown Court in 1983, led to the imprisonment of three of the accused and the release of four others. Serious doubts were expressed concerning the reliability of the **police** evidence. In Welsh, *wawr* (*gwawr*) means dawn.

WAYNE, Naunton (Henry Wayne Davies; 1901–70)
Actor

Born in Llanwonno (**Ynysybwl and Coed-y-cwm**), Wayne was a stalwart of British light comedy roles, with a speciality in blinkered unflappability, dyspepsia or petulance. With Basil Radford, he was half of the blimpish, **cricket**-loving pair Charters and Caldicott, first seen in Hitchcock's *The Lady Vanishes* (1939) and later revived in *Night Train to Munich* (1940), *Crooks Tour* (1941), *Next of Kin* (1942), *Millions Like Us* (1944), *Dead of Night* (1945) and *It's Not Cricket* (1948). On stage, Wayne enjoyed a long **London** run in *Arsenic and Old Lace* (1942–6).

'WE'LL KEEP A WELCOME'

A popular, if famously schmaltzy, song originally intended as a welcome for Welsh troops in the **Second World War**. It was first sung by the Lyrian Singers on BBC Radio's *Welsh Rarebit* on 29 February 1940, with words by Lyn Joshua and James Harper, to a melody by **Mai Jones**. Published in 1949, it was subsequently recorded by **Harry Secombe**.

WEBB, Harri (1920–94) Poet

Born in **Swansea** and educated at **Oxford**, Harri Webb served in the navy during the **Second World War**, and then worked with **Keidrych Rhys** at the Druid Press in **Carmarthen**. He was a librarian at Dowlais (**Merthyr Tydfil**) (1954–64), and subsequently at **Mountain Ash** (1964–74). He entered politics as a Welsh **Republican** but joined **Plaid [Genedlaethol] Cymru** in 1960. Between 1969 and 1983, he published four volumes of verse, which are gathered in his *Collected Poems*, (ed., Meic Stephens, 1995). He was a prolific writer of political and literary journalism, selections of which were published posthumously as *No Half-Way House* (1998) and *A Militant Muse* (1998).

Harri Webb described his work as having 'only one theme, one preoccupation' and as being 'unrepentantly nationalistic'. Although many of his poems are satirical squibs, such as 'Ode to the Severn Bridge', he was capable of writing more lyrically, and was fond of themes drawn from Welsh history, as in the poems 'A Crown for Branwen' and 'Dyffryn Woods'. Among his most famous verses are those of 'Colli Iaith' – one of his few **Welsh**-language poems – which has achieved the status of a folk song.

WEBBER brothers Newspaper managers

The **Barry**-born brothers Robert John Webber (1884–1962) and Frank Edward Webber (1893–1963) occupied key positions on the *Western Mail*. For a period, Robert was secretary to George Riddell, chairman of several groups of **newspapers**. In 1916, he was appointed manager of the *Western Mail* and its successful **printing** business. In 1923, he became the paper's director for life and co-managing-director with William Davies (editor, 1901–31). He steered the paper through a difficult period after the **First World War** and maintained publication throughout the **General Strike**, in addition to overseeing the merger, in 1928, with the Duncan family's company and newspapers the *South Wales Echo* and the *South Wales Daily News*. Among his aspirations was the building of a highway to connect north and south Wales (*see* **Roads**). His brother Frank Webber became general manager (1940) and director (1946) of the *Western Mail and Echo*.

Harri Webb

WEIGHTLIFTING

The Welsh Weightlifting Federation (initially the Welsh Amateur Weightlifters' Association) was founded in 1927, following interest generated by a display given in **Llanelli**'s Market Hall by the famous German strongman Herman Goerner. Since then, Wales has established an international reputation for its weightlifters, many of whom have represented **Britain** at European and world championship levels.

Mel Barnett won a bronze medal in the 1950 World Championships in Paris. Welsh weightlifters have been conspicuously successful at the **Commonwealth Games**, winning more medals than Welsh competitors have won in any other sport – 18 gold, 11 silver and 20 bronze. David Morgan won 9 gold and 3 silver medals. In the first competition for **women** in 2002, Michaela Breeze won a gold and two silver medals; in 2006, she won a gold medal.

WELCH, Edward (1806–68) and John (b.1810–pre-1857) Architects

The Welch brothers were born at **Overton**. Edward formed a partnership (1828) with Joseph Hansom, first in York and then **Liverpool**. After winning the competition to design Birmingham Town Hall, they became bankrupt and parted. Their work included remodelling **Bodelwyddan** Castle (c.1830) and Victoria Terrace, **Beaumaris** (1830–5). Edward Welch's later works included **Wrexham** Infirmary (1838) and Rhosymedre church (**Cefn**). After working in the Isle of **Man**, John Welch established an office in **St Asaph** (1839). He designed a number of churches in the north, as well as **Flint** Town Hall (1840) and the workhouse, later the **H. M. Stanley** Hospital, St Asaph (1838).

WELCH REGIMENT, The

Raised in 1719 as a regiment of invalids for garrison duty only, the 41st Foot became a line regiment in 1787. The 2nd battalion, linked to South Lincolnshire, was redesignated the 69th Foot. The 41st was titled 'the Welch Regiment' ('Welch' is the old English manner of spelling 'Welsh'). From 1831, a **Pembrokeshire** depot for both regiments was established and, in 1881, they became 1st/2nd Battalions, the Welsh Regiment. Expanded to 35 battalions during the **First World War**, the spelling 'Welch' was restored in 1920. Between 1939 and 1945, the regiment fought in North Africa, mainland Europe and Burma. In 1969, it was amalgamated with the **South Wales Borderers** to form the **Royal Regiment of Wales**.

WELFARE STATE, The

So great was the contribution of Welshmen to the creation of the British welfare state that the belief arose that concern for social justice was a particular trait of the Welsh. Indeed, during the 1979 referendum campaign on **devolution**, Leo Abse, MP for **Pontypool**, frequently expressed his fear that, if a Welsh assembly were established, **Britain** as a whole could be deprived of one of its greatest assets – the Welsh social conscience.

While **government**s have always been interested in social questions, historically their main involvement has been a readiness to provide sufficient succour to the poor to prevent serious unrest. More positive attitudes can be discerned in the 19th century, but it was not until the early 20th century that it was widely argued that the state could intervene decisively to relieve deprivation. The key figure in the implementation of that belief in Britain was **David Lloyd George**. As chancellor of the exchequer (1908–15), he was associated with the introduction of old age pensions (1908). His 'Peoples' Budget' (1909), imposing increased taxes upon unearned money, land values, high incomes and inherited money, was partly intended to raise revenue for an extensive programme of social reform. In 1911, he introduced **health** and unemployment **insurance**. Further developments occurred during his premiership (1916–22), including the establishment of the Ministry of Health, an ambitious programme of council-house building (see **housing**) and the passage of the Unemployment Insurance Act. As **Winston Churchill** put it in his obituary tribute, Lloyd George was responsible for the state's first 'efforts to set a balustrade along the crowded causeway of the people's life and … to fasten a lid over the abyss into which so many used to fall'.

In the 1920s and 1930s, attempts were made to build on Lloyd George's achievements, for the **Conservative**-dominated governments of the interwar years were not as reactionary as is sometimes thought. Of particular importance was the dismantling of the **Poor Law** system in 1929. As in the **First World War**, the **Second World War** saw a yearning for further social reform, which found expression in the publication of the Beveridge Report (1942). The **Labour Party**'s enthusiastic endorsement of the report contrasted with the Conservatives' lukewarm attitude, and was a major factor in Labour's remarkable victory in 1945.

The chief figures in implementing the post-war Labour government's social policy were **James Griffiths** and **Aneurin Bevan**. Griffiths's National Insurance Act (1946) and Industrial Injuries Act (1948) were, he claimed, directly inspired by his experience in the **South Wales Miners' Federation**. Aneurin Bevan's plans for a National Health Service were, he claimed, directly inspired by the example of the **Tredegar** Medical Aid Society (see **Miners' Medical Aid Societies**). Welsh doctors were more supportive of Bevan's efforts than were doctors in Britain as a whole, and the demands on the service proved greater in Wales than elsewhere in the United Kingdom. As past neglect was more extensive in Wales, as heavy industries – with their frequent accidents – were more important in the country's **economy**, and as the **population** tended to be older, it is hardly surprising that per capita health service expenditure in Wales tended to be up to 30% higher than it was in Britain as a whole.

The inequalities with which the founders of the welfare state were concerned were largely those of **class**. In the later 20th century, it became apparent that the welfare state, although improving conditions for the poorer sections of society, had neither eliminated poverty nor tackled inequalities such as those experienced by **women**. One of the responses to this was the establishment of Welsh Women's Aid and its network of refuges for women and children threatened with domestic violence – a feminist form of welfare provision, which is part of the voluntary sector of the welfare state.

Until 1979, there was a Labour–Conservative consensus on the need to sustain the welfare state. The election of Margaret Thatcher's Conservative government in that year initiated a new policy, which envisaged the state as guarantor rather than provider of social services and benefits. That policy led to two decades of state under-investment in welfare, which the Labour government elected in 1997 promised to reverse. However, its readiness to accept some of the concepts of Thatcherism suggested that there would be no return to the free and comprehensive welfare system envisaged by Aneurin Bevan. During the first two terms of the **National Assembly** (1999–2007), the Labour administration evidently saw itself as guardian of the traditions of Lloyd George, James Griffiths and Aneurin Bevan. With the reintroduction in 2007 of free prescriptions for all, it sought to substantiate such claims.

WELLS OF THE SAINTS

Throughout the Middle Ages, the holy wells of Wales were the focus of pious devotion, **pilgrimage** and superstition. Francis Jones, in his authoritative study, located over 1000 wells, of which nearly half are dedicated to **'saints'**. Some are almost certainly of pre-Christian origin. The **Celts'** veneration of water and water deities lived on in their descendants' adherence to the Christianized wells and their observance of pagan rituals.

More than a third of the wells are known to have been healing wells, where people flocked either to drink the water or to bathe, in the hope of being cured of various afflictions. The most famous example, and possibly the most important well in medieval **Britain**, is St **Winefride's**

at **Holywell**, with its striking chapel – one of the **'Seven Wonders of Wales'**. Ffynnon Fair, Penrhys (**Rhondda**), attracted hordes of pilgrims.

The well-cult survived the **Protestant Reformation**, despite the prohibition of well-pilgrimages and the destruction of many well-chapels along with their accompanying symbols of the **Roman Catholic** faith. The increasing influence of **Nonconformists** also failed to eradicate popular belief in the miraculous powers of the wells. Indeed, the water of some of them was analysed and proved to have medicinal properties, giving rise to the fame of several Welsh spas. The wells also acquired a new status through the interest shown in them by antiquaries such as **Thomas Pennant** and Lewis Morris (*see* **Morris Brothers**).

Some wells were used for purposes other than healing, such as divination and cursing. Ffynnon Eilian, Llan-yn-Rhos (**Betws yn Rhos**), was originally a healing well which later became a notorious cursing well, where people paid to have their enemies cursed or to have a curse removed. Two of its 'priests' were jailed in the 1820s and 1830s for fraud.

An array of rituals surrounded the well culture, such as drinking from skulls, incantation and the throwing of pins, coins and other objects into the well as offerings. Legends and ghost stories about wells abound. Some wells are still used today, especially for healing and baptism.

WELSH, Freddie (Frederick Hall Thomas; 1886–1927) Boxer

World lightweight champion from 1914 to 1917, Freddie Thomas left a comfortable home in **Pontypridd** in 1902 to seek a new life in **North America**. A few years living rough

The chapel of St Winefride's Well, Holywell

The Freddie Welsh–Jim Driscoll fight at Cardiff: Welsh's win, when Driscoll was disqualified, caused a riot

toughened him before he settled in Philadelphia and took up **boxing**; patriotically renaming himself Freddie Welsh, he fought his first bout in December 1905.

Standing 1.7-m tall and weighing 60.32 kg, Welsh had self-confidence, a lethal straight left, and no reservations about crouching, clinching, kidney-punching and using his head and elbows. By these controversial tactics, he defended his British lightweight title, won in 1909, against **Jim Driscoll** in **Cardiff** in 1910. In 1914, he beat Willie Ritchie of the United States for the world title and defended it strenuously until Benny Leonard knocked him out in New York in May 1917. Welsh, who prided himself on his literary interests, later founded a **health** farm in New Jersey where he sparred with F. Scott Fitzgerald.

WELSH ACADEMY, The
Founded in 1959 as Yr Academi Gymreig by a group of **Welsh-language** authors, including Bobi Jones (b.1929) and **Waldo Williams**, the Academy is the national association for writers. An **English-language** section was created in 1968, when the society first attracted the support of the Welsh Arts Council (*see* **Arts Council of Wales**). It adopted a new constitution in 1998 and, as Academi, is now the Welsh National **Literature** Promotion Agency. Three major works of reference have been produced under the Academy's aegis: *The Oxford Companion to the Literature of Wales* (1986), republished in 1998 as *The New Companion to the Literature of Wales*, *The Welsh Academy English–Welsh Dictionary* (1995) and this encyclopaedia.

WELSH ARMY CORPS, The
David Lloyd George encouraged the formation of a 'Welsh Army' in his Queen's Hall, **London** speech on 19 September 1914. Overcoming the hostility of the secretary of state for war, Lord Kitchener, he won cabinet approval for a volunteer corps comprised largely of 'Pals' battalions (*see* **First World War**). The Corps was formed on 10 October 1914, but recruitment never matched expectations, and just one division (38th Welsh), rather than the intended two, landed in France in December 1915, seeing action at Mametz Wood in July 1916.

WELSH BOARD OF HEALTH, The
Established under the Ministry of **Health** Act 1919 as a territorial arm of the new ministry, the Board absorbed the functions of the Welsh **Insurance** Commission (a product of **David Lloyd George**'s 1911 National Insurance Act), and additional public health responsibilities were delegated to it. Continuity in outlook as well as in personnel – a defining characteristic of the Board – was still in evidence in 1938, when new offices were opened in **Cardiff** in a building destined to become the post-war **Welsh Office**. Compared with its more autonomous Scottish counterpart, the Welsh Board of Health had a somewhat restricted role, and remained subservient to the ministry of health. It had insufficient power to address independently the multiple health issues arising from the interwar **depression**; it continued to act as the decentralized arm of the Whitehall ministry during the first two decades of the National Health Service, until its disappearance in 1969 when new powers were devolved to the Welsh Office. Thereafter,

executive responsibility for health and welfare services was vested in the **secretary of state for Wales**, and the administrative service was redesignated the Health Division of the Welsh Office. From 1999 onwards, the services were the responsibility of the **National Assembly**.

WELSH BOOKS COUNCIL, The

A public body established in 1961 through the efforts of the Union of Welsh Books Societies under the leadership of **Alun R. Edwards** and with the financial backing of five of Wales's **counties**. Initially, its main aims were to seek the provision of an ample supply of popular **Welsh-language** books and to promote book sales. Its main activities during the 1960s were the awarding of grants to the authors of popular Welsh-language books for adults, co-ordinating a standing orders scheme within **public libraries**, and managing the Books Distribution Centre.

At the beginning of the 1970s, the remit of the Welsh Books Council was extended to include Welsh-language books for children and also **English-language** books of Welsh interest. With the financial support of the Welsh Arts Council (*see* **Arts Council of Wales**), new departments were established to provide editing, **design** and marketing services in order to strengthen the various elements of the book trade in Wales. In the early 1980s, the administrative responsibility for distributing the **government**'s publishing grant for Welsh-language books and **periodicals** was transferred to the Welsh Books Council. Since then, the Welsh Books Council has taken advantage of developments in information technology to expand its range of services to the book trade and to the general public. In 2003, the responsibility for the allocation of production grants for books and periodicals of a literary nature, in both languages, was delegated by the Arts Council to the Welsh Books Council. Consequently, the Welsh Books Council plays the central role in the infrastructure of the book trade in Wales. Its main activities are directly funded by the **National Assembly**. Its headquarters at **Aberystwyth** offers a superb view of Cardigan Bay.

WELSH CAKES

Welsh cakes have been teatime favourites in most parts of Wales since the late 19th century. Traditionally, flat-breads were baked on a bakestone or griddle suspended over an open fire, and, in areas where refined flour was available, unleavened white batches were baked regularly. The addition of a little fat, sugar and dried fruit to this bread dough was a natural progression. The **Welsh** names given to them were usually based on the regional Welsh names for the bakestone; these included *tishan lechwan*, *tishan ar y ma'n* (bakestone cakes), *pice bach* or *cacenni cri*, but in **English** they generally became known as Welsh cakes. Eaten in farmhouses and cottages, miners would also expect to find them in their food boxes.

WELSH CENTRE FOR INTERNATIONAL AFFAIRS, The

Based at the Temple of Peace, **Cathays Park**, **Cardiff**, the centre was established in 1974 to foster an understanding of global issues and to encourage a sense of belonging to the international community (*see* **Internationalism**). It is involved in a wide range of activities – lectures, conferences, publications, school visits – and has several constituent organizations.

WELSH COSTUME, The

The popular image of Welsh national dress – of a woman in a red cloak and a tall black hat – developed during the

R Griffiths, *Welsh Fashions Taken on a Market Day in Wales* (1851)

19th century and is based on clothing worn by Welsh country**women** at the time: a striped flannel petticoat, worn under an open-fronted flannel bedgown, with an apron, a shawl and a kerchief or cap. There was no standard national or even **county** style of dress. Fabrics and styles varied widely, often according to the produce of local **woollen** mills. Women's hats were generally of the same kind as those worn by men. Eighteenth-century illustrations show both men and women wearing low-crowned hats with wide brims. Printed cotton sunbonnets were probably a more common sight in the countryside than the tall 'chimney' hat, even after it had become a recognized part of the costume in the mid-19th century. This style seems to have been based on an amalgamation of men's top hats and a form of high-crowned hat worn in some country areas *c*.1790–1820.

Lady Llanover (**Augusta Hall**), an enthusiastic supporter of Welsh culture, was highly influential in encouraging the wearing of a 'national' dress, both within her own household and at *eisteddfodau*. She first championed the idea of a distinct national costume, using Welsh tweeds, in a prize-winning essay at the **Gwent** and **Glamorgan** eisteddfod held at **Cardiff** in 1834; the 'Welsh costume' as it is known today was first seen in processions organized by her in *eisteddfodau* held in **Abergavenny** in the 1840s. Lady Llanover succeeded in her aim partly because many in a rapidly industrializing Wales felt that their national identity was under threat, and wearing a national costume made of Welsh wool was a visual declaration of that identity.

Prints produced by artists for the growing **tourism** trade popularized the notion of a Welsh costume, and later the work of photographers (*see* **Photography**) who produced postcards in their thousands contributed to the stereotyping of one style of costume, as opposed to the various styles which were worn earlier in the 19th century.

The costume is now worn only on ceremonial and patriotic occasions, such as St **David**'s Day. Lady Llanover's invention of a national costume for men failed to catch on, but in the 20th century a male fancy dress of flat cap, waistcoat, breeches and clogs began to exert some appeal, and the advocacy of a Welsh 'cilt' brought an element of dash and swagger to 'Cymric' couture.

WELSH COUNCIL OF THE LEAGUE OF NATIONS UNION, The

Inaugurated at Shrewsbury in January 1922, the Council was steeped in the traditional **Liberal** ethos. With David Davies (1880–1944; *see* **Davies family (Llandinam)**) as patron and **Gwilym Davies** as organizer, it emphasized the need for collective security and international co-operation in order to preserve peace. It was vehement in its assault on Welsh **nationalism**. Until the late 1930s, it was a significant force in Welsh life, as a non-party political body dedicated to the furtherance of the principles of the League of Nations.

From 1923 onwards, the Council organized an annual **pilgrimage** to **Tregaron**, birthplace of **Henry Richard**. It pressed constantly for a revision of the Treaty of Versailles, urging that Germany be readmitted to the 'comity of nations', and calling for a solution to the vexed question of

reparations payments. In the late 1920s, the Council powerfully advocated compulsory arbitration and disarmament. By 1925, there were 571 branches and an adult membership of 31,299, but the **Depression** took its toll; by 1931, membership had fallen to 13,570.

The Council canvassed Welsh candidates in the general election of October 1931, came out strongly in favour of David Davies's proposals for an international equity tribunal and **police** force, and helped to secure an impressive turnout in the peace ballot of June 1935, in which 62.3% of the Welsh electorate voted. (The proportion voting in **Britain** as a whole was 38%.) It circulated questionnaires to candidates again in the general election of 1935, but increasingly lost ground thereafter in the face of the **Spanish Civil War** and the ever-growing threat from Hitler and Mussolini. By 1938 – the year of the opening of the movement's iconic building, the Temple of Peace in **Cardiff**'s **Cathays Park** – widespread public apathy and disillusionment prevailed, with disastrous consequences for membership and morale.

WELSH COURTS ACT (1942), The

From the **Act of 'Union'** of 1536 until the 20th century, the use of the **Welsh language** in courts was an inescapable necessity, but the interjections of Judge W. H. P. Lewis at the **Penyberth** trial at **Caernarfon** in 1936 indicated that the right to use the language was ambiguous. The interjections gave rise to the National Welsh Language Petition (1938–41), which eventually led to the Welsh Courts Act (1942). The language clause of the Act of 'Union' was repealed. The Lord Chancellor was authorized to prepare Welsh versions of oaths and provide interpreters at public expense – provisions already existing for foreigners with an inadequate command of **English**. To be allowed to use Welsh, defendants and witnesses had to swear that they would be disadvantaged if they were obliged to use English. Thus, the Act hardly gave Welsh equal status with English and it was considered a betrayal by many language campaigners.

WELSH DAY DEBATE, The

The first House of Commons debate ever to be assigned exclusively to Welsh affairs took place on 17 October 1944; it was devoted almost entirely to the post-war problems of reconstruction facing Wales in the fields of employment, industry and transport. In October 1946, the **Labour government** agreed that the debate, regarded by the supporters of **devolution** as a grossly inadequate sop to Welsh national sentiment, should be an annual event. Although the debates – which continue to be held in the post-devolution era – have often been sparsely attended, and the standard of discussion has frequently been unimpressive, they have at least provided an annual forum for the airing of Welsh issues and problems.

WELSH DEPARTMENT OF THE BOARD OF EDUCATION, The

Created in 1907, the department fell short of the National Council of **Education** for Wales mooted in the 1906 Education Act; nevertheless, it constituted significant educational **devolution**. The first permanent secretary was

Alfred T. Davies, and the chief inspector – a post that disappeared on his death in 1920 – was **O. M. Edwards**. His promotion of what he believed to be best in Welsh life – communal concern, love of handi**crafts**, learning, and the **Welsh language** and culture – led to confrontation with the examining and inspecting body of the Welsh intermediate schools, the **Central Welsh Board**. The Welsh Department's 1909 report, suggesting that examinations caused a 'wooden and unintelligent type of mind', resulted in public antagonism between the two bodies. After Edwards's death, the department assumed a lower profile.

WELSH DEPARTMENT OF THE MINISTRY OF AGRICULTURE AND FISHERIES, The
When, in 1919, the Board of **Agriculture** was renamed the Ministry of Agriculture and Fisheries, a department was established for Wales. The distinct needs of Wales had already been recognized in 1912 with the inauguration of the Welsh Agricultural Council, whose first commissioner was **C. Bryner Jones**. In 1919, he was appointed secretary of the new department, which, under his leadership, became a strong administrative body. Its influential advisory system was crucial in securing increased home production during the **Second World War**. Full responsibilities for agriculture were transferred to the **Welsh Office** in 1979, and thence to the **National Assembly** in 1999.

WELSH DEVELOPMENT AGENCY, The
Established by the **Labour government** through the Welsh Development Agency Act 1975, the WDA came into existence on 1 January 1976. With a board of members appointed by the **secretary of state for Wales**, the WDA was charged with four objectives: furthering the economic development of Wales; promoting industrial efficiency and international competitiveness; developing employment; and improving the environment.

Politically, the WDA was one of Labour's responses to growing national consciousness in Wales and the increasing pressure for **devolution**. There was also an economic rationale for a more devolved and interventionist approach to regional development, because the traditional regional policy was becoming less effective. The WDA justified its existence by helping to modernize and diversify the **economy** and by enhancing the environment. In 1999, the agency became subject to the **National Assembly** and belatedly came to realize its responsibility for furthering indigenous economic growth. In a long-anticipated, post-devolution 'bonfire of the **quangos**', the WDA was abolished as a quango in 2006 and its functions brought in-house by the Assembly.

WELSH FOLK DANCE SOCIETY, The
Formed in Shrewsbury in 1949 by Lois Blake, **W. S. Gwynn Williams**, Emrys Cleaver and Enid Daniels Jones, the Welsh Folk Dance Society has been instrumental in the development of traditional **dance** in Wales. Launching its annual journal, *Dawns*, in 1953, the society has continued to promote folk dance activities through publications, demonstrations and instructional courses. Performances by affiliated groups at international events have raised its profile and placed the art on a world stage. The society regularly creates new dances based on historical steps and patterns, thereby imbuing them with a contemporary feel while maintaining links with the past.

WELSH FOLK-SONG SOCIETY, The (Cymdeithas Alawon Gwerin Cymru)
The society was founded in 1906 to collect folk **music**, as part of the movement to safeguard traditional elements of Welsh culture. By the mid-20th century, the society had published nearly 600 traditional songs, mainly in the **Welsh language**; it then began to concentrate its resources on research. The society's *Journal* (1909–77) and its successor *Canu Gwerin/Folk-Song* (1978–) have published over 400 songs; in 1988, the society reprinted **Maria Jane Williams**'s important collection of 1844, *Ancient National Airs of Gwent and Morganwg* (ed., Daniel Huws).

WELSH GRAND COMMITTEE, The
The idea of a Welsh Grand Committee was first broached in the **Labour Party**'s *Policy for Wales* (1954). It was set up in March 1960 by Henry Brooke, the **Conservative** minister for Welsh affairs, apparently because of pressure from the Labour MPs **Ness Edwards** and **Goronwy Roberts**, who were concerned at the inadequacy of the annual **Welsh Day** debate. The committee was to include all MPs representing Welsh constituencies, as well as five others reflecting the political complexion of the Commons. Its brief was to consider all bills and other matters 'relating exclusively to Wales'. Denied any real power and with even less significance in the post-**devolution** era, it meets on average on only four days of each parliamentary session.

Folk-dancing teams at the National Botanic Garden of Wales, 2007

WELSH GROUP, The

The Welsh Group of artists was founded in 1948 as the South Wales Group, under the chairmanship of **Evan Charlton**, to promote contemporary art and to unite the foremost practitioners of the day. In 1956, conflict between conformist and radical viewpoints led to the establishment of the 56 Group (*see* **Fifty-Six Group**). In 1975, the South Wales Group officially became the Welsh Group. At the beginning of the 21st century, the Group's 40 members were still exhibiting, although their original pioneering importance had been overtaken by events.

WELSH GUARDS, The

Following the establishment of the Irish Guards in 1900, calls (supported by George V and Lord Kitchener) were made for Wales to have its own regiment of guards, and the Welsh Guards were raised in February 1915. Recruits needed Welsh parentage on at least one side, Welsh domiciles or Welsh **surnames**. Blooded at Loos in the **First World War**, the Guards fought on the Western Front until the Armistice. During the **Second World War**, three battalions fought in mainland Europe and North Africa, the 2nd and 3rd Battalions being disbanded thereafter. The 1st Battalion has since served in Palestine, Germany, Egypt, Cyprus, Aden, Northern **Ireland**, Kenya, Belize and the **Falklands**. The Welsh Guards' regimental headquarters is Wellington Barracks in **London**. In 2003, the 1st Battalion moved from Aldershot to take up residence in Wales for the first time – at RAF **St Athan**. Welsh guardsmen are identifiable from the fact that the buttons on their tunics are in groups of five.

WELSH HOSPITAL BOARD, The

Created under the National **Health** Service Act 1946, the Welsh Hospital Board was responsible until 1974 for planning the development of public hospitals and specialist medical care throughout Wales. Its first major undertaking entailed assigning the formerly uncoordinated local authority and 'voluntary' (charitable) hospitals to local groupings, which could provide a comprehensive range of both in-patient and out-patient services. These groups were to be run on a day-to-day basis by part-time hospital management committees served by full-time officials.

Severe financial stringency during the early years of the NHS prevented the replacement of inefficient and outdated hospitals, and the board had to fall back on a strategy of make do and mend. In 1959, however, it formulated a long-term plan for a countrywide network of large district general hospitals, of between 400 and 800 beds each, retaining a number of small units in rural areas in order to balance the advantages of centralizing advanced medical skills and technology against the time and expense of long journeys to hospital.

The board was able to spend increasingly large sums of public money – in 1972–3 its capital projects were assigned a total of £8.6 million, while current expenditure reached £78.6 million. By then, central **government** had decided on a major administrative reorganization of the NHS, and the board was dissolved.

WELSH IN EDUCATION AND LIFE

A report, published in 1927, which played a significant role in the campaign to secure official status for the **Welsh language**. In 1925, the Board of Education established a committee to investigate the place of Welsh in the schools of Wales. With individuals such as **W. J. Gruffydd** and **D. Lleufer Thomas** among the committee's members, the report inevitably exceeded its brief, describing and analysing the language's standing, not only in the world of **education** but also in the domains of **law** and **broadcasting**.

The picture was a damning one. The report argued that without radical and immediate measures to improve the situation, Welsh faced a benighted future. Among its recommendations were: the classification of schools and their language policies into three categories, according to their linguistic and cultural environment; the repeal of the 'language clause' of the **Acts of 'Union'**; and the provision of Welsh translations of a range of legal forms. Although the report received a negative response from some **government** departments and from many local authorities, it succeeded in paving the way for significant advances. Chief among those advances were the eventual establishment of officially designated Welsh-medium schools, although the report did not advocate the establishment of such schools, largely because of fears that they would lead to the marginalization of the language in other schools.

WELSH INTERMEDIATE EDUCATION ACT, The (1889)

The Act of 1889, one of the first pieces of legislation of modern times to apply specifically to Wales, has been described as the 'Welsh **education** charter'. It empowered **counties** and **county boroughs** to set up joint education committees to establish intermediate (secondary) schools. By 1905, a network of 95 schools had been created throughout Wales; they contained over 8000 pupils, with girls exceeding boys in number. Notwithstanding the intention that the schools should promote a modern curriculum, technical and commercial subjects were largely neglected. However, low fees and a generous provision of scholarships made the schools accessible to children of the lower-middle **class** and even to many of the working class, sectors hitherto deprived of secondary education. The schools were thus a major force in promoting social mobility. The act put Wales ahead of **England** in terms of state secondary education.

WELSH JOINT EDUCATION COMMITTEE (WJEC)

Set up in 1949 with representation from each local **education** authority, the committee took over many of the responsibilities of the **Central Welsh Board**. The largest of its numerous sections is the examination department, responsible for examinations taken by those living in Wales and beyond, including the Entry Level Certificate, GCSE and Advanced Level. The WJEC also prepares a wide range of teaching resources, in **Welsh** and **English**, and administers the **National Youth Orchestra of Wales** and the **National Youth Theatre of Wales**.

WELSH LANGUAGE, The

Throughout the centuries, the Welsh language has been a central factor in the concept of Wales as a nation. It is undoubtedly the strongest of the **Celtic** languages and ranks high among those indigenous European languages – about 20 in all – which are not the chief language of a sovereign state. The 2001 census can be considered as indicating that 575,640 of the inhabitants of Wales over the age of three – 20.52% of the **population** – were able to speak Welsh.

However, interpreting that census is no easy task. The figure 575,640 includes three levels of competence in Welsh: the ability to speak Welsh unaccompanied by other skills in the language (79,310); the ability to speak and read Welsh, but not to write the language (38,384); the ability to speak, read and write Welsh (457,946) – people referred to in other entries in this encyclopaedia as those fully fluent in the language. In addition, the census recorded that there were in Wales 138,416 people who could understand Welsh but were unable to speak it. (This figure may well include many less competent speakers of Welsh, for the official nature of the census has always discouraged less fluent Welsh speakers from recording their knowledge of the language.)

Furthermore, 83,661 respondents stated that they had other combinations of skills, although those were not fully defined. The sum of the various categories yields a figure of 797,661 – 28.43% of Wales's population over three years old. Although these figures should be approached with great caution, they do suggest that the percentage decline consistently apparent since the late 19th century, and the absolute decline apparent since 1911, had ceased and that statistically the language was experiencing something of a revival.

The highest percentages of Welsh speakers were recorded in **Gwynedd** (68.7%; 76.11% with some skills), **Anglesey** (59.8%; 70.4% with some skills), **Ceredigion** (51.8%; 61.24% with some skills) and **Carmarthenshire** (51.1%; 63.59% with some skills), **counties** which, between them, were home to 237,766 Welsh speakers. The lowest percentages were recorded in the south-eastern counties: **Monmouthshire** (9.0%; 12.9% with some skills), **Blaenau Gwent** (9.0%; 13.3 with some skills) and **Newport** (9.6%; 13.4% with some skills). Yet, despite the generally low percentages in the south-eastern industrial areas, the absolute number of Welsh speakers in those areas is considerable, for there are 195,926 of them in the one-time county of **Glamorgan** and the pre-1974 county of Monmouth. Indeed, **Cardiff** has twice as many Welsh-speakers as live within the boundaries of the **Snowdonia National Park** (31,944, compared with 15,332).

The development of the language

As a Celtic language, Welsh belongs to the Indo-European family of languages. **Place names** such as Lyon, Leiden, Laon and Nantlle (all of them commemorating the Celtic god Lug; **Lleu** in Welsh), and **river** names such as Danube, Rhône and Rhine are proof that Celtic languages were once spoken over a very wide area. However, in mainland Europe (apart from **Brittany**), Celtic languages failed to survive the **Roman** era. Thus, Lepontic (spoken in northern Italy), Celtiberian (spoken in Spain) and Galatian (spoken in Anatolia, now part of Turkey) had become extinct by the 5th century AD. That was also the fate of the Gaulish of Gaul, although Breton, a language mainly originating from the speech of British migrants to Brittany, is believed to contain some Gaulish elements.

That was not the fate of the Celtic languages of **Britain** and **Ireland**. Those languages belong to two groups: the Goedelic languages – Irish, Scottish Gaelic and Manx – and the Brythonic languages – Welsh, Cumbric, Cornish and Breton. The groups are also referred to as Q-Celtic and P-Celtic, for the labial sound *kw* (or *qu*) in Indo-European was delabialized into *c* in the Goedelic languages and labialized into *p* in the Brythonic languages, a development which gave rise to *mac* (son) and *ceathoir* (four) in Irish, and *map* (later *mab*) and *pedwar* in Welsh.

Table 1: Cognate Celtic Words

Welsh	Breton	Irish	Gaelic
Tŷ (house)	Ti	Teach	Tigh
Ci (dog)	Ki	Cu	Cu
Du (black)	Du	Dubh	Dubh

At the time of the Roman invasion, Brythonic was spoken throughout southern Britain and as far north as the Firths of Forth and Clyde. Under the impact of Rome, Brythonic borrowed words from **Latin**, with many – such as *liber* (book), which survives in Welsh as *llyfr* – relating to things foreign to the British before the coming of the Romans. **Kenneth H. Jackson** argued that Brythonic underwent much more drastic changes from the early 5th century onwards, and that these culminated during the 6th century in the language's transformation, during a period of social pressures caused by the **Anglo-Saxon** invasions. A central element of the transformation was the loss of final syllables and case endings, with names such as the Brythonic *Cunobelinos* becoming the Welsh *Cynfelyn*. However, recent scholarship rejects the notion of a sudden transformation, preferring instead to assert that the main changes might long have been apparent in the spoken language, having occurred gradually over several centuries.

The period up to the end of the 8th century is that of Early or Archaic Welsh. It is possible that Welsh was a written language by at least the early 7th century but, apart from the famous stone at **Tywyn** (7th/9th centuries), which bears the earliest surviving inscription of the language, the surviving evidence consists only of names in insular Latin manuscripts and on Latin inscribed stones (*see* **Monuments, Early Christian**). The earliest surviving examples of continuous texts in Welsh date from the era of Old Welsh (late 8th to mid-12th centuries). Among the most important examples are the Surrexit Memorandum in *The Book of St Chad*, the **Juvencus** Manuscript, the **Computus Fragment** and material in *Liber Landavensis* (The Book of Llandaff). By the era of Middle Welsh (12th/15th centuries), evidence is plentiful, with a large body of **literature** providing ample sources for the study of the language.

The 15th century onwards is the era of Modern Welsh and, with the publication of the Welsh translation of the **Bible** in 1588, there existed a template ensuring the unity of the literary language. Although there are considerable differences between spoken and literary Welsh, its continuous use as a literary language was an enormous advantage when Welsh came to embrace the **printing** press and when, in a later age, it regained a role in **education**, **law** and public administration. In this respect, the history of Welsh differs from that of some of Europe's other non-state languages. In the Basque Country, for example, it was necessary to create a standard form of literary Basque which could bridge the differences between the various dialects, a task which did not need to be undertaken in Wales. At the beginning of the 21st century, the vocabulary of the language remains overwhelmingly Celtic in origin.

The Latin element of the Brythonic period was supplemented during the Middle Ages, mostly by scholarly borrowings such as *berf* (verb) from *verbum*. A few borrowings from Old Irish, *brechdan* (slice of bread and butter) for example, also survive as living words, as do *gardd* (garden) and *iarll* (earl), which derive from Old Norse. In the Middle-Welsh period, several hundred words of **French** origin, such as *pali* (brocaded silk) and *swmer* (pack), appear in the language, although many may have passed through **English** into Welsh. English, of course, is the source of most borrowed words in Welsh. However, the creation of Welsh technical terms has been vigorously and successfully pursued in recent times.

The Lord's Prayer in modern Welsh:

> *Ein Tad yn y nefoedd,*
> *Sancteiddier dy enw;*
> *deled dy deyrnas;*
> *gwneler dy ewyllys,*
> *ar y ddaear fel yn y nef.*
> *Dyro inni heddiw ein bara beunyddiol;*
> *a maddau inni ein troseddau,*
> *fel yr ŷm ni wedi maddau i'r rhai a droseddodd yn*
> *   ein herbyn;*
> *a phaid â'n dwyn i brawf,*
> *ond gwared ni rhag yr Un drwg.*

Dialects

Without a **London** or a Paris to impose its dialect as the standard, the socio-politics of Wales has not been conducive to the creation of a standardized and prestigious form of spoken Welsh, nor is there a received pronunciation comparable with 'Received English'. Although a spoken literary form of Welsh gained universal currency in the **Nonconformist** chapels of the 19th century (sometimes called 'pulpit Welsh'), and this remains – albeit in a much more flexible and modernized form – an important feature of public oration, education and the more formal aspects of **broadcasting**, the spontaneous speech of all native Welsh speakers has always been, to a greater or lesser extent, in dialect, and a delight in dialect is evident from medieval times. In medieval poetry, there are references to Gwentian (the dialect of **Gwent** and Glamorgan) and to Venedotian (the dialect of Gwynedd). In 1188, **Giraldus Cambrensis** noted that 'it is observed that the British language is more delicate and richer in north Wales ... [but] many assert that the language of Ceredigion ... is the most refined'.

Traditionally, Wales has been broadly divided into 4 dialect areas, namely north-west (Venedotian), north-east and mid (Powysian), south-west (Demetian), and south-east (Gwentian). Alan R. Thomas's work on lexical geography has identified 6 major speech areas, which can be further divided into 16 minor speech areas. Yet the emphasis has largely centred upon the differences between the speech of the *Gog* (northerner), and that of the *Hwntw* (southerner) (*see* **Gogs and Hwntws**). Nevertheless, it is difficult to be precise about the location of the boundary between the speech of the *Gog* and that of the *Hwntw*. A major difference is the absence in the south of any distinction between the pronunciation of *i* and of *u*; thus words such as *hin* (weather) and *hun* (sleep) sound exactly the same. The change occurs in the region of the **Dyfi** valley, but in the case of another well-recognized difference – the words for 'out' (*mâs* in the south and *allan* in the north) – the southern and northern forms co-exist across much of Ceredigion. Similarly, a northerner who enjoys a *panad* or *paned o de* (cup of **tea**) would have to travel to the banks of the **Llwchwr** before being offered a *dishglid* or a *dishgled o de*.

The inscribed stone at Tywyn, Meirionnydd

The coming of broadcasting, and the increase in numbers of those who acquired Welsh as a second language, has led to a significant erosion of Welsh dialects, and the language may well be entering a period of dialect convergence. There is certainly no longer any substance to the once widely proposed notion that northern and southern dialects are mutually incomprehensible. If the whole of Wales were Welsh-speaking, by far the most widely spoken dialect would be the Gwentian dialect of Gwent and east and mid Glamorgan, the home of over half the country's inhabitants. However, the revival of Welsh in those areas has not been accompanied by the revitalization of that dialect, which can now be heard only on the lips of the elderly in places such as **Rhymney** and **Aberdare**. With up to 90% of their pupils coming from Anglicized backgrounds, and with teachers hailing from many parts of Wales, the Welsh-medium schools of such areas inevitably introduce their pupils to a much more standardized version of Welsh, although the accent of pupils in such schools still remains broadly southern.

The social history of the language

The emergence of Welsh coincided with a massive contraction in the area in which it was spoken. By the late 7th century, Anglo-Saxon conquest had reached the estuaries of the **Dee** and the **Severn**. From the 8th century onwards, the territory of the Welsh language was essentially the territory later known as Wales, although the extinction of Welsh in what would become **England** may well have been a protracted process. The closest relation of Welsh was Cumbric, the language of the **Old North**. Cumbric may well have been spoken in **Strathclyde** until the extinction of that kingdom in the early 11th century, and is still evident in place names such as Ecclefechan (Welsh: *Eglwysfechan*).

Throughout the Middle Ages, Welsh was the dominant spoken language in most of Wales. Regions such as eastern **Flintshire**, an area of Anglo-Saxon settlement located east of **Offa's Dyke**, were re-Cymricized in the 11th century, and the language was spoken in places that later became part of **Shropshire** and **Herefordshire**. In religious matters, Welsh had a secondary position to Latin, the official language of the Church, but in legal matters, Welsh reigned supreme, for although the oldest surviving texts of the Welsh laws are in Latin, their original language was unquestionably Welsh.

The **Norman** invasions complicated the situation. While French was the language of the Norman knights, English was that of the yeoman settlers who colonized areas such as the **Vale of Glamorgan** and the **Gower** peninsula. It also eventually became that of the **Flemings** who settled in **Rhos** and **Daugleddau** in western **Dyfed**. Further rural settlement occurred in the wake of the **Edwardian conquest**, and the conquest increased the number of **boroughs**, which had been alien strongholds from their beginnings. Nevertheless, the degree of Anglicization should not be exaggerated. Despite the conquest, Welsh remained a major language in legal matters, and an increasing body of religious literature proves that it had a significant role in the Church. Above all, the patronage of the princes, and later of the **gentry**, gave rise to one of the major literatures of medieval

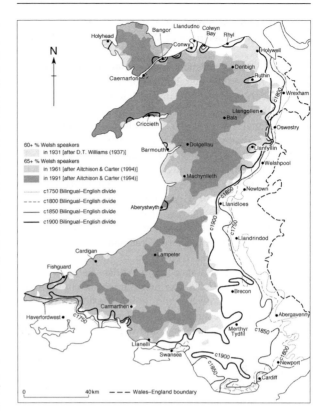

The Welsh language, c. 1750–1991

Europe. In the later Middle Ages, changing settlement patterns caused Welsh to return to previously Anglicized regions – in the Vale of Glamorgan particularly, but also in **border** lordships such as Oswestry and Whittington. Marriage with native Welsh gentry families caused the descendants of some of the *adventae* to become fully integrated into Welsh cultural life. Thus, while Roger de Puleston was hanged during the revolt of **Madog ap Llywelyn** (1294) because of his anti-Welsh arrogance, his 15th-century descendants were among the most prominent of the patrons of the bards and took pride in their kinship with **Owain Glyndŵr**. Similarly, the boroughs came to be settled by Welsh families from the surrounding countryside. By the 15th century, the majority of the inhabitants of **Aberystwyth** had Welsh **surnames**, and such names had also begun to appear in the records of long-Anglicized places such as **Tenby**.

Yet, if Welsh was being reinvigorated, so also was English. The replacement of Latin and French by English as the language of most legal documents in England coincided in Wales with the gradual abandonment of Welsh law and its replacement by English law. The drawing up of legal documents was becoming the work of professional scribes who, in Wales, naturally enough, used the same format and language as their fellows in England. Thus, decades before the **Act of 'Union'** outlawed Welsh from public affairs, English was well on the way to becoming Wales's official language. The Act placed the local administration of Wales in the hands of the Welsh gentry, who had to be fluent in English. That did not mean that gentry families were obliged to abandon Welsh, but that was what eventually happened – a process aided by education in

English public schools and universities, the appeal of London and the marriage of Welsh heiresses into English families.

Initially, the **Protestant Reformation** seemed likely to increase further the marginalization of Welsh. However, the publication of the Bible in Welsh in 1588 and the use of the Welsh Bible and the Welsh **Book of Common Prayer** in the great majority of Wales's churches meant that Welsh, shortly after being excluded from the official secular world, obtained a strong role in the official religious world. In subsequent centuries, through the growth of the unofficial religious world of Dissent and Nonconformity (*see* Nonconformists and Dissenters), it would find even greater succour – so much so, indeed, that many devotees of Welsh believe that it is axiomatic that its fortunes are closely intertwined with those of **religion**.

The initiator of the translation of the scriptures into Welsh was the **Renaissance** figure **William Salesbury**, who was eager to ensure that the new humanism should both enrich the Welsh language and find expression through it. The tradition he represented – the desire to ensure that it should be a learned language and that its richness should be explored and made known – became a tradition of great fecundity. It was fostered above all by the *hen bersoniaid llengar* (old literary parsons), the main upholders of the dignity of the language until the establishment of Wales's university colleges in the late 19th century.

Statistics concerning the prevalence of Welsh are, until the 1891 census, largely a matter of conjecture. Thomas Phillips estimated that in 1570 Wales had 325,000 inhabitants, around 250,000 of whom were Welsh-speaking – with the great majority, no doubt, having no knowledge of any other language. Over the following two centuries, there was a further strengthening of the language in the boroughs and in one-time Anglicized areas such as the Vale of Glamorgan, but that was accompanied by considerable erosion along the borderlands, particularly in **Radnorshire**, which had become largely English in speech by the late 18th century. Of particular importance was the work of **Griffith Jones** of **Llanddowror**, who, through his **circulating schools**, had ensured that, by the late 18th century, the majority of Welsh speakers possessed a degree of literacy in their language. It was a boon not enjoyed by any of the other non-state languages of Europe – or, for that matter, of hardly any of the continent's state languages.

The 1801 census revealed that Wales had 587,245 inhabitants of whom perhaps 470,000 spoke Welsh. In 1901, Wales had 1,864,696 inhabitants over the age of three, of whom 929,824 claimed to be able to speak Welsh. Thus, while the number speaking Welsh had almost doubled, the population as a whole had almost quadrupled. Those with a command of English increased from around 175,000 in 1801 to 1,583,791 in 1901 – a ninefold increase. Therefore, while the 19th century was a period of increase for Welsh in numerical terms (a marked contrast with Irish, the speakers of which more than halved during that century) it was a period of decline in proportional terms – from 80% to 50%. Furthermore, by 1901 English, a minority language in Wales in 1801, was the majority language: in 1901, 84% of Wales's inhabitants claimed that they had a

knowledge of English, although it may not have been a language which all of them used on a daily basis.

The 1870s was probably the decade when those with a knowledge of English first exceeded in number those with a knowledge of Welsh. The major factor causing language change was the industrialization of the **coal**fields of the south and the north-east. (The **slate**-quarrying areas of Gwynedd with their short-distance migration remained solidly Welsh-speaking.) Industrialization can be considered a positive factor in the history of Welsh, for without it the inhabitants of the over-populated countryside would have been obliged to leave Wales in order to secure a livelihood – the fate of millions of the Irish-speaking inhabitants of the west of Ireland. (There was also, however, considerable migration from Wales, causing Welsh-speaking communities to come into existence in places such as **Liverpool**, London, **Pennsylvania** and **Patagonia**.) The emergence of Welsh-speaking industrial areas, where incomes were higher than those of the countryside, was a major advantage for the language. The chief manifestations of 19th-century Welsh-language culture – the vigour of the Nonconformist chapels, the flourishing **periodical** press, **music**al activities such as choirs, and the success of the **eisteddfod** – would have been impossible had industrialization and urbanization not occurred.

However, the burgeoning industrial areas attracted English-speaking as well as Welsh-speaking immigrants. Initially, the former were assimilated by the latter, but, as the 19th century advanced, the number of English-speaking migrants came to exceed those who were Welsh-speaking. By 1901, the Rhymney **urban district** was the only part of Monmouthshire with a Welsh-speaking majority. Other factors hostile to the prospects of Welsh included: the assault on the language made by the authors of the Education Report of 1847 (*see* **Treason of the Blue Books**); the virtual exclusion of the language from the network of elementary schools created in the 1870s; the vast prestige of the British Empire and of its flagship language, English; and the notion that the embracing of English by Welsh-speakers represented no threat to their mother tongue, for that was securely anchored in the life of the chapel. As the celebrated minister Kilsby Jones (1813–89) put it, 'Be faithful to Welsh on Sunday … but when Monday morning comes, I advise you to learn English, for that is the language of trade and the language of the most adventurous people on earth.' The increasingly bitter struggles against employers created the need for social solidarity. Writing of the various peoples who were moving into the **Rhondda**, **Gwyn Thomas** (1913–91) declared, 'The Welsh language stood in the way of our fuller union, and we made ruthless haste to destroy it. We nearly did.'

The first half of the 20th century saw new threats to the Welsh language, among them the losses and dislocation caused by the **First** and **Second World War**s. Above all, there was the interwar **depression**, which resulted in Wales losing almost 400,000 people through emigration. There seemed little point in passing Welsh on to one's children if they were fated to move to Dagenham or Coventry – a consideration similar to that which, a century earlier, had caused multitudes of **Irish** to abandon their mother tongue. Those strongholds of the language, the Nonconformist chapels, became increasingly marginal. The **cinema** (*see* **Film**), a wholly English medium, became hugely popular, as did the English-language daily press and the largely English radio broadcasts of the BBC. It is hardly surprising, therefore, that by the 1930s there were many who confidently predicted the imminent demise of the Welsh language.

Yet the language showed remarkable resilience. **Urdd Gobaith Cymru**, founded in 1922, energetically sought to give Welsh a more appealing image among the young. Initially, **Plaid [Genedlaethol] Cymru**, founded in 1925, was primarily concerned to ensure that Welsh would be Wales's sovereign language. The government report *Welsh in Education and Life* (1927) argued in favour of enabling primary schools effectively to teach Welsh to all the country's children. Linguistic and literary scholarship increasingly made public the language's rich history. In the mid-1930s, Welsh secured a substantial share of the BBC's output in Wales. The **Welsh Courts Act (1942)** went some way to undo the restrictions enshrined in the language clause of the Act of 'Union'.

The decades following the Second World War saw even more dedicated efforts to foster the language. The establishment of the first specifically designated Welsh-medium local authority primary school (**Llanelli**, 1947) initiated the Welsh schools movement – a movement which would flourish mightily. The first Welsh-medium secondary school, Ysgol Glan Clwyd, was opened in **Flintshire** in 1956 and some rather tentative moves were made to provide Welsh-medium courses in the **University of Wales**. Far more dramatic was the growth of **Mudiad Ysgolion Meithrin** (the Welsh nursery school movement), whose work had by the early 21st century resulted in the establishment of schools and groups attended by over 15,000 children. In 1988, the National Curriculum enhanced the status of Welsh in all of the schools of Wales and a wide range of attractive teaching materials was produced, especially by the Resources Centre at **Aberystwyth**. Other initiatives included the foundation of the **Welsh Books Council** in 1961, the proliferation of *papurau bro* (Welsh-medium neighbourhood papers), the inauguration of the BBC Wales television channel (1964), the availability of grants to encourage the provision of Welsh-language **drama**, and the **Welsh Language Act 1967**. Perhaps more significant was the transformation of the popular culture of young people which began in the 1960s. The electric guitar was taken up with enthusiasm as Welsh-speaking Wales spawned a vigorous pop music scene, a development which coincided with the growing Welsh-language protest movement.

The first census to record the linguistic condition of Wales was that of 1891. (Such a census was first held in Ireland in 1851, in the Isle of **Man** in 1871 and in **Scotland** in 1881.) In holding it, the government's main motive was to discover to what extent Wales could be administered through the medium of English. Thus, the key question concerned English rather than Welsh. The unsatisfactory census of 1891 undoubtedly overstated the degree of Welsh

Students protesting in favour of Welsh-medium education at the University of Wales, Aberystwyth, early 21st century

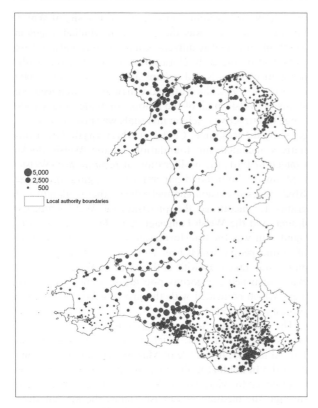

Numbers of Welsh speakers, 2001

monoglotism, but total reliance upon Welsh continued to be a marked phenomenon in much of Wales well into the 20th century. In 1921, when 6.3% of the inhabitants of Wales were monoglot Welsh, the figure was 31% in Anglesey and 22.1% in **Merioneth**. In the industrialized **parish** of **Llanddeiniolen**, 56% of the inhabitants had no knowledge of English and there was a parish in **Llŷn** (Bodferin, *see* **Aberdaron**) where everyone was monoglot Welsh. The 1960s was probably the decade which saw the passing of the last adult with no English at his – or more probably at her – command, although, inspired by **Saunders Lewis**, there continued to be patriots who declared themselves to be monoglot Welsh. The question concerning English was last asked in 1981. Thereafter, although monoglotism in young children continued, it was assumed – almost certainly correctly – that life-long monoglotism in Welsh was a thing of the past.

The decline in the number of Welsh speakers, apparent in successive censuses (*see* table right), was the context of Saunders Lewis's 1962 radio lecture *Tynged yr Iaith* (The fate of the language). The lecture resulted in the foundation of **Cymdeithas yr Iaith Gymraeg** (The Welsh Language Society), the members of which undertook a campaign of civil disobedience to secure official status for the language. Numerous court cases and periods of imprisonment followed, causing Welsh to become a major political issue. The society's campaigns led to significant victories, including the erection of bilingual **road** signs, a plethora of bilingual official forms, the **Welsh Language Act 1993**, the foundation of the **Welsh Language Board** and, above all, the establishment of the television channel *Sianel Pedwar Cymru* (**S4C**). Changed attitudes to the language became

particularly apparent at public meetings. Where once the presence of a single non-Welsh speaker would result in a meeting being held wholly in English, the availability of translation equipment means that discussions can be conducted bilingually. The system, pioneered by Gwynedd County Council, is particularly evident in the activities of the **National Assembly for Wales**.

Some of the fruits of these efforts became apparent in the findings of the 2001 census. They showed that in the period 1991–2001, there was an increase in the number of Welsh speakers in 14 of Wales's 22 counties. However, there was a sting in the tail. The counties showing increases had all long experienced significant Anglicization. No such increases were evident in the counties considered to be the language's heartland. In 1961, large tracts of the north-west and south-west, representing 36.8% of the surface area of Wales, consisted of parishes with proportions of Welsh speakers in excess of 80%. In 1974, Wales's civil parishes were replaced by **communities** (867 by 2001) of which only 9 had proportions of Welsh speakers in excess of 80% in 2001. They were **Llangefni** (Anglesey), **Bontnewydd, Caernarfon, Llanberis, Llanllyfni, Llanuwchllyn, Llanwnda, Llanycil** (all in Gwynedd) and **Ysbyty Ifan** (**Conwy**). (Professors Carter and Aitcheson, the leading commentators on Wales's linguistic condition, analyse the statistics in terms of wards, but as discussion of localities in this encyclopaedia is based on communities, that option would be inappropriate here.) Of Wales's communities, Caernarfon has the highest proportion of Welsh speakers (87.23%). That it is a town is significant, for Welsh, whose strongholds were once essentially rural, seems to be increasingly becoming an urban language.

In some of the language's heartlands – the Aman and Gwendraeth valleys, for example – percentage decline can

Table 2: Speakers of Welsh, 1901–2001

	Inhabitants of Wales over the age of 3	Welsh speakers	%
1901	1,864,696	929,824	49.9
1911	2,247,927	977,366	43.5
1921	2,486,740	922,092	37.1
1931	2,472,378	909,261	36.8
1951	2,472,429	714,686	28.9
1961	2,518,711	656,002	26.0
1971	2,602,955	542,425	20.9
1981	2,688,926	508,207	18.9
1991	2,723,623	508,098	18.6
2001	2,805,701	575,604	20.52

be attributed to linguistic slippage between the generations, but the chief cause in most of them is the influx of outsiders, mainly from England. Thus, in 2001, 41.1% of the population of Ceredigion had been born outside Wales and the equivalent figure for Anglesey was 32.5%. Although some incomers have learnt Welsh and have contributed to movements such as **CYD** (the Council of Learners of Welsh) and **Cymuned**, the great majority seem oblivious to the unique linguistic character of the country in which they have chosen to live.

Thus, despite the comfort that devotees of Welsh have derived from the findings of 2001 census, those findings raise important questions. With the decline in the language's heartlands still unchecked, can a language survive when the great majority of its speakers live in localities in which the language is increasingly that of a minority? In north-west Wales, the only area where consolidation is evident is Caernarfon and its environs, although it is well worth noting that in areas such as Anglesey, Ceredigion and **Meirionnydd**, which have all witnessed far-reaching population movements since the 1960s, there is still no discernible language shift among native Welsh speakers. The close proximity of Welsh speakers to each other in urban areas is also often overlooked; in parts of Cardiff, for example, there are over 350 Welsh speakers per sq km, a concentration which allows the creation of the social networks necessary for language maintenance.

Perhaps too much gloom has been expressed about the prospects for the Welsh language. Compared with a large number of other languages, it has considerable strengths. It can be prophesied with complete confidence that there are people still unborn who will have Welsh as their first language, an assertion that cannot be made in relation to over half the languages spoken at the beginning of the 21st century. Indeed, the language expert David Crystal has estimated that Welsh is among the top 15% of the world's languages in terms of its prospects. That is especially remarkable in view of the fact that, throughout its existence, it has been the closest neighbour of English, a language which has bulldozed into oblivion languages thousands of kilometres from the shores of England.

WELSH LANGUAGE ACT 1967, The

Based on the report (1965) of the committee appointed under Sir **David Hughes Parry** – 'to clarify the legal status of the **Welsh language** and to consider changes to the **law**' – the Act conferred the absolute right to speak Welsh in legal proceedings in Wales. It contained a statement that Welsh could be used with the same effect as **English** in public administration in Wales – the concept of equal validity. It empowered the making of a Welsh version of a statutory document, but in the case of discrepancy between the two texts, the English text would prevail. The Act enhanced the legal status of the Welsh language, but the implementation of the principle of equal validity was not mandatory on public bodies.

WELSH LANGUAGE ACT 1993, The

The guiding principle of the Act is that the **English** and **Welsh** languages should be treated on 'a basis of equality' in the conduct of public business and in the administration of justice in Wales. The principle of 'the basis of equality' replaced that of 'equal validity' given by the **Welsh Language Act 1967**. The Act, confined to the public sector, set up the statutory **Welsh Language Board**. It also broke new ground by establishing the concept of a scheme for the Welsh language to be prepared by every public body and to be approved by the Board. The language scheme sets out the services that a public body will provide through the medium of Welsh, in the light of what 'is both appropriate in the circumstances and reasonably practicable'.

The Act enables a person who has been directly affected to complain in writing to the board that a public body has failed to comply with its approved language scheme, and the board may at its discretion investigate such a complaint. The Act does not apply to a Crown Agent, but where such a body decides to adopt a language scheme it has to be approved by the Board. It authorizes subordinate legislation for the use of Welsh-language documents in legal proceedings. It repeals the provision that English be the language of record and the presumption that in the case of discrepancy between Welsh and English versions of a statutory document, the latter prevails.

The Act represents an important stage in ensuring that the Welsh language is in a position of equality in relation to English in Welsh public life. However, there are those who claim that it is not the end of the story, especially because Welsh has not been declared an official language of Wales – but, then, neither has English.

WELSH LANGUAGE BOARD, The

A statutory body, set up in 1993, to promote and facilitate the use of the **Welsh language** on the basis of equality with **English**. The relevant legislation is contained in the **Welsh Language Act 1993** and the **Government** of Wales Act 1998. It comprises a chairman and not more than 15 members, who are lay persons appointed by the **National Assembly** for three years. It is funded by the Assembly, has grant-making powers and publishes an annual statutory report.

The board is under a duty to require a public body to prepare for its approval a language scheme setting out the services it will provide through the medium of Welsh. By March 2006, it had approved 342 language schemes. The board may investigate a written complaint from a person claiming to be affected directly by the failure of a public body to comply with its language scheme. However, it has no power to enforce its recommendations upon a public body. Where there is a language scheme disagreement between it and a public body, the board may refer its recommendations to the Assembly, which may apply for a court order. In 2004, the Assembly Government announced that the board would be subsumed by the Assembly by April 2007. That subsumation did not occur and, in October 2007, it was announced that, for the time being, the existing arrangements would continue.

WELSH MAM, The

An archetypal image that originated in 19th-century industrial south Wales, the Welsh Mam was a hard-working and warm-hearted housewife whose husband and sons – and sometimes lodgers – proudly presented her with their weekly wages from their labour in the **coal**mines. She, in turn, devoted herself to their welfare, both physical and moral, and ran a household that was a model of thrift, cleanliness and godliness. This mythologized 'Mam' ruled the domestic scene and is often depicted as the real power in a matriarchal society. In reality, however, **women** were not given power but merely the responsibility and burden of maintaining a family on inadequate wages, and they suffered greatly from poverty and ill **health** exacerbated by constant childbearing.

WELSH NATIONAL OPERA, The

Founded in 1946 by amateur enthusiasts, notably Idloes Owen (1895–1954) of Merthyr Vale (**Merthyr Tydfil**), the WNO grew to be one of Europe's major opera companies (*see* **Music**). It became fully professional in the 1970s, further consolidating its international reputation with performances of the works of Janáček and of Michael Tippett's *Midsummer Marriage* (1976). The unique funding arrangement between the **Arts Council of Wales** and that of **England** has enabled the WNO to grow to full production strength, although the company has not been free from periodic financial problems. In 2004, the WNO moved into its first ever home theatre in the new £100 million Wales Millennium Centre in Cardiff. The company's artistic achievements in recent years have been recognised by a succession of prestigious international awards.

WELSH NOT(E)

A piece of wood or **slate** marked with 'W. N.' or 'Welsh Not(e)' and hung around the neck of a child caught talking **Welsh** during school hours. The child could transfer it to any other child heard speaking the language and, at the end of the day, the last pupil wearing it would be punished. It was already in use when the authors of the notorious **education** report of 1847 came to Wales (*see* **Treason of the Blue Books**). Other common names for it were the 'cwstom', the 'Welsh stick' and the 'Welsh lump' – a lump of **lead**, according to the traveller Richard Warner in the late 18th century. There is evidence that some teachers caned every pupil who was given the Not during the day.

Welsh patriots view the Welsh Not(e) as an instrument of cultural genocide, although it was welcomed by some parents as a way of ensuring that their children made daily use of **English**. It had parallels in other countries, such as **Ireland**, **Brittany** and Kenya. **Michael D. Jones** said that the educational system used it to destroy the language and make the Welsh 'more amenable to English aims' by reducing them to servility. According to **T. Gwynn Jones**, it taught children to be 'cowards and liars'. Of the many writers of the 19th and 20th centuries to have recorded their bitter experience of the Welsh Not, the best known is **O. M. Edwards**, who wrote in 1906 that 'that token was around my neck hundreds of times'; he called it 'a cursed method ... of destroying the basis of a child's character'. According to **Saunders Lewis**, however, Edwards's recollections are subject to a modicum of mythology, and some have argued that the Welsh Not was used less extensively than is popularly believed.

WELSH OFFICE, The

Although the **Conservatives** established an office known as the Welsh Office in **Cardiff** in 1963, the office's foundation as a department of state occurred in 1964, with the appointment of **James Griffiths** as the first **secretary of state for Wales**. Its offices were located in a massive building in **Cathays Park**; completed in 1979, the building conveys an impression of 'bureaucracy under siege'. The new institution progressively assumed powers devolved from a number of Whitehall departments: **housing**, local **government** and **roads** (1964); historic buildings and water (1968); **health** (1969); **education** (other than university level), industry, employment, **agriculture**, **fish**eries and assistance to urban areas (1970s). By 1992, when university education became its responsibility, the office was financed by an annual block grant of £6 billion. It had oversight of the activities in Wales of all government departments except the Home Office, the Foreign Office, the Lord Chancellor's Office, the Ministry of Defence and, crucially, the Treasury. In addition, the secretary of state had authority over the **Welsh Development Agency**, the **Development Board for Rural Wales** and the Welsh Land Authority.

Although the Welsh Office could seem remote from the needs and desires of the Welsh people, the institutional growth which followed its establishment added a new dimension to national consciousness. By the time of the

Friday 14th I feel at a loss to know the best method, to adopt in order to prevent the children generally, from speaking Welsh. Today, I have introduced a "Welsh Stick" into each of the Classes, and the child who has it last is to be kept in half an hour after School hours.

Welsh Not(e): how the 'Welsh stick' was used in the British School, Tywyn, 1863

devolution referendum of 1997, the anti-devolutionist argument that the establishment of a **National Assembly for Wales** would mean the creation of an additional layer of government had little substance, for that layer already existed. What was lacking was the means to allow the people of Wales to have any democratic control over it. On 1 July 1999, following the establishment of the National Assembly, most of the powers of the Welsh Office were transferred to the Welsh Assembly Government. The name Wales Office was given to the secretary of state's **London** office, located at Gwydyr House in Whitehall.

WELSH RABBIT Food

A dish still popular throughout Wales, consisting of **cheese**, melted with milk, butter or eggs, on toast. The name, often held to be a corruption of 'rarebit', was first recorded in 1725, and refers to the frugal diet of the Welsh. The poet John Skelton (c. 1460–1529) used the Welsh weakness for cheese to deride the influx of opportunist Welshmen to the **Tudor** court, recording a story in which St Peter, tired of all the Welsh clamouring for the best jobs in heaven, arranged for an angel to stand outside the celestial gates and shout 'caws pobi!' ('toasted cheese!') – whereupon the Welsh stampeded out of heaven, and the gates were slammed shut behind them.

WELSH RAREBIT Radio programme

This radio variety programme was the main **English**-language entertainment programme from the BBC in Wales during the **Second World War** and subsequent years. First transmitted on the Welsh Home Service in July 1938, it was transmitted during the war to the whole of the United Kingdom on the BBC unified Home Service; from 1948 until it came to an end in July 1951, it was heard on the BBC's network Light Programme. From 1941 onwards, it was produced by **Mai Jones**. During the war, it brought light-hearted entertainment to Welsh servicemen in France and elsewhere; there was an enthusiastic following for 'Dai's Letter to the Forces', read by Lyn Joshua. Other participants included Maudie Edwards, Albert and Les Ward, Stan Stennett, Ossie Morris, Gladys Morgan and **Harry Secombe**.

WELSH REVOLT, The (1294–5)

The revolt was led by descendants of the old Welsh royal houses. The leader in the north was **Madog ap Llywelyn**, son of the last lord of **Meirionnydd**, who assumed the title of **Prince of Wales**. In the south-west, it was led by **Maelgwn ap Rhys Fychan** of the house of **Deheubarth**, and in the south-east by Morgan ap Maredudd, a descendant of the rulers of **Caerleon**. It was provoked by the imposition of high taxes and by the heavy-handedness of Edward I's officials. It was eventually suppressed by a massive campaign led by the king in person; it ended on 5 March 1295 at the battle of **Maes Moydog** in **Caereinion**.

'WELSH REVOLT, The'

A protest against the **Conservative government**'s **Education** Act, 1902. Welsh (and English) **Nonconformists** objected to clauses enabling **Anglican** and **Roman Catholic** schools to be maintained by rates levied by the local education authorities, and insisted that no publicly funded school should be run on denominational lines. All but two education authorities refused full grants to denominational schools, although the extent of the defiance varied. Eventually, the government forced the local authorities to implement the act, but the dissension helped to consolidate support for the **Liberal Party** in the 1906 general election. His participation in the 'Revolt' did much to bring **David Lloyd George** to public attention.

WELSH ST DONATS (Llanddunwyd), Vale of Glamorgan (1207 ha; 485 inhabitants)

A **community** located in undulating land north-east of **Cowbridge**, the compact village contains the 18th-century Great House and a fine farm group. The late medieval church was modified in the 16th century. To the north lies Talyfan Castle, once the centre of one of the largest of the lordships of the **Vale of Glamorgan**.

WELSH SCHOOL OF ARCHITECTURE, The

Founded in 1920, the Welsh School of **Architecture** is based at **Cardiff University** and housed in the Bute Building, in **Cathays Park**. One of the largest architectural schools in **Britain**, its teaching is practically based and research led. It shares premises with the Design Research Unit and the Live Project Office (established in 1970 to undertake planning projects on a commercial basis), the offices of the **Royal Society of Architects in Wales**, the Centre for **Education** in the Built Environment, and a specialist architecture library available for use by the public. Since the **Second World War**, the school has had an important influence on architecture in Wales. Its first head was **Dewi-Prys Thomas**. In 2006, it had 470 students (350 undergraduates and 120 postgraduates).

WELSH SUNDAY, The

Special esteem for the Sunday in Wales emerged as a result of the increasing influence of **Nonconformists**, **Calvinistic Methodists** and evangelical **Anglicans** from the mid-18th century onwards. By 1815, games traditionally played on Sundays had been superseded by the **Sunday school**. The Calvinistic Methodist Confession of Faith (1823) emphasized that the Sabbath should be devoted to public worship, family prayers and the reading of works of piety. Sunday observance reached its peak in the third quarter of the 19th century. Thereafter, the rise of secularism, combined with social and demographic change, led to its decline. Nevertheless, that decline should not be predated; in **Cardiff**, it was not until the 1950s that the citizens voted in favour of opening **cinemas** on Sunday. Remnants of the Welsh Sunday survived in the rural areas until the 1960s, if not later; indeed, **Sunday closing** of public houses continued in **Dwyfor** until 1996.

WELSH TRUST, The

An educational enterprise of **Puritan** temper established in 1674 to evangelize among the Welsh. It was founded by the **London** clergyman Thomas Gouge, who had been deprived of his living because of his Puritan leanings. Along with his London patrons, Gouge desired to give Welsh children a knowledge of **English** so that they might read devotional

Powis Castle, Welshpool

literature. Between 1674 and 1681, the year of Gouge's death, about 3000 children attended the Trust's schools. **Stephen Hughes**, who resented the implication that salvation for the Welsh was attainable only if they learned English, persuaded the Trust to spend money on the publication of religious texts in **Welsh**; this gave a major stimulus to **printing and publishing** in Wales.

WELSH WOMEN'S HOSPITAL IN SERBIA, The
Following a visit by Dr Elsie Inglis to **women**'s suffrage groups in **Cardiff** and **Newport** in March 1915, to speak about her pioneering work in establishing the Scottish Women's Hospital in Serbia, the Welsh women's suffrage societies raised £4000 to fund a 100-bed Welsh Women's Hospital. A field hospital staffed by some 40 women doctors and nurses from Wales, the Welsh Women's Hospital (later renamed the Wales-**London** Hospital Unit) was based at Valjevo and was in operation until the end of the **First World War**.

WELSHPOOL (Y Trallwng), Montgomeryshire, Powys (3901 ha; 6269 inhabitants)
Located on the left bank of the **Severn**, the **community** is 11 km from north to south. 'Pool' derives from the Welsh *Trallwng* – a place that swallows water, dirty pool; 'Welsh' was added to differentiate the town from Poole, Dorset. Following the creation of **Montgomeryshire** in 1536, Welshpool became the *de facto*, if not the *de jure*, **county** town.

Welshpool's stronghold was Domen Castell, a still visible motte first mentioned in 1196, but it was under the shadow of Powis Castle that the town developed. The castle, which perhaps began as a stronghold of **Cadwgan ap Bleddyn** (d.1111), was rebuilt in stone by his descendant, Owain ap Gruffudd (Owen de la Pole; d.1309), lord of **Powys Wenwynwyn**. It remains essentially a medieval building, although the **Herbert** family, who purchased it in 1587, was responsible for many embellishments, including a magnificent long gallery (1590s) and a grand staircase (*c.*1668). In 1801, the Herbert inheritance passed by marriage to Edward, heir of Robert Clive – which explains Powis Castle's museum of Indian artefacts. The **gardens**, with their late 17th-century terraces, are world renowned and are, like the castle itself, in the care of the **National Trust**.

Welshpool received its charter *c.*1241 from **Gruffudd ap Gwenwynwyn**. On a hill in its centre stands St Mary's church. It has a 13th-century tower, but much of the original building was destroyed when **Owain Glyndŵr** overran the town in 1401. It was rebuilt in the late 15th century, enlarged in 1737, and restored in 1857 and 1871.

In the early 19th century, Welshpool was sixth in size among the towns of Wales. Shipping reached Pool Quay, 2 km to its north. The highest navigable point on the **Severn**, the quay lost its importance following the arrival of the Montgomeryshire **Canal** at Garthmyl, south of the town, in 1797. The town enjoyed considerable prosperity as a market town and as a centre of flannel making, malting and tanning (*see* **Woollen Industry**). The industries declined in the later 19th century, but Welshpool continued to flourish as an agricultural centre; until the foot-and-mouth epidemic of 2001, its livestock market was one of the largest in Europe. A fine stretch of the canal was restored in 1973. Adjoining it are the comprehensive Powysland Museum and the Canal Centre.

The site of the **Cistercian** monastery of Strata Marcella lies 4 km north of Welshpool. Founded by **Owain Cyfeiliog** in 1170, nothing of it is visible above ground. It was excavated in 1890 and found to have had a church 84 m long and a square central tower; the monastery was dissolved in 1536. **Tudur Aled** (d.*c.*1526) much appreciated the hospitality of its abbot, Dafydd ab Owain.

The important collection of bronze implements discovered in Crowther's Coppice is known as the **Guilsfield** Hoard. Trelydan Hall (originally 16th century) is an attractive half-timbered mansion. Cloddiau Cochion was the birthplace of the **Quaker** author and evangelist Richard Davies (1635–1708). Llanerchydol, a romantic, irregular pile (1776, 1820), perhaps occupies the site of the *llys* (court) of the **commote** of **Llannerch Hudol**. Montgomeryshire Mid Wales **Airport** is situated in the southern part of the community.

WENTLOOGE (Gwynllŵg), Newport
(1593 ha; 720 inhabitants)
Located across the Ebbw estuary immediately west of **Newport**, the **community** extends over the Wentlooge Levels (part of the **Gwent Levels**), and is crisscrossed by a network of reens or drainage channels. The name preserves that of the medieval *cantref* of **Gwynllŵg**, the region between the **Rhymney** and the **Usk**. Before the abolition of civil **parishes** in 1974, it consisted of the parishes of Peterstone Wentlooge and St Bride's Wentlooge. St Peter's church once belonged to St Augustine's Abbey, Bristol. With its noble west tower, finely proportioned arcades and attractive hammer-beam roof, it is the finest Perpendicular church in **Gwent**. The marshy land, barely above sea level, has caused St Bride's church to sink; its 15th-century tower is rakishly skewed. A tablet in the porch, 1.7 m above the ground, records the height of the great flood of 1606 (1607 by modern reckoning), which was probably a tsunami (*see* **Earthquakes**). West Usk **Lighthouse**, built in 1821 to guide ships approaching Newport, stands 2 km east of St Bride's. The lighthouse has been converted into an intriguing hotel.

WENVOE (Gwenfô), Vale of Glamorgan
(1863 ha; 2009 inhabitants)
Located west of **Cardiff** and south of the A48, the **community**'s chief attraction is Dyffryn **Gardens** (34 ha) landscaped between 1894 and 1909. Designed by Thomas H. Mawson for John **Cory**, they were acquired in 1937 by Cennydd Traherne who leased them to **Glamorgan County** Council in the hope that they would become the Welsh equivalent of Kew. In 1973, they were the setting for the garden party commemorating the demise of the **county** of Glamorgan. Dyffryn House (1893–4) – French Second

Dyffryn House and gardens, Wenvoe

Empire in style – was among the last massive country houses to be erected in Wales.

Wenvoe village has become an extensive commuter sprawl. Its church contains some interesting tombs. Wenvoe Castle, which includes a pavilion designed by Robert Adam, is now a **golf** course clubhouse. To its east is Wrinston Farm, once the site of a castle and a hamlet. At the community's north-west corner lies Whitton, an extensively excavated **Romano**-British farmstead site. St Bleiddian's church, St Lythans, has a west tower with a saddleback top. The nearby **Neolithic** chambered tomb lies within a 27-m long mound. The north-eastern part of the community is dominated by the developments around Culverhouse Cross, among them the headquarters of ITV Wales (*see* **Broadcasting**).

WESLEYANS

Members of the Church that emerged from the doctrine and organization developed by John Wesley (1703–91). The emphasis from the beginning was on justification by faith alone, and on the quest for holiness. Compared with that wing of the **Methodist Revival** which embraced **Calvinism**, Wesleyanism made few inroads into Wales during the 18th century. Although not dismissive of the **Welsh language**, John Wesley regarded it as a barrier to mission and, as a result, the sphere of his influence was restricted to **English**-speaking regions – south **Pembrokeshire**, east **Breconshire** and the environs of **Cardiff**. Concern among Wesleyans that they had achieved so little in Wales led to a resolution at their conference in **London** on 8 August 1800, moved by Thomas Coke (1747–1814) of **Brecon**, to establish a mission to the Welsh. That date is generally regarded as the day on which Welsh Wesleyanism came into existence, although Edward Jones (1778–1837) of Bathafarn (**Llanbedr Dyffryn Clwyd**) had already founded a Wesleyan **society** at **Ruthin**, a key development in ensuring that the north-east would be the heartland of Welsh Wesleyanism.

The Wesleyans had to compete with the **Calvinistic Methodists**, the **Baptists** and the **Congregationalists** – Calvinists deeply suspicious of their **Arminianism**. Although the Wesleyans remained the smallest of the mainstream **Nonconformist** denominations, their growth was remarkable, with 100 congregations in existence by 1810. By 1858, they had 11,839 members and 293 chapels. By 1905, membership had increased to 20,684; it peaked at 24,784 in 1925. Thereafter, the denomination went into decline. By 1976, membership had fallen below 10,000 and was continuing to fall at the beginning of the 21st century. The denomination's Welsh journal, *Yr Eurgrawn*, was published from 1809 to 1983.

WEST GLAMORGAN (Gorllewin Morgannwg)
One-time county

The **county** was established in 1974 following the abolition of the county of **Glamorgan**. It consisted of what had been the **county borough** of **Swansea**, the **boroughs** of **Neath** and **Port Talbot**, the **urban districts** of **Glyncorrwg** and **Llwchwr**, and the **rural districts** of **Gower**, **Neath** and **Pontardawe**. It was divided into the districts of **Lliw Valley**, Neath, Port Talbot and Swansea. Abolished in 1996, it was replaced by the county boroughs of **Neath Port Talbot** and Swansea.

WEST INDIANS

West Indians began to settle in Wales from the mid-19th century, arriving mainly as sailors. The community expanded as the result of shortages of seamen in the **First World War**. The largest group was in Butetown (**Cardiff**) where there were about 300 men in the 1920s, many of whom were married to local **women** and had families. The bulk came from Barbados and Trinidad but there was a spread of representation across the islands, including Jamaica, Montserrat and St Lucia.

They were notable for supplying much of the political leadership of the Cardiff black community between the wars, and after. Some were associated with the **Communist Party** and with Pan-African movements. Harry O'Connell and Alan Sheppard both came from British Guiana, while Jim Nurse was from Barbados. They were associated with a range of campaigning groups such as the Coloured Seamen's Union and the Colonial Defence Association. Sheppard was a friend and antagonist of the leading Communist and Pan-Africanist George Padmore. Some West Indians began to settle in Cardiff after the **Second World War**, but apparently there were antagonisms with the established group, and south Wales was not developing fast enough to attract many new immigrants. The community has not been renewed by newcomers and has tended to blend into the ethnic mix of inner-city Cardiff.

WHAITE, [Henry] Clarence (1828–1912) Painter

During his first tour in the 1840s, the English-born Clarence Whaite was captivated by the landscape and people of north Wales; he stayed regularly at **Betws-y-Coed**, becoming prominent in its burgeoning artistic culture. In 1870, he married a local woman, settling near **Conwy**. Their daughter, Lily F[lorence] Whaite (1876–1959), is a much under-rated artist, who exhibited with the **Gwynedd** Ladies' Arts Society and in **England**.

Whaite's wonderfully vibrant watercolours capture the rapidly changing weather as well as incidents from peasant life. Religious faith led him to attach moral significance to landscape, his **paintings** sometimes evoking an anxious religious wonder. His method of oil painting, with spots of pure colour – a consequence of his interest in colour theory – may have pre-empted the pointillist strand of Impressionism that developed elsewhere in Europe.

WHALES, DOLPHINS and PORPOISES

Of all the cetaceans, whales frequent Welsh waters the least, although such visits do occur. Since 1973, there have been sightings at sea or strandings of pilot, bottlenose, minke, killer and fin whales. Where strandings of cetaceans occur, the corpses often attract considerable public and media interest. Dolphins and porpoises are a more familiar presence, particularly in Cardigan Bay. The most frequently sighted are the harbour porpoise and the bottlenose dolphin, the conservation of which has been recognized to be of international importance. The bay also offers suitable habitats for the common dolphin and Risso's dolphin, with its distinctive sabre-like dorsal fin and grey body; the white-sided dolphin may be seen in midsummer. In 2005, an unprecedented 2000 common dolphins were seen, in a single school, off the **Pembrokeshire** coast. Porpoises are traditionally considered to be harbingers of fine weather in the coastal communities of Cardigan Bay where they are known as *pysgod duon* (black **fish**).

There has never been an indigenous Welsh whaling fleet, although Welsh seaman have been recruited to the crews of English whaling **ships**. The town of **Milford Haven** was founded in the 1790s by whalers from Nantucket, Massachusetts.

WHEELER, Mortimer [Robert Eric] (1890–1976)
Archaeologist
Brought up in **Scotland** and **England**, Mortimer Wheeler was one of the most influential archaeologists of the 20th century. He made a major contribution to establishing **archaeology** as an academic discipline in Wales. As keeper of archaeology (1920–4) at the **National Museum** and later as director of the museum (1924–6), he oversaw the extension, interpretation and exhibition of its collections. His excavations at Segontium (**Caernarfon**) and at **Caerleon** set a standard for innovation and meticulous recording. Between 1921 and 1924, he lectured in archaeology at **Cardiff** – the first lectureship of its kind in the **University of Wales**. His *Prehistoric and Roman Wales* (1925) is the first comprehensive synthesis of the subject, and his autobiography, *Still Digging* (1955), recalls his connection with Wales.

WHEELER, Olive [Annie] (1886–1963)
Psychologist and academic
Born in **Brecon** and educated at **Aberystwyth**, **London** and Paris, Olive Wheeler was professor of **women's education** at **Cardiff** (1925–32) and subsequently professor of the education department as a whole (1932–51). She was the first female head of department in the **University of Wales**. A fellow of the British Psychological Society, she was created DBE in 1950 for educational and social work with such institutions as the University of Wales, the **Workers' Educational Association** and the **Welsh Joint Education Committee**. Her numerous publications include *Youth: the Psychology of Adolescence* (1929), which relates psychology to public policy. In 1923, she stood as **Labour** candidate for the University of Wales constituency, one of the first women to contest a parliamentary election in Wales. (The first was Mrs H. M. Mackenzie, Labour candidate for the same seat in 1918.)

WHELDON, Huw [Pyrs] (1916–86) Broadcaster
Born in **Bangor**, Huw Weldon was a grandson of Thomas Jones Wheldon (1814–1916), a powerful **Calvinistic Methodist** minister devoted to **education**; his father was Sir Wynn Powell Wheldon (1879–1961), permanent secretary to the **Welsh Department of the Board of Education** (1923–45). The first organizer of the Arts Council in Wales (1946–52; *see* **Arts Council of Wales**), Huw Weldon joined the BBC in 1952, and from 1958 to 1964 he planned and presented *Monitor*, the first television series on the arts. The years 1969 to 1976, when he was managing director of the BBC, were a golden era, featuring programmes such as Kenneth Clark's *Civilization* and Alistair Cooke's *America*. In 1976, this tall, striking man was awarded a

Huw Wheldon

knighthood – becoming 'Sir Huge', according to his biographer, Paul Ferris.

WHIG PARTY, The
One of the two major parliamentary and political parties in Wales and **England** from the late 17th until the mid-19th century. The name comes from a Scots word applied to Scottish **Presbyterians** who were in conflict with the crown. The party had its origins in the exclusionists – those who sought to exclude James, duke of York (later James II), from the royal succession on the grounds that he was a **Roman Catholic**. The accession of William III and Mary II in 1688 initiated a long period of rule by the Whig Party, although, by the later 18th century, the ideological distinctions between that party and the **Tory Party** were slight. Supported by only a small minority of the Welsh landlord **class**, the party sympathized with the claims of Protestant Dissenters (*see* **Nonconformists**). By the 1830s, the name 'Whig' had largely been superseded by the name '**Liberal**', although, until the 1880s, the aristocratic elements within the Liberal Party were frequently referred to as Whigs.

WHISKY
Unlike **Ireland** and **Scotland**, Wales has no long tradition of distilling. Commercial development was inhibited by the **temperance movement**'s aversion to strong liquor. But that did not prevent the odd venture springing up. In 1887, R. J. Lloyd Price (*see* **Price family (Rhiwlas)**) established a distillery at Frongoch (**Llandderfel**) at a cost of £100,000. However, its Royal Welsh Whisky did not prove a success and the Welsh Whisky Distillery Company went bankrupt

in 1910. (In 1916, its buildings became the **Frongoch Internment Camp**.) In the 1970s, a venture in **Brecon** started producing 'Welsh' whisky, but its output was blended spirit from Scotland infused with local herbs. In 2000, a distillery was built at Penderyn (**Hirwaun**) by a new Welsh Whisky Company; the single malt whisky, Penderyn, which the company introduced on 1 March 2004, received warm approbation from whisky lovers.

WHITE, Eirene (1909–99) Politician
Eirene White, **Labour** MP for **Flintshire** East (1950–70), was the first **woman** to be a Foreign Office minister (1964–70). She inherited from her father, Dr **Thomas Jones** (1870–1955), a mandarin style and an interest in Welsh matters, especially **Coleg Harlech**. Enobled as Baroness White in 1970, she served as deputy speaker of the House of Lords.

WHITE, Lynette (1968–88) Murder victim
Of the five **Cardiff** men wrongly accused of the murder of the Butetown prostitute Lynette White on Valentine's Day 1988, three were found guilty after a 117-day trial, the longest until then in British history. 'The Cardiff Three' – Tony Parris, Yusef Abdullahi and Stephen Miller – spent four years in **prison** until their convictions were quashed on appeal in 1992. It was not until 2002 that DNA profiling led detectives to the killer, Jeffrey Gafoor (b.1966), who was sentenced to life imprisonment in 2003. It was the first time in British criminal history that a murder conviction was overturned and someone else later convicted.

WHITE BOOK OF RHYDDERCH, The
A mid-14th-century manuscript containing an important collection of medieval **Welsh** prose, including the tales of *The Mabinogion* and many religious works. It is thought that it was compiled *c.*1350 for Rhydderch ap Ieuan Llwyd, a gentleman of Parcrhydderch, **Llangeitho**, by a team of five scribes associated with Strata Florida Abbey (**Ystrad Fflur**). Bound in two volumes with covers of white **leather**, it forms part of the **National Library**'s Peniarth Collection (*see* **Llanegryn**).

WHITFORD (Chwitffordd), Flintshire
(2142 ha; 2247 inhabitants)
Located immediately north-west of **Holywell**, the **community** is rich in archaeological features, including Maen Achwyfan, a monolithic slab cross of *c.*1000 bearing Scandinavian and **Celtic** motifs (*see* **Monuments, Early Christian**). The community contains numerous houses dating from the 15th to 18th centuries, among them Plas Ucha (1603), the temporary home of the **Mostyn family** following the **Civil Wars**. Garreg Tower (early 17th century) was part of a chain of beacons built to warn of pirate raids (*see* **Piracy**). The landscape is heavily pocked with remnants of 18th- and 19th-century **lead** mines.

Downing Hall, burned in 1922 and demolished in 1953, was the home of **Thomas Pennant** (1726–98). His *History of the Parishes of Whiteford and Holywell* (1796) was a pioneering study of local history. His great-granddaughter married Lord Fielding, later the earl of **Denbigh**. In 1849, the couple commissioned T. H. Wyatt to build an **Anglican**

church at Pantasaph. Following their conversion in 1850, they transferred the building to the **Roman Catholic** Church. Uproar followed. An appeal throughout Wales and **England** produced sufficient funds to build Establishment churches at Gorsedd (Whitford) and **Brynford**. The Pantasaph church was completed by A. W. Pugin, who introduced several quirky features. A Franciscan **friar**y, completed in 1865, adjoins the church. Nearby is a range of buildings occupied from 1861 to 1977 by St Clare's convent.

WHITFORD, Arthur (1908–96) Gymnast
Arthur Whitford, of the **Swansea** YMCA gymnastic club, won 17 major titles between the late 1920s and early 1950s, and was the leading British men's gymnast of the period. His distinguished career included Olympic and World Championship gold medals, and his appointment as Welsh national and British Olympic coach.

WHITLAND (Hendy-gwyn), Carmarthenshire
(629 ha; 1643 inhabitants)
Straddling the **Taf** on the **Carmarthenshire–Pembrokeshire** border, the **community** contains the small town of Whitland on the north side of the **river** and the suburb of Trevaughan on the south. Whitland is traditionally considered to be the place to which **Hywel Dda**, *c.*940s, summoned representatives from all parts of Wales to codify Welsh **law**. The Hywel Dda centre, with its splendidly evocative **garden** designed by artist Peter Lord (b.1948), commemorates the tradition. The United Dairies Creamery, one of the largest in Europe, dealt in the 1960s with the milk produced by 2700 farms. The closure of the creamery in 1994 caused high local unemployment; its buildings were demolished in 2003. (For the **Cistercian** monastery of Whitland, *see* **Llanboidy**.)

WHITTON (Llanddewi-yn-Hwytyn), Radnorshire, Powys (3321 ha; 310 inhabitants)
Located immediately west of **Presteigne**, the **community** contains the settlements of Whitton, Discoed, Cascob and Pilleth, the last of which is one of the few places in Wales mentioned in Domesday Book. **Owain Glyndŵr**'s forces won a notable victory there in 1402. Heaps of bones discovered in 1870 near the beautifully sited church are believed to be the remains of those who fell in the battle. Cascob is on the edge of **Radnor Forest**; its **parish**ioners 'had free common of pasture there tyme out of minde in the said forrest' (W. H. Rouse, quoting a 16th-century charter in *Radnorshire*, 1949). William Jenkins Rees (1772–1855), the scholar and antiquary and one of the *hen bersoniaid llengar* (old literary clerics), was vicar of Cascob from 1805 to 1855. Goodhart-Rendel called the restored church at Discoed 'a poem in its way'.

WICK (Y Wig), Vale of Glamorgan
(683 ha; 694 inhabitants)
A windswept **community** in the western part of the **Vale of Glamorgan**, its originally Romanesque church was rebuilt in 1871. The 16th-century farmhouse of Lower Monkton has a large barn of *c.*1800. Broughton Maltings, now flats, was built as a kiln for turning barley into malt.

WILD BOAR

Wild boar, present in Wales in some interglacial periods, have been recorded archaeologically up to **Roman** times, when an increase in free-ranging domestic **pigs** may have put considerable pressure on the wild population. Sacred to the **Celts**, the wild boar's significance in medieval Wales, and the thrill and danger of the boar hunt, are echoed in 'Culhwch ac Olwen', *The Mabinogion* story of **Arthur**'s pursuit of the **Twrch Trwyth**, a king transformed into a mighty boar. A number of Wales's **river** names contain the elements *twrch*, *banw* and *gwythwch* (or similar). However, such names may refer figuratively to the water's flow rather than to any mythical connections.

According to the Welsh **laws**, a wild pig had the same value as a domesticated one, and its high productivity and varied diet predisposed it to domestication. The wild boar did not become extinct in **Britain** until the end of 16th century, but as a result of interbreeding with domesticated pigs there were probably no genuinely wild animals present in Wales after the end of the 13th century.

WILDE, Jimmy (1892–1969) Boxer

Flyweight champion of the world from 1916 to 1923, Jimmy Wilde was brought up in Tylorstown (**Rhondda**). By the time he turned professional in 1911, he was already a veteran of hundreds of unrecorded fights against bigger and heavier opponents in the fairground booths of the south Wales **coal**field. His various nicknames – 'the Tylorstown Terror', 'the Mighty Atom' and 'the Ghost with a Hammer in his Hands' – indicate that despite being only 1.57-m tall and weighing less than 112 kg, his spindly frame concealed enormous power. Through necessity an unorthodox fighter, he would bob around until he saw an opportunity to unleash the sudden and devastating fusillade of perfectly timed punches by which he scored 75 knockouts and suffered only 4 defeats in 145 recorded professional fights.

Already British and European flyweight champion, his 11th-round knockout of Young Zulu Kid brought him the world title in December 1916. He made his fourth and final defence of it in New York in June 1923 against the much younger Pancho Villa. In losing, he received £13,000, the largest purse of his career, which he then wasted on harebrained schemes for **London** musicals and Welsh **cinemas**, causing him to die in poverty.

WILIAM CYNWAL (fl. 1561–87) Poet

Born at **Ysbyty Ifan**, Wiliam was taught by the poet **Gruffudd Hiraethog**. A graduate of the 1567 **eisteddfod** at **Caerwys**, he later won the degree of *pencerdd* (chief poet). Some 230 of his *cywyddau* and *awdlau* are extant, mostly addressed to **gentry** patrons in the north. He was famous for his seven-year bardic dispute with **Edmwnd Prys**: conservative in outlook, he criticized Prys for his lack of bardic qualifications and for writing satire.

WILIAM LLŶN (1534/5–80) Poet

A native of **Llŷn** and a brother of the poet Huw Llŷn, he spent the last 16 years of his life at Oswestry, **Shropshire**. A graduate of the 1567 **eisteddfod** at **Caerwys**, he addressed numerous poems to patrons throughout Wales. He was a master craftsman, adept at composing polished epigrammatic couplets. He excelled in his elegies, which often display an acute awareness of life's transience. His elegies to his bardic teacher, **Gruffudd Hiraethog**, and to the priest-poet Owain ap Gwilym, both ingeniously utilizing the conventions of the serenade, are justly admired.

WILIEMS, Thomas (1545/6–1622)
Lexicographer and antiquary

A native of **Trefriw**, Thomas Wiliems was educated at **Oxford** and practised as a doctor; he probably took holy orders, but was an uneasy Protestant and reverted to **Roman Catholicism**. His chief interest was in the **Welsh language** and its **literature**, together with the antiquities of Wales, and he assiduously sought and copied earlier manuscripts. The main memorial to his scholarship is a **Latin**–Welsh **dictionary**, *Thesaurus Linguae Latinae et Cambrobritannicae*, a masterpiece completed in 1608. The work remains in manuscript, but an abbreviated version is contained in the *Dictionarium Duplex* (1632) of **John Davies** (*c.*1567–1644).

WILKINS, Charles (1813–1913) Historian

Gloucestershire-born Charles Wilkins spent most of his life in **Merthyr Tydfil**, as a librarian and postmaster, and came to identify strongly with the indigenous culture. He published widely in the local press and wrote pioneering works on the **coal** trade (1888) and the **iron** industry (1903) of Wales. His history of Merthyr (1867) remains the only attempt to present a comprehensive history of the town. He edited the *Red Dragon* (1882–5), an innovative **English-language periodical** aimed at stimulating the interest of non-**Welsh**-speakers in Welsh affairs.

WILKINSON, John (1728–1808) Ironmaster

Wilkinson came from a Cumbrian family of **iron**workers. He found employment in the English Midlands, where he used coke to fire the furnaces he acquired. His father,

John Wilkinson after Lemuel Francis Abbott (*c.*1795)

Isaac, bought the lease of the **Bersham Ironworks (Coedpoeth)** in 1753, and John managed the enterprise, specializing in the manufacture of cannon and cylinders for steam engines, and making a previously marginal ironworks successful. He was accused of selling cannon to the French during the **French Revolutionary and Napoleonic Wars** (though this was not proved), and was denounced by local **Tories** for his **radical** political views. An enthusiastic advocate of the use of iron for all conceivable purposes, he even had an iron coffin manufactured for himself – but his girth at death prevented its use. His fortune was subsequently squandered in litigation between his mistress, her children and his nephew.

WILLIAM AP THOMAS (d.1446) Patriarch

Originally a member of a minor **gentry** family in **Gwent**, William ap Thomas enriched himself to such an extent that among his descendants were the first and second lineages of the **Herbert earls of Pembroke**, the **Herbert earls of Powis**, the Herbert earls of Caernarvon, the dukes of Beaufort (*see* **Somerset family**) and the marquesses of Bute (*see* **Stuart family**). He fought at the battle of Agincourt (1415; *see* **Hundred Years War**), and after being knighted by Henry VI in 1426 was known as 'Y Marchog Glas o Went' (The Blue Knight of Gwent). His first wife, Elizabeth Bloet (d.1420), was heiress of the **manor** of **Raglan**. Following her death, he bought the manor, where he commissioned the castle's Great Tower. His second wife was Gwladys, the daughter of **Dafydd Gam** and widow of Rhosier Fychan (*see* **Vaughan family (Tretower)**). In his elegy to her, **Lewys Glyn Cothi** hailed her as as 'Y Seren o Efenni' (the Star of **Abergavenny**). Their eldest son was William, first Herbert earl of Pembroke. The tomb of William and Gwladys at St Mary's church, Abergavenny, is one of the finest monuments in that magnificent necropolis. Its location in the centre of what had been the burial chapel of the **Hastings family** is symbolic of the replacement of **march**er-lords by Welsh **gentry**.

WILLIAM, Thomas (Thomas William, Bethesda'r Fro; 1761–1844) Hymnwriter

The composer of some of the best-known **hymns** in **Welsh** – among them 'O'th flaen, O Dduw, 'rwy'n dyfod' and 'Adenydd fel c'lomen pe cawn' – William was born in **Pendoylan**. He left the **Calvinistic Methodists** following the expulsion of **Peter Williams** in 1791 and became minister of the Bethesda'r Fro **Congregationalist** chapel (**Llantwit Major**) in 1814. He lived to experience the retreat of **Revival** enthusiasm, which gives much of his writing a unique, regretful tone.

WILLIAMS, Alice (Alice Meirion; 1863–1957) Writer and organizer

The daughter of David Williams (1799–1869), **Liberal** MP for **Merioneth** (1868–9), of Castell Deudraeth (**Penrhyndeudraeth**), she was kept at home to care for her mother, only escaping at the age of 40 to study art in Paris. In 1917, she was honoured with membership of the **Gorsedd** for her play *Britannia*. One of the chief architects of the **Women's Institute**, she started the movement's magazine, *Home and Country*, which she edited from 1919 onwards. She was also a founder of the Forum, a **women**'s club in **London**, where she ran its lively Welsh section.

WILLIAMS, Alice Matilda Langland (Alis Mallt Williams; Y Dau Wynne; 1867–1950) Novelist

Born in Oystermouth, **Swansea**, to the Williams family of Aberclydach (**Talybont-on-Usk**), Alis Mallt Williams and her sister Gwenffreda (*c.*1860–1914), inspired by Lady Llanover (**Augusta Hall**), together published two patriotic novels, *One of the Royal Celts* (1889) and *A Maid of Cymru* (1901), under the pseudonym Y Dau Wynne. A pioneer feminist, Alis Mallt was also a fervent supporter of the nationalist and cultural movements of her day, including **Cymru Fydd**, **Plaid [Genedlaethol] Cymru** and **Urdd Gobaith Cymru**. It was she who coined the term 'bombing school' to describe the RAF station at **Penyberth**. Her brother, William Retlaw Williams (1863–1944), wrote the still indispensable *Parliamentary History of the Principality of Wales 1541–1895* (1895).

WILLIAMS, Beryl (1937–2004) Actress

Flame-haired, enigmatic Beryl Williams, described as the most distinguished of Welsh actresses in the second half of the 20th century, was a native of **Dolgellau** and studied at Rose Bruford College, **London**. One of the first three actors to join the newly formed Cwmni Theatr Cymru in 1968 (*see* **Drama**), she gave many fine performances with the company over the years. She also excelled on television, especially as the housewife Gwen Elis in the **S4C** series *Minafon*, the long-suffering mother in Meic Povey's play *Sul y Blodau* (1995) and the central character in Povey's *Nel* (1991).

WILLIAMS, Charles (1915–90)
Actor and entertainer

The gifted character actor Charles Williams was born in **Boddfordd** and worked in his youth as an **agricultural labourer**. He was discovered by **Sam Jones** at BBC **Bangor** and he made his mark, initially, as compere of the radio programme *Noson Lawen*. He later played Harri Parri in the television serial *Pobol y Cwm*, appeared opposite Flora Robson in **Rhydderch Jones**'s *Mr Lollipop MA* (1970 in **Welsh**; 1978 in **English**) and was Haydn Evans in *The Archers*, on BBC Radio 4.

WILLIAMS, Christopher [David] (1873–1934)
Painter

Williams's belief that 'the highest form of art is that which portrays the deep problems and aspirations of human life' was certainly tested in his **painting**, but his efforts were stranded between high Victorian sentiment and illustrative **romanticism**, and outpaced by rapid changes in the artistic taste of his times. He completed a number of commissions, notably the painting *The Charge of the Welsh Division at Mametz Wood* during the **First World War**.

Born in **Maesteg**, Williams was deeply committed to Welsh causes and resorted to Welsh literary sources for subject matter, but he was obliged to make his living in **London**. Primarily a portraitist, he claimed a particular visual sensibility for the Welsh artist. His painting *The Awakening of Wales*, adorns the **Gwynedd County** Council offices in **Caernarfon**.

WILLIAMS, D[avid] J[ohn] (1885–1970)
Writer and patriot

D. J. Williams, whose 'square mile' consisted of **Llansawel** and Rhydcymerau (**Llanybydder**) in **Carmarthenshire**, wrote the story of the first quarter century of his own life in the two volumes *Hen Dŷ Ffarm* (1953; translated by **Waldo Williams** as *The Old Farmhouse*, 1961) and *Yn Chwech ar Hugain Oed* (1959). After working on the land and as a **coal**miner in various parts of the south, he gained degrees from the **University of Wales** and from **Oxford**, and spent most of his life as a teacher of **English** at **Fishguard**. He was one of the earliest members of **Plaid [Genedlaethol] Cymru**, and, following his participation in the burning of the **Penyberth Bombing School** in 1936, he was imprisoned for nine months in Wormwood Scrubs. One of the author's most good-humoured volumes is his *Hen Wynebau* (1934), a portrait gallery of some of the characters and animals of his native district. His other works include *Storïau'r Tir* (1936, 1941, 1949). In retirement, he spent much of his time following the court cases of members of **Cymdeithas yr Iaith Gymraeg**.

WILLIAMS, David (1738–1816) Philosopher

Born at Waunwaelod (**Caerphilly**), David Williams was educated at **Carmarthen Nonconformist Academy**. Leaving in 1757, he had a chequered career in the **Nonconformist** ministry, which he abandoned in 1773, having rejected revealed **religion** in favour of a religion based upon reason and nature. Influential supporters of his Deist chapel (1776–80) at Margaret Street, **London** included Thomas Bentley, Josiah Wedgwood, James 'Athenian' Stuart and Benjamin Franklin. Williams emerged as an **Enlightenment** figure of international significance, distinguished by his forthright arguments for an ethical civil religion, complete toleration and intellectual liberty. Living by teaching and journalism, Williams developed original ideas on political and civil liberty (*Letters on Political Liberty*, 1782), and on civic **education** (*Lectures on Education*, 1789). In 1792, he accepted honorary French citizenship, but his advice on a new constitution was ignored. An individualistic but never an isolated intellectual, he wrote a *History of Monmouthshire* (1796), in which he was aided by Welsh antiquarians, most notably by his friend Iolo Morganwg (**Edward Williams**). Perhaps his most lasting achievement was his founding, in 1790, of the Literary Fund (later the Royal Literary Fund) to assist indigent writers and to promote intellectual liberty.

WILLIAMS, David (1900–78) Historian

A native of Llanycefn (**Maenclochog**), he was appointed a lecturer in history at **Cardiff** in 1930; from 1945 to 1967, he was professor of Welsh history at **Aberystwyth**. His early interests were in the revolutionary eras in American and French history. He pioneered the study of the social and working-**class** history of Wales in his two acclaimed books, *John Frost* (1939) and *The Rebecca Riots* (1955). Both were works of meticulous, balanced scholarship, as was his *A History of Modern Wales* (1950). Always the scholar in his interests and priorities, his writings reflect much of the man himself – his humanity, wit, scorn for conceit and hypocrisy, and his **Pembrokeshire** patriotism.

Christopher Williams, *The Charge of the Welsh Division at Mametz Wood* (1918)

WILLIAMS, Edward (Iolo Morganwg; 1747–1826)
Poet, antiquary and forger

'One of the ablest and most versatile men ever born in Wales', according to Professor Ceri W. Lewis, Iolo Morganwg was born at **Llancarfan**, and spent most of his life as a stonemason, either in **Glamorgan** – chiefly at Flemingston (**St Athan**), where he died – or, during the 1770s and 1790s, in **England**. In 1786–7, he spent a year in **Cardiff prison** as a debtor.

At an early age, he befriended the poets and other literary figures of his area, and began collecting and copying manuscripts, taking a delight in imitating their contents. Influenced by the 18th-century literary and antiquarian revival, he began writing poetry himself, both in **Welsh** and **English**. He rejoiced in the glory of the **literature** and history of Wales, particularly with reference to Glamorgan. He sought to enhance this glory, and in the absence of historical sources to support his claims, he utilized his formidable literary gifts and rich imagination to create some 'sources' of his own. Thus, he misled not only scholars of his own day, who were greatly inferior to him in knowledge and learning, but also, for many years, their successors. He interested himself in **Druid**ism, the **Gorsedd Beirdd Ynys Prydain** being one of his inventions: he held his first Gorsedd on Primrose Hill, London, in 1792, and in 1819, during an **eisteddfod** in **Carmarthen**, he made the Gorsedd an integral part of eisteddfodic proceedings. These activities, argued **G. J. Williams**, caused Iolo to be one of the fathers of the national movement.

Edward Williams (Iolo Morganwg), an engraving by Robert Cruikshank

From an early age, he became addicted to the drug laudanum (a tincture of opium), perhaps to relieve his chronic pain – backache made it impossible for him to sleep in a bed. The laudanum may well have affected his state of mind. Nevertheless, he was a scholar of genius, who took an interest in a wide range of subjects, including **agriculture**, **garden**ing, **architecture**, **geology**, botany, **theology**, folk **music**, and many more, often adding to general knowledge of them. A **radical** in politics, he began to style himself, during his time in London, 'The Bard of Liberty'.

He was a gifted poet of the romantic school, though little of his Welsh poetry was published during his lifetime; his English poetry was published in two volumes as *Poems Lyrical and Pastoral* (1794); as a **Unitarian**, he wrote and published many **hymns**. Some of his brilliant forgeries may be seen in such publications as *Barddoniaeth Dafydd ab Gwilym* (1789) and ***The Myvyrian Archaiology*** (1801–7). His treatise on Welsh metrics, *Cyfrinach Beirdd Ynys Prydain* (1829), another invention to the glory of Glamorgan, was published after his death by his son, Taliesin ab Iolo (1787–1847), who was an influential teacher in **Merthyr Tydfil** and a significant figure in the cultural life of Glamorgan. Taliesin was partially responsible for the publication of the *Iolo Manuscripts* (1848) and, following the **Merthyr Rising** (1831), was active in the petition against the execution of **Richard Lewis**.

WILLIAMS, Eliseus (Eifion Wyn; 1867–1926) Poet

Employed as a schoolteacher and later as a clerk with a **slate** company in his native **Porthmadog**, Eifion Wyn was an ardent **Liberal** who delighted in **angling** and **billiards**. He is best remembered for his nature lyrics, and especially for his series on the months of the year. He also wrote several popular **hymns**. A monument above his grave in Chwilog (**Llanystumdwy**) cemetery was unveiled by **David Lloyd George** in 1934.

WILLIAMS, Emlyn (George Emlyn Williams; 1905–87) Dramatist and actor

As he reminded his audience at **Rhyl** (1953), opening the most memorable speech ever delivered by a day-president at the National **Eisteddfod**, Emlyn Williams was a 'hogyn bach o Sir y Fflint' (a little **Flintshire** lad). Born at Pen-y-ffordd (**Llanasa**), he studied at **Oxford**, where, recovering from a nervous breakdown in 1926, he began to write plays. He wrote some 30 in all, achieving considerable success with *Night Must Fall* (1935), *The Corn is Green* (1938), *The Druid's Rest* (1944) and *The Wind of Heaven* (1945). He was the first to bring to the English stage an authentic representation of Welsh village life, in naturalistic plays whose chief purpose was entertainment. Two of his plays – *Night Must Fall* (1964) and *The Corn is Green* (1979) – were adapted for the screen, and he wrote, directed and starred in ***The Last Days of Dolwyn*** (1949).

Williams was a comic and sometimes sentimental writer with little taste for the tragic. From the 1950s onwards, he enjoyed enormous success on worldwide tours presenting the works of Dickens and **Dylan Thomas**. His engaging autobiography comes in two parts, *George* (1961) and *Emlyn* (1973), with the latter containing a convincing description of **homosexual** cruising.

WILLIAMS, Emlyn (1921–95) Trade unionist

The president of the South Wales district of the **National Union of Mineworkers** (NUM) from 1973 to 1985, it was he who led the southern miners during the 1984–5 **miners' strike**. Although deeply suspicious of Arthur Scargill, the president of the NUM as a whole, he succeeded during that unsuccessful strike in ensuring the almost total loyalty of the miners of the south Wales **coal**field to the NUM, and in leading them back to work with dignity and honour. Emlyn Williams was born in **Aberdare** and began working at the Nantmelyn colliery when only 14 years old. During the **Second World War**, he fought in North Africa against the forces of Rommel – later his nickname among some of his fellow **trade union**ists. His bitter experience of private ownership of the pits caused him to stay in the army until 1947, when he returned to an industry which by then had been nationalized.

WILLIAMS, Evan (1871–1959) Coalowner

In the interwar years, **coal** was the industry most at the centre of political storms, and **Pontarddulais**-born Evan Williams played a central role throughout. He was chairman of the **Monmouthshire** and South Wales **Coalowners' Association** (1913), and presided over its conciliation board from 1918.

He led the coalowners as president of the Mining Association of Great Britain (MAGB) from 1919 to 1944, transforming the presidency and converting the MAGB from a passive to a well-organized, assertive institution. His initial triumph was 'putting nationalization to sleep' by 1920, followed by the dismissal (notably in a famous, acrimonious confrontation with **Churchill**) of mild **government** attempts to soften the settlement of the 1926 **General Strike**. He was consistently unbending in opposing **Britain**-wide wage settlements, insisting on management's unfettered right to manage. Although the voice of the coalowners, Williams's only initial foothold in the industry was through the small family firm which owned Morlais Colliery, **Llangennech**. He was made baronet in 1935. **Thomas Jones** (1870–1955) considered him 'an insignificant little man'.

WILLIAMS, Evan [James] (1903–45) Physicist

Evan Williams, FRS, was one of the most brilliant physicists that Wales has ever produced. Born at Cwmsychbant (**Llanwenog**) (where the house is marked by an Institute of Physics plaque), he was one of **Swansea**'s first **science** graduates. He completed his PhD at Manchester, studying X-ray scatter under the supervision of Lawrence Bragg. He moved first to the Cavendish Laboratory, **Cambridge**, where he worked with Ernest Rutherford, and then to Copenhagen where he collaborated with Niels Bohr and was one of the first to interpret the quantum phenomenon of wave-particle duality. After a brief period at **Liverpool**, he was appointed to the chair of physics at **Aberystwyth** in 1938.

The field of particle physics witnessed rapid development from the mid-1930s onwards, and endeavours were fuelled by Hideki Yukawa's theory proposing the existence of a particle intermediate in weight between the electron and the proton – the pi-meson or pion as it is now called. Evan

Emlyn Williams, interpreting the novels of Charles Dickens

Williams sought evidence to substantiate Yukawa's theory. In 1940, he was the first to observe the decay of a particle now known as the muon, thus providing experimental proof that fundamental particles can be transformed into other particles. This experiment took place in a cloud chamber in the cellar of the Old College, Aberystwyth. After his death, an examination of his photographic plates suggested that he had acquired proof of Yukawa's proposed particle. However, his work was curtailed by the **Second World War**, and the first recorded identification of the pi-meson was achieved by a team in Bristol in 1947.

Seconded to Coastal Command during the Second World War, Williams introduced the degaussing or neutralizing of **ships** to protect them against magnetic mines, and he calculated the optimum depth for exploding depth charges. He also gave crucial advice that helped save Allied convoys from German U-boats. Evan Williams died of cancer at the age of 42, while at the peak of his intellectual powers. His brother, Dafydd or David Williams (1894–1970), was a renowned engineer who became an expert in the field of aircraft structures.

WILLIAMS, G[riffith] J[ohn] (1892–1963) Scholar

The leading authority on Iolo Morganwg (**Edward Williams**), G. J. Williams came to prominence with the publication of *Iolo Morganwg a Chywyddau'r Ychwanegiad* (1926), where he revealed how Iolo had ascribed some of his own poems to **Dafydd ap Gwilym**; his last major work was the first volume of an unfinished biography, *Iolo Morganwg* (1956). He also published a study of the literary tradition of **Glamorgan** as well as numerous articles on the history of Welsh scholarship and seminal studies of the works of 16th-century humanists. A native of Cellan (**Llanfair Clydogau**), he was educated at **Aberystwyth**. He was appointed to a lectureship in the **Welsh** department at **Cardiff** (1921), becoming professor in 1946. Y Mudiad Cymreig, one of the organizations which came together to form **Plaid [Genedlaethol] Cymru** in 1925, was founded in his house in **Penarth**.

WILLIAMS, G[wilym] O[wen] (1913–91)
Archbishop

Born in **London** of **Nonconformist** parents and brought up at Penisa'r Waun (**Llanddeiniolen**), 'G. O.', as he came to be known, became an **Anglican** following a brilliant academic career at **Oxford**. He was bishop of **Bangor** (1957–82) and archbishop of Wales (1971–82). He won widespread respect for his contribution to Welsh public life and, during his archepiscopate, it became evident that the **Church in Wales**, 60 years and more after **disestablishment**, was considered to be the country's quasi-official church. For instance, at the height of the agitation over a **Welsh** television channel, the deputation which met the home secretary, William Whitelaw, in 1980 consisted of the archbishop, **Cledwyn Hughes** (one-time **secretary of state for Wales**) and **Goronwy Daniel** (one-time vice-chancellor of the **University of Wales**). It was that meeting which led to the **government**'s decision to establish **S4C**, thus opening the way for **Gwynfor Evans** to abandon his intended fast.

Grace Williams

WILLIAMS, Glanmor (1920–2005) Historian

A native of Dowlais (**Merthyr Tydfil**), Glanmor Williams was the leading Welsh historian of the second half of the 20th century (*see* **Historiography of Wales, The**). A graduate of **Aberystwyth**, he was, from 1945 to 1982, a member of the history department of University College, **Swansea** (*see* **University of Wales Swansea**), where he was professor (1957–82) and vice-principal (1975–78). His many publications include his masterpiece, *The Welsh Church from Conquest to Reformation* (1962), *Welsh Reformation Essays* (1967), *Recovery, Reorientation and Reformation* (1987), *Grym Tafodau Tân* (1984), *Wales and the Reformation* (1997) and *Glanmor Williams: a Life* (2002). The leading figure in the remarkable flowering of Welsh **historiography** from the 1950s onwards, he was largely responsible for the establishment of the *Welsh History Review* and was the main mover in three multi-volume projects – the *Oxford History of Wales*, the *History of Glamorgan* and the 'Studies in Welsh History' series of monographs. As a teacher and as the mentor of young researchers, his contribution was immense; equally remarkable was his encouragement of amateur and local historians. He was a member of the committee on the legal status of the **Welsh language** and co-author of its report (1965). He was the BBC's National Governor for Wales from 1965 to 1971, a controversial period in the history of Welsh **broadcasting**. He was knighted in 1995.

WILLIAMS, Grace [Mary] (1906–77) Composer

Grace Williams, who was born and died in **Barry**, graduated at **Cardiff** before studying composition with Vaughan Williams and Gordon Jacob at the Royal College of Music, **London**, and then in Vienna, with Egon Wellensz. She spent many years teaching in schools and at teacher training college in London, before returning to Wales in 1947, where she spent the rest of her working life as a composer.

Most of her major works were in response to commissions from institutions such as BBC Wales and the **Welsh National Youth Orchestra**. She often exploited Welsh themes, such as *Fantasia on Welsh Nursery Tunes* (1941) and *Penillion for Orchestra* (1955). She wrote one opera, *The Parlour* (1966), but her most enduring output is found in her orchestral and vocal **music**, which shows her to have an individual voice and a convincing compositional technique.

WILLIAMS, Gwyn (1904–90) Translator
and writer

Port Talbot-born Gwyn Williams taught **English**, from 1935, at universities in North Africa and Turkey, returning to Wales in 1969. His translations into English of **Welsh** poetry, published in the 1950s, were the best available at the time; they were collected in the volume *To Look for a Word* (1976). A prolific writer in both Welsh and English, he published three novels, an autobiography, four travel books about Cyrenaica and Turkey, books on the history of Wales, and five volumes of his own verse; his *Collected Poems* appeared in 1987. His memoir on his period as a subsistence farmer at Trefenter (**Llangwyryfon**) was published in 2004.

WILLIAMS, Gwyn Alfred (1925–95) Historian

A native of Dowlais (**Merthyr Tydfil**), Gwyn A. Williams was successively lecturer at **Aberystwyth** (1954–65), and professor at York (1965–74) and **Cardiff** (1974–85); from 1985, he worked as a writer-presenter for television. His books on Welsh subjects include *The Merthyr Rising* (1978), *Madoc: the Making of a Myth* (1979), *The Search for Beulah Land* (1980), *The Welsh in their History* (1982) and *When Was Wales?* (1985). A Marxist, but in his later phase a member of **Plaid [Genedlaethol] Cymru**, he saw himself as 'a people's remembrancer'; his books, like his broadcasts, are characterized by passion, wide erudition and a fondness for the dramatic. The television series *The Dragon Has Two Tongues*, which he co-presented with **Wynford Vaughan Thomas**, is a notable example of history as dialectic.

WILLIAMS, Ifor (1881–1965) Scholar

Born in Tregarth (**Llandygai**), Ifor Williams made his major contribution as the primary authority on the *Cynfeirdd*. He devoted his academic life to studying this poetry and its background, publishing his research in a series of brilliant editions: *Canu Llywarch Hen* (1935), *Canu Aneirin* (1938) and *Canu Taliesin* (1960). He also prepared the first dependable editions of some of the stories of *The Mabinogion*, as well as the works of some of the **Poets of the Gentry**. He spent his entire career in the **Welsh** department at **Bangor**; (he was appointed to a chair there in 1920). He was a founder of the radical journal *Y Tyddynnwr*, a lay **preacher** and an effective essayist and broadcaster. Concern about the future of Welsh led him to try to establish a standard form of spoken Welsh, which he termed *Cymraeg Byw* (Living Welsh). He was knighted in 1947.

WILLIAMS, J[ohn] E[llis] Caerwyn (1912–99) Scholar

One of the foremost 20th-century experts on the Brythonic and Goedelic groups of languages (*see* **Welsh Language**), he was born in **Gwaun-Cae-Gurwen** and studied in **Bangor**, Dublin, **Aberystwyth** and **Bala**. In 1945, he was appointed lecturer in Welsh at Bangor, becoming professor in 1953. In 1965, he became professor of Irish at Aberystwyth, and was the first director of the **University of Wales Centre for Advanced Welsh and Celtic Studies**. The breadth of his scholarly contribution is remarkable – from the literary tradition of **Ireland** to the poetry of the *Gogynfeirdd*, and from the religious poetry of the Middle Ages to literary criticism.

WILLIAMS, J[ohn] G[riffith] (1915–87) Writer

A native of Llangwnadl (**Tudweiliog**), he was a carpenter who later became a woodwork teacher. He wrote two fine volumes of autobiography, *Pigau'r Sêr* (1969) and *Maes Mihangel* (1974), the second of which ends with an account of the author's imprisonment as a **conscientious objector** during the **Second World War** (he objected to the war on nationalistic grounds). He also wrote a historical novel set in the Wales of **Owain Glyndŵr**. His brother, Robin Williams (1923–2003), a **Presbyterian** minister, was an accomplished writer of literary essays who published several volumes, as well as being a well-known broadcaster and, during his youth, a member of the popular student trio Triawd y Coleg.

Gwyn Alfred Williams

WILLIAMS, J[ohn] Lloyd (1854–1945) Botanist and musician

After spending 18 years as head teacher at the elementary school in Garndolbenmaen (**Dolbenmaen**), **Llanrwst**-born J. Lloyd Williams left teaching to conduct research on seaweeds at the Royal College of **Science, London**. Appointed assistant lecturer in botany at **Bangor**, and later professor of botany at **Aberystwyth**, he was an authority on marine algae and the arctic-alpine **plants** of **Snowdonia**. Prominent in the **Welsh Folk-Song Society** from its foundation, he edited its journal from 1909 until his death, and trained his students at Bangor to record songs. He edited the journal *Y Cerddor* (The Musician) from 1930 to 1939, and published volumes of folk song arrangements and four volumes of autobiography.

WILLIAMS, J[ohn] O[wen] (1942–2000) Chemist

Porthmadog-born J. O. Williams studied **chemistry** at **Bangor**, where he was fortunate to find in John Meurig Thomas an inspirational mentor. On completion of his PhD on the solid-state behaviour of anthracene and its derivatives, and after a year at the department of biophysics in Michigan State University, he followed John Meurig Thomas to **Aberystwyth** as senior research fellow and then reader. There, and as professor at the University of Manchester Institute of **Science** and Technology, he became a world leader in studies of the structure of semiconductors, before returning to Wales in 1991 as principal of the **North East Wales Institute of Higher Education**. He was an amateur **football** international, **golf**er, sailor and singer.

WILLIAMS, Jac L[ewis] (1918–77)
Educationist and author

A native of Aberarth (**Dyffryn Arth**), Jac L. Williams became an authority on bilingual **education**. Educated at **Aberystwyth** and **London**, he lectured at **Trinity College, Carmarthen**, and was professor of education at Aberystwyth from 1960 until his death. He was highly independent in outlook, as demonstrated by the numerous articles he published in **periodicals** such as *Barn*, particularly on education and the **Welsh language**. He was passionately opposed to the establishment of a separate Welsh-language television channel (*see* **S4C**), arguing that it would distance the non-Welsh-speaking Welsh from Welsh-language culture. He published several volumes of stories and essays.

WILLIAMS, Jane (Ysgafell; 1806–85) Writer

London-born Jane Williams spent the early part of her life at **Talgarth**, where she took an interest in **Welsh literature** and learned the language. She first emerged as an **English-language** poet, but her published work also includes devotional essays, a scathing riposte to the 1847 **Education** Report (*see* **Treason of the Blue Books**) and a history of Wales (1869). Her forte was biography, as witness her volumes on Carnhuanawc (**Thomas Price**) (1854–5), Betsi Cadwaladr (**Elizabeth Davi(e)s**) (1857) and *The Literary Women of England* (1861).

WILLIAMS, John (1582–1650) Archbishop

Born at **Conwy**, he was consecrated archbishop of York in 1641, despite his opposition to Charles I's ecclesiastical policies and the enmity of Archbishop Laud, which had led to his im**prison**ment. He supported the king on the outbreak of the **Civil Wars**, renovating and defending Conwy Castle but, by 1646, he was assisting the Parliamentary forces in their attempt to capture it. He was buried at **Llandygai**. There are those who believe that, had Charles listened to Williams rather than Laud, the Civil Wars would not have occurred.

WILLIAMS, John (1732–95) Mineral surveyor

Born to a farming family in **Kerry**, John Williams started his career as a metalliferous miner in **Cardiganshire** and **Snowdonia**. On moving to **Scotland**, he soon became recognized as one of the most distinguished mineral surveyors of his generation. His guide to **coal** finding and mining, *The Natural History of the Mineral Kingdom* (2 vols, 1790; with German translation of parts of it, 1798), filled a vacuum in European technical **literature**. Catherine the Great of Russia granted him a gold medal. He died of typhoid at Verona, whose duke had invited him to undertake a survey of the minerals of the duchy.

WILLIAMS, John (1801–59) Naturalist

John Williams, of **Llanrwst**, was a professional **garden**er at Kew and Chelsea before turning to medicine. He was author of the trilingual *Faunula Grustensis* (1830), subtitled 'An Outline of the Natural Contents of the Parish of Llanrwst', and, as 'Corvinius', he wrote widely in **Welsh** on scientific topics, including a pioneer article on the rare **plants** of **Snowdon**.

WILLIAMS, John (Ab Ithel; 1811–62)
Antiquary and editor

A man of praiseworthy but uncritical industry, **Llangynhafal**-born and **Oxford**-educated Ab Ithel edited several **periodicals** and poetry and prose texts – work seriously marred by the influence of Iolo Morganwg (**Edward Williams**). Rector of Llanymawddwy (**Mawddwy**) from 1849 until his death, he was one of the *hen bersoniaid llengar* (old literary clerics), a leader of the **Oxford Movement** and co-founder, with **Harry Longueville Jones**, of the journal *Archaeologica Cambrensis* (1846–). He organized the **Eisteddfod** held at **Llangollen** in 1858, which, notoriously, denied **Thomas Stephens** the prize for his essay on **Madog ab Owain Gwynedd**, but which was also the forerunner of the National Eisteddfod.

WILLIAMS, John (1840–1926)
Physician and collector of manuscripts

John Williams was born in Gwynfe (**Llangadog**). After studying at Glasgow University, he worked in **Swansea** as a medical apprentice before entering University College Hospital, **London**, as a student. He practised as a doctor in Swansea before returning to the hospital in London. There, his surgical work opened new frontiers in gynaecological practice. Later, he became a professor at the University of London and, in 1886, was appointed physician to Queen Victoria, who made him a baronet in 1894. It was Williams who was largely responsible for the founding of the **National Library of Wales**, and was its first president. He also became president of the University College of Wales, **Aberystwyth** (**University of Wales, Aberystwyth**). His valuable collection of manuscripts and books was donated to the National Library, on condition that the institution be located in Aberystwyth. In 2005, a distant relative, Tony Williams, claimed in his book *Uncle Jack* that Williams was Jack the Ripper, the serial killer, in 1888, of five London prostitutes. As a result, the National Library received a flood of letters by cranks from all over the world.

WILLIAMS, John (Brynsiencyn; 1853–1921)
Minister

The most forceful **Calvinistic Methodist preacher** of his day, John Williams is remembered primarily for his controversial role in exhorting hundreds of young Welshman to enlist during the **First World War**. Born at Llandyfrydog (**Rhosybol**), and brought up in **Beaumaris**, he began preaching in 1873, was ordained in 1878 and ministered at Brynsiencyn (**Llanidan**) and **Liverpool**, before retiring to Brynsiencyn in 1906.

Politically he was a **Liberal**, but theologically he was conservative. He took an active part in promoting the formation of the **Welsh Army Corps** and was its honorary chaplain. Going so far as to conduct services dressed in military uniform, he was regarded as **David Lloyd George**'s greatest recruiting officer in Wales. But as the death toll mounted, so Williams's reputation crumbled. He is buried at Llanfaes (**Beaumaris**), near his hero **John Elias**.

WILLIAMS, [Laurence] John (1929– 2004)
Economist and historian

Cardiff-born and educated, in 1962 John Williams became a member of the department of economics at **Aberystwyth**, where he remained until his retirement in 1994; he was given a personal chair in 1989. His scholarly publications ranged widely and included studies of the decline of British manufacturing, the future of the European Union and the theories of Keynes and Beveridge. His work on Wales included *The South Wales Coal Industry, 1841–1875* (with J. H. Morris, 1958), a remarkable collection of essays (*Was Wales Industrialized?* 1995) and *Digest of Welsh Historical Statistics* (1985 and subsequent updates). As the census and other statistic-collecting bodies rarely treat Wales as a unit, the *Digest* rapidly became the most indispensable volume in the libraries of the historians of modern Wales. John Williams was the central figure in the founding and growth of the Welsh Labour History Society and its journal *Llafur*. A gentle but incisive man, he was probably the best loved of all those of his generation who worked in the field of Welsh social studies.

WILLIAMS, John Ellis (1901–75) Author

As dramatist, storyteller, essayist, satirist, journalist, translator and critic, John Ellis Williams was among the most prolific Welsh writers ever: he published over 70 books. Brought up in Penmachno (**Bro Machno**), he became a teacher in Blaenau **Ffestiniog**. His plays, the first of which he published at the age of 17, include the highly popular *Ceidwad y Porth* (1927), *Pen y Daith* (1932) and *Chwalu'r Nyth* (1939). He wrote two series of detective novels, and 12 books for children, including the adventure novel *Drwy Ddŵr a Thân* (1957). The satirist found scope in books such as *Sglodion* (1932) and *Whilmentan* (1961). The account of his literary career in *Inc yn fy Ngwaed* (1963) is valuable for its perspective on Welsh **drama** in the middle years of the 20th century.

WILLIAMS, John Roberts (1914–2004)
Journalist and broadcaster

Born in Llangybi (**Llanystumdwy**) and educated at **Bangor**, John Roberts Williams came to prominence as editor of *Y Cymro*, the weekly **Welsh-language newspaper** whose circulation he increased greatly between 1945 and 1962 by means of his populist approach. Along with the paper's photographer, **Geoff Charles**, he also produced the pioneering film **Yr Etifeddiaeth** (*The Heritage*; 1949). In 1963, he was appointed editor of BBC Wales's news programme *Heddiw*, a post which he held until 1970 when he became head of the BBC in north Wales. His shrewd view of both world and Welsh affairs found expression, until a few weeks before his death, in his popular weekly radio slot *Dros fy Sbectol* (Over My Spectacles).

WILLIAMS, [John] Kyffin (1918–2006)
Artist and author

Widely regarded as the nation's defining artist of the past century and, as he proposed himself, 'the first painter

Kyffin Williams, *Farmers on Glyder Fach* (1981)

that people in Wales have been able to relate to', **Llangefni**-born Kyffin Williams – known by all as simply Kyffin – became an artist as a result of illness. He embarked on a military career in 1937 but was invalided out of the **Royal Welch Fusiliers** in 1941 because of epilepsy, his doctor advising him to take up art for the sake of his **health**.

His studies at the Slade School of Art, evacuated during the **Second World War** to **Oxford**, qualified him for the post of senior art master at Highgate School, **London**, which he held from 1944 until 1973, returning to Wales to paint at every opportunity. In 1968, he travelled to **Patagonia** to record the Welsh community there. In his mid-fifties, he settled permanently in **Anglesey**, his home for many years being a cottage at **Llanfair Pwllgwyngylch** overlooking the **Menai Strait** and the **mountains** of **Snowdonia** – a landscape, especially in its brooding, overcast moods, which the artist made particularly his own.

A Kyffin oil **painting** – including his portraits, which he held in higher regard than his landscapes – is instantly recognizable as such, with its trademark palette-knife slabs of paint, bold delineations, restless energy and atmospheric drama; expressionism and the art of van Gogh were important influences. He also produced masterful work in pastels and watercolours. Having one of his paintings on their walls has become the hallmark of authentic members of the Welsh bourgeoisie.

Elected to the Royal Academy in 1974 and knighted in 1999, Kyffin used his status to campaign for a national gallery of Welsh art, although he could be scathing of many of the art world's contemporary pretensions. His apparent unassailability as the nation's premier artist prompted one of a younger generation to dub him 'the queen mother of Welsh art'. His publications include the autobiographical *Across the Straits* (1973) and *A Wider Sky* (1991).

WILLIAMS, [William] Llewelyn (1867–1922)
Journalist, politician and historian

Born into a prosperous **Congregationalist** family at Brownhill, **Llansadwrn**, Llewelyn Williams studied history at **Oxford**. After a career in journalism, which included editorship of the **Swansea**-based **radical newspaper** the *South Wales Post*, he turned to the **law** and politics. MP for **Carmarthen Boroughs** from 1906 until the constituency's abolition in 1918, he campaigned for **disestablishment** and **home rule**. A staunch **Liberal**, his detestation of military conscription caused him to loathe **David Lloyd George**. In the famous **Cardiganshire** by-election of 1921, he won 42.7% of the vote in his contest with the successful pro-Lloyd George Liberal. Among his publications were the children's story *Gwilym a Benni Bach* (1897) and his historical study *The Making of Modern Wales* (1919).

WILLIAMS, Margaret Lindsay (1888–1960) Painter
The daughter of a wealthy **Barry** shipowner (*see* **Ships and Shipowners**), she studied at **Cardiff** and at the Royal Academy of Art, **London**. Popular in her time for her romantic academic portraiture and her treatments of Welsh folktales, she used her accomplished drawing skills to manufacture highly melodramatic, allegorical scenes, which soon became historical anachronisms.

WILLIAMS, Maria Jane (Llinos; 1795–1873)
Singer and collector of folk songs

Born at Aberpergwm House (**Glynneath**), she was a **harp**ist and guitarist, but was especially acclaimed for her singing, acquiring the name *Llinos* (linnet). A friend of Lady Llanover (**Augusta Hall**), she was associated with the Welsh cultural society **Cymreigyddion Y Fenni**. Her home became a focus for 'Celtic Renaissance' enthusiasts. She studied and collected folk songs, publishing *Ancient National Airs of Gwent and Morganwg* (1844), which, despite later criticisms, remains an important contribution to knowledge of traditional Welsh **music**.

WILLIAMS, Meirion (1901–76) Composer
Born at **Dyffryn Ardudwy**, Williams studied at **Aberystwyth** under **Walford Davies** and at the Royal Academy of **Music**, **London**. He settled in London as a freelance pianist and accompanist, acting as organist and choirmaster to three **Welsh** chapels. He accompanied many well-known singers and was an established adjudicator at *eisteddfodau*, including the National Eisteddfod. Many of his songs for voice and piano remain popular, including 'Aros mae'r mynyddau mawr' and 'Gwynfyd'. His compositions are noted for their lyrical style and poetic sensitivity.

WILLIAMS, Morgan (1808–83)
Chartist and journalist

A **Merthyr Tydfil**-born master weaver and **Unitarian**, Morgan Williams became prominent with workers' movements and, in 1834, he co-edited the **periodical** *Y Gweithiwr/The Worker* with John Thomas. In March 1840, he and David John published *Udgorn Cymru* with the aim of promoting **Chartism**, and they also established the *Advocate and Merthyr Free Press* in July of the same year. Both papers caused alarm amongst the local magistrates, who urged the Home Office to prosecute their publishers. The *Advocate* ceased publication in April 1841, but the *Udgorn* continued until 1842. Morgan Williams, with whom **John Frost** corresponded from the **ship** which carried him into exile, became in 1842 one of the five directors of the National Association of the Charter. Registrar for marriages at Merthyr from 1853 until his death, he collected material relating to his fellow Unitarian Iolo Morganwg (**Edward Williams**).

WILLIAMS, Morris (Nicander; 1809–74) Poet
Born at Llangybi (**Llanystumdwy**), he was an **Oxford**-educated poet and an industrious promoter of the **Oxford Movement**. He won **eisteddfod** prizes but, as an epic poet in overlong religious and historical *pryddestau*, Nicander won no lasting fame. Yet the **Church in Wales Welsh-language hymn**al contains more contributions by Nicander than any other hymnwriter except **William Williams** (Pantycelyn; 1717–91).

WILLIAMS, Penry (1800–85) Painter
Penry Williams, who spent almost 60 years in Rome, was born in **Merthyr Tydfil**, the son of a stonemason. While

working in the drawing office of the Cyfarthfa **Iron**works, he came to the attention of his first patron, William **Crawshay** II, the **iron**master, who sent him to the Royal Academy Schools in **London**. His early work included studies of workers and of the Merthyr area; his **painting** of the 1816 riots, although lacking polish, shows talent and feeling. In Rome, he became very successful, painting scenes of the Campagna and portraits of the nobility.

WILLIAMS, Peter (1723–96) Methodist author
One of the most prominent Methodist leaders of the 18th century, Peter Williams was born at Llansadurnen (**Llanddowror**). He was ordained deacon in 1745 but was refused full orders because of his Methodist inclinations; he joined the Methodists in 1747, became an itinerant **preacher** and eventually settled at **Llandyfaelog**. Early Methodists could suffer severe persecution, and on one occasion Williams was imprisoned in the kennels of Sir Watkin **Williams Wynn**.

A prolific author of **hymns**, poetry, children's books and religious works, he is remembered chiefly for the annotated 'Peter Williams **Bible**' (1770), the first **Welsh** Bible to be printed in Wales, which found a place in thousands of Welsh homes. His biblical commentaries led to accusations of **Sabellianism** and to his expulsion from the ranks of the **Calvinistic Methodists** in 1791.

WILLIAMS, Phil[ip James Stradling] (1939–2003) Physicist and politician
Born in **Tredegar**, Phil Williams, as he was always known, was brought up in **Bargoed** and educated at Lewis School **Pengam**, and Clare College, **Cambridge**. Appointed a fellow of Clare in 1964, he became in 1967 a lecturer in the physics department at **Aberystwyth**; he was awarded a personal chair in 1991. Initially a radio astronomer, he published a pioneer catalogue of radio sources and was involved in the discovery of quasars (*see* **Astronomy**). He then turned to atmospheric physics and became a world authority on the incoherent scatter radar of the upper atmosphere. He played a key role in EISCAT (the European Incoherent-Scatter Facility), the radar system established in northern Sweden to study the impact of solar wind, and was recognized as a leading expert on the aurora borealis.

He joined **Plaid [Genedlaethol] Cymru** in 1960 and became the party's leading intellectual light, establishing its research group and turning what had been essentially a cultural movement into a fully functioning political party with a serious economic policy. In the **Caerphilly** by-election of 1968, he turned a **Labour** majority of 21,148 into one of merely 1874. Elected to the **National Assembly for Wales** in 1999 as one of the list members for the south-east, he became a trenchant analyst of the sources of **government**

Penry Williams, *The Procession to the Christening in l'Ariccia* (1831)

expenditure in Wales. His sudden death at the age of 64 was widely seen as a national calamity. In addition to his scientific and political interests, he was a skilled saxophone player, deeply versed in Russian **literature** and a tireless researcher into the Welsh contribution to **science** – work from which this encyclopaedia has greatly benefited. Phil Williams was, without doubt, the ablest Welshman of his generation.

WILLIAMS, Prysor (Robert John Williams; 1892–1967) Actor

A member of the BBC repertory radio company from 1946 to 1960, **Trawsfynydd**-born Prysor Williams made an impact as the ailing miner in Jill Craigie's cinema feature *Blue Scar* (1949). He enjoyed a scene-stealing cameo as a staunch **eisteddfod** attendant in the outstanding Welsh **film** *David* (1951).

WILLIAMS, R[hys] H[aydn] (1930–93) Rugby player and administrator

Cwmllynfell-born 'R. H.' was one of the outstanding second-row forwards of the post-war era. Massive in frame, he dominated the line-out, mauled ferociously and was a specialist in the controlled foot rush. An automatic selection for the British Lions in 1955 and 1959, he was acclaimed in **New Zealand** as the best in the world in his position. His later career as a Welsh **Rugby** Union administrator was blighted by controversy over links with apartheid **South Africa**, which forced his resignation.

Raymond Williams

WILLIAMS, Raymond [Henry] (1921–88) Social historian, critic and novelist

Raymond Williams was born near the **border** with **England** at Pandy (**Crucorney**), where his father was a **railway** worker. Educated at **Cambridge**, he took part in the Normandy landings and, after the **Second World War**, entered adult **education** as a teacher in **Oxford**. From 1974 to 1983, he was professor of **drama** at Cambridge. His early books, *Culture and Society* (1958) and *The Long Revolution* (1966), established his reputation as a cultural historian of the first rank. He had a lifelong engagement with politics, but resigned from the **Labour Party** in 1966, and was thereafter associated with the New Left; his writings had an influence on **Plaid [Genedlaethol] Cymru**.

Williams's main concern was to throw light on the modern concept of 'culture' as an expression, in both high and popular modes, of life in contemporary **Britain**; for his knowledge of working-**class** life he often drew on his boyhood in Pandy, which featured in his novel *Border Country* (1960). He wrote over 20 books, notably *May Day Manifesto* (1968), *The Country and the City* (1973), *Keywords* (1973), *Marxism and Literature* (1977) and *Writing in Society* (1983). A collection of interviews with staff of the *New Left Review*, to which he frequently contributed, was published as *Politics and Letters* (1979); after his death, there appeared *The Politics of Modernism* (1989) and two collections of shorter pieces, *Resources of Hope* (1989) and *What I Came to Say* (1989). His novels *Second Generation* (1964), *The Volunteers* (1978), *The Fight for Manod* (1979) and *Loyalties* (1985) are set partly or wholly in Wales. Of his projected massive novel *People of the Black Mountains*, only two parts were published: *The Beginning* (1989) and *The Eggs of the Eagle* (1990). His critical essays on Wales were collected by Daniel Williams in *Who Speaks for Wales?* (2003).

WILLIAMS, Rhydwen (1916–97) Poet and novelist

Rhydwen Williams, the **Welsh**-speaking voice of his native **Rhondda**, followed a career as a **Baptist** minister. He also worked in television and was a freelance actor and producer. He won the National **Eisteddfod** crown for his long poems in the free metres 'Yr Arloeswr' (1946) and 'Y Ffynhonnau' (1964). A complete collection of his poems (which were dramatic and colourful, as was his personality), *Barddoniaeth Rhydwen Williams: y casgliad cyflawn 1941–1991*, appeared in 1991. The most important of his many novels, the autobiographical trilogy *Cwm Hiraeth* (1969–73), is a kind of prose epic to the Rhondda. The Rhondda is also the theme of his **English** novel *The Angry Vineyard* (1975). *Amser i Wylo: Senghennydd 1913* (1986) is 'faction' based on Wales's worst ever **colliery disaster** (*see* **Senghenydd Colliery Disaster**). With his beautiful voice, his public readings – particularly from the works of **Daniel Owen** – enjoyed great success.

WILLIAMS, Richard Hughes (Dic Tryfan; ?1878–1919) Short-story writer

The pioneer of the Welsh short story came from Rhosgadfan (**Llanwnda**) – the same locality as his short-story writing successor **Kate Roberts** – and worked in the **slate** quarry before embarking on a career as a journalist.

He published widely in both **Welsh** and **English periodicals**, and a selection of his Welsh-language stories appeared as *Storïau Richard Hughes Williams* (1932; new edition, 1994). He studied the form of the short story, learning from Chekhov and others the art of subtle suggestion. His main subject matter was life in the slate quarries, and he made no attempt to avoid its harshness.

WILLIAMS, Richard Tecwyn (1909–79)
Pharmacologist

Born at **Abertillery**, of northern parentage, Richard Tecwyn Williams could not afford to train as a doctor, but entered the medical profession via a degree in **chemistry**, and research in physiology at **Cardiff**, Birmingham and **Liverpool**. With the publication of his *Detoxication Mechanisms* (1949 and 1956), he became an authority on the body's ability to metabolize drugs and toxins. He was professor of biochemistry at St Mary's Hospital Medical School, **London**, from 1949 to 1976.

WILLIAMS, Robert (Robert ap Gwilym Ddu; 1766–1850) Poet and hymnwriter

As a farmer of ample means in the **parish** of Llanystumdwy, Robert was able to devote himself to self-**education** and poetry. He learned his craft from the poets of **Eifionydd** and outshone them all in the strict metres (*see* **Cynghanedd**); but, unlike them, he was not a competitor, remaining independent of **eisteddfod** fashions and concentrating on everyday events. Like his predecessor, **Goronwy Owen**, he chose the *awdl* form for an elegy to his only daughter, Jane – a poem combining traditional discipline with deep feeling. The most famous of his many well-crafted **hymns** is 'Mae'r gwaed a redodd ar y Groes'.

WILLIAMS, Roger (?1540–95) Soldier and author

A member of the Williams family of Penrhos (**Llantilio Crossenny**), he fought for Holland against Spain and went to Flushing with Captain Thomas Morgan (*c.*1542–95) of **Glamorgan** (1572). He was expert in the martial arts and was knighted in 1586. His three publications include *A Brief Discourse of War* (1590). **Shakespeare** may have based Fluellen in *Henry V* on him.

WILLIAMS, Samuel (*c.*1660–*c.*1722) and Moses (1685–1742) Clergymen and scholars

This father and son were among several gifted clergymen, scholars and translators who were born in the vale of **Teifi** in the late 17th century. Samuel Williams was a clergyman in **Llandyfriog** and Llangynllo. Many of his **Welsh** translations remain unpublished, but he bequeathed his splendid collection of books and manuscripts to his son, who was born in the **parish** of Cellan (**Llanfair Clydogau**). At **Oxford**, Moses tried to follow in **Edward Lhuyd**'s footsteps by publishing a series of scholarly works as well as the first bibliography of Welsh books. During his journeys through Wales, he rescued many of the manuscripts that now adorn the shelves of the **National Library**. Not the least of his achievements was his edition of the Welsh **Bible**, published by the **Society for the Promotion of Christian Knowledge** (1717; reprinted 1727). Moses Williams would have made a first-rate bishop, but his burning patriotism and forthright

tongue were unacceptable in high places, and he died embittered in Bridgwater.

WILLIAMS, Stephen J[oseph] (1896–1992) Scholar

Ystradgynlais-born Stephen J. Williams was a schoolteacher before being appointed a lecturer in the **Welsh** department at **Swansea**, where he succeeded **Henry Lewis** as professor in 1954. He was the primary authority on the Welsh translations of some of the Old **French** Charlemagne epics (*Ystorya de Carolo Magno*, 1930) and he became one of the pioneers of the modern study of the **law** of **Hywel Dda**, with the publication (with J. Enoch Powell) of *Llyfr Blegywryd* (1942). He made his other important contribution as a grammarian. He was prominent in **drama** circles in Swansea and an ardent devotee of the **eisteddfod**. His literary interests were inherited by his sons, the author Urien Wiliam (1929–2006) and the poet and scholar Aled Rhys Wiliam (b.1926).

WILLIAMS, Stephen William (1837–89) Architect

Born in **Churchstoke**, Stephen William Williams was apprenticed as an engineer and worked on the Cambrian **Railway**. In 1862, he began practising from **Rhayader** as an architect, specializing in repairs to old houses and churches, and became **Radnorshire county** surveyor. He became an authority on Welsh monasteries and published *The Cistercian Abbey of Strata Florida* (1889).

WILLIAMS, Thomas (1737–1802) Copper magnate

A key entrepreneur of the **Industrial Revolution**, Williams came from yeoman stock at Cefn Coch, Llansadwrn (**Cwm Cadnant, Anglesey**), becoming a solicitor after apprenticeship at **Caerwys**. He became chief administrator of the **copper** mines on **Mynydd Parys** in the 1770s, developing them as the hub of a business empire that stretched to **London**. Williams not only mined copper but also smelted it (at **Swansea**, **Holywell** and in Lancashire), manufactured products from it, marketed them and developed **banking** interests (*see* **Anglesey Pennies**). He pioneered copper bolts as a more effective means of attaching copper sheathing onto wooden naval vessels to protect them from decay (hence the phrase 'copper bottomed'). The low cost of copper production on Mynydd Parys gave him a dominant position in the industry, enabling him to establish a stranglehold on the formerly dominant Cornish producers; his alleged monopoly position was investigated by a parliamentary Select Committee in 1799. With a reputation for fair dealing with his workers, he was known as 'Twm Chwarae Teg' (Tom Fair Play). He was MP for Great Marlow from 1790 until he died – worth, reputedly, half a million pounds, money that his descendants used to establish the **North and South Wales Bank**, later absorbed by the Midland Bank (HSBC). He acquired Plas **Llanidan** and is therefore often known as Thomas Williams Llanidan.

WILLIAMS, Thomas (Tom Nefyn; 1895–1958)
Minister

Born at Boduan (**Buan**) near **Nefyn**, Thomas Williams fought in the **First World War** before training for the ministry in the **Calvinistic Methodists**' colleges at **Bala** and **Aberystwyth**. Ordained in 1925, he became minister of

Ebenezer chapel, Tumble (**Llannon**), where he instigated a survey of local **housing**, experimented with various approaches to worship, and advocated uncompromising allegiance to **pacifism**. Judged to have departed from the historic faith, he was deprived of his pastorate at the denomination's **Association** held at Nantgaredig (**Llanegwad**) in August 1928. Rather than minister to his followers who had formed a new church at Tumble (Llain y Delyn), he spent some time in retreat with the **Quakers**. He was reinstated as a Methodist minister in 1932, subsequently serving in **Flintshire** and in **Caernarfonshire**. The controversy caused by his challenge to traditional religious practices, widely reported in the press, led many Calvinistic Methodists to regret the rigidly **Calvinist** character of the denomination's Confession of Faith.

WILLIAMS, Thomas (1923–2001)
Transport engineer

Brought up in Cwmtwrch (**Ystradgynlais**), and a graduate in civil **engineering** at **Swansea**, Tom Williams became an international authority on traffic engineering and policy, and an adviser to numerous British **government** agencies. His early publications on the **design** and construction of motorways (*see* **Roads**) had a far-reaching impact on the development of the embryonic British motorway system. From 1963 to 1983, he was head of the civil engineering department at Southampton University. A regular *eisteddfodwr*, he was an active supporter of the language and culture of Wales.

Waldo Williams

WILLIAMS, W[illiam] E[llis] (1881–1962)
Aerodynamic theorist

The son of a **Bethesda slate** quarryman, W. E. Williams was an academic at **Bangor** who was joint author, with Professor George H. Bryan, of important and original papers on aerodynamic theory during the early 20th century. After further studies at Glasgow and Munich, he was appointed a physics lectureship at Bangor. In 1910, he built his own experimental aircraft which, although not particularly successful, was the first British full-scale research aircraft. During the **First World War**, he conducted research for the Air Ministry, but he died without receiving full recognition for his achievements in the field of aerodynamics.

WILLIAMS, W[illiam] S[idney] Gwynn (1896–1978)
Musician

Llangollen-born W. S. Gwynn Williams trained as a lawyer and acted as **music** editor to Hughes and Son before establishing his own imprint, the Gwynn Publishing Company. A composer and arranger of songs and folk songs, he was secretary and editor of the **Welsh Folk-Song Society**, and played a prominent part in the foundation of the **Llangollen International Musical Eisteddfod** (1947) and the **Welsh Folk Dance Society** (1949).

WILLIAMS, Waldo (1904–71) Poet

Waldo Williams's early years were spent in the **Haverfordwest** area, but in 1911 the family moved north of the **Pembrokeshire** linguistic divide, and it was as a primary school pupil at **Mynachlog-Ddu** that he became fluent in **Welsh**. He graduated in **English** at **Aberystwyth**, and taught in schools mainly in Pembrokeshire; for a time he was an extramural lecturer. He suffered for his principles as a pacifist (*see* **Pacifism**), and was imprisoned for holding back his payment of income tax. Two bereavements left an indelible mark on him: the death of his sister Morfydd when she was still a young girl, and the death of his wife Linda only one year into their marriage. He had mystical experiences during his youth, and his mature expression of them in poetry transforms them into visions of the essential unity of mankind. He joined the **Quakers** and his key words were *brawdoliaeth* (brotherhood) and *cyfeillach* (fellowship).

Apart from *Cerddi'r Plant* (in collaboration with Llwyd Williams, 1970), he published only one volume of poems, *Dail Pren* (Leaves of a Tree, 1956). The title comes from his poem 'Mewn Dau Gae', and echoes a verse from the Book of Revelations, which mentions the leaves of the tree which were for 'the healing of nations'. There is remarkable variety within the comparatively short compass of his poems: strict-metre verses, free verse and poems in *vers libre*, Georgian lyrics such as 'Cofio', abstruse modern poems such as 'Cwmwl Haf', challenging poems such as 'Preseli' and poems teeming with humour and satire. All are united by one integral vision: from **Mynydd Preseli**, he saw an 'order', which was reflected in the unity of Wales and, ultimately, in the unity of the world under the governance of a God of love. He is the poet of a humane Christianity, and a civilized **nationalism** and pacifism run like a silver thread through his poems. He stood as **Plaid**

[Genedlaethol] Cymru candidate for Pembrokeshire in the general election of 1959.

WILLIAMS, Watkin Hezekiah (Watcyn Wyn; 1844–1905) Poet and teacher

A native of Brynamman (Quarter Bach), Watcyn Wyn began work underground at the age of eight, but later, having prepared for the Congregational ministry, founded the influential school Ysgol y Gwynfryn at Ammanford. Winner of both the National Eisteddfod crown (1881) and the chair (1885), he became one of the nation's loveable characters because of his ready and genial wit. He wrote the famous hymn 'Rwy'n gweld o bell y dydd yn dod'.

WILLIAMS, William (1634–1700)
Lawyer and landowner

The founder of the Williams Wynn family, and son of an Anglesey clergyman, he was elected MP for Chester in 1675, and speaker in 1680. Abandoning the 'Country Party', he became solicitor general in 1687 and a key figure in the last months of James II's reign. Despite his association with James II, he won the favour of the new monarchs, William III and Mary II. He bought the Llanforda (Shropshire) estate and married the heiress of the Glascoed (Denbighshire) estate, thus beginning the family tradition of amassing estates through marriage. His baronetcy, granted in 1688, was by the early 21st century held by the eleventh baronet.

WILLIAMS, William (William Williams, Pantycelyn or Pantycelyn; 1717–91)
Hymnwriter, poet and prose writer

The foremost Welsh literary figure of the 18th century, William Williams ranks with Isaac Watts (1674–1748) and Charles Wesley (1707–88) as a hymnwriter but, because the Nonconformists among the Welsh adopted the hymn as their liturgy, his influence on Wales far exceeded that of Watts and Wesley in England.

He was one of the three leaders – with Howel Harris and Daniel Rowland – of the Methodist Revival. He was born at Cefncoed, a small farm at Llanfair-ar-y-bryn; he later lived at Pantycelyn, a larger farm within the same parish, the original home of his mother and the place with which he is indelibly linked. He was to be a doctor and was sent to the Nonconformist Academy at Llwynllwyd (Llanigon). It was in Talgarth churchyard in 1737 or 1738 that, on hearing Howel Harris preach, he underwent his conversion experience. He was ordained deacon in 1740, but his work organizing the new Methodist societies (see Calvinistic Methodists and Society) preoccupied him to such an extent that the bishop refused to ordain him a priest. About 1748, he married Mary Francis ('Mali') and, over the years, she looked after the farm and their eight children as Williams, as an itinerant preacher, chief superintendent of the societies and seller of tea, toured the whole of Wales on horseback.

It is said that Harris laid down that 'Williams has the singing' and, in 1744, he published his first collection of hymns, Aleluia I, with five parts following in the next three years. He used over 25 different metrical patterns for the first time in Welsh, and gained increasing mastery over them in such collections as Caniadau y rhai sydd ar y Môr o Wydr (1762–73), Ffarwel Weledig (1763–6) and Gloria in Excelsis (1771–2). There were also two collections in English. He wrote over 800 hymns, 88 of which are included in the interdenominational hymnbook Caneuon Ffydd (2001). The hymns are characterized by intense emotion mediated through scriptural language, from time to time coloured with that of the marketplace. In the typological tradition of the Puritans, he saw Old Testament history flowing through the New into his circumstances and those of his flock: 'Guide me, O Thou great Jehovah, Pilgrim through this barren land.'

Of his long epic poems, Golwg ar Deyrnas Crist (1756) is an ambitious attempt at scriptural history set in the context of new scientific discoveries, and Theomemphus (1764) develops the theme of humanity's spiritual pilgrimage. Although the uniform metrical pattern palls, each epic contains passages of great power.

The author of nearly 90 publications, Williams was also a distinguished writer of prose, as may be seen in the volume Pantheologia (1762–79), a history of world religions, and in his other treatises, such as the guide to marriage, Ductor Nuptiarum (1777), with its broad-minded view of the position of women, and Templum Experientiae Apertum (1777), the summation of his pastoral experience.

Although pedagogy rather than literature was Williams's purpose, he was hailed by Saunders Lewis (in his major study Williams Pantycelyn, 1927) as the earliest exponent of Romanticism in European literature.

WILLIAMS, William (Llandygai; 1738–1817)
Writer and pioneer of industry

A native of Trefdraeth (Bodorgan), Williams became a steward on the Penrhyn estate, Llandygai, playing a key role in the development, from 1782 onwards, of the Penrhyn Quarry (see Slate), as it later became known. He left many writings, including some 100 poems. His Observations on the Snowdon Mountains (1802) is the first standard work on Snowdonia, and his Prydnawngwaith y Cymry (1822) is the first printed book in Welsh on the 'age of the princes'.

WILLIAMS, William (Williams o'r Wern; 1781–1840) Minister

Considered – with John Elias and Christmas Evans – one of the three greatest itinerant preachers of his age, Williams was born at Llanfachreth (Brithdir and Llanfachreth). In 1808, he was ordained a Congregationalist minister at Wern (Minera). He founded new chapels at Rhosllanerchrugog, Ruabon and Llangollen, ministered in Liverpool (1836–9) and spent his last days at Wern.

WILLIAMS, William (Crwys; 1875–1968) Poet

The author of some of the best-known poems in the Welsh language – 'Melin Trefin', 'Siôn a Siân', 'Y Border Bach', 'Y Sipsi' – Crwys was born at Craig-cefn-parc (Mawr), near Swansea. He was a Congregationalist minister (1898–1914) and the Bible Society's representative in the south (1915–1940). Thrice winner of the National Eisteddfod crown (1910, 1911, 1919), Crwys wrote highly crafted and often touching lyrical poetry that was popular and sold well. He was archdruid from 1938 to 1947.

WILLIAMS, William Nantlais (Nantlais; 1874–1959)
Poet and hymnwriter

An evangelical **preacher** deeply influenced by the 1904–5 religious **revival**, Nantlais was born in Gwyddgrug (**Llanfihangel-ar-arth**), and became a minister with the **Calvinistic Methodists** in **Ammanford**. He is best remembered for children's **hymns** such as 'Plant bach Iesu Grist ydym ni bob un', 'Uno wnawn â'r nefol gôr' and 'Draw draw yn China'.

WILLIAMS-ELLIS, [Bertram] Clough (1883–1978)
Architect and writer

Born at Gayton, Northamptonshire, the son of a Welsh rector, Clough Williams-Ellis opened his own office in **London** after minimal architectural training. Later, he inherited Plas Brondanw, **Llanfrothen**, and lived there. His practice mostly consisted of domestic work – loosely based on the Arts and Crafts style – and also included the occasional, more classically oriented public building and town planning. His best-known work is Portmeirion, **Penrhyndeudraeth**, which he developed into an Italianate holiday village (1925–76). He wrote numerous books, including an autobiography, *Architect Errant* (1971). He was knighted in 1972. His wife was the author Amabel Williams-Ellis (1894–1984), a sister of Lytton Strachey. His grandson is the **Welsh-language** novelist Robin Llywelyn (b.1958).

Clough Williams-Ellis at Portmeirion, 1969

WILLIAMS PARRY, R[obert] (1884–1956) Poet

A native of Talysarn (**Llanllyfni**), he studied at **Aberystwyth** and **Bangor**, and was a schoolteacher before becoming a lecturer in **Welsh** and in the extramural department at Bangor. He won the National **Eisteddfod** chair in 1910 for his strict-metre **awdl** 'Yr Haf' (Summer) – a poem which tries to justify pleasure for its own sake, and which can be interpreted as extolling art for art's sake. However, he renounced the aestheticism of this poem, and parodied it in 'Yr Hwyaden' (The Duck). With the **First World War**, during which he spent two unhappy years in army camps in **England**, there came a change of tone, and he wrote his famous **englynion** on the death of Hedd Wyn (**Ellis Humphrey Evans**). His first volume, *Yr Haf a Cherddi Eraill* (1924), established him as an important poet, but there came an interruption to his creativity when he went on a poetry-writing strike in protest at the terms of his employment at Bangor.

The strike was broken in 1936 by his elegy to A. E. Housman; but what reignited his muse most of all was the burning of **Penyberth Bombing School**, and the dismissal of **Saunders Lewis** for his part in it. He began writing committed poems, such as 'J.S.L.' and 'Cymru 1937', and deployed the *soned laes* (long or trailing sonnet) to castigate the Welsh for their supine indifference. Yet he never accepted the idea that the poet was a propagandist. Many of his mature poems express his fear of **death**, and he marvelled and despaired at the wonder of human existence: 'Marwolaeth nid yw'n marw: hyn sydd wae.' ('Death does not die: *this* is woe.') The work of his mature years was published as *Cerddi'r Gaeaf* (Winter Poems) in 1952.

WILLIAMS WYNN family (Wynnstay)
Landowners

The fortunes of the family that came to own the largest landed estate of 19th-century Wales were founded by **William Williams** (1634–1700), the first baronet. His son, William (1684–1740), married the heiress of Plas-y-Ward (**Llanynys, Denbighshire**), a descendant of the **Wynn family (Gwydir)**, and through her the family also acquired the Watstay estate (**Ruabon**, Denbighshire). Their son, Watkin Williams Wynn (d.1749), the third baronet, married the heiress of the **Vaughan family (Llwydiarth)**, adopted the **surname** Wynn and renamed Watstay as Wynnstay (for the mansion, *see* Ruabon). Thereafter, a succession of Watkin Williams Wynns lived at Wynnstay; known as 'the uncrowned kings of north Wales', they amassed an estate which, by the 1880s, extended over 57,000 ha and was by far the largest landed estate in Wales. The third baronet was a **Jacobite** and a persecutor of Methodists (*see* **Peter Williams**). The fourth (1748–89) was a friend of Handel and of Joshua Reynolds; he was president of the **Cymmrodorion**, as was his son, the fifth baronet (1772–1840), a prominent figure in **London** society. From 1716 to 1885, Denbighshire was represented in parliament by an almost unbroken succession of Williams Wynns, whose influence was also extensive in **Montgomeryshire** and **Merioneth**.

The fifth baronet, MP for Denbighshire (1796–1840), had a husky voice and his brother Charles, MP for Montgomeryshire (1799–1850), had a thin voice; they were

Wynnstay, Ruabon, the seat of the Williams Wynn family, before it was rebuilt in the 1860s

called 'bubble and squeak' by the cartoonist James Gillray. Charles Williams Wynn was one of the three 19th-century Welsh MPs to be a member of the British cabinet. (James Graham and **George Cornewall Lewis** were the other two.)

The sixth baronet died without a son in 1885; his daughter, Louisa Alexander, married her cousin, Herbert Lloyd Watkin Williams-Wynn (1860–1944), who became the seventh baronet. With his defeat by **George Osborne Morgan** in the East Denbighshire constituency in 1885, the family's political influence went into rapid decline. Following the death of the seventh baronet, Wynnstay was sold (it became a boarding school and was later converted into flats) and Glanllyn (**Llanuwchllyn**), the family's Merioneth mansion, became one of the centres of **Urdd Gobaith Cymru**. However, Plas-yn Cefn (**Cefnmeiriadog**) continues to be occupied by the eleventh baronet, David Watkin Williams-Wynn (b.1940).

WILLINGTON WORTHENBURY (Wrddymbre), Wrexham (2146 ha; 730 inhabitants)

Constituting the north-western part of **Maelor Saesneg**, the **community**'s fertile land sustains two small villages – Worthenbury and Tallarn Green. St Deiniol's church, Worthenbury (1739) is the most complete 18th-century church in Wales. Tallarn Green has a church, vicarage, almshouse and mansion built by the Kenyon family (*see* **Hanmer**). In the 1280s, the **Shropshire** knight Roger de Puleston settled at Emral, near Worthenbury. His descendant, Robert, married Lowri, sister of **Owain Glyndŵr**, and Robert joined the **Glyndŵr Revolt**. John Puleston (d.1659) built Worthenbury vicarage for Philip Henry (*see* **Bronington**) – its grounds contain a promising **vineyard**.

Other members of the family included John Henry Puleston, treasurer (1880–1907) of the National **Eisteddfod** Association and **David Lloyd George**'s **Conservative** opponent in 1892, and the popular blind **preacher John Puleston Jones**. The Puleston family home, Emral Hall (1727), was demolished in 1936. It contained a remarkable barrel-vaulted ceiling depicting the labours of Hercules, which was purchased by **Clough Williams-Ellis** for £13 and installed at Portmeirion (**Penrhyndeudraeth**). In 2001, 88.81% of the community's inhabitants had no knowledge at all of **Welsh**, making it, linguistically, the most Anglicized of the communities of the **county borough** of **Wrexham**.

WILLOWS, Ernest [Thompson] (1886–1926)
Airship pioneer

'The father of British airships', as Ernest Willows became known, was born in **Cardiff**. From 1905 – although untrained technically – he built six airships, developing a new steering method. His longest flight, in 1910, was in the Willows III, *The City of Cardiff*, from **London** to Paris. Although financially unsuccessful, Willows combined determination with ingenuity, and holds a secure place in **aviation** history. He and four passengers died in a spherical balloon disaster in Bedford. Willows School on Pengam Moors, the site from 1930 to 1954 of Cardiff's Municipal **Airport**, commemorates him.

WILSON, Richard (1713–82) Painter

Richard Wilson is the most distinguished painter Wales has ever produced and the first fully to appreciate the aesthetic possibilities of the landscape of his native country.

Richard Wilson, painted in Rome by Anton Raphael Mengs

He is considered to be the father of landscape **painting** in **Britain** and the precursor of Constable and **Turner**.

Richard Wilson was the son of an enlightened clergyman of Penegoes (**Cadfarch, Montgomeryshire**), who encouraged the boy's interest in art, while giving him a thorough classical **education**. His mother was a native of Leeswood and was a distant relation of prominent **gentry** families, the **Mostyn family** among them. Through the assistance of a relation, Sir George Wynne, Wilson went to **London** in 1729 and became the apprentice of an obscure artist, Thomas Wright. He became a skilful portraitist, but the turning point in his life was his visit to Italy in 1750. Inspired by the landscapes of the French painter Claude Lorraine (?1604–92), he combined a complete mastery of the grand style of painting with a love of nature and a regard for classical antiquity.

By 1757, Wilson had returned to London, and the following decade proved particularly prosperous for him. He continued to paint Italianate landscapes and landscapes based upon classical **literature**. His painting *The Destruction of the Children of Niobe* (*c.*1759–60) won special acclaim and he had many commissions from wealthy families seeking classical portrayals of their estates.

In 1768, Wilson was one of the 34 artists who founded the Royal Academy, and one of his apprentices in this period was **Thomas Jones** (1742–1803). Those years were also the period when he painted his best-known Welsh landscapes, among them *Snowdon from Llyn Nantlle* (two versions, *c.*1765–6 and *c.*1765–7) and *Cader Idris, Llyn y Cau* (*c.*1765–7). These paintings reflected the increasing interest in ancient Britain, and it is likely that Wilson embraced the same kind of British-Welsh patriotism as that which inspired the founders of the **Cymmrodorion**

(1751). Indeed, two of the presidents of that society, William Vaughan (*see* **Vaughan family (Cors y Gedol)**) and Watkin **Williams Wynn**, were among the purchasers of his Welsh landscapes.

In the 1770s, his prospects went into decline; he took to the bottle and was wracked with illness and poverty. His popularity as an artist declined, because, argues David H. Solkin, the leading Wilson specialist, of his inability to appeal to the taste of the emerging middle **class**es. In 1776, he was appointed librarian of the Royal Academy. In 1781, his failing **health** caused him to seek refuge among family members at **Mold**. In the following year he died at Colomendy (**Llanferres**) and was buried in the churchyard of St Mary's church, Mold. (In 1851, two lamentably poor *englynion* were carved on his tomb, verses which were the fruit of a competition organized by the Mold **Cymreigyddion**.) Shortly after his death, his achievement was reassessed and he came to be seen as a pioneer of **Romanticism** and as the precursor of the numerous painters who, from the 1790s onwards, portrayed the landscape of Wales.

WINDMILLS

Windmills first appeared in Wales during the 1260s, some 80 years after their probable invention in **England** or Flanders. The earliest windmills were small timber-framed structures, pivoted upon a stout oak post, which could be turned to face into the wind. By the 16th century, these were being replaced by small stone-built cylindrical tower mills. Later towers were taller and tapered. Most windmills were found in exposed areas such as **Anglesey**, and in the **limestone** cornlands of the south and the north-east, although even there they were far less numerous than **watermills**. Only the restored Llynon windmill at Llanddeusant (**Tref Alaw**), Anglesey, still operates.

A few windmills were used to drive farm machinery – winnowers, chaffers and threshing machines. Industrial applications included water pumps, ochre crushers for paint manufacture, oak bark crushers for the tanning industry and timber saws. The few surviving ruined shells are overwhelmed in size and number by the hundreds of electricity wind turbines – or 'cash-generators' as their critics call them – that began their controversial proliferation in upland areas towards the end of the 20th century (*see* **Energy**). Following the **oil** crisis of the mid-1970s, concerns about nuclear power and the decline in fossil fuels, experimental wind turbines were erected at Burry Port (**Pembrey and Burry Port**). By 2006, Wales had 24 wind farms capable of producing 300.60 MW of electricity. The most productive of them was Cefn Croes completed in 2005 (*see* **Pontarfynach**). The largest collection of turbines is at **Llandinam**, although its 104 turbines are far smaller than the 39 at Cefn Croes. There are others at **Llangwyryfon** and in exposed parts of Anglesey and **Glamorgan**. In 2004, Wales had 36% of all the United Kingdom turbines; as Wales consists only of 8.5% of the area of the United Kingdom, the concentration of windmills within its boundaries is a tribute to Wales's potential as a site of wind power. Offshore wind turbines are visible from the north-eastern coast, and the construction of others off **Porthcawl** and in Cardigan Bay is under discussion.

WINDSOR-CLIVE family (earls of Plymouth)
Landowners

The family became associated with Wales in 1730 when Other Windsor, third earl of Plymouth, married Elizabeth, heiress of the Lewis family of Fan, **Caerphilly**. The earldom became extinct on the death of the eighth earl in 1843, but was revived in 1905 in favour of Robert Windsor-Clive, grandson of Harriet Windsor and her husband Robert Clive, son of the earl of Powis. By the late 19th century, the family owned some 16,000 ha of land, half in **England** and half in Wales. The Welsh estates included considerable holdings in Llanwonno (**Ynysybwl and Coed-y-cwm**) and Eglwysilan (**Caerphilly**) and valuable land at Grangetown (**Cardiff**) and **Penarth,** where the Windsor-Clive impact on urban development is unmistakable. Much of the family's wealth was spent at St Fagans (Cardiff), where it had total dominance and where for three generations after 1850 a model estate and aristocratic household were maintained. In 1947, the third earl (of the second creation) gave St Fagans Castle and its park to the **National Museum [of] Wales** as the site for what became the National History Museum (*see* **St Fagans**).

WINEFRIDE (Gwenffrewi, Gwenfrewi or Winefred; 7th century) 'Saint'

Winefride is chiefly associated with **Holywell**, where her holy **well**, reputed to heal sick pilgrims, is considered to be one of the **'seven wonders of Wales'**. According to medieval Lives of Winefride, she was decapitated by a local prince called Caradog ab Alawog because she refused to have sexual intercourse with him, and a miraculous healing well issued forth from the pool of saintly blood spilled on the ground. Winefride was resurrected by St **Beuno** and later became abbess of a community of nuns at Gwytherin (**Llangernyw**). Her **relics** were moved to Shrewsbury Priory in 1138. Winefride's feast day is 3 November.

WINSTONE, Howard (1939–2000) Boxer

One of the most elegant, cultured and determined of British post-war boxers, Winstone was born in **Merthyr Tydfil**, of Welsh, **Irish** and **Jew**ish extraction. The loss, in a factory accident, of three fingertips on his right hand meant that he was never a great puncher but, trained by his neighbour **Eddie Thomas**, he won gold at the 1957 **Commonwealth Games** and then the Amateur **Boxing** Association championship. He turned professional after completing national service in 1959 and was undefeated British and European featherweight champion (1961–8). During these years, it emerged that Winstone was the second-best featherweight in the world, for he lost three times to the great southpaw Vicente Saldivar of Mexico, although most commentators thought that the Welsh fighter should have been given the verdict in **Cardiff** in 1967. Following Saldivar's retirement, Winstone won the world championship in 1968 by defeating Mitsunori Seki of Japan; but now clearly past his best and experiencing weight difficulties, he lost it to Jose Legra later in the same year. Always a modest champion and a model professional sportsman, he represented everything that was best in the sport.

WISTON (Cas-wis), Pembrokeshire
(4421 ha; 848 inhabitants)

Located in the heart of **Pembrokeshire**, north-east of **Haverfordwest**, the **community** contains the villages of Wiston, Clarbeston, Clarbeston Road and Walton East. Wiston Castle was originally built as a motte-and-bailey construction by a **Fleming**, Wizo (d. pre-1130), who seized much of the *cantref* of **Daugleddau**. After being all but destroyed by **Llywelyn ap Iorwerth** in 1220, Henry III ordered its rebuilding. What remains is an extensive bailey and a high motte, crowned with the remains of a shell keep. From the **Acts of 'Union'** until 1918, Wiston was one of the **boroughs** constituting the **Pembroke** Boroughs parliamentary constituency. St Mary's church, Wiston, retains some medieval features. In 1645, **Rowland Laugharne** defeated a Royalist force at Colby Moor. Penty Park, originally 1710, was one of the seats of the **Philipps family** of Picton Castle. Clarbeston Road developed around the **railway** junction where the line to **Fishguard** joins that to **Milford Haven**.

WITCHES and *DYNION HYSBYS* (Wise men)

For centuries, many Welsh believed, like other Europeans, in the power of witches. A **woman** could become a witch by giving communion bread to the first animal she saw after leaving church. When animals were sick, or crops withered, or milk failed to churn or a family suffered illness and misfortune, a witch was often blamed. Upsetting a witch or refusing her when she came begging might lead to bewitching. Witches cursed by making wax images and piercing them with pins while reciting charms. They could change their shape into that of a **hare** and if the animal was

Howard Winstone, featherweight world champion, 1968

wounded, then an identical wound, it was said, would be found on the witch's body when she returned to human form. It was believed that a piece of rowan, carried in the pocket or tied to a whip, could protect people from becoming bewitched; the baby's cradle and vessels for the dairy were made from this wood. Salt, **iron** and a stone with a natural hole in it were believed to keep witches at bay. A curse could be lifted, it was claimed, by bleeding the witch or getting her to bless the object bewitched.

In the Middle Ages, the right to punish witches belonged to the lord of the **manor** and to the Church, but between 1563 and 1736 witches were dealt with by the courts. The first **execution** of a Welsh witch occurred in 1594; she was Gwen ferch Ellis of **Llandyrnog**. Later, two sisters, Lowri and Agnes ferch Evan of **Llanbedrog**, and their brother, Rhydderch ab Evan of **Llannor**, were found guilty of murdering Margaret Hughes through witchcraft, and of causing her sister Mary to be lame and dumb; all three were hanged. There were other similar cases. However, a high proportion of those accused of witchcraft received not-guilty verdicts, and Wales did not experience the anti-witch hysteria that occurred in **Scotland** and New England.

A readier antidote to witchcraft was provided by the *dyn hysbys* (wise man or wizard), also known as *consuriwr* (conjuror), *swynwr* (charmer) or *dewin* (magician). *Dynion hysbys*, trained either by family members or through apprenticeship to reputable practitioners, performed various roles in their communities, in addition to breaking a witch's curse and safeguarding people. They were finders of lost objects, they placed a disclosing mark on thieves, they sold charms written on paper to protect property from being bewitched and to heal sick animals, and they predicted future events.

Welsh women in traditional costume, *c.*1900

The most famous *dyn hysbys* was Dr John Harris (1785–1839) of Cwrtycadno (**Cynwyl Gaeo**), who learned his art from books. Others, such as the *dynion hysbys* of Troed-y-Lôn (**Llangurig**) inherited the art from their forefathers. Such beliefs and practices survived in some parts of Wales well into the 20th century.

WOLVES

Remains from Pontnewydd **cave** in the Elwy valley (**Cefnmeiriadog**) prove the wolf's presence in Wales during an interglacial period 250,000 years ago. Principal ancestor of the domestic **dog**, the wolf reappeared in **Neolithic** times after the latest glacial retreat. It remained a well-known, if not numerous, animal throughout the historic period, as testified by the Welsh **laws**, by *blaidd* and wolf **place names** and by stories such as 'Culhwch ac Olwen' in *The Mabinogion*. In 1136, Florence of Worcester noted that wolves had feasted upon the bodies of **Norman** knights killed in **Gower** and, in a satirical poem by Ieuan ap Tudur Penllyn (fl.1475–1500), the poet claims that a wolf had eaten his father's genitals.

Although there is no reliable evidence as to the date of the wolf's extinction in Wales, it is likely that, owing to the wild and remote nature of much of the land, it survived in Wales for some time after its extinction in **England** at the beginning of the 17th century. In **Glascwm**, however, there was a tradition that Wales's last wolf was killed at Cregrina during the reign of Elizabeth I.

WOLFSCASTLE (Cas-blaidd), Pembrokeshire (2251 ha; 626 inhabitants)

Bisected by the **Haverfordwest–Fishguard road** (the A40) and halfway between the two towns, the **community**'s main feature is the Treffgarne Gorge through which flows the Western **Cleddau**. There is a **Neolithic** burial chamber at Garn Turne. The setting of the **Iron Age hill-fort** on Treffgarne Rocks is much enhanced by the weird shapes of the eroded rocks. The ruins of a 12th-century motte-and-bailey castle stand at the confluence of the Anghof with the Western Cleddau.

Joseph Harris (1773–1825), editor of *Seren Gomer,* the first **newspaper** in the **Welsh language**, was born in St Dogwells (Llantyddewi). St Dogwells' church (13th and 14th century), contains a memorial to Admiral Thomas Tucker (d.1766), a scourge of pirates (*see* **Piracy**). He lived at Sealyham (18th century), later the home of John Edwardes, who developed a breed of **dog** bearing the name of the house. In 2003, the investigation of the remains of a substantial **Roman** villa, originally discovered in 1806, contributed to growing speculation that Romano-British culture spread much further into the south-west of Wales than was previously thought.

WOMEN

In the history of Wales, as in that of most countries, the role of women has been marginalized. Of the entries in *The Dictionary of Welsh Biography*, a mere 1.8% are those of women, and of those chosen in a 2004 ballot for the hundred greatest heroes of the Welsh people, only nine were women. Nevertheless, the earliest evidence indicates that women were held in high regard. **Celt**ic religious tradition

Wives and daughters of striking Aberdare miners taking home coal from the tips in 1910

honoured goddesses such as Epona, Andraste and Brigit. **Roman** sources describe powerful female rulers in **Britain** – Boudicca and Cartimandua (AD 43–70) among them – and the **Celtic Church** in Wales provided an honourable role for holy women. However, with the growth of patriarchal Christianity, religious and lay authority became a masculine preserve. (**Gwenllian ferch Gruffudd ap Cynan**, who led an army against the **Normans** at **Kidwelly** in 1136, may have been a throwback to Boudicca.)

As elsewhere in Europe, the women of medieval Wales took their status from their father or, after marriage, from their husband. Under Welsh **law**, a woman could neither own land nor transfer rights in land to her children. However, the status of women under Welsh law was in some ways higher than it was under other legal systems of Europe. A daughter was not wholly without rights in the face of the authority of the father, as was the case in those countries that had inherited Roman law, and a husband did not gain unrestricted control over his wife's property, as he did under English law. The wife was entitled to some degree of compensation if her husband were unfaithful to her; if she in turn were unfaithful, her fate was less appalling than it was in most of the countries of Europe. For medieval Welsh rulers, marriage to highborn women – that of **Llywelyn ap Gruffudd** to Elinor de **Montfort**, for example – was central to their status. Among the lords of the **March**, it was marriages with heiresses that made and unmade the territories of families such as the **Clares** and **Mortimers**. With the decay of Welsh law, the women of Wales came increasingly to be subject to the same legal provisions as the women of **England**, a process that virtually came to completion through the **Acts of 'Union'**.

The centrality of marriage to the amassing of landed estates became more marked in the post-'Union' years, with upper-**class** women considered primarily as pawns in the battle to elevate a family's possessions and influence. Women of the lower orders had a more direct economic role. Sharing with men in agricultural tasks, a trading role often gave them control of the purse – a source of power within a developing cash **economy**. Before marriage, many were in agricultural or domestic service, but received less than half the male wage rate. Apprenticeships were restricted to boys, although spinsters – those who spun thread – were predominantly female. Some women invoked the supernatural in beneficial acts as white **witches** but, despite the fine line between this and the black arts – according to the authorities – during the 16th to 18th centuries, prosecution for witchcraft was less severe in Wales than in parts of England and **Scotland**.

Marriage was the norm, but independent unmarried women were perceptible by the mid-17th century. Among the well-born, property considerations dominated over **love**, but contemporary correspondence often reveals genuine tenderness. Some women emphasized physical attraction and, in the 17th century, **Puritan** influence elevated the role of individual will. The lower orders had greater freedom in choosing a marriage partner but, as couples were expected to survive as independent households, marriage was (in theory) postponed until sufficient assets had been acquired. Yet, as up to half the wives gave birth within fewer than nine months of the wedding, it would appear that the time of marriage was not always determined by prudence.

Childbearing frequently caused early death and it was common for women to marry widowers far older than themselves. During the 18th century, polite society demanded more refined masculine behaviour, a trend encouraged by philanthropic organizations and by the Methodists (*see* **Methodist Revival**) who were concerned to improve marital behaviour among the poor. These developments, along with the rise of **Romanticism**, helped to counter the disparaging references to the morals of Welsh women made by English satirists. Nevertheless, comments on their morals in the infamous **Education** Report of 1847 (*see* **Treason of the Blue Books**) received extensive publicity. Their advancement was the aim of the **periodical** *Y Gymraes* (1850–1), edited by **Evan Jones** (Ieuan Gwynedd) and financed by Lady Llanover (**Augusta Hall**). A similar task was undertaken by *Y Frythones* (1878–91) and *Y Gymraes* (1896–1934), publications that paid particular attention to the **temperance movement**, in which women were disproportionately represented.

With the onset of industrialization, women found employment in metalworking and **coal** extraction, becoming especially prominent in the **copper** and **tinplate** industries. The prohibition of underground work by females in 1842 caused grave hardships to families with numerous daughters. As coalmining, Wales's chief industry, offered virtually no employment to women, the concept of work was redefined in almost exclusively masculine terms – a

21st century women: working on an electronics assembly line in Pencoed

marked contrast with places such as the Lancashire mill towns, where paid employment for women was abundant. However, unpaid women's employment was abundant in the developing coalmining communities, where the absence of pit-head baths meant that the task of ensuring that the family home and the family's menfolk attained a decent level of cleanliness involved almost ceaseless labour – an issue on which **Elizabeth Andrews** was particularly vocal. Lack of female paid employment coincided with a patriarchal ideology which stressed the role of women in the private sphere of the home and the ideal of the 'angel of the hearth', giving rise to the stereotype of the stoic '**Welsh Mam**', much featured in periodicals, novels and, later, in **films**. The central role of coalmining in the Welsh economy meant that Wales exported women and imported men. As a result, it became the sole country in Europe in which females represented less than half the **population** – the situation revealed by the censuses of 1881, 1891, 1901, 1911 and 1921.

Lack of employment opportunities in industrial Wales caused girls to be more eager than boys to attain educational qualifications. Until the late 19th century, girls of all classes had received virtually no **education** beyond training in domestic virtues. With the growth of secondary schools from the 1890s onwards, girls seized their opportunity and female teachers became one of Wales's leading exports. Further openings came during the **First World War**, as women replaced men joining the armed forces. By then, Wales had a significant number of politically assertive women – the membership of the **Cardiff** branch of the Women's Suffrage Society was the highest in Britain outside **London**. The suffrage movement won a partial victory in 1918, when women over 30 gained the vote. They obtained the same voting rights as men in 1928, the year in which women became the majority of the electorate in every constituency apart from those within the southern coalfield. In 1929, **Megan Lloyd George**, elected in **Anglesey**, became Wales's first female MP. (Between 1929 and the 1990s, a further three women won Welsh seats – a poor record indeed.)

Other interwar advances included the appointment of women magistrates and barristers, the acknowledgement that the authority of mothers was equal to that of fathers, the acceptance that women had the same rights to property as men, and the demise of the prissy image of femininity promoted in the Victorian era. Even more significant was the tentative spread of family planning techniques; between 1921 and 1931, the birth rate in Wales per 1000 inhabitants declined from 25.2 to 16.7, thus reducing the number of women exhausted by child carrying and rearing. Yet, too much should not be claimed. The interwar years saw little advance in women's employment, their wages were generally half those of men, women were routinely dismissed when they got married, and in households dependent upon the dole, women would half starve themselves to ensure that their husbands and children were adequately fed.

The **Second World War** brought economic salvation to many, with hundreds of thousands of women working in the munitions factories (*see* **Royal Ordnance Factories**) or serving in the armed forces. Following the war,

Rhymney Valley women marching in support of their community's miners during the 1984–5 miners' strike

employment opportunities for women expanded dramatically and, by the end of the 20th century, almost half the Welsh workforce was female. The increase in female paid employment, the universal availability of contraceptive devices and the rise of an assertive feminist movement – which, admittedly, was slow to strike roots in Wales – transformed concepts of sexual morality and undermined traditional notions of the family. Although Welsh women still suffer considerable disadvantages, over the last century their economic and political status has undergone changes which are truly revolutionary.

In the elections to the **National Assembly** held in May 2003, Wales set a world record when the 60-strong Assembly became the first governing body with equal numbers of men and women. Increasing by five the number of women members, the Assembly overtook the Swedish parliament, where women accounted for 45.3% of members.

WOMEN'S INSTITUTES

The first **Women**'s Institute (WI) in **Britain** was established in 1915 at **Llanfair Pwllgwyngyll**, after Madge Watt, founder of the WI in Canada, addressed a meeting of the north Wales branch of the Agricultural Organization Society. The first meetings were held in a member's home; it was not until after the **First World War** that the group moved into the corrugated-**iron** hut that still stands in the

village. Within a month of Llanfair PG forming, five further branches had formed: **Cefn**, **Trefnant**, Chwilog, Glasfryn (both **Llanystumdwy**) and **Criccieth**; by the end of 1915, the first branches in **England** had been formed.

The largest voluntary organization for women in Wales, and indeed the United Kingdom, the WI offers opportunities for women to participate in community life, cultural projects and public campaigns. In 1967, however, members of the Parc (**Llanycil**) WI led a breakaway movement to form the fully **Welsh**-medium **Merched y Wawr**. In 2006, the WI in Wales had 500 branches and 16,000 members.

WOOD family Musicians and storytellers

The **parish** register of **Llangelynin** notes the death of Abram Wood, 'a travelling Egyptian', in 1799. There is little information concerning Abram, but so numerous were his descendants in mid and north Wales that the phrase *Teulu Abram Wood* (Abram Wood's Family) became synonymous with 'Gypsy' or **Romany**. In the 19th century, members of the family won prominence as **harp**ists and fiddlers on the basis of their skill in the **music** of their adopted country. One of the grandsons of Abram was Jeremiah Wood (*c.*1778–1867) – Jerry Bach Gogerddan – the harpist at Gogerddan (**Trefeurig**), and John Wood Jones (1800–44), the harpist of Lady Llanover (**Augusta Hall**), was his great-grandson. The most famous of his

An *Illustrated London News* engraving of John Roberts and his sons playing their harps before Queen Victoria at Palé Hall, Llandderfel, 1889

descendants was **John Roberts** (1816–94), Telynor Cymru (The Harpist of Wales), who collected much of the family lore. It was among the Wood family that **John Sampson** collected the greater part of the material for his study of the Romanies and the Romany language. Sampson's greatest source for Romany legends was Matthew Wood (1845–1929), who ended his life in **Bala**. His son, Howel (1882–1967), was one of the last of the family to speak Romany; his dancing ability gave him a role in the **film The Last Days of Dolwyn** (1949).

WOOD, Alan (1910–92) Geologist
Professor of **geology** at **Aberystwyth** (1947–77), Alan Wood, a **Liverpool** graduate, had numerous interests. He created the first school of micropalaeontology in the **University of Wales**, and his geomorphological knowledge led both to the initiation of marine studies and, with **A. W. Woodland**, to the siting of a deep borehole at Mochras (**Llanbedr**) in 1967. The resulting rock cores, revealing a wholly unexpected sequence of strata, transformed the understanding of the geological development of Wales.

WOODCARVING
The ancient **Celtic** stone crosses had their equivalents in timber, but the earliest extant woodcarving is found adorning the numerous 15th and 16th-century oak rood screens that have survived in remote locations. Elaborate examples are found at **Llangwm** Uchaf (**Monmouthshire**), Patrisio (**Vale of Grwyney**), Llananno (**Llanbadarn Fynydd**) and **Llanegryn**. In these churches, dragons and wyverns, and intertwining vines, oak leaves and water plants crowd each space in free and inventive patterns. Equal in quality and far more monumental is the 15th-century Sleeping Jesse in St Mary's church, **Abergavenny**, carved from a single oak.

Carving with armorial, zoomorphic and more purely decorative themes developed during the 16th and 17th centuries, and survives in the sumptuous panelling at Gregynog (**Tregynon**) and Gwydir (**Trefriw**), and in **furniture** at the National History Museum (*see* **St Fagans**).

In the 18th and 19th centuries, a vibrant tradition characterized rural life, with everyday objects, such as butter stamps and walking sticks, being ornamented in both traditional and innovative styles. Pre-eminent among such items was what became known by the 1930s as the **lovespoon**, whittled out of hedgerow timber into intricate shapes and designs. In the architectural use of wood, the most distinguished practitioner was **John Douglas** (1830–1911); houses and churches in the north-east offer numerous examples of his superb craftsmanship, which was derived from Jacobean furniture.

In the late 19th and early 20th centuries, woodcarving was fostered by local competitions, including *eisteddfodau*, for which gifted amateurs and professional carpenters, such as William Llewellyn Morris of Derwydd (**Llandybie**), were encouraged to produce furniture, especially ceremonial chairs, and small decorative objects carved with traditional **designs**. The cabinet maker Thomas John of **Cowbridge** was responsible for intricate carvings at **Cardiff** Castle, aided by a local team that included his two sons, the younger of whom, **William Goscombe John**, became Wales's foremost sculptor (*see* **Sculpture**).

WOODLAND, A[ustin] W[illiam] (1914–90)
Geologist

Born in **Mountain Ash** and educated at **Aberystwyth**, A. W. Woodland spent virtually the whole of his career with the Geological Survey of Great **Britain** (later the British Geological Survey), graduating from field geologist to director (*see* **Geology**). He was described as the 'doyen of the south Wales **coal**field geologists', on the basis of his 1950s survey, with W. B. Evans, of the **Pontypridd** and **Maesteg** districts, which included a reappraisal of the mining prospects of the southern part of the coalfield. The accolade was confirmed by his service as geological assessor at the **Aberfan disaster** tribunal of 1966–7.

WOODS, Stephen [Esslemont] (1912–94)
Metallurgist

Scientists who develop important industrial processes are rarely well known. Stephen Woods played a major part in developing the efficient blast-furnace production of zinc and **lead** as an alternative to electrolysis. Born and brought up in **Cardiff**, he completed a doctorate at **Oxford** before joining the research team of the Imperial Smelting Corporation in Avonmouth. He pioneered a series of improvements in the smelting process that greatly enhanced the **energy** and economic efficiency of furnaces. He was elected FRS in 1974.

WOODSTOCK, Treaty of (1247)

The treaty, concluded on 30 April 1247 between Henry III and Owain ap Gruffudd (d.*c.*1282) and **Llywelyn ap Gruffudd**, princes of **Gwynedd**, marked the highest point of the power of the English crown in Wales before the **Edwardian conquest** of 1282. The two princes agreed to hold Gwynedd west of the **Conwy** by military service, the first time that such a condition had been imposed on Gwynedd. The lands between the Conwy and the **Clwyd** were ceded to the crown. At the time, the position of Gwynedd was particularly weak and the brothers had no choice but to accept these humiliating terms.

WOOLLEN INDUSTRY, The

For much of the last 2000 years, woollen manufacture has been one of Wales's most important activities. In the 20th century, however, the industry declined drastically, and by the early 21st century there were fewer centres of production than at any time in the preceding six centuries.

In the Middle Ages, woollen manufacturing was particularly important in what is now **Pembrokeshire**, where the inhabitants – both those of Welsh and of Flemish ancestry (*see* **Flemings**) – spun yarn and wove cloth in their cottages and farmhouses. They worked the wool of local **sheep** primarily to provide themselves with blankets and rugs, tweeds and flannels. On occasion, they produced a surplus, which was sold at one of the many local fairs, or taken by **ship** to Bristol. From there, Welsh cloth was re-exported at considerable profit, especially to Gascony, **Brittany**, Portugal and Iceland. Despite the importance of the trade, the cloth was of poor quality. Designed more for hard wear than for appearance, it was thick, rough and drab; in English cities, it was deemed a suitable Ash Wednesday gift to the poor.

By the late 16th century, the decline in the demand for Pembrokeshire cloth had led to the virtual extinction of the industry in the **county**. The centre of cloth making in Wales moved to **Merioneth**, **Denbighshire** and **Montgomeryshire**. The trade was organized in the English **border** towns, especially in Shrewsbury, whose Drapers' Company sought to monopolize it. In 1624, parliament legislated against such a monopoly, but the weavers of Wales, isolated and lacking in capital as they were, failed to create structures that would have given them control over their industry.

By the 18th century, pre-eminence in flannel manufacture had been won by Montgomeryshire, and **Llanidloes**, **Newtown** and **Llanbrynmair** had become heavily dependent on textiles. **Agricultural labourers**, hired at the November fairs, were chosen as much for their weaving abilities as for their farming skills; employed in the fields from spring to autumn, they were expected to work at the loom in the weaving shed in the winter.

Initially a proto-industrial activity carried out in scattered farmsteads, flannel making was, by 1790s, becoming increasing centralized, especially at Newtown which was developing into one of Wales's most important manufacturing towns. The county flannel exchange (now the town leisure centre), erected in 1832, was the location of the weekly market at which local weavers met drapers from **Liverpool** and Shrewsbury, **London** and Manchester. In 1821, the Montgomeryshire **Canal** reached Newtown, enabling flannel to be transported to Manchester for 2s 11d (14–15 pence) per hundredweight (112 lbs or 51 kg).

As the town had 82 weaving factories and 35 spinning mills, it attracted a large number of immigrants, especially from Yorkshire and Lancashire. Welsh flannel was cheap; worn by the duke of Wellington's army as well as by **North American** slaves (*see* **Slavery**), it was known over much of the world. Four-storeyed buildings in Newtown and Llanidloes still bear witness to the importance of flannel in the history of Montgomeryshire. A weaving factory, occupying the third and fourth floors – and accessible via an outside staircase at the back of the terrace – stretched over dwellings occupying the first two storeys. Such factories could accommodate at least 10 looms. Frequently, their owners also owned shops. Those with large families were preferred as employees, for they would be better customers at the employer's shop. Weavers were paid an average wage of 11 shillings (55 pence) for a six-day week, much of which would be retained by the employer as payment for goods bought at his shop.

Montgomeryshire could have developed into one of the most important **textile** manufacturing districts in **Britain** had the county contained **coal** to fuel steam-powered looms and had not **road**, **railway** and canal links facilitated the swamping of mid Wales by the products of the coal-rich textile centres of Lancashire. Ill-advisedly, the Montgomeryshire manufacturers attempted to compete on the terms of the manufacturers of Lancashire and Yorkshire; in consequence, Montgomeryshire flannel could be indistinguishable from Rochdale imitations. By 1860, the industry was in serious difficulties, with bankruptcy rife and unemployment widespread. There was a slight revival in the 1870s, following the foundation in Newtown of the world's first mail order business. Sir Pryce

Pryce-Jones established the Royal Welsh Warehouse to sell the products of his two flannel mills, but he soon found that it was far cheaper for him to buy 'real Welch flannel' made in Rochdale. By 1900, the Montgomeryshire woollen industry was virtually moribund, and Newtown was reverting to being no more than a modest market town.

While the Montgomeryshire weaving industry was declining, that in the **Teifi** valley was expanding – and by the early 21st century, to the extent the industry survived at all, it survived in that valley. By the 1890s, **Cardiganshire**, **Carmarthenshire** and Pembrokeshire had 250 woollen mills, with Drefach-Felindre (**Llangeler**) alone having 23 mills in full production. In Drefach and in neighbouring villages, life revolved around the factory and the production of flannel shirts, underwear and blankets for the burgeoning southern coalfield, where the colliers appreciated the qualities of *brethyn cartref*.

The golden era lasted until the end of the **First World War**. Following the war, **government** surplus stocks of flannel and blankets were thrown on the market at absurdly low prices – unfair competition which forced woollen manufacturers to reduce costs and prices. Wages were cut and hundreds of workers were dismissed in a losing battle to make ends meet. Since the 1920s, the story of the Welsh woollen industry has been one of contraction, with the number of mills decreasing from 250 in 1926 to 81 in 1947 and to a mere half dozen at the opening of the 21st century. The industry is commemorated at the National Wool Museum at Drefach-Felindre (*see* **National Museum [of] Wales**).

WOOLLER, Wilfred (1912–97)
Rugby player, cricketer and cricket administrator
A dominant figure in Welsh sport for over half a century, Wooller was born in **Rhos-on-Sea** and first became famous as a schoolboy **rugby** player picked to play against **England** in 1933. His career with **Cambridge** University, Sale, **Cardiff** and Wales, as a forceful, individualist centre, brought him 18 caps and 6 international tries. But he is chiefly remembered for 2 tries he did not score – bad bounces resulting in wing Geoffrey Rees-Jones scoring, rather than Wooller himself, after twice breaking and kicking ahead in Wales's victory over **New Zealand** in 1935.

After the **Second World War**, and three years in Japanese captivity, he took over in 1947 as captain and secretary of **Glamorgan** County Cricket Club, leading the team to its first championship in 1948. Captain until 1960, he scored 13,593 runs and took 958 wickets; he continued his brand of fearless, abrasive autocracy as secretary until 1978.

WORKERS' EDUCATIONAL ASSOCIATION, The
The Workers' Educational Association, which owes its existence to the vision of Albert Mansbridge (1876–1952), was founded in **England** in 1903. The first class in Wales, at **Barry** in 1906, led to the founding of the South Wales District in 1906. Originally, the district had an ad hoc administration but, in 1911, John Thomas was appointed full-time secretary and, in 1915, **D. Lleufer Thomas** became president. In 1919, an all-Wales district was established; in

1925, this was divided into southern and northern districts. From 1919 to 1937, the south was the responsibility of **John Davies** (1882–1937), a dedicated **socialist** who ensured that the organization not only survived but flourished during the rigours of the interwar **depression**. R. [Silyn] Roberts, northern organizer 1925–30, was succeeded by his wife Mary, organizer 1930–51 (*see* **Robert Roberts and Mary Roberts**).

The aim of the WEA was to provide adults with a liberal **education**; history and economics were among the most popular subjects in the early years. The movement's magazine in Wales, *Lleufer* (meaning 'light', but also commemorating D. Lleufer Thomas), became an important **periodical** under the inspired editorship of **David Thomas** (1880–1967). In 1993, the WEA's North and South Wales Districts became independent of the central body in **London** and, in 2001, the North Wales District merged with **Coleg Harlech**. Several of the leading figures in the Wales of the early 21st century – Rhodri Morgan and Neil Kinnock among them – began their careers as WEA lecturers.

WORKS SCHOOLS
As Wales became dominated by heavy industry, some employers in the 19th century made a significant contribution to the provision of elementary **education**. The concern to produce a better-educated workforce, with higher literacy and numeracy skills, led to schools being established in conjunction with **iron**works, **copper**works, **tinplate** works, collieries and **slate** quarries. Although the first charity works school was founded as early as 1700, it was not until the early 19th century that the movement gathered momentum; eventually, Wales had some 130 works schools, the great majority in **Glamorgan** and **Monmouthshire**. The basis on which they were founded was that the employer provided a building, while a levy was imposed on the workers' wages. This was usually about 1d a week; when accommodation was available, children of non-workers were admitted for 2d.

The works schools were one of the few aspects of educational provision in Wales praised by the authors of the 1847 education report (*see* **Treason of the Blue Books**). The most notable of the works schools was that established by Sir John **Guest** and his wife Lady Charlotte Guest at Dowlais (*see* **Merthyr Tydfil**). Begun in 1828, it eventually accommodated over 2000 pupils of all ages, ranging from infants to adults. After the Education Act of 1870, the works schools were gradually taken over by the school boards.

WREXHAM, County Borough (Bwrdeistref Sirol Wrecsam) (50,379 ha; 128,476 inhabitants)
In 1974, the industrial areas of the **Denbighshire** were combined with the two detached areas of **Flintshire** to form the **Wrexham-Maelor** District, one of the six districts of the new **county** of **Clwyd**. In 1996, the district, together with four **communities** of the former district of **Glyndŵr**, became the **county borough** of Wrexham. The community of **Llangollen Rural** was added in 1998. In 2001, 22.90% of the inhabitants of the county borough had some knowledge of **Welsh**, with 10.9% wholly fluent in the language. (*See also* **Ceiriog Ucha** and **Willington Worthenbury**.)

WREXHAM, Town of (Wrecsam, Tref)

(1332 ha; 41,276 inhabitants)

The town of Wrexham lies within the **communities** of Acton, Caia Park, Offa and Rhosddu (*see* below).

The first mention of Wrexham (or rather Wristlesham) occurs in the Pipe Roll of 1161 (*see* **Marchwiel**). Located after 1282 in the **march**er-lordship of **Bromfield and Yale**, whose caput was at **Holt**, Wrexham developed as a trading centre devoid of any military role. Its large church of St Giles, originally built in the early 14th century and remodelled between about 1480 and 1520, is evidence of Wrexham's growing prosperity. The use of the Legs of Man motif in the church suggests that the remodelling was initiated by the **Stanley family** (*see* Isle of **Man**). Its crowning glory is its tower – one of the **'seven wonders of Wales'** – which was inspired by that of Gloucester Cathedral. There is a replica of the tower at Yale University, which was endowed by Elihu **Yale** who is buried in St Giles churchyard.

Wrexham became a centre for religious radicals, **Morgan Llwyd** among them; during the **Civil Wars** it was one of the few places in Wales with Parliamentary sympathies. By the late 17th century, it was probably Wales's largest urban centre, although – consisting as it did of 12 **townships** – it was bereft of municipal **government** until 1857 when it attained **borough** status. From the mid-18th century onwards, Wrexham, already the market town for a rich agricultural area, became the centre of **Denbighshire**'s **coal** and metal industries. It also developed a reputation as a brewing centre. By the late 19th century, it had 19 breweries, including that of the Wrexham **Beer** Lager Company, which operated from 1883, until the demise of the industry in 2000. The town also played its part in the history of **printing and publishing** in Wales; a press was established there in 1820 by Richard Hughes (1794–1871), and continued by his son, Charles Hughes (1823–86), under the name Hughes a'i Fab. The literary **periodical** *Y Llenor* and the novels of **Daniel Owen** were amongst the publications of the company, which is now owned by **S4C**.

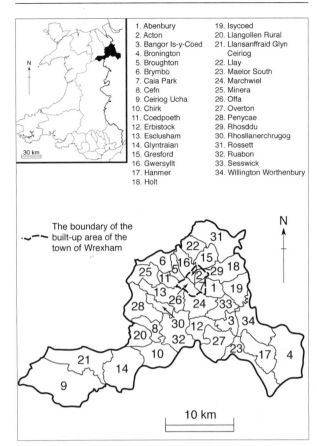

1. Abenbury	19. Isycoed
2. Acton	20. Llangollen Rural
3. Bangor Is-y-Coed	21. Llansantffraid Glyn
4. Bronington	Ceiriog
5. Broughton	22. Llay
6. Brymbo	23. Maelor South
7. Caia Park	24. Marchwiel
8. Cefn	25. Minera
9. Ceiriog Ucha	26. Offa
10. Chirk	27. Overton
11. Coedpoeth	28. Penycae
12. Erbistock	29. Rhosddu
13. Esclusham	30. Rhosllanerchrugog
14. Glyntraian	31. Rossett
15. Gresford	32. Ruabon
16. Gwersyllt	33. Sesswick
17. Hanmer	34. Willington Worthenbury
18. Holt	

The communities of the county borough of Wrexham

By the end of the 19th century, Wrexham's **population** was approaching 40,000, although only 15,000 lived within the borough's boundaries, which had been very tightly drawn. Its size found expression in its Hightown Barracks (1877; home of the **Royal Welch Fusiliers**), market halls, large banks and numerous places of worship – including Our Lady of Dolours, recognized in 1898 as the cathedral of the **Roman Catholic diocese** of Menevia. Yet, although by far the largest urban centre in northern Wales, Wrexham is not the location of any of the north's major institutions – the University College, for example, or the northern headquarters of the BBC in Wales. That may be because it was perceived to be an Anglicized **border** town; indeed, Wrexham's western boundary is 2 km east of **Offa's Dyke**. (In 2002, Wrexham was again snubbed over its claim to city status, a status that has been granted to all three of the major urban centres of the south.)

In the 20th century, the decline of Denbighshire's heavy industry proved a severe blow to Wrexham, although the town itself did not experience the appalling levels of unemployment suffered by the more outlying communities of the northern coalfield. Wrexham was fortunate in having an enlightened council, which proved to be the most progressive in Wales on matters such as slum clearance and the provision of council **housing**. In the later 20th century, the growth of service industries and general manufacturing, aided by Wrexham's accessibility, gave the town a considerable degree of prosperity. Wrexham has been especially fortunate in its historians, among them **A. N. Palmer**,

The chancel arch and wooden roof of St Giles's church, Wrexham

A. H. Dodd, Stanley Williamson and W. Alister Williams; through the work of the latter, Wrexham is the only place in Wales to have its own encyclopaedia (2001).

The communities of Wrexham

ACTON (Gwaunyterfyn) (344 ha; 12,960 inhabitants)
Constituting north-eastern Wrexham, the name recalls Acton Park, the birthplace in 1645 of the notorious Judge **Jeffreys**. The house, largely rebuilt in 1787, was demolished in 1956. Three of its lodges survive, as does the **lake** created in the 19th century. The much-esteemed Grove Park County School (1895–1983), which had developed from the Grove Academy (1823), was located alongside the old Chester Road.

CAIA PARK (Parc Caia) (282 ha; 11,882 inhabitants)
Constituting south-eastern Wrexham, the area contains the Queen's Park Housing Estate (1950 onwards), **Britain**'s earliest example of Radburn planning – a system conceived in Radburn, New Jersey, involving the segregation of vehicles and pedestrians (*see also* **Cwmbran**). Cefn Road was the original site of Cartrefle Training College, established in 1946. In 2000, its buildings became the home of Ysgol Morgan Llwyd, Wrexham's **Welsh**-medium secondary school founded in 1963. The southern part of the community is **National Trust** land bordering the Clywedog **River**. At King's Mills – the mills built in the 14th century to serve the township of Wrexham Regis – are a visitors' centre and the terminus of the Clywedog Way (*see* **Minera**).

OFFA (486 ha; 9852 inhabitants)
Constituting western Wrexham, the community also contains the town centre. The name recalls not the Dyke but the 19th-century mansion Bryn Offa. Lower Berse has 14th-century origins. Croesnewydd is a fine house built in 1696.

RHOSDDU (Rhos-ddu) (220 ha; 6582 inhabitants)
Constituting north-western Wrexham, the community contains Wrexham Garden Village. Founded in 1901, the village has a wealth of houses in an informal vernacular style. The Wrexham racecourse, established by the **Williams Wynn family** in 1807, was the location of the first match played by the Wrexham **Football** Club (1872). The racecourse has been the home of the club since 1887. Plas Coch is the main site of the **North East Wales Institute of Higher Education** (NEWI), a federation of colleges established in 1975.

WREXHAM-MAELOR (Wrecsam-Maelor)
One-time district
Following the abolition of **Denbighshire** and **Flintshire** in 1974, Wrexham-Maelor was created as one of the six districts of the new **county** of **Clwyd**. It consisted of what had been the **borough** of **Wrexham** and most of the **rural district** of Wrexham, in Denbighshire, and the rural district of **Maelor** and the detached **parish** of Marford and Horsley in Flintshire (*see* **Gresford**). In 1996, the district, together with four (later five) **communities** previously in the district of **Glyndŵr**, became **Wrexham County Borough**.

The Wye at Chepstow

WYATT family Architects
One of a large family of architects of Staffordshire origin, Benjamin Wyatt (1745–1818) became agent for Penrhyn (**Llandygai**) estate and had a practice in **Bangor**. In addition to works for Lord Penrhyn, he designed the Penrhyn Arms Hotel, Bangor, later the first home of the University College (**University of Wales, Bangor**). His older brother, Samuel (1737–1807), and younger brother, James (1746–1813), set up practices in **London** and designed a number of buildings in north Wales. Benjamin's son, Lewis William Wyatt (1777–1853), was born in Bangor, and, after studying at the Royal Academy and working for his uncles, set up his own practice in London, carrying out mainly country house commissions.

WYE (Gwy) River (209 km, 85 km wholly in Wales)
The Wye rises on the eastern slopes of **Pumlumon** (752 m) before flowing south-east to **Llangurig** and **Rhayader**. The Elan, with its remarkable series of **reservoirs**, joins the Wye south of Rhayader. The Ithon (Afon Ieithon), the Wye's chief Welsh tributary (60 km), which has its source south of **Newtown** in the **community** of **Kerry**, joins the Wye south of Newbridge-on-Wye (**Llanyre**). The Irfon, which rises near the source of the **Tywi**, joins the Wye at **Builth**. The Wye valley between Builth and **Hay** offers **river** scenery at its best. At Hay, the Wye flows into **England**; there, it receives water drained from the **Radnor Forest** carried by the Lugg (Afon Llugwy) and by its chief tributary, the Arrow (Afon Arwy). At **Crucorney**, one of the Wye's major tributaries, the Monnow (Afon Mynwy), forms the Wales–England **border**, a role undertaken by the Wye between **Monmouth** and the sea. The beauty of the lower Wye valley around **Tintern** was eulogized by William Wordsworth. The Wye flows into the Severn Sea at **Chepstow**, where the river is overlooked by the town's magnificent castle. **Brunel**'s **railway** bridge crossing the Wye at Chepstow is a remarkable structure. The first **Severn bridge** carried the **M4** (now the M48) across the mouth of the Wye.

WYLFA NUCLEAR POWER STATION,
Isle of Anglesey
Situated near Cemaes Bay (**Llanbadrig**), Wylfa nuclear power station began generating electricity in 1971, as the last of the Magnox stations to be built by the Central Electricity Generating Board. It has two reactors generating some 950 megawatts of electricity, sufficient to supply a **population** of around a million people. At its peak, employment at the plant totalled some 600. Its licence to produce electricity is due to come to an end in 2010. Much of its production is consumed by **Anglesey** Aluminium (*see* **Trearddur**), the future of which will be in doubt when the power station closes.

WYN, Eirug (1950–2004) Writer, language campaigner and entrepreneur
Eirug Wyn was brought up in his native Llan (**Llanbrynmair**), and in Deiniolen (**Llanddeiniolen**). Fined at the age of 17 for displaying a 'D' (for *Dysgwr*: 'learner') rather than an 'L' on his car whilst learning to drive – a right which was later conceded – he became a prominent

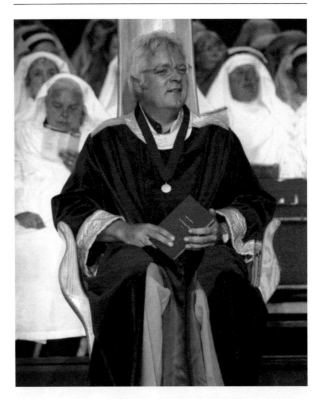
Eirug Wyn wearing the Eisteddfod prose medal

Welsh-language activist. He opened several Welsh bookshops and later worked in television. Anti-establishment and mischievous, he published satirical and parodic poems under the pseudonym Derec Tomos and edited the satirical magazine *Lol!* He published over 15 books, mostly novels, and twice won both the National **Eisteddfod**'s prose medal and the **Daniel Owen** memorial award.

WYNN family (Gwydir) Landowners
Claiming descent from **Gruffudd ap Cynan**, the family originated in **Eifionydd**. One of their number, Maredudd ap Ieuan, bought (*c*.1500) the Gwydir estate in the **Conwy** valley (*see* **Trefriw**). His heir, John Wyn ap Maredudd (d.1559), consolidated the estate, rebuilt the house and was, according to tradition, instrumental in the suppression of the **Red Bandits of Mawddwy**. His son, Maurice (d.1580), adopted the surname Wynn. Maurice's son, the celebrated, litigious and acquisitive Sir John Wynn (1553–1627), dominated **Caernarfonshire** politics for half a century. A scholar and a patron of poets, he became a baronet in 1611, wrote the *History of the Gwydir Family* (not published until 1770) to celebrate his distinguished lineage, and increased and consolidated the Gwydir estate. He was succeeded in the baronetcy by two of his ten sons, Richard (1588–1649), treasurer to Queen Henrietta Maria, and Owen (1592–1660). On the death of the fourth baronet – Owen's son, Richard (*c*.1625–74) – the title passed to Sir John Wynn, son of the first baronet's tenth son, Henry, and lapsed on his death in 1719. The estate, valued at about £3000, was inherited by Richard's daughter Mary, who married Baron Willoughby de Eresby in 1678. In the 1890s, their descendant, the earl of Ancaster, began to dispose of the 12,140-ha estate.

Edith Wynne, 'the Welsh Nightingale', *c.*1885

WYNN-WILLIAMS, [Charles] Eryl (1903–79)
Physicist

In the 1920s, the emerging fields of particle and nuclear physics required the development of much original and innovative equipment. This led Eryl Wynn-Williams, **Swansea** born, **Wrexham** bred and a graduate of **Bangor**, to devise the 'scale of two' concept for the electronic counters used in particle physics research. This principle forms the basis of almost all modern computers and digital electronics, and has been described as the greatest contribution to computation since humankind learnt to count with fingers and toes. He spent most of his career at Imperial College, **London**. During the **Second World War**, he made a significant contribution to the work of those at Bletchley Park, seeking to decode the messages of the German 'Enigma' machine.

WYNNE family (Peniarth) Landowners

The family came to prominence with Maurice ap Robert Wynne (d.1610) of Glyn (**Talsarnau**). The **Ormsby-Gore family**, later Barons **Harlech**, were descended from his eldest son. His fourth son, William Wynne I (d.1700), married Elizabeth, heiress of the Jones family of Wern (**Dolbenmaen**). William's descendant, William Wynn IV

(1745–96), acquired Peniarth (**Llanegryn**) by marriage. Hengwrt (**Llanelltyd**) and its famous library collected by **Robert Vaughan** were bequeathed to William Wynn IV's grandson, William Watkin Edward Wynne (1801–80), by Sir Robert Vaughan (d.1859). W. W. E. Wynne was a genealogist and antiquary, a prominent local administrator and a supporter of the **Oxford Movement**. He was president of the **Cambrian Archaeological Association** (1850) and contributed articles on Welsh history and antiquities to *Archaeologia Cambrensis*. Elected MP for **Merioneth** in 1852, he was challenged in 1859 by the **Liberal** David Williams. Wynne retained the seat by 40 votes, but a number of Liberal supporters were victimized by **Conservative** landlords.

His son, William Wynne VII (1840–1909), elected for Merioneth in 1865, withdrew in 1868 and David Williams was elected unopposed, initiating a long period of Liberal control of the **county**. In 1898, Sir **John Williams** (1840–1926) arranged to acquire the Hengwrt-Peniarth library on the death of the last to survive of the sons of W. W. E. Wynne. That came about in 1909, when Sir John donated the library to the **National Library of Wales** as its foundation collection.

WYNNE, [Thomas], David (1900–83) Composer
Born at Penderyn (**Hirwaun**), David Wynne was a miner before going to **Cardiff** to study **music**. He became a schoolteacher and then a lecturer at Cardiff, while developing his reputation as a composer. His compositional output was considerable and included four symphonies, several large-scale choral works, song cycles and chamber music.

WYNNE, Edith (Eos Cymru; 1842–97) Singer
The first icon of **The Land of Song**, Edith Wynne was born in **Holywell**. In the 1860s, she attended the Royal Academy of **Music**, **London** and became known, by a nation that idolized her, as 'the Welsh Nightingale'. A sparkling soprano, she starred in National *Eisteddfodau*, sang in **England**'s leading music festivals and received the royal command on at least three occasions. In 1874, she went to America and excelled in the Boston Music Festival.

WYNNE, Ellis (1671–1734) Writer
One of the most distinguished writers of prose in **Welsh**, Ellis Wynne was born at Y Lasynys, **Harlech**. He was a descendant of Maurice ap Robert Wynne (d.1610) (*see* **Ormsby-Gore family** and **Wynne family (Peniarth)**). Educated at Jesus College, **Oxford**, he was ordained in 1704 and was rector of Llandanwg (**Llanfair**) and **Llanbedr** (1705–11) and of Llanfair from 1711 until his death. His main work is the classic *Gweledigaetheu y Bardd Cwsc* (Visions of the Sleeping Bard; 1703), a creative adaptation of **English** versions of a work by the Spaniard Quevedo. In 1701, he published *Rheol Buchedd Sanctaidd*, a translation of Jeremy Taylor's *The Rule and Exercises of Holy Living* (1650), and in 1710 his edited version of the Welsh **Book of Common Prayer**. After his death, his son Edward published a collection of his father's religious pieces, *Prif Addysc y Cristion* (1755).

A Cardiff stoker of Yemeni descent

YALE, Thomas (c.1526–77) Canon lawyer
A member of the Yale family of Plas-yn-Iâl (*see* **Bryneglwys**), Thomas served successive archbishops of Canterbury, helped to enforce the **Protestant Reformation** settlement, and became Dean of the Arches – chief judge in the ecclesiastical courts of the province of Canterbury. His family produced several notable lawyers. His nephew was the lawyer David Yale (d.1626), whose great-grandson was the India merchant and philanthropist Elihu Yale, after whom Yale University in the United States is named.

YELLOW FEVER
The only epidemic of this tropical disease known to have broken out in **Britain** occurred in **Swansea** in 1865. When the barque *Hecla* arrived from Cuba, several of those on board had died from the acutely infectious disease. Subsequently, 17 people from the town also died.

YEMENIS
In the age of steam **ships**, Aden, seized by the British in 1839, became a major centre of **coal** bunkering. Ships conveying coal from the **ports** of south Wales returned with Yemenis, thus giving rise to the earliest Arab communities in **Britain**. Yemeni men worked mostly as ships' stokers, and many died in the convoys of the **First** and **Second World Wars**. Arriving in the ports of south Wales, Yemenis quickly founded communities. **Cardiff** was the location of Britain's first mosque (1860). Cardiff's docklands also became home to Britain's first Arab school, Muslim cemetery and Arab **newspaper** (*Al-Salam*, 1948–52). Lodging houses were numerous, the best known being the Cairo Café run by Ali Salaman and his wife Olive, who was a **Welsh**-speaker (Yemenis often married Welsh **women**). By the early 21st century, there were several thousand people of Yemeni ancestry in Wales, with communities in **Newport** and **Swansea** as well as in Cardiff. The links between Yemen and Cardiff are portrayed in Patricia Aithie's *The Burning Ashes of Time* (2005).

YNY LHYVYR HWNN (*In this Book*)
Probably rightly considered to be the first printed book in the **Welsh language** (1546), it is generally known by its opening words. It was printed in **London** by Edward Whitchurch for its author and publisher **John Price** – who gave it neither his name nor a title. Its main objective was to provide key religious texts, such as the Credo, the Lord's

979

Prayer, and the Ten Commandments, to Welsh people who could read Welsh but not **English** or **Latin**. It also includes a calendar, which notes the feast days of many Welsh **saints**, as well as providing agricultural advice for each month. The introductory discussion of Welsh orthography reveals the author's humanist interests. An attractive type-facsimile was published in 1902.

YNYSAWDRE, Bridgend
(192 ha; 3003 inhabitants)
Located north of **Bridgend**, the **community** contains the site of the Tondu **Iron**works, established in the 1820s. Its 100 or so beehive-shaped coking kilns represent one of the most extensive series remaining in **Britain**. The ironworks company shop is now an old-people's home. Of the **horse**-drawn tramroads of the 1820s, two bridges survive. Betharran, Brynmenyn, is a handsome chapel.

YNYSDDU (Ynys-ddu), Caerphilly
(1420 ha; 3698 inhabitants)
Straddling the bend in the Sirhowy, a tributary of the **Ebbw**, the **community** contains Cwmfelinfach, the site of the one-time colliery of Nine Mile Point, where a stay-down strike in 1935 dealt a deathblow to **company unionism** (unions financed by the employers) in the southern **coal**-field. Islwyn (**William Thomas**; 1832–78) was born in Ynysddu. Capel y Babell is now a museum devoted him. Mynyddislwyn church, located on the community's north-ern edge, was rebuilt on a large scale in 1819. Near it is the 12th-century motte of Twyn Tudur.

YNYSYBWL AND COED-Y-CWM (Ynys-y-bŵl a Choed-y-cwm), Rhondda Cynon Taff (1956 ha; 4787 inhabitants)
Located immediately north of **Pontypridd**, the **community** constitutes the basin of one of Wales's several Clydach **rivers**. It contains the villages of Ynysybwl and Coed-y-Cwm and the remote hamlet of Llanwonno, once the cen-tre of an extensive **parish**.

St Gwynno's church, although heavily restored in 1893, retains its medieval walls; ancient inscribed stones suggest that the place was an ecclesiastical centre as early as the 6th century (*see* **Monuments, Early Christian**). In the church-yard is the grave of the famous runner Guto Nyth Brân (**Griffith Morgan**; 1700–37). Urbanization reached the lower Clydach valley in the wake of the opening of the Lady Windsor Colliery in 1885. The colliery, which at its peak employed over 1000 workers, closed in 1988. While William Thomas (Glanffrwd; 1843–90) in his *Plwyf Llanwynno* (1888) admirably invoked the society of pre-industrial upland **Glamorgan**, John E. Morgan in his *A Village Workers' Council* (?1950) equally admirably invoked the way in which the miners of Ynysybwl created the social fabric of their community.

YORK family Marcher-lords
The founder of the family was Edmund, duke of York (d.1402), the fourth son of Edward III to attain adulthood. His son, Richard (d.1415), married Anne, sister and heiress of Edmund **Mortimer**, fifth earl of March (d.1425) and great-grandson of Lionel, duke of Clarence, the second son

of Edward III to attain adulthood. Their son, Richard, duke of York (d.1460), inherited from his mother both the Mortimer territories and the dynastic claims of the senior surviving line of the descendants of Edward III, and from his father the dynastic claims of the third surviving line. As Richard was – through the Mortimers – a descendant of Gwladus Ddu, daughter of **Llywelyn ap Iorwerth**, he was also a plausible heir to the rights of the princes of **Gwynedd**. The resources of the territories he had inherited from the Mortimer family – a series of lordships extending from **Denbigh** to **Caerleon** – were central to Richard's bid for the English crown (*see* **Wars of the Roses**). When in 1461 his son secured the crown as Edward IV, the York lordships became crown possessions. Royal ownership of so much of the Welsh **March** greatly facilitated state policy in Wales.

YOUNG, Gruffydd (fl.*c*.1391–1432)
Lawyer and chancellor
Among the ablest of Wales's medieval clerics, Gruffydd Young was probably an illegitimate member of a leading **Flintshire** family. Educated at **Oxford**, he became a canon lawyer and archdeacon of **Merioneth**. By *c*.1403, he had become a supporter of **Owain Glyndŵr** and was appointed his chancellor. In 1404, he was in Paris arranging an alliance between Owain and the French king. He was prob-ably responsible for the policy laid out in the **Pennal Letter** of 1406, the aims of which included the elevation of **St David's** to archiepiscopal status. In 1407, Young was the Avignon pope's nominee as archbishop, but Owain's wan-ing power meant that the appointment did not take effect. Young remained in touch with the insurgents until Owain's death. In 1418, he sought to convince the Council of Konstanz that the Welsh were a *natio particularis*.

YOUNG, [James] Jubilee (1887–1962) Minister
Born in **Maenclochog**, in the year of Queen Victoria's jubilee, Young was brought up in **Aberavon**. After working in an outfitter's shop in Tonypandy (**Rhondda**), he attended the **Carmarthen Presbyterian** College. He was ordained at Capel Rhondda **Baptist** church, **Pontypridd** (1910), before moving to Felinganol (**Solva**) (1914) and thereafter to Seion, **Llanelli** (1931), where he remained for the rest of his career. By then, he had become one of the best-known **preachers** of his time but, because of his propensity to imitate famous preachers of a bygone age, he was suspected of entertaining congregations rather than edifying or challenging them.

YOUNG FARMERS' CLUBS
This youth movement derives from the inspiration of Lord Northcliffe in the early 1920s. He was determined to estab-lish a rural youth movement in **Britain** comparable to the '4H' clubs in **North America**. Financial support from the Ministry of **Agriculture** and the Carnegie Trust enabled the formation of the British National Federation.

The network of clubs, which offered social opportuni-ties to rural young people between the ages of 10 and 20, expanded quickly. By the end of the **Second World War**, there were some 200 individual clubs with over 10,000 members in Wales. In 1945, the Federation in Wales decided to give equal status to the **Welsh** and **English**

The Wales Young Farmers' Clubs talent competition at the Royal Welsh Agricultural Show, Llanelwedd, near Builth, 2005

languages, a radical decision at a time when bilingualism was a novel concept. With the upper age limit for membership extended to 26, a pattern of activities developed. Practical rural skills, from hedging (*see* **Hedgerows**) to livestock judging, are complemented by amateur **dramat**ics, *eisteddfodau*, public speaking, cookery and dressmaking; the current membership of 6000 embraces young people from all backgrounds, not only farmers. Charitable fundraising is encouraged, and overseas exchange visits are arranged.

YSBYTY IFAN, Conwy (6798 ha; 221 inhabitants)
Constituting the upper reaches of the **Conwy** valley, the greater part of the **community** is owned by the **National Trust**, which acquired the land from the Douglas-**Pennant family**. Until 1974, the area was divided between the civil **parishes** of Tir Ifan in **Denbighshire** and Eidda in **Caernarfonshire**. The name Ysbyty Ifan derives from the Hospital of St John – a church and hospice established *c.*1190 by the crusading Knights of St John to offer hospitality to travellers. John Wynn (*see* **Wynn family (Gwydir)**) recorded that by the 15th century the hospice had become 'the receptacle of thieves and murderers'. Suppressed in 1537, parts of the hospice survived until 1858. Gwernhywel Ganol was the home of Sarah Jones (d.1864) whose elopement with the Methodist evangelist William Roberts (1784–1864) is the theme of their great-grandson **Saunders Lewis**'s novel *Merch Gwern Hywel* (1964). The skilful rural poet (*see* **beirdd gwlad**) Huw Selwyn Owen (1921–98) was a native of Ysbyty Ifan, which was also the birthplace of Orig Williams (b.1932 – El Bandito – among the most

famous of Wales's wrestlers). In 2001, 86.11% of the community's inhabitants had some knowledge of **Welsh**, with 79.11% being wholly fluent in the language – the highest percentages in the **county borough** of Conwy.

YSBYTY YSTWYTH, Ceredigion
(5613 ha; 454 inhabitants)
Constituting the southern bank of the upper **Ystwyth** valley and extending to the upper reaches of the Elan valley, the **community** contains the villages of Ysbyty Ystwyth and Pont-rhyd-y-groes, creations and relics of the **lead**-mining industry. St John's church (1876) has a prominent tower. The 1859 religious **revival** owed much to the leadership of David Morgan (1814–83), who became **Calvinistic Methodist** minister at Ysbyty Ystwyth. In the late 18th and early 19th centuries, the area proved attractive to squatters; remains of their *tai unnos* are still obvious in the landscape. On visiting Ysbyty Ystwyth, **George Borrow** was told to 'go back ... to your **goats** in **Anglesey**'.

YSCEIFIOG, Flintshire (2336 ha; 1181 inhabitants)
Located south-west of **Holywell**, the **community** contains the villages of Ysceifiog, Babell and Lixwm. Its **limestone** plateau is dotted with **Bronze Age** barrows. The 26-ha Penycloddiau **hill-fort** is one of the largest in Wales. Although always primarily agricultural, in the 19th century the area contained several **lead** mines. Among the community's historic houses is Gellilyfdy (or Gelli Loveday) with its superb barn (1586). **John Jones** (*c.*1580–1658/9), the tireless copier who saved much of Wales's medieval **literature**, was born at Gellilyfdy.

YSCIR (Ysgyr), Breconshire, Powys
(2241 ha; 483 inhabitants)
Located immediately west of **Brecon**, the **community** contains the **Roman** fort of Y Gaer. Built to accommodate a garrison of 500, it was excavated in 1925–6 by **Mortimer Wheeler**. The historian **William Rees** (1887–1978) was born in Aberyscir, a place associated with the 15th-century poet Hywel Swrdwal (*see* **Ieuan ap Hywel Swrdwal**). Battle stands on land owned by Brecon Priory, once a cell of Battle Abbey in Sussex. There is also a tradition that the name refers to the battle in which **Rhys ap Tewdwr** was killed by **Norman** invaders in 1093. Pennoyre, an incredible pile, was completed in 1848 at the then astronomical cost of £30,000; it is being converted into flats. There is a multivallate **hill-fort** at Pen y Crug.

YSGUBOR-Y-COED, Ceredigion
(4241 ha; 293 inhabitants)
Constituting the northernmost part of **Ceredigion**, the **community** contains the 12th-century motte Tomen Las, established by **Rhys ap Gruffudd** (The Lord Rhys; d.1197) to guard his northern boundary. Ynys-hir mansion, now a hotel, was the home of the Lloyd family who built the church of Llanfihangel-ynys-Edwin at Eglwys Fach in 1629. Largely rebuilt in 1833, **R. S. Thomas** was its vicar from 1954 to 1967.

Nearby is Ynys-hir **bird** sanctuary. Adjoining the **waterfall** on the Einon are the ruins of the 18th-century foundry, which gave the village of Furnace its name. Built to smelt **iron** using charcoal from the district's extensive woods, it is now in the care of **Cadw**. Glandyfi Castle (18th century),

occupying the site of a 12th-century motte, has attractive **gardens**. The scenic delights of the community include Cwm Einon (tourist-speak: Artists' Valley), Cwm Llyfnant and the **lakes** around Anglers' Retreat.

YSTALYFERA, Neath Port Talbot
(988 ha; 4499 inhabitants)
Straddling the west bank of the **Tawe** north of **Pontardawe**, the **community** was until 1974 part of the one-time civil **parish** of Llanguike. Exploitation of the local **coal** and **iron** ore began with the completion of the **Swansea Canal** in 1798; an impressive canal aqueduct survives. The Ystalyfera ironworks, founded in 1838, had a bank of 11 blast furnaces, second only to the 14 at Dowlais (**Merthyr Tydfil**). In 1969, Ystalyfera **County** School, established in 1895, became **Glamorgan**'s second **Welsh**-medium secondary school. Pantyffynnon near Godre'r Graig is notorious for its 'moving **mountain**', the consequence of its unstable hillside site.

YSTLWYF Commote
One of the **commotes** of **Cantref Gwarthaf**, it was located at the head of the estuary of the **Taf**. In the later Middle Ages, it was an area of contention between the earls of **Pembroke** and the royal **government** based at **Carmarthen**. The caput of the commote was at **Meidrim**.

YSTRAD ALUN Commote
A **commote** of **Powys Fadog**, it was converted into the lordship of Montalt or **Mold**esdale and linked with that of **Hawarden**. In 1536, the lordships became part of **Denbigh**shire, but were transferred to **Flintshire** in 1541.

The Furnace waterfall and old sluice gate on the Einon at Ysgubor-y-coed

YSTRAD FFLUR (Ystrad-fflur), Ceredigion
(9255 ha; 687 inhabitants)

Occupying a wide swathe of east central **Ceredigion**, the **community** extends to the upper reaches of the Claerwen **reservoir** and contains the **lakes** that are the source of the **Teifi**. While its chief settlement is Pontrhydfendigaid, home to the **eisteddfod** endowed by the **London** Welshman **David James**, its most distinctive feature is Strata Florida Abbey, a medieval site of primary importance. Originally founded under **Norman** patronage in 1164 as a daughter of the **Cistercian** monastery at **Whitland** (*see* **Llanboidy**), it was refounded a little later on a new site by **Rhys ap Gruffudd** (The Lord Rhys; d.1197). Of the abbey's buildings, which date in the main from c.1184–c.1220, the most endearing survival is the west doorway of the church, which contains motifs reminiscent of prehistoric **Celtic** art. Strata Florida became the spiritual heart of **Deheubarth**. It was the burial place of at least nine of the Lord Rhys's descendants, and also of **Dafydd ap Gwilym** who is commemorated by a bilingual (**Welsh** and **Latin**) memorial. (**Talyllychau** has a competing claim to the poet's grave.) The **Hendregadredd Manuscript** and *The White Book of Rhydderch* were almost certainly copied at Strata Florida, which was the home of the chronicle *Brut y Tywysogyon*. In 2005, work published by archaeologists from the **University of Wales, Lampeter**, suggested that the monastic site, in its 13th-century heyday, was much larger than the present ruins would suggest.

With the **dissolution** of the much-decayed monastery in 1538, the demesne land became the property of the Stedman family, who built the much-altered house that adjoins the abbey ruins. The abbey's extensive lands were a factor in the development of **sheep**-raising in Ceredigion, and the monks' fair may have given its name to Ffair Rhos, a hamlet famous for its poets. A leg was buried in the churchyard of Ystrad Fflur church in 1776, causing its owner, Henry Hughes, to spend the rest of his life with one foot in the grave. Pontrhydfendigaid may have come into existence as the home of the monastery's servants, although its later growth was the result of **lead** mining.

YSTRAD MARCHELL Commote
A **commote** of **Powys Wenwynwyn**, it was located west of the **Severn** and north of **Welshpool**. Together with **Deuddwr** and **Llannerch Hudol**, it was part of the district known as Teirswydd. The post-**Acts of 'Union' hundred** of Ystradmarchell also included the commotes of Llannerch Hudol and **Gorddwr**. (For the **Cistercian** monastery of Strata Marcella (Ystrad Marchell), *see* **Welshpool**.)

YSTRAD MEURIG (Ystradmeurig),
Ceredigion (3703 ha; 372 inhabitants)

Located immediately north-west of **Tregaron**, the **community** extends from the **Ystwyth** to the **Teifi**. It contains the villages of Ystrad Meurig, Swyddffynnon and Ty'n-y-graig. Ystrad Meurig Castle – one of **Ceredigion**'s three stone-built castles – was one of the fortifications built c.1110 following Gilbert de **Clare**'s invasion. St Gwnnws's church (1874) stands in splendid isolation; within it is a 7th-century inscribed stone. St John's church, once the property of the Knights of St John, was rebuilt in 1899.

Until 1974, the buildings in its churchyard were a school (1812), originally founded c.1736 by **Edward Richard**. Among those who studied there was **Evan Evans** (Ieuan Fardd; 1731–88), whose birthplace was Gwenhafdre, Swyddffynnon. The most distinctive feature of the area is the vast bog **Cors Caron**.

YSTRAD TYWI Kingdom
One of the kingdoms of early Wales, Ystrad **Tywi** constituted what would later be the central and eastern parts of **Carmarthenshire** and the westernmost part of the **county** of **Glamorgan**. It consisted of the *cantrefi* of **Cantref Bychan**, **Cantref Mawr** and **Eginog**. Nothing is known of its early rulers, but c.730, Seisyll, king of **Ceredigion**, united Ystrad Tywi with Ceredigion; the new kingdom came to be known as **Seisyllwg**. Under **Hywel Dda**, Seisyllwg, together with **Dyfed** and **Brycheiniog**, became the kingdom of **Deheubarth**. By the early 12th century, Eginog had been lost to the **Normans**, but Welsh possession of Cantref Mawr and Cantref Bychan was central to the revival of Deheubarth under **Rhys ap Gruffudd** (The Lord Rhys; d.1197).

YSTRAD YW Commote
Ystrad Yw, a **commote** of the *cantref* of **Blaenllynfi** or **Talgarth**, constituted south-eastern **Brycheiniog**. Following **Norman** incursions, it became the domain of the Picard family, who lived at Tretower (**Llanfihangel Cwmdu**), from whom it eventually passed to the **Vaughan family** (**Tretower**). Originally subject to the suzerainty of the lord of **Brecon**, after 1211 the lordships of Ystrad Yw (or Tretower) and **Crickhowell** became subject to that of the Fitz Herbert family, lords of Blaenllynfi.

YSTRADFELLTE, Breconshire, Powys
(8279 ha; 549 inhabitants)

The **community** constitutes the heart of the Fforest Fawr, the uplands between the **Black Mountain** and the **Brecon Beacons**. To the south, on the **Rivers** Hepste, Mellte, **Nedd** and Pyrddin, is the greatest concentration of **waterfalls** in Wales. The area also offers a variety of man-made sights. Maen Madoc, an inscribed stone pillar dating from c.500, probably marks a Christian burial site; close by is a fine stretch of **Roman road** – that part of **Sarn Helen** which connected the Gaer (**Yscir**) with the fort at Coelbren (**Onllwyn**). Castell Coch (13th century) is situated above the confluence of the Llia and the Dringarth. Hepste Fawr was one of the last of the Welsh **longhouses** to be inhabited by both farmers and **cattle**, with access to both dwelling and beast-house from the lobby; it was inhabited at least until the 1970s.

YSTRADGYNLAIS, Breconshire, Powys
(5496 ha; 8023 inhabitants)

In the late 18th century, Ystradgynlais, on the southern border of **Breconshire** and on the northern edge of the **coalfield**, was little more than a hamlet. The opening in 1798 of the **Swansea Canal** initiated the development of heavy industry in the upper **Tawe** valley. During the early phase of the **Industrial Revolution**, the slow-burning local anthracite was of limited use, a situation that changed following experiments at the Ynyscedwyn **Iron**works, which had been founded in 1628. **David Thomas** (1794–1882), who began working there in 1817, pioneered a method of using anthracite in smelting iron ore. Ironmaking came to an end at Ynyscedwyn in 1861, and the works were adapted to produce **tinplate**. They finally closed in 1903, but some of the buildings survive.

The coalmines of the area were hit by the interwar **depression**. Since the **Second World War**, the **community**'s major sources of employment have been open-cast mining and general manufacturing – **clock** making in particular. Ystradgynlais and its inhabitants are portrayed in the work of the artist **Josef Herman**. The National **Eisteddfod** was held at Ystradgynlais in 1954, only the second occasion (**Brecon** in 1889 was the other) for the festival to be held in Breconshire. Cwmgiedd was the setting for the **film** *Silent Village* (1943), depicting the destruction of the Czech village of Lidice during the Second World War. In 2001, 68.1% of the inhabitants of Ystradgynlais had some knowledge of **Welsh**, with 34.46% wholly fluent in the language –

the highest percentages of any of the communities of the former **county** of Breconshire.

YSTUMANNER Commote
The southernmost of the two **commotes** of the *cantref* of **Meirionnydd**, it was perhaps named after the *ystum* (bend) in the River Dysynni. Its centre was the rock eventually crowned by Castell y Bere (**Llanfihangel-y-Pennant**).

YSTWYTH River (70 km)
The Ystwyth rises in the central part of the **Elenydd Mountains**. It flows through a narrow glen past the village of Cwmystwyth (*see* **Pontarfynach**), once an important area of **copper** and **lead** mining. It then traverses a wooded glen between Pont-rhyd-y-groes and **Trawsgoed**, where the valley floor widens to create a more fertile farming area. Between Trawsgoed and **Llanilar**, the **river** has undergone a degree of **canal**ization; thereafter, it meanders past **Llanfarian** and joins the **Rheidol** in **Aberystwyth** harbour before flowing into Cardigan Bay. The river has no major tributaries.

Z ~ Z

Ivor Emmanuel (left) and Neil McCarthy in *Zulu* (1964)

ZIMMERN, Alfred [Eckhart] (1879–1957)
Academic and author
The son of a German-Jewish political exile, Alfred Zimmern had a distinguished career at **Oxford**, publishing his major scholarly book *The Greek Commonwealth* in 1911. During the **First World War**, his interest shifted towards contemporary world affairs. In 1919, he became the first Wilson Professor of International Affairs at **Aberystwyth**, the first chair of its kind in the world. There, he was a breath of fresh cosmopolitan air; in 1921, however, he was asked to leave because of his relationship with another professor's wife. He stood against **David Lloyd George** as a **Labour** candidate in the 1924 election. In 1921, he published his perceptive essay *My Impressions of Wales*, in which he advanced the influential concept of the **coal**-field as 'American Wales'.

ZOBOLE, Ernest (1927–99) Painter
Ernest Zobole, who studied at **Cardiff** and taught at **Newport** School of Art, was born into an **Italian** family at

Porth (**Rhondda**). A member of the Rhondda Group, he was influenced by the expressionism of Heinz Koppel and other **refugee artists**. The looming horizons and rearing perspectives of the southern **coal**field permeate Zobole's magical **paintings**, which often include the artist himself gazing into a world of secret dreams.

***ZULU* (1964)** Film
An eloquent Paramount screen feature, paying tribute to the **South Wales Borderers**' bravery and Pyrrhic victory in the battle of Rorke's Drift in 1879 (*see* **South African Wars**). Directed, co-produced and co-written (with John Prebble) by the American Cy Endfield, adroit in his handling of battle and crowd scenes, the **film** avoided too flagrant a display of jingoism. Endfield's co-producer was **Stanley Baker**, who played an initially tetchy Royal Engineer, proving a fine foil for Michael Caine's superficially cavalier officer. John Barry supplied highly affecting **music**, and the cast included Jack Hawkins, Ulla Jacobsson, Nigel Green, James Booth and the singer **Ivor Emmanuel**.

ILLUSTRATION ACKNOWLEDGEMENTS

Map artwork by Anna Ratcliffe based upon supplied references; maps prepared for publication by Alun Ceri Jones. Every effort has been made to secure the permission of copyright holders in reproducing images, the quality of which vary according to sources. Images are reproduced with the kind permission of the following individuals, institutions and copyright holders.

Abergavenny Museum: p. 7
Airbus UK: p. 888
Alamy: p. 939 (aberCPC); p. 422 (AKG-images); p. 268 (Content Mine International); p. 220 (Daniel Dempster Photography); p. 686 (floralimages); p. 654 (Paul Harvard Evans); p. 624 (Andre Jenny); p. 838 (Phil Holden); p. 798 (Mary Evans Picture Library); p. 1 (Jeff Morgan); p. 525 (Jeff Morgan/The Arts); pp. 626, 785, 833, 895 (Pictorial Press); pp. 295, 440, 548, 657, 861 (popperfoto); p. 632 (The Print Collector); p. 571 (Reflex Picture Library); p. 754 (Amoret Tanner); p. 608 (travelibUK); p. 258 (World History Archive)
BBC: pp. 89, 225, 431, 633, 651
BBC Wales: p. 86
Chris Bell: p. 629
Dave Berry: p. 144
Birmingham Museum and Art Gallery: p. 205
Andrea Bonazzi: p. 418
Breconshire Museum and Art Gallery: p. 865
British Museum: p. 91
Cadw (Historic Environment Service of the Welsh Assembly): pp. 352, 929, 851, 883
Camarthen County Council: p. 124
Canal+ Image UK Ltd: pp. 243, 417, 715
Cardiff Central Library: pp. 155, 299
Cardiff University: pp. 731, 788, 799
Carmarthen Museum Archives: p. 409
CCW/Llyr Gruffydd: p. 684
Contemporary Art Society for Wales/D. Garret/Estate of Alfred Janes: p. 410
Corus: p. 404
Courtaulds: p. 51
Mark Crampin: p. 85
Crown Copyright: pp. 29, 101, 369, 375, 723, 752, 797, 836, 877, 908 (Royal Commission on the Ancient and Historical Monuments of Wales); p. 522 (Visit Wales, 2007)
Cyfarthfa Castle Museum and Art Gallery: pp. 79, 678; p. 959 (Charles and Patricia Aithie/Ffotograff)
Cyfeillion Fenn: p. 320

Cyffeillion Cadw Tremadog: p. 529
Czech Lacrosse Union: p. 441
Ray Daniel: pp. 388, 461, 786
Ivor Davies: p. 646
J. K. Davies family: p. 201
Janet Davies: p. 679
Sara Lewis Davies and Alun Ceri Jones: p. 854
Robert S. Davey/GlynVivian Art Gallery: p. 573
Denbighshire Record Office: p. 965
Diversions Dance Company of Wales: p. 193
Eisteddfod Genedlaethol Cymru: p. 247
Essex Peabody Museum: p. 627
Mrs M. Evans/Glyn Vivian Art Gallery: p. 273
Ffotograff: pp. 8, 30, 70, 169, 463, 630, 737, 791, 802, 805, 975 (Charles Aithie); pp. 10, 103, 104, 115, 166, 175, 280, 322, 376, 442, 447, 479, 495, 517, 547, 565, 567, 594, 606, 658, 811, 842, 944, 979 (Patricia Aithie); p. 936 (Patricia Aithie/National Museum of Wales)
Flintshire Museum Services: p. 637
Forman Archives (Michael and Doreen Forman): p. 406
FotoLibra: pp. 647, 924 (Glyn Ackroyd); p. 744 (Richard Broady); p. 904 (Paul Brzenczek); p. 696 (Brian Carroll); p. 523 (Sarah Cody); p. 97 (Ted Edwards); pp. 233, 256, 618, 667, 697 (Kevin Fitzmaurice-Brown); p. 721 (Michael Gwynne); p. 501 (Michael Hayward); pp. 331, 738 (Gwyn Headley); p. 968 (Peter Herbert); pp. 81, 139, 143, 319, 598, 855, 915, 981 (Nick Jenkins); p. 511 (Alwyn Jones); pp. 454, 690, 982 (Phil Jones); pp. 73, 149, 231, 246, 306, 346, 504, 892 (William Jones); p. 872 (Stuart Jones); p. 68 (David Knowles); pp. 913, 919 (Kokoro/D. McCarthy); p. 821 (Stuart Lord); pp. 77, 127, 508, 660, 676 (Ken Mayled); p. 925 (Dan Ogden); pp. 338, 436 (Ros Pierson); p. 55 (David Poole); p. 183 (Gareth Price); p. 438 (Alex Ramsay); p. 62 (Mike Reda); p. 93 (Daniel Smethurst); p. 297 (Matthew Stoner); pp. 189, 862 (Peter Thomas); pp. 71, 643 (Simon Tilley); p. 722 (Gareth Williams); p. 218 (Linda Wright); p. 665 (David Young)
Francis Frith Collection: p. 49

Helen Fryer/Cardiff Devils: p. 389
George Eastman House: p. 279
Getty Images: pp. 43, 78, 87, 88, 98, 163, 325, 335, 435,
    467, 609, 640, 806, 827, 829, 863; p. 43 (AFP); p. 347
    (Mark Dadswell); p. 191 (Time & Life Pictures);
    p. 342 (Rob Taggart/Central Press/Hulton Archive)
Glamorgan Cricket Archives: p. 176; p. 760 (Andrew
    Hignell)
Glamorgan Records Office/Archives: pp. 52, 333, 340,
    382, 552, 765
Glyn Vivian Art Gallery: p. 573 (Robert S. Davey);
    p. 367 (Nina Herman)
Gren Group Holdings: p. 423
David Griffiths: p. 197
Nicky Griffiths: p. 619
Gwynedd Archives: pp. 301, 514, 653, 817, 942
Hill and Adamson: p. 317
HTV Cymru PLC: p. 47
International Institute for Sustainable Development
    Reporting Services: p. 675
ITV plc (Granada International)/LFI: pp. 469, 870
Jesus College, Oxford, Principal and Fellows: p. 641
Margaret Jones: p. 620
Kobal Collection/Picture Desk: p. 282 (Agenda/Figment/
    Polygram); p. 283 (Miramax/David James); pp. 379,
    985 (Columbia British); p. 558 (Coronado
    Productions); p. 636 (United Artists)
Lady Llanover Society: p. 350
Lambeth Palace: p. 740
B. J. Lee: p. 232
Alan W. Leigh: p. 923
Leonora Gwalia Historical Museum: p. 42
Llandough Hospital: p. 688
Don Llewellyn: p. 384
Peter Llewellyn: p. 685
London Features International: p. 769
Lord Roberts of Conwy: p. 165
Jeremy Lowe: pp. 34, 901
Magnum: p. 674
Martin Tinney Gallery: pp. 395, 706
Merthyr Tydfil Central Library: pp. 6, 45, 240
Bethan Miles: p. 334
Monmouth Museum: p. 773
Monmouth Regimental Museum: p. 285
Jeff Morgan: pp. 212, 600
Museum of the History of the Welsh Settlement in
    Gaiman and Glaniad: p. 623
National Library of Wales: pp. 11, 18, 64, 99, 109, 145,
    154, 161, 179, 184, 203, 214, 217, 226, 281, 290, 303,
    308, 324, 359, 372, 380, 383, 386, 387, 391, 399, 416,
    419, 458, 476, 482, 486, 490, 493, 515, 537, 560, 562,
    578, 580, 582, 617, 634, 639, 652, 655, 664, 673, 680,
    682, 704, 705, 709, 711, 724, 726, 730, 734, 739, 779,
    807, 816, 832, 857, 864, 868, 873, 882, 889, 890, 927,
    930, 952, 962, 972, 978; p. 645 (DACS Limited 2007):
    pp. 357, 902 (Geoff Charles); p. 957 (Estate of Kyffin
    Williams/DACS Limited 2007); p. 671 (Estate of
    John Petts/Brenda Chamberlain); p. 142 (Film
    Archives); p. 391 (Solo Syndication)
National Museums and Galleries on Merseyside (Lady
    Lever Gallery, Port Sunlight): p. 795
National Museum of Wales (formerly National Museum
    and Gallery of Wales): pp. 15, 28, 40, 46, 50, 53, 150,
171, 252, 269, 275, 281, 287, 315, 393, 403, 408, 432,
    450, 512, 521, 536, 540, 542, 555, 559, 583, 589, 595,
    596, 694, 700, 701, 741, 758, 774, 782, 813, 847, 853,
    856, 858, 866, 875, 886, 909, 926, 951, 966, 967, 971;
    p. 645 (DACS Ltd); p. 759 (Estate of Ceri Richards/
    DACS Ltd 2007); p. 420 (Trustees of the David Jones
    Estate)
National Physical Laboratory: p. 198
National Portrait Gallery, London: pp. 199, 564, 949;
    p. 947 (Estate of Bob Collins); p. 526 (Estate of
    Angus McBean)
National Showcaves Centre for Wales: p. 129
National Trust Photographic Library (Penrhyn Castle,
    The Douglas Pennant Collection): p. 818
National Union of Miners: p. 879
New Welsh Review: pp. 768, 907
Newport City Council: p. 33
Newport Museum and Art Gallery, South Wales: p. 137
    (Bridgeman Art Library); p. 893 (Bridgeman Art
    Library/Estate of C. F. Tunnicliffe); p. 156 (Rex
    Moreton)
The Old Stile Press: p. 405
PA Photos: pp. 277, 439, 586; p. 41 lower (Deutsche
    Presse-Agentur/DPA); p. 41 top (Gareth Copley)
Patrick Olner: p. 878
Pembrokeshire County Council: p. 16
Photolibrary Wales: pp. 2, 20, 25, 80, 121, 133, 140, 192,
    221, 229, 245, 276, 289, 326, 332, 346, 353, 356, 444,
    474, 477, 478, 496, 519, 544, 568, 584, 588, 591, 602,
    610, 611, 628, 648, 698, 703, 713, 718, 729, 732, 743,
    749, 750, 753, 763, 771, 783, 784, 789, 790, 792, 793,
    801, 803, 809, 810, 814, 822, 823, 825, 830, 835, 849,
    852, 871, 876, 897, 905, 910, 933, 945, 970
Pontypool Museum: p. 692
Pontypridd Museum: p. 693
Portmeirion Ltd: p. 964
Powysland Museum, Welshpool: p. 158
Radnorshire Museum: p. 775
Rhondda Cynon Taff Libraries: pp. 58, 209, 254, 424,
    532, 747, 880, 969
Alun Roberts: p. 414
Arwyn Roberts: p. 248
Huw Roberts: p. 931
Tegwyn Roberts: p. 128
Dylan Rowlands: p. 224
Royal Academy of Arts: p. 957
Royal Geographic Society: p. 274
Royal National Lifeboat Institution: pp. 272; p. 462
    (Rod Pace)
Royal Welch Regiment: p. 781
S4C: p. 787
Science Museum (Science and Society Picture Library):
    p. 767
Seren: p. 456
Sheffield Photo Company: p. 349
Snowdon Society: p. 114
South Wales Coalfield Collection, Swansea University:
    pp. 222, 828
South Wales Miners' Library: p. 541
Michael J. Stead: pp. 37, 407, 443, 473, 920
Meic Stephens: p. 271
Sutton Motorsport Images: p. 716
Swansea Museum: p. 841, 911

ILLUSTRATION ACKNOWLEDGEMENTS

Swansea University: p. 911
Tate Gallery: p. 576; p. 839 (Estate of the late Graham Sutherland)
Techniquest: p. 800
Theatr Fach Llangefni/Llangefni Library: p. 223
E. G. Thomas: p. 831
Topfoto: p. 65 (©2004 PA); p. 157 (Topham/PA); pp. 278, 561, 808 (Topham Picturepoint); p. 227 (Fortean Library); p. 585 (Arena PAL); p. 953 (Mander and Mitchenson/ArenaPAL)
University of Wales, Lampeter, Library Services: p. 900
University of Wales, Bangor, Department of Manuscripts and Archives: p. 254
Urdd Gobaith Cymru: p. 903

Philip Vale for Land Design Studio: p. 844
Roger Vitos: p. 796
Welsh Library, University of Wales, Bangor, Information Services: pp. 669, 770, 898
Welsh National Opera/Bill Cooper: p. 38
Welsh Whisky Company: p. 293
Western Mail: pp. 63, 411, 483, 702, 772, 867, 954, 955
R. G. Woods: p. 762
Yale College, Wrexham: p. 677

www.aberdareonline.co.uk: p. 5
www.johnnyowen.com: p. 638
www.ninnau.com/Arturo Roberts: p. 622
www.rhiannon.co.uk: p. 324
www.sporting-heroes.net: p. 691

ILLUSTRATION ACKNOWLEDGEMENTS

Swansea University, p. 91
Tate Galleys p. 376, p. 839 (Thanks of the late Graham Sutherland)
Technium, p. 900
Theatr Fach, Llangefni/Amgueddfa i Diwary p. 223
R. C. Thomas p. 431
Topfoto p. 654, 2004 PA p.c. 157/Topfoto/PA/
pp. 218, 561, 808 (Topham Picturepoint) p. 222
(Lorian Library), p. 585/Arena PA/ p. 953
(Manod and Nitrickson/Arena/PAL)
University of Wales, Lampeter, Library Services, p. 900
University of Wales, Bangor, Department of Manuscripts and Archives, p. 234
Urdd Gobaith Cymru p. 902

Philip Vale for Land Design Studio p. 841
Roger Vlitos p. 796
Welsh Library, University of Wales, Bangor, Information Services, pp. 669, 770, 888
Welsh National Opera/Bill Cooper p. 38
Welsh Whisky Company, p. 293
Western Mail, pp. 63, 111, 483, 702, 772, 867, 884, 935
R. G. Wode p. 765
Yale College, Wrexham p. 674

www.aberdulaisonline.co.uk p. 5
www.johnnyowen.com p. 638
www.rusnan.com/Arturo Roberts p. 622
www.rhiannon.co.uk p. 324
www.spring-heroes.net p. 951

INDEX

A

N

Z